GOOD NEWS

BIBLE

WITH

DEUTEROCANONICALS/

APOCRYPHA

GOOD NEWS  BIBLE

WITH

DEUTEROCANONICALS/

APOCRYPHA

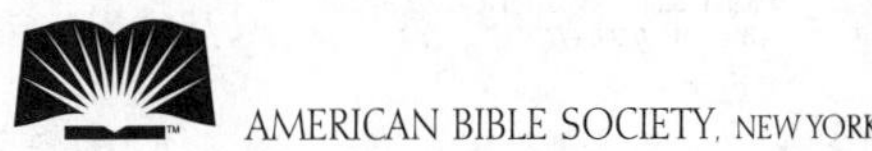

Good News Bible
African American Jubilee Edition

Imprimatur:
✠Most Reverend William H. Keeler, D.D.
President, National Conference of Catholic Bishops

March 10, 1993

Right of Quotation Statement

The American Bible Society is glad to grant authors and publishers the right to use up to one thousand (1,000) verses from the Good News Bible/*Today's English Version* text in church, religious and other publications without the need to seek and receive written permission. However, the extent of quotation must not comprise a complete book nor should it amount to more than 50% of the work. The proper copyright notice must appear on the title or copyright page.

When quotations from TEV are used in non-saleable media, such as church bulletins, orders of service, posters, transparencies or similar media, a complete copyright notice is not required, but the initials (TEV) must appear at the end of each quotation.

Requests for quotations in excess of one thousand (1,000) verses in any publication must be directed to, and written approval received from, the American Bible Society, 1865 Broadway, New York, NY 10023-7505

Visit the ABS website! www.americanbible.org

Page design concept by
The Williams Group, Inc., New York.

ISBN 1-58516-181-0
ISBN 1-58516-508-5
Printed in the United States of America
English Bible TEV053P/DC-109875-110806
ABS-1/01-20,000—QW1

Good News Bible

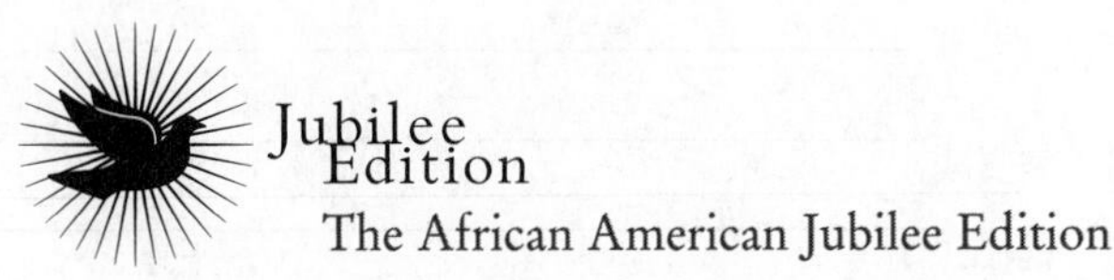

Salvation comes by Jesus Christ alone,
The only Son of God;
Redemption now to every one,
That love his holy Word.

–From *Penitential Cries To God* (1760) by Jupiter Hammon

Presented to ______________________

On ______________________

By ______________________

On the occasion of ______________________

____

____

Family History

Acknowledgments

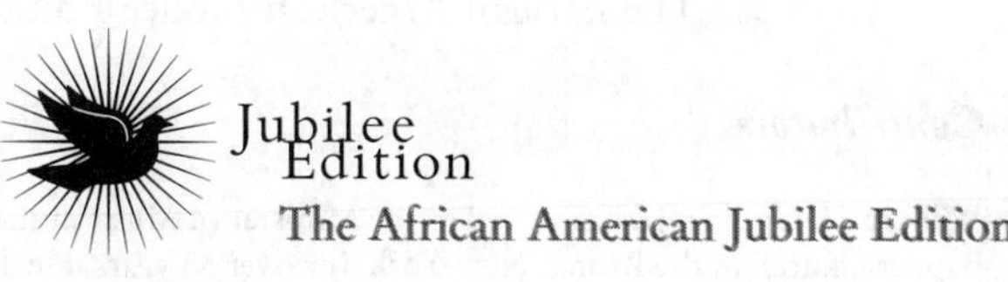

The African American Jubilee Edition

THE JUBILEE BIBLE PROJECT was championed by the Rev. Charles H. Smith, who saw the need to bridge the teachings of the Bible with the realities of African American day-to-day living. In his capacity as Assistant Director for Heritage Markets at the American Bible Society, Reverend Smith traveled extensively throughout the United States for ommunity and beyond. From such exhaustive research comes the Jubilee Bible. The American Bible Society gratefully acknowledges Reverend Smith's determination, indefatigable spirit, and deep commitment to the Bible cause.

The Society gratefully acknowledges the contributions of Dr. Virgil A. Wood, pastor, educator, and American Bible Society consultant, whose concept of a biblical jubilee was instrumental in laying the foundation for this project.

The Society also acknowledges the Rev. Dr. Thomas L. Hoyt, Jr., Presiding Bishop, Fourth Episcopal District, Christian Methodist Episcopal Church, Shreveport, Louisiana, and Dr. Dennis C. Dickerson, Professor of History at Vanderbilt University in Nashville, Tennessee, historiographer, ordained minister, and member of the Board of Trustees at the American Bible Society, for their roles as senior advisors for the Jubilee Bible.

The American Bible Society is deeply indebted to the Rev. Cyprian Davis, O.S.B., D. Hist. Sc., Professor of Church History at St. Meinrad School of Theology and Benedictine monk of St. Meinrad Archabbey in St. Meinrad, Indiana, for his role as advisor. Rev. Davis' guidance and extensive knowledge of the history of black Catholicism has been invaluable to the Jubilee Bible project. Rev. Davis is a founding member of the National Black Catholic Clergy Caucus and the summer degree faculty of the Institute for Black Catholic Studies of Xavier University in New Orleans, Louisiana. He earned an S.T.L. at the Catholic University of America in Washington, D.C., and received his L. Hist. Sc. and D. Hist. Sc. from the Catholic University of Louvain (Belgium). He is the author of several articles and books including the comprehensive work, *The History of Black Catholics in the United States.*

The Society also recognizes the contributions of the Most Reverend John H. Ricard, SSJ, Bishop of Pensacola-Tallahassee, Mr. Hilbert Stanley, President of the National Black Catholic Congress, the Rev. Martin J. Carter, SA of Our Lady of Victory Church, Brooklyn, New York, Ms. Therese Wilson-Favors, Director, African American Catholic Ministries, Archdiocese of Baltimore, and Mr. Joseph Powell, President of the National Association of Black Catholic Administrators, Chairman of the Commission for Black Catholic Ministry, Archdiocese of Metuchen, and member of the American Bible Society African American/Black Advisory group.

The Society owes much gratitude to the Rev. Diane M. Ritzie, consultant for the American Bible Society, for serving as editor and project manager for the Jubilee Bible.

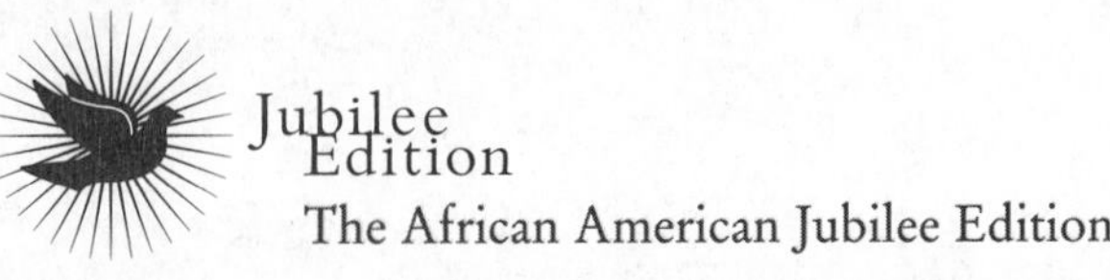

The African American Jubilee Edition

Contributors

William H. Collins, Jr. has served as the Minister of Music at the Mount Hermon Baptist Church in the Bronx, New York, for over 35 years. He directs his own music studio in Harlem. He received his Bachelor of Music degree from the Candell Conservatory of Music in Oakland, California, and his Master of Music degree from the Manhattan School of Music in New York City. Professor Collins is listed in *Distinguished Musicians in the United States.* He has served in the music ministry for more than 50 years.

Robert L. Cvornyek was formerly a Historical Researcher at the American Bible Society. He is the author of *The Bible in Slavery and Freedom: The American Bible Society and the Afro-American Community, 1816-1960.* He is currently an Associate Professor of History at Rhode Island College, Providence, Rhode Island.

Elliott Cuff is the pastor of the Mount Ararat Missionary Baptist Church in Brooklyn, New York. He received a Bachelor's degree from Harvard University, his Master of Divinity degree from New York Theological Seminary, and a Doctorate of Ministry from United Theological Seminary in Dayton, Ohio. His preaching motto is: "Be RADICAL, Be RELEVANT, but most of all, Be RIGHT!"

Michael I. N. Dash is an Associate Professor of Ministry and the Director of Field Education at the Interdenominational Theological Center in Atlanta, Georgia. He is currently serving as executive vice-president and academic dean at that institution. He received his Seminary Diploma from Union Theological Seminary in Kingston, Jamaica, a Diploma of Theology from the University of London, a Master of Sacred Theology from Christian Theological Seminary, and his Doctorate of Ministry from the School of Theology at Boston University. He has co-authored *Hidden Wholeness: An African American Spirituality for Individuals and Communities.*

Dennis C. Dickerson is Professor of History at Vanderbilt University in Nashville, Tennessee. He is also a member of the Board of Trustees at the American Bible Society. Dr. Dickerson is a historiographer and ordained minister in the African Methodist Episcopal Church and has served his denomination as a General Officer since 1988. He received his Bachelor's degree from Lincoln University in Pennsylvania, and earned an M.A. and Ph.D. from Washington University. Dr. Dickerson has also written extensively on African American Religious History, with his works appearing in many scholarly journals and anthologies, and is the author of several books, including *Militant Mediator: Whitney M. Young, Jr.*

Cain Hope Felder is Professor of New Testament Language and Literature at the Howard University School of Divinity in Washington, D.C., and Editor of *The Journal of Religious Thought.* He currently serves as Chair of the President's Implementation Panel for the Howard University African American Heritage and Cultural Center. He has been on Howard's faculty since 1981, having come to Washington from Princeton Theological Seminary. He is an ordained elder in the Methodist Church, and pastored Grace United Methodist Church in New York City.

Dr. Felder earned a Ph.D. in Biblical Languages and Literature from Columbia University, a Diploma of Theology from Oxford University in England, and a Master of Divinity and a Master of Philosophy from Union Theological Seminary in the City of New York. He is also the author of several works including *Troubling Biblical Waters: Race, Class, and Family,* and editor of *Stony the Road We Trod: African American Biblical Interpretation,* and *The Original African Heritage Study Bible.*

Frank L. Gipson is a Ph.D. candidate in Hebrew Bible and Ancient Near Eastern Studies, the Graduate School, Drew University, Madison, New Jersey. His dissertation, entitled "Local Authority in Ancient Israel," describes local leadership via social structure and organization visible within the text of the Hebrew Bible.

Diana L. Hayes is Associate Professor of Theology at Georgetown University and adjunct faculty at Howard University School of Divinity in Washington, D.C. and the Institute for Black Catholic Studies program at Xavier University in New Orleans, Louisiana. She specializes in systematic theology with emphasis on liberation theologies in the United States, particularly Black Liberation and Womanist Theologies. Dr. Hayes received her Bachelor's degree from the State University of New York at Buffalo. She earned a Juris Doctor (J.D.) degree from the National Law Center at George Washington University and Doctorate degrees (Ph.D. in Religious Studies and Doctor of Sacred Theology (S.T.D.) from the Catholic University of Louvain in Leuven, Belgium. She is the first African American woman to earn the S.T.D. degree. She is also the recipient of an honorary Doctor of Humane Letters degree from Ursuline College. She presently serves on the Policy Committee of the Common Ground Initiative and is a member of the International Grail, an ecumenical women's religious society. Dr. Hayes is the author of several books including *And Still We Rise: An Introduction to Black Liberation Theology* and *Taking Down Our Harps: Black Catholics in the United States* with Cyprian Davis, O.S.B.

Thomas L. Hoyt, Jr. is the Presiding Bishop of the Fourth Episcopal District of the Christian Methodist Episcopal Church in Louisiana and Mississippi. He received his Bachelor's degree from Lane College, Jackson, Tennessee, his Master of Divinity degree from the Interdenominational Theological Center, a Master of Sacred Theology degree from Union Theological Seminary in the City of New York, and his Ph.D. from Duke University. Bishop Hoyt also received a Doctor of Divinity degree from Trinity College, Hartford, Connecticut. He serves on the Faith and Order Commissions of the World Council of Churches and the National Council of Churches of Christ in the USA. He is a lecturer for the Lyman Beecher Series at Yale Divinity School.

Bryan N. Massingale is Associate Professor of Moral Theology at St. Francis Seminary in Milwaukee, Wisconsin, and a member of the summer degree faculty of the Institute for Black Catholic Studies of Xavier University in New Orleans. He earned his B.A. in Theology, Philosophy, and Psychology at Marquette University and an M.Div. from St. Francis Seminary. He received his S.T.L. in Moral Theology from The Catholic University of America, Washington, D.C., and his S.T.D., also in Moral Theology, from the Academia Alphonsianum, Rome, Italy. He is an ordained priest in the Roman Catholic Church, and a member of the Catholic Theological Society of America, the National Black Catholic Clergy Caucus, and the Black Catholic Theological Symposium.

Murray L. Newman was educated at Phillips University in Enid, Oklahoma, where he received his Bachelor's and Master of Arts degrees. He attended Union Theological Seminary in the City of New York where he received his B.D. and Th.D. He also attended the University of Basel in Switzerland and the University of Heidelberg in Germany. He is an ordained priest of the Episcopal Church. He was Professor of Old Testament at Virginia Theological Seminary, Alexandria, from 1955-1996; and Visiting Lecturer at Howard Divinity School, Howard University. Dr. Murray is the author of *People of the Covenant, The Continuing Quest for the Historical Covenant, Rahab and the Conquest*, and other articles and book reviews.

Prince Vuyani Ntintili is the Head of the Department of Biblical and Religious Studies at the University of Transkei in South Africa. Dr. Ntintili received a Master of Theology from Dallas Theological Seminary, a Master of Philosophy from Drew University, a Doctor of Theology from Christian Leadership University in Florida, and a Ph.D. in Ethics from Drew University. He is the founder and president of Christian Leadership Equipping and Networking (CLEAN) Ministries in South Africa.

James C. Okoye is Assistant Professor of Biblical Languages and Literature at the Catholic Theological Union in Chicago, Illinois. After receiving the L.S.S. at the Pontifical Biblical Institute in Rome, Italy, he proceeded to Oxford University, England, where he received a Master's in Classical Hebrew and a Doctorate in Targums (Aramaic translations of the Bible). He was appointed lecturer at the Catholic Institute of West Africa, Nigeria in 1981. He has also served as Provincial Superior of the Nigeria Province of the Holy Ghost Congregation and as General Councilor for the Holy Ghost Congregation in Rome, Italy. He was a member of the International Theological Commission. He worked for the Synod of Bishops in Rome in the preparation of the Synod for Africa. He is currently president of the Governing Council of the Spiritan International School of Theology in Enugu, Nigeria. He also teaches at the Institute of Black Catholic Studies at Xavier University, New Orleans, and has authored several scholarly articles which have appeared in such publications as the *Nigerian Journal of Theology; Spiritan Life; AFER; New Theology Review; Catholic Biblical Quarterly; Sedos Bulletin;* and *Bulletin of Ecumenical Theology.*

Gene Rice is Professor of Old Testament Language and Literature at the Howard University School of Divinity in Washington, D. C. He received his Bachelor's degree from Berea College, Berea, Kentucky, his Master of Divinity from Union Theological Seminary in the City of New York, and his Ph.D. from Columbia University. He is the author of *1 Kings: Nations Under God* and some twenty articles in various scholarly journals, among which is *Africans and the Origin of the Worship of Yahweh* which was published in *The Journal of Religious Thought* 50 (1993-94).

Diane M. Ritzie is a consultant for the American Bible Society. She received her Bachelor's degree from Lehman College of the City University of New York, a Master of Science degree from Columbia University, a Master of Divinity degree from Seminary of the East, and is currently a Ph.D. candidate in Biblical Studies–Old Testament at Drew University. She was the first African American to teach Old Testament at Nyack College. She also served as a New York State chaplain for the Department of Corrections

Jerome Clayton Ross is Assistant Professor of Old Testament and Hebrew at the Samuel DeWitt Proctor School of Theology, Virginia Union University. He is also the pastor of Providence Park Baptist Church in Richmond, Virginia. Dr. Ross received his Bachelor's degree from Randolph-Macon College, Ashland, Virginia, his Master of Divinity from Virginia Union, and his Ph.D. in Old Testament from the University of Pittsburgh. His dissertation is entitled *The Composition of the Holiness Code (Leviticus 17-26),* and his review of *Stony the Road We Trod* was published in *A Journal of Bible and Theology* (April 1993).

Mitzi Jane Smith is a Ph.D. candidate in New Testament at Harvard Divinity School. She received her Bachelor's degree in Theology from Columbia Union College, Takoma Park, Maryland, a Master of Arts in Black Studies from Ohio State University, and a Master of Divinity from Howard University School of Divinity. She is the author of *A Tale of Two Sisters: Am I My Sister's Keeper?* which was published in *The Journal of Religious Thought:* Volume 52:2/53:1 (June 1996).

Maxine M. Walker is the first African American chaplain for the entire hospital system of Greenville, South Carolina. She is also Minister of Pastoral Care and Counseling at Cedar Grove Baptist Church in Simpsonville, South Carolina. Chaplain Walker received her Bachelor's degree from the University of Central Florida in Orlando, and her Master of Divinity degree from the Interdenominational Theological Center. One of her sermons is featured in the third edition of *Those Preachin' Women.* She is also the author of *My Round Rainbow,* a children's story/activity book.

Virgil A. Wood is an ordained Baptist minister who became actively involved in the Civil Rights Movement. He served with Dr. Martin Luther King, Jr. as a member of his National Executive Board of the Southern Christian Leadership Conference for the last ten years of Dr. King's life and coordinated the state of Virginia in the historic March on Washington in 1963.
Dr. Wood received his Master of Divinity from Andover Newton Theological School in Newton, Massachusetts and his Doctorate in Education from Harvard University. He served as Dean and Director, the African American Institute, and Associate Professor at Virginia Seminary and College in Lynchburg, and a visiting Lecturer, Research and Teaching Fellow at Harvard University. Dr. Wood is the author of several books including *Introduction to Black Church Economic Studies.* He is currently the pastor of Pond Street Baptist Church in Providence, Rhode Island.

Edwina Maria Wright received her Bachelor's degree from Douglass College, Rutgers University, her Master of Arts degree from Eastern Baptist Seminary, Master of Divinity from McCormick Theological Seminary, and her Ph.D. in Comparative Semitic Philology from Harvard University. She is Assistant Professor of Old Testament at Union Theological Seminary in the City of New York. Prior to accepting the post at Union, Dr. Wright lectured at Rutgers University and was a teaching fellow at Harvard University.

Acknowledgments

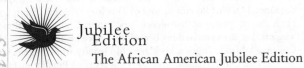

The African American Jubilee Edition

Reviewers

Shaykh Abd'Allah Latif Ali, *Amir, Admiral Family Circle Islamic Community, New York, New York*

Amir Al-Islam, *World Conference on Religion & Peace/USA, New York, New York*

Dr. Randall C. Bailey, Andrew W. Mellon Associate Professor of Old Testament and Hebrew, *Interdenominational Theological Center, Atlanta, Georgia*

Mr. Simon Barnes, Executive Director, *Fellowship of Christians in Universities and Schools, West Tisbury, Massachusetts*

The Rev. Frederick J. Bryant, Jr., Pastor, *Trinity Lutheran Church, Jersey City, New Jersey*

Dr. David G. Burke, Associate Vice President for Scripture Publications, *American Bible Society, New York, New York*

Bishop Clarence Carr, *African Methodist Episcopal Zion Church, Western District, St. Louis, Missouri*

The Rev. Martin J. Carter, SA, Pastor, *Our Lady of Victory Church, Brooklyn, New York*

Dr. Ronald M. Cunningham, General Secretary, Department of Christian Education, *Christian Methodist Episcopal Church, Memphis, Tennessee*

Dr. Michael I. N. Dash, Associate Professor of Ministry and Director of Field Education, *Interdenominational Theological Center, Atlanta, Georgia*

Ms. Charolette Davis, Director, *African American Catholic Ministries, Diocese of Galveston/Houston, Houston, Texas*

The Rev. Cyprian Davis, OSB, Professor of Church History, *St. Meinrad School of Theology, St. Meinrad, Indiana*

Dr. Cain Hope Felder, Professor of New Testament Language and Literature, *Howard University, School of Divinity,* Chairman, *Biblical Institute for Social Change, Washington, D.C.*

The Rev. Dr. Edward L. Foggs, General Secretary, *Leadership Council of the Church of God, Anderson, Indiana*

The Rev. Dr. Robert M. Franklin, President, *Interdenominational Theological Center, Atlanta, Georgia*

Ms. Vanessa Griffin-Campbell, Director, *African American Catholic Ministries, Diocese of Cleveland, Cleveland, Ohio*

Dr. Diana L. Hayes, Associate Professor of Theology, *Georgetown University, Washington, D.C.*

The Rev. Dr. Will Herzfeld, Director for Global Community and Overseas Operations, Division for Global Mission, *Evangelical Lutheran Church in America, Chicago, Illinois*

The Rev. Dr. Darcel M. Holloway, Former Director of the Church Desk, *Federation of Protestant Welfare Agencies, New York, New York*

Dr. Dwight N. Hopkins, Associate Professor of Theology, *The Divinity School, University of Chicago, Chicago, Illinois*

The Rev. Arnold W. Howard, Pastor, *Enon Baptist Church, Baltimore, Maryland*

Dr. David Matthews, past Vice President, *National Baptist Convention USA, Indianola, Mississippi*

The Rev. Bryan N. Massingale, Associate Professor of Moral Theology, *Saint Francis Seminary, Milwaukee, Wisconsin*

Bishop Felton Edwin May, *Baltimore-Washington Conference, The United Methodist Church, Washington, D.C.*

The Rev. Dr. Dale A. Meyer, Speaker, *The Lutheran Hour, St. Louis, Missouri*

Mrs. Bobbie Patterson, Associate Executive Director, *Southern Baptist Convention, Women's Missionary Union, Birmingham, Alabama*

Mr. Joseph Powell, President, *National Association of Black Catholic Administrators, Piscataway, New Jersey,* and Chairman of the *Commission for Black Catholic Ministry, Archdiocese of Metuchen, Metuchen, New Jersey*

The Rev. Dr. Staccato Powell, Executive Director, National Ministries Unit, *National Council of the Churches of Christ in the USA, New York, New York*

Dr. Gene Rice, Professor of Old Testament Language and Literature, *Howard University, School of Divinity, Washington, D.C.*

The Rev. Diane M. Ritzie, Consultant, *American Bible Society, New York, New York*

Dr. Jerome C. Ross, Assistant Professor of Old Testament and Hebrew, *The Samuel DeWitt Proctor School of Theology, Virginia Union University, Richmond, Virginia*

The Rev. Dr. John R. Scott, Jr., Pastor, *Gethsemane Baptist Church, Baltimore, Maryland*

Dr. Linda E. Thomas, Assistant Professor of Theology and Anthropology, *Garrett-Evangelical Theological Seminary, Evanston, Illinois*

The Rev. Dr. G. Ralph Thompson, Secretary, *General Conference of Seventh-Day Adventists, Silver Spring, Maryland*

The Rev. Eugene G. Turner, Director, Department of Governing Bodies, Ecumenical and Agency Relationships, *Presbyterian Church (USA), Louisville, Kentucky*

Dr. Angelique Walker-Smith, Executive Director, *The Church Federation of Greater Indianapolis, Indianapolis, Indiana*

Ms. Jacqueline Wilson, Executive Director, *Office of Black Catholics, Archdiocese of Washington, D.C., Washington, D.C.*

Ms. Therese Wilson-Favors, Director, *African American Catholic Ministries, Archdiocese of Baltimore, Baltimore, Maryland*

Preface

The African American Jubilee Edition

THE AFRICAN AMERICAN JUBILEE EDITION of the Bible heralds a call to engage anew the Holy Scriptures, through the lens of the African American experience, and to be renewed by the intentional moving of the Holy Spirit in the lives of a Covenant people.

The Jubilee Bible, with its supplementary material, presents a way for African Americans to see how they are inextricably connected to the ancient world of the Bible; it allows them to fully understand the inter-relatedness of the biblical stories and their own rich heritage by critically examining the elements of place, people, culture, and story. This culturally-relevant edition of the Bible invites readers to reconnect with the historic struggles of their ancestors whose lives were fashioned by Jubilee Laws; and it reminds them that despite dispersion, social dislocation, and disenfranchisement, God's enabling Spirit has been present all the time.

The supplementary material is designed to encourage readers, especially those of this contemporary generation, to read and, in some instances, re-read the Bible in light of their own cultural and social locations. As readers bring their own experiences to the biblical text and interact with the various stories, remarkable similarities will emerge between the issues they face today and those of the ancient world. Issues of race, gender, oppression, exploitation, prejudice, and xenophobia are all addressed in the Bible. God, who is God of all wisdom and all knowledge, reconciled those issues in Christ and has provided, through the Scriptures, guidance for our life in a faith community.

The Jubilee Bible challenges today's African Americans to move beyond religious rhetoric to more communal relationships. It encourages them to look within the sacred pages and unanimously define themselves as the Scriptures define them, "...God's own people, chosen to proclaim the wonderful acts of God..." (1 Peter 2.9a). It invites them to affirm God as the center of their being and urges them to move toward Jubilee by accepting God's plan of redemption, reconciliation and release.

As members of the body of Christ, we need to know one another's story. We embrace this opportunity to share the African American story as part of the restoration and healing that is needed to bring all of us into a Jubilee community. It is a story that bears repeating; it is the sacred history of a people and their engagement with the God of liberation; it is a story that bids us open wide the doors to Christ.

Contents

Jubilee Edition

The African American Jubilee Edition

Jubilee Biblical Mandates

Leviticus 25.8-12

Today's English Version

Count seven times seven years, a total of forty-nine years. Then, on the tenth day of the seventh month, the Day of Atonement, send someone to blow a trumpet throughout the whole land. In this way you shall set the fiftieth year apart and proclaim freedom to all the inhabitants of the land. During this year all property that has been sold shall be restored to the original owner or the descendants, and any who have been sold as slaves shall return to their families. You shall not plant your fields or harvest the grain that grows by itself or gather the grapes in your unpruned vineyards. The whole year shall be sacred for you; you shall eat only what the fields produce of themselves.

Isaiah 61.1-4

Today's English Version

The Sovereign LORD has filled me with his Spirit.
He has chosen me and sent me
To bring good news to the poor,
To heal the broken-hearted,
To announce release to captives
And freedom to those in prison.
He has sent me to proclaim
That the time has come
When the LORD will save his people
And defeat their enemies.
He has sent me to comfort all who mourn,
To give to those who mourn in Zion
Joy and gladness instead of grief,
A song of praise instead of sorrow.
They will be like trees
That the LORD himself has planted.
They will all do what is right,
And God will be praised for what he has done.
They will rebuild cities that have long been in ruins.

Luke 4.16-21

Today's English Version

Then Jesus went to Nazareth, where he had been brought up, and on the Sabbath he went as usual to the synagogue. He stood up to read the Scriptures and was handed the book of the prophet Isaiah. He unrolled the scroll and found the place where it is written,

"The Spirit of the Lord is upon me,
because he has chosen me to bring good news to the poor.
He has sent me to proclaim liberty to the captives
and recovery of sight to the blind,
to set free the oppressed
and announce that the time has come
when the Lord will save his people."

Jesus rolled up the scroll, gave it back to the attendant, and sat down. All the people in the synagogue had their eyes fixed on him, as he said to them, "This passage of scripture has come true today, as you heard it being read."

Questions for Reflection

(see also Deuteronomy 15.1-18)

1. How would you summarize the main aims of the "Jubilee Year?" Do you know of any attempts today to translate some of these aims into practical initiatives or policies?

2. So far as we know historically, the provisions of the Jubilee Year were never put into practice. Why do you think this was so? What would be the difficulties of carrying out this vision?

3. The Jubilee tradition mandates in Leviticus 25.11, "You shall not plant your fields or harvest the grain that grows by itself or gather the grapes in your unpruned vinyard." Why do you think the land needs to be left unplanted and unharvested? Can we relate this today to an ecological system in danger of collapse?

4. What themes from Jesus' proclamation in Luke 4.16-21 can you relate to the Jubilee tradition?

Source: Adapted from *"Turn to God: Rejoice in Hope,"* prepared for the Eighth World Council of Churches Assembly, held in Harare, Zimbabwe, December, 1998

Jubilee Edition

The African American Jubilee Edition

The Formation of the Biblical Canon

The Bible as Christians know it today did not begin as one large volume—with Old and New Testaments. It came into being as part of a selection process called "canonization." The Greek word for "canon" can mean many things, such as "measuring rod" or "ruler." At first, the early church leaders used "canon" to mean a "standard," and later a "list" or "catalog" of authoritative writings. There were many books circulating among the churches throughout the Roman world that were read and studied by the early church. It was important for the church leaders at that time to go through a process of deciding which books were holy and had authority for God's people. This process did not happen overnight. In some cases, it took hundreds of years from the time they were written to decide which of the many writings that were being read should be part of Holy Scripture, that is, the Bible.

The Hebrew Scriptures and the Old Testament

The books in the Old Testament are translations of the Hebrew Scriptures still used by the Jewish people in their worship services today. These books were written by many different authors over a period of hundreds of years.

It can be said that the Old Testament developed in stages and its books were collected in groups. Before the process of collecting books and putting them in some kind of order took place, individual manuscripts were hand-copied and passed among groups. The earliest literature of the Jewish people may date as far back as the time of Moses or earlier (about 1300 B.C.), while other literature found in the Old Testament (for instance *Daniel*) may have been written as late as the second century B.C. That would mean that the literature collected into the Old Testament was written over a period of 1,000 years or more!

While the writing of Hebrew manuscripts was taking place, the process of collecting and editing was also going on. One important collection of books was called "The Law," which included the first five books of the Bible. "The Law" is also called by its Hebrew name, *Torah*, and by the name *Pentateuch*, which is the Greek term for a five-volume book. Another collection was called "The Prophets." In the Jewish Bible, this collection includes certain books that Christians would call "history books." The last major group of books to be collected was simply called "The Writings." They contain books of poetry and wise sayings, and books that Christians would consider prophetic or historical in nature. Because different religious traditions arrange these books differently, a chart has been provided for easy reference.

BOOKS OF THE HEBREW SCRIPTURES, OR "TANAKH"		
TORAH (The Law)	NEVI'IM (The Prophets)	KETHUVIM (The Writings)
Genesis	Joshua	Psalms
Exodus	Judges	Job
Leviticus	Samuel (1 & 2 S)	Proverbs
Numbers	Kings (1 & 2 K)	Ruth
Deuteronomy	Isaiah	Song of Songs
	Jeremiah	Ecclesiastes
	Ezekiel	Lamentations
	BOOK OF THE TWELVE	Esther
	Hosea	Daniel
	Joel	Ezra-Nehemiah
	Amos	Chronicles (1 & 2 Ch)
	Obadiah	
	Jonah	
	Micah	
	Nahum	
	Habakkuk	
	Zephaniah	
	Haggai	
	Zechariah	
	Malachi	

It is not known exactly how or when the books of the Old Testament were selected and approved for inclusion in the Hebrew Scriptures, but it is certain that the books of the *Torah* were accepted as authoritative almost from the time they were written. There is also some evidence that the list of authoritative books was not finalized until after A.D. 100. Only the books on this final list were considered to be Scripture by the Jewish people.

The chart shows the three main sections of the Hebrew Scriptures: The Law, The Prophets, and The Writings. If you compare this list to the chart on pp. *xxiv*, *xxv*, you'll notice that all of these books are included in the Old Testaments of Christian Bibles, though they are grouped differently and placed in a slightly different order. The Hebrew word for Bible is *Tanak* (sometimes spelled *Tanakh*). This is an acronym, or a word made from the first letters of the Hebrew words for each of the three main sections: *Torah, Nevi'im,* and *Kethuvim*.

If you further examine the chart on pp. *xxiv*, *xxv*, you'll notice that some Christian traditions include other books in their Old Testaments as well. These additional writings are known as "Apocryphal" or "Deuterocanonical" books. The term "apocrypha" comes from a Greek word meaning "hidden," and today suggests books that have been "set aside" or given secondary status. The term "deuterocanonical," a word that Catholics prefer to use when referring to many of these same books, means books that came into the canon at a later (secondary) date, in order to distinguish them from the Hebrew Scriptures discussed above. In the 1600s, some Protestant Christians began to use only the Jewish list of Old Testament books, while the Roman Catholic and Eastern Orthodox Christians continued to use some or all of the Apocryphal/Deuterocanonical books as well. Some of these books are discussed in the following section on Greek versions of the Jewish Scriptures.

Greek Versions of the Jewish Scriptures

In the third century B.C. Jewish scholars in Alexandria, Egypt, translated the Hebrew Scriptures into Greek, since many Jewish people lived in Greek-speaking areas of the Mediterranean world, and spoke Greek on an everyday basis. This Greek version of the Jewish Scriptures is known as the Septuagint (commonly abbreviated LXX), the Roman numeral for seventy.

Some of the Jewish scholars in Egypt did not agree about what books should be included in the official list of Scriptures, even though a canon was being agreed upon by another group of Jewish scholars in Palestine. For example, some of the Egyptian scholars would allow only documents written in Hebrew or Aramaic (a Semitic language similar to Hebrew). Other Greek-speaking Jews included documents originally written in Greek (some of them from as late as the first century A.D.). These Greek writings included:

Historical writings: *1 Esdras* (a Greek version of Ezra in the Hebrew Bible, with some additions); *Judith; Tobit; 1-4 Maccabees;* and

Poetic and prophetic writings, wisdom, and tales: *Sirach* (sometimes called *Ecclesiasticus*); *Wisdom of Solomon; Baruch; Letter of Jeremiah; Susanna; Prayer of Azariah and the Song of the Three Young Men;* and *Bel and the Dragon.*

Though most of these titles may not sound familiar to many Christians today, many of the early Christians seem to have accepted them as part of their Scriptures. Aside from these documents, there were also additions to the Greek translation of the Hebrew book of *Esther* that were made in the second and first centuries B.C. And, some of the tales listed above were added to the Greek translation of *Daniel* (see the notes in the chart on pp.*xxiv*, *xxv*.

The Roman Catholic Bible still includes many of these books, along with the fuller versions of the books of *Esther* and *Daniel.* The Greek Orthodox Bible includes many of these books, plus a few others, such as the *Prayer of Manasseh* and an extra psalm (151). Most Protestant Bibles now follow the list called "Hebrew Scriptures" and exclude the "extra" books. Interconfessional editions include them but place them between the Old and New Testaments or at the end of the Bible.

THE OLD TESTAMENT IN CHRISTIAN BIBLES

The Old Testament in Christian Bibles contains all of the books included in the Jewish Scriptures. Some Christian traditions, however, also include books that are not part of the Hebrew Bible. Most of these books were included in the Septuagint, a Greek translation of the Hebrew Bible that was used by the apostles and the early Christians.

Protestant	Catholic	Orthodox
Genesis	Genesis	Genesis
Exodus	Exodus	Exodus
Leviticus	Leviticus	Leviticus
Numbers	Numbers	Numbers
Deuteronomy	Deuteronomy	Deuteronomy
Joshua	Joshua	Joshua
Judges	Judges	Judges
Ruth	Ruth	Ruth
1 Samuel	1 Samuel	1 Kingdoms (1 S)
2 Samuel	2 Samuel	2 Kingdoms (2 S)
1 Kings	1 Kings	3 Kingdoms (1 K)
2 Kings	2 Kings	4 Kingdoms (2 K)
1 Chronicles	1 Chronicles	1 Chronicles
2 Chronicles	2 Chronicles	2 Chronicles
Ezra	Ezra	***1 Esdras***
Nehemiah	Nehemiah	***2 Esdras*** (Ezra + Ne)
Esther	*Tobit*	*Esther (with additions)*[1]
Job	*Judith*	*Judith*
Psalms	*Esther (with additions)*[1]	*Tobit*
Proverbs	*1 Maccabees*	*1 Maccabees*
Ecclesiastes	*2 Maccabees*	*2 Maccabees*
Song of Songs	Job	***3 Maccabees***
Isaiah	Psalms	Psalms (+ Ps 151)
Jeremiah	Proverbs	***Prayer of Manasseh***
Lamentations	Ecclesiastes	Job
Ezekiel	Song of Songs	Proverbs
Daniel	*Wisdom of Solomon*	Ecclesiastes

Books listed in the Catholic and Orthodox columns that are printed in *red italics* are part of the traditional Protestant Apocrypha. Books that are printed in bold ***italics*** are traditionally included in Orthodox Bibles.

[1] *Esther* in Catholic and Orthodox Bibles includes six additional passages that are found in the Septuagint version of *Esther*.

The Protestant Old Testament contains only the books found in the Hebrew Bible, but arranges them in a different order. The Catholic Old Testament contains all of these books plus the other books that were part of the Septuagint. The Orthodox Old Testament includes all of these books, plus *3 & 4 Maccabees, Prayer of Manasseh*, *Psalm 151*, and *1 Esdras* which are included in the Orthodox Bible because they appear in some versions of the Septuagint.The list below shows the order in which these books usually appear in Bibles printed for each of these Christian communities.

Protestant	Catholic	Orthodox
Hosea	*Sirach*[2]	Song of Songs
Joel	Isaiah	*Wisdom of Solomon*
Amos	Jeremiah	*Sirach*[2]
Obadiah	Lamentations	Hosea
Jonah	*Baruch (with Letter of Jeremiah)*	Amos
Micah	Ezekiel	Micah
Nahum	*Daniel (with additions)*[3]	Joel
Habakkuk	Hosea	Obadiah
Zephaniah	Joel	Jonah
Haggai	Amos	Nahum
Zechariah	Obadiah	Habakkuk
Malachi	Jonah	Zephaniah
	Micah	Haggai
	Nahum	Zechariah
	Habakkuk	Malachi
	Zephaniah	Isaiah
	Haggai	Jeremiah
	Zechariah	*Baruch*
	Malachi	Lamentations
		Letter of Jeremiah
		Ezekiel
		Daniel (with additions)[3]
		4 Maccabees (in Appendix)

[2] *Sirach* is also known as *Ecclesiasticus*.

[3] *Daniel* in Catholic and Orthodox Bibles includes additional sections sometimes printed with the titles: "Prayer of Azariah and the Song of the Three Young Men," "Susanna," and "Bel and the Dragon."

The New Testament

Jesus and his disciples spoke Aramaic and used the Hebrew version of the Jewish Scriptures, but the apostle Paul and many other early Christians spoke Greek and used the Greek version of the Jewish Scriptures (Septuagint). Of the many Old Testament passages quoted or referred to in the New Testament, most are taken from the Septuagint. Though a small number of Christians, by the third and fourth centuries, thought that the Jewish Scriptures should not be part of the Christian Bible, most believed, as did the writers of the New Testament, that the Jewish Scriptures were the Word of God. They considered these writings to be holy and authoritative, and to be suitable for instructing Christians about God and faith (see Mark 7.13; Romans 3.2; 2 Timothy 3.16; Hebrews 1.1). After all, they would have argued, Jesus said that he did not come to do away with the Law and the Prophets, but to give them their full meaning (Matthew 5.17-19).

The twenty-seven books that are included in the present New Testament were written by a number of different authors, the earliest ones being written as early as A.D. 50 and none being written any later than the early part of the second century. Exact dating is not possible, but certain books give clues about when they may have been written. The letters of Paul are probably the oldest writings included in the New Testament. *Matthew, Mark, Luke,* and *John* (the Gospels) were probably written between A.D. 60, ten years before the Temple was destroyed in Jerusalem, and A.D. 100. Most scholars agree that *Mark* was probably the first Gospel written, since *Matthew* and *Luke* seem to take many of their details and the order of events directly from *Mark*. Some of the other letters and *Revelation* were probably some of the last books to be written, since they seem to give a picture of the situations Christians faced at the end of the first century and in the early part of the second century A.D.

The books included in the present New Testament were not the only letters or Gospels written by Christians during the first and second centuries. It took many years of debate between church leaders and scholars to finally settle on an accepted list (canon) of New Testament books. Various church leaders proposed different lists in the three hundred years that followed the writing of the New Testament books, but the list proposed in A.D. 367 by Athanasius, a bishop of Alexandria, is the accepted list that nearly all Christian traditions accept today.

How did the church leaders decide which books should become part of the accepted list? There were probably three "tests" they used to make their decision. First of all, a book had to have some connection with one of the early apostles. This meant that either the apostle was judged to be the writer of the book, or the material was thought to capture the key teachings of that apostle. Second, the book or letter had to be in agreement with the Jewish Scriptures and other accepted New Testament writings. The third test had to do with usage. Was the book or letter accepted and being used by a majority of Christians? If so, the case for including it as part of the New Testament was stronger.

The Protestant, Roman Catholic, and Eastern Orthodox churches all generally consider the twenty-seven books of the New Testament to be "canonical" and usually list them in the same order in their Bibles.

EQUAL
RIGH

Section One

The Biblical Jubilee

Virgil A. Wood

"And ye shall hallow the fiftieth year, and proclaim liberty throughout all the land unto all the inhabitants thereof: it shall be a *jubilee* unto you; and ye shall return every man unto his possession, and ye shall return every man unto his family" (Leviticus 25.10, *KJV*).

"... you shall set the fiftieth year apart and proclaim freedom to all the inhabitants of the land. During this year all property that has been sold shall be restored to the original owner or the descendants, and any who have been sold as slaves shall return to their families" (Leviticus 25.10, *TEV*).

◂ "400 Years of Our People," by Michael Escoffery. Mixed media 1994-1995. Art Resource, New York, NY.

The story of Jubilee is well established in both the Old and New Testaments, although the record of its practice is barely known. For African Americans, it was their slave ancestors' love for the Bible which drew them to embrace certain biblical beliefs which kept the spirit of Jubilee alive. The collective activity of enslaved blacks immediately after the emancipation in 1865 shows that those newly freed blacks created, within the first 50 years after slavery, the institutional framework for black churches, black colleges, the black press, and black businesses. The foundation has been so solidly laid that these institutions have been able to survive to the present time. (See Section Two: "A Hidden History: African American Contributions to the Bible Cause," by Robert L. Cvornyek.)

In modern society, the word Jubilee strikes an unfamiliar sound with little known historical connections. Most Americans would be surprised to learn that the Jubilee Scripture, Leviticus 25.10, is inscribed on the Liberty Bell, and that the British and American legal systems of bankruptcy laws come out of the Jubilee tradition.

The Jubilee tenets are practiced in some parts of the world to this day. The Gabbra, a nomadic people in the Northeast of Kenya, "live in one of the driest areas of East Africa. In 1981, they celebrated their year of Jubilee, ending another cycle of fifty years in their existence. In the year of Jubilee crooked affairs are straightened out, injustice is righted, debts are settled, cattle (the only property) are reallotted and sins are forgiven. This is not a myth; it is not a story; it is not an ideal that they believe should be fulfilled. It really happened in 1981 after a year of preparation."[1]

Provisions of Jubilee

The Jubilee provisions are cited in Leviticus 25, Isaiah 61, and Luke 4. The original text in Leviticus 25.10 in the King James Version (KJV) reads, "And ye shall hallow the fiftieth year, and proclaim liberty throughout all the land unto all the inhabitants thereof: it shall be a ***jubilee*** unto you; and ye shall return every man unto his possession, and ye shall return every man unto his family." The text focuses on provisions relative to land use, redemption of lost land, pricing and selling considerations in relation to Jubilee guidelines, and later gives the injunction "ye shall not therefore oppress one another" (v.17).

In the Leviticus account, we discover that God was preparing the various tribes who yearned to become the nation of God's original promise to Abraham, to move from a nomadic existence to a people of settlement (25.2). There were core beliefs which had to be observed if the People of Promise were to become the Nation of Promise with their own Land of Promise. However, the provisions of Jubilee were to be kept within the Hebrew nation.

▸ "Liberty Bell," by Kimanne Smith

We also note that the Jubilee is the fiftieth year, the year after the succession of seven sabbatical years*, in which all the land which had been taken from its owners, for whatever reason, was to be returned. The land was to lie fallow, and slaves were to be set free.[2]

Jubilee is a biblical concept and we begin a retrospective examination of Jubilee with the Leviticus passage which speaks to justice, freedom, restoration, and reparation. Much of this concept is mirrored by our Lord, as recorded in Luke 4.16-30. There, Jesus reads the well-known Scripture which begins, "the Spirit of the Lord is upon me, because he hath anointed me to preach the gospel to the poor." (v.18, *KJV*). After Jesus was finished reading, he sat down and said to the people, "This day is the Scripture fulfilled in your ears" (v. 21, *KJV*). In essence, at the end of this his inaugural sermon, Jesus endorses Jubilee.

There were six provisions set forth in Jesus' message: (1) to preach the gospel to the poor; (2) to heal the broken-hearted; (3) to proclaim liberty to the captives; (4) to restore sight to the blind; (5) to set at liberty those that are oppressed; and (6) to proclaim the acceptable year of the Lord.

Luke's account of Jubilee differs slightly from the passage in Isaiah 61 in that Luke adds, "recovery of sight to the blind," and

* Sabbatical year is defined as every seventh year during which time debts are forgiven, debtors/slaves are released and the land would remain uncultivated. See Deuteronomy 15.1-18.

Luke's liberation of the oppressed is rendered as "the opening of the prison to them that are bound," in the Isaiah text. When Jesus announced his central mission, he illustrated how the Jubilee would work by extending the traditional boundaries of family beyond the nation of Israel. Jesus now included foreigners and all the nations of the earth in the provisions of God's Jubilee. He went far beyond the concept of physical liberation to offer spiritual liberation—salvation through God's grace. (For further study, see Section Two: "The Message of Salvation," by Thomas L. Hoyt, Jr.)

Jubilee Now

What, then, are the implications for Jubilee today? As the Church moves toward a better understanding of the biblical Jubilee, some elements will be apparent. First, the Jubilee is always associated with the activity and presence of God's Spirit as explicitly stated in the Isaiah 61 and Luke 4 accounts; in the Leviticus account, the Lord speaks directly to Moses. The Church will yield abundant fruitfulness of Jubilee wisdom as it considers the biblical Jubilee through its consistent surrender to God's Holy Spirit.

Second, we will find the provisions of Jubilee as enduring objectives and outcomes in the life, ministry, and work of Jesus, especially following Jesus' announcement of Jubilee and its fulfillment in himself, in the Nazareth hometown synagogue. Thirdly, after the resurrection, the new band of Jesus' followers, first the twelve, then the 120, then the 3,000, committed themselves to these core beliefs by the day of Pentecost, just fifty days following Easter. In a sense, we find the first significant manifestation of the Jubilee in the life of the new community, as recorded in the following passage from the Acts of the Apostles.

God has raised this very Jesus from death, and we are all witnesses to this fact.... They spent their time in learning from the apostles, taking part in the fellowship, and sharing in the fellowship meals and the prayers. Many miracles and wonders were being done through the apostles, and everyone was filled with awe. All the believers continued together in close fellowship and shared their belongings with one another. They would sell their property and possessions, and distribute the money among all, according to what each one needed (Acts 2.32, 42-45).

Maria Harris, an author and professor of Religious Education, offers significant insight into the first century church by discussing the broad curriculum which they embraced, and which we, the current Church, would benefit from adopting.

Harris states:
"The first time these forms are named for us is in the book of Acts. There we find in one place the most detailed description of the first Christian community doing what will in time become the classical activities of ecclesial ministry: ***kerygma***, proclaiming the word of

▸ "Three Women of America," by Elizabeth Catlett, Hampton University Museum

Jesus' resurrection; ***didache***, the activity of teaching; ***leiturgia***, coming together to pray and to represent Jesus in the breaking of bread; ***koinonia***, or community; and ***diakonia***, caring for those in need."[3] If we are to engage in biblical Jubilee, those five elements need to be present in the life of the church and the community.

Finally, attaining Jubilee may be a painfully slow journey. However, as the Church makes its way on such a Jubilee pilgrimage, it will move every wall of religious separation and undertake this journey, beseeching and welcoming brothers and sisters of all faith communities to join in. The Church will share the message of salvation as it seeks the kingdom in the midst of a world filled with chaos and pain. As we journey together, we will make discovery after joyful discovery, many of which are beyond our imagination.

▸ **Detail "400 Years of Our People," by Michael Escoffery. Mixed media 1994-1995. Art Resource, NY.**

To understand our history as African Americans, as the people of America, we must understand our continuing need, if less than constant commitment, "to define and refine our common understanding of the very idea and fact of liberty."[4] It is this commitment to liberty that the Jubilee Bible invites and requires all of us to proclaim.

As a Church, as a nation, as a people, the whole polity, the whole family, the whole of humanity, we will remember to the profit of ourselves and our common future, that Jubilee is a universal mandate for a civil world and a civil society. No Jubilee, no justice. No justice, no Jubilee. No Jubilee, no civility. Despite neglect, disdain, and irreverence, earth shall have a Jubilee. Jubilee will not be denied. And, with our whole-hearted participation, it will be a Jubilee of justice, peace, security, and the kingdom of character. But there will also be judgment. Is not judgment already upon America and the world? Witness the conflicts and hatreds we once thought obsolete; the rash of violence now rampant and destructive, on a scale unmatched at home and abroad.

As we explore its practices we will discover that Jubilee *is* the guarantor of the Good Society, with its provisions for self-adjudication of every kind of injustice and hostility that builds up in individuals, families, and societies. Skeptics say that Jubilee cannot work. But, it can also be said that whether or not Jubilee can work, we will not know, until we have put its principles into practice.

As a People of Promise, *coming* into a Land of Promise, *having* in our hand the Book of Promise, we can do no better than study God's Word and pray earnestly that God who gives us the courage to keep faith in his promises, will show us the way to a bright, new Jubilee future.

Sources Cited

1. Joseph Donders, *Non-Bourgeois Theology, An African Experience of Jesus,* (Maryknoll, NY: Orbis Books, 1985), 75-79.

2. *Smith's Comprehensive Dictionary of the Bible,* Samuel Barnum, 1893.

3. Maria Harris, *Fashion Me A People,* (Louisville, KY: Westminster John Knox Press, 1989), 16, 17.

4. James McGregor Burns and Stewart Burns, *A People's Charter: The Pursuit of Rights in America*, (New York: Alfred A. Knopf), 1991.

The African American Experience

From Experience to Biblical Image

◄ "I'm Harriet Tubman. I Helped Hundreds to Freedom," linocut, 1975 © Elizabeth Catlett/Licensed by VAGA, New York, NY.

African Americans have known slavery. They have known it as brutally as the suffering Israelites in Pharaoh's Egypt. To speak of the African American experience is to speak of the experience of slavery. This horrific experience dates back to 1619 when Africans arrived in Jamestown, Virginia, and were thereafter forced into slavery. Their European captors were "Bible Christians" and, as noted by New Testament scholar, Vincent L. Wimbush, the Africans were quick to notice the influence the Bible had on the "self-image, culture, and orientation" of these slave owners. Slaves heard their captors refer to the Bible as "Holy Scripture" or "Holy Book," and they soon began to associate the Bible with power.[1] According to Wimbush, African slaves sought to engage "the Book" and thus demonstrated their "ability to adapt themselves to different understandings of reality."[2] Inasmuch as slaves were forbidden to read, they were denied access to "the Book;" hence, the biblical narratives they heard were filtered through the lens of their experience in bondage. The Bible came to represent a body of literature that contained stories of enslavement and liberation.

The events recorded in the book of Exodus concerning the escape of the Israelites from bondage in Egypt would have resonated with the African slaves. They would have identified with the struggles of the Hebrews and come to know God as one who heard their cries and who would deliver them from bondage. Clarice Martin, a New Testament scholar, points out that this particular biblical narrative (most notably, Exodus 14) "has functioned as a vivid and explicit symbol that confirms that God is a God who liberates, who secures justice for the people of God."[3]

Another New Testament scholar, Brian K. Blount, observes that, for the slaves, the critical starting point in any engagement with the Bible was their historical circumstance. According to Blount, "the interpretative move is from experience to biblical image, not the other way around... They begin with the horrors of their experience and then interpret those horrors through their understandings of biblical images. Their key intent is not so much to understand the Bible as it is to understand their historical circumstance."[4] The Exodus event, as noted above, is an example of this movement from experience to biblical image. As slaves became increasingly familiar with the Bible, they interpreted their experiences as parallel to the sufferings of the Israelites while they were in bondage in Egypt. Inasmuch as the slaves were illiterate, they had, as Blount points out, "but one interpretative lens through which they instinctively analyzed the Bible: their own historical experience," which led them into an interpersonal engagement with the biblical text and fostered their own spiritual formation.[5]

This interpersonal engagement, or interpretation of the Scriptures, was often done through song. Images drawn from the Bible were wedded to music, and the songs represented a voice against institutionalized slavery. The words from the following spirituals demonstrate interpretations of Scripture in light of the experience of African Americans as slaves and illustrate a "process of the transformation of the Book Religion of the dominant peoples into the religion reflective of the socio-political and economic status of African slaves:"[6]

Go down, Moses
'Way down in Egypt land,
Tell ole Pharaoh,
Let my people go.

◆ ◆ ◆

Dey crucified my Lord,
An' He never said a mumblin' word.
Dey crucified my Lord,
An' He never said a mumblin' word,
Not a word – not a word – not a word.

Katie Cannon in her book, "Womanism and the Soul of the Black Community," notes that the slaves, as spiritual singers, "were not bothered by the chronological distance between the biblical era and their present." They operated on "a sense of sacred time" and experienced "an immediate intimacy with biblical persons as faith relatives." People and events from the past world of the Bible came alive in the midst of their present circumstances.[7] And stories such as the Israelites' freedom from Egyptian bondage (Exodus 14) and Daniel being protected while in a lions' den (Daniel 6) represented stories of deliverance and hope.

▸ **"Death on the Cross," Society of African Missions, Tenafly, NJ.**

African Americans thus "saw themselves as *hermeneutically* free"[8]—that is, they were free to engage, interpret, and refashion Scripture in light of their experience. And since their engagement with the biblical texts was primarily based on oral transmissions, "a strict literalism did not characterize their engagement of the Bible."[9] As noted by Renita Weems, an Old Testament scholar, the illiteracy of the slaves liberated them from any "allegiance to any official text, translation, or interpretation; hence once they heard biblical passages read and interpreted to them, they in turn were free to remember and repeat in accordance with their own interests and tastes."[10] Thus, the slave experience became the interpretative lens or *hermeneutic* for engaging the biblical texts, and listening and remembering were the key *hermeneutical* tools.

Wimbush further points out that, during the eighteenth century revival movements in the North and the South, "Africans began to convert to Christianity in significant numbers," and they took "note of the diversity of views that reading the Bible could inspire" and "learned that they, too, could read 'the Book' freely" – reading certain parts and ignoring others.[11] Nowhere is this more vividly evidenced than in the account of Howard Thurman's story of his grandmother's listening habits and how in the early 1900s she would not let her grandson read from any of the Pauline letters (with the exception of 1 Corinthians 13) inasmuch as, when she was a slave, she often heard her master's white minister preach from the text: "Servants, be obedient to them that are your masters according to the flesh, with fear and trembling, in singleness of your heart, as unto Christ" (Ephesians 6.5, *KJV*). Because the minister had interpreted this passage to mean that the existence of slavery was God's will, the grandmother vowed that if ever she learned to read and became free she "would not read that part of the Bible."[12]

The ways in which African Americans have appropriated Scripture interpretation in light of their experiences illustrates what Wimbush has termed "a culture-specific reading of the Bible" which has shifted "the focus of interpretation away from objective text toward 'world' or culture" and has laid the foundation for continued African American and other culturalist readings of the Bible.[13]

The Word of God in African American Culture

The textual theme for this Jubilee Edition of the Bible is grounded in Scripture: Leviticus 25.8-12; Isaiah 61.1-4; and Luke 4.16-21.

(For a further examination of these textual themes, see the following articles in Section Two: "Jubilee in Leviticus 17-26," by Jerome C. Ross, and "The Message of Salvation," by Thomas L. Hoyt, Jr.) The Jubilee theme is rich in historic interpretation and offers a message of hope for all humankind to live as the family of God, as evidenced by the vision recorded in the Letter to the Ephesians 2.19b, "You are now citizens together with God's people and members of the family of God."

In addition to allowing the land to lie fallow, mortgage debts to be remitted, and slaves to be freed, as prescribed by Jewish law, the Year of Jubilee is described theologically to mean that all life and land belongs to God. The term "jubilee" has been used in Catholicism since 1300 in connection with the Holy Year, a time in which the Pope granted special spiritual benefits (indulgences) for those who made a pilgrimage to Rome and performed other religious acts.[14]

This jubilee, although appropriate for that time, was clearly not what the mandates in Leviticus intended. Pope John Paul II, in his 1994 Apostolic Letter, "The Coming of the Third Millennium," says, "The jubilee celebration should confirm the Christians of today in their *faith* in God, who has revealed himself in Christ, sustain their *hope*, which reaches out in expectations of eternal life, and rekindle their *charity,* in active service to their brothers and sisters."[15]

Further, Pope John Paul II mentions that "the joy of every Jubilee is above all a joy based upon the forgiveness of sins... which is the pre-condition for reconciliation with God on the part of both individuals and communities."[16]

In uplifting the Jubilee, "the year of God's favor" or the *tikkun olam*: (year of restoration of the world) as it was referred to in Jewish folklore,[17] the African American Jubilee Edition of the Bible helps readers connect their histories, cultural images, moral visions, and perspectives to the ancient Scriptures in such a way that the Word of God becomes authentic, relevant, and intimate. Readers are thus invited to examine and study the Bible through the lens of African American historic and culturally relevant understandings of the Scriptures.

In studying the Scriptures and exploring their connections to one's social reality, the reader is encouraged to examine the biblical text from four perspectives: **Place, People, Culture,** and **Story.**

1. Where does the event take **place**? Study the ancient lands and geography.

2. Who were the **people**? From where did they migrate and at what period in history?

3. What was the **culture**; e.g., habits, traits, language, occupations, survival skills, faith systems, judicial systems, and power relationships?

4. What was their "**story**?" The Bible is lived history—human stories, both oral and written—of pilgrimages, faith jouneys, struggles, triumphs, temptations, testings, stories of achievments and failures, of relationships, coping strategies, and spiritual encounters, to name a few.

New Testament scholar Brad Ronnell Braxton has drawn upon Jesus' parable of the Good Samaritan (Luke 10.25-37) as an example for examining a biblical text within the context of today's social reality. He points out the following:

> Historically, the ill will between blacks and whites in America has always been a useful point of connection, because social tension is at the heart of this text. African American preachers have drawn strong parallels between Samaritans and their own community. Both groups were considered racially inferior by the ruling culture. Both groups were objects of bitter feelings.
>
> In spite of his social status, the Samaritan in the text acted in a commendable manner. Many African American preachers have lifted up the Samaritan as an example for behavior. This example applies not only to some far-off time and setting. It applies now—to the real world of racism, second-class citizenship, police brutality, and economic exploitation.
>
> For African Americans this parable has been a weapon in the warfare for human rights and equality. It has served as a clarion call to act in an ethically responsible way, even if the wounded victim on the road is not part of one's social group. Even more, if the person is the oppressor.
>
> In the face of oppression, African Americans have found great solace in Jesus' story. Here was a man from society's margins who stopped on a dangerous road. He helped a traveler who appeared to be the other, but in reality was the brother.[18]

Read the parable of the Good Samaritan. Examine the story in light of the four perspectives outlined above. How does your interpretation of the story compare with Braxton's? What were your interpretative lenses? What insights did you gain? What connections do you see between this parable and the six provisions of the Jubilee set forth by Jesus in Luke 4?

Jesus introduced the final jubilee, the *tikkun olam*, the repair of the world. Through our baptism and eucharist, we are incorporated in him and the challenge is passed on to us!"[19]

By reading the stories and events in the Bible, discover ways in which they connect to your experiences. For a guide to interpreting the Scriptures, see the article in Section Two: "Interpretation of Scripture," by Murray L. Newman. And, for a more in-depth examination of the presence of Africans in the Bible, see also in Section Two: "The Presence and Role of Africans in the Bible," by Prince V. Ntintili, and "The Presence of Blacks in Biblical Antiquity," by Cain Hope Felder.

An exciting Jubilee journey awaits you! Discover the transforming power of God's Word and the insights God has in store for you as you engage the world of the Bible through the lens of your own unique experience.

Continue to grow in the grace and knowledge of our Lord and Savior Jesus Christ. To him be the glory, now and forever! Amen.
(2 Peter 3.18)

Africa

A discussion on the Jubilee concept would not be complete without the inclusion of Africa, the place where the history of African Americans began.

Africa was the seat of civilization, a continent of vast empires. Among its peoples were great prophets, teachers and leaders who had distinguished themselves through their visionary acuity, knowledge, and prowess.

Around the first century A.D., the great mountainous kingdom of Ethiopia arose. Its people were an indigenous group of blacks who were highly intellectual. Ethiopia was governed by kings who sought to trade with Egypt, Arabia, Greece, and other countries whose ports lay along the Indian Ocean. By the second century, this civilization was well established as a center of world trade and a written form of its language, Ge'ez, evolved. By the beginning of the fourth century, Ethiopia had become a Christian nation through the conversion of its king, Ezana. Ethiopia, then, is not only one of the oldest black Christian traditions, but it provides us with important information on the history of the biblical text through the Ethiopian biblical manuscripts which were written in Ge'ez. (See Section Two: "The Relationship Between Hebrew and African Languages," by Edwina M. Wright.)

Like Ethiopia, other mighty empires maintained their prominence by aggressively trading with faraway cities and expanding their territory through conquest of other lands. Thus, through commerce and wars, the people of Africa began a migratory pattern that took them away from their original regions. Such migration eventually spawned powerful kingdoms especially in West Africa. Ghana, Mali, Songhay, and the Mossi States are among the most notable.

Ghana dates back to the seventh century B.C. Long before A.D. 1000, it was a major, well-organized empire, which had intricate systems of democracy. Its riches came from an abundance of gold, a lively slave trade, and a tax system not unlike our own. Mining, farming, and artistry made the region thrive, but later internal

▸ **"Two Kings Shake Hands," Society of African Missions, Tenafly, NJ.**

strife, invasions from rival neighboring states, and severe climatic changes caused Ghana to fall in the thirteenth century.

With the collapse of Ghana came Mali, a more powerful state whose famous capital, Timbuktu, and equally famous city, Djenne, were highly regarded as Islamic centers of culture and education as well as trade and commerce. Mali's most famous emperor, Mansa Musa (who ruled 1312-1337), is remembered for making a pilgrimage to Mecca through Cairo dressed in full regalia, with a large entourage of slaves, elephants and camels who were ornately groomed, and several trunks filled with gold. Musa gave lavish presents of gold as he traveled, and it is believed that he caused the price of Egypt's gold to fall because of his actions. Although Musa was skilled in military tactics, he is also credited for boosting commerce and "proselytizing Islam more than any one of his predecessors."[20]

Despite Mali's military and commercial successes, it was eventually eclipsed by the Songhay empire. Like Mali, the Songhay empire profited greatly from shrewd trading. Its people, who were primarily traders, also flourished as farmers, fishermen, shepherds, and craftsmen. Their military skills kept them safe from attack but widespread rebellion, coupled with an invasion of Timbuktu by the Moroccans in 1591, caused the empire to collapse.

The Mossi States (later known as Upper Volta, and today as Burkino Faso) succeeded Songhay. It became the most powerful and most industrial state in the region. It survived as an African state for over 500 years and was the last of the great black West African states. When it was subjugated by the French in 1896, it opened the way to European dominance in West Africa, which was by then a major source for the Atlantic slave trade.

Diaspora

The word *diaspora* is defined as the scattering of people with a common origin, background, and belief. It has been used traditionally to describe the experience of the Jews who were dispersed from Judah in the sixth century and exiled in Babylonia (587- 483 B.C.). Diaspora is now also used to define the forcible dispersal of peoples of African descent beyond the boundaries of the continent of Africa. Unlike the Jews in captivity, the millions of uprooted and enslaved Africans were heterogeneous peoples from a wide range of tribal groups and cultures who spoke different languages.

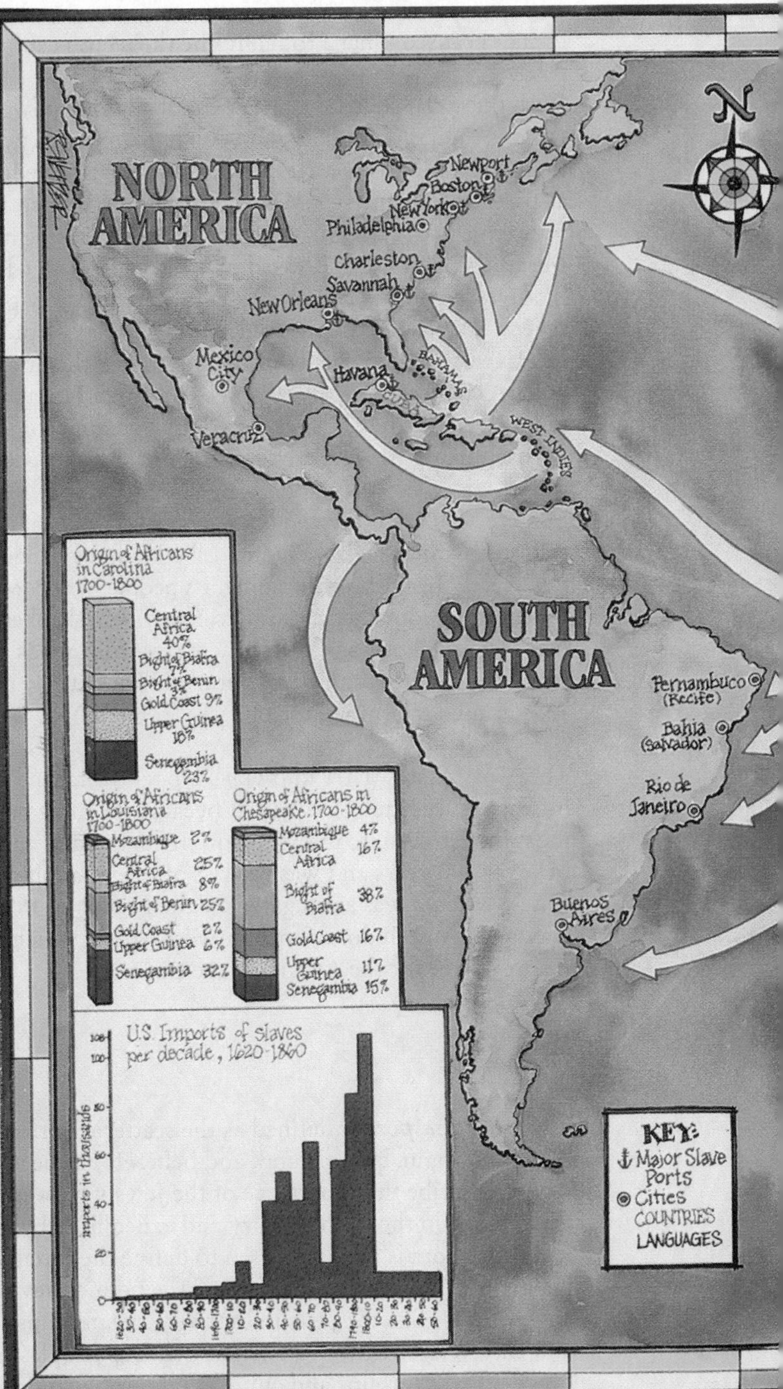
NORTH AMERICA
SOUTH AMERICA
N
Newport
Boston
New York
Philadelphia
Charleston
Savannah
New Orleans
Mexico City
Havana
Veracruz
BAHAMAS
CUBA
WEST INDIES
Pernambuco (Recife)
Bahia (Salvador)
Rio de Janeiro
Buenos Aires
Origin of Africans in Carolina 1700-1800
Central Africa 40%
Bight of Biafra 7%
Bight of Benin 3%
Gold Coast 9%
Upper Guinea 18%
Senegambia 23%
Origin of Africans in Louisiana 1700-1800
Mozambique 2%
Central Africa 25%
Bight of Biafra 8%
Bight of Benin 25%
Gold Coast 2%
Upper Guinea 6%
Senegambia 32%
Origin of Africans in Chesapeake, 1700-1800
Mozambique 4%
Central Africa 16%
Bight of Biafra 38%
Gold Coast 16%
Upper Guinea 11%
Senegambia 15%
U.S. Imports of slaves per decade, 1620-1860
imports in thousands
KEY:
Major Slave Ports
Cities
COUNTRIES
LANGUAGES

▸ "Diaspora Map," showing westward migration, by R. Sweitzer

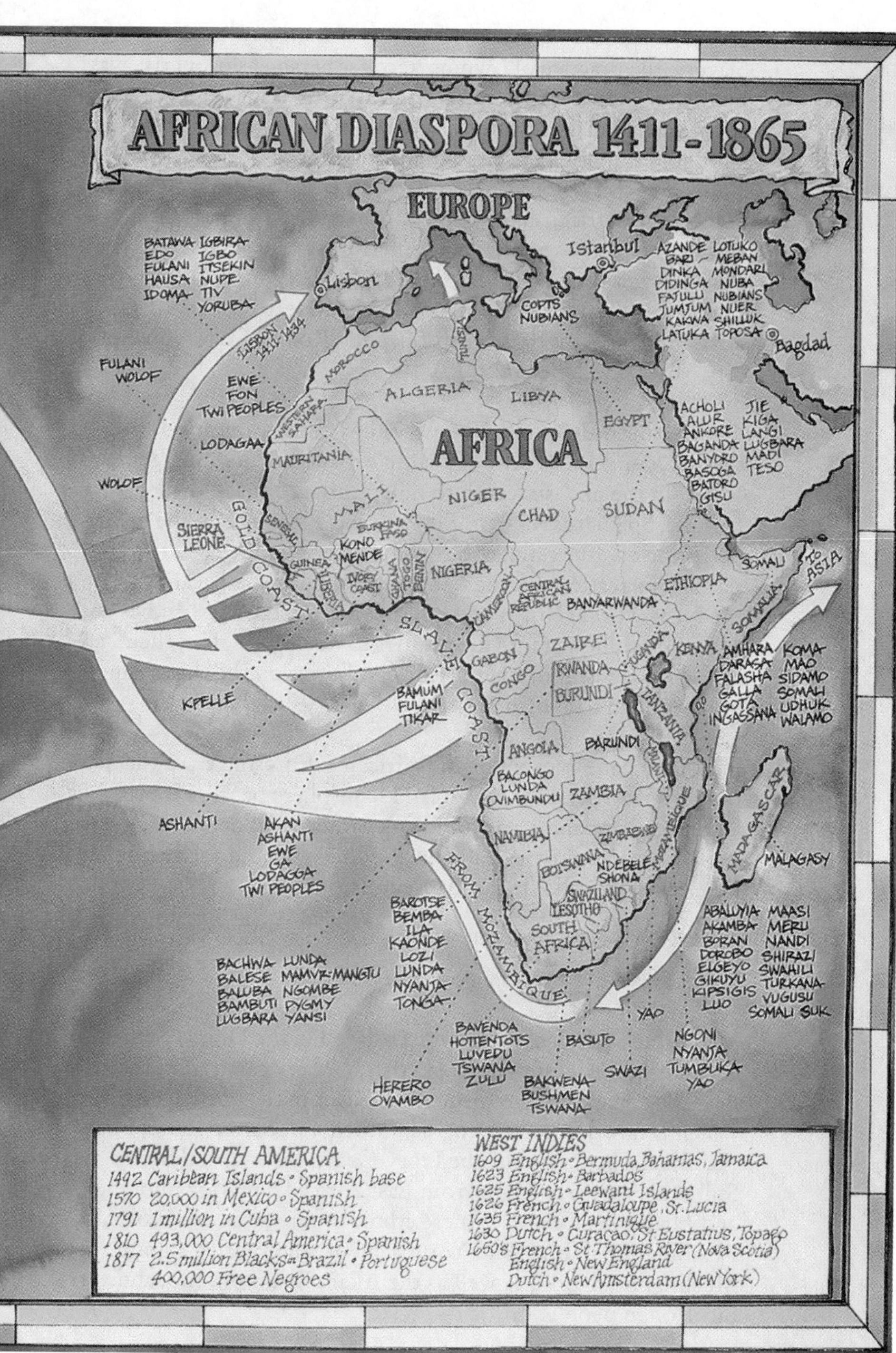
AFRICAN DIASPORA 1411-1865
EUROPE
Lisbon
Istanbul
Bagdad
AFRICA
BATAWA IGBIRA
EDO IGBO
FULANI ITSEKIN
HAUSA NUPE
IDOMA TIV
YORUBA
LISBON 1411-1434
FULANI
WOLOF
EWE
FON
TWI PEOPLES
LODAGAA
WOLOF
SIERRA LEONE
GOLD COAST
SLAVE COAST
KPELLE
BAMUM
FULANI
TIKAR
ASHANTI
AKAN
ASHANTI
EWE
GA
LODAGGA
TWI PEOPLES
AZANDE LOTUKO
BARI MEBAN
DINKA MONDARI
DIDINGA NUBA
FAJULU NUBIANS
JUMJUM NUER
KAKWA SHILLUK
LATUKA TOPOSA
COPTS
NUBIANS
MOROCCO
ALGERIA
LIBYA
EGYPT
TUNISIA
WESTERN SAHARA
MAURITANIA
MALI
NIGER
CHAD
SUDAN
SENEGAL
BURKINA FASO
KONO
MENDE
GUINEA
LIBERIA
IVORY COAST
GHANA
TOGO
BENIN
NIGERIA
CAMEROON
CENTRAL AFRICAN REPUBLIC
BANYARWANDA
ETHIOPIA
SOMALI
SOMALIA
TO ASIA
ACHOLI JIE
ALUR KIGA
ANKORE LANGI
BAGANDA LUGBARA
BANYORO MADI
BASOGA TESO
BATORO
GISU
GABON
CONGO
ZAIRE
RWANDA
BURUNDI
UGANDA
KENYA
TANZANIA
AMHARA KOMA
DARASA MAO
FALASHA SIDAMO
GALLA SOMALI
GOTA UDHUK
INGASSANA WALAMO
ANGOLA
BARUNDI
BACONGO
LUNDA
OVIMBUNDU
ZAMBIA
MALAWI
MOZAMBIQUE
MADAGASCAR
MALAGASY
NAMIBIA
ZIMBABWE
BOTSWANA
NDEBELE
SHONA
SWAZILAND
LESOTHO
SOUTH AFRICA
FROM MOZAMBIQUE
BAROTSE
BEMBA
ILA
KAONDE
LOZI
LUNDA
NYANJA
TONGA
BACHWA LUNDA
BALESE MAMVU-MANGTU
BALUBA NGOMBE
BAMBUTI PYGMY
LUGBARA YANSI
ABALUYIA MAASI
AKAMBA MERU
BORAN NANDI
DOROBO SHIRAZI
ELGEYO SWAHILI
GIKUYU TURKANA
KIPSIGIS VUGUSU
LUO SOMALI SUK
YAO
BAVENDA
HOTTENTOTS
LUVEDU
TSWANA
ZULU
BASUTO
NGONI
NYANJA
TUMBUKA
YAO
SWAZI
HERERO
OVAMBO
BAKWENA
BUSHMEN
TSWANA
CENTRAL/SOUTH AMERICA
1492 Caribbean Islands • Spanish base
1570 20,000 in Mexico • Spanish
1791 1 million in Cuba • Spanish
1810 493,000 Central America • Spanish
1817 2.5 million Blacks in Brazil • Portuguese
400,000 Free Negroes
WEST INDIES
1609 English • Bermuda, Bahamas, Jamaica
1623 English • Barbados
1625 English • Leewand Islands
1626 French • Guadaloupe, St. Lucia
1635 French • Martinique
1630 Dutch • Curacao, St Eustatius, Topago
1650's French • St Thomas River (Nova Scotia)
English • New England
Dutch • New Amsterdam (New York)

Slavery, the practice of owning another person as property, was not a new idea. The forcible dispersal of Africans can be traced as far back as classical antiquity when small numbers of Africans were sold into slavery in the Mediterranean region. Others were shipped to western India, southern Iraq, and as far away as China. The African slave trade, however, was not based on race and did not carry the stigma of inferiority. In fact, many of the enslaved were educated and skilled people. (For further study, see Section Two: "Slavery in the Ancient Near East and, Particularly, in Israel," by Frank Gipson, and "Roman Slavery in Antiquity," by Mitzi Jane Smith.)

The colonization of the New World by the Europeans during the 1500s and 1600s only served to expand the booming slave trade. In the mid-sixteenth to nineteenth centuries, the Portuguese, Spaniards, Dutch, English, and French were the main perpetrators. It is estimated that during these three centuries slave ships scattered some ten to twelve million Africans across the New World (North and South America, the West Indies and Mexico). Millions more died in Africa during, or after, their capture, or as a result of the horrific conditions on the ships transporting them to North America.

It is significant to examine the African culture and trace the diaspora from Africa to the Western Hemisphere because it provides a fuller understanding as to the importance and necessity of Jubilee. It also provides a historical link and cultural identity to the people we call African Americans.

From Africa to the United States

Most of the Africans who were enslaved in the United States came from the western part of Africa. Many came from the area near the seacoast, from the Senegal River in the north to the area which is now known as Angola. Others came from Zaire, Nigeria, Ghana, Senegambia, the Ivory Coast, Liberia, and Sudan. Still others were brought from East Africa from Mozambique and Madagascar. Among these ethnic groups were the Wolof, Mandingo, Bambara, and Yoruba, all of whom had a significant Muslim population, as well as the Akan, Kru, Fon, Ibo, and various Kongo people.

▸ "Poor Man's Cotton," by Hale Aspacio Woodruff, 1944 The Newark Museum/Art Resource, NY.

African slaves first arrived in the British North American colonies in 1619 in Virginia. Slavery spread to Maryland, the Carolinas, and later Georgia where Africans cultivated tobacco, rice, and indigo. South Carolina depended upon black labor to such an extent that by 1720 more Africans inhabited the colony than Europeans. This demographic reality caused one observer in 1737 to note that South Carolina "looks more like a Negro country than like a country settled by white people."[21] Although large scale agriculture required major importations of African slaves, farm and urban necessities in northern colonies also put Africans into bondage in New England and in the Middle Atlantic. The rhetoric of liberty during the Revolutionary War period, however, compelled the authors of the Declaration of Independence to proclaim slavery as incompatible with democratic ideas. As a result, slaves were increasingly manumitted in the North and in some parts of the Upper South, particularly in Virginia and Maryland. Nonetheless, the Constitution which established the United States in 1789 recognized black slaves as three-fifths of a person and permitted the slave trade to continue until 1808. The invention of the cotton gin in 1793 revived slavery in the South and inaugurated its spread elsewhere in the region and beyond.

From the beginning, African slaves worked without pay in grueling conditions. Freedom of movement, family disruption, ties to tribes, language, religion, and culture all yielded to the necessities of American slavery. A congressional gag rule forbade the discussion of slavery in the U.S. Capitol while fugitive slave provisions in the Constitution and in a congressional enactment seemed to fix the servile status of blacks into an indefinite future. No state in the Union had been immune from the practice of involuntary servitude. It took a Civil War from 1861 through 1865 to free slaves from permanent bondage in the United States. (See Section Two: "The Alleged Curse on Ham," by Gene Rice.)

From Africa to the West Indies and South America

One scholar has estimated that 9,566,100 Africans survived the "Middle Passage" and were enslaved in the Western Hemisphere.

Estimated Slave Imports into the Americas by Importing Region (1451-1870)

British North America	339,000
Spanish America	1,552,100
British Caribbean	1,665,000
French Caribbean	1,600,200
Dutch Caribbean	500,000
Brazil	28,000
Old World	175,000
Total	**9,566,100** [22]

▸ "Gathering Fruit," by Emile Private Collection/ Beth Hinckley/ Superstock.

Africans went in the largest numbers into the Caribbean while Brazil was the primary single destination for this tragic traffic in human beings. Slaves were shipped first to South America or the West Indies where they would be trained or "seasoned" for work in the United States. By 1700, the major Caribbean islands, including Jamaica and Barbados, enslaved thousands of slaves.[23] Sugar plantations flourished and many absentee masters had their slaves worked to death.

In South America, the Spanish and Portuguese colonists who practiced slavery met little opposition from the Roman Catholic Church. Slaves were considered a labor system, a part of the monarch's property and the Church sought to maintain some semblance of human rights for the enslaved. Marriage among slaves, for example, was recognized. Such "humane" treatment did not prevent uprising by some slaves. But, in Brazil especially, there was considerable intermingling between slaves and masters until a significant mulatto population emerged. After emancipation, this group occupied a higher status than blacks in Brazilian society.[24]

Since 1619: A Faith Journey

The articles in Section Two of the Jubilee Bible examine the ugly beginnings of slavery in American society and weave a story of torturous exile to one that continuously unfolds in triumphant exodus under the guidance of Almighty God.

Dr. Samuel D. Proctor in *The Substance of Things Hoped For: The Faith Epic of African Americans* describes a pilgrimage of "a handful of slaves (20) who disembarked in Jamestown to 32 million African American citizens, from 244 years of physical bondage of slavery to positions of trust and responsibility in the highest levels of government, religion, education, business, industry, sports, arts/entertainment, medicine, and jurisprudence." Proctor sees this journey as one that is unparalleled; an epic of a unique people of faith who persevered, endured, and maintained their spirituality despite the harshness of their lives.

Faith-based Freedom

The African Americans' view of the sacred and divine is inextricably linked to their African heritage, their inherent values of freedom, justice, and racial equality, and their early experiences in the U.S. Although many blacks voluntarily embraced Christianity, some whites used selected biblical teachings of obedience and suffering to keep the slaves submissive. Despite this, blacks adopted the salvation story as their own and were quick to accept the freedom it offered. Consequently, their music, dance, prayer and secret gatherings reflected the theme of freedom. (See Section Two: "The Bible in African American Spirituality," by Michael I. N. Dash.) They strongly identified with the suffering of Jesus and held the hope that one day Jesus' message of Jubilee—his proclamation of freedom from oppression—would eventually be realized. This faith lies at the heart of the African American experience.

"Faith became their bridge," says Proctor. "Their depth of faith required the special preparation for living on tirelessly, living on unfulfilled hopes and desires, which have not been paralleled. This faith brought them through sheer pain and brutality of the lash, the chains, the whip, and the burden; this faith sustained them in the anguish of the separation from their parents, children and spouses... More particularly, this faith enabled them to envision that a day of freedom would come, and they could begin that long trek toward an education, and respectability, independence, security, leisure, and personal privacy, which was the most cruel denial of all."[25]

What African Americans needed was not just freedom from servitude, but the freedom to make their own choices, to attain their full potential, and to knock on the doors of justice and be let in.

African Culture

Kinship

Most of the indigenous peoples of Africa live in clusters or units commonly called tribes. In modern times, the word "tribe" is viewed as derogatory and it is often replaced by the term "people." Each people is seen to have their own language, occupy a specific geographical region, share a common culture, and hold similar religious beliefs.

The African family includes the extended family, "a more or less close-knit group of relatives comprising several pairs of grandparents or possibly great-grandparents and all their living descendants except those who had married out of the group into another comparable group."[26] Family also includes those who were yet to be born.

As an individual, each person is a valued member of the group. The individual exists because of the community and people of present and past generations. This interdependence creates a strong bond within the community.

Religion

Long before Christianity arrived in the Scandinavian countries, at least a century before St. Patrick evangelized Ireland, and over two centuries before St. Augustine would arrive in Canterbury, and almost seven centuries before the conversion of the Poles and the establishment of the kingdom of Poland, the mountainous black kingdom (Ethiopia) was a Catholic nation with its own liturgy, its own spectacular religious art, its own monastic tradition, its saints, and its own spirituality. [27]

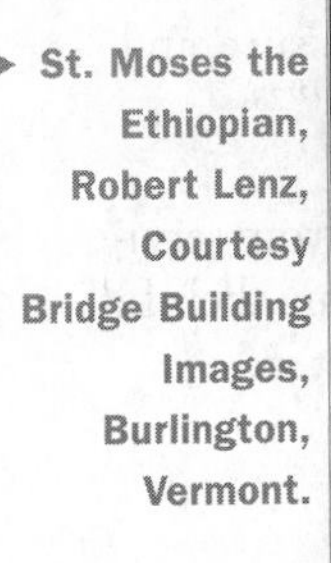

▸ St. Moses the Ethiopian, Robert Lenz, Courtesy Bridge Building Images, Burlington, Vermont.

Of the early saints of the Catholic church, St. Moses the Ethiopian (or Moses the Black) and St. Augustine, Bishop of Hippo, are among those described as being black African. Augustine, whose first language was Latin, was born in 354 near Carthage. Although not baptized in the Catholic faith in his youth, Augustine was converted when he was 32. Having been a highly intellectual student of rhetoric, he became an eloquent defender of the Christian faith and a brilliant theologian.

It is believed that three of the popes in the early church were Africans. St. Victor (ca. 186-ca. 197), St. Miltiades (311-14), and St. Gelasius I (492-96). Of the three, Pope Gelasius I is probably

▸ Pope Gelasius, Granger Collection, New York

best remembered for establishing the primacy of the Holy See. He ruled that the pontiff was outside the jurisdiction of the ruling emperor and therefore could not be judged by him. He also advocated that it was the right of the Pope, not the state, to oversee all areas of the church.

▸ St. Augustine, Pinacoteca Civica Castello Sforzesco, Milan, Italy, Mauro Magliani, SuperStock.

Most scholars agree that, while African American Christianity developed orthodox adherence either to Catholicism or Protestantism, preserved remnants drew from the African religious heritage. Some slaves in spiritual ecstasy engaged in ring shouts. Others decorated the graves of departed family members with items that would be useful to the deceased in the afterlife. However, "it is in Catholicism that the transplanted Africans found a home 'of sorts' that nurtured their traditional religiosity. The saints and sacramentals, feast days and fast days, processions and rituals were strikingly familiar to a people comfortable with the concept of a high God of intercessions and special rites and rituals in their life of worship."[28] Blacks integrated these and other practices with their Christian beliefs and developed the cultural richness that characterizes African American Christianity.

▸ **African Woman Praying, Society of African Missions, Tenafly, NJ**

Worship

"Africans in their act of worship live close to the land. Prayers to God relate directly to rain, fertility, and the welfare of humans, cattle and fields. Since animals and plants constitute food for humans, it is not surprising that Africans have many religious ceremonies associated with them. Their act of worship is aided by sacrifices, offerings, prayers, and invocations. God is the one who makes the sun rise and set, the rain fall, the mountains quake, and the rivers overflow. He heals the sick, helps the barren, and aids those in distress."[29]

Black Catholics have harkened to the voices of their ancestors and have brought their unique gifts of song, dance, and praise to the worship experience. They no longer ask, "How can we sing a song to the Lord in a foreign land?" (Psalm 137.4) but rather, they have claimed this land, America, as their own. They have sought acceptance and inclusivity within the broader Roman Catholic Church and have claimed the right to define themselves as "truly black and authentically Catholic" as an expression of their heritage as "people of African roots yet with American branches."[30]

They have begun to heed the words of Pope Paul VI who told the people of Africa and those of African descent, "You must now give your gifts of Blackness to the whole church."[31] Pope John Paul II also concurred with this statement in a meeting with black Catholics in 1987.

Music

Music played an integral role in the life of the African people. Oral history and traditions were recited and sung by traveling troubadours who would often perform in a public place. Laws, customs, national and family history, and even news were often handed down in this way by these professional ***griots*** or storytellers. Such singing invited rhythmic action. Singers would snap their fingers while onlookers would pat their feet, clap their hands, and move their bodies rhythmically to the beat. In most cases, dancing accompanied the singing. Africans are known to dance for all occasions: in happy or sad times, and simply to pass the time. These cultural practices are clearly a large part of the heritage of the African American people and have been incorporated into their religious experience. (See Section Two: "Music in the Black Church," by William H. Collins, Jr.)

Black Catholic liturgical practitioners and musicians found the music within their churches "bland" and "began to experiment

▸ **"Choir Procession," by Robert Steele, 1998. Copyright 1998 Frederick Douglass Designs. Used by Permission.**

with music, readings, symbols and gestures which more properly reflected the genius and spirit of African Americans and which would nurture their understanding of the challenge of the gospel."[32]

As a result, the liturgical music of black Catholics today proudly reflects the heritage and culture of its people. It is an indigenous music which is holistic, highly symbolic and celebratory. Contemporary black Catholic composers such as Leon Roberts (see hymn "Remember Me" in Chapter 15), Rawn Harbor, Clarence J. Rivers, Grayson Brown, and Eddie Bonnemere have taken the lead in composing sacred music that unifies the church at worship and engages the worshippers in a unique spiritual experience.

▸ **Our Lady of Victory Church, Brooklyn, NY. Photo: Michael Scott Studio, NY.**

The Black Church

"O, freedom over me.
And before I'd be a slave
I'll be buried in my grave
An' go home to my Lord
An' be free."

Negro Spiritual

If Jubilee is to be established, it must first start with the church. The church has been the bedrock of faith, a balm of healing for the hurting and weary, and a strong voice on behalf of the oppressed. The black church is not a single institution, but it can be identified as a distinctive community whose faith is rooted and grounded in an interpretation viewed through the lens of a people victimized by almost three centuries of slavery. The black church has sought to acquire justice and rights which have been enjoyed, primarily, by the dominant culture of this country.

At its inception, the black church has been the most important and dominant institutional reality in African American communities. The black church carries burdens, and performs roles and functions beyond the boundaries of spiritual nurturing, in politics, economics, education, music, and culture. It has been involved in missions that embrace domestic activities such as family, education, urban ministries, and the institutional church, to name a few.

Leadership and Politics

The black church is not just a building for the "gathering of the saints." It is a community whose influence is reflected in politics, civil rights, militancy, outreach programs and economic independence contributions. The fundamental values of survival and liberation are deeply embedded in the primary biblical doctrine of the "belief systems" of the black faith community, and involvement is motivated by convictions.

Historically, the black church was primarily the natural training ground for the development of leadership skills. This was seen especially in the areas of politics and community development.

This accounts for many of the famous historical figures who were involved in slave revolts, abolitionism, electoral politics and civil rights protests. These figures have been either clergy, or closely identified with black churches, and history reflects their accomplishments in the black community. Clergy leadership of the black church tends to be strong and decisive, though it is increasingly being shared with mission-driven laypersons who are being led into multiple ministries and are becoming more vocal in decision-making. Likewise, African American leaders from predominately white churches played significant roles. For example, Dr. Elder G. Hawkins, and many others like him, was a staunch supporter of the Civil Rights Movement. Dr. Gayraud S. Wilmore, a theologian and author, did much to advance black theology.

Preaching in the Black Church

The black preacher is integral to the nurture of the spiritual life of the black church. The preacher is often pastor, community leader, prophet, civil rights advocate, and the chief administrator of the black community's most independent enterprise, the black church. The preacher played a significant part in the social and religious development of "Negro" life. First, preaching was an outlet for leadership ability. It was the one position of leadership permitted Negroes, and the office carried prestige. The black preacher was able to communicate religion in a useful and intimate form to those enslaved. As one of the people suffering with them, the minister made religion not only a discipline but also a living ground of hope. The preacher could appeal to the people,

▸ "The Good Shepherd." 1978, Nigeria, unknown artist, Society of African Missions, Tenafly, NJ.

many of whom had lived in agrarian communities, by having them relate to Jesus as the "good shepherd" (John 10.11) who would "save" them and give them "life in all its fullness" (v. 9, 10).

This preacher was the first "shepherd" to the people of diverse languages and customs who were brought from diverse parts of Africa and thrown into slavery. Though the black church gave them their first sense of unity and solidarity, it was the "ole time" preacher who for generations was the mainspring of hope and inspiration for blacks in America. (For further study, see Section Two: "Black Preaching in the Church," by Elliott Cuff.)

The following excerpt of a sermon/poem by James Weldon Johnson pays tribute to all African American preachers who inspire their congregations with the excitement, the dramatic cadences, and the illuminating Word of God.

Go Down Death–A Funeral Sermon

Weep not, weep not,
She is not dead;
She's resting in the bosom of Jesus.
Heart-broken husband–weep no more;
Grief-stricken son–weep no more;
Left-lonesome daughter–weep no more
She's only just gone home.

Day before yesterday morning,
God was looking down from his great, high heaven,
Looking down on all his children,
And his eye fell on Sister Caroline,
Tossing on her bed of pain,
And God's big heart was touched with pity,
With the everlasting pity.

And God sat back on his throne,
And he commandeth that tall, bright angel standing at his right hand:
Call me Death!
And that tall, bright angel cried in a voice
That broke like a clap of thunder:
Call Death–Call Death!
And the echo sounded down the streets of heaven
Till it reached away back to that shadowy place.

▸ "Go Down Death," Aaron Douglas, 1934. Collection of Professor and Mrs. David C. Driskell

And death didn't say a word,
But he loosed the reins on his pale, white horse,
And he clamped the spurs on his bloodless sides,
And out and down he rode,
Through heaven's pearly gates,
Past suns and moons and stars;
On Death rode,
And the foam from his horse was like a comet in the sky;

While we were watching round her bed,
She turned her eyes and looked away,
She saw what we couldn't see;
She saw Old Death. She saw Old Death
Coming like a fallen star.
But death didn't frighten Sister Caroline;
He looked to her like a welcome friend.
And she whispered to us: I'm going home,
And she smiled and closed her eyes.

Weep not, weep not,
She is not dead;
She is resting in the bosom of Jesus.[33]

(See Section Two: "Homegoing," by Diane M. Ritzie.)

The Black Church and Education

Since the institution of slavery, the question of black education has been an important issue in the United States. Early slaveholders believed that if slaves received an education, it might inspire them to revolt, ultimately resulting in the destruction of the institution of slavery. If this had happened, the celebration of slavery's end would have been Jubilee! Rather than cause for celebration, the Reconstruction period proved to be an unplanned system that had no significant benefit for the slave, resulting in individuals who had not been prepared, socially or economically, to succeed in America.

No other area of black life received a higher priority from black churches than education. (See Section Two: "Ethiopia Shall Stretch Forth Her Arms: The Evangelization and Education of Black Catholics," by Diana L. Hayes.) Despite the fact that teaching a slave to read and write was illegal during slavery, one of the most persistent desires of the slaves was to be educated. Blacks knew instinctively that literacy would provide untold opportunities and it would give them access to reading the Bible for themselves.

▸ **"Scipio and Grandson," (murdered for teaching his grandson to read the Bible). Art by Kimanne Smith**

The Black Church and the Black Family

The church is the one institution in the community where its congregants can find a focal place to express their God-given gifts, receive recognition, develop raw talents, and cultivate inner strength for self-determination and worth. The church enables the family to find ways to give positive meaning to potentially stressful life events. The black church plays an indispensable role as "the extended family" where the roles of "brother, sister, aunt, and uncle" take on new meanings. Social outings, rituals, baptisms, graduation, celebrations, funerals, and other church-focused activities have provided cultural systems for church-centered lives. Church-sponsored meals have provided the elderly with fellowship and nourishment. The growth of whole life centers in urban settings attempts to recapture the holistic role of the church as the primary spiritual center for the entire life of the individual, thus, taking steps toward creating Jubilee. (For further study, see Section Two: "A History of the Black Church," by Dennis C. Dickerson, and "Black and Catholic: Elements of African American Catholic History," by James C. Okoye.)

Creating a Jubilee World

Practice Jubilee!

Throughout the Scriptures, the Jubilee refrain resounds with themes of forgiveness, liberty, and justice. To forgive and be forgiven; to be free to return to one's traditions and to remember bondage and freedom from bondage; to strive for justice in the biblical sense, both economically and socially, with regard to equitable distribution of the earth's resources and concern for the family—these tenets are at the heart of true Jubilee that culminates in gratitude to God, the source of every perfect gift (James 1.17). (See Section Two: "Racial Reconciliation and the Challenge of Jubilee Justice in the United States: A Black Catholic Perspective," by Bryan N. Massingale.)

In her book *"Proclaim Jubilee!"* Religious Education Professor Maria Harris states that she has "found no people more involved with living the Jubilee than African Americans" inasmuch as they "preserve in their own experience a history of the slavery and suffering and longing for liberation that the Jubilee sought to address."[34] From the Jubilee Emancipation of 1865, through the post-Civil War Reconstruction period, up to the Civil Rights' movements in the twentieth century, the Jubilee pilgrimage for African Americans has continued with the quest for forgiveness, liberty, and justice.

To apply the Jubilee model and understand its significance in daily life "requires that people dwell in God's creative presence" and "experience God's forgiveness; hope in God's promises; and practice God's justice." Such "religious wholeness characterizes Jubilee."[35]

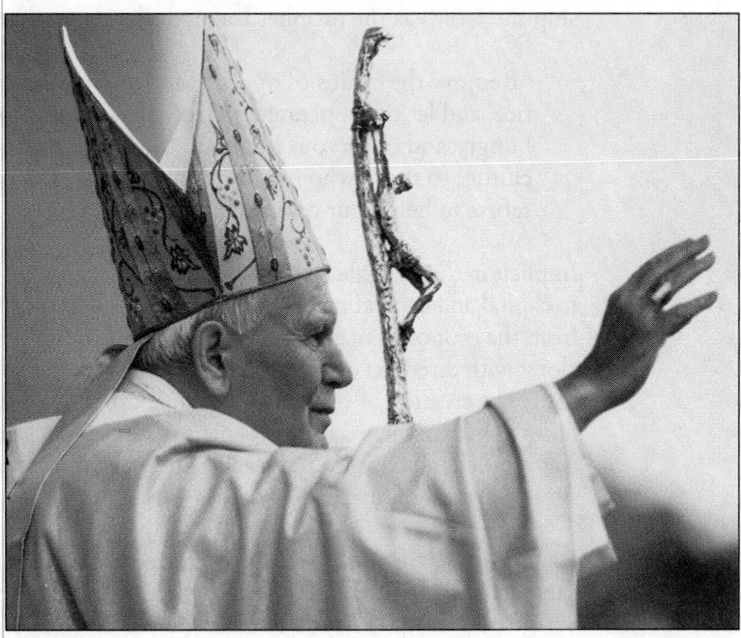

▸ **Pope John Paul II. Photo courtesy Gamma/Lochon**

To practice jubilee requires the people of God to engage in the struggle to "to do what is just" (Micah 6.8b)—locally, nationally, and globally. "Christians will have to raise their voice on behalf of all the poor of the world, proposing the Jubilee as an appropriate time to give thought, among other things, to reducing substantially, if not cancelling outright, the international debt which seriously threatens the future of many nations."[36]

In communities where people are oppressed, their cries echo the words of the prophet Habakkuk:

> O LORD, how long must I call for help before you listen, before you save us from violence? Why do you make me see such trouble? How can you stand to look on such wrongdoing? Destruction and violence are all around me, and there is fighting and quarreling everywhere. The law is weak and useless, and justice is never done. Evil people get the better of the righteous, and so justice is perverted. (Habakkuk 1.2-4)

To strive for justice now is what the prophets Micah, Amos, Isaiah and others are calling us to do if we are to understand the significance and relevance of jubilee today.[37] To practice Jubilee is to worship the LORD as the prophet Isaiah declares:

> "Remove the chains of oppression and the yoke of injustice, and let the oppressed go free. Share your food with the hungry and open your homes to the homeless poor. Give clothes to those who have nothing to wear, and do not refuse to help your own relatives" (Isaiah 58.6b, 7).

Implicit in the struggle is the call for economic justice—equal access to capital and expanding economic opportunities for those excluded from the economic mainstream. Church and community leaders, along with directors of financial institutions, are being challenged to foster the creation of equitable local financial policies so that communities are strengthened for the benefit of all people.[38] Such a challenge is grounded in Scripture and teaches the value of everyone becoming a wise steward of financial resources (see Matthew 25.14-30).

As you study the Holy Scriptures, reflect on ways in which you can participate in the struggle and practice Jubilee. Some suggested Scripture passages for you to examine are:[39]

Exodus 21.1-11 (giving freedom to slaves)
Exodus 22.25-27 (lending money to the poor without interest)
Exodus 23.10-13 (the sabbath year and providing for the poor)
Leviticus 25 (laws for observing the sabbath year)
Deuteronomy 15.1-18 (sharing with the poor and setting slaves free)
Nehemiah 5 (removing the burden of debt)
Isaiah 5.8-10 (condemnation of greed)
Isaiah 58 (true worship by striving for justice)

Isaiah 59 (social injustice condemned)
Amos 5 (justice demanded by the LORD)
Luke 3.11 (sharing with those in need)
Luke 7.18-23 (good news proclaimed to the poor)
Luke 10.25-37 (offering compassion to your neighbor)

How do these passages speak to you today? What are you called to do?

Celebrate Jubilee!

The ending of the twentieth century marks the beginning of a new millennium, and author Maria Harris calls humankind to celebrate Jubilee as a way of responding "to the challenges with which the twentieth century leaves us and the twenty-first century confronts us."[40] Her call is one of celebration and an acknowledgement "that the world continues to be charged with the grandeur of God," and that "proclaiming Jubilee is an act of faith, an act of hope, and an act of conviction that grace, goodness, and holiness exist, even though none of them has triumphed fully."[41]

To celebrate Jubilee is

- to proclaim Jubilee and announce a new social order is at hand
- to acknowledge one's sins and seek forgiveness from others
- to listen quietly and wait upon the Lord both privately and in community
- to give thanks to God and respond with songs of gratitude
- to make a commitment to strive for justice and freedom for all people.[42]

The Holy Scriptures invite you to celebrate Jubilee. Examine the following passages in light of the five points noted above:
Isaiah 61 (good news is proclaimed)
Isaiah 65.17-25 (a vision of the Lord's new creation)
Matthew 5-7 (Jesus outlines a vision for living in community)
Luke 4.16-19 (Jesus preaches good news to the poor)

How will ***you*** celebrate Jubilee?

▸ "Celebration, 1975," Charles Searles. Courtesy National Museum of American Art, Washington, DC, Art Resource, NY.

Pope John Paul II suggests that "we can celebrate the Great Jubilee, if not completely united, *at least much closer to overcoming the divisions of the second millenium*...but above all to be more committed to *prayer for Christian unity*."[43]

Empowered by the Holy Spirit, humanity can celebrate that the kingdom of God is truly at hand (Mark 1.15).

- Jubilee ushers in the new social order as ordained by God.
- Jubilee is a universal mandate for a civil society and a civil world.
- Jubilee can bring connectedness among all peoples.
- Jubilee empowers the Black Church, even in the midst of chaos and pain, to lead all Christians to a beloved Jubilee community as envisioned by Jesus and as recorded in the 4th chapter of the Gospel according to Luke.

Join hands with your neighbor and celebrate God's kingdom in your midst. Celebrate the fullness of life that is intended for all God's children (John 10.10). (See Section Two: "The Blessing: Restoring Hope for African American Youth," by Maxine Walker.)

Proclaim Jubilee!

Practice Jubilee!

Celebrate Jubilee!

Proclamation
ALL SLAVES
ARE FREE.

Selected Chronology (1565-2000)

Struggles and Victories

◂ "Juneteenth," (Emancipation Proclamation). Private collection. Art Resource, NY

1565 Establishment of the city of St. Augustine in Florida by Spain. Inhabitants are both white and black.

1619 The first Africans are brought to British North American colonies when a Dutch ship lands 20 black laborers in Jamestown, Virginia.

1638 Native Americans are transported from Salem, Massachusetts to the West Indies and exchanged for African laborers, opening the New England slave trade.

1639 Death of St. Martin de Porres in Lima, Peru.

1641 Massachusetts becomes the first colony to legalize slavery.

1738 Establishment of free black town of Santa Teresa de Mose in Florida for freed slaves converted to Catholicism.

1761 Jupiter Hammon, a New York slave, publishes his poem, "An Evening Thought: Salvation by Christ, with Penitential Cries." He is probably the first published slave poet.

▶ Courtesy Josephite Seminary, Washington, D.C.

1770 Runaway slave, Crispus Attucks, is the first of five killed in the Boston Massacre. Attucks is recognized as the leader of the action that eventually led to the American Revolution.

1776 United States Declaration of Independence.

1781 Settlement of Los Angeles by blacks and Indians from Mexico.

1787 Establishment of the Free African Society.

1793 Arrival of Haitian refugees at Fells' Point, near Baltimore.

1808 Ban on slave trade put into effect. In accordance with provisions of the Constitution, Congress outlaws the African slave trade. The slave trade continues illegally, with greatly reduced numbers of Africans being smuggled into the United States thereafter.

1820 Start of "Back to Africa" movement: 20,000 blacks will eventually leave the United States for Liberia.

1824 Unsuccessful foundation of a community of black women religious by Charles Nerinckx in Loretto, Kentucky.

1827 *Freedom's Journal*, the first black newspaper in America, is published in March in New York City.

1829 Elizabeth Lange, Marie Ballas, Rosine Boegue, and Almeide Duchemin Maxis begin religious life in Baltimore as the Oblate Sisters of Providence. First black congregation of women religious in the United States.

1829 In September, David Walker, a free black man from North Carolina living in Boston, publishes his militant anti-slavery tract ***An Appeal to the Colored People of the World.*** Its publication gives rise to panic in the South and there are efforts to restrict its circulation.

1839 Condemnation of the slave trade by Pope Gregory XVI in the bull *In Supremo Apostolatus.*

1842 Henriette Delille and Juliette Gaudin begin the Sisters of the Holy Family in New Orleans, Louisiana.

1843 Formation of the Society of the Holy Family in Baltimore, first known black Catholic society of lay persons.

1853 Death of Pierre Toussaint in New York. Toussaint, a slave in his native Haiti, was brought to the U.S. and worked as a hair - dresser. He was declared "Venerable" by Pope John Paul II, and when canonized will become the first African American saint.

1854 Ordination of James Augustine Healy in Paris. Ordinations of his brothers, Alexander Sherwood Healy in Rome (1858) and Francis Patrick Healy, S.J., in Liège (1864).

1857 In March, the Supreme Court of the United States renders the Dred Scott decision, declaring that black people are not and cannot be citizens of the United States. Dred Scott remains a slave even though he has lived for a long period outside the jurisdiction of slavery. It also ruled that Cogress has no right to bar slavery from western states.

1863 Lincoln's Emancipation Proclamation. On January 1, President Lincoln issues the Proclamation freeing slaves in areas then in rebellion against the United States. The Proclamation does not free slaves in areas under the control of the United States.

1865 Juneteenth is the oldest known celebration signaling the ending of slavery. On June 19th, Union soldiers at Galveston, Texas brought the news that the war had ended and that all slaves were to be freed. This was more than two years *after* the Emancipation Proclamation.

1871 Arrival of Mill Hill Fathers (Josephites) in Baltimore.

1874 Reverend Francis Patrick Healy is named president of Georgetown University in Washington, D.C.

1875 Reverend James Augustine Healy is consecrated second bishop of Portland, Maine. First black Catholic bishop in the United States.

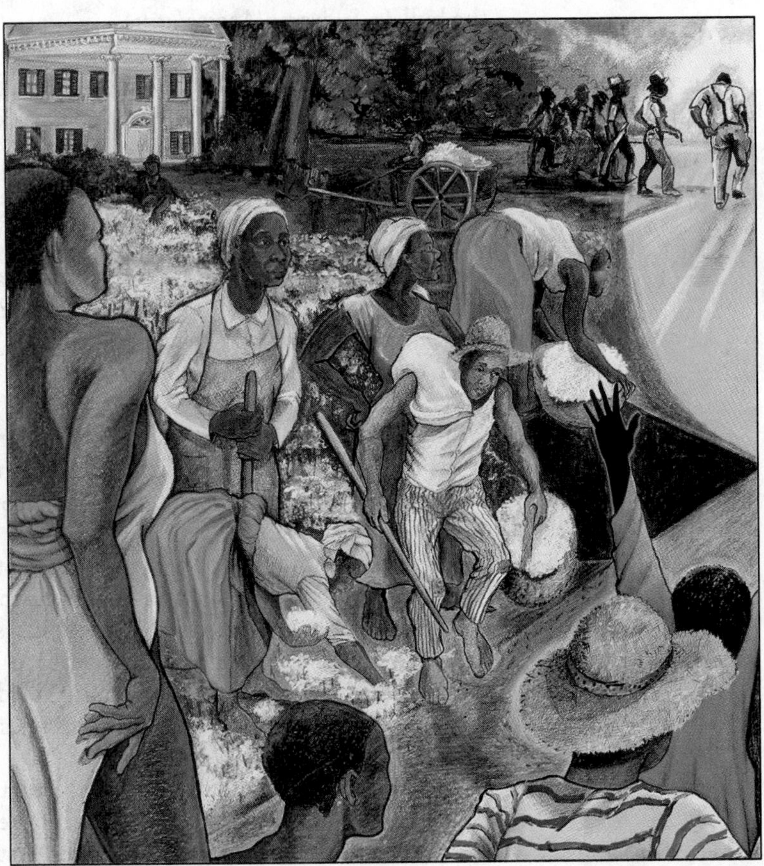

▸ **Detail "Juneteenth," (Emancipation Proclamation). Private Collection. Art Resource, NY**

1875 The Civil Rights Act concerns itself primarily with the prohibition of racial discrimination in places of public accommodation. In 1883, however, the Supreme Court rules the law unconstitutional. This decision virtually removes the federal government from the civil rights arena, particularly in regard to enforcement of the 14th Amendment.

1885 Reverend Samuel David Ferguson is consecrated as the first African American Protestant Episcopal Bishop in the United States.

1886 Ordination of Reverend Augustus Tolton in Rome. Tolton was denied ordination in the Catholic Church in the U.S. because he was black.

1886 Daniel Rudd, a former slave, establishes *The American Catholic Tribune*, a weekly black Catholic newspaper. The paper is currently being published by the National Black Catholic Congress as a newsletter, *The African American Catholic Tribune.*

1889 First black Catholic lay congress, in Washington, D.C. Other congresses are held in Cincinnati (1890), Philadelphia (1892), Chicago (1893), and Baltimore (1894).

1889 Black Lutherans in North Carolina organize the Alpha Evangelical Lutheran Synod of Freedmen in America, the first and only separate black Lutheran ecclesiastical organization in United States history.

1891 Ordination of Reverend Charles Uncles, S.S.J., in Baltimore. First black priest ordained in the United States.

1891 Foundation of the Sisters of the Blessed Sacrament for Indians and Colored People by Blessed Katherine Drexel.

1897 Death of Augustus Tolton in Chicago.

1905 W. E. B. DuBois, William Monroe Trotter and other blacks establish the Niagara Movement in Fort Erie, NY, forerunner of the integrated NAACP.

1908 Lincoln Vallé opens Catholic mission for the black community in Milwaukee.

1909 Establishment of the National Association for the Advancement of Colored People (NAACP) in New York City on the 100th Anniversary of Lincoln's birth.

1909 The Knights of St. Peter Claver is founded.

1910 Establishment of the National Urban League with support from Booker T. Washington and affluent whites.

1913 Thomas Wyatt Turner organizes a committee on behalf of black Catholic servicemen.

1914 Marcus Garvey founds the Universal Negro Improvement Association to promote racial pride and emigration to Africa.

1916 Mother Theodore Williams and Father Ignatius Lissner begin the Handmaids of Mary in Savannah, Georgia.

1920 First seminary for black candidates for the priesthood is started by the Society of the Divine Word in Greenville, Mississippi, later moved to Bay St. Louis (1923).

1921 Founding of the Ladies Auxiliary of The Knights of St. Peter Claver.

1924 Founding of the Federated Colored Catholics of the United States.

1931 Xavier University in New Orleans, Louisiana, is established by the Sisters of the Blessed Sacrament and becomes the first black Catholic university in the U.S.

1934 Organization of the first Catholic Interracial Council in New York City, by John LaFarge, S.J.

1935 Mary McLeod Bethune establishes the National Council of Negro Women.

1947 John Hope Franklin publishes his comprehensive black history, ***From Slavery to Freedom***.

1950 Ralph Bunche is awarded the Nobel Peace Prize for successful mediation between the Arabs and Israelis in Palestine.

1954 In the case of *Brown vs. Board of Education* of Topeka, the Supreme Court rules that segregation in public education is unconstitutional, declaring that separate is "inherently unequal."

1954 Dr. James Joshua Thomas becomes the first African American pastor of the Reformed Dutch Church.

1955 Rosa Parks refuses to surrender her seat in the front of a bus to a white man and is jailed, sparking the Montgomery Bus Boycott.

1957 Congress passes the first important civil rights legislation since 1857, protecting the right to vote.

1963 Medgar Evers, a prominent civil rights activist, is assassinated.

1964 Congress passes, and President Lyndon B. Johnson signs, the Civil Rights bill banning discrimination in education, employment, and public accommodations.

1964 Dr. Lena Edwards Madison (1901-1986), a social activist and Catholic obstetrician/gynecologist, receives the Medal of Freedom for her work and dedication to impoverished communities, especially among migrant workers.

1966 Dr. Ron Karenga introduces Kwaanza, the Nugzo Saba, an African cultural celebration.

1966 Episcopal ordination of Harold Perry, S.V.D., as the auxiliary bishop of New Orleans. Second black bishop in the history of the United States.

1966 Constance Baker Motley, former New York City Borough President and NAACP lawyer, is appointed the first black female federal judge.

1967 President Lyndon Johnson appoints Thurgood Marshall first black Justice to the U. S. Supreme Court.

▸ "Miracles, The Image of the Virgin," Gianni Giansanti, Sygma.

1968 Formation of the National Black Catholic Clergy Caucus in Detroit, results in the subsequent development of the National Black Sisters' Conference (1968) and the National Black Catholic Seminarians Association.

1968 Reverend Dr. Martin Luther King, Jr., civil rights leader, is assassinated in Memphis, Tennessee.

1969 Shirley Chisholm is elected as the first African American Congresswoman in the United States. She makes a bid for the presidency in 1972.

1971 The National Office of Black Catholics is founded in Washington, D.C.

1976 President-elect Jimmy Carter appoints Georgia Representative Andrew Young U. S. Ambassador to the United Nations.

1978 Death of Llewellyn Scott, a Catholic layman, who founded the Blessed Martin de Porres Hospice for poor black men.

1979 Congress honors the memory of Dr. Martin Luther King, Jr. by voting to make him the first African American with his likeness in the Capitol rotunda.

1983 President Ronald Reagan signs a bill into law making the third Monday in January a federal holiday honoring Dr. Martin Luther King, Jr.

1984 Reverend Jesse Jackson is the first African American male candidate in a presidential primary.

1987 James Goode, O.F.M., designates the first Sunday in February (Black History Month) as National Day of Prayer for the African American Family.

1987 The sixth National Black Catholic Congress is held in Washington, D.C. after a hiatus of 93 years. Other congresses held in New Orleans (1992) and Baltimore (1997).

1988 Reverend Barbara Harris is elected the first female Bishop of the Episcopal Church.

1989 Colin Powell is appointed Chairman of the Joint Chiefs of Staff.

1990 National Black Catholic Congress designates November as Black Catholic History Month.

1991 Barbara T. Christian, professor of African American studies at the University of California at Berkley, becomes the first black to win that University's Distinguished Teaching Award. She was also the first black woman to be granted tenure there (1978) and the first black to be promoted to full professor (1986).

1992 Mae Jemison becomes the first African American woman to venture into space when she boards the space shuttle Endeavor on a mission to study the effects of zero gravity on people and animals.

1993 Toni Morrison wins the Nobel Prize for Literature for her novel, ***Beloved***.

1994 Black and white Pentecostals meet in Memphis, Tennesse and plan a new association, The Pentecostal-Charismatic Churches of North America, to include predominantly black denominations such as the Church of God in Christ and predominantly white denominations such as the Assemblies of God.

1997 Reverend Frederick K. C. Price, televangelist and pastor of the 17,500-member FaithDome in Los Angeles, California, starts a nearly two-year series on Race, Religion, and Racism.

1998 Reverend Arnold I. Thomas, the first black pastor of the First Congregational Church of Williamstown, Massachusetts, becomes the Conference Minister of the Vermont Conference of United Church of Christ.

1998 Bishop Wilton D. Gregory, of the Diocese of Belleville, Illinois, is elected Vice President of the National Conference of Catholic Bishops.

1999 Reverend Jesse Jackson, accompanied by a delegation of American religious leaders, travels to Belgrade, Yugoslavia, and secures the release of three U. S. servicemen being held as prisoners in the Serbian-Albanian conflict.

1999 Rosa Parks is honored for her role in the civil rights movement with the Congressional Gold Medal. The Medal is the highest civilian award given by Congress.

2000 Reverend Vashti McKenzie is elected the first female bishop of the African Methodist Episcopal Church, the nation's oldest black church.

2000 Mother Josephine Bakhita becomes the first African woman to be cannonized by the Roman Catholic Church in the new millennium.

2000 Blessed Katherine Drexel, founder of the Sisters of the Blessed Sacrament for Indians and Colored People, is canonized by the Roman Catholic Church.

▸ "From Slavery to Freedom," Photo by Bro. Earl V. Kent S.S.J., Josephite Pastoral Center, Washington, D.C.

Sources Cited

1. Vincent L. Wimbush, "The Bible and African Americans. An Outline of an Interpretive History," *Stony the Road We Trod*, Cain Hope Felder, ed. (Minneapolis: Fortress Press, 1991), 85.
2. Ibid.
3. Clarice J. Martin, "Haustafeln (Household Codes) in African American Biblical Interpretation: 'Free Slaves' and 'Subordinate Women,'" *Stony the Road We Trod,* Cain Hope Felder, ed. (Minneapolis: Fortress Press, 1991), 226.
4. Brian K. Blount, *Cultural Interpretation: Reorienting New Testament Criticism* (Minneapolis: Fortress Press, 1995), 56.
5. Ibid., 56, 57.
6. Wimbush, op.cit., 87.
7. Katie Geneva Cannon, *Katie's Cannon: Womanism and the Soul of the Black Community,* (New York: Continuum, 1996), 36.

8. Wimbush, "Reading Texts as Reading Ourselves: A Chapter in the History of African-American Biblical Interpretation," *Reading from this Place: Social Location and Biblical Interpretation in the United States,* Fernando F. Segovia and Mary Ann Tolbert, eds. (Minneapolis: Fortress Press, 1995), 99.

9. Ibid.

10. Renita J. Weems, "Reading Her Way Through the Struggle: African American Women and the Bible," *Stony the Road We Trod,* Cain Hope Felder, ed. (Minneapolis: Fortress Press, 1991), 61.

11. Wimbush, *Stony the Road We Trod,* op.cit., 86.

12. Howard Thurman (1899-1981), author, pastor, and professor of Christian theology at Howard Divinity School, *Jesus and the Disinherited,* (Nashville: Abingdon Press, 1949), 30, 31 as cited by Weems, op. cit., 61-62.

13. Wimbush, *Reading from this Place*, op.cit., 99, 101.

14. Richard P. McBrien, General Editor, *The Harper Collins Encyclopedia of Catholicism*, (New York: Harper Collins, 1995), 720.

15. Pope John Paul II, Apostolic Letter, "*The Coming of the Third Millennium*" (Tertio Millennio Adveniente), November 10, 1994, (#31).

16. Ibid, (#32)

17. Joseph G. Donders, "*Countdown to 2000: Celebrating the Great Jubilee,*" (Mystic, CT: Twenty-Third Publications, 1999), 18.

18. Brad Ronnell Braxton, "The Good Samaritan in African American Culture," research paper prepared for *The Neighbor* video translation of Luke 10.25-37, (New York: American Bible Society, 1999), 2.

19. Donders, op. cit., p33).

20. Basil Davidson, *Africa in History* (New York, NY: MacMillan Publishing Co., 1974), 85.

21. Peter Wood, *Black Majority: Negroes in Colonial South Carolina from 1670 through the Stono Rebellion* (New York: W.W. Norton & Company, Inc., 1974), 131, 132.

22. Philip D. Curtin, *The Atlantic Slave Trade: A Census* (Madison: University of Wisconsin Press, 1969), 268.

23. Harry A. Ploski and Warren A. Marr, II, *The Negro Almanac: A Reference Work on the African American* (New York, NY: Bellweather Publishing Company, 1976), 1059.

24. Ibid., 1058.

25. Samuel D. Proctor, *The Substance of Things Hoped For: The Faith Epic of African Americans*, (New York: G.P. Putnam's Sons, 1995).

26. Davidson, op.cit., 53.

27. Cyprian Davis, O.S.B., "Black Spirituality: A Catholic Perspective," in "*One Faith, One Lord, One Baptism: The Hopes and Experiences of the Black Community in the Archdiocese of New York*, vol. 2 (New York: Archdiocese of New York, Office of Pastoral Research, 1988), 45.

28. Diana L. Hayes, "And When We Speak" in *Taking Down Our Harps, Black Catholics in the United States*, Diana Hayes and Cyprian Davis, eds., (Maryknoll, NY: Orbis Books, 1998), 112.

29. John S. Mbiti, *African Religions and Philosophy,* John S. White, ed., (New York, NY: Frederick A. Praeger Publishers, 1969), 29.

30. Hayes, "And When We Speak," op. cit., 110.

31. Hayes, "We've Come This Far By Faith," in *Taking Down Our Harps,* op. cit., 10.

32. Jamie T. Phelps, "Sources of Theology: African-American Catholic Experience" in *Black and Catholic, The Challenge and Gift of Black Folk*, Jamie T. Phelps, ed., (Milwaukee: Marquette University Press, 1997), 165.

33. James Weldon Johnson, *God's Trombones*, (New York, NY: Viking Press, 1927), 27-30.

34. Maria Harris, *Proclaim Jubilee!* (Louisville, KY: Westminster/John Knox Press, 1996), 98, 99.

35. Ibid., 81. See also "Jubilee, Year of" in *The Anchor Bible Dictionary: Volume 3,* David Noel Freedman, ed. (New York: Doubleday, 1992), 1029.

36. Pope John Paul II, op. cit., (#51).

37. David Wildman, "Jubilee: Hallowing the 50th," *Response*, July/August 1994, 8.

38. Denise Johnson Stovall, "Millennium role for churches: Become economics advocates," *The United Methodist Reporter,* 1/16/98, 1.

39. Wildman, op.cit., 10.

40. Harris, op. cit., 100.

41. Ibid., 100.

42. Ibid., 102-109

43. Pope John Paul II, op. cit., (#34).

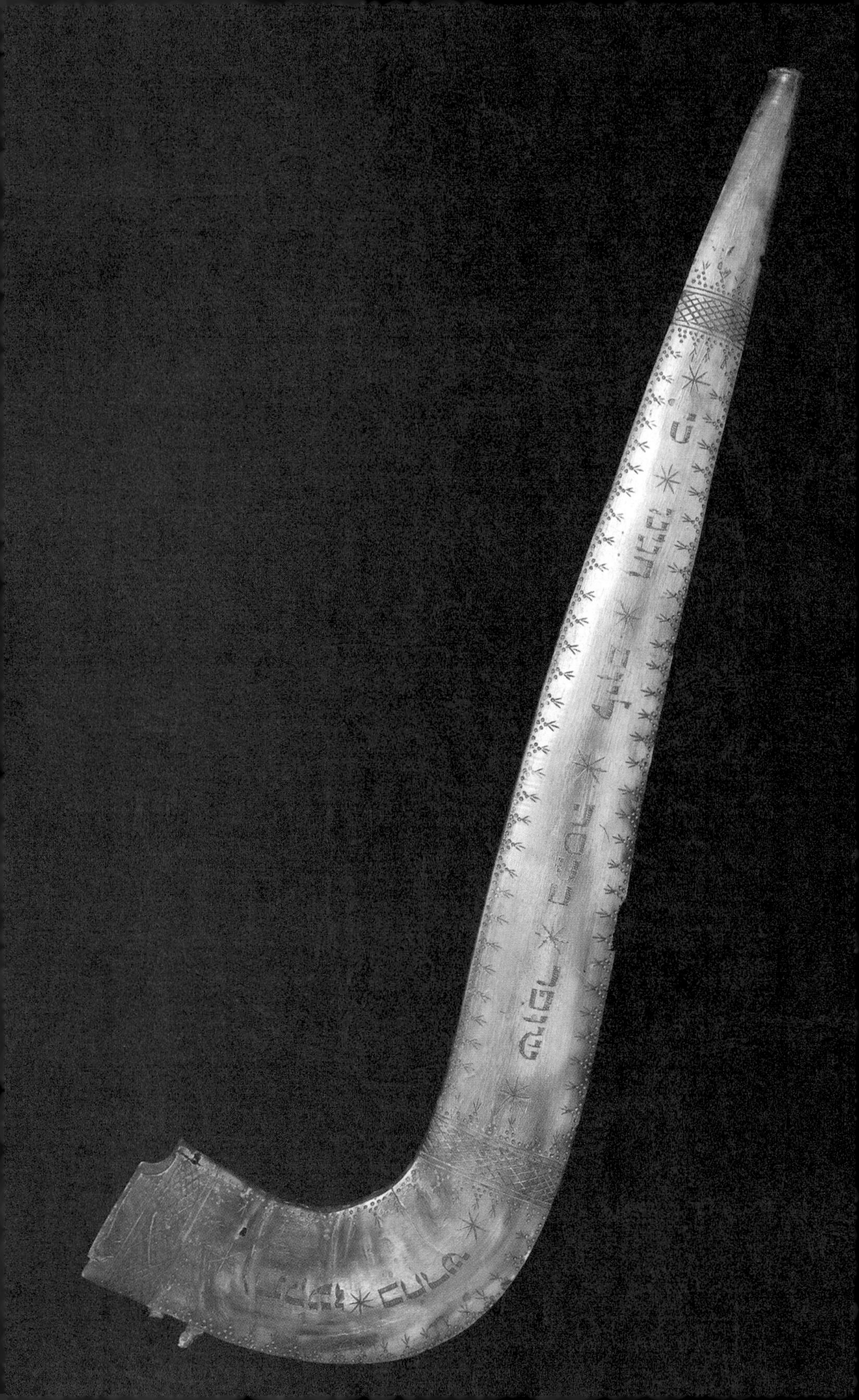

Section Two

"Then, on...the Day of Atonement, send someone to blow a trumpet throughout the whole land. In this way you shall set the fiftieth year apart and proclaim freedom to all the inhabitants of the land."

(Leviticus 25.9, *10)*

The preceding material gave an overview of the Jubilee system and some historical background on African American heritage. The nineteen articles that follow in Section Two extend an invitation to examine issues today in light of the Jubilee mandate and the Holy Scriptures. The articles are designed to help you explore your own connection between the world of the Bible and the social issues you face on a day-to-day basis.

If Jubilee must begin with the Church, how are Scriptures interpreted? What part does music play? What is spirituality? How does one view death? What legacy do we leave our youth? How does God's salvation impact our lives?

◂ **"A Ram's Horn Shofar." Photograph by David Harris**

Most of the articles are replete with Scripture references taken from the **Good News Bible/Today's English Version**. The topics, in conjunction with biblical citations, could well serve as the foundation for some lively discussions and Bible study. Readers are encouraged to examine the issues set forth and journey with God's people to "Proclaim Jubilee" and spread God's Word of liberation, justice, and reconciliation.

"...[T]he time has come when the Lord will save his people."

(Luke 4.19b)

One

Interpretation of Scripture

Murray L. Newman

The Bible may be viewed as the Word of God in the words of the people of God. Its focus and center is that stream of history which emerged with Abraham and Sarah, and flowed through the subsequent centuries to reach a climax in Jesus of Nazareth— his life, death, and resurrection. The thoughtful interpreter approaches the Bible with humility, always open to Christian insights of the centuries. In addition, the interpreter is sensitive to the literary composition of both the Old and New Testaments, their historical value, and above all their theological message. Jesus Christ, the incarnate Word, is the measure of all other words in the Bible.

◂ **"Jesus with the Elders," by Pheoris West. Collection, Mt. Vernon A.M.E. Church**

Interpretation of Scripture involves a knowledge of its contents, origin, nature, and authority, as well as principles and guidelines for understanding and applying its meaning for contemporary hearers and readers.

I. The Protestant Bible

For Protestant Christians, the Bible consists of 66 books, 39 in the Old Testament (almost all originally in Hebrew) and 27 in the New Testament (all originally in Greek). Although the canons of the Roman Catholic and Orthodox churches contain additional books, (See Section One: "The Formation of the Biblical Canon.") the 66 books are the ones assumed to comprise the Bible for purposes of this article.

The Scriptures of the Old and New Testaments represent a collection of writings authored by many different people in different historical periods from at least the 13th century B.C. to the first century A.D. Those of the Old Testament (or Old Covenant) come from the people of ancient Israel who stood in a covenant relation with God. Those of the New Testament (or New Covenant) were written by early Christians who recognized Jesus of Nazareth as the Jewish Messiah and were entrusted with the task of extending God's covenant to all the world.

II. The Word of God in the Words of the People of God

A basic assumption in this article is that the Bible is the Word of God in the words of the people of God.

A. The Word of God

Although not encompassing its totality, from a Christian perspective the central thrust of the Bible may be viewed as that stream of history witnessed to in the Book of Genesis that began with the call of Abraham. The account of Abraham's call is preceded by the narrative of creation and the disobedience of the first couple, which resulted in human estrangement from God and the breakthrough of evil in the world. This disobedience affected nature itself, as well as all human beings, who were not only estranged from God, but from one another.

Abraham's destiny under God was to become the father of a people with a land, from whom would come a blessing for all the families of the earth, thus counteracting human estrangement from God and neighbor (Genesis 12.1-3). This stream flowed from Abraham, Sarah, and the other ancestors, to Moses and Miriam, with the liberating events of the exodus and the covenant between the ancient Hebrews and God, with his commandments. It moved into the Promised Land under Joshua, then to the kingship of David, bringing order and security to God's people. There followed the Prophets with their messages of both judgment and salvation. From this same stream also emerged the Psalmists and Writers of Wisdom. It then flowed to the Exile and beyond, to reach a climax with God's perfect revelation in Jesus of Nazareth, whose life, death, and resurrection are recounted in the four Gospels and other writings of the New Testament Church. Both the Old and New Testaments unequivocally affirm that God was uniquely involved in this stream of biblical history to manifest his presence, power and purpose in the world, and to achieve human salvation. For this reason the biblical writings, which witness to these events of God's self-revelation, can be called the Word of God.

In this special history, God is revealed as the Creator, holy, righteous, commanding, and loving. He is concerned with saving people from all earthly bondage, as witnessed particularly by the Exodus event and the prophets of the Old Testament, as well as from the deeper bondages of sin and death, proclaimed with power by the New Testament.

B. In the Words of the People of God

Although the people of God who were responsible for the emergence, formulation, and transmission of the biblical writings were inspired by the Holy Spirit, their words, although also inspired, are human and fallible. These writings always point beyond themselves to the God who is the Creator and Lord of nature, acts in human history, and will bring all things to their consummation with the Second Coming of Christ.

The life of the Christian Church represents a continuation of the biblical history. The Bible, which the people of the covenants produced, is therefore indispensable for worship, discipline, theologizing, and the very existence of the Christian Church. Under the guidance of the Holy Spirit the members of the Church, individually and collectively, have the responsibility of interpreting the Scriptures. However, every interpretation is ultimately subject to reinterpretation in the light of new reading and hearing of its words in new historical situations.

III. Principles of Interpretation

A. The Principle of Humility

The first principle of biblical interpretation is *humility.* For the individual Christian, as well as the larger Christian community with its various leaders and scholars, humility is the point of departure. The Christian does not stand in authority above the Bible; rather, the Bible stands in authority over the Christian. All human beings, including all Christians, are sinful and fallible, and none can ever claim to have the final, infallible interpretation of any biblical passage.

▸ Bible Commentaries Photo: Michael Scott Studio

B. The Principle of Reason

At the same time, Christians do in fact have the responsibility of interpreting the Bible to the best of their intellectual ability. Christians are not called to stand passive before the Bible. Every human being has been granted the gift of *reason.* Reason is a human faculty that comes from being created in God's image. With the gift of reason, the believer will use his or her mind as responsibly as humanly possible in biblical interpretation.

C. The Principle of Tradition

A third principle of interpretation is the use of the *tradition* of the people of God. No one interprets Scripture in a vacuum. Both the Christian individual and the Christian community stand as members of the ongoing life of the covenant people and their tradition. Tradition includes the collective reflection of the Church on the biblical revelation through the centuries. This would encompass Christian thinkers and theologians from New Testament times to the present, as well as hymns, sermons, prayers, liturgies, creeds, biblical commentaries, and whatever else has helped people of the past to understand the nature and will of God as revealed in Holy Scripture.

D. The Literary Principle

Whatever else the Bible may be, it is certainly a *literary* document. Its books comprise the collection of a rich variety of literature. The thoughtful believer recognizes it as such, and uses principles employed for the study of any great work of literature.

Just as in reading a newspaper it is essential to distinguish among news articles, editorials, obituaries, cartoons, and other literary forms in order to understand each one and the role it plays in contemporary life, it is equally important to distinguish the many different literary forms in the Bible. There are too many different types to mention them all. Thus only a few are noted here.

Some are unique, such as the four Gospels in the New Testament. They tell of the life and ministry of Jesus, and in that sense are biographies. But they are more than biographies; they are proclamations of God's saving work through his only Son. They are Gospels, that is, proclamations of the Good News concerning the life, death, and resurrection of Jesus of Nazareth, the Messiah.

Within the Gospels there are the smaller units, termed pericopes, such as parables, sermons, teachings, miracle stories, the birth accounts, and especially the passion narratives. Each has its own meaning, but must also be considered in the larger context of the entire Gospel.

One should mention the apocalyptic passages in the Gospels, as well as the entire book of Revelation. These apocalyptic writings do not speak of the past, but of what God will do in the future with the Second Coming of Christ and the consummation of all things. The apocalyptic writings contain a great deal of highly symbolic language, which frequently is difficult to understand. The thoughtful person of faith will be slow to interpret the symbols too literally.

The Book of Acts appears as a history of the early Church, stressing particularly the activities of Peter and Paul. The letters, or epistles, of Paul and other early Christians provide yet another New Testament form.

In the Old Testament one is aware of an even greater variety of literary types. A great deal of the Old Testament comes in the form of historical narrative: Genesis– 2 Kings, as well as 1 and 2 Chronicles, Ezra and Nehemiah. Within these larger narratives are numerous smaller units, such as theological myths, sagas, parables, genealogies, liturgies, laws, sermons, and a number of others.

In addition to the writings that tell of past historical events, there are those that speak of the future. The oracles of Israel's Prophets spoke of the future, usually of the near future. Their primary concern was with God's righteousness and his desire for justice in Israel's life. Some, however, were inspired to look further into the future and anticipate a perfect messianic savior and leader of God's people.

On the other hand, the Book of Daniel, like the Book of Revelation, is an apocalyptic work which looks into the more distant future. Again, as in the apocalyptic writings of the New Testament, the thoughtful interpreter will avoid trying to press all the details of such writings, but will recognize that their final and most important message is the ultimate triumph of God in human history.

One should also mention the Psalms (a collection of Israel's hymns), traditionally ascribed to King David, and also the Wisdom literature (Proverbs, Job, Ecclesiastes), in which the writers of Wisdom reflect on order in nature and human life.

The discerning Christian is always sensitive to the literary character of each passage, and avoids interpreting it in the same way. The reader is also aware that each individual passage must finally be considered in the larger context of the book in which it appears, as well as the entire Old Testament in the case of Old Testament passages; the entire New Testament with New Testament passages; and finally the entire Bible; with its rich variety of literary forms.

E. The Historical Principle

Another principle of biblical interpretation has to do with *history*. By historical principle we mean that the biblical traditions are rooted in the actual events of human life. Scripture witnesses to real happenings in space and time involving the ancient Hebrews, Jesus of Nazareth, and the earliest Christians.

For the Christian, the historical point of departure in this regard is the Incarnation of Jesus Christ. *God was in Christ.* God acted uniquely in the life, death, and resurrection of Jesus of Nazareth, a real historical person. Jesus was born during the reign of Herod the Great, preached, taught, and healed in Galilee while Tiberius was the Roman Emperor, and was crucified and raised again while Pontius Pilate was Governor of Judea. In addition, the apostles who accompanied Jesus in his ministry and experienced his resurrection were actual historical people, as were Peter, Paul and the other Christians whose activity is recorded in the New Testament.

The same can be said of the historical people of ancient Israel, from Abraham and Sarah and the other ancestors, to Moses and Miriam, Joshua, David and the other kings, Amos and the other Prophets, the Psalmists and Wisdom writers. Further, the great events to which the Old Testament bears witness actually happened— the Exodus, the Covenant at Sinai, the entrance into the land of Canaan, the emergence of the kingship, the kingdoms of Judah and Israel, the Assyrian threat, the Babylonian exile and return, actually happened.

In this connection, the use of maps of the Holy Land, Jerusalem, the Ancient Near East, as a whole, as well as Greece and Italy, can be invaluable in understanding the geographical settings of the various biblical events.

To be sure, none of the books of the Old Testament or the New Testament were intended to be scientific, secular histories. They were composed as proclamations of God's involvement in the lives of the people of ancient Israel and new Israel. So the wise interpreter does not expect inerrant scientific accuracy in all respects. At the same time, the great biblical events can be accepted as basically historical, and certainly the traditions of the Bible were inspired by God in such a way that his nature and purposes for human life and its salvation are revealed.

F. The Theological Principle

The word *theology* comes from Greek and means the "word of God." Is the Bible really the Word of God in the words of the people of God? Is God living and active and the Bible his living and active Word? Is it the most important means of God's self-revelation to people? If the interpreter approaches the Bible with the openness of faith in the living and active God, it can indeed be a revelation of the nature and will of God, of his power and presence and purposes, of his Word for people today.

1. The Incarnate Word

God inspired many words from many different voices through the centuries of biblical history. The result was the unparalleled theological richness contained in the Holy Scriptures. These words have continued to speak to the faithful through the centuries following that special history to this very day. Since the Bible is so rich in theological content, it is self-evident that different words from God can come through its pages to different people in different circumstances. At the center of this richness, it must be emphasized, stands Jesus Christ in his incarnation, life, atoning death, and resurrection. The Word Incarnate is the measure of all other words in the Bible.

2. The Entire Bible as Authoritative

Although the Christian's knowledge of God's nature and will comes most fully through the witness of the New Testament to Christ, it must be recognized that all biblical books are authoritative for the Church— Old Testament as well as New Testament.

No Christian should undervalue the divine significance of the Old Testament. It was the Bible of Jesus and the earliest Christians, and their primary knowledge of God's nature and will came from its pages. One should note that the Old Testament contains a number of truths that are presupposed or not fully developed in the New Testament. Genesis 1, for example, speaks of God's creation of nature and its fundamental goodness. The Exodus event testifies to God's continuing concern to liberate people from all kinds of physical bondage, while the subsequent covenant at Sinai with the Ten Commandments reveals his unchanging moral will, commandments with continuing authority even for today. The prophecies of the prophets, such as the words of Amos, "...let justice flow like a stream, and righteousness like a river that never goes dry" (5.24), speak of God's demand for social justice in human society. Of special importance for the Christian believer is the fact that the Old Testament has preserved God's promises concerning the Messiah, the Suffering Servant, the Great High Priest, the Prophet to come, the Mediator of a new covenant, and others, which the New Testament sees as fulfilled in Jesus.

To be sure, if there seems to be a tension between the teachings of the Old Testament and the New Testament, the latter takes precedence for Christians. Through the biblical centuries God was progressively revealing his reality and will, as his people were able to appropriate them, to reach a climax with his perfect Word in Jesus Christ. For example, the destruction of Canaanite men, women, and children during the Conquest under Joshua, which the Hebrews believed to be in accordance with the will of God, may be understandable in certain ways in that time, but it is certainly not a warrant for such actions on the part of present followers of the One who commanded love, not only of neighbor, but of enemy as well.

3. Proof Texts and Theme Texts

In interpreting the entire Bible, one should distinguish between *proof* texts and *theme* texts. A *proof* text is a biblical passage that is taken out of context and is used in an attempt to prove a belief that is contrary to the fundamental thrust of the biblical revelation. An illustration would be the curse on Canaan in Genesis 9.25, originally directed against the immoral Canaanite religion, but which has been misinterpreted to claim the inferiority of black people or even to justify slavery. On the other hand, a *theme* text expresses a fundamental truth of biblical revelation. The statement in Genesis 1.27 affirming that "man" (*adam*, human being) has been created in the image of God reflects a basic theme that becomes ever clearer in the entire Bible. Every human being in God's creation has incomparable value, whose dignity must be respected.

Perhaps, however, the most important theme texts for Christians are John 3.16: "For God loved the world so much that he gave his only Son, so that everyone who believes in him may not die but have eternal life." And: "Love the Lord your God with all your heart, with all your soul, with all your mind, and with all your strength" ... and "Love your neighbor as you love yourself" (Mark 12.30, 31).

4. Different Words for Different People

The believer always seeks to be open to all of Scripture, while recognizing, of course, that it will speak different words to different people at different times, depending on their situation and needs.

For example, the traditions in the Book of Exodus concerning God's act of liberating the Hebrew people from bondage in Egypt have spoken powerfully to African Americans as well as to other oppressed racial and ethnic groups through the years. Slavery, segregation, prejudice, or any form of racial or ethnic bondage, are repugnant in the eyes of the God of Moses and of the Lord Jesus Christ.

Paul's affirmation in Galatians 3.28 that in Christ there is neither Jew nor Gentile, slave nor free, male nor *female* has spoken to contemporary women in their struggle to find their rightful place under God in the Church and larger society.

The biblical words from God come not only to groups but also to individuals. To one believer, as with Moses in the Old Testament, or to Paul in the New Testament, is addressed a call to a special vocation; to another, a word of judgment for wrongful conduct; to yet another, a word of forgiveness for the same; to a person in deep sorrow, a word of comfort and support; to one facing imminent death: "I am the resurrection and the life. Those who believe in me will live, even though they die; and those who live and

▸ "Prayer Meeting," ©Samella Lewis/ Licensed by VAGA, New York, NY

believe in me will never die." (John 11.25b, 26a). The biblical words do not answer all of life's questions, but they do speak to the deepest human needs.

5. A Few Final Guidelines

Perhaps the most important guidelines for the Christian interpreter are (a) to be continually immersed in reading and listening to the Bible; (b) to think about what each passage meant in biblical times and may mean in contemporary times; (c) to be humble before it as the Word of God; and, above all, (d) to be prayerfully open to the guidance of the Holy Spirit in its interpretation.

IV. A Prayer

Blessed Lord, who caused all Holy Scriptures to be written for our learning: Grant us so to hear them, read, mark, learn, and inwardly digest them, that by the power of your Holy Word, and guidance of your Holy Spirit, we may patiently embrace, ever hold fast, and faithfully proclaim the hope of everlasting life you have given us in our Savior Jesus Christ. In his name we pray. Amen.

זה קטרת ואהרן הטיב שמן בנירות·

Two

Jubilee in Leviticus 17-26

Jerome Clayton Ross

The primary text on Jubilee is Leviticus 25, which is contextualized in two respects. First, Leviticus 25 is part of Leviticus 17–26, a three-tiered, five-part manual of discipline that was designed for use by the Aaronite priests. Second, Jubilee is located within the discussion of survival of a post-exilic Judean, and minority, community during the Persian Period. When seen in this respect, Jubilee is a socio-political and economic measure that is intended to secure the survival of the Judean community by means of reconstitution of community, and reclamation of control. Thus, it may best be appropriated as a tool for critique of contemporary discriminatory practices, and for empowerment of equitous communal life.

◂ "Aaron Pouring Oil Into One of the Lamps of the Menorah." By permission of the British Library

Introduction

As we approach the 21st century, the biblical theme of Jubilee (pronounced *Yôbel*, from the Hebrew) has surfaced. The main text for this theme is Leviticus 25, which is part of the larger law collection called the Holiness Code (or "H"- Leviticus 17–26). Typically, "return" or "restoration" has been regarded as its focus. However, this depends upon the approach that one takes. This discussion of Jubilee takes a different focus, which examines the text from a literary critical approach.

Since our concern is with Jubilee, Leviticus 25 is the focal text for discussion. In the first section, **The Structure of Leviticus 25** is briefly described. In the second section, **The Structure and the Classification of Leviticus 17–26**, its "superstructure," is presented in order to show its levels and interconnections, and to classify it. In this respect, Leviticus 17–26 has a three-tiered, five-part structure, and is best classified as a manual of discipline for use by priests.

The third section, **The Theme of Holiness in Leviticus 17–26: Its Use**, discusses this key theme and shows that it is developed and utilized as a multi-faceted boundary-marker for the community, and as such is employed as a mechanism for survival. In this regard, faith constitutes a way of living that is manifested socially in customs, institutions, practices, and symbols, and conceptually in principles, statements, or theories. Being both theoretical and practical, it is complex, integrating matters pertaining to worship with sociopolitical affairs, all from the perspectives of its drafters. As an expression of biblical faith, Leviticus 17–26 is the indicator of a post-exilic Judean (and thereby minority) community, that was headed by priests, who led a struggle to survive, and secured the existence of their community by means of the "fence" of holiness.

The fourth section, **The Concern with Survival in Leviticus 17–26,** explains the circumstances that necessitated its provisions. Here, it is shown that these laws address the confusion regarding the standards for the community that had ensued due to competing priestly factions within their socially mixed community (which was under Persian supervision) by means of seven principles for survival. The fifth section, **The Message of Leviticus 17–26,** details its basic thrust: its argument is that anyone, regardless of origin or prior affiliations, who lives in the province of Judah, and follows its rulings, is a legitimate worshiper of the LORD, or a Yahwist, and is thereby holy.

In the last section, **Conclusion: The Implications of Jubilee according to Leviticus 17–26**, the key data is summarized, from which implications for living are considered. The premier thesis for understanding Jubilee, according to Leviticus 17–26, is that it is designed to ensure the survival of the Judean community by means of reconstitution of community and reclamation of control on the part of the descendants of the exiled Jews. It is not simply a "return" or "restoration."

The Structure of Leviticus 25

Leviticus 25 is the ninth in a series of ten lessons, of which Leviticus 17–26 is composed. It consists of two parts: 1. an introduction (vv. 1, 2aa); and 2. teachings (vv. 2ab-55), that are followed by an insert (Leviticus 26.1, 2).

The introduction follows the standard, introductory formula (cf. Leviticus 17.1, 2a; 18.1, 2a; 19.1, 2aa) that consists of a quotation formula and a two-fold command ("The LORD commanded Moses to give...the following regulations..."; and "The LORD told Moses to say to the people..." serves the typical function of bracketing, and commissioning, the practical instructions that follow. The teachings are very extensive, including two major sections (vv. 2ab-7, 8-55) that cover regulations pertaining to land sabbaths and Jubilee.

The Structure and the Classification of Leviticus 17-26

Leviticus 25, which contains the discussion of Jubilee, is found in Leviticus 17–26, which has the following structure:

Priestly Regulations
Leviticus 21, 22

Communal Regulations
Leviticus 18–20

Cultic Regulations
Leviticus 23–25

Introduction
Leviticus 17

Conclusion
Leviticus 26

This structure reveals that Leviticus 17–26 is a teaching for priests, having Leviticus 21, 22 as the point of reference for the other chapters, and the land as the pervading focus. First, the instructions in

Leviticus 18–20 have points of contact with Leviticus 21, 22, and Leviticus 18.6-23; 19.3, 4, 20, 22; and 20.9-21 correspond to the regulations on marriage for the priests (Leviticus 21.7-9, 13-15), presenting the rules in the forms of prohibitions, cases that have been deliberated, and punishments.

The morality of the priests is set in the context of communal morality. For example, the purity that is required of the people in marriage is correlated with that of the priests, since it is probable from the general context that wives were sought and taken for these priests. The purity of the priests is, then, partially premised upon the purity of the community.

Second, in Leviticus 25.13-55, the specific cases concerning redemption which build upon the general regulations (vv. 10b-12) for Jubilee have similarities with the passages in Leviticus 18, especially vv. 6-23 and vv. 24-30. The consideration of marital relations betrays an underlying concern: maintenance and protection of land-rights. These were formulated and proposed in order that land may not be lost through exogamous marriages. In this respect, Leviticus 25.13-55 probably served as precautionary measures against the accumulation of land in the hands of a few landowners to the detriment of peasant farmers (called latifundialization). Furthermore, the land is the focus in Leviticus 26, continuing the discussions of Leviticus 25, and thereby relating to the other references to the land (19.23aa; 23.10ab; 25.2ab).

Regardless of whether or not the land-sabbaths and the Jubilee regulations were implemented, the ideals are lifted up, and serve as themes that connect this chapter to the rest of Leviticus 17–26. Several other observations are important: 1. the situation of the Levites (Leviticus 25.32-34); 2. the references to the priests as the primary addressees in the introductory formulae (Leviticus 17.2a; 21.1a; 22.2aa); and 3. the references to the members of Israel as the primary addressees (Leviticus 18.2a; 19.2aa; 20.2aa; 23.2aa; 24.2aa; 25.2aa).

The first two observations present the Levites in a position that is subordinate to the sons of Aaron, suggesting that the Aaronite priests are in power. The latter observation reveals a structural connector for the respective units (Leviticus 18–20; 23–25). Throughout each unit the intended final recipients are the same, changing only beyond these sections, and thereby bracketing them. Third, further similarities may be seen in Leviticus 19 and 23, 24.

In spite of mixed concerns that relate to other sections, these chapters contain passages that regulate the participation of the people in worship, such as eating (cf. 19.5-10, 23-25; 23; 24.5-9) and worship practices (cf. 19.3, 4, 26-32; 23; 24.2ab-9), which are also handled in the central section (21.16-23; 22). The distinguishing feature is the primary addressees, that is, the intended final recipients, for whom the instructions are presented. The difference between these two audiences is the direction of their responsibilities: the priests are primarily responsible *for* the people, while the people are to be accountable to the priests. So, the similarities between Leviticus 18–20 and 23–25 also reveal identical parties that are responsible, as distinct from those in Leviticus 21, 22.

Though all of the material within each unit is not substantially related, the major portions are. Thus, Leviticus 18–20 and 23–25 have a common focal point (i. e., Leviticus 21, 22) that projects the priests as the center, and suggests that these priests are the proponents of all three units of instructions. Though the instructions are purportedly for the laity as the intended final recipients, the written collection is primarily designed for use by the priests in the form of catechism or professional training. In light of the discussions about holiness-unholiness, and the insights from examination of its structure, Leviticus 17–26 is best classified as a *manual of discipline* for some faction of the Aaronite priests.

The Theme of Holiness in Leviticus 17–26: Its Use

As noted above, Leviticus 23–25 is laterally related to Leviticus 18–20. Because of this, the concern with holiness in Leviticus 23–25 develops the themes that are found in Leviticus 18–20. The dominant concern in Leviticus 23–25 is the establishment of the economy of the community which involves regulation of communal life (23.1—24.9; 25.1-12), control of deviant behavior (24.10-16), legislation of discrepancies in legal affairs (24.17-23), and redemption of property and persons (25.3-55). The underlying focus is management of the communal resources. The deprivation that had ensued due to exploitation had materialized in indentured servitude and loss of land (cf. Nehemiah 5.1-13).

Regardless of whether or not the sabbatical years and Jubilee (25.1-13) were observed, the regulations regarding these times aim toward redemption of property, and persons, and prevention of permanent land-sales (25.23a). In response to poverty and debt-slavery, a traditio-literary context for its cases of redemption is created, that is, Jubilee, and the primary goal is reacquisition of land and relief from debts. Positing that the land is holy because it is the LORD's (25.23a), the different cases are adjudicated: 1. redemption of property/crops (25.14-18); 2. securing of the land (25.19-24); 3. redemption of property in general (25.25-28); 4. redemption of a house in a walled city (25.29, 30); 5. redemption of houses in unwalled villages (25.31); 6. redemption of the property of the Levites (25.32-34); 7. maintenance of the poor Israelites (25.35-38); 8. redemption of an Israelite from an Israelite (25.39-46); and 9. redemption of an Israelite from a non-Israelite (25.47-53).

These stipulations, then, presuppose that their proponents claim the political authority to enforce them. In other words, the cases of redemption assume the legalization of holiness, whereby their composers addressed the legal inconsistencies (24.17-23), and the deviant behavior (24.10-16), that had occurred due to the mixed population. This use of the theme of holiness marks an effort to establish uniformity in jurisprudence (24.22). These chapters and themes culminate in another dimension of holiness. Here, holiness is the "traditio-spatio-temporal boundary-marker" for the community, which regulates its occasions for worship and business, as well as legal affairs. The view is fostered that the politics, and the economics of the community are to be premised upon the understanding that the land, and therefore time in the land, is holy.

In sum, the logical progression of the development of the holiness theme is: the personification of holiness by the priests (Leviticus 21–22) initially led to the parochialization of holiness (Leviticus 18; 19.19-32; 20) and the legalization of holiness (Leviticus 18; 19.11-18, 33-37; 24.10-23; 25; 26), by which the localization of holiness (Leviticus17) and the periodization of holiness (Leviticus 19.5-10; 23.1—24.9) occurred. The goal of the whole effort, or the most essential development, is the parochialization of holiness as the mechanism for the definition, and the demarcation, of the post-exilic Jewish community.

The Concern with Survival in Leviticus 17–26

The composition of Leviticus 17–26 is located in post-exilic Judah, specifically during the late Persian Period (350-300 B.C.). It addresses several local problems that had persisted from the beginning of the period when Cyrus instituted his administration: 1. the weakened socioeconomic fabric of Judah which was reflected in indentured servitude of Jews to Jews due to loss of land and debts (Nehemiah 5.1-15); 2. the conflicts of interest between the Palestinian Jews that remained in the land and the Jews that returned, that were reflected in the interference of the Samaritans (Nehemiah 3.10, 19; 4.1-3, 7, 8; 6.1, 2, 6, 7), the interference of "adversaries" of Judah and Benjamin (Ezra 4.1-5), and the rivalry among the priesthoods (i. e., the Levites and the Aaronites); and 3. the thin population of Judah.

Specifically, at the time of Nehemiah and Ezra, Judah was still internally disorganized, reflecting: 1. loss of identity and rights to land due to uncontrolled syncretism caused by marriage to foreign women (Nehemiah 10.30; 13.23, 24; Ezra 9, 10); 2. unregulated market practices such as selling on the Sabbath (Nehemiah 10.31; 13.15-18); 3. neglect of the seventh-year land-rest (Nehemiah 10.31); 4. neglect of the Levites and the sanctuary (Haggai 1.1-11; Malachi 2.4-9; Nehemiah 10.32-39; 13.10); 5. abuse, or misuse, of the sanctuary and offerings (Malachi 1.1-14; 3.6ff; Nehemiah 13.4, 5); and 6. infidelity among the priests (Malachi 2.13-17).

These features were caused by: 1. the termination of the Davidic monarchy which had provided economic and political structure, including its royal officials and the temple; 2. the rivalry among the leaders that remained in the land, particularly the priests; 3. the lack of a politically-endorsed ideology for the community; and 4. the increased de-urbanization of the Jewish population. To address these matters, Aaronite priests composed Leviticus 17–26, employing the theme of holiness as a mechanism for survival.

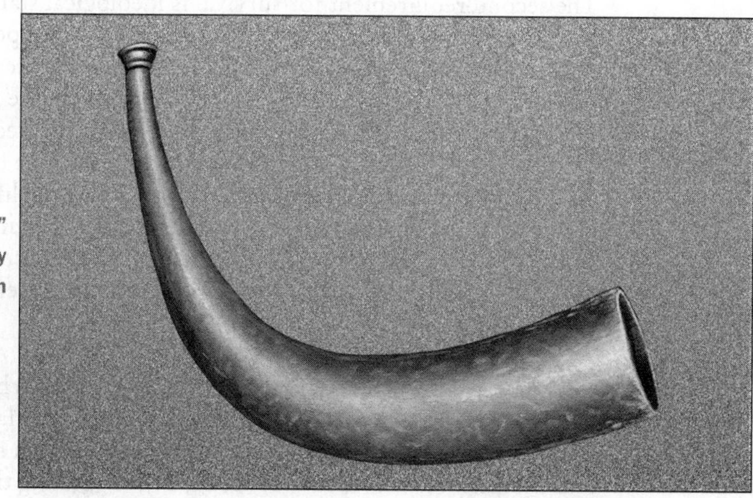

▸ **"Shofar," illustration by Steven Sullivan**

The primary concern of the post-exilic community, as throughout Israelite-Judean history, was survival, particularly since their community constituted a "minority culture" that was not politically self-determinant. The community, headed by its leaders, sought to address this concern in seven ways, which constitute categorically principles for survival. In this respect, both Ezra-Nehemiah and Leviticus 17–26 are reflections of the efforts of these post-exilic leaders.

First, survival required some administrative structure. This structure would account for the leadership, and provide the details of their positions and responsibilities. Ezra-Nehemiah shows that the Aaronite priests as well as non-priestly members of the exilic community were employed. While Nehemiah served as a governor, overseeing religious, political, and military affairs (cf. Nehemiah 8, 10, 11), Ezra's assignment was restricted to investigation of the central administration, which he scrutinized according to a Persian-endorsed version of Israelite laws (cf. Ezra 7.6, 11-21). The stylistic features of Ezra-Nehemiah betray two tendencies (i.e., that of the Aaronites, and that of the Levites), which reflect competing biblical traditions (i.e., some versions of the Priestly traditions and the Deuteronomic traditions). However, Leviticus 17–26 does not allude to such a tension, but assumes that the Aaronites are in control (cf. Leviticus 24.10-23), making only one reference to the Levites (Leviticus 25.32, 33), and building upon the extant traditions.

The second requirement for survival is ideological standardization, that is, establishment and determination of the policies for intra-communal organization. This was necessary because of the mixed composition of the community. These Israelite traditions, including possible law collections, that Ezra purportedly taught (cf. 9.1, 2, 10-15; 10.2, 10-14, 44), and that Nehemiah enforced (cf. 13.23-31a), provided the rules that regulated the life of the community. Similarly, the whole of Leviticus 17–26 instructs a priestly faction that would have been operative in a society like that of Nehemiah and Ezra, that is, a society that resembles that of Ezra-Nehemiah.

Leviticus 17–26 projects a heterogeneous society in which power struggles were occurring, that included concern over land-rights. This mixture is especially evident in the concern with morality and exogamy (cf. Leviticus 18, 20, 21, 24), suggesting that cultural clashes ensued in which conflicting standards were propagated.

Though the Aaronite priests were in power, they suffered from internecine struggles. However, that faction of their group that composed Leviticus 17–26 offers a more conciliatory view to the two polarized positions of the Levites (represented by Nehemiah) and the Aaronites (represented by Ezra).

The third requirement for survival is economic independence. This concern with acquisition and management of intra-communal resources is the underlying purpose behind Nehemiah's, and Ezra's, abolition of intermarriages, and the focus upon observance of Sabbath (cf. Nehemiah 5; 10; 13.15-22). Similarly, Leviticus 17–26 endorses the Sabbath, establishing its priority in the cultic calendar (cf. Leviticus 23.3), and Jubilee (cf. Leviticus 25.10-55), which appears as a development of the Sabbath-year (Leviticus 25.1-9). There, the rules pertaining to intermarriage, particularly those regarding familial relations (chapters 18, 20), are on the same structural level as those pertaining to worship matters (chapters 23–25).

By means of structural association, the rules concerning the social behavior of its community are related to those regarding its economic status and prevalent problems. The focus upon the worship-system, then, reveals the concern with establishment of the rules for the community, and the regulation of the life of the people. This, inevitably, included the effort to control the economics of the community (cf. Leviticus 17, 22, 23, 25). However, Leviticus 17–26 goes further than Ezra-Nehemiah by defining the familial relations, and detailing the cases of land-rights disputes, including their respective, legal decisions. Its focus upon purity constitutes its effort to preserve the solidarity and the identity of the Judean community, that is, to create a "culture of resistance," and thereby completes the missions of Ezra and Nehemiah.

The other four requirements for survival are implicit in the previous ones. They are: 1. selective appropriation; 2. common language; 3. population; and 4. land. The concern with land, especially maintenance and protection of land-rights (cf. Nehemiah 5; Leviticus 25), has been discussed. This preoccupation is understandable since agriculture was the basis for the economy of the community. Also, having a common language within the community was an obvious necessity for perpetuation of the governing and founding traditions of the community (cf. Nehemiah 13.23, 24). The concern with promotion of Israelite traditions inevitably included, and required, the preservation of the "mother tongue." This requirement is, thus, an ingredient of ideological standardization.

Regarding selective appropriation, the community had to balance the extra-communal influences and the intra-communal accommodation. In other words, they had to assimilate carefully the features of the dominant culture that they could adopt (cf. Nehemiah 7.6-72; 10.1, 2; Leviticus 18.1-5, 24-30; 20.22-26). This concern is particularly at stake in the area of ideological standardization, in which the norms for the community are determined. However, as a dominated culture, this concern was most acute. It is noteworthy, then, that Leviticus 17–26 addresses this concern that is prevalent in Ezra-Nehemiah, and promulgates legal decisions regarding cases of violation (cf. Leviticus 18, 20), of which Ezra and Nehemiah (and the writer of their work) were ignorant. Lastly, and most obvious, population was a primary concern. Nehemiah's efforts at debt-release, whereby land could be regained, served the purpose of relocation of the people to Jerusalem (cf. Nehemiah 5). Also, the efforts of both Nehemiah and Ezra entailed the fortification of Judah, which required the numbers of the people in the area to be increased.

Besides the concern with land-rights and familial relations, Leviticus 17–26 indirectly encourages (re)population in its definitions of inter-personal relations. For example, that homosexuality is forbidden (Leviticus 18.22; 20.13) suggests that, not only was it regarded as a "confusion" or an "unnatural mixture," it was unproductive; it did not contribute to the biological perpetuation of the community. Thus, Leviticus 17–26 is a comprehensive statement of the rulings that implicitly addresses the situation that is described in Ezra-Nehemiah, and is best seen as a law collection that is directed toward resolution of the lingering problems that the missions of Nehemiah and Ezra sought to handle. In this light, Jubilee is best understood.

The Message of Leviticus 17–26

Leviticus 17–26 has two general categories of addressees: the primary addressees and the intended final recipients. The Aaronite priests are the primary addressees in Leviticus 17.2a; 21.1a; and 22.2aa, while the members of Israel are the primary addressees in Leviticus 18.2a; 19.2aa; 20.2aa; 23.2aa; 24.2aa; 25.2aa. Also, the people are the intended final recipients in those chapters, where the priests are the primary addressees. Notice that the instructions are always initially directed to the Aaronite priests, who are charged with the responsibility of conveying the message to the people. This is understandable by virtue of the position of the priests who were numbered among the leadership of the community, and probably drafted the laws for the community.

▸ "Shofar Horn," carved dark brown ram's horn with Hebrew inscription. Mid 18th century, from Germany Erich Lessing/ Art Resource, NY

As a manual of discipline for its priests, Leviticus 17-26 was designed to establish uniformity in theory and practice regarding the governance of the cult and the community, specifically in the aftermath of the missions of Nehemiah and Ezra, which is reflected in Samaritan Yahwism (cf. Nehemiah 3.10, 19; 4.1-3, 7, 8; 6.1, 2, 6, 7) and Zionistic Yahwism (cf. references to "Jew[s]"—Ezra 5.1, 8; 7.14; Nehemiah 1.2; 2.16; 3.33, 34; 4.6; 5.1, 8, 17; 6.6; 13.23), respectively.

The situation that Leviticus 17–26 addresses was further complicated by those who may have been non-Israelites, or non-believers, and were categorized as: 1. "nation" (cf. Leviticus 18.24, 28; 20.23); 2. "stranger" (cf. Leviticus 22.10, 12, 13); 3. "native" (cf. Leviticus 17.15; 19.34; 24.22); 4. "resident" (cf. Leviticus 25.6, 23, 35, 40, 45, 47); 5. "day-laborer" (cf. Leviticus 22.10; 25.6, 40); and 6. "resident alien" (cf. Leviticus 17.8, 10, 12, 13, 15; 18.26; 19.33, 34; 20.2; 22.18; 23.22; 24.22 [cf. vv. 10-16, 23]; 25.23, 35, 45, 47 [cf. v. 6]).

"One of the nations" signifies "a political entity that is different from Israel," while "stranger" denotes "an individual who is not a member of Israel." These are used to refer to outsiders. "Native" is a generic term for "one who is born among (i.e., within the territory of) the member group," while "resident" indicates "one who resides in the vicinity of the member group" but is not necessarily a member of the group, such as a "day-laborer." In this sense, the "resident" is a foreigner, or non-Israelite, that is, one who is

▸ "Jubilee Justice," Illustration by Kimanne Smith

uncircumcised and thereby a non-proselyte. Now, the most frequent references are to the "resident alien." Its frequency reflects a concern with the welfare of the persons in this category. This label denotes "one who is fully integrated into Israel," that is, "a proselyte who has been circumcised, and thereby has obtained rights equal to any Israelite."

The various possible strands of Israelite faith, including their respective proponents, and the mixed composition of the community combined to create a situation in which confusion persisted regarding the aims of the Persian overlords, as presented by the local leaders, and the identification of the legitimate leaders. Specifically, the competing Israelite groups evidently differed regarding the degree of inclusivity that would be operative for determining the Israelite (here, Judean) community. So, Leviticus 17–26 informs the priests and the people, particularly the "newcomers" or proselytes, of the standards that are regarded as the administrative policy for the community. It is intended to enhance its support from the priests, and to solicit allegiance to its sponsoring priests from the populace, particularly the "resident aliens."

Leviticus 17–26 addresses the problem of confusion regarding the standards for the community that is due to competing priestly factions within the community. The mixed composition of the community fostered internecine struggles between competitors for control. In this context the identity, and the existence, of Israel were threatened due to unqualified accommodation of foreigners by the majority of the Aaronite priests.

Regionally, the Samaritan worshipers and the Judean worshipers — representatives of two forms of Israelite faith/Yahwism—argued for the legitimacy of their respective worship traditions and sites. Locally, the Aaronite priesthood was divided regarding a temple-focused worship-system as opposed to a popular-oriented one. The key issue was the degree of inclusion of outsiders, that is, to what extent the resident aliens were to be involved in the Judean community. This matter was, then, addressed through the theme of holiness. Leviticus 17–26 was compiled to train its priests in facilitating the education of the resident aliens, along with the other Israelites within the community, who suffered at the hands of the Aaronite priests who contended with the priests who composed it.

The solution that Leviticus 17–26 offers has several premises. First, it assumes that one's level/degree of holiness is commensurate with that of one's political power and status. In this respect, the high priest held the highest level/degree of holiness, since he permanently remained within the sanctuary confines (Leviticus 21.10-13) and headed the Aaronite priests. The Aaronite priests, then, constituted the second level. On the third, and lowest, level of holiness were the people of Israel, whose status as holy was contingent upon compliance with the regulations, and thereby maintenance of the purity of the land. Thus, it is posited that one's state of holiness is equivalent to one's social standing. The corollary, then, to the first premise is that the purity laws of Leviticus 17–26 are its norms for the community.

The central message of Leviticus 17–26 relates to the issue of survival, particularly in regard to the inclusion of the resident aliens. Through use of holiness as a multi-faceted boundary marker, in which the purity laws are utilized as the norms for the community, it argues that Israelite-monitored inclusivity is mandatory for Jewish existence. It perceives that foreigners, especially the resident aliens, are indispensable for the economic well-being of the Jewish community. However, these foreigners could not be unconditionally permitted to participate in the community, since they had acquired land and status within the community.

By means of parochialization of holiness, the legal mechanism to include and supervise the resident aliens is drafted. This stance is conciliatory: a line is drawn between the right-wing view of the Aaronite priests who advocated a temple-focus, and the left-wing view of the popular culture, which included the Samaritan worshipers of the Lord and the Levites, who advocated forms of Israelite faith that were different. This inclusion of the resident aliens, and the conciliatory stance, permitted the priests who composed Leviticus 17–26 to gain the dominance that was needed to control the community. Thus, the Judean community was redefined. Now, anyone, regardless of origin or prior affiliations, who lived in the province of Judah, and followed Leviticus 17–26, the rulings of a conciliatory faction of the Aaronite priests, was a legitimate member of Israel (i.e., a Yahwist), and thereby holy. The consequence of this movement was the survival (i.e., the establishment and the expansion) of the Judean community through the end of the Persian period.

Conclusion: The Implications of Jubilee according to Leviticus 17–26

This examination of Leviticus 17–26 has uncovered several things about Jubilee. First, the Jubilee regulations are developments of the principle of Sabbath, which is designed for control and management of the economics of the community. Second, the Jubilee regulations have several interrelated premises: 1. the land is the basis of the economy; 2. the land is the LORD's and thereby not marketable; and 3. the land is holy, and therefore time in the land is holy. Third, the Jubilee regulations have a two-fold design: 1. to prevent latifundialization, that is, the accumulation of land in the hands of a few landowners to the detriment of peasant farmers; and 2. to redeem land and people. These foci serve the larger goal of protecting and maintaining land-rights. Fourth, the Jubilee regulations directly counter the situation, mainly status, of the resident aliens, who owned land that had been confiscated due to debts, yet whose participation in the community was indispensable for its economic well-being. These resident aliens were the creditors, to whom the indebted Israelites, probably Jews, had been indentured slaves. The inclusion and the conversion of the resident aliens, then, served to facilitate reconstruction of the community by means of debt-release.

Several implications emerge for modern appropriation and practice of Jubilee. First, *people should not profit at the expense of others' integrity*. Economic exploitation is tabooed! Jubilee and Leviticus 17–26 as a whole employ a "principle of fairness/equality," which highlights the "connectedness" of all members of society. When the well-being of one is meaningfully tied to the well-being of another, welfare systems and government medical assistance become superfluous, for these programs would be supplied by the "grassroots movement" of the families. In other words, the "Social Security" commandment (Exodus 20.12; Deuteronomy 5.16) must constitute the basis for family life. On a larger scale, Jubilee demands economic cooperation between the suburbs and the inner cities, the rural areas and the urban areas!

Second, *integration must be integritous.* The lack of success of the prevalent attempts at integration, the various efforts at cooperation, and the diverse projects for reunification is due to the approaches that are taken, that is, the standards and the policies are not integrated, but the cards of color, race, and status as reflected in the people are shuffled, while the rules of the game remain the same! True integration, as suggested by Leviticus 17–26, requires genuine and mutual appreciation of others (i.e., peoples, races, ethnic groups. etc.). Just like the returning descendants of the exiled Jews needed the resident aliens, so do all the diverse facets of our citizenry need each other, not as political pawns but as partners! Those who are most socio-politically self-determinant must be compassionate and sensitive to those who are not, as expressed through thorough inclusivity, which cannot be legislated but must be self-motivatedly orchestrated at the nuclear (i.e., individual, personal, or family) level.

Third and final, *a sense of awe and wonder must be reembraced*, such that life and land are primary. Survival is simply people in some place with some sacred purpose. Jubilee is based upon the premise that life is holy. In this respect, life must be consecrated—not "worship life" or some compartmentalized portions, but all of life! Such sanctification of life has to include intentional transformation of all spheres of society—family, job, neighborhood, schools, hospitals, businesses! The only way that one may know that the Lord is holy, even that the Lord is present, is through holy living! In other words, holy—"holistic"—living *re-presents* the Lord's holy presence.

Selected Bibliography

Gerstenberger, Erhard S. *Leviticus. The Old Testament Library Series,* translated by Douglas W. Stott. Louisville: Westminster/John Knox Press, 1996.

Knohl, Israel. *The Sanctuary of Silence: The Priestly Torah and the Holiness School.* Minneapolis: Fortress Press, 1995.

Ross, Jerome C. *The Composition of the Holiness Code* (Lev. 17–26). (Dissertation: University of Pittsburgh, 1997) [UMI 9816816].

Wright, Christopher J. H. *"Jubilee, Year of"* in *The Anchor Bible Dictionary, Volume 3,* edited by David Noel Freedman and others. New York: Doubleday, 1992.

Wright, David P. *"Holiness (OT)" in The Anchor Bible Dictionary, Volume 3,* edited by David Noel Freedman and others. New York: Doubleday, 1992.

Three

The Message of Salvation

Thomas L. Hoyt, Jr.

The article on Luke 4.16-30 is written with the original readers in mind and with the realization that the re-enactment of traditions creates through the Spirit of God an ever new event in the life of new believers. This text is shown to be programmatic for the whole of Luke's Gospel. It connects Jesus' ministry to the Year of Jubilee, a time of care, redemption, and release. It shows how the ministry of Jesus epitomized a rejection-acceptance theme: Gentiles accept Jesus, Jewish religious leadership does not; poor, sinners, outcasts accept Jesus, but so-called rich, righteous ones, religious leaders, and others do not.

This message of salvation, so dear to the Lukan congregation, has functioned in the lives of African Americans, giving impetus for hope and motivation for positive action against oppression.

◂ "Young woman reading the Bible," ca. 1937, ABS Archives

Luke 4.16-30

Jesus and those who originally interpreted his mission were influenced by the prophetic tradition of Hebrew scripture. This Bible Study lifts up the salient features of the prophetic ministry of Jesus as described by one trajectory of the biblical text, Luke 4.16-30.

Importance of the Lukan Text

Luke 4.16-30 has been called the entire Gospel in a nutshell. It is the prelude to all that will come after. Robert C. Tannehill describes the event at Nazareth as having "typical and programmatic significance for the whole of Jesus' ministry as Luke understands it." [1] The introduction of themes which re-occur elsewhere in Luke-Acts is one major indication of the programmatic nature of Luke 4.16-30.

The importance of this text is further shown by the manner in which Luke borrowed the original story from Mark and determined its form and position within his Gospel to create his original version. In my opinion it seems reasonable to be allied with those scholars (Creed, Tannehill, Fitzmyer) who maintain, with Bultmann, that while vv. 25-27 have come to Luke from one tradition and v. 23 has been incorporated from another source (with its mention of Capernaum and the proverb), Luke has constructed the scene at Nazareth rewriting the Markan account (cf. the much shorter Mark 6.1-6). Verses 17-21 and 28-30 are probably from Luke's own pen.[2] In the words of Tannehill, "the most convincing view of the origin of this pericope is that Luke has rewritten the Markan account, supplementing it with fragments of tradition and with material of his own composition."[3]

Locating the story at this point has a programmatic character. Regardless of one's opinion concerning the origin of Luke's account, one thing is clear: the point of the Lukan pericope is no longer simply the rejection at Nazareth; it has been expanded to introduce what Jesus' ministry is all about. This passage is Jesus' kerygmatic announcement, substituted for Mark 1.14b,15, which Luke omits.

1 Robert C. Tannehill. "The Mission of Jesus according to Luke 4.16-30," in *Jesus in Nazareth*, Walther Elthester. ed. (Berlin: de Gruyter, 1972), 51.

2 Joseph Fitzmyer, "Luke," *Anchor Bible* (New York: Doubleday, 1981, 526-27).

3 Tannehill, op. cit., 52.

The Inaugural Sermon

Luke uses 4.16-30 as a launching pad for the further development of the story of Jesus and compels the reader to become arrested by that fact by utilizing it as the inaugural address of Jesus as he begins his public ministry. There seems to be scholarly unanimity that this passage is programmatic for Luke's two volumes.[4]

As Luke's plan develops, the sequence seems to be deliberate as seen in the cry of John the Baptist, the Baptism of Jesus, the establishment of Jesus' divine and human ancestry, aborted attempts of "Satan" to impede the divine plan of salvation, and Jesus travels from Jerusalem to Galilee (4.14a). Jesus has now come to the discovery of who he is and recognizes that the Spirit of God is upon him. His fame spreads throughout the entire region (4.14b) and his teaching is universally acclaimed (4.15). The next step seems obvious: the public announcement of his mission which takes place in the synagogue at Nazareth (4.16-30).

Luke emphasizes four major points which I shall discuss separately. First, the announcement of Jesus' ministry as the fulfillment of God's salvation time; second, a statement about the nature of fulfillment of Jesus' ministry based on the quotation from Isaiah; third, the foreshadowing of Jesus' final suffering and rejection; and fourth, the foreshadowing of the movement of the Gospel from Jew to Gentile.

The Today of God's Salvation

The opening section of this text emphasizes rather dramatically the "today" of Jesus appearance. Today is "salvation-time." The "today" is intended to emphasize the fact that the fulfillment of the Scriptures has actually come to pass. This appears to be the most prevalent meaning of this term in Luke's usage.[5] Today, the Old Testament prophecies reach their goal. Thus, the text does not seem to sustain the thesis of some interpreters that "today" indicates that Luke thought of it as belonging to past history in terms of fulfillment of hope for a future kingdom.

[4] Walter E. Pilgrim. *Good News to the Poor: Wealth and Poverty in Luke-Acts.* (Minneapolis: Augsburg, 1981), 64. See Howard Marshall, *The Gospel of Luke: A Commentary on the Greek Text.* (Grand Rapids: Eerdmans, 1978), 178.

[5] See William F. Moulton and A.S. Geden, *A Concordance to the Greek Testament*, 2nd ed. (New York: Charles Scribner's Sons, 1960), 891-2.

In fact, it appears that a basic element of Luke's belief about the end of the age is the documentation of the present as the fulfillment of the promises made long ago. The time of fulfillment of Luke 4.18, 19 is now.

Since the time of salvation is here, the kingdom of God has begun, and the setting of this word "today" is within the context of Isaiah 61.1, 2a, describing that in which the kingdom consists, it is important to study the quotation 4.18, 19 to see how the ministry of Jesus is portrayed.

The Nature of Fulfillment in 4.18,19

Jesus, on the Sabbath, went in the synagogue of his hometown of Nazareth. He was following both his own and the Jewish custom (4.16). He stood to read the scripture from the scroll of the prophet Isaiah. He opened the scroll and sought the passage which says:

> "The Spirit of the Lord is upon me,
> because he has chosen me to bring good news to the poor.
> He has sent me to proclaim liberty to the captives
> and recovery of sight to the blind,
> to set free the oppressed
> and announce that the time has come
> when the Lord will save his people."
>
> (Luke 4.18, 19)

The Greek word, *heuren* of verse 17 does not mean "he found," but "he sought till he found," a fact many commentators and translators have overlooked. The text which Jesus read, Isaiah 61.1, 2, is

▸ "Jesus Speaking in the Synagogue" by Kimanne Smith

so central to Jesus' teaching (and to the themes of Luke's Gospel) that it is unacceptable to ascribe its selection to a coincidence. No, when Jesus was handed the Isaian scroll, he deliberately searched for this passage. This must have taken some time. If we remember that the scroll was probably 30 feet long and that it had to be unwound from the left spindle on to the right one, that Isaiah 61.1,2b is almost at the end of the book, and that in Jesus' time the text had not been subdivided into chapters, verses, or paragraphs, we may well imagine that it took Jesus some minutes before he located the text he wanted! If indeed Jesus delivered this sermon, one does not wonder that Luke remarks that all eyes in the synagogue were fixed on him! Luke (or Jesus) wanted this text and no other, because in his search of the Scriptures he had identified this text as central to the message of Jesus.

Essentially, verses 18 and 19 are a loose quotation of Isaiah 61.1, 2a (LXX) and an additional clause from Isaiah 58.6. Since Luke probably had a fondness for the Septuagint (the Greek translation), we would expect a great deal of agreement with it. Luke 4.18,19 follows closely the Septuagint, including its word order and its variations from the Hebrew text; nevertheless, there are some significant differences between the Septuagint and the Lukan version of Isaiah.

Luke substitutes "bring" and "proclaim" for "announce" in verse 18. After "He has sent me," Luke omits "to heal the broken-hearted." Luke adds a phrase from Isaiah 58.6, "to set free the oppressed."[6] Finally, the quotation ends abruptly in the midst of Isaiah 61.2 and, consequently, omits a reference to a day of vengeance. The omission of this latter phrase from the quotation of Luke implies that Jesus spoke words of mercy and grace, which probably accounts for the reaction of the Jews to Jesus' works, and which might even have prompted John to inquire of Jesus' identity (7.22).

The differences between the Lukan version and the texts from which he quotes may be the result of combined or isolated factors. First, the quotation in Luke may have been taken from a tradition of the Septuagint that no longer exists; second, some or all of the variations may be due to an attempt by either Luke or the church to recall the Old Testament passages from memory; or third, the

[6] G. W. Lampe, "Luke," in *Peake's Commentary on the Bible*, ed. M. Black (rev. ed., London: Thomas Nelson and Sons, 1962), 828, stipulates that the clause added from Isaiah 58.6 enables Luke "to introduce his favorite theme of 'release,' a word generally used in the sense of 'forgiveness' (of sins), which for him is the essence of the gospel."

▸ **"The Righteous Path," John Holyfield, Holyfield Studio. Centreville, VA**

quotation may reflect evangelistic editorializing. A closer look at these Septuagintal changes suggests that Luke 4.18,19 is an interpretive rendering of the Isaianic passages designed to emphasize a particular point. Otherwise, how does one explain how Jesus, while reading, or Luke while composing, could omit two particular phrases? Even more important, how could he have added a phrase (58.6) that was not even in the text that he is purported to have read? Apparently, the quotation merely helps us see that early church tradition depicted Jesus' ministry in the light of Isaiah 61.1, 2. Whatever may be the reasons for the variations of the Septuagint,

those variations confirm that an interpretation of the use of the quotation must be done in the light of the messianic implications of the passage.[7]

"The Sovereign LORD has filled me with his Spirit." The opening line of Isaiah touches on a special theme of importance to Luke. In both the Gospel and Acts, the role of the Spirit is crucial. Jesus is conceived

[7] Cf. James Muilenburg, *The Book of Isaiah, Chapters 40-66: Introduction and Exegesis*, IB, V, 708-709. He sees that the Isaianic passages are descriptive of the anticipated mission of the Servant of Yahweh during the Messianic era.

by the Spirit, baptized by the Spirit, empowered by the Spirit, the bearer of the Spirit, and anointed by the Spirit; and the entire story of the Church in Acts is a continuation of the work of the Spirit.

Not only in this episode, but throughout the Gospel, Luke points out the effect of the Spirit in the people when Jesus is present. The people are astonished, filled with awe, and obedient to his commands as they see signs of the inbreaking of the kingdom and the Spirit's manifestation. One notes that where there is movement of the Spirit, there is always movement toward the neighbor (Luke 4.22; 5.25; 7.16; 13.13; 17.15; 18.43).

The Greek word for poor in 4.18 is *ptochos*. The Hebrew word that lay behind the Greek of Isaiah 61.1 is *anawim*. This latter word usually means pious, God-fearing fold. Probably the word used in 4.18 has religious significance. Manson postulated that "poor," as well as "captives," "blind," and "oppressed," meant victims of inward repressions and spiritual ills. Hence, Jesus was offering spiritual deliverance.[8] This observation appears to be only partially correct. It minimizes both the historical occasion and the Lukan context of the text. As the evangelist used this passage, the religious import is certainly less clear.

The nature of Isaiah 61.1 must be remembered in any interpretation of 4.18, 19. Gilmour says, "The original expressed some post-exilic prophet's consciousness of mission."[9] The mission was to herald a joyous return from Babylonian exile, with the imagery of the year of Jubilee saturating the whole. The phrase, "and announce that the time has come when the Lord will save his people" (4.19), suggests the imagery of the Old Testament's year of Jubilee. The year of Jubilee included the following four prescriptions: (1) leaving soil fallow, (2) the remission of debts, (3) the liberation of slaves, (4) the return of family property to each individual.

Paul Hollenbach offers a striking summary of this Sabbath-Jubilee tradition in other Torah texts. He summarizes as follows: There are to be no poor, i.e., disinherited, in Israel according to her covenant with Yahweh; however, if Israel breaks the covenant and Israelites wrong (i.e., dishonor) each other and Yahweh, and poor appear, their needs are to be met generously in three time frames—

[8] William Manson, *The Gospel of Luke* (New York: R.R. Smith, 1930), 41-42.

[9] S. M. Gilmour, "*The Gospel According to St. Luke*," IB, VIII (1952), 91.

their immediate need for food and clothing, their short-term need for family restoration, and their long-term need for total social reconstruction; in these ways the honor of the disinherited and of Yahweh will be restored.[10]

After this summary, Hollenbach sets up a schema which stems directly from the Sabbath-Jubilee tradition for understanding the thinking and deeds of Jesus. He says:

> The purpose of SJ (Sabbath-Jubilee) provisions is to prevent the permanent degradation of the poor by meeting their needs in these three time frames and in two social settings. Meeting needs in immediate, short-term, and long-term frames we may call care, redemption, and release. The social settings are kinship and politics. The first two time frames concern the kin of those in need, while the third concerns the total community. This is so because the first two kinds of need are largely individual, while the third is a matter of the structure of the whole society. The first two needs can be met by philanthropic acts, while the third can be met only through a reordering of the whole social structure. The first two are designed to prevent the need for the third, but the third is necessary because the first two do not do the job. In short, the SJ legislation is designed to prevent the development of an aristocratic-peasant society out of a covenantal egalitarian society, but should such a shift occur, the legislation also is designed to prevent its being permanently established.[11]

Claus Westermann agrees with the basic analysis of Hollenbach when he suggests that the passage from Isaiah refers, not to the exiles, but to persons imprisoned for indebtedness. Furthermore, he sees the suffering as actual in nature.[12] Thus, if Luke relates to the Isaianic text with the meaning as projected by Westermann, the year of Jubilee saturates the whole and speaks to physical destitution, possibly signifying the new age. Salvation is, therefore, not just spiritual, but also physical.

The question can be asked: Do we find in the ministry of Jesus the three responses of care, redemption, and release as displayed in the Sabbath-Jubilee? A brief look at each may show the following:

[10] See "Liberating Jesus for Social Involvement," *Biblical Theology Bulletin* Vol. XV, 153.

[11] Ibid.

[12] Claus Westermann, *Isaiah 40-66*, trans. David M.G. Stalker (Philadelphia: Westminster Press, 1969), 366-7.

Care, Redemption, and Release

While care for the poor was the basic character of the actions and teachings of Jesus, redemption and release certainly would flow from his compassionate ministry.

In the conversation with John's disciples, Jesus makes known the nature of his ministry which was in doubt by John. "Are you the one John said was going to come, or should we expect someone else?" The several tasks to be carried out by the one anointed by the Spirit are suggested in Luke 7.21,22 as presently being carried out in the ministry of Jesus.

At that very time Jesus healed many people from their sicknesses, diseases, and evil spirits, and gave sight to many blind people. He answered John's messengers, "Go back and tell John what you have seen and heard: the blind can see, the lame can walk, those who suffer from dreaded skin diseases are made clean, the deaf can hear, the dead are raised to life, and the Good News is preached to the poor."

The blind see:

This quotation fits perfectly the theme of the opening sermon of Jesus. What could it mean that the "blind receive their sight?" Allan Boesak of South Africa has some wonderful images of what these phrases in Luke really mean. The blind received their sight:

> What else can it mean but that people can now see themselves as God sees them. They can see their human possibilities as well as they see their present situation. They can see a future of freedom and human dignity to which they have been blind before.

The lame walk:

> What could it mean for those who for so long were lying by the wayside crippled by feelings of inferiority, fear and lack of vision?

Boesak says of his poor and oppressed fellow pilgrims:

> We got so used to our lowly position, we accepted our suffering as God's will. We stared ourselves blind against the white man's power and his guns. We were lame! Jesus is saying to us: the kingdom is yours. Get up and walk. Its power is yours: stand up and be strong.

Lepers are cleansed:

Means that God has touched the poor in Jesus the Messiah. God has given "untouchables" a new self image of "worthfulness".

The deaf hear: What do they hear?

They hear good news. No longer a pseudo-gospel designed to justify oppression and comfort for the oppressor. No longer a gospel so spiritualized that it has become anemic and incapable of dealing with the harsh realities… , but a word of liberation and freedom and human dignity.[13]

The dead are raised up:

There are various kinds of death. There is physical death; there is death which one experiences outside of the human community. This latter experience is the death of a person who is merely property and is not accepted by others. More importantly, there is a death in which one is not at peace with oneself, when one does not accept oneself as a vital link in the human community. Such has been the case of so many in the Third World and those in the first world living under Third World conditions.

To all these people Jesus preaches the good news that God, in Messiah Jesus, has seen the condition of the people, has taken upon God's self the condition of the people, and taken their cause as God's own. That is the good news:

"He has filled the hungry with good things,
and sent the rich away with empty hands."
(Luke 1.53)

The LORD judges in favor of the oppressed
and gives them their rights.
(Psalm 103.6)

The good news is that the Sovereign One is here to execute justice for the oppressed, to give food to the hungry, to uphold the widow and the fatherless, and to bring to ruin the way of the wicked.

[13] Allan Boesak, "Shall We Look For Another?" *The Reformed Journal* Vol. 31 (June, 1981), 19.

Rejection at home (4.22-30)

This announcement of a new age in 4.18,19 contained an inherent criticism of all those powers and agents of the present order. This was the time of release announced by Jesus. Walter Brueggemann summarizes concerning the ministry of Jesus:

> His message was to the poor, but others kept them poor and benefitted from their poverty. He addressed the captives (which meant bonded slaves). But others surely wanted that arrangement unchanged. He named the oppressed, but there are never oppressed without oppressors.[14]

We are surprised, therefore, by the initial reaction of the crowd: "They were all well impressed with him and marveled at the eloquent words that he spoke" (Luke 4.22a). The record of Matthew 13.57 and Mark 6.3 state that the crowd took offense at him. The initial reaction of the crowd in Luke later turned into the same reaction as recorded in Matthew and Mark.

The final rejection by the crowd ensued because Jesus continued to talk about prophets lacking honor in their own country (v. 24). He also recounted in a second sermon (vv. 25-28) the Old Testament stories of Elijah and Elisha. These two prophets, in their ministry to Gentiles, were used to illustrate the proverb: "Prophets are never welcomed in their hometown" (Luke 4.24). Both prophets were more successful with Gentiles (strangers) than with Jews. Elijah ministered to the widow at Zarephath, a Sidonian town and Elisha healed Namaan, a leper at Syria.

The implications are two-fold: (1) Those of Jesus' territory will not understand, and the Gentiles will. Luke once again stresses his universalism. (2) Jesus' way of salvation did not sustain the idea of preference, which some Jews had derived from their belief in God's election of them. God's love and redemption was on behalf of all. Poor and outcasts in one place were loved alike in another place by the God of Abraham, Isaac, and Jacob. God was free to love and choose whomever God desired. "The message of salvation" was for all people. Israel is called to be a light to the nations, and in Jesus that calling has become a reality.

[14] Walter Brueggemann, *The Prophetic Imagination.* (Philadelphia: Fortress Press, 1978), 83.

In this second sermon (4.25-28), if Israel rejects the gospel, the good news is preached to those who will hear, i.e., the Gentiles, the poor and outcast. In the first sermon, 4.18,19, Jesus' ministry was described in terms of a program in obedience to his calling, which had been sealed at baptism. The first sermon established a program for the whole of Luke's Gospel, and the second sermon laid out a basis for Acts.

The Scene Ends

The hometown folk rejected Jesus because they refused to believe that the village boy, the son of a carpenter, whom they had known from infancy, had a right to talk with them as a prophet. The crowd became incensed and wanted to cast him out of their village. They held his background against him, but, more importantly, their pride and prejudice stood in the way of their acceptance of his message and the universality of the good news that God had visited God's people.

▸ **"Elderly man reading the Bible," ca. 1949, ABS Archives**

In this section, we have attempted to show that Luke modified the tradition in order to accent the present fulfillment of Scriptures. The less-clear Markan summary of Jesus' beginning is replaced by a dramatic scene in which Jesus announces the presence of the messianic age, which is also described by Mark as "the Kingdom of God." The present kingdom is understood to be the coming of the anointed one in Jesus and his proclamation or evangelization of the physically and spiritually poor. Yet this present fulfillment in no way negates the consummation of the kingdom, which is characterized as "The End" (21.9). The kingdom is present and yet to come. We live between an "already" and a "not yet." In its present form, the poor are being evangelized. The deed and the word have combined to give power to the proclamation on behalf of the poor. There is release for the captives, sight for the blind, and liberty for the oppressed. They only have to receive what is being offered.

በስመ፡አብ፡ወወል
ድ፡ወመንፈስ፡ቅ
ዱስ፡አሐዱ፡አምላ
ክ፡ንወጥን፡ምስለ
ረድኤቱ፡እግዚአብ
ሔር፡ሎቱ፡ስብሐ
ት፡በእንተ፡ጽሒፈ፡
ሰዓታት፡ዘሌሊት
ወዘመዓልት፡ወ
እቱ፡ረዳኢነ፡በእ
ት፡ፈጽሞ፡ምስለ፡
ገቢር። ቀዳሚሁ፡
ለዝንቱ፡ይብል፡ዘይ
ጼሊ፡በውስተ፡ለ
ሊ፡ኵሉ፡ጸሎት። እ
ግዚኦ፡መሐረነ።
እግዚኦ፡መሐረነ፡እ
ግዚኦ፡ባርከነ። ሃ
ሌሉያ፡ስብሐት፡ለ
አብ፡ወወልድ፡ወ
መንፈስ፡ቅዱስ፡ይ

እዜኒ፡ወዘልፈኒ፡ለ
ዓለመ፡ዓለም፡አሜ
ን። ሶበ፡ንዘብጥ፡ደወ
ቅ፡ይትቀደስ፡ስም
ከ፡ትምጻእ፡መንግሥ
ትከ፡ወይኩን፡ፈቃ
ድከ፡በከመ፡በሰማ
ያት፡ከማሁ፡በምድር፡
ሲሳየነ፡ዘለለ፡ዕለት
ነ፡ሀበነ፡ዮም፡ኅድ
ግ፡ለነ፡አበሳነ፡ወጌጋ
የነ፡ከመ፡ንሕነኒ፡ን
ኅድግ፡ለዘ፡አበሰ፡ለ
ወኢታብአነ፡ውስ
ተ፡መንሱት፡አላ፡አድ
ኅነነ፡ወባልሐነ፡እ
ምኵሉ፡እኩይ፡በኢ
የሱስ፡ክርስቶስ፡
እግዚእነ፡እስመ፡ዚ
አከ፡ይእቲ፡መንግ
ሥት፡ኃይል፡ወስብ

Four

The Relationship between Hebrew and African Languages

Edwina M. Wright

◂ Ethiopian Psalter, 15th Century, Photo by Malcolm Varon

Very explicit linguistic connections can be made between the original language of the Old Testament, Hebrew, and certain African languages. Hebrew is a language of the Semitic family, as are certain languages of ancient and modern Ethiopia: Ancient Ethiopic and modern Ethiopian languages such as Amharic, Tigré and Tigrinya.

Another more fundamental linguistic connection between Hebrew and African languages is demonstrated by the fact that the Semitic language family itself is part of a larger language superfamily known as Afro-Asiatic. The Afro-Asiatic phylum is comprised of languages from the following language groups: Semitic, Berber, Egyptian, and the distinctly Black African language groups, Chadic and Cushitic.

This linguistic interrelationship between Hebrew and African languages allows for the discussion of further cultural linkages between the Old Testament and African reality.

The Hebrew language is the original language in which almost all of the Old Testament was written. Classical Hebrew is written from right to left, with vowel points written primarily below and above consonants.

Hebrew was first recorded around 1200 B.C. These first writings are ancient poetry which are found in the Old Testament in Exodus 15.1-18 and Judges 5.2-31 (referred to as "The Song of the Sea" and "The Song of Deborah" respectively).

In order to understand the historical relationship of languages, linguists have classified them according to families. The primary family, of which Hebrew is a part, is the Semitic language family. Of interest to those familiar with biblical genealogies, the term Semitic is derived from the biblical name Shem, Noah's eldest son.

Over the years there have been various classifications of the Semitic languages. One prominent classification system has been developed by Robert Hetzron, with modifications by John Huehnergard. According to this classification system, Semitic languages can be divided into three major groupings: East Semitic, South West Semitic and Central West Semitic.

Hebrew is classified as a part of the Central West Semitic subdivision. This grouping includes Arabian dialects and those languages which are most closely related to Hebrew (the Northwest Semitic subgroup). The Arabic subgrouping includes modern and ancient dialects. The ancient dialects include Pre-classical North dialects (5th century B.C.-4th century A.D.) and Classical Arabic, the language of the Qur'an (ca. 4th century A.D.). The North West Semitic subgroup includes Aramaic, Ugaritic, Hebrew, and other languages related to Hebrew. Ugaritic is the language of ancient Ugarit, a city of about sixty square kilometers located in Northern Syria, just one kilometer from the Mediterranean Sea. Aramaic is a language also closely related to Hebrew and is found in passages in Ezra and Daniel in the Old Testament. From the 8th to 4th centuries B.C., Aramaic became the universal language of diplomacy in the Ancient Near East. Certain Aramaic phrases are also found in the New Testament (e.g. Mark 5.41; 15.34).

East Semitic languages include Akkadian and Eblaite. Akkadian is the language which was spoken by peoples of the same name who settled in Mesopotamia (generally described as the land between the Tigris and Euphrates rivers). Eblaite texts have been discovered in Syria and date from the 24th to the 23rd centuries B.C.

The third major Semitic subgroup, the South West Semitic languages, include South Arabian and Ethiopian languages. Recorded ancient South Arabian languages (called Old Inscriptional South Arabian) date from the 8th to the 6th centuries B.C. An example of a modern South Arabian dialect is the language Mehri, which is spoken in Yemen.

It is in the South West Semitic subgrouping that we find Ethiopian languages. In any discussion of the interrelationship of the Hebrew language with African languages, the most obvious linkage to be discussed is that with the Semitic languages found in the African country of Ethiopia. Edward Ullendorff writes regarding Ethiopia: "In its long history the country has always formed a bridge between Africa and Asia" (p. 23).

Most scholars suggest that South Arabians (sometime during the first millennium B.C.), motivated in great part by trade concerns, migrated to the northern area of Ethiopia and commingled with the existing African Agaw population. The original Semitic South Arabian tongue was influenced by the Agaw dialect; this influence resulted over time in the development of Ethiopian Semitic languages. However, it is the opinion of other scholars that Ethiopian Semitic is more original.

These Semitic languages are divided into northern and southern dialects. Northern dialects include Ge'ez, Tigré, and Tigrinya. Ge'ez, also referred to as Ethiopic, is an ancient Ethiopian language for which texts exist which date from the 4th century A.D. While it is no longer a spoken language, Ge'ez is used as the liturgical language of the Ethiopian Orthodox Christian Church. Tigrinya is primarily spoken in the northern part of Ethiopia, particularly in the area of the old Axumite Kingdom; Tigré is primarily spoken in the northern province of Eritrea.

Southern dialects include Amharic, Gafat, Gurage, Harari, and Argobba. Amharic is spoken in the central part of Ethiopia and is the national language. It has been written since the 16th century in the script of Ge'ez. Gafat, a largely extinct dialect is spoken in the region of the Blue Nile. Gurage is a cluster of dialects (including for example, Chaha, Ennemor, and Muher) which is spoken in the area to the southwest of Addis Ababa, Ethiopia's capital. Harari is spoken in the city of Harar in eastern Ethiopia; Argobba is spoken to the northeast of Addis Ababa, and like Gafat, is nearly extinct.

An even closer connection can be suggested between Hebrew and African languages than that which is provided by the linkage between Hebrew and Ethiopian languages as members of the same language family. This closer association is indicated by the fact that most linguists consider the Semitic language family to be one branch of the larger Afro-Asiatic superfamily (or phylum). In addition to Semitic, the Afro-Asiatic phylum encompasses at least four other branches. These branches are Egyptian, Berber, Chadic and Cushitic. Some scholars also include the Omotic languages as a separate branch; these languages are spoken in the Omo Valley in Ethiopia and were formerly understood as part of the Cushitic language family.

The Egyptian branch is the only branch which includes one language. It began as Old Egyptian which was recorded from the third millennium B.C. and continued through its latest stage, Coptic. Coptic is known from the 2nd century B.C. to the 17th century A.D., and is still used to a small extent in the liturgy of the Egyptian Monophysite church.

The Berber (or Berbero-Libyan) branch is divided into various subgroups: 1) a northern subgroup spoken in Morocco, Algeria, and Tunisia, including, for example Tamazight; 2) an Eastern subgroup found in Libya; 3) Tuareg in the Sahara and Sahel, in Algeria, Niger, Mali; and 4) a Zenaga subgroup in Mauritania and possibly Senegal.

The Chadic branch contains about one hundred fifty living dialects in Nigeria, Chad, Cameroun, and Niger. Chadic languages are divided into Western, Central, and Eastern Chadic. Western Chadic includes the well-known and widely spoken language Hausa, as well as the Bauchi and Ron language groups. Central Chadic includes Logone-Kotoko, Higi, and Wandala among others; Eastern Chadic includes, for example, Dangla and Sokoro.

Cushitic languages are spoken primarily by peoples in Ethiopia, Somalia, and northwestern Kenya. This branch is divided into Northern, Central, and Eastern (which is further subdivided into Highland East and Lowland East Cushitic). Northern Cushitic includes the Beja language which is spoken in eastern Sudan and northern Ethiopia. The primary language of Central Cushitic is Agaw. Highland East Cushitic, a primary example of which is Sidamo, is spoken around the Ethiopian Great Rift Valley. Low-

▸ **Ethiopian Mandala Cross, 18th Century. Courtesy, Society of African Missions, Tenafly, NJ**

land East Cushitic languages are the most numerous and include Oromo, Afar-Saho, and Somali, which is the official language of Somalia.

Discussions regarding the classifying of languages into families or superfamilies almost always are accompanied by some discussion of how and where the family (or superfamily) may have originated. Scholars who work with the Afro-Asiatic superfamily have put forth numerous hypotheses concerning its geographical and linguistic origins. Suggestions for the geographic origin of Afro-Asiatic include Arabia, North Africa and East Africa.

The fact that Ethiopian languages are a blend of Cushitic and Semitic and that these two branches of the Afro-Asiatic family intersect in an African setting is certainly very suggestive as to the location of the original Afro-Asiatic language family. Scholars have noted as much. (See, for example, Ullendorff, p. 118.) No final determinations about origins, however, can be made at this time. In fact, scholars are not yet fully agreed on the facts of this superfamily. In comparing the various languages of the superfamily not every language contains all the same features. Significant similarities, however, have been found among various branches in vocabulary, in some sound patterns, and in some grammatical forms (especially in some verbal forms, pronouns and gender referents). Historical linguists, aided by archaeological finds, will continue to investigate these languages and perform the tasks that will make comparisons more valid.

While such investigation continues, however, those of us in the black church can note with great interest the significant familial relationship which most scholars acknowledge exists between the Hebrew language of the Old Testament Scriptures and languages which are spoken by peoples of African descent.

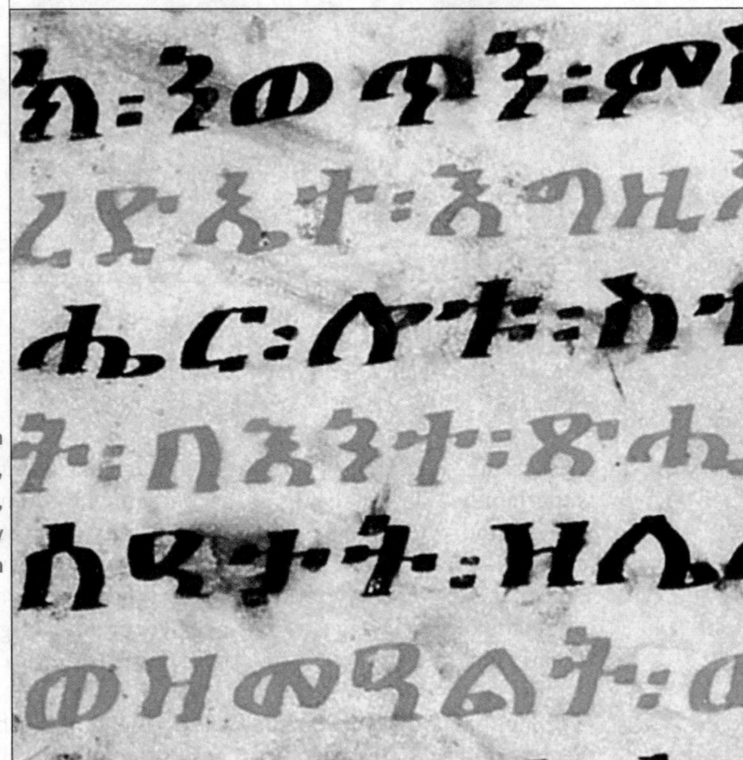

▸ **Detail, Ethiopian Psalter, 15th Century, Photo by Malcolm Varon**

Works Consulted

Diakonoff, Igor. *Afrasian Languages*. Moskow: Nauka, 1988.

Huehnergard, John. "Languages (Introductory)." in the *Anchor Bible Dictionary*, vol. 4, pp. 155-170. Edited by David Noel Freedman. New York: Doubleday, 1992.

________. *"Remarks on the Classification of the Northwest Semitic Languages,"* in The Balaam Text from Deir, 'Alla Re-Evaluated: Proceedings of the International Symposium held at Leiden 21-24 August 1989, pp. 282-293. Edited by J. Hoftijzer and G. Van der Kooij. Leiden: E. J. Brill, 1991.

Ullendorff, Edward. *The Ethiopians: An Introduction to Country and People.* London: Oxford University Press, 1965.

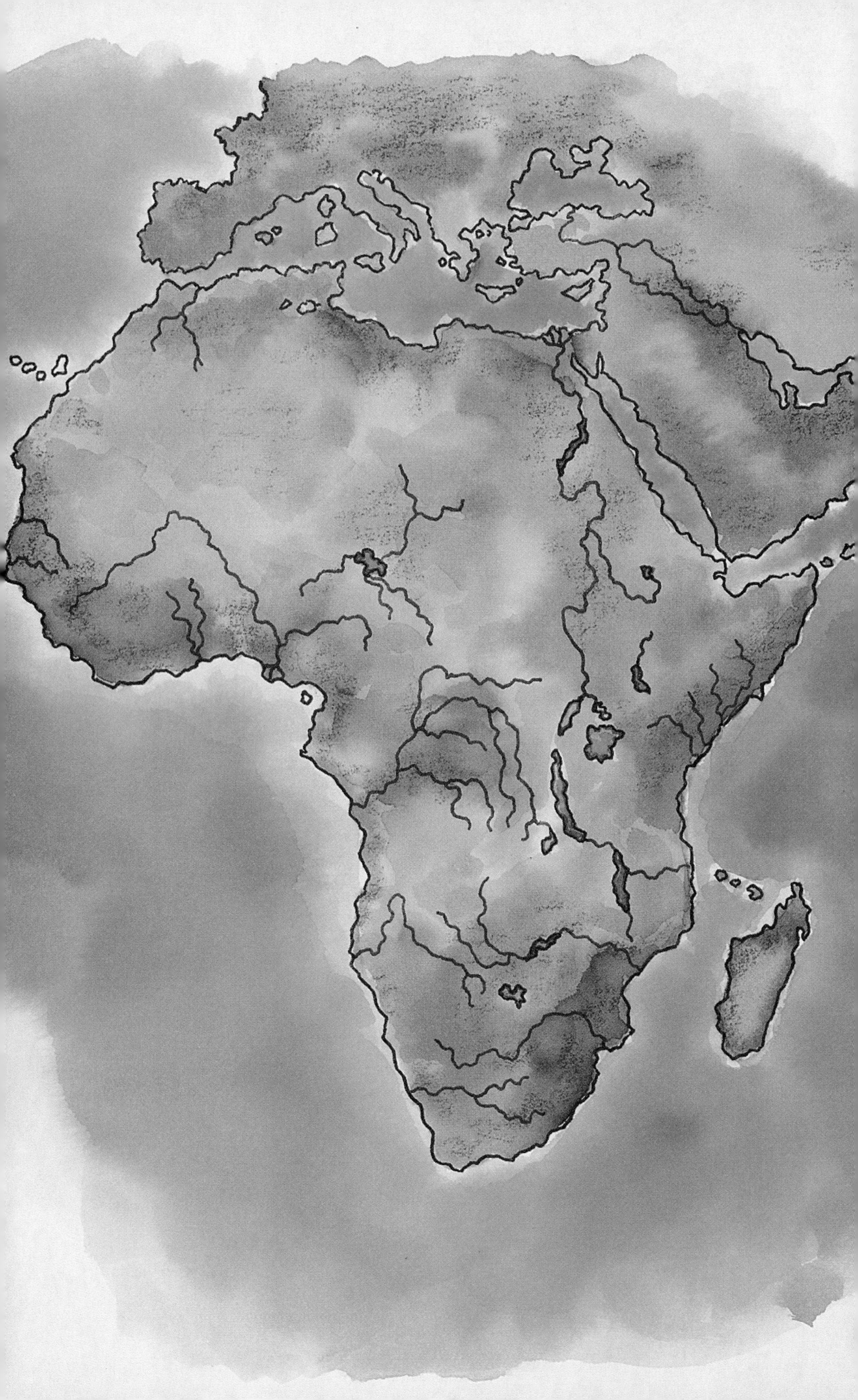

Five

The Presence and Role of Africans in the Bible

Prince Vuyani Ntintili

There is a perennial and widespread misconception that the Bible is a white person's book and thus excludes other people; particularly those of African descent. This insidious fallacy is based on innocent ignorance on the part of some and on deliberate and calculated distortion on the part of others. This article cuts through this murkiness and demonstrates the conspicuous presence of African people on the pages of the Bible. But their presence does not make the Bible a black person's book either. It is the Word of God (Ephesians. 6.17; Hebrews 4.12) which is written for the "teaching, rebuking, correcting, and training in righteousness" of all those who heed its precious instructions. THE BIBLE IS A BOOK FOR ALL HUMANITY. Let all freely drink from its fresh springs.

◂ **Map of Africa. Illustration by R. Sweitzer**

Introduction

If one were to ask most people if Africans are found in the Bible, the common answer one would get would be that they are not. There are several reasons for such an answer. First, there is the prevailing belief that the Bible is a caucasian person's book and, as such, people who are featured in it are caucasians. This belief is attributable to many factors. It is the result of a confusion between the authors of the Bible and the characters featured in the Bible.

One reason why the Bible is assumed to be a caucasian person's book is because it was brought to Africa by European, and later North American, missionaries. What complicates the matter is that the advent of Western missionaries coincided with the arrival of colonizers. Thus the two are associated and, in many instances, rightly so. It is for this reason that the Bible in many African/African American circles is viewed with suspicion because it is believed that it is a book that was brought to subjugate, colonize, and enslave African people.

The second reason often advanced for the belief of the absence of African people in the Bible is the mistaken but persistent belief that Africans, as descendants of Ham, are cursed. As such, they could not be featured in the Holy Scriptures. This view is based on innocent ignorance on the part of some and on deliberate distortion of biblical facts on the part of others. But it, unfortunately, this continues to feed the erroneous belief that there is no African presence in the Bible. This article seeks to demonstrate that there are African people who played very prominent roles in the Bible.

When one investigates the question of the presence and the role of African people in the Bible, one encounters two extremes. The first is the one already articulated in the preceding discussion, namely that there is no African presence whatsoever in the Bible. The other extreme is that of making almost every significant person in the Bible of African descent. This view is espoused by some scholars who are overly keen to prove that African people are featured in the Bible. In trying to achieve this, they overstate their point. Both extremes must be avoided if an investigation of the presence and role of Africans in the Bible is to remain objective.

This article purports, therefore, to do two things. First, it will prove that there is an African presence in the Bible. It will show that there are African countries and places that are actually mentioned in the Bible. Second, it will also show that there are places outside of Africa which were, nevertheless inhabited predominantly by African people. The presence of these territories in the Bible indicates the presence of African people who lived in them. This article will argue not only for the presence of African people in the Bible but also for the significant roles they played. The activities of Africans in the Bible, both positive and negative, reflect the strengths and frailties of humanity. The Bible is an account of the lives of those who obeyed God's commands and precepts and also those who flagrantly flouted them and the consequences they faced for doing so.

African Territories in the Bible

There are several territories geographically located in Africa that which are mentioned in the Bible. For illustrative purposes a few will be mentioned. First, Egypt is mentioned in many places in the Bible. In *Young's Analytical Concordance to the Bible*, Young explains that Egypt is "a country of the N[orth] E[astern] angle of Africa." There are more than 500 references to Egypt in the Bible. Egypt is mentioned from Genesis to Revelation (Genesis 12.10-14; Revelation 11.8).

Egypt is also referred to by other names. At times it is called Mizraim, which means "red mud." Mizraim was the second son of Ham (Genesis 10.6, 13; 1 Chronicles 1.8, 11). Young points out that Egypt "was colonized by the descendants of Ham." He further explains that the word Mizraim is dual, and indicates the natural division of the country into an upper and lower region—the plain of the Delta, and the narrow valley above.

When the singular form of Mizraim is used, it refers to lower Egypt only. When the plural form is used, it refers to the entire territory which extends from Migdol to Syene. The first king of Egypt was Menes. It is well known that Egypt enjoyed an advanced and thriving civilization for a long time and contributed much to the civilization of the world, particularly to the Greeks. Egypt and its people played a critical role, both positively and negatively, in the life of Israel (Exodus 1–15). It must not be forgotten that, according to Matthew 2.13-21, Joseph, Mary, and the child Jesus found refuge in Egypt when Herod was seeking to kill Jesus.

The second African territory mentioned in the Bible is Libya (Ezekiel 30.5; Daniel 11.43; Acts 2.10). Libya is a Greek word for this territory, which is situated west of Egypt along the African coast. *Young's Analytical Concordance to the Bible* states that "the inhabitants of Libya

▸ "Escape to Egypt. Nigeria," Osillorin, 1964. Courtesy, Society of African Missions, Tenafly, NJ

[are] supposed to have sprung from Phut, the son of Ham [in] B.C. 2300." Josephus also concurs that Phut was the founder of Libya. People of Libya were known as valiant warriors (Jeremiah 46.9) who could "carry the shield." The country specialized in producing mercenaries and supplying other countries with them (see Ezekiel 27.10). The people of Libya played an important role in the Bible.

The third African territory that is featured in the Bible is Ethiopia (Genesis 2.13; 2 Kings 19.9; Esther 1.1; 8.9; Job 28.19; Psalm 68.31; 87.4; Isaiah 18.1; 20.3, 5; 37.9; 43.3; 45.14; Ezekiel 29.10; 30.5; 38.5; Nahum 3.9; Zephaniah 3.10; Acts 8.27). The Bible also speaks of Ethiopian(s) (Numbers 12.1; 2 Chronicles 12.3; 14.9, 12, 13; 16.8; 21.16; Isaiah 20.4; Jeremiah 13.23; 38.7, 10, 12; 39.16; 46.9; Ezekiel 30.9; Daniel 11.43; Amos 9.7; Zephaniah 2.12; Acts 8.27). The word "Ethiopia" is used by both the Greeks and the Romans and it is derived from two Greek words—*ethios* which means "burned" and *opes* which means "face." It is the Greeks who referred to people of Ethiopia as those of "burned faces" to indicate the complexion of their faces. The Hebrew word for Ethiopia is Cush, named after Ham's first son. *Young's Analytical Concordance to the Bible* explains that this country "comprehended, in its widest sense, the modern Nubia, Sennar, Kordofan, and northern Abyssinia, but in its more limited sense, only the kingdom of Meroe, from the junction of the White and Blue branches of the Nile to the [Southern] border of Egypt."

Concerning the country of Ethiopia, it is notable that it is one of the first countries mentioned in Scripture. Genesis 2.13 describes one of the rivers that waters the garden of Eden as Gihon which "flows around the country of Cush." It is for this reason that some scholars argue that Eden was in Africa.

The Bible also mentions certain cities found in Africa. One such city is Alexandria, and this city is mentioned in Acts 6.9; 18.24; 27.6; 28.11. Alexandria is a city in Egypt founded by Alexander the Great in B.C. 332 near the western branch of the Nile where it flows to the Mediterranean. Young notes that "it was long one of the most celebrated cities in the world, the metropolis of Egypt, as well as a grand seat of commerce and wealth." Certain people from this African city played a role in biblical history. For example Apollos who is described as "a learned man, with thorough knowledge of the Scriptures" was a native of Alexandria.

Another African city mentioned in the Bible is that of Cyrene, a city in Libya in Cyranaica, North Africa. It was the chief of the five cities called Pentapolitana. Young points out that, under the Romans, Cyrene was connected with Crete. This city is mentioned in Matthew 27.32; Acts 2.10; 11.20; 13.1. Certain persons of this city also played significant roles in the Bible.

Territories Inhabited by African People

Apart from territories that are actually found in the continent of Africa, there are other territories which are outside of Africa but which were inhabited by African people. People who lived in these areas were predominately African and significantly participated in the events that took place in the Bible.

First, there is what is known as the "land of Shinar," which is probably referred to in Hebrew as Sumer. Shinar is the place where God confounded and confused the languages of the people and the place was, as a result, called Babel. Shinar is a kingdom which was founded by Nimrod, Cush's son. R. K. Harrison, in his book, *Old Testament Times,* writes as follows: "About 4000 B.C., a people of superior intellectual caliber, known as Sumerians, occupied Sumer…They were a swarthy (black), non-Semitic group."

Second, there is the land of Babylon. Babylon is a city, together with Erech, Ahkkad, and Calneh, which was founded by Nimrod, Cush's son. It is believed that there was a strong presence of the Hamitic people among the Assyrian people of Babylon. Clem Davies, in his book,

The Racial Streams of Mankind, argues that there were many people of Hamitic descent in Babylon.

Third, there is the territory of Phoenicia. The Bible refers to this area as Sidon. Canaan's firstborn son was named Sidon. (Genesis 10.15). Canaan, himself, was Ham's first son. Many scholars, including Young, Josephus, and Augustine, maintain that Ham's descendants occupied Sidon and that Phoenicians considered themselves Canaanites. Sidon is featured many times in the Gospels and in the Book of Acts (Matthew 11.21, 22; 15.21; Mark 3.8; 7.24; Luke 4.26; 6.17; 10.13, 14; Acts 12.20; 27.3). This shows that Christ ministered among people of African descent during his earthly ministry. It also speaks to Christ's attitude of inclusion toward people of other cultures and racial groupings.

Fourth, there are the territories of Canaan and Hebron which were occupied by the Hittites. The Hittites were of African descent because they were from Heth, Canaan's second son. R.K. Harrison, in his book, *Introduction to the Old Testament*, points out that Hittites "were in possession of advanced technological processes of smelting iron for all commercial purposes" and were also "renowned horsemen and were the first to manufacture chariots with iron fittings." These skilled people were all of African descent.

Fifth, there were the Jebusites, people of African descent who lived in Jerusalem. That explains why Jerusalem was called Jebus prior to David's conquest of that city (Joshua 18.16,28; Judges 19.10, 11; 1 Chronicles 11.4,5). Jebusites were descendants of Canaan, the son of Ham. The Jebusites, along with the Amorites and Girgashites, are described in the Bible as "tribes of the Canaanites" (Genesis 10.16-18). Since Jebusites came from Canaan, who was the son of Ham, it is correct to argue that they, too, were of African descent.

It must be noted that there are many other peoples who were fathered by Canaan, Ham's fourth son; peoples such as the Hivites, Arkites, and Sinites. The lineage of these people argues eloquently for the existence of a black or African presence in the Bible.

People of African Origin in the Bible

In the preceding section, the African presence in the territories mentioned in the Bible was discussed. This section will highlight some people from these areas who are mentioned in the Bible.

The Old Testament

People of African Origin in the Pentateuch

In Genesis 10.6-14, Nimrod is mentioned as the son of Cush and a descendant of Ham. The Bible says that Nimrod was "the world's first great conqueror." He was "a great hunter" for the Lord (Genesis 10.8, 9). He also built tremendous cities such as Babylon, Erech, Akkad, Calneh, Nineveh, Rohoboth-Ir, Calah and Resen.

▸ "Pastoral Fulani and Infant," by Cyrus L. Baldridge Watercolor Collection of Fisk University, Nashville, Tennessee

Jethro, Moses' father-in-law, who was a priest from Midian was probably of African descent. Midianites are believed to have descended from Ham through the line of Cush, (Exodus 18.1). Some scholars purport that Moses' Cushite wife (Numbers 12.1) was probably Zipporah, the daughter of Jethro. As noted in Habakkuk 3.7, Midian and Cush are linked, and this could lead one to conclude that both Jethro and his daughter, Zipporah, were of African origin.

The Bible explicitly tells us that Hagar was "an Egyptian maidservant." It is notable that God promised, in Genesis 21.13, to make the son of the (Egyptian) maidservant into a nation also, because he is Abraham's offspring. In verse 18, God promised to make Ishmael, this African woman's son, into a great nation. This shows that God is no respecter of persons. We, too, should emulate him.

Asenath, the wife of Joseph, was an Egyptian, and her father was Potiphera, the priest of On. On was the capital of Lower Egypt, about six miles northeast of Cairo and three miles north of modern Heliopolis. Asenath was the mother of Manasseh and Ephraim (Genesis 41.45; 46.20). These two sons played important roles in the history of the Israelites and became the eponymous ancestors of the tribes of Manasseh and Ephraim that inhabited the land of Canaan.

People of African Origin in the Historical Books

The queen of Sheba was of African descent. Sheba was the son of Raamah who was the son of Ham. Young, in his book, *Young's Analytical Concordance to the Bible*, explains that Sheba was "a land in the South West of Arabia, or in Africa near the Straits of Babel-mandeb." The queen of Sheba was a wealthy woman who played a prominent role in international trade and commerce. Thus, when she visited King Solomon, she was accorded the dignity and status of a head of state (1 Kings 10.10-13). This woman of African descent was bright, self-assertive, wealthy, and generous.

In addition, there is an unnamed slave who brought David the news of the death of his son, Absalom. This slave had the courage to tell David the truth concerning his son's death. According to 2 Samuel 18.21, the slave was a Cushite. Since it has already been established that Egypt is sometimes called Cush in the Bible, this brave slave was undoubtedly an African.

People of African Origin in the Prophetical Books

In Jeremiah 38.7-13 there is the account of Ebedmelech, the Ethiopian, who saved the life of the prophet Jeremiah. In Hebrew, the name Ebedmelech means royal servant. Ebedmelech feared God more than men. He alone, among the palace officials, stood up against the murder plot. His intervention on behalf of Jeremiah could have caused him his life, but he was willing and courageous enough to take the risk. The Bible reports that God remembered what Ebedmelech had done for Jeremiah; and when Babylon conquered Jerusalem, God protected him from the Babylonians (Jeremiah 39.15-18). This Scripture states that Ebedmelech rescued Jeremiah because he trusted God.

Another person of African origin in the Prophetic Books is Zephaniah. He was the son of Cushi (Zephaniah 1.1). Zephaniah prophesied around 630 B.C., and his prophecies fostered a religious revival in Judah.

In the book of the prophet Amos, Ethiopians are described as worshipers with Israel: The LORD says, "People of Israel, I think as much of the people of Ethiopia as I do of you." (Amos 9.7a). Similarly, the prophet Isaiah affirms that the blessings of God are extended to the people of Egypt (Isaiah 19.23-25).

People of African Origin in Wisdom or Poetic Literature

The Song of Solomon (also known as Song of Songs) is a collection of songs or poems in which a man and a woman express their love for each other. The woman describes her appearance as follows:

> Women of Jerusalem, I am dark but beautiful,
> dark as the desert tents of Kedar,
> but beautiful as the draperies in Solomon's palace.
> Don't look down on me because of my color,
> because the sun has tanned me.
> (Song of Songs 1.5, 6a)

In Psalm 68.31 the Psalmist says,

> Ambassadors will come from Egypt;
> the Ethiopians will raise their hands in prayer to God.

In this Scripture passage, the Bible is not talking about individual Africans, but a group of people, and God is promising to save them. Also, in Psalm 87 there is a reference to a universal understanding that Africans are included among the people who know the Lord God and belong to Zion (Psalm 87.4-6).

The New Testament

People of African Origin in the Gospels

Simon, the one who helped Jesus bear the cross, was from Cyrene, a major city in North Africa (Matthew 27.32; Mark 15.21; Luke 23.26). This was a unique opportunity for Simon to be selected to help bear the burden of our Lord and Savior on his way to Calvary. In recognition of the role he played in our Lord's passion, it is significant that all three synoptic gospels mention his name.

People of African Origin in the Historical Book

African presence is also found in the only historical book of the New Testament; namely the Book of Acts. In Acts 2.10 we are told that some of the visitors in Jerusalem who witnessed the Day of Pentecost were "from Egypt and the regions of Libya near Cyrene." On that eventful Day of Pentecost Africa too, had its representatives who were among the three thousand that responded to Peter's preaching.

Cyrenians are also mentioned in Acts 6.9 as among those who belonged to the synagogue of Freedman (also known as Libertines). In Acts 13.1, Lucius of Cyrene is mentioned as being one of the leaders in the church of Antioch which commissioned the apostle Paul for his first missionary journey. Simeon of Niger was also one of the leaders of the church in Antioch. The word Niger, in Latin, means "black."

In Acts 8.26-39 we are told of the Ethiopian eunuch to whom Philip was sent by the Spirit of God. What is striking is that Philip was engaged in a thriving revival and awakening in Samaria and people were coming to the Lord in large numbers. But this Ethiopian official was so important in God's program that God asked Philip to evangelize this African individual. This man was "an important official in charge of the treasury of the queen of Ethiopia" (Acts 8.27). He was a trusted and well-placed person in his nation's leadership. He was a highly learned man who could read the Scriptures in both Hebrew and Greek and who was able to converse with Philip. But more importantly, he was a devout man who not only attended the Jewish festivals but also read God's Word. He may have been a Gentile convert to Judaism. That day he became a follower of Christ.

People of African Origin in the Epistles

According to Mark 15.21, Rufus was the son of Simon of Cyrene who carried the cross of Jesus. In Romans 16.13, Rufus was chosen to do the Lord's work, and Paul said: "I send greetings to Rufus, that outstanding worker in the Lord's service, and to his mother, who has always treated me like a son." He came from a good family with a father and a mother who were committed to the Lord.

People of African Origin in the Book of Revelation

In Revelation 5.9, 10 the Bible speaks of Christ having "bought for God people from every tribe, language, nation, and race" and having "made them a kingdom of priests to serve our God, and they shall rule on earth." Africans are among those who have been bought with the precious blood of Christ. Revelation 14.6b speaks of the Gospel which will be proclaimed to "every race, tribe, language, and nation." These Scriptures do include Africans even though they are not specifically mentioned by name.

Conclusion

There are several reasons why the issue of the presence of Africans in the Bible is of importance. Proving the presence of Africans in the Bible is not meant to prove that the Bible is a black person's book; rather, it is meant to show that the Bible reveals the blessings God has for them. The Bible belongs to no particular race of people. It is God's book which unveils the plan that God has for all the peoples of the earth. No one is left out. Some groups may not be specifically mentioned by name but they are not excluded. The Bible says that God loved "the world" (John 3.16) and this means that everyone in the world is included. The Bible speaks of "everyone" which includes every racial and ethnic group; every individual on earth (Revelation 7.9). But because people of African descent have been enslaved and oppressed, it is easier for them to believe that they are not included. This study refutes the misinterpretation that Ham and his descendants are cursed. The Bible does not teach that. (cf. "The Alleged Curse on Ham" by Gene Rice). Africans have always been included in God's redemptive plan. This is amply demonstrated by their inclusion in the holy history so ably explicated in the Bible. Finally, this study should help blacks who may need to overcome a poor self-image which is caused by their sad history of oppression, slavery, and discrimination. The self-image of blacks must be based on what God says about them which is supported by God's redemptive acts. They need to espouse a biblical view of ethnicity which does not change. All other fads will come and go but the truth of God's Word does not change. This study should prove to be helpful to both black brothers and sisters as well as to white brothers and sisters. It ought to dispel myths which have been perpetuated for too many years.

Bibliography

Felder, Cain Hope, ed. *The Original African Heritage Study Bible, King James Version.* Nashville: The James C. Winston Publishing Company, 1993.

Harrison, R.K. *Introduction to the Old Testament.* Grand Rapids: Eerdmans, 1969.

McKissic, Sr., William Dwight and Evans, Anthony T. *Beyond Roots II: If Anybody Ask You Who I Am: A Deeper Look at Blacks in the Bible.* Wenonah, New Jersey: Renaissance Productions, 1994.

Tenney, Merrill C., ed. *Zondervan's Pictorial Encyclopedia of the Bible, Volume 2.* Grand Rapids: Zondervan Publishing House, 1975.

Unger, Merrill F. *Unger's Bible Dictionary.* Chicago: Moody Press, 1966.

Young, Robert. *Young's Analytical Concordance to the Bible.* Nashville: Thomas Nelson Publishers, 1982.

The Presence of Blacks in Biblical Antiquity

Cain Hope Felder

The view of Africa, that has evolved in recent centuries has little or no historical integrity inasmuch as it reflects Eurocentric interpretations of the Bible. However, new light is shining on biblical antiquity, and layers of unfavorable biases are being peeled away. In their place is a more congenial basis for inclusiveness and reconciliation in conjunction with an emergence of critical studies on the black presence in the Bible and the recovering of ancient African heritage in the Scriptures. Consequently, persons of African descent now have the opportunity to rediscover consistent and favorable mentioning of their forebears within the pages of the Bible. The Word of God shows itself to be a truly universal, inclusive, and multicultural message of salvation for the human race.

◂ **"The Creation," by Aaron Douglas, oil on canvas, 1935. The Howard University Gallery of Art, Permanant Collection, Washington, DC**

Then God commanded, "Let there be light"—and light appeared. God was pleased with what he saw. Then he separated the light from the darkness. (Genesis 1.3, 4)

This is the most exciting and intriguing time for Scripture study, especially by persons of immediate African descent. We, the people of the darker hue, are again at the turning point of a new millennium when God's ancient Word shows itself to be truly a universal, inclusive, and multicultural message of salvation for the human race. Evidence, ancient and modern, again and again confirms as fact that the human race began on the continent that is now known as Africa (a name derived from the Latin: "Africanus" –itself post-biblical). In the sweep of what has come to be called Western Civilization, Africa has often been dubbed "the Dark Continent," as if nothing good has ever, nor will ever, come out of this great land mass. The words of the ancient Psalmist resonate still in our ears: "Ambassadors will come from Egypt; the Ethiopians will raise their hands in prayer to God" (Psalm 68.31).

The view of Africa, that has evolved in recent centuries, has little or no historical integrity; rather it tells us much more about the ways that Europeans have re-interpreted the Bible along lines that have served mainly to affirm their own cultural identity and racial aggrandizement, particularly since the beginning of the seventeenth century at the onset of the Renaissance. Modern history has witnessed the painful consequences for blacks in Africa and the African "Diaspora" (the "scattering"/dispersal from Africa through the slave trade or voluntary migrations). Sadly, the black descendants of the continent have been too often stereotyped and even demonized. Nevertheless, thanks be to God, new light is beginning to shine on biblical antiquity.

Today, we are systematically peeling away layers of unfavorable biases that suggest that Black History consists only of the sad chapter of modern slavery. The latter-day negative overlays are disappearing; and in their place, one encounters a more congenial basis for inclusiveness and reconciliation. People of immediate African descent can see themselves once again in the Bible as an occasion for celebration, renewed spiritual motivation, and empowerment. Light is once more shining out of darkness. It can illumine the whole human race, if studied and taught with the right spirit— the spirit of love for all humanity.

The African Methodist Episcopal Church certainly has one of the more distinguished records for not only defending the dignity of black people, but also for celebrating the existence of blacks in biblical antiquity. Over the years, the denomination has taken strong stances on the protection of the rights of persons of African descent as human beings. This is well known. What is perhaps less familiar are the extraordinary ways in which leaders within this Protestant denomination have studied and systematically examined the Bible as a sacred record in which Africans have played a major role. Writing in 1895, for example, Daniel P. Seaton, D.D., M.D., a prominent leader in the A.M.E. Church, displayed considerable knowledge about ancient blacks within the Bible as well as the locations of biblical lands and religious sites. Seaton made several field trips to Palestine at his own expense and documented his findings in a mammoth study, published by the A.M.E. Church Publishing House, containing 443 pages of texts, maps, illustrations and notes. In a remarkably careful manner he provided extensive descriptions of tombs, villages, and artifacts that suggested strongly influences of African heritage.

Everywhere Dr. Seaton visited in Palestine at the close of the 19th century, he encountered signs of "Hamites" or Hamitic influence. He wrote:

> "Because these Hamites were an important people, attempts have been made to rob them of their proper place in the catalogue of the races. The Bible tells us plainly that the Phoenicians were descendants of Canaan, the son of Ham, and anyone who will take the time to read the Bible account of their lineage must concede the fact." (p. 377)

It is indeed noteworthy that Seaton was profoundly aware of scholarly racial bias on the part of the so-called bona-fide Bible scholars (i.e., products of the European academy and its American offshoots) of his day. Nevertheless, as much as we may applaud Dr. Seaton's constructive intent, he could clearly have benefited from the historical-critical methods of biblical study and a more substantial understanding of the evolution of race topologies, pseudo-scientific theories, and ideologies of racial supremacy in modern Western Civilization. Today, in the United States of America, other parts of the global African diaspora, and increasingly even on the continent of Africa herself, there is developing a proliferation of critical studies on the black presence in the Bible together with Afro-sensitive versions of the Bible with maps of the Holy Land in relation to the African land mass. These resources are often accompanied by study guides, illustrations, and supplemental essays designed to underscore the importance of African connections with the ancient biblical record. Even so, caution must be urged for anyone who might tend to construe the sons of Noah (Genesis. 9.18-29)—Ham, Shem, and Japheth—as somehow representing three different "races." Any conclusion of this type is highly flawed and moves in the opposite direction of the "Curse of Canaan" narrative. The intent of the story is really to provide the ancient Hebrews with a kind of theological justification for taking over the land of the Canaanites. The "Curse of Canaan" passage, after all, speaks of three brothers from the same family.

The Bible emerges out of the ancient world that knew nothing of racial types like Caucasoids, Mongoloids, or Africaoids. These arbitrary and pseudo-scientific categories are actually quite modern. They constitute little more than fraudulent mythologies created to further the social construct of racism and the dubious notion of Aryan supremacy and so-called Africaoid inferiority. African American and other scholars from Ashley Montague (*Man's Most Dangerous Myth*) to Martin Bernal (*Black Athena: The Afro-Asiatic Origin of Western Civilization*) have demonstrated that white racism is essentially a European by-product after 1492.

With the Renaissance (16th and 17th centuries) and the so-called European Enlightenment that followed (A.D. 1700-1899), we begin to see a carefully orchestrated pattern of European racially biased "scholarship," claiming to have an objective, empirical basis, but in fact having nothing of the sort. Still there emerged a Western "scholarly" consensus from Francois Bernier (1685), Carolus Linnaeus (1735), to the German social anthropologist Johann Blumenbach (1775-1795). The new consensus was that North Africa was to be seen as Caucasoid or non-black; this was clearly a subtle political decision. In this way, European scholarship literally de-Africanized the entire Nile Valley civilization! This woeful development still dominates the way in which American and European universities regard the people of North Africa. Despite even the color of these people (invariably shades of brown to black), the Western official race category for them is "honorary" Caucasians.

Revelations of this kind lend a certain urgency to recovering the ancient African heritage in Scripture. African Americans are fundamentally people of the Book even as they have adapted remnants of their traditional African religions with Hebraic/Jewish, Christian, or Islamic thought and practice. More black pastors today need to realize that Islam or the Muslim religion begins formally with Muhammad of Arabia in the mid-seventh century A.D., 600 years *after* Jesus of Nazareth, and that Muhammad had great respect for the Book on which his own Qur'an depended to some extent. That "Book" was the Holy Bible; and it is crucial for each generation of spiritual leaders, to people of immediate African descent, to celebrate the fact that they, by no means, are an "afterthought" in the plan of God.

On the contrary, the Bible constantly reminds us that not only did God bring light out of darkness, but that God also has made it clear that "(I) called him out of Egypt (Africa) as my son." This applies not just to the quotation in Hosea 11.1 and Matthew 2.15, but also to the Garden of Eden, which begins with the Nile (Gihon) River (Genesis 2.10-14), and extends through the Exodus Saga. Indeed it continues with notices from both the Old Testament prophetic literature and the Psalms that African people hasten to "raise their hands in prayer to God" (Psalm 68.31) or that they will bring offerings from "distant Ethiopia" (Zephaniah 3.10). Here, doubtless, is a reference to the Blue and White Nile Rivers which together make up the longest river in the world.

With the foregoing observations as general background, let us establish a basis for two propositions that will guide a six-fold survey of discrete segments of the Bible. The first proposition is that much of the material in the Old Testament or Hebrew Bible arises against the backdrop of ancient pre-historic Africa primarily, and Mesopotamia or the Fertile Crescent, secondarily. This claim opposes that championed by European scholarship which has so rigorously sought to de-Africanize not only Egypt but also Ethiopia. Consider, however, the simple preponderance of references in the Old Testament to Egypt, Ethiopia, Put, Punt, Libya and other lands known to be associated with the African continent, including Sheba and Havilah. (There are well over 1,500 such references in the Old Testament. This is far more than mentioning of lands in Mesopotamia.) Then too, whenever there was famine within or the threat of military invasion to Ancient Palestine/Israel, invariably the patriarch, including Abraham, would flee or otherwise seek relief in Africa – not Mesopotamia.

Of course, there were interactions between the peoples of Africa and Mesopotamia in the biblical world, and these were of a commercial, military, and cultural nature yielding similarities in language, folklore, and religious customs. It is for precisely this reason that we emphasize a second guiding proposition for our survey, namely that the best refer to the people of the Old Testament as being of Afro-Asiatic stock. Hebrew as well as Ethiopic are technically Afro-Asiatic languages. Thus, it should not be surprising that behind many of the Old Testament ways of life are architectural and cultural influences that originate in Africa, from the idea of an Ark/sacred boat to the "holy of holies" within the Temple. If the Hebrews spent as much as 400 years in Egyptian bondage, one would only naturally conclude that, despite a relatively brief interlude in the wilderness of Sinai, they would retain an enormous amount of cultural and social mores from the hundreds of years in Africa once they entered the Promised Land.

Once we understand the centrality of the ancient African ethos to the development of the Old Testament, the biblical world truly emerges as a world not only before any "color prejudice," but also as a world that had no notion of "race" based on the physical make-up of a person. The biblical world certainly practiced gender, class, tribe, and even religious bias, but not racial discrimination in any way comparable to that found in Western societies within the past few centuries after the rise of modern European imperial powers. As a consequence, persons of African descent have the opportunity to rediscover and recover today consistent and rather favorable mentioning of their forebears within the pages of the Bible, despite the fact that others have intentionally tried to obscure this important fact.

Part I. The African Heritage in the Old Testament

The Old Testament or Hebrew Bible may be divided into three parts. It is customary to divide the traditional Old Testament narratives into groupings known as the Law, the Prophets, and the Hagiographa (including the Psalms and the Wisdom Literature). Normally, the Law refers to the "Five Books of Moses" or the Pentateuch, although Moses did not literally write these books, any more than King David composed all of the Psalms. The Law, when seen as Genesis, Exodus, Leviticus, Numbers, and Deuteronomy, is merely a traditional way to recognize the opening Books of the Bible as having the giving of the Mosaic Law as a central feature. Moreover, these books provide the literary and quasi-historical context for the giving of the Law on Mount Sinai (some Hebrew sources say on Mount Horeb). After all, the Law epitomizes ancient Hebraic, and later, Jewish faith. The two other

"Out of Bondage," Illustration by Kimanne Smith

segments of the Old Testament are the Prophetic Literature (including the Major and Minor Prophets) and the Hagiographa ("holy writings"). In each of these three parts of the Old Testament, one encounters numerous favorable references to the lands and people of what later came to be called "Africa" by the Romans. Since the term Africa is not found in the Bible, one will need to become familiar with the biblical names of those areas within Africa, but too often construed to be somewhere other than in that continent to which we today routinely refer as Africa.

The presence of blacks in the Old Testament/Hebrew Bible is rather substantial; fortunately, ours is an age that increasingly allows such an important fact to be acknowledged more widely than perhaps ever before. Since this specific topic has long been studied by Dr. Gene Rice, Professor of Old Testament, he has supplied a representative listing of key Old Testament passages that mention, indeed often celebrate, the black biblical presence. He has graciously offered the following:

Nimrod, son of Cush, "the world's first great conqueror." Nimrod is also credited with founding and ruling the principal cities of Mesopotamia (Genesis 10.8-12).

Hagar, the Egyptian maid of Sarah (Genesis 16; 21.8-21). If Abraham had had his way, Hagar would have become the foremother of the covenant people (Genesis 17.18).

Asenath, daughter of Potiphera, priest of On (Heliopolis), wife of Joseph and mother of Ephraim and Manasseh (Genesis 41.45, 51,52; 46.20), whom Jacob claimed and adopted (Genesis 48.38).

Moses' Cushite wife (Numbers 12.1). She was probably Zipporah of the Kenite clan of the Midianites (Exodus 2.21-23). If Moses' Cushite wife is indeed Zipporah, then her father Jethro, (also called Reuel), would also have been an African. Since Jethro was the priest of Midian (Exodus 2.16; 3.1; 18.1) and the mountain of God where Moses was called was located in Midian (Exodus 3.1; 18.5), and Jethro presided at a meal where Aaron and the elders of Israel were guests (Exodus 18.12), the Kenites may have been the original worshipers of God by the name of the LORD, that is, Yahweh (YHWH). Jethro also instructed Moses in the governance of the newly liberated Israelites (Exodus 8.13-27).

Phinehas, the grandson of Aaron and a high priest (Exodus 6.25). The name, Phinehas, is Egyptian and means literally, "The Nubian," or "The Dark-skinned One."

The "large number of other people" that accompanied the Israelites when they left Egypt undoubtedly included various African and Asian peoples (Exodus 12.38).

The unnamed Ethiopian slave. He bore the news of Absalom's death to David and, in contrast to Ahimaaz, had the courage to tell David the truth about Absalom (2 Samuel 18.21, 31, 32).

Solomon's Egyptian wife. She was an Egyptian princess and by his marriage to her, Solomon sealed an alliance with Egypt (1 Kings 3.1; 11.1).

The Queen of Sheba. She ruled a kingdom that included territory in both Arabia and Africa. When she visited Solomon, she was accorded the dignity and status of a head of state (1 Kings 10.1-13).

Zerah, the Ethiopian. He commanded a military garrison at Gerar in Southwest Palestine and fought against King Asa of Judah and almost defeated him (2 Chronicles 14.9-15). After Egyptian influence ceased in Palestine, the Cushite soldiers stationed at Gerar settled down and became farmers. Some two centuries after the time of Zerah, the Simeonites took over Gerar where "they found plenty of fertile pasture lands there in a stretch of open country that was quiet and peaceful. The people who had lived there before were Hamites" (1 Chronicles 4.40).

Cush, a Benjaminite (heading to Psalm 7). He is identified as Saul in the Talmud.

The Ethiopian ambassadors who came to Jerusalem to establish diplomatic relations with Judah (Isaiah 18.1, 2). They represented the Ethiopian Pharaoh, Shabaka (716-702) of the Twenty-fifth Dynasty of Egypt.

The Ethiopian, Taharqa, spelled Tirhakah in the Bible. When Hezekiah revolted against Assyria in 705 B.C., he did so with the support of Shaboka and Shebitku (702-690), rulers of the Twenty-fifth Dynasty of Egypt. Tirhakah led an army in support of Judah during Hezekiah's revolt against Assyria (2 Kings 19.9; Isaiah 37.9). Tirhakah later ruled Egypt from 690-664.

The Prophet Zephaniah. Zephaniah's father was Cushi, his grandfather Gedaliah, his great-grandfather Amariah, and his great-great-grandfather (King) Hezekiah (Zephaniah 1.1). Zephaniah was active about 630 B.C. and sparked a religious revival in Judah.

Jehudi ben Nethaniah ben Shelemiah ben Cushi. The context in Jeremiah 36 indicates that Jehudi was a trusted member of the cabinet of King Jehoiakim of Judah (Jeremiah 36.14, 21, 23).

Ebedmelech ("Royal Servant"), the Ethiopian. He was an officer of King Zedekiah who, at great risk to himself, saved Jeremiah's life (Jeremiah 38.7-13), and was blessed by Jeremiah (Jeremiah 39.15-18).

Africans as Worshipers with Israel

"I will include Egypt and Babylonia
when I list the nations that obey me;
the people of Philistia, Tyre, and Ethiopia
I will number among the inhabitants of Jerusalem."
(Psalm 87.4)

Ambassadors will come from Egypt;
the Ethiopians will raise their hands in prayer to God.
(Psalm 68.31)

A time is coming when the LORD Almighty will receive offerings from this land divided by rivers, this strong and powerful nation, this tall and smooth-skinned people, who are feared all over the world. They will come to Mount Zion, where the LORD Almighty is worshiped (Isaiah 18.7).

When that time comes, there will be a highway between Egypt and Assyria. The people of these two countries will travel back and forth between them, and the two nations will worship together (Isaiah 19.23).

When that time comes, Israel will rank with Egypt and Assyria, and these three nations will be a blessing to all the world. The LORD Almighty will bless them and say, "I will bless you, Egypt, my people; you, Assyria, whom I created; and you, Israel, my chosen people" (Isaiah 19.24, 25).

"Then I will change the people of the nations, and they will pray to me alone and not to other gods. They will all obey me. Even from distant Ethiopia my scattered people will bring offerings to me" (Zephaniah 3.9, 10).

The LORD says, "People of Israel, I think as much of the people of Ethiopia as I do of you" (Amos 9.7a).

Africa as the Home of the Jewish Diaspora

When that day comes, the Lord will once again use his power and bring back home those of his people who are left in Assyria and Egypt, in the lands of Pathros, Ethiopia, Elam, Babylonia, and Hamath, and in the coastlands and on the islands of the sea (Isaiah 11.11).

"My people will come from far away,
from the north and the west,
and from Aswan in the south" (Isaiah 49.12).

The LORD spoke to me concerning all the Israelites living in Egypt, in the cities of Migdol, Tahpanhes, and Memphis, and in the southern part of the country (Jeremiah 44.1).

Part II. The African Heritage in the New Testament

As with the Hebrew Bible, the New Testament may be divided into three parts, namely the Gospels (including the Acts of the Apostles, as Luke's second volume), the Epistles, and the unique apocalyptic book, the Revelation to John, that closes the New Testament canon. Romans and Greeks are certainly part of the New Testament which frequently mentions them by name, military rank, or political title.

Yet, Africans, and persons of African descent, are fully represented as well. For years, persons of African descent have taken heart upon reading the celebrated passage in Psalm 68.31:

> Ambassadors will come from Egypt;
> the Ethiopians will raise their hands in prayer to God.

But today there is a much greater basis upon which blacks may celebrate and otherwise take seriously their rich ancient heritage with sacred Scripture, showing that long ago, their outstretched hand was fully accepted by God, despite what has happened to them in the intervening centuries. The substantial African presence in Scripture is by no means limited to an isolated verse here and there.

The African presence in the Bible is also by no means limited to the Old Testament. Indeed many Jews of the first century lived in regions where Africans intermingled freely with other racial and ethnic types. We too easily forget today that miscegenation or interracial marriage was an explicit part of Alexander the Great's policy; he wanted all subjects to have Greek blood flowing through their veins! Of course there was no notion of the modern idea of "race" during that time, but suffice it to say that the ancients had no problem with black people nor did the Greeks and Romans consider them to be inferior.

Consider a few inescapable factors that challenge the traditional Western perception of the Madonna and Child. In the Gospel of Matthew, we find the quotation from Hosea 11.1 which reads:

> "When Israel was a child, I loved him
> and called him out of Egypt as my son."

The passage is part of the notorious "Flight into Egypt" that describes the way in which Mary and Joseph fled to Egypt to hide the one that King Herod feared would displace him. Assuming that we can lend some historical credence to this report, it is difficult imagining, if the Holy Family were indeed persons who looked like typical "Europeans," that they could effectively "hide" in Africa. One must remember and take most seriously the fact that Egypt has always been and remains part of Africa. Her indigenous people are noticeably different from the European types, notwithstanding the Hellenistic cultural incursions, beginning in earnest just over 300 B.C. In fact, it has only been in recent centuries that the Egyptians and other North Americans have been officially racially classified as somehow "caucasians" (similar to the manner in which Western Civilization has come to regard all of the indigenous Africans north of the Sahara). Nevertheless, for thousands of years, Africans have migrated out of biblical Ethiopia and Egypt and have passed through Palestine en route to the Fertile Crescent

▸ **"Black Madonna and Child," by Joe Cauchi, oil on canvas. Courtesy of Superstock**

or Mesopotamia. Thus the term Afro-Asiatic emerged, and it is a fitting description of persons from Abraham to Jesus and his disciples.

Beyond this, we must also consider the hundreds of shrines of the Black Madonna that have existed in many parts of North Africa, Europe, Meso-America and Russia. These are not some weather-beaten misrepresentations of an original White Madonna. Rather, as recent studies of the oldest such Madonnas in Italy have shown, they are uncanny reminders of the diverse ethnography of those who inhabited Palestine at the time of Jesus of Nazareth and earlier. Today, in Western Civilization, many avoid the term Afro-Asiatic, due to negative modern attitudes that have been associated with Africa over the past three or four hundred years. Yet, it may not be going too far to suggest that the "Sweet Lil' Jesus Boy" of the negro spiritual is probably most accurately described as an Afro-Asiatic or "person of color." While the negro spiritual intones: "we didn't know who you was," it paradoxically reminds many modern Christians that what Jesus actually looked like may come as a surprise.

As long as one keeps in mind that, for the most part by modern standards of ethnicity, first-century Jews could be considered Afro-Asiatics. This is to say that Jesus, his family, his disciples and, doubtless, most of the fellow Jews that he encountered in his public ministry were persons of color. They would certainly not be Europeans. We stress this point only because it has become virtually axiomatic for people today to envision that somehow the ancient people of the New Testament were all Europeans. Without much reflection or critical analysis, people tend to project modern Jews back into antiquity as if two thousand years of assimilation never occurred. Having established this important interpretive principle, we can identify a few New Testament passages where there is an explicit African presence.

Matthew 1.1-14	The genealogy of Jesus in which four Afro-Asiatic women are included, viz. Rahab, Tamar, Ruth, and Bathsheba.
Matthew 2.13-18	Out of Egypt (Africa) I have called my son (see Hosea 11.1).
Matthew 12.42	The Queen of Sheba (parallel reference in Luke 11.31; compare 1 Kings 10.1-10 and 2 Chronicles 9.1-9).

Matthew 27.32	Simon of Cyrene compelled to carry the cross (parallel accounts in Mark 15.21 and Luke 23.26).
Mark 1.3	Note the mentioning of the "desert" as a reminder of the geographical context for the gospel and most of the biblical narratives.
Luke 13.29	Luke instructs us through his more inclusive editing of Jesus' sayings found in Matthew 8.11. Here, Luke adds "north and south," thereby underscoring the Lukan universalism of both the gospel and the plan of salvation.
Luke 19.41-44	Jesus weeps over the city and initiates change.
Acts 2.9, 10	The Jewish pilgrims gathered at Pentecost included persons of African descent, notably the Elamites of Mesopotamia and those from Egypt, Libya, and Cyrene.
Acts 8.26-40	The Ethiopian Finance Minister on a mission for the Queen of the Ethiopians, the Kandake or Candace; he is baptized as perhaps the first non-Jew (an early tradition that rivals the baptism of Cornelius).
Acts 13.1	Two of the four prophets and teachers at Antioch (where persons of the Way were first called Christians—11.26) were Africans, namely Lucius of Cyrene and Simeon who was called Niger, a Latinism for "the Black Man."
Acts 18.24, 25	Apollos, the Jew of Alexandria in North Africa, becomes converted (1 Corinthians 3).
John 4.7-39	The Samaritan as ancient outcast and here metaphor for victims of racial, ethnic, and gender bias today.
John 8.32	"You will know the truth, and the truth will set you free."

Galatians 5.1	Freedom is what we have—Christ has set us free! Stand, then, as free people, and do not allow yourselves to become slaves again.
1 Corinthians 3.5	Apollos, the African Preacher (He was from Alexandria on the Nile Delta.)
1 Corinthians 7.21c	Further evidence of Paul's dislike of slavery: If you have a chance to become free, use it. (2 Corinthians 11.20 and the Epistle to Philemon).
James 2.1-8	Outward appearances can lead to fraudulent judgments about people. (Although James principally has in mind class distinctions, the principle supports a wider application.)
1 Peter 2.4-10	Those who believe and do the will of God through humble service and self-sacrifice are the Chosen People and the true royal priesthood, and the recipients of God's mercy. No racial or ethnic basis for divine election!

▸ **Detail, "The Creation," by Aaron Douglas, oil on canvas, 1935. The Howard University Gallery of Art, Permanent Collection, Washington, DC**

As the Holy Scriptures testify, all people of faith are "one in union with Christ Jesus" and "descendants of Abraham and will receive what God has promised" (Galatians 3.28, 29). And as the apostle Paul stated, "No longer, then, do we judge anyone by human standards. Even if at one time we judged Christ according to human standards, we no longer do so. Anyone who is joined to Christ is a new being; the old is gone, the new has come. All this is done by God, who through Christ changed us from enemies into his friends and gave us the task of making others his friends also. Our message is that God was making all human beings his friends through Christ. God did not keep an account of their sins, and he has given us the message which tells how he makes them his friends" (2 Corinthians 5.16-19).

Bibliography

Bernal, Martin. *Black Athena: The Afroasiatic Roots of Classical Civilization, Vol. I.* London: Free Association Books, 1987.

Birnbaum, Lucia Chivola. *Black Madonnas: Feminism, Religion & Politics in Italy.* Boston: Northeastern University Press, 1991.

DeCoy, Robert H. *The Blue Book Manual of Nigritian History: American Descendants of African Origin.* New York: Nigritian, Inc., Publishers, 1969.

Featherman, A. *Social History of the Races of Mankind: First Division; Nigritians.* London: Trubner & Co., 1985.

Felder, Cain Hope, ed. *Stony the Road We Trod: African American Biblical Interpretation.* Minneapolis: Fortress Press, 1991.

______________. *Troubling Biblical Waters.* Maryknoll, New York: Orbis Books, 1989.

Harris, Joseph E. *Pillars in Ethiopian History: The William Leo Hansberry African History Notebook, Vol. I.* Washington, DC: Howard University Press, 1974.

Hughley, Ella J. *The Truth about Black Biblical Hebrew-Israel.* Springfield Gardens, NY: Hughley Publications, 1982.

James, George G. M. *The Stolen Legacy: Greek Philosophy is stolen Egyptian Philosophy.* New York: The African Publication Society, 1980.

Leslau, Wolf. *Falasha Anthology: The Black Jews of Ethiopia.* New York: Schocken Books, 1951.

Martin, Clarice J. "*A Chamberlain's Journey and the Challenge of Interpretation for Liberation,*" *Semeia.* Vol. 47, 1989.

McKissic, William Dwight., Sr. *Beyond Roots: In Search of Blacks in the Bible.* Wenonah, NJ: Renaissance Productions, 1990.

Montagu, Ashley M. F. *Most Dangerous Myth: The Fallacy of Race.* New York: Harper & Brothers Publishers, 1952.

Mosley, William. *What Color was Jesus?* Chicago: African-American Images,1987.

Nantambu, Kwame. *Egypt & Afrocentric Geopolitics: Essays on European Supremacy.* Kent, OH: Imhotep Publishing Company, 1996.

Onyewuenyi, Innocent C. *The African Origin of Greek Philosophy: An Exercise in Afrocentrism.* Nsukka, Nigeria: University of Nigeria Press, 1993.

Seaton, Daniel P. *African People of Bible Lands.* Nashville: The A. M. E. Church Publishing House, 1895.

Snowden, Frank M., Jr. *Blacks in Antiquity: Ethiopians in the Greco-Roman Experience.* Cambridge, MA: Harvard University Press, 1970.

_____________. *Before Color Prejudice: The Ancient View of Blacks.* Cambridge, MA: Harvard University, 1983.

Ullendorff, Edward. *Ethiopia in the Bible: The Schweich Lectures, 1967.* London: Oxford University Press, 1968.

Seven

The Alleged Curse on Ham

Gene Rice

Genesis 9.18-29 has been popularly understood to mean that Ham was cursed, and this understanding has often been used to justify oppression of African people, the descendants of Ham. The text gives the impression that Ham offended his father Noah and because of this was cursed, but a careful reading of the passage reveals that this is not so, but rather that Canaan was the offender and was the one cursed. Confusion has arisen because Genesis is not a book in the modern sense, but an editorial synthesis of different traditions of Noah's family. Genesis 9.18-29 is concerned with giving an account of the political relationships between the Israelites, the Philistines, and the Canaanites in biblical times and has nothing to do with race. In fact, the Bible knows nothing of a curse on Ham and nowhere does it have anything negative to say about Africans because of their race. The theological heartbeat of the Bible is that we are all sons and daughters of God, that we are all related to one another as members of a family, that each one of us, whatever our race, ethnicity, and nationality, is special and precious to God, and that we were created for companionship with God—and fellowship with one another.

◂ "Noah's Ark," by Aaron Douglas. Oil on canvas, 1944, Permanent Collection, Fisk University, Nashville, Tennessee

One of the most damaging misconceptions of the Bible is that it sanctions a curse on African people because Ham was cursed. Since Ham is regarded as the father of African people, this belief implies that Ham's descendants are also cursed. Incalculable harm has resulted from this supposition. It has provided a theological justification to Caucasian Americans and others for feelings of superiority, prejudice, and actions that are oppressive to African Americans. Conversely, this assumption has created resentment and anger among African Americans and caused many to reject the Bible. The tragedy is that the belief that Ham was cursed rests on an erroneous interpretation of the Bible. The authority claimed for the curse on Ham is Genesis 9.18-29, but this passage is complex and subject to misunderstanding.

A Careful Reading of Genesis 9.18-29

This passage is made up of three distinct parts. The centerpiece is a story in vv. 20-27 about Noah's discovery of wine and how this affected relationships between him and his sons. This story is framed by a summary statement in vv. 18,19 that the sons of Noah were the ancestors of all the peoples of the biblical world, and by the conclusion to the genealogy of Noah from Genesis 5.28,29.

According to Genesis 9.18,19, Shem, Ham, and Japheth went forth from the ark, and in obedience to God's command (9.1, 7), peopled the whole earth. These verses condense a long history but no details are given. The concern is to make clear the identity of the ancestors of the various peoples of the biblical world and to establish that it was only from "these three" that all the peoples of the world are descended. The results of the procreative activity of Shem, Ham, and Japheth are given in Genesis 10. There, some seventy different peoples are listed and all are identified as descendants of Shem, Ham, and Japheth. Thus Genesis 9.18,19 anticipate and prepare the reader for the extraordinary expansion of humankind from the three sons of Noah recorded in chapter 10.

Verses 28, 29 of chapter 9 connect back to Genesis 5, take up, and bring to a close the genealogy and the life of Noah. In keeping with the interest of Genesis 5, Genesis 9.28, 29 informs us that Noah lived 350 years after the flood, "and died at the age of 950." A regular feature of the genealogy of Noah's ancestors is that after their first-born, they all had "other children" (Genesis 5.4,7, 10, 13, 16 19, 22, 26, 30). Noticeable by its absence is any reference in

9.28, 29 to Noah having other sons and daughters after the birth of Shem, Ham, and Japheth. This relates 9.28, 29 to the emphasis in 9.18, 19 that it was only from "these three" sons of Noah that all humankind is descended.

The story of Noah's discovery of wine in Genesis 9.20-27 stands apart from its framing passages. Verses 18,19 of chapter 9 lead one to expect an account of the increase and dispersal of Noah's descendants following the flood. Instead, vv. 20-27 deal with the relationships of Noah's sons and their descendants in the land of Canaan or Palestine, and connect these relationships to Noah's discovery of wine. According to this story, Noah was the first to plant a vineyard and to discover wine. This new development has significant connections with the previous history of humankind.

Because of Adam's sin, the ground was cursed and Adam had to earn his livelihood by the sweat of his brow (Genesis 3.18,19). But with the birth of Noah, his father saw an omen in Noah's name and expressed the hope that "this child will bring us relief from all our hard work" (Genesis 5.29). Lamech's wish was inspired by the similarity of sound between the name Noah in Hebrew, *noach*, and the Hebrew word for relief or comfort, *nicham*. Thus Noah's discovery of wine, God's gift "to make us happy" (Psalm 104.15; Judges 9.13; Proverbs 31.6,7; Jeremiah 16.7), is regarded as the fulfillment of his father's wish and a blessing. But wine can be a mixed blessing (Proverbs 23.29-35; Hosea 4.11,18).

Ignorant of the properties of wine, Noah drank some, became drunk, uncovered himself because of the heat from the wine, and lay naked in his tent. Noah betrays no consciousness of wrongdoing in becoming drunk nor does the text condemn him, but his nakedness created problems for his sons.

From the references to nakedness in the Old Testament, it appears that the Israelites observed a modesty about their physical being comparable to that of Muslims today. Exposure of one's nakedness was a source of shame, humiliation, and degradation. To be clothed was the first need of the man and the woman after eating the forbidden fruit (Genesis 3.7). One was not to go up by steps to the altar because you might "expose" yourself as you go up the steps (Exodus 20.26). Prisoners were led away naked and barefoot, with buttocks uncovered (Isaiah 20). The degradation and humiliation of defeat and exile is likened to the exposure of a woman's nakedness (e. g., Hosea 2.10; Isaiah 47.3; Jeremiah 13.26; Ezekiel 16.37, 39; Nahum 3.5).

Thus Noah's nakedness posed a delicate problem for his sons, whose responsibility to respect and care for their parents is presupposed here and spelled out in Israelite tradition (Exodus 20.12; 21.15,17; Deuteronomy 27.16; Proverbs 30.17; Isaiah 51.17-19).

Ham, according to Genesis 9.22, behaved very badly. He discovered his father in his tent in his drunken condition, paused to look upon him, then went outside and told his brothers. Shem and Japheth, however, took an outer garment (*the garment* in Hebrew, probably Noah's discarded garment) which also served as a blanket (Exodus 22.26,27; Deuteronomy 24.12,13), put it over their shoulders and walked backward [gingerly, and awkwardly, no doubt] into the tent. Without looking at their father, they placed it over his body (Genesis 9.23). The detail and vividness of this scene emphasize the modesty, respect, and sense of duty of Shem and Japheth for their father and highlight, by contrast, the offense of Ham. Ham looked at Noah in his naked condition, made no effort to cover his father, and talked about his father's nakedness.

Some time later Noah awoke "and learned what his youngest son had done to him." Noah's son is not named in the Hebrew text of Genesis 9.24, but a few translations, as the *King James Version*, identify Noah's son in verse 24 as Ham by referring to him as the "younger son." The grammar permits either the comparative or the superlative degree, but the more natural construction because of the three sons, and the one adopted by most modern translators, is the superlative, "the youngest."

The text does not tell us how Noah came to know what had been done to him. Did Shem and Japheth tell Noah about their brother viewing and talking about their father's nakedness? Or was more involved than seeing and talking about it? In any case, Noah was highly offended and cursed his son.

In Hebrew mentality a curse has a self-fulfilling energy and power to bring about the malady prescribed in the curse. The king of Moab hired Balaam to curse Israel to prevent the Israelites from entering his land, confident that Balaam's curse was as effective as a military force (Numbers 22-24). After conquering and burning Jericho, Joshua pronounced a curse on anyone who would rebuild the city (Joshua 6.26). Centuries later in the days of Ahab, Hiel rebuilt Jericho and, because of Joshua's curse, lost his first-born and his youngest son (1 Kings 16.34). The text leads us to expect Ham to be cursed but takes us by surprise by naming Canaan as the one cursed and by identifying him as Noah's youngest son! Ham, however, is consistently referred to as Noah's middle son (Genesis 5.32; 6.10; 7.13; 9.18; 10.6). The curse is that Canaan is to be the lowest of slaves to his brothers. Canaan's brothers, whom he is to be subject to, are then named. Again the text takes us by surprise and mystifies us. The brothers Canaan is to be a slave to are Shem and Japheth! Shem and Japheth, however, are blessed and after each is blessed it is reiterated that Canaan is to be their slave, making the curse all the more binding, for repetition strengthens and intensifies (Genesis 41.32).

As a curse has a self-fulfilling energy and power, so does a blessing when rightly spoken. And the blessing, like the curse, has the power to determine destiny and to shape the future. Jacob's ascendancy over Esau (Genesis 27), Ephraim's pre-eminence over Manasseh, the first-born (Genesis 48.8-20), and the destinies of all Jacob's sons (Genesis 49.1-27) are attributed to blessing. So also the relationships of Noah's descendants in Canaan are understood in terms of curse and blessing. The motive for the blessing of Shem and Japheth is not stated, but from the context it is clearly because of their respect and care for their father.

Noah blesses Shem by way of blessing the Lord, the God of Shem. The thought here is that of Psalm 144.15 "Happy are the people whose God is the LORD!" To bless the Lord is to express thanksgiving and praise in acknowledgment of the Lord as God. Since among the descendants of Shem the Lord became the covenant God of Israel, Shem at this point in time represents the future Israelites. The blessing of Japheth takes the form of a wish that God may extend *yapht*, a play on Japheth, his territory and that he may dwell in the tents of Shem.

With the blessing of Japheth it becomes clear that we are not dealing with individuals alone but with groups of people and their political relationships to one another. Canaan obviously represents the Canaanites, Shem the Israelites, and Japheth, the ancestor of Greek peoples (Genesis 10.2), the Philistines, who were immigrants from the Aegean basin (Amos 9.7; Jeremiah 47.3,4). This way of referring to peoples in their relationships to one another is confirmed by Genesis 10. There, a combination of geographical, political, ethnic, racial, and linguistic relations among people are expressed in terms of genealogical relationships. When Canaan is said to be the son of Ham (Genesis 10.6), for example, this expressed the fact that Canaan is geographically adjacent to Egypt and was, from earliest times, either under the hegemony or directly ruled by Egypt. As the list of Canaan's descendants in Genesis 10.15-19 shows, the Canaanites were not properly an African people, but Semites and Indo-Europeans who all lived in Palestine.

Problems of Interpretation

One comes to the end of Genesis 9.18-29 perplexed and with a host of questions. Verse 22 implies that Ham was liable to be cursed for acting disrespectfully to his father, but it is Canaan who is cursed. One might infer that Canaan was cursed for the infraction of his father, but if this were so one would expect a reason to be given for it; but none is. In fact, Canaan is explicitly identified as the offender in verses 24, 25. When Noah sobered up and learned what his youngest son had done to him, he said, "A curse on Canaan! He will be a slave to his brothers." Since Canaan is called Noah's son, and the brothers he is to be subjected to are identified as Shem and Japheth, how does this accord with the statement in Genesis 9.18 that the sons of Noah were Shem, Ham, and Japheth? Moreover, the descendants of Shem, Ham, and Japheth are said to populate the whole earth in 9.19, but Shem and Japheth rule over, and jointly occupy, only the land of Canaan in 9.26,27. In the flood story, Shem, Ham, and Japheth have wives (Genesis 7.7,13; 8.15,18), but Noah's sons in 9.20-27 seem to be living at home with their father and there is no mention of their wives. Why is it said in 9.18 and 9.22 that Ham was the father of Canaan, but there is no reference to Ham's other sons, Cush, Egypt, and Put? And why is there no mention of Shem and Japheth being the father of anyone? How can Ham be the father of Canaan when according to 9.24,25, Noah was the father of Canaan? When did Shem (Israel) and Japheth (the Philistines) jointly rule Canaan and did these old enemies live in peace? Finally, what is the point of the passage?

The Literary Character of Genesis

One of the established results of biblical criticism is the recognition that Genesis speaks with not one, but four voices. By paying attention to the terms used for the deity, God (Hebrew, *Elohim*) and the Lord (Hebrew, YHWH, traditionally pronounced Yahweh) together with literary style and theological point of view, scholars have distinguished two creation stories, two lists of patriarchs before the flood, two versions of the flood, two versions of the family of nations in chapter 10, etc. These different voices continue throughout Genesis and into Exodus, Leviticus, and Numbers. Scholars call the voice that consistently refers to God as the Lord, J (from the German spelling, Jahweh), and a widely accepted date is ca. 950 B.C. Another voice begins with God (*Elohim*), changes to God All-Powerful (*El Shaddai*) at Genesis 17, and to the Lord in Exodus 6. This voice has a pronounced interest in priestly matters and for this reason is called P; it is generally dated to ca. 550-450 B.C. A third voice calls the deity God (*Elohim*) until the time of Moses, then the Lord (but not consistently), but it is fragmentary and difficult to date. Because of its preference for Elohim and its place of origin in the Northern Kingdom, also called Ephraim, this voice is named E. Proposed dates range from ca. 900-750 B.C. The fourth voice of Genesis is that of the one(s) who carefully and purposefully placed J, E, and P in the order in which we now find them.

While there is a profound theological harmony between these versions of the early history of humankind, they often differ in detail. The universe in Genesis 1.1—2.4a is brought into being by eight creative acts of God's Word over a period of six days. In Genesis 2.4b-25 creation is accomplished by four creative acts by the Lord's hands and there is no reference to the time involved. In the parallel genealogies of humankind before the flood in Genesis 4.17-26 and Genesis 5, the names are sometimes spelled differently and they do not consistently follow the same order of birth. (Note also the differences in the genealogy of Jesus in Matthew and Luke.) According to one version of the flood, Noah took two of every kind of animal into the ark (Genesis 6.19,20; 7.9,15). In the other version, Noah took seven pairs of clean and one pair of unclean animals and seven pairs of birds into the ark (Genesis 7.2, 3). Nor is this phenomenon confined to the Old Testament. We have not one, but four versions of the life and ministry of Jesus, and the differences between Mark and John are as striking as anything in Genesis. But whereas the New Testament Gospels have been preserved separately, the different literary sources in Genesis have been "braided" together.

These differences in detail are the inevitable results of the oral transmission of information and traditions for generations in different geographical locales and under different historical circumstances. The Bible leaves these differences uncensored and thereby indicates that it accepts and embraces them. The combined witness of the different voices in Genesis (and elsewhere in the Bible) gives us a fuller and better understanding than any one voice alone.

Two Versions of Noah's Family

The recognition of the composite nature of Genesis provides the key to the proper understanding of 9.18-29. As there are two versions of creation, two genealogies of humankind before the flood, and two versions of the flood, so there are two versions of Noah's family. Verses 18,19 represent one tradition; verses 20-27 embody another. Verses 18,19 and also 28,29 belong with Genesis 1, 5, and 10 (the P voice) and reflect the view that the (married) sons of Noah were Shem, Ham, and Japheth and that they were the ancestors of all the peoples of the biblical world. In 9.20-27, on the other hand, the (apparently unmarried) sons of Noah are Shem, Japheth, and Canaan. In this version of Noah's sons the one cursed is Canaan and the purpose of these verses is to account for relations between Israelites, Canaanites, and Philistines in the land of Canaan. These verses speak with the voice of J, also found in Genesis 2–4; 11.1-9, and chapter 12. This tradition of Noah's sons seems also to be reflected in Genesis 10.21 where Shem is referred to as the elder brother of Japheth.

The understanding of Genesis 9.18-29 is so confused because the Hebrew text at an early stage of its transmission has been edited to harmonize the two traditions of Noah's sons. This was done by adding the note in 9.18b, "Ham was the father of Canaan" (to give a literal translation of the Hebrew text), and by inserting the phrase, "Ham, the father of," before Canaan in 9.22a. These editorial additions interrupt the flow of the narrative and stand out like a bandaged thumb. The concern of 9.18, 19 is to establish that Shem, Ham, and Japheth, and only "these three," were the forebears of all the peoples of the biblical world. The note that explains Ham's relationship to Canaan in 9.18b introduces a new and unrelated subject. And this note is made conspicuous as an addition by the absence of similar information about Shem and Japheth.

The insertion of "Ham, the father of" in 9.22 is equally intrusive and stands in conflict with 9.24. This editorial note makes Ham, the middle son of Noah, the offender, but Noah explicitly identifies the guilty party as his youngest son (9.23,24).

The editorial nature of "Ham was the father of Canaan" in 9.18b is acknowledged in the translations of *The New International Version*, *The New American Bible*, and *Today's English Version* by placing these words in brackets or parentheses. The same should be done for "Ham, the father of" in 9.22, as in the *Moffatt Translation* and the *Confraternity Version.* Notes added to the Hebrew text by a later editor to explain changes in place names, etc. are found throughout the Bible. *The New Revised Standard Version,* the *New International Version,* and the *New King James Version* use parentheses to designate part of the following passages in Genesis as editorial additions: 14.8; 23.2,19; 35.6,19,27; 48.7. Other translations, including the *Contemporary English Version,* integrate these editorial additions into the text.

It is understandable that someone confronted by the two traditions of Noah's family in Genesis 9.18-29 would attempt to harmonize them, especially since Noah's sons are identified by name as Shem, Ham, and Japheth in the P version of the flood (Genesis 6.10; 7.13), and the P version of Noah's sons (9.18,19) stands immediately before Noah's curse and blessing (9.20-27). In the J version of the flood the sons of Noah are not named. When they are referred to, it is as Noah's "whole family" (Genesis 7.1) and "those who were with him in the boat" (7.23). The authority for the editorial additions in 9.18 and 9.22 is Genesis 10.6, where it is stated that Ham indeed was the father of Canaan. However, the author of these editorial notes overlooks the fact that in Genesis 9.24,25 Noah is the father of Canaan.

The recognition that there are two traditions of Noah's sons in Genesis 9.18-29 opens the way to the correct interpretation of the passage. The only basis for identifying Ham as the offender is the note in 9.18, (Ham was the father of Canaan) and the insertion in 9.22, "Ham, the father of." When it is understood that these notes were not a part of the original narrative but later, editorial additions to the Hebrew text, the offender as well as the one cursed is Canaan. Ham was not the one cursed because in Genesis 9.1 God blessed Ham and his brothers. As Baalam could not curse Israel whom God had blessed (Numbers 22.12; 23.8), so Noah could not have cursed Ham whom God had blessed.

If the editorial notes about Ham being the father of Canaan are accepted as original, no satisfactory explanation of Genesis 9.18-29 is possible. These notes make Ham the offender but give no reason why Canaan is cursed. There is the additional awkwardness that Ham is consistently referred to as Noah's middle son, but the one cursed is identified as Noah's youngest son. Those who interpret the passage on the assumption that the notes in 9.18 and 9.22 are an integral part of the narrative are forced to resort to speculation or to declare other portions of the passage secondary. This approach has achieved no consensus of interpretation and has led to widely diverging and sometimes bizarre expositions.

The Purpose of 9.18-29

In Genesis 12.7 God promises Abraham that the land of Canaan will be given to his descendants. Preceding and following this promise (12.6; 13.7) is the notation that the Canaanites were then living in the land and therefore were the native inhabitants of Canaan. This raises an important question: What right did the Israelites have to Canaan when its native population were Canaanites? In the course of time the Israelites did occupy Canaan and subjected the native population to forced labor (Joshua 16.10; 17.12,13; Judges 1.27-35; 1 Kings 9.20,21), but they shared possession of the land with the Philistines. If God promised the land to the Israelites, why did they share it with the Philistines?

Genesis 9.20-27 provides answers to these questions. According to this passage, the Canaanites lost their right to their land because of an inherent perversity in their ancestor Canaan which was perpetuated by his descendants. The Canaanites, especially those of Sodom, were considered "wicked" because they "sinned against the LORD" (Genesis 13.13; 15.16; 18.20,21; 19; Amorites in 15.16 is a synonymous term for Canaanites). According to Leviticus 18.24, 25, it was because of the abominable sexual practices of the native population of Canaan that the land rejected them (see also Deuteronomy 9.4, 5; 12.29-31; 1 Kings 14.24; 2 Kings 17.7, 11). Because of the notoriety of the Canaanites for sexual misconduct, it is tempting to infer that what was "done" to Noah (Genesis 9.24) was homosexual rape and that a fuller account of what happened has been curtailed to avoid offending readers. To see the nakedness of another leads naturally to sexual relations (Leviticus 20.17). And to look upon a forbidden object opens the way to succumbing to temptation, as in the case of Eve with the forbidden fruit (Genesis 3.6) and David with Bathsheba (2 Samuel 11.2-5). In whatever way we understand what was done to Noah, Canaan did not honor his father. And as the Fifth Commandment makes clear, honoring one's parents is the basis for maintaining the tenure of one's land.

Noah's curse and blessing are in effect a theological mandate for Israel's supremacy over Canaan. A remarkable feature of this mandate is that it also includes the Philistines. The Israelites and Philistines entered Canaan about the same time and at first were rivals for control of the land. Under David, the Israelites conquered the Philistines (2 Samuel 5.17-25; 8.1, 12; 2.15-22; 23.9-17), but the Philistines were allowed to retain their holding along the coastal plain of Canaan and to maintain their separate identity (see maps

3,4, and 6 in the back of the Bible). This is all the more remarkable in that the Israelites claimed the territory occupied by the Philistines. In the boundary lists of the Promised Land (Exodus 23.31; Numbers 34.3; Joshua 15.11; Ezekiel 47.20) the western boundary does not stop at Philistine territory but is placed at the Mediterranean Sea.

The wish that God may enlarge Japheth probably refers to an extension of Philistine territory in the direction of Egypt. This would not only be a blessing to Japheth but also a source of security to Israel from the threat of Egyptian incursion into Palestine.

David may have contributed to the Israelite acceptance of the Philistine presence "in the tents of Shem," for he had enduring relationships with the Philistines, especially Achish, king of Gath. David lived as a refugee with Achish for one year and four months (1 Samuel 27.7). Achish later gave David the city of Ziklag as a feudal holding (1 Samuel 27). After David became king of all Israel and conquered the Philistines, Achish continued to be king of Gath into the reign of Solomon (1 Kings 2.39). Also, there was in David's army a contingent of troops from Gath willing to follow him into exile (2 Samuel 15.18-22). And the royal bodyguard of David and Solomon was composed of Cherethites and Pelethites (2 Samuel 8.18; 23.23; 1 Kings 1.44), who were either components or relatives of the Philistines (Ezekiel 25.16; Zephaniah 2.5). In any case, it is true that personal relationships with the "enemy" and those who are different can lead to blessing and dwelling together in peace.

No Evidence of a Curse on Ham Anywhere in the Bible

Not only is there no shred of evidence in Genesis 9.18-29 of a curse on Ham; nowhere in the Bible is there any reference or even an allusion to such a curse. Genesis 10 contains a list of the descendants of Shem, Ham, and Japheth (from the P source; portions of the chapter also belong to J). If there were any negative thoughts and feelings toward Ham and his descendants, this passage, following immediately on Noah's curse and blessing, would have been the place to express them. But no disparaging remark is made about anyone. (In Deuteronomy 23.7,8 Israelites are expressly forbidden to be unkind to Egyptians because "you once lived in their land") Rather, all the descendants of Noah are listed as related to one another as brothers and sisters. The one person

▸ "Nubians carrying offerings, among them a giraffe." Tomb of Huy, Thebes, Egypt, Art Resource, NY

given special attention is Nimrod, the son of Cush, and he is credited with being the first to exercise imperial political power in Mesopotamia (Genesis 10.8-12). The point of Genesis 10 is that humankind is conceived as a unity, and the diversity of peoples "living in their different tribes and countries, each group speaking its own language" (vv. 5, 20, 31) is understood as the fulfillment of God's command to Noah and his sons to be fruitful and to multiply, and to fill the earth (Genesis 9.1, 7). As God inspected the creation in Genesis 1 and declared it to correspond exactly to the divine intention, that it is good, so Genesis 10 implies that humankind in all its ethnic and racial manifestations corresponds to God's intention and is good. Abraham had no reservation about going to Egypt, the land of Ham (Psalms 78.51; 105.23, 27; 106.22), when there was a famine in Canaan (Genesis 12.10-20). Nor did Abraham and Sarah have any qualms about using Hagar, an Egyptian, as a surrogate mother so they could have an heir (Genesis 16). In fact, Abraham would gladly have accepted Ishmael, Hagar's son, as the father of the covenant people (Genesis 17.18). The mother of the

tribes of Ephraim and Manasseh was Asenath, an Egyptian (Genesis 41.45, 50-52; 46.20), and Jacob was at pains to adopt her sons so that they could be recognized as fully Israelite (Genesis 48.5,6).

Moses was married to a Cushite (the Hebrew word for the peoples living south of Egypt whom the Greeks called Ethiopians, a word meaning literally, "burnt faces") and while Miriam and Aaron spoke out against her, the context shows that what they were really protesting was Moses' exclusive authority to speak for God (Numbers 12). If Moses' Cushite wife was Zipporah from the land of Midian where Moses found refuge (Exodus 2.11-22), then Moses accepted instruction in the administration of justice from his Cushite father-in-law, Jethro (Exodus 18.13-27). It is worthy of note that Aaron's grandson and successor as high priest (Exodus 6.25), and also one of the sons of Eli the priest (1 Samuel 1.3), given the Egyptian name, Phinehas, which means literally, "The Southerner" (in relation to Egypt), that is, the Ethiopian or the Nubian.

David had Ethiopian troops in his army (2 Samuel 18.19-32). Solomon made an alliance with Egypt and took an Egyptian wife (1 Kings 3.1). Solomon graciously received, and treated as an equal, the queen of Sheba whose kingdom embraced both Arabian and African territory (1 Kings 10.1-13).

Amos likens Israel to the Ethiopians to make the point that the distant and different Ethiopians were just as near and dear to God as the covenant people (Amos 9.7,8a). The Targum on this passage quotes God as saying: "Are you [the Ethiopians] not greatly beloved unto me."

Hezekiah made an alliance with Egypt, then ruled by the Twenty-fifth (Ethiopian) Dynasty, and with the support of his ally revolted against Assyria. Isaiah, who called for repentance and faith, objected to this alliance and makes some disparaging remarks about Egypt's help (e.g., Isaiah 30.5, 7) because the Egyptians were men and not God (31.3), but nowhere does he appeal to an ancient curse on Egypt (nor do other prophets who criticize Israel for turning to Egypt or who announce judgment on Egypt, e.g., Hosea 7.11; Jeremiah 2.18; Ezekiel 30). Hezekiah's revolt was not successful, but the Ethiopian general and later pharaoh, Tirhakah, stood by Hezekiah and fought for him (2 Kings 19.9; Isaiah 37.9).

As a result of Hezekiah's alliances with the Twenty-fifth Dynasty of Egypt, close contacts were established between the two peoples. Soon afterwards we find Ethiopians as members of Israelite society and Israelite settlers in Ethiopia. The father of the prophet Zephaniah was an Ethiopian as his name, Cushi, indicates, and Zephaniah's great-great grandfather was (King) Hezekiah of Judah (Zephaniah 1.1). Jehudi, son of Nethaniah, son of Shelemiah, son of Cushi, was a trusted member of King Jehoiakim's cabinet (Jeremiah 36.14, 21, 23). And Jeremiah's life was saved by the royal servant, Ebed-melech, "the Ethiopian" (Jeremiah 38.7-13; 39.15-18). Throughout Israel's history, Egypt and Ethiopia were places of refuge (e.g., Isaiah 11.11; Jeremiah 42–44; Matthew 2.13-15). But for Israelite refugees and converts to the religion of Israel, Zion was their spiritual home and those in foreign lands looked forward to worshipping in Zion. Isaiah 18.7 anticipates the time when gifts will be brought to the Lord by the Ethiopians. So does Zephaniah in 3.10 of his prophecy, and the Psalmist in Psalm 68.31. Psalm 87 pictures such a gathering of pilgrims in Zion, not only from Egypt and Ethiopia, but also from Babylon, Philistia, and Tyre, who all say, "In Zion is the source of all our blessings" (v. 7). And Isaiah 19.23b-25 anticipates the time when "The people of these two countries will travel back and forth between them, and the two nations will worship together. When that time comes, Israel will rank with Egypt and Assyria, and these three nations will be a blessing to all the world. The LORD Almighty will bless them and say, 'I will bless you, Egypt, my people; you, Assyria, whom I created; and you, Israel, my chosen people.'" Note also the diverse peoples gathered in Jerusalem at the time of Pentecost (Acts 2.5-11), and the "enormous crowd...from every race, tribe, nation and language" gathered before the throne and the Lamb in Revelation 7.9, 10.

Simon, from the North African city of Cyrene (Matthew 27.32; Mark 15.21; Luke 23.26), was not regarded as unworthy to carry Jesus' cross. Nor did Philip feel obligated to discuss Genesis 9.18-29 with the Ethiopian minister of Queen Candace before baptizing him (Acts 8.26-40).

Origin of the Idea of a Curse on Ham

If there is no basis in the Bible for a curse on Ham, how did this idea originate? It was not until the last quarter of the nineteenth century that biblical scholars convincingly clarified the composite literary character of Genesis. To one unaware of the two traditions of Noah's family and the editorial nature of the references to Ham as the father of Canaan in Genesis 9.18, 22, the offender is obviously Ham. And if Ham is the offender, the inference naturally suggests itself that Ham was also the one cursed. A few manuscripts of the early Greek translation, the Septuagint (ca. 250-100 B.C.), name Ham as the one cursed. Ham is also named as the one cursed in the Arabic version (13th century A.D.). In early rabbinic literature and the writings of the Church Fathers, one occasionally finds references to Ham as affected by Noah's curse. But it was not until the Middle Ages that Jewish, Christian, and Moslem authorities alike began generally to identify Ham as cursed. Luther and Calvin also name Ham as cursed, as well as Canaan. Still, the interpretation of Genesis 9.18-29 during the Middle Ages for the most part was homiletical and moralistic, not intentionally racist. Ham was criticized for his immodesty or for speaking disrespectfully about his father, or for failing to care for his father, or for causing dissension in the family. Nevertheless, the focus on Ham during the Middle Ages helped establish the popular notion that Ham was cursed and made it possible for racists to seize upon this passage and to use it as theological justification for the oppression of African people.

The misunderstanding and abuse of Genesis 9.18-29 illustrate what a responsibility it is to rightly interpret Scripture. The erroneous idea that there is a curse on Ham is not the fault of the Bible. At the least, it is poor exegesis and reflects lack of knowledge of biblical scholarship. Used in a racist sense, this erroneous idea is a reminder of the ingenuity and perversity with which humans find ways to justify to themselves and to others; their sin. However one reads Genesis 9.18-29, it is absolutely clear that there is no basis for a curse on Ham in this passage. The curse is on Canaan and it is because of behavior, not race. And the passage is concerned with political relationships between Israelites,

▸ **Detail, "Nubians carrying offerings, among them a giraffe." Tomb of Huy, Thebes, Egypt, Art Resource, NY**

Canaanites, and Philistines in Canaan in the 10th century B.C., not with Africans or African Americans. Even if the passage is accepted as an organic literary unit speaking with a single, coherent voice, it has nothing to do with race. Read this way, its point is that the behavior of parents may bring a curse on their children. The erroneous idea of a curse on Ham stands in violent conflict with the theological heartbeat of the Bible that we are all sons and daughters of God, that we are all related to one another as members of a family, that each one of us, whatever our race, ethnicity, and nationality, is special and precious to God, and that we were created for companionship with God—and fellowship with one another.

Eight

Slavery in the Ancient Near East and, Particularly, in Israel

Frank L. Gipson

◂ "The Ancient Israelites as Slaves in Egypt," Wood engraving, 19th century, courtesy of The Granger Collection, New York

In ancient Israel and the Near East, slavery had a vital role in the household. The household that was successful, having a thriving dynasty and growing wealth, also had slaves. Slaves were an economic sign of strength and political power. The patriarchs, or propertied members of society, and their households were the social paradigm for society. Although a particular deity was acknowledged as the owner of the land and its people, the king or ruler was recognized as an owner of the land and its people as well; his or her subjects and vassals were considered servants of their sovereign. Economically, the mode of production in the ancient Near East, and particularly in monarchic Israel, was tributary. This mode of production was conducive to slavery, owing to the honorific status it gave to conquerors, royalty, and ruling classes at the top of society who, by their status and power, were due tribute in exchange for protection, life, and peace.

Terminology

The Hebrew term for "slave" that often translates as "a male slave" carries a range of meaning from *servant, royal subject, to minister* and even a theological title, such as *Moses, the servant of God.* The terms designating a female slave describe a female servant or a concubine in the household (Genesis 29.24, 29; 30.3; 31.33). Yet, in some references, the terms imply humility in consideration of the lowly and vulnerable status of a female slave (Ruth 3.9; 2 Samuel 14.15). The Hebrew term for *boy, lad,* or *youth* has a secondary meaning of a "young male slave, servant or retainer." This word can describe a household servant (Numbers 22.22; Judges 7.10, 11). As with all the terms the translation of the Hebrew words for "slave" depends upon the context in which they are used.

The Definition

Slavery is when one person or party has ownership over another. It is an institution when such ownership is legal and sanctioned politically as a right and privilege within a given society.

While slavery is not by definition a way of obtaining free labor, it is a means of obtaining labor at little cost, often involving mental coercion, physical force, and without any reasonable and just compensation to the person(s) producing the labor and its byproduct. In slavery, the laborers are owned and their productivity belongs to their owner(s).

In most cases slavery was a perpetual institution in the ancient Near East; e.g., a person who was born into such status would, in most cases, die in that social status. So also, the descendants of the slave remained in their station generation after generation. According to Exodus 21.2, (also Deuteronomy 15.12 and Jeremiah 34.14) however, the servitude of a Hebrew debt-slave was limited to six years.[1] Any act of manumission (release from bondage) was an official one, executed in courts or public forums. In some cases, slaves could purchase their freedom or even that of kin, but technically whatever slaves owned belonged to their masters. This would mean that owners primarily held the right of manumission. There are records of

[1] Barry Lee Eichler. "*Slavery*" *Harper Bible Dictionary*, ed. Paul J. Achtemeier. (San Francisco: Harper, 1985), 959.

owners manumitting slaves and adopting them which would entitle them to an inheritance. In Israel, there was opportunity for one to intervene and redeem a relative from debt slavery or purchase the enslaved relative out of slavery. One could become a slave through various means, such as by capture in battle, punishment for crimes committed, or debt slavery. A family member could sell a person into slavery, as was the case with Joseph, who was sold by his brothers (Genesis 37.12-36). It is well narrated in the Old Testament that the Israelites had been slaves in Egypt (Exodus 13.3, 14; Deuteronomy 5.15; 16.1; 24.18). The Egyptian officials made them slaves in order to contain and control the Israelites' population growth and their political and military potential (Exodus 1.10, 11). Foreigners were slaves in Israel as well.

The general mode of production in ancient Near Eastern societies was tributary, especially in the first and second millennia, B.C. The word "tributary" means that a ruler or country pays a conqueror for protection or peace. Slaves were used as a commodity in this arrangement. The conditions of enslavement accommodated this tributary mode of obtaining labor.

Conditions for Slavery

As a society grows in population and political and economic strength, its needs for labor availability and utilization increase. In human societies, the expansion and development of the production forces are often "due to advances and changes in at least three areas: the geopolitical arrangements; regional specialization of productive activities; and labor availability and utilization."[2] For example, a despot, overlord or nobility maximizes productivity, amasses wealth, and becomes dominant through labor availability and utilization, as well as through the use of military capability and political and class superiority. Slaves and peasants can best supply labor availability and utilization within a tributary mode of production. Slave labor or forced labor aided in producing the great monuments of the ancient Africa, such as palaces, pyramids and temples. Even King Solomon is among the rulers who used forced labor (1 Kings 9.15, 20, 21; 12.4), in part, to build the great temple, the king's palace, and the many shrines for his multitude of foreign wives.

[2] Itumeleng J. Mosala, *Bible Hermeneutics and Black Theology in South Africa.* (Grand Rapids: Wm. B. Eerdmans Publishing Co., 1989), 108.

In such places such as Egypt, Asia Minor, Mesopotamia, Achaemenid Iran and Palestine, slavery was an institution that played a major economic role. Within these societies there existed a tributary mode of production wherein the status of the societal majority ranged from peasantry to slavery. A mode of production identifies how labor is produced, how goods are exchanged, and the value given to labor and the goods that are produced. The mode of production is tributary (1) when it subsists upon tributes paid for protection, imposed by a feudal overlord who rules by intimidation, terror, oppression and/or a popular hegemonic ideology, and (2) when the tribute payments determine who is rich or poor and what status societal members hold and inherit.

Furthermore, the prophet Samuel describes this mode of production and links it with the rise of the monarchy (1 Samuel 8.11-18). It is a

▸ "Slave Trade in Morocco." Prospective buyers examining one of the captured slaves. Woodcut by R. Canton Woodville. Courtesy of Corbis-Bettman, New York

political and economic reality where one person maximizes his rule over the many which he, along with the ruling classes, reduces to servants of the state and to slavery. Also, his personage is identified with the spirit of the country he rules; consequently, what is good for him is deemed good for the country and its entire citizenry. This type of dominance over human labor and identity takes its example from the household of the patriarch or propertied member of society. Therefore, a description of the patriarchal household and explanation of slavery practiced therein follows.

Slavery in the Household[3]

Not only did kings, overlords and nobility have slaves, but slavery also existed within the households. Although scholars report that "privately owned slaves functioned more as domestic servants than as an agricultural or industrial labor force,"[4] the household in Israel was a commonwealth wherein such division of labor did not apply.

> The Family (household), in fact, was a Corporation; and he (the patriarch) was its (chief) representative or, we might almost say, its Public officer. He enjoyed rights and stood under duties, but the rights and duties were, in the contemplation of his fellow-citizens (kinsmen and others under his rule) and in the eye of the law, quite as much those of the collective body as his own.[5]

Exodus 20.17 and Deuteronomy 5.21 (in the Ten Commandments or Decalogue) describe your neighbor or Israelite compatriots to be propertied members of society holding estates. The Ten Commandments were addressed to and for these propertied members of Israelite society. Listed among their properties, which were not to be coveted by another compatriot, are slaves, wives, livestock, and other property. Their households were not nuclear families. Here, and elsewhere, the household appears to be kinship

[3] The present writer's dissertation in progress is on the subject of local authority; from that dissertation the understanding of the patriarchal household presented here is borrowed and developed.

[4] Barry Lee Eichler, "*Slavery,*" *Harper Bible Dictionary, 959.*

[5] Henry S. Maine, "The Primitive Family and the Corporation," *Readings in Kinship and Social Structure,* ed. Nelson Graburn. (New York: Harper & Row, Publishers, 1971), 11. Here, Maine describes a patriarch in the classical Roman household primarily, yet the description is appropriate for a patriarch within the ancient Israelite household as well.

groups organized into extended families (numbering up to fifty members or more, and may extend over four generations of living relatives), as Leviticus 18.7-16 describes.[6]

However, both the family, as the smallest segment of Israelite society, and extended families are indicated in the Hebrew term for "family." Because the household was the model social unit for all other types, this term can describe a range of social units, such as clan, tribe, and nation. The household it describes is often dynastic in leadership. The eldest son is the rightful heir of its leadership, just as the leadership was inherited in the dynasty of the Davidic monarchy, for example.

Slaves were an important part of the household and their owners did not restrict their work to "domestic" areas. The slave was not left at home while the owner of the house went to engage in agricultural or industrial labor. For example, in Judges 6.27a, "So Gideon took ten of his servants and did what the LORD had told him." Genesis 32.16 calls Jacob's shepherds, slaves. This point is highly significant when one recognizes that much of Jacob's wealth was in his flocks of sheep and goats. Jacob's slaves managed his wealth. In addition, Genesis 26.15 and 19 describe Abraham's and Isaac's slaves as digging wells to sustain the households and flocks of these patriarchs. Saul's herdsman was an Edomite slave (1 Samuel 21.7). There is also record of "the use of slave labor in cultivating the land (Ruth 2.5; 2 Samuel 9.10)."[7]

The place of slaves was of immense significance in every aspect of Israelite society because, regardless of their status, they were fully functional human persons within the society. For example, in Genesis 16, Sarai gave the Egyptian slave-girl Hagar to Abraham in order to produce an heir. Of course, without an heir, the ancient Near Eastern patriarch and his household would have died out. According to the psalmist, children (sons) were a blessing from the LORD; particularly, they were a great accomplishment and source of strength (Psalm 127.3-5). Hence, Hagar's son, Ishmael, is counted among the descendants of

[6] In a series of injunctions, all sexual contact with individuals related by kin (literally "flesh") are prohibited. Mother, sister, granddaughter, half-sister, paternal aunt, maternal aunt, daughter-in-law, and sister-in-law are listed as illicit sexual partners for a man; father and paternal uncle are prohibited as sexual partners for a woman. The persons mentioned would probably be members of the household unit.

[7] Muhammah A. Dandamayev, "Slavery (OT)" *The Anchor Bible Dictionary, Volume Six, 64.*

Abraham (Genesis 25.9, 12). As recorded in Genesis 17.23, Ishmael was circumcised along with all the male slaves: "On that same day Abraham obeyed God and circumcised his son Ishmael and all the other males in his household, including the slaves born in his home and those he had bought." This inclusion of Abraham's slaves as covenant members demonstrates that their importance was considerable to the patriarch. They were significant members of that household because of their irreducible contributions of vital service on its behalf. Of course, it was not possible for men like Abraham to be a patriarch or propertied member of society without owning slaves and receiving their considerable compliance and assistance.

Clearly, the owner used the slaves to provide whatever was needed or desired for the perceived good of his household. This, of course, is the message found in the story of Joseph (Genesis 39.1-6a). He was among the category of a servant or slave in Potiphar's household, which illustrates, in part, the range of possible roles and status of such a person. Upon Potiphar's purchase, he first became a slave in Potiphar's household. However, his gifts and skills led Potiphar to promote him to increasingly higher levels of status and authority, by which promotions he ultimately became the chief household steward. The status of slave, in this case, is transformed by the roles that Joseph performed. Through his role performance he transcended slavery until he met disfavor (Genesis 39.6b-20). While disfavor degraded his status, he again rebounded and became the chief minister to the Pharaoh of Egypt (Genesis 39.21— 41.57). As the story of Joseph illustrates, through the humility of a slave, Joseph's character transformed him into a savior figure. It is material that Joseph worked within the context of a household, because that is where slavery existed most acutely in the ancient Near East. However, it needs to be emphasized that the household was not a nuclear family but a commonwealth; that is, a corporation that represented a microcosm of society.

In the ancient Near East, slavery was endemic and indispensable in every society or country. If it had not been such, then allowing captives of wars to remain alive and permitting those in egregious debt to sell themselves or relatives into slavery would not have been notable social conventions or viable options. Why capture a kingdom or territory that is not strategically located and/or without the means to pay tribute? Because inexpensive sources of labor were needed, slaves were a socially sanctioned and desirable commodity; and ownership was legally enforced. Slavery was prevalent

▸ "Joseph, overseer of pharoah's granaries." Ancient Egypt, Courtesy of North Wind Picture Archives

because it was essential to the economic mode of production in every kingdom of the ancient Near East. Among these kingdoms Israel is included, but the difference was that the humanity of the slave was more recognized and respected in Israel.

Ideally, the master of the household was to govern in the best interest of all the members of the household, including the slaves, because they may be all that he could rely on for support, everyday survival, productivity and well being. Without this household, who would provide for him in his old age? If he were sonless, then his male slave might marry his daughter and become his heir, or he might father an heir through a female slave or concubine. Laws were in place to ensure that the highest ethical considerations were accorded slaves. Hence, there were laws that restricted the punishment and abuse that a master could mete out upon slaves (Leviticus 25.46, Deuteronomy 23.15,16, and also Job 31.13-15).

Laws Regarding Slavery

Within the Old Testament, there is a marked distinction between the status of the Israelite and foreign slaves. "Non-Israelite slaves were legally considered movable property of their masters who could dispose of them as they wished."[8]

Nonetheless, every slave was to rest on the Sabbath (Exodus 20.10; 23.12; Deuteronomy 5.14). It was a crime to premeditatedly kill the slave (Exodus 21.20), but if a slave died two days after being beaten by the owner, then the owner escaped without legal penalty. If the owner knocked out a slave's tooth or put out a slave's eye, then the slave was granted freedom to compensate for the loss (Exodus 21.26,27).

In contrast to all the laws of the ancient Near East, "Deuteronomy (23.15,16) forbade the handing over of a fugitive slave who had sought asylum from his owner."[9] In other kingdoms, abetting an escaped slave was a punishable offense; and thus it carried a heavy penalty. Under such laws, slaves remained slaves with no real protection. Slavery, regardless of its benign appearance in some texts, was very cruel and inhumane. During the period of the exile (ca. 587-539 B.C.), this point was made very clear (Isaiah 14.3,4; 47.6; Ezra 9.9). Even in Israelite society slaves were deemed inferior inasmuch as they had to honor their masters (Malachi 1.6).

Conclusion

What the Old Testament reveals about the nature of slavery and its view upon slavery is informative, but the practice of slavery is not a standard for human rights today. Full human rights and equality were not concepts or social values that dominated the Old Testament. As one reads the Old Testament through the eyes of faith, one must be guided by the Torah (law), by the prophets who point to Jesus Christ, and by Jesus Christ himself,

[8] *Ibid.*
[9] *Ibid, 65.*

for true standards of full human rights and equality. Furthermore, the Scriptures (both the Old and New Testaments) are to be interpreted through the life and teaching of Jesus and the on-going work of the Holy Spirit, who is to lead us into all truth.

According to Matthew 5.17-20, Jesus said,

> "Do not think that I have come to do away with the Law of Moses and the teachings of the prophets. I have not come to do away with them, but to make their teachings come true. Remember that as long as heaven and earth last, not the least point nor the smallest detail of the Law will be done away with—not until the end of all things. So then, whoever disobeys even the least important of the commandments and teaches others to do the same, will be least in the Kingdom of heaven. On the other hand, whoever obeys the Law and teaches others to do the same, will be great in the Kingdom of heaven. I tell you, then, that you will be able to enter the Kingdom of heaven only if you are more faithful than the teachers of the Law and the Pharisees in doing what God requires."

The remaining verses in chapter 5 (21-48) show the relationship between the Law and Jesus' teachings and reflect Jesus' standard of piety. Jesus came to fulfill the Law and the Prophets. He retells those teachings, but in light of the spirit of the Law so that there are no ethical loopholes. According to Jesus, for example, Moses allowed the bill of divorce because of the hardness of the human heart (Matthew 19.3-9); yet the Israelite custom of giving a bill of divorce was a practice never meant to be. The institution of slavery should be understood from this vantage point. This is the interpretive aim of Jesus' teaching and is the starting point for understanding the issues of slavery and human rights in the ancient Near East and, in particular, Israel. God did not intend for people to be in bondage to others; rather humankind, created in God's image, is created to "have life—life in all its fullness" (John 10.10b). As children of promise, freedom in Christ "has set us free" (Galatians 5.1). Slavery is a part of the pollution of sin; and to protect the disenfranchised, God created Jubilee and provided for the emancipation of those who had been in bondage (Leviticus 25.40).

Bibliography

Dandamayev, Muhammad A. "Slavery (ANE and OT)," *The Anchor Bible Dictionary, Volume Six,* ed. David Noel Freedman. New York: Doubleday, 1992.

Eichler, Barry Lee. "Slavery" *Harper Bible Dictionary,* 959, ed. Paul J. Achtemeier. San Francisco: Harper, 1985.

Mosala, Itumeleng J. *Biblical Hermeneutics and Black Theology in South Africa.* Grand Rapids: Wm. B. Eerdmans Publishing Co., 1989.

Maine, Henry S. "The Primitive Family and the Corporation," *Readings in Kinship and Social Structure,* ed. Nelson Graburn. New York: Harper & Row, Publishers, 1971.

Nine

Roman Slavery in Antiquity

Mitzi Jane Smith

Racist ideologies have been sacralized by tendentious interpretations of New Testament references to slaves and slavery. Historically, some have conveniently glossed over the most salient feature distinguishing New World slavery from slavery in antiquity (200 B.C. to 200 A.D.): New Testament slavery was not based on color prejudice. The Romans enslaved prisoners of war and foreigners, uprooting and transplanting them to foreign and hostile communities, which in praxis and in law treated them as "human property." Concessions provided to loyal, obedient slaves, i.e., manumission and "marriage," operated to encourage productive servile behavior and thus to insure the perpetuity of the institution.

◂ "Slave-markets of ancient Rome." Courtesy of North Wind Picture Archives

> I had no rod wherewith to smite the stream, and thereby divide the waters. I had no Moses to go before me and lead the way from bondage to a promised land. . . . I thought of the fishes of the water, the fowls of the air, the wild beasts of the forest, all appeared to be free, to go just where they pleased, and I was an unhappy slave.
>
> —Henry Bibb, *former slave*[1]

When African Americans encounter biblical texts about slaves, it is difficult for us to dismiss mental pictures of slaves in Roman antiquity as persons of African descent who by divine decree happily and contentedly served their masters. Pro-slavery advocates have distorted history and manipulated biblical texts from the Pauline corpus (i.e., 1 Corinthians and Philemon) and from the Deutero-Pauline epistles (i.e., 1 Timothy, Colossians and Ephesians) to undergird racist ideologies that have sanctioned the enslavement of Africans in America. As a youngster, Howard Thurman read the Psalms, Isaiah and the Gospels to his grandmother, an illiterate former slave, but she forbade him to read to her from the Pauline epistles. She later explained to him the reasons for her dislike of these Pauline passages:

> During the days of slavery . . . the master's minister would occasionally hold services for the slaves. Old man McGhee was so mean that he would not let a Negro minister preach to his slaves. Always the white minister used as his text something from Paul. At least three or four times a year he used as a text: "Slaves, be obedient to them that are your masters… as unto Christ." Then he would go on to show how it was God's will that we were slaves and how, if we were good and happy slaves, God would bless us. I promised my Maker that if I ever learned to read and if freedom ever came, I would not read that part of the Bible.[2]

The significance of Roman slavery in antiquity to the American slavery debate is apparent in Josiah Priest's 1851 defense of slavery in which he justified slavery based on racist presuppositions about Roman slavery and the fallacious curse of Ham theory. (See Section Two: "The Alleged Curse on Ham," by Gene Rice.) Priest wrote:

> . . . for the *Romans*, who were also the descendants of Japheth [white race], as well as all the Grecian tribes and nations,

> bought and sold negroes, even down to the time of the apostles, and for many ages after; by thousands and millions.[3]

Priest depicted Roman slavery as the enslavement of "negroes" and asserted that biblical slavery was analogous to and prescriptive for the enslavement of Africans in America. Conversely, Rev. Charles Elliott in his *The Bible and Slavery* (1851) analyzed Pauline biblical references to slaves in the historical context of Roman slavery, and concluded that "Christian slaves are bound . . . to do their utmost to be free" and that the Bible condemns slavery.[4]

African Americans, with spiritual tenacity and steadfast faith in God, have responded to racist interpretations of Scripture and one-sided accounts of history with both a hermeneutic of suspicion and a hermeneutic for liberation. The suspicions and spiritual tenacity of African Americans, and others, have stirred renewed investigations of biblical texts and historical contexts in order to uncover and recover liberating truths about God and slavery.

This article represents such an uncovering and provides a glimpse of slavery in Roman antiquity (ca. 200 B.C. to 200 A.D.).[5] Roman slavery is a necessary socio-historical context for understanding biblical texts that are traditionally used to corroborate the modern practice of slavery. As a social institution, Roman slavery uprooted and socially marginalized slaves, subjugating them to the lowest level of society. Slaves in antiquity were treated subhumanly and juridically categorized as property. Slave resistance existed alongside slaveowners' attempts to placate slaves with concessions designed to promote the servile behavior necessary to perpetuate the institution. The most salient feature that distinguished Roman slavery from American slavery was that Roman slavery was not racially motivated in the modern sense of the term. Although this is not a comparative study, the reader will recognize similarities and differences between American slavery and Roman slavery. While it is impossible to provide here a thorough overview of Roman slavery, I have attempted a provocative treatment of specific aspects of Roman slavery. I briefly cover the following topics: (1) slave ideology: Aristotle and Stoicism; (2) the acquisition and nationality of slaves; (3) the treatment of slaves; (4) slave resistance; and (5) the manumission or freedom of slaves. Finally, I provide brief comments on 1 Corinthians 7.21 and Philemon.

While African American slave narratives and testimonies relate the experience of slavery from the slave's perspective, slavery in antiquity left few, if any, biographies or autobiographies. Historians rely on epigraphs or inscriptions, the works of Greek and Roman historians and writers, Roman law, and Egyptian papyri for information about slavery in antiquity. Thus, the information available is from the slave owner's point of view. We know little of what it was like to be a slave in antiquity from the slave's perspective.

I. Roman Slavery

1. Slave Ideology

Aristotle. The Romans inherited the slave trade from the Greeks and the Phoenicians.[6] Greek ideas of slavery preceded, and to some extent influenced, Roman slave ideology. The Greek philosopher Aristotle (384-322 B.C.) propounded a classical view of "natural slavery." In his *Politica*, Aristotle asserted that nature intended for some persons to be slaves and others to be masters. Masters were born to rule and slaves were born to be in subjection. From the relationship between man and woman and master and slave, the family developed. Thus, a complete household consisted of slaves and freepersons. In the family structure, a slave existed as a "living possession," and as such he took "precedence of all other instruments." Slaves were instruments of action for maintaining life—the life of the family and the state. The slave belonged "wholly" to the master. He was a human being and a possession. (This concept is similar to the chattel nature of slavery that was practiced in the American South.) Nature normally blessed slaves with strong bodies that were suited for labor but the freedmen's bodies were fit for political life. However, sometimes nature messed up and the opposite occurred. Since slaves are inferior to their superiors, it was best for them to be under the rule of masters.[7] Natural slave theory neither originated nor ended with Aristotle, but he "was undoubtedly the high priest of natural slave theory, he elaborated it, and it was his canonical version which reverberated down the ages."[8]

Stoicism. The Stoics believed that all men shared a common logos or reason (rationality). All human beings were slaves in the sense that all persons had masters. The Roman writer Seneca (ca. 4 B.C. to 65 A.D.), a stoic, former slave, and slave owner, referred to slaves as "fellow slaves (*conservi*)," for "Fortune has equal rights over slaves and free men alike."[9] Slaves originate from the "same stock," are "smiled upon by the same skies," breathe, live, and die just as do other humans.[10] Human beings acquire character, "but accident assigns his duties."[11] The Stoics moralized slavery. The physical condition of slavery was of no consequence. A slave may possess a soul of a free person and vice versa. All persons are slaves to something — to lust, greed or ambition; all persons are slaves to fear (*timori*).[12] The Stoic theme of universality, i.e., all humans came from the same source, "sits uneasily with the notion of natural slaves and natural masters, which rests on the principle that the human race is not a unity, but includes a category of subhumans, and subrational people."[13] Stoicism, a minority position, preceded and existed contemporaneously with Christianity, but the full extent of its influence upon Christian thought is not certain.

Roman Slave Ideology: Person or Property? The Romans possessed no slave law *per se*, but laws that addressed slavery were incorporated within their *Corpus Iuris Civilis* (Body of Civil Law). One can gain only an impression of Roman slave ideology from Roman law. Generally, persons were categorized as either "free" or "slaves." Roman law defined slavery as "an institution of the law of all peoples; it makes a man the property (*dominio*) of another, *contrary to the law of nature*" (emphasis mine).[14] Contrary to Aristotle, Roman law stated that persons were not slaves by nature. The legal impression is that slaves are human property. Noted historian, M. I. Finley asserts that "[a]s a commodity, the slave is property," and the slave's human status is irrelevant, merely revealing that "he is a peculiar property."[15] Orlando Patterson offers a more vivid characterization of slavery in general: "slavery is the . . . violent domination of naturally alienated and generally dishonored persons" (emphasis Patterson's).[16] Patterson addresses the ambiguities inherent in the fact that slavery coexisted with other property relationships. The ownership of people as property extended to a number of relationships, including husband and wife.[17] Slavery must be understood as a "social institution" that tied master to slave and represented one of many asymmetrical relationships in Roman society.[18] Much like Aristotle's model, slaves as members of the *familia* or household represented the lowest property relationship to the master/father or *paterfamilias*.

2. *The Acquisition and Nationality of Roman Slaves*

According to Roman law, slaves, in Latin *servi*, are so called because it is the practice of army commanders to order captives to be sold and thus saved . . . instead of killed. Another Latin word for slaves is *mancipia,* derived from the fact that they are captured by hand from the enemy, in Latin *manu capiuntur.* They are either born slaves or enslaved afterwards. The off-spring of slave women are born slaves.[19]

Relatives or other persons could ransom captured foreigners to prevent their enslavement or murder. Thus, if not ransomed, the only alternative for the captured foreigner, short of death, was slavery. Warfare was a constant source, but *not* the only source, of slave supply throughout the central period. The Romans generally maintained the slave population by "a combination of complementary sources, warfare, trade and breeding, each of which was a constant contributor but of fluctuating relative significance . . ."[20] *Vernae* (children born to slave women) and war captives served as "mutually supportive strategies."[21] Given the demand for slaves and the effect of frequent manumissions and deaths (infant and maternal) upon the slave pool, no single source could have sufficed as a means of replenishment. Some are of the opinion that after the *Pax Romana of* 27 B.C. under Augustus, warfare ceased to be a significant source of slave supply; however, this is not the case.[22] The Jewish historian Josephus relates how the city of Japha was destroyed by the Romans under Vespasian and "the number of the slain, both now in the city and at the former fight, was fifteen thousand, and the captives were two thousand one hundred and thirty." [23] Another war under Vespasian resulted in the enslavement of 30,400 Jews, notwithstanding that "six thousand of the strongest" were sent to Nero to "dig through the Isthmus."[24] The prisoners of war or foreigners captured by the Romans included women and children, as well as men.

In addition to warfare and children born to slave women, the Romans acquired slaves by means of piracy, kidnapping (brigandage), infant exposure (the abandonment and sale of infants into slavery), and family members sold into slavery because of poverty. While the means of acquisition of slaves can be stated with certainty, the specific nationality of the slaves cannot. One would expect that slave names would be a reliable means of determining a slave's nationality, but it is difficult to ascertain a slave's nationality or race by virtue of nomenclature (naming of slaves). Slave nomenclature became Graeco-Romanized:

> The typical slave of the early empire belonged to neither east nor west: he was a product of Graeco-Roman civilisation [sic],

> an example of Rome's strange power of absorbing and assimilating aliens. His name was Greek or Roman; his speech, Latin;... He lost the great gifts of nationality, its inheritances and inspirations, its vigorous creativeness, its unique, individual quality; but he also escaped the limitations of race and tradition . . ."[25]

The following factors contribute to the difficulty of determining a slave's nationality based on nomenclature: A slave who retained her/his native name likely retained it in a Latinized or Graecized form; Greek was the language of the slave trade, and slaves could conceivably be given Greek names for ease of pronunciation; masters could arbitrarily rename slaves as they pleased; vernae (home born slaves) were likely named by their masters; early nomenclature reflected the master's identity rather than the identity of the slave; names sometimes indicated the physical and moral qualities of the "ideal slave."[26] "The nationality of the slave mattered little, so long as his physical strength sufficed for the most exacting work. (Syrians, for example, were proverbially strong)."[27] Despite the assimilation of names, it remains that the slaves were a highly heterogeneous group. The slave population consisted of many nationalities, including "Phrygians, Cappadocians, Syrians, Jews, Egyptians, Ethiopians, Numidians, Spaniards, Gauls, Germans, Thracians and Greeks."[28] With few exceptions, Romans generally were not enslaved because the slave was an "outsider" and "the earliest Roman law code explicitly provided that if a Roman were subject to enslavement as a punishment, he had to be sold abroad . . ."[29]

Although slavery in antiquity was not racially motivated in the modern sense of the term, some Romans appear to have believed that certain nationalities were more suitable for slavery than others, which is reminiscent of Aristotle's natural slave law. The Roman orator Livy (ca. 59 B.C. to 17 A.D.) wrote:

> . . . the different kinds of weapons, the many names of unheard-of peoples, Dahae and Medes and Cadusians and Elymaeans—these were all Syrians, far better fitted to be slaves, on account of their servile dispositions, than to be a race of warriors.[30]
>
> There were Macedonians and Thracians and Illyrians, all most warlike nations, here Syrians and Asiatic Greeks, the most worthless peoples among mankind and born for slavery (*servituti*).[31]

Nevertheless, Roman slave society was not racialized, that is one's nationality was not deemed superior or inferior to another because of the complexion of one's skin.

The slave's new and strange position in the family structure of Roman society required loyalty and obedience to the master's every whim and fancy. The slave's sole purpose was to please his/her master for the benefit of family and society.

3. The Treatment of Slaves

Slaves were integrated into the social structure of the Roman family hierarchy of father/master, mother, children, and slaves. According to the household codes (*Haustafeln*), the father of the family (*paterfamilias*) was entitled to complete submission by the other members of the household.[32] The slave was the lowest member of the family, and his/her purpose was to sustain and maintain the family by performing any or all tasks assigned to him/her by the master of the house.

Slaves were relegated to one of two categories according to the tasks they performed: *Rustici* referred to agricultural slaves who resided in the rural districts of the *polis* (city) and performed duties associated with the maintenance of the land. The *urbani* or domestic slaves generally lived in the households of the city districts of the *polis* and performed tasks necessary for the upkeep of the family and household. The vast majority of slaves were *rustici* who lived "in relative seclusion, at subsistence or near subsistence level" with few prospects for social mobility.[33] Whether slaves were categorized as a *rustici* or *urbani* depended solely on the type of job they performed and not where they lived. Slaves performed precise and diversified tasks. A rural slave could function as a ploughman, shepherd, herdsman, pruner, hunter, tracker, overseer (*vilicus*), maidservant, steward, potter, doorkeeper, sweeper, furniture supervisor, gardener, vilicus' wife, poultry fattener, pig breeder, agent, and provisions keeper. A domestic slave could be a water-carrier, silversmith, furniture polisher, pet child, secretary, doctor, supervisor of doctors, wetnurse, servant in charge of ceremonial dress, cook, footman, clothes mender, masseuse, servant in charge of pictures, oculist, architect, surgeon, waiter, singer, food-taster and tailor. Military service was the only occupation in Roman society off limits to slaves. Slaves could move from one job to another of greater responsibility during their lifetimes; conversely, a slaveowner could demote a slave.

Occupational hierarchy existed among domestic slaves within the urban households as well as between rural and urban slaves, the former being inferior to the latter. Diversity served to disperse and not to unite the slave population.[34]

Whether a master dealt with an urban or rural slave, his overall motives were the same. The slaveowner concerned himself with what was advantageous for the slave only if by so doing he was benefitted as well.[35] Any humane or inhumane treatment of slaves always had the ultimate physical and economic well being of the master in mind. Slaveowning served to constantly "validate and enhance the status of those who were free."[36] Seneca advised that if slaves were treated as men, rather than cruelly and inhumanely, they would readily "bare their necks for their master, to bring upon their own heads any danger that threatened him; they spoke at the feast, but kept silence during torture."[37]

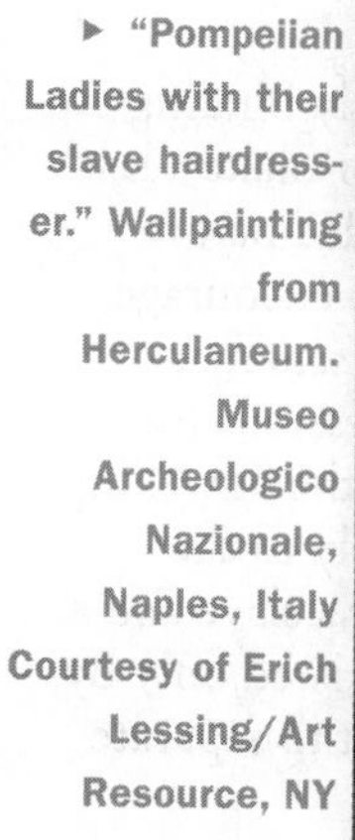

▸ "Pompeiian Ladies with their slave hairdresser." Wallpainting from Herculaneum. Museo Archeologico Nazionale, Naples, Italy Courtesy of Erich Lessing/Art Resource, NY

Columella (middle late to first century A.D.), the famous agriculturalist, advised that *rustici* (rural slaves) should be cared for and clothed to enhance their "usefulness" and not their appearance. Slaves' clothing should keep them "fortified against wind, cold, and rain" so that no matter how "unbearable" the weather, they might be able to work in the field uninterrupted. The overseer (*vilicus*), himself a slave, is not to resort to cruelty but is to keep the slaves in line by "strict enforcement of labor," for slaves "when smarting under cruelty and greed . . . are more to be feared." Female slaves who are "unusually prolific" and bear a certain number of children are to be rewarded with "exemption from work and sometimes even freedom after they reared many children." If a mother had three sons, she would be exempted from work; for more than three sons she might be given her freedom. Such concessions would contribute to the profitability of the estate.[38]

Slaveowners attempted to achieve the optimum usefulness from their slaves through positive concessions or benefits (*beneficium*). The rewards for slave loyalty (*fides*) and obedience (*obsequium*) ranged from permission to enter into a *de facto* marriage to the promise of manumission.

Roman law prohibited slaves from entering into legally binding contracts. Therefore, slaves could not legally marry or make a last will and testament.[39] Nevertheless, slaveowners dangled before slaves the prospects for a semblance of married life to encourage the desired level of production and profitability. *De facto* marriages or *contubernium* often served as positive concessions for slave loyalty and obedience. *Contubernium* denoted the "dwelling together" of soldiers or animals, but referred especially to the quasi-marital and illegal union between two slaves or a slave and a free person. *Contubernium* as a "factual situation" existed only by permission of the slaveowner who reserved the "right to separate slave family members, and commonly did so."[40]

It must be noted that regardless of a slave's "marital status," slaves, male and female, were constantly subjected to sexual exploitation. Slaves were answerable "with their bodies," which meant that slaveowners had unrestricted access to slave bodies for sexual exploitation.[41] Slave dealers often catered to the sexual desires and demands of slaveowners for homosexual partners, and the practice of castrating young male slaves confirms that slaves were the "object of capricious sexual abuse."[42] Seneca, writing of the ill-treatment of slaves, relates how a slave whose task it was to serve wine had to "dress like a woman" and was forced to "remain awake throughout the night, dividing his time between his master's drunkenness and his lust; in the chamber he must be a man, at the feast a boy."[43] Not only did slaveowners exploit slaves for their own gratification (young girls and boys were purchased expressly to serve as sexual partners), but male and female slaves were forced into prostitution for as long as a master determined.[44]

Slaveowners often permitted slaves the privilege of access to *peculium.* Peculium referred to property and assets at the slave's disposal, such as cash, land, clothing, and other slaves. Peculium could be placed in the slave's possession for the purpose of conducting business transactions for the master. If a slave were offered his freedom in exchange for a sum of money (*statuliber*), the slave could use his/her peculium to pay the fee.[45] Since slaves could not own property, the peculium legally belonged to the slaveowner, but in practice it belonged to the slave.

It is of critical significance that the slaveowner's failure to "exercise all his rights over his slave-property was always a unilateral act on his part, never binding, always revocable."[46] The slaveowner could renege on any concession, including the promise of manumission.

In addition to positive concessions, slaveowners used negative reinforcement to maintain servile relations and to achieve optimum profitability from their slaves. Negative reinforcement ranged from flogging to murder. The flogging of slaves was ubiquitous and apparently required little justification.[47] Some slaveowners are said to have inflicted their slaves with 300 lashes if they were "slow in bringing the hot water."[48] Seneca admits that "we Romans are excessively haughty, cruel, and insulting" in the treatment of slaves.[49]

Cases of "extreme cruelty" by masters have been documented. One must bear in mind that it was the slaveowner who determined what constituted extreme cruelty. One recorded instance involved a friend of Emperor Augustus, Vedius Pollio, who "was allowed to punish his slaves by throwing them into his fishpond as food for his lampreys with complete impunity."[50] Slaves and criminals were regularly forced to fight against other gladiators and with wild beasts in the arena.[51]

The Romans enacted laws apparently aimed at improving the abusive nature of slavery. The Emperor Claudius declared that all sick slaves who were abandoned and survived would be freed rather than returned to their masters; if the master killed the slave instead of abandoning him/her, then he would be liable for homicide. Vespasian (emperor A.D. 69-79) passed a law that a female slave would be freed if forced into prostitution after being purchased under the condition that she would not be subjected to prostitution. Hadrian (emperor A.D. 117-138) decreed that a slaveowner could not arbitrarily kill a slave; a slave must be found deserving of death by the courts. A slave could only be sold to fight as a gladiator for good cause shown. If a slaveowner was murdered by one of his slaves, only those slaves who were "near enough to notice anything" could be questioned under torture. Antonius (emperor A.D. 138-161) declared that a master's power over his slaves must remain "unimpaired," but it is in the master's interest for slaves to be permitted relief from "cruelty" and "intolerable wrong," of course, "with just cause shown." Slaves found to have been "treated more harshly than is just" were to be sold to another owner.[52] Keith Bradley cautions that "[t]he arbitrary physical abuse of slaves cannot be said to have been dramatically alleviated by legislation of an improving kind;" lower social categories were discriminated against with regard to the application of punishment.[53] One must also bear in mind that the court officials who decided whether a slaveowner's treatment of his slave was "intolerable" were most likely slaveowners themselves and members of the higher social order, thus their decisions would not be without bias.

4. Slave Resistance

Slaves responded to the conditions of slavery in a variety of ways. Slave resistance ranged from less extreme incidents of lying, cheating, stealing, feigning sickness, working at a slow pace, petty sabotage and running away to violent acts of suicide and homicide.[54] Dio Chrysostom (ca. 40/50 A.D. to after 110 A.D.) reported that slave women (doulas) destroyed their own children before and after birth, sometimes in collusion with their husbands so as "'not [to] be involved in trouble by being compelled to raise children in addition to their enduring slavery.'"[55]

There is evidence that slaves sometimes resorted to murdering their masters. One incident involved a city prefect, Lucius Pedanius Secundus, who was murdered by one of his slaves possibly because Secundus either reneged on an agreed upon manumission price or because of rivalry in a homosexual relationship involving the slave.

In any case, Secundus' 400 slaves, women and children included, were sentenced to death because they failed to prevent the murder of their master. Gaius Cassius, a member of the senate, representing a majority opinion, declared that there was no excuse for the slaves not to have protected Secundus from death. The slaves should have suspected something or noticed "antecedent symptoms" of the crime. The slaves' failure to protect their master showed that they were not fearful for their own lives. "So long as our slaves disclose them [threats of violence and murder against masters], we may live solitary amid their numbers, secure amid their anxieties, and finally–if die we must–certain of our vengeance amid the guilty crowd." Slaves must be coerced to protect their masters by means of "terror."[56]

Slaves often resorted to running away. Escape was a direct form of resistance and a rejection of subjugation.[57] These runaways showed the inability of some slaves to endure the degradation of slavery and the uncertainty of manumission. Some slaveowners used every means to retrieve a fugitive, including the help of friends and associates, public advertisements, public officials, diviners and professional "slave catchers" (*fugitivarii*).[58] The fact that runaway slaves tried to pass as free persons serves as a reminder that "Roman slavery had no association with skin colour."[59] Fugitives could be successful in creating a new life for themselves. Their "success depended on . . . a suitable moment for departure, the ability to elude detection and to find safe refuge, . . . the capacity to cover terrain and to survive independently."[60] Fugitives were constantly exposed to the dangers of recapture no matter how great the distance achieved between master and slave and the amount of time lapsed since the escape.[61] Slave resistance served as a constant reminder that Roman slaves were by no means content with their servile status even though manumission was a legal possibility.

5. The Manumission of Slaves: Freed at Last?

There were three formal ways to manumit a slave that simultaneously conferred Roman citizenship on the freedman/freedwoman: (1) by *vindicta* (or rod) in which the owner declared his intention before the appropriate magistrate; (2) by census in which the slave was enrolled on the census list of Roman citizens by the owner's permission (taking of census was largely abandoned after 166 B.C.); and (3) by last will and testament. The *lex Fufia Caninia* (2 B.C.) required that the specific names of slaves to be manumitted must appear in the will, and it limited the number of slaves that could be manumitted at one time. A person who owned 3 to10 slaves could manumit up to one-half of his slaves; 11 to 30, one-third; 31 to 100, one-fourth; 101 to 500, one-fifth; no one could manumit more than 100 slaves at one time. An owner of less than two slaves had full freedom of manumission.[62]

The informal methods of manumission, by letter and *inter amicos* (among friends or witnesses), did not grant Roman citizenship but conferred the inferior Junian Latin status. Some slaveowners probably preferred the informal methods of manumission because it meant greater succession rights for the former master. For instance, if a freedman with full Roman citizenship died testate and at least three freeborn children survived, the patron (former master) was excluded from any access to the freedman's inheritance. But the inheritance of a freedperson with Junian Latin status would pass to the patron's heirs, since the freedman Latin's heirs were excluded from succession.[63]

The *lex Aelia Sentia* (4 A.D.) established age requirements for manumission. A slave could not be manumitted under age 30 except by *vindicta* for good cause shown before a *consilium* (council), and the master must be at least 20 years of age to manumit a slave, except by *vindicta* for good cause shown.[64] It is instructive that the life expectancy at birth of the slave was likely not more than 20 years. Thirty years was a far more advanced age than in modern times.[65] Even if a slave lived to the age of 30, this alone did not guarantee manumission—all powers of manumission rested with the master.

There existed no Roman laws that restricted manumission by virtue of race or nationality. The nationality of the slave was not a determinant for manumission and the nationality of the freedwoman/mother did not delimit the status of her freeborn child.

In theory manumission nullified the slave's former relationship with the slaveowner. Roman citizenship, which accompanied formal manumission, bestowed legal and political rights on the freedperson, and any children born to the freedwoman thereafter acquired the social status of freeborn children. However, legal obligations (*operae*) continued to bind freedpersons and women to their former masters. Under these obligations, the freedpersons were to perform certain services for a specific amount of time. Although the slave as a freedperson entered a higher social category, the master did not experience severe economic loss.[66]

The new relationship was formed with the former slave as the client of the patron (the former master). Theoretically, this new relationship was to be characterized by mutual respect. If a freedperson's patron (former owner) fell into poverty, the freedperson was expected to support the patron. Any delinquency in performing services due to the patron could result in punishment or even a return to slavery.[67] Freedpersons were expected to retain their freedom by "the same obedience (*obsequium*) which [he/she] had earned it," and "notorious offenders" "deserved to be brought back to their bondage (*servitutem*), so that fear might coerce those whom kindness had not reformed."[68] Manumission was subject to restrictions and could be revoked.

Although manumission occurred frequently, the great majority of slaves "especially those who were engaged in menial, non-domestic tasks, probably had no realistic hope of changing their status."[69] The promise of manumission was reserved as a reward for loyalty and obedience. The hope of freedom, while regularly available to all slaves, like other incentives was another means to exploit and regulate the behavior of slaves.[70] However, most of the "servile population probably never achieved freedom at all."[71]

Slavery was ubiquitous and pervasive in Roman society. Slaves, as foreigners, were forced to contribute to the social and economic well being of a society that deemed them unworthy of participation in that society. This exploitation, however, was indiscriminate in that the Romans did not enslave persons based on nationality or skin color. A slave's nationality neither delimited his/her access to the benefits proffered to obedient and loyal slaves, nor did it increase the incidence of exploitation and abuse. While slaveowners in antiquity at times treated slaves humanely, such treatment was economically motivated. Widespread and constant resistance existed in spite of the constant dangling of concessions before slaves to encourage servile behavior. Slave resistance testifies to the unbearable nature of the institution. The most coveted benefit, freedom, was restricted, uncertain and often withheld. When a slaveowner did grant manumission, a "new" servile relationship awaited the former slave, one which required loyalty and obedience to the former master, now his patron, for as long as life should continue. Although a slaveowner might celebrate the manumission of a slave, it did not always represent a personal Jubilee for the slave. Besides, the master could celebrate with the assurance that the freedperson's place had already been filled by another slave.

▸ The Forum was Rome's religious, political, and business center. Photo: American Bible Society

II. Hermeneutical Considerations

A Note on 1 Corinthians 7.21

> Were you called when you were a slave? Do not let it worry you. But if you are provided with the opportunity to become a freedperson (*eleutheros*), then [certainly] make use (*mallon chrésai*) [of the opportunity to become a freedperson].

1 Corinthians 7.21 is one of the most controversial passages in the New Testament. Translations of the text in which Paul advises the slave to remain a slave have been used to provide divine sanction for the enslavement of Africans in America. Unfortunately, most readers, especially African Americans, have not had access to translations that depict Paul as advising the slaves to make use of the opportunity to become freedpersons. I will briefly address the general context of 1 Corinthians 7.21 (verses 1-16), the immediate context (verses 17-20), and the interpretation of the text itself.

The General Context of 1 Corinthians

Pauline Christian groups consisted of individuals from various social categories, including men and women, freeborn persons, freedpersons, and slaves.[72] The Corinthian group was no different in this respect. The New Testament city of Corinth was a Roman colony whose first settlers were mostly freedpersons.[73] While Paul is addressing a heterogeneous group, quite a number of them either had experienced slavery or were slaves. 1 Corinthians 7 is Paul's response to a letter he received from the Corinthian group requesting advice about specific concerns relating to male and female relationships in the world (7.1).

Paul's first advice is to husbands and wives so that they might avoid sexual immorality (7.2). Each one is to have their own husband or wife. Each party is to make sure the other receives their conjugal rights within the marriage; one partner should not withhold their affections from the other partner. Paul, however, provides an exception to this rule: Husband and wife may deprive one another of their conjugal rights but only by agreement and for the purpose of engaging in prayer (v. 5). Paul admits that everyone is not like him, presumably single and celibate, because everyone does not have the same gift (*charisma*) as God has given to him (v. 7). Paul sets down a rule and then provides an exception to the rule, and he continues this pattern in the following verses.

Next Paul advises the unmarried and the widows (vv. 8,9). The general rule is that they should "continue to live alone." The exception to the rule is: "But if" they lack self-control, then they should get married.

The third category to whom Paul offers advice is wives who are contemplating leaving their husbands (vv. 10, 11). Husbands and wives are not to separate. The exception to the rule is: "But if" the wife does leave her husband, she should not remarry and should eventually reconcile with her husband.

Finally, Paul offers his own personal advice to the "others," those marriages in which one spouse is an unbeliever (vv. 12-16). The rule is that a believing spouse should not divorce his/her unbelieving spouse if the unbelieving spouse consents to stay in the marriage relationship. The exception is, "But if," the unbeliever leaves, so be it. The believing spouse is not bound to the marriage once the unbeliever leaves the marriage. Paul's advice is based on the fact that God has called (*kekléken*) the Corinthians to peace (v. 15). The objective is to live in the peace that God has called one.

Verses 17-20. The "golden rule" for all four situations is that each one is to live in the assignment in which God has called them (v. 17). This is the rule among the churches (*ekklésias*) (v.17). The Greek word translated 'assigned' or 'given' is *emerisen* from the root word *merizo* meaning to divide or apportion. It is used two other times in the Pauline corpus, Romans 12.3 and 2 Corinthians 10.13. In Romans 12.3 Paul admonishes the saints not to think more highly of themselves than they ought to but to think soberly "according to the amount of faith that God has *given* you." The verses that follow Romans 12.3 refer to God's giving of spiritual gifts in the church. Paul is obviously referring to a spiritual gift or grace from God, a spiritual endowment and not a social status. In defense of his apostolic ministry, Paul asserts in 2 Corinthians 10.13 that "As for us, however, our boasting will not go beyond certain limits; it will stay within the limits of the work which God has set for us, and this includes our work among you." Paul is referring to his evangelistic mission to the Gentiles as a "work which God has set for us." This is the assignment he received from God (Galatians 1.11, 12).

The word translated "called" in 1 Corinthians 7.17 is *kekléken,* the perfect form of *kaleo* meaning "to call." Allan Callahan notes that when Paul speaks of those who are called he does not refer to one's social or religious position in the world.[74] Paul uses another form of *kaleo* at 1 Corinthians 1.9, the Corinthians were "called...to have fellowship with his Son Jesus Christ, our Lord." Nowhere in Paul's writings does he refer to marriage as a gift from God. God has called the Corinthians into fellowship with Jesus Christ and this is a free gift.

Paul now provides examples for the advice he has given. Paul admonishes one who is circumcised not to try to not get circumcised (v. 18) and one who is not circumcised to "seek circumcision." But on the other hand, "whether or not a man is circumcised means nothing; what matters is to obey God's commandments"(v. 19). Paul follows the same pattern here that he has in the preceding verses by setting a rule and then introducing an exception to the rule. It seems apparent that Paul's point is that what is important is that one maintains one's relationship of obedience to God. In verse 20 when Paul says "Each of you should remain as you were when you accepted God's call," he is referring to a relationship of fellowship with Jesus Christ, which is freely "given." Whether one decides to remain celibate, marry or separate, one should remain true to the fellowship to which you were called in Jesus Christ by being obedient to his commandments. It seems that Paul's intention is to clarify the position he has taken that social status does not affect one's calling.

Paul's Admonition to Slaves: 1 Corinthians 7.21

"Were you a slave when God called you? Well, never mind..." (v. 21a). While Paul's slave example serves the same purpose as his circumcision example, the examples are not without dissimilarities. Circumcision is normally a voluntary act which is physically irreversible. Circumcision is permanent. As we have shown above, slavery in the Graeco-Roman Empire was not necessarily a permanent, irreversible condition. When manumitted by formal means, a slave became a Roman citizen. (There also existed means by which an informally manumitted slave could achieve citizenship.) Manumission was a frequent occurrence, the promise of which was a combination of humanitarian gestures and exploitation to perpetuate servile behavior in those who remained in slavery. As evidenced by the constant widespread slave resistance, slaves, like anyone else, wanted to be free. To say otherwise would be to deny their humanity. Paul is not saying be happy in your servile status, but he is saying your slave status does not deny you access to the gifts and participation in the calling of God. Paul asserts that, "there is no difference between Jews and Gentiles, between slaves and free people, between men and women; you are all one in union with Christ Jesus"(Galatians 3.28), and he maintains that "in the same way, all of us, whether Jews or Gentiles, whether slaves or free, have been baptized into the one body by the same Spirit, and we have all been given the one Spirit to drink" (1 Corinthians 12.13). Paul is reassuring the slaves of their place and equality in the body. Vincent Wimbush asserts that Paul is saying that worldly status does not "determine status with God," and Paul provides this advice to "counter what Paul took to be the Corinthians' antiworldly understanding of Christian existence."[75]

"But if you have a chance to become free, **use it**." (v. 21b). The second half of verse 21b presents the challenge. I have translated the subordinate clause emphatically. This represents the translation of only two Greek words, *mallon chrésai*. *Mallon* literally means "rather," and *chrésai* is the aorist middle imperative form of the deponent verb *chraomai* meaning "to make use of." The problem is that the Greek text does not supply a subject with which to complete the subordinate clause. So what is it that the slave is to make use of, freedom or slavery? J. Albert Harrill analyzes the text in the context of chapter 7, its social-historical context, and also provides a philological analysis (comparison with analogous literature). He asserts that *mallon* with *chraomai* carries the adversative sense with respect to the previous apodosis, "never mind."[76] The slave is not to dismiss any opportunity to become freed, but to take advantage of freedom. Paul was obviously referring to the achievement of a concrete legal status, for in v. 22 he uses the proper juridical designation, "freedman" (*apeleutheros*).

Paul is consistent with his rule and exception pattern established in the previous verses. "[T]he context does not exclude the 'use freedom' interpretation . . . To the contrary, this reading naturally fits Paul's argumentative and rhetorical structure in 1 Corinthians 7 of granting particular exceptions to general principles."[77] As a rule, if you were a slave when you were called, do not worry about it. Conversely, the exception is but if you can become free, take advantage of the opportunity to become a freedperson.

A Note on Philemon

Traditional scholarship has bequeathed to us a conservative reading of Philemon as the story of the "runaway-slave—Onesimus."

Onesimus is said to have found refuge with the Apostle Paul who himself is in bondage. After Onesimus has benefitted from Paul's ministry, Paul sends him back to his master Philemon. Onesimus has been so stigmatized as the "runaway-slave" of Philemon, that it is difficult for many to read the text with an untainted and open mind. However, in the text itself there is nothing that conclusively warrants labeling Onesimus as a runaway, and it is questionable as to whether he is even a slave. The major evidence used by most scholars to call Onesimus a slave is the phrase in verse 16. Philemon is to receive Onesimus no longer as a slave but above a slave, [as] a beloved brother *(ouketi hōs doulon all' hyper doulon, adelphon agapāton).*

If we presume that Onesimus was a runaway slave, we must ask why he would flee to Paul. Paul was imprisoned under guard and would have to explain Onesimus' presence to the authorities. Thus, as a runaway slave, Onesimus would not have been safe with Paul. Paul would be guilty of harboring a runaway slave. Under Roman law, Paul was obligated to immediately notify Philemon of Onesimus' whereabouts and to send Onesimus back to his owner posthaste. Places of refuge existed for runaway slaves who ran away for just cause shown (extreme cruelty). A certain Julius Sabinus' slaves fled and sought refuge at the statue of the deified Emperor Antonius. Sabinus was found to be extremely cruel to his slaves and they were sold to another owner.[78] As a runaway slave, the wisest thing to do would be to put as many miles between oneself and one's master, and as quickly as possible.

Onesimus certainly would not seek refuge with a friend of his slaveowner. If caught, Onesimus would be severely punished for running away, and his master would likely brand him and "adorn" him with an iron collar. While Onesimus' service to Paul can be described as Christian ministry (*diakoné*), even a Christian slave was not oblivious to the Roman laws delimiting his status as a slave and the lowest member of the family and one who was under the total power (*dominium*) of the master of the house. If he was a slave, Christian or not, he knew if he were to abscond, he had better succeed or suffer severe consequences. If Onesimus were a runaway slave, it would have been almost as radical for Paul to harbor him as a runaway slave for any length of time as it would have been for Paul to encourage Philemon to manumit a runaway slave (manumission was generally withheld from runaway slaves).

I believe it is plausible to believe that Onesimus and Philemon were brothers. In his book T*he Embassy of Onesimus: The Letter of Paul to Philemon*, Alan Callahan retells the story as the story of two brothers whom Paul attempts to reconcile.[79] In light of the socio-historical context of slavery, it is more likely that Onesimus was an estranged brother, possibly a younger brother under Philemon's guardianship. As *paterfamilias*, Philemon had the right to treat anyone under his roof like mere property. Even sons were sometimes treated as slaves, and conversely slaves were treated humanely at times. It is possible that Philemon had previously treated his brother as a slave, and not as a brother. Social historical considerations and the paucity of evidence favoring the depiction of Onesimus as a runaway-slave, warrant a retelling of the story.

> Once upon a time there was a man named Paul. He had a colleague named Philemon, who worked together with him in the service of their common lord, Jesus Christ. Philemon had a brother named Onesimus . . .[80]

Notes

1. Henry Bibb, *Narrative of the Life and Adventures of Henry Bibb, an American Slave, Written by Himself*, (New York, published by the author, 1850), 29-30.
2. Howard Thurman, *Jesus and the Disinherited* (Boston: Beacon Press, 1976). On rare occasions he could read the thirteenth chapter of I Corinthians, 30, 31. Howard Thurman was a theologian, preacher, and former Dean of the Howard University Rankin Chapel.
3. Josiah Priest, *Bible Defense of Slavery or the Origin, History, and Fortunes of the Negro Race, as Deduced from History, both Sacred and Profane, their Natural Relations – Moral, Mental, and Physical – to the Other Races and Mankind, Compared and Illustrated – Their Future Destiny Predicted, etc.* (Louisville, Kentucky: J. F. Bennan, 1851), 287, 309 (quotation); Priest refers to Ham as the Negro race and Japheth as the white race. For a thorough treatment of the curse of Ham theory, see Gene Rice, "The Curse That Never Was (Genesis 9.18-27)," *Journal of Religious Thought* 29 (1972).
4. Charles Elliott, *The Bible and Slavery: in which the Abrahamic and Mosaic Discipline is Considered in Connection with the Most Ancient Forms of Slavery; and the Pauline Code on Slavery as Related to Roman Slavery and the Discipline of the Apostolic Churches* (Cincinnati: L. Swormstedt & A. Poe, 1857), 298 (quotation) - 302. This was published by the Methodist Episcopal Church "to show the relation of the church to slavery, so as to point out the duties of the church in the present state of affairs," 31. While Elliott clearly found Scripture to be against slavery, he also moralized slavery.
5. Rome constitutes one of four "genuine slave societies" in the world (the other three are classical Greece (except Sparta), the Caribbean [some say Brazil], and the American South. Other societies owned slaves but are not considered to be slave societies. M. I. Finley, "The Extent of Slavery," *Slavery: A Comparative*

Perspective: Readings on Slavery from Ancient Times to the Present, ed. Robin W. Winks, (New York: New York Univ. Press, 1972), 5.

6. Mary L. Gordon, "The Nationality of Slaves Under the Early Roman Empire," *Slavery in Classical Antiquity*, ed. M. I. Finley, (Cambridge: W. Heffer & Sons, Ltd., 1964), 171.

7. Aristotle, "Politica," *The Works of Aristotle*, Vol. X (London: Oxford University Press, 1946), trans. by Benjamin Jowett, 1252a30-35, 1252b1-15 (quotation), 1253b1-5 (quotation), 253b30-35, 1254a1-25, 1254b15-40.

8. Peter Garnsey, *Ideas of Slavery from Aristotle to Augustine* (Cambridge, Great Britain: Cambridge University Press, 1996), 15.

9. Seneca, *Ad Lucilium Epistulae Morales* (Cambridge: Harvard University Press, The Loeb Classical Library, 1979), 47.1.

10. Seneca, *Epistulae Morales,* 47.10.

11. *Ibid.,* 47.15.

12. *Ibid.,* 47.17.

13. Peter Garnsey, *Ideas of Slavery from Aristotle to Augustine,* 144.

14. *Justinian's Institutes*, trans. by Peter Birks & Grand McLeod, Latin text of Paul Krueger (London: Gerald Duckworth & Co. Ltd., 1987), 1.3.2.

15 M. I. Finley, *Ancient Slavery and Modern Ideology* (New York: The Viking Press, 1980), 73.

16. Orlando Patterson, *Slavery and Social Death: A Comparative Study* (Cambridge: Harvard University Press, 1982), 13. Patterson's book is a comparative analysis of slavery. His study is based on 66 of the 186 slaveholding societies listed by George P. Murdock's sample of world societies. The 66 societies are listed in Patterson's Appendix B, 350-352.

17. Patterson, *Slavery and Social Death,* 21. While it is "impolite" to call one's spouse one's property, "[w]ith slaves politeness is unnecessary," 22.

18. Keith Bradley, *Slavery and Society,* 4.

19. *Institutes,* 1.3.3-4.

20. Keith Bradley, "On the Roman Slave Supply and Slave Breeding," *Classical Slavery,* ed. M. I. Finley, (London: Frank Cass & Co., Ltd., 1987), 58, 59 (quotation).

21. Bradley, "On the Roman Slave Supply and Slave Breeding," 50.

22. *Ibid.*, 49.

23. Josephus, *Jewish Wars,* 3.305.

24. Josephus, *Wars,* 3.540.

25. Gordon, "The Nationality of Slaves . . .," 188.

26. *Ibid.*, 178-186.

27. *Ibid.*, 181.

28. T. G. Tucker, *Life in the Roman World of Nero and St. Paul* (New York: The MacMillan Company, 1911), 68.

29. M. I. Finley, "The Extent of Slavery: M. I. Finlay [*sic]*," *Slavery: A Comparative*

Perspective, ed. Robin W. Winks, (New York: New York University Press, 1972), 5-6.

30. *Livy,* trans. by Evan T. Sage (Cambridge: Harvard Univ. Press, The Loeb Classical Library, 1965), 35.49.8.

31. *Ibid.,* 36.17.5.

32. Household codes that specifically govern the slave-master relationship are found in Ephesians 5.21–6.9, Colossians 3.18–4.1, 1 Timothy 6.1,2, Titus 2.1-10, 1 Peter 2.18–3.7. *See* Clarice J. Martin, "The Haustafeln (Household Codes) in African American Biblical Interpretation: 'Free Slaves' and 'Subordinate Women'," *Stony the Road We Trod: African American Biblical Interpretation.* (Minneapolis: Fortress Press, 1991) ed. Cain Hope Felder.

33. Bradley, *Slavery and Society at Rome,* (Cambridge: Cambridge University Press, 1994), 71.

34. Bradley, *Slavery and Society at Rome,* 58-60, 62, 63, 65, 68, 69, 70, 73.

35. Dio Chrysostom, "The Fourteenth Discourse: Slavery I," (Cambridge: Harvard University Press, The Loeb Classical Library, 1977), § 10.

36. Bradley, *Slavery and Society at Rome,* 29.

37. Seneca, *Epistulae Morales,* 47.4. Evidently some masters forbade their slaves to speak at feasts; the slaves were ordered to serve food all night "hungry and dumb." "The slightest murmur is repressed by the rod . . . " 47.3.

38. Columella, *De Re Rustica: I-IV on Agriculture,* Vol. I (Cambridge: Harvard University Press, The Loeb Classical Library, 1977) §§ I.8.9, 10 (quotation), 11, 16, 17 (quotation), 18, 19 (quotation).

39. Under Roman law marriage was legally binding only between Roman citizens, *Institutes* 1.10; Women, children or slaves did not have the capacity to make a will or serve as witnesses to a will. *Institutes* 2.10.6.; 2.12

40. M. I. Finley and K.R.Bradley, "Contubernium," *The Oxford Classical Dictionary* Third Edition, eds. Simon Hornblower and Antony Spawforth, (New York: Oxford University Press, 1996), 388. Since slaves could not enter into legal marriages, they were never guilty of adultery.

41. Finley, *Ancient Slavery and Modern Ideology,* 95, 96.

42. Keith Bradley, *Slaves and Masters in the Roman Empire: A Study in Social Control* (Bruxelles: Latomus Revue D'Etudes Latines, 1984), 115, 116 (quotation).

43. Seneca, *Epistulae Morales,* 47.7, 8.

44. Bradley, *Slaves and Masters,* 116, 117.

45. Alan Ferguson Rodger, "Peculium," *The Oxford Classical Dictionary* Third Edition, eds. Simon Hornblower and Antony Spawforth, (New York: Oxford University Press, 1996), 110.

46. Finley, *Ancient Slavery and Modern Ideology,* 74.

47. Bradley, *Slaves and Masters,* 119.

48. Ammianus Marcellinus, "Valentinianus Valens Gratianus," Vol. 3 (3 vols.: Cambridge: Harvard University Press, The Loeb Classical Library, 1972), 28.4.16.

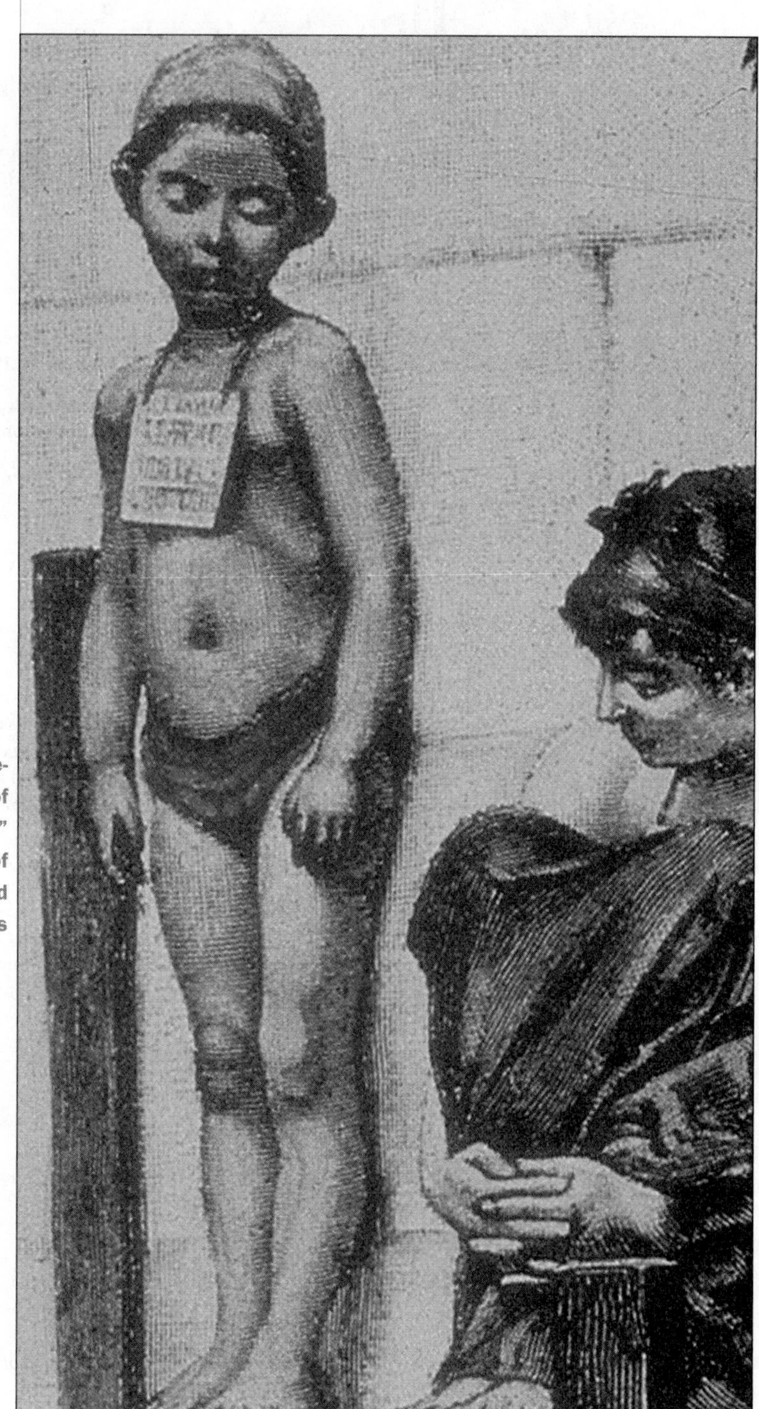

▸ Detail, "Slave-markets of ancient Rome." Courtesy of North Wind Picture Archives

49. Seneca, *Epistulae Morales,* 47.11.

50. Joseph Vogt, *Ancient Slavery and the Ideal of Man* (Cambridge: Harvard University Press, 1975),104.

51. Naphtali Lewis and Meyer Reinhold, eds., *Roman Civilization Sourcebook II: The Empire* (New York: Harper & Row Publishers, 1966), 229.

52. Lewis, *Roman Civilization*, 268, 69.

53. Bradley, *Slaves and Masters*, 129.

54. Bradley, *Slavery and Society at Rome,* 110, 117.

55. Dio Chrysostom, "The Fifteenth Discourse: On Slavery & Freedom II" (Cambridge: Harvard University Press, The Loeb Classical Library, 1977) § 8.

56. Tacitus, *The Annals,* Books 13-16 (Cambridge: Harvard University Press, The Loeb Classical Library, 1981), 14.42-45 , 14.44 (quotations).

57. Keith R. Bradley, *Slavery and Rebellion in the Roman World, 140 B.C.-70 B.C.* (Indianapolis: Indiana University Press, 1989), 37, 38.

58. Finley, *Ancient Slavery and Modern Ideology,* 111.

59. Bradley, *Slavery and Society at Rome,* 121.

60. Bradley, *Slavery and Rebellion*, 38.

61. *Ibid.*, 35.

62. Alan Watson, *Roman Slave Law* (Baltimore: The John Hopkins University Press, 1987), 2434. Keith Bradley notes that formal manumission was subject to taxation and this was a means by which the Roman state exploited slavery to its own pecuniary advantage. The slave might be required to pay the price of manumission as well as the extra burden of the tax. *Slaves and Masters,* 104-106.

63. Watson, *Roman Slave Law,* 35-42.

64. *Ibid.*, 29-30. The *lex Aelia Sentia* also prohibited the manumission with full citizenship or Latin status to slaves who had been chained or branded as punishment (regardless of guilt or innocence), questioned under torture for wrongdoing and found guilty, or put in the arena to fight with men or beasts, *id.*

65. Bradley, *Slaves and Masters*, 96.

66. *Ibid.*, 81, 82.

67. Lewis, *Roman Civilization*, 256.

68. Tacitus, *The Annals*, Books 13-16 (Cambridge: Harvard University Press, The Loeb Classical Library, 1981), 13.26.4, 5.

69. Watson, *Roman Slave Law*, 23.

70. Bradley, *Slaves and Masters,* 104.

71. *Ibid.*, 83.

72. Wayne A. Meeks, *The First Urban Christians: The Social World of the Apostle Paul* (New Haven: Yale Univ. Press, 1983), 79.

73. Meeks, *The First Urban Christians,* 55.

74. Allan Callahan, "A Note on 1 Corinthians 7.21," *Journal of Interdenominational Theological Center* 17 (Fall 1989 - Spring 1990), 111.

75. Vincent L. Wimbush, *Paul, The Worldly Ascetic: Response to the World and Self-Understanding according to 1 Corinthians 7* (Macon, Georgia: Mercer University Press, 1987), 16.

76. J. Albert Harrill, *The Manumission of Slaves in Early Christianity* (Tübingen: J. C. B. Mohr (Paul Siebeck), 1995), 120.

77. J. Albert Harrill, *The Manumission of Slaves in Early Christianity*,126.

78. Lewis, *Roman Civilization*, 270.

79. Dwight Allan Callahan, *Embassy of Onesimus: The Letter of Paul to Philemon.* (Valley Forge, PA: Trinity Press International, 1997), 69, 70.

80. Callahan, *Embassy of Onesimus,* 69.

Bibliography

Aristotle. "Politica," *The Works of Aristotle Translated into English,* Vol. X , Benjamin Jowett, trans. London: Oxford University Press, 1946.

Barrett, C. K. *A Commentary on the First Epistle to the Corinthians.* New York: Harper & Row, 1968.

Bartchy, S. Scott. "Slavery (Greco-Roman): New Testament," *Anchor Bible Dictionary: Si-Z* Vol. 6. David Noel Freeman, ed. New York: Doubleday, 1992.

____________. *First-Century Slavery and the Interpretation of 1 Corinthians 7.21.* Atlanta: Scholars Press/Society of Biblical Literature, 1985.

Birks, Peter and Grand McLeod, trans. *Justinian's Institutes.* London: Duckworth & Co., Ltd., 1987.

Bradley, Keith R. "Slavery (Roman)," *The Oxford Classical Dictionary,* Third Edition. Simon Hornblower and Antony Spawforth, eds. New York: Oxford University Press, 1996.

______________. *Slavery and Society at Rome.* Cambridge: Cambridge University Press, 1994.

______________. *Slavery and Rebellion in the Roman World, 140 B.C.—70 B.C.* Bloomington: Indiana University Press, 1989.

________________. "On the Roman Slave Supply and Slavebreeding," *Classical Slavery.* M. I. Finley, ed. London: Frank Cass & Co., Ltd., 1987.

________________. *Slave and Masters in the Roman Empire: A Study in Social Control.* Bruxelles: Latomus Revue D'Etudes Latines, 1984.

Callahan, Allen Dwight, *Embassy of Onesimus: The Letter of Paul to Philemon.* Valley Forge, Penn.: Trinity Press International, 1997.

________________. "A Note on 1 Corinthians 7.21," *Journal of Interdenominational Theological Center* 17 (Fall 1989—Spring 1990), 110-114.

Columella. *De Re Rustica: IV On Agriculture,* Harrison Boyd Ash, trans. The Loeb Classical Library, 1977.

Conzelmann, Hans. *1 Corinthians: A Commentary on the First Epistle to the Corinthians,* Philadelphia: Fortress Press.

Dawes, Gregory W. "But If You Can Gain Your Freedom (1 Corinthians 7.17-24)," *The Catholic Biblical Quarterly,* Vol. 52:681-97, October, 1990.

Dio Chrysostom. "Thirty-First Discourse," *Discourses 31-36,* Vol. III, The Loeb Classical Library, 1979.

______________. "The Fourteenth Discourse: On Slavery and Freedom I," *Discourses 12-30,* Vol. II, The Loeb Classical Library, 1977.

______________,."The Fifteenth Discourse: On Slavery and Freedom I," *Discourses 12-30,* Vol. II. 5 vols. Cambridge: Harvard University Press, The Loeb Classical Library, 1977.

Elliott, Charles. *The Bible and Slavery: in which the Abrahamic and Mosaic Discipline is Considered in Connection with the Most Ancient Forms of Slavery; and the Pauline Code on Slavery as Related to Roman Slavery and the Discipline of the Apostolic Churches.* Cincinnati: L. Swormstedt & A. Poe, 1857.

Feldstein, Stanley. *Once a Slave: The Slave's View of Slavery,* Narrative of the Life and Adventures of Henry Bibb, an American Slave Written by Himself, New York, 1850. New York: William Morrow & Co., Inc., 1971.

Finley, M.I. *Ancient Slavery and Modern Ideology.* New York: The Viking Press, 1980.

______________. "The Extent of Slavery," *Slavery: A Comparative Perspective: Readings on Slavery from Ancient Times to the Present,* Robin W. Winks, ed. New York: New York University Press, 1972.

Finley, M. I. and K. R.Bradley. "Contubernium," *The Oxford Classical Dictionary,* Third Edition. Simon Hornblower and Antony Spawforth, eds. New York: Oxford University Press, 1996 , 386.

Garnsey, Peter. *Ideas of Slavery from Aristotle to Augustine.* Cambridge, Great Britain: Cambridge University Press, 1996.

Gordon, Mary L. "The Nationality of Slaves under the Early Roman Empire,"(originally appeared in *Journal of Roman Studies* 14 (1924), 93-11) *Slavery in classical Antiquity*. M. I. Finley, ed. Cambridge: W. Heffer & Sons, Ltd., 1964.

Harrill, J. Albert. "Paul and Slavery: The Problem of 1 Corinthians 7.21," *Biblical Research,* Vol. 39-5-28, 1994.

______________. *The Manumission of Slaves in Early Christianity.* Tübingen: J. C. B. Mohr (Paul Siebeck), 1995.

Jones, Amos. Jr. *Paul's Message of Freedom: What Does It Mean to the Black Church?* Valley Forge: Judson Press, 1984.

Kisembo, Benezeri. "The Free Man and the Freedman," *The Bible Translator,* Vol. 46, No. 2, April, 1995.

Lewis, Naphtali and Reinhold Meyer. *Roman Civilization: Sourcebook II: The Empire.* New York: Harper & Row Publishers, 1955.

Martin, Dale B. *Slavery as Salvation: A Metaphor for Slavery in Pauline Christianity.* New Haven: Yale University Press, 1990.

Martin, Clarice J. "The *Haustafeln* (Household Codes) in African American Biblical Interpretation: 'Free Slaves' and 'Subordinate Women'," *Stony the Road We Trod: African American Biblical Interpretation.* Cain Hope Felder, ed., Minneapolis: Fortress Press, 1991.

Meeks, Wayne A. *The First Urban Christians: The Social World of the Apostle Paul.* New Haven: Yale University Press, 1983.

Patterson, Orlando. *Slavery and Social Death: A Comparative Study.* Cambridge: Harvard University Press, 1982.

Priest, Josiah. *Bible Defence of Slavery; or the Origin, History, and Fortunes of the Negro Race as Deduced from History, Both Sacred and Profane. Their Natural Relations —Moral, Mental, and Physical - to the Other Races of Mankind, Compared and Illustrated - Their Future Destiny Predicted, etc.* Louisville, Kentucky: J. F. Bennan, 1851.

Rice, Gene. "The Curse That Never Was (Genesis 9.18-27)," *Journal of Religious Thought* 29 (1972).

Robertson, Archibold and Plummer Alfred. *International Critical Commentary: 1 Corinthians.* New York: Charles Scribner's Sons, 1911.

Rodger, Alan Ferguson. "Peculium," *The Oxford Classical Dictionary,* Third Edition. Simon Hornblower and Antony Spawforth, eds., New York: Oxford University Press, 1996.

Saller, Richard. "Slavery and the Roman Family," *Classical Slavery.* M. I. Finley, ed., London: Frank Cass & Co., Ltd., 1987.

Ste. Croix, G. E. M. De. *The Class Struggle in the Ancient Greek World from the Archaic Age to the Arab Conquests.* Ithaca, New York: Cornell University Press, 1981.

Seneca. *Ad Lucilium Epistulae Morales,* The Loeb Classical Library, 1979, 47.1-21.

Tacitus. *The Annals,* The Loeb Classical Library, 1981, 14.42-45.

Talbert, Charles H. *Reading Corinthians: A Literary and Theological Commentary on 1 and 2 Corinthians.* New York: Crossroad Publising Company, 1987.

Thurman, Howard. *Jesus and the Disinherited.* Boston: Beacon Press, 1976.

Tucker, T. G. *Life in the Roman World of Nero and St. Paul.* New York: The MacMillan Company, 1911.

Vogt, Joseph. *Ancient Slavery and the Ideal of Man*. Cambridge: Harvard University Press, 1975.

Watson, Alan. *Roman Slave Law*. Baltimore: John Hopkins University Press, 1987.

Wimbush, Vincent L. *Paul, the Worldly Ascetic: Response to the World and Self-Understanding according to 1 Corinthians 7.* Macon, Georgia: Mercer University Press, 1987.

Ten

A History of the Black Church

Dennis C. Dickerson

Several scholars in recent years have identified salient themes that have defined the development of the black church and the black religious experience. Charles Long, for example, indicated that the phenomena of the black church and the black religious experience are explained by the involuntary presence of blacks. Another scholar, Albert Raboteau, contended that America represented Egypt, whereas Canada, Africa, and the northern cities of America represented Israel. These symbolic destinations helped shape the sermons, speeches and songs of black Christians. Although the Anglicans started catechesis among blacks before other Christian denominations, the evangelistic successes of the Baptists and Methodists determined the religious inclinations of blacks. The rise of independent black churches and denominations provided places and personnel for the fight against slavery and its ultimate demise during the Civil War. In the first few decades during the twentieth century, the spread of pentecostalism created additional black denominations, and the black migration from the South to the North spearheaded social gospel programs within many black congregations. Support of the Civil Rights movement, and the espousal of black theology brought black clergy and black churches into the forefront of activism from the 1950s through the 1970s. When Jarena Lee started to preach in the African Methodist Episcopal Church in the 1810s and Nannie Burroughs organized the Women's Auxiliary of the National Baptist Convention in 1900, they developed precedents, during the 1980s, that brought to frontline church leadership such women as Bishop Leontine E. C. Kelly in the United Methodist Church and Bishop Barbara Harris in the Protestant Episcopal Church.

◂ **"A Negro camp meeting in the South, 1892." Hand-colored woodcut, courtesy North Wind Picture Archives**

African American Christianity emerged out of the crucible of slavery. In fact "the involuntary presence of the black community in America," according to Charles Long, has been a formative and persistent factor in shaping the African American religious experience. Although Long also argues that the African background influenced African American Christianity, he and other scholars, some of whom discount the importance of the African heritage, agree that as blacks grappled with slavery, segregation, and other forms of racial oppression, they developed theological perspectives that differed significantly from those of whites.

Albert Raboteau, for example, observed that blacks interpreted "the language, symbols, and worldview" found in the Bible to explain their peculiar fate. Often African Americans turned to the story of Exodus and applied it to themselves. White Christians who fled religious persecution in the Old World also used Exodus events to explain their journey to the New World. For them Europe was the Egypt that they left behind to go to a Promised Land, an Israel that was America. Blacks found similar hermeneutical possibilities in the Exodus story. Blacks were captured and shipped from their homeland in Africa on crowded and disease-infested slave ships headed for America. Although America was an Israel for white Christians, it was a different place for blacks. America, where oppression and persecution awaited them, was like the biblical Egypt. Hence, they longed to escape Egypt in order to go to a Promised Land. Israel for southern slaves was located in the North or in Canada or in Africa. Israel was any place to which they could journey to end their bondage and become free from racial subjugation. The views of African American Christians differed from those of whites in other respects. As blacks tried to make sense of their enslaved and segregated status they developed a deeper understanding of forgiveness, reconciliation, and other fundamental tenets of Christian doctrine.

Timothy Smith, for example, observed that blacks who converted to Christianity "knew they had a lot to forgive." Those who were serious and steadfast understood better than most whites the depth of desire, discipline, and fortitude required to forgive others for their wrongful acts toward African Americans. Similarly, black Christians demonstrated their spiritual resilience when, in the face of physical persecution and abuse, they counselled reconciliation with whites rather than revenge. Moreover, they viewed God as active in history. Hence, they waited for deliverance either directly from God from divinely appointed agents on the Underground Railroad, or from Civil War soldiers in the Union Army.[1]

The founding in 1701 of the Society for the Propagation of the Gospel in Foreign Parts started the Anglican mission to evangelize African American slaves. These initiatives, mainly in the South, predated other denominational efforts to introduce Christianity to blacks. Opposition from slave owners, failure to condemn human bondage, and a tedious method of catechesis limited the number of slave converts. The Dutch Reformed Church made similar efforts in the North, principally in New York, to Christianize blacks. This pro-slavery denomination, like the Anglicans, emphasized strict "catechetical instruction," but these factors restricted its evangelical effectiveness.[2]

Most scholars have agreed that the 18th century revivals and camp meetings of the Baptists and Methodists proved more successful than the evangelical efforts of their Anglican and Dutch Reformed counterparts. Winthrop Hudson, for example, offered three explanations why most blacks became Baptists and Methodists. Aggressive and extensive evangelization, acceptance of black members on a somewhat equal basis, and opportunities to become preachers pulled African Americans into these denominations in large numbers both in the North and in the South. Their acceptance into the ministry enabled black preachers, especially in the North, when faced with racial discrimination in white churches, to form separate congregations and denominations. Between 1787 and 1822 in several northern and some southern cities, blacks withdrew to found their own Baptist, Methodist, Episcopal, Congregational, and Presbyterian churches.[3]

Will B. Gravely has contended that the rise of independent black congregations and denominations was traceable to three crucial circumstances: discriminatory behavior by whites, the desire of blacks for religious independence and autonomy, and white clergy distancing themselves from previous anti-slavery positions. As a result black Baptists started congregations in Silver Bluff, South Carolina in the 1770s, Savannah, Georgia in 1782, and Augusta, Georgia in 1793. Richard Allen, a Delaware slave converted by a Methodist circuit rider, purchased his freedom and founded the Free African Society (FAS) in Philadelphia in 1787. An ugly racial incident at St. George Methodist Episcopal Church moved Allen and his followers to become completely autonomous. Out of the FAS emerged two black congregations, St. Thomas Protestant Episcopal Church and Bethel African Methodist Episcopal Church, both dedicated in 1794. Since Allen declined to serve St. Thomas, his associate, Absalom Jones, became its priest.

Allen's Bethel congregation eventually severed all ties with Wesleyan whites and led other congregations in Pennsylvania, Maryland, and New Jersey to form the African Methodist Episcopal Church in Philadelphia in 1816.

Similar racial tensions led Peter Spencer to found another black Wesleyan denomination in Wilmington, Delaware in 1813, the Union Church of Africans. James Varick, Christopher Rush, and others established another denomination, the African Methodist Episcopal Zion Church in 1821 in New York City.[4] Although some African Americans remained within white religious structures, they, like their Baptist and African Methodist counterparts, worshiped in separate congregations. In 1807, black Presbyterians founded the First African Presbyterian Church with John Gloucester as pastor, in Philadelphia. Black Calvinist congregations spread to other cities in Pennsylvania, New Jersey, and New York. Black Congregational churches started in New Haven, Hartford, Pittsfield, Providence and other cities in New England. After the Disciples of Christ began in 1820 in Kentucky, several black congregations started in Kentucky, Ohio, North Carolina, Georgia, and Tennessee prior to 1862. Although most Roman Catholic missionaries ministered among slaves in Baltimore, Maryland; Savannah, Georgia; Mobile, Alabama; New Orleans, Louisiana; and their environs, free blacks sometimes attended mixed congregations in Pittsburgh, Washington, D.C., New York City, St. Louis, and Chicago prior to the Civil War.[5]

Black pastors and their parishioners, particularly in the North, used their churches to advance abolitionism and to support emancipation efforts during the Civil War. Samuel Cornish and Theodore S. Wright, both black Presbyterian ministers, through their own newspapers, and through cooperation with white anti-slavery groups, advocated freedom for the slaves, denounced the colonization of free blacks, and supported the establishment of black schools. J. W. C. Pennington, an escaped slave, Amos G. Beman, and Charles B. Ray, all black Congregational clergymen, joined Cornish and Wright in these endeavors. Perhaps the most prominent preacher-turned-abolitionist was Frederick Douglass who ran away from bondage in Maryland and settled in New Bedford, Massachusetts. There he became a local preacher in the African Methodist Episcopal Zion Church. Some clergy opened their churches to abolitionist meetings and offered them as stations on the Underground Railroad. Fleeing slaves often stopped at any one of several Baptist, A.M.E. and A.M.E. Zion churches in the Midwest, the Middle Atlantic and

New England states to hide from marauding slave catchers and bounty hunters anxious to recapture them and return them to bondage in the South.

A divinely inspired slave preacher, Nat Turner, in Southampton County, Virginia, believed that Old Testament justice required him to lead a slave revolt in 1831. Henry Highland Garnet, a former slave from Maryland, and a Presbyterian pastor, in 1843 called upon slaves to break the chains of their oppression using whatever means were at their disposal. During the Civil War numerous black ministers recruited soldiers to fight in the Union Army against the Confederacy. Fourteen black clergy served in the Union Army as chaplains. They performed marriages, improved morale, tended to the wounded, and taught illiterate recruits how to read and write.[6]

The Civil War destroyed slavery and freed four million persons, many of whom were without a formal church affiliation. Northern white denominations sent preachers and teachers, both white and black, into the South to evangelize among the newly emancipated. However, the Baptists and the Methodist Episcopal Church in the north outdistanced the Presbyterians, Episcopalians, and Congregationalists in their recruitment of black members. All of these denominations, however, made major educational contributions through the many secondary, collegiate, and professional

▸ **"The Family of the Hampton Institute graduates, ca. 1900." Oil-colored photograph, courtesy, The Granger Collection, New York**

institutions that they established to train black ministers, teachers, doctors, and lawyers. Similarly, black Baptists, the African Methodist Episcopal Church, and the African Methodist Episcopal Zion Church outpaced the white denominations in their numerical success. They also founded schools and colleges for the former slaves and their children. With assistance from the American Baptist Home Mission Society, black Baptists supported Wayland Seminary in Virginia, Shaw in North Carolina, Atlanta Baptist (Morehouse) and Spelman in Georgia, and Leland in Louisiana. The A.M.E. Church established Morris Brown in Georgia, Allen in South Carolina, Kittrell in North Carolina, Edward Waters in Florida, and Paul Quinn in Texas. The A.M.E. Zion Church founded Livingstone in North Carolina as its flagship institution. Additionally, black voters in several southern states elected black ministers in significant numbers to Reconstruction legislatures and they also served as local and state officials.[7]

Southern white denominations that had slave members before the Civil War encouraged them to start separate denominations and congregations. The Methodist Episcopal, South in response to their black members agreed to establish the Colored Methodist Episcopal Church in Jackson, Tennessee, in 1870. Similarly, in 1874 in Nashville, Tennessee, the Cumberland Presbyterian Church endorsed the founding of the Colored Cumberland Presbyterian Church. Although blacks remained a part of the southern-based Presbyterian Church in the U.S., they were organized into separate synods, presbyteries, and congregations. Similar structures existed within other northern and southern white denominations. In 1889 blacks within the Evangelical Lutheran Synodical Conference of North America, for example, established the Alpha Synod of the Evangelical Lutheran Church of Freedmen in America consisting of five North Carolina congregations. Nonetheless, the vast majority of African Americans belonged to black controlled Baptist and Methodist churches.[8]

After Reconstruction, newly enfranchised blacks lost their right to vote and faced increased violence and hostility from whites. At the same time, a surge of millennial thought characterized the perspectives of leading black churchmen. They reached into their ancient past for sources of hope and assurance that the suffering that blacks endured would culminate in a golden age in which freedom for all would become a reality. Some believed their glorious African past heralded an equally promising future in which God would rebuke western society for its ill treatment of blacks.

Benjamin W. Arnett, a bishop in the African Methodist Episcopal Church and a bibliophile of black history, in an 1893 address to the World's Parliament of Religions, credited Africa with helping to spread Christianity. "In the first days of Christianity," he said, "it contributed more than its proportion of the early agents." He cited Luke of Cyrene in North Africa as the author of one of the gospels. He mentioned Simon, also of Cyrene, "who became the cross-bearer of the Son of God on his way to Calvary." Arnett's colleague, Bishop Benjamin T. Tanner published *The Color of Solomon—What?* in 1895. He argued that Solomon, through his parents, David and Bathsheba, had a Hamitic or a black origin. He also cited Solomon's "passion for women manifestly of darker hue than were the women of Israel." Tanner's point in advancing these contentions was that most translations of the Bible made "Solomon to be white when it is absolutely certain that according to the division of the human family. . . he did not belong to the white race, and all things being equal could not personally have been white, as that word is popularly understood." Arnett and Tanner believed that Christianity's ancient anchors among people of color argued for their equality in 19th century American society.[9]

The millennialism of black clergy did not obscure another influential movement among the African American community. William Seymour, a black Holiness preacher born in Louisiana, inaugurated a marathon series of revivals at the Azusa Street Mission in Los Angeles, California. Seymour preached sanctification and speaking in tongues (glossolalia). As word spread about Seymour's powerful preaching, blacks and whites flocked to Azusa Street to receive these spiritual gifts that Seymour enthusiastically espoused. The founders of numerous Pentecostal denominations drew their spiritual authority from Azusa Street to establish Holiness churches. One pilgrim to Azusa Street was Charles Harrison Mason who formally founded the Church of God in Christ in 1914. Another was G. T. Haywood, head of the interracial Pentecostal Assemblies of the World started in 1914. R. C. Lawson, a Haywood follower, founded the Church of Our Lord Jesus Christ of the Apostolic Faith in 1919. Lawson trained other clergy including Sherrod Johnson, Henry C. Brooks, J. P. Shields, Smallwood E. Williams, and Lymus Johnson who started their own Pentecostal denominations.[10]

During the era of the two World Wars the labor needs of northern industry drew millions of African Americans away from the South to major urban areas of the Northeast, Midwest, and Pacific Coast.

▸ "Baptism" (detail), painting by Ana Bel Lee Washington, Superstock

Beginning in the first decades of the 1900s through the 1960s, African Americans populated plants, factories, and foundries that manufactured steel, automobiles, rubber, ships, and electrical products. As a result, African American congregations in numerous denominations experienced phenomenal growth and financial support from their blue collar parishioners. Consequently, such model congregations as Reverdy C. Ransom's Institutional A.M.E. Church and Social Settlement in Chicago, J. C. Austin's Ebenezer Baptist Church in Pittsburgh, Pilgrim Baptist Church in Chicago, and Robert Bradby's Second Baptist Church in Detroit established social gospel programs that addressed the housing, employment, and child care needs of their respective communities. Such pastors as Adam Clayton Powell, Jr. at Abyssinian Baptist Church in New York City and Archibald J. Carey, Jr. at Woodlawn A.M.E. Church and Quinn Chapel A.M.E. Church in Chicago respectively launched successful careers in national and municipal politics.[11]

African American clergy and congregations were also conspicuous in spearheading the Civil Rights Movement in the 1950s and 1960s. The landmark 1954 Supreme Court decision in *Brown vs. Board of Education* owed its origin to suits that two A.M.E. ministers, Reverend Oliver Brown of Topeka, Kansas, and Reverend Joseph A. DeLaine of Clarendon County, South Carolina, initiated. Bus boycott leaders in Baton Rouge in 1953, Montgomery in 1955, and Tallahassee in 1956 were Baptist ministers, Theodore Jemison, Martin Luther King, Jr., and C. K. Steele, respectively. Their congregations, along with several others in their respective cities, provided sites for rallies and financial support to these grassroots movements. The Southern Christian Leadership Conference, founded in Atlanta in 1957 with Martin Luther King, Jr. as president, gave material support to numerous southern communities that fought against legalized racial segregation and discrimination in the region and in the nation.[12]

Civil Rights clergy owed their activism to an earlier generation of black religious intellectuals who pressed black congregations to reinterpret Jesus and his relationship to social struggle and the place of the church in movements for social change. In the 1930s, 1940s, and 1950s the perspectives of Howard Thurman, Mordecai W. Johnson, Benjamin E. Mays, and George D. Kelsey inspired a succeeding generation of black activist clergy that included Martin Luther King, Jr. and others. Similarly, the millenialist black theology of Benjamin W. Arnett and Benjamin T. Tanner resonated in the late 1960s with James Cone, Cecil Cone, J. Deotis Roberts,

Gayraud S. Wilmore, and others who promulgated the view that African American Christianity required commitments to critique racist biblical interpretations, to oppose oppressive religious and economic institutions, and to support the black freedom struggle. Jacqueline Grant, Pauli Murray, and other black feminist writers condemned both the racism and sexism practiced by American society and black and white churches.[13]

Women also sought a place in the African American clergy. Jarena Lee whom Bishop Richard Allen initially rebuffed was licensed to preach in the A.M.E. Church in 1817. Although Bishop Henry M. Turner ordained Sarah A. Hughes as an itinerant deacon in the A.M.E. Church's North Carolina Annual Conference in 1885, his successor, Bishop Jabaz P. Campbell, rescinded this action. The denomination authorized that women could be ordained as local deacons in 1948, then as local elders in 1956, and finally as itinerant deacons and elders in 1960. The A.M.E. Zion Church authorized the full ordination of Mary Blair Smalls in 1898 in the Philadelphia-Baltimore Annual Conference. The C.M.E. Church followed the other two black Wesleyan bodies with the full ordination of women in 1966.

The election of Leontine T. C. Kelly as a United Methodist bishop in 1984, and the the elevation of Barbara Harris as suffragan bishop of the Episcopal Diocese of Massachusetts in 1989 represented significant achievements for black women in the ministry. Women also spearheaded several Pentecostal/Holiness denominations. Mary Magdalena Lewis Tate, the founder of the Church of the Living God, the Pillar and Ground of Truth, is the best example. After some Alabama revivals in 1908, Mother Tate became a Bishop and later ordained four others, including her two sons to help her supervise the growing denomination. Additionally, church mothers within Pentecostal/Holiness churches developed into important positions at the local, regional, and national levels. Their substantial influence upon clergy drew from their moral guidance and rhetorical abilities. Women assumed other leadership positions in numerous auxiliaries, especially in the historic black denominations. All the Baptist, Methodist, and Pentecostal bodies had women's missionary societies. Perhaps, Nannie H. Burrough's Women's Auxiliary of the National Baptist Convention established in 1900 is the best known.[14]

African American churches have cooperated primarily through several interdenominational groups. The Fraternal Council of Negro Churches which started in 1934, with A.M.E. Bishop Reverdy C. Ransom as president is one such group.

A.M.E. Bishop John Hurst Adams spearheaded the Congress of National Black Churches in 1978. The National Association for the Advancement of Colored People, the National Urban League, and the Southern Christian Leadership Conference were black betterment groups that have drawn consistent support from black churches throughout the 20th century.[15]

The impact of black churches also stretched elsewhere within the Americas and to Africa where major denominations established churches, schools, and hospitals. Black Baptists established the Baptist Foreign Missionary Convention of the United States of America in 1880. This body, which helped to create the National Baptist Convention in 1895, became the denomination's Foreign Mission Board. The Board founded the Providence Industrial Mission in Nyasaland in Central Africa, with Lewis G. Jordan as Corresponding Secretary between 1896 and 1921. In 1923 there were ten mission stations in Liberia and fourteen in South Africa. Bishop Henry M. Turner of the African Methodist Episcopal Church established the Sierra Leone and Liberia Annual Conferences in 1891, and he brought into this denomination the Ethiopian Church of South Africa in 1896. While he presided as the Bishop of Georgia from 1896 through 1908, Turner also launched missions in Cuba and Mexico. The A.M.E. Zion Church, the C.M.E. Church, and the Church of God in Christ inaugurated similar efforts to expand within the Americas and to Africa. Hence, black churches that have functioned as meeting places for abolitionists, as stations on the Underground Railroad, and as sites for civil rights activism also embraced a Pan African vision to include persons of color throughout the African diaspora.[16]

Three trends will likely define the future direction of black churches. First, the growing influence of mega-churches probably will continue. Such congregations as First A.M.E. Church and West Angeles Church of God in Christ in Los Angeles, California, Full Gospel A.M.E. Zion Church in Temple Hills and Clinton, Maryland, Windsor Village United Methodist Church in Houston, Texas, and Greater St. Stephen Full Gospel Baptist Church in New Orleans, Louisiana, all boast memberships in the multiple thousands and they support a broad range of social outreach, media, and housing ministries. Second, blacks in predominantly white denominations will continue to ascend to important executive positions such as Bishop Wilton D. Gregory, the Vice President of the National Conference of Catholic Bishops, and Reverend Arnold I. Thomas, the conference minister of the Vermont Conference of the United Church of Christ. Third, non-denominational churches such as Frederick K.C. Price's Crenshaw Christian Center in Los Angeles, California, Johnnie Colemon's Christ Universal Temple in Chicago, Illinois, and T.D. Jake's Potter's House in Dallas, Texas will continue to attract increasing numbers of black parishioners.

Selected Chronology

A History of the Black Church

1701 The Society for the Propagation of the Gospel in Foreign Parts started the Anglican mission to evangelize African American slaves.

1782 Several black Baptist congregations are started in Savannah, Georgia.

1787 Richard Allen, a Delaware slave converted by a Methodist circuit rider, purchased his freedom and founded the Free African Society (FAS) in Philadelphia.

1787-1822 Blacks in several northern and southern cities founded their own Baptist, Methodist, Episcopal, Congregational, and Presbyterian churches.

1813 The Union Church of Africans was founded by Peter Spencer in Wilmington, Delaware.

1816 The African Methodist Episcopal Church was founded in Philadelphia, Pennsylvania.

1831 Nat Turner, a slave preacher in Southampton County, Virginia, leads a revolt.

1843 Henry Highland Garnet, a former slave from Maryland and a Presbyterian pastor, called upon slaves to break the chains of their oppression.

1870 The Colored Methodist Episcopal Church was established in Jackson, Tennessee.

1880 The Baptist Foreign Missionary Convention of the United States was formed by black Baptists.

1895 Bishop Benjamin T. Tanner publishes *The Color of Solomon—What?* Tanner argued that Solomon had a Hamitic or a black origin through his parents, David and Bathsheba.

1900 Nannie H. Burroughs established the Women's Auxiliary of the National Baptist Convention.

1906 William Seymour, a black Holiness preacher, organized what became known as the Azusa Street Mission.

1914 The Church of God in Christ was formally founded by Charles Harrison Mason.

1948 The African Methodist Episcopal Church began ordaining women as local deacons.

1957 The Southern Christian Leadership Conference (SCLC) was founded in Atlanta, Georgia, with the Rev. Dr. Martin Luther King, Jr. as president.

1978 The Congress of National Black Churches was spearheaded by Bishop John Hurst Adams.

Notes

1. Charles H. Long, "Perspectives for a Study of Afro-American Religion in the United States" *Significations: Signs, Symbols, and Images in the Interpretation of Religion,* Charles H. Long, ed. (Philadelphia: Fortress Press,1986), 176-179; Albert J. Raboteau, "African Americans, Exodus, and the American Israel," *A Fire in the Bones: Reflections on African American Religious History,* Albert J. Raboteau, ed. (Boston: Beacon Press, 1995), 17-36; Timothy L. Smith, "Slavery and Theology: The Emergence of Black Christian Consciousness in Nineteenth Century America," *Church History*, 41 (December 1972), 498-499.

2. Harold T. Lewis, *Yet With a Steady Beat: The African American Struggle for Recognition in the Episcopal Church* (Valley Forge, Pennsylvania: Trinity Press International, 1996), 19-23; Gerald F. DeJong, "The Dutch Reformed Church and Negro Slavery in Colonial America," *Church History,* 40, (December 1971), 430-436.

3. Winthrop S. Hudson,"The American Context as an Area for Research in Black Church Studies," *Church History*, 52, (June 1983), 157-171; Will B. Gravely,"The Rise of African Churches in America (1786-1822): Re-examining the Contexts," *African-American Religion: Interpretive Essays in History and Culture*, Timothy E. Fulop and Albert J. Raboteau, editors, (New York: Routledge, 1997), 135-151.

4. Ibid., 137-140; 144-146.

5. Andrew E. Murray, *Presbyterians and the Negro: A History.* (Philadelphia: Presbyterian Historical Society, 1966), 30-39; David E. Swift, *Black Prophets of Justice: Activist Clergy Before the Civil War,* (Baton Rouge: Louisiana State University Press, 1989), 182-185; 215; Dennis C. Dickerson, "Samuel Harrison, A Nineteenth Century Black Clergyman," *Black Apostles at Home and Abroad: The Black Christian Mission from the Revolution to Reconstruction,* David W. Wills and Richard Newman, editors, (Boston: G. K. Hall & Co., 1982), 148, 149; 151; Hap Lyda, "A History of Black Christian Churches (Disciples of Christ)

in the United States Through 1899," Ph.D. dissertation, Vanderbilt University, 1972, 23; Cyprian Davis, *The History of Black Catholics in the United States*, (New York: Crossroad Publishing Company, 1990), 67-97.

6. Swift, *Black Prophets of Freedom*, 2-4; 7-18; William L. Andrews, "Frederick Douglass, Preacher," *American Literature* 54, (December 1982), 592-597; Benjamin Quarles, *Black Abolitionists*, (New York: Oxford University Press, 1969), 83, 84; Gayraud S. Wilmore, *Black Religion and Black Radicalism*, (Maryknoll, New York: Orbis Books, 1973), 62-73; Henry Highland Garnet, "Address to the Slaves of the United States of America," (1843), *The Black Abolitionist Papers*, Volume III, The United States, 1830-1846, C. Peter Ripley, editor, (Chapel Hill, North Carolina: University of North Carolina Press, 1991), 403-411; Edwin S. Redkey, "Black Chaplains in the Union Army," *Civil War History* 33, (December 1987), 331-350.

7. William E. Montgomery, *Under Our Own Vine and Fig Tree: The African American Church in the South, 1865-1900*, (Baton Rouge: Louisiana State University Press, 1993), 38-190. On black denominational involvement in higher education see Paul R. Griffin, *Black Theology as the Foundation of Three Methodist Colleges*, (Lanham, Maryland: University Press of America, 1984) and Leroy Fitts, *A History of Black Baptists,* (Nashville: Broadman Press, 1985).

8. Othal H. Lakey, *A History of the CME Church,* (Memphis: The CME Publishing House, 1985), 131-163; Thomas D. Campbell, *One Family Under God: A Story of Cumberland Presbyterians in Black and White,* (Memphis: Frontier Press,1982), 38-40; Ernest Trice Thompson, "Black Presbyterians, Education and Evangelism After the Civil War," *Journal of Presbyterian History* 51, (Summer 1973), 174-198.

9. Timothy E. Fulop, "'The Future Golden Day of the Race': Millenialism and Black Americans in the Nadir, 1877-1901," *Harvard Theological Review* 84, (1991), 75-99; Benjamin W. Arnett, "Christianity and the Negro," *The World's Congress of Religions: Addresses and Papers Delivered Before the Parliament*, J. W. Hanson, editor, (Chicago: W. B. Conkey Company, 1894), 748-750; Benjamin T. Tanner, *The Color of Solomon—What?* (Philadelphia: A.M.E. Book Concern, 1895), 16-18; 31-38.

10. James S. Tinney, "William J. Seymour: Father of Modern Day Pentecostalism," *Black Apostles: Afro-American Clergy Confront the Twentieth Century*, Randall K. Burkett and Richard Newman, editors, (Boston: G. K. Hall & Co., 1978), 213-225; Elsie W. Mason, *The Man... Charles Harrison Mason*, (Memphis: Privately Printed, 1979); Robert C. Spellman, A Chart on Pentecostal History: Partial Development of Predominantly Black Pentecostal Organizations, U.S.A.

11. Milton Sernett, *Bound for the Promised Land: African American Religion and the Great Migration*, (Durham: Duke University Press, 1997), 87-121; 154-179; Dennis C. Dickerson, "The Black Church in Industrializing Western Pennsylvania, 1870-1950," *African Americans in Pennsylvania*, Joe William Trotter, Jr. and Eric Ledell Smith, editors, (University Park: Pennsylvania State University Press, 1997), 388-402; Reverdy C. Ransom, *The Pilgrimage of Harriet Ransom's Son*, (Nashville, A.M.E. Sunday School Union, n.d.), pp. 104-118; Randall K. Burkett, "The Baptist Church in the Years of Crisis: J.C. Austin and Pilgrim Baptist Church, 1926-1950," *African American Christianity*, Paul E. Johnson, editor, (Berkeley: University of California Press, 1994), 134-158; Cara L. Shelly, "Brad-

by's Baptists: Second Baptist Church of Detroit, 1910-1946," *Michigan Historical Review* 17, (Spring1991), 1-33; Charles V. Hamilton, *Adam Clayton Powell: The Political Biography of an American Dilemma*, (New York: Atheneum, 1991), "Archibald J. Carey, Jr.," *Encyclopedia of African Methodism*, Richard R.Wright, Jr., editor, (Philadelphia: A.M.E. Book Concern, 1947), 62, 63; Biographical Data in *Archibald J. Carey, Jr.* Papers, Chicago Historical Society, Chicago, Illinois.

12. Howard D. Gregg, *The A.M.E. Church and the Current Negro Revolt*, (Nashville: A.M.E. Sunday School Union, n.d.), 17-24; Aldon D. Morris, *The Origins of the Civil Rights Movement*, (New York: The Free Press, 1984), 40-119.

13. Thomas I. S. Mikelson, "Mays, King, and The Negro's God," *Walking Integrity: Benjamin Elijah Mays, Mentor to Martin Luther King, Jr.*, Lawrence Edward Carter, Sr., editor, (Macon: Mercer University Press, 1998), 153-184; Walter Earl Fluker and Catherine Tumber, editors, *A Strange Freedom: The Best of Howard Thurman on Religious Experience and Public Life*, (Boston: Beacon Press,1998), 6, 13, 131; Clayborne Carson, editor, *The Autobiography of Martin Luther King, Jr.*, (New York: Warner Books, 1998), 16, 23; Gayraud S. Wilmore and James H. Cone, editors, *Black Theology: A Documentary History, 1966-1979*, (Maryknoll, New York: Orbis Books, 1979), 1-11; 398-414; 418-431.

14. Dennis C. Dickerson, "'Did Not Mary First Preach the Risen Savior': Women Preachers Within Wesleyan Black Denominations," *Historical Bulletin of the World Methodist Historical Society*, Fourth Quarter 1997, 5-9; "Barbara Harris," "Leontine T. C. Kelly," *Black Women in America: An Historical Encyclopedia*, Volume I, Darlene Clark Hine, editor, (Brooklyn: Carlson Publishing Company, 1993), 537; 675; Evelyn Brooks Higginbotham, *Righteous Discontent: The Women's Movement in the Black Baptist Church, 1880-1920,* (Cambridge, Massachusetts: Harvard University Press, 1993), 150-184.

15. Mary R. Sawyer, "The Fraternal Council of Negro Churches, 1934-1964," *Church History* 59, (March 1990), 51-64; Also see the following: Mary R. Sawyer, B*lack Ecumenism: Implementing the Demands of Justice*, (Valley Forge, Pennsylvania: Trinity Press International, 1994), and Dennis C. Dickerson, "Black Ecumenicism: Efforts to Establish a United Methodist Episcopal Church, 1918-1932," *Church History* 52, (December 1983), 479-491.

16. William J. Harvey, III, *Bridges of Faith Across the Seas: The Story of the Foreign Mission Board of the National Baptist Convention, USA, Inc.*, (Warminster, Pennsylvania: Neibauer Peeress, 1989), 22; 29-33; 44, 75, 76; Stephen W. Angell, *Bishop Henry McNeal Turner and African American Religion in the South*, (Knoxville: University of Tennessee Press, 1992), 215-237; Dennis C. Dickerson, *Religion, Race, and Region: Research Notes on A.M.E. Church History* (Nashville: A.M.E. Sunday School Union/Legacy Publishing, 1995), 121-130.

Eleven

Black and Catholic: Elements of African American Catholic History

James C. Okoye

The story of black Catholics in the American church is one of deep loyalty amidst the painful struggle to hold together both black truth and Catholic truth. Four periods are considered: The Antebellum Period; The Civil War and Reconstruction; The Age of Black Power and Black Civil Rights; and The Abiding Question: 1960s to the Present.

◂ "Our Mother of Africa holding the Christ Child." Photo by Bro. Earl V. Kent, S.S.J., Josephite Pastoral Center, Washington, D.C.

African American experiences of Catholicism are diverse, yet share the one element of "blackness." The end of the 19th century saw African American laypersons fighting the benign neglect of their church and tackling the issues facing blacks in the "Jim Crow" period. In the late 1960s black clergy and religious responded to "Black Power" by beginning to trace an African American Catholic praxis and theology. The very history paints a picture of what an African American Catholic church should look like. It shows also an ongoing struggle to balance black pride with Catholic truth.

Black Catholicism

The black church is not just an institution. It crosses denominational boundaries and has no formal structure; it is the result of a common experience and history (cf. US Black Bishops, 1984: 15). "Black" signifies more than color, it depicts a situation. The situation is that of blacks in this country who have been subjected to slavery and/or racial discrimination. If "the inclusion of African Americans as full and equal citizens within the American journey of the United States has been fraught with rejection, ambiguity, and struggle" (Phelps, 1997: 17), the situation has also been the same within the church. As one writer succinctly put it, "the continued presence of Black Catholics in the Catholic Church in the United States serves as a subversive memory…for it is a memory of hope brought forth from pain, of perseverance maintained in the face of bloody opposition, of faith born of tortured struggle" (Hayes/ Davis, 1998: 3).

Why would one become Christian and Catholic and persist in that faith in the face of rejection or a grudging acceptance that relegated one to the aisles and galleries of the church? Some people have characterized the religion of black slaves in America as "folk religion" in the service of freedom and equality: "missionaries preached the next world; the slave seized on the religion of the whites

▸ "Swing Low Sweet Chariot," William H. Johnson, Courtesy National Museum of American Art, Washington, D.C./Art Resource, NY.

to achieve freedom in this world" (Washington, 1964: 30-42). The emotionalism of the camp meetings, the emphasis on feeling as the root of conversion, has been seen as suited to the religious experience of the black slave (cf. Frazier, 1963:16). Further, emotional conversion experience was a leveler which conferred dignity on the slave: it was accessible to all and made all equally acceptable in the eyes of God. In evangelical religion, it conferred on converted blacks the right to preach, even to whites (cf. Raboteau, 1978: 133). As no conversion is devoid of human elements, some of these elements may have been present; however, conversion to Catholicism usually invokes little of the emotions. The persistence of blacks in the Catholic faith would seem to be more closely explained by three factors. In the first place, religion is as much part of the identity of the African American, as it is of his/her counterpart in Africa. "It is … the religious consciousness of the black in America which is the repository of who he is, where he has been, and where he is going" (Long, 1971: 66). Slavery left only two social institutions under the slaves' control: religion and the family. These they adapted and structured in a self-defining manner. In his new environment, the slave could not re-create the forms of his traditional religion; he could, however, adapt the Christian religion to his own religious consciousness; "the new orientation to the world was provided by Christianity" (Frazier, 1963: 17).

Secondly, blacks accepted Christianity "because it explained their unique situation: God saw a suffering people; Jesus took up their burden, and he changed the world, changed the history of the African American slave, lifting it and pointing it toward divine expectations" (*Plenty Good Room: no. 56*).

Finally, having become Catholic, the slaves found this faith bore similarities to, and was strengthened by, their African heritage. Because the Catholic sacramental system evokes the African symbolic approach to life, the slave could continue to live "all of life in the context of the encounter with the divine" (Phelps, 1998: 179). All through their history, black Catholics in America have held together the quest for God and the quest for human dignity. Segregation forced them to draw upon the African village ethos to provide for the temporal and spiritual needs of the members. They built churches and schools in the same breath as they established burial and insurance/credit societies. Since the Bible and authentic Catholic tradition decried slavery and racial discrimination, they could seize upon these as elements of hope against hope and allies in their undying struggle for liberation and dignity.

The Antebellum Period

The African Heritage of Black Catholicism

Africans from different parts of the continent were enslaved and subjected to the inhuman conditions of the "Middle Passage." Those who survived were sold on the slave markets of the Caribbean and other places. In Brazil they were grouped according to similar ethnic and linguistic backgrounds, while on the American continent, masters took care to mix people of different backgrounds in order to forestall any hopes of rebellion. E. Frazier has argued that the brutal enslavement stripped the slaves of their African heritage; M. Herskovits, on the contrary, insisted that they carried over "Africanisms" into the new environment. It would, however, be truer to say that they created a new culture by re-modeling both what they brought with them and what they received from the new environment (cf. Mintz/Price, 1992: 81-84). African American culture is a symbiosis of the African and American worldviews. It is this culture that African American Catholics bring to their profession of the Catholic faith.

The Spanish Element in Black Catholicism

Blacks were among the first explorers in the New World in 1492 and not all of them were slaves. Pedro Alonza was captain of Columbus' flagship, the Niña; Estevanico led an expedition into what is now New Mexico and Arizona; there, he discovered the Zuni Indians and planted the first wheat crop in America in 1539 (cf. Lincoln, 1973: 299). In 1501, the Spanish throne approved the use of black slaves in this New World. It would seem that the first group of blacks to arrive on the American continent were Catholics. In 1526, a Spanish explorer brought some blacks with him to make a settlement in South Carolina, but they fled to the interior and settled with the Indians. It was the policy of Spain and Portugal, both Catholic countries, to baptize their slaves either at the port of embarkation or at entry, and so these were probably black Catholics. We are on surer ground with the Spanish colony of St. Augustine established in 1565 in north Florida, the oldest parish in America; blacks, slave and free, were part of this settlement (cf. Davis, 1990: 30). Florida was Spanish territory until 1763, and again from 1784 until 1821, when it finally reverted to the United States. As the English settled in the Carolinas and Georgia and used these areas as a base for attacks on the Spanish territory, Spain encouraged slaves in those territories to escape to Florida, convert to Catholicism, and be granted their freedom. In 1738, those who had escaped settled north of St. Augustine in a place called Santa Teresa de Mose (cf. Davis, 1990: 30). With the restoration of Spanish rule in 1784, many of the British emigrated from St. Augustine leaving room for the ingress of Americans, slaves and free, who were expected to convert to Catholicism (cf. Davis, 1990: 68). Mobile, Alabama was captured by Spain in 1763. When Bishop Cirilo of Barcelona visited in 1790, black Catholics numbered 419 against 165 whites. By the time of the Civil War, the registers in Mobile show about 1,000 black Catholics (Davis, 1990: 77). In 1781, the eleven founding families of Nuestra Señora de Los Angeles were all Catholic. They were mostly mulatto and black; only two were Spanish (cf. Davis, 1990: 34). Church registers were either segregated or clearly identified one's racial identity.

The Spanish system of slavery recognized the humanity of those it enslaved. Blacks, slave and free, carried arms and fought alongside the Spanish. Slaves had the dignity of a name and were buried in the church cemetery. There was sometimes intermarriage between Spaniards and blacks.

The French Element in Black Catholicism

The French established a colony in Louisiana at the end of the 17th century and settled in much of the territory along the

▸ "Going to Church," William H. Johnson, National Museum of American Art, Washington, D.C./Art Resource, NY.

Mississippi River, in Missouri and Illinois; most of their slaves were black and Catholic. Louisiana would become briefly Spanish (1769-1803) before finally reverting to the United States in 1803. The *Code Noir*, established for the French West Indies in 1685, and in New Orleans in 1724, governed slavery in the French dominions. Like Spain and Portugal, France was a Catholic country. Masters were to assure the religious instruction of their slaves, and slaves were not to be put to work on Sundays and holy days. Intermarriage was permitted but mulatto children could not be freed at age 21 if their mothers were still enslaved. The settlers largely ignored legislation about religious practice for slaves, though they availed themselves of the license for intermarriage. As French women were few, intermarriage and concubinage with black and Indian women produced offspring of different hues of light skin who became "free people of color" or creoles. Similar situations were common also in the Spanish colonies. In 1727, Ursuline nuns arrived at New Orleans to educate young French women, but they also attended to black and Indian girls. Registers at St. John the Baptist parish, Savannah, Georgia, detail the baptisms and burials of both white and black Catholics from 1796 to 1816. The first entries were in French, then in English. There were many free blacks here, mostly with French names, and probably escapees from Haiti (Davis, 1990: 80). In 1842, the second black religious congregation of women, the Sisters of the Holy Family, was founded in New Orleans. The founder, Henriette Delille, was creole, as was the core of the group who were French-speaking women of color. They devoted themselves to the education of black children and the service of destitute blacks.

The English Element in Black Catholicism

The English period began in 1619 with the arrival of 20 blacks at Jamestown, Virginia. These blacks arrived by ship as indentured servants. Indentured servants, white and black, usually served for seven years and were then assigned their own portion of land. There was as yet parity in the situation of black and white indentured servants. At that time, Britain had nothing in its laws to address slavery. Besides, it was the tradition in Christendom that baptism rendered one free, for "Freedom is what we have...Christ has set us free..." (Galatians 5.1). But then the colonies had joined in the continental slave traffic and the mother country would establish a *Slave Code for the British Plantations* in 1667. Slaves could not leave the plantation without a pass fixing the duration of absence. They could not carry weapons. An owner who accidentally flogged a slave to death was not liable. Slaves could convert and be baptized, but this does not "alter the condition of the person as to his bondage or freedom." It was thought that masters would be more willing to have their slaves baptized if freedom did not come with baptism. The English system of slavery in this country was joined with debates about the full humanity of the African.

Maryland had the largest community of black Catholics. In Spring 1785, Fr. John Carroll, the superior of the mission, reported to the Cardinal Prefect of the Congregation for the Propagation of the Faith in Rome, that the Catholic population in Maryland was then 15,800, of whom 3,000 were slaves of all ages who had come from Africa. The French Revolution of 1789 set off ripples in the colonies, leading to an uprising in Santo Domingo (now Haiti), led by Toussaint L'Ouverture, a self-educated slave. The battle-cry was "Freedom or Death." In July 1793, 619 refugees, white and black, arrived at Fells Point, Baltimore. Baltimore was the site of the first black religious congregation of women, the Oblate Sisters of Providence, founded in 1829, by a French Sulpician, Fr. Jacques H. Joubert. The first four members were women of color, part of the refugee colony from Haiti. Their goal was the education of black children. In addition to their work in Baltimore, the group established, in 1863, a school for black children and a night school for black women in Philadelphia (cf. Davis, 1990: 99-104). It is also in Baltimore that we find the oldest extant document of a black Catholic society in the United States, the Holy Family Society of Colored People. This Society operated from 1843 till 1845. It should be noted that the first settler, in what would become Chicago, was Jean-Baptiste du Sable, a black Catholic who married into the Indian tribe of Potowatomi.

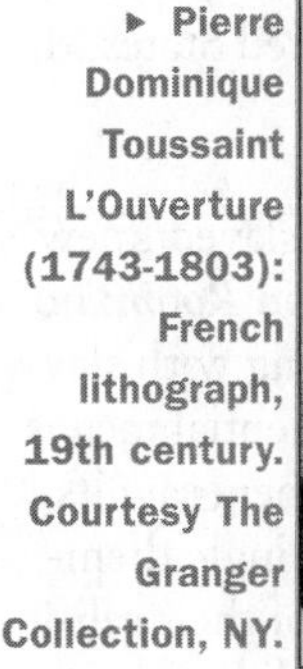

▸ **Pierre Dominique Toussaint L'Ouverture (1743-1803): French lithograph, 19th century. Courtesy The Granger Collection, NY.**

The 18th century was foundational for the identity of African Americans. In the 1730s and 1740s (the "Great Awakening") the revivalist movement of white Baptists and Methodists led many black slaves to the "mourners' bench" and conversion experience. On the plantations, these converted blacks began to articulate their faith in the light of their social and religious experience. Focusing on certain texts of the Bible and ignoring others, they brought to bear on Scripture the interpretative dimension of the spirituals, their songs, sermons, testimonies, and prayers—a hermeneutics controlled not by the words of the text but by their social and religious experience (cf. Wimbush, 1991: 85-89). The Bible became a subversive text that mandated the efforts of the slave at freedom, so much so that attempts were made to restrict his reading of the Bible to portions, like Ephesians 6.5a ("slaves, obey your human masters with fear and trembling..."). Many of the slaves learned to read from the Bible. In fact, in 1834, South Carolina enacted a law forbidding the teaching of black children, slave or free! Religion and resistance joined hands: the idea of the "happy and indifferent Negro slave" was a myth (cf. Harding, 1997: 109). In 1782, several black Baptist congregations started in Savannah, Georgia; thus began the black church. In 1787, Richard Allen and followers withdrew in protest from St. George Methodist Church, Philadelphia, to form the first independent black society in the United States, the Free Black Society.

When the black church was developed, most of the enslaved knew almost nothing about the Catholic church (*Plenty Good Room*: no. 62). The Catholic church of the time saw nothing wrong with slavery; on the contrary, some divines touted it as a providential means to evangelize and civilize the black race. The church, then, saw its unity in terms of uniformity; black Catholics did not single themselves out in bringing to bear on the Bible the wealth of their religious experience; as such a distinct black Catholicism did not yet emerge. Nor were black Catholics conspicuous in the black struggle for freedom in this period. The Cato and Stono rebellions in South Carolina in 1739 may have been led by black Catholics from the former kingdom of the Congo (now Angola) (cf. Davis, 1998: 21), but their Catholic faith was not in the forefront. It would seem that, rather than liberation, black Catholics of the period sought amelioration of their condition through various sodalities and through the provision of opportunities for education and the acquisition of working skills. The few available records of their worship showed little of the dynamic re-modeling of western Christianity evident in the institution of the black church, but it contained some elements that were remarkable in the light of the Catholic practice at the time. For example, the Holy Family Society of Colored People in Baltimore, a group of some 270 black Catholics who met weekly, on Sunday evening, from December 1843 till September 1845, went beyond the Catholic horizons of the time. Their devotion was quite traditional, but some features stood out. Singing was so important that practice sessions were held during the week. There was spontaneous prayer. There was the usual black concern for proper burial and contributions for masses for the dead. The group maintained a lending library and contributed towards the support of the poor (cf. Davis, 1990: 86-89).

In 1688, the Quakers of Germantown, Pennsylvannia, were the first Christian body to raise a protest against slavery. In 1839, Gregory XVI condemned slavery in his bull, *In Supremo Apostolatus Fastigio* (In the Supreme Labor of the Apostolate). However, in America many bishops and religious orders were slave owners. The First Plenary Council of Baltimore in 1854 ignored the slavery issue. Auguste Marie Martin, made bishop of Nachitoches in north Louisiana in 1853, wrote a Pastoral Letter at the dawn of the Civil War in which he called the faithful to arms *against* the abolitionists. He advocated that blacks being descended from Canaan, were cursed; slavery was therefore a blessing in disguise, God's own plan for the conversion and redemption of the black race (cf. Davis, 1990: 56-57). Martin's missive was put on the Index of Forbidden Books but the Civil War supervened before the author could be made to recant.

The Civil War and Reconstruction

The Civil War began on April 12, 1861 when the Confederate forces attacked Fort Sumter, South Carolina. The southern states argued that slavery was necessary for self-preservation. A regiment of some 10,000 black soldiers served in the continental armies. On January 1, 1863, President Lincoln declared all slaves in rebel areas free. The War ended on April 9, 1865; on December 18 of the same year, the 13th Amendment proscribed slavery. On April 9, 1866, the Civil Rights Bill nullified the Black Codes and recognized the full citizenship of blacks. In most southern states, blacks had majority vote. On March 2, 1867, the Reconstruction Act imposed military rule in the south until governments loyal to the Union could be formed. This lasted until 1877 and was known as the Reconstruction Period. Meanwhile, from 1870 until 1875, a series of southern states introduced "Jim Crow" laws, beginning with the banning of intermarriage in Tennessee. They also imposed segregation in trains, hotels and restaurants, and schools. Gradually, white political control of the south was re-established. The legal and economic condition of blacks deteriorated, leading to mass emigration of blacks to the north and west. In the north, they formed a pool of cheap labor and were used as strike breakers. Lynchings became a common tool of oppression in the south: in the ten years between 1889 and 1899, there were no less than 1,240 lynchings.

In 1896, in *Plessy vs. Ferguson*, the Supreme Court gave the "separate but equal" judgment which legalized the situation in the south. The black response was split. Booker T.Washington advocated success through acceptance of white domination: blacks should seek neither social equality nor a college education, but rather they should apply themselves to the acquisition

▸ **"Booker T. Washington Legend," William H. Johnson, Courtesy National Museum of American Art, Washington, D.C., Art Resource, NY.**

of technical and working skills. He founded the Tuskegee Institute in Alabama for this purpose. William DuBois and a number of black intellectuals, on the contrary, founded the Niagara Movement in 1905, which in 1909 became the National Association for the Advancement of Colored People (NAACP) to fight legal abuse of blacks and to promote their civil rights.

The mass movement of blacks northward created an urgent situation of evangelization. In the north, the black freed slave was uprooted: the black church, a southern phenomenon, was absent.

The black church provided more than spiritual care, it also afforded sickness and burial societies, education and improvement projects of all types. In the north, a variety of religious options, including Catholicism, were open, and many turned to the church. Something needed to be done to address the social and spiritual situation of blacks in general, and black Catholics, in particular. Archbishop Spalding of Baltimore obtained permission for the Second Plenary Council of Baltimore which met in 1866. The bishops could agree neither on separate churches for black Catholics nor on the question of an Ordinary (perhaps a Prefect Apostolic) to be responsible for the care of African Americans. Each bishop, with blacks in his diocese, was to procure his pastoral care in concert with provincial synods. A plea was sent to Europe for missionaries for the evangelization of African Americans. Spalding would call the 10th provincial synod of Baltimore in 1868. It recommended separate churches for blacks and whites, and a vigorous black mission.

The plea for missionaries was speedily heard. In 1866, the Jesuits founded the black parish of St. Ann and a school in Cincinnati. Francis Weninger, a Jesuit, obtained a donation of $4,000 from King Ludwig of Bavaria. Weninger advocated a national collection for Indians and African Americans; this was eventually instituted in the name of the Society for the Propagation of the Faith on the First Sunday of Lent by the Third Plenary Council of Baltimore, 1884 (Davis, 1990: 131). In 1871, the first four members of the Mill Hill Fathers arrived in Baltimore to run the black parish of St. Francis Xavier. The American branch of Mill Hill would separate in 1893 as the Society of St. Joseph of the Sacred Heart (Josephites); their first superior general, Fr. John Slattery, played a pivotal role in promoting the black apostolate. In 1872, the German Spiritans (Congregation of the Holy Spirit) arrived in Kentucky, but later set up their center in Pittsburgh. In 1912, they took over St. Mark's Parish in Harlem, New York as a parish for blacks. In Savannah, the Benedictines opened a parish and industrial school for blacks in 1878. Their monastic community of seven included at various times three African Americans, Siricius Palmer (a cleric who later left), Brother Rbaban Canonge, and Arthur Mason who left them, but would take part in the first Catholic Congress in 1889 (cf. Davis, 1990: 123). Katherine Drexel (canonized in 2000), born in Philadelphia in 1858 of Austrian and German parents, used her entire inheritance for the promotion of Native Americans and blacks. In 1891, she founded the Sisters of the Blessed Sacrament for Indians and Colored People. In 1916,

Mother Theodore Williams cooperated with Fr. Ignatius Lissner, S.M.A., in founding the Handmaids of Mary in Savannah, Georgia.

But if the black apostolate would take off, an urgent need would seem to be a black clergy. The first black priests in the United States had been the three Healy brothers, sons of Michael Morris Healy, an Irishman who settled in Georgia and a light-skinned slave, called Mary Eliza. James Augustine Healy was ordained in Notre Dame, Paris on June 10, 1854 and was named the second bishop of Portland, Maine in 1875, and the first African American Catholic bishop in the United States. Alexander Sherwood Healy studied Canon Law at the Lateran University in Rome and was ordained there in December 1858. Patrick Francis Healy became a Jesuit. He studied in Rome and Louvain and was ordained in 1864. In 1874, he became president of Georgetown University, a university which would not admit African Americans until the success of the Civil Rights Movement in the 1960s! The Healy brothers did not identify with the black cause and generally passed as whites; so recognition as the first black Catholic priest generally goes to Augustus Tolton. Tolton could find no bishop in the United States to admit him, so he learned Latin, Greek, German, English, geography, and ancient and modern European history through tutorials by various German priests. He was then given admission in the Urbiana in Rome in 1880, and was ordained on April 24, 1886. Again he was to have been sent as missionary to Africa because of doubts about his reception in the United States, were it not that Cardinal Simeoni of the Propaganda insisted: "America has been called the most enlightened nation; we will see if it deserves that honor. If America has never seen a black priest, it has to see one now" (Davis, 1990: 155). Tolton started a black parish at Quincy, but had to move to Chicago because of tension with some priests since many whites were coming to his church. He founded the parish of St. Monica in 1894, the first black Catholic church in Chicago. In 1925, St. Monica combined with St. Elizabeth as "mother church" of the black Catholic community in Chicago.

In 1888, Fr. Slattery opened St. Joseph's seminary in Baltimore to train whites and blacks for the ordained ministry among African Americans. The first black Josephite was Fr. Charles Uncles, who was ordained in Baltimore in 1891. In 1893, the Mill Hill Fathers in the United States would separate as Josephites, entirely dedicated to the evangelization of African Americans.

▸ "Daniel Rudd," Courtesy of The National Black Catholic Congress, Baltimore, MD.

The glorious chapter in African American Catholic history is the leadership given by an active black Catholic laity, often against opposition, or at best neglect, by most of the hierarchy. Against the backdrop of segregation and "Jim Crow" laws, the Holy Spirit stirred Daniel Rudd, born in Bardstown, Kentucky in 1854, to engineer the First Black Catholic Congress, January 1-4, 1889. This was the very year that the bishops founded the Catholic University of America in Washington. After the Civil War, Rudd moved to Springfield, Ohio, where in 1886 he began a weekly paper called the *American Catholic Tribune*. He used this paper to trail the growth of lynching and segregation laws, and also to argue that the Catholic church was the best hope of the black person. All American bishops were invited to the Congress; all black Catholic societies and each black parish were to send one delegate for every 500 members. Rudd was elected president. In his speech he outlined the need for schools, for training in labor skills and for family virtues. The Congress decried the discrimination in renting of property and appealed to factory owners to give employment without racial discrimination (cf. Davis, 1990: 173). The Congress Movement continued in Cincinnati in July 1890, Philadelphia in January 1892, Chicago in September 1893, and Baltimore in 1894. It would not be revived till the 6th Congress in 1987, the 7th in July 1992, and the 8th in August 1997, but then under close episcopal supervision and management. At the 3rd Congress held in Philadelphia in 1892, Rudd spoke of the attrition wrought by the imprisonment of black youth for long terms for minor offenses. A delegate called for a moratorium on churches for blacks and the construction of more schools. It was clear that the black school fulfilled a double aim: evangelization and the necessary ushering of black youth into American society. The 4th Congress appointed a Committee of Grievances. It regretted the neglect of the evangelization of blacks

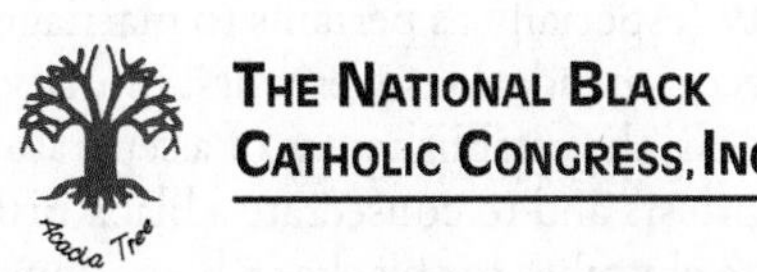

▸ Logo of the National Black Catholic Congress

who had emigrated from the south, while on the contrary Protestants from the north were flooding the south with colleges and industrial schools for blacks. In 1909, some Josephite pastors in Mobile, Alabama, cooperated in founding the Knights of St. Peter Claver as a charitable and insurance society for black Catholics (the Knights of Columbus had been founded for whites in 1884).

Initiative now passed to the Congregation of the Propagation of the Faith in Rome. America was treated as a mission country until 1908. The report of the Committee of Grievances was at hand; also circulating was a pamphlet in Latin published in 1903 in Namur, Belgium by Fr. Joseph Anciaux, entitled, *The Miserable Condition of Black Catholics in America*. It depicted the social situation and the general prejudice of the clergy, and the refusal to admit blacks to Catholic schools, colleges and universities. Except for two bishops, none of the hierarchy was bold enough to defend the rights of blacks. In fact, John Marion Laval, vice general of New Orleans, was quoted as being of the opinion that "in America no black man should be ordained. Just as illegitimate sons are declared irregular in Canon Law...so blacks can be declared irregular because they are held in such contempt by whites" (Davis, 1990: 197). This contrasted sharply with the fact that at the time both the Protestant churches and the black church had thousands of black clergy. Under Roman pressure, the bishops, in 1907, created the Catholic Board of Negro Missions with Fr. John Burke of the New York diocese as the first director. Burke's report (1913), at the instance of the Apostolic Delegation, outlined the following obstacles to the conversion of blacks: lack of priests (there were only four black priests in the United States); secret societies which blacks joined for the insurance benefits; lack of trust between white priests and blacks; and low standards of morality (especially as pertains to marriage) (Davis, 1990: 201-202). His recommendations were: first priority was to be given to Catholic schools; the establishment of a separate college and seminary for black priests and to consecrate a black bishop as soon as possible; separate churches for blacks (who no longer accepted segregated seating in white churches); and permission for converts to retain membership of secret societies (which did not pose the same threat to the church as white secret societies). The church should also create similar financial societies for blacks.

Another tract by John Albert, a Josephite, suggested reviving the permanent diaconate so black married deacons could take charge of particular communities under white priests. He pointed to the massive withdrawal of blacks, especially light-skinned blacks, from the church in Louisiana and the Gulf coast. The delegate reported to the Cardinal Prefect of the Propagation of the Faith in May 1914. He did not agree with a special jurisdiction for black Catholics nor with the retention of membership of secret societies. He did not favor the ordination of blacks for it was a "fact confirmed by experience" that blacks preferred white priests who were considered to be "from a superior race and hence had greater trust placed in them" (Davis, 1990: 206). Cardinal De Lai in his reply recommended, among other things: that catechists be encouraged and developed; schools be increased; hospitals and diverse associations, even of an economic nature, be established for the exclusive needs of blacks. However, all efforts were to be under the exclusive direction of the bishops.

The Age of Black Power and Black Civil Rights

The massive exodus of blacks from the south to the north continued during the First World War. In the north, they found jobs in the munitions factories and were free of some of the ugly elements of racial discrimination. In 1915, the weevil devastation of cotton led to the exodus of 350,000 blacks from the south within a year and a half. The end of the First World War and the return of black G.I.'s precipitated a black consciousness movement leading to great interracial strife. In 1919 alone, there were twenty-five riots and seventy-five lynchings. A movement of black pride was to blossom in the 1920s known as the "Harlem Renaissance." The Immigration Act of 1924 pretty much shut the borders, in particular excluding blacks of African descent from entering the country. In the same year, the Ku Klux Klan in America had a membership of five million (Brophy/Westenhaver, 1978: 102). On May 17, 1954, by nine to zero, in *Brown vs. Board of Education* (of Topeka) the Supreme Court declared "separate but equal" educational facilities "inherently unequal." The following year, Rosa Parks refused to sit in the back of a bus; four days later, Martin Luther King, Jr., organized the Montgomery Bus Boycott, and the Civil Rights Movement was afoot. The Civil Rights Bill was signed in 1964 and the Voting Rights Bill on May 26, 1965.

Thomas Wyatt Turner was born in 1877 in Charles County, Maryland; he became professor of biology at Howard University. During the First World War, the Knights of Columbus cared for white soldiers. Turner brought together a group of five black laymen, made a representation to the War Council, and secured pastoral care for black soldiers. The original group of laymen increased to twenty-five by 1919 to form the Committee for the

Advancement of Colored Catholics (patterned on the NAACP). In 1924, they developed into the Federated Colored Catholics, with the goal of uniting black Catholics, increasing Catholic education for blacks, raising the position of blacks within the church, and ensuring the greater participation of black Catholics in the fight for racial justice. Turner complained to the Apostolic Delegate about the policy of Catholic University to reject applications from blacks (changing its original open policy). The result was that black sisters could not attend summer school to improve themselves. He also decried the continued neglect of Catholic education for black children (cf. Davis, 1990: 218-219). Two Jesuits had collaborated with Turner, William Markoe and John LaFarge. In 1932 they differed about the aims of the society, with a faction under LaFarge opting for promoting interracial relations instead of the fight for justice, and becoming the National Interracial Federation. Turner's group continued until 1952.

Many American bishops still refused to admit blacks into the seminary or ordain black priests. The Josephites after some time seemed to have put a hold on black vocations. Father Slattery opened a school for black catechists near Montgomery, Alabama, which he hoped would blossom into a preparatory seminary. It failed and was closed in 1921. In 1920, the Divine Word Missionaries opened a seminary for blacks in Greensville, Mississippi which in 1923 moved to Bay St. Louis. In 1958, a Pastoral Letter of the American bishops condemned racial discrimination for the first time.

The Abiding Question: 1960s to the Present

The aftermath of the Second World War was to affect both the nation and the church profoundly. The exodus from the south continued: from 1940 to 1970 it totaled 4.4 million. The G.I. Bill of Rights guaranteed a free college education to ex-servicemen. The mass education of former immigrants moved the church towards the mainstream, from an immigrant church to an American church. It also had an effect in the black community. For blacks, the opportunity to attend college became the most important factor in achieving middle class status. A black middle class began to develop and with it, a certain fragmentation of the black community. For some middle class blacks, "integration ...means the loss of racial identity" (Frazier, 1963: 82). They tend to reject identification with Africa, wanting to be just Americans. For them the church is no longer the center of social life as it is for the lower classes. Frazier remarked that such

▸ "The Library," Jacob Lawrence, Courtesy National Museum of American Art, Washington, D.C. Art Resource, NY.

middle class blacks have been joining the Catholic church as well as the Presbyterian and Episcopal churches. A force in these conversions has been the acclaimed excellence of Catholic education. Many inner-city Catholic schools for blacks generally have a majority of non-Catholics, and some of these become interested in the Catholic faith.

The 1960s and 1970s saw a veritable Black Revolution. Stokely Carmichael articulated the concept of "Black Power" in 1966. Departments of Black Studies began to proliferate in colleges and universities. In 1969, James Cone published *Black Theology and Black Power*. In Gary, Indiana, in 1972, the first National Black Political Convention produced a National Black Political Agenda, although opinions were divided. There was a continuing racial divide in America as the passage of Proposition 209 banning Affirmative Action in California on November 7, 1996, indicated.

The Second Vatican Council of 1962-65 had allowed fresh winds to blow in the church. Further, black Catholics could not be isolated from the ferment of Black Power and the struggle for Civil Rights going on in the society. In April 1968, in Detroit, black priests formed the National Black Catholic Clergy Caucus. Among their demands of the hierarchy was that black priests be placed to work directly with the black community and that greater efforts be made to recruit black men for the priesthood; white priests who work in the black community should be given formation in black ministry; funds should be set aside on a permanent basis for leadership training of black laypersons; bishops should choose black persons, including married ones, for the permanent diaconate; and a department should be opened in the National Episcopal Conference for the Affairs of African Americans (cf. Cone/Wilmore, 1996: 231-232). In other words, they served notice that it was time to recognize and promote black Catholicism as a contribution to the very catholicity of the church. Not long afterwards, the National Black Sisters Conference was formed. In 1971, the National Office of Black Catholics was established in Washington, D.C. by Br. Joseph M. Davis, S.M. The Black Catholic Theological Symposium was founded in 1978 by Thaddeus Posey, O.F.M. Cap. (*Theology: A Portrait in Black,* 1980) and re-established in 1991 by Sr. Jamie Phelps, O.P. In 1984, the black bishops of the United States issued a Pastoral Letter, *What We Have Seen and Heard*. The schism of George Stallings, a black priest of the Washington archdiocese, who in 1989 founded the Imani Temple for authentic African American worship, has only made the quest for an authentically black Catholic experience more urgent. Islam, especially the Nation of Islam, has proved very effective in redirecting youth through their prison and street ministries, showing thereby a vast field of evangelization for the church. Over twenty-five percent of African American youth have a brush with the law which results in incarceration; heavy and relatively long sentences are given for minor crimes, keeping the industry of prison construction booming. In 1991, the Secretariat for Black Catholics issued *Plenty Good Room: The Spirit and Truth of African American Catholic Worship*. This document, while accepting diversity in the African American Catholic experience, nevertheless outlines the elements of an African American worship: "to be Catholic is to be universal. To be universal is not to be uniform" (no. 46). There is *room* in the Catholic church for African American worship.

Conclusion

At the end of this survey, it is clear that the black Catholic community in the United States finds itself at a crossroads. Many of the issues and debates raised in the history are still with us. Some of the most pressing questions can be sifted from a document

(*Summoned by the Holy Spirit–A Call to New Life*) prepared for the Black Catholic Convention of the Archdiocese of Chicago which was held in November 2000. The current number of black Catholics, African and African American, in the United States is difficult to estimate because they are not found only in predominantly black parishes. However, the Gallup Survey and *The New York Times,* July 15, 1989 gave the figure as 2 million, being 8.4% of Catholics (Lincoln/Mamiya, 1990: 407). It is possible that since then, with the influx of blacks from Africa and the Caribbean, and allowing for natural growth, the figure may now be more than 2.5 million.

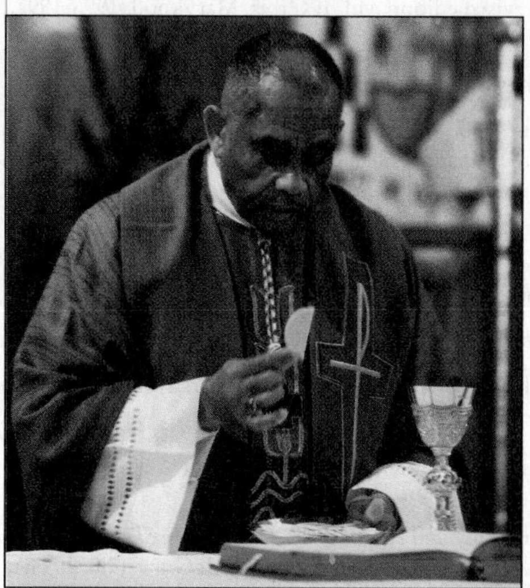

▸ **Catholic Communion, Courtesy UNIPHOTO Picture Agency, Washington, D.C.**

Although the number of black Catholics in Chicago is estimated at 100,000, there is a dearth of Catholic clergy in general, and an even smaller number of African Americans in particular. Statistics show that in 1995, no African American Catholic seminarians were enrolled in undergraduate study, and only one (along with three Africans) was enrolled in Mundelein Major Seminary. Similarly, using the Chicago Archdiocese as an example, the number of Catholic schools has declined, with the number of black Catholic students comprising only about fifteen percent of the elementary and secondary school population (nbccongress.org/facts/statistics).

It is evident that the upward movement of the black community into the middle class has strengthened the black Protestant churches, especially the mega churches, which seem to be the attraction for the 1980s and 1990s. Becoming a Catholic would seem to be no longer representative of upward mobility nor an enhancement of black identity. Blacks looking for identification with black enterprise tend to join the churches of the black tradition (*Summoned by the Spirit*: 15-19). This suggests that the present task is that of a search for a Catholic experience that is at the same time authentically African American.

Selected Bibliography

Robert J. Bennett, "Black Experience and the Bible," *Theology Today* 27 (1970-71) 422-433.

Black Bishops of the United States, *What We Have Seen and Heard*, Pastoral Letter on Evangelization, September 9, 1984. St. Anthony Messenger Press, 1984.

Don Brophy and Edythe Westenhaver, *The Story of Catholics in America*, Paulist Press, New York, 1978.

James Cone and Gayraud Wilmore, Black Theology: A Documentary History, second revised edition, vol. 1, Orbis, Maryknoll, 1996-1997.

Cyprian Davis, *The History of Black Catholics in the United States*, Crossroad Publishing Co., New York, 1990.

Cyprian Davis, "God of Our Weary Years: Black Catholics in American Catholic History," Diana Hayes and Cyprian Davis, eds., *Taking Down Our Harps: Black Catholics in the United States*, Orbis, N.Y., 1998.

Cyprian Davis, "Roman Catholicism," in Larry G. Murphy et al., *Encyclopaedia of African American Religions*, Garland Publishing, Inc., N.Y. and London, 1993, 656-660.

Jay Dolan, *The American Catholic Experience*, Doubleday, New York, 1985.

John Tracy Ellis, *American Catholicism*, University of Chicago Press, 1956, second revised edition, 1969.

John Tracy Ellis, ed., *Documents of American Catholic History*, 3 vols. Michael Glazier, Wilmington, Delaware, 1987.

John Hope Franklin, and Alfred A.Moss, Jr., *From Slavery to Freedom: A History of African Americans*, seventh edition, McGraw-Hill, 1994.

E. Franklin Frazier, *The Negro Church in America*, Shocken Books, New York, 1963.

Peter Guilday, ed., *The National Pastorals of the American Hierarchy* (1792-1919), National Catholic Welfare Council, Washington, 1923.

Vincent Harding, "Religion and Resistance Among Antebellum Slaves,1800-1860," in Raboteau and Fulop, eds., *African American Religion*, Routledge, New York and London, 1997, 107-130.

Diana Hayes, "We Have Come This Far by Faith: Black Catholics and Their Church," Diana Hayes and Cyprian Davis, eds., *Taking Down Our Harps: Black Catholics in the United States*, Orbis, N.Y., 1998, 1-14.

Diana Hayes and Cyprian Davis, eds., *Taking Down Our Harps: Black Catholics in the United States*, Orbis, N.Y., 1998.

James Hennessy, *American Catholics: A History of the Roman Catholic Community in the United States*, Oxford University Press, N.Y., 1981.

C. Eric Lincoln, "The Development of Black Religion in America," *Review and Expositor*, 70 (1973) 295-308.

C. Eric Lincoln and Lawrence H.Mamiya, *The Black Church in African American Experience*, Duke University Press, Durham and London, 1990.

Charles H. Long, "Perspectives for a Study of African-American Religion in the United States," *History of Religions* 11 (1971) 54-66.

Sidney W. Mintz and Richard Price, *The Birth of African-American Culture: An Anthropological Perspective*, Beacon Press, Boston, 1992.

Peter J. Paris, "The Bible and the Black Churches," Ernest R.Sandeen, ed., *The Bible and Social Reform*, Fortress Press, Philadelphia, 1982, 133-154.

Jamie Phelps, "*Black Spirituality*," Diana Hayes and Cyprian Davis, eds., *Taking Down Our Harps: Black Catholics in the United States*, Orbis, N.Y., 1998, 179-198.

Jamie Phelps, ed., *Black and Catholic: The Challenge and Gift of Black Folk*, Marquette University Press, 1997.

Jamie Phelps, "African American Catholics: The Struggles, Contributions and Gifts of a Marginalized Community," *Black and Catholic: The Challenge and Gift of Black Folk*, Marquette University Press, 1997, 19-42.

Plenty Good Room: The Spirit and Truth of African American Catholic Worship, Secretariat for Black Catholics, National Conference of Catholic Bishops, 1990.

Albert J. Raboteau, *Slave Religion: The "Invisible Institution" in the Antebellum South*, Oxford University Press, 1978.

Albert J. Raboteau, "Minority Within a Minority: The History of Black Catholics in America," *A Fire in My Bones: Reflections on African American Religious History*, Beacon Press, Boston, 1995, 117-137.

Albert J. Raboteau, "The Black Church: Continuity Within Change," *A Fire in My Bones: Reflections on African American Religious History*, Beacon Press, Boston, 1995, 103-116.

Albert J. Raboteau and Timothy E. Fulop, eds., *African American Religion*, Routledge, N.Y. and London, 1997.

"*Summoned by the Holy Spirit—A Call to New Life*," Archdiocese of Chicago, Black Catholic Convocation, Nov. 3-4, 2000.

Theology: A Portrait in Black, Proceedings of the Black Catholic Theological Symposium, 1978. National Black Catholic Clergy Caucus, 1980.

Joseph R. Washington, "Folk Religion and Negro Congregations: The Fifth Religion," *Black Religion*, 1964, 30-42.

G.S.Wilmore, *African American Religious Studies: An Interdisciplinary Anthology*, Duke University Press, Durham and London, 1989.

G.S. Wilmore, *Black Religion and Black Radicalism: An Interpretation of the Religious History of Afro-American People*, second revised and enlarged edition, Orbis, Maryknoll, 1983.

Vincent L. Wimbush, "The Bible and African Americans: An Outline of an Interpretive History," Cain Hope Felder, ed., *Stony the Road We Trod: African American Biblical Interpretation*, Fortress Press, Minneapolis, 1991, 81-97.

Twelve

Ethiopia Shall Stretch Forth Her Arms: The Evangelization and Education of African American Catholics

Diana L. Hayes

For the Catholic church, evangelization has, historically, been not only the means of introducing others to the faith, but of providing basic literacy skills as well. This understanding can be seen in the efforts the church undertook, both during and after slavery, to educate persons of African descent. Although records reveal that education, both religious and secular, was provided as early as the 17th century in the Americas, racism, lack of finance and teachers, played a critical role in limiting educational efforts until well into the 19th century. Today, however, the Catholic church in the United States is one of the leading educators of persons of African descent, Catholic and non-Catholic. It has been successful in guiding students, especially those from the inner-city, from grade school through college. A critical factor in this success has been the leadership of black religious women who fought overwhelming obstacles to found and staff schools throughout the country.

(The reference to Ethiopia in the title of the article is based on Psalm 68.31.)

"Phillip the Deacon Baptizes the Eunuch of the Queen of Ethiopia," Theodore Chasseriau, Courtesy SuperStock.

The history of Catholics of African descent in the United States is intertwined with the histories of both the United States itself and the Catholic church in the U.S. It is a history of oppression and perseverance as black Catholics struggled for recognition of their humanity and for acceptance in both church and society. Their persistent presence is a testimony of faith that serves as a constant challenge to the church to live up to the liberating gospel message of Christ, Savior of all who believe in him, regardless of race, ethnicity or gender. The narrative of how African American Catholics have been evangelized–taught the faith, and educated, and taught intellectual, trade, and manual skills–reveals both human failings and the working of the Holy Spirit in their lives and the lives of those with whom they interacted.

An Historical Journey

The African presence in the Catholic church is not recent but dates back to the earliest beginnings of Christianity. As revealed in Acts 8.26-40, a black man (identified by the Greek word, *ethiope*, meaning "burnt face" or "dark-skinned") was the first Gentile convert to the Christian faith. With his conversion begins the almost 2,000-year association between Christianity, in its various expressions, and Africa. From this association, the East African churches of Ethiopia, Egypt, and Nubia, emerged as well as many of the early Church Fathers such as Augustine (354–430), Tertullian (c.160–c.225) and Origen (c.185–c.254), all of whom were defenders of Christianity, and a host of martyrs and saints (Davis, pp. 10ff). The church in West Africa became influential in the 15th and later centuries for it is here that the ancestors of most African Americans can be found. Catholic Christianity was introduced in the West by the Portuguese who were instrumental in the establishment of what became its most profitable business endeavor, the Atlantic Slave Trade. This was done initially with the cooperation of local African rulers already familiar with slavery in their lands as a result of war and poverty. They were unprepared, however, and opposed, often to their and their peoples' peril, the massive drainage of men, women, and children which took place over the next three hundred or more years and resulted in the collapse and destruction of peoples, cultures, and traditions.

King Afonso of the Congo (1506–1543) was a devout Catholic ruler who sought to bring his people into the church "and to profit from the technological knowledge of the Europeans"

(Davis, p. 16). However, his efforts to have his people evangelized and educated were often thwarted by the desire of his fellow Christians for "black gold" regardless of the costs to his country. Afonso quickly learned that his faith and that of his people did not make them the equals of their Portuguese benefactors. He sought to establish the Catholic church in his kingdom, independent of the Europeans, and to do so sent his eldest son, Henrique, to study for the priesthood in Portugal. Henrique was ordained and later installed as Bishop in the Congo but died prematurely. With his death and the continuing rise of the slave trade, the hope of an independent Congolese church died (Davis, p.18).

> In the end, slavery meant the undoing of all that Afonso had tried to accomplish. It must be admitted that Afonso had agreed from the beginning to supply slaves as part of the regular trade agreement. Slavery was found in practically all of the African civilizations. The African form of slavery resulted primarily from being captured in war or being punished for crimes. It might be said on Afonso's behalf that he probably did not know that slavery in Portugal meant something other than the kind of slavery found in Africa. The king soon found out that the appetite for slaves was insatiable. He found out also that nothing would stop the Portuguese from expanding the slave trade, even if it meant seizing Afonso's own people, and even members of his family (Davis, p.17).

The Catholic church gave not only Africa (1452), but also the Americas and the Caribbean (1493), to the Kings of Portugal and Spain and gave them permission to enslave their inhabitants who were viewed as pagans. Many Africans became Christian but were not spared capture and enslavement because slavery was seen as a "natural state" in accordance with the natural law of God, which could not be changed. It was believed everyone had a particular role and status that was ordained by God, and persons of African descent soon found themselves ordained to be servants in perpetuity to the Europeans.

The millions of Africans stolen from Africa were followers of traditional African religions, of Islam, and of Christianity. However, they usually found themselves enslaved by plantation owners who gave little thought to their former faith and either left them unchurched or, especially in the North American colonies, introduced them to Protestant Christianity. It is the history of African American Protestants that we are most familiar with in the United States because that is the faith of most of the founders. However, many Africans were and remained Roman Catholic, or even became Catholic, after being enslaved because they were on Catholic plantations or had Catholic owners some of whom were religious, and priests (See Hayes, Ch. 2).

This history starts earlier than that of the eastern colonies. It is a history of the French and Spanish settlements of the southwest and west, as well as Louisiana and Florida. It begins in the 16th century with a black Catholic scout, Estevanico, who, with the Spanish conquistadors, helped to open up what became the country of Mexico. It is not known whether he was a slave or free man, but well-kept baptismal records reveal that blacks, both free and slave, were instrumental not only in exploring the Americas, but in establishing such cities as St. Augustine, FL and Los Angeles, CA. It appears that in these early settlements, issues of race and skin color, though present, were of lesser significance than in the east.

▸ "Field Workers," Ellis Wilson, Courtesy National Museum of American Art, Washington, D.C./Art Resource, NY.

Church records document that blacks and whites lived and worked together, intermarried, and were baptized and confirmed within the church. They also show that in the latter part of the 17th century, in Louisiana, French Catholics provided education for all laborers, regardless of race.

It has been asserted that because of the sacramental nature of the Roman Catholic church, slavery was less harsh in Catholic colonies. Marriage was a sacrament that had to be honored and therefore families could not be split, husband or wife separated, children sold away. The reality, of course, is that slavery in any form is a denial of the dignity that all humans possess through their creation by God. Thus, even though the church affirmed the humanity of African peoples, it still denied them self-determination. As noted earlier, a hierarchy of status existed which many Catholic slaveholders were able to exploit to their economic benefit. The sacraments, especially that of marriage, were often denied or, citing a greater (usually financial) good, overlooked.

The colony of Maryland, the only English-speaking colony founded by Roman Catholics, is an example of what came to be an entrenched dualistic perspective which separated the spiritual and sacred realm from that of the material and secular. Thus, one's actual physical status was irrelevant as long as one's soul had been saved. Although the church insisted on the baptism and catechizing of all slaves, many Catholic slave owners felt that the status of the slaves put them outside the realm of the Divine. Owning a fellow Catholic was not seen as a conflict of faith since slaveowners quickly pointed out the beneficial aspects for both master and slave as the former profited from the slave's labor and the slave was exposed to the "civilizing" influences of Christianity. The long and rich history of the African presence and the contributions of people of African descent to the church were either ignored or, for the most part, unknown. Christianity and sacred Scripture were used to justify a social, economic, and political institution–slavery–whose negative aspects, racism, persist to this day. Evangelization and education became a means to an end, the pacification and civilizing of a labor force.

Despite the harshly negative ways in which African slaves and their descendants were introduced to Christianity in the Americas, many accepted the faith and their descendants maintain it to the present day. However, their understanding of Christianity and the Jesus to whom they prayed was critically different from that which was being taught to them. Although they were taught to see themselves as intended for eternal servitude, the African slaves were able, instead, to recognize and be affirmed by a God who created them as well as their masters, as free human beings. Jesus, for them, was the Savior who promised not just spiritual but physical freedom as well. They saw themselves, in many ways, as a leaven within the church, a witness to its failures and a challenge to its complacency. In this belief, they were eventually joined by the Vatican, which condemned their enslavement and sought to convert the hearts and minds of their fellow Catholics on their behalf, but too often with little success until well into the 20th century.

Evangelization and Catholic Education: Before 1900

Evangelization means the spreading of the Word of God by teaching the foundational beliefs of Christianity. Historically, it meant spreading the New Testament message of Jesus Christ and his life, death, and resurrection. Evangelization was a means of educating people not simply about their faith, but how to live that faith in their own cultures and worlds. For the slaves, the rudiments of the faith were often coupled with education in manual skills and basic literacy in order to help them to understand the Christian message in its various forms. However, little effort was made to evangelize and educate slaves in any organized or institutionalized form until the latter part of the 19th century. The exceptions were in Maryland and Louisiana where two pioneering black women's religious communities whose vocation was the education of black children, slave and free, were founded.

The first of these communities was the Oblate Sisters of Providence founded in 1829 in Baltimore, Maryland, under the guidance of Sulpician Fr. Jacques Joubert. The founders were Mary Elizabeth Lange, Marie Balas, Rosine Boegue, and Almeide Duchemin Maxis, free women of color, from the island of Santo Domingo. These four courageous women came together in 1828 to found the Colored School, which later became St. Frances Academy for girls, (which currently exists as a co-ed school). The Academy had both boarders and day students and was open to Catholics and non-Catholics alike, an openness that today remains a mark of Catholic schools. It was the first successful black Catholic school in the United States and served as a model for all others. Mother Lange, who became the first Superior General of the Oblates, strongly believed that the only way to strengthen African Americans in their faith was to provide them with a strong foundation in basic reading, writing, domestic science, and other skills. In this way, they would hopefully be prepared to move from lives of domestic drudgery, which was the fate of most black women, free or slave, into higher callings, including the religious life.

> While experiencing poverty, racism and untold hardships, the Oblate Sisters labored to evangelize the black Catholic community through Catholic education. The Sisters opened and staffed schools for young people, conducted night classes for women, provided homes for widows and orphans, offered vocational and career training, opened a free school for children whose parents could not afford Catholic education and started an institution for Civil War orphans (Geddes/USCH, p. 83).

Often opposed by those in positions of leadership in the church, shunned and ridiculed by their fellow Catholics who refused to accept black women in religious garb, the Oblate Sisters of Providence persevered in their efforts to provide an educational foundation for black Catholic men, women, and children. By the end of the 19th century, they had founded schools and orphanages not only in Baltimore but also in Philadelphia (where it was illegal to teach blacks in public schools), St. Louis, and New Orleans. Often their success depended not only on their own resourcefulness but also on the support, financial and otherwise, and leadership of the black Catholic community in which they lived. They also sought benefactors from within the broader Catholic community:

> In order to sustain and protect themselves, these women religious created alliances and political affiliations with white women and men (both lay and clerical), with wealthy and well-situated free persons of color, and with a few influential members of the hierarchy, in order to receive legal and social support for their endeavors.
>
> In many places, these black women religious built long-lasting institutions of educational benevolence and social development that are the Catholic equivalent of the great institutions created by the black Protestant churches (Brown, p. 146).

▸ "Men exist for the sake of one another. Teach them then or bear with them." Jacob Lawence, Courtesy National Museum of American Art, Washington, D.C./Art Resource, NY.

The Sisters believed so strongly in their calling to serve their own people that, after the Civil War when many whites urged them to stop teaching former slaves, they persevered on their own. "One of the greatest pains for us after emancipation was that those owners who had previously sent their slaves to us to be instructed wished us to refuse to give them any more lessons. But that was asking too much of our sisters when our dear Lord said, 'Go and teach all nations.' And we as sisters are more obliged than others to teach all to know their God. And the day that we would refuse would be the day of sin for us, for our dear Lord said in another place that He had not come for the just but to save sinners. This would have been preaching one thing and practicing another, for the rich have many friends when they have money. We would work in vain if we were to seek to please them and to neglect the poor, for he that is in health has no need of a doctor" (Brown, p. 144).

The second black women's religious congregation, the Sisters of the Holy Family, was founded in New Orleans around1842 by Henriette Delille. They also saw their mission to be the education of black children and service to the needy, regardless of faith. In time, they too founded schools throughout Louisiana and eventually, like their sisters in Baltimore, throughout the nation, serving in black parishes at parochial schools on every level. They survived and thrived in the face of countless challenges to their faith and obstacles set in their path.

Evangelization and Catholic Education: After 1900

At the Second Plenary Conference of Catholic Bishops, held in Baltimore in 1866, a major topic of discussion was the evangelization and continued education of the freed slaves. The Vatican took the lead once again and argued for a concerted effort to be made to ensure that black Catholics would not be lost to the church. Most of the Bishops, however, were not supportive of the proposed apostolic prefecture, which would have established a vicar especially for black Catholics. Instead, each agreed to develop programs within their respective dioceses.

Sadly, the church in the United States was not exempt from the racism that burdened the entire country. Many Bishops did little to encourage Catholics of African descent who sought to join the church or remain in it. With limited resources and manpower, it was felt that more attention should be paid to the ever-growing population of European immigrants who were themselves in danger of faltering in their faith. Encouragement and some support was given, however, by some Bishops to missionary congregations to become active in the black communities, and many did. Some were American branches of already-established organizations such as the Society of Jesus (Jesuits), while others were founded with a specific mission to the black Catholic apostolate, such as the Society of St. Joseph (Josephites), the Society of the Divine Word, the Holy Ghost Fathers (Spiritans) and others.

▸ Founder of the Sisters of the Blessed Sacrament, Saint Katherine Drexel, Courtesy Josephite Archives.

The same was true of women's religious orders, most importantly the Sisters of the Blessed Sacrament founded in 1890 by Saint Katherine Drexel (who was canonized on October 1, 2000), a wealthy heiress from Philadelphia.

These missionary outreach efforts were both burdensome and beneficial in their approach to the evangelization and education of African Americans. For the most part they were developed to support and maintain black Catholic communities. Like the black women's orders, but unlike the black Sisters, they often fell victim to the common beliefs of their times regarding African Americans. Thus, while encouraging blacks to attain education, they often restricted the scope of that education assuming their parishioners were not intellectually capable of achieving higher levels of education or were not morally or emotionally fit for religious life or the priesthood. The education offered, both religious and secular, was Eurocentric in content and often patronizing in expression.

African Americans were the recipients of missionary evangelization and, as such, were directed into worship communities that were deemed appropriate by external determinants. Often the best and most humane compromise black Catholics could expect, in the face of being treated "worse than heathens" was the establishment of a separate chapel for their use, to be staffed by the same clerics who pastored in the "real" (white) church. Such oppressive treatment ranged from segregated worship spaces, to the segregation of cemeteries, to the withholding of adequate instruction and to the absence of compassionate and consistent pastoral care (Brown, p. 135).

At the same time, however, these "segregated" parishes, which were very similar to the national (ethnic) parishes the church established throughout the U.S. (although the former were never acknowledged as such), and the segregated schools, were beneficial to the development of strong black Catholic communities. They served as sites of transformation and affirmation for a people ostracized and discriminated against in both their church and the American society at large. The schools served not just as places of religious and secular education, but as training grounds for leadership within the black community and, over time, as incubators for black vocations to the religious life and priesthood. Black Catholic parishes and schools were safe havens where, as in the black Protestant churches, black Catholics could engage in religious, social, intellectual, and even political activities without being overly concerned about the perceptions and approval of others. Many of the schools and parishes were built without the financial support of the local church, but with the blood, sweat, and tears of the faithful themselves. From them emerged sodalities and societies such as the Knights and Ladies of St. Peter Claver and the Knights and Ladies of St. John. They were the foundation for the thriving black Catholic communities of today.

Evangelization and Education Today

The twin pillars of evangelization and a Catholic education still serve, despite the obstacles that had to be overcome, not just the black Catholic community, but the greater black community today, as black Christians begin to recognize the ties that bind them together as people of faith. The foundations laid in the past, the recognition of the need for on-going education, not just in the faith but across the board, has been a constant. The openness to, and acceptance of, all blacks, both Catholic and non-Catholic, was always present as was the recognition that black sisters, brothers and priests were necessary to serve as role models and to provide hope and encouragement at every level.

In the late 1800s, five lay Black Catholic Congresses were held, forerunners of the contemporary National Black Catholic Congress Movement. Then, as now, the representatives at these Congresses called for the church's support in evangelizing and educating black Catholics, grounding their demands not in benevolence but in conscience. It was the responsibility of the church, they asserted, to care and provide for the well-being of all of its members regardless of race, ethnicity, class or gender, as all were created in the image and likeness of God, and therefore shared in the same humanity and dignity. The demand was for all forms of education, manual, industrial, and intellectual. These lay leaders recognized that there were many paths to success for persons of African descent. Not only were teachers and preachers needed but also farmers, laborers, mechanics, and industrial workers so that they could gain independence from the confines of American society.

> (Dr. William S. Lofton) spoke to the issue of education, affirming, "I dare today to insist upon the education, manual, industrial, and intellectual of our down-trodden race." Discussing these three types of education, Lofton spoke of the necessity of creating schools for black youth in all three areas. His point was that most trade unions were closed to blacks and apprenticeship in a trade was therefore practically inaccessible. Schools of the manual arts might be the only way to open up certain trades to black workers....Lofton deplored the fact that the Catholic Church provided few schools for black children. "The Church teaches that we must send our children to Catholic schools. We value our religion and Catholic training; we marvel that the Divines of the Church do not support their teaching by having Catholic colleges and schools open their doors to at least those of our Colored children who are well behaved and able to pay." Since this is the state of affairs, he went on to say, "It behooves us for the love of God, our race and children, to establish schools of a high order ourselves" (Davis, p. 175-176).

And this they proceeded to do and have continued to do to the present day, but not with the support of their church.

Today, black Catholics continue to challenge the Roman Catholic church to live up to its social justice and gospel teachings. As a result of the Great Migration of the 1930s and 1940s, which saw an overwhelming shift in the black population from south to north, mid-west and west, the need for expansion of black parishes and schools rapidly increased. Yet many black Catholics, both "cradle" and convert, were greeted with hostility rather than open arms by their fellow immigrant Catholics. Once again, the local church failed them, but they were undeterred. Again, they built their own parishes and schools and invited their

▸ "The 1920's... The Migrants Cast Their Ballots." Jacob Lawrence. Courtesy The Newark Museum, Newark, NJ/Art Resource, NY.

black sisters in the Oblate, Holy Family, and Franciscan Handmaid (a newer group founded in the 1900s) communities to maintain them and teach; they encouraged black vocations and raised up lay leaders for the church. Many of these parishes still exist today.

Confronted with old and new challenges of financial shortfalls, racial prejudice, and general ignorance about them and their history in the church, the constant call of black Catholics for recognition and affirmation as truly black and authentically Catholic, is finally being heard. African American Catholics are reclaiming their history, both in the church and in the United States. They are calling for a re-orientation in evangelization and Catholic education in keeping with their self-affirmation as a people both black and Catholic. They see themselves as a people who have "come of age" in their church and must now move forward. They are a witness to the changes taking place within the church and the United States where persons of color are becoming the majority, thereby challenging the status quo.

Black Catholics are calling for the inculturation of their faith into their culture and traditions, a reclamation of the African roots of the church universally and locally as well as a recognition of their ongoing black presence and the world-view that presence has fostered.

> The nature and purpose of catechesis is to pass on the tradition of the Christ-event, the "story" of God's love as manifested in salvation history, and to do it in such a manner that students and seekers of truth see themselves as participants in that history and as objects of that divine love....Black catechesis has the additional responsibility of showing the interconnectedness—in fact, the fusion—of salvation history with African American history. Each ethnic group, indeed, each individual, must see how the universal salvation history applies to its own life in all the particularity that might entail (Conwill, p. 214).

Much needs to be done to insure that such an effort is not only developed but encouraged and supported by the church as a whole. There is growing evidence that the church, beginning with Rome to the smallest parish, is slowly coming to understand the need for such inculturation at every level. This is being aided by the demographic shifts taking place as noted. It is also a reflection on the shifts taking place at the highest levels of the church, which acknowledge the legitimacy of the church's message being transmitted in ways and forms familiar to those receiving it. The story of Catholic schools today, especially those being maintained in the too-often abandoned urban core, serves as an illustrious example of

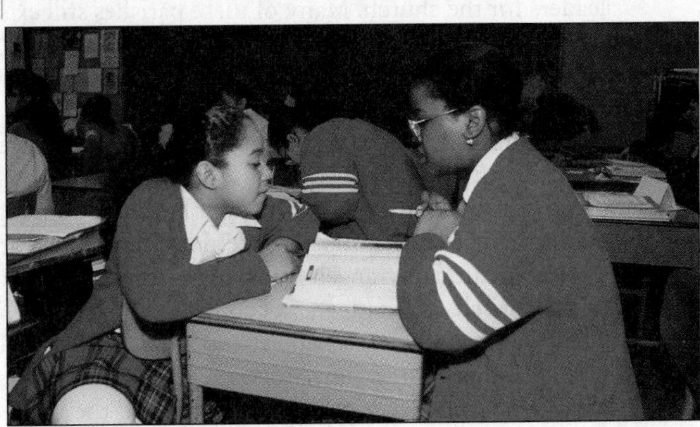

▸ **Catholic school children. Courtesy Woodfin Camp & Associates, Inc., NY.**

how this can be successfully done. Unlike urban public schools, and with greatly reduced financial resources, Catholic schools have been, and continue to be, effective in educating disadvantaged children and children of color. The statistics speak for themselves: the drop-out rate is significantly lower whether students are from one- or two-parent families; 76% of the students take college preparatory courses; 59% attend college, while 27% achieve degrees, as opposed to only 11% of public school students of similar means and background. Why is this so?

> The curriculum of a Catholic school...is based upon a communal organization with specific characteristics that lend themselves to greater educational achievement. Socially, the internal life of the Catholic school is structured to promote many different opportunities for personal interaction and shared experiences among those who work in the school, attend it and support it. The small size of the typical Catholic school fosters the creation of social intimacy, while a host of activities engage students and supporters (athletic events, fund-raisers, rallies, school plays, alumni gatherings, retreats, liturgy, and other forms of religious ritual and prayer). These and other formal and informal events foster a community spirit that supports the school's academic mission (Manno, p. 3).

Although many of the religious have moved into other professional roles, those who remain, as well as the lay teachers who have replaced them, continue to be inspired by an understanding of teaching, not as a job, but "as a vocation, a ministry of service" which fosters "collegial relationships" among faculty leading to a "shared sense of purpose and social interaction..." (Manno, p. 4).

Many of these schools are now mostly non-Catholic in student body but offer a disciplined and rigorous academic curriculum and ethos which many parents find attractive and for which they are willing to sacrifice, as many black parents did in the past — investing in the futures of their children. Catholic schools are "one of the primary institutions in the community that assist in the moral education of youth." They assist the community "in creating a more educated citizenry" with not only sound and solidly prepared minds, but also with upright and moral character (Manno, p. 4).

Thus, the Catholic school of today is helping to prepare young black men and women to lead lives that "give back" to their respective communities, that instill in them a sense of responsibility for the betterment of themselves and those around them, and that encourage them to achieve goals which they often think is unattainable. These schools are following in the footsteps of those Catholics—black and white—who so long ago believed that persons of African descent were both capable of attaining educational success and were deserving and desirous of it.

An excellent example of this educational legacy can be seen in Xavier University of New Orleans, Louisiana. Founded initially as a high school in 1915 by Saint Katherine Drexel and the Sisters of the Blessed Sacrament, Xavier became a university in 1933. It was the first, and remains today, the only black Catholic university in the United States. It is a monument both to the faith and perseverance of black Catholics who knew they were capable of more than was expected of them in their church and society, and to the religious communities, black and white, that dedicated themselves to the education of African American Catholics in the face of constant opposition and often overwhelming obstacles.

▸ Xavier University of Louisiana, Courtesy Xavier University, New Orleans, LA. Photo: Irving Johnson III

Today Xavier is a leader in the field of science education producing one-fourth of the black pharmacists in the United States. Its graduates teach in medical and dental schools throughout the country. Xavier also serves as a home for the Institute of Black Catholic Studies which provides theological, historical, pastoral, and catechetical education from a black perspective to Catholics, regardless of race or ethnicity, who serve in the black Catholic community. It also serves as a training ground for high school students in summer achievement programs.

Conclusion

The history of the evangelization and education of African American Catholics is one of highs and lows, successes and failures, prejudice

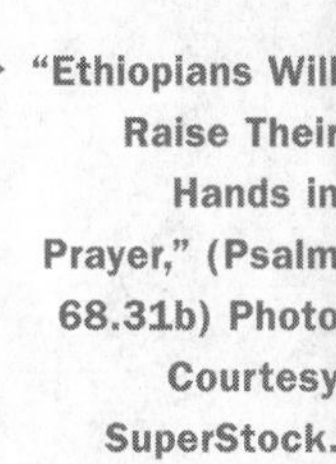

▸ "Ethiopians Will Raise Their Hands in Prayer," (Psalm 68.31b) Photo Courtesy SuperStock.

and faith. It is God's message written in crooked lines. The church has not always succeeded in living up to its mandate "Go ye therefore and teach all nations," but it has been consistently faithful in its proclamation of the liberating gospel of Jesus Christ, distorted as it may have been by some of the faithful. Initially advocates of slavery, the church eventually condemned the traffic in human lives and affirmed the God-given human dignity of all. Black Catholics have been persistent in their faith and have witnessed the working of the Holy Spirit in their lives over the centuries. Today, black Catholics in the United States and throughout the world are taking their rightful place in the church as preachers and teachers, prophets and healers, prayers and singers. They have kept the faith given them by a righteous and loving God, and have faithfully pursued the uplift of their people. There is still much to be done, but African American Catholics and their church are working together, as never before, to insure a beneficial future for all.

Selected Bibliography

1. Brown, Joseph A., *To Stand on the Rock: Meditations on Black Catholic Identity* (Maryknoll, NY: Orbis Books, 1998).

2. Conwill, Giles, *"Black Catechesis: Catching the Flame and Passing It On"* in Diana L. Hayes and Cyprian Davis, eds., *Taking Down Our Harps: Black Catholics in the United States* (Maryknoll, NY: Orbis Books, 1998), pp. 199-231.

3. Davis, Cyprian, OSB, *The History of Black Catholics in the United States* (New York: Crossroad, 1990).

4. Geddes, Sr. M. Reginald, OSP, *"To Educate and Evangelize: Black Catholic Schools of the Oblate Sisters of Providence (1828-1880)"* in U.S. Catholic Historian, vol. 7, #2/3, Spring/Summer 1988, pp. 183-199.

5. Hayes, Diana L., *And Still We Rise: An Introduction To Black Liberation Theology* (Mahwah, NY: Paulist Press, 1996).

6. Manno, Bruno V., *"What Public Education Can Learn From Catholic Schools"* in Crisis, 1999, pp. 20-25.

309½

Thirteen

A Hidden History: African American Contributions to the Bible Cause

Robert L. Cvornyek

Despite laws forbidding them to read, African American slaves yearned to read the Bible for themselves. After the Civil War, several religious and charitable organizations supported the freed blacks in their quest for literacy. The American Bible Society was one of those organizations that not only championed the right of African Americans to an education, but also intentionally focused on providing African Americans with the Bible, "the book which must be the great educator of the Colored people of the South." In addition, the American Bible Society trained blacks as *colporteurs* or door-to-door distributors who could reach their own people with the Word of God.

◂ "From Door to Door," ca. 1933, ABS Archives

▸ "1890 Graduating Class," ABS Archives

The American Bible Society has worked actively to share the Word of God with the African American community since its founding in 1816, occasionally against great odds.

Before the Civil War, African American slaves in virtually every southern state were forbidden by law to read. During the Civil War, as many African Americans sought protection in Union forts and garrisons, many forts established primary schools and churches to help educate people on the path to freedom.

In the decade following the war, more than four dozen religious and benevolent organizations raised money and sent teachers to establish schools among the freed African Americans. The American Bible Society worked in conjunction with these organizations to furnish "the book which must be the great educator of the Colored people of the South." Correspondence to the Society revealed a strong desire among African Americans to learn for themselves. Individuals sometimes traveled several miles to obtain a Bible and many preferred to purchase one rather than receive it as a gift.

For the remainder of the century, though, distribution of the Bible to the African American community was spotty, due in part to the lack of structured distribution channels and in part to conflict over who was responsible for distribution.

The ABS Agency Among the Colored People of the South

In 1900, leaders of the American Bible Society responded to the new situations created by the Supreme Court's "separate but equal" decision in 1896 and the uneven distribution of the Bible in the southern states by launching the "Agency Among the Colored People of the South," a new Agency devoted solely to the distribution of the Bible among African Americans in the South.

The Rev. Dr. John Percy Wragg of Atlanta, Georgia, a pastor and presiding elder in the Savannah and Atlanta Conferences of the Methodist Episcopal Church, was chosen to lead the new Agency in June 1901. Dr. Wragg, a seminary-trained clergyman, pledged his total support and dedication to the Bible cause. Historical documents reveal Dr. Wragg's deep concern for many African American families who were without Bibles.

Dr. Wragg focused particularly on African Americans living in urban areas as a target group for ABS work. He maintained that many "drifted" into the cities, fell into bad habits, and, at last, became "lost in the great sea of city sins." Their only salvation, in Dr. Wragg's view, rested in spiritual rebirth through the Scriptures. He wanted the African American churches to take an active role in Bible work by recognizing and supporting the work of the American Bible Society.

ABS Colporteurs reading the Bible with a southern family, ca. 1900, ABS Archives

▸ Dr. and Mrs. Wragg, June 1929, ABS Archives

From 1901-1929, Dr. Wragg supervised the Agency's operation from his home at Gammon Seminary, an African American Methodist seminary in Atlanta. During that time, the Agency distributed more than 625,000 Bibles and countless portions. Public distribution was undertaken by an initial group of six colporteurs (Bible distributors) at work in six states: Georgia, Alabama, Mississippi, Tennessee, Louisiana, and South Carolina. By 1920, 16 colporteurs were at work for the Agency in 13 states.

Most of the colporteurs were seminary-trained members of the Methodist Episcopal Church. Their outreach extended to many other traditional African American denominations, including the African Methodist Episcopal Church, the African Methodist Episcopal Zion Church, the former Colored Methodist Episcopal Church (now Christian Methodist Episcopal Church), and the National Baptist Convention, U.S.A., Inc., and they reaped great rewards in distribution.

▸ Miss S.E. Harris. First female African-American colporteur, ca. 1911, ABS Archives

In 1911, Dr. Wragg hired the first African American woman colporteur, Miss S. E. Harris. As a student at Atlanta University, Miss Harris had been an active volunteer for the Agency, and she became a salaried colporteur in Mississippi immediately after her graduation.

All Agency colporteurs followed the same basic Bible Society rules. They systematically visited all African American households in a neighborhood and specifically sought out families likely to be neglected. They sold Bibles at standard ABS discounted rates, giving free volumes only to the most destitute, in accordance with regular ABS policy.

Each colporteur developed his or her own style and found the approach most effective in the communities they served. They understood that the difficult work of spreading God's Word could not depend upon comfortable accommodations or good roads.

Most people received the colporteurs warmly, gathered their families together, and requested them to read selections aloud. A colporteur's arrival was a special event, which helped overcome feelings of separation and isolation for rural families.

▸ A young boy sells a New Testament in St. Petersburg, FL, ca. 1934, ABS Archives

In the cities, colporteurs found established African American neighborhoods with thriving local institutions. The local African American church usually provided a focal point for introducing and carrying out the work of the Society. Bible distributors frequently entered a particular city by train, canvassed the area, and then reboarded the same line to visit other cities. The cities offered a special opportunity to visit the workplaces of many African American residents and to reach out to larger groups.

The Agency Among the Colored People of the United States

In 1919, the American Bible Society formed the National Church Advisory Council (NCAC). This inter-denominational group was formed to enhance and strengthen collaboration between the American Bible Society and Christian churches and organizations that are committed to sharing the gospel. Currently, the National Church Advisory Council provides counsel and feedback on ABS projects and programs, and helps to educate denominational staff in using and distributing ABS Scripture resources in and around their churches and communities.

In 1920, Dr. Wragg sought to extend his territory to include the whole United States. Hundreds of thousands of African Americans had fled the South since 1900 in search of economic opportunity in the North. World War I greatly accelerated this exodus as African Americans, especially those from the deep South, headed North for jobs in factories producing war materials.

Dr. Wragg's proposal was approved by the ABS, and the name of the Agency changed to reflect the new territory. Dr. Wragg moved to Bible House in New York City, establishing five regional administrative centers throughout the country.

In just ten years, the Agency distributed 1,367,828 pieces of Scripture to African Americans nationwide. More than 134,000 people received complete Bibles during that time.

A relatively new form of transportation, the automobile, became a vital element in distribution, with colporteurs relying on the vehicles not only for mobility but also to attract interest and arouse curiosity wherever they stopped.

In 1927, a major flood devastated communities along the Mississippi River. African Americans constituted a disproportionately high number of the victims who lost their homes and belongings. ABS efforts to help those affected by the flood included the production of a special edition of the Bible. During the relief period, more than 50,000 Gospels, thousands of portions and New Testaments, and more than 2,000 Bibles were distributed to African American families affected by the flooding. Agency officials contended that the prompt and generous response from the ABS strengthened the organization's appeal and legitimacy to the communities it served.

The William Ingraham Haven Memorial Agency Among the Colored People of the United States

In 1929, Dr. Wragg retired. But before leaving, he renamed the Agency for William Ingraham Haven, the ABS general secretary who had created it. Dr. Wragg and his wife, Jessie Elizabeth, also established a sizable personal endowment to continue the work of the Agency.

The reorganized Haven Agency embarked on its mission during the worst financial depression in American history. Factory shutdowns and slowdowns resulted in massive industrial unemployment, and the fall in the price of cotton and other agricultural products forced many farmers and tenants off the land. In 1931, the Agency's annual report noted "that the Negro is the last to get a job and the first to be dropped, other things being equal." African Americans suffered more acutely than any other group, with most possessing meager resources for Scripture purchase. Consequently, sales dropped precipitously during the early years of the decade and they leveled off to about 180,000 copies annually in 1941.

The Agency again sought new and creative ways to share the Word of God, turning to the business community and govern-

▸ **Children distributing the Scriptures, Houston, TX, ca. 1927, ABS Archives**

ment programs as avenues of distribution. As unemployment and poverty escalated among African American youth, the Agency instituted special Bible study programs to increase the Bible-mindedness of the young.World War II ended the depression, but created new problems for the Bible Society. Periodic paper shortages and paper rationing restricted the production of Bibles, and transportation problems delayed shipments and limited colporteur travel within the United States.

Despite these obstacles, the Agency continued its domestic work and initiated new and expanded services to the Armed Forces. Although units were segregated in the Armed Forces, the Agency frequently donated scriptural materials to military personnel without regard to race, continuing a policy begun by Dr. Wragg during the First World War.

After the war, the program emphasized youth work, especially among the students and recent graduates of African American colleges in the South, until 1959, when ABS leaders declared the segregated work an anachronism, and an internal reorganization ended the Society's special mission among African Americans in the United States.

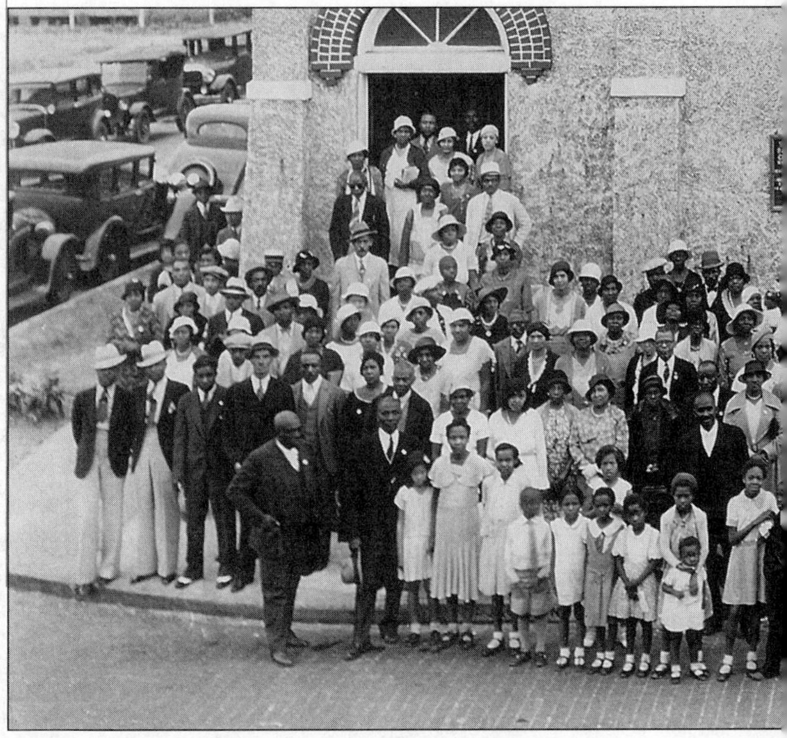

▸ "Conference at Orlando," FL, ca. 1933, ABS Archives

The Stirrings of the Civil Rights Movement

Intensified protests against segregation and the legal movement to banish discrimination from society during the 1950s exerted a profound impact on the Bible movement. The ABS confronted its own part in the fight for human rights and chose to eliminate any aspect of its operation that bore "any semblance to segregation."

Within the context of the African American churches, the Bible played an essential role in shaping and guiding the work of civil rights leaders such as the Rev. Dr. Martin Luther King, Jr., and the Rev. Joseph Lowery of the Southern Christian Leadership Conference.

In 1968 Dr. Gilbert Darlington, a General Officer of the ABS, undertook a personal mission to distribute Dr. King's "Letter from a Birmingham Jail" in an attempt to raise public awareness of injustices to the African American community.

In the late 1960s, the ABS increased its efforts to distribute Scripture in inner-city areas, particularly to African Americans living in the cities, and it placed special emphasis on building relations with and among various African American groups.

The ABS Heritage Program

In keeping with its commitment to build a strong relationship with America's racial and ethnic heritage groups, the American Bible Society launched the Heritage Program in 1991. This inter-denominational effort invites people of all races to partner with ABS in carrying out its mission of sharing the gospel.

Participants in the Heritage Program, along with the members of the inter-racial National Church Advisory Council, help the American Bible Society to spread God's Word to every man, woman, and child – of every race and nation—so that all may come to know the saving grace of our Lord Jesus Christ.

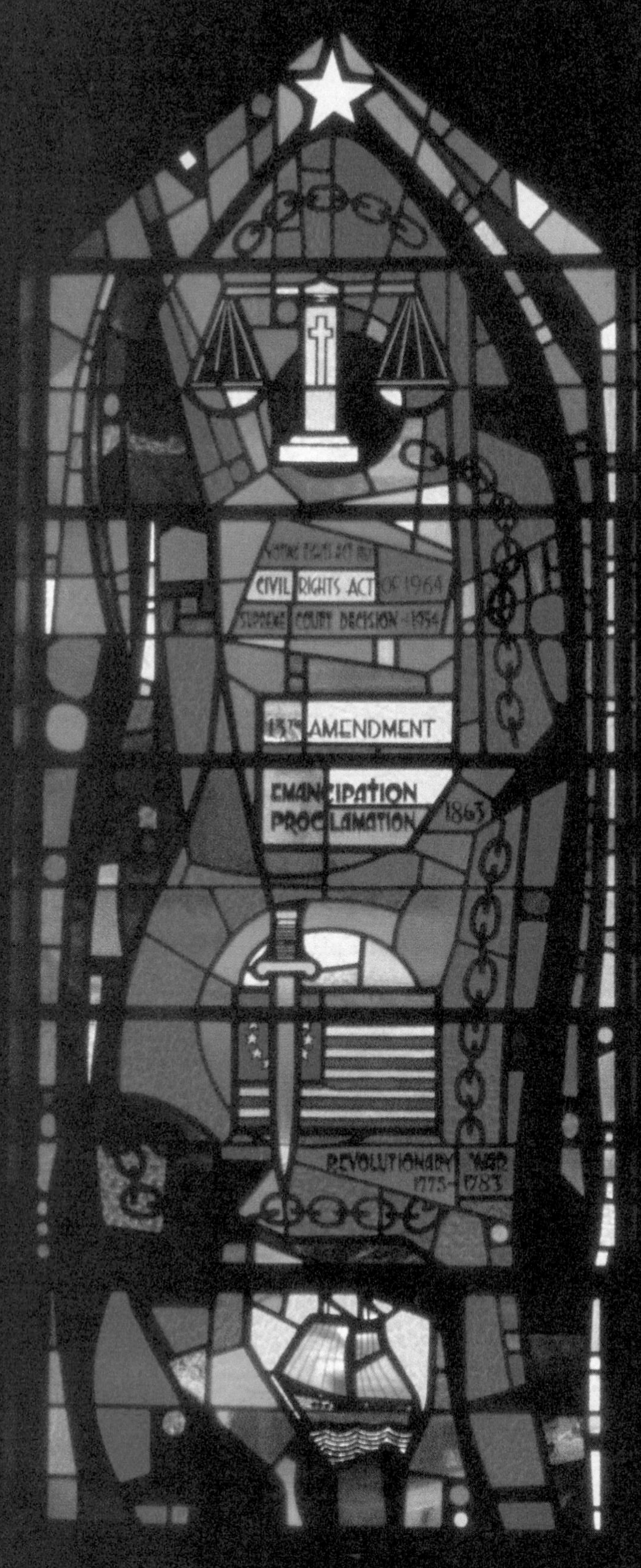
CIVIL RIGHTS ACT OF 1964
13TH AMENDMENT
EMANCIPATION
PROCLAMATION
1863
REVOLUTIONARY WAR
1775-1783

Fourteen

Black Preaching in the Church

Elliott Cuff

The role of black preaching in the spiritual and social history and lives of African Americans in America is inestimable. Additionally, the strengths of the black church in America cannot be known without relevant and relative considerations being given to the contributions made by black preaching in developing those strengths. Black preaching continues to be the predominant art and literary form that the black church has derived from the Bible for the maintenance of its spiritual consciousness and moral conscience. The following article briefly summarizes the relationship the Bible and black preaching have enjoyed in America.

"Freedom Window." First Baptist Church, Huntington, West Virginia, Designed by Pastor Charles H. Smith (1966). Fabricated by Pittsburgh Stained Glass Studio. Photo:Bias Photography

The publication of the Jubilee Bible by the American Bible Society presents a good opportunity to talk about the relationship of the Bible and black preaching in America; that is, black preaching in the church in America. This article will briefly examine that relationship historically, culturally, and theologically.

First, it needs to be understood what is meant by the term "black preaching." In this article the term, black preaching refers to the preaching done by those persons of African descent who have, for the most part, done most of their preaching in what is commonly understood as the Protestant black church in America (Lincoln and Mamiya, 1990). In other instances, the term "black preaching" has been called African American preaching. The black church, however, is not a monolithic religious institution. The black church is made up of many Protestant denominations as well as a few non-Protestant denominations. They vary in their sociological descriptions, class, and cultural definitions. Black preaching is also a significant part of Roman Catholic worship experiences and liturgy. Therefore, black preaching in the church is not a monolithic proclamation driven solely by cultural, racial, or class interests. Black preaching is simply the spiritual, artistic, and linguistic expression used by the preacher to help those persons in the black church and in the church in general to hear the Word of God (Romans 10.14, 17).

It also needs to be understood that while black preaching is mostly done by black preachers in the black church, there have been preachers of other nationalities and racial backgrounds who have done what can be called "black preaching." This "non-black" black preaching is marked primarily by its acceptance among black preachers and congregations and not by any definable literary or artistic form (Brueggemann, 1978; Buttrick, 1994). Also, many black preachers have done black preaching in other churches not commonly understood as being black nor interracial. Moreover, due to the historical and the relevant societal concerns of people of African descent in America, the pulpit for black preaching has been set up in the political and social forums beyond the conventional and traditional trappings of the church (Abernathy, 1970). Black preaching has become known by its cultural theater, its biblical and theological emphasis, and its spiritual acceptance among those persons in the church who have come to recognize what is and what is not black preaching (Mitchell, 1979). This generalization can be borne out more succinctly by reviewing black preaching in the church historically.

In many ways, the role of black preaching in the church historically parallels the major doctrinal and historical themes set forth in the Bible. Themes such as creation, redemption, restoration, liberation, nation building, exile, new creation, and community building mark the emphasis of the earliest black preaching done in the church. While there are no exact records about when or where the first black preaching was done, it is commonly believed that the earliest black preaching emerged and evolved during slavery in America (Franklin, 1967; Woodson, 1921).

Slaves who had heard the preaching of white preachers, white missionaries, and white abolitionists soon grew in knowledge, although limited, of the Bible and began to preach to other slaves about God. Imbued with the power of the Holy Spirit, the earliest black preaching was directed at sustaining the hopes of a people for a new day of freedom and liberation from slavery in heaven (Franklin, 1967). It was this "otherworldliness" of black preaching that initially characterized and shaped the literary forms of black preaching. It is indeed remarkable how black preachers were able to shape and hone an idiom and language for preaching, given the near universal bar, both by legal and societal consensus, against slaves learning to read and write. Moreover, there was a general fear among white slave owners and the free masses that any forms of free association and public speaking by slaves, be it for religious purposes or otherwise, were dangerous to law and order. Into such a societal context, black preaching was created. To echo and embellish a preaching dictum attributed to a famous European preacher in the preceding century, "...with the Bible in one hand and [the power of God] in the other hand," black preachers helped to create fluid and elastic spheres of faith among a people whose hopes were anchored in the God of their oppressors. While much of what black preachers initially preached was a mimic of what they heard white preachers say about God, it was not long before an identifiable context of biblical content became the distinguishing characteristic of black preaching.

There appeared to be, and understandably so, more spiritual fervor and emotional passion derived in black preaching when the content of the preaching focused on biblical stories of creation, redemption, restoration, liberation, and the like that mirrored the plight of the slaves. So, black preachers preached about Daniel being delivered by God while in the lions den (Daniel 6), the three Hebrew boys escaping the fiery furnace (Daniel 3), the children of Israel being led by Moses from Egypt to the Promised Land (Exodus 3–24), and other biblical stories and themes that emphasized hope

▸ "George Liele," 1750 - 1820. Art by Kimanne Smith

in God. In nearly every instance, black preachers paralleled the context of the situations faced by their hearers. In most cases, due to the lack of access to the language of the King James Bible and to the language of their oppressors, black preachers were forced to compensate rational linguistic forms with their own imagination, language creativity, and retained African cultural art forms that would eventually set black preaching apart from all other forms of the white evangelistic and missionary preaching that the slaves first heard (Franklin, 1967). This is not to say that early black preaching was not eloquent nor heard more widely. The very opposite is true.

Recent scholarship has reported that there were "so-called slave preachers" whose preaching had become so effective and so eloquent that the general masses longed to hear them. There are now verifiable stories and folklore about such black preachers as Harry Hoosier or "Black Harry" (1750-1810) who became such a great orator of the Bible that many of the famed leaders of that generation marveled at the incomparable speaking skills that he possessed. Then there was George Liele. Liele was a slave converted to Christianity around 1772. Liele would later be recognized for his worship skills and would be ordained as a preacher and granted the privilege to preach to slaves on a plantation near Silver Bluff, Georgia. The influence of Liele's preaching is attributed to the establishing of the first Baptist church in America (Woodson, 1921).

Henry Highland Garnet was one of the most famous Negro orators in the period before the Civil War. He was born a slave in New Market, Maryland, about 1815, and escaped with his family to New York City in 1824. Two years later he entered New York African Free School where his schoolmates included S.R. Ward (who was Garnet's second cousin) and Alexander Crummell, both of whom were to become active in the anti-slavery movement. From 1828 to 1830, Garnet worked as a cabin boy on a ship to Cuba and as a bound-out servant. In 1831 he entered the high school for Negro youth in New York City and also attended the Sunday school of the First Colored Presbyterian Church where he came under the influence of the Rev. Theodore S. Wright. Garnet attended the academy in Canaan, New Hampshire, but this school was destroyed by an anti-Negro riot and students were forced to flee. From 1838 to 1840, he studied at the Oneida Institute, which was under the direction of Beriah Green, a noted anti-slavery leader. While editing an abolitionist paper, *The Clarion*, at Troy, New York, Garnet turned to the study of theology. After several years of study under Dr. Berman, he was licensed by the Presbytery of Troy in 1842. From 1842 to 1848 he served as pastor of the Liberty Street Presbyterian Church of Troy while continuing his anti-slavery activities.

▸ "Richard Allen," 1760-1831, was the first bishop of the African Methodist Episcopal Church and the first recognized national leader of the black community. Art by Kimanne Smith

The African Methodist Episcopal (A.M.E.) Church, among other things, largely owes its origins to the preaching of Richard Allen (1760-1831). Allen, who first gained acceptance as a preacher among whites, was involved in one of the most triumphant socio-religious movements in American religious history at the St. George's Methodist Church in Philadelphia, Pennsylvania. It was out of this movement at St. George's that the A.M.E. Church was born and for which Allen was revered for his powerful preaching and his dynamic leadership. There were other black preachers, many of them slave preachers, who were respected both for their preaching abilities as well as their leadership abilities. Again, mirroring their historical African roots and paralleling the preachers and prophets of the Bible, especially the Old Testament, the development of black preaching, historically in the church in America, would give the black preacher the prime responsibility as the leader of his community. As the Israelites looked to Moses and others (Exodus 3–24), the black church and the black community would recognize the black preacher in a similar way. This historical current in black preaching is still very prevalent today in many churches. However, there may be indications that the traditional cultural aspects of black preaching are on the decline.

Culturally speaking, black preaching has always been at home in what is commonly understood as the black spiritual cultural context. This is a context that is derived largely from the traditional African religious expression (Herskovits, 1958). It is a spiritual context shaped by what is understood about God through the verbal declaration, the physical demonstration, and the imaginative storytelling. First, the context was socially innate in the slaves, slavery notwithstanding, and then maintained and sustained by the black church throughout its history (Franklin, 1967; Lincoln 1974). So, then, the earliest cultural expressions in the religious experience of black people were focused around prayer, song, and dance. While some have mistakenly marked the cultural accentuation of this experience as "illiterate, slavish, or backward," these expressions have shaped and formed the foundations for black preaching in the church (Johnston, 1974; Woodson, 1921).

▸ **"The Pastor's visit to an African American family," 1800's hand-colored woodcut. Courtesy of North Wind Picture Archives**

In Africa and also in the Caribbean (Wilmore, 1983) the contexts of the celebrations were feasts, songs, fellowship, and adoration (praise) to the Supreme Being or God. As the slaves were converted to Christianity, they continued this tradition in their expressions of Christian faith. Black preaching connected to this experience by incorporating, in many instances, the song-style, the physical dramatic expression, the fellowship, and the praise of the recognizable cultural context in telling stories or preaching about God. The fellowship of black preaching is understood as the interaction between the preacher and the hearers as both interact in the Spirit. This interaction in black preaching was and is still audibly recognized by the antiphonal or "call and response" attribute associated with black church worship.

In this regard, the fellowship aspect of black preaching is very critical in how preaching is viewed and defined culturally by both preachers and congregations. Although many black congregations and preachers have not recognized this aspect of black preaching, they seem to favor a cultural aspect that is accompanied by song, prayer, and praise. It is also shaped by distinct religious interests based upon class and social status preferences. On the other hand, the most recognized traditional and cultural aspect of black preaching is sometimes referred to as "tuning up," "pulling it," "gravy," or "whooping."

"Tuning up" usually happens near the conclusion of the sermon, although in any given church context it might occur at any point in the sermon. Sometimes, the "tuning up" aspect of black preaching today is accompanied by musical intonations, usually from the Hammond organ or a piano in the church. Before black churches could afford to have musical instruments, "tuning up" was accompanied by the vocal musical tonal inflections of the members of the church. These vocal musical tonal inflections were similar to the chants associated with West African and Caribbean religions (Wilmore, 1983). In many churches today this aspect of the fellowship in black preaching still exists and is formally recognized by many, preachers and congregations alike, as the measure of the ability to preach. In fact, there are some denominations in the black church experience who have developed recognizable subcultures for this type of preaching (commonly referred to as the Late Night Services) where the whole subculture is contrived on "tuning up." Others, usually more interested in the more substantive aspects of Christian Education, have called this continued preaching practice of "tuning up" as only being done in response to the itching ears of the culture rather than as preaching being done to the glory of God (1 Timothy 4.1-3). Again, with the new preaching being done in the black religious context, there is a clear break from the traditional and conventional forms of black preaching as it is historically understood. This might be further underscored by briefly looking at the theological aspects of black preaching.

Theologically, the heart and mind of black preaching are, and always have been, Jesus, Calvary, and "the third day." While it is true that, historically, the great character and theme stories of the Old Testament in the Bible have a large place in the canon of the black preaching experience, there is more identification theologically with Jesus, Calvary, and "early Sunday morning" as understood from the perspective of the New Testament. Regardless of the style or type of black preaching that was and is being done, and no matter where the black preacher takes a preaching text in the Bible, at some point in the preaching, usually at the end, the preaching must go by Jesus at Calvary. In black preaching, Jesus must die, be buried, and then be resurrected. This resurrected Jesus is the most practical theology of hope understood universally in the black church experience. The whole of the black experience can be understood in preaching, biblically and theologically, by identifying with what happened to Jesus.

Jesus suffered needlessly, and black people suffer needlessly. Jesus received injustice, and black people receive injustice. Jesus was marginalized by the majority, and black people, too, are marginalized by the majority in America. Jesus identified more readily with the oppressed, the downcast, the poor, the imprisoned, and the powerless minorities in societies (Luke 4.18,19; 15); and black people hold their theological identity more closely being associated with what happened to Jesus.

Jesus would eventually be triumphant over every form of sin, sickness, and evil; and black people believe that with Jesus they, too, can be as triumphant. This is at the heart and mind, theologically, of the black preaching experience. Jesus was crucified, buried, and has risen triumphantly; and Jesus has all power over the kingdoms of this world and the next (1 Corinthians 15). This is the holistic aspect of the black preaching experience where every aspect of broken humanity in black life is hermeneutically, that is, biblically interpreted, through the contexts of what Jesus went through. Therefore, the struggles, setbacks, hurts, and hopes of a people, historically denied and yet still denied, have been addressed in the proclamation of a triumphant Jesus as set forth in the Bible. It was this type of theological understanding that underscored the black preaching done in one of the most telling periods in our nation's history, the Civil Rights Movement.

▸ **Dr. Martin Luther King, Jr. speaking to civil rights marchers in Alabama. Photo, UPI/Corbis Bettman, New York, NY**

Martin Luther King, Jr., as well as others who believed in the movement, helped to shape a black preaching ethic based on the liberation and freedom grounded in a theology primarily shaped by what happened to Jesus. Although not roundly received with great popularity during that time, nonetheless it was the liberation and redemptive preaching done by a host of others that moved an entire nation toward its true biblical identity with God (Proverbs 14.34; 29.18).

As we celebrate the publication of the Jubilee Edition of the Bible, the relevance of preaching a triumphant Jesus is still existent in our world today. There are hard questions black preaching must face in and for the next millennium. For instance, how will the rapid increases in the continued impersonalization of ministry through the electronic media affect how conventional preaching forms are used? Will the reliance upon a type of preaching that pays almost

▸ "The Black Church." Art by Kimanne Smith

no attention to any of the classical preachers or the historical scholarship of black preaching create a new understanding of Romans 10.14-17? With the continuing social formation of the "mega-churches" around the nation, where the boundaries of race, nationality, class (in some instances), and denominational preferences are becoming less distinguishable, will it mean that black preaching, as it is known, will soon meet its mainstream demise? What, if any, effect will the availability and proliferation of Christian information among the masses have on the demand for biblically relevant expository preaching in the church?

Even before the dawn of a new millennium, more and more black female preachers have been making their voices heard. Modern society, as a result of civil and equal rights laws and policies, is increasingly elevating the status and role of women in virtually all areas of professional secular life. A similar, albeit protracted and hesitant, parallel of such elevation of women in the proclamation ministries can also be seen in the black church. Thus, the gospel of Jesus Christ is now increasingly being proclaimed in the pulpits of churches and seminaries by female voices which had previously been silent or suppressed. While society and the black church (as well as the church in general) have yet a long way to go in this regard, black preaching is already reaping the benefits. Further, an increasing number of articles and books championing the contributions of black female preachers are now available. This new vista can only strengthen the future of black preaching, theologically, biblically, and culturally.

For the most part, black preaching has had a glorious past, enjoys a good, but unpredictable and amorphous present, yet still has hope for a bright future in God! As long as black preaching in the church can have the Bible in the church and keep the Bible in its preaching, God shall be victorious in all of humanity!

Bibliography

Abernathy, Ralph. "Our Lives Were Filled With Action," in *Martin Luther King, Jr.* C. Eric Lincoln, ed. New York: Hill & Wang, 1970.

Brueggemann, Walter. *The Prophetic Imagination.* Minneapolis: Fortress Press, 1978.

Buttrick, David. *A Captive Voice: The Liberation of Preaching.* Louisville: John Know/Westminster Press, 1994.

________. *Preaching Jesus Christ.* Philadelphia: Fortress, 1988.

Franklin, John Hope. *From Slavery to Freedman.* New York: Alfred A. Knopf, 1967.

Herskovits, Melville. *The Myth of the Negro Past.* Boston: Beacon Press, 1958.

Johnston, Rubye F. *The Development of Negro Religion.* Garden City, NY: Anchor/Doubleday, 1974.

_________ and Lawrence H. Mamiya. *The Black Church in the African American Experience.* Durham: North Carolina University Press, 1990.

Mitchell, Henry. *Black Preaching.* New York: Harper & Row, 1979.

_________. *Celebration and Experience in Preaching.* Nashville: Abingdon Press, 1990.

Wilmore, Gayraud S. *Black Religion and Black Radicalism.* 2nd Ed. Maryknoll, NY: Orbis, 1983.

Woodson, Carter G. *The History of the Negro Church.* Washington, DC: Associated Publishers, 1921.

Voices of Black Women Who Have Proclaimed the Gospel

Amanda Berry Smith (1837-1915)

▸ Fisk University Library, Special Collections

Amanda Smith was first a preacher in the African Methodist Church. Later, she became a missionary evangelist who preached in the United States, as well as in England, Scotland, Africa, and India. Against the most adverse circumstances, beginning her life as a slave, she not only preached God's Word, but she lived it. She also encouraged Christians to achieve "spiritual perfection." Amanda dedicated her life to helping women and children. She was referred to as "God's image carved in ebony."

Lulu (Louise Cecilia) Fleming (1862-1899)

▸ From the photographic archives of the Board of International Ministries, American Baptist Churches USA, courtesy of the American Baptist Historical Society

Lulu Fleming was born during slavery, but became a career missionary in the Women's American Baptist Foreign Mission Society of the West. During her short life, she served God in Africa. Miss Fleming was the valedictorian of her class at Shaw University. She also received a medical degree from the Pennsylvania Women's Medical College, in preparation for a position as a medical missionary in the Congo.

Jarena Lee (1783-1857)

▸ Photo courtesy of the Billy Graham Center Museum

Jarena Lee was born a free person in New Jersey. Against much opposition, she was the first black woman to preach the gospel in the African Methodist Episcopal Church in 1809. When she first requested a license from Richard Allen to preach the gospel, he discouraged her, but later, because of her persistence, he became supportive of her ministry.

Zilpha Elaw (c. 1790) *(Photo not available.)*

Zilpha Elaw was converted at a camp meeting in 1817. At the same time, she received a call to the ministry. Zilpha Elaw ministered in the south to congregations of slaves even though she was a free black woman from the north. There was a danger of her being captured and sold as a slave, but this did not deter her. Eventually, she joined with Jarena Lee to form a preaching team.

Julia A. Foote (1823-1900)

▸ Permission from the Woodruff Library of Clark-Atlanta University; Photograph from Fisk University Library, Special Collections

Julia A. Foote was the first black woman to be ordained a deacon in the African Methodist Episcopal Zion Church. She was the second black woman to be ordained an elder in 1900. She had a very special conversion experience and received a call to a preaching ministry. Julia overcame much resistance to answer the Lord's call to service.

Bertha "Thea" Bowman (1937-1990)

▸ Photo courtesy of Boston College, Chestnut Hill, MA.

Sr. Thea Bowman, F.S.P.A., Ph.D., was born in Yazoo City, Mississippi. She joined the Franciscan Sisters of Perpetual Adoration in La Crosse, Wisconsin and professed her vows in 1958. The granddaughter of a slave, Sr. Thea earned her Doctorate at the Catholic University of America in Washington, D.C. She taught for several years at Viterbo and helped to organize the Institute of Black Catholic Studies at Xavier University in New Orleans, Louisiana. A woman of many talents and deep spirituality, Sr. Thea was a liturgist, a preacher, a gospel singer (among her favorite songs were "Done Made My Vow to the Lord" and "Every Time I feel the Spirit"—see lyrics in Chapter 15), whose exuberant love for Christ and the Catholic church never waned. Her commitment to multiculturalism and the ease in which she infused black culture into Catholic liturgy is part of her extraordinary legacy.

Sources Cited

Deen, Edith. *Great Women of the Christian Faith.* New Jersey: Barbour & Co., 1959.

Ruether, Rosemary R. and Skinner, Rosemary K. *In Our Own Voices: Four Centuries of American Women's Religious Writing.* San Francisco: Harper Collins, 1996.

__________. *Women and Religion in America.* Vol. 3: 1900-1968. San Francisco: Harper & Row, 1986.

Riggs, Marcia Y. *Can I Get A Witness? Prophetic Religious Voices of African American Women: An Anthology.* Maryknoll, NY: Orbis Books, 1997.

"The Gallery: Thumbnail Sketches of Significant Leaders, Evangelists, Thinkers, and Movers in Baptist History." Christian History Magazine. Vol. IV, No. 2, Issue #6.

Black Women Educators

Mary Jane Patterson (? -1894)

▸ Used with Permission from Oberlin College Archives

Mary Jane Patterson was the first black woman in America to receive a bachelor's degree in 1862. She attended Oberlin College in Ohio. Oberlin was well known for its abolitionist policies. Charles Finney, the great revivalist of the nineteenth century was also president of Oberlin at that time, and advocated coed classes. Oberlin College was a "station on the Underground Railroad" and helped many slaves achieve freedom. Mary Jane Patterson, from a family of slaves, graduated and pursued a teaching career in the north.

Mary McCleod Bethune (1875 - 1955)

▸ Photo courtesy of Bethune - Cookman College

Mary McCleod Bethune was an outstanding educator and humanitarian, as well as an eloquent lecturer. She was an advisor to Franklin D. Roosevelt and she was the Founder-President of Bethune-Cookman College in Florida. She availed herself of every opportunity to crusade on behalf of decent public schools and civil rights.

Virginia W. Broughton (c. 1850) *(Photo not available.)*

Virginia W. Broughton, the first black woman to receive a college degree in the south (Fisk University), dedicated her life to home missions and forming Bible study groups for women. She was very active in Sunday School work, and what was called the "Bible Band." Virginia W. Broughton was a fine example of a person who combined her faith with her teaching.

Nannie Helen Burroughs (1883 - 1961)

▸ Fisk University Library, Special Collections

Nannie Helen Burroughs devoted her life to working on behalf of and for black women in their struggle for visibility and recognition of their gifts and talents in the Black Church. She was instrumental in forming the Women's Convention of the National Baptist Convention; and her great achievement was her role as the founder of Women's Day in the Black Church.

Mary Elizabeth Lange (c. 1784-1882)

▸ Photo courtesy of The Josephite Archives, Washington, D.C.

Mary Elizabeth Lange, O.S.P., was born in Cuba of Haitian parents. She came to the United States around 1817 and settled in Baltimore. As a young woman, she considered consecrating her life to God. Mary Elizabeth Lange met two other black Haitians, Marie Madeleine Balas, and Rosine Boegue, who held similar views about beginning a religious life. Together, the three women started a free school for children. They were later joined by Almeide Duchemin Maxis. In 1829, Mary Elizabeth Lange and the others took their vows and were named the Oblate Sisters of Providence. The sisters devoted themselves to educating blacks by founding several schools, and by caring for the sick. Under the leadership of Mary Elizabeth Lange, the Oblate Sisters of Providence became the first successful foundation of black women religious.

Sources Cited

Davis, Cyprian, OSB, *The History of Black Catholics in the United States.* New York: Crossroad, 1990

"God's College and Radical Change." Christian History Magazine. Vol. VII, No. 4, Issue #20.

Ruether, Rosemary R. and Skinner, Rosemary K. *In Our Own Voices: Four Centuries of American Women's Religious Writing.* San Francisco: HarperCollins, 1996.

_________. *Women and Religion in America.* Vol. 3: 1900-1968. San Francisco: Harper & Row, 1986.

Riggs, Marcia Y. *Can I Get A Witness? Prophetic Voices of African American Women: An Anthology.* Maryknoll, NY: Orbis Books, 1997.

Fifteen

Music in the Black Church

William H. Collins, Jr.

All great music finds its roots in the church, and in the black experience, it is no different. The music of black people—rhythm and blues, soul, jazz, and folk—finds its origin in the black church. Music in the forms of spirituals, hymns, anthems, traditional gospel, contemporary gospel, and praise and worship is the root and inspiration of the sound of music in the Black community. The melodies, rhythms, and harmonies are born out of a desire to give God the glory due him and to lift up the name of Jesus, our Lord and Savior.

◂ "The Jubilee Singers," by Edward Havel, (British, 1835-1908). Oil on canvas, Fisk University Galleries, Nashville, Tennessee

Music has always been an integral part in the lives of black people. It carries over from everyday life into the church and has been very important in helping to keep the emotional balance necessary for the joy, peace, and spirituality of the individual. Its purpose is, therefore, that God may be glorified and people edified. "I will sing to the LORD all my life; as long as I live I will sing praises to my God"(Psalm 104.33).

In 1619, a Dutch vessel landed twenty Africans at Jamestown, Virginia. They were bought by colonial settlers. This was the beginning of the African slave trade in the American colonies. Slaves came from various localities in Africa. In this country they were cut off from the moorings of their culture, having to adjust to a completely alien way of life, having to learn a strange language, and having to endure a barbaric system of slavery. Yet, it was within this cruel milieu, and from these oppressed people, that beautiful melodious spirituals originated. The music and words of the black spirituals are noble and their sentiments are exalted.

Many of the spirituals used in worship in the black church grew out of the everyday struggles for existence and survival. Songs were sung to ease the adverse circumstances—uncertainties of the future, harsh and painful treatment, and the wounding of the psyche. These circumstances characterized the lives of the slaves; yet, they were able to communicate with their Maker through the spirituals.

Some of the spirituals were also sung to transport messages to one another in their endeavors to escape from slavery by way of the Underground Railroad. Songs such as "Go Down Moses," "Deep River," "Stan, Still Jordan," "Walk Together Children," and "Swing Low, Sweet Chariot."

The slaves came to America endowed with musical talent to begin with; and the spirituals possess many of the fundamental characteristics of African music. African-American spirituals are built upon this foundation, but they contain a higher melodic quality and an added harmonic development.

All great music finds its roots in the church, and in the black experience, it is no different. The music of black people—folk, rhythm and blues, soul, and jazz—finds its origin in the black church. The black church has always been a breeding ground for the talent, gifts, and creativity of its community. Its music, found in the forms of spirituals, hymns, gospel, contemporary gospel, and praise and worship songs are very prominent in the church— "Speak to one another with the words of psalms, hymns, and sacred songs; sing hymns and psalms to the Lord with praise in your hearts"(Ephesians 5.19). The melodies, rhythms, and harmonies are born out of a desire to give God the glory due him and to lift up the name of Jesus, our Lord and Savior.

The only difference between the root of gospel and its offspring is the lyrical content and the focus of the music. In the best of gospel, the lyrical content is Word-based, right out of the Scriptures. The focus of the music is the Lord, Jesus Christ, "the only God our Savior" (Jude 25), to the glory of God the Father.

During the 1730s, the Great Awakening brought with it a demand for the use of livelier music (rather than anthems and canticles) in the worship services. These "livelier"songs were called hymns. The new style of texts by Dr. Isaac Watts (1674-1748) and Charles Wesley (1707-1788) appealed to blacks because of the vitality of the words, wider use of intervals than in psalm tunes, and their rhythmic freedom. The book, *Hymns and Spiritual Songs*, was published by Dr. Watts in 1707, and *A Collection of Psalms and Hymns* (1742) was published by John Wesley (1703-1791) together with his brother, Charles. These hymnbooks became the most widely used; and the latter book ultimately became the forerunner of the official *Methodist Hymnal.*

Toward the end of the eighteenth century, blacks began to break away from white congregations to establish their own places of worship. They brought to their own worship services some semblance of the white church worship format; however, the music gained another dimension by the addition of the African-Americans' indigenous experiences. The creation of new musical forms began—black hymns and spirituals.

The most prolific writer of the black hymn was Dr. Charles Albert Tindley (1856-1933). For many years, he pastored the Tindley Temple United Methodist Church in Philadelphia, PA. His period as a composer was from 1901-1906. However, his hymns did not become well known in the black churches until after World War I. Some of the hymns written by Dr. Tindley are: "Some Day" (Beams of Heaven), "Nothing Between," "Leave It There," "I'll Overcome Someday," "Stand by Me," "We'll Understand It Better By and By," among others.

Black gospel music came into existence during the latter part of the nineteenth century. This music was generally classified as "gospel" songs because they were inspired by the four gospels of the New Testament. They dealt with the teachings of Jesus and the life of the believer. Some black ministers, at first, did not permit gospel singing in their churches because of the rhythmic beat and its close relationship to the blues. Eventually, however, gospel began seeping into the churches.

Eileen Southern states in her book, *The Music of Black Americans,* "When the black people began pouring into the nation's cities during the second decade of the twentieth century, they took their joyful spirituals with them, but found the rural born music to be unsatisfactory in urban settings and unresponsive to their needs." Consequently, the church singers created a more expressive music to which they applied the term, gospel, but which displayed little resemblance to the traditional gospel song of the whites. Composer Thomas A. Dorsey developed and made popular the "gospel blues." His "Precious Lord, Take My Hand" became a musical staple of the black churches across the U.S. Black gospel music, then, became essentially the sacred counterpart of the city blues, sung in the same improvisatory tradition with piano, guitar, or instrumental accompaniment.

The music of the black church is also born out of its experience and relationship with the Lord, Jesus Christ. Our thanksgiving, praise, and worship is heartfelt and soulful because God has shown himself to be a great and good God unto us as a people. The love, care, and compassion of God toward us causes us to sing the way we do. We have experienced God as Savior, Liberator, Deliverer, Redeemer, Creator, Great Emancipator, Protector, Master, King, Judge, Supplier, etc., and the music in the black church reflects it. Black music addresses God for his keeping power through our formidable and toilsome past and our current struggles in today's burdensome society. The strength of African Americans can be viewed in light of the music that has been generated from their history.

God has graced the black church musician with creativity, ingenuity, and a wonderful ability of improvisation. Black worshipers join in, and celebrate with them in, the joyous renditions to magnify and glorify the Lord, for the Lord is the great source of music. All of the diversity within the musical realm emanates from God, who possesses multi-faceted and manifold wisdom in and through his creation, and music is just one of the examples.

"Rise, shine for thy light has come!" Gouache on paper by Aaron Douglas, ca. 1930. The Howard University Gallery of Art Permanent Collection, Washington, DC

God uses the experiences of the gospel psalmists in the church. The black church, although joined universally with those in Christ, does not have the same heritage, culture, experiences, or history as others, so its music is unique and diverse in its forms.

One of the primary reasons for the black church service is for the people of God to come together to worship God for who he is and all that he has done. Therefore, the music, lyrics, and presentation must reflect the purpose of worship and be conducive to setting such an atmosphere in the house of the Lord. One must know what worship, praise, thanksgiving, and supplication are before being able to offer them worthily to the Lord. The music in the black church, through its lyrics, melodies, rhythms, and harmonies, enables and inspires these expressions in the service of the Lord.

Music must have the ability to open the hearts of the worshipers so they may yield and be available to God, to express praises and thanksgiving for his glory. Music, in many instances, enables the repentant to confess sorrow about sin. Music can be utilized to entreat God's presence among the people, and ushers the people into the presence of God. The music itself must be fitting and of a spiritual quality that welcomes the presence of a holy God. It must anticipate the anointing of the Holy Spirit to empower, deliver, and prosper the people of God, and whoever may be in the midst. Music should prepare our hearts and minds to hear from God so that we "might have life—life in all its fullness" (John 10.10b).

Music in the black church aids us in expressing ourselves in a way that is uniquely our own. As we sing, leap, dance, and shout praises, give thanks, and worship, the Lord God enthrones himself in our midst. It is reminiscent of Moses as he sang a song of victory (Exodus 15.1, 19), Miriam and the women who sang, danced, and played the timbrels (Exodus 15.20, 21), and David who danced before the Lord because the Ark had been carried safely into Jerusalem (2 Samuel 6.12-16). The liberty and freedom that we, as a people, have found in God's presence has long kept us sane and alive in the midst of the worst social injustices and oppression against humanity. Our music has been most instrumental in bringing us near to the great God our Savior, Jesus the Lord.

As a background accompaniment, music aids the preacher in proclaiming the Word of God in the worship service, especially near the climax of the message or sermon. When the Holy Spirit begins to move upon the preacher to speak the Word of God, there is a flow in the way the message is being spoken. Hence, the phrase, "the flow of conversation." In the moving of the Holy Spirit, there is sensitivity and timing; and hearts are open and receptive to the Word of God. Music inspired by the Holy Spirit assists the preaching moment by fostering sensitivity to God, as well as providing the timing necessary through its Word-based lyrics, melodies, rhythms, and harmonies. Music helps the anointing mount higher and higher as God uses his preaching instrument to sound his message to the people. The preacher can focus, tune in, tune up, and hear accurately from God. Music has prepared the atmosphere with the spiritual ambiance necessary for worship. Can the preacher preach by the Spirit of God without music? Yes, but it is very sweet with musical accompaniment. Consecrated music stills the soul of the preacher so that he or she may hear from God and proclaim the Word.

> All the priests present, regardless of the group to which they belonged, had consecrated themselves. And all the Levite musicians—Asaph, Heman, and Jeduthun, and the members of their clans—were wearing linen clothing. The Levites stood near the east side of the altar with cymbals and harps, and with them were 120 priests playing trumpets. The singers were accompanied in perfect harmony by trumpets, cymbals, and other instruments, as they praised the LORD singing:
>
> "Praise the LORD, because he is good,
> And his love is eternal."
>
> As the priests were leaving the Temple, it was suddenly filled with a cloud shining with the dazzling light of the LORD's presence, and they could not continue the service of worship.
>
> (2 Chronicles 5.11-14)

Dr. William B. McClain states, "the Spirit has descended often when slaves and ex-slaves have gathered in worship and sung the Negro spirituals. These spirituals reveal the rich culture and the ineffable beauty and creativity of the black soul and intimate the uniqueness of the black religious tradition."

The slaves—having found themselves far from their native land, despised by those among whom they lived, experiencing the hurt of their separation from loved ones on the auction block, knowing the hard task master, feeling the lash—seized Christianity, the religion of compensations in the life to come, to help them endure the hurts suffered in their current existence. For the black slaves, Christianity gave them the hope that in the heavenly world there would be a complete reversal of conditions.

"Instruments," art by Kimanne Smith

Having experienced the heartaches and struggles of everyday life, black people enter their churches with much hope and trust in the God who sends the sunshine and the rain, the God who is very much alive and active, and who has not forsaken those who are poor, oppressed, and out of work. Fear is turned to hope as they burst into songs of praise and celebration in sanctuaries large and small, and in storefronts. They did not need the services of psychologists, psychiatrists, or analysts because all of their inner frustrations were released to Almighty God in their outbursts of singing, shouting, dancing, and praises.

The importance of music in the black church can be seen through its ability to unify people. Group singing is done in practically every black church. It is a way of sharing joy, grief, and love. Congregations that sing together are brought closer through this experience. God has placed emphasis on music in his Word because it has a tremendous power to unify his people. "Those who guard the city are shouting, shouting together for joy. They can see with their own eyes the return of the LORD to Zion. Break into shouts of joy, you ruins of Jerusalem! The LORD will rescue his city and comfort his people" (Isaiah 52.8, 9).

The song of the Christian ought to include meaningful praise and thanksgiving to the LORD if the scriptural examples of music in worship and life are to be followed; e.g., Romans 15.9; Colossians 3.16; Hebrews 2.12.

"TO GOD BE THE GLORY"

Bibliography

Cleveland, J. Jefferson. *Songs of Zion*. Nashville: Abingdon/Parthenon Press, 1981.

DuBois, W.E.B. *Suppression of the African Slave-Trade*. New York: Longmans, 1896.

Garlock, Frank and Woetzel, Kurt. *Music in the Balance.* Greenville: Majesty Music, 1992.

Heilbut, Tony. *The Gospel Sound: Good News and Bad Times*. New York: Simon and Schuster, 1971.

Johnson, James Weldon and Johnson, J. Rosamond. *The Book of American Negro Spirituals*. New York: Da Capo Press, 1954.

Katz, Bernard. *The Social Implications of Early Negro Music in the United States.* New York: Arno/The New York Times, 1969.

National Baptist Publishing Board. *The New National Baptist Hymnal.* Nashville: National Baptist Publishing Board, 1977.

Southern, Eileen. *The Music of Black Americans*. New York: W. W. Norton, 1971.

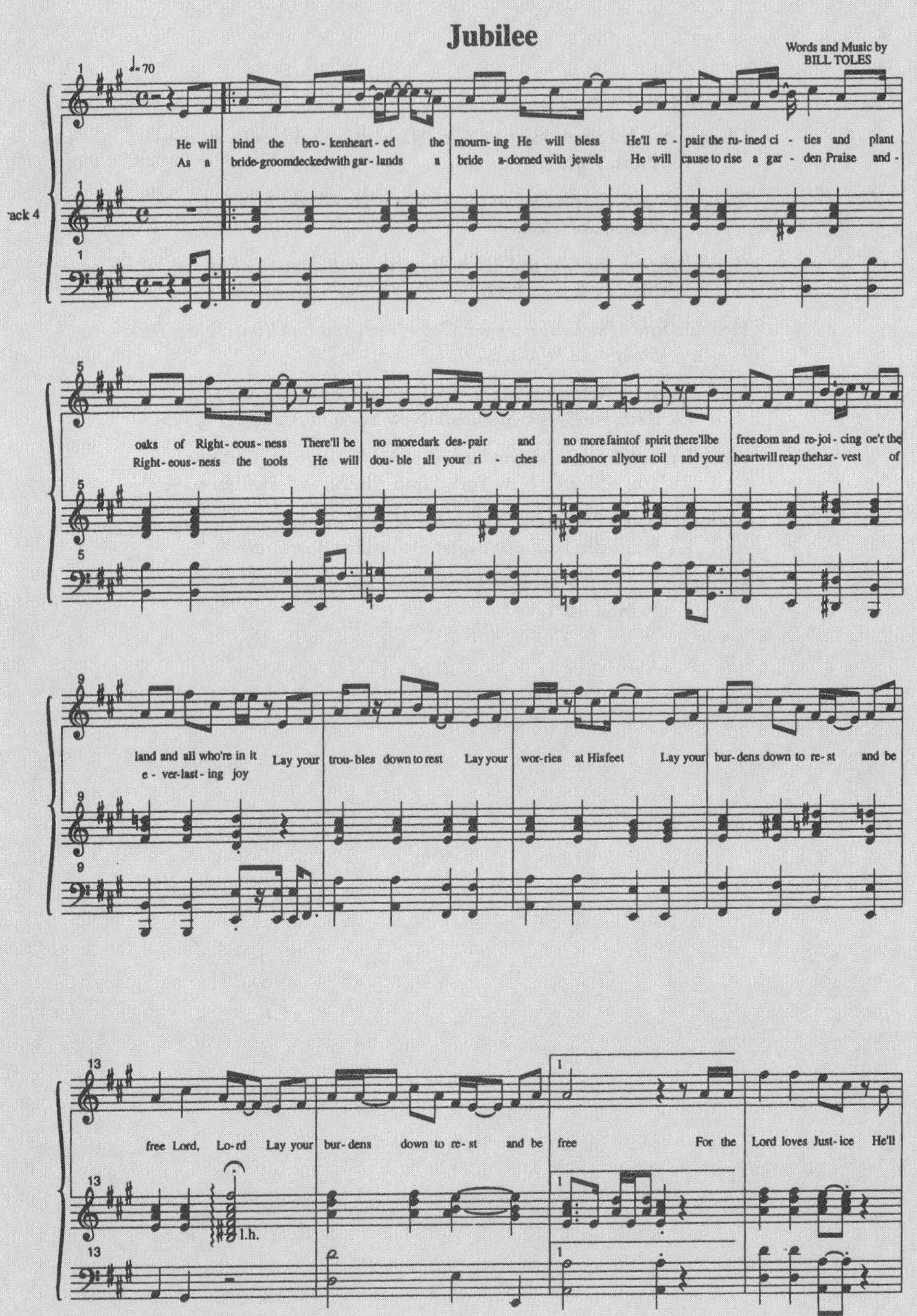
Jubilee
Words and Music by
BILL TOLES
♩. = 70
He will bind the bro- kenheart- ed the mourn- ing He will bless He'll re - pair the ru- ined ci - ties and plant
As a bride-groomdeckedwith gar- lands a bride a-dorned with jewels He will cause to rise a gar - den Praise and -
rack 4
oaks of Right- eous- ness There'll be no moredark des- pair and no more faintof spirit there'llbe freedom and re-joi- cing oe'r the
Right- eous- ness the tools He will dou- ble all your ri - ches andhonor allyour toil and your heartwill reap theharvest of
land and all who're in it Lay your trou- bles down to rest Lay your wor- ries at His feet Lay your bur- dens down to re- st and be
e - ver-last- ing joy
free Lord, Lo-rd Lay your bur- dens down to re- st and be free For the Lord loves Just- ice He'll
l.h.

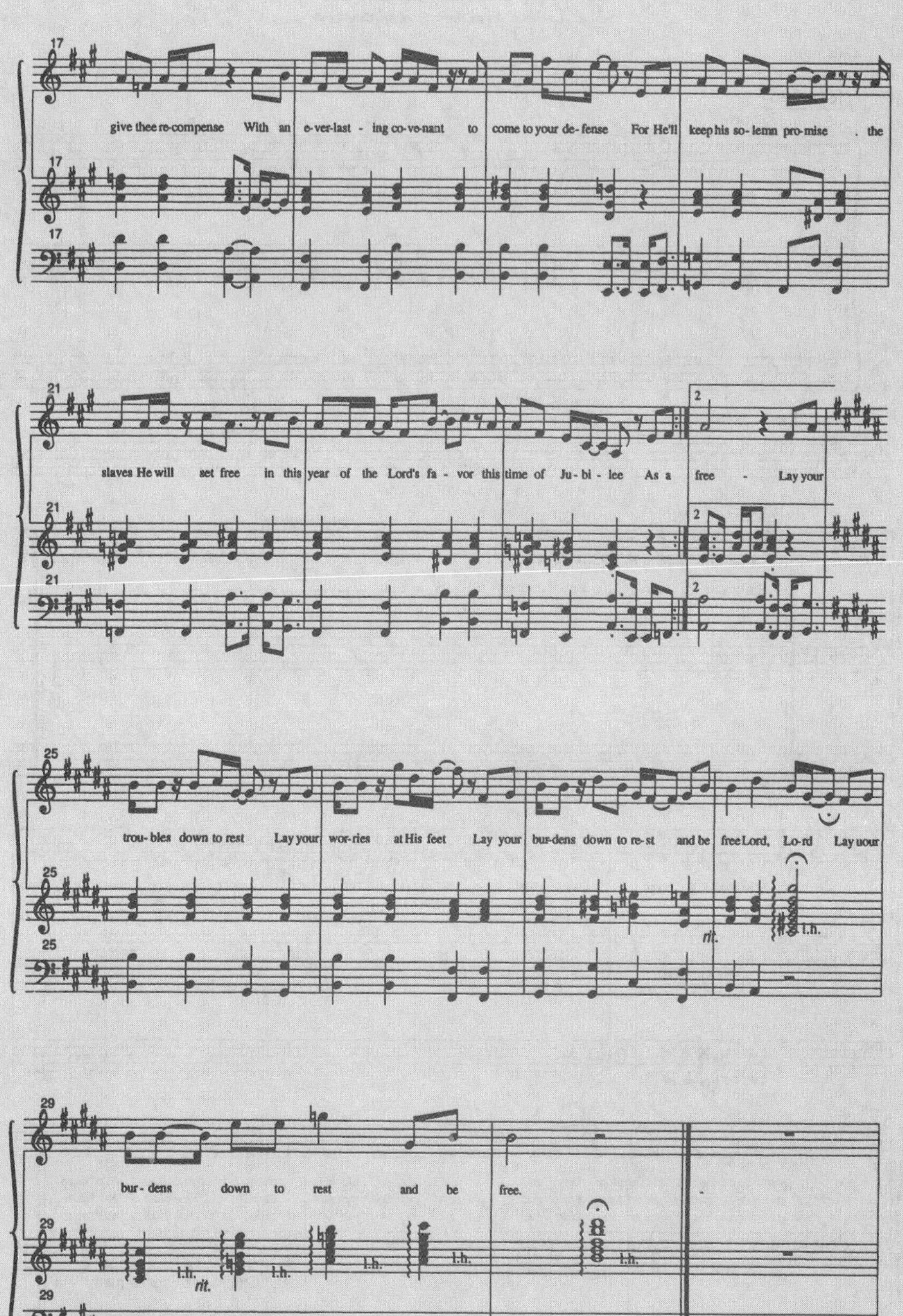
17
give thee re-compense With an e-ver-last - ing co-ve-nant to come to your de- fense For He'll keep his so- lemn pro-mise . the
21
slaves He will set free in this year of the Lord's fa- vor this time of Ju- bi- lee As a free - Lay your
2
25
trou- bles down to rest Lay your wor-ries at His feet Lay your bur-dens down to re- st and be free Lord, Lo-rd Lay uour
rit.
l.h.
29
bur- dens down to rest and be free.
l.h.
rit.

Trouble Don't Last Always

Traditional arr. by Aaron F. Brown and Dennis Hilliman

Vocal arr. Lawrence Vincent Poole Score: Dr. Carol Lewis

BRIDGE
24
3.
ti - me What shall I do?
29
34
VAMP
I'm so glad trou - ble don't last always I'm so glad trou - ble don't last al ways (Hey)
38
TAG
I'm so glad trou- ble don't last al- ways I'm so glad trou- ble don't last al- ways (Hey)
I'm so- glad I got a hi- ding place I'm so glad I got a hi- ding place.

Witness For My Lord.
COPYRIGHT, 1921, BY WILLA A. TOWNSEND. USED BY PERMISSION.
Joyfully.
Arr. by Willa A. Townsend.
Wit-ness,..for my Lord,.... Wit-ness,...for my Lord,....
Wit-ness for my Lord, Wit-ness for my Lord,
Wit-ness, for my Lord;.... O, my soul is a wit-ness
Wit-ness for my Lord;
1
2
FINE.
for my Lord. My soul, is a wit-ness for my Lord.
LEADER.
1. O, I haven't been to Heav'n but I've been told,.....My soul is a witness for my Lord;
2. I want to go to Heaven and I want to go right,.....My soul is a witness for my Lord;
3. There isn't but the one thing that grieves my mind,.....My soul is a witness for my Lord;
Hum..
D. C.
That the streets are pearl and the gates are gold,...My soul is a witness for my Lord.
I want to go to Heav'n all dressed in white,...My soul is a witness for my Lord.
My mother's gone to Heav'n and left me be-hind,...My soul is a witness for my Lord.
Hum..

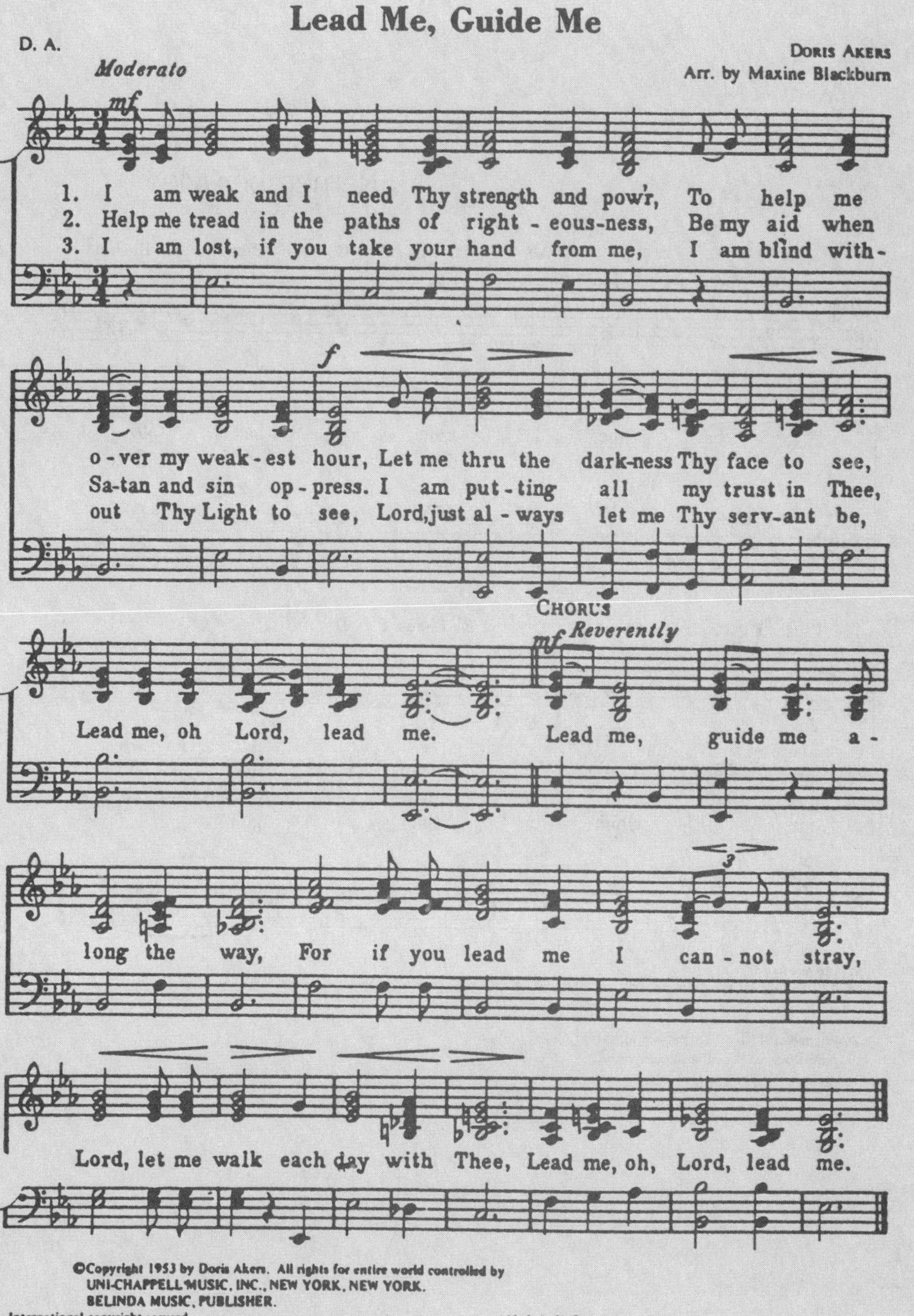
Lead Me, Guide Me
D. A.
Doris Akers
Arr. by Maxine Blackburn
Moderato
1. I am weak and I need Thy strength and pow'r, To help me o-ver my weak-est hour, Let me thru the dark-ness Thy face to see,
2. Help me tread in the paths of right-eous-ness, Be my aid when Sa-tan and sin op-press. I am put-ting all my trust in Thee,
3. I am lost, if you take your hand from me, I am blind with-out Thy Light to see, Lord, just al-ways let me Thy serv-ant be,
Lead me, oh Lord, lead me.
Chorus
Reverently
Lead me, guide me a-long the way, For if you lead me I can-not stray,
Lord, let me walk each day with Thee, Lead me, oh, Lord, lead me.
©Copyright 1953 by Doris Akers. All rights for entire world controlled by UNI-CHAPPELL MUSIC, INC., NEW YORK, NEW YORK.
BELINDA MUSIC, PUBLISHER.
International copyright secured.
Any copying, arranging, or adapting of this composition without consent of the owner is infringement of the copyright.
Used by permission.
Made in U. S. A.

Remember Me

G G A/B B Emsus E G A Bmsus Bm B♭ Em7
p p ff
Re - mem - ber me, re - mem - ber
Fa - ther I stretch my hands to
If thou with - draw thy self from
Fsus F C/E D7/F♯ Gsus G Cm F/E♭ E♭sus E♭ D G7sus C/G G
addD/E♭
p mf p pp
me, Oh Lord, re - mem - ber me.
thee, no oth - er help I know.
me, Oh whith - er shall I go?

Text: Afro-American Spiritual
Tune: Afro-American Spiritual; Harm. by Leon C. Roberts, from *The Mass of St. Augustine,* © 1981, GIA Publications, Inc.

Every Time I Feel the Spirit

Ev - 'ry time I feel the spir - it, mov - ing
in my heart, I will pray. Ev - 'ry - time I feel the
spir - it, mov - ing in my heart, I will pray.
Up - on the moun - tain my Lord spoke,
All a - round me looked so shine,
Jor - dan riv - er, chilly and cold,
D.C.
(Out of) His mouth came fire and smoke.
Asked my Lord if all was mine.
Chills the bod - y but not the soul.

Text: Afro-American Spiritual
Tune: Afro-American Spiritual

Done Made My Vow to the Lord

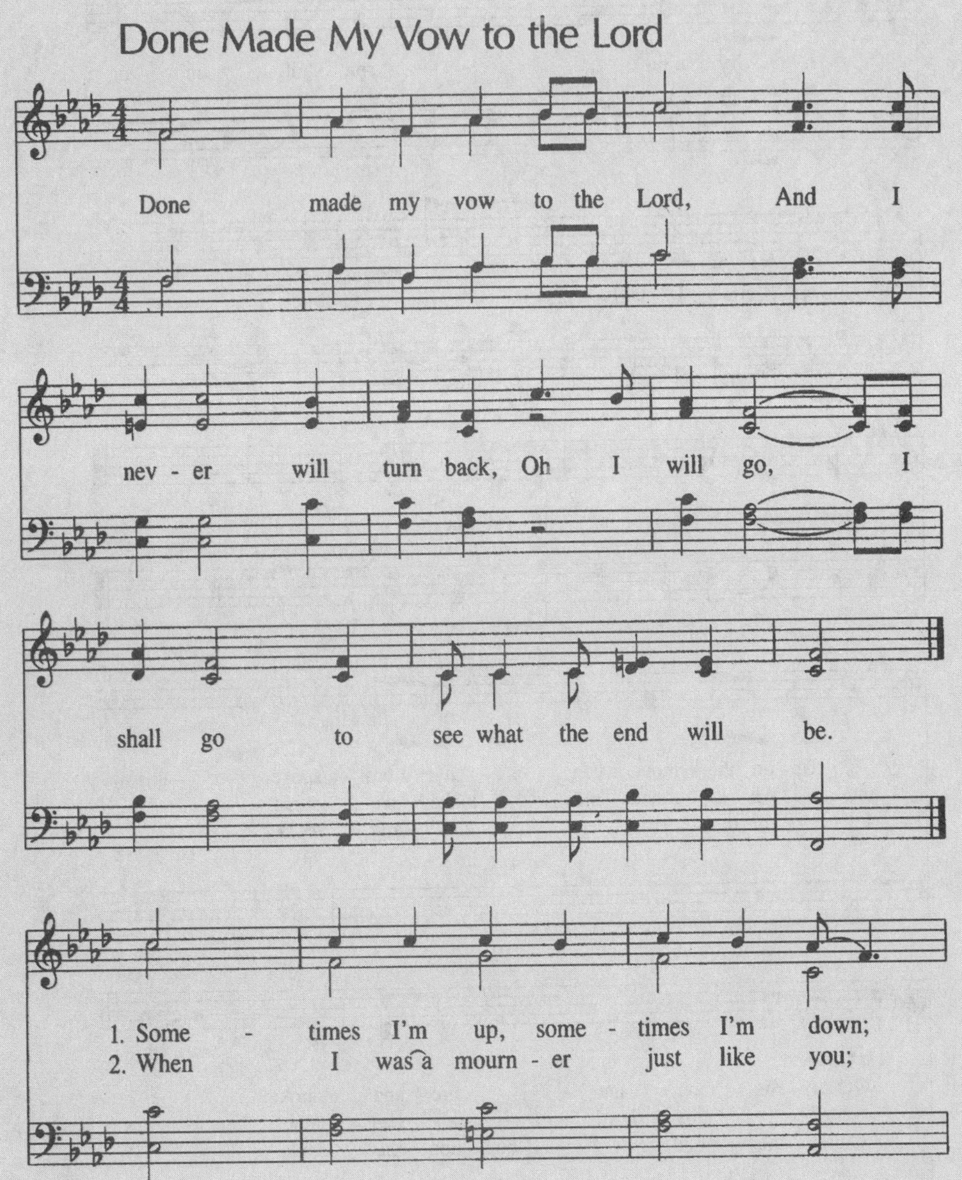
Done made my vow to the Lord, And I
nev - er will turn back, Oh I will go, I
shall go to see what the end will be.
1. Some - times I'm up, some - times I'm down;
2. When I was a mourn - er just like you;

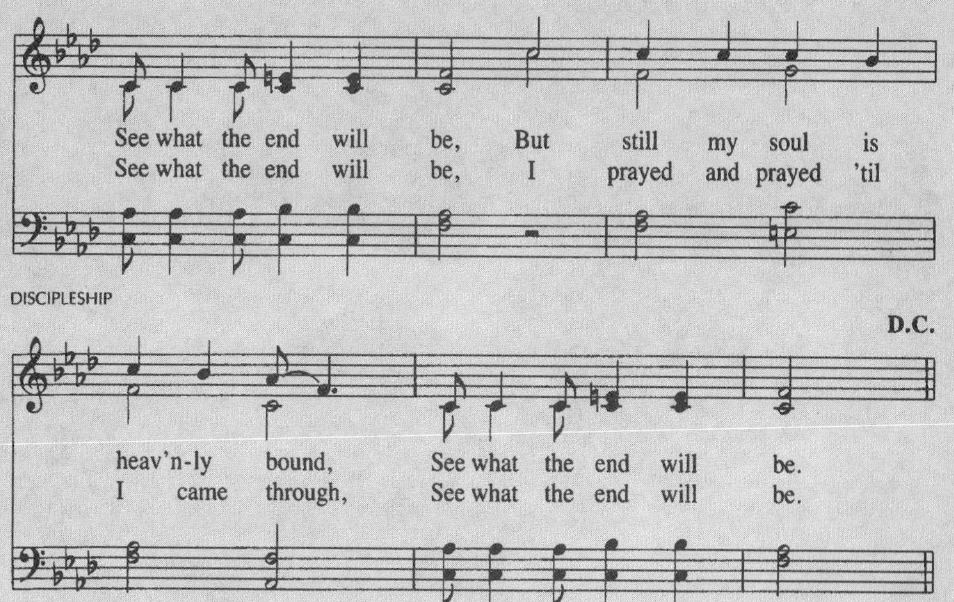
See what the end will be, But still my soul is
See what the end will be, I prayed and prayed 'til
DISCIPLESHIP
D.C.
heav'n-ly bound, See what the end will be.
I came through, See what the end will be.

Text: Afro-American Spiritual
Tune: Afro-American Spiritual; Harm. by Evelyn Davidson White

Holyfield

Sixteen

The Bible in African American Spirituality

Michael I. N. Dash

The Bible has always had a place in the religious experience of African Americans. It was through the Bible that many of their slave ancestors learned to read. Indeed, the Bible became the primary source book for their devotion to the Christian faith and their life journey. The Bible is equally foundational in sustaining them amidst challenges today. African Americans' spirituality is woven into the texture of everyday living. Their knowledge and use of the Bible is a significant resource that helped their ancestors make meaning out of dehumanizing conditions in the slave society. That meaning is enriched through their identification with biblical characters and the story of the drama of the divine-human encounter.

◂ "Family Reunion." Painting by John Holyfield, Holyfield Studio, Centreville, VA

There is a persistent impression which has imprinted itself into my consciousness—a pencil drawing that hung on an office wall. It was the picture of an old black woman. She must have been in her late eighties, perhaps even nineties. She is seated in a chair, bent over with a distinct curvature of her back at the shoulders, a hump, as if stricken with osteoporosis. She has woolly white hair. One of her fingers is placed, perhaps marking the spot in the book she is reading. It is the Bible.

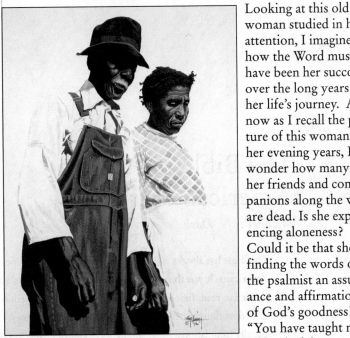

▸ "Bless Us O'Lord," by Tom McKinney Prints

Looking at this old woman studied in her attention, I imagined how the Word must have been her succor over the long years of her life's journey. And now as I recall the picture of this woman in her evening years, I wonder how many of her friends and companions along the way are dead. Is she experiencing aloneness? Could it be that she is finding the words of the psalmist an assurance and affirmation of God's goodness? "You have taught me ever since I was young, and I still tell of your wonderful acts. ...Your righteousness, God, reaches the skies. You have done great things; there is no one like you" (Psalm 71.17, 19).

Then my mind turned to imagine a similar scene in the period of the slave society. Our ancestors too, like that woman in my picture, were acquainted with the Book, both through an oral tradition and later through the text itself. It was in the Bible that our ancestors found the promise of deliverance from the bondage to slavery and sin. It was in the Bible that they found inspiration, solace, and a word of hope. Albert Raboteau reminds us that, "the biblical orientation of slave religion was one of its central characteristics" (Raboteau, 1978, 239).

In this brief article, I will examine the use of the Bible by African Americans and how that use helped to inform and shape their spirituality, indeed their lives. For Africans, as well as African Americans, life is life in the Spirit. Life, as understood by our ancestors, and experienced by us, their children, is always in the totality of our beings—body, mind, and spirit. How then did, and does, the Bible impact and influence the totality of our lives and the tales that we tell? This is the question that is being explored in this article.

The Bible for Us

As Christians, we would claim that the Bible is the source book of our faith. It is the story of humankind's response to God's actions. That response has sometimes been rejection and rebellion, sometimes acceptance and obedience. Jesus Christ is God's act of acts. The acts of God are narrated in the Old Testament (Hebrew Bible) and lead us to Jesus Christ. In the New Testament, the acts of God recorded there flow from him, so that Jesus himself is revealed in his full meaning, or as we see him, in the total context of the biblical witness.

We affirm that the Bible is both a word in a particular historical situation, as well as word for us today. Our challenge in using the Bible is to rediscover the faith of the Bible. This rediscovery will lead us to meet the God of the Bible who reveals who God is in the Word. So as we engage the Bible, we pray:

> Break Thou the bread of life, dear Lord, to me,
> As Thou didst break the loaves beside the sea;
> Beyond the sacred page, I seek Thee, Lord,
> My spirit pants for Thee, O living Word.
>
> Mary Artemisia Lathbury, *The Bread of Life*

Jesus said"You study the Scriptures, because you think that in them you will find eternal life. And these very Scriptures speak about me! Yet you are not willing to come to me in order to have life" (John 5.39, 40). It is the witness of the Scriptures that is the determining factor. They point beyond themselves. Eternal life is not in them but in him to whom they point. When we have finished using all the critical tools available to us for a study of the Bible, we still have to wrestle with the witness of the passage that we are studying. The genius of African American spirituality, and its inheritance from our slave ancestors, is that there is this openness to discover God as revealed in the Word. It is a witness to a concern for every single aspect and area of our daily human existence.

Biblical Christianity enabled our slave ancestors not only to deal with the contradictions of their life, but also to make affirmations about God. This spirituality that enabled their survival was no escapism from their everyday existence. Rather it expressed in those conditions a transcendence that affirmed the presence of the divine-human encounter and relationship.

The Bible has always occupied a significant place in the lives of African Americans. It was from the Bible that many of the slave ancestors learned to read. This ability to read was both dangerous and liberating. Those slaves who could read kept this knowledge secret for fear of bodily harm. Indeed, many had been known, to lose parts of their bodies because they could read. Still others, recognizing the values of learning, were prepared to take that and other risks. They stole out at nights for meetings in deep gullies, to study there by torchlight and have a little time "wid Jesus."

This knowledge gained through reading the text for themselves enabled them to reject the interpretations that contradicted their own sense of humanity and justice. They sought to embrace those interpretations that helped them to make sense and meaning of their harsh daily realities. A sense of community, of belonging to one another is also evident in the slave period. Stories are told of how they learned from one another and shared this learning with others.

On the other hand, there were masters who were anxious for their slaves to learn to read. Slaveholders hoped that if slaves were taught the Bible that they would become docile and obedient slaves. The admonition from Ephesians 6.5 is often offered to support this viewpoint: "Slaves, obey your human masters." It is ironic that, observing how the masters used the Bible, some slaves made clear distinctions between their own experiences of the Christian faith through the Bible and the "Bible Christianity" of their masters. The slaves' response was a freedom-oriented faith.

"It was in the spirituals, above all, that the characters, themes, and lessons of the Bible became dramatically real and took on special meaning for the slaves" (Raboteau, 1978, 243). Those "sorrow" songs forged out of the crucible of pain and suffering, were affirmations of God out of the experience of brutality. Through those spirituals slaves sang of a hope that "trouble don't last always." For them, the present harshness they were experiencing could be endured, and become meaningful, in light of a different and better future to which they looked forward.

Throughout the history of African Americans in this society, the Bible has continued to be influential and affective in their lives. A supercilious visitor once said to a young uneducated black woman in one of the southern small towns, "I see you are reading the Bible." "No, sir," she replied, "the Bible is reading me." She was expressing a profound understanding, that the Word has that capacity to lay bare our souls. "The word of God is alive and active, sharper than any double-edged sword. It cuts all the way through, to where soul and spirit meet, to where joints and marrow come together. It judges the desires and thoughts of the heart. There is nothing that can be hid from God; everything in all creation is exposed and lies open before his eyes. And it is to him that we must all give an account of ourselves" (Hebrews 4.12, 13). It is this awareness of who God is and who we are in God that makes the Christian life possible, because it is a life lived before, in and with God. God is always working on us. The assertion is always being made that "God isn't finished with us yet." These perspectives of life that inform the spirituality of African Americans find their source in the Bible.

Spirituality

Explorations into Meaning

Within the last decade there has been a heightened interest in spirituality. It is often characterized by a deep hunger for meaning in empty lives. Henri Nouwen, one of the spiritual guides of our age, has written,

"One way to express the spiritual crisis of our time is to say that most of us have an address but cannot be found there" (Durback, 1997, 60). There is an ongoing frenetic search for that meaning in many places except where it could ultimately be found, that is, in the center of one's being. "Too many of us seem to be searching for something 'out there' to make our lives complete. We feel alienated, lonely, and empty. No matter what we do or have, we never feel fulfilled. This feeling of emptiness or intense loneliness is our clue that we are off course, and that we need to correct our direction.

Often we think the correction lies in a new mate, house, car, job or whatever. Not so. I believe that what all of us are really searching for is this divine essence within ourselves" (bell hooks, 1995, 342).

Many people's lives are like huge warehouses filled with a variety of things that refuse to suggest why they are there and what is their purpose. Yet we continue to warehouse our addictions, obsessions, violence, failures, fantasies, narcissism, disillusionment about marriage, family, relationships. Such lives are no homes. Very often the hidden cause of the emptiness we sense is a result of a painful and essential alienation from our spiritual selves, the integrating center of our beings. The manifestation of this reality is a truly spiritual experience, a movement of the Spirit in our lives. The Spirit needs a home with large spaces, a home where it is free to move, to grow, to expand. This quest for spirituality is only properly realized as we empty our lives of all the bitterness that we possess, cherish, cling to; and open them to become living spaces for the Spirit. God fills every empty space. Jesus offered the following counsel to someone who was obsessed with filling life with an abundance of things: "your true life is not made up of the things you own, no matter how rich you may be" (Luke 12.15b).

As we discover the need and the way to let go of the "stuff" of everyday living, then the real meaning in our lives is found. "The spiritual life is like making prints from negatives. Often it is the dark forest that makes us speak about the open field. Frequently prison makes us think about freedom, hunger helps us to appreciate food, and war gives us words for peace...often someone's careful and honest articulation of ambiguities, uncertainties and painful conditions of life gives us new hope. The paradox is indeed that new life is born out of the pains of the old" (Durback, 1997, 53).

The spiritual life is simply a life in which all that we do comes from the center of that life in God. It is a life in which we acknowledge God's reality and claim, and yield ourselves to God's will. Spirituality is living life in the Spirit and discovering there the presence of God as love, who challenges us to find and manifest that love through our relationship with others and in God's world. Indeed it is the ordering of our lives so that the Holy Spirit has a chance. It is a way of being open to God in Jesus Christ through the Spirit.

Self-awareness, discovery, discernment, meaning making, attention, journey, relationship, integration, love, justice, community, wholeness, are words that may be used when exploring spirituality. All these words reflect how effective the Bible has been in shaping our life and our behavior. One does not have to labor at making the point that the strong sense of family and community and belonging to one another, being fellow travelers on the journey through life, are evidences of the way in which life is ordered for Africans and African Americans.

This sense of discovering God in the center of one's being and living out of that center is at the core of African and African American spirituality. It is holistic and encompasses the totality of being for African Americans—who we are, what we know, what we feel, and what we do. The conventions of African American spirituality embrace and encompass the totality of our beings. They are unconfined to any exclusively religious expression. One important reason for this is that the distinction between sacred and secular disappears in the African and African American experiences. We are affirming that the encounter with God and the expression of the meaning of that encounter is a total human experience. It calls forth every part of our being—body, mind, and spirit—for expression. This is equally true of the biblical admonition: to love God "with all your heart, with all your soul, with all your strength, and with all your mind; and love your neighbor as you love yourself"(Luke 10.27b).

A fundamental understanding of spirituality both for Africans and African Americans is that it is woven into the texture of everyday life and living. Spirituality is not experienced, discussed, nor relegated exclusively to the religious or sacred realm. Howard Thurman, who continues to be influential in any discussion on spirituality, writes about using "the raw materials of everyday life" as sources for reflection on the meaning of life's experiences. For Africans, the dichotomy between "sacred" and "profane" was never present. Indeed, one might claim that in every aspect of the slave's life in community, fusion and linkage occurred such that the ordinary was pervaded by the sacred.

It is impossible to discuss spirituality without referencing how it impacts the totality of one's life. "For the African, life is one integral whole. There is an interrelationship among the several aspects of life. Social life, politics, economics, morality, spirituality all constitute the "stuff" of life. Human life and existence are guided by religion as a motive principle" (Dash et. al., 1997, 24).

This is equally so for African Americans. There is an inherent unity of personality that illustrates integration created by self-awareness which is inclusive of who they are, what they do, what they know, and what they feel. This configuration also reflects a totality of being and informs any spirituality that may be described. "It is no accident that our ancestors' songs were called 'spirituals'; that others describe us as a 'spiritual' people, 'spirited' people, or 'soulful' people when the context, they assume, is secular rather than spiritual..."(Wade-Gayles,1995, 4).

When Jesus declared that "the Kingdom of God is within you" (Luke 17.21b), he was suggesting that this search for one's identity and integrity finds its fulfillment in the discovery of God within the center of one's being. The actual Greek for "within you" is *entos umon*. One interpretation of the Greek here is that the kingdom is fundamentally a spiritual experience. Its discovery is recognition of God within. The movement of the Spirit in one's life, especially at those points of difficulty and trouble, are opportunities for the discovery of God within and with us through the power of the Spirit to sustain and give hope. George Cummings observes: "The Spirit's sustaining power/presence was nurtured in the secret meetings where black slaves disobeyed their masters' orders and served God, sustained their sense of personal identity and well being, and provided mutual support for each other by giving meaning and hope to their tragic existence" (Cummings, 1991, 49).

The ancestors of African Americans were herded together with others, with their fellow tribespeople from the motherland, with whom they came to share a common condition of servitude. To be sure there was some degree of cultural overlap. These enslaved Africans were compelled to create a new language, a new religion, and a precarious new lifestyle. This lifestyle was to exert a formidable influence on American religious culture. It emerged as a significant force in the shaping of a people and their lives, and consequently, their spirituality.

Spirituality and the Bible

The African American Experience

Slave religion was a continuity of African ancestral religion. In contact with European Christianity on American soil, African American religion became an inventiveness within a tradition. The discussion about cultural continuities reflects not only expressions but content as well. In North America, African culture traits are

▸ West African wood sculpture. "Christ with Crown of Thorns." Photo courtesy Lee Boltin.

evident in transformations more than in survivals. African American spirituality, birthed under conditions of travail and suffering, provided, and continues to provide, a means of survival and hope for a people who claim wholeness for their lives. This claim is grounded in the belief in a God whom they encounter in the totality of their daily existence, at work, at play, and in worship.

The Bible gave them a language to articulate their thoughts, ideas, and feelings about their life and their lives in God, who was for them very present in their daily journey. On the plantation, in their labors in the fields, from sunup to sundown, the slave ancestors were on the journey to freedom. It began when the first shackles were placed on their hands and feet, and our slave ancestors sought to break loose or cast themselves overboard during the Middle Passage. As Theophus Smith contends, "the black story... [is] the pilgrimage of a people toward freedom." (Smith, 1991, 373.) The words of one of the old songs remind us that the slave ancestors "woke up this mornin' wid my mind stayed on freedom." Emancipation, when it came for the slaves, was celebrated with great jubilation. Indeed, that day of deliverance was spoken of as the "day of Jubilee."

Biblical concepts of freedom are significant in themes, in the preaching, in the songs. "Before I'd be a slave, I'll be buried in my grave, an' go home to my Lord and be free." We may assert and indeed suggest that African American spirituality is a liberating spirituality. "In slave religion the figural vision of the emancipation as a type of biblical exodus provides the paradigm for subsequent strategies and acts of political imagination. The exodus figure has informed Afro-American political projects from the post-Reconstruction period to the recent civil rights..." (Smith, 1991, 391).

In the New Testament Jesus teaches about the Holy Spirit in a farewell discourse to his disciples. He promises them that the Spirit will be for them what he was to them. Caleb Oladipo offers some interesting insights into this passage. "There are two words for 'another' in Greek. One is *allos*, and the other is *heteros*. In John 14.16, Jesus promised 'another' paraclete to stay with believers forever. His word 'another' here was *allos* (not *heteros*). Thus, Jesus Christ was describing the Holy Spirit as distinct or separate, but not different or strange from him." Oladipo concludes that "the function of the Holy Spirit...[is] to help the believers attain both the subjective and the objective Christian experience" (Oladipo, October 1989, 39).

African American spirituality is expressed through many conventions. They all illustrate the inclusiveness and totality of life experience for African Americans as it is for Africans. A common core of its expression is the black religious experience, which manifests itself, among other ways, in full sensory engaging worship, triumphant singing, religious education, and prophetic imaginative preaching. We must be reminded that the religious experience profoundly affects the whole of life for African Americans.

Perhaps it is the worship experience that is a most readily observable expression of African American spirituality. This sense of experiencing God during worship through the Spirit is in our heritage. "The spirit realm is conceived as one of freedom. Slaves who were shackled could experience a bit of absolute freedom by abandoning themselves to God's spirit. Through the careful coordination of visual, audio, olfactory, and tactile stimuli, good worship becomes a form of spiritual therapy in which human wholeness is actualized through communion with God" (Franklin, 1997, 31).

Much has been written about the "spirituals." But no exploration of spirituality can avoid some commentary about them and their enduring significance for African American life and culture. Indeed, their contribution is equally an important part of the larger American cultural heritage. They reflect both individual and communal religious experiences and hopes. The spirituals helped to affirm an identity with God for the slave ancestors. Central to that identity was their several understandings of the relationship they had with Jesus. "It is out of this sense of being a child of God that the genius of the religious folk songs is born. There were three major sources from which the raw materials of the Negro spirituals were derived: the Old and New Testaments, the world of nature, and the personal experiences of religion that were the common lot of the people, emerging from their inner life. Echoes from each source are present in practically all the songs" (Thurman, 1975, 18). The spirituals were also creatively adapted and used as freedom songs during the civil rights period (Spencer, 1990, 83-105).

Summary

African ancestors, transported as slaves to labor on American plantations, brought their beliefs, practices, and culture to their life on this continent. These beliefs in God had always informed their daily existence. Indeed, there was no division of life into sacred and secular. For them all life was sacred, filled with the presence of the divine. The individual discovered identity in community and this became a means of survival. It is these aspects of a worldview that were to shape and influence their response to the brutal and dehumanizing experiences during the slave period and a heritage that they bequeathed to their descendants. There was an interconnecting unity in the rhythm of life for our slave ancestors. It was manifest in the totality of human experience—work, play, and worship.

Toward the end of the eighteenth and in the early decades of the nineteenth century, vigorous efforts were pursued to spread

▸ **"The Thankful Poor." Painting by Henry O. Tanner, Art Resource/NY**

Christianity among those early African Americans, both slave and free. For them, the Bible became a significant source of spirituality. This spirituality was evident in all of their lives and found expression in their appropriation of the Bible story—the divine-human encounter and the characters through whom that drama was played. The major character in that drama was Jesus, with whom they identified in many ways. Jesus became not only a personal friend and brother, Jesus was also the subject of sermons and songs, which became known as "spirituals." Jesus became the symbol of suffering, survival, salvation, and hope.

A Concluding Reflection and an Invitation

Carolyn C. Denard tells the story of her grandmother who was dying with Alzheimer's. Communication between them had become impossible. She attempted to address this challenge by, as she puts it, talking "around her so that she could hear the conversation." In the middle of such an engagement, Denard and her sister began to recall old songs that they used to sing, one of which was "A Charge To Keep I Have." When neither of them could recall the second line, Denard "leaned over to Grandmother in a half-hearted gesture to include her in the conversation and asked, 'What were those other words, Grandmother?' 'A charge to keep I have...charge to keep I have...' I repeated searchingly, not expecting a response. And then a miracle happened: as clear as a bell with no stuttering or moaning, and from a woman who had not spoken even her name clearly in almost a year, she answered, 'A God to Glorify'" (Denard, 1995, 131f). The spirit within a body and mind deteriorating spoke loudly of who she was and affirmed an understanding of who God was for her and the commitment she had made to that God. The anticipation of coming face to face with Jesus is heard in that plaintive cry, "Oh, when I come to die, Give me Jesus."

Spirituality is inclusive of the whole of life for African Americans. It reflects interrelationships between body, mind, and spirit; work, worship, and play. An important characteristic is the discovery of self in relation to God and inevitably to others. It is the kind of life of which the Bible speaks and a demand that God makes on our lives. We are free to make that choice in response.

Sources Cited

Cone, James H. *The Spirituals and the Blues: An Interpretation*. New York: Seabury, 1972.

Cummings, George. "The Slave Narratives as a Source of Black Theological Discourse: The Spirit and Eschatology," *Cut Loose Your Stammering Tongue: Black Theology in the Slave Narratives*, Dwight N. Hopkins and George Cummings, eds. Maryknoll, New York: Orbis Books, 1991.

Dash, Michael I. N., Jonathan Jackson and Stephen C. Rasor. *Hidden Wholeness: An African American Spirituality for Individuals and Communities*. Cleveland, Ohio: The United Church Press, 1997.

Denard, Carolyn C. "Defying Alzheimer's: Saving Her Spirit in Song," *My Soul Is A Witness: African American Women's Spirituality*, Gloria Wade-Gayles, ed. Boston: Beacon Press, 1995, 131f.

Durback, Robert, ed. *Seeds of Hope: A Henri Nouwen Reader.* New York: Bantam Books, 1989.

Franklin, Robert M. *Another Day's Journey: Black Churches Confronting the American Crisis*. Minneapolis: Fortress Press, 1997.

hooks, bell. "Walking in the Spirit," *My Soul Is A Witness: African American Women's Spirituality*, Gloria Wade-Gayles, ed. Boston: Beacon Press, 1995, 342.

Oladipo, Caleb Remi. "The Holy Spirit: Distinct but not different from Jesus" *International Christian Digest* (October 1989), 39.

Raboteau, Albert J. *Slave Religion: "The Invisible Institution in the Antebellum South."* New York: Oxford University Press, 1978.

Smith, Theophus H. "The Spirituality of Afro-American Traditions," *Christian Spirituality: Post Reformation and Modern*, Louis Dupre and Don E. Saliers, eds. New York: The Crossroad Publishing Company, 1991, 373, 396.

Spencer, Jon Michael. *Protest and Praise: Sacred Music of Black Religion*. Minneapolis: Fortress Press, 1990.

Thurman, Howard. *Deep River and The Negro Spiritual Speaks of Life and Death*. Richmond, Indiana: Friends United Press, 1975.

Wade-Gayles, Gloria, ed. *My Soul Is A Witness: African American Women' s Spirituality.* Boston: Beacon Press, 1995.

Seventeen

Homegoing

Diane M. Ritzie

◂ "Funeral Procession," painting by Ellis Wilson, 1940. Aaron Douglas Collection. The Amistad Research Center, Tulane University, New Orleans, Louisiana

During America's darkest hour, slavery, with its devastating physical afflictions upon enslaved Africans, was probably the leading cause of death. Escapes, attempted escapes, challenging the slave owners, or standing up for one's rights, could result in death. Learning to read, needing or wanting the neccesities of life—things that were taken for granted by others—also could lead to death.

This article attempts to discuss how death is viewed in the Bible, in the ancient world, and how Africans enslaved in America perceived death in light of their horrific circumstances. The stages of death, based on Kubler-Ross' classic work, are illustrated with biblical examples. A few Negro spirituals that deal with death as a release from bondage are also cited. For the slaves, as well as for African Americans today, homegoing marks the entrance to a blessed, peaceful eternity with the Lord.

Introduction

When I was a child, my grandmother told me all about my mother. My mother had a terminal illness when she gave birth to me and my twin sister. She lived for two more years and then died at the age of nineteen. My mother had received medical care, but to no avail. She refused drastic medical means to prolong her life, and she would not go south to change her environment. My grandmother explained that my mother said she was satisfied with the life she had. It was very difficult for me to understand as a young child, and even now sometimes, how my mother could have been satisfied with her life at such a young age. I wanted to know what was the substance of her life—what she had experienced with God in her life that allowed her to accept death at an early age. As I grew up and learned about the Lord that my mother loved, I began to experience the rich satisfaction of the presence of the Lord in my life. My grandmother told me that my mother prayed for me and for my sister very much before she died. So, her prayers in life, and her acceptance of God's will in death, have given me spiritual strength for experiences with dying and death in my life and in my ministry.

From the moment that a newborn baby takes the first breath, that child is on the road to deterioration and, finally, death. One's life is headed in that direction in spite of whatever achievements may have been accomplished during that lifetime. The human condition, as we know it, mandates the continuation of life and also demands its cessation. One looks optimistically at the processes of growth, maturation and self-actualization; yet these stages of life eventually lead to death.

The Yearning for Death: Release from Bondage

During the period of bondage in the United States, slaves were not permitted to read; nor were they even allowed to learn to read. As they heard the stories from the Old Testament that bore witness to release from bondage by a God who delivers, and as they heard of a Savior called Jesus who promised release from their torturous way of life into an eternal life of peace and joy, the emotions and musical abilities of the slaves ignited the sparks for their beautiful spirituals that emanated from their existence. In this way, slaves became familiar with stories from the Bible which they re-interpreted through song in light of their experience of enslavement.

Many of the Negro spirituals gave affirmation to the fact that slaves were overwhelmed in their plight of bondage. They were without earthly hope and, through song, they expressed a desire for death as a means of release from their oppressive conditions. Howard Thurman, in *Deep River and the Negro Spiritual Speaks of Life and Death,* states "the other-worldly hope looms large, and this of course is not strange; the other-worldly hope is always available when groups of people find themselves completely frustrated in the present. When all hope for release in this world seems unrealistic and groundless, the heart turns to a way of escape beyond the present order. The options are very few for those who are thus circumstanced. Their belief in God leads quite definitely to a position that fixes their hope on deliverance beyond the grave... There is desolation, fear, loneliness, but hope, at once desperate and profound!" Thus death and the afterlife are prominent themes in Negro spirituals. "Soon—a Will Be Done a—with the troubles of the world," a mournful Negro spiritual, communicates the weariness of life for a slave who had no earthly hope. He or she would sing, as this spiritual goes on, "I want t' meet my Jesus, I'm goin' to live with God." Death was viewed as a release from this life and an entrance to a blessed, peaceful eternity with the Lord.

These spirituals—intense with desires, expressions, and yearnings to journey to the afterlife—were also a form of criticism that gave the slaves voice to rail against the intolerable conditions of slavery in everyday life. Yet the spirituals overwhelmingly speak to the blessed hope that is centered in Christ Jesus—a "hope we have of sharing God's glory!" (Romans 5.2b). This is a hope that emanates from suffering, endurance and character (Romans 5.3-5), and the slaves drew their strength from Jesus who suffered, endured shame, and conquered death. The hope of the slaves was grounded in their trust in the Lord and the assurance that they had redemption through his blood and would inherit spiritual blessings (Ephesians 1.3-14).

The Ancient World

In the ancient world, biblical people, including those in the surrounding cultures, lived with the reality of death (Psalm 49.10-12). Most cultures were preoccupied with the "hereafter" — a destiny that they could not control. Quite frequently they were involved with appeasing the gods and caring for the burial places of their deceased loved ones.

Death was accepted in the Ancient Near East as the end of life—be it full or wanting. Although death was unavoidable, people still looked forward to long lives. It is characteristic of humans everywhere to make all attempts to postpone the inevitable; the survival instinct is innate in our humanity.

If one escaped the dangers associated with childbirth (mother and/or child), experienced success against the rigors of life, and eluded deadly illnesses, one generally lived to a "good old age," a term which renders a sense of maturity and completeness. In the Old Testament, there are accounts of people living to a "good old age"—ages which are never reached in our lifetimes. Chapter five of the Book of Genesis records the lifetimes of Adam and his descendants: Adam lived for 930 years, Seth lived for 912 years, Enosh for 905 years, Kenan for 910 years, and Enoch lived for 365 years (which was not very long at that time). According to the Bible, the oldest person who ever lived was Methuselah—969 years. These were all remarkable life spans.

Well after the period of the flood and soon after the patriarchal period, the human life span was shortened. Psalm 90, a prayer attributed to Moses, records these words in verse 10:

> Seventy years is all we have—
> eighty years, if we are strong;
> yet all they bring us is trouble and sorrow;
> life is soon over, and we are gone.

This is approximately what the normal life expectancy is today, and life spans of seventy, eighty, or even ninety years of age are not uncommon.

The biblical record also makes mention of persons whose significant contributions to Bible history, in terms of their callings, did not occur until late adulthood: Abraham was seventy-five years of age when the LORD called him out of his father's house; he was one hundred years old when Isaac was born, and he died at one hundred and seventy-five years of age (Genesis 12.4; 21.5; 25.7). Sarah was ninety years old when she gave birth to Isaac, and she died at one hundred and twenty-seven years of age (Genesis 17.17; 23.1). Moses and Aaron were eighty years old and eighty-three years old respectively when they spoke to Pharaoh about freeing the people of Israel from the bondage of slavery (Exodus 7.7). Moses died at one hundred and twenty years of age in his full strength (Deuteronomy 34.7).

Daily life was difficult in the Ancient Near East. Many times this caused people to cry out to God in their times of distress when they desired the end of life. The ancients believed that the locus of death was the nether world. The "direction" of the grave was downward, leading to the nether world. The grave, referred to as *Sheol* in Hebrew, was considered the abode of the dead. It was not considered just a place for the wicked in the Hebrew mindset, but it was a refuge for respite from a weary, troubled, and undignified life.

Jacob said in his great sadness, when he believed that Joseph was dead, "I will go down to the world of the dead still mourning for my son" (Genesis 37.35b). When Jacob did not want Benjamin to return to Egypt with his brothers for fear of losing him, he told them, "the sorrow you would cause me would kill me, as old as I am" (Genesis 44.29b). Job asked the unanswerable question, "Why let people go on living in misery? Why give light to those in grief? They wait for death, but it never comes; they prefer a grave to any treasure. They are not happy till they are dead and buried"(Job 3.20-22).

In the Old Testament there is no consistent view of death. There are divergent views which are expressed, for the Bible also contains accounts of persons who cry out to God for deliverance from death. The psalmist cried out to God to spare his life, saying, "Come and save me, LORD; in your mercy rescue me from death. In the world of the dead you are not remembered; no one can praise you there"(Psalm 6.4, 5). Psalm 88 is a prayer psalm, a strong cry for deliverance from death. The psalmist implores the Lord to spare his life because: (a) Sheol is a place where he would be separated from God who could save his life (verses 1-3); (b) he did not want to be just another number (verse 4); and (c) he would not be remembered anymore (verse 5).

King Hezekiah was told by the prophet Isaiah that the Lord had set the time of his death. So he prayed diligently to the Lord, saying "Remember, LORD, that I have served you faithfully and loyally and that I have always tried to do what you wanted me to" (2 Kings 20.3). The Lord heard Hezekiah's prayer and added fifteen extra years to his life (2 Kings 20.1-7). As these accounts illustrate, whether the people were seeking death or trying to avoid it, they acknowledged that life and death were in the hands of God. Yet humans, in their sometimes desperate attempts to prolong life and prevent death, protest against the discretion of the Lord who has control over human destiny.

Resurrection in the Old Testament

The Old Testament teaching of the resurrection can be found in a few Scriptures. The writers did not have a complete understanding of what the resurrection was or how it would occur. They had some knowledge, which included the anticipation of eternal life. Job said, "I wish you would hide me in the world of the dead; let me be hidden until your anger is over, and then set a time to remember me"(Job 14.13). Job had a hope of the resurrection, that God would not leave him in the grave forever. Job looked forward to life after death when he said,

> But I know there is someone in heaven
> who will come at last to my defense.
> Even after my skin is eaten by disease,
> while still in this body I will see God.
> I will see him with my own eyes,
> and he will not be a stranger.
>
> (Job 19.25-27)

The Book of Daniel has the major teaching of the resurrection in the Old Testament. The angel told Daniel, "Many of those who have already died will live again: some will enjoy eternal life, and some will suffer eternal disgrace"(Daniel 12.2). The meaning was not revealed to Daniel for "these words are to be kept secret and hidden until the end comes" (Daniel 12.9b).

The Old Testament records several resurrection events. The widow of Zarephath had a son who was raised by Elijah (1Kings 17.17-22); a Shunammite woman had a son who was restored to life by Elisha (2 Kings 4.18-37); and an unnamed man, who was cast into Elisha's sepulchre, was raised to life when his body touched Elisha's bones (2 Kings 13.20, 21). The ancient Hebrews trusted in God and knew that the grave did not have the power to hold them forever.

The Hebrews' views and attitudes toward death constitute a theological issue with which to wrestle—the tension between the desire to die and the hope to live. One can examine these perspectives and consider how they may relate to our thinking about dying and death in today's world.

▸ "Building More Stately Mansions" by Aaron Douglas, oil on canvas, 1944. The Carl Van Vechten Gallery of Fine Arts of Fisk University, Alfred Stieglitz Collection, Nashville, Tennessee

Resurrection in the New Testament

At God's appointed time, Jesus Christ entered humanity's history to announce the Kingdom of God and to confront the works of Satan's kingdom. Salvation is totally God's work in which a right relationship is effected between God and humankind through the sacrifice of Jesus Christ. Through Christ's death and resurrection, believers receive salvation and the assurance of eternal life (1 Corinthians 15.12-19). During his ministry, Jesus raised people from the dead. These miracles accompanied his preaching of the gospel in order to demonstrate the power of God through Christ Jesus.

Jesus had compassion on the widow of Nain and restored to life her only son (Luke 7.11-17). The most detailed account of a resurrection is that of Jesus' calling Lazarus out of a tomb (John 11.1-44). Lazarus had been dead four days, and his body had already begun to decompose (verse 39). Yet, Jesus resurrected Lazarus, thus demonstrating that he had power over Satan who had the power of death. This was when Jesus declared, "I am the resurrection and the life" (verse 25a).

Our resurrection is based on Jesus Christ's resurrection from the dead. His resurrection seals the believers' resurrection. "But the truth is that Christ has been raised from death, as the guarantee that those who sleep in death will also be raised. For just as death came by means of a man, in the same way the rising from death comes by means of a man. For just as all people die because of their union with Adam, in the same way all will be raised to life because of their union with Christ. But each one will be raised in proper order: Christ, first of all; then, at the time of his coming, those who belong to him"(1 Corinthians 15.20-23). This is the hope for the believer—the only hope. Christ's resurrection was accomplished because it was not possible that death's power should be able to hold the Son of God (Acts 2.24). The Holy Spirit raised up Jesus Christ and the Spirit will also give life to believers (Romans 8.11).

Humanity's dilemma over death has been conquered by Jesus Christ. We have a great hope and anticipation before us because "through his death he might destroy the Devil, who has the power over death, and in this way set free those who were slaves all their lives because of their fear of death" (Hebrews 2.14b, 15). The wonderful achievement is that one no longer has to be in bondage to the fear of death (Hebrews 2.15). Fear forces people to do things that they may not desire to do. So, this freedom in Christ enables the believer to live holy before God and, as life ends, to go to God in great anticipation of the blessed hope of the resurrection (Romans 6.5-11).

The Different Stages of Dying and Death

As we read the Bible, we meet persons who express various views concerning death at different stages of their dying process. Each one speaks according to his or her situation. For example, Rachel dies giving birth to her second son. In her last words, she names him *Benoni*, meaning "son of my sorrow" (Genesis 35.18). This must have been heartbreaking for her—she is dying while giving birth and will not be able to participate in her son's upbringing, nor experience the joys of his childhood. The psalmist who cries out in Psalm 88 must have been suffering for a long time. For he says to God, "Why do you turn away from me?" (Psalm 88.14b). So people are at different places along the road to the end.

Dr. Elizabeth Kubler-Ross, in her classic treatise on death and dying, established five stages of the dying process. The first stage is **denial and isolation** in which a person refuses to accept the prognosis of a terminal illness. Kubler-Ross states that this is a psychological defense mechanism which allows the person to gradually get used to the idea of dying. The **isolation** aspect of this stage is that family members and close friends begin to stay away from a dying person because they do not want to face the reality that their loved one is in the final stage of life. This is especially difficult for the dying person who feels rejected because of his or her impending death. Jesus himself experienced such rejection at the time of his betrayal and arrest (Matthew 26.56).

A dying person may also isolate him/herself from family and friends. Jephthah's daughter, who had to be sacrificed to the LORD because of her father's careless vow in return for a military victory (Judges 11.30,31), went away from her father to be alone with her friends for two months to mourn the life that she would never have (Judges 11.37-40). The essence of her life would have been the rearing of children, for this was a vital responsibility for the female in the ancient world, and also a sense of accomplishment and achievement. What Jephthah's daughter mourned was the loss of a fulfilled life. It was not just her impending death itself for which she and her friends grieved, but life's essence or potential that death brings to a halt.

The second stage is **anger** in which a dying person resents him/herself, family, friends, the doctors, and even God. The anger may be suppressed or expressed in strong words and/or actions. A number of psalms express such anger. For example, the psalmist writes: "How much longer will you forget me, LORD? Forever? How much longer will you hide yourself from me? How long must I endure trouble? How long will sorrow fill my heart day and night? How long will my enemies triumph over me? Look at me, O LORD my God, and answer me. Restore my strength; don't let me die" (Psalm 13.1-3).

The third stage is the **bargaining process** in which the person begins to realize that it does no good to be angry with God. So promises are made to God if God will let the person live. Many times people promise to change their lives for the better if God will heal them. But many times these promises are short-lived. When requests for physical healing are not granted, it does not mean that God is uncaring, even though some may interpret it as such. There are many questions for which there are no sufficient answers. Then there is the point in each and every life when it will be "the end."

In the biblical text, Hezekiah denies the termination of his life and prays to the Lord for an extension of time. He bargains with God by explaining how faithful he has been, and God chooses to extend his life (2 Kings 20.1-7). When God told Moses that he would not be permitted to enter the Promised Land and that he would die, Moses sought to bargain with God. But God told Moses to stop asking for what he wanted; rather Moses was instructed to encourage and strengthen Joshua because God had chosen Joshua to lead the people across the Jordan, and had decreed that Moses would die on the mountain overlooking Canaan (Deuteronomy 3.23-29; 32.48-52; 34.4-8).

The examples of Hezekiah and Moses illustrate how people bargained with God and how God dealt with each one individually according to God's own purpose. In the case of Moses, whose request was denied, we learn from the New Testament that Moses appeared at Jesus' transfiguration. Luke's account tells us that Moses and Elijah spoke with Jesus concerning Jesus' impending suffering, death, and resurrection (Luke 9.28-31).

The fourth stage is **depression** in which a dying person becomes physically exhausted and emotionally depleted. There are two types of depression—one in which the person has lost self-esteem, a job, etc., and also the type of depression in which loss and separation is anticipated. King Saul experienced both types of depression after being told of his impending death. He was very weak and refused to eat (1 Samuel 28.20-25).

The fifth and final stage is **acceptance**, in which a person accepts death. When Jacob was near death, he outlined the plans for his burial (Genesis 47.30; 48.29-33) and blessed his family (Genesis 48, 49).

In the New Testament it is recorded that, when Jesus was about to go to the cross, he prayed diligently in the Garden of Gethsemane. He...threw himself face downward on the ground, and prayed, "My Father, if it is possible, take this cup of suffering from me! Yet not what I want, but what you want" (Matthew 26.39b). The cup could not pass from Jesus. In him was humanity's only hope. The thief on the cross asked Jesus to remember him when Jesus came into his kingdom (Luke 23.42). This thief had accepted his fate and his hope was centered in Christ.

We are not sure whether or not the people of the Bible cited above went through all five stages outlined by Kubler-Ross. These are but a few examples from the Bible that depict how some people reacted to impending death. From these witnesses of the faith, we learn that their experiences were not unlike those of people today.

Conclusion

Even with the modern scientific competence to examine the dying and analyze the different stages of death, its process cannot be understood completely. The fetus in the womb can be examined before birth, and an autopsy can be performed on a body after death, but the complete knowledge of dying and death still rests with God.

People today are no different from ancient men and women. The same perplexities about dying and death also plague us. As believers, the difference is our belief in Christ with the hope of the resurrection and the promises of God that are revealed in the Bible. We will receive glorified bodies (Romans 8.23; 1 Corinthians 15.35-57; Philippians 3.21); new heavens and a new earth (Isaiah 65.17-25; 2 Peter 3.13); and the physical and emotional healing promised in Isaiah 25.6-10a and in Revelation 21 and 22.

Mother and Son

As a prison chaplain, I receive requests for different types of assistance from family members of inmates. One day I received a request to help a dying mother who desperately wanted to see her son for the last time. The son was in prison many miles away, and it was very difficult to arrange for a compassionate visit. Although the authorities were working on arranging it, the mother was deteriorating rapidly. Yet she was holding on with everything she had to be granted her last request. Due to some intractable circumstances, I was told that the visit could not be arranged. I was asked to go to the hospital to break this dismal, heart-wrenching news to the mother. I felt helpless and weak—I did not have the strength to do it. I fell to my knees and prayed for strength and wisdom to carry out this request. My prayer to God was for this mother not to die in disappointment and sadness. As I was about to leave for the hospital, the phone rang, and I was told to delay giving her the news because the authorities were going to make one more attempt. I felt encouraged and went on to the hospital to minister to the mother.

When I arrived at the hospital, the mother and I were introduced to each other. She was extremely weak, and I knew that she was using all her strength to hold on. She asked me if any progress had been made regarding the visit. I told her that we were still trying. She told me she was trying to accept whatever the outcome would be. I asked her if she knew the Lord Jesus Christ. She said "no" and then asked me if I thought it was now time. I said "yes" and she said she wanted to know the Lord. So I read some Scriptures and then we prayed. She received Jesus Christ as her Lord and Savior. She told me she experienced a sense of release and relief and was at peace.

The mother's sister called me the next morning to tell me that the mother had the first night of a complete peaceful sleep. She was praising God on her deathbed. Within a few days, the mother died. She never had the opportunity to see her son, but she did meet the Son, the Son of Righteousness, Jesus Christ our Lord and Savior. She experienced "homegoing" and the joy of being welcomed by Jesus into his loving arms.

The song, "Goin' Home" by William Arms Fisher (1861-1948) and sung to Anton Dvorak's "Largo" from his "New World Symphony," captures the hope shared by those who believe and trust in God's everlasting love.

"Goin' Home"

Goin' home, goin' home, I'm a-goin' home;
Quiet like, some still day, I'm jes' goin' home.

It's not far, jes' close by, Through an open door;
Work all done, care laid by, Gwine to fear no more.

Mother's there 'spectin' me, Father's waitin' too;
Lots o' folks gathered there, All the friends I knew.
All the friends I knew.

(Home, home, I'm goin' home!)

Nothin' lost, all's gain, No more fret nor pain.
No more stumblin' on the way,
No more longin' for the day,
Gwine to roam no more!

Mornin' star lights the way, Res'less dream all done;
Shadows gone, break o' day, Real life jes' begun.

Dere's no break, ain't no end, Jes' a-liv-in' on,
Wide awake, with a smile, Goin' on and on.

Goin' home, goin' home, I'm jes' goin' home;
It's not far, jes' close by, Through an open door.
I'm jes' goin' home.
Goin' home.

Jesus said, "I am the gate. Those who come in by me will be saved; they will come in and go out and find pasture" (John 10.9). Jesus is the open door for our "homegoing." The apostle Paul counsels that we are not to grieve as "...those who have no hope. We believe that Jesus died and rose again, and so we believe that God will take back with Jesus those who have died believing in him....So then, encourage one another with these words" (1 Thessalonians 4.13, 14, 18). Our hope is indeed grounded in "goin' home" to the Lord.

Works Consulted

Cooper, John W. *Body, Soul, & Life Everlasting.* Grand Rapids: Eerdmans, 1989.

Kubler-Ross, Elizabeth. *On Death and Dying.* New York: Macmillan, 1969.

Miller, Patrick D. *They Cried to the Lord: The Form and Theology of Biblical Prayer.* Minneapolis: Fortress Press, 1994.

Thurman, Howard. *Deep River and the Negro Spiritual Speaks of Life and Death.* Richmond: Friends United Press, 1990.

Eighteen

The Blessing: Restoring Hope for African American Youth

Maxine M. Walker

According to *Harper's Bible Dictionary* hope is "the expectation of a favorable future under God's direction." The four components of hope mentioned in the article, Promise, Purpose, Perseverance, and Prosperity, are pregnant with the activity of God and are waiting to be delivered toward the fulfillment of purpose in the lives of our youth. It is the intent of this article to encourage our youth to see themselves partnered with God to work toward the fulfillment of purpose in their lives. The Blessing is the extension of the lifeline of hope to present and future generations and encourages them to seek their place in salvation history.

◂ "Family," by Charles Alston, 1955, oil on canvas. Photograph 1997, Whitney Museum of American Art, New York

Historically, African Americans have found comfort and direction from the generational sharing of ancestral stories. In addition to chronicling vivid and moving accounts of slave journeys, these stories have also been sources of strength and lessons in motivation, pride, determination, and perseverance to many generations. The value of the stories is enhanced by their poignant rehearsal of motivation, pride, determination and perseverance which enabled our ancestors not only to survive, but also to bequeath a legacy of uncompromising faith, an unsurpassed love for God, and a blessing of promise. This legacy is ours. Our ancestral parents lived their existence in hope. This is the blessing they handed down to us, and to our youth.

Living in an era of mixed media and mixed messages, our young people often find it difficult to embrace the legacy of their ancestral history and yet be fully in tune with today's society. Because of peer pressure and other outside influences, there is an ambivalence on the part of our youth to link the rich history of their heritage with the social norms of the prevailing culture.

As we witness many of our neighborhoods being torn apart by domestic and societal violence and inadequate community services, it is imperative that we teach our youth that hope is alive. Hope makes room for creative resources in reconciling brokenness and conflictual messages. Hope is a gift from God and part of the legacy bequeathed to us from our ancestral parents. Yes, there is still hope. Despite the enemy's desire to rob our youth of this knowledge, the Bible reminds us that without vision (or hope) our people will perish (Proverbs 29.18). In hope, God created order out of chaos. The message to our youth, then, should be that God is still creating order.

Our young people who have grasped a glimmer of this hope are doing marvelous things! We watch proudly as our youth excel in city or statewide exams; we beam at those who at year's end throw their mortar boards high in the air—graduates of some fine institution of learning; we stand in the wings as we see our young people become lawyers, sanitation workers, entrepreneurs, carpenters, teachers, secretaries, nurses, construction workers, army personnel, loving home-makers, professional athletes, historians. Like the village elders, we pat our chests because we know it takes a village to raise a child. We know how important the stories are; we know just how important the blessing of hope is.

As a benefactor of this blessing, I remember the indelible impact that my great-grandmother made on me at the tender age of five.

When I was five years old my great-grandmother was an awesome figure for me. I would spend hours on end listening to her fascinating and rich stories. Her hopes, her faith, and her love for God were paramount in shaping my reality. At five years of age I was inserted into the age-old story that is lineal. My great-grandmother's stories were strong and full of traditional and cultural truth. Her truth, which later became my own, had its foundation in pride and hope. This is indeed the blessing of an old, illiterate African American woman who was very articulate and powerfully eloquent in expressing her faith and hope.

Our historical theological concept is rich in hope, born out of our grief, pain and suffering, and our belief in the eternal hope of God. It is a transformative hope, which takes its historical context from our desire for change. This context was no louder heard than from the traditional black church with its consciousness relating to dynamic social change and cultural transformation.

Not all our youth have fully understood the blessing. Parents, as well as the church, have an awesome responsibility in keeping the message of hope alive. We need to challenge those young people who have not claimed their blessing to believe in a God who is bigger than any system. Our God can provide them with a future and give them a reason to prepare themselves for one. As we hand down the wisdom we were taught, and expect more from our youth, they will, in turn expect more of themselves, and hope will become visible.

In order to secure the survival of generations to follow, African American youth must be steered toward renewed spiritual values. The answer is not in a *new* way of worship, but rather a worship that would incorporate cultural identity, reestablish strong and nurturing faith communities, grounded in hope. Moreover, they can be proud of a culture and heritage that instill good work ethics, strong moral character, and a steadfast faith nurtured in hope. This is the blessing of our ancestral parents. This is the gift we continue to offer our youth. If the story grows weak, and the faces of our ancestral parents grow dim, then the stain of their blood fades into oblivion, and we lose our purpose and direction.

Purpose or direction is vital for survival. Our youth are inheritors of the blessing handed down to them from ancestors who believed that their offspring would continue to spread the good news of love and forgiveness; that each generation would find its purpose and persevere; that they not be tainted by the ignorance of the hatred they experience because of the color of their skin; that they would fight for justice and a chance to move forward toward a prosperous future. The fight must continue; but without hope, it is impossible. We, as adults, must continue to echo the message from the past by telling them to "press on." African American youth must be encouraged to receive the blessing and not be deceived by the enemy.

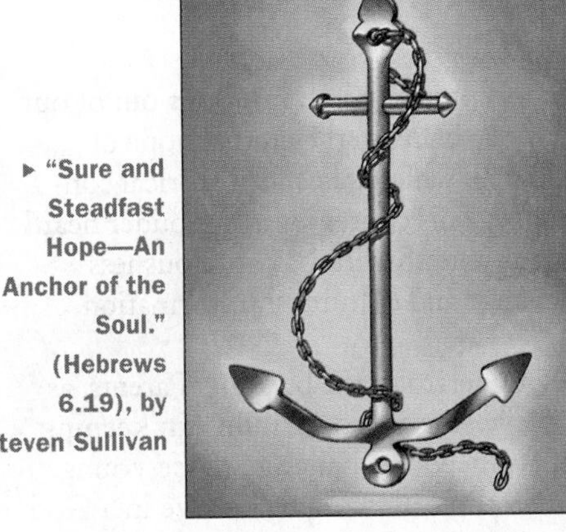

▸ "Sure and Steadfast Hope—An Anchor of the Soul." (Hebrews 6.19), by Steven Sullivan

Hebrews 6.19 says that hope is the anchor of the soul. The hope that Hebrews speaks of, and our ancestral parents left us, is Christ. This hope extends the scope of forgiveness of sins, love, liberation, justice, peace, and eternal life. In other words, it is a hope of inner and outer transformation that anchors our faith in Jesus Christ. If this hope is not solidly anchored, our youth will wander without direction. As adults, we must not neglect our responsibility to serve as prophetic voices for our youth.

The message of the gospel is good news and it is available for everyone. Our youth are entitled to hear all of the good news. Surely, the most important is salvation and eternal life, but Christ promises more. In hope, young people can find the liberation of spirit, mind, body, talent, and the ability to succeed in life. They are entitled to hear, and choose to claim as their own, the message, because the message of hope will keep them grounded, focused, and confident toward the fulfillment of their purpose. It affords them the opportunity to live in expectation of things to come: "I wait eagerly for the LORD's help, and in his word I trust" (Psalm 130.5).

Hence, African American youth should be encouraged to embrace moral living, to have ambition, to dream dreams and to keep the faith. Hope liberates and frees one's spirit to breathe life into one's aspirations. It can grow out of the doubt that one experiences in failure. Hopelessness and a sense of powerlessness find no home where hope abides. So, then, hope grows out of faith and is sustained by faith which undergirds its birth. "Thus in the Christian life faith has the priority, but hope becomes a utopia and remains hanging in the air. But without hope, faith falls to pieces, becomes fainthearted and ultimately a dead faith." (*Moltmann, Theology of Hope,* p. 20)

African American youth have been dealt a devastating blow. They have been left without direction but are expected to move ahead. They are told how they shouldn't be, but they have no clear understanding of how they should be. They feel betrayed by a God who promises to protect and by Christians who don't practice what they preach. They have been robbed of their blessing, the message of hope, and they should have it back; and it is our responsibility to see to it that they do. I would encourage our youth to become more accountable, seek God's grace, and experience hope in the act of love on the cross; and for us as adults to be accountable to our responsibility for their care and nurture, to support and to encourage them toward restored wholeness.

The church has the awesome responsibility of keeping the message of hope alive in the lives of young people despite the many distractions they face. It is challenged to nurture them in the faith, instill in them a pride that makes them cognizant of who they are in Christ, and remind them of the history of their race.

First, our youth must discover the **promise in hope.** The transforming power, grounded in the promise, encourages one to strive toward where one desires to be. Where can youth discover this except in seeing themselves as part of that promise and a part of the same story, which began many years ago? It was in Israel's hope-giving promise that Israel found its truth. As African Americans we need to know that the promise speaks to us from the cross as we participate in salvation history. This promise we bring to our youth—a promise that is sustained in the tests of present perils. Our youth must be able to see the transcendence of God through Jesus Christ and Christ transcendent through African American adult Christians. The transforming promise that Christ offers is liberation, inclusivity, and a social order that opposes the injustices of society. To live in the promise of hope is to live positively in the present. The promise serves as a healing salve for the pain and betrayal that has been inflicted on our youth. It becomes imperative that youth are receptive and forgiving.

Secondly, our youth must be able to discover the **purpose in hope.** Why should we hope? Purpose gives reason to continue in one's efforts toward attaining one's goals. Purpose deters doubt and keeps one focused in spite of obstacles. Hope gives one a base from which to work, and purpose gives one a target for which to aim.

▸ **"The Banjo Lesson," by Henry O. Tanner, oil on canvas, Hampton University Museum, Virginia**

The restlessness, hopelessness, and the belief that nothing will change for the better makes a powerful impact on how one perceives him/herself and the future. Purpose teaches one how to build and not destroy, to hope rather than to despair, to work for peace rather than warring against each other, to love rather than to hate. This is the purpose in hope. It builds strong and lasting stories to be handed down proudly to one's children's children. It sustains life. There are times when the purpose in hope teaches us to wait, and there are other times when it teaches us to seek. This is part of the blessing our forebears handed down through generations.

When to wait and when to seek was thematic in the mentality of our slave mothers and fathers. The purpose in hope became their focus for survival. They believed in the eschatological teaching of Christ who promised to liberate them from the cruelty of slavery. The slaves believed in a God who loved them, accepted them, and identified with their suffering. This gave them purpose toward survival, that purpose in part, being reason enough to work toward securing our race and our rightful place in salvation history. Their purpose was to secure the blessing for generations to come.

Hope does not accept things as they are, but Moltmann surmises that it is alive and progressing with reason to believe that change can take place. Our youth today can be proud of such a rich history, a story not told often enough. They should be encouraged to see the importance of having such a legacy on which to build and to live out their purpose. There is a need to hear the prophetic voices from the past as they speak from the riverbanks of old. Our youth have a right and a responsibility to continue the blessing. They must be **taught** that they are the continuance of salvation history. They must **believe** that with every generation, God will bring forth leaders who will carry on the traditions of the African American race, and who will have a positive impact on every race, color, and creed. As they are endowed with the blessing, these voices of young, strong, visionary African Americans will speak with fervor, wisdom of revelation, renewed strength and restored hope.

Thirdly, our youth are encouraged to seek assurance and conviction which wills them to **persevere,** all the time recognizing God's grace to enable them in their struggles. They must stay focused, remain steady, and tune out negative influences. To help them, we must build a strong bridge of positive, open communication in which they feel free to share their aspirations as well as their fears.

It is imperative for the survival of our youth that they experience God's redeeming love and the nurture of a caring community.

I recall my great-grandmother's teaching and nurturing, her confidence in me, and her belief in a loving God to protect me. Because of the hope she instilled in me at an early age, I have persevered. She blessed me with the good news and continued to assure me of God's love, and I always needed to hear it.We can never remind our youth too much that the same is true for them. Too many of our youth do not have the same reference as I and many others of my generation had, but we, as adults, should see each child as an extension of ourselves and instill in him/her the tools for success. Further, each child should be encouraged to live and to persevere towards his/her purpose in life. For example, the emerging of a butterfly from a cocoon signifies life and celebration. The message of hope is new life. The cross and the resurrection stand as reminders that all can be recipients of new life. For this reason our youth should be directed to look to the cross and the resurrection, to embrace them both in order to become empowered to persevere so that they may grow in God's grace and fulfill their purpose and gain eternal life.

I also encourage our youth to explore the certainty of **prosperity in hope.** Prosperity assures them of a favorable future with God. They can invest in that future under God's direction to build a trust fund that reaches maturity at the consummation of the last day. As long as they are fully confident of its payoff, hope will never fail them (Romans 5.5).

Long after my great-grandmother died, hope continued to find its way through stories told within my faith community. This community helped me build a dream so vivid I was compelled to make it my reality. We must help young people build dreams, teach them how to succeed, allow them the freedom to explore and to exercise hope for themselves.

Young people are included in God's plan for the world. For God so loved the world that God gave God's best to the world—the gift of life, now and eternal. Youth have within themselves all the potential to be the best they can be. It is important that young people's lives be so impacted by the message to persevere that they will experience the fulfillment of hope.

The author of Hebrews tells us what hope is and what hope does. Jurgen Moltmann brings hope from the eschatological to the present.

▸ "Children of the World," photo composite by Ed Horowitz/ Tony Stone Images

In order to move forward and to remain a part of salvation history, young people must continue the blessing of their ancestral parents, seek after justice, live in hope, and share the good news of the gospel. In other words, they must be willing agents and catalysts for a transforming change for all humankind.

As African Americans, we learned this sitting at the feet of our ancestors. In their own way, they were articulate and eloquent in living out their belief system. As an emotional people (no apology) we have always been able to achieve spiritual health and wholeness through our cultural practices, which included stories, dance, and exerting other kinds of motion or physical energy. We have been affirmed by these stories handed down through generations, and we have been empowered through Jesus Christ. This has always made sense in our culture. This was and should always be the premise by which we "live and move and exist" (Acts 17.28b). This is the blessing we hand down to our young people. It is in the hope of this premise that they find coherence, balance, and fortitude.

Hope keeps us connected to Jesus Christ. Our ancestral parents knew this, no matter where they were: in the fields, in the big house, or under the slavemaster's whip; somehow, they were able to feel the nearness of God. The anchor of hope liberates us and transforms us to meet the ultimate challenge of experiencing the fulfillment of God's promise of eternal life while keeping us in the presence of today. Soren Kierkegaard called hope the passion for what is possible. It complements our faith.

Our young people are our most precious resource. We must continue to instill in them that faith undergirds hope, and hope is the ***promise*** that allows us to live in expectation of eternal life and all the blessings of God; ***purpose*** allows us to remain focused toward eternal life and all the blessings of God, ***perseverance*** teaches us to remain constant so that we can experience eternal life and all the blessings of God, and ***prosperity*** is the reaping of the harvest. This is the blessing.

▸ "Roots," oil on board by Walter Williams, Fisk University Collection, Nashville, Tennessee

The Scriptures (Proverbs 14.26,27) tell us that the blessings of prosperity involve the fear of the Lord and that this fear or "aweness" not only secures a place for the parents, but the children are also promised a fortress and a refuge. The children will reap the rewards of the faith of the parents, and the children are encouraged to embrace the promise that God will be their protector and will cover them in honor of the parents' faith, trust and hope.

Young people, this is your legacy. This is your blessing. Be wise enough to accept it graciously, and in return, hand it down for generations to come. You have been endowed with the richest inheritance which cannot be compared to any other. Guard it carefully. Proverbs says it best, "Reverence for the LORD gives confidence and security" (Proverbs 14.26) and, like a secure fortress, reverence or fear of the Lord will be a refuge for our children and youth.

Sources Cited

Evans, C. Stephen. *Soren Kierkegaard's Christian Psychology*. Bellingham, WA: Regent College, 1995.

Moltmann, Jurgen. *Theology of Hope*, New York: Harper & Row, Publishers, 1976.

Valeriana
Salvia

Nineteen

Racial Reconciliation and the Challenge of Jubilee Justice in the United States: A Black Catholic Perspective

Bryan N. Massingale

The work of justice and social restoration is one of the principal themes of the biblical jubilee. This article explores what taking this jubilee summons seriously might entail for American believers. The basic point made is this: virtually every form of injustice in the United States either stems from, or is aggravated by, a pervasive consumer mentality and a pernicious, enduring racism. Therefore, American individuals and communities of faith cannot answer the call to justice without combating racism and committing themselves to the cause of racial reconciliation. Using insights rooted in the Catholic social tradition and the biblical narratives of the Jubilee year, one sees that embracing and speaking the truth about our social situation is an indispensable component of authentic racial justice and healing. This arduous task is not optional for believers. Yet, we are inspired and sustained by the witness of those who have gone before us and the steadfastness of a promise-keeping God.

◂ **Saint Martin de Porres, Robert Lentz, Courtesy Bridge Building Images, Burlington, VT.**

I. The Context: The Existence of "Permissible Victims"

On the weekend of July 4, 1999, a young man named Benjamin Smith went on a shooting spree in Illinois and Indiana. Before his rampage of hate ended with his suicide, he killed two men—one African American, the other Asian American—and wounded nine others. Smith targeted these victims because he considered them inferior. Why? Because they differed from the norm of "Christian whiteness" he and others believe essential to "true" American identity.

A week later, President Clinton visited regions of the United States untouched by the current boom of economic prosperity so celebrated by Wall Street. Among his stops was the Pine Ridge Indian Reservation in South Dakota. While the national unemployment rate is about 4%, the unemployment rate of this reservation is 73%. It is noteworthy that the last American president to visit an Indian reservation was Franklin Roosevelt (over *nine* presidents ago). This pointedly illustrates the history of neglect endured by Native Americans.[1]

Newsweek magazine on July 5, 1999 reported that in several Silicon Valley companies, 25% of the employees are millionaires—a reflection of the information-based economic expansion. Not noted, however, is that the same percentage of American children—25%—live in poverty.

These events are more than random, isolated coincidences. They bear witness to a disturbing reality: we live in a nation with "*permissible victims,*" that is, those whose lives, dignity, and life opportunities can be violated with little social outrage, public notice, or civic protest.[2] For example, it is because some are "permissible victims" that the nation will bail out savings and loans, banks, and corporations, rescuing them from the consequences of corporate irresponsibility . . . and yet tens of millions of America's poor can be written off, neglected and cast aside under the pretext of "personal responsibility." The existence of such "permissible victims" in American society is America's greatest justice challenge.

II. The Reasons: The Ideology of Consumerism and Endemic Racism

It is not enough merely to note the existence of this reality. We must push deeper, and ask, "Why?" Why, especially in the midst of unprecedented economic prosperity, do such groups exist? Of the many reasons, I will focus upon two.

The first reason: "Permissible victims" are a reflection and consequence of an American culture of consumerism. Consumerism, simply defined, is a mentality or worldview which measures one's personal worth primarily by *what* one has, *how much* one has, and one's *ability to get more*. In a consumer culture, one is defined by what one has; the consumer culture's credo is: "I have; therefore, I am."[3]

As a result, in a consumer culture the poor are "worthless." Why? They don't have much. What they have isn't worth much. And, they lack the resources to get more. Hence, the poor are unwanted, irrelevant, nonessential, and expendable—in a word, "permissible victims." In a consumer society, the plight of the poor is unworthy of sustained civic attention or public concern.

However, we must push this analysis still further, for while 25% of America's children are seemingly trapped in poverty, a disproportionate number of these are children of color. Though 25% of Silicon Valley's employees are millionaires, their ranks are overwhelmingly white.[4] Finally, though all hate crimes are heinous, we must not overlook the fact that the vast majority of hate crimes are racially motivated, with the preponderance being perpetrated by whites upon blacks.[5]

My point is this: a second—and perhaps the *major*—reason for the existence of "permissible victims" in American society is *racism*: the collective conviction that people with darker skin are less important and more expendable than those with lighter skin. Wherever we turn, whatever the particular justice struggle which most concerns us, we cannot be long engaged in it without encountering the brick wall of racism. This is because virtually every pressing social concern facing the United States—education, care for the environment, access to health care, gun control, capital punishment, immigration, refugees, migrant farm workers, right-to-life, HIV/AIDS, criminal justice, workers' rights, concern for women—is entangled with or aggravated by racial bias against people of color. In fact, Pope John Paul II recently reminded American citizens: "As the new millennium approaches, there remains another great challenge facing . . . [your] country: *to put an end to every form of racism, a plague which [is] one of the most persistent and destructive evils of the nation.*"[6]

In short, the challenge of jubilee justice cannot be met unless American believers confront squarely the issue lurking beneath all national justice concerns: the enduring reality of racial injustice and privilege in American life. Unless we attend to and combat racism, domestic struggles for justice will be partial, inadequate, and doomed to failure.

III. The Challenge: Racial Reconciliation

Hence, the major task of domestic jubilee justice is racial reconciliation. Reconciliation is more than mere racial "integration," which very often results in lives that intersect without real connection.[7] Racial reconciliation entails a fundamental transformation of American society by eliminating the social stigma or privilege assigned to racial differences. The aim of genuine racial reconciliation is the building of a society where race is no longer a basis for social hierarchy.

IV. The Strategy: Seeking and Embracing the Truth

But how? How do faith-filled individuals and communities of faith facilitate such a major social transformation? The jubilee narrative of Leviticus 25 gives important insight into this question.

The Jubilee Year was to be a time when the social divisions between the rich and poor were healed through a process of communal remembering. Everyone was to return to his or her familial lands (Leviticus 25.10). The community was then to remember the ancestral claims upon the land, and in light of that memory, to restore what was lost or taken away to its rightful owners. Through a collective remembering of the past, the social wounds of the present were healed. The key catalyst to social reconciliation in the Jubilee Year was a communal act of remembering.

What does this mean for America at the beginning of the twenty-first century? The pursuit of jubilee justice in the United States—especially the task of racial reconciliation—must be grounded in an honest engagement with our past, so that we can heal the present and create a new future. As a nation, we have not made peace with our past; we are so eager to get beyond it and put it behind us. "Get over it" has become a national mantra, directed especially

▸ "The Past," Ana Bel Lee Washington, Courtesy SuperStock.

toward the victims of historic social injustices. But we cannot be reconciled as a people by telling each other, "Get over it! Let bygones be bygones," for our past is not "past," but present as an enduring legacy and oppressive burden. The past will not let us go unless we face it and tell the truth about it. A just society can only be built on truth. As James Cone, a preeminent black theologian, so rightly notes, "Amnesia is an enemy of justice."[8] If we seek a harvest of justice, we must sow seeds of truth.

To be racial reconcilers, then, as believers and citizens we must forthrightly face the legacy of our not so distant past. We must embrace the truth about and remember:

- the *Chinese laborers* who suffered cruel indignities while building the western railroads;

- the *Japanese citizens* forcibly removed to prisoner of war camps, victims of national hysteria and paranoia;

- the *Latino peoples* persecuted, displaced, uprooted, and twice-colonized in their own land;

- the *American Indians* shamelessly massacred, culturally denuded, and systematically hunted and exterminated —an American instance of "ethnic cleansing" never fully acknowledged or properly named;

- *the enslavement of African peoples:* the national "shadow" over American life which subtly directs the course of America's race relations, stamping a stigmata of inferiority upon the descendants of these slaves which endures even today. In fact, no other group in U.S. history has been as thoroughly and relentlessly denied the status of humanity;

- and the *Civil Rights Movement:* that faith-based saga of how both blacks and *whites* gave their lives standing with and for the dispossessed. We need to recall and embrace the truth about those white Americans who were reviled as "race traitors" but who found ways to reject and move beyond the false promises of racial privilege. Their stories must be told and remembered, but not in a facile attempt at premature absolution. Rather, this truth must be recalled in order to show that there are alternative and just ways of being "white," and to inspire future possibilities for genuine interracial solidarity.[9]

How, then, can faith communities promote racial justice and reconciliation? By becoming communities consecrated in truth (John 17.17), that is, places of memory where the truth is spoken, embraced, and acted upon. Places where the lies of racial supremacy and inferiority are exposed and challenged. Places where justice is cultivated because truth is sown.

This will not be easy. Pursuing and embracing the truths of the past will be disconcerting, disorienting, confusing, challenging, even excruciating. It means facing and confessing personal collusion, ancestral culpability, and institutional complicity.[10] It means suffering the hostility of those who benefit from the racial myths and dishonesties that plague American society. It means risking mistakes, for all human accounts of truth are partial and incomplete. We have this comfort though: Christians are not called to infallibility, only to greater honesty and deeper integrity. As the Catholic Bishops of the United States stated in 1992, "Our religious organizations, schools, and other educational efforts must tell the truth about how [racial groups] have been treated and how they endured in this land. *History can be healing if we will face up to its lessons.*"[11]

▸ "Jesus of the People," Janet McKenzie, Bridge Building Images, Burlington, VT.

▸ "Equality, Freedom, Justice, Peace." Photo: Michael Scott Studio, NY.

Pope Paul VI once said, "If you want peace, work for justice." I summarize my convictions by expanding on this insight:

- If you want peace, work for justice.
- If you want justice, combat racism.
- If you want to combat racism, seek reconciliation.
- If you want reconciliation, pursue and speak the truth.

Speaking the truth for the sake of reconciliation is an indispensable component of the call to jubilee justice.

V. The Reasons for Our Hope

As a new century dawns, the need for racial reconciliation and social transformation becomes ever more urgent. The twenty-first century will see an America where no single racial or ethnic group will be the majority. The United States will become a nation of "minorities." This is a seismic demographic shift for which our past has ill-prepared us. The need for racial healing is real. But where is the hope? Upon what grounds can people of faith remain committed to the costly and seemingly endless struggle for a justice which constantly eludes us?

I conclude, then, by singling out two grounds for our hope. The first is that those who are justice-seekers are part of a long, broad, and deep tradition. When we act for justice, we are surrounded and sustained by a "crowd of witnesses" who have gone before us (Hebrews 12.1). Some of these witnesses are well-known and celebrated; for example, Martin Luther King, Jr. and Fannie Lou Hamer, Caesar Chavez and Oscar Romero, Dorothy Day and Ita Ford, Sitting Bull and Crazy Horse. Many others, however, are unschooled, unskilled, unlettered, and unknown. With quiet courage and dogged determination they pushed, resisted, marched, and prayed. Thus they kept hopes, dreams, and spirits alive. . . and changed history. We do not know their names, but we stand on their shoulders. In turn, we become the shoulders upon which future justice-seekers will stand. As part of a tradition of struggle and transformation, we draw hope from the witness of those who have gone before us.

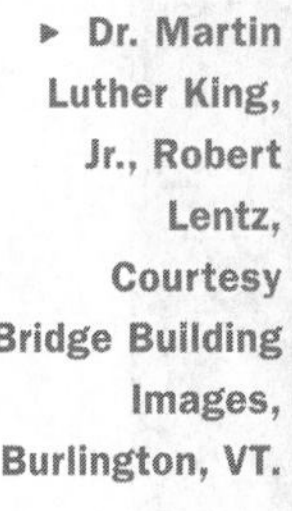
▸ Dr. Martin Luther King, Jr., Robert Lentz, Courtesy Bridge Building Images, Burlington, VT.

The second, and most significant, ground for our hope, is that we are people of faith. Ultimately, our hope for future justice rests not on human wisdom, but on the power of God (1 Corinthians 2.5). The power of God, who brings life out of death (John 11.1-44); who makes "all things new" (Revelation 21.5; see also Isaiah 42.18,19); who can do far more than we can ask or imagine (Ephesians 3.21); who thus assures us that "things need not be what they have been [and] that the future need not repeat the past."[12] Our hope, then, stems from a radical trust in the Divine Promise-Giver who is ever faithful.

This stance of hope is well articulated in the Catholic Church's liturgy. In the second "Eucharistic Prayer for Reconciliation" one finds this petition: "In that new world, where the fullness of your peace will be revealed, gather people from every race, language, and way of life to share in the one eternal banquet with Jesus Christ the Lord." I want to highlight the phrase, "*in that new world ....*" Implicit in this prayer is a recognition that human efforts at reconciling estranged racial groups will prove inadequate, incomplete, and lacking. To put it bluntly, we cannot save ourselves. Yet we

▸ "Come to me and I'll give you rest." Courtesy Father Fernando Aritzi, S.J., St. Brigid Catholic Church, Los Angeles, CA.

pray from a stance of trust, confident in the good news that we don't have to save ourselves. Racial healing, justice, and reconciliation are, ultimately, God's doing. They stem from God's initiative, and are brought to completion in the fullness of time known to God alone. The Christians' challenge is to become God's co-workers and cooperators, grounding our faltering present efforts in the assurance of a divinely-given future. Thus, we can dare to sow seeds of justice and truth in the confidence that God will yield an abundant harvest (1 Corinthians 3.6-9). Inspired and sustained by this hope, the Catholic community—indeed every community of faith and goodwill—can strive to become a more truly universal body of believers, a foretaste of the "New Jerusalem" where all are welcome and where all are at home.

Selected Bibliography

1. Jonathan Alter, "*Trade Mission to Misery, USA,*" Newsweek (July 19, 1999) 34.

2. Frances E. Wood defines "permissible victims" as "those groups or individuals who can be harmed with little or no negative consequence befalling the perpetrator." She further notes that the least permissible victim in American society is "a white, wealthy, heterosexual male." See her essay, "*Take My Yoke upon You: The Role of the Church in the Oppression of African American Women,*" in Emile M. Townes (ed.), *A Troubling In My Soul* (Maryknoll, NY: Orbis Books, 1993) 46 at note 3.

3. Pope John Paul II has developed an insightful critique of consumer culture's equation of personal worth with the ability to possess. See his encyclical letters *Sollicitudo Rei Socialis, #28 (1987);* and *Centesimus Annus, #36 (1991)*. These documents can be found in a collection edited by David J. O'Brien and Thomas A. Shannon, *Catholic Social Thought: The Documentary Heritage* (Maryknoll, NY: Orbis Books, 1992).

4. For example, only 3 of the Fortune 500 companies—0.6%—are headed by an African American. See Ernest Holsendolph, "*Minding our Business,*" Emerge 10 (July/August 1999) 28.

5. Cf. the comments of Michael Marcum, "*Interview,*" CNN Talkback Live (24 February 1999); see also Joe R. Feagin and Hernan Vera, *White Racism: The Basics* (New York: Routledge, 1995).

6. Pope John Paul II, "*Homily in the Trans World Dome,*" Origins 28 (February 11, 1999) 601; emphasis added.

7. Interracial contact and cross-cultural "borrowing" do not, in and of themselves, lead to racial justice and reconciliation. This is typified in the words of a white "rapper" who notes, "You can love what black people represent without loving black people." See N'Gai Croal, "*Long Live Rock 'n' Rap,*" Newsweek (July 19, 1999) 60-62.

8. James H. Cone, *Black Theology and Black Power, 20th Anniversary Edition* (New York: Harper and Row, 1969, 1989) xi.

9. There are numerous resources for the sort of historical confrontation and embrace of which I speak. Some of the more accessible for the general reader are: Howard Zinn, *A People's History of the United States* (New York: HarperCollins, 1980); Vincent Harding, *Hope and History: Why We Must Share the Story of the Movement* (Maryknoll, NY: Orbis Books, 1990); Juan Williams, *Eyes on the Prize: America's Civil Rights Years* (New York: Penguin Books, 1987); from a Catholic perspective, Cyprian Davis, *The History of Black Catholics in the United States* (New York: Crossroad, 1992; and Stephen J. Ochs, *Desegregating the Altar: The Josephites and the Struggle for Black Priests 1871-1960* (Baton Rouge, LA: Louisiana State University Press, 1990).

10. For an account of one family's struggle in coming to terms with its slaveholding past, see Edward Ball, *Slaves in the Family* (New York: Ballatine Publishing, 1999). For an account of Catholic complicity in anti-black racism, see John T. McGreevy, *Parish Boundaries: The Catholic Encounter with Race in the Twentieth Century Urban North* (Chicago, IL: University of Chicago Press, 1996).

11. National Conference of Catholic Bishops, 1992: *A Time for Remembering, Reconciling, and Recommitting Ourselves as People* (Washington, DC: United States Catholic Conference, 1992) 2; emphasis added.

12. Cardinal Roger Mahony, "*Gather Faithfully Together: A Guide for Sunday Mass,*" Origins 27 (September 25, 1997) 243.

GOOD NEWS

BIBLE

WITH

DEUTEROCANONICALS/

APOCRYPHA

FOREWORD

The Bible in Today's English Version is a new translation which seeks to state clearly and accurately the meaning of the original texts in words and forms that are widely accepted by all people who use English as a means of communication. This translation does not follow the traditional vocabulary and style found in the historic English Bible versions. Rather it attempts in this century to set forth the Biblical content and message in a standard, everyday, natural form of English.

The aim of this Bible is to give today's readers maximum understanding of the content of the original texts. The Preface explains the nature of special aids for readers which are included in the volume. It also sets forth the basic principles which the translators followed in their work.

The Bible in Today's English Version was translated and published by the United Bible Societies for use throughout the world. The Bible Societies trust that people everywhere will not only find increased understanding through the reading and study of this translation, but will also find a saving hope through faith in God, who made possible this message of Good News for all people.

PREFACE

In September 1966 the American Bible Society published *The New Testament in Today's English Version*, a translation intended for people everywhere for whom English is either their mother tongue or an acquired language. Shortly thereafter the United Bible Societies requested the American Bible Society to undertake on its behalf a translation of the Old Testament following the same principles. Accordingly the American Bible Society appointed a group of translators to prepare the translation. In 1971 this group added a British consultant recommended by the British and Foreign Bible Society. The translation of the Old Testament, which was completed in 1976, was joined to the fourth edition New Testament, thus completing the first edition of the *Good News Bible*.

In a separate section before the New Testament this Bible contains two series of books: (1) Tobit, Judith, Esther (Greek text), Wisdom of Solomon, Sirach, Baruch, Letter of Jeremiah, Song of the Three Young Men, Susanna, Bel and the Dragon, 1 Maccabees, and 2 Maccabees, and (2) 1 Esdras, 2 Esdras, and the Prayer of Manasseh. With the exception of 2 Esdras, these books formed part of the Septuagint Greek text of the Old Testament which was in circulation at the time of Christ. The first series of books, generally known as deuterocanonicals, are accepted by Roman Catholics and most Eastern Orthodox communions as part of the canon of the Old Testament; and both series, together generally known by Protestants as Apocrypha, are regarded by many Protestants (including especially Anglicans, Episcopalians, and Lutherans) as worthy of at least private reading, though they are not regarded as a basis for doctrine. For further information about these books, see the Introductions to the respective series.

The translation of the books of the Deuterocanonicals/Apocrypha was completed in 1978, and the first edition of *Today's English Version* with Deuterocanonicals/Apocrypha was published in 1979, with the Imprimatur of the Most Reverend John F. Whealon, Archbishop of Hartford, Connecticut.

The basic text for the Old Testament is the Masoretic Text made available through printed editions, published by the UBS, and since 1977 under the title of *Biblia Hebraica Stuttgartensia*. In some instances the words of the printed consonantal text have been divided differently or have been read with a different set of vowels; at times a variant reading in the margin of the Hebrew text (qere) has been followed instead of the reading in the text (kethiv); and in other instances a variant reading supported by one or more Hebrew manuscripts has been adopted. Where no Hebrew source yields a satisfactory meaning in the context, the translation has either followed one or more of the ancient versions (e.g. Greek, Syriac, Latin) or has adopted a reconstructed text (technically referred to as a conjectural emendation) based on scholarly consensus; such departures from the Hebrew are indicated in footnotes.

With the exception of 2 Esdras, the basic text for the two sections of books occurring before the New Testament is the Greek text printed in the Septuagint (3rd edition, 1949), edited by Alfred Rahlfs. For some of these books the more recently published Goettingen edition of the Septuagint has also been consulted. For 2 Esdras the translation is based on the Latin text printed in *Biblia Sacra* (lst edition, 1969), edited by Robert Weber.

The basic text for the translation of the New Testament is *The Greek New Testament* published by the United Bible Societies (3rd edition, 1975), but in a few instances the translation is based on a variant reading supported by one or more Greek manuscripts.

Drafts of the translation in its early stages were sent for comments and suggestions to a Review Panel consisting of prominent theologians and Biblical scholars appointed by the American Bible Society Board of Managers in its capacity as trustee for the translation. In addition, drafts were sent to major English-speaking Bible Societies throughout the world. Final approval of the translation on behalf of the United Bible Societies was given by the American Bible Society's Board of Managers upon recommendation of its Translations Committee.

The primary concern of the translators has been to provide a faithful translation of the meaning of the Hebrew, Aramaic, and Greek texts. Their first task was to understand correctly the meaning of the original. At times the original meaning cannot be precisely known, not only because the meaning of some words and phrases cannot be determined with a great degree of assurance, but also because the underlying cultural and historical context is sometimes beyond recovery. All aids available were used in this task, including the ancient versions and the modern translations in English and other languages. After ascertaining as accurately as possible the meaning of the original, the translators' next task was to express that meaning in a manner and form easily understood by the readers. Since this translation is intended for all who use English as a means of communication, the translators have tried to avoid words and forms not in current or widespread use; but no artificial limit has been set to the range of the vocabulary employed. Every effort has been made to use language that is natural, clear, simple, and unambiguous. Consequently there has been no attempt to reproduce in English the parts of speech, sentence structure, word order and grammatical devices of the original languages. Faithfulness in translation also includes a faithful representation of the cultural and historical features of the original. Certain features, however, such as the hours of the day and the measures of weight, capacity, distance, and area, are given their modern equivalents, since the information in those terms conveys more meaning to the reader than the Biblical form of those terms.

In cases where a person or place is called by two or more different names in the original, this translation has normally used only the more familiar name in all places; e.g. King Jehoiachin of Judah (Jeremiah 52.31), also called Jeconiah (Jeremiah 24.1) and Coniah (Jeremiah 37.1). Where a proper name is spelled two or more different ways in the original text, this translation has used only one spelling; e.g. Nebuchadnezzar, also spelled Nebuchadrezzar (compare Jeremiah 29.3 and 29.21), and Priscilla, also spelled Prisca (compare Acts 18.26 and Romans 16.3).

In view of the differences in vocabulary and form which exist between the American and the British use of the English language, a British edition has been published, which incorporates changes that are in keeping with British usage.

Following an ancient tradition, begun by the first translation of the Hebrew

Scriptures into Greek (the Septuagint) and followed by the vast majority of English translations, the distinctive Hebrew name for God (usually transliterated *Jehovah* or *Yahweh*) is in this translation represented by "LORD." When *Adonai*, normally translated "Lord," is followed by *Yahweh*, the combination is rendered by the phrase "Sovereign LORD."

Since the appearance of the full Bible in *Today's English Version* in 1976, some minor editorial changes and corrections of printing errors have been introduced into the text in connection with various printings. The New Testament was already in its fourth edition at the time the full Bible appeared, but for the Old Testament and the Deuterocanonicals/Apocrypha there has been no revised edition. The preparation and publication of this second edition of the full TEV Bible in two formats, with and without the Deuterocanonicals/Apocrypha, is the result of a broad international process of careful review and evaluation of the TEV translation by many scholars and experts over a period of several years.

In December 1986, acting in response to a mounting perception of a need for TEV revisions, the ABS Board of Managers approved the undertaking of a revision of the TEV translation. The revision is restricted to two main areas of concern that have been raised and discussed over the years since the first appearance of *Today's English Version*: (1) passages in which the English style has been unnecessarily exclusive and inattentive to gender concerns, and (2) passages in which the translation has been seen as problematic or insensitive from either a stylistic or an exegetical viewpoint.

The process followed in preparing this revised edition was one of first inviting and collecting proposals for needed revisions from all English-language Bible Societies and English-speaking UBS translations consultants around the world, as well as numerous scholarly consultants in the USA and representatives of various American churches. The proposals received were then assembled for review and evaluation by the same broad array of experts whose specializations included translation, linguistics, English usage, literary and poetic style, biblical studies, and theology. In a series of four stages, consensus was sought on which proposals were necessary and valid, and at each of these review stages the number of proposals under consideration was reduced until widespread agreement was reached. On the recommendation of the program committee of the ABS Board of Trustees, and its Translations subcommittee, the ABS Board acted to approve the revisions for the TEV Second Edition in September, 1990. These revisions have also been adapted for use in British usage editions of the TEV.

In the decade and a half since publication of the full TEV Bible, many Bible readers have become sensitive to the negative effects of exclusive language; that is, to the ways in which the built-in linguistic biases of the ancient languages and the English language toward the masculine gender has led some Bible readers to feel excluded from being addressed by the scriptural Word. This concern has led to the revision of most major English translations during the 1980s, and, increasingly, TEV readers have written to request that the Bible Society take this concern into consideration in preparing any revision. In practical terms what this means is that, where references in particular passages are to both men and women, the revision aims at language that is not exclusively masculine-oriented. At the same time, however, great care was taken not to distort the historical situation of the ancient patriarchal culture of Bible times.

In order to make the text easier to understand, various kinds of readers' helps are supplied. The text itself has been divided into sections, and headings are provided which indicate the contents of the section. Where there are parallel accounts elsewhere in the Bible, a reference to such a passage appears within parentheses below the heading. There are, in addition, several kinds of notes which appear at the bottom of the page. (1) *Cultural or Historical Notes.* These provide information required to enable the reader to understand the meaning of the text in terms of its original setting (e.g. the explanation of *Rahab* in Psalm 89.10; the explanation of *Day of Atonement* in Acts 27.9). (2) *Textual Notes.* In the Old Testament these indicate primarily those places where the translators were compelled for a variety of reasons to base the translation on some text other than the Hebrew. Where one or more of the ancient versions were followed, the note indicates this by *One ancient translation* (e.g. Genesis 1.26) or *Some ancient translations* (e.g. Genesis 4.8); where a conjectural emendation was adopted, the note reads *Probable text* (e.g. Genesis 10.14). In the New Testament, as well as in the Deuterocanonicals and other books of the Apocrypha, there are textual notes indicating some of the places where there are significant differences among the ancient manuscripts. These differences may consist of additions to the text (e.g. Matthew 21.43), deletions (e.g. Matthew 24.36), or substitutions (e.g. Mark 1.41). (3) *Alternative Renderings.* In many places the precise meaning of the original text is in dispute, and there are two or more different ways in which the text may be understood. In some of the more important of such instances an alternative rendering is given (e.g. Genesis 2.9; Matthew 6.11).

There are several appendices at the end of the volume. A *Word List* identifies many objects or cultural features whose meaning may not be known to all readers. A *Chronological Chart* gives the approximate dates of the major events recorded in the Bible. The *Maps* are designed to help the reader to visualize the geographical setting of countries and localities mentioned in the Bible.

The numbering of chapters and verses in this translation follows the traditional system of major English translations of the Bible. In some instances, however, where the order of thought or events in two or more verses is more clearly represented by a rearrangement of the material, two or more verse numbers are joined (e.g. Exodus 2.15,16; Acts 1.21,22).

No one knows better than the translators how difficult has been their task. But they have performed it gladly, conscious always of the presence of the Holy Spirit and of the tremendous debt which they owe to the dedication and scholarship of those who have preceded them. The Bible is not simply great literature to be admired and revered; it is Good News for all people everywhere—a message both to be understood and to be applied in daily life. It is with the prayer that the Lord of the Scriptures will be pleased to use this translation for his sovereign purpose that the United Bible Societies has published the Bible in *Today's English Version.* And to Christ be the glory forever and ever!

CONTENTS

OLD TESTAMENT

DEUTEROCANONICALS/APOCRYPHA

NEW TESTAMENT

HELPS FOR THE READER

ALPHABETICAL LIST OF BIBLICAL BOOKS AND ABBREVIATIONS

OTHER ABBREVIATIONS

Circa (around)	c.
Old Testament	OT
New Testament	NT
Septuagint	LXX

HOLY BIBLE

Today's English Version

The Old Testament

GENESIS

Introduction

The name Genesis means "origin." The book tells about the creation of the universe, the origin of human beings, the beginning of sin and suffering in the world, and about God's way of dealing with people. Genesis can be divided into two main parts:

1) Chapters 1–11 *The creation of the world and the early history of the human race. Here are the accounts of Adam and Eve, Cain and Abel, Noah and the flood, and the Tower of Babylon.*

2) Chapters 12–50 *The history of the early ancestors of the Israelites. The first is Abraham, who was notable for his faith and his obedience to God. Then follow the stories of his son Isaac, and grandson Jacob (also called Israel), and of Jacob's twelve sons, the founders of the twelve tribes of Israel. Special attention is given to one of the sons, Joseph, and the events that brought Jacob and his other sons with their families to live in Egypt.*

While this book tells stories about people, it is first and foremost an account of what God has done. It begins with the affirmation that God created the universe, and it ends with a promise that God will continue to show his concern for his people. Throughout the book the main character is God, who judges and punishes those who do wrong, leads and helps his people, and shapes their history. This ancient book was written to record the story of a people's faith and to help keep that faith alive.

Outline of Contents

The Story of Creation

1 In the beginning, when God created
the universe,[a] 2 the earth was form-
less and desolate. The raging ocean that
covered everything was engulfed in total
darkness, and the Spirit of God[b] was
moving over the water. 3 Then God commanded, "Let there be light" – and light
appeared. 4 God was pleased with what
he saw. Then he separated the light from
the darkness, 5 and he named the light
"Day" and the darkness "Night." Evening
passed and morning came – that was the
first day.
6-7 Then God commanded, "Let there
be a dome to divide the water and to keep
it in two separate places" – and it was
done. So God made a dome, and it separated the water under it from the water
above it. 8 He named the dome "Sky."
Evening passed and morning came –
that was the second day.
9 Then God commanded, "Let the water below the sky come together in one
place, so that the land will appear" – and
it was done. 10 He named the land
"Earth," and the water which had come
together he named "Sea." And God was
pleased with what he saw. 11 Then he
commanded, "Let the earth produce all
kinds of plants, those that bear grain and
those that bear fruit" – and it was done.
12 So the earth produced all kinds of
plants, and God was pleased with what
he saw. 13 Evening passed and morning
came – that was the third day.
14 Then God commanded, "Let lights

[a] In the beginning . . . the universe; *or* In the beginning God created the universe; *or* When God began to create the universe. [b] the Spirit of God; *or* the power of God; *or* a wind from God; *or* an awesome wind.

appear in the sky to separate day from
night and to show the time when days,
years, and religious festivals[c] begin;
15they will shine in the sky to give light
to the earth"—and it was done. 16So God
made the two larger lights, the sun to rule
over the day and the moon to rule over
the night; he also made the stars. 17He
placed the lights in the sky to shine on
the earth, 18to rule over the day and the
night, and to separate light from darkness. And God was pleased with what he
saw. 19Evening passed and morning
came—that was the fourth day.
20Then God commanded, "Let the water be filled with many kinds of living
beings, and let the air be filled with
birds." 21So God created the great sea
monsters, all kinds of creatures that live
in the water, and all kinds of birds. And
God was pleased with what he saw. 22He
blessed them all and told the creatures
that live in the water to reproduce and to
fill the sea, and he told the birds to increase in number. 23Evening passed and
morning came—that was the fifth day.
24Then God commanded, "Let the
earth produce all kinds of animal life:
domestic and wild, large and small"—
and it was done. 25So God made them all,
and he was pleased with what he saw.
26Then God said, "And now we will
make human beings; they will be like us
and resemble us. They will have power
over the fish, the birds, and all animals,
domestic and wild,[d] large and small."
27So God created human beings, making
them to be like himself. He created them
male and female, 28blessed them, and
said, "Have many children, so that your
descendants will live all over the earth
and bring it under their control. I am putting you in charge of the fish, the birds,
and all the wild animals. 29I have provided all kinds of grain and all kinds of
fruit for you to eat; 30but for all the wild
animals and for all the birds I have provided grass and leafy plants for food"—
and it was done. 31God looked at
everything he had made, and he was
very pleased. Evening passed and morning came—that was the sixth day.

2 And so the whole universe was completed. 2By the seventh day God finished what he had been doing and
stopped working. 3He blessed the seventh day and set it apart as a special day,
because by that day he had completed
his creation[e] and stopped working.
4And that is how the universe was
created.

The Garden of Eden

When the LORD[f] God made the universe, 5there were no plants on the earth
and no seeds had sprouted, because he
had not sent any rain, and there was no
one to cultivate the land; 6but water
would come up from beneath the surface
and water the ground.
7Then the LORD God took some soil
from the ground[g] and formed a man[g]
out of it; he breathed life-giving breath
into his nostrils and the man began to
live.
8Then the LORD God planted a garden
in Eden, in the East, and there he put the
man he had formed. 9He made all kinds
of beautiful trees grow there and produce good fruit. In the middle of the garden stood the tree that gives life and the
tree that gives knowledge of what is
good and what is bad.[h]
10A stream flowed in Eden and watered the garden; beyond Eden it divided
into four rivers. 11The first river is the
Pishon; it flows around the country of
Havilah. (12Pure gold is found there and
also rare perfume and precious stones.)
13The second river is the Gihon; it flows
around the country of Cush.[i] 14The
third river is the Tigris, which flows east
of Assyria, and the fourth river is the
Euphrates.
15Then the LORD God placed the man in
the Garden of Eden to cultivate it and
guard it. 16He told him, "You may eat the
fruit of any tree in the garden, 17except
the tree that gives knowledge of what is
good and what is bad.[j] You must not eat

[c] religious festivals; *or* seasons. [d] *One ancient translation* animals, domestic and wild; *Hebrew* domestic animals and all the earth. [e] by that day he had completed his creation; *or* on that day he completed his creation. [f] THE LORD: *Where the Hebrew text has Yahweh, traditionally transliterated as Jehovah, this translation employs* LORD *with capital letters, following a usage which is widespread in English versions.* [g] GROUND . . . MAN: *The Hebrew words for "man" and "ground" have similar sounds.* [h] knowledge of what is good and what is bad; *or* knowledge of everything. [i] Cush (of Mesopotamia); *or* Ethiopia. [j] knowledge of what is good and what is bad; *or* knowledge of everything.

the fruit of that tree; if you do, you will
die the same day."
18 Then the LORD God said, "It is not
good for the man to live alone. I will
make a suitable companion to help him."
19 So he took some soil from the ground
and formed all the animals and all the
birds. Then he brought them to the man
to see what he would name them; and
that is how they all got their names. 20 So
the man named all the birds and all the
animals; but not one of them was a suitable companion to help him.
21 Then the LORD God made the man fall
into a deep sleep, and while he was sleeping, he took out one of the man's ribs and
closed up the flesh. 22 He formed a
woman out of the rib and brought her to
him. 23 Then the man said,

"At last, here is one of my own
kind—
Bone taken from my bone, and
flesh from my flesh.
'Woman' is her name because she
was taken out of man."[k]

24 That is why a man leaves his father and
mother and is united with his wife, and
they become one.
25 The man and the woman were both
naked, but they were not embarrassed.

Human Disobedience

3 Now the snake was the most cunning animal that the LORD God had
made. The snake asked the woman, "Did
God really tell you not to eat fruit from
any tree in the garden?"
2 "We may eat the fruit of any tree in
the garden," the woman answered, 3 "except the tree in the middle of it. God told
us not to eat the fruit of that tree or even
touch it; if we do, we will die."
4 The snake replied, "That's not true;
you will not die. 5 God said that because
he knows that when you eat it, you will
be like God[l] and know what is good and
what is bad."[m]
6 The woman saw how beautiful the
tree was and how good its fruit would be
to eat, and she thought how wonderful it
would be to become wise. So she took
some of the fruit and ate it. Then she gave
some to her husband, and he also ate it.
7 As soon as they had eaten it, they were
given understanding and realized that
they were naked; so they sewed fig
leaves together and covered themselves.
8 That evening they heard the LORD God
walking in the garden, and they hid from
him among the trees. 9 But the LORD God
called out to the man, "Where are you?"
10 He answered, "I heard you in the garden; I was afraid and hid from you, because I was naked."
11 "Who told you that you were naked?" God asked. "Did you eat the fruit
that I told you not to eat?"
12 The man answered, "The woman
you put here with me gave me the fruit,
and I ate it."
13 The LORD God asked the woman,
"Why did you do this?"
She replied, "The snake tricked me
into eating it."

God Pronounces Judgment

14 Then the LORD God said to the snake,
"You will be punished for this; you alone
of all the animals must bear this curse:
From now on you will crawl on your
belly, and you will have to eat dust as
long as you live. 15 I will make you and
the woman hate each other; her offspring and yours will always be enemies.
Her offspring will crush your head, and
you will bite her offspring's[n] heel."
16 And he said to the woman, "I will
increase your trouble in pregnancy and
your pain in giving birth. In spite of this,
you will still have desire for your husband, yet you will be subject to him."
17 And he said to the man, "You listened to your wife and ate the fruit which
I told you not to eat. Because of what you
have done, the ground will be under a
curse. You will have to work hard all
your life to make it produce enough food
for you. 18 It will produce weeds and
thorns, and you will have to eat wild
plants. 19 You will have to work hard and
sweat to make the soil produce anything,
until you go back to the soil from which
you were formed. You were made from
soil, and you will become soil again."
20 Adam[o] named his wife Eve,[p] because she was the mother of all human

[k] WOMAN . . . MAN: *The Hebrew words for "woman" and "man" have rather similar sounds.*
[l] God; *or* the gods. [m] know what is good and what is bad; *or* know everything. [n] her offspring's; *or* their. [o] ADAM: *This name in Hebrew means "all human beings."* [p] EVE: *This name sounds similar to the Hebrew word for "living," which is rendered in this context as "human beings."*

beings. 21 And the LORD God made clothes
out of animal skins for Adam and his
wife, and he clothed them.

Adam and Eve Are Sent Out of the Garden

22 Then the LORD God said, "Now these
human beings have become like one of
us and have knowledge of what is good
and what is bad.[q] They must not be allowed to take fruit from the tree that
gives life, eat it, and live forever." 23 So
the LORD God sent them out of the Garden
of Eden and made them cultivate the soil
from which they had been formed.
24 Then at the east side of the garden he
put living creatures[r] and a flaming
sword which turned in all directions.
This was to keep anyone from coming
near the tree that gives life.

Cain and Abel

4 Then Adam had intercourse with
his wife, and she became pregnant.
She bore a son and said, "By the LORD's
help I have gotten a son." So she named
him Cain.[s] 2 Later she gave birth to another son, Abel. Abel became a shepherd, but Cain was a farmer. 3 After some
time Cain brought some of his harvest
and gave it as an offering to the LORD.
4 Then Abel brought the first lamb born
to one of his sheep, killed it, and gave the
best parts of it as an offering. The LORD
was pleased with Abel and his offering,
5 but he rejected Cain and his offering.
Cain became furious, and he scowled in
anger. 6 Then the LORD said to Cain, "Why
are you angry? Why that scowl on your
face? 7 If you had done the right thing,
you would be smiling;[t] but because you
have done evil, sin is crouching at your
door. It wants to rule you, but you must
overcome it."

8 Then Cain said to his brother Abel,
"Let's go out in the fields."[u] When they
were out in the fields, Cain turned on his
brother and killed him.

9 The LORD asked Cain, "Where is your
brother Abel?"

He answered, "I don't know. Am I supposed to take care of my brother?"

10 Then the LORD said, "Why have you
done this terrible thing? Your brother's
blood is crying out to me from the
ground, like a voice calling for revenge.
11 You are placed under a curse and can
no longer farm the soil. It has soaked up
your brother's blood as if it had opened
its mouth to receive it when you killed
him. 12 If you try to grow crops, the soil
will not produce anything; you will be a
homeless wanderer on the earth."

13 And Cain said to the LORD, "This punishment is too hard for me to bear. 14 You
are driving me off the land and away
from your presence. I will be a homeless
wanderer on the earth, and anyone who
finds me will kill me."

15 But the LORD answered, "No. If anyone kills you, seven lives will be taken in
revenge." So the LORD put a mark on Cain
to warn anyone who met him not to kill
him. 16 And Cain went away from the
LORD's presence and lived in a land called
"Wandering," which is east of Eden.

The Descendants of Cain

17 Cain and his wife had a son and
named him Enoch. Then Cain built a city
and named it after his son. 18 Enoch had
a son named Irad, who was the father of
Mehujael, and Mehujael had a son
named Methushael, who was the father
of Lamech. 19 Lamech had two wives,
Adah and Zillah. 20 Adah gave birth to
Jabal, who was the ancestor of those
who raise livestock and live in tents.
21 His brother was Jubal, the ancestor of
all musicians who play the harp and the
flute. 22 Zillah gave birth to Tubal Cain,
who made all kinds of tools[v] out of
bronze and iron. The sister of Tubal Cain
was Naamah.

23 Lamech said to his wives,
"Adah and Zillah, listen to me:
I have killed a young man because
he struck me.
24 If seven lives are taken to pay for
killing Cain,
Seventy-seven will be taken if
anyone kills me."

Seth and Enosh

25 Adam and his wife had another son.
She said, "God has given me a son to

[q] knowledge of what is good and what is bad; *or* knowledge of everything. [r] LIVING CREATURES: *See Word List.* [s] CAIN: *This name sounds like the Hebrew for "gotten."* [t] you would be smiling; *or* I would have accepted your offering. [u] *Some ancient translations* Let's go out in the fields; *Hebrew does not have these words.* [v] who made all kinds of tools; *one ancient translation* ancestor of all metalworkers.

replace Abel, whom Cain killed." So she
named him Seth.[w] 26 Seth had a son
whom he named Enosh. It was then that
people began using the LORD's holy name
in worship.

The Descendants of Adam

(1 Chronicles 1.1-4)

5 This is the list of the descendants of
Adam. (When God created human
beings, he made them like himself. 2 He
created them male and female, blessed
them, and named them "Human Beings.") 3 When Adam was 130 years old,
he had a son who was like him, and he
named him Seth. 4 After that, Adam lived
another 800 years. He had other children
5 and died at the age of 930.
6 When Seth was 105, he had a son,
Enosh, 7 and then lived another 807
years. He had other children 8 and died at
the age of 912.
9 When Enosh was 90, he had a son,
Kenan, 10 and then lived another 815
years. He had other children 11 and died
at the age of 905.
12 When Kenan was 70, he had a son,
Mahalalel, 13 and then lived another 840
years. He had other children 14 and died
at the age of 910.
15 When Mahalalel was 65, he had a
son, Jared, 16 and then lived another 830
years. He had other children 17 and died
at the age of 895.
18 When Jared was 162, he had a son,
Enoch, 19 and then lived another 800
years. He had other children 20 and died
at the age of 962.
21 When Enoch was 65, he had a son,
Methuselah. 22 After that, Enoch lived in
fellowship with God for 300 years and
had other children. 23 He lived to be 365
years old. 24 He spent his life in fellowship with God, and then he disappeared,
because God took him away.
25 When Methuselah was 187, he had a
son, Lamech, 26 and then lived another
782 years. He had other children 27 and
died at the age of 969.
28 When Lamech was 182, he had a son
29 and said, "From the very ground on
which the LORD put a curse, this child will
bring us relief from all our hard work";
so he named him Noah.[x] 30 Lamech lived
another 595 years. He had other children
31 and died at the age of 777.
32 After Noah was 500 years old, he had
three sons, Shem, Ham, and Japheth.

Human Wickedness

6 When people had spread all over the
world, and daughters were being
born, 2 some of the heavenly beings[y]
saw that these young women were beautiful, so they took the ones they liked.
3 Then the LORD said, "I will not allow
people to live forever; they are mortal.
From now on they will live no longer
than 120 years." 4 In those days, and even
later, there were giants on the earth who
were descendants of human women and
the heavenly beings. They were the great
heroes and famous men of long ago.
5 When the LORD saw how wicked
everyone on earth was and how evil their
thoughts were all the time, 6 he was sorry
that he had ever made them and put them
on the earth. He was so filled with regret
7 that he said, "I will wipe out these people I have created, and also the animals
and the birds, because I am sorry that I
made any of them." 8 But the LORD was
pleased with Noah.

Noah

9-10 This is the story of Noah. He had
three sons, Shem, Ham, and Japheth.
Noah had no faults and was the only
good man of his time. He lived in fellowship with God, 11 but everyone else was
evil in God's sight, and violence had
spread everywhere. 12 God looked at the
world and saw that it was evil, for the
people were all living evil lives.
13 God said to Noah, "I have decided to
put an end to all people. I will destroy
them completely, because the world is
full of their violent deeds. 14 Build a boat
for yourself out of good timber; make
rooms in it and cover it with tar inside
and out. 15 Make it 450 feet long, 75 feet
wide, and 45 feet high. 16 Make a roof[z]
for the boat and leave a space of 18
inches between the roof[z] and the sides.
Build it with three decks and put a door
in the side. 17 I am going to send a flood
on the earth to destroy every living being. Everything on the earth will die,
18 but I will make a covenant with you. Go

[w] SETH: *This name sounds like the Hebrew for "has given."* [x] NOAH: *This name sounds like the Hebrew for "relief."* [y] heavenly beings; *or* sons of the gods; *or* sons of God. [z] roof; *or* window.

into the boat with your wife, your sons,
and their wives. 19-20 Take into the boat
with you a male and a female of every
kind of animal and of every kind of bird,
in order to keep them alive. 21 Take along
all kinds of food for you and for them."
22 Noah did everything that God
commanded.

The Flood

7 The LORD said to Noah, "Go into the
boat with your whole family; I have
found that you are the only one in all the
world who does what is right. 2 Take with
you seven pairs of each kind of ritually
clean animal, but only one pair of each
kind of unclean animal. 3 Take also seven
pairs of each kind of bird. Do this so that
every kind of animal and bird will be
kept alive to reproduce again on the
earth. 4 Seven days from now I am going
to send rain that will fall for forty days
and nights, in order to destroy all the
living beings that I have made." 5 And
Noah did everything that the LORD
commanded.

6 Noah was six hundred years old
when the flood came on the earth. 7 He
and his wife, and his sons and their
wives, went into the boat to escape the
flood. 8 A male and a female of every
kind of animal and bird, whether ritually
clean or unclean, 9 went into the boat
with Noah, as God had commanded.
10 Seven days later the flood came.

11 When Noah was six hundred years
old, on the seventeenth day of the second
month all the outlets of the vast body of
water beneath the earth burst open, all
the floodgates of the sky were opened,
12 and rain fell on the earth for forty days
and nights. 13 On that same day Noah and
his wife went into the boat with their
three sons, Shem, Ham, and Japheth,
and their wives. 14 With them went every
kind of animal, domestic and wild, large
and small, and every kind of bird.
15 A male and a female of each kind of
living being went into the boat with
Noah, 16 as God had commanded. Then
the LORD shut the door behind Noah.

17 The flood continued for forty days,
and the water became deep enough for
the boat to float. 18 The water became
deeper, and the boat drifted on the surface. 19 It became so deep that it covered
the highest mountains; 20 it went on rising until it was about twenty-five feet
above the tops of the mountains. 21 Every
living being on the earth died — every
bird, every animal, and every person.
22 Everything on earth that breathed
died. 23 The LORD destroyed all living beings on the earth — human beings, animals, and birds. The only ones left were
Noah and those who were with him in
the boat. 24 The water did not start going
down for a hundred and fifty days.

The End of the Flood

8 God had not forgotten Noah and all
the animals with him in the boat; he
caused a wind to blow, and the water
started going down. 2 The outlets of the
water beneath the earth and the floodgates of the sky were closed. The rain
stopped, 3 and the water gradually went
down for 150 days. 4 On the seventeenth
day of the seventh month the boat came
to rest on a mountain in the Ararat range.
5 The water kept going down, and on the
first day of the tenth month the tops of
the mountains appeared.

6 After forty days Noah opened a window 7 and sent out a raven. It did not
come back, but kept flying around until
the water was completely gone. 8 Meanwhile, Noah sent out a dove to see if the
water had gone down, 9 but since the water still covered all the land, the dove did
not find a place to light. It flew back to
the boat, and Noah reached out and took
it in. 10 He waited another seven days and
sent out the dove again. 11 It returned to
him in the evening with a fresh olive leaf
in its beak. So Noah knew that the water
had gone down. 12 Then he waited another seven days and sent out the dove
once more; this time it did not come
back.

13 When Noah was 601 years old, on
the first day of the first month, the water
was gone. Noah removed the covering of
the boat, looked around, and saw that the
ground was getting dry. 14 By the twenty-
seventh day of the second month the
earth was completely dry.

15 God said to Noah, 16 "Go out of the
boat with your wife, your sons, and their
wives. 17 Take all the birds and animals
out with you, so that they may reproduce
and spread over all the earth." 18 So Noah
went out of the boat with his wife, his
sons, and their wives. 19 All the animals
and birds went out of the boat in groups
of their own kind.

Noah Offers a Sacrifice

20 Noah built an altar to the LORD; he
took one of each kind of ritually clean
animal and bird, and burned them whole
as a sacrifice on the altar. 21 The odor of
the sacrifice pleased the LORD, and he
said to himself, "Never again will I put
the earth under a curse because of what
people do; I know that from the time they
are young their thoughts are evil. Never
again will I destroy all living beings, as I
have done this time. 22 As long as the
world exists, there will be a time for
planting and a time for harvest. There
will always be cold and heat, summer
and winter, day and night."

God's Covenant with Noah

9 God blessed Noah and his sons and
said, "Have many children, so that
your descendants will live all over the
earth. 2 All the animals, birds, and fish
will live in fear of you. They are all
placed under your power. 3 Now you can
eat them, as well as green plants; I give
them all to you for food. 4 The one thing
you must not eat is meat with blood still
in it; I forbid this because the life is in the
blood. 5 If anyone takes human life, he
will be punished. I will punish with death
any animal that takes a human life. 6 Human beings were made like God, so whoever murders one of them will be killed
by someone else.

7 "You must have many children, so
that your descendants will live all over
the earth."

8 God said to Noah and his sons, 9 "I am
now making my covenant with you and
with your descendants, 10 and with all living beings — all birds and all animals —
everything that came out of the boat with
you. 11 With these words I make my covenant with you: I promise that never again
will all living beings be destroyed by a
flood; never again will a flood destroy
the earth. 12 As a sign of this everlasting
covenant which I am making with you
and with all living beings, 13 I am putting
my bow in the clouds. It will be the sign
of my covenant with the world. 14 Whenever I cover the sky with clouds and the
rainbow appears, 15 I will remember my
promise to you and to all the animals that
a flood will never again destroy all living
beings. 16 When the rainbow appears in
the clouds, I will see it and remember the
everlasting covenant between me and all
living beings on earth. 17 That is the sign
of the promise which I am making to all
living beings."

Noah and His Sons

18 The sons of Noah who went out of
the boat were Shem, Ham, and Japheth.
(Ham was the father of Canaan.) 19 These
three sons of Noah were the ancestors of
all the people on earth.

20 Noah, who was a farmer, was the
first man to plant a vineyard. 21 After he
drank some of the wine, he became
drunk, took off his clothes, and lay naked
in his tent. 22 When Ham, the father of
Canaan, saw that his father was naked,
he went out and told his two brothers.
23 Then Shem and Japheth took a robe
and held it behind them on their shoulders. They walked backward into the
tent and covered their father, keeping
their faces turned away so as not to see
him naked. 24 When Noah sobered up
and learned what his youngest son had
done to him, 25 he said,

"A curse on Canaan!
He will be a slave to his brothers.
26 Give praise to the LORD, the God
of Shem!
Canaan will be the slave of Shem.
27 May God cause Japheth[a] to
increase!
May his descendants live with the
people of Shem!
Canaan will be the slave of
Japheth."

28 After the flood Noah lived 350 years
29 and died at the age of 950.

The Descendants of Noah's Sons

(1 Chronicles 1.5-23)

10 These are the descendants of
Noah's sons, Shem, Ham, and Japheth. These three had sons after the
flood.

2 The sons of Japheth — Gomer, Magog, Madai, Javan, Tubal, Meshech, and
Tiras — were the ancestors of the peoples
who bear their names. 3 The descendants
of Gomer were the people of Ashkenaz,
Riphath, and Togarmah. 4 The descendants of Javan were the people of Elishah,
Spain, Cyprus, and Rhodes; 5 they were
the ancestors of the people who live

[a] JAPHETH: *This name sounds like the Hebrew for "increase."*

along the coast and on the islands. These
are the descendants of Japheth, living in
their different tribes and countries, each
group speaking its own language.
6 The sons of Ham—Cush, Egypt,
Libya, and Canaan—were the ancestors
of the peoples who bear their names.
7 The descendants of Cush were the people of Seba, Havilah, Sabtah, Raamah,
and Sabteca. The descendants of Raamah were the people of Sheba and Dedan. 8 Cush had a son named Nimrod,
who became the world's first great conqueror. 9 By the LORD's help he was a
great hunter, and that is why people say,
"May the LORD make you as great a
hunter as Nimrod!" 10 At first his kingdom included Babylon, Erech, and Ac-
cad, all three of them in Babylonia.
11 From that land he went to Assyria and
built the cities of Nineveh, Rehoboth Ir,
Calah, 12 and Resen, which is between
Nineveh and the great city of Calah.
13 The descendants of Egypt were the
people of Lydia, Anam, Lehab, Naphtuh,
14 Pathrus, Casluh, and of Crete, from
whom the Philistines are descended.[b]
15 Canaan's sons—Sidon, the oldest,
and Heth—were the ancestors of the
peoples who bear their names. 16 Canaan
was also the ancestor of the Jebusites,
the Amorites, the Girgashites, 17 the Hivites, the Arkites, the Sinites, 18 the Ar-
vadites, the Zemarites, and the
Hamathites. The different tribes of the
Canaanites spread out, 19 until the Canaanite borders reached from Sidon
southward to Gerar near Gaza, and eastward to Sodom, Gomorrah, Admah, and
Zeboiim near Lasha. 20 These are the
descendants of Ham, living in their different tribes and countries, each group
speaking its own language.
21 Shem, the older brother of Japheth,
was the ancestor of all the Hebrews.
22 Shem's sons—Elam, Asshur, Arpachshad, Lud, and Aram—were the ancestors of the peoples who bear their names.
23 The descendants of Aram were the
people of Uz, Hul, Gether, and Meshek.
24 Arpachshad was the father of Shelah,
who was the father of Eber. 25 Eber had
two sons: one was named Peleg,[c] because during his time the people of the
world were divided; and the other was
named Joktan. 26 The descendants of
Joktan were the people of Almodad, Sheleph, Hazarmaveth, Jerah, 27 Hadoram,
Uzal, Diklah, 28 Obal, Abimael, Sheba,
29 Ophir, Havilah, and Jobab. All of them
were descended from Joktan. 30 The land
in which they lived extended from Mesha to Sephar in the eastern hill country.
31 These are the descendants of Shem,
living in their different tribes and countries, each group speaking its own
language.
32 All these peoples are the descendants of Noah, nation by nation, according to their different lines of descent.
After the flood all the nations of the earth
were descended from the sons of Noah.

The Tower of Babylon

11 At first, the people of the whole
world had only one language and
used the same words. 2 As they wandered
about in the East, they came to a plain in
Babylonia and settled there. 3 They said
to one another, "Come on! Let's make
bricks and bake them hard." So they had
bricks to build with and tar to hold them
together. 4 They said, "Now let's build a
city with a tower that reaches the sky, so
that we can make a name for ourselves
and not be scattered all over the earth."
5 Then the LORD came down to see the
city and the tower which they had built,
6 and he said, "Now then, these are all
one people and they speak one language;
this is just the beginning of what they are
going to do. Soon they will be able to do
anything they want! 7 Let us go down and
mix up their language so that they will
not understand each other." 8 So the LORD
scattered them all over the earth, and
they stopped building the city. 9 The city
was called Babylon,[d] because there the
LORD mixed up the language of all the
people, and from there he scattered them
all over the earth.

The Descendants of Shem

(1 Chronicles 1.24-27)

10 These are the descendants of Shem.
Two years after the flood, when Shem
was 100 years old, he had a son, Arpachshad. 11 After that, he lived another 500
years and had other children.
12 When Arpachshad was 35 years old,

[b] *Probable text* and of Crete . . . descended; *Hebrew* from whom the Philistines are descended, and Crete. [c] PELEG: *This name sounds like the Hebrew for "divide."* [d] BABYLON: *This name sounds like the Hebrew for "mixed up."*

he had a son, Shelah; 13 after that, he
lived another 403 years and had other
children.
14 When Shelah was 30 years old, he
had a son, Eber; 15 after that, he lived another 403 years and had other children.
16 When Eber was 34 years old, he had
a son, Peleg; 17 after that, he lived another 430 years and had other children.
18 When Peleg was 30 years old, he had
a son, Reu; 19 after that, he lived another
209 years and had other children.
20 When Reu was 32 years old, he had
a son, Serug; 21 after that, he lived another 207 years and had other children.
22 When Serug was 30 years old, he had
a son, Nahor; 23 after that, he lived another 200 years and had other children.
24 When Nahor was 29 years old, he
had a son, Terah; 25 after that, he lived
another 119 years and had other
children.
26 After Terah was 70 years old, he became the father of Abram, Nahor, and
Haran.

The Descendants of Terah

27 These are the descendants of Terah,
who was the father of Abram, Nahor,
and Haran. Haran was the father of Lot,
28 and Haran died in his hometown of Ur
in Babylonia, while his father was still
living. 29 Abram married Sarai, and Nahor married Milcah, the daughter of Haran, who was also the father of Iscah.
30 Sarai was not able to have children.
31 Terah took his son Abram, his
grandson Lot, who was the son of Haran,
and his daughter-in-law Sarai, Abram's
wife, and with them he left the city of Ur
in Babylonia to go to the land of Canaan.
They went as far as Haran and settled
there. 32 Terah died there at the age
of 205.

God's Call to Abram

12 The LORD said to Abram, "Leave
your country, your relatives, and
your father's home, and go to a land that
I am going to show you. 2 I will give you
many descendants, and they will become
a great nation. I will bless you and make
your name famous, so that you will be a
blessing.
3 I will bless those who bless you,
But I will curse those who
curse you.
And through you I will bless all
the nations."[e]
4 When Abram was seventy-five years
old, he started out from Haran, as the
LORD had told him to do; and Lot went
with him. 5 Abram took his wife Sarai,
his nephew Lot, and all the wealth and
all the slaves they had acquired in Haran,
and they started out for the land of
Canaan.
When they arrived in Canaan, 6 Abram
traveled through the land until he came
to the sacred tree of Moreh, the holy
place at Shechem. (At that time the Canaanites were still living in the land.)
7 The LORD appeared to Abram and said
to him, "This is the country that I am
going to give to your descendants." Then
Abram built an altar there to the LORD,
who had appeared to him. 8 After that, he
moved on south to the hill country east of
the city of Bethel and set up his camp
between Bethel on the west and Ai on the
east. There also he built an altar and worshiped the LORD. 9 Then he moved on
from place to place, going toward the
southern part of Canaan.

Abram in Egypt

10 But there was a famine in Canaan,
and it was so bad that Abram went farther south to Egypt, to live there for a
while. 11 When he was about to cross the
border into Egypt, he said to his wife Sarai, "You are a beautiful woman. 12 When
the Egyptians see you, they will assume
that you are my wife, and so they will kill
me and let you live. 13 Tell them that you
are my sister; then because of you they
will let me live and treat me well."
14 When he crossed the border into
Egypt, the Egyptians did see that his wife
was beautiful. 15 Some of the court officials saw her and told the king how beautiful she was; so she was taken to his
palace. 16 Because of her the king treated
Abram well and gave him flocks of sheep
and goats, cattle, donkeys, slaves, and
camels.
17 But because the king had taken Sarai, the LORD sent terrible diseases on him
and on the people of his palace. 18 Then
the king sent for Abram and asked him,
"What have you done to me? Why didn't

[e] And through ... nations; *or* All the nations will ask me to bless them as I have blessed you.

you tell me that she was your wife?
19 Why did you say that she was your sister, and let me take her as my wife? Here
is your wife; take her and get out!" 20 The
king gave orders to his men, so they took
Abram and put him out of the country,
together with his wife and everything he
owned.

Abram and Lot Separate

13 Abram went north out of Egypt
to the southern part of Canaan
with his wife and everything he owned,
and Lot went with him. 2 Abram was a
very rich man, with sheep, goats, and
cattle, as well as silver and gold. 3 Then
he left there and moved from place to
place, going toward Bethel. He reached
the place between Bethel and Ai where
he had camped before 4 and had built an
altar. There he worshiped the LORD.

5 Lot also had sheep, goats, and cattle,
as well as his own family and servants.
6 And so there was not enough pasture
land for the two of them to stay together,
because they had too many animals. 7 So
quarrels broke out between the men who
took care of Abram's animals and those
who took care of Lot's animals. (At that
time the Canaanites and the Perizzites
were still living in the land.)

8 Then Abram said to Lot, "We are relatives, and your men and my men
shouldn't be quarreling. 9 So let's separate. Choose any part of the land you
want. You go one way, and I'll go the
other."

10 Lot looked around and saw that the
whole Jordan Valley, all the way to Zoar,
had plenty of water, like the Garden of
the LORD[f] or like the land of Egypt. (This
was before the LORD had destroyed the
cities of Sodom and Gomorrah.) 11 So Lot
chose the whole Jordan Valley for himself and moved away toward the east.
That is how the two men parted.
12 Abram stayed in the land of Canaan,
and Lot settled among the cities in the
valley and camped near Sodom, 13 whose
people were wicked and sinned against
the LORD.

Abram Moves to Hebron

14 After Lot had left, the LORD said to
Abram, "From where you are, look carefully in all directions. 15 I am going to give
you and your descendants all the land
that you see, and it will be yours forever.
16 I am going to give you so many
descendants that no one will be able to
count them all; it would be as easy to
count all the specks of dust on earth!
17 Now, go and look over the whole land,
because I am going to give it all to you."
18 So Abram moved his camp and settled
near the sacred trees of Mamre at Hebron, and there he built an altar to the
LORD.

Abram Rescues Lot

14 Four kings, Amraphel of Babylonia, Arioch of Ellasar, Chedorlaomer of Elam, and Tidal of Goiim, 2 went
to war against five other kings: Bera of
Sodom, Birsha of Gomorrah, Shinab of
Admah, Shemeber of Zeboiim, and the
king of Bela (or Zoar). 3 These five kings
had formed an alliance and joined forces
in Siddim Valley, which is now the Dead
Sea. 4 They had been under the control of
Chedorlaomer for twelve years, but in
the thirteenth year they rebelled against
him. 5 In the fourteenth year Chedorlaomer and his allies came with their armies
and defeated the Rephaim in Ashteroth
Karnaim, the Zuzim in Ham, the Emim in
the plain of Kiriathaim, 6 and the Horites
in the mountains of Edom, pursuing
them as far as Elparan on the edge of the
desert. 7 Then they turned around and
came back to Kadesh (then known as En-
mishpat). They conquered all the land of
the Amalekites and defeated the Amorites who lived in Hazazon Tamar.

8 Then the kings of Sodom, Gomorrah,
Admah, Zeboiim, and Bela drew up their
armies for battle in Siddim Valley and
fought 9 against the kings of Elam,
Goiim, Babylonia, and Ellasar, five kings
against four. 10 The valley was full of tar
pits, and when the kings of Sodom and
Gomorrah tried to run away from the
battle, they fell into the pits; but the other
three kings escaped to the mountains.
11 The four kings took everything in
Sodom and Gomorrah, including the
food, and went away. 12 Lot, Abram's
nephew, was living in Sodom, so they
took him and all his possessions.

13 But a man escaped and reported all
this to Abram, the Hebrew, who was living near the sacred trees belonging to

[f] GARDEN OF THE LORD: *a reference to the Garden of Eden.*

Mamre the Amorite. Mamre and his
brothers Eshcol and Aner were Abram's
allies. 14When Abram heard that his
nephew had been captured, he called together all the fighting men in his camp,
318 in all, and pursued the four kings all
the way to Dan. 15There he divided his
men into groups, attacked the enemy by
night, and defeated them. He chased
them as far as Hobah, north of Damascus, 16and got back all the loot that had
been taken. He also brought back his
nephew Lot and his possessions, together with the women and the other
prisoners.

Melchizedek Blesses Abram

17When Abram came back from his
victory over Chedorlaomer and the other
kings, the king of Sodom went out to
meet him in Shaveh Valley (also called
King's Valley). 18And Melchizedek, who
was king of Salem and also a priest of the
Most High God, brought bread and wine
to Abram, 19blessed him, and said, "May
the Most High God, who made heaven
and earth, bless Abram! 20May the Most
High God, who gave you victory over
your enemies, be praised!" And Abram
gave Melchizedek a tenth of all the loot
he had recovered.

21The king of Sodom said to Abram,
"Keep the loot, but give me back all my
people."

22Abram answered, "I solemnly swear
before the LORD, the Most High God,
Maker of heaven and earth, 23that I will
not keep anything of yours, not even a
thread or a sandal strap. Then you can
never say, 'I am the one who made
Abram rich.' 24I will take nothing for
myself. I will accept only what my men
have used. But let my allies, Aner, Eshcol, and Mamre, take their share."

God's Covenant with Abram

15 After this, Abram had a vision
and heard the LORD say to him,
"Do not be afraid, Abram. I will shield
you from danger and give you a great
reward."

2But Abram answered, "Sovereign
LORD, what good will your reward do me,
since I have no children? My only heir is
Eliezer of Damascus.[g] 3You have given
me no children, and one of my slaves will
inherit my property."

4Then he heard the LORD speaking to
him again: "This slave Eliezer will not
inherit your property; your own son will
be your heir." 5The LORD took him outside and said, "Look at the sky and try to
count the stars; you will have as many
descendants as that."

6Abram put his trust in the LORD, and
because of this the LORD was pleased
with him and accepted him.

7Then the LORD said to him, "I am the
LORD, who led you out of Ur in Babylonia,
to give you this land as your own."

8But Abram asked, "Sovereign LORD,
how can I know that it will be mine?"

9He answered, "Bring me a cow, a
goat, and a ram, each of them three years
old, and a dove and a pigeon." 10Abram
brought the animals to God, cut them in
half, and placed the halves opposite each
other in two rows; but he did not cut up
the birds. 11Vultures came down on the
bodies, but Abram drove them off.

12When the sun was going down,
Abram fell into a deep sleep, and fear
and terror came over him. 13The LORD
said to him, "Your descendants will be
strangers in a foreign land; they will be
slaves there and will be treated cruelly
for four hundred years. 14But I will punish the nation that enslaves them, and
when they leave that foreign land, they
will take great wealth with them. 15You
yourself will live to a ripe old age, die in
peace, and be buried. 16It will be four
generations before your descendants
come back here, because I will not drive
out the Amorites until they become so
wicked that they must be punished."

17When the sun had set and it was
dark, a smoking fire pot and a flaming
torch suddenly appeared and passed between the pieces of the animals. 18Then
and there the LORD made a covenant with
Abram. He said, "I promise to give your
descendants all this land from the border
of Egypt to the Euphrates River, 19in-
cluding the lands of the Kenites, the Ken-
izzites, the Kadmonites, 20the Hittites,
the Perizzites, the Rephaim, 21the Amorites, the Canaanites, the Girgashites,
and the Jebusites."

[g] My . . . Damascus; *Hebrew unclear.*

Hagar and Ishmael

16 Abram's wife Sarai had not borne him any children. But she had an Egyptian slave woman named Hagar, 2 and so she said to Abram, "The LORD has kept me from having children. Why don't you sleep with my slave? Perhaps she can have a child for me." Abram agreed with what Sarai said. 3 So she gave Hagar to him to be his concubine. (This happened after Abram had lived in Canaan for ten years.) 4 Abram had intercourse with Hagar, and she became pregnant. When she found out that she was pregnant, she became proud and despised Sarai.

5 Then Sarai said to Abram, "It's your fault that Hagar despises me.[h] I myself gave her to you, and ever since she found out that she was pregnant, she has despised me. May the LORD judge which of us is right, you or me!"

6 Abram answered, "Very well, she is your slave and under your control; do whatever you want with her." Then Sarai treated Hagar so cruelly that she ran away.

7 The angel of the LORD met Hagar at a spring in the desert on the road to Shur 8 and said, "Hagar, slave of Sarai, where have you come from and where are you going?"

She answered, "I am running away from my mistress."

9 He said, "Go back to her and be her slave." 10 Then he said, "I will give you so many descendants that no one will be able to count them. 11 You are going to have a son, and you will name him Ishmael,[i] because the LORD has heard your cry of distress. 12 But your son will live like a wild donkey; he will be against everyone, and everyone will be against him. He will live apart from all his relatives."

13 Hagar asked herself, "Have I really seen God and lived to tell about it?"[j] So she called the LORD, who had spoken to her, "A God Who Sees." 14 That is why people call the well between Kadesh and Bered "The Well of the Living One Who Sees Me."

15 Hagar bore Abram a son, and he named him Ishmael. 16 Abram was eighty-six years old at the time.

Circumcision, the Sign of the Covenant

17 When Abram was ninety-nine years old, the LORD appeared to him and said, "I am the Almighty God. Obey me and always do what is right. 2 I will make my covenant with you and give you many descendants." 3 Abram bowed down with his face touching the ground, and God said, 4 "I make this covenant with you: I promise that you will be the ancestor of many nations. 5 Your name will no longer be Abram, but Abraham,[k] because I am making you the ancestor of many nations. 6 I will give you many descendants, and some of them will be kings. You will have so many descendants that they will become nations.

7 "I will keep my promise to you and to your descendants in future generations as an everlasting covenant. I will be your God and the God of your descendants. 8 I will give to you and to your descendants this land in which you are now a foreigner. The whole land of Canaan will belong to your descendants forever, and I will be their God."

9 God said to Abraham, "You also must agree to keep the covenant with me, both you and your descendants in future generations. 10 You and your descendants must all agree to circumcise every male among you. 11-12 From now on you must circumcise every baby boy when he is eight days old, including slaves born in your homes and slaves bought from foreigners. This will show that there is a covenant between you and me. 13 Each one must be circumcised, and this will be a physical sign to show that my covenant with you is everlasting. 14 Any male who has not been circumcised will no longer be considered one of my people, because he has not kept the covenant with me."

15 God said to Abraham, "You must no longer call your wife Sarai; from now on her name is Sarah.[l] 16 I will bless her, and I will give you a son by her. I will bless her, and she will become the

[h] It's your fault . . . me; *or* May you suffer for this wrong done against me. [i] ISHMAEL: *This name in Hebrew means "God hears."* [j] *Probable text* lived to tell about it?; *Hebrew unclear.* [k] ABRAHAM: *This name sounds like the Hebrew for "ancestor of many nations."* [l] SARAH: *This name in Hebrew means "princess."*

mother of nations, and there will be
kings among her descendants."
17 Abraham bowed down with his face
touching the ground, but he began to
laugh when he thought, "Can a man have
a child when he is a hundred years old?
Can Sarah have a child at ninety?" 18 He
asked God, "Why not let Ishmael be my
heir?"
19 But God said, "No. Your wife Sarah
will bear you a son and you will name
him Isaac.[m] I will keep my covenant with
him and with his descendants forever. It
is an everlasting covenant. 20 I have
heard your request about Ishmael, so I
will bless him and give him many children and many descendants. He will be
the father of twelve princes, and I will
make a great nation of his descendants.
21 But I will keep my covenant with your
son Isaac, who will be born to Sarah
about this time next year." 22 When God
finished speaking to Abraham, he
left him.
23 On that same day Abraham obeyed
God and circumcised his son Ishmael
and all the other males in his household,
including the slaves born in his home
and those he had bought. 24 Abraham
was ninety-nine years old when he was
circumcised, 25 and his son Ishmael was
thirteen. 26 They were both circumcised
on the same day, 27 together with all of
Abraham's slaves.

A Son Is Promised to Abraham

18 The LORD appeared to Abraham
at the sacred trees of Mamre. As
Abraham was sitting at the entrance of
his tent during the hottest part of the day,
2 he looked up and saw three men standing there. As soon as he saw them, he ran
out to meet them. Bowing down with his
face touching the ground, 3 he said, "Sirs,
please do not pass by my home without
stopping; I am here to serve you. 4 Let me
bring some water for you to wash your
feet; you can rest here beneath this tree.
5 I will also bring a bit of food; it will give
you strength to continue your journey.
You have honored me by coming to my
home, so let me serve you."
They replied, "Thank you; we accept."
6 Abraham hurried into the tent and
said to Sarah, "Quick, take a sack of your
best flour, and bake some bread." 7 Then
he ran to the herd and picked out a calf
that was tender and fat, and gave it to a
servant, who hurried to get it ready. 8 He
took some cream, some milk, and the
meat, and set the food before the men.
There under the tree he served them himself, and they ate.
9 Then they asked him, "Where is your
wife Sarah?"
"She is there in the tent," he answered.
10 One of them said, "Nine months from
now[n] I will come back, and your wife
Sarah will have a son."
Sarah was behind him, at the door of
the tent, listening. 11 Abraham and Sarah
were very old, and Sarah had stopped
having her monthly periods. 12 So Sarah
laughed to herself and said, "Now that I
am old and worn out, can I still enjoy
sex? And besides, my husband is
old too."
13 Then the LORD asked Abraham,
"Why did Sarah laugh and say, 'Can I
really have a child when I am so old?' 14 Is
anything too hard for the LORD? As I said,
nine months from now I will return, and
Sarah will have a son."
15 Because Sarah was afraid, she denied it. "I didn't laugh," she said.
"Yes, you did," he replied. "You
laughed."

Abraham Pleads for Sodom

16 Then the men left and went to a place
where they could look down at Sodom,
and Abraham went with them to send
them on their way. 17 And the LORD said
to himself, "I will not hide from Abraham
what I am going to do. 18 His descendants
will become a great and mighty nation,
and through him I will bless all the nations.[o] 19 I have chosen him in order that
he may command his sons and his
descendants to obey me and to do what
is right and just. If they do, I will do
everything for him that I have
promised."
20 Then the LORD said to Abraham,
"There are terrible accusations against
Sodom and Gomorrah, and their sin is
very great. 21 I must go down to find out
whether or not the accusations which I
have heard are true."
22 Then the two men left and went on

[m] ISAAC: *This name in Hebrew means "he laughs."* [n] Nine months from now; *or* This time next year. [o] through . . . nations; *or* all the nations will ask me to bless them as I have blessed him.

toward Sodom, but the LORD remained
with Abraham. 23 Abraham approached
the LORD and asked, "Are you really going to destroy the innocent with the
guilty? 24 If there are fifty innocent people in the city, will you destroy the whole
city? Won't you spare it in order to save
the fifty? 25 Surely you won't kill the innocent with the guilty. That's impossible! You can't do that. If you did, the
innocent would be punished along with
the guilty. That is impossible. The judge
of all the earth has to act justly."
26 The LORD answered, "If I find fifty
innocent people in Sodom, I will spare
the whole city for their sake."
27 Abraham spoke again: "Please forgive my boldness in continuing to speak
to you, Lord. I am only a man and have
no right to say anything. 28 But perhaps
there will be only forty-five innocent
people instead of fifty. Will you destroy
the whole city because there are five
too few?"
The LORD answered, "I will not destroy
the city if I find forty-five innocent
people."
29 Abraham spoke again: "Perhaps
there will be only forty."
He replied, "I will not destroy it if there
are forty."
30 Abraham said, "Please don't be angry, Lord, but I must speak again. What
if there are only thirty?"
He said, "I will not do it if I find thirty."
31 Abraham said, "Please forgive my
boldness in continuing to speak to you,
Lord. Suppose that only twenty are
found?"
He said, "I will not destroy the city if I
find twenty."
32 Abraham said, "Please don't be angry, Lord, and I will speak only once
more. What if only ten are found?"
He said, "I will not destroy it if there
are ten." 33 After he had finished speaking with Abraham, the LORD went away,
and Abraham returned home.

The Sinfulness of Sodom

19 When the two angels came to
Sodom that evening, Lot was sitting at the city gate. As soon as he saw
them, he got up and went to meet them.
He bowed down before them 2 and said,
"Sirs, I am here to serve you. Please come
to my house. You can wash your feet and
spend the night. In the morning you can
get up early and go on your way."
But they answered, "No, we will spend
the night here in the city square."
3 He kept on urging them, and finally
they went with him to his house. Lot ordered his servants to bake some bread
and prepare a fine meal for the guests.
When it was ready, they ate it.
4 Before the guests went to bed, the
men of Sodom surrounded the house. All
the men of the city, both young and old,
were there. 5 They called out to Lot and
asked, "Where are the men who came to
stay with you tonight? Bring them out to
us!" The men of Sodom wanted to have
sex with them.
6 Lot went outside and closed the door
behind him. 7 He said to them, "Friends,
I beg you, don't do such a wicked thing!
8 Look, I have two daughters who are still
virgins. Let me bring them out to you,
and you can do whatever you want with
them. But don't do anything to these
men; they are guests in my house, and I
must protect them."
9 But they said, "Get out of our way,
you foreigner! Who are you to tell us
what to do? Out of our way, or we will
treat you worse than them." They pushed
Lot back and moved up to break down
the door. 10 But the two men inside
reached out, pulled Lot back into the
house, and shut the door. 11 Then they
struck all the men outside with blindness, so that they couldn't find the door.

Lot Leaves Sodom

12 The two men said to Lot, "If you have
anyone else here—sons, daughters,
sons-in-law, or any other relatives living
in the city—get them out of here, 13 because we are going to destroy this place.
The LORD has heard the terrible accusations against these people and has sent
us to destroy Sodom."
14 Then Lot went to the men that his
daughters were going to marry, and said,
"Hurry up and get out of here; the LORD
is going to destroy this place." But they
thought he was joking.
15 At dawn the angels tried to make Lot
hurry. "Quick!" they said. "Take your
wife and your two daughters and get out,
so that you will not lose your lives when
the city is destroyed." 16 Lot hesitated.
The LORD, however, had pity on him; so
the men took him, his wife, and his two

daughters by the hand and led them out
of the city. 17 Then one of the angels said,
"Run for your lives! Don't look back and
don't stop in the valley. Run to the hills,
so that you won't be killed."
18 But Lot answered, "No, please don't
make us do that, sir. 19 You have done me
a great favor and saved my life. But the
hills are too far away; the disaster will
overtake me, and I will die before I get
there. 20 Do you see that little town? It is
near enough. Let me go over there—you
can see it is just a small place—and I will
be safe."
21 He answered, "All right, I agree. I
won't destroy that town. 22 Hurry! Run! I
can't do anything until you get there."
Because Lot called it small, the town
was named Zoar.[p]

The Destruction of Sodom and Gomorrah

23 The sun was rising when Lot reached
Zoar. 24 Suddenly the LORD rained burning sulfur on the cities of Sodom and Gomorrah 25 and destroyed them and the
whole valley, along with all the people
there and everything that grew on the
land. 26 But Lot's wife looked back and
was turned into a pillar of salt.
27 Early the next morning Abraham
hurried to the place where he had stood
in the presence of the LORD. 28 He looked
down at Sodom and Gomorrah and the
whole valley and saw smoke rising from
the land, like smoke from a huge furnace. 29 But when God destroyed the cities of the valley where Lot was living, he
kept Abraham in mind and allowed Lot
to escape to safety.

The Origin of the Moabites and Ammonites

30 Because Lot was afraid to stay in
Zoar, he and his two daughters moved up
into the hills and lived in a cave. 31 The
older daughter said to her sister, "Our
father is getting old, and there are no
men in the whole world[q] to marry us so
that we can have children. 32 Come on,
let's get our father drunk, so that we can
sleep with him and have children by
him." 33 That night they gave him wine to
drink, and the older daughter had intercourse with him. But he was so drunk
that he didn't know it.
34 The next day the older daughter said
to her sister, "I slept with him last night;
now let's get him drunk again tonight,
and you sleep with him. Then each of us
will have a child by our father." 35 So that
night they got him drunk, and the
younger daughter had intercourse with
him. Again he was so drunk that he
didn't know it. 36 In this way both of Lot's
daughters became pregnant by their own
father. 37 The older daughter had a son,
whom she named Moab.[r] He was the
ancestor of the present-day Moabites.
38 The younger daughter also had a son,
whom she named Benammi.[s] He was
the ancestor of the present-day Ammonites.

Abraham and Abimelech

20 Abraham moved from Mamre to
the southern part of Canaan and
lived between Kadesh and Shur. Later,
while he was living in Gerar, 2 he said
that his wife Sarah was his sister. So
King Abimelech of Gerar had Sarah
brought to him. 3 One night God appeared to him in a dream and said, "You
are going to die, because you have taken
this woman; she is already married."
4 But Abimelech had not come near
her, and he said, "Lord, I am innocent!
Would you destroy me and my people?
5 Abraham himself said that she was his
sister, and she said the same thing. I did
this with a clear conscience, and I have
done no wrong."
6 God replied in the dream, "Yes, I
know that you did it with a clear conscience; so I kept you from sinning
against me and did not let you touch her.
7 But now, give the woman back to her
husband. He is a prophet, and he will
pray for you, so that you will not die. But
if you do not give her back, I warn you
that you are going to die, you and all your
people."
8 Early the next morning Abimelech
called all his officials and told them what
had happened, and they were terrified.
9 Then Abimelech called Abraham and
asked, "What have you done to us? What
wrong have I done to you to make you

[p] ZOAR: *This name sounds like the Hebrew for "small."* [q] the whole world; *or* this land.
[r] MOAB: *This name sounds like the Hebrew for "from my father."* [s] BENAMMI: *This name in Hebrew means "son of my relative" and sounds like the Hebrew for "Ammonite."*

bring this disaster on me and my kingdom? No one should ever do what you
have done to me. 10 Why did you do it?"
11 Abraham answered, "I thought that
there would be no one here who has reverence for God and that they would kill
me to get my wife. 12 She really is my
sister. She is the daughter of my father,
but not of my mother, and I married her.
13 So when God sent me from my father's
house into foreign lands, I said to her,
'You can show how loyal you are to me
by telling everyone that I am your
brother.' "
14 Then Abimelech gave Sarah back to
Abraham, and at the same time he gave
him sheep, cattle, and slaves. 15 He said
to Abraham, "Here is my whole land; live
anywhere you like." 16 He said to Sarah,
"I am giving your brother a thousand
pieces of silver as proof to all who are
with you that you are innocent; everyone
will know that you have done no wrong."
17-18 Because of what had happened to
Sarah, Abraham's wife, the LORD had
made it impossible for any woman in
Abimelech's palace to have children. So
Abraham prayed for Abimelech, and
God healed him. He also healed his wife
and his slave women, so that they could
have children.

The Birth of Isaac

21 The LORD blessed Sarah, as he
had promised, 2 and she became
pregnant and bore a son to Abraham
when he was old. The boy was born at
the time God had said he would be born.
3 Abraham named him Isaac, 4 and when
Isaac was eight days old, Abraham circumcised him, as God had commanded.
5 Abraham was a hundred years old
when Isaac was born. 6 Sarah said, "God
has brought me joy and laughter.[t]
Everyone who hears about it will laugh
with me." 7 Then she added, "Who would
have said to Abraham that Sarah would
nurse children? Yet I have borne him a
son in his old age."
8 The child grew, and on the day that he
was weaned, Abraham gave a great
feast.

Hagar and Ishmael Are Sent Away

9 One day Ishmael, whom Hagar the
Egyptian had borne to Abraham, was
playing with[u] Sarah's son Isaac.[v]
10 Sarah saw them and said to Abraham,
"Send this slave and her son away. The
son of this woman must not get any part
of your wealth, which my son Isaac
should inherit." 11 This troubled Abraham very much, because Ishmael also
was his son. 12 But God said to Abraham,
"Don't be worried about the boy and
your slave Hagar. Do whatever Sarah
tells you, because it is through Isaac that
you will have the descendants I have
promised. 13 I will also give many children to the son of the slave woman, so
that they will become a nation. He too is
your son."
14 Early the next morning Abraham
gave Hagar some food and a leather bag
full of water. He put the child on her back
and sent her away. She left and wandered about in the wilderness of Beersheba. 15 When the water was all gone,
she left the child under a bush 16 and sat
down about a hundred yards away. She
said to herself, "I can't bear to see my
child die." While she was sitting there,
she[w] began to cry.
17 God heard the boy crying, and from
heaven the angel of God spoke to Hagar,
"What are you troubled about, Hagar?
Don't be afraid. God has heard the boy
crying. 18 Get up, go and pick him up, and
comfort him. I will make a great nation
out of his descendants." 19 Then God
opened her eyes, and she saw a well. She
went and filled the leather bag with water and gave some to the boy. 20 God was
with the boy as he grew up; he lived in
the wilderness of Paran and became a
skillful hunter. 21 His mother got an
Egyptian wife for him.

The Agreement between Abraham and Abimelech

22 At that time Abimelech went with
Phicol, the commander of his army, and
said to Abraham, "God is with you in
everything you do. 23 So make a vow here
in the presence of God that you will not
deceive me, my children, or my descendants. I have been loyal to you, so promise
that you will also be loyal to me and to

[t] LAUGHTER: *The name Isaac in Hebrew means "he laughs" (see also 17.17-19).* [u] playing with; *or* making fun of. [v] *Some ancient translations* with Sarah's son Isaac; *Hebrew does not have these words.* [w] she; *one ancient translation* the child.

this country in which you are living."
24 Abraham said, "I promise."
25 Abraham complained to Abimelech
about a well which the servants of Abimelech had seized. 26 Abimelech said, "I
don't know who did this. You didn't tell
me about it, and this is the first I have
heard of it." 27 Then Abraham gave some
sheep and cattle to Abimelech, and the
two of them made an agreement. 28 Abraham separated seven lambs from his
flock, 29 and Abimelech asked him, "Why
did you do that?"
30 Abraham answered, "Accept these
seven lambs. By doing this, you admit
that I am the one who dug this well."
31 And so the place was called Beersheba,[x] because it was there that the two
of them made a vow.
32 After they had made this agreement
at Beersheba, Abimelech and Phicol
went back to Philistia. 33 Then Abraham
planted a tamarisk tree in Beersheba and
worshiped the LORD, the Everlasting God.
34 Abraham lived in Philistia for a long
time.

God Commands Abraham to Offer Isaac

22 Some time later God tested Abraham; he called to him, "Abraham!" And Abraham answered, "Yes,
here I am!"
2 "Take your son," God said, "your only
son, Isaac, whom you love so much, and
go to the land of Moriah. There on a
mountain that I will show you, offer him
as a sacrifice to me."
3 Early the next morning Abraham cut
some wood for the sacrifice, loaded his
donkey, and took Isaac and two servants
with him. They started out for the place
that God had told him about. 4 On the
third day Abraham saw the place in the
distance. 5 Then he said to the servants,
"Stay here with the donkey. The boy and
I will go over there and worship, and
then we will come back to you."
6 Abraham made Isaac carry the wood
for the sacrifice, and he himself carried a
knife and live coals for starting the fire.
As they walked along together, 7 Isaac
spoke up, "Father!"
He answered, "Yes, my son?"
Isaac asked, "I see that you have the
coals and the wood, but where is the
lamb for the sacrifice?"
8 Abraham answered, "God himself
will provide one." And the two of them
walked on together.
9 When they came to the place which
God had told him about, Abraham built
an altar and arranged the wood on it. He
tied up his son and placed him on the
altar, on top of the wood. 10 Then he
picked up the knife to kill him. 11 But the
angel of the LORD called to him from
heaven, "Abraham, Abraham!"
He answered, "Yes, here I am."
12 "Don't hurt the boy or do anything to
him," he said. "Now I know that you
honor and obey God, because you have
not kept back your only son from
him."
13 Abraham looked around and saw a
ram caught in a bush by its horns. He
went and got it and offered it as a burnt
offering instead of his son. 14 Abraham
named that place "The LORD Provides."[y]
And even today people say, "On the
LORD's mountain he provides."[z]
15 The angel of the LORD called to Abraham from heaven a second time, 16 "I
make a vow by my own name—the LORD
is speaking—that I will richly bless you.
Because you did this and did not keep
back your only son from me, 17 I promise
that I will give you as many descendants
as there are stars in the sky or grains of
sand along the seashore. Your descendants will conquer their enemies. 18 All the
nations will ask me to bless them as I
have blessed your descendants—all because you obeyed my command."
19 Abraham went back to his servants,
and they went together to Beersheba,
where Abraham settled.

The Descendants of Nahor

20 Some time later Abraham learned
that Milcah had borne eight children to
his brother Nahor: 21 Uz the first-born,
Buz his brother, Kemuel the father of
Aram, 22 Chesed, Hazo, Pildash, Jidlaph,
and Bethuel, 23 Rebecca's father. Milcah
bore these eight sons to Nahor, Abraham's brother. 24 Reumah, Nahor's concubine, bore Tebah, Gaham, Tahash, and
Maacah.

[x] BEERSHEBA: *This name in Hebrew means "Well of the Vow" or "Well of Seven" (see also 26.33).*
[y] Provides; *or* Sees. [z] provides; *or* is seen.

Sarah Dies and Abraham Buys a Burial Ground

23 Sarah lived to be 127 years old.
2 She died in Hebron in the land
of Canaan, and Abraham mourned her
death.
3 He left the place where his wife's
body was lying, went to the Hittites, and
said, 4 "I am a foreigner living here
among you; sell me some land, so that I
can bury my wife."
5 They answered, 6 "Listen to us, sir.
We look upon you as a mighty leader;
bury your wife in the best grave that we
have. Any of us would be glad to give you
a grave, so that you can bury her."
7 Then Abraham bowed before them
8 and said, "If you are willing to let me
bury my wife here, please ask Ephron
son of Zohar 9 to sell me Machpelah
Cave, which is near the edge of his field.
Ask him to sell it to me for its full price,
here in your presence, so that I can own
it as a burial ground."
10 Ephron himself was sitting with the
other Hittites at the meeting place at the
city gate; he answered in the hearing of
everyone there, 11 "Listen, sir; I will give
you the whole field and the cave that is
in it. Here in the presence of my own
people, I will give it to you, so that you
can bury your wife."
12 But Abraham bowed before the Hittites 13 and said to Ephron, so that everyone could hear, "May I ask you, please, to
listen. I will buy the whole field. Accept
my payment, and I will bury my wife
there."
14 Ephron answered, 15 "Sir, land worth
only four hundred pieces of silver—what
is that between us? Bury your wife in it."
16 Abraham agreed and weighed out the
amount that Ephron had mentioned in
the hearing of the people—four hundred
pieces of silver, according to the standard weights used by the merchants.
17 That is how the property which had
belonged to Ephron at Machpelah east of
Mamre, became Abraham's. It included
the field, the cave which was in it, and all
the trees in the field up to the edge of the
property. 18 It was recognized as Abraham's property by all the Hittites who
were there at the meeting.
19 Then Abraham buried his wife Sarah
in that cave in the land of Canaan. 20 So
the field which had belonged to the Hittites, and the cave in it, became the property of Abraham for a burial ground.

A Wife for Isaac

24 Abraham was now very old, and
the LORD had blessed him in
everything he did. 2 He said to his oldest
servant, who was in charge of all that he
had, "Place your hand between my
thighs[a] and make a vow. 3 I want you to
make a vow in the name of the LORD, the
God of heaven and earth, that you will
not choose a wife for my son from the
people here in Canaan. 4 You must go
back to the country where I was born and
get a wife for my son Isaac from among
my relatives."
5 But the servant asked, "What if the
young woman will not leave home to
come with me to this land? Shall I send
your son back to the land you came
from?"
6 Abraham answered, "Make sure that
you don't send my son back there! 7 The
LORD, the God of heaven, brought me
from the home of my father and from the
land of my relatives, and he solemnly
promised me that he would give this land
to my descendants. He will send his angel before you, so that you can get a wife
there for my son. 8 If the young woman is
not willing to come with you, you will be
free from this promise. But you must not
under any circumstances take my son
back there." 9 So the servant put his hand
between the thighs of Abraham, his master, and made a vow to do what Abraham
had asked.
10 The servant, who was in charge of
Abraham's property, took ten of his master's camels and went to the city where
Nahor had lived in northern Mesopotamia. 11 When he arrived, he made the
camels kneel down at the well outside
the city. It was late afternoon, the time
when women came out to get water. 12 He
prayed, "LORD, God of my master Abraham, give me success today and keep
your promise to my master. 13 Here I am
at the well where the young women of
the city will be coming to get water.
14 I will say to one of them, 'Please, lower
your jar and let me have a drink.' If she
says, 'Drink, and I will also bring water
for your camels,' may she be the one that

[a] PLACE . . . THIGHS: *This was the way in which a vow was made absolutely unchangeable.*

you have chosen for your servant Isaac.
If this happens, I will know that you have
kept your promise to my master."
15 Before he had finished praying, Rebecca arrived with a water jar on her
shoulder. She was the daughter of Bethuel, who was the son of Abraham's
brother Nahor and his wife Milcah.
16 She was a very beautiful young woman
and still a virgin. She went down to the
well, filled her jar, and came back. 17 The
servant ran to meet her and said, "Please
give me a drink of water from your jar."
18 She said, "Drink, sir," and quickly
lowered her jar from her shoulder and
held it while he drank. 19 When he had
finished, she said, "I will also bring water
for your camels and let them have all
they want." 20 She quickly emptied her
jar into the animals' drinking trough and
ran to the well to get more water, until
she had watered all his camels. 21 The
man kept watching her in silence, to see
if the LORD had given him success.
22 When she had finished, the man took
an expensive gold ring and put it in her
nose and put two large gold bracelets on
her arms. 23 He said, "Please tell me who
your father is. Is there room in his house
for my men and me to spend the night?"
24 "My father is Bethuel son of Nahor
and Milcah," she answered. 25 "There is
plenty of straw and fodder at our house,
and there is a place for you to stay."
26 Then the man knelt down and worshiped the LORD. 27 He said, "Praise the
LORD, the God of my master Abraham,
who has faithfully kept his promise to
my master. The LORD has led me straight
to my master's relatives."
28 The young woman ran to her
mother's house and told the whole story.
29 Now Rebecca had a brother named Laban, and he ran outside to go to the well
where Abraham's servant was. 30 Laban
had seen the nose ring and the bracelets
on his sister's arms and had heard her
say what the man had told her. He went
to Abraham's servant, who was standing
by his camels at the well, 31 and said,
"Come home with me. You are a man
whom the LORD has blessed. Why are you
standing out here? I have a room ready
for you in my house, and there is a place
for your camels."
32 So the man went into the house, and
Laban unloaded the camels and gave
them straw and fodder. Then he brought
water for Abraham's servant and his
men to wash their feet. 33 When food was
brought, the man said, "I will not eat until
I have said what I have to say."
Laban said, "Go on and speak."
34 "I am the servant of Abraham," he
began. 35 "The LORD has greatly blessed
my master and made him a rich man. He
has given him flocks of sheep and goats,
cattle, silver, gold, male and female
slaves, camels, and donkeys. 36 Sarah,
my master's wife, bore him a son when
she was old, and my master has given
everything he owns to him. 37 My master
made me promise with a vow to obey his
command. He said, 'Do not choose a wife
for my son from the young women in the
land of Canaan. 38 Instead, go to my
father's people, to my relatives, and
choose a wife for him.' 39 And I asked my
master, 'What if she will not come with
me?' 40 He answered, 'The LORD, whom I
have always obeyed, will send his angel
with you and give you success. You will
get for my son a wife from my own people, from my father's family. 41 There is
only one way for you to be free from your
vow: if you go to my relatives and they
refuse you, then you will be free.'
42 "When I came to the well today, I
prayed, 'LORD, God of my master Abraham, please give me success in what I am
doing. 43 Here I am at the well. When a
young woman comes out to get water, I
will ask her to give me a drink of water
from her jar. 44 If she agrees and also offers to bring water for my camels, may
she be the one that you have chosen as
the wife for my master's son.' 45 Before I
had finished my silent prayer, Rebecca
came with a water jar on her shoulder
and went down to the well to get water.
I said to her, 'Please give me a drink.'
46 She quickly lowered her jar from her
shoulder and said, 'Drink, and I will also
water your camels.' So I drank, and she
watered the camels. 47 I asked her, 'Who
is your father?' And she answered, 'My
father is Bethuel son of Nahor and Milcah.' Then I put the ring in her nose and
the bracelets on her arms. 48 I knelt down
and worshiped the LORD. I praised the
LORD, the God of my master Abraham,
who had led me straight to my master's
relative, where I found his daughter for
my master's son. 49 Now, if you intend to
fulfill your responsibility toward my
master and treat him fairly, please tell

me; if not, say so, and I will decide what
to do."
50 Laban and Bethuel answered, "Since
this matter comes from the LORD, it is not
for us to make a decision. 51 Here is Rebecca; take her and go. Let her become
the wife of your master's son, as the LORD
himself has said." 52 When the servant of
Abraham heard this, he bowed down and
worshiped the LORD. 53 Then he brought
out clothing and silver and gold jewelry,
and gave them to Rebecca. He also gave
expensive gifts to her brother and to her
mother.
54 Then Abraham's servant and the
men with him ate and drank, and spent
the night there. When they got up in the
morning, he said, "Let me go back to my
master."
55 But Rebecca's brother and her
mother said, "Let her stay with us a week
or ten days, and then she may go."
56 But he said, "Don't make us stay. The
LORD has made my journey a success; let
me go back to my master."
57 They answered, "Let's call her and
find out what she has to say." 58 So they
called Rebecca and asked, "Do you want
to go with this man?"
"Yes," she answered.
59 So they let Rebecca and her old family servant go with Abraham's servant
and his men. 60 And they gave Rebecca
their blessing in these words:

"May you, sister, become the
mother of millions!
May your descendants conquer the
cities of their enemies!"

61 Then Rebecca and her young women
got ready and mounted the camels to go
with Abraham's servant, and they all
started out.
62 Isaac had come into the wilderness
of[b] "The Well of the Living One Who
Sees Me" and was staying in the southern part of Canaan. 63 He went out in the
early evening to take a walk in the fields
and saw camels coming. 64 When Rebecca saw Isaac, she got down from her
camel 65 and asked Abraham's servant,
"Who is that man walking toward us in
the field?"
"He is my master," the servant answered. So she took her scarf and covered her face.
66 The servant told Isaac everything he
had done. 67 Then Isaac brought Rebecca
into the tent that his mother Sarah had
lived in, and she became his wife. Isaac
loved Rebecca, and so he was comforted
for the loss of his mother.

Other Descendants of Abraham

(1 Chronicles 1.32, 33)

25 Abraham married another
woman, whose name was Keturah. 2 She bore him Zimran, Jokshan,
Medan, Midian, Ishbak, and Shuah.
3 Jokshan was the father of Sheba and
Dedan, and the descendants of Dedan
were the Asshurim, the Letushim, and
the Leummim. 4 The sons of Midian were
Ephah, Epher, Hanoch, Abida, and
Eldaah. All these were Keturah's
descendants.
5 Abraham left everything he owned to
Isaac; 6 but while he was still alive, he
gave presents to the sons his other wives
had borne him. Then he sent these sons
to the land of the East, away from his son
Isaac.

The Death and Burial of Abraham

7-8 Abraham died at the ripe old age of
175. 9 His sons Isaac and Ishmael buried
him in Machpelah Cave, in the field east
of Mamre that had belonged to Ephron
son of Zohar the Hittite. 10 It was the field
that Abraham had bought from the Hittites; both Abraham and his wife Sarah
were buried there. 11 After the death of
Abraham, God blessed his son Isaac,
who lived near "The Well of the Living
One Who Sees Me."

The Descendants of Ishmael

(1 Chronicles 1.28-31)

12 Ishmael, whom Hagar, the Egyptian
slave of Sarah, bore to Abraham, 13 had
the following sons, listed in the order of
their birth: Nebaioth, Kedar, Adbeel,
Mibsam, 14 Mishma, Dumah, Massa,
15 Hadad, Tema, Jetur, Naphish, and
Kedemah. 16 They were the ancestors of
twelve tribes, and their names were
given to their villages and camping
places. 17 Ishmael was 137 years old
when he died. 18 The descendants of Ishmael lived in the territory between Havilah and Shur, to the east of Egypt on the
way to Assyria. They lived apart from
the other descendants of Abraham.

[b] *Some ancient translations* into the wilderness of; *Hebrew* from coming.

The Birth of Esau and Jacob

19 This is the story of Abraham's son
Isaac. 20 Isaac was forty years old when
he married Rebecca, the daughter of Bethuel (an Aramean from Mesopotamia)
and sister of Laban. 21 Because Rebecca
had no children, Isaac prayed to the LORD
for her. The LORD answered his prayer,
and Rebecca became pregnant. 22 She
was going to have twins, and before they
were born, they struggled against each
other in her womb. She said, "Why
should something like this happen to
me?" So she went to ask the LORD for an
answer.
23 The LORD said to her,

"Two nations are within you;
You will give birth to two rival
peoples.
One will be stronger than the
other;
The older will serve the younger."

24 The time came for her to give birth,
and she had twin sons. 25 The first one
was reddish, and his skin was like a
hairy robe, so he was named Esau.[c]
26 The second one was born holding on
tightly to the heel of Esau, so he was
named Jacob.[d] Isaac was sixty years old
when they were born.

Esau Sells His Rights as the First-Born Son

27 The boys grew up, and Esau became
a skilled hunter, a man who loved the
outdoors, but Jacob was a quiet man who
stayed at home. 28 Isaac preferred Esau,
because he enjoyed eating the animals
Esau killed, but Rebecca preferred
Jacob.
29 One day while Jacob was cooking
some bean soup, Esau came in from
hunting. He was hungry 30 and said to
Jacob, "I'm starving; give me some of
that red stuff." (That is why he was
named Edom.[e])
31 Jacob answered, "I will give it to you
if you give me your rights as the first-
born son."
32 Esau said, "All right! I am about to
die; what good will my rights do me?"
33 Jacob answered, "First make a vow
that you will give me your rights."
Esau made the vow and gave his rights
to Jacob. 34 Then Jacob gave him some
bread and some of the soup. He ate and
drank and then got up and left. That was
all Esau cared about his rights as the
first-born son.

Isaac Lives at Gerar

26 There was another famine in the
land besides the earlier one during the time of Abraham. Isaac went to
Abimelech, king of the Philistines, at Gerar. 2 The LORD had appeared to Isaac and
had said, "Do not go to Egypt; stay in this
land, where I tell you to stay. 3 Live here,
and I will be with you and bless you. I am
going to give all this territory to you and
to your descendants. I will keep the
promise I made to your father Abraham.
4 I will give you as many descendants as
there are stars in the sky, and I will give
them all this territory. All the nations will
ask me to bless them as I have blessed
your descendants. 5 I will bless you, because Abraham obeyed me and kept all
my laws and commands."
6 So Isaac lived at Gerar. 7 When the
men there asked about his wife, he said
that she was his sister. He would not admit that she was his wife, because he was
afraid that the men there would kill him
to get Rebecca, who was very beautiful.
8 When Isaac had been there for some
time, King Abimelech looked down from
his window and saw Isaac and Rebecca
making love. 9 Abimelech sent for Isaac
and said, "So she is your wife! Why did
you say she was your sister?"
He answered, "I thought I would be
killed if I said she was my wife."
10 "What have you done to us?" Abimelech said. "One of my men might easily
have slept with your wife, and you would
have been responsible for our guilt."
11 Abimelech warned all the people:
"Anyone who mistreats this man or his
wife will be put to death."
12 Isaac sowed crops in that land, and
that year he harvested a hundred times
as much as he had sown, because the
LORD blessed him. 13 He continued to
prosper and became a very rich man.
14 Because he had many herds of sheep
and cattle and many servants, the Philistines were jealous of him. 15 So they filled
in all the wells which the servants of his

[c] ESAU: *This name is taken to refer to Seir, the territory later inhabited by Esau's descendants; Seir sounds like the Hebrew for "hairy."* [d] JACOB: *This name sounds like the Hebrew for "heel."* [e] EDOM: *This name sounds like the Hebrew for "red."*

father Abraham had dug while Abraham
was alive.
16 Then Abimelech said to Isaac,
"Leave our country. You have become
more powerful than we are." 17 So Isaac
left and set up his camp in Gerar Valley,
where he stayed for some time. 18 He dug
once again the wells which had been dug
during the time of Abraham and which
the Philistines had stopped up after
Abraham's death. Isaac gave the wells
the same names that his father had given
them.
19 Isaac's servants dug a well in the valley and found water. 20 The shepherds of
Gerar quarreled with Isaac's shepherds
and said, "This water belongs to us." So
Isaac named the well "Quarrel."
21 Isaac's servants dug another well,
and there was a quarrel about that one
also, so he named it "Enmity." 22 He
moved away from there and dug another
well. There was no dispute about this
one, so he named it "Freedom." He said,
"Now the LORD has given us freedom to
live in the land, and we will be prosperous here."
23 Isaac left and went to Beersheba.
24 That night the LORD appeared to him
and said, "I am the God of your father
Abraham. Do not be afraid; I am with
you. I will bless you and give you many
descendants because of my promise to
my servant Abraham." 25 Isaac built an
altar there and worshiped the LORD. Then
he set up his camp there, and his servants
dug another well.

The Agreement between Isaac and Abimelech

26 Abimelech came from Gerar with
Ahuzzath his adviser and Phicol the
commander of his army to see Isaac.
27 So Isaac asked, "Why have you now
come to see me, when you were so un-
friendly to me before and made me leave
your country?"
28 They answered, "Now we know that
the LORD is with you, and we think that
there should be a solemn agreement between us. We want you to promise 29 that
you will not harm us, just as we did not
harm you. We were kind to you and let
you go peacefully. Now it is clear that the
LORD has blessed you." 30 Isaac prepared
a feast for them, and they ate and drank.
31 Early next morning each man made his
promise and sealed it with a vow. Isaac
said good-bye to them, and they parted
as friends.
32 On that day Isaac's servants came
and told him about the well which they
had dug. They said, "We have found water." 33 He named the well "Vow." That is
how the city of Beersheba[f] got its name.

Esau's Foreign Wives

34 When Esau was forty years old, he
married two Hittites, Judith the daughter
of Beeri, and Basemath the daughter of
Elon. 35 They made life miserable for
Isaac and Rebecca.

Isaac Blesses Jacob

27 Isaac was now old and had become blind. He sent for his older
son Esau and said to him, "Son!"
"Yes," he answered.
2 Isaac said, "You see that I am old and
may die soon. 3 Take your bow and arrows, go out into the country, and kill an
animal for me. 4 Cook me some of that
tasty food that I like, and bring it to me.
After I have eaten it, I will give you my
final blessing before I die."
5 While Isaac was talking to Esau, Rebecca was listening. So when Esau went
out to hunt, 6 she said to Jacob, "I have
just heard your father say to Esau,
7 'Bring me an animal and cook it for me.
After I have eaten it, I will give you my
blessing in the presence of the LORD before I die.' 8 Now, son," Rebecca continued, "listen to me and do what I say. 9 Go
to the flock and pick out two fat young
goats, so that I can cook them and make
some of that food your father likes so
much. 10 You can take it to him to eat, and
he will give you his blessing before he
dies."
11 But Jacob said to his mother, "You
know that Esau is a hairy man, but I have
smooth skin. 12 Perhaps my father will
touch me and find out that I am deceiving
him; in this way, I will bring a curse on
myself instead of a blessing."
13 His mother answered, "Let any curse
against you fall on me, my son; just do as
I say, and go and get the goats for me."
14 So he went to get them and brought
them to her, and she cooked the kind of
food that his father liked. 15 Then she

f BEERSHEBA: *This name in Hebrew means "Well of the Vow" or "Well of Seven" (see also 21.31).*

took Esau's best clothes, which she kept
in the house, and put them on Jacob.
16 She put the skins of the goats on his
arms and on the hairless part of his neck.
17 She handed him the tasty food, along
with the bread she had baked.

18 Then Jacob went to his father and
said, "Father!"

"Yes," he answered. "Which of my
sons are you?"

19 Jacob answered, "I am your older
son Esau; I have done as you told me.
Please sit up and eat some of the meat
that I have brought you, so that you can
give me your blessing."

20 Isaac said, "How did you find it so
quickly, son?"

Jacob answered, "The LORD your God
helped me find it."

21 Isaac said to Jacob, "Please come
closer so that I can touch you. Are you
really Esau?" 22 Jacob moved closer to his
father, who felt him and said, "Your
voice sounds like Jacob's voice, but your
arms feel like Esau's arms." 23 He did not
recognize Jacob, because his arms were
hairy like Esau's. He was about to give
him his blessing, 24 but asked again, "Are
you really Esau?"

"I am," he answered.

25 Isaac said, "Bring me some of the
meat. After I eat it, I will give you my
blessing." Jacob brought it to him, and he
also brought him some wine to drink.
26 Then his father said to him, "Come
closer and kiss me, son." 27 As he came up
to kiss him, Isaac smelled his clothes—so
he gave him his blessing. He said, "The
pleasant smell of my son is like the smell
of a field which the LORD has blessed.
28 May God give you dew from heaven
and make your fields fertile! May he give
you plenty of grain and wine! 29 May nations be your servants, and may peoples
bow down before you. May you rule over
all your relatives, and may your mother's
descendants bow down before you. May
those who curse you be cursed, and may
those who bless you be blessed."

Esau Begs for Isaac's Blessing

30 Isaac finished giving his blessing,
and as soon as Jacob left, his brother
Esau came in from hunting. 31 He also
cooked some tasty food and took it to his
father. He said, "Please, father, sit up and
eat some of the meat that I have brought
you, so that you can give me your
blessing."

32 "Who are you?" Isaac asked.

"Your older son Esau," he answered.

33 Isaac began to tremble and shake all
over, and he asked, "Who was it, then,
who killed an animal and brought it to
me? I ate it just before you came. I gave
him my final blessing, and so it is his
forever."

34 When Esau heard this, he cried out
loudly and bitterly and said, "Give me
your blessing also, father!"

35 Isaac answered, "Your brother came
and deceived me. He has taken away
your blessing."

36 Esau said, "This is the second time
that he has cheated me. No wonder his
name is Jacob.[g] He took my rights as the
first-born son, and now he has taken
away my blessing. Haven't you saved a
blessing for me?"

37 Isaac answered, "I have already
made him master over you, and I have
made all his relatives his slaves. I have
given him grain and wine. Now there is
nothing that I can do for you, son!"

38 Esau continued to plead with his
father: "Do you have only one blessing,
father? Bless me too, father!" He began
to cry.

39 Then Isaac said to him,

"No dew from heaven for you,
No fertile fields for you.
40 You will live by your sword,
But be your brother's slave.
Yet when you rebel,[h]
You will break away from his
control."

41 Esau hated Jacob, because his father
had given Jacob the blessing. He
thought, "The time to mourn my father's
death is near; then I will kill Jacob."

42 But when Rebecca heard about
Esau's plan, she sent for Jacob and said,
"Listen, your brother Esau is planning to
get even with you and kill you. 43 Now,
son, do what I say. Go at once to my
brother Laban in Haran, 44 and stay with
him for a while, until your brother's anger cools down 45 and he forgets what
you have done to him. Then I will send
someone to bring you back. Why should
I lose both of my sons on the same day?"

[g] JACOB: *This name sounds like the Hebrew for "cheat."* [h] rebel; *or* grow restless.

Isaac Sends Jacob to Laban

46 Rebecca said to Isaac, "I am sick and
tired of Esau's foreign wives. If Jacob
also marries one of these Hittites, I might
as well die."

28 Isaac called Jacob, greeted him,
and told him, "Don't marry a Canaanite. 2 Go instead to Mesopotamia, to
the home of your grandfather Bethuel,
and marry one of the young women
there, one of your uncle Laban's daughters. 3 May Almighty God bless your marriage and give you many children, so that
you will become the father of many nations! 4 May he bless you and your
descendants as he blessed Abraham, and
may you take possession of this land, in
which you have lived and which God
gave to Abraham!" 5 Isaac sent Jacob
away to Mesopotamia, to Laban, who
was the son of Bethuel the Aramean and
the brother of Rebecca, the mother of Jacob and Esau.

Esau Takes Another Wife

6 Esau learned that Isaac had blessed
Jacob and sent him away to Mesopotamia to find a wife. He also learned that
when Isaac blessed him, he commanded
him not to marry a Canaanite woman.
7 He found out that Jacob had obeyed his
father and mother and had gone to Mesopotamia. 8 Esau then understood that his
father Isaac did not approve of Canaanite women. 9 So he went to Ishmael son of
Abraham and married his daughter Mahalath, who was the sister of Nebaioth.

Jacob's Dream at Bethel

10 Jacob left Beersheba and started toward Haran. 11 At sunset he came to a
holy place[i] and camped there. He lay
down to sleep, resting his head on a
stone. 12 He dreamed that he saw a stairway reaching from earth to heaven, with
angels going up and coming down on it.
13 And there was the LORD standing beside him.[j] "I am the LORD, the God of
Abraham and Isaac," he said. "I will give
to you and to your descendants this land
on which you are lying. 14 They will be as
numerous as the specks of dust on the
earth. They will extend their territory in
all directions, and through you and your
descendants I will bless all the nations.[k]
15 Remember, I will be with you and protect you wherever you go, and I will
bring you back to this land. I will not
leave you until I have done all that I have
promised you."

16 Jacob woke up and said, "The LORD is
here! He is in this place, and I didn't
know it!" 17 He was afraid and said,
"What a terrifying place this is! It must
be the house of God; it must be the gate
that opens into heaven."

18 Jacob got up early next morning,
took the stone that was under his head,
and set it up as a memorial. Then he
poured olive oil on it to dedicate it to
God. 19 He named the place Bethel.[l]
(The town there was once known as
Luz.) 20 Then Jacob made a vow to the
LORD: "If you will be with me and protect
me on the journey I am making and give
me food and clothing, 21 and if I return
safely to my father's home, then you will
be my God. 22 This memorial stone which
I have set up will be the place where you
are worshiped, and I will give you a tenth
of everything you give me."

Jacob Arrives at Laban's Home

29 Jacob continued on his way and
went toward the land of the East.
2 Suddenly he came upon a well out in the
fields with three flocks of sheep lying
around it. The flocks were watered from
this well, which had a large stone over
the opening. 3 Whenever all the flocks
came together there, the shepherds
would roll the stone back and water
them. Then they would put the stone
back in place.

4 Jacob asked the shepherds, "My
friends, where are you from?"

"From Haran," they answered.

5 He asked, "Do you know Laban,
grandson of Nahor?"

"Yes, we do," they answered.

6 "Is he well?" he asked.

"He is well," they answered. "Look,
here comes his daughter Rachel with his
flock."

7 Jacob said, "Since it is still broad daylight and not yet time to bring the flocks
in, why don't you water them and take
them back to pasture?"

8 They answered, "We can't do that until all the flocks are here and the stone

[i] a holy place; *or* a place. [j] beside him; *or* on it. [k] through you . . . nations; *or* all the nations will ask me to bless them as I have blessed you and your descendants. [l] BETHEL: *This name in Hebrew means "house of God."*

has been rolled back; then we will water
the flocks."
9 While Jacob was still talking with
them, Rachel arrived with the flock.
10 When Jacob saw Rachel with his uncle
Laban's flock, he went to the well, rolled
the stone back, and watered the sheep.
11 Then he kissed her and began to cry for
joy. 12 He told her, "I am your father's
relative, the son of Rebecca."
She ran to tell her father; 13 and when
he heard the news about his nephew Jacob, he ran to meet him, hugged him and
kissed him, and brought him into the
house. When Jacob told Laban everything that had happened, 14 Laban said,
"Yes, indeed, you are my own flesh and
blood." Jacob stayed there a whole
month.

Jacob Serves Laban for Rachel and Leah

15 Laban said to Jacob, "You shouldn't
work for me for nothing just because you
are my relative. How much pay do you
want?" 16 Laban had two daughters; the
older was named Leah, and the younger
Rachel. 17 Leah had lovely[m] eyes, but Rachel was shapely and beautiful.
18 Jacob was in love with Rachel, so he
said, "I will work seven years for you, if
you will let me marry Rachel."
19 Laban answered, "I would rather
give her to you than to anyone else; stay
here with me." 20 Jacob worked seven
years so that he could have Rachel, and
the time seemed like only a few days to
him, because he loved her.
21 Then Jacob said to Laban, "The time
is up; let me marry your daughter." 22 So
Laban gave a wedding feast and invited
everyone. 23 But that night, instead of Rachel, he took Leah to Jacob, and Jacob
had intercourse with her. (24 Laban gave
his slave woman Zilpah to his daughter
Leah as her maid.) 25 Not until the next
morning did Jacob discover that it was
Leah. He went to Laban and said, "Why
did you do this to me? I worked to get
Rachel. Why have you tricked me?"
26 Laban answered, "It is not the custom here to give the younger daughter in
marriage before the older. 27 Wait until
the week's marriage celebrations are
over, and I will give you Rachel, if you
will work for me another seven years."
28 Jacob agreed, and when the week of
marriage celebrations was over, Laban
gave him his daughter Rachel as his wife.
(29 Laban gave his slave woman Bilhah
to his daughter Rachel as her maid.)
30 Jacob had intercourse with Rachel
also, and he loved her more than Leah.
Then he worked for Laban another
seven years.

The Children Born to Jacob

31 When the LORD saw that Leah was
loved less than Rachel, he made it possible for her to have children, but Rachel
remained childless. 32 Leah became pregnant and gave birth to a son. She said,
"The LORD has seen my trouble, and now
my husband will love me"; so she named
him Reuben.[n] 33 She became pregnant
again and gave birth to another son. She
said, "The LORD has given me this son
also, because he heard that I was not
loved"; so she named him Simeon.[o]
34 Once again she became pregnant and
gave birth to another son. She said,
"Now my husband will be bound more
tightly to me, because I have borne him
three sons"; so she named him Levi.[p]
35 Then she became pregnant again and
gave birth to another son. She said, "This
time I will praise the LORD"; so she named
him Judah.[q] Then she stopped having
children.

30 But Rachel had not borne Jacob
any children, and so she became
jealous of her sister and said to Jacob,
"Give me children, or I will die."
2 Jacob became angry with Rachel and
said, "I can't take the place of God. He is
the one who keeps you from having
children."
3 She said, "Here is my slave Bilhah;
sleep with her, so that she can have a
child for me. In this way I can become a
mother through her." 4 So she gave Bilhah to her husband, and he had intercourse with her. 5 Bilhah became
pregnant and bore Jacob a son. 6 Rachel
said, "God has judged in my favor. He
has heard my prayer and has given me a
son"; so she named him Dan.[r] 7 Bilhah
became pregnant again and bore Jacob a

[m] lovely; *or* weak. [n] REUBEN: *This name sounds like the Hebrew for "see, a son" and "has seen my trouble."* [o] SIMEON: *This name sounds like the Hebrew for "hear."* [p] LEVI: *This name sounds like the Hebrew for "bound."* [q] JUDAH: *This name sounds like the Hebrew for "praise."* [r] DAN: *This name sounds like the Hebrew for "judge in favor."*

second son. 8 Rachel said, "I have fought
a hard fight with my sister, but I have
won"; so she named him Naphtali.[s]
9 When Leah realized that she had
stopped having children, she gave her
slave Zilpah to Jacob as his wife. 10 Then
Zilpah bore Jacob a son. 11 Leah said, "I
have been lucky"; so she named him
Gad.[t] 12 Zilpah bore Jacob another son,
13 and Leah said, "How happy I am! Now
women will call me happy"; so she
named him Asher.[u]
14 During the wheat harvest Reuben
went into the fields and found mandrakes,[v] which he brought to his mother
Leah. Rachel said to Leah, "Please give
me some of your son's mandrakes."
15 Leah answered, "Isn't it enough that
you have taken away my husband? Now
you are even trying to take away my
son's mandrakes."
Rachel said, "If you will give me your
son's mandrakes, you can sleep with Jacob tonight."
16 When Jacob came in from the fields
in the evening, Leah went out to meet
him and said, "You are going to sleep
with me tonight, because I have paid for
you with my son's mandrakes." So he
had intercourse with her that night.
17 God answered Leah's prayer, and
she became pregnant and bore Jacob a
fifth son. 18 Leah said, "God has given me
my reward, because I gave my slave to
my husband"; so she named her son Issachar.[w] 19 Leah became pregnant again
and bore Jacob a sixth son. 20 She said,
"God has given me a fine gift. Now my
husband will accept me, because I have
borne him six sons"; so she named him
Zebulun.[x] 21 Later she bore a daughter,
whom she named Dinah.
22 Then God remembered Rachel; he
answered her prayer and made it possible for her to have children. 23 She became pregnant and gave birth to a son.
She said, "God has taken away my disgrace by giving me a son. 24 May the LORD
give me another son"; so she named him
Joseph.[y]

Jacob's Bargain with Laban

25 After the birth of Joseph, Jacob said
to Laban, "Let me go, so that I can return
home. 26 Give me my wives and children
that I have earned by working for you,
and I will leave. You know how well I
have served you."
27 Laban said to him, "Let me say this:
I have learned by divination that the
LORD has blessed me because of you.
28 Name your wages, and I will pay
them."
29 Jacob answered, "You know how I
have worked for you and how your
flocks have prospered under my care.
30 The little you had before I came has
grown enormously, and the LORD has
blessed you wherever I went.[z] Now it is
time for me to look out for my own interests."
31 "What shall I pay you?" Laban
asked.
Jacob answered, "I don't want any
wages. I will continue to take care of
your flocks if you agree to this suggestion: 32 Let me go through all your flocks
today and take every black lamb[a] and
every spotted or speckled young goat.
That is all the wages I want. 33 In the future you can easily find out if I have been
honest. When you come to check up on
my wages, if I have any goat that isn't
speckled or spotted or any sheep that
isn't black, you will know that it has been
stolen."
34 Laban answered, "Agreed. We will
do as you suggest." 35 But that day Laban
removed the male goats that had stripes
or spots and all the females that were
speckled and spotted or which had white
on them; he also removed all the black
sheep. He put his sons in charge of them,
36 and then went away from Jacob with
this flock as far as he could travel in
three days. Jacob took care of the rest of
Laban's flocks.
37 Jacob got green branches of poplar,
almond, and plane trees and stripped off
some of the bark so that the branches
had white stripes on them. 38 He placed
these branches in front of the flocks at

[s] NAPHTALI: *This name sounds like the Hebrew for "fight."* [t] GAD: *This name in Hebrew means "luck."* [u] ASHER: *This name in Hebrew means "happy."* [v] MANDRAKES: *Plants which were believed to produce fertility and were used as love charms.* [w] ISSACHAR: *This name sounds like the Hebrew for "a man is hired" and "there is reward."* [x] ZEBULUN: *This name sounds like the Hebrew for "accept" and "gift."* [y] JOSEPH: *This name sounds like the Hebrew for "may he give another" and "he has taken away."* [z] wherever I went; *or* because of me. [a] *One ancient translation* every black lamb; *Hebrew* every spotted and speckled lamb, and every black lamb.

their drinking troughs. He put them
there, because the animals mated when
they came to drink. 39 So when the goats
bred in front of the branches, they produced young that were streaked, speckled, and spotted.

40 Jacob kept the sheep separate from
the goats and made them face in the direction of the streaked and black animals of Laban's flock. In this way he
built up his own flock and kept it apart
from Laban's.

41 When the healthy animals were mating, Jacob put the branches in front of
them at the drinking troughs, so that
they would breed among the branches.
42 But he did not put the branches in front
of the weak animals. Soon Laban had all
the weak animals, and Jacob all the
healthy ones. 43 In this way Jacob became very wealthy. He had many flocks,
slaves, camels, and donkeys.

Jacob Flees from Laban

31 Jacob heard that Laban's sons
were saying, "Jacob has taken
everything that belonged to our father.
He got all his wealth from what our
father owned." 2 He also saw that Laban
was no longer as friendly as he had been
earlier. 3 Then the LORD said to him, "Go
back to the land of your fathers and to
your relatives. I will be with you."

4 So Jacob sent word to Rachel and
Leah to meet him in the field where his
flocks were. 5 He said to them, "I have
noticed that your father is not as friendly
toward me as he used to be; but my
father's God has been with me. 6 You
both know that I have worked for your
father with all my strength. 7 Yet he has
cheated me and changed my wages ten
times. But God did not let him harm me.
8 Whenever Laban said, 'The speckled
goats shall be your wages,' all the flocks
produced speckled young. When he said,
'The striped goats shall be your wages,'
all the flocks produced striped young.
9 God has taken flocks away from your
father and given them to me.

10 "During the breeding season I had a
dream, and I saw that the male goats that
were mating were striped, spotted, and
speckled. 11 The angel of God spoke to
me in the dream and said, 'Jacob!' 'Yes,'
I answered. 12 'Look,' he continued, 'all
the male goats that are mating are
striped, spotted, and speckled. I am making this happen because I have seen all
that Laban is doing to you. 13 I am the
God who appeared to you at Bethel,
where you dedicated a stone as a memorial by pouring olive oil on it and where
you made a vow to me. Now get ready
and go back to the land where you were
born.' "

14 Rachel and Leah answered Jacob,
"There is nothing left for us to inherit
from our father. 15 He treats us like foreigners. He sold us, and now he has spent
all the money he was paid for us. 16 All
this wealth which God has taken from
our father belongs to us and to our children. Do whatever God has told you."

17-18 So Jacob got ready to go back to
his father in the land of Canaan. He put
his children and his wives on the camels,
and drove all his flocks ahead of him,
with everything that he had gotten in
Mesopotamia. 19 Laban had gone to
shear his sheep, and during his absence
Rachel stole the household gods that belonged to her father. 20 Jacob deceived
Laban by not letting him know that he
was leaving. 21 He took everything he
owned and left in a hurry. He crossed the
Euphrates River and started for the hill
country of Gilead.

Laban Pursues Jacob

22 Three days later Laban was told that
Jacob had fled. 23 He took his men with
him and pursued Jacob for seven days
until he caught up with him in the hill
country of Gilead. 24 In a dream that
night God came to Laban and said to
him, "Be careful not to threaten Jacob in
any way." 25 Jacob had set up his camp
on a mountain, and Laban set up his
camp with his relatives in the hill country
of Gilead.

26 Laban said to Jacob, "Why did you
deceive me and carry off my daughters
like women captured in war? 27 Why did
you deceive me and slip away without
telling me? If you had told me, I would
have sent you on your way with rejoicing
and singing to the music of tambourines
and harps. 28 You did not even let me kiss
my grandchildren and my daughters
good-bye. That was a foolish thing to do!
29 I have the power to do you harm, but
last night the God of your father warned
me not to threaten you in any way.
30 I know that you left because you were

so anxious to get back home, but why did
you steal my household gods?"
31 Jacob answered, "I was afraid, because I thought that you might take your
daughters away from me. 32 But if you
find that anyone here has your gods, he
will be put to death. Here, with our men
as witnesses, look for anything that belongs to you and take what is yours." Jacob did not know that Rachel had stolen
Laban's gods.
33 Laban went and searched Jacob's
tent; then he went into Leah's tent, and
the tent of the two slave women, but he
did not find his gods. Then he went into
Rachel's tent. 34 Rachel had taken the
household gods and put them in a
camel's saddlebag and was sitting on
them. Laban searched through the whole
tent, but did not find them. 35 Rachel said
to her father, "Do not be angry with me,
sir, but I am not able to stand up in your
presence; I am having my monthly period." Laban searched but did not find
his household gods.
36 Then Jacob lost his temper. "What
crime have I committed?" he asked angrily. "What law have I broken that gives
you the right to hunt me down? 37 Now
that you have searched through all my
belongings, what household article have
you found that belongs to you? Put it out
here where your men and mine can see
it, and let them decide which one of us is
right. 38 I have been with you now for
twenty years; your sheep and your goats
have not failed to reproduce, and I have
not eaten any rams from your flocks.
39 Whenever a sheep was killed by wild
animals, I always bore the loss myself. I
didn't take it to you to show that it was
not my fault. You demanded that I make
good anything that was stolen during the
day or during the night. 40 Many times I
suffered from the heat during the day
and from the cold at night. I was not able
to sleep. 41 It was like that for the whole
twenty years I was with you. For fourteen years I worked to win your two
daughters – and six years for your
flocks. And even then, you changed my
wages ten times. 42 If the God of my
fathers, the God of Abraham and Isaac,
had not been with me, you would have
already sent me away empty-handed.
But God has seen my trouble and the
work I have done, and last night he gave
his judgment."

The Agreement between Jacob and Laban

43 Laban answered Jacob, "These
young women are my daughters; their
children belong to me, and these flocks
are mine. In fact, everything you see here
belongs to me. But since I can do nothing
to keep my daughters and their children,
44 I am ready to make an agreement with
you. Let us make a pile of stones to remind us of our agreement."
45 So Jacob got a stone and set it up as
a memorial. 46 He told his men to gather
some rocks and pile them up. Then they
ate a meal beside the pile of rocks. 47 Laban named it Jegar Sahadutha,[b] while
Jacob named it Galeed.[c] 48 Laban said to
Jacob, "This pile of rocks will be a reminder for both of us." That is why that
place was named Galeed. 49 Laban also
said, "May the LORD keep an eye on us
while we are separated from each other."
So the place was also named Mizpah.[d]
50 Laban went on, "If you mistreat my
daughters or if you marry other women,
even though I don't know about it, remember that God is watching us. 51 Here
are the rocks that I have piled up between us, and here is the memorial stone.
52 Both this pile and this memorial stone
are reminders. I will never go beyond
this pile to attack you, and you must
never go beyond it or beyond this memorial stone to attack me. 53 The God of
Abraham and the God of Nahor[e] will
judge between us." Then, in the name of
the God whom his father Isaac worshiped, Jacob solemnly vowed to keep
this promise. 54 He killed an animal,
which he offered as a sacrifice on the
mountain, and he invited his men to the
meal. After they had eaten, they spent
the night on the mountain. 55 Early the
next morning Laban kissed his grandchildren and his daughters good-bye,
and left to go back home.

[b] JEGAR SAHADUTHA: *This name in Aramaic means "a pile to remind us."* [c] GALEED: *This name in Hebrew means "a pile to remind us."* [d] MIZPAH: *This name sounds like the Hebrew for "place from which to watch."* [e] ABRAHAM . . . NAHOR: *Abraham was Jacob's grandfather and Nahor was Laban's grandfather.*

Jacob Prepares to Meet Esau

32 As Jacob went on his way, some
angels met him. 2 When he saw
them, he said, "This is God's camp"; so he
named the place Mahanaim.[f]
3 Jacob sent messengers ahead of him
to his brother Esau in the country of
Edom. 4 He instructed them to say: "I, Jacob, your obedient servant, report to my
master Esau that I have been staying
with Laban and that I have delayed my
return until now. 5 I own cattle, donkeys,
sheep, goats, and slaves. I am sending
you word, sir, in the hope of gaining your
favor."
6 When the messengers came back to
Jacob, they said, "We went to your
brother Esau, and he is already on his
way to meet you. He has four hundred
men with him." 7 Jacob was frightened
and worried. He divided into two groups
the people who were with him, and also
his sheep, goats, cattle, and camels. 8 He
thought, "If Esau comes and attacks the
first group, the other may be able to
escape."
9 Then Jacob prayed, "God of my
grandfather Abraham and God of my
father Isaac, hear me! You told me, LORD,
to go back to my land and to my relatives,
and you would make everything go well
for me. 10 I am not worth all the kindness
and faithfulness that you have shown
me, your servant. I crossed the Jordan
with nothing but a walking stick, and
now I have come back with these two
groups. 11 Save me, I pray, from my
brother Esau. I am afraid—afraid that he
is coming to attack us and destroy us all,
even the women and children. 12 Remember that you promised to make everything go well for me and to give me more
descendants than anyone could count, as
many as the grains of sand along the
seashore."
13-15 After spending the night there, Jacob chose from his livestock as a present
for his brother Esau: 200 female goats
and 20 males, 200 female sheep and 20
males, 30 milk camels with their young,
40 cows and 10 bulls, 20 female donkeys
and 10 males. 16 He divided them into
herds and put one of his servants in
charge of each herd. He said to them, "Go
ahead of me, and leave a space between
each herd and the one behind it." 17 He
ordered the first servant, "When my
brother Esau meets you and asks, 'Who
is your master? Where are you going?
Who owns these animals in front of you?'
18 you must answer, 'They belong to your
servant Jacob. He sends them as a
present to his master Esau. Jacob himself is right behind us.' " 19 He gave the
same order to the second, the third, and
to all the others who were in charge of
the herds: "This is what you must say to
Esau when you meet him. 20 You must
say, 'Yes, your servant Jacob is right behind us.' " Jacob was thinking, "I will win
him over with the gifts, and when I meet
him, perhaps he will forgive me." 21 He
sent the gifts on ahead of him and spent
that night in camp.

Jacob Wrestles at Peniel

22 That same night Jacob got up, took
his two wives, his two concubines, and
his eleven children, and crossed the Jabbok River. 23 After he had sent them
across, he also sent across all that he
owned, 24 but he stayed behind, alone.
Then a man came and wrestled with
him until just before daybreak. 25 When
the man saw that he was not winning the
struggle, he hit Jacob on the hip, and it
was thrown out of joint. 26 The man said,
"Let me go; daylight is coming."
"I won't, unless you bless me," Jacob
answered.
27 "What is your name?" the man
asked.
"Jacob," he answered.
28 The man said, "Your name will no
longer be Jacob. You have struggled
with God and with men, and you have
won; so your name will be Israel."[g]
29 Jacob said, "Now tell me your
name."
But he answered, "Why do you want to
know my name?" Then he blessed Jacob.
30 Jacob said, "I have seen God face-to-
face, and I am still alive"; so he named
the place Peniel.[h] 31 The sun rose as Jacob was leaving Peniel, and he was limp-
ing because of his hip. 32 Even today the
descendants of Israel do not eat the muscle which is on the hip joint, because it
was on this muscle that Jacob was hit.

[f] MAHANAIM: *This name in Hebrew means "two camps."* [g] ISRAEL: *This name sounds like the Hebrew for "he struggles with God" or "God struggles."* [h] PENIEL: *This name sounds like the Hebrew for "the face of God."*

Jacob Meets Esau

33 Jacob saw Esau coming with his four hundred men, so he divided the children among Leah, Rachel, and the two concubines. 2 He put the concubines and their children first, then Leah and her children, and finally Rachel and Joseph at the rear. 3 Jacob went ahead of them and bowed down to the ground seven times as he approached his brother. 4 But Esau ran to meet him, threw his arms around him, and kissed him. They were both crying. 5 When Esau looked around and saw the women and the children, he asked, "Who are these people with you?"

"These, sir, are the children whom God has been good enough to give me," Jacob answered. 6 Then the concubines came up with their children and bowed down; 7 then Leah and her children came, and last of all Joseph and Rachel came and bowed down.

8 Esau asked, "What about that other group I met? What did that mean?"

Jacob answered, "It was to gain your favor."

9 But Esau said, "I have enough, my brother; keep what you have."

10 Jacob said, "No, please, if I have gained your favor, accept my gift. To see your face is for me like seeing the face of God, now that you have been so friendly to me. 11 Please accept this gift which I have brought for you; God has been kind to me and given me everything I need." Jacob kept on urging him until he accepted.

12 Esau said, "Let's get ready and leave. I will go ahead of you."

13 Jacob answered, "You know that the children are weak, and I must think of the sheep and livestock with their young. If they are driven hard for even one day, the whole herd will die. 14 Please go on ahead of me, and I will follow slowly, going as fast as I can with the livestock and the children until I catch up with you in Edom."

15 Esau said, "Then let me leave some of my men with you."

But Jacob answered, "There is no need for that for I only want to gain your favor."[i] 16 So that day Esau started on his way back to Edom. 17 But Jacob went to Sukkoth, where he built a house for himself and shelters for his livestock. That is why the place was named Sukkoth.[j]

18 On his return from Mesopotamia Jacob arrived safely at the city of Shechem in the land of Canaan and set up his camp in a field near the city. 19 He bought that part of the field from the descendants of Hamor father of Shechem for a hundred pieces of silver. 20 He put up an altar there and named it for El, the God of Israel.

The Rape of Dinah

34 One day Dinah, the daughter of Jacob and Leah, went to visit some of the Canaanite women. 2 When Shechem son of Hamor the Hivite, who was chief of that region, saw her, he took her and raped her. 3 But he found the young woman so attractive that he fell in love with her and tried to win her affection.[k] 4 He told his father, "I want you to get Dinah for me as my wife."

5 Jacob learned that his daughter had been disgraced, but because his sons were out in the fields with his livestock, he did nothing until they came back. 6 Shechem's father Hamor went out to talk with Jacob, 7 just as Jacob's sons were coming in from the fields. When they heard about it, they were shocked and furious that Shechem had done such a thing and had insulted the people of Israel by raping Jacob's daughter. 8 Hamor said to him, "My son Shechem has fallen in love with your daughter; please let him marry her. 9 Let us make an agreement that there will be intermarriage between our people and yours. 10 Then you may stay here in our country with us; you may live anywhere you wish, trade freely, and own property."

11 Then Shechem said to Dinah's father and brothers, "Do me this favor, and I will give you whatever you want. 12 Tell me what presents you want, and set the payment for the bride as high as you wish; I will give you whatever you ask, if you will only let me marry her."

13 Because Shechem had disgraced their sister Dinah, Jacob's sons answered Shechem and his father Hamor in a deceitful way. 14 They said to him, "We cannot let our sister marry a man

[i] for I only want to gain your favor; *or* if it's all right with you. [j] SUKKOTH: *This name in Hebrew means "shelters."* [k] tried to win her affection; *or* comforted her.

who is not circumcised; that would be a
disgrace for us. 15 We can agree only on
the condition that you become like us by
circumcising all your males. 16 Then we
will agree to intermarriage. We will settle among you and become one people
with you. 17 But if you will not accept our
terms and be circumcised, we will take
her and leave."

18 These terms seemed fair to Hamor
and his son Shechem, 19 and the young
man lost no time in doing what was suggested, because he was in love with
Jacob's daughter. He was the most
important member of his family.

20 Hamor and his son Shechem went to
the meeting place at the city gate and
spoke to the people of the town: 21 "These
men are friendly; let them live in the land
with us and travel freely. The land is
large enough for them also. Let us marry
their daughters and give them ours in
marriage. 22 But these men will agree to
live among us and be one people with us
only on the condition that we circumcise
all our males, as they are circumcised.
23 Won't all their livestock and everything else they own be ours? So let us
agree that they can live among us." 24 All
the citizens of the city agreed with what
Hamor and Shechem proposed, and all
the males were circumcised.

25 Three days later, when the men were
still sore from their circumcision, two of
Jacob's sons, Simeon and Levi, the
brothers of Dinah, took their swords,
went into the city without arousing suspicion, and killed all the men, 26 including Hamor and his son Shechem. Then
they took Dinah from Shechem's house
and left. 27 After the slaughter Jacob's
other sons looted the town to take revenge for their sister's disgrace. 28 They
took the flocks, the cattle, the donkeys,
and everything else in the city and in the
fields. 29 They took everything of value,
captured all the women and children,
and carried off everything in the houses.

30 Jacob said to Simeon and Levi, "You
have gotten me into trouble; now the Canaanites, the Perizzites, and everybody
else in the land will hate me. I do not have
many men; if they all band together
against me and attack me, our whole
family will be destroyed."

31 But they answered, "We cannot let
our sister be treated like a common
whore."

God Blesses Jacob at Bethel

35 God said to Jacob, "Go to Bethel
at once, and live there. Build an
altar there to me, the God who appeared
to you when you were running away
from your brother Esau."

2 So Jacob said to his family and to all
who were with him, "Get rid of the foreign gods that you have; purify yourselves and put on clean clothes. 3 We are
going to leave here and go to Bethel,
where I will build an altar to the God who
helped me in the time of my trouble and
who has been with me everywhere I have
gone." 4 So they gave Jacob all the foreign gods that they had and also the earrings that they were wearing. He buried
them beneath the oak tree near
Shechem.

5 When Jacob and his sons started to
leave, great fear fell on the people of the
nearby towns, and they did not pursue
them. 6 Jacob came with all his people to
Luz, which is now known as Bethel, in
the land of Canaan. 7 He built an altar
there and named the place for the God of
Bethel, because God had revealed himself to him there when he was running
away from his brother. 8 Rebecca's nurse
Deborah died and was buried beneath
the oak south of Bethel. So it was named
"Oak of Weeping."

9 When Jacob returned from Mesopotamia, God appeared to him again and
blessed him. 10 God said to him, "Your
name is Jacob, but from now on it will be
Israel." So God named him Israel. 11 And
God said to him, "I am Almighty God.
Have many children. Nations will be descended from you, and you will be the
ancestor of kings. 12 I will give you the
land which I gave to Abraham and to
Isaac, and I will also give it to your
descendants after you." 13 Then God left
him. 14 There, where God had spoken to
him, Jacob set up a memorial stone and
consecrated it by pouring wine and olive
oil on it. 15 He named the place Bethel.

The Death of Rachel

16 Jacob and his family left Bethel, and
when they were still some distance from
Ephrath, the time came for Rachel to
have her baby, and she was having difficult labor. 17 When her labor pains were
at their worst, the midwife said to her,
"Don't be afraid, Rachel; it's another

boy." 18 But she was dying, and as she
breathed her last, she named her son
Benoni,[l] but his father named him
Benjamin.[m]
19 When Rachel died, she was buried
beside the road to Ephrath, now known
as Bethlehem. 20 Jacob set up a memorial
stone there, and it still marks Rachel's
grave to this day. 21 Jacob moved on and
set up his camp on the other side of the
tower of Eder.

The Sons of Jacob

(1 Chronicles 2.1, 2)

22 While Jacob was living in that land,
Reuben had sexual intercourse with Bilhah, one of his father's concubines; Jacob heard about it and was furious.[n]
Jacob had twelve sons. 23 The sons of
Leah were Reuben (Jacob's oldest son),
Simeon, Levi, Judah, Issachar, and Zebulun. 24 The sons of Rachel were Joseph
and Benjamin. 25 The sons of Rachel's
slave Bilhah were Dan and Naphtali.
26 The sons of Leah's slave Zilpah were
Gad and Asher. These sons were born in
Mesopotamia.

The Death of Isaac

27 Jacob went to his father Isaac at
Mamre, near Hebron, where Abraham
and Isaac had lived. 28 Isaac lived to be a
hundred and eighty years old 29 and died
at a ripe old age; and his sons Esau and
Jacob buried him.

The Descendants of Esau

(1 Chronicles 1.34-37)

36 These are the descendants of
Esau, also called Edom. 2 Esau
married Canaanite women: Adah, the
daughter of Elon the Hittite; Oholibamah, the daughter of Anah son[o] of Zibeon the Hivite; 3 and Basemath, the
daughter of Ishmael and sister of Nebaioth. 4 Adah bore Eliphaz; Basemath bore
Reuel; 5 and Oholibamah bore Jeush, Jalam, and Korah. All these sons were born
to Esau in the land of Canaan.
6 Then Esau took his wives, his sons,
his daughters, and all the people of his
house, along with all his livestock and all
the possessions he had gotten in the land
of Canaan, and went away from his
brother Jacob to another land. 7 He left
because the land where he and Jacob
were living was not able to support them;
they had too much livestock and could
no longer stay together. 8 So Esau lived in
the hill country of Edom.
9 These are the descendants of Esau,
the ancestor of the Edomites. 10-13 Esau's
wife Adah bore him one son, Eliphaz,
and Eliphaz had five sons: Teman, Omar,
Zepho, Gatam, and Kenaz. And by another wife, Timna, he had one more son,
Amalek.
Esau's wife Basemath bore him one
son, Reuel, and Reuel had four sons: Nahath, Zerah, Shammah, and Mizzah.
14 Esau's wife Oholibamah, the daughter of Anah son[o] of Zibeon, bore him
three sons: Jeush, Jalam, and Korah.
15 These are the tribes descended from
Esau. Esau's first son Eliphaz was the
ancestor of the following tribes: Teman,
Omar, Zepho, Kenaz, 16 Korah, Gatam,
and Amalek. These were all descendants
of Esau's wife Adah.
17 Esau's son Reuel was the ancestor of
the following tribes: Nahath, Zerah,
Shammah, and Mizzah. These were all
descendants of Esau's wife Basemath.
18 The following tribes were descended
from Esau by his wife Oholibamah, the
daughter of Anah: Jeush, Jalam, and Korah. 19 All these tribes were descended
from Esau.

The Descendants of Seir

(1 Chronicles 1.38-42)

20-21 The original inhabitants of the
land of Edom were divided into tribes
which traced their ancestry to the following descendants of Seir, a Horite: Lotan,
Shobal, Zibeon, Anah, Dishon, Ezer, and
Dishan.
22 Lotan was the ancestor of the clans
of Hori and Heman. (Lotan had a sister
named Timna.)
23 Shobal was the ancestor of the clans
of Alvan, Manahath, Ebal, Shepho, and
Onam.
24 Zibeon had two sons, Aiah and
Anah. (This is the Anah who found the
hot springs in the wilderness when he
was taking care of his father's donkeys.)
25-26 Anah was the father of Dishon, who
was the ancestor of the clans of Hemdan,

[l] BENONI: *This name in Hebrew means "son of my sorrow."* [m] BENJAMIN: *This name in Hebrew means "son who will be fortunate."* [n] *One ancient translation* and was furious; *Hebrew does not have these words.* [o] *Some ancient translations* son; *Hebrew* daughter; *or* granddaughter.

Eshban, Ithran, and Cheran. Anah also
had a daughter named Oholibamah.
27 Ezer was the ancestor of the clans of
Bilhan, Zaavan, and Akan.
28 Dishan was the ancestor of the clans
of Uz and Aran.
29-30 These are the Horite tribes in the
land of Edom: Lotan, Shobal, Zibeon,
Anah, Dishon, Ezer, and Dishan.

The Kings of Edom

(1 Chronicles 1.43-54)

31-39 Before there were any kings in Israel, the following kings ruled the land of
Edom in succession:

Bela son of Beor from Dinhabah
Jobab son of Zerah from Bozrah
Husham from the region of Teman
Hadad son of Bedad from Avith
(he defeated the Midianites in
a battle in the country of
Moab)
Samlah from Masrekah
Shaul from Rehoboth-on-the-River
Baal Hanan son of Achbor
Hadad from Pau (his wife was
Mehetabel, the daughter of
Matred and granddaughter of
Mezahab)

40-43 Esau was the ancestor of the following Edomite tribes: Timna, Alvah, Jetheth, Oholibamah, Elah, Pinon, Kenaz,
Teman, Mibzar, Magdiel, and Iram. The
area where each of these tribes lived was
known by the name of the tribe.

Joseph and His Brothers

37 Jacob continued to live in the
land of Canaan, where his father
had lived, 2 and this is the story of Jacob's
family.
Joseph, a young man of seventeen,
took care of the sheep and goats with his
brothers, the sons of Bilhah and Zilpah,
his father's concubines. He brought bad
reports to his father about what his
brothers were doing.
3 Jacob loved Joseph more than all his
other sons, because he had been born to
him when he was old. He made a long
robe with full sleeves[p] for him. 4 When
his brothers saw that their father loved
Joseph more than he loved them, they
hated their brother so much that they
would not speak to him in a friendly
manner.

5 One time Joseph had a dream, and
when he told his brothers about it, they
hated him even more. 6 He said, "Listen
to the dream I had. 7 We were all in the
field tying up sheaves of wheat, when my
sheaf got up and stood up straight. Yours
formed a circle around mine and bowed
down to it."
8 "Do you think you are going to be a
king and rule over us?" his brothers
asked. So they hated him even more because of his dreams and because of what
he said about them.
9 Then Joseph had another dream and
told his brothers, "I had another dream,
in which I saw the sun, the moon, and
eleven stars bowing down to me."
10 He also told the dream to his father,
and his father scolded him: "What kind
of a dream is that? Do you think that your
mother, your brothers, and I are going to
come and bow down to you?" 11 Joseph's
brothers were jealous of him, but his
father kept thinking about the whole
matter.

Joseph Is Sold and Taken to Egypt

12 One day when Joseph's brothers had
gone to Shechem to take care of their
father's flock, 13 Jacob said to Joseph, "I
want you to go to Shechem, where your
brothers are taking care of the flock."
Joseph answered, "I am ready."
14 His father told him, "Go and see if
your brothers are safe and if the flock is
all right; then come back and tell me." So
his father sent him on his way from Hebron Valley.
Joseph arrived at Shechem 15 and was
wandering around in the country when a
man saw him and asked him, "What are
you looking for?"
16 "I am looking for my brothers, who
are taking care of their flock," he
answered. "Can you tell me where
they are?"
17 The man said, "They have already
left. I heard them say that they were going to Dothan." So Joseph went after his
brothers and found them at Dothan.
18 They saw him in the distance, and
before he reached them, they plotted
against him and decided to kill him.
19 They said to one another, "Here comes

[p] robe with full sleeves; *or* decorated robe.

that dreamer. 20 Come on now, let's kill
him and throw his body into one of the
dry wells. We can say that a wild animal
killed him. Then we will see what becomes of his dreams."

21 Reuben heard them and tried to save
Joseph. "Let's not kill him," he said.
22 "Just throw him into this well in the
wilderness, but don't hurt him." He said
this, planning to save him from them and
send him back to his father. 23 When Joseph came up to his brothers, they ripped
off his long robe with full sleeves.[p]
24 Then they took him and threw him into
the well, which was dry.

25 While they were eating, they suddenly saw a group of Ishmaelites traveling from Gilead to Egypt. Their camels
were loaded with spices and resins. 26 Judah said to his brothers, "What will we
gain by killing our brother and covering
up the murder? 27 Let's sell him to these
Ishmaelites. Then we won't have to hurt
him; after all, he is our brother, our own
flesh and blood." His brothers agreed,
28 and when some Midianite traders
came by, the brothers[q] pulled Joseph
out of the well and sold him for twenty
pieces of silver to the Ishmaelites, who
took him to Egypt.

29 When Reuben came back to the well
and found that Joseph was not there, he
tore his clothes in sorrow. 30 He returned
to his brothers and said, "The boy is not
there! What am I going to do?"

31 Then they killed a goat and dipped
Joseph's robe in its blood. 32 They took
the robe to their father and said, "We
found this. Does it belong to your
son?"

33 He recognized it and said, "Yes, it is
his! Some wild animal has killed him. My
son Joseph has been torn to pieces!"
34 Jacob tore his clothes in sorrow and
put on sackcloth. He mourned for his son
a long time. 35 All his sons and daughters
came to comfort him, but he refused to be
comforted and said, "I will go down to
the world of the dead still mourning for
my son." So he continued to mourn for
his son Joseph.

36 Meanwhile, in Egypt the Midianites
had sold Joseph to Potiphar, one of the
king's officers, who was the captain of
the palace guard.

Judah and Tamar

38 About that time Judah left his
brothers and went to stay with a
man named Hirah, who was from the
town of Adullam. 2 There Judah met a
young Canaanite woman whose father
was named Shua. He married her, 3 and
she bore him a son, whom he named Er.
4 She became pregnant again and bore
another son and named him Onan.
5 Again she had a son and named him
Shelah. Judah was at Achzib when the
boy was born.

6 For his first son Er, Judah got a wife
whose name was Tamar. 7 Er's conduct
was evil, and it displeased the LORD, so
the LORD killed him. 8 Then Judah said to
Er's brother Onan, "Go and sleep with
your brother's widow. Fulfill your obligation to her as her husband's brother,
so that your brother may have descendants." 9 But Onan knew that the children
would not belong to him, so when he had
intercourse with his brother's widow, he
let the semen spill on the ground, so that
there would be no children for his
brother. 10 What he did displeased the
LORD, and the LORD killed him also.
11 Then Judah said to his daughter-in-law
Tamar, "Return to your father's house
and remain a widow until my son Shelah
grows up." He said this because he was
afraid that Shelah would be killed, as his
brothers had been. So Tamar went back
home.

12 After some time Judah's wife died.
When he had finished the time of mourning, he and his friend Hirah of Adullam
went to Timnah, where his sheep were
being sheared. 13 Someone told Tamar
that her father-in-law was going to Timnah to shear his sheep. 14 So she changed
from the widow's clothes she had been
wearing, covered her face with a veil,
and sat down at the entrance to Enaim, a
town on the road to Timnah. As she well
knew, Judah's youngest son Shelah was
now grown up, and yet she had not been
given to him in marriage.

15 When Judah saw her, he thought
that she was a prostitute, because she
had her face covered. 16 He went over to
her at the side of the road and said, "All
right, how much do you charge?" (He did
not know that she was his daughter-in-
law.)

[p] robe with full sleeves; *or* decorated robe. [q] the brothers; *Hebrew* they.

She said, "What will you give me?"
17 He answered, "I will send you a
young goat from my flock."
She said, "All right, if you will give me
something to keep as a pledge until you
send the goat."
18 "What shall I give you as a pledge?"
he asked.
She answered, "Your seal with its cord
and the walking stick you are carrying."
He gave them to her. Then they had intercourse, and she became pregnant.
19 Tamar went home, took off her veil,
and put her widow's clothes back on.
20 Judah sent his friend Hirah to take
the goat and get back from the woman
the articles he had pledged, but Hirah
could not find her. 21 He asked some men
at Enaim, "Where is the prostitute who
was here by the road?"
"There has never been a prostitute
here," they answered.
22 He returned to Judah and said, "I
couldn't find her. The men of the place
said that there had never been a prostitute there."
23 Judah said, "Let her keep the things.
We don't want people to laugh at us. I did
try to pay her, but you couldn't find her."
24 About three months later someone
told Judah, "Your daughter-in-law Tamar has been acting like a whore, and
now she is pregnant."
Judah ordered, "Take her out and burn
her to death."
25 As she was being taken out, she sent
word to her father-in-law: "I am pregnant by the man who owns these things.
Look at them and see whose they are—
this seal with its cord and this walking
stick."
26 Judah recognized them and said,
"She is in the right. I have failed in my
obligation to her—I should have given
her to my son Shelah in marriage." And
Judah never had intercourse with her
again.
27 When the time came for her to give
birth, it was discovered that she was going to have twins. 28 While she was in
labor, one of them put out an arm; the
midwife caught it, tied a red thread
around it, and said, "This one was born
first." 29 But he pulled his arm back, and
his brother was born first. Then the midwife said, "So this is how you break your
way out!" So he was named Perez.[r]
30 Then his brother was born with the red
thread on his arm, and he was named
Zerah.[s]

Joseph and Potiphar's Wife

39 Now the Ishmaelites had taken
Joseph to Egypt and sold him to
Potiphar, one of the king's officers, who
was the captain of the palace guard. 2 The
LORD was with Joseph and made him successful. He lived in the house of his Egyptian master, 3 who saw that the LORD was
with Joseph and had made him successful in everything he did. 4 Potiphar was
pleased with him and made him his personal servant; so he put him in charge of
his house and everything he owned.
5 From then on, because of Joseph the
LORD blessed the household of the Egyptian and everything that he had in his
house and in his fields. 6 Potiphar turned
over everything he had to the care of Joseph and did not concern himself with
anything except the food he ate.
Joseph was well-built and good-
looking, 7 and after a while his master's
wife began to desire Joseph and asked
him to go to bed with her. 8 He refused
and said to her, "Look, my master does
not have to concern himself with anything in the house, because I am here. He
has put me in charge of everything he
has. 9 I have as much authority in this
house as he has, and he has not kept
back anything from me except you. How
then could I do such an immoral thing
and sin against God?" 10 Although she
asked Joseph day after day, he would
not go to bed with her.
11 But one day when Joseph went into
the house to do his work, none of the
house servants was there. 12 She caught
him by his robe and said, "Come to bed
with me." But he escaped and ran outside, leaving his robe in her hand.
13 When she saw that he had left his robe
and had run out of the house, 14 she called
to her house servants and said, "Look at
this! This Hebrew that my husband
brought to the house is insulting us. He
came into my room and tried to rape me,
but I screamed as loud as I could. 15 When

[r] PEREZ: *This name in Hebrew means "breaking out."* [s] ZERAH: *This name sounds like a Hebrew word for the red brightness of dawn.*

he heard me scream, he ran outside, leaving his robe beside me."

16 She kept his robe with her until Joseph's master came home. 17 Then she told him the same story: "That Hebrew slave that you brought here came into my room and insulted me. 18 But when I screamed, he ran outside, leaving his robe beside me."

19 Joseph's master was furious 20 and had Joseph arrested and put in the prison where the king's prisoners were kept, and there he stayed. 21 But the LORD was with Joseph and blessed him, so that the jailer was pleased with him. 22 He put Joseph in charge of all the other prisoners and made him responsible for everything that was done in the prison. 23 The jailer did not have to look after anything for which Joseph was responsible, because the LORD was with Joseph and made him succeed in everything he did.

Joseph Interprets the Prisoners' Dreams

40 Some time later the king of Egypt's wine steward and his chief baker offended the king. 2 He was angry with these two officials 3 and put them in prison in the house of the captain of the guard, in the same place where Joseph was being kept. 4 They spent a long time in prison, and the captain assigned Joseph as their servant.

5 One night there in prison the wine steward and the chief baker each had a dream, and the dreams had different meanings. 6 When Joseph came to them in the morning, he saw that they were upset. 7 He asked them, "Why do you look so worried today?"

8 They answered, "Each of us had a dream, and there is no one here to explain what the dreams mean."

"It is God who gives the ability to interpret dreams," Joseph said. "Tell me your dreams."

9 So the wine steward said, "In my dream there was a grapevine in front of me 10 with three branches on it. As soon as the leaves came out, the blossoms appeared, and the grapes ripened. 11 I was holding the king's cup; so I took the grapes and squeezed them into the cup and gave it to him."

12 Joseph said, "This is what it means: the three branches are three days. 13 In three days the king will release you, pardon you, and restore you to your position. You will give him his cup as you did before when you were his wine steward. 14 But please remember me when everything is going well for you, and please be kind enough to mention me to the king and help me get out of this prison. 15 After all, I was kidnapped from the land of the Hebrews, and even here in Egypt I didn't do anything to deserve being put in prison."

16 When the chief baker saw that the interpretation of the wine steward's dream was favorable, he said to Joseph, "I had a dream too; I was carrying three breadbaskets on my head. 17 In the top basket there were all kinds of baked goods for the king, and the birds were eating them."

18 Joseph answered, "This is what it means: the three baskets are three days. 19 In three days the king will release you—and have your head cut off! Then he will hang your body on a pole, and the birds will eat your flesh."

20 On his birthday three days later the king gave a banquet for all his officials; he released his wine steward and his chief baker and brought them before his officials. 21 He restored the wine steward to his former position, 22 but he executed the chief baker. It all happened just as Joseph had said. 23 But the wine steward never gave Joseph another thought—he forgot all about him.

Joseph Interprets the King's Dreams

41 After two years had passed, the king of Egypt dreamed that he was standing by the Nile River, 2 when seven cows, fat and sleek, came up out of the river and began to feed on the grass. 3 Then seven other cows came up; they were thin and bony. They came and stood by the other cows on the riverbank, 4 and the thin cows ate up the fat cows. Then the king woke up. 5 He fell asleep again and had another dream. Seven heads of grain, full and ripe, were growing on one stalk. 6 Then seven other heads of grain sprouted, thin and scorched by the desert wind, 7 and the thin heads of grain swallowed the full ones. The king woke up and realized that he had been dreaming. 8 In the morning he was worried, so he sent for all the magicians and wise men of Egypt. He

told them his dreams, but no one could
explain them to him.
9 Then the wine steward said to the
king, "I must confess today that I have
done wrong. 10 You were angry with the
chief baker and me, and you put us in
prison in the house of the captain of the
guard. 11 One night each of us had a
dream, and the dreams had different
meanings. 12 A young Hebrew was there
with us, a slave of the captain of the
guard. We told him our dreams, and he
interpreted them for us. 13 Things turned
out just as he said: you restored me to my
position, but you executed the baker."
14 The king sent for Joseph, and he was
immediately brought from the prison.
After he had shaved and changed his
clothes, he came into the king's presence. 15 The king said to him, "I have had
a dream, and no one can explain it. I have
been told that you can interpret dreams."
16 Joseph answered, "I cannot, Your
Majesty, but God will give a favorable
interpretation."
17 The king said, "I dreamed that I was
standing on the bank of the Nile, 18 when
seven cows, fat and sleek, came up out of
the river and began feeding on the grass.
19 Then seven other cows came up which
were thin and bony. They were the poorest cows I have ever seen anywhere in
Egypt. 20 The thin cows ate up the fat
ones, 21 but no one would have known it,
because they looked just as bad as before. Then I woke up. 22 I also dreamed
that I saw seven heads of grain which
were full and ripe, growing on one stalk.
23 Then seven heads of grain sprouted,
thin and scorched by the desert wind,
24 and the thin heads of grain swallowed
the full ones. I told the dreams to the
magicians, but none of them could explain them to me."
25 Joseph said to the king, "The two
dreams mean the same thing; God has
told you what he is going to do. 26 The
seven fat cows are seven years, and the
seven full heads of grain are also seven
years; they have the same meaning.
27 The seven thin cows which came up
later and the seven thin heads of grain
scorched by the desert wind are seven
years of famine. 28 It is just as I told you—
God has shown you what he is going to
do. 29 There will be seven years of great
plenty in all the land of Egypt. 30 After
that, there will be seven years of famine,
and all the good years will be forgotten,
because the famine will ruin the country.
31 The time of plenty will be entirely forgotten, because the famine which follows will be so terrible. 32 The repetition
of your dream means that the matter is
fixed by God and that he will make it
happen in the near future.
33 "Now you should choose some man
with wisdom and insight and put him in
charge of the country. 34 You must also
appoint other officials and take a fifth of
the crops during the seven years of
plenty. 35 Order them to collect all the
food during the good years that are coming, and give them authority to store up
grain in the cities and guard it. 36 The
food will be a reserve supply for the
country during the seven years of famine
which are going to come on Egypt. In this
way the people will not starve."

Joseph Is Made Governor over Egypt

37 The king and his officials approved
this plan, 38 and he said to them, "We will
never find a better man than Joseph, a
man who has God's spirit in him." 39 The
king said to Joseph, "God has shown you
all this, so it is obvious that you have
greater wisdom and insight than anyone
else. 40 I will put you in charge of my
country, and all my people will obey
your orders. Your authority will be second only to mine. 41 I now appoint you
governor over all Egypt." 42 The king removed from his finger the ring engraved
with the royal seal and put it on Joseph's
finger. He put a fine linen robe on him,
and placed a gold chain around his neck.
43 He gave him the second royal chariot
to ride in, and his guard of honor went
ahead of him and cried out, "Make way!
Make way!" And so Joseph was appointed governor over all Egypt. 44 The
king said to him, "I am the king—and no
one in all Egypt shall so much as lift a
hand or a foot without your permission."
45-46 He gave Joseph the Egyptian name
Zaphenath Paneah, and he gave him a
wife, Asenath, the daughter of Potiphera,
a priest in the city of Heliopolis.

Joseph was thirty years old when he
began to serve the king of Egypt. He left
the king's court and traveled all over the
land. 47 During the seven years of plenty
the land produced abundant crops, 48 all

of which Joseph collected and stored in
the cities. In each city he stored the food
from the fields around it. 49 There was so
much grain that Joseph stopped measuring it—it was like the sand of the sea.
50 Before the years of famine came, Joseph had two sons by Asenath. 51 He said,
"God has made me forget all my sufferings and all my father's family"; so he
named his first son Manasseh.[t] 52 He
also said, "God has given me children in
the land of my trouble"; so he named his
second son Ephraim.[u]
53 The seven years of plenty that the
land of Egypt had enjoyed came to an
end, 54 and the seven years of famine began, just as Joseph had said. There was
famine in every other country, but there
was food throughout Egypt. 55 When the
Egyptians began to be hungry, they cried
out to the king for food. So he ordered
them to go to Joseph and do what he told
them. 56 The famine grew worse and
spread over the whole country, so Joseph opened all the storehouses and sold
grain to the Egyptians. 57 People came to
Egypt from all over the world to buy
grain from Joseph, because the famine
was severe everywhere.

Joseph's Brothers Go to Egypt to Buy Grain

42 When Jacob learned that there
was grain in Egypt, he said to his
sons, "Why don't you do something? 2 I
hear that there is grain in Egypt; go there
and buy some to keep us from starving to
death." 3 So Joseph's ten half brothers
went to buy grain in Egypt, 4 but Jacob
did not send Joseph's full brother Benjamin with them, because he was afraid
that something might happen to him.
5 The sons of Jacob came with others to
buy grain, because there was famine in
the land of Canaan. 6 Joseph, as governor
of the land of Egypt, was selling grain to
people from all over the world. So Joseph's brothers came and bowed down
before him with their faces to the ground.
7 When Joseph saw his brothers, he recognized them, but he acted as if he did
not know them. He asked them harshly,
"Where do you come from?"
"We have come from Canaan to buy
food," they answered.
8 Although Joseph recognized his
brothers, they did not recognize him.
9 He remembered the dreams he had
dreamed about them and said, "You are
spies; you have come to find out where
our country is weak."
10 "No, sir," they answered. "We have
come as your slaves, to buy food. 11 We
are all brothers. We are not spies, sir, we
are honest men."
12 Joseph said to them, "No! You have
come to find out where our country is
weak."
13 They said, "We were twelve brothers
in all, sir, sons of the same man in the
land of Canaan. One brother is dead, and
the youngest is now with our father."
14 "It is just as I said," Joseph answered.
"You are spies. 15 This is how you will be
tested: I swear by the name of the king
that you will never leave unless your
youngest brother comes here. 16 One of
you must go and get him. The rest of you
will be kept under guard until the truth of
what you say can be tested. Otherwise,
as sure as the king lives, you are spies."
17 With that, he put them in prison for
three days.
18 On the third day Joseph said to them,
"I am a God-fearing man, and I will spare
your lives on one condition. 19 To prove
that you are honest, one of you will stay
in the prison where you have been kept;
the rest of you may go and take back to
your starving families the grain that you
have bought. 20 Then you must bring
your youngest brother to me. This will
prove that you have been telling the
truth, and I will not put you to death."
They agreed to this 21 and said to one
another, "Yes, now we are suffering the
consequences of what we did to our
brother; we saw the great trouble he was
in when he begged for help, but we
would not listen. That is why we are in
this trouble now."
22 Reuben said, "I told you not to harm
the boy, but you wouldn't listen. And
now we are being paid back for his
death." 23 Joseph understood what they
said, but they did not know it, because
they had been speaking to him through
an interpreter. 24 Joseph left them and began to cry. When he was able to speak

[t] MANASSEH: *This name sounds like the Hebrew for "cause to forget."* [u] EPHRAIM: *This name sounds like the Hebrew for "give children."*

again, he came back, picked out Simeon, and had him tied up in front of
them.

Joseph's Brothers Return to Canaan

25 Joseph gave orders to fill his brothers' packs with grain, to put each man's
money back in his sack, and to give them
food for the trip. This was done. 26 The
brothers loaded their donkeys with the
grain they had bought, and then they left.
27 At the place where they spent the
night, one of them opened his sack to
feed his donkey and found his money at
the top of the sack. 28 "My money has
been returned to me," he called to his
brothers. "Here it is in my sack!" Their
hearts sank, and in fear they asked one
another, "What has God done to us?"
29 When they came to their father Jacob in Canaan, they told him all that had
happened to them: 30 "The governor of
Egypt spoke harshly to us and accused
us of spying against his country. 31 'We
are not spies,' we answered, 'we are honest men. 32 We were twelve brothers in
all, sons of the same father. One brother
is dead, and the youngest is still in Canaan with our father.' 33 The man answered, 'This is how I will find out if you
are honest men: One of you will stay with
me; the rest will take grain for your
starving families and leave. 34 Bring your
youngest brother to me. Then I will know
that you are not spies, but honest men; I
will give your brother back to you, and
you can stay here and trade.' "
35 Then when they emptied out their
sacks, every one of them found his bag of
money; and when they saw the money,
they and their father Jacob were afraid.
36 Their father said to them, "Do you
want to make me lose all my children?
Joseph is gone; Simeon is gone; and now
you want to take away Benjamin. I am
the one who suffers!"
37 Reuben said to his father, "If I do not
bring Benjamin back to you, you can kill
my two sons. Put him in my care, and I
will bring him back."
38 But Jacob said, "My son cannot go
with you; his brother is dead, and he is
the only one left. Something might happen to him on the way. I am an old man,
and the sorrow you would cause me
would kill me."

Joseph's Brothers Return to Egypt with Benjamin

43 The famine in Canaan got worse,
2 and when the family of Jacob
had eaten all the grain which had been
brought from Egypt, Jacob said to his
sons, "Go back and buy a little food
for us."
3 Judah said to him, "The man sternly
warned us that we would not be admitted
to his presence unless we had our
brother with us. 4 If you are willing to
send our brother with us, we will go and
buy food for you. 5 If you are not willing,
we will not go, because the man told us
we would not be admitted to his presence
unless our brother was with us."
6 Jacob said, "Why did you cause me so
much trouble by telling the man that you
had another brother?"
7 They answered, "The man kept asking about us and our family, 'Is your
father still living? Do you have another
brother?' We had to answer his questions. How could we know that he would
tell us to bring our brother with us?"
8 Judah said to his father, "Send the
boy with me, and we will leave at once.
Then none of us will starve to death.
9 I will pledge my own life, and you can
hold me responsible for him. If I do not
bring him back to you safe and sound, I
will always bear the blame. 10 If we had
not waited so long, we could have been
there and back twice by now."
11 Their father said to them, "If that is
how it has to be, then take the best products of the land in your packs as a
present for the governor: a little resin, a
little honey, spices, pistachio nuts, and
almonds. 12 Take with you also twice as
much money, because you must take
back the money that was returned in the
top of your sacks. Maybe it was a mistake. 13 Take your brother and return at
once. 14 May Almighty God cause the
man to have pity on you, so that he will
give Benjamin and your other brother
back to you. As for me, if I must lose my
children, I must lose them."
15 So the brothers took the gifts and
twice as much money, and set out for
Egypt with Benjamin. There they presented themselves to Joseph. 16 When Joseph saw Benjamin with them, he said to
the servant in charge of his house, "Take
these men to my house. They are going to

eat with me at noon, so kill an animal and
prepare it." 17 The servant did as he was
commanded and took the brothers to Joseph's house.

18 As they were being brought to the
house, they were afraid and thought,
"We are being brought here because of
the money that was returned in our sacks
the first time. They will suddenly attack
us, take our donkeys, and make us his
slaves." 19 So at the door of the house,
they said to the servant in charge, 20 "If
you please, sir, we came here once before
to buy food. 21 When we set up camp on
the way home, we opened our sacks, and
each man found his money in the top
of his sack – every bit of it. We have
brought it back to you. 22 We have also
brought some more money with us to
buy more food. We do not know who put
our money back in our sacks."

23 The servant said, "Don't worry.
Don't be afraid. Your God, the God of
your father, must have put the money in
your sacks for you. I received your payment." Then he brought Simeon to them.

24 The servant took the brothers into
the house. He gave them water so that
they could wash their feet, and he fed
their donkeys. 25 They got their gifts
ready to present to Joseph when he arrived at noon, because they had been told
that they were to eat with him. 26 When
Joseph got home, they took the gifts into
the house to him and bowed down to the
ground before him. 27 He asked about
their health and then said, "You told me
about your old father – how is he? Is he
still alive and well?"

28 They answered, "Your humble servant, our father, is still alive and well."
And they knelt and bowed down before him.

29 When Joseph saw his brother Benjamin, he said, "So this is your youngest
brother, the one you told me about. God
bless you, my son." 30 Then Joseph left
suddenly, because his heart was full of
tender feelings for his brother. He was
about to break down, so he went to his
room and cried. 31 After he had washed
his face, he came out, and controlling
himself, he ordered the meal to be
served. 32 Joseph was served at one table
and his brothers at another. The Egyptians who were eating there were served
separately, because they considered it
beneath their dignity to eat with Hebrews. 33 The brothers had been seated at
the table, facing Joseph, in the order of
their age from the oldest to the youngest.
When they saw how they had been
seated, they looked at one another in
amazement. 34 Food was served to them
from Joseph's table, and Benjamin was
served five times as much as the rest of
them. So they ate and drank with Joseph
until they were drunk.

The Missing Cup

44 Joseph commanded the servant
in charge of his house, "Fill the
men's sacks with as much food as they
can carry, and put each man's money in
the top of his sack. 2 Put my silver cup in
the top of the youngest brother's sack,
together with the money for his grain."
He did as he was told. 3 Early in the morning the brothers were sent on their way
with their donkeys. 4 When they had
gone only a short distance from the city,
Joseph said to the servant in charge of
his house, "Hurry after those men. When
you catch up with them, ask them, 'Why
have you paid back evil for good? 5 Why
did you steal my master's silver cup?[v] It
is the one he drinks from, the one he uses
for divination. You have committed a serious crime!' "

6 When the servant caught up with
them, he repeated these words. 7 They
answered him, "What do you mean, sir,
by talking like this? We swear that we
have done no such thing. 8 You know that
we brought back to you from the land of
Canaan the money we found in the top of
our sacks. Why then should we steal silver or gold from your master's house?
9 Sir, if any one of us is found to have it,
he will be put to death, and the rest of us
will become your slaves."

10 He said, "I agree; but only the one
who has taken the cup will become my
slave, and the rest of you can go free."
11 So they quickly lowered their sacks to
the ground, and each man opened his
sack. 12 Joseph's servant searched carefully, beginning with the oldest and ending with the youngest, and the cup was
found in Benjamin's sack. 13 The broth-

[v] *One ancient translation* Why did you steal my master's silver cup?; *Hebrew does not have these words.*

ers tore their clothes in sorrow, loaded
their donkeys, and returned to the city.
14 When Judah and his brothers came
to Joseph's house, he was still there.
They bowed down before him, 15 and Joseph said, "What have you done? Didn't
you know that a man in my position
could find you out by practicing divination?"
16 "What can we say to you, sir?" Judah
answered. "How can we argue? How can
we clear ourselves? God has uncovered
our guilt. All of us are now your slaves
and not just the one with whom the cup
was found."
17 Joseph said, "Oh, no! I would never
do that! Only the one who had the cup
will be my slave. The rest of you may go
back safe and sound to your father."

Judah Pleads for Benjamin

18 Judah went up to Joseph and said,
"Please, sir, allow me to speak with you
freely. Don't be angry with me; you are
like the king himself. 19 Sir, you asked us,
'Do you have a father or another
brother?' 20 We answered, 'We have a
father who is old and a younger brother,
born to him in his old age. The boy's
brother is dead, and he is the only one of
his mother's children still alive; his
father loves him very much.' 21 Sir, you
told us to bring him here, so that you
could see him, 22 and we answered that
the boy could not leave his father; if he
did, his father would die. 23 Then you
said, 'You will not be admitted to my
presence again unless your youngest
brother comes with you.'
24 "When we went back to our father,
we told him what you had said. 25 Then
he told us to return and buy a little food.
26 We answered, 'We cannot go; we will
not be admitted to the man's presence
unless our youngest brother is with us.
We can go only if our youngest brother
goes also.' 27 Our father said to us, 'You
know that my wife Rachel bore me only
two sons. 28 One of them has already left
me. He must have been torn to pieces by
wild animals, because I have not seen
him since he left. 29 If you take this one
from me now and something happens to
him, the sorrow you would cause me
would kill me, as old as I am.'
30-31 "And now, sir," Judah continued,
"if I go back to my father without the boy,
as soon as he sees that the boy is not with
me, he will die. His life is wrapped up
with the life of the boy, and he is so old
that the sorrow we would cause him
would kill him. 32 What is more, I pledged
my life to my father for the boy. I told him
that if I did not bring the boy back to him,
I would bear the blame all my life. 33 And
now, sir, I will stay here as your slave in
place of the boy; let him go back with his
brothers. 34 How can I go back to my
father if the boy is not with me? I cannot
bear to see this disaster come upon my
father."

Joseph Tells His Brothers Who He Is

45 Joseph was no longer able to
control his feelings in front of his
servants, so he ordered them all to leave
the room. No one else was with him
when Joseph told his brothers who he
was. 2 He cried with such loud sobs that
the Egyptians heard it, and the news was
taken to the king's palace. 3 Joseph said
to his brothers, "I am Joseph. Is my
father still alive?" But when his brothers
heard this, they were so terrified that
they could not answer. 4 Then Joseph
said to them, "Please come closer." They
did, and he said, "I am your brother Joseph, whom you sold into Egypt. 5 Now
do not be upset or blame yourselves because you sold me here. It was really God
who sent me ahead of you to save people's lives. 6 This is only the second year
of famine in the land; there will be five
more years in which there will be neither
plowing nor reaping. 7 God sent me
ahead of you to rescue you in this amazing way and to make sure that you and
your descendants survive. 8 So it was not
really you who sent me here, but God. He
has made me the king's highest official.
I am in charge of his whole country; I am
the ruler of all Egypt.
9 "Now hurry back to my father and tell
him that this is what his son Joseph says:
'God has made me ruler of all Egypt;
come to me without delay. 10 You can live
in the region of Goshen, where you can
be near me – you, your children, your
grandchildren, your sheep, your goats,
your cattle, and everything else that you
have. 11 If you are in Goshen, I can take
care of you. There will still be five years
of famine; and I do not want you, your
family, and your livestock to starve.'"
12 Joseph continued, "Now all of you,
and you too, Benjamin, can see that I am

really Joseph. 13 Tell my father how powerful I am here in Egypt and tell him
about everything that you have seen.
Then hurry and bring him here."

14 He threw his arms around his
brother Benjamin and began to cry; Benjamin also cried as he hugged him.
15 Then, still weeping, he embraced each
of his brothers and kissed them. After
that, his brothers began to talk with him.

16 When the news reached the palace
that Joseph's brothers had come, the
king and his officials were pleased. 17 He
said to Joseph, "Tell your brothers to
load their animals and to return to the
land of Canaan. 18 Let them get their
father and their families and come back
here. I will give them the best land in
Egypt, and they will have more than
enough to live on. 19 Tell them also to
take wagons with them from Egypt for
their wives and small children and to
bring their father with them. 20 They are
not to worry about leaving their possessions behind; the best in the whole land
of Egypt will be theirs."

21 Jacob's sons did as they were told.
Joseph gave them wagons, as the king
had ordered, and food for the trip. 22 He
also gave each of them a change of
clothes, but he gave Benjamin three hundred pieces of silver and five changes of
clothes. 23 He sent his father ten donkeys
loaded with the best Egyptian goods and
ten donkeys loaded with grain, bread,
and other food for the trip. 24 He sent his
brothers off and as they left, he said to
them, "Don't quarrel on the way."

25 They left Egypt and went back home
to their father Jacob in Canaan. 26 "Joseph is still alive!" they told him. "He is
the ruler of all Egypt!" Jacob was
stunned and could not believe them.

27 But when they told him all that Joseph had said to them, and when he saw
the wagons which Joseph had sent to
take him to Egypt, he recovered from the
shock. 28 "My son Joseph is still alive!" he
said. "This is all I could ask for! I must go
and see him before I die."

Jacob and His Family Go to Egypt

46 Jacob packed up all he had and
went to Beersheba, where he offered sacrifices to the God of his father
Isaac. 2 God spoke to him in a vision at
night and called, "Jacob, Jacob!"

"Yes, here I am," he answered.

3 "I am God, the God of your father," he
said. "Do not be afraid to go to Egypt; I
will make your descendants a great nation there. 4 I will go with you to Egypt,
and I will bring your descendants back to
this land. Joseph will be with you when
you die."

5 Jacob set out from Beersheba. His
sons put him, their small children, and
their wives in the wagons which the king
of Egypt had sent. 6 They took their livestock and the possessions they had acquired in Canaan and went to Egypt.
Jacob took all his descendants with him:
7 his sons, his grandsons, his daughters,
and his granddaughters.

8 The members of Jacob's family who
went to Egypt with him were his oldest
son Reuben 9 and Reuben's sons: Hanoch, Pallu, Hezron, and Carmi. 10 Simeon and his sons: Jemuel, Jamin, Ohad,
Jachin, Zohar, and Shaul, the son of a
Canaanite woman. 11 Levi and his sons:
Gershon, Kohath, and Merari. 12 Judah
and his sons: Shelah, Perez, and Zerah.
(Judah's other sons, Er and Onan, had
died in Canaan.) Perez' sons were Hezron and Hamul. 13 Issachar and his sons:
Tola, Puah, Jashub, and Shimron. 14 Zebulun and his sons: Sered, Elon, and Jahleel. 15 These are the sons that Leah had
borne to Jacob in Mesopotamia, besides
his daughter Dinah. In all, his descendants by Leah numbered thirty-three.

16 Gad and his sons: Zephon, Haggi,
Shuni, Ezbon, Eri, Arod, and Areli.
17 Asher and his sons: Imnah, Ishvah,
Ishvi, Beriah, and their sister Serah. Be-
riah's sons were Heber and Malchiel.
18 These sixteen are the descendants of
Jacob by Zilpah, the slave woman whom
Laban gave to his daughter Leah.

19 Jacob's wife Rachel bore him two
sons: Joseph and Benjamin. 20 In Egypt
Joseph had two sons, Manasseh and
Ephraim, by Asenath, the daughter of
Potiphera, a priest in Heliopolis. 21 Benjamin's sons were Bela, Becher, Ashbel,
Gera, Naaman, Ehi, Rosh, Muppim, Huppim, and Ard. 22 These fourteen are the
descendants of Jacob by Rachel.

23 Dan and his son Hushim. 24 Naphtali
and his sons: Jahzeel, Guni, Jezer, and
Shillem. 25 These seven are the descendants of Jacob by Bilhah, the slave woman
whom Laban gave to his daughter
Rachel.

26 The total number of the direct

descendants of Jacob who went to Egypt
was sixty-six, not including his sons'
wives. 27 Two sons were born to Joseph
in Egypt, bringing to seventy the total
number of Jacob's family who went
there.

Jacob and His Family in Egypt

28 Jacob sent Judah ahead to ask Joseph to meet them in Goshen. When they
arrived, 29 Joseph got in his chariot and
went to Goshen to meet his father. When
they met, Joseph threw his arms around
his father's neck and cried for a long
time. 30 Jacob said to Joseph, "I am ready
to die, now that I have seen you and
know that you are still alive."

31 Then Joseph said to his brothers and
the rest of his father's family, "I must go
and tell the king that my brothers and all
my father's family, who were living in
Canaan, have come to me. 32 I will tell
him that you are shepherds and take care
of livestock and that you have brought
your flocks and herds and everything
else that belongs to you. 33 When the king
calls for you and asks what your occupation is, 34 be sure to tell him that you have
taken care of livestock all your lives, just
as your ancestors did. In this way he will
let you live in the region of Goshen." Joseph said this because Egyptians will
have nothing to do with shepherds.

47 So Joseph took five of his brothers and went to the king. He told
him, "My father and my brothers have
come from Canaan with their flocks,
their herds, and all that they own. They
are now in the region of Goshen." 2 He
then presented his brothers to the king.
3 The king asked them, "What is your occupation?"

"We are shepherds, sir, just as our ancestors were," they answered. 4 "We have
come to live in this country, because in
the land of Canaan the famine is so severe that there is no pasture for our
flocks. Please give us permission to live
in the region of Goshen." 5 The king said
to Joseph, "Now that your father and
your brothers have arrived, 6 the land of
Egypt is theirs. Let them settle in the region of Goshen, the best part of the land.
And if there are any capable men among
them, put them in charge of my own
livestock."

7 Then Joseph brought his father Jacob
and presented him to the king. Jacob
gave the king his blessing, 8 and the king
asked him, "How old are you?"

9 Jacob answered, "My life of wandering has lasted a hundred and thirty
years. Those years have been few and
difficult, unlike the long years of my ancestors in their wanderings." 10 Jacob
gave the king a farewell blessing and left.
11 Then Joseph settled his father and his
brothers in Egypt, giving them property
in the best of the land near the city of
Rameses, as the king had commanded.
12 Joseph provided food for his father, his
brothers, and all the rest of his father's
family, including the very youngest.

The Famine

13 The famine was so severe that there
was no food anywhere, and the people of
Egypt and Canaan became weak with
hunger. 14 As they bought grain, Joseph
collected all the money and took it to the
palace. 15 When all the money in Egypt
and Canaan was spent, the Egyptians
came to Joseph and said, "Give us food!
Don't let us die. Do something! Our
money is all gone."

16 Joseph answered, "Bring your livestock; I will give you food in exchange
for it if your money is all gone." 17 So they
brought their livestock to Joseph, and he
gave them food in exchange for their
horses, sheep, goats, cattle, and donkeys.
That year he supplied them with food in
exchange for all their livestock.

18 The following year they came to him
and said, "We will not hide the fact from
you, sir, that our money is all gone and
our livestock belongs to you. There is
nothing left to give you except our bodies
and our lands. 19 Don't let us die. Do
something! Don't let our fields be deserted. Buy us and our land in exchange
for food. We will be the king's slaves, and
he will own our land. Give us grain to
keep us alive and seed so that we can
plant our fields."

20 Joseph bought all the land in Egypt
for the king. Every Egyptian was forced
to sell his land, because the famine was
so severe; and all the land became the
king's property. 21 Joseph made slaves of
the people from one end of Egypt to the
other. 22 The only land he did not buy was
the land that belonged to the priests.
They did not have to sell their lands, because the king gave them an allowance
to live on. 23 Joseph said to the people,

"You see, I have now bought you and
your lands for the king. Here is seed for
you to sow in your fields. 24 At the time of
harvest you must give one-fifth to the
king. You can use the rest for seed and
for food for yourselves and your
families."
25 They answered, "You have saved our
lives; you have been good to us, sir, and
we will be the king's slaves." 26 So Joseph
made it a law for the land of Egypt that
one-fifth of the harvest should belong to
the king. This law still remains in force
today. Only the lands of the priests did
not become the king's property.

Jacob's Last Request

27 The Israelites lived in Egypt in the
region of Goshen, where they became
rich and had many children. 28 Jacob
lived in Egypt seventeen years, until he
was a hundred and forty-seven years old.
29 When the time drew near for him to
die, he called for his son Joseph and said
to him, "Place your hand between my
thighs[w] and make a solemn vow that you
will not bury me in Egypt. 30 I want to be
buried where my fathers are; carry me
out of Egypt and bury me where they are
buried."

Joseph answered, "I will do as
you say."
31 Jacob said, "Make a vow that you
will." Joseph made the vow, and Jacob
gave thanks there on his bed.

Jacob Blesses Ephraim and Manasseh

48 Some time later Joseph was told
that his father was ill. So he took
his two sons, Manasseh and Ephraim,
and went to see Jacob. 2 When Jacob was
told that his son Joseph had come to see
him, he gathered his strength and sat up
in bed. 3 Jacob said to Joseph, "Almighty
God appeared to me at Luz in the land of
Canaan and blessed me. 4 He said to me,
'I will give you many children, so that
your descendants will become many nations; I will give this land to your
descendants as their possession
forever.' "
5 Jacob continued, "Joseph, your two
sons, who were born to you in Egypt before I came here, belong to me; Ephraim
and Manasseh are just as much my sons
as Reuben and Simeon. 6 If you have any
more sons, they will not be considered
mine; the inheritance they get will come
through Ephraim and Manasseh. 7 I am
doing this because of your mother Rachel. To my great sorrow she died in the
land of Canaan, not far from Ephrath, as
I was returning from Mesopotamia.
I buried her there beside the road to
Ephrath." (Ephrath is now known as
Bethlehem.)
8 When Jacob saw Joseph's sons, he
asked, "Who are these boys?"
9 Joseph answered, "These are my
sons, whom God has given me here in
Egypt."

Jacob said, "Bring them to me so that
I may bless them." 10 Jacob's eyesight
was failing because of his age, and he
could not see very well. Joseph brought
the boys to him, and he hugged them and
kissed them. 11 Jacob said to Joseph, "I
never expected to see you again, and
now God has even let me see your children." 12 Then Joseph took them from Jacob's lap and bowed down before him
with his face to the ground.
13 Joseph put Ephraim at Jacob's left
and Manasseh at his right. 14 But Jacob
crossed his hands, and put his right hand
on the head of Ephraim, even though he
was the younger, and his left hand on the
head of Manasseh, who was the older.
15 Then he blessed Joseph:[x]

"May God, whom my fathers
Abraham and Isaac served,
bless these boys!
May God, who has led me to this
very day, bless them!
16 May the angel, who has rescued
me from all harm, bless them!
May my name and the name of my
fathers Abraham and Isaac
live on through these boys!
May they have many children,
many descendants!"

17 Joseph was upset when he saw that
his father had put his right hand on
Ephraim's head; so he took his father's
hand to move it from Ephraim's head to
the head of Manasseh. 18 He said to his
father, "Not that way, father. This is the
older boy; put your right hand on his
head."

[w] PLACE . . . THIGHS: *See 24.2.* [x] JOSEPH: *In blessing Ephraim and Manasseh, Jacob was in fact blessing Joseph.*

19His father refused, saying, "I know,
son, I know. Manasseh's descendants
will also become a great people. But his
younger brother will be greater than he,
and his descendants will become great
nations."
20So he blessed them that day, saying,
"The Israelites will use your names when
they pronounce blessings. They will say,
'May God make you like Ephraim and
Manasseh.'" In this way Jacob put
Ephraim before Manasseh.
21Then Jacob said to Joseph, "As you
see, I am about to die, but God will be
with you and will take you back to the
land of your ancestors. 22It is to you and
not to your brothers that I am giving Shechem, that fertile region which I took
from the Amorites with my sword and
my bow."

The Last Words of Jacob

49 Jacob called for his sons and said, "Gather around, and I will tell you what will happen to you in the future:

2"Come together and listen, sons of
Jacob.
Listen to your father Israel.

3"Reuben, my first-born, you are
my strength
And the first child of my
manhood,
The proudest and strongest of all
my sons.
4You are like a raging flood,
But you will not be the most
important,
For you slept with my concubine
And dishonored your father's bed.

5"Simeon and Levi are brothers.
They use their weapons to commit
violence.
6I will not join in their secret talks,
Nor will I take part in their
meetings,
For they killed people in anger
And they crippled bulls for sport.
7A curse be on their anger, because
it is so fierce,
And on their fury, because it is so
cruel.
I will scatter them throughout the
land of Israel.
I will disperse them among its
people.

8"Judah, your brothers will
praise you.
You hold your enemies by the
neck.
Your brothers will bow down
before you.
9Judah is like a lion,
Killing his victim and returning to
his den,
Stretching out and lying down.
No one dares disturb him.
10Judah will hold the royal scepter,
And his descendants will always
rule.
Nations will bring him tribute[y]
And bow in obedience before him.
11He ties his young donkey to a
grapevine,
To the very best of the vines.
He washes his clothes in blood-red
wine.
12His eyes are bloodshot from
drinking wine,
His teeth white from drinking
milk.[z]

13"Zebulun will live beside the sea.
His shore will be a haven for
ships.
His territory will reach as far as
Sidon.

14"Issachar is no better than a
donkey
That lies stretched out between its
saddlebags.
15But he sees that the resting place
is good
And that the land is delightful.
So he bends his back to carry the
load
And is forced to work as a slave.

16"Dan will be a ruler for his people.
They will be like the other tribes
of Israel.
17Dan will be a snake at the side of
the road,
A poisonous snake beside the
path,

[y] *Probable text* Nations . . . tribute; *Hebrew unclear.*

[z] His eyes . . . milk; *or* His eyes are darker than wine, his teeth are whiter than milk.

That strikes at the horse's heel,
So that the rider is thrown off
backward.

18 "I wait for your deliverance, LORD.

19 "Gad will be attacked by a band of
robbers,
But he will turn and pursue them.

20 "Asher's land will produce rich
food.
He will provide food fit for a king.

21 "Naphtali is a deer that runs free,
Who bears lovely fawns.[a]

22 "Joseph is like a wild donkey by a
spring,
A wild colt on a hillside.[b]
23 His enemies attack him fiercely
And pursue him with their bows
and arrows.
24 But his bow remains steady,
And his arms are made strong[c]
By the power of the Mighty God of
Jacob,
By the Shepherd, the Protector of
Israel.
25 It is your father's God who
helps you,
The Almighty God who
blesses you
With blessings of rain from above
And of deep waters from beneath
the ground,
Blessings of many cattle and
children,
26 Blessings of grain and flowers,[d]
Blessings of ancient mountains,[e]
Delightful things from everlasting
hills.
May these blessings rest on the
head of Joseph,
On the brow of the one set apart
from his brothers.

27 "Benjamin is like a vicious wolf.
Morning and evening he kills and
devours."

28 These are the twelve tribes of Israel,
and this is what their father said as he
spoke a suitable word of farewell to
each son.

The Death and Burial of Jacob

29 Then Jacob commanded his sons,
"Now that I am going to join my people
in death, bury me with my fathers in the
cave that is in the field of Ephron the
Hittite, 30 at Machpelah east of Mamre in
the land of Canaan. Abraham bought
this cave and field from Ephron for a burial ground. 31 That is where they buried
Abraham and his wife Sarah; that is
where they buried Isaac and his wife Rebecca; and that is where I buried Leah.
32 The field and the cave in it were bought
from the Hittites. Bury me there."
33 When Jacob had finished giving instructions to his sons, he lay back down
and died.

50 Joseph threw himself on his
father, crying and kissing his
face. 2 Then Joseph gave orders to em-
balm his father's body. 3 It took forty
days, the normal time for embalming.
The Egyptians mourned for him seventy
days.

4 When the time of mourning was over,
Joseph said to the king's officials,
"Please take this message to the king:
5 'When my father was about to die, he
made me promise him that I would bury
him in the tomb which he had prepared
in the land of Canaan. So please let me go
and bury my father, and then I will come
back.' "
6 The king answered, "Go and bury
your father, as you promised you would."
7 So Joseph went to bury his father. All
the king's officials, the senior men of his
court, and all the leading men of Egypt
went with Joseph. 8 His family, his brothers, and the rest of his father's family all
went with him. Only their small children
and their sheep, goats, and cattle stayed
in the region of Goshen. 9 Men in chariots
and men on horseback also went with
him; it was a huge group.
10 When they came to the threshing
place at Atad east of the Jordan, they
mourned loudly for a long time, and Joseph performed mourning ceremonies
for seven days. 11 When the citizens of

[a] Naphtali . . . fawns; *or* Naphtali is a spreading tree that puts out lovely branches. [b] Joseph . . . hillside; *or* Joseph is like a tree by a spring, a fruitful tree that spreads over a wall. [c] But . . . strong; *or* But their bows were broken and splintered, the muscles of their arms torn apart. [d] *Probable text* grain and flowers; *Hebrew* your fathers are mightier than. [e] *One ancient translation* ancient mountains; *Hebrew* my ancestors to.

Canaan saw those people mourning at
Atad, they said, "What a solemn ceremony of mourning the Egyptians are
holding!" That is why the place was
named Abel Mizraim.[f]
12 So Jacob's sons did as he had commanded them; 13 they carried his body to
Canaan and buried it in the cave at
Machpelah east of Mamre in the field
which Abraham had bought from
Ephron the Hittite for a burial ground.
14 After Joseph had buried his father, he
returned to Egypt with his brothers and
all who had gone with him for the
funeral.

Joseph Reassures His Brothers

15 After the death of their father, Joseph's brothers said, "What if Joseph still
hates us and plans to pay us back for all
the harm we did to him?" 16 So they sent
a message to Joseph: "Before our father
died, 17 he told us to ask you, 'Please forgive the crime your brothers committed
when they wronged you.' Now please
forgive us the wrong that we, the servants of your father's God, have done."
Joseph cried when he received this
message.
18 Then his brothers themselves came
and bowed down before him. "Here we
are before you as your slaves," they said.
19 But Joseph said to them, "Don't be
afraid; I can't put myself in the place of
God. 20 You plotted evil against me, but
God turned it into good, in order to preserve the lives of many people who are
alive today because of what happened.
21 You have nothing to fear. I will take
care of you and your children." So he
reassured them with kind words that
touched their hearts.

The Death of Joseph

22 Joseph continued to live in Egypt
with his father's family; he was a hundred and ten years old when he died.
23 He lived to see Ephraim's children and
grandchildren. He also lived to receive
the children of Machir son of Manasseh
into the family. 24 He said to his brothers,
"I am about to die, but God will certainly
take care of you and lead you out of this
land to the land he solemnly promised to
Abraham, Isaac, and Jacob." 25 Then Joseph asked his people to make a vow.
"Promise me," he said, "that when God
leads you to that land, you will take my
body with you." 26 So Joseph died in
Egypt at the age of a hundred and ten.
They embalmed his body and put it in a
coffin.

[f] ABEL MIZRAIM: *This name sounds like the Hebrew for "mourning of the Egyptians."*

EXODUS

Introduction

The name Exodus *means "departure," and refers to the most important event in Israel's history, which is described in this book—the departure of the people of Israel from Egypt, where they had been slaves. The book has four main parts: 1) the freeing of the Hebrews from slavery; 2) their journey to Mount Sinai; 3) God's covenant with his people at Sinai, which gave them moral, civil, and religious laws to live by; and 4) the building and furnishing of a place of worship for Israel, and laws regarding the priests and the worship of God.*

Above all, this book describes what God did, as he liberated his enslaved people and formed them into a nation with hope for the future.

The central human figure in the book is Moses, the man whom God chose to lead his people from Egypt. The most widely known part of the book is the list of the Ten Commandments in chapter 20.

Outline of Contents

The Israelites Are Treated Cruelly in Egypt

1 The sons of Jacob who went to
Egypt with him, each with his family, were 2 Reuben, Simeon, Levi, Judah,
3 Issachar, Zebulun, Benjamin, 4 Dan,
Naphtali, Gad, and Asher. 5 The total
number of these people directly descended from Jacob was seventy.[a] His
son Joseph was already in Egypt. 6 In the
course of time Joseph, his brothers, and
all the rest of that generation died, 7 but
their descendants, the Israelites, had
many children and became so numerous
and strong that Egypt was filled with
them.

8 Then, a new king, who knew nothing
about Joseph, came to power in Egypt.
9 He said to his people, "These Israelites
are so numerous and strong that they are
a threat to us. 10 In case of war they might
join our enemies in order to fight against
us, and might escape from[b] the country.
We must find some way to keep them
from becoming even more numerous."
11 So the Egyptians put slave drivers over
them to crush their spirits with hard labor. The Israelites built the cities of Pi-
thom and Rameses to serve as supply
centers for the king. 12 But the more the
Egyptians oppressed the Israelites, the
more they increased in number and the
farther they spread through the land.
The Egyptians came to fear the Israelites
13-14 and made their lives miserable by
forcing them into cruel slavery. They
made them work on their building
projects and in their fields, and they had
no pity on them.

15 Then the king of Egypt spoke to
Shiphrah and Puah, the two midwives
who helped the Hebrew women.
16 "When you help the Hebrew women
give birth," he said to them, "kill the baby
if it is a boy; but if it is a girl, let it live."
17 But the midwives were God-fearing
and so did not obey the king; instead,
they let the boys live. 18 So the king sent
for the midwives and asked them, "Why
are you doing this? Why are you letting
the boys live?"

19 They answered, "The Hebrew
women are not like Egyptian women;
they give birth easily, and their babies

[a] *One ancient translation* seventy-five *(see Ac 7.14).* [b] escape from; *or* take control of.

are born before either of us gets there."
20-21 Because the midwives were God-
fearing, God was good to them and gave
them families of their own. And the Israelites continued to increase and become
strong. 22 Finally the king issued a command to all his people: "Take every newborn Hebrew boy and throw him into the
Nile, but let all the girls live."

The Birth of Moses

2 During this time a man from the
tribe of Levi married a woman of his
own tribe, 2 and she bore him a son.
When she saw what a fine baby he was,
she hid him for three months. 3 But when
she could not hide him any longer, she
took a basket made of reeds and covered
it with tar to make it watertight. She put
the baby in it and then placed it in the tall
grass at the edge of the river. 4 The baby's
sister stood some distance away to see
what would happen to him.

5 The king's daughter came down to
the river to bathe, while her servants
walked along the bank. Suddenly she noticed the basket in the tall grass and sent
a slave woman to get it. 6 The princess
opened it and saw a baby boy. He was
crying, and she felt sorry for him. "This
is one of the Hebrew babies," she said.
7 Then his sister asked her, "Shall I go
and call a Hebrew woman to nurse the
baby for you?"

8 "Please do," she answered. So the girl
went and brought the baby's own
mother. 9 The princess told the woman,
"Take this baby and nurse him for me,
and I will pay you." So she took the baby
and nursed him. 10 Later, when the child
was old enough, she took him to the
king's daughter, who adopted him as her
own son. She said to herself, "I pulled
him out of the water, and so I name him
Moses."[c]

Moses Escapes to Midian

11 When Moses had grown up, he went
out to visit his people, the Hebrews, and
he saw how they were forced to do hard
labor. He even saw an Egyptian kill a
Hebrew, one of Moses' own people.
12 Moses looked all around, and when he
saw that no one was watching, he killed
the Egyptian and hid his body in the
sand. 13 The next day he went back and
saw two Hebrew men fighting. He said to
the one who was in the wrong, "Why are
you beating up a fellow Hebrew?"

14 The man answered, "Who made you
our ruler and judge? Are you going to kill
me just as you killed that Egyptian?"
Then Moses was afraid and said to himself, "People have found out what I have
done." 15-16 When the king heard about
what had happened, he tried to have
Moses killed, but Moses fled and went to
live in the land of Midian.

One day, when Moses was sitting by a
well, seven daughters of Jethro, the
priest of Midian, came to draw water and
fill the troughs for their father's sheep
and goats. 17 But some shepherds drove
Jethro's daughters away. Then Moses
went to their rescue and watered their
animals for them. 18 When they returned
to their father, he asked, "Why have you
come back so early today?"

19 "An Egyptian rescued us from the
shepherds," they answered, "and he even
drew water for us and watered our
animals."

20 "Where is he?" he asked his daughters. "Why did you leave the man out
there? Go and invite him to eat with us."

21 So Moses decided to live there, and
Jethro gave him his daughter Zipporah
in marriage, 22 who bore him a son.
Moses said to himself, "I am a foreigner
in this land, and so I name him
Gershom."[d]

23 Years later the king of Egypt died,
but the Israelites were still groaning under their slavery and cried out for help.
Their cry went up to God, 24 who heard
their groaning and remembered his covenant with Abraham, Isaac, and Jacob.
25 He saw the slavery of the Israelites and
was concerned for them.[e]

God Calls Moses

3 One day while Moses was taking
care of the sheep and goats of his
father-in-law Jethro, the priest of Midian, he led the flock across the desert and
came to Sinai, the holy mountain. 2 There
the angel of the LORD appeared to him as
a flame coming from the middle of a

[c] MOSES: *This name sounds like the Hebrew for "pull out."* [d] GERSHOM: *This name sounds like the Hebrew for "foreigner."* [e] was concerned for them; *one ancient translation* revealed himself to them.

bush. Moses saw that the bush was on
fire but that it was not burning up. 3“This
is strange,” he thought. “Why isn’t the
bush burning up? I will go closer
and see.”
4When the LORD saw that Moses was
coming closer, he called to him from the
middle of the bush and said, “Moses!
Moses!”
He answered, “Yes, here I am.”
5God said, “Do not come any closer.
Take off your sandals, because you are
standing on holy ground. 6I am the God
of your ancestors, the God of Abraham,
Isaac, and Jacob.” So Moses covered his
face, because he was afraid to look
at God.
7Then the LORD said, “I have seen how
cruelly my people are being treated in
Egypt; I have heard them cry out to be
rescued from their slave drivers. I know
all about their sufferings, 8and so I have
come down to rescue them from the
Egyptians and to bring them out of Egypt
to a spacious land, one which is rich and
fertile and in which the Canaanites, the
Hittites, the Amorites, the Perizzites, the
Hivites, and the Jebusites now live.
9I have indeed heard the cry of my people, and I see how the Egyptians are oppressing them. 10Now I am sending you
to the king of Egypt so that you can lead
my people out of his country.”
11But Moses said to God, “I am nobody.
How can I go to the king and bring the
Israelites out of Egypt?”
12God answered, “I will be with you,
and when you bring the people out of
Egypt, you will worship me on this
mountain. That will be the proof that I
have sent you.”
13But Moses replied, “When I go to the
Israelites and say to them, ‘The God of
your ancestors sent me to you,’ they will
ask me, ‘What is his name?’ So what can
I tell them?”
14God said, “I am who I am. You must
tell them: ‘The one who is called I AM[f]
has sent me to you.’ 15Tell the Israelites
that I, the LORD, the God of their ancestors, the God of Abraham, Isaac, and Jacob, have sent you to them. This is my
name forever; this is what all future generations are to call me. 16Go and gather
the leaders of Israel together and tell
them that I, the LORD, the God of their
ancestors, the God of Abraham, Isaac,
and Jacob, appeared to you. Tell them
that I have come to them and have seen
what the Egyptians are doing to them.
17I have decided that I will bring them
out of Egypt, where they are being
treated cruelly, and will take them to a
rich and fertile land—the land of the Canaanites, the Hittites, the Amorites, the
Perizzites, the Hivites, and the Jebusites.
18“My people will listen to what you
say to them. Then you must go with the
leaders of Israel to the king of Egypt and
say to him, ‘The LORD, the God of the
Hebrews, has revealed himself to us.
Now allow us to travel three days into the
desert to offer sacrifices to the LORD, our
God.’ 19I know that the king of Egypt will
not let you go unless he is forced to do so.
20But I will use my power and will punish
Egypt by doing terrifying things there.
After that he will let you go.
21“I will make the Egyptians respect
you so that when my people leave, they
will not go empty-handed. 22Every Israelite woman will go to her Egyptian
neighbors and to any Egyptian woman
living in her house and will ask for clothing and for gold and silver jewelry. The
Israelites will put these things on their
sons and daughters and carry away the
wealth of the Egyptians.”

God Gives Moses Miraculous Power

4 Then Moses answered the LORD,
“But suppose the Israelites do not
believe me and will not listen to what I
say. What shall I do if they say that you
did not appear to me?”
2So the LORD asked him, “What are you
holding?”
“A walking stick,” he answered.
3The LORD said, “Throw it on the
ground.” When Moses threw it down, it
turned into a snake, and he ran away
from it. 4Then the LORD said to Moses,
“Reach down and pick it up by the tail.”
So Moses reached down and caught it,
and it became a walking stick again.
5The LORD said, “Do this to prove to the
Israelites that the LORD, the God of their

[f] I am who I am . . . I AM; *or* I will be who I will be . . . I WILL BE. *“I am” sounds like the Hebrew name Yahweh traditionally transliterated as Jehovah. This name is represented in this translation by “the* LORD*” in capital letters, following a usage which is widespread in English versions.*

ancestors, the God of Abraham, Isaac,
and Jacob, has appeared to you."
6The LORD spoke to Moses again, "Put
your hand inside your robe." Moses
obeyed; and when he took his hand out,
it was diseased, covered with white
spots, like snow. 7Then the LORD said,
"Put your hand inside your robe again."
He did so, and when he took it out this
time, it was healthy, just like the rest of
his body. 8The LORD said, "If they will not
believe you or be convinced by the first
miracle, then this one will convince
them. 9If in spite of these two miracles
they still will not believe you, and if they
refuse to listen to what you say, take
some water from the Nile and pour it on
the ground. The water will turn into
blood."
10But Moses said, "No, LORD, don't
send me. I have never been a good
speaker, and I haven't become one since
you began to speak to me. I am a poor
speaker, slow and hesitant."
11The LORD said to him, "Who gives
man his mouth? Who makes him deaf or
dumb? Who gives him sight or makes
him blind? It is I, the LORD. 12Now, go! I
will help you to speak, and I will tell you
what to say."
13But Moses answered, "No, Lord,
please send someone else."
14At this the LORD became angry with
Moses and said, "What about your
brother Aaron, the Levite? I know that he
can speak well. In fact, he is now coming
to meet you and will be glad to see you.
15You can speak to him and tell him what
to say. I will help both of you to speak,
and I will tell you both what to do. 16He
will be your spokesman and speak to the
people for you. Then you will be like
God, telling him what to say. 17Take this
walking stick with you; for with it you
will perform miracles."

Moses Returns to Egypt

18Then Moses went back to Jethro, his
father-in-law, and said to him, "Please let
me go back to my relatives in Egypt to
see if they are still alive." Jethro agreed
and told him good-bye.
19While Moses was still in Midian, the
LORD said to him, "Go back to Egypt, for
all those who wanted to kill you are
dead." 20So Moses took his wife and his
sons, put them on a donkey, and set out
with them for Egypt, carrying the walking stick that God had told him to take.
21Again the LORD said to Moses, "Now
that you are going back to Egypt, be sure
to perform before the king all the miracles which I have given you the power to
do. But I will make the king stubborn,
and he will not let the people go. 22Then
you must tell him that I, the LORD, say,
'Israel is my first-born son. 23I told you to
let my son go, so that he might worship
me, but you refused. Now I am going to
kill your first-born son.' "
24At a camping place on the way to
Egypt, the LORD met Moses and tried to
kill him. 25-26Then Zipporah, his wife,
took a sharp stone, cut off the foreskin of
her son, and touched Moses' feet[g] with
it. Because of the rite of circumcision she
said to Moses, "You are a husband of
blood to me." And so the LORD spared
Moses' life.
27Meanwhile the LORD had said to
Aaron, "Go into the desert to meet
Moses." So he went to meet him at the
holy mountain; and when he met him, he
kissed him. 28Then Moses told Aaron
everything that the LORD had said when
he told him to return to Egypt; he also
told him about the miracles which the
LORD had ordered him to perform. 29So
Moses and Aaron went to Egypt and
gathered all the Israelite leaders together. 30Aaron told them everything
that the LORD had said to Moses, and then
Moses performed all the miracles in
front of the people. 31They believed, and
when they heard that the LORD had come
to them and had seen how they were being treated cruelly, they bowed down
and worshiped.

Moses and Aaron before the King of Egypt

5 Then Moses and Aaron went to the
king of Egypt and said, "The LORD,
the God of Israel, says, 'Let my people
go, so that they can hold a festival in the
desert to honor me.' "
2"Who is the LORD?" the king demanded. "Why should I listen to him and
let Israel go? I do not know the LORD; and
I will not let Israel go."
3Moses and Aaron replied, "The God
of the Hebrews has revealed himself to

[g] FEET: *This reference to "feet" is thought by some to be a euphemism for the genitals.*

us. Allow us to travel three days into the
desert to offer sacrifices to the LORD our
God. If we don't do so, he will kill us with
disease or by war."
4 The king said to Moses and Aaron,
"What do you mean by making the people neglect their work? Get those slaves
back to work! 5 You people have become
more numerous than the Egyptians. And
now you want to stop working!"
6 That same day the king commanded
the Egyptian slave drivers and the Israelite foremen: 7 "Stop giving the people
straw for making bricks. Make them go
and find it for themselves. 8 But still require them to make the same number of
bricks as before, not one brick less. They
don't have enough work to do, and that
is why they keep asking me to let them
go and offer sacrifices to their God!
9 Make them work harder and keep them
busy, so that they won't have time to listen to a pack of lies."
10 The slave drivers and the Israelite
foremen went out and said to the Israelites, "The king has said that he will not
supply you with any more straw. 11 He
says that you must go and get it for yourselves wherever you can find it, but you
must still make the same number of
bricks." 12 So the people went all over
Egypt looking for straw. 13 The slave
drivers kept trying to force them to make
the same number of bricks every day as
they had made when they were given
straw. 14 The Egyptian slave drivers beat
the Israelite foremen, whom they had put
in charge of the work. They demanded,
"Why aren't you people making the same
number of bricks that you made before?"
15 Then the foremen went to the king
and complained, "Why do you do this to
us, Your Majesty? 16 We are given no
straw, but we are still ordered to make
bricks! And now we are being beaten. It
is your people that are at fault."
17 The king answered, "You are lazy
and don't want to work, and that is why
you ask me to let you go and offer sacrifices to the LORD. 18 Now get back to
work! You will not be given any straw,
but you must still make the same number
of bricks." 19 The foremen realized that
they were in trouble when they were told
that they had to make the same number
of bricks every day as they had made
before.
20 As they were leaving, they met
Moses and Aaron, who were waiting for
them. 21 They said to Moses and Aaron,
"The LORD has seen what you have done
and will punish you for making the king
and his officers hate us. You have given
them an excuse to kill us."

Moses Complains to the LORD

22 Then Moses turned to the LORD again
and said, "Lord, why do you mistreat
your people? Why did you send me here?
23 Ever since I went to the king to speak
for you, he has treated them cruelly. And
you have done nothing to help them!"
6 Then the LORD said to Moses, "Now
you are going to see what I will do to
the king. I will force him to let my people
go. In fact, I will force him to drive them
out of his land."

God Calls Moses

2 God spoke to Moses and said, "I am
the LORD. 3 I appeared to Abraham, to
Isaac, and to Jacob as Almighty God, but
I did not make myself known to them by
my holy name, the LORD.[h] 4 I also made
my covenant with them, promising to
give them the land of Canaan, the land in
which they had lived as foreigners. 5 Now
I have heard the groaning of the Israelites, whom the Egyptians have enslaved,
and I have remembered my covenant.
6 So tell the Israelites that I say to them,
'I am the LORD; I will rescue you and set
you free from your slavery to the Egyptians. I will raise my mighty arm to bring
terrible punishment upon them, and I
will save you. 7 I will make you my own
people, and I will be your God. You will
know that I am the LORD your God when
I set you free from slavery in Egypt.
8 I will bring you to the land that I solemnly promised to give to Abraham,
Isaac, and Jacob; and I will give it to you
as your own possession. I am the LORD.' "
9 Moses told this to the Israelites, but they
would not listen to him, because their
spirit had been broken by their cruel
slavery.
10 Then the LORD said to Moses, 11 "Go
and tell the king of Egypt that he must let
the Israelites leave his land."
12 But Moses replied, "Even the Israel-

[h] THE LORD: *See 3.14.*

ites will not listen to me, so why should
the king? I am such a poor speaker."
13 The LORD commanded Moses and
Aaron: "Tell the Israelites and the king of
Egypt that I have ordered you to lead the
Israelites out of Egypt."

The Family Record of Moses and Aaron

14 Reuben, Jacob's first-born, had four
sons: Hanoch, Pallu, Hezron, and Carmi;
they were the ancestors of the clans that
bear their names. 15 Simeon had six sons:
Jemuel, Jamin, Ohad, Jachin, Zohar, and
Shaul, the son of a Canaanite woman;
they were the ancestors of the clans that
bear their names. 16 Levi had three sons:
Gershon, Kohath, and Merari; they were
the ancestors of the clans that bear their
names. Levi lived 137 years. 17 Gershon
had two sons: Libni and Shimei, and
they had many descendants. 18 Kohath
had four sons: Amram, Izhar, Hebron,
and Uzziel. Kohath lived 133 years. 19 Merari had two sons: Mahli and Mushi.
These are the clans of Levi with their
descendants.
20 Amram married his father's sister
Jochebed, who bore him Aaron and
Moses. Amram lived 137 years. 21 Izhar
had three sons: Korah, Nepheg, and
Zichri. 22 Uzziel also had three sons:
Mishael, Elzaphan, and Sithri.
23 Aaron married Elisheba, the daughter of Amminadab and sister of Nahshon; she bore him Nadab, Abihu,
Eleazar, and Ithamar. 24 Korah had three
sons: Assir, Elkanah, and Abiasaph;
they were the ancestors of the divisions
of the clan of Korah. 25 Eleazar, Aaron's
son, married one of Putiel's daughters,
who bore him Phinehas. These were the
heads of the families and the clans of the
tribe of Levi.
26 Aaron and Moses were the ones to
whom the LORD said, "Lead the tribes of
Israel out of Egypt." 27 They were the
men who told the king of Egypt to free
the Israelites.

The LORD's Command to Moses and Aaron

28 When the LORD spoke to Moses in the
land of Egypt, 29 he said, "I am the LORD.
Tell the king of Egypt everything I
tell you."
30 But Moses answered, "You know
that I am such a poor speaker; why
should the king listen to me?"

7 The LORD said, "I am going to make
you like God to the king, and your
brother Aaron will speak to him as your
prophet. 2 Tell Aaron everything I command you, and he will tell the king to let
the Israelites leave his country. 3-4 But I
will make the king stubborn, and he will
not listen to you, no matter how many
terrifying things I do in Egypt. Then I will
bring severe punishment on Egypt and
lead the tribes of my people out of the
land. 5 The Egyptians will then know that
I am the LORD, when I raise my hand
against them and bring the Israelites out
of their country." 6 Moses and Aaron did
what the LORD commanded. 7 At the time
when they spoke to the king, Moses was
eighty years old, and Aaron was eighty-
three.

Aaron's Walking Stick

8 The LORD said to Moses and Aaron,
9 "If the king demands that you prove
yourselves by performing a miracle, tell
Aaron to take his walking stick and
throw it down in front of the king, and it
will turn into a snake." 10 So Moses and
Aaron went to the king and did as the
LORD had commanded. Aaron threw his
walking stick down in front of the king
and his officers, and it turned into a
snake. 11 Then the king called for his wise
men and magicians, and by their magic
they did the same thing. 12 They threw
down their walking sticks, and the sticks
turned into snakes. But Aaron's stick
swallowed theirs. 13 The king, however,
remained stubborn and, just as the LORD
had said, the king would not listen to
Moses and Aaron.

Disasters Strike Egypt

Blood

14 Then the LORD said to Moses, "The
king is very stubborn and refuses to let
the people go. 15 So go and meet him in
the morning when he goes down to the
Nile. Take with you the walking stick
that was turned into a snake, and wait for
him on the riverbank. 16 Then say to the
king, 'The LORD, the God of the Hebrews,
sent me to tell you to let his people go, so
that they can worship him in the desert.
But until now you have not listened.
17 Now, Your Majesty, the LORD says that

you will find out who he is by what he is
going to do. Look, I am going to strike the
surface of the river with this stick, and
the water will be turned into blood. 18 The
fish will die, and the river will stink so
much that the Egyptians will not be able
to drink from it.' "
19 The LORD said to Moses, "Tell Aaron
to take his stick and hold it out over all
the rivers, canals, and pools in Egypt.
The water will become blood, and all
over the land there will be blood, even in
the wooden tubs and stone jars."
20 Then Moses and Aaron did as the
LORD commanded. In the presence of the
king and his officers, Aaron raised his
stick and struck the surface of the river,
and all the water in it was turned into
blood. 21 The fish in the river died, and it
smelled so bad that the Egyptians could
not drink from it. There was blood everywhere in Egypt. 22 Then the king's magicians did the same thing by means of
their magic, and the king was as stubborn as ever. Just as the LORD had said,
the king refused to listen to Moses and
Aaron. 23 Instead, he turned and went
back to his palace without paying any
attention even to this. 24 All the Egyptians dug along the bank of the river for
drinking water, because they were not
able to drink water from the river.
25 Seven days passed after the LORD
struck the river.

Frogs

8 Then the LORD said to Moses, "Go to
the king and tell him that the LORD
says, 'Let my people go, so that they can
worship me. 2 If you refuse, I will punish
your country by covering it with frogs.
3 The Nile will be so full of frogs that they
will leave it and go into your palace, your
bedroom, your bed, the houses of your
officials and your people, and even into
your ovens and baking pans. 4 They will
jump up on you, your people, and all
your officials.' "
5 The LORD said to Moses, "Tell Aaron
to hold out his walking stick over the
rivers, the canals, and the pools, and
make frogs come up and cover the land
of Egypt." 6 So Aaron held it out over all
the water, and the frogs came out and
covered the land. 7 But the magicians
used magic, and they also made frogs
come up on the land.
8 The king called for Moses and Aaron
and said, "Pray to the LORD to take away
these frogs, and I will let your people go,
so that they can offer sacrifices to the
LORD."
9 Moses replied, "I will be glad to pray
for you. Just set the time when I am to
pray for you, your officers, and your people. Then you will be rid of the frogs, and
there will be none left except in the Nile."
10 The king answered, "Pray for me
tomorrow."
Moses said, "I will do as you ask, and
then you will know that there is no other
god like the LORD, our God. 11 You, your
officials, and your people will be rid of
the frogs, and there will be none left except in the Nile." 12 Then Moses and
Aaron left the king, and Moses prayed to
the LORD to take away the frogs which he
had brought on the king. 13 The LORD did
as Moses asked, and the frogs in the
houses, the courtyards, and the fields
died. 14 The Egyptians piled them up in
great heaps, until the land stank with
them. 15 When the king saw that the frogs
were dead, he became stubborn again
and, just as the LORD had said, the king
would not listen to Moses and Aaron.

Gnats

16 The LORD said to Moses, "Tell Aaron
to strike the ground with his stick, and all
over the land of Egypt the dust will
change into gnats." 17 So Aaron struck
the ground with his stick, and all the dust
in Egypt was turned into gnats, which
covered the people and the animals.
18 The magicians tried to use their magic
to make gnats appear, but they failed.
There were gnats everywhere, 19 and the
magicians said to the king, "God has
done this!" But the king was stubborn
and, just as the LORD had said, the king
would not listen to Moses and Aaron.

Flies

20 The LORD said to Moses, "Early tomorrow morning go and meet the king as
he goes to the river, and tell him that the
LORD says, 'Let my people go, so that they
can worship me. 21 I warn you that if you
refuse, I will punish you by sending flies
on you, your officials, and your people.
The houses of the Egyptians will be full
of flies, and the ground will be covered
with them. 22 But I will spare the region of
Goshen, where my people live, so that
there will be no flies there. I will do this

so that you will know that I, the LORD, am
at work in this land. 23 I will make a distinction[i] between my people and your
people. This miracle will take place tomorrow.' " 24 The LORD sent great swarms
of flies into the king's palace and the
houses of his officials. The whole land of
Egypt was brought to ruin by the flies.
25 Then the king called for Moses and
Aaron and said, "Go and offer sacrifices
to your God here in this country."
26 "It would not be right to do that,"
Moses answered, "because the Egyptians would be offended by our sacrificing the animals that we offer to the LORD
our God. If we use these animals and offend the Egyptians by sacrificing them
where they can see us, they will stone us
to death. 27 We must travel three days
into the desert to offer sacrifices to the
LORD our God, just as he commanded us."
28 The king said, "I will let you go to
sacrifice to the LORD, your God, in the
desert, if you do not go very far. Pray
for me."
29 Moses answered, "As soon as I leave,
I will pray to the LORD that tomorrow the
flies will leave you, your officials, and
your people. But you must not deceive us
again and prevent the people from going
to sacrifice to the LORD."
30 Moses left the king and prayed to the
LORD, 31 and the LORD did as Moses asked.
The flies left the king, his officials, and
his people; not one fly remained. 32 But
even this time the king became stubborn,
and again he would not let the people go.

Death of the Animals

9 The LORD said to Moses, "Go to the
king and tell him that the LORD, the
God of the Hebrews, says, 'Let my people
go, so that they may worship me. 2 If you
again refuse to let them go, 3 I will punish
you by sending a terrible disease on all
your animals—your horses, donkeys,
camels, cattle, sheep, and goats. 4 I will
make a distinction between the animals
of the Israelites and those of the Egyptians, and no animal that belongs to the
Israelites will die. 5 I, the LORD, have set
tomorrow as the time when I will do
this.' "
6 The next day the LORD did as he had
said, and all the animals of the Egyptians
died, but not one of the animals of the
Israelites died. 7 The king asked what
had happened and was told that none of
the animals of the Israelites had died. But
he was stubborn and would not let the
people go.

Boils

8 Then the LORD said to Moses and
Aaron, "Take a few handfuls of ashes
from a furnace; Moses is to throw them
into the air in front of the king. 9 They
will spread out like fine dust over all the
land of Egypt, and everywhere they will
produce boils that become open sores on
the people and the animals." 10 So they
got some ashes and stood before the
king; Moses threw them into the air, and
they produced boils that became open
sores on the people and the animals.
11 The magicians were not able to appear
before Moses, because they were covered with boils, like all the other Egyptians. 12 But the LORD made the king
stubborn and, just as the LORD had said,
the king would not listen to Moses and
Aaron.

Hail

13 The LORD then said to Moses, "Early
tomorrow morning meet with the king
and tell him that the LORD, the God of the
Hebrews, says, 'Let my people go, so that
they may worship me. 14 This time I will
punish not only your officials and your
people, but I will punish you as well, so
that you may know that there is no one
like me in all the world. 15 If I had raised
my hand to strike you and your people
with disease, you would have been completely destroyed. 16 But to show you my
power I have let you live so that my fame
might spread over the whole world.
17 Yet you are still arrogant and refuse to
let my people go. 18 This time tomorrow
I will cause a heavy hailstorm, such as
Egypt has never known in all its history.
19 Now give orders for your livestock and
everything else you have in the open to
be put under shelter. Hail will fall on the
people and animals left outside unpro-
tected, and they will all die.' " 20 Some of
the king's officials were afraid because
of what the LORD had said, and they
brought their slaves and animals indoors
for shelter. 21 Others, however, paid no
attention to the LORD's warning and left

[i] *Some ancient translations* a distinction; *Hebrew* redemption.

their slaves and animals out in the open.
22 Then the LORD said to Moses, "Raise
your hand toward the sky, and hail will
fall over the whole land of Egypt — on the
people, the animals, and all the plants in
the fields." 23 So Moses raised his stick
toward the sky, and the LORD sent thunder and hail, and lightning struck the
ground. The LORD sent 24 a heavy hailstorm, with lightning flashing back and
forth. It was the worst storm that Egypt
had ever known in all its history. 25 All
over Egypt the hail struck down everything in the open, including all the people
and all the animals. It beat down all the
plants in the fields and broke all the
trees. 26 The region of Goshen, where the
Israelites lived, was the only place where
there was no hail.

27 The king sent for Moses and Aaron
and said, "This time I have sinned; the
LORD is in the right, and my people and I
are in the wrong. 28 Pray to the LORD! We
have had enough of this thunder and
hail! I promise to let you go; you don't
have to stay here any longer."

29 Moses said to him, "As soon as I go
out of the city, I will lift up my hands in
prayer to the LORD. The thunder will stop,
and there will be no more hail, so that
you may know that the earth belongs to
the LORD. 30 But I know that you and your
officials do not yet fear the LORD God."

31 The flax and the barley were ruined,
because the barley was ripe, and the flax
was budding. 32 But none of the wheat
was ruined, because it ripens later.

33 Moses left the king, went out of the
city, and lifted up his hands in prayer to
the LORD. The thunder, the hail, and the
rain all stopped. 34 When the king saw
what had happened, he sinned again. He
and his officials remained as stubborn as
ever 35 and, just as the LORD had foretold
through Moses, the king would not let
the Israelites go.

Locusts

10 Then the LORD said to Moses, "Go
and see the king. I have made
him and his officials stubborn, in order
that I may perform these miracles among
them 2 and in order that you may be able
to tell your children and grandchildren
how I made fools of the Egyptians when
I performed the miracles. All of you will
know that I am the LORD."

3 So Moses and Aaron went to the king
and said to him, "The LORD, the God of
the Hebrews, says, 'How much longer
will you refuse to submit to me? Let my
people go, so that they may worship me.
4 If you keep on refusing, then I will bring
locusts into your country tomorrow.
5 There will be so many that they will
completely cover the ground. They will
eat everything that the hail did not destroy, even the trees that are left. 6 They
will fill your palaces and the houses of all
your officials and all your people. They
will be worse than anything your ancestors ever saw.' " Then Moses turned and
left.

7 The king's officials said to him, "How
long is this man going to give us trouble?
Let the Israelite men go, so that they can
worship the LORD their God. Don't you
realize that Egypt is ruined?"

8 So Moses and Aaron were brought
back to the king, and he said to them,
"You may go and worship the LORD your
God. But exactly who will go?"

9 Moses answered, "We will all go, including our children and our old people.
We will take our sons and daughters, our
sheep and goats, and our cattle, because
we must hold a festival to honor the
LORD."

10 The king said, "I swear by the LORD
that I will never let you take your women
and children! It is clear that you are plotting to revolt. 11 No! Only the men may go
and worship the LORD if that is what you
want." With that, Moses and Aaron were
driven out of the king's presence.

12 Then the LORD said to Moses, "Raise
your hand over the land of Egypt to bring
the locusts. They will come and eat
everything that grows, everything that
has survived the hail." 13 So Moses raised
his stick, and the LORD caused a wind
from the east to blow on the land all that
day and all that night. By morning it had
brought the locusts. 14 They came in
swarms and settled over the whole country. It was the largest swarm of locusts
that had ever been seen or that ever
would be seen again. 15 They covered the
ground until it was black with them; they
ate everything that the hail had left, including all the fruit on the trees. Not a
green thing was left on any tree or plant
in all the land of Egypt.

16 Then the king hurriedly called
Moses and Aaron and said, "I have
sinned against the LORD your God and

against you. 17 Now forgive my sin this
one time and pray to the LORD your God
to take away this fatal punishment from
me." 18 Moses left the king and prayed to
the LORD. 19 And the LORD changed the
east wind into a very strong west wind,
which picked up the locusts and blew
them into the Gulf of Suez.[j] Not one
locust was left in all of Egypt. 20 But the
LORD made the king stubborn, and he did
not let the Israelites go.

Darkness

21 The LORD then said to Moses, "Raise
your hand toward the sky, and a darkness thick enough to be felt will cover the
land of Egypt." 22 Moses raised his hand
toward the sky, and there was total darkness throughout Egypt for three days.
23 The Egyptians could not see each
other, and no one left his house during
that time. But the Israelites had light
where they were living.

24 The king called Moses and said,
"You may go and worship the LORD; even
your women and children may go with
you. But your sheep, goats, and cattle
must stay here."

25 Moses answered, "Then you would
have to provide us with animals for sacrifices and burnt offerings to offer to the
LORD our God. 26 No, we will take our animals with us; not one will be left behind.
We ourselves must select the animals
with which to worship the LORD our God.
And until we get there, we will not know
what animals to sacrifice to him."

27 The LORD made the king stubborn,
and he would not let them go. 28 He said
to Moses, "Get out of my sight! Don't let
me ever see you again! On the day I do,
you will die!"

29 "You are right," Moses answered.
"You will never see me again."

Moses Announces the Death of the First-Born

11 Then the LORD said to Moses, "I
will send only one more punishment on the king of Egypt and his people.
After that he will let you leave. In fact, he
will drive all of you out of here. 2 Now
speak to the people of Israel and tell all
of them to ask their neighbors for gold
and silver jewelry." 3 The LORD made the
Egyptians respect the Israelites. Indeed,
the officials and all the people considered Moses to be a very great man.

4 Moses then said to the king, "The
LORD says, 'At about midnight I will go
through Egypt, 5 and every first-born son
in Egypt will die, from the king's son,
who is heir to the throne, to the son of the
slave woman who grinds grain. The first-
born of all the cattle will die also. 6 There
will be loud crying all over Egypt, such
as there has never been before or ever
will be again. 7 But not even a dog will
bark at the Israelites or their animals.
Then you will know that I, the LORD,
make a distinction between the Egyptians and the Israelites.' " 8 Moses concluded by saying, "All your officials will
come to me and bow down before me,
and they will beg me to take all my people and go away. After that, I will leave."
Then in great anger Moses left the king.

9 The LORD had said to Moses, "The
king will continue to refuse to listen to
you, in order that I may do more of my
miracles in Egypt." 10 Moses and Aaron
performed all these miracles before the
king, but the LORD made him stubborn,
and he would not let the Israelites leave
his country.

The Passover

12 The LORD spoke to Moses and
Aaron in Egypt: 2 "This month is
to be the first month of the year for you.
3 Give these instructions to the whole
community of Israel: On the tenth day of
this month each man must choose either
a lamb or a young goat for his household.
4 If his family is too small to eat a whole
animal, he and his next-door neighbor
may share an animal, in proportion to
the number of people and the amount
that each person can eat. 5 You may
choose either a sheep or a goat, but it
must be a one-year-old male without any
defects. 6 Then, on the evening of the
fourteenth day of the month, the whole
community of Israel will kill the animals.
7 The people are to take some of the blood
and put it on the doorposts and above the
doors of the houses in which the animals
are to be eaten. 8 That night the meat is to
be roasted, and eaten with bitter herbs
and with bread made without yeast. 9 Do
not eat any of it raw or boiled, but eat it
roasted whole, including the head, the

[j] GULF OF SUEZ: *See Red Sea in 13.18.*

legs, and the internal organs. 10 You must
not leave any of it until morning; if any
is left over, it must be burned. 11 You are
to eat it quickly, for you are to be dressed
for travel, with your sandals on your feet
and your walking stick in your hand. It is
the Passover Festival to honor me, the
LORD.

12 "On that night I will go through the
land of Egypt, killing every first-born
male, both human and animal, and punishing all the gods of Egypt. I am the
LORD. 13 The blood on the doorposts will
be a sign to mark the houses in which
you live. When I see the blood, I will pass
over you and will not harm you when I
punish the Egyptians. 14 You must celebrate this day as a religious festival to
remind you of what I, the LORD, have
done. Celebrate it for all time to come."

The Festival of Unleavened Bread

15 The LORD said, "For seven days you
must not eat any bread made with
yeast—eat only unleavened bread. On
the first day you are to get rid of all the
yeast in your houses, for if anyone during those seven days eats bread made
with yeast, he shall no longer be considered one of my people. 16 On the first day
and again on the seventh day you are to
meet for worship. No work is to be done
on those days, but you may prepare food.
17 Keep this festival, because it was on
this day that I brought your tribes out of
Egypt. For all time to come you must celebrate this day as a festival. 18 From the
evening of the fourteenth day of the first
month to the evening of the twenty-first
day, you must not eat any bread made
with yeast. 19-20 For seven days no yeast
must be found in your houses, for if anyone, native-born or foreign, eats bread
made with yeast, he shall no longer be
considered one of my people."

The First Passover

21 Moses called for all the leaders of
Israel and said to them, "Each of you is
to choose a lamb or a young goat and kill
it, so that your families can celebrate
Passover. 22 Take a sprig of hyssop, dip it
in the bowl containing[k] the animal's
blood, and wipe the blood on the doorposts and the beam above the door of
your house. Not one of you is to leave the
house until morning. 23 When the LORD
goes through Egypt to kill the Egyptians,
he will see the blood on the beams and
the doorposts and will not let the Angel
of Death enter your houses and kill you.
24 You and your children must obey these
rules forever. 25 When you enter the land
that the LORD has promised to give you,
you must perform this ritual. 26 When
your children ask you, 'What does this
ritual mean?' 27 you will answer, 'It is the
sacrifice of Passover to honor the LORD,
because he passed over the houses of the
Israelites in Egypt. He killed the Egyptians, but spared us.' "

The Israelites knelt down and worshiped. 28 Then they went and did what
the LORD had commanded Moses and
Aaron.

The Death of the First-Born

29 At midnight the LORD killed all the
first-born sons in Egypt, from the king's
son, who was heir to the throne, to the
son of the prisoner in the dungeon; all
the first-born of the animals were also
killed. 30 That night, the king, his officials, and all the other Egyptians were
awakened. There was loud crying
throughout Egypt, because there was not
one home in which there was not a dead
son. 31 That same night the king sent for
Moses and Aaron and said, "Get out, you
and your Israelites! Leave my country;
go and worship the LORD, as you asked.
32 Take your sheep, goats, and cattle, and
leave. Also pray for a blessing on me."

33 The Egyptians urged the people to
hurry and leave the country; they said,
"We will all be dead if you don't leave."
34 So the people filled their baking pans
with unleavened dough, wrapped them
in clothing, and carried them on their
shoulders. 35 The Israelites had done as
Moses had said, and had asked the Egyptians for gold and silver jewelry and for
clothes. 36 The LORD made the Egyptians
respect the people and give them what
they asked for. In this way the Israelites carried away the wealth of the
Egyptians.

The Israelites Leave Egypt

37 The Israelites set out on foot from
Rameses for Sukkoth. There were about
600,000 men, not counting women and

[k] dip it in the bowl containing; *or* put it on the threshold covered with.

children. 38 A large number of other people and many sheep, goats, and cattle
also went with them. 39 They baked unleavened bread from the dough that they
had brought out of Egypt, for they had
been driven out of Egypt so suddenly
that they did not have time to get their
food ready or to prepare leavened dough.
40 The Israelites had lived in Egypt for
430 years. 41 On the day the 430 years
ended, all the tribes of the LORD's people
left Egypt. 42 It was a night when the LORD
kept watch to bring them out of Egypt;
this same night is dedicated to the LORD
for all time to come as a night when the
Israelites must keep watch.

Regulations about Passover

43 The LORD said to Moses and Aaron,
"These are the Passover regulations: No
foreigner shall eat the Passover meal,
44 but any slave that you have bought
may eat it if you circumcise him first.
45 No temporary resident or hired worker
may eat it. 46 The whole meal must be
eaten in the house in which it was prepared; it must not be taken outside. And
do not break any of the animal's bones.
47 The whole community of Israel must
celebrate this festival, 48 but no uncircumcised man may eat it. If a foreigner
has settled among you and wants to celebrate Passover to honor the LORD, you
must first circumcise all the males of his
household. He is then to be treated like a
native-born Israelite and may join in the
festival. 49 The same regulations apply to
native-born Israelites and to foreigners
who settle among you." 50 All the Israelites obeyed and did what the LORD had
commanded Moses and Aaron. 51 On that
day the LORD brought the Israelite tribes
out of Egypt.

Dedication of the First-Born

13 The LORD said to Moses, 2 "Dedicate all the first-born males to
me, for every first-born male Israelite
and every first-born male animal belongs to me."

The Festival of Unleavened Bread

3 Moses said to the people, "Remember
this day—the day on which you left
Egypt, the place where you were slaves.
This is the day the LORD brought you out
by his great power. No leavened bread is
to be eaten. 4 You are leaving Egypt on
this day in the first month, the month of
Abib. 5 The LORD solemnly promised your
ancestors to give you the land of the Canaanites, the Hittites, the Amorites, the
Hivites, and the Jebusites. When he
brings you into that rich and fertile land,
you must celebrate this festival in the
first month of every year. 6 For seven
days you must eat unleavened bread and
on the seventh day there is to be a festival
to honor the LORD. 7 For seven days you
must not eat any bread made with yeast;
there must be no yeast or leavened bread
anywhere in your land. 8 When the festival begins, explain to your sons that you
do all this because of what the LORD did
for you when you left Egypt. 9 This observance will be a reminder, like something tied on your hand or on your
forehead; it will remind you to continue
to recite and study the Law of the LORD,
because the LORD brought you out of
Egypt by his great power. 10 Celebrate
this festival at the appointed time each
year.

The First-Born

11 "The LORD will bring you into the
land of the Canaanites, which he solemnly promised to you and your ancestors. When he gives it to you, 12 you must
offer every first-born male to the LORD.
Every first-born male of your animals
belongs to the LORD, 13 but you must buy
back from him every first-born male
donkey by offering a lamb in its place. If
you do not want to buy back the donkey,
break its neck. You must buy back every
first-born male child of yours. 14 In the
future, when your son asks what this observance means, you will answer him,
'By using great power the LORD brought
us out of Egypt, the place where we were
slaves. 15 When the king of Egypt was
stubborn and refused to let us go, the
LORD killed every first-born male in the
land of Egypt, both human and animal.
That is why we sacrifice every first-born
male animal to the LORD, but buy back
our first-born sons. 16 This observance
will be a reminder, like something tied
on our hands or on our foreheads; it will
remind us that the LORD brought us out of
Egypt by his great power.'"

The Pillar of Cloud and the Pillar of Fire

17 When the king of Egypt let the people go, God did not take them by the road that goes up the coast to Philistia, although it was the shortest way. God thought, "I do not want the people to change their minds and return to Egypt when they see that they are going to have to fight." 18 Instead, he led them in a roundabout way through the desert toward the Red Sea.[l] The Israelites were armed for battle.

19 Moses took the body of Joseph with him, as Joseph had made the Israelites solemnly promise to do. Joseph had said, "When God rescues you, you must carry my body with you from this place."

20 The Israelites left Sukkoth and camped at Etham on the edge of the desert. 21 During the day the LORD went in front of them in a pillar of cloud to show them the way, and during the night he went in front of them in a pillar of fire to give them light, so that they could travel night and day. 22 The pillar of cloud was always in front of the people during the day, and the pillar of fire at night.

Crossing the Red Sea

14 Then the LORD said to Moses, 2 "Tell the Israelites to turn back and camp in front of Pi Hahiroth, between Migdol and the Red Sea, near Baal Zephon. 3 The king will think that the Israelites are wandering around in the country and are closed in by the desert. 4 I will make him stubborn, and he will pursue you, and my victory over the king and his army will bring me honor. Then the Egyptians will know that I am the LORD." The Israelites did as they were told.

5 When the king of Egypt was told that the people had escaped, he and his officials changed their minds and said, "What have we done? We have let the Israelites escape, and we have lost them as our slaves!" 6 The king got his war chariot and his army ready. 7 He set out with all his chariots, including the six hundred finest, commanded by their officers. 8 The LORD made the king stubborn, and he pursued the Israelites, who were leaving triumphantly.[m] 9 The Egyptian army, with all the horses, chariots, and drivers, pursued them and caught up with them where they were camped by the Red Sea near Pi Hahiroth and Baal Zephon.

10 When the Israelites saw the king and his army marching against them, they were terrified and cried out to the LORD for help. 11 They said to Moses, "Weren't there any graves in Egypt? Did you have to bring us out here in the desert to die? Look what you have done by bringing us out of Egypt! 12 Didn't we tell you before we left that this would happen? We told you to leave us alone and let us go on being slaves of the Egyptians. It would be better to be slaves there than to die here in the desert."

13 Moses answered, "Don't be afraid! Stand your ground, and you will see what the LORD will do to save you today; you will never see these Egyptians again. 14 The LORD will fight for you, and all you have to do is keep still."

15 The LORD said to Moses, "Why are you crying out for help? Tell the people to move forward. 16 Lift up your walking stick and hold it out over the sea. The water will divide, and the Israelites will be able to walk through the sea on dry ground. 17 I will make the Egyptians so stubborn that they will go in after them, and I will gain honor by my victory over the king, his army, his chariots, and his drivers. 18 When I defeat them, the Egyptians will know that I am the LORD."

19 The angel of God, who had been in front of the army of Israel, moved and went to the rear. The pillar of cloud also moved until it was 20 between the Egyptians and the Israelites. The cloud made it dark for the Egyptians, but gave light to the people of Israel,[n] and so the armies could not come near each other all night.

21 Moses held out his hand over the sea, and the LORD drove the sea back with a strong east wind. It blew all night and turned the sea into dry land. The water was divided, 22 and the Israelites went through the sea on dry ground, with

[l] RED SEA: *(in Hebrew literally "Sea of Reeds") evidently referred to (1) a series of lakes and marshes between the head of the Gulf of Suez and the Mediterranean, the region generally regarded as the site of the events described in Exodus 13, and was also used to designate (2) the Gulf of Suez, and (3) the Gulf of Aqaba.* [m] triumphantly; *or* under the protection of the LORD. [n] *Probable text* The cloud . . . Israel; *Hebrew unclear.*

walls of water on both sides. 23 The Egyptians pursued them and went after them
into the sea with all their horses, chariots, and drivers. 24 Just before dawn the
LORD looked down from the pillar of fire
and cloud at the Egyptian army and
threw them into a panic. 25 He made the
wheels of their chariots get stuck, so that
they moved with great difficulty. The
Egyptians said, "The LORD is fighting for
the Israelites against us. Let's get out of
here!"

26 The LORD said to Moses, "Hold out
your hand over the sea, and the water
will come back over the Egyptians and
their chariots and drivers." 27 So Moses
held out his hand over the sea, and at
daybreak the water returned to its normal level. The Egyptians tried to escape
from the water, but the LORD threw them
into the sea. 28 The water returned and
covered the chariots, the drivers, and all
the Egyptian army that had followed the
Israelites into the sea; not one of them
was left. 29 But the Israelites walked
through the sea on dry ground, with
walls of water on both sides.

30 On that day the LORD saved the people of Israel from the Egyptians, and the
Israelites saw them lying dead on the
seashore. 31 When the Israelites saw the
great power with which the LORD had defeated the Egyptians, they stood in awe
of the LORD; and they had faith in the
LORD and in his servant Moses.

The Song of Moses

15 Then Moses and the Israelites
sang this song to the LORD:

"I will sing to the LORD, because he
has won a glorious victory;
he has thrown the horses and
their riders into the sea.
2 The LORD is my strong defender;
he is the one who has saved me.
He is my God, and I will
praise him,
my father's God, and I will sing
about his greatness.
3 The LORD is a warrior;
the LORD is his name.

4 "He threw Egypt's army and its
chariots into the sea;
the best of its officers were
drowned in the Red Sea.
5 The deep sea covered them;
they sank to the bottom like a
stone.
6 "Your right hand, LORD, is
awesome in power;
it breaks the enemy in pieces.
7 In majestic triumph you overthrow
your foes;
your anger blazes out and burns
them up like straw.
8 You blew on the sea and the water
piled up high;
it stood up straight like a wall;
the deepest part of the sea
became solid.
9 The enemy said, 'I will pursue
them and catch them;
I will divide their wealth and
take all I want;
I will draw my sword and take
all they have.'
10 But one breath from you, LORD,
and the Egyptians were
drowned;
they sank like lead in the
terrible water.

11 "LORD, who among the gods is
like you?
Who is like you, wonderful in
holiness?
Who can work miracles and
mighty acts like yours?
12 You stretched out your right hand,
and the earth swallowed our
enemies.
13 Faithful to your promise, you led
the people you had rescued;
by your strength you guided
them to your sacred land.
14 The nations have heard, and they
tremble with fear;
the Philistines are seized with
terror.
15 The leaders of Edom are terrified;
Moab's mighty men are
trembling;
the people of Canaan lose their
courage.
16 Terror and dread fall upon them.
They see your strength, O LORD,
and stand helpless with fear
until your people have marched
past—
the people you set free from
slavery.
17 You bring them in and plant them
on your mountain,

the place that you, LORD, have
chosen for your home,
the Temple that you yourself
have built.
18 You, LORD, will be king forever
and ever."

The Song of Miriam

19 The Israelites walked through the
sea on dry ground. But when the Egyptian chariots with their horses and drivers went into the sea, the LORD brought
the water back, and it covered them.
20 The prophet Miriam, Aaron's sister,
took her tambourine, and all the women
followed her, playing tambourines and
dancing. 21 Miriam sang for them:
"Sing to the LORD, because he has
won a glorious victory;
he has thrown the horses and
their riders into the sea."

Bitter Water

22 Then Moses led the people of Israel
away from the Red Sea into the desert of
Shur. For three days they walked
through the desert, but found no water.
23 Then they came to a place called Marah, but the water there was so bitter that
they could not drink it. That is why it was
named Marah.[o] 24 The people complained to Moses and asked, "What are
we going to drink?" 25 Moses prayed earnestly to the LORD, and the LORD showed
him a piece of wood, which he threw into
the water; and the water became fit to
drink.
There the LORD gave them laws to live
by, and there he also tested them. 26 He
said, "If you will obey me completely by
doing what I consider right and by keeping my commands, I will not punish you
with any of the diseases that I brought on
the Egyptians. I am the LORD, the one
who heals you."
27 Next they came to Elim, where there
were twelve springs and seventy palm
trees; there they camped by the water.

The Manna and the Quails

16 The whole Israelite community
set out from Elim, and on the fifteenth day of the second month after
they had left Egypt, they came to the
desert of Sin, which is between Elim and
Sinai. 2 There in the desert they all complained to Moses and Aaron 3 and said to
them, "We wish that the LORD had killed
us in Egypt. There we could at least sit
down and eat meat and as much other
food as we wanted. But you have brought
us out into this desert to starve us all to
death."
4 The LORD said to Moses, "Now I am
going to cause food to rain down from
the sky for all of you. The people must go
out every day and gather enough for that
day. In this way I can test them to find out
if they will follow my instructions. 5 On
the sixth day they are to bring in twice as
much as usual and prepare it."
6 So Moses and Aaron said to all the
Israelites, "This evening you will know
that it was the LORD who brought you out
of Egypt. 7 In the morning you will see the
dazzling light of the LORD's presence. He
has heard your complaints against him—
yes, against him, because we are only
carrying out his instructions." 8 Then
Moses said, "It is the LORD who will give
you meat to eat in the evening and as
much bread as you want in the morning,
because he has heard how much you
have complained against him. When you
complain against us, you are really complaining against the LORD."
9 Moses said to Aaron, "Tell the whole
community to come and stand before the
LORD, because he has heard their complaints." 10 As Aaron spoke to the whole
community, they turned toward the
desert, and suddenly the dazzling light of
the LORD appeared in a cloud. 11 The LORD
said to Moses, 12 "I have heard the complaints of the Israelites. Tell them that at
twilight they will have meat to eat, and in
the morning they will have all the bread
they want. Then they will know that I,
the LORD, am their God."
13 In the evening a large flock of quails
flew in, enough to cover the camp, and in
the morning there was dew all around
the camp. 14 When the dew evaporated,
there was something thin and flaky on
the surface of the desert. It was as delicate as frost. 15 When the Israelites saw
it, they didn't know what it was and
asked each other, "What is it?"
Moses said to them, "This is the food
that the LORD has given you to eat. 16 The
LORD has commanded that each of you
is to gather as much of it as he needs,

[o] MARAH: *This name in Hebrew means "bitter."*

two quarts for each member of his
household."
17 The Israelites did this, some gathering more, others less. 18 When they measured it, those who gathered much did not
have too much, and those who gathered
less did not have too little. Each had
gathered just what he needed. 19 Moses
said to them, "No one is to keep any of it
for tomorrow." 20 But some of them did
not listen to Moses and saved part of it.
The next morning it was full of worms
and smelled rotten, and Moses was angry with them. 21 Every morning each
one gathered as much as he needed; and
when the sun grew hot, what was left on
the ground melted.
22 On the sixth day they gathered twice
as much food, four quarts for each person. All the leaders of the community
came and told Moses about it, 23 and he
said to them, "The LORD has commanded
that tomorrow is a holy day of rest, dedicated to him. Bake today what you want
to bake and boil what you want to boil.
Whatever is left should be put aside and
kept for tomorrow." 24 As Moses had
commanded, they kept what was left until the next day; it did not spoil or get
worms in it. 25 Moses said, "Eat this today, because today is the Sabbath, a day
of rest dedicated to the LORD, and you will
not find any food outside the camp.
26 You must gather food for six days, but
on the seventh day, the day of rest, there
will be none."
27 On the seventh day some of the people went out to gather food, but they did
not find any. 28 Then the LORD said to
Moses, "How much longer will you people refuse to obey my commands? 29 Remember that I, the LORD, have given you
a day of rest, and that is why on the sixth
day I will always give you enough food
for two days. Everyone is to stay where
he is on the seventh day and not leave his
home." 30 So the people did no work on
the seventh day.
31 The people of Israel called the food
manna.[p] It was like a small white seed,
and tasted like thin cakes made with
honey. 32 Moses said, "The LORD has commanded us to save some manna, to be
kept for our descendants, so that they
can see the food which he gave us to eat
in the desert when he brought us out of
Egypt." 33 Moses said to Aaron, "Take a
jar, put two quarts of manna in it, and
place it in the LORD's presence to be kept
for our descendants." 34 As the LORD had
commanded Moses, Aaron put it in front
of the Covenant Box, so that it could be
kept. 35 The Israelites ate manna for the
next forty years, until they reached the
land of Canaan, where they settled.
(36 The standard dry measure then in use
equaled twenty quarts.)

Water from the Rock

(Numbers 20.1-13)

17 The whole Israelite community
left the desert of Sin, moving
from one place to another at the command of the LORD. They camped at Rephidim, but there was no water there to
drink. 2 They complained to Moses and
said, "Give us water to drink."
Moses answered, "Why are you complaining? Why are you putting the LORD
to the test?"
3 But the people were very thirsty and
continued to complain to Moses. They
said, "Why did you bring us out of Egypt?
To kill us and our children and our livestock with thirst?"
4 Moses prayed earnestly to the LORD
and said, "What can I do with these people? They are almost ready to stone me."
5 The LORD said to Moses, "Take some
of the leaders of Israel with you, and go
on ahead of the people. Take along the
stick with which you struck the Nile.
6 I will stand before you on a rock at
Mount Sinai. Strike the rock, and water
will come out of it for the people to
drink." Moses did so in the presence of
the leaders of Israel.
7 The place was named Massah and
Meribah,[q] because the Israelites complained and put the LORD to the test when
they asked, "Is the LORD with us or not?"

War with the Amalekites

8 The Amalekites came and attacked
the Israelites at Rephidim. 9 Moses said
to Joshua, "Pick out some men to go and
fight the Amalekites tomorrow. I will
stand on top of the hill holding the stick
that God told me to carry." 10 Joshua did
as Moses commanded him and went out
to fight the Amalekites, while Moses,

[p] MANNA: *This word sounds like the Hebrew for "what is it?" (see verse 15).*
[q] MASSAH . . . MERIBAH: *These names in Hebrew mean "testing" and "complaining."*

Aaron, and Hur went up to the top of the
hill. 11 As long as Moses held up his arms,
the Israelites won, but when he put his
arms down, the Amalekites started winning. 12 When Moses' arms grew tired,
Aaron and Hur brought a stone for him
to sit on, while they stood beside him and
held up his arms, holding them steady
until the sun went down. 13 In this way
Joshua totally defeated the Amalekites.
14 Then the LORD said to Moses, "Write
an account of this victory, so that it will
be remembered. Tell Joshua that I will
completely destroy the Amalekites."
15 Moses built an altar and named it "The
LORD is my Banner." 16 He said, "Hold
high the banner of the LORD![r] The LORD
will continue to fight against the Amalekites forever!"

Jethro Visits Moses

18 Moses' father-in-law Jethro, the
priest of Midian, heard about
everything that God had done for Moses
and the people of Israel when he led
them out of Egypt. 2 So he came to Moses,
bringing with him Moses' wife Zipporah,
who had been left behind, 3 and Gershom
and Eliezer, her two sons. (Moses had
said, "I have been a foreigner in a strange
land"; so he had named one son Gershom.[s] 4 He had also said, "The God of
my father helped me and saved me from
being killed by the king of Egypt"; so he
had named the other son Eliezer.[t])
5 Jethro came with Moses' wife and her
two sons into the desert where Moses
was camped at the holy mountain. 6 He
had sent word to Moses that they were
coming, 7 so Moses went out to meet him,
bowed before him, and kissed him. They
asked about each other's health and then
went into Moses' tent. 8 Moses told Jethro
everything that the LORD had done to the
king and the people of Egypt in order to
rescue the Israelites. He also told him
about the hardships the people had faced
on the way and how the LORD had saved
them. 9 When Jethro heard all this, he
was happy 10 and said, "Praise the LORD,
who saved you from the king and the
people of Egypt! Praise the LORD, who
saved his people from slavery! 11 Now I
know that the LORD is greater than all the
gods, because he did this when the Egyptians treated the Israelites with such
contempt." 12 Then Jethro brought an
offering to be burned whole and other
sacrifices to be offered to God; and
Aaron and all the leaders of Israel went
with him to eat the sacred meal as an act
of worship.

The Appointment of Judges

(Deuteronomy 1.9-18)

13 The next day Moses was settling disputes among the people, and he was kept
busy from morning till night. 14 When
Jethro saw everything that Moses had to
do, he asked, "What is all this that you
are doing for the people? Why are you
doing this all alone, with people standing
here from morning till night to consult you?"
15 Moses answered, "I must do this because the people come to me to learn
God's will. 16 When two people have a
dispute, they come to me, and I decide
which one of them is right, and I tell them
God's commands and laws."
17 Then Jethro said, "You are not doing
this right. 18 You will wear yourself out
and these people as well. This is too
much for you to do alone. 19 Now let me
give you some good advice, and God will
be with you. It is right for you to represent the people before God and bring
their disputes to him. 20 You should teach
them God's commands and explain to
them how they should live and what they
should do. 21 But in addition, you should
choose some capable men and appoint
them as leaders of the people: leaders of
thousands, hundreds, fifties, and tens.
They must be God-fearing men who can
be trusted and who cannot be bribed.
22 Let them serve as judges for the people
on a permanent basis. They can bring all
the difficult cases to you, but they themselves can decide all the smaller disputes. That will make it easier for you, as
they share your burden. 23 If you do this,
as God commands, you will not wear
yourself out, and all these people can go
home with their disputes settled."
24 Moses took Jethro's advice 25 and
chose capable men from among all the
Israelites. He appointed them as leaders
of thousands, hundreds, fifties, and tens.
26 They served as judges for the people on

[r] *Probable text* Hold . . . LORD; *Hebrew unclear.* [s] GERSHOM: *This name sounds like the Hebrew for "foreigner."* [t] ELIEZER: *This name sounds like the Hebrew for "God helps me."*

a permanent basis, bringing the difficult
cases to Moses but deciding the smaller
disputes themselves.
27 Then Moses said good-bye to Jethro,
and Jethro went back home.

The Israelites at Mount Sinai

19 1-2 The people of Israel left Rephidim, and on the first day of the
third month after they had left Egypt
they came to the desert of Sinai. There
they set up camp at the foot of Mount
Sinai, 3 and Moses went up the mountain
to meet with God.
The LORD called to him from the mountain and told him to say to the Israelites,
Jacob's descendants: 4 "You saw what I,
the LORD, did to the Egyptians and how I
carried you as an eagle carries her young
on her wings, and brought you here to
me. 5 Now, if you will obey me and keep
my covenant, you will be my own people.
The whole earth is mine, but you will be
my chosen people, 6 a people dedicated to
me alone, and you will serve me as
priests." 7 So Moses went down and
called the leaders of the people together
and told them everything that the LORD
had commanded him. 8 Then all the people answered together, "We will do
everything that the LORD has said," and
Moses reported this to the LORD.
9 The LORD said to Moses, "I will come
to you in a thick cloud, so that the people
will hear me speaking with you and will
believe you from now on."
Moses told the LORD what the people
had answered, 10 and the LORD said to
him, "Go to the people and tell them to
spend today and tomorrow purifying
themselves for worship. They must wash
their clothes 11 and be ready the day after
tomorrow. On that day I will come down
on Mount Sinai, where all the people can
see me. 12 Mark a boundary around the
mountain that the people must not cross,
and tell them not to go up the mountain
or even get near it. If any of you set foot
on it, you are to be put to death; 13 you
must either be stoned or shot with arrows, without anyone touching you. This
applies to both people and animals; they
must be put to death. But when the trumpet is blown, then the people are to go up
to the mountain."
14 Then Moses came down the mountain and told the people to get ready for
worship. So they washed their clothes,
15 and Moses told them, "Be ready by the
day after tomorrow and don't have sexual intercourse in the meantime."
16 On the morning of the third day there
was thunder and lightning, a thick cloud
appeared on the mountain, and a very
loud trumpet blast was heard. All the
people in the camp trembled with fear.
17 Moses led them out of the camp to meet
God, and they stood at the foot of the
mountain. 18 All of Mount Sinai was covered with smoke, because the LORD had
come down on it in fire. The smoke went
up like the smoke of a furnace, and all the
people trembled violently. 19 The sound
of the trumpet became louder and
louder. Moses spoke, and God answered
him with thunder. 20 The LORD came
down on the top of Mount Sinai and
called Moses to the top of the mountain.
Moses went up 21 and the LORD said to
him, "Go down and warn the people not
to cross the boundary to come and look
at me; if they do, many of them will die.
22 Even the priests who come near me
must purify themselves, or I will punish
them."
23 Moses said to the LORD, "The people
cannot come up, because you commanded us to consider the mountain sacred and to mark a boundary around it."
24 The LORD replied, "Go down and
bring Aaron back with you. But the
priests and the people must not cross the
boundary to come up to me, or I will punish them." 25 Moses then went down to
the people and told them what the LORD
had said.

The Ten Commandments

(Deuteronomy 5.1-21)

20 God spoke, and these were his
words: 2 "I am the LORD your God
who brought you out of Egypt, where
you were slaves.
3 "Worship no god but me.
4 "Do not make for yourselves images
of anything in heaven or on earth or in
the water under the earth. 5 Do not bow
down to any idol or worship it, because
I am the LORD your God and I tolerate no
rivals. I bring punishment on those
who hate me and on their descendants
down to the third and fourth generation.
6 But I show my love to thousands of

generations[u] of those who love me
and obey my laws.
7“Do not use my name for evil purposes, for I, the LORD your God, will punish anyone who misuses my name.
8“Observe the Sabbath and keep it
holy. 9You have six days in which to do
your work, 10but the seventh day is a day
of rest dedicated to me. On that day no
one is to work—neither you, your children, your slaves, your animals, nor the
foreigners who live in your country. 11In
six days I, the LORD, made the earth, the
sky, the seas, and everything in them, but
on the seventh day I rested. That is why
I, the LORD, blessed the Sabbath and
made it holy.
12“Respect your father and your
mother, so that you may live a long time
in the land that I am giving you.
13“Do not commit murder.
14“Do not commit adultery.
15“Do not steal.
16“Do not accuse anyone falsely.
17“Do not desire another man's house;
do not desire his wife, his slaves, his cattle, his donkeys, or anything else that he
owns."

The People's Fear

(Deuteronomy 5.22-33)

18When the people heard the thunder
and the trumpet blast and saw the lightning and the smoking mountain, they
trembled with fear and stood a long way
off. 19They said to Moses, “If you speak
to us, we will listen; but we are afraid
that if God speaks to us, we will die.”
20Moses replied, “Don't be afraid; God
has only come to test you and make you
keep on obeying him, so that you will not
sin.” 21But the people continued to stand
a long way off, and only Moses went near
the dark cloud where God was.

Laws about Altars

22The LORD commanded Moses to tell
the Israelites: “You have seen how I, the
LORD, have spoken to you from heaven.
23Do not make for yourselves gods of silver or gold to be worshiped in addition to
me. 24Make an altar of earth for me, and
on it sacrifice your sheep and your cattle
as offerings to be completely burned and
as fellowship offerings. In every place
that I set aside for you to worship me, I
will come to you and bless you. 25If you
make an altar of stone for me, do not
build it out of cut stones, because when
you use a chisel on stones, you make
them unfit for my use. 26Do not build an
altar for me with steps leading up to it; if
you do, you will expose yourselves as
you go up the steps.

The Treatment of Slaves

(Deuteronomy 15.12-18)

21 “Give the Israelites the following
laws: 2If you buy a Hebrew slave,
he shall serve you for six years. In the
seventh year he is to be set free without
having to pay anything. 3If he was unmarried when he became your slave, he
is not to take a wife with him when he
leaves; but if he was married when he
became your slave, he may take his wife
with him. 4If his master gave him a wife
and she bore him sons or daughters, the
woman and her children belong to the
master, and the man is to leave by himself. 5But if the slave declares that he
loves his master, his wife, and his children and does not want to be set free,
6then his master shall take him to the
place of worship. There he is to make
him stand against the door or the door-
post and put a hole through his ear. Then
he will be his slave for life.
7“If a man sells his daughter as a slave,
she is not to be set free, as male slaves
are. 8If she is sold to someone who intends to make her his wife, but he doesn't
like her, then she is to be sold back to her
father; her master cannot sell her to foreigners, because he has treated her unfairly. 9If a man buys a female slave to
give to his son, he is to treat her like a
daughter. 10If a man takes a second wife,
he must continue to give his first wife the
same amount of food and clothing and
the same rights that she had before. 11If
he does not fulfill these duties to her, he
must set her free and not receive any
payment.

Laws about Violent Acts

12“Whoever hits someone and kills
him is to be put to death. 13But if it was
an accident and he did not mean to kill
him, he can escape to a place which I will
choose for you, and there he will be safe.
14But when someone gets angry and

[u] thousands of generations; *or* thousands.

deliberately kills someone else, he is to
be put to death, even if he has run to
my altar for safety.
15 "Whoever hits his father or his
mother is to be put to death.
16 "Whoever kidnaps someone, either
to sell him or to keep him as a slave, is to
be put to death.
17 "Whoever curses his father or his
mother is to be put to death.
18-19 "If there is a fight and someone
hits someone else with a stone or with his
fist, but does not kill him, he is not to be
punished. If the one who was hit has to
stay in bed, but later is able to get up and
walk outside with the help of a cane, the
one who hit him is to pay for his lost time
and take care of him until he gets well.
20 "If a slave owner takes a stick and
beats his slave, whether male or female,
and the slave dies on the spot, the owner
is to be punished. 21 But if the slave does
not die for a day or two, the master is not
to be punished. The loss of his property
is punishment enough.
22 "If some men are fighting and hurt a
pregnant woman so that she loses her
child, but she is not injured in any other
way, the one who hurt her is to be fined
whatever amount the woman's husband
demands, subject to the approval of the
judges. 23 But if the woman herself is injured, the punishment shall be life for
life, 24 eye for eye, tooth for tooth, hand
for hand, foot for foot, 25 burn for burn,
wound for wound, bruise for bruise.
26 "If someone hits his male or female
slave in the eye and puts it out, he is to
free the slave as payment for the eye. 27 If
he knocks out a tooth, he is to free the
slave as payment for the tooth.

The Responsibility of Owners

28 "If a bull gores someone to death, it
is to be stoned, and its flesh shall not be
eaten; but its owner is not to be punished.
29 But if the bull had been in the habit of
attacking people and its owner had been
warned, but did not keep it penned up—
then if it gores someone to death, it is to
be stoned, and its owner is to be put to
death also. 30 However, if the owner is
allowed to pay a fine to save his life, he
must pay the full amount required. 31 If
the bull kills a boy or a girl, the same rule
applies. 32 If the bull kills a male or female slave, its owner shall pay the owner
of the slave thirty pieces of silver, and the
bull shall be stoned to death.
33 "If someone takes the cover off a pit
or if he digs one and does not cover it,
and a bull or a donkey falls into it, 34 he
must pay for the animal. He is to pay the
money to the owner and may keep the
dead animal. 35 If someone's bull kills
someone else's bull, the two of them shall
sell the live bull and divide the money;
they shall also divide up the meat from
the dead animal. 36 But if it was known
that the bull had been in the habit of attacking and its owner did not keep it
penned up, he must make good the loss
by giving the other man a live bull, but he
may keep the dead animal.

Laws about Repayment

22 "If someone steals a cow or a
sheep and kills it or sells it, he
must pay five cows for one cow and four
sheep for one sheep. 2-4 He must pay for
what he stole. If he owns nothing, he
shall be sold as a slave to pay for what he
has stolen. If the stolen animal, whether
a cow, a donkey, or a sheep, is found
alive in his possession, he shall pay two
for one.
"If a thief is caught breaking into a
house at night and is killed, the one who
killed him is not guilty of murder. But if
it happens during the day, he is guilty of
murder.
5 "If someone lets his animals graze in
a field or a vineyard and they stray away
and eat up the crops[v] growing in someone else's field, he must make good the
loss with the crops from his own fields or
vineyards.
6 "If someone starts a fire in his own
field and it spreads through the weeds to
someone else's field and burns up grain
that is growing or that has been cut and
stacked, the one who started the fire is to
pay for the damage.
7 "If anyone agrees to keep someone
else's money or other valuables for him
and they are stolen from his house, the
thief, if found, shall repay double. 8 But if
the thief is not found, the one who was
keeping the valuables is to be brought to
the place of worship and there he must

[v] If . . . crops; *or* If someone burns off a field or a vineyard, and lets the fire get out of control and burn up the crops.

take an oath that he has not stolen the
other one's property.
9 "In every case of a dispute about
property, whether it involves cattle, donkeys, sheep, clothing, or any other lost
object, the two people claiming the property shall be taken to the place of worship. The one whom God declares to be
guilty shall pay double to the other one.
10 "If anyone agrees to keep someone
else's donkey, cow, sheep, or other animal for him, and the animal dies or is
injured or is carried off in a raid, and if
there was no witness, 11 the man must go
to the place of worship and take an oath
that he has not stolen the other man's
animal. If the animal was not stolen, the
owner shall accept the loss, and the other
man need not repay him; 12 but if the animal was stolen, the man must repay the
owner. 13 If it was killed by wild animals,
the man is to bring the remains as evidence; he need not pay for what has been
killed by wild animals.
14 "If anyone borrows an animal from
someone else and it is injured or dies
when its owner is not present, he must
pay for it. 15 But if that happens when the
owner is present, he need not repay. If it
is a rented animal, the loss is covered by
the rental price.

Moral and Religious Laws

16 "If a man seduces a virgin who is not
engaged, he must pay the bride price for
her and marry her. 17 But if her father
refuses to let him marry her, he must pay
the father a sum of money equal to the
bride price for a virgin.
18 "Put to death any woman who practices magic.
19 "Put to death any man who has sexual relations with an animal.
20 "Condemn to death anyone who offers sacrifices to any god except to me,
the LORD.
21 "Do not mistreat or oppress a foreigner; remember that you were foreigners in Egypt. 22 Do not mistreat any
widow or orphan. 23 If you do, I, the LORD,
will answer them when they cry out to
me for help, 24 and I will become angry
and kill you in war. Your wives will become widows, and your children will be
fatherless.
25 "If you lend money to any of my people who are poor, do not act like a
moneylender and require him to pay interest. 26 If you take someone's cloak as a
pledge that he will pay you, you must
give it back to him before the sun sets,
27 because it is the only covering he has to
keep him warm. What else can he sleep
in? When he cries out to me for help, I
will answer him because I am merciful.
28 "Do not speak evil of God,[w] and do
not curse a leader of your people.
29 "Give me the offerings from your
grain, your wine, and your olive oil when
they are due.
"Give me your first-born sons. 30 Give
me the first-born of your cattle and your
sheep. Let the first-born male stay with
its mother for seven days, and on the
eighth day offer it to me.
31 "You are my people, so you must not
eat the meat of any animal that has been
killed by wild animals; instead, give it to
the dogs.

Justice and Fairness

23 "Do not spread false rumors, and
do not help a guilty person by
giving false testimony. 2 Do not follow
the majority when they do wrong or
when they give testimony that perverts
justice. 3 Do not show partiality to a poor
person at his trial.
4 "If you happen to see your enemy's
cow or donkey running loose, take it
back to him. 5 If his donkey has fallen
under its load, help him get the donkey to
its feet again; don't just walk off.
6 "Do not deny justice to a poor person
when he appears in court. 7 Do not make
false accusations, and do not put an innocent person to death, for I will condemn
anyone who does such an evil thing. 8 Do
not accept a bribe, for a bribe makes people blind to what is right and ruins the
cause of those who are innocent.
9 "Do not mistreat a foreigner; you
know how it feels to be a foreigner, because you were foreigners in Egypt.

The Seventh Year and the Seventh Day

10 "For six years plant your land and
gather in what it produces. 11 But in the
seventh year let it rest, and do not harvest anything that grows on it. The poor
may eat what grows there, and the wild

[w] God; *or* the judges.

animals can have what is left. Do the
same with your vineyards and your olive
trees.
12 "Work six days a week, but do no
work on the seventh day, so that your
slaves and the foreigners who work for
you and even your animals can rest.
13 "Listen to everything that I, the LORD,
have said to you. Do not pray to other
gods; do not even mention their names.

The Three Great Festivals

(Exodus 34.18-26; Deuteronomy 16.1-17)

14 "Celebrate three festivals a year to
honor me. 15 In the month of Abib, the
month in which you left Egypt, celebrate
the Festival of Unleavened Bread in the
way that I commanded you. Do not eat
any bread made with yeast during the
seven days of this festival. Never come
to worship me without bringing an
offering.
16 "Celebrate the Harvest Festival
when you begin to harvest your crops.
"Celebrate the Festival of Shelters in
the autumn, when you gather the fruit
from your vineyards and orchards.
17 Every year at these three festivals all
your men must come to worship me, the
Lord your God.
18 "Do not offer bread made with yeast
when you sacrifice an animal to me. The
fat of animals sacrificed to me during
these festivals is not to be left until the
following morning.
19 "Each year bring to the house of the
LORD your God the first grain that you
harvest.
"Do not cook a young sheep or goat in
its mother's milk.

Promises and Instructions

20 "I will send an angel ahead of you to
protect you as you travel and to bring
you to the place which I have prepared.
21 Pay attention to him and obey him. Do
not rebel against him, for I have sent him,
and he will not pardon such rebellion.
22 But if you obey him and do everything
I command, I will fight against all your
enemies. 23 My angel will go ahead of you
and take you into the land of the Amorites, the Hittites, the Perizzites, the Canaanites, the Hivites, and the Jebusites,
and I will destroy them. 24 Do not bow
down to their gods or worship them, and
do not adopt their religious practices.
Destroy their gods and break down their
sacred stone pillars. 25 If you worship me,
the LORD your God, I will bless you with
food and water and take away all your
sicknesses. 26 In your land no woman will
have a miscarriage or be without children. I will give you long lives.
27 "I will make the people who oppose
you afraid of me; I will bring confusion
among the people against whom you
fight, and I will make all your enemies
turn and run from you. 28 I will throw
your enemies into panic;[x] I will drive out
the Hivites, the Canaanites, and the Hittites as you advance. 29 I will not drive
them out within a year's time; if I did, the
land would become deserted, and the
wild animals would be too many for you.
30 Instead, I will drive them out little by
little, until there are enough of you to
take possession of the land. 31 I will make
the borders of your land extend from the
Gulf of Aqaba to the Mediterranean Sea
and from the desert to the Euphrates
River. I will give you power over the inhabitants of the land, and you will drive
them out as you advance. 32 Do not make
any agreement with them or with their
gods. 33 Do not let those people live in
your country; if you do, they will make
you sin against me. If you worship their
gods, it will be a fatal trap for you."

The Covenant Is Sealed

24 The LORD said to Moses, "Come
up the mountain to me, you and
Aaron, Nadab, Abihu, and seventy of the
leaders of Israel; and while you are still
some distance away, bow down in worship. 2 You alone, and none of the others,
are to come near me. The people are not
even to come up the mountain."
3 Moses went and told the people all the
LORD's commands and all the ordinances,
and all the people answered together,
"We will do everything that the LORD has
said." 4 Moses wrote down all the LORD's
commands. Early the next morning he
built an altar at the foot of the mountain
and set up twelve stones, one for each of
the twelve tribes of Israel. 5 Then he sent
young men, and they burned sacrifices to
the LORD and sacrificed some cattle as
fellowship offerings. 6 Moses took half of
the blood of the animals and put it in

[x] I will . . . panic; *or* I will send hornets among your enemies.

bowls; and the other half he threw
against the altar. 7Then he took the book
of the covenant, in which the LORD's commands were written, and read it aloud to
the people. They said, "We will obey the
LORD and do everything that he has
commanded."
8Then Moses took the blood in the
bowls and threw it on the people. He
said, "This is the blood that seals the covenant which the LORD made with you
when he gave all these commands."
9Moses, Aaron, Nadab, Abihu, and
seventy of the leaders of Israel went up
the mountain 10and they saw the God of
Israel. Beneath his feet was what looked
like a pavement of sapphire, as blue as
the sky. 11God did not harm these leading men of Israel; they saw God, and then
they ate and drank together.

Moses on Mount Sinai

12The LORD said to Moses, "Come up
the mountain to me, and while you are
here, I will give you two stone tablets
which contain all the laws that I have
written for the instruction of the people."
13Moses and his helper Joshua got ready,
and Moses began[y] to go up the holy
mountain. 14Moses said to the leaders,
"Wait here in the camp for us until we
come back. Aaron and Hur are here with
you; and so whoever has a dispute to settle can go to them."
15Moses went up Mount Sinai, and a
cloud covered it. 16-17The dazzling light
of the LORD's presence came down on the
mountain. To the Israelites the light
looked like a fire burning on top of the
mountain. The cloud covered the mountain for six days, and on the seventh day
the LORD called to Moses from the cloud.
18Moses went on up the mountain into
the cloud. There he stayed for forty days
and nights.

Offerings for the Sacred Tent

(Exodus 35.4-9)

25 The LORD said to Moses, 2"Tell
the Israelites to make an offering
to me. Receive whatever offerings anyone wishes to give. 3These offerings are
to be: gold, silver, and bronze; 4fine
linen; blue, purple, and red wool; cloth
made of goats' hair; 5rams' skin dyed
red; fine leather; acacia wood; 6oil for
the lamps; spices for the anointing oil
and for the sweet-smelling incense; 7car-
nelians and other jewels to be set in the
ephod[z] of the High Priest and in his
breastpiece. 8The people must make a
sacred Tent for me, so that I may live
among them. 9Make it and all its furnishings according to the plan that I will
show you.

The Covenant Box

(Exodus 37.1-9)

10"Make a Box out of acacia wood, 45
inches long, 27 inches wide, and 27
inches high. 11Cover it with pure gold
inside and out and put a gold border all
around it. 12Make four carrying rings of
gold for it and attach them to its four
legs, with two rings on each side. 13Make
carrying poles of acacia wood and cover
them with gold 14and put them through
the rings on each side of the Box. 15The
poles are to be left in the rings and must
not be taken out. 16Then put in the Box
the two stone tablets that I will give you,
on which the commandments are
written.
17"Make a lid of pure gold, 45 inches
long and 27 inches wide. 18Make two
winged creatures[a] of hammered gold,
19one for each end of the lid. Make them
so that they form one piece with the lid.
20The winged creatures are to face each
other across the lid, and their outspread
wings are to cover it. 21Put the two stone
tablets inside the Box and put the lid on
top of it. 22I will meet you there, and
from above the lid between the two
winged creatures I will give you all my
laws for the people of Israel.

The Table for the Bread Offered to God

(Exodus 37.10-16)

23"Make a table out of acacia wood, 36
inches long, 18 inches wide, and 27
inches high. 24Cover it with pure gold
and put a gold border around it. 25Make
a rim 3 inches wide around it and a gold
border around the rim. 26Make four carrying rings of gold for it and put them at
the four corners, where the legs are.

[y] Moses began; *one ancient translation* they began. [z] EPHOD: *In most contexts the term ephod refers to a type of shoulder garment, in certain respects resembling a vest. It was made of costly and colorful cloth and to it was attached a kind of pouch containing the Urim and Thummim, two objects used in determining God's will.* [a] WINGED CREATURES: *See Word List.*

27 The rings to hold the poles for carrying
the table are to be placed near the rim.
28 Make the poles of acacia wood and
cover them with gold. 29 Make plates,
cups, jars, and bowls to be used for the
wine offerings. All of these are to be
made of pure gold. 30 The table is to be
placed in front of the Covenant Box, and
on the table there is always to be the
sacred bread offered to me.

The Lampstand

(Exodus 37.17-24)

31 "Make a lampstand of pure gold.
Make its base and its shaft of hammered
gold; its decorative flowers, including
buds and petals, are to form one piece
with it. 32 Six branches shall extend from
its sides, three from each side. 33 Each of
the six branches is to have three decorative flowers shaped like almond blossoms with buds and petals. 34 The shaft of
the lampstand is to have four decorative
flowers shaped like almond blossoms
with buds and petals. 35 There is to be one
bud below each of the three pairs of
branches. 36 The buds, the branches, and
the lampstand are to be a single piece of
pure hammered gold. 37 Make seven
lamps for the lampstand and set them up
so that they shine toward the front.
38 Make its tongs and trays of pure gold.
39 Use seventy-five pounds of pure gold
to make the lampstand and all this equipment. 40 Take care to make them according to the plan that I showed you on the
mountain.

The Tent of the LORD's Presence[b]

(Exodus 36.8-38)

26 "Make the interior of the sacred
Tent, the Tent of my presence,
out of ten pieces of fine linen woven with
blue, purple, and red wool. Embroider
them with figures of winged creatures.
2 Make each piece the same size, 14 yards
long and 2 yards wide. 3 Sew five of them
together in one set, and do the same with
the other five. 4 Make loops of blue cloth
on the edge of the outside piece in each
set. 5 Put fifty loops on the first piece of
the first set and fifty loops matching
them on the last piece of the second set.
6 Make fifty gold hooks with which to
join the two sets into one piece.
7 "Make a cover for the Tent out of
eleven pieces of cloth made of goats'
hair. 8 Make them all the same size, 15
yards long and 2 yards wide. 9 Sew five of
them together in one set, and the other
six in another set. Fold the sixth piece
double over the front of the Tent. 10 Put
fifty loops on the edge of the last piece of
one set, and fifty loops on the edge of the
other set. 11 Make fifty bronze hooks and
put them in the loops to join the two sets
so as to form one cover. 12 Hang the extra
half piece over the back of the Tent.
13 The extra half yard on each side of the
length is to hang over the sides of the
Tent to cover it.
14 "Make two more coverings, one of
rams' skin dyed red and the other of fine
leather, to serve as the outer cover.
15 "Make upright frames for the Tent
out of acacia wood. 16 Each frame is to be
15 feet long and 27 inches wide, 17 with
two matching projections, so that the
frames can be joined together. All the
frames are to have these projections.
18 Make twenty frames for the south side
19 and forty silver bases to go under them,
two bases under each frame to hold its
two projections. 20 Make twenty frames
for the north side of the Tent 21 and forty
silver bases, two under each frame. 22 For
the back of the Tent on the west, make
six frames, 23 and two frames for the corners. 24 These corner frames are to be
joined at the bottom and connected all
the way to the top. The two frames that
form the two corners are to be made in
this way. 25 So there will be eight frames
with their sixteen silver bases, two under
each frame.
26 "Make fifteen crossbars of acacia
wood, five for the frames on one side of
the Tent, 27 five for the frames on the
other side, and five for the frames on the
west end, at the back. 28 The middle
crossbar, set halfway up the frames, is to
extend from one end of the Tent to the
other. 29 Cover the frames with gold and
fit them with gold rings to hold the crossbars, which are also to be covered with
gold. 30 Set up the Tent according to the
plan that I showed you on the mountain.
31 "Make a curtain of fine linen woven
with blue, purple, and red wool. Embroider it with figures of winged creatures.
32 Hang it on four posts of acacia wood
covered with gold, fitted with hooks, and

[b] TENT OF THE LORD'S PRESENCE: *See Word List.*

set in four silver bases. 33 Place the curtain under the row of hooks in the roof of
the Tent, and put behind the curtain the
Covenant Box containing the two stone
tablets. The curtain will separate the
Holy Place from the Most Holy Place.
34 Put the lid on the Covenant Box. 35 Outside the Most Holy Place put the table
against the north side of the Tent and the
lampstand against the south side.

36 "For the entrance of the Tent make a
curtain of fine linen woven with blue,
purple, and red wool and decorated with
embroidery. 37 For this curtain make five
posts of acacia wood covered with gold
and fitted with gold hooks; make five
bronze bases for these posts.

The Altar

(Exodus 38.1-7)

27 "Make an altar out of acacia
wood. It is to be square, 7½ feet
long and 7½ feet wide, and it is to be 4½
feet high. 2 Make projections at the top of
the four corners. They are to form one
piece with the altar, and the whole is to
be covered with bronze. 3 Make pans for
the greasy ashes, and make shovels,
bowls, hooks, and fire pans. All this
equipment is to be made of bronze.
4 Make a bronze grating and put four
bronze carrying rings on its corners.
5 Put the grating under the rim of the altar, so that it reaches halfway up the altar. 6 Make carrying poles of acacia
wood, cover them with bronze, 7 and put
them in the rings on each side of the altar
when it is carried. 8 Make the altar out of
boards and leave it hollow, according to
the plan that I showed you on the
mountain.

The Enclosure for the Tent of the LORD's Presence

(Exodus 38.9-20)

9 "For the Tent of my presence make an
enclosure out of fine linen curtains. On
the south side the curtains are to be 50
yards long, 10 supported by twenty
bronze posts in twenty bronze bases,
with hooks and rods made of silver. 11 Do
the same on the north side of the enclosure. 12 On the west side there are to be
curtains 25 yards long, with ten posts
and ten bases. 13 On the east side, where
the entrance is, the enclosure is also to be
25 yards wide. 14-15 On each side of the
entrance there are to be 7½ yards of curtains, with three posts and three bases.
16 For the entrance itself there is to be a
curtain 10 yards long made of fine linen
woven with blue, purple, and red wool,
and decorated with embroidery. It is to
be supported by four posts in four bases.
17 All the posts around the enclosure are
to be connected with silver rods, and
their hooks are to be made of silver and
their bases of bronze. 18 The enclosure is
to be 50 yards long, 25 yards wide, and
2½ yards high. The curtains are to be
made of fine linen and the bases of
bronze. 19 All the equipment that is used
in the Tent and all the pegs for the Tent
and for the enclosure are to be made of
bronze.

Taking Care of the Lamp

(Leviticus 24.1-4)

20 "Command the people of Israel to
bring you the best olive oil for the lamp,
so that it can be lit each evening. 21 Aaron
and his sons are to set up the lamp in the
Tent of my presence outside the curtain
which is in front of the Covenant Box.
There in my presence it is to burn from
evening until morning. This command is
to be kept forever by the Israelites and
their descendants.

Garments for the Priests

(Exodus 39.1-7)

28 "Summon your brother Aaron
and his sons, Nadab, Abihu, Eleazar, and Ithamar. Separate them from
the people of Israel, so that they may
serve me as priests. 2 Make priestly garments for your brother Aaron, to provide
him with dignity and beauty. 3 Call all the
skilled workers to whom I have given
ability, and tell them to make Aaron's
clothes, so that he may be dedicated as a
priest in my service. 4 Tell them to make
a breastpiece, an ephod, a robe, an embroidered shirt, a turban, and a sash.
They are to make these priestly garments for your brother Aaron and his
sons, so that they can serve me as priests.
5 The skilled workers are to use blue, purple, and red wool, gold thread, and fine
linen.

6 "They are to make the ephod of blue,
purple, and red wool, gold thread, and
fine linen, decorated with embroidery.
7 Two shoulder straps, by which it can be
fastened, are to be attached to the sides.
8 A finely woven belt made of the same

materials is to be attached to the ephod
so as to form one piece with it. 9Take two
carnelian stones and engrave on them
the names of the twelve sons of Jacob,
10in the order of their birth, with six on
one stone and six on the other. 11Have a
skillful jeweler engrave on the two
stones the names of the sons of Jacob,
and mount the stones in gold settings.
12Put them on the shoulder straps of the
ephod to represent the twelve tribes of
Israel. In this way Aaron will carry their
names on his shoulders, so that I, the
LORD, will always remember my people.
13Make two gold settings 14and two
chains of pure gold twisted like cords,
and attach them to the settings.

The Breastpiece

(Exodus 39.8-21)

15"Make a breastpiece for the High
Priest to use in determining God's will. It
is to be made of the same materials as the
ephod and with similar embroidery. 16It
is to be square and folded double, 9
inches long and 9 inches wide. 17Mount
four rows of precious stones on it; in the
first row mount a ruby, a topaz, and a
garnet; 18in the second row, an emerald,
a sapphire, and a diamond; 19in the third
row, a turquoise, an agate, and an amethyst; 20and in the fourth row, a beryl, a
carnelian, and a jasper. These are to be
mounted in gold settings. 21Each of these
twelve stones is to have engraved on it
the name of one of the sons of Jacob, to
represent the tribes of Israel. 22For the
breastpiece make chains of pure gold,
twisted like cords. 23Make two gold rings
and attach them to the upper corners of
the breastpiece, 24and fasten the two
gold cords to the two rings. 25Fasten the
other two ends of the cords to the two
settings, and in this way attach them in
front to the shoulder straps of the ephod.
26Then make two rings of gold and attach them to the lower corners of the
breastpiece on the inside edge next to the
ephod. 27Make two more gold rings and
attach them to the lower part of the front
of the two shoulder straps of the ephod,
near the seam and above the finely woven belt. 28Tie the rings of the breastpiece to the rings of the ephod with a blue
cord, so that the breastpiece rests above
the belt and does not come loose.
29"When Aaron enters the Holy Place,
he will wear this breastpiece engraved
with the names of the tribes of Israel, so
that I, the LORD, will always remember
my people. 30Put the Urim and Thummim[c] in the breastpiece, so that Aaron
will carry them when he comes into my
holy presence. At such times he must always wear this breastpiece, so that he
can determine my will for the people of
Israel.

The Other Priestly Garments

(Exodus 39.22-31)

31"The robe that goes under the ephod
is to be made entirely of blue wool. 32It is
to have a hole for the head, and this hole
is to be reinforced with a woven binding
to keep it from tearing. 33-34All around its
lower hem put pomegranates of blue,
purple, and red wool, alternating with
gold bells. 35Aaron is to wear this robe
when he serves as priest. When he comes
into my presence in the Holy Place or
when he leaves it, the sound of the bells
will be heard, and he will not be killed.
36"Make an ornament of pure gold and
engrave on it 'Dedicated to the LORD.'
37Tie it to the front of the turban with a
blue cord. 38Aaron is to wear it on his
forehead, so that I, the LORD, will accept
all the offerings that the Israelites dedicate to me, even if the people commit
some error in offering them.
39"Weave Aaron's shirt of fine linen
and make a turban of fine linen and also
a sash decorated with embroidery.
40"Make shirts, sashes, and caps for
Aaron's sons, to provide them with dignity and beauty. 41Put these clothes on
your brother Aaron and his sons. Then
ordain them and dedicate them by
anointing them with olive oil, so that
they may serve me as priests. 42Make
linen shorts for them, reaching from the
waist to the thighs, so that they will not
expose themselves. 43Aaron and his sons
must always wear them when they go
into the Tent of my presence or approach
the altar to serve as priests in the Holy
Place, so that they will not be killed for
exposing themselves. This is a permanent rule for Aaron and his descendants.

[c] URIM AND THUMMIM: *Two objects used by the priest to determine God's will; it is not known precisely how they were used.*

Instructions for Ordaining Aaron and His Sons as Priests

(Leviticus 8.1-36)

29 “This is what you are to do to
Aaron and his sons to dedicate
them as priests in my service. Take one
young bull and two rams without any defects. 2 Use the best wheat flour, but no
yeast, and make some bread with olive
oil, some without it, and some in the form
of thin cakes brushed with oil. 3 Put them
in a basket and offer them to me when
you sacrifice the bull and the two rams.
4 “Bring Aaron and his sons to the entrance of the Tent of my presence, and
have them take a ritual bath. 5 Then dress
Aaron in the priestly garments — the
shirt, the robe that goes under the ephod,
the ephod, the breastpiece, and the belt.
6 Put the turban on him and tie on it the
sacred sign of dedication engraved ‘Dedicated to the LORD.’ 7 Then take the
anointing oil, pour it on his head, and
anoint him.
8 “Bring his sons and put shirts on
them; 9 put sashes around their waists
and tie caps on their heads. That is how
you are to ordain Aaron and his sons.
They and their descendants are to serve
me as priests forever.
10 “Bring the bull to the front of the
Tent of my presence and tell Aaron and
his sons to put their hands on its head.
11 Kill the bull there in my holy presence
at the entrance of the Tent. 12 Take some
of the bull’s blood and with your finger
put it on the projections of the altar. Then
pour out the rest of the blood at the base
of the altar. 13 Next, take all the fat which
covers the internal organs, the best part
of the liver, and the two kidneys with the
fat on them, and burn them on the altar
as an offering to me. 14 But burn the bull’s
flesh, its skin, and its intestines outside
the camp. This is an offering to take
away the sins of the priests.
15 “Take one of the rams and tell Aaron
and his sons to put their hands on its
head. 16 Kill it, and take its blood and
throw it against all four sides of the altar.
17 Cut the ram in pieces; wash its internal
organs and its hind legs, and put them on
top of the head and the other pieces.
18 Burn the whole ram on the altar as a
food offering. The odor of this offering
pleases me.
19 “Take the other ram — the ram used
for dedication — and tell Aaron and his
sons to put their hands on its head. 20 Kill
it, and take some of its blood and put it
on the lobes of the right ears of Aaron
and his sons, on the thumbs of their right
hands and on the big toes of their right
feet. Throw the rest of the blood against
all four sides of the altar. 21 Take some of
the blood that is on the altar and some of
the anointing oil, and sprinkle it on
Aaron and his clothes and on his sons
and their clothes. He, his sons, and their
clothes will then be dedicated to me.
22 “Cut away the ram’s fat, the fat tail,
the fat covering the internal organs, the
best part of the liver, the two kidneys
with the fat on them, and the right thigh.
23 From the basket of bread which has
been offered to me, take one loaf of each
kind: one loaf made with olive oil and
one made without it and one thin cake.
24 Put all this food in the hands of Aaron
and his sons and have them dedicate it to
me as a special gift. 25 Then take it from
them and burn it on the altar, on top of
the burnt offering, as a food offering to
me. The odor of this offering pleases me.
26 “Take the breast of this ram and dedicate it to me as a special gift. This part
of the animal will be yours.
27 “When a priest is ordained, the
breast and the thigh of the ram being
used for the ordination are to be dedicated to me as a special gift and set aside
for the priests. 28 It is my unchanging decision that when my people make their
fellowship offerings, the breast and the
thigh of the animal belong to the priests.
This is the people’s gift to me, the LORD.
29 “Aaron’s priestly garments are to be
handed on to his sons after his death, for
them to wear when they are ordained.
30 The son of Aaron who succeeds him as
priest and who goes into the Tent of my
presence to serve in the Holy Place is to
wear these garments for seven days.
31 “Take the meat of the ram used for
the ordination of Aaron and his sons and
boil it in a holy place. 32 At the entrance
of the Tent of my presence they are to eat
it along with the bread left in the basket.
33 They shall eat what was used in the
ritual of forgiveness at their ordination.
Only priests may eat this food, because it
is sacred. 34 If some of the meat or some
of the bread is not eaten by morning, it is
to be burned; it is not to be eaten, for it
is sacred.

35 "Perform the rites of ordination for Aaron and his sons for seven days exactly as I have commanded you. 36 Each day you must offer a bull as a sacrifice, so that sin may be forgiven. This will purify the altar. Then anoint it with olive oil to make it holy. 37 Do this every day for seven days. Then the altar will be completely holy, and anyone or anything that touches it will be harmed by the power of its holiness.[d]

The Daily Offerings

(Numbers 28.1-8)

38 "Every day for all time to come, sacrifice on the altar two one-year-old lambs. 39 Sacrifice one of the lambs in the morning and the other in the evening. 40 With the first lamb offer two pounds of fine wheat flour mixed with one quart of pure olive oil. Pour out one quart of wine as an offering. 41 Sacrifice the second lamb in the evening, and offer with it the same amounts of flour, olive oil, and wine as in the morning. This is a food offering to me, the LORD, and its odor pleases me. 42 For all time to come, this burnt offering is to be offered in my presence at the entrance of the Tent of my presence. That is where I will meet my people and speak to you. 43 There I will meet the people of Israel, and the dazzling light of my presence will make the place holy. 44 I will make the Tent and the altar holy, and I will set Aaron and his sons apart to serve me as priests. 45 I will live among the people of Israel, and I will be their God. 46 They will know that I am the LORD their God who brought them out of Egypt so that I could live among them. I am the LORD their God.

The Altar for Burning Incense

(Exodus 37.25-28)

30 "Make an altar out of acacia wood, for burning incense. 2 It is to be square, 18 inches long and 18 inches wide, and it is to be 36 inches high. Its projections at the four corners are to form one piece with it. 3 Cover its top, all four sides, and its projections with pure gold, and put a gold border around it. 4 Make two gold carrying rings for it and attach them below the border on two sides to hold the poles with which it is to be carried. 5 Make these poles of acacia wood and cover them with gold. 6 Put this altar outside the curtain which hangs in front of the Covenant Box. That is the place where I will meet you. 7 Every morning when Aaron comes to take care of the lamps, he is to burn sweet-smelling incense on it. 8 He must do the same when he lights the lamps in the evening. This offering of incense is to continue without interruption for all time to come. 9 Do not offer on this altar any forbidden incense, any animal offering, or any grain offering, and do not pour out any wine offering on it. 10 Once a year Aaron is to perform the ritual for purifying the altar by putting on its four projections the blood of the animal sacrificed for sin. This is to be done every year for all time to come. This altar is to be completely holy, dedicated to me, the LORD."

The Tax for the Tent of the LORD's Presence

11 The LORD said to Moses, 12 "When you take a census of the people of Israel, each man is to pay me a price for his life, so that no disaster will come on him while the census is being taken. 13 Everyone included in the census must pay the required amount of money, weighed according to the official standard. Everyone must pay this as an offering to me. 14 Everyone being counted in the census, that is, every man twenty years old or older, is to pay me this amount. 15 The rich man is not to pay more, nor the poor man less, when they pay this amount for their lives. 16 Collect this money from the people of Israel and spend it for the upkeep of the Tent of my presence. This tax will be the payment for their lives, and I will remember to protect them."

The Bronze Basin

17 The LORD said to Moses, 18 "Make a bronze basin with a bronze base. Place it between the Tent and the altar, and put water in it. 19 Aaron and his sons are to use the water to wash their hands and feet 20 before they go into the Tent or approach the altar to offer the food

[d] BE HARMED BY THE POWER OF ITS HOLINESS: *It was believed that ordinary people or things would be harmed by touching something holy.*

offering. Then they will not be killed.
21 They must wash their hands and feet,
so that they will not die. This is a rule
which they and their descendants are to
observe forever."

The Anointing Oil

22 The LORD said to Moses, 23 "Take the
finest spices — 12 pounds of liquid myrrh,
6 pounds of sweet-smelling cinnamon, 6
pounds of sweet-smelling cane, 24 and 12
pounds of cassia (all weighed according
to the official standard). Add one gallon
of olive oil, 25 and make a sacred anointing oil, mixed like perfume. 26 Use it to
anoint the Tent of my presence, the Covenant Box, 27 the table and all its equipment, the lampstand and its equipment,
the altar for burning incense, 28 the altar
for burning offerings, together with all
its equipment, and the washbasin with
its base. 29 Dedicate these things in this
way, and they will be completely holy,
and anyone or anything that touches
them will be harmed by the power of its
holiness.[e] 30 Then anoint Aaron and his
sons, and ordain them as priests in my
service. 31 Say to the people of Israel,
'This holy anointing oil is to be used in
my service for all time to come. 32 It must
not be poured on ordinary men, and you
must not use the same formula to make
any mixture like it. It is holy, and you
must treat it as holy. 33 Whoever makes
any like it or uses any of it on anyone
who is not a priest will no longer be considered one of my people.' "

The Incense

34 The LORD said to Moses, "Take an
equal part of each of the following sweet
spices — stacte, onycha, galbanum, and
pure frankincense. 35 Use them to make
incense, mixed like perfume. Add salt to
keep it pure and holy. 36 Beat part of it
into a fine powder, take it into the Tent
of my presence, and sprinkle it in front of
the Covenant Box. Treat this incense as
completely holy. 37 Do not use the same
formula to make any incense like it for
yourselves. Treat it as a holy thing dedicated to me. 38 If anyone makes any like
it for use as perfume, he will no longer be
considered one of my people."

Craftsmen for the Tent of the LORD's Presence

(Exodus 35.30 – 36.1)

31 The LORD said to Moses, 2 "I have
chosen Bezalel, the son of Uri
and grandson of Hur, from the tribe of
Judah, 3 and I have filled him with my
power.[f] I have given him understanding, skill, and ability for every kind
of artistic work — 4 for planning skillful
designs and working them in gold, silver,
and bronze; 5 for cutting jewels to be set;
for carving wood; and for every other
kind of artistic work. 6 I have also selected Oholiab son of Ahisamach, from
the tribe of Dan, to work with him. I have
also given great ability to all the other
skilled workers, so that they can make
everything I have commanded to be
made: 7 the Tent of my presence, the Covenant Box and its lid, all the furnishings
of the Tent, 8 the table and its equipment,
the lampstand of pure gold and all its
equipment, the altar for burning incense,
9 the altar for burnt offerings and all its
equipment, the washbasin and its base,
10 the magnificent priestly garments for
Aaron and his sons to use when they
serve as priests, 11 the anointing oil, and
the sweet-smelling incense for the Holy
Place. In making all these things, they
are to do exactly as I have commanded you."

Sabbath, the Day of Rest

12 The LORD commanded Moses 13 to tell
the people of Israel, "Keep the Sabbath,
my day of rest, because it is a sign between you and me for all time to come, to
show that I, the LORD, have made you my
own people. 14 You must keep the day of
rest, because it is sacred. Whoever does
not keep it, but works on that day, is to
be put to death. 15 You have six days in
which to do your work, but the seventh
day is a solemn day of rest dedicated to
me. Whoever does any work on that day
is to be put to death. 16 The people of Israel are to keep this day as a sign of the
covenant. 17 It is a permanent sign between the people of Israel and me, because I, the LORD, made heaven and earth
in six days, and on the seventh day I
stopped working and rested."

18 When God had finished speaking to
Moses on Mount Sinai, he gave him the

[e] HARMED BY THE POWER OF ITS HOLINESS: *See* 29.37. [f] power; *or* spirit.

two stone tablets on which God himself
had written the commandments.

The Gold Bull-Calf

(Deuteronomy 9.6-29)

32 When the people saw that Moses
had not come down from the
mountain but was staying there a long
time, they gathered around Aaron and
said to him, "We do not know what has
happened to this man Moses, who led
us out of Egypt; so make us a god[g] to
lead us."

2 Aaron said to them, "Take off the gold
earrings which your wives, your sons,
and your daughters are wearing, and
bring them to me." 3 So all the people
took off their gold earrings and brought
them to Aaron. 4 He took the earrings,
melted them, poured the gold into a
mold, and made a gold bull-calf.

The people said, "Israel, this is our god,
who led us out of Egypt!"

5 Then Aaron built an altar in front of
the gold bull-calf and announced, "Tomorrow there will be a festival to honor
the LORD." 6 Early the next morning they
brought some animals to burn as sacrifices and others to eat as fellowship offerings. The people sat down to a feast,
which turned into an orgy of drinking
and sex.

7 The LORD said to Moses, "Hurry and
go back down, because your people,
whom you led out of Egypt, have sinned
and rejected me. 8 They have already left
the way that I commanded them to follow; they have made a bull-calf out of
melted gold and have worshiped it and
offered sacrifices to it. They are saying
that this is their god, who led them out of
Egypt. 9 I know how stubborn these people are. 10 Now, don't try to stop me. I am
angry with them, and I am going to destroy them. Then I will make you and
your descendants into a great nation."

11 But Moses pleaded with the LORD his
God and said, "LORD, why should you be
so angry with your people, whom you
rescued from Egypt with great might and
power? 12 Why should the Egyptians be
able to say that you led your people out
of Egypt, planning to kill them in the
mountains and destroy them completely? Stop being angry; change your
mind and do not bring this disaster on
your people. 13 Remember your servants
Abraham, Isaac, and Jacob. Remember
the solemn promise you made to them to
give them as many descendants as there
are stars in the sky and to give their
descendants all that land you promised
would be their possession forever." 14 So
the LORD changed his mind and did not
bring on his people the disaster he had
threatened.

15 Moses went back down the mountain, carrying the two stone tablets with
the commandments written on both
sides. 16 God himself had made the tablets and had engraved the commandments on them.

17 Joshua heard the people shouting
and said to Moses, "I hear the sound of
battle in the camp."

18 Moses said, "That doesn't sound like
a shout of victory or a cry of defeat; it's
the sound of singing."

19 When Moses came close enough to
the camp to see the bull-calf and to see
the people dancing, he became furious.
There at the foot of the mountain, he
threw down the tablets he was carrying
and broke them. 20 He took the bull-calf
which they had made, melted it, ground
it into fine powder, and mixed it with
water. Then he made the people of Israel
drink it. 21 He said to Aaron, "What did
these people do to you, that you have
made them commit such a terrible sin?"

22 Aaron answered, "Don't be angry
with me; you know how determined
these people are to do evil. 23 They said to
me, 'We don't know what has happened
to this man Moses, who brought us out of
Egypt; so make us a god to lead us.'
24 I asked them to bring me their gold ornaments, and those who had any took
them off and gave them to me. I threw the
ornaments into the fire and out came this
bull-calf!"

25 Moses saw that Aaron had let the
people get out of control and make fools
of themselves in front of their enemies.
26 So he stood at the gate of the camp and
shouted, "Everyone who is on the LORD's
side come over here!" So all the Levites
gathered around him, 27 and he said to
them, "The LORD God of Israel commands
every one of you to put on your sword
and go through the camp from this gate
to the other and kill your brothers, your

[g] a god; *or* some gods.

friends, and your neighbors." 28 The Levites obeyed, and killed about three
thousand men that day. 29 Moses said to
the Levites, "Today you have consecrated yourselves[h] as priests in the service of the LORD by killing your sons and
brothers, so the LORD has given you his
blessing."
30 The next day Moses said to the people, "You have committed a terrible sin.
But now I will again go up the mountain
to the LORD; perhaps I can obtain forgiveness for your sin." 31 Moses then returned
to the LORD and said, "These people have
committed a terrible sin. They have
made a god out of gold and worshiped it.
32 Please forgive their sin; but if you
won't, then remove my name from the
book in which you have written the
names of your people."
33 The LORD answered, "It is those who
have sinned against me whose names I
will remove from my book. 34 Now go,
lead the people to the place I told you
about. Remember that my angel will
guide you, but the time is coming when
I will punish these people for their sin."
35 So the LORD sent a disease on the people, because they had caused Aaron to
make the gold bull-calf.

The LORD Orders Israel to Leave Mount Sinai

33 The LORD said to Moses, "Leave
this place, you and the people
you brought out of Egypt, and go to the
land that I promised to give to Abraham,
Isaac, and Jacob and to their descendants. 2 I will send an angel to guide you,
and I will drive out the Canaanites, the
Amorites, the Hittites, the Perizzites, the
Hivites, and the Jebusites. 3 You are going to a rich and fertile land. But I will not
go with you myself, because you are a
stubborn people, and I might destroy you
on the way."
4 When the people heard this, they began to mourn and did not wear jewelry
any more. 5 For the LORD had commanded
Moses to tell them, "You are a stubborn
people. If I were to go with you even for
a moment, I would completely destroy
you. Now take off your jewelry, and I will
decide what to do with you." 6 So after
they left Mount Sinai, the people of Israel
no longer wore jewelry.

The Tent of the LORD's Presence

7 Whenever the people of Israel set up
camp, Moses would take the sacred Tent
and put it up some distance outside the
camp. It was called the Tent of the LORD's
presence, and anyone who wanted to
consult the LORD would go out to it.
8 Whenever Moses went out there, the
people would stand at the door of their
tents and watch Moses until he entered
it. 9 After Moses had gone in, the pillar of
cloud would come down and stay at the
door of the Tent, and the LORD would
speak to Moses from the cloud. 10 As
soon as the people saw the pillar of cloud
at the door of the Tent, they would bow
down. 11 The LORD would speak with
Moses face-to-face, just as someone
speaks with a friend. Then Moses would
return to the camp. But the young man
who was his helper, Joshua son of Nun,
stayed in the Tent.

The LORD Promises to Be with His People

12 Moses said to the LORD, "It is true that
you have told me to lead these people to
that land, but you did not tell me whom
you would send with me. You have said
that you know me well and are pleased
with me. 13 Now if you are, tell me your
plans, so that I may serve you and continue to please you. Remember also that
you have chosen this nation to be
your own."
14 The LORD said, "I will go with you,
and I will give you victory."
15 Moses replied, "If you do not go with
us, don't make us leave this place. 16 How
will anyone know that you are pleased
with your people and with me if you do
not go with us? Your presence with us
will distinguish us from any other people
on earth."
17 The LORD said to Moses, "I will do just
as you have asked, because I know you
very well and I am pleased with you."
18 Then Moses requested, "Please, let
me see the dazzling light of your
presence."
19 The LORD answered, "I will make all
my splendor pass before you and in your

[h] *Some ancient translations* Today you have consecrated yourselves; *Hebrew* Consecrate yourselves today; *or* You have been consecrated today.

presence I will pronounce my sacred
name. I am the LORD, and I show compassion and pity on those I choose. 20 I will
not let you see my face, because no one
can see me and stay alive, 21 but here is a
place beside me where you can stand on
a rock. 22 When the dazzling light of my
presence passes by, I will put you in an
opening in the rock and cover you with
my hand until I have passed by. 23 Then
I will take my hand away, and you will
see my back but not my face."

The Second Set of Stone Tablets

(Deuteronomy 10.1-5)

34 The LORD said to Moses, "Cut two
stone tablets like the first ones,
and I will write on them the words that
were on the first tablets, which you
broke. 2 Get ready tomorrow morning,
and come up Mount Sinai to meet me
there at the top. 3 No one is to come up
with you; no one is to be seen on any part
of the mountain; and no sheep or cattle
are to graze at the foot of the mountain."
4 So Moses cut two more stone tablets,
and early the next morning he carried
them up Mount Sinai, just as the LORD
had commanded.
5 The LORD came down in a cloud, stood
with him there, and pronounced his holy
name, the LORD.[i] 6 The LORD then passed
in front of him and called out, "I, the
LORD, am a God who is full of compassion
and pity, who is not easily angered and
who shows great love and faithfulness.
7 I keep my promise for thousands of
generations[j] and forgive evil and sin;
but I will not fail to punish children and
grandchildren to the third and fourth
generation for the sins of their parents."
8 Moses quickly bowed down to the
ground and worshiped. 9 He said, "Lord,
if you really are pleased with me, I ask
you to go with us. These people are stubborn, but forgive our evil and our sin, and
accept us as your own people."

The Covenant Is Renewed

(Exodus 23.14-19; Deuteronomy 7.1-5; 16.1-17)

10 The LORD said to Moses, "I now make
a covenant with the people of Israel. In
their presence I will do great things such
as have never been done anywhere on
earth among any of the nations. All the
people will see what great things I, the
LORD, can do, because I am going to do an
awesome thing for you. 11 Obey the laws
that I am giving you today. I will drive
out the Amorites, the Canaanites, the
Hittites, the Perizzites, the Hivites, and
the Jebusites, as you advance. 12 Do not
make any treaties with the people of the
country into which you are going, because this could be a fatal trap for you.
13 Instead, tear down their altars, destroy
their sacred pillars, and cut down their
symbols of the goddess Asherah.
14 "Do not worship any other god, because I, the LORD, tolerate no rivals. 15 Do
not make any treaties with the people of
the country, because when they worship
their pagan gods and sacrifice to them,
they will invite you to join them, and you
will be tempted to eat the food they offer
to their gods. 16 Your sons might marry
those foreign women, who would lead
them to be unfaithful to me and to worship their pagan gods.
17 "Do not make gods of metal and worship them.
18 "Keep the Festival of Unleavened
Bread. As I have commanded you, eat
unleavened bread for seven days in the
month of Abib, because it was in that
month that you left Egypt.
19 "Every first-born son and first-born
male domestic animal belongs to me,
20 but you are to buy back every first-
born donkey by offering a lamb in its
place. If you do not buy it back, break its
neck. Buy back every first-born son.
"No one is to appear before me without
an offering.
21 "You have six days in which to do
your work, but do not work on the seventh day, not even during plowing time
or harvest.
22 "Keep the Harvest Festival when you
begin to harvest the first crop of your
wheat, and keep the Festival of Shelters
in the autumn when you gather your
fruit.
23 "Three times a year all of your men
must come to worship me, the LORD, the
God of Israel. 24 After I have driven out
the nations before you and extended
your territory, no one will try to conquer
your country during the three festivals.
25 "Do not offer bread made with yeast

[i] THE LORD: *See 3.14, and Word List.* [j] thousands of generations; *or* thousands.

when you sacrifice an animal to me. Do
not keep until the following morning any
part of the animal killed at the Passover
Festival.
26 "Each year bring to the house of the
LORD the first grain that you harvest.
"Do not cook a young sheep or goat in
its mother's milk."
27 The LORD said to Moses, "Write these
words down, because it is on the basis of
these words that I am making a covenant
with you and with Israel." 28 Moses
stayed there with the LORD forty days and
nights, eating and drinking nothing. He
wrote on the tablets the words of the
covenant—the Ten Commandments.

Moses Goes Down from Mount Sinai

29 When Moses went down from Mount
Sinai carrying the Ten Commandments,
his face was shining because he had been
speaking with the LORD; but he did not
know it. 30 Aaron and all the people
looked at Moses and saw that his face
was shining, and they were afraid to go
near him. 31 But Moses called them, and
Aaron and all the leaders of the community went to him, and Moses spoke with
them. 32 After that, all the people of Israel
gathered around him, and Moses gave
them all the laws that the LORD had given
him on Mount Sinai. 33 When Moses had
finished speaking with them, he covered
his face with a veil. 34 Whenever Moses
went into the Tent of the LORD's presence
to speak to the LORD, he would take the
veil off. When he came out, he would tell
the people of Israel everything that he
had been commanded to say, 35 and they
would see that his face was shining.
Then he would put the veil back on until
the next time he went to speak with the
LORD.

Regulations for the Sabbath

35 Moses called together the whole
community of the people of Israel
and said to them, "This is what the LORD
has commanded you to do: 2 You have six
days in which to do your work, but the
seventh day is to be sacred, a solemn day
of rest dedicated to me, the LORD. Anyone
who does any work on that day is to be
put to death. 3 Do not even light a fire in
your homes on the Sabbath."

Offerings for the Sacred Tent

(Exodus 25.1-9)

4 Moses said to all the people of Israel,
"This is what the LORD has commanded:
5 Make an offering to the LORD. Everyone
who wishes to do so is to bring an offering of gold, silver, or bronze; 6 fine linen;
blue, purple, and red wool; cloth made of
goats' hair; 7 rams' skin dyed red; fine
leather; acacia wood; 8 oil for the lamps;
spices for the anointing oil and for the
sweet-smelling incense; 9 carnelians and
other jewels to be set in the High Priest's
ephod and in his breastpiece.

Articles for the Tent of the LORD's Presence

(Exodus 39.32-43)

10 "All the skilled workers among you
are to come and make everything that
the LORD commanded: 11 the Tent, its covering and its outer covering, its hooks
and its frames, its crossbars, its posts,
and its bases; 12 the Covenant Box, its
poles, its lid, and the curtain to screen it
off; 13 the table, its poles, and all its equipment; the bread offered to God; 14 the
lampstand for the light and its equipment; the lamps with their oil; 15 the altar
for burning incense and its poles; the
anointing oil; the sweet-smelling incense; the curtain for the entrance of the
Tent; 16 the altar on which to burn offerings, with its bronze grating attached, its
poles, and all its equipment; the washbasin and its base; 17 the curtains for the
enclosure, its posts and bases; the curtain for the entrance of the enclosure;
18 the Tent pegs and ropes for the Tent
and the enclosure; 19 and the magnificent
garments the priests are to wear when
they serve in the Holy Place—the sacred
clothes for Aaron the priest and for his
sons."

The People Bring Their Offerings

20 All the people of Israel left, 21 and
everyone who wished to do so brought
an offering to the LORD for making the
Tent of the LORD's presence. They
brought everything needed for use in
worship and for making the priestly garments. 22 All who wanted to, both men
and women, brought decorative pins,
earrings, rings, necklaces, and all kinds
of gold jewelry and dedicated them to the
LORD. 23 Everyone who had fine linen;

blue, purple, or red wool; cloth of goats' hair; rams' skin dyed red; or fine leather, brought it. 24 All who were able to contribute silver or bronze brought their offering for the LORD, and all who had acacia wood which could be used for any of the work brought it. 25 All the skilled women brought fine linen thread and thread of blue, purple, and red wool, which they had made. 26 They also made thread of goats' hair. 27 The leaders brought carnelians and other jewels to be set in the ephod and the breastpiece 28 and spices and oil for the lamps, for the anointing oil, and for the sweet-smelling incense. 29 All the people of Israel who wanted to brought their offering to the LORD for the work which he had commanded Moses to do.

Workers to Make the Tent of the LORD's Presence

(Exodus 31.1-11)

30 Moses said to the Israelites, "The LORD has chosen Bezalel, the son of Uri and grandson of Hur from the tribe of Judah. 31 God has filled him with his power[k] and given him skill, ability, and understanding for every kind of artistic work, 32 for planning skillful designs and working them in gold, silver, and bronze; 33 for cutting jewels to be set; for carving wood; and for every other kind of artistic work. 34 The LORD has given to him and to Oholiab son of Ahisamach, from the tribe of Dan, the ability to teach their crafts to others. 35 He has given them skill in all kinds of work done by engravers, designers, and weavers of fine linen; blue, purple, and red wool; and other cloth. They are able to do all kinds of work and are skillful designers.

36 "Bezalel, Oholiab, and all the other workers to whom the LORD has given skill and understanding, who know how to make everything needed to build the sacred Tent, are to make everything just as the LORD has commanded."

The People Bring Many Gifts

2 Moses called Bezalel, Oholiab, and all the other skilled men to whom the LORD had given ability and who were willing to help, and Moses told them to start working. 3 They received from him all the offerings which the Israelites had brought for constructing the sacred Tent. But the people of Israel continued to bring Moses their offerings every morning. 4 Then the skilled men who were doing the work went 5 and told Moses, "The people are bringing more than is needed for the work which the LORD commanded to be done."

6 So Moses sent a command throughout the camp that no one was to make any further contribution for the sacred Tent; so the people did not bring any more. 7 What had already been brought was more than enough to finish all the work.

Making the Tent of the LORD's Presence

(Exodus 26.1-37)

8 The most skilled men among those doing the work made the Tent of the LORD's presence. They made it out of ten pieces of fine linen woven with blue, purple, and red wool and embroidered with figures of winged creatures. 9 Each piece was the same size, 14 yards long and 2 yards wide. 10 They sewed five of them together in one set and did the same with the other five. 11 They made loops of blue cloth on the edge of the outside piece in each set. 12 They put fifty loops on the first piece of the first set and fifty loops matching them on the last piece of the second set. 13 They made fifty gold hooks, with which to join the two sets into one piece.

14 Then they made a cover for the Tent out of eleven pieces of cloth made of goats' hair. 15 They made them all the same size, 15 yards long and 2 yards wide. 16 They sewed five of them together in one set and the other six in another set. 17 They put fifty loops on the edge of the last piece of one set and fifty loops on the edge of the other set. 18 They made fifty bronze hooks to join the two sets, so as to form one cover. 19 They made two more coverings, one of rams' skin dyed red and the other of fine leather, to serve as an outer cover.

20 They made upright frames of acacia wood for the Tent. 21 Each frame was 15 feet tall and 27 inches wide, 22 with two matching projections, so that the frames could be joined together. All the frames had these projections. 23 They made

[k] power; *or* spirit.

twenty frames for the south side 24 and
forty silver bases to go under them, two
bases under each frame to hold its two
projections. 25 They made twenty frames
for the north side of the Tent 26 and forty
silver bases, two under each frame. 27 For
the back of the Tent, on the west, they
made six frames 28 and two frames for
the corners. 29 These corner frames were
joined at the bottom and connected all
the way to the top. The two frames that
formed the two corners were made in
this way. 30 So there were eight frames
and sixteen silver bases, two under each
frame.

31 They made fifteen crossbars of acacia wood, five for the frames on one side
of the Tent, 32 five for the frames on the
other side, and five for the frames on the
west end, at the back. 33 The middle
crossbar, set halfway up the frames, extended from one end of the Tent to the
other. 34 They covered the frames with
gold and fitted them with gold rings to
hold the crossbars, which were also covered with gold.

35 They made a curtain of fine linen,
woven with blue, purple, and red wool
and embroidered it with figures of
winged creatures. 36 They made four
posts of acacia wood to hold the curtain,
covered them with gold, and fitted them
with gold hooks. Then they made four
silver bases to hold the posts. 37 For the
entrance of the Tent they made a curtain
of fine linen woven with blue, purple,
and red wool and decorated with embroidery. 38 For this curtain they made five
posts fitted with hooks, covered their
tops and their rods with gold, and made
five bronze bases for the posts.

Making the Covenant Box

(Exodus 25.10-22)

37 Bezalel made the Covenant Box
out of acacia wood, 45 inches
long, 27 inches wide, and 27 inches high.
2 He covered it with pure gold inside and
out and put a gold border all around it.
3 He made four carrying rings of gold for
it and attached them to its four feet, with
two rings on each side. 4 He made carrying poles of acacia wood, covered them
with gold, 5 and put them through the
rings on each side of the Box. 6 He made
a lid of pure gold, 45 inches long and 27
inches wide. 7 He made two winged creatures of hammered gold, 8 one for each
end of the lid. He made them so that they
formed one piece with the lid. 9 The
winged creatures faced each other
across the lid, and their outspread wings
covered it.

Making the Table for the Bread Offered to God

(Exodus 25.23-30)

10 He made the table out of acacia
wood, 36 inches long, 18 inches wide,
and 27 inches high. 11 He covered it with
pure gold and put a gold border around
it. 12 He made a rim 3 inches wide around
it and put a gold border around the rim.
13 He made four carrying rings of gold for
it and put them at the four corners, where
the legs were. 14 The rings to hold the
poles for carrying the table were placed
near the rim. 15 He made the poles of acacia wood and covered them with gold.
16 He made the dishes of pure gold for
the table: the plates, the cups, the jars,
and the bowls to be used for the wine
offering.

Making the Lampstand

(Exodus 25.31-40)

17 He made the lampstand of pure gold.
He made its base and its shaft of hammered gold; its decorative flowers, including buds and petals, formed one
piece with it. 18 Six branches extended
from its sides, three from each side.
19 Each of the six branches had three decorative flowers shaped like almond blossoms with buds and petals. 20 The shaft
of the lampstand had four decorative
flowers shaped like almond blossoms
with buds and petals. 21 There was one
bud below each of the three pairs of
branches. 22 The buds, the branches, and
the lampstand were a single piece of pure
hammered gold. 23 He made seven lamps
for the lampstand, and he made its tongs
and trays of pure gold. 24 He used
seventy-five pounds of pure gold to make
the lampstand and all its equipment.

Making the Altar for Burning Incense

(Exodus 30.1-5)

25 He made an altar out of acacia wood,
for burning incense. It was square, 18
inches long and 18 inches wide, and it
was 36 inches high. Its projections at the
four corners formed one piece with it.

26 He covered its top, all four sides, and
its projections with pure gold and put a
gold border around it. 27 He made two
gold carrying rings for it and attached
them below the border on the two sides,
to hold the poles with which it was to be
carried. 28 He made the poles of acacia
wood and covered them with gold.

Making the Anointing Oil and the Incense

(Exodus 30.22-38)

29 He also made the sacred anointing
oil and the pure sweet-smelling incense,
mixed like perfume.

Making the Altar for Burning Offerings

(Exodus 27.1-8)

38 For burning offerings, he made
an altar out of acacia wood. It
was square, 7½ feet long and 7½ feet
wide, and it was 4½ feet high. 2 He made
the projections at the top of the four corners, so that they formed one piece with
the altar. He covered it all with bronze.
3 He also made all the equipment for the
altar: the pans, the shovels, the bowls,
the hooks, and the fire pans. All this
equipment was made of bronze. 4 He
made a bronze grating and put it under
the rim of the altar, so that it reached
halfway up the altar. 5 He made four carrying rings and put them on the four corners. 6 He made carrying poles of acacia
wood, covered them with bronze, 7 and
put them in the rings on each side of the
altar. The altar was made of boards and
was hollow.

Making the Bronze Basin

(Exodus 30.18)

8 He made the bronze basin and its
bronze base out of the mirrors belonging
to the women who served at the entrance
of the Tent of the LORD's presence.

The Enclosure for the Tent of the LORD's Presence

(Exodus 27.9-19)

9 For the Tent of the LORD's presence he
made the enclosure out of fine linen curtains. On the south side the curtains were
50 yards long, 10 supported by twenty
bronze posts in twenty bronze bases,
with hooks and rods made of silver.
11 The enclosure was the same on the
north side. 12 On the west side there were
curtains 25 yards long, with ten posts
and ten bases and with hooks and rods
made of silver. 13 On the east side, where
the entrance was, the enclosure was also
25 yards wide. 14-15 On each side of the
entrance there were 7½ yards of curtains, with three posts and three bases.
16 All the curtains around the enclosure
were made of fine linen. 17 The bases for
the posts were made of bronze, and the
hooks, the rods, and the covering of the
tops of the posts were made of silver. All
the posts around the enclosure were connected with silver rods. 18 The curtain for
the entrance of the enclosure was made
of fine linen woven with blue, purple,
and red wool and decorated with embroidery. It was 10 yards long and 2½ yards
high, like the curtains of the enclosure.
19 It was supported by four posts in four
bronze bases. Their hooks, the covering
of their tops, and their rods were made of
silver. 20 All the pegs for the Tent and for
the surrounding enclosure were made of
bronze.

Metals Used in the Tent of the LORD's Presence

21 Here is a list of the amounts of the
metals used in the Tent of the LORD's
presence, where the two stone tablets
were kept on which the Ten Commandments were written. The list was ordered
by Moses and made by the Levites who
worked under the direction of Ithamar
son of Aaron the priest.
22 Bezalel, the son of Uri and grandson
of Hur from the tribe of Judah, made
everything that the LORD had commanded. 23 His helper, Oholiab son of
Ahisamach, from the tribe of Dan, was
an engraver, a designer, and a weaver of
fine linen and of blue, purple, and red
wool.
24 All the gold that had been dedicated
to the LORD for the sacred Tent weighed
2,195 pounds, weighed according to the
official standard. 25 The silver from the
census of the community weighed 7,550
pounds, weighed according to the official standard. 26 This amount equaled the
total paid by all persons enrolled in the
census, each one paying the required
amount, weighed according to the official standard. There were 603,550 men
twenty years old or older enrolled in the

census. 27 Of the silver, 7,500 pounds
were used to make the hundred bases for
the sacred Tent and for the curtain, 75
pounds for each base. 28 With the remaining 50 pounds of silver Bezalel made the
rods, the hooks for the posts, and the
covering for their tops. 29 The bronze
which was dedicated to the LORD
amounted to 5,310 pounds. 30 With it he
made the bases for the entrance of the
Tent of the LORD's presence, the bronze
altar with its bronze grating, all the
equipment for the altar, 31 the bases for
the surrounding enclosure and for the
entrance of the enclosure, and all the
pegs for the Tent and the surrounding
enclosure.

Making the Garments for the Priests

(Exodus 28.1-14)

39 With the blue, purple, and red
wool they made the magnificent
garments which the priests were to wear
when they served in the Holy Place. They
made the priestly garments for Aaron, as
the LORD had commanded Moses.

2 They made the ephod of fine linen;
blue, purple, and red wool; and gold
thread. 3 They hammered out sheets of
gold and cut them into thin strips to be
worked into the fine linen and into the
blue, purple, and red wool. 4 They made
two shoulder straps for the ephod and
attached them to its sides, so that it could
be fastened. 5 The finely woven belt,
made of the same materials, was attached to the ephod so as to form one
piece with it, as the LORD had commanded Moses. 6 They prepared the carnelians and mounted them in gold
settings; they were skillfully engraved
with the names of the twelve sons of Jacob. 7 They put them on the shoulder
straps of the ephod to represent the
twelve tribes of Israel, just as the LORD
had commanded Moses.

Making the Breastpiece

(Exodus 28.15-30)

8 They made the breastpiece of the
same materials as the ephod and with
similar embroidery. 9 It was square and
folded double, 9 inches long and 9 inches
wide. 10 They mounted four rows of precious stones on it: in the first row they
mounted a ruby, a topaz, and a garnet;
11 in the second row, an emerald, a sapphire, and a diamond; 12 in the third row,
a turquoise, an agate, and an amethyst;
13 and in the fourth row, a beryl, a carnelian, and a jasper. These were mounted in
gold settings. 14 Each of the twelve stones
had engraved on it the name of one of the
sons of Jacob, in order to represent the
twelve tribes of Israel. 15 For the breastpiece they made chains of pure gold,
twisted like cords. 16 They made two gold
settings and two gold rings and attached
the two rings to the upper corners of the
breastpiece. 17 They fastened the two
gold cords to the two rings 18 and fastened the other two ends of the cords to
the two settings and in this way attached
them in front to the shoulder straps of the
ephod. 19 They made two rings of gold
and attached them to the lower corners
of the breastpiece, on the inside edge
next to the ephod. 20 They made two
more gold rings and attached them to the
lower part of the front of the two shoulder straps of the ephod, near the seam
and above the finely woven belt. 21 Just
as the LORD had commanded Moses, they
tied the rings of the breastpiece to the
rings of the ephod with a blue cord, so
that the breastpiece rested above the belt
and did not come loose.

Making the Other Priestly Garments

(Exodus 28.31-43)

22 The robe that goes under the ephod
was made entirely of blue wool. 23 The
hole for the head was reinforced with a
woven binding to keep it from tearing.
24-26 All around its lower hem they put
pomegranates of fine linen and of blue,
purple, and red wool, alternating with
bells of pure gold, just as the LORD had
commanded Moses.

27 They made the shirts for Aaron and
his sons, 28 and the turban, the caps, the
linen shorts, 29 and the sash of fine linen
and of blue, purple, and red wool, decorated with embroidery, as the LORD had
commanded Moses. 30 They made the ornament, the sacred sign of dedication,
out of pure gold, and they engraved on it
"Dedicated to the LORD." 31 They tied it to
the front of the turban with a blue cord,
just as the LORD had commanded Moses.

The Completion of the Work

(Exodus 35.10-19)

32 All the work on the Tent of the LORD's
presence was finally completed. The Is-

raelites made everything just as the LORD
had commanded Moses. 33 They brought
to Moses the Tent and all its equipment,
its hooks, its frames, its crossbars, its
posts, and its bases; 34 the covering of
rams' skin dyed red; the covering of fine
leather; the curtain; 35 the Covenant Box
containing the stone tablets, its poles,
and its lid; 36 the table and all its equipment, and the bread offered to God; 37 the
lampstand of pure gold, its lamps, all its
equipment, and the oil for the lamps;
38 the gold altar; the anointing oil; the
sweet-smelling incense; the curtain for
the entrance of the Tent; 39 the bronze
altar with its bronze grating, its poles,
and all its equipment; the washbasin and
its base; 40 the curtains for the enclosure
and its posts and bases; the curtain for
the entrance of the enclosure and its
ropes; the Tent pegs; all the equipment to
be used in the Tent; 41 and the magnificent garments the priests were to wear in
the Holy Place—the sacred clothes for
Aaron the priest and for his sons. 42 The
Israelites had done all the work just as
the LORD had commanded Moses.
43 Moses examined everything and saw
that they had made it all just as the LORD
had commanded. So Moses blessed
them.

Setting Up and Dedicating the Tent of the LORD's Presence

40 The LORD said to Moses, 2 "On the
first day of the first month set up
the Tent of the LORD's presence. 3 Place in
it the Covenant Box containing the Ten
Commandments and put the curtain in
front of it. 4 Bring in the table and place
the equipment on it. Also bring in the
lampstand and set up the lamps on it.
5 Put the gold altar for burning incense in
front of the Covenant Box and hang the
curtain at the entrance of the Tent. 6 Put
in front of the Tent the altar for burning
offerings. 7 Put the washbasin between
the Tent and the altar and fill it with water. 8 Put up the surrounding enclosure
and hang the curtain at its entrance.

9 "Then dedicate the Tent and all its
equipment by anointing it with the sacred oil, and it will be holy. 10 Next, dedicate the altar and all its equipment by
anointing it, and it will be completely
holy. 11 Also dedicate the washbasin and
its base in the same way.

12 "Bring Aaron and his sons to the entrance of the Tent, and have them take a
ritual bath. 13 Dress Aaron in the priestly
garments, anoint him, and in this way
consecrate him, so that he can serve me
as priest. 14 Bring his sons and put the
shirts on them. 15 Then anoint them, just
as you anointed their father, so that they
can serve me as priests. This anointing
will make them priests for all time to
come."

16 Moses did everything just as the
LORD had commanded. 17 So on the first
day of the first month of the second year
after they left Egypt, the Tent of the
LORD's presence was set up. 18 Moses put
down its bases, set up its frames, attached its crossbars, and put up its posts.
19 He spread out the covering over the
Tent and put the outer covering over it,
just as the LORD had commanded. 20 Then
he took the two stone tablets and put
them in the Covenant Box. He put the
poles in the rings of the Box and put the
lid on it. 21 Then he put the Box in the
Tent and hung up the curtain. In this way
he screened off the Covenant Box, just as
the LORD had commanded.

22 He put the table in the Tent, on the
north side outside the curtain, 23 and
placed on it the bread offered to the LORD,
just as the LORD had commanded. 24 He
put the lampstand in the Tent, on the
south side, opposite the table, 25 and
there in the LORD's presence he lit the
lamps, just as the LORD had commanded.
26 He put the gold altar in the Tent, in
front of the curtain, 27 and burned the
sweet-smelling incense, just as the LORD
had commanded. 28 He hung the curtain
at the entrance of the Tent, 29 and there in
front of the curtain he placed the altar for
burning offerings. On it he sacrificed the
burnt offering and the grain offering, just
as the LORD had commanded. 30 He put
the washbasin between the Tent and the
altar and filled it with water. 31 Moses,
Aaron, and his sons washed their hands
and their feet there 32 whenever they
went into the Tent or to the altar, just as
the LORD had commanded. 33 Moses set
up the enclosure around the Tent and the
altar and hung the curtain at the entrance of the enclosure. So he finished all
the work.

The Cloud over the Tent of the LORD's Presence

(Numbers 9.15-23)

34 Then the cloud covered the Tent and
the dazzling light of the LORD's presence
filled it. 35 Because of this, Moses could
not go into the Tent. 36 The Israelites moved their camp to another place
only when the cloud lifted from the
Tent. 37 As long as the cloud stayed
there, they did not move their camp.
38 During all their wanderings they
could see the cloud of the LORD's presence over the Tent during the day and
a fire burning above it during the
night.

LEVITICUS

Introduction

Leviticus contains regulations for worship and religious ceremonies in ancient Israel, and for the priests who were responsible for carrying out these instructions.

The main theme of the book is the holiness of God and the ways in which his people were to worship and live so as to maintain their relationship with "the holy God of Israel."

The best known words from the book, found in 19.18, are those which Jesus called the second great commandment: "Love your neighbors as you love yourself."

Outline of Contents

Laws about offerings and sacrifices 1.1–7.38
The ordination of Aaron and his sons as priests 8.1–10.20
Laws about ritual cleanness and uncleanness 11.1–15.33
The Day of Atonement 16.1-34
Laws about holiness in life and worship 17.1–27.34

Sacrifices Burned Whole

1 The LORD called to Moses from the
Tent of the LORD's presence and
gave him the following rules 2 for the Israelites to observe when they offer their
sacrifices.
When you offer an animal sacrifice, it
may be one of your cattle or one of your
sheep or goats. 3 If you are offering one of
your cattle as a burnt offering, you must
bring a bull without any defects. You
must present it at the entrance of the
Tent of the LORD's presence so that the
LORD will accept you. 4 You shall put your
hand on its head, and it will be accepted
as a sacrifice to take away your sins.
5 You shall kill the bull there, and the
Aaronite priests shall present the blood
to the LORD and then throw it against all
four sides of the altar located at the entrance of the Tent. 6 Then you shall skin
the animal and cut it up, 7 and the priests
shall arrange firewood on the altar and
light it. 8 They shall put on the fire the
pieces of the animal, including the head
and the fat. 9 You must wash the internal
organs and the hind legs, and the officiating priest will burn the whole sacrifice
on the altar. The odor of this food offering is pleasing to the LORD.
10 If you are offering one of your sheep
or goats, it must be a male without any
defects. 11 You shall kill it on the north
side of the altar, and the priests shall
throw its blood on all four sides of the
altar. 12 After you cut it up, the officiating
priest shall put on the fire all the parts,
including the head and the fat. 13 You
must wash the internal organs and the
hind legs, and the priest will present the
sacrifice to the LORD and burn all of it on
the altar. The odor of this food offering is
pleasing to the LORD.
14 If you are offering a bird as a burnt
offering, it must be a dove or a pigeon.
15 The priest shall present it at the altar,
wring its neck, and burn its head on the
altar. Its blood shall be drained out
against the side of the altar. 16 He shall
remove the crop and its contents and
throw them away on the east side of the
altar where the ashes are put. 17 He shall
take hold of its wings and tear its body
open, without tearing the wings off, and
then burn it whole on the altar. The odor
of this food offering is pleasing to the
LORD.

Grain Offerings

2 When any of you present an offering of grain to the LORD, you must
first grind it into flour. You must put

olive oil and incense on it 2 and bring it to the Aaronite priests. The officiating priest shall take a handful of the flour and oil and all of the incense and burn it on the altar as a token that it has all been offered to the LORD. The odor of this food offering is pleasing to the LORD. 3 The rest of the grain offering belongs to the priests; it is very holy, since it is taken from the food offered to the LORD.

4 If the offering is bread baked in an oven, it must be made without yeast. It may be thick loaves made of flour mixed with olive oil or thin cakes brushed with olive oil.

5 If the offering is bread cooked on a griddle, it is to be made of flour mixed with olive oil but without yeast. 6 Crumble it up and pour the oil on it when you present it as an offering.

7 If the offering is bread cooked in a pan, it is to be made of flour and olive oil. 8 Bring it as an offering to the LORD and present it to the priest, who will take it to the altar. 9 The priest will take part of it as a token that it has all been offered to the LORD, and he will burn it on the altar. The odor of this food offering is pleasing to the LORD. 10 The rest of the offering belongs to the priests; it is very holy, since it is taken from the food offered to the LORD.

11 None of the grain offerings which you present to the LORD may be made with yeast; you must never use yeast or honey in food offered to the LORD. 12 An offering of the first grain that you harvest each year shall be brought to the LORD, but it is not to be burned on the altar. 13 Put salt on every grain offering, because salt represents the covenant between you and God. (You must put salt on all your offerings.) 14 When you bring to the LORD an offering of the first grain harvested, offer roasted grain or ground meal. 15 Add olive oil and put incense on it. 16 The priest will burn that part of the meal and oil that is to serve as a token, and also all the incense, as a food offering to the LORD.

Fellowship Offerings

3 When any of you offer one of your cattle as a fellowship offering, it is to be a bull or a cow without any defects. 2 You shall put your hand on the head of the animal and kill it at the entrance of the Tent of the LORD's presence. The Aaronite priests shall throw the blood against all four sides of the altar 3 and present the following parts of the animal as a food offering to the LORD: all the fat on the internal organs, 4 the kidneys and the fat on them, and the best part of the liver. 5 The priests shall burn all this on the altar along with the burnt offerings. The odor of this food offering is pleasing to the LORD.

6 If a sheep or goat is used as a fellowship offering, it may be male or female, but it must be without any defects. 7 If you offer a sheep, 8 you shall put your hand on its head and kill it in front of the Tent. The priests shall throw its blood against all four sides of the altar 9 and present the following parts of the animal as a food offering to the LORD: the fat, the entire fat tail cut off near the backbone, all the fat covering the internal organs, 10 the kidneys and the fat on them, and the best part of the liver. 11 The officiating priest shall burn all this on the altar as a food offering to the LORD.

12 If you offer a goat, 13 you shall put your hand on its head and kill it in front of the Tent. The priests shall throw its blood against all four sides of the altar 14 and present the following parts as a food offering to the LORD: all the fat on the internal organs, 15 the kidneys and the fat on them, and the best part of the liver. 16 The priest shall burn all this on the altar as a food offering pleasing to the LORD. All the fat belongs to the LORD. 17 No Israelite may eat any fat or any blood; this is a rule to be kept forever by all Israelites wherever they live.

Offerings for Unintentional Sins

4 The LORD commanded Moses 2 to tell the people of Israel that anyone who sinned and broke any of the LORD's commands without intending to, would have to observe the following rules.

3 If it is the High Priest who sins and so brings guilt on the people, he shall present a young bull without any defects and sacrifice it to the LORD for his sin. 4 He shall bring the bull to the entrance of the Tent, put his hand on its head, and kill it

there in the LORD's presence. 5 Then the
High Priest shall take some of the bull's
blood and carry it into the Tent. 6 He shall
dip his finger in the blood and sprinkle it
in front of the sacred curtain seven times.
7 Then he shall put some of the blood on
the projections at the corners of the incense altar in the Tent. He shall pour out
the rest of the blood at the base of the
altar used for burning sacrifices, which
is at the entrance of the Tent. 8 From this
bull he shall take all the fat, the fat on the
internal organs, 9 the kidneys and the fat
on them, and the best part of the liver.
10 The priest shall take this fat and burn
it on the altar used for the burnt offerings, just as he does with the fat from the
animal killed for the fellowship offering.
11 But he shall take its skin, all its flesh,
its head, its legs, and its internal organs,
including the intestines, 12 carry it all
outside the camp to the ritually clean
place where the ashes are poured out,
and there he shall burn it on a wood
fire.

13 If it is the whole community of Israel
that sins and becomes guilty of breaking
one of the LORD's commands without intending to, 14 then as soon as the sin becomes known, the community shall
bring a young bull as a sin offering. They
shall bring it to the Tent of the LORD's
presence; 15 the leaders of the community
shall put their hands on its head, and it
shall be killed there. 16 The High Priest
shall take some of the bull's blood into
the Tent, 17 dip his finger in it, and sprinkle it in front of the curtain seven times.
18 He shall put some of the blood on the
projections at the corners of the incense
altar inside the Tent and pour out the rest
of it at the base of the altar used for burning sacrifices, which is at the entrance of
the Tent. 19 Then he shall take all its fat
and burn it on the altar. 20 He shall do the
same thing with this bull as he does with
the bull for the sin offering, and in this
way he shall make the sacrifice for the
people's sin, and they will be forgiven.
21 Then he shall take the bull outside the
camp and burn it, just as he burns the
bull offered for his own sin. This is an
offering to take away the sin of the
community.

22 If it is a ruler who sins and becomes
guilty of breaking one of the LORD's commands without intending to, 23 then as
soon as the sin is called to his attention,
he shall bring as his offering a male goat
without any defects. 24 He shall put his
hand on its head and kill it on the north
side of the altar, where the animals for
the burnt offerings are killed. This is an
offering to take away sin. 25 The priest
shall dip his finger in the blood of the
animal, put it on the projections at the
corners of the altar, and pour out the rest
of it at the base of the altar. 26 Then he
shall burn all of its fat on the altar, just
as he burns the fat of the animals killed
for the fellowship offerings. In this way
the priest shall offer the sacrifice for the
sin of the ruler, and he will be forgiven.

27 If any of you people sin and become
guilty of breaking one of the LORD's commands without intending to, 28 then as
soon as the sin is called to your attention,
you shall bring as your offering a female
goat without any defects. 29 You shall put
your hand on its head and kill it on the
north side of the altar, where the animals
for the burnt offerings are killed. 30 The
priest shall dip his finger in the blood of
the animal, put it on the projections at
the corners of the altar, and pour out the
rest of it at the base of the altar. 31 Then
he shall remove all its fat, just as the fat
is removed from the animals killed for
the fellowship offerings, and he shall
burn it on the altar as an odor pleasing to
the LORD. In this way the priest shall offer
the sacrifice for the man's sin, and he will
be forgiven.

32 If you bring a sheep as a sin offering,
it must be a female without any defects.
33 You shall put your hand on its head
and kill it on the north side of the altar,
where the animals for the burnt offerings
are killed. 34 The priest shall dip his finger in the blood of the animal, put it on
the projections at the corners of the altar,
and pour out the rest of it at the base of
the altar. 35 Then he shall remove all its
fat, just as the fat is removed from the
sheep killed for the fellowship offerings,
and he shall burn it on the altar along
with the food offerings given to the LORD.
In this way the priest shall offer the sacrifice for your sin, and you will be
forgiven.

Cases Requiring Sin Offerings

5 Sin offerings are required in the following cases.
If you are officially summoned to give
evidence in court and do not give information about something you have seen
or heard, you must suffer the consequences.
2 If you unintentionally touch anything
ritually unclean, such as a dead animal,
you are unclean and guilty as soon as
you realize what you have done.
3 If you unintentionally touch anything
of human origin that is unclean, whatever it may be, you are guilty as soon as
you realize what you have done.
4 If you make a careless vow, no matter
what it is about, you are guilty as soon as
you realize what you have done.
5 When you are guilty, you must confess the sin, 6 and as the penalty for your
sin you must bring to the LORD a female
sheep or goat as an offering. The priest
shall offer the sacrifice for your sin.
7 If you cannot afford a sheep or a goat,
you shall bring to the LORD as the payment for your sin two doves or two pigeons, one for a sin offering and the
other for a burnt offering. 8 You shall
bring them to the priest, who will first
offer the bird for the sin offering. He will
break its neck without pulling off its
head 9 and sprinkle some of its blood
against the side of the altar. The rest of
the blood will be drained out at the base
of the altar. This is an offering to take
away sin. 10 Then he shall offer the second bird as a burnt offering, according to
the regulations. In this way the priest
shall offer the sacrifice for your sin, and
you will be forgiven.
11 If you cannot afford two doves or
two pigeons, you shall bring two pounds
of flour as a sin offering. You shall not
put any olive oil or any incense on it,
because it is a sin offering, not a grain
offering. 12 You shall bring it to the priest,
who will take a handful of it as a token
that it has all been offered to the LORD,
and he will burn it on the altar as a food
offering. It is an offering to take away
sin. 13 In this way the priest shall offer the
sacrifice for your sin, and you will be
forgiven. The rest of the flour belongs to
the priest, just as in the case of a grain
offering.

Repayment Offerings

14 The LORD gave the following regulations to Moses. 15 If any of you sin unintentionally by failing to hand over the
payments that are sacred to the LORD,
you shall bring as your repayment offering to the LORD a male sheep or goat without any defects. Its value is to be
determined according to the official
standard. 16 You must make the payments you have failed to hand over and
must pay an additional 20 percent. You
shall give it to the priest, and the priest
shall offer the animal as a sacrifice for
your sin, and you will be forgiven.
17 If any of you sin unintentionally by
breaking any of the LORD's commands,
you are guilty and must pay the penalty.
18 You must bring to the priest as a repayment offering a male sheep or goat without any defects. Its value is to be
determined according to the official
standard. The priest shall offer the sacrifice for the sin which you committed unintentionally, and you will be forgiven.
19 It is a repayment offering for the sin
you committed against the LORD.
6 The LORD gave the following regulations to Moses. 2 An offering is to be
made if any of you sin against the LORD
by refusing to return what another Israelite has left as a deposit or by stealing
something from him or by cheating him
3 or by lying about something that has
been lost and swearing that you did not
find it. 4-5 When you sin in any of these
ways, you must repay whatever you got
by dishonest means. On the day you are
found guilty, you must repay the owner
in full, plus an additional 20 percent.
6 You shall bring to the priest as your
repayment offering to the LORD a male
sheep or goat without any defects. Its
value is to be determined according to
the official standard. 7 The priest shall offer the sacrifice for your sin, and you will
be forgiven.

Sacrifices Burned Whole

8 The LORD commanded Moses 9 to give
Aaron and his sons the following regulations for burnt offerings. A burnt offering is to be left on the altar all night long,
and the fire is to be kept burning. 10 Then
the priest, wearing his linen robe and
linen shorts, shall remove the greasy
ashes left on the altar and put them at the

side of the altar. 11 Then he shall change his clothes and take the ashes outside the camp to a ritually clean place. 12 The fire on the altar must be kept burning and never allowed to go out. Every morning the priest shall put firewood on it, arrange the burnt offering on it, and burn the fat of the fellowship offering. 13 The fire must always be kept burning on the altar and never allowed to go out.

Grain Offerings

14 The following are the regulations for grain offerings. An Aaronite priest shall present the grain offering to the LORD in front of the altar. 15 Then he shall take a handful of the flour and oil, and the incense on it, and burn it on the altar as a token that all of it has been offered to the LORD. The odor of this offering is pleasing to the LORD. 16-17 The priests shall eat the rest of it. It shall be made into bread baked without yeast and eaten in a holy place, the courtyard of the Tent of the LORD's presence. The LORD has given it to the priests as their part of the food offerings. It is very holy, like the sin offerings and the repayment offerings. 18 For all time to come any of the male descendants of Aaron may eat it as their continuing share of the food offered to the LORD. Anyone else who touches a food offering will be harmed by the power of its holiness.

19 The LORD gave Moses the following regulations 20 for the ordination of an Aaronite priest. On the day he is ordained, he shall present as an offering to the LORD two pounds of flour (the same amount as the daily grain offering), half in the morning and half in the evening. 21 It is to be mixed with oil and cooked on a griddle and then crumbled and presented as a grain offering, an odor pleasing to the LORD. 22 For all time to come this offering is to be made by every descendant of Aaron who is serving as High Priest. It shall be completely burned as a sacrifice to the LORD. 23 No part of a grain offering that a priest makes may be eaten; all of it must be burned.

Sin Offerings

24 The LORD commanded Moses 25 to give Aaron and his sons the following regulations for sin offerings. The animal for a sin offering shall be killed on the north side of the altar, where the animals for the burnt offerings are killed. This is a very holy offering. 26 The priest who sacrifices the animal shall eat it in a holy place, the courtyard of the Tent of the LORD's presence. 27 Anyone or anything that touches the flesh of the animal will be harmed by the power of its holiness. If any article of clothing is spattered with the animal's blood, it must be washed in a holy place. 28 Any clay pot in which the meat is boiled must be broken, and if a metal pot is used, it must be scrubbed and rinsed with water. 29 Any male of the priestly families may eat this offering; it is very holy. 30 But if any of the blood is brought into the Tent and used in the ritual to take away sin, the animal must not be eaten; it must be burned.

Repayment Offerings

7 The following are the regulations for repayment offerings, which are very holy. 2 The animal for this offering is to be killed on the north side of the altar, where the animals for the burnt offerings are killed, and its blood is to be thrown against all four sides of the altar. 3 All of its fat shall be removed and offered on the altar: the fat tail, the fat covering the internal organs, 4 the kidneys and the fat on them, and the best part of the liver. 5 The priest shall burn all the fat on the altar as a food offering to the LORD. It is a repayment offering. 6 Any male of the priestly families may eat it, but it must be eaten in a holy place, because it is very holy.

7 There is one regulation that applies to both the sin offering and the repayment offering: the meat belongs to the priest who offers the sacrifice. 8 The skin of an animal offered as a burnt offering belongs to the priest who offers the sacrifice. 9 Every grain offering that has been baked in an oven or prepared in a pan or on a griddle belongs to the priest who has offered it to God. 10 But all uncooked grain offerings, whether mixed with oil or dry, belong to all the Aaronite priests and must be shared equally among them.

Fellowship Offerings

11 The following are the regulations for the fellowship offerings presented to the LORD. 12 If you make this offering as a thanksgiving offering to God, you shall present, together with the animal to be sacrificed, an offering of bread made

without yeast: either thick loaves made
of flour mixed with olive oil or thin cakes
brushed with olive oil or cakes made of
flour mixed with olive oil. 13In addition,
you shall offer loaves of bread baked
with yeast. 14You shall present one part
of each kind of bread as a special contribution to the LORD; it belongs to the priest
who takes the blood of the animal and
throws it against the altar. 15The flesh of
the animal must be eaten on the day it is
sacrificed; none of it may be left until the
next morning.

16If you bring a fellowship offering as
fulfillment of a vow or as your own freewill offering, not all of it has to be eaten
on the day it is offered, but any that is left
over may be eaten on the following day.
17Any meat that still remains on the third
day must be burned. 18If any of it is eaten
on the third day, God will not accept your
offering. The offering will not be counted
to your credit but will be considered unclean, and whoever eats it will suffer the
consequences. 19If the meat comes into
contact with anything ritually unclean, it
must not be eaten, but must be burned.

Any of you that are ritually clean may
eat the meat, 20but if any of you who are
not clean eat it, you shall no longer be
considered one of God's people. 21Also,
if you eat the meat of this offering after
you have touched anything ritually unclean, whether from a person or an animal, you shall no longer be considered
one of God's people.

22The LORD gave Moses the following
regulations 23for the people of Israel. No
fat of cattle, sheep, or goats shall be
eaten. 24The fat of an animal that has
died a natural death or has been killed by
a wild animal must not be eaten, but it
may be used for any other purpose.
25Anyone who eats the fat of an animal
that may be offered as a food offering to
the LORD will no longer be considered one
of God's people. 26No matter where the
Israelites live, they must never use the
blood of birds or animals for food.
27Anyone who breaks this law will no
longer be considered one of God's
people.

28The LORD gave Moses the following
regulations 29for the people of Israel.
When any of you offer a fellowship offering you must bring part of it as a special
gift to the LORD, 30bringing it with your
own hands as a food offering. You shall
bring the fat of the animal with its breast
and present it as a special gift to the LORD.
31The priest shall burn the fat on the altar, but the breast shall belong to the
priests. 32The right hind leg of the animal
shall be given as a special contribution
33to the priest who offers the blood and
the fat of the fellowship offering. 34The
breast of the animal is a special gift, and
the right hind leg is a special contribution that the LORD has taken from the
people of Israel and given to the priests.
This is what the people of Israel must
give to the priests for all time to come.
35This is the part of the food offered to
the LORD that was given to Aaron and his
sons on the day they were ordained as
priests. 36On that day the LORD commanded the people of Israel to give them
this part of the offering. It is a regulation
that the people of Israel must obey for all
time to come.

37These, then, are the regulations for
the burnt offerings, the grain offerings,
the sin offerings, the repayment offerings, the ordination offerings, and the
fellowship offerings. 38There on Mount
Sinai in the desert, the LORD gave these
commands to Moses on the day he told
the people of Israel to make their offerings.

The Ordination of Aaron and His Sons

(Exodus 29.1-37)

8 The LORD said to Moses, 2"Take
Aaron and his sons to the entrance
of the Tent of my presence and bring the
priestly garments, the anointing oil, the
young bull for the sin offering, the two
rams, and the basket of unleavened
bread. 3Then call the whole community
together there."

4Moses did as the LORD had commanded, and when the community had
assembled, 5he said to them, "What I am
now about to do is what the LORD has
commanded."

6Moses brought Aaron and his sons
forward and had them take a ritual bath.
7He put the shirt and the robe on Aaron
and the sash around his waist. He put the
ephod[a] on him and fastened it by put-

[a] EPHOD: *See Word List.*

ting its finely woven belt around his
waist. 8 He put the breastpiece on him
and put the Urim and Thummim[b] in it.
9 He placed the turban on his head, and
on the front of it he put the gold ornament, the sacred sign of dedication, just
as the LORD had commanded him.
10 Then Moses took the anointing oil
and put it on the Tent of the LORD's presence and everything that was in it, and in
this way he dedicated it all to the LORD.
11 He took some of the oil and sprinkled
it seven times on the altar and its equipment and on the basin and its base, in
order to dedicate them to the LORD. 12 He
ordained Aaron by pouring some of the
anointing oil on his head. 13 Next, Moses
brought the sons of Aaron forward and
put shirts on them, put sashes around
their waists, and tied caps on their heads,
just as the LORD had commanded.
14 Then Moses brought the young bull
for the sin offering, and Aaron and his
sons put their hands on its head. 15 Moses
killed it and took some of the blood, and
with his finger put it on the projections at
the corners of the altar, in order to dedicate it. He then poured out the rest of the
blood at the base of the altar. In this way
he dedicated it and purified it. 16 Moses
took all the fat on the internal organs, the
best part of the liver, and the kidneys
with the fat on them, and burned it all on
the altar. 17 He took the rest of the bull,
including its skin, flesh, and intestines,
and burned it outside the camp, just as
the LORD had commanded.
18 Next, Moses brought the ram for the
burnt offering, and Aaron and his sons
put their hands on its head. 19 Moses
killed it and threw the blood on all four
sides of the altar. 20-21 He cut the ram in
pieces, washed the internal organs and
the hind legs with water, and burned the
head, the fat, and all the rest of the ram
on the altar, just as the LORD had commanded. This burnt offering was a food
offering, and its odor was pleasing to the
LORD.
22 Then Moses brought the second ram,
which was for the ordination of priests,
and Aaron and his sons put their hands
on its head. 23 Moses killed it and took
some of the blood and put it on the lobe
of Aaron's right ear, on the thumb of his
right hand, and on the big toe of his right
foot. 24 Then he brought Aaron's sons
forward and put some of the blood on the
lobes of their right ears, on the thumbs of
their right hands, and on the big toes of
their right feet. Moses then threw the rest
of the blood on all four sides of the altar.
25 He took the fat, the fat tail, all the fat
covering the internal organs, the best
part of the liver, the kidneys with the fat
on them, and the right hind leg. 26 Then
he took one loaf of bread from the basket
of unleavened bread dedicated to the
LORD, one loaf made with oil, and one
thin cake, and he put them on top of the
fat and the right hind leg. 27 He put all of
this food in the hands of Aaron and his
sons, and they presented it as a special
gift to the LORD. 28 Then Moses took the
food from them and burned it on the altar, on top of the burnt offering, as an
ordination offering. This was a food offering, and its odor was pleasing to the
LORD. 29 Then Moses took the breast and
presented it as a special gift to the LORD.
It was Moses' part of the ordination ram.
Moses did everything just as the LORD
had commanded.
30 Moses took some of the anointing oil
and some of the blood that was on the
altar and sprinkled them on Aaron and
his sons and on their clothes. In this way
he consecrated them and their clothes to
the LORD.
31 Moses said to Aaron and his sons,
"Take the meat to the entrance of the
Tent of the LORD's presence, boil it, and
eat it there with the bread that is in the
basket of ordination offerings, just as the
LORD commanded. 32 Burn up any meat or
bread that is left over. 33 You shall not
leave the entrance of the Tent for seven
days, until your ordination rites are completed. 34 The LORD commanded us to do
what we have done today, in order to
take away your sin. 35 You must stay at
the entrance of the Tent day and night
for seven days, doing what the LORD has
commanded. If you don't, you will die.
This is what the LORD has commanded
me." 36 So Aaron and his sons did everything that the LORD had commanded
through Moses.

[b] URIM AND THUMMIM: *Two objects used by the priest to determine God's will; it is not known precisely how they were used.*

Aaron Offers Sacrifices

9 The day after the ordination rites
were completed, Moses called
Aaron and his sons and the leaders of
Israel. 2He said to Aaron, "Take a young
bull and a ram without any defects and
offer them to the LORD, the bull for a sin
offering and the ram for a burnt offering.
3Then tell the people of Israel to take a
male goat for a sin offering, a one-year-
old calf, and a one-year-old lamb without
any defects for a burnt offering, 4and a
bull and a ram for a fellowship offering.
They are to sacrifice them to the LORD
with the grain offering mixed with oil.
They must do this because the LORD will
appear to them today."
5They brought to the front of the Tent
everything that Moses had commanded,
and the whole community assembled
there to worship the LORD. 6Moses said,
"The LORD has commanded you to do all
this, so that the dazzling light of his presence can appear to you." 7Then he said to
Aaron, "Go to the altar and offer the sin
offering and the burnt offering to take
away your sins and the sins of the people. Present this offering to take away
the sins of the people, just as the LORD
commanded."
8Aaron went to the altar and killed the
young bull which was for his own sin
offering. 9His sons brought him the
blood, and he dipped his finger in it, put
some of it on the projections at the corners of the altar, and poured out the rest
of it at the base of the altar. 10Then he
burned on the altar the fat, the kidneys,
and the best part of the liver, just as the
LORD had commanded Moses. 11But he
burned the meat and the skin outside the
camp.
12He killed the animal which was for
his own burnt offering. His sons brought
him the blood, and he threw it on all four
sides of the altar. 13They handed him the
head and the other pieces of the animal,
and he burned them on the altar. 14Then
he washed the internal organs and the
hind legs and burned them on the altar
on top of the rest of the burnt offering.
15After that, he presented the people's
offerings. He took the goat that was to be
offered for the people's sins, killed it, and
offered it, as he had done with his own
sin offering. 16He also brought the animal for the burnt offering and offered it
according to the regulations. 17He presented the grain offering and took a
handful of flour and burned it on the altar. (This was in addition to the daily
burnt offering.) 18He killed the bull and
the ram as a fellowship offering for the
people. His sons brought him the blood,
and he threw it on all four sides of the
altar. 19Aaron put the fat parts of the bull
and the ram 20on top of the breasts of the
animals and carried it all to the altar. He
burned the fat on the altar 21and presented the breasts and the right hind legs
as the special gift to the LORD for the
priests, as Moses had commanded.
22When Aaron had finished all the sacrifices, he raised his hands over the people and blessed them, and then stepped
down. 23Moses and Aaron went into the
Tent of the LORD's presence, and when
they came out, they blessed the people,
and the dazzling light of the LORD's
presence appeared to all the people.
24Suddenly the LORD sent a fire, and it
consumed the burnt offering and the fat
parts on the altar. When the people saw
it, they all shouted and bowed down with
their faces to the ground.

The Sin of Nadab and Abihu

10 Aaron's sons, Nadab and Abihu,
each took his fire pan, put live
coals in it, added incense, and presented
it to the LORD. But this fire was not holy,
because the LORD had not commanded
them to present it. 2Suddenly the LORD
sent fire, and it burned them to death
there in the presence of the LORD. 3Then
Moses said to Aaron, "This is what the
LORD was speaking about when he said,
'All who serve me must respect my holiness; I will reveal my glory to my people.' "[c] But Aaron remained silent.
4Moses called Mishael and Elzaphan,
the sons of Uzziel, Aaron's uncle, and
said to them, "Come here and carry your
cousins' bodies away from the sacred
Tent and put them outside the camp."
5So they came and took hold of the clothing on the corpses and carried them outside the camp, just as Moses had
commanded.
6Then Moses said to Aaron and to his
sons Eleazar and Ithamar, "Do not leave
your hair uncombed or tear your clothes

[c] I will reveal my glory to my people; *or* my people must honor me.

to show that you are in mourning. If you
do, you will die, and the LORD will be angry with the whole community. But all
other Israelites are allowed to mourn this
death caused by the fire which the LORD
sent. 7 Do not leave the entrance of the
Tent or you will die, because you have
been consecrated by the anointing oil of
the LORD." So they did as Moses said.

Rules for Priests

8 The LORD said to Aaron, 9 "You and
your sons are not to enter the Tent of my
presence after drinking wine or beer; if
you do, you will die. This is a law to be
kept by all your descendants. 10 You must
distinguish between what belongs to
God and what is for general use, between
what is ritually clean and what is unclean. 11 You must teach the people of
Israel all the laws which I have given to
you through Moses."

12 Moses said to Aaron and his two remaining sons, Eleazar and Ithamar,
"Take the grain offering that is left over
from the food offered to the LORD, make
unleavened bread with it and eat it beside the altar, because this offering is
very holy. 13 Eat it in a holy place; it is the
part that belongs to you and your sons
from the food offered to the LORD. That is
what the LORD commanded me. 14 But you
and your families may eat the breast and
the hind leg that are presented as the
special gift and the special contribution
to the LORD for the priests. You may eat
them in any ritually clean place. These
offerings have been given to you and
your children as the part that belongs to
you from the fellowship offerings of the
people of Israel. 15 They shall bring the
hind leg and the breast at the time the
fat is presented as a food offering to
the LORD. These parts belong to you and
your children forever, just as the LORD
commanded."

16 Moses asked about the goat for the
sin offering and learned that it had already been burned. This made him angry
at Eleazar and Ithamar, and he demanded, 17 "Why didn't you eat the sin
offering in a sacred place? It is very holy,
and the LORD has given it to you in order
to take away the sin of the community.
18 Since its blood was not brought into
the sacred Tent, you should have eaten
the sacrifice there, as I commanded."

19 Aaron answered, "If I had eaten the
sin offering today, would the LORD have
approved? The people presented their
sin offering to the LORD today, and they
brought their burnt offering, but still
these terrible things have happened to
me." 20 When Moses heard this, he was
satisfied.

Animals That May Be Eaten

(Deuteronomy 14.3-21)

11 The LORD gave Moses and Aaron
the following regulations 2 for the
people of Israel. You may eat any land
animal 3 that has divided hoofs and that
also chews the cud, 4-6 but you must not
eat camels, rock badgers, or rabbits.
These must be considered unclean; they
chew the cud, but do not have divided
hoofs. 7 Do not eat pigs. They must be
considered unclean; they have divided
hoofs, but do not chew the cud. 8 Do not
eat these animals or even touch their
dead bodies; they are unclean.

9 You may eat any kind of fish that has
fins and scales, 10 but anything living in
the water that does not have fins and
scales must not be eaten. 11 Such creatures must be considered unclean. You
must not eat them or even touch their
dead bodies. 12 You must not eat anything that lives in the water and does not
have fins and scales.

13-19 You must not eat any of the following birds: eagles, owls, hawks, falcons;
buzzards, vultures, crows; ostriches;
seagulls, storks, herons, pelicans, cormorants;[d] hoopoes; or bats.

20 All winged insects are unclean, 21 except those that hop. 22 You may eat locusts, crickets, or grasshoppers. 23 But all
other small things that have wings and
also crawl must be considered unclean.

24-28 If you touch the dead bodies of the
following animals, you will be unclean
until evening: all animals with hoofs, unless their hoofs are divided and they
chew the cud, and all four-footed animals with paws. If you carry their dead
bodies, you must wash your clothes, but
you will still be unclean until evening.

29-30 Moles, rats, mice, and lizards must
be considered unclean. 31 Whoever
touches them or their dead bodies will be

[d] *The identification of some of the birds in verses 13-19 is uncertain.*

unclean until evening. 32 And if their
dead bodies fall on anything, it will be
unclean. This applies to any article of
wood, cloth, leather, or sacking, no matter what it is used for. It shall be dipped
in water, but it will remain unclean until
evening. 33 And if their bodies fall into a
clay pot, everything that is in it shall be
unclean, and you must break the pot.
34 Any food which could normally be
eaten, but on which water from such a
pot has been poured, will be unclean, and
anything drinkable in such a pot is unclean. 35 Anything on which the dead
bodies fall is unclean; a clay stove or
oven shall be broken, 36 but a spring or a
cistern remains clean, although anything
else that touches their dead bodies is unclean. 37 If one of them falls on seed that
is going to be planted, the seed remains
clean. 38 But if the seed is soaking in water and one of them falls on it, the seed is
unclean.

39 If any animal that may be eaten dies,
anyone who touches it will be unclean
until evening. 40 And if any of you eat any
part of the animal, you must wash your
clothes, but you will still be unclean until
evening; any of you who carry the dead
body must wash your clothes, but you
will still be unclean until evening.

41 You must not eat any of the small
animals that move on the ground,
42 whether they crawl, or walk on four
legs, or have many legs. 43 Do not make
yourselves unclean by eating any of
these. 44 I am the LORD your God, and you
must keep yourselves holy, because I am
holy. 45 I am the LORD who brought you
out of Egypt so that I could be your God.
You must be holy, because I am holy.

46 This, then, is the law about animals
and birds, about everything that lives in
the water, and everything that moves on
the ground. 47 You must be careful to distinguish between what is ritually clean
and unclean, between animals that may
be eaten and those that may not.

The Purification of Women after Childbirth

12 The LORD gave Moses the following regulations 2 for the people of
Israel. For seven days after a woman
gives birth to a son, she is ritually unclean, as she is during her monthly period. 3 On the eighth day, the child shall
be circumcised. 4 Then it will be thirty-
three more days until she is ritually clean
from her loss of blood; she must not
touch anything that is holy or enter the
sacred Tent until the time of her purification is completed.

5 For fourteen days after a woman
gives birth to a daughter, she is ritually
unclean, as she is during her monthly
period. Then it will be sixty-six more
days until she is ritually clean from her
loss of blood.

6 When the time of her purification is
completed, whether for a son or daughter, she shall bring to the priest at the
entrance of the Tent of the LORD's presence a one-year-old lamb for a burnt offering and a pigeon or a dove for a sin
offering. 7 The priest shall present her offering to the LORD and perform the ritual
to take away her impurity, and she will
be ritually clean. This, then, is what a
woman must do after giving birth.

8 If the woman cannot afford a lamb,
she shall bring two doves or two pigeons,
one for a burnt offering and the other for
a sin offering, and the priest shall perform the ritual to take away her impurity, and she will be ritually clean.

Laws concerning Skin Diseases

13 The LORD gave Moses and Aaron
these regulations. 2 If any of you
have a sore on your skin or a boil or an
inflammation which could develop into a
dreaded skin disease, you shall be
brought to the Aaronite priest. 3 The
priest shall examine the sore, and if the
hairs in it have turned white and the sore
appears to be deeper than the surrounding skin, it is a dreaded skin disease, and
the priest shall pronounce you unclean.
4 But if the sore is white and does not
appear to be deeper than the skin around
it and the hairs have not turned white,
the priest shall isolate you for seven
days. 5 The priest shall examine you
again on the seventh day, and if in his
opinion the sore looks the same and has
not spread, he shall isolate you for another seven days. 6 The priest shall examine you again on the seventh day, and if
the sore has faded and has not spread, he
shall pronounce you ritually clean; it is
only a sore. You shall wash your clothes
and be ritually clean. 7 But if the sore
spreads after the priest has examined
you and pronounced you clean, you must

appear before the priest again. 8 The
priest will examine you again, and if it
has spread, he shall pronounce you unclean; it is a dreaded skin disease.
9 If any of you have a dreaded skin disease, you shall be brought to the priest,
10 who will examine you. If there is a
white sore on your skin which turns the
hairs white and is full of pus, 11 it is a
chronic skin disease. The priest shall
pronounce you unclean; there is no need
to isolate you, because you are obviously
unclean. 12 If the skin disease spreads
and covers you from head to foot, 13 the
priest shall examine you again. If he
finds that it actually has covered the
whole body, he shall pronounce you ritually clean. If your whole skin has turned
white, you are ritually clean. 14 But from
the moment an open sore appears, you
are unclean. 15 The priest shall examine
you again, and if he sees an open sore, he
shall pronounce you unclean. An open
sore means a dreaded skin disease, and
you are unclean. 16 But when the sore
heals and becomes white again, you
shall go to the priest, 17 who will examine
you again. If the sore has turned white,
you are ritually clean, and the priest shall
pronounce you clean.
18 If any of you have a boil that has
healed 19 and if afterward a white swelling or a reddish-white spot appears
where the boil was, you shall go to the
priest. 20 The priest shall examine you,
and if the spot seems to be deeper than
the surrounding skin and the hairs in it
have turned white, he shall pronounce
you unclean. It is a dreaded skin disease
that has started in the boil. 21 But if the
priest examines it and finds that the hairs
in it have not turned white and that it is
not deeper than the surrounding skin,
but is light in color, the priest shall isolate you for seven days. 22 If the spot
spreads, the priest shall pronounce you
unclean; you are diseased. 23 But if it remains unchanged and does not spread, it
is only the scar left from the boil, and the
priest shall pronounce you ritually clean.
24 In case any of you have been burned,
if the raw flesh becomes white or
reddish-white, 25 the priest shall examine
you. If the hairs in the spot have turned
white and it appears deeper than the surrounding skin, it is a dreaded skin disease that has started in the burn, and the
priest shall pronounce you unclean.
26 But if the hairs in it have not turned
white and it is not deeper than the surrounding skin, but is light in color, the
priest shall isolate you for seven days.
27 The priest shall examine you again on
the seventh day, and if it is spreading, it
is a dreaded skin disease, and the priest
shall pronounce you unclean. 28 But if the
spot remains unchanged and does not
spread and is light in color, it is not a
dreaded skin disease. The priest shall
pronounce you ritually clean, because it
is only a scar from the burn.
29 When any of you, male or female,
have a sore on your head or chin, 30 the
priest shall examine it. If it seems to be
deeper than the surrounding skin and
the hairs in it are yellowish and thin, it is
a dreaded skin disease, and he shall pronounce you unclean. 31 If, when the priest
examines you, the sore does not appear
to be deeper than the surrounding skin,
but there are still no healthy hairs in it,
he shall isolate you for seven days. 32 The
priest shall examine the sore again on
the seventh day, and if it has not spread
and there are no yellowish hairs in it and
it does not seem to be deeper than the
surrounding skin, 33 you shall shave the
head except the area around the sore.
The priest shall then isolate you for another seven days. 34 On the seventh day
the priest shall again examine the sore,
and if it has not spread and does not
seem to be deeper than the surrounding
skin, he shall pronounce you ritually
clean. You shall wash your clothes, and
you will be clean. 35 But if the sore
spreads after you have been pronounced
clean, 36 the priest shall examine you
again. If the sore has spread, he need not
look for yellowish hairs; you are obviously unclean. 37 But if in the priest's
opinion the sore has not spread and
healthy hairs are growing in it, the sore
has healed, and the priest shall pronounce you ritually clean.
38 When any of you, male or female,
have white spots on the skin, 39 the priest
shall examine you. If the spots are dull
white, it is only a blemish that has broken out on the skin; you are ritually
clean.
40-41 If you lose your hair at the back or
the front of your head, this does not
make you unclean. 42 But if a reddish-
white sore appears on the bald spot, it is
a dreaded skin disease. 43 The priest shall

examine you, and if there is a reddish-
white sore, 44 the priest shall pronounce
you unclean, because of the dreaded skin
disease on your head.
45 If you have a dreaded skin disease,
you must wear torn clothes, leave your
hair uncombed, cover the lower part of
your face, and call out, "Unclean, unclean!" 46 You remain unclean as long as
you have the disease, and you must live
outside the camp, away from others.

Laws concerning Mildew

47 When there is mildew[e] on clothing,
whether wool or linen, 48 or on any piece
of linen or wool cloth or on leather or
anything made of leather, 49 if it is greenish or reddish, it is a spreading mildew
and must be shown to the priest. 50 The
priest shall examine it and put the object
away for seven days. 51 He shall examine
it again on the seventh day, and if the
mildew has spread, the object is unclean.
52 The priest shall burn it, because it is a
spreading mildew which must be destroyed by fire.
53 But if, when he examines it, the
priest finds that the mildew has not
spread on the object, 54 he shall order
that it be washed and put away for another seven days. 55 Then he shall examine it, and if the mildew has not changed
color, even though it has not spread, it is
still unclean; you must burn the object,
whether the rot is on the front or the
back. 56 But if, when the priest examines
it again, the mildew has faded, he shall
tear it out of the clothing or leather.
57 Then, if the mildew reappears, it is
spreading again, and the owner shall
burn the object. 58 If he washes the object
and the spot disappears, he shall wash it
again, and it will be ritually clean.
59 This, then, is the law about mildew
on clothing, whether it is wool or linen,
or on linen or wool cloth or on anything
made of leather; this is how the decision
is made as to whether it is ritually clean
or unclean.

Purification after Having Skin Diseases

14 The LORD gave Moses 2 the following regulations about the ritual purification of those of you cured of
a dreaded skin disease. On the day you
are to be pronounced clean, you shall be
brought to the priest, 3 and the priest
shall take you outside the camp and examine you. If the disease is healed, 4 the
priest shall order that two ritually clean
birds be brought, along with a piece of
cedar wood, a red cord, and a sprig of
hyssop. 5 Then the priest shall order that
one of the birds be killed over a clay bowl
containing fresh spring water. 6 He shall
take the other bird and dip it, together
with the cedar wood, the red cord, and
the hyssop, in the blood of the bird that
was killed. 7 He shall sprinkle the blood
seven times on the one of you who is to
be purified from your skin disease, and
then he shall pronounce you clean. He
shall let the live bird fly away over the
open fields. 8 You shall wash your
clothes, shave off all your hair, and take
a bath; you will then be ritually clean.
You may enter the camp, but you must
live outside your tent for seven days. 9 On
the seventh day you shall again shave
your head, your beard, your eyebrows,
and all the rest of the hair on your body;
you shall wash your clothes and take a
bath, and then you will be ritually clean.
10 On the eighth day you shall bring
two male lambs and one female lamb a
year old that are without any defects, five
pounds of flour mixed with olive oil, and
half a pint of olive oil. 11 The priest shall
take you and these offerings to the entrance of the Tent of the LORD's presence.
12 Then the priest shall take one of the
male lambs and together with the half
pint of oil he shall offer it as a repayment
offering. He shall present them as a special gift to the LORD for the priest. 13 He
shall kill the lamb in the holy place
where the animals for the sin offerings
and the burnt offerings are killed. He
must do this because the repayment offering, like the sin offering, belongs to
the priest and is very holy. 14 The priest
shall take some of the blood of the lamb
and put it on the lobe of the right ear, on
the thumb of the right hand, and on the
big toe of the right foot of the one of you
to be declared ritually clean. 15 The priest
shall take some of the olive oil and pour
it in the palm of his own left hand, 16 dip
a finger of his right hand in it, and sprinkle some of it seven times there in the
LORD's presence. 17 He shall take some of

[e] MILDEW: *The Hebrew word for "dreaded skin disease" and "mildew" is the same.*

the oil that is in the palm of his hand and
some of the blood of the lamb and put
them on the lobe of the right ear, on the
thumb of the right hand, and on the big
toe of the right foot of the one of you to
be declared ritually clean. 18 He shall put
the rest of the oil that is in the palm of his
hand on your head. In this way he shall
perform the ritual of purification.

19 Then the priest shall offer the sin offering and perform the ritual of purification. After that, he shall kill the animal
for the burnt offering 20 and offer it with
the grain offering on the altar. In this
way the priest shall perform the ritual of
purification, and you will be ritually
clean.

21 If you are poor and cannot afford any
more, you shall bring for your purification only one male lamb as your repayment offering, a special gift to the LORD
for the priest. You shall bring only two
pounds of flour mixed with olive oil for a
grain offering and half a pint of olive oil.
22 You shall also bring two doves or two
pigeons, one for the sin offering and one
for the burnt offering. 23 On the eighth
day of your purification you shall bring
them to the priest at the entrance of the
Tent. 24 The priest shall take the lamb
and the olive oil and present them as a
special gift to the LORD for the priest.
25 He shall kill the lamb and take some of
the blood and put it on the lobe of your
right ear, on the thumb of your right
hand, and on the big toe of your right
foot. 26 The priest shall pour some of the
oil into the palm of his own left hand
27 and with a finger of his right hand
sprinkle some of it seven times there in
the LORD's presence. 28 He shall put some
of the oil on the same places he put the
blood: on the lobe of your right ear, on
the thumb of your right hand, and on the
big toe of your right foot. 29 The rest of
the oil that is in his palm he shall put on
your head and in this way perform the
ritual of purification. 30 Then he shall offer one of the doves or pigeons 31 as the
sin offering and the other as the burnt
offering with the grain offering. In this
way the priest shall perform the ritual of
purification. 32 This is the law for those
who have a dreaded skin disease but
who cannot afford the normal offerings
required for his purification.

Mildew in Houses

33 The LORD gave Moses and Aaron
34-35 the following regulations about
houses affected by spreading mildew.
(These were to apply after the people of
Israel entered the land of Canaan, which
the LORD was going to give them as their
possession.) If any of you find that the
LORD has sent mildew on your house,
then you must go and tell the priest about
it. 36 The priest shall order everything to
be moved out of the house before he goes
to examine the mildew; otherwise everything in the house will be declared unclean. Then he shall go to the house
37 and examine the mildew. If there are
greenish or reddish spots that appear to
be eating into the wall, 38 he shall leave
the house and lock it up for seven days.
39 On the seventh day he shall return and
examine it again. If the mildew has
spread, 40 he shall order that the stones
on which the mildew is found be removed and thrown into some unclean
place outside the city. 41 After that he
must have all the interior walls scraped
and the plaster dumped in an unclean
place outside the city. 42 Then other
stones are to be used to replace the
stones that were removed, and new plaster will be used to cover the walls.

43 If the mildew breaks out again in the
house after the stones have been removed and the house has been scraped
and plastered, 44 the priest shall go and
look. If it has spread, the house is unclean. 45 It must be torn down, and its
stones, its wood, and all its plaster must
be carried out of the city to an unclean
place. 46 Any who enter the house while
it is locked up will be unclean until evening. 47 Any who lie down or eat in the
house must wash their clothes.

48 If, when the priest comes to look, the
mildew has not reappeared after the
house has been replastered, he shall pronounce the house ritually clean, because
the mildew has been completely removed. 49 To purify the house, he shall
take two birds, some cedar wood, a red
cord, and a sprig of hyssop. 50 He shall
kill one of the birds over a clay bowl containing fresh spring water. 51 Then he
shall take the cedar wood, the hyssop,
the red cord, and the live bird and shall
dip them in the blood of the bird that was
killed and in the fresh water. And he

shall sprinkle the house seven times. 52 In
this way he shall purify the house with
the bird's blood, the fresh water, the live
bird, the cedar wood, the hyssop, and the
red cord. 53 Then he shall let the live bird
fly away outside the city over the open
fields. In this way he shall perform the
ritual of purification for the house, and it
will be ritually clean.

54 These are the laws about dreaded
skin diseases; 55-56 sores, boils, or inflam-
mations; and about mildew in clothes or
houses. 57 These laws determine when
something is unclean and when it is
clean.

Unclean Bodily Discharges

15 The LORD gave Moses and Aaron
the following regulations 2 for the
people of Israel. When any man has a
discharge from his penis, the discharge
is unclean, 3 whether the penis runs with
it or is stopped up by it. 4 Any bed on
which he sits or lies is unclean. 5 Anyone
who touches his bed 6 or sits on anything
the man has sat on must wash his clothes
and take a bath, and he remains unclean
until evening. 7 Anyone who touches the
man with the discharge must wash his
clothes and take a bath, and he remains
unclean until evening. 8 If the man with
the discharge spits on anyone who is
ritually clean, that person must wash his
clothes and take a bath, and he remains
unclean until evening. 9 Any saddle or
seat on which the man with the discharge sits is unclean. 10 Anyone who
touches anything on which the man sat is
unclean until evening. Anyone who carries anything on which the man sat must
wash his clothes and take a bath, and he
remains unclean until evening. 11 If a
man who has a discharge touches one of
you without first having washed his
hands, you must wash your clothes and
take a bath, and you remain unclean until evening. 12 Any clay pot that the man
touches must be broken, and any
wooden bowl that he touches must be
washed.

13 After the man is cured of his discharge, he must wait seven days and
then wash his clothes and take a bath in
fresh spring water, and he will be ritually
clean. 14 On the eighth day he shall take
two doves or two pigeons to the entrance
of the Tent of the LORD's presence and
give them to the priest. 15 The priest shall
offer one of them as a sin offering and the
other as a burnt offering. In this way he
will perform the ritual of purification for
the man.

16 When a man has an emission of semen, he must bathe his whole body, and
he remains unclean until evening.
17 Anything made of cloth or leather on
which the semen falls must be washed,
and it remains unclean until evening.
18 After sexual intercourse both the man
and the woman must take a bath, and
they remain unclean until evening.

19 When a woman has her monthly period, she remains unclean for seven
days. Anyone who touches her is unclean until evening. 20 Anything on
which she sits or lies during her monthly
period is unclean. 21-23 Any who touch
her bed or anything on which she has sat
must wash their clothes and take a bath,
and they remain unclean until evening.
24 If a man has sexual intercourse with
her during her period, he is contaminated by her impurity and remains unclean for seven days, and any bed on
which he lies is unclean.

25 If a woman has a flow of blood for
several days outside her monthly period
or if her flow continues beyond her regular period, she remains unclean as long
as the flow continues, just as she is during her monthly period. 26 Any bed on
which she lies and anything on which
she sits during this time is unclean.
27 Any who touch them are unclean and
must wash their clothes and take a bath;
they remain unclean until evening. 28 After her flow stops, she must wait seven
days, and then she will be ritually clean.
29 On the eighth day she shall take two
doves or two pigeons to the priest at the
entrance of the Tent of the LORD's presence. 30 The priest shall offer one of them
as a sin offering and the other as a burnt
offering, and in this way he will perform
the ritual of purification for her.

31 The LORD told Moses to warn the people of Israel about their uncleanness, so
that they would not defile the Tent of his
presence, which was in the middle of the
camp. If they did, they would be killed.

32 These are the regulations about a
man who has a discharge or an emission
of semen, 33 a woman during her monthly
period, or a man who has sexual intercourse with a woman who is ritually
unclean.

The Day of Atonement

16 The LORD spoke to Moses after
the death of the two sons of
Aaron who were killed when they offered unholy fire to the LORD. 2He said,
"Tell your brother Aaron that only at the
proper time is he to go behind the curtain
into the Most Holy Place, because that is
where I appear in a cloud above the lid
on the Covenant Box. If he disobeys, he
will be killed. 3He may enter the Most
Holy Place only after he has brought a
young bull for a sin offering and a ram
for a burnt offering."
4Then the LORD gave the following instructions. Before Aaron goes into the
Most Holy Place, he must take a bath and
put on the priestly garments: the linen
robe and shorts, the belt, and the turban.
5The community of Israel shall give
Aaron two male goats for a sin offering
and a ram for a burnt offering. 6He shall
offer a bull as a sacrifice to take away his
own sins and those of his family. 7Then
he shall take the two goats to the entrance of the Tent of the LORD's presence.
8There he shall draw lots, using two
stones, one marked "for the LORD" and
the other "for Azazel."[f] 9Aaron shall
sacrifice the goat chosen by lot for the
LORD and offer it as a sin offering. 10The
goat chosen for Azazel shall be presented alive to the LORD and sent off into
the desert to Azazel, in order to take
away the sins of the people.
11When Aaron sacrifices the bull as
the sin offering for himself and his family, 12he shall take a fire pan full of burning coals from the altar and two handfuls
of fine incense and bring them into the
Most Holy Place. 13There in the LORD's
presence he shall put the incense on the
fire, and the smoke of the incense will
hide the lid of the Covenant Box so that
he will not see it and die. 14He shall take
some of the bull's blood and with his finger sprinkle it on the front of the lid and
then sprinkle some of it seven times in
front of the Covenant Box.
15After that, he shall kill the goat for
the sin offering for the people, bring its
blood into the Most Holy Place, and
sprinkle it on the lid and then in front of
the Covenant Box, as he did with the
bull's blood. 16In this way he will perform the ritual to purify the Most Holy
Place from the uncleanness of the people
of Israel and from all their sins. He must
do this to the Tent, because it stands in
the middle of the camp, which is ritually
unclean. 17From the time Aaron enters
the Most Holy Place to perform the ritual
of purification until he comes out, there
must be no one in the Tent. When he has
performed the ritual for himself, his family, and the whole community, 18he must
then go out to the altar for burnt offerings and purify it. He must take some of
the bull's blood and some of the goat's
blood and put it all over the projections
at the corners of the altar. 19With his finger he must sprinkle some of the blood
on the altar seven times. In this way he
is to purify it from the sins of the people
of Israel and make it holy.

The Scapegoat

20When Aaron has finished performing the ritual to purify the Most Holy
Place, the rest of the Tent of the LORD's
presence, and the altar, he shall present
to the LORD the live goat chosen for Azazel.[g] 21He shall put both of his hands on
the goat's head and confess over it all the
evils, sins, and rebellions of the people of
Israel, and so transfer them to the goat's
head. Then the goat is to be driven off
into the desert by someone appointed to
do it. 22The goat will carry all their sins
away with him into some uninhabited
land.
23Then Aaron shall go into the Tent,
take off the priestly garments that he had
put on before entering the Most Holy
Place, and leave them there. 24He must
take a bath in a holy place and put on his
own clothes. After that, he shall go out
and offer the burnt offering to remove
his own sins and those of the people.
25He shall burn on the altar the fat of the
animal for the sin offering. 26The man
who drove the goat into the desert to
Azazel must wash his clothes and take a
bath before he comes back into camp.
27The bull and the goat used for the sin
offering, whose blood was brought into
the Most Holy Place to take away sin,
shall be carried outside the camp and
burned. Skin, meat, and intestines shall
all be burned. 28The one who burns them

[f] AZAZEL: *The meaning of this Hebrew word is unknown; it may be the name of a desert demon.*
[g] AZAZEL: *See 16.8.*

must wash his clothes and take a bath
before he returns to camp.

Observing the Day of Atonement

29 The following regulations are to be
observed for all time to come. On the
tenth day of the seventh month the Israelites and the foreigners living among
them must fast and must not do any
work. 30 On that day the ritual is to be
performed to purify them from all their
sins, so that they will be ritually clean.
31 That day is to be a very holy day, one
on which they fast and do no work at all.
These regulations are to be observed for
all time to come. 32 The High Priest, properly ordained and consecrated to succeed his father, is to perform the ritual of
purification. He shall put on the priestly
garments 33 and perform the ritual to purify the Most Holy Place, the rest of the
Tent of the LORD's presence, the altar, the
priests, and all the people of the community. 34 These regulations are to be observed for all time to come. This ritual
must be performed once a year to purify
the people of Israel from all their sins.
So Moses[h] did as the LORD had
commanded.

The Sacredness of Blood

17 The LORD commanded Moses 2 to
give Aaron and his sons and all
the people of Israel the following regulations. 3-4 Any Israelites who kill a cow or
a sheep or a goat as an offering to the
LORD anywhere except at the entrance of
the Tent of the LORD's presence have broken the Law. They have shed blood and
shall no longer be considered God's people. 5 The meaning of this command is
that the people of Israel shall now bring
to the LORD the animals which they used
to kill in the open country. They shall
now bring them to the priest at the entrance of the Tent and kill them as fellowship offerings. 6 The priest shall
throw the blood against the sides of the
altar at the entrance of the Tent and burn
the fat to produce an odor that is pleasing
to the LORD. 7 The people of Israel must no
longer be unfaithful to the LORD by killing
their animals in the fields as sacrifices to
the goat demons. The people of Israel
must keep this regulation for all time to
come.
8 Any Israelites or any foreigners living
in the community who offer a burnt offering or any other sacrifice 9 as an offering to the LORD anywhere except at the
entrance of the Tent shall no longer be
considered God's people.
10 If any Israelites or any foreigners living in the community eat meat with
blood still in it, the LORD will turn against
them and no longer consider them his
people. 11 The life of every living thing is
in the blood, and that is why the LORD has
commanded that all blood be poured out
on the altar to take away the people's
sins. Blood, which is life, takes away
sins. 12 That is why the LORD has told the
people of Israel that neither they nor any
foreigner living among them shall eat
any meat with blood still in it.
13 If any Israelites or any foreigners living in the community catch an animal or
a bird which is ritually clean, they must
pour its blood out on the ground and
cover it with dirt. 14 The life of every living thing is in the blood, and that is why
the LORD has told the people of Israel that
they shall not eat any meat with blood
still in it and that anyone who does so
will no longer be considered one of his
people.
15 Any people, Israelites or foreigners,
who eat meat from an animal that has
died a natural death or has been killed by
wild animals must wash their clothes,
take a bath, and wait until evening before they are ritually clean. 16 If they do
not, they must suffer the consequences.

Forbidden Sexual Practices

18 The LORD told Moses 2 to say to
the people of Israel, "I am the
LORD your God. 3 Do not follow the practices of the people of Egypt, where you
once lived, or of the people in the land of
Canaan, where I am now taking you.
4 Obey my laws and do what I command.
I am the LORD your God. 5 Follow the
practices and the laws that I give you;
you will save your life by doing so. I am
the LORD."
6 The LORD gave the following regulations. Do not have sexual intercourse
with any of your relatives. 7 Do not disgrace your father by having intercourse
with your mother. You must not disgrace
your own mother. 8 Do not disgrace your

[h] Moses; *or* Aaron.

father by having intercourse with any of
his other wives. 9 Do not have intercourse with your sister or your stepsis-
ter, whether or not she was brought up in
the same house with you. 10 Do not have
intercourse with your granddaughter;
that would be a disgrace to you. 11 Do not
have intercourse with a half sister; she,
too, is your sister. 12-13 Do not have intercourse with an aunt, whether she is your
father's sister or your mother's sister.
14 Do not have intercourse with your uncle's wife; she, too, is your aunt. 15 Do not
have intercourse with your daughter-in-
law 16 or with your brother's wife. 17 Do
not have intercourse with the daughter
or granddaughter of a woman with
whom you have had intercourse; they
may be related to you, and that would be
incest. 18 Do not take your wife's sister as
one of your wives, as long as your wife is
living.

19 Do not have intercourse with a
woman during her monthly period, because she is ritually unclean. 20 Do not
have intercourse with another man's
wife; that would make you ritually unclean. 21 Do not hand over any of your
children to be used in the worship of the
god Molech, because that would bring
disgrace on the name of God, the LORD.
22 No man is to have sexual relations with
another man; God hates that. 23 No man
or woman is to have sexual relations
with an animal; that perversion makes
you ritually unclean.

24 Do not make yourselves unclean by
any of these acts, for that is how the pagans made themselves unclean, those
pagans who lived in the land before you
and whom the LORD is driving out so that
you can go in. 25 Their actions made the
land unclean, and so the LORD is punishing the land and making it reject the people who lived there. 26-27 They did all
these disgusting things and made the
land unclean, but you must not do them.
All of you, whether Israelites or foreigners living with you, must keep the LORD's
laws and commands, 28 and then the land
will not reject you, as it rejected the pagans who lived there before you. 29 You
know that whoever does any of these disgusting things will no longer be considered one of God's people.

30 And the LORD said, "Obey the commands I give and do not follow the practices of the people who lived in the land
before you, and do not make yourselves
unclean by doing any of these things. I
am the LORD your God."

Laws of Holiness and Justice

19 The LORD told Moses 2 to say to
the community of Israel, "Be
holy, because I, the LORD your God, am
holy. 3 Each of you must respect your
mother and your father, and must keep
the Sabbath, as I have commanded. I am
the LORD your God.

4 "Do not abandon me and worship
idols; do not make gods of metal and
worship them. I am the LORD your God.

5 "When you kill an animal for a fellowship offering, keep the regulations that I
have given you, and I will accept the offering. 6 The meat must be eaten on the
day the animal is killed or on the next
day. Any meat left on the third day must
be burned, 7 because it is ritually unclean, and if anyone eats it, I will not
accept the offering. 8 Any who eat it will
be guilty of treating as ordinary what is
dedicated to me, and they will no longer
be considered my people.

9 "When you harvest your fields, do not
cut the grain at the edges of the fields,
and do not go back to cut the heads of
grain that were left. 10 Do not go back
through your vineyard to gather the
grapes that were missed or to pick up the
grapes that have fallen; leave them for
poor people and foreigners. I am the
LORD your God.

11 "Do not steal or cheat or lie. 12 Do not
make a promise in my name if you do not
intend to keep it; that brings disgrace on
my name. I am the LORD your God.

13 "Do not rob or take advantage of
anyone. Do not hold back the wages of
someone you have hired, not even for
one night. 14 Do not curse the deaf or put
something in front of the blind so as to
make them stumble over it. Obey me; I
am the LORD your God.

15 "Be honest and just when you make
decisions in legal cases; do not show favoritism to the poor or fear the rich. 16 Do
not spread lies about anyone, and when
someone is on trial for his life, speak out
if your testimony can help him. I am the
LORD.

17 "Do not bear a grudge against others, but settle your differences with
them, so that you will not commit a sin

because of them.[i] 18 Do not take revenge
on others or continue to hate them, but
love your neighbors as you love yourself.
I am the LORD.

19 "Obey my commands. Do not cross-
breed domestic animals. Do not plant
two kinds of seed in the same field. Do
not wear clothes made of two kinds of
material.

20 "If a slave woman is the recognized
concubine of a man and she has not been
paid for and freed, then if another man
has sexual relations with her, they will
be punished, but not[j] put to death, since
she is a slave. 21 The man shall bring a
ram to the entrance of the Tent of my
presence as his repayment offering,
22 and with it the priest shall perform the
ritual of purification to remove the man's
sin, and God will forgive him.

23 "When you come into the land of Canaan and plant any kind of fruit tree,
consider the fruit ritually unclean for the
first three years. During that time you
must not eat it. 24 In the fourth year all the
fruit shall be dedicated as an offering to
show your gratitude to me,[k] the LORD.
25 But in the fifth year you may eat the
fruit. If you do all this, your trees will
bear more fruit. I am the LORD your God.

26 "Do not eat any meat with blood still
in it. Do not practice any kind of magic.
27 Do not cut the hair on the sides of your
head or trim your beard 28 or tattoo yourselves or cut gashes in your body to
mourn for the dead. I am the LORD.

29 "Do not disgrace your daughters by
making them temple prostitutes;[l] if you
do, you will turn to other gods and the
land will be full of immorality. 30 Keep
the Sabbath, and honor the place where
I am worshiped. I am the LORD.

31 "Do not go for advice to people who
consult the spirits of the dead. If you do,
you will be ritually unclean. I am the
LORD your God.

32 "Show respect for old people and
honor them. Reverently obey me; I am
the LORD.

33 "Do not mistreat foreigners who are
living in your land. 34 Treat them as you
would an Israelite, and love them as you
love yourselves. Remember that you
were once foreigners in the land of
Egypt. I am the LORD your God.

35 "Do not cheat anyone by using false
measures of length, weight, or quantity.
36 Use honest scales, honest weights, and
honest measures. I am the LORD your
God, and I brought you out of Egypt.
37 Obey all my laws and commands. I am
the LORD."

Penalties for Disobedience

20 The LORD told Moses 2 to say to
the people of Israel, "Any of you
or any foreigner living among you who
gives any children to be used in the worship of the god Molech shall be stoned to
death by the whole community. 3 If any of
you give one of your children to Molech
and make my sacred Tent unclean and
disgrace my holy name, I will turn
against you and will no longer consider
you my people. 4 But if the community
ignores what you have done and does not
put you to death, 5 I myself will turn
against you and your whole family and
against all who join you in being unfaithful to me and worshiping Molech. I will
no longer consider any of you my people.

6 "If any of you go for advice to people
who consult the spirits of the dead, I will
turn against you and will no longer consider you one of my people. 7 Keep yourselves holy, because I am the LORD your
God. 8 Obey my laws, because I am the
LORD and I make you holy."

9 The LORD gave the following regulations. Any of you that curse your father
or mother shall be put to death; you are
responsible for your own death.

10 If a man commits adultery with the
wife of an Israelite, both he and the
woman shall be put to death. 11 A man
who has intercourse with one of his
father's wives disgraces his father, and
both he and the woman shall be put to
death. They are responsible for their own
death. 12 If a man has intercourse with his
daughter-in-law, they shall both be put to
death. They have committed incest and
are responsible for their own death. 13 If
a man has sexual relations with another
man, they have done a disgusting thing,
and both shall be put to death. They are

[i] so ... them; *or* so that you do not commit this sin against them. [j] they ... not; *or* an investigation will be made but they will not be. [k] to show your gratitude to me; *or* in praise of me. [l] TEMPLE PROSTITUTES: *These women were found in Canaanite temples, where fertility gods were worshiped. It was believed that intercourse with these prostitutes assured fertile fields and herds.*

responsible for their own death. 14 If a man marries a woman and her mother, all three shall be burned to death because of the disgraceful thing they have done; such a thing must not be permitted among you. 15 If a man has sexual relations with an animal, he and the animal shall be put to death. 16 If a woman tries to have sexual relations with an animal, she and the animal shall be put to death. They are responsible for their own death.

17 If a man marries his sister or half sister, they shall be publicly disgraced and driven out of the community. He has had intercourse with his sister and must suffer the consequences. 18 If a man has intercourse with a woman during her monthly period, both of them are to be driven out of the community, because they have broken the regulations about ritual uncleanness.

19 If a man has intercourse with his aunt, both of them must suffer the consequences for incest. 20 If a man has intercourse with his uncle's wife, he disgraces his uncle, and he and the woman will pay the penalty; neither one will have children. 21 If a man takes his brother's wife, they will die childless. He has done a ritually unclean thing and has disgraced his brother.

22 The LORD said, "Keep all my laws and commands, so that you will not be rejected by the land of Canaan, into which I am bringing you. 23 Do not adopt the customs of the people who live there; I am driving out those pagans so that you can enter the land. They have disgusted me with all their evil practices. 24 But I have promised you this rich and fertile land as your possession, and I will give it to you. I am the LORD your God, and I have set you apart from the other nations. 25 So then, you must make a clear distinction between animals and birds that are ritually clean and those that are not. Do not eat unclean animals or birds. I have declared them unclean, and eating them would make you unclean. 26 You shall be holy and belong only to me, because I am the LORD and I am holy. I have set you apart from the other nations so that you would belong to me alone.

27 "Any man or woman who consults the spirits of the dead shall be stoned to death; any of you that do this are responsible for your own death."

The Holiness of the Priests

21 The LORD commanded Moses to tell the Aaronite priests, "No priest is to make himself ritually unclean by taking part in the funeral ceremonies when a relative dies, 2 unless it is his mother, father, son, daughter, brother, 3 or unmarried sister living in his house. 4 He shall not make himself unclean at the death of those related to him by marriage.[m]

5 "No priest shall shave any part of his head or trim his beard or cut gashes on his body to show that he is in mourning. 6 He must be holy and must not disgrace my name. He offers food offerings to me, and he must be holy. 7 A priest shall not marry a woman who has been a prostitute or a woman who is not a virgin or who is divorced; he is holy. 8 The people must consider the priest holy, because he presents the food offerings to me. I am the LORD; I am holy and I make my people holy. 9 If a priest's daughter becomes a prostitute, she disgraces her father; she shall be burned to death.

10 "The High Priest has had the anointing oil poured on his head and has been consecrated to wear the priestly garments, so he must not leave his hair uncombed or tear his clothes to show that he is in mourning. 11-12 He has been dedicated to me and is not to make himself ritually unclean nor is he to defile my sacred Tent by leaving it and entering a house where there is a dead person, even if it is his own father or mother. 13 He shall marry a virgin, 14 not a widow or a divorced woman or a woman who has been a prostitute. He shall marry only a virgin from his own clan. 15 Otherwise, his children, who ought to be holy, will be ritually unclean. I am the LORD and I have set him apart as the High Priest."

16 The LORD commanded Moses 17 to tell Aaron, "None of your descendants who has any physical defects may present the food offering to me. This applies for all time to come. 18 No man with any physical defects may make the offering: no one who is blind, lame, disfigured, or deformed; 19 no one with a crippled hand or foot; 20 no one who is a hunchback or a

[m] *Verse 4 in Hebrew is unclear.*

dwarf; no one with any eye or skin disease; and no eunuch. 21 No descendant of
Aaron the priest who has any physical
defects may present the food offering to
me. 22 Such a man may eat the food offered to me, both the holy food offering
and the very holy food offering, 23 but because he has a physical defect, he shall
not come near the sacred curtain or approach the altar. He must not profane
these holy things, because I am the LORD
and I make them holy."

24 This, then, is what Moses said to
Aaron, the sons of Aaron, and to all the
people of Israel.

The Holiness of the Offerings

22 The LORD commanded Moses 2 to
tell Aaron and his sons, "You
must not bring disgrace on my holy
name, so treat with respect the sacred
offerings that the people of Israel dedicate to me. I am the LORD. 3 If any of your
descendants, while he is ritually unclean,
comes near the sacred offerings which
the people of Israel have dedicated to me,
he can never again serve at the altar.
This applies for all time to come. I am the
LORD.

4 "None of the descendants of Aaron
who has a dreaded skin disease or a discharge may eat any of the sacred offerings until he is ritually clean. Any priest
is unclean if he touches anything which
is unclean through contact with a corpse
or if he has an emission of semen 5 or if
he has touched an unclean animal or person. 6 Any priest who becomes unclean
remains unclean until evening, and even
then he may not eat any of the sacred
offerings until he has taken a bath. 7 After the sun sets he is clean, and then he
may eat the sacred offerings, which are
his food. 8 He shall not eat the meat of
any animal that has died a natural death
or has been killed by wild animals; it will
make him unclean. I am the LORD.

9 "All priests shall observe the regulations that I have given. Otherwise, they
will become guilty and die, because they
have disobeyed the sacred regulations. I
am the LORD and I make them holy.

10 "Only a member of a priestly family
may eat any of the sacred offerings; no
one else may eat them — not even someone staying with a priest or hired by him.
11 But a priest's slaves, bought with his
own money or born in his home, may eat
the food the priest receives. 12 A priest's
daughter who marries someone who is
not a priest may not eat any of the sacred
offerings. 13 But a widowed or divorced
daughter who has no children and who
has returned to live in her father's house
as a dependent may eat the food her
father receives as a priest. Only a member of a priestly family may eat any of it.

14 "If any people who are not members
of a priestly family eat any of the sacred
offerings without intending to, they must
repay the priest its full value plus an additional 20 percent. 15 The priests shall
not profane the sacred offerings 16 by letting any unauthorized people eat them;
this would bring guilt and punishment on
such people. I am the LORD and I make
the offerings holy."

17 The LORD commanded Moses 18 to
give Aaron and his sons and all the people of Israel the following regulations.
When any Israelite or any foreigner living in Israel presents a burnt offering,
whether as fulfillment of a vow or as a
freewill offering, the animal must not
have any defects. 19 To be accepted, it
must be a male without any defects. 20 If
you offer any animal that has any defects, the LORD will not accept it. 21 When
anyone presents a fellowship offering to
the LORD, whether as fulfillment of a vow
or as a freewill offering, the animal must
be without any defects if it is to be accepted. 22 Do not offer to the LORD any
animal that is blind or crippled or mutilated, or that has a running sore or a skin
eruption or scabs. Do not offer any such
animals on the altar as a food offering.
23 As a freewill offering you may offer an
animal that is stunted or not perfectly
formed, but it is not acceptable in fulfillment of a vow. 24 Do not offer to the LORD
any animal whose testicles have been
crushed, cut, bruised, or torn off. This is
not permitted in your land.

25 Do not offer as a food offering any
animal obtained from a foreigner. Such
animals are considered defective and are
not acceptable.

26-27 When a calf or a lamb or a kid is
born, it must not be taken from its
mother for seven days, but after that it is
acceptable as a food offering. 28 Do not
sacrifice a cow and its calf or a sheep and
its lamb or a goat and its kid on the same
day. 29 When you offer a sacrifice of
thanksgiving to the LORD, follow the rules

so that you will be accepted; 30 eat it the same day and leave none of it until the next morning.

31 The LORD said, "Obey my commands; I am the LORD. 32 Do not bring disgrace on my holy name; all the people of Israel must acknowledge me to be holy. I am the LORD and I make you holy; 33 and I brought you out of Egypt to become your God. I am the LORD."

The Religious Festivals

23 The LORD gave Moses 2 the following regulations for the religious festivals, when the people of Israel are to gather for worship. 3 You have six days in which to do your work, but remember that the seventh day, the Sabbath, is a day of rest. On that day do not work, but gather for worship. The Sabbath belongs to the LORD, no matter where you live. 4 Proclaim the following festivals at the appointed times.

Passover and Unleavened Bread

(Numbers 28.16-25)

5 The Passover, celebrated to honor the LORD, begins at sunset on the fourteenth day of the first month. 6 On the fifteenth day the Festival of Unleavened Bread begins, and for seven days you must not eat any bread made with yeast. 7 On the first of these days you shall gather for worship and do none of your daily work. 8 Offer your food offerings to the LORD for seven days. On the seventh day you shall again gather for worship, but you shall do none of your daily work.

9-10 When you come into the land that the LORD is giving you and you harvest your grain, take the first sheaf to the priest. 11 He shall present it as a special offering to the LORD, so that you may be accepted. The priest shall present it the day after the Sabbath. 12 On the day you present the offering of grain, also sacrifice as a burnt offering a one-year-old male lamb that has no defects. 13 With it you shall present four pounds of flour mixed with olive oil as a food offering. The odor of this offering is pleasing to the LORD. You shall also present with it an offering of one quart of wine. 14 Do not eat any of the new grain, whether raw, roasted, or baked into bread, until you have brought this offering to God. This regulation is to be observed by all your descendants for all time to come.

The Harvest Festival

(Numbers 28.26-31)

15 Count seven full weeks from the day after the Sabbath on which you bring your sheaf of grain to present to the LORD. 16 On the fiftieth day, the day after the seventh Sabbath, present to the LORD another new offering of grain. 17 Each family is to bring two loaves of bread and present them to the LORD as a special gift. Each loaf shall be made of four pounds of flour baked with yeast and shall be presented to the LORD as an offering of the first grain to be harvested. 18 And with the bread the community is to present seven one-year-old lambs, one bull, and two rams, none of which may have any defects. They shall be offered as a burnt offering to the LORD, along with a grain offering and a wine offering. The odor of this offering is pleasing to the LORD. 19 Also offer one male goat as a sin offering and two one-year-old male lambs as a fellowship offering. 20 The priest shall present the bread with the two lambs as a special gift to the LORD for the priests. These offerings are holy. 21 On that day do none of your daily work, but gather for worship. Your descendants are to observe this regulation for all time to come, no matter where they live.

22 When you harvest your fields, do not cut the grain at the edges of the fields, and do not go back to cut the heads of grain that were left; leave them for poor people and foreigners. The LORD is your God.

The New Year Festival

(Numbers 29.1-6)

23-24 On the first day of the seventh month observe a special day of rest, and come together for worship when the trumpets sound. 25 Present a food offering to the LORD and do none of your daily work.

The Day of Atonement

(Numbers 29.7-11)

26-27 The tenth day of the seventh month is the day when the annual ritual is to be performed to take away the sins of the people. On that day do not eat anything at all; come together for worship, and present a food offering to the LORD. 28 Do no work on that day, because it is

the day for performing the ritual to take
away sin. 29 Any who eat anything on
that day will no longer be considered
God's people. 30 And if any do any work
on that day, the LORD himself will put
them to death. 31 This regulation applies
to all your descendants, no matter where
they live. 32 From sunset on the ninth day
of the month to sunset on the tenth observe this day as a special day of rest,
during which nothing may be eaten.

The Festival of Shelters

(Numbers 29.12-40)

33-34 The Festival of Shelters begins on
the fifteenth day of the seventh month
and continues for seven days. 35 On the
first of these days come together for worship and do none of your daily work.
36 Each day for seven days you shall
present a food offering. On the eighth
day come together again for worship and
present a food offering. It is a day for
worship, and you shall do no work.
(37 These are the religious festivals on
which you honor the LORD by gathering
together for worship and presenting food
offerings, burnt offerings, grain offerings, sacrifices, and wine offerings, as
required day by day. 38 These festivals
are in addition to the regular Sabbaths,
and these offerings are in addition to
your regular gifts, your offerings as fulfillment of vows, and your freewill offerings that you give to the LORD.)
39 When you have harvested your
fields, celebrate this festival for seven
days, beginning on the fifteenth day of
the seventh month. The first day shall be
a special day of rest. 40 On that day take
some of the best fruit from your trees,
take palm branches and limbs from leafy
trees, and begin a religious festival to
honor the LORD your God. 41 Celebrate it
for seven days. This regulation is to be
kept by your descendants for all time to
come. 42 All the people of Israel shall live
in shelters for seven days, 43 so that your
descendants may know that the LORD
made the people of Israel live in simple
shelters when he led them out of Egypt.
He is the LORD your God.
44 So in this way Moses gave the people
of Israel the regulations for observing the religious festivals to honor the
LORD.

Taking Care of the Lamps

(Exodus 27.20, 21)

24 The LORD told Moses 2 to give the
following orders to the people of
Israel: Bring pure olive oil of the finest
quality for the lamps in the Tent, so that
a light might be kept burning regularly.
3 Each evening Aaron shall light them
and keep them burning until morning,
there in the LORD's presence outside the
curtain in front of the Covenant Box,
which is in the Most Holy Place. This
regulation is to be observed for all time
to come. 4 Aaron shall take care of the
lamps on the lampstand of pure gold and
must see that they burn regularly in the
LORD's presence.

The Bread Offered to God

5 Take twenty-four pounds of flour and
bake twelve loaves of bread. 6 Put the
loaves in two rows, six in each row, on
the table covered with pure gold, which
is in the LORD's presence. 7 Put some pure
incense on each row, as a token food offering to the LORD to take the place of the
bread. 8 Every Sabbath, for all time to
come, the bread must be placed in the
presence of the LORD. This is Israel's duty
forever. 9 The bread belongs to Aaron
and his descendants, and they shall eat it
in a holy place, because this is a very
holy part of the food offered to the LORD
for the priests.

An Example of Just and Fair Punishment

10-11 There was a man whose father was
an Egyptian and whose mother was an
Israelite named Shelomith, the daughter
of Dibri from the tribe of Dan. There in
the camp this man quarreled with an Israelite. During the quarrel he cursed the
LORD, so they took him to Moses, 12 put
him under guard, and waited for the LORD
to tell them what to do with him.
13 The LORD said to Moses, 14 "Take that
man out of the camp. Everyone who
heard him curse shall put his hands on
the man's head to testify that he is guilty,
and then the whole community shall
stone him to death. 15 Then tell the people
of Israel that anyone who curses God
must suffer the consequences 16 and be
put to death. Any Israelite or any foreigner living in Israel who curses the

LORD shall be stoned to death by the
whole community.
17 “Any who commit murder shall be
put to death, 18 and any who kill an animal belonging to someone else must replace it. The principle is a life for a life.
19 “If any of you injure another person,
whatever you have done shall be done to
you. 20 If you break a bone, one of your
bones shall be broken; if you put out an
eye, one of your eyes shall be put out; if
you knock out a tooth, one of your teeth
shall be knocked out. Whatever injury
you cause another person shall be done
to you in return. 21 Whoever kills an animal shall replace it, but whoever kills a
human being shall be put to death. 22 This
law applies to all of you, to Israelites and
to foreigners living among you, because
I am the LORD your God.”
23 When Moses had said this to the people of Israel, they took the man outside
the camp and stoned him to death. In this
way the people of Israel did what the
LORD had commanded Moses.

The Seventh Year

(Deuteronomy 15.1-11)

25 The LORD spoke to Moses on
Mount Sinai and commanded
him 2 to give the following regulations to
the people of Israel. When you enter the
land that the LORD is giving you, you shall
honor the LORD by not cultivating the
land every seventh year. 3 You shall plant
your fields, prune your vineyards, and
gather your crops for six years. 4 But the
seventh year is to be a year of complete
rest for the land, a year dedicated to the
LORD. Do not plant your fields or prune
your vineyards. 5 Do not even harvest the
grain that grows by itself without being
planted, and do not gather the grapes
from your unpruned vines; it is a year of
complete rest for the land. 6 Although the
land has not been cultivated during that
year, it will provide food for you, your
slaves, your hired men, the foreigners
living with you, 7 your domestic animals,
and the wild animals in your fields.
Everything that it produces may be
eaten.

The Year of Restoration

8 Count seven times seven years, a total
of forty-nine years. 9 Then, on the tenth
day of the seventh month, the Day of
Atonement, send someone to blow a
trumpet throughout the whole land. 10 In
this way you shall set the fiftieth year
apart and proclaim freedom to all the inhabitants of the land. During this year all
property that has been sold shall be restored to the original owner or the
descendants, and any who have been
sold as slaves shall return to their families. 11 You shall not plant your fields or
harvest the grain that grows by itself or
gather the grapes in your unpruned vineyards. 12 The whole year shall be sacred
for you; you shall eat only what the fields
produce of themselves.
13 In this year all property that has
been sold shall be restored to its original
owner. 14 So when you sell land to an Israelite or buy land, do not deal unfairly.
15 The price is to be set according to the
number of years the land can produce
crops before the next Year of Restoration. 16 If there are many years, the price
shall be higher, but if there are only a few
years, the price shall be lower, because
what is being sold is the number of crops
the land can produce. 17 Do not cheat an
Israelite, but obey the LORD your God.

The Problem of the Seventh Year

18 Obey all the LORD's laws and commands, so that you may live in safety in
the land. 19 The land will produce its
crops, and you will have all you want to
eat and will live in safety.
20 But someone may ask what there
will be to eat during the seventh year,
when no fields are planted and no crops
gathered. 21 The LORD will bless the land
in the sixth year so that it will produce
enough food for two years. 22 When you
plant your fields in the eighth year, you
will still be eating what you harvested
during the sixth year, and you will have
enough to eat until the crops you plant
that year are harvested.

Restoration of Property

23 Your land must not be sold on a permanent basis, because you do not own it;
it belongs to God, and you are like foreigners who are allowed to make use
of it.
24 When land is sold, the right of the
original owner to buy it back must be
recognized. 25 If any of you Israelites become poor and are forced to sell your

land, your closest relative is to buy it
back. 26 If you have no relative to buy it
back, you may later become prosperous
and have enough to buy it back yourself.
27 In that case you must pay to the one
who bought it a sum that will make up for
the years remaining until the next Year
of Restoration, when you would in any
event recover your land. 28 But if you do
not have enough money to buy the land
back, it remains under the control of the
one who bought it until the next Year of
Restoration. In that year it will be returned to its original owner.
29 If you sell a house in a walled city,
you have the right to buy it back during
the first full year from the date of sale.
30 But if you do not buy it back within the
year, you lose the right of repurchase,
and the house becomes the permanent
property of the purchasers and their
descendants; it will not be returned in the
Year of Restoration. 31 But houses in unwalled villages are to be treated like
fields; the original owner has the right to
buy them back, and they are to be returned in the Year of Restoration.
32 However, Levites have the right to buy
back at any time their property in the
cities assigned to them. 33 If a house in
one of these cities is sold by a Levite and
is not bought back, it must be returned in
the Year of Restoration,[n] because the
houses which the Levites own in their
cities are their permanent property
among the people of Israel. 34 But the
pasture land around the Levite cities
shall never be sold; it is their property
forever.

Loans to the Poor

35 If any Israelites living near you become poor and cannot support themselves, you must provide for them as you
would for a hired worker, so that they
can continue to live near you. 36 Do not
charge Israelites any interest, but obey
God and let them live near you. 37 Do not
make them pay interest on the money
you lend them, and do not make a profit
on the food you sell them. 38 This is the
command of the LORD your God, who
brought you out of Egypt in order to give
you the land of Canaan and to be
your God.

Release of Slaves

39 If any Israelites living near you become so poor that they sell themselves to
you as a slave, you shall not make them
do the work of a slave. 40 They shall stay
with you as hired workers and serve you
until the next Year of Restoration. 41 At
that time they and their children shall
leave you and return to their family and
to the property of their ancestors. 42 The
people of Israel are the LORD's slaves, and
he brought them out of Egypt; they must
not be sold into slavery. 43 Do not treat
them harshly, but obey your God. 44 If
you need slaves, you may buy them from
the nations around you. 45 You may also
buy the children of the foreigners who
are living among you. Such children
born in your land may become your
property, 46 and you may leave them as
an inheritance to your children, whom
they must serve as long as they live. But
you must not treat any Israelites harshly.
47 Suppose a foreigner living with you
becomes rich, while some Israelites become poor and sell themselves as slaves
to that foreigner or to a member of that
foreigner's family. 48 After they are sold,
they still have the right to be bought
back. A brother 49 or an uncle or a cousin
or another close relative may buy them
back; or if they themselves earn enough,
they may buy their own freedom. 50 They
must consult the one who bought them,
and they must count the years from the
time they sold themselves until the next
Year of Restoration and must set the
price for their release on the basis of the
wages paid hired workers. 51-52 They
must refund a part of the purchase price
according to the number of years left,
53 as if they had been hired on an annual
basis. Their master must not treat them
harshly. 54 If they are not set free in any
of these ways, they and their children
must be set free in the next Year of Restoration. 55 Israelites cannot be permanent slaves, because the people of Israel
are the LORD's slaves. He brought them
out of Egypt; he is the LORD their God.

Blessings for Obedience

(Deuteronomy 7.12-24; 28.1-14)

26 The LORD said, "Do not make
idols or set up statues, stone pillars, or carved stones to worship. I am

[n] *Probable text* If a house . . . Restoration; *Hebrew unclear.*

the LORD your God. 2 Keep the religious festivals and honor the place where I am worshiped. I am the LORD.

3 "If you live according to my laws and obey my commands, 4 I will send you rain at the right time, so that the land will produce crops and the trees will bear fruit. 5 Your crops will be so plentiful that you will still be harvesting grain when it is time to pick grapes, and you will still be picking grapes when it is time to plant grain. You will have all that you want to eat, and you can live in safety in your land.

6 "I will give you peace in your land, and you can sleep without being afraid of anyone. I will get rid of the dangerous animals in the land, and there will be no more war there. 7 You will be victorious over your enemies; 8 five of you will be able to defeat a hundred, and a hundred will be able to defeat ten thousand. 9 I will bless you and give you many children; I will keep my part of the covenant that I made with you. 10 Your harvests will be so plentiful that they will last for a year, and even then you will have to throw away what is left of the old harvest to make room for the new. 11 I will live among you in my sacred Tent, and I will never turn away from you. 12 I will be with you; I will be your God, and you will be my people. 13 I, the LORD your God, brought you out of Egypt so that you would no longer be slaves. I broke the power that held you down and I let you walk with your head held high."

Punishment for Disobedience

(Deuteronomy 28.15-68)

14 The LORD said, "If you will not obey my commands, you will be punished. 15 If you refuse to obey my laws and commands and break the covenant I have made with you, 16 I will punish you. I will bring disaster on you—incurable diseases and fevers that will make you blind and cause your life to waste away. You will plant your crops, but it will do you no good, because your enemies will conquer you and eat what you have grown. 17 I will turn against you, so that you will be defeated, and those who hate you will rule over you; you will be so terrified that you will run when no one is chasing you.

18 "If even after all of this you still do not obey me, I will increase your punishment seven times. 19 I will break your stubborn pride; there will be no rain, and your land will be dry and as hard as iron. 20 All your hard work will do you no good, because your land will not produce crops and the trees will not bear fruit.

21 "If you still continue to resist me and refuse to obey me, I will again increase your punishment seven times. 22 I will send dangerous animals among you, and they will kill your children, destroy your livestock, and leave so few of you that your roads will be deserted.

23 "If after all of this punishment you still do not listen to me, but continue to defy me, 24 then I will turn on you and punish you seven times harder than before. 25 I will bring war on you to punish you for breaking our covenant, and if you gather in your cities for safety, I will send incurable diseases among you, and you will be forced to surrender to your enemies. 26 I will cut off your food supply, so that ten women will need only one oven to bake all the bread they have. They will ration it out, and when you have eaten it all, you will still be hungry.

27 "If after all of this you still continue to defy me and refuse to obey me, 28 then in my anger I will turn on you and again make your punishment seven times worse than before. 29 Your hunger will be so great that you will eat your own children. 30 I will destroy your places of worship on the hills, tear down your incense altars, and throw your dead bodies on your fallen idols. In utter disgust 31 I will turn your cities into ruins, destroy your places of worship, and refuse to accept your sacrifices. 32 I will destroy your land so completely that the enemies who occupy it will be shocked at the destruction. 33 I will bring war on you and scatter you in foreign lands. Your land will be deserted, and your cities left in ruins. 34-35 Then the land will enjoy the years of complete rest that you would not give it; it will lie abandoned and get its rest while you are in exile in the land of your enemies.

36 "I will make those of you who are in exile so terrified that the sound of a leaf blowing in the wind will make you run. You will run as if you were being pursued in battle, and you will fall when there is no enemy near you. 37 You will stumble over one another when no one is chasing you, and you will be unable to fight against any enemy. 38 You will die

in exile, swallowed up by the land of
your enemies. 39 The few of you who survive in the land of your enemies will
waste away because of your own sin and
the sin of your ancestors.
40 "But your descendants will confess
their sins and the sins of their ancestors,
who resisted me and rebelled against me,
41 and caused me to turn against them
and send them into exile in the land of
their enemies. At last, when your
descendants are humbled and they have
paid the penalty for their sin and rebellion, 42 I will remember my covenant with
Jacob and with Isaac and with Abraham,
and I will renew my promise to give my
people the land. 43 First, however, the
land must be rid of its people, so that it
can enjoy its complete rest, and they
must pay the full penalty for having rejected my laws and my commands. 44 But
even then, when they are still in the land
of their enemies, I will not completely
abandon them or destroy them. That
would put an end to my covenant with
them, and I am the LORD their God.
45 I will renew the covenant that I made
with their ancestors when I showed all
the nations my power by bringing my
people out of Egypt, in order that I, the
LORD, might be their God."
46 All these are the laws and commands
that the LORD gave to Moses on Mount
Sinai for the people of Israel.

Laws concerning Gifts to the LORD

27 The LORD gave Moses 2 the following regulations for the people
of Israel. When any of you have been
given to the LORD in fulfillment of a special vow, you may be set free by the payment of the following sums of money,
3-7 according to the official standard:
–adult male, twenty to sixty years
old: 50 pieces of silver
–adult female: 30 pieces of silver
–young male, five to twenty years
old: 20 pieces of silver
–young female: 10 pieces of silver
–infant male under five: 5 pieces
of silver
–infant female: 3 pieces of silver
–male above sixty years of age:
15 pieces of silver
–female above sixty: 10 pieces of
silver
8 If any of you make a vow and are too
poor to pay the standard price, you shall
bring the person to the priest, and the
priest will set a lower price, according to
your ability to pay.
9 If your vow concerns an animal that
is acceptable as an offering to the LORD,
then every gift made to the LORD is sacred, 10 and you may not substitute another animal for it. If you do, both
animals belong to the LORD. 11 But if your
vow concerns a ritually unclean animal,
which is not acceptable as an offering to
the LORD, you shall take the animal to the
priest. 12 The priest shall set a price for it,
according to its good or bad qualities,
and the price will be final. 13 If you wish
to buy it back, you must pay the price
plus an additional 20 percent.
14 When any of you dedicate your
house to the LORD, the priest shall set the
price according to its good or bad points,
and the price will be final. 15 If you wish
to buy your house back, you must pay the
price plus an additional 20 percent.
16 If any of you dedicate part of your
land to the LORD, the price shall be set
according to the amount of seed it takes
to sow it, at the rate of ten pieces of silver
per bushel of barley. 17 If you dedicate the
land immediately after a Year of Restoration, the full price applies. 18 If you dedicate it any time later, the priest shall
estimate the cash value according to the
number of years left until the next Year
of Restoration, and set a reduced price.
19 If you wish to buy your field back, you
must pay the price plus an additional 20
percent. 20 If you sell the field to someone
else without first buying it back from the
LORD, you lose the right to buy it back.
21 At the next Year of Restoration the
field will become the LORD's permanent
property; it shall belong to the priests.
22 If you dedicate to the LORD a field that
you have bought, 23 the priest shall estimate its value according to the number
of years until the next Year of Restoration, and you must pay the price that very
day; the money belongs to the LORD. 24 At
the Year of Restoration the field shall be
returned to the original owner or to the
descendants.
25 All prices shall be set according to
the official standard.
26 The first-born of an animal already
belongs to the LORD, so no one may dedicate it to him as a freewill offering. A
calf, a lamb, or a kid belongs to the LORD,

27 but the first-born of an unclean animal
may be bought back at the standard price
plus an additional 20 percent. If it is not
bought back, it may be sold to someone
else at the standard price.

28 None of you may sell or buy back
what you have unconditionally dedicated[o] to the LORD, whether it is a human
being, an animal, or land. It belongs permanently to the LORD. 29 Not even human
beings who have been unconditionally
dedicated may be bought back; they
must be put to death.

30 One tenth of all the produce of the
land, whether grain or fruit, belongs to
the LORD. 31 If you wish to buy any of it
back, you must pay the standard price
plus an additional 20 percent. 32 One of
every ten domestic animals belongs to
the LORD. When the animals are counted,
every tenth one belongs to the LORD.
33 You may not arrange the animals so
that the poor animals are chosen, and
you may not make any substitutions. If
you do substitute one animal for another,
then both animals will belong to the LORD
and may not be bought back.

34 These are the commands that the
LORD gave Moses on Mount Sinai for the
people of Israel.

[o] UNCONDITIONALLY DEDICATED: *Anything dedicated in this way belonged completely to the LORD and could not be used; it had to be destroyed.*

NUMBERS

Introduction

The book of Numbers *tells the story of the Israelites during the nearly forty years from the time they left Mount Sinai until they reached the eastern border of the land that God had promised to give them. The name of the book refers to a prominent feature of the story, that is, the census which Moses took of the Israelites at Mount Sinai before their departure, and again in Moab, east of the Jordan, about a generation later. In the period between the two censuses the Israelites went to Kadesh Barnea on the southern border of Canaan, but failed to enter the promised land from there. After spending many years in that area, they went to the region east of the Jordan River, where part of the people settled and where the rest prepared to cross the river into Canaan.*

The book of Numbers *is an account of a people who were often discouraged and afraid in the face of hardship, and who rebelled against God and against Moses, the man God appointed to lead them. It is the story of God's faithful, persistent care for his people in spite of their weakness and disobedience, and of Moses' steadfast, if sometimes impatient, devotion both to God and to his people.*

Outline of Contents

The First Census of Israel

1 On the first day of the second month
in the second year after the people
of Israel left Egypt, the LORD spoke to
Moses there in the Tent of his presence in
the Sinai Desert. He said, 2 "You and
Aaron are to take a census of the people
of Israel by clans and families. List the
names of all the men 3 twenty years old
or older who are fit for military service.
4 Ask one clan chief from each tribe to
help you." 5-16 These are the men, leaders
within their tribes, who were chosen
from the community for this work:

Tribe	*Clan chief*
Reuben	Elizur son of Shedeur
Simeon	Shelumiel son of Zurishaddai
Judah	Nahshon son of Amminadab
Issachar	Nethanel son of Zuar
Zebulun	Eliab son of Helon
Ephraim	Elishama son of Ammihud
Manasseh	Gamaliel son of Pedahzur
Benjamin	Abidan son of Gideoni
Dan	Ahiezer son of Ammishaddai
Asher	Pagiel son of Ochran
Gad	Eliasaph son of Deuel
Naphtali	Ahira son of Enan

17 With the help of these twelve men
Moses and Aaron 18 called together the
whole community on the first day of the
second month and registered all the people by clans and families. The names of
all the men twenty years old or older
were recorded and counted, 19 as the
LORD had commanded. In the Sinai
Desert, Moses registered the people.
20-46 The men twenty years old or older
who were fit for military service were
registered by name according to clan

and family, beginning with the tribe of Reuben, Jacob's oldest son. The totals were as follows:

Tribe	*Number*
Reuben	46,500
Simeon	59,300
Gad	45,650
Judah	74,600
Issachar	54,400
Zebulun	57,400
Ephraim	40,500
Manasseh	32,200
Benjamin	35,400
Dan	62,700
Asher	41,500
Naphtali	53,400
Total:	603,550

47 The Levites were not registered with
the other tribes, 48 because the LORD had
said to Moses, 49 "When you take a census of the men fit for military service, do
not include the tribe of Levi. 50 Instead,
put the Levites in charge of the Tent of my presence and all its equipment. They shall carry it and its equipment, serve in it, and set up their camp around it.
51 Whenever you move your camp, the Levites shall take the Tent down and set it up again at each new campsite. Anyone else who comes near the Tent shall
be put to death. 52 The rest of the Israelites shall set up camp, company by company, each man with his own group and
under his own banner. 53 But the Levites shall camp around the Tent to guard it, so that no one may come near and cause my anger to strike the community of Israel."
54 So the people of Israel did everything that the LORD had commanded Moses.

The Arrangement of the Tribes in Camp

2 The LORD gave Moses and Aaron the
following instructions. 2 When the
Israelites set up camp, each man will camp under the banner of his division and the flag of his own clan. The camp is to be set up all around the Tent.
3-9 On the east side, those under the banner of the division of Judah shall camp in their groups, under their leaders, as follows:

Tribe	*Leader*	*Number*
Judah	Nahshon son of Amminadab	74,600
Issachar	Nethanel son of Zuar	54,400
Zebulun	Eliab son of Helon	57,400
	Total:	186,400

The division of Judah shall march first.
10-16 On the south, those under the banner of the division of Reuben shall camp in their groups, under their leaders, as follows:

Tribe	*Leader*	*Number*
Reuben	Elizur son of Shedeur	46,500
Simeon	Shelumiel son of Zurishaddai	59,300
Gad	Eliasaph son of Deuel	45,650
	Total:	151,450

The division of Reuben shall march second.
17 Then, between the first two divisions and the last two the Levites are to march carrying the Tent. Each division shall march in the same order as they camp, each in position under its banner.
18-24 On the west, those under the banner of the division of Ephraim shall camp in their groups, under their leaders, as follows:

Tribe	*Leader*	*Number*
Ephraim	Elishama son of Ammihud	40,500
Manasseh	Gamaliel son of Pedahzur	32,200
Benjamin	Abidan son of Gideoni	35,400
	Total:	108,100

The division of Ephraim shall march third.
25-31 On the north, those under the banner of the division of Dan shall camp in their groups, under their leaders, as follows:

Tribe	*Leader*	*Number*
Dan	Ahiezer son of Ammishaddai	62,700
Asher	Pagiel son of Ochran	41,500
Naphtali	Ahira son of Enan	53,400
	Total:	157,600

The division of Dan shall march last.
32 The total number of the people of

Israel enrolled in the divisions, group by
group, was 603,550. 33 As the LORD had
commanded Moses, the Levites were not
registered with the rest of the Israelites.
34 So the people of Israel did everything the LORD had commanded Moses.
They camped, each under his own banner, and they marched, each with his
own clan.

Aaron's Sons

3 This is the family of Aaron and
Moses at the time the LORD spoke to
Moses on Mount Sinai. 2 Aaron had four
sons: Nadab, the oldest, Abihu, Eleazar,
and Ithamar. 3 They were anointed and
ordained as priests, 4 but Nadab and
Abihu were killed when they offered unholy fire to the LORD in the Sinai Desert.
They had no children, so Eleazar and Ithamar served as priests during Aaron's
lifetime.

The Levites Are Appointed to Serve the Priests

5 The LORD said to Moses, 6 "Bring forward the tribe of Levi and appoint them
as servants of Aaron the priest. 7 They
shall do the work required for the Tent of
my presence and perform duties for the
priests and for the whole community.
8 They shall take charge of all the equipment of the Tent and perform the duties
for the rest of the Israelites. 9 The only
responsibility the Levites have is to serve
Aaron and his sons. 10 You shall appoint
Aaron and his sons to carry out the duties of the priesthood; anyone else who
tries to do so shall be put to death."
11 The LORD said to Moses, 12-13 "The Levites are now to be mine. When I killed
all the first-born of the Egyptians, I consecrated as my own the oldest son of
each Israelite family and the first-born of
every animal. Now, instead of having the
first-born sons of Israel as my own, I
have the Levites; they will belong to me.
I am the LORD."

The Census of the Levites

14 In the Sinai Desert the LORD commanded Moses 15 to register the Levites
by clans and families, enrolling every
male a month old or older, 16 and Moses
did so. 17-20 Levi had three sons: Gershon,
Kohath, and Merari, who were the ancestors of the clans that bear their names.
Gershon had two sons: Libni and
Shimei; Kohath had four sons: Amram,
Izhar, Hebron, and Uzziel; and Merari
had two sons: Mahli and Mushi. They
were the ancestors of the families that
bear their names.
21 The clan of Gershon was composed
of the families of Libni and Shimei. 22 The
total number of males one month old or
older that were enrolled was 7,500.
23 This clan was to camp on the west behind the Tent, 24 with Eliasaph son of
Lael as chief of the clan. 25 They were
responsible for the Tent, its inner cover,
its outer cover, the curtain for the entrance, 26 the curtains for the court which
is around the Tent and the altar, and the
curtain for the entrance of the court.
They were responsible for all the service
connected with these items.
27 The clan of Kohath was composed of
the families of Amram, Izhar, Hebron,
and Uzziel. 28 The total number of males
one month old or older that were enrolled was 8,600. 29 This clan was to camp
on the south side of the Tent, 30 with Elizaphan son of Uzziel as chief of the clan.
31 They were responsible for the Covenant Box, the table, the lampstand, the
altars, the utensils the priests use in the
Holy Place, and the curtain at the entrance to the Most Holy Place. They were
responsible for all the service connected
with these items.
32 The chief of the Levites was Eleazar
son of Aaron the priest. He was in charge
of those who carried out the duties in the
Holy Place.
33 The clan of Merari was composed of
the families of Mahli and Mushi. 34 The
total number of males one month old or
older that were enrolled was 6,200.
35 This clan was to camp on the north side
of the Tent, with Zuriel son of Abihail as
chief of the clan. 36 They were assigned
responsibility for the frames for the Tent,
its bars, posts, bases, and all its fittings.
They were responsible for all the service
connected with these items. 37 They were
also responsible for the posts, bases,
pegs, and ropes for the outer court.
38 Moses and Aaron and his sons were
to camp in front of the Tent on the east.
They were responsible for carrying out
the services performed in the Holy Place
for the people of Israel. Anyone else who
tried to do so was to be put to death.
39 The total number of all the Levite
males one month old or older that Moses

enrolled by clans at the command of the
LORD, was 22,000.

The Levites Take the Place of the First-Born Sons

40-41 The LORD said to Moses, "All of Israel's first-born sons belong to me. So
register by name every first-born male
Israelite, one month old or older. But in
place of them I claim all the Levites as
mine! I am the LORD! I also claim the livestock of the Levites in place of all the
first-born of the livestock." 42 Moses
obeyed, and registered all the first-born
males 43 one month old or older; the total
was 22,273.
44 The LORD said to Moses, 45 "Now dedicate the Levites as mine in place of all
the first-born Israelite sons, and dedicate
the livestock of the Levites in place of the
first-born of the Israelites' livestock.
46 Since the first-born Israelite sons outnumber the Levites by 273, you must buy
back the extra sons. 47 For each one pay
five pieces of silver, according to the official standard, 48 and give this money to
Aaron and his sons." 49 Moses obeyed
and took 50 the 1,365 pieces of silver
51 and gave them to Aaron and his sons.

The Duties of the Levite Clan of Kohath

4 The LORD told Moses 2 to take a census of the Levite clan of Kohath by
subclans and families, 3 and to register
all the men between the ages of thirty
and fifty who were qualified to work in
the Tent of the LORD's presence. 4 Their
service involves the most holy things.
5 The LORD gave Moses the following
instructions. When it is time to break
camp, Aaron and his sons shall enter the
Tent, take down the curtain in front of
the Covenant Box, and cover the Box
with it. 6 They shall put a fine leather
cover over it, spread a cloth of solid blue
on top, and then insert the carrying
poles.
7 They shall spread a blue cloth over
the table for the bread offered to the LORD
and put on it the dishes, the incense
bowls, the offering bowls, and the jars
for the wine offering. There shall always
be bread on the table. 8 They shall spread
a red cloth over all of this, put a fine
leather cover over it, and then insert the
carrying poles.
9 They shall take a blue cloth and cover
the lampstand, with its lamps, tongs,
trays, and all the olive oil containers.
10 They shall wrap it and all its equipment
in a fine leather cover and place it on a
carrying frame.
11 Next they shall spread a blue cloth
over the gold altar, put a fine leather
cover over it, and then insert the carrying
poles. 12 They shall take all the utensils
used in the Holy Place, wrap them in a
blue cloth, put a fine leather cover over
them, and place them on a carrying
frame. 13 They shall remove the greasy
ashes from the altar and spread a purple
cloth over it. 14 They shall put on it all the
equipment used in the service at the altar: fire pans, hooks, shovels, and basins.
Then they shall put a fine leather cover
over it and insert the carrying poles.
15 When it is time to break camp, the clan
of Kohath shall come to carry the sacred
objects only after Aaron and his sons
have finished covering them and all their
equipment. The Kohath clan must not
touch the sacred objects, or they will die.
These are the responsibilities of the
Kohath clan whenever the Tent is
moved.
16 Eleazar son of Aaron the priest shall
be responsible for the whole Tent and for
the oil for the lamps, the incense, the
grain offerings, the anointing oil, and
everything else in the Tent that has been
consecrated to the LORD.
17 The LORD said to Moses and Aaron,
18 "Do not let the clan of Kohath 19 be
killed by coming near these most sacred
objects. To prevent this from happening,
Aaron and his sons shall go in and assign
each man his task and tell him what
to carry. 20 But if the Kohathites enter
the Tent and see the priests preparing
the sacred objects for moving,[a] they
will die."

The Duties of the Levite Clan of Gershon

21 The LORD told Moses 22 to take a census of the Levite clan of Gershon by subclans and families, 23 and to register all
the men between the ages of thirty and
fifty who were qualified to work in the
Tent of the LORD's presence. 24 They shall

[a] see . . . moving; *or* see the sacred objects even for a moment.

be responsible for carrying the following objects: 25 the Tent, its inner cover, its outer cover, the fine leather cover on top of it, the curtain for the entrance, 26 the curtains and ropes for the court that is around the Tent and the altar, the curtains for the entrance of the court, and all the fittings used in setting up these objects. They shall perform all the tasks required for these things. 27 Moses and Aaron shall see to it that the Gershonites perform all the duties and carry everything that Aaron and his sons assign to them. 28 These are the responsibilities of the Gershon clan in the Tent; they shall carry them out under the direction of Ithamar son of Aaron the priest.

The Duties of the Levite Clan of Merari

29 The LORD told Moses to take a census of the Levite clan of Merari by subclans and families, 30 and to register all the men between the ages of thirty and fifty who were qualified to work in the Tent of the LORD's presence. 31 They shall be responsible for carrying the frames, bars, posts, and bases of the Tent, 32 and the posts, bases, pegs, and ropes of the court around the Tent, with all the fittings used in setting them up. Each man will be responsible for carrying specific items. 33 These are the responsibilities of the Merari clan in their service in the Tent; they shall carry them out under the direction of Ithamar son of Aaron the priest.

The Census of the Levites

34-48 Following the LORD's command, Moses, Aaron, and the leaders of the community took a census of the three Levite clans, Kohath, Gershon, and Merari. They did this by subclans and families and registered all the men between the ages of thirty and fifty who were qualified to work in the Tent of the LORD's presence, as follows:

Clan	*Number*
Kohath	2,750
Gershon	2,630
Merari	3,200
Total:	8,580

49 Each man was registered as the LORD had commanded Moses; and at the command of the LORD given through Moses, each man was assigned responsibility for his task of serving or carrying.

Unclean People

5 The LORD said to Moses, 2 "Command the people of Israel to expel from the camp everyone with a dreaded skin disease or a bodily discharge and everyone who is unclean by contact with a corpse. 3 Send all these ritually unclean people out, so that they will not defile the camp, where I live among my people." 4 The Israelites obeyed and expelled them all from the camp.

Repayment for Wrongs Done

5 The LORD gave Moses 6 the following instructions for the people of Israel. When any of you are unfaithful to the LORD and commit a wrong against someone, 7 you must confess your sin and make full repayment, plus an additional 20 percent, to the person you have wronged. 8 But if that person has died and has no near relative to whom payment can be made, it shall be given to the LORD for the priest. This payment is in addition to the ram used to perform the ritual of purification for the guilty person. 9 Also every special contribution which the Israelites offer to the LORD belongs to the priest to whom they present it. 10 Each priest shall keep the offerings presented to him.

Cases of Wives with Suspicious Husbands

11 The LORD commanded Moses 12-14 to give the Israelites the following instructions. It may happen that a man becomes suspicious that his wife is unfaithful to him and has defiled herself by having intercourse with another man. But the husband may not be certain, for his wife may have kept it secret—there was no witness, and she was not caught in the act. Or it may happen that a husband becomes suspicious of his wife, even though she has not been unfaithful. 15 In either case the man shall take his wife to the priest. He shall also take the required offering of two pounds of barley flour, but he shall not pour any olive oil on it or put any incense on it, because it is an offering from a suspicious husband, made to bring the truth to light.

16 The priest shall bring the woman forward and have her stand in front of the

altar. 17 He shall pour some holy water
into a clay bowl and take some of the
earth that is on the floor of the Tent of the
LORD's presence and put it in the water to
make it bitter. 18 Then he shall loosen the
woman's hair and put the offering of
flour in her hands. In his hands the priest
shall hold the bowl containing the bitter
water that brings a curse. 19 Then the
priest shall make the woman agree to
this oath spoken by the priest: "If you
have not committed adultery, you will
not be harmed by the curse that this water brings. 20 But if you have committed
adultery, 21 may the LORD make your
name a curse among your people. May
he cause your genital organs to shrink
and your stomach to swell up. 22 May this
water enter your stomach and cause it to
swell up and your genital organs to
shrink."

The woman shall respond, "I agree;
may the LORD do so."

23 Then the priest shall write this curse
down and wash the writing off into the
bowl of bitter water. 24 Before he makes
the woman drink the water, which may
then cause her bitter pain, 25 the priest
shall take the offering of flour out of the
woman's hands, hold it out in dedication
to the LORD, and present it on the altar.
26 Then he shall take a handful of it as a
token offering and burn it on the altar.
Finally, he shall make the woman drink
the water. 27 If she has committed adultery, the water will cause bitter pain; her
stomach will swell up and her genital organs will shrink. Her name will become
a curse among her people. 28 But if she is
innocent, she will not be harmed and will
be able to bear children.

29-30 This is the law in cases where a
man is jealous and becomes suspicious
that his wife has committed adultery.
The woman shall be made to stand in
front of the altar, and the priest shall perform this ritual. 31 The husband shall be
free of guilt, but the woman, if guilty,
must suffer the consequences.

Rules for Nazirites

6 The LORD commanded Moses 2 to
give the following instructions to
the people of Israel. Any of you, male or
female, who make a special vow to become a nazirite and dedicate yourself to
the LORD 3 shall abstain from wine and
beer. You shall not drink any kind of
drink made from grapes or eat any
grapes or raisins. 4 As long as you are a
nazirite, you shall not eat anything that
comes from a grapevine, not even the
seeds or skins of grapes.

5 As long as you are under the nazirite
vow, you must not cut your hair or shave.
You are bound by the vow for the full
time that you are dedicated to the LORD,
and you shall let your hair grow. 6-7 Your
hair is the sign of your dedication to God,
and so you must not defile yourself by
going near a corpse, not even that of your
father, mother, brother, or sister. 8 As
long as you are a nazirite, you are consecrated to the LORD.

9 If your consecrated hair is defiled because you are right beside someone who
suddenly dies, you must wait seven days
and then shave your head; and so you
become ritually clean. 10 On the eighth
day you shall bring two doves or two pigeons to the priest at the entrance of the
Tent of the LORD's presence. 11 The priest
shall offer one as a sin offering and the
other as a burnt offering, to perform the
ritual of purification for you because of
your contact with a corpse. On the same
day you shall reconsecrate your hair
12 and rededicate to the LORD your time as
a nazirite. The previous period of time
doesn't count, because your consecrated
hair was defiled. As a repayment offering you shall bring a one-year-old lamb.

13 When you complete your nazirite
vow, you shall perform this ritual. You
shall go to the entrance of the Tent 14 and
present to the LORD three animals without any defects: a one-year-old male
lamb for a burnt offering, a one-year-old
ewe lamb for a sin offering, and a ram for
a fellowship offering. 15 You shall also offer a basket of bread made without yeast:
thick loaves made of flour mixed with
olive oil and thin cakes brushed with olive oil, and in addition the required offerings of grain and wine.

16 The priest shall present all these to
the LORD and offer the sin offering and
the burnt offering. 17 He shall sacrifice
the ram to the LORD as a fellowship offering, and offer it with the basket of bread;
he shall also present the offerings of
grain and wine. 18 At the entrance of the
Tent you nazirites shall shave off your
hair and put it on the fire on which the
fellowship offering is being burned.

19 Then, when the shoulder of the ram

is boiled, the priest shall take it and put
it, together with one thick loaf of bread
and one thin cake from the basket, into
the hands of the nazirite. 20 Next, the
priest shall present them as a special gift
to the LORD; they are a sacred offering for
the priest, in addition to the breast and
the leg of the ram which by law belong to
the priest. After that, the nazirite may
drink wine.
21 These are the regulations for you
nazirites; but if you promise an offering
beyond what your vow requires you to
give, you must fulfill exactly the promise
you made.

The Priestly Blessing

22 The LORD commanded Moses 23 to tell
Aaron and his sons to use the following
words in blessing the people of Israel:

24 May the LORD bless you and take
care of you;
25 May the LORD be kind and
gracious to you;
26 May the LORD look on you with
favor and give you peace.

27 And the LORD said, "If they pronounce my name as a blessing upon the
people of Israel, I will bless them."

The Offerings of the Leaders

7 On the day Moses finished setting
up the Tent of the LORD's presence,
he anointed and dedicated the Tent and
all its equipment, and the altar and all its
equipment. 2 Then the clan chiefs who
were leaders in the tribes of Israel, the
same men who were in charge of the census, 3 brought their offerings to the LORD:
six wagons and twelve oxen, a wagon for
every two leaders and an ox for each
leader. After they had presented them,
4 the LORD said to Moses, 5 "Accept these
gifts for use in the work to be done for the
Tent; give them to the Levites according
to the work they have to do." 6 So Moses
gave the wagons and the oxen to the Levites. 7 He gave two wagons and four
oxen to the Gershonites, 8 and four wagons and eight oxen to the Merarites. All
their work was to be done under the direction of Ithamar son of Aaron. 9 But
Moses gave no wagons or oxen to the
Kohathites, because the sacred objects
they took care of had to be carried on
their shoulders.
10 The leaders also brought offerings to
celebrate the dedication of the altar.
When they were ready to present their
gifts at the altar, 11 the LORD said to
Moses, "Tell them that each day for a
period of twelve days one of the leaders
is to present his gifts for the dedication of
the altar."
12-83 They presented their offerings in
the following order:

Day	*Tribe*	*Leader*
1st	Judah	Nahshon son of Amminadab
2nd	Issachar	Nethanel son of Zuar
3rd	Zebulun	Eliab son of Helon
4th	Reuben	Elizur son of Shedeur
5th	Simeon	Shelumiel son of Zurishaddai
6th	Gad	Eliasaph son of Deuel
7th	Ephraim	Elishama son of Ammihud
8th	Manasseh	Gamaliel son of Pedahzur
9th	Benjamin	Abidan son of Gideoni
10th	Dan	Ahiezer son of Ammishaddai
11th	Asher	Pagiel son of Ochran
12th	Naphtali	Ahira son of Enan

The offerings each one brought were
identical: one silver bowl weighing 50
ounces and one silver basin weighing 30
ounces, by the official standard, both of
them full of flour mixed with oil for the
grain offering; one gold dish weighing 4
ounces, full of incense; one young bull,
one ram, and a one-year-old lamb, for
the burnt offering; one goat for the sin
offering; and two bulls, five rams, five
goats, and five one-year-old lambs, for
the fellowship offering.
84-88 The totals of the offerings brought
by the twelve leaders for the dedication
of the altar were as follows:

–twelve silver bowls and twelve silver basins weighing a total of 60 pounds
–twelve gold dishes weighing a total of 48 ounces, filled with incense
–twelve bulls, twelve rams, and twelve one-year-old lambs, plus the grain offerings that go with them, for the burnt offerings

–twelve goats for the sin offerings
–twenty-four bulls, sixty rams,
sixty goats, sixty one-year-old
lambs, for the fellowship
offerings
89 When Moses went into the Tent to
talk with the LORD, he heard the LORD
speaking to him from above the lid on the
Covenant Box, between the two winged
creatures.[b]

Placing the Lamps

8 The LORD said to Moses, 2 "Tell
Aaron that when he puts the seven
lamps on the lampstand, he should place
them so that the light shines toward the
front." 3 Aaron obeyed and placed the
lamps facing the front of the lampstand.
4 From top to bottom the lampstand was
made of hammered gold, according to
the pattern that the LORD had shown
Moses.

The Purification and Dedication of the Levites

5 The LORD said to Moses, 6 "Separate
the Levites from the rest of the people of
Israel and purify them 7 in the following
way: sprinkle them with the water of purification and have them shave their
whole bodies and have them wash their
clothes. Then they will be ritually clean.
8 Then they are to take a young bull and
the required grain offering of flour
mixed with olive oil; and you are to take
another bull for the sin offering. 9 Then
assemble the whole community of Israel
and have the Levites stand in front of the
Tent of my presence. 10 The people of Israel are to place their hands on the heads
of the Levites, 11 and then Aaron shall
dedicate the Levites to me as a special
gift from the Israelites, so that they may
do my work. 12 The Levites shall then put
their hands on the heads of the two bulls;
one is to be offered as a sin offering and
the other as a burnt offering, in order to
perform the ritual of purification for the
Levites.
13 "Dedicate the Levites as a special gift
to me, and put Aaron and his sons in
charge of them. 14 Separate the Levites in
this way from the rest of the Israelites, so
that they will belong to me. 15 After you
have purified and dedicated the Levites,
they will be qualified to work in the Tent.
16 I have claimed them in the place of all
the first-born sons of the Israelites, and
they belong to me alone. 17 When I killed
all the first-born in Egypt, I consecrated
as my own the oldest son of each Israelite
family and the first-born of every animal.
18 I am now taking the Levites instead of
all the first-born of the Israelites, 19 and I
assign the Levites to Aaron and his sons,
as a gift from the Israelites, to work in the
Tent for the people of Israel and to protect the Israelites from the disaster that
would strike them if they came too near
the Holy Place."
20 So Moses, Aaron, and all the people
of Israel dedicated the Levites, as the
LORD commanded Moses. 21 The Levites
purified themselves and washed their
clothes, and Aaron dedicated them as a
special gift to the LORD. He also performed the ritual of purification for
them. 22 The people did everything the
LORD had commanded Moses concerning
the Levites. And so the Levites were
qualified to work in the Tent under
Aaron and his sons.
23 The LORD said to Moses, 24 "From the
age of twenty-five each Levite shall perform his duties in the Tent of my presence, 25 and at the age of fifty he shall
retire. 26 After that, he may help his fellow Levites in performing their duties in
the Tent, but he must not perform any
service by himself. This is how you are to
regulate the duties of the Levites."

The Second Passover

9 The LORD spoke to Moses in the Sinai Desert in the first month of the
second year after the people of Israel had
left Egypt. He said, 2-3 "On the fourteenth
day of this month, beginning at sunset,
the people of Israel are to observe the
Passover according to all the rules and
regulations for it." 4 So Moses told the
people to observe the Passover, 5 and on
the evening of the fourteenth day of the
first month they did so in the Sinai
Desert. The people did everything just as
the LORD had commanded Moses.
6 But there were some people who were
ritually unclean because they had
touched a corpse, and they were not able
to keep the Passover on that day. They
went to Moses and Aaron 7 and said, "We
are unclean because we have touched a

[b] WINGED CREATURES: *See Word List.*

corpse, but why should we be excluded
from presenting the LORD's offering with
the rest of the Israelites?"
8 Moses answered, "Wait until I receive
instructions from the LORD."
9 The LORD told Moses 10 to say to the
people of Israel, "When any of you or
your descendants are unclean from
touching a corpse or are far away on a
journey, but still want to keep the Passover, 11 you are permitted to observe it
one month later instead, on the evening
of the fourteenth day of the second
month. Celebrate it with unleavened
bread and bitter herbs. 12 Do not leave
any of the food until the following morning and do not break any of the animal's
bones. Observe the Passover according
to all the regulations. 13 But if any of you
are ritually clean and not away on a journey and do not observe the Passover, you
shall no longer be considered my people,
because you did not present the offering
to me at the appointed time. You must
suffer the consequences of your sin.
14 "If foreigners living among you want
to keep the Passover, they must observe
it according to all the rules and regulations. The same law applies to everyone,
whether native or foreigner."

The Fiery Cloud

(Exodus 40.34-38)

15-16 On the day the Tent of the LORD's
presence was set up, a cloud came and
covered it. At night the cloud looked like
fire. 17 Whenever the cloud lifted, the
people of Israel broke camp, and they set
up camp again in the place where the
cloud came down. 18 The people broke
camp at the command of the LORD, and at
his command they set up camp. As long
as the cloud stayed over the Tent, they
stayed in the same camp. 19 When the
cloud stayed over the Tent for a long
time, they obeyed the LORD and did not
move on. 20 Sometimes the cloud remained over the Tent for only a few days;
in any case, they remained in camp or
moved, according to the command of the
LORD. 21 Sometimes the cloud remained
only from evening until morning, and
they moved on as soon as the cloud lifted.
Whenever the cloud lifted, they moved
on. 22 Whether it was two days, a month,
a year, or longer, as long as the cloud
remained over the Tent, they did not
move on; but when it lifted, they moved.
23 They set up camp and broke camp in
obedience to the commands which the
LORD gave through Moses.

The Silver Trumpets

10 The LORD said to Moses, 2 "Make
two trumpets of hammered silver
to use for calling the people together and
for breaking camp. 3 When long blasts
are sounded on both trumpets, the whole
community is to gather around you at the
entrance to the Tent of my presence.
4 But when only one trumpet is sounded,
then only the leaders of the clans are to
gather around you. 5 When short blasts
are sounded, the tribes camped on the
east will move out. 6 When short blasts
are sounded a second time, the tribes on
the south will move out. So short blasts
are to be sounded to break camp, 7 but in
order to call the community together,
long blasts are to be sounded. 8 The trumpets are to be blown by Aaron's sons, the
priests.
"The following rule is to be observed
for all time to come. 9 When you are at
war in your land, defending yourselves
against an enemy who has attacked you,
sound the signal for battle on these trumpets. I, the LORD your God, will help you
and save you from your enemies. 10 Also
on joyful occasions — at your New Moon
Festivals and your other religious
festivals — you are to blow the trumpets
when you present your burnt offerings
and your fellowship offerings. Then I
will help you. I am the LORD your God."

The Israelites Break Camp

11 On the twentieth day of the second
month in the second year after the people
left Egypt, the cloud over the Tent of the
LORD's presence lifted, 12 and the Israelites started on their journey out of the
Sinai Desert. The cloud came to rest in
the wilderness of Paran.
13 They began to march at the command of the LORD through Moses, 14 and
each time they moved, they were in the
same order. Those under the banner of
the division led by the tribe of Judah
started out first, company by company,
with Nahshon son of Amminadab in
command. 15 Nethanel son of Zuar was in
command of the tribe of Issachar, 16 and
Eliab son of Helon was in command of
the tribe of Zebulun.
17 Then the Tent would be taken down,

and the clans of Gershon and Merari,
who carried it, would start out.
18 Next, those under the banner of the
division led by the tribe of Reuben would
start out, company by company, with Eli-
zur son of Shedeur in command. 19 She-
lumiel son of Zurishaddai was in
command of the tribe of Simeon, 20 and
Eliasaph son of Deuel was in command
of the tribe of Gad.
21 Then the Levite clan of Kohath
would start out, carrying the sacred objects. By the time they arrived at the next
camp, the Tent had been set up again.
22 Next, those under the banner of the
division led by the tribe of Ephraim
would start out, company by company,
with Elishama son of Ammihud in command. 23 Gamaliel son of Pedahzur was
in command of the tribe of Manasseh,
24 and Abidan son of Gideoni was in command of the tribe of Benjamin.
25 Finally, those under the banner of
the division led by the tribe of Dan, serving as the rear guard of all the divisions,
would start out, company by company,
with Ahiezer son of Ammishaddai in
command. 26 Pagiel son of Ochran was in
command of the tribe of Asher, 27 and
Ahira son of Enan was in command of
the tribe of Naphtali. 28 This, then, was
the order of march, company by company, whenever the Israelites broke
camp and set out.
29 Moses said to his brother-in-law Hobab son of Jethro the Midianite, "We are
about to start out for the place which the
LORD said he would give us. He has promised to make Israel prosperous, so come
with us, and we will share our prosperity
with you."
30 Hobab answered, "No, I am going
back to my native land."
31 "Please don't leave us," Moses said.
"You know where we can camp in the
wilderness, and you can be our guide.
32 If you come with us, we will share with
you all the blessings that the LORD
gives us."

The People Set Out

33 When the people left Sinai, the holy
mountain, they traveled three days. The
LORD's Covenant Box always went ahead
of them to find a place for them to camp.
34 As they moved on from each camp, the
cloud of the LORD was over them by day.
35 Whenever the Covenant Box started
out, Moses would say, "Arise, LORD; scatter your enemies and put to flight those
who hate you!" 36 And whenever it
stopped, he would say, "Return, LORD, to
the thousands of families of Israel."[c]

The Place Named Taberah

11 The people began to complain to
the LORD about their troubles.
When the LORD heard them, he became
angry and sent fire on the people. It
burned among them and destroyed one
end of the camp. 2 The people cried out to
Moses for help; he prayed to the LORD,
and the fire died down. 3 So the place was
named Taberah,[d] because there the fire
of the LORD burned among them.

Moses Chooses Seventy Leaders

4 There were foreigners traveling with
the Israelites. They had a strong craving
for meat, and even the Israelites themselves began to complain: "If only we
could have some meat! 5 In Egypt we
used to eat all the fish we wanted, and it
cost us nothing. Remember the cucum-
bers, the watermelons, the leeks, the onions, and the garlic we had? 6 But now
our strength is gone. There is nothing at
all to eat – nothing but this manna day
after day!"
(7 Manna was like small seeds, whitish
yellow in color. 8-9 It fell on the camp at
night along with the dew. The next morning the people would go around and
gather it, grind it or pound it into flour,
and then boil it and make it into flat
cakes. It tasted like bread baked with olive oil.)
10 Moses heard all the people complaining as they stood around in groups
at the entrances of their tents. He was
distressed because the LORD had become
angry with them, 11 and he said to the
LORD, "Why have you treated me so
badly? Why are you displeased with me?
Why have you given me the responsibility for all these people? 12 I didn't create
them or bring them to birth! Why should
you ask me to act like a nurse and carry
them in my arms like babies all the way
to the land you promised to their ancestors? 13 Where could I get enough meat

[c] Return . . . Israel; *or* Return, LORD, you who are like an army of millions for Israel.
[d] TABERAH: *This name sounds like the Hebrew for "burning."*

for all these people? They keep whining
and asking for meat. 14 I can't be responsible for all these people by myself; it's
too much for me! 15 If you are going to
treat me like this, have pity on me and
kill me, so that I won't have to endure
your cruelty any longer."

16 The LORD said to Moses, "Assemble
seventy respected men who are recognized as leaders of the people, bring
them to me at the Tent of my presence,
and tell them to stand there beside you.
17 I will come down and speak with you
there, and I will take some of the spirit I
have given you and give it to them. Then
they can help you bear the responsibility
for these people, and you will not have to
bear it alone. 18 Now tell the people, 'Purify yourselves for tomorrow; you will
have meat to eat. The LORD has heard you
whining and saying that you wished you
had some meat and that you were better
off in Egypt. Now the LORD will give you
meat, and you will have to eat it. 19 You
will have to eat it not just for one or two
days, or five, or ten, or even twenty days,
20 but for a whole month, until it comes
out of your ears, until you are sick of it.
This will happen because you have rejected the LORD who is here among you
and have complained to him that you
should never have left Egypt.' "

21 Moses said to the LORD, "Here I am
leading 600,000 people, and you say that
you will give them enough meat for a
month? 22 Could enough cattle and sheep
be killed to satisfy them? Are all the fish
in the sea enough for them?"

23 "Is there a limit to my power?" the
LORD answered. "You will soon see
whether what I have said will happen
or not!"

24 So Moses went out and told the people what the LORD had said. He assembled seventy of the leaders and placed
them around the Tent. 25 Then the LORD
came down in the cloud and spoke to
him. He took some of the spirit he had
given to Moses and gave it to the seventy
leaders. When the spirit came on them,
they began to shout like prophets, but
not for long.

26 Two of the seventy leaders, Eldad
and Medad, had stayed in the camp and
had not gone out to the Tent. There in the
camp the spirit came on them, and they
too began to shout like prophets.
27 A young man ran out to tell Moses
what Eldad and Medad were doing.

28 Then Joshua son of Nun, who had
been Moses' helper since he was a young
man, spoke up and said to Moses, "Stop
them, sir!"

29 Moses answered, "Are you concerned about my interests? I wish that
the LORD would give his spirit to all his
people and make all of them shout like
prophets!" 30 Then Moses and the seventy leaders of Israel went back to camp.

The LORD Sends Quails

31 Suddenly the LORD sent a wind that
brought quails from the sea, flying three
feet above the ground. They settled on
the camp and all around it for miles and
miles in every direction.[e] 32 So all that
day, all night, and all the next day, the
people worked catching quails; no one
gathered less than fifty bushels. They
spread them out to dry all around the
camp. 33 While there was still plenty of
meat for them to eat, the LORD became
angry with the people and caused an epidemic to break out among them. 34 That
place was named Kibroth Hattaavah
(which means "Graves of Craving"), because there they buried the people who
had craved meat.

35 From there the people moved to Hazeroth, where they made camp.

Miriam Is Punished

12 Moses had married a Cushite[f]
woman, and Miriam and Aaron
criticized him for it. 2 They said, "Has the
LORD spoken only through[g] Moses?
Hasn't he also spoken through[g] us?"
The LORD heard what they said. (3 Moses
was a humble man, more humble than
anyone else on earth.)

4 Suddenly the LORD said to Moses,
Aaron, and Miriam, "I want the three of
you to come out to the Tent of my presence." They went, 5 and the LORD came
down in a pillar of cloud, stood at the
entrance of the Tent, and called out,
"Aaron! Miriam!" The two of them
stepped forward, 6 and the LORD said,
"Now hear what I have to say! When

[e] sea, flying . . . direction; *or* sea. They settled in the camp and all around it for miles and miles in every direction, until they were piled up three feet deep on the ground. [f] Cushite *(compare Hb 3.7); or* Midianite; *or* Ethiopian. [g] through; *or* to.

there are prophets among you,[h] I reveal
myself to them in visions and speak to
them in dreams. 7 It is different when I
speak with my servant Moses; I have put
him in charge of all my people Israel.[i]
8 So I speak to him face-to-face, clearly
and not in riddles; he has even seen my
form! How dare you speak against my
servant Moses?"
9 The LORD was angry with them; and
so as he departed 10 and the cloud left the
Tent, Miriam's skin was suddenly covered with a dreaded disease and turned
as white as snow. When Aaron looked at
her and saw that she was covered with
the disease, 11 he said to Moses, "Please,
sir, do not make us suffer this punishment for our foolish sin. 12 Don't let her
become like something born dead with
half its flesh eaten away."
13 So Moses cried out to the LORD,
"O God, heal her!"
14 The LORD answered, "If her father
had spit in her face, she would have to
bear her disgrace for seven days. So let
her be shut out of the camp for a week,
and after that she can be brought back
in." 15 Miriam was shut out of the camp
for seven days, and the people did not
move on until she was brought back in.
16 Then they left Hazeroth and set up
camp in the wilderness of Paran.

The Spies

(Deuteronomy 1.19-33)

13 The LORD said to Moses,
2 "Choose one of the leaders from
each of the twelve tribes and send them
as spies to explore the land of Canaan,
which I am giving to the Israelites."
3-15 Moses obeyed and from the wilderness of Paran he sent out leaders, as
follows:

Tribe	*Leader*
Reuben	Shammua son of Zaccur
Simeon	Shaphat son of Hori
Judah	Caleb son of Jephunneh
Issachar	Igal son of Joseph
Ephraim	Hoshea son of Nun
Benjamin	Palti son of Raphu
Zebulun	Gaddiel son of Sodi
Manasseh	Gaddi son of Susi
Dan	Ammiel son of Gemalli
Asher	Sethur son of Michael
Naphtali	Nahbi son of Vophsi
Gad	Geuel son of Machi

16 These are the spies Moses sent to explore the land. He changed the name of
Hoshea son of Nun to Joshua.
17 When Moses sent them out, he said
to them, "Go north from here into the
southern part of the land of Canaan and
then on into the hill country. 18 Find out
what kind of country it is, how many people live there, and how strong they are.
19 Find out whether the land is good or
bad and whether the people live in open
towns or in fortified cities. 20 Find out
whether the soil is fertile and whether
the land is wooded. And be sure to bring
back some of the fruit that grows there."
(It was the season when grapes were beginning to ripen.)
21 So the men went north and explored
the land from the wilderness of Zin in the
south all the way to Rehob, near Hamath
Pass in the north. 22 They went first into
the southern part of the land and came to
Hebron, where the clans of Ahiman, Sheshai, and Talmai, the descendants of a
race of giants called the Anakim, lived.
(Hebron was founded seven years before
Zoan in Egypt.) 23 They came to Eshcol
Valley, and there they cut off a branch
which had one bunch of grapes on it so
heavy that it took two men to carry it on
a pole between them. They also brought
back some pomegranates and figs.
(24 That place was named Eshcol[j] Valley because of the bunch of grapes the
Israelites cut off there.)
25 After exploring the land for forty
days, the spies returned 26 to Moses,
Aaron, and the whole community of Israel at Kadesh in the wilderness of Paran. They reported what they had seen
and showed them the fruit they had
brought. 27 They told Moses, "We explored the land and found it to be rich
and fertile; and here is some of its fruit.
28 But the people who live there are powerful, and their cities are very large and
well fortified. Even worse, we saw the
descendants of the giants there. 29 Amalekites live in the southern part of the
land; Hittites, Jebusites, and Amorites
live in the hill country; and Canaanites

[h] *Some ancient translations* When ... you; *Hebrew unclear.* [i] I have put ... Israel; *or* he can be trusted with all my affairs. [j] ESHCOL: *This name in Hebrew means "bunch of grapes."*

live by the Mediterranean Sea and along
the Jordan River."
30 Caleb silenced the people who were
complaining against[k] Moses, and said,
"We should attack now and take the
land; we are strong enough to conquer it."
31 But the men who had gone with Caleb said, "No, we are not strong enough
to attack them; the people there are more
powerful than we are." 32 So they spread
a false report among the Israelites about
the land they had explored. They said,
"That land doesn't even produce enough
to feed the people who live there. Everyone we saw was very tall, 33 and we even
saw giants there, the descendants of
Anak. We felt as small as grasshoppers,
and that is how we must have looked to
them."

The People Complain

14 All night long the people cried
out in distress. 2 They complained against Moses and Aaron, and
said, "It would have been better to die in
Egypt or even here in the wilderness!
3 Why is the LORD taking us into that
land? We will be killed in battle, and our
wives and children will be captured.
Wouldn't it be better to go back to
Egypt?" 4 So they said to one another,
"Let's choose a leader and go back to
Egypt!"
5 Then Moses and Aaron bowed to the
ground in front of all the people. 6 And
Joshua son of Nun and Caleb son of Jephunneh, two of the spies, tore their
clothes in sorrow 7 and said to the people,
"The land we explored is an excellent
land. 8 If the LORD is pleased with us, he
will take us there and give us that rich
and fertile land. 9 Do not rebel against the
LORD and don't be afraid of the people
who live there. We will conquer them
easily. The LORD is with us and has defeated the gods who protected them; so
don't be afraid." 10 The whole community
was threatening to stone them to death,
but suddenly the people saw the dazzling
light of the LORD's presence appear over
the Tent.

Moses Prays for the People

11 The LORD said to Moses, "How much
longer will these people reject me? How
much longer will they refuse to trust in
me, even though I have performed so
many miracles among them? 12 I will
send an epidemic and destroy them, but
I will make you the father of a nation
that is larger and more powerful than
they are!"
13 But Moses said to the LORD, "You
brought these people out of Egypt by
your power. When the Egyptians hear
what you have done to your people,
14 they will tell it to the people who live in
this land. These people have already
heard that you, LORD, are with us, that
you appear in plain sight when your
cloud stops over us, and that you go before us in a pillar of cloud by day and a
pillar of fire by night. 15 Now if you kill all
your people, the nations who have heard
of your fame will say 16 that you killed
your people in the wilderness because
you were not able to bring them into the
land you promised to give them. 17 So
now, LORD, I pray, show us your power
and do what you promised when you
said, 18 'I, the LORD, am not easily angered, and I show great love and faithfulness and forgive sin and rebellion. Yet I
will not fail to punish children and
grandchildren to the third and fourth
generation for the sins of their parents.'
19 And now, LORD, according to the greatness of your unchanging love, forgive, I
pray, the sin of these people, just as you
have forgiven them ever since they left
Egypt."
20 The LORD answered, "I will forgive
them, as you have asked. 21 But I promise
that as surely as I live and as surely as my
presence fills the earth, 22 none of these
people will live to enter that land. They
have seen the dazzling light of my presence and the miracles that I performed in
Egypt and in the wilderness, but they
have tried my patience over and over
again and have refused to obey me.
23 They will never enter the land which I
promised to their ancestors. None of
those who have rejected me will ever enter it. 24 But because my servant Caleb
has a different attitude and has remained
loyal to me, I will bring him into the land
which he explored, and his descendants
will possess the land 25 in whose valleys
the Amalekites and the Canaanites now
live. Turn back tomorrow and go into the

[k] complaining against; *or* gathered around.

wilderness in the direction of the Gulf
of Aqaba."

The Lord Punishes the People for Complaining

26 The Lord said to Moses and Aaron,
27 "How much longer are these wicked
people going to complain against me? I
have heard enough of these complaints!
28 Now give them this answer: 'I swear
that as surely as I live, I will do to you just
what you have asked. I, the Lord, have
spoken. 29 You will die and your corpses
will be scattered across this wilderness.
Because you have complained against
me, none of you over twenty years of age
will enter that land. 30 I promised to let
you live there, but not one of you will,
except Caleb and Joshua. 31 You said that
your children would be captured, but I
will bring them into the land that you
rejected, and it will be their home. 32 You
will die here in this wilderness. 33 Your
children will wander in the wilderness
for forty years, suffering for your unfaithfulness, until the last one of you
dies. 34 You will suffer the consequences
of your sin for forty years, one year for
each of the forty days you spent exploring the land. You will know what it
means to have me against you! 35 I swear
that I will do this to you wicked people
who have gathered together against me.
Here in the wilderness every one of you
will die. I, the Lord, have spoken.' "

36-37 The men Moses had sent to explore the land brought back a false report which caused the people to
complain against the Lord. And so the
Lord struck them with a disease, and
they died. 38 Of the twelve spies only
Joshua and Caleb survived.

The First Attempt to Invade the Land

(Deuteronomy 1.41-46)

39 When Moses told the Israelites what
the Lord had said, they mourned bitterly.
40 Early the next morning they started
out to invade the hill country, saying,
"Now we are ready to go to the place
which the Lord told us about. We admit
that we have sinned."

41 But Moses said, "Then why are you
disobeying the Lord now? You will not
succeed! 42 Don't go. The Lord is not with
you, and your enemies will defeat you.
43 When you face the Amalekites and the
Canaanites, you will die in battle; the
Lord will not be with you, because you
have refused to follow him."

44 Yet they still dared to go up into the
hill country, even though neither the
Lord's Covenant Box nor Moses left
the camp. 45 Then the Amalekites and
the Canaanites who lived there attacked
and defeated them, and pursued them
as far as Hormah.

Laws about Sacrifice

15 The Lord gave Moses 2 the following regulations for the people
of Israel to observe in the land that he
was going to give them. 3 A bull, a ram, a
sheep, or a goat may be presented to the
Lord as a burnt offering or as a sacrifice
in fulfillment of a vow or as a freewill
offering or as an offering at your regular
religious festivals; the odor of these food
offerings is pleasing to the Lord.
4-5 Whoever presents a sheep or a goat as
a burnt offering to the Lord is to bring
with each animal 2 pounds of flour
mixed with 2 pints of olive oil as a grain
offering, together with 2 pints of wine.
6 When a ram is offered, 4 pounds of flour
mixed with 3 pints of olive oil are to be
presented as a grain offering, 7 together
with 3 pints of wine. The odor of these
sacrifices is pleasing to the Lord. 8 When
a bull is offered to the Lord as a burnt
offering or as a sacrifice in fulfillment of
a vow or as a fellowship offering, 9 a
grain offering of 6 pounds of flour mixed
with 4 pints of olive oil is to be presented,
10 together with 4 pints of wine. The
odor of this sacrifice is pleasing to the
Lord.

11 That is what shall be offered with
each bull, ram, sheep, or goat. 12 When
more than one animal is offered, the ac-
companying offering is to be increased
proportionately. 13 All native Israelites
are to do this when they present a food
offering, an odor pleasing to the Lord.
14 And if at any time foreigners living
among you, whether on a temporary or a
permanent basis, make a food offering,
an odor that pleases the Lord, they are
to observe the same regulations. 15 For
all time to come, the same[l] rules are

[l] *Some ancient translations* the same; *Hebrew* the congregation the same.

binding on you and on the foreigners who
live among you. You and they are alike
in the LORD's sight; 16the same laws and
regulations apply to you and to them.
17The LORD gave Moses 18the following
regulations for the people of Israel to observe in the land that he was going to
give them. 19When any food produced
there is eaten, some of it is to be set aside
as a special contribution to the LORD.
20When you bake bread, the first loaf of
the first bread made from the new grain
is to be presented as a special contribution to the LORD. This is to be presented
in the same way as the special contribution you make from the grain you thresh.
21For all time to come, this special gift is
to be given to the LORD from the bread
you bake.
22But suppose someone unintentionally fails to keep some of these regulations which the LORD has given Moses.
23And suppose that in the future the community fails to do everything that the
LORD commanded through Moses. 24If
the mistake was made because of the ignorance of the community, they are to
offer a bull as a burnt offering, an odor
that pleases the LORD, with the proper
grain offering and wine offering. In addition, they are to offer a male goat as a sin
offering. 25The priest shall perform the
ritual of purification for the community,
and they will be forgiven, because the
mistake was unintentional and they
brought their sin offering as a food offering to the LORD. 26The whole community
of Israel and the foreigners living among
them will be forgiven, because everyone
was involved in the mistake.
27If any of you sin unintentionally, you
are to offer a one-year-old female goat as
a sin offering. 28At the altar the priest
shall perform the ritual of purification to
purify you from your sin, and you will be
forgiven. 29The same regulation applies
to all who unintentionally commit a sin,
whether they are native Israelites or resident foreigners.
30But any who sin deliberately,
whether they are natives or foreigners,
are guilty of treating the LORD with contempt, and they shall be put to death,
31because they have rejected what the
LORD said and have deliberately broken
one of his commands. They are responsible for their own death.

The Man Who Broke the Sabbath

32Once, while the Israelites were still
in the wilderness, a man was found gathering firewood on the Sabbath. 33He was
taken to Moses, Aaron, and the whole
community, 34and was put under guard,
because it was not clear what should be
done with him. 35Then the LORD said to
Moses, "The man must be put to death;
the whole community is to stone him to
death outside the camp." 36So the whole
community took him outside the camp
and stoned him to death, as the LORD had
commanded.

Rules about Tassels

37The LORD commanded Moses 38to
say to the people of Israel: "Make tassels
on the corners of your garments and put
a blue cord on each tassel. You are to do
this for all time to come. 39The tassels
will serve as reminders, and each time
you see them you will remember all my
commands and obey them; then you will
not turn away from me and follow your
own wishes and desires. 40The tassels
will remind you to keep all my commands, and you will belong completely
to me. 41I am the LORD your God; I
brought you out of Egypt to be your God.
I am the LORD."

The Rebellion of Korah, Dathan, and Abiram

16 1-2Korah son of Izhar, from the
Levite clan of Kohath, rebelled
against the leadership of Moses. He was
joined by three members of the tribe of
Reuben—Dathan and Abiram, the sons
of Eliab, and On son of Peleth—and by
250 other Israelites, well-known leaders
chosen by the community. 3They assembled before Moses and Aaron and said to
them, "You have gone too far! All the
members of the community belong to the
LORD, and the LORD is with all of us. Why,
then, Moses, do you set yourself above
the LORD's community?"
4When Moses heard this, he threw
himself on the ground and prayed. 5Then
he said to Korah and his followers, "Tomorrow morning the LORD will show us
who belongs to him; he will let the one
who belongs to him, that is, the one he
has chosen, approach him at the altar.
6-7Tomorrow morning you and your followers take fire pans, put live coals and

incense on them, and take them to the
altar. Then we will see which of us the
LORD has chosen. You Levites are the
ones who have gone too far!"
8 Moses continued to speak to Korah.
"Listen, you Levites! 9 Do you consider it
a small matter that the God of Israel has
set you apart from the rest of the community, so that you can approach him, perform your service in the LORD's Tent, and
minister to the community and serve
them? 10 He has let you and all the other
Levites have this honor—and now you
are trying to get the priesthood too!
11 When you complain against Aaron, it
is really against the LORD that you and
your followers are rebelling."
12 Then Moses sent for Dathan and
Abiram, but they said, "We will not
come! 13 Isn't it enough that you have
brought us out of the fertile land of Egypt
to kill us here in the wilderness? Do you
also have to lord it over us? 14 You certainly have not brought us into a fertile
land or given us fields and vineyards as
our possession, and now you are trying
to deceive us. We will not come!"
15 Moses became angry and said to the
LORD, "Do not accept any offerings these
men bring. I have not wronged any of
them; I have not even taken one of their
donkeys."
16 Moses said to Korah, "Tomorrow
you and your 250 followers must come to
the Tent of the LORD's presence; Aaron
will also be there. 17 Each of you will take
his fire pan, put incense on it, and then
present it at the altar." 18 So they each
took their fire pans, put live coals and
incense on them, and stood at the entrance of the Tent with Moses and Aaron.
19 Then Korah gathered the whole community, and they stood facing Moses and
Aaron at the entrance of the Tent. Suddenly the dazzling light of the LORD's
presence appeared to the whole community, 20 and the LORD said to Moses and
Aaron, 21 "Move back from these people,
and I will destroy them immediately."
22 But Moses and Aaron bowed down
with their faces to the ground and said,
"O God, you are the source of all life.
When one of us sins, do you become angry with the whole community?"
23 The LORD said to Moses, 24 "Tell the
people to move away from the tents of
Korah, Dathan, and Abiram."
25 Then Moses, accompanied by the
leaders of Israel, went to Dathan and
Abiram. 26 He said to the people, "Get
away from the tents of these wicked men
and don't touch anything that belongs to
them. Otherwise, you will be wiped out
with them for all their sins." 27 So they
moved away from the tents of Korah, Dathan, and Abiram.
Dathan and Abiram had come out and
were standing at the entrance of their
tents, with their wives and children.
28 Moses said to the people, "This is how
you will know that the LORD has sent me
to do all these things and that it is not by
my own choice that I have done them.
29 If these men die a natural death without some punishment from God, then the
LORD did not send me. 30 But if the LORD
does something unheard of, and the
earth opens up and swallows them with
all they own, so that they go down alive
to the world of the dead, you will know
that these men have rejected the LORD."
31 As soon as he had finished speaking,
the ground under Dathan and Abiram
split open 32 and swallowed them and
their families, together with all of Korah's followers and their possessions.
33 So they went down alive to the world of
the dead, with their possessions. The
earth closed over them, and they vanished. 34 All the people of Israel who were
there fled when they heard their cry.
They shouted, "Run! The earth might
swallow us too!"
35 Then the LORD sent a fire that blazed
out and burned up the 250 men who had
presented the incense.

The Fire Pans

36 Then the LORD said to Moses, 37 "Tell
Eleazar son of Aaron the priest to remove the bronze fire pans from the remains of those who have been burned,
and scatter the coals from the fire pans
somewhere else, because the fire pans
are holy. 38 They became holy when they
were presented at the LORD's altar. So
take the fire pans of these who were put
to death for their sin, beat them into thin
plates, and make a covering for the altar.
It will be a warning to the people of Israel." 39 So Eleazar the priest took the fire
pans and had them beaten into thin
plates to make a covering for the altar.
40 This was a warning to the Israelites
that no one who was not a descendant of
Aaron should come to the altar to burn

incense for the LORD. Otherwise he would
be destroyed like Korah and his men. All
this was done as the LORD had commanded Eleazar through Moses.

Aaron Saves the People

41 The next day the whole community
complained against Moses and Aaron
and said, "You have killed some of the
LORD's people." 42 After they had all gathered to protest to Moses and Aaron, they
turned toward the Tent and saw that the
cloud was covering it and that the dazzling light of the LORD's presence had appeared. 43 Moses and Aaron went and
stood in front of the Tent, 44 and the LORD
said to Moses, 45 "Move back from these
people, and I will destroy them on the
spot!"

The two of them bowed down with
their faces to the ground, 46 and Moses
said to Aaron, "Take your fire pan, put
live coals from the altar in it, and put
some incense on the coals. Then hurry
with it to the people and perform the ritual of purification for them. Hurry! The
LORD's anger has already broken out
and an epidemic has already begun."
47 Aaron obeyed, took his fire pan and
ran into the middle of the assembled people. When he saw that the plague had
already begun, he put the incense on the
coals and performed the ritual of purification for the people. 48 This stopped the
plague, and he was left standing between
the living and the dead. 49 The number of
people who died was 14,700, not counting those who died in Korah's rebellion.
50 When the plague had stopped, Aaron
returned to Moses at the entrance of the
Tent.

Aaron's Walking Stick

17 The LORD said to Moses, 2 "Tell
the people of Israel to give you
twelve walking sticks, one from the
leader of each tribe. Write each man's
name on his stick 3 and then write
Aaron's name on the stick representing
Levi. There will be one stick for each
tribal leader. 4 Take them to the Tent of
my presence and put them in front of the
Covenant Box, where I meet you. 5 Then
the stick of the man I have chosen will
sprout. In this way I will put a stop to the
constant complaining of these Israelites
against you."

6 So Moses spoke to the Israelites, and
each of their leaders gave him a stick,
one for each tribe, twelve in all, and
Aaron's stick was put with them. 7 Moses
then put all the sticks in the Tent in front
of the LORD's Covenant Box.

8 The next day, when Moses went into
the Tent, he saw that Aaron's stick, representing the tribe of Levi, had sprouted.
It had budded, blossomed, and produced
ripe almonds! 9 Moses took all the sticks
and showed them to the Israelites. They
saw what had happened, and each leader
took his own stick back. 10 The LORD said
to Moses, "Put Aaron's stick back in
front of the Covenant Box. It is to be kept
as a warning to the rebel Israelites that
they will die unless their complaining stops." 11 Moses did as the LORD
commanded.

12 The people of Israel said to Moses,
"Then that's the end of us! 13 If anyone
who even comes near the Tent must die,
then we are all as good as dead!"

Duties of Priests and Levites

18 The LORD said to Aaron, "You,
your sons, and the Levites must
suffer the consequences of any guilt connected with serving in the Tent of my
presence; but only you and your sons
will suffer the consequences of service in
the priesthood. 2 Bring in your relatives,
the tribe of Levi, to work with you and
help you while you and your sons are
serving at the Tent. 3 They are to fulfill
their duties to you and their responsibilities for the Tent, but they must not have
any contact with sacred objects in the
Holy Place or with the altar. If they do,
both they and you will be put to death.
4 They are to work with you and fulfill
their responsibilities for all the service in
the Tent, but no unqualified person may
work with you. 5 You and your sons
alone must fulfill the responsibilities for
the Holy Place and the altar, so that my
anger will not again break out against
the people of Israel. 6 I am the one who
has chosen your relatives the Levites
from among the Israelites as a gift to you.
They are dedicated to me, so that they
can carry out their duties in the Tent.
7 But you and your sons alone shall fulfill
all the responsibilities of the priesthood
that concern the altar and what is in the
Most Holy Place. These things are your

responsibility, because I have given you
the gift of the priesthood. Any unqualified person who comes near the sacred
objects shall be put to death."

The Share of the Priests

8 The LORD said to Aaron, "Remember
that I am giving you all the special contributions made to me that are not burned
as sacrifices. I am giving them to you and
to your descendants as the part assigned
to you forever. 9 Of the most sacred offerings not burned on the altar, the following belong to you: the grain offerings, the
sin offerings, and the repayment offerings. Everything that is presented to me
as a sacred offering belongs to you and
your sons. 10 You must eat these things in
a holy place, and only males may eat
them; consider them holy.

11 "In addition, any other special contributions that the Israelites present to
me shall be yours. I am giving them to
you, your sons, and your daughters for
all time to come. Every member of your
family who is ritually clean may eat
them.

12 "I am giving you all the best of the
first produce which the Israelites give me
each year: olive oil, wine, and grain. 13 It
all belongs to you. Every member of your
family who is ritually clean may eat it.

14 "Everything in Israel that has been
unconditionally dedicated to me belongs
to you.

15 "Every first-born child or animal that
the Israelites present to me belongs to
you. But you must accept payment to buy
back every first-born child, and must
also accept payment for every first-born
animal that is ritually unclean. 16 Children shall be bought back at the age of
one month for the fixed price of five
pieces of silver, according to the official
standard. 17 But the first-born of cows,
sheep, and goats are not to be bought
back; they belong completely to me and
are to be sacrificed. Throw their blood
against the altar and burn their fat as a
food offering, an odor pleasing to me.
18 The meat from them belongs to you,
like the breast and the right hind leg of
the special offering.

19 "I am giving to you, to your sons, and
to your daughters, for all time to come,
all the special contributions which the
Israelites present to me. This is an unbreakable covenant that I have made
with you and your descendants."

20 The LORD said to Aaron, "You will not
receive any property that can be inherited, and no part of the land of Israel will
be assigned to you. I, the LORD, am all you
need."

The Share of the Levites

21 The LORD said, "I have given to the
Levites every tithe that the people of Israel present to me. This is in payment for
their service in taking care of the Tent of
my presence. 22 The other Israelites must
no longer approach the Tent and in this
way bring on themselves the penalty of
death. 23 From now on only the Levites
will take care of the Tent and bear the
full responsibility for it. This is a permanent rule that applies also to your
descendants. The Levites shall have no
permanent property in Israel, 24 because
I have given to them as their possession
the tithe which the Israelites present to
me as a special contribution. That is why
I told them that they would have no permanent property in Israel."

The Levites' Tithe

25 The LORD commanded Moses 26 to
say to the Levites: "When you receive
from the Israelites the tithe that the LORD
gives you as your possession, you must
present a tenth of it as a special contribution to the LORD. 27 This special contribution will be considered as the equivalent
of the offering which the farmer makes
of new grain and new wine. 28 In this way
you also will present the special contribution that belongs to the LORD from all
the tithes which you receive from the Israelites. You are to give this special contribution for the LORD to Aaron the priest.
29 Give it from the best that you receive.
30 When you have presented the best
part, you may keep the rest, just as the
farmer keeps what is left after he makes
his offering. 31 You and your families
may eat the rest anywhere, because it is
your wages for your service in the Tent.
32 You will not become guilty when you
eat it, as long as you have presented the
best of it to the LORD. But be sure not to
profane the sacred gifts of the Israelites
by eating any of the gifts before the best
part is offered; if you do, you will be put
to death."

Ashes of the Red Cow

19 The LORD commanded Moses and
Aaron 2to give the Israelites the
following regulations. Bring to Moses
and Aaron a red cow which has no defects and which has never been worked,
3and they will give it to Eleazar the
priest. It is to be taken outside the camp
and killed in his presence.[m] 4Then Eleazar is to take some of its blood and with
his finger sprinkle it seven times in the
direction of the Tent. 5The whole animal,
including skin, meat, blood, and intestines, is to be burned in the presence of
the priest. 6Then he is to take some cedar
wood, a sprig of hyssop, and a red cord
and throw them into the fire. 7After that,
he is to wash his clothes and pour water
over himself, and then he may enter the
camp; but he remains ritually unclean
until evening. 8The one who burned the
cow must also wash his clothes and pour
water over himself, but he also remains
unclean until evening. 9Then someone
who is ritually clean is to collect the
ashes of the cow and put them in a ritually clean place outside the camp, where
they are to be kept for the Israelite community to use in preparing the water for
removing ritual uncleanness. This ritual
is performed to remove sin. 10The one
who collected the ashes must wash his
clothes, but he remains unclean until
evening. This regulation is valid for all
time to come, both for the Israelites and
for the foreigners living among them.

Contact with a Corpse

11Those who touch a corpse are ritually unclean for seven days. 12They must
purify themselves with the water for purification on the third day and on the seventh day, and then they will be clean. But
if they do not purify themselves on both
the third and the seventh day, they will
not be clean. 13Those who touch a corpse
and do not purify themselves remain unclean, because the water for purification
has not been thrown over them. They defile the LORD's Tent, and they will no
longer be considered God's people.

14In the case of a person who dies in a
tent, anyone who is in the tent at the time
of death or who enters it becomes ritually unclean for seven days. 15Every jar
and pot in the tent that has no lid[n] on it
also becomes unclean. 16If any touch a
person who has been killed or has died a
natural death outdoors or if any touch a
human bone or a grave, they become unclean for seven days.

17To remove the uncleanness, some
ashes from the red cow which was
burned to remove sin shall be taken and
put in a pot, and fresh water added. 18In
the first case, someone who is ritually
clean is to take a sprig of hyssop, dip it
in the water, and sprinkle the tent, everything in it, and the people who were
there. In the second case, someone who
is ritually clean is to sprinkle the water
on those who had touched the human
bone or the dead body or the grave. 19On
the third day and on the seventh the person who is ritually clean is to sprinkle the
water on the unclean persons. On the
seventh day he is to purify those, who,
after washing their clothes and pouring
water over themselves, become ritually
clean at sunset.

20Those who have become ritually unclean and do not purify themselves remain unclean, because the water for
purification has not been thrown over
them. They defile the LORD's Tent and
will no longer be considered God's people. 21You are to observe this rule for all
time to come. The person who sprinkles
the water for purification must also wash
his clothes; anyone who touches the water remains ritually unclean until evening. 22Whatever an unclean person
touches is unclean, and anyone else who
touches it remains unclean until evening.

Events at Kadesh

(Exodus 17.1-7)

20 In the first month the whole community of Israel came to the wilderness of Zin and camped at Kadesh.
There Miriam died and was buried.

2There was no water where they
camped, so the people gathered around
Moses and Aaron 3and complained: "It
would have been better if we had died in
front of the LORD's Tent along with the
other Israelites. 4Why have you brought
us out into this wilderness? Just so that
we can die here with our animals? 5Why
did you bring us out of Egypt into this

[m] It . . . presence; *or* He is to take it outside to the east of the camp and kill it. [n] no lid; *or* no lid fastened.

miserable place where nothing will
grow? There's no grain, no figs, no
grapes, no pomegranates. There is not
even any water to drink!" 6 Moses and
Aaron moved away from the people and
stood at the entrance of the Tent. They
bowed down with their faces to the
ground, and the dazzling light of the
LORD's presence appeared to them.
7 The LORD said to Moses, 8 "Take the
stick that is in front of the Covenant Box,
and then you and Aaron assemble the
whole community. There in front of them
all speak to that rock over there, and water will gush out of it. In this way you will
bring water out of the rock for the people, for them and their animals to drink."
9 Moses went and got the stick, as the
LORD had commanded.
10 He and Aaron assembled the whole
community in front of the rock, and
Moses said, "Listen, you rebels! Do we
have to get water out of this rock for
you?" 11 Then Moses raised the stick and
struck the rock twice with it, and a great
stream of water gushed out, and all the
people and animals drank.
12 But the LORD reprimanded Moses
and Aaron. He said, "Because you did not
have enough faith to acknowledge my
holy power before the people of Israel,
you will not lead them into the land that
I promised to give them."
13 This happened at Meribah,[o] where
the people of Israel complained against
the LORD and where he showed them that
he is holy.

The King of Edom Refuses to Let Israel Pass

14 Moses sent messengers from Kadesh
to the king of Edom. They said, "This
message is from your kinsmen, the tribes
of Israel. You know the hardships we
have suffered, 15 how our ancestors went
to Egypt, where we lived many years.
The Egyptians mistreated our ancestors
and us, 16 and we cried to the LORD for
help. He heard our cry and sent an angel,
who led us out of Egypt. Now we are at
Kadesh, a town at the border of your territory. 17 Please permit us to pass through
your land. We and our cattle will not
leave the road or go into your fields or
vineyards, and we will not drink from
your wells. We will stay on the main
road[p] until we are out of your territory."
18 But the Edomites answered, "We refuse to let you pass through our country!
If you try, we will march out and attack you."
19 The people of Israel said, "We will
stay on the main road, and if we or our
animals drink any of your water, we
will pay for it—all we want is to pass
through."
20 The Edomites repeated, "We refuse!"
and they marched out with a powerful
army to attack the people of Israel. 21 Because the Edomites would not let the Israelites pass through their territory, the
Israelites turned and went another way.

The Death of Aaron

22 The whole community of Israel left
Kadesh and arrived at Mount Hor, 23 on
the border of Edom. There the LORD said
to Moses and Aaron, 24 "Aaron is not going to enter the land which I promised to
give to Israel; he is going to die, because
the two of you rebelled against my command at Meribah. 25 Take Aaron and his
son Eleazar up Mount Hor, 26 and there
remove Aaron's priestly robes and put
them on Eleazar. Aaron is going to die
there." 27 Moses did what the LORD had
commanded. They went up Mount Hor in
the sight of the whole community, 28 and
Moses removed Aaron's priestly robes
and put them on Eleazar. There on the
top of the mountain Aaron died, and
Moses and Eleazar came back down.
29 The whole community learned that
Aaron had died, and they all mourned for
him for thirty days.

Victory over the Canaanites

21 When the Canaanite king of
Arad in the southern part of Canaan heard that the Israelites were coming by way of Atharim, he attacked them
and captured some of them. 2 Then the
Israelites made a vow to the LORD: "If you
will let us conquer these people, we will
unconditionally dedicate[q] them and
their cities to you and will destroy them."
3 The LORD heard them and helped them
conquer the Canaanites. So the Israelites

[o] MERIBAH: *This name in Hebrew means "complaining."* [p] main road; *or* King's Highway.
[q] UNCONDITIONALLY DEDICATE: *Anything dedicated in this way belonged completely to the LORD and could not be used; it had to be destroyed.*

completely destroyed them and their cities, and named the place Hormah.[r]

The Snake Made of Bronze

4 The Israelites left Mount Hor by the
road that leads to the Gulf of Aqaba, in
order to go around the territory of Edom.
But on the way the people lost their patience 5 and spoke against God and
Moses. They complained, "Why did you
bring us out of Egypt to die in this desert,
where there is no food or water? We
can't stand any more of this miserable
food!" 6 Then the LORD sent poisonous
snakes among the people, and many Israelites were bitten and died. 7 The people came to Moses and said, "We sinned
when we spoke against the LORD and
against you. Now pray to the LORD to take
these snakes away." So Moses prayed for
the people. 8 Then the LORD told Moses to
make a metal snake and put it on a pole,
so that anyone who was bitten could look
at it and be healed. 9 So Moses made a
bronze snake and put it on a pole. Anyone who had been bitten would look at
the bronze snake and be healed.

From Mount Hor to the Valley of the Moabites

10 The Israelites moved on and camped
at Oboth. 11 After leaving that place, they
camped at the ruins of Abarim in the wilderness east of Moabite territory. 12 Then
they camped in Zered Valley. 13 From
there they moved again and camped on
the north side of the Arnon River, in the
wilderness which extends into Amorite
territory. (The Arnon was the border between the Moabites and the Amorites.)
14 That is why *The Book of the LORD's
Battles* speaks of ". . . the town of Waheb
in the area of Suphah, and the valleys;
the Arnon River, 15 and the slope of the
valleys that extend to the town of Ar and
toward the border of Moab."
16 From there they went on to a place
called Wells, where the LORD said to
Moses, "Bring the people together, and I
will give them water." 17 At that time the
people of Israel sang this song:

"Wells, produce your water;
And we will greet it with a song—
18 The well dug by princes
And by leaders of the people,
Dug with a royal scepter
And with their walking sticks."

They moved from the wilderness to
Mattanah, 19 and from there they went on
to Nahaliel, and from Nahaliel to Bamoth, 20 and from Bamoth to the valley in
the territory of the Moabites, below the
top of Mount Pisgah, looking out over the
desert.

Victory over King Sihon and King Og

(*Deuteronomy 2.26–3.11*)

21 Then the people of Israel sent messengers to the Amorite king Sihon to say:
22 "Let us pass through your land. We and
our cattle will not leave the road and go
into your fields or vineyards, and we will
not drink water from your wells; we will
stay on the main road[s] until we are out
of your territory." 23 But Sihon would not
permit the people of Israel to pass
through his territory. He gathered his
army and went out to Jahaz in the wilderness and attacked the Israelites. 24 But
the Israelites killed many of the enemy in
battle and occupied their land from the
Arnon River north to the Jabbok, that is,
to the Ammonites, because the Ammonite border was strongly defended.[t] 25 So
the people of Israel captured all the Amorite cities, including Heshbon and all the
surrounding towns, and settled in them.
26 Heshbon was the capital city of the
Amorite king Sihon, who had fought
against the former king of Moab and had
captured all his land as far as the Arnon
River. 27 That is why the poets sing,

"Come to Heshbon, to King
Sihon's city!
We want to see it rebuilt and
restored.
28 Once from this city of Heshbon
Sihon's army went forth like a
fire;
It destroyed the city of Ar in Moab
And devoured[u] the hills of the
upper Arnon.
29 How terrible for you, people of
Moab!
You worshipers of Chemosh are
brought to ruin!

[r] HORMAH: *This name in Hebrew means "destruction."* [s] main road; *or* King's Highway.
[t] because . . . strongly defended; *some ancient translations* as far as Jazer on the Ammonite border. [u] *One ancient translation* devoured; *Hebrew* the lords of.

Your god let the men become
refugees,
And the women became captives
of the Amorite king.
30 But now their descendants are
destroyed,
All the way from Heshbon to
Dibon,
From Nashim to Nophah, near
Medeba."[v]

31 So the people of Israel settled in the
territory of the Amorites, 32 and Moses
sent men to find the best way to attack
the city of Jazer. The Israelites captured
it and its surrounding towns and drove
out the Amorites living there.
33 Then the Israelites turned and took
the road to Bashan, and King Og of Bashan marched out with his army to attack them at Edrei. 34 The LORD said to
Moses, "Do not be afraid of him. I will
give you victory over him, all his people,
and his land. Do to him what you did to
Sihon, the Amorite king who ruled at
Heshbon." 35 So the Israelites killed Og,
his sons, and all his people, leaving no
survivors, and then they occupied his
land.

The King of Moab Sends for Balaam

22 The Israelites moved on and set
up camp in the plains of Moab
east of the Jordan and opposite Jericho.
2 When the king of Moab, Balak son of
Zippor, heard what the Israelites had
done to the Amorites and how many Israelites there were, 3 he and all his people
became terrified. 4 The Moabites said to
the leaders of the Midianites, "This horde
will soon destroy everything around us,
like a bull eating the grass in a pasture."
So King Balak 5 sent messengers to summon Balaam son of Beor, who was at
Pethor near the Euphrates River in the
land of Amaw. They brought him this
message from Balak: "I want you to
know that a whole nation has come from
Egypt; its people are spreading out
everywhere and threatening to take over
our land. 6 They outnumber us, so please
come and put a curse on them for me.
Then perhaps we will be able to defeat
them and drive them out of the land. I
know that when you pronounce a blessing, people are blessed, and when you
pronounce a curse, they are placed under
a curse."
7 So the Moabite and Midianite leaders
took with them the payment for the
curse, went to Balaam, and gave him Balak's message. 8 Balaam said to them,
"Spend the night here, and tomorrow I
will report to you whatever the LORD tells
me." So the Moabite leaders stayed with
Balaam.
9 God came to Balaam and asked,
"Who are these people that are staying
with you?"
10 He answered, "King Balak of Moab
has sent them to tell me 11 that a people
who came from Egypt has spread out
over the whole land. He wants me to
curse them for him, so that he can fight
them and drive them out."
12 God said to Balaam, "Do not go with
them, and do not put a curse on the people of Israel, because they have my
blessing."
13 The next morning Balaam went to
Balak's messengers and said, "Go back
home; the LORD has refused to let me go
with you." 14 So they returned to Balak
and told him that Balaam had refused to
come with them.
15 Then Balak sent a larger number of
leaders, who were more important than
the first. 16 They went to Balaam and
gave him this message from Balak:
"Please don't let anything prevent you
from coming to me! 17 I will reward you
richly and do anything you say. Please
come and curse these people for me."
18 But Balaam answered, "Even if Balak gave me all the silver and gold in his
palace, I could not disobey the command
of the LORD my God in even the smallest
matter. 19 But please spend the night, as
the others did, so that I may learn
whether or not the LORD has something
else to tell me."
20 That night God came to Balaam and
said, "If these men have come to ask you
to go with them, get ready and go, but do
only what I tell you." 21 So the next morning Balaam saddled his donkey and went
with the Moabite leaders.

Balaam and His Donkey

22 God was angry that Balaam was going, and as Balaam was riding along on
his donkey, accompanied by his two

[v] *Verse 30 in Hebrew is unclear.*

servants, the angel of the LORD stood in
the road to bar his way. 23When the donkey saw the angel standing there holding
a sword, it left the road and turned into
the fields. Balaam beat the donkey and
brought it back onto the road. 24Then the
angel stood where the road narrowed between two vineyards and had a stone
wall on each side. 25When the donkey
saw the angel, it moved over against the
wall and crushed Balaam's foot against
it. Again Balaam beat the donkey.
26Once more the angel moved ahead; he
stood in a narrow place where there was
no room at all to pass on either side.
27This time, when the donkey saw the
angel, it lay down. Balaam lost his temper and began to beat the donkey with
his stick. 28Then the LORD gave the donkey the power of speech, and it said to
Balaam, "What have I done to you? Why
have you beaten me these three times?"
29Balaam answered, "Because you
have made a fool of me! If I had a sword,
I would kill you."
30The donkey replied, "Am I not the
same donkey on which you have ridden
all your life? Have I ever treated you like
this before?"

"No," he answered.

31Then the LORD let Balaam see the angel standing there with his sword; and
Balaam threw himself face downward on
the ground. 32The angel demanded,
"Why have you beaten your donkey
three times like this? I have come to bar
your way, because you should not be
making this journey.[w] 33But your donkey saw me and turned aside three times.
If it hadn't, I would have killed you and
spared the donkey."
34Balaam replied, "I have sinned. I did
not know that you were standing in the
road to oppose me; but now if you think
it is wrong for me to go on, I will return
home."
35But the angel said, "Go on with these
men, but say only what I tell you to say."
So Balaam went on with them.

Balak Welcomes Balaam

36When Balak heard that Balaam was
coming, he went to meet him at Ar, a city
on the Arnon River at the border of
Moab. 37Balak said to him, "Why didn't
you come when I sent for you the first
time? Did you think I wasn't able to reward you enough?"
38Balaam answered, "I came, didn't I?
But now, what power do I have? I can say
only what God tells me to say." 39So Balaam went with Balak to the town of Hu-
zoth, 40where Balak slaughtered cattle
and sheep and gave some of the meat to
Balaam and the leaders who were
with him.

Balaam's First Prophecy

41The next morning Balak took Balaam up to Bamoth Baal, from where Balaam could see a part of the people of
23 Israel. 1He said to Balak, "Build
seven altars here for me, and
bring me seven bulls and seven rams."
2Balak did as he was told, and he and
Balaam offered a bull and a ram on each
altar. 3Then Balaam said to Balak,
"Stand here by your burnt offering, while
I go to see whether or not the LORD will
meet me. I will tell you whatever he reveals to me." So he went alone to the top
of a hill, 4and God met him. Balaam said
to him, "I have built the seven altars and
offered a bull and a ram on each."
5The LORD told Balaam what to say and
sent him back to Balak to give him his
message. 6So he went back and found
Balak still standing by his burnt offering
with all the leaders of Moab.
7Balaam uttered this prophecy:

"Balak king of Moab has
brought me
From Syria, from the eastern
mountains.
'Come speak for me,' he said.
'Put a curse on the people of
Israel.'
8How can I curse what God has
not cursed,
Or speak of doom when the LORD
has not?
9From the high rocks I can see
them;
I can watch them from the hills.
They are a nation that lives alone;
They know they are blessed more
than other nations.
10The descendants of Israel are like
the dust—
There are too many of them to
be counted.

[w] *Probable text* you should . . . journey; *Hebrew unclear.*

Let me end my days like one of
God's people;
Let me die in peace like the
righteous."

11 Then Balak said to Balaam, "What
have you done to me? I brought you here
to curse my enemies, but all you have
done is bless them."
12 He answered, "I can say only what
the LORD tells me to say."

Balaam's Second Prophecy

13 Then Balak said to Balaam, "Come
with me to another place from which you
can see only some of the Israelites. Curse
them for me from there." 14 He took him
to the field of Zophim on the top of
Mount Pisgah. There also he built seven
altars and offered a bull and a ram on
each of them.
15 Balaam said to Balak, "Stand here by
your burnt offering, and I will meet God
over there."
16 The LORD met Balaam, told him what
to say, and sent him back to Balak to give
him his message. 17 So he went back and
found Balak still standing by his burnt
offering, with the leaders of Moab. Balak
asked what the LORD had said, 18 and Balaam uttered this prophecy:

"Come, Balak son of Zippor,
And listen to what I have to say.
19 God is not like people, who lie;
He is not a human who changes
his mind.
Whatever he promises, he does;
He speaks, and it is done.
20 I have been instructed to bless,
And when God blesses, I cannot
call it back.
21 I foresee that Israel's future
Will bring her no misfortune or
trouble.
The LORD their God is with them;
They proclaim that he is their
king.
22 God has brought them out of
Egypt;
He fights for them like a wild ox.
23 There is no magic charm, no
witchcraft,
That can be used against the
nation of Israel.[x]
Now people will say about Israel,
'Look what God has done!'
24 The nation of Israel is like a
mighty lion:
It doesn't rest until it has torn and
devoured,
Until it has drunk the blood of
those it has killed."

25 Then Balak said to Balaam, "You refuse to curse the people of Israel, but at
least don't bless them!"
26 Balaam answered, "Didn't I tell you
that I had to do everything that the LORD
told me?"

Balaam's Third Prophecy

27 Balak said, "Come with me, and I will
take you to another place. Perhaps God
will be willing to let you curse them for
me from there." 28 So he took Balaam to
the top of Mount Peor overlooking the
desert. 29 Balaam said to him, "Build
seven altars for me here and bring me
seven bulls and seven rams." 30 Balak did
as he was told, and offered a bull and a
ram on each altar.

24 By now Balaam knew that the
LORD wanted him to bless the
people of Israel, so he did not go to look
for omens, as he had done before. He
turned toward the desert 2 and saw the
people of Israel camped tribe by tribe.
The spirit of God took control of him,
3 and he uttered this prophecy:

"The message of Balaam son of
Beor,
The words of the man who can
see clearly,[y]
4 Who can hear what God is saying.
With staring eyes I see in a trance
A vision from Almighty God.
5 The tents of Israel are beautiful,
6 Like long rows of palms
Or gardens beside a river,
Like aloes planted by the LORD
Or cedars beside the water.
7 They will have abundant rainfall
And plant their seed in
well-watered fields.[z]
Their king shall be greater than
Agag,
And his rule shall be extended
far and wide.

[x] There . . . Israel; *or* No magic charms are used in Israel, no witchcraft is practiced there.
[y] who can see clearly; *or* whose eyes are closed. [z] *One ancient translation* They . . . fields; *Hebrew unclear.*

8 God brought them out of Egypt;
He fights for them like a wild ox.
They devour their enemies,
Crush their bones, smash their
arrows.
9 The nation is like a mighty lion;
When it is sleeping, no one dares
wake it.
Whoever blesses Israel will be
blessed,
And whoever curses Israel will
be cursed."

10 Balak clenched his fists in anger and
said to Balaam, "I called you to curse my
enemies, but three times now you have
blessed them instead. 11 Now get on
home! I promised to reward you, but
the LORD has kept you from getting the
reward."
12 Balaam answered, "I told the messengers you sent to me that 13 even if you
gave me all the silver and gold in your
palace, I could not disobey the command
of the LORD by doing anything of myself.
I will say only what the LORD tells me
to say."

Balaam's Final Prophecies

14 Balaam said to Balak, "Now I am going back to my own people, but before I
go, I am warning you what the people of
Israel will do to your people in the future." 15 Then he uttered this prophecy:

"The message of Balaam son of
Beor,
The words of the man who can
see clearly,[a]
16 Who can hear what God is saying
And receive the knowledge that
comes from the Most High.
With staring eyes I see in a trance
A vision from Almighty God.
17 I look into the future,
And I see the nation of Israel.
A king, like a bright star, will
arise in that nation.
Like a comet he will come from
Israel.
He will strike the leaders of Moab
And beat down all the people of
Seth.[b]
18 He will conquer his enemies in
Edom
And make their land his property,
While Israel continues victorious.
19 The nation of Israel will trample
them down
And wipe out the last survivors."

20 Then in his vision Balaam saw the
Amalekites and uttered this prophecy:
"Amalek was the most powerful
nation of all,
But at the end it will perish
forever."
21 In his vision he saw the Kenites, and
uttered this prophecy:
"The place where you live is
secure,
Safe as a nest set high on a cliff,
22 But you Kenites will be destroyed
When Assyria takes you
captive."[c]
23 Balaam uttered this prophecy:
"Who are these people gathering
in the north?[d]
24 Invaders will sail from Cyprus;
They will conquer Assyria and
Eber,
But they, in turn, will perish
forever."
25 Then Balaam got ready and went
back home, and Balak went on his way.

The People of Israel at Peor

25 When the Israelites were camped
at Acacia Valley, the men began
to have sexual intercourse with the Moabite women who were there. 2 These
women invited them to sacrificial feasts,
where the god of Moab was worshiped.
The Israelites ate the food and worshiped
the god 3 Baal of Peor. So the LORD was
angry with them 4 and said to Moses,
"Take all the leaders of Israel and, in obedience to me, execute them in broad daylight,[e] and then I will no longer be angry
with the people." 5 Moses said to the officials, "Each of you is to kill every man in
your tribe who has become a worshiper
of Baal of Peor."
6 One of the Israelites took a Midianite
woman into his tent in the sight of Moses
and the whole community, while they
were mourning at the entrance of the
Tent of the LORD's presence. 7 When Phinehas, the son of Eleazar and grandson of
Aaron the priest, saw this, he got up and
left the assembly. He took a spear, 8 fol-

[a] who can see clearly; *or* whose eyes are closed. [b] the people of Seth; *or* who are proud and violent. [c] *Verse 22 in Hebrew is unclear.* [d] *Probable text* Who . . . north; *Hebrew unclear.* [e] in broad daylight; *or* publicly.

lowed the man and the woman into the
tent, and drove the spear through both of
them. In this way the epidemic that was
destroying Israel was stopped, 9 but it
had already killed twenty-four thousand
people.
10 The LORD said to Moses, 11 "Because
of what Phinehas has done, I am no
longer angry with the people of Israel.
He refused to tolerate the worship of any
god but me, and that is why I did not
destroy them in my anger. 12 So tell him
that I am making a covenant with him
that is valid for all time to come. 13 He and
his descendants are permanently established as priests, because he did not tolerate any rivals to me and brought about
forgiveness for the people's sin."
14 The name of the Israelite who was
killed with the Midianite woman was
Zimri son of Salu, the head of a family in
the tribe of Simeon. 15 The woman's
name was Cozbi. Zur, her father, was
chief of a group of Midianite clans.
16 The LORD commanded Moses, 17 "Attack the Midianites and destroy them,
18 because of the evil they did to you
when they deceived you at Peor, and because of Cozbi, who was killed at the
time of the epidemic at Peor."

The Second Census

26 After the epidemic the LORD said
to Moses and Eleazar son of
Aaron, 2 "Take a census by families of the
whole community of Israel, of all men
twenty years old or older who are fit for
military service." 3-4 Moses and Eleazar
obeyed and called together all the men of
that age group. They assembled in the
plains of Moab across the Jordan River
from Jericho.
These were the Israelites who came
out of Egypt:
5 The tribe of Reuben (Reuben was the
oldest son of Jacob): the clans of Hanoch,
Pallu, 6 Hezron, and Carmi. 7 These clans
numbered 43,730 men. 8 The descendants
of Pallu were Eliab 9 and his sons Nemuel, Dathan, and Abiram. (These are the
Dathan and Abiram who were chosen by
the community. They defied Moses and
Aaron and joined the followers of Korah
when they rebelled against the LORD.
10 The ground opened and swallowed
them, and they died with Korah and his
followers when fire destroyed 250 men;
they became a warning to the people.
11 But the sons of Korah were not killed.)
12 The tribe of Simeon: the clans of
Nemuel, Jamin, Jachin, 13 Zerah, and
Shaul. 14 These clans numbered
22,200 men.
15 The tribe of Gad: the clans of Zephon, Haggi, Shuni, 16 Ozni, Eri, 17 Arod,
and Areli. 18 These clans numbered
40,500 men.
19-21 The tribe of Judah: the clans of
Shelah, Perez, Zerah, Hezron, and Hamul. (Two of Judah's sons, Er and Onan,
had died in the land of Canaan.) 22 These
clans numbered 76,500 men.
23 The tribe of Issachar: the clans of
Tola, Puah, 24 Jashub, and Shimron.
25 These clans numbered 64,300 men.
26 The tribe of Zebulun: the clans of Sered, Elon, and Jahleel. 27 These clans
numbered 60,500 men.
28 The tribes of Joseph, who was the
father of two sons, Manasseh and
Ephraim.
29 The tribe of Manasseh. Machir son of
Manasseh was the father of Gilead, and
the following clans traced their ancestry
to Gilead: 30 the clans of Iezer, Helek,
31 Asriel, Shechem, 32 Shemida, and Hepher. 33 Zelophehad son of Hepher had
no sons, but only daughters; their names
were Mahlah, Noah, Hoglah, Milcah,
and Tirzah. 34 These clans numbered
52,700 men.
35 The tribe of Ephraim: the clans of
Shuthelah, Becher, and Tahan. 36 The
clan of Eran traced its descent from
Shuthelah. 37 These clans numbered
32,500 men.
These are the clans descended from
Joseph.
38 The tribe of Benjamin: the clans of
Bela, Ashbel, Ahiram, 39 Shephupham,
and Hupham. 40 The clans of Ard and Naaman traced their descent from Bela.
41 These clans numbered 45,600 men.
42 The tribe of Dan: the clan of Shu-
ham, 43 which numbered 64,400 men.
44 The tribe of Asher: the clans of Imnah, Ishvi, and Beriah. 45 The clans of Heber and Malchiel traced their descent
from Beriah. 46 Asher had a daughter
named Serah. 47 These clans numbered
53,400 men.
48 The tribe of Naphtali: the clans of
Jahzeel, Guni, 49 Jezer, and Shillem.
50 These clans numbered 45,400 men.
51 The total number of the Israelite men
was 601,730.

52 The LORD said to Moses, 53 "Divide
the land among the tribes, according to
their size. 54-56 Divide the land by drawing lots, and give a large share to a large
tribe and a small one to a small tribe."

57 The tribe of Levi consisted of the
clans of Gershon, Kohath, and Merari.
58 Their descendants included the subclans of Libni, Hebron, Mahli, Mushi,
and Korah. Kohath was the father of Amram, 59 who was married to Levi's daughter Jochebed, who was born in Egypt.
She bore Amram two sons, Aaron and
Moses, and a daughter, Miriam. 60 Aaron
had four sons, Nadab, Abihu, Eleazar,
and Ithamar. 61 Nadab and Abihu died
when they offered unholy fire to the
LORD. 62 The male Levites who were one
month old or older numbered 23,000.
They were listed separately from the rest
of the Israelites, because they were not
given any property in Israel.

63 All these clans were listed by Moses
and Eleazar when they took a census of
the Israelites in the plains of Moab
across the Jordan River from Jericho.
64 There was not even one man left
among those whom Moses and Aaron
had listed in the first census in the Sinai
Desert. 65 The LORD had said that all of
them would die in the wilderness, and
except for Caleb son of Jephunneh and
Joshua son of Nun they all did.

The Daughters of Zelophehad

27 Mahlah, Noah, Hoglah, Milcah,
and Tirzah were the daughters of
Zelophehad son of Hepher, son of Gilead, son of Machir, son of Manasseh, son
of Joseph. 2 They went and stood before
Moses, Eleazar the priest, the leaders,
and the whole community at the entrance of the Tent of the LORD's presence
and said, 3 "Our father died in the wilderness without leaving any sons. He was
not among the followers of Korah, who
rebelled against the LORD; he died because of his own sin. 4 Just because he
had no sons, why should our father's
name disappear from Israel? Give us
property among our father's relatives."

5 Moses presented their case to the
LORD, 6 and the LORD said to him, 7 "What
the daughters of Zelophehad request is
right; give them property among their
father's relatives. Let his inheritance
pass on to them. 8 Tell the people of Israel
that whenever a man dies without leaving a son, his daughter is to inherit his
property. 9 If he has no daughter, his
brothers are to inherit it. 10 If he has no
brothers, his father's brothers are to inherit it. 11 If he has no brothers or uncles,
then his nearest relative is to inherit it
and hold it as his own property. The people of Israel are to observe this as a legal
requirement, just as I, the LORD, have
commanded you."

Joshua Is Chosen as Successor to Moses

(Deuteronomy 31.1-8)

12 The LORD said to Moses, "Go up the
Abarim Mountains and look out over the
land that I am giving to the Israelites.
13 After you have seen it, you will die, as
your brother Aaron did, 14 because both
of you rebelled against my command in
the wilderness of Zin. When the whole
community complained against me at
Meribah, you refused to acknowledge
my holy power before them." (Meribah is
the spring at Kadesh in the wilderness
of Zin.)

15 Moses prayed, 16 "LORD God, source
of all life, appoint, I pray, a man who can
lead the people 17 and can command
them in battle, so that your community will not be like sheep without a
shepherd."

18 The LORD said to Moses, "Take
Joshua son of Nun, a capable man, and
place your hands on his head. 19 Have
him stand in front of Eleazar the priest
and the whole community, and there before them all proclaim him as your successor. 20 Give him some of your own
authority, so that the whole community
of Israel will obey him. 21 He will depend
on Eleazar the priest, who will learn my
will by using the Urim and Thummim.[f]
In this way Eleazar will direct Joshua
and the whole community of Israel in all
their affairs." 22 Moses did as the LORD
had commanded him. He had Joshua
stand before Eleazar the priest and the
whole community. 23 As the LORD had
commanded, Moses put his hands on
Joshua's head and proclaimed him as his
successor.

[f] URIM AND THUMMIM: *Two objects used by the priest to determine God's will; it is not known precisely how they were used.*

The Regular Offerings

(Exodus 29.38-46)

28 The LORD commanded Moses 2 to instruct the Israelites to present to God at the appointed times the required food offerings that are pleasing to him.

3 These are the food offerings that are to be presented to the LORD: for the daily burnt offering, two one-year-old male lambs without any defects. 4 Offer the first lamb in the morning, and the second in the evening, 5 each with a grain offering of 2 pounds of flour, mixed with 2 pints of the best olive oil. 6 This is the daily offering that is completely burned, which was first offered at Mount Sinai as a food offering, an odor pleasing to the LORD. 7 As the wine offering with the first lamb, pour out at the altar 2 pints of wine. 8 In the evening offer the second lamb in the same way as the morning offering, together with its wine offering. It also is a food offering, an odor pleasing to the LORD.

The Sabbath Offering

9 On the Sabbath day offer two one-year-old male lambs without any defects, 4 pounds of flour mixed with olive oil as a grain offering, and the wine offering. 10 This burnt offering is to be offered every Sabbath in addition to the daily offering with its wine offering.

The Offering on the First Day of the Month

11 Present a burnt offering to the LORD at the beginning of each month: two young bulls, one ram, seven one-year-old male lambs, all without any defects. 12 As a grain offering, offer flour mixed with olive oil: with each bull, 6 pounds of flour; with the ram, 4 pounds; 13 and with each lamb, 2 pounds. These burnt offerings are food offerings, an odor pleasing to the LORD. 14 The proper wine offering is 4 pints of wine with each bull, 3 pints with the ram, and 2 pints with each lamb. This is the regulation for the burnt offering for the first day of each month throughout the year. 15 And in addition to the daily burnt offering with its wine offering, offer one male goat as a sin offering.

The Offerings at the Festival of Unleavened Bread

(Leviticus 23.5-14)

16 The Passover Festival in honor of the LORD is to be held on the fourteenth day of the first month. 17 On the fifteenth day a religious festival begins which lasts seven days, during which only bread prepared without yeast is to be eaten. 18 On the first day of the festival you are to gather for worship, and no work is to be done. 19 Offer a burnt offering as a food offering to the LORD: two young bulls, one ram, and seven one-year-old male lambs, all without any defects. 20 Offer the proper grain offering of flour mixed with olive oil: 6 pounds with each bull, 4 pounds with the ram, 21 and 2 pounds with each lamb. 22 Also offer one male goat as a sin offering, and in this way perform the ritual of purification for the people. 23 Offer these in addition to the regular morning burnt offering. 24 In the same way, for seven days offer to the LORD a food offering, an odor pleasing to him. Offer this in addition to the daily burnt offering and wine offering. 25 Meet for worship on the seventh day and do no work.

The Offerings at the Harvest Festival

(Leviticus 23.15-22)

26 On the first day of the Harvest Festival, when you present the offering of new grain to the LORD, you are to gather for worship, and no work is to be done. 27 Offer a burnt offering as an odor pleasing to the LORD: two young bulls, one ram, and seven one-year-old male lambs, all without any defects. 28 Offer the proper grain offering of flour mixed with olive oil: 6 pounds with each bull, 4 pounds with the ram, 29 and 2 pounds with each lamb. 30 Also offer one male goat as a sin offering, and in this way perform the ritual of purification for the people. 31 Offer these and the wine offering in addition to the daily burnt offering and grain offering.

The Offerings at the New Year Festival

(Leviticus 23.23-25)

29 On the first day of the seventh month you are to gather for worship, and no work is to be done. On that

day trumpets are to be blown. 2 Present a
burnt offering to the LORD, an odor pleasing to him: one young bull, one ram, and
seven one-year-old male lambs, all without any defects. 3 Offer the proper grain
offering of flour mixed with olive oil: 6
pounds of flour with the bull, 4 pounds
with the ram, 4 and 2 pounds with each
lamb. 5 Also offer one male goat as a sin
offering, and in this way perform the ritual of purification for the people. 6 Offer
these in addition to the regular burnt offering for the first day of the month with
its grain offering, and the daily burnt offering with its grain offering and wine
offering. These food offerings are an
odor pleasing to the LORD.

The Offerings at the Day of Atonement

(Leviticus 23.26-32)

7 Gather for worship on the tenth day
of the seventh month; eat no food and do
no work. 8 Offer a burnt offering to the
LORD, an odor pleasing to him: one young
bull, one ram, and seven one-year-old
male lambs, all without any defects. 9 Offer the proper grain offering of flour
mixed with olive oil: 6 pounds of flour
with the bull, 4 pounds with the ram,
10 and 2 pounds with each lamb. 11 Also
offer one male goat as a sin offering, in
addition to the goat offered in the ritual
of purification for the people, and the
daily burnt offering with its grain offering and wine offering.

The Offerings at the Festival of Shelters

(Leviticus 23.33-44)

12 Gather for worship on the fifteenth
day of the seventh month. Celebrate this
festival in honor of the LORD for seven
days and do no work. 13 On this first day
offer a food offering to the LORD, an odor
pleasing to him: thirteen young bulls,
two rams, and fourteen one-year-old
male lambs, all without any defects.
14 Offer the proper grain offering of flour
mixed with olive oil: 6 pounds of flour
with each bull, 4 pounds with each ram,
15 and 2 pounds with each lamb, with the
required wine offerings. 16 Also offer one
male goat as a sin offering. Offer these in
addition to the daily burnt offering with
its grain offering and wine offering.
17 On the second day offer twelve
young bulls, two rams, and fourteen one-
year-old male lambs, all without any defects. 18-19 Offer with them all the other
offerings required for the first day.
20 On the third day offer eleven young
bulls, two rams, and fourteen one-year-
old male lambs, all without any defects.
21-22 Offer with them all the other offerings required for the first day.
23 On the fourth day offer ten young
bulls, two rams, and fourteen one-year-
old male lambs, all without any defects.
24-25 Offer with them all the other offerings required for the first day.
26 On the fifth day offer nine young
bulls, two rams, and fourteen one-year-
old male lambs, all without any defects.
27-28 Offer with them all the other offerings required for the first day.
29 On the sixth day offer eight young
bulls, two rams, and fourteen one-year-
old male lambs, all without any defects.
30-31 Offer with them all the other offerings required for the first day.
32 On the seventh day offer seven
young bulls, two rams, and fourteen one-
year-old male lambs, all without any defects. 33-34 Offer with them all the other
offerings required for the first day.
35 On the eighth day gather for worship
and do no work. 36 Offer a burnt offering
as a food offering to the LORD, an odor
pleasing to him: one young bull, one ram,
and seven one-year-old male lambs, all
without any defects. 37-38 Offer with them
all the other offerings required for the
first day.
39 These are the regulations concerning the burnt offerings, grain offerings,
wine offerings, and fellowship offerings
that you are to make to the LORD at your
appointed festivals. These are in addition
to the offerings you give in fulfillment of
a vow or as freewill offerings.
40 So Moses told the people of Israel
everything that the LORD had commanded him.

Rules about Vows

30 Moses gave the following instructions to the leaders of the
tribes of Israel. 2 When a man makes a
vow to give something to the LORD or
takes an oath to abstain from something,
he must not break his promise, but must
do everything that he said he would.
3 When a young woman still living in
her father's house makes a vow to give

something to the LORD or promises to abstain from something, 4 she must do everything that she vowed or promised unless her father raises an objection when he hears about it. 5 But if her father forbids her to fulfill the vow when he hears about it, she is not required to keep it. The LORD will forgive her, because her father refused to let her keep it.

6 If an unmarried woman makes a vow, whether deliberately or carelessly, or promises to abstain from something, and then marries, 7 she must do everything that she vowed or promised unless her husband raises an objection when he hears about it. 8 But if her husband forbids her to fulfill the vow when he hears about it, she is not required to keep it. The LORD will forgive her.

9 A widow or a divorced woman must keep every vow she makes and every promise to abstain from something.

10 If a married woman makes a vow or promises to abstain from something, 11 she must do everything that she vowed or promised unless her husband raises an objection when he hears about it. 12 But if her husband forbids her to fulfill the vow when he hears about it, she is not required to keep it. The LORD will forgive her, because her husband prevented her from keeping her vow. 13 Her husband has the right to affirm or to annul any vow or promise that she has made. 14 But if, by the day after he hears of the vow, he has raised no objection, she must do everything that she has vowed or promised. He has affirmed the vow by not objecting on the day he heard of it. 15 But if he later annuls the vow, he must suffer the consequences for the failure to fulfill the vow.

16 These are the rules that the LORD gave Moses concerning vows made by an unmarried woman living in her father's house or by a married woman.

The Holy War against Midian

31 The LORD said to Moses, 2 "Punish the Midianites for what they did to the people of Israel. After you have done that, you will die."

3 So Moses said to the people, "Get ready for war, so that you can attack Midian and punish them for what they did to the LORD. 4 From each tribe of Israel send a thousand men to war."

5 So a thousand men were chosen from each tribe, a total of twelve thousand men ready for battle. 6 Moses sent them to war under the command of Phinehas son of Eleazar the priest, who took charge of the sacred objects and the trumpets for giving signals. 7 They attacked Midian, as the LORD had commanded Moses, and killed all the men, 8 including the five kings of Midian: Evi, Rekem, Zur, Hur, and Reba. They also killed Balaam son of Beor.

9 The people of Israel captured the Midianite women and children, took their cattle and their flocks, plundered all their wealth, 10 and burned all their cities and camps. 11 They took all the loot that they had captured, including the prisoners and the animals, 12 and brought them to Moses and Eleazar and to the community of the people of Israel, who were at the camp on the plains of Moab across the Jordan from Jericho.

The Army Returns

13 Moses, Eleazar, and all the other leaders of the community went out of the camp to meet the army. 14 Moses became angry with the officers, the commanders of battalions and companies, who had returned from the war. 15 He asked them, "Why have you kept all the women alive? 16 Remember that it was the women who followed Balaam's instructions and at Peor led the people to be unfaithful to the LORD. That was what brought the epidemic on the LORD's people. 17 So now kill every boy and kill every woman who has had sexual intercourse, 18 but keep alive for yourselves all the girls and all the women who are virgins. 19 Now all of you who have killed anyone or have touched a corpse must stay outside the camp for seven days. On the third day and on the seventh day purify yourselves and the women you have captured. 20 You must also purify every piece of clothing and everything made of leather, goats' hair, or wood."

21 Eleazar the priest said to the men who had returned from battle, "These are the regulations that the LORD has given to Moses. 22-23 Everything that will not burn, such as gold, silver, bronze, iron, tin, or lead, is to be purified by passing it through fire. Everything else is to be purified by the water for purification. 24 On the seventh day you must wash your

clothes; then you will be ritually clean
and will be permitted to enter the camp."

Division of the Loot

25 The LORD said to Moses, 26 "You and
Eleazar, together with the other leaders
of the community, are to count everything that has been captured, including
the prisoners and the animals. 27 Divide
what was taken into two equal parts, one
part for the soldiers and the other part
for the rest of the community. 28 From the
part that belongs to the soldiers, withhold as a tax for the LORD one out of every
five hundred prisoners and the same proportion of the cattle, donkeys, sheep, and
goats. 29 Give them to Eleazar the priest
as a special contribution to the LORD.
30 From the part given to the rest of the
people, take one out of every fifty prisoners and the same proportion of the cattle,
donkeys, sheep, and goats. Give them to
the Levites who are in charge of the
LORD's Tent." 31 Moses and Eleazar did
what the LORD commanded.

32-35 The following is a list of what was
captured by the soldiers, in addition to
what they kept for themselves: 675,000
sheep and goats, 72,000 cattle, 61,000
donkeys, and 32,000 virgins. 36-40 The
half share of the soldiers was 337,500
sheep and goats, of which 675 were the
tax for the LORD; 36,000 cattle for the soldiers, of which 72 were the tax for the
LORD; 30,500 donkeys for the soldiers, of
which 61 were the tax for the LORD; and
16,000 virgins for the soldiers, of which
32 were the tax for the LORD. 41 So Moses
gave Eleazar the tax as a special contribution to the LORD, as the LORD had
commanded.

42-46 The share of the community was
the same as that for the soldiers: 337,500
sheep and goats, 36,000 cattle, 30,500
donkeys, and 16,000 virgins. 47 From this
share Moses took one out of every fifty
prisoners and animals, and as the LORD
had commanded, gave them to the Levites who were in charge of the LORD's
Tent.

48 Then the officers who had commanded the army went to Moses 49 and
reported, "Sir, we have counted the soldiers under our command and not one of
them is missing. 50 So we are bringing the
gold ornaments, armlets, bracelets,
rings, earrings, and necklaces that each
of us has taken. We offer them to the
LORD as a payment for our lives, so that
he will protect us." 51 Moses and Eleazar
received the gold, all of which was in the
form of ornaments. 52 The total contribution of the officers weighed over four
hundred pounds. 53 Those who were not
officers kept the loot they had taken.
54 So Moses and Eleazar took the gold to
the Tent, so that the LORD would protect
the people of Israel.

The Tribes East of the Jordan

(Deuteronomy 3.12-22)

32 The tribes of Reuben and Gad
had a lot of livestock. When they
saw how suitable the land of Jazer and
Gilead was for cattle, 2 they went to
Moses, Eleazar, and the other leaders of
the community and said, 3-4 "This region
which the LORD has helped the Israelites
occupy – the towns of Ataroth, Dibon,
Jazer, Nimrah, Heshbon, Elealeh, Sibmah, Nebo, and Beon – is good land for
livestock, and we have so much livestock. 5 Please give us this land as our
property, and do not make us cross the
Jordan River and settle there."

6 Moses replied, "Do you want to stay
here while the other Israelites go to war?
7 How dare you try to discourage the people of Israel from crossing the Jordan
into the land which the LORD has given
them? 8 That is what your fathers did
when I sent them from Kadesh Barnea to
explore the land. 9 They went as far as
Eshcol Valley and saw the land, but
when they returned, they discouraged
the people from entering the land which
the LORD had given them. 10 The LORD became angry that day and made a promise: 11 'I swear that because they did not
remain loyal to me, none of the men
twenty years old or older who came out
of Egypt will enter the land that I promised to Abraham, Isaac, and Jacob.'
12 This included everyone, except Caleb
son of Jephunneh the Kenizzite and
Joshua son of Nun; they remained loyal
to the LORD. 13 The LORD became angry
with the people and made them wander
in the wilderness forty years until that
whole generation that had displeased
him was dead. 14 And now you have
taken your ancestors' place, a new generation of sinful people ready to bring
down the fierce anger of the LORD on Israel again. 15 If you people of Reuben and
Gad refuse to follow him now, he will

once again abandon all these people in
the wilderness, and you will be responsible for their destruction."
16 They approached Moses and said,
"First, allow us to build stone enclosures
here for our sheep and fortified towns for
our dependents. 17 Then we will be ready
to go with the other Israelites into battle
and lead the attack until we have settled
them in the land that will be theirs. In the
meantime, our dependents can live here
in the fortified towns, safe from the people of this land. 18 We will not return to
our homes until all the other Israelites
have taken possession of the land assigned to them. 19 We will not take possession of any property among them on
the other side of the Jordan, because we
have received our share here east of the
Jordan."
20 Moses answered, "If you really mean
what you say, then here in the presence
of the LORD get ready to go into battle.
21 All your fighting men are to cross the
Jordan and under the command of the
LORD they are to attack our enemies until
the LORD defeats them 22 and takes possession of the land. After that, you may
return, because you will have fulfilled
your obligation to the LORD and to the
other Israelites. Then the LORD will acknowledge that this land east of the Jordan is yours. 23 But if you do not keep
your promise, I warn you that you will be
sinning against the LORD. Make no mistake about it; you will be punished for
your sin. 24 So build your towns and the
enclosures for your sheep, but do what
you have promised!"
25 The men of Gad and Reuben said,
"Sir, we will do as you command. 26 Our
wives and children and our cattle and
sheep will remain here in the towns of
Gilead. 27 But all of us are ready to go into
battle under the LORD's command. We
will cross the Jordan and fight, just as
you have said."
28 So Moses gave these commands to
Eleazar, Joshua, and the other leaders of
Israel: 29 "If the men of Gad and Reuben
cross the Jordan ready for battle at the
LORD's command and if with their help
you are able to conquer the land, then
give them the land of Gilead as their
property. 30 But if they do not cross the
Jordan and go into battle with you, they
are to receive their share of the property in the land of Canaan, as you do."
31 The men of Gad and Reuben answered, "Sir, we will do as the LORD has
commanded. 32 Under his command we
will cross into the land of Canaan and go
into battle, so that we can retain our
property here east of the Jordan."
33 So Moses assigned to the tribes of
Gad and Reuben and to half the tribe of
Manasseh all the territory of King Sihon
of the Amorites and King Og of Bashan,
including the towns and the country
around them. 34 The tribe of Gad rebuilt
the fortified towns of Dibon, Ataroth,
Aroer, 35 Atroth Shophan, Jazer, Jogbehah, 36 Beth Nimrah, and Beth Haran.
37 The tribe of Reuben rebuilt Heshbon,
Elealeh, Kiriathaim, 38 Nebo, Baal Meon
(this name was changed), and Sibmah.
They gave new names to the towns they
rebuilt.
39 The clan of Machir son of Manasseh
invaded the land of Gilead, occupied it,
and drove out the Amorites who were
there. 40 So Moses gave Gilead to the clan
of Machir, and they lived there. 41 Jair, of
the tribe of Manasseh, attacked and captured some villages and named them
"Villages of Jair." 42 Nobah attacked and
captured Kenath and its villages, and he
renamed it Nobah, after himself.

The Journey from Egypt to Moab

33 The following account gives the
names of the places where the Israelites set up camp after they left Egypt
in their tribes under the leadership of
Moses and Aaron. 2 At the command of
the LORD, Moses wrote down the name
of the place each time they set up
camp.
3 The people of Israel left Egypt on the
fifteenth day of the first month of the
year, the day after the first Passover. Under the LORD's protection they left the city
of Rameses in full view of the Egyptians,
4 who were burying the first-born sons
that the LORD had killed. By doing this,
the LORD showed that he was more powerful than the gods of Egypt.
5 The people of Israel left Rameses and
set up camp at Sukkoth. 6 Their next
camp was at Etham on the edge of the
desert. 7 From there they turned back to
Pi Hahiroth, east of Baal Zephon, and
camped near Migdol. 8 They left Pi Hahiroth and passed through the Red

Sea[g] into the desert of Shur; after a three
days' march they camped at Marah.
9 From there they went to Elim,
where they camped, because there
were twelve springs of water and seventy palm trees there.

10 They left Elim and camped near the
Gulf of Suez. 11 Their next camp was in
the desert of Sin. 12 Then they camped at
Dophkah, 13 and after that at Alush.
14 Next was Rephidim, where there was
no water for them to drink.

15-37 From Rephidim to Mount Hor they
set up camp at the following places: the
Sinai Desert, Kibroth Hattaavah (or
"Graves of Craving"), Hazeroth, Rith-
mah, Rimmon Perez, Libnah, Rissah, Ke-
helathah, Mount Shepher, Haradah,
Makheloth, Tahath, Terah, Mithkah,
Hashmonah, Moseroth, Bene Jaakan,
Hor Haggidgad, Jotbathah, Abronah,
Eziongeber, the wilderness of Zin (that
is, Kadesh), and Mount Hor, at the edge
of the land of Edom.

38-39 At the command of the LORD,
Aaron the priest climbed Mount Hor. At
the age of 123 he died there on the first
day of the fifth month of the fortieth year
after the Israelites had left Egypt.

40 The king of Arad in southern Canaan
heard that the Israelites were coming.

41-49 From Mount Hor to the plains of
Moab the Israelites set up camp at the
following places: Zalmonah, Punon,
Oboth, the ruins of Abarim in the territory of Moab, Dibon Gad, Almon Diblathaim, the Abarim Mountains near
Mount Nebo, and in the plains of Moab
across the Jordan River from Jericho,
between Beth Jeshimoth and Acacia
Valley.

Instructions before Crossing the Jordan

50 There in the plains of Moab across
the Jordan from Jericho the LORD gave
Moses 51 the following instructions for Israel: "When you cross the Jordan into
the land of Canaan, 52 you must drive out
all the inhabitants of the land. Destroy all
their stone and metal idols and all their
places of worship. 53 Occupy the land and
settle in it, because I am giving it to you.
54 Divide the land among the various
tribes and clans by drawing lots, giving
a large piece of property to a large clan
and a small one to a small clan. 55 But if
you do not drive out the inhabitants of
the land, those that are left will be as
troublesome as splinters in your eyes
and thorns in your sides, and they will
fight against you. 56 If you do not drive
them out, I will destroy you, as I planned
to destroy them."

The Boundaries of the Land

34 The LORD gave Moses 2 the following instructions for the people of Israel: "When you enter Canaan,
the land which I am giving you, the borders of your territory will be as follows.
3 The southern border will extend from
the wilderness of Zin along the border of
Edom. It will begin on the east at the
southern end of the Dead Sea. 4 Then it
will turn southward toward Akrabbim
Pass and continue on through Zin as far
south as Kadesh Barnea. Then it will turn
northwest to Hazar Addar and on to Azmon, 5 where it will turn toward the valley at the border of Egypt and end at the
Mediterranean.

6 "The western border will be the Mediterranean Sea.

7 "The northern border will follow a
line from the Mediterranean to Mount
Hor 8 and from there to Hamath Pass. It
will continue to Zedad 9 and to Ziphron,
and will end at Hazar Enan.

10 "The eastern border will follow a line
from Hazar Enan to Shepham. 11 It will
then go south to Harbel, east of Ain, and
on to the hills on the eastern shore of
Lake Galilee, 12 then south along the Jordan River to the Dead Sea.

"These will be the four borders of your
land."

13 So Moses said to the Israelites, "This
is the land that you will receive by drawing lots, the land that the LORD has assigned to the nine and one-half tribes.
14 The tribes of Reuben and Gad and the
eastern half of Manasseh have received
their property, divided according to their
families, 15 on the eastern side of the Jordan, opposite Jericho."

The Leaders Responsible for Dividing the Land

16 The LORD said to Moses, 17 "Eleazar
the priest and Joshua son of Nun will

[g] RED SEA: *See Word List.*

divide the land for the people. 18 Take also one leader from each tribe to help them divide it." 19-28 These are the men the LORD chose:

Tribe	*Leader*
Judah	Caleb son of Jephunneh
Simeon	Shelumiel son of Ammihud
Benjamin	Elidad son of Chislon
Dan	Bukki son of Jogli
Manasseh	Hanniel son of Ephod
Ephraim	Kemuel son of Shiphtan
Zebulun	Elizaphan son of Parnach
Issachar	Paltiel son of Azzan
Asher	Ahihud son of Shelomi
Naphtali	Pedahel son of Ammihud

29 These are the men that the LORD assigned to divide the property for the people of Israel in the land of Canaan.

The Cities Assigned to the Levites

35 In the plains of Moab across the Jordan from Jericho the LORD said to Moses, 2 "Tell the Israelites that from the property they receive they must give the Levites some cities to live in and pasture land around the cities. 3 These cities will belong to the Levites, and they will live there. The pasture land will be for their cattle and all their other animals. 4 The pasture land is to extend outward from the city walls five hundred yards in each direction, 5 so that there is a square area measuring one thousand yards on each side, with the city in the middle. 6 You are to give the Levites six cities of refuge to which any of you can escape if you kill someone accidentally. In addition, give them forty-two other cities 7 with their pasture land, making a total of forty-eight. 8 The number of Levite cities in each tribe is to be determined according to the size of its territory."

The Cities of Refuge

(Deuteronomy 19.1-13; Joshua 20.1-9)

9 The LORD told Moses 10 to say to the people of Israel: "When you cross the Jordan River and enter the land of Canaan, 11 you are to choose cities of refuge to which any of you can escape if you kill someone accidentally. 12 There you will be safe from the dead person's relative who seeks revenge. No one accused of manslaughter is to be put to death without a public trial. 13 Choose six cities, 14 three east of the Jordan and three in the land of Canaan. 15 These will serve as cities of refuge for Israelites and for foreigners who are temporary or permanent residents. Anyone who kills someone accidentally can escape to one of them.

16-18 "If, however, any of you use a weapon of iron or stone or wood to kill someone, you are guilty of murder and are to be put to death. 19 The dead person's nearest relative has the responsibility for putting the murderer to death. When he finds you, he is to kill you.

20 "If you hate someone and kill him by pushing him down or by throwing something at him 21 or by striking him with your fist, you are guilty of murder and are to be put to death. The dead person's nearest relative has the responsibility for putting the murderer to death. When he finds you, he is to kill you.

22 "But suppose you accidentally kill someone you do not hate, whether by pushing him down or by throwing something at him. 23 Or suppose that, without looking, you throw a stone that kills someone whom you did not intend to hurt and who was not your enemy. 24 In such cases the community shall judge in your favor and not in favor of the dead person's relative who is seeking revenge. 25 You are guilty only of manslaughter, and the community is to rescue you from the dead person's relative, and they are to return you to the city of refuge to which you had escaped. You must live there until the death of the man who is then High Priest. 26 If you leave the city of refuge to which you have escaped 27 and if the dead person's relative finds you and kills you, this act of revenge is not murder. 28 Any of you guilty of manslaughter must remain in the city of refuge until the death of the High Priest, but after that you may return home. 29 These rules apply to you and your descendants wherever you may live.

30 "Those accused of murder may be found guilty and put to death only on the evidence of two or more witnesses; the evidence of one witness is not sufficient

to support an accusation of murder.
31 Murderers must be put to death. They
cannot escape this penalty by the payment of money. 32 If they have fled to a
city of refuge, do not allow them to make
a payment in order to return home before
the death of the High Priest. 33 If you did
this, you would defile the land where you
are living. Murder defiles the land, and
except by the death of the murderer
there is no way to perform the ritual of
purification for the land where someone
has been murdered. 34 Do not defile the
land where you are living, because I am
the LORD and I live among the people of
Israel."

The Inheritance of Married Women

36 The heads of the families in the
clan of Gilead, the son of Machir
and grandson of Manasseh son of Joseph, went to Moses and the other leaders. 2 They said, "The LORD commanded
you to distribute the land to the people of
Israel by drawing lots. He also commanded you to give the property of our
relative Zelophehad to his daughters.
3 But remember, if they marry men of another tribe, their property will then belong to that tribe, and the total allotted to
us will be reduced. 4 In the Year of Restoration, when all property that has been
sold is restored to its original owners, the
property of Zelophehad's daughters will
be permanently added to the tribe into
which they marry and will be lost to our
tribe."

5 So Moses gave the people of Israel the
following command from the LORD. He
said, "What the tribe of Manasseh says is
right, 6 and so the LORD says that the
daughters of Zelophehad are free to
marry anyone they wish but only within
their own tribe. 7 The property of every
Israelite will remain attached to his tribe.
8 Every woman who inherits property in
an Israelite tribe must marry a man belonging to that tribe. In this way all Israelites will inherit the property of their
ancestors, 9 and the property will not
pass from one tribe to another. Each
tribe will continue to possess its own
property."

10-11 So Mahlah, Tirzah, Hoglah, Milcah, and Noah, the daughters of Zelophehad, did as the LORD had commanded
Moses, and they married their cousins.
12 They married within the clans of the
tribe of Manasseh son of Joseph, and
their property remained in their father's
tribe.

13 These are the rules and regulations
that the LORD gave the Israelites through
Moses in the plains of Moab across the
Jordan River from Jericho.

DEUTERONOMY

Introduction

The book of Deuteronomy *is organized as a series of addresses given by Moses to the people of Israel in the land of Moab, where they had stopped at the end of the long wilderness journey and were about to enter and occupy Canaan.*

Some of the most important matters recorded in the book are as follows: 1) Moses recalls the great events of the past forty years. He appeals to the people to remember how God has led them through the wilderness and to be obedient and loyal to God. 2) Moses reviews the Ten Commandments and emphasizes the meaning of the First Commandment, calling the people to devotion to the Lord alone. Then he reviews the various laws that are to govern Israel's life in the promised land. 3) Moses reminds the people of the meaning of God's covenant with them, and calls for them to renew their commitment to its obligations. 4) Joshua is commissioned as the next leader of God's people. After singing a song celebrating God's faithfulness, and pronouncing a blessing on the tribes of Israel, Moses dies in Moab, east of the Jordan River.

The great theme of the book is that God has saved and blessed his chosen people, whom he loves; so his people are to remember this, and love and obey him, so that they may have life and continued blessing.

The key verses of the book are 6.4-6, and contain the words that Jesus called the greatest of all commandments: "Love the LORD *your God with all your heart, with all your soul, and with all your strength."*

Outline of Contents

Introduction

1 In this book are the words that
Moses spoke to the people of Israel
when they were in the wilderness east of
the Jordan River. They were in the Jordan Valley near Suph, between the town
of Paran on one side and the towns of
Tophel, Laban, Hazeroth, and Dizahab
on the other. (2 It takes eleven days to
travel from Mount Sinai to Kadesh Barnea by way of the hill country of Edom.)
3 On the first day of the eleventh month of
the fortieth year after they had left
Egypt, Moses told the people everything
the LORD had commanded him to tell
them. 4 This was after the LORD[a] had defeated King Sihon of the Amorites, who
ruled in the town of Heshbon, and King
Og of Bashan, who ruled in the towns of
Ashtaroth and Edrei. 5 It was while the
people were east of the Jordan in the territory of Moab that Moses began to explain God's laws and teachings.

He said, 6 "When we were at Mount Si-
nai, the LORD our God said to us, 'You
have stayed long enough at this mountain. 7 Break camp and move on. Go to
the hill country of the Amorites and to all
the surrounding regions—to the Jordan
Valley, to the hill country and the lowlands, to the southern region, and to the
Mediterranean coast. Go to the land of
Canaan and on beyond the Lebanon
Mountains as far as the great Euphrates
River. 8 All of this is the land which I, the
LORD, promised to give to your ancestors,
Abraham, Isaac, and Jacob, and to their
descendants. Go and occupy it.' "

[a] the LORD; *or* Moses.

Moses Appoints Judges

(Exodus 18.13-27)

9 Moses said to the people, "While we
were still at Mount Sinai, I told you, 'The
responsibility for leading you is too
much for me. I can't do it alone. 10 The
LORD your God has made you as numerous as the stars in the sky. 11 May the
LORD, the God of your ancestors, make
you increase a thousand times more and
make you prosperous, as he promised!
12 But how can I alone bear the heavy
responsibility for settling your disputes?
13 Choose some wise, understanding, and
experienced men from each tribe, and I
will put them in charge of you.' 14 And
you agreed that this was a good thing to
do. 15 So I took the wise and experienced
leaders you chose from your tribes, and
I placed them in charge of you. Some
were responsible for a thousand people,
some for a hundred, some for fifty, and
some for ten. I also appointed other officials throughout the tribes.
16 "At that time I instructed them, 'Listen to the disputes that come up among
your people. Judge every dispute fairly,
whether it concerns only your own people or involves foreigners who live
among you. 17 Show no partiality in your
decisions; judge everyone on the same
basis, no matter who they are. Do not be
afraid of anyone, for the decisions you
make come from God. If any case is too
difficult for you, bring it to me, and I will
decide it.' 18 At the same time I gave you
instructions for everything else you were
to do.

The Spies Are Sent Out from Kadesh Barnea

(Numbers 13.1-33)

19 "We did what the LORD our God commanded us. We left Mount Sinai and
went through that vast and fearful desert
on the way to the hill country of the Amorites. When we reached Kadesh Barnea,
20-21 I told you, 'You have now come to
the hill country of the Amorites, which
the LORD our God, the God of our ancestors, is giving us. Look, there it is. Go and
occupy it as he commanded. Do not hesitate or be afraid.'
22 "But you came to me and said, 'Let's
send men ahead of us to spy out the land,
so that they can tell us the best route to
take and what kind of cities are there.'
23 "That seemed like a good thing to do,
so I selected twelve men, one from each
tribe. 24 They went into the hill country as
far as Eshcol Valley and explored it.
25 They brought us back some fruit they
found there, and reported that the land
which the LORD our God was giving us
was very fertile.
26 "But you rebelled against the command of the LORD your God, and you
would not enter the land. 27 You grumbled to one another: 'The LORD hates us.
He brought us out of Egypt just to hand
us over to these Amorites, so that they
could kill us. 28 Why should we go there?
We are afraid. The men we sent tell us
that the people there are stronger and
taller than we are, and that they live in
cities with walls that reach the sky. They
saw giants there!'
29 "But I told you, 'Don't be afraid of
those people. 30 The LORD your God will
lead you, and he will fight for you, just as
you saw him do in Egypt 31 and in the
desert. You saw how he brought you
safely all the way to this place, just as a
father would carry his son.' 32 But in spite
of what I said, you still would not trust
the LORD, 33 even though he always went
ahead of you to find a place for you to
camp. To show you the way, he went in
front of you in a pillar of fire by night and
in a pillar of cloud by day.

The LORD Punishes Israel

(Numbers 14.20-45)

34 "The LORD heard your complaints
and became angry, and so he solemnly
declared, 35 'Not one of you from this evil
generation will enter the fertile land that
I promised to give your ancestors. 36 Only
Caleb son of Jephunneh will enter it. He
has remained faithful to me, and I will
give him and his descendants the land
that he has explored.' 37 Because of you
the LORD also became angry with me and
said, 'Not even you, Moses, will enter the
land. 38 But strengthen the determination
of your helper, Joshua son of Nun. He
will lead Israel to occupy the land.'
39 "Then the LORD said to all of us, 'Your
children, who are still too young to know
right from wrong, will enter the land—
the children you said would be seized by
your enemies. I will give the land to
them, and they will occupy it. 40 But as for
you people, turn around and go back into

the desert on the road to the Gulf of
Aqaba.’
41 “You replied, ‘Moses, we have
sinned against the LORD. But now we will
attack, just as the LORD our God commanded us.’ Then each one of you got
ready to fight, thinking it would be easy
to invade the hill country.
42 “But the LORD said to me, ‘Warn them
not to attack, for I will not be with them,
and their enemies will defeat them.’
43 I told you what the LORD had said, but
you paid no attention. You rebelled
against him, and in your pride you
marched into the hill country. 44 Then the
Amorites who lived in those hills came
out against you like a swarm of bees.
They chased you as far as Hormah and
defeated you there in the hill country of
Edom. 45 So you cried out to the LORD for
help, but he would not listen to you or
pay any attention to you.

The Years in the Desert

46 “So then, after we had stayed at Ka-
2 desh for a long time, 1 we finally
turned and went into the desert, on
the road to the Gulf of Aqaba, as the LORD
had commanded, and we spent a long
time wandering about in the hill country
of Edom.
2 “Then the LORD told me 3 that we had
spent enough time wandering about in
those hills and that we should go north.
4 He told me to give you the following
instructions: ‘You are about to go
through the hill country of Edom, the territory of your distant relatives, the
descendants of Esau. They will be afraid
of you, 5 but you must not start a war with
them, because I am not going to give you
so much as a square foot of their land. I
have given Edom to Esau’s descendants.
6 You may buy food and water from
them.’
7 “Remember how the LORD your God
has blessed you in everything that you
have done. He has taken care of you as
you wandered through this vast desert.
He has been with you these forty years,
and you have had everything you
needed.
8 “So we moved on and left the road
that goes from the towns of Elath and
Eziongeber to the Dead Sea, and we
turned northeast toward Moab. 9 The
LORD said to me, ‘Don’t trouble the people
of Moab, the descendants of Lot, or start
a war against them. I have given them
the city of Ar, and I am not going to give
you any of their land.’ ”
(10 A mighty race of giants called the
Emim used to live in Ar. They were as tall
as the Anakim, another race of giants.
11 Like the Anakim they were also known
as Rephaim; but the Moabites called
them Emim. 12 The Horites used to live in
Edom, but the descendants of Esau
chased them out, destroyed their nation,
and settled there themselves, just as the
Israelites later chased their enemies out
of the land that the LORD gave them.)
13 “Then we crossed the Zered River as
the LORD told us to do. 14 This was thirty-
eight years after we had left Kadesh Barnea. All the fighting men of that
generation had died, as the LORD had said
they would. 15 The LORD kept on opposing
them until he had destroyed them all.
16 “After they had all died, 17 the LORD
said to us, 18 ‘Today you are to pass
through the territory of Moab by way of
Ar. 19 You will then be near the land of
the Ammonites, the descendants of Lot.
Don’t trouble them or start a war against
them, because I am not going to give you
any of the land that I have given them.’ ”
(20 This territory is also known as the
land of the Rephaim, the name of the
people who used to live there; the Ammonites called them Zamzummim.
21 They were as tall as the Anakim. There
were many of them, and they were a
mighty race. But the LORD destroyed
them, so that the Ammonites took over
their land and settled there. 22 The LORD
had done the same thing for the Edomites, the descendants of Esau, who live in
the hill country of Edom. He destroyed
the Horites, so that the Edomites took
over their land and settled there, where
they still live. 23 The land along the Mediterranean coast had been settled by people from the island of Crete. They had
destroyed the Avvim, the original inhabitants, and had taken over all their land
as far south as the city of Gaza.)
24 “After we had passed through Moab,
the LORD told us, ‘Now, start out and
cross the Arnon River. I am placing in
your power Sihon, the Amorite king of
Heshbon, along with his land. Attack
him, and begin occupying his land.
25 From today on I will make people
everywhere afraid of you. Everyone will

tremble with fear at the mention of your
name.'

Israel Defeats King Sihon

(Numbers 21.21-30)

26 “Then I sent messengers from the
desert of Kedemoth to King Sihon of
Heshbon with the following offer of
peace: 27 ‘Let us pass through your country. We will go straight through and not
leave the road. 28 We will pay for the food
we eat and the water we drink. All we
want to do is to pass through your country, 29 until we cross the Jordan River into
the land that the LORD our God is giving
us. The descendants of Esau, who live in
Edom, and the Moabites, who live in
Ar, allowed us to pass through their
territory.'

30 “But King Sihon would not let us
pass through his country. The LORD your
God had made him stubborn and rebellious, so that we could defeat him and
take his territory, which we still occupy.

31 “Then the LORD said to me, ‘Look, I
have made King Sihon and his land helpless before you; take his land and occupy
it.' 32 Sihon came out with all his men to
fight us near the town of Jahaz, 33 but the
LORD our God put him in our power, and
we killed him, his sons, and all his men.
34 At the same time we captured and destroyed every town, and put everyone to
death, men, women, and children. We
left no survivors. 35 We took the livestock
and plundered the towns. 36 The LORD our
God let us capture all the towns from
Aroer, on the edge of the Arnon Valley,
and the city in the middle of that valley,
all the way to Gilead. No town had walls
too strong for us. 37 But we did not go
near the territory of the Ammonites or to
the banks of the Jabbok River or to the
towns of the hill country or to any other
place where the LORD our God had commanded us not to go.

Israel Conquers King Og

(Numbers 21.31-35)

3 “Next, we moved north toward the
region of Bashan, and King Og
came out with all his men to fight us near
the town of Edrei. 2 But the LORD said to
me, ‘Don't be afraid of him. I am going to
give him, his men, and all his territory to
you. Do the same thing to him that you
did to Sihon the Amorite king who ruled
in Heshbon.'

3 “So the LORD also placed King Og and
his people in our power, and we slaughtered them all. 4 At the same time we captured all his towns – there was not one
that we did not take. In all we captured
sixty towns – the whole region of Argob,
where King Og of Bashan ruled. 5 All
these towns were fortified with high
walls, gates, and bars to lock the gates,
and there were also many villages without walls. 6 We destroyed all the towns
and put to death all the men, women, and
children, just as we did in the towns that
belonged to King Sihon of Heshbon. 7 We
took the livestock and plundered the
towns.

8 “At that time we took from those two
Amorite kings the land east of the Jordan
River, from the Arnon River to Mount
Hermon. (9 Mount Hermon is called Sir-
ion by the Sidonians, and Senir by the
Amorites.) 10 We took all the territory of
King Og of Bashan: the cities on the pla-
teau, the regions of Gilead and of Ba-
shan, as far east as the towns of Salecah
and Edrei.”

(11 King Og was the last of the Rephaim. His coffin,[b] made of stone,[c] was
six feet wide and almost fourteen feet
long, according to standard measurements. It can still be seen in the Ammonite city of Rabbah.)

The Tribes That Settled East of the Jordan

(Numbers 32.1-42)

12 “When we took possession of the
land, I assigned to the tribes of Reuben
and Gad the territory north of the town
of Aroer near the Arnon River and part
of the hill country of Gilead, along with
its towns. 13 To half the tribe of Manasseh
I assigned the rest of Gilead and also all
of Bashan, where Og had ruled, that is,
the entire Argob region.”

(Bashan was known as the land of the
Rephaim. 14 Jair, from the tribe of Manasseh, took the entire region of Argob,
that is, Bashan, as far as the border of
Geshur and Maacah. He named the villages after himself, and they are still
known as the villages of Jair.)

15 “I assigned Gilead to the clan of Machir of the tribe of Manasseh. 16 And to

[b] coffin; *or* bed. [c] stone; *or* iron.

the tribes of Reuben and Gad I assigned
the territory from Gilead to the Arnon
River. The middle of the river was their
southern boundary, and their northern
boundary was the Jabbok River, part of
which formed the Ammonite border.
17 On the west their territory extended to
the Jordan River, from Lake Galilee in
the north down to the Dead Sea in the
south and to the foot of Mount Pisgah on
the east.
18 "At the same time, I gave them the
following instructions: 'The LORD our
God has given you this land east of the
Jordan to occupy. Now arm your fighting
men and send them across the Jordan
ahead of the other tribes of Israel, to help
them occupy their land. 19 Only your
wives, children, and livestock—I know
you have a lot of livestock—will remain
behind in the towns that I have assigned
to you. 20 Help the other Israelites until
they occupy the land that the LORD is giving them west of the Jordan and until the
LORD lets them live there in peace, as he
has already done here for you. After that,
you may return to this land that I have
assigned to you.'
21 "Then I instructed Joshua: 'You have
seen all that the LORD your God did to
those two kings, Sihon and Og; and he
will do the same thing to everyone else
whose land you invade. 22 Don't be afraid
of them, for the LORD your God will fight
for you.'

Moses Is Not Permitted to Enter Canaan

23 "At that time I earnestly prayed,
24 'Sovereign LORD, I know that you have
shown me only the beginning of the
great and wonderful things you are going to do. There is no god in heaven or on
earth who can do the mighty things that
you have done! 25 Let me cross the Jordan River, LORD, and see the fertile land
on the other side, the beautiful hill country and the Lebanon Mountains.'
26 "But because of you people the LORD
was angry with me and would not listen.
Instead, he said, 'That's enough! Don't
mention this again! 27 Go to the peak of
Mount Pisgah and look to the north and
to the south, to the east and to the west.
Look carefully at what you see, because
you will never go across the Jordan.
28 Give Joshua his instructions.
Strengthen his determination, because
he will lead the people across to occupy
the land that you see.'
29 "So we remained in the valley opposite the town of Bethpeor."

Moses Urges Israel to Be Obedient

4 Then Moses said to the people,
"Obey all the laws that I am teaching
you, and you will live and occupy the
land which the LORD, the God of your ancestors, is giving you. 2 Do not add anything to what I command you, and do not
take anything away. Obey the commands of the LORD your God that I have
given you. 3 You yourselves saw what the
LORD did at Mount Peor. He destroyed
everyone who worshiped Baal there,
4 but those of you who were faithful to the
LORD your God are still alive today.
5 "I have taught you all the laws, as the
LORD my God told me to do. Obey them in
the land that you are about to invade and
occupy. 6 Obey them faithfully, and this
will show the people of other nations
how wise you are. When they hear of
all these laws, they will say, 'What wisdom and understanding this great nation has!'
7 "No other nation, no matter how
great, has a god who is so near when they
need him as the LORD our God is to us. He
answers us whenever we call for help.
8 No other nation, no matter how great,
has laws so just as those that I have
taught you today. 9 Be on your guard!
Make certain that you do not forget, as
long as you live, what you have seen with
your own eyes. Tell your children and
your grandchildren 10 about the day you
stood in the presence of the LORD your
God at Mount Sinai,[d] when he said to
me, 'Assemble the people. I want them to
hear what I have to say, so that they will
learn to obey me as long as they live and
so that they will teach their children to do
the same.'
11 "Tell your children how you went
and stood at the foot of the mountain
which was covered with thick clouds of
dark smoke and fire blazing up to the
sky. 12 Tell them how the LORD spoke to
you from the fire, how you heard him
speaking but did not see him in any form
at all. 13 He told you what you must do to

[d] Sinai; *or* Horeb.

keep the covenant he made with you—
you must obey the Ten Commandments,
which he wrote on two stone tablets.
14 The LORD told me to teach you all the
laws that you are to obey in the land that
you are about to invade and occupy.

Warning against Idolatry

15 "When the LORD spoke to you from
the fire on Mount Sinai, you did not see
any form. For your own good, then,
make certain 16 that you do not sin by
making for yourselves an idol in any
form at all—whether man or woman,
17 animal or bird, 18 reptile or fish. 19 Do
not be tempted to worship and serve
what you see in the sky—the sun, the
moon, and the stars. The LORD your God
has given these to all other peoples for
them to worship. 20 But you are the people he rescued from Egypt, that blazing
furnace. He brought you out to make you
his own people, as you are today. 21 Because of you the LORD your God was angry with me and solemnly declared that
I would not cross the Jordan River to enter the fertile land which he is giving you.
22 I will die in this land and never cross
the river, but you are about to go across
and occupy that fertile land. 23 Be certain
that you do not forget the covenant that
the LORD your God made with you. Obey
his command not to make yourselves
any kind of idol, 24 because the LORD your
God is like a flaming fire; he tolerates no
rivals.

25 "Even when you have been in the
land a long time and have children and
grandchildren, do not sin by making for
yourselves an idol in any form at all. This
is evil in the LORD's sight, and it will make
him angry. 26 I call heaven and earth as
witnesses against you today that, if you
disobey me, you will soon disappear
from the land. You will not live very long
in the land across the Jordan that you are
about to occupy. You will be completely
destroyed. 27 The LORD will scatter you
among other nations, where only a few
of you will survive. 28 There you will
serve gods made by human hands, gods
of wood and stone, gods that cannot see
or hear, eat or smell. 29 There you will
look for the LORD your God, and if you
search for him with all your heart, you
will find him. 30 When you are in trouble
and all those things happen to you, then
you will finally turn to the LORD and obey
him. 31 He is a merciful God. He will not
abandon you or destroy you, and he will
not forget the covenant that he himself
made with your ancestors.

32 "Search the past, the time before you
were born, all the way back to the time
when God created human beings on the
earth. Search the entire earth. Has anything as great as this ever happened before? Has anyone ever heard of anything
like this? 33 Have any people ever lived
after hearing a god speak to them from a
fire, as you have? 34 Has any god ever
dared to go and take a people from another nation and make them his own, as
the LORD your God did for you in Egypt?
Before your very eyes he used his great
power and strength; he brought plagues
and war, worked miracles and wonders,
and caused terrifying things to happen.
35 The LORD has shown you this, to prove
to you that he alone is God and that there
is no other. 36 He let you hear his voice
from heaven so that he could instruct
you; and here on earth he let you see his
holy fire, and he spoke to you from it.
37 Because he loved your ancestors, he
chose you, and by his great power he
himself brought you out of Egypt. 38 As
you advanced, he drove out nations
greater and more powerful than you, so
that he might bring you in and give you
their land, the land which still belongs to
you. 39 So remember today and never forget: the LORD is God in heaven and on
earth. There is no other god. 40 Obey all
his laws that I have given you today, and
all will go well with you and your
descendants. You will continue to live in
the land that the LORD your God is giving
you to be yours forever."

The Cities of Refuge East of the Jordan

41 Then Moses set aside three cities
east of the Jordan River 42 to which a man
could escape and be safe if he had accidentally killed someone who had not
been his enemy. He could escape to one
of these cities and not be put to death.
43 For the tribe of Reuben there was the
city of Bezer, on the desert plateau; for
the tribe of Gad there was Ramoth, in the
territory of Gilead; and for the tribe of
Manasseh there was Golan, in the territory of Bashan.

Introduction to the Giving of God's Law

44 Moses gave God's laws and teachings to the people of Israel. 45-46 It was
after they had come out of Egypt and
were in the valley east of the Jordan
River, opposite the town of Bethpeor,
that he gave them these laws. This was in
the territory that had belonged to King
Sihon of the Amorites, who had ruled in
the town of Heshbon. Moses and the people of Israel defeated him when they
came out of Egypt. 47 They occupied his
land and the land of King Og of Bashan,
the other Amorite king who lived east of
the Jordan. 48 This land extended from
the town of Aroer, on the edge of the
Arnon River, all the way north to Mount
Sirion,[e] that is, Mount Hermon. 49 It also
included all the region east of the Jordan
River as far south as the Dead Sea and
east to the foot of Mount Pisgah.

The Ten Commandments

(Exodus 20.1-17)

5 Moses called together all the people
of Israel and said to them, "People of
Israel, listen to all the laws that I am giving you today. Learn them and be sure
that you obey them. 2 At Mount Sinai the
LORD our God made a covenant, 3 not only
with our fathers, but with all of us who
are living today. 4 There on the mountain
the LORD spoke to you face-to-face from
the fire. 5 I stood between you and the
LORD at that time to tell you what he said,
because you were afraid of the fire and
would not go up the mountain.
"The LORD said, 6 'I am the LORD your
God, who rescued you from Egypt,
where you were slaves.
7 " 'Worship no god but me.
8 " 'Do not make for yourselves images
of anything in heaven or on earth or in
the water under the earth. 9 Do not bow
down to any idol or worship it, for I am
the LORD your God and I tolerate no rivals. I bring punishment on those who
hate me and on their descendants down
to the third and fourth generation. 10 But
I show my love to thousands of generations[f] of those who love me and obey
my laws.
11 " 'Do not use my name for evil purposes, for I, the LORD your God, will punish anyone who misuses my name.
12 " 'Observe the Sabbath and keep it
holy, as I, the LORD your God, have commanded you. 13 You have six days in
which to do your work, 14 but the seventh
day is a day of rest dedicated to me. On
that day no one is to work—neither you,
your children, your slaves, your animals,
nor the foreigners who live in your country. Your slaves must rest just as you do.
15 Remember that you were slaves in
Egypt, and that I, the LORD your God, rescued you by my great power and
strength. That is why I command you to
observe the Sabbath.
16 " 'Respect your father and your
mother, as I, the LORD your God, command you, so that all may go well with
you and so that you may live a long time
in the land that I am giving you.
17 " 'Do not commit murder.
18 " 'Do not commit adultery.
19 " 'Do not steal.
20 " 'Do not accuse anyone falsely.
21 " 'Do not desire another man's wife;
do not desire his house, his land, his
slaves, his cattle, his donkeys, or anything else that he owns.'
22 "These are the commandments the
LORD gave to all of you when you were
gathered at the mountain. When he
spoke with a mighty voice from the fire
and from the thick clouds, he gave these
commandments and no others. Then he
wrote them on two stone tablets and
gave them to me.

The People's Fear

(Exodus 20.18-21)

23 "When the whole mountain was on
fire and you heard the voice from the
darkness, your leaders and the chiefs of
your tribes came to me 24 and said, 'The
LORD our God showed us his greatness
and his glory when we heard him speak
from the fire! Today we have seen that it
is possible for people to continue to live,
even though God has spoken to them.
25 But why should we risk death again?
That terrible fire will destroy us. We are
sure to die if we hear the LORD our God
speak again. 26 Has any human being
ever lived after hearing the living God
speak from a fire? 27 Go back, Moses, and
listen to everything that the LORD our
God says. Then return and tell us what he
said to you. We will listen and obey.'

[e] *One ancient translation* Sirion; *Hebrew* Sion.

[f] thousands of generations; *or* thousands.

28 "When the LORD heard this, he said to
me, 'I have heard what these people said,
and they are right. 29 If only they would
always feel this way! If only they would
always honor me and obey all my commands, so that everything would go well
with them and their descendants forever.
30 Go and tell them to return to their tents.
31 But you, Moses, stay here with me, and
I will give you all my laws and commands. Teach them to the people, so that
they will obey them in the land that I am
giving them.'
32 "People of Israel, be sure that you do
everything that the LORD your God has
commanded you. Do not disobey any of
his laws. 33 Obey them all, so that everything will go well with you and so that
you will continue to live in the land that
you are going to occupy.

The Great Commandment

6 "These are all the laws that the LORD
your God commanded me to teach
you. Obey them in the land that you are
about to enter and occupy. 2 As long as
you live, you and your descendants are
to honor the LORD your God and obey all
his laws that I am giving you, so that you
may live in that land a long time. 3 Listen
to them, people of Israel, and obey them!
Then all will go well with you, and you
will become a mighty nation and live in
that rich and fertile land, just as the LORD,
the God of our ancestors, has promised.
4 "Israel, remember this! The LORD—
and the LORD alone—is our God.[g] 5 Love
the LORD your God with all your heart,
with all your soul, and with all your
strength. 6 Never forget these commands
that I am giving you today. 7 Teach them
to your children. Repeat them when you
are at home and when you are away,
when you are resting and when you are
working. 8 Tie them on your arms and
wear them on your foreheads as a reminder. 9 Write them on the doorposts of
your houses and on your gates.

Warning against Disobedience

10 "Just as the LORD your God promised
your ancestors, Abraham, Isaac, and Jacob, he will give you a land with large
and prosperous cities which you did not
build. 11 The houses will be full of good
things which you did not put in them, and
there will be wells that you did not dig,
and vineyards and olive orchards that
you did not plant. When the LORD brings
you into this land and you have all you
want to eat, 12 make certain that you do
not forget the LORD who rescued you
from Egypt, where you were slaves.
13 Honor the LORD your God, worship
only him, and make your promises in his
name alone. 14 Do not worship other
gods, any of the gods of the peoples
around you. 15 If you do worship other
gods, the LORD's anger will come against
you like fire and will destroy you completely, because the LORD your God, who
is present with you, tolerates no rivals.
16 "Do not put the LORD your God to the
test, as you did at Massah. 17 Be sure that
you obey all the laws that he has given
you. 18 Do what the LORD says is right and
good, and all will go well with you. You
will be able to take possession of the fertile land that the LORD promised your ancestors, 19 and you will drive out your
enemies, as he promised.
20 "In times to come your children will
ask you, 'Why did the LORD our God command us to obey all these laws?' 21 Then
tell them, 'We were slaves of the king of
Egypt, and the LORD rescued us by his
great power. 22 With our own eyes we
saw him work miracles and do terrifying
things to the Egyptians and to their king
and to all his officials. 23 He freed us from
Egypt to bring us here and give us this
land, as he had promised our ancestors
he would. 24 Then the LORD our God commanded us to obey all these laws and to
honor him. If we do, he will always watch
over our nation and keep it prosperous.
25 If we faithfully obey everything that
God has commanded us, he will be
pleased with us.'[h]

The LORD's Own People

(Exodus 34.11-16)

7 "The LORD your God will bring you
into the land that you are going to
occupy, and he will drive many nations
out of it. As you advance, he will drive
out seven nations larger and more powerful than you: the Hittites, the Girgashites, the Amorites, the Canaanites, the
Perizzites, the Hivites, and the Jebusites.

[g] The LORD . . . is our God; *or* The LORD, our God, is the only God; *or* The LORD our God is one.
[h] If we faithfully . . . with us; *or* The right thing for us to do is to obey faithfully everything that God has commanded us.

2When the LORD your God places these
people in your power and you defeat
them, you must put them all to death. Do
not make an alliance with them or show
them any mercy. 3Do not marry any of
them, and do not let your children marry
any of them, 4because then they would
lead your children away from the LORD to
worship other gods. If that happens, the
LORD will be angry with you and destroy
you at once. 5So then, tear down their
altars, break their sacred stone pillars in
pieces, cut down their symbols of the
goddess Asherah, and burn their idols.
6Do this because you belong to the LORD
your God. From all the peoples on earth
he chose you to be his own special
people.
7"The LORD did not love you and
choose you because you outnumbered
other peoples; you were the smallest nation on earth. 8But the LORD loved you
and wanted to keep the promise that he
made to your ancestors. That is why he
saved you by his great might and set you
free from slavery to the king of Egypt.
9Remember that the LORD your God is the
only God and that he is faithful. He will
keep his covenant and show his constant
love to a thousand generations of those
who love him and obey his commands,
10but he will not hesitate to punish those
who hate him. 11Now then, obey what
you have been taught; obey all the laws
that I have given you today.

The Blessings of Obedience

(Deuteronomy 28.1-14)

12"If you listen to these commands and
obey them faithfully, then the LORD your
God will continue to keep his covenant
with you and will show you his constant
love, as he promised your ancestors.
13He will love you and bless you, so that
you will increase in number and have
many children; he will bless your fields,
so that you will have grain, wine, and
olive oil; and he will bless you by giving
you many cattle and sheep. He will give
you all these blessings in the land that he
promised your ancestors he would give
to you. 14No people in the world will be
as richly blessed as you. None of you nor
any of your livestock will be sterile.
15The LORD will protect you from all sickness, and he will not bring on you any of
the dreadful diseases that you experienced in Egypt, but he will bring them on
all your enemies. 16Destroy every nation
that the LORD your God places in your
power, and do not show them any mercy.
Do not worship their gods, for that would
be fatal.
17"Do not tell yourselves that these
peoples outnumber you and that you
cannot drive them out. 18Do not be afraid
of them; remember what the LORD your
God did to the king of Egypt and to all his
people. 19Remember the terrible plagues
that you saw with your own eyes, the
miracles and wonders, and the great
power and strength by which the LORD
your God set you free. In the same way
that he destroyed the Egyptians, he will
destroy all these people that you now
fear. 20He will even cause panic[l] among
them and will destroy those who escape
and go into hiding. 21So do not be afraid
of these people. The LORD your God is
with you; he is a great God and one to be
feared. 22Little by little he will drive out
these nations as you advance. You will
not be able to destroy them all at once,
for, if you did, the number of wild animals would increase and be a threat to
you. 23The LORD will put your enemies in
your power and make them panic until
they are destroyed. 24He will put their
kings in your power. You will kill them,
and they will be forgotten. No one will be
able to stop you; you will destroy everyone. 25Burn their idols. Do not desire the
silver or gold that is on them, and do not
take it for yourselves. If you do, that will
be fatal, because the LORD hates idolatry.
26Do not bring any of these idols into
your homes, or the same curse will be on
you that is on them. You must hate and
despise these idols, because they are under the LORD's curse.

A Good Land to Be Possessed

8 "Obey faithfully all the laws that I
have given you today, so that you
may live, increase in number, and occupy the land that the LORD promised to
your ancestors. 2Remember how the
LORD your God led you on this long journey through the desert these past forty
years, sending hardships to test you, so
that he might know what you intended to
do and whether you would obey his

[l] cause panic; *or* send hornets, *or* send plagues.

commands. 3 He made you go hungry,
and then he gave you manna to eat, food
that you and your ancestors had never
eaten before. He did this to teach you that
you must not depend on bread alone to
sustain you, but on everything that the
LORD says. 4 During these forty years
your clothes have not worn out, nor have
your feet swollen up. 5 Remember that
the LORD your God corrects and punishes you just as parents discipline their
children. 6 So then, do as the LORD has
commanded you: live according to his
laws and obey him. 7 The LORD your God
is bringing you into a fertile land—a
land that has rivers and springs, and
underground streams gushing out into
the valleys and hills; 8 a land that produces wheat and barley, grapes, figs,
pomegranates, olives, and honey. 9 There
you will never go hungry or ever be
in need. Its rocks have iron in them, and
from its hills you can mine copper. 10 You
will have all you want to eat, and you
will give thanks to the LORD your God for
the fertile land that he has given you.

Warnings against Forgetting the LORD

11 "Make certain that you do not forget
the LORD your God; do not fail to obey
any of his laws that I am giving you today. 12 When you have all you want to eat
and have built good houses to live in
13 and when your cattle and sheep, your
silver and gold, and all your other possessions have increased, 14 be sure that
you do not become proud and forget the
LORD your God who rescued you from
Egypt, where you were slaves. 15 He led
you through that vast and terrifying
desert where there were poisonous
snakes and scorpions. In that dry and
waterless land he made water flow out of
solid rock for you. 16 In the desert he gave
you manna to eat, food that your ancestors had never eaten. He sent hardships
on you to test you, so that in the end he
could bless you with good things. 17 So
then, you must never think that you have
made yourselves wealthy by your own
power and strength. 18 Remember that it
is the LORD your God who gives you the
power to become rich. He does this because he is still faithful today to the covenant that he made with your ancestors.
19 Never forget the LORD your God or turn
to other gods to worship and serve them.
If you do, then I warn you today that you
will certainly be destroyed. 20 If you do
not obey the LORD, then you will be destroyed just like those nations that he is
going to destroy as you advance.

The People's Disobedience

9 "Listen, people of Israel! Today you
are about to cross the Jordan River
and occupy the land belonging to nations
greater and more powerful than you.
Their cities are large, with walls that
reach the sky. 2 The people themselves
are tall and strong; they are giants, and
you have heard it said that no one can
stand against them. 3 But now you will
see for yourselves that the LORD your God
will go ahead of you like a raging fire. He
will defeat them as you advance, so that
you will drive them out and destroy them
quickly, as he promised.
4 "After the LORD your God has driven
them out for you, do not say to yourselves that he brought you in to possess
this land because you deserved it. No, the
LORD is going to drive these people out for
you because they are wicked. 5 It is not
because you are good and do what is
right that the LORD is letting you take
their land. He will drive them out because they are wicked and because he
intends to keep the promise that he made
to your ancestors, Abraham, Isaac, and
Jacob. 6 You can be sure that the LORD is
not giving you this fertile land because
you deserve it. No, you are a stubborn
people.
7 "Never forget how you made the LORD
your God angry in the desert. From the
day that you left Egypt until the day you
arrived here, you have rebelled against
him. 8 Even at Mount Sinai you made the
LORD angry—angry enough to destroy
you. 9 I went up the mountain to receive
the stone tablets on which was written
the covenant that the LORD had made
with you. I stayed there forty days and
nights and did not eat or drink anything.
10 Then the LORD gave me the two stone
tablets on which he had written with his
own hand what he had said to you from
the fire on the day that you were gathered there at the mountain. 11 Yes, after
those forty days and nights the LORD gave
me the two stone tablets on which he had
written the covenant.
12 "Then the LORD said to me, 'Go down

the mountain at once, because your people, whom you led out of Egypt, have
become corrupt and have done evil. They
have already turned away from what I
commanded them to do, and they have
made an idol for themselves.'
13 "The LORD also said to me, 'I know
how stubborn these people are. 14 Don't
try to stop me. I intend to destroy them so
that no one will remember them any
longer. Then I will make you the father of
a nation larger and more powerful than
they are.'
15 "So I turned and went down the
mountain, carrying the two stone tablets
on which the covenant was written.
Flames of fire were coming from the
mountain. 16 I saw that you had already
disobeyed the command that the LORD
your God had given you, and that you
had sinned against him by making yourselves a metal idol in the form of a bull-
calf. 17 So there in front of you I threw the
stone tablets down and broke them to
pieces. 18 Then once again I lay face
downward in the LORD's presence for
forty days and nights and did not eat or
drink anything. I did this because you
had sinned against the LORD and had
made him angry. 19 I was afraid of the
LORD's fierce anger, because he was furious enough to destroy you; but once
again the LORD listened to me. 20 The LORD
was also angry enough with Aaron to kill
him, so I prayed for Aaron at the same
time. 21 I took that sinful thing that you
had made—that metal bull-calf—and
threw it into the fire. Then I broke it in
pieces, ground it to dust, and threw the
dust into the stream that flowed down
the mountain.
22 "You also made the LORD your God
angry when you were at Taberah, Massah, and Kibroth Hattaavah. 23 And when
he sent you from Kadesh Barnea with
orders to go and take possession of the
land that he was giving you, you rebelled
against him; you did not trust him or
obey him. 24 Ever since I have known
you, you have rebelled against the LORD.
25 "So I lay face downward in the
LORD's presence those forty days and
nights, because I knew that he was determined to destroy you. 26 And I prayed,
'Sovereign LORD, don't destroy your own
people, the people you rescued and
brought out of Egypt by your great
strength and power. 27 Remember your
servants, Abraham, Isaac, and Jacob,
and do not pay any attention to the stubbornness, wickedness, and sin of this
people. 28 Otherwise, the Egyptians will
say that you were unable to take your
people into the land that you had promised them. They will say that you took
your people out into the desert to kill
them, because you hated them. 29 After
all, these are the people whom you chose
to be your own and whom you brought
out of Egypt by your great power and
might.'

Moses Receives the Commandments Again

(Exodus 34.1-10)

10 "Then the LORD said to me, 'Cut
two stone tablets like the first
ones and make a wooden Box to put
them in. Come up to me on the mountain,
2 and I will write on those tablets what I
wrote on the tablets that you broke, and
then you are to put them in the Box.'
3 "So I made a Box of acacia wood and
cut two stone tablets like the first ones
and took them up the mountain. 4 Then
the LORD wrote on those tablets the same
words that he had written the first time,
the Ten Commandments that he gave
you when he spoke from the fire on the
day you were gathered at the mountain.
The LORD gave me the tablets, 5 and I
turned and went down the mountain.
Then, just as the LORD had commanded,
I put them in the Box that I had made—
and they have been there ever since."
(6 The Israelites set out from the wells
that belonged to the people of Jaakan,
and went to Moserah. There Aaron died
and was buried, and his son Eleazar succeeded him as priest. 7 From there they
went to Gudgodah and then on to Jotbathah, a well-watered place. 8 At the
mountain[j] the LORD appointed the men
of the tribe of Levi to be in charge of the
Covenant Box, to serve him as priests,
and to pronounce blessings in his name.
And these are still their duties. 9 That is
why the tribe of Levi received no land as
the other tribes did; what they received
was the privilege of being the LORD's
priests, as the LORD your God promised.)
10 "I stayed on the mountain forty days

[j] the mountain; *or* that time.

and nights, as I did the first time. The
LORD listened to me once more and
agreed not to destroy you. 11 Then he told
me to go and lead you, so that you could
take possession of the land that he had
promised to give to your ancestors.

What God Demands

12 "Now, people of Israel, listen to what
the LORD your God demands of you: Worship the LORD and do all that he commands. Love him, serve him with all your
heart, 13 and obey all his laws. I am giving
them to you today for your benefit. 14 To
the LORD belong even the highest heavens; the earth is his also, and everything
on it. 15 But the LORD's love for your ancestors was so strong that he chose you
instead of any other people, and you are
still his chosen people. 16 So then, from
now on be obedient to the LORD and stop
being stubborn. 17 The LORD your God is
supreme over all gods and over all powers. He is great and mighty, and he is to
be obeyed. He does not show partiality,
and he does not accept bribes. 18 He
makes sure that orphans and widows are
treated fairly; he loves the foreigners
who live with our people, and gives them
food and clothes. 19 So then, show love
for those foreigners, because you were
once foreigners in Egypt. 20 Have reverence for the LORD your God and worship
only him. Be faithful to him and make
your promises in his name alone.
21 Praise him—he is your God, and you
have seen with your own eyes the great
and astounding things that he has done
for you. 22 When your ancestors went to
Egypt, there were only seventy of them.
But now the LORD your God has made
you as numerous as the stars in the sky.

The LORD's Greatness

11 "Love the LORD your God and always obey all his laws. 2 Remember today what you have learned about
the LORD through your experiences with
him. It was you, not your children, who
had these experiences. You saw the
LORD's greatness, his power, his might,
3 and his miracles. You saw what he did
to the king of Egypt and to his entire
country. 4 You saw how the LORD completely wiped out the Egyptian army,
along with their horses and chariots, by
drowning them in the Red Sea[k] when
they were pursuing you. 5 You know
what the LORD did for you in the desert
before you arrived here. 6 You recall
what he did to Dathan and Abiram, the
sons of Eliab of the tribe of Reuben. In
the sight of everyone the earth opened up
and swallowed them, along with their
families, their tents, and all their servants and animals. 7 Yes, you are the ones
who have seen all these great things that
the LORD has done.

The Blessings of the Promised Land

8 "Obey everything that I have commanded you today. Then you will be able
to cross the river and occupy the land
that you are about to enter. 9 And you will
live a long time in the rich and fertile
land that the LORD promised to give your
ancestors and their descendants. 10 The
land that you are about to occupy is not
like the land of Egypt, where you lived
before. There, when you planted grain,
you had to work hard to irrigate the
fields; 11 but the land that you are about
to enter is a land of mountains
and valleys, a land watered by rain.
12 The LORD your God takes care of this
land and watches over it throughout the
year.

13 "So then, obey the commands that I
have given you today; love the LORD your
God and serve him with all your heart.
14 If you do, he will send rain on your land
when it is needed, in the autumn and in
the spring, so that there will be grain,
wine, and olive oil for you, 15 and grass
for your livestock. You will have all the
food you want. 16 Do not let yourselves be
led away from the LORD to worship and
serve other gods. 17 If you do, the LORD
will become angry with you. He will hold
back the rain, and your ground will become too dry for crops to grow. Then you
will soon die there, even though it is a
good land that he is giving you.

18 "Remember these commands and
cherish them. Tie them on your arms and
wear them on your foreheads as a reminder. 19 Teach them to your children.
Talk about them when you are at home
and when you are away, when you are
resting and when you are working.
20 Write them on the doorposts of your
houses and on your gates. 21 Then you

[k] RED SEA: *See Word List.*

and your children will live a long time in
the land that the LORD your God promised to give to your ancestors. You will
live there as long as there is a sky above
the earth.

22 “Obey faithfully everything that I
have commanded you: Love the LORD
your God, do everything he commands,
and be faithful to him. 23 Then he will
drive out all those nations as you advance, and you will occupy the land belonging to nations greater and more
powerful than you. 24 All the ground that
you march over will be yours. Your territory will extend from the desert in the
south to the Lebanon Mountains in the
north, and from the Euphrates River in
the east to the Mediterranean Sea in the
west. 25 Wherever you go in that land, the
LORD your God will make the people fear
you, as he has promised, and no one will
be able to stop you.

26 “Today I am giving you the choice
between a blessing and a curse—27 a
blessing, if you obey the commands of
the LORD your God that I am giving you
today; 28 but a curse, if you disobey these
commands and turn away to worship
other gods that you have never worshiped before. 29 When the LORD brings
you into the land that you are going to
occupy, you are to proclaim the blessing
from Mount Gerizim and the curse from
Mount Ebal. (30 These two mountains are
west of the Jordan River in the territory
of the Canaanites who live in the Jordan
Valley. They are toward the west, not far
from the sacred trees of Moreh near the
town of Gilgal.) 31 You are about to cross
the Jordan River and occupy the land
that the LORD your God is giving you.
When you take it and settle there, 32 be
sure to obey all the laws that I am giving
you today.

The One Place for Worship

12 “Here are the laws that you are to
obey as long as you live in the
land that the LORD, the God of your ancestors, is giving you. Listen to them! 2 In
the land that you are taking, destroy all
the places where the people worship
their gods on high mountains, on hills,
and under green trees. 3 Tear down their
altars and smash their sacred stone pillars to pieces. Burn their symbols of the
goddess Asherah and chop down their
idols, so that they will never again be
worshiped at those places.

4 “Do not worship the LORD your God in
the way that these people worship their
gods. 5 Out of the territory of all your
tribes the LORD will choose the one place
where the people are to come into his
presence and worship him. 6 There you
are to offer your sacrifices that are to be
burned and your other sacrifices, your
tithes and your offerings, the gifts that
you promise to the LORD, your freewill
offerings, and the first-born of your cattle and sheep. 7 There, in the presence of
the LORD your God, who has blessed
you, you and your families will eat and
enjoy the good things that you have
worked for.

8 “When that time comes, you must not
do as you have been doing. Until now
you have all been worshiping as you
please, 9 because you have not yet entered the land that the LORD your God is
giving you, where you can live in peace.
10 When you cross the Jordan River, the
LORD will let you occupy the land and live
there. He will keep you safe from all your
enemies, and you will live in peace.
11 The LORD will choose a single place
where he is to be worshiped, and there
you must bring to him everything that I
have commanded: your sacrifices that
are to be burned and your other sacrifices, your tithes and your offerings, and
those special gifts that you have promised to the LORD. 12 Be joyful there in his
presence, together with your children,
your servants, and the Levites who live
in your towns; remember that the Levites
will have no land of their own. 13 You are
not to offer your sacrifices wherever you
choose; 14 you must offer them only in the
one place that the LORD will choose in the
territory of one of your tribes. Only there
are you to offer your sacrifices that are to
be burned and do all the other things that
I have commanded you.

15 “But you are free to kill and eat your
animals wherever you live. You may eat
as many as the LORD gives you. All of you,
whether ritually clean or unclean, may
eat them, just as you would eat the meat
of deer or antelope. 16 But you must not
eat their blood; you must pour it out on
the ground like water. 17 Nothing that
you offer to the LORD is to be eaten in the
places where you live: neither the tithes
of your grain, your wine, or your olive

oil, nor the first-born of your cattle and sheep, the gifts that you promise to the LORD, your freewill offerings, or any other offerings. 18 You and your children, together with your servants and the Levites who live in your towns, are to eat these offerings only in the presence of the LORD your God, in the one place of worship chosen by the LORD your God. And you are to be happy there over everything that you have done. 19 Be sure, also, not to neglect the Levites, as long as you live in your land.

20 “When the LORD your God enlarges your territory, as he has promised, you may eat meat whenever you want to. 21 If the one place of worship is too far away, then, whenever you wish, you may kill any of the cattle or sheep that the LORD has given you, and you may eat the meat at home, as I have told you. 22 Anyone, ritually clean or unclean, may eat that meat, just as he would eat the meat of deer or antelope. 23 Only do not eat meat with blood still in it, for the life is in the blood, and you must not eat the life with the meat. 24 Do not use the blood for food; instead, pour it out on the ground like water. 25 If you obey this command, the LORD will be pleased, and all will go well for you and your descendants. 26 Take to the one place of worship your offerings and the gifts that you have promised the LORD. 27 Offer there the sacrifices which are to be completely burned on the LORD’s altar. Also offer those sacrifices in which you eat the meat and pour the blood out on the altar. 28 Obey faithfully everything that I have commanded you, and all will go well for you and your descendants forever, because you will be doing what is right and what pleases the LORD your God.

Warning against Idolatry

29 “The LORD your God will destroy the nations as you invade their land, and you will occupy it and settle there. 30 After the LORD destroys those nations, make sure that you don’t follow their religious practices, because that would be fatal. Don’t try to find out how they worship their gods, so that you can worship in the same way. 31 Do not worship the LORD your God in the way they worship their gods, for in the worship of their gods they do all the disgusting things that the LORD hates. They even sacrifice their children in the fires on their altars.

32 “Do everything that I have commanded you; do not add anything to it or take anything from it.

13 “Prophets or interpreters of dreams may promise a miracle or a wonder, 2 in order to lead you to worship and serve gods that you have not worshiped before. Even if what they promise comes true, 3 do not pay any attention to them. The LORD your God is using them to test you, to see if you love the LORD with all your heart. 4 Follow the LORD and honor him; obey him and keep his commands; worship him and be faithful to him. 5 But put to death any interpreters of dreams or prophets that tell you to rebel against the LORD, who rescued you from Egypt, where you were slaves. Such people are evil and are trying to lead you away from the life that the LORD has commanded you to live. They must be put to death, in order to rid yourselves of this evil.

6 “Even your brother or your son or your daughter or the wife you love or your closest friend may secretly encourage you to worship other gods, gods that you and your ancestors have never worshiped. 7 Some of them may encourage you to worship the gods of the people who live near you or the gods of those who live far away. 8 But do not let any of them persuade you; do not even listen to them. Show them no mercy or pity, and do not protect them. 9 Kill them! Be the first to stone them, and then let everyone else stone them too. 10 Stone them to death! They tried to lead you away from the LORD your God, who rescued you from Egypt, where you were slaves. 11 Then all the people of Israel will hear what happened; they will be afraid, and no one will ever again do such an evil thing.

12 “When you are living in the towns that the LORD your God gives you, you may hear 13 that some worthless people of your nation have misled the people of their town to worship gods that you have never worshiped before. 14 If you hear such a rumor, investigate it thoroughly; and if it is true that this evil thing did happen, 15 then kill all the people in that town and all their livestock too. Destroy that town completely. 16 Bring together all the possessions of the people who live

there and pile them up in the town
square. Then burn the town and everything in it as an offering to the LORD your
God. It must be left in ruins forever and
never again be rebuilt. 17 Do not keep for
yourselves anything that was condemned to destruction, and then the LORD
will turn from his fierce anger and show
you mercy. He will be merciful to you
and make you a numerous people, as he
promised your ancestors, 18 if you obey
all his commands that I have given you
today, and do what he requires.

A Forbidden Mourning Practice

14 "You are the people of the LORD
your God. So when you mourn
for the dead, don't gash yourselves or
shave the front of your head, as other
people do. 2 You belong to the LORD your
God; he has chosen you to be his own
people from among all the peoples who
live on earth.

Clean and Unclean Animals

(Leviticus 11.1-47)

3 "Do not eat anything that the LORD
has declared unclean. 4 You may eat
these animals: cattle, sheep, goats, 5 deer,
wild sheep, wild goats, or antelopes—
6 any animals that have divided hoofs
and that also chew the cud. 7 But no animals may be eaten unless they have divided hoofs and also chew the cud. You
may not eat camels, rabbits, or rock
badgers. They must be considered unclean; they chew the cud but do not have
divided hoofs. 8 Do not eat pigs. They
must be considered unclean; they have
divided hoofs but do not chew the cud.
Do not eat any of these animals or even
touch their dead bodies.

9 "You may eat any kind of fish that has
fins and scales, 10 but anything living in
the water that does not have fins and
scales may not be eaten; it must be considered unclean.

11 "You may eat any clean bird. 12-18 But
these are the kinds of birds you are not
to eat: eagles, owls, hawks, falcons;
buzzards, vultures, crows; ostriches;
seagulls, storks, herons, pelicans,
cormorants;[l] hoopoes; and bats.

19 "All winged insects are unclean; do
not eat them. 20 You may eat any clean
insect.

21 "Do not eat any animal that dies a
natural death. You may let the foreigners
who live among you eat it, or you may
sell it to other foreigners. But you belong
to the LORD your God; you are his people.

"Do not cook a young sheep or goat in
its mother's milk.

The Law of the Tithe

22 "Set aside a tithe—a tenth of all that
your fields produce each year. 23 Then go
to the one place where the LORD your God
has chosen to be worshiped; and there in
his presence eat the tithes of your grain,
wine, and olive oil, and the first-born of
your cattle and sheep. Do this so that you
may learn to honor the LORD your God
always. 24 If the place of worship is too
far from your home for you to carry there
the tithe of the produce that the LORD has
blessed you with, then do this: 25 Sell
your produce and take the money with
you to the one place of worship. 26 Spend
it on whatever you want—beef, lamb,
wine, beer—and there, in the presence of
the LORD your God, you and your families
are to eat and enjoy yourselves.

27 "Do not neglect the Levites who live
in your towns; they have no property of
their own. 28 At the end of every third
year bring the tithe of all your crops and
store it in your towns. 29 This food is for
the Levites, since they own no property,
and for the foreigners, orphans, and widows who live in your towns. They are to
come and get all they need. Do this, and
the LORD your God will bless you in
everything you do.

The Seventh Year

(Leviticus 25.1-7)

15 "At the end of every seventh year
you are to cancel the debts of
those who owe you money. 2 This is how
it is to be done. Each of you who has lent
money to any Israelite is to cancel the
debt; you must not try to collect the
money; the LORD himself has declared
the debt canceled. 3 You may collect
what a foreigner owes you, but you must
not collect what any of your own people
owe you.

4 "The LORD your God will bless you in
the land that he is giving you. Not one of
your people will be poor 5 if you obey him
and carefully observe everything that I

[l] *The identification of some of these birds is uncertain.*

command you today. 6 The LORD will
bless you, as he has promised. You will
lend money to many nations, but you
will not have to borrow from any; you
will have control over many nations, but
no nation will have control over you.
7 "If in any of the towns in the land that
the LORD your God is giving you there are
Israelites in need, then do not be selfish
and refuse to help them. 8 Instead, be
generous and lend them as much as they
need. 9 Do not refuse to lend them something, just because the year when debts
are canceled is near. Do not let such an
evil thought enter your mind. If you refuse to make the loan, they will cry out to
the LORD against you, and you will be
held guilty. 10 Give to them freely and un-
selfishly, and the LORD will bless you in
everything you do. 11 There will always
be some Israelites who are poor and in
need, and so I command you to be generous to them.

The Treatment of Slaves

(Exodus 21.1-11)

12 "If any Israelites, male or female, sell
themselves[m] to you as slaves, you are to
release them after they have served you
for six years. When the seventh year
comes, you must let them go free.
13 When you set them free, do not send
them away empty-handed. 14 Give to
them generously from what the LORD has
blessed you with — sheep, grain, and
wine. 15 Remember that you were slaves
in Egypt and the LORD your God set you
free; that is why I am now giving you this
command.
16 "But your slave may not want to
leave; he may love you and your family
and be content to stay. 17 Then take him
to the door of your house and there
pierce his ear; he will then be your slave
for life. Treat your female slave in the
same way. 18 Do not be resentful when
you set slaves free; after all, they have
served you for six years at half the cost
of hired servants.[n] Do this, and the LORD
your God will bless you in all that
you do.

The First-Born Cattle and Sheep

19 "Set aside for the LORD your God all
the first-born males of your cattle and
sheep; don't use any of these cattle for
work and don't shear any of these sheep.
20 Each year you and your family are to
eat them in the LORD's presence at the one
place of worship. 21 But if there is anything wrong with the animals, if they are
crippled or blind or have any other serious defect, you must not sacrifice them to
the LORD your God. 22 You may eat such
animals at home. All of you, whether
ritually clean or unclean, may eat them,
just as you eat deer or antelope. 23 But do
not use their blood for food; instead, you
must pour it out on the ground like water.

The Passover

(Exodus 12.1-20)

16 "Honor the LORD your God by celebrating Passover in the month
of Abib; it was on a night in that month
that he rescued you from Egypt. 2 Go to
the one place of worship and slaughter
there one of your sheep or cattle for the
Passover meal to honor the LORD your
God. 3 When you eat this meal, do not eat
bread prepared with yeast. For seven
days you are to eat bread prepared without yeast, as you did when you had to
leave Egypt in such a hurry. Eat this
bread — it will be called the bread of
suffering — so that as long as you live you
will remember the day you came out of
Egypt, that place of suffering. 4 For seven
days no one in your land is to have any
yeast in the house; and the meat of the
animal killed on the evening of the first
day must be eaten that same night.
5-6 "Slaughter the Passover animals at
the one place of worship — and nowhere
else in the land that the LORD your God
will give you. Do it at sunset, the time of
day when you left Egypt. 7 Boil the meat
and eat it at the one place of worship; and
the next morning return home. 8 For the
next six days you are to eat bread prepared without yeast, and on the seventh
day assemble to worship the LORD your
God, and do no work on that day.

The Harvest Festival

(Exodus 34.22; Leviticus 23.15-21)

9 "Count seven weeks from the time
that you begin to harvest the grain, 10 and
then celebrate the Harvest Festival, to
honor the LORD your God, by bringing
him a freewill offering in proportion to
the blessing he has given you. 11 Be joyful

[m] sell themselves; *or* are sold. [n] at half . . . servants; *or* and have worked twice as hard as hired servants.

in the LORD's presence, together with
your children, your servants, and the Levites, foreigners, orphans, and widows
who live in your towns. Do this at the one
place of worship. 12 Be sure that you obey
these commands; do not forget that you
were slaves in Egypt.

The Festival of Shelters

(Leviticus 23.33-43)

13 "After you have threshed all your
grain and pressed all your grapes, celebrate the Festival of Shelters for seven
days. 14 Enjoy it with your children, your
servants, and the Levites, foreigners, orphans, and widows who live in your
towns. 15 Honor the LORD your God by
celebrating this festival for seven days at
the one place of worship. Be joyful, because the LORD has blessed your harvest
and your work.
16 "All the men of your nation are to
come to worship the LORD three times a
year at the one place of worship: at Passover, Harvest Festival, and the Festival
of Shelters. Each man is to bring a gift
17 as he is able, in proportion to the blessings that the LORD your God has
given him.

The Administration of Justice

18 "Appoint judges and other officials
in every town that the LORD your God
gives you. These men are to judge the
people impartially. 19 They are not to be
unjust or show partiality in their judgments; and they are not to accept bribes,
for gifts blind the eyes even of wise and
honest men, and cause them to give
wrong decisions. 20 Always be fair and
just, so that you will occupy the land that
the LORD your God is giving you and so
that you will continue to live there.
21 "When you make an altar for the
LORD your God, do not put beside it a
wooden symbol of the goddess Asherah.
22 And do not set up any stone pillar for
idol worship; the LORD hates them.

17 "Do not sacrifice to the LORD your
God cattle or sheep that have any
defects; the LORD hates this.
2 "Suppose you hear that in one of your
towns some men or women have sinned
against the LORD and broken his covenant 3 by worshiping and serving other
gods or the sun or the moon or the stars,
contrary to the LORD's command. 4 If you
hear such a report, then investigate it
thoroughly. If it is true that this evil thing
has happened in Israel, 5 then take them
outside the town and stone them to
death. 6 However, they may be put to
death only if two or more witnesses testify against them; they are not to be put
to death if there is only one witness. 7 The
witnesses are to throw the first stones,
and then the rest of the people are to
stone them; in this way you will get rid of
this evil.
8 "It may be that some cases will be too
difficult for the local judges to decide,
such as certain cases of property rights
or of bodily injury or those cases that
involve a distinction between murder
and manslaughter. When this happens,
go to the one place of worship chosen by
the LORD your God, 9 and present your
case to the levitical priests and to the
judge who is in office at that time, and let
them decide the case. 10 They will give
their decision, and you are to do exactly
as they tell you. 11 Accept their verdict
and follow their instructions in every detail. 12 Anyone who dares to disobey either the judge or the priest on duty is to
be put to death; in this way you will remove this evil from Israel. 13 Then everyone will hear of it and be afraid, and no
one else will dare to act in such a way.

Instructions concerning a King

14 "After you have taken possession of
the land that the LORD your God is going
to give you and have settled there, then
you will decide you need a king like all
the nations around you. 15 Be sure that
the man you choose to be king is the one
whom the LORD has chosen. He must be
one of your own people; do not make a
foreigner your king. 16 The king is not to
have a large number of horses for his
army, and he is not to send people to
Egypt to buy horses,[o] because the LORD
has said that his people are never to return there. 17 The king is not to have
many wives, because this would make
him turn away from the LORD; and he is
not to make himself rich with silver and
gold. 18 When he becomes king, he is to
have a copy of the book of God's laws
and teachings made from the original
copy kept by the levitical priests. 19 He is

[o] to buy horses; *or* in exchange for horses.

to keep this book near him and read from
it all his life, so that he will learn to honor
the LORD and to obey faithfully everything that is commanded in it. 20This will
keep him from thinking that he is better
than other Israelites and from disobeying the LORD's commands in any way.
Then he will reign for many years, and
his descendants will rule Israel for many
generations.

The Share of the Priests

18 "The priestly tribe of Levi is not
to receive any share of land in
Israel; instead, they are to live on the offerings and other sacrifices given to the
LORD. 2They are to own no land, as the
other tribes do; their share is the privilege of being the LORD's priests, as the
LORD has promised.
3"Whenever cattle or sheep are sacrificed, the priests are to be given the
shoulder, the jaw, and the stomach.
4They are to receive the first share of the
grain, wine, olive oil, and wool. 5The
LORD chose from all your tribes the tribe
of Levi to serve him as priests forever.
6"Any Levite who wants to may come
from any town in Israel to the one place
of worship 7and may serve there as a
priest of the LORD his God, like the other
Levites who are serving there. 8He is to
receive the same amount of food as the
other priests, and he may keep whatever
his family sends him.[p]

Warning against Pagan Practices

9"When you come into the land that
the LORD your God is giving you, don't
follow the disgusting practices of the nations that are there. 10Don't sacrifice
your children in the fires on your altars;
and don't let your people practice divination or look for omens or use spells 11or
charms, and don't let them consult the
spirits of the dead. 12The LORD your God
hates people who do these disgusting
things, and that is why he is driving those
nations out of the land as you advance.
13Be completely faithful to the LORD."

The Promise to Send a Prophet

14Then Moses said, "In the land you
are about to occupy, people follow the
advice of those who practice divination
and look for omens, but the LORD your
God does not allow you to do this. 15In-
stead, he will send you a prophet like me
from among your own people, and you
are to obey him.[q]
16"On the day that you were gathered
at Mount Sinai, you begged not to hear
the LORD speak again or to see his fiery
presence any more, because you were
afraid you would die. 17So the LORD said
to me, 'They have made a wise request.
18I will send them a prophet like you
from among their own people; I will tell
him what to say, and he[r] will tell the
people everything I command. 19He will
speak in my name, and I[s] will punish
anyone who refuses to obey him. 20But if
any prophet dares to speak a message in
my name when I did not command him
to do so, he must die for it, and so must
any prophet who speaks in the name of
other gods.'
21"You may wonder how you can tell
when a prophet's message does not come
from the LORD. 22If a prophet speaks in
the name of the LORD and what he says
does not come true, then it is not the
LORD's message. That prophet has spoken on his own authority, and you are
not to fear him.

The Cities of Refuge

(Numbers 35.9-34; Joshua 20.1-9)

19 "After the LORD your God has destroyed the people whose land he
is giving you and after you have taken
their cities and houses and settled there,
2-3divide the territory into three parts,
each with a city that can be easily
reached. Then any of you that kill will be
able to escape to one of them for protection. 4If you accidentally kill someone
who is not your enemy, you may escape
to any of these cities and be safe. 5For
example, if two of you go into the forest
together to cut wood and if, as one of you
is chopping down a tree, the ax head
comes off the handle and kills the other,
you can run to one of those three cities
and be safe. 6If there were only one city,
the distance to it might be too great, and
the relative who is responsible for taking
revenge for the killing might catch you
and angrily kill an innocent person. After all, it was by accident that you killed

[p] *Probable text* and he may keep . . . sends him; *Hebrew unclear.* [q] a prophet . . . him; *or* prophets . . . them. [r] a prophet . . . him . . . he; *or* prophets . . . them . . . they. [s] He will speak . . . and I; *or* When a prophet speaks in my name, I.

someone who was not your enemy. 7This
is why I order you to set aside three
cities.
8"When the LORD your God enlarges
your territory, as he told your ancestors
he would, and gives you all the land he
has promised, 9then you are to select
three more cities. (He will give you this
land if you do everything that I command
you today and if you love the LORD your
God and live according to his teachings.)
10Do this, so that innocent people will
not die and so that you will not be guilty
of putting them to death in the land that
the LORD is giving you.
11"But suppose you deliberately murder your enemy in cold blood and then
escape to one of those cities for protection. 12In that case, the leaders of your
own town are to send for you and hand
you over to the relative responsible for
taking revenge for the murder, so that
you may be put to death. 13No mercy will
be shown to you. Israel must rid itself of
murderers, so that all will go well.

Ancient Property Lines

14"Do not move your neighbor's property line, established long ago in the land
that the LORD your God is giving you.

Concerning Witnesses

15"One witness is not enough to con-
vict someone of a crime; at least two witnesses are necessary to prove that
someone is guilty. 16If any of you try to
harm another by false accusations,
17both of you are to go to the one place
of worship and be judged by the priests
and judges who are then in office. 18The
judges will investigate the case thoroughly; and if you have made a false
accusation, 19you are to receive the
punishment the accused would have received. In this way your nation will get
rid of this evil. 20Then everyone else will
hear what happened; they will be afraid,
and no one will ever again do such an
evil thing. 21In such cases show no
mercy; the punishment is to be a life for
a life, an eye for an eye, a tooth for a
tooth, a hand for a hand, and a foot for a
foot.

Concerning War

20 "When you go out to fight against
your enemies and you see chariots and horses and an army that outnum-
bers yours, do not be afraid of them. The
LORD your God, who rescued you from
Egypt, will be with you. 2Before you start
fighting, a priest is to come forward and
say to the army, 3'Men of Israel, listen!
Today you are going into battle. Do not
be afraid of your enemies or lose courage
or panic. 4The LORD your God is going
with you, and he will give you victory.'
5"Then the officers will address the
men and say, 'Is there any man here who
has just built a house, but has not yet
dedicated it? If so, he is to go home.
Otherwise, if he is killed in battle, someone else will dedicate his house. 6Is there
any man here who has just planted a
vineyard, but has not yet had the chance
to harvest its grapes? If so, he is to go
home. Otherwise, if he is killed in battle,
someone else will enjoy the wine. 7Is
there anyone here who is engaged to be
married? If so, he is to go home. Otherwise, if he is killed in battle, someone
else will marry the woman he is engaged to.'
8"The officers will also say to the men,
'Is there any man here who has lost his
nerve and is afraid? If so, he is to go
home. Otherwise, he will destroy the morale of the others.' 9When the officers
have finished speaking to the army, leaders are to be chosen for each unit.
10"When you go to attack a city, first
give its people a chance to surrender. 11If
they open the gates and surrender, they
are all to become your slaves and do
forced labor for you. 12But if the people
of that city will not surrender, but choose
to fight, surround it with your army.
13Then, when the LORD your God lets you
capture the city, kill every man in it.
14You may, however, take for yourselves
the women, the children, the livestock,
and everything else in the city. You may
use everything that belongs to your enemies. The LORD has given it to you. 15That
is how you are to deal with those cities
that are far away from the land you will
settle in.
16"But when you capture cities in the
land that the LORD your God is giving
you, kill everyone. 17Completely destroy
all the people: the Hittites, the Amorites,
the Canaanites, the Perizzites, the Hivites, and the Jebusites, as the LORD ordered you to do. 18Kill them, so that they
will not make you sin against the LORD by
teaching you to do all the disgusting

things that they do in the worship of their
gods.
19 "When you are trying to capture a
city, do not cut down its fruit trees, even
though the siege lasts a long time. Eat the
fruit, but do not destroy the trees; the
trees are not your enemies. 20 You may
cut down the other trees and use them in
the siege mounds until the city is
captured.

Concerning Unsolved Murders

21 "Suppose someone is found murdered in a field in the land that
the LORD your God is going to give you,
and you do not know who killed him.
2 Your leaders and judges are to go out
and measure the distance from the place
where the body was found to each of the
nearby towns. 3 Then the leaders of the
town nearest to where the body was
found are to select a young cow that has
never been used for work. 4 They are to
take it down to a spot near a stream that
never runs dry and where the ground has
never been plowed or planted, and there
they are to break its neck. 5 The levitical
priests are to go there also, because they
are to decide every legal case involving
violence. The LORD your God has chosen
them to serve him and to pronounce
blessings in his name. 6 Then all the leaders from the town nearest the place
where the murdered person was found
are to wash their hands over the cow
7 and say, 'We did not murder this one,
and we do not know who did it. 8 LORD,
forgive your people Israel, whom you
rescued from Egypt. Forgive us and do
not hold us responsible for the murder of
an innocent person.' 9 And so, by doing
what the LORD requires, you will not be
held responsible for the murder.

Concerning Women Prisoners of War

10 "When the LORD your God gives you
victory in battle and you take prisoners,
11 you may see among them a beautiful
woman that you like and want to marry.
12 Take her to your home, where she will
shave her head,[t] cut her fingernails,
13 and change her clothes. She is to stay
in your home and mourn for her parents
for a month; after that, you may marry
her. 14 Later, if you no longer want her,
you are to let her go free. Since you
forced her to have intercourse with you,
you cannot treat her as a slave and
sell her.

Concerning the First Son's Inheritance

15 "Suppose a man has two wives and
they both bear him sons, but the first son
is not the child of his favorite wife.
16 When the man decides how he is going
to divide his property among his children, he is not to show partiality to the
son of his favorite wife by giving him the
share that belongs to the first-born son.
17 He is to give a double share of his possessions to his first son, even though he
is not the son of his favorite wife. A man
must acknowledge his first son and give
him the share he is legally entitled to.

Concerning a Disobedient Son

18 "Suppose someone has a son who is
stubborn and rebellious, a son who will
not obey his parents, even though they
punish him. 19 His parents are to take him
before the leaders of the town where he
lives and make him stand trial. 20 They
are to say to them, 'Our son is stubborn
and rebellious and refuses to obey us; he
wastes money and is a drunkard.' 21 Then
the men of the city are to stone him to
death, and so you will get rid of this evil.
Everyone in Israel will hear what has
happened and be afraid.

Various Laws

22 "If someone has been put to death for
a crime and the body is hung on a post,
23 it is not to remain there overnight. It
must be buried the same day, because a
dead body hanging on a post brings
God's curse on the land. Bury the body,
so that you will not defile the land that
the LORD your God is giving you.
22 "If you see an Israelite's cow or
sheep running loose, do not ignore it; take it back. 2 But if its owner
lives a long way off or if you don't know
who owns it, then take it home with you.
When its owner comes looking for it,
give it to him. 3 Do the same thing if you
find a donkey, a piece of clothing, or anything else that an Israelite may have lost.
4 "If an Israelite's donkey or cow has

[t] shave her head; *or* trim her hair.

fallen down, don't ignore it; help him get
the animal to its feet again.
5 "Women are not to wear men's clothing, and men are not to wear women's
clothing; the LORD your God hates people
who do such things.
6 "If you happen to find a bird's nest in
a tree or on the ground with the mother
bird sitting either on the eggs or with her
young, you are not to take the mother
bird. 7 You may take the young birds, but
you must let the mother bird go, so that
you will live a long and prosperous life.
8 "When you build a new house, be sure
to put a railing around the edge of the
roof. Then you will not be responsible if
someone falls off and is killed.
9 "Do not plant any crop in the same
field with your grapevines; if you do, you
are forbidden to use either the grapes or
the produce of the other crop.
10 "Do not hitch an ox and a donkey
together for plowing.
11 "Do not wear cloth made by weaving
wool and linen together.
12 "Sew tassels on the four corners of
your clothes.

Laws concerning Sexual Purity

13 "Suppose a man marries a young
woman and later he decides he doesn't
want her. 14 So he makes up false charges
against her, accusing her of not being a
virgin when they got married.
15 "If this happens, the young woman's
parents are to take the blood-stained
wedding sheet that proves she was a virgin, and they are to show it in court to the
town leaders. 16 Her father will say to
them, 'I gave my daughter to this man in
marriage, and now he doesn't want her.
17 He has made false charges against her,
saying that she was not a virgin when he
married her. But here is the proof that my
daughter was a virgin; look at the blood-
stains on the wedding sheet!' 18 Then the
town leaders are to take the husband and
beat him. 19 They are also to fine him a
hundred pieces of silver and give the
money to the young woman's father, because the man has brought disgrace on
an Israelite woman. Moreover, she will
continue to be his wife, and he can never
divorce her as long as he lives.
20 "But if the charge is true and there is
no proof that she was a virgin, 21 then
they are to take her out to the entrance of
her father's house, where the men of her
city are to stone her to death. She has
done a shameful thing among our people
by having intercourse before she was
married, while she was still living in her
father's house. In this way you will get
rid of this evil.
22 "If a man is caught having intercourse with another man's wife, both of
them are to be put to death. In this way
you will get rid of this evil.
23 "Suppose a man is caught in a town
having intercourse with a young woman
who is engaged to someone else. 24 You
are to take them outside the town and
stone them to death. She is to die because
she did not cry out for help, although she
was in a town, where she could have
been heard. And the man is to die because he had intercourse with someone
who was engaged. In this way you will
get rid of this evil.
25 "Suppose a man out in the countryside rapes a young woman who is engaged to someone else. Then only the
man is to be put to death; 26 nothing is to
be done to the woman, because she has
not committed a sin worthy of death.
This case is the same as when one man
attacks another man and murders him.
27 The man raped the engaged woman in
the countryside, and although she cried
for help, there was no one to help her.
28 "Suppose a man is caught raping a
young woman who is not engaged. 29 He
is to pay her father the bride price of fifty
pieces of silver, and she is to become his
wife, because he forced her to have intercourse with him. He can never divorce
her as long as he lives.
30 "No man is to disgrace his father by
having intercourse with any of his
father's wives.

Exclusion from the LORD's People

23 "No man who has been castrated
or whose penis has been cut off
may be included among the LORD's
people.
2 "No one born out of wedlock or any
descendant of such a person, even in the
tenth generation, may be included
among the LORD's people.
3 "No Ammonite or Moabite — or any of
their descendants, even in the tenth
generation — may be included among the
LORD's people. 4 They refused to provide
you with food and water when you were
on your way out of Egypt, and they hired

Balaam son of Beor, from the city of Pethor in Mesopotamia, to curse you. 5 But
the LORD your God would not listen to
Balaam; instead he turned the curse into
a blessing, because he loved you. 6 As
long as you are a nation, never do anything to help these nations or to make
them prosperous.
7 “Do not despise the Edomites; they
are your relatives. And do not despise
the Egyptians; you once lived in their
land. 8 From the third generation onward
their descendants may be included
among the LORD's people.

Keeping the Military Camp Clean

9 “When you are in camp in time of
war, you are to avoid anything that
would make you ritually unclean. 10 If a
man becomes unclean because he has
had a wet dream during the night, he is
to go outside the camp and stay there.
11 Toward evening he is to wash himself,
and at sunset he may come back into
camp.
12 “You are to have a place outside the
camp where you can go when you need
to relieve yourselves. 13 Carry a stick as
part of your equipment, so that when you
have a bowel movement you can dig a
hole and cover it up. 14 Keep your camp
ritually clean, because the LORD your God
is with you in your camp to protect you
and to give you victory over your enemies. Do not do anything indecent that
would cause the LORD to turn his back
on you.

Various Laws

15 “If slaves run away from their owners and come to you for protection, do
not send them back. 16 They may live in
any of your towns that they choose, and
you are not to treat them harshly.
17 “No Israelite, man or woman, is to
become a temple prostitute. 18 Also, no
money earned in this way may be
brought into the house of the LORD your
God in fulfillment of a vow. The LORD
hates temple prostitutes.
19 “When you lend money or food or
anything else to Israelites, do not charge
them interest. 20 You may charge interest
on what you lend to foreigners, but not
on what you lend to Israelites. Obey this
rule, and the LORD your God will bless
everything you do in the land that you
are going to occupy.
21 “When you make a vow to the LORD
your God, do not put off doing what you
promised; the LORD will hold you to your
vow, and it is a sin not to keep it. 22 It is
no sin not to make a vow to the LORD,
23 but if you make one voluntarily, be
sure that you keep it.
24 “When you walk along a path in
someone else's vineyard, you may eat all
the grapes you want, but you must not
carry any away in a container. 25 When
you walk along a path in someone else's
grainfield, you may eat all the grain you
can pull off with your hands, but you
must not cut any grain with a sickle.

Divorce and Remarriage

24 “Suppose a man marries a
woman and later decides that he
doesn't want her, because he finds something about her that he doesn't like.[u] So
he writes out divorce papers, gives them
to her, and sends her away from his
home. 2 Then suppose she marries another man, 3 and he also decides that he
doesn't want her, so he also writes out
divorce papers, gives them to her, and
sends her away from his home. Or suppose her second husband dies. 4 In either
case, her first husband is not to marry
her again; he is to consider her defiled. If
he married her again, it would be offensive to the LORD. You are not to commit
such a terrible sin in the land that the
LORD your God is giving you.

Various Laws

5 “When a man is newly married, he is
not to be drafted into military service or
any other public duty; he is to be excused
from duty for one year, so that he can
stay at home and make his wife happy.[v]
6 “When you lend someone something,
you are not to take as security his mill-
stones used for grinding his grain. This
would take away the family's means of
preparing food to stay alive.
7 “If any of you kidnap Israelites and
make them your slaves or sell them into
slavery, you are to be put to death. In this
way your nation will get rid of this evil.
8 “When you are suffering from a
dreaded skin disease, be sure to do exactly what the levitical priests tell you;

[u] something . . . like; *or* that she is guilty of some shameful conduct. [v] make his wife happy; *or* be happy with his wife.

follow the instructions that I have given
them. 9 Remember what the LORD your
God did to Miriam as you were coming
from Egypt.
10 "When you lend someone something, do not go into his house to get the
garment he is going to give you as security; 11 wait outside and let him bring it to
you himself. 12 If he is poor, do not keep
it overnight; 13 return it to him each evening, so that he can have it to sleep in.
Then he will be grateful, and the LORD
your God will be pleased with you.
14 "Do not cheat poor and needy hired
servants, whether they are Israelites or
foreigners living in one of your towns.
15 Each day before sunset pay them for
that day's work; they need the money
and have counted on getting it. If you do
not pay them, they will cry out against
you to the LORD, and you will be guilty
of sin.
16 "Parents are not to be put to death for
crimes committed by their children, and
children are not to be put to death for
crimes committed by their parents; people are to be put to death only for a crime
they themselves have committed.
17 "Do not deprive foreigners and orphans of their rights; and do not take a
widow's garment as security for a loan.
18 Remember that you were slaves in
Egypt and that the LORD your God set you
free; that is why I have given you this
command.
19 "When you gather your crops and
fail to bring in some of the grain that you
have cut, do not go back for it; it is to be
left for the foreigners, orphans, and widows, so that the LORD your God will bless
you in everything you do. 20 When you
have picked your olives once, do not go
back and get those that are left; they are
for the foreigners, orphans, and widows.
21 When you have gathered your grapes
once, do not go back over the vines a
second time; the grapes that are left are
for the foreigners, orphans, and widows.
22 Never forget that you were slaves in
Egypt; that is why I have given you this
command.

25 "Suppose two Israelites go to
court to settle a dispute, and one
is declared innocent and the other guilty.
2 If the guilty one is sentenced to be
beaten, the judge is to make him lie face
downward and have him whipped. The
number of lashes will depend on the
crime he has committed. 3 He may be
given as many as forty lashes, but no
more; more than that would humiliate
him publicly.
4 "Do not muzzle an ox when you are
using it to thresh grain.

Duty to a Dead Brother

5 "If two brothers live on the same
property and one of them dies, leaving
no son, then his widow is not to be married to someone outside the family; it is
the duty of the dead man's brother to
marry her. 6 The first son that they have
will be considered the son of the dead
man, so that his family line will continue
in Israel. 7 But if the dead man's brother
does not want to marry her, she is to go
before the town leaders and say, 'My
husband's brother will not do his duty;
he refuses to give his brother a descendant among the people of Israel.' 8 Then
the town leaders are to summon him and
speak to him. If he still refuses to marry
her, 9 his brother's widow is to go up to
him in the presence of the town leaders,
take off one of his sandals, spit in his
face, and say, 'This is what happens to
the man who refuses to give his brother
a descendant.' 10 His family will be
known in Israel as 'the family of the man
who had his sandal pulled off.'

Other Laws

11 "If two men are having a fight and
the wife of one tries to help her husband
by grabbing hold of the other man's genitals, 12 show her no mercy; cut off her
hand.
13-14 "Do not cheat when you use
weights and measures. 15 Use true and
honest weights and measures, so that
you may live a long time in the land that
the LORD your God is giving you. 16 The
LORD hates people who cheat.

The Command to Kill the Amalekites

17 "Remember what the Amalekites did
to you as you were coming from Egypt.
18 They had no fear of God, and so they
attacked you from the rear when you
were tired and exhausted, and killed all
who were straggling behind. 19 So then,
when the LORD your God has given you
the land and made you safe from all your
enemies who live around you, be sure to
kill all the Amalekites, so that no one will

remember them any longer. Do not
forget!

Harvest Offerings

26 "After you have occupied the
land that the LORD your God is
giving you and have settled there, 2 each
of you must place in a basket the first
part of each crop that you harvest and
you must take it with you to the one place
of worship. 3 Go to the priest in charge at
that time and say to him, 'I now acknowledge to the LORD my God that I have entered the land that he promised our
ancestors to give us.'

4 "The priest will take the basket from
you and place it before the altar of the
LORD your God. 5 Then, in the LORD's presence you will recite these words: 'My ancestor was a wandering Aramean, who
took his family to Egypt to live. They
were few in number when they went
there, but they became a large and powerful nation. 6 The Egyptians treated us
harshly and forced us to work as slaves.
7 Then we cried out for help to the LORD,
the God of our ancestors. He heard us
and saw our suffering, hardship, and
misery. 8 By his great power and strength
he rescued us from Egypt. He worked
miracles and wonders, and caused terrifying things to happen. 9 He brought us
here and gave us this rich and fertile
land. 10 So now I bring to the LORD the
first part of the harvest that he has
given me.'

"Then set the basket down in the
LORD's presence and worship there. 11 Be
grateful for the good things that the LORD
your God has given you and your family;
and let the Levites and the foreigners
who live among you join in the celebration.

12 "Every third year give the tithe—a
tenth of your crops—to the Levites, the
foreigners, the orphans, and the widows,
so that in every community they will
have all they need to eat. When you have
done this, 13 say to the LORD, 'None of the
sacred tithe is left in my house; I have
given it to the Levites, the foreigners, the
orphans, and the widows, as you commanded me to do. I have not disobeyed
or forgotten any of your commands concerning the tithe. 14 I have not eaten any
of it when I was mourning; I have not
taken any of it out of my house when I
was ritually unclean; and I have not
given any of it as an offering for the
dead.[w] I have obeyed you, O LORD; I
have done everything you commanded
concerning the tithe. 15 Look down from
your holy place in heaven and bless your
people Israel; bless also the rich and fertile land that you have given us, as you
promised our ancestors.'

The LORD's Own People

16 "Today the LORD your God commands you to obey all his laws; so obey
them faithfully with all your heart. 17 Today you have acknowledged the LORD as
your God; you have promised to obey
him, to keep all his laws, and to do all
that he commands. 18 Today the LORD has
accepted you as his own people, as he
promised you; and he commands you to
obey all his laws. 19 He will make you
greater than any other nation that he has
created, and you will bring praise and
honor to his name.[x] You will be his own
people, as he promised."

God's Laws Written on Stones

27 Then Moses, together with the
leaders of Israel, said to the people, "Obey all the instructions that I am
giving you today. 2 On the day you cross
the Jordan River and enter the land that
the LORD your God is giving you, you are
to set up some large stones, cover them
with plaster, 3 and write on them all these
laws and teachings. When you have entered the rich and fertile land that the
LORD, the God of your ancestors, promised you, 4 and you are on the other side
of the Jordan, set up these stones on
Mount Ebal, as I am instructing you today, and cover them with plaster. 5 Build
an altar there made of stones that have
had no iron tools used on them, 6 because
any altar you build for the LORD your God
must be made of uncut stones. There you
are to offer the sacrifices that are to be
burned, 7 and there you are to sacrifice
and eat your fellowship offerings and be
grateful in the presence of the LORD your
God. 8 On the stones covered with plaster
write clearly every word of God's laws."

9 Then Moses, together with the levitical priests, said to all the people of Israel,
"Give me your attention, people of Israel,

[w] for the dead; *or* to the dead. [x] bring praise . . . name; *or* receive praise and honor.

and listen to me. Today you have become
the people of the LORD your God; 10 so
obey him and keep all his laws that I am
giving you today."

The Curses on Disobedience

11 Then Moses said to the people of Israel, 12 "After you have crossed the Jordan, the following tribes are to stand on
Mount Gerizim when the blessings are
pronounced on the people: Simeon, Levi,
Judah, Issachar, Joseph, and Benjamin.
13 And the following tribes will stand on
Mount Ebal when the curses are pronounced: Reuben, Gad, Asher, Zebulun,
Dan, and Naphtali. 14 The Levites will
speak these words in a loud voice:

15 " 'God's curse on anyone who makes
an idol of stone, wood, or metal and secretly worships it; the LORD hates
idolatry.'

"And all the people will answer,
'Amen!'

16 " 'God's curse on anyone who dishonors his father or mother.'

"And all the people will answer,
'Amen!'

17 " 'God's curse on anyone who moves
a neighbor's property line.'

"And all the people will answer,
'Amen!'

18 " 'God's curse on anyone who leads a
blind person in the wrong direction.'

"And all the people will answer,
'Amen!'

19 " 'God's curse on anyone who de-
prives foreigners, orphans, and widows
of their rights.'

"And all the people will answer,
'Amen!'

20 " 'God's curse on anyone who disgraces his father by having intercourse
with any of his father's wives.'

"And all the people will answer,
'Amen!'

21 " 'God's curse on anyone who has
sexual relations with an animal.'

"And all the people will answer,
'Amen!'

22 " 'God's curse on anyone who has intercourse with his sister or half sister.'

"And all the people will answer,
'Amen!'

23 " 'God's curse on anyone who has intercourse with his mother-in-law.'

"And all the people will answer,
'Amen!'

24 " 'God's curse on anyone who secretly commits murder.'

"And all the people will answer,
'Amen!'

25 " 'God's curse on anyone who accepts money to murder an innocent
person.'

"And all the people will answer,
'Amen!'

26 " 'God's curse on anyone who does
not obey all of God's laws and teachings.'

"And all the people will answer,
'Amen!'

The Blessings of Obedience

(Leviticus 26.3-13; Deuteronomy 7.12-24)

28 "If you obey the LORD your God
and faithfully keep all his commands that I am giving you today, he will
make you greater than any other nation
on earth. 2 Obey the LORD your God and
all these blessings will be yours:

3 "The LORD will bless your towns and
your fields.

4 "The LORD will bless you with many
children, with abundant crops, and with
many cattle and sheep.

5 "The LORD will bless your grain crops
and the food you prepare from them.

6 "The LORD will bless everything
you do.

7 "The LORD will defeat your enemies
when they attack you. They will attack
from one direction, but they will run
from you in all directions.

8 "The LORD your God will bless your
work and fill your barns with grain. He
will bless you in the land that he is giving you.

9 "If you obey the LORD your God and do
everything he commands, he will make
you his own people, as he has promised.
10 Then all the peoples on earth will see
that the LORD has chosen you to be his
own people, and they will be afraid of
you. 11 The LORD will give you many children, many cattle, and abundant crops in
the land that he promised your ancestors
to give you. 12 He will send rain in season
from his rich storehouse in the sky and
bless all your work, so that you will lend
to many nations, but you will not have to
borrow from any. 13 The LORD your God
will make you the leader among the nations and not a follower; you will always
prosper and never fail if you obey faithfully all his commands that I am giving
you today. 14 But you must never disobey

them in any way, or worship and serve
other gods.

The Consequences of Disobedience

(Leviticus 26.14-46)

15 "But if you disobey the LORD your
God and do not faithfully keep all his
commands and laws that I am giving you
today, all these evil things will happen
to you:
16 "The LORD will curse your towns and
your fields.
17 "The LORD will curse your grain
crops and the food you prepare from
them.
18 "The LORD will curse you by giving
you only a few children, poor crops, and
few cattle and sheep.
19 "The LORD will curse everything
you do.
20 "If you do evil and reject the LORD, he
will bring on you disaster, confusion,
and trouble in everything you do, until
you are quickly and completely destroyed. 21 He will send disease after disease on you until there is not one of you
left in the land that you are about to occupy. 22 The LORD will strike you with in-
fectious diseases, with swelling and
fever; he will send drought and scorching winds to destroy your crops. These
disasters will be with you until you die.
23 No rain will fall, and your ground will
become as hard as iron. 24 Instead of rain,
the LORD will send down duststorms and
sandstorms until you are destroyed.
25 "The LORD will give your enemies victory over you. You will attack them from
one direction, but you will run from them
in all directions, and all the people on
earth will be terrified when they see
what happens to you. 26 When you die,
birds and wild animals will come and eat
your bodies, and there will be no one to
scare them off. 27 The LORD will send boils
on you, as he did on the Egyptians. He
will make your bodies break out with
sores. You will be covered with scabs,
and you will itch, but there will be no
cure. 28 The LORD will make you lose your
mind; he will strike you with blindness
and confusion. 29 You will grope about in
broad daylight like someone blind, and
you will not be able to find your way.
You will not prosper in anything you do.
You will be constantly oppressed and
robbed, and there will be no one to
help you.
30 "You will be engaged to a young
woman—but someone else will marry
her. You will build a house—but never
live in it. You will plant a vineyard—but
never eat its grapes. 31 Your cattle will be
butchered before your very eyes, but you
will not eat any of the meat. Your donkeys will be dragged away while you
look on, and they will not be given back
to you. Your sheep will be given to your
enemies, and there will be no one to help
you. 32 Your sons and daughters will be
given as slaves to foreigners while you
look on. Every day you will strain your
eyes, looking in vain for your children to
return. 33 A foreign nation will take all
the crops that you have worked so hard
to grow, while you receive nothing but
constant oppression and harsh treatment. 34 Your sufferings will make you
lose your mind. 35 The LORD will cover
your legs with incurable, painful sores;
boils will cover you from head to foot.
36 "The LORD will take you and your
king away to a foreign land, where neither you nor your ancestors ever lived
before; there you will serve gods made of
wood and stone. 37 In the countries to
which the LORD will scatter you, the people will be shocked at what has happened to you; they will make fun of you
and ridicule you.
38 "You will plant plenty of seed, but
reap only a small harvest, because the
locusts will eat your crops. 39 You will
plant vineyards and take care of them,
but you will not gather their grapes or
drink wine from them, because worms
will eat the vines. 40 Olive trees will grow
everywhere in your land, but you will not
have any olive oil, because the olives will
drop off. 41 You will have sons and
daughters, but you will lose them, because they will be taken away as prisoners of war. 42 All your trees and crops will
be devoured by insects.
43 "Foreigners who live in your land
will gain more and more power, while
you gradually lose yours. 44 They will
have money to lend you, but you will
have none to lend them. In the end they
will be your rulers.
45 "All these disasters will come on you,
and they will be with you until you are
destroyed, because you did not obey the
LORD your God and keep all the laws that
he gave you. 46 They will be the evidence
of God's judgment on you and your

descendants forever. 47 The LORD blessed
you in every way, but you would not
serve him with glad and joyful hearts.
48 So then, you will serve the enemies
that the LORD is going to send against
you. You will be hungry, thirsty, and
naked—in need of everything. The
LORD[y] will oppress you harshly until you
are destroyed. 49 The LORD will bring
against you a nation from the ends of the
earth, a nation whose language you do
not know. They will swoop down on you
like an eagle. 50 They will be ruthless and
show no mercy to anyone, young or old.
51 They will eat your livestock and your
crops, and you will starve to death. They
will not leave you any grain, wine, olive
oil, cattle, or sheep; and you will die.
52 They will attack every town in the land
that the LORD your God is giving you, and
the high, fortified walls in which you
trust will fall.

53 "When your enemies are besieging
your towns, you will become so desperate for food that you will even eat the
children that the LORD your God has
given you. 54-55 Even the most refined
man of noble birth will become so desperate during the siege that he will eat
some of his own children because he has
no other food. He will not even give any
to his brother or to the wife he loves or
to any of his children who are left.
56-57 Even the most refined woman of noble birth, so rich that she has never had
to walk anywhere, will behave in the
same way. When the enemy besieges her
town, she will become so desperate for
food that she will secretly eat her newborn child and the afterbirth as well. She
will not share them with the husband she
loves or with any of her children.

58 "If you do not obey faithfully all of
God's teachings that are written in this
book and if you do not honor the wonderful and awesome name of the LORD your
God, 59 he will send on you and on your
descendants incurable diseases and horrible epidemics that can never be
stopped. 60 He will bring on you once
again all the dreadful diseases you experienced in Egypt, and you will never recover. 61 He will also send all kinds of
diseases and epidemics that are not mentioned in this book of God's laws and
teachings, and you will be destroyed.
62 Although you become as numerous as
the stars in the sky, only a few of you will
survive, because you did not obey the
LORD your God. 63 Just as the LORD took
delight in making you prosper and in
making you increase in number, so he
will take delight in destroying you and in
bringing ruin on you. You will be uprooted from the land that you are about
to occupy.

64 "The LORD will scatter you among all
the nations, from one end of the earth to
the other, and there you will serve gods
made of wood and stone, gods that neither you nor your ancestors have ever
worshiped before. 65 You will find no
peace anywhere, no place to call your
own; the LORD will overwhelm you with
anxiety, hopelessness, and despair.
66 Your life will always be in danger. Day
and night you will be filled with terror,
and you will live in constant fear of
death. 67 Your hearts will pound with fear
at everything you see. Every morning
you will wish for evening; every evening
you will wish for morning. 68 The LORD
will send you back to Egypt in ships,
even though he[z] said that you would
never have to go there again. There you
will try to sell yourselves to your enemies
as slaves, but no one will want to
buy you."

The LORD's Covenant with Israel in the Land of Moab

29 These are the terms of the covenant that the LORD commanded
Moses to make with the people of Israel
in the land of Moab; all this was in addition to the covenant which the LORD had
made with them at Mount Sinai.

2 Moses called together all the people
of Israel and said to them, "You saw for
yourselves what the LORD did to the king
of Egypt, to his officials, and to his entire
country. 3 You saw the terrible plagues,
the miracles, and the great wonders that
the LORD performed. 4 But to this very day
he has not let you understand what you
have experienced. 5 For forty years the
LORD led you through the desert, and
your clothes and sandals never wore out.
6 You did not have bread to eat or wine or
beer to drink, but the LORD provided for
your needs in order to teach you that he
is your God. 7 And when we came to this

[y] The LORD; *or* Your enemies. [z] he; *or* I.

place, King Sihon of Heshbon and King
Og of Bashan came out to fight against
us. But we defeated them, 8took their
land, and divided it among the tribes of
Reuben and Gad, and half the tribe of
Manasseh. 9Obey faithfully all the terms
of this covenant, so that you will be successful in everything you do.

10“Today you are standing in the presence of the LORD your God, all of you—
your leaders and officials, your men,
11women, and children, and the foreigners who live among you and cut wood
and carry water for you. 12You are here
today to enter into this covenant that the
LORD your God is making with you and to
accept its obligations, 13so that the LORD
may now confirm you as his people and
be your God, as he promised you and
your ancestors, Abraham, Isaac, and Jacob. 14You are not the only ones with
whom the LORD is making this covenant
with its obligations. 15He is making it
with all of us who stand here in his presence today and also with our descendants who are not yet born.

16“You remember what life was like in
Egypt and what it was like to travel
through the territory of other nations.
17You saw their disgusting idols made of
wood, stone, silver, and gold. 18Make
sure that no man, woman, family, or
tribe standing here today turns from the
LORD our God to worship the gods of
other nations. This would be like a root
that grows to be a bitter and poisonous
plant. 19Make sure that there is no one
here today who hears these solemn demands and yet convinces himself that all
will be well with him, even if he stubbornly goes his own way. That would destroy all of you, good and evil alike.
20The LORD will not forgive such a man.
Instead, the LORD's burning anger will
flame up against him, and all the disasters written in this book will fall on him
until the LORD has destroyed him completely. 21The LORD will make an example of him before all the tribes of Israel
and will bring disaster on him in accordance with all the curses listed in the covenant that is written in this book of the
LORD's teachings.

22“In future generations your descendants and foreigners from distant lands
will see the disasters and sufferings that
the LORD has brought on your land. 23The
fields will be a barren waste, covered
with sulfur and salt; nothing will be
planted, and not even weeds will grow
there. Your land will be like the cities of
Sodom and Gomorrah, of Admah and
Zeboiim, which the LORD destroyed when
he was furiously angry. 24Then the
whole world will ask, 'Why did the LORD
do this to their land? What was the reason for his fierce anger?' 25And the answer will be, 'It is because the LORD's
people broke the covenant they had
made with him, the God of their ancestors, when he brought them out of Egypt.
26They served other gods that they had
never worshiped before, gods that the
LORD had forbidden them to worship.
27And so the LORD became angry with his
people and brought on their land all the
disasters written in this book. 28The LORD
became furiously angry, and in his great
anger he uprooted them from their land
and threw them into a foreign land, and
there they are today.'

29“There are some things that the LORD
our God has kept secret; but he has revealed his Law, and we and our descendants are to obey it forever.

Conditions for Restoration and Blessing

30 “I have now given you a choice
between a blessing and a curse.
When all these things have happened to
you, and you are living among the nations where the LORD your God has scattered you, you will remember the choice
I gave you. 2If you and your descendants
will turn back to the LORD and with all
your heart obey his commands that I am
giving you today, 3then the LORD your
God will have mercy on you. He will
bring you back from the nations where
he has scattered you, and he will make
you prosperous again. 4Even if you are
scattered to the farthest corners of the
earth, the LORD your God will gather you
together and bring you back, 5so that
you may again take possession of the
land where your ancestors once lived.
And he will make you more prosperous
and more numerous than your ancestors
ever were. 6The LORD your God will give
you and your descendants obedient
hearts, so that you will love him with all
your heart, and you will continue to live
in that land. 7He will turn all these curses
against your enemies, who hated you

and oppressed you, 8 and you will again
obey him and keep all his commands
that I am giving you today. 9 The LORD
will make you prosperous in all that you
do; you will have many children and a lot
of livestock, and your fields will produce
abundant crops. He will be as glad to
make you prosperous as he was to make
your ancestors prosperous, 10 but you
will have to obey him and keep all his
laws that are written in this book of his
teachings. You will have to turn to him
with all your heart.

11 "The command that I am giving you
today is not too difficult or beyond your
reach. 12 It is not up in the sky. You do not
have to ask, 'Who will go up and bring it
down for us, so that we can hear it and
obey it?' 13 Nor is it on the other side of
the ocean. You do not have to ask, 'Who
will go across the ocean and bring it to
us, so that we may hear it and obey it?'
14 No, it is here with you. You know it and
can quote it, so now obey it.

15 "Today I am giving you a choice between good and evil, between life and
death. 16 If you obey the commands of the
LORD your God,[a] which I give you today,
if you love him, obey him, and keep all
his laws, then you will prosper and become a nation of many people. The LORD
your God will bless you in the land that
you are about to occupy. 17 But if you disobey and refuse to listen, and are led
away to worship other gods, 18 you will
be destroyed—I warn you here and now.
You will not live long in that land across
the Jordan that you are about to occupy.
19 I am now giving you the choice between life and death, between God's
blessing and God's curse, and I call
heaven and earth to witness the choice
you make. Choose life. 20 Love the LORD
your God, obey him and be faithful to
him, and then you and your descendants
will live long in the land that he promised
to give your ancestors, Abraham, Isaac,
and Jacob."

Joshua Becomes Moses' Successor

31 Moses continued speaking to the
people of Israel, 2 and said, "I am
now a hundred and twenty years old and
am no longer able to be your leader. And
besides this, the LORD has told me that I
will not cross the Jordan. 3 The LORD your
God himself will go before you and destroy the nations living there, so that you
can occupy their land; and Joshua will be
your leader, as the LORD has said. 4 The
LORD will destroy those people, just as he
defeated Sihon and Og, kings of the Amorites, and destroyed their country. 5 The
LORD will give you victory over them, and
you are to treat them exactly as I have
told you. 6 Be determined and confident.
Do not be afraid of them. Your God, the
LORD himself, will be with you. He will
not fail you or abandon you."

7 Then Moses called Joshua and said to
him in the presence of all the people of
Israel, "Be determined and confident;
you are the one who will lead these people to occupy the land that the LORD
promised to their ancestors. 8 The LORD
himself will lead you and be with you. He
will not fail you or abandon you, so do
not lose courage or be afraid."

The Law Is to Be Read Every Seven Years

9 So Moses wrote down God's Law and
gave it to the levitical priests, who were
in charge of the LORD's Covenant Box,
and to the leaders of Israel. 10 He commanded them, "At the end of every seven
years, when the year that debts are canceled comes around, read this aloud at
the Festival of Shelters. 11 Read it to the
people of Israel when they come to worship the LORD your God at the one place
of worship. 12 Call together all the men,
women, and children, and the foreigners
who live in your towns, so that everyone
may hear it and learn to honor the LORD
your God and to obey his teachings faithfully. 13 In this way your descendants
who have never heard the Law of the
LORD your God will hear it. And so they
will learn to obey him as long as they live
in the land that you are about to occupy
across the Jordan."

The LORD's Last Instructions to Moses

14 Then the LORD said to Moses, "You do
not have much longer to live. Call Joshua
and bring him to the Tent, so that I may
give him his instructions." Moses and
Joshua went to the Tent, 15 and the LORD

[a] *One ancient translation* If you obey the commands of the LORD your God; *Hebrew does not have these words.*

appeared to them there in a pillar of
cloud that stood by the door of the Tent.
16 The LORD said to Moses, "You will
soon die, and after your death the people
will become unfaithful to me and break
the covenant that I made with them.
They will abandon me and worship the
pagan gods of the land they are about to
enter. 17 When that happens, I will become angry with them; I will abandon
them, and they will be destroyed. Many
terrible disasters will come upon them,
and then they will realize that these
things are happening to them because I,
their God, am no longer with them.
18 And I will refuse to help them then,
because they have done evil and worshiped other gods.
19 "Now, write down this song. Teach it
to the people of Israel, so that it will stand
as evidence against them. 20 I will take
them into this rich and fertile land, as I
promised their ancestors. There they will
have all the food they want, and they will
live comfortably. But they will turn away
and worship other gods. They will reject
me and break my covenant, 21 and many
terrible disasters will come on them. But
this song will still be sung, and it will
stand as evidence against them. Even
now, before I take them into the land that
I promised to give them, I know what
they are thinking."
22 That same day Moses wrote down
the song and taught it to the people of
Israel.
23 Then the LORD spoke to Joshua son of
Nun and told him, "Be confident and determined. You will lead the people of Israel into the land that I promised them,
and I will be with you."
24 Moses wrote God's Law in a book,
taking care not to leave out anything.
25 When he finished, he said to the levitical priests, who were in charge of the
LORD's Covenant Box, 26 "Take this book
of God's Law and place it beside the Covenant Box of the LORD your God, so that
it will remain there as a witness against
his people. 27 I know how stubborn and
rebellious they are. They have rebelled
against the LORD during my lifetime, and
they will rebel even more after I am dead.
28 Assemble all your tribal leaders and
officials before me, so that I can tell them
these things; I will call heaven and earth
to be my witnesses against them.
29 I know that after my death the people
will become wicked and reject what I
have taught them. And in time to come
they will meet with disaster, because
they will have made the LORD angry by
doing what he has forbidden."

The Song of Moses

30 Then Moses recited the entire song
while all the people of Israel listened.

32 "Earth and sky, hear my words,
listen closely to what I say.
2 My teaching will fall like drops of
rain
and form on the earth like dew.
My words will fall like showers on
young plants,
like gentle rain on tender grass.
3 I will praise the name of the LORD,
and his people will tell of his
greatness.

4 "The LORD is your mighty
defender,
perfect and just in all his ways;
Your God is faithful and true;
he does what is right and fair.
5 But you are unfaithful, unworthy
to be his people,[b]
a sinful and deceitful nation.
6 Is this the way you should treat
the LORD,
you foolish, senseless people?
He is your father, your Creator,
he made you into a nation.

7 "Think of the past, of the time
long ago;
ask your parents to tell you
what happened,
ask the old people to tell of the
past.
8 The Most High assigned nations
their lands;
he determined where peoples
should live.
He assigned to each nation a
heavenly being,
9 but Jacob's descendants he
chose for himself.

10 "He found them wandering
through the desert,

[b] *Probable text* But you . . . people; *Hebrew unclear.*

a desolate, wind-swept
wilderness.
He protected them and cared for
them,
as he would protect himself.
11 Like an eagle teaching its young
to fly,[c]
catching them safely on its
spreading wings,
the LORD kept Israel from falling.
12 The LORD alone led his people
without the help of a
foreign god.

13 "He let them rule the highlands,
and they ate what grew in the
fields.
They found wild honey among the
rocks;
their olive trees flourished in
stony ground.
14 Their cows and goats gave plenty
of milk;
they had the best sheep, goats,
and cattle,
the finest wheat, and the
choicest wine.

15 "The LORD's people grew rich, but
rebellious;
they were fat and stuffed with
food.
They abandoned God their Creator
and rejected their mighty savior.
16 Their idolatry made the LORD
jealous;
the evil they did made him
angry.
17 They sacrificed to gods that are
not real,
new gods their ancestors had
never known,
gods that Israel had never
obeyed.
18 They forgot their God, their
mighty savior,
the one who had given them life.

19 "When the LORD saw this, he was
angry
and rejected his sons and
daughters.
20 'I will no longer help them,' he
said;
'then I will see what happens to
them,
those stubborn, unfaithful
people.
21 With their idols they have made
me angry,
jealous with their so-called gods,
gods that are really not gods.
So I will use a so-called nation to
make them angry;
I will make them jealous with a
nation of fools.
22 My anger will flame up like fire
and burn everything on earth.
It will reach to the world below[d]
and consume the roots of the
mountains.

23 " 'I will bring on them endless
disasters
and use all my arrows against
them.
24 They will die from hunger and
fever;
they will die from terrible
diseases.
I will send wild animals to attack
them,
and poisonous snakes to bite
them.
25 War will bring death in the streets;
terrors will strike in the homes.
Young men and young women
will die;
neither babies nor old people
will be spared.
26 I would have destroyed them
completely,
so that no one would remember
them.
27 But I could not let their enemies
boast
that they had defeated my
people,
when it was I myself who had
crushed them.'

28 "Israel is a nation without sense;
they have no wisdom at all.
29 They fail to see why they were
defeated;
they cannot understand what
happened.
30 Why were a thousand defeated
by one,

[c] teaching its young to fly; *or* watching over its young.
[d] THE WORLD BELOW: *This refers to the world of the dead.*

and ten thousand by only two?
The LORD, their God, had
abandoned them;
their mighty God had given
them up.
31 Their enemies know that their
own gods are weak,
not mighty like Israel's God.
32 Their enemies, corrupt as Sodom
and Gomorrah,
are like vines that bear bitter
and poisonous grapes,
33 like wine made from the venom
of snakes.
34 "The LORD remembers what their
enemies have done;
he waits for the right time to
punish them.
35 The LORD will take revenge and
punish them;
the time will come when they
will fall;
the day of their doom is near.
36 The LORD will rescue his people
when he sees that their strength
is gone.
He will have mercy on those who
serve him,
when he sees how helpless
they are.
37 Then the LORD will ask his people,
'Where are those mighty gods
you trusted?
38 You fed them the fat of your
sacrifices
and offered them wine to drink.
Let them come and help you now;
let them run to your rescue.

39 " 'I, and I alone, am God;
no other god is real.
I kill and I give life, I wound and
I heal,
and no one can oppose what
I do.
40 As surely as I am the living God,
I raise my hand and I vow
41 that I will sharpen my flashing
sword
and see that justice is done.
I will take revenge on my enemies
and punish those who hate me.
42 My arrows will drip with their
blood,
and my sword will kill all who
oppose me.
I will spare no one who fights
against me;
even the wounded and prisoners
will die.'
43 "Nations, you must praise the
LORD's people —
he punishes all who kill them.
He takes revenge on his enemies
and forgives the sins of his
people."

44 Moses and Joshua son of Nun recited
this song, so that the people of Israel
could hear it.

Moses' Final Instructions

45 When Moses had finished giving
God's teachings to the people, 46 he said,
"Be sure to obey all these commands that
I have given you today. Repeat them to
your children, so that they may faithfully
obey all of God's teachings. 47 These
teachings are not empty words; they are
your very life. Obey them and you will
live long in that land across the Jordan
that you are about to occupy."
48 That same day the LORD said to
Moses, 49 "Go to the Abarim Mountains
in the land of Moab opposite the city of
Jericho; climb Mount Nebo and look at
the land of Canaan that I am about to
give the people of Israel. 50 You will die
on that mountain as your brother Aaron
died on Mount Hor, 51 because both of
you were unfaithful to me in the presence
of the people of Israel. When you were at
the waters of Meribah, near the town of
Kadesh in the wilderness of Zin, you dishonored me in the presence of the people. 52 You will look at the land from a
distance, but you will not enter the land
that I am giving the people of Israel."

Moses Blesses the Tribes of Israel

33 These are the blessings that
Moses, the man of God, pronounced on the people of Israel before he
died.

2 The LORD came from Mount Sinai;
he rose like the sun over Edom
and shone on his people from
Mount Paran.
Ten thousand angels were
with him,

a flaming fire at his right
hand.[e]
3 The LORD loves his people[f]
and protects those who belong
to him.
So we bow at[g] his feet
and obey his commands.
4 We obey the Law that Moses
gave us,
our nation's most treasured
possession.
5 The LORD became king of his
people Israel
when their tribes and leaders
were gathered together.

6 Moses said about the tribe of Reuben:
"May Reuben never die out,
Although their people are few."

7 About the tribe of Judah he said:
"LORD, listen to their cry for help;
Unite them again with the other
tribes.
Fight for them, LORD,
And help them against their
enemies."[h]

8 About the tribe of Levi he said:
"You, LORD, reveal your will by the
Urim and Thummim[i]
Through your faithful servants, the
Levites;
You put them to the test at
Massah
And proved them true at the
waters of Meribah.
9 They showed greater loyalty
to you
Than to parents, brothers, or
children.
They obeyed your commands
And were faithful to your
covenant.
10 They will teach your people to
obey your Law;
They will offer sacrifices on your
altar.
11 LORD, help their tribe to grow
strong;
Be pleased with what they do.
Crush all their enemies;
Let them never rise again."

12 About the tribe of Benjamin he said:
"This is the tribe the LORD loves
and protects;
He guards them all the day long,
And he dwells in their midst."[j]

13 About the tribe of Joseph he said:
"May the LORD bless their land
with rain
And with water from under the
earth.
14 May their land be blessed with
sun-ripened fruit,
Rich with the best fruits of each
season.
15 May their ancient hills be covered
with choice fruit.
16 May their land be filled with all
that is good,
Blessed by the goodness of the
LORD,
Who spoke from the burning bush.
May these blessings come to the
tribe of Joseph,
Because he was the leader among
his brothers.
17 Joseph has the strength of a bull,
The horns of a wild ox.
His horns are Manasseh's
thousands
And Ephraim's ten thousands.
With them he gores the nations
And pushes them to the ends of
the earth."

18 About the tribes of Zebulun and Issachar he said:
"May Zebulun be prosperous in
their trade on the sea,
And may Issachar's wealth
increase at home.
19 They invite foreigners to their
mountain
And offer the right sacrifices
there.
They get their wealth from the sea
And from the sand along the
shore."

20 About the tribe of Gad he said:

[e] *Probable text* Ten thousand . . . right hand; *Hebrew unclear.* [f] *One ancient translation* his people; *Hebrew* the peoples. [g] *Probable text* bow at; *Hebrew unclear.* [h] *Probable text* Fight for . . . enemies; *Hebrew* The tribe of Judah will fight for itself, and the LORD will help it against its enemies. [i] URIM AND THUMMIM: *Two objects used by the priest to determine God's will; it is not known precisely how they were used.* [j] And he . . . midst; *or* They live under his protection.

"Praise God, who made their
territory large.
Gad waits like a lion
To tear off an arm or a scalp.
21 They took the best of the land for
themselves;
A leader's share was assigned to
them.
They obeyed the LORD's commands
and laws
When the leaders of Israel were
gathered together."[k]

22 About the tribe of Dan he said:
"Dan is a young lion;
He leaps out from Bashan."

23 About the tribe of Naphtali he said:
"Naphtali is richly blessed by the
LORD's good favor;
Their land reaches to the south
from Lake Galilee."

24 About the tribe of Asher he said:
"Asher is blessed more than the
other tribes.
May he be the favorite of his
brothers,
And may his land be rich with
olive trees.
25 May his towns be protected with
iron gates,
And may he always live secure."
26 People of Israel, no god is like
your God,
riding in splendor across
the sky,
riding through the clouds to
come to your aid.
27 God has always been your
defense;
his eternal arms are your
support.
He drove out your enemies as you
advanced,
and told you to destroy them all.
28 So Jacob's descendants live in
peace,
secure in a land full of grain and
wine,
where dew from the sky waters
the ground.
29 Israel, how happy you are!
There is no one like you,
a nation saved by the LORD.
The LORD himself is your shield
and your sword,
to defend you and give you
victory.
Your enemies will come begging
for mercy,
and you will trample them
down.

The Death of Moses

34 Moses went up from the plains of
Moab to Mount Nebo, to the top
of Mount Pisgah east of Jericho, and
there the LORD showed him the whole
land: the territory of Gilead as far north
as the town of Dan; 2 the entire territory
of Naphtali; the territories of Ephraim
and Manasseh; the territory of Judah as
far west as the Mediterranean Sea; 3 the
southern part of Judah; and the plain
that reaches from Zoar to Jericho, the
city of palm trees. 4 Then the LORD said to
Moses, "This is the land that I promised
Abraham, Isaac, and Jacob I would give
to their descendants. I have let you see it,
but I will not let you go there."
5 So Moses, the LORD's servant, died
there in the land of Moab, as the LORD
had said he would. 6 The LORD buried him
in a valley in Moab, opposite the town of
Bethpeor, but to this day no one knows
the exact place of his burial. 7 Moses was
a hundred and twenty years old when he
died; he was as strong as ever, and his
eyesight was still good. 8 The people of
Israel mourned for him for thirty days in
the plains of Moab.
9 Joshua son of Nun was filled with
wisdom, because Moses had appointed
him to be his successor. The people of
Israel obeyed Joshua and kept the commands that the LORD had given them
through Moses.
10 There has never been a prophet in
Israel like Moses; the LORD spoke with
him face-to-face. 11 No other prophet has
ever done miracles and wonders like
those that the LORD sent Moses to perform against the king of Egypt, his officials, and the entire country. 12 No other
prophet has been able to do the great and
terrifying things that Moses did in the
sight of all Israel.

[k] *One ancient translation* When the leaders . . . together; *Hebrew unclear.*

The Book of
JOSHUA

Introduction

The Book of Joshua *is the story of the Israelite invasion of Canaan under the leadership of Joshua, the successor of Moses. Notable events recorded in this book include the crossing of the Jordan, the fall of Jericho, the battle at Ai, and the renewal of the covenant between God and his people. One of the best-known passages in the book is, "Decide today whom you will serve . . . . As for my family and me, we will serve the* Lord*" (24.15).*

Outline of Contents

The conquest of Canaan 1.1 – 12.24
The division of the land 13.1 – 21.45
- *a. The land east of the Jordan 13.1-33*
- *b. The land west of the Jordan 14.1 – 19.51*
- *c. The cities of refuge 20.1-9*
- *d. The cities of the Levites 21.1-45*

The eastern tribes return to their territory 22.1-34
Joshua's farewell address 23.1-16
The covenant renewed at Shechem 24.1-33

God Commands Joshua to Conquer Canaan

1 After the death of the Lord's servant
Moses, the Lord spoke to Moses'
helper, Joshua son of Nun. 2 He said, "My
servant Moses is dead. Get ready now,
you and all the people of Israel, and cross
the Jordan River into the land that I am
giving them. 3 As I told Moses, I have
given you and all my people the entire
land that you will be marching over.
4 Your borders will reach from the desert
in the south to the Lebanon Mountains in
the north; from the great Euphrates
River in the east, through the Hittite
country, to the Mediterranean Sea in the
west. 5 Joshua, no one will be able to defeat you as long as you live. I will be with
you as I was with Moses. I will always be
with you; I will never abandon you. 6 Be
determined and confident, for you will be
the leader of these people as they occupy
this land which I promised their ancestors. 7 Just be determined, be confident;
and make sure that you obey the whole
Law that my servant Moses gave you. Do
not neglect any part of it and you will
succeed wherever you go. 8 Be sure that
the book of the Law is always read in
your worship. Study it day and night,
and make sure that you obey everything
written in it. Then you will be prosperous
and successful. 9 Remember that I have
commanded you to be determined and
confident! Do not be afraid or discouraged, for I, the Lord your God, am with
you wherever you go."

Joshua Gives Orders to the People

10 Then Joshua ordered the leaders to
11 go through the camp and say to the
people, "Get some food ready, because in
three days you are going to cross the Jordan River to occupy the land that the
Lord your God is giving you."

12 Joshua said to the tribes of Reuben
and Gad and to half the tribe of Manasseh, 13 "Remember how the Lord's servant Moses told you that the Lord your
God would give you this land on the east
side of the Jordan as your home. 14 Your
wives, your children, and your livestock
will stay here, but your soldiers, armed
for battle, will cross over ahead of the
other Israelites in order to help them
15 until they have occupied the land west
of the Jordan that the Lord your God has
given them. When he has given safety to
all the tribes of Israel, then you may
come back and settle here in your own
land east of the Jordan, which Moses, the
Lord's servant, gave to you."

16 They answered Joshua, "We will do
everything you have told us and will go
anywhere you send us. 17 We will obey

you, just as we always obeyed Moses,
and may the LORD your God be with you
as he was with Moses! 18 Whoever questions your authority or disobeys any of
your orders will be put to death. Be determined and confident!"

Joshua Sends Spies into Jericho

2 Then Joshua sent two spies from the
camp at Acacia with orders to go
and secretly explore the land of Canaan,
especially the city of Jericho. When they
came to the city, they went to spend the
night in the house of a prostitute named
Rahab. 2 The king of Jericho heard that
some Israelites had come that night to
spy out the country, 3 so he sent word to
Rahab: "The men in your house have
come to spy out the whole country! Bring
them out!"
4-6 "Some men did come to my house,"
she answered, "but I don't know where
they were from. They left at sundown
before the city gate was closed. I didn't
find out where they were going, but if
you start after them quickly, you can
catch them." (Now Rahab had taken the
two spies up on the roof and hidden them
under some stalks of flax that she had
put there.) 7 The king's men left the city,
and then the gate was shut. They went
looking for the Israelite spies as far as
the place where the road crosses the
Jordan.
8 Before the spies settled down for the
night, Rahab went up on the roof 9 and
said to them, "I know that the LORD has
given you this land. Everyone in the
country is terrified of you. 10 We have
heard how the LORD dried up the Red Sea
in front of you when you were leaving
Egypt. We have also heard how you
killed Sihon and Og, the two Amorite
kings east of the Jordan. 11 We were
afraid as soon as we heard about it; we
have all lost our courage because of you.
The LORD your God is God in heaven
above and here on earth. 12 Now swear
by him that you will treat my family as
kindly as I have treated you, and give me
some sign that I can trust you. 13 Promise
me that you will save my father and
mother, my brothers and sisters, and all
their families! Don't let us be killed!"
14 The men said to her, "May God take
our lives if we don't do as we say![a] If you
do not tell anyone what we have been
doing, we promise you that when the
LORD gives us this land, we will treat you
well."
15 Rahab lived in a house built into the
city wall, so she let the men down from
the window by a rope. 16 "Go into the hill
country," she said, "or the king's men
will find you. Hide there for three days
until they come back. After that, you can
go on your way."
17 The men said to her, "We will keep
the promise that you have made us give.
18 This is what you must do. When we
invade your land, tie this red cord to the
window you let us down from. Get your
father and mother, your brothers, and all
your father's family together in your
house. 19 If anyone goes out of the house,
his death will be his own fault, and we
will not be responsible; but if anyone in
the house with you is harmed, then we
will be responsible. 20 However, if you
tell anyone what we have been doing,
then we will not have to keep our promise which you have made us give you."
21 She agreed and sent them away. When
they had gone, she tied the red cord to
the window.
22 The spies went into the hills and hid.
The king's men looked for them all over
the countryside for three days, but they
did not find them, so they returned to
Jericho. 23 Then the two spies came down
from the hills, crossed the river, and
went back to Joshua. They told him
everything that had happened, 24 and
then said, "We are sure that the LORD has
given us the whole country. All the people there are terrified of us."

The People of Israel Cross the Jordan

3 The next morning Joshua and all the
people of Israel got up early, left the
camp at Acacia, and went to the Jordan,
where they camped while waiting to
cross it. 2 Three days later the leaders
went through the camp 3 and told the
people, "When you see the priests carrying the Covenant Box of the LORD your
God, break camp and follow them. 4 You
have never been here before, so they will
show you the way to go. But do not get
near the Covenant Box; stay about half a
mile behind it."

[a] May God . . . say; *or* We will protect you if you protect us.

5 Joshua told the people, "Purify yourselves, because tomorrow the LORD will
perform miracles among you." 6 Then he
told the priests to take the Covenant Box
and go with it ahead of the people. They
did as he said.
7 The LORD said to Joshua, "What I do
today will make all the people of Israel
begin to honor you as a great man, and
they will realize that I am with you as I
was with Moses. 8 Tell the priests carrying the Covenant Box that when they
reach the river, they must wade in and
stand near the bank."
9 Then Joshua said to the people,
"Come here and listen to what the LORD
your God has to say. 10 As you advance,
he will surely drive out the Canaanites,
the Hittites, the Hivites, the Perizzites,
the Girgashites, the Amorites, and the
Jebusites. You will know that the living
God is among you 11 when the Covenant
Box of the Lord of all the earth crosses
the Jordan ahead of you. 12 Now choose
twelve men, one from each of the tribes
of Israel. 13 When the priests who carry
the Covenant Box of the LORD of all the
earth put their feet in the water, the Jordan will stop flowing, and the water coming downstream will pile up in one
place."
14-15 It was harvest time, and the river
was in flood.
When the people left the camp to cross
the Jordan, the priests went ahead of
them, carrying the Covenant Box. As
soon as the priests stepped into the river,
16 the water stopped flowing and piled
up, far upstream at Adam, the city beside
Zarethan. The flow downstream to the
Dead Sea was completely cut off, and the
people were able to cross over near Jericho. 17 While the people walked across
on dry ground, the priests carrying the
LORD's Covenant Box stood on dry
ground in the middle of the Jordan until
all the people had crossed over.

Memorial Stones Are Set Up

4 When the whole nation had crossed
the Jordan, the LORD said to Joshua,
2 "Choose twelve men, one from each
tribe, 3 and command them to take twelve
stones out of the middle of the Jordan,
from the very place where the priests
were standing. Tell them to carry these
stones with them and to put them down
where you camp tonight."
4 Then Joshua called the twelve men he
had chosen, 5 and he told them, "Go into
the Jordan ahead of the Covenant Box of
the LORD your God. Each one of you take
a stone on your shoulder, one for each of
the tribes of Israel. 6 These stones will
remind the people of what the LORD has
done. In the future, when your children
ask what these stones mean to you, 7 you
will tell them that the water of the Jordan
stopped flowing when the LORD's Covenant Box crossed the river. These stones
will always remind the people of Israel of
what happened here."
8 The men followed Joshua's orders.
As the LORD had commanded Joshua,
they took twelve stones from the middle
of the Jordan, one for each of the tribes
of Israel, carried them to the camping
place, and put them down there. 9 Joshua
also set up twelve stones in the middle of
the Jordan, where the priests carrying
the Covenant Box had stood. (Those
stones are still there.) 10 The priests stood
in the middle of the Jordan until everything had been done that the LORD ordered Joshua to tell the people to do. This
is what Moses had commanded.
The people hurried across the river.
11 When they were all on the other side,
the priests with the LORD's Covenant Box
went on ahead of the people. 12 The men
of the tribes of Reuben and Gad and of
half the tribe of Manasseh, ready for battle, crossed ahead of the rest of the people, as Moses had told them to do. 13 In
the presence of the LORD about forty
thousand men ready for war crossed
over to the plain near Jericho. 14 What
the LORD did that day made the people of
Israel consider Joshua a great man. They
honored him all his life, just as they had
honored Moses.
15 Then the LORD told Joshua 16 to command the priests carrying the Covenant
Box to come up out of the Jordan.
17 Joshua did so, 18 and when the priests
reached the riverbank, the river began
flowing once more and flooded its banks
again.
19 The people crossed the Jordan on the
tenth day of the first month and camped
at Gilgal, east of Jericho. 20 There Joshua
set up the twelve stones taken from the
Jordan. 21 And he said to the people of
Israel, "In the future, when your children
ask you what these stones mean, 22 you
will tell them about the time when Israel

crossed the Jordan on dry ground. 23 Tell them that the LORD your God dried up the water of the Jordan for you until you had crossed, just as he dried up the Red Sea for us. 24 Because of this everyone on earth will know how great the LORD's power is, and you will honor the LORD your God forever."

5 All the Amorite kings west of the Jordan and all the Canaanite kings along the Mediterranean Sea heard that the LORD had dried up the Jordan until the people of Israel had crossed it. They became afraid and lost their courage because of the Israelites.

The Circumcision at Gilgal

2 Then the LORD told Joshua, "Make some knives out of flint and circumcise the Israelites." 3 So Joshua did as the LORD had commanded, and he circumcised the Israelites at a place called Circumcision Hill. 4-6 When the people of Israel left Egypt, all the males were already circumcised. However, during the forty years the people spent crossing the desert, none of the baby boys had been circumcised. Also, by the end of that time all the men who were of fighting age when they left Egypt had died because they had disobeyed the LORD. Just as he had sworn, they were not allowed to see the rich and fertile land that he had promised their ancestors. 7 The sons of these men had never been circumcised, and it was this new generation that Joshua circumcised.

8 After the circumcision was completed, the whole nation stayed in the camp until the wounds had healed. 9 The LORD said to Joshua, "Today I have removed from you the disgrace of being slaves in Egypt." That is why the place was named Gilgal,[b] the name it still has.

10 While the Israelites were camping at Gilgal on the plain near Jericho, they observed Passover on the evening of the fourteenth day of the month. 11 The next day was the first time they ate food grown in Canaan: roasted grain and bread made without yeast. 12 The manna stopped falling then, and the Israelites no longer had any. From that time on they ate food grown in Canaan.

Joshua and the Man with a Sword

13 While Joshua was near Jericho, he suddenly saw a man standing in front of him, holding a sword. Joshua went up to him and asked, "Are you one of our soldiers, or an enemy?"

14 "Neither," the man answered. "I am here as the commander of the LORD's army."

Joshua threw himself on the ground in worship and said, "I am your servant, sir. What do you want me to do?"

15 And the commander of the LORD's army told him, "Take your sandals off; you are standing on holy ground." And Joshua did as he was told.

The Fall of Jericho

6 The gates of Jericho were kept shut and guarded to keep the Israelites out. No one could enter or leave the city. 2 The LORD said to Joshua, "I am putting into your hands Jericho, with its king and all its brave soldiers. 3 You and your soldiers are to march around the city once a day for six days. 4 Seven priests, each carrying a trumpet, are to go in front of the Covenant Box. On the seventh day you and your soldiers are to march around the city seven times while the priests blow the trumpets. 5 Then they are to sound one long note. As soon as you hear it, all the people are to give a loud shout, and the city walls will collapse. Then the whole army will go straight into the city."

6 Joshua called the priests and told them, "Take the Covenant Box, and seven of you go in front of it, carrying trumpets." 7 Then he ordered the people to start marching around the city, with an advance guard going on ahead of the LORD's Covenant Box.

8-9 So, just as Joshua had ordered, an advance guard started out ahead of the priests who were blowing trumpets; behind these came the priests who were carrying the Covenant Box, followed by a rear guard. All this time the trumpets were sounding. 10 But Joshua had ordered the people not to shout, not to say a word until he gave the order. 11 So he had this group of men take the LORD's Covenant Box around the city one time. Then they came back to camp and spent the night there.

[b] GILGAL: *This name sounds like the Hebrew for "removed."*

12-13 Joshua got up early the next morning, and for the second time the priests
and soldiers marched around the city in
the same order as the day before: first,
the advance guard; next, the seven
priests blowing the seven trumpets; then,
the priests carrying the LORD's Covenant
Box; and finally, the rear guard. All this
time the trumpets were sounding. 14 On
this second day they again marched
around the city one time and then returned to camp. They did this for six
days.

15 On the seventh day they got up at
daybreak and marched seven times
around the city in the same way—this
was the only day that they marched
around it seven times. 16 The seventh
time around, when the priests were
about to sound the trumpets, Joshua ordered the people to shout, and he said,
"The LORD has given you the city! 17 The
city and everything in it must be totally
destroyed as an offering to the LORD.
Only the prostitute Rahab and her household will be spared, because she hid our
spies. 18 But you are not to take anything
that is to be destroyed; if you do, you will
bring trouble and destruction on the Israelite camp. 19 Everything made of silver,
gold, bronze, or iron is set apart for
the LORD. It is to be put in the LORD's
treasury."

20 So the priests blew the trumpets. As
soon as the people heard it, they gave a
loud shout, and the walls collapsed. Then
all the army went straight up the hill into
the city and captured it. 21 With their
swords they killed everyone in the
city, men and women, young and old.
They also killed the cattle, sheep, and
donkeys.

22 Joshua then told the two men who
had served as spies, "Go into the prostitute's house, and bring her and her family out, as you promised her." 23 So they
went and brought Rahab out, along with
her father and mother, her brothers, and
the rest of her family. They took them all,
family and slaves, to safety near the Israelite camp. 24 Then they set fire to the city
and burned it to the ground, along with
everything in it, except the things made
of gold, silver, bronze, and iron, which
they took and put in the LORD's treasury.
25 But Joshua spared the lives of the prostitute Rahab and all her relatives, because she had hidden the two spies that
he had sent to Jericho. (Her descendants
have lived in Israel to this day.)

26 At this time Joshua issued a solemn
warning: "Anyone who tries to rebuild
the city of Jericho will be under the
LORD's curse.

Whoever lays the foundation will
lose his oldest son;
Whoever builds the gates will lose
his youngest."

27 So the LORD was with Joshua, and his
fame spread through the whole country.

Achan's Sin

7 The LORD's command to Israel not to
take from Jericho anything that was
to be destroyed was not obeyed. A man
named Achan disobeyed that order, and
so the LORD was furious with the Israelites. (Achan was the son of Carmi and
grandson of Zabdi, and belonged to the
clan of Zerah, a part of the tribe of
Judah.)

2 Joshua sent some men from Jericho
to Ai, a city east of Bethel, near Bethaven, with orders to go and explore the
land. When they had done so, 3 they reported back to Joshua: "There is no need
for everyone to attack Ai. Send only
about two or three thousand men. Don't
send the whole army up there to fight; it
is not a large city." 4 So about three thousand Israelites made the attack, but they
were forced to retreat. 5 The men of Ai
chased them from the city gate as far as
some quarries and killed about thirty-six
of them on the way down the hill. Then
the Israelites lost their courage and were
afraid.

6 Joshua and the leaders of Israel tore
their clothes in grief, threw themselves
to the ground before the LORD's Covenant
Box, and lay there till evening, with dust
on their heads to show their sorrow.
7 And Joshua said, "Sovereign LORD!
Why did you bring us across the Jordan
at all? To turn us over to the Amorites?
To destroy us? Why didn't we just stay
on the other side of the Jordan? 8 What
can I say, O Lord, now that Israel has
retreated from the enemy? 9 The Canaanites and everyone else in the country will
hear about it. They will surround us and
kill every one of us! And then what will
you do to protect your honor?"

10 The LORD said to Joshua, "Get up!
Why are you lying on the ground like
this? 11 Israel has sinned! They have

broken the agreement with me that I
ordered them to keep. They have taken
some of the things condemned to destruction. They stole them, lied about
it, and put them with their own things.
12 This is why the Israelites cannot stand
against their enemies. They retreat from
them because they themselves have
now been condemned to destruction! I
will not stay with you any longer unless
you destroy the things you were ordered
not to take! 13 Get up! Purify the people
and get them ready to come before me.
Tell them to be ready tomorrow, because
I, the LORD God of Israel, have this to say:
'Israel, you have in your possession some
things that I ordered you to destroy!
You cannot stand against your enemies
until you get rid of these things!' 14 So tell
them that in the morning they will be
brought forward, tribe by tribe. The
tribe that I pick out will then come forward, clan by clan. The clan that I pick
out will come forward, family by family.
The family that I pick out will come forward, one by one. 15 The one who is then
picked out and found with the condemned goods will be burned, along with
his family and everything he owns, for
he has brought terrible shame on Israel
and has broken my covenant."

16 Early the next morning Joshua
brought Israel forward, tribe by tribe,
and the tribe of Judah was picked out.
17 He brought the tribe of Judah forward,
clan by clan, and the clan of Zerah was
picked out. Then he brought the clan of
Zerah forward, family by family, and the
family of Zabdi was picked out. 18 He
then brought Zabdi's family forward,
one by one, and Achan, the son of Carmi
and grandson of Zabdi, was picked out.
19 Joshua said to him, "My son, tell the
truth here before the LORD, the God of
Israel, and confess. Tell me now what
you have done. Don't try to hide it
from me."

20 "It's true," Achan answered. "I have
sinned against the LORD, Israel's God,
and this is what I did. 21 Among the
things we seized I saw a beautiful Babylonian cloak, about five pounds of silver,
and a bar of gold weighing over one
pound. I wanted them so much that I took
them. You will find them buried inside
my tent, with the silver at the bottom."

22 So Joshua sent some men, who ran
to the tent and found that the condemned
things really were buried there, with the
silver at the bottom. 23 They brought
them out of the tent, took them to Joshua
and all the Israelites, and laid them down
in the presence of the LORD. 24 Joshua,
along with all the people of Israel, seized
Achan, the silver, the cloak, the bar of
gold, together with Achan's sons and
daughters, his cattle, donkeys, and
sheep, his tent, and everything else he
owned; and they took them to Trouble
Valley. 25 And Joshua said, "Why have
you brought such trouble on us? The
LORD will now bring trouble on you!" All
the people then stoned Achan to death;
they also stoned and burned his family
and possessions. 26 They put a huge pile
of stones over him, which is there to this
day. That is why that place is still called
Trouble Valley.

Then the LORD was no longer furious.

The Capture and Destruction of Ai

8 The LORD said to Joshua, "Take all
the soldiers with you and go on up to
Ai. Don't be afraid or discouraged. I will
give you victory over the king of Ai; his
people, city, and land will be yours. 2 You
are to do to Ai and its king what you did
to Jericho and its king, but this time you
may keep its goods and livestock for
yourselves. Prepare to attack the city by
surprise from the rear."

3 So Joshua got ready to go to Ai with
all his soldiers. He picked out thirty thousand of his best troops and sent them out
at night 4 with these orders: "Hide on the
other side of the city, but not too far away
from it; be ready to attack. 5 My men and
I will approach the city. When the men of
Ai come out against us, we will turn and
run, just as we did the first time. 6 They
will pursue us until we have led them
away from the city. They will think that
we are running from them, as we did before. 7 Then you will come out of hiding
and capture the city. The LORD your God
will give it to you. 8 After you have taken
the city, set it on fire, just as the LORD has
commanded. These are your orders." 9 So
Joshua sent them out, and they went to
their hiding place and waited there, west
of Ai, between Ai and Bethel. Joshua
spent the night in camp.

10 Early in the morning Joshua got up
and called the soldiers together. Then he
and the leaders of Israel led them to Ai.
11 The soldiers with him went toward the

main entrance to the city and set up
camp on the north side, with a valley between themselves and Ai. 12 He took
about five thousand men and put them in
hiding west of the city, between Ai and
Bethel. 13 The soldiers were arranged for
battle with the main camp north of the
city and the rest of the men to the west.
Joshua spent the night in the valley.
14 When the king of Ai saw Joshua's men,
he acted quickly. He and all his men went
out toward the Jordan Valley to fight the
Israelites at the same place as before, not
knowing that he was about to be attacked from the rear. 15 Joshua and his
men pretended that they were retreating,
and ran away toward the barren country.
16 All the men in the city had been called
together to go after them, and as they
pursued Joshua, they kept getting farther away from the city. 17 Every man in
Ai[c] went after the Israelites, and the city
was left wide open, with no one to defend it.

18 Then the LORD said to Joshua, "Point
your spear at Ai; I am giving it to you."
Joshua did as he was told, 19 and as soon
as he lifted his hand, the men who had
been hiding got up quickly, ran into the
city and captured it. They immediately
set the city on fire. 20 When the men of Ai
looked back, they saw the smoke rising
to the sky. There was no way for them to
escape, because the Israelites who had
run toward the barren country now
turned around to attack them. 21 When
Joshua and his men saw that the others
had taken the city and that it was on fire,
they turned around and began killing the
men of Ai. 22 The Israelites in the city
now came down to join the battle. So the
men of Ai found themselves completely
surrounded by Israelites, and they were
all killed. No one got away, and no one
lived through it 23 except the king of Ai.
He was captured and taken to Joshua.

24 The Israelites killed every one of
the enemy in the barren country where
they had chased them. Then they went
back to Ai and killed everyone there.
25-26 Joshua kept his spear pointed at Ai
and did not put it down until every person there had been killed. The whole
population of Ai was killed that day—
twelve thousand men and women. 27 The
Israelites kept for themselves the livestock and goods captured in the city, as
the LORD had told Joshua. 28 Joshua
burned Ai and left it in ruins. It is still like
that today. 29 He hanged the king of Ai
from a tree and left his body there until
evening. At sundown Joshua gave orders
for the body to be removed, and it was
thrown down at the entrance to the city
gate. They covered it with a huge pile of
stones, which is still there today.

The Law Is Read at Mount Ebal

30 Then Joshua built on Mount Ebal an
altar to the LORD, the God of Israel. 31 He
made it according to the instructions that
Moses, the LORD's servant, had given the
Israelites, as it says in the Law of Moses:
"an altar made of stones which have not
been cut with iron tools." On it they offered burnt sacrifices to the LORD, and
they also presented their fellowship offerings. 32 There, with the Israelites looking on, Joshua made on the stones[d] a
copy of the Law which Moses had written. 33 The Israelites, with their leaders,
officers, and judges, as well as the foreigners among them, stood on two sides
of the LORD's Covenant Box, facing the
levitical priests who carried it. Half of the
people stood with their backs to Mount
Gerizim and the other half with their
backs to Mount Ebal. The LORD's servant
Moses had commanded them to do this
when the time came for them to receive
the blessing. 34 Joshua then read aloud
the whole Law, including the blessings
and the curses, just as they are written in
the book of the Law. 35 Every one of the
commandments of Moses was read by
Joshua to the whole gathering, which included women and children, as well as
the foreigners living among them.

The Gibeonites Deceive Joshua

9 The victories of Israel became
known to all the kings west of the
Jordan—in the hills, in the foothills, and
all along the coastal plain of the Mediterranean Sea as far north as Lebanon;
these were the kings of the Hittites, the
Amorites, the Canaanites, the Perizzites,
the Hivites, and the Jebusites. 2 They all
came together and joined forces to fight
against Joshua and the Israelites.

3 But the people of Gibeon, who were
Hivites, heard what Joshua had done to

[c] *One ancient translation* Ai; *Hebrew* Ai and Bethel. [d] the stones; *or* stones.

Jericho and Ai, 4 and they decided to deceive him. They went and got some food and loaded their donkeys with worn-out sacks and patched-up wineskins. 5 They put on ragged clothes and worn-out sandals that had been mended. The bread they took with them was dry and moldy. 6 Then they went to the camp at Gilgal and said to Joshua and the Israelites, "We have come from a distant land. We want you to make a treaty with us."

7 But the Israelites said, "Why should we make a treaty with you? Maybe you live nearby."

8 They said to Joshua, "We are at your service."

Joshua asked them, "Who are you? Where do you come from?"

9 Then they told him this story: "We have come from a very distant land, sir, because we have heard of the LORD your God. We have heard about everything that he did in Egypt 10 and what he did to the two Amorite kings east of the Jordan: King Sihon of Heshbon and King Og of Bashan, who lived in Ashtaroth. 11 Our leaders and all the people that live in our land told us to get some food ready for a trip and to go and meet you. We were told to put ourselves at your service and ask you to make a treaty with us. 12 Look at our bread. When we left home with it and started out to meet you, it was still warm. But look! Now it is dry and moldy. 13 When we filled these wineskins, they were new, but look! They are torn. Our clothes and sandals are worn out from the long trip."

14 The Israelites accepted some food from them, but did not consult the LORD about it. 15 Joshua made a treaty of friendship with the people of Gibeon and allowed them to live. The leaders of the community of Israel gave their solemn promise to keep the treaty.

16 Three days after the treaty had been made, the Israelites learned that these people did indeed live nearby. 17 So the people of Israel started out and three days later arrived at the cities where these people lived: Gibeon, Chephirah, Beeroth, and Kiriath Jearim. 18 But the Israelites could not kill them, because their leaders had made a solemn promise to them in the name of the LORD, Israel's God. All the people complained to the leaders about this, 19 but they answered, "We have made our solemn promise to them in the name of the LORD God of Israel. Now we cannot harm them. 20 We must let them live because of our promise; if we don't, God will punish us. 21 Let them live, but they will have to cut wood and carry water for us." This was what the leaders suggested.

22 Joshua ordered the people of Gibeon to be brought to him, and he asked them, "Why did you deceive us and tell us that you were from far away, when you live right here? 23 Because you did this, God has condemned you. Your people will always be slaves, cutting wood and carrying water for the sanctuary of my God."

24 They answered, "We did it, sir, because we learned that it was really true that the LORD your God had commanded his servant Moses to give you the whole land and to kill the people living in it as you advanced. We did it because we were terrified of you; we were in fear of our lives. 25 Now we are in your power; do with us what you think is right." 26 So this is what Joshua did: he protected them and did not allow the people of Israel to kill them. 27 But at the same time he made them slaves, to cut wood and carry water for the people of Israel and for the LORD's altar. To this day they have continued to do this work in the place where the LORD has chosen to be worshiped.

The Amorites Are Defeated

10 Adonizedek, the king of Jerusalem,[e] heard that Joshua had captured and totally destroyed Ai and had killed its king, just as he had done to Jericho and its king. He also heard that the people of Gibeon had made peace with the Israelites and were living among them. 2 The people of Jerusalem were greatly alarmed at this because Gibeon was as large as any of the cities that had a king; it was larger than Ai, and its men were good fighters. 3 So Adonizedek sent the following message to King Hoham of Hebron, King Piram of Jarmuth, King Japhia of Lachish, and to King Debir of Eglon: 4 "Come and help me attack Gibeon, because its people have made peace with Joshua and the Israelites." 5 These five Amorite kings,

[e] JERUSALEM: *At that time it was a Jebusite city.*

the kings of Jerusalem, Hebron, Jarmuth, Lachish, and Eglon, joined forces,
surrounded Gibeon, and attacked it.
6 The men of Gibeon sent word to
Joshua at the camp in Gilgal: "Do not
abandon us, sir! Come at once and help
us! Save us! All the Amorite kings in the
hill country have joined forces and have
attacked us!"
7 So Joshua and his whole army, including the best troops, started out from
Gilgal. 8 The LORD said to Joshua, "Do not
be afraid of them. I have already given
you the victory. Not one of them will be
able to stand against you." 9 All night
Joshua and his army marched from Gilgal to Gibeon, and they made a surprise
attack on the Amorites. 10 The LORD made
the Amorites panic at the sight of Israel's
army. The Israelites slaughtered them at
Gibeon and pursued them down the
mountain pass at Beth Horon, keeping
up the attack as far south as Azekah and
Makkedah. 11 While the Amorites were
running down the pass from the Israelite
army, the LORD made large hailstones fall
down on them all the way to Azekah.
More were killed by the hailstones than
by the Israelites.
12 On the day that the LORD gave the
men of Israel victory over the Amorites,
Joshua spoke to the LORD. In the presence
of the Israelites he said,
"Sun, stand still over Gibeon;
Moon, stop over Aijalon Valley."
13 The sun stood still and the moon did
not move until the nation had conquered
its enemies. This is written in The Book
of Jashar. The sun stood still in the middle of the sky and did not go down for a
whole day. 14 Never before, and never
since, has there been a day like it, when
the LORD obeyed a human being. The
LORD fought on Israel's side!
15 After this, Joshua and his army went
back to the camp at Gilgal.

Joshua Captures the Five Amorite Kings

16 The five Amorite kings, however,
had escaped and were hiding in the cave
at Makkedah. 17 Someone found them,
and Joshua was told where they were
hiding. 18 He said, "Roll some big stones
in front of the entrance to the cave. Place
some guards there, 19 but don't stay there
yourselves. Keep on after the enemy and
attack them from the rear; don't let them
get to their cities! The LORD your God has
given you victory over them." 20 Joshua
and the men of Israel slaughtered them,
although some managed to find safety
inside their city walls and were not
killed. 21 Then all of Joshua's men came
back safe to him at the camp at Makkedah.
No one in the land dared even to speak
against the Israelites.
22 Then Joshua said, "Open the entrance to the cave and bring those five
kings out to me." 23 So the cave was
opened, and the kings of Jerusalem, Hebron, Jarmuth, Lachish, and Eglon were
brought out 24 and taken to Joshua.
Joshua then called all the men of Israel to
him and ordered the officers who had
gone with him to come and put their feet
on the necks of the kings. They did so.
25 Then Joshua said to his officers, "Don't
be afraid or discouraged. Be determined
and confident because this is what the
LORD is going to do to all your enemies."
26 Then Joshua killed the kings and
hanged them on five trees, where their
bodies stayed until evening. 27 At sundown Joshua gave orders, and their bodies were taken down and thrown into the
same cave where they had hidden earlier. Large stones were placed at the entrance to the cave, and they are still
there.

Joshua Captures More Amorite Territory

28 Joshua attacked and captured Makkedah and its king that day. He put
everyone in the city to death; no one was
left alive. He did to the king of Makkedah
what he had done to the king of Jericho.
29 After this, Joshua and his army went
on from Makkedah to Libnah and attacked it. 30 The LORD also gave the Israelites victory over this city and its king.
They spared no one, but killed every person in it. They did to the king what they
had done to the king of Jericho.
31 After this, Joshua and his army went
on from Libnah to Lachish, surrounded it
and attacked it. 32 The LORD gave the Israelites victory over Lachish on the second
day of the battle. Just as they had done at
Libnah, they spared no one, but killed
every person in the city. 33 King Horam of
Gezer came to the aid of Lachish, but

Joshua defeated him and his army and
left none of them alive.
34 Next, Joshua and his army went on
from Lachish to Eglon, surrounded it and
attacked it. 35 They captured it the same
day and put everyone there to death, just
as they had done at Lachish.
36 After this, Joshua and his army went
from Eglon up into the hills to Hebron,
attacked it 37 and captured it. They killed
the king and everyone else in the city as
well as in the nearby towns. Joshua condemned the city to total destruction, just
as he had done to Eglon. No one in it was
left alive.
38 Then Joshua and his army turned
back to Debir and attacked it. 39 He captured it, with its king and all the nearby
towns. They put everyone there to death.
Joshua did to Debir and its king what he
had done to Hebron and to Libnah and
its king.
40 Joshua conquered the whole land.
He defeated the kings of the hill country,
the eastern slopes, and the western foothills, as well as those of the dry country
in the south. He spared no one; everyone
was put to death. This was what the
LORD God of Israel had commanded.
41 Joshua's campaign took him from Kadesh Barnea in the south to Gaza near
the coast, including all the area of Goshen, and as far north as Gibeon.
42 Joshua conquered all these kings and
their territory in one campaign because
the LORD, Israel's God, was fighting for
Israel. 43 After this, Joshua and his army
went back to the camp at Gilgal.

Joshua Defeats Jabin and His Allies

11 When the news of Israel's victories reached King Jabin of Hazor,
he sent word to King Jobab of Madon, to
the kings of Shimron and Achshaph,
2 and to the kings in the hill country in the
north, in the Jordan Valley south of Lake
Galilee, in the foothills, and on the coast
near Dor. 3 He also sent word to the Canaanites on both sides of the Jordan, to
the Amorites, the Hittites, the Perizzites,
and the Jebusites in the hill country, as
well as to the Hivites who lived at the foot
of Mount Hermon in the land of Mizpah.
4 They came with all their soldiers – an
army with as many men as there are
grains of sand on the seashore. They also
had many horses and chariots. 5 All of
these kings joined forces and came together and set up camp at Merom Brook
to fight against Israel.
6 The LORD said to Joshua, "Do not be
afraid of them. By this time tomorrow I
will have killed all of them for Israel. You
are to cripple their horses and burn their
chariots." 7 So Joshua and all his men attacked them by surprise at Merom
Brook. 8 The LORD gave the Israelites victory over them; the Israelites attacked
and pursued them as far north as Misrephoth Maim and Sidon, and as far east as
the valley of Mizpah. The fight continued
until none of the enemy was left alive.
9 Joshua did to them what the LORD had
commanded: he crippled their horses
and burned their chariots.
10 Joshua then turned back, captured
Hazor and killed its king. (At that time
Hazor was the most powerful of all those
kingdoms.) 11 They put everyone there to
death; no one was left alive, and the city
was burned.
12 Joshua captured all these cities and
their kings, putting everyone to death,
just as Moses, the LORD's servant, had
commanded. 13 However, the Israelites
did not burn any of the cities built on
mounds, except Hazor, which Joshua did
burn. 14 The people of Israel took all the
valuables and livestock from these cities
and kept them for themselves. But they
put every person to death; no one was
left alive. 15 The LORD had given his commands to his servant Moses, Moses had
given them to Joshua, and Joshua
obeyed them. He did everything that the
LORD had commanded Moses.

The Territory Taken by Joshua

16 Joshua captured all the land – the
hill country and foothills, both north and
south, all the area of Goshen and the dry
country south of it, as well as the Jordan
Valley. 17-18 The territory extended from
Mount Halak in the south near Edom, as
far as Baalgad in the north, in the valley
of Lebanon south of Mount Hermon.
Joshua was at war with the kings of this
territory for a long time, but he captured
them all and put them to death. 19 The
only city that made peace with the people
of Israel was Gibeon, where some of the
Hivites lived. All the others were conquered in battle. 20 The LORD had made
them determined to fight the Israelites,
so that they would be condemned to total
destruction and all be killed without

mercy. This was what the LORD had commanded Moses.
21 At this time Joshua went and destroyed the race of giants called the Anakim who lived in the hill country—in
Hebron, Debir, Anab, and in all the hill
country of Judah and Israel. Joshua completely destroyed them and their cities.
22 None of the Anakim were left in the
land of Israel; a few, however, were left
in Gaza, Gath, and Ashdod.
23 Joshua captured the whole land, as
the LORD had commanded Moses. Joshua
gave it to the Israelites as their own and
divided it into portions, one for each
tribe.

So the people rested from war.

The Kings Defeated by Moses

12 The people of Israel had already
conquered and occupied the land
east of the Jordan, from the Arnon Valley up the Jordan Valley and as far north
as Mount Hermon. They defeated two
kings. 2 One was Sihon, the Amorite king
who ruled at Heshbon. His kingdom included half of Gilead: from Aroer (on the
edge of the Arnon Valley) and from the
city in[f] the middle of that valley, as far
as the Jabbok River, the border of Ammon; 3 it included the Jordan Valley from
Lake Galilee south to Beth Jeshimoth
(east of the Dead Sea) and on toward the
foot of Mount Pisgah.
4 They also defeated King Og of Bashan, who was one of the last of the
Rephaim; he ruled at Ashtaroth and Edrei. 5 His kingdom included Mount Hermon, Salecah, and all of Bashan as far as
the boundaries of Geshur and Maacah,
as well as half of Gilead, as far as the
territory of King Sihon of Heshbon.
6 These two kings were defeated by
Moses and the people of Israel. Moses,
the LORD's servant, gave their land to the
tribes of Reuben and Gad and to half the
tribe of Manasseh, to be their possession.

The Kings Defeated by Joshua

7 Joshua and the people of Israel defeated all the kings in the territory west
of the Jordan, from Baalgad in the valley
of Lebanon to Mount Halak in the south
near Edom. Joshua divided this land
among the tribes and gave it to them as
a permanent possession. 8 This portion
included the hill country, the western
foothills, the Jordan Valley and its foothills, the eastern slopes, and the dry
country in the south. This land had been
the home of the Hittites, the Amorites,
the Canaanites, the Perizzites, the Hivites, and the Jebusites. 9 The people of
Israel defeated the kings of the following
cities: Jericho, Ai (near Bethel), 10 Jerusalem, Hebron, 11 Jarmuth, Lachish, 12 Eglon, Gezer, 13 Debir, Geder, 14 Hormah,
Arad, 15 Libnah, Adullam, 16 Makkedah,
Bethel, 17 Tappuah, Hepher, 18 Aphek,
Lasharon, 19 Madon, Hazor, 20 Shimron
Meron, Achshaph, 21 Taanach, Megiddo,
22 Kedesh, Jokneam (in Carmel), 23 Dor
(on the coast), Goiim (in Galilee[g]), 24 and
Tirzah—thirty-one kings in all.

The Land Still to Be Taken

13 Joshua was now very old. The
LORD said to him, "You are very
old, but there is still much land to be
taken: 2 all the territory of Philistia and
Geshur, 3 as well as all the territory of the
Avvim to the south. (The land from the
stream Shihor, at the Egyptian border, as
far north as the border of Ekron was considered Canaanite; the kings of the Philistines lived at Gaza, Ashdod, Ashkelon,
Gath, and Ekron.) 4 There is still all the
Canaanite country, and Mearah (which
belonged to the Sidonians), as far as
Aphek, at the Amorite border; 5 the land
of the Gebalites; all of Lebanon to the
east, from Baalgad, which is south of
Mount Hermon, to Hamath Pass. 6 This
includes all the territory of the Sidonians, who live in the hill country between
the Lebanon Mountains and Misrephoth
Maim. I will drive all these peoples out as
the people of Israel advance. You must
divide the land among the Israelites, just
as I have commanded you to do. 7 Now
then, divide this land among the other
nine tribes and half of the tribe of Manasseh, for them to possess as their own."

The Division of the Territory East of the Jordan

8 The tribes of Reuben and Gad and the
other half of the tribe of Manasseh had
already received the land that Moses, the
LORD's servant, had given them; it was on
the east side of the Jordan River. 9 Their

[f] *Probable text (see 13.16; Dt 2.36)* the city in; *Hebrew does not have these words.* [g] *One ancient translation* Galilee; *Hebrew* Gilgal.

territory extended to Aroer (on the edge
of the Arnon Valley) and the city in the
middle of that valley and included all of
the plateau from Medeba to Dibon. 10 It
went as far as the border of Ammon and
included all the cities that had been ruled
by the Amorite king Sihon, who had
ruled at Heshbon. 11 It included Gilead,
the regions of Geshur and Maacah, all of
Mount Hermon, and all of Bashan as far
as Salecah. 12 It included the kingdom of
Og, the last of the Rephaim, who had
ruled at Ashtaroth and Edrei. Moses had
defeated these people and driven them
out. 13 However, the Israelites did not
drive out the people of Geshur and Maacah; they still live in Israel.

14 Moses had given no land to the tribe
of Levi. As the LORD had told Moses, they
were to receive as their possession a
share of the sacrifices burned on the altar to the LORD God of Israel.

The Territory Assigned to Reuben

15 Moses had given a part of the land to
the families of the tribe of Reuben as
their possession. 16 Their territory extended to Aroer (on the edge of the Arnon Valley) and the city in the middle of
that valley and included all the plateau
around Medeba. 17 It included Heshbon
and all the cities on the plateau: Dibon,
Bamoth Baal, Beth Baalmeon, 18 Jahaz,
Kedemoth, Mephaath, 19 Kiriathaim, Sibmah, Zereth Shahar on the hill in the
valley, 20 Bethpeor, the slopes of Mount
Pisgah, and Beth Jeshimoth. 21 It included all the cities of the plateau and the
whole kingdom of the Amorite king Sihon, who had ruled at Heshbon. Moses
defeated him, as well as the rulers of
Midian: Evi, Rekem, Zur, Hur, and Reba.
All of them had ruled the land for King
Sihon. 22 Among those whom the people
of Israel killed was the fortune teller Balaam son of Beor. 23 The Jordan was the
western border of the tribe of Reuben.
These were the cities and towns given to
the families of the tribe of Reuben as
their possession.

The Territory Assigned to Gad

24 Moses had also given a part of the
land to the families of the tribe of Gad as
their possession. 25 Their territory included Jazer and all the cities of Gilead,
half the land of Ammon as far as Aroer,
which is east of Rabbah; 26 their land extended from Heshbon to Ramath Mizpeh
and Betonim, from Mahanaim to the border of Lodebar. 27 In the Jordan Valley it
included Beth Haram, Bethnimrah, Sukkoth, and Zaphon, the rest of the kingdom of King Sihon of Heshbon. Their
western border was the Jordan River as
far north as Lake Galilee. 28 These were
the cities and towns given to the families
of the tribe of Gad as their possession.

The Territory Assigned to East Manasseh

29 Moses had given a part of the land to
the families of half the tribe of Manasseh
as their possession. 30 Their territory extended to Mahanaim and included all of
Bashan—the whole kingdom of Og, the
king of Bashan, as well as all sixty of the
villages of Jair in Bashan. 31 It included
half of Gilead, as well as Ashtaroth and
Edrei, the capital cities of Og's kingdom
in Bashan. All this was given to half the
families descended from Machir son of
Manasseh.

32 This is how Moses divided the land
east of Jericho and the Jordan when he
was in the plains of Moab. 33 But Moses
did not assign any land to the tribe of
Levi. He told them that their possession
was to be a share of the offerings to the
LORD God of Israel.

The Division of the Territory West of the Jordan

14 What follows is an account of
how the land of Canaan west of
the Jordan was divided among the people of Israel. Eleazar the priest, Joshua
son of Nun, and the leaders of the families of the Israelite tribes divided it
among the population. 2 As the LORD had
commanded Moses, the territories of the
nine and one-half tribes west of the Jordan were determined by drawing lots.[h]
3-4 Moses had already assigned the land
east of the Jordan to the other two and
one-half tribes. (The descendants of Joseph were divided into two tribes: Manasseh and Ephraim.) However, Moses
gave the Levites no portion of the territory. Instead, they received cities to live
in, with fields for their cattle and flocks.

[h] DRAWING LOTS: *This was usually done by using specially marked stones to determine God's will.*

5 The people of Israel divided the land as
the LORD had commanded Moses.

Hebron Is Given to Caleb

6 One day some people from the tribe of
Judah came to Joshua at Gilgal. One of
them, Caleb son of Jephunneh the Kenizzite, said to him, "You know what the
LORD said in Kadesh Barnea about you
and me to Moses, the man of God. 7 I was
forty years old when the LORD's servant
Moses sent me from Kadesh Barnea to
spy out this land. I brought an honest
report back to him. 8 The men who went
with me, however, made our people
afraid. But I faithfully obeyed the LORD
my God. 9 Because I did, Moses promised
me that my children and I would certainly receive as our possession the land
which I walked over. 10 But now, look. It
has been forty-five years since the LORD
said that to Moses. That was when Israel
was going through the desert, and the
LORD, as he promised, has kept me alive
ever since. Look at me! I am eighty-five
years old 11 and am just as strong today
as I was when Moses sent me out. I am
still strong enough for war or for anything else. 12 Now then, give me the hill
country that the LORD promised me on
that day when my men and I reported.
We told you then that the race of giants
called the Anakim were there in large
walled cities. Maybe the LORD will be
with me, and I will drive them out, just as
the LORD said."

13 Joshua blessed Caleb son of Jephunneh and gave him the city of Hebron as
his possession. 14 Hebron still belongs to
the descendants of Caleb son of Jephunneh the Kenizzite, because he faithfully
obeyed the LORD, the God of Israel. 15 Before this, Hebron was called the city of
Arba. (Arba had been the greatest of the
Anakim.)

There was now peace in the land.

The Territory Assigned to Judah

15 The families of the tribe of Judah
received a part of the land described as follows:

The land reached south to the south-
ernmost point of the wilderness of Zin, at
the border of Edom. 2 This southern border ran from the south end of the Dead
Sea, 3 went southward from the Akrabbim Pass and on to Zin. It ran south of
Kadesh Barnea, past Hezron and up to
Addar, turned toward Karka, 4 went on to
Azmon, and followed the stream on the
border of Egypt to the Mediterranean
Sea, where the border ended. That was
the southern border of Judah.

5 The eastern border was the Dead Sea,
all the way up to the inlet where the Jordan empties into it.

The northern border began there, 6 extended up to Beth Hoglah, and went
north of the ridge overlooking the Jordan Valley. Then it went up to the Stone
of Bohan (Bohan was a son of Reuben),
7 from Trouble Valley up to Debir, and
then turned north toward Gilgal, which
faces Adummim Pass on the south side
of the valley. It then went on to the
springs of Enshemesh, out to Enrogel,
8 and up through Hinnom Valley on the
south side of the hill where the Jebusite
city of Jerusalem was located. The border then proceeded up to the top of the
hill on the west side of Hinnom Valley, at
the northern end of Rephaim Valley.
9 From there it went to the Springs of
Nephtoah and out to the cities near
Mount Ephron. There it turned toward
Baalah (or Kiriath Jearim), 10 where it
circled west of Baalah toward the hill
country of Edom, went on the north side
of Mount Jearim (or Chesalon), down to
Beth Shemesh, and on past Timnah.
11 The border then went out to the hill
north of Ekron, turned toward Shikke-
ron, past Mount Baalah, and on to Jamnia. It ended at the Mediterranean Sea,
12 which formed the western border.

Within these borders lived the people
of the families of Judah.

Caleb Conquers Hebron and Debir

(Judges 1.11-15)

13 As the LORD commanded Joshua,
part of the territory of Judah was given
to Caleb son of Jephunneh, from the
tribe of Judah. He received Hebron, the
city belonging to Arba, father of Anak.
14 Caleb drove the descendants of Anak
out of the city—the clans of Sheshai,
Ahiman, and Talmai. 15 From there he
went to attack the people living in Debir.
(This city used to be called Kiriath Sepher.) 16 Caleb said, "I will give my
daughter Achsah in marriage to the man
who succeeds in capturing Kiriath Sepher." 17 Othniel, the son of Caleb's
brother Kenaz, captured the city, so Caleb gave him his daughter Achsah in

marriage. 18 On the wedding day Othniel
urged her[i] to ask her father for a field.
She got down from her donkey, and Caleb asked her what she wanted. 19 She
answered, "I want some water holes. The
land you have given me is in the dry
country." So Caleb gave her the upper
and lower springs.

The Cities of Judah

20 This is the land that the families of
the tribe of Judah received as their possession. 21 The cities farthest south that
belonged to them, those that were near
the border of Edom, were Kabzeel, Eder,
Jagur, 22 Kinah, Dimonah, Adadah, 23 Kedesh, Hazor, Ithnan, 24 Ziph, Telem, Bealoth, 25 Hazor Hadattah, Kerioth Hezron
(or Hazor), 26 Amam, Shema, Moladah,
27 Hazar Gaddah, Heshmon, Bethpelet,
28 Hazar Shual, Beersheba, Biziothiah,
29 Baalah, Iim, Ezem, 30 Eltolad, Chesil,
Hormah, 31 Ziklag, Madmannah, San-
sannah, 32 Lebaoth, Shilhim, Ain, and
Rimmon: twenty-nine cities in all, along
with the towns around them.

33 The cities in the foothills were Eshtaol, Zorah, Ashnah, 34 Zanoah, Engannim, Tappuah, Enam, 35 Jarmuth,
Adullam, Socoh, Azekah, 36 Shaaraim,
Adithaim, Gederah, and Gederothaim:
fourteen cities, along with the towns
around them.

37 There were also Zenan, Hadashah,
Migdalgad, 38 Dilean, Mizpah, Joktheel,
39 Lachish, Bozkath, Eglon, 40 Cabbon,
Lahmam, Chitlish, 41 Gederoth, Bethdagon, Naamah, and Makkedah: sixteen
cities, along with the towns around them.

42 There were also Libnah, Ether,
Ashan, 43 Iphtah, Ashnah, Nezib, 44 Keilah, Achzib, and Mareshah: nine cities,
along with the towns around them.

45 There was Ekron with its towns and
villages, 46 and all the cities and towns
near Ashdod, from Ekron to the Mediterranean Sea.

47 There were Ashdod and Gaza, with
their towns and villages, reaching to the
stream on the border of Egypt and the
coast of the Mediterranean Sea.

48 In the hill country there were Shamir, Jattir, Socoh, 49 Dannah, Kiriath Sepher (or Debir), 50 Anab, Eshtemoa,
Anim, 51 Goshen, Holon, and Giloh:
eleven cities, along with the towns
around them.

52 There were Arab, Dumah, Eshan,
53 Janim, Beth Tappuah, Aphekah,
54 Humtah, Hebron, and Zior: nine cities,
along with the towns around them.

55 There were Maon, Carmel, Ziph, Juttah, 56 Jezreel, Jokdeam, Zanoah, 57 Kain,
Gibeah, and Timnah: ten cities, along
with the towns around them.

58 There were Halhul, Bethzur, Gedor,
59 Maarath, Bethanoth, and Eltekon: six
cities, along with the towns around them.

60 There were Kiriath Baal (or Kiriath
Jearim) and Rabbah: two cities, along
with the towns around them.

61 In the desert there were Beth Arabah, Middin, Secacah, 62 Nibshan, Salt
City, and Engedi: six cities, along with
the towns around them.

63 But the people of Judah were not
able to drive out the Jebusites, who lived
in Jerusalem. The Jebusites still live
there with the people of Judah.

The Territory Assigned to Ephraim and West Manasseh

16 The southern boundary of the
land assigned to the descendants
of Joseph started from the Jordan near
Jericho, at a point east of the springs of
Jericho, and went into the desert. It went
from Jericho up into the hill country as
far as Bethel. 2 From Bethel it went to
Luz, passing on to Ataroth Addar, where
the Archites lived. 3 It then went west to
the area of the Japhletites, as far as the
area of Lower Beth Horon. It went on
from there to Gezer and ended at the
Mediterranean Sea.

4 The descendants of Joseph, the tribes
of Ephraim and West Manasseh, received this land as their possession.

Ephraim

5 This was the territory of the Ephraimite families: their border ran from Ataroth Addar eastward to Upper Beth
Horon, 6 and from there to the Mediterranean Sea. Michmethath was on their
north. East of there the border bent toward Taanath Shiloh and went past it on
the east to Janoah. 7 Then it went down
from Janoah to Ataroth and Naarah,
reaching Jericho and ending at the Jordan. 8 The border went west from Tap-

[i] *Probable text (see Jg 1.14)* Othniel urged her; *Hebrew* she urged Othniel.

puah to the stream Kanah and ended at
the Mediterranean Sea. This was the
land given to the families of the tribe of
Ephraim as their possession, 9 along with
some towns and villages that were
within the borders of Manasseh, but
given to the Ephraimites. 10 But they did
not drive out the Canaanites who lived in
Gezer, so the Canaanites have lived
among the Ephraimites to this day, but
they have been forced to work as slaves.

West Manasseh

17 A part of the land west of the Jordan was assigned to some of the
families descended from Joseph's older
son Manasseh. Machir, the father of Gilead, was Manasseh's oldest son and a
military hero, so Gilead and Bashan, east
of the Jordan, were assigned to him.
2 Land west of the Jordan was assigned
to the rest of the families of Manasseh:
Abiezer, Helek, Asriel, Shechem, Hepher, and Shemida. These were male
descendants of Manasseh son of Joseph,
and they were heads of families. 3 Zelophehad, son of Hepher, son of Gilead,
son of Machir, son of Manasseh, did not
have any sons, but only daughters. Their
names were Mahlah, Noah, Hoglah, Milcah, and Tirzah. 4 They went to Eleazar
the priest and to Joshua son of Nun and
to the leaders, and said, "The LORD commanded Moses to give us, as well as our
male relatives, a part of the land to possess." So, as the LORD had commanded,
they were given land along with their
male relatives. 5 This is why Manasseh
received ten shares in addition to Gilead
and Bashan on the east side of the Jordan, 6 since his female descendants as
well as his male descendants were assigned land. The land of Gilead was assigned to the rest of the descendants of
Manasseh.

7 The territory of Manasseh reached
from Asher to Michmethath, east of Shechem. The border then went south to include the people of Entappuah. 8 The
land around Tappuah belonged to Manasseh, but the town of Tappuah, on the
border, belonged to the descendants of
Ephraim. 9 The border then went down to
the stream Kanah. The cities south of the
stream belonged to Ephraim, even
though they were in the territory of Manasseh. The border of Manasseh proceeded along the north side of the stream
and ended at the Mediterranean Sea.
10 Ephraim was to the south, and Manasseh was to the north, with the Mediterranean Sea as their western border. Asher
was to the northwest, and Issachar to the
northeast. 11 Within the territories of Issachar and Asher, Manasseh possessed
Beth Shan and Ibleam, along with their
surrounding towns, as well as Dor (the
one on the coast),[j] Endor, Taanach, Megiddo, and their surrounding towns.
12 The people of Manasseh, however,
were not able to drive out the people living in those cities, so the Canaanites continued to live there. 13 Even when the
Israelites became stronger, they did not
drive out all the Canaanites, but they did
force them to work for them.

Ephraim and West Manasseh Request More Land

14 The descendants of Joseph said to
Joshua, "Why have you given us only
one part of the land to possess as our
own? There are very many of us because
the LORD has blessed us."

15 Joshua answered, "If there are so
many of you and the hill country of
Ephraim is too small for you, then go into
the forests and clear ground for yourselves in the land of the Perizzites and
the Rephaim."

16 They replied, "The hill country is not
big enough for us, but the Canaanites in
the plains have iron chariots, both those
who live in Beth Shan and its surrounding towns and those who live in Jezreel
Valley."

17 Joshua said to the tribes of Ephraim
and West Manasseh, "There are indeed
many of you, and you are very powerful.
You shall have more than one share.
18 The hill country will be yours. Even
though it is a forest, you will clear it and
take possession of it from one end to the
other. As for the Canaanites, you will
drive them out, even though they do have
iron chariots and are a strong people."

The Division of the Rest of the Land

18 After they had conquered the
land, the entire community of Israel assembled at Shiloh and set up the
Tent of the LORD's presence. 2 There were

[j] *Probable text* Dor (the one on the coast); *Hebrew unclear.*

still seven tribes of the people of Israel
who had not yet been assigned their
share of the land. 3 So Joshua said to the
people of Israel, "How long are you going
to wait before you go in and take the land
that the LORD, the God of your ancestors,
has given you? 4 Let me have three men
from each tribe. I will send them out over
the whole country to map out the territory that they would like to have as their
possession. Then they are to come back
to me. 5 The land will be divided among
them in seven parts; Judah will stay in its
territory in the south, and Joseph in its
territory in the north. 6 Write down a description of these seven divisions and
bring it to me. Then I will draw lots[k] to
consult the LORD our God for you. 7 The
Levites, however, will not receive a share
of the land with the rest of you, because
their share is to serve as the LORD's
priests. And of course, the tribes of Gad,
Reuben, and East Manasseh have already received their land east of the Jordan, which Moses, the LORD's servant,
gave to them."
8 The men went on their way to map
out the land after Joshua had given them
these instructions: "Go all over the land
and map it out, and come back to me.
And then here in Shiloh I will consult the
LORD for you by drawing lots." 9 So the
men went all over the land and set down
in writing how they divided it into seven
parts, making a list of the towns. Then
they went back to Joshua in the camp at
Shiloh. 10 Joshua drew lots to consult the
LORD for them, and assigned each of the
remaining tribes of Israel a certain part
of the land.

The Territory Assigned to Benjamin

11 The territory belonging to the families of the tribe of Benjamin was the first
to be assigned. Their land lay between
the tribes of Judah and Joseph. 12 On the
north their border began at the Jordan
and then went up the slope north of Jericho and westward through the hill country as far as the desert of Bethaven. 13 The
border then went to the slope on the
south side of Luz (also called Bethel),
then down to Ataroth Addar, on the
mountain south of Lower Beth Horon.
14 The border then went in another direction, turning south from the western side
of this mountain and going to Kiriath
Baal (or Kiriath Jearim), which belongs
to the tribe of Judah. This was the western border. 15 The southern border
started on the edge of Kiriath Jearim and
went[l] to the Springs of Nephtoah. 16 It
then went down to the foot of the mountain that overlooks Hinnom Valley, at the
north end of Rephaim Valley. It then
went south through Hinnom Valley,
south of the Jebusite ridge, toward Enrogel. 17 It then turned north to Enshemesh
and then on to Geliloth, opposite Adummim Pass. The border then went down to
the Stone of Bohan (Bohan was a son of
Reuben) 18 and passed north of the ridge
overlooking the Jordan Valley. It then
went down into the valley, 19 passing
north of the ridge of Beth Hoglah, and
ended at the northern inlet on the Dead
Sea, where the Jordan River empties into
it. This was the southern border. 20 The
Jordan was the eastern border. These
were the borders of the land which the
families of the tribe of Benjamin received
as their possession.
21 The cities belonging to the families
of the tribe of Benjamin were Jericho,
Beth Hoglah, Emek Keziz, 22 Beth Arabah, Zemaraim, Bethel, 23 Avvim, Parah,
Ophrah, 24 Chepharammoni, Ophni, and
Geba: twelve cities, along with the towns
around them. 25 There were also Gibeon,
Ramah, Beeroth, 26 Mizpah, Chephirah,
Mozah, 27 Rekem, Irpeel, Taralah, 28 Zela,
Haeleph, Jebus (or Jerusalem), Gibeah,
and Kiriath Jearim: fourteen cities, along
with the towns around them. This is the
land which the families of the tribe of
Benjamin received as their possession.

The Territory Assigned to Simeon

19 The second assignment made
was for the families of the tribe of
Simeon. Its territory extended into the
land assigned to the tribe of Judah. 2 It
included Beersheba, Sheba, Moladah,
3 Hazar Shual, Balah, Ezem, 4 Eltolad,
Bethul, Hormah, 5 Ziklag, Beth Marca-
both, Hazar Susah, 6 Beth Lebaoth, and
Sharuhen: thirteen cities, along with the
towns around them.
7 There were also Ain, Rimmon, Ether,
and Ashan: four cities, along with the
towns around them. 8 This included all
the towns around these cities as far as

[k] DRAW LOTS: *See 14.2.* [l] *Probable text* and went; *Hebrew* and went westward.

Baalath Beer (or Ramah), in the south.
This was the land which the families of
the tribe of Simeon received as their possession. 9 Since Judah's assignment was
larger than was needed, part of its territory was given to the tribe of Simeon.

The Territory Assigned to Zebulun

10 The third assignment made was for
the families of the tribe of Zebulun. The
land which they received reached as far
as Sarid. 11 From there the border went
west to Mareal, touching Dabbesheth
and the stream east of Jokneam. 12 On the
other side of Sarid it went east to the
border of Chisloth Tabor, then to Daberath and up to Japhia. 13 It continued east
from there to Gath Hepher and Ethkazin,
turning in the direction of Neah on the
way to Rimmon. 14 On the north the border turned toward Hannathon, ending at
Iphtahel Valley. 15 It included Kattath,
Nahalal, Shimron, Idalah, and Bethlehem: twelve cities, along with the towns
around them. 16 These cities and their
towns were in the land which the families of the tribe of Zebulun received as
their possession.

The Territory Assigned to Issachar

17 The fourth assignment made was for
the families of the tribe of Issachar. 18 Its
area included Jezreel, Chesulloth, Shunem, 19 Hapharaim, Shion, Anaharath,
20 Rabbith, Kishion, Ebez, 21 Remeth, Engannim, Enhaddah, and Bethpazzez.
22 The border also touched Tabor, Shaha-
zumah, and Beth Shemesh, ending at the
Jordan. It included sixteen cities along
with the towns around them. 23 These cities and their towns were in the land
which the families of the tribe of Issachar
received as their possession.

The Territory Assigned to Asher

24 The fifth assignment made was for
the families of the tribe of Asher. 25 Its
area included Helkath, Hali, Beten, Achshaph, 26 Allam Melech, Amad, and Mishal. On the west it touched Carmel and
Shihor Libnath. 27 As it turned east, the
border went to Bethdagon, touching
Zebulun and Iphtahel Valley on the way
north to Bethemek and Neiel. It continued north to Cabul, 28 Ebron, Rehob,
Hammon, and Kanah, as far as Sidon.
29 The border then turned to Ramah,
reaching the fortified city of Tyre; then it
turned to Hosah and ended at the Mediterranean Sea. It included Mahalab,
Achzib, 30 Ummah, Aphek, and Rehob:
twenty-two cities, along with the towns
around them. 31 These cities and their
towns were in the land which the families of the tribe of Asher received as their
possession.

The Territory Assigned to Naphtali

32 The sixth assignment made was for
the families of the tribe of Naphtali. 33 Its
border went from Heleph to the oak in
Zaanannim, on to Adaminekeb and to
Jamnia, as far as Lakkum, and ended at
the Jordan. 34 There the border turned
west to Aznoth Tabor, from there to Huk-
kok, touching Zebulun on the south,
Asher on the west, and the Jordan[m] on
the east. 35 The fortified cities were Zid-
dim, Zer, Hammath, Rakkath, Chinne-
reth, 36 Adamah, Ramah, Hazor,
37 Kedesh, Edrei, Enhazor, 38 Yiron, Mig-
dalel, Horem, Bethanath, and Beth Shemesh: nineteen cities, along with the
towns around them. 39 These cities and
their towns were in the land which the
families of the tribe of Naphtali received
as their possession.

The Territory Assigned to Dan

40 The seventh assignment made was
for the families of the tribe of Dan. 41 Its
area included Zorah, Eshtaol, Irshe-
mesh, 42 Shaalbim, Aijalon, Ithlah,
43 Elon, Timnah, Ekron, 44 Eltekeh, Gibbethon, Baalath, 45 Jehud, Beneberak,
Gathrimmon, 46 Mejarkon, and Rakkon,
as well as the territory around Joppa.
47 When the people of Dan lost their land,
they went to Laish and attacked it. They
captured it, killed its people, and claimed
it for themselves. They settled there and
changed the name of the city from Laish
to Dan, naming it after their ancestor
Dan. 48 These cities and their towns were
in the land which the families of the tribe
of Dan received as their possession.

The Final Assignment of the Land

49 When the people of Israel finished
dividing up the land, they gave Joshua
son of Nun a part of the land as his own.
50 As the LORD had commanded, they

[m] *One ancient translation* the Jordan; *Hebrew* Judah at the Jordan.

gave him the city he asked for: Timnath
Serah, in the hill country of Ephraim. He
rebuilt the city and settled there.
51 Eleazar the priest, Joshua son of
Nun, and the leaders of the families of
the tribes of Israel assigned these parts
of the land by drawing lots[n] to consult
the LORD at Shiloh, at the entrance of the
Tent of the LORD's presence. In this way
they finished dividing the land.

The Cities of Refuge

20 Then the LORD told Joshua 2 to say
to the people of Israel, "Choose
the cities of refuge that I had Moses tell
you about. 3 If any of you accidentally
kills someone, you can go there and escape the one who is looking for revenge.
4 You can run away to one of these cities,
go to the place of judgment at the entrance to the city, and explain to the leaders what happened. Then they will let
you into the city and give you a place to
live in, so that you can stay there. 5 If the
one looking for revenge follows you
there, the people of the city must not
hand you over to that one. They must
protect you because you killed the person accidentally and not out of anger.
6 You may stay in the city until you have
received a public trial and until the death
of the man who is then the High Priest.
Then you may go back home to your own
town, from which you had run away."
7 So, on the west side of the Jordan they
set aside Kedesh in Galilee, in the hill
country of Naphtali; Shechem, in the hill
country of Ephraim; and Hebron, in the
hill country of Judah. 8 East of the Jordan, on the desert plateau east of Jericho,
they chose Bezer in the territory of Reuben; Ramoth in Gilead, in the territory of
Gad; and Golan in Bashan, in the territory of Manasseh. 9 These were the cities
of refuge chosen for all the people of Israel and for any foreigner living among
them. Any who killed a person accidentally could find protection there from the
one looking for revenge; they could not
be killed unless they had first received a
public trial.

The Cities of the Levites

21 The leaders of the Levite families
went to Eleazar the priest,
Joshua son of Nun, and to the heads of
the families of all the tribes of Israel.
2 There at Shiloh in the land of Canaan
they said to them, "The LORD commanded
through Moses that we were to be given
cities to live in, as well as pasture land
around them for our livestock." 3 So in
accordance with the LORD's command
the people of Israel gave the Levites certain cities and pasture lands out of their
own territories.
4 The families of the Levite clan of Kohath were the first to be assigned cities.
The families who were descended from
Aaron the priest were assigned thirteen
cities from the territories of Judah, Simeon, and Benjamin. 5 The rest of the clan
of Kohath was assigned ten cities from
the territories of Ephraim, Dan, and
West Manasseh.
6 The clan of Gershon was assigned
thirteen cities from the territories of
Issachar, Asher, Naphtali, and East
Manasseh.
7 The families of the clan of Merari
were assigned twelve cities from the territories of Reuben, Gad, and Zebulun.
8 By drawing lots,[n] the people of Israel
assigned these cities and their pasture
lands to the Levites, as the LORD had commanded through Moses.
9 These are the names of the cities from
the territories of Judah and Simeon
which were given 10 to the descendants of
Aaron who were of the clan of Kohath,
which was descended from Levi. Their
assignment was the first to be made.
11 They were given the city of Arba (Arba
was Anak's father), now called Hebron,
in the hill country of Judah, along with
the pasture land surrounding it. 12 However, the fields of the city, as well as its
towns, had already been given to Caleb
son of Jephunneh as his possession.
13 In addition to Hebron (one of the cities of refuge), the following cities were
assigned to the descendants of Aaron the
priest: Libnah, 14 Jattir, Eshtemoa, 15 Holon, Debir, 16 Ain, Juttah, and Beth Shemesh, with their pasture lands: nine
cities from the tribes of Judah and Simeon. 17 From the territory of Benjamin
they were given four cities: Gibeon,
Geba, 18 Anathoth, and Almon, with their
pasture lands. 19 Thirteen cities in all,
with their pasture lands, were given to
the priests, the descendants of Aaron.

[n] DRAWING LOTS: *See 14.2.*

20 The other families of the Levite clan of Kohath were assigned some cities from the territory of Ephraim. 21 They were given four cities: Shechem and its pasture lands in the hill country of Ephraim (one of the cities of refuge), Gezer, 22 Kibzaim, and Beth Horon, with their pasture lands. 23 From the territory of Dan they were given four cities: Eltekeh, Gibbethon, 24 Aijalon, and Gathrimmon, with their pasture lands. 25 From the territory of West Manasseh they were given two cities: Taanach and Gathrimmon, with their pasture lands. 26 These families of the clan of Kohath received ten cities in all, with their pasture lands.

27 Another group of Levites, the clan of Gershon, received from the territory of East Manasseh two cities: Golan in Bashan (one of the cities of refuge) and Beeshterah, with their pasture lands. 28 From the territory of Issachar they received four cities: Kishion, Daberath, 29 Jarmuth, and Engannim, with their pasture lands. 30 From the territory of Asher they received four cities: Mishal, Abdon, 31 Helkath, and Rehob, with their pasture lands. 32 From the territory of Naphtali they received three cities: Kedesh in Galilee, with its pasture lands (one of the cities of refuge), Hammoth Dor, and Kartan, with their pasture lands. 33 The various families of the clan of Gershon received a total of thirteen cities with their pasture lands.

34 The rest of the Levites, the clan of Merari, received from the territory of Zebulun four cities: Jokneam, Kartah, 35 Dimnah, and Nahalal, with their pasture lands. 36 From the territory of Reuben they received four cities: Bezer, Jahaz, 37 Kedemoth, and Mephaath, with their pasture lands. 38 From the tribe of Gad they received four cities: Ramoth in Gilead, with its pasture lands (one of the cities of refuge), Mahanaim, 39 Heshbon, and Jazer, with their pasture lands. 40 So the clan of Merari was assigned a total of twelve cities.

41-42 From the land that the people of Israel possessed, a total of forty-eight cities, with the pasture lands around them, was given to the Levites.

Israel Takes Possession of the Land

43 So the LORD gave to Israel all the land that he had solemnly promised their ancestors he would give them. When they had taken possession of it, they settled down there. 44 The LORD gave them peace throughout the land, just as he had promised their ancestors. Not one of all their enemies had been able to stand against them, because the LORD gave the Israelites the victory over all their enemies. 45 The LORD kept every one of the promises that he had made to the people of Israel.

Joshua Sends the Eastern Tribes Home

22 Then Joshua called together the people of the tribes of Reuben, Gad, and East Manasseh. 2 He said to them, "You have done everything that Moses the LORD's servant ordered you to do, and you have obeyed all my commands. 3 All this time you have never once deserted the other Israelites. You have been careful to obey the commands of the LORD your God. 4 Now, as he promised, the LORD your God has given the other Israelites peace. So go back home to the land which you claimed for your own, the land on the east side of the Jordan, that Moses, the LORD's servant, gave you. 5 Make sure you obey the law that Moses commanded you: love the LORD your God, do his will, obey his commandments, be faithful to him, and serve him with all your heart and soul." 6-8 Joshua sent them home with his blessing and with these words: "You are going back home very rich, with a lot of livestock, silver, gold, bronze, iron, and many clothes. Share with your fellow tribesmen what you took from your enemies." Then they left for home.

Moses had given land east of the Jordan to one half of the tribe of Manasseh, but to the other half Joshua had given land west of the Jordan, along with the other tribes.

9 So the people of the tribes of Reuben, Gad, and East Manasseh went back home. They left the rest of the people of Israel at Shiloh in the land of Canaan and started out for their own land, the land of Gilead, which they had taken as the LORD had commanded them through Moses.

The Altar by the Jordan

10 When the tribes of Reuben, Gad, and East Manasseh arrived at Geliloth, still

on the west side[o] of the Jordan, they
built a large, impressive altar there by
the river. 11 The rest of the people of Israel were told, "Listen! The people of the
tribes of Reuben, Gad, and East Manasseh have built an altar at Geliloth, on our
side of the Jordan!" 12 When the people of
Israel heard this, the whole community
came together at Shiloh to go to war
against the eastern tribes.

13 Then the people of Israel sent Phinehas, the son of Eleazar the priest, to the
people of the tribes of Reuben, Gad, and
East Manasseh in the land of Gilead.
14 Ten leading men went with Phinehas,
one from each of the western tribes and
each one the head of a family among the
clans. 15 They came to the land of Gilead,
to the people of Reuben, Gad, and East
Manasseh, 16 and speaking for the whole
community of the LORD, they said to
them, "Why have you done this evil thing
against the God of Israel? You have rebelled against the LORD by building this
altar for yourselves! You are no longer
following him! 17 Remember our sin at
Peor, when the LORD punished his own
people with an epidemic? We are still
suffering because of that. Wasn't that sin
enough? 18 Are you going to refuse to follow him now? If you rebel against the
LORD today, he will be angry with everyone in Israel tomorrow. 19 Now then, if
your land is not fit to worship in, come
over into the LORD's land, where his Tent
is. Claim some land among us. But don't
rebel against the LORD or make rebels out
of us by building an altar in addition to
the altar of the LORD our God. 20 Remember how Achan son of Zerah refused to
obey the command about the things condemned to destruction; the whole community of Israel was punished for that.
Achan was not the only one who died
because of his sin."

21 The people of the tribes of Reuben,
Gad, and East Manasseh answered the
heads of the families of the western
tribes: 22 "The Mighty One is God! He is
the LORD! The Mighty One is God! He is
the LORD! He knows why we did this, and
we want you to know too! If we rebelled
and did not keep faith with the LORD, do
not let us live any longer! 23 If we disobeyed the LORD and built our own altar
to burn sacrifices on or to use for grain
offerings or fellowship offerings, let the
LORD himself punish us. 24 No! We did it
because we were afraid that in the future
your descendants would say to ours,
'What do you have to do with the LORD,
the God of Israel? 25 He made the Jordan
a boundary between us and you people
of Reuben and Gad. You have nothing to
do with the LORD.' Then your descendants might make our descendants stop
worshiping the LORD. 26 So we built an
altar, not to burn sacrifices or make offerings, 27 but instead, as a sign for our
people and yours, and for the generations after us, that we do indeed worship
the LORD before his sacred Tent with our
offerings to be burned and with sacrifices and fellowship offerings. This was
to keep your descendants from saying
that ours have nothing to do with the
LORD. 28 It was our idea that, if this should
ever happen, our descendants could say,
'Look! Our ancestors made an altar just
like the LORD's altar. It was not for burning offerings or for sacrifice, but as a sign
for our people and yours.' 29 We would
certainly not rebel against the LORD or
stop following him now by building an
altar to burn offerings on or for grain
offerings or sacrifices. We would not
build any other altar than the altar of the
LORD our God that stands in front of the
Tent of his presence."

30 Phinehas the priest and the ten leading men of the community who were
with him, the heads of families of the
western tribes, heard what the people of
the tribes of Reuben, Gad, and East Manasseh had to say, and they were satisfied. 31 Phinehas, the son of Eleazar the
priest, said to them, "Now we know that
the LORD is with us. You have not rebelled
against him, and so you have saved the
people of Israel from the LORD's punishment."

32 Then Phinehas and the leaders left
the people of Reuben and Gad in the land
of Gilead and went back to Canaan, to
the people of Israel, and reported to
them. 33 The Israelites were satisfied and
praised God. They no longer talked
about going to war to devastate the land
where the people of Reuben and Gad had
settled.

34 The people of Reuben and Gad said,
"This altar is a witness to all of us that the

[o] still on the west side; *or* on the east side.

LORD is God." And so they named it
"Witness."

Joshua's Farewell Address

23 Much later the LORD gave Israel
security from their enemies
around them. By that time Joshua was
very old, 2 so he called all Israel, the elders, leaders, judges, and officers of the
people, and said, "I am very old now.
3 You have seen everything that the LORD
your God has done to all these nations
because of you. The LORD your God has
been fighting for you. 4 I have assigned
as the possession of your tribes the land
of the nations that are still left, as well as
of all the nations that I have already conquered, from the Jordan River in the east
to the Mediterranean Sea in the west.
5 The LORD your God will make them retreat from you, and he will drive them
away as you advance. You shall have
their land, as the LORD your God has
promised you. 6 So be careful to obey and
do everything that is written in the book
of the Law of Moses. Do not neglect any
part of it, 7 and then you will not associate with these peoples left among you or
speak the names of their gods or use
those names in taking vows or worship
those gods or bow down to them. 8 Instead, be faithful to the LORD, as you have
been till now. 9 The LORD has driven great
and powerful nations out as you advanced, and no one has ever been able to
stand against you. 10 Any one of you can
make a thousand men run away, because
the LORD your God is fighting for you, just
as he promised. 11 Be careful, then, to
love the LORD your God. 12 If you are disloyal and join with the nations that are
still left among you and intermarry with
them, 13 you may be sure that the LORD
your God will no longer drive these nations out as you advance. Rather, they
will be as dangerous for you as a trap or
a pit and as painful as a whip on your
back or thorns in your eyes. And this will
last until none of you are left in this good
land which the LORD your God has
given you.

14 "Now my time has come to die. Every
one of you knows in his heart and soul
that the LORD your God has given you all
the good things that he promised. Every
promise he made has been kept; not one
has failed. 15 But just as he kept every
promise that he made to you, so he will
carry out every threat. 16 If you do not
keep the covenant which the LORD your
God commanded you to keep and if you
serve and worship other gods, then in his
anger he will punish you, and soon none
of you will be left in this good land that
he has given you."

Joshua Speaks to the People at Shechem

24 Joshua gathered all the tribes of
Israel together at Shechem. He
called the elders, the leaders, the judges,
and the officers of Israel, and they came
into the presence of God. 2 Joshua said to
all the people, "This is what the LORD, the
God of Israel, has to say: 'Long ago your
ancestors lived on the other side of the
Euphrates River and worshiped other
gods. One of those ancestors was Terah,
the father of Abraham and Nahor. 3 Then
I took Abraham, your ancestor, from the
land across the Euphrates and led him
through the whole land of Canaan. I gave
him many descendants. I gave him Isaac,
4 and to Isaac I gave Jacob and Esau. I
gave Esau the hill country of Edom as his
possession, but your ancestor Jacob and
his children went down to Egypt. 5 Later
I sent Moses and Aaron, and I brought
great trouble on Egypt. But I led you out;
6 I brought your ancestors out of Egypt,
and the Egyptians pursued them with
chariots and cavalry. But when your ancestors got to the Red Sea 7 they cried out
to me for help, and I put darkness between them and the Egyptians. I made
the sea come rolling over the Egyptians
and drown them. You know what I did to
Egypt.

" 'You lived in the desert a long time.
8 Then I brought you to the land of the
Amorites, who lived on the east side of
the Jordan. They fought you, but I gave
you victory over them. You took their
land, and I destroyed them as you advanced. 9 Then the king of Moab, Balak
son of Zippor, fought against you. He
sent word to Balaam son of Beor and
asked him to put a curse on you. 10 But I
would not listen to Balaam, so he blessed
you, and in this way I rescued you from
Balak. 11 You crossed the Jordan and
came to Jericho. The men of Jericho
fought you, as did the Amorites, the Perizzites, the Canaanites, the Hittites, the

Girgashites, the Hivites, and the Jebusites. But I gave you victory over them
all. 12 As you advanced, I threw them into
panic in order to drive out the two Amorite kings. Your swords and bows had
nothing to do with it. 13 I gave you a land
that you had never worked and cities
that you had not built. Now you are living there and eating grapes from vines
that you did not plant, and olives from
trees that you did not plant.'

14 "Now then," Joshua continued,
"honor the LORD and serve him sincerely
and faithfully. Get rid of the gods which
your ancestors used to worship in Mesopotamia and in Egypt, and serve only the
LORD. 15 If you are not willing to serve
him, decide today whom you will serve,
the gods your ancestors worshiped in
Mesopotamia or the gods of the Amorites, in whose land you are now living.
As for my family and me, we will serve
the LORD."

16 The people replied, "We would never
leave the LORD to serve other gods! 17 The
LORD our God brought our fathers and us
out of slavery in Egypt, and we saw the
miracles that he performed. He kept us
safe wherever we went among all the nations through which we passed. 18 As we
advanced into this land, the LORD drove
out all the Amorites who lived here. So
we also will serve the LORD; he is
our God."

19 Joshua said to the people, "But you
may not be able to serve the LORD. He is
a holy God and will not forgive your sins.
He will tolerate no rivals, 20 and if you
leave him to serve foreign gods, he will
turn against you and punish you. He will
destroy you, even though he was good to
you before."

21 The people said to Joshua, "No! We
will serve the LORD."

22 Joshua told them, "You are your own
witnesses to the fact that you have chosen to serve the LORD."

"Yes," they said, "we are witnesses."

23 "Then get rid of those foreign gods
that you have," he demanded, "and
pledge your loyalty to the LORD, the God
of Israel."

24 The people then said to Joshua, "We
will serve the LORD our God. We will obey
his commands."

25 So Joshua made a covenant for [p] the
people that day, and there at Shechem he
gave them laws and rules to follow.
26 Joshua wrote these commands in the
book of the Law of God. Then he took a
large stone and set it up under the oak
tree in the LORD's sanctuary. 27 He said to
all the people, "This stone will be our
witness. It has heard all the words that
the LORD has spoken to us. So it will be a
witness against you, to keep you from
rebelling against your God." 28 Then
Joshua sent the people away, and everyone returned to their own part of the
land.

Joshua and Eleazar Die

29 After that, the LORD's servant Joshua
son of Nun died at the age of a hundred
and ten. 30 They buried him on his own
land at Timnath Serah in the hill country
of Ephraim north of Mount Gaash.

31 As long as Joshua lived, the people of
Israel served the LORD, and after his
death they continued to do so as long as
those leaders were alive who had seen
for themselves everything that the LORD
had done for Israel.

32 The body of Joseph, which the people of Israel had brought from Egypt,
was buried at Shechem, in the piece of
land that Jacob had bought from the sons
of Hamor, the father of Shechem, for a
hundred pieces of silver. This land was
inherited by Joseph's descendants.

33 Eleazar son of Aaron died and was
buried at Gibeah, the town in the hill
country of Ephraim which had been
given to his son Phinehas.

[p] for; *or* with.

The Book of
JUDGES

Introduction

The Book of Judges *is composed of stories from the lawless period of Israel's history between the invasion of Canaan and the establishment of the monarchy. These stories are about the exploits of national heroes called "judges," most of whom were military leaders rather than judges in the legal sense of the word. One of the better known of them is Samson, whose deeds are recorded in chapters 13–16.*

The great lesson of the book is that Israel's survival depended on loyalty to God, while disloyalty always led to disaster. But there was more than this: even when the nation was disloyal to God and disaster came, God was always ready to save his people when they repented and turned to him again.

Outline of Contents

The Tribes of Judah and Simeon Capture Adonibezek

1 After Joshua's death the people of
Israel asked the LORD, "Which of our
tribes should be the first to go and attack
the Canaanites?"
2 The LORD answered, "The tribe of Judah will go first. I am giving them control
of the land."
3 The people of Judah said to the people of Simeon, "Go with us into the territory assigned to us, and we will fight the
Canaanites together. Then we will go
with you into the territory assigned to
you." So the tribes of Simeon 4 and Judah
went into battle together. The LORD gave
them victory over the Canaanites and the
Perizzites, and they defeated ten thousand men at Bezek. 5 They found Adonibezek there and fought him. 6 He ran
away, but they chased him, caught him,
and cut off his thumbs and big toes.
7 Adonibezek said, "Seventy kings with
their thumbs and big toes cut off have
picked up scraps under my table. God
has now done to me what I did to them."
He was taken to Jerusalem, where he
died.

The Tribe of Judah Conquers Jerusalem and Hebron

8 The people of Judah attacked Jerusalem and captured it. They killed its people and set fire to the city. 9 After this
they went on to fight the Canaanites who
lived in the hill country, in the foothills,
and in the dry country to the south.
10 They marched against the Canaanites
living in the city of Hebron, which used
to be called Kiriath Arba. There they defeated the clans of Sheshai, Ahiman, and
Talmai.

Othniel Conquers the City of Debir

(Joshua 15.13-19)

11 From there the men of Judah
marched against the city of Debir, at that
time called Kiriath Sepher. 12 One of
them, called Caleb, said, "I will give my
daughter Achsah in marriage to the man
who succeeds in capturing Kiriath Sepher." 13 Othniel, the son of Caleb's
younger brother Kenaz, captured the
city, so Caleb gave him his daughter
Achsah in marriage. 14 On the wedding
day Othniel urged her[a] to ask her father
for a field. She got down from her donkey, and Caleb asked her what she
wanted. 15 She answered, "I want some
water holes. The land you have given me
is in the dry country." So Caleb gave her
the upper and lower springs.

The Victories of the Tribes of Judah and Benjamin

16 The descendants of Moses' father-in-
law, the Kenite, went on with the people

[a] *Some ancient translations* Othniel urged her; *Hebrew* she urged Othniel.

of Judah from Jericho, the city of palm
trees, into the barren country south of
Arad in Judah. There they settled among
the Amalekites.[b] 17 The people of Judah
went with the people of Simeon, and together they defeated the Canaanites who
lived in the city of Zephath. They put a
curse on the city, destroyed it, and
named it Hormah.[c] 18-19 The LORD helped
the people of Judah, and they took possession of the hill country. But they did
not capture[d] Gaza, Ashkelon, or Ekron,
with their surrounding territories. These
people living along the coast had iron
chariots, and so the people of Judah were
not able to drive them out. 20 As Moses
had commanded, Hebron was given to
Caleb, who drove out of the city the three
clans descended from Anak. 21 But the
people of the tribe of Benjamin did not
drive out the Jebusites living in Jerusalem, and the Jebusites have continued to
live there with the people of Benjamin
ever since.

The Tribes of Ephraim and Manasseh Conquer Bethel

22-23 The tribes of Ephraim and Manasseh went to attack the city of Bethel, at
that time called Luz. The LORD helped
them. They sent spies to the city, 24 who
saw a man leaving and said to him,
"Show us how to get into the city, and we
won't hurt you." 25 So he showed them,
and the people of Ephraim and Manasseh killed everyone in the city, except
this man and his family. 26 He later went
to the land of the Hittites, built a city
there, and named it Luz, which is still its
name.

People Who Were Not Driven Out by the Israelites

27 The tribe of Manasseh did not drive
out the people living in the cities of Beth
Shan, Taanach, Dor, Ibleam, Megiddo,
and the nearby towns; the Canaanites
continued to live there. 28 When the Israelites became stronger, they forced the
Canaanites to work for them, but still
they did not drive them all out.
29 The tribe of Ephraim did not drive
out the Canaanites living in the city of
Gezer, and so the Canaanites continued
to live there with them.
30 The tribe of Zebulun did not drive
out the people living in the cities of Kit-
ron and Nahalal, and so the Canaanites
continued to live there with them and
were forced to work for them.
31 The tribe of Asher did not drive out
the people living in the cities of Acco,
Sidon, Ahlab, Achzib, Helbah, Aphek,
and Rehob. 32 The people of Asher lived
with the local Canaanites, since they had
not been driven out.
33 The tribe of Naphtali did not drive
out the people living in the cities of Beth
Shemesh and Bethanath. The people of
Naphtali lived with the local Canaanites,
but forced them to work for them.
34 The Amorites forced the people of
the tribe of Dan into the hill country and
did not let them come down to the plain.
35 The Amorites continued to live at Aijalon, Shaalbim, and Mount Heres, but the
tribes of Ephraim and Manasseh kept
them under their rule and forced them to
work for them.
36 North of Sela, the Edomite[e] border
ran through Akrabbim Pass.

The Angel of the LORD at Bochim

2 The angel of the LORD went from Gilgal to Bochim and said to the Israelites, "I took you out of Egypt and brought
you to the land that I promised to your
ancestors. I said, 'I will never break my
covenant with you. 2 You must not make
any covenant with the people who live in
this land. You must tear down their altars.' But you have not done what I told
you. You have done just the opposite!
3 So I tell you now that I will not drive
these people out as you advance. They
will be your enemies,[f] and you will be
trapped by the worship of their gods."
4 When the angel had said this, all the
people of Israel began to cry, 5 and that is
why the place is called Bochim.[g] There
they offered sacrifices to the LORD.

The Death of Joshua

6 Joshua sent the people of Israel on
their way, and each man went to take
possession of his own share of the land.
7 As long as Joshua lived, the people of

[b] *Some ancient translations* Amalekites; *Hebrew* people. [c] HORMAH: *This name in Hebrew means "destruction."* [d] *One ancient translation* But they did not capture; *Hebrew* And they captured. [e] *One ancient translation* Edomite; *Hebrew* Amorite. [f] *Some ancient translations* enemies; *Hebrew* sides. [g] BOCHIM: *This name in Hebrew means "those who cry."*

Israel served the LORD, and even after his
death they continued to do so as long as
the leaders were alive who had seen for
themselves all the great things that the
LORD had done for Israel. 8 The LORD's
servant Joshua son of Nun died at the
age of a hundred and ten. 9 He was buried
in his own part of the land at Timnath
Serah in the hill country of Ephraim
north of Mount Gaash. 10 That whole
generation also died, and the next generation forgot the LORD and what he had
done for Israel.

Israel Stops Worshiping the LORD

11 Then the people of Israel sinned
against the LORD and began to serve the
Baals. 12 They stopped worshiping the
LORD, the God of their ancestors, the God
who had brought them out of Egypt, and
they began to worship other gods, the
gods of the peoples around them. They
bowed down to them and made the LORD
angry. 13 They stopped worshiping the
LORD and served the Baals and the Astartes. 14 And so the LORD became furious
with Israel and let raiders attack and rob
them. He let the enemies all around overpower them, and the Israelites could no
longer protect themselves. 15 Every time
they would go into battle, the LORD was
against them, just as he had said he
would be. They were in great distress.
16 Then the LORD gave the Israelites
leaders who saved them from the raiders. 17 But the Israelites paid no attention
to their leaders. Israel was unfaithful to
the LORD and worshiped other gods.
Their fathers had obeyed the LORD's commands, but this new generation soon
stopped doing so. 18 Whenever the LORD
gave Israel a leader, the LORD would help
that leader and would save the people
from their enemies as long as that leader
lived. The LORD would have mercy on
them because they groaned under their
suffering and oppression. 19 But when
the leader died, the people would return
to the old ways and behave worse than
the previous generation. They would
serve and worship other gods, and stubbornly continue their own evil ways.
20 Then the LORD would become furious
with Israel and say, "This nation has broken the covenant that I commanded their
ancestors to keep. Because they have not
obeyed me, 21 I will no longer drive out
any of the nations that were still in the
land when Joshua died. 22 I will use them
to find out whether or not these Israelites
will follow my ways, as their ancestors
did." 23 So the LORD allowed these nations
to remain in the land; he did not give
Joshua victory over them, nor did he
drive them out soon after Joshua's death.

The Nations Remaining in the Land

3 So then, the LORD left some nations
in the land to test the Israelites who
had not been through the wars in Canaan. 2 He did this only in order to teach
each generation of Israelites about war,
especially those who had never been in
battle before. 3 Those left in the land were
the five Philistine cities, all the Canaanites, the Sidonians, and the Hivites who
lived in the Lebanon Mountains from
Mount Baal Hermon as far as Hamath
Pass. 4 They were to be a test for Israel,
to find out whether or not the Israelites
would obey the commands that the LORD
had given their ancestors through
Moses. 5 And so the people of Israel settled down among the Canaanites, the
Hittites, the Amorites, the Perizzites, the
Hivites, and the Jebusites. 6 They intermarried with them and worshiped their
gods.

Othniel

7 The people of Israel forgot the LORD
their God; they sinned against him and
worshiped the idols of Baal and Asherah.
8 So the LORD became angry with Israel
and let King Cushan Rishathaim of Mesopotamia conquer them. They were subject to him for eight years. 9 Then the
Israelites cried out to the LORD, and he
sent someone to free them. This was Othniel, the son of Caleb's younger brother
Kenaz. 10 The spirit of the LORD came
upon him, and he became Israel's leader.
Othniel went to war, and the LORD gave
him the victory over the king of Mesopotamia. 11 There was peace in the land for
forty years, and then Othniel died.

Ehud

12 The people of Israel sinned against
the LORD again. Because of this the LORD
made King Eglon of Moab stronger than
Israel. 13 Eglon joined the Ammonites
and the Amalekites; they defeated Israel
and captured Jericho, the city of palm
trees. 14 The Israelites were subject to Eglon for eighteen years.

15 Then the Israelites cried out to the
LORD, and he sent someone to free them.
This was Ehud, a left-handed man, who
was the son of Gera, from the tribe of
Benjamin. The people of Israel sent Ehud
to King Eglon of Moab with gifts for him.
16 Ehud had made himself a double-
edged sword about a foot and a half long.
He had it fastened on his right side under
his clothes. 17 Then he took the gifts to
Eglon, who was a very fat man. 18 When
Ehud had given him the gifts, he told the
men who had carried them to go back
home. 19 But Ehud himself turned back at
the carved stones near Gilgal, went back
to Eglon, and said, "Your Majesty, I have
a secret message for you."
So the king ordered his servants,
"Leave us alone!" And they all went out.
20 Then, as the king was sitting there
alone in his cool room on the roof, Ehud
went over to him and said, "I have a message from God for you." The king stood
up. 21 With his left hand Ehud took the
sword from his right side and plunged it
into the king's belly. 22 The whole sword
went in, handle and all, and the fat covered it up. Ehud did not pull it out of the
king's belly, and it stuck out behind, between his legs.[h] 23 Then Ehud went outside, closed the doors behind him, locked
them, 24 and left. The servants came and
saw that the doors were locked, but they
only thought that the king was inside,
relieving himself. 25 They waited as long
as they thought they should, but when he
still did not open the door, they took the
key and opened it. And there was their
master, lying dead on the floor.
26 Ehud got away while they were waiting. He went past the carved stones and
escaped to Seirah. 27 When he arrived
there in the hill country of Ephraim, he
blew a trumpet to call the people of Israel
to battle; then he led them down from the
hills. 28 He told them, "Follow me! The
LORD has given you victory over your enemies, the Moabites." So they followed
Ehud down and captured the place
where the Moabites were to cross the
Jordan; they did not allow anyone to
cross. 29 That day they killed about ten
thousand of the best Moabite soldiers;
none of them escaped. 30 That day the Israelites defeated Moab, and there was
peace in the land for eighty years.

Shamgar

31 The next leader was Shamgar son of
Anath. He too rescued Israel, and did so
by killing six hundred Philistines with an
oxgoad.

Deborah and Barak

4 After Ehud died, the people of Israel
sinned against the LORD again. 2 So
the LORD let them be conquered by Jabin,
a Canaanite king who ruled in the city of
Hazor. The commander of his army was
Sisera, who lived at Harosheth-of-the-
Gentiles. 3 Jabin had nine hundred iron
chariots, and he ruled the people of Israel
with cruelty and violence for twenty
years. Then the people of Israel cried out
to the LORD for help.
4 Now Deborah, the wife of Lappidoth,
was a prophet, and she was serving as a
judge for the Israelites at that time. 5 She
would sit under a certain palm tree between Ramah and Bethel in the hill country of Ephraim, and the people of Israel
would go there for her decisions. 6 One
day she sent for Barak son of Abinoam
from the city of Kedesh in Naphtali and
said to him, "The LORD, the God of Israel,
has given you this command: 'Take ten
thousand men from the tribes of Naphtali and Zebulun and lead them to Mount
Tabor. 7 I will bring Sisera, the commander of Jabin's army, to fight you at
the Kishon River. He will have his chariots and soldiers, but I will give you victory over him.' "
8 Then Barak replied, "I will go if you
go with me, but if you don't go with me,
I won't go either."
9 She answered, "All right, I will go
with you, but you won't get any credit for
the victory, because the LORD will hand
Sisera over to a woman." So Deborah set
off for Kedesh with Barak. 10 Barak
called the tribes of Zebulun and Naphtali
to Kedesh, and ten thousand men followed him. Deborah went with him.
11 In the meantime Heber the Kenite
had set up his tent close to Kedesh near
the oak tree at Zaanannim. He had
moved away from the other Kenites, the
descendants of Hobab, the brother-in-
law of Moses.
12 When Sisera learned that Barak had
gone up to Mount Tabor, 13 he called out
his nine hundred iron chariots and all his

[h] *Probable text* it stuck . . . legs; *Hebrew unclear.*

men, and sent them from Harosheth-of-
the-Gentiles to the Kishon River.
14 Then Deborah said to Barak, "Go!
The LORD is leading you! Today he has
given you victory over Sisera." So Barak
went down from Mount Tabor with his
ten thousand men. 15 When Barak attacked with his army, the LORD threw Sisera into confusion together with all his
chariots and men. Sisera got down from
his chariot and fled on foot. 16 Barak pursued the chariots and the army to
Harosheth-of-the-Gentiles, and Sisera's
whole army was killed. Not a man was
left.
17 Sisera ran away to the tent of Jael,
the wife of Heber the Kenite, because
King Jabin of Hazor was at peace with
Heber's family. 18 Jael went out to meet
Sisera and said to him, "Come in, sir;
come into my tent. Don't be afraid." So
he went in, and she hid him behind a
curtain.[i] 19 He said to her, "Please give
me a drink of water; I'm thirsty." She
opened a leather bag of milk, gave him a
drink, and hid him again. 20 Then he told
her, "Stand at the door of the tent, and if
anyone comes and asks you if anyone is
here, say no."
21 Sisera was so tired that he fell sound
asleep. Then Jael took a hammer and a
tent peg, quietly went up to him, and
killed him by driving the peg right
through the side of his head and into the
ground. 22 When Barak came looking for
Sisera, Jael went out to meet him and
said to him, "Come here! I'll show you
the man you're looking for." So he went
in with her, and there was Sisera on the
ground, dead, with the tent peg through
his head.
23 That day God gave the Israelites victory over Jabin, the Canaanite king.
24 They pressed harder and harder
against him until they destroyed him.

The Song of Deborah and Barak

5 On that day Deborah and Barak son of Abinoam sang this song:

2 Praise the LORD!
The Israelites were determined to fight;
the people gladly volunteered.
3 Listen, you kings!
Pay attention, you rulers!
I will sing and play music
to Israel's God, the LORD.
4 LORD, when you left the mountains of Seir,
when you came out of the region of Edom,
the earth shook, and rain fell from the sky.
Yes, water poured down from the clouds.
5 The mountains quaked before the LORD of Sinai,
before the LORD, the God of Israel.

6 In the days of Shamgar son of Anath,
in the days of Jael,
caravans no longer went through the land,
and travelers used the back roads.
7 The towns of Israel stood abandoned, Deborah;
they stood empty until you came,[j]
came like a mother for Israel.
8 Then there was war in the land
when the Israelites chose new gods.
Of the forty thousand men in Israel,
did anyone carry shield or spear?
9 My heart is with the commanders of Israel,
with the people who gladly volunteered.
Praise the LORD!
10 Tell of[k] it, you that ride on white donkeys,
sitting on saddles,
and you that must walk wherever you go.
11 Listen! The noisy crowds around the wells
are telling of the LORD's victories,
the victories of Israel's people!

Then the LORD's people marched down from their cities.[l]
12 Lead on, Deborah, lead on!
Lead on! Sing a song! Lead on!

[i] hid him behind a curtain; *or* covered him with a rug. [j] abandoned, Deborah . . . you came; *or* abandoned; they stood empty until I, Deborah, came. [k] Tell of; *or* Think about. [l] from their cities; *or* to their gates.

Forward, Barak son of Abinoam,
lead your captives away!
13 Then the faithful ones came down
to their leaders;
the LORD's people came to him[m]
ready to fight.
14 They came[n] from Ephraim into
the valley,[o]
behind the tribe of Benjamin
and its people.
The commanders came down from
Machir,
the officers down from Zebulun.
15 The leaders of Issachar came with
Deborah;
yes, Issachar came and
Barak too,
and they followed him into the
valley.
But the tribe of Reuben was
divided;
they could not decide to come.
16 Why did they stay behind with the
sheep?
To listen to shepherds calling
the flocks?
Yes, the tribe of Reuben was
divided;
they could not decide to come.
17 The tribe of Gad stayed east of the
Jordan,
and the tribe of Dan remained
by the ships.
The tribe of Asher stayed by the
seacoast;
they remained along the shore.
18 But the people of Zebulun and
Naphtali
risked their lives on the
battlefield.

19 At Taanach, by the stream of
Megiddo,
the kings came and fought;
the kings of Canaan fought,
but they took no silver away.
20 The stars fought from the sky;
as they moved across the sky,
they fought against Sisera.
21 A flood in the Kishon swept them
away—
the onrushing Kishon River.
I shall march, march on, with
strength!

22 Then the horses came
galloping on,
stamping the ground with their
hoofs.

23 "Put a curse on Meroz," says the
angel of the LORD,
"a curse, a curse on those who
live there.
They did not come to help the
LORD,
come as soldiers to fight
for him."

24 The most fortunate of women is
Jael,
the wife of Heber the Kenite—
the most fortunate of women
who live in tents.
25 Sisera asked for water, but she
gave him milk;
she brought him cream in a
beautiful bowl.
26 She took a tent peg in one hand,
a worker's hammer in the other;
she struck Sisera and crushed his
skull;
she pierced him through the
head.
27 He sank to his knees,
fell down and lay still at her
feet.
At her feet he sank to his knees
and fell;
he fell to the ground, dead.

28 Sisera's mother looked out of the
window;
she gazed[p] from behind the
lattice.
"Why is his chariot so late in
coming?" she asked.
"Why are his horses so slow to
return?"
29 Her wisest friends answered her,
and she told herself over and
over,
30 "They are only finding things to
capture and divide,
a woman or two for every
soldier,
rich cloth for Sisera,
embroidered pieces for the neck
of the queen."[q]

[m] *One ancient translation* him; *Hebrew* me. [n] *Probable text* They came; *Hebrew* Their root. [o] *One ancient translation* into the valley; *Hebrew* in Amalek. [p] *Some ancient translations* gazed; *Hebrew* cried out. [q] *Probable text* queen; *Hebrew* plunder.

31 So may all your enemies die like
that, O LORD,
but may your friends shine like
the rising sun!

And there was peace in the land for forty years.

Gideon

6 Once again the people of Israel
sinned against the LORD, so he let the
people of Midian rule them for seven
years. 2 The Midianites were stronger
than Israel, and the people of Israel hid
from them in caves and other safe places
in the hills. 3 Whenever the Israelites
would plant their crops, the Midianites
would come with the Amalekites and the
desert tribes and attack them. 4 They
would camp on the land and destroy the
crops as far south as the area around
Gaza. They would take all the sheep, cattle, and donkeys, and leave nothing for
the Israelites to live on. 5 They would
come with their livestock and tents, as
thick as locusts. They and their camels
were too many to count. They came and
devastated the land, 6 and Israel was
helpless against them.
7 Then the people of Israel cried out to
the LORD for help against the Midianites,
8 and he sent them a prophet who
brought them this message from the
LORD, the God of Israel: "I brought you
out of slavery in Egypt. 9 I rescued you
from the Egyptians and from the people
who fought you here in this land. I drove
them out as you advanced, and I gave
you their land. 10 I told you that I am the
LORD your God and that you should not
worship the gods of the Amorites, whose
land you are now living in. But you have
not listened to me."
11 Then the LORD's angel came to the
village of Ophrah and sat under the oak
tree that belonged to Joash, a man of the
clan of Abiezer. His son Gideon was
threshing some wheat secretly in a wine
press, so that the Midianites would not
see him. 12 The LORD's angel appeared to
him there and said, "The LORD is with
you, brave and mighty man!"
13 Gideon said to him, "If I may ask, sir,
why has all this happened to us if the
LORD is with us? What happened to all the
wonderful things that our fathers told us
the LORD used to do—how he brought
them out of Egypt? The LORD has abandoned us and left us to the mercy of the
Midianites."
14 Then the LORD ordered him, "Go with
all your great strength and rescue Israel
from the Midianites. I myself am sending you."
15 Gideon replied, "But Lord, how can I
rescue Israel? My clan is the weakest in
the tribe of Manasseh, and I am the least
important member of my family."
16 The LORD answered, "You can do it
because I will help you. You will crush
the Midianites as easily as if they were
only one man."
17 Gideon replied, "If you are pleased
with me, give me some proof that you are
really the LORD. 18 Please do not leave until I bring you an offering of food."
He said, "I will stay until you come
back."
19 So Gideon went into his house and
cooked a young goat and used a bushel
of flour to make bread without any yeast.
He put the meat in a basket and the broth
in a pot, brought them to the LORD's angel
under the oak tree, and gave them to him.
20 The angel told him, "Put the meat and
the bread on this rock, and pour the
broth over them." Gideon did so. 21 Then
the LORD's angel reached out and touched
the meat and the bread with the end of
the stick he was holding. Fire came out
of the rock and burned up the meat and
the bread. Then the angel disappeared.
22 Gideon then realized that it was the
LORD's angel he had seen, and he said in
terror, "Sovereign LORD! I have seen your
angel face-to-face!"
23 But the LORD told him, "Peace. Don't
be afraid. You will not die." 24 Gideon
built an altar to the LORD there and
named it "The LORD is Peace." (It is still
standing at Ophrah, which belongs to the
clan of Abiezer.)
25 That night the LORD told Gideon,
"Take your father's bull and another bull
seven years old,[r] tear down your
father's altar to Baal, and cut down the
symbol of the goddess Asherah, which is
beside it. 26 Build a well-constructed altar
to the LORD your God on top of this
mound. Then take the second bull[s] and

[r] bull and another bull seven years old; *or* bull, the seven-year-old one. [s] the second bull; *or* the bull.

burn it whole as an offering, using for
firewood the symbol of Asherah you
have cut down." 27 So Gideon took ten of
his servants and did what the LORD had
told him. He was too afraid of his family
and the people in town to do it by day, so
he did it at night.

28 When the people in town got up early
the next morning, they found that the altar to Baal and the symbol of Asherah
had been cut down, and that the second
bull had been burned on the altar that
had been built there. 29 They asked each
other, "Who did this?" They investigated
and found out that Gideon son of Joash
had done it. 30 Then they said to Joash,
"Bring your son out here, so that we can
kill him! He tore down the altar to Baal
and cut down the symbol of Asherah beside it."

31 But Joash said to all those who confronted him, "Are you arguing for Baal?
Are you defending him? Anyone who argues for him will be killed before morning. If Baal is a god, let him defend
himself. It is his altar that was torn
down." 32 From then on Gideon was
known as Jerubbaal,[t] because Joash
said, "Let Baal defend himself; it is his
altar that was torn down."

33 Then all the Midianites, the Amalekites, and the desert tribes assembled,
crossed the Jordan River, and camped in
Jezreel Valley. 34 The spirit of the LORD
took control of Gideon, and he blew a
trumpet to call the men of the clan of
Abiezer to follow him. 35 He sent messengers throughout the territory of both
parts of Manasseh to call them to follow
him. He sent messengers to the tribes of
Asher, Zebulun, and Naphtali, and they
also came to join him.

36 Then Gideon said to God, "You say
that you have decided to use me to rescue
Israel. 37 Well, I am putting some wool on
the ground where we thresh the wheat. If
in the morning there is dew only on the
wool but not on the ground, then I will
know that you are going to use me to
rescue Israel." 38 That is exactly what
happened. When Gideon got up early the
next morning, he squeezed the wool and
wrung enough dew out of it to fill a bowl
with water. 39 Then Gideon said to God,
"Don't be angry with me; let me speak
just once more. Please let me make one
more test with the wool. This time let the
wool be dry, and the ground be wet."
40 That night God did that very thing. The
next morning the wool was dry, but the
ground was wet with dew.

Gideon Defeats the Midianites

7 One day Gideon and all his men got
up early and camped beside Harod
Spring. The Midianite camp was in the
valley to the north of them by Moreh Hill.

2 The LORD said to Gideon, "The men
you have are too many for me to give
them victory over the Midianites. They
might think that they had won by themselves, and so give me no credit. 3 Announce to the people, 'Anyone who is
afraid should go back home, and we will
stay here at Mount Gilead.'" So twenty-
two thousand went back, but ten thousand stayed.

4 Then the LORD said to Gideon, "You
still have too many men. Take them
down to the water, and I will separate
them for you there. If I tell you a man
should go with you, he will go. If I tell you
a man should not go with you, he will not
go." 5 Gideon took the men down to the
water, and the LORD told him, "Separate
everyone who laps up the water with his
tongue like a dog, from everyone who
gets down on his knees to drink." 6 There
were three hundred men who scooped up
water in their hands and lapped it; all the
others got down on their knees to drink.
7 The LORD said to Gideon, "I will rescue
you and give you victory over the Midianites with the three hundred men who
lapped the water. Tell everyone else to go
home." 8 So Gideon sent all the Israelites
home, except the three hundred, who
kept all the supplies and trumpets. The
Midianite camp was below them in the
valley.

9 That night the LORD commanded Gideon, "Get up and attack the camp; I am
giving you victory over it. 10 But if you are
afraid to attack, go down to the camp
with your servant Purah. 11 You will hear
what they are saying, and then you will
have the courage to attack." So Gideon
and his servant Purah went down to the
edge of the enemy camp. 12 The Midianites, the Amalekites, and the desert
tribesmen were spread out in the valley
like a swarm of locusts, and they had as

[t] JERUBBAAL: *This name in Hebrew means "Let Baal defend himself."*

many camels as there are grains of sand
on the seashore.
13 When Gideon arrived, he heard a
man telling a friend about a dream. He
was saying, "I dreamed that a loaf of barley bread rolled into our camp and hit a
tent. The tent collapsed and lay flat on
the ground."
14 His friend replied, "It's the sword of
the Israelite, Gideon son of Joash! It can't
mean anything else! God has given him
victory over Midian and our whole
army!"
15 When Gideon heard about the man's
dream and what it meant, he fell to his
knees and worshiped the LORD. Then he
went back to the Israelite camp and said,
"Get up! The LORD is giving you victory
over the Midianite army!" 16 He divided
his three hundred men into three groups
and gave each man a trumpet and a jar
with a torch inside it. 17 He told them,
"When I get to the edge of the camp,
watch me, and do what I do. 18 When my
group and I blow our trumpets, then you
blow yours all around the camp and
shout, 'For the LORD and for Gideon!' "
19 Gideon and his one hundred men
came to the edge of the camp a while
before midnight, just after the guard had
been changed. Then they blew the trumpets and broke the jars they were holding, 20 and the other two groups did the
same. They all held the torches in their
left hands, the trumpets in their right,
and shouted, "A sword for the LORD and
for Gideon!" 21 Every man stood in his
place around the camp, and the whole
enemy army ran away yelling. 22 While
Gideon's men were blowing their trumpets, the LORD made the enemy troops
attack each other with their swords.
They ran toward Zarethan as far as Beth
Shittah, as far as the town of Abel Meholah near Tabbath.
23 Then men from the tribes of Naphtali, Asher, and both parts of Manasseh
were called out, and they pursued the
Midianites. 24 Gideon sent messengers
through all the hill country of Ephraim to
say, "Come down and fight the Midianites. Hold the Jordan River and the
streams as far as Bethbarah, to keep the
Midianites from crossing them." The
men of Ephraim were called together,
and they held the Jordan River and the
streams as far as Bethbarah. 25 They captured the two Midianite chiefs, Oreb and
Zeeb; they killed Oreb at Oreb Rock, and
Zeeb at the Winepress of Zeeb. They
continued to pursue the Midianites and
brought the heads of Oreb and Zeeb to
Gideon, who was now east of the Jordan.

The Final Defeat of the Midianites

8 Then the people of Ephraim said to
Gideon, "Why didn't you call us
when you went to fight the Midianites?
Why did you treat us like this?" They
complained bitterly about it.
2 But he told them, "What I was able to
do is nothing compared with what you
have done. Even the little that you people
of Ephraim did is worth more than what
my whole clan has done. 3 After all,
through the power of God you killed the
two Midianite chiefs, Oreb and Zeeb.
What have I done to compare with that?"
When he said this, they were no longer
so angry.
4 By this time Gideon and his three
hundred men had come to the Jordan
River and had crossed it. They were exhausted, but were still pursuing the enemy. 5 When they arrived at Sukkoth, he
said to the men of the town, "Please give
my men some loaves of bread. They are
exhausted, and I am chasing Zebah and
Zalmunna, the Midianite kings."
6 But the leaders of Sukkoth said,
"Why should we give your army any
food? You haven't captured Zebah and
Zalmunna yet."
7 So Gideon said, "All right! When the
LORD has handed Zebah and Zalmunna
over to me, I will beat you with thorns
and briers from the desert!" 8 Gideon
went on to Penuel and made the same
request of the people there, but the men
of Penuel gave the same answer as the
men of Sukkoth. 9 So he said to them, "I
am going to come back safe and sound,
and when I do, I will tear this tower
down!"
10 Zebah and Zalmunna were at Kar-
kor with their army. Of the whole army
of desert tribesmen, only about 15,000
were left; 120,000 soldiers had been
killed. 11 Gideon went on the road along
the edge of the desert, east of Nobah and
Jogbehah, and attacked the army by surprise. 12 The two Midianite kings, Zebah
and Zalmunna, ran away, but he pursued
them and captured them, and caused
their whole army to panic.
13 When Gideon was returning from

the battle by way of Heres Pass, 14 he captured a young man from Sukkoth and questioned him. The young man wrote down for Gideon the names of the seventy-seven leading men of Sukkoth. 15 Then Gideon went to the men of Sukkoth and said, "Remember when you refused to help me? You said that you couldn't give any food to my exhausted army because I hadn't captured Zebah and Zalmunna yet. Well, here they are!" 16 He then took thorns and briers from the desert and used them to punish the leaders of Sukkoth. 17 He also tore down the tower at Penuel and killed the men of that city.

18 Then Gideon asked Zebah and Zalmunna, "What about the men you killed at Tabor?"

They answered, "They looked like you—every one of them like the son of a king."

19 Gideon said, "They were my brothers, my own mother's sons. I solemnly swear that if you had not killed them, I would not kill you." 20 Then he said to Jether, his oldest son, "Go ahead, kill them!" But the boy did not draw his sword. He hesitated, because he was still only a boy.

21 Then Zebah and Zalmunna said to Gideon, "Come on, kill us yourself. It takes a man to do a man's job." So Gideon killed them and took the ornaments that were on the necks of their camels.

22 After that, the Israelites said to Gideon, "Be our ruler—you and your descendants after you. You have saved us from the Midianites."

23 Gideon answered, "I will not be your ruler, nor will my son. The LORD will be your ruler." 24 But he went on to say, "Let me ask one thing of you. Every one of you give me the earrings you took." (The Midianites, like other desert people, wore gold earrings.)

25 The people answered, "We'll be glad to give them to you." They spread out a cloth, and everyone put on it the earrings that he had taken. 26 The gold earrings that Gideon got weighed over forty pounds, and this did not include the ornaments, necklaces, and purple clothes that the kings of Midian wore, nor the collars that were around the necks of their camels. 27 Gideon made an idol from the gold and put it in his hometown, Ophrah. All the Israelites abandoned God and went there to worship the idol. It was a trap for Gideon and his family.

28 So Midian was defeated by the Israelites and was no longer a threat. The land was at peace for forty years, until Gideon died.

The Death of Gideon

29 Gideon went back to his own home and lived there. 30 He had seventy sons, because he had many wives. 31 He also had a concubine in Shechem; she bore him a son, and he named him Abimelech. 32 Gideon son of Joash died at a ripe old age and was buried in the tomb of his father Joash, at Ophrah, the town of the clan of Abiezer.

33 After Gideon's death the people of Israel were unfaithful to God again and worshiped the Baals. They made Baal-of-the-Covenant their god, 34 and no longer served the LORD their God, who had saved them from all their enemies around them. 35 They were not grateful to the family of Gideon for all the good that he had done for Israel.

Abimelech

9 Gideon's son Abimelech went to the town of Shechem, where all his mother's relatives lived, and told them 2 to ask the men of Shechem, "Which would you prefer? To have all seventy of Gideon's sons govern you or to have just one man? Remember that Abimelech is your own flesh and blood." 3 His mother's relatives talked to the men of Shechem about this for him, and the men of Shechem decided to follow Abimelech because he was their relative. 4 They gave him seventy pieces of silver from the temple of Baal-of-the-Covenant, and with this money he hired a bunch of worthless scoundrels to join him. 5 He went to his father's house at Ophrah, and there on top of a single stone he killed his seventy brothers, Gideon's sons. But Jotham, Gideon's youngest son, hid and was not killed. 6 Then all the men of Shechem and Bethmillo got together and went to the sacred oak tree at Shechem, where they made Abimelech king.

7 When Jotham heard about this, he went and stood on top of Mount Gerizim and shouted out to them, "Listen to me, you men of Shechem, and God may listen to you! 8 Once upon a time the trees went out to choose a king for themselves.

They said to the olive tree, 'Be our king.'
9The olive tree answered, 'In order to
govern you, I would have to stop producing my oil, which is used to honor gods
and human beings.' 10Then the trees said
to the fig tree, 'You come and be our
king.' 11But the fig tree answered, 'In order to govern you, I would have to stop
producing my good sweet fruit.' 12So the
trees then said to the grapevine, 'You
come and be our king.' 13But the vine
answered, 'In order to govern you, I
would have to stop producing my wine,
that makes gods and human beings
happy.' 14So then all the trees said to the
thorn bush, 'You come and be our king.'
15The thorn bush answered, 'If you really
want to make me your king, then come
and take shelter in my shade. If you
don't, fire will blaze out of my thorny
branches and burn up the cedars of
Lebanon.'
16"Now then," Jotham continued,
"were you really honest and sincere
when you made Abimelech king? Did
you respect Gideon's memory and treat
his family properly, as his actions deserved? 17Remember that my father
fought for you. He risked his life to save
you from the Midianites. 18But today you
turned against my father's family. You
killed his sons — seventy men on a single
stone — and just because Abimelech, his
son by his servant woman, is your relative, you have made him king of Shechem. 19Now then, if what you did today
to Gideon and his family was sincere and
honest, then be happy with Abimelech
and let him be happy with you. 20But if
not, may fire blaze out from Abimelech
and burn up the men of Shechem and
Bethmillo. May fire blaze out from the
men of Shechem and Bethmillo and burn
Abimelech up." 21Then because he was
afraid of his brother Abimelech, Jotham
ran away and went to live at Beer.
22Abimelech ruled Israel for three
years. 23Then God made Abimelech and
the men of Shechem hostile to each
other, and they rebelled against Abimelech. 24This happened so that Abimelech
and the men of Shechem, who encouraged him to murder Gideon's seventy
sons, would pay for their crime. 25The
men of Shechem put men in ambush
against Abimelech on the mountaintops,
and they robbed everyone who passed
their way. Abimelech was told about
this.
26Then Gaal son of Ebed came to Shechem with his brothers, and the men of
Shechem put their confidence in him.
27They all went out into their vineyards
and picked the grapes, made wine from
them, and held a festival. They went into
the temple of their god, where they ate
and drank and made fun of Abimelech.
28Gaal said, "What kind of men are we in
Shechem? Why are we serving Abimelech? Who is he, anyway? The son of
Gideon! And Zebul takes orders from
him, but why should we serve him? Be
loyal to your ancestor Hamor, who
founded your clan! 29I wish I were leading this people! I would get rid of Abimelech! I would tell[u] him, 'Reinforce your
army, come on out and fight!' "
30Zebul, the ruler of the city, became
angry when he heard what Gaal had
said. 31He sent messengers to Abimelech
at Arumah[v] to say, "Gaal son of Ebed
and his brothers have come to Shechem,
and they are not going to let you into the
city. 32Now then, you and your men
should move by night and hide in the
fields. 33Get up tomorrow morning at
sunrise and make a sudden attack on the
city. Then when Gaal and his men come
out against you, hit them with all
you've got!"
34So Abimelech and all his men made
their move at night and hid outside Shechem in four groups. 35When Abimelech
and his men saw Gaal come out and
stand at the city gate, they got up from
their hiding places. 36Gaal saw them and
said to Zebul, "Look! There are men
coming down from the mountaintops!"
"Those are not men," Zebul answered.
"They are just shadows on the
mountains."
37Gaal said again, "Look! There are
men coming down the crest of the mountain and one group is coming along the
road from the oak tree of the fortunetellers!"
38Then Zebul said to him, "Where is all
your big talk now? You were the one who
asked why we should serve this man
Abimelech. These are the men you were

[u] *One ancient translation* I would tell; *Hebrew* He told. [v] *Probable text* Arumah; *Hebrew unclear.*

making fun of. Go on out now and fight
them." 39 Gaal led the men of Shechem
out and fought Abimelech. 40 Abimelech
started after Gaal, and Gaal ran. Many
were wounded, even at the city gate.
41 Abimelech lived in Arumah, and Zebul
drove Gaal and his brothers out of Shechem, so that they could no longer live
there.

42 The next day Abimelech found out
that the people of Shechem were planning to go out into the fields, 43 so he took
his men, divided them into three groups,
and hid in the fields, waiting. When he
saw the people coming out of the city, he
came out of hiding to kill them. 44 While
Abimelech and his group hurried forward to guard the city gate, the other two
companies attacked the people in the
fields and killed them all. 45 The fighting
continued all day long. Abimelech captured the city, killed its people, tore it
down, and covered the ground with salt.

46 When all the leading men in the fort
at Shechem heard about this, they
sought safety in the stronghold of the
temple of Baal-of-the-Covenant. 47 Abimelech was told that they had gathered
there, 48 so he went up to Mount Zalmon
with his men. There he took an ax, cut a
limb off a tree, and put it on his shoulder.
He told his men to hurry and do the same
thing. 49 So everyone cut off a tree limb;
then they followed Abimelech and piled
the wood up against the stronghold.
They set it on fire, with the people inside,
and all the people of the fort died – about
a thousand men and women.

50 Then Abimelech went to Thebez,
surrounded that city, and captured it.
51 There was a strong tower there, and
every man and woman in the city, including the leaders, ran to it. They locked
themselves in and went up to the roof.
52 When Abimelech came to attack the
tower, he went up to the door to set the
tower on fire. 53 But a woman threw a
millstone down on his head and frac-
tured his skull. 54 Then he quickly called
the young man who was carrying his
weapons and told him, "Draw your
sword and kill me. I don't want it said
that a woman killed me." So the young
man ran him through, and he died.
55 When the Israelites saw that Abimelech was dead, they all went home.

56 And so it was that God paid Abimelech back for the crime that he committed against his father in killing his
seventy brothers. 57 God also made the
men of Shechem suffer for their wickedness, just as Jotham, Gideon's son, said
they would when he cursed them.

Tola

10 After Abimelech's death Tola,
the son of Puah and grandson of
Dodo, came to free Israel. He was from
the tribe of Issachar and lived at Shamir
in the hill country of Ephraim. 2 He was
Israel's leader for twenty-three years.
Then he died and was buried at Shamir.

Jair

3 After Tola came Jair from Gilead. He
led Israel for twenty-two years. 4 He had
thirty sons who rode thirty donkeys.
They had thirty cities in the land of Gilead, which are still called the villages
of Jair. 5 Jair died and was buried at
Kamon.

Jephthah

6 Once again the Israelites sinned
against the LORD by worshiping the Baals
and the Astartes, as well as the gods of
Syria, of Sidon, of Moab, of Ammon, and
of Philistia. They abandoned the LORD
and stopped worshiping him. 7 So the
LORD became angry with the Israelites,
and let the Philistines and the Ammonites conquer them. 8 For eighteen years
they oppressed and persecuted all the Israelites who lived in Amorite country
east of the Jordan River in Gilead. 9 The
Ammonites even crossed the Jordan to
fight the tribes of Judah, Benjamin, and
Ephraim. Israel was in great distress.

10 Then the Israelites cried out to the
LORD and said, "We have sinned against
you, for we left you, our God, and worshiped the Baals."

11 The LORD gave them this answer:
"The Egyptians, the Amorites, the Ammonites, the Philistines, 12 the Sidonians,
the Amalekites, and the Maonites oppressed you in the past, and you cried out
to me. Did I not save you from them?
13 But you still left me and worshiped
other gods, so I am not going to rescue
you again. 14 Go and cry out to the gods
you have chosen. Let them rescue you
when you get in trouble."

15 But the people of Israel said to the
LORD, "We have sinned. Do whatever you
like, but please, save us today." 16 So they

got rid of their foreign gods and worshiped the LORD; and he became troubled
over Israel's distress.
17 Then the Ammonite army prepared
for battle and camped in Gilead. The people of Israel came together and camped
at Mizpah in Gilead. 18 There the people
and the leaders of the Israelite tribes
asked one another, "Who will lead the
fight against the Ammonites? Whoever
does will be the leader of everyone in
Gilead."

11 Jephthah, a brave soldier from
Gilead, was the son of a prostitute. His father Gilead 2 had other sons by
his wife, and when they grew up, they
forced Jephthah to leave home. They
told him, "You will not inherit anything
from our father; you are the son of another woman." 3 Jephthah fled from his
brothers and lived in the land of Tob.
There he attracted a group of worthless
men, and they went around with him.
4 It was some time later that the Ammonites went to war against Israel.
5 When this happened, the leaders of Gilead went to bring Jephthah back from
the land of Tob. 6 They told him, "Come
and lead us, so that we can fight the Ammonites."
7 But Jephthah answered, "You hated
me so much that you forced me to leave
my father's house. Why come to me now
that you're in trouble?"
8 They said to Jephthah, "We are turning to you now because we want you to
go with us and fight the Ammonites and
lead all the people of Gilead."
9 Jephthah said to them, "If you take
me back home to fight the Ammonites
and the LORD gives me victory, I will be
your ruler."
10 They replied, "We agree. The LORD is
our witness." 11 So Jephthah went with
the leaders of Gilead, and the people
made him their ruler and leader. Jephthah stated his terms at Mizpah in the
presence of the LORD.
12 Then Jephthah sent messengers to
the king of Ammon to say, "What is your
quarrel with us? Why have you invaded
our country?"
13 The king of Ammon answered Jephthah's messengers, "When the Israelites
came out of Egypt, they took away my
land from the Arnon River to the Jabbok
River and the Jordan River. Now you
must give it back peacefully."
14 Jephthah sent messengers back to
the king of Ammon 15 with this answer:
"It is not true that Israel took away the
land of Moab or the land of Ammon.
16 This is what happened: when the Israelites left Egypt, they went through the
desert to the Gulf of Aqaba and came to
Kadesh. 17 Then they sent messengers to
the king of Edom to ask permission to go
through his land. But the king of Edom
would not let them. They also asked the
king of Moab, but neither would he let
them go through his land. So the Israelites stayed at Kadesh. 18 Then they went
on through the desert, going around the
land of Edom and the land of Moab until
they came to the east side of Moab, on
the other side of the Arnon River. They
camped there, but they did not cross the
Arnon because it was the boundary of
Moab. 19 Then the Israelites sent messengers to Sihon, the Amorite king of Heshbon, and asked him for permission to go
through his country to their own land.
20 But Sihon would not let Israel do it. He
brought his whole army together,
camped at Jahaz, and attacked Israel.
21 But the LORD, the God of Israel, gave
the Israelites victory over Sihon and his
army. So the Israelites took possession
of all the territory of the Amorites who
lived in that country. 22 They occupied all
the Amorite territory from the Arnon in
the south to the Jabbok in the north and
from the desert on the east to the Jordan
on the west. 23 So it was the LORD, the God
of Israel, who drove out the Amorites for
his people, the Israelites. 24 Are you going to try to take it back? You can keep
whatever your god Chemosh has given
you. But we are going to keep everything
that the LORD, our God, has taken for us.
25 Do you think you are any better than
Balak son of Zippor, king of Moab? He
never challenged Israel, did he? Did he
ever go to war against us? 26 For three
hundred years Israel has occupied Heshbon and Aroer, and the towns around
them, and all the cities on the banks of
the Arnon River. Why haven't you taken
them back in all this time? 27 No, I have
not done you any wrong. You are doing
wrong by making war on me. The LORD is
the judge. He will decide today between
the Israelites and the Ammonites." 28 But
the king of Ammon paid no attention to
this message from Jephthah.
29 Then the spirit of the LORD came

upon Jephthah. He went through Gilead
and Manasseh and returned to Mizpah in
Gilead and went on to Ammon. 30 Jephthah promised the LORD: "If you will give
me victory over the Ammonites, 31 I will
burn as an offering the first person that
comes out of my house to meet me, when
I come back from the victory. I will offer
that person to you as a sacrifice."
32 So Jephthah crossed the river to
fight the Ammonites, and the LORD gave
him victory. 33 He struck at them from
Aroer to the area around Minnith,
twenty cities in all, and as far as Abel
Keramim. There was a great slaughter,
and the Ammonites were defeated by
Israel.

Jephthah's Daughter

34 When Jephthah went back home to
Mizpah, there was his daughter coming
out to meet him, dancing and playing the
tambourine. She was his only child.
35 When he saw her, he tore his clothes in
sorrow and said, "Oh, my daughter! You
are breaking my heart! Why must it be
you that causes me pain? I have made a
solemn promise to the LORD, and I cannot
take it back!"
36 She told him, "If you have made a
promise to the LORD, do what you said
you would do to me, since the LORD has
given you revenge on your enemies, the
Ammonites." 37 But she asked her father,
"Do this one thing for me. Leave me
alone for two months, so that I can go
with my friends to wander in the mountains and grieve that I must die a virgin."
38 He told her to go and sent her away for
two months. She and her friends went up
into the mountains and grieved because
she was going to die unmarried and
childless. 39 After two months she came
back to her father. He did what he had
promised the LORD, and she died still a
virgin.
This was the origin of the custom in
Israel 40 that the Israelite women would
go out for four days every year to grieve
for the daughter of Jephthah of Gilead.

Jephthah and the Ephraimites

12 The men of Ephraim prepared
for battle; they crossed the Jordan River to Zaphon and said to Jephthah, "Why did you cross the border to
fight the Ammonites without calling us
to go with you? We'll burn the house
down over your head!"
2 But Jephthah told them, "My people
and I had a serious quarrel with the Ammonites. I did call you, but you would not
rescue me from them. 3 When I saw that
you were not going to, I risked my life
and crossed the border to fight them, and
the LORD gave me victory over them. So
why are you coming up to fight me now?"
4 Then Jephthah brought all the men of
Gilead together, fought the men of
Ephraim and defeated them. (The Ephraimites had said, "You Gileadites in
Ephraim and Manasseh, you are desert-
ers from Ephraim!") 5 In order to keep the
Ephraimites from escaping, the Gileadites captured the places where the Jordan could be crossed. When any
Ephraimite who was trying to escape
would ask permission to cross, the men
of Gilead would ask, "Are you an Ephraimite?" If he said, "No," 6 they would tell
him to say "Shibboleth." But he would
say "Sibboleth," because he could not
pronounce it correctly. Then they would
grab him and kill him there at one of the
Jordan River crossings. At that time
forty-two thousand of the Ephraimites
were killed.
7 Jephthah led Israel for six years.
Then he died and was buried in his
hometown[w] in Gilead.

Ibzan, Elon, and Abdon

8 After Jephthah, Ibzan from Bethlehem led Israel. 9 He had thirty sons and
thirty daughters. He gave his daughters
in marriage outside the clan and brought
thirty young women from outside the
clan for his sons to marry. Ibzan led Israel for seven years, 10 then he died and
was buried at Bethlehem.
11 After Ibzan, Elon from Zebulun led
Israel for ten years. 12 Then he died and
was buried at Aijalon in the territory of
Zebulun.
13 After Elon, Abdon son of Hillel from
Pirathon led Israel. 14 He had forty sons
and thirty grandsons, who rode on seventy donkeys. Abdon led Israel for eight
years, 15 then he died and was buried at
Pirathon in the territory of Ephraim in
the hill country of the Amalekites.

w *One ancient translation* his hometown; *Hebrew* the towns.

The Birth of Samson

13 The Israelites sinned against the
LORD again, and he let the Philistines rule them for forty years.
2 At that time there was a man named
Manoah from the town of Zorah. He was
a member of the tribe of Dan. His wife
had never been able to have children.
3 The LORD's angel appeared to her and
said, "You have never been able to have
children, but you will soon be pregnant
and have a son. 4 Be sure not to drink any
wine or beer, or eat any forbidden food;
5 and after your son is born, you must
never cut his hair, because from the day
of his birth he will be dedicated to God as
a nazirite.[x] He will begin the work of
rescuing Israel from the Philistines."
6 Then the woman went and told her
husband, "A man of God has come to me,
and he looked as frightening as the angel[y] of God. I didn't ask him where he
came from, and he didn't tell me his
name. 7 But he did tell me that I would
become pregnant and have a son. He told
me not to drink any wine or beer, or eat
any forbidden food, because the boy is to
be dedicated to God as a nazirite as long
as he lives."
8 Then Manoah prayed to the LORD,
"Please, LORD, let the man of God that you
sent come back to us and tell us what we
must do with the boy when he is born."
9 God did what Manoah asked, and his
angel came back to the woman while she
was sitting in the field. Her husband Manoah was not with her, 10 so she ran at
once and told him, "Look! The man who
came to me the other day has appeared
to me again."
11 Manoah got up and followed his
wife. He went to the man and asked, "Are
you the man who talked to my wife?"
"Yes," he answered.
12 Then Manoah said, "Now then, when
your words come true, what must the boy
do? What kind of a life must he lead?"
13 The LORD's angel answered, "Your
wife must be sure to do everything that I
have told her. 14 She must not eat anything that comes from the grapevine; she
must not drink any wine or beer, or eat
any forbidden food. She must do everything that I have told her."
15-16 Not knowing that it was the LORD's
angel, Manoah said to him, "Please do
not go yet. Let us cook a young goat
for you."
But the angel said, "If I do stay, I will
not eat your food. But if you want to prepare it, burn it as an offering to the LORD."
17 Manoah replied, "Tell us your name,
so that we can honor you when your
words come true."
18 The angel asked, "Why do you want
to know my name? It is a name of
wonder."[z]
19 So Manoah took a young goat and
some grain, and offered them on the rock
altar to the LORD who works wonders.[a]
20-21 While the flames were going up from
the altar, Manoah and his wife saw the
LORD's angel go up toward heaven in the
flames. Manoah realized then that the
man had been the LORD's angel, and he
and his wife threw themselves face
downward on the ground. They never
saw the angel again.
22 Manoah said to his wife, "We are
sure to die, because we have seen God!"
23 But his wife answered, "If the LORD
had wanted to kill us, he would not have
accepted our offerings; he would not
have shown us all this or told us such
things at this time."
24 The woman gave birth to a son and
named him Samson. The child grew and
the LORD blessed him. 25 And the LORD's
power began to strengthen him while he
was between Zorah and Eshtaol in the
Camp of Dan.

Samson and the Woman from Timnah

14 One day Samson went down to
Timnah, where he noticed a certain young Philistine woman. 2 He went
back home and told his father and
mother, "There is a Philistine woman
down at Timnah who caught my attention. Get her for me; I want to marry
her."
3 But his father and mother asked him,
"Why do you have to go to those heathen
Philistines to get a wife? Can't you find
someone in our own clan, among all our
people?"
But Samson told his father, "She is the

[x] NAZIRITE: *A person who showed devotion to God by taking vows not to drink wine or beer or allow any hair to be cut or touch corpses (see Nu 6.1-8).* [y] the angel; *or* an angel. [z] name of wonder; *or* mysterious name. [a] *Some ancient translations* who works wonders; *Hebrew* and working wonders while Manoah and his wife watched.

one I want you to get for me. I like her."
4 His parents did not know that it was
the LORD who was leading Samson to do
this, for the LORD was looking for a
chance to fight the Philistines. At this
time the Philistines were ruling Israel.
5 So Samson went down to Timnah
with his father and mother. As they were
going through the vineyards there, he
heard a young lion roaring. 6 Suddenly
the power of the LORD made Samson
strong, and he tore the lion apart with his
bare hands, as if it were a young goat.
But he did not tell his parents what he
had done.
7 Then he went and talked to the young
woman, and he liked her. 8 A few days
later Samson went back to marry her. On
the way he left the road to look at the lion
he had killed, and he was surprised to
find a swarm of bees and some honey
inside the dead body. 9 He scraped the
honey out into his hands and ate it as he
walked along. Then he went to his father
and mother and gave them some. They
ate it, but Samson did not tell them that
he had taken the honey from the dead
body of a lion.
10 His father went to the woman's
house, and Samson gave a banquet
there. This was a custom among the
young men. 11 When the Philistines saw
him, they sent thirty young men to stay
with him. 12-13 Samson said to them, "Let
me tell you a riddle. I'll bet each one of
you a piece of fine linen and a change of
fine clothes that you can't tell me its
meaning before the seven days of the
wedding feast are over."

"Tell us your riddle," they said. "Let's
hear it."
14 He said,

> "Out of the eater came something
> to eat;
> Out of the strong came something
> sweet."

Three days later they had still not figured
out what the riddle meant.
15 On the fourth[b] day they said to Samson's wife, "Trick your husband into telling us what the riddle means. If you
don't, we'll set fire to your father's house
and burn you with it.[c] You two invited
us so that you could rob us, didn't you?"
16 So Samson's wife went to him in
tears and said, "You don't love me! You
just hate me! You told my friends a riddle
and didn't tell me what it means!"

He said, "Look, I haven't even told my
father and mother. Why should I tell
you?" 17 She cried about it for the whole
seven days of the feast. But on the seventh day he told her what the riddle
meant, for she nagged him so about it.
Then she told the Philistines. 18 So on the
seventh day, before Samson went into
the bedroom,[d] the men of the city said
to him,

> "What could be sweeter than
> honey?
> What could be stronger than a
> lion?"

Samson replied,

> "If you hadn't been plowing with
> my cow,
> You wouldn't know the
> answer now."

19 Suddenly the power of the LORD made
him strong, and he went down to Ashkelon, where he killed thirty men, stripped
them, and gave their fine clothes to the
men who had solved the riddle. After
that, he went back home, furious about
what had happened, 20 and his wife was
given to the man that had been his best
man at the wedding.

15 Some time later Samson went to
visit his wife during the wheat
harvest and took her a young goat. He
told her father, "I want to go to my wife's
room."

But he wouldn't let him go in. 2 He told
Samson, "I really thought that you hated
her, so I gave her to your friend. But her
younger sister is prettier, anyway. You
can have her, instead."
3 Samson said, "This time I'm not going
to be responsible for what I do to the
Philistines!" 4 So he went and caught
three hundred foxes. Two at a time, he
tied their tails together and put torches in
the knots. 5 Then he set fire to the torches
and turned the foxes loose in the Philistine wheat fields. In this way he burned
up not only the wheat that had been harvested but also the wheat that was still in
the fields. The olive orchards were also
burned. 6 When the Philistines asked
who had done this, they learned that
Samson had done it because his father-

[b] *Some ancient translations* fourth; *Hebrew* seventh. [c] set fire . . . you with it; *or* burn you and your family. [d] *Probable text* bedroom; *Hebrew* sun.

in-law, a man from Timnah, had given
Samson's wife to a friend of Samson's.
So the Philistines went and burned the
woman to death and burned down her
father's house.[e]
7 Samson told them, "So this is how
you act! I swear that I won't stop until I
pay you back!" 8 He attacked them
fiercely and killed many of them. Then
he went and stayed in the cave in the cliff
at Etam.

Samson Defeats the Philistines

9 The Philistines came and camped in
Judah, and attacked the town of Lehi.
10 The men of Judah asked them, "Why
are you attacking us?"
They answered, "We came to take
Samson prisoner and to treat him as he
treated us." 11 So these three thousand
men of Judah went to the cave in the cliff
at Etam and said to Samson, "Don't you
know that the Philistines are our rulers?
What have you done to us?"
He answered, "I did to them just what
they did to me."
12 They told him, "We have come here
to tie you up, so we can hand you over to
them."
Samson said, "Give me your word that
you won't kill me yourselves."
13 "All right," they said, "we are only
going to tie you up and hand you over to
them. We won't kill you." So they tied
him up with two new ropes and brought
him back from the cliff.
14 When he got to Lehi, the Philistines
came running toward him, shouting at
him. Suddenly the power of the LORD
made him strong, and he broke the ropes
around his arms and hands as if they
were burnt thread. 15 Then he found a
jawbone of a donkey that had recently
died. He reached down and picked it up,
and killed a thousand men with it. 16 So
Samson sang,

"With the jawbone of a donkey I
killed a thousand men;
With the jawbone of a donkey I
piled them up in piles."[f]

17 After that, he threw the jawbone away.
The place where this happened was
named Ramath Lehi.[g]
18 Then Samson became very thirsty,
so he called to the LORD and said, "You
gave me this great victory; am I now going to die of thirst and be captured by
these heathen Philistines?" 19 Then God
opened a hollow place in the ground
there at Lehi, and water came out of it.
Samson drank it and began to feel much
better. So the spring was named Hakkore;[h] it is still there at Lehi.
20 Samson led Israel for twenty years
while the Philistines ruled the land.

Samson at Gaza

16 One day Samson went to the Philistine city of Gaza, where he met
a prostitute and went to bed with her.
2 The people of Gaza found out that Samson was there, so they surrounded the
place and waited for him all night long at
the city gate. They were quiet all night,
thinking to themselves, "We'll wait until
daybreak, and then we'll kill him." 3 But
Samson stayed in bed only until midnight. Then he got up and took hold of
the city gate and pulled it up—doors,
posts, lock, and all. He put them on his
shoulders and carried them far off to the
top of the hill overlooking Hebron.

Samson and Delilah

4 After this, Samson fell in love with a
woman named Delilah, who lived in So-
rek Valley. 5 The five Philistine kings
went to her and said, "Trick Samson into
telling you why he is so strong and how
we can overpower him, tie him up, and
make him helpless. Each one of us will
give you eleven hundred pieces of
silver."
6 So Delilah said to Samson, "Please
tell me what makes you so strong. If
someone wanted to tie you up and make
you helpless, how could he do it?"
7 Samson answered, "If they tie me up
with seven new bowstrings that are not
dried out, I'll be as weak as anybody
else."
8 So the Philistine kings brought Delilah seven new bowstrings that were not
dried out, and she tied Samson up. 9 She
had some men waiting in another room,
so she shouted, "Samson! The Philistines
are coming!" But he snapped the bowstrings just as thread breaks when fire
touches it. So they still did not know the
secret of his strength.

[e] burned the woman . . . house; *or* burned the woman and her family to death. [f] PILES: *This word sounds like the Hebrew for "donkey."* [g] RAMATH LEHI: *This name in Hebrew means "Jawbone Hill."* [h] HAKKORE: *This name in Hebrew means "caller."*

10 Delilah told Samson, "Look, you've
been making a fool of me and not telling
me the truth. Please tell me how someone
could tie you up."

11 He told her, "If they tie me with new
ropes that have never been used, I'll be as
weak as anybody else."

12 So Delilah got some new ropes and
tied him up. Then she shouted, "Samson!
The Philistines are coming!" The men
were waiting in another room. But he
snapped the ropes off his arms like
thread.

13 Delilah said to Samson, "You're still
making a fool of me and not telling me
the truth. Tell me how someone could tie
you up."

He told her, "If you weave my seven
locks of hair into a loom, and make it
tight with a peg, I'll be as weak as anybody else."

14 Delilah then lulled him to sleep, took
his seven locks of hair, and wove them
into the loom.[i] She made it tight with a
peg and shouted, "Samson! The Philistines are coming!" But he woke up and
pulled his hair loose from the loom.

15 So she said to him, "How can you say
you love me, when you don't mean it?
You've made a fool of me three times,
and you still haven't told me what makes
you so strong." 16 She kept on asking
him, day after day. He got so sick and
tired of her bothering him about it 17 that
he finally told her the truth. "My hair has
never been cut," he said. "I have been
dedicated to God as a nazirite[j] from the
time I was born. If my hair were cut, I
would lose my strength and be as weak
as anybody else."

18 When Delilah realized that he had
told her the truth, she sent a message to
the Philistine kings and said, "Come
back one more time. He has told me the
truth." Then they came and brought the
money with them. 19 Delilah lulled Samson to sleep in her lap and then called a
man, who cut off[k] Samson's seven locks
of hair. Then she began to torment him,
for he had lost his strength. 20 Then she
shouted, "Samson! The Philistines are
coming!" He woke up and thought, "I'll
get loose and go free, as always." He did
not know that the LORD had left him.
21 The Philistines captured him and put
his eyes out. They took him to Gaza,
chained him with bronze chains, and put
him to work grinding at the mill in the
prison. 22 But his hair started growing
back.

The Death of Samson

23 The Philistine kings met together to
celebrate and offer a great sacrifice to
their god Dagon. They sang, "Our god
has given us victory over our enemy
Samson!" 24-25 They were enjoying themselves, and so they said, "Call Samson,
and let's make him entertain us!"[l] When
they brought Samson out of the prison,
they made him entertain them[m] and
made him stand between the columns.
When the people saw him, they sang
praise to their god: "Our god has given us
victory over our enemy, who devastated
our land and killed so many of us!"
26 Samson said to the boy who was leading him by the hand, "Let me touch the
columns that hold up the building. I want
to lean on them." 27 The building was
crowded with men and women. All five
Philistine kings were there, and there
were about three thousand men and
women on the roof, watching Samson
entertain them.[n]

28 Then Samson prayed, "Sovereign
LORD, please remember me; please, God,
give me my strength just this one time
more, so that with this one blow I can get
even with the Philistines for putting out
my two eyes." 29 So Samson took hold of
the two middle columns holding up the
building. Putting one hand on each column, he pushed against them 30 and
shouted, "Let me die with the Philistines!" He pushed with all his might, and
the building fell down on the five kings
and everyone else. Samson killed more
people at his death than he had killed
during his life.

31 His brothers and the rest of his family came down to get his body. They took
him back and buried him between Zorah
and Eshtaol in the tomb of his father Manoah. He had been Israel's leader for
twenty years.

[i] *One ancient translation* and make it tight *(in verse 13)* . . . into the loom *(in verse 14)*; *Hebrew does not have these words.* [j] NAZIRITE: *See 13.5.* [k] *Probable text* who cut off; *Hebrew* and she cut off. [l] make him entertain us; *or* make fun of him. [m] made him entertain them; *or* made fun of him. [n] entertain them; *or* and making fun of him.

Micah's Idols

17 There was once a man named Micah, who lived in the hill country
of Ephraim. 2 He told his mother, "When
someone stole those eleven hundred
pieces of silver from you, you put a curse
on the robber. I heard you do it. Look, I
have the money. I am the one who
took it."
His mother said, "May the LORD bless
you, my son!" 3 He gave the money back
to his mother, and she said, "To keep the
curse from falling on my son, I myself am
solemnly dedicating the silver to the
LORD. It will be used to make a wooden
idol covered with silver. So now I will
give the pieces of silver back to you."
4 Then he gave them back to his mother.
She took two hundred of the pieces of
silver and gave them to a metalworker,
who made an idol, carving it from wood
and covering it with the silver. It was
placed in Micah's house.
5 This man Micah had his own place of
worship. He made some idols and an
ephod,[o] and appointed one of his sons
as his priest. 6 There was no king in Israel
at that time; everyone did whatever they
wanted.
7 At that same time there was a young
Levite who had been living in the town of
Bethlehem in Judah. 8 He left Bethlehem
to find another place to live. While he
was traveling, he came to Micah's house
in the hill country of Ephraim. 9 Micah
asked him, "Where do you come from?"
He answered, "I am a Levite from
Bethlehem in Judah. I am looking for a
place to live."
10 Micah said, "Stay with me. Be my
adviser and priest, and I will give you ten
pieces of silver a year, some clothes, and
your food."[p] 11 The young Levite agreed
to stay with Micah and became like a son
to him. 12 Micah appointed him as his
priest, and he lived in Micah's home.
13 Micah said, "Now that I have a Levite
as my priest, I know that the LORD will
make things go well for me."

Micah and the Tribe of Dan

18 There was no king in Israel at
that time. In those days the tribe
of Dan was looking for territory to claim
and settle in because they had not yet
received any land of their own among
the tribes of Israel. 2 So the people of Dan
chose five qualified[q] men out of all the
families in the tribe and sent them from
the towns of Zorah and Eshtaol with instructions to explore the land and spy on
it. When they arrived in the hill country
of Ephraim, they stayed at Micah's
house. 3 While they were there, they recognized the accent of the young Levite,
so they went up to him and asked, "What
are you doing here? Who brought you
here?"
4 He answered, "I have an arrangement
with Micah, who pays me to serve as his
priest."
5 They said to him, "Please ask God if
we are going to be successful on our
trip."
6 The priest answered, "You have nothing to worry about. The LORD is taking
care of you on this trip."
7 So the five men left and went to the
town of Laish. They saw how the people
there lived in security like the Sidonians.
They were a peaceful, quiet people, with
no argument with anyone; they had all
they needed.[r] They lived far away from
the Sidonians and had no dealings with
any other people. 8 When the five men
returned to Zorah and Eshtaol, the people asked them what they had found out.
9 "Come on," they replied. "Let's attack
Laish. We saw the land, and it's very
good. Don't stay here doing nothing;
hurry! Go on in and take it over! 10 When
you get there, you will find that the people don't suspect a thing. It is a big country; it has everything a person could
want, and God has given it to you."
11 So six hundred men from the tribe of
Dan left Zorah and Eshtaol, ready for
battle. 12 They went up and camped west
of Kiriath Jearim in Judah. That is why
the place is still called Camp of Dan.
13 They went on from there and came to
Micah's house in the hill country of
Ephraim.
14 Then the five men who had gone to
spy on the country around Laish said to
their companions, "Did you know that
here in one of these houses there is a
wooden idol covered with silver? There
are also other idols and an ephod. What
do you think we should do?" 15 So they

[o] EPHOD: *See Word List.* [p] *Probable text* your food; *Hebrew* your food. So the Levite went.
[q] qualified; *or* brave. [r] *Probable text* They were . . . needed; *Hebrew unclear.*

went into Micah's house, where the
young Levite lived, and asked the Levite
how he was getting along. 16 Meanwhile
the six hundred Danite soldiers, ready
for battle, were standing at the gate.
17 The five spies went straight on into the
house and took the wooden idol covered
with silver, the other idols, and the
ephod, while the priest stayed at the gate
with the six hundred armed men.
18 When the men went into Micah's
house and took the sacred objects, the
priest asked them, "What are you
doing?"
19 They told him, "Keep quiet. Don't
say a word. Come with us and be our
priest and adviser. Wouldn't you rather
be a priest for a whole Israelite tribe than
for the family of one man?" 20 This made
the priest very happy, so he took the sacred objects and went along with them.
21 They turned around and started off,
with their children, their livestock, and
their belongings going ahead. 22 They
had traveled a good distance from the
house when Micah called his neighbors
out for battle. They caught up with the
Danites 23 and shouted at them. The Danites turned around and asked Micah,
"What's the matter? Why all this mob?"
24 Micah answered, "What do you
mean, 'What's the matter?' You take my
priest and the gods that I made, and walk
off! What have I got left?"
25 The Danites told him, "You had better not say anything else unless you want
these men to get angry and attack you.
You and your whole family would die."
26 Then the Danites went on. Micah saw
that they were too strong for him, so he
turned and went back home.
27-28 After the Danites had taken the
priest and the things that Micah had
made, they went and attacked Laish, that
town of peaceful, quiet people which was
in the same valley as Bethrehob. They
killed the inhabitants and burned the
town. There was no one to save them,
because Laish was a long way from Sidon, and they had no dealings with any
other people. The Danites rebuilt the
town and settled down there. 29 They
changed its name from Laish to Dan, after their ancestor Dan, the son of Jacob.
30 The Danites set up the idol to be worshiped, and Jonathan, the son of Gershom and grandson of Moses, served as
a priest for the Danites, and his descendants served as their priests until the people were taken away into exile.
31 Micah's idol remained there as long as
the Tent where God was worshiped remained at Shiloh.

The Levite and His Concubine

19 In those days before Israel had a
king, there was a Levite living far
back in the hill country of Ephraim. He
took a young woman from Bethlehem in
Judah to be his concubine. 2 But she became angry with him, went back to her
father's house in Bethlehem, and stayed
there four months. 3 Then the man decided to go after her and try to persuade
her to return to him. He took his servant
and two donkeys with him. The woman
showed the Levite into the house, and
when her father saw him, he gave him a
hearty greeting. 4 The father insisted that
he stay, and so he stayed for three days.
The couple had their meals and spent the
nights there. 5 On the morning of the
fourth day they woke up early and got
ready to go. But the woman's father said
to the Levite, "Have something to eat
first. You'll feel better. You can go later."
6 So the two men sat down and ate and
drank together. Then the woman's father
told him, "Please spend the night and enjoy yourself."
7 The Levite got up to go, but the father
urged him to stay, so he spent another
night there. 8 Early in the morning of the
fifth day he started to leave, but the
woman's father said, "Eat something,
please. Wait until later in the day." So the
two men ate together.
9 When the man, his concubine, and
the servant once more started to leave,
the father said, "Look, it's almost evening now; you might as well stay all
night. It will be dark soon; stay here and
have a good time. Tomorrow you can get
up early for the trip and go home."
10-11 But the man did not want to spend
another night there, so he and his concubine started on their way, with their servant and two donkeys with pack saddles.
It was late in the day when they came
near Jebus (that is, Jerusalem), so the
servant said to his master, "Why don't
we stop and spend the night here in this
Jebusite city?"
12-13 But his master said, "We're not going to stop in a city where the people are
not Israelites. We'll pass on by and go a

little farther and spend the night at Gibeah or Ramah." 14 So they passed by Jebus and continued on their way. It was
sunset when they came to Gibeah in the
territory of the tribe of Benjamin. 15 They
turned off the road to go and spend the
night there. They went into town and sat
down in the city square, but no one offered to take them home for the night.

16 While they were there, an old man
came by at the end of a day's work on the
farm. He was originally from the hill
country of Ephraim, but he was now living in Gibeah. (The other people there
were from the tribe of Benjamin.) 17 The
old man noticed the traveler in the city
square and asked him, "Where do you
come from? Where are you going?"

18 The Levite answered, "We have been
in Bethlehem in Judah, and now we are
on our way home[s] deep in the hill country of Ephraim. No one will put us up for
the night, 19 even though we have fodder
and straw for our donkeys, as well as
bread and wine for my concubine and me
and for my servant. We have everything
we need."

20 The old man said, "You are welcome
in my home! I'll take care of you; you
don't have to spend the night in the
square." 21 So he took them home with
him and fed their donkeys. His guests
washed their feet and had a meal.

22 They were enjoying themselves
when all of a sudden some sexual perverts from the town surrounded the
house and started beating on the door.
They said to the old man, "Bring out that
man that came home with you! We want
to have sex with him!"

23 But the old man went outside and
said to them, "No, my friends! Please!
Don't do such an evil, immoral thing!
This man is my guest. 24 Look! Here is his
concubine and my own virgin daughter.
I'll bring them out now, and you can have
them. Do whatever you want to with
them. But don't do such an awful thing to
this man!" 25 But the men would not listen
to him. So the Levite took his concubine
and put her outside with them. They
raped her and abused her all night long
and didn't stop until morning.

26 At dawn the woman came and fell
down at the door of the old man's house,
where her husband was. She was still
there when daylight came. 27 Her husband got up that morning, and when he
opened the door to go on his way, he
found his concubine lying in front of the
house with her hands reaching for the
door. 28 He said, "Get up. Let's go." But
there was no answer. So he put her body
across the donkey and started on his way
home. 29 When he arrived, he went in the
house and got a knife. He took his concubine's body, cut it into twelve pieces, and
sent one piece to each of the twelve tribes
of Israel. 30 Everyone who saw it said,
"We have never heard of such a thing!
Nothing like this has ever happened
since the Israelites left Egypt! We have to
do something about this! What will
it be?"

Israel Prepares for War

20 All the people of Israel from Dan
in the north to Beersheba in the
south, as well as from the land of Gilead
in the east, answered the call. They gathered in one body in the LORD's presence
at Mizpah. 2 The leaders of all the tribes
of Israel were present at this gathering of
God's people, and there were 400,000
foot soldiers. 3 Meanwhile the people of
Benjamin heard that all the other Israelites had gathered at Mizpah.

The Israelites asked, "Tell us, how was
this crime committed?" 4 The Levite
whose concubine had been murdered answered, "My concubine and I went to
Gibeah in the territory of Benjamin to
spend the night. 5 The men of Gibeah
came to get me and surrounded the
house at night. They intended to kill
me; instead they raped my concubine,
and she died. 6 I took her body, cut it in
pieces, and sent one piece to each of the
twelve tribes of Israel. These people have
committed an evil and immoral act
among us. 7 All of you here are Israelites.
What are we going to do about this?"

8 All the people stood up together and
said, "None of us, whether he lives in a
tent or in a house, will go home. 9 This is
what we will do: we will draw lots and
choose some men to attack Gibeah.[t]
10 One tenth of the men in Israel will provide food for the army, and the others
will go and punish Gibeah[u] for this

[s] *One ancient translation* home; *Hebrew* to the house of the LORD. [t] *One ancient translation* to attack Gibeah; *Hebrew* to Gibeah. [u] *One ancient translation* Gibeah; *Hebrew* Geba.

immoral act that they have committed in Israel." 11 So all the men in Israel assembled with one purpose—to attack the town.

12 The Israelite tribes sent messengers all through the territory of the tribe of Benjamin to say, "What is this crime that you have committed? 13 Now hand over those perverts in Gibeah, so that we can kill them and remove this evil from Israel." But the people of Benjamin paid no attention to the other Israelites. 14 From all the cities of Benjamin they came to Gibeah to fight the other people of Israel. 15-16 They called out twenty-six thousand soldiers from their cities that day. Besides these, the citizens of Gibeah gathered seven hundred specially chosen men[v] who were left-handed. Every one of them could sling a stone at a strand of hair and never miss. 17 Not counting the tribe of Benjamin, the Israelites gathered 400,000 trained soldiers.

The War against the Benjaminites

18 The Israelites went to the place of worship at Bethel, and there they asked God, "Which tribe should attack the Benjaminites first?"

The LORD answered, "The tribe of Judah."

19 So the Israelites started out the next morning and camped near the city of Gibeah. 20 They went to attack the army of Benjamin, and placed the soldiers in position facing the city. 21 The army of Benjamin came out of the city, and before the day was over they had killed twenty-two thousand Israelite soldiers. 22-23 Then the Israelites went to the place of worship and mourned in the presence of the LORD until evening. They asked him, "Should we go again into battle against our brothers the Benjaminites?"

The LORD answered, "Yes."

So the Israelite army was encouraged, and they placed their soldiers in position again, where they had been the day before. 24 They marched against the army of Benjamin a second time. 25 And for the second time the Benjaminites came out of Gibeah, and this time they killed eighteen thousand trained Israelite soldiers. 26 Then all the people of Israel went up to Bethel and mourned. They sat there in the LORD's presence and did not eat until evening. They offered fellowship sacrifices and burned some sacrifices whole—all in the presence of the LORD. 27-28 God's Covenant Box was there at Bethel in those days, and Phinehas, the son of Eleazar and grandson of Aaron, was in charge of it. The people asked the LORD, "Should we go out to fight our brothers the Benjaminites again, or should we give up?"

The LORD answered, "Fight. Tomorrow I will give you victory over them."

29 So the Israelites put some soldiers in hiding around Gibeah. 30 Then for the third straight day they marched against the army of Benjamin and placed their soldiers in battle position facing Gibeah, as they had done before. 31 The Benjaminites came out to fight and were led away from the city. As they had before, they began killing some Israelites in the open country, on the road to Bethel and on the road to Gibeah. They killed about thirty Israelites. 32 The Benjaminites said, "We've beaten them just as before."

But the Israelites had planned to retreat and lead them away from the city onto the roads. 33 So when the main army of the Israelites pulled back and regrouped at Baaltamar, the men surrounding Gibeah suddenly rushed out of their hiding places in the rocky country around the city.[w] 34 Ten thousand men, specially chosen out of all Israel, attacked Gibeah, and the fighting was hard. The Benjaminites had not realized that they were about to be destroyed. 35 The LORD gave Israel victory over the army of Benjamin. The Israelites killed 25,100 of the enemy that day, 36 and the Benjaminites realized they were defeated.

How the Israelites Won

The main body of the Israelite army had retreated from the Benjaminites because they were relying on the men that they had put in hiding around Gibeah. 37 These men ran quickly toward Gibeah; they spread out in the city and killed everyone there. 38 The main Israelite

[v] *Some ancient translations* men; *Hebrew* men. In all this number there were seven hundred specially chosen men. [w] *One ancient translation* the city *(that is, Gibeah)*; *Hebrew* Geba.

army and the men in hiding had arranged a signal. When they saw a big cloud of smoke going up from the town, 39 the Israelites out on the battlefield were to turn around. By this time the Benjaminites had already killed the thirty Israelites. They told themselves, "Yes, we've beaten them just as before." 40 Then the signal appeared; a cloud of smoke began to go up from the town. The Benjaminites looked behind them and were amazed to see the whole city going up in flames. 41 Then the Israelites turned around, and the Benjaminites were thrown into panic because they realized that they were about to be destroyed. 42 They retreated from the Israelites and ran toward the open country, but they could not escape. They were caught between the main army and the men who were now coming out of the city,[x] and they were destroyed. 43 The Israelites had the enemy trapped, and without stopping they pursued them as far as a point east of Gibeah, killing them as they went.[y] 44 Eighteen thousand of the best Benjaminite soldiers were killed. 45 The others turned and ran toward the open country to Rimmon Rock. Five thousand of them were killed on the roads. The Israelites continued to pursue the rest to Gidom, killing two thousand. 46 In all, twenty-five thousand Benjaminites were killed that day—all of them brave soldiers.

47 But six hundred men were able to escape to the open country to Rimmon Rock, and they stayed there four months. 48 The Israelites turned back against the rest of the Benjaminites and killed them all—men, women, and children, and animals as well. They burned every town in the area.

Wives for the Tribe of Benjamin

21 When the Israelites had gathered at Mizpah, they had made a solemn promise to the LORD: "None of us will allow a Benjaminite to marry a daughter of ours." 2 So now the people of Israel went to Bethel and sat there in the presence of God until evening. Loudly and bitterly they mourned: 3 "LORD God of Israel, why has this happened? Why is the tribe of Benjamin about to disappear from Israel?"

4 Early the next morning the people got up and built an altar there. They offered fellowship sacrifices and burned some sacrifices whole. 5 They asked, "Is there any group out of all the tribes of Israel that did not go to the gathering in the LORD's presence at Mizpah?" (They had taken a solemn oath that anyone who had not gone to Mizpah would be put to death.) 6 The people of Israel felt sorry for their brothers the Benjaminites and said, "Today Israel has lost one of its tribes. 7 What shall we do to provide wives for the men of Benjamin who are left? We have made a solemn promise to the LORD that we will not give them any of our daughters."

8 When they asked if there was some group out of the tribes of Israel that had not gone to the gathering at Mizpah, they found out that no one from Jabesh in Gilead had been there; 9 at the roll call of the army no one from Jabesh had responded. 10 So the assembly sent twelve thousand of their bravest men with the orders, "Go and kill everyone in Jabesh, including women and children. 11 Kill all the males, and also every woman who is not a virgin." 12 They found four hundred young virgins among the people in Jabesh, so they brought them to the camp at Shiloh, which is in the land of Canaan.

13 Then the whole assembly sent word to the Benjaminites who were at Rimmon Rock and offered to end the war. 14 The Benjaminites came back, and the other Israelites gave them the young women from Jabesh whom they had not killed. But there were not enough of them.

15 The people felt sorry for the Benjaminites because the LORD had broken the unity of the tribes of Israel. 16 So the leaders of the gathering said, "There are no more women in the tribe of Benjamin. What shall we do to provide wives for the men who are left? 17 Israel must not lose one of its twelve tribes. We must find a way for the tribe of Benjamin to survive, 18 but we cannot allow them to marry our daughters, because we have put a curse on anyone who allows a Benjaminite to marry one of our daughters."

[x] *Probable text* city; *Hebrew* cities. [y] *Verse 43 in Hebrew is unclear.*

19 Then they thought, "The yearly festival of the LORD at Shiloh is coming soon."
(Shiloh is north of Bethel, south of Lebo-
nah, and east of the road between Bethel
and Shechem.) 20 They told the Benjaminites, "Go and hide in the vineyards
21 and watch. When the young women of
Shiloh come out to dance during the festival, you come out of the vineyards.
Each of you take a wife by force from
among them and take her back to the
territory of Benjamin with you. 22 If their
fathers or brothers come to you[z] and
protest, you[a] can tell them, 'Please let us
keep them, because we did not take them
from you in battle to be our wives. And
since you did not give them to us, you are
not guilty of breaking your promise.' "

23 The Benjaminites did this; each of
them chose a wife from the young
women who were dancing at Shiloh and
carried her away. Then they went back
to their own territory, rebuilt their towns,
and lived there. 24 At the same time the
rest of the Israelites left, and every man
went back to his own tribe and family
and to his own property.

25 There was no king in Israel at that
time. Everyone did whatever they
pleased.

[z] *One ancient translation* you; *Hebrew* us. [a] *Probable text* you; *Hebrew* we.

The Book of
RUTH

Introduction

The peaceful story of Ruth *is set in the violent times of* The Book of Judges. *Ruth, a Moabite woman, is married to an Israelite. When he dies, Ruth shows uncommon loyalty to her Israelite mother-in-law and deep devotion to the God of Israel. In the end she finds a new husband among her former husband's relatives, and through this marriage becomes the great-grandmother of David, Israel's greatest king.*

The stories of Judges show the disaster that came when God's people turned away from him. Ruth *shows the blessing that came to a foreigner who turned to Israel's God and so became part of his faithful people.*

Outline of Contents

Naomi returns to Bethlehem with Ruth 1.1-22
Ruth meets Boaz 2.1—3.18
Boaz marries Ruth 4.1-22

Elimelech and His Family Move to Moab

1 1-2 Long ago, in the days before Israel had a king, there was a famine
in the land. So a man named Elimelech,
who belonged to the clan of Ephrath and
who lived in Bethlehem in Judah, went
with his wife Naomi and their two sons
Mahlon and Chilion to live for a while in
the country of Moab. While they were
living there, 3 Elimelech died, and Naomi
was left alone with her two sons, 4 who
married Moabite women, Orpah and
Ruth. About ten years later 5 Mahlon and
Chilion also died, and Naomi was left all
alone, without husband or sons.

Naomi and Ruth Return to Bethlehem

6 Some time later Naomi heard that the
LORD had blessed his people by giving
them good crops; so she got ready to
leave Moab with her daughters-in-law.
7 They started out together to go back to
Judah, but on the way 8 she said to them,
"Go back home and stay with your mothers. May the LORD be as good to you as
you have been to me and to those who
have died. 9 And may the LORD make it
possible for each of you to marry again
and have a home."

So Naomi kissed them good-bye. But
they started crying 10 and said to her,
"No! We will go with you to your people."
11 "You must go back, my daughters,"
Naomi answered. "Why do you want to
come with me? Do you think I could have
sons again for you to marry? 12 Go back
home, for I am too old to get married
again. Even if I thought there was still
hope, and so got married tonight and had
sons, 13 would you wait until they had
grown up? Would this keep you from
marrying someone else? No, my daughters, you know that's impossible. The
LORD has turned against me, and I feel
very sorry for you."[a]

14 Again they started crying. Then Orpah kissed her mother-in-law good-bye
and went back home,[b] but Ruth held on
to her. 15 So Naomi said to her, "Ruth,
your sister-in-law has gone back to her
people and to her god.[c] Go back home
with her."

16 But Ruth answered, "Don't ask me to
leave you! Let me go with you. Wherever
you go, I will go; wherever you live, I will
live. Your people will be my people, and
your God will be my God. 17 Wherever
you die, I will die, and that is where I will
be buried. May the LORD's worst punishment come upon me if I let anything but
death[d] separate me from you!"

18 When Naomi saw that Ruth was determined to go with her, she said nothing
more.

[a] sorry for you; *or* bitter about what has happened to you. [b] *One ancient translation* and went back home; *Hebrew does not have these words.* [c] god; *or* gods. [d] anything but death; *or* even death.

19 They went on until they came to
Bethlehem. When they arrived, the
whole town became excited, and the
women there exclaimed, "Is this really
Naomi?"

20 "Don't call me Naomi," she answered; "call me Marah,[e] because
Almighty God has made my life bitter.
21 When I left here, I had plenty, but the
LORD has brought me back without a
thing. Why call me Naomi when the LORD
Almighty has condemned me and sent
me trouble?"

22 This, then, was how Naomi came
back from Moab with Ruth, her Moabite
daughter-in-law. When they arrived in
Bethlehem, the barley harvest was just
beginning.

Ruth Works in the Field of Boaz

2 Naomi had a relative named Boaz, a
rich and influential man who belonged to the family of her husband
Elimelech. 2 One day Ruth said to Naomi,
"Let me go to the fields to gather the
grain that the harvest workers leave. I
am sure to find someone who will let me
work with him."

Naomi answered, "Go ahead,
daughter."

3 So Ruth went out to the fields and
walked behind the workers, picking up
the heads of grain which they left. It so
happened that she was in a field that belonged to Boaz.

4 Some time later Boaz himself arrived
from Bethlehem and greeted the workers. "The LORD be with you!" he said.

"The LORD bless you!" they answered.

5 Boaz asked the man in charge, "Who
is that young woman?"

6 The man answered, "She is the foreigner who came back from Moab with
Naomi. 7 She asked me to let her follow
the workers and gather grain. She has
been working since early morning and
has just now stopped to rest for a while
under the shelter."

8 Then Boaz said to Ruth, "Let me give
you some advice. Don't gather grain anywhere except in this field. Work with the
women here; 9 watch them to see where
they are reaping and stay with them. I
have ordered my men not to molest you.
And whenever you are thirsty, go and
drink from the water jars that they have
filled."

10 Ruth bowed down with her face
touching the ground, and said to Boaz,
"Why should you be so concerned about
me? Why should you be so kind to a
foreigner?"

11 Boaz answered, "I have heard about
everything that you have done for your
mother-in-law since your husband died.
I know how you left your father and
mother and your own country and how
you came to live among a people you had
never known before. 12 May the LORD reward you for what you have done. May
you have a full reward from the LORD God
of Israel, to whom you have come for
protection!"

13 Ruth answered, "You are very kind[f]
to me, sir. You have made me feel better
by speaking gently to me, even though
I am not the equal of one of your
servants."

14 At mealtime Boaz said to Ruth,
"Come and have a piece of bread, and dip
it in the sauce." So she sat with the workers, and Boaz passed some roasted grain
to her. She ate until she was satisfied,
and she still had some food left over.
15-16 After she had left to go and gather
grain, Boaz ordered the workers, "Let
her gather grain even where the bundles
are lying, and don't say anything to stop
her. Besides that, pull out some heads of
grain from the bundles and leave them
for her to pick up."

17 So Ruth gathered grain in the field
until evening, and when she had beaten
it out, she found she had nearly twenty-
five pounds. 18 She took the grain back
into town and showed her mother-in-law
how much she had gathered. She also
gave her the food left over from the meal.
19 Naomi asked her, "Where did you
gather all this grain today? Whose field
have you been working in? May God
bless the man who took an interest
in you!"

So Ruth told Naomi that she had been
working in a field belonging to a man
named Boaz.

20 "May the LORD bless Boaz!" Naomi
exclaimed. "The LORD always keeps his
promises to the living and the dead." And
she went on, "That man is a close relative

[e] NAOMI . . . MARAH: *In Hebrew Naomi means "pleasant" and Marah means "bitter."* [f] You are very kind; *or* Please be kind.

of ours, one of those responsible for taking care of us."
21 Then Ruth said, "Best of all, he told
me to keep gathering grain with his
workers until they finish the harvest."
22 Naomi said to Ruth, "Yes, daughter,
it will be better for you to work with the
women in Boaz' field. You might be molested if you went to someone else's
field." 23 So Ruth worked with them and
gathered grain until all the barley and
wheat had been harvested. And she continued to live with her mother-in-law.

Ruth Finds a Husband

3 Some time later Naomi said to Ruth,
"I must find a husband for you, so
that you will have a home of your own.
2 Remember that this man Boaz, whose
women you have been working with, is
our relative. Now listen. This evening he
will be threshing the barley. 3 So wash
yourself, put on some perfume, and get
dressed in your best clothes. Then go
where he is threshing, but don't let him
know you are there until he has finished
eating and drinking. 4 Be sure to notice
where he lies down, and after he falls
asleep, go and lift the covers and lie
down at his feet. He will tell you what
to do."
5 Ruth answered, "I will do everything
you say."
6 So Ruth went to the threshing place
and did just what her mother-in-law had
told her. 7 When Boaz had finished eating
and drinking, he was in a good mood. He
went to the pile of barley and lay down
to sleep. Ruth slipped over quietly, lifted
the covers and lay down at his feet. 8 During the night he woke up suddenly,
turned over, and was surprised to find a
woman lying at his feet. 9 "Who are you?"
he asked.
"It's Ruth, sir," she answered. "Because you are a close relative, you are
responsible for taking care of me. So
please marry me."
10 "The LORD bless you," he said. "You
are showing even greater family loyalty
in what you are doing now than in what
you did for your mother-in-law. You
might have gone looking for a young
man, either rich or poor, but you haven't.
11 Now don't worry, Ruth. I will do everything you ask; as everyone in town
knows, you are a fine woman. 12 It is true
that I am a close relative and am responsible for you, but there is a man who is a
closer relative than I am. 13 Stay here the
rest of the night, and in the morning we
will find out whether or not he will take
responsibility for you. If so, well and
good; if not, then I swear by the living
LORD that I will take the responsibility.
Now lie down and stay here till
morning."
14 So she lay there at his feet, but she
got up before it was light enough for her
to be seen, because Boaz did not want
anyone to know that she had been there.
15 Boaz said to her, "Take off your cloak
and spread it out here." She did, and he
poured out almost fifty pounds of barley
and helped her lift it to her shoulder.
Then she returned to town with it.
16 When she arrived home, her mother-
in-law asked her, "How did you get
along, daughter?"
Ruth told her everything that Boaz had
done for her. 17 She added, "He told me I
must not come back to you empty-
handed, so he gave me all this barley."
18 Naomi said to her, "Now be patient,
Ruth, until you see how this all turns out.
Boaz will not rest today until he settles
the matter."

Boaz Marries Ruth

4 Boaz went to the meeting place at
the town gate and sat down there.
Then Elimelech's nearest relative, the
man whom Boaz had mentioned, came
by, and Boaz called to him, "Come over
here, my friend, and sit down." So he
went over and sat down. 2 Then Boaz got
ten of the leaders of the town and asked
them to sit down there too. When they
were seated, 3 he said to his relative,
"Now that Naomi has come back from
Moab, she wants to sell the field that belonged to our relative Elimelech, 4 and I
think you ought to know about it. Now
then, if you want it, buy it in the presence
of these men sitting here. But if you don't
want it, say so, because the right to buy
it belongs first to you and then to me."
The man said, "I will buy it."
5 Boaz said, "Very well, if you buy the
field from Naomi, then you are also buying Ruth,[g] the Moabite widow, so that

[g] *Some ancient translations* Naomi . . . Ruth; *Hebrew* Naomi and from Ruth.

the field will stay in the dead man's
family."
6 The man answered, "In that case I will
give up my right to buy the field, because
it would mean that my own children
would not inherit it. You buy it; I would
rather not."
7 Now in those days, to settle a sale or
an exchange of property, it was the custom for the seller to take off his sandal
and give it to the buyer. In this way the
Israelites showed that the matter was
settled.
8 So when the man said to Boaz, "You
buy it," he took off his sandal and gave it
to Boaz.[h] 9 Then Boaz said to the leaders
and all the others there, "You are all witnesses today that I have bought from
Naomi everything that belonged to
Elimelech and to his sons Chilion and
Mahlon. 10 In addition, Ruth the Moabite,
Mahlon's widow, becomes my wife. This
will keep the property in the dead man's
family, and his family line will continue
among his people and in his hometown.
You are witnesses to this today."
11 The leaders and the others said,
"Yes, we are witnesses. May the LORD
make your wife become like Rachel and
Leah, who bore many children to Jacob.
May you become rich in the clan of Ephrath and famous in Bethlehem. 12 May
the children that the LORD will give you
by this young woman make your family
like the family of Perez, the son of Judah
and Tamar."

Boaz and His Descendants

13 So Boaz took Ruth home as his wife.
The LORD blessed her, and she became
pregnant and had a son. 14 The women
said to Naomi, "Praise the LORD! He has
given you a grandson today to take care
of you. May the boy become famous in
Israel! 15 Your daughter-in-law loves
you, and has done more for you than
seven sons. And now she has given you
a grandson, who will bring new life to
you and give you security in your old
age." 16 Naomi took the child, held him
close,[i] and took care of him.
17 The women of the neighborhood
named the boy Obed. They told everyone, "A son has been born to Naomi!"
Obed became the father of Jesse, who
was the father of David.
18-22 This is the family line from Perez
to David: Perez, Hezron, Ram, Amminadab, Nahshon, Salmon, Boaz, Obed,
Jesse, David.

[h] *One ancient translation* and gave it to Boaz; *Hebrew does not have these words.* [i] held him close; *or* adopted him.

The First Book of
SAMUEL

Introduction

The book of First Samuel *records the transition in Israel from the period of the judges to the monarchy. This change in Israel's national life revolved mainly around three men: Samuel, the last of the great judges; Saul, Israel's first king; and David, whose early adventures before coming to power are interwoven with the accounts of Samuel and Saul.*

The theme of this book, like that of other historical writings in the Old Testament, is that faithfulness to God brings success, while disobedience brings disaster. This is stated clearly in the Lord's message to the priest Eli in 2.30: "I will honor those who honor me, and I will treat with contempt those who despise me."

The book records mixed feelings about the establishment of the monarchy. The Lord himself was regarded as the real king of Israel, but in response to the people's request the Lord chose a king for them. The important fact was that both the king and the people of Israel lived under the sovereignty and judgment of God (2.7-10). Under God's laws the rights of all people, rich and poor alike, were to be maintained.

Outline of Contents

Elkanah and His Family at Shiloh

1 There was a man named Elkanah,
from the tribe of Ephraim, who
lived in the town of Ramah in the hill
country of Ephraim. He was the son of
Jeroham and grandson of Elihu, and belonged to the family of Tohu, a part of
the clan of Zuph. 2Elkanah had two
wives, Hannah and Peninnah. Peninnah
had children, but Hannah did not.
3Every year Elkanah went from Ramah
to worship and offer sacrifices to the
LORD Almighty at Shiloh, where Hophni
and Phinehas, the two sons of Eli, were
priests of the LORD. 4Each time Elkanah
offered his sacrifice, he would give one
share of the meat to Peninnah and one
share to each of her children. 5And even
though he loved Hannah very much he
would give her only one share, because[a] the LORD had kept her from having children. 6Peninnah, her rival,
would torment and humiliate her, because the LORD had kept her childless.
7This went on year after year; whenever
they went to the house of the LORD, Peninnah would upset Hannah so much
that she would cry and refuse to eat anything. 8Her husband Elkanah would ask
her, "Hannah, why are you crying? Why
won't you eat? Why are you always so
sad? Don't I mean more to you than ten
sons?"

Hannah and Eli

9-10One time, after they had finished
their meal in the house of the LORD at
Shiloh, Hannah got up. She was deeply
distressed, and she cried bitterly as she
prayed to the LORD. Meanwhile, Eli the
priest was sitting in his place by the
door. 11Hannah made a solemn promise:
"LORD Almighty, look at me, your servant! See my trouble and remember me!
Don't forget me! If you give me a son, I
promise that I will dedicate him to you
for his whole life and that he will never
have his hair cut."[b]
12Hannah continued to pray to the
LORD for a long time, and Eli watched her
lips. 13She was praying silently; her lips

[a] And even ... because; *or* To Hannah, however, he would give a special share, because he loved her very much, even though. [b] NEVER HAVE HIS HAIR CUT: *A sign of dedication to the* LORD *(see Nu 6.5).*

were moving, but she made no sound. So
Eli thought that she was drunk, 14 and he
said to her, "Stop making a drunken
show of yourself! Stop your drinking
and sober up!"
15 "No, I'm not drunk, sir," she answered.
"I haven't been drinking! I am
desperate, and I have been praying,
pouring out my troubles to the LORD.
16 Don't think I am a worthless woman. I
have been praying like this because I'm
so miserable."
17 "Go in peace," Eli said, "and may the
God of Israel give you what you have
asked him for."
18 "May you always think kindly of
me," she replied. Then she went away,
ate some food, and was no longer sad.

Samuel's Birth and Dedication

19 The next morning Elkanah and his
family got up early, and after worshiping
the LORD, they went back home to
Ramah. Elkanah had intercourse with
his wife Hannah, and the LORD answered
her prayer. 20 So it was that she became
pregnant and gave birth to a son. She
named him Samuel,[c] and explained, "I
asked the LORD for him."
21 The time came again for Elkanah
and his family to go to Shiloh and offer
to the LORD the yearly sacrifice and the
special sacrifice he had promised. 22 But
this time Hannah did not go. She told
her husband, "As soon as the child is
weaned, I will take him to the house of
the LORD, where he will stay all his life."
23 Elkanah answered, "All right, do
whatever you think best; stay at home
until you have weaned him. And may
the LORD make your[d] promise come
true." So Hannah stayed at home and
nursed her child.
24 After she had weaned him, she took
him to Shiloh, taking along a three-year-old
bull,[e] a bushel of flour, and a leather
bag full of wine. She took Samuel,
young as he was, to the house of the
LORD at Shiloh. 25 After they had killed
the bull, they took the child to Eli.
26 Hannah said to him, "Excuse me, sir.
Do you remember me? I am the woman
you saw standing here, praying to the
LORD. 27 I asked him for this child, and he
gave me what I asked for. 28 So I am dedicating
him to the LORD. As long as he
lives, he will belong to the LORD."
Then they[f] worshiped the LORD there.

Hannah's Prayer

2 Hannah prayed:

"The LORD has filled my heart
with joy;
how happy I am because of
what he has done!
I laugh at my enemies;
how joyful I am because God
has helped me!

2 "No one is holy like the LORD;
there is none like him,
no protector like our God.
3 Stop your loud boasting;
silence your proud words.
For the LORD is a God who knows,
and he judges all that people do.
4 The bows of strong soldiers are
broken,
but the weak grow strong.
5 The people who once were
well fed
now hire themselves out to get
food,
but the hungry are hungry no
more.
The childless wife has borne seven
children,
but the mother of many is left
with none.
6 The LORD kills and restores to life;
he sends people to the world of
the dead
and brings them back again.
7 He makes some people poor and
others rich;
he humbles some and makes
others great.
8 He lifts the poor from the dust
and raises the needy from their
misery.
He makes them companions of
princes
and puts them in places of
honor.
The foundations of the earth
belong to the LORD;
on them he has built the world.

[c] SAMUEL: *This name, which in Hebrew means "name of God," is here related to the Hebrew verb for "ask."* [d] *Some ancient translations* your; *Hebrew* his. [e] *Some ancient translations* a three-year-old bull; *Hebrew* three bulls. [f] *Some ancient translations* they; *Hebrew* he.

9 "He protects the lives of his
faithful people,
but the wicked disappear in
darkness;
a man does not triumph by his
own strength.
10 The LORD's enemies will be
destroyed;
he will thunder against them
from heaven.
The LORD will judge the whole
world;
he will give power to his king,
he will make his chosen king
victorious."

11 Then Elkanah went back home to
Ramah, but the boy Samuel stayed in
Shiloh and served the LORD under the
priest Eli.

The Sons of Eli

12 The sons of Eli were scoundrels.
They paid no attention to the LORD 13 or
to the regulations concerning what the
priests could demand from the people.
Instead, when someone was offering a
sacrifice, the priest's servant would
come with a three-pronged fork. While
the meat was still cooking, 14 he would
stick the fork into the cooking pot, and
whatever the fork brought out belonged
to the priest. All the Israelites who came
to Shiloh to offer sacrifices were treated
like this. 15 In addition, even before the
fat was taken off and burned, the priest's
servant would come and say to the one
offering the sacrifice, "Give me some
meat for the priest to roast; he won't accept boiled meat from you, only raw
meat."
16 If the person answered, "Let us do
what is right and burn the fat first; then
take what you want," the priest's servant
would say, "No! Give it to me now! If you
don't, I will have to take it by force!"
17 This sin of the sons of Eli was extremely serious in the LORD's sight, because they treated the offerings to the
LORD with such disrespect.

Samuel at Shiloh

18 In the meantime the boy Samuel
continued to serve the LORD, wearing a
sacred linen apron. 19 Each year his
mother would make a little robe and
take it to him when she accompanied
her husband to offer the yearly sacrifice.
20 Then Eli would bless Elkanah and his
wife, and say to Elkanah, "May the LORD
give you other children by this woman
to take the place of the one you dedicated to him."
After that they would go back home.
21 The LORD did bless Hannah, and she
had three more sons and two daughters.
The boy Samuel grew up in the service
of the LORD.

Eli and His Sons

22 Eli was now very old. He kept hearing about everything his sons were doing to the Israelites and that they were
even sleeping with the women who
worked at the entrance to the Tent of the
LORD's presence. 23 So he said to them,
"Why are you doing these things? Everybody tells me about the evil you are doing. 24 Stop it, my sons! This is an awful
thing the people of the LORD are talking
about! 25 If anyone sins against someone
else, God can defend the one who is
wrong; but who can defend someone
who sins against the LORD?"
But they would not listen to their
father, for the LORD had decided to kill
them.
26 The boy Samuel continued to grow
and to gain favor both with the LORD and
with people.

The Prophecy against Eli's Family

27 A prophet came to Eli with this message from the LORD: "When your ancestor Aaron and his family were slaves of
the king of Egypt, I revealed myself to
Aaron. 28 From all the tribes of Israel I
chose his family to be my priests, to
serve at the altar, to burn the incense,
and to wear the ephod[g] to consult me.
And I gave them the right to keep a
share of the sacrifices burned on the altar. 29 Why, then, do you look with
greed[h] at the sacrifices and offerings
which I require from my people? Why,
Eli, do you honor your sons more than
me by letting them fatten themselves on
the best parts of all the sacrifices my
people offer to me? 30 I, the LORD God of
Israel, promised in the past that your

[g] EPHOD: *See Word List.* [h] *One ancient translation* look with greed; *Hebrew unclear.*

family and your clan would serve me as
priests for all time. But now I say that I
won't have it any longer! Instead, I will
honor those who honor me, and I will
treat with contempt those who despise
me. 31 Listen, the time is coming when I
will kill all the young men in your family
and your clan, so that no man in your
family will live to be old. 32 You will be
troubled and look with envy[i] on all the
blessings I will give to the other people
of Israel, but no one in your family will
ever again live to old age. 33 Yet I will
keep one of your descendants alive, and
he will serve me as priest. But he[j] will
become blind and lose all hope, and all
your other descendants will die a violent
death. 34 When your two sons Hophni
and Phinehas both die on the same day,
this will show you that everything I have
said will come true. 35 I will choose a
priest who will be faithful to me and do
everything I want him to. I will give him
descendants, who will always serve in
the presence of my chosen king. 36 Any
of your descendants who survive will
have to go to that priest and ask him for
money and food, and beg to be allowed
to help the priests, in order to have
something to eat."

The Lord Appears to Samuel

3 In those days, when the boy Samuel
was serving the Lord under the direction of Eli, there were very few messages from the Lord, and visions from
him were quite rare. 2 One night Eli, who
was now almost blind, was sleeping in
his own room; 3 Samuel was sleeping in
the sanctuary, where the sacred Covenant Box was. Before dawn, while the
lamp was still burning, 4 the Lord called
Samuel. He answered, "Yes, sir!" 5 and
ran to Eli and said, "You called me, and
here I am."

But Eli answered, "I didn't call you; go
back to bed." So Samuel went back
to bed.

6-7 The Lord called Samuel again. The
boy did not know that it was the Lord,
because the Lord had never spoken to
him before. So he got up, went to Eli,
and said, "You called me, and here
I am."

But Eli answered, "My son, I didn't call
you; go back to bed."

8 The Lord called Samuel a third time;
he got up, went to Eli, and said, "You
called me, and here I am."

Then Eli realized that it was the Lord
who was calling the boy, 9 so he said to
him, "Go back to bed; and if he calls you
again, say, 'Speak, Lord, your servant is
listening.'" So Samuel went back
to bed.

10 The Lord came and stood there, and
called as he had before, "Samuel!
Samuel!"

Samuel answered, "Speak; your servant is listening."

11 The Lord said to him, "Some day I
am going to do something to the people
of Israel that is so terrible that everyone
who hears about it will be stunned. 12 On
that day I will carry out all my threats
against Eli's family, from beginning to
end. 13 I have already told him[k] that I
am going to punish his family forever
because his sons have spoken evil things
against me. Eli knew they were doing
this, but he did not stop them. 14 So I solemnly declare to the family of Eli that no
sacrifice or offering will ever be able to
remove the consequences of this terrible sin."

15 Samuel stayed in bed until morning;
then he got up and opened the doors of
the house of the Lord. He was afraid to
tell Eli about the vision. 16 Eli called him,
"Samuel, my boy!"

"Yes, sir," answered Samuel.

17 "What did the Lord tell you?" Eli
asked. "Don't keep anything from me.
God will punish you severely if you
don't tell me everything he said." 18 So
Samuel told him everything; he did not
keep anything back. Eli said, "He is the
Lord; he will do whatever seems best
to him."

19 As Samuel grew up, the Lord was
with him and made come true everything that Samuel said. 20 So all the people of Israel, from one end of the country
to the other, knew that Samuel was indeed a prophet of the Lord. 21 The Lord
continued to reveal himself at Shiloh,
where he had appeared to Samuel and
had spoken to him. And when Samuel
spoke, all Israel listened.

[i] *Probable text* look with envy; *Hebrew unclear.* [j] *One ancient translation* he; *Hebrew* you.
[k] *One ancient translation* I have already told him; *Hebrew* I will tell him.

The Capture of the Covenant Box

4 At that time the Philistines gathered to go to war against Israel, so[l] the Israelites set out to fight them. The Israelites set up their camp at Ebenezer and the Philistines at Aphek. 2 The Philistines attacked, and after fierce fighting they defeated the Israelites and killed about four thousand men on the battlefield. 3 When the survivors came back to camp, the leaders of Israel said, "Why did the LORD let the Philistines defeat us today? Let's go and bring the LORD's Covenant Box from Shiloh, so that he[m] will go with us and save us from our enemies." 4 So they sent messengers to Shiloh and got the Covenant Box of the LORD Almighty, who is enthroned above the winged creatures.[n] And Eli's two sons, Hophni and Phinehas, came along with the Covenant Box.

5 When the Covenant Box arrived, the Israelites gave such a loud shout of joy that the earth shook. 6 The Philistines heard the shouting and said, "Listen to all that shouting in the Hebrew camp! What does it mean?" When they found out that the LORD's Covenant Box had arrived in the Hebrew camp, 7 they were afraid, and said, "A god has come into their camp! We're lost! Nothing like this has ever happened to us before! 8 Who can save us from those powerful gods? They are the gods who slaughtered the Egyptians in the desert! 9 Be brave, Philistines! Fight like men, or we will become slaves to the Hebrews, just as they were our slaves. So fight like men!"

10 The Philistines fought hard and defeated the Israelites, who went running to their homes. There was a great slaughter: thirty thousand Israelite soldiers were killed. 11 God's Covenant Box was captured, and Eli's sons, Hophni and Phinehas, were both killed.

The Death of Eli

12 A man from the tribe of Benjamin ran all the way from the battlefield to Shiloh and arrived there the same day. To show his grief, he had torn his clothes and put dirt on his head. 13 Eli, who was very worried about the Covenant Box, was sitting in his seat beside the road, staring. The man spread the news throughout the town, and everyone cried out in fear. 14 Eli heard the noise and asked, "What is all this noise about?" The man hurried to Eli to tell him the news. (15 Eli was now ninety-eight years old and almost completely blind.) 16 The man said, "I have escaped from the battle and have run all the way here today."

Eli asked him, "What happened, my son?"

17 The messenger answered, "Israel ran away from the Philistines; it was a terrible defeat for us! Besides that, your sons Hophni and Phinehas were killed, and God's Covenant Box was captured!"

18 When the man mentioned the Covenant Box, Eli fell backward from his seat beside the gate. He was so old and fat that the fall broke his neck, and he died. He had been a leader in Israel for forty years.

The Death of the Widow of Phinehas

19 Eli's daughter-in-law, the wife of Phinehas, was pregnant, and it was almost time for her baby to be born. When she heard that God's Covenant Box had been captured and that her father-in-law and her husband were dead, she suddenly went into labor and gave birth. 20 As she was dying, the women helping her said to her, "Be brave! You have a son!" But she paid no attention and did not answer. 21 She named the boy Ichabod,[o] explaining, "God's glory has left Israel"—referring to the capture of the Covenant Box and the death of her father-in-law and her husband. 22 "God's glory has left Israel," she said, "because God's Covenant Box has been captured."

The Covenant Box among the Philistines

5 After the Philistines captured the Covenant Box, they carried it from Ebenezer to their city of Ashdod, 2 took it into the temple of their god Dagon, and set it up beside his statue. 3 Early the next morning the people of Ashdod saw that the statue of Dagon had fallen face downward on the ground in front of the LORD's Covenant Box. So they lifted it up and put it back in its place. 4 Early the

[l] *One ancient translation* the Philistines . . . so; *Hebrew does not have these words.* [m] he; *or* it.
[n] WINGED CREATURES: *See Word List.* [o] ICHABOD: *This name in Hebrew means "no glory."*

following morning they saw that the statue had again fallen down in front of the Covenant Box. This time its head and both its arms were broken off and were lying in the doorway; only the body was left. (5 That is why even today the priests of Dagon and all his worshipers in Ashdod step over that place and do not walk on it.)

6 The LORD punished the people of Ashdod severely and terrified them. He punished them and the people in the surrounding territory by causing them to have tumors.[p] 7 When they saw what was happening, they said, "The God of Israel is punishing us and our god Dagon. We can't let the Covenant Box stay here any longer." 8 So they sent messengers and called together all five of the Philistine kings and asked them, "What shall we do with the Covenant Box of the God of Israel?"

"Take it over to Gath," they answered; so they took it to Gath, another Philistine city. 9 But after it arrived there, the LORD punished that city too and caused a great panic. He punished them with tumors which developed in all the people of the city, young and old alike. 10 So they sent the Covenant Box to Ekron, another Philistine city; but when it arrived there, the people cried out, "They have brought the Covenant Box of the God of Israel here, in order to kill us all!" 11 So again they sent for all the Philistine kings and said, "Send the Covenant Box of Israel back to its own place, so that it won't kill us and our families." There was panic throughout the city because God was punishing them so severely. 12 Even those who did not die developed tumors and the people cried out to their gods for help.

The Return of the Covenant Box

6 After the LORD's Covenant Box had been in Philistia for seven months, 2 the people called the priests and the magicians and asked, "What shall we do with the Covenant Box of the LORD? If we send it back where it belongs, what shall we send with it?"

3 They answered, "If you return the Covenant Box of the God of Israel, you must, of course, send with it a gift to him to pay for your sin. The Covenant Box must not go back without a gift. In this way you will be healed, and you will find out why he has kept on punishing you."

4 "What gift shall we send him?" the people asked.

They answered, "Five gold models of tumors and five gold mice, one of each for each Philistine king. The same plague was sent on all of you and on the five kings. 5 You must make these models of the tumors and of the mice that are ravaging your country, and you must give honor to the God of Israel. Perhaps he will stop punishing you, your gods, and your land. 6 Why should you be stubborn, as the king of Egypt and the Egyptians were? Don't forget how God made fools of them until they let the Israelites leave Egypt. 7 So prepare a new wagon and two cows that have never been yoked; hitch them to the wagon and drive their calves back to the barn. 8 Take the LORD's Covenant Box, put it on the wagon, and place in a box beside it the gold models that you are sending to him as a gift to pay for your sins. Start the wagon on its way and let it go by itself. 9 Then watch it go; if it goes toward the town of Beth Shemesh, this means that it is the God of the Israelites who has sent this terrible disaster on us. But if it doesn't, then we will know that he did not send the plague; it was only a matter of chance."

10 They did what they were told: they took two cows and hitched them to the wagon, and shut the calves in the barn. 11 They put the Covenant Box in the wagon, together with the box containing the gold models of the mice and of the tumors. 12 The cows started off on the road to Beth Shemesh and headed straight toward it, without turning off the road. They were mooing as they went. The five Philistine kings followed them as far as the border of Beth Shemesh.

13 The people of Beth Shemesh were reaping wheat in the valley, when suddenly they looked up and saw the Covenant Box. They were overjoyed at the sight. 14 The wagon came to a field belonging to a man named Joshua, who lived in Beth Shemesh, and it stopped

[p] TUMORS: *The association of tumors with an abundance of mice suggests that this was a case of bubonic plague (see 6.5).*

there near a large rock. The people
chopped up the wooden wagon and
killed the cows and burned them as a
burnt sacrifice to the LORD. 15The Levites
lifted off the Covenant Box of the LORD
and the box with the gold models in it,
and placed them on the large rock. Then
the people of Beth Shemesh offered
burnt sacrifices and other sacrifices to
the LORD. 16The five Philistine kings
watched them do this and then went
back to Ekron that same day.
17The Philistines sent the five gold tumors to the LORD as a gift to pay for their
sins, one each for the cities of Ashdod,
Gaza, Ashkelon, Gath, and Ekron.
18They also sent gold mice, one for each
of the cities ruled by the five Philistine
kings, both the fortified towns and the
villages without walls. The large rock in
the field of Joshua of Beth Shemesh, on
which they placed the LORD's Covenant
Box, is still there as a witness to what
happened.
19The LORD killed seventy of the men
of Beth Shemesh because they looked
inside the Covenant Box. And the people
mourned because the LORD had caused
such a great slaughter among them.

The Covenant Box at Kiriath Jearim

20So the men of Beth Shemesh said,
"Who can stand before the LORD, this
holy God? Where can we send him to get
him away from us?" 21They sent messengers to the people of Kiriath Jearim
to say, "The Philistines have returned
the LORD's Covenant Box. Come down
and get it."
7 So the people of Kiriath Jearim got
the LORD's Covenant Box and took it
to the house of a man named Abinadab,
who lived on a hill. They consecrated his
son Eleazar to be in charge of it.

Samuel Rules Israel

2The Covenant Box of the LORD stayed
in Kiriath Jearim a long time, some
twenty years. During this time all the Israelites cried to the LORD for help.
3Samuel said to the people of Israel,
"If you are going to turn to the LORD with
all your hearts, you must get rid of all
the foreign gods and the images of the
goddess Astarte. Dedicate yourselves
completely to the LORD and worship only
him, and he will rescue you from the
power of the Philistines." 4So the Israelites got rid of their idols of Baal and Astarte, and worshiped only the LORD.
5Then Samuel called for all the Israelites to meet at Mizpah, telling them, "I
will pray to the LORD for you there." 6So
they all gathered at Mizpah. They drew
some water and poured it out as an offering to the LORD and fasted that whole
day. They said, "We have sinned against
the LORD." (It was at Mizpah where Samuel settled disputes among the Israelites.)
7When the Philistines heard that the
Israelites had gathered at Mizpah, the
five Philistine kings started out with
their men to attack them. The Israelites
heard about it and were afraid, 8and
said to Samuel, "Keep praying to the
LORD our God to save us from the Philistines." 9Samuel killed a young lamb and
burned it whole as a sacrifice to the
LORD. Then he prayed to the LORD to help
Israel, and the LORD answered his
prayer. 10While Samuel was offering the
sacrifice, the Philistines moved forward
to attack; but just then the LORD thundered from heaven against them. They
became completely confused and fled in
panic. 11The Israelites marched out from
Mizpah and pursued the Philistines almost as far as Bethcar, killing them
along the way.
12Then Samuel took a stone, set it up
between Mizpah and Shen, and said,
"The LORD has helped us all the way"—
and he named it "Stone of Help." 13So
the Philistines were defeated, and the
LORD prevented them from invading Israel's territory as long as Samuel lived.
14All the cities which the Philistines had
captured between Ekron and Gath were
returned to Israel, and so Israel got back
all its territory. And there was peace
also between the Israelites and the Canaanites.
15Samuel ruled Israel as long as he
lived. 16Every year he would go around
to Bethel, Gilgal, and Mizpah, and in
these places he would settle disputes.
17Then he would go back to his home in
Ramah, where also he would serve as
judge. In Ramah he built an altar to the
LORD.

The People Ask for a King

8 When Samuel grew old, he made
his sons judges in Israel. 2The older
son was named Joel and the younger

one Abijah; they were judges in Beersheba. 3 But they did not follow their
father's example; they were interested
only in making money, so they accepted
bribes and did not decide cases honestly.
4 Then all the leaders of Israel met together, went to Samuel in Ramah, 5 and
said to him, "Look, you are getting old
and your sons don't follow your example. So then, appoint a king to rule over
us, so that we will have a king, as other
countries have." 6 Samuel was displeased with their request for a king; so
he prayed to the LORD, 7 and the LORD
said, "Listen to everything the people
say to you. You are not the one they
have rejected; I am the one they have
rejected as their king. 8 Ever since I
brought them out of Egypt, they have
turned away from me and worshiped
other gods; and now they are doing to
you what they have always done to me.
9 So then, listen to them, but give them
strict warnings and explain how their
kings will treat them."
10 Samuel told the people who were
asking him for a king everything that
the LORD had said to him. 11 "This is how
your king will treat you," Samuel explained. "He will make soldiers of your
sons; some of them will serve in his war
chariots, others in his cavalry, and others will run before his chariots. 12 He will
make some of them officers in charge of
a thousand men, and others in charge of
fifty men. Your sons will have to plow
his fields, harvest his crops, and make
his weapons and the equipment for his
chariots. 13 Your daughters will have to
make perfumes for him and work as his
cooks and his bakers. 14 He will take
your best fields, vineyards, and olive
groves, and give them to his officials.
15 He will take a tenth of your grain and
of your grapes for his court officers and
other officials. 16 He will take your servants and your best cattle[q] and donkeys,
and make them work for him. 17 He will
take a tenth of your flocks. And you
yourselves will become his slaves.
18 When that time comes, you will complain bitterly because of your king,
whom you yourselves chose, but the
LORD will not listen to your complaints."
19 The people paid no attention to
Samuel, but said, "No! We want a king,
20 so that we will be like other nations,
with our own king to rule us and to lead
us out to war and to fight our battles."
21 Samuel listened to everything they
said and then went and told it to the
LORD. 22 The LORD answered, "Do what
they want and give them a king." Then
Samuel told all the men of Israel to go
back home.

Saul Meets Samuel

9 There was a wealthy and influential
man named Kish, from the tribe of
Benjamin; he was the son of Abiel and
grandson of Zeror, and belonged to the
family of Becorath, a part of the clan of
Aphiah. 2 He had a son named Saul, a
handsome man in the prime of life. Saul
was a foot taller than anyone else in Israel and more handsome as well.
3 Some donkeys belonging to Kish had
wandered off, so he said to Saul, "Take
one of the servants with you and go and
look for the donkeys." 4 They went
through the hill country of Ephraim and
the region of Shalishah, but did not find
them; so they went on through the region of Shaalim, but the donkeys were
not there. Then they went through the
territory of Benjamin, but still did not
find them. 5 When they came into the region of Zuph, Saul said to his servant,
"Let's go back home, or my father might
stop thinking about the donkeys and
start worrying about us."
6 The servant answered, "Wait! In this
town there is a holy man who is highly
respected because everything he says
comes true. Let's go to him, and maybe
he can tell us where we can find the
donkeys."
7 "If we go to him, what can we give
him?" Saul asked. "There is no food left
in our packs, and we don't have a thing
to give him, do we?"
8 The servant answered, "I have a
small silver coin. I can give him that, and
then he will tell us where we can find
them."
9-11 Saul replied, "A good idea! Let's
go." So they went to the town where the
holy man lived. As they were going up
the hill to the town, they met some
young women who were coming out to
draw water. They asked these women,
"Is the seer in town?"

[q] *One ancient translation* cattle; *Hebrew* young men.

(At that time a prophet was called a
seer, and so whenever someone wanted
to ask God a question, he would say,
“Let’s go to the seer.”)
12-13“Yes, he is,” the young women answered. “In fact, he is just ahead of you.
If you hurry, you will catch up with him.
As soon as you go into town, you will
find him. He arrived in town today because the people are going to offer a sacrifice on the altar on the hill. The people
who are invited won’t start eating until
he gets there, because he has to bless the
sacrifice first. If you go now, you will
find him before he goes up the hill to
eat.” 14So Saul and his servant went on
to the town, and as they were going in,
they saw Samuel coming out toward
them on his way to the place of worship.
15Now on the previous day the LORD
had told Samuel, 16“Tomorrow about
this time I will send you a man from the
tribe of Benjamin; anoint him as ruler of
my people Israel, and he will rescue
them from the Philistines. I have seen
the suffering of my people and have
heard their cries for help.”
17When Samuel caught sight of Saul,
the LORD said to him, “This is the man I
told you about. He will rule my people.”
18Then Saul went over to Samuel, who
was near the gate, and asked, “Tell me,
where does the seer live?”
19Samuel answered, “I am the seer. Go
on ahead of me to the place of worship.
Both of you are to eat with me today.
Tomorrow morning I will answer all
your questions and send you on your
way. 20As for the donkeys that were lost
three days ago, don’t worry about them;
they have already been found. But who
is it that the people of Israel want so
much?[r] It is you – you and your father’s
family.”
21Saul answered, “I belong to the tribe
of Benjamin, the smallest tribe in Israel,
and my family is the least important one
in the tribe. Why, then, do you talk like
this to me?”
22Then Samuel led Saul and his servant into the large room and gave them a
place at the head of the table where the
guests, about thirty in all, were seated.
23Samuel said to the cook, “Bring the
piece of meat I gave you, which I told
you to set aside.” 24So the cook brought
the choice piece of the leg and placed it
before Saul. Samuel[s] said, “Look, here
is the piece that was kept for you. Eat it.
I saved it for you to eat at this time with
the people I invited.”[t]
So Saul ate with Samuel that day.
25When they went down from the place
of worship to the town, they fixed up a
bed for Saul[u] on the roof,[v] 26and he
slept there.[w]

Samuel Anoints Saul as Ruler

At dawn Samuel called to Saul on the
roof, “Get up, and I will send you on
your way.” Saul got up, and he and Samuel went out to the street together.
27When they arrived at the edge of town,
Samuel said to Saul, “Tell the servant to
go on ahead of us.” The servant left, and
Samuel continued, “Stay here a minute,
and I will tell you what God has said.”
10 Then Samuel took a jar of olive
oil and poured it on Saul’s head,
kissed him, and said, “The LORD anoints
you as ruler of his people Israel. You will
rule his people and protect them from all
their enemies. And this is the proof to
you that the LORD has chosen you[x] to be
the ruler of his people: 2When you leave
me today, you will meet two men near
Rachel’s tomb at Zelzah in the territory
of Benjamin. They will tell you that the
donkeys you were looking for have been
found, so that your father isn’t worried
any more about them but about you, and
he keeps asking, ‘What shall I do about
my son?’ 3You will go on from there until you come to the sacred tree at Tabor,
where you will meet three men on their
way to offer a sacrifice to God at Bethel.
One of them will be leading three young
goats, another one will be carrying three
loaves of bread, and the third one will
have a leather bag full of wine. 4They
will greet you and offer you two of the
loaves, which you are to accept. 5Then
you will go to the Hill of God in Gibeah,

[r] who is it . . . much?; *or* who is to have the most desirable thing in Israel? [s] *Some ancient translations* Samuel; *Hebrew* He (that is, the cook). [t] *Probable text* I saved it . . . invited; *Hebrew unclear.* [u] *One ancient translation* they fixed up a bed for Saul; *Hebrew* he spoke with Saul. [v] ON THE ROOF: *At that time houses had flat roofs, and it was common for people to sleep on them.* [w] *Some ancient translations* and he slept there; *Hebrew* and they got up early. [x] *Some ancient translations* as ruler of his people . . . the LORD has chosen you; *Hebrew does not have these words.*

where there is a Philistine camp. At the
entrance to the town you will meet a
group of prophets coming down from
the altar on the hill, playing harps,
drums, flutes, and lyres. They will be
dancing and shouting. 6 Suddenly the
spirit of the LORD will take control of
you, and you will join in their religious
dancing and shouting and will become a
different person. 7 When these things
happen, do whatever God leads you to
do. 8 You will go ahead of me to Gilgal,
where I will meet you and offer burnt
sacrifices and fellowship sacrifices.
Wait there seven days until I come and
tell you what to do."

9 When Saul turned to leave Samuel,
God gave Saul a new nature. And everything Samuel had told him happened
that day. 10 When Saul and his servant
arrived at Gibeah, a group of prophets
met him. Suddenly the spirit of God took
control of him, and he joined in their ec-
static dancing and shouting. 11 People
who had known him before saw him doing this and asked one another, "What
has happened to the son of Kish? Has
Saul become a prophet?" 12 A man who
lived there asked, "How about these
other prophets — who do you think their
fathers are?" This is how the saying originated, "Has even Saul become a
prophet?" 13 When Saul finished his ec-
static dancing and shouting, he went to
the altar on the hill.

14 Saul's uncle saw him and the servant, and he asked them, "Where have
you been?"

"Looking for the donkeys," Saul answered. "When we couldn't find them,
we went to see Samuel."

15 "And what did he tell you?" Saul's
uncle asked.

16 "He told us that the animals had
been found," Saul answered — but he did
not tell his uncle what Samuel had said
about his becoming king.

Saul Is Acclaimed as King

17 Samuel called the people together
for a religious gathering at Mizpah
18 and said to them, "The LORD, the God
of Israel, says, 'I brought you out of
Egypt and rescued you from the Egyptians and all the other peoples who were
oppressing you. 19 I am your God, the
one who rescues you from all your troubles and difficulties, but today you have
rejected me and have asked me to give
you a king. Very well, then, gather yourselves before the LORD by tribes and by
clans.' "

20 Then Samuel had each tribe come
forward, and the LORD picked the tribe of
Benjamin. 21 Then Samuel had the families of the tribe of Benjamin come forward, and the family of Matri was
picked out. Then the men of the family
of Matri came forward,[y] and Saul son of
Kish was picked out. They looked for
him, but when they could not find him,
22 they asked the LORD, "Is there still
someone else?"

The LORD answered, "Saul is over
there, hiding behind the supplies."

23 So they ran and brought Saul out to
the people, and they could see that he
was a foot taller than anyone else.
24 Samuel said to the people, "Here is the
man the LORD has chosen! There is no
one else among us like him."

All the people shouted, "Long live the
king!"

25 Samuel explained to the people the
rights and duties of a king, and then
wrote them in a book, which he deposited in a holy place. Then he sent everyone home. 26 Saul also went back home
to Gibeah. Some powerful men,[z] whose
hearts God had touched, went with him.
27 But some worthless people said, "How
can this fellow do us any good?" They
despised Saul and did not bring him any
gifts.

Saul Defeats the Ammonites

11 About a month later King Nahash of Ammon led his army
against the town of Jabesh in the territory of Gilead and besieged it. The men
of Jabesh said to Nahash, "Make a treaty
with us, and we will accept you as our
ruler."

2 Nahash answered, "I will make a
treaty with you on one condition: I will
put out everyone's right eye and so bring
disgrace on all Israel."

3 The leaders of Jabesh said, "Give us

[y] *One ancient translation* Then the men of the family of Matri came forward; *Hebrew does not have these words.* [z] *One ancient translation* Some powerful men; *Hebrew* The army.

seven days to send messengers throughout the land of Israel. If no one will help
us, then we will surrender to you."
4 The messengers arrived at Gibeah,
where Saul lived, and when they told the
news, the people started crying in despair. 5 Saul was just then coming in
from the field with his oxen, and he
asked, "What's wrong? Why is everyone
crying?" They told him what the messengers from Jabesh had reported. 6 When
Saul heard this, the spirit of God took
control of him, and he became furious.
7 He took two oxen, cut them in pieces,
and had messengers carry the pieces
throughout the land of Israel with this
warning: "Whoever does not follow Saul
and Samuel into battle will have this
done to his oxen!"

The people of Israel were afraid of
what the LORD might do, and all of them,
without exception, came out together.
8 Saul gathered them at Bezek: there
were 300,000 from Israel and 30,000
from Judah. 9 They said to the messengers from Jabesh, "Tell your people that
before noon tomorrow they will be rescued." When the people of Jabesh received the message, they were overjoyed
10 and said to Nahash, "Tomorrow we
will surrender to you, and you can do
with us whatever you wish."
11 That night Saul divided his men into
three groups, and at dawn the next day
they rushed into the enemy camp and
attacked the Ammonites. By noon they
had slaughtered them. The survivors
scattered, each man running off by
himself.
12 Then the people of Israel said to
Samuel, "Where are the people who
said that Saul should not be our king?
Hand them over to us, and we will kill
them!"
13 But Saul said, "No one will be put to
death today, for this is the day the LORD
rescued Israel." 14 And Samuel said to
them, "Let us all go to Gilgal and once
more proclaim Saul as our king." 15 So
they all went to Gilgal, and there at the
holy place they proclaimed Saul king.
They offered fellowship sacrifices, and
Saul and all the people of Israel celebrated the event.

Samuel Addresses the People

12 Then Samuel said to the people
of Israel, "I have done what you
asked me to do. I have given you a king
to rule you, 2 and now you have him to
lead you. As for me, I am old and gray,
and my sons are with you. I have been
your leader from my youth until now.
3 Here I am. If I have done anything
wrong, accuse me now in the presence
of the LORD and the king he has chosen.
Have I taken anybody's cow or anybody's donkey? Have I cheated or oppressed anyone? Have I accepted a bribe
from anyone? If I have done any of these
things, I will pay back what I have
taken."
4 The people answered, "No, you have
not cheated us or oppressed us; you
have not taken anything from anyone."
5 Samuel replied, "The LORD and the
king he has chosen are witnesses today
that you have found me to be completely
innocent."

"Yes, the LORD is our witness," they
answered.
6 Samuel continued, "The LORD is the
one who chose Moses and Aaron and
who brought your ancestors out of
Egypt. 7 Now stand where you are, and I
will accuse you before the LORD by reminding you[a] of all the mighty actions
the LORD did to save you and your ancestors. 8 When Jacob and his family went
to Egypt and the Egyptians oppressed
them,[b] your ancestors cried to the LORD
for help, and he sent Moses and Aaron,
who brought them out of Egypt and settled them in this land. 9 But the people
forgot the LORD their God, and so he let
the Philistines and the king of Moab and
Sisera, commander of the army of the
city of Hazor, fight against your ancestors and conquer them. 10 Then they
cried to the LORD for help and said, 'We
have sinned, because we turned away
from you, LORD, and worshiped the idols
of Baal and Astarte. Rescue us from our
enemies, and we will worship you!'
11 And the LORD sent Gideon, Barak,[c]
Jephthah, and finally me. Each of us rescued you from your enemies, and you
lived in safety. 12 But when you saw that
King Nahash of Ammon was about to

[a] *One ancient translation* by reminding you; *Hebrew does not have these words.*
[b] *One ancient translation* and the Egyptians oppressed them; *Hebrew does not have these words.*
[c] *Some ancient translations* Barak; *Hebrew* Bedan.

attack you, you rejected the LORD as your
king and said to me, 'We want a king to
rule us.'
13 "Now here is the king you chose;
you asked for him, and now the LORD has
given him to you. 14 All will go well with
you if you honor the LORD your God,
serve him, listen to him, and obey his
commands, and if you and your king follow him. 15 But if you do not listen to the
LORD but disobey his commands, he will
be against you and your king.[d] 16 So
then, stand where you are, and you will
see the great thing which the LORD is going to do. 17 It's the dry season, isn't it?
But I will pray, and the LORD will send
thunder and rain. When this happens,
you will realize that you committed a
great sin against the LORD when you
asked him for a king."
18 So Samuel prayed, and on that same
day the LORD sent thunder and rain.
Then all the people became afraid of the
LORD and of Samuel, 19 and they said to
Samuel, "Please, sir, pray to the LORD
your God for us, so that we won't die.
We now realize that, besides all our
other sins, we have sinned by asking for
a king."
20 "Don't be afraid," Samuel answered.
"Even though you have done such an
evil thing, do not turn away from the
LORD, but serve him with all your heart.
21 Don't go after[e] false gods; they cannot help you or save you, for they are not
real. 22 The LORD has made a solemn
promise, and he will not abandon you,
for he has decided to make you his own
people. 23 As for me, the LORD forbid that
I should sin against him by no longer
praying for you. Instead, I will teach you
what is good and right for you to do.
24 Obey the LORD and serve him faithfully
with all your heart. Remember the great
things he has done for you. 25 But if you
continue to sin, you and your king will
be destroyed."

War against the Philistines

13[f] 2 Saul picked three thousand
men, keeping two thousand of
them with him in Michmash and in the
hill country of Bethel and sending one
thousand with his son Jonathan to Gibeah, in the territory of the tribe of Benjamin. The rest of the men Saul sent home.
3 Jonathan killed the Philistine commander[g] in Geba, and all the Philistines
heard about it. Then Saul sent messengers to call the Hebrews to war by blowing a trumpet throughout the whole
country. 4 All the Israelites were told that
Saul had killed the Philistine commander and that the Philistines hated
them. So the people answered the call to
join Saul at Gilgal.
5 The Philistines assembled to fight the
Israelites; they had thirty thousand war
chariots, six thousand cavalry troops,
and as many soldiers as there are grains
of sand on the seashore. They went to
Michmash, east of Bethaven, and
camped there. 6 Then they launched a
strong attack against the Israelites, putting them in a desperate situation. Some
of the Israelites hid in caves and holes or
among the rocks or in pits and wells;
7 others crossed the Jordan River into
the territories of Gad and Gilead.
Saul was still at Gilgal, and the people
with him were trembling with fear. 8 He
waited seven days for Samuel, as Samuel had instructed him to do, but Samuel
still had not come to Gilgal. The people
began to desert Saul, 9 so he said to
them, "Bring me the burnt sacrifices and
the fellowship sacrifices." He offered a
burnt sacrifice, 10 and just as he was finishing, Samuel arrived. Saul went out to
meet him and welcome him, 11 but Samuel said, "What have you done?"
Saul answered, "The people were deserting me, and you had not come when
you said you would; besides that, the
Philistines are gathering at Michmash.
12 So I thought, 'The Philistines are going
to attack me here in Gilgal, and I have
not tried to win the LORD's favor.' So I
felt I had to offer a sacrifice."
13 "That was a foolish thing to do,"
Samuel answered. "You have not
obeyed the command the LORD your God
gave you. If you had obeyed, he would
have let you and your descendants rule
over Israel forever. 14 But now your rule
will not continue. Because you have dis-

[d] *One ancient translation* your king; *Hebrew* your ancestors. [e] *Some ancient translations* after; *Hebrew* because after. [f] *One ancient translation does not have verse 1; Hebrew has as verse 1* Saul was . . . years old when he became king, and he was king of Israel for two years. *The Hebrew text is defective at two points in this verse.* [g] killed the Philistine commander; *or* defeated the Philistines camping.

obeyed him, the LORD will find the kind
of man he wants and make him ruler of
his people."
15 Samuel left Gilgal and went on his
way. The rest of the people followed
Saul as he went to join his soldiers. They
went from Gilgal[h] to Gibeah in the territory of Benjamin. Saul inspected his
troops, about six hundred men. 16 Saul,
his son Jonathan, and their men camped
in Geba in the territory of Benjamin; the
Philistine camp was at Michmash. 17 The
Philistine soldiers went out on raids
from their camp in three groups: one
group went toward Ophrah in the territory of Shual, 18 another went toward
Beth Horon, and the other one went to
the border overlooking Zeboim Valley
and the wilderness.
19 There were no blacksmiths in Israel
because the Philistines were determined
to keep the Hebrews from making
swords and spears. (20 The Israelites had
to go to the Philistines to get their plows,
hoes, axes, and sickles[i] sharpened;
21 the charge was one small coin for
sharpening axes and for fixing goads,[j]
and two coins for sharpening plows or
hoes.) 22 And so on the day of battle none
of the Israelite soldiers except Saul and
his son Jonathan had swords or spears.
23 The Philistines sent a group of soldiers to defend Michmash Pass.

Jonathan's Daring Deed

14 One day Jonathan said to the
young man who carried his
weapons, "Let's go across to the Philistine camp." But Jonathan did not tell his
father Saul, 2 who was camping under a
pomegranate tree in Migron, not far
from Gibeah; he had about six hundred
men with him. 3 (The priest carrying the
ephod was Ahijah, the son of Ichabod's
brother Ahitub, who was the son of
Phinehas and grandson of Eli, the priest
of the LORD in Shiloh.) The men did not
know that Jonathan had left.
4 In Michmash Pass, which Jonathan
had to go through to get over to the Philistine camp, there were two large jagged rocks, one on each side of the pass:
one was called Bozez and the other Se-
neh. 5 One was on the north side of the
pass, facing Michmash, and the other
was on the south side, facing Geba.
6 Jonathan said to the young man,
"Let's cross over to the camp of those
heathen Philistines. Maybe the LORD will
help us; if he does, nothing can keep him
from giving us the victory, no matter
how few of us there are."
7 The young man answered, "Whatever you want to do,[k] I'm with you."
8 "All right," Jonathan said. "We will
go across and let the Philistines see us.
9 If they tell us to wait for them to come
to us, then we will stay where we are.
10 But if they tell us to go to them, then
we will, because that will be the sign that
the LORD has given us victory over
them."
11 So they let the Philistines see them,
and the Philistines said, "Look! Some
Hebrews are coming out of the holes
they have been hiding in!" 12 Then they
called out to Jonathan and the young
man, "Come on up here! We have something to tell[l] you!"
Jonathan said to the young man, "Follow me. The LORD has given Israel victory over them." 13 Jonathan climbed up
out of the pass on his hands and knees,
and the young man followed him. Jonathan attacked the Philistines and
knocked them down, and the young man
killed them. 14 In that first slaughter Jonathan and the young man killed about
twenty men in an area of about half an
acre.[m] 15 All the Philistines in the
countryside were terrified; the raiders
and the soldiers in the camp trembled
with fear; the earth shook, and there
was great panic.

The Defeat of the Philistines

16 Saul's men on watch at Gibeah in
the territory of Benjamin saw the Philistines running in confusion. 17 So Saul
said to his men, "Count the soldiers and
find out who is missing." They did so
and found that Jonathan and the young
man who carried his weapons were
missing. 18 "Bring the ephod[n] here,"
Saul said to Ahijah the priest. (On that
day Ahijah was carrying it in front of the

[h] *Some ancient translations* on his way . . . went from Gilgal; *Hebrew does not have these words.* [i] *One ancient translation* sickles; *Hebrew* plows. [j] *Probable text* the charge . . . fixing goads; *Hebrew unclear.* [k] *One ancient translation* you want to do; *Hebrew* you want to do. Turn. [l] tell; *or* show. [m] *Probable text* in an area of about half an acre; *Hebrew unclear.* [n] *One ancient translation* ephod *(see 2.28); Hebrew* Covenant Box.

people of Israel.)[o] 19 As Saul was speaking to the priest, the confusion in the
Philistine camp kept getting worse, so
Saul said to him, "There's no time to
consult the LORD!" 20 Then he and his
men marched into battle against the Philistines, who were fighting each other in
complete confusion. 21 Some Hebrews,
who had been on the Philistine side and
had gone with them to the camp,
changed sides again[p] and joined Saul
and Jonathan. 22 Others, who had been
hiding in the hills of Ephraim, heard that
the Philistines were running away, so
they also joined in and attacked the Philistines, 23 fighting all the way beyond
Bethaven. The LORD saved Israel
that day.

Events after the Battle

24 The Israelites were weak with hunger that day, because Saul, with a solemn oath, had given the order: "A curse
be on anyone who eats any food today
before I take revenge on my enemies."
So nobody had eaten anything all day.
25 They all[q] came into a wooded area
and found honey everywhere. 26 The
woods were full of honey, but no one ate
any of it because they were all afraid of
Saul's curse. 27 But Jonathan had not
heard his father threaten the people with
a curse; so he reached out with the stick
he was carrying, dipped it in a honeycomb, and ate some honey. At once he
felt much better. 28 But one of the men
told him, "We are all weak from hunger,
but your father threatened us and said,
'A curse be on anyone who eats any food
today.' "

29 Jonathan answered, "What a terrible thing my father has done to our people! See how much better I feel because
I ate some honey! 30 How much better it
would have been today if our people had
eaten the food they took when they defeated the enemy. Just think how many
more Philistines they would have
killed!"

31 That day the Israelites defeated the
Philistines, fighting all the way from
Michmash to Aijalon. By this time the
Israelites were very weak from hunger,
32 and so they rushed over to what they
had captured from the enemy, took
sheep and cattle, slaughtered them on
the spot, and ate the meat with the blood
still in it. 33 Saul was told, "Look, the people are sinning against the LORD by eating meat with the blood in it."

"You are traitors!" Saul cried out.
"Roll a big stone over here[r] to me."
34 Then he gave another order: "Go
among the people and tell them all to
bring their cattle and sheep here. They
are to slaughter them and eat them here;
they must not sin against the LORD by
eating meat with blood in it." So that
night they all brought their cattle and
slaughtered them there. 35 Saul built an
altar to the LORD, the first one that he
built.

36 Saul said to his men, "Let's go down
and attack the Philistines in the night,
plunder them until dawn, and kill
them all."

"Do whatever you think best," they
answered.

But the priest said, "Let's consult God
first."

37 So Saul asked God, "Shall I attack
the Philistines? Will you give us victory?" But God did not answer that day.
38 Then Saul said to the leaders of the
people, "Come here and find out what
sin was committed today. 39 I promise by
the living LORD, who gives Israel victory,
that the guilty one will be put to death,
even if he is my son Jonathan." But no
one said anything. 40 Then Saul said to
them, "All of you stand over there, and
Jonathan and I will stand over here."

"Do whatever you think best," they
answered.

41 Saul said to the LORD, the God of Israel, "LORD, why have you not answered
me today? LORD, God of Israel, answer
me by the sacred stones. If the guilt is
Jonathan's or mine, answer by the Urim;
but if it belongs to your people Israel,[s]
answer by the Thummim."[t] The answer
indicated Jonathan and Saul; and the
people were cleared. 42 Then Saul said,
"Decide between my son Jonathan and

[o] *One ancient translation* On that day ... Israel; *Hebrew* Because on that day God's Covenant Box and the people of Israel. [p] *Some ancient translations* changed sides again; *Hebrew* around also. [q] *Probable text* They all; *Hebrew* All the land. [r] *One ancient translation* here; *Hebrew* today. [s] *Some ancient translations* answer me by the sacred stones ... your people Israel; *Hebrew does not have these words.* [t] URIM ... THUMMIM: *Two stones used by the priest to determine God's will; it is not known precisely how they were used.*

me." And Jonathan was indicated.
43 Then Saul asked Jonathan, "What
have you done?"
Jonathan answered, "I ate a little
honey with the stick I was holding. Here
I am—I am ready to die."
44 Saul said to him, "May God strike
me dead if you are not put to death!"
45 But the people said to Saul, "Will
Jonathan, who won this great victory for
Israel, be put to death? No! We promise
by the living LORD that he will not lose
even a hair from his head. What he did
today was done with God's help." So the
people saved Jonathan from being put to
death.
46 After that, Saul stopped pursuing
the Philistines, and they went back to
their own territory.

Saul's Reign and Family

47 After Saul became king of Israel, he
fought all his enemies everywhere: the
people of Moab, of Ammon, and of
Edom, the kings of Zobah, and the Philistines. Wherever he fought he was victorious.[u] 48 He fought heroically and
defeated even the people of Amalek. He
saved the Israelites from all attacks.
49 Saul's sons were Jonathan, Ishvi,
and Malchishua. His older daughter was
named Merab, and the younger one Michal. 50 His wife was Ahinoam, the
daughter of Ahimaaz; his army commander was his cousin Abner, the son of
his uncle Ner. 51 Saul's father Kish and
Abner's father Ner were sons of Abiel.
52 As long as he lived, Saul had to fight
fiercely against the Philistines. So whenever he found a man who was strong or
brave, he would enlist him in his army.

War against the Amalekites

15 Samuel said to Saul, "I am the
one whom the LORD sent to
anoint you king of his people Israel.
Now listen to what the LORD Almighty
says. 2 He is going to punish the people
of Amalek because their ancestors opposed the Israelites when they were
coming from Egypt. 3 Go and attack the
Amalekites and completely destroy
everything they have. Don't leave a
thing; kill all the men, women, children,
and babies; the cattle, sheep, camels,
and donkeys."
4 Saul called his forces together and inspected them at Telem: there were
200,000 soldiers from Israel and 10,000
from Judah. 5 Then he and his men went
to the city of Amalek and waited in ambush
in a dry riverbed. 6 He sent a warning to the
Kenites, a people whose ancestors had
been kind to the Israelites when they
came from Egypt: "Go away and leave
the Amalekites, so that I won't kill you
along with them." So the Kenites left.
7 Saul defeated the Amalekites, fighting all the way from Havilah to Shur,
east of Egypt; 8 he captured King Agag
of Amalek alive and killed all the people.
9 But Saul and his men spared Agag's life
and did not kill the best sheep and cattle,
the best calves and lambs,[v] or anything
else that was good; they destroyed only
what was useless or worthless.[w]

Saul Is Rejected as King

10 The LORD said to Samuel, 11 "I am
sorry that I made Saul king; he has
turned away from me and disobeyed my
commands." Samuel was angry, and all
night long he pleaded with the LORD.
12 Early the following morning he went
off to find Saul. He heard that Saul had
gone to the town of Carmel, where he
had built a monument to himself, and
then had gone on to Gilgal. 13 Samuel
went up to Saul, who greeted him, saying, "The LORD bless you, Samuel! I have
obeyed the LORD's command."
14 Samuel asked, "Why, then, do I hear
cattle mooing and sheep bleating?"
15 Saul answered, "My men took them
from the Amalekites. They kept the best
sheep and cattle to offer as a sacrifice to
the LORD your God, and the rest we have
destroyed completely."[x]
16 "Stop," Samuel ordered, "and I will
tell you what the LORD said to me last
night."
"Tell me," Saul said.
17 Samuel answered, "Even though
you consider yourself of no importance,
you are the leader of the tribes of Israel.
The LORD anointed you king of Israel,
18 and he sent you out with orders to destroy those wicked people of Amalek.

[u] *One ancient translation* was victorious; *Hebrew* acted wickedly. [v] *One ancient translation* the best calves and lambs; *Hebrew unclear.* [w] *Some ancient translations* useless or worthless; *Hebrew unclear.* [x] DESTROYED COMPLETELY: *These animals had been unconditionally dedicated to the LORD and had to be destroyed (see Lv 27.28).*

He told you to fight until you had killed
them all. 19 Why, then, did you not obey
him? Why did you rush to grab the loot,
and so do what displeases the LORD?"
20 "I did obey the LORD," Saul replied. "I
went out as he told me to, brought back
King Agag, and killed all the Amalekites. 21 But my men did not kill the best
sheep and cattle that they captured; instead, they brought them here to Gilgal
to offer as a sacrifice to the LORD
your God."
22 Samuel said, "Which does the LORD
prefer: obedience or offerings and sacrifices? It is better to obey him than to sacrifice the best sheep to him. 23 Rebellion
against him is as bad as witchcraft, and
arrogance is as sinful as idolatry. Because you rejected the LORD's command,
he has rejected you as king."
24 "Yes, I have sinned," Saul replied. "I
disobeyed the LORD's command and your
instructions. I was afraid of my men and
did what they wanted. 25 But now I beg
you, forgive my sin and go back with
me, so that I can worship the LORD."
26 "I will not go back with you," Samuel answered. "You rejected the LORD's
command, and he has rejected you as
king of Israel."
27 Then Samuel turned to leave, but
Saul caught hold of his cloak, and it tore.
28 Samuel said to him, "The LORD has
torn the kingdom of Israel away from
you today and given it to someone who
is a better man than you. 29 Israel's majestic God does not lie or change his
mind. He is not a human being—he does
not change his mind."
30 "I have sinned," Saul replied. "But at
least show me respect in front of the
leaders of my people and all of Israel. Go
back with me so that I can worship the
LORD your God." 31 So Samuel went back
with him, and Saul worshiped the LORD.
32 "Bring King Agag here to me," Samuel ordered. Agag came to him, trembling with fear, thinking to himself,
"What a bitter thing it is to die!"[y]
33 Samuel said, "As your sword has
made many mothers childless, so now
your mother will become childless." And
he cut Agag to pieces in front of the altar
in Gilgal.
34 Then Samuel went to Ramah, and
King Saul went home to Gibeah. 35 As
long as Samuel lived, he never again
saw the king; but he grieved over him.
The LORD was sorry that he had made
Saul king of Israel.

David Is Anointed King

16 The LORD said to Samuel, "How
long will you go on grieving over
Saul? I have rejected him as king of Israel. But now get some olive oil and go
to Bethlehem, to a man named Jesse, because I have chosen one of his sons to be
king."
2 "How can I do that?" Samuel asked.
"If Saul hears about it, he will kill me!"
The LORD answered, "Take a calf with
you and say that you are there to offer a
sacrifice to the LORD. 3 Invite Jesse to the
sacrifice, and I will tell you what to do.
You will anoint as king the man I tell
you to."
4 Samuel did what the LORD told him to
do and went to Bethlehem, where the
city leaders came trembling to meet him
and asked, "Is this a peaceful visit,
seer?"
5 "Yes," he answered. "I have come to
offer a sacrifice to the LORD. Purify yourselves and come with me." He also told
Jesse and his sons to purify themselves,
and he invited them to the sacrifice.
6 When they arrived, Samuel saw
Jesse's son Eliab and said to himself,
"This man standing here in the LORD's
presence is surely the one he has chosen." 7 But the LORD said to him, "Pay no
attention to how tall and handsome he
is. I have rejected him, because I do not
judge as people judge. They look at the
outward appearance, but I look at the
heart."
8 Then Jesse called his son Abinadab
and brought him to Samuel. But Samuel
said, "No, the LORD hasn't chosen him either." 9 Jesse then brought Shammah.
"No, the LORD hasn't chosen him either,"
Samuel said. 10 In this way Jesse brought
seven of his sons to Samuel. And Samuel said to him, "No, the LORD hasn't chosen any of these." 11 Then he asked him,
"Do you have any more sons?"
Jesse answered, "There is still the
youngest, but he is out taking care of the
sheep."

y trembling with fear . . . die; *or* confidently, thinking to himself, "Surely the bitter danger of death is past!"

"Tell him to come here," Samuel said.
"We won't offer the sacrifice until he
comes." 12 So Jesse sent for him. He was
a handsome, healthy young man, and
his eyes sparkled. The LORD said to Samuel, "This is the one—anoint him!"
13 Samuel took the olive oil and anointed
David in front of his brothers. Immediately the spirit of the LORD took control
of David and was with him from that day
on. Then Samuel returned to Ramah.

David in Saul's Court

14 The LORD's spirit left Saul, and an
evil spirit sent by the LORD tormented
him. 15 His servants said to him, "We
know that an evil spirit sent by God is
tormenting you. 16 So give us the order,
sir, and we will look for a man who
knows how to play the harp. Then when
the evil spirit comes on you, the man can
play his harp, and you will be all right
again."

17 Saul ordered them, "Find me a man
who plays well and bring him to me."
18 One of his attendants said, "Jesse of
the town of Bethlehem has a son who is
a good musician. He is also a brave and
handsome man, a good soldier, and an
able speaker. The LORD is with him."
19 So Saul sent messengers to Jesse to
say, "Send me your son David, the one
who takes care of the sheep." 20 Jesse
sent David to Saul with a young goat, a
donkey loaded with bread, and a leather
bag full of wine. 21 David came to Saul
and entered his service. Saul liked him
very much and chose him as the man to
carry his weapons. 22 Then Saul sent a
message to Jesse: "I like David. Let him
stay here in my service." 23 From then
on, whenever the evil spirit sent by God
came on Saul, David would get his harp
and play it. The evil spirit would leave,
and Saul would feel better and be all
right again.

Goliath Challenges the Israelites

17 The Philistines gathered for battle in Socoh, a town in Judah;
they camped at a place called Ephes
Dammim, between Socoh and Azekah.
2 Saul and the Israelites assembled and
camped in Elah Valley, where they got
ready to fight the Philistines. 3 The Philistines lined up on one hill and the Israelites on another, with a valley between
them.

4 A man named Goliath, from the city
of Gath, came out from the Philistine
camp to challenge the Israelites. He was
over nine feet[z] tall 5 and wore bronze
armor that weighed about 125 pounds
and a bronze helmet. 6 His legs were also
protected by bronze armor, and he carried a bronze javelin slung over his
shoulder. 7 His spear was as thick as the
bar on a weaver's loom, and its iron
head weighed about fifteen pounds. A
soldier walked in front of him carrying
his shield. 8 Goliath stood and shouted at
the Israelites, "What are you doing
there, lined up for battle? I am a Philistine, you slaves of Saul! Choose one of
your men to fight me. 9 If he wins and
kills me, we will be your slaves; but if I
win and kill him, you will be our slaves.
10 Here and now I challenge the Israelite
army. I dare you to pick someone to
fight me!" 11 When Saul and his men
heard this, they were terrified.

David in Saul's Camp

12 David was the son of Jesse, who was
an Ephrathite from Bethlehem in Judah.
Jesse had eight sons, and at the time
Saul was king, he was already a very old
man.[a] 13 His three oldest sons had gone
with Saul to war. The oldest was Eliab,
the next was Abinadab, and the third
was Shammah. 14 David was the youngest son, and while the three oldest brothers stayed with Saul, 15 David would go
back to Bethlehem from time to time, to
take care of his father's sheep.

16 Goliath challenged the Israelites
every morning and evening for forty
days.

17 One day Jesse said to David, "Take a
half-bushel of this roasted grain and
these ten loaves of bread, and hurry with
them to your brothers in the camp.
18 And take these ten cheeses to the commanding officer. Find out how your
brothers are getting along and bring
back something to show that you saw
them and that they are well. 19 King Saul,
your brothers, and all the other Israelites are in Elah Valley fighting the Philistines."

20 David got up early the next morn-

[z] *Hebrew* nine feet; *one ancient Hebrew manuscript and one ancient translation* seven feet.
[a] *Some ancient translations* a very old man; *Hebrew unclear.*

ing, left someone else in charge of the
sheep, took the food, and went as Jesse
had told him to. He arrived at the camp
just as the Israelites were going out to
their battle line, shouting the war cry.
21 The Philistine and the Israelite armies
took positions for battle, facing each
other. 22 David left the food with the officer in charge of the supplies, ran to the
battle line, went to his brothers, and
asked how they were getting along. 23 As
he was talking with them, Goliath came
forward and challenged the Israelites as
he had done before. And David heard
him. 24 When the Israelites saw Goliath,
they ran away in terror. 25 "Look at him!"
they said to each other. "Listen to his
challenge! King Saul has promised to
give a big reward to the man who kills
him; the king will also give him his
daughter to marry and will not require
his father's family to pay taxes."[b]

26 David asked the men who were near
him, "What will the man get who kills
this Philistine and frees Israel from this
disgrace? After all, who is this heathen
Philistine to defy the army of the living
God?" 27 They told him what would be
done for the man who killed Goliath.

28 Eliab, David's oldest brother, heard
David talking to the men. He became angry with David and said, "What are you
doing here? Who is taking care of those
sheep of yours out there in the wilderness? You smart aleck, you! You just
came to watch the fighting!"

29 "Now what have I done?" David
asked. "Can't I even ask a question?"
30 He turned to another man and asked
him the same question, and every time
he asked, he got the same answer.

31 Some men heard what David had
said, and they told Saul, who sent for
him. 32 David said to Saul, "Your Majesty, no one should be afraid of this Philistine! I will go and fight him."

33 "No," answered Saul. "How could
you fight him? You're just a boy, and he
has been a soldier all his life!"

34 "Your Majesty," David said, "I take
care of my father's sheep. Any time a
lion or a bear carries off a lamb, 35 I go
after it, attack it, and rescue the lamb.
And if the lion or bear turns on me, I
grab it by the throat and beat it to death.
36 I have killed lions and bears, and I will
do the same to this heathen Philistine,
who has defied the army of the living
God. 37 The LORD has saved me from lions and bears; he will save me from this
Philistine."

"All right," Saul answered. "Go, and
the LORD be with you." 38 He gave his
own armor to David for him to wear: a
bronze helmet, which he put on David's
head, and a coat of armor. 39 David
strapped Saul's sword over the armor
and tried to walk, but he couldn't, because he wasn't used to wearing them. "I
can't fight with all this," he said to Saul.
"I'm not used to it." So he took it all off.
40 He took his shepherd's stick and then
picked up five smooth stones from the
stream and put them in his bag. With his
sling ready, he went out to meet Goliath.

David Defeats Goliath

41 The Philistine started walking toward David, with his shield bearer walking in front of him. He kept coming
closer, 42 and when he got a good look at
David, he was filled with scorn for him
because he was just a nice, good-looking
boy. 43 He said to David, "What's that
stick for? Do you think I'm a dog?" And
he called down curses from his god on
David. 44 "Come on," he challenged David, "and I will give your body to the
birds and animals to eat."

45 David answered, "You are coming
against me with sword, spear, and javelin, but I come against you in the name
of the LORD Almighty, the God of the Israelite armies, which you have defied.
46 This very day the LORD will put you in
my power; I will defeat you and cut off
your head. And I will give the bodies of
the Philistine soldiers to the birds and
animals to eat. Then the whole world
will know that Israel has a God, 47 and
everyone here will see that the LORD
does not need swords or spears to save
his people. He is victorious in battle, and
he will put all of you in our power."

48 Goliath started walking toward David again, and David ran quickly toward
the Philistine battle line to fight him.
49 He reached into his bag and took out a
stone, which he slung at Goliath. It hit
him on the forehead and broke his skull,
and Goliath fell face downward on the
ground. 50 And so, without a sword, Da-

[b] to pay taxes; *or* either to pay taxes or serve him.

vid defeated and killed Goliath with a
sling and a stone! 51 He ran to him, stood
over him, took Goliath's sword out of its
sheath, and cut off his head and
killed him.

When the Philistines saw that their
hero was dead, they ran away. 52 The
men of Israel and Judah shouted and ran
after them, pursuing them all the way to
Gath[c] and to the gates of Ekron. The
Philistines fell wounded all along the
road that leads to Shaaraim, as far as
Gath and Ekron. 53 When the Israelites
came back from pursuing the Philistines, they looted their camp. 54 David
got Goliath's head and took it to Jerusalem, but he kept Goliath's weapons in
his own tent.

David Is Presented to Saul

55 When Saul saw David going out to
fight Goliath, he asked Abner, the commander of his army, "Abner, whose son
is he?"

"I have no idea, Your Majesty," Abner
answered.

56 "Then go and find out," Saul
ordered.

57 So when David returned to camp after killing Goliath, Abner took him to
Saul. David was still carrying Goliath's
head. 58 Saul asked him, "Young man,
whose son are you?"

"I am the son of your servant Jesse
from Bethlehem," David answered.

18 Saul and David finished their
conversation. After that, Saul's
son Jonathan was deeply attracted to
David and came to love him as much as
he loved himself. 2 Saul kept David with
him from that day on and did not let him
go back home. 3 Jonathan swore eternal
friendship with David because of his
deep affection for him. 4 He took off the
robe he was wearing and gave it to David, together with his armor and also his
sword, bow, and belt. 5 David was successful in all the missions on which Saul
sent him, and so Saul made him an officer in his army. This pleased all of
Saul's officers and men.

Saul Becomes Jealous of David

6 As David was returning after killing
Goliath and as the soldiers were coming
back home, women from every town in
Israel came out to meet King Saul. They
were singing joyful songs, dancing, and
playing tambourines and lyres. 7 In their
celebration the women sang, "Saul has
killed thousands, but David tens of thousands." 8 Saul did not like this, and he
became very angry. He said, "For David
they claim tens of thousands, but only
thousands for me. They will be making
him king next!" 9 And so he was jealous
and suspicious of David from that
day on.

10 The next day an evil spirit from God
suddenly took control of Saul, and he
raved in his house like a madman. David
was playing the harp, as he did every
day, and Saul was holding a spear. 11 "I'll
pin him to the wall," Saul said to himself,
and he threw the spear at him twice; but
David dodged each time.

12 Saul was afraid of David because
the LORD was with David but had abandoned him. 13 So Saul sent him away and
put him in command of a thousand men.
David led his men in battle 14 and was
successful in all he did, because the LORD
was with him. 15 Saul noticed David's
success and became even more afraid of
him. 16 But everyone in Israel and Judah
loved David because he was such a successful leader.

David Marries Saul's Daughter

17 Then Saul said to David, "Here is my
older daughter Merab. I will give her to
you as your wife on condition that you
serve me as a brave and loyal soldier,
and fight the LORD's battles." (Saul was
thinking that in this way the Philistines
would kill David, and he would not have
to do it himself.)

18 David answered, "Who am I and
what is my family that I should become
the king's son-in-law?" 19 But when the
time came for Merab to be given to David, she was given instead to a man
named Adriel from Meholah.

20 Saul's daughter Michal, however,
fell in love with David, and when Saul
heard of this, he was pleased. 21 He said
to himself, "I'll give Michal to David; I
will use her to trap him, and he will be
killed by the Philistines." So for the second time Saul said to David, "You will be
my son-in-law." 22 He ordered his officials to speak privately with David and

[c] *One ancient translation* Gath; *Hebrew* a valley.

tell him, "The king is pleased with you
and all his officials like you; now is a
good time for you to marry his
daughter."
23 So they told this to David, and he
answered, "It's a great honor to become
the king's son-in-law, too great for
someone poor and insignificant
like me."
24 The officials told Saul what David
had said, 25 and Saul ordered them to tell
David: "All the king wants from you as
payment for the bride are the foreskins
of a hundred dead Philistines, as revenge on his enemies." (This was how
Saul planned to have David killed by the
Philistines.) 26 Saul's officials reported to
David what Saul had said, and David
was delighted with the thought of becoming the king's son-in-law. Before the
day set for the wedding, 27 David and his
men went and killed two hundred Philistines. He took their foreskins to the king
and counted them all out to him, so that
he might become his son-in-law. So Saul
had to give his daughter Michal in marriage to David.
28 Saul realized clearly that the LORD
was with David and also that his daughter Michal loved him. 29 So he became
even more afraid of David and was his
enemy as long as he lived.
30 The Philistine armies would come
and fight, but in every battle David was
more successful than any of Saul's other
officers. As a result David became very
famous.

David Is Persecuted by Saul

19 Saul told his son Jonathan and
all his officials that he planned to
kill[d] David. But Jonathan was very fond
of David, 2 and so he told him, "My
father is trying to kill you. Please be
careful tomorrow morning; hide in some
secret place and stay there. 3 I will go
and stand by my father in the field
where you are hiding, and I will speak to
him about you. If I find out anything, I
will let you know."
4 Jonathan praised David to Saul and
said, "Sir, don't do wrong to your servant David. He has never done you any
wrong; on the contrary, everything he
has done has been a great help to you.
5 He risked his life when he killed Goliath, and the LORD won a great victory for
Israel. When you saw it, you were glad.
Why, then, do you now want to do
wrong to an innocent man and kill David for no reason at all?"
6 Saul was convinced by what Jonathan said and made a vow in the LORD's
name that he would not kill David. 7 So
Jonathan called David and told him
everything; then he took him to Saul,
and David served the king as he had
before.
8 War with the Philistines broke out
again. David attacked them and defeated them so thoroughly that they fled.
9 One day an evil spirit from the LORD
took control of Saul. He was sitting in
his house with his spear in his hand, and
David was there, playing his harp.
10 Saul tried to pin David to the wall with
his spear, but David dodged, and the
spear stuck in the wall. David ran away
and escaped.
11 That same night Saul sent some men
to watch David's house and kill him the
next morning. Michal, David's wife,
warned him, "If you don't get away tonight, tomorrow you will be dead."
12 She let him down from a window, and
he ran away and escaped. 13 Then she
took the household idol, laid it on the
bed, put a pillow made of goats' hair at
its head, and put a cover over it. 14 When
Saul's men came to get David, Michal
told them that he was sick. 15 But Saul
sent them back to see David for themselves. He ordered them, "Carry him
here in his bed, and I will kill him."
16 They went inside and found the household idol in the bed and the goats' hair
pillow at its head. 17 Saul asked Michal,
"Why have you tricked me like this and
let my enemy escape?"
She answered, "He said he would kill
me if I didn't help him escape."
18 David escaped and went to Samuel
in Ramah and told him everything that
Saul had done to him. Then he and Samuel went to Naioth and stayed there.
19 Saul was told that David was in Naioth
in Ramah, 20 so he sent some men to arrest him. They saw[e] the group of prophets dancing and shouting, with Samuel
as their leader. Then the spirit of God
took control of Saul's men, and they also
began to dance and shout. 21 When Saul

[d] that he planned to kill; *or* to kill. [e] *Some ancient translations* They saw; *Hebrew* He saw.

heard of this, he sent more messengers,
and they also began to dance and shout.
He sent messengers the third time, and
the same thing happened to them.
22 Then he himself started out to Ramah.
When he came to the large well in Secu,
he asked where Samuel and David were
and was told that they were at Naioth.
23 As he was going there, the spirit of
God took control of him also, and he
danced and shouted all the way to Naioth. 24 He took off his clothes and danced
and shouted in Samuel's presence, and
lay naked all that day and all that night.
(This is how the saying originated, "Has
even Saul become a prophet?")

Jonathan Helps David

20 Then David fled from Naioth in
Ramah and went to Jonathan.
"What have I done?" he asked. "What
crime have I committed? What wrong
have I done to your father to make him
want to kill me?"
2 Jonathan answered, "God forbid that
you should die! My father tells me everything he does, important or not, and he
would not hide this from me. It just
isn't so!"
3 But David answered,[f] "Your father
knows very well how much you like me,
and he has decided not to let you know
what he plans to do, because you would
be deeply hurt. I swear to you by the living LORD that I am only a step away from
death!"
4 Jonathan said, "I'll do anything you
want."
5 "Tomorrow is the New Moon Festival," David replied, "and I am supposed
to eat with the king. But if it's all right
with you, I will go and hide in the fields
until the evening of the day after tomorrow. 6 If your father notices that I am not
at the table, tell him that I begged your
permission to hurry home to Bethlehem,
since it's the time for the annual sacrifice there for my whole family. 7 If he
says, 'All right,' I will be safe; but if he
becomes angry, you will know that he is
determined to harm me. 8 Please do me
this favor, and keep the sacred promise
you made to me. But if I'm guilty, kill me
yourself! Why take me to your father to
be killed?"
9 "Don't even think such a thing!" Jonathan answered. "If I knew for sure that
my father was determined to harm you,
wouldn't I tell you?"
10 David then asked, "Who will let me
know if your father answers you
angrily?"
11 "Let's go out to the fields," Jonathan
answered. So they went, 12 and Jonathan
said to David, "May the LORD God of Israel be our witness![g] At this time tomorrow and on the following day I will
question my father. If his attitude toward you is good, I will send you word.
13 If he intends to harm you, may the
LORD strike me dead if I don't let you
know about it and get you safely away.
May the LORD be with you as he was with
my father! 14 And if I remain alive, please
keep your sacred promise and be loyal
to me; but if I die,[h] 15 show the same
kind of loyalty to my family forever.
And when the LORD has completely destroyed all your enemies, 16 may our
promise to each other still be unbroken.
If it is broken, the LORD will punish you."[i]
17 Once again Jonathan made David
promise to love him, for Jonathan loved
David as much as he loved himself.
18 Then Jonathan said to him, "Since tomorrow is the New Moon Festival, your
absence will be noticed if you aren't at
the meal. 19 The day after tomorrow your
absence will be noticed[j] even more; so
go to the place where you hid yourself
the other time, and hide behind the pile
of stones there.[k] 20 I will then shoot
three arrows at it, as though it were a
target. 21 Then I will tell my servant to go
and find them. And if I tell him, 'Look,
the arrows are on this side of you; get
them,' that means that you are safe and
can come out. I swear by the living LORD
that you will be in no danger. 22 But if I
tell him, 'The arrows are on the other
side of you,' then leave, because the
LORD is sending you away. 23 As for the
promise we have made to each other, the
LORD will make sure that we will keep it
forever."

[f] *One ancient translation* answered; *Hebrew* made a vow again. [g] *One ancient translation* be our witness; *Hebrew does not have these words.* [h] *Some ancient translations* if I die; *Hebrew* that I may not die. [i] *Verses 15-16 in Hebrew are unclear.* [j] *Some ancient translations* your absence will be noticed; *Hebrew* go down. [k] *Probable text* the pile of stones there; *Hebrew* the Ezel Stone.

24 So David hid in the fields. At the
New Moon Festival, King Saul came to
the meal 25 and sat in his usual place by
the wall. Abner sat next to him, and Jonathan sat across the table from him.[l]
David's place was empty, 26 but Saul said
nothing that day, because he thought,
"Something has happened to him, and
he is not ritually pure." 27 On the following day, the day after the New Moon
Festival, David's place was still empty,
and Saul asked Jonathan, "Why didn't
David come to the meal either yesterday
or today?"
28 Jonathan answered, "He begged me
to let him go to Bethlehem. 29 'Please let
me go,' he said, 'because our family is
celebrating the sacrificial feast in town,
and my brother ordered me to be there.
So then, if you are my friend, let me go
and see my relatives.' That is why he
isn't in his place at your table."
30 Saul became furious with Jonathan
and said to him, "How rebellious and
faithless your mother was! Now I know
you are taking sides with David and are
disgracing yourself and that mother of
yours! 31 Don't you realize that as long as
David is alive, you will never be king of
this country? Now go and bring him
here—he must die!"
32 "Why should he die?" Jonathan replied. "What has he done?"
33 At that, Saul threw his spear at Jonathan to kill him, and Jonathan realized
that his father was really determined to
kill David. 34 Jonathan got up from the
table in a rage and ate nothing that
day—the second day of the New Moon
Festival. He was deeply distressed about
David, because Saul had insulted him.
35 The following morning Jonathan went
to the fields to meet David, as they had
agreed. He took a young boy with him
36 and said to him, "Run and find the arrows I'm going to shoot." The boy ran,
and Jonathan shot an arrow beyond
him. 37 When the boy reached the place
where the arrow had fallen, Jonathan
shouted to him, "The arrow is farther on!
38 Don't just stand there! Hurry up!" The
boy picked up the arrow and returned to
his master, 39 not knowing what it all
meant; only Jonathan and David knew.
40 Jonathan gave his weapons to the boy
and told him to take them back to town.
41 After the boy had left, David got up
from behind the pile of stones,[m] fell on
his knees and bowed with his face to the
ground three times. Both he and Jonathan were crying as they kissed each
other; David's grief was even greater
than Jonathan's.[n] 42 Then Jonathan said
to David, "God be with you. The LORD
will make sure that you and I, and your
descendants and mine, will forever keep
the sacred promise we have made to
each other." Then David left, and Jonathan went back to the town.

David Flees from Saul

21 David went to the priest Ahimelech in Nob. Ahimelech came out
trembling to meet him and asked, "Why
did you come here all by yourself?"
2 "I am here on the king's business,"
David answered. "He told me not to let
anyone know what he sent me to do. As
for my men, I have told them to meet me
at a certain place. 3 Now, then, what supplies do you have? Give me five loaves of
bread or anything else you have."
4 The priest said, "I don't have any ordinary bread, only sacred bread; you
can have it if your men haven't had sexual relations recently."
5 "Of course they haven't," answered
David. "My men always keep themselves ritually pure even when we go out
on an ordinary mission; how much more
this time when we are on a special
mission!"
6 So the priest gave David the sacred
bread, because the only bread he had
was the loaves offered to God, which
had been removed from the sacred table
and replaced by fresh bread.
(7 Saul's chief herdsman, Doeg, who
was from Edom, happened to be there
that day, because he had to fulfill a religious obligation.)
8 David said to Ahimelech, "Do you
have a spear or a sword you can give
me? The king's orders made me leave in
such a hurry that I didn't have time to
get my sword or any other weapon."
9 Ahimelech answered, "I have the
sword of Goliath the Philistine, whom
you killed in Elah Valley; it is behind the

[l] *One ancient translation* sat across the table from him; *Hebrew* stood up. [m] *Probable text* the pile of stones; *Hebrew* the south. [n] *Probable text* David's grief was even greater than Jonathan's; *Hebrew unclear.*

ephod, wrapped in a cloth. If you want it,
take it—it's the only weapon here."
"Give it to me," David said. "There is
not a better sword anywhere!"
10 So David left, fleeing from Saul, and
went to King Achish of Gath. 11 The
king's officials said to Achish, "Isn't this
David, the king of his country? This is
the man about whom the women sang,
as they danced, 'Saul has killed thousands, but David has killed tens of
thousands.' "
12 Their words made a deep impression on David, and he became very
much afraid of King Achish. 13 So whenever David was around them, he pretended to be insane and acted like a
madman when they tried to restrain
him; he would scribble on the city[o]
gates and let spit drool down his beard.
14 So Achish said to his officials, "Look!
The man is crazy! Why did you bring
him to me? 15 Don't I have enough madmen already? Why bring another one to
bother me with his crazy actions right
here in my own house?"

The Slaughter of the Priests

22 David fled from the city of Gath
and went to a cave near the town
of Adullam. When his brothers and the
rest of the family heard that he was
there, they joined him. 2 People who
were oppressed or in debt or dissatisfied
went to him, about four hundred men in
all, and he became their leader.
3 David went on from there to Mizpah
in Moab and said to the king of Moab,
"Please let my father and mother come
and stay with you until I find out what
God is going to do for me." 4 So David
left his parents with the king of Moab,
and they stayed there as long as David
was hiding out in the cave.
5 Then the prophet Gad came to David
and said, "Don't stay here; go at once to
the land of Judah." So David left and
went to the forest of Hereth.
6 One day Saul was in Gibeah, sitting
under a tamarisk tree on a hill, with his
spear in his hand, and all his officers
were standing around him. He was told
that David and his men had been located, 7 and he said to his officers, "Listen, men of Benjamin! Do you think that
David will give fields and vineyards to
all of you, and make you officers in his
army? 8 Is that why you are plotting
against me? Not one of you told me that
my own son had made an alliance with
David. No one is concerned about me or
tells me that David, one of my own men,
is right now looking for a chance to kill
me, and that my son has encouraged him!"
9 Doeg was standing there with Saul's
officers, and he said, "I saw David when
he went to Ahimelech son of Ahitub in
Nob. 10 Ahimelech asked the LORD what
David should do, and then he gave David some food and the sword of Goliath
the Philistine."
11 So King Saul sent for the priest
Ahimelech and all his relatives, who
were also priests in Nob, and they came
to him. 12 Saul said to Ahimelech, "Listen, Ahimelech!"
"At your service, sir," he answered.
13 Saul asked him, "Why are you and
David plotting against me? Why did you
give him some food and a sword, and
consult God for him? Now he has turned
against me and is waiting for a chance to
kill me!"
14 Ahimelech answered, "David is the
most faithful officer you have! He is
your own son-in-law, captain of[p] your
bodyguard, and highly respected by
everyone in the royal court. 15 Yes, I consulted God for him, and it wasn't the first
time.[q] As for plotting against you, Your
Majesty must not accuse me or anyone
else in my family. I don't know anything
about this matter!"
16 The king said, "Ahimelech, you and
all your relatives must die." 17 Then he
said to the guards standing near him,
"Kill the LORD's priests! They conspired
with David and did not tell me that he
had run away, even though they knew it
all along." But the guards refused to lift
a hand to kill the LORD's priests. 18 So
Saul said to Doeg, "You kill them!"—
and Doeg killed them all. On that day he
killed eighty-five priests who were qualified to carry the ephod. 19 Saul also had
all the other inhabitants of Nob, the city
of priests, put to death: men and women,
children and babies, cattle, donkeys,
and sheep—they were all killed.

[o] city; *or* palace. [p] *Some ancient translations* captain of; *Hebrew* he turned to. [q] Yes, I consulted . . . time; *or* Now, have I done something wrong today by consulting God for him? Not at all!

20 But Abiathar, one of Ahimelech's
sons, escaped, and went and joined David. 21 He told him how Saul had slaughtered the priests of the LORD. 22 David
said to him, "When I saw Doeg there
that day, I knew that he would be sure to
tell Saul. So I am responsible[r] for the
death of all your relatives. 23 Stay with
me and don't be afraid. Saul wants to kill
both you and me, but you will be safe
with me."

David Saves the Town of Keilah

23 David heard that the Philistines
were attacking the town of Keilah and were stealing the newly harvested grain. 2 So he asked the LORD,
"Shall I go and attack the Philistines?"
"Yes," the LORD answered. "Attack
them and save Keilah."
3 But David's men said to him, "We
have enough to be afraid of here in Judah; it will be much worse if we go to
Keilah and attack the Philistine forces!"
4 So David consulted the LORD again, and
the LORD said to him, "Go and attack Keilah, because I will give you victory over
the Philistines." 5 So David and his men
went to Keilah and attacked the Philistines; they killed many of them and took
their livestock. And so it was that David
saved the town.
6 When Abiathar son of Ahimelech escaped and joined David in Keilah, he
took the ephod with him.
7 Saul was told that David had gone to
Keilah, and he said, "God has put him in
my power. David has trapped himself by
going into a walled town with fortified
gates." 8 So Saul called his troops to war,
to march against Keilah and besiege David and his men.
9 When David heard that Saul was
planning to attack him, he said to the
priest Abiathar, "Bring the ephod here."
10 Then David said, "LORD, God of Israel,
I have heard that Saul is planning to
come to Keilah and destroy it on account
of me, your servant. 11 Will the citizens
of Keilah hand me over to Saul? Will
Saul really come, as I have heard? LORD,
God of Israel, I beg you to answer me!"
The LORD answered, "Saul will come."
12 "And will the citizens of Keilah hand
my men and me over to Saul?" David
asked again.
"They will," the LORD answered.
13 So David and his men—about six
hundred in all—left Keilah at once and
kept on the move. When Saul heard that
David had escaped from Keilah, he gave
up his plan.

David in the Hill Country

14 David stayed in hiding in the hill
country, in the wilderness near Ziph.
Saul was always trying to find him, but
God did not turn David over to him.
15 David saw that Saul was out to
kill him.
David was at Horesh, in the wilderness near Ziph. 16 Jonathan went to him
there and encouraged him with assurances of God's protection, 17 saying to
him, "Don't be afraid. My father Saul
won't be able to harm you. He knows
very well that you are the one who will
be the king of Israel and that I will be
next in rank to you." 18 The two of them
made a sacred promise of friendship to
each other. David stayed at Horesh, and
Jonathan went home.
19 Some people from Ziph went to Saul
at Gibeah and said, "David is hiding out
in our territory at Horesh on Mount Hachilah, in the southern part of the Judean wilderness. 20 We know, Your
Majesty, how much you want to capture
him; so come to our territory, and we
will make sure that you catch him."
21 Saul answered, "May the LORD bless
you for being so kind to me! 22 Go and
make sure once more; find out for certain where he is and who has seen him
there. I hear that he is very cunning.
23 Find out exactly the places where he
hides, and be sure to bring back a report
to me right away. Then I will go with
you, and if he is still in the region, I will
hunt him down, even if I have to search
the whole land of Judah."
24 So they left and returned to Ziph
ahead of Saul. David and his men were
in the wilderness of Maon, in a desolate
valley in the southern part of the Judean
wilderness. 25 Saul and his men set out to
look for David, but he heard about it and
went to a rocky hill in the wilderness of
Maon and stayed there. When Saul
heard about this, he went after David.
26 Saul and his men were on one side of
the hill, separated from David and his

[r] *Some ancient translations* I am responsible; *Hebrew* I have turned.

men, who were on the other side. They
were hurrying to get away from Saul
and his men, who were closing in on
them and were about to capture them.
27 Just then a messenger arrived and said
to Saul, "Come back at once! The Philistines are invading the country!" 28 So
Saul stopped pursuing David and went
to fight the Philistines. That is why that
place is called Separation Hill. 29 David
left and went to the region of Engedi,
where he stayed in hiding.

David Spares Saul's Life

24 When Saul came back from
fighting the Philistines, he was
told that David was in the wilderness
near Engedi. 2 Saul took three thousand
of the best soldiers in Israel and went
looking for David and his men east of
Wild Goat Rocks. 3 He came to a cave
close to some sheep pens by the road
and went in to relieve himself. It happened to be the very cave in which David and his men were hiding far back in
the cave. 4 They said to him, "This is your
chance! The LORD has told you that he
would put your enemy in your power
and you could do to him whatever you
wanted to." David crept over and cut off
a piece of Saul's robe without Saul's
knowing it. 5 But then David's conscience began to hurt, 6 and he said to his
men, "May the LORD keep me from doing
any harm to my master, whom the LORD
chose as king! I must not harm him in
the least, because he is the king chosen
by the LORD!" 7 So David convinced his
men that they should not attack Saul.

Saul got up, left the cave, and started
away. 8 Then David went out after him
and called to him, "Your Majesty!" Saul
turned around, and David bowed down
to the ground in respect 9 and said, "Why
do you listen to people who say that I am
trying to harm you? 10 You can see for
yourself that just now in the cave the
LORD put you in my power. Some of my
men told me to kill you, but I felt sorry
for you and said that I would not harm
you in the least, because you are the one
whom the LORD chose to be king. 11 Look,
my father, look at the piece of your robe
I am holding! I could have killed you, but
instead I only cut this off. This should
convince you that I have no thought of
rebelling against you or of harming you.
You are hunting me down to kill me,
even though I have not done you any
wrong. 12 May the LORD judge which one
of us is wrong! May he punish you for
your action against me, for I will not
harm you in the least. 13 You know the
old saying, 'Evil is done only by evil people.' And so I will not harm you. 14 Look
at what the king of Israel is trying to kill!
Look at what he is chasing! A dead dog,
a flea! 15 The LORD will judge, and he will
decide which one of us is wrong. May he
look into the matter, defend me, and
save me from you."

16 When David had finished speaking,
Saul said, "Is that really you, David my
son?" And he started crying. 17 Then he
said to David, "You are right, and I am
wrong. You have been so good to me,
while I have done such wrong to you!
18 Today you have shown how good you
are to me, because you did not kill me,
even though the LORD put me in your
power. 19 How often does someone catch
an enemy and then let him get away unharmed? The LORD bless you for what
you have done to me today! 20 Now I am
sure that you will be king of Israel and
that the kingdom will continue under
your rule. 21 But promise me in the
LORD's name that you will spare my
descendants, so that my name and my
family's name will not be completely
forgotten." 22 David promised that he
would.

Then Saul went back home, and David
and his men went back to their hiding
place.

The Death of Samuel

25 Samuel died, and all the Israelites came together and mourned
for him. Then they buried him at his
home in Ramah.

David and Abigail

After this, David went to the wilderness of Paran. 2-3 There was a man of the
clan of Caleb named Nabal, who was
from the town of Maon, and who owned
land near the town of Carmel. He was a
very rich man, the owner of three thousand sheep and one thousand goats.
His wife Abigail was beautiful and intelligent, but he was a mean, bad-
tempered man.

Nabal was shearing his sheep in Carmel, 4 and David, who was in the wilderness, heard about it, 5 so he sent ten

young men with orders to go to Carmel,
find Nabal, and give him his greetings.
6 He instructed them to say to Nabal:
"David sends you greetings, my friend,
with his best wishes for you, your family, and all that is yours. 7 He heard that
you were shearing your sheep, and he
wants you to know that your shepherds
have been with us and we did not harm
them. Nothing that belonged to them
was stolen all the time they were at Carmel. 8 Just ask them, and they will tell
you. We have come on a feast day, and
David asks you to receive us kindly.
Please give what you can to us your
servants and to your dear friend David."
9 David's men delivered this message
to Nabal in David's name. Then they
waited there, 10 and Nabal finally answered, "David? Who is he? I've never
heard of him! The country is full of runaway slaves nowadays! 11 I'm not going
to take my bread and water, and the animals I have butchered for my sheep-
shearers, and give them to people who
come from I don't know where!"
12 David's men went back to him and
told him what Nabal had said. 13 "Buckle
on your swords!" he ordered, and they
all did. David also buckled on his sword
and left with about four hundred of his
men, leaving two hundred behind with
the supplies.
14 One of Nabal's servants said to Nabal's wife Abigail, "Have you heard? David sent some messengers from the
wilderness with greetings for our master, but he insulted them. 15 Yet they
were very good to us; they never bothered us, and all the time we were with
them in the fields, nothing that belonged
to us was stolen. 16 They protected us
day and night the whole time we were
with them looking after our flocks.
17 Please think this over and decide what
to do. This could be disastrous for our
master and all his family. He is so mean
that he won't listen to anybody!"
18 Abigail quickly gathered two hundred loaves of bread, two leather bags
full of wine, five roasted sheep, two
bushels of roasted grain, a hundred
bunches of raisins, and two hundred
cakes of dried figs, and loaded them on
donkeys. 19 Then she said to the servants, "You go on ahead and I will follow
you." But she said nothing to her
husband.
20 She was riding her donkey around a
bend on a hillside when suddenly she
met David and his men coming toward
her. 21 David had been thinking, "Why
did I ever protect that fellow's property
out here in the wilderness? Not a thing
that belonged to him was stolen, and this
is how he pays me back for the help I
gave him! 22 May God strike me[s] dead if
I don't kill every last one of those men
before morning!"
23 When Abigail saw David, she
quickly dismounted and threw herself
on the ground 24 at David's feet, and said
to him, "Please, sir, listen to me! Let me
take the blame. 25 Please, don't pay any
attention to Nabal, that good-for-
nothing! He is exactly what his name
means—a fool![t] I wasn't there when
your servants arrived, sir. 26 It is the LORD
who has kept you from taking revenge
and killing your enemies. And now I
swear to you by the living LORD that your
enemies and all who want to harm you
will be punished like Nabal. 27 Please,
sir, accept this present I have brought
you, and give it to your men. 28 Please
forgive me, sir, for any wrong I have
done. The LORD will make you king, and
your descendants also, because you are
fighting his battles; and you will not do
anything evil[u] as long as you live. 29 If
anyone should attack you and try to kill
you, the LORD your God will keep you
safe, as someone guards a precious
treasure. As for your enemies, however,
he will throw them away, as someone
hurls stones with a sling. 30 And when
the LORD has done all the good things he
has promised you and has made you
king of Israel, 31 then you will not have to
feel regret or remorse, sir, for having
killed without cause or for having taken
your own revenge. And when the LORD
has blessed you, sir, please do not forget me."
32 David said to her, "Praise the LORD,
the God of Israel, who sent you today to
meet me! 33 Thank God for your good
sense and for what you have done today
in keeping me from the crime of murder
and from taking my own revenge. 34 The

[s] *One ancient translation* me; *Hebrew* my enemies. [t] A FOOL: *This is the meaning of the Hebrew name Nabal.* [u] you will not do anything evil; *or* no evil will happen to you.

LORD has kept me from harming you. But
I swear by the living God of Israel that if
you had not hurried to meet me, all of
Nabal's men would have been dead by
morning!" 35 Then David accepted what
she had brought him and said to her,
"Go back home and don't worry. I will
do what you want."
36 Abigail went back to Nabal, who
was at home having a feast fit for a king.
He was drunk and in a good mood, so
she did not tell him anything until the
next morning. 37 Then, after he had sobered up, she told him everything. He
suffered a stroke and was completely
paralyzed. 38 Some ten days later the
LORD struck Nabal and he died.
39 When David heard that Nabal had
died, he said, "Praise the LORD! He has
taken revenge on Nabal for insulting me
and has kept me his servant from doing
wrong. The LORD has punished Nabal for
his evil."

Then David sent a proposal of marriage to Abigail. 40 His servants went to
her at Carmel and said to her, "David
sent us to take you to him to be his wife."
41 Abigail bowed down to the ground
and said, "I am his servant, ready to
wash the feet of his servants." 42 She rose
quickly and mounted her donkey. Accompanied by her five maids, she went
with David's servants and became his
wife.
43 David had married Ahinoam from
Jezreel, and now Abigail also became
his wife. 44 Meanwhile, Saul had given
his daughter Michal, who had been David's wife, to Palti son of Laish, who was
from the town of Gallim.

David Spares Saul's Life Again

26 Some men from Ziph came to
Saul at Gibeah and told him that
David was hiding on Mount Hachilah at
the edge of the Judean wilderness. 2 Saul
went at once with three thousand of the
best soldiers in Israel to the wilderness
of Ziph to look for David, 3 and camped
by the road on Mount Hachilah. David
was still in the wilderness, and when he
learned that Saul had come to look for
him, 4 he sent spies and found out that
Saul was indeed there. 5 He went at once
and located the exact place where Saul
and Abner son of Ner, commander of
Saul's army, slept. Saul slept inside the
camp, and his men camped around him.
6 Then David asked Ahimelech the
Hittite, and Abishai the brother of Joab
(their mother was Zeruiah), "Which of
you two will go to Saul's camp
with me?"

"I will," Abishai answered.
7 So that night David and Abishai entered Saul's camp and found Saul sleeping in the center of the camp with his
spear stuck in the ground near his head.
Abner and the troops were sleeping
around him. 8 Abishai said to David,
"God has put your enemy in your power
tonight. Now let me plunge his own
spear through him and pin him to the
ground with just one blow—I won't have
to strike twice!"
9 But David said, "You must not harm
him! The LORD will certainly punish
whoever harms his chosen king. 10 By
the living LORD," David continued, "I
know that the LORD himself will kill Saul,
either when his time comes to die a natural death or when he dies in battle. 11 The
LORD forbid that I should try to harm the
one whom the LORD has made king! Let's
take his spear and his water jar, and go."
12 So David took the spear and the water
jar from right beside Saul's head, and he
and Abishai left. No one saw it or knew
what had happened or even woke up—
they were all sound asleep, because the
LORD had sent a heavy sleep on them all.
13 Then David crossed over to the
other side of the valley to the top of the
hill, a safe distance away, 14 and shouted
to Saul's troops and to Abner, "Abner!
Can you hear me?"

"Who is that shouting and waking up
the king?" Abner asked.
15 David answered, "Abner, aren't you
the greatest man in Israel? So why aren't
you protecting your master, the king?
Just now someone entered the camp to
kill your master. 16 You failed in your
duty, Abner! I swear by the living LORD
that all of you deserve to die, because
you have not protected your master,
whom the LORD made king. Look! Where
is the king's spear? Where is the water
jar that was right by his head?"
17 Saul recognized David's voice and
asked, "David, is that you, my son?"

"Yes, Your Majesty," David answered.
18 And he added, "Why, sir, are you still
pursuing me, your servant? What have I
done? What crime have I committed?
19 Your Majesty, listen to what I have to

say. If it is the LORD who has turned you
against me, an offering to him will make
him change his mind; but if some people
have done it, may the LORD's curse fall
on them. For they have driven me out
from the LORD's land to a country where
I can only worship foreign gods. 20 Don't
let me be killed on foreign soil, away
from the LORD. Why should the king of
Israel come to kill a flea like me? Why
should he hunt me down like a wild
bird?"

21 Saul answered, "I have done wrong.
Come back, David, my son! I will never
harm you again, because you have
spared my life tonight. I have been a
fool! I have done a terrible thing!"

22 David replied, "Here is your spear,
Your Majesty. Let one of your men come
over and get it. 23 The LORD rewards
those who are faithful and righteous. Today he put you in my power, but I did not
harm you, whom the LORD made king.
24 Just as I have spared your life today,
may the LORD do the same to me and free
me from all troubles!"

25 Saul said to David, "God bless you,
my son! You will succeed in everything
you do!"

So David went on his way, and Saul
returned home.

David among the Philistines

27 David said to himself, "One of
these days Saul will kill me. The
best thing for me to do is to escape to
Philistia. Then Saul will give up looking
for me in Israel, and I will be safe." 2 So
David and his six hundred men went
over at once to Achish son of Maoch,
king of Gath. 3 David and his men settled
there in Gath with their families. David
had his two wives with him, Ahinoam
from Jezreel, and Abigail, Nabal's
widow, from Carmel. 4 When Saul heard
that David had fled to Gath, he gave up
trying to find him.

5 David said to Achish, "If you are my
friend, let me have a small town to live
in. There is no need, sir, for me to live
with you in the capital city." 6 So Achish
gave him the town of Ziklag, and for this
reason Ziklag has belonged to the kings
of Judah ever since. 7 David lived in Philistia for sixteen months.

8 During that time David and his men
would attack the people of Geshur,
Girzi, and Amalek, who had been living
in the region a very long time. He would
raid their land as far as Shur, all the way
down to Egypt, 9 killing all the men and
women and taking the sheep, cattle,
donkeys, camels, and even the clothes.
Then he would come back to Achish,
10 who would ask him, "Where did you
go on a raid this time?" and David would
tell him that he had gone to the southern
part of Judah or to the territory of the
clan of Jerahmeel or to the territory
where the Kenites lived. 11 David would
kill everyone, men and women, so that
no one could go back to Gath and report
what he and his men had really done.
This is what David did the whole time he
lived in Philistia. 12 But Achish trusted
David and said to himself, "He is hated
so much by his own people the Israelites
that he will have to serve me all his life."

28 Some time later the Philistines
gathered their troops to fight Israel, and Achish said to David, "Of
course you understand that you and
your men are to fight on my side."

2 "Of course," David answered. "I am
your servant, and you will see for yourself what I can do."

Achish said, "Good! I will make you
my permanent bodyguard."

Saul Consults a Medium

3 Now Samuel had died, and all the Israelites had mourned for him and had
buried him in his hometown of Ramah.
Saul had forced all the fortunetellers
and mediums to leave Israel.

4 The Philistine troops assembled and
camped near the town of Shunem; Saul
gathered the Israelites and camped at
Mount Gilboa. 5 When Saul saw the Philistine army, he was terrified, 6 and so he
asked the LORD what to do. But the LORD
did not answer him at all, either by
dreams or by the use of Urim and Thummim or by prophets. 7 Then Saul ordered
his officials, "Find me a woman who is a
medium, and I will go and consult her."

"There is one in Endor," they
answered.

8 So Saul disguised himself; he put on
different clothes, and after dark he went
with two of his men to see the woman.
"Consult the spirits for me and tell me
what is going to happen," he said to her.
"Call up the spirit of the man I name."

9 The woman answered, "Surely you
know what King Saul has done, how he

forced the fortunetellers and mediums to
leave Israel.[v] Why, then, are you trying
to trap me and get me killed?"
10 Then Saul made a sacred vow. "By
the living LORD I promise that you will
not be punished for doing this," he
told her.
11 "Whom shall I call up for you?" the
woman asked.
"Samuel," he answered.
12 When the woman saw Samuel, she
screamed and said to Saul, "Why have
you tricked me? You are King Saul!"
13 "Don't be afraid!" the king said to
her. "What do you see?"
"I see a spirit coming up from the
earth," she answered.
14 "What does it look like?" he asked.
"It's an old man coming up," she answered. "He is wearing a cloak."
Then Saul knew that it was Samuel,
and he bowed to the ground in respect.
15 Samuel said to Saul, "Why have you
disturbed me? Why did you make me
come back?"
Saul answered, "I am in great trouble!
The Philistines are at war with me, and
God has abandoned me. He doesn't answer me any more, either by prophets or
by dreams. And so I have called you, for
you to tell me what I must do."
16 Samuel said, "Why do you call me
when the LORD has abandoned you and
become your enemy? 17 The LORD has
done to you what he told you through
me: he has taken the kingdom away
from you and given it to David instead.
18 You disobeyed the LORD's command
and did not completely destroy the Amalekites and all they had. That is why the
LORD is doing this to you now. 19 He will
give you and Israel over to the Philistines. Tomorrow you and your sons will
join me, and the LORD will also give the
army of Israel over to the Philistines."
20 At once Saul fell down and lay
stretched out on the ground, terrified by
what Samuel had said. He was weak, because he had not eaten anything all day
and all night. 21 The woman went over to
him and saw that he was terrified, so she
said to him, "Please, sir, I risked my life
by doing what you asked. 22 Now please
do what I ask. Let me fix you some food.
You must eat so that you will be strong
enough to travel."
23 Saul refused and said he would not
eat anything. But his officers also urged
him to eat. He finally gave in, got up
from the ground, and sat on the bed.
24 The woman quickly killed a calf which
she had been fattening. Then she took
some flour, prepared it, and baked some
bread without yeast. 25 She set the food
before Saul and his officers, and they ate
it. And they left that same night.

David Is Rejected by the Philistines

29 The Philistines brought all their
troops together at Aphek, while
the Israelites camped at the spring in
Jezreel Valley. 2 The five Philistine kings
marched out with their units of a hundred and of a thousand men; David and
his men marched in the rear with King
Achish. 3 The Philistine commanders
saw them and asked, "What are these
Hebrews doing here?"
Achish answered, "This is David, an
official of King Saul of Israel. He has
been with me for quite some time now.
He has done nothing I can find fault with
since the day he came over to me."
4 But the Philistine commanders were
angry with Achish and said to him,
"Send that fellow back to the town you
gave him. Don't let him go into battle
with us; he might turn against us during
the fighting. What better way is there for
him to win back his master's favor than
by the death of our men? 5 After all, this
is David, the one about whom the
women sang, as they danced, 'Saul has
killed thousands, but David has killed
tens of thousands.' "
6 Achish called David and said to him,
"I swear by the living God of Israel that
you have been loyal to me; and I would
be pleased to have you go with me and
fight in this battle. I have not found any
fault in you from the day you came over
to me. But the other kings don't approve
of you. 7 So go back home in peace, and
don't do anything that would displease
them."
8 David answered, "What have I done
wrong, sir? If, as you say, you haven't
found any fault in me since the day I
started serving you, why shouldn't I go
with you, my master and king, and fight
your enemies?"
9 "I agree," Achish replied. "I consider

[v] he forced . . . Israel; *or* he put to death the fortunetellers and mediums in Israel.

you as loyal as an angel of God. But the
other kings have said that you can't go
with us into battle. 10 So then, David, tomorrow morning all of you who left Saul
and came over to me will have to get up
early and leave as soon as it's light."
11 So David and his men started out
early the following morning to go back
to Philistia, and the Philistines went on
to Jezreel.

The War against the Amalekites

30 Two days later David and his
men arrived back at Ziklag. The
Amalekites had raided southern Judah
and attacked Ziklag. They had burned
down the town 2 and captured all the
women; they had not killed anyone, but
had taken everyone with them when
they left. 3 When David and his men arrived, they found that the town had been
burned down and that their wives, sons,
and daughters had been carried away.
4 David and his men started crying and
did not stop until they were completely
exhausted. 5 Even David's two wives,
Ahinoam and Abigail, had been taken
away.
6 David was now in great trouble, because his men were all very bitter about
losing their children, and they were
threatening to stone him; but the LORD
his God gave him courage. 7 David said
to the priest Abiathar son of Ahimelech,
"Bring me the ephod," and Abiathar
brought it to him. 8 David asked the
LORD, "Shall I go after those raiders?
And will I catch them?"
He answered, "Go after them; you will
catch them and rescue the captives."
9 So David and his six hundred men
started out, and when they arrived at Besor Brook, some of them stayed there.
10 David continued on his way with four
hundred men; the other two hundred
men were too tired to cross the brook
and so stayed behind. 11 The men with
David found a young Egyptian out in the
country and brought him to David. They
gave him some food and water, 12 some
dried figs, and two bunches of raisins.
After he had eaten, his strength returned; he had not had anything to eat or
drink for three full days. 13 David asked
him, "Who is your master, and where
are you from?"
"I am an Egyptian, the slave of an Amalekite," he answered. "My master left
me behind three days ago because I got
sick. 14 We had raided the territory of the
Cherethites in the southern part of Judah and the territory of the clan of Caleb, and we burned down Ziklag."
15 "Will you lead me to those raiders?"
David asked him.
He answered, "I will if you promise me
in God's name that you will not kill me
or hand me over to my master." 16 And
he led David to them.
The raiders were scattered all over the
place, eating, drinking, and celebrating
because of the enormous amount of loot
they had captured from Philistia and Judah. 17 At dawn the next day David attacked them and fought until evening.
Except for four hundred young men who
mounted camels and got away, none of
them escaped. 18 David rescued everyone and everything the Amalekites had
taken, including his two wives; 19 nothing at all was missing. David got back all
his men's sons and daughters, and all
the loot the Amalekites had taken. 20 He
also recovered all the flocks and herds;
his men drove all the livestock in front of
them[w] and said, "This belongs to
David!"
21 Then David went back to the two
hundred men who had been too weak to
go with him and had stayed behind at
Besor Brook. They came forward to
meet David and his men, and David
went up to them and greeted them
warmly. 22 But some mean and worthless
men who had gone with David said,
"They didn't go with us, and so we won't
give them any of the loot. They can take
their wives and children and go away."
23 But David answered, "My brothers,
you can't do this with what the LORD has
given us! He kept us safe and gave us
victory over the raiders. 24 No one can
agree with what you say! All must share
alike: whoever stays behind with the
supplies gets the same share as the one
who goes into battle." 25 David made this
a rule, and it has been followed in Israel
ever since.
26 When David returned to Ziklag, he
sent part of the loot to his friends, the
leaders of Judah, with the message,
"Here is a present for you from the loot

[w] *Probable text* his men . . . front of them; *Hebrew unclear.*

we took from the LORD's enemies." 27 He
sent it to the people in Bethel, to the people in Ramah in the southern part of Judah, and to the people in the towns of
Jattir, 28 Aroer, Siphmoth, Eshtemoa,
29 and Racal; to the clan of Jerahmeel, to
the Kenites, 30 and to the people in the
towns of Hormah, Borashan, Athach,
31 and Hebron. He sent it to all the places
where he and his men had roamed.

The Death of Saul and His Sons

(1 Chronicles 10.1-12)

31 The Philistines fought a battle
against the Israelites on Mount
Gilboa. Many Israelites were killed
there, and the rest of them, including
King Saul and his sons, fled. 2 But the
Philistines caught up with them and
killed three of Saul's sons, Jonathan,
Abinadab, and Malchishua. 3 The fighting was heavy around Saul, and he himself was hit by enemy arrows and badly
wounded. 4 He said to the young man
carrying his weapons, "Draw your
sword and kill me, so that these godless
Philistines won't gloat over me and kill
me." But the young man was too terrified to do it. So Saul took his own sword
and threw himself on it. 5 The young
man saw that Saul was dead, so he too
threw himself on his own sword and
died with Saul. 6 And that is how Saul,
his three sons, and the young man died;
all of Saul's men died that day. 7 When
the Israelites on the other side of Jezreel
Valley and east of the Jordan River
heard that the Israelite army had fled
and that Saul and his sons had been
killed, they abandoned their towns and
fled. Then the Philistines came and occupied the towns.

8 The day after the battle the Philistines went to plunder the corpses, and
they found the bodies of Saul and his
three sons lying on Mount Gilboa. 9 They
cut off Saul's head, stripped off his armor, and sent messengers with them
throughout Philistia to tell the good
news to their idols and to their people.
10 Then they put his weapons in the temple of the goddess Astarte, and they
nailed his body to the wall of the city of
Beth Shan.

11 When the people of Jabesh in Gilead
heard what the Philistines had done to
Saul, 12 the bravest men started out and
marched all night to Beth Shan. They
took down the bodies of Saul and his
sons from the wall, brought them back
to Jabesh, and burned them there.
13 Then they took the bones and buried
them under the tamarisk tree in town,
and fasted for seven days.

The Second Book of
SAMUEL

Introduction

Second Samuel, *the sequel to* First Samuel, *is the history of David's reign as king, first over Judah in the south (chapters 1–4) and then over the whole nation, including Israel in the north (chapters 5–24). It is a vivid account of how David, in order to extend his kingdom and consolidate his position, had to struggle with enemies within the nation as well as with foreign powers. David is shown to be a man of deep faith and devotion to God, and one who was able to win the loyalty of his people. Yet he is also shown as being sometimes ruthless and willing to commit terrible sins to serve his own desires and ambitions. But when he is confronted with his sins by the Lord's prophet Nathan, he confesses them and accepts the punishment that God sends.*

The life and achievements of David impressed the people of Israel so much that in later times of national distress, when they longed for another king, it was for one who would be "a son of David," that is, a descendant of David who would be like him.

Outline of Contents

David Learns of Saul's Death

1 After Saul's death David came back
from his victory over the Amalekites and stayed in Ziklag for two days.
2 The next day a young man arrived from
Saul's camp. To show his grief, he had
torn his clothes and put dirt on his head.
He went to David and bowed to the
ground in respect. 3 David asked him,
"Where have you come from?"
"I have escaped from the Israelite
camp," he answered.
4 "Tell me what happened," David
said.
"Our army ran away from the battle,"
he replied, "and many of our men were
killed. Saul and his son Jonathan were
also killed."
5 "How do you know that Saul and
Jonathan are dead?" David asked him.
6 He answered, "I happened to be on
Mount Gilboa, and I saw that Saul was
leaning on his spear and that the chariots and cavalry of the enemy were closing in on him. 7 Then he turned around,
saw me, and called to me. I answered,
'Yes, sir!' 8 He asked who I was, and I
told him that I was an Amalekite. 9 Then
he said, 'Come here and kill me! I have
been badly wounded, and I'm about to
die.' 10 So I went up to him and killed
him, because I knew that he would die
anyway as soon as he fell. Then I took
the crown from his head and the brace-
let from his arm, and I have brought
them to you, sir."
11 David tore his clothes in sorrow, and
all his men did the same. 12 They grieved
and mourned and fasted until evening
for Saul and Jonathan and for Israel, the
people of the LORD, because so many had
been killed in battle.
13 David asked the young man who
had brought him the news, "Where are
you from?"
He answered, "I'm an Amalekite, but I
live in your country."
14 David asked him, "How is it that you
dared kill the LORD's chosen king?"
15 Then David called one of his men and
said, "Kill him!" The man struck the Amalekite and mortally wounded him,
16 and David said to the Amalekite, "You
brought this on yourself. You condemned yourself when you confessed
that you killed the one whom the LORD
chose to be king."

David's Lament for Saul and Jonathan

17 David sang this lament for Saul and
his son Jonathan, 18 and ordered it[a] to
be taught to the people of Judah. (It is
recorded in *The Book of Jashar*.)

19 "On the hills of Israel our leaders
are dead!
The bravest of our soldiers have
fallen!
20 Do not announce it in Gath
or in the streets of Ashkelon.
Do not make the women of
Philistia glad;
do not let the daughters of
pagans rejoice.

21 "May no rain or dew fall on
Gilboa's hills;
may its fields be always barren!
For the shields of the brave lie
there in disgrace;
the shield of Saul is no longer
polished with oil.
22 Jonathan's bow was deadly,
the sword of Saul was merciless,
striking down the mighty, killing
the enemy.

23 "Saul and Jonathan, so wonderful
and dear;
together in life, together in
death;
swifter than eagles, stronger
than lions.

[a] *One ancient translation* it; *Hebrew* the bow.

24 "Women of Israel, mourn for Saul!
He clothed you in rich scarlet dresses
and adorned you with jewels and gold.

25 "The brave soldiers have fallen,
they were killed in battle.
Jonathan lies dead in the hills.

26 "I grieve for you, my brother Jonathan;
how dear you were to me!
How wonderful was your love for me,
better even than the love of women.

27 "The brave soldiers have fallen,
their weapons abandoned and useless."

David Is Made King of Judah

2 After this, David asked the LORD,
"Shall I go and take control of one
of the towns of Judah?"
"Yes," the LORD answered.
"Which one?" David asked.
"Hebron," the LORD said. 2 So David
went to Hebron, taking with him his two
wives: Ahinoam, who was from Jezreel,
and Abigail, Nabal's widow, who was
from Carmel. 3 He also took his men and
their families, and they settled in the
towns around Hebron. 4 Then the men of
Judah came to Hebron and anointed David as king of Judah.

When David heard that the people of
Jabesh in Gilead had buried Saul, 5 he
sent some men there with the message:
"May the LORD bless you for showing
your loyalty to your king by burying
him. 6 And now may the LORD be kind
and faithful to you. I too will treat you
well because of what you have done. 7 Be
strong and brave! Saul your king is
dead, and the people of Judah have
anointed me as their king."

Ishbosheth Is Made King of Israel

8 The commander of Saul's army, Abner son of Ner, had fled with Saul's son
Ishbosheth across the Jordan to Mahanaim. 9 There Abner made Ishbosheth
king of the territories of Gilead, Asher,[b]
Jezreel, Ephraim, and Benjamin, and indeed over all Israel. 10 He was forty years
old when he was made king of Israel,
and he ruled for two years.

But the tribe of Judah was loyal to David, 11 and he ruled in Hebron over Judah for seven and a half years.

War between Israel and Judah

12 Abner and the officials of Ishbosheth went from Mahanaim to the city of
Gibeon. 13 Joab, whose mother was Zeruiah, and David's other officials met
them at the pool, where they all sat
down, one group on one side of the pool
and the other group on the opposite side.
14 Abner said to Joab, "Let's have some
of the young men from each side fight an
armed contest."
"All right," Joab answered.
15 So twelve men, representing Ishbosheth and the tribe of Benjamin, fought
twelve of David's men. 16 Each man
caught his opponent by the head and
plunged his sword into his opponent's
side, so that all twenty-four of them fell
down dead together. And so that place
in Gibeon is called "Field of Swords."
17 Then a furious battle broke out, and
Abner and the Israelites were defeated
by David's men. 18 The three sons of Zeruiah were there: Joab, Abishai, and Asahel. Asahel, who could run as fast as a
wild deer, 19 started chasing Abner, running straight for him. 20 Abner looked
back and said, "Is that you, Asahel?"
"Yes," he answered.
21 "Stop chasing me!" Abner said. "Run
after one of the soldiers and take what
he has." But Asahel kept on chasing him.
22 Once more Abner said to him, "Stop
chasing me! Why force me to kill you?
How could I face your brother Joab?"
23 But Asahel would not quit; so Abner,
with a backward thrust[c] of his spear,
struck him through the stomach so that
the spear came out at his back. Asahel
dropped to the ground dead, and everyone who came to the place where he was
lying stopped and stood there.
24 But Joab and Abishai started out after Abner, and at sunset they came to the
hill of Ammah, which is to the east of
Giah on the road to the wilderness of
Gibeon. 25 The men from the tribe of
Benjamin gathered around Abner again

[b] *One ancient translation* Asher; *Hebrew* Assyria. *Hebrew unclear.*

[c] *Probable text* with a backward thrust;

and took their stand on the top of a hill.
26 Abner called out to Joab, "Do we have
to go on fighting forever? Can't you see
that in the end there will be nothing but
bitterness? We are your relatives. How
long will it be before you order your men
to stop chasing us?"
27 "I swear by the living God," Joab answered, "that if you had not spoken, my
men would have kept on chasing you
until tomorrow morning." 28 Then Joab
blew the trumpet as a signal for his men
to stop pursuing the Israelites; and so
the fighting stopped.
29 Abner and his men marched
through the Jordan Valley all that night;
they crossed the Jordan River, and after
marching all the next morning, they arrived back at Mahanaim.
30 When Joab gave up the chase, he
gathered all his men and found that
nineteen of them were missing, in addition to Asahel. 31 David's men had killed
360 of Abner's men from the tribe of
Benjamin. 32 Joab and his men took Asahel's body and buried it in the family
tomb at Bethlehem. Then they marched
all night and at dawn arrived back at
Hebron.

3 The fighting between the forces supporting Saul's family and those supporting David went on for a long time. As David became stronger and stronger, his opponents became weaker and weaker.

David's Sons

2 The following six sons, in order of
their birth, were born to David at Hebron: Amnon, whose mother was Ahinoam, from Jezreel; 3 Chileab, whose
mother was Abigail, Nabal's widow,
from Carmel; Absalom, whose mother
was Maacah, the daughter of King Talmai of Geshur; 4 Adonijah, whose
mother was Haggith; Shephatiah, whose
mother was Abital; 5 Ithream, whose
mother was Eglah. All of these sons
were born in Hebron.

Abner Joins David

6 As the fighting continued between
David's forces and the forces loyal to
Saul's family, Abner became more and
more powerful among Saul's followers.
7 One day Ishbosheth son of Saul accused Abner of sleeping with Saul's concubine Rizpah, the daughter of Aiah.
8 This made Abner furious. "Do you
think that I would betray Saul? Do you
really think I'm serving Judah?" he exclaimed. "From the very first I have been
loyal to the cause of your father Saul, his
brothers, and his friends, and I have
kept you from being defeated by David;
yet today you find fault with me about a
woman! 9-10 The LORD promised David
that he would take the kingdom away
from Saul and his descendants and
would make David king of both Israel
and Judah, from one end of the country
to the other. Now may God strike me
dead if I don't make this come true!"
11 Ishbosheth was so afraid of Abner that
he could not say a word.
12 Abner sent messengers to David,
who at that time was at Hebron,[d] to say,
"Who is going to rule this land? Make an
agreement with me, and I will help you
win all Israel over to your side."
13 "Good!" David answered. "I will
make an agreement with you on one
condition: you must bring Saul's daughter Michal to me when you come to see
me." 14 And David also sent messengers
to Ishbosheth to say, "Give me back my
wife Michal. I paid a hundred Philistine
foreskins in order to marry her." 15 So
Ishbosheth had her taken from her husband Paltiel son of Laish. 16 Paltiel followed her all the way to the town of
Bahurim, crying as he went. But when
Abner said, "Go back home," he did.
17 Abner went to the leaders of Israel
and said to them, "For a long time you
have wanted David to be your king.
18 Now here is your chance. Remember
that the LORD has said, 'I will use my
servant David to rescue my people Israel
from the Philistines and from all their
other enemies.'" 19 Abner spoke also to
the people of the tribe of Benjamin and
then went to Hebron to tell David what
the people of Benjamin and of Israel had
agreed to do.
20 When Abner came to David at Hebron with twenty men, David gave a
feast for them. 21 Abner told David, "I
will go now and win all Israel over to
Your Majesty. They will accept you
as king, and then you will get what you
have wanted and will rule over the

[d] *One ancient translation* at Hebron; *Hebrew* where he (Abner) was.

whole land." David gave Abner a guarantee of safety and sent him on his way.

Abner Is Murdered

22 Later on Joab and David's other officials returned from a raid, bringing a
large amount of loot with them. Abner,
however, was no longer there at Hebron
with David, because David had sent him
away with a guarantee of safety.
23 When Joab and his men arrived, he
was told that Abner had come to King
David and had been sent away with a
guarantee of safety. 24 So Joab went to
the king and said to him, "What have
you done? Abner came to you—why did
you let him go like that? 25 He came here
to deceive you and to find out everything
you do and everywhere you go. Surely
you know that!"
26 After leaving David, Joab sent messengers to get Abner, and they brought
him back from Sirah Well; but David
knew nothing about it. 27 When Abner
arrived in Hebron, Joab took him aside
at the gate, as though he wanted to
speak privately with him, and there he
stabbed him in the stomach. And so Abner was murdered because he had killed
Joab's brother Asahel. 28 When David
heard the news, he said, "The LORD
knows that my subjects and I are completely innocent of the murder of Abner.
29 May the punishment for it fall on Joab
and all his family! In every generation
may there be some man in his family
who has gonorrhea or a dreaded skin
disease or is fit only to do a woman's
work or is killed in battle or doesn't have
enough to eat!" 30 So Joab and his
brother Abishai took revenge on Abner
for killing their brother Asahel in the
battle at Gibeon.

Abner Is Buried

31 Then David ordered Joab and his
men to tear their clothes, wear sackcloth, and mourn for Abner. And at the
funeral King David himself walked behind the coffin. 32 Abner was buried at
Hebron, and the king wept aloud at the
grave, and so did all the people. 33 David
sang this lament for Abner:

"Why did Abner have to die like a
fool?
34 His hands were not tied,
And his feet were not bound;
He died like someone killed by
criminals!"

And the people wept for him again.
35 All day long the people tried to get
David to eat something, but he made a
solemn promise, "May God strike me
dead if I eat anything before the day is
over!" 36 They took note of this and were
pleased. Indeed, everything the king did
pleased the people. 37 All of David's people and all the people in Israel understood that the king had no part in the
murder of Abner. 38 The king said to his
officials, "Don't you realize that this day
a great leader in Israel has died? 39 Even
though I am the king chosen by God, I
feel weak today. These sons of Zeruiah
are too violent for me. May the LORD
punish these criminals as they deserve!"

Ishbosheth Is Murdered

4 When Saul's son Ishbosheth heard
that Abner had been killed in Hebron, he was afraid, and all the people of
Israel were alarmed. 2 Ishbosheth had
two officers who were leaders of raiding
parties, Baanah and Rechab, sons of
Rimmon, from Beeroth in the tribe of
Benjamin. (Beeroth is counted as part of
Benjamin. 3 Its original inhabitants had
fled to Gittaim, where they have lived
ever since.)
4 Another descendant of Saul was Jonathan's son Mephibosheth, who was five
years old when Saul and Jonathan were
killed. When the news about their death
came from the city of Jezreel, his nurse
picked him up and fled; but she was in
such a hurry that she dropped him, and
he became crippled.
5 Rechab and Baanah set out for Ishbosheth's house and arrived there about
noon, while he was taking his midday
rest. 6 The woman at the door had become drowsy while she was sifting
wheat and had fallen asleep, so Rechab
and Baanah slipped in.[e] 7 Once inside,
they went to Ishbosheth's bedroom,
where he was sound asleep, and killed
him. Then they cut off his head, took it
with them, and walked all night through
the Jordan Valley. 8 They presented the
head to King David at Hebron and said
to him, "Here is the head of Ishbosheth,

[e] *Verse 6 follows one ancient translation; Hebrew* They went on into the house carrying wheat, and struck him in the belly. Then Rechab and his brother Baanah escaped.

the son of your enemy Saul, who tried to
kill you. Today the LORD has allowed
Your Majesty to take revenge on Saul
and his descendants."
9 David answered them, "I take a vow
by the living LORD, who has saved me
from all dangers! 10 The messenger who
came to me at Ziklag and told me of
Saul's death thought he was bringing
good news. I seized him and had him put
to death. That was the reward I gave him
for his good news! 11 How much worse it
will be for evil men who murder an innocent man asleep in his own house! I will
now take revenge on you for murdering
him and will wipe you off the face of the
earth!" 12 David gave the order, and his
soldiers killed Rechab and Baanah and
cut off their hands and feet, which they
hung up near the pool in Hebron. They
took Ishbosheth's head and buried it in
Abner's tomb there at Hebron.

David Becomes King of Israel and Judah

(1 Chronicles 11.1-9; 14.1-7)

5 Then all the tribes of Israel went to
David at Hebron and said to him,
"We are your own flesh and blood. 2 In
the past, even when Saul was still our
king, you led the people of Israel in battle, and the LORD promised you that you
would lead his people and be their
ruler." 3 So all the leaders of Israel came
to King David at Hebron. He made a sacred alliance with them, they anointed
him, and he became king of Israel. 4 David was thirty years old when he became
king, and he ruled for forty years. 5 He
ruled in Hebron over Judah for seven
and a half years, and in Jerusalem over
all Israel and Judah for thirty-three
years.
6 The time came when King David and
his men set out to attack Jerusalem. The
Jebusites, who lived there, thought that
David would not be able to conquer the
city, and so they said to him, "You will
never get in here; even the blind and the
crippled could keep you out." (7 But David did capture their fortress of Zion,
and it became known as "David's City.")
8 That day David said to his men,
"Does anybody here hate the Jebusites
as much as I do? Enough to kill them?
Then go up through the water tunnel
and attack those poor blind cripples."
(That is why it is said, "The blind and
the crippled cannot enter the LORD's
house.")[f]
9 After capturing the fortress, David
lived in it and named it "David's City."
He built the city around it, starting at the
place where land was filled in on the
east side of the hill. 10 He grew stronger
all the time, because the LORD God
Almighty was with him.
11 King Hiram of Tyre sent a trade mission to David; he provided him with cedar logs and with carpenters and stone
masons to build a palace. 12 And so David realized that the LORD had established him as king of Israel and was
making his kingdom prosperous for the
sake of his people.
13 After moving from Hebron to Jerusalem, David took more concubines and
wives, and had more sons and daughters. 14 The following children were born
to him in Jerusalem: Shammua, Shobab,
Nathan, Solomon, 15 Ibhar, Elishua, Nepheg, Japhia, 16 Elishama, Eliada, and
Eliphelet.

Victory over the Philistines

(1 Chronicles 14.8-17)

17 The Philistines were told that David
had been made king of Israel, so their
army set out to capture him. When David heard of it, he went down to a fortified place. 18 The Philistines arrived at
Rephaim Valley and occupied it. 19 David asked the LORD, "Shall I attack the
Philistines? Will you give me the
victory?"
"Yes, attack!" the LORD answered. "I
will give you the victory!"
20 So David went to Baal Perazim and
there he defeated the Philistines. He
said, "The LORD has broken through my
enemies like a flood." And so that place
is called Baal Perazim.[g] 21 When the
Philistines fled, they left their idols behind, and David and his men carried
them away.
22 Then the Philistines went back to
Rephaim Valley and occupied it again.
23 Once more David consulted the LORD,
who answered, "Don't attack them from
here, but go around and get ready to at-

[f] *Verse 8 in Hebrew is unclear.* [g] BAAL PERAZIM: *This name in Hebrew means "Lord of the Breakthrough."*

tack them from the other side, near the
balsam trees. 24 When you hear the
sound of marching in the treetops, then
attack because I will be marching ahead
of you to defeat the Philistine army."
25 David did what the LORD had commanded, and was able to drive the Philistines back from Geba all the way to
Gezer.

The Covenant Box Is Brought to Jerusalem

(1 Chronicles 13.1-14; 15.25 – 16.6, 43)

6 Once more David called together
the best soldiers in Israel, a total of
thirty thousand men, 2 and led them to
Baalah[h] in Judah, in order to bring from
there God's Covenant Box, bearing the
name of the LORD Almighty, whose
throne is above the winged creatures.[i]
3 They took it from Abinadab's home on
the hill and placed it on a new cart. Uzzah and Ahio, sons of Abinadab, were
guiding the cart, 4 with Ahio walking in
front. 5 David and all the Israelites were
dancing and singing with all their
might[j] to honor the LORD. They were
playing harps, lyres, drums, rattles, and
cymbals.
6 As they came to the threshing place
of Nacon, the oxen stumbled, and Uzzah
reached out and took hold of the Covenant Box. 7 At once the LORD God became angry with Uzzah and killed him
because of his irreverence.[k] Uzzah died
there beside the Covenant Box, 8 and so
that place has been called Perez Uzzah[l]
ever since. David was furious because
the LORD had punished Uzzah in anger.
9 Then David was afraid of the LORD
and said, "How can I take the Covenant
Box with me now?" 10 So he decided not
to take it with him to Jerusalem; instead,
he turned off the road and took it to the
house of Obed Edom, a native of the city
of Gath. 11 It stayed there three months,
and the LORD blessed Obed Edom and his
family.
12 King David heard that because of
the Covenant Box the LORD had blessed
Obed Edom's family and all that he had;
so he got the Covenant Box from Obed's
house to take it to Jerusalem with a
great celebration. 13 After the men carrying the Covenant Box had gone six
steps, David had them stop while he offered the LORD a sacrifice of a bull and a
fattened calf. 14 David, wearing only a
linen cloth around his waist, danced
with all his might to honor the LORD.
15 And so he and all the Israelites took
the Covenant Box up to Jerusalem with
shouts of joy and the sound of trumpets.
16 As the Box was being brought into
the city, Michal, Saul's daughter, looked
out of the window and saw King David
dancing and jumping around in the sacred dance, and she was disgusted with
him. 17 They brought the Box and put it
in its place in the Tent that David had set
up for it. Then he offered sacrifices and
fellowship offerings to the LORD. 18 When
he had finished offering the sacrifices,
he blessed the people in the name of the
LORD Almighty 19 and distributed food to
them all. He gave each man and woman
in Israel a loaf of bread, a piece of
roasted meat,[m] and some raisins. Then
everyone went home.
20 Afterward, when David went home
to greet his family, Michal came out to
meet him. "The king of Israel made a big
name for himself today!" she said. "He
exposed himself like a fool in the sight of
the servant women of his officials!"
21 David answered, "I was dancing to
honor the LORD, who chose me instead of
your father and his family to make me
the leader of his people Israel. And I will
go on dancing to honor the LORD, 22 and
will disgrace myself even more. You[n]
may think I am nothing, but those
women will think highly of me!"
23 Michal, Saul's daughter, never had
any children.

Nathan's Message to David

(1 Chronicles 17.1-15)

7 King David was settled in his palace, and the LORD kept him safe
from all his enemies. 2 Then the king
said to the prophet Nathan, "Here I am
living in a house built of cedar, but God's
Covenant Box is kept in a tent!"
3 Nathan answered, "Do whatever you
have in mind, because the LORD is with

[h] *Probable text (see 1 Ch 13.6)* to Baalah; *Hebrew* from Baaley, or from the leaders. [i] WINGED CREATURES: *See Word List.* [j] *One ancient translation (and see 1 Ch 13.8)* and singing with all their might; *Hebrew* with all the fir trees. [k] *Probable text* his irreverence; *Hebrew unclear.* [l] PEREZ UZZAH: *This name in Hebrew means "Punishment of Uzzah."* [m] a piece of roasted meat; *or* a cake of dates. [n] *One ancient translation* You; *Hebrew* I.

you." 4 But that night the LORD said to Nathan, 5 "Go and tell my servant David
that I say to him, 'You are not the one to
build a temple for me to live in. 6 From
the time I rescued the people of Israel
from Egypt until now, I have never lived
in a temple; I have traveled around living in a tent. 7 In all my traveling with
the people of Israel I never asked any of
the leaders[o] that I appointed why they
had not built me a temple made of
cedar.'

8 "So tell my servant David that I, the
LORD Almighty, say to him, 'I took you
from looking after sheep in the fields
and made you the ruler of my people Israel. 9 I have been with you wherever
you have gone, and I have defeated all
your enemies as you advanced. I will
make you as famous as the greatest
leaders in the world. 10-11 I have chosen a
place for my people Israel and have settled them there, where they will live
without being oppressed any more. Ever
since they entered this land, they have
been attacked by violent people, but this
will not happen again. I promise to keep
you safe from all your enemies and to
give you descendants. 12 When you die
and are buried with your ancestors, I
will make one of your sons king and will
keep his kingdom strong. 13 He will be
the one to build a temple for me, and I
will make sure that his dynasty continues forever. 14 I will be his father, and he
will be my son. When he does wrong, I
will punish him as a father punishes his
son. 15 But I will not withdraw my support from him as I did from Saul, whom
I removed so that you could be king.
16 You will always have descendants,
and I will make your kingdom last forever. Your dynasty will never end.' "

17 Nathan told David everything that
God had revealed to him.

David's Prayer of Thanksgiving

(1 Chronicles 17.16-27)

18 Then King David went into the Tent
of the LORD's presence, sat down and
prayed, "Sovereign LORD, I am not worthy of what you have already done for
me, nor is my family. 19 Yet now you are
doing even more, Sovereign LORD; you
have made promises about my descendants in the years to come. And you let a
man see this,[p] Sovereign LORD! 20 What
more can I say to you! You know me,
your servant. 21 It was your will and purpose to do this; you have done all these
great things in order to instruct me.
22 How great you are, Sovereign LORD!
There is none like you; we have always
known that you alone are God. 23 There
is no other nation on earth like Israel,
whom you rescued from slavery to make
them your own people. The great and
wonderful things you did for them[q]
have spread your fame throughout the
world. You drove out[r] other nations
and their gods as your people advanced,
the people whom you set free from
Egypt to be your own. 24 You have made
Israel your own people forever, and you,
LORD, have become their God.

25 "And now, LORD God, fulfill for all
time the promise you made about me
and my descendants, and do what you
said you would. 26 Your fame will be
great, and people will forever say, 'The
LORD Almighty is God over Israel.' And
you will preserve my dynasty for all
time. 27 LORD Almighty, God of Israel! I
have the courage to pray this prayer to
you, because you have revealed all this
to me, your servant, and have told me
that you will make my descendants
kings.

28 "And now, Sovereign LORD, you are
God; you always keep your promises,
and you have made this wonderful
promise to me. 29 I ask you to bless my
descendants so that they will continue to
enjoy your favor. You, Sovereign LORD,
have promised this, and your blessing
will rest on my descendants forever."

David's Military Victories

(1 Chronicles 18.1-17)

8 Some time later King David attacked the Philistines again, defeated them, and ended their control
over the land.[s]

2 Then he defeated the Moabites. He
made the prisoners lie down on the
ground and put two out of every three of

[o] *Probable text (see 1 Ch 17.6)* leaders; *Hebrew* tribes. [p] *Probable text* you let a man see this; *Hebrew* this is a law for human beings. [q] *Probable text* them; *Hebrew* you *(plural)*. [r] *One ancient translation (and see 1 Ch 17.21)* You drove out; *Hebrew* for your land. [s] *Probable text* over the land; *Hebrew unclear.*

them to death. So the Moabites became
his subjects and paid taxes to him.
3 Then he defeated the king of the Syrian state of Zobah, Hadadezer son of Rehob, as Hadadezer was on his way to
restore his control over the territory by
the upper Euphrates River. 4 David captured seventeen hundred of his cavalry
and twenty thousand of his foot soldiers.
He kept enough horses for a hundred
chariots and crippled all the rest.
5 When the Syrians of Damascus sent
an army to help King Hadadezer, David
attacked it and killed twenty-two thousand men. 6 Then he set up military
camps in[t] their territory, and they became his subjects and paid taxes to him.
The LORD made David victorious everywhere. 7 David captured the gold shields
carried by Hadadezer's officials and
took them to Jerusalem. 8 He also took a
great quantity of bronze from Betah and
Berothai, cities ruled by Hadadezer.
9 King Toi of Hamath heard that David
had defeated all of Hadadezer's army.
10 So he sent his son Joram to greet King
David and congratulate him for his victory over Hadadezer, against whom Toi
had fought many times. Joram took David presents made of gold, silver, and
bronze. 11 King David dedicated them for
use in worship, along with the silver and
gold he took from the nations he had
conquered—12 Edom, Moab, Ammon,
Philistia, and Amalek—as well as part of
the loot he had taken from Hadadezer.
13 David became even more famous
when he returned from killing eighteen
thousand Edomites in Salt Valley. 14 He
set up military camps[u] throughout
Edom, and the people there became his
subjects. The LORD made David victorious everywhere.
15 David ruled over all of Israel and
made sure that his people were always
treated fairly and justly. 16 Joab, whose
mother was Zeruiah, was the commander of the army; Jehoshaphat son of
Ahilud was in charge of the records;
17 Zadok son of Ahitub and Ahimelech
son of Abiathar were priests; Seraiah
was the court secretary; 18 Benaiah son
of Jehoiada was in charge of[v] David's
bodyguards; and David's sons were
priests.

David and Mephibosheth

9 One day David asked, "Is there any-
one left of Saul's family? If there is,
I would like to show him kindness for
Jonathan's sake."
2 There was a servant of Saul's family
named Ziba, and he was told to go to
David. "Are you Ziba?" the king asked.
"At your service, sir," he answered.
3 The king asked him, "Is there anyone
left of Saul's family to whom I can show
loyalty and kindness, as I promised God
I would?"
Ziba answered, "There is still one of
Jonathan's sons. He is crippled."
4 "Where is he?" the king asked.
"At the home of Machir son of Ammiel
in Lodebar," Ziba answered. 5 So King
David sent for him.
6 When Mephibosheth, the son of Jonathan and grandson of Saul, arrived, he
bowed down before David in respect.
David said, "Mephibosheth," and he answered, "At your service, sir."
7 "Don't be afraid," David replied. "I
will be kind to you for the sake of your
father Jonathan. I will give you back all
the land that belonged to your grandfather Saul, and you will always be welcome at my table."
8 Mephibosheth bowed again and said,
"I am no better than a dead dog, sir!
Why should you be so good to me?"
9 Then the king called Ziba, Saul's
servant, and said, "I am giving Mephibosheth, your master's grandson, everything that belonged to Saul and his
family. 10 You, your sons, and your servants will farm the land for your master
Saul's family and bring in the harvest, to
provide food for them. But Mephibosheth himself will always be a guest at
my table." (Ziba had fifteen sons and
twenty servants.)
11 Ziba answered, "I will do everything
Your Majesty commands."
So Mephibosheth ate at the king's[w]
table, just like one of the king's sons.
12 Mephibosheth had a young son named
Mica. All the members of Ziba's family
became servants of Mephibosheth. 13 So
Mephibosheth, who was crippled in both
feet, lived in Jerusalem, eating all his
meals at the king's table.

[t] set up military camps in; *or* placed military commanders over. [u] set up military camps; *or* placed military commanders. [v] *Some ancient translations* was in charge of; *Hebrew does not have these words.* [w] *One ancient translation* the king's; *Hebrew* my.

David Defeats the Ammonites and the Syrians

(1 Chronicles 19.1-19)

10 Some time later King Nahash of
Ammon died, and his son Hanun
became king. 2 King David said, "I must
show loyal friendship to Hanun, as his
father Nahash did to me." So David sent
messengers to express his sympathy.
When they arrived in Ammon, 3 the
Ammonite leaders said to the king, "Do
you think that it is in your father's honor
that David has sent these men to express
sympathy to you? Of course not! He has
sent them here as spies to explore the
city, so that he can conquer us!"
4 Hanun seized David's messengers,
shaved off one side of their beards, cut
off their clothes at the hips, and sent
them away. 5 They were too ashamed to
return home. When David heard about
what had happened, he sent word for
them to stay in Jericho and not return
until their beards had grown again.
6 The Ammonites realized that they
had made David their enemy, so they
hired twenty thousand Syrian soldiers
from Bethrehob and Zobah, twelve
thousand men from Tob, and the king of
Maacah with a thousand men. 7 David
heard of it and sent Joab against them
with the whole army. 8 The Ammonites
marched out and took up their position
at the entrance to Rabbah, their capital
city, while the others, both the Syrians
and the men from Tob and Maacah,
took up their position in the open
countryside.
9 Joab saw that the enemy troops
would attack him in front and from the
rear, so he chose the best of Israel's soldiers and put them in position facing the
Syrians. 10 He placed the rest of his
troops under the command of his
brother Abishai, who put them in position facing the Ammonites. 11 Joab said
to him, "If you see that the Syrians are
defeating me, come and help me, and if
the Ammonites are defeating you, I will
go and help you. 12 Be strong and courageous! Let's fight hard for our people
and for the cities of our God. And may
the LORD's will be done!"
13 Joab and his men advanced to attack, and the Syrians fled. 14 When the
Ammonites saw the Syrians running
away, they fled from Abishai and retreated into the city. Then Joab turned
back from fighting the Ammonites and
went back to Jerusalem.
15 The Syrians realized that they had
been defeated by the Israelites, and so
they called all their troops together.
16 King Hadadezer sent for the Syrians
who were on the east side of the Euphrates River, and they came to Helam under
the command of Shobach, commander
of the army of King Hadadezer of Zobah. 17 When David heard of it, he gathered the Israelite troops, crossed the
Jordan River, and marched to Helam,
where the Syrians took up their position
facing him. The fighting began, 18 and
the Israelites drove the Syrian army
back. David and his men killed seven
hundred Syrian chariot drivers and forty
thousand cavalry, and they wounded
Shobach, the enemy commander, who
died on the battlefield. 19 When the kings
who were subject to Hadadezer realized
that they had been defeated by the Israelites, they made peace with them and
became their subjects. And the Syrians
were afraid to help the Ammonites any
more.

David and Bathsheba

11 The following spring, at the time
of the year when kings usually
go to war, David sent out Joab with his
officers and the Israelite army; they defeated the Ammonites and besieged the
city of Rabbah. But David himself
stayed in Jerusalem.
2 One day, late in the afternoon, David
got up from his nap and went to the palace roof. As he walked around up there,
he saw a woman taking a bath in her
house. She was very beautiful. 3 So he
sent a messenger to find out who she
was, and learned that she was Bathsheba, the daughter of Eliam and the
wife of Uriah the Hittite. 4 David sent
messengers to get her; they brought her
to him and he made love to her. (She had
just finished her monthly ritual of purification.) Then she went back home.
5 Afterward she discovered that she was
pregnant and sent a message to David to
tell him.
6 David then sent a message to Joab:
"Send me Uriah the Hittite." So Joab
sent him to David. 7 When Uriah arrived,
David asked him if Joab and the troops
were well, and how the fighting was go-

ing. 8Then he said to Uriah, "Go on
home and rest a while." Uriah left, and
David had a present sent to his home.
9But Uriah did not go home; instead he
slept at the palace gate with the king's
guards. 10When David heard that Uriah
had not gone home, he asked him, "You
have just returned after a long absence;
why didn't you go home?"

11Uriah answered, "The men of Israel
and Judah are away in battle, and the
Covenant Box is with them; my commander Joab and his officers are camping out in the open. How could I go
home, eat and drink, and sleep with my
wife? By all that's sacred, I swear that I
could never do such a thing!"

12So David said, "Then stay here the
rest of the day, and tomorrow I'll send
you back." So Uriah stayed in Jerusalem
that day and the next. 13David invited
him to supper and got him drunk. But
again that night Uriah did not go home;
instead he slept on his blanket[x] in the
palace guardroom.

14The next morning David wrote a letter to Joab and sent it by Uriah. 15He
wrote: "Put Uriah in the front line,
where the fighting is heaviest, then retreat and let him be killed." 16So while
Joab was besieging the city, he sent
Uriah to a place where he knew the enemy was strong. 17The enemy troops
came out of the city and fought Joab's
forces; some of David's officers were
killed, and so was Uriah.

18Then Joab sent a report to David
telling him about the battle, 19and he instructed the messenger, "After you have
told the king all about the battle, 20he
may get angry and ask you, 'Why did
you go so near the city to fight them?
Didn't you realize that they would shoot
arrows from the walls? 21Don't you remember how Abimelech son of Gideon
was killed? It was at Thebez, where a
woman threw a millstone down from the
wall and killed him. Why, then, did you
go so near the wall?' If the king asks you
this, tell him, 'Your officer Uriah was
also killed.' "

22So the messenger went to David and
told him what Joab had commanded him
to say. 23He said, "Our enemies were
stronger than we were and came out of
the city to fight us in the open, but we
drove them back to the city gate. 24Then
they shot arrows at us from the wall, and
some of Your Majesty's officers were
killed; your officer Uriah was also
killed."

25David said to the messenger, "Encourage Joab and tell him not to be upset, since you never can tell who will die
in battle. Tell him to launch a stronger
attack on the city and capture it."

26When Bathsheba heard that her husband had been killed, she mourned for
him. 27When the time of mourning was
over, David had her brought to the palace; she became his wife and bore him a
son. But the LORD was not pleased with
what David had done.

Nathan's Message and David's Repentance

12 The LORD sent the prophet Nathan to David. Nathan went to
him and said, "There were two men who
lived in the same town; one was rich and
the other poor. 2The rich man had many
cattle and sheep, 3while the poor man
had only one lamb, which he had
bought. He took care of it, and it grew up
in his home with his children. He would
feed it some of his own food, let it drink
from his cup, and hold it in his lap. The
lamb was like a daughter to him. 4One
day a visitor arrived at the rich man's
home. The rich man didn't want to kill
one of his own animals to fix a meal for
him; instead, he took the poor man's
lamb and prepared a meal for his guest."

5David became very angry at the rich
man and said, "I swear by the living
LORD that the man who did this ought to
die! 6For having done such a cruel thing,
he must pay back four times as much as
he took."

7"You are that man," Nathan said to
David. "And this is what the LORD God of
Israel says: 'I made you king of Israel
and rescued you from Saul. 8I gave you
his kingdom and his wives; I made you
king over Israel and Judah. If this had
not been enough, I would have given
you twice as much. 9Why, then, have
you disobeyed my commands? Why did
you do this evil thing? You had Uriah
killed in battle; you let the Ammonites
kill him, and then you took his wife!
10Now, in every generation some of your

[x] blanket; *or* cot.

descendants will die a violent death because you have disobeyed me and have
taken Uriah's wife. 11 I swear to you that
I will cause someone from your own family to bring trouble on you. You will see it when I take your wives from you and give them to another man; and he will have intercourse with them in broad
daylight. 12 You sinned in secret, but I
will make this happen in broad daylight for all Israel to see.'"
13 "I have sinned against the LORD," David said.

Nathan replied, "The LORD forgives
you; you will not die. 14 But because you
have shown such contempt for the LORD
in doing this, your child will die." 15 Then
Nathan went home.

David's Son Dies

The LORD caused the child that Uriah's wife had borne to David to become very
sick. 16 David prayed to God that the
child would get well. He refused to eat anything, and every night he went into his room and spent the night lying on the
floor. 17 His court officials went to him
and tried to make him get up, but he refused and would not eat anything with
them. 18 A week later the child died, and
David's officials were afraid to tell him the news. They said, "While the child was living, David wouldn't answer us when we spoke to him. How can we tell him that his child is dead? He might do himself some harm!"
19 When David noticed them whispering to each other, he realized that the child had died. So he asked them, "Is the child dead?"

"Yes, he is," they answered.
20 David got up from the floor, took a
bath, combed his hair, and changed his clothes. Then he went and worshiped in the house of the LORD. When he returned to the palace, he asked for food and ate
it as soon as it was served. 21 "We don't
understand this," his officials said to him. "While the child was alive, you wept for him and would not eat; but as soon as he died, you got up and ate!"
22 "Yes," David answered, "I did fast and weep while he was still alive. I thought that the LORD might be merciful
to me and not let the child die. 23 But now
that he is dead, why should I fast? Could I bring the child back to life? I will some day go to where he is, but he can never come back to me."

Solomon Is Born

24 Then David comforted his wife Bathsheba. He had intercourse with her, and she bore a son, whom David named
Solomon. The LORD loved the boy 25 and
commanded the prophet Nathan to name the boy Jedidiah,[y] because the LORD loved him.

David Captures Rabbah

(1 Chronicles 20.1-3)

26 Meanwhile Joab continued his campaign against Rabbah, the capital city of Ammon, and was about to capture it.
27 He sent messengers to David to report:
"I have attacked Rabbah and have captured its water supply. 28 Now gather the
rest of your forces, attack the city and take it yourself. I don't want to get the
credit for capturing it." 29 So David gath-
ered his forces, went to Rabbah, attacked it, and conquered it. 30 From the
head of the idol of the Ammonite god Molech[z] David took a gold crown which weighed about seventy-five pounds and had a jewel in it. David took the jewel and put it in his own crown.[a] He also took a large amount of loot from
the city 31 and put its people to work with
saws, iron hoes, and iron axes, and forced them to work at[b] making bricks. He did the same to the people of all the other towns of Ammon. Then he and his men returned to Jerusalem.

Amnon and Tamar

13 David's son Absalom had a beautiful unmarried sister named Tamar. Amnon, another of David's sons, fell in love with her. 2 He was
so much in love with her that he became sick, because it seemed impossible for him to have her; as a virgin, she was
kept from meeting men. 3 But he had a
friend, a very shrewd man named Jonadab, the son of David's brother Shammah. 4 Jonadab said to Amnon, "You are
the king's son, yet day after day I see you looking sad. What's the matter?"

"I'm in love with Tamar, the sister of

[y] JEDIDIAH: *This name in Hebrew means "Beloved of the LORD."* [z] idol of the Ammonite god Molech; *or* Ammonite king. [a] jewel . . . crown; *or* crown and put it on his own head.
[b] *Probable text (see 1 Ch 20.3)* work at; *Hebrew* pass through.

my half brother Absalom," he answered.
5 Jonadab said to him, "Pretend that
you are sick and go to bed. When your
father comes to see you, say to him,
'Please ask my sister Tamar to come and
feed me. I want her to fix the food here
where I can see her, and then serve it to
me herself.' " 6 So Amnon pretended that
he was sick and went to bed.

King David went to see him, and Amnon said to him, "Please let Tamar come
and make a few cakes here where I can
see her, and then serve them to me
herself."

7 So David sent word to Tamar in the
palace: "Go to Amnon's house and fix
him some food." 8 She went there and
found him in bed. She took some dough,
prepared it, and made some cakes there
where he could see her. Then she baked
the cakes 9 and emptied them out of the
pan for him to eat, but he wouldn't. He
said, "Send everyone away"—and they
all left. 10 Then he said to her, "Bring the
cakes here to my bed and serve them to
me yourself." She took the cakes and
went over to him. 11 As she offered them
to him, he grabbed her and said, "Come
to bed with me!"

12 "No," she said. "Don't force me to do
such a degrading thing! That's awful!
13 How could I ever hold up my head in
public again? And you—you would be
completely disgraced in Israel. Please,
speak to the king, and I'm sure that he
will give me to you." 14 But he would not
listen to her; and since he was stronger
than she was, he overpowered her and
raped her.

15 Then Amnon was filled with a deep
hatred for her; he hated her now even
more than he had loved her before. He
said to her, "Get out!"

16 "No," she answered. "To send me
away like this is a greater crime[c] than
what you just did!"

But Amnon would not listen to her;
17 he called in his personal servant and
said, "Get this woman out of my sight!
Throw her out and lock the door!" 18 The
servant put her out and locked the door.

Tamar was wearing a long robe with
full sleeves,[d] the usual clothing for an
unmarried princess in those days.[e]
19 She sprinkled ashes on her head, tore
her robe, and with her face buried in her
hands went away crying. 20 When her
brother Absalom saw her, he asked,
"Has Amnon molested you? Please, sister, don't let it upset you so much. He is
your half brother, so don't tell anyone
about it." So Tamar lived in Absalom's
house, sad and lonely.

21 When King David heard what had
happened, he was furious. 22 And Absalom hated Amnon so much for having
raped his sister Tamar that he would no
longer even speak to him.

Absalom's Revenge

23 Two years later Absalom was having his sheep sheared at Baal Hazor,
near the town of Ephraim, and he invited all the king's sons to be there. 24 He
went to King David and said, "Your Majesty, I am having my sheep sheared.
Will you and your officials come and
take part in the festivities?"

25 "No, my son," the king answered. "It
would be too much trouble for you if we
all went." Absalom insisted, but the king
would not give in, and he asked Absalom to leave.

26 But Absalom said, "Well, then, will
you at least let my brother Amnon
come?"

"Why should he?" the king asked.
27 But Absalom kept on insisting until
David finally let Amnon and all his other
sons go with Absalom.

Absalom prepared a banquet fit for a
king[f] 28 and instructed his servants:
"Notice when Amnon has had too much
to drink, and then when I give the order,
kill him. Don't be afraid. I will take the
responsibility myself. Be brave and
don't hesitate!" 29 So the servants followed Absalom's instructions and killed
Amnon. All the rest of David's sons
mounted their mules and fled.

30 While they were on their way home,
David was told: "Absalom has killed all
your sons—not one of them is left!"
31 The king stood up, tore his clothes in
sorrow, and threw himself to the
ground. The servants who were there
with him tore their clothes also. 32 But
Jonadab, the son of David's brother

[c] *Probable text* To send me . . . crime; *Hebrew unclear.* [d] long robe with full sleeves; *or* decorated robe *(see Gn 37.3).* [e] *Probable text* in those days; *Hebrew* garments. [f] *Some ancient translations* Absalom prepared a banquet fit for a king; *Hebrew does not have these words.*

Shammah, said, "Your Majesty, they
haven't killed all your sons. Only Amnon is dead. You could tell by looking at
Absalom that he had made up his mind
to do this from the time that Amnon
raped his sister Tamar. 33 So don't believe the news that all your sons are
dead; only Amnon was killed."

34 In the meantime Absalom had fled.
Just then the soldier on sentry duty
saw a large crowd coming down the hill
on the road from Horonaim.[g] He went
to the king and reported what he had
seen.[h] 35 Jonadab said to David, "Those
are your sons coming, just as I said they
would." 36 As soon as he finished saying
this, David's sons came in; they started
crying, and David and his officials also
cried bitterly.

37-38 Absalom fled and went to the king
of Geshur, Talmai son of Ammihud,
and stayed there three years. David
mourned a long time for his son Amnon;
39 but when he got over Amnon's death,
he was filled with longing for his son
Absalom.

Joab Arranges for Absalom's Return

14 Joab knew that King David
missed Absalom very much, 2 so
he sent for a clever woman who lived in
Tekoa. When she arrived, he said to her,
"Pretend that you are in mourning; put
on your mourning clothes, and don't
comb your hair. Act like a woman who
has been in mourning for a long time.
3 Then go to the king and say to him
what I tell you to say." Then Joab told
her what to say.

4 The woman went to the king, bowed
down to the ground in respect, and said,
"Help me, Your Majesty!"

5 "What do you want?" he asked her.

"I am a poor widow, sir," she answered. "My husband is dead. 6 Sir, I had
two sons, and one day they got into a
quarrel out in the fields, where there
was no one to separate them, and one of
them killed the other. 7 And now, sir, all
my relatives have turned against me and
are demanding that I hand my son over
to them, so that they can kill him for
murdering his brother. If they do this, I
will be left without a son. They will destroy my last hope and leave my husband without a son to keep his name
alive."

8 "Go back home," the king answered,
"and I will take care of the matter."

9 "Your Majesty," she said, "whatever
you do, my family and I will take the
blame; you and the royal family are
innocent."

10 The king replied, "If anyone threatens you, bring him to me, and he will
never bother you again."

11 She said, "Your Majesty, please pray
to the LORD your God, so that my relative
who is responsible for avenging the
death of my son will not commit a
greater crime by killing my other son."

"I promise by the living LORD," David
replied, "that your son will not be
harmed in the least."

12 "Please, Your Majesty, let me say
just one more thing," the woman said.

"All right," he answered.

13 She said to him, "Why have you
done such a wrong to God's people? You
have not allowed your own son to return
from exile, and so you have condemned
yourself by what you have just said.
14 We will all die; we are like water
spilled on the ground, which can't be
gathered again. Even God does not
bring the dead back to life, but the king
can at least find a way to bring a man
back from exile.[i] 15 Now, Your Majesty,
the reason I have come to speak to you is
that the people threatened me, and so I
said to myself that I would speak to you
in the hope that you would do what I
ask. 16 I thought you would listen to me
and save me from the one who is trying
to kill my son and me and so remove us
from the land God gave his people. 17 I
said to myself that your promise, sir,
would make me safe, because the king is
like God's angel and can distinguish
good from evil.[j] May the LORD your God
be with you!"

18 The king answered, "I'm going to
ask you a question, and you must tell me
the whole truth."

"Ask me anything, Your Majesty," she
answered.

19 "Did Joab put you up to this?" he
asked her.

She answered, "I swear by all that is
sacred, Your Majesty, that there is no

[g] *Probable text* from Horonaim; *Hebrew* behind him. [h] *One ancient translation* He went . . . had seen; *Hebrew does not have these words.* [i] *Probable text* Even God . . . from exile; *Hebrew unclear.* [j] can distinguish good from evil; *or* knows everything.

way to avoid answering your question.[k]
It was indeed your officer Joab who told
me what to do and what to say. 20 But he
did it in order to straighten out this
whole matter. Your Majesty is as wise as
the angel of God and knows everything
that happens."
21 Later on the king said to Joab, "I
have decided to do what you want. Go
and get the young man Absalom and
bring him back here."
22 Joab threw himself to the ground in
front of David in respect, and said, "God
bless you, Your Majesty! Now I know
that you are pleased with me, because
you have granted my request." 23 Then
he got up and went to Geshur and
brought Absalom back to Jerusalem.
24 The king, however, gave orders that
Absalom should not live in the palace. "I
don't want to see him," the king said. So
Absalom lived in his own house and did
not appear before the king.

Absalom Is Reconciled to David

25 There was no one in Israel as famous for his good looks as Absalom; he
had no defect from head to toe. 26 His
hair was very thick, and he had to cut it
once a year, when it grew too long and
heavy. It would weigh about five pounds
according to the royal standard of
weights. 27 Absalom had three sons and
one daughter named Tamar, a very
beautiful woman.
28 Absalom lived two years in Jerusalem without seeing the king. 29 Then he
sent for Joab, to ask him to go to the
king for him; but Joab would not come.
Again Absalom sent for him, and again
Joab refused to come. 30 So Absalom
said to his servants, "Look, Joab's field
is next to mine, and it has barley growing in it. Go and set fire to it." So they
went and set the field on fire.
31 Joab went to Absalom's house and
demanded, "Why did your servants set
fire to my field?"
32 Absalom answered, "Because you
wouldn't come when I sent for you. I
wanted you to go to the king and ask for
me: 'Why did I leave Geshur and come
here? It would have been better for me to
have stayed there.' " And Absalom went
on, "I want you to arrange for me to see
the king, and if I'm guilty, then let him
put me to death."
33 So Joab went to King David and told
him what Absalom had said. The king
sent for Absalom, who went to him and
bowed down to the ground in front of
him. The king welcomed him with a kiss.

Absalom Plans Rebellion

15 After this, Absalom provided a
chariot and horses for himself,
and an escort of fifty men. 2 He would get
up early and go and stand by the road at
the city gate. Whenever someone came
there with a dispute that he wanted the
king to settle, Absalom would call him
over and ask him where he was from.
And after the man had told him what
tribe he was from, 3 Absalom would say,
"Look, the law is on your side, but there
is no representative of the king to hear
your case." 4 And he would add, "How I
wish I were a judge! Then anyone who
had a dispute or a claim could come to
me, and I would give him justice."
5 When the man would approach Absalom to bow down before him, Absalom
would reach out, take hold of him, and
kiss him. 6 Absalom did this with every
Israelite who came to the king for judgment, and so he won their loyalty.
7 After four[l] years Absalom said to
King David, "Sir, let me go to Hebron
and keep a promise I made to the LORD.
8 While I was living in Geshur in Syria, I
promised the LORD that if he would take
me back to Jerusalem, I would worship
him in Hebron."[m]
9 "Go in peace," the king said. So Absalom went to Hebron. 10 But he sent messengers to all the tribes of Israel to say,
"When you hear the sound of trumpets,
shout, 'Absalom has become king at Hebron!' " 11 There were two hundred men
who at Absalom's invitation had gone
from Jerusalem with him; they knew
nothing of the plot and went in all good
faith. 12 And while he was offering sacrifices, Absalom also sent to the town of
Gilo for Ahithophel, who was one of
King David's advisers. The plot against
the king gained strength, and Absalom's
followers grew in number.

[k] there is . . . question; *or* you are absolutely right. [l] *Some ancient translations* four; *Hebrew* forty. [m] *One ancient translation* in Hebron; *Hebrew does not have these words.*

David Flees from Jerusalem

13 A messenger reported to David,
"The Israelites are pledging their loyalty
to Absalom."
14 So David said to all his officials who
were with him in Jerusalem, "We must
get away at once if we want to escape
from Absalom! Hurry! Or else he will
soon be here and defeat us and kill
everyone in the city!"
15 "Yes, Your Majesty," they answered.
"We are ready to do whatever you say."
16 So the king left, accompanied by all
his family and officials, except for ten
concubines, whom he left behind to take
care of the palace.
17 As the king and all his men were
leaving the city, they stopped at the last
house. 18 All his officials stood[n] next to
him as the royal bodyguards passed by
in front of him. The six hundred soldiers
who had followed him from Gath also
passed by, 19 and the king said to Ittai,
their leader, "Why are you going with
us? Go back and stay with the new king.
You are a foreigner, a refugee away
from your own country. 20 You have
lived here only a short time, so why
should I make you wander around with
me? I don't even know where I'm going.
Go back and take all your people with
you—and may the LORD be kind and
faithful to you."[o]
21 But Ittai answered, "Your Majesty, I
swear to you in the LORD's name that I
will always go with you wherever you
go, even if it means death."
22 "Fine!" David answered. "March
on!" So Ittai went on with all his men
and their dependents. 23 The people cried
loudly as David's followers left. The
king crossed Kidron Brook, followed by
his men, and together they went out toward the wilderness.
24 Zadok the priest was there, and with
him were the Levites, carrying the sacred Covenant Box. They set it down[p]
and didn't pick it up again until all the
people had left the city. The priest Abiathar was there too.[q] 25 Then the king
said to Zadok, "Take the Covenant Box
back to the city. If the LORD is pleased
with me, some day he will let me come
back to see it and the place where it
stays. 26 But if he isn't pleased with me—
well, then, let him do to me what he
wishes." 27 And he went on to say to Zadok, "Look,[r] take your son Ahimaaz
and Abiathar's son Jonathan and go
back to the city in peace. 28 Meanwhile, I
will wait at the river crossings in the wilderness until I receive news from you."
29 So Zadok and Abiathar took the Covenant Box back into Jerusalem and
stayed there.
30 David went on up the Mount of Olives crying; he was barefoot and had his
head covered as a sign of grief. All who
followed him covered their heads and
cried also. 31 When David was told[s] that
Ahithophel had joined Absalom's rebellion, he prayed, "Please, LORD, turn
Ahithophel's advice into nonsense!"
32 When David reached the top of the
hill, where there was a place of worship,
his trusted friend Hushai the Archite
met him with his clothes torn and with
dirt on his head. 33 David said to him,
"You will be of no help to me if you come
with me, 34 but you can help me by returning to the city and telling Absalom
that you will now serve him as faithfully
as you served his father. And do all you
can to oppose any advice that Ahithophel gives. 35 The priests Zadok and Abiathar will be there; tell them everything
you hear in the king's palace. 36 They
have their sons Ahimaaz and Jonathan
with them, and you can send them to me
with all the information you gather."
37 So Hushai, David's friend, returned
to the city just as Absalom was arriving.

David and Ziba

16 When David had gone a little beyond the top of the hill, he was
suddenly met by Ziba, the servant of Mephibosheth, who had with him a couple
of donkeys loaded with two hundred
loaves of bread, a hundred bunches of
raisins, a hundred bunches of fresh fruit,
and a leather bag full of wine. 2 King David asked him, "What are you going to
do with all that?"
Ziba answered, "The donkeys are for
Your Majesty's family to ride, the bread
and the fruit are for the men to eat, and

[n] *Probable text* stood; *Hebrew* passed. [o] *One ancient translation* and may the LORD be kind and faithful to you; *Hebrew* kindness and faithfulness. [p] *Probable text* set it down; *Hebrew* poured it out. [q] *Probable text* was there too; *Hebrew* went up. [r] *Some ancient translations* Look; *Hebrew* Are you the seer? [s] *One ancient translation* was told; *Hebrew* told.

the wine is for them to drink when they
get tired in the wilderness."
3 "Where is Mephibosheth, the grandson of your master Saul?" the king
asked him.
"He is staying in Jerusalem," Ziba answered, "because he is convinced that
the Israelites will now restore to him the
kingdom of his grandfather Saul."
4 The king said to Ziba, "Everything
that belonged to Mephibosheth is
yours."
"I am your servant," Ziba replied.
"May I always please Your Majesty!"

David and Shimei

5 When King David arrived at Bahurim, one of Saul's relatives, Shimei son
of Gera, came out to meet him, cursing
him as he came. 6 Shimei started throwing stones at David and his officials,
even though David was surrounded by
his men and his bodyguards. 7 Shimei
cursed him and said, "Get out! Get out!
Murderer! Criminal! 8 You took Saul's
kingdom, and now the LORD is punishing
you for murdering so many of Saul's
family. The LORD has given the kingdom
to your son Absalom, and you are ruined, you murderer!"
9 Abishai, whose mother was Zeruiah,
said to the king, "Your Majesty, why do
you let this dog curse you? Let me go
over there and cut off his head!"
10 "This is none of your business," the
king said to Abishai and his brother
Joab. "If he curses me because the LORD
told him to, who has the right to ask why
he does it?" 11 And David said to Abishai
and to all his officials, "My own son is
trying to kill me; so why should you be
surprised at this Benjaminite? The LORD
told him to curse; so leave him alone and
let him do it. 12 Perhaps the LORD will notice my misery[t] and give me some
blessings to take the place of his curse."
13 So David and his men continued along
the road. Shimei kept up with them,
walking on the hillside; he was cursing
and throwing stones and dirt at them as
he went. 14 The king and all his men
were worn out when they reached the
Jordan,[u] and there they rested.

Absalom in Jerusalem

15 Absalom and all the Israelites with
him entered Jerusalem, and Ahithophel
was with them. 16 When Hushai, David's
trusted friend, met Absalom, he shouted,
"Long live the king! Long live the king!"
17 "What has happened to your loyalty
to your friend David?" Absalom asked
him. "Why didn't you go with him?"
18 Hushai answered, "How could I? I
am for the one chosen by the LORD, by
these people, and by all the Israelites. I
will stay with you. 19 After all, whom
should I serve, if not my master's son?
As I served your father, so now I will
serve you."
20 Then Absalom turned to Ahithophel
and said, "Now that we are here, what
do you advise us to do?"
21 Ahithophel answered, "Go and have
intercourse with your father's concubines whom he left behind to take care
of the palace. Then everyone in Israel
will know that your father regards you
as his enemy, and your followers will be
greatly encouraged." 22 So they set up a
tent for Absalom on the palace roof, and
in the sight of everyone Absalom went
in and had intercourse with his father's
concubines.
23 Any advice that Ahithophel gave in
those days was accepted as though it
were the very word of God; both David
and Absalom followed it.

Hushai Misleads Absalom

17 Not long after that, Ahithophel
said to Absalom, "Let me choose
twelve thousand men, and tonight I will
set out after David. 2 I will attack him
while he is tired and discouraged. He
will be frightened, and all his men will
run away. I will kill only the king 3 and
then bring back all his men to you, like
a bride returning to her husband. You
want to kill only one man;[v] the rest of
the people will be safe." 4 This seemed
like good advice to Absalom and all the
Israelite leaders.
5 Absalom said, "Now call Hushai, and
let us hear what he has to say." 6 When
Hushai arrived, Absalom said to him,
"This is the advice that Ahithophel has

[t] *Some ancient translations* misery; *Hebrew* wickedness. [u] *One ancient translation* the Jordan; *Hebrew does not have these words.* [v] *One ancient translation* like a bride . . . only one man; *Hebrew* like the return of the whole, so is the man you seek.

given us; shall we follow it? If not, you
tell us what to do."
7 Hushai answered, "The advice Ahithophel gave you this time is no good.
8 You know that your father David and
his men are hard fighters and that they
are as fierce as a mother bear robbed of
her cubs. Your father is an experienced
soldier and does not stay with his men at
night. 9 Right now he is probably hiding
in a cave or some other place. As soon as
David attacks your men, whoever hears
about it will say that your men have
been defeated. 10 Then even the bravest
men, as fearless as lions, will be afraid
because everyone in Israel knows that
your father is a great soldier and that his
men are hard fighters. 11 My advice is
that you bring all the Israelites together
from one end of the country to the other,
as many as the grains of sand on the seashore, and that you lead them personally
in battle. 12 We will find David wherever
he is, and attack him before he knows
what's happening. Neither he nor any of
his men will survive. 13 If he retreats into
a city, our people will all bring ropes and
just pull the city[w] into the valley below.
Not a single stone will be left there on
top of the hill."
14 Absalom and all the Israelites said,
"Hushai's advice is better than Ahithophel's." The LORD had decided that
Ahithophel's good advice would not be
followed, so that disaster would come on
Absalom.

David Is Warned and Escapes

15 Then Hushai told the priests Zadok
and Abiathar what advice he had given
to Absalom and the Israelite leaders and
what advice Ahithophel had given.
16 Hushai added, "Quick, now! Send a
message to David not to spend the night
at the river crossings in the wilderness,
but to cross the Jordan at once, so that
he and his men won't all be caught and
killed."
17 Abiathar's son Jonathan and Zadok's son Ahimaaz were waiting at the
spring of Enrogel, on the outskirts of Jerusalem, because they did not dare be
seen entering the city. A servant woman
would regularly go and tell them what
was happening, and then they would go
and tell King David. 18 But one day a boy
happened to see them, and he told Absalom; so they hurried off to hide in the
house of a certain man in Bahurim. He
had a well near his house, and they got
down in it. 19 The man's wife took a covering, spread it over the opening of the
well and scattered grain over it, so that
no one would notice anything. 20 Absalom's officials came to the house and
asked the woman, "Where are Ahimaaz
and Jonathan?"
"They crossed the river," she answered.
The men looked for them but could
not find them, and so they returned to
Jerusalem. 21 After they left, Ahimaaz
and Jonathan came up out of the well
and went and reported to King David.
They told him what Ahithophel had
planned against him and said, "Hurry up
and cross the river." 22 So David and his
men started crossing the Jordan, and by
daybreak they had all gone across.
23 When Ahithophel saw that his advice had not been followed, he saddled
his donkey and went back to his hometown. After putting his affairs in order,
he hanged himself. He was buried in the
family grave.
24 David had reached the town of Mahanaim by the time Absalom and the Israelites had crossed the Jordan.
(25 Absalom had put Amasa in command
of the army in the place of Joab. Amasa
was the son of Jether the Ishmaelite;[x]
his mother was Abigail, the daughter of
Nahash and the sister of Joab's mother
Zeruiah.) 26 Absalom and his men
camped in the land of Gilead.
27 When David arrived at Mahanaim,
he was met by Shobi son of Nahash,
from the city of Rabbah in Ammon, and
by Machir son of Ammiel, from Lodebar, and by Barzillai, from Rogelim in
Gilead. 28-29 They brought bowls, clay
pots, and bedding, and also food for David and his men: wheat, barley, meal,
roasted grain, beans, peas,[y] honey,
cheese, cream, and some sheep. They
knew that David and his men would get
hungry, thirsty, and tired in the wilderness.

[w] *Some ancient translations* the city; *Hebrew* him. [x] *One ancient translation (and see 1 Ch 2.17)* Ishmaelite; *Hebrew* Israelite. [y] *Some ancient translations* peas; *Hebrew* peas and roasted grain.

Absalom Is Defeated and Killed

18 King David brought all his men
together, divided them into units
of a thousand and of a hundred, and
placed officers in command of them.
2Then he sent them out in three groups,
with Joab and Joab's brother Abishai
and Ittai from Gath, each in command of
a group. And the king said to his men, "I
will go with you myself."
3"You mustn't go with us," they answered. "It won't make any difference to
the enemy if the rest of us turn and run,
or even if half of us are killed; but you
are worth ten thousand of us. It will be
better if you stay here in the city and
send us help."
4"I will do whatever you think best,"
the king answered. Then he stood by the
side of the gate as his men marched out
in units of a thousand and of a hundred.
5He gave orders to Joab, Abishai, and
Ittai: "For my sake don't harm the young
man Absalom." And all the troops heard
David give this command to his officers.
6David's army went out into the
countryside and fought the Israelites in
Ephraim Forest. 7The Israelites were defeated by David's men; it was a terrible
defeat, with twenty thousand men killed
that day. 8The fighting spread over the
countryside, and more men died in the
forest than were killed in battle.
9Suddenly Absalom met some of David's men. Absalom was riding a mule,
and as it went under a large oak tree,
Absalom's head got caught in the
branches. The mule ran on and Absalom
was left hanging in midair. 10One of David's men saw him and reported to Joab,
"Sir, I saw Absalom hanging in an oak
tree!"
11Joab answered, "If you saw him,
why didn't you kill him on the spot? I
myself would have given you ten pieces
of silver and a belt."
12But the man answered, "Even if you
gave me a thousand pieces of silver, I
wouldn't lift a finger against the king's
son. We all heard the king command
you and Abishai and Ittai, 'For my sake
don't harm the young man Absalom.'
13But if I had disobeyed the king and
killed Absalom, the king would have
heard about it—he hears about
everything—and you would not have
defended me."
14"I'm not going to waste any more
time with you," Joab said. He took three
spears and plunged them into Absalom's
chest while he was still alive, hanging in
the oak tree. 15Then ten of Joab's soldiers closed in on Absalom and finished
killing him.
16Joab had the trumpet blown to stop
the fighting, and his troops came back
from pursuing the Israelites. 17They
took Absalom's body, threw it into a
deep pit in the forest, and covered it with
a huge pile of stones. All the Israelites
fled to their own hometowns.
18During his lifetime Absalom had
built a monument for himself in King's
Valley, because he had no son to keep
his name alive. So he named it after himself, and to this day it is known as Absalom's Monument.

David Is Told of Absalom's Death

19Then Ahimaaz son of Zadok said to
Joab, "Let me run to the king with the
good news that the LORD has saved him
from his enemies."
20"No," Joab said, "today you will not
take any good news. Some other day
you may do so, but not today, for the
king's son is dead." 21Then he said to his
Ethiopian[z] slave, "Go and tell the king
what you have seen." The slave bowed
and ran off.
22Ahimaaz insisted, "I don't care what
happens; please let me take the news
also."
"Why do you want to do it, my son?"
Joab asked. "You will get no reward
for it."
23"Whatever happens," Ahimaaz said
again, "I want to go."
"Then go," Joab said. So Ahimaaz ran
off down the road through the Jordan
Valley, and soon he passed the slave.
24David was sitting in the space between the inner and outer gates of the
city. The lookout went up to the top of
the wall and stood on the roof of the
gateway; he looked out and saw a man
running alone. 25He called down and
told the king, and the king said, "If he is

[z] *Hebrew* Cushite: *Cush is the ancient name of the extensive territory south of the First Cataract of the Nile River. This region was called Ethiopia in Graeco-Roman times, and included within its borders most of modern Sudan and some of present-day Ethiopia (Abyssinia).*

alone, he is bringing good news." The
runner kept coming closer.
26 Then the lookout saw another man
running alone, and he called down to the
gatekeeper, "Look! There's another man
running!"
The king answered, "This one also is
bringing good news."
27 The lookout said, "I can see that the
first man runs like Ahimaaz."
"He's a good man," the king said, "and
he is bringing good news."
28 Ahimaaz called out a greeting to the
king, threw himself down to the ground
before him, and said, "Praise the LORD
your God, who has given you victory
over the men who rebelled against Your
Majesty!"
29 "Is the young man Absalom all
right?" the king asked.
Ahimaaz answered, "Sir, when your
officer Joab sent me, I saw a great commotion, but I couldn't tell what it was."
30 "Stand over there," the king told
him; and he went over and stood there.
31 Then the Ethiopian[z] slave arrived
and said to the king, "I have good news
for Your Majesty! Today the LORD has
given you victory over all who rebelled
against you!"
32 "Is the young man Absalom all
right?" the king asked.
The slave answered, "I wish that what
has happened to him would happen to
all your enemies, sir, and to all who
rebel against you."
33 The king was overcome with grief.
He went up to the room over the gateway and wept. As he went, he cried,
"O my son! My son Absalom! Absalom,
my son! If only I had died in your place,
my son! Absalom, my son!"

Joab Reprimands David

19 Joab was told that King David
was weeping and mourning for
Absalom. 2 And so the joy of victory was
turned into sadness for all of David's
troops that day, because they heard that
the king was mourning for his son.
3 They went back into the city quietly,
like soldiers who are ashamed because
they are running away from battle. 4 The
king covered his face and cried loudly,
"O my son! My son Absalom! Absalom,
my son!"
5 Joab went to the king's house and
said to him, "Today you have humiliated
your men—the men who saved your life
and the lives of your sons and daughters
and of your wives and concubines. 6 You
oppose those who love you and support
those who hate you! You have made it
clear that your officers and men mean
nothing to you. I can see that you would
be quite happy if Absalom were alive today and all of us were dead. 7 Now go
and reassure your men. I swear by the
LORD's name that if you don't, not one of
them will be with you by tomorrow
morning. That would be the worst disaster you have suffered in all your life."
8 Then the king got up, and went and sat
near the city gate. His men heard that
he was there, and they all gathered
around him.

David Starts Back to Jerusalem

Meanwhile all the Israelites had fled
to their own hometowns. 9 All over the
country they started quarreling among
themselves. "King David saved us from
our enemies," they said to one another.
"He rescued us from the Philistines, but
now he has fled from Absalom and left
the country. 10 We anointed Absalom as
our king, but he has been killed in battle.
So why doesn't somebody try to bring
King David back?"
11 The news of what the Israelites were
saying reached King David.[a] So he sent
the priests Zadok and Abiathar to ask
the leaders of Judah, "Why should you
be the last to help bring the king back to
his palace? 12 You are my relatives, my
own flesh and blood; why should you be
the last to bring me back?" 13 David also
told them to say to Amasa, "You are my
relative. From now on I am putting you
in charge of the army in place of Joab.
May God strike me dead if I don't!"
14 David's words won the complete loyalty of all the men of Judah, and they
sent him word to return with all his officials.
15 On his way back the king was met at

[z] *Hebrew* Cushite: *Cush is the ancient name of the extensive territory south of the First Cataract of the Nile River. This region was called Ethiopia in Graeco-Roman times, and included within its borders most of modern Sudan and some of present-day Ethiopia (Abyssinia).* [a] *Some ancient translations* The news . . . David; *Hebrew* The news . . . David, to his palace, *and places this sentence at the end of the verse.*

the Jordan River by the men of Judah,
who had come to Gilgal to escort him
across the river. 16 At the same time the
Benjaminite Shimei son of Gera from
Bahurim hurried to the Jordan to meet
King David. 17 He had with him a thousand men from the tribe of Benjamin.
And Ziba, the servant of Saul's family,
also came with his fifteen sons and
twenty servants, and they arrived at the
Jordan before the king. 18 They crossed[b]
the river to escort the royal party across
and to do whatever the king wanted.

David Shows Kindness to Shimei

As the king was getting ready to cross,
Shimei threw himself down in front of
him 19 and said, "Your Majesty, please
forget the wrong I did that day you left
Jerusalem. Don't hold it against me or
think about it any more. 20 I know, sir,
that I have sinned, and this is why I am
the first one from the northern tribes to
come and meet Your Majesty today."

21 Abishai son of Zeruiah spoke up:
"Shimei should be put to death because
he cursed the one whom the LORD chose
as king."

22 But David said to Abishai and his
brother Joab, "Who asked your opinion?
Are you going to give me trouble? I am
the one who is king of Israel now, and no
Israelite will be put to death today."
23 And he said to Shimei, "I give you my
word that you will not be put to death."

David Shows Kindness to Mephibosheth

24 Then Mephibosheth, Saul's grandson, came down to meet the king. He
had not washed his feet, trimmed his
beard, or washed his clothes from the
time the king left Jerusalem until he returned victorious. 25 When Mephibosheth arrived from[c] Jerusalem to meet
the king, the king said to him, "Mephibosheth, you didn't go with me. Why not?"

26 He answered, "As you know, Your
Majesty, I am crippled. I told my servant
to saddle my donkey so that I could ride
along with you, but he betrayed me.
27 He lied about me to Your Majesty, but
you are like God's angel, so do what
seems right to you. 28 All of my father's
family deserved to be put to death by
Your Majesty, but you gave me the right
to eat at your table. I have no right to ask
for any more favors from Your Majesty."

29 The king answered, "You don't have
to say anything more. I have decided
that you and Ziba will share Saul's
property."

30 "Let Ziba have it all," Mephibosheth
answered. "It's enough for me that Your
Majesty has come home safely."

David Shows Kindness to Barzillai

31 Barzillai, from Gilead, had also
come down from Rogelim to escort the
king across the Jordan. 32 Barzillai was a
very old man, eighty years old. He was
very rich and had supplied the king with
food while he was staying at Mahanaim.
33 The king said to him, "Come with me
to Jerusalem, and I will take care of
you."

34 But Barzillai answered, "I don't have
long to live; why should I go with Your
Majesty to Jerusalem? 35 I am already
eighty years old, and nothing gives me
pleasure any more. I can't taste what I
eat and drink, and I can't hear the voices
of singers. I would only be a burden to
Your Majesty. 36 I don't deserve such a
great reward. So I will go just a little way
with you beyond the Jordan. 37 Then let
me go back home and die near my parents' grave. Here is my son Chimham,
who will serve you; take him with you,
Your Majesty, and do for him as you
think best."

38 The king answered, "I will take him
with me and do for him whatever you
want. And I will do for you anything you
ask." 39 Then David and all of his men
crossed the Jordan. He kissed Barzillai
and gave him his blessing, and Barzillai
went back home.

Judah and Israel Argue over the King

40 When the king had crossed, escorted by all the people of Judah and
half the people of Israel, he went on to
Gilgal, and Chimham went with him.
41 Then all the Israelites went to the king
and said to him, "Your Majesty, why did
our brothers, the men of Judah, think
they had the right to take you away and

[b] *Probable text* They crossed; *Hebrew* The crossing crossed. [c] *One ancient translation* from; *Hebrew* at.

escort you, your family, and your men
across the Jordan?"
42 The men of Judah answered, "We
did it because the king is one of us. So
why should this make you angry? He
hasn't paid for our food nor has he given
us anything."
43 The Israelites replied, "We have ten
times as many claims on King David as
you have, even if he is one of you. Why
do you look down on us? Don't forget
that we were the first to talk about
bringing the king back!"

But the men of Judah were more violent in making their claims than the men
of Israel.

Sheba's Rebellion

20 There happened to be in Gilgal a
worthless character named
Sheba son of Bikri, of the tribe of Benjamin. He blew the trumpet and called out,
"Down with David! We won't follow
him! Men of Israel, let's go home!" 2 So
the Israelites deserted David and went
with Sheba, but the men of Judah remained loyal and followed David from
the Jordan to Jerusalem.
3 When David arrived at his palace in
Jerusalem, he took the ten concubines
he had left to take care of the palace, and
put them under guard. He provided for
their needs, but did not have intercourse
with them. They were kept confined for
the rest of their lives, living like widows.
4 The king said to Amasa, "Call the
men of Judah together and be back here
with them by the day after tomorrow."
5 Amasa went to call them, but he did not
get back by the time the king had told
him to. 6 So the king said to Abishai,
"Sheba will give us more trouble than
Absalom. Take my men and go after
him, or else he may occupy some fortified towns and escape from us." 7 So
Joab's men, the royal bodyguards, and
all the other soldiers left Jerusalem with
Abishai to go after Sheba. 8 When they
reached the large rock at Gibeon, Amasa met them. Joab was dressed for battle, with a sword in its sheath fastened to
his belt. As he came forward, the sword
fell out. 9 Joab said to Amasa, "How are
you, my friend?" and took hold of his
beard with his right hand in order to kiss
him. 10 Amasa was not on guard against
the sword that Joab was holding in his
other hand, and Joab stabbed him in the
belly, and his insides spilled out on the
ground. He died immediately, and Joab
did not have to strike again.

Then Joab and his brother Abishai
went on after Sheba. 11 One of Joab's
men stood by Amasa's body and called
out, "Everyone who is for Joab and David follow Joab!" 12 Amasa's body, covered with blood, was lying in the middle
of the road. Joab's man saw that everybody was stopping, so he dragged the
body from the road out into the field and
threw a blanket over it. 13 After the body
had been removed from the road, everyone followed Joab in pursuit of Sheba.
14 Sheba passed through the territory
of all the tribes of Israel and came to the
city of Abel Beth Maacah, and all the
members of the clan of Bikri[d] assembled and followed him into the city.
15 Joab's men heard that Sheba was
there, and so they went and besieged the
city. They built ramps of earth against
the outer wall and also began to dig under the wall to make it fall down.
16 There was a wise woman in the city
who shouted from the wall, "Listen! Listen! Tell Joab to come here; I want to
speak with him." 17 Joab went, and she
asked, "Are you Joab?"

"Yes, I am," he answered.

"Listen to me, sir," she said.

"I'm listening," he answered.

18 She said, "Long ago they used to
say, 'Go and get your answer in the city
of Abel'—and that's just what they did.
19 Ours is a great city, one of the most
peaceful and loyal in Israel. Why are
you trying to destroy it? Do you want to
ruin what belongs to the LORD?"
20 "Never!" Joab answered. "I will
never ruin or destroy your city! 21 That is
not our plan. A man named Sheba son of
Bikri, who is from the hill country of
Ephraim, started a rebellion against
King David. Hand over this one man,
and I will withdraw from the city."

"We will throw his head over the wall
to you," she said. 22 Then she went to the
people of the city with her plan, and they
cut off Sheba's head and threw it over
the wall to Joab. He blew the trumpet as
a signal for his men to leave the city, and

[d] *Probable text* Bikri; *Hebrew* Beri.

they went back home. And Joab returned to Jerusalem to the king.

David's Officials

23 Joab was in command of the army of
Israel; Benaiah son of Jehoiada was in
charge of David's bodyguards; 24 Adoniram was in charge of the forced labor;
Jehoshaphat son of Ahilud was in
charge of the records; 25 Sheva was the
court secretary; Zadok and Abiathar
were the priests, 26 and Ira from the town
of Jair was also one of David's priests.

Saul's Descendants Are Put to Death

21 During David's reign there was a
severe famine which lasted for
three full years. So David consulted the
LORD about it, and the LORD said, "Saul
and his family are guilty of murder; he
put the people of Gibeon to death."
(2 The people of Gibeon were not Israelites; they were a small group of Amorites whom the Israelites had promised
to protect, but Saul had tried to destroy
them because of his zeal for the people
of Israel and Judah.) 3 So David summoned the people of Gibeon and said to
them, "What can I do for you? I want to
make up for the wrong that was done to
you, so that you will bless the LORD's
people."

4 They answered, "Our quarrel with
Saul and his family can't be settled with
silver or gold, nor do we want to kill any
Israelite."

"What, then, do you think I should do
for you?" David asked.

5 They answered, "Saul wanted to destroy us and leave none of us alive anywhere in Israel. 6 So hand over seven of
his male descendants, and we will hang
them before the LORD at Gibeah, the
hometown of Saul, the LORD's chosen
king."

"I will hand them over," the king
answered.

7 But because of the sacred promise
that he and Jonathan had made to each
other, David spared Jonathan's son
Mephibosheth, the grandson of Saul.
8 However, he took Armoni and
Mephibosheth, the two sons that Rizpah
the daughter of Aiah had borne to Saul;
he also took the five sons of Saul's
daughter Merab, whom she had borne to
Adriel son of Barzillai, who was from
Meholah. 9 David handed them over to
the people of Gibeon, who hanged them
on the mountain before the LORD—and
all seven of them died together. It was
late in the spring, at the beginning of the
barley harvest, when they were put to
death.

10 Then Saul's concubine Rizpah, the
daughter of Aiah, used sackcloth to
make a shelter for herself on the rock
where the corpses were, and she stayed
there from the beginning of harvest until
the autumn rains came. During the day
she would keep the birds away from the
corpses, and at night she would protect
them from wild animals.

11 When David heard what Rizpah had
done, 12 he went and got the bones of
Saul and of his son Jonathan from the
people of Jabesh in Gilead. (They had
stolen them from the public square in
Beth Shan, where the Philistines had
hanged the bodies on the day they killed
Saul on Mount Gilboa.) 13 David took the
bones of Saul and Jonathan and also
gathered up the bones of the seven men
who had been hanged. 14 Then they buried the bones of Saul and Jonathan in
the grave of Saul's father Kish, in Zela in
the territory of Benjamin, doing all that
the king had commanded. And after
that, God answered their prayers for the
country.

Battles against Philistine Giants

(1 Chronicles 20.4-8)

15 There was another war between the
Philistines and Israel, and David and his
men went and fought the Philistines.
During one of the battles David grew
tired. 16 A giant named Ishbibenob, who
was carrying a bronze spear that
weighed about seven and a half pounds
and who was wearing a new sword,
thought he could kill David. 17 But
Abishai son of Zeruiah came to David's
help, attacked the giant, and killed him.
Then David's men made David promise
that he would never again go out with
them to battle. "You are the hope of Israel, and we don't want to lose you,"
they said.

18 After this there was a battle with the
Philistines at Gob, during which Sibbe-
cai from Hushah killed a giant named
Saph.

19 There was another battle with the
Philistines at Gob, and Elhanan son of

Jair[e] from Bethlehem killed Goliath
from Gath, whose spear had a shaft as
thick as the bar on a weaver's loom.
20 Then there was another battle at
Gath, where there was a giant who loved
to fight. He had six fingers on each hand
and six toes on each foot. 21 He defied the
Israelites, and Jonathan, the son of David's brother Shammah, killed him.
22 These four were descendants of the
giants of Gath, and they were killed by
David and his men.

David's Song of Victory

(Psalm 18)

22 When the LORD saved David
from Saul and his other enemies,
David sang this song to the LORD:

2 The LORD is my protector;
he is my strong fortress.
3 My God is my protection,
and with him I am safe.
He protects me like a shield;
he defends me and keeps me safe.
He is my savior;
he protects me and saves me from violence.
4 I call to the LORD,
and he saves me from my enemies.
Praise the LORD!

5 The waves of death were all around me;
the waves of destruction rolled over me.
6 The danger of death was around me,
and the grave set its trap for me.
7 In my trouble I called to the LORD;
I called to my God for help.
In his temple he heard my voice;
he listened to my cry for help.

8 Then the earth trembled and shook;
the foundations of the sky rocked and quivered
because God was angry!
9 Smoke poured out of his nostrils,
a consuming flame and burning coals from his mouth.
10 He tore the sky open and came down,
with a dark cloud under his feet.
11 He flew swiftly on his winged creature;[f]
he traveled on the wings of the wind.
12 He covered himself with darkness;
thick clouds, full of[g] water, surrounded him;
13 burning coals flamed up from the lightning before him.

14 Then the LORD thundered from the sky,
and the voice of Almighty God was heard.
15 He shot his arrows and scattered his enemies;
with flashes of lightning he sent them running.
16 The floor of the ocean was laid bare,
and the foundations of the earth were uncovered
when the LORD rebuked his enemies
and roared at them in anger.

17 The LORD reached down from above and took hold of me;
he pulled me out of the deep waters.
18 He rescued me from my powerful enemies
and from all those who hate me—
they were too strong for me.
19 When I was in trouble, they attacked me,
but the LORD protected me.
20 He helped me out of danger;
he saved me because he was pleased with me.

21 The LORD rewards me because I do what is right;
he blesses me because I am innocent.
22 I have obeyed the law of the LORD;
I have not turned away from my God.
23 I have observed all his laws;
I have not disobeyed his commands.

[e] *Probable text (see 1 Ch 20.5)* Jair; *Hebrew* Jaareoregim. [f] WINGED CREATURE: *See Word List.*
[g] *Some ancient translations (and see Ps 18.11)* full of; *Hebrew unclear.*

24 He knows that I am faultless,
that I have kept myself from doing wrong.
25 And so he rewards me because I do what is right,
because he knows that I am innocent.

26 O LORD, you are faithful to those who are faithful to you,
and completely good to those[h] who are perfect.
27 You are pure to those who are pure,
but hostile to those who are wicked.
28 You save those who are humble,
but you humble those who are proud.

29 You, LORD, are my light;
you dispel my darkness.
30 You give me strength to attack my enemies
and power to overcome their defenses.

31 This God—how perfect are his deeds,
how dependable his words!
He is like a shield
for all who seek his protection.
32 The LORD alone is God;
God alone is our defense.
33 This God is my strong refuge;
he makes[i] my pathway safe.
34 He makes me sure-footed as a deer;
he keeps me safe on the mountains.
35 He trains me for battle,
so that I can use the strongest bow.

36 O LORD, you protect me and save me;
your help has made me great.
37 You have kept me from being captured,
and I have never fallen.
38 I pursue my enemies and defeat them;
I do not stop until I destroy them.
39 I strike them down, and they cannot rise;
they lie defeated before me.
40 You give me strength for the battle
and victory over my enemies.
41 You make my enemies run from me;
I destroy those who hate me.
42 They look for help, but no one saves them;
they call to the LORD, but he does not answer.
43 I crush them, and they become like dust;
I trample on them like mud in the streets.

44 You saved me from my rebellious people
and maintained my rule over the nations;
people I did not know have now become my subjects.
45 Foreigners bow before me;
when they hear me, they obey.
46 They lose their courage
and come trembling[j] from their fortresses.

47 The LORD lives! Praise my defender!
Proclaim the greatness of the strong God who saves me!
48 He gives me victory over my enemies;
he subdues the nations under me
49 and saves me from my foes.

O LORD, you give me victory over my enemies
and protect me from violent men.
50 And so I praise you among the nations;
I sing praises to you.
51 God gives great victories to his king;
he shows constant love to the one he has chosen,
to David and his descendants forever.

[h] *Probable text (see Ps 18.25)* those; *Hebrew* the strong. [i] *Probable text (see Ps 18.32)* he makes; *Hebrew unclear.* [j] *Probable text (see Ps 18.45)* come trembling; *Hebrew* come ready to fight.

David's Last Words

23 David son of Jesse was the man
whom God made great, whom
the God of Jacob chose to be king, and
who was the composer of beautiful
songs for Israel. These are David's last
words:

2 The spirit of the LORD speaks
through me;
his message is on my lips.
3 The God of Israel has spoken;
the protector of Israel said
to me:
"The king who rules with justice,
who rules in obedience to God,
4 is like the sun shining on a
cloudless dawn,
the sun that makes the grass
sparkle after rain."

5 And that is how God will bless my
descendants,
because he has made an eternal
covenant with me,
an agreement that will not be
broken,
a promise that will not be
changed.
That is all I desire;
that will be my victory,
and God will surely bring it
about.
6 But godless people are like thorns
that are thrown away;
no one can touch them
barehanded.
7 You must use an iron tool or a
spear;
they will be burned
completely.[k]

David's Famous Soldiers

(1 Chronicles 11.10-41)

8 These are the names of David's famous soldiers: the first was Josheb Bas-
shebeth from Tachemon, who was the
leader of "The Three";[l] he fought with
his spear[m] against eight hundred men
and killed them all in one battle.
9 The second of the famous three was
Eleazar son of Dodo, of the clan of
Ahoh. One day he and David challenged
the Philistines who had gathered for battle. The Israelites fell back, 10 but he
stood his ground and fought the Philistines until his hand was so cramped that
he could not let go of his sword. The
LORD won a great victory that day. After
it was over, the Israelites returned to
where Eleazar was and stripped the armor from the dead.
11 The third of the famous three was
Shammah son of Agee from Harar. The
Philistines had gathered at Lehi, where
there was a field of peas. The Israelites
fled from the Philistines, 12 but Shammah stood his ground in the field, defended it, and killed the Philistines. The
LORD won a great victory that day.
13 Near the beginning of harvest time[n]
three of "The Thirty" went down to
Adullam Cave, where David was, while
a band of Philistines was camping in
Rephaim Valley. 14 At that time David
was on a fortified hill, and a group of
Philistines had occupied Bethlehem.
15 David grew homesick and said, "How
I wish someone would bring me a drink
of water from the well by the gate at
Bethlehem!" 16 The three famous soldiers forced their way through the Philistine camp, drew some water from the
well, and brought it back to David. But
he would not drink it; instead he poured
it out as an offering to the LORD 17 and
said, "LORD, I could never drink this! It
would be like drinking the blood of these
men who risked their lives!" So he refused to drink it.

Those were the brave deeds of the
three famous soldiers.
18 Joab's brother Abishai (their mother
was Zeruiah) was the leader of "The Famous Thirty." He fought with his spear
against three hundred men and killed
them, and became famous among "The
Thirty."[o] 19 He was the most famous of
"The Thirty"[p] and became their leader,
but he was not as famous as "The
Three."
20 Benaiah son of Jehoiada from Kabzeel was another famous soldier; he did
many brave deeds, including killing two
great Moabite warriors. He once went
down into a pit on a snowy day and
killed a lion. 21 He also killed an Egyptian, a huge man who was armed with a

[k] *Verses 6-7 in Hebrew are unclear.* [l] *One ancient translation* "The Three"; *Hebrew* the third. [m] *Probable text (see 1 Ch 11.11)* he fought with his spear; *Hebrew unclear.* [n] *Probable text* Near the beginning of harvest time; *Hebrew unclear.* [o] *One ancient translation* "The Thirty"; *Hebrew* "The Three." [p] *Probable text* "The Thirty"; *Hebrew* "The Three."

spear. Benaiah attacked him with his club, snatched the spear from the Egyptian's hand, and killed him with it.
22 Those were the brave deeds of Benaiah, who was one of "The Thirty."[p]
23 He was outstanding among them, but was not as famous as "The Three." David put him in charge of his bodyguard.

24-39 Other members of "The Thirty" included:

Asahel, Joab's brother
Elhanan son of Dodo from Bethlehem
Shammah and Elika from Harod
Helez from Pelet
Ira son of Ikkesh from Tekoa
Abiezer from Anathoth
Mebunnai from Hushah
Zalmon from Ahoh
Maharai from Netophah
Heleb son of Baanah from Netophah
Ittai son of Ribai from Gibeah in Benjamin
Benaiah from Pirathon
Hiddai from the valleys near Gaash
Abialbon from Arabah
Azmaveth from Bahurim
Eliahba from Shaalbon
The sons of Jashen
Jonathan
Shammah from Harar
Ahiam son of Sharar from Harar
Eliphelet son of Ahasbai from Maacah
Eliam son of Ahithophel from Gilo
Hezro from Carmel
Paarai from Arab
Igal son of Nathan from Zobah
Bani from Gad
Zelek from Ammon
Naharai from Beeroth, Joab's armorbearer
Ira and Gareb from Jattir
Uriah the Hittite.

There were thirty-seven famous soldiers in all.

David Takes a Census

(1 Chronicles 21.1-27)

24 On another occasion the LORD was angry with Israel, and he made David bring trouble on them. The LORD said to him, "Go and count the people of Israel and Judah."
2 So David gave orders to Joab, the commander of his army: "Go with your officers through all the tribes of Israel from one end of the country to the other, and count the people. I want to know how many there are."

3 But Joab answered the king, "Your Majesty, may the LORD your God make the people of Israel a hundred times more numerous than they are now, and may you live to see him do it. But why does Your Majesty want to do this?"
4 But the king made Joab and his officers obey his order; they left his presence and went out to count the people of Israel.

5 They crossed the Jordan and camped south of Aroer, the city in the middle of the valley, in the territory of Gad.[q] From there they went north to Jazer,
6 and on to Gilead and to Kadesh, in Hittite territory.[r] Then they went to Dan, and from Dan they went[s] west to Sidon.
7 Then they went south to the fortified city of Tyre, on to all the cities of the Hivites and the Canaanites, and finally to Beersheba, in the southern part of Judah.
8 So after nine months and twenty days they returned to Jerusalem, having traveled through the whole country.
9 They reported to the king the total number of men capable of military service: 800,000 in Israel and 500,000 in Judah.

10 But after David had taken the census, his conscience began to hurt, and he said to the LORD, "I have committed a terrible sin in doing this! Please forgive me. I have acted foolishly."

11-12 The LORD said to Gad, David's prophet, "Go and tell David that I am giving him three choices. I will do whichever he chooses." The next morning, after David had gotten up,
13 Gad went to him, told him what the LORD had said, and asked, "Which is it to be? Three[t] years of famine in your land or three months of running away from your enemies or three days of an epidemic in your land? Now think it over, and tell me what answer to take back to the LORD."

[p] *Probable text* "The Thirty"; *Hebrew* "The Three." [q] *Probable text* Aroer ... Gad; *Hebrew unclear.* [r] *One ancient translation* Kadesh, in Hittite territory; *Hebrew* to the land of Tahtim, Hodshi. [s] *Probable text* and from Dan they went; *Hebrew unclear.* [t] *Some ancient translations (and see 1 Ch 21.12)* Three; *Hebrew* Seven.

14 David answered, "I am in a desperate situation! But I don't want to be punished by people. Let the LORD himself be the one to punish us, for he is merciful."
15 So the LORD sent an epidemic on Israel, which lasted from that morning until the time that he had chosen. From one end of the country to the other seventy thousand Israelites died. 16 When the LORD's angel was about to destroy Jerusalem, the LORD changed his mind about punishing the people and said to the angel who was killing them, "Stop! That's enough!" The angel was by the threshing place of Araunah, a Jebusite.
17 David saw the angel who was killing the people, and said to the LORD, "I am the guilty one. I am the one who did wrong. What have these poor people done? You should punish me and my family."
18 That same day Gad went to David and said to him, "Go up to Araunah's threshing place and build an altar to the LORD." 19 David obeyed the LORD's command and went as Gad had told him to.
20 Araunah looked down and saw the king and his officials coming up to him. He threw himself on the ground in front of David 21 and asked, "Your Majesty, why are you here?"

David answered, "To buy your threshing place and build an altar for the LORD, in order to stop the epidemic."
22 "Take it, Your Majesty," Araunah said, "and offer to the LORD whatever you wish. Here are these oxen to burn as an offering on the altar; here are their yokes and the threshing boards to use as fuel." 23 Araunah gave it all to the king[u] and said to him, "May the LORD your God accept your offering."
24 But the king answered, "No, I will pay you for it. I will not offer to the LORD my God sacrifices that have cost me nothing." And he bought the threshing place and the oxen for fifty pieces of silver. 25 Then he built an altar to the LORD and offered burnt offerings and fellowship offerings. The LORD answered his prayer, and the epidemic in Israel was stopped.

[u] *Probable text* to the king; *Hebrew* to the king the king.

The First Book of
KINGS

Introduction

First Kings *continues the history of the Israelite monarchy begun in the books of* Samuel. *It may be divided into three parts: 1) The succession of Solomon as king of Israel and Judah, and the death of his father David. 2) The reign and achievements of Solomon. Especially noteworthy is the building of the Temple in Jerusalem. 3) The division of the nation into the northern and southern kingdoms, and the stories of the kings who ruled them down to the middle of the ninth century B.C.*

In the two books of Kings each ruler is judged according to his loyalty to God, and national success is seen as depending on this loyalty, while idolatry and disobedience lead to disaster. The kings of the northern kingdom all fail the test, while the record of Judah's kings is mixed.

Prominent in the book of First Kings are the prophets of the Lord, those courageous spokesmen for God who warned the people not to worship idols and not to disobey God. Especially notable is Elijah and the story of his contest with the priests of Baal (chapter 18).

Outline of Contents

The end of David's reign 1.1–2.12
Solomon becomes king 2.13-46
Solomon's reign 3.1–11.43
- a. *The early years* 3.1–4.34
- b. *The Temple is built* 5.1–8.66
- c. *The later years* 9.1–11.43

The divided kingdom 12.1–22.53
- a. *The revolt of the northern tribes* 12.1–14.20
- b. *The kings of Judah and of Israel* 14.21–16.34
- c. *The prophet Elijah* 17.1–19.21
- d. *King Ahab of Israel* 20.1–22.40
- e. *Jehoshaphat of Judah and Ahaziah of Israel* 22.41-53

King David in His Old Age

1 King David was now a very old
man, and although his servants covered him with blankets, he could not
keep warm. 2 So his officials said to him,
"Your Majesty, let us find a young
woman to stay with you and take care of
you. She will lie close to you and keep
you warm." 3 A search was made all
over Israel for a beautiful young woman,
and in Shunem they found such a
woman named Abishag, and brought
her to the king. 4 She was very beautiful,
and waited on the king and took care of
him, but he did not have intercourse
with her.

Adonijah Claims the Throne

5-6 Now that Absalom was dead, Adonijah, the son of David and Haggith, was
the oldest surviving son. He was a very
handsome man. David had never reprimanded him about anything, and he was
ambitious to be king. He provided for
himself chariots, horses, and an escort
of fifty men. 7 He talked with Joab
(whose mother was Zeruiah) and with
Abiathar the priest, and they agreed to
support his cause. 8 But Zadok the priest,
Benaiah son of Jehoiada, Nathan the
prophet, Shimei, Rei, and David's bodyguards were not on Adonijah's side.

9 One day Adonijah offered a sacrifice
of sheep, bulls, and fattened calves at
Snake Rock, near the spring of Enrogel.
He invited the other sons of King David
and the king's officials who were from
Judah to come to this sacrificial feast,
10 but he did not invite his half brother
Solomon or Nathan the prophet or Benaiah or the king's bodyguards.

Solomon Is Made King

11 Then Nathan went to Bathsheba,
Solomon's mother, and asked her,

"Haven't you heard that Haggith's son
Adonijah has made himself king? And
King David doesn't know anything
about it! 12 If you want to save your life
and the life of your son Solomon, I
would advise you to 13 go at once to King
David and ask him, 'Your Majesty,
didn't you solemnly promise me that my
son Solomon would succeed you as
king? How is it, then, that Adonijah has
become king?'" 14 And Nathan added,
"Then, while you are still talking with
King David, I will come in and confirm
your story."

15 So Bathsheba went to see the king in
his bedroom. He was very old, and Abishag, the young woman from Shunem,
was taking care of him. 16 Bathsheba
bowed low before the king, and he
asked, "What do you want?"

17 She answered, "Your Majesty, you
made me a solemn promise in the name
of the LORD your God that my son Solomon would be king after you. 18 But Adonijah has already become king, and you
don't know anything about it. 19 He has
offered a sacrifice of many bulls, sheep,
and fattened calves, and he invited your
sons, and Abiathar the priest, and Joab
the commander of your army to the
feast, but he did not invite your son Solomon. 20 Your Majesty, all the people of
Israel are looking to you to tell them
who is to succeed you as king. 21 If you
don't, as soon as you are dead, my son
Solomon and I will be treated as
traitors."

22 She was still speaking, when Nathan arrived at the palace. 23 The king
was told that the prophet was there, and
Nathan went in and bowed low before
the king. 24 Then he said, "Your Majesty,
have you announced that Adonijah
would succeed you as king? 25 This very
day he has gone and offered a sacrifice
of many bulls, sheep, and fattened
calves. He invited all your sons, Joab the
commander of your army,[a] and Abiathar the priest, and right now they are
feasting with him and shouting, 'Long
live King Adonijah!' 26 But he did not invite me, sir, or Zadok the priest or Benaiah or Solomon. 27 Did Your Majesty
approve all this and not even tell your
officials who is to succeed you as king?"

28 King David said, "Ask Bathsheba to
come back in"—and she came and stood
before him. 29 Then he said to her, "I
promise you by the living LORD, who has
rescued me from all my troubles, 30 that
today I will keep the promise I made to
you in the name of the LORD, the God of
Israel, that your son Solomon would
succeed me as king."

31 Bathsheba bowed low and said,
"May my lord the king live forever!"

32 Then King David sent for Zadok,
Nathan, and Benaiah. When they came
in, 33 he said to them, "Take my court officials with you; have my son Solomon
ride my own mule, and escort him down
to Gihon Spring, 34 where Zadok and Nathan are to anoint him as king of Israel.
Then blow the trumpet and shout, 'Long
live King Solomon!' 35 Follow him back
here when he comes to sit on my throne.
He will succeed me as king, because he
is the one I have chosen to be the ruler of
Israel and Judah."

36 "It shall be done," answered Benaiah, "and may the LORD your God confirm it! 37 As the LORD has been with
Your Majesty, may he also be with Solomon and make his reign even more prosperous than yours."

38 So Zadok, Nathan, Benaiah, and the
royal bodyguards put Solomon on King
David's mule and escorted him to Gihon
Spring. 39 Zadok took the container of olive oil which he had brought from the
Tent of the LORD's presence, and
anointed Solomon. They blew the trumpet, and all the people shouted, "Long
live King Solomon!" 40 Then they all followed him back, shouting for joy and
playing flutes, making enough noise to
shake the ground.

41 As Adonijah and all his guests were
finishing the feast, they heard the noise.
And when Joab heard the trumpet, he
asked, "What's the meaning of all that
noise in the city?" 42 Before he finished
speaking, Jonathan, the son of the priest
Abiathar, arrived. "Come on in," Adonijah said. "You're a good man—you must
be bringing good news."

43 "I'm afraid not," Jonathan answered. "His Majesty King David has
made Solomon king. 44 He sent Zadok,
Nathan, Benaiah, and the royal bodyguards to escort him. They had him ride
on the king's mule, 45 and Zadok and Na-

[a] *One ancient translation* Joab the commander of your army; *Hebrew* your army commanders.

than anointed him as king at Gihon
Spring. Then they went into the city,
shouting for joy, and the people are now
in an uproar. That's the noise you just
heard. 46 Solomon is now the king.
47 What is more, the court officials went
in to pay their respects to His Majesty
King David and said, 'May your God
make Solomon even more famous than
you, and may Solomon's reign be even
more prosperous than yours.' Then King
David bowed in worship on his bed
48 and prayed, 'Let us praise the LORD,
the God of Israel, who has today made
one of my descendants succeed me as
king, and has let me live to see it!' "

49 Then Adonijah's guests were afraid,
and they all got up and left, each going
his own way. 50 Adonijah, in great fear of
Solomon, went to the Tent of the LORD's
presence and took hold of the corners of
the altar.[b] 51 King Solomon was told
that Adonijah was afraid of him and that
he was holding on to the corners of the
altar and had said, "First, I want King
Solomon to swear to me that he will not
have me put to death."

52 Solomon replied, "If he is loyal, not
even a hair on his head will be touched;
but if he is not, he will die." 53 King Solomon then sent for Adonijah and had him
brought down from the altar. Adonijah
went to the king and bowed low before
him, and the king said to him, "You may
go home."

David's Last Instructions to Solomon

2 When David was about to die, he
called his son Solomon and gave
him his last instructions: 2 "My time to
die has come. Be confident and determined, 3 and do what the LORD your God
orders you to do. Obey all his laws and
commands, as written in the Law of
Moses, so that wherever you go you may
prosper in everything you do. 4 If you
obey him, the LORD will keep the promise
he made when he told me that my
descendants would rule Israel as long as
they were careful to obey his commands
faithfully with all their heart and soul.

5 "There is something else. You remember what Joab did to me by killing
the two commanders of Israel's armies,
Abner son of Ner and Amasa son of Jether. You remember how he murdered
them in time of peace as revenge for
deaths they had caused in time of war.
He killed innocent men,[c] and now I
bear the responsibility for what he did,
and I suffer[d] the consequences. 6 You
know what to do; you must not let him
die a natural death.

7 "But show kindness to the sons of
Barzillai from Gilead and take care of
them, because they were kind to me
when I was fleeing from your brother
Absalom.

8 "There is also Shimei son of Gera,
from the town of Bahurim in Benjamin.
He cursed me bitterly the day I went to
Mahanaim, but when he met me at the
Jordan River, I gave him my solemn
promise in the name of the LORD that I
would not have him killed. 9 But you
must not let him go unpunished. You
know what to do, and you must see to it
that he is put to death."

The Death of David

10 David died and was buried in David's City. 11 He had been king of Israel
for forty years, ruling seven years in Hebron and thirty-three years in Jerusalem. 12 Solomon succeeded his father
David as king, and his royal power was
firmly established.

The Death of Adonijah

13 Then Adonijah, whose mother was
Haggith, went to Bathsheba, who was
Solomon's mother. "Is this a friendly
visit?" she asked.

"It is," he answered, 14 and then he
added, "I have something to ask of you."

"What is it?" she asked.

15 He answered, "You know that I
should have become king and that
everyone in Israel expected it. But it
happened differently, and my brother
became king because it was the LORD's
will. 16 And now I have one request to
make; please do not refuse me."

"What is it?" Bathsheba asked.

17 He answered, "Please ask King
Solomon—I know he won't refuse you—
to let me have Abishag, the young
woman from Shunem, as my wife."

[b] CORNERS OF THE ALTAR: *Small projections at the four corners of the altar that looked like horns. Anyone holding on to them was safe from being killed.* [c] *Some ancient translations* innocent men; *Hebrew* men in battle. [d] *Some ancient translations* I bear . . . and I suffer; *Hebrew* he bears . . . and he suffers.

18 "Very well," she answered. "I will
speak to the king for you."
19 So Bathsheba went to the king to
speak to him on behalf of Adonijah. The
king stood up to greet his mother and
bowed to her. Then he sat on his throne
and had another one brought in on
which she sat at his right. 20 She said, "I
have a small favor to ask of you; please
do not refuse me."
"What is it, mother?" he asked. "I will
not refuse you."
21 She answered, "Let your brother
Adonijah have Abishag as his wife."
22 "Why do you ask me to give Abishag
to him?" the king asked. "You might as
well ask me to give him the throne too.
After all, he is my older brother, and
Abiathar the priest and Joab are on his
side!"[e] 23 Then Solomon made a solemn
promise in the LORD's name, "May God
strike me dead if I don't make Adonijah
pay with his life for asking this! 24 The
LORD has firmly established me on the
throne of my father David; he has kept
his promise and given the kingdom to
me and my descendants. I swear by the
living LORD that Adonijah will die this
very day!"
25 So King Solomon gave orders to
Benaiah, who went out and killed
Adonijah.

Abiathar's Banishment and Joab's Death

26 Then King Solomon said to Abiathar
the priest, "Go to your country home in
Anathoth. You deserve to die, but I will
not have you put to death now, for you
were in charge of the LORD's Covenant
Box while you were with my father David, and you shared in all his troubles."
27 Then Solomon dismissed Abiathar
from serving as a priest of the LORD, and
so made come true what the LORD had
said in Shiloh about the priest Eli and
his descendants.
28 Joab heard what had happened. (He
had supported Adonijah, but not Absalom.) So he fled to the Tent of the LORD's
presence and took hold of the corners of
the altar.[f] 29 When the news reached
King Solomon that Joab had fled to the
Tent and was by the altar, Solomon sent
a messenger to Joab to ask him why he
had fled to the altar. Joab answered that
he had fled to the LORD because he was
afraid of Solomon. So King Solomon
sent Benaiah[g] to kill Joab. 30 He went to
the Tent of the LORD's presence and said
to Joab, "The king orders you to
come out."
"No," Joab answered. "I will die here."
Benaiah went back to the king and
told him what Joab had said.
31 "Do what Joab says," Solomon answered. "Kill him and bury him. Then
neither I nor any other of David's
descendants will any longer be held responsible for what Joab did when he
killed innocent men. 32 The LORD will
punish Joab for those murders, which he
committed[h] without my father David's
knowledge. Joab killed two innocent
men who were better men than he: Abner, commander of the army of Israel,
and Amasa, commander of the army of
Judah. 33 The punishment for their murders will fall on Joab and on his
descendants forever. But the LORD will
always give success to David's descendants who sit on his throne."
34 So Benaiah went to the Tent of the
LORD's presence and killed Joab, and he
was buried at his home in the open country. 35 The king made Benaiah commander of the army in Joab's place and
put Zadok the priest in Abiathar's place.

The Death of Shimei

36 Then the king sent for Shimei and
said to him, "Build a house for yourself
here in Jerusalem. Live in it and don't
leave the city. 37 If you ever leave and go
beyond Kidron Brook, you will certainly
die — and you yourself will be to blame."
38 "Very well, Your Majesty," Shimei
answered. "I will do what you say." So
he lived in Jerusalem a long time.
39 Three years later, however, two of
Shimei's slaves ran away to the king of
Gath, Achish son of Maacah. When
Shimei heard that they were in Gath,
40 he saddled his donkey and went to
King Achish in Gath, to find his slaves.
He found them and brought them back
home. 41 When Solomon heard what
Shimei had done, 42 he sent for him and

[e] *Some ancient translations* and Abiathar the priest . . . on his side; *Hebrew unclear.* [f] CORNERS OF THE ALTAR: *See 1.50.* [g] *One ancient translation* Solomon sent a messenger . . . sent Benaiah; *Hebrew* Solomon sent Benaiah. [h] will punish . . . committed; *or* will kill Joab, because he committed those murders.

said, "I made you promise in the LORD's
name not to leave Jerusalem. And I
warned you that if you ever did, you
would certainly die. Did you not agree to
it and say that you would obey me?
43 Why, then, have you broken your
promise and disobeyed my command?
44 You know very well all the wrong that
you did to my father David. The LORD
will punish you for it. 45 But he will bless
me, and he will make David's kingdom
secure forever."
46 Then the king gave orders to Benaiah, who went out and killed Shimei.
Solomon was now in complete control.

Solomon Prays for Wisdom

(2 Chronicles 1.3-12)

3 Solomon made an alliance with the
king of Egypt by marrying his
daughter. He brought her to live in David's City until he had finished building
his palace, the Temple, and the wall
around Jerusalem. 2 A temple had not
yet been built for the LORD, and so the
people were still offering sacrifices at
many different altars. 3 Solomon loved
the LORD and followed the instructions of
his father David, but he also slaughtered
animals and offered them as sacrifices
on various altars.
4 On one occasion he went to Gibeon
to offer sacrifices because that was
where the most famous altar was. He
had offered hundreds of burnt offerings
there in the past. 5 That night the LORD
appeared to him in a dream and asked
him, "What would you like me to
give you?"
6 Solomon answered, "You always
showed great love for my father David,
your servant, and he was good, loyal,
and honest in his relation with you. And
you have continued to show him your
great and constant love by giving him a
son who today rules in his place.
7 O LORD God, you have let me succeed
my father as king, even though I am very
young and don't know how to rule.
8 Here I am among the people you have
chosen to be your own, a people who are
so many that they cannot be counted.
9 So give me the wisdom I need to rule
your people with justice and to know the
difference between good and evil. Otherwise, how would I ever be able to rule
this great people of yours?"
10 The Lord was pleased that Solomon
had asked for this, 11 and so he said to
him, "Because you have asked for the
wisdom to rule justly, instead of long life
for yourself or riches or the death of
your enemies, 12 I will do what you have
asked. I will give you more wisdom and
understanding than anyone has ever
had before or will ever have again.
13 I will also give you what you have not
asked for: all your life you will have
wealth and honor, more than that of any
other king. 14 And if you obey me and
keep my laws and commands, as your
father David did, I will give you a long
life."
15 Solomon woke up and realized that
God had spoken to him in the dream.
Then he went to Jerusalem and stood in
front of the LORD's Covenant Box and offered burnt offerings and fellowship offerings to the LORD. After that he gave a
feast for all his officials.

Solomon Judges a Difficult Case

16 One day two prostitutes came and
presented themselves before King Solomon. 17 One of them said, "Your Majesty,
this woman and I live in the same house,
and I gave birth to a baby boy at home
while she was there. 18 Two days after
my child was born, she also gave birth to
a baby boy. Only the two of us were
there in the house—no one else was
present. 19 Then one night she accidentally rolled over on her baby and smothered it. 20 She got up during the night,
took my son from my side while I was
asleep, and carried him to her bed; then
she put the dead child in my bed. 21 The
next morning, when I woke up and was
going to nurse my baby, I saw that it was
dead. I looked at it more closely and saw
that it was not my child."
22 But the other woman said, "No! The
living child is mine, and the dead one is
yours!"

The first woman answered back, "No!
The dead child is yours, and the living
one is mine!"

And so they argued before the king.
23 Then King Solomon said, "Each of
you claims that the living child is hers
and that the dead child belongs to the
other one." 24 He sent for a sword, and
when it was brought, 25 he said, "Cut the
living child in two and give each woman
half of it."
26 The real mother, her heart full of

love for her son, said to the king, "Please, Your Majesty, don't kill the child! Give it to her!"

But the other woman said, "Don't give it to either of us; go on and cut it in two."
27 Then Solomon said, "Don't kill the child! Give it to the first woman—she is its real mother."
28 When the people of Israel heard of Solomon's decision, they were all filled with deep respect for him, because they knew then that God had given him the wisdom to settle disputes fairly.

Solomon's Officials

4 Solomon was king of all Israel,
2 and these were his high officials:
The priest: Azariah son of Zadok
3 The court secretaries: Elihoreph and Ahijah, sons of Shisha
In charge of the records: Jehoshaphat son of Ahilud
4 Commander of the army: Benaiah son of Jehoiada
Priests: Zadok and Abiathar
5 Chief of the district governors: Azariah son of Nathan
Royal Adviser: the priest Zabud son of Nathan
6 In charge of the palace servants: Ahishar
In charge of the forced labor: Adoniram son of Abda
7 Solomon appointed twelve men as district governors in Israel. They were to provide food from their districts for the king and his household, each man being responsible for one month out of the year.
8 The following are the names of these twelve officers and the districts they were in charge of:
Benhur: the hill country of Ephraim
9 Bendeker: the cities of Makaz, Shaalbim, Beth Shemesh, Elon, and Beth Hanan
10 Benhesed: the cities of Arubboth and Socoh and all the territory of Hepher
11 Benabinadab, who was married to Solomon's daughter Taphath: the whole region of Dor
12 Baana son of Ahilud: the cities of Taanach, Megiddo, and all the region near Beth Shan, near the town of Zarethan, south of the town of Jezreel, as far as the city of Abel Meholah and the city of Jokmeam
13 Bengeber: the city of Ramoth in Gilead, and the villages in Gilead belonging to the clan of Jair, a descendant of Manasseh, and the region of Argob in Bashan, sixty large towns in all, fortified with walls and with bronze bars on the gates
14 Ahinadab son of Iddo: the district of Mahanaim
15 Ahimaaz, who was married to Basemath, another of Solomon's daughters: the territory of Naphtali
16 Baana son of Hushai: the region of Asher and the town of Bealoth
17 Jehoshaphat son of Paruah: the territory of Issachar
18 Shimei son of Ela: the territory of Benjamin
19 Geber son of Uri: the region of Gilead, which had been ruled by King Sihon of the Amorites and King Og of Bashan

Besides these twelve, there was one governor over the whole land.

Solomon's Prosperous Reign

20 The people of Judah and Israel were as numerous as the grains of sand on the seashore; they ate and drank, and were
happy. 21 Solomon's kingdom included all the nations from the Euphrates River to Philistia and the Egyptian border. They paid him taxes and were subject to him all his life.
22 The supplies Solomon needed each day were 150 bushels of fine flour and
300 bushels of meal; 23 10 stall-fed cattle, 20 pasture-fed cattle, and 100 sheep, besides deer, gazelles, roebucks, and poultry.
24 Solomon ruled over all the land west of the Euphrates River, from Tiphsah on the Euphrates as far west as the city of Gaza. All the kings west of the Euphrates were subject to him, and he was at peace with all the neighboring countries.
25 As long as he lived, the people throughout Judah and Israel lived in safety, each family with its own grapevines and fig trees.

26 Solomon had forty thousand stalls
for his chariot horses and twelve thousand cavalry horses. 27 His twelve governors, each one in the month assigned to
him, supplied the food King Solomon
needed for himself and for all who ate in
the palace; they always supplied everything needed. 28 Each governor also supplied his share of barley and straw,
where it was needed,[i] for the chariot
horses and the work animals.

29 God gave Solomon unusual wisdom
and insight, and knowledge too great to
be measured. 30 Solomon was wiser than
the wise men of the East or the wise men
of Egypt. 31 He was the wisest of all men:
wiser than Ethan the Ezrahite, and Heman, Calcol, and Darda, the sons of Ma-
hol, and his fame spread throughout all
the neighboring countries. 32 He composed three thousand proverbs and
more than a thousand songs. 33 He spoke
of trees and plants, from the Lebanon
cedars to the hyssop that grows on
walls; he talked about animals, birds,
reptiles, and fish. 34 Kings all over the
world heard of his wisdom and sent people to listen to him.

Solomon Prepares to Build the Temple

(2 Chronicles 2.1-18)

5 King Hiram of Tyre had always
been a friend of David's, and when
he heard that Solomon had succeeded
his father David as king, he sent ambassadors to him. 2 Solomon sent back this
message to Hiram: 3 "You know that because of the constant wars my father
David had to fight against the enemy
countries all around him, he could not
build a temple for the worship of the
LORD his God until the LORD had given
him victory over all his enemies. 4 But
now the LORD my God has given me
peace on all my borders. I have no enemies, and there is no danger of attack.
5 The LORD promised my father David,
'Your son, whom I will make king after
you, will build a temple for me.' And I
have now decided to build that temple
for the worship of the LORD my God. 6 So
send your men to Lebanon to cut down
cedars for me. My men will work with
them, and I will pay your men whatever
you decide. As you well know, my men
don't know how to cut down trees as
well as yours do."

7 Hiram was extremely pleased when
he received Solomon's message, and he
said, "Praise the LORD today for giving
David such a wise son to succeed him as
king of that great nation!" 8 Then Hiram
sent Solomon the following message: "I
have received your message, and I am
ready to do what you ask. I will provide
the cedars and the pine trees. 9 My men
will bring the logs down from Lebanon
to the sea and will tie them together in
rafts to float them down the coast to the
place you choose. There my men will untie them, and your men will take charge
of them. On your part, I would like you
to supply the food for my men."

10 So Hiram supplied Solomon with all
the cedar and pine logs that he wanted,
11 and Solomon provided Hiram with
100,000 bushels of wheat and 110,000
gallons[j] of pure olive oil every year to
feed his men.

12 The LORD kept his promise and gave
Solomon wisdom. There was peace between Hiram and Solomon, and they
made a treaty with each other.

13 King Solomon drafted 30,000 men as
forced labor from all over Israel, 14 and
put Adoniram in charge of them. He divided them into three groups of 10,000
men, and each group spent one month in
Lebanon and two months back home.
15 Solomon also had 80,000 stone cutters
in the hill country, with 70,000 men to
carry the stones, 16 and he placed 3,300
foremen in charge of them to supervise
their work. 17 At King Solomon's command they cut fine large stones for the
foundation of the Temple. 18 Solomon's
and Hiram's workers and men from the
city of Byblos prepared the stones and
the timber to build the Temple.

Solomon Builds the Temple

6 Four hundred and eighty years after the people of Israel left Egypt,
during the fourth year of Solomon's
reign over Israel, in the second month,
the month of Ziv, Solomon began work
on the Temple. 2 Inside it was 90 feet

[i] where it was needed; *or* wherever King Solomon was. [j] *Some ancient translations (and see 2 Ch 2.10)* 110,000 gallons; *Hebrew* 1,100 gallons.

long, 30 feet wide, and 45 feet high. 3 The
entrance room was 15 feet deep and 30
feet wide, as wide as the sanctuary itself.
4 The walls of the Temple had openings
in them, narrower on the outside than on
the inside. 5 Against the outside walls, on
the sides and the back of the Temple, a
three-storied annex was built, each story
7½ feet high. 6 Each room in the lowest
story was 7½ feet wide, in the middle
story 9 feet wide, and in the top story
10½ feet wide. The Temple wall on each
floor was thinner than on the floor below, so that the rooms could rest on the
wall without having their beams built
into it.

7 The stones with which the Temple
was built had been prepared at the
quarry, so that there was no noise made
by hammers, axes, or any other iron
tools as the Temple was being built.

8 The entrance to the lowest[k] story of
the annex was on the south side of the
Temple, with stairs leading up to the second and third stories. 9 So King Solomon
finished building the Temple. He put in a
ceiling made of beams and boards of cedar. 10 The three-storied annex, each
story[l] 7½ feet high, was built against
the outside walls of the Temple, and was
joined to them by cedar beams.

11 The LORD said to Solomon, 12 "If you
obey all my laws and commands, I will
do for you what I promised your father
David. 13 I will live among my people Israel in this Temple that you are building,
and I will never abandon them."

14 So Solomon finished building the
Temple.

The Interior Furnishings of the Temple

(2 Chronicles 3.8-14)

15 The inside walls were covered with
cedar panels from the floor to the ceiling, and the floor was made of pine.
16 An inner room, called the Most Holy
Place, was built in the rear of the Temple. It was 30 feet long and was parti-
tioned off by cedar boards reaching
from the floor to the ceiling.[m] 17 The
room in front of the Most Holy Place was
60 feet long. 18 The cedar panels were
decorated with carvings of gourds and
flowers; the whole interior was covered
with cedar, so that the stones of the
walls could not be seen.

19 In the rear of the Temple an inner
room was built, where the LORD's Covenant Box was to be placed. 20 This inner
room was 30 feet long, 30 feet wide, and
30 feet high, all covered with pure gold.
The altar was covered with cedar panels.[n] 21 The inside of the Temple was
covered with gold, and gold chains were
placed across the entrance of the inner
room, which was also covered with gold.
22 The whole interior of the Temple was
covered with gold, as well as the altar in
the Most Holy Place.

23 Two winged creatures were made of
olive wood and placed in the Most Holy
Place, each one 15 feet tall. 24-26 Both
were of the same size and shape. Each
had two wings, each wing 7½ feet long,
so that the distance from one wing tip to
the other was 15 feet. 27 They were
placed side by side in the Most Holy
Place, so that two of their outstretched
wings touched each other in the middle
of the room, and the other two wings
touched the walls. 28 The two winged
creatures were covered with gold.

29 The walls of the main room and of
the inner room were all decorated with
carved figures of winged creatures,
palm trees, and flowers. 30 Even the floor
was covered with gold.

31 A double door made of olive wood
was set in place at the entrance of the
Most Holy Place; the top of the doorway
was a pointed arch. 32 The doors were
decorated with carved figures of winged
creatures, palm trees, and flowers. The
doors, the winged creatures, and the
palm trees were covered with gold. 33 For
the entrance to the main room a rectangular doorframe of olive wood was
made. 34 There were two folding doors
made of pine 35 and decorated with
carved figures of winged creatures,
palm trees, and flowers, which were
evenly covered with gold.

36 An inner court was built in front of
the Temple, enclosed with walls which
had one layer of cedar beams for every
three layers of stone.

37 The foundation of the Temple was
laid in the second month, the month of

[k] *Some ancient translations* lowest; *Hebrew* middle. [l] *Probable text* three-storied annex, each story; *Hebrew* three-storied annex. [m] *One ancient translation* ceiling; *Hebrew* walls. [n] *Verse 20 in Hebrew is unclear.*

Ziv, in the fourth year of Solomon's reign. 38 In the eighth month, the month of Bul, in the eleventh year of Solomon's reign, the Temple was completely finished exactly as it had been planned. It had taken Solomon seven years to build it.

Solomon's Palace

7 Solomon also built a palace for himself, and it took him thirteen years. 2-3 The Hall of the Forest of Lebanon[o] was 150 feet long, 75 feet wide, and 45 feet high. It had three[p] rows of cedar pillars, 15 in each row, with cedar beams resting on them. The ceiling was of cedar, extending over storerooms, which were supported by the pillars. 4 On each of the two side walls there were three rows of windows. 5 The doorways and the windows[q] had rectangular frames, and the three rows of windows in each wall faced the opposite rows.

6 The Hall of Columns was 75 feet long and 45 feet wide. It had a covered porch, supported by columns.

7 The Throne Room, also called the Hall of Judgment, where Solomon decided cases, had cedar panels from the floor to the rafters.[r]

8 Solomon's own quarters, in another court behind the Hall of Judgment, were made like the other buildings. He also built the same kind of house for his wife, the daughter of the king of Egypt.

9 All these buildings and the great court were made of fine stones from the foundations to the eaves. The stones were prepared at the quarry and cut to measure, with their inner and outer sides trimmed with saws. 10 The foundations were made of large stones prepared at the quarry, some of them twelve feet long and others fifteen feet long. 11 On top of them were other stones, cut to measure, and cedar beams. 12 The palace court, the inner court of the Temple, and the entrance room of the Temple had walls with one layer of cedar beams for every three layers of cut stones.

Huram's Task

13 King Solomon sent for a man named Huram, a craftsman living in the city of Tyre, who was skilled in bronze work. 14 His father, who was no longer living, was from Tyre, and had also been a skilled bronze craftsman; his mother was from the tribe of Naphtali. Huram was an intelligent and experienced craftsman. He accepted King Solomon's invitation to be in charge of all the bronze work.

The Two Bronze Columns

(2 Chronicles 3.15-17)

15 Huram cast two bronze columns, each one 27 feet tall and 18 feet in circumference,[s] and placed them at the entrance of the Temple. 16 He also made two bronze capitals, each one 7½ feet tall, to be placed on top of the columns. 17 The top of each column was decorated with a design of interwoven chains[t] 18 and two rows of bronze pomegranates.

19 The capitals were shaped like lilies, 6 feet tall, 20 and were placed on a rounded section which was above the chain design. There were 200 pomegranates in two rows around each[u] capital.

21 Huram placed these two bronze columns in front of the entrance of the Temple: the one on the south side was named Jachin[v] and the one on the north was named Boaz.[w] 22 The lily-shaped bronze capitals were on top of the columns.

And so the work on the columns was completed.

The Bronze Tank

(2 Chronicles 4.2-5)

23 Huram made a round tank of bronze, 7½ feet deep, 15 feet in diameter, and 45 feet in circumference. 24 All around the outer edge of the rim of the tank[x] were two rows of bronze gourds, which had been cast all in one piece with the rest of the tank. 25 The tank rested on the backs of twelve bronze bulls that faced outward, three facing in each

[o] HALL OF THE FOREST OF LEBANON: *A large ceremonial hall in the palace, probably so called because it was paneled in cedar.* [p] *One ancient translation* three; *Hebrew* four. [q] *One ancient translation* windows; *Hebrew* doorposts. [r] *Some ancient translations* rafters; *Hebrew* floor. [s] *Some ancient translations* each one . . . circumference; *Hebrew* the first column was 27 feet tall and the second column was 18 feet in circumference. [t] *Verse 17 in Hebrew is unclear.* [u] *One ancient translation* each; *Hebrew* the second. [v] JACHIN: *This name sounds like the Hebrew for "he (God) establishes."* [w] BOAZ: *This name sounds like the Hebrew for "by his (God's) strength."* [x] *Probable text* All around . . . tank; *Hebrew unclear.*

direction. 26 The sides of the tank were 3
inches thick. Its rim was like the rim of a
cup, curving outward like the petals of a
lily. The tank held about 10,000 gallons.

The Bronze Carts

27 Huram also made ten bronze carts;
each was 6 feet long, 6 feet wide, and 4½
feet high. 28 They were made of square
panels which were set in frames, 29 with
the figures of lions, bulls, and winged
creatures on the panels; and on the
frames, above and underneath the lions
and bulls, there were spiral figures in relief. 30 Each cart had four bronze wheels
with bronze axles. At the four corners
were bronze supports for a basin; the
supports were decorated with spiral figures in relief. 31 There was a circular
frame on top for the basin. It projected
upward 18 inches from the top of the
cart and 7 inches down into it. It had
carvings around it. 32 The wheels were
25 inches high; they were under the panels, and the axles were of one piece with
the carts. 33 The wheels were like chariot
wheels; their axles, rims, spokes, and
hubs were all of bronze. 34 There were
four supports at the bottom corners of
each cart, which were of one piece with
the cart. 35 There was a 9-inch band
around the top of each cart; its supports
and the panels were of one piece with
the cart. 36 The supports and panels were
decorated with figures of winged creatures, lions, and palm trees, wherever
there was space for them, with spiral figures all around. 37 This, then, is how the
carts were made; they were all alike,
having the same size and shape.
38 Huram also made ten basins, one for
each cart. Each basin was 6 feet in diameter and held 200 gallons. 39 He placed
five of the carts on the south side of the
Temple, and the other five on the north
side; the tank he placed at the southeast
corner.

Summary List of Temple Furnishings

(2 Chronicles 4.11 – 5.1)

40-45 Huram also made pots, shovels,
and bowls. He completed all his work
for King Solomon for the LORD's Temple.
This is what he made:

The two columns
The two bowl-shaped capitals on top of the columns
The design of interwoven chains on each capital
The 400 bronze pomegranates, in two rows of 100 each around the design on each capital
The ten carts
The ten basins
The tank
The twelve bulls supporting the tank
The pots, shovels, and bowls

All this equipment for the Temple,
which Huram made for King Solomon,
was of polished bronze. 46 The king had
it all made in the foundry between Sukkoth and Zarethan, in the Jordan Valley.
47 Solomon did not have these bronze
objects weighed, because there were too
many of them, and so their weight was
never determined.
48 Solomon also had gold furnishings
made for the Temple: the altar, the table
for the bread offered to God, 49 the ten
lampstands that stood in front of the
Most Holy Place, five on the south side
and five on the north; the flowers,
lamps, and tongs; 50 the cups, lamp
snuffers, bowls, dishes for incense, and
the pans used for carrying live coals;
and the hinges for the doors of the Most
Holy Place and of the outer doors of the
Temple. All these furnishings were
made of gold.
51 When King Solomon finished all the
work on the Temple, he placed in the
Temple storerooms all the things that
his father David had dedicated to the
LORD – the silver, gold, and other
articles.

The Covenant Box Is Brought to the Temple

(2 Chronicles 5.2 – 6.2)

8 Then King Solomon summoned all
the leaders of the tribes and clans of
Israel to come to him in Jerusalem in order to take the LORD's Covenant Box
from Zion, David's City, to the Temple.
2 They all assembled during the Festival
of Shelters in the seventh month, in the
month of Ethanim. 3 When all the leaders had gathered, the priests lifted the
Covenant Box 4 and carried it to the
Temple. The Levites and the priests also
moved the Tent of the LORD's presence
and all its equipment to the Temple.
5 King Solomon and all the people of Is-

rael assembled in front of the Covenant
Box and sacrificed a large number of
sheep and cattle—too many to count.
6 Then the priests carried the Covenant
Box into the Temple and put it in the
Most Holy Place, beneath the winged
creatures. 7 Their outstretched wings
covered the box and the poles it was carried by. 8 The ends of the poles could be
seen by anyone standing directly in
front of the Most Holy Place, but from
nowhere else. (The poles are still there
today.) 9 There was nothing inside the
Covenant Box except the two stone tablets which Moses had placed there at
Mount Sinai, when the LORD made a covenant with the people of Israel as they
were coming from Egypt.

10 As the priests were leaving the Temple, it was suddenly filled with a cloud
11 shining with the dazzling light of the
LORD's presence, and they could not go
back in to perform their duties. 12 Then
Solomon prayed:

"You, LORD, have placed the sun in the sky,[y]
yet you have chosen to live in clouds and darkness.
13 Now I have built a majestic temple for you,
a place for you to live in forever."

Solomon's Address to the People

(2 Chronicles 6.3-11)

14 As the people stood there, King Solomon turned to face them, and he asked
God's blessing on them. 15 He said,
"Praise the LORD God of Israel! He has
kept the promise he made to my father
David, when he told him, 16 'From the
time I brought my people out of Egypt, I
have not chosen any city in all the land
of Israel in which a temple should be
built where I would be worshiped. But I
chose you, David, to rule my people.' "

17 And Solomon continued, "My father
David planned to build a temple for the
worship of the LORD God of Israel, 18 but
the LORD said to him, 'You were right in
wanting to build a temple for me, 19 but
you will never build it. It is your son,
your own son, who will build my
temple.'

20 "And now the LORD has kept his
promise. I have succeeded my father as
king of Israel, and I have built the Temple for the worship of the LORD God of
Israel. 21 I have also provided a place in
the Temple for the Covenant Box containing the stone tablets of the covenant
which the LORD made with our ancestors
when he brought them out of Egypt."

Solomon's Prayer

(2 Chronicles 6.12-42)

22 Then in the presence of the people
Solomon went and stood in front of the
altar, where he raised his arms 23 and
prayed, "LORD God of Israel, there is no
god like you in heaven above or on earth
below! You keep your covenant with
your people and show them your love
when they live in wholehearted obedience to you. 24 You have kept the promise you made to my father David; today
every word has been fulfilled. 25 And
now, LORD God of Israel, I pray that you
will also keep the other promise you
made to my father when you told him
that there would always be one of his
descendants ruling as king of Israel, provided they obeyed you as carefully as he
did. 26 So now, O God of Israel, let everything come true that you promised to my
father David, your servant.

27 "But can you, O God, really live on
earth? Not even all of heaven is large
enough to hold you, so how can this
Temple that I have built be large
enough? 28 LORD my God, I am your servant. Listen to my prayer, and grant the
requests I make to you today. 29 Watch
over this Temple day and night, this
place where you have chosen to be worshiped. Hear me when I face this Temple
and pray. 30 Hear my prayers and the
prayers of your people when they face
this place and pray. In your home in
heaven hear us and forgive us.

31 "When a person is accused of
wronging another and is brought to your
altar in this Temple to take an oath that
he is innocent, 32 O LORD, listen in
heaven and judge your servants. Punish
the guilty one as he deserves, and acquit
the one who is innocent.

33 "When your people Israel are defeated by their enemies because they
have sinned against you, and then
when they turn to you and come to this
Temple, humbly praying to you for

[y] *One ancient translation* You . . . sky; *Hebrew does not have these words.*

forgiveness, 34 listen to them in heaven.
Forgive the sins of your people and
bring them back to the land which you
gave to their ancestors.

35 "When you hold back the rain because your people have sinned against
you, and then when they repent and face
this Temple, humbly praying to you,
36 listen to them in heaven. Forgive the
sins of the king and of the people of Israel, and teach them to do what is right.
Then, O LORD, send rain on this land of
yours, which you gave to your people as
a permanent possession.

37 "When there is famine in the land or
an epidemic or the crops are destroyed
by scorching winds or swarms of locusts, or when your people are attacked
by their enemies, or when there is disease or sickness among them, 38 listen to
their prayers. If any of your people Israel, out of heartfelt sorrow, stretch out
their hands in prayer toward this Temple, 39 hear their prayer. Listen to them
in your home in heaven, forgive them,
and help them. You alone know the
thoughts of the human heart. Deal with
each person as he deserves, 40 so that
your people may obey you all the time
they live in the land which you gave to
our ancestors.

41-42 "When a foreigner who lives in a
distant land hears of your fame and of
the great things you have done for your
people and comes to worship you and to
pray at this Temple, 43 listen to his
prayer. In heaven, where you live, hear
him and do what he asks you to do, so
that all the peoples of the world may
know you and obey you, as your people
Israel do. Then they will know that this
Temple I have built is the place where
you are to be worshiped.

44 "When you command your people to
go into battle against their enemies and
they pray to you, wherever they are, facing this city which you have chosen and
this Temple which I have built for you,
45 listen to their prayers. Hear them in
heaven and give them victory.

46 "When your people sin against
you — and there is no one who does not
sin — and in your anger you let their enemies defeat them and take them as prisoners to some other land, even if that
land is far away, 47 listen to your people's prayers. If there in that land they
repent and pray to you, confessing how
sinful and wicked they have been, hear
their prayers, O LORD. 48 If in that land
they truly and sincerely repent and pray
to you as they face toward this land
which you gave to our ancestors, this
city which you have chosen, and this
Temple which I have built for you,
49 then listen to their prayers. In your
home in heaven hear them and be merciful to them. 50 Forgive all their sins and
their rebellion against you, and make
their enemies treat them with kindness.
51 They are your own people, whom you
brought out of Egypt, that blazing
furnace.

52 "Sovereign LORD, may you always
look with favor on your people Israel
and their king, and hear their prayer
whenever they call to you for help.
53 You chose them from all the peoples to
be your own people, as you told them
through your servant Moses when you
brought our ancestors out of Egypt."

The Final Prayer

54 After Solomon had finished praying
to the LORD, he stood up in front of the
altar, where he had been kneeling with
uplifted hands. 55 In a loud voice he
asked God's blessings on all the people
assembled there. He said, 56 "Praise the
LORD who has given his people peace, as
he promised he would. He has kept all
the generous promises he made through
his servant Moses. 57 May the LORD our
God be with us as he was with our ancestors; may he never leave us or abandon us; 58 may he make us obedient to
him, so that we will always live as he
wants us to live, keeping all the laws and
commands he gave our ancestors. 59 May
the LORD our God remember at all times
this prayer and these petitions I have
made to him. May he always be merciful
to the people of Israel and to their king,
according to their daily needs. 60 And so
all the nations of the world will know
that the LORD alone is God — there is no
other. 61 May you, his people, always be
faithful to the LORD our God, obeying all
his laws and commands as you do
today."

The Dedication of the Temple

(2 Chronicles 7.4-10)

62 Then King Solomon and all the people there offered sacrifices to the LORD.
63 He sacrificed 22,000 head of cattle and

120,000 sheep as fellowship offerings.
And so the king and all the people dedicated the Temple. 64 That same day he
also consecrated the central part of the
courtyard, the area in front of the Temple, and then he offered there the sacrifices burned whole, the grain offerings,
and the fat of the animals for the fellowship offerings. He did this because the
bronze altar was too small for all these
offerings.
65 There at the Temple, Solomon and
all the people of Israel celebrated the
Festival of Shelters for seven[z] days.
There was a huge crowd of people from
as far away as Hamath Pass in the north
and the Egyptian border in the south.
66 On the eighth day Solomon sent
the people home. They all praised him
and went home happy because of all
the blessings that the LORD had given
his servant David and his people Israel.

God Appears to Solomon Again

(2 Chronicles 7.11-22)

9 After King Solomon had finished
building the Temple and the palace
and everything else he wanted to build,
2 the LORD appeared to him again, as he
had in Gibeon. 3 The LORD said to him, "I
have heard your prayer. I consecrate
this Temple which you have built as the
place where I shall be worshiped forever. I will watch over it and protect it
for all time. 4 If you will serve me in honesty and integrity, as your father David
did, and if you obey my laws and do
everything I have commanded you, 5 I
will keep the promise I made to your
father David when I told him that Israel
would always be ruled by his descendants. 6 But if you or your descendants
stop following me, disobey the laws and
commands I have given you, and worship other gods, 7 then I will remove my
people Israel from the land that I have
given them. I will also abandon this
Temple which I have consecrated as the
place where I am to be worshiped. People everywhere will ridicule Israel and
treat her with contempt. 8 This Temple
will become a pile of ruins,[a] and everyone who passes by will be shocked and
amazed. 'Why did the LORD do this to
this land and this Temple?' they will ask.
9 People will answer, 'It is because they
abandoned the LORD their God, who
brought their ancestors out of Egypt.
They gave their allegiance to other gods
and worshiped them. That is why the
LORD has brought this disaster on
them.' "

Solomon's Agreement with Hiram

(2 Chronicles 8.1, 2)

10 It took Solomon twenty years to
build the Temple and his palace. 11 King
Hiram of Tyre had provided him with all
the cedar and pine and with all the gold
he wanted for this work. After it was finished, King Solomon gave Hiram twenty
towns in the region of Galilee. 12 Hiram
went to see them, and he did not like
them. 13 So he said to Solomon, "So
these, my brother, are the towns you
have given me!" For this reason the area
is still called Cabul.[b] 14 Hiram had sent
Solomon almost five tons of gold.

Further Achievements of Solomon

(2 Chronicles 8.3-18)

15 King Solomon used forced labor to
build the Temple and the palace, to fill in
land on the east side of the city, and to
build the city wall. He also used it to rebuild the cities of Hazor, Megiddo, and
Gezer. (16 The king of Egypt had attacked Gezer and captured it, killing its
inhabitants and setting fire to the city.
Then he gave it as a wedding present to
his daughter when she married Solomon, 17 and Solomon rebuilt it.) Using
his forced labor, Solomon also rebuilt
Lower Beth Horon, 18 Baalath, Tamar in
the wilderness of Judah, 19 the cities
where his supplies were kept, the cities
for his horses and chariots, and everything else he wanted to build in Jerusalem, in Lebanon, and elsewhere in his
kingdom. 20-21 For his forced labor Solomon used the descendants of the people
of Canaan whom the Israelites had not
killed when they took possession of
their land. These included Amorites, Hittites, Perizzites, Hivites, and Jebusites,
whose descendants continue to be slaves
down to the present time. 22 Solomon did
not make slaves of Israelites; they
served as his soldiers, officers, commanders, chariot captains, and cavalry.
23 There were 550 officials in charge of

[z] *One ancient translation* seven; *Hebrew* fourteen. [a] *Some ancient translations* a pile of ruins; *Hebrew* high. [b] CABUL: *This name sounds like "ke-bal," the Hebrew for "worthless."*

the forced labor working on Solomon's various building projects.

24 Solomon filled in the land on the east side of the city, after his wife, the daughter of the king of Egypt, had moved from David's City to the palace Solomon built for her.

25 Three times a year Solomon offered burnt offerings and fellowship offerings on the altar he had built to the LORD. He also burned incense[c] to the LORD. And so he finished building the Temple.

26 King Solomon also built a fleet of ships at Eziongeber, which is near Elath on the shore of the Gulf of Aqaba, in the land of Edom. 27 King Hiram sent some experienced sailors from his fleet to serve with Solomon's men. 28 They sailed to the land of Ophir and brought back to Solomon about sixteen tons of gold.

The Visit of the Queen of Sheba

(2 Chronicles 9.1-12)

10 The queen of Sheba heard of Solomon's fame,[d] and she traveled to Jerusalem to test him with difficult questions. 2 She brought with her a large group of attendants, as well as camels loaded with spices, jewels, and a large amount of gold. When she and Solomon met, she asked him all the questions that she could think of. 3 He answered them all; there was nothing too difficult for him to explain. 4 The queen of Sheba heard Solomon's wisdom and saw the palace he had built. 5 She saw the food that was served at his table, the living quarters for his officials, the organization of his palace staff and the uniforms they wore, the servants who waited on him at feasts, and the sacrifices he offered in the Temple. It left her breathless and amazed. 6 She said to King Solomon, "What I heard in my own country about you[e] and your wisdom is true! 7 But I couldn't believe it until I had come and seen it all for myself. But I didn't hear even half of it; your wisdom and wealth are much greater than what I was told. 8 How fortunate are your wives![f] And how fortunate your servants, who are always in your presence and are privileged to hear your wise sayings! 9 Praise the LORD your God! He has shown how pleased he is with you by making you king of Israel. Because his love for Israel is eternal, he has made you their king so that you can maintain law and justice."

10 She presented to King Solomon the gifts she had brought: almost five tons of gold and a very large amount of spices and jewels. The amount of spices she gave him was by far the greatest that he ever received at any time.

(11 Hiram's fleet, which had brought gold from Ophir, also brought from there a large amount of juniper wood and jewels. 12 Solomon used the wood to build railings in the Temple and the palace, and also to make harps and lyres for the musicians. It was the finest juniper wood ever imported into Israel; none like it has ever been seen again.)

13 King Solomon gave the queen of Sheba everything she asked for, besides all the other customary gifts that he had generously given her. Then she and her attendants returned to the land of Sheba.

King Solomon's Wealth

(2 Chronicles 9.13-29)

14 Every year King Solomon received over twenty-five tons of gold, 15 in addition to the taxes[g] paid by merchants, the profits from trade, and tribute paid by the Arabian kings and the governors of the Israelite districts.

16 Solomon made two hundred large shields and had each one overlaid with almost fifteen pounds of gold. 17 He also made three hundred smaller shields, overlaying each one of them with nearly four pounds of gold. He had all these shields placed in the Hall of the Forest of Lebanon.[h]

18 He also had a large throne made. Part of it was covered with ivory and the rest of it was covered with the finest gold. 19-20 The throne had six steps leading up to it, with the figure of a lion at each end of every step, a total of twelve lions. At the back of the throne was the figure of a bull's head, and beside each of the two armrests was the figure of a lion. No throne like this had ever existed in any other kingdom.

[c] *Hebrew has two additional words, the meaning of which is unclear.* [d] *Probable text (see 2 Ch 9.1)* Solomon's fame; *Hebrew* Solomon's fame concerning the name of the LORD. [e] you; *or* your deeds. [f] *Some ancient translations* wives; *Hebrew* men. [g] *Some ancient translations* taxes; *Hebrew* men. [h] HALL OF THE FOREST OF LEBANON: *See 7.2-3.*

21 All of Solomon's drinking cups were
made of gold, and all the utensils in the
Hall of the Forest of Lebanon were of
pure gold. No silver was used, since it
was not considered valuable in Solomon's day. 22 He had a fleet of ocean-
going ships sailing with Hiram's fleet.
Every three years his fleet would return,
bringing gold, silver, ivory, apes, and
monkeys.
23 King Solomon was richer and wiser
than any other king, 24 and the whole
world wanted to come and listen to the
wisdom that God had given him.
25 Everyone who came brought him a
gift—articles of silver and gold, robes,
weapons, spices, horses, and mules. This
continued year after year.
26 Solomon built up a force of fourteen
hundred chariots and twelve thousand
cavalry horses. Some of them he kept in
Jerusalem and the rest he stationed in
various other cities. 27 During his reign
silver was as common in Jerusalem as
stone, and cedar was as plentiful as ordinary sycamore in the foothills of Judah.
28 The king's agents controlled the export of horses from Musri[i] and Cilicia,[j] 29 and the export of chariots from
Egypt. They supplied the Hittite and
Syrian kings with horses and chariots,
selling chariots for 600 pieces of silver
each and horses for 150 each.

Solomon Turns Away from God

11 Solomon loved many foreign
women. Besides the daughter of
the king of Egypt he married Hittite
women and women from Moab, Ammon, Edom, and Sidon. 2 He married
them even though the LORD had commanded the Israelites not to intermarry
with these people, because they would
cause the Israelites to give their loyalty
to other gods. 3 Solomon married seven
hundred princesses and also had three
hundred concubines. They made him
turn away from God, 4 and by the time he
was old they had led him into the worship of foreign gods. He was not faithful
to the LORD his God, as his father David
had been. 5 He worshiped Astarte, the
goddess of Sidon, and Molech, the disgusting god of Ammon. 6 He sinned
against the LORD and was not true to him
as his father David had been. 7 On the
mountain east of Jerusalem he built a
place to worship Chemosh, the disgusting god of Moab, and a place to worship
Molech, the disgusting god of Ammon.
8 He also built places of worship where
all his foreign wives could burn incense
and offer sacrifices to their own gods.
9-10 Even though the LORD, the God of
Israel, had appeared to Solomon twice
and had commanded him not to worship
foreign gods, Solomon did not obey the
LORD but turned away from him. So the
LORD was angry with Solomon 11 and
said to him, "Because you have deliberately broken your covenant with me and
disobeyed my commands, I promise that
I will take the kingdom away from you
and give it to one of your officials.
12 However, for the sake of your father
David I will not do this in your lifetime,
but during the reign of your son. 13 And
I will not take the whole kingdom away
from him; instead, I will leave him one
tribe for the sake of my servant David
and for the sake of Jerusalem, the city I
have made my own."

Solomon's Enemies

14 So the LORD caused Hadad, of the
royal family of Edom, to turn against
Solomon. 15-16 Long before this, when
David had conquered Edom, Joab the
commander of his army had gone there
to bury the dead. He and his men remained in Edom six months, and during
that time they killed every male in Edom
17 except Hadad and some of his father's
Edomite servants, who escaped to
Egypt. (At that time Hadad was just a
child.) 18 They left Midian and went to
Paran, where some other men joined
them. Then they traveled to Egypt and
went to the king, who gave Hadad some
land and a house and provided him with
food. 19 Hadad won the friendship of the
king, and the king gave his sister-in-law,
the sister of Queen Tahpenes, to Hadad
in marriage. 20 She bore him a son, Ge-
nubath, who was raised by the queen in
the palace, where he lived with the
king's sons.
21 When the news reached Hadad in
Egypt that David had died and that Joab
the commander of the army was dead,

[i] *Probable text* Musri; *Hebrew* Egypt. [j] MUSRI AND CILICIA: *Two ancient countries in what is now southeast Turkey which were centers of horse breeding in Solomon's time.*

Hadad said to the king, "Let me go back
to my own country."
22 "Why?" the king asked. "Have I
failed to give you something? Is that why
you want to go back home?"
"Just let me go," Hadad answered the
king. And he went back to his country.[k]
As king of Edom, Hadad was an evil,
bitter enemy of Israel.[l]
23 God also caused Rezon son of Eliada
to turn against Solomon. Rezon had fled
from his master, King Hadadezer of Zobah, 24 and had become the leader of a
gang of outlaws. (This happened after
David had defeated Hadadezer and had
slaughtered his Syrian allies.) Rezon
and his gang went and lived in Damascus, where his followers made him king
of Syria. 25 He was an enemy of Israel
during the lifetime of Solomon.

God's Promise to Jeroboam

26 Another man who turned against
King Solomon was one of his officials,
Jeroboam son of Nebat, from Zeredah in
Ephraim. His mother was a widow
named Zeruah. 27 This is the story of the
revolt.
Solomon was filling in the land on the
east side of Jerusalem and repairing the
city walls. 28 Jeroboam was an able
young man, and when Solomon noticed
how hard he worked, he put him in
charge of all the forced labor in the territory of the tribes of Manasseh and
Ephraim. 29 One day, as Jeroboam was
traveling from Jerusalem, the prophet
Ahijah from Shiloh met him alone on the
road in the open country. 30 Ahijah took
off the new robe he was wearing, tore it
into twelve pieces, 31 and said to Jeroboam, "Take ten pieces for yourself, because the LORD, the God of Israel, says to
you, 'I am going to take the kingdom
away from Solomon, and I will give you
ten tribes. 32 Solomon will keep one tribe
for the sake of my servant David and for
the sake of Jerusalem, the city I have
chosen to be my own from the whole
land of Israel. 33 I am going to do this because Solomon has rejected me and
has[m] worshiped foreign gods: Astarte,
the goddess of Sidon; Chemosh, the god
of Moab; and Molech, the god of Ammon. Solomon has[n] disobeyed me; he
has done wrong and has not kept my
laws and commands as his father David
did. 34 But I will not take the whole kingdom away from Solomon, and I will
keep him in power as long as he lives.
This I will do for the sake of my servant
David, whom I chose and who obeyed
my laws and commands. 35 I will take
the kingdom away from Solomon's son
and will give you ten tribes, 36 but I will
let Solomon's son keep one tribe, so that
I will always have a descendant of my
servant David ruling in Jerusalem, the
city I have chosen as the place where I
am worshiped. 37 Jeroboam, I will make
you king of Israel, and you will rule over
all the territory that you want. 38 If you
obey me completely, live by my laws,
and win my approval by doing what I
command, as my servant David did, I
will always be with you. I will make you
king of Israel and will make sure that
your descendants rule after you, just as I
have done for David. 39 Because of Solomon's sin I will punish the descendants
of David, but not for all time.' "
40 And so Solomon tried to kill Jeroboam, but he escaped to King Shishak of
Egypt and stayed there until Solomon's
death.

The Death of Solomon

(*2 Chronicles 9.29-31*)

41 Everything else that Solomon did,
his career, and his wisdom, are all recorded in *The History of Solomon.* 42 He
was king in Jerusalem over all Israel for
forty years. 43 He died and was buried in
David's City, and his son Rehoboam
succeeded him as king.

The Northern Tribes Revolt

(*2 Chronicles 10.1-19*)

12 Rehoboam went to Shechem,
where all the people of northern
Israel had gathered to make him king.
2 When Jeroboam son of Nebat, who had
gone to Egypt to escape from King Solomon, heard this news, he returned

[k] *One ancient translation* And he went back to his country; *Hebrew does not have these words.* [l] *One ancient translation* As king . . . Israel; *in Hebrew this sentence, with some differences, comes at the end of verse 25.* [m] *Some ancient translations* Solomon has . . . and has; *Hebrew* they have . . . and have. [n] *Some ancient translations* Solomon has; *Hebrew* They have.

from[o] Egypt. 3 The people of the northern tribes sent for him, and then they all
went together to Rehoboam and said to
him, 4 "Your father Solomon treated us
harshly and placed heavy burdens on us.
If you make these burdens lighter and
make life easier for us, we will be your
loyal subjects."
5 "Come back in three days and I will
give you my answer," he replied. So they
left.
6 King Rehoboam consulted the older
men who had served as his father Solomon's advisers. "What answer do you
advise me to give these people?" he
asked.
7 They replied, "If you want to serve
this people well, give a favorable answer
to their request, and they will always
serve you loyally."
8 But he ignored the advice of the older
men and went instead to the young men
who had grown up with him and who
were now his advisers. 9 "What do you
advise me to do?" he asked. "What shall
I say to the people who are asking me to
make their burdens lighter?"
10 They replied, "This is what you
should tell them: 'My little finger is
thicker than my father's waist!' 11 Tell
them, 'My father placed heavy burdens
on you; I will make them even heavier.
He beat you with whips; I'll flog you
with bullwhips!' "
12 Three days later Jeroboam and all
the people returned to King Rehoboam,
as he had instructed them. 13 The king
ignored the advice of the older men and
spoke harshly to the people, 14 as the
younger men had advised. He said, "My
father placed heavy burdens on you; I
will make them even heavier. He beat
you with whips; I'll flog you with bullwhips!" 15 It was the will of the LORD to
bring about what he had spoken to Jeroboam son of Nebat through the prophet
Ahijah from Shiloh. This is why the king
did not pay any attention to the people.
16 When the people saw that the king
would not listen to them, they shouted,
"Down with David and his family! What
have they ever done for us? People of
Israel, let's go home! Let Rehoboam
look out for himself!"
So the people of Israel rebelled,
17 leaving Rehoboam as king only of the
people who lived in the territory of
Judah.
18 Then King Rehoboam sent Adoniram, who was in charge of the forced
labor, to go to the Israelites, but they
stoned him to death. At this, Rehoboam
hurriedly got in his chariot and escaped
to Jerusalem. 19 Ever since that time the
people of the northern kingdom of Israel
have been in rebellion against the dynasty of David.
20 When the people of Israel heard that
Jeroboam had returned from Egypt,
they invited him to a meeting of the people and made him king of Israel. Only
the tribe of Judah remained loyal to David's descendants.

Shemaiah's Prophecy

(2 Chronicles 11.1-4)

21 When Rehoboam arrived in Jerusalem, he called together 180,000 of the
best soldiers from the tribes of Judah
and Benjamin. He intended to go to war
and restore his control over the northern
tribes of Israel. 22 But God told the
prophet Shemaiah 23 to give this message to Rehoboam and to all the people
of the tribes of Judah and Benjamin:
24 "Do not attack your own relatives, the
people of Israel. Go home, all of you.
What has happened is my will." They all
obeyed the LORD's command and went
back home.

Jeroboam Turns Away from God

25 King Jeroboam of Israel fortified the
town of Shechem in the hill country of
Ephraim and lived there for a while.
Then he left and fortified the town of Penuel. 26-27 He said to himself, "As things
are now, if my people go to Jerusalem
and offer sacrifices to the LORD in the
Temple there, they will transfer their allegiance to King Rehoboam of Judah
and will kill me."
28 After thinking it over, he made two
bull-calves of gold and said to his people, "You have been going long enough
to Jerusalem to worship. People of Israel, here are your gods who brought
you out of Egypt!" 29 He placed one of the
gold bull-calves in Bethel and the other
in Dan. 30 And so the people sinned, going to worship in Bethel and in Dan.[p]

[o] *Some ancient translations (and see 2 Ch 10.2)* returned from; *Hebrew* remained in.
[p] *One ancient translation* in Bethel and in Dan; *Hebrew* in Dan.

31 Jeroboam also built places of worship
on hilltops, and he chose priests from
families who were not of the tribe of
Levi.

Worship at Bethel Is Condemned

32 Jeroboam also instituted a religious
festival on the fifteenth day of the eighth
month, like the festival in Judah. On the
altar in Bethel he offered sacrifices to
the gold bull-calves he had made, and he
placed there in Bethel the priests serving
at the places of worship he had built.
33 And on the fifteenth day of the eighth
month, the day that he himself had set,
he went to Bethel and offered a sacrifice
on the altar in celebration of the festival
he had instituted for the people of Israel.

13 At the LORD's command a
prophet from Judah went to
Bethel and arrived there as Jeroboam
stood at the altar to offer the sacrifice.
2 Following the LORD's command, the
prophet denounced the altar: "O altar,
altar, this is what the LORD says: A child,
whose name will be Josiah, will be born
to the family of David. He will slaughter
on you the priests serving at the pagan
altars who offer sacrifices on you, and
he will burn human bones on you." 3 And
the prophet went on to say, "This altar
will fall apart, and the ashes on it will be
scattered. Then you will know that the
LORD has spoken through me."

4 When King Jeroboam heard this, he
pointed at him and ordered, "Seize that
man!" At once the king's arm became
paralyzed so that he couldn't pull it
back. 5 The altar suddenly fell apart and
the ashes spilled to the ground, as the
prophet had predicted in the name of the
LORD. 6 King Jeroboam said to the
prophet, "Please pray for me to the LORD
your God, and ask him to heal my arm!"

The prophet prayed to the LORD, and
the king's arm was healed. 7 Then the
king said to the prophet, "Come home
with me and have something to eat. I
will reward you for what you have
done."

8 The prophet answered, "Even if you
gave me half of your wealth, I would not
go with you or eat or drink anything
with you. 9 The LORD has commanded me
not to eat or drink a thing, and not to
return home the same way I came." 10 So
he did not go back the same way he had
come, but by another road.

The Old Prophet of Bethel

11 At that time there was an old
prophet living in Bethel. His sons[q] came
and told him what the prophet from Judah had done in Bethel that day and
what he had said to King Jeroboam.
12 "Which way did he go when he left?"
the old prophet asked them. They
showed him[r] the road 13 and he told
them to saddle his donkey for him. They
did so, and he rode off 14 down the road
after the prophet from Judah and found
him sitting under an oak tree. "Are you
the prophet from Judah?" he asked.

"I am," the man answered.

15 "Come home and have a meal with
me," he said.

16 But the prophet from Judah answered, "I can't go home with you or accept your hospitality. And I won't eat or
drink anything with you here, 17 because
the LORD has commanded me not to eat
or drink a thing, and not to return home
the same way I came."

18 Then the old prophet from Bethel
said to him, "I, too, am a prophet just like
you, and at the LORD's command an angel told me to take you home with me
and offer you my hospitality." But the
old prophet was lying.

19 So the prophet from Judah went
home with the old prophet and had a
meal with him. 20 As they were sitting at
the table, the word of the LORD came to
the old prophet, 21 and he cried out to the
prophet from Judah, "The LORD says that
you disobeyed him and did not do what
he commanded. 22 Instead, you returned
and ate a meal in a place he had ordered
you not to eat in. Because of this you will
be killed, and your body will not be buried in your family grave."

23 After they had finished eating, the
old prophet saddled the donkey for the
prophet from Judah, 24 who rode off. On
the way a lion met him and killed him.
His body lay on the road, and the donkey and the lion stood beside it. 25 Some

[q] *Some ancient translations* sons; *Hebrew* son.
[r] *Some ancient translations* showed him; *Hebrew* saw.

men passed by and saw the body on the
road, with the lion standing near by.
They went on into Bethel and reported
what they had seen.
26 When the old prophet heard about
it, he said, "That is the prophet who disobeyed the LORD's command! And so the
LORD sent the lion to attack and kill him,
just as the LORD said he would." 27 Then
he said to his sons, "Saddle my donkey
for me." They did so, 28 and he rode off
and found the prophet's body lying on
the road, with the donkey and the lion
still standing by it. The lion had not
eaten the body or attacked the donkey.
29 The old prophet picked up the body,
put it on the donkey, and brought it back
to Bethel to mourn over it and bury it.
30 He buried it in his own family grave,
and he and his sons mourned over it,
saying, "Oh my brother, my brother!"
31 After the burial the prophet said to his
sons, "When I die, bury me in this grave
and lay my body next to his. 32 The
words that he spoke at the LORD's command against the altar in Bethel and
against all the places of worship in the
towns of Samaria will surely come
true."

Jeroboam's Fatal Sin

33 King Jeroboam of Israel still did not
turn from his evil ways but continued to
choose priests from ordinary families to
serve at the altars he had built. He ordained as priest anyone who wanted to
be one. 34 This sin on his part brought
about the ruin and total destruction of
his dynasty.

The Death of Jeroboam's Son

14 At that time King Jeroboam's
son Abijah got sick. 2 Jeroboam
said to his wife, "Disguise yourself so
that no one will recognize you, and go to
Shiloh, where the prophet Ahijah lives,
the one who said I would be king of Israel. 3 Take him ten loaves of bread,
some cakes, and a jar of honey. Ask him
what is going to happen to our son, and
he will tell you."
4 So she went to Ahijah's home in Shiloh. Old age had made Ahijah blind.
5 The LORD had told him that Jeroboam's
wife was coming to ask him about her
son, who was sick. And the LORD told
Ahijah what to say.
When Jeroboam's wife arrived, she
pretended to be someone else. 6 But
when Ahijah heard her coming in the
door, he said, "Come in. I know you are
Jeroboam's wife. Why are you pretending to be someone else? I have bad news
for you. 7 Go and tell Jeroboam that this
is what the LORD, the God of Israel, says
to him: 'I chose you from among the people and made you the ruler of my people
Israel. 8 I took the kingdom away from
David's descendants and gave it to you.
But you have not been like my servant
David, who was completely loyal to me,
obeyed my commands, and did only
what I approve of. 9 You have committed
far greater sins than those who ruled before you. You have rejected me and have
aroused my anger by making idols and
metal images to worship. 10 Because of
this I will bring disaster on your dynasty
and will kill all your male descendants,
young and old alike. I will get rid of your
family; they will be swept away like
dung. 11 Any members of your family
who die in the city will be eaten by dogs,
and any who die in the open country will
be eaten by vultures. I, the LORD, have
spoken.' "
12 And Ahijah went on to say to Jeroboam's wife, "Now go back home. As
soon as you enter the town, your son will
die. 13 All the people of Israel will mourn
for him and bury him. He will be the
only member of Jeroboam's family who
will be properly buried, because he is the
only one with whom the LORD, the God of
Israel, is pleased. 14 The LORD is going to
place a king over Israel who will put an
end to Jeroboam's dynasty.[s] 15 The LORD
will punish Israel, and she will shake
like a reed shaking in a stream. He will
uproot the people of Israel from this
good land which he gave to their ancestors, and he will scatter them beyond the
Euphrates River, because they have
aroused his anger by making idols of the
goddess Asherah. 16 The LORD will abandon Israel because Jeroboam sinned and
led the people of Israel into sin."
17 Jeroboam's wife went back to Tirzah. Just as she entered her home, the
child died. 18 The people of Israel
mourned for him and buried him, as the

[s] *Hebrew has five additional words, the meaning of which is unclear.*

LORD had said through his servant, the
prophet Ahijah.

The Death of Jeroboam

19 Everything else that King Jeroboam
did, the wars he fought and how he
ruled, are all recorded in *The History of
the Kings of Israel.* 20 Jeroboam ruled as
king for twenty-two years. He died and
was buried, and his son Nadab succeeded him as king.

King Rehoboam of Judah

(2 Chronicles 11.5 – 12.15)

21 Solomon's son Rehoboam was forty-
one years old when he became king of
Judah, and he ruled seventeen years in
Jerusalem, the city which the LORD had
chosen from all the territory of Israel as
the place where he was to be worshiped.
Rehoboam's mother was Naamah from
Ammon.

22 The people of Judah sinned against
the LORD and did more to arouse his anger against them than all their ancestors
had done. 23 They built places of worship
for false gods and put up stone pillars
and symbols of Asherah to worship on
the hills and under shady trees. 24 Worst
of all, there were men and women who
served as prostitutes at those pagan
places of worship. The people of Judah
practiced all the shameful things done
by the people whom the LORD had driven
out of the land as the Israelites advanced
into the country.

25 In the fifth year of Rehoboam's reign
King Shishak of Egypt attacked Jerusalem. 26 He took away all the treasures in
the Temple and in the palace, including
the gold shields Solomon had made.
27 To replace them, King Rehoboam
made bronze shields and entrusted them
to the officers responsible for guarding
the palace gates. 28 Every time the king
went to the Temple, the guards carried
the shields and then returned them to
the guardroom.

29 Everything else that King Rehoboam did is recorded in *The History of
the Kings of Judah.* 30 During all this
time Rehoboam and Jeroboam were
constantly at war with each other. 31 Rehoboam died and was buried in the royal
tombs in David's City and his son Abijah
succeeded him as king.

King Abijah of Judah

(2 Chronicles 13.1 – 14.1)

15 In the eighteenth year of the
reign of King Jeroboam of Israel,
Abijah became king of Judah, 2 and he
ruled three years in Jerusalem. His
mother was Maacah, the daughter of
Absalom. 3 He committed the same sins
as his father and was not completely
loyal to the LORD his God, as his great-
grandfather David had been. 4 But for
David's sake the LORD his God gave Abijah a son to rule after him in Jerusalem
and to keep Jerusalem secure. 5 The LORD
did this because David had done what
pleased him and had never disobeyed
any of his commands, except in the case
of Uriah the Hittite. 6 The war which had
begun between Rehoboam and Jeroboam continued throughout Abijah's
lifetime. 7 And everything else that Abijah did is recorded in *The History of the
Kings of Judah.*

8 Abijah died and was buried in David's City, and his son Asa succeeded
him as king.

King Asa of Judah

(2 Chronicles 15.16 – 16.6)

9 In the twentieth year of the reign of
King Jeroboam of Israel, Asa became
king of Judah, 10 and he ruled forty-one
years in Jerusalem. His grandmother
was Maacah, the daughter of Absalom.
11 Asa did what pleased the LORD, as his
ancestor David had done. 12 He expelled
from the country all the male and female
prostitutes serving at the pagan places
of worship, and he removed all the idols
his predecessors had made. 13 He removed his grandmother Maacah from
her position as queen mother, because
she had made an obscene idol of the fertility goddess Asherah. Asa cut down
the idol and burned it in Kidron Valley.
14 Even though Asa did not destroy all
the pagan places of worship, he remained faithful to the LORD all his life.
15 He placed in the Temple all the objects
his father had dedicated to God, as well
as the gold and silver objects that he
himself dedicated.

16 King Asa of Judah and King Baasha
of Israel were constantly at war with
each other as long as they were in
power. 17 Baasha invaded Judah and
started to fortify Ramah in order to cut

off all traffic in and out of Judah. 18 So
King Asa took all the silver and gold that
was left in the Temple and the palace,
and sent it by some of his officials to Damascus, to King Benhadad of Syria, the
son of Tabrimmon and grandson of He-
zion, with this message: 19 "Let us be allies, as our fathers were. This silver and
gold is a present for you. Now break
your alliance with King Baasha of Israel,
so that he will have to pull his troops out
of my territory."

20 King Benhadad agreed to Asa's proposal and sent his commanding officers
and their armies to attack the cities of
Israel. They captured Ijon, Dan, Abel
Beth Maacah, the area near Lake Galilee, and the whole territory of Naphtali.
21 When King Baasha heard what had
happened, he stopped fortifying Ramah
and went to Tirzah.

22 Then King Asa sent out an order
throughout all of Judah requiring everyone, without exception, to help carry
away from Ramah the stones and timber
that Baasha had been using to fortify it.
With this material Asa fortified Mizpah
and Geba, a city in the territory of
Benjamin.

23 Everything else that King Asa did,
his brave deeds and the towns he fortified, are all recorded in *The History of
the Kings of Judah.* But in his old age he
was crippled by a foot disease. 24 Asa
died and was buried in the royal tombs
in David's City, and his son Jehoshaphat
succeeded him as king.

King Nadab of Israel

25 In the second year of the reign of
King Asa of Judah, King Jeroboam's son
Nadab became king of Israel, and he
ruled for two years. 26 Like his father before him, he sinned against the LORD and
led Israel into sin.

27 Baasha son of Ahijah, of the tribe of
Issachar, plotted against Nadab and
killed him as Nadab and his army were
besieging the city of Gibbethon in Philistia. 28 This happened during the third
year of the reign of King Asa of Judah.
And so Baasha succeeded Nadab as king
of Israel. 29 At once he began killing all
the members of Jeroboam's family. In
accordance with what the LORD had said
through his servant, the prophet Ahijah
from Shiloh, all of Jeroboam's family
were killed; not one survived. 30 This
happened because Jeroboam aroused
the anger of the LORD, the God of Israel,
by the sins that he committed and that
he caused Israel to commit.

31 Everything else that Nadab did is recorded in *The History of the Kings of
Israel.* 32 King Asa of Judah and King Baasha of Israel were constantly at war
with each other as long as they were in
power.

King Baasha of Israel

33 In the third year of the reign of King
Asa of Judah, Baasha son of Ahijah be-
came king of all Israel, and he ruled in
Tirzah for twenty-four years. 34 Like
King Jeroboam before him, he sinned
against the LORD and led Israel into sin.

16 The LORD spoke to the prophet
Jehu son of Hanani and gave
him this message for Baasha: 2 "You
were a nobody, but I made you the
leader of my people Israel. And now you
have sinned like Jeroboam and have led
my people into sin. Their sins have
aroused my anger, 3 and so I will do
away with you and your family, just as I
did with Jeroboam. 4 Any members of
your family who die in the city will be
eaten by dogs, and any who die in the
open country will be eaten by vultures."

5 Everything else that Baasha did and
all his brave deeds are recorded in *The
History of the Kings of Israel.* 6 Baasha
died and was buried in Tirzah, and his
son Elah succeeded him as king.

7 That message from the LORD against
Baasha and his family was given by the
prophet Jehu because of the sins that
Baasha committed against the LORD. He
aroused the LORD's anger not only because of the evil he did, just as King Jeroboam had done before him, but also
because he killed all of Jeroboam's
family.

King Elah of Israel

8 In the twenty-sixth year of the reign
of King Asa of Judah, Elah son of Baasha became king of Israel, and he ruled
in Tirzah for two years. 9 Zimri, one of
his officers who was in charge of half of
the king's chariots, plotted against him.
One day in Tirzah, Elah was getting
drunk in the home of Arza, who was in
charge of the palace. 10 Zimri entered the
house, assassinated Elah, and succeeded
him as king. This happened in the

twenty-seventh year of the reign of King
Asa of Judah.
11 As soon as Zimri became king he
killed off all the members of Baasha's
family. Every male relative and friend
was put to death. 12 And so, in accordance with what the LORD had said
against Baasha through the prophet
Jehu, Zimri killed all the family of Baasha. 13 Because of their idolatry and because they led Israel into sin, Baasha
and his son Elah had aroused the anger
of the LORD, the God of Israel. 14 Everything else that Elah did is recorded in
The History of the Kings of Israel.

King Zimri of Israel

15 In the twenty-seventh year of the
reign of King Asa of Judah, Zimri ruled
in Tirzah over Israel for seven days. The
Israelite troops were besieging the city
of Gibbethon in Philistia, 16 and when
they heard that Zimri had plotted
against the king and assassinated him,
then and there they all proclaimed their
commander Omri king of Israel. 17 Omri
and his troops left Gibbethon and went
and besieged Tirzah. 18 When Zimri saw
that the city had fallen, he went into the
palace's inner fortress, set the palace on
fire, and died in the flames. 19 This happened because of his sins against the
LORD. Like his predecessor Jeroboam, he
displeased the LORD by his own sins and
by leading Israel into sin. 20 Everything
else that Zimri did, including the account of his conspiracy, is recorded in
The History of the Kings of Israel.

King Omri of Israel

21 The people of Israel were divided:
some of them wanted to make Tibni son
of Ginath king, and the others were in
favor of Omri. 22 In the end, those in favor of Omri won out; Tibni died and
Omri became king. 23 So in the thirty-
first year of the reign of King Asa of Judah, Omri became king of Israel, and he
ruled for twelve years. The first six years
he ruled in Tirzah, 24 and then he bought
the hill of Samaria for six thousand
pieces of silver from a man named Shemer. Omri fortified the hill, built a town
there, and named it Samaria, after Shemer, the former owner of the hill.
25 Omri sinned against the LORD more
than any of his predecessors. 26 Like Jeroboam before him, he aroused the anger
of the LORD, the God of Israel, by his sins
and by leading the people into sin and
idolatry. 27 Everything else that Omri did
and all his accomplishments are recorded in *The History of the Kings of
Israel.* 28 Omri died and was buried in Samaria, and his son Ahab succeeded him
as king.

King Ahab of Israel

29 In the thirty-eighth year of the reign
of King Asa of Judah, Ahab son of Omri
became king of Israel, and he ruled in
Samaria for twenty-two years. 30 He
sinned against the LORD more than any
of his predecessors. 31 It was not enough
for him to sin like King Jeroboam; he
went further and married Jezebel, the
daughter of King Ethbaal of Sidon, and
worshiped Baal. 32 He built a temple to
Baal in Samaria, made an altar for him,
and put it in the temple. 33 He also put up
an image of the goddess Asherah. He did
more to arouse the anger of the LORD, the
God of Israel, than all the kings of Israel
before him. 34 During his reign Hiel from
Bethel rebuilt Jericho. As the LORD had
foretold through Joshua son of Nun,
Hiel lost his oldest son Abiram when he
laid the foundation of Jericho, and his
youngest son Segub when he built the
gates.

Elijah and the Drought

17 A prophet named Elijah, from
Tishbe in Gilead, said to King
Ahab, "In the name of the LORD, the living God of Israel, whom I serve, I tell
you that there will be no dew or rain for
the next two or three years until I
say so."
2 Then the LORD said to Elijah, 3 "Leave
this place and go east and hide yourself
near Cherith Brook, east of the Jordan.
4 The brook will supply you with water
to drink, and I have commanded ravens
to bring you food there."
5 Elijah obeyed the LORD's command,
and went and stayed by Cherith Brook.
6 He drank water from the brook, and ravens brought him bread and meat every
morning and every evening. 7 After a
while the brook dried up because of the
lack of rain.

Elijah and the Widow in Zarephath

8 Then the LORD said to Elijah, 9 "Now
go to the town of Zarephath, near Sidon,

and stay there. I have commanded a
widow who lives there to feed you." 10 So
Elijah went to Zarephath, and as he
came to the town gate, he saw a widow
gathering firewood. "Please bring me a
drink of water," he said to her. 11 And as
she was going to get it, he called out,
"And please bring me some bread, too."
12 She answered, "By the living LORD
your God I swear that I don't have any
bread. All I have is a handful of flour in
a bowl and a bit of olive oil in a jar. I
came here to gather some firewood to
take back home and prepare what little I
have for my son and me. That will be our
last meal, and then we will starve to
death."
13 "Don't worry," Elijah said to her.
"Go on and prepare your meal. But first
make a small loaf from what you have
and bring it to me, and then prepare the
rest for you and your son. 14 For this is
what the LORD, the God of Israel, says:
'The bowl will not run out of flour or the
jar run out of oil before the day that I,
the LORD, send rain.' "
15 The widow went and did as Elijah
had told her, and all of them had enough
food for many days. 16 As the LORD had
promised through Elijah, the bowl did
not run out of flour nor did the jar run
out of oil.
17 Some time later the widow's son got
sick; he got worse and worse, and finally
he died. 18 She said to Elijah, "Man of
God, why did you do this to me? Did you
come here to remind God of my sins and
so cause my son's death?"
19 "Give the boy to me," Elijah said. He
took the boy from her arms, carried him
upstairs to the room where he was staying, and laid him on the bed. 20 Then he
prayed aloud, "O LORD my God, why
have you done such a terrible thing to
this widow? She has been kind enough
to take care of me, and now you kill her
son!" 21 Then Elijah stretched himself
out on the boy three times and prayed,
"O LORD my God, restore this child to
life!" 22 The LORD answered Elijah's
prayer; the child started breathing again
and revived.
23 Elijah took the boy back downstairs
to his mother and said to her, "Look,
your son is alive!"
24 She answered, "Now I know that
you are a man of God and that the LORD
really speaks through you!"

Elijah and the Prophets of Baal

18 After some time, in the third year
of the drought, the LORD said to
Elijah, "Go and present yourself to King
Ahab, and I will send rain." 2 So Elijah
started out.
The famine in Samaria was at its
worst, 3 so Ahab called in Obadiah, who
was in charge of the palace. (Obadiah
was a devout worshiper of the LORD,
4 and when Jezebel was killing the
LORD's prophets, Obadiah took a hundred of them, hid them in caves in two
groups of fifty, and provided them with
food and water.) 5 Ahab said to Obadiah,
"Let us go and look[t] at every spring and
every stream bed in the land to see if we
can find enough grass to keep the horses
and mules alive. Maybe we won't have
to kill any of our animals." 6 They agreed
on which part of the land each one
would explore, and set off in different
directions.
7 As Obadiah was on his way, he suddenly met Elijah. He recognized him,
bowed low before him, and asked, "Is it
really you, sir?"
8 "Yes, I'm Elijah," he answered. "Go
and tell your master the king that I am
here."
9 Obadiah answered, "What have I
done that you want to put me in danger
of being killed by King Ahab? 10 By the
living LORD, your God, I swear that the
king has made a search for you in every
country in the world. Whenever the
ruler of a country reported that you were
not in his country, Ahab would require
that ruler to swear that you could not be
found. 11 And now you want me to go
and tell him that you are here? 12 What if
the spirit of the LORD carries you off to
some unknown place as soon as I leave?
Then, when I tell Ahab that you are here
and he can't find you, he will put me to
death. Remember that I have been a devout worshiper of the LORD ever since I
was a boy. 13 Haven't you heard that
when Jezebel was killing the prophets of
the LORD I hid a hundred of them in
caves, in two groups of fifty, and supplied them with food and water? 14 So
how can you order me to go and tell the

[t] *One ancient translation* Let us go and look; *Hebrew* You go and look.

king that you are here? He will kill me!"
15 Elijah answered, "By the living LORD
Almighty, whom I serve, I promise that I
will present myself to the king today."

16 So Obadiah went to King Ahab and
told him, and Ahab set off to meet Elijah.
17 When Ahab saw him, he said, "So
there you are—the worst troublemaker
in Israel!"

18 "I'm not the troublemaker," Elijah
answered. "You are—you and your
father. You are disobeying the LORD's
commands and worshiping the idols of
Baal. 19 Now order all the people of Israel to meet me at Mount Carmel. Bring
along the 450 prophets of Baal and the
400 prophets of the goddess Asherah
who are supported by Queen Jezebel."

20 So Ahab summoned all the Israelites
and the prophets of Baal to meet at
Mount Carmel. 21 Elijah went up to the
people and said, "How much longer will
it take you to make up your minds? If the
LORD is God, worship him; but if Baal is
God, worship him!" But the people didn't
say a word. 22 Then Elijah said, "I am the
only prophet of the LORD still left, but
there are 450 prophets of Baal. 23 Bring
two bulls; let the prophets of Baal take
one, kill it, cut it in pieces, and put it on
the wood—but don't light the fire. I will
do the same with the other bull. 24 Then
let the prophets of Baal pray to their
god, and I will pray to the LORD, and the
one who answers by sending fire—he
is God."

The people shouted their approval.

25 Then Elijah said to the prophets of
Baal, "Since there are so many of you,
you take a bull and prepare it first. Pray
to your god, but don't set fire to the
wood."

26 They took the bull that was brought
to them, prepared it, and prayed to Baal
until noon. They shouted, "Answer us,
Baal!" and kept dancing around the altar
they had built. But no answer came.

27 At noon Elijah started making fun of
them: "Pray louder! He is a god! Maybe
he is day-dreaming or relieving himself,
or perhaps he's gone off on a trip! Or
maybe he's sleeping, and you've got to
wake him up!" 28 So the prophets prayed
louder and cut themselves with knives
and daggers, according to their ritual,
until blood flowed. 29 They kept on rant-
ing and raving until the middle of the
afternoon; but no answer came, not a
sound was heard.

30 Then Elijah said to the people,
"Come closer to me," and they all gathered around him. He set about repairing
the altar of the LORD which had been torn
down. 31 He took twelve stones, one for
each of the twelve tribes named for the
sons of Jacob, the man to whom the LORD
had given the name Israel. 32 With these
stones he rebuilt the altar for the worship of the LORD. He dug a trench around
it, large enough to hold about four gallons of water. 33 Then he placed the
wood on the altar, cut the bull in pieces,
and laid it on the wood. He said, "Fill
four jars with water and pour it on the
offering and the wood." They did so,
34 and he said, "Do it again"—and they
did. "Do it once more," he said—and
they did. 35 The water ran down around
the altar and filled the trench.

36 At the hour of the afternoon sacrifice the prophet Elijah approached the
altar and prayed, "O LORD, the God of
Abraham, Isaac, and Jacob, prove now
that you are the God of Israel and that I
am your servant and have done all this
at your command. 37 Answer me, LORD,
answer me, so that this people will know
that you, the LORD, are God and that you
are bringing them back to yourself."[u]

38 The LORD sent fire down, and it
burned up the sacrifice, the wood, and
the stones, scorched the earth and dried
up the water in the trench. 39 When the
people saw this, they threw themselves
on the ground and exclaimed, "The LORD
is God; the LORD alone is God!"

40 Elijah ordered, "Seize the prophets
of Baal; don't let any of them get away!"
The people seized them all, and Elijah
led them down to Kishon Brook and
killed them.

The End of the Drought

41 Then Elijah said to King Ahab,
"Now, go and eat. I hear the roar of rain
approaching." 42 While Ahab went to eat,
Elijah climbed to the top of Mount Carmel, where he bowed down to the
ground, with his head between his
knees. 43 He said to his servant, "Go and
look toward the sea."

The servant went and returned, say-

[u] you are bringing them back to yourself; *or* you yourself made them turn away from you.

ing, "I didn't see a thing." Seven times in
all Elijah told him to go and look. 44The
seventh time he returned and said, "I
saw a little cloud no bigger than a man's
hand, coming up from the sea."

Elijah ordered his servant, "Go to King
Ahab and tell him to get in his chariot
and go back home before the rain
stops him."

45In a little while the sky was covered
with dark clouds, the wind began to
blow, and a heavy rain began to fall.
Ahab got in his chariot and started back
to Jezreel. 46The power of the LORD came
on Elijah; he fastened his clothes tight
around his waist and ran ahead of Ahab
all the way to Jezreel.

Elijah on Mount Sinai

19 King Ahab told his wife Jezebel
everything that Elijah had done
and how he had put all the prophets of
Baal to death. 2She sent a message to
Elijah: "May the gods strike me dead if
by this time tomorrow I don't do the
same thing to you that you did to the
prophets." 3Elijah was afraid and fled
for his life; he took his servant and went
to Beersheba in Judah.

Leaving the servant there, 4Elijah
walked a whole day into the wilderness.
He stopped and sat down in the shade of
a tree and wished he would die. "It's too
much, LORD," he prayed. "Take away my
life; I might as well be dead!"

5He lay down under the tree and fell
asleep. Suddenly an angel touched him
and said, "Wake up and eat." 6He looked
around and saw a loaf of bread and a jar
of water near his head. He ate and
drank, and lay down again. 7The LORD's
angel returned and woke him up a second time, saying, "Get up and eat, or the
trip will be too much for you." 8Elijah
got up, ate and drank, and the food gave
him enough strength to walk forty days
to Sinai, the holy mountain. 9There he
went into a cave to spend the night.

Suddenly the LORD spoke to him, "Elijah, what are you doing here?"

10He answered, "LORD God Almighty, I
have always served you—you alone. But
the people of Israel have broken their
covenant with you, torn down your altars, and killed all your prophets. I am
the only one left—and they are trying to
kill me!"

11"Go out and stand before me on top
of the mountain," the LORD said to him.
Then the LORD passed by and sent a furious wind that split the hills and shattered the rocks—but the LORD was not in
the wind. The wind stopped blowing,
and then there was an earthquake—but
the LORD was not in the earthquake.
12After the earthquake there was a
fire—but the LORD was not in the fire.
And after the fire there was the soft
whisper of a voice.

13When Elijah heard it, he covered his
face with his cloak and went out and
stood at the entrance of the cave. A voice
said to him, "Elijah, what are you doing
here?"

14He answered, "LORD God Almighty, I
have always served you—you alone. But
the people of Israel have broken their
covenant with you, torn down your altars, and killed all your prophets. I am
the only one left—and they are trying to
kill me."

15The LORD said, "Return to the wilderness near Damascus, then enter the city
and anoint Hazael as king of Syria;
16anoint Jehu son of Nimshi as king of
Israel, and anoint Elisha son of Shaphat
from Abel Meholah to succeed you as
prophet. 17Anyone who escapes being
put to death by Hazael will be killed by
Jehu, and anyone who escapes Jehu will
be killed by Elisha. 18Yet I will leave
seven thousand people alive in Israel—
all those who are loyal to me and have
not bowed to Baal or kissed his idol."

The Call of Elisha

19Elijah left and found Elisha plowing
with a team of oxen; there were eleven
teams ahead of him, and he was plowing
with the last one. Elijah took off his
cloak and put it on Elisha. 20Elisha then
left his oxen, ran after Elijah, and said,
"Let me kiss my father and mother good-
bye, and then I will go with you."

Elijah answered, "All right, go back.
I'm not stopping you!"[v]

21Then Elisha went to his team of
oxen, killed them, and cooked the meat,
using the yoke as fuel for the fire. He
gave the meat to the people, and they ate

[v] All right . . . you; *or* Go on, but come back, because what I have just done to you is important.

it. Then he went and followed Elijah as
his helper.

War with Syria

20 King Benhadad of Syria gathered all his troops, and supported by thirty-two other rulers with
their horses and chariots, he marched
up, laid siege to Samaria, and launched
attacks against it. 2 He sent messengers
into the city to King Ahab of Israel to
say, "King Benhadad demands that 3 you
surrender to him your silver and gold,
your women and the strongest of your
children."

4 "Tell my lord, King Benhadad, that I
agree; he can have me and everything I
own," Ahab answered.

5 Later the messengers came back to
Ahab with another demand from Benhadad: "I sent you word that you were to
hand over to me your silver and gold,
your women and your children. 6 Now,
however, I will send my officers to
search your palace and the homes of
your officials, and to take everything
they[w] consider valuable. They will be
there about this time tomorrow."

7 King Ahab called in all the leaders of
the country and said, "You see that this
man wants to ruin us. He sent me a message demanding my wives and children,
my silver and gold, and I agreed."

8 The leaders and the people answered, "Don't pay any attention to him;
don't give in."

9 So Ahab replied to Benhadad's messengers, "Tell my lord the king that I
agreed to his first demand, but I cannot
agree to the second."

The messengers left and then returned
with another message 10 from Benhadad:
"I will bring enough men to destroy this
city of yours and carry off the rubble in
their hands. May the gods strike me
dead if I don't!"

11 King Ahab answered, "Tell King
Benhadad that a real soldier does his
bragging *after* a battle, not before it."

12 Benhadad received Ahab's answer
as he and his allies, the other rulers,
were drinking in their tents. He ordered
his men to get ready to attack the city,
and so they moved into position.

13 Meanwhile, a prophet went to King
Ahab and said, "The LORD says, 'Don't be
afraid of that huge army! I will give you
victory over it today, and you will know
that I am the LORD.' "

14 "Who will lead the attack?" Ahab
asked.

The prophet answered, "The LORD says
that the young soldiers under the command of the district governors are to
do it."

"Who will command the main force?"
the king asked.

"You," the prophet answered.

15 So the king called out the young soldiers who were under the district commanders, 232 in all. Then he called out
the Israelite army, a total of seven thousand men.

16 The attack began at noon, as Benhadad and his thirty-two allies were getting drunk in their tents. 17 The young
soldiers advanced first. Scouts sent out
by Benhadad reported to him that a
group of soldiers was coming out of Samaria. 18 He ordered, "Take them alive,
no matter whether they are coming to
fight or to ask for peace."

19 The young soldiers led the attack,
followed by the Israelite army, 20 and
each one killed the man he fought. The
Syrians fled, with the Israelites in hot
pursuit, but Benhadad escaped on horseback, accompanied by some of the cavalry. 21 King Ahab took to the field,
captured[x] the horses and chariots, and
inflicted a severe defeat on the Syrians.

22 Then the prophet went to King Ahab
and said, "Go back and build up your
forces and make careful plans, because
the king of Syria will attack again next
spring."

The Second Syrian Attack

23 King Benhadad's officials said to
him, "The gods of Israel are mountain
gods, and that is why the Israelites defeated us. But we will certainly defeat
them if we fight them in the plains.
24 Now, remove the thirty-two rulers
from their commands and replace them
with field commanders. 25 Then call up
an army as large as the one that deserted
you, with the same number of horses
and chariots. We will fight the Israelites

[w] *Some ancient translations* they; *Hebrew* you.
[x] *One ancient translation* captured; *Hebrew* destroyed.

in the plains, and this time we will defeat
them."
King Benhadad agreed and followed
their advice. 26 The following spring he
called up his men and marched with
them to the city of Aphek to attack the
Israelites. 27 The Israelites were called
up and equipped; they marched out and
camped in two groups facing the Syrians. The Israelites looked like two small
flocks of goats compared to the Syrians,
who spread out over the countryside.
28 A prophet went to King Ahab and
said, "This is what the LORD says: 'Because the Syrians say that I am a god of
the hills and not of the plains, I will give
you victory over their huge army, and
you and your people will know that I am
the LORD.' "
29 For seven days the Syrians and the
Israelites stayed in their camps, facing
each other. On the seventh day they
started fighting, and the Israelites killed
a hundred thousand Syrians. 30 The survivors fled into the city of Aphek, where
the city walls fell on twenty-seven thousand of them.
Benhadad also escaped into the city
and took refuge in the back room of a
house. 31 His officials went to him and
said, "We have heard that the Israelite
kings are merciful. Give us permission
to go to the king of Israel with sackcloth
around our waists and ropes around our
necks, and maybe he will spare your
life." 32 So they wrapped sackcloth
around their waists and ropes around
their necks, went to Ahab and said,
"Your servant Benhadad pleads with
you for his life."
Ahab answered, "Is he still alive?
Good! He's like a brother to me!"
33 Benhadad's officials were watching
for a good sign, and when Ahab said
"brother," they took it up at once, and
said, "As you say, Benhadad is your
brother!"
"Bring him to me," Ahab ordered.
When Benhadad arrived, Ahab invited
him to get in the chariot with him. 34 Benhadad said to him, "I will restore to you
the towns my father took from your
father, and you may set up a commercial
center for yourself in Damascus, just as
my father did in Samaria."
Ahab replied, "On these terms, then, I
will set you free." He made a treaty with
him and let him go.

A Prophet Condemns Ahab

35 At the LORD's command a member of
a group of prophets ordered a fellow
prophet to hit him. But he refused, 36 so
he said to him, "Because you have disobeyed the LORD's command, a lion will
kill you as soon as you leave me." And as
soon as he left, a lion came along and
killed him.
37 Then this same prophet went to another man and said, "Hit me!" This man
did so; he hit him a hard blow and hurt
him. 38 The prophet bandaged his face
with a cloth, to disguise himself, and
went and stood by the road, waiting for
the king of Israel to pass. 39 As the king
was passing by, the prophet called out to
him and said, "Your Majesty, I was fighting in the battle when a soldier brought
a captured enemy to me and said,
'Guard this man; if he escapes, you will
pay for it with your life or else pay a fine
of three thousand pieces of silver.' 40 But
I got busy with other things, and the
man escaped."
The king answered, "You have pronounced your own sentence, and you
will have to pay the penalty."
41 The prophet tore the cloth from his
face, and at once the king recognized
him as one of the prophets. 42 The
prophet then said to the king, "This is
the word of the LORD: 'Because you allowed the man to escape whom I had
ordered to be killed, you will pay for it
with your life, and your army will be destroyed for letting his army escape.' "
43 The king went back home to Samaria, worried and depressed.

Naboth's Vineyard

21 Near King Ahab's palace in Jezreel there was a vineyard owned
by a man named Naboth. 2 One day
Ahab said to Naboth, "Let me have your
vineyard; it is close to my palace, and I
want to use the land for a vegetable garden. I will give you a better vineyard for
it or, if you prefer, I will pay you a fair
price."
3 "I inherited this vineyard from my
ancestors," Naboth replied. "The LORD
forbid that I should let you have it!"
4 Ahab went home, depressed and angry over what Naboth had said to him.
He lay down on his bed, facing the wall,
and would not eat. 5 His wife Jezebel

went to him and asked, "Why are you so
depressed? Why won't you eat?"
6He answered, "Because of what Naboth said to me. I offered to buy his vineyard or, if he preferred, to give him
another one for it, but he told me that I
couldn't have it!"
7"Well, are you the king or aren't
you?" Jezebel replied. "Get out of bed,
cheer up, and eat. I will get you Naboth's
vineyard!"
8Then she wrote some letters, signed
Ahab's name to them, sealed them with
his seal, and sent them to the officials
and leading citizens of Jezreel. 9The letters said: "Proclaim a day of fasting, call
the people together, and give Naboth the
place of honor. 10Get a couple of scoundrels to accuse him to his face of cursing
God and the king. Then take him out of
the city and stone him to death."
11The officials and leading citizens of
Jezreel did what Jezebel had commanded. 12They proclaimed a day of
fasting, called the people together, and
gave Naboth the place of honor. 13The
two scoundrels publicly accused him of
cursing God and the king, and so he was
taken outside the city and stoned to
death. 14The message was sent to Jezebel: "Naboth has been put to death."
15As soon as Jezebel received the message, she said to Ahab, "Naboth is dead.
Now go and take possession of the vineyard which he refused to sell to you."
16At once Ahab went to the vineyard to
take possession of it.
17Then the LORD said to Elijah, the
prophet from Tishbe, 18"Go to King
Ahab of Samaria. You will find him in
Naboth's vineyard, about to take possession of it. 19Tell him that I, the LORD, say
to him, 'After murdering the man, are
you taking over his property as well?'
Tell him that this is what I say: 'In the
very place that the dogs licked up Naboth's blood they will lick up your
blood!'"
20When Ahab saw Elijah, he said,
"Have you caught up with me, my
enemy?"
"Yes, I have," Elijah answered. "You
have devoted yourself completely to doing what is wrong in the LORD's sight.
21So the LORD says to you, 'I will bring
disaster on you. I will do away with you
and get rid of every male in your family,
young and old alike. 22Your family will
become like the family of King Jeroboam son of Nebat and like the family of
King Baasha son of Ahijah, because you
have stirred up my anger by leading Israel into sin.' 23And concerning Jezebel,
the LORD says that dogs will eat her body
in the city of Jezreel. 24Any of your relatives who die in the city will be eaten by
dogs, and any who die in the open country will be eaten by vultures."
(25There was no one else who had devoted himself so completely to doing
wrong in the LORD's sight as Ahab—all
at the urging of his wife Jezebel. 26He
committed the most shameful sins by
worshiping idols, as the Amorites had
done, whom the LORD had driven out
of the land as the people of Israel
advanced.)
27When Elijah finished speaking,
Ahab tore his clothes, took them off, and
put on sackcloth. He refused food, slept
in the sackcloth, and went about gloomy
and depressed.
28The LORD said to the prophet Elijah,
29"Have you noticed how Ahab has
humbled himself before me? Since he
has done this, I will not bring disaster on
him during his lifetime; it will be during
his son's lifetime that I will bring disaster on Ahab's family."

The Prophet Micaiah Warns Ahab

(2 Chronicles 18.2-27)

22 There was peace between Israel
and Syria for the next two years,
2but in the third year King Jehoshaphat of Judah went to see King Ahab
of Israel.
3Ahab asked his officials, "Why is it
that we have not done anything to get
back Ramoth in Gilead from the king of
Syria? It belongs to us!" 4And Ahab
asked Jehoshaphat, "Will you go with
me to attack Ramoth?"
"I am ready when you are," Jehoshaphat answered, "and so are my soldiers
and my cavalry. 5But first let's consult
the LORD."
6So Ahab called in the prophets, about
four hundred of them, and asked them,
"Should I go and attack Ramoth, or
not?"
"Attack it," they answered. "The Lord
will give you victory."
7But Jehoshaphat asked, "Isn't there
another prophet through whom we can
consult the LORD?"

8 Ahab answered, "There is one more,
Micaiah son of Imlah. But I hate him
because he never prophesies anything good for me; it's always something bad."
"You shouldn't say that!" Jehoshaphat
replied.
9 Then Ahab called in a court official
and told him to go and get Micaiah at
once.
10 The two kings, dressed in their royal
robes, were sitting on their thrones at
the threshing place just outside the gate
of Samaria, and all the prophets were
prophesying in front of them. 11 One of
them, Zedekiah son of Chenaanah,
made iron horns and said to Ahab, "This
is what the LORD says: 'With these you
will fight the Syrians and totally defeat
them.' " 12 All the other prophets said the
same thing. "March against Ramoth and
you will win," they said. "The LORD will
give you victory."
13 Meanwhile, the official who had
gone to get Micaiah said to him, "All the
other prophets have prophesied success
for the king, and you had better do the
same."
14 But Micaiah answered, "By the living LORD I promise that I will say what he
tells me to!"
15 When he appeared before King
Ahab, the king asked him, "Micaiah,
should King Jehoshaphat and I go and
attack Ramoth, or not?"
"Attack!" Micaiah answered. "Of
course you'll win. The LORD will give you
victory."
16 But Ahab replied, "When you speak
to me in the name of the LORD, tell the
truth! How many times do I have to tell
you that?"
17 Micaiah answered, "I can see the
army of Israel scattered over the hills
like sheep without a shepherd. And the
LORD said, 'These men have no leader; let
them go home in peace.' "
18 Ahab said to Jehoshaphat, "Didn't I
tell you that he never prophesies anything good for me? It's always something bad!"
19 Micaiah went on: "Now listen to
what the LORD says! I saw the LORD sitting on his throne in heaven, with all his
angels standing beside him. 20 The LORD
asked, 'Who will deceive Ahab so that
he will go and be killed at Ramoth?'
Some of the angels said one thing, and
others said something else, 21 until a
spirit stepped forward, approached the
LORD, and said, 'I will deceive him.'
22 'How?' the LORD asked. The spirit replied, 'I will go and make all of Ahab's
prophets tell lies.' The LORD said, 'Go
and deceive him. You will succeed.' "
23 And Micaiah concluded: "This is
what has happened. The LORD has made
these prophets of yours lie to you. But he
himself has decreed that you will meet
with disaster!"
24 Then the prophet Zedekiah went up
to Micaiah, slapped his face, and asked,
"Since when did the LORD's spirit leave
me and speak to you?"
25 "You will find out when you go into
some back room to hide," Micaiah
replied.
26 Then King Ahab ordered one of his
officers, "Arrest Micaiah and take him to
Amon, the governor of the city, and to
Prince Joash. 27 Tell them to throw him
in prison and to put him on bread and
water until I return safely."
28 "If you return safely," Micaiah exclaimed, "then the LORD has not spoken
through me!" And he added, "Listen,
everyone, to what I have said!"

The Death of Ahab

(2 Chronicles 18.28-34)

29 Then King Ahab of Israel and King
Jehoshaphat of Judah went to attack the
city of Ramoth in Gilead. 30 Ahab said to
Jehoshaphat, "As we go into battle, I will
disguise myself, but you wear your royal
garments." So the king of Israel went
into battle in disguise.
31 The king of Syria had ordered his
thirty-two chariot commanders to attack
no one else except the king of Israel.
32 So when they saw King Jehoshaphat,
they all thought that he was the king of
Israel, and they turned to attack him.
But when he cried out, 33 they realized
that he was not the king of Israel, and
they stopped their attack. 34 By chance,
however, a Syrian soldier shot an arrow
which struck King Ahab between the
joints of his armor. "I'm wounded!" he
cried out to his chariot driver. "Turn
around and pull out of the battle!"
35 While the battle raged on, King
Ahab remained propped up in his chariot, facing the Syrians. The blood from
his wound ran down and covered the
bottom of the chariot, and at evening he

died. 36 Near sunset the order went out
through the Israelite ranks: "Each of you
go back to your own country and city!"
37 So died King Ahab. His body was
taken to Samaria and buried. 38 His chariot was cleaned up at the pool of Samaria, where dogs licked up his blood
and prostitutes washed themselves, as
the LORD had said would happen.
39 Everything else that King Ahab did,
including an account of his palace decorated with ivory and of all the cities he
built, is recorded in *The History of the*
Kings of Israel. 40 At his death his son
Ahaziah succeeded him as king.

King Jehoshaphat of Judah

(2 Chronicles 20.31 – 21.1)

41 In the fourth year of the reign of
King Ahab of Israel, Jehoshaphat son of
Asa became king of Judah 42 at the age
of thirty-five, and he ruled in Jerusalem
for twenty-five years. His mother was
Azubah, the daughter of Shilhi. 43 Like
his father Asa before him, he did what
was right in the sight of the LORD; but the
places of worship were not destroyed,
and the people continued to offer sacrifices and burn incense there. 44 Jehoshaphat made peace with the king of Israel.
45 Everything else that Jehoshaphat
did, all his bravery and his battles, are
recorded in *The History of the Kings of*
Judah. 46 He got rid of all the male and
female prostitutes serving at the pagan
altars who were still left from the days of
his father Asa.
47 The land of Edom had no king; it
was ruled by a deputy appointed by the
king of Judah.
48 King Jehoshaphat had ocean-going
ships built to sail to the land of Ophir for
gold; but they were wrecked at Eziongeber and never sailed. 49 Then King
Ahaziah of Israel offered to let his men
sail with Jehoshaphat's men, but Jehoshaphat refused the offer.
50 Jehoshaphat died and was buried in
the royal tombs in David's City, and his
son Jehoram succeeded him as king.

King Ahaziah of Israel

51 In the seventeenth year of the reign
of King Jehoshaphat of Judah, Ahaziah
son of Ahab became king of Israel, and
he ruled in Samaria for two years. 52 He
sinned against the LORD, following the
wicked example of his father Ahab, his
mother Jezebel, and King Jeroboam,
who had led Israel into sin. 53 He worshiped and served Baal, and like his
father before him, he aroused the anger
of the LORD, the God of Israel.

The Second Book of KINGS

Introduction

Second Kings *continues the history of the two Israelite kingdoms where* First Kings *leaves off. The book may be divided into two parts: 1) The story of the two kingdoms from the middle of the ninth century B.C. down to the fall of Samaria and the end of the northern kingdom in 722 B.C. 2) The story of the kingdom of Judah from the fall of the kingdom of Israel down to the capture and destruction of Jerusalem by King Nebuchadnezzar of Babylonia in 586 B.C. The book ends with an account of Gedaliah as governor of Judah under the Babylonians and a report of the release of King Jehoiachin of Judah from prison in Babylon.*

These national disasters took place because of the unfaithfulness of the kings and people of Israel and Judah. The destruction of Jerusalem and the exile of many of the people of Judah was one of the great turning points of Israelite history.

The prophet who stands out in Second Kings *is Elijah's successor Elisha.*

Outline of Contents

Elijah and King Ahaziah

1 After the death of King Ahab of Israel the country of Moab rebelled
against Israel.
2 King Ahaziah of Israel fell off the bal-
cony on the roof of his palace in Samaria
and was seriously injured. So he sent
some messengers to consult Baalzebub,
the god of the Philistine city of Ekron, in
order to find out whether or not he
would recover. 3 But an angel of the LORD
commanded Elijah, the prophet from
Tishbe, to go and meet the messengers
of King Ahaziah and ask them, "Why
are you going to consult Baalzebub, the
god of Ekron? Is it because you think
there is no god in Israel? 4 Tell the king
that the LORD says, 'You will not recover
from your injuries; you will die!' "
Elijah did as the LORD commanded,
5 and the messengers returned to the
king. "Why have you come back?" he
asked.
6 They answered, "We were met by a
man who told us to come back and tell
you that the LORD says to you, 'Why are
you sending messengers to consult Baalzebub, the god of Ekron? Is it because
you think there is no god in Israel? You
will not recover from your injuries; you
will die!' "
7 "What did the man look like?" the
king asked.
8 "He was wearing a cloak made of animal skins, tied with[a] a leather belt,"
they answered.
"It's Elijah!" the king exclaimed.
9 Then he sent an officer with fifty men
to get Elijah. The officer found him sitting on a hill and said to him, "Man of
God, the king orders you to come down."
10 "If I am a man of God," Elijah answered, "may fire come down from
heaven and kill you and your men!" At
once fire came down and killed the officer and his men.
11 The king sent another officer with
fifty men, who went up[b] and said to Elijah, "Man of God, the king orders you to
come down at once!"
12 "If I am a man of God," Elijah answered, "may fire come down from
heaven and kill you and your men!" At
once the fire of God came down and
killed the officer and his men.
13 Once more the king sent an officer
with fifty men. He went up the hill, fell
on his knees in front of Elijah, and
pleaded, "Man of God, be merciful to me
and my men. Spare our lives! 14 The two
other officers and their men were killed
by fire from heaven; but please be merciful to me!"
15 The angel of the LORD said to Elijah,
"Go down with him, and don't be
afraid." So Elijah went with the officer to
the king 16 and said to him, "This is what
the LORD says: 'Because you sent messengers to consult Baalzebub, the god of
Ekron – as if there were no god in Israel
to consult – you will not get well; you
will die!' "
17 Ahaziah died, as the LORD had said
through Elijah. Ahaziah had no sons, so
his brother[c] Joram succeeded him as
king in the second year of the reign of
Jehoram son of Jehoshaphat, king of
Judah.
18 Everything else that King Ahaziah
did is recorded in *The History of the
Kings of Israel.*

Elijah Is Taken Up to Heaven

2 The time came for the LORD to take
Elijah up to heaven in a whirlwind.
Elijah and Elisha set out from Gilgal,

[a] was wearing ... with; *or* was a hairy man and wore. [b] *One ancient translation* went up; *Hebrew* answered. [c] *Some ancient translations* his brother; *Hebrew does not have these words.*

2 and on the way Elijah said to Elisha,
"Now stay here; the LORD has ordered
me to go to Bethel."
But Elisha answered, "I swear by my
loyalty to the living LORD and to you that
I will not leave you." So they went on to
Bethel.
3 A group of prophets who lived there
went to Elisha and asked him, "Do you
know that the LORD is going to take your
master away from you today?"
"Yes, I know," Elisha answered. "But
let's not talk about it."
4 Then Elijah said to Elisha, "Now stay
here; the LORD has ordered me to go to
Jericho."
But Elisha answered, "I swear by my
loyalty to the living LORD and to you that
I will not leave you." So they went on to
Jericho.
5 A group of prophets who lived there
went to Elisha and asked him, "Do you
know that the LORD is going to take your
master away from you today?"
"Yes, I know," Elisha answered. "But
let's not talk about it."
6 Then Elijah said to Elisha, "Now stay
here; the LORD has ordered me to go to
the Jordan River."
But Elisha answered, "I swear by my
loyalty to the living LORD and to you that
I will not leave you." So they went on,
7 and fifty of the prophets followed them
to the Jordan. Elijah and Elisha stopped
by the river, and the fifty prophets stood
a short distance away. 8 Then Elijah took
off his cloak, rolled it up, and struck the
water with it; the water divided, and he
and Elisha crossed to the other side on
dry ground. 9 There, Elijah said to Elisha, "Tell me what you want me to do for
you before I am taken away."
"Let me receive the share of your
power that will make me your successor,"[d] Elisha answered.
10 "That is a difficult request to grant,"
Elijah replied. "But you will receive it if
you see me as I am being taken away
from you; if you don't see me, you won't
receive it."
11 They kept talking as they walked
on; then suddenly a chariot of fire pulled
by horses of fire came between them,
and Elijah was taken up to heaven by a
whirlwind. 12 Elisha saw it and cried out
to Elijah, "My father, my father! Mighty
defender of Israel! You are gone!" And
he never saw Elijah again.
In grief Elisha tore his cloak in two.
13 Then he picked up Elijah's cloak that
had fallen from him, and went back and
stood on the bank of the Jordan. 14 He
struck the water with Elijah's cloak and
said, "Where is the LORD, the God of Elijah?" Then he struck the water again,
and it divided, and he walked over to the
other side. 15 The fifty prophets from Jericho saw him and said, "The power of
Elijah is on Elisha!" They went to meet
him, bowed down before him, 16 and
said, "There are fifty of us here, all
strong men. Let us go and look for your
master. Maybe the spirit of the LORD has
carried him away and left him on some
mountain or in some valley."
"No, you must not go," Elisha
answered.
17 But they insisted until he gave in and
let them go. The fifty of them went and
looked high and low for Elijah for three
days, but didn't find him. 18 Then they
returned to Elisha, who had waited at
Jericho, and he said to them, "Didn't I
tell you not to go?"

Miracles of Elisha

19 Some men from Jericho went to Elisha and said, "As you know, sir, this is a
fine city, but the water is bad and causes
miscarriages."
20 "Put some salt in a new bowl and
bring it to me," he ordered. They
brought it to him, 21 and he went to the
spring, threw the salt in the water, and
said, "This is what the LORD says: 'I make
this water pure, and it will not cause any
more deaths or miscarriages.' " 22 And
that water has been pure ever since, just
as Elisha said it would be.
23 Elisha left Jericho to go to Bethel,
and on the way some boys came out of a
town and made fun of him. "Get out of
here, baldy!" they shouted.
24 Elisha turned around, glared at
them, and cursed them in the name of
the LORD. Then two she-bears came out
of the woods and tore forty-two of the
boys to pieces.
25 Elisha went on to Mount Carmel and
later returned to Samaria.

[d] THE SHARE . . . SUCCESSOR: *Elisha asked for the share that the first-born son inherited by law from his father (see Dt 21.17).*

War between Israel and Moab

3 In the eighteenth year of the reign
of King Jehoshaphat of Judah, Joram son of Ahab became king of Israel,
and he ruled in Samaria for twelve
years. 2He sinned against the LORD, but
he was not as bad as his father or his
mother Jezebel; he pulled down the image his father had made for the worship
of Baal. 3Yet, like King Jeroboam son of
Nebat before him, he led Israel into sin
and would not stop.
4King Mesha of Moab raised sheep,
and every year he gave as tribute to the
king of Israel 100,000 lambs and the
wool from 100,000 sheep. 5But when
King Ahab of Israel died, Mesha rebelled against Israel. 6At once King Joram left Samaria and gathered all his
troops. 7He sent word to King Jehoshaphat of Judah: "The king of Moab has
rebelled against me; will you join me in
war against him?"
"I will," King Jehoshaphat replied. "I
am at your disposal, and so are my men
and my horses. 8What route shall we
take for the attack?"
"We will go the long way through the
wilderness of Edom," Joram answered.
9So King Joram and the kings of Judah and Edom set out. After marching
seven days, they ran out of water, and
there was none left for the men or the
pack animals. 10"We're done for!" King
Joram exclaimed. "The LORD has put the
three of us at the mercy of the king of
Moab!"
11King Jehoshaphat asked, "Is there a
prophet here through whom we can consult the LORD?"
An officer of King Joram's forces answered, "Elisha son of Shaphat is here.
He was Elijah's assistant."
12"He is a true prophet," King Jehoshaphat said. So the three kings went to
Elisha.
13"Why should I help you?" Elisha
said to the king of Israel. "Go and consult those prophets that your father and
mother consulted."
"No!" Joram replied. "It is the LORD
who has put us three kings at the mercy
of the king of Moab."
14Elisha answered, "By the living
LORD, whom I serve, I swear that I would
have nothing to do with you if I didn't
respect your ally, King Jehoshaphat of
Judah. 15Now get me a musician."
As the musician played his harp, the
power of the LORD came on Elisha, 16and
he said, "This is what the LORD says: 'Dig
ditches all over this dry stream bed.
17Even though you will not see any rain
or wind, this stream bed will be filled
with water, and you, your livestock, and
your pack animals will have plenty to
drink.' " 18And Elisha continued, "But
this is an easy thing for the LORD to do;
he will also give you victory over the
Moabites. 19You will conquer all their
beautiful fortified cities; you will cut
down all their fruit trees, stop all their
springs, and ruin all their fertile fields by
covering them with stones."
20The next morning, at the time of the
regular morning sacrifice, water came
flowing from the direction of Edom and
covered the ground.
21When the Moabites heard that the
three kings had come to attack them, all
the men who could bear arms, from the
oldest to the youngest, were called out
and stationed at the border. 22When
they got up the following morning, the
sun was shining on the water, making it
look as red as blood. 23"It's blood!" they
exclaimed. "The three enemy armies
must have fought and killed each other!
Let's go and loot their camp!"
24But when they reached the camp,
the Israelites attacked them and drove
them back. The Israelites kept up the
pursuit,[e] slaughtering the Moabites
25and destroying their cities. As they
passed by a fertile field, every Israelite
would throw a stone on it until finally all
the fields were covered; they also
stopped up the springs and cut down the
fruit trees. At last only the capital city of
Kir Heres[f] was left, and the slingers
surrounded it and attacked it.
26When the king of Moab realized that
he was losing the battle, he took seven
hundred swordsmen with him and tried
to force his way through the enemy lines
and escape to the king of Syria,[g] but he
failed. 27So he took his oldest son, who
was to succeed him as king, and offered
him on the city wall as a sacrifice to the
god of Moab. The Israelites were terri-

[e] *One ancient translation* kept up the pursuit; *Hebrew unclear.* [f] *Probable text* only the capital city of Kir Heres; *Hebrew unclear.* [g] *One ancient translation* Syria; *Hebrew* Edom.

fied[h] and so they drew back from the
city and returned to their own country.

Elisha Helps a Poor Widow

4 The widow of a member of a group
of prophets went to Elisha and said,
“Sir, my husband has died! As you
know, he was a God-fearing man, but
now a man he owed money to has come
to take away my two sons as slaves in
payment for my husband’s debt.”
2 “What shall I do for you?” he asked.
“Tell me, what do you have at home?”
“Nothing at all, except a small jar of
olive oil,” she answered.
3 “Go to your neighbors and borrow as
many empty jars as you can,” Elisha told
her. 4 “Then you and your sons go into
the house, close the door, and start pouring oil into the jars. Set each one aside as
soon as it is full.”
5 So the woman went into her house
with her sons, closed the door, took the
small jar of olive oil, and poured oil into
the jars as her sons brought them to her.
6 When they had filled all the jars, she
asked if there were any more. “That was
the last one,” one of her sons answered.
And the olive oil stopped flowing. 7 She
went back to Elisha, the prophet, who
said to her, “Sell the olive oil and pay all
your debts, and there will be enough
money left over for you and your sons to
live on.”

Elisha and the Rich Woman from Shunem

8 One day Elisha went to Shunem,
where a rich woman lived. She invited
him to a meal, and from then on every
time he went to Shunem he would have
his meals at her house. 9 She said to her
husband, “I am sure that this man who
comes here so often is a holy man.
10 Let’s build a small room on the roof,
put a bed, a table, a chair, and a lamp in
it, and he can stay there whenever he
visits us.”
11 One day Elisha returned to Shunem
and went up to his room to rest. 12 He
told his servant Gehazi to go and call the
woman. When she came, 13 he said to
Gehazi, “Ask her what I can do for her in
return for all the trouble she has had in
providing for our needs. Maybe she
would like me to go to the king or the
army commander and put in a good
word for her.”
“I have all I need here among my own
people,” she answered.
14 Elisha asked Gehazi, “What can I do
for her then?”
He answered, “Well, she has no son,
and her husband is an old man.”
15 “Tell her to come here,” Elisha ordered. She came and stood in the doorway, 16 and Elisha said to her, “By this
time next year you will be holding a son
in your arms.”
“Oh!” she exclaimed. “Please, sir,
don’t lie to me. You are a man of God!”
17 But, as Elisha had said, at about that
time the following year she gave birth to
a son.
18 Some years later, at harvest time,
the boy went out one morning to join his
father, who was in the field with the harvest workers. 19 Suddenly he cried out to
his father, “My head hurts! My head
hurts!”
“Carry the boy to his mother,” the
father said to a servant. 20 The servant
carried the boy back to his mother, who
held him in her lap until noon, at which
time he died. 21 She carried him up to Elisha’s room, put him on the bed and left,
closing the door behind her. 22 Then she
called her husband and said to him,
“Send a servant here with a donkey. I
need to go to the prophet Elisha. I’ll be
back as soon as I can.”
23 “Why do you have to go today?” her
husband asked. “It’s neither a Sabbath
nor a New Moon Festival.”[i]
“Never mind,” she answered. 24 Then
she had the donkey saddled, and ordered the servant, “Make the donkey go
as fast as it can, and don’t slow down
unless I tell you to.” 25 So she set out and
went to Mount Carmel, where Eli-
sha was.
Elisha saw her coming while she was
still some distance away, and he said to
his servant Gehazi, “Look, there comes
the woman from Shunem! 26 Hurry to
her and find out if everything is all right
with her, her husband, and her son.”
She told Gehazi that everything was
all right, 27 but when she came to Elisha,
she bowed down before him and took

[h] TERRIFIED, *either because of what Chemosh, the god of the Moabites, might do,* or *because of what the* LORD, *the God of the Israelites, might do.* [i] SABBATH . . . NEW MOON FESTIVAL: *Such holy days were thought to be the best time to consult a prophet.*

hold of his feet. Gehazi was about to
push her away, but Elisha said, "Leave
her alone. Can't you see she's deeply distressed? And the LORD has not told me a
thing about it."
28 The woman said to him, "Sir, did I
ask you for a son? Didn't I tell you not to
get my hopes up?"
29 Elisha turned to Gehazi and said,
"Hurry! Take my walking stick and go.
Don't stop to greet anyone you meet,
and if anyone greets you, don't take time
to answer. Go straight to the house and
hold my stick over the boy."
30 The woman said to Elisha, "I swear
by my loyalty to the living LORD and to
you that I will not leave you!" So the two
of them started back together. 31 Gehazi
went on ahead and held Elisha's stick
over the child, but there was no sound or
any other sign of life. So he went back to
meet Elisha and said, "The boy didn't
wake up."
32 When Elisha arrived, he went alone
into the room and saw the boy lying
dead on the bed. 33 He closed the door
and prayed to the LORD. 34 Then he lay
down on the boy, placing his mouth,
eyes, and hands on the boy's mouth,
eyes, and hands. As he lay stretched out
over the boy, the boy's body started to
get warm. 35 Elisha got up, walked
around the room, and then went back
and again stretched himself over the
boy. The boy sneezed seven times and
then opened his eyes. 36 Elisha called Gehazi and told him to call the boy's
mother. When she came in, he said to
her, "Here's your son." 37 She fell at Elisha's feet, with her face touching the
ground; then she took her son and left.

Two More Miracles

38 Once, when there was a famine
throughout the land, Elisha returned to
Gilgal. While he was teaching a group of
prophets, he told his servant to put a big
pot on the fire and make some stew for
them. 39 One of them went out in the
fields to get some herbs. He found a wild
vine and picked as many gourds as he
could carry. He brought them back and
sliced them up into the stew, not knowing what they were. 40 The stew was
poured out for the men to eat, but as
soon as they tasted it they exclaimed to
Elisha, "It's poisoned!"—and wouldn't
eat it. 41 Elisha asked for some meal,
threw it into the pot, and said, "Pour out
some more stew for them." And then
there was nothing wrong with it.
42 Another time, a man came from
Baal Shalishah, bringing Elisha twenty
loaves of bread made from the first barley harvested that year, and some
freshly-cut heads of grain. Elisha told
his servant to feed the group of prophets
with this, 43 but he answered, "Do you
think this is enough for a hundred men?"
Elisha replied, "Give it to them to eat,
because the LORD says that they will eat
and still have some left over." 44 So the
servant set the food before them, and as
the LORD had said, they all ate, and there
was still some left over.

Naaman Is Cured

5 Naaman, the commander of the
Syrian army, was highly respected
and esteemed by the king of Syria, because through Naaman the LORD had
given victory to the Syrian forces. He
was a great soldier, but he suffered from
a dreaded skin disease. 2 In one of their
raids against Israel, the Syrians had carried off a little Israelite girl, who became
a servant of Naaman's wife. 3 One day
she said to her mistress, "I wish that my
master could go to the prophet who lives
in Samaria! He would cure him of his
disease." 4 When Naaman heard of this,
he went to the king and told him what
the girl had said. 5 The king said, "Go to
the king of Israel and take this letter
to him."
So Naaman set out, taking thirty thousand pieces of silver, six thousand
pieces of gold, and ten changes of fine
clothes. 6 The letter that he took read:
"This letter will introduce my officer Naaman. I want you to cure him of his
disease."
7 When the king of Israel read the letter, he tore his clothes in dismay and exclaimed, "How can the king of Syria
expect me to cure this man? Does he
think that I am God,[j] with the power of
life and death? It's plain that he is trying
to start a quarrel with me!"
8 When the prophet Elisha heard what
had happened, he sent word to the king:

[j] God; *or* a god.

"Why are you so upset? Send the man to
me, and I'll show him that there is a
prophet in Israel!"
9 So Naaman went with his horses and
chariot and stopped at the entrance to
Elisha's house. 10 Elisha sent a servant
out to tell him to go and wash himself
seven times in the Jordan River, and he
would be completely cured of his disease. 11 But Naaman left in a rage, saying, "I thought that he would at least
come out to me, pray to the LORD his
God, wave his hand over the diseased
spot,[k] and cure me! 12 Besides, aren't the
rivers Abana and Pharpar, back in Damascus, better than any river in Israel? I
could have washed in them and been
cured!"

13 His servants went up to him and
said, "Sir, if the prophet had told you to
do something difficult, you would have
done it. Now why can't you just wash
yourself, as he said, and be cured?" 14 So
Naaman went down to the Jordan,
dipped himself in it seven times, as Elisha had instructed, and he was completely cured. His flesh became firm and
healthy like that of a child. 15 He returned to Elisha with all his men and
said, "Now I know that there is no god
but the God of Israel; so please, sir, accept a gift from me."

16 Elisha answered, "By the living
LORD, whom I serve, I swear that I will
not accept a gift."

Naaman insisted that he accept it, but
he would not. 17 So Naaman said, "If you
won't accept my gift, then let me have
two mule-loads of earth to take home
with me,[l] because from now on I will
not offer sacrifices or burnt offerings to
any god except the LORD. 18 So I hope
that the LORD will forgive me when I accompany my king to the temple of Rimmon, the god of Syria, and worship him.
Surely the LORD will forgive me!"

19 "Go in peace," Elisha said. And Naaman left.

He had gone only a short distance,
20 when Elisha's servant Gehazi said to
himself, "My master has let Naaman get
away without paying a thing! He should
have accepted what that Syrian offered
him. By the living LORD I will run after
him and get something from him." 21 So
he set off after Naaman. When Naaman
saw a man running after him, he got
down from his chariot to meet him, and
asked, "Is something wrong?"

22 "No," Gehazi answered. "But my
master sent me to tell you that just now
two members of the group of prophets in
the hill country of Ephraim arrived, and
he would like you to give them three
thousand pieces of silver and two
changes of fine clothes."

23 "Please take six thousand pieces of
silver," Naaman replied. He insisted on
it, tied up the silver in two bags, gave
them and two changes of fine clothes to
two of his servants, and sent them on
ahead of Gehazi. 24 When they reached
the hill where Elisha lived, Gehazi took
the two bags and carried them into the
house. Then he sent Naaman's servants
back. 25 He went back into the house,
and Elisha asked him, "Where have you
been?"

"Oh, nowhere, sir," he answered.

26 But Elisha said, "Wasn't I there in
spirit when the man got out of his chariot to meet you? This is no time to accept
money and clothes, olive groves and
vineyards, sheep and cattle, or servants!
27 And now Naaman's disease will come
upon you, and you and your descendants will have it forever!"

When Gehazi left, he had the disease—his skin was as white as snow.

The Recovery of the Ax Head

6 One day the group of prophets that
Elisha was in charge of complained
to him, "The place where we live is too
small! 2 Give us permission to go to the
Jordan and cut down some trees, so that
we can build a place to live."

"All right," Elisha answered.

3 One of them urged him to go with
them; he agreed, 4 and they set out together. When they arrived at the Jordan,
they began to work. 5 As one of them
was cutting down a tree, suddenly his
iron ax head fell in the water. "What
shall I do, sir?" he exclaimed to Elisha.
"It was a borrowed ax!"

6 "Where did it fall?" Elisha asked.

The man showed him the place, and
Elisha cut off a stick, threw it in the water, and made the ax head float. 7 "Take

[k] the diseased spot; *or* this place. [l] EARTH TO TAKE HOME WITH ME: *It was then believed that a god could be worshiped only on his own land.*

it out," he ordered, and the man reached
down and picked it up.

The Syrian Army Is Defeated

8 The king of Syria was at war with
Israel. He consulted his officers and
chose a place to set up his camp. 9 But
Elisha sent word to the king of Israel,
warning him not to go near that place,
because the Syrians were waiting in ambush there. 10 So the king of Israel
warned the people who lived in that
place, and they were on guard. This happened several times.
11 The Syrian king became greatly upset over this; he called in his officers and
asked them, "Which one of you is on the
side of the king of Israel?"
12 One of them answered, "No one is,
Your Majesty. The prophet Elisha tells
the king of Israel what you say even in
the privacy of your own room."
13 "Find out where he is," the king ordered, "and I will capture him."
When he was told that Elisha was in
Dothan, 14 he sent a large force there
with horses and chariots. They reached
the town at night and surrounded it.
15 Early the next morning Elisha's servant got up, went out of the house, and
saw the Syrian troops with their horses
and chariots surrounding the town. He
went back to Elisha and exclaimed, "We
are doomed, sir! What shall we do?"
16 "Don't be afraid," Elisha answered.
"We have more on our side than they
have on theirs." 17 Then he prayed,
"O LORD, open his eyes and let him see!"
The LORD answered his prayer, and Elisha's servant looked up and saw the hillside covered with horses and chariots of
fire all around Elisha.
18 When the Syrians attacked, Elisha
prayed, "O LORD, strike these men
blind!" The LORD answered his prayer
and struck them blind. 19 Then Elisha
went to them and said, "You are on the
wrong road; this is not the town you are
looking for. Follow me, and I will lead
you to the man you are after." And he
led them to Samaria.
20 As soon as they had entered the city,
Elisha prayed, "Open their eyes, LORD,
and let them see." The LORD answered
his prayer; he restored their sight, and
they saw that they were inside Samaria.
21 When the king of Israel saw the Syrians, he asked Elisha, "Shall I kill them,
sir? Shall I kill them?"
22 "No," he answered. "Not even soldiers you had captured in combat would
you put to death. Give them something
to eat and drink, and let them return to
their king." 23 So the king of Israel provided a great feast for them; and after
they had eaten and drunk, he sent them
back to the king of Syria. From then on
the Syrians stopped raiding the land of
Israel.

The Siege of Samaria

24 Some time later King Benhadad of
Syria led his entire army against Israel
and laid siege to the city of Samaria.
25 As a result of the siege the food shortage in the city was so severe that a donkey's head cost eighty pieces of silver,
and half a pound of dove's dung[m] cost
five pieces of silver.
26 The king of Israel was walking by on
the city wall when a woman cried out,
"Help me, Your Majesty!"
27 He replied, "If the LORD won't help
you, what help can I provide? Do I have
any wheat or wine? 28 What's your
trouble?"
She answered, "The other day this
woman here suggested that we eat my
child, and then eat her child the next
day. 29 So we cooked my son and ate
him. The next day I told her that we
would eat her son, but she had hidden him!"
30 Hearing this, the king tore his
clothes in dismay, and the people who
were close to the wall could see that he
was wearing sackcloth under his
clothes. 31 He exclaimed, "May God
strike me dead if Elisha is not beheaded
before the day is over!" 32 And he sent a
messenger to get Elisha.
Meanwhile Elisha was at home with
some elders who were visiting him. Before the king's messenger arrived, Elisha said to the elders, "That murderer is
sending someone to kill me! Now, when
he gets here, shut the door and don't let
him come in. The king himself will be
right behind him." 33 He had hardly finished saying this, when the king[n]

[m] DOVE'S DUNG: *This may be a popular term for a vegetable such as wild onions.* [n] *Probable text* king; *Hebrew* messenger.

arrived and said, "It's the LORD who has
brought this trouble on us! Why should
I wait any longer for him to do something?"

7 Elisha answered, "Listen to what
the LORD says! By this time tomorrow you will be able to buy in Samaria
ten pounds of the best wheat or twenty
pounds of barley for one piece of silver."
2 The personal attendant of the king
said to Elisha, "That can't happen—not
even if the LORD himself were to send
grain[o] at once!"

"You will see it happen, but you won't
get to eat any of the food," Elisha
replied.

The Syrian Army Leaves

3 Four men who were suffering from a
dreaded skin disease were outside the
gates of Samaria, and they said to each
other, "Why should we wait here until
we die? 4 It's no use going into the city,
because we would starve to death in
there; but if we stay here, we'll die also.
So let's go to the Syrian camp; the worst
they can do is kill us, but maybe they
will spare our lives." 5 So, as it began to
get dark, they went to the Syrian camp,
but when they reached it, no one was
there. 6 The Lord had made the Syrians
hear what sounded like the advance of a
large army with horses and chariots,
and the Syrians thought that the king of
Israel had hired Hittite and Egyptian
kings and their armies to attack them.
7 So that evening the Syrians had fled for
their lives, abandoning their tents,
horses, and donkeys, and leaving the
camp just as it was.
8 When the four men reached the edge
of the camp, they went into a tent, ate
and drank what was there, grabbed the
silver, gold, and clothing they found,
and went off and hid them; then they returned, entered another tent, and did the
same thing. 9 But then they said to each
other, "We shouldn't be doing this! We
have good news, and we shouldn't keep
it to ourselves. If we wait until morning
to tell it, we are sure to be punished.
Let's go right now and tell the king's officers!" 10 So they left the Syrian camp,
went back to Samaria, and called out to
the guards at the gates: "We went to the
Syrian camp and didn't see or hear anybody; the horses and donkeys have not
been untied, and the tents are just as the
Syrians left them."
11 The guards announced the news,
and it was reported in the palace. 12 It
was still night, but the king got out of
bed and said to his officials, "I'll tell you
what the Syrians are planning! They
know about the famine here, so they
have left their camp to go and hide in the
countryside. They think that we will
leave the city to find food, and then they
will take us alive and capture the city."
13 One of his officials said, "The people
here in the city are doomed anyway, like
those that have already died. So let's
send some men with five of the horses
that are left, so that we can find out what
has happened."[p] 14 They chose some
men, and the king sent them in two chariots with instructions to go and find out
what had happened to the Syrian army.
15 The men went as far as the Jordan,
and all along the road they saw the
clothes and equipment that the Syrians
had abandoned as they fled. Then they
returned and reported to the king. 16 The
people of Samaria rushed out and looted
the Syrian camp. And as the LORD had
said, ten pounds of the best wheat or
twenty pounds of barley were sold for
one piece of silver.
17 It so happened that the king of Israel
had put the city gate under the command of the officer who was his personal attendant. The officer was
trampled to death there by the people
and died, as Elisha had predicted when
the king went to see him. 18 Elisha had
told the king that by that time the following day ten pounds of the best wheat or
twenty pounds of barley would be sold
in Samaria for one piece of silver, 19 to
which the officer had answered, "That
can't happen—not even if the LORD himself were to send grain[q] at once!" And
Elisha had replied, "You will see it happen, but you won't get to eat any of the
food." 20 And that is just what happened
to him—he died, trampled to death by
the people at the city gate.

The Woman from Shunem Returns

8 Now Elisha had told the woman
who lived in Shunem, whose son he
had brought back to life, that the LORD

[o] grain; *or* rain. [p] *Verse 13 in Hebrew is unclear.* [q] grain; *or* rain.

was sending a famine on the land, which
would last for seven years, and that she
should leave with her family and go and
live somewhere else. 2 She had followed
his instructions and had gone with her
family to live in Philistia for the seven
years.
3 At the end of the seven years she returned to Israel and went to the king to
ask that her house and her land be restored to her. 4 She found the king talking with Gehazi, Elisha's servant; the
king wanted to know about Elisha's miracles. 5 While Gehazi was telling the
king how Elisha had brought a dead person back to life, the woman made her
appeal to the king. Gehazi said to him,
"Your Majesty, here is the woman and
here is her son whom Elisha brought
back to life!" 6 In answer to the king's
question, she confirmed Gehazi's story,
and so the king called an official and
told him to give back to her everything
that was hers, including the value of all
the crops that her fields had produced
during the seven years she had been
away.

Elisha and King Benhadad of Syria

7 Elisha went to Damascus at a time
when King Benhadad of Syria was sick.
When the king was told that Elisha was
there, 8 he said to Hazael, one of his officials, "Take a gift to the prophet and ask
him to consult the LORD to find out
whether or not I am going to get well."
9 So Hazael loaded forty camels with all
kinds of the finest products of Damascus
and went to Elisha. When Hazael met
him, he said, "Your servant King Benhadad has sent me to ask you whether or
not he will recover from his sickness."
10 Elisha answered, "The LORD has revealed to me that he will die; but go to
him and tell him that he will recover."
11 Then Elisha stared at him with a horrified look on his face until Hazael became ill at ease. Suddenly Elisha burst
into tears. 12 "Why are you crying, sir?"
Hazael asked.
"Because I know the horrible things
you will do against the people of Israel,"
Elisha answered. "You will set their fortresses on fire, slaughter their finest
young men, batter their children to
death, and rip open their pregnant
women."
13 "How could I ever be that powerful?"
Hazael asked. "I'm a nobody!"
"The LORD has shown me that you will
be king of Syria," Elisha replied.
14 Hazael went back to Benhadad, who
asked him, "What did Elisha say?"
"He told me that you would certainly
get well," Hazael answered. 15 But on the
following day Hazael took a blanket,
soaked it in water, and smothered the
king.
And Hazael succeeded Benhadad as
king of Syria.

King Jehoram of Judah

(2 Chronicles 21.1-20)

16 In the fifth year of the reign of Joram
son of Ahab as king of Israel,[r] Jehoram
son of Jehoshaphat became king of Judah 17 at the age of thirty-two, and he
ruled in Jerusalem for eight years. 18 His
wife was Ahab's daughter, and like the
family of Ahab he followed the evil ways
of the kings of Israel. He sinned against
the LORD, 19 but the LORD was not willing
to destroy Judah, because he had promised his servant David that his descendants would always continue to rule.
20 During Jehoram's reign Edom revolted against Judah and became an independent kingdom. 21 So Jehoram set
out with all his chariots to Zair, where
the Edomite army surrounded them.
During the night he and his chariot commanders managed to break out and escape, and his soldiers scattered to their
homes. 22 Edom has been independent
of[s] Judah ever since. During this same
period the city of Libnah also revolted.
23 Everything else that Jehoram did is
recorded in *The History of the Kings of
Judah.* 24 Jehoram died and was buried
in the royal tombs in David's City, and
his son Ahaziah succeeded him as king.

King Ahaziah of Judah

(2 Chronicles 22.1-6)

25 In the twelfth year of the reign of
Joram son of Ahab as king of Israel,
Ahaziah son of Jehoram became king of
Judah 26 at the age of twenty-two, and he
ruled in Jerusalem for one year. His
mother was Athaliah, the daughter of
King Ahab and granddaughter of King

[r] *Some ancient translations* Israel; *Hebrew* Israel, Jehoshaphat being king of Judah.
[s] independent of; *or* in revolt against.

Omri of Israel. 27 Since Ahaziah was related to King Ahab by marriage, he
sinned against the LORD, just as Ahab's
family did.
28 King Ahaziah joined King Joram of
Israel in a war against King Hazael of
Syria. The armies clashed at Ramoth in
Gilead, and Joram was wounded in battle. 29 He returned to the city of Jezreel to
recover from his wounds, and Ahaziah
went there to visit him.

Jehu Is Anointed King of Israel

9 Meanwhile the prophet Elisha
called one of the young prophets
and said to him, "Get ready and go to
Ramoth in Gilead. Take this jar of olive
oil with you, 2 and when you get there
look for Jehu, the son of Jehoshaphat
and grandson of Nimshi. Take him to a
private room away from his companions, 3 pour this olive oil on his head, and
say, 'The LORD proclaims that he anoints
you king of Israel.' Then leave there as
fast as you can."
4 So the young prophet went to Ramoth, 5 where he found the army officers
in a conference. He said, "Sir, I have a
message for you."
Jehu asked, "Which one of us are you
speaking to?"
"To you, sir," he replied. 6 Then the
two of them went indoors, and the
young prophet poured the olive oil on
Jehu's head and said to him, "The LORD,
the God of Israel, proclaims: 'I anoint
you king of my people Israel. 7 You are
to kill your master the king, that son of
Ahab, so that I may punish Jezebel for
murdering my prophets and my other
servants. 8 All of Ahab's family and
descendants are to die; I will get rid of
every male in his family, young and old
alike. 9 I will treat his family as I did the
families of King Jeroboam of Israel and
of King Baasha of Israel. 10 Jezebel will
not be buried; her body will be eaten by
dogs in the territory of Jezreel.' " After
saying this, the young prophet left the
room and fled.
11 Jehu went back to his fellow officers, who asked him, "Is everything all
right? What did that crazy fellow want
with you?"
"You know what he wanted," Jehu
answered.
12 "No we don't!" they replied. "Tell us
what he said!"
"He told me that the LORD proclaims: 'I
anoint you king of Israel.' "
13 At once Jehu's fellow officers spread
their cloaks at the top of the steps for
Jehu to stand on, blew trumpets, and
shouted, "Jehu is king!"

King Joram of Israel Is Killed

14-15 Then Jehu plotted against King
Joram, who was in Jezreel, where he
had gone to recover from the wounds
which he had received in the battle at
Ramoth against King Hazael of Syria.
So Jehu said to his fellow officers, "If
you are with me, make sure that no one
slips out of Ramoth to go and warn the
people in Jezreel." 16 Then he got into his
chariot and set off for Jezreel. Joram
had still not recovered, and King Ahaziah of Judah was there, visiting him.
17 A guard on duty in the watchtower
at Jezreel saw Jehu and his men approaching. "I see some men riding up!"
he called out.
Joram replied, "Send a rider to find
out if they are friends or enemies."
18 The messenger rode out to Jehu and
said to him, "The king wants to know if
you come as a friend."
"That's none of your business!" Jehu
answered. "Fall in behind me."
The guard on the watchtower reported
that the messenger had reached the
group but was not returning. 19 Another
messenger was sent out, who asked
Jehu the same question. Again Jehu answered, "That's none of your business!
Fall in behind me."
20 Once more the guard reported that
the messenger had reached the group
but was not returning. And he added,
"The leader of the group is driving his
chariot like a madman, just like Jehu!"
21 "Get my chariot ready," King Joram
ordered. It was done, and he and King
Ahaziah rode out, each in his own chariot, to meet Jehu. They met him at the
field which had belonged to Naboth.
22 "Are you coming in peace?" Joram
asked him.
"How can there be peace," Jehu answered, "when we still have all the
witchcraft and idolatry that your mother
Jezebel started?"
23 "It's treason, Ahaziah!" Joram cried
out, as he turned his chariot around and
fled. 24 Jehu drew his bow, and with all
his strength shot an arrow that struck

Joram in the back and pierced his heart. Joram fell dead in his chariot, 25 and Jehu said to his aide Bidkar, "Get his body and throw it in the field that belonged to Naboth. Remember that when you and I were riding together behind King Joram's father Ahab, the LORD spoke these words against Ahab: 26 'I saw the murder of Naboth and his sons yesterday. And I promise that I will punish you here in this same field.' So take Joram's body," Jehu ordered his aide, "and throw it in the field that belonged to Naboth, so as to fulfill the LORD's promise."

King Ahaziah of Judah Is Killed

27 King Ahaziah saw what happened, so he fled in his chariot toward the town of Beth Haggan, pursued by Jehu. "Kill him too!" Jehu ordered his men, and they wounded him[t] as he drove his chariot on the road up to Gur, near the town of Ibleam. But he managed to keep on going until he reached the city of Megiddo, where he died. 28 His officials took his body back to Jerusalem in a chariot and buried him in the royal tombs in David's City.

29 Ahaziah had become king of Judah in the eleventh year that Joram son of Ahab was king of Israel.

Queen Jezebel Is Killed

30 Jehu arrived in Jezreel. Jezebel, having heard what had happened, put on eye shadow, arranged her hair, and stood looking down at the street from a window in the palace. 31 As Jehu came through the gate, she called out, "You Zimri![u] You assassin! Why are you here?"

32 Jehu looked up and shouted, "Who is on my side?" Two or three palace officials looked down at him from a window, 33 and Jehu said to them, "Throw her down!" They threw her down, and her blood spattered on the wall and on the horses. Jehu drove his horses and chariot over her body, 34 entered the palace, and had a meal. Only then did he say, "Take that cursed woman and bury her; after all, she is a king's daughter." 35 But the men who went out to bury her found nothing except her skull and the bones of her hands and feet. 36 When they reported this to Jehu, he said, "This is what the LORD said would happen, when he spoke through his servant Elijah: 'Dogs will eat Jezebel's body in the territory of Jezreel. 37 Her remains will be scattered there like dung, so that no one will be able to identify them.' "

The Descendants of Ahab Are Killed

10 There were seventy descendants of King Ahab living in the city of Samaria. Jehu wrote a letter and sent copies to the rulers of the city,[v] to the leading citizens, and to the guardians of Ahab's descendants. The letter read: 2 "You are in charge of the king's descendants, and you have at your disposal chariots, horses, weapons, and fortified cities. So then, as soon as you receive this letter, 3 you are to choose the best qualified of the king's descendants, make him king, and fight to defend him."

4 The rulers of Samaria were terrified. "How can we oppose Jehu," they said, "when neither King Joram nor King Ahaziah could?" 5 So the officer in charge of the palace and the official in charge of the city, together with the leading citizens and the guardians, sent this message to Jehu: "We are your servants, and we are ready to do anything you say. But we will not make anyone king; do whatever you think best."

6 Jehu wrote them another letter: "If you are with me and are ready to follow my orders, bring the heads of King Ahab's descendants to me at Jezreel by this time tomorrow."

The seventy descendants of King Ahab were under the care of the leading citizens of Samaria, who were bringing them up. 7 When Jehu's letter was received, the leaders of Samaria killed all seventy of Ahab's descendants, put their heads in baskets, and sent them to Jehu at Jezreel.

8 When Jehu was told that the heads of Ahab's descendants had been brought, he ordered them to be piled up in two heaps at the city gate and to be left there until the following morning. 9 In the morning he went out to the gate and said to the people who were there, "I was the

[t] *Some ancient translations* and they wounded him; *Hebrew does not have these words.*
[u] ZIMRI: *An Israelite army officer who assassinated the king of Israel (see 1 K 16.8-12).*
[v] *Some ancient translations* the city; *Hebrew* Jezreel.

one who plotted against King Joram and
killed him; you are not responsible for
that. But who killed all these? 10 This
proves that everything that the LORD said
about the descendants of Ahab will
come true. The LORD has done what he
promised through his prophet Elijah."
11 Then Jehu put to death all the other
relatives of Ahab living in Jezreel, and
all his officers, close friends, and priests;
not one of them was left alive.

The Relatives of King Ahaziah Are Killed

12 Jehu left Jezreel to go to Samaria.
On the way, at a place called "Shepherds' Camp," 13 he met some relatives
of the late King Ahaziah of Judah and
asked them, "Who are you?"

"Ahaziah's relatives," they answered.
"We are going to Jezreel to pay our respects to the children of Queen Jezebel
and to the rest of the royal family."
14 Jehu ordered his men, "Take them
alive!" They seized them, and he put
them to death near a pit there. There
were forty-two people in all, and not one
of them was left alive.

All Remaining Relatives of Ahab Are Killed

15 Jehu started out again, and on his
way he was met by Jonadab son of Rechab. Jehu greeted him and said, "You
and I think alike. Will you support me?"

"I will," Jonadab answered.

"Give me your hand, then," Jehu replied. They clasped hands, and Jehu
helped him up into the chariot, 16 saying,
"Come with me and see for yourself how
devoted I am to the LORD." And they rode
on together to Samaria. 17 When they arrived there, Jehu killed all of Ahab's relatives, not sparing even one. This is
what the LORD had told Elijah would
happen.

The Worshipers of Baal Are Killed

18 Jehu called the people of Samaria
together and said, "King Ahab served
the god Baal a little, but I will serve him
much more. 19 Call together all the
prophets of Baal, all his worshipers, and
all his priests. No one is excused; I am
going to offer a great sacrifice to Baal,
and whoever is not present will be put to
death." (This was a trick on the part of
Jehu by which he meant to kill all the
worshipers of Baal.) 20 Then Jehu ordered, "Proclaim a day of worship in
honor of Baal!" The proclamation was
made, 21 and Jehu sent word throughout
all the land of Israel. All who worshiped
Baal came; not one of them failed to
come. They all went into the temple of
Baal, filling it from one end to the other.
22 Then Jehu ordered the priest in charge
of the sacred robes to bring the robes out
and give them to the worshipers. 23 After
that, Jehu himself went into the temple
with Jonadab son of Rechab and said to
the people there, "Make sure that only
worshipers of Baal are present and that
no worshiper of the LORD has come in."
24 Then he and Jonadab went in to offer
sacrifices and burnt offerings to Baal.
He had stationed eighty men outside the
temple and had instructed them: "You
are to kill all these people; anyone who
lets one of them escape will pay for it
with his life!"

25 As soon as Jehu had presented the
offerings, he said to the guards and officers, "Go in and kill them all; don't let
anyone escape!" They went in with
drawn swords, killed them all, and
dragged the bodies outside. Then they
went on into the inner sanctuary of the
temple, 26 brought out the sacred pillar
that was there, and burned it. 27 So they
destroyed the sacred pillar and the temple, and turned the temple into a
latrine—which it still is today.

28 That was how Jehu wiped out the
worship of Baal in Israel. 29 But he imitated the sin of King Jeroboam, who led
Israel into the sin of worshiping the gold
bull-calves he set up in Bethel and in
Dan. 30 The LORD said to Jehu, "You have
done to Ahab's descendants everything I
wanted you to do. So I promise you that
your descendants, down to the fourth
generation, will be kings of Israel." 31 But
Jehu did not obey with all his heart the
Law of the LORD, the God of Israel; instead, he followed the example of Jeroboam, who led Israel into sin.

The Death of Jehu

32 At that time the LORD began to reduce the size of Israel's territory. King
Hazael of Syria conquered all the Israelite territory 33 east of the Jordan, as far
south as the town of Aroer on the Arnon
River—this included the territories of

Gilead and Bashan, where the tribes
of Gad, Reuben, and East Manasseh
lived.
34 Everything else that Jehu did, including his brave deeds, is recorded in
The History of the Kings of Israel. 35 He
died and was buried in Samaria, and his
son Jehoahaz succeeded him as king.
36 Jehu had ruled in Samaria as king of
Israel for twenty-eight years.

Queen Athaliah of Judah

(2 Chronicles 22.10 – 23.15)

11 As soon as King Ahaziah's
mother Athaliah learned of her
son's murder, she gave orders for all the
members of the royal family to be killed.
2 Only Ahaziah's son Joash escaped. He
was about to be killed with the others,
but was rescued by his aunt Jehosheba,
who was King Jehoram's daughter and
Ahaziah's half sister. She took him and
his nurse into a bedroom in the Temple
and hid him from Athaliah, so that he
was not killed. 3 For six years Jehosheba
took care of the boy and kept him hidden in the Temple, while Athaliah ruled
as queen.
4 But in the seventh year Jehoiada the
priest sent for the officers in charge of
the royal bodyguard and of the palace
guards, and told them to come to the
Temple, where he made them agree under oath to what he planned to do. He
showed them King Ahaziah's son Joash
5 and gave them the following orders:
"When you come on duty on the Sabbath, one third of you are to guard the
palace; 6 another third are to stand guard
at the Sur Gate, and the other third are
to stand guard at the gate behind the
other guards.[w] 7 The two groups that go
off duty on the Sabbath are to stand
guard at the Temple to protect the king.
8 You are to guard King Joash with
drawn swords and stay with him wherever he goes. Anyone who comes near
you is to be killed."
9 The officers obeyed Jehoiada's instructions and brought their men to
him—those going off duty on the Sabbath and those going on duty. 10 He gave
the officers the spears[x] and shields that
had belonged to King David and had
been kept in the Temple, 11 and he stationed the men with drawn swords all
around the front of the Temple, to protect the king. 12 Then Jehoiada led Joash
out, placed the crown on his head, and
gave him a copy of the laws governing
kingship. Then Joash was anointed and
proclaimed king. The people clapped
their hands and shouted, "Long live the
king!"
13 Queen Athaliah heard the noise being made by the guards and the people,
so she hurried to the Temple, where the
crowd had gathered. 14 There she saw
the new king standing by the column at
the entrance of the Temple, as was the
custom. He was surrounded by the officers and the trumpeters, and the people
were all shouting joyfully and blowing
trumpets. Athaliah tore her clothes
in distress and shouted, "Treason!
Treason!"
15 Jehoiada did not want Athaliah
killed in the Temple area, so he ordered
the army officers: "Take her out between the rows of guards, and kill anyone who tries to rescue her." 16 They
seized her, took her to the palace, and
there at the Horse Gate they killed
her.

Jehoiada's Reforms

(2 Chronicles 23.16-21)

17 The priest Jehoiada had King Joash
and the people make a covenant with the
LORD that they would be the LORD's people; he also made a covenant between
the king and the people. 18 Then the people went to the temple of Baal and tore it
down; they smashed the altars and the
idols, and killed Mattan, the priest of
Baal, in front of the altars.
Jehoiada put guards on duty at the
Temple, 19 and then he, the officers, the
royal bodyguard, and the palace guards
escorted the king from the Temple to the
palace, followed by all the people. Joash
entered by the Guard Gate and took his
place on the throne. 20 All the people
were filled with happiness, and the city
was quiet, now that Athaliah had been
killed in the palace.
21 Joash became king of Judah at the
age of seven.

[w] *Hebrew has an additional word, the meaning of which is unclear.* [x] *Some ancient translations (and see 2 Ch 23.9)* spears; *Hebrew* spear.

King Joash of Judah

(2 Chronicles 24.1-16)

12 In the seventh year of the reign of King Jehu of Israel, Joash became king of Judah, and he ruled in Jerusalem for forty years. His mother was Zibiah from the city of Beersheba. 2 Throughout his life he did what pleased the LORD, because Jehoiada the priest instructed him. 3 However, the pagan places of worship were not destroyed, and the people continued to offer sacrifices and burn incense there.

4 Joash called the priests and ordered them to save up the money paid in connection with the sacrifices in the Temple, both the dues paid for the regular sacrifices and the money given as freewill gifts. 5 Each priest was to be responsible for the money brought by those he served, and the money was to be used to repair the Temple, as needed.

6 But by the twenty-third year of Joash's reign the priests still had not made any repairs in the Temple. 7 So he called in Jehoiada and the other priests and asked them, "Why aren't you repairing the Temple? From now on you are not to keep the money you receive; you must hand it over, so that the repairs can be made." 8 The priests agreed to this and also agreed not to make the repairs in the Temple.

9 Then Jehoiada took a box, made a hole in the lid, and placed the box by the altar, on the right side as one enters the Temple. The priests on duty at the entrance put in the box all the money given by the worshipers. 10 Whenever there was a large amount of money in the box, the royal secretary and the High Priest would come, melt down the silver, and weigh it.[y] 11 After recording the exact amount, they would hand the silver over to the men in charge of the work in the Temple, and these would pay the carpenters, the builders, 12 the masons, and the stone cutters, buy the timber and the stones used in the repairs, and pay all other necessary expenses. 13 None of the money, however, was used to pay for making silver cups, bowls, trumpets, or tools for tending the lamps, or any other article of silver or of gold. 14 It was all used to pay the workers and to buy the materials used in the repairs. 15 The men in charge of the work were thoroughly honest, so there was no need to require them to account for the funds. 16 The money given for the repayment offerings and for the offerings for sin was not deposited in the box; it belonged to the priests.

17 At that time King Hazael of Syria attacked the city of Gath and conquered it; then he decided to attack Jerusalem. 18 King Joash of Judah took all the offerings that his predecessors Jehoshaphat, Jehoram, and Ahaziah had dedicated to the LORD, added to them his own offerings and all the gold in the treasuries of the Temple and the palace, and sent them all as a gift to King Hazael, who then led his army away from Jerusalem.

19 Everything else that King Joash did is recorded in *The History of the Kings of Judah*.

20-21 King Joash's officials plotted against him, and two of them, Jozacar son of Shimeath and Jehozabad son of Shomer, killed him at the house built on the land that was filled in on the east side of Jerusalem, on the road that goes down to Silla. Joash was buried in the royal tombs in David's City, and his son Amaziah succeeded him as king.

King Jehoahaz of Israel

13 In the twenty-third year of the reign of Joash son of Ahaziah as king of Judah, Jehoahaz son of Jehu became king of Israel, and he ruled in Samaria for seventeen years. 2 Like King Jeroboam before him, he sinned against the LORD and led Israel into sin; he never gave up his evil ways. 3 So the LORD was angry with Israel, and he allowed King Hazael of Syria and his son Benhadad to defeat Israel time after time. 4 Then Jehoahaz prayed to the LORD, and the LORD, seeing how harshly the king of Syria was oppressing the Israelites, answered his prayer. 5 The LORD sent Israel a leader, who freed them from the Syrians, and so the Israelites lived in peace, as before. 6 But they still did not give up the sins into which King Jeroboam had led Israel, but kept on[z] committing them; and the image of the goddess Asherah remained in Samaria.

[y] melt down the silver, and weigh it; *or* count the money, and tie it up in bags.
[z] *Some ancient translations* kept on; *Hebrew* he kept on.

7 Jehoahaz had no armed forces left
except fifty cavalry troops, ten chariots,
and ten thousand foot soldiers, because
the king of Syria had destroyed the rest,
trampling them down like dust.
8 Everything else that Jehoahaz did
and all his brave deeds are recorded in
The History of the Kings of Israel. 9 He
died and was buried in Samaria, and his
son Jehoash succeeded him as king.

King Jehoash of Israel

10 In the thirty-seventh year of the
reign of King Joash of Judah, Jehoash
son of Jehoahaz became king of Israel,
and he ruled in Samaria for sixteen
years. 11 He too sinned against the LORD
and followed the evil example of King
Jeroboam, who had led Israel into sin.
12 Everything else that Jehoash did, including his bravery in the war against
King Amaziah of Judah, is recorded in
The History of the Kings of Israel. 13 Jehoash died and was buried in the royal
tombs in Samaria, and his son Jeroboam II succeeded him as king.

The Death of Elisha

14 The prophet Elisha was sick with a
fatal disease, and as he lay dying, King
Jehoash of Israel went to visit him. "My
father, my father!" he exclaimed as he
wept. "You have been the mighty defender of Israel!"
15 "Get a bow and some arrows," Elisha ordered him. Jehoash got them,
16 and Elisha told him to get ready to
shoot. The king did so, and Elisha placed
his hands on the king's hands. 17 Then,
following the prophet's instructions, the
king opened the window that faced toward Syria. "Shoot the arrow!" Elisha
ordered. As soon as the king shot the
arrow, the prophet exclaimed, "You are
the LORD's arrow, with which he will win
victory over Syria. You will fight the
Syrians in Aphek until you defeat them."
18 Then Elisha told the king to take the
other arrows and strike the ground with
them. The king struck the ground three
times, and then stopped. 19 This made
Elisha angry, and he said to the king,
"You should have struck five or six
times, and then you would have won
complete victory over the Syrians; but
now you will defeat them only three
times."
20 Elisha died and was buried.
Every year bands of Moabites used to
invade the land of Israel. 21 One time
during a funeral, one of those bands was
seen, and the people threw the corpse
into Elisha's tomb and ran off.[a] As soon
as the body came into contact with Elisha's bones, the man came back to life
and stood up.

War between Israel and Syria

22 King Hazael of Syria oppressed the
Israelites during all of Jehoahaz' reign,
23 but the LORD was kind and merciful to
them. He would not let them be destroyed, but helped them because of his
covenant with Abraham, Isaac, and Jacob. He has never forgotten his people.
24 At the death of King Hazael of Syria
his son Benhadad became king. 25 Then
King Jehoash of Israel defeated Benhadad three times and recaptured the cities
that had been taken by Benhadad during
the reign of Jehoahaz, the father of
Jehoash.

King Amaziah of Judah

(2 Chronicles 25.1-24)

14 In the second year of the reign of
Jehoash son of Jehoahaz as king
of Israel, Amaziah son of Joash became
king of Judah 2 at the age of twenty-five,
and he ruled in Jerusalem for twenty-
nine years. His mother was Jehoaddin
from Jerusalem. 3 He did what was
pleasing to the LORD, but he was not like
his ancestor King David; instead, he did
what his father Joash had done. 4 He did
not tear down the pagan places of worship, and the people continued to offer
sacrifices and burn incense there.
5 As soon as Amaziah was firmly in
power, he executed the officials who had
killed his father, the king. 6 However, he
did not kill their children but followed
what the LORD had commanded in the
Law of Moses: "Parents are not to be put
to death for crimes committed by their
children, and children are not to be put
to death for crimes committed by their
parents; people are to be put to death
only for a crime they themselves have
committed."

[a] *One ancient translation* and ran off; *Hebrew* and he ran off.

7 Amaziah killed ten thousand Edomite soldiers in Salt Valley; he captured
the city of Sela in battle and called it
Joktheel, the name it still has.
8 Then Amaziah sent messengers to
King Jehoash of Israel, challenging him
to fight.[b] 9 But King Jehoash sent back
the following reply: "Once a thorn bush
on the Lebanon Mountains sent a message to a cedar: 'Give your daughter in
marriage to my son.' A wild animal
passed by and trampled the bush down.
10 Now Amaziah, you have defeated the
Edomites, and you are filled with pride.
Be satisfied with your fame and stay at
home. Why stir up trouble that will only
bring disaster on you and your people?"
11 But Amaziah refused to listen, so
King Jehoash marched out with his men
and fought against him at Beth Shemesh
in Judah. 12 Amaziah's army was defeated, and all his soldiers fled to their
homes. 13 Jehoash took Amaziah prisoner, advanced on Jerusalem, and tore
down the city wall from Ephraim Gate to
the Corner Gate, a distance of two hundred yards. 14 He took all the silver and
gold he could find, all the Temple equipment and all the palace treasures, and
carried them back to Samaria. He also
took hostages with him.
15 Everything else that Jehoash did, including his bravery in the war against
King Amaziah of Judah, is recorded in
The History of the Kings of Israel. 16 Jehoash died and was buried in the royal
tombs in Samaria, and his son Jeroboam II succeeded him as king.

The Death of King Amaziah of Judah

(2 Chronicles 25.25-28)

17 King Amaziah of Judah lived fifteen
years after the death of King Jehoash of
Israel. 18 Everything else that Amaziah
did is recorded in *The History of the
Kings of Judah.*
19 There was a plot in Jerusalem to assassinate Amaziah, so he fled to the city
of Lachish, but his enemies followed
him there and killed him. 20 His body
was carried back to Jerusalem on a
horse and was buried in the royal tombs
in David's City. 21 The people of Judah
then crowned his sixteen-year-old son
Uzziah as king. 22 Uzziah reconquered
and rebuilt Elath after his father's death.

King Jeroboam II of Israel

23 In the fifteenth year of the reign of
Amaziah son of Joash as king of Judah,
Jeroboam son of Jehoash became king
of Israel, and he ruled in Samaria for
forty-one years. 24 He sinned against the
LORD, following the wicked example of
his predecessor King Jeroboam son of
Nebat, who led Israel into sin. 25 He reconquered all the territory that had belonged to Israel, from Hamath Pass in
the north to the Dead Sea in the south.
This was what the LORD, the God of Israel, had promised through his servant
the prophet Jonah son of Amittai from
Gath Hepher.
26 The LORD saw the terrible[c] suffering
of the Israelites; there was no one at all
to help them. 27 But it was not the LORD's
purpose to destroy Israel completely and
forever, so he rescued them through
King Jeroboam II.
28 Everything else that Jeroboam II
did, his brave battles, and how he restored Damascus and Hamath to Israel,[d] are all recorded in *The History of
the Kings of Israel.* 29 Jeroboam died and
was buried in the royal tombs, and his
son Zechariah succeeded him as king.

King Uzziah of Judah

(2 Chronicles 26.1-23)

15 In the twenty-seventh year of the
reign of King Jeroboam II of Israel, Uzziah son of Amaziah became
king of Judah 2 at the age of sixteen, and
he ruled in Jerusalem for fifty-two years.
His mother was Jecoliah from Jerusalem. 3 Following the example of his
father, he did what was pleasing to the
LORD. 4 But the pagan places of worship
were not destroyed, and the people continued to offer sacrifices and burn incense there. 5 The LORD struck Uzziah
with a dreaded skin disease that stayed
with him the rest of his life. He lived in a
separate house, relieved of all duties,
while his son Jotham governed the
country.
6 Everything else that Uzziah did is recorded in *The History of the Kings of
Judah.* 7 Uzziah died and was buried in
the royal burial ground in David's City,

[b] challenging him to fight; *or* inviting him to a conference. [c] *Some ancient translations* terrible; *Hebrew* rebellious. [d] *One ancient translation* to Israel; *Hebrew* for Judah in Israel.

and his son Jotham succeeded him as
king.

King Zechariah of Israel

8 In the thirty-eighth year of the reign
of King Uzziah of Judah, Zechariah son
of Jeroboam II became king of Israel,
and he ruled in Samaria for six months.
9 He, like his predecessors, sinned
against the LORD. He followed the
wicked example of King Jeroboam son
of Nebat, who led Israel into sin. 10 Shallum son of Jabesh conspired against
King Zechariah, assassinated him at Ibleam,[e] and succeeded him as king.
11 Everything else that Zechariah did
is recorded in *The History of the Kings
of Israel.*
12 So the promise was fulfilled which
the LORD had made to King Jehu: "Your
descendants down to the fourth generation[f] will be kings of Israel."

King Shallum of Israel

13 In the thirty-ninth year of the reign
of King Uzziah of Judah, Shallum son of
Jabesh became king of Israel, and he
ruled in Samaria for one month.
14 Menahem son of Gadi went from
Tirzah to Samaria, assassinated Shallum, and succeeded him as king.
15 Everything else that Shallum did, including an account of his conspiracy, is
recorded in *The History of the Kings of
Israel.* 16 As Menahem was on his way
from Tirzah, he completely destroyed
the city of Tappuah,[g] its inhabitants,
and the surrounding territory, because
the city did not surrender to him. He
even ripped open the bellies of all the
pregnant women.

King Menahem of Israel

17 In the thirty-ninth year of the reign
of King Uzziah of Judah, Menahem son
of Gadi became king of Israel, and he
ruled in Samaria for ten years. 18 He
sinned against the LORD, for until the day
of his death he followed the wicked example of King Jeroboam son of Nebat,
who led Israel into sin. 19 Tiglath Pileser,
the emperor of Assyria, invaded Israel,
and Menahem gave him thirty-eight tons
of silver to gain his support in strengthening Menahem's power over the country. 20 Menahem got the money from the
rich men of Israel by forcing each one
to contribute fifty pieces of silver. So
Tiglath Pileser went back to his own
country.
21 Everything else that Menahem did is
recorded in *The History of the Kings of
Israel.* 22 He died and was buried, and his
son Pekahiah succeeded him as king.

King Pekahiah of Israel

23 In the fiftieth year of the reign of
King Uzziah of Judah, Pekahiah son of
Menahem became king of Israel, and he
ruled in Samaria for two years. 24 He
sinned against the LORD, following the
wicked example of King Jeroboam son
of Nebat, who led Israel into sin. 25 An
officer of Pekahiah's forces, Pekah son
of Remaliah, plotted with fifty men from
Gilead, assassinated Pekahiah in the
palace's inner fortress[h] in Samaria, and
succeeded him as king.
26 Everything else that Pekahiah did is
recorded in *The History of the Kings of
Israel.*

King Pekah of Israel

27 In the fifty-second year of the reign
of King Uzziah of Judah, Pekah son of
Remaliah became king of Israel, and he
ruled in Samaria for twenty years. 28 He
sinned against the LORD, following the
wicked example of King Jeroboam son
of Nebat, who led Israel into sin.
29 It was while Pekah was king that
Tiglath Pileser, the emperor of Assyria,
captured the cities of Ijon, Abel Beth
Maacah, Janoah, Kedesh, and Hazor,
and the territories of Gilead, Galilee, and
Naphtali, and took the people to Assyria
as prisoners.
30 In the twentieth year of the reign of
Jotham son of Uzziah as king of Judah,
Hoshea son of Elah plotted against King
Pekah, assassinated him, and succeeded
him as king. 31 Everything else that Pekah did is recorded in *The History of the
Kings of Israel.*

King Jotham of Judah

(2 Chronicles 27.1-9)

32 In the second year of the reign of Pekah son of Remaliah as king of Israel,
Jotham son of Uzziah became king of

[e] *One ancient translation* at Ibleam; *Hebrew* before people. [f] FOURTH GENERATION: *Zechariah was Jehu's great-great-grandson.* [g] *One ancient translation* Tappuah; *Hebrew* Tiphsah.
[h] *Hebrew has two additional words, the meaning of which is unclear.*

Judah 33 at the age of twenty-five, and he
ruled in Jerusalem for sixteen years. His
mother was Jerusha, the daughter of Zadok. 34 Following the example of his
father Uzziah, Jotham did what was
pleasing to the LORD. 35 But the pagan
places of worship were not destroyed,
and the people continued to offer sacrifices and burn incense there. It was Jotham who built the North Gate of the
Temple.
36 Everything else that Jotham did is
recorded in *The History of the Kings of
Judah.* 37 It was while he was king that
the LORD first sent King Rezin of Syria
and King Pekah of Israel to attack Judah. 38 Jotham died and was buried in
the royal tombs in David's City, and his
son Ahaz succeeded him as king.

King Ahaz of Judah

(2 Chronicles 28.1-27)

16 In the seventeenth year of the
reign of Pekah son of Remaliah
as king of Israel, Ahaz son of Jotham
became king of Judah 2 at the age of
twenty, and he ruled in Jerusalem for
sixteen years. He did not follow the good
example of his ancestor King David; instead, he did what was not pleasing to
the LORD his God 3 and followed the example of the kings of Israel. He even sacrificed his own son as a burnt offering to
idols, imitating the disgusting practice of
the people whom the LORD had driven
out of the land as the Israelites advanced. 4 At the pagan places of worship, on the hills, and under every shady
tree, Ahaz offered sacrifices and burned
incense.
5 King Rezin of Syria and King Pekah
of Israel attacked Jerusalem and besieged it, but could not defeat Ahaz. (6 At
the same time the king of Edom[i] regained control of the city of Elath and
drove out the Judeans who lived there.
The Edomites settled in Elath and still
live there.) 7 Ahaz sent men to Tiglath
Pileser, the emperor of Assyria, with this
message: "I am your devoted servant.
Come and rescue me from the kings of
Syria and of Israel, who are attacking
me." 8 Ahaz took the silver and gold
from the Temple and the palace treasury, and sent it as a present to the emperor. 9 Tiglath Pileser, in answer to
Ahaz' plea, marched out with his army
against Damascus, captured it, killed
King Rezin, and took the people to Kir
as prisoners.
10 When King Ahaz went to Damascus
to meet Emperor Tiglath Pileser, he saw
the altar there and sent back to Uriah
the priest an exact model of it, down to
the smallest details. 11 So Uriah built an
altar just like it and finished it before
Ahaz returned. 12 On his return from Damascus, Ahaz saw that the altar was finished, 13 so he burned animal sacrifices
and grain offerings on it and poured a
wine offering and the blood of a fellowship offering on it. 14 The bronze altar
dedicated to the LORD was between the
new altar and the Temple, so Ahaz
moved it to the north side of his new altar. 15 Then he ordered Uriah: "Use this
large altar of mine for the morning burnt
offerings and the evening grain offerings, for the burnt offerings and grain
offerings of the king and the people, and
for the people's wine offerings. Pour on
it the blood of all the animals that are
sacrificed. But keep the bronze altar for
me to use for divination." 16 Uriah did as
the king commanded.
17 King Ahaz took apart the bronze
carts used in the Temple and removed
the basins that were on them. He also
took the bronze tank from the backs of
the twelve bronze bulls and placed it on
a stone foundation. 18 And in order to
please the Assyrian emperor, Ahaz also
removed from the Temple the platform
for the royal throne and closed up the
king's private entrance to the Temple.[j]
19 Everything else that King Ahaz did
is recorded in *The History of the Kings
of Judah.* 20 Ahaz died and was buried in
the royal tombs in David's City, and his
son Hezekiah succeeded him as king.

King Hoshea of Israel

17 In the twelfth year of the reign of
King Ahaz of Judah, Hoshea son
of Elah became king of Israel, and he
ruled in Samaria for nine years. 2 He
sinned against the LORD, but not as much
as the kings who had ruled Israel before
him. 3 Emperor Shalmaneser of Assyria
made war against him; Hoshea surren-

[i] *Probable text* the king of Edom; *Hebrew* King Rezin of Syria. [j] *Verse 18 in Hebrew is unclear.*

dered to Shalmaneser and paid him tribute every year. 4 But one year Hoshea
sent messengers to So, king of Egypt,[k]
asking for his help, and stopped paying
the annual tribute to Assyria. When
Shalmaneser learned of this, he had Hoshea arrested and put in prison.

The Fall of Samaria

5 Then Shalmaneser invaded Israel
and besieged Samaria. In the third year
of the siege, 6 which was the ninth year
of the reign of Hoshea, the Assyrian emperor[l] captured Samaria, took the Israelites to Assyria as prisoners, and settled
some of them in the city of Halah, some
near the Habor River in the district of
Gozan and some in the cities of Media.
7 Samaria fell because the Israelites
sinned against the LORD their God, who
had rescued them from the king of Egypt
and had led them out of Egypt. They
worshiped other gods, 8 followed the
customs of the people whom the LORD
had driven out as his people advanced,
and adopted customs introduced by the
kings of Israel.[m] 9 The Israelites did[n]
things that the LORD their God disapproved of. They built pagan places of
worship in all their towns, from the
smallest village to the largest city. 10 On
all the hills and under every shady tree
they put up stone pillars and images of
the goddess Asherah, 11 and they burned
incense on all the pagan altars, following the practice of the people whom the
LORD had driven out of the land. They
aroused the LORD's anger with all their
wicked deeds 12 and disobeyed the
LORD's command not to worship idols.
13 The LORD had sent his messengers
and prophets to warn Israel and Judah:
"Abandon your evil ways and obey my
commands, which are contained in the
Law I gave to your ancestors and which
I handed on to you through my servants
the prophets." 14 But they would not
obey; they were stubborn like their ancestors, who had not trusted in the LORD
their God. 15 They refused to obey his instructions, they did not keep the covenant he had made with their ancestors,
and they disregarded his warnings.
They worshiped worthless idols and became worthless themselves, and they
followed the customs of the surrounding
nations, disobeying the LORD's command
not to imitate them. 16 They broke all the
laws of the LORD their God and made two
metal bull-calves to worship; they also
made an image of the goddess Asherah,
worshiped the stars, and served the god
Baal. 17 They sacrificed their sons and
daughters as burnt offerings to pagan
gods; they consulted mediums and fortunetellers, and they devoted themselves
completely to doing what is wrong in the
LORD's sight, and so aroused his anger.
18 The LORD was angry with the Israelites
and banished them from his sight, leaving only the kingdom of Judah.
19 But even the people of Judah did not
obey the laws of the LORD their God; they
imitated the customs adopted by the
people of Israel. 20 The LORD rejected all
the Israelites, punishing them and handing them over to cruel enemies until at
last he had banished them from his
sight.
21 After the LORD had separated Israel
from Judah, the Israelites made Jeroboam son of Nebat their king. Jeroboam
caused them to abandon the LORD and
led them into terrible sins. 22 They followed Jeroboam and continued to practice all the sins he had committed,
23 until at last the LORD banished them
from his sight, as he had warned
through his servants the prophets that
he would do. So the people of Israel
were taken into exile to Assyria, where
they still live.

The Assyrians Settle in Israel

24 The emperor of Assyria took people
from the cities of Babylon, Cuth, Ivvah,
Hamath, and Sepharvaim, and settled
them in the cities of Samaria[o] in place
of the exiled Israelites. They took possession of these cities and lived there.
25 When they first settled there, they did
not worship the LORD, and so he sent lions, which killed some of them. 26 The
emperor of Assyria was told that the
people he had settled in the cities of Samaria did not know the law of the god
of that land, and so the god had sent lions, which were killing them. 27 So the

[k] So, king of Egypt; *or* the king of Egypt at Sais. [l] ASSYRIAN EMPEROR: *Probably Sargon II, the successor of Shalmaneser.* [m] *Probable text* and adopted ... Israel; *Hebrew unclear.* [n] did; *or* said. [o] SAMARIA: *The name of the capital city was applied to the territory of the former kingdom of Israel.*

emperor commanded: "Send back one of
the priests we brought as prisoners;
have him[p] go back and live there, in order to teach the people the law of the god
of that land." 28 So an Israelite priest who
had been deported from Samaria went
and lived in Bethel, where he taught the
people how to worship the LORD.

29 But the people who settled in Samaria continued to make their own
idols, and they placed them in the
shrines that the Israelites had built. Each
different group made idols in the cities
they were living in: 30 the people of
Babylon made idols of the god Succoth
Benoth; the people of Cuth, idols of Nergal; the people of Hamath, idols of
Ashima; 31 the people of Ivvah, idols of
Nibhaz and Tartak; and the people of
Sepharvaim sacrificed their children as
burnt offerings to their gods Adrammelech and Anammelech. 32 These people
also worshiped the LORD and chose from
among their own number all sorts of
people to serve as priests at the pagan
places of worship and to offer sacrifices
for them there. 33 So they worshiped
the LORD, but they also worshiped their
own gods according to the customs
of the countries from which they had
come.

34 They still carry on their old customs
to this day. They do not worship the
LORD nor do they obey the laws and commands which he gave to the descendants
of Jacob, whom he named Israel. 35 The
LORD had made a covenant with them
and had ordered them: "Do not worship
other gods; do not bow down to them or
serve them or offer sacrifices to them.
36 You shall obey me, the LORD, who
brought you out of Egypt with great
power and strength; you are to bow
down to me and offer sacrifices to me.
37 You shall always obey the laws and
commands that I wrote for you. You
shall not obey other gods, 38 and you
shall not forget the covenant I made
with you. 39 You shall obey me, the LORD
your God, and I will rescue you from
your enemies." 40 But those people would
not listen, and they continued to follow
their old customs.

41 So those people worshiped the LORD,
but they also worshiped their idols; and
to this day their descendants continue to
do the same.

King Hezekiah of Judah

(2 Chronicles 29.1, 2; 31.1)

18 In the third year of the reign of
Hoshea son of Elah as king of Israel, Hezekiah son of Ahaz became king
of Judah 2 at the age of twenty-five, and
he ruled in Jerusalem for twenty-nine
years. His mother was Abijah, the
daughter of Zechariah. 3 Following the
example of his ancestor King David, he
did what was pleasing to the LORD. 4 He
destroyed the pagan places of worship,
broke the stone pillars, and cut down the
images of the goddess Asherah. He also
broke in pieces the bronze snake that
Moses had made, which was called Ne-
hushtan. Up to that time the people of
Israel had burned incense in its honor.
5 Hezekiah trusted in the LORD, the God
of Israel; Judah never had another king
like him, either before or after his time.
6 He was faithful to the LORD and never
disobeyed him, but carefully kept all the
commands that the LORD had given
Moses. 7 So the LORD was with him, and
he was successful in everything he did.
He rebelled against the emperor of Assyria and refused to submit to him. 8 He
defeated the Philistines and raided their
settlements, from the smallest village to
the largest city, including Gaza and its
surrounding territory.

9 In the fourth year of Hezekiah's
reign—which was the seventh year of
King Hoshea's reign over Israel—
Emperor Shalmaneser of Assyria invaded Israel and besieged Samaria. 10 In
the third year of the siege Samaria fell;
this was the sixth year of Hezekiah's
reign and the ninth year of Hoshea's
reign. 11 The Assyrian emperor[q] took
the Israelites to Assyria as prisoners and
settled some of them in the city of Halah,
some near the Habor River in the district
of Gozan, and some in the cities of
Media.

12 Samaria fell because the Israelites
did not obey the LORD their God, but
broke the covenant he had made with
them and disobeyed all the laws given
by Moses, the servant of the LORD. They
would not listen and they would not
obey.

[p] *Some ancient translations* him; *Hebrew* them.

[q] ASSYRIAN EMPEROR: *See 17.6.*

The Assyrians Threaten Jerusalem

(2 Chronicles 32.1-19; Isaiah 36.1-22)

13 In the fourteenth year of the reign of
King Hezekiah, Sennacherib, the emperor of Assyria, attacked the fortified
cities of Judah and conquered them.
14 Hezekiah sent a message to Sennacherib, who was in Lachish: "I have done
wrong; please stop your attack, and I
will pay whatever you demand." The
emperor's answer was that Hezekiah
should send him ten tons of silver and
one ton of gold. 15 Hezekiah sent him all
the silver in the Temple and in the palace treasury; 16 he also stripped the gold
from the temple doors and the gold with
which he himself had covered the doorposts, and he sent it all to Sennacherib.
17 The Assyrian emperor sent a large
army from Lachish to attack Hezekiah
at Jerusalem; it was commanded by his
three highest officials. When they arrived at Jerusalem, they occupied the
road where the cloth makers work by
the ditch that brings water from the upper pool. 18 Then they sent for King Hezekiah, and three of his officials went out
to meet them: Eliakim son of Hilkiah,
who was in charge of the palace;
Shebna, the court secretary; and Joah
son of Asaph, who was in charge of the
records. 19 One of the Assyrian officials
told them that the emperor wanted to
know what made King Hezekiah so confident. 20 He demanded, "Do you think
that words can take the place of military
skill and might? Who do you think will
help you rebel against Assyria? 21 You
are expecting Egypt to help you, but that
would be like using a reed as a walking
stick – it would break and jab your
hand. That is what the king of Egypt is
like when anyone relies on him."

22 The Assyrian official went on, "Or
will you tell me that you are relying on
the LORD your God? It was the LORD's
shrines and altars that Hezekiah destroyed, when he told the people of Judah and Jerusalem to worship only at
the altar in Jerusalem. 23 I will make a
bargain with you in the name of the emperor. I will give you two thousand
horses if you can find that many men to
ride them! 24 You are no match for even
the lowest ranking Assyrian official, and
yet you expect the Egyptians to send you
chariots and cavalry! 25 Do you think I
have attacked your country and destroyed it without the LORD's help? The
LORD himself told me to attack it and destroy it."

26 Then Eliakim, Shebna, and Joah
told the official, "Speak Aramaic to us,
sir. We understand it. Don't speak Hebrew; all the people on the wall are
listening."

27 He replied, "Do you think you and
the king are the only ones the emperor
sent me to say all these things to? No, I
am also talking to the people who are
sitting on the wall, who will have to eat
their excrement and drink their urine,
just as you will."

28 Then the official stood up and
shouted in Hebrew, "Listen to what the
emperor of Assyria is telling you! 29 He
warns you not to let Hezekiah deceive
you. Hezekiah can't save you. 30 And
don't let him persuade you to rely on the
LORD. Don't think that the LORD will save
you and that he will stop our Assyrian
army from capturing your city. 31 Don't
listen to Hezekiah. The emperor of Assyria commands you to come out of the
city and surrender. You will all be allowed to eat grapes from your own vines
and figs from your own trees, and to
drink water from your own wells –
32 until the emperor resettles you in a
country much like your own, where
there are vineyards to give wine and
there is grain for making bread; it is a
land of olives, olive oil, and honey. If you
do what he commands, you will not die,
but live. Don't let Hezekiah fool you into
thinking that the LORD will rescue you.
33 Did the gods of any other nations save
their countries from the emperor of Assyria? 34 Where are they now, the gods of
Hamath and Arpad? Where are the gods
of Sepharvaim, Hena, and Ivvah? Did
anyone save Samaria? 35 When did any
of the gods of all these countries ever
save their country from our emperor?
Then what makes you think the LORD
can save Jerusalem?"

36 The people kept quiet, just as King
Hezekiah had told them to; they did not
say a word. 37 Then Eliakim, Shebna,
and Joah tore their clothes in grief, and
went and reported to the king what the
Assyrian official had said.

The King Asks Isaiah's Advice

(Isaiah 37.1-7)

19 As soon as King Hezekiah heard
their report, he tore his clothes in
grief, put on sackcloth, and went to the
Temple of the LORD. 2He sent Eliakim,
the official in charge of the palace,
Shebna, the court secretary, and the senior priests to the prophet Isaiah son of
Amoz. They also were wearing sackcloth. 3This is the message which he told
them to give Isaiah: "Today is a day of
suffering; we are being punished and
are in disgrace. We are like a woman
who is ready to give birth, but is too
weak to do it. 4The Assyrian emperor
has sent his chief official to insult the
living God. May the LORD your God hear
these insults and punish those who
spoke them. So pray to God for those of
our people who survive."
5When Isaiah received King Hezekiah's message, 6he sent back this answer: "The LORD tells you not to let the
Assyrians frighten you with their claims
that he cannot save you. 7The LORD will
cause the emperor to hear a rumor that
will make him go back to his own country, and the LORD will have him killed
there."

The Assyrians Send Another Threat

(Isaiah 37.8-20)

8The Assyrian official learned that the
emperor had left Lachish and was fighting against the nearby city of Libnah; so
he went there to consult him. 9Word
reached the Assyrians that the Egyptian
army, led by King Tirhakah of Ethiopia,[r] was coming to attack them. When
the emperor heard this, he sent a letter
to King Hezekiah of Judah 10to tell him,
"The god you are trusting in has told you
that you will not fall into my hands, but
don't let that deceive you. 11You have
heard what an Assyrian emperor does to
any country he decides to destroy. Do
you think that you can escape? 12My ancestors destroyed the cities of Gozan,
Haran, and Rezeph, and killed the people of Betheden who lived in Telassar,
and none of their gods could save them.
13Where are the kings of the cities of Hamath, Arpad, Sepharvaim, Hena, and
Ivvah?"
14King Hezekiah took the letter from
the messengers and read it. Then he
went to the Temple, placed the letter
there in the presence of the LORD, 15and
prayed, "O LORD, the God of Israel,
seated on your throne above the winged
creatures, you alone are God, ruling all
the kingdoms of the world. You created
the earth and the sky. 16Now, LORD, look
at what is happening to us. Listen to all
the things that Sennacherib is saying to
insult you, the living God. 17We all
know, LORD, that the emperors of Assyria have destroyed many nations,
made their lands desolate, 18and burned
up their gods—which were no gods at
all, only images of wood and stone made
by human hands. 19Now, LORD our God,
rescue us from the Assyrians, so that all
the nations of the world will know that
only you, O LORD, are God."

Isaiah's Message to the King

(Isaiah 37.21-38)

20Then Isaiah sent a message telling
King Hezekiah that in answer to the
king's prayer 21the LORD had said, "The
city of Jerusalem laughs at you, Sennacherib, and makes fun of you.
22Whom do you think you have been insulting and ridiculing? You have been
disrespectful to me, the holy God of Israel. 23You sent your messengers to
boast to me that with all your chariots
you had conquered the highest mountains of Lebanon. You boasted that there
you cut down the tallest cedars and the
finest cypress trees and that you reached
the deepest parts of the forests. 24You
boasted that you dug wells and drank
water in foreign lands and that the feet
of your soldiers tramped the Nile
River dry.
25"Have you never heard that I
planned all this long ago? And now I
have carried it out. I gave you the power
to turn fortified cities into piles of rubble. 26The people who lived there were
powerless; they were frightened and
stunned. They were like grass in a field
or weeds growing on a roof when the hot
east wind blasts them.[s]

[r] *Hebrew* Cush: *Cush is the ancient name of the extensive territory south of the First Cataract of the Nile River. This region was called Ethiopia in Graeco-Roman times, and included within its borders most of modern Sudan and some of present-day Ethiopia (Abyssinia).* [s] *Probable text* when the hot east wind blasts them; *Hebrew* blasted before they are grown.

27 “But I know everything about you,
what you do and where you go. I know
how you rage against me. 28 I have received the report of that rage and that
pride of yours, and now I will put a hook
through your nose and a bit in your
mouth, and take you back by the same
road you came.”

29 Then Isaiah said to King Hezekiah,
“Here is a sign of what will happen. This
year and next you will have only wild
grain to eat, but the following year you
will be able to plant your grain and harvest it, and plant vines and eat grapes.
30 Those in Judah who survive will flourish like plants that send roots deep into
the ground and produce fruit. 31 There
will be people in Jerusalem and on
Mount Zion who will survive, because
the LORD is determined to make this
happen.

32 “And this is what the LORD has said
about the Assyrian emperor: ‘He will not
enter this city or shoot a single arrow
against it. No soldiers with shields will
come near the city, and no siege mounds
will be built around it. 33 He will go back
by the same road he came, without entering this city. I, the LORD, have spoken.
34 I will defend this city and protect it, for
the sake of my own honor and because
of the promise I made to my servant
David.’ ”

35 That night an angel of the LORD went
to the Assyrian camp and killed 185,000
soldiers. At dawn the next day there
they lay, all dead! 36 Then the Assyrian
emperor Sennacherib withdrew and returned to Nineveh. 37 One day, when he
was worshiping in the temple of his god
Nisroch, two of his sons, Adrammelech
and Sharezer, killed him with their
swords and then escaped to the land of
Ararat. Another of his sons, Esarhaddon, succeeded him as emperor.

King Hezekiah's Illness and Recovery

(Isaiah 38.1-8, 21, 22; 2 Chronicles 32.24-26)

20 About this time King Hezekiah
became sick and almost died.
The prophet Isaiah son of Amoz went to
see him and said to him, “The LORD tells
you that you are to put everything in order, because you will not recover. Get
ready to die.”

2 Hezekiah turned his face to the wall
and prayed: 3 “Remember, LORD, that I
have served you faithfully and loyally
and that I have always tried to do what
you wanted me to.” And he began to cry
bitterly.

4 Isaiah left the king, but before he had
passed through the central courtyard of
the palace the LORD told him 5 to go back
to Hezekiah, ruler of the LORD's people,
and say to him, “I, the LORD, the God of
your ancestor David, have heard your
prayer and seen your tears. I will heal
you, and in three days you will go to the
Temple. 6 I will let you live fifteen years
longer. I will rescue you and this city Jerusalem from the emperor of Assyria. I
will defend this city, for the sake of my
own honor and because of the promise I
made to my servant David.”

7 Then Isaiah told the king's attendants to put on his boil a paste made of
figs, and he would get well.[t] 8 King Hezekiah asked, “What is the sign to prove
that the LORD will heal me and that three
days later I will be able to go to the
Temple?”

9 Isaiah replied, “The LORD will give
you a sign to prove that he will keep his
promise. Now, would you prefer to have
the shadow on the stairway go forward
ten steps or go back ten steps?”[u]

10 Hezekiah answered, “It's easy to
have the shadow go forward ten steps![v]
Have it go back ten steps.”[v]

11 Isaiah prayed to the LORD, and the
LORD made the shadow go back ten
steps[v] on the stairway[w] set up by King
Ahaz.

Messengers from Babylonia

(Isaiah 39.1-8)

12 About that same time the king of
Babylonia, Merodach Baladan, the son
of Baladan, heard that King Hezekiah
had been sick, so he sent him a letter and
a present. 13 Hezekiah welcomed the
messengers and showed them his
wealth—his silver and gold, his spices
and perfumes, and all his military equipment. There was nothing in his storerooms or anywhere in his kingdom that

[t] *One ancient translation (and see Is 38.21)* figs, and he would get well; *Hebrew* figs. They did so, and he got well. [u] stairway . . . steps . . . steps . . . ; *or* sundial . . . degrees . . . degrees.
[v] steps; *or* degrees. [w] stairway; *or* sundial. *Archaeological evidence suggests that the stairway referred to in this passage was one specially constructed to tell time.*

he did not show them. 14 Then the
prophet Isaiah went to King Hezekiah
and asked, "Where did these men come
from and what did they say to you?"
Hezekiah answered, "They came from
a very distant country, from Babylonia."
15 "What did they see in the palace?"
"They saw everything. There is nothing in the storerooms that I didn't show
them."
16 Isaiah then told the king, "The LORD
Almighty says that 17 a time is coming
when everything in your palace, everything that your ancestors have stored up
to this day, will be carried off to Babylonia. Nothing will be left. 18 Some of your
own direct descendants will be taken
away and made eunuchs to serve in the
palace of the king of Babylonia."
19 King Hezekiah understood this to
mean that there would be peace and security during his lifetime, so he replied,
"The message you have given me from
the LORD is good."

The End of Hezekiah's Reign

(2 Chronicles 32.32, 33)

20 Everything else that King Hezekiah
did, his brave deeds, and an account of
how he built a reservoir and dug a tunnel to bring water into the city, are all
recorded in *The History of the Kings of
Judah*. 21 Hezekiah died, and his son Manasseh succeeded him as king.

King Manasseh of Judah

(2 Chronicles 33.1-20)

21 Manasseh was twelve years old
when he became king of Judah,
and he ruled in Jerusalem for fifty-five
years. His mother was Hephzibah. 2 Following the disgusting practices of the
nations whom the LORD had driven out of
the land as his people advanced, Manasseh sinned against the LORD. 3 He rebuilt
the pagan places of worship that his
father Hezekiah had destroyed; he built
altars for the worship of Baal and made
an image of the goddess Asherah, as
King Ahab of Israel had done. Manasseh
also worshiped the stars. 4 He built pagan altars in the Temple, the place that
the LORD had said was where he should
be worshiped. 5 In the two courtyards of
the Temple he built altars for the worship of the stars. 6 He sacrificed his son
as a burnt offering. He practiced divination and magic and consulted[x] fortunetellers and mediums. He sinned greatly
against the LORD and stirred up his anger. 7 He placed the symbol of the goddess Asherah in the Temple, the place
about which the LORD had said to David
and his son Solomon: "Here in Jerusalem, in this Temple, is the place that I
have chosen out of all the territory of the
twelve tribes of Israel as the place where
I am to be worshiped. 8 And if the people
of Israel will obey all my commands and
keep the whole Law that my servant
Moses gave them, then I will not allow
them to be driven out of the land that I
gave to their ancestors." 9 But the people
of Judah did not obey the LORD, and Manasseh led them to commit even greater
sins than those committed by the nations whom the LORD had driven out of
the land as his people advanced.
10 Through his servants the prophets
the LORD said, 11 "King Manasseh has
done these disgusting things, things far
worse than what the Canaanites did;
and with his idols he has led the people
of Judah into sin. 12 So I, the LORD God of
Israel, will bring such a disaster on Jerusalem and Judah that everyone who
hears about it will be stunned. 13 I will
punish Jerusalem as I did Samaria, as I
did King Ahab of Israel and his descendants. I will wipe Jerusalem clean of its
people, as clean as a plate that has been
wiped and turned upside down. 14 I will
abandon the people who survive, and
will hand them over to their enemies,
who will conquer them and plunder
their land. 15 I will do this to my people
because they have sinned against me
and have stirred up my anger from the
time their ancestors came out of Egypt
to this day."
16 Manasseh killed so many innocent
people that the streets of Jerusalem
were flowing with blood; he did this in
addition to leading the people of Judah
into idolatry, causing them to sin against
the LORD.
17 Everything else that Manasseh did,
including the sins he committed, is recorded in *The History of the Kings of
Judah*. 18 Manasseh died and was buried
in the palace garden, the garden of

x consulted; *or* brought back.

Uzza, and his son Amon succeeded him
as king.

King Amon of Judah

(2 Chronicles 33.21-25)

19 Amon was twenty-two years old
when he became king of Judah, and he
ruled in Jerusalem for two years. His
mother was Meshullemeth, the daughter
of Haruz from the town of Jotbah. 20 Like
his father Manasseh, he sinned against
the LORD; 21 he imitated his father's actions, and he worshiped the idols that
his father had worshiped. 22 He rejected
the LORD, the God of his ancestors, and
disobeyed the LORD's commands.
23 Amon's officials plotted against him
and assassinated him in the palace.
24 The people of Judah killed Amon's as-
sassins and made his son Josiah king.
25 Everything else that Amon did is recorded in *The History of the Kings of
Judah.* 26 Amon was buried in the tomb
in the garden of Uzza, and his son Josiah
succeeded him as king.

King Josiah of Judah

(2 Chronicles 34.1, 2)

22 Josiah was eight years old when
he became king of Judah, and he
ruled in Jerusalem for thirty-one years.
His mother was Jedidah, the daughter of
Adaiah from the town of Bozkath. 2 Josiah did what was pleasing to the LORD;
he followed the example of his ancestor
King David, strictly obeying all the laws
of God.

The Book of the Law Is Discovered

(2 Chronicles 34.8-28)

3 In the eighteenth year of his reign,
King Josiah sent the court secretary
Shaphan, the son of Azaliah and grandson of Meshullam, to the Temple with
the order: 4 "Go to the High Priest Hilkiah and get a report on the amount of
money that the priests on duty at the entrance to the Temple have collected from
the people. 5 Tell him to give the money
to the men who are in charge of the repairs in the Temple. They are to pay 6 the
carpenters, the builders, and the masons, and buy the timber and the stones
used in the repairs. 7 The men in charge
of the work are thoroughly honest, so
there is no need to require them to account for the funds."
8 Shaphan delivered the king's order
to Hilkiah, and Hilkiah told him that he
had found the book of the Law in the
Temple. Hilkiah gave him the book, and
Shaphan read it. 9 Then he went back to
the king and reported: "Your servants
have taken the money that was in the
Temple and have handed it over to the
men in charge of the repairs." 10 And
then he said, "I have here a book that
Hilkiah gave me." And he read it aloud
to the king.
11 When the king heard the book being
read, he tore his clothes in dismay, 12 and
gave the following order to Hilkiah the
priest, to Ahikam son of Shaphan, to
Achbor son of Micaiah, to Shaphan, the
court secretary, and to Asaiah, the
king's attendant: 13 "Go and consult the
LORD for me and for all the people of Judah about the teachings of this book.
The LORD is angry with us because our
ancestors have not done what this book
says must be done."
14 Hilkiah, Ahikam, Achbor, Shaphan,
and Asaiah went to consult a woman
named Huldah, a prophet who lived in
the newer part of Jerusalem. (Her husband Shallum, the son of Tikvah and
grandson of Harhas, was in charge of
the Temple robes.) They described to
her what had happened, 15 and she told
them to go back to the king and give him
16 the following message from the LORD:
"I am going to punish Jerusalem and all
its people, as written in the book that the
king has read. 17 They have rejected me
and have offered sacrifices to other
gods, and so have stirred up my anger
by all they have done. My anger is
aroused against Jerusalem, and it will
not die down. 18 As for the king himself,
this is what I, the LORD God of Israel, say:
You listened to what is written in the
book, 19 and you repented and humbled
yourself before me, tearing your clothes
and weeping, when you heard how I
threatened to punish Jerusalem and its
people. I will make it a terrifying sight, a
place whose name people will use as a
curse. But I have heard your prayer,
20 and the punishment which I am going
to bring on Jerusalem will not come until after your death. I will let you die in
peace."
The men returned to King Josiah with
this message.

Josiah Does Away with Pagan Worship

(2 Chronicles 34.3-7, 29-33)

23 King Josiah summoned all the
leaders of Judah and Jerusalem,
2 and together they went to the Temple,
accompanied by the priests and the
prophets and all the rest of the people,
rich and poor alike. Before them all the
king read aloud the whole book of the
covenant which had been found in the
Temple. 3 He stood by the royal column
and made a covenant with the LORD to
obey him, to keep his laws and commands with all his heart and soul, and to
put into practice the demands attached
to the covenant, as written in the book.
And all the people promised to keep the
covenant.
4 Then Josiah ordered the High Priest
Hilkiah, his assistant priests, and the
guards on duty at the entrance to the
Temple to bring out of the Temple all the
objects used in the worship of Baal, of
the goddess Asherah, and of the stars.
The king burned all these objects outside the city near Kidron Valley and
then had the ashes taken to Bethel. 5 He
removed from office the priests that the
kings of Judah had ordained to offer
sacrifices[y] on the pagan altars in the
cities of Judah and in places near
Jerusalem—all the priests who offered
sacrifices to Baal, to the sun, the moon,
the planets, and the stars. 6 He removed
from the Temple the symbol of the goddess Asherah, took it out of the city to
Kidron Valley, burned it, pounded its
ashes to dust, and scattered it over the
public burying ground. 7 He destroyed
the living quarters in the Temple occupied by the temple prostitutes.[z] (It was
there that women wove robes used in
the worship of Asherah.) 8 He brought to
Jerusalem the priests who were in the
cities of Judah, and throughout the
whole country he desecrated the altars
where they had offered sacrifices. He
also tore down the altars dedicated to
the goat demons near the gate built by
Joshua, the city governor, which was to
the left of the main gate as one enters the
city. 9 Those priests were not allowed to
serve in the Temple, but they could eat
the unleavened bread provided for their
fellow priests.
10 King Josiah also desecrated Topheth, the pagan place of worship in
Hinnom Valley, so that no one could sacrifice his son or daughter as a burnt offering to the god Molech. 11 He also
removed the horses that the kings of Judah had dedicated to the worship of the
sun, and he burned the chariots used in
this worship. (These were kept in the
temple courtyard, near the gate and not
far from the living quarters of Nathan
Melech, a high official.) 12 The altars
which the kings of Judah had built on
the palace roof above King Ahaz' quarters, King Josiah tore down, along with
the altars put up by King Manasseh in
the two courtyards of the Temple; he
smashed the altars to bits[a] and threw
them into Kidron Valley. 13 Josiah desecrated the altars that King Solomon had
built east of Jerusalem, south of the
Mount of Olives,[b] for the worship of disgusting idols—Astarte the goddess of Sidon, Chemosh the god of Moab, and
Molech the god of Ammon. 14 King Josiah broke the stone pillars to pieces,
cut down the symbols of the goddess
Asherah, and the ground where
they had stood he covered with human
bones.
15 Josiah also tore down the place of
worship in Bethel, which had been built
by King Jeroboam son of Nebat, who led
Israel into sin. Josiah pulled down the
altar, broke its stones into pieces,[c] and
pounded them to dust; he also burned
the image of Asherah. 16 Then Josiah
looked around and saw some tombs
there on the hill; he had the bones taken
out of them and burned on the altar. In
this way he desecrated the altar, doing
what the prophet had predicted long before during the festival as King Jeroboam was standing by the altar. King
Josiah looked around and saw the tomb
of the prophet[d] who had made this pre-

[y] *Some ancient translations* to offer sacrifices; *Hebrew* and he offered sacrifices.
[z] TEMPLE PROSTITUTES: *Men and women who practiced prostitution in the worship of fertility gods.*
[a] *Probable text* smashed . . . to bits; *Hebrew unclear.* [b] MOUNT OF OLIVES: *Hebrew here refers to it as "Mount of Destruction" or "Mount of Sin."* [c] *One ancient translation* broke its stones into pieces; *Hebrew* burned the altar. [d] *One ancient translation* during the festival . . . the prophet; *Hebrew does not have these words.*

diction. 17 “Whose tomb is that?” he
asked.
The people of Bethel answered, “It is
the tomb of the prophet who came from
Judah and predicted these things that
you have done to this altar.”
18 “Leave it as it is,” Josiah ordered.
“His bones are not to be moved.”
So his bones were not moved, neither
were those of the prophet who had come
from Samaria.
19 In every city of Israel King Josiah
tore down all the pagan places of worship
which had been built by the kings
of Israel, who thereby aroused the
LORD's anger. He did to all those altars
what he had done in Bethel. 20 He killed
all the pagan priests on the altars where
they served, and he burned human
bones on every altar. Then he returned
to Jerusalem.

Josiah Celebrates the Passover

(2 Chronicles 35.1-19)

21 King Josiah ordered the people to
celebrate the Passover in honor of the
LORD their God, as written in the book of
the covenant. 22 No Passover like this
one had ever been celebrated by any of
the kings of Israel or of Judah, since the
time when judges ruled the nation.
23 Now at last, in the eighteenth year of
the reign of Josiah, the Passover was
celebrated in Jerusalem.

Other Changes Made by Josiah

24 In order to enforce the laws written
in the book that the High Priest Hilkiah
had found in the Temple, King Josiah
removed from Jerusalem and the rest of
Judah all the mediums and fortunetellers,
and all the household gods, idols,
and all other pagan objects of worship.
25 There had never been a king like him
before, who served the LORD with all his
heart, mind, and strength, obeying all
the Law of Moses; nor has there been a
king like him since.
26 But the LORD's fierce anger had been
aroused against Judah by what King
Manasseh had done, and even now it did
not die down. 27 The LORD said, “I will do
to Judah what I have done to Israel: I
will banish the people of Judah from my
sight, and I will reject Jerusalem, the city
I chose, and the Temple, the place I said
was where I should be worshiped.”

The End of Josiah's Reign

(2 Chronicles 35.20 – 36.1)

28 Everything else that King Josiah did
is recorded in *The History of the Kings
of Judah*. 29 While Josiah was king, King
Neco of Egypt led an army to the Euphrates
River to help the emperor of Assyria.
King Josiah tried to stop the
Egyptian army at Megiddo and was
killed in battle. 30 His officials placed his
body in a chariot and took it back to Jerusalem,
where he was buried in the
royal tombs.
The people of Judah chose Josiah's
son Joahaz and anointed him king.

King Joahaz of Judah

(2 Chronicles 36.2-4)

31 Joahaz was twenty-three years old
when he became king of Judah, and he
ruled in Jerusalem for three months. His
mother was Hamutal, the daughter of
Jeremiah from the city of Libnah. 32 Following
the example of his ancestors, he
sinned against the LORD. 33 His reign
ended when King Neco of Egypt took
him prisoner in Riblah, in the land of
Hamath, and made Judah pay 7,500
pounds of silver and 75 pounds of gold
as tribute. 34 King Neco made Josiah's
son Eliakim king of Judah as successor
to Josiah, and changed his name to Jehoiakim.
Joahaz was taken to Egypt by
King Neco, and there he died.

King Jehoiakim of Judah

(2 Chronicles 36.5-8)

35 King Jehoiakim collected a tax from
the people in proportion to their wealth,
in order to raise the amount needed to
pay the tribute demanded by the king of
Egypt.
36 Jehoiakim was twenty-five years old
when he became king of Judah, and he
ruled in Jerusalem for eleven years. His
mother was Zebidah, the daughter of Pedaiah
from the town of Rumah. 37 Following
the example of his ancestors,
Jehoiakim sinned against the LORD.

24 While Jehoiakim was king, King
Nebuchadnezzar of Babylonia
invaded Judah, and for three years Jehoiakim
was forced to submit to his rule;
then he rebelled. 2 The LORD sent armed
bands of Babylonians, Syrians, Moabites,
and Ammonites against Jehoiakim
to destroy Judah, as the LORD had said
through his servants the prophets that

he would do. 3This happened at the
LORD's command, in order to banish the
people of Judah from his sight because
of all the sins that King Manasseh had
committed, 4and especially because of
all the innocent people he had killed.
The LORD could not forgive Manasseh for
that.

5Everything that Jehoiakim did is recorded in *The History of the Kings of*
Judah. 6Jehoiakim died, and his son Jehoiachin succeeded him as king.

7The king of Egypt and his army never
marched out of Egypt again, because the
king of Babylonia now controlled all the
territory that had belonged to Egypt,
from the Euphrates River to the northern border of Egypt.

King Jehoiachin of Judah

(2 Chronicles 36.9, 10)

8Jehoiachin was eighteen years old
when he became king of Judah, and he
ruled in Jerusalem for three months. His
mother was Nehushta, the daughter of
Elnathan from Jerusalem. 9Following
the example of his father, Jehoiachin
sinned against the LORD.

10It was during his reign that the
Babylonian army, commanded by King
Nebuchadnezzar's officers, marched
against Jerusalem and besieged it.
11During the siege Nebuchadnezzar
himself came to Jerusalem, 12and King
Jehoiachin, along with his mother, his
sons, his officers, and the palace officials, surrendered to the Babylonians. In
the eighth year of Nebuchadnezzar's
reign he took Jehoiachin prisoner 13and
carried off to Babylon all the treasures
in the Temple and the palace. As the
LORD had foretold, Nebuchadnezzar
broke up all the gold utensils which
King Solomon had made for use in the
Temple. 14Nebuchadnezzar carried
away as prisoners the people of Jerusalem, all the royal princes, and all the
leading men, ten thousand in all. He also
deported all the skilled workers, including the blacksmiths, leaving only the
poorest of the people behind in Judah.

15Nebuchadnezzar took Jehoiachin to
Babylon as a prisoner, together with Jehoiachin's mother, his wives, his officials, and the leading men of Judah.
16Nebuchadnezzar deported all the important men to Babylonia, seven thousand in all, and one thousand skilled
workers, including the blacksmiths, all
of them able-bodied men fit for military
duty.

17Nebuchadnezzar made Jehoiachin's
uncle Mattaniah king of Judah and
changed his name to Zedekiah.

King Zedekiah of Judah

(2 Chronicles 36.11, 12; Jeremiah 52.1-3a)

18Zedekiah was twenty-one years old
when he became king of Judah, and he
ruled in Jerusalem for eleven years. His
mother was Hamutal, the daughter of
Jeremiah from the city of Libnah. 19King
Zedekiah sinned against the LORD, just
as King Jehoiakim had done. 20The LORD
became so angry with the people of Jerusalem and Judah that he banished
them from his sight.

The Fall of Jerusalem

(2 Chronicles 36.13-21; Jeremiah 52.3b-11)

25 Zedekiah rebelled against King
Nebuchadnezzar of Babylonia,
and so Nebuchadnezzar came with all
his army and attacked Jerusalem on the
tenth day of the tenth month of the ninth
year of Zedekiah's reign. They set up
camp outside the city, built siege walls
around it, 2and kept it under siege until
Zedekiah's eleventh year. 3On the ninth
day of the fourth month[e] of that same
year, when the famine was so bad that
the people had nothing left to eat, 4the
city walls were broken through. Although the Babylonians were surrounding the city, all the soldiers escaped
during the night. They left by way of the
royal garden, went through the gateway
connecting the two walls, and fled in the
direction of the Jordan Valley. 5But the
Babylonian army pursued King Zedekiah, captured him in the plains near
Jericho, and all his soldiers deserted
him. 6Zedekiah was taken to King Nebuchadnezzar, who was in the city of Riblah, and there Nebuchadnezzar passed
sentence on him. 7While Zedekiah was
looking on, his sons were put to death;
then Nebuchadnezzar had Zedekiah's
eyes put out, placed him in chains, and
took him to Babylon.

[e] *Probable text (see Jr 52.6)* the fourth month; *Hebrew* the month.

The Destruction of the Temple

(Jeremiah 52.12-33)

8 On the seventh day of the fifth month
of the nineteenth year of King Nebuchadnezzar of Babylonia, Nebuzaradan,
adviser to the king and commander of
his army, entered Jerusalem. 9 He
burned down the Temple, the palace,
and the houses of all the important people in Jerusalem, 10 and his soldiers tore
down the city walls. 11 Then Nebuzaradan took away to Babylonia the people
who were left in the city, the remaining
skilled workers,[f] and those who had
deserted to the Babylonians. 12 But he
left in Judah some of the poorest people,
who owned no property, and put them to
work in the vineyards and fields.
13 The Babylonians broke in pieces the
bronze columns and the carts that were
in the Temple, together with the large
bronze tank, and they took all the
bronze to Babylon. 14 They also took
away the shovels and the ash containers
used in cleaning the altar, the tools used
in tending the lamps, the bowls used for
catching the blood from the sacrifices,
the bowls used for burning incense, and
all the other bronze articles used in the
Temple service. 15 They took away
everything that was made of gold or silver, including the small bowls and the
pans used for carrying live coals. 16 The
bronze objects that King Solomon had
made for the Temple—the two columns,
the carts, and the large tank—were too
heavy to weigh. 17 The two columns were
identical: each one was 27 feet high,
with a bronze capital on top, 4½ feet
high. All around each capital was a
bronze grillwork decorated with pomegranates made of bronze.

The People of Judah Are Taken to Babylonia

(Jeremiah 52.24-27)

18 In addition, Nebuzaradan, the commanding officer, took away as prisoners
Seraiah the High Priest, Zephaniah the
priest next in rank, and the three other
important Temple officials. 19 From the
city he took the officer who had been in
command of the troops, five of the king's
personal advisers who were still in
the city, the commander's assistant,
who was in charge of military records,
and sixty other important men. 20 Nebuzaradan took them to the king of Babylonia, who was in the city of Riblah
21 in the territory of Hamath. There
the king had them beaten and put to
death.

So the people of Judah were carried
away from their land into exile.

Gedaliah, Governor of Judah

(Jeremiah 40.7-9; 41.1-3)

22 King Nebuchadnezzar of Babylonia
made Gedaliah, the son of Ahikam and
grandson of Shaphan, governor of Judah, and placed him in charge of all
those who had not been taken away to
Babylonia. 23 When the Judean officers
and soldiers who had not surrendered
heard about this, they joined Gedaliah at
Mizpah. These officers were Ishmael
son of Nethaniah, Johanan son of Kareah, Seraiah son of Tanhumeth from
the town of Netophah, and Jezaniah
from Maacah. 24 Gedaliah said to them,
"I give you my word that there is no need
for you to be afraid of the Babylonian
officials. Settle in this land, serve the
king of Babylonia, and all will go well
with you."
25 But in the seventh month of that
year, Ishmael, the son of Nethaniah and
grandson of Elishama, a member of the
royal family, went to Mizpah with ten
men, attacked Gedaliah, and killed him.
He also killed the Israelites and Babylonians who were there with him. 26 Then
all the Israelites, rich and poor alike, together with the army officers, left and
went to Egypt, because they were afraid
of the Babylonians.

Jehoiachin Is Released from Prison

(Jeremiah 52.31-34)

27 In the year that Evilmerodach became king of Babylonia, he showed
kindness to King Jehoiachin of Judah by
releasing him from prison. This happened on the twenty-seventh day of the
twelfth month of the thirty-seventh year
after Jehoiachin had been taken away
as prisoner. 28 Evilmerodach treated
him kindly and gave him a position of

[f] *Probable text (see Jr 52.15)* skilled workers; *Hebrew* crowd.

greater honor than he gave the other
kings who were exiles with him in Babylonia. 29 So Jehoiachin was permitted to
change from his prison clothes and to
dine at the king's table for the rest of his
life. 30 Each day, for as long as he lived,
he was given a regular allowance for his
needs.

The First Book of
CHRONICLES

Introduction

First *and* Second Chronicles *are largely a retelling of events recorded in the books of* Samuel *and* Kings, *but from a different point of view. Two main purposes govern the account of the history of the Israelite monarchy in the books of* Chronicles:

1) To show that in spite of the disasters that had fallen upon the kingdoms of Israel and Judah, God was still keeping his promises to the nation and was working out his plan for his people through those who were living in Judah. As a basis for this assurance, the writer looked to the great achievements of David and Solomon, to the reforms of Jehoshaphat, Hezekiah, and Josiah, and to the people who remained faithful to God.

2) To describe the origin of the worship of God in the Temple at Jerusalem and especially the organization of the priests and Levites, by which the worship was carried out. David is presented as the real founder of the Temple and its ritual, even though it is Solomon who builds the Temple.

Outline of Contents

Genealogies and lists 1.1–9.44
The death of Saul 10.1-14
The reign of David 11.1–29.30
  a. *Troubles and achievements* 11.1–22.1
  b. *Preparations for building the Temple* 22.2–29.30

From Adam to Abraham
(Genesis 5.1-32; 10.1-32; 11.10-26)

1 Adam was the father of Seth, Seth
was the father of Enosh, Enosh the
father of Kenan, 2 Kenan the father of
Mahalalel, Mahalalel the father of Jared.
3 Jared was the father of Enoch, who was
the father of Methuselah; Methuselah
was the father of Lamech, 4 who was the
father of Noah. Noah had three sons:
Shem, Ham, and Japheth.
5 The sons of Japheth – Gomer, Magog, Madai, Javan, Tubal, Meshech, and
Tiras – were the ancestors of the peoples
who bear their names. 6 The descendants
of Gomer were the people of Ashkenaz,
Riphath, and Togarmah. 7 The descendants of Javan were the people of Elishah,
Spain, Cyprus, and Rhodes.
8 The sons of Ham – Cush, Egypt,
Libya, and Canaan – were the ancestors
of the peoples who bear their names.
9 The descendants of Cush were the people of Seba, Havilah, Sabtah, Raamah,
and Sabteca. The descendants of Raamah were the people of Sheba and Dedan. (10 Cush had a son named Nimrod,
who became the world's first great conqueror.) 11 The descendants of Egypt
were the people of Lydia, Anam, Lehab,
Naphtuh, 12 Pathrus, Casluh, and of
Crete (from whom the Philistines were
descended). 13 Canaan's sons – Sidon,
the oldest, and Heth – were the ancestors of the peoples who bear their
names. 14 Canaan was also the ancestor
of the Jebusites, the Amorites, Girgashites, 15 Hivites, Arkites, Sinites, 16 Ar-
vadites, Zemarites, and Hamathites.
17 Shem's sons – Elam, Asshur, Arpachshad, Lud, Aram, Uz, Hul, Gether,
and Meshek – were the ancestors of the
peoples who bear their names. 18 Arpachshad was the father of Shelah, who
was the father of Eber. 19 Eber had two
sons; one was named Peleg,[a] because
during his time the people of the world
were divided, and the other was named
Joktan. 20 The descendants of Joktan
were the people of Almodad, Sheleph,
Hazarmaveth, Jerah, 21 Hadoram, Uzal,
Diklah, 22 Ebal, Abimael, Sheba,
23 Ophir, Havilah, and Jobab.
24 The family line from Shem to Abram
is as follows: Shem, Arpachshad, Shelah, 25 Eber, Peleg, Reu, 26 Serug, Nahor,
Terah, 27 and Abram (also known as
Abraham).

[a] PELEG: *This name sounds like the Hebrew for "divide."*

The Descendants of Ishmael

(Genesis 25.12-16)

28 Abraham had two sons, Isaac and
Ishmael. 29 The sons of Ishmael became
the heads of twelve tribes: Nebaioth
(from the name of Ishmael's oldest son),
Kedar, Adbeel, Mibsam, 30 Mishma, Dumah, Massa, Hadad, Tema, 31 Jetur, Naphish, and Kedemah.

32 Abraham had a concubine named
Keturah, who bore him six sons: Zimran, Jokshan, Medan, Midian, Ishbak,
and Shuah. Jokshan had two sons:
Sheba and Dedan. 33 Midian had five
sons: Ephah, Epher, Hanoch, Abida, and
Eldaah.

The Descendants of Esau

(Genesis 36.1-19)

34 Abraham's son Isaac had two sons,
Esau and Jacob. 35 Esau's sons were Eliphaz, Reuel, Jeush, Jalam, and Korah.
36 Eliphaz became the ancestor of the following tribes: Teman, Omar, Zephi, Gatam, Kenaz, Timna, and Amalek. 37 And
Reuel became the ancestor of the tribes
of Nahath, Zerah, Shammah, and
Mizzah.

The Original Inhabitants of Edom

(Genesis 36.20-30)

38-42 The original inhabitants of Edom were descended from the following sons of Seir:

Lotan, who was the ancestor of the clans of Hori and Homam. (Lotan had a sister named Timna.)

Shobal, who was the ancestor of the clans of Alvan, Manahath, Ebal, Shephi, and Onam.

Zibeon, who had two sons, Aiah and Anah. Anah was the father of Dishon, and Dishon was the ancestor of the clans of Hamran, Eshban, Ithran, and Cheran.

Ezer, who was the ancestor of the clans of Bilhan, Zaavan, and Jaakan.

Dishan, who was the ancestor of the clans of Uz and Aran.

The Kings of Edom

(Genesis 36.31-43)

43-50 The following kings ruled the land of Edom one after the other, in the time before there were any kings in Israel:

Bela son of Beor from Dinhabah
Jobab son of Zerah from Bozrah
Husham from the region of Teman
Hadad son of Bedad from Avith (he defeated the Midianites in a battle in the country of Moab)
Samlah from Masrekah
Shaul from Rehoboth-on-the-River
Baal Hanan son of Achbor
Hadad from Pau (his wife was Mehetabel, the daughter of Matred and granddaughter of Mezahab)

51 The people of Edom were divided
into the following tribes: Timna, Alvah,
Jetheth, 52 Oholibamah, Elah, Pinon,
53 Kenaz, Teman, Mibzar, 54 Magdiel,
and Iram.

The Descendants of Judah

2 Jacob had twelve sons: Reuben,
Simeon, Levi, Judah, Issachar, Zeb-
ulun, 2 Dan, Joseph, Benjamin, Naphtali,
Gad, and Asher.

3 Judah had five sons in all. By his wife
Bathshua, a Canaanite, he had three
sons: Er, Onan, and Shelah. His oldest
son, Er, was so evil that the LORD killed
him. 4 By his daughter-in-law Tamar, Judah had two more sons, Perez and
Zerah.

5 Perez had two sons, Hezron and Hamul. 6 His brother Zerah had five sons:
Zimri, Ethan, Heman, Calcol, and
Darda. 7 Achan[b] son of Carmi, one of
Zerah's descendants, brought disaster
on the people of Israel by keeping loot
that had been devoted to God.
8 Ethan had one son, Azariah.

The Family Tree of King David

9 Hezron had three sons: Jerahmeel,
Ram, and Caleb.

10 The family line from Ram to Jesse is
as follows: Ram, Amminadab, Nahshon
(a prominent man of the tribe of Judah),
11 Salmon, Boaz, 12 Obed, and Jesse.

13 Jesse had seven sons. In order of age
they were: Eliab, Abinadab, Shammah,
14 Nethanel, Raddai, 15 Ozem, and David.
16 He also had two daughters, Zeruiah
and Abigail.

Jesse's daughter Zeruiah had three
sons: Abishai, Joab, and Asahel. 17 His

[b] ACHAN: *This is his name in Js 7.1. The Hebrew text here calls him "Achar," which means "disaster."*

other daughter Abigail married Jether, a descendant of Ishmael, and they had a son named Amasa.

The Descendants of Hezron

18 Hezron's son Caleb married Azubah and had a daughter named Jerioth. She had[c] three sons: Jesher, Shobab, and Ardon. 19 After the death of Azubah, Caleb married Ephrath, and they had a son named Hur. 20 Hur's son was Uri, and his grandson was Bezalel.

21 When Hezron was sixty years old, he married Machir's daughter, the sister of Gilead. They had a son named Segub, 22 and Segub had a son named Jair. Jair ruled[d] twenty-three cities in the territory of Gilead. 23 But the kingdoms of Geshur and Aram conquered sixty towns there, including the villages of Jair and Kenath, and the towns nearby. All the people who lived there were descendants of Machir, the father of Gilead. 24 After Hezron died, his son Caleb married Ephrath, his father's widow.[e] They had a son named Ashhur, who founded the town of Tekoa.

The Descendants of Jerahmeel

25 Jerahmeel, the oldest son of Hezron, had five sons: Ram, the oldest, Bunah, Oren, Ozem, and Ahijah. 26-27 Ram had three sons: Maaz, Jamin, and Eker. Jerahmeel had another wife, a woman named Atarah, and they had a son, Onam. 28 Onam had two sons, Shammai and Jada, and Shammai also had two sons, Nadab and Abishur.

29 Abishur married a woman named Abihail, and they had two sons, Ahban and Molid. 30 Abishur's brother Nadab had two sons, Seled and Appaim, but Seled died without having any sons. 31 Appaim was the father of Ishi, Ishi was the father of Sheshan, and Sheshan the father of Ahlai.

32 Jada, the brother of Shammai, had two sons, Jether and Jonathan, but Jether died without having any sons. 33 Jonathan had two sons, Peleth and Zaza. All these were descendants of Jerahmeel.

34 Sheshan had no sons, only daughters. He had an Egyptian servant named Jarha, 35 to whom he gave one of his daughters in marriage. They had a son named Attai. 36 The family line from Attai to Elishama is as follows: Attai, Nathan, Zabad, 37 Ephlal, Obed, 38 Jehu, Azariah, 39 Helez, Eleasah, 40 Sismai, Shallum, 41 Jekamiah, and Elishama.

Other Descendants of Caleb

42 The oldest son of Caleb, Jerahmeel's brother, was named Mesha. Mesha was the father of Ziph, who was the father of Mareshah, who was the father of Hebron.[f] 43 Hebron had four sons: Korah, Tappuah, Rekem, and Shema. 44 Shema was the father of Raham and the grandfather of Jorkeam. Rekem, Shema's brother, was the father of Shammai, 45 who was the father of Maon, who was the father of Bethzur.

46 Caleb had a concubine named Ephah, and by her he had three more sons: Haran, Moza, and Gazez. Haran also had a son named Gazez.

(47 A man named Jahdai had six sons: Regem, Jotham, Geshan, Pelet, Ephah, and Shaaph.)

48 Caleb had another concubine, Maacah, who bore him two sons, Sheber and Tirhanah. 49 Later she had two more sons: Shaaph, who founded the town of Madmannah; and Shevah, who founded the towns of Machbenah and Gibea.

In addition, Caleb had a daughter named Achsah.

50 The following are also descendants of Caleb.

Hur was the oldest son of Caleb and his wife Ephrath. Hur's son Shobal founded Kiriath Jearim, 51 his second son Salma founded Bethlehem, and his third son Hareph founded Bethgader.

52 Shobal, the founder of Kiriath Jearim, was the ancestor of the people of Haroeh, of half the inhabitants of Menuhoth, 53 and of the following clans that lived in Kiriath Jearim: the Ithrites, Puthites, Shumathites, and Mishraites. (The people of the cities of Zorah and Eshtaol were members of these clans.)

54 Salma, the founder of Bethlehem, was the ancestor of the people of Netophath, of Atroth Beth Joab, and of the Zorites, who were one of the two clans in Manahath.

(55 The following clans of experts in

[c] *Some ancient translations* had a daughter.... She had; *Hebrew unclear.* [d] ruled; *or* owned.
[e] *Some ancient translations* his son ... widow; *Hebrew unclear.* [f] *Probable text* father of Mareshah ... Hebron; *Hebrew unclear.*

writing and copying documents lived in
the town of Jabez: the Tirathites, Shime-
athites, and Sucathites. They were Kenites who had intermarried with the
Rechabites.)

King David's Children

3 1-3 The following, in order of age,
are David's sons who were born
while he was in Hebron:
Amnon, whose mother was
Ahinoam from Jezreel
Daniel, whose mother was
Abigail from Carmel
Absalom, whose mother was
Maacah, daughter of King
Talmai of Geshur
Adonijah, whose mother was
Haggith
Shephatiah, whose mother was
Abital
Ithream, whose mother was
Eglah
4 All six were born in Hebron during the
seven and a half years that David ruled
there.

In Jerusalem he ruled as king for
thirty-three years, 5 and many sons were
born to him there.

His wife Bathsheba, daughter of Ammiel, bore him four sons: Shimea, Shobab, Nathan, and Solomon.

6 He had nine other sons: Ibhar, Elishua, Elpelet, 7 Nogah, Nepheg, Japhia,
8 Elishama, Eliada, and Eliphelet. 9 In addition to all these sons, David had sons
by his concubines. He also had a daughter, Tamar.

The Descendants of King Solomon

10 This is the line of King Solomon's
descendants from father to son: Solomon, Rehoboam, Abijah, Asa, Jehoshaphat, 11 Jehoram, Ahaziah, Joash,
12 Amaziah, Uzziah, Jotham, 13 Ahaz,
Hezekiah, Manasseh, 14 Amon, and Josiah. 15 Josiah had four sons: Johanan,
Jehoiakim, Zedekiah, and Joahaz. 16 Jehoiakim had two sons: Jehoiachin and
Zedekiah.

The Descendants of King Jehoiachin

17 These are the descendants of King
Jehoiachin, who was taken prisoner by
the Babylonians. Jehoiachin had seven
sons: Shealtiel, 18 Malchiram, Pedaiah,
Shenazzar, Jekamiah, Hoshama, and
Nedabiah. 19 Pedaiah had two sons, Ze-
rubbabel and Shimei. Zerubbabel was
the father of two sons, Meshullam and
Hananiah, and one daughter, Shelomith.
20 He had five other sons: Hashubah,
Ohel, Berechiah, Hasadiah, and Jushab
Hesed.

21 Hananiah had two sons, Pelatiah
and Jeshaiah. Jeshaiah was the father of
Rephaiah, who was the father of Arnan,
the father of Obadiah, the father of
Shecaniah.[g] 22 Shecaniah had one son,
Shemaiah, and five grandsons: Hattush,
Igal, Bariah, Neariah, and Shaphat.
23 Neariah had three sons: Elioenai, Hiz-
kiah, and Azrikam. 24 Elioenai had seven
sons: Hodaviah, Eliashib, Pelaiah, Akkub, Johanan, Delaiah, and Anani.

The Descendants of Judah

4 These are some of the descendants
of Judah: Perez, Hezron, Carmi,
Hur, and Shobal. 2 Shobal was the father
of Reaiah, who was the father of Jahath,
the father of Ahumai and Lahad, the ancestors of the people who lived in Zorah.

3-4 Hur was the oldest son of his father
Caleb's wife Ephrath, and his descendants founded the city of Bethlehem. Hur
had three sons: Etam, Penuel, and Ezer.
Etam had three sons:[h] Jezreel, Ishma,
and Idbash, and one daughter, Hazzelel-
poni. Penuel founded the city of Gedor,
and Ezer founded Hushah.

5 Ashhur, who founded the town of Tekoa, had two wives, Helah and Naarah.
6 He and Naarah had four sons: Ahuz-
zam, Hepher, Temeni, and Haahashtari.
7 Ashhur and Helah had three sons: Zereth, Izhar, and Ethnan.

8 Koz was the father of Anub and Zo-
bebah, and the ancestor of the clans descended from Aharhel son of Harum.

9 There was a man named Jabez, who
was the most respected member of his
family. His mother had given him the
name Jabez,[i] because his birth had
been very painful. 10 But Jabez prayed to
the God of Israel, "Bless me, God, and
give me much land. Be with me and keep
me from anything evil that might cause
me pain." And God gave him what he
prayed for.

[g] *Verse 21 in Hebrew is unclear.* [h] *Some ancient translations* sons; *Hebrew* fathers.
[i] JABEZ: *This name sounds like the Hebrew for "pain."*

Other Family Lists

11 Caleb, the brother of Shuhah, had a
son, Mehir. Mehir was the father of Esh-
ton, 12 who had three sons: Bethrapha,
Paseah, and Tehinnah. Tehinnah was
the founder of the city of Nahash. The
descendants of these men lived in
Recah.
13 Kenaz had two sons, Othniel and Seraiah. Othniel also had two sons, Ha-
thath and Meonothai.[j] 14 Meonothai
was the father of Ophrah.
Seraiah was the father of Joab, the
founder of Handcraft Valley, where all
the people were skilled workers.
15 Caleb son of Jephunneh had three
sons: Iru, Elah, and Naam. And Elah
was the father of Kenaz.
16 Jehallelel had four sons: Ziph, Zi-
phah, Tiria, and Asarel.
17-18 Ezrah had four sons: Jether, Mered, Epher, and Jalon. Mered married
Bithiah, a daughter of the king of Egypt,
and they had a daughter, Miriam, and
two sons, Shammai and Ishbah. Ishbah
founded the town of Eshtemoa. Mered
also married a woman from the tribe of
Judah, and they had three sons: Jered,
who founded the town of Gedor; Heber,
founder of the town of Soco; and Jeku-
thiel, founder of the town of Zanoah.
19 Hodiah married the sister of Naham.
Their descendants founded the clan of
Garm, which lived in the town of Keilah,
and the clan of Maacath, which lived in
the town of Eshtemoa.[k]
20 Shimon had four sons: Amnon, Rin-
nah, Benhanan, and Tilon.
Ishi had two sons: Zoheth and Ben-zoheth.

The Descendants of Shelah

21 Shelah was one of Judah's sons. His
descendants included Er, who founded
the town of Lecah; Laadah, founder of
the town of Mareshah; the clan of linen
weavers, who lived in the town of Beth
Ashbea; 22 Jokim and the people who
lived in the town of Cozeba; and Joash
and Saraph, who married Moabite
women and then settled in Bethlehem.[l]
(These traditions are very old.) 23 They
were potters in the service of the king
and lived in the towns of Netaim and
Gederah.

The Descendants of Simeon

24 Simeon had five sons: Nemuel, Jamin, Jarib, Zerah, and Shaul. 25 Shaul's
son was Shallum, his grandson was Mibsam, and his great-grandson was
Mishma. 26 Then from Mishma the line
descended through Hammuel, Zaccur,
and Shimei. 27 Shimei had sixteen sons
and six daughters, but his relatives had
fewer children, and the tribe of Simeon
did not grow as much as the tribe of Judah did.
28 Down to the time of King David the
descendants of Simeon lived in the following towns: Beersheba, Moladah, Hazarshual, 29 Bilhah, Ezem, Tolad,
30 Bethuel, Hormah, Ziklag, 31 Beth Mar-
caboth, Hazarsusim, Bethbiri, and Shaaraim. 32 They also lived in five other
places: Etam, Ain, Rimmon, Tochen,
and Ashan, 33 and the surrounding villages, as far southwest as the town of
Baalath. These are the records which
they kept of their families and of the
places where they lived.
34-38 The following men were the heads
of their clans:

Meshobab, Jamlech, Joshah son of Amaziah, Joel,
Jehu (the son of Joshibiah, the son of Seraiah, the son of Asiel),
Elioenai, Jaakobah, Jeshohaiah, Asaiah, Adiel, Jesimiel, Benaiah,
Ziza (the son of Shiphi, the son of Allon, a descendant of Jedaiah, Shimri, and Shemaiah).

Because their families continued to
grow, 39 they spread out westward almost to Gerar[m] and pastured their sheep
on the eastern side of the valley in which
that city is located. 40 They found plenty
of fertile pasture lands there in a stretch
of open country that was quiet and
peaceful. The people who had lived
there before were Hamites.
41 In the time of King Hezekiah of Judah, the men named above went to Gerar and destroyed the tents and huts of
the people who lived there.[n] They drove

[j] *Some ancient translations* Meonothai; *Hebrew does not have this name.* [k] *Verse 19 in Hebrew is unclear.* [l] *Probable text* settled in Bethlehem; *Hebrew unclear.* [m] *Some ancient translations* Gerar; *Hebrew* Gedor. [n] the tents and huts . . . there; *or* the tents of the people who lived there, and the Meunites also.

the people out and settled there permanently because there was plenty of pasture for their sheep. 42 Five hundred
other members of the tribe of Simeon
went east to Edom. They were led by the
sons of Ishi: Pelatiah, Neariah, Rephaiah, and Uzziel. 43 There they killed the
surviving Amalekites, and they have
lived there ever since.

The Descendants of Reuben

5 These are the descendants of Reuben, the oldest of Jacob's sons. (Because he had sex with one of his father's
concubines, he lost the rights belonging
to the first-born son, and those rights
were given to Joseph. 2 It was the tribe of
Judah, however, that became the strongest and provided a ruler for all the
tribes.) 3 Reuben, the oldest of Jacob's
sons, had four sons: Hanoch, Pallu, Hezron, and Carmi.

4-6 These are the descendants of Joel
from generation to generation: Shemaiah, Gog, Shimei, Micah, Reaiah, Baal,
and Beerah. The Assyrian emperor, Tiglath Pileser, captured Beerah, a leader of
the tribe, and deported him.

7 The family records list the following
clan leaders in the tribe of Reuben: Jeiel,
Zechariah, 8 and Bela, the son of Azaz
and grandson of Shema, of the clan of
Joel. This clan lived in Aroer and in the
territory from there north to Nebo and
Baal Meon. 9 They had large herds in the
land of Gilead, and so they occupied the
land as far east as the desert that
stretches all the way to the Euphrates
River.

10 In the time of King Saul the tribe of
Reuben attacked the Hagrites, killed
them in battle, and occupied their land
in the eastern part of Gilead.

The Descendants of Gad

11 The tribe of Gad lived to the north of
Reuben in the land of Bashan as far east
as Salecah. 12 Joel was the founder of the
leading clan, and Shapham of the second most important clan. Janai and Shaphat were founders of other clans in
Bashan. 13 The other members of the
tribe belonged to the following seven
clans: Michael, Meshullam, Sheba, Jo-
rai, Jacan, Zia, and Eber. 14 They were
descendants of Abihail son of Huri,
whose ancestors were traced back as
follows: Abihail, Huri, Jaroah, Gilead,
Michael, Jeshishai, Jahdo, Buz. 15 Ahi,
the son of Abdiel and grandson of Guni,
was head of these clans. 16 They lived in
the territory of Bashan and Gilead, in
the towns there and all over the pasture
lands of Sharon. (17 These records were
compiled in the days of King Jotham
of Judah and King Jeroboam II of
Israel.)

The Armies of the Eastern Tribes

18 In the tribes of Reuben, Gad, and
East Manasseh there were 44,760 soldiers, well-trained in the use of shields,
swords, and bows. 19 They went to war
against the Hagrite tribes of Jetur, Naphish, and Nodab. 20 They put their trust
in God and prayed to him for help, and
God answered their prayers and made
them victorious over the Hagrites and
their allies. 21 They captured from the enemy 50,000 camels, 250,000 sheep, and
2,000 donkeys, and took 100,000 prisoners of war. 22 They killed many of the enemy, because the war was God's will.
And they went on living in that territory
until the exile.[o]

The People of East Manasseh

23 The people of East Manasseh settled
in the territory of Bashan as far north as
Baal Hermon, Senir, and Mount Hermon, and their population increased
greatly. 24 The following were the heads
of their clans: Epher, Ishi, Eliel, Azriel,
Jeremiah, Hodaviah, and Jahdiel. They
were all outstanding soldiers, well-
known leaders of their clans.

The Eastern Tribes Are Deported

25 But the people were unfaithful to the
God of their ancestors and deserted him
to worship the gods of the nations whom
God had driven out of the land. 26 So God
caused Emperor Pul of Assyria (also
known as Tiglath Pileser) to invade their
country. He deported the tribes of
Reuben, Gad, and East Manasseh and
settled them permanently in Halah,
Habor, and Hara, and by the Gozan
River.

[o] THE EXILE: *About 733 B.C. the Assyrians conquered northern Israel and the Israelite territory east of the Jordan River and deported the people (see 2 K 15.29).*

The Family Line of the High Priests

6 Levi had three sons: Gershon, Kohath, and Merari. 2 Kohath had four sons: Amram, Izhar, Hebron, and Uzziel.

3 Amram had two sons, Aaron and Moses, and one daughter, Miriam.

Aaron had four sons: Nadab, Abihu, Eleazar, and Ithamar.

4 The descendants of Eleazar from generation to generation are as follows: Phinehas, Abishua, 5 Bukki, Uzzi, 6 Zerahiah, Meraioth, 7 Amariah, Ahitub, 8 Zadok, Ahimaaz, 9 Azariah, Johanan, 10 Azariah (the one who served in the Temple which King Solomon built in Jerusalem), 11 Amariah, Ahitub, 12 Zadok, Shallum, 13 Hilkiah, Azariah, 14 Seraiah, Jehozadak. 15 King Nebuchadnezzar deported Jehozadak along with the other people of Judah and Jerusalem whom the LORD sent into exile.

Other Descendants of Levi

16 Levi had three sons: Gershon, Kohath, and Merari. 17 Each of them also had sons. Gershon was the father of Libni and Shimei; 18 Kohath was the father of Amram, Izhar, Hebron, and Uzziel; 19 and Merari was the father of Mahli and Mushi.

20 These are the descendants of Gershon from generation to generation: Libni, Jahath, Zimmah, 21 Joah, Iddo, Zerah, Jeatherai.

22 These are the descendants of Kohath from generation to generation: Amminadab, Korah, Assir, 23 Elkanah, Ebiasaph, Assir, 24 Tahath, Uriel, Uzziah, Shaul.

25 Elkanah had two sons, Amasai and Ahimoth. 26 These are Ahimoth's descendants from generation to generation: Elkanah, Zophai, Nahath, 27 Eliab, Jeroham, Elkanah.

28 Samuel had two sons: Joel,[p] the older, and Abijah, the younger.

29 These are the descendants of Merari from generation to generation: Mahli, Libni, Shimei, Uzzah, 30 Shimea, Haggiah, Asaiah.

The Temple Musicians

31 These are the men whom King David put in charge of the music at the place of worship in Jerusalem after the Covenant Box was moved there. 32 They took regular turns of duty at the Tent of the LORD's presence during the time before King Solomon built the Temple. 33 The family lines of those who held this office are as follows:

The clan of Kohath: Heman, the leader of the first choir, was the son of Joel. His family line went back to Jacob as follows: Heman, Joel, Samuel, 34 Elkanah, Jeroham, Eliel, Toah, 35 Zuph, Elkanah, Mahath, Amasai, 36 Elkanah, Joel, Azariah, Zephaniah, 37 Tahath, Assir, Ebiasaph, Korah, 38 Izhar, Kohath, Levi, Jacob.

39 Asaph was leader of the second choir. His family line went back to Levi as follows: Asaph, Berechiah, Shimea, 40 Michael, Baaseiah, Malchijah, 41 Ethni, Zerah, Adaiah, 42 Ethan, Zimmah, Shimei, 43 Jahath, Gershon, Levi.

44 Ethan of the clan of Merari was the leader of the third choir. His family line went back to Levi as follows: Ethan, Kishi, Abdi, Malluch, 45 Hashabiah, Amaziah, Hilkiah, 46 Amzi, Bani, Shemer, 47 Mahli, Mushi, Merari, Levi.

48 The other Levites were assigned all the other duties at the place of worship.

The Descendants of Aaron

49 Aaron and his descendants presented the offerings of incense and offered the sacrifices that were burnt on the altar. They were responsible for all the worship in the Most Holy Place and for the sacrifices by which God forgives Israel's sins. They did all this in accordance with the instructions given by Moses, God's servant. 50 This is the line of Aaron's descendants: Eleazar, Phinehas, Abishua, 51 Bukki, Uzzi, Zerahiah, 52 Meraioth, Amariah, Ahitub, 53 Zadok, Ahimaaz.

Where the Levites Lived

54 This is the territory assigned to the descendants of Aaron of the clan of Kohath. They received the first share of the land assigned to the Levites. 55 This included Hebron in the territory of Judah and the pasture lands around it. 56 The fields and villages, however, that belonged to the city were assigned to Caleb son of Jephunneh. 57-59 The following towns were assigned to Aaron's

[p] *Some ancient translations (see also 1 S 8.2)* Joel; *Hebrew does not have this name.*

descendants: Hebron, a city of refuge,[q]
Jattir, and the towns of Libnah, Eshtemoa, Hilen, Debir, Ashan, and Beth Shemesh, with their pasture lands. 60 In the
territory of Benjamin they were assigned the following towns with their
pasture lands: Geba, Alemeth, and Anathoth. This made a total of thirteen
towns for all their families to live in.
61 Ten towns in the territory of West
Manasseh were assigned by lot to the
rest of the clan of Kohath, family by
family.

62 To the clan of Gershon, family by
family, were assigned thirteen towns in
the territories of Issachar, Asher, Naphtali, and East Manasseh in Bashan. 63 In
the same way, twelve towns in the territories of Reuben, Gad, and Zebulun
were assigned to the clan of Merari, family by family. 64 In this way the people of
Israel assigned towns for the Levites to
live in, together with the pasture lands
around the towns. (65 The towns in the
territories of Judah, Simeon, and Benjamin, mentioned above, were also assigned by drawing lots.)

66 Some of the families of the clan of
Kohath were assigned towns and pasture lands in the territory of Ephraim:
67 Shechem, the city of refuge in the hills
of Ephraim, Gezer, 68 Jokmeam, Beth
Horon, 69 Aijalon, and Gath Rimmon.
70 In the territory of West Manasseh they
were assigned the towns of Aner and
Bileam with the surrounding pasture
lands.

71 The families of the clan of Gershon
were assigned the following towns, with
the surrounding pasture lands:

In the territory of East Manasseh: Golan in Bashan, and Ashtaroth.

72 In the territory of Issachar: Kedesh,
Daberath, 73 Ramoth, and Anem.

74 In the territory of Asher: Mashal,
Abdon, 75 Hukok, and Rehob.

76 In the territory of Naphtali: Kedesh
in Galilee, Hammon, and Kiriathaim.

77 The remaining families of the clan of
Merari were assigned the following
towns with the surrounding pasture
lands:

In the territory of Zebulun: Rimmono
and Tabor.

78 In the territory of Reuben, east of the
Jordan River beyond Jericho: Bezer on
the plateau, Jahzah, 79 Kedemoth, and
Mephaath.

80 In the territory of Gad: Ramoth in
Gilead, Mahanaim, 81 Heshbon, and
Jazer.

The Descendants of Issachar

7 Issachar had four sons: Tola, Puah,
Jashub, and Shimron.

2 Tola had six sons: Uzzi, Rephaiah,
Jeriel, Jahmai, Ibsam, and Shemuel.
They were heads of families of the clan
of Tola and were famous soldiers. At the
time of King David their descendants
numbered 22,600.

3 Uzzi had one son, Izrahiah. Izrahiah
and his four sons, Michael, Obadiah,
Joel, and Isshiah, were all heads of families. 4 They had so many wives and children that their descendants were able to
provide 36,000 men for military duty.

5 The official records of all the families
of the tribe of Issachar listed 87,000 men
eligible for military duty.

The Descendants of Benjamin and Dan

6 Benjamin had three sons: Bela, Becher, and Jediael.

7 Bela had five sons: Ezbon, Uzzi, Uzziel, Jerimoth, and Iri. They were heads
of families in the clan and were all famous soldiers. Their descendants included 22,034 men eligible for military
duty.

8 Becher had nine sons: Zemirah, Joash, Eliezer, Elioenai, Omri, Jeremoth,
Abijah, Anathoth, and Alemeth. 9 The official record of their descendants by
families listed 20,200 men eligible for
military duty.

10 Jediael had one son, Bilhan, and Bilhan had seven sons: Jeush, Benjamin,
Ehud, Chenaanah, Zethan, Tarshish,
and Ahishahar. 11 They were heads of
families in the clan and were all famous
soldiers. Their descendants included
17,200 men eligible for military duty.
12 Shuppim and Huppim also belonged
to this tribe.

Dan had one son, Hushim.[r]

[q] CITY OF REFUGE: *If anyone accidentally killed someone, he could escape to one of these cities and be safe from revenge (see Js 20.1-9).* [r] *Probable text* Shuppim . . . Hushim *(see Gn 46.23; Nu 26.39, 42); Hebrew* And Shuppim and Huppim, sons of Ir; Hushim son of Aher.

The Descendants of Naphtali

13 Naphtali had four sons: Jahziel,
Guni, Jezer, and Shallum. (They were
descendants of Bilhah.[s])

The Descendants of Manasseh

14 By his Aramean concubine, Manasseh had two sons, Asriel and Machir.
Machir was the father of Gilead. 15 Machir found a wife for Huppim and one
for Shuppim. His sister's name was Maacah. Machir's second son was Zelophehad, and he had only daughters.
16 Maacah, Machir's wife, gave birth to
two sons, whom they named Peresh and
Sheresh. Peresh had two sons, Ulam and
Rakem, 17 and Ulam had a son named
Bedan. These are all descendants of Gilead, the son of Machir and grandson of
Manasseh.
18 Gilead's sister Hammolecheth had
three sons: Ishod, Abiezer, and Mahlah.
(19 Shemida had four sons: Ahian, Shechem, Likhi, and Aniam.)

The Descendants of Ephraim

20 These are the descendants of
Ephraim from generation to generation:
Shuthelah, Bered, Tahath, Eleadah, Tahath, 21 Zabad, Shuthelah. Ephraim had
two other sons besides Shuthelah: Ezer
and Elead, who were killed when they
tried to steal the livestock belonging to
the native inhabitants of Gath. 22 Their
father Ephraim mourned for them for
many days, and his relatives came to
comfort him. 23 Then he had intercourse
with his wife again, and she became
pregnant and had a son. They named
him Beriah,[t] because of the trouble that
had come to their family.
24 Ephraim had a daughter named
Sheerah. She built the towns of Upper
and Lower Beth Horon, and Uzzen
Sheerah.
25 Ephraim also had a son named Re-
phah, whose descendants were as follows: Resheph, Telah, Tahan, 26 Ladan,
Ammihud, Elishama, 27 Nun, Joshua.
28 The territory which they took and
settled included Bethel and the towns
around it, as far east as Naaran and as
far west as Gezer and the towns around
it. It also included the cities of Shechem
and Ayyah, and the towns around them.
29 The descendants of Manasseh controlled the cities of Beth Shan, Taanach,
Megiddo, and Dor, and the towns
around them.

All these are the places where the descendants of Joseph son of Jacob lived.

The Descendants of Asher

30 These are the descendants of Asher.
He had four sons: Imnah, Ishvah, Ishvi,
and Beriah; and one daughter, Serah.
31 Beriah had two sons, Heber and
Malchiel. (Malchiel founded the city of
Birzaith.)
32 Heber had three sons: Japhlet, Shomer, and Hotham; and one daughter,
Shua.
33 Japhlet also had three sons: Pasach,
Bimhal, and Ashvath.
34 His brother Shomer had three sons:
Rohgah, Jehubbah, and Aram.
35 His brother Hotham[u] had four sons:
Zophah, Imna, Shelesh, and Amal.
36 The descendants of Zophah were
Suah, Harnepher, Shual, Beri, Imrah,
37 Bezer, Hod, Shamma, Shilshah, Ithran, and Beera.
38 The descendants of Jether were Jephunneh, Pispa, and Ara, 39 and the
descendants of Ulla were Arah, Hanniel,
and Rizia.
40 All of these were descendants of
Asher. They were heads of families, famous fighting men, outstanding leaders.
Asher's descendants included 26,000
men eligible for military duty.

The Descendants of Benjamin

8 Benjamin had five sons. In order
of age they were Bela, Ashbel,
Aharah, 2 Nohah, and Rapha.
3 The descendants of Bela were Addar,
Gera, Abihud, 4 Abishua, Naaman,
Ahoah, 5 Gera, Shephuphan, and
Huram.
6-7 The descendants of Ehud were Naaman, Ahijah, and Gera. They were heads
of families that lived in Geba, but which
were forced out and went to live in Manahath. Gera, the father of Uzza and Ahi-
hud, led them in this move.
8-9 Shaharaim divorced two wives, Hushim and Baara. Later, when he lived in
the country of Moab, he married Hodesh

[s] BILHAH: *A concubine of Jacob and the mother of his two sons Dan and Naphtali.* [t] BERIAH: *This name sounds like the Hebrew for "in trouble."* [u] *Probable text (see verse 32)* Hotham; *Hebrew* Helem.

and had seven sons: Jobab, Zibia, Mesha, Malcam, 10 Jeuz, Sachia, and Mirmah. His sons all became heads of families.

11 He also had two sons by Hushim: Abitub and Elpaal.

12 Elpaal had three sons: Eber, Misham, and Shemed. It was Shemed who built the cities of Ono and Lod and the surrounding villages.

The Benjaminites in Gath and Aijalon

13 Beriah and Shema were heads of families that settled in the city of Aijalon and drove out the people who lived in the city of Gath. 14 Beriah's descendants included Ahio, Shashak, Jeremoth, 15 Zebadiah, Arad, Eder, 16 Michael, Ishpah, and Joha.

The Benjaminites in Jerusalem

17 Elpaal's descendants included Zebadiah, Meshullam, Hizki, Heber, 18 Ishmerai, Izliah, and Jobab.

19 Shimei's descendants included Jakim, Zichri, Zabdi, 20 Elienai, Zillethai, Eliel, 21 Adaiah, Beraiah, and Shimrath.

22 Shashak's descendants included Ishpan, Eber, Eliel, 23 Abdon, Zichri, Hanan, 24 Hananiah, Elam, Anthothijah, 25 Iphdeiah, and Penuel.

26 Jeroham's descendants included Shamsherai, Shehariah, Athaliah, 27 Jaareshiah, Elijah, and Zichri.

28 These were the ancestral heads of families and their principal descendants who lived in Jerusalem.

The Benjaminites in Gibeon and Jerusalem

29 Jeiel[v] founded the city of Gibeon and settled there. His wife was named Maacah, 30 and his oldest son, Abdon. His other sons were Zur, Kish, Baal, Ner,[w] Nadab, 31 Gedor, Ahio, Zechariah, 32 and Mikloth, the father of Shimeah. Their descendants lived in Jerusalem near other families of their clan.

The Family of King Saul

33 Ner was the father of Kish, and Kish was the father of King Saul. Saul had four sons: Jonathan, Malchishua, Abinadab, and Eshbaal.[x] 34 Jonathan was the father of Meribbaal,[y] who was the father of Micah.

35 Micah had four sons: Pithon, Melech, Tarea, and Ahaz. 36 Ahaz was the father of Jehoaddah, who was the father of three sons: Alemeth, Azmaveth, and Zimri. Zimri was the father of Moza, 37 Moza the father of Binea, Binea of Raphah, Raphah of Eleasah, and Eleasah of Azel.

38 Azel had six sons: Azrikam, Bocheru, Ishmael, Sheariah, Obadiah, and Hanan. 39 Azel's brother Eshek had three sons: Ulam, Jeush, and Eliphelet.

40 Ulam's sons were outstanding soldiers and archers. He had a hundred and fifty sons and grandsons in all. All those named above were members of the tribe of Benjamin.

The People Who Returned from Captivity

9 All the people of Israel were listed according to their families, and this information was recorded in *The Book of the Kings of Israel.*

The people of Judah had been deported to Babylon as punishment for their sins. 2 The first to return to their property in the cities included Israelite citizens, priests, Levites, and Temple workers. 3 People from the tribes of Judah, Benjamin, Ephraim, and Manasseh went to live in Jerusalem.

4-6 There were 690 families of the tribe of Judah who lived in Jerusalem.

The descendants of Judah's son Perez had as their leader Uthai, the son of Ammihud and grandson of Omri. His other ancestors included Imri and Bani.

The descendants of Judah's son Shelah had as their leader Asaiah, who was the head of his family.

The descendants of Judah's son Zerah had Jeuel as their leader.

7-8 The following members of the tribe of Benjamin lived in Jerusalem:

Sallu son of Meshullam, who was the son of Hodaviah, the son of Hassenuah
Ibneiah son of Jeroham
Elah, the son of Uzzi and grandson of Michri

[v] *Probable text (and see 9.35)* Jeiel; *Hebrew does not have this name.* [w] *One ancient translation (and see 9.36)* Ner; *Hebrew does not have this name.* [x] ESHBAAL: *Called Ishbosheth in 2 S 2.8 and elsewhere in 2 Samuel.* [y] MERIBBAAL: *Called Mephibosheth in 2 S 4.4 and elsewhere in 2 Samuel.*

Meshullam son of Shephatiah,
who was the son of Reuel, the
son of Ibnijah

9 There were 956 families of this tribe
living there. All the men named above
were heads of families.

The Priests Who Lived in Jerusalem

10-12 The following priests lived in Jerusalem:

Jedaiah, Jehoiarib, and Jachin
Azariah son of Hilkiah (the chief official in the Temple), whose ancestors included Meshullam, Zadok, Meraioth, and Ahitub
Adaiah son of Jeroham, whose ancestors included Pashhur and Malchijah
Maasai son of Adiel, whose ancestors included Jahzerah, Meshullam, Meshillemith, and Immer

13 The priests who were heads of families totaled 1,760. They were experts in
all the work carried on in the Temple.

The Levites Who Lived in Jerusalem

14-16 The following Levites lived in Jerusalem:

Shemaiah son of Hasshub, whose ancestors included Azrikam and Hashabiah, of the clan of Merari
Bakbakkar, Heresh, and Galal
Mattaniah son of Mica, whose ancestors included Zichri and Asaph
Obadiah son of Shemaiah, whose ancestors included Galal and Jeduthun
Berechiah, the son of Asa and grandson of Elkanah, who lived in the territory that belonged to the town of Netophah

The Temple Guards Who Lived in Jerusalem

17 The following Temple guards lived
in Jerusalem: Shallum, Akkub, Talmon,
and Ahiman. Shallum was their leader.
18 Down to that time members of their
clans had been stationed at the eastern
entrance to the King's Gate.[z] Formerly
they had stood guard at the gates to the
camps of the Levites.
19 Shallum, the son of Kore and grandson of Ebiasaph, together with his fellow
members of the clan of Korah, was responsible for guarding the entrance to
the Tent of the LORD's presence, just as
their ancestors had been when they
were in charge of the LORD's camp.
20 Phinehas son of Eleazar—may the
LORD be with him!—had supervised
them at one time.
21 Zechariah son of Meshelemiah was
also a guard at the entrance to the Tent
of the LORD's presence.
22 In all, 212 men were chosen as
guards for the entrances and gates. They
were registered according to the villages
where they lived. It was King David and
the prophet Samuel who had put their
ancestors in these responsible positions.
23 They and their descendants continued
to guard the gates to the Temple.
24 There was a gate facing in each direction, north, south, east, and west, and
each had a chief guard. 25 These guards
were assisted by their relatives, who
lived in the villages and who had to take
turns at guard duty for seven days at a
time. 26 The four chief guards were Levites and had the final responsibility.
They were also responsible for the
rooms in the Temple and for the supplies
kept there. 27 They lived near the Temple, because it was their duty to guard it
and to open the gates every morning.

The Other Levites

28 Other Levites were responsible for
the utensils used in worship. They
checked them out and checked them
back in every time they were used.
29 Others were in charge of the other sacred equipment, and of the flour, wine,
olive oil, incense, and spices. 30 But the
responsibility for mixing the spices belonged to the priests.
31 A Levite named Mattithiah, oldest
son of Shallum, of the clan of Korah,
was responsible for preparing the baked
offerings.[a] 32 Members of the clan of Kohath were responsible for preparing the
sacred bread[b] for the Temple every
Sabbath.

[z] KING'S GATE: *The east gate of the Temple, through which the king usually entered.* [a] BAKED OFFERINGS: *Thin cakes of flour and olive oil which were baked and then presented as offerings to God (see Lv 2.4-6).* [b] SACRED BREAD: *Twelve loaves of bread which were placed on a table in the Temple each Sabbath as an offering to God (see Lv 24.5-9).*

33 Some Levite families were responsible for the Temple music. The heads of
these families lived in some of the Temple buildings and were free from other
duties, because they were on call day
and night.
34 The men named above were heads
of Levite families, according to their ancestral lines. They were the leaders who
lived in Jerusalem.

The Ancestors and Descendants of King Saul

(1 Chronicles 8.29-38)

35 Jeiel founded the city of Gibeon and
settled there. His wife was named Maacah. 36 His oldest son was Abdon, and his
other sons were Zur, Kish, Baal, Ner,
Nadab, 37 Gedor, Ahio, Zechariah, and
Mikloth, 38 the father of Shimeah. Their
descendants lived in Jerusalem near
other families of their clan.
39 Ner was the father of Kish, and Kish
was the father of Saul. Saul had four
sons: Jonathan, Malchishua, Abinadab,
and Eshbaal.[c] 40 Jonathan was the
father of Meribbaal,[d] who was the
father of Micah. 41 Micah had four sons:
Pithon, Melech, Tarea, and Ahaz.[e]
42 Ahaz was the father of Jarah, who was
the father of three sons: Alemeth, Azmaveth, and Zimri. Zimri was the father of
Moza, 43 Moza the father of Binea, Binea
of Rephaiah, Rephaiah of Eleasah, and
Eleasah of Azel.
44 Azel had six sons: Azrikam, Bocheru, Ishmael, Sheariah, Obadiah, and
Hanan.

The Death of King Saul

(1 Samuel 31.1-13)

10 The Philistines fought a battle
against the Israelites on Mount
Gilboa. Many Israelites were killed
there, and the rest of them, including
King Saul and his sons, fled. 2 But the
Philistines caught up with them and
killed three of Saul's sons, Jonathan,
Abinadab, and Malchishua. 3 The fighting was heavy around Saul, and he was
hit by enemy arrows and badly
wounded. 4 He said to the young man
carrying his weapons, "Draw your
sword and kill me, to keep these godless
Philistines from gloating over me." But
the young man was too terrified to do it.
So Saul took his own sword and threw
himself on it. 5 The young man saw that
Saul was dead, so he too threw himself
on his sword and died. 6 So Saul and his
three sons all died together, and none of
his descendants ever ruled. 7 When the
Israelites who lived in Jezreel Valley
heard that the army had fled and that
Saul and his sons had died, they abandoned their towns and ran off. Then the
Philistines came and occupied them.
8 The day after the battle the Philistines went to plunder the corpses, and
they found the bodies of Saul and his
sons lying on Mount Gilboa. 9 They cut
off Saul's head, stripped off his armor,
and sent messengers with them throughout Philistia to tell the good news to their
idols and to their people. 10 They put his
weapons in one of their temples and
hung his head in the temple of their god
Dagon. 11 When the people of Jabesh in
Gilead heard what the Philistines had
done to Saul, 12 the bravest men went
and got the bodies of Saul and his sons
and took them to Jabesh. They buried
them there under an oak and fasted for
seven days.
13 Saul died because he was unfaithful
to the LORD. He disobeyed the LORD's
commands; he tried to find guidance by
consulting the spirits of the dead 14 instead of consulting the LORD. So the LORD
killed him and gave control of the kingdom to David son of Jesse.

David Becomes King of Israel and Judah

(2 Samuel 5.1-10)

11 All the people of Israel went to
David at Hebron and said to him,
"We are your own flesh and blood. 2 In
the past, even when Saul was still our
king, you led the people of Israel in battle, and the LORD your God promised you
that you would lead his people and be
their ruler." 3 So all the leaders of Israel
came to King David at Hebron. He made
a sacred alliance with them, they
anointed him, and he became king of Israel, just as the LORD had promised
through Samuel.
4 King David and all the Israelites went

[c] ESHBAAL: *Called Ishbosheth in 2 S 2.8 and elsewhere in 2 Samuel.* [d] MERIBBAAL: *Called Mephibosheth in 2 S 4.4 and elsewhere in 2 Samuel.* [e] *Some ancient translations* Ahaz *(see 1 Ch 8.35); Hebrew does not have this name.*

and attacked the city of Jerusalem. It
was then known as Jebus, and the Jebusites, the original inhabitants of the
land, were still living there. 5 The Jebusites told David he would never get inside the city, but David captured their
fortress of Zion, and it became known as
"David's City." 6 David said, "The first
man to kill a Jebusite will be commander of the army!" Joab, whose
mother was Zeruiah, led the attack and
became commander. 7 Because David
went to live in the fortress, it came to be
called "David's City." 8 He rebuilt the
city, starting at the place where land was
filled in on the east side of the hill, and
Joab restored the rest of the city. 9 David
grew stronger and stronger, because the
LORD Almighty was with him.

David's Famous Soldiers

(2 Samuel 23.8-39)

10 This is the list of David's famous soldiers. Together with the rest of the people of Israel, they helped him become
king, as the LORD had promised, and they
kept his kingdom strong.
11 First was Jashobeam of the clan of
Hachmon, the leader of "The Three."[f]
He fought with his spear against three
hundred men and killed them all in one
battle. 12 Next among the famous
"Three" was Eleazar son of Dodo, of the
clan of Ahoh. 13 He fought on David's
side against the Philistines at the battle
of Pas Dammim. He was in a barley field
when the Israelites started to run away,
14 so he and his men took a stand in the
middle of the field and fought the Philistines. The LORD gave him a great victory.
15 One day three of the thirty leading
soldiers went to a rock where David was
staying near Adullam Cave, while a
band of Philistines was camping in
Rephaim Valley. 16 At that time David
was on a fortified hill, and a group of
Philistines had occupied Bethlehem.
17 David got homesick and said, "How I
wish someone would bring me a drink of
water from the well by the gate in Bethlehem!" 18 The three famous soldiers
forced their way through the Philistine
camp, drew some water from the well,
and brought it back to David. But he
would not drink it; instead he poured it
out as an offering to the LORD 19 and said,
"I could never drink this! It would be like
drinking the blood of these men who
risked their lives!" So he refused to
drink it. These were the brave deeds of
the three famous soldiers.
20 Joab's brother Abishai was the
leader of "The Famous Thirty."[g] He
fought with his spear against three hundred men and killed them, and became
famous among "The Thirty."[h] 21 He was
the most famous of "The Thirty"[i] and
became their leader, but he was not as
famous as "The Three."
22 Benaiah son of Jehoiada from Kabzeel was a famous soldier; he did many
brave deeds, including killing two great
Moabite warriors. He once went down
into a pit on a snowy day and killed a
lion. 23 He also killed an Egyptian, a
huge man seven and a half feet tall, who
was armed with a gigantic spear. Benaiah attacked him with a club, snatched
the spear from the Egyptian's hand, and
killed him with it. 24 Those were the
brave deeds of Benaiah, who was one of
"The Thirty."[j] 25 He was outstanding
among "The Thirty," but not as famous
as "The Three." David put him in charge
of his bodyguard.
26-47 These are the other outstanding
soldiers:

Asahel, Joab's brother
Elhanan son of Dodo from Bethlehem
Shammoth from Harod
Helez from Pelet
Ira son of Ikkesh from Tekoa
Abiezer from Anathoth
Sibbecai from Hushah
Ilai from Ahoh
Maharai from Netophah
Heled son of Baanah from Netophah
Ithai son of Ribai from Gibeah in Benjamin
Benaiah from Pirathon
Hurai from the valleys near Gaash
Abiel from Arbah
Azmaveth from Bahurum
Eliahba from Shaalbon

[f] *One ancient translation (see also 2 S 23.8)* "The Three"; *Hebrew* "The Thirty." [g] *One ancient translation* Thirty; *Hebrew* Three. [h] *One ancient translation (see also 2 S 23.18)* "The Thirty"; *Hebrew* "The Three." [i] *Probable text (see 2 S 23.19)* most famous of "The Thirty"; *Hebrew unclear.* [j] *Probable text* "The Thirty"; *Hebrew* "The Three."

Hashem[k] from Gizon
Jonathan son of Shagee from Harar
Ahiam son of Sachar from Harar
Eliphal son of Ur
Hepher from Mecherah
Ahijah from Pelon
Hezro from Carmel
Naarai son of Ezbai
Joel brother of Nathan
Mibhar son of Hagri
Zelek from Ammon
Naharai, Joab's armorbearer, from Beeroth
Ira and Gareb from Jattir
Uriah the Hittite
Zabad son of Ahlai
Adina son of Shiza (a leading member of the tribe of Reuben, with his own group of thirty soldiers)
Hanan son of Maacah
Joshaphat from Mithan
Uzzia from Ashterah
Shamma and Jeiel, sons of Hotham, from Aroer
Jediael and Joha, sons of Shimri, from Tiz
Eliel from Mahavah
Jeribai and Joshaviah, sons of Elnaam
Ithmah from Moab
Eliel, Obed, and Jaasiel from Zobah[l]

David's Early Followers from the Tribe of Benjamin

12 David was living in Ziklag,
where he had gone to escape
from King Saul. There he was joined by
many experienced, reliable soldiers,
2 members of the tribe of Benjamin, to
which Saul belonged. They could shoot
arrows and sling stones either right-
handed or left-handed. 3-7 They were under the command of Ahiezer and Joash,
sons of Shemaah, from Gibeah.

These were the soldiers:

Jeziel and Pelet, sons of Azmaveth
Beracah and Jehu from Anathoth
Ishmaiah from Gibeon, a famous soldier and one of the leaders of "The Thirty"
Jeremiah, Jahaziel, Johannan, and Jozabad, from Gederah
Eluzai, Jerimoth, Bealiah, Shemariah, and Shephatiah, from Hariph
Elkanah, Isshiah, Azarel, Joezer, and Jashobeam, of the clan of Korah
Joelah and Zebadiah, sons of Jeroham, from Gedor

David's Followers from the Tribe of Gad

8 These are the names of the famous,
experienced soldiers from the tribe of
Gad who joined David's troops when he
was at the desert fort. They were experts
with shields and spears, as fierce looking as lions and as quick as mountain
deer. 9-13 They were ranked in the following order: Ezer, Obadiah, Eliab, Mish-
mannah, Jeremiah, Attai, Eliel,
Johanan, Elzabad, Jeremiah, and
Machbannai.

14 Some of these men from the tribe of
Gad were senior officers in command of
a thousand men, and others were junior
officers in command of a hundred. 15 In
the first month of one year, the time
when the Jordan River overflowed its
banks, they crossed the river, scattering
the people who lived in the valleys both
east and west of the river.

Followers from Benjamin and Judah

16 Once a group of men from the tribes
of Benjamin and Judah went out to the
fort where David was. 17 David went to
meet them and said, "If you are coming
as friends to help me, you are welcome
here. Join us! But if you intend to betray
me to my enemies, even though I have
not tried to hurt you, the God of our ancestors will know it and punish you."

18 God's spirit took control of one of
them, Amasai, who later became the
commander of "The Thirty," and he
called out,

"David son of Jesse, we are yours!
Success to you and those who help you!
God is on your side."

[k] *Probable text* Hashem; *Hebrew* the sons of Hashem. [l] *Probable text* from Zobah; *Hebrew* unclear.

David welcomed them and made them
officers in his army.

Followers from Manasseh

19 Some soldiers from the tribe of Manasseh went over to David's side when
he was marching out with the Philistines
to fight King Saul. Actually he did not
help the Philistines, for their kings were
afraid that he would betray them to his
former master Saul, so they sent him
back to Ziklag. 20 These are the soldiers
from Manasseh who went over to David's side when he was returning: Ad-
nah, Jozabad, Jediael, Michael,
Jozabad, Elihu, and Zillethai. In Manasseh they had all commanded units of a
thousand men. 21 They served David as
officers over his troops,[m] because they
were all outstanding soldiers. Later they
were officers in the Israelite army. 22 Almost every day new men joined David's
forces, so that his army was soon
enormous.

List of David's Forces

23-37 When David was at Hebron, many
trained soldiers joined his army to help
make him king in place of Saul, as the
LORD had promised. Their numbers were
as follows:

Judah: 6,800 well-equipped men,
armed with shields and spears;

Simeon: 7,100 well-trained men;

Levi: 4,600 men;

Followers of Jehoiada,
descendant of Aaron:
3,700 men;

Relatives of Zadok, an able
young fighter: 22 leading men;

Benjamin (Saul's own tribe): 3,000
men (most of the people of Benjamin
had remained loyal to Saul);

Ephraim: 20,800 men famous in their
own clans;

West Manasseh: 18,000 men chosen to
go and make David king;

Issachar: 200 leaders, together with
the men under their command (these
leaders knew what Israel should do and
the best time to do it);

Zebulun: 50,000 loyal and reliable
men ready to fight, trained to use all
kinds of weapons;

Naphtali: 1,000 leaders, together with
37,000 men armed with shields and
spears;

Dan: 28,600 trained men;

Asher: 40,000 men ready for battle;

Tribes east of the Jordan—Reuben,
Gad, and East Manasseh: 120,000 men
trained to use all kinds of weapons.

38 All these soldiers, ready for battle,
went to Hebron, determined to make
David king over all Israel. All the rest of
the people of Israel were united in the
same purpose. 39 They spent three days
there with David, feasting on the food
and drink which their relatives had prepared for them. 40 From as far away as
the northern tribes of Issachar, Zebulun,
and Naphtali, people came bringing
donkeys, camels, mules, and oxen
loaded with food—flour, figs, raisins,
wine, and olive oil. They also brought
cattle and sheep to kill and eat. All this
was an expression of the joy that was
felt throughout the whole country.

The Covenant Box Is Moved from Kiriath Jearim

(2 Samuel 6.1-11)

13 King David consulted with all
the officers in command of units
of a thousand men and units of a hundred men. 2 Then he announced to all the
people of Israel, "If you give your approval and if it is the will of the LORD our
God, let us send messengers to the rest
of our people and to the priests and Levites in their towns, and tell them to assemble here with us. 3 Then we will go
and get God's Covenant Box, which was
ignored while Saul was king." 4 The people were pleased with the suggestion
and agreed to it.

5 So David assembled the people of Israel from all over the country, from the
Egyptian border in the south to Hamath
Pass in the north, in order to bring the
Covenant Box from Kiriath Jearim to Jerusalem. 6 David and the people went to
the city of Baalah, that is, to Kiriath Jearim, in the territory of Judah, to get the
Covenant Box of God, which bears the
name of the LORD enthroned above the
winged creatures. 7 At Abinadab's house
they brought out the Covenant Box and
put it on a new cart. Uzzah and Ahio
guided the cart, 8 while David and all the
people danced with all their might to

[m] They served David . . . troops; *or* They helped David fight against the bands of raiders.

honor God. They sang and played musical instruments—harps, drums, cymbals, and trumpets.
9 As they came to the threshing place
of Chidon, the oxen stumbled, and Uzzah reached out and took hold of the
Covenant Box. 10 At once the LORD became angry with Uzzah and killed him
for touching the Box. He died there in
God's presence, 11 and so that place has
been called Perez Uzzah[n] ever since.
David was furious because the LORD had
punished Uzzah in anger.
12 Then David was afraid of God and
said, "How can I take the Covenant Box
with me now?" 13 So David did not take it
with him to Jerusalem. Instead, he left it
at the house of a man named Obed
Edom, a native of the city of Gath. 14 It
stayed there three months, and the LORD
blessed Obed Edom's family and everything that belonged to him.

David's Activities in Jerusalem

(2 Samuel 5.11-16)

14 King Hiram of Tyre sent a trade
mission to David; he provided
him with cedar logs and with stonemasons and carpenters to build a palace.
2 And so David realized that the LORD
had established him as king of Israel and
was making his kingdom prosperous for
the sake of his people.
3 There in Jerusalem, David married
more wives and had more sons and
daughters. 4 The following children were
born to him in Jerusalem: Shammua,
Shobab, Nathan, Solomon, 5 Ibhar, Elishua, Elpelet, 6 Nogah, Nepheg, Japhia,
7 Elishama, Beeliada,[o] and Eliphelet.

Victory over the Philistines

(2 Samuel 5.17-25)

8 When the Philistines heard that David had now been made king over the
whole country of Israel, their army went
out to capture him. So David marched
out to meet them. 9 The Philistines arrived at Rephaim Valley and began
plundering. 10 David asked God, "Shall I
attack the Philistines? Will you give me
the victory?"
The LORD answered, "Yes, attack! I
will give you the victory!"
11 So David attacked them at Baal Perazim and defeated them. He said, "God
has used me to break through the enemy
army like a flood." So that place is called
Baal Perazim.[p] 12 When the Philistines
fled, they left their idols behind, and David gave orders for them to be burned.
13 Soon the Philistines returned to the
valley and started plundering it again.
14 Once more David consulted God, who
answered, "Don't attack them from here,
but go around and get ready to attack
them from the other side, near the balsam trees. 15 When you hear the sound of
marching in the treetops, then attack,
because I will be marching ahead of you
to defeat the Philistine army." 16 David
did what God had commanded, and so
he drove the Philistines back from Gibeon all the way to Gezer. 17 David's fame
spread everywhere, and the LORD made
every nation afraid of him.

Getting Ready to Move the Covenant Box

15 For his own use, David built
houses in David's City.[q] He also
prepared a place for God's Covenant
Box and put up a tent for it. 2 Then he
said, "Only Levites should carry the
Covenant Box, because they are the
ones the LORD chose to carry it and to
serve him forever." 3 So David summoned all the people of Israel to Jerusalem in order to bring the Covenant Box
to the place he had prepared for it. 4 Next
he sent for the descendants of Aaron
and for the Levites. 5 From the Levite
clan of Kohath came Uriel, in charge of
120 members of his clan; 6 from the clan
of Merari came Asaiah, in charge of 220;
7 from the clan of Gershon, Joel, in
charge of 130; 8 from the clan of Elizaphan, Shemaiah, in charge of 200; 9 from
the clan of Hebron, Eliel, in charge of 80;
10 and from the clan of Uzziel, Amminadab, in charge of 112.
11 David called in the priests Zadok
and Abiathar and the six Levites, Uriel,
Asaiah, Joel, Shemaiah, Eliel, and Amminadab. 12 He said to the Levites, "You
are the leaders of the Levite clans. Purify
yourselves and your fellow Levites, so
that you can bring the Covenant Box of

[n] PEREZ UZZAH: *This name in Hebrew means "Punishment of Uzzah."* [o] BEELIADA: *Called Eliada in 3.8.* [p] BAAL PERAZIM: *This name in Hebrew means "Lord of the Breakthrough."* [q] DAVID'S CITY: *That part of Jerusalem which David had captured from the original inhabitants, the Jebusites (see 2 S 5.6-10).*

the LORD God of Israel to the place I have
prepared for it. 13 Because you were not
there to carry it the first time, the LORD
our God punished us for not worshiping
him as we should have done."

14 Then the priests and the Levites purified themselves in order to move the
Covenant Box of the LORD God of Israel.
15 The Levites carried it on poles on their
shoulders, as the LORD had commanded
through Moses.

16 David commanded the leaders of the
Levites to assign various Levites to sing
and to play joyful music on harps and
cymbals. 17-21 From the clans of singers
they chose the following men to play the
brass cymbals: Heman son of Joel, his
relative Asaph son of Berechiah, and
Ethan son of Kushaiah, of the clan of
Merari. To assist them they chose the
following Levites to play the high-
pitched harps: Zechariah, Jaaziel, Shemiramoth, Jehiel, Unni, Eliab, Maaseiah, and Benaiah.

To play the low-pitched harps they
chose the following Levites: Mattithiah,
Eliphelehu, Mikneiah, Azaziah, and the
Temple guards, Obed Edom and Jeiel.

22 Because of his skill in music Chenaniah was chosen to be in charge of the
levitical musicians. 23-24 Berechiah and
Elkanah, along with Obed Edom and Je-
hiah, were chosen as guards for the Covenant Box. The priests Shebaniah,
Joshaphat, Nethanel, Amasai, Zechariah, Benaiah, and Eliezer were chosen
to blow trumpets in front of the Covenant Box.

Moving the Covenant Box to Jerusalem

(2 Samuel 6.12-22)

25 So King David, the leaders of Israel,
and the military commanders went to
the house of Obed Edom to get the Covenant Box, and they had a great celebration. 26 They sacrificed seven bulls and
seven sheep, to make sure that God
would help the Levites who were carrying the Covenant Box. 27 David was
wearing a robe made of the finest linen,
and so were the musicians, Chenaniah
their leader, and the Levites who carried
the Box. David also wore a linen ephod.
28 So all the Israelites accompanied the
Covenant Box up to Jerusalem with
shouts of joy, the sound of trumpets,
horns, and cymbals, and the music of
harps.

29 As the Box was being brought into
the city, Michal, Saul's daughter, looked
out of the window and saw King David
dancing and leaping for joy, and she was
disgusted with him.

16 They took the Covenant Box to
the tent which David had prepared for it and put it inside. Then they
offered sacrifices and fellowship offerings to God. 2 After David had finished
offering the sacrifices, he blessed the
people in the name of the LORD 3 and distributed food to them all. He gave each
man and woman in Israel a loaf of bread,
a piece of roasted meat,[r] and some
raisins.

4 David appointed some of the Levites
to lead the worship of the LORD, the God
of Israel, in front of the Covenant Box,
by singing and praising him. 5 Asaph
was appointed leader, with Zechariah as
his assistant. Jeiel, Shemiramoth, Jehiel,
Mattithiah, Eliab, Benaiah, Obed Edom,
and Jeiel were to play harps. Asaph was
to sound the cymbals, 6 and two priests,
Benaiah and Jahaziel, were to blow
trumpets regularly in front of the Covenant Box. 7 It was then that David first
gave Asaph and the other Levites the responsibility for singing praises to the
LORD.

A Song of Praise

(Psalms 105.1-15; 96.1-13; 106.1, 47, 48)

8 Give thanks to the LORD, proclaim
his greatness;
tell the nations what he has
done.
9 Sing praise to the LORD;
tell the wonderful things he has
done.
10 Be glad that we belong to him;
let all who worship him rejoice!
11 Go to the LORD for help,
and worship him continually.
12-13 You descendants of Jacob, God's
servant,
descendants of Israel, whom
God chose,
remember the miracles that God
performed
and the judgments that he gave.
14 The LORD is our God;

[r] a piece of roasted meat; *or* a cake of dates.

his commands are for all the
world.
15 Never forget God's covenant,
which he made to last forever,
16 the covenant he made with
Abraham,
the promise he made to Isaac.
17 The LORD made a covenant with
Jacob,
one that will last forever.
18 "I will give you the land of
Canaan," he said.
"It will be your own possession."
19 God's people were few in number,
strangers in the land of Canaan.
20 They wandered from country to
country,
from one kingdom to another.
21 But God let no one oppress them;
to protect them, he warned the
kings:
22 "Don't harm my chosen servants;
do not touch my prophets."

23 Sing to the LORD, all the world!
Proclaim every day the good
news that he has saved us.
24 Proclaim his glory to the nations,
his mighty deeds to all peoples.

25 The LORD is great and is to be
highly praised;
he is to be honored more than
all the gods.
26 The gods of all other nations are
only idols,
but the LORD created the
heavens.
27 Glory and majesty surround him,
power and joy fill his Temple.

28 Praise the LORD, all people on
earth,
praise his glory and might.
29 Praise the LORD's glorious name;
bring an offering and come into
his Temple.
Bow down before the Holy One
when he appears;[s]
30 tremble before him, all the
earth!
The earth is set firmly in place
and cannot be moved.
31 Be glad, earth and sky!
Tell the nations that the LORD
is king.
32 Roar, sea, and every creature
in you;
be glad, fields, and everything
in you!
33 The trees in the woods will shout
for joy
when the LORD comes to rule the
earth.

34 Give thanks to the LORD, because
he is good;
his love is eternal.
35 Say to him, "Save us, O God our
Savior;
gather us together; rescue us
from the nations,
so that we may be thankful
and praise your holy name."
36 Praise the LORD, the God of Israel!
Praise him now and forever!

Then all the people said, "Amen," and praised the LORD.

Worship at Jerusalem and Gibeon

37 King David put Asaph and the other
Levites in permanent charge of the worship that was held at the place where the
Covenant Box was kept. They were to
perform their duties there day by day.
38 Obed Edom son of Jeduthun and sixty-
eight men of his clan were to assist
them. Hosah and Obed Edom were in
charge of guarding the gates.
39 Zadok the priest and his fellow
priests, however, were in charge of the
worship of the LORD at the place of worship in Gibeon. 40 Every morning and
evening they were to burn sacrifices
whole on the altar in accordance with
what was written in the Law which the
LORD gave to Israel. 41 There with them
were Heman and Jeduthun and the others who were specifically chosen to sing
praises to the LORD for his eternal love.
42 Heman and Jeduthun also had charge
of the trumpets and cymbals and the
other instruments which were played
when the songs of praise were sung. The
members of Jeduthun's clan were in
charge of guarding the gates.
43 Then everyone went home, and David went home to spend some time with
his family.

[s] when he appears; *or* in garments of worship.

Nathan's Message to David

(2 Samuel 7.1-17)

17 King David was now living in his
palace. One day he sent for the
prophet Nathan and said to him, "Here I
am living in a house built of cedar, but
the LORD's Covenant Box is kept in a
tent!"
2 Nathan answered, "Do whatever
you have in mind, because God is with
you."
3 But that night God said to Nathan,
4 "Go and tell my servant David that I
say to him, 'You are not the one to build
a temple for me to live in. 5 From the time
I rescued the people of Israel from Egypt
until now I have never lived in a temple;
I have always lived in tents and moved
from place to place. 6 In all my traveling
with the people of Israel I never asked
any of the leaders that I appointed why
they had not built me a temple made of
cedar.'
7 "So tell my servant David that I, the
LORD Almighty, say to him, 'I took you
from looking after sheep in the fields
and made you the ruler of my people Israel. 8 I have been with you wherever
you have gone, and I have defeated all
your enemies as you advanced. I will
make you as famous as the greatest
leaders in the world. 9-10 I have chosen a
place for my people Israel and have settled them there, where they will live
without being oppressed any more. Ever
since they entered this land they have
been attacked by violent people, but this
will not happen again. I promise to defeat all your enemies and to give you
descendants. 11 When you die and are
buried with your ancestors, I will make
one of your sons king and will keep
his kingdom strong. 12 He will be the
one to build a temple for me, and I
will make sure that his dynasty continues forever. 13 I will be his father, and
he will be my son. I will not withdraw my support from him as I did
from Saul, whom I removed so that
you could be king. 14 I will put him in
charge of my people and my kingdom
forever. His dynasty will never
end.' "
15 Nathan told David everything that
God had revealed to him.

David's Prayer of Thanksgiving

(2 Samuel 7.18-29)

16 Then King David went into the Tent
of the LORD's presence, sat down, and
prayed, "I am not worthy of what you
have already done for me, LORD God, nor
is my family. 17 Yet now you are doing
even more; you have made promises
about my descendants in the years to
come, and you, LORD God, are already
treating me like someone great.[t]
18 What more can I say to you! You know
me well, and yet you honor me, your
servant. 19 It was your will and purpose
to do this for me and to show me my
future greatness. 20 LORD, there is none
like you; we have always known that
you alone are God. 21 There is no other
nation on earth like Israel, whom you
rescued from slavery to make them your
own people. The great and wonderful
things you did for them spread your
fame throughout the world. You rescued
your people from Egypt and drove out
other nations as your people advanced.
22 You have made Israel your own people forever, and you, LORD, have become
their God.
23 "And now, O LORD, fulfill for all time
the promise you made about me and my
descendants, and do what you said you
would. 24 Your fame will be great, and
people will forever say, 'The LORD
Almighty is God over Israel.' And you
will preserve my dynasty for all time.
25 I have the courage to pray this prayer
to you, my God, because you have revealed all this to me, your servant, and
have told me that you will make my
descendants kings. 26 You, LORD, are
God, and you have made this wonderful
promise to me. 27 I ask you to bless my
descendants so that they will continue to
enjoy your favor. You, LORD, have
blessed them, and your blessing will rest
on them forever."

David's Military Victories

(2 Samuel 8.1-18)

18 Some time later King David attacked the Philistines again and
defeated them. He took out of their control the city of Gath and its surrounding
villages. 2 He also defeated the Moabites,
who became his subjects and paid taxes
to him.

[t] *Probable text* and you, LORD God . . . great; *Hebrew unclear.*

3 Next, David attacked King Hadadezer of the Syrian state of Zobah, near the
territory of Hamath, because Hadadezer
was trying to gain control of the territory by the upper Euphrates River. 4 David captured a thousand of his chariots,
seven thousand cavalry troops, and
twenty thousand foot soldiers. He kept
enough horses for a hundred chariots
and crippled all the rest.

5 When the Syrians of Damascus sent
an army to help King Hadadezer, David
attacked it and killed twenty-two thousand men. 6 Then he set up military
camps in their territory, and they became his subjects and paid taxes to him.
The LORD made David victorious everywhere. 7 David captured the gold shields
carried by Hadadezer's officials and
took them to Jerusalem. 8 He also took a
great quantity of bronze from Tibhath
and Kun, cities ruled by Hadadezer.
(Solomon later used this bronze to make
the tank, the columns, and the bronze
utensils for the Temple.)

9 King Toi of Hamath heard that David
had defeated Hadadezer's entire army.
10 So he sent his son Joram to greet King
David and congratulate him for his victory over Hadadezer, against whom Toi
had fought many times. Joram brought
David presents made of gold, silver, and
bronze. 11 King David dedicated them for
use in worship, along with the silver and
gold he took from the nations he
conquered—Edom, Moab, Ammon, Philistia, and Amalek.

12 Abishai, whose mother was Zeruiah,
defeated the Edomites in Salt Valley and
killed eighteen thousand of them. 13 He
set up military camps throughout Edom,
and the people there became King David's subjects. The LORD made David victorious everywhere.

14 David ruled over all Israel and made
sure that his people were always treated
fairly and justly. 15 Abishai's brother
Joab was commander of the army; Jehoshaphat son of Ahilud was in charge
of the records; 16 Zadok son of Ahitub
and Ahimelech son of Abiathar were
priests; Seraiah[u] was court secretary;
17 Benaiah son of Jehoiada was in charge
of David's bodyguards; and King David's sons held high positions in his
service.

David Defeats the Ammonites and the Syrians

(2 Samuel 10.1-19)

19 Some time later King Nahash of
Ammon died, and his son Hanun
became king. 2 King David said, "I must
show loyal friendship to Hanun, as his
father Nahash did to me." So David sent
messengers to express his sympathy.

When they arrived in Ammon and
called on King Hanun, 3 the Ammonite
leaders said to the king, "Do you think
that it is in your father's honor that David has sent these men to express sympathy to you? Of course not! He has sent
them here as spies to explore the land,
so that he can conquer it!"

4 Hanun seized David's messengers,
shaved off their beards, cut off their
clothes at the hips, and sent them away.
5 They were too ashamed to return
home. When David heard what had happened, he sent word for them to stay in
Jericho and not return until their beards
had grown again.

6 King Hanun and the Ammonites realized that they had made David their enemy, so they paid nearly forty tons of
silver to hire chariots and charioteers
from Upper Mesopotamia and from the
Syrian states of Maacah and Zobah.
7 The thirty-two thousand chariots they
hired and the army of the king of Maacah came and camped near Medeba. The
Ammonites too came out from all their
cities and got ready to fight.

8 When David heard what was happening, he sent out Joab and the whole
army. 9 The Ammonites marched out
and took up their position at the entrance to Rabbah, their capital city, and
the kings who had come to help took up
their position in the open countryside.

10 Joab saw that the enemy troops
would attack him in front and from the
rear, so he chose the best of Israel's soldiers and put them in position facing the
Syrians. 11 He placed the rest of his
troops under the command of his
brother Abishai, who put them in position facing the Ammonites. 12 Joab said
to him, "If you see that the Syrians are
defeating me, come and help me, and if
the Ammonites are defeating you, I will
go and help you. 13 Be strong and courageous! Let's fight hard for our people

[u] *Probable text (see 2 S 8.17)* Seraiah; *Hebrew* Shavsha.

and for the cities of our God. And may
the LORD's will be done."
14 Joab and his men advanced to attack, and the Syrians fled. 15 When the
Ammonites saw the Syrians running
away, they fled from Abishai and retreated into the city. Then Joab went
back to Jerusalem.
16 The Syrians realized that they had
been defeated by the Israelites, so they
brought troops from the Syrian states on
the east side of the Euphrates River and
placed them under the command of Shobach, commander of the army of King
Hadadezer of Zobah. 17 When David
heard of it, he gathered the Israelite
troops, crossed the Jordan River, and
put them in position facing the Syrians.
The fighting began, 18 and the Israelites
drove the Syrian army back. David and
his men killed seven thousand Syrian
chariot drivers and forty thousand foot
soldiers. They also killed the Syrian
commander, Shobach. 19 When the kings
who were subject to Hadadezer realized
that they had been defeated by Israel,
they made peace with David and became his subjects. 20 The Syrians were
never again willing to help the Ammonites.

David Captures Rabbah

(2 Samuel 12.26-31)

20 The following spring, at the time
of the year when kings usually
go to war, Joab led out the army and
invaded the land of Ammon; King David, however, stayed in Jerusalem. They
besieged the city of Rabbah, attacked it,
and destroyed it. 2 The Ammonite idol
Molech[v] had a gold crown which
weighed about seventy-five pounds. In it
there was a jewel, which David took and
put in his own crown. He also took a
large amount of loot from the city. 3 He
took the people of the city and put them
to work with saws, iron hoes, and axes.
He did the same to the people of all the
other towns of Ammon. Then he and his
men returned to Jerusalem.

Battles against Philistine Giants

(2 Samuel 21.15-22)

4 Later on, war broke out again with
the Philistines at Gezer. This was when
Sibbecai from Hushah killed a giant
named Sippai, and the Philistines were
defeated.
5 There was another battle with the
Philistines, and Elhanan son of Jair
killed Lahmi, the brother of Goliath
from Gath, whose spear had a shaft as
thick as the bar on a weaver's loom.
6 Another battle took place at Gath,
where there was a giant with six fingers
on each hand and six toes on each foot.
He was a descendant of the ancient giants. 7 He defied the Israelites, and Jonathan, the son of David's brother Shammah, killed him.
8 These three, who were killed by David and his men, were descendants of
the giants at Gath.

David Takes a Census

(2 Samuel 24.1-25)

21 Satan wanted to bring trouble on
the people of Israel, so he made
David decide to take a census. 2 David
gave orders to Joab and the other officers, "Go through Israel, from one end of
the country to the other, and count the
people. I want to know how many
there are."
3 Joab answered, "May the LORD make
the people of Israel a hundred times
more numerous than they are now! Your
Majesty, they are all your servants. Why
do you want to do this and make the
whole nation guilty?" 4 But the king
made Joab obey the order. Joab went
out, traveled through the whole country
of Israel, and then returned to Jerusalem. 5 He reported to King David the total number of men capable of military
service: 1,100,000 in Israel and 470,000
in Judah. 6 Because Joab disapproved of
the king's command, he did not take
any census of the tribes of Levi and
Benjamin.
7 God was displeased with what had
been done, so he punished Israel. 8 David
said to God, "I have committed a terrible
sin in doing this! Please forgive me. I
have acted foolishly."
9 Then the LORD said to Gad, David's
prophet, 10 "Go and tell David that I am
giving him three choices. I will do
whichever he chooses."
11 Gad went to David, told him what
the LORD had said, and asked, "Which is
it to be? 12 Three years of famine? Or

[v] Ammonite idol Molech; *or* Ammonite king.

three months of running away from the
armies of your enemies? Or three days
during which the LORD attacks you with
his sword and sends an epidemic on
your land, using his angel to bring death
throughout Israel? What answer shall I
give the LORD?"

13 David replied to Gad, "I am in a desperate situation! But I don't want to be
punished by people. Let the LORD himself
be the one to punish me, because he is
merciful."

14 So the LORD sent an epidemic on the
people of Israel, and seventy thousand
of them died. 15 Then he sent an angel to
destroy Jerusalem, but he changed his
mind and said to the angel, "Stop! That's
enough!" The angel was standing by the
threshing place of Araunah, a Jebusite.

16 David saw the angel standing in
midair, holding his sword in his hand,
ready to destroy Jerusalem. Then David
and the leaders of the people—all of
whom were wearing sackcloth—bowed
low, with their faces touching the
ground. 17 David prayed, "O God, I am
the one who did wrong. I am the one
who ordered the census. What have
these poor people done? LORD, my God,
punish me and my family, and spare
your people."

18 The angel of the LORD told Gad to
command David to go and build an altar
to the LORD at Araunah's threshing
place. 19 David obeyed the LORD's command and went, as Gad had told him to.
20 There at the threshing place Araunah
and his four sons were threshing wheat,
and when they saw the angel, the sons
ran and hid. 21 As soon as Araunah saw
King David approaching, he left the
threshing place and bowed low, with his
face touching the ground. 22 David said
to him, "Sell me your threshing place, so
that I can build an altar to the LORD, to
stop the epidemic. I'll give you the full
price."

23 "Take it, Your Majesty," Araunah
said, "and do whatever you wish. Here
are these oxen to burn as an offering on
the altar, and here are the threshing
boards to use as fuel, and wheat to give
as an offering. I give it all to you."

24 But the king answered, "No, I will
pay you the full price. I will not give as
an offering to the LORD something that
belongs to you, something that costs me
nothing." 25 And he paid Araunah six
hundred gold coins for the threshing
place. 26 He built an altar to the LORD
there and offered burnt offerings and
fellowship offerings. He prayed, and the
LORD answered him by sending fire from
heaven to burn the sacrifices on the
altar.

27 The LORD told the angel to put his
sword away, and the angel obeyed.
28 David saw by this that the LORD had
answered his prayer, so he offered sacrifices on the altar at Araunah's threshing
place. 29 The Tent of the LORD's presence
which Moses had made in the wilderness, and the altar on which sacrifices
were burned were still at the place of
worship at Gibeon at this time; 30 but David was not able to go there to worship
God, because he was afraid of the sword
of the LORD's angel.

22 So David said, "This is where the
Temple of the LORD God will be.
Here is the altar where the people of Is-
rael are to offer burnt offerings."

Preparations for Building the Temple

2 King David gave orders for all the
foreigners living in the land of Israel to
assemble, and he put them to work.
Some of them prepared stone blocks for
building the Temple. 3 He supplied a
large amount of iron for making nails
and clamps for the wooden gates, and so
much bronze that no one could weigh it.
4 He had the people of Tyre and Sidon
bring him a large number of cedar logs.
5 David thought, "The Temple that my
son Solomon is to build must be splendid
and world-famous. But he is young and
inexperienced, so I must make preparations for it." So David got large amounts
of the materials ready before he died.

6 He sent for his son Solomon and
commanded him to build a temple for
the LORD, the God of Israel. 7 David said
to him, "Son, I wanted to build a temple
to honor the LORD my God. 8 But the LORD
told me that I had killed too many people
and fought too many wars. And so, because of all the bloodshed I have caused,
he would not let me build a temple for
him. 9 He did, however, make me a
promise. He said, 'You will have a son
who will rule in peace, because I will
give him peace from all his enemies. His

name will be Solomon,[w] because during
his reign I will give Israel peace and security. 10 He will build a temple for me.
He will be my son, and I will be his
father. His dynasty will rule Israel
forever.' "
11 David continued, "Now, son, may
the LORD your God be with you, and may
he keep his promise to make you successful in building a temple for him.
12 And may the LORD your God give you
insight and wisdom so that you may
govern Israel according to his Law. 13 If
you obey all the laws which the LORD
gave to Moses for Israel, you will be successful. Be determined and confident,
and don't let anything make you afraid.
14 As for the Temple, by my efforts I have
accumulated almost four thousand tons
of gold and nearly forty thousand tons of
silver to be used in building it. Besides
that, there is an unlimited supply of
bronze and iron. I also have wood and
stone ready, but you must get more.
15 You have many workers. There are
stonecutters to work in the quarries, and
there are masons and carpenters, as well
as a large number of skilled workers of
every sort who can work 16 with gold, silver, bronze, and iron. Now begin the
work, and may the LORD be with you."
17 David commanded all the leaders of
Israel to help Solomon. 18 He said, "The
LORD your God has been with you and
given you peace on all sides. He let me
conquer all the people who used to live
in this land, and they are now subject to
you and to the LORD. 19 Now serve the
LORD your God with all your heart and
soul. Start building the Temple, so that
you can place in it the Covenant Box of
the LORD and all the other sacred objects
used in worshiping him."

23 When David was very old, he
made his son Solomon king of
Israel.

The Work of the Levites

2 King David brought together all the
Israelite leaders and all the priests and
Levites. 3 He took a census of all the
male Levites aged thirty or older. The
total was thirty-eight thousand. 4 The
king assigned twenty-four thousand to
administer the work of the Temple, six
thousand to keep records and decide disputes, 5 four thousand to do guard duty,
and four thousand to praise the LORD, using the musical instruments provided by
the king for this purpose.
6 David divided the Levites into three
groups, according to their clans: Gershon, Kohath, and Merari.
7 Gershon had two sons: Ladan and
Shimei. 8 Ladan had three sons: Jehiel,
Zetham, and Joel, 9 who were the heads
of the clans descended from Ladan.
(Shimei had three sons: Shelomoth, Ha-
ziel, and Haran.)[x] 10-11 Shimei had four
sons: Jahath, Zina, Jeush, and Beriah, in
order of age. Jeush and Beriah did not
have many descendants, so they were
counted as one clan.
12 Kohath had four sons: Amram, Izhar, Hebron, and Uzziel. 13 His oldest
son, Amram, was the father of Aaron
and Moses. (Aaron and his descendants
were set apart to be in charge of the sacred objects forever, to burn incense in
the worship of the LORD, to serve him,
and to bless the people in his name.
14 But the sons of Moses, the man of God,
were included among the Levites.)
15 Moses had two sons, Gershom and Eliezer. 16 The leader among Gershom's
sons was Shebuel. 17 Eliezer had only
one son, Rehabiah, but Rehabiah had
many descendants.
18 Kohath's second son, Izhar, had a
son, Shelomith, the head of the clan.
19 Kohath's third son, Hebron, had four
sons: Jeriah, Amariah, Jahaziel, and
Jekameam. 20 Kohath's fourth son, Uzziel, had two sons, Micah and Isshiah.
21 Merari had two sons, Mahli and Mushi. Mahli also had two sons, Eleazar
and Kish, 22 but Eleazar died without
having any sons, only daughters. His
daughters married their cousins, the
sons of Kish. 23 Merari's second son, Mushi, had three sons: Mahli, Eder, and
Jeremoth.
24 These were the descendants of Levi,
by clans and families, every one of them
registered by name. Each of his
descendants, twenty years of age or
older, had a share in the work of the
LORD's Temple.
25 David said, "The LORD God of Israel
has given peace to his people, and he

[w] SOLOMON: *This name is formed from the Hebrew word "shalom," which means "peace and security."* [x] SHIMEI ... HARAN: *The relation of this list to the list of Shimei's sons in verse 10 is not clear.*

himself will live in Jerusalem forever.
26 So there is no longer any need for the
Levites to carry the Tent of the LORD's
presence and all the equipment used in
worship." 27 On the basis of David's final
instructions all Levites were registered
for service when they reached the age of
twenty, 28 and were assigned the following duties: to help the priests descended
from Aaron with the Temple worship, to
take care of its courtyards and its rooms,
and to keep undefiled everything that is
sacred; 29 to be responsible for the bread
offered to God, the flour used in offerings, the wafers made without yeast, the
baked offerings, and the flour mixed
with olive oil; to weigh and measure the
Temple offerings; 30 and to praise and
glorify the LORD every morning and
every evening 31 and whenever offerings
to the LORD are burned on the Sabbath,
the New Moon Festival, and other festivals. Rules were made specifying the
number of Levites assigned to do this
work each time. The Levites were assigned the duty of worshiping the LORD
for all time. 32 They were given the responsibility of taking care of the Tent of
the LORD's presence and the Temple, and
of assisting their relatives, the priests
descended from Aaron, in the Temple
worship.

The Work Assigned to the Priests

24 These are the groups to which
the descendants of Aaron belong. Aaron had four sons: Nadab,
Abihu, Eleazar, and Ithamar. 2 Nadab
and Abihu died before their father did,
and left no descendants, so their brothers Eleazar and Ithamar became priests.
3 King David organized the descendants
of Aaron into groups according to their
duties. He was assisted in this by Zadok,
a descendant of Eleazar, and by Ahimelech, a descendant of Ithamar. 4 The
descendants of Eleazar were organized
into sixteen groups, while the descendants of Ithamar were organized into
eight; this was done because there were
more male heads of families among the
descendants of Eleazar. 5 Since there
were Temple officials and spiritual leaders among the descendants of both Eleazar and Ithamar, assignments were
made by drawing lots. 6 The descendants
of Eleazar and of Ithamar took turns
drawing lots. Then they were registered
by Shemaiah son of Nethanel, a Levite
secretary. The king, his officials, the
priest Zadok, Ahimelech son of Abiathar, and the heads of the priestly families and of the Levite families, were all
witnesses.

7-18 This is the order in which the
twenty-four family groups were given
their assignments: 1) Jehoiarib; 2) Jedaiah; 3) Harim; 4) Seorim; 5) Malchijah;
6) Mijamin; 7) Hakkoz; 8) Abijah;
9) Jeshua; 10) Shecaniah; 11) Eliashib;
12) Jakim; 13) Huppah; 14) Jeshebeab;
15) Bilgah; 16) Immer; 17) Hezir;
18) Happizzez; 19) Pethahiah; 20) Je-
hezkel; 21) Jachin; 22) Gamul; 23) Delaiah; 24) Maaziah.

19 These men were registered according to their assignments for going to the
Temple and performing the duties established by their ancestor Aaron in obedience to the commands of the LORD God
of Israel.

The List of the Levites

20 These are other heads of families descended from Levi:

Jehdeiah, a descendant of Amram
through Shebuel;

21 Isshiah, a descendant of Rehabiah;

22 Jahath, a descendant of Izhar
through Shelomith;

23 Jeriah, Amariah, Jehaziel, and Jekameam, sons of Hebron, in order of age;

24 Shamir, a descendant of Uzziel
through Micah;

25 Zechariah, a descendant of Uzziel
through Isshiah, Micah's brother;

26 Mahli, Mushi, and Jaaziah, descendants of Merari. 27 Jaaziah had three sons
Shoham, Zaccur, and Ibri. 28-29 Mahli
had two sons, Eleazar and Kish. Eleazar
had no sons, but Kish had one son, Je
rahmeel. 30 Mushi had three sons: Mahli
Eder, and Jeremoth.

These are the families of the Levites

31 The head of each family and one of
his younger brothers drew lots for their
assignments, just as their relatives, the
priests descended from Aaron, had
done. King David, Zadok, Ahimelech
and the heads of families of the priests
and of the Levites were witnesses.

The Temple Musicians

25 King David and the leaders of
the Levites chose the following
Levite clans to lead the worship serv

ices: Asaph, Heman, and Jeduthun.
They were to proclaim God's messages,
accompanied by the music of harps and
cymbals. This is the list of persons chosen to lead the worship, with the type of
service that each group performed:
2 The four sons of Asaph: Zaccur, Joseph, Nethaniah, and Asharelah. They
were under the direction of Asaph, who
proclaimed God's messages whenever
the king commanded.
3 The six sons of Jeduthun: Gedaliah,
Zeri, Jeshaiah, Shimei, Hashabiah, and
Mattithiah. Under the direction of their
father they proclaimed God's message,
accompanied by the music of harps, and
sang praise and thanks to the LORD.
4 The fourteen sons of Heman: Bukkiah, Mattaniah, Uzziel, Shebuel, Jerimoth, Hananiah, Hanani, Eliathah,
Giddalti, Romamti Ezer, Joshbekashah,
Mallothi, Hothir, and Mahazioth. 5 God
gave to Heman, the king's prophet, these
fourteen sons and also three daughters,
as he had promised, in order to give
power to Heman. 6 All of his sons played
cymbals and harps under their father's
direction, to accompany the Temple
worship. And Asaph, Jeduthun, and Heman were under orders from the king.
7 All these twenty-four men were experts; and their fellow Levites were
trained musicians. There were 288 men
in all.
8 To determine the assignment of duties they all drew lots, whether they
were young or old, experts or beginners.
9-31 These 288 men were divided according to families into twenty-four
groups of twelve, with a leader in charge
of each group. This is the order in which
they were on duty: 1) Joseph of the family of Asaph; 2) Gedaliah; 3) Zaccur;
4) Zeri; 5) Nethaniah; 6) Bukkiah;
7) Asharelah; 8) Jeshaiah; 9) Mattaniah;
10) Shimei; 11) Uzziel; 12) Hashabiah;
13) Shebuel; 14) Mattithiah; 15) Jerimoth; 16) Hananiah; 17) Joshbekashah;
18) Hanani; 19) Mallothi; 20) Eliathah;
21) Hothir; 22) Giddalti; 23) Mahazioth;
24) Romamti Ezer.

The Temple Guards

26 These are the assignments of
work for the Levites who served
as Temple guards. From the clan of Korah there was Meshelemiah son of Kore,
of the family of Asaph. 2 He had seven
sons, listed in order of age: Zechariah,
Jediael, Zebadiah, Jathniel, 3 Elam, Jehohanan, and Eliehoenai.
4 There was also Obed Edom, whom
God blessed by giving him eight sons,
listed in order of age: Shemaiah, Jehozabad, Joah, Sachar, Nethanel, 5 Ammiel,
Issachar, and Peullethai.
6-7 Obed Edom's oldest son, Shemaiah,
had six sons: Othni, Rephael, Obed, Elzabad, Elihu, and Semachiah. They
were important men in their clan because of their great ability; the last two
were especially talented.
8 Obed Edom's family furnished a total
of sixty-two highly qualified men for this
work.
9 Meshelemiah's family furnished
eighteen qualified men.
10 From the clan of Merari there was
Hosah, who had four sons: Shimri (his
father made him the leader, even though
he was not the oldest son), 11 Hilkiah,
Tebaliah, and Zechariah. In all there
were thirteen members of Hosah's family who were Temple guards.
12 The Temple guards were divided
into groups, according to families, and
they were assigned duties in the Temple,
just as the other Levites were. 13 Each
family, regardless of size, drew lots to
see which gate it would be responsible
for. 14 Shelemiah drew the east gate, and
his son Zechariah, a man who always
gave good advice, drew the north gate.
15 Obed Edom was allotted the south
gate, and his sons were allotted to guard
the storerooms. 16 Shuppim and Hosah
were allotted the west gate and the Shal-
lecheth Gate on the upper road. Guard
duty was divided into assigned periods,
one after another. 17 On the east, six
guards were on duty each day, on the
north, four, and on the south, four. Four
guards were stationed at the storerooms
daily, two at each storeroom. 18 Near the
western pavilion there were four guards
by the road and two at the pavilion itself.
19 This is the assignment of guard duty to
the clan of Korah and the clan of Merari.

Other Temple Duties

20 Others of their fellow Levites[y] were
in charge of the Temple treasury and the

[y] *One ancient translation* fellow Levites; *Hebrew* Levites, Ahijah.

storerooms for gifts dedicated to God.
21 Ladan, one of the sons of Gershon,
was the ancestor of several family
groups, including the family of his son
Jehiel. 22 Ladan's two other sons, Zetham and Joel, had charge of the Temple
treasury and storerooms.
23 Duties were also assigned to the
descendants of Amram, Izhar, Hebron,
and Uzziel.
24 Shebuel, of the clan of Moses' son
Gershom, was the chief official responsible for the Temple treasury. 25 Through
Gershom's brother Eliezer he was related to Shelomith. Eliezer was the
father of Rehabiah, who was the father
of Jeshaiah, the father of Joram, the
father of Zichri, the father of Shelomith.
26 Shelomith and the members of his
family were in charge of all the gifts dedicated to God by King David, the heads
of families, leaders of clan groups, and
army officers. 27 They took some of the
loot they captured in battle and dedicated it for use in the Temple. 28 Shelomith and his family were in charge of
everything that had been dedicated for
use in the Temple, including the gifts
brought by the prophet Samuel, by King
Saul, by Abner son of Ner, and by Joab
son of Zeruiah.

Duties of Other Levites

29 Among the descendants of Izhar,
Chenaniah and his sons were assigned
administrative duties: keeping records
and settling disputes for the people of
Israel.
30 Among the descendants of Hebron,
Hashabiah and seventeen hundred of
his relatives, all outstanding men, were
put in charge of the administration of all
religious and civil matters in Israel west
of the Jordan River. 31 Jeriah was the
leader of the descendants of Hebron. In
the fortieth year that David was king, an
investigation was made of the family
line of Hebron's descendants, and outstanding soldiers belonging to this family were found living at Jazer in the
territory of Gilead. 32 King David chose
twenty-seven hundred outstanding
heads of families from Jeriah's relatives
and put them in charge of administering
all religious and civil matters in Israel
east of the Jordan River—the territories
of Reuben, Gad, and East Manasseh.

Military and Civil Organization

27 This is the list of the Israelite
heads of families and clan leaders and their officials who administered
the work of the kingdom. Each month of
the year a different group of twenty-four
thousand men was on duty under the
commander for that month.
2-15 The following were the commanders for each month:

First month: Jashobeam son of Zabdiel (he was a member of the clan of Perez, a part of the tribe of Judah)
Second month: Dodai, a descendant of Ahohi (Mikloth was his second in command)[z]
Third month: Benaiah son of Jehoiada the priest; he was the leader of "The Thirty" (his son Ammizabad succeeded him as commander of this group)
Fourth month: Asahel, brother of Joab (his son Zebadiah succeeded him)
Fifth month: Shamhuth, a descendant of Izhar
Sixth month: Ira son of Ikkesh from Tekoa
Seventh month: Helez, an Ephraimite from Pelon
Eighth month: Sibbecai from Hushah (he was a member of the clan of Zerah, a part of the tribe of Judah)
Ninth month: Abiezer from Anathoth in the territory of the tribe of Benjamin
Tenth month: Maharai from Netophah (he was a member of the clan of Zerah)
Eleventh month: Benaiah from Pirathon in the territory of the tribe of Ephraim
Twelfth month: Heldai from Netophah (he was a descendant of Othniel)

Administration of the Tribes of Israel

16-22 This is the list of the administrators of the tribes of Israel:

[z] *Probable text* Mikloth . . . command; *Hebrew unclear.*

Tribe	*Administrator*
Reuben	Eliezer son of Zichri
Simeon	Shephatiah son of Maacah
Levi	Hashabiah son of Kemuel
Aaron	Zadok
Judah	Elihu, one of King David's brothers
Issachar	Omri son of Michael
Zebulun	Ishmaiah son of Obadiah
Naphtali	Jeremoth son of Azriel
Ephraim	Hoshea son of Azaziah
West Manasseh	Joel son of Pedaiah
East Manasseh	Iddo son of Zechariah
Benjamin	Jaasiel son of Abner
Dan	Azarel son of Jeroham

23 King David did not take a census of
the people who were under the age of
twenty, because of the LORD's promise to
make the people of Israel as numerous
as the stars in the sky. 24 Joab, whose
mother was Zeruiah, began to take a
census, but he did not complete it. God
punished Israel because of this census,
so the final figures were never recorded
in King David's official records.

Administrators of the Royal Property

25-31 This is the list of those who administered the royal property:

Royal storerooms: Azmaveth son of Adiel
Local storerooms: Jonathan son of Uzziah
Farm labor: Ezri son of Chelub
Vineyards: Shimei from Ramah
Wine cellars: Zabdi from Shepham
Olive and sycamore trees (in the western foothills): Baal Hanan from Geder
Olive oil storage: Joash
Cattle in the Plain of Sharon: Shitrai from Sharon
Cattle in the valleys: Shaphat son of Adlai
Camels: Obil, an Ishmaelite
Donkeys: Jehdeiah from Meronoth
Sheep and goats: Jaziz, a Hagrite

David's Personal Advisers

32 Jonathan, King David's uncle, was a
skillful adviser and a scholar. He and Jehiel son of Hachmoni were in charge of
the education of the king's sons.
33 Ahithophel was adviser to the king,
and Hushai the Archite was the king's
friend and counselor. 34 After Ahithophel died, Abiathar and Jehoiada son of
Benaiah became advisers. Joab was
commander of the royal army.

David's Instructions for the Temple

28 King David commanded all the
officials of Israel to assemble in
Jerusalem. So all the officials of the
tribes, the officials who administered
the work of the kingdom, the leaders of
the clans, the supervisors of the property
and livestock that belonged to the king
and his sons—indeed all the palace officials, leading soldiers, and important
men—gathered in Jerusalem.

2 David stood before them and addressed them: "My friends, listen to me.
I wanted to build a permanent home for
the Covenant Box, the footstool of the
LORD our God. I have made preparations
for building a temple to honor him, 3 but
he has forbidden me to do it, because I
am a soldier and have shed too much
blood. 4 The LORD, the God of Israel,
chose me and my descendants to rule Israel forever. He chose the tribe of Judah
to provide leadership, and out of Judah
he chose my father's family. From all
that family it was his pleasure to take me
and make me king over all Israel. 5 He
gave me many sons, and out of them all
he chose Solomon to rule over Israel, the
LORD's kingdom.

6 "The LORD said to me, 'Your son Solomon is the one who will build my Temple. I have chosen him to be my son, and
I will be his father. 7 I will make his kingdom last forever if he continues to obey
carefully all my laws and commands as
he does now.'

8 "So now, my people, in the presence
of our God and of this assembly of all
Israel, the LORD's people, I charge you to
obey carefully everything that the LORD
our God has commanded us, so that you
may continue to possess this good land

and so that you may hand it on to succeeding generations forever."
9 And to Solomon he said, "My son, I
charge you to acknowledge your
father's God and to serve him with an
undivided heart and a willing mind. He
knows all our thoughts and desires. If
you go to him, he will accept you; but if
you turn away from him, he will abandon you forever. 10 You must realize that
the LORD has chosen you to build his holy
Temple. Now do it—and do it with determination."
11 David gave Solomon the plans for
all the Temple buildings, for the storerooms and all the other rooms, and for
the Most Holy Place, where sins are forgiven. 12 He also gave him the plans for
all he had in mind for the courtyards and
the rooms around them, and for the
storerooms for the Temple equipment
and the gifts dedicated to the LORD. 13 David also gave him the plans for organiz-
ing the priests and Levites to perform
their duties, to do the work of the Temple, and to take care of all the Temple
utensils. 14 He gave instructions as to
how much silver and gold was to be used
for making the utensils, 15 for each lamp
and lampstand, 16 for the silver tables,
and for each gold table on which were
placed the loaves of bread offered to
God. 17 He also gave instructions as to
how much pure gold was to be used in
making forks, bowls, and jars, how
much silver and gold in making dishes,
18 and how much pure gold in making
the altar on which incense was burned
and in making the chariot for the winged
creatures that spread their wings over
the LORD's Covenant Box. 19 King David
said, "All this is contained in the plan
written according to the instructions
which the LORD himself gave me to
carry out."
20 King David said to his son Solomon,
"Be confident and determined. Start the
work and don't let anything stop you.
The LORD God, whom I serve, will be
with you. He will not abandon you, but
he will stay with you until you finish the
work to be done on his Temple. 21 The
priests and the Levites have been assigned duties to perform in the Temple.
Workers with every kind of skill are eager to help you, and all the people and
their leaders are at your command."

Gifts for Building the Temple

29 King David announced to the
whole assembly: "My son Solomon is the one whom God has chosen,
but he is still young and lacks experience. The work to be done is tremendous, because this is not a palace for
people but a temple for the LORD God.
2 I have made every effort to prepare
materials for the Temple—gold, silver,
bronze, iron, timber, precious stones
and gems, stones for mosaics, and quantities of marble. 3 Over and above all this
that I have provided, I have given silver
and gold from my personal property because of my love for God's Temple.
4 I have given 115 tons of the finest gold
and 265 tons of pure silver for decorat-
ing the walls of the Temple 5 and for all
the objects which the skilled workers
are to make. Now who else is willing to
give a generous offering to the LORD?"
6 Then the heads of the clans, the officials of the tribes, the commanders of
the army, and the administrators of the
royal property volunteered to give 7 the
following for the work on the Temple:
190 tons of gold, 380 tons of silver, 675
tons of bronze, and 3,750 tons of iron.
8 Those who had precious stones gave
them to the Temple treasury, which was
administered by Jehiel of the Levite clan
of Gershon. 9 The people had given willingly to the LORD, and they were happy
that so much had been given. King David also was extremely happy.

David Praises God

10 There in front of the whole assembly
King David praised the LORD. He said,
"LORD God of our ancestor Jacob, may
you be praised forever and ever! 11 You
are great and powerful, glorious, splendid, and majestic. Everything in heaven
and earth is yours, and you are king, supreme ruler over all. 12 All riches and
wealth come from you; you rule everything by your strength and power; and
you are able to make anyone great and
strong. 13 Now, our God, we give you
thanks, and we praise your glorious
name.
14 "Yet my people and I cannot really
give you anything, because everything is
a gift from you, and we have only given
back what is yours already. 15 You know,
O LORD, that we pass through life like ex-

iles and strangers, as our ancestors did.
Our days are like a passing shadow, and
we cannot escape death. 16 O LORD, our
God, we have brought together all this
wealth to build a temple to honor your
holy name, but it all came from you and
all belongs to you. 17 I know that you test
everyone's heart and are pleased with
people of integrity. In honesty and sincerity I have willingly given all this to
you, and I have seen how your people
who are gathered here have been happy
to bring offerings to you. 18 LORD God of
our ancestors Abraham, Isaac, and Jacob, keep such devotion forever strong
in your people's hearts and keep them
always faithful to you. 19 Give my son
Solomon a wholehearted desire to obey
everything that you command and to
build the Temple for which I have made
these preparations."

20 Then David commanded the people,
"Praise the LORD your God!" And the
whole assembly praised the LORD, the
God of their ancestors, and they bowed
low and gave honor to the LORD and also
to the king.

21 The following day they killed animals as sacrifices, dedicating them to
the LORD, and then gave them to the people to eat. In addition, they sacrificed a
thousand bulls, a thousand rams, and a
thousand lambs, which they burned
whole on the altar. They also brought
the offerings of wine. 22 So that day they
were very happy as they ate and drank
in the presence of the LORD.

For a second time they proclaimed
Solomon king. In the name of the LORD
they anointed him as their ruler and Zadok as priest. 23 So Solomon succeeded
his father David on the throne which the
LORD had established. He was a successful king, and the whole nation of Israel
obeyed him. 24 All the officials and soldiers, and even all of David's other sons,
promised to be loyal to Solomon as king.
25 The LORD made the whole nation stand
in awe of Solomon, and he made him
more glorious than any other king that
had ruled Israel.

Summary of David's Reign

26 David son of Jesse ruled over all Israel 27 for forty years. He ruled in Hebron for seven years and in Jerusalem
for thirty-three. 28 He died at a ripe old
age, wealthy and respected, and his son
Solomon succeeded him as king. 29 The
history of King David from beginning to
end is recorded in the records of the
three prophets, Samuel, Nathan, and
Gad. 30 The records tell how he ruled,
how powerful he was, and all the things
that happened to him, to Israel, and to
the surrounding kingdoms.

The Second Book of CHRONICLES

Introduction

Second Chronicles *begins where* First Chronicles *ends. It describes the rule of King Solomon, records the revolt of the northern tribes led by Jeroboam against Rehoboam, King Solomon's son and successor, and continues an account of the history of the kingdom of Judah until the fall of Jerusalem in 586 B.C.*

Outline of Contents

King Solomon Prays for Wisdom

(1 Kings 3.1-15)

1 Solomon, the son of King David,
took firm control of the kingdom of
Israel, and the LORD his God blessed him
and made him very powerful.
2 King Solomon gave an order to all
the officers in charge of units of a thousand men and of a hundred men, all the
government officials, all the heads of
families, and all the rest of the people,
3 commanding them to go with him to
the place of worship at Gibeon. They
went there because that was where the
Tent of the LORD's presence was located,
which Moses, the LORD's servant, had
made in the wilderness. (4 The Covenant
Box, however, was in Jerusalem, kept in
a tent which King David had set up
when he brought the Box from Kiriath
Jearim.) 5 The bronze altar which had
been made by Bezalel, the son of Uri and
grandson of Hur, was also in Gibeon in
front of the Tent of the LORD's presence.
King Solomon and all the people worshiped the LORD there. 6 In front of the
Tent the king worshiped the LORD by offering sacrifices on the bronze altar; he
had a thousand animals killed and
burned whole on it.
7 That night God appeared to Solomon
and asked, "What would you like me to
give you?"
8 Solomon answered, "You always
showed great love for my father David,
and now you have let me succeed him as
king. 9 O LORD God, fulfill the promise
you made to my father. You have made
me king over a people who are so many
that they cannot be counted, 10 so give
me the wisdom and knowledge I need to
rule over them. Otherwise, how would I
ever be able to rule this great people of
yours?"
11 God replied to Solomon, "You have
made the right choice. Instead of asking
for wealth or treasure or fame or the
death of your enemies or even for long
life for yourself, you have asked for wisdom and knowledge so that you can rule
my people, over whom I have made you
king. 12 I will give you wisdom and
knowledge. And in addition, I will give
you more wealth, treasure, and fame
than any king has ever had before or
will ever have again."

King Solomon's Power and Wealth

(1 Kings 10.26-29)

13 So Solomon left[a] the place of worship at Gibeon, where the Tent of the
LORD's presence was, and returned to Jerusalem. There he ruled over Israel.
14 He built up a force of fourteen hundred
chariots and twelve thousand cavalry
horses. Some of them he kept in Jerusalem, and the rest he stationed in various
other cities. 15 During his reign silver
and gold became as common in Jerusalem as stone, and cedar was as plentiful
as ordinary sycamore in the foothills of
Judah. 16 The king's agents controlled
the export of horses from Musri[b] and
Cilicia,[c] 17 and the export of chariots
from Egypt. They supplied the Hittite
and Syrian kings with horses and chariots, selling chariots for 600 pieces of silver each and horses for 150 each.[d]

Preparations for Building the Temple

(1 Kings 5.1-18)

2 King Solomon decided to build a
temple where the LORD would be
worshiped, and also to build a palace for
himself. 2 He put 70,000 men to work
transporting materials, and 80,000 to
work cutting stone in the hill country.
There were 3,600 others responsible for
supervising the work.
3 Solomon sent a message to King Hiram of Tyre: "Do business with me as
you did with my father, King David,
when you sold him cedar logs for building his palace. 4 I am building a temple
to honor the LORD my God. It will be a
holy place where my people and I will
worship him by burning incense of fragrant spices, where we will present
offerings of sacred bread to him
continuously, and where we will offer
burnt offerings every morning and evening, as well as on Sabbaths, New Moon
Festivals, and other holy days honoring
the LORD our God. He has commanded
Israel to do this forever. 5 I intend to
build a great temple, because our God is
greater than any other god. 6 Yet no one
can really build a temple for God, because even all the vastness of heaven

[a] *Some ancient translations* left; *Hebrew* came to. [b] *Probable text* Musri; *Hebrew* Egypt.
[c] MUSRI AND CILICIA: *Two ancient countries in what is now southeast Turkey which were centers of horse breeding in Solomon's time.* [d] *Verses 16-17 in Hebrew are unclear.*

cannot contain him. How then can I
build a temple that would be anything
more than a place to burn incense to
God? 7 Now send me a man with skill in
engraving, in working gold, silver,
bronze, and iron, and in making blue,
purple, and red cloth. He will work with
the craftsmen of Judah and Jerusalem
whom my father David selected.
8 I know how skillful your lumbermen
are, so send me cedar, cypress, and juniper logs from Lebanon. I am ready to
send my men to assist yours 9 in preparing large quantities of timber, because
this temple I intend to build will be large
and magnificent. 10 As provisions for
your lumbermen, I will send you 100,000
bushels of wheat, 100,000 bushels of barley, 110,000 gallons of wine, and 110,000
gallons of olive oil."
11 King Hiram sent Solomon a letter in
reply. He wrote, "Because the LORD loves
his people, he has made you their king.
12 Praise the LORD God of Israel, Creator
of heaven and earth! He has given King
David a wise son, full of understanding
and skill, who now plans to build a temple for the LORD and a palace for himself.
13 I am sending you a wise and skillful
master metalworker named Huram.
14 His mother was a member of the tribe
of Dan and his father was a native of
Tyre. He knows how to make things out
of gold, silver, bronze, iron, stone, and
wood. He can work with blue, purple,
and red cloth, and with linen. He can do
all sorts of engraving and can follow any
design suggested to him. Let him work
with your skilled workers and with
those who worked for your father, King
David. 15 So now send us the wheat, barley, wine, and olive oil that you promised. 16 In the mountains of Lebanon we
will cut down all the cedars you need, tie
them together in rafts, and float them by
sea as far as Joppa. From there you can
take them to Jerusalem."

Construction of the Temple Begins

(1 Kings 6.1-38)

17 King Solomon took a census of all
the foreigners living in the land of Israel,
similar to the census his father David
had taken. There were 153,600 resident
foreigners. 18 He assigned 70,000 of them
to transport materials and 80,000 to cut
stones in the mountains, and appointed
3,600 supervisors to make sure the work
was done.

3 King David, Solomon's father, had
already prepared a place for the
Temple. It was in Jerusalem, on Mount
Moriah, where the LORD appeared to David, at the place which Araunah the Jebusite had used as a threshing place. King
Solomon began the construction 2 in the
second month of the fourth year that he
was king. 3 The Temple which King Solomon built was 90 feet long and 30 feet
wide. 4 The entrance room was the full
width of the Temple, 30 feet, and was
180 feet high. The inside of the room was
overlaid with pure gold. 5 The main room
was paneled with cedar and overlaid
with fine gold, in which were worked designs of palm trees and chain patterns.
6 The king decorated the Temple with
beautiful precious stones and with gold
imported from the land of Parvaim. 7 He
used the gold to overlay the Temple
walls, the rafters, the entryways, and the
doors. On the walls the workers carved
designs of winged creatures.[e] 8 The inner room, called the Most Holy Place,
was 30 feet long and 30 feet wide, which
was the full width of the Temple.
Twenty-five tons of gold were used to
cover the walls of the Most Holy Place;
9 twenty ounces of gold were used for
making nails, and the walls of the upper
rooms were also covered with gold.
10 The king also had his workers make
two winged creatures out of metal, cover
them with gold, and place them in the
Most Holy Place, 11-13 where they stood
side by side facing the entrance. Each
had two wings, each wing 7½ feet long,
which were spread out so that they
touched each other in the center of the
room and reached to the wall on either
side of the room, stretching across the
full width of 30 feet. 14 A curtain for the
Most Holy Place was made of linen and
of other material, which was dyed blue,
purple, and red, with designs of the
winged creatures worked into it.

The Two Bronze Columns

(1 Kings 7.15-22)

15 The king had two columns made,
each one 52 feet tall, and placed them
in front of the Temple. Each one had a

[e] WINGED CREATURES: *See Word List.*

capital 7½ feet tall. 16 The tops of the
columns were decorated with a design of
interwoven chains and one hundred
bronze pomegranates.[f] 17 The columns
were set at the sides of the Temple entrance: the one on the south side was
named Jachin[g] and the one on the north
side was named Boaz.[h]

Equipment for the Temple

(1 Kings 7.23-51)

4 King Solomon had a bronze altar
made, which was 30 feet square and
15 feet high. 2 He also made a round tank
of bronze, 7½ feet deep, 15 feet in diameter, and 45 feet in circumference. 3 All
around the outer edge of the rim of the
tank[i] were two rows of decorations,
one above the other. The decorations
were in the shape of bulls, which had
been cast all in one piece with the rest of
the tank. 4 The tank rested on the backs
of twelve bronze bulls that faced outward, three facing in each direction.
5 The sides of the tank were 3 inches
thick. Its rim was like the rim of a cup,
curving outward like the petals of a
flower. The tank held about 15,000 gallons. 6 They also made ten basins, five to
be placed on the south side of the Temple and five on the north side. They were
to be used to rinse the parts of the animals that were burned as sacrifices. The
water in the large tank was for the
priests to use for washing.

7-8 They made ten gold lampstands according to the usual pattern, and ten tables, and placed them in the main room
of the Temple, five lampstands and five
tables on each side. They also made a
hundred gold bowls.

9 They made an inner courtyard for the
priests, and also an outer courtyard. The
doors in the gates between the courtyards were covered with bronze. 10 The
tank was placed near the southeast corner of the Temple.

11-16 Huram also made pots, shovels,
and bowls. He completed all the objects
that he had promised King Solomon he
would make for the Temple:

The two columns
The two bowl-shaped capitals on top of the columns
The design of interwoven chains on each capital
The 400 bronze pomegranates arranged in two rows around the design of each capital
The ten[j] carts
The ten basins
The tank
The twelve bulls supporting the tank
The pots, shovels, and forks

Huram the master metalworker made all
these objects[k] out of polished bronze, as
King Solomon had commanded, for use
in the Temple of the LORD.

17 The king had them all made in the
foundry between Sukkoth and Zeredah[l] in the Jordan Valley. 18 So many
objects were made that no one determined the total weight of the bronze
used.

19 King Solomon also had gold furnishings made for the Temple: the altar and
the tables for the bread offered to God;
20 the lampstands and the lamps of fine
gold that were to burn in front of the
Most Holy Place, according to plan;
21 the flower decorations, the lamps, and
the tongs; 22 the lamp snuffers, the
bowls, the dishes for incense, and the
pans used for carrying live coals. All
these objects were made of pure gold.
The outer doors of the Temple and the
doors to the Most Holy Place were overlaid with gold.

5 When King Solomon finished all
the work on the Temple, he placed
in the Temple storerooms all the things
that his father David had dedicated to
the LORD—the silver, gold, and other
articles.

The Covenant Box Is Brought to the Temple

(1 Kings 8.1-9)

2 Then King Solomon summoned all
the leaders of the tribes and clans of Israel to assemble in Jerusalem, in order
to take the LORD's Covenant Box from
Zion, David's City,[m] to the Temple.
3 They all assembled at the time of the

[f] *Verse 16 in Hebrew is unclear.* [g] JACHIN: *This name sounds like the Hebrew for "he (God) establishes."* [h] BOAZ: *This name sounds like the Hebrew for "by his (God's) strength."*
[i] *Probable text* All around . . . tank; *Hebrew unclear.* [j] *Probable text (see 1 K 7.40-45)* ten; *Hebrew* he made. [k] *One ancient translation* all these objects; *Hebrew* all their objects.
[l] ZEREDAH *(see Zarethan, 1 K 7.46).* [m] DAVID'S CITY: *See Word List.*

Festival of Shelters. 4 When all the leaders had gathered, then the Levites lifted
the Covenant Box 5 and carried it to the
Temple. The priests and the Levites also
moved the Tent of the LORD's presence
and all its equipment to the Temple.
6 King Solomon and all the people of Israel assembled in front of the Covenant
Box and sacrificed a large number of
sheep and cattle—too many to count.
7 Then the priests carried the Covenant
Box of the LORD into the Temple and put
it in the Most Holy Place, beneath the
winged creatures. 8 Their outstretched
wings covered the Box and the poles it
was carried by. 9 The ends of the poles
could be seen by anyone standing directly in front of the Most Holy Place,
but from nowhere else. (The poles are
still there today.) 10 There was nothing
inside the Covenant Box except the two
stone tablets which Moses had placed
there at Mount Sinai, when the LORD
made a covenant with the people of Israel as they were coming from Egypt.

The Glory of the LORD

11-14 All the priests present, regardless of the group to which they belonged, had consecrated themselves. And all the Levite musicians—Asaph, Heman, and Jeduthun, and the members of their clans—were wearing linen clothing. The Levites stood near the east side of the altar with cymbals and harps, and with them were 120 priests playing trumpets. The singers were accompanied in perfect harmony by trumpets, cymbals, and other instruments, as they praised the LORD singing:

"Praise the LORD, because he is
good,
And his love is eternal."

As the priests were leaving the Temple, it was suddenly filled with a cloud shining with the dazzling light of the LORD's presence, and they could not continue the service of worship.

Solomon's Address to the People

(1 Kings 8.12-21)

6 Then King Solomon prayed,
"LORD, you have chosen to live
in clouds and darkness.
2 Now I have built a majestic temple
for you,
a place for you to live in
forever."

3 All the people of Israel were standing
there. The king turned to face them and
asked God's blessing on them. 4 He said,
"Praise the LORD God of Israel! He has
kept the promise he made to my father
David when he said to him, 5 'From the
time I brought my people out of Egypt
until now, I did not choose any city in
the land of Israel as the place to build a
temple where I would be worshiped, and
I did not choose anyone to lead my people Israel. 6 But now I have chosen Jerusalem as the place where I will be
worshiped, and you, David, to rule my
people.' "
7 And Solomon continued, "My father
David planned to build a temple for the
worship of the LORD God of Israel, 8 but
the LORD said to him, 'You were right in
wanting to build a temple for me, 9 but
you will never build it. It is your son,
your own son, who will build my
temple.'
10 "Now the LORD has kept his promise:
I have succeeded my father as king of
Israel, and I have built a temple for the
worship of the LORD God of Israel.
11 I have placed in the Temple the Covenant Box, which contains the stone tablets of the covenant which the LORD
made with the people of Israel."

Solomon's Prayer

(1 Kings 8.22-53)

12 Then in the presence of the people
Solomon went and stood in front of the
altar and raised his arms in prayer.
(13 Solomon had made a bronze platform
and put it in the middle of the courtyard.
It was eight feet square and five feet
high. He mounted this platform, knelt
down where everyone could see him,
and raised his hands toward heaven.)
14 He prayed, "LORD God of Israel, in all
heaven and earth there is no god like
you. You keep your covenant with your
people and show them your love when
they live in wholehearted obedience to
you. 15 You have kept the promise you
made to my father David; today every
word has been fulfilled. 16 Now, LORD
God of Israel, keep the other promise
you made to my father when you told
him that there would always be one of
his descendants ruling as king of Israel,
provided that they carefully obeyed
your Law just as he did. 17 So now, LORD
God of Israel, let everything come true

that you promised to your servant
David.
18 "But can you, O God, really live on
earth among men and women? Not even
all of heaven is large enough to hold
you, so how can this Temple that I have
built be large enough? 19 LORD my God, I
am your servant. Listen to my prayer
and grant the requests I make to you.
20 Watch over this Temple day and night.
You have promised that this is where
you will be worshiped, so hear me when
I face this Temple and pray. 21 Hear my
prayers and the prayers of your people
Israel when they face this place and
pray. In your home in heaven hear us
and forgive us.
22 "When people are accused of wronging others and are brought to your altar
in this Temple to take an oath that they
are innocent, 23 O LORD, listen in heaven
and judge your servants. Punish the
guilty ones as they deserve and acquit
the innocent.
24 "When your people Israel are defeated by their enemies because they
have sinned against you and then when
they turn to you and come to this Temple, humbly praying to you for forgiveness, 25 listen to them in heaven. Forgive
the sins of your people and bring them
back to the land which you gave to them
and to their ancestors.
26 "When you hold back the rain because your people have sinned against
you and then when they repent and face
this Temple, humbly praying to you,
27 O LORD, listen to them in heaven and
forgive the sins of your servants,
the people of Israel, and teach them
to do what is right. Then, O LORD, send
rain on this land of yours, which you
gave to your people as a permanent
possession.
28 "When there is famine in the land or
an epidemic or the crops are destroyed
by scorching winds or swarms of locusts, or when your people are attacked
by their enemies, or when there is disease or sickness among them, 29 listen to
their prayers. If any of your people Israel, out of heartfelt sorrow, stretch out
their hands in prayer toward this Temple, 30 hear their prayer. Listen to them
in your home in heaven and forgive
them. You alone know the thoughts of
the human heart. Deal with each of us as
we deserve, 31 so that your people may
honor you and obey you all the time they
live in the land which you gave to our
ancestors.
32 "When foreigners who live in a distant land hear how great and powerful
you are and how you are always ready
to act, and then they come to pray at this
Temple, 33 listen to their prayers. In
heaven, where you live, hear them and
do what they ask you to do, so that all
the peoples of the world may know you
and obey you, as your people Israel do.
Then they will know that this Temple I
have built is where you are to be
worshiped.
34 "When you command your people to
go into battle against their enemies and
they pray to you, wherever they are, facing this city which you have chosen and
this Temple which I have built for you,
35 listen to their prayers. Hear them in
heaven and give them victory.
36 "When your people sin against
you—and there is no one who does not
sin—and in your anger you let their enemies defeat them and take them as prisoners to some other land, even if that
land is far away, 37 listen to your people's prayers. If there in that land they
repent and pray to you, confessing how
sinful and wicked they have been, hear
their prayers, O LORD. 38 If in that land
they truly and sincerely repent and pray
to you as they face toward this land
which you gave to our ancestors, this
city which you have chosen, and this
Temple which I have built for you,
39 then listen to their prayers. In your
home in heaven hear them and be merciful to them and forgive all the sins of
your people.
40 "Now, O my God, look on us and listen to the prayers offered in this place.
41 Rise up now, LORD God, and with the
Covenant Box, the symbol of your
power, enter the Temple and stay here
forever. Bless your priests in all they do,
and may all your people be happy because of your goodness to them. 42 LORD
God, do not reject the king you have
chosen. Remember the love you had for
your servant David."[n]

[n] the love you ... David; *or* your servant David's loyal service.

The Dedication of the Temple

(1 Kings 8.62-66)

7 When King Solomon finished his
prayer, fire came down from
heaven and burned up the sacrifices that
had been offered, and the dazzling light
of the LORD's presence filled the Temple.
2 Because the Temple was full of the dazzling light, the priests could not enter it.
3 When the people of Israel saw the fire
fall from heaven and the light fill the
Temple, they fell face downward on the
pavement, worshiping God and praising
him for his goodness and his eternal
love. 4 Then Solomon and all the people
offered sacrifices to the LORD. 5 He sacrificed 22,000 head of cattle and 120,000
sheep as fellowship offerings. And so he
and all the people dedicated the Temple.
6 The priests stood in the places that
were assigned to them, and facing them
stood the Levites, praising the LORD with
the musical instruments that King David
had provided and singing the hymn,
"His Love Is Eternal!" as they had been
commissioned by David. The priests
blew trumpets while all the people
stood.

7 Solomon consecrated the central part
of the courtyard, the area in front of the
Temple, and then offered there the sacrifices burned whole, the grain offerings,
and the fat from the fellowship offerings. He did this because the bronze altar which he had made was too small for
all these offerings.

8 Solomon and all the people of Israel
celebrated the Festival of Shelters for
seven days. There was a huge crowd of
people from as far away as Hamath Pass
in the north and the Egyptian border in
the south. 9 They had spent seven days
for the dedication of the altar and then
seven more days for the festival. On the
last day they had a closing celebration,
10 and on the following day, the twenty-
third day of the seventh month, Solomon
sent the people home. They were happy
about all the blessings that the LORD had
given to his people Israel, to David, and
to Solomon.

God Appears to Solomon Again

(1 Kings 9.1-9)

11 After King Solomon had finished the
Temple and the palace, successfully
completing all his plans for them, 12 the
LORD appeared to him at night. He said to
him, "I have heard your prayer, and I
accept this Temple as the place where
sacrifices are to be offered to me.
13 Whenever I hold back the rain or send
locusts to eat up the crops or send an
epidemic on my people, 14 if they pray to
me and repent and turn away from the
evil they have been doing, then I will
hear them in heaven, forgive their sins,
and make their land prosperous again.
15 I will watch over this Temple and be
ready to hear all the prayers that are offered here, 16 because I have chosen it
and consecrated it as the place where I
will be worshiped forever. I will watch
over it and protect it for all time. 17 If you
serve me faithfully as your father David
did, obeying my laws and doing everything I have commanded you, 18 I will
keep the promise I made to your father
David when I told him that Israel would
always be ruled by his descendants.
19 But if you and your people ever disobey the laws and commands I have
given you and worship other gods,
20 then I will remove you from the land
that I gave you, and I will abandon this
Temple that I have consecrated as the
place where I am to be worshiped. People everywhere will ridicule it and treat
it with contempt.

21 "The Temple is now greatly honored, but then everyone who passes by it
will be amazed and will ask, 'Why did
the LORD do this to this land and this
Temple?' 22 People will answer, 'It is because they abandoned the LORD their
God, who brought their ancestors out of
Egypt. They gave their allegiance to
other gods and worshiped them. That is
why the LORD has brought this disaster
on them.' "

Solomon's Achievements

(1 Kings 9.10-28)

8 It took Solomon twenty years to
build the Temple and his palace.
2 He also rebuilt the cities that King Hiram had given him, and sent Israelites to
settle in them. 3 He captured the territory
of Hamath and Zobah 4 and fortified the
city of Palmyra in the desert. He rebuilt
all the cities in Hamath that were centers
for storing supplies. 5 Solomon also rebuilt the following cities: Upper Beth
Horon and Lower Beth Horon (fortified
cities with gates that could be barred),

6 the city of Baalath, all the cities where
he stored supplies, and the cities where
his horses and chariots were stationed.
He carried out all his plans for building
in Jerusalem, in Lebanon, and throughout the territory that he ruled over.
7-8 Solomon employed at forced labor all
the descendants of the people of Canaan
whom the Israelites had not killed when
they took possession of the land. These
included Hittites, Amorites, Perizzites,
Hivites, and Jebusites, whose descendants continue to be slaves down to the
present time. 9 Israelites were not used at
forced labor, but served as soldiers, officers, chariot commanders, and cavalry
troops. 10 There were 250 officials in
charge of the forced labor working on
the various building projects.

11 Solomon moved his wife, the daughter of the king of Egypt, from David's
City to a house he built for her. He said,
"She must not live in the palace of King
David of Israel, because any place
where the Covenant Box has been is
holy."

12 Solomon offered sacrifices to the
LORD on the altar which he had built in
front of the Temple. 13 He offered burnt
offerings according to the requirements
of the Law of Moses for each holy day:
Sabbaths, New Moon Festivals, and the
three annual festivals—the Festival of
Unleavened Bread, the Harvest Festival,
and the Festival of Shelters. 14 Following
the rules laid down by his father David,
he organized the daily work of the
priests and of the Levites who assisted
the priests in singing hymns and in doing their work. He also organized the
Temple guards in sections for performing their daily duties at each gate, in accordance with the commands of David,
the man of God. 15 The instructions
which David had given the priests and
the Levites concerning the storehouses
and other matters were carried out in
detail.

16 By this time all of Solomon's
projects had been completed. From the
laying of the foundation of the LORD's
Temple to its completion, all the work
had been successful.

17 Then Solomon went to Eziongeber
and Elath, ports on the shore of the Gulf
of Aqaba, in the land of Edom. 18 King
Hiram sent him ships under the command of his own officers and with experienced sailors. They sailed with
Solomon's officers to the land of Ophir
and brought back to Solomon about sixteen tons of gold.

The Visit of the Queen of Sheba

(1 Kings 10.1-13)

9 The queen of Sheba heard of King
Solomon's fame, and she traveled
to Jerusalem to test him with difficult
questions. She brought with her a large
group of attendants, as well as camels
loaded with spices, jewels, and a large
amount of gold. When she and Solomon
met, she asked him all the questions that
she could think of. 2 He answered them
all; there was nothing too difficult for
him to explain. 3 The queen of Sheba
heard Solomon's wisdom and saw the
palace he had built. 4 She saw the food
that was served at his table, the living
quarters for his officials, the organization of his palace staff and the uniforms
they wore, the clothing of the servants
who waited on him at feasts, and the
sacrifices he offered[o] in the Temple. It
left her breathless and amazed.

5 She said to the king, "What I heard in
my own country about you[p] and your
wisdom is true! 6 I did not believe what
they told me until I came and saw for
myself. I had not heard of even half your
wisdom. You are even wiser than people
say. 7 How fortunate are those who serve
you, who are always in your presence
and are privileged to hear your wise sayings! 8 Praise the LORD your God! He has
shown how pleased he is with you by
making you king, to rule in his name.
Because he loves his people Israel and
wants to preserve them forever, he has
made you their king so that you can
maintain law and justice."

9 She presented to King Solomon the
gifts she had brought: almost five tons of
gold and a very large amount of spices
and jewels. There have never been any
other spices as fine as those that the
queen of Sheba gave to King Solomon.

(10 The sailors of King Hiram and of
King Solomon who brought gold from
Ophir also brought juniper wood and

o *Probable text (see 1 K 10.5)* sacrifices he offered; *Hebrew* his upper rooms. p you; *or* your deeds.

jewels. 11 Solomon used the wood to
make stairs for the Temple and for his
palace, and to make harps and lyres for
the musicians. Nothing like that had
ever been seen before in the land of
Judah.)
12 King Solomon gave the queen of
Sheba everything she asked for. This
was in addition to what he gave her in
exchange for the gifts[q] she brought to
him. Then she and her attendants returned to the land of Sheba.

King Solomon's Wealth

(1 Kings 10.14-25)

13 Every year King Solomon received
over twenty-five tons of gold, 14 in addition to the taxes paid by the traders and
merchants. The kings of Arabia and the
governors of the Israelite districts also
brought him silver and gold. 15 Solomon
made two hundred large shields, each of
which was covered with about fifteen
pounds of beaten gold, 16 and three hundred smaller shields, each covered with
about eight pounds of beaten gold. He
had them all placed in the Hall of the
Forest of Lebanon.[r]
17 The king also had a large throne
made. Part of it was covered with ivory
and the rest of it was covered with pure
gold. 18 Six steps led up to the throne,
and there was a footstool attached to it,
covered with gold. There were arms on
each side of the throne, and the figure of
a lion stood at each side. 19 Twelve figures of lions were on the steps, one at
either end of each step. No throne like
this had ever existed in any other
kingdom.
20 All of King Solomon's drinking cups
were made of gold, and all the utensils in
the Hall of the Forest of Lebanon were of
pure gold. Silver was not considered valuable in Solomon's day. 21 He had a fleet
of ocean-going ships sailing with King
Hiram's fleet. Every three years his fleet
would return, bringing gold, silver,
ivory, apes, and monkeys.
22 King Solomon was richer and wiser
than any other king in the world. 23 They
all consulted him, to hear the wisdom
that God had given him. 24 Each of them
brought Solomon gifts—articles of silver and gold, robes, weapons, spices,
horses, and mules. This continued year
after year.
25 King Solomon also had four thousand stalls for his chariots and horses,
and had twelve thousand cavalry
horses. Some of them he kept in Jerusalem and the rest he stationed in various
other cities. 26 He was supreme ruler of
all the kings in the territory from the Euphrates River to Philistia and the Egyptian border. 27 During his reign silver
was as common in Jerusalem as stone,
and cedar was as plentiful as ordinary
sycamore in the foothills of Judah.
28 Solomon imported horses from
Musri[s] and from every other country.

Summary of Solomon's Reign

(1 Kings 11.41-43)

29 The rest of the history of Solomon
from beginning to end is recorded in *The
History of Nathan the Prophet,* in *The
Prophecy of Ahijah of Shiloh,* and in *The
Visions of Iddo the Prophet,* which also
deal with the reign of King Jeroboam of
Israel. 30 Solomon ruled in Jerusalem
over all Israel for forty years. 31 He died
and was buried in David's City, and his
son Rehoboam succeeded him as king.

The Northern Tribes Revolt

(1 Kings 12.1-20)

10 Rehoboam went to Shechem,
where all the people of northern
Israel had gathered to make him king.
2 When Jeroboam son of Nebat, who had
gone to Egypt to escape from King Solomon, heard this news, he returned home.
3 The people of the northern tribes sent
for him, and they all went together to
Rehoboam and said to him, 4 "Your
father placed heavy burdens on us. If
you make these burdens lighter and
make life easier for us, we will be your
loyal subjects."
5 Rehoboam replied, "Give me three
days to consider the matter. Then come
back." So the people left.
6 King Rehoboam consulted the older
men who had served as his father Solomon's advisers. "What answer do you
advise me to give these people?" he
asked.
7 They replied, "If you are kind to these
people and try to please them by giving

[q] *Probable text* he gave her in exchange for the gifts; *Hebrew unclear.* [r] HALL OF THE FOREST OF LEBANON: *A large ceremonial hall in the palace, probably so called because it was paneled in cedar.* [s] *Probable text (see 1.16)* Musri; *Hebrew* Egypt.

a considerate answer, they will always
serve you loyally."
8 But he ignored the advice of the older
men and went instead to the young men
who had grown up with him and who
were now his advisers. 9 "What do you
advise me to do?" he asked. "What shall
I say to the people who are asking me to
make their burdens lighter?"
10 They replied, "This is what you
should tell them: 'My little finger is
thicker than my father's waist.' 11 Tell
them, 'My father placed heavy burdens
on you; I will make them even heavier.
He beat you with whips; I'll flog you
with bullwhips!'"
12 Three days later Jeroboam and all
the people returned to King Rehoboam,
as he had instructed them. 13 The king
ignored the advice of the older men and
spoke harshly to the people, 14 as the
younger men had advised. He said, "My
father placed heavy burdens on you; I
will make them even heavier. He beat
you with whips; I'll flog you with bullwhips!" 15 It was the will of the LORD God
to bring about what he had spoken to
Jeroboam son of Nebat through the
prophet Ahijah from Shiloh. This is why
the king did not pay any attention to the
people.
16 When the people saw that the king
would not listen to them, they shouted,
"Down with David and his family! What
have they ever done for us? People of
Israel, let's go home! Let Rehoboam
look out for himself!"
So the people of Israel rebelled,
17 leaving Rehoboam as king only of the
people who lived in the territory of
Judah.
18 Then King Rehoboam sent Adoniram, who was in charge of the forced
labor, to go to the Israelites, but they
stoned him to death. At this, Rehoboam
hurriedly got in his chariot and escaped
to Jerusalem. 19 Ever since that time the
people of the northern kingdom of Israel
have been in rebellion against the dynasty of David.

Shemaiah's Prophecy

(1 Kings 12.21-24)

11 When King Rehoboam arrived in
Jerusalem, he called together
180,000 of the best soldiers from the
tribes of Benjamin and Judah. He intended to go to war and restore his control over the northern tribes of Israel.
2 But the LORD told the prophet Shemaiah
3 to give this message to King Rehoboam
and to all the people of the tribes of Judah and Benjamin: 4 "Do not attack your
own relatives. Go home, all of you. What
has happened is my will." They obeyed
the LORD's command and did not go to
fight Jeroboam.

Rehoboam Fortifies the Cities

5 Rehoboam remained in Jerusalem
and had fortifications built for the following cities of Judah and Benjamin:
6 Bethlehem, Etam, Tekoa, 7 Bethzur,
Soco, Adullam, 8 Gath, Mareshah, Ziph,
9 Adoraim, Lachish, Azekah, 10 Zorah,
Aijalon, and Hebron. 11 He had them
strongly fortified and appointed a commander for each of them, and in each
one he placed supplies of food, olive oil,
and wine, 12 and also shields and spears.
In this way he kept Judah and Benjamin
under his control.

Priests and Levites Come to Judah

13 From all the territory of Israel
priests and Levites came south to Judah.
14 The Levites abandoned their pastures
and other land and moved to Judah and
Jerusalem, because King Jeroboam of
Israel and his successors would not let
them serve as priests of the LORD. 15 Jeroboam appointed priests of his own to
serve at the pagan places of worship and
to worship demons and the idols he
made in the form of bull-calves. 16 From
all the tribes of Israel people who sincerely wanted to worship the LORD, the
God of Israel, followed the Levites to Jerusalem, so that they could offer sacrifices to the LORD, the God of their
ancestors. 17 This strengthened the kingdom of Judah, and for three years they
supported Rehoboam son of Solomon
and lived as they had under the rule of
King David and King Solomon.

Rehoboam's Family

18 Rehoboam married Mahalath,
whose father was Jerimoth son of David
and whose mother was Abihail, the
daughter of Eliab and granddaughter of
Jesse. 19 They had three sons, Jeush,
Shemariah, and Zaham. 20 Later he married Maacah, the daughter of Absalom,
and they had four sons: Abijah, Attai,
Ziza, and Shelomith. 21 In all, Rehoboam

had eighteen wives and sixty concubines, and he fathered twenty-eight sons
and sixty daughters. Of all his wives and
concubines he loved Maacah best, 22 and
he favored her son Abijah over all his
other children, choosing him as the one
to succeed him as king. 23 Rehoboam
wisely assigned responsibilities to his
sons and stationed them throughout Judah and Benjamin in the fortified cities.
He provided generously for them and
also secured many wives for them.

An Egyptian Invasion of Judah

(1 Kings 14.25-28)

12 As soon as Rehoboam had established his authority as king, he
and all his people abandoned the Law of
the LORD. 2 In the fifth year of Rehoboam's reign their disloyalty to the LORD
was punished. King Shishak of Egypt attacked Jerusalem 3 with an army of
twelve hundred chariots, sixty thousand
cavalry, and more soldiers than could be
counted, including Libyan, Sukkite, and
Ethiopian[t] troops. 4 He captured the
fortified cities of Judah and advanced as
far as Jerusalem.
5 Shemaiah the prophet went to King
Rehoboam and the Judean leaders who
had gathered in Jerusalem to escape
Shishak. He said to them, "This is the
LORD's message to you: 'You have abandoned me, so now I have abandoned you
to Shishak.' "
6 The king and the leaders admitted
that they had sinned, and they said,
"What the LORD is doing is just."
7 When the LORD saw this, he spoke
again to Shemaiah and said to him, "Because they admit their sin, I will not destroy them. But when Shishak attacks,
they will barely survive. Jerusalem will
not feel the full force of my anger, 8 but
Shishak will conquer them, and they
will learn the difference between serving me and serving earthly rulers."
9 King Shishak came to Jerusalem and
took the treasures from the Temple and
from the palace. He took everything, including the gold shields that King Solomon had made. 10 To replace them,
Rehoboam made bronze shields and entrusted them to the officers responsible
for guarding the palace gates. 11 Every
time the king went to the Temple, the
guards carried the shields and then returned them to the guardroom. 12 Because he submitted to the LORD, the
LORD's anger did not completely destroy
him, and things went well for Judah.

Summary of Rehoboam's Reign

13 Rehoboam ruled in Jerusalem and
increased his power as king. He was
forty-one years old when he became
king, and he ruled for seventeen years in
Jerusalem, the city which the LORD had
chosen from all the territory of Israel as
the place where he was to be worshiped.
Rehoboam's mother was Naamah, from
the land of Ammon. 14 He did what was
evil, because he did not try to find the
LORD's will.
15 Rehoboam's acts from beginning to
end and his family records are found in
The History of Shemaiah the Prophet
and *The History of Iddo the Prophet*. Rehoboam and Jeroboam were constantly
at war with each other. 16 Rehoboam
died and was buried in the royal tombs
in David's City and his son Abijah succeeded him as king.

Abijah's War with Jeroboam

(1 Kings 15.1-8)

13 In the eighteenth year of the
reign of King Jeroboam of Israel,
Abijah became king of Judah, 2 and he
ruled three years in Jerusalem. His
mother was Micaiah daughter of Uriel,
from the city of Gibeah.
War broke out between Abijah and
Jeroboam. 3 Abijah raised an army of
400,000 soldiers, and Jeroboam opposed
him with an army of 800,000.
4 The armies met in the hill country of
Ephraim. King Abijah went up Mount
Zemaraim and called out to Jeroboam
and the Israelites: "Listen to me!" he
said. 5 "Don't you know that the LORD,
the God of Israel, made an unbreakable
covenant with David, giving him and his
descendants kingship over Israel forever? 6 Jeroboam son of Nebat rebelled
against Solomon, his king. 7 Later he
gathered together a group of worthless
scoundrels, and they forced their will on

[t] Hebrew Cushite(s): *Cush is the ancient name of the extensive territory south of the First Cataract of the Nile River. This region was called Ethiopia in Graeco-Roman times, and included within its borders most of modern Sudan and some of present-day Ethiopia (Abyssinia).*

Rehoboam son of Solomon, who was too
young and inexperienced to resist them.
8 Now you propose to fight against the
royal authority that the LORD gave to David's descendants. You have a huge
army and have with you the gold bull-
calves that Jeroboam made to be your
gods. 9 You drove out the LORD's priests,
the descendants of Aaron, and you
drove out the Levites. In their place you
appointed priests in the same way that
other nations do. Anybody who comes
along with a bull or seven sheep can get
himself consecrated as a priest of those
so-called gods of yours.

10 "But we still serve the LORD our God
and have not abandoned him. Priests descended from Aaron perform their duties, and Levites assist them. 11 Every
morning and every evening they offer
him incense and animal sacrifices
burned whole. They present the offerings of bread on a table that is ritually
clean, and every evening they light the
lamps on the gold lampstand. We do
what the LORD has commanded, but you
have abandoned him. 12 God himself is
our leader and his priests are here with
trumpets, ready to blow them and call us
to battle against you. People of Israel,
don't fight against the LORD, the God of
your ancestors! You can't win!"

13 Meanwhile Jeroboam had sent some
of his troops to ambush the Judean army
from the rear, while the rest faced them
from the front. 14 The Judeans looked
around and saw that they were surrounded. They cried to the LORD for help,
and the priests blew the trumpets. 15 The
Judeans gave a loud shout, and led by
Abijah, they attacked; God defeated Jeroboam and the Israelite army. 16 The Israelites fled from the Judeans, and God
let the Judeans overpower them. 17 Abijah and his army dealt the Israelites a
crushing defeat—half a million of Israel's best soldiers were killed. 18 And so
the people of Judah were victorious over
Israel, because they relied on the LORD,
the God of their ancestors.

19 Abijah pursued Jeroboam's army
and occupied some of his cities: Bethel,
Jeshanah, and Ephron, and the villages
near each of these cities. 20 Jeroboam
never regained his power during Abijah's reign. Finally the LORD struck him
down, and he died.

21 Abijah, however, grew more powerful. He had fourteen wives and fathered
twenty-two sons and sixteen daughters.
22 The rest of the history of Abijah, what
he said and what he did, is written in
The History of Iddo the Prophet.

King Asa Defeats the Ethiopians

14 King Abijah died and was buried
in the royal tombs in David's
City. His son Asa succeeded him as king,
and under Asa the land enjoyed peace
for ten years. 2 Asa pleased the LORD, his
God, by doing what was right and good.
3 He removed the foreign altars and the
pagan places of worship, broke down
the sacred stone columns, and cut down
the symbols of the goddess Asherah.
4 He commanded the people of Judah to
do the will of the LORD, the God of their
ancestors, and to obey his teachings and
commands. 5 Because he abolished the
pagan places of worship and the incense
altars from all the cities of Judah, the
kingdom was at peace under his rule.
6 He built fortifications for the cities of
Judah during this time, and for several
years there was no war, because the
LORD gave him peace. 7 He told the people of Judah, "Let us fortify the cities by
building walls and towers, and gates
that can be shut and barred. We have
control of the land because we have
done the will of the LORD our God. He
has protected us and given us security
on every side." And so they built and
prospered. 8 King Asa had an army of
300,000 men from Judah, armed with
shields and spears, and 280,000 men
from Benjamin, armed with shields and
bows. All of them were brave, well-
trained men.

9 An Ethiopian[t] named Zerah invaded Judah with an army of a million
men and three hundred chariots and advanced as far as Mareshah. 10 Asa went
out to fight him, and both sides took up
their positions at Zephathah Valley near
Mareshah. 11 Asa prayed to the LORD his
God, "O LORD, you can help a weak army
as easily as a powerful one. Help us now,

[t] *Hebrew* Cushite(s): *Cush is the ancient name of the extensive territory south of the First Cataract of the Nile River. This region was called Ethiopia in Graeco-Roman times, and included within its borders most of modern Sudan and some of present-day Ethiopia (Abyssinia).*

O LORD our God, because we are relying
on you, and in your name we have come
out to fight against this huge army. LORD,
you are our God; no one can hope to defeat you."
12 The LORD defeated the Ethiopian[t]
army when Asa and the Judean army attacked them. They fled, 13 and Asa and
his troops pursued them as far as Gerar.
So many of the Ethiopians[t] were killed
that the army was unable to rally and
fight.[u] They were overpowered by the
LORD and his army, and the army took
large amounts of loot. 14 Then they were
able to destroy the cities in the area
around Gerar, because the people there
were terrified of the LORD. The army
plundered all those cities and captured
large amounts of loot. 15 They also attacked the camps of some shepherds,
capturing large numbers of sheep and
camels. Then they returned to Jerusalem.

Asa's Reforms

15 The spirit of God came upon Azariah son of Oded, 2 and he went
to meet King Asa. He called out, "Listen
to me, King Asa, and all you people of
Judah and Benjamin! The LORD is with
you as long as you are with him. If you
look for him, he will let you find him, but
if you turn away, he will abandon you.
3 For a long time Israel lived without the
true God, without priests to teach them,
and without a law. 4 But when trouble
came, they turned to the LORD, the God
of Israel. They searched for him and
found him. 5 In those days no one could
come and go in safety, because there
was trouble and disorder in every land.
6 One nation oppressed another nation,
and one city oppressed another city, because God was bringing trouble and distress on them. 7 But you must be strong
and not be discouraged. The work that
you do will be rewarded."
8 When Asa heard the prophecy that
Azariah son of[v] Oded had spoken, he
was encouraged. He did away with all
the idols in the land of Judah and Benjamin and all the idols in the cities he had
captured in the hill country of Ephraim.
He also repaired the altar of the LORD
that stood in the Temple courtyard.
9 Many people had come over to Asa's
side from Ephraim, Manasseh, and Simeon, and were living in his kingdom, because they had seen that the LORD was
with him. Asa summoned all of them
and the people of Judah and Benjamin.
10 They assembled in Jerusalem in the
third month of the fifteenth year that
Asa was king. 11 On that day they offered
sacrifices to the LORD from the loot they
had brought back: seven hundred head
of cattle and seven thousand sheep.
12 They made a covenant in which they
agreed to worship the LORD, the God of
their ancestors, with all their heart and
soul. 13 Anyone, young or old, male or
female, who did not worship him was to
be put to death. 14 In a loud voice they
took an oath in the LORD's name that
they would keep the covenant, and then
they shouted and blew trumpets. 15 All
the people of Judah were happy because
they had made this covenant with all
their heart. They took delight in worshiping the LORD, and he accepted them
and gave them peace on every side.
16 King Asa removed his grandmother
Maacah from her position as queen
mother, because she had made an obscene idol of the fertility goddess Asherah. Asa cut down the idol, chopped it
up, and burned the pieces in Kidron Valley. 17 Even though Asa did not destroy
all the pagan places of worship in the
land, he remained faithful to the LORD all
his life. 18 He placed in the Temple all the
objects his father Abijah had dedicated
to God, as well as the gold and silver
objects that he himself dedicated.
19 There was no more war until the
thirty-fifth year of his reign.

Troubles with Israel

(1 Kings 15.17-22)

16 In the thirty-sixth year of the
reign of King Asa of Judah, King
Baasha of Israel invaded Judah and
started to fortify Ramah in order to cut
off all traffic in and out of Judah. 2 So

[t] *Hebrew* Cushite(s): *Cush is the ancient name of the extensive territory south of the First Cataract of the Nile River. This region was called Ethiopia in Graeco-Roman times, and included within its borders most of modern Sudan and some of present-day Ethiopia (Abyssinia).* [u] So many of the Ethiopians . . . fight; *or* The Ethiopians were completely defeated; not one of them was left alive. [v] *Some ancient translations* Azariah son of; *Hebrew does not have these words.*

Asa took silver and gold from the treasuries of the Temple and the palace and sent it to Damascus, to King Benhadad of Syria, with this message: [3]"Let us be allies, as our fathers were. This silver and gold is a present for you. Now break your alliance with King Baasha of Israel so that he will have to pull his troops out of my territory."

[4]Benhadad agreed to Asa's proposal and sent his commanding officers and their armies to attack the cities of Israel. They captured Ijon, Dan, Abel Beth Maacah, and all the cities of Naphtali where supplies were stored. [5]When King Baasha heard what was happening, he stopped fortifying Ramah and abandoned the work. [6]Then King Asa gathered men from throughout Judah and had them carry off the stones and timbers that Baasha had been using at Ramah, and they used them to fortify the cities of Geba and Mizpah.

The Prophet Hanani

[7]At that time the prophet Hanani went to King Asa and said, "Because you relied on the king of Syria instead of relying on the LORD your God, the army of the king of Israel[w] has escaped from you. [8]Didn't the Ethiopians[x] and the Libyans have large armies with many chariots and cavalry troops? But because you relied on the LORD, he gave you victory over them. [9]The LORD keeps close watch over the whole world, to give strength to those whose hearts are loyal to him. You have acted foolishly, and so from now on you will always be at war." [10]This made Asa so angry with the prophet that he had him put in chains. It was at this same time that Asa began treating some of the people cruelly.

The End of Asa's Reign

(1 Kings 15.23, 24)

[11]All the events of Asa's reign from beginning to end are recorded in *The History of the Kings of Judah and Israel.* [12]In the thirty-ninth year that Asa was king, he was crippled by a severe foot disease; but even then he did not turn to the LORD for help, but to doctors. [13]Two years later he died [14]and was buried in the rock tomb which he had carved out for himself in David's City. They used spices and perfumed oils to prepare his body for burial, and they built a huge bonfire to mourn his death.

Jehoshaphat Becomes King

17 Jehoshaphat succeeded his father Asa as king and strengthened his position against Israel. [2]He stationed troops in the fortified cities of Judah, in the Judean countryside, and in the cities which Asa had captured in the territory of Ephraim. [3]The LORD blessed Jehoshaphat because he followed the example of his father's early life and did not worship Baal. [4]He served his father's God, obeyed God's commands, and did not act the way the kings of Israel did. [5]The LORD gave Jehoshaphat firm control over the kingdom of Judah, and all the people brought him gifts, so that he became wealthy and highly honored. [6]He took pride in serving the LORD and destroyed all the pagan places of worship and the symbols of the goddess Asherah in Judah.

[7]In the third year of his reign he sent out the following officials to teach in the cities of Judah: Benhail, Obadiah, Zechariah, Nethanel, and Micaiah. [8]They were accompanied by nine Levites and two priests. The Levites were Shemaiah, Nethaniah, Zebadiah, Asahel, Shemiramoth, Jehonathan, Adonijah, Tobijah, and Tobadonijah; and the priests were Elishama and Jehoram. [9]They took the book of the Law of the LORD and went through all the towns of Judah, teaching it to the people.

Jehoshaphat's Greatness

[10]The LORD made all the surrounding kingdoms afraid to go to war against King Jehoshaphat. [11]Some of the Philistines brought Jehoshaphat a large amount of silver and other gifts, and some Arabs brought him 7,700 sheep and 7,700 goats. [12]So Jehoshaphat continued to grow more and more powerful. Throughout Judah he built fortifications and cities, [13]where supplies were stored in huge amounts.

[w] *One ancient translation* Israel; *Hebrew* Syria. [x] *Hebrew* Cushites: *Cush is the ancient name of the extensive territory south of the First Cataract of the Nile River. This region was called Ethiopia in Graeco-Roman times, and included within its borders most of modern Sudan and some of present-day Ethiopia (Abyssinia).*

In Jerusalem he stationed outstanding
officers, 14 according to their clans. Ad-
nah was the commander of the troops
from the clans of Judah, and he had
300,000 soldiers under him. 15 Second in
rank was Jehohanan, with 280,000 soldiers, 16 and third was Amasiah son of
Zichri, with 200,000. (Amasiah had volunteered to serve the LORD.) 17 The commander of the troops from the clans of
Benjamin was Eliada, an outstanding
soldier, in command of 200,000 men
armed with shields and bows. 18 His second in command was Jehozabad with
180,000 men, well-equipped for battle.
19 These soldiers served the king in Jerusalem, and in addition he stationed others in the other fortified cities of Judah.

The Prophet Micaiah Warns Ahab

(1 Kings 22.1-28)

18 When King Jehoshaphat of Judah became rich and famous, he
arranged a marriage between a member
of his family and the family of King
Ahab of Israel. 2 A number of years later
Jehoshaphat went to the city of Samaria
to visit Ahab. To honor Jehoshaphat and
those with him, Ahab had a large number of sheep and cattle slaughtered for a
feast. He tried to persuade Jehoshaphat
to join him in attacking the city of Ramoth in Gilead. 3 He asked, "Will you go
with me to attack Ramoth?"

Jehoshaphat replied, "I am ready
when you are, and so is my army. We
will join you." 4 Then he added, "But first
let's consult the LORD."

5 So Ahab called in the prophets, about
four hundred of them, and asked them,
"Should I go and attack Ramoth, or
not?"

"Attack it," they answered. "God will
give you victory."

6 But Jehoshaphat asked, "Isn't there
another prophet through whom we can
consult the LORD?"

7 Ahab answered, "There is one more,
Micaiah son of Imlah. But I hate him
because he never prophesies anything good for me; it's always something bad."

"You shouldn't say that!" Jehoshaphat
replied.

8 So King Ahab called in a court official and told him to go and get Micaiah
at once.

9 The two kings, dressed in their royal
robes, were sitting on their thrones at
the threshing place just outside the gate
of Samaria, and all the prophets were
prophesying in front of them. 10 One of
them, Zedekiah son of Chenaanah,
made iron horns and said to Ahab, "This
is what the LORD says, 'With these you
will fight the Syrians and totally defeat
them.' " 11 All the other prophets said the
same thing. "March against Ramoth and
you will win," they said. "The LORD will
give you victory."

12 Meanwhile, the official who had
gone to get Micaiah said to him, "All the
other prophets have prophesied success
for the king, and you had better do the
same."

13 But Micaiah answered, "By the living LORD I will say what my God tells
me to!"

14 When he appeared before King
Ahab, the king asked him, "Micaiah,
should King Jehoshaphat and I go and
attack Ramoth, or not?"

"Attack!" Micaiah answered. "Of
course you'll win. The LORD will give you
victory."

15 But Ahab replied, "When you speak
to me in the name of the LORD, tell the
truth! How many times do I have to tell
you that?"

16 Micaiah answered, "I can see the
army of Israel scattered over the hills
like sheep without a shepherd. And the
LORD said, 'These men have no leader; let
them go home in peace.' "

17 Ahab said to Jehoshaphat, "I told
you that he never prophesies anything
good for me; it's always something
bad!"

18 Micaiah went on: "Now listen to
what the LORD says! I saw the LORD sitting on his throne in heaven, with all his
angels standing beside him. 19 The LORD
asked, 'Who will deceive Ahab so that
he will go and get killed at Ramoth?'
Some of the angels said one thing, and
others said something else, 20 until a
spirit stepped forward, approached the
LORD, and said, 'I will deceive him.'
'How?' the LORD asked. 21 The spirit replied, 'I will go and make all of Ahab's
prophets tell lies.' The LORD said, 'Go
and deceive him. You will succeed.' "

22 And Micaiah concluded: "This is
what has happened. The LORD has made
these prophets of yours lie to you. But he

himself has decreed that you will meet
with disaster!"
23 Then the prophet Zedekiah went up
to Micaiah, slapped his face, and asked,
"Since when did the LORD's spirit leave
me and speak to you?"
24 "You will find out when you go into
some back room to hide," Micaiah
replied.
25 Then King Ahab ordered one of his
officers, "Arrest Micaiah and take him to
Amon, the governor of the city, and to
Prince Joash. 26 Tell them to throw him
in prison and to put him on bread and
water until I return safely."
27 "If you return safely," Micaiah exclaimed, "then the LORD has not spoken
through me!" And he added, "Listen,
everyone, to what I have said!"

The Death of Ahab

(1 Kings 22.29-35)

28 Then King Ahab of Israel and King
Jehoshaphat of Judah went to attack the
city of Ramoth in Gilead. 29 Ahab said to
Jehoshaphat, "As we go into battle, I will
disguise myself, but you wear your royal
garments." So the king of Israel went
into battle in disguise.
30 The king of Syria had ordered his
chariot commanders to attack no one
else except the king of Israel. 31 So when
they saw King Jehoshaphat, they all
thought that he was the king of Israel,
and they turned to attack him. But Jehoshaphat gave a shout, and the LORD
God rescued him and turned the attack
away from him. 32 The chariot commanders saw that he was not the king of
Israel, so they stopped pursuing him.
33 By chance, however, a Syrian soldier
shot an arrow which struck King Ahab
between the joints of his armor. "I'm
wounded!" he cried out to his chariot
driver. "Turn around and pull out of the
battle!" 34 While the battle raged on,
King Ahab remained propped up in his
chariot, facing the Syrians. At sunset he
died.

A Prophet Reprimands Jehoshaphat

19 King Jehoshaphat of Judah returned safely to his palace in Jerusalem. 2 A prophet, Jehu son of
Hanani, went to meet the king and said
to him, "Do you think it is right to help
those who are wicked and to take the
side of those who hate the LORD? What
you have done has brought the LORD's
anger on you. 3 But even so, there is
some good in you. You have removed all
the symbols of the goddess Asherah
which people worshiped, and you have
tried to follow God's will."

Jehoshaphat's Reforms

4 Even though King Jehoshaphat lived
in Jerusalem, he traveled regularly
among the people, from Beersheba in
the south to the edge of the hill country
of Ephraim in the north, in order to call
the people back to the LORD, the God of
their ancestors. 5 He appointed judges in
each of the fortified cities of Judah 6 and
instructed them: "Be careful in pronouncing judgment; you are not acting
on human authority, but on the authority of the LORD, and he is with you when
you pass sentence. 7 Honor the LORD and
act carefully, because the LORD our God
does not tolerate fraud or partiality or
the taking of bribes."
8 In Jerusalem Jehoshaphat appointed
Levites, priests, and some of the leading
citizens as judges in cases involving a
violation of the Law of the LORD or legal
disputes between inhabitants of the
city.[y] 9 He gave them the following instructions: "You must perform your duties in reverence for the LORD, faithfully
obeying him in everything you do.
10 Whenever your fellow citizens from
any of the cities bring before you a case
of homicide or any other violation of a
law or commandment, you must instruct
them carefully how to conduct themselves during the trial, so that they do
not become guilty of sinning against the
LORD. Unless you do, you and your fellow citizens will feel the force of the
LORD's anger. But if you do your duty,
you will not be guilty. 11 Amariah the
High Priest will have final authority in
all religious cases, and Zebadiah son of
Ishmael, governor of Judah, will have final authority in all civil cases. The Levites have the responsibility of seeing
that the decisions of the courts are carried out. Be courageous and carry out
these instructions, and may the LORD be
on the side of the right!"

[y] *Some ancient translations* between . . . city; *Hebrew unclear.*

War against Edom

20 Some time later the armies of Moab and Ammon, together with their allies, the Meunites,[z] invaded Judah. 2 Some messengers came and announced to King Jehoshaphat: "A large army from Edom has come from the other side of the Dead Sea to attack you. They have already captured Hazazon Tamar." (This is another name for Engedi.) 3 Jehoshaphat was frightened and prayed to the LORD for guidance. Then he gave orders for a fast to be observed throughout the country. 4 From every city of Judah people hurried to Jerusalem to ask the LORD for guidance, 5 and they and the people of Jerusalem gathered in the new courtyard of the Temple. King Jehoshaphat went and stood before them 6 and prayed aloud, "O LORD God of our ancestors, you rule in heaven over all the nations of the world. You are powerful and mighty, and no one can oppose you. 7 You are our God. When your people Israel moved into this land, you drove out the people who were living here and gave the land to the descendants of Abraham, your friend, to be theirs forever. 8 They have lived here and have built a temple to honor you, knowing 9 that if any disaster struck them to punish them—a war,[a] an epidemic, or a famine—then they could come and stand in front of this Temple where you are worshiped. They could pray to you in their trouble, and you would hear them and rescue them.

10 "Now the people of Ammon, Moab, and Edom have attacked us. When our ancestors came out of Egypt, you did not allow them to enter those lands, so our ancestors went around them and did not destroy them. 11 This is how they repay us—they come to drive us out of the land that you gave us. 12 You are our God! Punish them, for we are helpless in the face of this large army that is attacking us. We do not know what to do, but we look to you for help."

13 All the men of Judah, with their wives and children, were standing there at the Temple. 14 The spirit of the LORD came upon a Levite who was present in the crowd. His name was Jahaziel son of Zechariah; he was a member of the clan of Asaph and was descended from Asaph through Mattaniah, Jeiel, and Benaiah. 15 Jahaziel said, "Your Majesty and all you people of Judah and Jerusalem, the LORD says that you must not be discouraged or be afraid to face this large army. The battle depends on God, not on you. 16 Attack them tomorrow as they come up the pass at Ziz. You will meet them at the end of the valley that leads to the wild country near Jeruel. 17 You will not have to fight this battle. Just take up your positions and wait; you will see the LORD give you victory. People of Judah and Jerusalem, do not hesitate or be afraid. Go out to battle, and the LORD will be with you!"

18 Then King Jehoshaphat bowed low, with his face touching the ground, and all the people bowed with him and worshiped the LORD. 19 The members of the Levite clans of Kohath and Korah stood up and with a loud shout praised the LORD, the God of Israel.

20 Early the next morning the people went out to the wild country near Tekoa. As they were starting out, Jehoshaphat addressed them with these words: "People of Judah and Jerusalem! Put your trust in the LORD your God, and you will stand your ground. Believe what his prophets tell you, and you will succeed." 21 After consulting with the people, the king ordered some musicians to put on the robes they wore on sacred occasions and to march ahead of the army, singing: "Praise the LORD! His love is eternal!"

22 When they began to sing, the LORD threw the invading armies into a panic. 23 The Ammonites and the Moabites attacked the Edomite army and completely destroyed it, and then they turned on each other in savage fighting. 24 When the Judean army reached a tower that was in the desert, they looked toward the enemy and saw that they were all lying on the ground dead. Not one had escaped.

25 Jehoshaphat and his troops moved in to take the loot, and they found many cattle,[b] supplies, clothing, and other valuable objects. They spent three days gathering the loot, but there was so much that they could not take

[z] *One ancient translation* Meunites; *Hebrew* Ammonites. [a] struck . . . war; *or* struck them—a devastating war. [b] *One ancient translation* cattle; *Hebrew* among them.

everything. 26 On the fourth day they assembled in Beracah Valley and praised
the LORD for all he had done. That is why
the valley is called "Beracah."[c] 27 Jehoshaphat led his troops back to Jerusalem in triumph, because the LORD had
defeated their enemies. 28 When they
reached the city, they marched to the
Temple to the music of harps and trumpets. 29 Every nation that heard how the
LORD had defeated Israel's enemies
was terrified, 30 so Jehoshaphat ruled
in peace, and God gave him security
on every side.

The End of Jehoshaphat's Reign

(1 Kings 22.41-50)

31 Jehoshaphat had become king of Judah at the age of thirty-five and had
ruled in Jerusalem for twenty-five years.
His mother was Azubah, the daughter of
Shilhi. 32 Like his father Asa before him,
he did what was right in the sight of the
LORD; 33 but the pagan places of worship
were not destroyed. The people still did
not turn wholeheartedly to the worship
of the God of their ancestors.

34 Everything else that Jehoshaphat
did, from the beginning of his reign to its
end, is recorded in *The History of Jehu
Son of Hanani,* which is a part of *The
History of the Kings of Israel.*

35 At one time King Jehoshaphat of Judah made an alliance with King Ahaziah
of Israel, who did many wicked things.
36 At the port of Eziongeber they built
ocean-going ships. 37 But Eliezer son of
Dodavahu, from the town of Mareshah,
warned Jehoshaphat, "Because you
have made an alliance with Ahaziah, the
LORD will destroy what you have built."
And the ships were wrecked and never
sailed.

21 Jehoshaphat died and was buried in the royal tombs in David's
City and his son Jehoram succeeded him
as king.

King Jehoram of Judah

(2 Kings 8.17-24)

2 Jehoram son of King Jehoshaphat of
Judah had six brothers: Azariah, Jehiel,
Zechariah, Azariahu, Michael, and
Shephatiah. 3 Their father gave them
large amounts of gold, silver, and other
valuable possessions, and placed each
one in charge of one of the fortified cities
of Judah. But because Jehoram was the
oldest, Jehoshaphat made him his successor. 4 When Jehoram was in firm control of the kingdom, he had all his
brothers killed, and also some Israelite
officials.

5 Jehoram became king at the age of
thirty-two, and he ruled in Jerusalem for
eight years. 6 He followed the wicked example of King Ahab and the other kings
of Israel, because he had married one of
Ahab's daughters. He sinned against the
LORD, 7 but the LORD was not willing to
destroy the dynasty of David, because
he had made a covenant with David and
promised that his descendants would always continue to rule.

8 During Jehoram's reign Edom revolted against Judah and became an independent kingdom. 9 So Jehoram and
his officers set out with chariots and invaded Edom. There the Edomite army
surrounded them, but during the night
they managed to break out and escape.
10 Edom has been independent of[d] Judah ever since. During this same period
the city of Libnah also revolted, because
Jehoram had abandoned the LORD, the
God of his ancestors. 11 He even built pagan places of worship in the Judean
highlands and led the people of Judah
and Jerusalem to sin against the
LORD.

12 The prophet Elijah sent Jehoram a
letter, which read as follows: "The LORD,
the God of your ancestor David, condemns you, because you did not follow
the example of your father, King Jehoshaphat, or that of your grandfather,
King Asa. 13 Instead, you have followed
the example of the kings of Israel and
have led the people of Judah and Jerusalem into being unfaithful to God, just as
Ahab and his successors led Israel into
unfaithfulness. You even murdered your
brothers, who were better men than you
are. 14 As a result, the LORD will severely
punish your people, your children, and
your wives, and will destroy your possessions. 15 You yourself will suffer a
painful intestinal disease that will grow
worse day by day."

16 Some Philistines and Arabs lived

[c] BERACAH: *This name in Hebrew means "praise."*

[d] independent of; *or* in revolt against.

near where some Ethiopians[e] had settled along the coast. The LORD caused
them to go to war against Jehoram.
17 They invaded Judah, looted the royal
palace, and carried off as prisoners all
the king's wives and sons except Ahaziah, his youngest son.
18 Then after all this, the LORD brought
on the king a painful disease of the intestines. 19 For almost two years it grew
steadily worse until finally the king died
in agony. His subjects did not light a
bonfire in mourning for him as had been
done for his ancestors.
20 Jehoram had become king at the age
of thirty-two and had ruled in Jerusalem
for eight years. Nobody was sorry when
he died. They buried him in David's
City, but not in the royal tombs.

King Ahaziah of Judah

(2 Kings 8.25-29; 9.21-28)

22 Some Arabs had led a raid and
killed all of King Jehoram's sons
except Ahaziah, the youngest. So now
the people of Jerusalem made Ahaziah
king as his father's successor.
2-3 Ahaziah became king at the age of
twenty-two,[f] and he ruled in Jerusalem
for one year. Ahaziah also followed the
example of King Ahab's family, since his
mother Athaliah—the daughter of King
Ahab and granddaughter of King Omri
of Israel—gave him advice that led him
into evil. 4 He sinned against the LORD,
because after his father's death other
members of King Ahab's family became
his advisers, and they led to his downfall. 5 Following their advice, he joined
King Joram of Israel in a war against
King Hazael of Syria. The armies
clashed at Ramoth in Gilead, and Joram
was wounded in battle. 6 He returned to
the city of Jezreel to recover from his
wounds, and Ahaziah went there to
visit him.
7 God used this visit to Joram to bring
about Ahaziah's downfall. While Ahaziah was there, he and Joram were confronted by a man named Jehu son of
Nimshi, whom the LORD had chosen to
destroy the dynasty of Ahab. 8 As Jehu
was carrying out God's sentence on the
dynasty, he came across a group made
up of Judean leaders and of Ahaziah's
nephews that had accompanied Ahaziah
on his visit. Jehu killed them all.
9 A search was made for Ahaziah, and
he was found hiding in Samaria. They
took him to Jehu and put him to death.
But they did bury his body out of respect
for his grandfather King Jehoshaphat,
who had done all he could to serve the
LORD.

No member of Ahaziah's family was
left who could rule the kingdom.

Queen Athaliah of Judah

(2 Kings 11.1-3)

10 As soon as King Ahaziah's mother
Athaliah learned of her son's murder,
she gave orders for all the members of
the royal family of Judah to be killed.
11 Ahaziah had a half sister, Jehosheba,
who was married to a priest named Jehoiada. She secretly rescued one of Ahaziah's sons, Joash, took him away from
the other princes who were about to be
murdered and hid him and a nurse in a
bedroom at the Temple. By keeping him
hidden, she saved him from death at the
hands of Athaliah. 12 For six years he remained there in hiding, while Athaliah
ruled as queen.

The Revolt against Athaliah

(2 Kings 11.4-16)

23 After waiting six years Jehoiada
the priest decided that it was
time to take action. He made a pact with
five army officers: Azariah son of Jeroham, Ishmael son of Jehohanan, Azariah son of Obed, Maaseiah son of
Adaiah, and Elishaphat son of Zichri.
2 They traveled to all the cities of Judah
and brought back with them to Jerusalem the Levites and all the heads of the
clans.
3 They all gathered in the Temple, and
there they made a covenant with Joash,
the king's son. Jehoiada said to them,
"Here is the son of the late king. He is
now to be king, as the LORD promised
that King David's descendants would be.
4 This is what we will do. When the
priests and Levites come on duty on the

[e] *Hebrew* Cushites: *Cush is the ancient name of the extensive territory south of the First Cataract of the Nile River. This region was called Ethiopia in Graeco-Roman times, and included within its borders most of modern Sudan and some of present-day Ethiopia (Abyssinia).* [f] *Some ancient translations (and see 2 K 8.26)* twenty-two; *Hebrew* forty-two.

Sabbath, one third of them will guard
the Temple gates, 5 another third will
guard the royal palace, and the rest will
be stationed at the Foundation Gate. All
the people will assemble in the Temple
courtyard. 6 No one is to enter the Temple buildings except the priests and the
Levites who are on duty. They may enter, because they are consecrated, but
the rest of the people must obey the
LORD's instructions and stay outside.
7 The Levites are to stand guard around
the king, with their swords drawn, and
are to stay with the king wherever he
goes. Anyone who tries to enter the
Temple is to be killed."

8 The Levites and the people of Judah
carried out Jehoiada's instructions. The
men were not dismissed when they went
off duty on the Sabbath, so the commanders had available both those coming on duty and those going off.
9 Jehoiada gave the officers the spears
and shields that had belonged to King
David and had been kept in the Temple.
10 He stationed the men with drawn
swords all around the front of the Temple, to protect the king. 11 Then Jehoiada
led Joash out, placed the crown on his
head, and gave him a copy of the laws
governing kingship. And so he was
made king. Jehoiada the priest and his
sons anointed Joash, and everyone
shouted, "Long live the king!"

12 Athaliah heard the people cheering
for the king, so she hurried to the Temple, where the crowd had gathered.
13 There she saw the new king at the
Temple entrance, standing by the column reserved for kings and surrounded
by the army officers and the trumpeters.
All the people were shouting joyfully
and blowing trumpets, and the Temple
musicians with their instruments were
leading the celebration. She tore her
clothes in distress and shouted, "Treason! Treason!"

14 Jehoiada did not want Athaliah
killed in the Temple area, so he called
out the army officers and said, "Take her
out between the rows of guards, and kill
anyone who tries to rescue her."

15 They seized her, took her to the palace, and there at the Horse Gate they
killed her.

Jehoiada's Reforms

(2 Kings 11.17-20)

16 The priest Jehoiada had King Joash
and the people join him in making a covenant that they would be the LORD's people. 17 Then they all went to the temple of
Baal and tore it down. They smashed the
altars and idols there and killed Mattan,
the priest of Baal, in front of the altars.
18 Jehoiada put the priests and Levites in
charge of the work of the Temple. They
were to carry out the duties assigned to
them by King David and to burn the sacrifices offered to the LORD in accordance
with the Law of Moses. They were also
in charge of the music and the celebrations. 19 Jehoiada also put guards on
duty at the Temple gates to keep out
anyone who was ritually unclean.

20 The army officers, the leading citizens, the officials, and all the rest of the
people joined Jehoiada in a procession
that brought the king from the Temple to
the palace. They entered by the main
gate, and the king took his place on the
throne. 21 All the people were filled with
happiness, and the city was quiet, now
that Athaliah had been killed.

King Joash of Judah

(2 Kings 12.1-16)

24 Joash became king of Judah at
the age of seven, and he ruled in
Jerusalem for forty years. His mother
was Zibiah from the city of Beersheba.
2 He did what was pleasing to the LORD as
long as Jehoiada the priest was alive.
3 Jehoiada chose two wives for King Joash, and they bore him sons and
daughters.

4 After he had been king for a while,
Joash decided to have the Temple repaired. 5 He ordered the priests and the
Levites to go to the cities of Judah and
collect from all the people enough
money to make the annual repairs on
the Temple. He told them to act
promptly, but the Levites delayed, 6 so
he called in Jehoiada, their leader, and
demanded, "Why haven't you seen to it
that the Levites collect from Judah and
Jerusalem the tax which Moses, the
servant of the LORD, required the people[g] to pay for support of the Tent of the
LORD's presence?"

(7 The followers of Athaliah, that cor-

[g] *Probable text* required the people; *Hebrew unclear.*

rupt woman,[h] had damaged the Temple and had used many of the sacred objects in the worship of Baal.)

8 The king ordered the Levites to make a box for contributions and to place it at the Temple gate. 9 They sent word throughout Jerusalem and Judah for everyone to bring to the LORD the tax which Moses, God's servant, had first collected in the wilderness. 10 This pleased the people and their leaders, and they brought their tax money and filled the box with it. 11 Every day the Levites would take the box to the royal official who was in charge of it. Whenever it was full, the royal secretary and the High Priest's representative would take the money out and return the box to its place. And so they collected a large sum of money.

12 The king and Jehoiada would give the money to those who were in charge of repairing the Temple, and they hired stonemasons, carpenters, and metalworkers to make the repairs. 13 All of them worked hard, and they restored the Temple to its original condition, as solid as ever. 14 When the repairs were finished, the remaining gold and silver was given to the king and Jehoiada, who used it to have bowls and other utensils made for the Temple.

Jehoiada's Policies Are Reversed

As long as Jehoiada was alive, sacrifices were offered regularly at the Temple. 15 After reaching the very old age of a hundred and thirty, he died. 16 They buried him in the royal tombs in David's City in recognition of the service he had done for the people of Israel, for God, and for the Temple.

17 But once Jehoiada was dead, the leaders of Judah persuaded King Joash to listen to them instead. 18 And so the people stopped worshiping in the Temple of the LORD, the God of their ancestors, and began to worship idols and the images of the goddess Asherah. Their guilt for these sins brought the LORD's anger on Judah and Jerusalem. 19 The LORD sent prophets to warn them to return to him, but the people refused to listen. 20 Then the spirit of God took control of Zechariah son of Jehoiada the priest. He stood where the people could see him and called out, "The LORD God asks why you have disobeyed his commands and are bringing disaster on yourselves! You abandoned him, so he has abandoned you!" 21 King Joash joined in a conspiracy against Zechariah, and on the king's orders the people stoned Zechariah in the Temple courtyard. 22 The king forgot about the loyal service that Zechariah's father Jehoiada had given him, and he had Zechariah killed. As Zechariah was dying, he called out, "May the LORD see what you are doing and punish you!"

The End of Joash's Reign

23 When autumn came that year, the Syrian army attacked Judah and Jerusalem, killed all the leaders, and took large amounts of loot back to Damascus. 24 The Syrian army was small, but the LORD let them defeat a much larger Judean army because the people had abandoned him, the LORD God of their ancestors. In this way King Joash was punished. 25 He was severely wounded, and when the enemy withdrew, two of his officials plotted against him and killed him in his bed to avenge the murder of the son[i] of Jehoiada the priest. He was buried in David's City, but not in the royal tombs. (26 Those who plotted against him were Zabad, the son of an Ammonite woman named Shimeath, and Jehozabad, the son of a Moabite woman named Shimrith.) 27 The *Commentary on the Book of Kings* contains the stories of the sons of Joash, the prophecies spoken against him, and the record of how he rebuilt the Temple. His son Amaziah succeeded him as king.

King Amaziah of Judah

(2 Kings 14.2-6)

25 Amaziah became king at the age of twenty-five, and he ruled in Jerusalem for twenty-nine years. His mother was Jehoaddin from Jerusalem. 2 He did what was pleasing to the LORD, but did it reluctantly. 3 As soon as he was firmly in power, he executed the officials who had murdered his father. 4 He did not, however, execute their children, but followed what the LORD had commanded in the Law of Moses: "Parents are not to

[h] that corrupt woman; *or* whom she corrupted.

[i] *Some ancient translations* son; *Hebrew* sons.

be put to death for crimes committed by
their children, and children are not to be
put to death for crimes committed by
their parents; people are to be put to
death only for crimes they themselves
have committed."

War against Edom

(*2 Kings 14.7*)

5 King Amaziah organized all the men
of the tribes of Judah and Benjamin into
army units, according to the clans they
belonged to, and placed officers in command of units of a thousand and units of
a hundred. This included all men twenty
years of age or older, 300,000 in all. They
were picked troops, ready for battle,
skilled in using spears and shields. 6 In
addition, he hired 100,000 soldiers from
Israel at a cost of about four tons of silver. 7 But a prophet went to the king and
said to him, "Don't take these Israelite
soldiers with you. The LORD is not with
these people from the Northern Kingdom. 8 You may think that they will
make you stronger[j] in battle, but it is
God who has the power to give victory
or defeat, and he will let your enemies
defeat you."

9 Amaziah asked the prophet, "But
what about all that silver I have already
paid for them?"

The prophet replied, "The LORD can
give you back more than that!" 10 So Amaziah sent the hired troops away and
told them to go home. At this they went
home, bitterly angry with the people of
Judah.

11 Amaziah summoned up his courage
and led his army to Salt Valley. There
they fought and killed ten thousand
Edomite soldiers 12 and captured another ten thousand. They took the prisoners to the top of the cliff at the city of
Sela and threw them off, so that they
were killed on the rocks below.

13 Meanwhile the Israelite soldiers that
Amaziah had not allowed to go into battle with him attacked the Judean cities
between Samaria and Beth Horon, killed
three thousand men, and captured quantities of loot.

14 When Amaziah returned from defeating the Edomites, he brought their
idols back with him, set them up, worshiped them, and burned incense to
them. 15 This made the LORD angry, so he
sent a prophet to Amaziah. The prophet
demanded, "Why have you worshiped
foreign gods that could not even save
their own people from your power?"

16 "Since when," Amaziah interrupted,
"have we made you adviser to the king?
Stop talking, or I'll have you killed!"

The prophet stopped, but not before
saying, "Now I know that God has decided to destroy you because you have
done all this and have ignored my
advice."

War against Israel

(*2 Kings 14.8-20*)

17 King Amaziah of Judah and his advisers plotted against Israel. He then
sent a message to King Jehoash of Israel, who was the son of Jehoahaz and
grandson of Jehu, challenging him to
fight.[k] 18 Jehoash sent this answer to
Amaziah: "Once a thorn bush in the Lebanon Mountains sent a message to a cedar: 'Give your daughter in marriage to
my son.' A wild animal passed by and
trampled the bush down. 19 Now Amaziah, you boast that you have defeated
the Edomites, but I advise you to stay at
home. Why stir up trouble that will only
bring disaster on you and your people?"

20 But Amaziah refused to listen. It was
God's will for Amaziah to be defeated,
because he had worshiped the Edomite
idols. 21 So King Jehoash of Israel went
into battle against King Amaziah of Judah. They met at Beth Shemesh in Judah, 22 the Judean army was defeated,
and the soldiers fled to their homes.
23 Jehoash captured Amaziah and took
him to Jerusalem. There he tore down
the city wall from Ephraim Gate to the
Corner Gate, a distance of two hundred
yards. 24 He took back to Samaria as loot
all the gold and silver in the Temple, the
Temple equipment guarded by the
descendants of Obed Edom, and the palace treasures. He also took hostages
with him.

25 King Amaziah of Judah outlived
King Jehoash of Israel by fifteen years.
26 All the other things that Amaziah did
from the beginning to the end of his
reign are recorded in *The History of the*

[j] *Some ancient translations* You may . . . stronger; *Hebrew unclear.* [k] challenging him to fight; *or* inviting him to a conference.

Kings of Judah and Israel. 27 Ever since
the time when he rebelled against the
LORD, there had been a plot against him
in Jerusalem. Finally he fled to the city
of Lachish, but his enemies followed
him there and killed him. 28 His body
was carried to Jerusalem on a horse, and
he was buried in the royal tombs in David's City.

King Uzziah of Judah

(2 Kings 14.21, 22; 15.1-7)

26 All the people of Judah chose
Amaziah's sixteen-year-old son
Uzziah to succeed his father as king. (2 It
was after the death of Amaziah that Uzziah recaptured Elath and rebuilt the
city.)
3 Uzziah became king at the age of sixteen, and he ruled in Jerusalem for fifty-
two years. His mother was Jecoliah from
Jerusalem. 4 Following the example of
his father, he did what was pleasing to
the LORD. 5 As long as Zechariah, his religious adviser, was living, he served the
LORD faithfully, and God blessed him.
6 Uzziah went to war against the Philistines. He tore down the walls of the
cities of Gath, Jamnia, and Ashdod, and
built fortified cities near Ashdod and in
the rest of Philistia. 7 God helped him defeat the Philistines, the Arabs living at
Gurbaal, and the Meunites. 8 The Ammonites paid tribute to Uzziah, and he
became so powerful that his fame
spread even to Egypt.
9 Uzziah strengthened the fortifications of Jerusalem by building towers at
the Corner Gate, at the Valley Gate, and
where the wall turned. 10 He also built
fortified towers in the open country and
dug many cisterns, because he had large
herds of livestock in the western foothills and plains. Because he loved farming, he encouraged the people to plant
vineyards in the hill country and to farm
the fertile land.
11 He had a large army ready for battle.
Its records were kept by his secretaries
Jeiel and Maaseiah under the supervision of Hananiah, a member of the
king's staff. 12 The army was commanded by 2,600 officers. 13 Under them
were 307,500 soldiers able to fight effectively for the king against his enemies.
14 Uzziah supplied the army with shields,
spears, helmets, coats of armor, bows
and arrows, and stones for slinging. 15 In
Jerusalem his inventors made equipment for shooting arrows and for throwing large stones from the towers and
corners of the city wall. His fame spread
everywhere, and he became very powerful because of the help he received
from God.

Uzziah Is Punished for His Pride

16 But when King Uzziah became
strong, he grew arrogant, and that led to
his downfall. He defied the LORD his God
by going into the Temple to burn incense
on the altar of incense. 17 Azariah the
priest, accompanied by eighty strong
and courageous priests, followed the
king 18 to resist him. They said, "Uzziah!
You have no right to burn incense to the
LORD. Only the priests who are descended from Aaron have been consecrated to do this. Leave this holy place.
You have offended the LORD God, and
you no longer have his blessing."
19 Uzziah was standing there in the
Temple beside the incense altar and was
holding an incense burner. He became
angry with the priests, and immediately
a dreaded skin disease broke out on his
forehead. 20 Azariah and the other
priests stared at the king's forehead in
horror and then forced him to leave the
Temple. He hurried to get out, because
the LORD had punished him.
21 For the rest of his life King Uzziah
was ritually unclean because of his disease. Unable to enter the Temple again,
he lived in his own house, relieved of all
duties, while his son Jotham governed
the country.
22 The prophet Isaiah son of Amoz recorded all the other things that King Uzziah did during his reign. 23 Uzziah died
and was buried in the royal burial
ground, but because of his disease he
was not buried in the royal tombs. His
son Jotham succeeded him as king.

King Jotham of Judah

(2 Kings 15.32-38)

27 Jotham became king at the age
of twenty-five, and he ruled in
Jerusalem for sixteen years. His mother
was Jerushah, the daughter of Zadok.
2 He did what was pleasing to the LORD,
just as his father had done; but unlike
his father he did not sin by burning

incense[l] in the Temple. The people,
however, went on sinning.
3 It was Jotham who built the North
Gate of the Temple and did extensive
work on the city wall in the area of Jerusalem called Ophel. 4 In the mountains of
Judah he built cities, and in the forests
he built forts and towers. 5 He fought
against the king of Ammon and his army
and defeated them. Then he forced the
Ammonites to pay him the following
tribute each year for three years: four
tons of silver, fifty thousand bushels of
wheat, and fifty thousand bushels of
barley. 6 Jotham grew powerful because
he faithfully obeyed the LORD his God.
7 The other events of Jotham's reign, his
wars, and his policies, are all recorded in
*The History of the Kings of Israel and
Judah*. 8 Jotham was twenty-five years
old when he became king, and he ruled
in Jerusalem for sixteen years. 9 He died
and was buried in David's City and his
son Ahaz succeeded him as king.

King Ahaz of Judah

(2 Kings 16.1-4)

28 Ahaz became king at the age of
twenty, and he ruled in Jerusalem for sixteen years. He did not follow
the good example of his ancestor King
David; instead, he did what was not
pleasing to the LORD 2 and followed the
example of the kings of Israel. He had
metal images of Baal made, 3 burned incense in Hinnom Valley, and even sacrificed his own sons as burnt offerings to
idols, imitating the disgusting practice of
the people whom the LORD had driven
out of the land as the Israelites advanced. 4 At the pagan places of worship, on the hills, and under every shady
tree Ahaz offered sacrifices and burned
incense.

War with Syria and Israel

(2 Kings 16.5)

5-6 Because King Ahaz sinned, the LORD
his God let the king of Syria defeat him
and take a large number of Judeans
back to Damascus as prisoners. The
LORD also let the king of Israel, Pekah
son of Remaliah, defeat Ahaz and kill
120,000 of the bravest Judean soldiers
in one day. The LORD, the God of their
ancestors, permitted this to happen,
because the people of Judah had
abandoned him. 7 An Israelite soldier
named Zichri killed King Ahaz' son Maaseiah, the palace administrator Azrikam, and Elkanah, who was second in
command to the king. 8 Even though the
Judeans were their own relatives, the Israelite army captured 200,000 women
and children as prisoners and took them
back to Samaria, along with large
amounts of loot.

The Prophet Oded

9 A man named Oded, a prophet of the
LORD, lived in the city of Samaria. He
met the returning Israelite army with its
Judean prisoners as it was about to enter
the city, and he said, "The LORD God of
your ancestors was angry with Judah
and let you defeat them, but now he has
heard of the vicious way you slaughtered them. 10 And now you intend to
make the men and women of Jerusalem
and Judah your slaves. Don't you know
that you also have committed sins
against the LORD your God? 11 Listen to
me! These prisoners are your brothers
and sisters. Let them go, or the LORD will
punish you in his anger."
12 Four of the leading men of the
Northern Kingdom, Azariah son of Jehohanan, Berechiah son of Meshillemoth, Jehizkiah son of Shallum, and
Amasa son of Hadlai also opposed the
actions of the army. 13 They said, "Don't
bring those prisoners here! We have already sinned against the LORD and made
him angry enough to punish us. Now
you want to do something that will increase our guilt." 14 So then the army
handed the prisoners and the loot over
to the people and their leaders, 15 and the
four men were appointed to provide the
prisoners with clothing from the captured loot. They gave them clothes and
sandals to wear, gave them enough to
eat and drink, and put olive oil on their
wounds. Those who were too weak to
walk were put on donkeys, and all the
prisoners were taken back to Judean territory at Jericho, the city of palm trees.
Then the Israelites returned home to
Samaria.

[l] he did not sin by burning incense; *or* he did not take part in the worship.

Ahaz Asks Assyria for Help

(2 Kings 16.7-9)

16-17 The Edomites began to raid Judah
again and captured many prisoners, so
King Ahaz asked Tiglath Pileser, the
emperor of Assyria, to send help. 18 At
this same time the Philistines were raiding the towns in the western foothills
and in southern Judah. They captured
the cities of Beth Shemesh, Aijalon, and
Gederoth, and the cities of Soco, Timnah, and Gimzo with their villages, and
settled there permanently. 19 Because
King Ahaz of Judah had violated the
rights of his people and had defied the
LORD, the LORD brought troubles on Judah. 20 The Assyrian emperor, instead of
helping Ahaz, opposed him and caused
him trouble. 21 So Ahaz took the gold
from the Temple, the palace, and the
homes of the leaders of the people, and
gave it to the emperor, but even this did
not help.

The Sins of Ahaz

22 When his troubles were at their
worst, that man Ahaz sinned against the
LORD more than ever. 23 He offered sacrifices to the gods of the Syrians, who had
defeated him. He said, "The Syrian gods
helped the kings of Syria, so if I sacrifice
to them, they may help me too." This
brought disaster on him and on his nation. 24 In addition, he took all the Temple equipment and broke it in pieces. He
closed the Temple and set up altars in
every part of Jerusalem. 25 In every city
and town in Judah he built pagan places
of worship, where incense was to be
burned to foreign gods. In this way he
brought on himself the anger of the
LORD, the God of his ancestors.

26 All the other events of his reign,
from beginning to end, are recorded in
*The History of the Kings of Judah and
Israel.* 27 King Ahaz died and was buried
in Jerusalem, but not in the royal tombs.
His son Hezekiah succeeded him as
king.

King Hezekiah of Judah

(2 Kings 18.1-3)

29 Hezekiah became king of Judah
at the age of twenty-five, and he
ruled in Jerusalem for twenty-nine
years. His mother was Abijah, the
daughter of Zechariah. 2 Following the
example of his ancestor King David, he
did what was pleasing to the LORD.

The Purification of the Temple

3 In the first month of the year after
Hezekiah became king, he reopened the
gates of the Temple and had them repaired. 4 He assembled a group of priests
and Levites in the east courtyard of the
Temple 5 and spoke to them there. He
said, "You Levites are to consecrate
yourselves and purify the Temple of the
LORD, the God of your ancestors. Remove from the Temple everything that
defiles it. 6 Our ancestors were unfaithful
to the LORD our God and did what was
displeasing to him. They abandoned him
and turned their backs on the place
where he dwells. 7 They closed the doors
of the Temple, let the lamps go out, and
failed to burn incense or offer burnt offerings in the Temple of the God of Israel. 8 Because of this the LORD has been
angry with Judah and Jerusalem, and
what he has done to them has shocked
and frightened everyone. You know this
very well. 9 Our fathers were killed in
battle, and our wives and children have
been taken away as prisoners.

10 "I have now decided to make a covenant with the LORD, the God of Israel, so
that he will no longer be angry with us.
11 My sons, do not lose any time. You are
the ones that the LORD has chosen to
burn incense to him and to lead the people in worshiping him."

12-14 The following Levites were there:

From the clan of Kohath, Mahath son of Amasai and Joel son of Azariah
From the clan of Merari, Kish son of Abdi and Azariah son of Jehallelel
From the clan of Gershon, Joah son of Zimmah and Eden son of Joah
From the clan of Elizaphan, Shimri and Jeuel
From the clan of Asaph, Zechariah and Mattaniah
From the clan of Heman, Jehuel and Shimei
From the clan of Jeduthun, Shemaiah and Uzziel

15 These men assembled their fellow
Levites, and they all made themselves
ritually clean. Then, as the king had
commanded them to do, they began to

make the Temple ritually clean, according to the Law of the LORD.[m] 16The
priests went inside the Temple to purify
it, and they carried out into the Temple
courtyard everything that was ritually
unclean. From there the Levites took it
all outside the city to Kidron Valley.

17The work was begun on the first day
of the first month, and by the eighth day
they had finished it all, including the entrance room to the Temple. Then they
worked for the next eight days, until the
sixteenth of the month, preparing the
Temple for worship.

The Temple Is Rededicated

18The Levites made the following report to King Hezekiah: "We have completed the ritual purification of the
whole Temple, including the altar for
burnt offerings, the table for the sacred
bread, and all their equipment. 19We
have also brought back all the equipment which King Ahaz took away during those years he was unfaithful to God,
and we have rededicated it. It is all in
front of the LORD's altar."

20Without delay King Hezekiah assembled the leading men of the city, and
together they went to the Temple. 21As
an offering to take away the sins of the
royal family and of the people of Judah
and to purify the Temple, they took
seven bulls, seven sheep, seven lambs,
and seven goats. The king told the
priests, who were descendants of Aaron,
to offer the animals as sacrifices on the
altar. 22The priests killed the bulls first,
then the sheep, and then the lambs, and
sprinkled the blood of each sacrifice on
the altar. 23Finally they took the goats to
the king and to the other worshipers,
who laid their hands on them. 24Then
the priests killed the goats and poured
their blood on the altar as a sacrifice to
take away the sin of all the people, for
the king had commanded that burnt offerings and sin offerings be made for all
Israel.

25The king followed the instructions
that the LORD had given to King David
through Gad, the king's prophet, and
through the prophet Nathan; he stationed Levites in the Temple, with harps
and cymbals, 26instruments like those
that King David had used. The priests
also stood there with trumpets. 27Heze-
kiah gave the order for the burnt offering to be presented; and as the offering
began, the people sang praise to the
LORD, and the musicians began to play
the trumpets and all the other instruments. 28Everyone who was there joined
in worship, and the singing and the rest
of the music continued until all the sacrifices had been burned. 29Then King Hezekiah and all the people knelt down and
worshiped God. 30The king and the leaders of the nation told the Levites to sing
to the LORD the songs of praise that were
written by David and by Asaph the
prophet. So everyone sang with great
joy as they knelt and worshiped God.

31Hezekiah said to the people, "Now
that you are ritually clean, bring sacrifices as offerings of thanksgiving to the
LORD." They obeyed, and some of them
also voluntarily brought animals to be
sacrificed as burnt offerings. 32They
brought 70 bulls, 100 sheep, and 200
lambs as burnt offerings for the LORD;
33they also brought 600 bulls and 3,000
sheep as sacrifices for the people to eat.
34Since there were not enough priests to
kill all these animals, the Levites helped
them until the work was finished. By
then more priests had made themselves
ritually clean. (The Levites were more
faithful in keeping ritually clean than
the priests were.) 35In addition to offering the sacrifices that were burned
whole, the priests were responsible for
burning the fat that was offered from the
sacrifices which the people ate, and for
pouring out the wine that was presented
with the burnt offerings.

And so worship in the Temple was begun again. 36King Hezekiah and the people were happy, because God had helped
them to do all this so quickly.

Preparations for Passover

30 1-3The people had not been able
to celebrate the Passover Festival at the proper time in the first month,
because not enough priests were ritually
clean and not many people had assembled in Jerusalem. So King Hezekiah,
his officials, and the people of Jerusalem
agreed to celebrate it in the second

m Then, as the king . . . LORD; *or* Then they began to make the Temple ritually clean, as the king, who was acting at the LORD's command, had ordered them to do.

month, and the king sent word to all the
people of Israel and Judah. He took special care to send letters to the tribes of
Ephraim and Manasseh, inviting them to
come to the Temple in Jerusalem to celebrate the Passover in honor of the LORD,
the God of Israel. 4 The king and the people were pleased with their plan, 5 so
they invited all the Israelites, from Dan
in the north to Beersheba in the south, to
come together in Jerusalem and celebrate the Passover according to the Law,
in larger numbers than ever before.
6 Messengers went out at the command
of the king and his officials through all
Judah and Israel with the following invitation:
"People of Israel, you have survived
the Assyrian conquest of the land. Now
return to the LORD, the God of Abraham,
Isaac, and Jacob, and he will return to
you. 7 Do not be like your ancestors and
your Israelite relatives who were unfaithful to the LORD their God. As you
can see, he punished them severely. 8 Do
not be stubborn as they were, but obey
the LORD. Come to the Temple in Jerusalem, which the LORD your God has made
holy forever, and worship him so that he
will no longer be angry with you. 9 If you
return to the LORD, then those who have
taken your relatives away as prisoners
will take pity on them and let them come
back home. The LORD your God is kind
and merciful, and if you return to him,
he will accept you."
10 The messengers went to every city
in the territory of the tribes of Ephraim
and Manasseh, and as far north as the
tribe of Zebulun, but people laughed at
them and made fun of them. 11 Still, there
were some from the tribes of Asher, Manasseh, and Zebulun who were willing
to come to Jerusalem. 12 God was also at
work in Judah and united the people in
their determination to obey his will by
following the commands of the king and
his officials.

Passover Is Celebrated

13 A great number of people gathered
in Jerusalem in the second month to celebrate the Festival of Unleavened Bread.
14 They took all the altars that had been
used in Jerusalem for offering sacrifices
and burning incense and threw them
into Kidron Valley. 15 And on the fourteenth day of the month they killed the
lambs for the Passover sacrifice. The
priests and Levites who were not ritually
clean became so ashamed that they dedicated themselves to the LORD, and now
they could sacrifice burnt offerings in
the Temple. 16 They took their places in
the Temple according to the instructions
in the Law of Moses, the man of God.
The Levites gave the blood of the sacrifices to the priests, who sprinkled it on
the altar. 17 Because many of the people
were not ritually clean, they could not
kill the Passover lambs, so the Levites
did it for them and dedicated the lambs
to the LORD. 18 In addition, many of those
who had come from the tribes of
Ephraim, Manasseh, Issachar, and Zebulun had not performed the ritual of purification, and so they were observing
Passover improperly. King Hezekiah offered this prayer for them: 19 "O LORD,
the God of our ancestors, in your goodness forgive those who are worshiping
you with all their heart, even though
they are not ritually clean." 20 The LORD
answered Hezekiah's prayer; he forgave
the people and did not harm them. 21 For
seven days the people who had gathered
in Jerusalem celebrated the Festival of
Unleavened Bread with great joy, and
day after day the Levites and the priests
praised the LORD with all their
strength.[n] 22 Hezekiah praised the Levites for their skill in conducting the
worship of the LORD.

A Second Celebration

After the seven days during which
they offered sacrifices in praise of the
LORD, the God of their ancestors, 23 they
all decided to celebrate for another
seven days. So they celebrated with joy.
24 King Hezekiah contributed 1,000 bulls
and 7,000 sheep for the people to kill and
eat, and the officials gave them another
1,000 bulls and 10,000 sheep. A large
number of priests went through the ritual of purification. 25 So everyone was
happy—the people of Judah, the priests,
the Levites, the people who had come
from the north, and the foreigners who
had settled permanently in Israel and
Judah. 26 The city of Jerusalem was filled
with joy, because nothing like this had

[n] *Probable text* with all their strength; *Hebrew* with mighty instruments.

happened since the days of King Solomon, the son of David. 27 The priests and the Levites asked the LORD's blessing on the people. In his home in heaven God heard their prayers and accepted them.

Hezekiah Reforms Religious Life

31 After the festival ended, all the people of Israel went to every city in Judah and broke the stone pillars, cut down the symbols of the goddess Asherah, and destroyed the altars and the pagan places of worship. They did the same thing throughout the rest of Judah, and the territories of Benjamin, Ephraim, and Manasseh; then they all returned home.

2 King Hezekiah reestablished the organization of the priests and Levites, under which they each had specific duties. These included offering the burnt offerings and the fellowship offerings, taking part in the Temple worship, and giving praise and thanks in the various parts of the Temple. 3 From his own flocks and herds he provided animals for the burnt offerings each morning and evening, and for those offered on the Sabbath, at the New Moon Festival, and at the other festivals which are required by the Law of the LORD.

4 In addition, the king told the people of Jerusalem to bring the offerings to which the priests and the Levites were entitled, so that they could give all their time to the requirements of the Law of the LORD. 5 As soon as the order was given, the people of Israel brought gifts of their finest grain, wine, olive oil, honey, and other farm produce, and they also brought the tithes[o] of everything they had. 6 All the people who lived in the cities of Judah brought tithes of their cattle and sheep, and they also brought large quantities of gifts which they dedicated to the LORD their God. 7 The gifts started arriving in the third month and continued to pile up for the next four months. 8 When King Hezekiah and his officials saw how much had been given, they praised the LORD and praised his people Israel. 9 The king spoke to the priests and the Levites about these gifts, 10 and Azariah the High Priest, a descendant of Zadok, said to him, "Since the people started bringing their gifts to the Temple, there has been enough to eat and a large surplus besides. We have all this because the LORD has blessed his people."

11 On the king's orders they prepared storerooms in the Temple area 12 and put all the gifts and tithes in them for safekeeping. They placed a Levite named Conaniah in charge and made his brother Shimei his assistant. 13 Ten Levites were assigned to work under them: Jehiel, Azaziah, Nahath, Asahel, Jerimoth, Jozabad, Eliel, Ismachiah, Mahath, and Benaiah. All this was done under the authority of King Hezekiah and Azariah the High Priest. 14 Kore son of Imnah, a Levite who was chief guard at the East Gate of the Temple, was in charge of receiving the gifts offered to the LORD and of distributing them. 15 In the other cities where priests lived, he was faithfully assisted in this by other Levites: Eden, Miniamin, Jeshua, Shemaiah, Amariah, and Shecaniah. They distributed the food equally to their fellow Levites according to what their duties were, 16 and not by clans. They gave a share to all males thirty[p] years of age or older who had daily responsibilities in the Temple in accordance with their positions. 17 The priests were assigned their duties by clans, and the Levites twenty years of age or older were assigned theirs by work groups. 18 They were all registered together with their wives, children, and other dependents, because they were required to be ready to perform their sacred duties at any time. 19 Among the priests who lived in the cities assigned to Aaron's descendants or in the pasture lands belonging to these cities, there were responsible men who distributed the food to all the males in the priestly families and to everyone who was on the rolls of the Levite clans.

20 Throughout all Judah, King Hezekiah did what was right and what was pleasing to the LORD his God. 21 He was successful, because everything he did for the Temple or in observance of the Law, he did in a spirit of complete loyalty and devotion to his God.

[o] GIFTS . . . TITHES: *The gifts were for the priests, and the tithes for the Levites (see Nu 18).*
[p] *Probable text* thirty; *Hebrew* three.

The Assyrians Threaten Jerusalem

(2 Kings 18.13-37; 19.14-19, 35-37; Isaiah 36.1-22; 37.8-38)

32 After these events, in which King
Hezekiah served the LORD faithfully, Sennacherib, the emperor of Assyria, invaded Judah. He besieged the
fortified cities and gave orders for his
army to break their way through the
walls. 2 When Hezekiah saw that Sennacherib intended to attack Jerusalem
also, 3-4 he and his officials decided to cut
off the supply of water outside the city in
order to keep the Assyrians from having
any water when they got near Jerusalem. The officials led a large number of
people out and stopped up all the
springs, so that no more water flowed
out of them. 5 The king strengthened the
city's defenses by repairing the wall,
building towers on it,[q] and building an
outer wall. In addition, he repaired the
defenses built on the land that was filled
in on the east side of the old part of Jerusalem. He also had a large number of
spears and shields made. 6 He placed all
the men in the city under the command
of army officers and had them assemble
in the open square at the city gate. He
said to them, 7 "Be determined and confident, and don't be afraid of the Assyrian
emperor or of the army he is leading. We
have more power on our side than he
has on his. 8 He has human power, but
we have the LORD our God to help us and
to fight our battles." The people were encouraged by these words of their king.
9 Some time later, while Sennacherib
and his army were still at Lachish, he
sent the following message to Hezekiah
and the people of Judah who were with
him in Jerusalem: 10 "I, Sennacherib,
Emperor of Assyria, ask what gives you
people the confidence to remain in Jerusalem under siege. 11 Hezekiah tells you
that the LORD your God will save you
from our power, but Hezekiah is deceiving you and will let you die of hunger
and thirst. 12 He is the one who destroyed
the LORD's shrines and altars and then
told the people of Judah and Jerusalem
to worship and burn incense at one altar
only. 13 Don't you know what my ancestors and I have done to the people of
other nations? Did the gods of any other
nation save their people from the emperor of Assyria? 14 When did any of the
gods of all those countries ever save
their country from us? Then what makes
you think that your god can save you?
15 Now don't let Hezekiah deceive you or
mislead you like that. Don't believe him!
No god of any nation has ever been able
to save his people from any Assyrian
emperor. So certainly this god of yours
can't save you!"
16 The Assyrian officials said even
worse things about the LORD God and
Hezekiah, the LORD's servant. 17 The letter that the emperor wrote defied the
LORD, the God of Israel. It said, "The gods
of the nations have not saved their people from my power, and neither will
Hezekiah's god save his people from
me." 18 The officials shouted this in Hebrew in order to frighten and discourage
the people of Jerusalem who were on the
city wall, so that it would be easier to
capture the city. 19 They talked about the
God of Jerusalem in the same way that
they talked about the gods of the other
peoples, idols made by human hands.
20 Then King Hezekiah and the
prophet Isaiah son of Amoz prayed to
God and cried out to him for help. 21 The
LORD sent an angel that killed the soldiers and officers of the Assyrian army.
So the emperor went back to Assyria
disgraced. One day when he was in the
temple of his god, some of his sons killed
him with their swords.
22 In this way the LORD rescued King
Hezekiah and the people of Jerusalem
from the power of Sennacherib, the emperor of Assyria, and also from their
other enemies. He let the people live in
peace[r] with all the neighboring countries. 23 Many people came to Jerusalem,
bringing offerings to the LORD and gifts
to Hezekiah, so that from then on all the
nations held Hezekiah in honor.

Hezekiah's Illness and Pride

(2 Kings 20.1-3, 12-19; Isaiah 38.1-3; 39.1-8)

24 About this time King Hezekiah became sick and almost died. He prayed,
and the LORD gave him a sign that he
would recover. 25 But Hezekiah was too
proud to show gratitude for what the
LORD had done for him, and Judah and

[q] *Some ancient translations* building towers on it; *Hebrew* building on the towers.
[r] *Some ancient translations* He let the people live in peace; *Hebrew* He led the people.

Jerusalem suffered for it. 26 Finally, however, Hezekiah and the people of Jerusalem humbled themselves, and so the
LORD did not punish the people until after Hezekiah's death.

Hezekiah's Wealth and Splendor

27 King Hezekiah became very
wealthy, and everyone held him in
honor. He had storerooms built for his
gold, silver, precious stones, spices,
shields, and other valuable objects. 28 In
addition, he had storehouses built for his
grain, wine, and olive oil; barns for his
cattle; and pens for his sheep. 29 Besides
all this, God gave him sheep and cattle
and so much other wealth that he built
many cities. 30 It was King Hezekiah who
blocked the outlet for Gihon Spring and
channeled the water to flow through a
tunnel to a point inside the walls of Jerusalem. Hezekiah succeeded in everything he did, 31 and even when the
Babylonian ambassadors came to inquire about the unusual event that had
happened in the land, God let Hezekiah
go his own way only in order to test his
character.

The End of Hezekiah's Reign

(2 Kings 20.20, 21)

32 Everything else that King Hezekiah
did and his devotion to the LORD are recorded in *The Vision of the Prophet Isaiah Son of Amoz* and in *The History of
the Kings of Judah and Israel.* 33 Hezekiah died and was buried in the upper
section of the royal tombs. All the people
of Judah and Jerusalem paid him great
honor at his death. His son Manasseh
succeeded him as king.

King Manasseh of Judah

(2 Kings 21.1-9)

33 Manasseh was twelve years old
when he became king of Judah,
and he ruled in Jerusalem for fifty-five
years. 2 Following the disgusting practices of the nations whom the LORD had
driven out of the land as his people advanced, Manasseh sinned against the
LORD. 3 He rebuilt the pagan places of
worship that his father Hezekiah had destroyed. He built altars for the worship
of Baal, made images of the goddess
Asherah, and worshiped the stars. 4 He
built pagan altars in the Temple, the
place that the LORD had said was where
he should be worshiped forever. 5 In the
two courtyards of the Temple he built
altars for the worship of the stars. 6 He
sacrificed his sons in Hinnom Valley as
burnt offerings. He practiced divination
and magic and consulted fortunetellers
and mediums. He sinned greatly against
the LORD and stirred up his anger. 7 He
placed an image in the Temple, the place
about which God had said to David and
his son Solomon: "Here in Jerusalem, in
this Temple, is the place that I have chosen out of all the territory of the twelve
tribes of Israel as the place where I am to
be worshiped. 8 And if the people of Israel will obey all my commands and
keep the whole Law that my servant
Moses gave them, then I will not allow
them to be driven out of the land that I
gave to their ancestors." 9 Manasseh led
the people of Judah to commit even
greater sins than those committed by the
nations whom the LORD had driven out of
the land as his people advanced.

Manasseh Repents

10 Although the LORD warned Manasseh and his people, they refused to listen. 11 So the LORD let the commanders of
the Assyrian army invade Judah. They
captured Manasseh, stuck hooks in him,
put him in chains, and took him to Babylon. 12 In his suffering he became humble, turned to the LORD his God, and
begged him for help. 13 God accepted
Manasseh's prayer and answered it by
letting him go back to Jerusalem and
rule again. This convinced Manasseh
that the LORD was God.

14 After this, Manasseh increased the
height of the outer wall on the east side
of David's City, from a point in the valley near Gihon Spring north to the Fish
Gate and the area of the city called
Ophel. He also stationed an army officer
in command of a unit of troops in each of
the fortified cities of Judah. 15 He removed from the Temple the foreign gods
and the image that he had placed there,
and the pagan altars that were on the
hill where the Temple stood and in other
places in Jerusalem; he took all these
things outside the city and threw them
away. 16 He also repaired the altar where
the LORD was worshiped, and he sacrificed fellowship offerings and thanksgiving offerings on it. He commanded all
the people of Judah to worship the LORD,

the God of Israel. 17 Although the people
continued to offer sacrifices at other
places of worship, they offered them
only to the LORD.

The End of Manasseh's Reign

(2 Kings 21.17, 18)

18 Everything else that Manasseh did,
the prayer he made to his God, and the
messages of the prophets who spoke to
him in the name of the LORD, the God of
Israel, are all recorded in *The History of
the Kings of Israel.* 19 The king's prayer
and God's answer to it, and an account
of the sins he committed before he
repented—the evil he did, the pagan
places of worship and the symbols of the
goddess Asherah that he made and the
idols that he worshiped—are all recorded in *The History of the Prophets.*
20 Manasseh died and was buried at the
palace, and his son Amon succeeded
him as king.

King Amon of Judah

(2 Kings 21.19-26)

21 Amon was twenty-two years old
when he became king of Judah, and he
ruled in Jerusalem for two years. 22 Like
his father Manasseh, he sinned against
the LORD, and he worshiped the idols
that his father had worshiped. 23 But unlike his father, he did not become humble and turn to the LORD; he was even
more sinful than his father had been.
24 Amon's officials plotted against him
and assassinated him in the palace.
25 The people of Judah killed Amon's as-
sassins and made his son Josiah king.

King Josiah of Judah

(2 Kings 22.1, 2)

34 Josiah was eight years old when
he became king of Judah, and he
ruled in Jerusalem for thirty-one years.
2 He did what was pleasing to the LORD;
he followed the example of his ancestor
King David, strictly obeying all the laws
of God.

Josiah Attacks Pagan Worship

3 In the eighth year that Josiah was
king, while he was still very young, he
began to worship the God of his ancestor King David. Four years later he began to destroy the pagan places of
worship, the symbols of the goddess
Asherah, and all the other idols. 4 Under
his direction the altars where Baal was
worshiped were smashed, and the incense altars near them were torn down.
They ground to dust the images of Asherah and all the other idols and then scattered the dust on the graves of the
people who had sacrificed to them. 5 He
burned the bones of the pagan priests on
the altars where they had worshiped. By
doing all this, he made Judah and Jerusalem ritually clean again. 6 He did the
same thing in the cities and the devastated areas of Manasseh, Ephraim, and
Simeon, and as far north as Naphtali.
7 Throughout the territory of the Northern Kingdom he smashed the altars and
the symbols of Asherah, ground the
idols to dust, and broke into bits all the
incense altars. Then he returned to Jerusalem.

The Book of the Law Is Discovered

(2 Kings 22.3-20)

8 In the eighteenth year of his reign,
after he had purified the land and the
Temple by ending pagan worship, King
Josiah sent three men to repair the Temple of the LORD God: Shaphan son of Azaliah, Maaseiah, the governor of Jerusalem, and Joah son of Joahaz, a high
official. 9 The money that the Levite
guards had collected in the Temple was
turned over to Hilkiah the High Priest.
(It had been collected from the people of
Ephraim and Manasseh and the rest of
the Northern Kingdom, and from the
people of Judah, Benjamin, and Jerusalem.) 10 This money was then handed
over to the three men in charge of the
Temple repairs, and they gave it to 11 the
carpenters and the builders to buy the
stones and the timber used to repair
the buildings that the kings of Judah
had allowed to decay. 12 The men who
did the work were thoroughly honest.
They were supervised by four Levites: Jahath and Obadiah of the clan of Merari,
and Zechariah and Meshullam of the
clan of Kohath. (The Levites were all
skillful musicians.) 13 Other Levites
were in charge of transporting materials
and supervising the workers on various jobs, and others kept records or
served as guards.

14 While the money was being taken
out of the storeroom, Hilkiah found the
book of the Law of the LORD, the Law
that God had given to Moses. 15 He said

to Shaphan, "I have found the book of
the Law here in the Temple." He gave
Shaphan the book, 16 and Shaphan took
it to the king. He reported, "We have
done everything that you commanded.
17 We have taken the money that was
kept in the Temple and handed it over to
the workers and their supervisors."
18 Then he added, "I have here a book
that Hilkiah gave me." And he read it
aloud to the king.
19 When the king heard the book being
read, he tore his clothes in dismay 20 and
gave the following order to Hilkiah, to
Ahikam son of Shaphan, to Abdon[s] son
of Micaiah, to Shaphan, the court secretary, and to Asaiah, the king's attendant:
21 "Go and consult the LORD for me and
for the people who still remain in Israel
and Judah. Find out about the teachings
of this book. The LORD is angry with us
because our ancestors have not obeyed
the word of the LORD and have not done
what this book says must be done."
22 At the king's command, Hilkiah and
the others went to consult a woman
named Huldah, a prophet who lived in
the newer part of Jerusalem. (Her husband Shallum, the son of Tikvah and
grandson of Harhas, was in charge of
the Temple robes.) They described to
her what had happened, 23 and she told
them to go back to the king and give him
24 the following message from the LORD:
"I am going to punish Jerusalem and all
its people with the curses written in the
book that was read to the king. 25 They
have rejected me and have offered sacrifices to other gods, and so have stirred
up my anger by all they have done. My
anger is aroused against Jerusalem, and
it will not die down. 26 As for the king
himself, this is what I, the LORD God of
Israel, say: You listened to what is written in the book, 27 and you repented and
humbled yourself before me, tearing
your clothes and weeping, when you
heard how I threatened to punish Jerusalem and its people. I have heard your
prayer, 28 and the punishment which I
am going to bring on Jerusalem will not
come until after your death. I will let you
die in peace."
The men returned to King Josiah with
this message.

Josiah Makes a Covenant to Obey the LORD

(2 Kings 23.1-20)

29 King Josiah summoned all the leaders of Judah and Jerusalem, 30 and together they went to the Temple,
accompanied by the priests and the Levites and all the rest of the people, rich
and poor alike. Before them all the king
read aloud the whole book of the covenant, which had been found in the Temple. 31 He stood by the royal column[t]
and made a covenant with the LORD to
obey him, to keep his laws and commands with all his heart and soul, and to
put into practice the demands attached
to the covenant, as written in the book.
32 He made the people of Benjamin and
everyone else present in Jerusalem
promise to keep the covenant. And so
the people of Jerusalem obeyed the requirements of the covenant they had
made with the God of their ancestors.
33 King Josiah destroyed all the disgusting idols that were in the territory belonging to the people of Israel, and as
long as he lived, he required the people
to serve the LORD, the God of their ancestors.

Josiah Celebrates the Passover

(2 Kings 23.21-23)

35 King Josiah celebrated the Passover at Jerusalem in honor of the
LORD; on the fourteenth day of the first
month they killed the animals for the
festival. 2 He assigned to the priests the
duties they were to perform in the Temple and encouraged them to do them
well. 3 He also gave these instructions to
the Levites, the teachers of Israel, who
were dedicated to the LORD: "Put the sacred Covenant Box in the Temple that
King Solomon, the son of David, built.
You are no longer to carry it from place
to place, but you are to serve the LORD
your God and his people Israel. 4 Take
your places in the Temple by clans, according to the responsibilities assigned
to you by King David and his son King
Solomon, 5 and arrange yourselves so
that some of you will be available to help
each family of the people of Israel. 6 You
are to kill the Passover lambs and goats.
Now make yourselves ritually clean and

[s] ABDON: *Achbor in 2 K 22.12.* [t] *Probable text (see 2 K 23.3)* by the royal column; *Hebrew* in his place.

prepare the sacrifices in order that your
fellow Israelites may follow the instructions which the LORD gave through
Moses."
7 For the use of the people at the Passover, King Josiah contributed from his
own herds and flocks 30,000 sheep,
lambs, and young goats, and 3,000 bulls.
8 His officials also made contributions
for the people, the priests, and the Levites to use. And the officials in charge
of the Temple – Hilkiah, the High Priest,
Zechariah, and Jehiel – gave the priests
2,600 lambs and young goats and 300
bulls for sacrifices during the festival.
9 The leaders of the Levites – Conaniah,
Shemaiah and his brother Nethanel,
Hashabiah, Jeiel, and Jozabad –
contributed 5,000 lambs and young
goats and 500 bulls for the Levites to offer as sacrifices.
10 When everything was arranged for
the Passover, the priests and the Levites
took their posts, as commanded by the
king. 11 After the lambs and goats had
been killed, the Levites skinned them,
and the priests sprinkled the blood on
the altar. 12 Then they divided among the
people, by family groups, the animals
for burnt offerings, so that they could offer them according to the instructions in
the Law of Moses. 13 The Levites roasted
the Passover sacrifices over the fire, according to the regulations, and boiled
the sacred offerings in pots, kettles, and
pans, and quickly distributed the meat to
the people. 14 After this was done, the Levites provided meat for themselves and
for the priests descended from Aaron,
for the priests were kept busy until
night, burning the animals that were
burned whole and the fat of the sacrifices. 15 The following musicians of the
Levite clan of Asaph were in the places
assigned to them by King David's instructions: Asaph, Heman, and Jeduthun, the king's prophet. The guards at
the Temple gates did not need to leave
their posts, because the other Levites
prepared the Passover for them. 16 So, as
King Josiah had commanded, everything was done that day for the worship
of the LORD, the keeping of the Passover
Festival, and the offering of burnt offerings on the altar. 17 For seven days all the
people of Israel who were present celebrated the Passover and the Festival of
Unleavened Bread. 18 Since the days of
the prophet Samuel, the Passover had
never been celebrated like this. None of
the former kings had ever celebrated a
Passover like this one celebrated by
King Josiah, the priests, the Levites, and
the people of Judah, Israel, and Jerusalem 19 in the eighteenth year of Josiah's
reign.

The End of Josiah's Reign

(2 Kings 23.28-30)

20 After King Josiah had done all this
for the Temple, King Neco of Egypt led
an army to fight at Carchemish on the
Euphrates River. Josiah tried to stop
him, 21 but Neco sent Josiah this message: "This war I am fighting does not
concern you, King of Judah. I have not
come to fight you, but to fight my enemies, and God has told me to hurry. God
is on my side, so don't oppose me, or he
will destroy you." 22 But Josiah was determined to fight. He refused to listen to
what God was saying through King
Neco, so he disguised himself and went
into battle on the plain of Megiddo.
23 During the battle King Josiah was
struck by Egyptian arrows. He ordered
his servants, "Take me away; I'm badly
hurt!" 24 They lifted him out of his chariot, placed him in a second chariot which
he had there, and took him to Jerusalem.
There he died and was buried in the
royal tombs. All the people of Judah and
Jerusalem mourned his death.
25 The prophet Jeremiah composed a
lament for King Josiah. It has become a
custom in Israel for the singers, both
men and women, to use this song when
they mourn for him. The song is found in
the collection of laments.
26 Everything that Josiah did – his devotion to the LORD, his obedience to the
Law, 27 and his history from beginning to
end – is all recorded in *The History of
the Kings of Israel and Judah.*

King Joahaz of Judah

(2 Kings 23.30-35)

36 The people of Judah chose Josiah's son Joahaz and anointed
him king in Jerusalem. 2 Joahaz was
twenty-three years old when he became
king of Judah, and he ruled in Jerusalem
for three months. 3 King Neco of Egypt
took him prisoner and made Judah pay
7,500 pounds of silver and 75 pounds of
gold as tribute. 4 Neco made Joahaz'

brother Eliakim king of Judah and changed his name to Jehoiakim. Joahaz was taken to Egypt by Neco.

King Jehoiakim of Judah

(2 Kings 23.36 – 24.7)

5 Jehoiakim was twenty-five years old when he became king of Judah, and he ruled in Jerusalem for eleven years. He sinned against the LORD his God.
6 King Nebuchadnezzar of Babylonia invaded Judah, captured Jehoiakim, and took him to Babylonia in chains.
7 Nebuchadnezzar carried off some of the treasures of the Temple and put them in his palace in Babylon.
8 Everything that Jehoiakim did, including his disgusting practices and the evil he committed, is recorded in *The History of the Kings of Israel and Judah*. His son Jehoiachin succeeded him as king.

King Jehoiachin of Judah

(2 Kings 24.8-17)

9 Jehoiachin was eighteen[u] years old when he became king of Judah, and he ruled in Jerusalem for three months and ten days. He too sinned against the LORD.
10 When spring came, King Nebuchadnezzar took Jehoiachin to Babylonia as a prisoner and carried off the treasures of the Temple. Then Nebuchadnezzar made Jehoiachin's uncle[v] Zedekiah king of Judah and Jerusalem.

King Zedekiah of Judah

(2 Kings 24.18-20; Jeremiah 52.1-3a)

11 Zedekiah was twenty-one years old when he became king of Judah, and he ruled in Jerusalem for eleven years.
12 He sinned against the LORD and did not listen humbly to the prophet Jeremiah, who spoke the word of the LORD.

The Fall of Jerusalem

(2 Kings 25.1-21; Jeremiah 52.3b-11)

13 Zedekiah rebelled against King Nebuchadnezzar, who had forced him to swear in God's name that he would be loyal. He stubbornly refused to repent and return to the LORD, the God of Israel.
14 In addition, the leaders of Judah, the priests, and the people followed the sinful example of the nations around them in worshiping idols, and so they defiled the Temple, which the LORD himself had made holy.
15 The LORD, the God of their ancestors, had continued to send prophets to warn his people, because he wanted to spare them and the Temple.
16 But they made fun of God's messengers, ignoring his words and laughing at his prophets, until at last the LORD's anger against his people was so great that there was no escape.

17 So the LORD brought the king of Babylonia to attack them. The king killed the young men of Judah even in the Temple. He had no mercy on anyone, young or old, man or woman, sick or healthy. God handed them all over to him.
18 The king of Babylonia looted the Temple, the Temple treasury, and the wealth of the king and his officials, and took everything back to Babylon.
19 He burned down the Temple and the city, with all its palaces and its wealth, and broke down the city wall.
20 He took all the survivors to Babylonia, where they served him and his descendants as slaves until the rise of the Persian Empire.
21 And so what the LORD had foretold through the prophet Jeremiah was fulfilled: "The land will lie desolate for seventy years, to make up for the Sabbath rest[w] that has not been observed."

Cyrus Commands the Jews to Return

(Ezra 1.1-4)

22 In the first year that Cyrus of Persia was emperor,[x] the LORD made what he had said through the prophet Jeremiah come true. He prompted Cyrus to issue the following command and send it out in writing to be read aloud everywhere in his empire:

23 "This is the command of Cyrus, Emperor of Persia. The LORD, the God of Heaven, has made me ruler over the whole world and has given me the responsibility of building a temple for him in Jerusalem in Judah. Now, all of you who are God's people, go there, and may the LORD your God be with you."

[u] *Some ancient translations (and see 2 K 24.8)* eighteen; *Hebrew* eight. [v] *Some ancient translations (and see 2 K 24.17)* uncle; *Hebrew* brother. [w] SABBATH REST: *A reference to the requirement of the Law that every seventh year the land was not to be farmed (see Lv 25.1-7).*
[x] EMPEROR: *King Cyrus of Persia occupied the city of Babylon in 539 B.C. and began to reign as the emperor of Babylonia.*

The Book of
EZRA

Introduction

The Book of Ezra, *as a sequel to Chronicles, describes the return of some of the Jewish exiles from Babylon and the restoration of life and worship in Jerusalem. These events are presented in the following stages: 1) The first group of Jewish exiles returns from Babylonia at the order of Cyrus, the Persian emperor. 2) The Temple is rebuilt and dedicated, and the worship of God restored in Jerusalem. 3) Years later another group of Jews returns to Jerusalem under the leadership of Ezra, an expert in the Law of God, who helps the people reorganize their religious and social life in order to safeguard the spiritual heritage of Israel.*

Outline of Contents

Cyrus Commands the Jews to Return

1 In the first year that Cyrus of Persia
was emperor,[a] the LORD made what
he had said through the prophet Jeremiah come true. He prompted Cyrus to
issue the following command and send it
out in writing to be read aloud everywhere in his empire:
2 “This is the command of Cyrus,
Emperor of Persia. The LORD, the
God of Heaven, has made me ruler
over the whole world and has given
me the responsibility of building a
temple for him in Jerusalem in Judah. 3 May God be with all of you
who are his people. You are to go to
Jerusalem and rebuild the Temple of
the LORD, the God of Israel, the God
who is worshiped in Jerusalem. 4 If
any of his people in exile need help
to return, their neighbors are to give
them this help. They are to provide
them with silver and gold, supplies
and pack animals, as well as offerings to present in the Temple of God
in Jerusalem.”
5 Then the heads of the clans of the
tribes of Judah and Benjamin, the
priests and Levites, and everyone else
whose heart God had moved got ready
to go and rebuild the LORD's Temple in
Jerusalem. 6 All their neighbors helped
them by giving them many things: silver
utensils, gold, supplies, pack animals,
other valuables, and offerings for the
Temple.
7 Emperor Cyrus gave them back the
bowls and cups that King Nebuchadnezzar had taken from the Temple in Jerusalem and had put in the temple of his
gods. 8 He handed them over to Mithredath, chief of the royal treasury, who
made an inventory of them for Sheshbazzar, the governor of Judah, 9-10 as
follows:

gold bowls for offerings	30
silver bowls for offerings	1,000
other bowls	29
small gold bowls	30
small silver bowls	410
other utensils	1,000

11 In all there were 5,400 gold and silver bowls and other articles which
Sheshbazzar took with him when he and
the other exiles went from Babylon to
Jerusalem.

The List of Those Who Returned from Exile

(Nehemiah 7.4-73)

2 Many of the exiles left the province of Babylon and returned to Jerusalem and Judah, all to their own hometowns. Their families had been living in exile in Babylonia ever since King Nebuchadnezzar had taken them there as

[a] EMPEROR: *King Cyrus of Persia occupied the city of Babylon in 539 B.C. and began to reign as the emperor of Babylonia.*

prisoners. [2]Their leaders were Zerubbabel, Joshua, Nehemiah, Seraiah, Reelaiah, Mordecai, Bilshan, Mispar, Bigvai, Rehum, and Baanah.

This is the list of the clans of Israel, with the number of those from each clan who returned from exile:

3-20 Parosh - 2,172
Shephatiah - 372
Arah - 775
Pahath Moab (descendants of Jeshua and Joab) - 2,812
Elam - 1,254
Zattu - 945
Zaccai - 760
Bani - 642
Bebai - 623
Azgad - 1,222
Adonikam - 666
Bigvai - 2,056
Adin - 454
Ater (also called Hezekiah) - 98
Bezai - 323
Jorah - 112
Hashum - 223
Gibbar - 95

21-35 People whose ancestors had lived in the following towns also returned:
Bethlehem - 123
Netophah - 56
Anathoth - 128
Azmaveth - 42
Kiriath Jearim, Chephirah, and Beeroth - 743
Ramah and Geba - 621
Michmash - 122
Bethel and Ai - 223
Nebo - 52
Magbish - 156
The other Elam - 1,254
Harim - 320
Lod, Hadid, and Ono - 725
Jericho - 345
Senaah - 3,630

36-39 This is the list of the priestly clans that returned from exile:
Jedaiah (descendants of Jeshua) - 973
Immer - 1,052
Pashhur - 1,247
Harim - 1,017

40-42 Clans of Levites who returned from exile:
Jeshua and Kadmiel (descendants of Hodaviah) - 74
Temple musicians (descendants of Asaph) - 128
Temple guards (descendants of Shallum, Ater, Talmon, Akkub, Hatita, and Shobai) - 139

43-54 Clans of Temple workers who returned from exile:
Ziha, Hasupha, Tabbaoth,
Keros, Siaha, Padon,
Lebanah, Hagabah, Akkub,
Hagab, Shamlai, Hanan,
Giddel, Gahar, Reaiah,
Rezin, Nekoda, Gazzam,
Uzza, Paseah, Besai,
Asnah, Meunim, Nephisim,
Bakbuk, Hakupha, Harhur,
Bazluth, Mehida, Harsha,
Barkos, Sisera, Temah,
Neziah, and Hatipha

55-57 Clans of Solomon's servants who returned from exile:
Sotai, Hassophereth, Peruda,
Jaalah, Darkon, Giddel,
Shephatiah, Hattil, Pochereth Hazzebaim, and Ami

58 The total number of descendants of the Temple workers and of Solomon's servants who returned from exile was 392.

59-60 There were 652 belonging to the clans of Delaiah, Tobiah, and Nekoda who returned from the towns of Tel Melah, Tel Harsha, Cherub, Addan, and Immer; but they could not prove that they were descendants of Israelites.

61-62 The following priestly clans could find no record to prove their ancestry: Habaiah, Hakkoz, and Barzillai. (The ancestor of the priestly clan of Barzillai had married a woman from the clan of Barzillai of Gilead and had taken the name of his father-in-law's clan.) Since they were unable to prove who their ancestors were, they were not accepted as priests. [63]The Jewish governor told them that they could not eat the food offered to God until there was a priest who could use the Urim and Thummim.[b]

64-67 Total number of exiles who returned - 42,360
Their male and female servants - 7,337
Male and female musicians - 200
Horses - 736
Mules - 245

[b] URIM AND THUMMIM: *Two objects used by the priest to determine God's will; it is not known precisely how they were used.*

Camels - 435
Donkeys - 6,720
68 When the exiles arrived at the
LORD's Temple in Jerusalem, some of the
leaders of the clans gave freewill offerings to help rebuild the Temple on its old
site. 69 They gave as much as they could
for this work, and the total came to 1,030
pounds of gold, 5,740 pounds of silver,
and 100 robes for priests.
70 The priests, the Levites, and some of
the people settled in or near Jerusalem;[c] the musicians, the Temple guards,
and the Temple workers settled in
nearby towns; and the rest of the Israelites settled in the towns where their ancestors had lived.

Worship Begins Again

3 By the seventh month the people of
Israel were all settled in their
towns. Then they all assembled in Jerusalem, 2 and Joshua son of Jehozadak,
his fellow priests, and Zerubbabel son of
Shealtiel, together with his relatives, rebuilt the altar of the God of Israel, so
that they could burn sacrifices on it according to the instructions written in the
Law of Moses, the man of God. 3 Even
though[d] the returning exiles were
afraid of the people who were living in
the land, they rebuilt the altar where it
had stood before. Then they began once
again to burn on it the regular morning
and evening sacrifices. 4 They celebrated
the Festival of Shelters according to the
regulations; each day they offered the
sacrifices required for that day; 5 and in
addition they offered the regular sacrifices to be burned whole and those to be
offered at the New Moon Festival and at
all the other regular assemblies at which
the LORD is worshiped, as well as all the
offerings that were given to the LORD voluntarily. 6 Although the people had not
yet started to rebuild the Temple, they
began on the first day of the seventh
month to burn sacrifices to the LORD.

The Rebuilding of the Temple Begins

7 The people gave money to pay the
stonemasons and the carpenters and
gave food, drink, and olive oil to be sent
to the cities of Tyre and Sidon in exchange for cedar trees from Lebanon,
which were to be brought by sea to
Joppa. All this was done with the permission of Emperor Cyrus of Persia. 8 So
in the second month of the year after
they came back to the site of the Temple
in Jerusalem, they began work. Zerubbabel, Joshua, and the rest of their people, the priests, and the Levites, in fact
all the exiles who had come back to Jerusalem, joined in the work. All the Levites twenty years of age or older were
put in charge of the work of rebuilding
the Temple. 9 The Levite Jeshua and his
sons and relatives, and Kadmiel and his
sons (the clan of Hodaviah[e]) joined together in taking charge of the rebuilding
of the Temple. (They were helped by the
Levites of the clan of Henadad.)
10 When the builders started to lay the
foundation of the Temple, the priests in
their robes took their places with trumpets in their hands, and the Levites of
the clan of Asaph stood there with cymbals. They praised the LORD according to
the instructions handed down from the
time of King David. 11 They sang the
LORD's praises, repeating the refrain:
"The LORD is good, and his love for
Israel is eternal."
Everyone shouted with all their might,
praising the LORD, because the work on
the foundation of the Temple had been
started. 12 Many of the older priests, Levites, and heads of clans had seen the
first Temple, and as they watched the
foundation of this Temple being laid,
they cried and wailed. But the others
who were there shouted for joy. 13 No
one could distinguish between the joyful
shouts and the crying, because the noise
they made was so loud that it could be
heard for miles.

Opposition to the Rebuilding of the Temple

4 The enemies of the people of Judah
and Benjamin heard that those who
had returned from exile were rebuilding
the Temple of the LORD, the God of Israel. 2 So they went to see Zerubbabel
and the heads of the clans and said, "Let
us join you in building the Temple. We
worship the same God you worship, and
we have been offering sacrifices to him
ever since Emperor Esarhaddon of Assyria sent us here to live."

[c] *One ancient translation* in or near Jerusalem; *Hebrew does not have these words.*
[d] Even though; *or* Because. [e] *Probable text (see 2.40)* Hodaviah; *Hebrew* Judah.

3 Zerubbabel, Joshua, and the heads of
the clans told them, "We don't need your
help to build a temple for the LORD our
God. We will build it ourselves, just
as Emperor Cyrus of Persia commanded us."
4 Then the people who had been living
in the land tried to discourage and
frighten the Jews and keep them from
building. 5 They also bribed Persian government
officials to work against them.
They kept on doing this throughout the
reign of Emperor Cyrus and into the
reign of Emperor Darius.[f]

Opposition to the Rebuilding of Jerusalem

6 At the beginning of the reign of Emperor
Xerxes, the enemies of the people
living in Judah and Jerusalem brought
written charges against them.
7 Again in the reign of Emperor Artaxerxes
of Persia, Bishlam, Mithredath,
Tabeel, and their associates wrote a letter
to the emperor. The letter was
written in Aramaic[g] and was to be
translated when read.[h]
8 Also Rehum, the governor, and
Shimshai, the secretary of the province,
wrote the following letter to Emperor
Artaxerxes about Jerusalem:
9 "From Rehum, the governor,
from Shimshai, secretary of the
province, from their associates, the
judges, and from all the other officials,
who are originally from Erech,
Babylon, and Susa in the land of
Elam, 10 together with the other peoples
whom the great and powerful
Ashurbanipal moved from their
homes and settled in the city of Samaria
and elsewhere in West-of-Euphrates
Province."[i]
11 This is the text of the letter:
"To Emperor Artaxerxes from his
servants who live in West-of-Euphrates.
12 "We want Your Majesty to
know that the Jews who came here
from your other territories have settled
in Jerusalem and are rebuilding
that evil and rebellious city. They
have begun to rebuild the walls and
will soon finish them. 13 Your Majesty,
if this city is rebuilt and its
walls are completed, the people will
stop paying taxes, and your royal
revenues will decrease. 14 Now, because
we are under obligation to
Your Majesty, we do not want to see
this happen, and so we suggest
15 that you order a search to be made
in the records your ancestors kept.
If you do, you will discover that this
city has always been rebellious and
that from ancient times it has given
trouble to kings and to rulers of
provinces. Its people have always
been hard to govern. This is why the
city was destroyed. 16 We therefore
are convinced that if this city is rebuilt
and its walls are completed,
Your Majesty will no longer be able
to control West-of-Euphrates
Province."
17 The emperor sent this answer:
"To Rehum, the governor, to
Shimshai, secretary of the province,
and to their associates who live in
Samaria and in the rest of West-of-Euphrates,
greetings.
18 "The letter which you sent has
been translated and read to me.
19 I gave orders for an investigation
to be made, and it has indeed been
found that from ancient times Jerusalem
has revolted against royal authority
and that it has been full of
rebels and troublemakers. 20 Powerful
kings have reigned there and
have ruled over the entire province
of West-of-Euphrates, collecting
taxes and revenue. 21 Therefore you
are to issue orders that those men
are to stop rebuilding the city until I
give further commands. 22 Do this at
once, so that no more harm may be
done to my interests."
23 As soon as this letter from Emperor
Artaxerxes was read to Rehum, Shimshai,
and their associates, they hurried

[f] EMPEROR DARIUS: *The account of these events is continued at verse 24. The material in verses 6-23 describes events which took place almost a century later.* [g] ARAMAIC: *From 4.8 to 6.18 this book is not in Hebrew, but Aramaic, the official language of the Persian Empire.*
[h] The letter . . . read; *or* It was in Aramaic and was written in the Aramaic script.
[i] WEST-OF-EUPHRATES PROVINCE: *Under Persian rule the land of Judah was part of this large Persian province west of the Euphrates River.*

to Jerusalem and forced the Jews to stop
rebuilding the city.

Work on the Temple Begins Again

24 Work on the Temple had been
stopped and had remained at a standstill
until the second year of the reign of Em-
5 peror Darius of Persia. 1 At that
time two prophets, Haggai and
Zechariah son of Iddo, began to speak in
the name of the God of Israel to the Jews
who lived in Judah and Jerusalem.
2 When Zerubbabel son of Shealtiel and
Joshua son of Jehozadak heard their
messages, they began to rebuild the
Temple in Jerusalem, and the two
prophets helped them.
3 Almost at once Governor Tattenai of
West-of-Euphrates, Shethar Bozenai,
and their fellow officials came to Jerusalem and demanded: "Who gave you orders to build this Temple and equip it?"
4 They[j] also asked for the names of all
the men who were helping build the
Temple. 5 But God was watching over
the Jewish leaders, and the Persian officials decided to take no action until they
could write to Emperor Darius and receive a reply. 6 This is the report that
they sent to the emperor:
7 "To Emperor Darius, may you
rule in peace.
8 "Your Majesty should know that
we went to the province of Judah
and found that the Temple of the
great God is being rebuilt with large
stone blocks and with wooden
beams set in the wall. The work is
being done with great care and is
moving ahead steadily.
9 "We then asked the leaders of the
people to tell us who had given them
authority to rebuild the Temple and
to equip it. 10 We also asked them
their names so that we could inform
you who the leaders of this work
are.
11 "They answered, 'We are servants of the God of heaven and earth,
and we are rebuilding the Temple
which was originally built and
equipped many years ago by a powerful king of Israel. 12 But because
our ancestors made the God of
Heaven angry, he let them be conquered by King Nebuchadnezzar of
Babylonia, a king of the Chaldean
dynasty. The Temple was destroyed,
and the people were taken into exile
in Babylonia. 13 Then in the first
year of the reign of King Cyrus as
emperor of Babylonia, Cyrus issued
orders for the Temple to be rebuilt.
14 He restored the gold and silver
Temple utensils which Nebuchadnezzar had taken from the Temple
in Jerusalem and had placed in the
temple in Babylon. Emperor Cyrus
turned these utensils over to a man
named Sheshbazzar, whom he appointed governor of Judah. 15 The
emperor told him to take them and
return them to the Temple in Jerusalem, and to rebuild the Temple
where it had stood before. 16 So
Sheshbazzar came and laid its foundation; construction has continued
from then until the present, but it is
still not finished.'
17 "Now, if it please Your Majesty,
have a search made in the royal
records in Babylon to find whether
or not Emperor Cyrus gave orders
for this Temple in Jerusalem to be
rebuilt, and then inform us what
your will is in this matter."

Emperor Cyrus' Order Is Rediscovered

6 So Emperor Darius issued orders
for a search to be made in the royal
records that were kept in Babylon. 2 But
it was in the city of Ecbatana in the province of Media that a scroll was found,
containing the following record:
3 "In the first year of his reign Emperor Cyrus commanded that the
Temple in Jerusalem be rebuilt as a
place where sacrifices are made and
offerings are burned. The Temple is
to be ninety feet high and ninety feet
wide. 4 The walls are to be built with
one layer of wood on top of each
three layers of stone. All expenses
are to be paid by the royal treasury.
5 Also the gold and silver utensils
which King Nebuchadnezzar
brought to Babylon from the Temple
in Jerusalem are to be returned to
their proper place in the Jerusalem
Temple."

[j] *Some ancient translations* They; *Aramaic* We.

Emperor Darius Orders the Work to Continue

6 Then Emperor Darius sent the following reply:

"To Tattenai, governor of West-of-Euphrates, Shethar Bozenai, and your fellow officials in West-of-Euphrates.

"Stay away from the Temple 7 and do not interfere with its construction. Let the governor of Judah and the Jewish leaders rebuild the Temple of God where it stood before. 8 I hereby command you to help them rebuild it. Their expenses are to be paid promptly out of the royal funds received from taxes in West-of-Euphrates, so that the work is not interrupted. 9 Day by day, without fail, you are to give the priests in Jerusalem whatever they tell you they need: young bulls, sheep, or lambs to be burned as offerings to the God of Heaven, or wheat, salt, wine, or olive oil. 10 This is to be done so that they can offer sacrifices that are acceptable to the God of Heaven and pray for his blessing on me and my sons. 11 I further command that if any disobey this order, a wooden beam is to be torn out of their houses, sharpened on one end, and then driven through their bodies. And their houses are to be made a rubbish heap. 12 May the God who chose Jerusalem as the place where he is to be worshiped overthrow any king or nation that defies this command and tries to destroy the Temple there. I, Darius, have commanded. My command is to be fully obeyed."

The Temple Is Dedicated

13 Then Governor Tattenai, Shethar Bozenai, and their fellow officials did exactly as the emperor had commanded. 14 The Jewish leaders made good progress with the building of the Temple, encouraged by the prophets Haggai and Zechariah. They completed the Temple as they had been commanded by the God of Israel and by Cyrus, Darius, and Artaxerxes, emperors of Persia. 15 They finished the Temple on the third day of the month Adar in the sixth year of the reign of Emperor Darius. 16 Then the people of Israel—the priests, the Levites, and all the others who had returned from exile—joyfully dedicated the Temple. 17 For the dedication they offered 100 bulls, 200 sheep, and 400 lambs as sacrifices, and 12 goats as offerings for sin, one for each tribe of Israel. 18 They also organized the priests and the Levites for the Temple services in Jerusalem, according to the instructions contained in the book of Moses.

The Passover

19 The people who had returned from exile celebrated Passover on the fourteenth day of the first month of the following year. 20 All the priests and the Levites had purified themselves and were ritually clean. The Levites killed the animals for the Passover sacrifices for all the people who had returned, for the priests, and for themselves. 21 The sacrifices were eaten by all the Israelites who had returned from exile and by all those who had given up the pagan ways of the other people who were living in the land and who had come to worship the LORD God of Israel. 22 For seven days they joyfully celebrated the Festival of Unleavened Bread. They were full of joy because the LORD had made the emperor of Assyria[k] favorable to them, so that he supported them in their work of rebuilding the Temple of the God of Israel.

Ezra Arrives in Jerusalem

7 Many years later, when Artaxerxes was emperor of Persia, there was a man named Ezra. He traced his ancestors back to Aaron, the High Priest, as follows: Ezra was the son of Seraiah, son of Azariah, son of Hilkiah, 2 son of Shallum, son of Zadok, son of Ahitub, 3 son of Amariah, son of Azariah, son of Meraioth, 4 son of Zerahiah, son of Uzzi, son of Bukki, 5 son of Abishua, son of Phinehas, son of Eleazar, son of Aaron.

6-7 Ezra was a scholar with a thorough knowledge of the Law which the LORD, the God of Israel, had given to Moses. Because Ezra had the blessing of the LORD his God, the emperor gave him everything he asked for. In the seventh year of the reign of Artaxerxes, Ezra set

[k] EMPEROR OF ASSYRIA: *Apparently a reference to the Persian emperor who then also ruled the territory once occupied by Assyria, Israel's ancient enemy.*

out from Babylonia for Jerusalem with a
group of Israelites which included
priests, Levites, Temple musicians, Temple guards, and workers. 8-9 They left
Babylonia on the first day of the first
month, and with God's help they arrived
in Jerusalem on the first day of the fifth
month. 10 Ezra had devoted his life to
studying the Law of the LORD, to practicing it, and to teaching all its laws and
regulations to the people of Israel.

The Document Which Emperor Artaxerxes Gave to Ezra

11 Emperor Artaxerxes gave the following document to Ezra, the priest and
scholar, who had a thorough knowledge
of the laws and commands which the
LORD had given to Israel:

12 "From Emperor Artaxerxes[l] to
the priest Ezra, scholar in the Law
of the God of Heaven.[m]

13 "I command that throughout my
empire all the Israelite people,
priests, and Levites that so desire be
permitted to go with you to Jerusalem. 14 I, together with my seven
counselors, send you to investigate
the conditions in Jerusalem and Judah in order to see how well the Law
of your God, which has been entrusted to you, is being obeyed.
15 You are to take with you the gold
and silver offerings which I and my
counselors desire to give to the God
of Israel, whose Temple is in Jerusalem. 16 You are also to take all the
silver and gold which you collect
throughout the province of Babylon
and the offerings which the Israelite
people and their priests give for the
Temple of their God in Jerusalem.

17 "You are to spend this money
carefully and buy bulls, rams,
lambs, grain, and wine and offer
them on the altar of the Temple in
Jerusalem. 18 You may use the silver
and gold that is left over for whatever you and your people desire, in
accordance with the will of your
God. 19 You are to present to God in
Jerusalem all the utensils that have
been given to you for use in the
Temple services. 20 And anything
else which you need for the Temple,
you may get from the royal treasury.

21 "I command all the treasury officials in West-of-Euphrates Province
to provide promptly for Ezra, the
priest and scholar in the Law of the
God of Heaven, everything he asks
you for, 22 up to a limit of 7,500
pounds of silver, 500 bushels of
wheat, 550 gallons of wine, 550 gallons of olive oil, and as much salt as
needed. 23 You must be careful to
provide everything which the God
of Heaven requires for his Temple,
and so make sure that he is never
angry with me or with those who
reign after me. 24 You are forbidden
to collect any taxes from the priests,
Levites, musicians, guards, workers,
or anyone else connected with this
Temple.

25 "You, Ezra, using the wisdom
which your God has given you, are
to appoint administrators and
judges to govern all the people in
West-of-Euphrates who live by the
Law of your God. You must teach
that Law to anyone who does not
know it. 26 If any disobey the laws of
your God or the laws of the empire,
they are to be punished promptly:
by death or by exile or by confisca-
tion of their property or by imprisonment."

Ezra Praises God

27 Ezra said, "Praise the LORD, the God
of our ancestors! He has made the emperor willing to honor in this way the
Temple of the LORD in Jerusalem. 28 By
God's grace I have won the favor of the
emperor, of his counselors, and of all his
powerful officials; the LORD my God has
given me courage, and I have been able
to persuade many of the heads of the
clans of Israel to return with me."

The People Who Returned from Exile

8 This is the list of the heads of the
clans who had been in exile in
Babylonia and who returned with Ezra
to Jerusalem when Artaxerxes was
emperor:

2-14 Gershom, of the clan of Phinehas
Daniel, of the clan of Ithamar

[l] *Verses 12-26 are in Aramaic (see also 4.7).* [m] *Aramaic has an additional word, the meaning of which is unclear.*

Hattush son of Shecaniah, of the clan of David
Zechariah, of the clan of Parosh, with 150 men of his clan (there were records of their family lines)
Eliehoenai son of Zerahiah, of the clan of Pahath Moab, with 200 men
Shecaniah son of Jahaziel, of the clan of Zattu,[n] with 300 men
Ebed son of Jonathan, of the clan of Adin, with 50 men
Jeshaiah son of Athaliah, of the clan of Elam, with 70 men
Zebadiah son of Michael, of the clan of Shephatiah, with 80 men
Obadiah son of Jehiel, of the clan of Joab, with 218 men
Shelomith son of Josiphiah, of the clan of Bani,[o] with 160 men
Zechariah son of Bebai, of the clan of Bebai, with 28 men
Johanan son of Hakkatan, of the clan of Azgad, with 110 men
Eliphelet, Jeuel, and Shemaiah, of the clan of Adonikam, with 60 men (they returned at a later date)
Uthai and Zaccur, of the clan of Bigvai, with 70 men

Ezra Finds Levites for the Temple

15 I assembled the entire group by the
canal that runs to the town of Ahava,
and we camped there three days. I found
that there were priests in the group, but
no Levites. 16 I sent for nine of the leaders: Eliezer, Ariel, Shemaiah, Elnathan,
Jarib, Elnathan, Nathan, Zechariah, and
Meshullam, and for two teachers, Joiarib and Elnathan. 17 I sent them to Iddo,
head of the community at Casiphia, to
ask him and his associates, the Temple
workers, to send us people to serve God
in the Temple. 18 Through God's grace
they sent us Sherebiah, an able man, a
Levite from the clan of Mahli; and eighteen of his sons and brothers came with
him. 19 They also sent Hashabiah and Jeshaiah of the clan of Merari, with twenty
of their relatives. 20 In addition there
were 220 Temple workers whose ancestors had been designated by King David
and his officials to assist the Levites.
They were all listed by name.

Ezra Leads the People in Fasting and Prayer

21 There by the Ahava Canal I gave orders for us all to fast and humble ourselves before our God and to ask him to
lead us on our journey and protect us
and our children and all our possessions. 22 I would have been ashamed to
ask the emperor for a troop of cavalry to
guard us from any enemies during our
journey, because I had told him that our
God blesses everyone who trusts him,
but that he is displeased with and punishes anyone who turns away from him.
23 So we fasted and prayed for God to
protect us, and he answered our prayers.

The Gifts for the Temple

24 From among the leading priests I
chose Sherebiah, Hashabiah, and ten
others. 25 Then I weighed out the silver,
the gold, and the utensils which the emperor, his advisers and officials, and the
people of Israel had given to be used in
the Temple, and I gave it to the priests.
26-27 This is what I gave them:

silver - 25 tons
100 silver utensils - 150 pounds
gold - 7,500 pounds
20 gold bowls - 270 ounces
2 fine bronze bowls, equal in value to gold bowls

28 I said to them, "You are sacred to
the LORD, the God of your ancestors, and
so are all the silver and gold utensils
brought to him as freewill offerings.
29 Guard them carefully until you reach
the Temple. There in the priests' rooms
weigh them and turn them over to the
leaders of the priests and of the Levites,
and to the leaders of the people of Israel
in Jerusalem." 30 So the priests and the
Levites took charge of the silver, the
gold, and the utensils, to take them to
the Temple in Jerusalem.

The Return to Jerusalem

31 It was on the twelfth day of the first
month that we left the Ahava Canal to
go to Jerusalem. Our God was with us
and protected us from enemy attacks
and from ambush as we traveled.
32 When we reached Jerusalem, we
rested three days. 33 Then on the fourth
day we went to the Temple, weighed the

[n] *One ancient translation (see also 2.8)* Zattu; *Hebrew does not have this name.*
[o] *One ancient translation (see also 2.10)* Bani; *Hebrew does not have this name.*

silver, the gold, and the utensils, and
turned them over to Meremoth the
priest, son of Uriah. With him were Eleazar son of Phinehas and two Levites,
Jozabad son of Jeshua and Noadiah son
of Binnui. 34 Everything was counted
and weighed, and a complete record was
made at the same time.
35 All those who had returned from exile then brought offerings to be burned
as sacrifices to the God of Israel. They
offered 12 bulls for all Israel, 96 rams,
and 77 lambs; they also offered 12 goats
to purify themselves from sin. All these
animals were burned as sacrifices to the
LORD. 36 They also took the document the
emperor had given them and gave it to
the governors and officials of West-of-
Euphrates Province, who then gave their
support to the people and the Temple
worship.

Ezra Learns of Intermarriages with Non-Jews

9 After all this had been done, some
of the leaders of the people of Israel
came and told me that the people, the
priests, and the Levites had not kept
themselves separate from the people in
the neighboring countries of Ammon,
Moab, and Egypt or from the Canaanites, Hittites, Perizzites, Jebusites, and
Amorites. They were doing the same
disgusting things which these people
did. 2 Jewish men were marrying foreign
women, and so God's holy people had
become contaminated. The leaders and
officials were the chief offenders.
3 When I heard this, I tore my clothes in
despair, tore my hair and my beard, and
sat down crushed with grief. 4 I sat there
grieving until the time for the evening
sacrifice to be offered, and people began
to gather around me—all those who
were frightened because of what the
God of Israel had said about the sins of
those who had returned from exile.
5 When the time came for the evening
sacrifice, I got up from where I had been
grieving, and still wearing my torn
clothes, I knelt in prayer and stretched
out my hands to the LORD my God.
6 I said, "O God, I am too ashamed to
raise my head in your presence. Our sins
pile up higher than our heads; they
reach as high as the heavens. 7 From the
days of our ancestors until now, we,
your people, have sinned greatly. Because of our sins we, our kings, and our
priests have fallen into the hands of foreign kings, and we have been slaughtered, robbed, and carried away as
prisoners. We have been totally disgraced, as we still are today. 8 Now for a
short time, O LORD our God, you have
been gracious to us and have let some of
us escape from slavery and live in safety
in this holy place. You have let us escape
from slavery and have given us new life.
9 We were slaves, but you did not leave
us in slavery. You made the emperors of
Persia favor us and permit us to go on
living and to rebuild your Temple, which
was in ruins, and to find safety here in
Judah and Jerusalem.
10 "But now, O God, what can we say
after all that has happened? We have
again disobeyed the commands 11 that
you gave us through your servants, the
prophets. They told us that the land we
were going to occupy was an impure
land because the people who lived in it
filled it from one end to the other with
disgusting, filthy actions. 12 They told us
that we were never to intermarry with
those people and never to help them
prosper or succeed if we wanted to enjoy
the land and pass it on to our descendants forever. 13 Even after everything
that has happened to us in punishment
for our sins and wrongs, we know that
you, our God, have punished us less than
we deserve and have allowed us to survive. 14 Then how can we ignore your
commandments again and intermarry
with these wicked people? If we do, you
will be so angry that you will destroy us
completely and let no one survive.
15 LORD God of Israel, you are just, but
you have let us survive. We confess our
guilt to you; we have no right to come
into your presence."

The Plan for Ending Mixed Marriages

10 While Ezra was bowing in
prayer in front of the Temple,
weeping and confessing these sins, a
large group of Israelites—men, women,
and children—gathered around him,
weeping bitterly. 2 Then Shecaniah son
of Jehiel, of the clan of Elam, said to
Ezra, "We have broken faith with God
by marrying foreign women, but even so

there is still hope for Israel. 3 Now we
must make a solemn promise to our God
that we will send these women and their
children away. We will do what you and
the others who honor God's commands
advise us to do. We will do what God's
Law demands. 4 It is your responsibility
to act. We are behind you, so go ahead
and get it done."

5 So Ezra began by making the leaders
of the priests, of the Levites, and of the
rest of the people take an oath that they
would do what Shecaniah had proposed.
6 Then he went from in front of the Temple into the living quarters of Jehohanan
son of Eliashib, and spent the night[p]
there grieving over the unfaithfulness of
the exiles. He did not eat or drink
anything.

7 A message was sent throughout Jerusalem and Judah that all those who
had returned from exile were to meet in
Jerusalem 8 by order of the leaders of the
people. If any failed to come within three
days, all their property would be confiscated, and they would lose their right to
be members of the community. 9 Within
the three days, on the twentieth day of
the ninth month, all the men living in the
territory of Judah and Benjamin came to
Jerusalem and assembled in the Temple
square. It was raining hard, and because
of the weather and the importance of the
meeting everyone was trembling.

10 Ezra the priest stood up and spoke
to them. He said, "You have been faithless and have brought guilt on Israel by
marrying foreign women. 11 Now then,
confess your sins to the LORD, the God of
your ancestors, and do what pleases
him. Separate yourselves from the foreigners living in our land and get rid of
your foreign wives."

12 The people shouted in answer, "We
will do whatever you say." 13 But they
added, "The crowd is too big, and it's
raining hard. We can't stand here in the
open like this. This isn't something that
can be done in one or two days, because
so many of us are involved in this sin.
14 Let our officials stay in Jerusalem and
take charge of the matter. Then let anyone who has a foreign wife come at a set
time, together with the leaders and the
judges of his city. In this way God's anger over this situation will be turned
away." 15 No one was opposed to the
plan except Jonathan son of Asahel and
Jahzeiah son of Tikvah, who had the
support of Meshullam and of Shabbethai, a Levite.

16 The returned exiles accepted the
plan, so Ezra the priest appointed[q] men
from among the heads of the clans and
recorded their names. On the first day of
the tenth month they began their investigation, 17 and within the next three
months they investigated all the cases of
men with foreign wives.

The Men Who Had Foreign Wives

18 This is the list of the men who had
foreign wives:

Priests, listed by clans:

Clan of Joshua and his brothers, sons
of Jehozadak: Maaseiah, Eliezer, Jarib,
and Gedaliah. 19 They promised to divorce their wives, and they offered a
ram as a sacrifice for their sins.

20 Clan of Immer: Hanani and
Zebadiah

21 Clan of Harim: Maaseiah, Elijah,
Shemaiah, Jehiel, and Uzziah

22 Clan of Pashhur: Elioenai, Maaseiah, Ishmael, Nethanel, Jozabad, and
Elasah

23 *Levites:*

Jozabad, Shimei, Kelaiah (also called
Kelita), Pethahiah, Judah, and Eliezer

24 *Musicians:*

Eliashib

Temple guards:

Shallum, Telem, and Uri

25 *Others:*

Clan of Parosh: Ramiah, Izziah, Malchijah, Mijamin, Eleazar, Malchijah, and
Benaiah

26 Clan of Elam: Mattaniah, Zechariah,
Jehiel, Abdi, Jeremoth, and Elijah

27 Clan of Zattu: Elioenai, Eliashib,
Mattaniah, Jeremoth, Zabad, and Aziza

28 Clan of Bebai: Jehohanan, Hananiah, Zabbai, and Athlai

29 Clan of Bani: Meshullam, Malluch,

[p] *One ancient translation* spent the night; *Hebrew* went. [q] *Some ancient translations* appointed; *Hebrew unclear.*

Adaiah, Jashub, Sheal, and Jeremoth
30 Clan of Pahath Moab: Adna, Chelal,
Benaiah, Maaseiah, Mattaniah, Bezalel,
Binnui, and Manasseh
31-32 Clan of Harim: Eliezer, Isshijah,
Malchijah, Shemaiah, Shimeon, Benjamin, Malluch, and Shemariah
33 Clan of Hashum: Mattenai, Mattattah, Zabad, Eliphelet, Jeremai, Manasseh, and Shimei
34-37 Clan of Bani: Maadai, Amram,
Uel, Benaiah, Bedeiah, Cheluhi, Vaniah,
Meremoth, Eliashib, Mattaniah, Mattenai, and Jaasu
38-42 Clan of Binnui: Shimei, Shelemiah, Nathan, Adaiah, Machnadebai,
Shashai, Sharai, Azarel, Shelemiah,
Shemariah, Shallum, Amariah, and
Joseph
43 Clan of Nebo: Jeiel, Mattithiah, Zabad, Zebina, Jaddai, Joel, and Benaiah
44 All these men had foreign wives.
They divorced them and sent them and their children away.[r]

[r] *Verse 44 in Hebrew is unclear.*

The Book of NEHEMIAH

Introduction

The Book of Nehemiah *may be divided into four parts: 1) The return of Nehemiah to Jerusalem, where he has been sent by the Persian emperor to govern Judah. 2) The rebuilding of the walls of Jerusalem. 3) The solemn reading of the Law of God by Ezra and the people's confession of sin. 4) Further activities of Nehemiah as governor of Judah.*

A notable feature of the book is the record of Nehemiah's deep dependence on God and his frequent prayers to him.

Outline of Contents

---

1 This is the account of what Nehemiah son of Hacaliah accomplished.

Nehemiah's Concern for Jerusalem

In the month of Kislev in the twentieth
year that Artaxerxes was emperor of
Persia, I, Nehemiah, was in Susa, the
capital city. 2 Hanani, one of my brothers, arrived from Judah with another
group, and I asked them about Jerusalem and about the other Jews who had
returned from exile in[a] Babylonia.
3 They told me that those who had survived and were back in the homeland[b]
were in great difficulty and that the foreigners who lived nearby looked down
on them. They also told me that the
walls of Jerusalem were still broken
down and that the gates had not been
restored since the time they were
burned. 4 When I heard all this, I sat
down and wept.

For several days I mourned and did
not eat. I prayed to God, 5 "LORD God of
Heaven! You are great, and we stand in
fear of you. You faithfully keep your
covenant with those who love you and
do what you command. 6 Look at me,
LORD, and hear my prayer, as I pray day
and night for your servants, the people
of Israel. I confess that we, the people of

[a] had returned from exile in; *or* had not been exiled to. [b] had survived and . . . homeland; *or* had remained in the homeland and had not gone into exile.

Israel, have sinned. My ancestors and I have sinned. 7 We have acted wickedly against you and have not done what you commanded. We have not kept the laws which you gave us through Moses, your servant. 8 Remember now what you told Moses: 'If you people of Israel are unfaithful to me, I will scatter you among the other nations. 9 But then if you turn back to me and do what I have commanded you, I will bring you back to the place where I have chosen to be worshiped, even though you are scattered to the ends of the earth.'

10 "Lord, these are your servants, your own people. You rescued them by your great power and strength. 11 Listen now to my prayer and to the prayers of all your other servants who want to honor you. Give me success today and make the emperor merciful to me."

In those days I was the emperor's wine steward.

Nehemiah Goes to Jerusalem

2 One day four months later, when Emperor Artaxerxes was dining, I took the wine to him. He had never seen me look sad before, 2 so he asked, "Why are you looking so sad? You aren't sick, so it must be that you're unhappy."

I was startled 3 and answered, "May Your Majesty live forever! How can I keep from looking sad when the city where my ancestors are buried is in ruins and its gates have been destroyed by fire?"

4 The emperor asked, "What is it that you want?"

I prayed to the God of Heaven, 5 and then I said to the emperor, "If Your Majesty is pleased with me and is willing to grant my request, let me go to the land of Judah, to the city where my ancestors are buried, so that I can rebuild the city."

6 The emperor, with the empress sitting at his side, approved my request. He asked me how long I would be gone and when I would return, and I told him.

7 Then I asked him to grant me the favor of giving me letters to the governors of West-of-Euphrates Province,[c] instructing them to let me travel to Judah. 8 I asked also for a letter to Asaph, keeper of the royal forests, instructing him to supply me with timber for the gates of the fort that guards the Temple, for the city walls, and for the house I was to live in. The emperor gave me all I asked for, because God was with me.

9 The emperor sent some army officers and a troop of cavalry with me, and I made the journey to West-of-Euphrates. There I gave the emperor's letters to the governors. 10 But Sanballat, from the town of Beth Horon, and Tobiah, an official in the province of Ammon, heard that someone had come to work for the good of the people of Israel, and they were highly indignant.

11 I went on to Jerusalem, and for three days 12 I did not tell anyone what God had inspired me to do for Jerusalem. Then in the middle of the night I got up and went out, taking a few of my companions with me. The only animal we took was the donkey that I rode on. 13 It was still night as I left the city through the Valley Gate on the west and went south past Dragon's Fountain to the Rubbish Gate. As I went, I inspected the broken walls of the city and the gates that had been destroyed by fire. 14 Then on the east side of the city I went north to the Fountain Gate and the King's Pool. The donkey I was riding could not find any path through the rubble, 15 so I went down into Kidron Valley and rode along, looking at the wall. Then I returned the way I had come and went back into the city through the Valley Gate.

16 None of the local officials knew where I had gone or what I had been doing. So far I had not said anything to any of the other Jews—the priests, the leaders, the officials, or anyone else who would be taking part in the work. 17 But now I said to them, "See what trouble we are in because Jerusalem is in ruins and its gates are destroyed! Let's rebuild the city walls and put an end to our disgrace." 18 And I told them how God had been with me and helped me, and what the emperor had said to me.

They responded, "Let's start rebuilding!" And they got ready to start the work.

19 When Sanballat, Tobiah, and an Arab named Geshem heard what we

[c] WEST-OF-EUPHRATES PROVINCE: *Under Persian rule the land of Israel was part of this large Persian province west of the Euphrates River.*

were planning to do, they laughed at us
and said, "What do you think you're doing? Are you going to rebel against the
emperor?"
20 I answered, "The God of Heaven
will give us success. We are his servants,
and we are going to start building. But
you have no right to any property in Jerusalem, and you have no share in its
traditions."

Rebuilding the Wall of Jerusalem

3 This is how the city wall was rebuilt.[d] The High Priest Eliashib
and his fellow priests rebuilt the Sheep
Gate, dedicated it, and put the gates in
place. They dedicated the wall as far as
the Tower of the Hundred and the Tower
of Hananel.
2 The men of Jericho built the next
section.
Zaccur son of Imri built the next
section.
3 The clan of Hassenaah built the Fish
Gate. They put the beams and the gates
in place, and put in the bolts and bars for
locking the gate.
4 Meremoth, the son of Uriah and
grandson of Hakkoz, built the next
section.
Meshullam, the son of Berechiah and
grandson of Meshezabel, built the next
section.
Zadok son of Baana built the next
section.
5 The men of Tekoa built the next section, but the leading men of the town refused to do the manual labor assigned
them by the supervisors.
6 Joiada son of Paseah and Meshullam
son of Besodeiah rebuilt Jeshanah
Gate.[e] They put the beams and the
gates in place, and put in the bolts and
bars for locking the gate.
7 Melatiah from Gibeon, Jadon from
Meronoth, and the men of Gibeon and
Mizpah built the next section, as far as
the residence of the governor of West-
of-Euphrates.
8 Uzziel son of Harhaiah, a goldsmith,
built the next section.
Hananiah, a maker of perfumes, built
the next section, as far as Broad Wall.
9 Rephaiah son of Hur, ruler of half of
the Jerusalem District, built the next
section.
10 Jedaiah son of Harumaph built the
next section, which was near his own
house.
Hattush son of Hashabneiah built the
next section.
11 Malchijah son of Harim and Hasshub son of Pahath Moab built both the
next section and the Tower of the Ovens.
12 Shallum son of Hallohesh, ruler of
the other half of the Jerusalem District,
built the next section. (His daughters
helped with the work.)
13 Hanun and the inhabitants of the
city of Zanoah rebuilt the Valley Gate.
They put the gates in place, put in the
bolts and the bars for locking the gate,
and repaired the wall for fifteen hundred
feet, as far as the Rubbish Gate.
14 Malchijah son of Rechab, ruler of
the Beth Haccherem District, rebuilt the
Rubbish Gate. He put the gates in place,
and put in the bolts and the bars for
locking the gate.
15 Shallum son of Colhozeh, ruler of
the Mizpah District, rebuilt the Fountain
Gate. He covered the gateway, put the
gates in place, and put in the bolts and
the bars. At the Pool of Shelah he built
the wall next to the royal garden, as far
as the stairs leading down from David's
City.
16 Nehemiah son of Azbuk, ruler of
half of the Bethzur District, built the
next section, as far as David's tomb, the
pool, and the barracks.

Levites Who Worked on the Wall

17 The following Levites rebuilt the
next several sections of the wall:
Rehum son of Bani built the next
section;
Hashabiah, ruler of half of the Keilah
District, built the next section on behalf
of his district;
18 Bavvai son of Henadad, ruler of the
other half of the Keilah District, built the
next section;
19 Ezer son of Jeshua, ruler of Mizpah,
built the next section in front of the ar-
mory, as far as the place where the wall
turns;
20 Baruch son of Zabbai built the next

[d] CITY WALL WAS REBUILT: *According to the following report, the rebuilding of the wall started at the middle of the north side and proceeded counterclockwise around the city. Many of the places mentioned cannot be identified.* [e] Jeshanah Gate; *or* the Old Gate.

section, as far as the entrance to the
house of the High Priest Eliashib;
21 Meremoth, the son of Uriah and
grandson of Hakkoz, built the next section, up to the far end of Eliashib's
house.

Priests Who Worked on the Wall

22 The following priests rebuilt the
next several sections of the wall:
Priests from the area around Jerusalem built the next section;
23 Benjamin and Hasshub built the
next section, which was in front of their
houses;
Azariah, the son of Maaseiah and
grandson of Ananiah, built the next section, which was in front of his house;
24 Binnui son of Henadad built the next
section, from Azariah's house to the corner of the wall;
25-26 Palal son of Uzai built the next
section, beginning at the corner of the
wall and the tower of the upper palace
near the court of the guard;
Pedaiah son of Parosh built the next
section, to a point on the east near the
Water Gate and the tower guarding the
Temple. (This was near that part of the
city called Ophel, where the Temple
workers lived.)

Other Builders

27 The men of Tekoa built the next section, their second one, from a point opposite the large tower guarding the
Temple as far as the wall near Ophel.
28 A group of priests built the next section, going north from the Horse Gate,
each one building in front of his own
house.
29 Zadok son of Immer built the next
section, which was in front of his house.
Shemaiah son of Shecaniah, keeper of
the East Gate, built the next section.
30 Hananiah son of Shelemiah and Hanun, the sixth son of Zalaph, built the
next section, their second one.
Meshullam son of Berechiah built the
next section, which was in front of his
house.
31 Malchijah, a goldsmith, built the
next section, as far as the building used
by the Temple workers and the merchants, which was by the Miphkad[f]
Gate to the Temple, near the room on
top of the northeast corner of the wall.
32 The goldsmiths and the merchants
built the last section, from the room at
the corner as far as the Sheep Gate.

Nehemiah Overcomes Opposition to His Work

4 When Sanballat heard that we Jews
had begun rebuilding the wall, he
became furious and began to ridicule us.
2 In front of his companions and the Samaritan troops he said, "What do these
miserable Jews think they're doing? Do
they intend to rebuild the city? Do they
think that by offering sacrifices they can
finish the work in one day? Can they
make building stones out of heaps of
burnt rubble?"
3 Tobiah was standing there beside
him, and he added, "What kind of wall
could they ever build? Even a fox could
knock it down!"
4 I prayed, "Hear how they make fun
of us, O God! Let their ridicule fall on
their own heads. Let them be robbed of
everything they have, and let them be
taken as prisoners to a foreign land.
5 Don't forgive the evil they do and don't
forget their sins, for they have insulted
us who are building."
6 So we went on rebuilding the wall,
and soon it was half its full height, because the people were eager to work.
7 Sanballat, Tobiah, and the people of
Arabia, Ammon, and Ashdod heard that
we were making progress in rebuilding
the wall of Jerusalem and that the gaps
in the wall were being closed, and they
became very angry. 8 So they all plotted
together to come and attack Jerusalem
and create confusion, 9 but we prayed to
our God and kept men on guard against
them day and night.
10 The people of Judah had a song they
sang:

"We grow weak carrying burdens;
There's so much rubble to take
away.
How can we build the wall today?"

11 Our enemies thought we would not
see them or know what was happening
until they were already upon us, killing
us and putting an end to our work. 12 But
time after time Jews who were living
among our enemies came to warn us of
the plans our enemies were making

[f] Miphkad; *or* Mustering, *or* Watch.

against us.[g] 13 So I armed the people with swords, spears, and bows, and stationed them by clans behind the wall, wherever it was still unfinished.

14 I saw that the people were worried, so I said to them and to their leaders and officials, "Don't be afraid of our enemies. Remember how great and terrifying the Lord is, and fight for your relatives, your children, your wives, and your homes." 15 Our enemies heard that we had found out what they were plotting, and they realized that God had defeated their plans. Then all of us went back to rebuilding the wall.

16 From then on half of my men worked and half stood guard, wearing coats of armor and armed with spears, shields, and bows. And our leaders gave their full support to the people 17 who were rebuilding the wall. Even those who carried building materials worked with one hand and kept a weapon in the other, 18 and everyone who was building kept a sword strapped to their waist. The man who was to sound the alarm on the bugle stayed with me. 19 I told the people and their officials and leaders, "The work is spread out over such a distance that we are widely separated from one another on the wall. 20 If you hear the bugle, gather around me. Our God will fight for us." 21 So every day, from dawn until the stars came out at night, half of us worked on the wall, while the other half stood guard with spears.

22 During this time I told the men in charge that they and all their helpers had to stay in Jerusalem at night, so that we could guard the city at night as well as work in the daytime. 23 I didn't take off my clothes even at night, neither did any of my companions nor my servants nor my bodyguards. And we all kept our weapons at hand.[h]

Oppression of the Poor

5 Some time later many of the people, both men and women, began to complain against the other Jews. 2 Some said, "We have large families, we need grain to keep us alive."

3 Others said, "We have had to mortgage our fields and vineyards and houses to get enough grain to keep us from starving."

4 Still others said, "We had to borrow money to pay the royal tax on our fields and vineyards. 5 We are of the same race as the other Jews. Aren't our children just as good as theirs? But we have to make slaves of our children. Some of our daughters have already been sold as slaves. We are helpless because our fields and vineyards have been taken away from us."

6 When I heard their complaints, I grew angry 7 and decided to act. I denounced the leaders and officials of the people and told them, "You are oppressing your own relatives!"

I called a public assembly to deal with the problem 8 and said, "As far as we have been able, we have been buying back our Jewish relatives who had to sell themselves to foreigners. Now you are forcing your own relatives to sell themselves to you, their own people!" The leaders were silent and could find nothing to say.

9 Then I said, "What you are doing is wrong! You ought to obey God and do what's right. Then you would not give our enemies, the Gentiles, any reason to ridicule us. 10 I have let the people borrow money and grain from me, and so have my companions and those who work for me. Now let's give up all our claims to repayment. 11 Cancel all the debts[i] they owe you—money or grain or wine or olive oil. And give them back their fields, vineyards, olive groves, and houses right now!"

12 The leaders replied, "We'll do as you say. We'll give the property back and not try to collect the debts."

I called in the priests and made the leaders swear in front of them to keep the promise they had just made. 13 Then I took off the sash[j] I was wearing around my waist and shook it out. "This is how God will shake any of you who don't keep your promise," I said. "God will take away your houses and everything you own, and will leave you with nothing."

[g] *Probable text* the plans our enemies were making against us; *Hebrew unclear.*
[h] *Probable text* weapons at hand; *Hebrew unclear.* [i] *One ancient translation* debts; *Hebrew unclear.* [j] SASH: *Clothing in those days had no pockets, so small items were tucked into the sash that was worn like a belt around the waist. Shaking it out was a symbol of losing everything.*

Everyone who was present said,
"Amen!" and praised the LORD. And the
leaders kept their promise.

Nehemiah's Unselfishness

14 During all the twelve years that I
was governor of the land of Judah, from
the twentieth year that Artaxerxes was
emperor until his thirty-second year,
neither my relatives nor I ate the food I
was entitled to have as governor.
15 Every governor who had been in office
before me had been a burden to the people and had demanded forty silver coins
a day[k] for food and wine. Even their
servants had oppressed the people. But I
acted differently, because I honored
God. 16 I put all my energy into rebuilding the wall and did not acquire any
property. Everyone who worked for me
joined in the rebuilding. 17 I regularly fed
at my table a hundred and fifty of the
Jewish people and their leaders, besides
all the people who came to me from the
surrounding nations. 18 Every day I
served one beef, six of the best sheep,
and many chickens, and every ten days
I provided a fresh supply of wine. But I
knew what heavy burdens the people
had to bear, and so I did not claim the
allowance that the governor is entitled to.

19 I pray you, O God, remember to my
credit everything that I have done for
this people.

Plots against Nehemiah

6 Sanballat, Tobiah, Geshem, and the
rest of our enemies heard that we
had finished building the wall and that
there were no gaps left in it, although we
still had not set up the gates in the gateways. 2 So Sanballat and Geshem sent
me a message, suggesting that I meet
with them in one of the villages in the
Plain of Ono. This was a trick of theirs to
try to harm me. 3 I sent messengers to
say to them, "I am doing important work
and can't go down there. I am not going
to let the work stop just to go and
see you."

4 They sent me the same message four
times, and each time I sent them the
same reply.

5 Then Sanballat sent one of his servants to me with a fifth message, this one
in the form of an unsealed letter.[l] 6 It
read:

"Geshem tells me that a rumor is going around among the neighboring
peoples that you and the Jewish
people intend to revolt and that this
is why you are rebuilding the wall.
He also says you plan to make yourself king 7 and that you have arranged for some prophets to
proclaim in Jerusalem that you are
the king of Judah. His Majesty is
certain to hear about this, so I suggest that you and I meet to talk the
situation over."

8 I sent a reply to him: "Nothing of
what you are saying is true. You have
made it all up yourself."

9 They were trying to frighten us into
stopping work. I prayed, "But now, God,
make me strong!"

10 About this time I went to visit Shemaiah, the son of Delaiah and grandson
of Mehetabel, who was unable to leave
his house. He said to me, "You and I
must go and hide together in the Holy
Place of the Temple and lock the doors,
because they are coming to kill you. Any
night now they will come to kill you."

11 I answered, "I'm not the kind of person that runs and hides. Do you think I
would try to save my life by hiding in the
Temple? I won't do it."

12 When I thought it over, I realized
that God had not spoken to Shemaiah,
but that Tobiah and Sanballat had
bribed him to give me this warning.
13 They hired him to frighten me into sinning, so that they could ruin my reputation and humiliate me.

14 I prayed, "God, remember what Tobiah and Sanballat have done and punish them. Remember that woman
Noadiah and all the other prophets who
tried to frighten me."

The Conclusion of the Work

15 After fifty-two days of work the entire wall was finished on the twenty-fifth
day of the month of Elul. 16 When our
enemies in the surrounding nations
heard this, they realized that they had
lost face, since everyone knew that the
work had been done with God's help.

17 During all this time the Jewish lead-

[k] *One ancient translation* a day; *Hebrew unclear.* [l] UNSEALED LETTER: *Leaving a letter unsealed was a deliberate way of making certain that its contents would become widely known.*

ers had been in correspondence with Tobiah. 18 Many people in Judah were on
his side because of his Jewish father-in-
law, Shecaniah son of Arah. In addition,
his son Jehohanan had married the
daughter of Meshullam son of Berechiah. 19 People would talk in front of me
about all the good deeds Tobiah had
done and would tell him everything I
said. And he kept sending me letters to
try to frighten me.

7 And now the wall had been rebuilt,
the gates had all been put in place,
and the Temple guards, the members of
the sacred choir, and the other Levites
had been assigned their work. 2 I put two
men in charge of governing the city of
Jerusalem: my brother Hanani and Hananiah, commanding officer of the fortress. Hananiah was a reliable and
God-fearing man without equal. 3 I told
them not to have the gates of Jerusalem
opened in the morning until well after
sunrise and to have them closed and
barred before the guards went off duty
at sunset. I also told them to appoint
guards from among the people who
lived in Jerusalem and to assign some of
them to specific posts and others to patrol the area around their own houses.

The List of Those Who Returned from Exile

(Ezra 2.1-70)

4 Jerusalem was a large city, but not
many people were living in it, and not
many houses had been built yet. 5 God
inspired me to assemble the people and
their leaders and officials and to check
their family records. I located the
records of those who had first returned
from captivity, and this is the information I found:

6 Many of the exiles left the province of
Babylon and returned to Jerusalem and
Judah, each to his own hometown. Their
families had been living in exile in Babylonia ever since King Nebuchadnezzar
had taken them there as prisoners.
7 Their leaders were Zerubbabel,
Joshua, Nehemiah, Azariah, Raamiah,
Nahamani, Mordecai, Bilshan, Mispe-
reth, Bigvai, Nehum, and Baanah.

8-25 This is the list of the clans of Israel,
with the number of those from each clan
who returned from exile:

Parosh - 2,172
Shephatiah - 372
Arah - 652
Pahath Moab (descendants of Jeshua and Joab) - 2,818
Elam - 1,254
Zattu - 845
Zaccai - 760
Binnui - 648
Bebai - 628
Azgad - 2,322
Adonikam - 667
Bigvai - 2,067
Adin - 655
Ater (also called Hezekiah) - 98
Hashum - 328
Bezai - 324
Hariph - 112
Gibeon - 95

26-38 People whose ancestors had lived in
the following towns also returned:

Bethlehem and Netophah - 188
Anathoth - 128
Beth Azmaveth - 42
Kiriath Jearim, Chephirah, and Beeroth - 743
Ramah and Geba - 621
Michmash - 122
Bethel and Ai - 123
The other Nebo - 52
The other Elam - 1,254
Harim - 320
Jericho - 345
Lod, Hadid, and Ono - 721
Senaah - 3,930

39-42 This is the list of the priestly clans
that returned from exile:

Jedaiah (descendants of Jeshua) - 973
Immer - 1,052
Pashhur - 1,247
Harim - 1,017

43-45 Clans of Levites who returned from
exile:

Jeshua and Kadmiel (descendants of Hodaviah) - 74
Temple musicians (descendants of Asaph) - 148
Temple guards (descendants of Shallum, Ater, Talmon, Akkub, Hatita, and Shobai) - 138

46-56 Clans of Temple workers who returned from exile:

Ziha, Hasupha, Tabbaoth,
Keros, Sia, Padon,
Lebana, Hagaba, Shalmai,
Hanan, Giddel, Gahar,
Reaiah, Rezin, Nekoda,
Gazzam, Uzza, Paseah,

Besai, Meunim, Nephushesim,
Bakbuk, Hakupha, Harhur,
Bazlith, Meḥida, Harsha,
Barkos, Sisera, Temah,
Neziah, and Hatipha.

57-59 Clans of Solomon's servants who re-
turned from exile:
Sotai, Sophereth, Perida,
Jaalah, Darkon, Giddel,
Shephatiah, Hattil, Pochereth
Hazzebaim, and Amon.

60 The total number of descendants of
the Temple workers and of Solomon's
servants who returned from exile
was 392.

61-62 There were 642 belonging to the
clans of Delaiah, Tobiah, and Nekoda
who returned from the towns of Tel Melah, Tel Harsha, Cherub, Addon, and Immer; but they could not prove that they
were descendants of Israelites.

63-64 The following priestly clans could
find no record to prove their ancestry:
Hobaiah, Hakkoz, and Barzillai. (The
ancestor of the priestly clan of Barzillai
had married a woman from the clan of
Barzillai of Gilead and taken the name
of his father-in-law's clan.) Since they
were unable to prove who their ancestors were, they were not accepted as
priests. 65 The Jewish governor told
them that they could not eat the food offered to God until there was a priest who
could use the Urim and Thummim.[m]

66-69 Total number of exiles who
returned - 42,360.
Their male and female
servants - 7,337
Male and female musicians - 245
Horses - 736
Mules - 245
Camels - 435
Donkeys - 6,720

70-72 Many of the people contributed to
help pay the cost of restoring the
Temple:

The governor	270	ounces of gold
	50	ceremonial bowls
	530	robes for priests
Heads of clans	337	pounds of gold
	3,215	pounds of silver
The rest of the people	337	pounds of gold
	2,923	pounds of silver
	67	robes for priests

73 The priests, the Levites, the Temple
guards, the musicians, many of the ordinary people, the Temple workers—all
the people of Israel—settled in the
towns and cities of Judah.

Ezra Reads the Law to the People

8 By the seventh month the people of
Israel were all settled in their
towns. On the first day of that month
they all assembled in Jerusalem, in the
square just inside the Water Gate. They
asked Ezra, the priest and scholar of the
Law which the LORD had given Israel
through Moses, to get the book of the
Law. 2 So Ezra brought it to the place
where the people had gathered—men,
women, and the children who were old
enough to understand. 3 There in the
square by the gate he read the Law to
them from dawn until noon, and they all
listened attentively.

4 Ezra was standing on a wooden platform that had been built for the occasion. The following men stood at his
right: Mattithiah, Shema, Anaiah, Uriah,
Hilkiah, and Maaseiah; and the following stood at his left: Pedaiah, Mishael,
Malchijah, Hashum, Hashbaddanah,
Zechariah, and Meshullam.

5 As Ezra stood there on the platform
high above the people, they all kept their
eyes fixed on him. As soon as he opened
the book, they all stood up. 6 Ezra said,
"Praise the LORD, the great God!"

All the people raised their arms in the
air and answered, "Amen! Amen!" They
knelt in worship, with their faces to the
ground.

7 Then they rose and stood in their
places, and the following Levites explained the Law to them: Jeshua, Bani,
Sherebiah, Jamin, Akkub, Shabbethai,
Hodiah, Maaseiah, Kelita, Azariah, Jozabad, Hanan, and Pelaiah. 8 They gave
an oral translation[n] of God's Law and

[m] URIM AND THUMMIM: *Two objects used by the priest to determine God's will; it is not known precisely how they were used.* [n] TRANSLATION: *The Law was written in Hebrew, but in Babylonia the Jews had adopted Aramaic as the language for daily life. Because of this a translation was necessary.*

explained[o] it so that the people could
understand it.
9 When the people heard what the Law
required, they were so moved that they
began to cry. So Nehemiah, who was the
governor, Ezra, the priest and scholar of
the Law, and the Levites who were explaining the Law told all the people,
"This day is holy to the LORD your God,
so you are not to mourn or cry. 10 Now go
home and have a feast. Share your food
and wine with those who don't have
enough. Today is holy to our Lord, so
don't be sad. The joy that the LORD gives
you will make you strong."
11 The Levites went around calming
the people and telling them not to be sad
on such a holy day. 12 So all the people
went home and ate and drank joyfully
and shared what they had with others,
because they understood what had been
read to them.

The Festival of Shelters

13 The next day the heads of the clans,
together with the priests and the Levites,
went to Ezra to study the teachings of
the Law. 14 They discovered that the
Law, which the LORD gave through
Moses, ordered the people of Israel to
live in temporary shelters during the
Festival of Shelters. 15 So they gave the
following instructions and sent them[p]
all through Jerusalem and the other cities and towns: "Go out to the hills and
get branches from pines, olives, myrtles,
palms, and other trees to make shelters
according to the instructions written in
the Law."
16 So the people got branches and built
shelters on the flat roofs of their houses,
in their yards, in the Temple courtyard,
and in the public squares by the Water
Gate and by the Ephraim Gate. 17 All the
people who had come back from captivity built shelters and lived in them. This
was the first time it had been done since
the days of Joshua son of Nun, and
everybody was excited and happy.
18 From the first day of the festival to the
last they read a part of God's Law every
day. They celebrated for seven days, and
on the eighth day there was a closing
ceremony, as required in the Law.

The People Confess Their Sins

9 1-2 On the twenty-fourth day of the
same month the people of Israel
gathered to fast in order to show sorrow
for their sins. They had already separated themselves from all foreigners.
They wore sackcloth and put dust on
their heads as signs of grief. Then they
stood and began to confess the sins that
they and their ancestors had committed.
3 For about three hours the Law of the
LORD their God was read to them, and for
the next three hours they confessed their
sins and worshiped the LORD their God.
4 There was a platform for the Levites,
and on it stood Jeshua, Bani, Kadmiel,
Shebaniah, Bunni, Sherebiah, Bani, and
Chenani. They prayed aloud to the LORD
their God.
5 The following Levites gave a call to
worship: Jeshua, Kadmiel, Bani, Hashabneiah, Sherebiah, Hodiah, Shebaniah,
and Pethahiah. They said:

"Stand up and praise the LORD
your God;
praise him forever and ever!
Let everyone praise his glorious
name,
although no human praise is
great enough."

The Prayer of Confession

6 And then the people of Israel prayed
this prayer:

"You, LORD, you alone are LORD;
you made the heavens and the
stars of the sky.
You made land and sea and
everything in them;
you gave life to all.
The heavenly powers bow down
and worship you.
7 You, LORD God, chose Abram
and led him out of Ur in
Babylonia;
you changed his name to
Abraham.
8 You found that he was faithful
to you,
and you made a covenant
with him.
You promised to give him the land
of the Canaanites,

[o] They gave ... explained; *or* They read God's Law and then translated it, explaining.
[p] *Probable text* So they ... sent them; *Hebrew* It also ordered that the following instructions be sent.

the land of the Hittites and the
Amorites,
the land of the Perizzites, the
Jebusites, the Girgashites,
to be a land where his
descendants would live.
You kept your promise, because
you are faithful.

9 "You saw how our ancestors
suffered in Egypt;
you heard their call for help at
the Red Sea.
10 You worked amazing miracles
against the king,
against his officials and the
people of his land,
because you knew how they
oppressed your people.
You won then the fame you still
have today.
11 Through the sea you made a path
for your people
and led them through on dry
ground.
Those who pursued them drowned
in deep water,
as a stone sinks in the
raging sea.
12 With a cloud you led them in
daytime,
and at night you lighted their
way with fire.
13 At Mount Sinai you came down
from heaven;
you spoke to your people
and gave them good laws and
sound teachings.
14 You taught them to keep your
Sabbaths holy,
and through your servant Moses
you gave them your laws.

15 "When they were hungry, you
gave them bread from heaven,
and water from a rock when
they were thirsty.
You told them to take control of
the land
which you had promised to give
them.
16 But our ancestors grew proud and
stubborn
and refused to obey your
commands.
17 They refused to obey; they forgot
all you did;
they forgot the miracles you had
performed.
In their pride they chose a leader
to take them back to slavery in
Egypt.
But you are a God who forgives;
you are gracious and loving,
slow to be angry.
Your mercy is great; you did not
forsake them.
18 They made an idol in the shape of
a bull-calf
and said it was the god who led
them from Egypt!
How much they insulted you,
LORD!
19 But you did not abandon them
there in the desert,
for your mercy is great.
You did not take away the cloud
or the fire
that showed them the path by
day and night.
20 In your goodness you told them
what they should do;
you fed them manna and gave
them water to drink.
21 Through forty years in the desert
you provided all that they
needed;
their clothing never wore out,
and their feet were not swollen
with pain.

22 "You let them conquer nations and
kingdoms,
lands that bordered their own.
They conquered the land of
Heshbon, where Sihon ruled,
and the land of Bashan, where
Og was king.
23 You gave them as many children
as there are stars in the sky,
and let them conquer and live in
the land
that you had promised their
ancestors to give them.
24 They conquered the land of
Canaan;
you overcame the people living
there.
You gave your people the power
to do as they pleased
with the people and kings of
Canaan.
25 Your people captured fortified
cities,

fertile land, houses full of
wealth,
cisterns already dug,
olive trees, fruit trees, and
vineyards.
They ate all they wanted and
grew fat;
they enjoyed all the good things
you gave them.

26 "But your people rebelled and
disobeyed you;
they turned their backs on
your Law.
They killed the prophets who
warned them,
who told them to turn back
to you.
They insulted you time after time,
27 so you let their enemies conquer
and rule them.
In their trouble they called to you
for help,
and you answered them from
heaven.
In your great mercy you sent them
leaders
who rescued them from their
foes.
28 When peace returned, they sinned
again,
and again you let their enemies
conquer them.
Yet when they repented and asked
you to save them,
in heaven you heard, and time
after time
you rescued them in your great
mercy.
29 You warned them to obey your
teachings,
but in pride they rejected your
laws,
although keeping your Law is
the way to life.
Hard-headed and stubborn, they
refused to obey.
30 Year after year you patiently
warned them.
You inspired your prophets to
speak,
but your people were deaf,
so you let them be conquered
by other nations.
31 And yet, because your mercy is
great,
you did not forsake or destroy
them.
You are a gracious and
merciful God!

32 "O God, our God, how great
you are!
How terrifying, how powerful!
You faithfully keep your covenant
promises.
From the time when Assyrian
kings oppressed us,
even till now, how much we
have suffered!
Our kings, our leaders, our priests
and prophets,
our ancestors, and all our people
have suffered.
Remember how much we have
suffered!
33 You have done right to punish us;
you have been faithful, even
though we have sinned.
34 Our ancestors, our kings, leaders,
and priests
have not kept your Law.
They did not listen to your
commands and warnings.
35 With your blessing, kings ruled
your people
when they lived in the broad,
fertile land you gave them;
but they failed to turn from sin
and serve you.
36 And now we are slaves in the land
that you gave us,
this fertile land which gives us
food.
37 What the land produces goes to
the kings
that you put over us because we
sinned.
They do as they please with us
and our livestock,
and we are in deep distress!"

The People Sign an Agreement

38 Because of all that has happened,
we, the people of Israel, hereby make a
solemn written agreement, and our leaders, our Levites, and our priests put their
seals to it.

10 The first to sign was the governor, Nehemiah son of Hacaliah,
and then Zedekiah signed. The following also signed:

2-8 *Priests:*
Seraiah, Azariah, Jeremiah,
Pashhur, Amariah, Malchijah,

Hattush, Shebaniah, Malluch,
Harim, Meremoth, Obadiah,
Daniel, Ginnethon, Baruch,
Meshullam, Abijah, Mijamin,
Maaziah, Bilgai, and Shemaiah.

9-13 *Levites:*
Jeshua son of Azaniah,
Binnui of the clan of Henadad,
Kadmiel, Shebaniah, Hodiah,
Kelita, Pelaiah, Hanan,
Mica, Rehob, Hashabiah,
Zaccur, Sherebiah, Shebaniah,
Hodiah, Bani, and Beninu.

14-27 *Leaders of the people:*
Parosh, Pahath Moab,
Elam, Zattu, Bani,
Bunni, Azgad, Bebai,
Adonijah, Bigvai, Adin,
Ater, Hezekiah, Azzur,
Hodiah, Hashum, Bezai,
Hariph, Anathoth, Nebai,
Magpiash, Meshullam, Hezir,
Meshezabel, Zadok, Jaddua,
Pelatiah, Hanan, Anaiah,
Hoshea, Hananiah, Hasshub,
Hallohesh, Pilha, Shobek,
Rehum, Hashabnah, Maaseiah,
Ahiah, Hanan, Anan,
Malluch, Harim, and Baanah.

The Agreement

28 We, the people of Israel, the priests,
the Levites, the Temple guards, the Temple musicians, the Temple workers, and
all others who in obedience to God's
Law have separated themselves from
the foreigners living in our land, we, together with our wives and all our children old enough to understand, 29 do
hereby join with our leaders in an oath,
under penalty of a curse if we break it,
that we will live according to God's Law,
which God gave through his servant
Moses; that we will obey all that the
LORD, our Lord, commands us; and that
we will keep all his laws and requirements.

30 We will not intermarry with the foreigners living in our land.

31 If foreigners bring grain or anything
else to sell to us on the Sabbath or on
any other holy day, we will not buy from
them.

Every seventh year we will not farm
the land, and we will cancel all debts.

32 Every year we will each contribute
one-eighth of an ounce of silver to help
pay the expenses of the Temple.

33 We will provide for the Temple worship the following: the sacred bread, the
daily grain offering, the animals to be
burned each day as sacrifices, the sacred
offerings for Sabbaths, New Moon Festivals, and other festivals, the other sacred offerings, the offerings to take
away the sins of Israel, and anything
else needed for the Temple.

34 We, the people, priests, and Levites,
will draw lots each year to determine
which clans are to provide wood to burn
the sacrifices offered to the LORD our
God, according to the requirements of
the Law.

35 We will take to the Temple each
year an offering of the first grain we harvest and of the first fruit that ripens on
our trees.

36 The first son born to each of us we
will take to the priests in the Temple and
there, as required by the Law, dedicate
him to God. We will also dedicate the
first calf born to each of our cows, and
the first lamb or kid born to each of our
sheep or goats.

37 We will take to the priests in the
Temple the dough made from the first
grain harvested each year and our other
offerings of wine, olive oil, and all kinds
of fruit.

We will take to the Levites, who collect tithes in our farming villages, the
tithes from the crops that grow on our
land. 38 Priests who are descended from
Aaron are to be with the Levites when
tithes are collected, and for use in the
Temple the Levites are to take to the
Temple storerooms one-tenth of all the
tithes they collect. 39 The people of Israel
and the Levites are to take the contributions of grain, wine, and olive oil to the
storerooms where the utensils for the
Temple are kept and where the priests
who are on duty, the Temple guards, and
the members of the Temple choir have
their quarters.

We will not neglect the house of
our God.

The People Who Lived in Jerusalem

11 The leaders settled in Jerusalem,
and the rest of the people drew
lots to choose one family out of every ten
to go and live in the holy city of Jerusalem, while the rest were to live in the

other cities and towns. 2 The people
praised anyone else who volunteered to
live in Jerusalem. 3 In the other towns
and cities the people of Israel, the
priests, the Levites, the Temple workers,
and the descendants of Solomon's servants lived on their own property in their
own towns.

The following is the list of the leading
citizens of the province of Judah who
lived in Jerusalem:

4 *Members of the tribe of Judah:*

Athaiah, the son of Uzziah and grandson of Zechariah. His other ancestors included Amariah, Shephatiah, and
Mahalalel, descendants of Judah's son
Perez.

5 Maaseiah, the son of Baruch and
grandson of Colhozeh. His other ancestors included Hazaiah, Adaiah, Joiarib,
and Zechariah, descendants of Judah's
son Shelah.

6 Of the descendants of Perez, 468 outstanding soldiers lived in Jerusalem.

7 *Members of the tribe of Benjamin:*

Sallu, the son of Meshullam and
grandson of Joed. His other ancestors
included Pedaiah, Kolaiah, Maaseiah,
Ithiel, and Jeshaiah.

8 Gabbai and Sallai, close relatives[q] of
Sallu.

In all, 928 Benjaminites lived in Jerusalem. 9 Joel son of Zichri was their
leader, and Judah son of Hassenuah was
the second ranking official in the city.

10 *Priests:*

Jedaiah son of Joiarib, and Jachin.

11 Seraiah, the son of Hilkiah and
grandson of Meshullam. His ancestors
included Zadok, Meraioth, and Ahitub,
who was the High Priest. 12 In all, 822
members of this clan served in the
Temple.

Adaiah, the son of Jeroham and
grandson of Pelaliah. His ancestors included Amzi, Zechariah, Pashhur, and
Malchijah. 13 In all, 242 members of this
clan were heads of families.

Amashsai, the son of Azarel and
grandson of Ahzai. His ancestors included Meshillemoth and Immer.
14 There were 128 members of this clan
who were outstanding soldiers. Their
leader was Zabdiel, a member of a leading family.[r]

15 *Levites:*

Shemaiah, the son of Hasshub and
grandson of Azrikam. His ancestors included Hashabiah and Bunni.

16 Shabbethai and Jozabad, prominent
Levites in charge of the work outside the
Temple.

17 Mattaniah, the son of Mica and
grandson of Zabdi, a descendant of
Asaph. He led the Temple choir in singing the prayer of thanksgiving.

Bakbukiah, who was Mattaniah's assistant.

Abda, the son of Shammua and grandson of Galal, a descendant of Jeduthun.

18 In all, 284 Levites lived in the holy
city of Jerusalem.

19 *Temple guards:*

Akkub, Talmon, and their relatives,
172 in all.

20 The rest of the people of Israel and
the remaining priests and Levites lived
on their own property in the other cities
and towns of Judah. 21 The Temple
workers lived in the part of Jerusalem
called Ophel and worked under the supervision of Ziha and Gishpa.

22 The supervisor of the Levites who
lived in Jerusalem was Uzzi, the son of
Bani and grandson of Hashabiah. His
ancestors included Mattaniah and Mica,
and he belonged to the clan of Asaph,
the clan that was responsible for the music in the Temple services. 23 There were
royal regulations stating how the clans
should take turns in leading the Temple
music each day.

24 Pethahiah son of Meshezabel, of the
clan of Zerah and the tribe of Judah, represented the people of Israel at the Persian court.

The People in Other Towns and Cities

25 Many of the people lived in towns
near their farms. Those who were of the
tribe of Judah lived in Kiriath Arba, Dibon, and Jekabzeel, and in the villages
near these cities. 26 They also lived in the
cities of Jeshua, Moladah, Bethpelet,

[q] *One ancient translation* close relatives; *Hebrew* after him. [r] a member of a leading family; *or* son of Haggedolim.

27 and Hazarshual, and in Beersheba and
the villages around it. 28 They lived in the
city of Ziklag, in Meconah and its villages, 29 in Enrimmon, in Zorah, in Jarmuth, 30 in Zanoah, in Adullam, and in
the villages near these towns. They lived
in Lachish and on the farms nearby, and
in Azekah and its villages. That is to say,
the people of Judah lived in the territory
between Beersheba in the south and
Hinnom Valley in the north.
31 The people of the tribe of Benjamin
lived in Geba, Michmash, Ai, Bethel and
the nearby villages, 32 Anathoth, Nob,
Ananiah, 33 Hazor, Ramah, Gittaim,
34 Hadid, Zeboim, Neballat, 35 Lod, and
Ono, and in Craftsmen's Valley. 36 Some
groups of Levites that had lived in the
territory of Judah were assigned to live
with the people of Benjamin.

List of Priests and Levites

12 The following is a list of the
priests and Levites who returned
from exile with Zerubbabel son of Shealtiel and with the High Priest Joshua:

2-7 *Priests:*
Seraiah, Jeremiah, Ezra,
Amariah, Malluch, Hattush,
Shecaniah, Rehum, Meremoth,
Iddo, Ginnethoi, Abijah,
Mijamin, Maadiah, Bilgah,
Shemaiah, Joiarib, Jedaiah,
Sallu, Amok, Hilkiah, and Jedaiah.
These men were leaders among all
their fellow priests in the days of Joshua.

8 *Levites:*
The following were in charge of the
singing of hymns of thanksgiving:
Jeshua, Binnui, Kadmiel, Sherebiah, Judah, and Mattaniah.
9 The following formed the choir that
sang the responses: Bakbukiah, Unno,
and their fellow Levites.

Descendants of the High Priest Joshua

10 Joshua was the father of Joiakim;
Joiakim was the father of Eliashib; Eliashib was the father of Joiada; 11 Joiada
was the father of Jonathan; and Jonathan was the father of Jaddua.

Heads of the Priestly Clans

12-21 When Joiakim was High Priest,
the following priests were the heads of
the priestly clans:

Priest	*Clan*
Meraiah	Seraiah
Hananiah	Jeremiah
Meshullam	Ezra
Jehohanan	Amariah
Jonathan	Malluchi
Joseph	Shebaniah
Adna	Harim
Helkai	Meraioth
Zechariah	Iddo
Meshullam	Ginnethon
Zichri	Abijah
. . . [s]	Miniamin
Piltai	Moadiah
Shammua	Bilgah
Jehonathan	Shemaiah
Mattenai	Joiarib
Uzzi	Jedaiah
Kallai	Sallai
Eber	Amok
Hashabiah	Hilkiah
Nethanel	Jedaiah

Record of the Priestly and Levite Families

22 A record was kept of the heads of
the Levite families and of the priestly
families during the lifetimes of the following High Priests: Eliashib, Joiada,
Jonathan, and Jaddua. This record was
finished when Darius was emperor of
Persia.
23 The heads of the Levite families,
however, were recorded in the official
records only until the time of Jonathan,
the grandson of Eliashib.

Assignment of Duties in the Temple

24 Under the direction of Hashabiah,
Sherebiah, Jeshua, Binnui,[t] and Kadmiel, the Levites were organized into
groups. Two groups at a time praised
God responsively and gave thanks to
him, in accordance with the instructions
given by King David, the man of God.
25 The following Temple guards were
in charge of guarding the storerooms by
the gates to the Temple: Mattaniah, Bakbukiah, Obadiah, Meshullam, Talmon,
and Akkub.

[s] *In Hebrew a name is missing from the list.* [t] *Probable text (see 10.9 and 12.8)* Binnui; *Hebrew* son of.

26 These people lived during the time
of Joiakim, the son of Joshua and grandson of Jehozadak, and the time of Nehemiah the governor, and the time of Ezra,
the priest who was a scholar of the Law.

Nehemiah Dedicates the City Wall

27 When the city wall of Jerusalem was
dedicated, the Levites were brought in
from wherever they were living, so that
they could join in celebrating the dedication with songs of thanksgiving and with
the music of cymbals and harps. 28 The
Levite families of singers gathered from
the area where they had settled around
Jerusalem and from the towns around
Netophah, 29 and from Bethgilgal, Geba,
and Azmaveth. 30 The priests and the Levites performed ritual purification for
themselves, the people, the gates, and
the city wall.

31 I assembled the leaders of Judah on
top of the wall and put them in charge of
two large groups to march around the
city, giving thanks to God.

The first group went to the right on top
of the wall toward the Rubbish Gate.[u]
32 Hoshaiah marched behind the singers,
followed by half the leaders of Judah.
33-35 The following priests, blowing trumpets, marched next: Azariah, Ezra, Meshullam, Judah, Benjamin, Shemaiah,
and Jeremiah. Next came Zechariah, the
son of Jonathan and grandson of Shemaiah. (His ancestors also included Mattaniah, Micaiah, and Zaccur, of the clan
of Asaph.) 36 He was followed by other
members of his clan — Shemaiah, Azarel, Milalai, Gilalai, Maai, Nethanel, Judah, and Hanani — all of whom carried
musical instruments of the kind played
by King David, the man of God. Ezra the
scholar led this group in the procession.
37 At the Fountain Gate they went up the
steps that led to David's City, past David's palace, and back to the wall at the
Water Gate, on the east side of the city.

38 The other group of those who gave
thanks went to the left along the top of
the wall, and I followed with half of the
people. We marched past the Tower of
the Ovens to the Broad Wall, 39 and from
there we went past Ephraim Gate, Jeshanah Gate,[v] the Fish Gate, the Tower of
Hananel, and the Tower of the Hundred,
to the Sheep Gate. We ended our march
near the gate to the Temple.

40 So both the groups that were giving
thanks to God reached the Temple area.

In addition to the leaders who were
with me, 41 my group included the following priests, blowing trumpets: Eliakim, Maaseiah, Miniamin, Micaiah,
Elioenai, Zechariah, and Hananiah;
42 and they were followed by Maaseiah,
Shemaiah, Eleazar, Uzzi, Jehohanan,
Malchijah, Elam, and Ezer. The singers,
led by Jezrahiah, sang at the top of their
voices.

43 That day many sacrifices were offered, and the people were full of joy because God had made them very happy.
The women and the children joined in
the celebration, and the noise they all
made could be heard for miles.

Providing for Worship in the Temple

44 At that time men were put in charge
of the storerooms where contributions
for the Temple were kept, including the
tithes and the first grain and fruit that
ripened each year. These men were responsible for collecting from the farms
near the various cities the contributions
for the priests and the Levites which the
Law required. All the people of Judah
were pleased with the priests and the Levites, 45 because they performed the ceremonies of purification and the other
rituals that God had commanded. The
Temple musicians and the Temple
guards also performed their duties in accordance with the regulations made by
King David and his son Solomon.
46 From the time of King David and the
musician Asaph long ago, the musicians
have led songs of praise and thanksgiving to God. 47 In the time of Zerubbabel and also in the time of Nehemiah, all
the people of Israel gave daily gifts for
the support of the Temple musicians and
the Temple guards. The people gave a
sacred offering to the Levites, and the
Levites gave the required portion to the
priests.

Separation from Foreigners

13 When the Law of Moses was being read aloud to the people,
they came to the passage that said that

[u] RUBBISH GATE: *The two groups started somewhere on the southwestern part of the city wall and went in opposite directions until they met in front of the Temple in the northeastern part of the city.* [v] Ephraim Gate, Jeshanah Gate; *or* Ephraim Gate (also called the Old Gate).

no Ammonite or Moabite was ever to be
permitted to join God's people. 2 This
was because the people of Ammon and
Moab did not give food and water to the
Israelites on their way out of Egypt. Instead, they paid money to Balaam to
curse Israel, but our God turned the
curse into a blessing. 3 When the people
of Israel heard this law read, they excluded all foreigners from the
community.

Nehemiah's Reforms

4 The priest Eliashib, who was in
charge of the Temple storerooms, had
for a long time been on good terms with
Tobiah. 5 He allowed Tobiah to use a
large room that was intended only for
storing offerings of grain and incense,
the equipment used in the Temple, the
offerings for the priests, and the tithes of
grain, wine, and olive oil given to the
Levites, to the Temple musicians, and to
the Temple guards. 6 While this was going on, I was not in Jerusalem, because
in the thirty-second year that Artaxerxes[w] was king of Babylon I had gone
back to report to him. After some time I
received his permission 7 and returned to
Jerusalem. There I was shocked to find
that Eliashib had allowed Tobiah to use
a room in the Temple. 8 I was furious
and threw out all of Tobiah's belongings. 9 I gave orders for the rooms to be
ritually purified and for the Temple
equipment, grain offerings, and incense
to be put back.

10 I also learned that the Temple musicians and other Levites had left Jerusalem and gone back to their farms,
because the people had not been giving
them enough to live on. 11 I reprimanded
the officials for letting the Temple be neglected. And I brought the Levites and
musicians back to the Temple and put
them to work again. 12 Then all the people of Israel again started bringing to the
Temple storerooms their tithes of grain,
wine, and olive oil. 13 I put the following
men in charge of the storerooms: Shelemiah, a priest; Zadok, a scholar of the
Law; and Pedaiah, a Levite. Hanan, the
son of Zaccur and grandson of Mattaniah, was to be their assistant. I knew I
could trust these men to be honest in distributing the supplies to the other
workers.

14 Remember, my God, all these things
that I have done for your Temple and its
worship.

15 At that time I saw people in Judah
pressing juice from grapes on the Sabbath. Others were loading grain, wine,
grapes, figs, and other things on their
donkeys and taking them into Jerusalem; I warned them not to sell anything
on the Sabbath. 16 Some people from the
city of Tyre were living in Jerusalem,
and they brought fish and all kinds of
goods into the city to sell to our people
on the Sabbath. 17 I reprimanded the
Jewish leaders and told them, "Look at
the evil you're doing! You're making the
Sabbath unholy. 18 This is exactly why
God punished your ancestors when he
brought destruction on this city. And yet
you insist on bringing more of God's anger down on Israel by profaning the
Sabbath."

19 So I gave orders for the city gates to
be shut at the beginning of every Sabbath, as soon as evening[x] began to fall,
and not to be opened again until the Sabbath was over. I stationed some of my
men at the gates to make sure that nothing was brought into the city on the Sabbath. 20 Once or twice merchants who
sold all kinds of goods spent Friday
night outside the city walls. 21 I warned
them, "It's no use waiting out there for
morning to come. If you try this again,
I'll use force on you." From then on they
did not come back on the Sabbath.
22 I ordered the Levites to purify themselves and to go and guard the gates to
make sure that the Sabbath was kept
holy.

Remember me, O God, for this also,
and spare me because of your great love.

23 At that time I also discovered that
many of the Jewish men had married
women from Ashdod, Ammon, and
Moab. 24 Half of their children spoke the
language of Ashdod or some other language and didn't know how to speak our
language. 25 I reprimanded the men,
called down curses on them, beat them,
and pulled out their hair. Then I made
them take an oath in God's name that

[w] ARTAXERXES: *As emperor of Persia, Artaxerxes also had the title "King of Babylon."*
[x] EVENING: *The Jewish day begins at sunset.*

never again would they or their children
intermarry with foreigners. [26]I told
them, "It was foreign women that made
King Solomon sin. Here was a man who
was greater than any of the kings of
other nations. God loved him and made
him king over all of Israel, and yet he fell
into this sin. [27]Are we then to follow
your example and disobey our God by
marrying foreign women?"
[28]Joiada was the son of Eliashib the
High Priest, but one of Joiada's sons
married the daughter of Sanballat, from
the town of Beth Horon, so I made Joiada leave Jerusalem.

[29]Remember, God, how those people
defiled both the office of priest and the
covenant you made with the priests and
the Levites.
[30]I purified the people from everything foreign; I prepared regulations for
the priests and the Levites so that all
of them would know their duties;
[31]I arranged for the wood used for burning the offerings to be brought at the
proper times, and for the people to bring
their offerings of the first grain and the
first fruits that ripened.
Remember all this, O God, and give
me credit for it.

The Book of ESTHER

Introduction

The events of The Book of Esther, *which take place at the winter residence of the Persian emperor, center around a Jewish heroine named Esther, who by her great courage and devotion to her people saved them from being exterminated by their enemies. The book explains the background and meaning of the Jewish festival of Purim.*

Outline of Contents

Queen Vashti Defies King Xerxes

1 [1-2]From his royal throne in Persia's
capital city of Susa, King Xerxes
ruled 127 provinces, all the way from India to Ethiopia.[a]
[3]In the third year of his reign he gave
a banquet for all his officials and administrators. The armies of Persia and
Media were present, as well as the
governors and noblemen of the provinces. [4]For six whole months he made a
show of the riches of the imperial court
with all its splendor and majesty.
[5]After that, the king gave a banquet
for all the people in the capital city of
Susa, rich and poor alike. It lasted a
whole week and was held in the gardens
of the royal palace. [6]The courtyard there
was decorated with blue and white cotton curtains, tied by cords of fine purple
linen to silver rings on marble columns.
Couches made of gold and silver had
been placed in the courtyard, which was
paved with white marble, red feldspar,
shining mother-of-pearl, and blue turquoise. [7]Drinks were served in gold
cups, no two of them alike, and the king
was generous with the royal wine.
[8]There were no limits on the drinks;
the king had given orders to the palace

[a] *Hebrew* Cush: *Cush is the ancient name of the extensive territory south of the First Cataract of the Nile River. This region was called Ethiopia in Graeco-Roman times, and included within its borders most of modern Sudan and some of present-day Ethiopia (Abyssinia).*

servants that everyone could have as
much as they wanted.[b]
9 Meanwhile, inside the royal palace
Queen Vashti was giving a banquet for
the women.
10 On the seventh day of his banquet
the king was drinking and feeling
happy, so he called in the seven eunuchs
who were his personal servants, Mehu-
man, Biztha, Harbona, Bigtha, Abagtha,
Zethar, and Carkas. 11 He ordered them
to bring in Queen Vashti, wearing her
royal crown. The queen was a beautiful
woman, and the king wanted to show off
her beauty to the officials and all his
guests. 12 But when the servants told
Queen Vashti of the king's command,
she refused to come. This made the king
furious.
13 Now it was the king's custom to ask
for expert opinion on questions of law
and order, so he called for his advisers,
who would know what should be done.
14 Those he most often turned to for advice were Carshena, Shethar, Admatha,
Tarshish, Meres, Marsena, and
Memucan – seven officials of Persia and
Media who held the highest offices in
the kingdom. 15 He said to these men, "I,
King Xerxes, sent my servants to Queen
Vashti with a command, and she refused
to obey it! What does the law say that we
should do with her?"
16 Then Memucan declared to the king
and his officials: "Queen Vashti has insulted not only the king but also his
officials – in fact, every man in the empire! 17 Every woman in the empire will
start looking down on her husband as
soon as she hears what the queen has
done. They'll say, 'King Xerxes commanded Queen Vashti to come to him,
and she refused.' 18 When the wives of
the royal officials of Persia and Media
hear about the queen's behavior, they
will be telling their husbands about it before the day is out. Wives everywhere
will have no respect for their husbands,
and husbands will be angry with their
wives. 19 If it please Your Majesty, issue
a royal proclamation that Vashti may
never again appear before the king.
Have it written into the laws of Persia
and Media, so that it can never be
changed. Then give her place as queen
to some better woman. 20 When your
proclamation is made known all over
this huge empire, every woman will
treat her husband with proper respect,
whether he's rich or poor."
21 The king and his officials liked this
idea, and the king did what Memucan
suggested. 22 To each of the royal provinces he sent a message in the language
and the system of writing of that province, saying[c] that every husband should
be the master of his home and speak
with final authority.

Esther Becomes Queen

2 Later, even after the king's anger
had cooled down, he kept thinking
about what Vashti had done and about
his proclamation against her. 2 So some
of the king's advisers who were close to
him suggested, "Why don't you make a
search to find some beautiful young virgins? 3 You can appoint officials in every
province of the empire and have them
bring all these beautiful young women
to your harem here in Susa, the capital
city. Put them in the care of Hegai, the
eunuch who is in charge of your women,
and let them be given a beauty treatment. 4 Then take the young woman you
like best and make her queen in Vashti's
place."
The king thought this was good advice, so he followed it.
5 There in Susa lived a Jew named
Mordecai son of Jair; he was from the
tribe of Benjamin and was a descendant
of Kish and Shimei. 6 When King Nebuchadnezzar of Babylon took King Jehoiachin of Judah into exile from
Jerusalem, along with a group of captives, Mordecai was among them. 7 He
had a cousin, Esther, whose Hebrew
name was Hadassah; she was a beautiful
young woman, and had a good figure. At
the death of her parents, Mordecai had
adopted her and brought her up as his
own daughter.
8 When the king had issued his new
proclamation and many young women
were being brought to Susa, Esther was
among them. She too was put in the
royal palace in the care of Hegai, who
had charge of the harem. 9 Hegai liked
Esther, and she won his favor. He lost no

[b] There were no limits . . . wanted; *or* But no one was forced to drink; the king had given orders to the palace servants that everyone could have as much or as little as they wanted.
[c] saying; *or* in order.

time in beginning her beauty treatment
of massage and special diet. He gave her
the best place in the harem and assigned
seven young women specially chosen
from the royal palace to serve her.
10 Now, on the advice of Mordecai, Esther had kept it secret that she was Jewish. 11 Every day Mordecai would walk
back and forth in front of the courtyard
of the harem, in order to find out how
she was getting along and what was going to happen to her.
12 The regular beauty treatment for the
women lasted a year — massages with oil
of myrrh for six months and with oil of
balsam for six more. After that, each
woman would be taken in turn to King
Xerxes. 13 When she went from the
harem to the palace, she could wear
whatever she wanted. 14 She would go
there in the evening, and the next morning she would be taken to another harem
and put in the care of Shaashgaz, the
eunuch in charge of the king's concubines. She would not go to the king
again unless he liked her enough to ask
for her by name.
15 The time came for Esther to go to the
king. Esther — the daughter of Abihail
and the cousin of Mordecai, who had
adopted her as his daughter; Esther —
admired by everyone who saw her.
When her turn came, she wore just what
Hegai, the eunuch in charge of the
harem, advised her to wear. 16 So in Xerxes' seventh year as king, in the tenth
month, the month of Tebeth, Esther was
brought to King Xerxes in the royal palace. 17 The king liked her more than any
of the other women, and more than any
of the others she won his favor and affection. He placed the royal crown on
her head and made her queen in place of
Vashti. 18 Then the king gave a great
banquet in Esther's honor and invited all
his officials and administrators. He proclaimed a holiday[d] for the whole empire
and distributed gifts worthy of a king.

Mordecai Saves the King's Life

19 Meanwhile Mordecai had been appointed by the king to an administrative
position. 20 As for Esther, she had still
not let it be known that she was Jewish.
Mordecai had told her not to tell anyone,
and she obeyed him in this, just as she
had obeyed him when she was a little
girl under his care.
21 During the time that Mordecai held
office in the palace, Bigthana and Teresh, two of the palace eunuchs who
guarded the entrance to the king's
rooms, became hostile to King Xerxes
and plotted to assassinate him. 22 Mordecai learned about it and told Queen Esther, who then told the king what
Mordecai had found out. 23 There was an
investigation, and it was discovered that
the report was true, so both men were
hanged on the gallows. The king ordered an account of this to be written
down in the official records of the
empire.

Haman Plots to Destroy the Jews

3 Some time later King Xerxes promoted a man named Haman to the
position of prime minister. Haman was
the son of Hammedatha, a descendant of
Agag.[e] 2 The king ordered all the officials in his service to show their respect
for Haman by kneeling and bowing to
him. They all did so, except for Mordecai, who refused to do it. 3 The other officials in the royal service asked him why
he was disobeying the king's command;
4 day after day they urged him to give in,
but he would not listen to them. "I am a
Jew," he explained, "and I cannot bow to
Haman." So they told Haman about this,
wondering if he would tolerate Mordecai's conduct. 5 Haman was furious
when he realized that Mordecai was not
going to kneel and bow to him, 6 and
when he learned that Mordecai was a
Jew, he decided to do more than punish
Mordecai alone. He made plans to kill
every Jew in the whole Persian Empire.
7 In the twelfth year of King Xerxes'
rule, in the first month, the month of Nisan, Haman ordered the lots to be cast
("purim," they were called) to find out
the right day and month to carry out his
plot. The thirteenth day of the twelfth
month, the month of Adar, was decided on.
8 So Haman told the king, "There is a
certain race of people scattered all over
your empire and found in every province. They observe customs that are not

[d] holiday; *or* remission of taxes. [e] AGAG: *An Amalekite king; his people were traditional enemies of the people of Israel.*

like those of any other people. Moreover, they do not obey the laws of the
empire, so it is not in your best interests
to tolerate them. 9 If it please Your Majesty, issue a decree that they are to be
put to death. If you do, I guarantee that
I will be able to put 375 tons of silver into
the royal treasury for the administration
of the empire."

10 The king took off his ring, which
was used to stamp proclamations and
make them official, and gave it to the
enemy of the Jewish people, Haman son
of Hammedatha, the descendant of
Agag. 11 The king told him, "The people
and their money are yours; do as you
like with them."

12 So on the thirteenth day of the first
month Haman called the king's secretaries and dictated a proclamation to be
translated into every language and system of writing used in the empire and to
be sent to all the rulers, governors, and
officials. It was issued in the name of
King Xerxes and stamped with his ring.
13 Runners took this proclamation to
every province of the empire. It contained the instructions that on a single
day, the thirteenth day of Adar, all
Jews — young and old, women and
children — were to be killed. They were
to be slaughtered without mercy and
their belongings were to be taken. 14 The
contents of the proclamation were to be
made public in every province, so that
everyone would be prepared when that
day came.

15 At the king's command the decree
was made public in the capital city of
Susa, and runners carried the news to
the provinces. The king and Haman sat
down and had a drink while the city of
Susa was being thrown into confusion.

Mordecai Asks for Esther's Help

4 When Mordecai learned of all that
had been done, he tore his clothes
in anguish. Then he dressed in sackcloth, covered his head with ashes, and
walked through the city, wailing loudly
and bitterly, 2 until he came to the entrance of the palace. He did not go in
because no one wearing sackcloth was
allowed inside. 3 Throughout all the
provinces, wherever the king's proclamation was made known, there was
loud mourning among the Jews. They
fasted, wept, wailed, and most of them
put on sackcloth and lay in ashes.

4 When Esther's servant women and
eunuchs told her what Mordecai was doing, she was deeply disturbed. She sent
Mordecai some clothes to put on instead
of the sackcloth, but he would not accept
them. 5 Then she called Hathach, one of
the palace eunuchs appointed as her
servant by the king, and told him to go to
Mordecai and find out what was happening and why. 6 Hathach went to Mordecai in the city square at the entrance
of the palace. 7 Mordecai told him everything that had happened to him and just
how much money Haman had promised
to put into the royal treasury if all the
Jews were killed. 8 He gave Hathach a
copy of the proclamation that had been
issued in Susa, ordering the destruction
of the Jews. Mordecai asked him to take
it to Esther, explain the situation to her,
and have her go and plead with the king
and beg him to have mercy on her people. 9 Hathach did this, 10 and Esther
gave him this message to take back to
Mordecai: 11 "If anyone, man or woman,
goes to the inner courtyard and sees the
king without being summoned, that person must die. That is the law; everyone,
from the king's advisers to the people in
the provinces, knows that. There is only
one way to get around this law: if the
king holds out his gold scepter to someone, then that person's life is spared. But
it has been a month since the king sent
for me."

12 When Mordecai received Esther's
message, 13 he sent her this warning:
"Don't imagine that you are safer than
any other Jew just because you are in
the royal palace. 14 If you keep quiet at a
time like this, help will come from
heaven to the Jews, and they will be
saved, but you will die and your father's
family will come to an end. Yet who
knows — maybe it was for a time like this
that you were made queen!"

15 Esther sent Mordecai this reply:
16 "Go and get all the Jews in Susa together; hold a fast and pray for me.
Don't eat or drink anything for three
days and nights. My servant women and
I will be doing the same. After that, I will
go to the king, even though it is against
the law. If I must die for doing it, I
will die."

17 Mordecai then left and did everything that Esther had told him to do.

Esther Invites the King and Haman to a Banquet

5 On the third day of her fast Esther
put on her royal robes and went and
stood in the inner courtyard of the palace, facing the throne room. The king
was inside, seated on the royal throne,
facing the entrance. 2 When the king saw
Queen Esther standing outside, she won
his favor, and he held out to her the gold
scepter. She then came up and touched
the tip of it. 3 "What is it, Queen Esther?"
the king asked. "Tell me what you want,
and you shall have it—even if it is half
my empire."
4 Esther replied, "If it please Your Majesty, I would like you and Haman to be
my guests tonight at a banquet I am preparing for you."
5 The king then ordered Haman to
come quickly, so that they could be Esther's guests. So the king and Haman
went to Esther's banquet. 6 Over the
wine the king asked her, "Tell me what
you want, and you shall have it. I will
grant your request, even if you ask for
half my empire."
7 Esther replied, 8 "If Your Majesty is
kind enough to grant my request, I
would like you and Haman to be my
guests tomorrow at another banquet
that I will prepare for you. At that time I
will tell you what I want."

Haman Plots to Kill Mordecai

9 When Haman left the banquet he was
happy and in a good mood. But then he
saw Mordecai at the entrance of the palace, and when Mordecai did not rise or
show any sign of respect as he passed,
Haman was furious with him. 10 But he
controlled himself and went on home.
Then he invited his friends to his house
and asked his wife Zeresh to join them.
11 He boasted to them about how rich he
was, how many sons he had, how the
king had promoted him to high office,
and how much more important he was
than any of the king's other officials.
12 "What is more," Haman went on,
"Queen Esther gave a banquet for no
one but the king and me, and we are invited back tomorrow. 13 But none of this
means a thing to me as long as I see that
Jew Mordecai sitting at the entrance of
the palace."
14 So his wife and all his friends suggested, "Why don't you have a gallows
built, seventy-five feet tall? Tomorrow
morning you can ask the king to have
Mordecai hanged on it, and then you can
go to the banquet happy."
Haman thought this was a good idea,
so he had the gallows built.

The King Honors Mordecai

6 That same night the king could not
get to sleep, so he had the official
records of the empire brought and read
to him. 2 The part they read included the
account of how Mordecai had uncovered
a plot to assassinate the king—the plot
made by Bigthana and Teresh, the two
palace eunuchs who had guarded the
king's rooms. 3 The king asked, "How
have we honored and rewarded Mordecai for this?"
His servants answered, "Nothing has
been done for him."
4 "Are any of my officials in the palace?" the king asked.
Now Haman had just entered the
courtyard; he had come to ask the king
to have Mordecai hanged on the gallows
that was now ready. 5 So the servants answered, "Haman is here, waiting to
see you."
"Show him in," said the king.
6 So Haman came in, and the king said
to him, "There is someone I wish very
much to honor. What should I do for
this man?"
Haman thought to himself, "Now who
could the king want to honor so much?
Me, of course."
7-8 So he answered the king, "Have
royal robes brought for this man—robes
that you yourself wear. Have a royal ornament[f] put on your own horse. 9 Then
have one of your highest noblemen
dress the man in these robes and lead
him, mounted on the horse, through the
city square. Have the nobleman announce as they go: 'See how the king
rewards someone he wishes to honor!' "
10 Then the king said to Haman,
"Hurry and get the robes and the horse,
and provide these honors for Mordecai
the Jew. Do everything for him that you

[f] ORNAMENT: *Probably a type of crown.*

have suggested. You will find him sitting
at the entrance of the palace."
11 So Haman got the robes and the
horse, and he put the robes on Mordecai.
Mordecai got on the horse, and Haman
led him through the city square, announcing to the people as they went:
"See how the king rewards a man he
wishes to honor!"
12 Mordecai then went back to the palace entrance while Haman hurried
home, covering his face in embarrassment. 13 He told his wife and all his
friends everything that had happened to
him. Then she and those wise friends of
his told him, "You are beginning to lose
power to Mordecai. He is a Jew, and you
cannot overcome him. He will certainly
defeat you."

Haman Is Put to Death

14 While they were still talking, the
palace eunuchs arrived in a hurry to
7 take Haman to Esther's banquet.
1 And so the king and Haman went
to eat with Esther 2 for a second time.
Over the wine the king asked her again,
"Now, Queen Esther, what do you want?
Tell me and you shall have it. I'll even
give you half the empire."
3 Queen Esther answered, "If it please
Your Majesty to grant my humble request, my wish is that I may live and that
my people may live. 4 My people and I
have been sold for slaughter. If it were
nothing more serious than being sold
into slavery, I would have kept quiet and
not bothered you about it;[g] but we are
about to be destroyed—exterminated!"
5 Then King Xerxes asked Queen Esther, "Who dares to do such a thing?
Where is this man?"
6 Esther answered, "Our enemy, our
persecutor, is this evil man Haman!"
Haman faced the king and queen with
terror. 7 The king got up in a fury, left the
room, and went outside to the palace
gardens. Haman could see that the king
was determined to punish him for this,
so he stayed behind to beg Queen Esther
for his life. 8 He had just thrown himself
down on Esther's couch to beg for
mercy, when the king came back into
the room from the gardens. Seeing this,
the king cried out, "Is this man going to
rape the queen right here in front of me,
in my own palace?"
The king had no sooner said this than
the eunuchs covered Haman's head.
9 Then one of them, who was named
Harbonah, said, "Haman even went so
far as to build a gallows at his house so
that he could hang Mordecai, who saved
Your Majesty's life. And it's seventy-five
feet tall!"
"Hang Haman on it!" the king
commanded.
10 So Haman was hanged on the gallows that he had built for Mordecai.
Then the king's anger cooled down.

The Jews Are Told to Fight Back

8 That same day King Xerxes gave
Queen Esther all the property of
Haman, the enemy of the Jews. Esther
told the king that Mordecai was related
to her, and from then on Mordecai was
allowed to enter the king's presence.
2 The king took off his ring with his seal
on it (which he had taken back from Haman) and gave it to Mordecai. Esther
put Mordecai in charge of Haman's
property.
3 Then Esther spoke to the king again,
throwing herself at his feet and crying.
She begged him to do something to stop
the evil plot that Haman, the descendant
of Agag,[h] had made against the Jews.
4 The king held out the gold scepter to
her, so she stood up and said, 5 "If it
please Your Majesty, and if you care
about me and if it seems right to you,
please issue a proclamation to keep
Haman's orders from being carried
out—those orders that the son of
Hammedatha the descendant of Agag
gave for the destruction of all the Jews
in the empire. 6 How can I endure it if
this disaster comes on my people, and
my own relatives are killed?"
7 King Xerxes then said to Queen Esther and Mordecai, the Jew, "Look, I
have hanged Haman for his plot against
the Jews, and I have given Esther his
property. 8 But a proclamation issued in
the king's name and stamped with the
royal seal cannot be revoked. You may,
however, write to the Jews whatever
you like; and you may write it in my
name and stamp it with the royal seal."
9 This happened on the twenty-third

[g] *Probable text* and not . . . it; *Hebrew unclear.*

[h] AGAG: *See 3.1.*

day of the third month, the month of Sivan. Mordecai called the king's secretaries and dictated letters to the Jews and
to the governors, administrators, and officials of all the 127 provinces from India
to Ethiopia.[i] The letters were written to
each province in its own language and
system of writing and to the Jews in
their language and system of writing.
10 Mordecai had the letters written in the
name of King Xerxes, and he stamped
them with the royal seal. They were delivered by riders mounted on fast horses
from the royal stables.

11 These letters explained that the king
would allow the Jews in every city to organize for self-defense. If armed men of
any nationality in any province attacked
the Jewish men, their children, or their
women, the Jews could fight back and
destroy the attackers; they could slaughter them to the last man and take their
possessions. 12 This decree was to take
effect throughout the Persian Empire on
the day set for the slaughter of the Jews,
the thirteenth of Adar, the twelfth
month. 13 It was to be proclaimed as law
and made known to everyone in every
province, so that the Jews would be
ready to take revenge on their enemies
when that day came. 14 At the king's
command the riders mounted royal
horses and rode off at top speed. The decree was also made public in Susa, the
capital city.

15 Mordecai left the palace, wearing
royal robes of blue and white, a cloak of
fine purple linen, and a magnificent gold
crown. Then the streets of Susa rang
with cheers and joyful shouts. 16 For the
Jews there was joy and relief, happiness
and a sense of victory. 17 In every city
and province, wherever the king's proclamation was read, the Jews held a joyful holiday with feasting and happiness.
In fact, many other people became Jews,
because they were afraid of them now.

The Jews Destroy Their Enemies

9 The thirteenth day of Adar came,
the day on which the royal proclamation was to take effect, the day when
the enemies of the Jews were hoping to
get them in their power. But instead, the
Jews triumphed over them. 2 In the
Jewish quarter of every city[j] in the empire the Jews organized to attack anyone who tried to harm them. People
everywhere were afraid of them, and
no one could stand against them. 3 In
fact, all the provincial officials—governors, administrators, and royal
representatives—helped the Jews because they were all afraid of Mordecai.
4 It was well-known throughout the empire that Mordecai was now a powerful
man in the palace and was growing
more powerful. 5 So the Jews could do
what they wanted with their enemies.
They attacked them with swords and
slaughtered them.

6 In Susa, the capital city itself, the
Jews killed five hundred people.
7-10 Among them were the ten sons of
Haman son of Hammedatha, the enemy
of the Jews: Parshandatha, Dalphon,
Aspatha, Poratha, Adalia, Aridatha,
Parmashta, Arisai, Aridai, and Vaizatha.
However, there was no looting.

11 That same day the number of people
killed in Susa was reported to the king.
12 He then said to Queen Esther, "In Susa
alone the Jews have killed five hundred
people, including Haman's ten sons.
What must they have done out in the
provinces! What do you want now? You
shall have it. Tell me what else you
want, and you shall have it."

13 Esther answered, "If it please Your
Majesty, let the Jews in Susa do again
tomorrow what they were allowed to do
today. And have the bodies of Haman's
ten sons hung from the gallows." 14 The
king ordered this to be done, and the
proclamation was issued in Susa. The
bodies of Haman's ten sons were publicly displayed. 15 On the fourteenth day
of Adar the Jews of Susa got together
again and killed three hundred more
people in the city. But again, they did no
looting.

16 The Jews in the provinces also organized and defended themselves. They
rid themselves of their enemies by killing seventy-five thousand people who
hated them. But they did no looting.
17 This was on the thirteenth day of
Adar. On the next day, the fourteenth,

[i] *Hebrew* Cush: *Cush is the ancient name of the extensive territory south of the First Cataract of the Nile River. This region was called Ethiopia in Graeco-Roman times, and included within its borders most of modern Sudan and some of present-day Ethiopia (Abyssinia).*

[j] In the Jewish quarter of every city; *or* In every Jewish city.

there was no more killing, and they
made it a joyful day of feasting. 18 The
Jews of Susa, however, made the fifteenth a holiday, since they had slaughtered their enemies on the thirteenth and
fourteenth and then stopped on the fifteenth. 19 This is why Jews who live in
small towns observe the fourteenth day
of the month of Adar as a joyous holiday, a time for feasting and giving gifts
of food to one another.

The Festival of Purim

20 Mordecai had these events written
down and sent letters to all the Jews,
near and far, throughout the Persian
Empire, 21 telling them to observe the
fourteenth and fifteenth days of Adar as
holidays every year. 22 These were the
days on which the Jews had rid themselves of their enemies; this was a month
that had been turned from a time of grief
and despair into a time of joy and happiness. They were told to observe these
days with feasts and parties, giving gifts
of food to one another and to the poor.
23 So the Jews followed Mordecai's instructions, and the celebration became
an annual custom.
24 Haman son of Hammedatha—the
descendant of Agag and the enemy of
the Jewish people—had cast lots ("purim," they were called) to determine the
day for destroying the Jews; he had
planned to wipe them out. 25 But Esther
went to the king, and the king issued
written orders with the result that Haman suffered the fate he had planned for
the Jews—he and his sons were hanged
from the gallows. 26 That is why the holidays are called Purim. Because of Mordecai's letter and because of all that had
happened to them, 27 the Jews made it a
rule for themselves, their descendants,
and anyone who might become a Jew,
that at the proper time each year these
two days would be regularly observed
according to Mordecai's instructions.
28 It was resolved that every Jewish family of every future generation in every
province and every city should remember and observe the days of Purim for all
time to come.
29 Then Queen Esther, the daughter of
Abihail, along with Mordecai, also wrote
a letter, putting her full authority behind
the letter about Purim, which Mordecai
had written earlier. 30 The letter was addressed to all the Jews, and copies were
sent to all the 127 provinces of the Persian Empire. It wished the Jews peace
and security 31 and directed them and
their descendants to observe the days of
Purim at the proper time, just as they
had adopted rules for the observance of
fasts and times of mourning. This was
commanded by both Mordecai and
Queen Esther. 32 Esther's command, confirming the rules for Purim, was written
down on a scroll.

The Greatness of Xerxes and Mordecai

10 King Xerxes imposed forced labor on the people of the coastal
regions of his empire as well as on those
of the interior. 2 All the great and wonderful things he did, as well as the whole
story of how he promoted Mordecai to
high office, are recorded in the official
records of the kings of Persia and Media.
3 Mordecai the Jew was second in rank
only to King Xerxes himself. He was
honored and well-liked by his fellow
Jews. He worked for the good of his people and for the security of all their
descendants.

The Book of
JOB

Introduction

The Book of Job *is the story of a good man who suffers total disaster—he loses all his children and property and is afflicted with a repulsive disease. Then in three series of poetic dialogues the author shows how Job's friends and Job himself react to these calamities. In the end, God himself, whose dealings with the human race have been a prominent part of the discussion, appears to Job.*

The friends of Job explain his suffering in traditional religious terms. Since God, so they assume, always rewards good and punishes evil, the sufferings of Job can only mean that he has sinned. But for Job this is too simple; he does not deserve such cruel punishment, because he has been an unusually good and righteous man. He cannot understand how God can let so much evil happen to one like himself, and he boldly challenges God. Job does not lose his faith, but he does long to be justified before God and to regain his honor as a good man.

God does not give an answer to Job's questions, but he does respond to Job's faith by overwhelming him with a poetic picture of his divine power and wisdom. Job then humbly acknowledges God as wise and great, and repents of the wild and angry words he had used.

The prose conclusion records how Job is restored to his former condition, with even greater prosperity than before. God reprimands Job's friends for failing to understand the meaning of Job's suffering. Only Job had really sensed that God is greater than traditional religion had depicted him.

Outline of Contents

Satan Tests Job

1 There was a man named Job, living
in the land of Uz,[a] who worshiped
God and was faithful to him. He was a
good man, careful not to do anything
evil. 2 He had seven sons and three
daughters, 3 and owned seven thousand
sheep, three thousand camels, one thousand head of cattle, and five hundred
donkeys. He also had a large number of
servants and was the richest man in the
East.
4 Job's sons used to take turns giving a
feast, to which all the others would
come, and they always invited their
three sisters to join them. 5 The morning
after each feast, Job would get up early
and offer sacrifices for each of his children in order to purify them. He always
did this because he thought that one of
them might have sinned by insulting
God unintentionally.
6 When the day came for the heavenly
beings[b] to appear before the LORD, Satan[c] was there among them. 7 The LORD
asked him, "What have you been
doing?"
Satan answered, "I have been walking
here and there, roaming around the
earth."
8 "Did you notice my servant Job?" the

---

[a] UZ: *An area whose exact location is unknown.* [b] HEAVENLY BEINGS: *Supernatural beings who serve God in heaven.* [c] SATAN: *A supernatural being whose name indicates he was regarded as the opponent of human beings.*

LORD asked. "There is no one on earth as
faithful and good as he is. He worships
me and is careful not to do anything
evil."
9 Satan replied, "Would Job worship
you if he got nothing out of it? 10 You
have always protected him and his family and everything he owns. You bless
everything he does, and you have given
him enough cattle to fill the whole country. 11 But now suppose you take away
everything he has—he will curse you to
your face!"
12 "All right," the LORD said to Satan,
"everything he has is in your power, but
you must not hurt Job himself." So Satan
left.

Job's Children and Wealth Are Destroyed

13 One day when Job's children were
having a feast at the home of their oldest
brother, 14 a messenger came running to
Job. "We were plowing the fields with
the oxen," he said, "and the donkeys
were in a nearby pasture. 15 Suddenly
the Sabeans[d] attacked and stole them
all. They killed every one of your servants except me. I am the only one who
escaped to tell you."
16 Before he had finished speaking, another servant came and said, "Lightning
struck the sheep and the shepherds and
killed them all. I am the only one who
escaped to tell you."
17 Before he had finished speaking, another servant came and said, "Three
bands of Chaldean[e] raiders attacked us,
took away the camels, and killed all
your servants except me. I am the only
one who escaped to tell you."
18 Before he had finished speaking, another servant came and said, "Your children were having a feast at the home of
your oldest son, 19 when a storm swept in
from the desert. It blew the house down
and killed them all. I am the only one
who escaped to tell you."
20 Then Job got up and tore his clothes
in grief. He shaved his head and threw
himself face downward on the ground.
21 He said, "I was born with nothing, and
I will die with nothing. The LORD gave,
and now he has taken away. May his
name be praised!"
22 In spite of everything that had happened, Job did not sin by blaming God.

Satan Tests Job Again

2 When the day came for the heavenly beings to appear before the
LORD again, Satan was there among
them. 2 The LORD asked him, "Where
have you been?"
Satan answered, "I have been walking
here and there, roaming around the
earth."
3 "Did you notice my servant Job?" the
LORD asked. "There is no one on earth as
faithful and good as he is. He worships
me and is careful not to do anything evil.
You persuaded me to let you attack him
for no reason at all, but Job is still as
faithful as ever."
4 Satan replied, "A person will give up
everything in order to stay alive. 5 But
now suppose you hurt his body—he will
curse you to your face!"
6 So the LORD said to Satan, "All right,
he is in your power, but you are not to
kill him."
7 Then Satan left the LORD's presence
and made sores break out all over Job's
body. 8 Job went and sat by the garbage
dump and took a piece of broken pottery
to scrape his sores. 9 His wife said to
him, "You are still as faithful as ever,
aren't you? Why don't you curse God
and die?"
10 Job answered, "You are talking nonsense! When God sends us something
good, we welcome it. How can we complain when he sends us trouble?" Even
in all this suffering Job said nothing
against God.

Job's Friends Come

11 Three of Job's friends were Eliphaz,
from the city of Teman, Bildad, from the
land of Shuah, and Zophar, from the
land of Naamah. When they heard how
much Job had been suffering, they decided to go and comfort him. 12 While
they were still a long way off they saw
Job, but did not recognize him. When
they did, they began to weep and wail,
tearing their clothes in grief and throwing dust into the air and on their heads.
13 Then they sat there on the ground with
him for seven days and nights without

[d] SABEANS: *A tribe of wandering raiders from the south.* [e] CHALDEANS: *A tribe of wandering raiders from the north.*

saying a word, because they saw how much he was suffering.

Job's Complaint to God

3 Finally Job broke the silence and cursed the day on which he had been born.

Job

2-3 O God, put a curse on the day I was born;
put a curse on the night when I was conceived!
4 Turn that day into darkness, God.
Never again remember that day;
never again let light shine on it.
5 Make it a day of gloom and thick darkness;
cover it with clouds, and blot out the sun.
6 Blot that night out of the year,
and never let it be counted again;
7 make it a barren, joyless night.
8 Tell the sorcerers to curse that day,
those who know how to control Leviathan.[f]
9 Keep the morning star from shining;
give that night no hope of dawn.
10 Curse that night for letting me be born,
for exposing me to trouble and grief.

11 I wish I had died in my mother's womb
or died the moment I was born.
12 Why did my mother hold me on her knees?
Why did she feed me at her breast?
13 If I had died then, I would be at rest now,
14 sleeping like the kings and rulers
who rebuilt ancient palaces.
15 Then I would be sleeping like princes
who filled their houses with gold and silver,
16 or sleeping like a stillborn child.
17 In the grave wicked people stop their evil,
and tired workers find rest at last.
18 Even prisoners enjoy peace,
free from shouts and harsh commands.
19 Everyone is there, the famous and the unknown,
and slaves at last are free.

20 Why let people go on living in misery?
Why give light to those in grief?
21 They wait for death, but it never comes;
they prefer a grave to any treasure.
22 They are not happy till they are dead and buried;
23 God keeps their future hidden
and hems them in on every side.
24 Instead of eating, I mourn,
and I can never stop groaning.
25 Everything I fear and dread comes true.
26 I have no peace, no rest,
and my troubles never end.

The First Dialogue

(4.1–14.22)

4

Eliphaz

1-2 Job, will you be annoyed if I speak?
I can't keep quiet any longer.
3 You have taught many people
and given strength to feeble hands.
4 When someone stumbled, weak and tired,
your words encouraged him to stand.
5 Now it's your turn to be in trouble,
and you are too stunned to face it.
6 You worshiped God, and your life was blameless;
and so you should have confidence and hope.
7 Think back now. Name a single case
where someone righteous met with disaster.
8 I have seen people plow fields of evil

[f] LEVIATHAN: *Some take this to be the crocodile, others a legendary monster. Magicians were thought to be able to make him cause eclipses of the sun.*

and plant wickedness like seed;
now they harvest wickedness
and evil.
9 Like a storm, God destroys them
in his anger.
10 The wicked roar and growl like
lions,
but God silences them and
breaks their teeth.
11 Like lions with nothing to kill
and eat,
they die, and all their children
are scattered.

12 Once a message came quietly,
so quietly I could hardly hear it.
13 Like a nightmare it disturbed my
sleep.
14 I trembled and shuddered;
my whole body shook with fear.
15 A light breeze touched my face,
and my skin crawled with fright.
16 I could see something standing
there;
I stared, but couldn't tell what
it was.
Then I heard a voice out of the
silence:
17 "Can anyone be righteous in the
sight of[g] God
or be pure before[h] his Creator?
18 God does not trust his heavenly
servants;
he finds fault even with his
angels.
19 Do you think he will trust a
creature of clay,
a thing of dust that can be
crushed like a moth?
20 We may be alive in the morning,
but die unnoticed before evening
comes.
21 All that we have is taken away;
we die, still lacking wisdom."

5 Call out, Job. See if anyone
answers.
Is there any angel to whom you
can turn?
2 To worry yourself to death with
resentment
would be a foolish, senseless
thing to do.
3 I have seen fools who looked
secure,
but I called down a sudden curse
on their homes.
4 Their children can never find
safety;
no one stands up to defend them
in court.
5 Hungry people will eat the fool's
crops—
even the grain growing among
thorns[i]—
and thirsty people will envy his
wealth.
6 Evil does not grow in the soil,
nor does trouble grow out of the
ground.
7 No indeed! We bring trouble on
ourselves,
as surely as sparks fly up from
a fire.[j]

8 If I were you, I would turn to God
and present my case to him.
9 We cannot understand the great
things he does,
and to his miracles there is
no end.
10 He sends rain on the land
and he waters the fields.
11 Yes, it is God who raises the
humble
and gives joy to all who mourn.
12-13 He upsets the plans of cunning
people,
and traps the wise in their own
schemes,
so that nothing they do
succeeds;
14 even at noon they grope in
darkness.
15 But God saves the poor[k] from
death;
he saves the needy from
oppression.
16 He gives hope to the poor and
silences the wicked.

17 Happy is the person whom God
corrects!
Do not resent it when he
rebukes you.
18 God bandages the wounds he
makes;
his hand hurts you, and his
hand heals.

[g] righteous in the sight of; *or* more righteous than. [h] be pure before; *or* be more pure than. [i] *Probable text* even . . . thorns; *Hebrew unclear.* [j] sparks fly up from a fire; *or* birds fly up to the sky. [k] *Probable text* poor; *Hebrew unclear.*

19 Time after time he will save you
from harm;
20 when famine comes, he will
keep you alive,
and in war protect you from
death.
21 God will rescue you from slander;
he will save you when
destruction comes.
22 You will laugh at violence and
hunger
and not be afraid of wild
animals.
23 The fields you plow will be free
of rocks;
wild animals will never
attack you.
24 Then you will live at peace in your
tent;
when you look at your sheep,
you will find them safe.
25 You will have as many children
as there are blades of grass in a
pasture.
26 Like wheat that ripens till harvest
time,
you will live to a ripe old age.
27 Job, we have learned this by long
study.
It is true, so now accept it.

6

Job

1-2 If my troubles and griefs were
weighed on scales,
3 they would weigh more than the
sands of the sea,
so my wild words should not
surprise you.
4 Almighty God has shot me with
arrows,
and their poison spreads
through my body.
God has lined up his terrors
against me.

5 A donkey is content when eating
grass,
and a cow is quiet when
eating hay.
6 But who can eat flat, unsalted
food?
What taste is there in the white
of an egg?
7 I have no appetite for food like
that,
and everything I eat makes me
sick.[l]

8 Why won't God give me what
I ask?
Why won't he answer my
prayer?
9 If only he would go ahead and
kill me!
10 If I knew he would, I would leap
for joy,
no matter how great my pain.
I know that God is holy;
I have never opposed what he
commands.
11 What strength do I have to keep
on living?
Why go on living when I have
no hope?
12 Am I made of stone? Is my body
bronze?
13 I have no strength left to save
myself;
there is nowhere I can turn for
help.

14 In trouble[m] like this I need loyal
friends—
whether I've forsaken God
or not.
15 But you, my friends, you deceive
me like streams
that go dry when no rain comes.
16 The streams are choked with snow
and ice,
17 but in the heat they disappear,
and the stream beds lie bare
and dry.
18 Caravans get lost looking for
water;
they wander and die in the
desert.
19 Caravans from Sheba and Tema
search,
20 but their hope dies beside dry
streams.
21 You are like[n] those streams
to me,[o]
you see my fate and draw back
in fear.

[l] *Probable text* sick; *Hebrew unclear.* [m] *Probable text* trouble; *Hebrew unclear.*
[n] *Probable text* like; *Hebrew* because. [o] *Some ancient translations* and one; *Hebrew manuscript* to me; *most Hebrew manuscripts have two different expressions:* nothing *in the text and* to him *in the margin.*

22 Have I asked you to give me a gift
or to bribe someone on my
behalf
23 or to save me from some enemy
or tyrant?

24 All right, teach me; tell me my
faults.
I will be quiet and listen to you.
25 Honest words are convincing,
but you are talking nonsense.
26 You think I am talking nothing but
wind;
then why do you answer my
words of despair?
27 You would even roll dice for
orphan slaves
and make yourselves rich off
your closest friends!
28 Look me in the face. I won't lie.
29 You have gone far enough. Stop
being unjust.
Don't condemn me. I'm in the
right.
30 But you think I am lying—
you think I can't tell right from
wrong.

7

Human life is like forced army
service,
like a life of hard manual labor,
2 like a slave longing for cool
shade;
like a worker waiting to be paid.
3 Month after month I have nothing
to live for;
night after night brings me grief.
4 When I lie down to sleep, the
hours drag;
I toss all night and long for
dawn.
5 My body is full of worms;
it is covered with scabs;
pus runs out of my sores.
6 My days pass by without hope,
pass faster than a weaver's
shuttle.[p]

7 Remember, O God, my life is only
a breath;
my happiness has already
ended.
8 You see me now, but never again.
If you look for me, I'll be gone.
9-10 Like a cloud that fades and is
gone,
we humans die and never
return;
we are forgotten by all who
knew us.
11 No! I can't be quiet!
I am angry and bitter.
I have to speak.

12 Why do you keep me under
guard?
Do you think I am a sea
monster?[q]
13 I lie down and try to rest;
I look for relief from my pain.
14 But you—you terrify me with
dreams;
you send me visions and
nightmares
15 until I would rather be strangled
than live in this miserable body.
16 I give up; I am tired of living.
Leave me alone. My life makes no
sense.

17 Why are people so important
to you?
Why pay attention to what
they do?
18 You inspect them every morning
and test them every minute.
19 Won't you look away long enough
for me to swallow my spit?
20 Are you harmed by my sin, you
jailer?
Why use me for your target
practice?
Am I so great a burden to you?
21 Can't you ever forgive my sin?
Can't you pardon the wrong
I do?
Soon I will be in my grave,
and I'll be gone when you look
for me.

8

Bildad

1-2 Are you finally through with your
windy speech?
3 God never twists justice;
he never fails to do what is
right.

[p] WEAVER'S SHUTTLE: *A small device in the loom which carries threads back and forth rapidly in weaving cloth.* [q] SEA MONSTER: *A reference to ancient stories in which sea monsters had to be guarded so that they would not escape and do damage.*

4 Your children must have sinned
against God,
and so he punished them as they
deserved.
5 But turn now and plead with
Almighty God;
6 if you are so honest and pure,
then God will come and
help you
and restore your household as
your reward.
7 All the wealth you lost will be
nothing
compared with what God will
give you then.

8 Look for a moment at ancient
wisdom;
consider the truths our ancestors
learned.
9 Our life is short, we know nothing
at all;
we pass like shadows across the
earth.
10 But let the ancient wise people
teach you;
listen to what they had to say:

11 "Reeds can't grow where there is
no water;
they are never found outside a
swamp.
12 If the water dries up, they are the
first to wither,
while still too small to be cut
and used.
13 Godless people are like those
reeds;
their hope is gone, once God is
forgotten.
14 They trust a thread – a
spider's web.
15 If they lean on a web, will it
hold them up?
If they grab for a thread, will it
help them stand?"

16 Evil people sprout like weeds in
the sun,
like weeds that spread all
through the garden.
17 Their roots wrap around the
stones
and hold fast to[r] every rock.
18 But then pull them up –
no one will ever know they were
there.
19 Yes, that's all the joy evil people
have;
others now come and take their
places.

20 But God will never abandon the
faithful
or ever give help to evil people.
21 He will let you laugh and shout
again,
22 but he will bring disgrace on
those who hate you,
and the homes of the wicked
will vanish.

9

Job

1-2 Yes, I've heard all that before.
But how can a human being win
a case against God?
3 How can anyone argue with him?
He can ask a thousand questions
that no one could ever answer.[s]
4 God is so wise and powerful;
no one can stand up
against him.
5 Without warning he moves
mountains
and in anger he destroys them.
6 God sends earthquakes and
shakes the ground;
he rocks the pillars that support
the earth.
7 He can keep the sun from rising,
and the stars from shining at
night.
8 No one helped God spread out the
heavens
or trample the sea monster's
back.[t]
9 God hung the stars in the sky – the
Dipper,
Orion, the Pleiades, and the
stars of the south.
10 We cannot understand the great
things he does,
and to his miracles there is
no end.

11 God passes by, but I cannot
see him.

[r] *Probable text* hold fast to; *Hebrew* see. [s] He can ask . . . answer; *or* Someone could ask him a thousand questions, and he would not answer. [t] TRAMPLE THE SEA MONSTER'S BACK: *A reference to ancient stories in which a sea monster was killed and then trampled (see also 26.13).*

12 He takes what he wants, and no
one can stop him;
no one dares ask him, "What are
you doing?"
13 God's anger is constant. He
crushed his enemies
who helped Rahab,[u] the sea
monster, oppose him.
14 So how can I find words to
answer God?
15 Though I am innocent, all I can do
is beg for mercy from God my
judge.
16 Yet even then, if he lets me speak,
I can't believe he would listen
to me.
17 He sends storms to batter and
bruise me
without any reason at all.
18 He won't let me catch my breath;
he has filled my life with
bitterness.
19 Should I try force? Try force
on God?
Should I take him to court? Could
anyone make him go?[v]
20 I am innocent and faithful, but my
words sound guilty,
and everything I say seems to
condemn me.
21-22 I am innocent, but I no longer
care.
I am sick of living. Nothing
matters;
innocent or guilty, God will
destroy us.
23 When an innocent person
suddenly dies,
God laughs.
24 God gave the world to the wicked.
He made all the judges blind.
And if God didn't do it, who did?

25 My days race by, not one of them
good.
26 My life passes like the swiftest
boat,
as fast as an eagle swooping
down on a rabbit.
27-28 If I smile and try to forget my
pain,
all my suffering comes back to
haunt me;
I know that God does hold me
guilty.
29 Since I am held guilty, why should
I bother?
30 No soap can wash away my
sins.
31 God throws me into a pit with
filth,
and even my clothes are
ashamed of me.
32 If God were human, I could
answer him;
we could go to court to decide
our quarrel.
33 But there is no one to step
between us—
no one to judge both God
and me.
34 Stop punishing me, God!
Keep your terrors away!
35 I am not afraid. I am going to talk
because I know my own heart.

10 I am tired of living.
Listen to my bitter complaint.
2 Don't condemn me, God.
Tell me! What is the charge
against me?
3 Is it right for you to be so cruel?
To despise what you yourself
have made?
And then to smile on the
schemes of wicked people?
4 Do you see things as we do?
5 Is your life as short as ours?
6 Then why do you track down all
my sins
and hunt down every fault I
have?
7 You know that I am not guilty,
that no one can save me
from you.

8 Your hands formed and
shaped me,
and now[w] those same hands
destroy me.
9 Remember that you made me from
clay;[x]
are you going to crush me back
to dust?
10 You gave my father strength to
beget me;
you made me grow in my
mother's womb.
11 You formed my body with bones
and sinews

[u] RAHAB: *A legendary sea monster which represented the forces of chaos and evil.*
[v] *Probable text* make him go; *Hebrew* make me go. [w] *Some ancient translations* and now; *Hebrew* together. [x] *One ancient translation* from clay; *Hebrew* like clay.

and covered the bones with
muscles and skin.
12 You have given me life and
constant love,
and your care has kept me alive.
13 But now I know that all that time
you were secretly planning to
harm me.
14 You were watching to see if I
would sin,
so that you could refuse to
forgive me.
15 As soon as I sin, I'm in trouble
with you,
but when I do right, I get no
credit.
I am miserable and covered with
shame.[y]
16 If I have any success at all,
you hunt me down like a lion;
to hurt me you even work
miracles.
17 You always have some witness
against me;
your anger toward me grows
and grows;
you always plan some new
attack.

18 Why, God, did you let me be born?
I should have died before
anyone saw me.
19 To go from the womb straight to
the grave
would have been as good as
never existing.
20 Isn't my life almost over? Leave
me alone!
Let me enjoy the time I have
left.
21 I am going soon and will never
come back—
going to a land that is dark and
gloomy,
22 a land of darkness, shadows,
and confusion,
where the light itself is
darkness.

11

Zophar

1-2 Will no one answer all this
nonsense?
Does talking so much put you in
the right?
3 Job, do you think we can't
answer you?
That your mocking words will
leave us speechless?
4 You claim that what you say is
true;
you claim you are pure in the
sight of God.
5 How I wish God would
answer you!
6 He would tell you there are many
sides to wisdom;
there are things too deep for
human knowledge.
God is punishing you less than
you deserve.

7 Can you discover the limits and
bounds
of the greatness and power
of God?
8 The sky is no limit for God,
but it lies beyond your reach.
God knows the world of the dead,
but you do not know it.
9 God's greatness is broader than
the earth,
wider than the sea.
10 If God arrests you and brings you
to trial,
who is there to stop him?
11 God knows which people are
worthless;
he sees all their evil deeds.
12 Stupid people will start being wise
when wild donkeys are born
tame.

13 Put your heart right, Job. Reach
out to God.
14 Put away evil and wrong from
your home.
15 Then face the world again, firm
and courageous.
16 Then all your troubles will fade
from your memory,
like floods that are past and
remembered no more.
17 Your life will be brighter than
sunshine at noon,
and life's darkest hours will
shine like the dawn.
18 You will live secure and full of
hope;
God will protect you and give
you rest.

[y] *Probable text* covered with shame; *Hebrew* see my shame.

19 You won't be afraid of your
enemies;
many people will ask you for
help.
20 But the wicked will look around in
despair
and find that there is no way to
escape.
Their one hope is that death will
come.

12

Job

1-2 Yes, you are the voice of the
people.
When you die, wisdom will die
with you.
3 But I have as much sense as you
have;
I am in no way inferior to you;
everyone knows all that you
have said.
4 Even my friends laugh at me now;
they laugh, although I am
righteous and blameless;
but there was a time when God
answered my prayers.
5 You have no troubles, and yet you
make fun of me;
you hit someone who is about to
fall.
6 But thieves and godless people live
in peace,
though their only god is their
own strength.

7 Even birds and animals have
much they could teach you;
8 ask the creatures of earth and
sea for their wisdom.
9 All of them know that the LORD's
hand made them.
10 It is God who directs the lives of
his creatures;
everyone's life is in his power.
11 But just as your tongue enjoys
tasting food,
your ears enjoy hearing words.

12-13 Old people have wisdom,
but God has wisdom and power.
Old people have insight;
God has insight and power
to act.
14 When God tears down, who can
rebuild,
and who can free those God
imprisons?
15 Drought comes when God
withholds rain;
floods come when he turns
water loose.

16 God is strong and always
victorious;
both deceived and deceiver are
in his power.
17 He takes away the wisdom of
rulers
and makes leaders act like fools.
18 He dethrones kings and makes
them prisoners;
19 he humbles priests and men of
power.
20 He silences those who are trusted,
and takes the wisdom of old
people away.
21 He disgraces those in power
and puts an end to the strength
of rulers.
22 He sends light to places dark as
death.
23 He makes nations strong and
great,
but then he defeats and destroys
them.
24 He makes their leaders foolish
and lets them wander confused
and lost;
25 they grope in the dark and
stagger like drunkards.

13

1-2 Everything you say, I have
heard before.
I understand it all; I know as
much as you do.
I'm not your inferior.
3 But my dispute is with God,
not you;
I want to argue my case
with him.
4 You cover up your ignorance with
lies;
you are like doctors who can't
heal anyone.
5 Say nothing, and someone may
think you are wise!

6 Listen while I state my case.
7 Why are you lying?
Do you think your lies will
benefit God?
8 Are you trying to defend him?

Are you going to argue his case
in court?
9 If God looks at you closely, will he
find anything good?
Do you think you can fool God
the way you fool others?
10 Even though your prejudice is
hidden,
he will reprimand you,
11 and his power will fill you with
terror.
12 Your proverbs are as useless as
ashes;
your arguments are as weak as
clay.
13 Be quiet and give me a chance to
speak,
and let the results be what they
will.

14 I am[z] ready to risk my life.
15 I've lost all hope, so what if God
kills me?
I am going to state my case
to him.
16 It may even be that my boldness
will save me,
since no wicked person would
dare to face God.
17 Now listen to my words of
explanation.
18 I am ready to state my case,
because I know I am in the
right.

19 Are you coming to accuse
me, God?
If you do, I am ready to be silent
and die.
20 Let me ask for two things; agree
to them,
and I will not try to hide
from you:
21 stop punishing me, and don't
crush me with terror.

22 Speak first, O God, and I will
answer.
Or let me speak, and you
answer me.
23 What are my sins? What wrongs
have I done?
What crimes am I charged with?

24 Why do you avoid me?
Why do you treat me like an
enemy?
25 Are you trying to frighten me? I'm
nothing but a leaf;
you are attacking a piece of dry
straw.

26 You bring bitter charges
against me,
even for what I did when I was
young.
27 You bind chains on my feet;
you watch every step I take,
and even examine my footprints.
28 As a result, I crumble like rotten
wood,
like a moth-eaten coat.

14 We are all born weak and
helpless.
All lead the same short, troubled
life.
2 We grow and wither as quickly as
flowers;
we disappear like shadows.
3 Will you even look at me, God,
or put me on trial and judge me?
4 Nothing clean can ever come
from anything as unclean as
human beings.
5 The length of our lives is decided
beforehand—
the number of months we will
live.
You have settled it, and it can't be
changed.
6 Look away from us and leave us
alone;[a]
let us enjoy our hard life—if
we can.[b]

7 There is hope for a tree that has
been cut down;
it can come back to life and
sprout.
8 Even though its roots grow old,
and its stump dies in the ground,
9 with water it will sprout like a
young plant.
10 But we die, and that is the end
of us;
we die, and where are we then?

11 Like rivers that stop running,
and lakes that go dry,

[z] *One ancient translation* I am; *Hebrew* Why am I. [a] *One Hebrew manuscript* and leave us alone; *most Hebrew manuscripts* so that we may rest. [b] let us ... can; *or* until we finish our day of hard work.

12 people die, never to rise.
They will never wake up while the sky endures;
they will never stir from their sleep.

13 I wish you would hide me in the world of the dead;
let me be hidden until your anger is over,
and then set a time to remember me.
14 If a man dies, can he come back to life?
But I will wait for better times,
wait till this time of trouble is ended.
15 Then you will call, and I will answer,
and you will be pleased with me, your creature.
16 Then you will watch every step I take,
but you will not keep track of my sins.
17 You will forgive them and put them away;
you will wipe out all the wrongs I have done.

18 There comes a time when mountains fall
and solid cliffs are moved away.
19 Water will wear down rocks,
and heavy rain will wash away the soil;
so you destroy our hope for life.
20 You overpower us and send us away forever;
our faces are twisted in death.
21 Our children win honor, but we never know it,
nor are we told when they are disgraced.
22 We feel only the pain of our own bodies
and the grief of our own minds.

The Second Dialogue

(15.1 – 21.34)

15

Eliphaz

1-2 Empty words, Job! Empty words!
3 No one who is wise would talk the way you do
or defend himself with such meaningless words.
4 If you had your way, no one would fear God;
no one would pray to him.
5 Your wickedness is evident by what you say;
you are trying to hide behind clever words.
6 There is no need for me to condemn you;
you are condemned by every word you speak.

7 Do you think you were the first person born?
Were you there when God made the mountains?
8 Did you overhear the plans God made?
Does human wisdom belong to you alone?
9 There is nothing you know that we don't know.
10 We learned our wisdom from gray-haired people —
those born before your father.

11 God offers you comfort; why still reject it?
We have spoken for him with calm, even words.
12 But you are excited and glare at us in anger.
13 You are angry with God and denounce him.

14 Can any human being be really pure?
Can anyone be right with God?
15 Why, God does not trust even his angels;
even they are not pure in his sight.
16 And we drink evil as if it were water;
yes, we are corrupt; we are worthless.

17 Now listen, Job, to what I know.
18 Those who are wise have taught me truths
which they learned from their ancestors,
and they kept no secrets hidden.
19 Their land was free from foreigners;

there was no one to lead them
away from God.

20 The wicked who oppress others
will be in torment as long as
they live.
21 Voices of terror will scream in
their ears,
and robbers attack when they
think they are safe.
22 They have no hope of escaping
from darkness,
for somewhere a sword is
waiting to kill them,
23 and vultures[c] are waiting[d] to
eat their corpses.
They know their future is dark;
24 disaster, like a powerful king,
is waiting to attack them.

25 That is the fate of those
who shake their fists at God
and defy the Almighty.
26-27 They are proud and rebellious;
they stubbornly hold up their
shields
and rush to fight against God.

28 They are the ones who captured
cities
and seized houses whose owners
had fled,
but war will destroy those cities
and houses.
29 They will not remain rich for long;
nothing they own will last.
Even their shadows[e] will vanish,
30 and they will not escape from
darkness.
They will be like trees
whose branches are burned by
fire,
whose blossoms[f] are blown
away by the wind.
31 If they are foolish enough to trust
in evil,
then evil will be their reward.
32 Before their time is up they will
wither,[g]
wither like a branch and never
be green again.
33 They will be like vines that lose
their unripe grapes;
like olive trees that drop their
blossoms.
34 There will be no descendants for
godless people,
and fire will destroy the homes
built by bribery.
35 These are the ones who plan
trouble and do evil;
their hearts are always full of
deceit.

16

Job

1-2 I have heard words like that
before;
the comfort you give is only
torment.
3 Are you going to keep on talking
forever?
Do you always have to have the
last word?
4 If you were in my place and I in
yours,
I could say everything you are
saying.
I could shake my head wisely
and drown you with a flood of
words.
5 I could strengthen you with advice
and keep talking to comfort you.

6 But nothing I say helps,
and being silent does not calm
my pain.
7 You have worn me out, God;
you have let my family be killed.
8 You have seized me; you are my
enemy.
I am skin and bones,
and people take that as proof of
my guilt.[h]

9 In anger God tears me limb from
limb;
he glares at me with hate.
10 People sneer at me;
they crowd around me and slap
my face.
11 God has handed me over to evil
people.

[c] *One ancient translation* vultures; *Hebrew* where is he? [d] *One ancient translation* are waiting; *Hebrew* he wanders. [e] *One ancient translation* shadows; *Hebrew unclear.* [f] *One ancient translation* blossoms; *Hebrew* mouth. [g] *Some ancient translations* wither; *Hebrew* be filled. [h] *Verses 7-8 in Hebrew are unclear.*

12 I was living in peace,
but God took me by the throat
and battered me and
crushed me.
God uses me for target practice
13 and shoots arrows at me from
every side—
arrows that pierce and
wound me;
and even then he shows no pity.
14 He wounds me again and again;
he attacks like a soldier gone
mad with hate.

15 I mourn and wear clothes made of
sackcloth,
and I sit here in the dust
defeated.
16 I have cried until my face is red,
and my eyes are swollen and
circled with shadows,
17 but I am not guilty of any
violence,
and my prayer to God is sincere.

18 O Earth, don't hide the wrongs
done to me!
Don't let my call for justice be
silenced!
19 There is someone in heaven
to stand up for me and take my
side.
20 My friends scorn me;
my eyes pour out tears to God.
21 I want someone to plead with God
for me,
as one pleads for a friend.
22 My years are passing now,
and I walk the road of no return.

17

1 The end of my life is near. I
can hardly breathe;
there is nothing left for me but
the grave.
2 I watch how bitterly everyone
mocks me.
3 I am being honest, God. Accept
my word.
There is no one else to support
what I say.
4 You have closed their minds to
reason;
don't let them triumph over
me now.
5 In the old proverb someone
betrays his friends for money,
and his children suffer for it.[i]
6 And now people use this proverb
against me;
they come and spit in my face.
7 My grief has almost made me
blind;
my arms and legs are as thin as
shadows.
8 Those who claim to be honest are
shocked,
and they all condemn me as
godless.
9 Those who claim to be respectable
are more and more convinced
they are right.
10 But if all of them came and stood
before me,
I would not find even one of
them wise.

11 My days have passed; my plans
have failed;
my hope is gone.
12 But my friends say night is
daylight;
they say that light is near,
but I know I remain in darkness.
13 My only hope is the world of the
dead,
where I will lie down to sleep in
the dark.
14 I will call the grave my father,
and the worms that eat me
I will call my mother and my
sisters.
15 Where is there any hope for me?
Who sees any?
16 Hope will not go with me[j]
when I go down to the world of
the dead.

18

Bildad

1-2 Job, can't people like you ever be
quiet?
If you stopped to listen, we
could talk to you.
3 What makes you think we are as
stupid as cattle?
4 You are only hurting yourself with
your anger.

[i] someone . . . suffer for it; *or* someone entertains his friends while his children go hungry.
[j] *One ancient translation* with me; *Hebrew unclear.*

Will the earth be deserted
because you are angry?
Will God move mountains to
satisfy you?

5 The light of the wicked will still be
put out;
its flame will never burn again.
6 The lamp in their tents will be
darkened.
7 Their steps were firm, but now
they stumble;
they fall—victims of their own
advice.
8 They walk into a net, and their
feet are caught;
9 a trap catches their heels and
holds them.
10 On the ground a snare is hidden;
a trap has been set in their path.

11 All around them terror is waiting;
it follows them at every step.
12 They used to be rich, but now they
go hungry;
disaster stands and waits at their
side.
13 A deadly disease spreads over
their bodies
and causes their arms and legs
to rot.
14 They are torn from the tents
where they lived secure,
and are dragged off to face King
Death.
15 Now anyone may live in their
tents—[k]
after sulfur is sprinkled to
disinfect them![l]
16 Their roots and branches are
withered and dry.
17 Their fame is ended at home and
abroad;
no one remembers them any
more.
18 They will be driven out of the land
of the living,
driven from light into darkness.
19 They have no descendants, no
survivors.
20 From east to west, all who hear of
their fate
shudder and tremble with fear.
21 That is the fate of evil people,
the fate of those who care
nothing for God.

19

Job

1-2 Why do you keep tormenting me
with words?
3 Time after time you insult me
and show no shame for the way
you abuse me.
4 Even if I have done wrong,
how does that hurt you?
5 You think you are better than
I am,
and regard my troubles as proof
of my guilt.
6 Can't you see it is God who has
done this?
He has set a trap to catch me.
7 I protest his violence,
but no one is listening;
no one hears my cry for justice.
8 God has blocked the way, and I
can't get through;
he has hidden my path in
darkness.
9 He has taken away all my wealth
and destroyed my reputation.
10 He batters me from every side.
He uproots my hope
and leaves me to wither and die.
11 God is angry and rages
against me;
he treats me like his worst
enemy.
12 He sends his army to attack me;
they dig trenches and lay siege
to my tent.

13 God has made my own family
forsake me;
I am a stranger to those who
knew me;
14 my relatives and friends are
gone.
15 Those who were guests in my
house have forgotten me;
my servant women treat me like
a stranger and a foreigner.
16 When I call a servant, he doesn't
answer—
even when I beg him to help me.
17 My wife can't stand the smell of
my breath,
and my own brothers won't
come near me.

[k] Now anyone may live in their tents; *Hebrew unclear.* [l] TO DISINFECT THEM: *Sulfur was used in the ancient world as a disinfectant and to clean rooms that had contained corpses.*

18 Children despise me and laugh
when they see me.
19 My closest friends look at me with
disgust;
those I loved most have turned
against me.
20 My skin hangs loose on my bones;
I have barely escaped with my
life.[m]
21 You are my friends! Take pity
on me!
The hand of God has struck me
down.
22 Why must you persecute me the
way God does?
Haven't you tormented me
enough?

23 How I wish that someone would
remember my words
and record them in a book!
24 Or with a chisel carve my words
in stone
and write them so that they
would last forever.[n]

25 But I know there is someone in
heaven
who will come at last to my
defense.
26 Even after my skin is eaten by
disease,
while still in this body[o] I will
see God.[p]
27 I will see him with my own eyes,
and he will not be a stranger.

My courage failed because you
said,
28 "How can we torment him?"
You looked for some excuse to
attack me.
29 But now, be afraid of the sword—
the sword that brings God's
wrath on sin,
so that you will know there is
one who judges.[q]

20

Zophar

1-2 Job, you upset me. Now I'm
impatient to answer.
3 What you have said is an insult,
but I know how to reply to you.
4 Surely you know that from ancient
times,
when we humans were first
placed on earth,
5 no wicked people have been
happy for long.
6 They may grow great, towering to
the sky,
so great that their heads reach
the clouds,
7 but they will be blown away like
dust.
Those who used to know them
will wonder where they have
gone.
8 They will vanish like a dream, like
a vision at night,
and never be seen again.
9 The wicked will disappear from
the place where they used to
live;
10 and their children will make
good what they stole from the
poor.
11 Their bodies used to be young and
vigorous,
but soon they will turn to dust.

12-13 Evil tastes so good to them
that they keep some in their
mouths to enjoy its flavor.
14 But in their stomachs the food
turns bitter,
as bitter as any poison could be.
15 The wicked vomit up the wealth
they stole;
God takes it back, even out of
their stomachs.
16 What the evil people swallow is
like poison;
it kills them like the bite of a
deadly snake.
17 They will not live to see rivers of
olive oil[r]
or streams that flow with milk
and honey.
18 They will have to give up all they
have worked for;
they will have no chance to
enjoy their wealth,
19 because they oppressed and
neglected the poor

[m] *Verse 20 in Hebrew is unclear.* [n] last forever; *or* be on record. [o] while still in this body; *or* although not in this body. [p] *Verse 26 in Hebrew is unclear.* [q] one who judges; *or* a judgment. [r] *Probable text* They will ... oil; *Hebrew unclear.*

and seized houses someone else
had built.
20 Their greed is never satisfied.
21 When they eat, there is nothing
left over,
but now their prosperity comes
to an end.
22 At the height of their success
all the weight of misery will
crush them.
23 Let them eat all they want!
God will punish them in fury
and anger.
24 When they try to escape from an
iron sword,
a bronze bow will shoot them
down.
25 Arrows stick through their bodies;
the shiny points drip with their
blood,
and terror grips their hearts.
26 Everything they have saved is
destroyed;
a fire not lit by human hands
burns them and all their family.
27 Heaven reveals their sin,
and the earth gives testimony
against them.
28 All their wealth will be destroyed
in the flood of God's anger.

29 This is the fate of wicked people,
the fate that God assigns to
them.

21

Job

1-2 Listen to what I am saying;
that is all the comfort I ask
from you.
3 Give me a chance to speak and
then,
when I am through, sneer if you
like.

4 My quarrel is not with mortals;
I have good reason to be
impatient.
5 Look at me. Isn't that enough
to make you stare in shocked
silence?
6 When I think of what has
happened to me,
I am stunned, and I tremble and
shake.

7 Why does God let evil people live,
let them grow old and prosper?
8 They have children and
grandchildren,
and live to watch them all
grow up.
9 God does not bring disaster on
their homes;
they never have to live in terror.
10 Yes, all their cattle breed
and give birth without trouble.
11 Their children run and play like
lambs
12 and dance to the music of harps
and flutes.
13 They live out their lives in peace
and quietly die without
suffering.

14 The wicked tell God to leave them
alone;
they don't want to know his will
for their lives.
15 They think there is no need to
serve God
nor any advantage in praying
to him.
16 They claim they succeed by their
own strength,
but their way of thinking I can't
accept.

17 Was a wicked person's light ever
put out?
Did one of them ever meet with
disaster?
Did God ever punish the wicked in
anger
18 and blow them away like straw
in the wind,
or like dust carried away in a
storm?

19 You claim God punishes a child
for the sins of his father.
No! Let God punish the sinners
themselves;
let him show that he does it
because of *their* sins.
20 Let sinners bear their own
punishment;
let them feel the wrath of
Almighty God.
21 When our lives are over,
do we really care whether our
children are happy?
22 Can anyone teach God,

who judges even those in high
places?

23-24 Some people stay healthy till the
day they die;
they die happy and at ease,
their bodies well-nourished.
25 Others have no happiness at all;
they live and die with bitter
hearts.
26 But all alike die and are buried;
they all are covered with worms.

27 I know what spiteful thoughts you
have.
28 You ask, "Where are the homes of
great people now,
those who practiced evil?"

29 Haven't you talked with people
who travel?
Don't you know the reports they
bring back?
30 On the day God is angry and
punishes,
it is the wicked who are always
spared.
31 There is no one to accuse the
wicked
or pay them back for all they
have done.
32 When they are carried to the
graveyard,
to their well-guarded tombs,
33 thousands join the funeral
procession,
and even the earth lies gently on
their bodies.

34 And you! You try to comfort me
with nonsense!
Every answer you give is a lie!

The Third Dialogue

(22.1 – 27.23)

22

Eliphaz

1-2 Is there anyone, even the wisest,
who could ever be of use
to God?
3 Does your doing right benefit God,
or does your being good help
him at all?
4 It is not because you stand in awe
of God
that he reprimands you and
brings you to trial.
5 No, it's because you have sinned
so much;
it's because of all the evil
you do.
6 To make a brother repay you the
money he owed,
you took away his clothes and
left him nothing to wear.
7 You refused water to those who
were tired,
and refused to feed those who
were hungry.
8 You used your power and your
position
to take over the whole land.
9 You not only refused to help
widows,
but you also robbed and
mistreated orphans.
10 So now there are pitfalls all
around you,
and suddenly you are full of
fear.
11 It has grown so dark that you
cannot see,
and a flood overwhelms you.

12 Doesn't God live in the highest
heavens
and look down on the stars,
even though they are high?
13 And yet you ask, "What does God
know?
He is hidden by clouds — how
can he judge us?"
14 You think the thick clouds keep
him from seeing,
as he walks on the dome of
the sky.

15 Are you determined to walk in the
paths
that evil people have always
followed?
16 Even before their time had come,
they were washed away by a
flood.
17 These are the ones who
rejected God
and believed that he could do
nothing to them.
18 And yet it was God who made
them prosperous —
I can't understand the thoughts
of the wicked.

19 Good people are glad and the
innocent laugh
when they see the wicked
punished.
20 All that the wicked own is
destroyed,
and fire burns up anything that
is left.

21 Now, Job, make peace with God
and stop treating him like an
enemy;
if you do, then he will bless you.
22 Accept the teaching he gives;
keep his words in your heart.
23 Yes, you must humbly[s] return
to God
and put an end to all the evil
that is done in your house.
24 Throw away your gold;
dump your finest gold in the dry
stream bed.
25 Let Almighty God be your gold,
and let him be silver, piled high
for you.
26 Then you will always trust in God
and find that he is the source of
your joy.
27 When you pray, he will
answer you,
and you will keep the vows you
made.
28 You will succeed in all you do,
and light will shine on your
path.
29 God brings down the proud[t]
and saves the humble.
30 He will rescue you if you are
innocent,[u]
if what you do is right.[v]

23

Job

1-2 I still rebel and complain
against God;
I cannot keep from groaning.
3 How I wish I knew where to
find him,
and knew how to go where
he is.
4 I would state my case before him
and present all the arguments in
my favor.
5 I want to know what he would say
and how he would answer me.
6 Would God use all his strength
against me?
No, he would listen as I spoke.
7 I am honest; I could reason
with God;
he would declare me innocent[w]
once and for all.

8 I have searched in the East, but
God is not there;
I have not found him when I
searched in the West.
9 God has been at work in the North
and the South,
but still I have not seen him.
10 Yet God knows every step I take;
if he tests me, he will find me
pure.
11 I follow faithfully the road he
chooses,
and never wander to either side.
12 I always do what God commands;
I follow his will, not my own
desires.

13 He never changes. No one can
oppose him
or stop him from doing what he
wants to do.
14 He will fulfill what he has planned
for me;
that plan is just one of the many
he has;
15 I tremble with fear before him.
16-17 Almighty God has destroyed my
courage.
It is God, not the dark, that makes
me afraid—
even though the darkness has
made me blind.

24

Why doesn't God set a time for
judging,
a day of justice for those who
serve him?

2 People move property lines to get
more land;
they steal sheep and put them
with their own flocks.
3 They take donkeys that belong to
orphans,

[s] *One ancient translation* humbly; *Hebrew* be built up. [t] *Probable text* proud; *Hebrew unclear.* [u] *Some ancient translations* innocent; *Hebrew* not innocent. [v] *Verse 30 in Hebrew is unclear.* [w] he would declare me innocent; *or* then my rights would be safe.

and keep a widow's ox till she
pays her debts.
4 They prevent the poor from
getting their rights
and force the needy to run and
hide.

5 So the poor, like wild donkeys,
search for food in the dry
wilderness;
nowhere else can they find food
for their children.
6 They have to harvest fields they
don't own,[x]
and gather grapes in vineyards
of the wicked.
7 At night they sleep with nothing to
cover them,
nothing to keep them from the
cold.
8 They are drenched by the rain that
falls on the mountains,
and they huddle beside the rocks
for shelter.

9 Evil people make slaves of
fatherless infants
and take the children of the poor
in payment for debts.
10 But the poor must go out with no
clothes to protect them;
they must go hungry while
harvesting wheat.
11 They press olives for oil, and
grapes for wine,
but they themselves are thirsty.
12 In the cities the wounded and
dying cry out,
but God ignores their prayers.

13 There are those who reject the
light;
they don't understand it or go
where it leads.
14 At dawn the murderer gets up
and goes out to kill the poor,
and at night he steals.
15 The adulterer waits for twilight to
come;
he covers his face so that no one
can see him.
16 At night thieves break into houses,
but by day they hide and avoid
the light.
17 They fear the light of day,
but darkness holds no terror for
them.

[Zophar][y]

18 The wicked are swept away by
floods,
and the land they own is under
God's curse;
they no longer go to work in
their vineyards.
19 As snow vanishes in heat and
drought,
so sinners vanish from the land
of the living.
20 Not even their mothers remember
them now;
they are eaten by worms and
destroyed like fallen trees.
21 That happens because they
mistreated widows
and showed no kindness to
childless women.
22 God, in his strength, destroys the
mighty;
God acts — and the wicked die.
23 God may let them live secure,
but keeps an eye on them all the
time.
24 For a while the wicked prosper,
but then they wither like weeds,
like stalks of grain that have
been cut down.
25 Can anyone deny that this is so?
Can anyone prove that my words
are not true?

25

Bildad

1-2 God is powerful; all must stand in
awe of him;
he keeps his heavenly kingdom
in peace.
3 Can anyone count the angels who
serve him?
Is there any place where God's
light does not shine?
4 Can anyone be righteous or pure
in God's sight?
5 In his eyes even the moon is not
bright,
or the stars pure.
6 Then what about a human being,
that worm, that insect?

[x] FIELDS THEY DON'T OWN: *Having been cheated out of their own land, the poor are forced to work for others for very small pay.* [y] Zophar *is not named in the text, but this speech is usually assigned to him.*

What is a human life worth in
God's eyes?

26

Job

1-2 What a big help you are to me—
poor, weak man that I am!
3 You give such good advice
and share your knowledge with
a fool like me!
4 Who do you think will hear all
your words?
Who inspired you to speak like
this?

[Bildad][z]

5 The spirits of the dead tremble
in the waters under the earth.
6 The world of the dead lies open
to God;
no covering shields it from his
sight.
7 God stretched out the northern sky
and hung the earth in empty
space.
8 It is God who fills the clouds with
water
and keeps them from bursting
with the weight.
9 He hides the full moon behind a
cloud.
10 He divided light from darkness
by a circle drawn on the face of
the sea.
11 When he threatens the pillars that
hold up the sky,
they shake and tremble with
fear.
12 It is his strength that conquered
the sea;[a]
by his skill he destroyed the
monster Rahab.[b]
13 It is his breath that made the sky
clear,
and his hand that killed the
escaping monster.[c]
14 But these are only hints of his
power,
only the whispers that we have
heard.
Who can know how truly great
God is?

27

Job

1-2 I swear by the living
Almighty God,
who refuses me justice and
makes my life bitter—
3 as long as God gives me breath,
4 my lips will never say anything
evil,
my tongue will never tell a lie.
5 I will never say that you men are
right;
I will insist on my innocence to
my dying day.
6 I will never give up my claim to be
right;
my conscience is clear.

7 May all who oppose me and fight
against me
be punished like the wicked and
the unrighteous.
8 What hope is there for the godless
in the hour when God demands
their life?
9 When trouble comes, will God
hear their cries?
10 They should have desired the joy
he gives;
they should have constantly
prayed to him.

11 Let me teach you how great is
God's power,
and explain what Almighty God
has planned.
12 But no, after all, you have seen for
yourselves;
so why do you talk such
nonsense?

[Zophar][d]

13 This is how Almighty God
punishes wicked, violent people.
14 They may have many sons,
but all will be killed in war;
their children never have
enough to eat.
15 Those who survive will die from
disease,
and even their widows will not
mourn their death.

[z] Bildad *is not named in the text, but this speech is usually assigned to him.*
[a] CONQUERED THE SEA: *A reference to an ancient story in which the sea fought against God.*
[b] RAHAB: *See 9.13.* [c] ESCAPING MONSTER: *See 9.8.* [d] Zophar *is not named in the text, but this speech is usually assigned to him.*

16 The wicked may have too much
silver to count
and more clothes than anyone
needs;
17 but some good person will wear
the clothes,
and someone honest will get the
silver.
18 The wicked build houses like a
spider's web[e]
or like the hut of a slave
guarding the fields.
19 One last time[f] they will lie down
rich,
and when they wake up, they
will find their wealth gone.
20 Terror will strike like a sudden
flood;
a wind in the night will blow
them away;
21 the east wind will sweep them
from their homes;
22 it will blow down on them
without pity
while they try their best to
escape.
23 The wind howls at them as
they run,
frightening them with
destructive power.

In Praise of Wisdom[g]

28 There are mines where silver
is dug;
There are places where gold is
refined.
2 We dig iron out of the ground
And melt copper out of the stones.
3 Miners explore the deepest
darkness.
They search the depths of the
earth
And dig for rocks in the darkness.
4 Far from where anyone lives
Or human feet ever travel,
They dig the shafts of mines.
There they work in loneliness,
Clinging to ropes in the pits.
5 Food grows out of the earth,
But underneath the same earth
All is torn up and crushed.
6 The stones of the earth contain
sapphires,
And its dust contains gold.
7 No hawk sees the roads to the
mines,
And no vulture ever flies over
them.
8 No lion or other fierce beast
Ever travels those lonely roads.

9 Miners dig the hardest rocks,
Dig mountains away at their base.
10 As they tunnel through the rocks,
They discover precious stones.
11 They dig to the sources of[h] rivers
And bring to light what is hidden.
12 But where can wisdom be found?
Where can we learn to
understand?

13 Wisdom is not to be found among
mortals;
No one knows its true value.
14 The depths of the oceans and seas
Say that wisdom is not found
there.
15 It cannot be bought with silver or
gold.
16 The finest gold and jewels
Cannot equal its value.
17 It is worth more than gold,
Than a gold vase or finest glass.
18 The value of wisdom is more
Than coral or crystal or rubies.
19 The finest topaz and the purest
gold
Cannot compare with the value of
wisdom.

20 Where, then, is the source of
wisdom?
Where can we learn to
understand?
21 No living creature can see it,
Not even a bird in flight.
22 Even death and destruction
Admit they have heard only
rumors.

23 God alone knows the way,
Knows the place where wisdom is
found,
24 Because he sees the ends of the
earth,
Sees everything under the sky.
25 When God gave the wind its
power

[e] *Some ancient translations* spider's web; *Hebrew* moth *or* bird's nest.
[f] *Some ancient translations* One last time; *Hebrew* They will not be gathered.
[g] *The Hebrew text does not indicate who is speaking in this chapter.*
[h] *Some ancient translations* dig to the sources of; *Hebrew* bind from trickling.

And determined the size of
the sea;
26 When God decided where the rain
would fall,
And the path that the
thunderclouds travel;
27 It was then he saw wisdom and
tested its worth—
He gave it his approval.

28 God said to us humans,
"To be wise, you must have
reverence for the Lord.
To understand, you must turn
from evil."

Job's Final Statement of His Case

29 Job began speaking again.

2 If only my life could once again
be as it was when God watched
over me.
3 God was always with me then
and gave me light as I walked
through the darkness.
4 Those were the days when I was
prosperous,
and the friendship of God
protected my home.
5 Almighty God was with me then,
and I was surrounded by all my
children.
6 My cows and goats gave plenty of
milk,
and my olive trees grew in the
rockiest soil.
7 Whenever the city elders met
and I took my place among
them,
8 young men stepped aside as
soon as they saw me,
and old men stood up to show
me respect.
9 The leaders of the people would
stop talking;
10 even the most important men
kept silent.

11 Everyone who saw me or heard
of me
had good things to say about
what I had done.
12 When the poor cried out, I helped
them;
I gave help to orphans who had
nowhere to turn.
13 People who were in deepest
misery praised me,
and I helped widows find
security.
14 I have always acted justly and
fairly.
15 I was eyes for the blind,
and feet for the lame.
16 I was like a father to the poor
and took the side of strangers in
trouble.
17 I destroyed the power of cruel men
and rescued their victims.

18 I always expected to live a long
life
and to die at home in comfort.
19 I was like a tree whose roots
always have water
and whose branches are wet
with dew.
20 Everyone was always praising me,
and my strength never
failed me.
21 When I gave advice, people were
silent
and listened carefully to what I
said;
22 they had nothing to add when I
had finished.
My words sank in like drops of
rain;
23 everyone welcomed them
just as farmers welcome rain in
spring.
24 I smiled on them when they had
lost confidence;
my cheerful face encouraged
them.
25 I took charge and made the
decisions;
I led them as a king leads his
troops,
and gave them comfort in their
despair.

30 But men younger than I am
make fun of me now!
Their fathers have always been so
worthless
that I wouldn't let them help my
dogs guard sheep.
2 They were a bunch of
worn-out men,
too weak to do any work for me.
3 They were so poor and hungry
that they would gnaw dry
roots—

at night, in wild, desolate places.
4 They pulled up the plants of the
desert and ate them,
even the tasteless roots of the
broom tree!
5 Everyone drove them away with
shouts,
as if they were shouting at
thieves.
6 They had to live in caves,
in holes dug in the sides of cliffs.
7 Out in the wilds they howled like
animals
and huddled together under the
bushes.
8 A worthless bunch of nameless
nobodies!
They were driven out of the
land.

9 Now they come and laugh at me;
I am nothing but a joke to them.
10 They treat me with disgust;
they think they are too good
for me,
and even come and spit in my
face.
11 Because God has made me weak
and helpless,
they turn against me with all
their fury.
12 This mob attacks me head-on;
they send me running; they
prepare their final assault.
13 They cut off my escape and try to
destroy me;
and there is no one to stop[i]
them.
14 They pour through the holes in my
defenses
and come crashing down on top
of me;
15 I am overcome with terror;
my dignity is gone like a puff of
wind,
and my prosperity like a cloud.

16 Now I am about to die;
there is no relief for my
suffering.
17 At night my bones all ache;
the pain that gnaws me never
stops.
18 God seizes me by my collar
and twists my clothes out of
shape.
19 He throws me down in the mud;
I am no better than dirt.

20 I call to you, O God, but you never
answer;
and when I pray, you pay no
attention.
21 You are treating me cruelly;
you persecute me with all your
power.
22 You let the wind blow me away;
you toss me about in a raging
storm.
23 I know you are taking me off to
my death,
to the fate in store for everyone.
24 Why do you attack a ruined man,
one who can do nothing but beg
for pity?[j]
25 Didn't I weep with people in
trouble
and feel sorry for those in need?
26 I hoped for happiness and light,
but trouble and darkness came
instead.
27 I am torn apart by worry and
pain;
I have had day after day of
suffering.
28 I go about in gloom, without any
sunshine;
I stand up in public and plead
for help.
29 My voice is as sad and lonely
as the cries of a jackal or an
ostrich.
30 My skin has turned dark; I am
burning with fever.
31 Where once I heard joyful music,
now I hear only mourning and
weeping.

31 I have made a solemn promise
never to look with lust at a
woman.

2 What does Almighty God do to us?
How does he repay human
deeds?
3 He sends disaster and ruin
to those who do wrong.
4 God knows everything I do;
he sees every step I take.

5 I swear I have never acted
wickedly

[i] *Probable text* stop; *Hebrew* help. [j] *Verse 24 in Hebrew is unclear.*

and never tried to deceive
others.
6 Let God weigh me on honest
scales,
and he will see how innocent
I am.
7 If I have turned from the right
path
or let myself be attracted to evil,
if my hands are stained with sin,
8 then let my crops be destroyed,
or let others eat the food I grow.

9 If I have been attracted to my
neighbor's wife,
and waited, hidden, outside her
door,
10 then let my wife cook another
man's food
and sleep in another man's bed.
11 Such wickedness should be
punished by death.
12 It would be like a destructive,
hellish fire,
consuming everything I have.

13 When any of my servants
complained against me,
I would listen and treat them
fairly.
14 If I did not, how could I then
face God?
What could I say when God
came to judge me?
15 The same God who created me
created my servants also.

16 I have never refused to help the
poor;
never have I let widows live in
despair
17 or let orphans go hungry while
I ate.
18 All my life I have taken care of
them.[k]

19 When I found someone in need,
too poor to buy clothes,
20 I would give him clothing made
of wool
that had come from my own
flock of sheep.
Then he would praise me with all
his heart.

21 If I have ever cheated an orphan,
knowing I could win in court,
22 then may my arms be broken;
may they be torn from my
shoulders.
23 Because I fear God's punishment,
I could never do such a thing.

24 I have never trusted in riches
25 or taken pride in my wealth.
26 I have never worshiped the sun in
its brightness
or the moon in all its beauty.
27 I have not been led astray to
honor them
by kissing my hand in reverence
to them.
28 Such a sin should be punished by
death;
it denies Almighty God.

29 I have never been glad when my
enemies suffered,
or pleased when they met with
disaster;
30 I never sinned by praying for
their death.
31 All those who work for me know
that I have always welcomed
strangers.
32 I invited travelers into my home
and never let them sleep in the
streets.

33 Others try to hide their sins,
but I have never concealed mine.
34 I have never feared what people
would say;
I have never kept quiet or stayed
indoors
because I feared their scorn.

35 Will no one listen to what I am
saying?
I swear that every word is true.
Let Almighty God answer me.

If the charges my opponent brings
against me
were written down so that I
could see them,
36 I would wear them proudly on my
shoulder
and place them on my head like
a crown.
37 I would tell God everything I have
done,

[k] All my life . . . them; *Hebrew unclear.*

and hold my head high in his
presence.
38 If I have stolen the land I farm
and taken it from its rightful
owners—
39 if I have eaten the food that
grew there
but let the farmers that grew
it starve—
40 then instead of wheat and
barley,
may weeds and thistles grow.

The words of Job are ended.

The Speeches of Elihu

(32.1–37.24)

32 Because Job was convinced of
his own innocence, the three
men gave up trying to answer him. 2 But
a bystander named Elihu could not control his anger any longer, because Job
was justifying himself and blaming God.
(Elihu was the son of Barakel, a
descendant of Buz, and belonged to the
clan of Ram.) 3 He was also angry with
Job's three friends. They could not find
any way to answer Job, and this made it
appear that God was in the wrong. 4 Because Elihu was the youngest one there,
he had waited until everyone finished
speaking. 5 When he saw that the three
men could not answer Job, he was angry
6 and began to speak.

Elihu

I am young, and you are old,
so I was afraid to tell you what I
think.
7 I told myself that you ought to
speak,
that you older men should share
your wisdom.
8 But it is the spirit of Almighty God
that comes to us and gives us
wisdom.
9 It is not growing old that makes us
wise
or helps us to know what is
right.
10 So now I want you to listen to me;
let me tell you what I think.

11 I listened patiently while you were
speaking
and waited while you searched
for wise phrases.
12 I paid close attention and heard
you fail;
you have not disproved what
Job has said.
13 How can you claim you have
discovered wisdom?
God must answer Job, for you
have failed.
14 Job was speaking to you, not
to me,
but I would never answer the
way you did.

15 Words have failed them, Job;
they have no answer for you.
16 Shall I go on waiting when they
are silent?
They stand there with nothing
more to say.
17 No, I will give my own
answer now
and tell you what I think.
18 I can hardly wait to speak.
I can't hold back the words.
19 If I don't get a chance to speak,
I will burst like a wineskin full
of new wine.
20 I can't stand it; I have to speak.
21 I will not take sides in this debate;
I am not going to flatter anyone.
22 I don't know how to flatter,
and God would quickly punish
me if I did.

33 And now, Job, listen carefully
to all that I have to say.
2 I am ready to say what's on my
mind.
3 All my words are sincere,
and I am speaking the truth.
4 God's spirit made me and gave
me life.

5 Answer me if you can. Prepare
your arguments.
6 You and I are the same in God's
sight,
both of us were formed from
clay.
7 So you have no reason to fear me;
I will not overpower you.

8 Now this is what I heard you say:
9 "I am not guilty; I have done
nothing wrong.
I am innocent and free from sin.

10 But God finds excuses for
attacking me
and treats me like an enemy.
11 He binds chains on my feet;
he watches every move I make."

12 But I tell you, Job, you are wrong.
God is greater than any human
being.
13 Why do you accuse God
of never answering our
complaints?
14 Although God speaks again and
again,
no one pays attention to what he
says.
15 At night when people are asleep,
God speaks in dreams and
visions.
16 He makes them listen to what he
says,
and they are frightened at his
warnings.
17 God speaks to make them stop
their sinning
and to save them from becoming
proud.
18 He will not let them be destroyed;
he saves them from death itself.
19 God corrects us by sending
sickness
and filling our bodies with pain.
20 Those who are sick lose their
appetites,
and even the finest food looks
revolting.
21 Their bodies waste away to
nothing;
you can see all their bones;
22 they are about to go to the world
of the dead.

23 Perhaps an angel may come to
their aid—
one of God's thousands of
angels,
who remind us of our duty.
24 In mercy the angel will say,
"Release them!
They are not to go down to the
world of the dead.
Here is the ransom to set them
free."
25 Their bodies will grow young and
strong again;
26 when they pray, God will
answer;
they will worship God with joy;
God will set things right for
them again.
27 Each one will say in public, "I
have sinned.
I have not done right, but God
spared me.
28 He kept me from going to the
world of the dead,
and I am still alive."

29 God does all this again and again;
30 each one saves a person's life,
and gives him the joy of living.

31 Now, Job, listen to what I am
saying;
be quiet and let me speak.
32 But if you have something to say,
let me hear it;
I would gladly admit you are in
the right.
33 But if not, be quiet and listen
to me,
and I will teach you how to be
wise.

34

1-2 You men are so wise, so
clever;
listen now to what I am saying.
3 You know good food when you
taste it,
but not wise words when you
hear them.
4 It is up to us to decide the case.
5 Job claims that he is innocent,
that God refuses to give him
justice.
6 He asks, "How could I lie and say
I am wrong?
I am fatally wounded, but I am
sinless."

7 Have you ever seen anyone like
this man Job?
He never shows respect for God.
8 He likes the company of evil
people
and goes around with sinners.
9 He says that it never does any
good
to try to follow God's will.

10 Listen to me, you men who
understand!
Will Almighty God do what is
wrong?
11 He rewards people for what
they do

and treats them as they deserve.
12 Almighty God does not do evil;
he is never unjust to anyone.
13 Did God get his power from
someone else?
Did someone put him in charge
of the world?
14 If God took back the breath of life,
15 then everyone living would die
and turn into dust again.

16 Now listen to me, if you are wise.
17 Are you condemning the
righteous God?
Do you think that *he* hates
justice?
18 God condemns kings and rulers
when they are worthless or
wicked.
19 He does not take the side of rulers
nor favor the rich over the poor,
for he created everyone.
20 We may suddenly die at night.
God strikes us down and we
perish;
he kills the mighty with no
effort at all.
21 He watches every step we take.
22 There is no darkness dark enough
to hide a sinner from God.
23 God does not need to set a time[l]
for us to go and be judged
by him.
24 He does not need an investigation
to remove leaders and replace
them with others.
25 Because he knows what they do;
he overthrows them and crushes
them by night.
26 He punishes sinners where all can
see it,
27 because they have stopped
following him
and ignored all his commands.
28 They forced the poor to cry out
to God,
and he heard their calls for help.

29 If God decided to do nothing at all,
no one could criticize him.
If he hid his face, we would be
helpless.
30 There would be nothing that
nations could do
to keep godless oppressors from
ruling them.

[l] *Probable text* a time; *Hebrew* yet.

31 Job, have you confessed your sins
to God
and promised not to sin again?
32 Have you asked God to show you
your faults,
and have you agreed to stop
doing evil?
33 Since you object to what God
does,
can you expect him to do what
you want?
The decision is yours, not mine;
tell us now what you think.

34 Any sensible person will surely
agree;
and the wise who hear me
will say
35 that Job is speaking from
ignorance
and that nothing he says makes
sense.
36 Think through everything that Job
says;
you will see that he talks like an
evil man.
37 To his sins he adds rebellion;
in front of us all he mocks God.

35

1-2 It is not right, Job, for you
to say
that you are innocent in God's
sight,
3 or to ask God, "How does my sin
affect you?
What have I gained by not
sinning?"
4 I am going to answer you and
your friends too.

5 Look at the sky! See how high the
clouds are!
6 If you sin, that does no harm
to God.
If you do wrong many times,
does that affect him?
7 Do you help God by being so
righteous?
There is nothing God needs
from you.
8 Others suffer from your sins,
and the good you do helps them.

9 When people are oppressed, they
groan;

they cry for someone to save
them.
10 But they don't turn to God, their
Creator,
who gives them hope in their
darkest hours.
11 They don't turn to God, who
makes us wise,
wiser than any animal or bird.
12 They cry for help, but God doesn't
answer,
for they are proud and evil.
13 It is useless for them to cry out;
Almighty God does not see or
hear them.

14 Job, you say you can't see God;
but wait patiently—your case is
before him.
15 You think that God does not
punish,
that he pays little attention
to sin.
16 It is useless for you to go on
talking;
it is clear you don't know what
you are saying.

36

1-2 Be patient and listen a little
longer
to what I am saying on God's
behalf.
3 My knowledge is wide; I will use
what I know
to show that God, my Creator, is
just.
4 Nothing I say to you is false;
you see before you a truly
wise man.

5 How strong God is! He despises
no one;
there is nothing he doesn't
understand.
6 He does not let sinners live on,
and he always treats the poor
with justice.
7 He protects those who are
righteous;
he allows them to rule like kings
and lets them be honored
forever.
8 But if people are bound in chains,
suffering for what they have
done,
9 God shows them their sins and
their pride.
10 He makes them listen to his
warning
to turn away from evil.
11 If they obey God and serve him,
they live out their lives in peace
and prosperity.
12 But if not, they will die in
ignorance
and cross the stream into the
world of the dead.

13 Those who are godless keep on
being angry,
and even when punished, they
don't pray for help.
14 They die while they are still
young,
worn out by a life of disgrace.
15 But God teaches people through
suffering
and uses distress to open their
eyes.

16 God brought you out of trouble,
and let you enjoy security;
your table was piled high with
food.
17 But now you are being punished
as you deserve.
18 Be careful not to let bribes
deceive you,
or riches lead you astray.
19 It will do you no good to cry out
for help;
all your strength can't help
you now.
20 Don't wish for night to come,
the time when nations will
perish.
21 Be careful not to turn to evil;
your suffering was sent to keep
you from it.

22 Remember how great is God's
power;
he is the greatest teacher of all.
23 No one can tell God what to do
or accuse him of doing evil.
24 He has always been praised for
what he does;
you also must praise him.
25 Everyone has seen what he has
done;
but we can only watch from a
distance.[m]

[m] but we can only watch from a distance; *or* no one understands it all.

26 We cannot fully know his greatness
or count the number of his years.
27 It is God who takes water from the earth
and turns it into drops of rain.
28 He lets the rain pour from the clouds
in showers for all human beings.
29 No one knows how the clouds move
or how the thunder roars through the sky, where God dwells.
30 He sends lightning through all the sky,
but the depths of the sea remain dark.
31 This is how he feeds[n] the people
and provides an abundance of food.
32 He seizes the lightning with his hands
and commands it to hit the mark.
33 Thunder announces the approaching storm,
and the cattle know it is coming.

37 1 The storm makes my heart beat wildly.
2 Listen, all of you, to the voice of God,
to the thunder that comes from his mouth.
3 He sends the lightning across the sky,
from one end of the earth to the other.
4 Then the roar of his voice is heard,
the majestic sound of thunder,
and all the while the lightning flashes.
5 At God's command amazing things happen,
wonderful things that we can't understand.
6 He commands snow to fall on the earth,
and sends torrents of drenching rain.
7 He brings our work to a stop;
he shows us what he can do.[o]
8 The wild animals go to their dens.
9 The storm winds come from the south,
and the biting cold from the north.
10 The breath of God freezes the waters,
and turns them to solid ice.
11 Lightning flashes from the clouds,[p]
12 as they move at God's will.
They do all that God commands,
everywhere throughout the world.
13 God sends rain to water the earth;
he may send it to punish us,
or to show us his favor.

14 Pause a moment, Job, and listen;
consider the wonderful things God does.
15 Do you know how God gives the command
and makes lightning flash from the clouds?
16 Do you know how clouds float in the sky,
the work of God's amazing skill?
17 No, you can only suffer in the heat
when the south wind oppresses the land.
18 Can you help God stretch out the sky
and make it as hard as polished metal?
19 Teach us what to say to God;
our minds are blank; we have nothing to say.
20 I won't ask to speak with God;
why should I give him a chance to destroy me?

21 And now the light in the sky is dazzling,
too bright for us to look at it;
and the sky has been swept clean by the wind.
22 A golden glow is seen in the north,
and the glory of God fills us with awe.
23 God's power is so great that we cannot come near him;
he is righteous and just in his dealings with us.

[n] *Probable text* feeds; *Hebrew* judges. [o] *One ancient translation* us what he can do; *Hebrew* this to those whom he has made. [p] *Verse 11 in Hebrew is unclear.*

[24]No wonder, then, that everyone is
awed by him,
and that he ignores those who
claim to be wise.

The LORD Answers Job

38 Then out of the storm the LORD
spoke to Job.

The LORD

[2]Who are you to question my
wisdom
with your ignorant, empty
words?
[3]Now stand up straight
and answer the questions I
ask you.
[4]Were you there when I made the
world?
If you know so much, tell me
about it.
[5]Who decided how large it
would be?
Who stretched the measuring
line over it?
Do you know all the answers?
[6]What holds up the pillars that
support the earth?
Who laid the cornerstone of the
world?
[7]In the dawn of that day the stars
sang together,
and the heavenly beings[q]
shouted for joy.

[8]Who closed the gates to hold back
the sea[r]
when it burst from the womb of
the earth?
[9]It was I who covered the sea with
clouds
and wrapped it in darkness.
[10]I marked a boundary for the sea
and kept it behind bolted gates.
[11]I told it, "So far and no farther!
Here your powerful waves must
stop."
[12]Job, have you ever in all your life
commanded a day to dawn?
[13]Have you ordered the dawn to
seize the earth
and shake the wicked from their
hiding places?
[14]Daylight makes the hills and
valleys stand out
like the folds of a garment,
clear as the imprint of a seal on
clay.
[15]The light of day is too bright for
the wicked
and restrains them from doing
violence.

[16]Have you been to the springs in
the depths of the sea?
Have you walked on the floor of
the ocean?
[17]Has anyone ever shown you the
gates
that guard the dark world of the
dead?
[18]Have you any idea how big the
world is?
Answer me if you know.

[19]Do you know where the light
comes from
or what the source of
darkness is?
[20]Can you show them how far to go,
or send them back again?
[21]I am sure you can, because you're
so old
and were there when the world
was made!

[22]Have you ever visited the
storerooms,
where I keep the snow and the
hail?
[23]I keep them ready for times of
trouble,
for days of battle and war.
[24]Have you been to the place where
the sun comes up,
or the place from which the east
wind blows?

[25]Who dug a channel for the
pouring rain
and cleared the way for the
thunderstorm?
[26]Who makes rain fall where no one
lives?
[27]Who waters the dry and thirsty
land,
so that grass springs up?
[28]Does either the rain or the dew
have a father?
[29]Who is the mother of the ice and
the frost,
[30]which turn the waters to stone

[q] HEAVENLY BEINGS: *See* 1.6. [r] TO HOLD BACK THE SEA: *See* 26.12.

and freeze the face of the sea?

31 Can you tie the Pleiades together
or loosen the bonds that hold
Orion?
32 Can you guide the stars season by
season
and direct the Big and the Little
Dipper?
33 Do you know the laws that govern
the skies,
and can you make them apply to
the earth?

34 Can you shout orders to the clouds
and make them drench you with
rain?
35 And if you command the lightning
to flash,
will it come to you and say, "At
your service"?
36 Who tells the ibis[s] when the Nile
will flood,
or who tells the rooster that rain
will fall?[t]
37 Who is wise enough to count the
clouds
and tilt them over to pour out
the rain,
38 rain that hardens the dust into
lumps?

39 Do you find food for lions to eat,
and satisfy hungry young lions
40 when they hide in their caves,
or lie in wait in their dens?
41 Who is it that feeds the ravens
when they wander about
hungry,
when their young cry to me for
food?

39

1 Do you know when mountain
goats are born?
Have you watched wild deer
give birth?
2 Do you know how long they carry
their young?
Do you know the time for their
birth?
3 Do you know when they will
crouch down
and bring their young into the
world?
4 In the wilds their young grow
strong;
they go away and don't come
back.

5 Who gave the wild donkeys their
freedom?
Who turned them loose and let
them roam?
6 I gave them the desert to be their
home,
and let them live on the salt
plains.
7 They keep far away from the
noisy cities,
and no one can tame them and
make them work.
8 The mountains are the pastures
where they feed,
where they search for anything
green to eat.

9 Will a wild ox work for you?
Is he willing to spend the night
in your stable?
10 Can you hold one with a rope and
make him plow?
Or make him pull a harrow in
your fields?
11 Can you rely on his great strength
and expect him to do your heavy
work?
12 Do you expect him to bring in
your harvest
and gather the grain from your
threshing place?

13 How fast the wings of an ostrich
beat!
But no ostrich can fly like a
stork.[u]
14 The ostrich leaves her eggs on the
ground
for the heat in the soil to warm
them.
15 She is unaware that a foot may
crush them
or a wild animal break them.
16 She acts as if the eggs were not
hers,
and is unconcerned that her
efforts were wasted.
17 It was I who made her foolish
and did not give her wisdom.
18 But when she begins to run,[v]
she can laugh at any horse and
rider.

[s] IBIS: *A bird in ancient Egypt that was believed to announce the flooding of the Nile River.*
[t] *Verse 36 in Hebrew is unclear.* [u] *Verse 13 in Hebrew is unclear.* [v] *Probable text* run; *Hebrew unclear.*

19 Was it you, Job, who made horses
so strong
and gave them their flowing
manes?
20 Did you make them leap like
locusts
and frighten people with their
snorting?
21 They eagerly paw the ground in
the valley;
they rush into battle with all
their strength.
22 They do not know the meaning of
fear,
and no sword can turn them
back.
23 The weapons which their riders
carry
rattle and flash in the
sun.
24 Trembling with excitement, the
horses race ahead;
when the trumpet blows, they
can't stand still.
25 At each blast of the trumpet they
snort;
they can smell a battle before
they get near,
and they hear the officers
shouting commands.

26 Does a hawk learn from you how
to fly
when it spreads its wings toward
the south?
27 Does an eagle wait for your
command
to build its nest high in the
mountains?
28 It makes its home on the highest
rocks
and makes the sharp peaks its
fortress.
29 From there it watches near and
far
for something to kill and
eat.
30 Around dead bodies the eagles
gather,
and the young eagles drink the
blood.

40 1-2 Job, you challenged
Almighty God;
will you give up now, or will you
answer?

Job

3-4 I spoke foolishly, LORD. What can I
answer?
I will not try to say anything
else.
5 I have already said more than I
should.

6 Then out of the storm the LORD spoke
to Job once again.

The LORD

7 Now stand up straight,
and answer my questions.
8 Are you trying to prove that I am
unjust—
to put me in the wrong and
yourself in the right?
9 Are you as strong as I am?
Can your voice thunder as loud
as mine?
10 If so, stand up in your honor and
pride;
clothe yourself with majesty and
glory.
11 Look at those who are proud;
pour out your anger and humble
them.
12 Yes, look at them and bring them
down;
crush the wicked where they
stand.
13 Bury them all in the ground;
bind them in the world of the
dead.
14 Then I will be the first to
praise you
and admit that you won the
victory yourself.

15 Look at the monster Behemoth;[w]
I created him and I created you.
He eats grass like a cow,
16 but what strength there is in his
body,
and what power there is in his
muscles!
17 His tail stands up like a cedar,
and the muscles in his legs are
strong.
18 His bones are as strong as bronze,
and his legs are like iron bars.
19 The most amazing of all my
creatures!
Only his Creator can defeat him.

[w] BEHEMOTH: *Some identify this with the hippopotamus, others with a legendary creature.*

20 Grass to feed him grows
on the hills where wild beasts
play.[x]
21 He lies down under the thorn
bushes,
and hides among the reeds in
the swamp.
22 The thorn bushes and the willows
by the stream
give him shelter in their shade.
23 He is not afraid of a rushing river;
he is calm when the Jordan
dashes in his face.
24 Who can blind his eyes and
capture him?
Or who can catch his snout in a
trap?

41 Can you catch Leviathan[y] with
a fishhook
or tie his tongue down with a
rope?
2 Can you put a rope through his
snout
or put a hook through his jaws?
3 Will he beg you to let him go?
Will he plead with you for
mercy?
4 Will he make an agreement
with you
and promise to serve you
forever?
5 Will you tie him like a pet bird,
like something to amuse your
servant women?
6 Will fishermen bargain over him?
Will merchants cut him up to
sell?
7 Can you fill his hide with fishing
spears
or pierce his head with a
harpoon?
8 Touch him once and you'll never
try it again;
you'll never forget the fight!

9 Anyone who sees Leviathan
loses courage and falls to the
ground.
10 When he is aroused, he is fierce;
no one would dare to stand
before him.
11 Who can attack him and still be
safe?
No one in all the world can
do it.[z]

12 Let me tell you about Leviathan's
legs
and describe how great and
strong he is.
13 No one can tear off his outer coat
or pierce the armor[a] he wears.
14 Who can make him open his jaws,
ringed with those terrifying
teeth?
15 His back[b] is made of rows of
shields,
fastened together and hard as
stone.
16 Each one is joined so tight to the
next,
not even a breath can come
between.
17 They all are fastened so firmly
together
that nothing can ever pull them
apart.
18 Light flashes when he sneezes,
and his eyes glow like the
rising sun.
19 Flames blaze from his mouth,
and streams of sparks fly out.
20 Smoke comes pouring out of his
nose,
like smoke from weeds burning
under a pot.
21 His breath starts fires burning;
flames leap out of his mouth.
22 His neck is so powerful
that all who meet him are
terrified.
23 There is not a weak spot in his
skin;
it is as hard and unyielding as
iron.
24 His stony heart is without fear,
as unyielding and hard as a
millstone.
25 When he rises up, even the
strongest[c] are frightened;
they are helpless with fear.
26 There is no sword that can
wound him;
no spear or arrow or lance that
can harm him.
27 For him iron is as flimsy as straw,
and bronze as soft as rotten
wood.

[x] *Verse 20 in Hebrew is unclear.* [y] LEVIATHAN: *See 3.8.* [z] *Verse 11 in Hebrew is unclear.*
[a] *One ancient translation* armor; *Hebrew* bridle. [b] *Some ancient translations* back; *Hebrew* pride. [c] strongest; *or* gods.

[28]There is no arrow that can make
him run;
rocks thrown at him are like bits
of straw.
[29]To him a club is a piece of straw,
and he laughs when men throw
spears.
[30]The scales on his belly are like
jagged pieces of pottery;
they tear up the muddy ground
like a threshing sledge.[d]
[31]He churns up the sea like boiling
water
and makes it bubble like a pot
of oil.
[32]He leaves a shining path
behind him
and turns the sea to white foam.
[33]There is nothing on earth to
compare with him;
he is a creature that has no fear.
[34]He looks down on even the
proudest animals;
he is king of all wild beasts.

42

Then Job answered the LORD.

Job

[2]I know, LORD, that you are
all-powerful;
that you can do everything you
want.
[3]You ask how I dare question your
wisdom
when I am so very ignorant.
I talked about things I did not
understand,
about marvels too great for me
to know.
[4]You told me to listen while you
spoke
and to try to answer your
questions.
[5]In the past I knew only what
others had told me,
but now I have seen you with
my own eyes.
[6]So I am ashamed of all I have said
and repent in dust and ashes.

Conclusion

[7]After the LORD had finished speaking
to Job, he said to Eliphaz, "I am angry
with you and your two friends, because
you did not speak the truth about me,
the way my servant Job did. [8]Now take
seven bulls and seven rams to Job and
offer them as a sacrifice for yourselves.
Job will pray for you, and I will answer
his prayer and not disgrace you the way
you deserve. You did not speak the truth
about me as he did."
[9]Eliphaz, Bildad, and Zophar did what
the LORD had told them to do, and the
LORD answered Job's prayer.
[10]Then, after Job had prayed for his
three friends, the LORD made him prosperous again and gave him twice as
much as he had had before. [11]All Job's
brothers and sisters and former friends
came to visit him and feasted with him
in his house. They expressed their sympathy and comforted him for all the
troubles the LORD had brought on him.
Each of them gave him some money and
a gold ring.
[12]The LORD blessed the last part of
Job's life even more than he had blessed
the first. Job owned fourteen thousand
sheep, six thousand camels, two thousand head of cattle, and one thousand
donkeys. [13]He was the father of seven
sons and three daughters. [14]He called
the oldest daughter Jemimah, the second Keziah, and the youngest Keren
Happuch.[e] [15]There were no other
women in the whole world as beautiful
as Job's daughters. Their father gave
them a share of the inheritance along
with their brothers.
[16]Job lived a hundred and forty years
after this, long enough to see his grandchildren and great-grandchildren.
[17]And then he died at a very great age.

[d] THRESHING SLEDGES: *These had sharp pieces of iron or stone fastened beneath them.*
[e] *In Hebrew the names of Job's daughters suggest beauty both by their sound and by their meaning.* JEMIMAH *means "dove";* KEZIAH *means "cassia," a variety of cinnamon used as a perfume; and* KEREN HAPPUCH *means a small box used for eye make-up.*

PSALMS

Introduction

The book of Psalms is the hymnbook and prayer book of the Bible. Composed by different authors over a long period of time, these hymns and prayers were collected and used by the people of Israel in their worship, and eventually this collection was included in their Scriptures.

These religious poems are of many kinds: there are hymns of praise and worship of God; prayers for help, protection, and salvation; pleas for forgiveness; songs of thanksgiving for God's blessings; and petitions for the punishment of enemies. These prayers are both personal and national; some portray the most intimate feelings of one person, while others represent the needs and feelings of all the people of God.

The psalms were used by Jesus, quoted by the writers of the New Testament, and became the treasured book of worship of the Christian Church from its beginning.

Outline of Contents

The 150 psalms are grouped into five collections, or books, as follows:

BOOK ONE

(*Psalms 1–41*)

True Happiness

1 Happy are those
who reject the advice of evil people,
who do not follow the example of sinners
or join those who have no use for God.
2 Instead, they find joy in obeying the Law of the LORD,
and they study it day and night.
3 They are like trees that grow beside a stream,
that bear fruit at the right time,
and whose leaves do not dry up.
They succeed in everything they do.

4 But evil people are not like this at all;
they are like straw that the wind blows away.
5 Sinners will be condemned by God
and kept apart from God's own people.
6 The righteous are guided and protected by the LORD,
but the evil are on the way to their doom.

God's Chosen King

2 Why do the nations plan rebellion?
Why do people make their useless plots?
2 Their kings revolt,
their rulers plot together against the LORD
and against the king he chose.
3 "Let us free ourselves from their rule," they say;
"let us throw off their control."

4 From his throne in heaven the Lord laughs
and mocks their feeble plans.
5 Then he warns them in anger
and terrifies them with his fury.
6 "On Zion,[a] my sacred hill," he says,
"I have installed my king."

[a] ZION: *The term "Zion" (originally a designation for "David's City," the Jebusite stronghold captured by King David's forces) was later extended in meaning to refer to the hill on which the Temple stood.*

7 “I will announce,” says the king,
“what the LORD has declared.
He said to me: ‘You are my son;
today I have become your
father.
8 Ask, and I will give you all the
nations;
the whole earth will be yours.
9 You will break them with an
iron rod;
you will shatter them in pieces
like a clay pot.’ ”

10 Now listen to this warning, you
kings;
learn this lesson, you rulers of
the world:
11 Serve the LORD with fear;
tremble 12 and bow down
to him;[b]
or else his anger will be quickly
aroused,
and you will suddenly die.
Happy are all who go to him for
protection.

Morning Prayer for Help[c]

3 I have so many enemies, LORD,
so many who turn against me!
2 They talk about me and say,
“God will not help him.”

3 But you, O LORD, are always my
shield from danger;
you give me victory
and restore my courage.
4 I call to the LORD for help,
and from his sacred hill[d] he
answers me.

5 I lie down and sleep,
and all night long the LORD
protects me.
6 I am not afraid of the thousands of
enemies
who surround me on every side.

7 Come, LORD! Save me, my God!
You punish all my enemies
and leave them powerless to
harm me.
8 Victory comes from the LORD—
may he bless his people.

Evening Prayer for Help[e]

4 Answer me when I pray,
O God, my defender!
When I was in trouble, you
helped me.
Be kind to me now and hear my
prayer.

2 How long will you people
insult me?
How long will you love what is
worthless
and go after what is false?
3 Remember that the LORD has
chosen the righteous for
his own,
and he hears me when I call
to him.

4 Tremble with fear and stop
sinning;
think deeply about this,
when you lie in silence on your
beds.
5 Offer the right sacrifices to the
LORD,
and put your trust in him.

6 There are many who pray:
“Give us more blessings, O LORD.
Look on us with kindness!”
7 But the joy that you have
given me
is more than they will ever have
with all their grain and wine.

8 When I lie down, I go to sleep in
peace;
you alone, O LORD, keep me
perfectly safe.

A Prayer for Protection[e]

5 Listen to my words, O LORD,
and hear my sighs.
2 Listen to my cry for help,
my God and king!

I pray to you, O LORD;
3 you hear my voice in the
morning;
at sunrise I offer my prayer[f]
and wait for your answer.

[b] *Probable text* tremble . . . him; *some other possible texts* with trembling kiss his feet *and* with trembling kiss the Son *and* tremble and kiss the mighty one; *Hebrew unclear.*
[c] HEBREW TITLE: *A psalm by David, after he ran away from his son Absalom.* [d] SACRED HILL: *See 2.6.*
[e] HEBREW TITLE: *A psalm by David.* [f] prayer; *or* sacrifice.

4 You are not a God who is pleased
with wrongdoing;
you allow no evil in your
presence.
5 You cannot stand the sight of the
proud;
you hate all wicked people.
6 You destroy all liars
and despise violent, deceitful
people.
7 But because of your great love
I can come into your house;
I can worship in your holy Temple
and bow down to you in
reverence.
8 LORD, I have so many enemies!
Lead me to do your will;
make your way plain for me to
follow.

9 What my enemies say can never
be trusted;
they only want to destroy.
Their words are flattering and
smooth,
but full of deadly deceit.
10 Condemn and punish them,
O God;
may their own plots cause their
ruin.
Drive them out of your presence
because of their many sins
and their rebellion against you.

11 But all who find safety in you will
rejoice;
they can always sing for joy.
Protect those who love you;
because of you they are truly
happy.
12 You bless those who obey you,
LORD;
your love protects them like a
shield.

A Prayer for Help in Time of Trouble[g]

6 LORD, don't be angry and
rebuke me!
Don't punish me in your anger!
2 I am worn out, O LORD; have pity
on me!
Give me strength; I am
completely exhausted
3 and my whole being is deeply
troubled.
How long, O LORD, will you wait
to help me?

4 Come and save me, LORD;
in your mercy rescue me from
death.
5 In the world of the dead you are
not remembered;
no one can praise you there.

6 I am worn out with grief;
every night my bed is damp
from my weeping;
my pillow is soaked with tears.
7 I can hardly see;
my eyes are so swollen
from the weeping caused by my
enemies.

8 Keep away from me, you evil
people!
The LORD hears my weeping;
9 he listens to my cry for help
and will answer my prayer.
10 My enemies will know the bitter
shame of defeat;
in sudden confusion they will be
driven away.

A Prayer for Justice[h]

7 O LORD, my God, I come to you for
protection;
rescue me and save me from all
who pursue me,
2 or else like a lion they will carry
me off
where no one can save me,
and there they will tear me to
pieces.

3-4 O LORD, my God, if I have wronged
anyone,
if I have betrayed a friend
or without cause done violence
to my enemy[i]—
if I have done any of these
things—
5 then let my enemies pursue me
and catch me,
let them cut me down and
kill me

[g] HEBREW TITLE: *A psalm by David.* [h] HEBREW TITLE: *A song which David sang to the LORD because of Cush the Benjaminite.* [i] without cause done violence to my enemy; *or* shown mercy to someone who wronged me unjustly.

and leave me lifeless on the
ground!

6 Rise in your anger, O LORD!
Stand up against the fury of my
enemies;
rouse yourself and help me!
Justice is what you demand,
7 so bring together all the peoples
around you,
and rule over them from
above.[j]
8 You are the judge of all people.
Judge in my favor, O LORD;
you know that I am innocent.
9 You are a righteous God
and judge our thoughts and
desires.
Stop the wickedness of evildoers
and reward those who are good.

10 God is my protector;
he saves those who obey him.
11 God is a righteous judge
and always condemns the
wicked.
12 If they do not change their ways,
God will sharpen his sword.
He bends his bow and makes it
ready;
13 he takes up his deadly weapons
and aims his burning arrows.

14 See how wicked people think up
evil;
they plan trouble and practice
deception.
15 But in the traps they set for others,
they themselves get caught.
16 So they are punished by their own
evil
and are hurt by their own
violence.

17 I thank the LORD for his justice;
I sing praises to the LORD, the
Most High.

God's Glory and Human Dignity[k]

8 O LORD, our Lord,
your greatness is seen in all the
world!
Your praise reaches up to the
heavens;
2 it is sung by children and
babies.
You are safe and secure from all
your enemies;
you stop anyone who
opposes you.

3 When I look at the sky, which you
have made,
at the moon and the stars, which
you set in their places—
4 what are human beings, that you
think of them;
mere mortals, that you care for
them?

5 Yet you made them inferior only
to yourself;[l]
you crowned them with glory
and honor.
6 You appointed them rulers over
everything you made;
you placed them over all
creation:
7 sheep and cattle, and the wild
animals too;
8 the birds and the fish
and the creatures in the seas.

9 O LORD, our Lord,
your greatness is seen in all the
world!

Thanksgiving to God for His Justice[m]

9 I will praise you, LORD, with all my
heart;
I will tell of all the wonderful
things you have done.
2 I will sing with joy because of you.
I will sing praise to you,
Almighty God.

3 My enemies turn back when you
appear;
they fall down and die.
4 You are fair and honest in your
judgments,
and you have judged in my
favor.

5 You have condemned the heathen
and destroyed the wicked;

[j] *Probable text* rule over them from above; *Hebrew* return above over them.
[k] HEBREW TITLE: *A psalm by David.*
[l] yourself; *or* the gods, *or* the angels.
[m] HEBREW TITLE: *A psalm by David.*

they will be remembered no
more.
6 Our enemies are finished forever;
you have destroyed their cities,
and they are completely
forgotten.

7 But the LORD is king forever;
he has set up his throne for
judgment.
8 He rules the world with
righteousness;
he judges the nations with
justice.

9 The LORD is a refuge for the
oppressed,
a place of safety in times of
trouble.
10 Those who know you, LORD, will
trust you;
you do not abandon anyone who
comes to you.

11 Sing praise to the LORD, who rules
in Zion!
Tell every nation what he has
done!
12 God remembers those who suffer;
he does not forget their cry,
and he punishes those who
wrong them.

13 Be merciful to me, O LORD!
See the sufferings my enemies
cause me!
Rescue me from death, O LORD,
14 that I may stand before the
people of Jerusalem
and tell them all the things for
which I praise you.
I will rejoice because you
saved me.

15 The heathen have dug a pit and
fallen in;
they have been caught in their
own trap.
16 The LORD has revealed himself by
his righteous judgments,
and the wicked are trapped by
their own deeds.

17 Death is the destiny of all the
wicked,
of all those who reject God.
18 The needy will not always be
neglected;
the hope of the poor will not be
crushed forever.

19 Come, LORD! Do not let anyone
defy you!
Bring the heathen before you
and pronounce judgment on
them.
20 Make them afraid, O LORD;
make them know that they are
only mortal beings.

A Prayer for Justice

10 Why are you so far away,
O LORD?
Why do you hide yourself when
we are in trouble?
2 The wicked are proud and
persecute the poor;
catch them in the traps they
have made.

3 The wicked are proud of their evil
desires;
the greedy curse and reject the
LORD.
4 The wicked do not care about the
LORD;
in their pride they think that
God doesn't matter.

5 The wicked succeed in everything.
They cannot understand God's
judgments;
they sneer at their enemies.
6 They say to themselves, "We will
never fail;
we will never be in trouble."
7 Their speech is filled with curses,
lies, and threats;
they are quick to speak hateful,
evil words.

8 They hide themselves in the
villages,
waiting to murder innocent
people.
They spy on their helpless victims;
9 they wait in their hiding place
like lions.
They lie in wait for the poor;
they catch them in their traps
and drag them away.

10 The helpless victims lie crushed;
brute strength has defeated
them.

11 The wicked say to themselves,
"God doesn't care!
He has closed his eyes and will never see me!"

12 O LORD, punish those wicked people!
Remember those who are suffering!
13 How can the wicked despise God
and say to themselves, "He will not punish me"?

14 But you do see; you take notice of trouble and suffering
and are always ready to help.
The helpless commit themselves to you;
you have always helped the needy.

15 Break the power of wicked and evil people;
punish them for the wrong they have done
until they do it no more.

16 The LORD is king forever and ever.
Those who worship other gods will vanish from his land.

17 You will listen, O LORD, to the prayers of the lowly;
you will give them courage.
18 You will hear the cries of the oppressed and the orphans;
you will judge in their favor,
so that mortal men may cause terror no more.

Confidence in the LORD[n]

11 I trust in the LORD for safety.
How foolish of you to say to me,
"Fly away like a bird to the mountains,[o]
2 because the wicked have drawn their bows and aimed their arrows
to shoot from the shadows at good people.
3 There is nothing a good person can do
when everything falls apart."

4 The LORD is in his holy temple;
he has his throne in heaven.
He watches people everywhere
and knows what they are doing.
5 He examines the good and the wicked alike;
the lawless he hates with all his heart.

6 He sends down flaming coals[p]
and burning sulfur on the wicked;
he punishes them with scorching winds.
7 The LORD is righteous and loves good deeds;
those who do them will live in his presence.

A Prayer for Help[q]

12 Help us, LORD!
There is not a good person left;
honest people can no longer be found.
2 All of them lie to one another;
they deceive each other with flattery.

3 Silence those flattering tongues, O LORD!
Close those boastful mouths that say,
4 "With our words we get what we want.
We will say what we wish,
and no one can stop us."

5 "But now I will come," says the LORD,
"because the needy are oppressed
and the persecuted groan in pain.
I will give them the security they long for."

6 The promises of the LORD can be trusted;
they are as genuine as silver refined seven times in the furnace.

7-8 The wicked are everywhere,

[n] HEBREW TITLE: *By David.* [o] *Some ancient translations* like a bird to the mountains; *Hebrew* bird, to your *(plural)* mountain. [p] *One ancient translation* coals; *Hebrew* traps.
[q] HEBREW TITLE: *A psalm by David.*

and everyone praises what is
evil.
Keep us always safe, O LORD,
and preserve us from such
people.

A Prayer for Help[q]

13 How much longer will you
forget me, LORD? Forever?
How much longer will you hide
yourself from me?
2 How long must I endure trouble?
How long will sorrow fill my
heart day and night?
How long will my enemies
triumph over me?

3 Look at me, O LORD my God, and
answer me.
Restore my strength; don't let
me die.
4 Don't let my enemies say, "We
have defeated him."
Don't let them gloat over my
downfall.

5 I rely on your constant love;
I will be glad, because you will
rescue me.
6 I will sing to you, O LORD,
because you have been good
to me.

Human Wickedness[r]

(Psalm 53)

14 Fools say to themselves,
"There is no God!"
They are all corrupt,
and they have done terrible
things;
there is no one who does what is
right.

2 The LORD looks down from heaven
at us humans
to see if there are any who are
wise,
any who worship him.
3 But they have all gone wrong;
they are all equally bad.
Not one of them does what is
right,
not a single one.

4 "Don't they know?" asks the LORD.
"Are all these evildoers
ignorant?
They live by robbing my people,
and they never pray to me."

5 But then they will be terrified,
for God is with those who
obey him.
6 Evildoers frustrate the plans of the
humble,
but the LORD is their protection.

7 How I pray that victory
will come to Israel from Zion.
How happy the people of Israel
will be
when the LORD makes them
prosperous again!

What God Requires[s]

15 LORD, who may enter your
Temple?
Who may worship on Zion, your
sacred hill?[t]

2 Those who obey God in everything
and always do what is right,
whose words are true and sincere,
3 and who do not slander others.
They do no wrong to their friends
nor spread rumors about their
neighbors.
4 They despise those whom God
rejects,
but honor those who obey the
LORD.
They always do what they
promise,
no matter how much it may cost.
5 They make loans without charging
interest
and cannot be bribed to testify
against the innocent.

Whoever does these things will
always be secure.

A Prayer of Confidence[u]

16 Protect me, O God; I trust in
you for safety.
2 I say to the LORD, "You are my
Lord;
all the good things I have come
from you."

[q] HEBREW TITLE: *A psalm by David.* [r] HEBREW TITLE: *By David.* [s] HEBREW TITLE: *A psalm by David.*
[t] SACRED HILL: *See 2.6.* [u] HEBREW TITLE: *A psalm by David.*

3 How excellent are the LORD's
faithful people!
My greatest pleasure is to be
with them.

4 Those who rush to other gods
bring many troubles on
themselves.[v]
I will not take part in their
sacrifices;
I will not worship their gods.

5 You, LORD, are all I have,
and you give me all I need;
my future is in your hands.
6 How wonderful are your gifts
to me;
how good they are!

7 I praise the LORD, because he
guides me,
and in the night my conscience
warns me.
8 I am always aware of the LORD's
presence;
he is near, and nothing can
shake me.

9 And so I am thankful and glad,
and I feel completely secure,
10 because you protect me from the
power of death.
I have served you faithfully,
and you will not abandon me to
the world of the dead.

11 You will show me the path that
leads to life;
your presence fills me with joy
and brings me pleasure
forever.

The Prayer of an Innocent Person[w]

17 Listen, O LORD, to my plea for
justice;
pay attention to my cry
for help!
Listen to my honest prayer.
2 You will judge in my favor,
because you know what is right.

3 You know my heart.
You have come to me at night;
you have examined me
completely
and found no evil desire
in me.
I speak no evil, 4 as others do;
I have obeyed your command
and have not followed paths of
violence.
5 I have always walked in
your way
and have never strayed from it.

6 I pray to you, O God, because you
answer me;
so turn to me and listen to my
words.
7 Reveal your wonderful love and
save me;
at your side I am safe from my
enemies.

8 Protect me as you would your very
eyes;
hide me in the shadow of your
wings
9 from the attacks of the wicked.

Deadly enemies surround me;
10 they have no pity and speak
proudly.
11 They are around me now,
wherever I turn,
watching for a chance to pull me
down.
12 They are like lions, waiting
for me,
wanting to tear me to pieces.

13 Come, LORD! Oppose my enemies
and defeat them!
Save me from the wicked by your
sword;
14 save me from those who in this
life have all they want.
Punish them with the sufferings
you have stored up
for them;
may there be enough for their
children
and some left over for their
children's children!

15 But I will see you, because I have
done no wrong;
and when I awake, your
presence will fill me
with joy.

[v] *Probable text* Those . . . themselves; *Hebrew unclear.* [w] HEBREW TITLE: *A prayer by David.*

David's Song of Victory[x]

(2 Samuel 22.1-51)

18 How I love you, LORD!
You are my defender.

2 The LORD is my protector;
he is my strong fortress.
My God is my protection,
and with him I am safe.
He protects me like a shield;
he defends me and keeps me safe.
3 I call to the LORD,
and he saves me from my enemies.
Praise the LORD!

4 The danger of death was all around me;
the waves of destruction rolled over me.
5 The danger of death was around me,
and the grave set its trap for me.
6 In my trouble I called to the LORD;
I called to my God for help.
In his temple he heard my voice;
he listened to my cry for help.

7 Then the earth trembled and shook;
the foundations of the mountains rocked and quivered,
because God was angry.
8 Smoke poured out of his nostrils,
a consuming flame and burning coals from his mouth.
9 He tore the sky open and came down
with a dark cloud under his feet.
10 He flew swiftly on his winged creature;[y]
he traveled on the wings of the wind.
11 He covered himself with darkness;
thick clouds, full of water, surrounded him.
12 Hailstones and flashes of fire
came from the lightning before him
and broke through the dark clouds.

13 Then the LORD thundered from the sky;
and the voice of the Most High was heard.[z]
14 He shot his arrows and scattered his enemies;
with flashes of lightning he sent them running.
15 The floor of the ocean was laid bare,
and the foundations of the earth were uncovered,
when you rebuked your enemies, LORD,
and roared at them in anger.

16 The LORD reached down from above and took hold of me;
he pulled me out of the deep waters.
17 He rescued me from my powerful enemies
and from all those who hate me—
they were too strong for me.
18 When I was in trouble, they attacked me,
but the LORD protected me.
19 He helped me out of danger;
he saved me because he was pleased with me.

20 The LORD rewards me because I do what is right;
he blesses me because I am innocent.
21 I have obeyed the law of the LORD;
I have not turned away from my God.
22 I have observed all his laws;
I have not disobeyed his commands.
23 He knows that I am faultless,
that I have kept myself from doing wrong.
24 And so he rewards me because I do what is right,
because he knows that I am innocent.

25 O LORD, you are faithful to those who are faithful to you;
completely good to those who are perfect.

[x] HEBREW TITLE: *The words that David, the LORD's servant, sang to the LORD on the day the LORD saved him from Saul and all his other enemies.* [y] WINGED CREATURE: *See Word List.*
[z] *One ancient translation (and see 2 S 22.14)* was heard; *Hebrew* was heard hailstones and flashes of fire.

26 You are pure to those who are
pure,
but hostile to those who are
wicked.
27 You save those who are humble,
but you humble those who are
proud.

28 O LORD, you give me light;
you dispel my darkness.
29 You give me strength to attack
my enemies
and power to overcome their
defenses.

30 This God—how perfect are his
deeds!
How dependable his words!
He is like a shield
for all who seek his protection.
31 The LORD alone is God;
God alone is our defense.
32 He is the God who makes me
strong,
who makes my pathway safe.
33 He makes me sure-footed as a
deer;
he keeps me safe on the
mountains.
34 He trains me for battle,
so that I can use the
strongest bow.

35 O LORD, you protect me and
save me;
your care has made me great,
and your power has kept me
safe.
36 You have kept me from being
captured,
and I have never fallen.
37 I pursue my enemies and catch
them;
I do not stop until I destroy
them.
38 I strike them down, and they
cannot rise;
they lie defeated before me.
39 You give me strength for the battle
and victory over my enemies.
40 You make my enemies run
from me;
I destroy those who hate me.
41 They cry for help, but no one
saves them;
they call to the LORD, but he does
not answer.
42 I crush them, so that they become
like dust
which the wind blows away.
I trample on them like mud in the
streets.

43 You saved me from a rebellious
people
and made me ruler over the
nations;
people I did not know have now
become my subjects.
44 Foreigners bow before me;
when they hear me, they obey.
45 They lose their courage
and come trembling from their
fortresses.

46 The LORD lives! Praise my
defender!
Proclaim the greatness of the
God who saves me.
47 He gives me victory over my
enemies;
he subdues the nations under me
48 and saves me from my foes.

O LORD, you give me victory over
my enemies
and protect me from violent
people.
49 And so I praise you among the
nations;
I sing praises to you.

50 God gives great victories to his
king;
he shows constant love to the
one he has chosen,
to David and his descendants
forever.

God's Glory in Creation[a]

19 How clearly the sky reveals
God's glory!
How plainly it shows what he
has done!
2 Each day announces it to the
following day;
each night repeats it to the next.
3 No speech or words are used,
no sound is heard;
4 yet their message[b] goes out to all
the world

[a] HEBREW TITLE: *A psalm by David.* [b] *Some ancient translations* message; *Hebrew* line.

and is heard to the ends of the
earth.
God made a home in the sky for
the sun;
5 it comes out in the morning like
a happy bridegroom,
like an athlete eager to run a
race.
6 It starts at one end of the sky
and goes across to the other.
Nothing can hide from its heat.

The Law of the Lord

7 The law of the Lord is perfect;
it gives new strength.
The commands of the Lord are
trustworthy,
giving wisdom to those who
lack it.
8 The laws of the Lord are right,
and those who obey them are
happy.
The commands of the Lord are
just
and give understanding to the
mind.
9 Reverence for the Lord is good;
it will continue forever.
The judgments of the Lord are
just;
they are always fair.
10 They are more desirable than the
finest gold;
they are sweeter than the purest
honey.
11 They give knowledge to me, your
servant;
I am rewarded for obeying them.

12 None of us can see our own
errors;
deliver me, Lord, from hidden
faults!
13 Keep me safe, also, from willful
sins;
don't let them rule over me.
Then I shall be perfect
and free from the evil of sin.

14 May my words and my thoughts
be acceptable to you,
O Lord, my refuge and my
redeemer!

A Prayer for Victory[c]

20 May the Lord answer you when
you are in trouble!
May the God of Jacob
protect you!
2 May he send you help from his
Temple
and give you aid from Mount
Zion.
3 May he accept all your offerings
and be pleased with all your
sacrifices.
4 May he give you what you desire
and make all your plans
succeed.
5 Then we will shout for joy over
your victory
and celebrate your triumph by
praising our God.
May the Lord answer all your
requests.

6 Now I know that the Lord gives
victory to his chosen king;
he answers him from his holy
heaven
and by his power gives him
great victories.
7 Some trust in their war chariots
and others in their horses,
but we trust in the power of the
Lord our God.
8 Such people will stumble and fall,
but we will rise and stand firm.

9 Give victory to the king, O Lord;
answer[d] us when we call.

Praise for Victory[e]

21 The king is glad, O Lord,
because you gave him
strength;
he rejoices because you made
him victorious.
2 You have given him his heart's
desire;
you have answered his request.

3 You came to him with great
blessings
and set a crown of gold on his
head.
4 He asked for life, and you gave it,
a long and lasting life.

[c] HEBREW TITLE: *A psalm by David.* [d] *Some ancient translations* answer; *Hebrew* he will answer.
[e] HEBREW TITLE: *A psalm by David.*

5 His glory is great because of your
help;
you have given him fame and
majesty.
6 Your blessings are with him
forever,
and your presence fills him
with joy.

7 The king trusts in the LORD
Almighty;
and because of the LORD's
constant love
he will always be secure.
8 The king will capture all his
enemies;
he will capture everyone who
hates him.
9 He will destroy them like a blazing
fire
when he appears.

The LORD will devour them in his
anger,
and fire will consume them.
10 None of their descendants will
survive;
the king will kill them all.

11 They make their plans, and plot
against him,
but they will not succeed.
12 He will shoot his arrows at them
and make them turn and run.

13 We praise you, LORD, for your
great strength!
We will sing and praise your
power.

A Cry of Anguish and a Song of Praise[e]

22 My God, my God, why have
you abandoned me?
I have cried desperately for help,
but still it does not come.
2 During the day I call to you,
my God,
but you do not answer;
I call at night,
but get no rest.
3 But you are enthroned as the
Holy One,
the one whom Israel
praises.
4 Our ancestors put their trust
in you;
they trusted you, and you saved
them.
5 They called to you and escaped
from danger;
they trusted you and were not
disappointed.

6 But I am no longer a human
being; I am a worm,
despised and scorned by
everyone!
7 All who see me make fun of me;
they stick out their tongues and
shake their heads.
8 "You relied on the LORD,"
they say.
"Why doesn't he save you?
If the LORD likes you,
why doesn't he help you?"

9 It was you who brought me safely
through birth,
and when I was a baby, you
kept me safe.
10 I have relied on you since the day
I was born,
and you have always been
my God.
11 Do not stay away from me!
Trouble is near,
and there is no one to help.

12 Many enemies surround me like
bulls;
they are all around me,
like fierce bulls from the land of
Bashan.
13 They open their mouths like lions,
roaring and tearing at me.

14 My strength is gone,
gone like water spilled on the
ground.
All my bones are out of joint;
my heart is like melted wax.
15 My throat[f] is as dry as dust,
and my tongue sticks to the roof
of my mouth.
You have left me for dead in the
dust.

16 An evil gang is around me;
like a pack of dogs they close in
on me;

[e] HEBREW TITLE: *A psalm by David.* [f] *Probable text* throat; *Hebrew* strength.

they tear at[g] my hands and feet.
17 All my bones can be seen.
My enemies look at me and stare.
18 They gamble for my clothes
and divide them among themselves.

19 O LORD, don't stay away from me!
Come quickly to my rescue!
20 Save me from the sword;
save my life from these dogs.
21 Rescue me from these lions;
I am helpless[h] before these wild bulls.

22 I will tell my people what you have done;
I will praise you in their assembly:
23 "Praise him, you servants of the LORD!
Honor him, you descendants of Jacob!
Worship him, you people of Israel!
24 He does not neglect the poor or ignore their suffering;
he does not turn away from them,
but answers when they call for help."

25 In the full assembly I will praise you for what you have done;
in the presence of those who worship you
I will offer the sacrifices I promised.
26 The poor will eat as much as they want;
those who come to the LORD will praise him.
May they prosper forever!

27 All nations will remember the LORD.
From every part of the world they will turn to him;
all races will worship him.
28 The LORD is king,
and he rules the nations.
29 All proud people will bow down to him;[i]
all mortals will bow down before him.
30 Future generations will serve him;
they will speak of the Lord to the coming generation.
31 People not yet born will be told:
"The Lord saved his people."

The LORD Our Shepherd[j]

23 The LORD is my shepherd;
I have everything I need.
2 He lets me rest in fields of green grass
and leads me to quiet pools of fresh water.
3 He gives me new strength.
He guides me in the right paths,
as he has promised.
4 Even if I go through the deepest darkness,
I will not be afraid, LORD,
for you are with me.
Your shepherd's rod and staff protect me.

5 You prepare a banquet for me,
where all my enemies can see me;
you welcome me as an honored guest
and fill my cup to the brim.
6 I know that your goodness and love will be with me all my life;
and your house will be my home as long as I live.

The Great King[j]

24 The world and all that is in it belong to the LORD;
the earth and all who live on it are his.
2 He built it on the deep waters beneath the earth
and laid its foundations in the ocean depths.

3 Who has the right to go up the LORD's hill?[k]
Who may enter his holy Temple?

[g] *Some ancient translations* they tear at; *others* they tie; *Hebrew* like a lion.
[h] *Some ancient translations* I am helpless; *Hebrew* you answered me. [i] *Probable text* will bow down to him; *Hebrew* will eat and bow down. [j] HEBREW TITLE: *A psalm by David.*
[k] THE LORD'S HILL: *The hill in Jerusalem on which the Temple was built.*

4 Those who are pure in act and in thought,
who do not worship idols
or make false promises.
5 The LORD will bless them and save them;
God will declare them innocent.
6 Such are the people who come to God,
who come into the presence of the God of Jacob.

7 Fling wide the gates,
open the ancient doors,
and the great king will come in.
8 Who is this great king?
He is the LORD, strong and mighty,
the LORD, victorious in battle.

9 Fling wide the gates,
open the ancient doors,
and the great king will come in.
10 Who is this great king?
The triumphant LORD—he is the great king!

A Prayer for Guidance and Protection[l]

25 To you, O LORD, I offer my prayer;
2 in you, my God, I trust.
Save me from the shame of defeat;
don't let my enemies gloat over me!
3 Defeat does not come to those who trust in you,
but to those who are quick to rebel against you.

4 Teach me your ways, O LORD;
make them known to me.
5 Teach me to live according to your truth,
for you are my God, who saves me.
I always trust in you.
6 Remember, O LORD, your kindness and constant love
which you have shown from long ago.
7 Forgive the sins and errors of my youth.
In your constant love and goodness,
remember me, LORD!
8 Because the LORD is righteous and good,
he teaches sinners the path they should follow.
9 He leads the humble in the right way
and teaches them his will.
10 With faithfulness and love he leads
all who keep his covenant and obey his commands.

11 Keep your promise, LORD, and forgive my sins,
for they are many.
12 Those who have reverence for the LORD
will learn from him the path they should follow.
13 They will always be prosperous,
and their children will possess the land.
14 The LORD is the friend of those who obey him
and he affirms his covenant with them.

15 I look to the LORD for help at all times,
and he rescues me from danger.
16 Turn to me, LORD, and be merciful to me,
because I am lonely and weak.
17 Relieve me of my worries
and save me from all my troubles.
18 Consider my distress and suffering
and forgive all my sins.

19 See how many enemies I have;
see how much they hate me.
20 Protect me and save me;
keep me from defeat.
I come to you for safety.
21 May my goodness and honesty preserve me,
because I trust in you.

22 From all their troubles, O God,
save your people Israel!

The Prayer of a Good Person[l]

26 Declare me innocent, O LORD,
because I do what is right
and trust you completely.
2 Examine me and test me, LORD;

[l] HEBREW TITLE: *By David.*

judge my desires and thoughts.
3 Your constant love is my guide;
your faithfulness always
leads me.[m]

4 I do not keep company with
worthless people;
I have nothing to do with
hypocrites.
5 I hate the company of the evil
and avoid the wicked.

6 LORD, I wash my hands to show
that I am innocent
and march in worship around
your altar.
7 I sing a hymn of thanksgiving
and tell of all your wonderful
deeds.

8 I love the house where you live,
O LORD,
the place where your glory
dwells.
9 Do not destroy me with the
sinners;
spare me from the fate of
murderers—
10 those who do evil all the time
and are always ready to take
bribes.

11 As for me, I do what is right;
be merciful to me and
save me!

12 I am safe from all dangers;
in the assembly of his people I
praise the LORD.

A Prayer of Praise[n]

27 The LORD is my light and my
salvation;
I will fear no one.
The LORD protects me from all
danger;
I will never be afraid.

2 When evil people attack me and
try to kill me,
they stumble and fall.
3 Even if a whole army
surrounds me,
I will not be afraid;
even if enemies attack me,
I will still trust God.[o]

4 I have asked the LORD for one
thing;
one thing only do I want:
to live in the LORD's house all my
life,
to marvel there at his goodness,
and to ask for his guidance.
5 In times of trouble he will
shelter me;
he will keep me safe in his
Temple
and make me secure on a high
rock.
6 So I will triumph over my enemies
around me.
With shouts of joy I will offer
sacrifices in his Temple;
I will sing, I will praise the LORD.

7 Hear me, LORD, when I call to you!
Be merciful and answer me!
8 When you said, "Come
worship me,"
I answered, "I will come, LORD."
9 Don't hide yourself from me!

Don't be angry with me;
don't turn your servant away.
You have been my help;
don't leave me, don't
abandon me,
O God, my savior.
10 My father and mother may
abandon me,
but the LORD will take care
of me.

11 Teach me, LORD, what you want
me to do,
and lead me along a safe path,
because I have many
enemies.
12 Don't abandon me to my enemies,
who attack me with lies and
threats.

13 I know that I will live to see
the LORD's goodness in this
present life.
14 Trust in the LORD.
Have faith, do not despair.
Trust in the LORD.

[m] your faithfulness always leads me; *or* I live in loyalty to you.
[n] HEBREW TITLE: *By David.*
[o] still trust God; *or* not lose courage.

A Prayer for Help[p]

28 O LORD, my defender, I call
to you.
Listen to my cry!
If you do not answer me,
I will be among those who go
down to the world of the dead.
2 Hear me when I cry to you for
help,
when I lift my hands toward
your holy Temple.
3 Do not condemn me with the
wicked,
with those who do evil—
those whose words are friendly,
but who have hatred in their
hearts.

4 Punish them for what they have
done,
for the evil they have committed.
Punish them for all their deeds;
give them what they deserve!
5 They take no notice of what the
LORD has done
or of what he has made;
so he will punish them
and destroy them forever.

6 Give praise to the LORD;
he has heard my cry for help.
7 The LORD protects and defends me;
I trust in him.
He gives me help and makes me
glad;
I praise him with joyful songs.

8 The LORD protects his people;
he defends and saves his chosen
king.
9 Save your people, LORD,
and bless those who are yours.
Be their shepherd,
and take care of them forever.

The Voice of the LORD in the Storm[q]

29 Praise the LORD, you heavenly
beings;
praise his glory and power.
2 Praise the LORD's glorious name;
bow down before the Holy One
when he appears.[r]

3 The voice of the LORD is heard on
the seas;
the glorious God thunders,
and his voice echoes over the
ocean.
4 The voice of the LORD is heard
in all its might and majesty.

5 The voice of the LORD breaks the
cedars,
even the cedars of Lebanon.
6 He makes the mountains of
Lebanon jump like calves
and makes Mount Hermon leap
like a young bull.

7 The voice of the LORD makes the
lightning flash.
8 His voice makes the desert shake;
he shakes the desert of Kadesh.
9 The LORD's voice shakes the oaks[s]
and strips the leaves from the
trees
while everyone in his Temple
shouts, "Glory to God!"

10 The LORD rules over the deep
waters;
he rules as king forever.
11 The LORD gives strength to his
people
and blesses them with peace.

A Prayer of Thanksgiving[t]

30 I praise you, LORD, because you
have saved me
and kept my enemies from
gloating over me.
2 I cried to you for help, O LORD
my God,
and you healed me;
3 you kept me from the grave.
I was on my way to the depths
below,[u]
but you restored my life.

4 Sing praise to the LORD,
all his faithful people!
Remember what the Holy One has
done,
and give him thanks!
5 His anger lasts only a moment,
his goodness for a lifetime.
Tears may flow in the night,

[p] HEBREW TITLE: *By David.* [q] HEBREW TITLE: *A psalm by David.* [r] when he appears; *or* in garments of worship; *or* in his beautiful Temple. [s] *Probable text* shakes the oaks; *Hebrew* makes the deer give birth. [t] HEBREW TITLE: *A song for the dedication of the Temple; a psalm by David.* [u] THE DEPTHS BELOW: *The world of the dead (see 6.5).*

but joy comes in the morning.

6 I felt secure and said to myself,
"I will never be defeated."
7 You were good to me, LORD;
you protected me like a
mountain fortress.
But then you hid yourself
from me,
and I was afraid.

8 I called to you, LORD;
I begged for your help:
9 "What will you gain from my
death?
What profit from my going to
the grave?
Are dead people able to
praise you?
Can they proclaim your
unfailing goodness?
10 Hear me, LORD, and be merciful!
Help me, LORD!"

11 You have changed my sadness
into a joyful dance;
you have taken away my sorrow
and surrounded me with joy.
12 So I will not be silent;
I will sing praise to you.
LORD, you are my God;
I will give you thanks forever.

A Prayer of Trust in God[v]

31 I come to you, LORD, for
protection;
never let me be defeated.
You are a righteous God;
save me, I pray!
2 Hear me! Save me now!
Be my refuge to protect me;
my defense to save me.

3 You are my refuge and defense;
guide me and lead me as you
have promised.
4 Keep me safe from the trap that
has been set for me;
shelter me from danger.
5 I place myself in your care.
You will save me, LORD;
you are a faithful God.

6 You hate those who worship false
gods,
but I trust in you.
7 I will be glad and rejoice
because of your constant love.
You see my suffering;
you know my trouble.
8 You have not let my enemies
capture me;
you have given me freedom to
go where I wish.

9 Be merciful to me, LORD,
for I am in trouble;
my eyes are tired from so much
crying;
I am completely worn out.
10 I am exhausted by sorrow,
and weeping has shortened my
life.
I am weak from all my troubles;[w]
even my bones are wasting
away.

11 All my enemies, and especially my
neighbors,
treat me with contempt.
Those who know me are afraid
of me;
when they see me in the street,
they run away.
12 Everyone has forgotten me, as
though I were dead;
I am like something thrown
away.
13 I hear many enemies whispering;
terror is all around me.
They are making plans
against me,
plotting to kill me.

14 But my trust is in you, O LORD;
you are my God.
15 I am always in your care;
save me from my enemies,
from those who persecute me.
16 Look on your servant with
kindness;
save me in your constant love.
17 I call to you, LORD;
don't let me be disgraced.
May the wicked be disgraced;
may they go silently down to the
world of the dead.
18 Silence those liars—
all the proud and arrogant
who speak with contempt about
the righteous.

[v] HEBREW TITLE: *A psalm by David.* [w] *Some ancient translations* troubles; *Hebrew* iniquity.

19 How wonderful are the good
things
you keep for those who
honor you!
Everyone knows how good
you are,
how securely you protect those
who trust you.
20 You hide them in the safety of
your presence
from the plots of others;
in a safe shelter you hide them
from the insults of their enemies.

21 Praise the LORD!
How wonderfully he showed his
love for me
when I was surrounded and
attacked!
22 I was afraid and thought
that he had driven me out of his
presence.
But he heard my cry,
when I called to him for help.

23 Love the LORD, all his faithful
people.
The LORD protects the faithful,
but punishes the proud as they
deserve.
24 Be strong, be courageous,
all you that hope in the LORD.

Confession and Forgiveness[x]

32 Happy are those whose sins are
forgiven,
whose wrongs are pardoned.
2 Happy is the one whom the LORD
does not accuse of doing
wrong
and who is free from all deceit.

3 When I did not confess my sins,
I was worn out from crying all
day long.
4 Day and night you punished me,
LORD;
my strength was completely
drained,
as moisture is dried up by the
summer heat.

5 Then I confessed my sins to you;
I did not conceal my
wrongdoings.
I decided to confess them to you,
and you forgave all my sins.

6 So all your loyal people should
pray to you in times of need;[y]
when a great flood of trouble
comes rushing in,
it will not reach them.
7 You are my hiding place;
you will save me from trouble.
I sing aloud of your salvation,
because you protect me.

8 The LORD says, "I will teach you
the way you should go;
I will instruct you and
advise you.
9 Don't be stupid like a horse or a
mule,
which must be controlled with a
bit and bridle
to make it submit."

10 The wicked will have to suffer,
but those who trust in the LORD
are protected by his constant
love.
11 You that are righteous, be glad
and rejoice
because of what the LORD has
done.
You that obey him, shout for joy!

A Song of Praise

33 All you that are righteous,
shout for joy for what the
LORD has done;
praise him, all you that
obey him.
2 Give thanks to the LORD with
harps,
sing to him with stringed
instruments.
3 Sing a new song to him,
play the harp with skill, and
shout for joy!

4 The words of the LORD are true,
and all his works are
dependable.
5 The LORD loves what is righteous
and just;
his constant love fills the earth.
6 The LORD created the heavens by
his command,

[x] HEBREW TITLE: *A poem by David.* [y] *Some ancient translations* need; *Hebrew* finding only.

the sun, moon, and stars by his
spoken word.
7 He gathered all the seas into one
place;
he shut up the ocean depths in
storerooms.

8 Worship the LORD, all the earth!
Honor him, all peoples of the
world!
9 When he spoke, the world was
created;
at his command everything
appeared.

10 The LORD frustrates the purposes
of the nations;
he keeps them from carrying out
their plans.
11 But his plans endure forever;
his purposes last eternally.
12 Happy is the nation whose God is
the LORD;
happy are the people he has
chosen for his own!

13 The LORD looks down from
heaven
and sees all of us humans.
14 From where he rules, he looks
down
on all who live on earth.
15 He forms all their thoughts
and knows everything they do.

16 A king does not win because of
his powerful army;
a soldier does not triumph
because of his strength.
17 War horses are useless for
victory;
their great strength cannot save.

18 The LORD watches over those who
obey him,
those who trust in his constant
love.
19 He saves them from death;
he keeps them alive in times of
famine.

20 We put our hope in the LORD;
he is our protector and our help.
21 We are glad because of him;
we trust in his holy name.

22 May your constant love be with
us, LORD,
as we put our hope in you.

In Praise of God's Goodness[z]

34 I will always thank the LORD;
I will never stop praising him.
2 I will praise him for what he has
done;
may all who are oppressed listen
and be glad!
3 Proclaim with me the LORD's
greatness;
let us praise his name together!

4 I prayed to the LORD, and he
answered me;
he freed me from all my fears.
5 The oppressed look to him and are
glad;
they will never be disappointed.
6 The helpless call to him, and he
answers;
he saves them from all their
troubles.
7 His angel guards those who honor
the LORD
and rescues them from danger.

8 Find out for yourself how good the
LORD is.
Happy are those who find safety
with him.
9 Honor the LORD, all his people;
those who obey him have all
they need.
10 Even lions go hungry for lack of
food,
but those who obey the LORD
lack nothing good.

11 Come, my young friends, and
listen to me,
and I will teach you to honor the
LORD.
12 Would you like to enjoy life?
Do you want long life and
happiness?
13 Then keep from speaking evil
and from telling lies.
14 Turn away from evil and do good;
strive for peace with all your
heart.

[z] HEBREW TITLE: *By David, who left the presence of Abimelech after pretending to be crazy and being sent away by him.*

15 The LORD watches over the
righteous
and listens to their cries;
16 but he opposes those who do evil,
so that when they die, they are
soon forgotten.
17 The righteous call to the LORD, and
he listens;
he rescues them from all their
troubles.
18 The LORD is near to those who are
discouraged;
he saves those who have lost all
hope.

19 Good people suffer many troubles,
but the LORD saves them from
them all;
20 the LORD preserves them
completely;
not one of their bones is broken.
21 Evil will kill the wicked;
those who hate the righteous
will be punished.

22 The LORD will save his people;
those who go to him for
protection will be spared.

A Prayer for Help[a]

35 Oppose those who oppose me,
LORD,
and fight those who fight
against me!
2 Take your shield and armor
and come to my rescue.
3 Lift up your spear and war ax
against those who pursue me.
Promise that you will save me.

4 May those who try to kill me
be defeated and disgraced!
May those who plot against me
be turned back and confused!
5 May they be like straw blown by
the wind
as the angel of the LORD pursues
them!
6 May their path be dark and
slippery
while the angel of the LORD
strikes them down!

7 Without any reason they laid a
trap for me
and dug a deep hole to
catch me.
8 But destruction will catch them
before they know it;
they will be caught in their own
trap
and fall to their destruction!

9 Then I will be glad because of the
LORD;
I will be happy because he
saved me.
10 With all my heart I will say to the
LORD,
"There is no one like you.
You protect the weak from the
strong,
the poor from the oppressor."

11 Evil people testify against me
and accuse me of crimes I know
nothing about.
12 They pay me back evil for good,
and I sink in despair.
13 But when they were sick, I dressed
in mourning;
I deprived myself of food;
I prayed with my head bowed low,
14 as I would pray for a friend or a
brother.
I went around bent over in
mourning,
as one who mourns for his
mother.

15 But when I was in trouble, they
were all glad
and gathered around to make
fun of me;
strangers beat me
and kept striking me.
16 Like those who would mock a
cripple,[b]
they glared at me with hate.

17 How much longer, Lord, will you
just look on?
Rescue me from their attacks;
save my life from these lions!
18 Then I will thank you in the
assembly of your people;
I will praise you before them all.

19 Don't let my enemies, those liars,
gloat over my defeat.

[a] HEBREW TITLE: *By David.* [b] *Probable text* Like those . . . cripple; *Hebrew unclear.*

Don't let those who hate me for no
reason
smirk with delight over my
sorrow.
20 They do not speak in a
friendly way;
instead they invent all kinds of
lies about peace-loving people.
21 They accuse me, shouting,
"We saw what you did!"
22 But you, O LORD, have seen this.
So don't be silent, Lord;
don't keep yourself far away!
23 Rouse yourself, O Lord, and
defend me;
rise up, my God, and plead my
cause.
24 You are righteous, O LORD, so
declare me innocent;
don't let my enemies gloat
over me.
25 Don't let them say to themselves,
"We are rid of him!
That's just what we wanted!"

26 May those who gloat over my
suffering
be completely defeated and
confused;
may those who claim to be better
than I am
be covered with shame and
disgrace.

27 May those who want to see me
acquitted
shout for joy and say again and
again,
"How great is the LORD!
He is pleased with the success of
his servant."
28 Then I will proclaim your
righteousness,
and I will praise you all day
long.

Human Wickedness[c]

36 Sin speaks to the wicked deep
in their hearts;
they reject God and do not have
reverence for him.
2 Because they think so highly of
themselves,
they think that God will not
discover their sin and
condemn it.
3 Their speech is wicked and full of
lies;
they no longer do what is wise
and good.
4 They make evil plans as they lie
in bed;
nothing they do is good,
and they never reject anything
evil.

The Goodness of God

5 LORD, your constant love reaches
the heavens;
your faithfulness extends to the
skies.
6 Your righteousness is towering
like the mountains;
your justice is like the depths of
the sea.
People and animals are in your
care.

7 How precious, O God, is your
constant love!
We find[d] protection under the
shadow of your wings.
8 We feast on the abundant food
you provide;
you let us drink from the river
of your goodness.
9 You are the source of all life,
and because of your light we see
the light.

10 Continue to love those who
know you
and to do good to those who are
righteous.
11 Do not let proud people attack me
or the wicked make me run
away.
12 See where evil people have fallen.
There they lie, unable to rise.

The Destiny of the Wicked and of the Good[e]

37 Don't be worried on account of
the wicked;
don't be jealous of those who do
wrong.

[c] HEBREW TITLE: *By David, the LORD's servant.* [d] precious, O God, is . . . find; *or* precious is your constant love! Gods and people find. [e] HEBREW TITLE: *By David.*

2 They will soon disappear like
grass that dries up;
they will die like plants that
wither.

3 Trust in the LORD and do good;
live in the land and be safe.
4 Seek your happiness in the LORD,
and he will give you your heart's
desire.

5 Give yourself to the LORD;
trust in him, and he will
help you;
6 he will make your righteousness
shine like the noonday sun.

7 Be patient and wait for the LORD
to act;
don't be worried about those
who prosper
or those who succeed in their
evil plans.

8 Don't give in to worry or anger;
it only leads to trouble.
9 Those who trust in the LORD will
possess the land,
but the wicked will be
driven out.

10 Soon the wicked will disappear;
you may look for them, but you
won't find them;
11 but the humble will possess the
land
and enjoy prosperity and peace.

12 The wicked plot against good
people
and glare at them with hate.
13 But the Lord laughs at wicked
people,
because he knows they will soon
be destroyed.

14 The wicked draw their swords and
bend their bows
to kill the poor and needy,
to slaughter those who do what
is right;
15 but they will be killed by their
own swords,
and their bows will be smashed.

16 The little that a good person owns
is worth more than the wealth of
all the wicked,
17 because the LORD will take away
the strength of the wicked,
but protect those who are good.

18 The LORD takes care of those who
obey him,
and the land will be theirs
forever.
19 They will not suffer when times
are bad;
they will have enough in time of
famine.
20 But the wicked will die;
the enemies of the LORD will
vanish like wild flowers;
they will disappear like smoke.

21 The wicked borrow and never pay
back,
but good people are generous
with their gifts.
22 Those who are blessed by the LORD
will possess the land,
but those who are cursed by him
will be driven out.

23 The LORD guides us in the way we
should go
and protects those who
please him.
24 If they fall, they will not stay
down,
because the LORD will help
them up.

25 I am old now; I have lived a long
time,
but I have never seen good
people abandoned by the LORD
or their children begging for
food.
26 At all times they give freely and
lend to others,
and their children are a blessing.

27 Turn away from evil and do good,
and your descendants will
always live in the land;
28 for the LORD loves what is right
and does not abandon his
faithful people.
He protects them forever,
but the descendants of the
wicked will be driven out.
29 The righteous will possess the land
and live in it forever.

30 The words of good people are
wise,
and they are always fair.
31 They keep the law of their God in
their hearts
and never depart from it.

32 Wicked people watch good people
and try to kill them;
33 but the LORD will not abandon
them to their enemy's power
or let them be condemned when
they are on trial.

34 Put your hope in the LORD and
obey his commands;
he will honor you by giving you
the land,
and you will see the wicked
driven out.

35 I once knew someone wicked who
was a tyrant;
he towered over everyone like a
cedar of Lebanon;[f]
36 but later I[g] passed by, and he
wasn't there;
I looked for him, but couldn't
find him.

37 Notice good people, observe the
righteous;
peaceful people have
descendants,
38 but sinners are completely
destroyed,
and their descendants are
wiped out.

39 The LORD saves the righteous
and protects them in times of
trouble.
40 He helps them and rescues them;
he saves them from the wicked,
because they go to him for
protection.

The Prayer of a Sufferer[h]

38 O LORD, don't punish me in
your anger!
2 You have wounded me with your
arrows;
you have struck me down.
3 Because of your anger, I am in
great pain;
my whole body is diseased
because of my sins.
4 I am drowning in the flood of my
sins;
they are a burden too heavy to
bear.

5 Because I have been foolish,
my sores stink and rot.
6 I am bent over, I am crushed;
I mourn all day long.
7 I am burning with fever
and I am near death.
8 I am worn out and utterly crushed;
my heart is troubled, and I
groan with pain.

9 O Lord, you know what I long for;
you hear all my groans.
10 My heart is pounding, my strength
is gone,
and my eyes have lost their
brightness.
11 My friends and neighbors will not
come near me,
because of my sores;
even my family keeps away
from me.
12 Those who want to kill me lay
traps for me,
and those who want to hurt me
threaten to ruin me;
they never stop plotting
against me.

13 I am like the deaf and cannot
hear,
like the dumb and cannot speak.
14 I am like those who do not
answer,
because they cannot hear.

15 But I trust in you, O LORD;
and you, O Lord my God, will
answer me.
16 Don't let my enemies gloat over
my distress;
don't let them boast about my
downfall!
17 I am about to fall
and am in constant pain.

18 I confess my sins;

[f] *One ancient translation* like a cedar of Lebanon; *Hebrew unclear.*
[g] *Some ancient translations* I; *Hebrew* he. [h] HEBREW TITLE: *A psalm by David; a lament.*

they fill me with anxiety.
19 My enemies are healthy and strong;
there are many who hate me for no reason.
20 Those who pay back evil for good are against me because I try to do right.

21 Do not abandon me, O LORD;
do not stay away, my God!
22 Help me now, O Lord my savior!

The Confession of a Sufferer[i]

39 I said, "I will be careful about what I do
and will not let my tongue make me sin;
I will not say anything
while evil people are near."
2 I kept quiet, not saying a word,
not even about anything good!
But my suffering only grew worse,
3 and I was overcome with anxiety.
The more I thought, the more troubled I became;
I could not keep from asking:
4 "LORD, how long will I live?
When will I die?
Tell me how soon my life will end."

5 How short you have made my life!
In your sight my lifetime seems nothing.
Indeed every living being is no more than a puff of wind,
6 no more than a shadow.
All we do is for nothing;
we gather wealth, but don't know who will get it.

7 What, then, can I hope for, Lord?
I put my hope in you.
8 Save me from all my sins,
and don't let fools make fun of me.
9 I will keep quiet, I will not say a word,
for you are the one who made me suffer like this.
10 Don't punish me any more!
I am about to die from your blows.
11 You punish our sins by your rebukes,
and like a moth you destroy what we love.
Indeed we are no more than a puff of wind!

12 Hear my prayer, LORD,
and listen to my cry;
come to my aid when I weep.
Like all my ancestors
I am only your guest for a little while.
13 Leave me alone so that I may have some happiness
before I go away and am no more.

A Song of Praise[i]

40 I waited patiently for the LORD's help;
then he listened to me and heard my cry.
2 He pulled me out of a dangerous pit,
out of the deadly quicksand.
He set me safely on a rock
and made me secure.
3 He taught me to sing a new song,
a song of praise to our God.
Many who see this will take warning
and will put their trust in the LORD.

4 Happy are those who trust the LORD,
who do not turn to idols
or join those who worship false gods.
5 You have done many things for us, O LORD our God;
there is no one like you!
You have made many wonderful plans for us.
I could never speak of them all—
their number is so great!

6 You do not want sacrifices and offerings;
you do not ask for animals burned whole on the altar
or for sacrifices to take away sins.
Instead, you have given me ears to hear you,

[i] HEBREW TITLE: *A psalm by David.*

7 and so I answered, "Here I am;
your instructions for me are in
the book of the Law.[j]
8 How I love to do your will,
my God!
I keep your teaching in my
heart."

9 In the assembly of all your people,
LORD,
I told the good news that you
save us.
You know that I will never stop
telling it.
10 I have not kept the news of
salvation to myself;
I have always spoken of your
faithfulness and help.
In the assembly of all your people
I have not been silent
about your loyalty and constant
love.

11 LORD, I know you will never stop
being merciful to me.
Your love and loyalty will
always keep me safe.

A Prayer for Help

(Psalm 70)

12 I am surrounded by many
troubles—
too many to count!
My sins have caught up with me,
and I can no longer see;
they are more than the hairs of
my head,
and I have lost my courage.
13 Save me, LORD! Help me now!
14 May those who try to kill me
be completely defeated and
confused.
May those who are happy because
of my troubles
be turned back and disgraced.
15 May those who make fun of me
be dismayed by their defeat.

16 May all who come to you
be glad and joyful.
May all who are thankful for your
salvation
always say, "How great is the
LORD!"

17 I am weak and poor, O Lord,
but you have not forgotten me.
You are my savior and my God—
hurry to my aid!

A Prayer in Sickness[k]

41 Happy are those who are
concerned for the poor;
the LORD will help them when
they are in trouble.
2 The LORD will protect them and
preserve their lives;
he will make them happy in the
land;
he will not abandon them to the
power of their enemies.
3 The LORD will help them when
they are sick
and will restore them to health.

4 I said, "I have sinned against you,
LORD;
be merciful to me and heal me."
5 My enemies say cruel things
about me.
They want me to die and be
forgotten.
6 Those who come to see me are not
sincere;
they gather bad news about me
and then go out and tell it
everywhere.
7 All who hate me whisper to each
other about me,
they imagine the worst
about[l] me.
8 They say, "He is fatally ill;
he will never leave his bed
again."
9 Even my best friend, the one I
trusted most,
the one who shared my food,
has turned against me.

10 Be merciful to me, LORD, and
restore my health,
and I will pay my enemies back.
11 They will not triumph over me,
and I will know that you are
pleased with me.
12 You will help me, because I do
what is right;
you will keep me in your
presence forever.

[j] your instructions . . . Law; *or* my devotion to you is recorded in your book.
[k] HEBREW TITLE: *A psalm by David.* [l] imagine the worst about; *or* make evil plans to harm.

13 Praise the LORD, the God of Israel!
Praise him now and forever!

Amen! Amen!

BOOK TWO

(Psalms 42–72)

The Prayer of Someone in Exile[m]

42 As a deer longs for a stream of cool water,
so I long for you, O God.
2 I thirst for you, the living God.
When can I go and worship in your presence?
3 Day and night I cry,
and tears are my only food;
all the time my enemies ask me,
"Where is your God?"

4 My heart breaks when I remember the past,
when I went with the crowds to the house of God
and led them as they walked along,
a happy crowd, singing and shouting praise to God.
5 Why am I so sad?
Why am I so troubled?
I will put my hope in God,
and once again I will praise him,
my savior and my God.

6-7 Here in exile my heart is breaking,
and so I turn my thoughts to him.
He has sent waves of sorrow over my soul;
chaos roars at me like a flood,
like waterfalls thundering down to the Jordan
from Mount Hermon and Mount Mizar.
8 May the LORD show his constant love during the day,
so that I may have a song at night,
a prayer to the God of my life.

9 To God, my defender, I say,
"Why have you forgotten me?
Why must I go on suffering
from the cruelty of my enemies?"
10 I am crushed by their insults,
as they keep on asking me,
"Where is your God?"

11 Why am I so sad?
Why am I so troubled?
I will put my hope in God,
and once again I will praise him,
my savior and my God.

The Prayer of Someone in Exile

(Continuation of Psalm 42)

43 O God, declare me innocent,
and defend my cause against the ungodly;
deliver me from lying and evil people!
2 You are my protector;
why have you abandoned me?
Why must I go on suffering
from the cruelty of my enemies?

3 Send your light and your truth;
may they lead me
and bring me back to Zion, your sacred hill,[n]
and to your Temple, where you live.
4 Then I will go to your altar, O God;
you are the source of my happiness.
I will play my harp and sing praise to you,
O God, my God.

5 Why am I so sad?
Why am I so troubled?
I will put my hope in God,
and once again I will praise him,
my savior and my God.

A Prayer for Protection[o]

44 With our own ears we have heard it, O God—
our ancestors have told us about it,
about the great things you did in their time,
in the days of long ago:
2 how you yourself drove out the heathen
and established your people in their land;
how you punished the other nations

[m] HEBREW TITLE: *A poem by the clan of Korah.* [n] SACRED HILL: *See* 2.6. [o] HEBREW TITLE: *A poem by the clan of Korah.*

and caused your own to prosper.
3 Your people did not conquer the land with their swords;
they did not win it by their own power;
it was by your power and your strength,
by the assurance of your presence,
which showed that you loved them.

4 You are my king and my God;
you give[p] victory to your people,
5 and by your power we defeat our enemies.
6 I do not trust in my bow
or in my sword to save me;
7 but you have saved us from our enemies
and defeated those who hate us.
8 We will always praise you
and give thanks to you forever.

9 But now you have rejected us and let us be defeated;
you no longer march out with our armies.
10 You made us run from our enemies,
and they took for themselves what was ours.
11 You allowed us to be slaughtered like sheep;
you scattered us in foreign countries.
12 You sold your own people for a small price
as though they had little value.[q]

13 Our neighbors see what you did to us,
and they mock us and laugh at us.
14 You have made us a joke among the nations;
they shake their heads at us in scorn.
15 I am always in disgrace;
I am covered with shame
16 from hearing the sneers and insults
of my enemies and those who hate me.

17 All this has happened to us,
even though we have not forgotten you
or broken the covenant you made with us.
18 We have not been disloyal to you;
we have not disobeyed your commands.
19 Yet you left us helpless among wild animals;
you abandoned us in deepest darkness.

20 If we had stopped worshiping our God
and prayed to a foreign god,
21 you would surely have discovered it,
because you know our secret thoughts.
22 But it is on your account that we are being killed all the time,
that we are treated like sheep to be slaughtered.

23 Wake up, Lord! Why are you asleep?
Rouse yourself! Don't reject us forever!
24 Why are you hiding from us?
Don't forget our suffering and trouble!

25 We fall crushed to the ground;
we lie defeated in the dust.
26 Come to our aid!
Because of your constant love save us!

A Royal Wedding Song[r]

45 Beautiful words fill my mind,
as I compose this song for the king.
Like the pen of a good writer
my tongue is ready with a poem.

2 You are the most handsome of men;
you are an eloquent speaker.
God has always blessed you.
3 Buckle on your sword, mighty king;
you are glorious and majestic.

4 Ride on in majesty to victory

[p] *Some ancient translations* and my God; you give; *Hebrew* O God; give. [q] as . . . value; *or* and made no profit from the sale. [r] HEBREW TITLE: *A poem by the clan of Korah; a love song.*

for the defense of truth and
justice![s]
Your strength will win you great
victories!
5 Your arrows are sharp,
they pierce the hearts of your
enemies;
nations fall down at your feet.

6 The kingdom that God has given
you[t]
will last forever and ever.
You rule over your people with
justice;
7 you love what is right and hate
what is evil.
That is why God, your God, has
chosen you
and has poured out more
happiness on you
than on any other king.
8 The perfume of myrrh and aloes is
on your clothes;
musicians entertain you in
palaces decorated with ivory.
9 Among the women of your court
are daughters of kings,
and at the right of your throne
stands the queen,
wearing ornaments of finest
gold.

10 Bride of the king, listen to what
I say—
forget your people and your
relatives.
11 Your beauty will make the king
desire you;
he is your master, so you must
obey him.
12 The people of Tyre will bring you
gifts;
rich people will try to win your
favor.

13 The princess is in the palace—how
beautiful she is!
Her gown is made of gold
thread.
14 In her colorful gown she is led to
the king,
followed by her bridesmaids,
and they also are brought
to him.
15 With joy and gladness they come
and enter the king's palace.
16 You, my king, will have many
sons
to succeed your ancestors as
kings,
and you will make them rulers
over the whole earth.
17 My song will keep your fame alive
forever,
and everyone will praise you for
all time to come.

God Is with Us[u]

46 God is our shelter and strength,
always ready to help in times
of trouble.
2 So we will not be afraid, even if
the earth is shaken
and mountains fall into the
ocean depths;
3 even if the seas roar and rage,
and the hills are shaken by the
violence.

4 There is a river that brings joy to
the city of God,
to the sacred house of the Most
High.
5 God is in that city, and it will
never be destroyed;
at early dawn he will come to
its aid.
6 Nations are terrified, kingdoms are
shaken;
God thunders, and the earth
dissolves.

7 The LORD Almighty is with us;
the God of Jacob is our refuge.

8 Come and see what the LORD has
done.
See what amazing things he has
done on earth.
9 He stops wars all over the world;
he breaks bows, destroys spears,
and sets shields on fire.
10 "Stop fighting," he says, "and
know that I am God,
supreme among the nations,
supreme over the world."
11 The LORD Almighty is with us;
the God of Jacob is our refuge.

[s] *Probable text* and justice; *Hebrew* and meekness of justice. [t] The kingdom that God has given you; *or* Your kingdom, O God; *or* Your divine kingdom. [u] HEBREW TITLE: *A song by the clan of Korah.*

The Supreme Ruler[v]

47 Clap your hands for joy, all peoples!
Praise God with loud songs!
2 The LORD, the Most High, is to be feared;
he is a great king, ruling over all the world.
3 He gave us victory over the peoples;
he made us rule over the nations.
4 He chose for us the land where we live,
the proud possession of his people, whom he loves.

5 God goes up to his throne.
There are shouts of joy and the blast of trumpets,
as the LORD goes up.
6 Sing praise to God;
sing praise to our king!
7 God is king over all the world;
praise him with songs!

8 God sits on his sacred throne;
he rules over the nations.
9 The rulers of the nations assemble
with the people[w] of the God of Abraham.
More powerful than all armies is he;
he rules supreme.

Zion, the City of God[x]

48 The LORD is great and is to be highly praised
in the city of our God, on his sacred hill.[y]
2 Zion, the mountain of God, is high and beautiful;
the city of the great king brings joy to all the world.
3 God has shown that there is safety with him
inside the fortresses of the city.

4 The kings gathered together
and came to attack Mount Zion.
5 But when they saw it, they were amazed;
they were afraid and ran away.
6 There they were seized with fear and anguish,
like a woman about to bear a child,
7 like ships tossing in a furious storm.

8 We have heard what God has done,
and now we have seen it
in the city of our God, the LORD Almighty;
he will keep the city safe forever.

9 Inside your Temple, O God,
we think of your constant love.
10 You are praised by people everywhere,
and your fame extends over all the earth.
You rule with justice;
11 let the people of Zion be glad!
You give right judgments;
let there be joy in the cities of Judah!

12 People of God, walk around Zion
and count the towers;
13 take notice of the walls and examine the fortresses,
so that you may tell the next generation:
14 "This God is our God forever and ever;
he will lead us for all time to come."

The Foolishness of Trusting in Riches[z]

49 Hear this, everyone!
Listen, all people everywhere,
2 great and small alike,
rich and poor together.
3 My thoughts will be clear;
I will speak words of wisdom.
4 I will turn my attention to proverbs
and explain their meaning as I play the harp.

5 I am not afraid in times of danger
when I am surrounded by enemies,

[v] HEBREW TITLE: *A psalm by the clan of Korah.* [w] *Probable text* with the people; *Hebrew* the people.
[x] HEBREW TITLE: *A psalm by the clan of Korah; a song.* [y] SACRED HILL: *See 2.6.*
[z] HEBREW TITLE: *A psalm by the clan of Korah.*

6 by evil people who trust in their riches
and boast of their great wealth.
7 We can never redeem ourselves;
we cannot pay God the price for our lives,
8 because the payment for a human life is too great.
What we could pay would never be enough
9 to keep us from the grave,
to let us live forever.

10 Anyone can see that even the wise die,
as well as the foolish and stupid.
They all leave their riches to their descendants.
11 Their graves[a] are their homes forever;
there they stay for all time,
though they once had lands of their own.
12 Our greatness cannot keep us from death;
we will still die like the animals.

13 See what happens to those who trust in themselves,
the fate of those[b] who are satisfied with their wealth—
14 they are doomed to die like sheep,
and Death will be their shepherd.
The righteous will triumph over them,
as their bodies quickly decay
in the world of the dead far from their homes.[c]
15 But God will rescue me;
he will save me from the power of death.

16 Don't be upset when someone becomes rich,
when his wealth grows even greater;
17 he cannot take it with him when he dies;
his wealth will not go with him to the grave.
18 Even if someone is satisfied with this life
and is praised because he is successful,
19 he will join all his ancestors in death,
where the darkness lasts forever.
20 Our greatness cannot keep us from death;
we will still die like the animals.

True Worship[d]

50 The Almighty God, the LORD, speaks;
he calls to the whole earth from east to west.
2 God shines from Zion,
the city perfect in its beauty.

3 Our God is coming, but not in silence;
a raging fire is in front of him,
a furious storm around him.
4 He calls heaven and earth as witnesses
to see him judge his people.
5 He says, "Gather my faithful people to me,
those who made a covenant with me by offering a sacrifice."
6 The heavens proclaim that God is righteous,
that he himself is judge.

7 "Listen, my people, and I will speak;
I will testify against you, Israel.
I am God, your God.
8 I do not reprimand you because of your sacrifices
and the burnt offerings you always bring me.
9 And yet I do not need bulls from your farms
or goats from your flocks;
10 all the animals in the forest are mine
and the cattle on thousands of hills.
11 All the wild birds are mine
and all living things in the fields.

12 "If I were hungry, I would not ask you for food,
for the world and everything in it is mine.
13 Do I eat the flesh of bulls
or drink the blood of goats?

[a] *Some ancient translations* graves; *Hebrew* inner thoughts. [b] *One ancient translation* the fate of those; *Hebrew* after them. [c] in . . . homes.; *Hebrew unclear.* [d] HEBREW TITLE: *A psalm by Asaph.*

[14] Let the giving of thanks be your
sacrifice to God,[e]
and give the Almighty all that
you promised.
[15] Call to me when trouble comes;
I will save you,
and you will praise me."

[16] But God says to the wicked,
"Why should you recite my
commandments?
Why should you talk about my
covenant?
[17] You refuse to let me correct you;
you reject my commands.
[18] You become the friend of every
thief you see,
and you associate with
adulterers.

[19] "You are always ready to speak
evil;
you never hesitate to tell lies.
[20] You are ready to accuse your own
relatives
and to find fault with them.
[21] You have done all this, and I have
said nothing,
so you thought that I am
like you.
But now I reprimand you
and make the matter plain
to you.

[22] "Listen to this, you that ignore me,
or I will destroy you,
and there will be no one to
save you.
[23] Giving thanks is the sacrifice that
honors me,
and I will surely save all who
obey me."

A Prayer for Forgiveness[f]

51 Be merciful to me, O God,
because of your constant
love.
Because of your great mercy
wipe away my sins!
[2] Wash away all my evil
and make me clean from my sin!

[3] I recognize my faults;
I am always conscious of my
sins.
[4] I have sinned against you—only
against you—
and done what you consider
evil.
So you are right in judging me;
you are justified in
condemning me.
[5] I have been evil from the day I
was born;
from the time I was conceived, I
have been sinful.

[6] Sincerity and truth are what you
require;
fill my mind with your wisdom.
[7] Remove my sin, and I will be
clean;
wash me, and I will be whiter
than snow.
[8] Let me hear the sounds of joy and
gladness;
and though you have crushed
me and broken me,
I will be happy once again.
[9] Close your eyes to my sins
and wipe out all my evil.

[10] Create a pure heart in me, O God,
and put a new and loyal spirit
in me.
[11] Do not banish me from your
presence;
do not take your holy spirit
away from me.
[12] Give me again the joy that comes
from your salvation,
and make me willing to
obey you.
[13] Then I will teach sinners your
commands,
and they will turn back to you.

[14] Spare my life, O God, and
save me,[g]
and I will gladly proclaim your
righteousness.
[15] Help me to speak, Lord,
and I will praise you.

[16] You do not want sacrifices,
or I would offer them;
you are not pleased with burnt
offerings.
[17] My sacrifice is a humble spirit,
O God;

[e] Let the giving . . . to God; *or* Offer your thanksgiving sacrifice to God. [f] HEBREW TITLE: *A psalm by David, after the prophet Nathan had spoken to him about his adultery with Bathsheba.*
[g] Spare my life . . . me; *or* O God my savior, keep me from the crime of murder.

you will not reject a humble
and repentant heart.

18 O God, be kind to Zion and
help her;
rebuild the walls of
Jerusalem.
19 Then you will be pleased with
proper sacrifices
and with our burnt
offerings;
and bulls will be sacrificed on
your altar.

God's Judgment and Grace[h]

52 Why do you boast, great one,
of your evil?
God's faithfulness is eternal.
2 You make plans to ruin others;
your tongue is like a sharp
razor.
You are always inventing lies.
3 You love evil more than good
and falsehood more than truth.
4 You love to hurt people with your
words, you liar!

5 So God will ruin you forever;
he will take hold of you and
snatch you from your home;
he will remove you from the
world of the living.
6 Righteous people will see this and
be afraid;
then they will laugh at you
and say,
7 "Look, here is someone who did
not depend on God for safety,
but trusted instead in great
wealth
and looked for security in being
wicked."

8 But I am like an olive tree growing
in the house of God;
I trust in his constant love
forever and ever.
9 I will always thank you, God, for
what you have done;
in the presence of your
people
I will proclaim that you are
good.

Human Wickedness[i]

(Psalm 14)

53 Fools say to themselves,
"There is no God."
They are all corrupt,
and they have done terrible
things;
there is no one who does what
is right.

2 God looks down from heaven at
people
to see if there are any who are
wise,
any who worship him.
3 But they have all turned away;
they are all equally bad.
Not one of them does what is
right,
not a single one.

4 "Don't they know?" God asks.
"Are these evildoers ignorant?
They live by robbing my people,
and they never pray to me."

5 But then they will become
terrified,
as they have never been before,
for God will scatter the bones of
the enemies of his people.
God has rejected them,
and so Israel will totally defeat
them.

6 How I pray that victory
will come to Israel from Zion.
How happy the people of Israel
will be
when God makes them
prosperous again!

A Prayer for Protection from Enemies[j]

54 Save me by your power,
O God;
set me free by your might!
2 Hear my prayer, O God;
listen to my words!
3 Proud people are coming to
attack me;
cruel people are trying to
kill me—

[h] HEBREW TITLE: *A poem by David, after Doeg the Edomite went to Saul and told him that David had gone to the house of Ahimelech.* [i] HEBREW TITLE: *A poem by David.* [j] HEBREW TITLE: *A poem by David, after the men from Ziph went to Saul and told him that David was hiding in their territory.*

those who do not care
about God.

4 But God is my helper.
The Lord is my defender.
5 May God use their own evil to
punish my enemies.
He will destroy them because he
is faithful.

6 I will gladly offer you a sacrifice,
O LORD;
I will give you thanks
because you are good.
7 You have rescued me from all my
troubles,
and I have seen my enemies
defeated.

The Prayer of Someone Betrayed by a Friend[k]

55 Hear my prayer, O God;
don't turn away from my
plea!
2 Listen to me and answer me;
I am worn out by my worries.
3 I am terrified by the threats of my
enemies,
crushed by the oppression of the
wicked.
They bring trouble on me;
they are angry with me and
hate me.

4 I am terrified,
and the terrors of death
crush me.
5 I am gripped by fear and
trembling;
I am overcome with horror.
6 I wish I had wings like a dove.
I would fly away and find rest.
7 I would fly far away
and make my home in the
desert.
8 I would hurry and find myself a
shelter
from the raging wind and the
storm.
9 Confuse the speech of my
enemies, O Lord!

I see violence and riots in the city,
10 surrounding it day and night,
filling it with crime and trouble.
11 There is destruction everywhere;
the streets are full of oppression
and fraud.

12 If it were an enemy making fun
of me,
I could endure it;
if it were an opponent boasting
over me,
I could hide myself from him.
13 But it is you, my companion,
my colleague and close friend.
14 We had intimate talks with each
other
and worshiped together in the
Temple.
15 May my enemies die before their
time;
may they go down alive into the
world of the dead!
Evil is in their homes and in their
hearts.

16 But I call to the LORD God for help,
and he will save me.
17 Morning, noon, and night
my complaints and groans go up
to him,
and he will hear my voice.
18 He will bring me safely back
from the battles that I fight
against so many enemies.
19 God, who has ruled from eternity,
will hear me and defeat them;
for they refuse to change,
and they do not fear him.

20 My former companion attacked his
friends;
he broke his promises.
21 His words were smoother than
cream,
but there was hatred in his
heart;
his words were as soothing as oil,
but they cut like sharp swords.

22 Leave your troubles with the LORD,
and he will defend you;
he never lets honest people be
defeated.

23 But you, O God, will bring those
murderers and liars to their
graves
before half their life is over.
As for me, I will trust in you.

[k] HEBREW TITLE: *A poem by David.*

A Prayer of Trust in God[l]

56 Be merciful to me, O God,
because I am under attack;
my enemies persecute me all the time.
2 All day long my opponents attack me.
There are so many who fight against me.
3 When I am afraid, O LORD Almighty,
I put my trust in you.
4 I trust in God and am not afraid;
I praise him for what he has promised.
What can a mere human being do to me?

5 My enemies make trouble for me all day long;
they are always thinking up some way to hurt me!
6 They gather in hiding places
and watch everything I do,
hoping to kill me.
7 Punish[m] them, O God, for their evil;
defeat those people in your anger!

8 You know how troubled I am;
you have kept a record of my tears.
Aren't they listed in your book?
9 The day I call to you,
my enemies will be turned back.
I know this: God[n] is on my side—
10 the LORD, whose promises I praise.
11 In him I trust, and I will not be afraid.
What can a mere human being do to me?

12 O God, I will offer you what I have promised;
I will give you my offering of thanksgiving,
13 because you have rescued me from death
and kept me from defeat.
And so I walk in the presence of God,
in the light that shines on the living.

A Prayer for Help[o]

57 Be merciful to me, O God, be merciful,
because I come to you for safety.
In the shadow of your wings I find protection
until the raging storms are over.

2 I call to God, the Most High,
to God, who supplies my every need.
3 He will answer from heaven and save me;
he will defeat my oppressors.
God will show me his constant love and faithfulness.

4 I am surrounded by enemies,
who are like lions hungry for human flesh.
Their teeth are like spears and arrows;
their tongues are like sharp swords.

5 Show your greatness in the sky, O God,
and your glory over all the earth.

6 My enemies have spread a net to catch me;
I am overcome with distress.
They dug a pit in my path,
but fell into it themselves.

7 I have complete confidence, O God;
I will sing and praise you!
8 Wake up, my soul!
Wake up, my harp and lyre!
I will wake up the sun.
9 I will thank you, O Lord, among the nations.
I will praise you among the peoples.
10 Your constant love reaches the heavens;
your faithfulness touches the skies.
11 Show your greatness in the sky, O God,

[l] HEBREW TITLE: *A psalm by David, after the Philistines captured him in Gath.*
[m] *Probable text* Punish; *Hebrew* Save. [n] I know this: God; *or* Because I know that God.
[o] HEBREW TITLE: *A psalm by David, after he fled from Saul in the cave.*

and your glory over all the
earth.

A Prayer for God to Punish the Wicked[p]

58 Do you rulers[q] ever give a just
decision?
Do you judge everyone fairly?
2 No! You think only of the evil you
can do,
and commit crimes of violence
in the land.

3 Evildoers go wrong all their lives;
they tell lies from the day they
are born.
4 They are full of poison like
snakes;
they stop up their ears like a
deaf cobra,
5 which does not hear the voice of
the snake charmer,
or the chant of the clever
magician.

6 Break the teeth of these fierce
lions, O God.
7 May they disappear like water
draining away;
may they be crushed like weeds
on a path.[r]
8 May they be like snails that
dissolve into slime;
may they be like a baby born
dead that never sees the light.
9 Before they know it, they are cut
down like weeds;
in his fierce anger God will blow
them away
while they are still living.[s]

10 The righteous will be glad when
they see sinners punished;
they will wade through the
blood of the wicked.
11 People will say, "The righteous are
indeed rewarded;
there is indeed a God who
judges the world."

A Prayer for Safety[t]

59 Save me from my enemies,
my God;
protect me from those who
attack me!
2 Save me from those evil people;
rescue me from those
murderers!
3 Look! They are waiting to kill me;
cruel people are gathering
against me.
It is not because of any sin or
wrong I have done,
4 nor because of any fault of mine,
O LORD,
that they hurry to their places.

5 Rise, LORD God Almighty, and
come to my aid;
see for yourself, God of Israel!
Wake up and punish the heathen;
show no mercy to evil traitors!

6 They come back in the evening,
snarling like dogs as they go
about the city.
7 Listen to their insults and threats.
Their tongues are like swords in
their mouths,
yet they think that no one hears
them.

8 But you laugh at them, LORD;
you mock all the heathen.
9 I have confidence in your strength;
you are my refuge, O God.
10 My God loves me and will come
to me;
he will let me see my enemies
defeated.

11 Do not kill them, O God, or my
people may forget.
Scatter them by your strength
and defeat them,
O Lord, our protector.
12 Sin is on their lips; all their words
are sinful;
may they be caught in their
pride!
Because they curse and lie,
13 destroy them in your anger;
destroy them completely.
Then everyone will know that God
rules in Israel,
that his rule extends over all the
earth.

[p] HEBREW TITLE: *A psalm by David.* [q] rulers; *or* gods. [r] *Probable text* may . . . path; *Hebrew unclear.* [s] *Verse 9 in Hebrew is unclear.* [t] HEBREW TITLE: *A psalm by David, after Saul sent men to watch his house in order to kill him.*

14 My enemies come back in the evening,
snarling like dogs as they go about the city,
15 like dogs roaming about for food
and growling if they do not find enough.

16 But I will sing about your strength;
every morning I will sing aloud of your constant love.
You have been a refuge for me,
a shelter in my time of trouble.
17 I will praise you, my defender.
My refuge is God,
the God who loves me.

A Prayer for Deliverance[u]

60 You have rejected us, God, and defeated us;
you have been angry with us—
but now turn back to us.[v]
2 You have made the land tremble,
and you have cut it open;
now heal its wounds, because it is falling apart.
3 You have made your people suffer greatly;
we stagger around as though we were drunk.
4 You have warned those who have reverence for you,
so that they might escape destruction.
5 Save us by your might; answer our prayer,
so that the people you love may be rescued.

6 From his sanctuary[w] God has said,
"In triumph I will divide Shechem
and distribute Sukkoth Valley to my people.
7 Gilead is mine, and Manasseh too;
Ephraim is my helmet
and Judah my royal scepter.
8 But I will use Moab as my washbowl,
and I will throw my sandals on Edom,
as a sign that I own it.
Did the Philistines think they would shout in triumph over me?"

9 Who, O God, will take me into the fortified city?
Who will lead me to Edom?
10 Have you really rejected us?
Aren't you going to march out with our armies?
11 Help us against the enemy;
human help is worthless.
12 With God on our side we will win;
he will defeat our enemies.

A Prayer for Protection[x]

61 Hear my cry, O God;
listen to my prayer!
2 In despair and far from home
I call to you!

Take me to a safe refuge,
3 for you are my protector,
my strong defense against my enemies.

4 Let me live in your sanctuary all my life;
let me find safety under your wings.
5 You have heard my promises, O God,
and you have given me what belongs to those who honor you.

6 Add many years to the king's life;
let him live on and on!
7 May he rule forever in your presence, O God;
protect him with your constant love and faithfulness.

8 So I will always sing praises to you,
as I offer you daily what I have promised.

Confidence in God's Protection[y]

62 I wait patiently for God to save me;
I depend on him alone.
2 He alone protects and saves me;
he is my defender,

[u] HEBREW TITLE: *A psalm by David, for teaching, when he fought against the Arameans from Naharaim and from Zobah, and Joab turned back and killed 12,000 Edomites in Salt Valley.*
[v] angry with us . . . us; *or* angry with us and turned your back on us. [w] From his sanctuary; *or* In his holiness. [x] HEBREW TITLE: *By David.* [y] HEBREW TITLE: *A psalm by David.*

and I shall never be defeated.

3 How much longer will all of you
attack someone
who is no stronger than a
broken-down fence?
4 You only want to bring him down
from his place of honor;
you take pleasure in lies.
You speak words of blessing,
but in your heart you curse him.

5 I depend on God alone;
I put my hope in him.
6 He alone protects and saves me;
he is my defender,
and I shall never be defeated.
7 My salvation and honor depend
on God;
he is my strong protector;
he is my shelter.

8 Trust in God at all times, my
people.
Tell him all your troubles,
for he is our refuge.

9 Human beings are all like a puff
of breath;
great and small alike are
worthless.
Put them on the scales, and they
weigh nothing;
they are lighter than a mere
breath.
10 Don't put your trust in violence;
don't hope to gain anything by
robbery;
even if your riches increase,
don't depend on them.

11 More than once I have heard
God say
that power belongs to him
12 and that his love is constant.
You yourself, O Lord, reward
everyone according to their
deeds.

Longing for God[z]

63 O God, you are my God,
and I long for you.
My whole being desires you;
like a dry, worn-out, and
waterless land,
my soul is thirsty for you.
2 Let me see you in the sanctuary;
let me see how mighty and
glorious you are.
3 Your constant love is better than
life itself,
and so I will praise you.
4 I will give you thanks as long as I
live;
I will raise my hands to you in
prayer.
5 My soul will feast and be satisfied,
and I will sing glad songs of
praise to you.

6 As I lie in bed, I remember you;
all night long I think of you,
7 because you have always been
my help.
In the shadow of your wings I sing
for joy.
8 I cling to you,
and your hand keeps me safe.

9 Those who are trying to kill me
will go down into the world of
the dead.
10 They will be killed in battle,
and their bodies eaten by
wolves.
11 Because God gives him victory,
the king will rejoice.
Those who make promises in
God's name will praise him,
but the mouths of liars will be
shut.

A Prayer for Protection[a]

64 I am in trouble, God—listen to
my prayer!
I am afraid of my enemies—save
my life!
2 Protect me from the plots of the
wicked,
from mobs of evil people.
3 They sharpen their tongues like
swords
and aim cruel words like arrows.
4 They are quick to spread their
shameless lies;
they destroy good people with
cowardly slander.
5 They encourage each other in their
evil plots;

z HEBREW TITLE: *A psalm by David, when he was in the desert of Judea.* a HEBREW TITLE: *A psalm by David.*

they talk about where they will
place their traps.
"No one can see them," they say.
6 They make evil plans and say,
"We have planned a perfect
crime."
The human heart and mind are a
mystery.

7 But God shoots his arrows at
them,
and suddenly they are wounded.
8 He will destroy them because of
those words;[b]
all who see them will shake
their heads.
9 They will all be afraid;
they will think about what God
has done
and tell about his deeds.
10 All righteous people will rejoice
because of what the LORD has
done.
They will find safety in him;
all good people will praise him.

Praise and Thanksgiving[c]

65 O God, it is right for us to
praise you in Zion
and keep our promises to you,
2 because you answer prayers.
People everywhere will come
to you
3 on account of their sins.
Our faults defeat us,[d]
but you forgive them.
4 Happy are those whom you
choose,
whom you bring to live in your
sanctuary.
We shall be satisfied with the
good things of your house,
the blessings of your sacred
Temple.

5 You answer us by giving us
victory,
and you do wonderful things to
save us.
People all over the world
and across the distant seas trust
in you.
6 You set the mountains in place by
your strength,
showing your mighty power.
7 You calm the roar of the seas
and the noise of the waves;
you calm the uproar of the
peoples.
8 The whole world stands in awe
of the great things that you have
done.
Your deeds bring shouts of joy
from one end of the earth to the
other.

9 You show your care for the land
by sending rain;
you make it rich and fertile.
You fill the streams with water;
you provide the earth with
crops.
This is how you do it:
10 you send abundant rain on the
plowed fields
and soak them with water;
you soften the soil with showers
and cause the young plants to
grow.
11 What a rich harvest your goodness
provides!
Wherever you go there is plenty.
12 The pastures are filled with flocks;
the hillsides are full of joy.
13 The fields are covered with sheep;
the valleys are full of wheat.
Everything shouts and sings
for joy.

A Song of Praise and Thanksgiving[e]

66 Praise God with shouts of joy,
all people!
2 Sing to the glory of his name;
offer him glorious praise!
3 Say to God, "How wonderful are
the things you do!
Your power is so great
that your enemies bow down in
fear before you.
4 Everyone on earth worships you;
they sing praises to you,
they sing praises to your
name."

5 Come and see what God has done,
his wonderful acts among
people.
6 He changed the sea into dry
land;

[b] *Probable text* He will destroy them because of those words; *Hebrew* They will destroy him, those words are against them. [c] HEBREW TITLE: *A psalm by David; a song.*
[d] *One ancient translation* us; *Hebrew* me. [e] HEBREW TITLE: *A song.*

our ancestors crossed the river
on foot.
There we rejoiced because of what
he did.
7 He rules forever by his might
and keeps his eyes on the
nations.
Let no rebels rise against
him.
8 Praise our God, all nations;
let your praise be heard.
9 He has kept us alive
and has not allowed us to fall.

10 You have put us to the test,
God;
as silver is purified by fire,
so you have tested us.
11 You let us fall into a trap
and placed heavy burdens on
our backs.
12 You let our enemies trample us;
we went through fire and
flood,
but now you have brought us to
a place of safety.[f]

13 I will bring burnt offerings to your
house;
I will offer you what I promised.
14 I will give you what I said I would
when I was in trouble.
15 I will offer sheep to be burned on
the altar;
I will sacrifice bulls and goats,
and the smoke will go up to
the sky.

16 Come and listen, all who
honor God,
and I will tell you what he has
done for me.
17 I cried to him for help;
I praised him with songs.
18 If I had ignored my sins,
the Lord would not have listened
to me.
19 But God has indeed heard me;
he has listened to my prayer.

20 I praise God,
because he did not reject my
prayer
or keep back his constant love
from me.

A Song of Thanksgiving[g]

67 God, be merciful to us and
bless us;
look on us with kindness,
2 so that the whole world may know
your will;
so that all nations may know
your salvation.

3 May the peoples praise you,
O God;
may all the peoples praise you!

4 May the nations be glad and sing
for joy,
because you judge the peoples
with justice
and guide every nation on earth.

5 May the peoples praise you,
O God;
may all the peoples praise you!

6 The land has produced its harvest;
God, our God, has blessed us.
7 God has blessed us;
may all people everywhere
honor him.

A National Song of Triumph[h]

68 God rises up and scatters his
enemies.
Those who hate him run away
in defeat.
2 As smoke is blown away, so he
drives them off;
as wax melts in front of the fire,
so do the wicked perish in God's
presence.
3 But the righteous are glad and
rejoice in his presence;
they are happy and shout
for joy.

4 Sing to God, sing praises to his
name;
prepare a way for him who rides
on the clouds.[i]
His name is the LORD—be glad
in his presence!

5 God, who lives in his sacred
Temple,
cares for orphans and protects
widows.

[f] *Some ancient translations* safety; *Hebrew* overflowing. [g] HEBREW TITLE: *A psalm; a song.*
[h] HEBREW TITLE: *A psalm by David; a song.* [i] on the clouds; *or* across the desert.

6 He gives the lonely a home to
live in
and leads prisoners out into
happy freedom,
but rebels will have to live in a
desolate land.

7 O God, when you led your people,
when you marched across the
desert,
8 the earth shook, and the sky
poured down rain,
because of the coming of the
God of Sinai,[j]
the coming of the God of Israel.
9 You caused abundant rain to fall
and restored your worn-out
land;
10 your people made their home
there;
in your goodness you provided
for the poor.

11 The Lord gave the command,
and many women carried the
news:
12 "Kings and their armies are
running away!"
The women at home divided
what was captured:
13 figures of doves covered with
silver,
whose wings glittered with fine
gold.
(Why did some of you stay among
the sheep pens on the day of
battle?)
14 When Almighty God scattered the
kings on Mount Zalmon,
he caused snow to fall there.

15 What a mighty mountain is
Bashan,
a mountain of many peaks!
16 Why from your mighty peaks do
you look with scorn
on the mountain[k] on which God
chose to live?
The LORD will live there forever!

17 With his many thousands of
mighty chariots
the Lord comes from Sinai[l]
into the holy place.
18 He goes up to the heights,
taking many captives with him;
he receives gifts from rebellious
people.
The LORD God will live there.

19 Praise the Lord,
who carries our burdens day
after day;
he is the God who saves us.
20 Our God is a God who saves;
he is the LORD, our Lord,
who rescues us from death.

21 God will surely break the heads of
his enemies,
of those who persist in their
sinful ways.
22 The Lord has said, "I will bring
your enemies back from
Bashan;
I will bring them back from the
depths of the ocean,
23 so that you may wade in their
blood,
and your dogs may lap up as
much as they want."

24 O God, your march of triumph is
seen by all,
the procession of God, my king,
into his sanctuary.
25 The singers are in front, the
musicians are behind,
in between are the young
women beating the
tambourines.
26 "Praise God in the meeting of his
people;
praise the LORD, all you
descendants of Jacob!"
27 First comes Benjamin, the smallest
tribe,
then the leaders of Judah with
their group,
followed by the leaders of
Zebulun and Naphtali.

28 Show your power, O God,
the power you have used on our
behalf
29 from your Temple in Jerusalem,
where kings bring gifts to you.
30 Rebuke Egypt, that wild animal in
the reeds;

[j] GOD OF SINAI: *As the people of Israel went from Egypt to Canaan, God revealed himself to them at Mount Sinai (see Ex 19.16-25).* [k] MOUNTAIN: *See 2.6.* [l] *Probable text* comes from Sinai; *Hebrew* in them, Sinai.

rebuke the nations, that herd of
bulls with their calves,
until they all bow down and
offer you their silver.
Scatter those people who love to
make war![m]
31 Ambassadors[n] will come from
Egypt;
the Ethiopians[o] will raise their
hands in prayer to God.

32 Sing to God, kingdoms of the
world,
sing praise to the Lord,
33 to him who rides in the sky,
the ancient sky.
Listen to him shout with a mighty
roar.
34 Proclaim God's power;
his majesty is over Israel,
his might is in the skies.
35 How awesome is God as he comes
from his sanctuary—
the God of Israel!
He gives strength and power to his
people.

Praise God!

A Cry for Help[p]

69 Save me, O God!
The water is up to my neck;
2 I am sinking in deep mud,
and there is no solid ground;
I am out in deep water,
and the waves are about to
drown me.
3 I am worn out from calling for
help,
and my throat is aching.
I have strained my eyes,
looking for your help.

4 Those who hate me for no reason
are more numerous than the
hairs of my head.
My enemies tell lies against me;
they are strong and want to
kill me.
They made me give back things I
did not steal.
5 My sins, O God, are not hidden
from you;
you know how foolish I have
been.
6 Don't let me bring shame on those
who trust in you,
Sovereign LORD Almighty!
Don't let me bring disgrace to
those who worship you,
O God of Israel!
7 It is for your sake that I have been
insulted
and that I am covered with
shame.
8 I am like a stranger to my
relatives,
like a foreigner to my family.

9 My devotion to your Temple burns
in me like a fire;
the insults which are hurled at
you fall on me.
10 I humble myself[q] by fasting,
and people insult me;
11 I dress myself in clothes of
mourning,
and they laugh at me.
12 They talk about me in the streets,
and drunkards make up songs
about me.

13 But as for me, I will pray to you,
LORD;
answer me, God, at a time you
choose.
Answer me because of your great
love,
because you keep your promise
to save.
14 Save me from sinking in the mud;
keep me safe from my enemies,
safe from the deep water.
15 Don't let the flood come over me;
don't let me drown in the depths
or sink into the grave.

16 Answer me, LORD, in the goodness
of your constant love;
in your great compassion turn
to me!
17 Don't hide yourself from your
servant;

[m] *Verse 30 in Hebrew is unclear.* [n] *Some ancient translations* Ambassadors; *Hebrew unclear.*
[o] *Hebrew* Cushites: *Cush is the ancient name of the extensive territory south of the First Cataract of the Nile River. This region was called Ethiopia in Graeco-Roman time, and included within its borders most of modern Sudan and some of present-day Ethiopia (Abyssinia).* [p] HEBREW TITLE: *By David.* [q] *Some ancient translations* humble myself; *Hebrew* cry.

I am in great trouble—answer
me now!
18 Come to me and save me;
rescue me from my enemies.

19 You know how I am insulted,
how I am disgraced and
dishonored;
you see all my enemies.
20 Insults have broken my heart,
and I am in despair.
I had hoped for sympathy, but
there was none;
for comfort, but I found none.
21 When I was hungry, they gave me
poison;
when I was thirsty, they offered
me vinegar.

22 May their banquets cause their
ruin;
may their sacred feasts cause
their downfall.
23 Strike them with blindness!
Make their backs always weak!
24 Pour out your anger on them;
let your indignation overtake
them.
25 May their camps be left deserted;
may no one be left alive in their
tents.
26 They persecute those whom you
have punished;
they talk about the sufferings of
those you have wounded.
27 Keep a record of all their sins;
don't let them have any part in
your salvation.
28 May their names be erased from
the book of the living;
may they not be included in the
list of your people.

29 But I am in pain and despair;
lift me up, O God, and save me!

30 I will praise God with a song;
I will proclaim his greatness by
giving him thanks.
31 This will please the LORD more
than offering him cattle,
more than sacrificing a
full-grown bull.
32 When the oppressed see this, they
will be glad;
those who worship God will be
encouraged.
33 The LORD listens to those in need
and does not forget his people in
prison.

34 Praise God, O heaven and earth,
seas and all creatures in them.
35 He will save Jerusalem
and rebuild the towns of Judah.
His people will live there and
possess the land;
36 the descendants of his servants
will inherit it,
and those who love him will live
there.

A Prayer for Help[r]

(Psalm 40.13-17)

70 Save me, O God!
LORD, help me now!
2 May those who try to kill me
be defeated and confused.
May those who are happy because
of my troubles
be turned back and disgraced.
3 May those who make fun of me
be dismayed by their defeat.

4 May all who come to you
be glad and joyful.
May all who are thankful for your
salvation
always say, "How great is God!"

5 I am weak and poor;
come to me quickly, O God.
You are my savior and my LORD—
hurry to my aid!

The Prayer of an Elderly Person

71 LORD, I have come to you for
protection;
never let me be defeated!
2 Because you are righteous, help
me and rescue me.
Listen to me and save me!
3 Be my secure shelter
and a strong fortress[s] to
protect me;
you are my refuge and defense.

4 My God, rescue me from wicked
people,
from the power of cruel and evil
people.

[r] HEBREW TITLE: *A psalm by David; a lament.* [s] *One ancient translation* a strong fortress; *Hebrew* to go always you commanded.

5 Sovereign LORD, I put my hope
in you;
I have trusted in you since I was
young.
6 I have relied on you all my
life;
you have protected[t] me since
the day I was born.
I will always praise you.

7 My life has been an example to
many,
because you have been my
strong defender.
8 All day long I praise you
and proclaim your glory.
9 Do not reject me now that I
am old;
do not abandon me now that I
am feeble.
10 My enemies want to kill me;
they talk and plot against me.
11 They say, "God has abandoned
him;
let's go after him and catch
him;
there is no one to rescue him."

12 Don't stay so far away, O God;
my God, hurry to my aid!
13 May those who attack me
be defeated and destroyed.
May those who try to hurt me
be shamed and disgraced.
14 I will always put my hope in you;
I will praise you more and more.
15 I will tell of your goodness;
all day long I will speak of your
salvation,
though it is more than I can
understand.
16 I will go in the strength of the
LORD God;
I will proclaim your goodness,
yours alone.

17 You have taught me ever since I
was young,
and I still tell of your wonderful
acts.
18 Now that I am old and my hair is
gray,
do not abandon me, O God!
Be with me while I proclaim your
power and might
to all generations to come.
19 Your righteousness, God, reaches
the skies.
You have done great things;
there is no one like you.
20 You have sent troubles and
suffering on me,
but you will restore my strength;
you will keep me from the
grave.
21 You will make me greater than
ever;
you will comfort me again.

22 I will indeed praise you with the
harp;
I will praise your faithfulness,
my God.
On my harp I will play hymns
to you,
the Holy One of Israel.
23 I will shout for joy as I play
for you;
with my whole being I will sing
because you have saved me.
24 I will speak of your righteousness
all day long,
because those who tried to
harm me
have been defeated and
disgraced.

A Prayer for the King[u]

72 Teach the king to judge with
your righteousness, O God;
share with him your own justice,
2 so that he will rule over your
people with justice
and govern the oppressed with
righteousness.
3 May the land enjoy prosperity;
may it experience righteousness.
4 May the king judge the poor
fairly;
may he help the needy
and defeat their oppressors.
5 May your people worship you as
long as the sun shines,
as long as the moon gives light,
for ages to come.

6 May the king be like rain on the
fields,
like showers falling on the land.
7 May righteousness flourish in his
lifetime,

[t] *Some ancient translations* protected; *Hebrew unclear.*

[u] HEBREW TITLE: *By Solomon.*

and may prosperity last as long
as the moon gives light.
8 His kingdom will reach from sea
to sea,
from the Euphrates to the ends
of the earth.
9 The peoples of the desert will bow
down before him;
his enemies will throw
themselves to the ground.
10 The kings of Spain and of the
islands will offer him gifts;
the kings of Sheba and Seba[v]
will bring him offerings.
11 All kings will bow down
before him;
all nations will serve him.

12 He rescues the poor who call
to him,
and those who are needy and
neglected.
13 He has pity on the weak and poor;
he saves the lives of those in
need.
14 He rescues them from oppression
and violence;
their lives are precious to him.

15 Long live the king!
May he be given gold from
Sheba;[w]
may prayers be said for him at
all times;
may God's blessings be on him
always!
16 May there be plenty of grain in the
land;
may the hills be covered with
crops,
as fruitful as those of Lebanon.
May the cities be filled with
people,
like fields full of grass.
17 May the king's name never be
forgotten;
may his fame last as long as
the sun.
May all nations ask God to bless
them
as he has blessed the king.[x]

18 Praise the LORD, the God of Israel!
He alone does these wonderful
things.
19 Praise his glorious name forever!
May his glory fill the whole world.

Amen! Amen!

20 This is the end of the prayers of
David son of Jesse.

BOOK THREE

(Psalms 73–89)

The Justice of God[y]

73 God is indeed good to Israel,
to those who have pure
hearts.
2 But I had nearly lost confidence;
my faith was almost gone
3 because I was jealous of the proud
when I saw that things go well
for the wicked.

4 They do not suffer pain;
they are strong and healthy.
5 They do not suffer as other
people do;
they do not have the troubles
that others have.
6 And so they wear pride like a
necklace
and violence like a robe;
7 their hearts pour out evil,[z]
and their minds are busy with
wicked schemes.
8 They laugh at other people and
speak of evil things;
they are proud and make plans
to oppress others.
9 They speak evil of God in heaven
and give arrogant orders to
everyone on earth,
10 so that even God's people turn to
them
and eagerly believe whatever
they say.[a]
11 They say, "God will not know;
the Most High will not find out."
12 That is what the wicked are like.
They have plenty and are
always getting more.

[v] SHEBA AND SEBA: *Sheba was toward the south in Arabia and Seba was on the opposite side of the Red Sea.* [w] SHEBA: *See* 72.10. [x] as he has blessed the king; *or* and may they wish happiness for the king. [y] HEBREW TITLE: *By Asaph.* [z] *Some ancient translations* their hearts pour out evil; *Hebrew unclear.* [a] *Verse 10 in Hebrew is unclear.*

13 Is it for nothing, then, that I have
kept myself pure
and have not committed sin?
14 O God, you have made me suffer
all day long;
every morning you have
punished me.

15 If I had said such things,
I would not be acting as one of
your people.
16 I tried to think this problem
through,
but it was too difficult for me
17 until I went into your Temple.
Then I understood what will
happen to the wicked.

18 You will put them in slippery
places
and make them fall to
destruction!
19 They are instantly destroyed;
they go down to a horrible end.
20 They are like a dream that goes
away in the morning;
when you rouse yourself,
O Lord, they disappear.

21 When my thoughts were bitter
and my feelings were hurt,
22 I was as stupid as an animal;
I did not understand you.
23 Yet I always stay close to you,
and you hold me by the hand.
24 You guide me with your
instruction
and at the end you will receive
me with honor.
25 What else do I have in heaven
but you?
Since I have you, what else
could I want on earth?
26 My mind and my body may grow
weak,
but God is my strength;
he is all I ever need.

27 Those who abandon you will
certainly perish;
you will destroy those who are
unfaithful to you.
28 But as for me, how wonderful to
be near God,
to find protection with the
Sovereign LORD
and to proclaim all that he has
done!

A Prayer for National Deliverance[b]

74 Why have you abandoned us
like this, O God?
Will you be angry with your
own people forever?
2 Remember your people, whom you
chose for yourself long ago,
whom you brought out of
slavery to be your own tribe.
Remember Mount Zion, where
once you lived.
3 Walk over these total ruins;
our enemies have destroyed
everything in the Temple.

4 Your enemies have shouted in
triumph in your Temple;
they have placed their flags
there as signs of victory.
5 They looked like woodsmen
cutting down trees with their
axes.[c]
6 They smashed all the wooden
panels
with their axes and sledge
hammers.
7 They wrecked your Temple and
set it on fire;
they desecrated the place where
you are worshiped.
8 They wanted to crush us
completely;
they burned down every holy
place in the land.

9 All our sacred symbols are gone;
there are no prophets left,
and no one knows how long this
will last.
10 How long, O God, will our
enemies laugh at you?
Will they insult your name
forever?
11 Why have you refused to help us?
Why do you keep your hands
behind you?[d]

12 But you have been our king from
the beginning, O God;
you have saved us many times.

[b] HEBREW TITLE: *A poem by Asaph.* [c] *Verse 5 in Hebrew is unclear.* [d] *Probable text* Why do you keep your hands behind you; *Hebrew unclear.*

13 With your mighty strength you
divided the sea
and smashed the heads of the
sea monsters;
14 you crushed the heads of the
monster Leviathan[e]
and fed his body to desert
animals.[f]
15 You made springs and fountains
flow;
you dried up large rivers.
16 You created the day and the night;
you set the sun and the moon in
their places;
17 you set the limits of the earth;
you made summer and winter.

18 But remember, O LORD, that your
enemies laugh at you,
that they are godless and
despise you.
19 Don't abandon your helpless
people to their cruel enemies;
don't forget your persecuted
people!

20 Remember the covenant you made
with us.
There is violence in every dark
corner of the land.
21 Don't let the oppressed be put to
shame;
let those poor and needy people
praise you.

22 Rouse yourself, God, and defend
your cause!
Remember that godless people
laugh at you all day long.
23 Don't forget the angry shouts of
your enemies,
the continuous noise made by
your foes.

God the Judge[g]

75 We give thanks to you, O God,
we give thanks to you!
We proclaim how great you are
and tell of[h] the wonderful
things you have done.

2 "I have set a time for judgment,"
says God,
"and I will judge with fairness.
3 Though every living creature
tremble
and the earth itself be shaken,
I will keep its foundations firm.
4 I tell the wicked not to be
arrogant;
5 I tell them to stop their
boasting."

6 Judgment does not come from the
east or from the west,
from the north or from the
south;[i]
7 it is God who is the judge,
condemning some and acquitting
others.
8 The LORD holds a cup in his hand,
filled with the strong wine of his
anger.
He pours it out, and all the wicked
drink it;
they drink it down to the last
drop.

9 But I will never stop speaking of
the God of Jacob
or singing praises to him.
10 He will break the power of the
wicked,
but the power of the righteous
will be increased.

God the Victor[j]

76 God is known in Judah;
his name is honored in Israel.
2 He has his home in Jerusalem;
he lives on Mount Zion.
3 There he broke the arrows of the
enemy,
their shields and swords, yes, all
their weapons.

4 How glorious you are, O God!
How majestic, as you return
from the mountains
where you defeated your foes.
5 Their brave soldiers have been
stripped of all they had
and now are sleeping the sleep
of death;
all their strength and skill was
useless.

[e] LEVIATHAN: *A legendary monster which was a symbol of the forces of chaos and evil.*
[f] animals; *or* people. [g] HEBREW TITLE: *A psalm by Asaph; a song.* [h] *Some ancient translations* We proclaim how great you are and tell of; *Hebrew* Your name is near and they tell of.
[i] *Probable text* from the north or from the south; *Hebrew* from the wilderness of the mountains.
[j] HEBREW TITLE: *A psalm by Asaph; a song.*

6 When you threatened them, O God
of Jacob,
the horses and their riders fell
dead.
7 But you, LORD, are feared by all.
No one can stand in your
presence
when you are angry.
8 You made your judgment known
from heaven;
the world was afraid and kept
silent,
9 when you rose up to pronounce
judgment,
to save all the oppressed on
earth.

10 Human anger only results in more
praise for you;
those who survive the wars will
keep your festivals.[k]

11 Give the LORD your God what you
promised him;
bring gifts to him, all you
nearby nations.
God makes everyone fear him;
12 he humbles proud princes
and terrifies great kings.

Comfort in Time of Distress[l]

77 I cry aloud to God;
I cry aloud, and he hears me.
2 In times of trouble I pray to the
Lord;
all night long I lift my hands in
prayer,
but I cannot find comfort.
3 When I think of God, I sigh;
when I meditate, I feel
discouraged.

4 He keeps me awake all night;
I am so worried that I cannot
speak.
5 I think of days gone by
and remember years of
long ago.
6 I spend the night in deep
thought;[m]
I meditate, and this is what I ask
myself:
7 "Will the Lord always reject us?
Will he never again be pleased
with us?
8 Has he stopped loving us?
Does his promise no longer
stand?
9 Has God forgotten to be merciful?
Has anger taken the place of his
compassion?"
10 Then I said, "What hurts me most
is this—
that God is no longer
powerful."[n]

11 I will remember your great deeds,
LORD;
I will recall the wonders you did
in the past.
12 I will think about all that you have
done;
I will meditate on all your
mighty acts.

13 Everything you do, O God, is holy.
No god is as great as you.
14 You are the God who works
miracles;
you showed your might among
the nations.
15 By your power you saved your
people,
the descendants of Jacob and of
Joseph.

16 When the waters saw you, O God,
they were afraid,
and the depths of the sea
trembled.
17 The clouds poured down rain;
thunder crashed from the sky,
and lightning flashed in all
directions.
18 The crash of your thunder
rolled out,
and flashes of lightning lit up
the world;
the earth trembled and shook.
19 You walked through the waves;
you crossed the deep sea,
but your footprints could not be
seen.
20 You led your people like a
shepherd,
with Moses and Aaron in
charge.

[k] *One ancient translation* will keep your festivals; *verse 10 in Hebrew is unclear.*
[l] HEBREW TITLE: *A psalm by Asaph.* [m] *Some ancient translations* deep thought; *Hebrew* song.
[n] *Verse 10 in Hebrew is unclear.*

God and His People[o]

78 Listen, my people, to my teaching,
and pay attention to what I say.
2 I am going to use wise sayings
and explain mysteries from the past,
3 things we have heard and known,
things that our ancestors told us.
4 We will not keep them from our children;
we will tell the next generation
about the LORD's power and his great deeds
and the wonderful things he has done.

5 He gave laws to the people of Israel
and commandments to the descendants of Jacob.
He instructed our ancestors
to teach his laws to their children,
6 so that the next generation might learn them
and in turn should tell their children.
7 In this way they also will put their trust in God
and not forget what he has done,
but always obey his commandments.
8 They will not be like their ancestors,
a rebellious and disobedient people,
whose trust in God was never firm
and who did not remain faithful to him.

9 The Ephraimites, armed with bows and arrows,
ran away on the day of battle.
10 They did not keep their covenant with God;
they refused to obey his law.
11 They forgot what he had done,
the miracles they had seen him perform.
12 While their ancestors watched,
God performed miracles
in the plain of Zoan in the land of Egypt.
13 He divided the sea and took them through it;
he made the waters stand like walls.
14 By day he led them with a cloud
and all night long with the light of a fire.
15 He split rocks open in the desert
and gave them water from the depths.
16 He caused a stream to come out of the rock
and made water flow like a river.

17 But they continued to sin against God,
and in the desert they rebelled against the Most High.
18 They deliberately put God to the test
by demanding the food they wanted.
19 They spoke against God and said,
"Can God supply food in the desert?
20 It is true that he struck the rock,
and water flowed out in a torrent;
but can he also provide us with bread
and give his people meat?"

21 And so the LORD was angry when he heard them;
he attacked his people with fire,
and his anger against them grew,
22 because they had no faith in him
and did not believe that he would save them.
23 But he spoke to the sky above
and commanded its doors to open;
24 he gave them grain from heaven,
by sending down manna for them to eat.
25 So they ate the food of angels,
and God gave them all they wanted.
26 He also caused the east wind to blow,
and by his power he stirred up the south wind;
27 and to his people he sent down birds,

[o] HEBREW TITLE: *A poem by Asaph.*

as many as the grains of sand
on the shore;
28 they fell in the middle of the camp
all around the tents.
29 So the people ate and were
satisfied;
God gave them what they
wanted.
30 But they had not yet satisfied their
craving
and were still eating,
31 when God became angry with
them
and killed their strongest men,
the best young men of Israel.

32 In spite of all this the people kept
sinning;
in spite of his miracles they did
not trust him.
33 So he ended their days like a
breath
and their lives with sudden
disaster.
34 Whenever he killed some of them,
the rest would turn to him;
they would repent and pray
earnestly to him.
35 They remembered that God was
their protector,
that the Almighty came to
their aid.
36 But their words were all lies;
nothing they said was sincere.
37 They were not loyal to him;
they were not faithful to their
covenant with him.

38 But God was merciful to his
people.
He forgave their sin
and did not destroy them.
Many times he held back his
anger
and restrained his fury.
39 He remembered that they were
only mortal beings,
like a wind that blows by and is
gone.

40 How often they rebelled against
him in the desert;
how many times they made
him sad!
41 Again and again they put God to
the test
and brought pain to the Holy
God of Israel.
42 They forgot his great power
and the day when he saved them
from their enemies
43 and performed his mighty acts
and miracles
in the plain of Zoan in the land
of Egypt.
44 He turned the rivers into blood,
and the Egyptians had no water
to drink.
45 He sent flies among them, that
tormented them,
and frogs that ruined their land.
46 He sent locusts to eat their crops
and to destroy their fields.
47 He killed their grapevines with
hail
and their fig trees with frost.
48 He killed their cattle with hail
and their flocks with lightning.[p]
49 He caused them great distress
by pouring out his anger and
fierce rage,
which came as messengers of
death.
50 He did not restrain his anger
or spare their lives,
but killed them with a plague.
51 He killed the first-born sons
of all the families of Egypt.

52 Then he led his people out like a
shepherd
and guided them through the
desert.
53 He led them safely, and they were
not afraid;
but the sea came rolling over
their enemies.
54 He brought them to his holy land,
to the mountains which he
himself conquered.
55 He drove out the inhabitants as his
people advanced;
he divided their land among the
tribes of Israel
and gave their homes to his
people.

56 But they rebelled against
Almighty God
and put him to the test.
They did not obey his
commandments,

[p] hail . . . lightning; *or* terrible disease . . . deadly plague.

57 but were rebellious and disloyal
like their ancestors,
unreliable as a crooked arrow.
58 They angered him with their
heathen places of worship,
and with their idols they made
him furious.
59 God was angry when he saw it,
so he rejected his people
completely.
60 He abandoned his tent in Shiloh,[q]
the home where he had lived
among us.
61 He allowed our enemies to capture
the Covenant Box,
the symbol of his power and
glory.
62 He was angry with his own people
and let them be killed by their
enemies.
63 Young men were killed in war,
and young women had no one to
marry.
64 Priests died by violence,
and their widows were not
allowed to mourn.

65 At last the Lord woke up as
though from sleep;
he was like a strong man excited
by wine.
66 He drove his enemies back
in lasting and shameful defeat.
67 But he rejected the descendants of
Joseph;
he did not select the tribe of
Ephraim.
68 Instead he chose the tribe of Judah
and Mount Zion, which he
dearly loves.
69 There he built his Temple
like his home in heaven;
he made it firm like the earth
itself,
secure for all time.

70 He chose his servant David;
he took him from the pastures,
71 where he looked after his flocks,
and he made him king of Israel,
the shepherd of the people
of God.
72 David took care of them with
unselfish devotion
and led them with skill.

A Prayer for the Nation's Deliverance[r]

79 O God, the heathen have
invaded your land.
They have desecrated your holy
Temple
and left Jerusalem in ruins.
2 They left the bodies of your people
for the vultures,
the bodies of your servants for
wild animals to eat.
3 They shed your people's blood like
water;
blood flowed like water all
through Jerusalem,
and no one was left to bury the
dead.
4 The surrounding nations insult us;
they laugh at us and mock us.

5 LORD, will you be angry with us
forever?
Will your anger continue to burn
like fire?
6 Turn your anger on the nations
that do not worship you,
on the people who do not pray
to you.
7 For they have killed your people;
they have ruined your country.

8 Do not punish us for the sins of
our ancestors.
Have mercy on us now;
we have lost all hope.
9 Help us, O God, and save us;
rescue us and forgive our sins
for the sake of your own honor.
10 Why should the nations ask us,
"Where is your God?"
Let us see you punish the nations
for shedding the blood of your
servants.

11 Listen to the groans of the
prisoners,
and by your great power free
those who are condemned
to die.
12 Lord, pay the other nations back
seven times
for all the insults they have
hurled at you.
13 Then we, your people, the sheep of
your flock,

[q] SHILOH: *The central place of worship for the people of Israel before the time of King David.*
[r] HEBREW TITLE: *A psalm by Asaph.*

will thank you forever
and praise you for all time to
come.

A Prayer for the Nation's Restoration[s]

80 Listen to us, O Shepherd of
Israel;
hear us, leader of your flock.
Seated on your throne above the
winged creatures,
2 reveal yourself to the tribes of
Ephraim, Benjamin, and
Manasseh.
Show us your strength;
come and save us!

3 Bring us back, O God!
Show us your mercy, and we
will be saved!

4 How much longer, LORD God
Almighty,
will you be angry with your
people's prayers?
5 You have given us sorrow to eat,
a large cup of tears to drink.
6 You let the surrounding nations
fight over our land;
our enemies insult us.

7 Bring us back, Almighty God!
Show us your mercy, and we
will be saved!

8 You brought a grapevine out of
Egypt;
you drove out other nations and
planted it in their land.
9 You cleared a place for it to grow;
its roots went deep, and it
spread out over the whole
land.
10 It covered the hills with its shade;
its branches overshadowed the
giant cedars.
11 It extended its branches to the
Mediterranean Sea
and as far as the Euphrates
River.
12 Why did you break down the
fences around it?
Now anyone passing by can
steal its grapes;
13 wild hogs trample it down,
and wild animals feed on it.
14 Turn to us, Almighty God!
Look down from heaven at us;
come and save your people!
15 Come and save this grapevine that
you planted,
this young vine you made grow
so strong!

16 Our enemies have set it on fire
and cut it down;
look at them in anger and
destroy them!
17 Preserve and protect the people
you have chosen,
the nation you made so strong.
18 We will never turn away from you
again;
keep us alive, and we will
praise you.

19 Bring us back, LORD God Almighty.
Show us your mercy, and we
will be saved.

A Song for a Festival[t]

81 Shout for joy to God our
defender;
sing praise to the God of Jacob!
2 Start the music and beat the
tambourines;
play pleasant music on the harps
and the lyres.
3 Blow the trumpet for the festival,
when the moon is new and
when the moon is full.
4 This is the law in Israel,
an order from the God of Jacob.
5 He gave it to the people of Israel
when he attacked the land of
Egypt.

I hear an unknown voice saying,
6 "I took the burdens off your backs;
I let you put down your loads of
bricks.
7 When you were in trouble, you
called to me, and I saved you.
From my hiding place in the
storm, I answered you.
I put you to the test at the
springs of Meribah.
8 Listen, my people, to my warning;
Israel, how I wish you would
listen to me!
9 You must never worship
another god.

[s] HEBREW TITLE: *A psalm by Asaph; a testimony.*

[t] HEBREW TITLE: *By Asaph.*

10 I am the LORD your God,
who brought you out of Egypt.
Open your mouth, and I will
feed you.
11 "But my people would not listen
to me;
Israel would not obey me.
12 So I let them go their stubborn
ways
and do whatever they wanted.
13 How I wish my people would
listen to me;
how I wish they would obey me!
14 I would quickly defeat their
enemies
and conquer all their foes.
15 Those who hate me would bow in
fear before me;
their punishment would last
forever.
16 But I would feed you with the
finest wheat
and satisfy you with wild
honey."

God the Supreme Ruler[u]

82 God presides in the heavenly
council;
in the assembly of the gods he
gives his decision:
2 "You must stop judging unjustly;
you must no longer be partial to
the wicked!
3 Defend the rights of the poor and
the orphans;
be fair to the needy and the
helpless.
4 Rescue them from the power of
evil people.

5 "How ignorant you are! How
stupid!
You are completely corrupt,
and justice has disappeared from
the world.
6 'You are gods,' I said;
'all of you are children of the
Most High.'
7 But you will die like mortals;
your life will end like that of any
prince."

8 Come, O God, and rule the world;
all the nations are yours.

A Prayer for the Defeat of Israel's Enemies[v]

83 O God, do not keep silent;
do not be still, do not be
quiet!
2 Look! Your enemies are in revolt,
and those who hate you are
rebelling.
3 They are making secret plans
against your people;
they are plotting against those
you protect.
4 "Come," they say, "let us destroy
their nation,
so that Israel will be forgotten
forever."

5 They agree on their plan
and form an alliance
against you:
6 the people of Edom and the
Ishmaelites;
the people of Moab and the
Hagrites;
7 the people of Gebal, Ammon, and
Amalek,
and of Philistia and Tyre.
8 Assyria has also joined them
as a strong ally of the
Ammonites and Moabites, the
descendants of Lot.

9 Do to them what you did to the
Midianites,
and to Sisera and Jabin at the
Kishon River.
10 You defeated them at Endor,
and their bodies rotted on the
ground.
11 Do to their leaders what you did
to Oreb and Zeeb;
defeat all their rulers as you did
Zebah and Zalmunna,
12 who said, "We will take for
our own
the land that belongs to God."

13 Scatter them like dust, O God,
like straw blown away by the
wind.
14 As fire burns the forest,
as flames set the hills on fire,
15 chase them away with your storm
and terrify them with your fierce
winds.

[u] HEBREW TITLE: *A psalm by Asaph.* [v] HEBREW TITLE: *A psalm by Asaph; a song.*

16 Cover their faces with shame,
O LORD,
and make them acknowledge
your power.
17 May they be defeated and terrified
forever;
may they die in complete
disgrace.
18 May they know that you alone are
the LORD,
supreme ruler over all the earth.

Longing for God's House[w]

84 How I love your Temple, LORD
Almighty!
2 How I want to be there!
I long to be in the LORD's
Temple.
With my whole being I sing for joy
to the living God.
3 Even the sparrows have built a
nest,
and the swallows have their own
home;
they keep their young near your
altars,
LORD Almighty, my king and
my God.
4 How happy are those who live in
your Temple,
always singing praise to you.

5 How happy are those whose
strength comes from you,
who are eager to make the
pilgrimage to Mount Zion.
6 As they pass through the dry
valley of Baca,
it becomes a place of springs;
the autumn rain fills it with
pools.
7 They grow stronger as they go;
they will see the God of gods on
Zion.

8 Hear my prayer, LORD God
Almighty.
Listen, O God of Jacob!
9 Bless our king, O God,
the king you have chosen.

10 One day spent in your Temple
is better than a thousand
anywhere else;
I would rather stand at the gate of
the house of my God
than live in the homes of the
wicked.
11 The LORD is our protector and
glorious king,
blessing us with kindness and
honor.
He does not refuse any good thing
to those who do what is right.
12 LORD Almighty, how happy are
those who trust in you!

A Prayer for the Nation's Welfare[w]

85 LORD, you have been merciful to
your land;
you have made Israel
prosperous again.
2 You have forgiven your people's
sins
and pardoned all their wrongs.
3 You stopped being angry with
them
and held back your furious rage.

4 Bring us back, O God our savior,
and stop being displeased
with us!
5 Will you be angry with us forever?
Will your anger never cease?
6 Make us strong again,
and we, your people, will
praise you.
7 Show us your constant love,
O LORD,
and give us your saving help.

8 I am listening to what the LORD
God is saying;
he promises peace to us, his own
people,
if we do not go back to our
foolish ways.
9 Surely he is ready to save those
who honor him,
and his saving presence will
remain in our land.

10 Love and faithfulness will meet;
righteousness and peace will
embrace.
11 Human loyalty will reach up from
the earth,
and God's righteousness will
look down from heaven.
12 The LORD will make us prosperous,
and our land will produce rich
harvests.

[w] HEBREW TITLE: *A psalm by the clan of Korah.*

[13] Righteousness will go before the
LORD
and prepare the path for him.

A Prayer for Help[x]

86 Listen to me, LORD, and
answer me,
for I am helpless and weak.
[2] Save me from death, because I am
loyal to you;
save me, for I am your servant
and I trust in you.

[3] You are my God, so be merciful
to me;
I pray to you all day long.
[4] Make your servant glad, O Lord,
because my prayers go up
to you.
[5] You are good to us and forgiving,
full of constant love for all who
pray to you.

[6] Listen, LORD, to my prayer;
hear my cries for help.
[7] I call to you in times of trouble,
because you answer my prayers.

[8] There is no god like you, O Lord,
not one has done what you have
done.
[9] All the nations that you have
created
will come and bow down to you;
they will praise your greatness.
[10] You are mighty and do wonderful
things;
you alone are God.

[11] Teach me, LORD, what you want
me to do,
and I will obey you faithfully;
teach me to serve you with
complete devotion.
[12] I will praise you with all my heart,
O Lord my God;
I will proclaim your greatness
forever.
[13] How great is your constant love
for me!
You have saved me from the
grave itself.

[14] Proud people are coming against
me, O God;
a cruel gang is trying to
kill me—
people who pay no attention
to you.
[15] But you, O Lord, are a merciful
and loving God,
always patient, always kind and
faithful.
[16] Turn to me and have mercy
on me;
strengthen me and save me,
because I serve you just as my
mother did.
[17] Show me proof of your goodness,
LORD;
those who hate me will be
ashamed
when they see that you have
given me comfort and help.

In Praise of Jerusalem[y]

87 The LORD built his city on the
sacred hill;[z]
[2] more than any other place in
Israel
he loves the city of Jerusalem.
[3] Listen, city of God,
to the wonderful things he says
about you:

[4] "I will include Egypt and
Babylonia
when I list the nations that
obey me;
the people of Philistia, Tyre, and
Ethiopia[a]
I will number among the
inhabitants of Jerusalem."

[5] Of Zion it will be said
that all nations belong there
and that the Almighty will make
her strong.
[6] The LORD will write a list of the
peoples
and include them all as citizens
of Jerusalem.
[7] They dance and sing,
"In Zion is the source of all our
blessings."

[x] HEBREW TITLE: *A prayer by David.* [y] HEBREW TITLE: *A psalm by the clan of Korah; a song.*
[z] SACRED HILL: *See 2.6.* [a] *Hebrew* Cush: *Cush is the ancient name of the extensive territory south of the First Cataract of the Nile River. This region was called Ethiopia in Graeco-Roman time, and included within its borders most of modern Sudan and some of present-day Ethiopia (Abyssinia).*

A Cry for Help[b]

88 LORD God, my savior, I cry out
all day,
and at night I come before you.
2 Hear my prayer;
listen to my cry for help!
3 So many troubles have fallen
on me
that I am close to death.
4 I am like all others who are about
to die;
all my strength is gone.[c]
5 I am abandoned among the dead;
I am like the slain lying in their
graves,
those you have forgotten
completely,
who are beyond your help.
6 You have thrown me into the
depths of the tomb,
into the darkest and deepest pit.
7 Your anger lies heavy on me,
and I am crushed beneath its
waves.

8 You have caused my friends to
abandon me;
you have made me repulsive to
them.
I am closed in and cannot escape;
9 my eyes are weak from
suffering.
LORD, every day I call to you
and lift my hands to you in
prayer.

10 Do you perform miracles for the
dead?
Do they rise up and praise you?
11 Is your constant love spoken of in
the grave
or your faithfulness in the place
of destruction?
12 Are your miracles seen in that
place of darkness
or your goodness in the land of
the forgotten?

13 LORD, I call to you for help;
every morning I pray to you.
14 Why do you reject me, LORD?
Why do you turn away
from me?
15 Ever since I was young, I have
suffered and been near death;
I am worn out[d] from the burden
of your punishments.
16 Your furious anger crushes me;
your terrible attacks destroy me.
17 All day long they surround me like
a flood;
they close in on me from every
side.
18 You have made even my closest
friends abandon me,
and darkness is my only
companion.

A Hymn in Time of National Trouble[e]

89 O LORD, I will always sing of
your constant love;
I will proclaim your faithfulness
forever.
2 I know that your love will last for
all time,
that your faithfulness is as
permanent as the sky.
3 You said, "I have made a covenant
with the man I chose;
I have promised my servant
David,
4 'A descendant of yours will always
be king;
I will preserve your dynasty
forever.'"

5 The heavens sing of the wonderful
things you do;
the holy ones sing of your
faithfulness, LORD.
6 No one in heaven is like you,
LORD;
none of the heavenly beings is
your equal.
7 You are feared in the council of
the holy ones;
they all stand in awe of you.

8 LORD God Almighty, none is as
mighty as you;
in all things you are faithful,
O LORD.
9 You rule over the powerful sea;
you calm its angry waves.
10 You crushed the monster Rahab[f]
and killed it;

[b] HEBREW TITLE: *A psalm by the clan of Korah; a song. A poem by Heman the Ezrahite.*
[c] all my strength is gone; *or* there is no help for me. [d] *Probable text* I am worn out; *Hebrew unclear.* [e] HEBREW TITLE: *A poem by Ethan the Ezrahite.* [f] RAHAB: *A legendary sea monster which represented the forces of chaos and evil.*

with your mighty strength you
defeated your enemies.
11 Heaven is yours, the earth also;
you made the world and
everything in it.
12 You created the north and the
south;
Mount Tabor and Mount
Hermon sing to you for joy.
13 How powerful you are!
How great is your strength!
14 Your kingdom is founded on
righteousness and justice;
love and faithfulness are shown
in all you do.

15 How happy are the people who
worship you with songs,
who live in the light of your
kindness!
16 Because of you they rejoice all day
long,
and they praise you for your
goodness.
17 You give us great victories;
in your love you make us
triumphant.
18 You, O LORD, chose our protector;
you, the Holy God of Israel,
gave us our king.

God's Promise to David

19 In a vision long ago you said to
your faithful servants,
"I have given help to a famous
soldier;
I have given the throne to one I
chose from the people.
20 I have made my servant David
king
by anointing him with holy oil.
21 My strength will always be
with him,
my power will make him strong.
22 His enemies will never succeed
against him;
the wicked will not defeat him.
23 I will crush his foes
and kill everyone who
hates him.
24 I will love him and be loyal
to him;
I will make him always
victorious.
25 I will extend his kingdom
from the Mediterranean to the
Euphrates River.
26 He will say to me,
'You are my father and my God;
you are my protector and
savior.'
27 I will make him my first-born son,
the greatest of all kings.
28 I will always keep my promise
to him,
and my covenant with him will
last forever.
29 His dynasty will be as permanent
as the sky;
a descendant of his will always
be king.

30 "But if his descendants disobey
my law
and do not live according to my
commands,
31 if they disregard my instructions
and do not keep my
commandments,
32 then I will punish them for their
sins;
I will make them suffer for their
wrongs.
33 But I will not stop loving David
or fail to keep my promise
to him.
34 I will not break my covenant
with him
or take back even one promise I
made him.

35 "Once and for all I have promised
by my holy name:
I will never lie to David.
36 He will always have descendants,
and I will watch over his
kingdom as long as the sun
shines.
37 It will be as permanent as the
moon,
that faithful witness in the sky."

Lament over the Defeat of the King

38 But you are angry with your
chosen king;
you have deserted and
rejected him.
39 You have broken your covenant
with your servant
and thrown his crown in the
dirt.
40 You have torn down the walls of
his city
and left his forts in ruins.
41 All who pass by steal his
belongings;

all his neighbors laugh at him.
42 You have given the victory to his enemies;
you have made them all happy.
43 You have made his weapons useless
and let him be defeated in battle.
44 You have taken away his royal scepter[g]
and knocked his throne to the ground.
45 You have made him old before his time
and covered him with disgrace.

A Prayer for Deliverance

46 LORD, will you hide yourself forever?
How long will your anger burn like fire?
47 Remember how short my life is;
remember that you created all of us mortal!
48 Who can live and never die?
How can we humans keep ourselves from the grave?

49 Lord, where are the former proofs of your love?
Where are the promises you made to David?
50 Don't forget how I, your servant, am insulted,
how I endure all the curses[h] of the heathen.
51 Your enemies insult your chosen king, O LORD!
They insult him wherever he goes.

52 Praise the LORD forever!

Amen! Amen!

BOOK FOUR

(Psalms 90–106)

Of God and Human Beings[i]

90 O Lord, you have always been our home.
2 Before you created the hills
or brought the world into being,
you were eternally God,
and will be God forever.
3 You tell us to return to what we were;
you change us back to dust.
4 A thousand years to you are like one day;
they are like yesterday, already gone,
like a short hour in the night.
5 You carry us away like a flood;
we last no longer than a dream.
We are like weeds that sprout in the morning,
6 that grow and burst into bloom,
then dry up and die in the evening.

7 We are destroyed by your anger;
we are terrified by your fury.
8 You place our sins before you,
our secret sins where you can see them.

9 Our life is cut short by your anger;
it fades away like a whisper.
10 Seventy years is all we have—
eighty years, if we are strong;
yet all they bring us is trouble and sorrow;
life is soon over, and we are gone.

11 Who has felt the full power of your anger?
Who knows what fear your fury can bring?
12 Teach us how short our life is,
so that we may become wise.

13 How much longer will your anger last?
Have pity, O LORD, on your servants!
14 Fill us each morning with your constant love,
so that we may sing and be glad all our life.
15 Give us now as much happiness as the sadness you gave us
during all our years of misery.
16 Let us, your servants, see your mighty deeds;
let our descendants see your glorious might.

[g] *Probable text* royal scepter; *Hebrew* purity. [h] *Probable text* curses; *Hebrew* crowds.
[i] HEBREW TITLE: *A prayer by Moses, the man of God.*

17 Lord our God, may your blessings
be with us.
Give us success in all we do!

God Our Protector

91 Whoever goes to the LORD for
safety,
whoever remains under the
protection of the Almighty,
2 can say to him,
"You are my defender and
protector.
You are my God; in you I trust."
3 He will keep you safe from all
hidden dangers
and from all deadly diseases.
4 He will cover you with his wings;
you will be safe in his care;
his faithfulness will protect and
defend you.
5 You need not fear any dangers at
night
or sudden attacks during the day
6 or the plagues that strike in the
dark
or the evils that kill in daylight.

7 A thousand may fall dead
beside you,
ten thousand all around you,
but you will not be harmed.
8 You will look and see
how the wicked are punished.

9 You have made the LORD your[j]
defender,
the Most High your protector,
10 and so no disaster will strike you,
no violence will come near your
home.
11 God will put his angels in charge
of you
to protect you wherever you go.
12 They will hold you up with their
hands
to keep you from hurting your
feet on the stones.
13 You will trample down lions and
snakes,
fierce lions and poisonous
snakes.

14 God says, "I will save those who
love me
and will protect those who
acknowledge me as LORD.
15 When they call to me, I will
answer them;
when they are in trouble, I will
be with them.
I will rescue them and honor
them.
16 I will reward them with long life;
I will save them."

A Song of Praise[k]

92 How good it is to give thanks
to you, O LORD,
to sing in your honor, O Most
High God,
2 to proclaim your constant love
every morning
and your faithfulness every
night,
3 with the music of stringed
instruments
and with melody on the harp.
4 Your mighty deeds, O LORD, make
me glad;
because of what you have done,
I sing for joy.

5 How great are your actions, LORD!
How deep are your thoughts!
6 This is something a fool cannot
know;
someone who is stupid cannot
understand:
7 the wicked may grow like weeds,
those who do wrong may
prosper;
yet they will be totally destroyed,
8 because you, LORD, are supreme
forever.

9 We know that your enemies
will die,
and all the wicked will be
defeated.
10 You have made me as strong as a
wild ox;
you have blessed me with
happiness.
11 I have seen the defeat of my
enemies
and heard the cries of the
wicked.

12 The righteous will flourish like
palm trees;
they will grow like the cedars of
Lebanon.

[j] *Probable text* your; *Hebrew* my. [k] HEBREW TITLE: *A psalm; a song for the Sabbath.*

13 They are like trees planted in the
house of the LORD,
that flourish in the Temple of
our God,
14 that still bear fruit in old age
and are always green and
strong.
15 This shows that the LORD is just,
that there is no wrong in my
protector.

God the King

93 The LORD is king.
He is clothed with majesty
and strength.
The earth is set firmly in place
and cannot be moved.
2 Your throne, O LORD, has been
firm from the beginning,
and you existed before time
began.

3 The ocean depths raise their voice,
O LORD;
they raise their voice and roar.
4 The LORD rules supreme in heaven,
greater than the roar of the
ocean,
more powerful than the waves of
the sea.

5 Your laws are eternal, LORD,
and your Temple is holy indeed,
forever and ever.

God the Judge of All

94 LORD, you are a God who
punishes;
reveal your anger!
2 You are the judge of us all;
rise and give the proud what
they deserve!
3 How much longer will the wicked
be glad?
How much longer, LORD?
4 How much longer will criminals
be proud
and boast about their crimes?

5 They crush your people, LORD;
they oppress those who belong
to you.
6 They kill widows and orphans,
and murder the strangers who
live in our land.
7 They say, "The LORD does not
see us;
the God of Israel does not
notice."

8 My people, how can you be such
stupid fools?
When will you ever learn?
9 God made our ears—can't he
hear?
He made our eyes—can't he see?
10 He scolds the nations—won't he
punish them?[l]
He is the teacher of us all—
hasn't he any knowledge?
11 The LORD knows what we think;
he knows how senseless our
reasoning is.

12 LORD, how happy are those you
instruct,
the ones to whom you teach
your law!
13 You give them rest from days of
trouble
until a pit is dug to trap the
wicked.
14 The LORD will not abandon his
people;
he will not desert those who
belong to him.
15 Justice will again be found in the
courts,
and all righteous people will
support it.

16 Who stood up for me against the
wicked?
Who took my side against the
evildoers?
17 If the LORD had not helped me,
I would have gone quickly to the
land of silence.[m]
18 I said, "I am falling";
but your constant love, O LORD,
held me up.
19 Whenever I am anxious and
worried,
you comfort me and make me
glad.

20 You have nothing to do with
corrupt judges,
who make injustice legal,
21 who plot against good people

[l] them?; *or* our wicked leaders? [m] LAND OF SILENCE: *The world of the dead (see 6.5).*

and sentence the innocent to
death.
22 But the LORD defends me;
my God protects me.
23 He will punish them for their
wickedness
and destroy them for their sins;
the LORD our God will destroy
them.

A Song of Praise

95 Come, let us praise the LORD!
Let us sing for joy to God,
who protects us!
2 Let us come before him with
thanksgiving
and sing joyful songs of praise.
3 For the LORD is a mighty God,
a mighty king over all the gods.
4 He rules over the whole earth,
from the deepest caves to the
highest hills.
5 He rules over the sea, which he
made;
the land also, which he himself
formed.

6 Come, let us bow down and
worship him;
let us kneel before the LORD, our
Maker!
7 He is our God;
we are the people he cares for,
the flock for which he provides.

Listen today to what he says:
8 "Don't be stubborn, as your
ancestors were at Meribah,
as they were that day in the
desert at Massah.
9 There they put me to the test and
tried me,
although they had seen what I
did for them.
10 For forty years I was disgusted
with those people.
I said, 'How disloyal they are!
They refuse to obey my
commands.'
11 I was angry and made a solemn
promise:
'You will never enter the land
where I would have given you
rest.'"

God the Supreme King

(1 Chronicles 16.23-33)

96 Sing a new song to the LORD!
Sing to the LORD, all the
world!
2 Sing to the LORD, and praise
him!
Proclaim every day the good
news that he has saved us.
3 Proclaim his glory to the
nations,
his mighty deeds to all peoples.

4 The LORD is great and is to be
highly praised;
he is to be honored more than
all the gods.
5 The gods of all other nations are
only idols,
but the LORD created the
heavens.
6 Glory and majesty surround
him;
power and beauty fill his
Temple.

7 Praise the LORD, all people on
earth;
praise his glory and might.
8 Praise the LORD's glorious
name;
bring an offering and come into
his Temple.
9 Bow down before the Holy One
when he appears;[n]
tremble before him, all the
earth!

10 Say to all the nations, "The LORD
is king!
The earth is set firmly in place
and cannot be moved;
he will judge the peoples with
justice."
11 Be glad, earth and sky!
Roar, sea, and every creature
in you;
12 be glad, fields, and everything
in you!
The trees in the woods will shout
for joy
13 when the LORD comes to rule the
earth.
He will rule the peoples of the
world
with justice and fairness.

[n] when he appears; *or* in garments of worship.

God the Supreme Ruler

97 The LORD is king! Earth, be glad!
Rejoice, you islands of the seas!
2 Clouds and darkness surround him;
he rules with righteousness and justice.
3 Fire goes in front of him
and burns up his enemies around him.
4 His lightning lights up the world;
the earth sees it and trembles.
5 The hills melt like wax before the LORD,
before the Lord of all the earth.
6 The heavens proclaim his righteousness,
and all the nations see his glory.

7 Everyone who worships idols is put to shame;
all the gods bow down[o] before the LORD.
8 The people of Zion are glad,
and the cities of Judah rejoice
because of your judgments, O LORD.
9 LORD Almighty, you are ruler of all the earth;
you are much greater than all the gods.

10 The LORD loves those who hate evil;[p]
he protects the lives of his people;
he rescues them from the power of the wicked.
11 Light shines on the righteous,
and gladness on the good.
12 All you that are righteous be glad
because of what the LORD has done!
Remember what the holy God has done,
and give thanks to him.

God the Ruler of the World[q]

98 Sing a new song to the LORD;
he has done wonderful things!
By his own power and holy strength
he has won the victory.
2 The LORD announced his victory;
he made his saving power known to the nations.
3 He kept his promise to the people of Israel
with loyalty and constant love for them.
All people everywhere have seen the victory of our God.

4 Sing for joy to the LORD, all the earth;
praise him with songs and shouts of joy!
5 Sing praises to the LORD!
Play music on the harps!
6 Blow trumpets and horns,
and shout for joy to the LORD, our king.

7 Roar, sea, and every creature in you;
sing, earth, and all who live on you!
8 Clap your hands, you rivers;
you hills, sing together with joy before the LORD,
9 because he comes to rule the earth.
He will rule the peoples of the world
with justice and fairness.

God the Supreme King

99 The LORD is king,
and the people tremble.
He sits on his throne above the winged creatures,
and the earth shakes.
2 The LORD is mighty in Zion;
he is supreme over all the nations.
3 Everyone will praise his great and majestic name.
Holy is he!

4 Mighty king,[r] you love what is right;
you have established justice in Israel;
you have brought righteousness and fairness.
5 Praise the LORD our God;

[o] all the gods bow down; *or* bow down, all gods. [p] *Probable text* The LORD loves those who hate evil; *Hebrew* Hate evil, you who love the LORD. [q] HEBREW TITLE: *A psalm.*
[r] *Probable text* Mighty king; *Hebrew* The might of the king.

worship before his throne!
Holy is he!
6 Moses and Aaron were his priests,
and Samuel was one who prayed to him;
they called to the LORD, and he answered them.
7 He spoke to them from the pillar of cloud;
they obeyed the laws and commands that he gave them.

8 O LORD, our God, you answered your people;
you showed them that you are a God who forgives,
even though you punished them for their sins.
9 Praise the LORD our God,
and worship at his sacred hill![s]
The LORD our God is holy.

A Hymn of Praise[t]

100 Sing to the LORD, all the world!
2 Worship the LORD with joy;
come before him with happy songs!

3 Acknowledge that the LORD is God.
He made us, and we belong to him;
we are his people, we are his flock.

4 Enter the Temple gates with thanksgiving;
go into its courts with praise.
Give thanks to him and praise him.

5 The LORD is good;
his love is eternal
and his faithfulness lasts forever.

A King's Promise[u]

101 My song is about loyalty and justice,
and I sing it to you, O LORD.
2 My conduct will be faultless.
When will you come to me?

I will live a pure life in my house
3 and will never tolerate evil.
I hate the actions of those who turn away from God;
I will have nothing to do with them.
4 I will not be dishonest[v]
and will have no dealings with evil.[w]
5 I will get rid of anyone
who whispers evil things about someone else;
I will not tolerate anyone
who is proud and arrogant.

6 I will approve of those who are faithful to God
and will let them live in my palace.
Those who are completely honest
will be allowed to serve me.

7 No liar will live in my palace;
no hypocrite will remain in my presence.
8 Day after day I will destroy
the wicked in our land;
I will expel all who are evil
from the city of the LORD.

The Prayer of a Troubled Youth[x]

102 Listen to my prayer, O LORD,
and hear my cry for help!
2 When I am in trouble,
don't turn away from me!
Listen to me,
and answer me quickly when I call!

3 My life is disappearing like smoke;
my body is burning like fire.
4 I am beaten down like dry grass;
I have lost my desire for food.
5 I groan aloud;
I am nothing but skin and bones.
6 I am like a wild bird in the desert,
like an owl in abandoned ruins.
7 I lie awake;
I am like a lonely bird on a housetop.
8 All day long my enemies insult me;
those who mock me use my name in cursing.

9-10 Because of your anger and fury,

[s] SACRED HILL: *See 2.6.* [t] HEBREW TITLE: *A psalm of thanksgiving.* [u] HEBREW TITLE: *A psalm by David.* [v] not be dishonest; *or* stay away from dishonest people. [w] evil; *or* evil people.
[x] HEBREW TITLE: *A prayer by a weary sufferer who pours out his complaints to the LORD.*

ashes are my food.
and my tears are mixed with my drink.
You picked me up and threw me away.
11 My life is like the evening shadows;
I am like dry grass.

12 But you, O LORD, are king forever;
all generations will remember you.
13 You will rise and take pity on Zion;
the time has come to have mercy on her;
this is the right time.
14 Your servants love her,
even though she is destroyed;
they have pity on her,
even though she is in ruins.

15 The nations will fear the LORD;
all the kings of the earth will fear his power.
16 When the LORD rebuilds Zion,
he will reveal his greatness.
17 He will hear his forsaken people
and listen to their prayer.

18 Write down for the coming generation what the LORD has done,
so that people not yet born will praise him.
19 The LORD looked down from his holy place on high,
he looked down from heaven to earth.
20 He heard the groans of prisoners
and set free those who were condemned to die.
21 And so his name will be proclaimed in Zion,
and he will be praised in Jerusalem
22 when nations and kingdoms come together
and worship the LORD.

23 The LORD has made me weak while I am still young;
he has shortened my life.
24 O God, do not take me away now before I grow old.
O LORD, you live forever;
25 long ago you created the earth,
and with your own hands you made the heavens.
26 They will disappear, but you will remain;
they will all wear out like clothes.
You will discard them like clothes,
and they will vanish.
27 But you are always the same,
and your life never ends.
28 Our children will live in safety,
and under your protection
their descendants will be secure.

The Love of God[y]

103 Praise the LORD, my soul!
All my being, praise his holy name!
2 Praise the LORD, my soul,
and do not forget how kind he is.
3 He forgives all my sins
and heals all my diseases.
4 He keeps me from the grave
and blesses me with love and mercy.
5 He fills my life[z] with good things,
so that I stay young and strong like an eagle.

6 The LORD judges in favor of the oppressed
and gives them their rights.
7 He revealed his plans to Moses
and let the people of Israel see his mighty deeds.
8 The LORD is merciful and loving,
slow to become angry and full of constant love.
9 He does not keep on rebuking;
he is not angry forever.
10 He does not punish us as we deserve
or repay us according to our sins and wrongs.
11 As high as the sky is above the earth,
so great is his love for those who honor him.
12 As far as the east is from the west,
so far does he remove our sins from us.
13 As a father is kind to his children,

[y] HEBREW TITLE: *By David.* [z] *Probable text* my life; *Hebrew unclear.*

so the LORD is kind to those who
honor him.
14 He knows what we are made of;
he remembers that we are dust.

15 As for us, our life is like grass.
We grow and flourish like a wild
flower;
16 then the wind blows on it, and it
is gone—
no one sees it again.
17 But for those who honor the LORD,
his love lasts forever,
and his goodness endures for all
generations
18 of those who are true to his
covenant
and who faithfully obey his
commands.

19 The LORD placed his throne in
heaven;
he is king over all.
20 Praise the LORD, you strong and
mighty angels,
who obey his commands,
who listen to what he says.
21 Praise the LORD, all you heavenly
powers,
you servants of his, who do his
will!
22 Praise the LORD, all his creatures
in all the places he rules.
Praise the LORD, my soul!

In Praise of the Creator

104 Praise the LORD, my soul!
O LORD, my God, how
great you are!
You are clothed with majesty and
glory;
2 you cover yourself with light.
You have spread out the heavens
like a tent
3 and built your home on the
waters above.[a]
You use the clouds as your chariot
and ride on the wings of the
wind.
4 You use the winds as your
messengers
and flashes of lightning as your
servants.

5 You have set the earth firmly on
its foundations,
and it will never be moved.
6 You placed the ocean over it like a
robe,
and the water covered the
mountains.
7 When you rebuked the waters,
they fled;
they rushed away when they
heard your shout of command.
8 They flowed over the mountains
and into the valleys,
to the place you had made for
them.
9 You set a boundary they can never
pass,
to keep them from covering the
earth again.

10 You make springs flow in the
valleys,
and rivers run between the hills.
11 They provide water for the wild
animals;
there the wild donkeys quench
their thirst.
12 In the trees near by,
the birds make their nests and
sing.

13 From the sky you send rain on the
hills,
and the earth is filled with your
blessings.
14 You make grass grow for the
cattle
and plants for us to use,
so that we can grow our crops
15 and produce wine to make us
happy,
olive oil to make us cheerful,
and bread to give us strength.

16 The cedars of Lebanon get plenty
of rain—
the LORD's own trees, which he
planted.
17 There the birds build their nests;
the storks nest in the fir trees.
18 The wild goats live in the high
mountains,
and the rock badgers hide in the
cliffs.

19 You created the moon to mark the
months;
the sun knows the time to set.

[a] THE WATERS ABOVE: *A reference to the waters above the celestial dome (Gn 1.6, 7).*

20 You made the night, and in the darkness
all the wild animals come out.
21 The young lions roar while they hunt,
looking for the food that God provides.
22 When the sun rises, they go back
and lie down in their dens.
23 Then people go out to do their work
and keep working until evening.

24 LORD, you have made so many things!
How wisely you made them all!
The earth is filled with your creatures.
25 There is the ocean, large and wide,
where countless creatures live,
large and small alike.
26 The ships sail on it, and in it plays Leviathan,
that sea monster which you made.[b]

27 All of them depend on you
to give them food when they need it.
28 You give it to them, and they eat it;
you provide food, and they are satisfied.
29 When you turn away, they are afraid;
when you take away your breath, they die
and go back to the dust from which they came.
30 But when you give them breath,[c]
they are created;
you give new life to the earth.

31 May the glory of the LORD last forever!
May the LORD be happy with what he has made!
32 He looks at the earth, and it trembles;
he touches the mountains, and they pour out smoke.

33 I will sing to the LORD all my life;
as long as I live I will sing praises to my God.
34 May he be pleased with my song,
for my gladness comes from him.
35 May sinners be destroyed from the earth;
may the wicked be no more.

Praise the LORD, my soul!
Praise the LORD!

God and His People

(1 Chronicles 16.8-22)

105 Give thanks to the LORD,
proclaim his greatness;
tell the nations what he has done.
2 Sing praise to the LORD;
tell the wonderful things he has done.
3 Be glad that we belong to him;
let all who worship him rejoice.
4 Go to the LORD for help;
and worship him continually.
5-6 You descendants of Abraham, his servant;
you descendants of Jacob, the man he chose:
remember the miracles that God performed
and the judgments that he gave.

7 The LORD is our God;
his commands are for all the world.
8 He will keep his covenant forever,
his promises for a thousand generations.
9 He will keep the agreement he made with Abraham
and his promise to Isaac.
10 The LORD made a covenant with Jacob,
one that will last forever.
11 "I will give you the land of Canaan," he said.
"It will be your own possession."

12 God's people were few in number,
strangers in the land of Canaan.
13 They wandered from country to country,
from one kingdom to another.
14 But God let no one oppress them;
to protect them, he warned the kings:

[b] in it plays . . . made; *or* Leviathan is there, that sea monster you made to amuse you.
[c] give them breath; *or* send out your spirit.

15 "Don't harm my chosen servants;
do not touch my prophets."

16 The LORD sent famine to their country
and took away all their food.
17 But he sent a man ahead of them,
Joseph, who had been sold as a slave.
18 His feet were kept in chains,
and an iron collar was around his neck,
19 until what he had predicted came true.
The word of the LORD proved him right.
20 Then the king of Egypt had him released;
the ruler of nations set him free.
21 He put him in charge of his government
and made him ruler over all the land,
22 with power over the king's officials
and authority to instruct his advisers.

23 Then Jacob went to Egypt
and settled in that country.
24 The LORD gave many children to his people
and made them stronger than their enemies.
25 He made the Egyptians hate his people
and treat his servants with deceit.

26 Then he sent his servant Moses,
and Aaron, whom he had chosen.
27 They did God's mighty acts
and performed miracles in Egypt.
28 God sent darkness on the country,
but the Egyptians did not obey[d] his command.
29 He turned their rivers into blood
and killed all their fish.
30 Their country was overrun with frogs;
even the palace was filled with them.
31 God commanded, and flies and gnats
swarmed throughout the whole country.
32 He sent hail and lightning on their land
instead of rain;
33 he destroyed their grapevines and fig trees
and broke down all the trees.
34 He commanded, and the locusts came,
countless millions of them;
35 they ate all the plants in the land;
they ate all the crops.
36 He killed the first-born sons
of all the families of Egypt.

37 Then he led the Israelites out;
they carried silver and gold,
and all of them were healthy and strong.
38 The Egyptians were afraid of them
and were glad when they left.
39 God put a cloud over his people
and a fire at night to give them light.
40 They[e] asked, and he sent quails;
he gave them food from heaven to satisfy them.
41 He opened a rock, and water gushed out,
flowing through the desert like a river.
42 He remembered his sacred promise
to Abraham his servant.

43 So he led his chosen people out,
and they sang and shouted for joy.
44 He gave them the lands of other peoples
and let them take over their fields,
45 so that his people would obey his laws
and keep all his commands.

Praise the LORD!

[d] *Some ancient translations* did not obey; *Hebrew* obeyed. [e] *Some ancient translations* They; *Hebrew* He.

The LORD*'s Goodness to His People*

106 Praise the LORD!
Give thanks to the LORD,
because he is good;
his love is eternal.
2 Who can tell all the great things
he has done?
Who can praise him enough?
3 Happy are those who obey his
commands,
who always do what is right.

4 Remember me, LORD, when you
help your people;
include me when you save them.
5 Let me see the prosperity of your
people
and share in the happiness of
your nation,
in the glad pride of those who
belong to you.

6 We have sinned as our
ancestors did;
we have been wicked and evil.
7 Our ancestors in Egypt did not
understand God's wonderful
acts;
they forgot the many times he
showed them his love,
and they rebelled against the
Almighty[f] at the Red Sea.
8 But he saved them, as he had
promised,
in order to show his great
power.
9 He gave a command to the
Red Sea,
and it dried up;
he led his people across on dry
land.
10 He saved them from those who
hated them;
he rescued them from their
enemies.
11 But the water drowned their
enemies;
not one of them was left.
12 Then his people believed his
promises
and sang praises to him.

13 But they quickly forgot what he
had done
and acted without waiting for
his advice.
14 They were filled with craving in
the desert
and put God to the test;
15 so he gave them what they
asked for,
but also sent a terrible disease
among them.

16 There in the desert they were
jealous of Moses
and of Aaron, the LORD's holy
servant.
17 Then the earth opened up and
swallowed Dathan
and buried Abiram and his
family;
18 fire came down on their followers
and burned up those wicked
people.

19 They made a gold bull-calf at
Sinai
and worshiped that idol;
20 they exchanged the glory of God
for the image of an animal that
eats grass.
21 They forgot the God who had
saved them
by his mighty acts in Egypt.
22 What wonderful things he did
there!
What amazing things at the
Red Sea!
23 When God said that he would
destroy his people,
his chosen servant, Moses, stood
up against God
and kept his anger from
destroying them.

24 Then they rejected the pleasant
land,
because they did not believe
God's promise.
25 They stayed in their tents and
grumbled
and would not listen to the LORD.
26 So he gave them a solemn
warning
that he would make them die in
the desert
27 and scatter their descendants
among the heathen,

[f] *Probable text* the Almighty; *Hebrew* the sea.

letting them die in foreign
countries.
28 Then at Peor, God's people joined
in the worship of Baal
and ate sacrifices offered to
dead gods.
29 They stirred up the LORD's anger
by their actions,
and a terrible disease broke out
among them.
30 But Phinehas stood up and
punished the guilty,
and the plague was stopped.
31 This has been remembered in his
favor ever since
and will be for all time to come.

32 At the springs of Meribah the
people made the LORD angry,
and Moses was in trouble on
their account.
33 They made him so bitter
that he spoke without stopping
to think.

34 They did not kill the heathen,
as the LORD had commanded
them to do,
35 but they intermarried with them
and adopted their pagan ways.
36 God's people worshiped idols,
and this caused their
destruction.
37 They offered their own sons and
daughters
as sacrifices to the idols of
Canaan.
38 They killed those innocent
children,
and the land was defiled by
those murders.
39 They made themselves impure by
their actions
and were unfaithful to God.

40 So the LORD was angry with his
people;
he was disgusted with them.
41 He abandoned them to the power
of the heathen,
and their enemies ruled over
them.
42 They were oppressed by their
enemies
and were in complete subjection
to them.
43 Many times the LORD rescued his
people,
but they chose to rebel
against him
and sank deeper into sin.
44 Yet the LORD heard them when
they cried out,
and he took notice of their
distress.
45 For their sake he remembered his
covenant,
and because of his great love he
relented.
46 He made all their oppressors
feel sorry for them.

47 Save us, O LORD our God,
and bring us back from among
the nations,
so that we may be thankful
and praise your holy name.

48 Praise the LORD, the God of Israel;
praise him now and forever!
Let everyone say, "Amen!"

Praise the LORD!

BOOK FIVE

(Psalms 107–150)

In Praise of God's Goodness

107 "Give thanks to the LORD,
because he is good;
his love is eternal!"
2 Repeat these words in praise to
the LORD,
all you whom he has saved.
He has rescued you from your
enemies
3 and has brought you back from
foreign countries,
from east and west, from north
and south.[g]

4 Some wandered in the trackless
desert
and could not find their way to a
city to live in.
5 They were hungry and thirsty
and had given up all hope.
6 Then in their trouble they called to
the LORD,

[g] *Probable text* south; *Hebrew* the Mediterranean Sea *(meaning "west")*.

and he saved them from their
distress.
7 He led them by a straight road
to a city where they could live.
8 They must thank the LORD for his
constant love,
for the wonderful things he did
for them.
9 He satisfies those who are thirsty
and fills the hungry with good
things.

10 Some were living in gloom and
darkness,
prisoners suffering in chains,
11 because they had rebelled against
the commands of
Almighty God
and had rejected his
instructions.
12 They were worn out from hard
work;
they would fall down, and no
one would help.
13 Then in their trouble they called to
the LORD,
and he saved them from their
distress.
14 He brought them out of their
gloom and darkness
and broke their chains in pieces.
15 They must thank the LORD for his
constant love,
for the wonderful things he did
for them.
16 He breaks down doors of bronze
and smashes iron bars.

17 Some were fools, suffering
because of their sins
and because of their evil;
18 they couldn't stand the sight of
food
and were close to death.
19 Then in their trouble they called to
the LORD,
and he saved them from their
distress.
20 He healed them with his command
and saved them from the grave.
21 They must thank the LORD for his
constant love,
for the wonderful things he did
for them.
22 They must thank him with
sacrifices,
and with songs of joy must tell
all that he has done.

23 Some sailed over the ocean in
ships,
earning their living on the seas.
24 They saw what the LORD can do,
his wonderful acts on the seas.
25 He commanded, and a mighty
wind began to blow
and stirred up the waves.
26 The ships were lifted high in
the air
and plunged down into the
depths.
In such danger the sailors lost
their courage;
27 they stumbled and staggered
like drunks —
all their skill was useless.
28 Then in their trouble they called to
the LORD,
and he saved them from their
distress.
29 He calmed the raging storm,
and the waves became quiet.
30 They were glad because of the
calm,
and he brought them safe to the
port they wanted.
31 They must thank the LORD for his
constant love,
for the wonderful things he did
for them.
32 They must proclaim his greatness
in the assembly of the people
and praise him before the
council of the leaders.

33 The LORD made rivers dry up
completely
and stopped springs from
flowing.
34 He made rich soil become a salty
wasteland
because of the wickedness of
those who lived there.
35 He changed deserts into pools of
water
and dry land into flowing
springs.
36 He let hungry people settle there,
and they built a city to live in.
37 They sowed the fields and planted
grapevines
and reaped an abundant harvest.
38 He blessed his people, and they
had many children;
he kept their herds of cattle
from decreasing.

39 When God's people were defeated
and humiliated
by cruel oppression and
suffering,
40 he showed contempt for their
oppressors
and made them wander in
trackless deserts.
41 But he rescued the needy from
their misery
and made their families increase
like flocks.
42 The righteous see this and are
glad,
but all the wicked are put to
silence.

43 May those who are wise think
about these things;
may they consider the LORD's
constant love.

A Prayer for Help against Enemies[h]

(Psalm 57.7-11; 60.5-12)

108 I have complete confidence,
O God!
I will sing and praise you!
Wake up, my soul!
2 Wake up, my harp and lyre!
I will wake up the sun.
3 I will thank you, O LORD, among
the nations.
I will praise you among the
peoples.
4 Your constant love reaches above
the heavens;
your faithfulness touches the
skies.

5 Show your greatness in the sky,
O God,
and your glory over all the
earth.
6 Save us by your might; answer my
prayer,
so that the people you love may
be rescued.

7 From his sanctuary[i] God has
said,
"In triumph I will divide
Shechem
and distribute Sukkoth Valley to
my people.
8 Gilead is mine, and Manasseh too;
Ephraim is my helmet
and Judah my royal scepter.
9 But I will use Moab as my
washbowl,
and I will throw my sandals on
Edom,
as a sign that I own it.
I will shout in triumph over the
Philistines."

10 Who, O God, will take me into the
fortified city?
Who will lead me to Edom?
11 Have you really rejected us?
Aren't you going to march out
with our armies?
12 Help us against the enemy;
human help is worthless.
13 With God on our side we will win;
he will defeat our enemies.

The Complaint of Someone in Trouble[j]

109 I praise you, God; don't
remain silent!
2 Wicked people and liars have
attacked me.
They tell lies about me,
3 and they say evil things
about me,
attacking me for no reason.
4 They oppose me, even though I
love them
and have prayed for them.[k]
5 They pay me back evil for good
and hatred for love.

6 Choose some corrupt judge to try
my enemy,
and let one of his own enemies
accuse him.
7 May he be tried and found guilty;
may even his prayer be
considered a crime!
8 May his life soon be ended;
may someone else take his job!
9 May his children become orphans,
and his wife a widow!
10 May his children be homeless
beggars;
may they be driven from[l] the
ruins they live in!
11 May his creditors take away all
his property,

[h] HEBREW TITLE: *A psalm by David; a song.* [i] From his sanctuary; *or* In his holiness.
[j] HEBREW TITLE: *A psalm by David.* [k] *Probable text* have prayed for them; *Hebrew unclear.*
[l] *One ancient translation* be driven from; *Hebrew* seek.

and may strangers get
everything he worked for.
12 May no one ever be kind to him
or care for the orphans he
leaves behind.
13 May all his descendants die,
and may his name be forgotten
in the next generation.
14 May the LORD remember the evil of
his ancestors
and never forgive his mother's
sins.
15 May the LORD always remember
their sins,
but may they themselves be
completely forgotten!

16 That man never thought of being
kind;
he persecuted and killed
the poor, the needy, and the
helpless.
17 He loved to curse—may he be
cursed!
He hated to give blessings—may
no one bless him!
18 He cursed as naturally as he
dressed himself;
may his own curses soak into
his body like water
and into his bones like oil!
19 May they cover him like clothes
and always be around him like
a belt!
20 LORD, punish my enemies in
that way—
those who say such evil things
against me!
21 But my Sovereign LORD, help me
as you have promised,
and rescue me because of the
goodness of your love.
22 I am poor and needy;
I am hurt to the depths of my
heart.
23 Like an evening shadow I am
about to vanish;
I am blown away like an insect.
24 My knees are weak from lack of
food;
I am nothing but skin and
bones.
25 When people see me, they laugh
at me;
they shake their heads in scorn.

26 Help me, O LORD my God;
because of your constant love,
save me!
27 Make my enemies know
that you are the one who
saves me.
28 They may curse me, but you will
bless me.
May my persecutors be
defeated,[m]
and may I, your servant, be
glad.
29 May my enemies be covered with
disgrace;
may they wear their shame like
a robe.

30 I will give loud thanks to the LORD;
I will praise him in the assembly
of the people,
31 because he defends the poor
and saves them from those who
condemn them to death.

The LORD and His Chosen King[n]

110 The LORD said to my lord,
"Sit here at my right side
until I put your enemies under
your feet."
2 From Zion the LORD will extend
your royal power.
"Rule over your enemies," he
says.
3 On the day you fight your
enemies,
your people will volunteer.
Like the dew of early morning
your young men will come to
you on the sacred hills.[o]

4 The LORD made a solemn promise
and will not take it back:
"You will be a priest forever
in the priestly order of
Melchizedek."[p]

5 The Lord is at your right side;
when he becomes angry, he will
defeat kings.

[m] *One ancient translation* May my persecutors be defeated; *Hebrew* They persecuted me and were defeated. [n] HEBREW TITLE: *A psalm by David.* [o] *Verse 3 in Hebrew is unclear.*
[p] in the priestly order of Melchizedek; *or* like Melchizedek; *or* in the line of succession to Melchizedek.

6 He will pass judgment on the
nations
and fill the battlefield with
corpses;
he will defeat kings all over the
earth.
7 The king will drink from the
stream by the road,
and strengthened, he will stand
victorious.

In Praise of the LORD

111 Praise the LORD!
With all my heart I will thank the
LORD
in the assembly of his
people.
2 How wonderful are the things the
LORD does!
All who are delighted with them
want to understand them.
3 All he does is full of honor and
majesty;
his righteousness is eternal.
4 The LORD does not let us forget his
wonderful actions;
he is kind and merciful.
5 He provides food for those who
honor him;
he never forgets his
covenant.
6 He has shown his power to his
people
by giving them the lands of
foreigners.

7 In all he does he is faithful and
just;
all his commands are
dependable.
8 They last for all time;
they were given in truth and
righteousness.
9 He set his people free
and made an eternal covenant
with them.
Holy and mighty is he!
10 The way to become wise is to
honor the LORD;[q]
he gives sound judgment
to all who obey his commands.
He is to be praised forever.

The Happiness of a Good Person

112 Praise the LORD!
Happy is the person who honors
the LORD,
who takes pleasure in obeying
his commands.
2 The good man's children will be
powerful in the land;
his descendants will be blessed.
3 His family will be wealthy and
rich,
and he will be prosperous
forever.

4 Light shines in the darkness for
good people,
for those who are merciful, kind,
and just.
5 Happy is the person who is
generous with his loans,
who runs his business honestly.
6 A good person will never fail;
he will always be remembered.

7 He is not afraid of receiving bad
news;
his faith is strong, and he trusts
in the LORD.
8 He is not worried or afraid;
he is certain to see his enemies
defeated.
9 He gives generously to the needy,
and his kindness never fails;
he will be powerful and
respected.
10 The wicked see this and are angry;
they glare in hate and disappear;
their hopes are gone forever.

In Praise of the LORD's Goodness

113 Praise the LORD!
You servants of the LORD,
praise his name!
2 May his name be praised,
now and forever.
3 From the east to the west
praise the name of the LORD!
4 The LORD rules over all nations;
his glory is above the heavens.

5 There is no one like the LORD
our God.
He lives in the heights above,
6 but he bends down

[q] The way . . . the LORD; *or* The most important part of wisdom is honoring the LORD.

to see the heavens and the earth.
7 He raises the poor from the dust;
he lifts the needy from their misery
8 and makes them companions of princes,
the princes of his people.
9 He honors the childless wife in her home;
he makes her happy by giving her children.

Praise the LORD!

A Passover Song

114 When the people of Israel left Egypt,
when Jacob's descendants left that foreign land,
2 Judah became the Lord's holy people,
Israel became his own possession.

3 The Red Sea looked and ran away;
the Jordan River stopped flowing.
4 The mountains skipped like goats;
the hills jumped around like lambs.

5 What happened, Sea, to make you run away?
And you, O Jordan, why did you stop flowing?
6 You mountains, why did you skip like goats?
You hills, why did you jump around like lambs?

7 Tremble, earth, at the Lord's coming,
at the presence of the God of Jacob,
8 who changes rocks into pools of water
and solid cliffs into flowing springs.

The One True God

115 To you alone, O LORD, to you alone,
and not to us, must glory be given
because of your constant love and faithfulness.
2 Why should the nations ask us,
"Where is your God?"
3 Our God is in heaven;
he does whatever he wishes.
4 Their gods are made of silver and gold,
formed by human hands.
5 They have mouths, but cannot speak,
and eyes, but cannot see.
6 They have ears, but cannot hear,
and noses, but cannot smell.
7 They have hands, but cannot feel,
and feet, but cannot walk;
they cannot make a sound.
8 May all who made them and who trust in them
become[r] like the idols they have made.

9 Trust in the LORD, you people of Israel.
He helps you and protects you.
10 Trust in the LORD, you priests of God.
He helps you and protects you.
11 Trust in the LORD, all you that worship him.
He helps you and protects you.

12 The LORD remembers us and will bless us;
he will bless the people of Israel
and all the priests of God.
13 He will bless everyone who honors him,
the great and the small alike.

14 May the LORD give you children—
you and your descendants!
15 May you be blessed by the LORD,
who made heaven and earth!

16 Heaven belongs to the LORD alone,
but he gave the earth to us humans.
17 The LORD is not praised by the dead,
by any who go down to the land of silence.[s]

[r] May all . . . become; *or* All who made them and who trust in them will become.
[s] LAND OF SILENCE: *The world of the dead (see 6.5).*

18 But we, the living, will give thanks
to him
now and forever.

Praise the LORD!

Someone Saved from Death Praises God

116 I love the LORD, because he
hears me;
he listens to my prayers.
2 He listens to me
every time I call to him.
3 The danger of death was all
around me;
the horrors of the grave closed
in on me;
I was filled with fear and
anxiety.
4 Then I called to the LORD,
"I beg you, LORD, save me!"

5 The LORD is merciful and good;
our God is compassionate.
6 The LORD protects the helpless;
when I was in danger, he
saved me.
7 Be confident, my heart,
because the LORD has been good
to me.

8 The LORD saved me from death;
he stopped my tears
and kept me from defeat.
9 And so I walk in the presence of
the LORD
in the world of the living.
10 I kept on believing, even when I
said,
"I am completely crushed,"
11 even when I was afraid and said,
"No one can be trusted."

12 What can I offer the LORD
for all his goodness to me?
13 I will bring a wine offering to the
LORD,
to thank him for saving me.
14 In the assembly of all his people
I will give him what I have
promised.

15 How painful it is to the LORD
when one of his people dies!
16 I am your servant, LORD;
I serve you just as my
mother did.
You have saved me from death.
17 I will give you a sacrifice of
thanksgiving
and offer my prayer to you.
18-19 In the assembly of all your people,
in the sanctuary of your Temple
in Jerusalem,
I will give you what I have
promised.

Praise the LORD!

In Praise of the LORD

117 Praise the LORD, all nations!
Praise him, all peoples!
2 His love for us is strong,
and his faithfulness is eternal.

Praise the LORD!

A Prayer of Thanks for Victory

118 Give thanks to the LORD,
because he is good,
and his love is eternal.
2 Let the people of Israel say,
"His love is eternal."
3 Let the priests of God say,
"His love is eternal."
4 Let all who worship him say,
"His love is eternal."

5 In my distress I called to the LORD;
he answered me and set me free.
6 The LORD is with me, I will not be
afraid;
what can anyone do to me?
7 It is the LORD who helps me,
and I will see my enemies
defeated.
8 It is better to trust in the LORD
than to depend on people.
9 It is better to trust in the LORD
than to depend on human
leaders.

10 Many enemies were around me;
but I destroyed them by the
power of the LORD!
11 They were around me on every
side;
but I destroyed them by the
power of the LORD!
12 They swarmed around me like
bees,
but they burned out as quickly
as a brush fire;
by the power of the LORD I
destroyed them.

13 I was fiercely attacked and was being defeated,
but the LORD helped me.
14 The LORD makes me powerful and strong;
he has saved me.

15 Listen to the glad shouts of victory
in the tents of God's people:
"The LORD's mighty power has done it!
16 His power has brought us victory—
his mighty power in battle!"

17 I will not die; instead, I will live
and proclaim what the LORD has done.
18 He has punished me severely,
but he has not let me die.

19 Open to me the gates of the Temple;
I will go in and give thanks to the LORD!

20 This is the gate of the LORD;
only the righteous can come in.

21 I praise you, LORD, because you heard me,
because you have given me victory.

22 The stone which the builders rejected as worthless
turned out to be the most important of all.
23 This was done by the LORD;
what a wonderful sight it is!
24 This is the day of the LORD's victory;
let us be happy, let us celebrate!
25 Save us, LORD, save us!
Give us success, O LORD!

26 May God bless the one who comes in the name of the LORD!
From the Temple of the LORD we bless you.
27 The LORD is God; he has been good to us.
With branches in your hands, start the festival
and march around the altar.

28 You are my God, and I give you thanks;
I will proclaim your greatness.

29 Give thanks to the LORD, because he is good,
and his love is eternal.

The Law of the LORD

119 Happy are those whose lives are faultless,
who live according to the law of the LORD.
2 Happy are those who follow his commands,
who obey him with all their heart.
3 They never do wrong;
they walk in the LORD's ways.
4 LORD, you have given us your laws
and told us to obey them faithfully.
5 How I hope that I shall be faithful
in keeping your instructions!
6 If I pay attention to all your commands,
then I will not be put to shame.
7 As I learn your righteous judgments,
I will praise you with a pure heart.
8 I will obey your laws;
never abandon me!

Obedience to the Law of the LORD

9 How can young people keep their lives pure?
By obeying your commands.
10 With all my heart I try to serve you;
keep me from disobeying your commandments.
11 I keep your law in my heart,
so that I will not sin against you.
12 I praise you, O LORD;
teach me your ways.
13 I will repeat aloud
all the laws you have given.
14 I delight in following your commands
more than in having great wealth.
15 I study your instructions;
I examine your teachings.
16 I take pleasure in your laws;
your commands I will not forget

Happiness in the Law of the Lord

17 Be good to me, your servant,
so that I may live and obey your teachings.
18 Open my eyes, so that I may see
the wonderful truths in your law.
19 I am here on earth for just a little while;
do not hide your commands from me.
20 My heart aches with longing;
I want to know your judgments at all times.
21 You reprimand the proud;
cursed are those who disobey your commands.
22 Free me from their insults and scorn,
because I have kept your laws.
23 The rulers meet and plot against me,
but I will study your teachings.
24 Your instructions give me pleasure;
they are my advisers.

Determination to Obey the Law of the Lord

25 I lie defeated in the dust;
revive me, as you have promised.
26 I confessed all I have done, and you answered me;
teach me your ways.
27 Help me to understand your laws,
and I will meditate on your wonderful teachings.[t]
28 I am overcome by sorrow;
strengthen me, as you have promised.
29 Keep me from going the wrong way,
and in your goodness teach me your law.
30 I have chosen to be obedient;
I have paid attention to your judgments.
31 I have followed your instructions, Lord;
don't let me be put to shame.
32 I will eagerly obey your commands,
because you will give me more understanding.

A Prayer for Understanding

33 Teach me, Lord, the meaning of your laws,
and I will obey them at all times.
34 Explain your law to me, and I will obey it;
I will keep it with all my heart.
35 Keep me obedient to your commandments,
because in them I find happiness.
36 Give me the desire to obey your laws
rather than to get rich.
37 Keep me from paying attention to what is worthless;
be good to me, as you have promised.
38 Keep your promise to me, your servant—
the promise you make to those who obey you.
39 Save me from the insults I fear;
how wonderful are your judgments!
40 I want to obey your commands;
give me new life, for you are righteous.

Trusting the Law of the Lord

41 Show me how much you love me, Lord,
and save me according to your promise.
42 Then I can answer those who insult me
because I trust in your word.
43 Enable me to speak the truth at all times,
because my hope is in your judgments.
44 I will always obey your law,
forever and ever.
45 I will live in perfect freedom,
because I try to obey your teachings.
46 I will announce your commands to kings
and I will not be ashamed.
47 I find pleasure in obeying your commands,
because I love them.
48 I respect and love your commandments;
I will meditate on your instructions.

[t] teachings; *or* deeds.

Confidence in the Law of the LORD

49 Remember your promise to me,
your servant;
it has given me hope.
50 Even in my suffering I was
comforted
because your promise gave me
life.
51 The proud are always scornful
of me,
but I have not departed from
your law.
52 I remember your judgments of
long ago,
and they bring me comfort,
O LORD.
53 When I see the wicked breaking
your law,
I am filled with anger.
54 During my brief earthly life
I compose songs about your
commands.
55 In the night I remember you, LORD,
and I think about your law.
56 I find my happiness
in obeying your commands.

Devotion to the Law of the LORD

57 You are all I want, O LORD;
I promise to obey your laws.
58 I ask you with all my heart
to have mercy on me, as you
have promised!
59 I have considered my conduct,
and I promise to follow your
instructions.
60 Without delay I hurry
to obey your commands.
61 The wicked have laid a trap
for me,
but I do not forget your law.
62 In the middle of the night I
wake up
to praise you for your righteous
judgments.
63 I am a friend of all who serve you,
of all who obey your laws.
64 LORD, the earth is full of your
constant love;
teach me your commandments.

The Value of the Law of the LORD

65 You have kept your promise, LORD,
and you are good to me, your
servant.
66 Give me wisdom and knowledge,
because I trust in your
commands.
67 Before you punished me, I used to
go wrong,
but now I obey your word.
68 How good you are—how kind!
Teach me your commands.
69 The proud have told lies about me,
but with all my heart I obey
your instructions.
70 They have no understanding,
but I find pleasure in your law.
71 My punishment was good for me,
because it made me learn your
commands.
72 The law that you gave means
more to me
than all the money in the world.

The Justice of the Law of the LORD

73 You created me, and you keep me
safe;
give me understanding, so that I
may learn your laws.
74 Those who honor you will be glad
when they see me,
because I trust in your promise.
75 I know that your judgments are
righteous, LORD,
and that you punished me
because you are faithful.
76 Let your constant love comfort me,
as you have promised me, your
servant.
77 Have mercy on me, and I will live
because I take pleasure in
your law.
78 May the proud be ashamed for
falsely accusing me;
as for me, I will meditate on
your instructions.
79 May those who honor you come
to me—
all those who know your
commands.
80 May I perfectly obey your
commandments
and be spared the shame of
defeat.

A Prayer for Deliverance

81 I am worn out, LORD, waiting for
you to save me;
I place my trust in your word.
82 My eyes are tired from watching
for what you promised,
while I ask, "When will you
help me?"
83 I am as useless as a discarded
wineskin;

yet I have not forgotten your
commands.
84 How much longer must I wait?
When will you punish those who
persecute me?
85 The proud, who do not obey
your law,
have dug pits to trap me.
86 Your commandments are all
trustworthy;
people persecute me with lies—
help me!
87 They have almost succeeded in
killing me,
but I have not neglected your
commands.
88 Because of your constant love be
good to me,
so that I may obey your laws.

Faith in the Law of the Lord

89 Your word, O Lord, will last
forever;
it is eternal in heaven.
90 Your faithfulness endures through
all the ages;
you have set the earth in place,
and it remains.
91 All things remain to this day
because of your command,
because they are all your
servants.
92 If your law had not been the
source of my joy,
I would have died from my
sufferings.
93 I will never neglect your
instructions,
because by them you have kept
me alive.
94 I am yours—save me!
I have tried to obey your
commands.
95 The wicked are waiting to kill me,
but I will meditate on your laws.
96 I have learned that everything has
limits;
but your commandment is
perfect.

Love for the Law of the Lord

97 How I love your law!
I think about it all day long.
98 Your commandment is with me all
the time
and makes me wiser than my
enemies.
99 I understand more than all my
teachers,
because I meditate on your
instructions.
100 I have greater wisdom than those
who are old,
because I obey your commands.
101 I have avoided all evil conduct,
because I want to obey your
word.
102 I have not neglected your
instructions,
because you yourself are my
teacher.
103 How sweet is the taste of your
instructions—
sweeter even than honey!
104 I gain wisdom from your laws,
and so I hate all bad conduct.

Light from the Law of the Lord

105 Your word is a lamp to guide me
and a light for my path.
106 I will keep my solemn promise
to obey your just instructions.
107 My sufferings, Lord, are terrible
indeed;
keep me alive, as you have
promised.
108 Accept my prayer of thanks,
O Lord,
and teach me your commands.
109 I am always ready to risk my life;
I[u] have not forgotten your law.
110 The wicked lay a trap for me,
but I have not disobeyed your
commands.
111 Your commandments are my
eternal possession;
they are the joy of my heart.
112 I have decided to obey your laws
until the day I die.

Safety in the Law of the Lord

113 I hate those who are not
completely loyal to you,
but I love your law.
114 You are my defender and
protector;
I put my hope in your promise.
115 Go away from me, you sinful
people.
I will obey the commands of
my God.

[u] I am always ready to risk my life; I; *or* My life is in constant danger, but I.

116 Give me strength, as you
promised, and I shall live;
don't let me be disappointed in
my hope!
117 Hold me, and I will be safe,
and I will always pay attention
to your commands.
118 You reject everyone who disobeys
your laws;
their deceitful schemes are
useless.
119 You treat all the wicked like
rubbish,
and so I love your instructions.
120 Because of you I am afraid;
I am filled with fear because of
your judgments.

Obedience to the Law of the LORD

121 I have done what is right and
good;
don't abandon me to my
enemies!
122 Promise that you will help your
servant;
don't let the arrogant
oppress me!
123 My eyes are tired from watching
for your saving help,
for the deliverance you
promised.
124 Treat me according to your
constant love,
and teach me your commands.
125 I am your servant; give me
understanding,
so that I may know your
teachings.
126 LORD, it is time for you to act,
because people are disobeying
your law.
127 I love your commands more than
gold,
more than the finest gold.
128 And so I follow all your
instructions;[v]
I hate all wrong ways.

Desire to Obey the Law of the LORD

129 Your teachings are wonderful;
I obey them with all my heart.
130 The explanation of your teachings
gives light
and brings wisdom to the
ignorant.
131 In my desire for your commands
I pant with open mouth.
132 Turn to me and have mercy on me
as you do on all those who
love you.
133 As you have promised, keep me
from falling;
don't let me be overcome by
evil.
134 Save me from those who
oppress me,
so that I may obey your
commands.
135 Bless me with your presence
and teach me your laws.
136 My tears pour down like a river,
because people do not obey
your law.

The Justice of the Law of the LORD

137 You are righteous, LORD,
and your laws are just.
138 The rules that you have given
are completely fair and right.
139 My anger burns in me like a fire,
because my enemies disregard
your commands.
140 How certain your promise is!
How I love it!
141 I am unimportant and despised,
but I do not neglect your
teachings.
142 Your righteousness will last
forever,
and your law is always true.
143 I am filled with trouble and
anxiety,
but your commandments bring
me joy.
144 Your instructions are always just;
give me understanding, and I
shall live.

A Prayer for Deliverance

145 With all my heart I call to you;
answer me, LORD, and I will obey
your commands!
146 I call to you;
save me, and I will keep your
laws.
147 Before sunrise I call to you for
help;
I place my hope in your
promise.
148 All night long I lie awake,
to meditate on your instructions.

[v] *Some ancient translations* all your instructions; *Hebrew unclear.*

149 Because your love is constant,
hear me, O LORD;
show your mercy, and preserve
my life!
150 My cruel persecutors are coming
closer,
people who never keep
your law.
151 But you are near to me, LORD,
and all your commands are
permanent.
152 Long ago I learned about your
instructions;
you made them to last forever.

A Plea for Help

153 Look at my suffering, and
save me,
because I have not neglected
your law.
154 Defend my cause, and set me free;
save me, as you have promised.
155 The wicked will not be saved,
for they do not obey your laws.
156 But your compassion, LORD, is
great;
show your mercy and save me!
157 I have many enemies and
oppressors,
but I do not fail to obey your
laws.
158 When I look at those traitors, I am
filled with disgust,
because they do not keep your
commands.
159 See how I love your instructions,
LORD.
Your love never changes, so
save me!
160 The heart of your law is truth,
and all your righteous judgments
are eternal.

Dedication to the Law of the LORD

161 Powerful people attack me
unjustly,
but I respect your law.
162 How happy I am because of your
promises—
as happy as someone who finds
rich treasure.
163 I hate and detest all lies,
but I love your law.
164 Seven times each day I thank you
for your righteous judgments.
165 Those who love your law have
perfect security,
and there is nothing that can
make them fall.
166 I wait for you to save me, LORD,
and I do what you command.
167 I obey your teachings;
I love them with all my heart.
168 I obey your commands and your
instructions;
you see everything I do.

A Prayer for Help

169 Let my cry for help reach you,
LORD!
Give me understanding, as you
have promised.
170 Listen to my prayer,
and save me according to your
promise!
171 I will always praise you,
because you teach me your laws.
172 I will sing about your law,
because your commands are
just.
173 Always be ready to help me,
because I follow your
commands.
174 How I long for your saving help,
O LORD!
I find happiness in your law.
175 Give me life, so that I may
praise you;
may your instructions help me.
176 I wander about like a lost sheep;
so come and look for me, your
servant,
because I have not neglected
your laws.

A Prayer for Help

120

When I was in trouble, I
called to the LORD,
and he answered me.
2 Save me, LORD,
from liars and deceivers.

3 You liars, what will God do
to you?
How will he punish you?
4 With a soldier's sharp arrows,
with red-hot coals!

5 Living among you is as bad as
living in Meshech
or among the people of Kedar.[w]

[w] MESHECH . . . KEDAR: *Two distant regions, whose people were regarded as savages.*

6 I have lived too long
with people who hate peace!
7 When I speak of peace,
they are for war.

The Lord Our Protector

121 I look to the mountains;
where will my help come
from?
2 My help will come from the Lord,
who made heaven and earth.

3 He will not let you fall;
your protector is always awake.

4 The protector of Israel
never dozes or sleeps.
5 The Lord will guard you;
he is by your side to protect you.
6 The sun will not hurt you during
the day,
nor the moon during the night.

7 The Lord will protect you from all
danger;
he will keep you safe.
8 He will protect you as you come
and go
now and forever.

In Praise of Jerusalem[x]

122 I was glad when they said
to me,
"Let us go to the Lord's house."
2 And now we are here,
standing inside the gates of
Jerusalem!

3 Jerusalem is a city restored
in beautiful order and harmony.
4 This is where the tribes come,
the tribes of Israel,
to give thanks to the Lord
according to his command.
5 Here the kings of Israel
sat to judge their people.

6 Pray for the peace of Jerusalem:
"May those who love you
prosper.
7 May there be peace inside your
walls
and safety in your palaces."
8 For the sake of my relatives and
friends
I say to Jerusalem, "Peace be
with you!"
9 For the sake of the house of the
Lord our God
I pray for your prosperity.

A Prayer for Mercy

123 Lord, I look up to you,
up to heaven, where you
rule.
2 As a servant depends on his
master,
as a maid depends on her
mistress,
so we will keep looking to you,
O Lord our God,
until you have mercy on us.

3 Be merciful to us, Lord, be
merciful;
we have been treated with so
much contempt.
4 We have been mocked too long by
the rich
and scorned by proud
oppressors.

God the Protector of His People[x]

124 What if the Lord had not
been on our side?
Answer, O Israel!

2 "If the Lord had not been on our
side
when our enemies attacked us,
3 then they would have swallowed
us alive
in their furious anger against us;
4 then the flood would have carried
us away,
the water would have
covered us,
5 the raging torrent would have
drowned us."

6 Let us thank the Lord,
who has not let our enemies
destroy us.
7 We have escaped like a bird from
a hunter's trap;
the trap is broken, and we are
free!
8 Our help comes from the Lord,
who made heaven and earth.

[x] HEBREW TITLE: *By David.*

The Security of God's People

125 Those who trust in the LORD
are like Mount Zion,
which can never be shaken,
never be moved.
2 As the mountains surround
Jerusalem,
so the LORD surrounds his
people,
now and forever.

3 The wicked will not always rule
over the land of the righteous;
if they did, the righteous
themselves might do evil.
4 LORD, do good to those who are
good,
to those who obey your
commands.
5 But when you punish the wicked,
punish also those who abandon
your ways.

Peace be with Israel!

A Prayer for Deliverance

126 When the LORD brought us
back to Jerusalem,[y]
it was like a dream!
2 How we laughed, how we sang
for joy!
Then the other nations said
about us,
"The LORD did great things for
them."
3 Indeed he did great things for us;
how happy we were!

4 LORD, make us prosperous again,[z]
just as the rain brings water
back to dry riverbeds.
5 Let those who wept as they
planted their crops,
gather the harvest with joy!

6 Those who wept as they went out
carrying the seed
will come back singing for joy,
as they bring in the harvest.

In Praise of God's Goodness[a]

127 If the LORD does not build
the house,
the work of the builders is
useless;
if the LORD does not protect the
city,
it does no good for the sentries
to stand guard.
2 It is useless to work so hard for a
living,
getting up early and going to
bed late.
For the LORD provides for those he
loves,
while they are asleep.

3 Children are a gift from the LORD;
they are a real blessing.
4 The sons a man has when he is
young
are like arrows in a soldier's
hand.
5 Happy is the man who has many
such arrows.
He will never be defeated
when he meets his enemies in
the place of judgment.

The Reward of Obedience to the LORD

128 Happy are those who obey
the LORD,
who live by his commands.

2 Your work will provide for your
needs;
you will be happy and
prosperous.
3 Your wife will be like a fruitful
vine in your home,
and your children will be like
young olive trees around
your table.
4 A man who obeys the LORD
will surely be blessed like this.

5 May the LORD bless you from Zion!
May you see Jerusalem prosper
all the days of your life!
6 May you live to see your
grandchildren!

Peace be with Israel!

A Prayer against Israel's Enemies

129 Israel, tell us how your
enemies have
persecuted you
ever since you were young.

[y] brought us back to Jerusalem; *or* made Jerusalem prosperous again. [z] make us prosperous again; *or* take us back to our land. [a] HEBREW TITLE: *By Solomon.*

2 "Ever since I was young,
my enemies have persecuted me cruelly,
but they have not overcome me.
3 They cut deep wounds in my back
and made it like a plowed field.
4 But the LORD, the righteous one,
has freed me from slavery."

5 May everyone who hates Zion
be defeated and driven back.
6 May they all be like grass growing on the housetops,
which dries up before it can grow;
7 no one gathers it up
or carries it away in bundles.
8 No one who passes by will say,
"May the LORD bless you!
We bless you in the name of the LORD."

A Prayer for Help

130 From the depths of my despair I call to you, LORD.
2 Hear my cry, O Lord;
listen to my call for help!
3 If you kept a record of our sins,
who could escape being condemned?
4 But you forgive us,
so that we should stand in awe of you.

5 I wait eagerly for the LORD's help,
and in his word I trust.
6 I wait for the Lord
more eagerly than sentries wait for the dawn—
than sentries wait for the dawn.

7 Israel, trust in the LORD,
because his love is constant
and he is always willing to save.
8 He will save his people Israel
from all their sins.

A Prayer of Humble Trust[b]

131 LORD, I have given up my pride
and turned away from my arrogance.
I am not concerned with great matters
or with subjects too difficult for me.
2 Instead, I am content and at peace.
As a child lies quietly in its mother's arms,
so my heart is quiet within me.
3 Israel, trust in the LORD
now and forever!

In Praise of the Temple

132 LORD, do not forget David
and all the hardships he endured.
2 Remember, LORD, what he promised,
the vow he made to you, the Mighty God of Jacob:
3 "I will not go home or go to bed;
4 I will not rest or sleep,
5 until I provide a place for the LORD,
a home for the Mighty God of Jacob."

6 In Bethlehem we heard about the Covenant Box,
and we found it in the fields of Jearim.
7 We said, "Let us go to the LORD's house;
let us worship before his throne."

8 Come to the Temple, LORD, with the Covenant Box,
the symbol of your power,
and stay here forever.
9 May your priests do always what is right;
may your people shout for joy!

10 You made a promise to your servant David;
do not reject your chosen king, LORD.
11 You made a solemn promise to David—
a promise you will not take back:
"I will make one of your sons king,
and he will rule after you.
12 If your sons are true to my covenant

[b] HEBREW TITLE: *By David.*

and to the commands I give
them,
their sons, also, will succeed you
for all time as kings."

13 The LORD has chosen Zion;
he wants to make it his
home:
14 "This is where I will live forever;
this is where I want to rule.
15 I will richly provide Zion with all
she needs;
I will satisfy her poor with
food.
16 I will bless her priests in all
they do,
and her people will sing and
shout for joy.
17 Here I will make one of David's
descendants a great king;
here I will preserve the rule of
my chosen king.
18 I will cover his enemies with
shame,
but his kingdom will prosper
and flourish."

In Praise of Living in Peace[b]

133 How wonderful it is, how
pleasant,
for God's people to live together
in harmony!
2 It is like the precious anointing oil
running down from Aaron's
head and beard,
down to the collar of his
robes.
3 It is like the dew on Mount
Hermon,
falling on the hills of Zion.
That is where the LORD has
promised his blessing—
life that never ends.

A Call to Praise God

134 Come, praise the LORD,
all his servants,
all who serve in his Temple at
night.
2 Raise your hands in prayer in the
Temple,
and praise the LORD!

3 May the LORD, who made heaven
and earth,
bless you from Zion!

A Hymn of Praise

135 Praise the LORD!

Praise his name, you servants of
the LORD,
2 who stand in the LORD's house,
in the Temple of our God.
3 Praise the LORD, because he is
good;
sing praises to his name,
because he is kind.[c]
4 He chose Jacob for himself,
the people of Israel for his own.

5 I know that our LORD is great,
greater than all the gods.
6 He does whatever he wishes
in heaven and on earth,
in the seas and in the depths
below.
7 He brings storm clouds from the
ends of the earth;
he makes lightning for the
storms,
and he brings out the wind from
his storeroom.

8 In Egypt he killed all the first-born
of people and animals alike.
9 There he performed miracles and
wonders
to punish the king and all his
officials.
10 He destroyed many nations
and killed powerful kings:
11 Sihon, king of the Amorites,
Og, king of Bashan,
and all the kings in Canaan.
12 He gave their lands to his people;
he gave them to Israel.

13 LORD, you will always be
proclaimed as God;
all generations will
remember you.
14 The LORD will defend his people;
he will take pity on his servants.

15 The gods of the nations are made
of silver and gold;
they are formed by human
hands.
16 They have mouths, but cannot
speak,
and eyes, but cannot see.
17 They have ears, but cannot hear;

[b] HEBREW TITLE: *By David.* [c] he is kind; *or* it is pleasant to do so.

they are not even able to
breathe.
18 May all who made them and who
trust in them
become [d] like the idols they
have made!

19 Praise the LORD, people of Israel;
praise him, you priests of God!
20 Praise the LORD, you Levites;
praise him, all you that
worship him!
21 Praise the LORD in Zion,
in Jerusalem, his home.

Praise the LORD!

A Hymn of Thanksgiving

136 Give thanks to the LORD,
because he is good;
his love is eternal.
2 Give thanks to the greatest of all
gods;
his love is eternal.
3 Give thanks to the mightiest of all
lords;
his love is eternal.

4 He alone performs great miracles;
his love is eternal.
5 By his wisdom he made the
heavens;
his love is eternal;
6 he built the earth on the deep
waters;
his love is eternal.
7 He made the sun and the moon;
his love is eternal;
8 the sun to rule over the day;
his love is eternal;
9 the moon and the stars to rule
over the night;
his love is eternal.

10 He killed the first-born sons of the
Egyptians;
his love is eternal.
11 He led the people of Israel out of
Egypt;
his love is eternal;
12 with his strong hand, his
powerful arm;
his love is eternal.
13 He divided the Red Sea;
his love is eternal;
14 he led his people through it;
his love is eternal;
15 but he drowned the king of Egypt
and his army;
his love is eternal.

16 He led his people through the
desert;
his love is eternal.
17 He killed powerful kings;
his love is eternal;
18 he killed famous kings;
his love is eternal;
19 Sihon, king of the Amorites;
his love is eternal;
20 and Og, king of Bashan;
his love is eternal.
21 He gave their lands to his people;
his love is eternal;
22 he gave them to Israel, his servant;
his love is eternal.

23 He did not forget us when we
were defeated;
his love is eternal;
24 he freed us from our enemies;
his love is eternal.
25 He gives food to every living
creature;
his love is eternal.

26 Give thanks to the God of heaven;
his love is eternal.

A Lament of Israelites in Exile

137 By the rivers of Babylon we
sat down;
there we wept when we
remembered Zion.
2 On the willows near by
we hung up our harps.
3 Those who captured us told us to
sing;
they told us to entertain them:
"Sing us a song about Zion."

4 How can we sing a song to the
LORD
in a foreign land?
5 May I never be able to play the
harp again
if I forget you, Jerusalem!
6 May I never be able to sing again
if I do not remember you,
if I do not think of you as my
greatest joy!

[d] May all . . . become; *or* All who made them and who trust in them will become.

7 Remember, LORD, what the
Edomites did
the day Jerusalem was captured.
Remember how they kept saying,
"Tear it down to the ground!"

8 Babylon, you will be destroyed.
Happy are those who pay you
back
for what you have done to us—
9 who take your babies
and smash them against a rock.

A Prayer of Thanksgiving[e]

138 I thank you, LORD, with all
my heart;
I sing praise to you before the
gods.
2 I face your holy Temple,
bow down, and praise your
name
because of your constant love and
faithfulness,
because you have shown that
your name and your
commands are supreme.[f]
3 You answered me when I called
to you;
with your strength you
strengthened me.

4 All the kings in the world will
praise you, LORD,
because they have heard your
promises.
5 They will sing about what you
have done
and about your great glory.
6 Even though you are so high
above,
you care for the lowly,
and the proud cannot hide
from you.

7 When I am surrounded by
troubles,
you keep me safe.
You oppose my angry enemies
and save me by your power.
8 You will do everything you have
promised;
LORD, your love is eternal.
Complete the work that you
have begun.

God's Complete Knowledge and Care[g]

139 LORD, you have examined me
and you know me.
2 You know everything I do;
from far away you understand
all my thoughts.
3 You see me, whether I am
working or resting;
you know all my actions.
4 Even before I speak,
you already know what I
will say.
5 You are all around me on every
side;
you protect me with your power.
6 Your knowledge of me is too deep;
it is beyond my understanding.

7 Where could I go to escape
from you?
Where could I get away from
your presence?
8 If I went up to heaven, you would
be there;
if I lay down in the world of the
dead, you would be there.
9 If I flew away beyond the east
or lived in the farthest place in
the west,
10 you would be there to lead me,
you would be there to help me.
11 I could ask the darkness to
hide me
or the light around me to turn
into night,
12 but even darkness is not dark
for you,
and the night is as bright as
the day.
Darkness and light are the same
to you.

13 You created every part of me;
you put me together in my
mother's womb.
14 I praise you because you are to be
feared;
all you do is strange and
wonderful.
I know it with all my heart.
15 When my bones were being
formed,
carefully put together in my
mother's womb,

[e] HEBREW TITLE: *By David.* [f] *Probable text* your name and your commands are supreme; *Hebrew* your command is greater than all your name. [g] HEBREW TITLE: *A psalm by David.*

when I was growing there in
secret,
you knew that I was there—
16 you saw me before I was born.
The days allotted to me
had all been recorded in your
book,
before any of them ever began.
17 O God, how difficult I find your
thoughts;[h]
how many of them there are!
18 If I counted them, they would be
more than the grains of sand.
When I awake, I am still
with you.

19 O God, how I wish you would kill
the wicked!
How I wish violent people would
leave me alone!
20 They say wicked things about you;
they speak evil things against
your name.[i]
21 O LORD, how I hate those who
hate you!
How I despise those who rebel
against you!
22 I hate them with a total hatred;
I regard them as my enemies.

23 Examine me, O God, and know
my mind;
test me, and discover my
thoughts.
24 Find out if there is any evil in me
and guide me in the
everlasting way.[j]

A Prayer for Protection[k]

140 Save me, LORD, from
evildoers;
keep me safe from violent
people.
2 They are always plotting evil,
always stirring up quarrels.
3 Their tongues are like deadly
snakes;
their words are like a cobra's
poison.

4 Protect me, LORD, from the power
of the wicked;
keep me safe from violent
people
who plot my downfall.
5 The proud have set a trap for me;
they have laid their snares,
and along the path they have set
traps to catch me.

6 I say to the LORD, "You are
my God."
Hear my cry for help, LORD!
7 My Sovereign LORD, my strong
defender,
you have protected me in battle.
8 LORD, don't give the wicked what
they want;
don't let their plots succeed.

9 Don't let my enemies be
victorious;[l]
make their threats against me
fall back on them.
10 May red-hot coals fall on them;
may they be thrown into a pit
and never get out.
11 May those who accuse others
falsely not succeed;
may evil overtake violent people
and destroy them.

12 LORD, I know that you defend the
cause of the poor
and the rights of the needy.
13 The righteous will praise you
indeed;
they will live in your presence.

An Evening Prayer[m]

141 I call to you, LORD; help
me now!
Listen to me when I call to you.
2 Receive my prayer as incense,
my uplifted hands as an evening
sacrifice.

3 LORD, place a guard at my mouth,
a sentry at the door of my lips.
4 Keep me from wanting to do
wrong
and from joining evil people in
their wickedness.
May I never take part in their
feasts.

5 Good people may punish me and
rebuke me in kindness,

[h] how difficult I find your thoughts; *or* how precious are your thoughts to me.
[i] *Probable text* they speak . . . name; *Hebrew unclear.* [j] the everlasting way; *or* the ways of my ancestors. [k] HEBREW TITLE: *A psalm by David.* [l] *Probable text* Don't let my enemies be victorious; *Hebrew unclear.* [m] HEBREW TITLE: *A psalm by David.*

but I will never accept honor
from evil people,
because I am always praying
against their evil deeds.
6 When their rulers are thrown
down from rocky cliffs,
the people will admit that my
words were true.
7 Like wood that is split and
chopped into bits,
so their bones are scattered at
the edge of the grave.[n]

8 But I keep trusting in you, my
Sovereign LORD.
I seek your protection;
don't let me die!
9 Protect me from the traps they
have set for me,
from the snares of those
evildoers.
10 May the wicked fall into their own
traps
while I go by unharmed.

A Prayer for Help[o]

142 I call to the LORD for help;
I plead with him.
2 I bring him all my complaints;
I tell him all my troubles.
3 When I am ready to give up,
he knows what I should do.
In the path where I walk,
my enemies have hidden a trap
for me.
4 When I look beside me,
I see that there is no one to
help me,
no one to protect me.
No one cares for me.

5 LORD, I cry to you for help;
you, LORD, are my protector;
you are all I want in this
life.
6 Listen to my cry for help,
for I am sunk in despair.
Save me from my enemies;
they are too strong for me.
7 Set me free from my distress;[p]
then in the assembly of your
people I will praise you
because of your goodness to me.

A Prayer for Help[q]

143 LORD, hear my prayer!
In your righteousness listen
to my plea;
answer me in your faithfulness!
2 Don't put me, your servant, on
trial;
no one is innocent in your sight.

3 My enemies have hunted me down
and completely defeated me.
They have put me in a dark
prison,
and I am like those who died
long ago.
4 So I am ready to give up;
I am in deep despair.

5 I remember the days gone by;
I think about all that you have
done,
I bring to mind all your deeds.
6 I lift up my hands to you in
prayer;
like dry ground my soul is
thirsty for you.

7 Answer me now, LORD!
I have lost all hope.
Don't hide yourself from me,
or I will be among those who go
down to the world of the dead.
8 Remind me each morning of your
constant love,
for I put my trust in you.
My prayers go up to you;
show me the way I should go.

9 I go to you for protection, LORD;
rescue me from my enemies.
10 You are my God;
teach me to do your will.
Be good to me, and guide me on a
safe path.

11 Rescue me, LORD, as you have
promised;
in your goodness save me from
my troubles!
12 Because of your love for me, kill
my enemies
and destroy all my oppressors,
for I am your servant.

[n] *Verses 5-7 in Hebrew are unclear.* [o] HEBREW TITLE: *A poem by David, when he was in the cave; a prayer.* [p] distress; *or* prison. [q] HEBREW TITLE: *A psalm by David.*

A King Thanks God for Victory[r]

144 Praise the LORD, my protector!
He trains me for battle
and prepares me for war.
2 He is my protector and defender,
my shelter and savior,
in whom I trust for safety.
He subdues the nations under me.

3 LORD, what are mortals, that you notice them;
mere mortals, that you pay attention to us?
4 We are like a puff of wind;
our days are like a passing shadow.

5 O LORD, tear the sky open and come down;
touch the mountains, and they will pour out smoke.
6 Send flashes of lightning and scatter your enemies;
shoot your arrows and send them running.
7 Reach down from above,
pull me out of the deep water,
and rescue me;
save me from the power of foreigners,
8 who never tell the truth
and lie even under oath.

9 I will sing you a new song, O God;
I will play the harp and sing to you.
10 You give victory to kings
and rescue your servant David.
11 Save me from my cruel enemies;
rescue me from the power of foreigners,
who never tell the truth
and lie even under oath.

12 May our sons in their youth
be like plants that grow up strong.
May our daughters be like stately columns
which adorn the corners of a palace.
13 May our barns be filled
with crops of every kind.
May the sheep in our fields
bear young by the tens of thousands.
14 May our cattle reproduce plentifully
without miscarriage or loss.
May there be no cries of distress
in our streets.

15 Happy is the nation of whom this is true;
happy are the people whose God is the LORD!

A Hymn of Praise[s]

145 I will proclaim your greatness, my God and king;
I will thank you forever and ever.
2 Every day I will thank you;
I will praise you forever and ever.
3 The LORD is great and is to be highly praised;
his greatness is beyond understanding.

4 What you have done will be praised from one generation to the next;
they will proclaim your mighty acts.
5 They will speak of your glory and majesty,
and I will meditate on your wonderful deeds.
6 People will speak of your mighty deeds,
and I will proclaim your greatness.
7 They will tell about all your goodness
and sing about your kindness.
8 The LORD is loving and merciful,
slow to become angry and full of constant love.
9 He is good to everyone
and has compassion on all he made.

10 All your creatures, LORD, will praise you,
and all your people will give you thanks.
11 They will speak of the glory of your royal power

[r] HEBREW TITLE: *By David.* [s] HEBREW TITLE: *A song of praise by David.*

and tell of your might,
12 so that everyone will know your
mighty deeds
and the glorious majesty of your
kingdom.
13 Your rule is eternal,
and you are king forever.

The LORD is faithful to his
promises;
he is merciful in all his acts.
14 He helps those who are in trouble;
he lifts those who have fallen.

15 All living things look hopefully
to you,
and you give them food when
they need it.
16 You give them enough
and satisfy the needs of all.

17 The LORD is righteous in all he
does,
merciful in all his acts.
18 He is near to those who call
to him,
who call to him with sincerity.
19 He supplies the needs of those
who honor him;
he hears their cries and saves
them.
20 He protects everyone who
loves him,
but he will destroy the wicked.

21 I will always praise the LORD;
let all his creatures praise his
holy name forever.

In Praise of God the Savior

146 Praise the LORD!
Praise the LORD, my soul!
2 I will praise him as long as I live;
I will sing to my God all my life.

3 Don't put your trust in human
leaders;
no human being can save you.
4 When they die, they return to the
dust;
on that day all their plans come
to an end.

5 Happy are those who have the
God of Jacob to help them
and who depend on the LORD
their God,
6 the Creator of heaven, earth,
and sea,
and all that is in them.
He always keeps his promises;
7 he judges in favor of the
oppressed
and gives food to the hungry.

The LORD sets prisoners free
8 and gives sight to the blind.
He lifts those who have fallen;
he loves his righteous people.
9 He protects the strangers who live
in our land;
he helps widows and orphans,
but takes the wicked to their
ruin.

10 The LORD is king forever.
Your God, O Zion, will reign for
all time.

Praise the LORD!

In Praise of God the Almighty

147 Praise the LORD!

It is good to sing praise to
our God;
it is pleasant and right to
praise him.
2 The LORD is restoring Jerusalem;
he is bringing back the exiles.
3 He heals the broken-hearted
and bandages their wounds.

4 He has decided the number of the
stars
and calls each one by name.
5 Great and mighty is our Lord;
his wisdom cannot be measured.
6 He raises the humble,
but crushes the wicked to the
ground.

7 Sing hymns of praise to the LORD;
play music on the harp to
our God.
8 He spreads clouds over the sky;
he provides rain for the earth
and makes grass grow on the
hills.
9 He gives animals their food
and feeds the young ravens
when they call.

10 His pleasure is not in strong
horses,

nor his delight in brave soldiers;
11 but he takes pleasure in those who
honor him,
in those who trust in his
constant love.

12 Praise the LORD, O Jerusalem!
Praise your God, O Zion!
13 He keeps your gates strong;
he blesses your people.
14 He keeps your borders safe
and satisfies you with the finest
wheat.

15 He gives a command to the
earth,
and what he says is quickly
done.
16 He spreads snow like a blanket
and scatters frost like dust.
17 He sends hail like gravel;
no one can endure the cold he
sends!
18 Then he gives a command, and the
ice melts;
he sends the wind, and the
water flows.

19 He gives his message to his
people,
his instructions and laws to
Israel.
20 He has not done this for other
nations;
they do not know his laws.

Praise the LORD!

A Call for the Universe to Praise God

148

Praise the LORD!

Praise the LORD from
heaven,
you that live in the heights
above.
2 Praise him, all his angels,
all his heavenly armies.

3 Praise him, sun and moon;
praise him, shining stars.
4 Praise him, highest heavens,
and the waters above the sky.[t]
5 Let them all praise the name of
the LORD!
He commanded, and they were
created;
6 by his command they were fixed
in their places forever,
and they cannot disobey.[u]

7 Praise the LORD from the earth,
sea monsters and all ocean
depths;
8 lightning and hail, snow and
clouds,
strong winds that obey his
command.

9 Praise him, hills and mountains,
fruit trees and forests;
10 all animals, tame and wild,
reptiles and birds.

11 Praise him, kings and all
peoples,
princes and all other rulers;
12 young women and young men,
old people and children too.

13 Let them all praise the name of
the LORD!
His name is greater than all
others;
his glory is above earth and
heaven.
14 He made his nation strong,
so that all his people
praise him—
the people of Israel, so dear
to him.

Praise the LORD!

A Hymn of Praise

149

Praise the LORD!

Sing a new song to the LORD;
praise him in the assembly of
his faithful people!
2 Be glad, Israel, because of your
Creator;
rejoice, people of Zion, because
of your king!
3 Praise his name with
dancing;
play drums and harps in praise
of him.

[t] WATERS ABOVE THE SKY: *See Gn 1.6, 7.* [u] by his command . . . disobey; *or* he has fixed them in their places for all time, by a command that lasts forever.

4 The LORD takes pleasure in his
people;
he honors the humble with
victory.
5 Let God's people rejoice in their
triumph
and sing joyfully all night
long.
6 Let them shout aloud as they
praise God,
with their sharp swords in their
hands
7 to defeat the nations
and to punish the peoples;
8 to bind their kings in chains,
their leaders in chains of iron;
9 to punish the nations as God has
commanded.
This is the victory of God's people.

Praise the LORD!

Praise the LORD!

150

Praise the LORD!

Praise God in his Temple!
Praise his strength in heaven!
2 Praise him for the mighty things
he has done.
Praise his supreme greatness.

3 Praise him with trumpets.
Praise him with harps and lyres.
4 Praise him with drums and
dancing.
Praise him with harps and
flutes.
5 Praise him with cymbals.
Praise him with loud cymbals.
6 Praise the LORD, all living
creatures!

Praise the LORD!

PROVERBS

Introduction

The book of Proverbs *is a collection of moral and religious teachings in the form of sayings and proverbs. Much of it has to do with practical, everyday concerns. It begins with the reminder that "To have knowledge, you must first have reverence for the* Lord,*" and then goes on to deal with matters not only of religious morality, but also of common sense and good manners. Its many short sayings reveal the insights of ancient Israelite teachers about what a wise person will do in certain situations. Some of these concern family relations, others, business dealings. Some deal with matters of etiquette in social relationships, and others with the need of self-control. Much is said about such qualities as humility, patience, respect for the poor, and loyalty to friends.*

Outline of Contents

The Value of Proverbs

1 The proverbs of Solomon, son of
David and king of Israel.
2 Here are proverbs that will help you
recognize wisdom and good advice, and
understand sayings with deep meaning.
3 They can teach you how to live intelligently and how to be honest, just, and
fair. 4 They can make an inexperienced
person clever and teach young people
how to be resourceful. 5 These proverbs
can even add to the knowledge of the
wise and give guidance to the educated,
6 so that they can understand the hidden
meanings of proverbs and the problems
that the wise raise.

Advice to the Young

7 To have knowledge, you must first
have reverence for the Lord.[a] Stupid
people have no respect for wisdom and
refuse to learn.
8 My child, pay attention to what your
father and mother tell you. 9 Their teaching will improve your character as a
handsome turban or a necklace improves your appearance.
10 My child, when sinners tempt you,
don't give in. 11 Suppose they say, "Come
on; let's find someone to kill! Let's attack some innocent people for the fun of
it! 12 They may be alive and well when
we find them, but they'll be dead when
we're through with them! 13 We'll find all
kinds of riches and fill our houses with
loot! 14 Come and join us, and we'll all
share what we steal."
15 My child, don't go with people like
that. Stay away from them. 16 They can't
wait to do something bad. They're always ready to kill. 17 It does no good to
spread a net when the bird you want to
catch is watching, 18 but people like that
are setting a trap for themselves, a trap
in which they will die. 19 Robbery always
claims the life of the robber—this is
what happens to[b] anyone who lives by
violence.

Wisdom Calls

20 Listen! Wisdom is calling out in the
streets and marketplaces, 21 calling
loudly at the city gates and wherever
people come together:
22 "Foolish people! How long do you
want to be foolish? How long will you
enjoy making fun of knowledge? Will
you never learn? 23 Listen when I reprimand you; I will give you good advice
and share my knowledge with you.
24 I have been calling you, inviting you to
come, but you would not listen. You paid

[a] To . . . Lord; *or* The most important part of knowledge is having reverence for the Lord.
[b] *One ancient translation* what happens to; *Hebrew* the path of.

no attention to me. 25 You have ignored
all my advice and have not been willing
to let me correct you. 26 So when you get
into trouble, I will laugh at you. I will
make fun of you when terror strikes—
27 when it comes on you like a storm,
bringing fierce winds of trouble, and you
are in pain and misery. 28 Then you will
call for wisdom, but I will not answer.
You may look for me everywhere, but
you will not find me. 29 You have never
had any use for knowledge and have always refused to obey the LORD. 30 You
have never wanted my advice or paid
any attention when I corrected you. 31 So
then, you will get what you deserve, and
your own actions will make you sick.
32 Inexperienced people die because they
reject wisdom. Stupid people are destroyed by their own lack of concern.
33 But whoever listens to me will have security. He will be safe, with no reason to
be afraid."

The Rewards of Wisdom

2 My child, learn what I teach you
and never forget what I tell you to
do. 2 Listen to what is wise and try to
understand it. 3 Yes, beg for knowledge;
plead for insight. 4 Look for it as hard as
you would for silver or some hidden
treasure. 5 If you do, you will know what
it means to fear the LORD and you will
succeed in learning about God. 6 It is the
LORD who gives wisdom; from him come
knowledge and understanding. 7 He provides help and protection for those who
are righteous and honest. 8 He protects
those who treat others fairly, and guards
those who are devoted to him.

9 If you listen to me, you will know
what is right, just, and fair. You will
know what you should do. 10 You will become wise, and your knowledge will
give you pleasure. 11 Your insight and
understanding will protect you 12 and
prevent you from doing the wrong thing.
They will keep you away from people
who stir up trouble by what they say—
13 those who have abandoned a righteous life to live in the darkness of sin,
14 those who find pleasure in doing
wrong and who enjoy senseless evil,
15 unreliable people who cannot be
trusted.

16 You will be able to resist any immoral woman who tries to seduce you
with her smooth talk, 17 who is faithless
to her own husband and forgets her sacred vows. 18 If you go to her house, you
are traveling the road to death. To go
there is to approach the world of the
dead. 19 No one who visits her ever
comes back. He never returns to the
road to life. 20 So you must follow the example of good people and live a righteous life. 21 Righteous people—people of
integrity—will live in this land of ours.
22 But God will snatch the wicked from
the land and pull sinners out of it like
plants from the ground.

Advice to the Young

3 My child, don't forget what I teach
you. Always remember what I tell
you to do. 2 My teaching will give you a
long and prosperous life. 3 Never let go
of loyalty and faithfulness. Tie them
around your neck; write them on your
heart. 4 If you do this, both God and people will be pleased with you.

5 Trust in the LORD with all your heart.
Never rely on what you think you know.
6 Remember the LORD in everything you
do, and he will show you the right way.
7 Never let yourself think that you are
wiser than you are; simply obey the LORD
and refuse to do wrong. 8 If you do, it will
be like good medicine, healing your
wounds and easing your pains. 9 Honor
the LORD by making him an offering
from the best of all that your land produces. 10 If you do, your barns will be
filled with grain, and you will have too
much wine to store it all.

11 My child, when the LORD corrects
you, pay close attention and take it as a
warning. 12 The LORD corrects those he
loves, as parents correct a child of whom
they are proud. 13 Happy is anyone who
becomes wise—who comes to have
understanding. 14 There is more profit in
it than there is in silver; it is worth more
to you than gold. 15 Wisdom is more valuable than jewels; nothing you could
want can compare with it. 16 Wisdom offers you long life, as well as wealth and
honor. 17 Wisdom can make your life
pleasant and lead you safely through it.
18 Those who become wise are happy;
wisdom will give them life.

19 The LORD created the earth by his
wisdom;
by his knowledge he set the sky
in place.

20 His wisdom caused the rivers to
flow
and the clouds to give rain to
the earth.

21 My child, hold on to your wisdom
and insight. Never let them get away
from you. 22 They will provide you with
life—a pleasant and happy life. 23 You
can go safely on your way and never
even stumble. 24 You will not be afraid
when you go to bed, and you will sleep
soundly through the night. 25 You will
not have to worry about sudden disasters, such as come on the wicked like a
storm. 26 The LORD will keep you safe. He
will not let you fall into a trap.

27 Whenever you possibly can, do good
to those who need it. 28 Never tell your
neighbors to wait until tomorrow if you
can help them now. 29 Don't plan anything that will hurt your neighbors; they
live beside you, trusting you. 30 Don't argue with others for no reason when they
have never done you any harm. 31 Don't
be jealous of violent people or decide to
act as they do, 32 because the LORD hates
people who do evil, but he takes righteous people into his confidence. 33 The
LORD puts a curse on the homes of the
wicked, but blesses the homes of the
righteous. 34 He has no use for conceited
people, but shows favor to those who are
humble. 35 Wise people will gain an honorable reputation, but stupid people will
only add to their own disgrace.

The Benefits of Wisdom

4 My children, listen to what your
father teaches you. Pay attention,
and you will have understanding. 2 What
I am teaching you is good, so remember
it all. 3 When I was only a little boy, my
parents' only son, 4 my father would
teach me. He would say, "Remember
what I say and never forget it. Do as I tell
you, and you will live. 5 Get wisdom and
insight! Do not forget or ignore what I
say. 6 Do not abandon wisdom, and she
will protect you; love her, and she will
keep you safe. 7 Getting wisdom is the
most important thing you can do. Whatever else you get, get insight. 8 Love wisdom, and she will make you great.
Embrace her,[c] and she will bring you
honor. 9 She will be your crowning
glory."

10 Listen to me, my child. Take seriously what I am telling you, and you will
live a long life. 11 I have taught you wisdom and the right way to live. 12 Nothing
will stand in your way if you walk
wisely, and you will not stumble when
you run. 13 Always remember what you
have learned. Your education is your
life—guard it well. 14 Do not go where
evil people go. Do not follow the example of the wicked. 15 Don't do it! Keep
away from evil! Refuse it and go on your
way. 16 Wicked people cannot sleep unless they have done something wrong.
They lie awake unless they have hurt
someone. 17 Wickedness and violence
are like food and drink to them.

18 The road the righteous travel is like
the sunrise, getting brighter and
brighter until daylight has come. 19 The
road of the wicked, however, is dark as
night. They fall, but cannot see what
they have stumbled over.

20 My child, pay attention to what I
say. Listen to my words. 21 Never let
them get away from you. Remember
them and keep them in your heart.
22 They will give life and health to anyone who understands them. 23 Be careful
how you think; your life is shaped by
your thoughts. 24 Never say anything
that isn't true. Have nothing to do with
lies and misleading words. 25 Look
straight ahead with honest confidence;
don't hang your head in shame. 26 Plan
carefully what you do, and whatever you
do will turn out right. 27 Avoid evil and
walk straight ahead. Don't go one step
off the right way.

Warning against Adultery

5 My child, pay attention and listen to
my wisdom and insight. 2 Then you
will know how to behave properly, and
your words will show that you have
knowledge. 3 The lips of another man's
wife may be as sweet as honey and her
kisses as smooth as olive oil, 4 but when
it is all over, she leaves you nothing but
bitterness and pain. 5 She will take you
down to the world of the dead; the road
she walks is the road to death. 6 She does
not stay on the road to life; but wanders
off, and does not realize what is
happening.

7 Now listen to me, sons, and never

[c] Embrace her; *or* Prize her highly.

forget what I am saying. 8Keep away
from such a woman! Don't even go near
her door! 9If you do, others will gain the
respect that you once had, and you will
die young at the hands of merciless people. 10Yes, strangers will take all your
wealth, and what you have worked for
will belong to someone else. 11You will
lie groaning on your deathbed, your
flesh and muscles being eaten away,
12and you will say, "Why would I never
learn? Why would I never let anyone
correct me? 13I wouldn't listen to my
teachers. I paid no attention to them.
14And suddenly I found myself[d] publicly disgraced."

15Be faithful to your own wife and
give your love to her alone. 16Children
that you have by other women will do
you no good. 17Your children should
grow up to help you, not strangers. 18So
be happy with your wife and find your
joy with the woman you married—
19pretty and graceful as a deer. Let her
charms keep you happy; let her surround you with her love. 20Son, why
should you give your love to another
woman? Why should you prefer the
charms of another man's wife? 21The
LORD sees everything you do. Wherever
you go, he is watching. 22The sins of the
wicked are a trap. They get caught in the
net of their own sin. 23They die because
they have no self-control. Their utter
stupidity will send them to their graves.

More Warnings

6 My child, have you promised to be
responsible for someone else's
debts? 2Have you been caught by your
own words, trapped by your own promises? 3Well then, my child, you are in
that person's power, but this is how to
get out of it: hurry to him, and beg him to
release you. 4Don't let yourself go to
sleep or even stop to rest. 5Get out of the
trap like a bird or a deer escaping from
a hunter.

6Lazy people should learn a lesson
from the way ants live. 7They have no
leader, chief, or ruler, 8but they store up
their food during the summer, getting
ready for winter. 9How long is the lazy
man going to lie around? When is he
ever going to get up? 10"I'll just take a
short nap," he says; "I'll fold my hands
and rest a while." 11But while he sleeps,
poverty will attack him like an armed
robber.

12Worthless, wicked people go around
telling lies. 13They wink and make gestures to deceive you, 14all the while planning evil in their perverted minds,
stirring up trouble everywhere. 15Be-
cause of this, disaster will strike them
without warning, and they will be fatally
wounded.

16-19There are seven things that the
LORD hates and cannot tolerate:
A proud look,
a lying tongue,
hands that kill innocent people,
a mind that thinks up wicked plans,
feet that hurry off to do evil,
a witness who tells one lie after
another,
and someone who stirs up trouble
among friends.

Warning against Adultery

20Son, do what your father tells you
and never forget what your mother
taught you. 21Keep their words with you
always, locked in your heart. 22Their
teaching will lead you when you travel,
protect you at night, and advise you during the day. 23Their instructions are a
shining light; their correction can teach
you how to live. 24It can keep you away
from bad women, from the seductive
words of other men's wives. 25Don't be
tempted by their beauty; don't be
trapped by their flirting eyes. 26A man
can hire a prostitute for the price of a
loaf of bread, but adultery will cost him
all he has.

27Can you carry fire against your
chest without burning your clothes?
28Can you walk on hot coals without
burning your feet? 29It is just as dangerous to sleep with another man's wife.
Whoever does it will suffer. 30People
don't despise a thief if he steals food
when he is hungry;[e] 31yet if he is
caught, he must pay back seven times
more—he must give up everything
he has. 32But a man who commits adultery doesn't have any sense. He is just
destroying himself. 33He will be dishonored and beaten up; he will be

[d] And suddenly . . . myself; *or* I was about to be.

[e] People don't despise . . . hungry; *or* Don't
people despise . . . hungry?

permanently disgraced. 34 A husband is
never angrier than when he is jealous;
his revenge knows no limits. 35 He will
not accept any payment; no amount of
gifts will satisfy his anger.

7 My child, remember what I say and
never forget what I tell you to do.
2 Do what I say, and you will live. Be as
careful to follow my teaching as you are
to protect your eyes. 3 Keep my teaching
with you all the time; write it on your
heart. 4 Treat wisdom as your sister, and
insight as your closest friend. 5 They will
keep you away from other men's wives,
from women with seductive words.

The Immoral Woman

6 Once I was looking out the window of
my house, 7 and I saw many inexperienced young men, but noticed one foolish fellow in particular. 8 He was
walking along the street near the corner
where a certain woman lived. He was
passing near her house 9 in the evening
after it was dark. 10 And then she met
him; she was dressed like a prostitute
and was making plans. 11 She was a bold
and shameless woman who always
walked the streets 12 or stood waiting at
a corner, sometimes in the streets, sometimes in the marketplace. 13 She threw
her arms around the young man, kissed
him, looked him straight in the eye, and
said, 14 "I made my offerings today and
have the meat from the sacrifices. 15 So I
came out looking for you. I wanted to
find you, and here you are! 16 I've covered my bed with sheets of colored linen
from Egypt. 17 I've perfumed it with
myrrh, aloes, and cinnamon. 18 Come on!
Let's make love all night long. We'll be
happy in each other's arms. 19 My husband isn't at home. He's on a long trip.
20 He took plenty of money with him and
won't be back for two weeks." 21 So she
tempted him with her charms, and he
gave in to her smooth talk. 22 Suddenly
he was going with her like an ox on the
way to be slaughtered, like a deer prancing into a trap[f] 23 where an arrow would
pierce its heart. He was like a bird going
into a net—he did not know that his life
was in danger.

24 Now then, sons, listen to me. Pay attention to what I say. 25 Do not let such a
woman win your heart; don't go wandering after her. 26 She has been the ruin
of many men and caused the death of
too many to count. 27 If you go to her
house, you are on the way to the world
of the dead. It is a shortcut to death.

In Praise of Wisdom

8 Listen! Wisdom is calling out.
Reason is making herself heard.
2 On the hilltops near the road
and at the crossroads she
stands.
3 At the entrance to the city,
beside the gates, she calls:
4 "I appeal to all of you;
I call to everyone on earth.
5 Are you immature? Learn to be
mature.
Are you foolish? Learn to have
sense.
6 Listen to my excellent words;
all I tell you is right.
7 What I say is the truth;
lies are hateful to me.
8 Everything I say is true;
nothing is false or misleading.
9 To those with insight, it is all
clear;
to the well-informed, it is all
plain.
10 Choose my instruction instead of
silver;
choose knowledge rather than
the finest gold.

11 "I am Wisdom, I am better than
jewels;
nothing you want can compare
with me.
12 I am Wisdom, and I have insight;
I have knowledge and sound
judgment.
13 To honor the LORD is to hate evil;
I hate pride and arrogance,
evil ways and false words.
14 I make plans and carry them out.
I have understanding, and I am
strong.
15 I help kings to govern
and rulers to make good laws.
16 Every ruler on earth governs with
my help,
officials and nobles alike.
17 I love those who love me;
whoever looks for me can
find me.

f *Probable text* like a deer prancing into a trap; *Hebrew unclear.*

18 I have riches and honor to give,
prosperity and success.
19 What you get from me is better
than the finest gold,
better than the purest silver.
20 I walk the way of righteousness;
I follow the paths of justice,
21 giving wealth to those who
love me,
filling their houses with
treasures.

22 "The LORD created me first of all,
the first of his works, long ago.
23 I was made in the very beginning,
at the first, before the world
began.
24 I was born before the oceans,
when there were no springs of
water.
25 I was born before the mountains,
before the hills were set in
place,
26 before God made the earth and its
fields
or even the first handful of soil.
27 I was there when he set the sky in
place,
when he stretched the horizon
across the ocean,
28 when he placed the clouds in
the sky,
when he opened the springs of
the ocean
29 and ordered the waters of the sea
to rise no further than he said.
I was there when he laid the
earth's foundations.
30 I was beside him like an
architect,[g]
I was his daily source of joy,
always happy in his presence—
31 happy with the world
and pleased with the human
race.

32 "Now, young people, listen to me.
Do as I say, and you will be
happy.
33 Listen to what you are taught.
Be wise; do not neglect it.
34 Those who listen to me will be
happy—
those who stay at my door
every day,
waiting at the entrance to my
home.
35 Those who find me find life,
and the LORD will be pleased
with them.
36 Those who do not find me hurt
themselves;
anyone who hates me loves
death."

Wisdom and Stupidity

9 Wisdom has built her house and
made seven columns for it. 2 She
has had an animal killed for a feast,
mixed spices in the wine, and set the table. 3 She has sent her servant women to
call out from the highest place in town:
4 "Come in, ignorant people!" And to the
foolish she says, 5 "Come, eat my food
and drink the wine that I have mixed.
6 Leave the company of ignorant people,
and live. Follow the way of knowledge."
7 If you correct conceited people, you
will only be insulted. If you reprimand
evil people, you will only get hurt.
8 Never correct conceited people; they
will hate you for it. But if you correct the
wise, they will respect you. 9 Anything
you say to the wise will make them
wiser. Whatever you tell the righteous
will add to their knowledge.
10 To be wise you must first have reverence for the LORD. If you know the Holy
One, you have understanding. 11 Wisdom will add years to your life. 12 You
are the one who will profit if you have
wisdom, and if you reject it, you are the
one who will suffer.
13 Stupidity is like a loud, ignorant,
shameless woman.[h] 14 She sits at the
door of her house or on a seat in the
highest part of town, 15 and calls out to
people passing by, who are minding
their own business: 16 "Come in, ignorant people!" To the foolish she says,
17 "Stolen water is sweeter. Stolen bread
tastes better." 18 Her victims do not know
that the people die who go to her house,
that those who have already entered are
now deep in the world of the dead.

Solomon's Proverbs

10 These are Solomon's proverbs:
Wise children make their
fathers proud of them; foolish ones
bring their mothers grief.

[g] an architect; *or* a little child. [h] *Verse 13 in Hebrew is unclear.*

2 Wealth you get by dishonesty will do
you no good, but honesty can save your
life.
3 The LORD will not let good people go
hungry, but he will keep the wicked
from getting what they want.
4 Being lazy will make you poor, but
hard work will make you rich.
5 A sensible person gathers the crops
when they are ready; it is a disgrace to
sleep through the time of harvest.
6 Good people will receive blessings.
The words of the wicked hide a violent
nature.
7 Good people will be remembered as a
blessing, but the wicked will soon be
forgotten.
8 Sensible people accept good advice.
People who talk foolishly will come to
ruin.
9 Honest people are safe and secure,
but the dishonest will be caught.
10 Someone who holds back the truth
causes trouble, but one who openly criticizes works for peace.[i]
11 A good person's words are a fountain of life, but a wicked person's words
hide a violent nature.
12 Hate stirs up trouble, but love forgives all offenses.
13 Intelligent people talk sense, but stupid people need to be punished.
14 The wise get all the knowledge they
can, but when fools speak, trouble is not
far off.
15 Wealth protects the rich; poverty destroys the poor.
16 The reward for doing good is life,
but sin leads only to more sin.
17 People who listen when they are
corrected will live, but those who will
not admit that they are wrong are in
danger.
18 Anyone who hides hatred is a liar.
Anyone who spreads gossip is a fool.
19 The more you talk, the more likely
you are to sin. If you are wise, you will
keep quiet.
20 A good person's words are like pure
silver; a wicked person's ideas are
worthless.
21 A good person's words will benefit
many people, but you can kill yourself
with stupidity.
22 It is the LORD's blessing that makes
you wealthy. Hard work can make you
no richer.[j]
23 It is foolish to enjoy doing wrong.
Intelligent people take pleasure in
wisdom.
24 The righteous get what they want,
but the wicked will get what they fear
most.
25 Storms come, and the wicked are
blown away, but honest people are always safe.
26 Never get a lazy person to do something for you; he will be as irritating as
vinegar on your teeth or smoke in your
eyes.
27 Obey the LORD, and you will live
longer. The wicked die before their time.
28 The hopes of good people lead to
joy, but wicked people can look forward
to nothing.
29 The LORD protects honest people, but
destroys those who do wrong.
30 Righteous people will always have
security, but the wicked will not survive
in the land.
31 Righteous people speak wisdom, but
the tongue that speaks evil will be
stopped.
32 Righteous people know the kind
thing to say, but the wicked are always
saying things that hurt.

11 The LORD hates people who use
dishonest scales. He is happy
with honest weights.
2 People who are proud will soon be
disgraced. It is wiser to be modest.
3 If you are good, you are guided by
honesty. People who can't be trusted are
destroyed by their own dishonesty.
4 Riches will do you no good on the
day you face death, but honesty can save
your life.
5 Honesty makes a good person's life
easier, but the wicked will cause their
own downfall.
6 Righteousness rescues those who are
honest, but those who can't be trusted
are trapped by their own greed.
7 When the wicked die, their hope dies
with them. Confidence placed in riches
comes to nothing.
8 The righteous are protected from
trouble; it comes to the wicked instead.
9 You can be ruined by the talk of god

[i] *One ancient translation* but one . . . peace; *Hebrew repeats verse 8b.* [j] Hard work . . . richer; *or* And the LORD does not add sorrow to your wealth.

less people, but the wisdom of the righteous can save you.
10 A city is happy when honest people
have good fortune, and there are joyful
shouts when the wicked die.
11 A city becomes great when the
righteous give it their blessing; but a city
is brought to ruin by the words of the
wicked.
12 It is foolish to speak scornfully of
others. If you are smart, you will keep
quiet.
13 No one who gossips can be trusted
with a secret, but you can put confidence
in someone who is trustworthy.
14 A nation will fall if it has no guidance. Many advisers mean security.
15 If you promise to pay a stranger's
debt, you will regret it. You are better off
if you don't get involved.
16 A gracious woman is respected, but
a woman without virtue is a disgrace.
Lazy people will never have money,[k]
but aggressive people will get rich.
17 You do yourself a favor when you
are kind. If you are cruel, you only hurt
yourself.
18 Wicked people do not really gain
anything, but if you do what is right, you
are certain to be rewarded.
19 Anyone who is determined to do
right will live, but anyone who insists on
doing wrong will die.
20 The LORD hates evil-minded people,
but loves those who do right.
21 You can be sure that evil people will
be punished, but the righteous will
escape.
22 Beauty in a woman without good
judgment is like a gold ring in a pig's
snout.
23 What good people want always results in good; when the wicked get what
they want, everyone is angry.[l]
24 Some people spend their money
freely and still grow richer. Others are
cautious, and yet grow poorer.
25 Be generous, and you will be prosperous. Help others, and you will be
helped.
26 People curse someone who hoards
grain, waiting for a higher price, but
they praise the one who puts it up for
sale.
27 If your goals are good, you will be
respected, but if you are looking for
trouble, that is what you will get.
28 Those who depend on their wealth
will fall like the leaves of autumn, but
the righteous will prosper like the leaves
of summer.
29 Those who bring trouble on their
families will have nothing at the end.
Foolish people will always be servants
to the wise.
30 Righteousness[m] gives life, but violence[n] takes it away.
31 Those who are good are rewarded
here on earth, so you can be sure that
wicked and sinful people will be
punished.

12 Any who love knowledge want
to be told when they are wrong.
It is stupid to hate being corrected.
2 The LORD is pleased with good people, but condemns those who plan evil.
3 Wickedness does not give security,
but righteous people stand firm.
4 A good wife is her husband's pride
and joy; but a wife who brings shame on
her husband is like a cancer in his
bones.
5 Honest people will treat you fairly;
the wicked only want to deceive you.
6 The words of the wicked are murderous, but the words of the righteous rescue those who are threatened.
7 The wicked meet their downfall and
leave no descendants, but the families of
the righteous live on.
8 If you are intelligent, you will be
praised; if you are stupid, people will
look down on you.
9 It is better to be an ordinary person
working for a living than to play the part
of someone great but go hungry.
10 Good people take care of their animals, but wicked people are cruel to
theirs.
11 A hard-working farmer has plenty
to eat, but it is stupid to waste time on
useless projects.
12 All that wicked people want is to
find evil things to do, but the righteous
stand firm.[o]
13 The wicked are trapped by their own
words, but honest people get themselves
out of trouble.

[k] *One ancient translation* but a woman . . . money; *Hebrew does not have these words.*
[l] everyone is angry; or God punishes them. [m] *One ancient translation* Righteousness; *Hebrew* A righteous person. [n] *Probable text* violence; *Hebrew* a wise person. [o] *Verse 12 in Hebrew is unclear.*

14 Your reward depends on what you
say and what you do; you will get what
you deserve.
15 Stupid people always think they are
right. Wise people listen to advice.
16 When a fool is annoyed, he quickly
lets it be known. Smart people will ignore an insult.
17 When you tell the truth, justice is
done, but lies lead to injustice.
18 Thoughtless words can wound as
deeply as any sword, but wisely spoken
words can heal.
19 A lie has a short life, but truth lives
on forever.
20 Those who plan evil are in for a rude
surprise, but those who work for good
will find happiness.
21 Nothing bad happens to righteous
people, but the wicked have nothing but
trouble.
22 The LORD hates liars, but is pleased
with those who keep their word.
23 Smart people keep quiet about what
they know, but stupid people advertise
their ignorance.
24 Hard work will give you power; being lazy will make you a slave.
25 Worry can rob you of happiness, but
kind words will cheer you up.
26 The righteous person is a guide to
his friend, but the path of the wicked
leads them astray.
27 If you are lazy, you will never get
what you are after, but if you work hard,
you will get a fortune.[p]
28 Righteousness is the road to life;
wickedness[q] is the road to death.

13 Wise children pay attention
when their parents correct them,
but arrogant people never admit they
are wrong.
2 Good people will be rewarded for
what they say, but those who are deceitful are hungry for violence.
3 Be careful what you say and protect
your life. A careless talker destroys
himself.
4 No matter how much a lazy person
may want something, he will never get
it. A hard worker will get everything he
wants.
5 Honest people hate lies, but the
words of wicked people are shameful
and disgraceful.
6 Righteousness protects the innocent;
wickedness is the downfall of sinners.
7 Some people pretend to be rich, but
have nothing. Others pretend to be poor,
but own a fortune.
8 The rich have to use their money to
save their lives, but no one threatens the
poor.
9 The righteous are like a light shining
brightly; the wicked are like a lamp
flickering out.
10 Arrogance causes nothing but trouble. It is wiser to ask for advice.
11 The more easily you get your
wealth, the sooner you will lose it. The
harder it is to earn, the more you will
have.
12 When hope is crushed, the heart is
crushed, but a wish come true fills you
with joy.
13 If you refuse good advice, you are
asking for trouble; follow it and you are
safe.
14 The teachings of the wise are a fountain of life; they will help you escape
when your life is in danger.
15 Intelligence wins respect, but those
who can't be trusted are on the road to
ruin.[r]
16 Sensible people always think before
they act, but stupid people advertise
their ignorance.
17 Unreliable messengers cause trouble, but those who can be trusted bring
peace.
18 Someone who will not learn will be
poor and disgraced. Anyone who listens
to correction is respected.
19 How good it is to get what you want!
Stupid people refuse to turn away from
evil.
20 Keep company with the wise and
you will become wise. If you make
friends with stupid people, you will be
ruined.
21 Trouble follows sinners everywhere,
but righteous people will be rewarded
with good things.
22 Good people will have wealth to
leave to their grandchildren, but the
wealth of sinners will go to the
righteous.
23 Unused fields could yield plenty of
food for the poor, but unjust people keep
them from being farmed.[s]

[p] *Verse 27 in Hebrew is unclear.* [q] *One ancient translation* wickedness; *Hebrew* path.
[r] *One ancient translation* road to ruin; *Hebrew* permanent road. [s] *Verse 23 in Hebrew is unclear.*

24 If you don't punish your children, you don't love them. If you do love them, you will correct them.

25 The righteous have enough to eat, but the wicked are always hungry.

14 Homes are made by the wisdom of women, but are destroyed by foolishness.

2 Be honest and you show that you have reverence for the LORD; be dishonest and you show that you do not.

3 Proud fools talk too much; the words of the wise protect them.

4 Without any oxen to pull the plow your barn will be empty, but with them it will be full of grain.[t]

5 A reliable witness always tells the truth, but an unreliable one tells nothing but lies.

6 Conceited people can never become wise, but intelligent people learn easily.

7 Stay away from foolish people; they have nothing to teach you.

8 Why is a clever person wise? Because he knows what to do. Why is a stupid person foolish? Because he only thinks he knows.

9 Foolish people don't care if they sin, but good people want to be forgiven.[u]

10 Your joy is your own; your bitterness is your own. No one can share them with you.

11 A good person's house will still be standing after an evildoer's house has been destroyed.

12 What you think is the right road may lead to death.

13 Laughter may hide sadness. When happiness is gone, sorrow is always there.

14 Bad people will get what they deserve. Good people will be rewarded for their deeds.[v]

15 A fool will believe anything; smart people watch their step.

16 Sensible people are careful to stay out of trouble, but stupid people are careless and act too quickly.

17 People with a hot temper do foolish things; wiser people remain calm.[w]

18 Ignorant people get what their foolishness deserves, but the clever are rewarded with knowledge.

19 Evil people will have to bow down to the righteous and humbly beg their favor.

20 No one likes the poor, not even their neighbors, but the rich have many friends.

21 If you want to be happy, be kind to the poor; it is a sin to despise anyone.

22 You will earn the trust and respect of others if you work for good; if you work for evil, you are making a mistake.

23 Work and you will earn a living; if you sit around talking you will be poor.

24 Wise people are rewarded with wealth, but fools are known by[x] their foolishness.

25 A witness saves lives when he tells the truth; when he tells lies, he betrays people.

26 Reverence for the LORD gives confidence and security to a man and his family.

27 Do you want to avoid death? Reverence for the LORD is a fountain of life.

28 A king's greatness depends on how many people he rules; without them he is nothing.

29 If you stay calm, you are wise, but if you have a hot temper, you only show how stupid you are.

30 Peace of mind makes the body healthy, but jealousy is like a cancer.

31 If you oppress poor people, you insult the God who made them; but kindness shown to the poor is an act of worship.

32 Wicked people bring about their own downfall by their evil deeds, but good people are protected by their integrity.[y]

33 Wisdom is in every thought of intelligent people; fools know nothing[z] about wisdom.

34 Righteousness makes a nation great; sin is a disgrace to any nation.

35 Kings are pleased with competent officials, but they punish those who fail them.

15 A gentle answer quiets anger, but a harsh one stirs it up.

2 When wise people speak, they make knowledge attractive, but stupid people spout nonsense.

[t] your barn will be . . . grain; *or* you may grow a little grain, but with them you can grow much more. [u] *Verse 9 in Hebrew is unclear.* [v] *Probable text* for their deeds; *Hebrew* from upon them. [w] *One ancient translation* remain calm; *Hebrew* are hated. [x] *Probable text* are known by; *Hebrew unclear.* [y] *Some ancient translations* integrity; *Hebrew* death. [z] *One ancient translation* nothing; *Hebrew does not have this word.*

3 The LORD sees what happens everywhere; he is watching us, whether we do
good or evil.
4 Kind words bring life, but cruel
words crush your spirit.
5 It is foolish to ignore what your parents taught you; it is wise to accept their
correction.
6 Righteous people keep their wealth,
but the wicked lose theirs when hard
times come.
7 Knowledge is spread by people who
are wise, not by fools.
8 The LORD is pleased when good people pray, but hates the sacrifices that the
wicked bring him.
9 The LORD hates the ways of evil people, but loves those who do what is right.
10 If you do what is wrong, you will be
severely punished; you will die if you do
not let yourself be corrected.
11 Not even the world of the dead can
keep the LORD from knowing what is
there; how then can we hide our
thoughts from God?
12 Conceited people do not like to be
corrected; they never ask for advice
from those who are wiser.
13 When people are happy, they smile,
but when they are sad, they look depressed.
14 Intelligent people want to learn, but
stupid people are satisfied with ignorance.
15 The life of the poor is a constant
struggle, but happy people always enjoy
life.
16 Better to be poor and fear the LORD
than to be rich and in trouble.
17 Better to eat vegetables with people
you love than to eat the finest meat
where there is hate.
18 Hot tempers cause arguments, but
patience brings peace.
19 If you are lazy, you will meet difficulty everywhere, but if you are honest,
you will have no trouble.
20 Wise children make their fathers
happy. Only fools despise their mothers.
21 Stupid people are happy with their
foolishness, but the wise will do what is
right.
22 Get all the advice you can, and you
will succeed; without it you will fail.
23 What a joy it is to find just the right
word for the right occasion!
24 Wise people walk the road that leads
upward to life, not the road that leads
downward to death.
25 The LORD will destroy the homes of
arrogant men, but he will protect a
widow's property.
26 The LORD hates evil thoughts, but he
is pleased with friendly words.
27 Try to make a profit dishonestly,
and you get your family in trouble. Don't
take bribes and you will live longer.
28 Good people think before they answer. Evil people have a quick reply, but
it causes trouble.
29 When good people pray, the LORD
listens, but he ignores those who are
evil.
30 Smiling faces make you happy, and
good news makes you feel better.
31 If you pay attention when you are
corrected, you are wise.
32 If you refuse to learn, you are hurting yourself. If you accept correction,
you will become wiser.
33 Reverence for the LORD is an education in itself. You must be humble before
you can ever receive honors.

16 We may make our plans, but
God has the last word.[a]
2 You may think everything you do is
right, but the LORD judges your motives.
3 Ask the LORD to bless your plans, and
you will be successful in carrying
them out.
4 Everything the LORD has made has its
destiny; and the destiny of the wicked is
destruction.
5 The LORD hates everyone who is arrogant; he will never let them escape punishment.
6 Be loyal and faithful, and God will
forgive your sin. Obey the LORD and
nothing evil will happen to you.
7 When you please the LORD, you can
make[b] your enemies into friends.
8 It is better to have a little, honestly
earned, than to have a large income, dishonestly gained.
9 You may make your plans, but God
directs your actions.
10 The king speaks with divine authority; his decisions are always right.
11 The LORD wants weights and measures to be honest and every sale to be
fair.

[a] God . . . word; *or* God inspires our words. [b] you can make; *or* he will make.

12 Kings cannot tolerate evil,[c] because
justice is what makes a government
strong.
13 A king wants to hear the truth and
will favor those who speak it.
14 A wise person will try to keep the
king happy; if the king becomes angry,
someone may die.
15 The king's favor is like the clouds
that bring rain in the springtime—life is
there.
16 It is better—much better—to have
wisdom and knowledge than gold and
silver.
17 Those who are good travel a road
that avoids evil; so watch where you are
going—it may save your life.
18 Pride leads to destruction, and arrogance to downfall.
19 It is better to be humble and stay
poor than to be one of the arrogant and
get a share of their loot.
20 Pay attention to what you are
taught, and you will be successful; trust
in the LORD and you will be happy.
21 A wise, mature person is known for
his understanding. The more pleasant
his words, the more persuasive he is.
22 Wisdom is a fountain of life to the
wise, but trying to educate stupid people
is a waste of time.
23 Intelligent people think before they
speak; what they say is then more persuasive.
24 Kind words are like honey—sweet
to the taste and good for your health.
25 What you think is the right road
may lead to death.
26 A laborer's appetite makes him
work harder, because he wants to satisfy
his hunger.
27 Evil people look for ways to harm
others; even their words burn with evil.
28 Gossip is spread by wicked people;
they stir up trouble and break up
friendships.
29 Violent people deceive their friends
and lead them to disaster.
30 Watch out for people who grin and
wink at you; they have thought of something evil.
31 Long life is the reward of the righteous; gray hair is a glorious crown.
32 It is better to be patient than powerful. It is better to win control over yourself than over whole cities.
33 People cast lots to learn God's
will, but God himself determines the
answer.

17

Better to eat a dry crust of bread
with peace of mind than have a
banquet in a house full of trouble.
2 A shrewd servant will gain authority
over a master's worthless son and receive a part of the inheritance.
3 Gold and silver are tested by fire, and
a person's heart is tested by the LORD.
4 Evil people listen to evil ideas, and
liars listen to lies.
5 If you make fun of poor people, you
insult the God who made them. You will
be punished if you take pleasure in
someone's misfortune.
6 Grandparents are proud of their
grandchildren, just as children are
proud of their parents.
7 Respected people do not tell lies, and
fools have nothing worthwhile to say.
8 Some people think a bribe works
like magic; they believe it can do
anything.
9 If you want people to like you, forgive them when they wrong you. Remembering wrongs can break up a
friendship.
10 An intelligent person learns more
from one rebuke than a fool learns from
being beaten a hundred times.
11 Death will come like a cruel messenger to wicked people who are always
stirring up trouble.
12 It is better to meet a mother bear
robbed of her cubs than to meet some
fool busy with a stupid project.
13 If you repay good with evil, you will
never get evil out of your house.
14 The start of an argument is like the
first break in a dam; stop it before it goes
any further.
15 Condemning the innocent or letting
the wicked go—both are hateful to the
LORD.
16 It does a fool no good to spend
money on an education, because he has
no common sense.
17 Friends always show their love.
What are relatives for if not to share
trouble?
18 Only someone with no sense would
promise to be responsible for someone
else's debts.
19 To like sin is to like making trouble.

[c] Kings . . . evil; *or* It is intolerable for kings to do evil.

If you brag all the time,[d] you are asking
for trouble.
20 Anyone who thinks and speaks evil
can expect to find nothing good—only
disaster.
21 There is nothing but sadness and
sorrow for parents whose children do
foolish things.
22 Being cheerful keeps you healthy. It
is slow death to be gloomy all the time.
23 Corrupt judges accept secret bribes,
and then justice is not done.
24 An intelligent person aims at wise
action, but a fool starts off in many directions.
25 Foolish children bring grief to their
fathers and bitter regrets to their
mothers.
26 It is not right to make an innocent
person pay a fine; justice is perverted
when good people are punished.
27 Those who are sure of themselves do
not talk all the time. People who stay
calm have real insight. 28 After all, even
fools may be thought wise and intelligent if they stay quiet and keep their
mouths shut.

18 People who do not get along with
others are interested only in
themselves; they will disagree with what
everyone else knows is right.
2 A fool does not care whether he
understands a thing or not; all he wants
to do is show how smart he is.
3 Sin and shame go together. Lose
your honor, and you will get scorn in its
place.
4 A person's words can be a source of
wisdom, deep as the ocean, fresh as a
flowing stream.
5 It is not right to favor the guilty and
keep the innocent from receiving justice.
6 When some fool starts an argument,
he is asking for a beating.
7 When a fool speaks, he is ruining
himself; he gets caught in the trap of his
own words.
8 Gossip is so tasty—how we love to
swallow it!
9 A lazy person is as bad as someone
who is destructive.
10 The LORD is like a strong tower,
where the righteous can go and be safe.
11 Rich people, however, imagine that
their wealth protects them like high,
strong walls around a city.
12 No one is respected unless he is
humble; arrogant people are on the way
to ruin.
13 Listen before you answer. If you
don't, you are being stupid and insulting.
14 Your will to live can sustain you
when you are sick, but if you lose it, your
last hope is gone.
15 Intelligent people are always eager
and ready to learn.
16 Do you want to meet an important
person? Take a gift and it will be easy.
17 The first person to speak in court always seems right until his opponent begins to question him.
18 If two powerful people are opposing
each other in court, casting lots can settle the issue.
19 Help your relatives and they will
protect you like a strong city wall,[e] but
if you quarrel with them, they will close
their doors to you.
20 You will have to live with the consequences of everything you say. 21 What
you say can preserve life or destroy it; so
you must accept the consequences of
your words.
22 Find a wife and you find a good
thing; it shows that the LORD is good
to you.
23 When the poor speak, they have to
be polite, but when the rich answer, they
are rude.
24 Some friendships do[f] not last, but
some friends are more loyal than
brothers.

19 It is better to be poor but honest
than to be a lying fool.
2 Enthusiasm without knowledge is
not good; impatience will get you into
trouble.
3 Some people ruin themselves by their
own stupid actions and then blame the
LORD.
4 Rich people are always finding new
friends, but the poor cannot keep the
few they have.
5 If you tell lies in court, you will be
punished—there will be no escape.
6 Everyone tries to gain the favor of
important people; everyone claims the
friendship of those who give out favors.

[d] brag ... time; *or* make a show of your wealth. *Hebrew unclear.* [e] *Some ancient translations* Help ... wall; *Hebrew* Someone with friends does. [f] *Some ancient translations* Some friendships do; *Hebrew* Someone with friends does.

7 Even the relatives of a poor person have no use for him; no wonder he has no friends. No matter how hard he tries, he cannot win any.[g]
8 Do yourself a favor and learn all you can; then remember what you learn and you will prosper.
9 No one who tells lies in court can escape punishment; he is doomed.
10 Fools should not live in luxury, and slaves should not rule over noblemen.
11 If you are sensible, you will control your temper. When someone wrongs you, it is a great virtue to ignore it.
12 The king's anger is like the roar of a lion, but his favor is like welcome rain.
13 Stupid children can bring their parents to ruin. A nagging wife is like water going drip-drip-drip.
14 A man can inherit a house and money from his parents, but only the LORD can give him a sensible wife.
15 Go ahead and be lazy; sleep on, but you will go hungry.
16 Keep God's laws and you will live longer; if you ignore them, you will die.
17 When you give to the poor, it is like lending to the LORD, and the LORD will pay you back.
18 Discipline your children while they are young enough to learn. If you don't, you are helping them destroy themselves.[h]
19 If someone has a hot temper, let him take the consequences. If you get him out of trouble once, you will have to do it again.[i]
20 If you listen to advice and are willing to learn, one day you will be wise.
21 People may plan all kinds of things, but the LORD's will is going to be done.
22 It is a disgrace to be greedy;[j] poor people are better off than liars.
23 Obey the LORD and you will live a long life, content and safe from harm.
24 Some people are too lazy to put food in their own mouths.
25 Arrogance should be punished, so that people who don't know any better can learn a lesson. If you are wise, you will learn when you are corrected.
26 Only a shameful, disgraceful person would mistreat his father or turn his mother away from his home.
27 My child, when you stop learning, you will soon neglect what you already know.
28 There is no justice where a witness is determined to hurt someone. Wicked people love the taste of evil.
29 A conceited fool is sure to get a beating.

20 Drinking too much makes you loud and foolish. It's stupid to get drunk.
2 Fear an angry king as you would a growling lion; making him angry is suicide.
3 Any fool can start arguments; the honorable thing is to stay out of them.
4 A farmer too lazy to plow his fields at the right time will have nothing to harvest.
5 A person's thoughts are like water in a deep well, but someone with insight can draw them out.
6 Everyone talks about how loyal and faithful he is, but just try to find someone who really is!
7 Children are fortunate if they have a father who is honest and does what is right.
8 The king sits in judgment and knows evil when he sees it.
9 Can anyone really say that his conscience is clear, that he has gotten rid of his sin?
10 The LORD hates people who use dishonest weights and measures.
11 Even children show what they are by what they do; you can tell if they are honest and good.
12 The LORD has given us eyes to see with and ears to listen with.
13 If you spend your time sleeping, you will be poor. Keep busy and you will have plenty to eat.
14 The customer always complains that the price is too high, but then he goes off and brags about the bargain he got.
15 If you know what you are talking about, you have something more valuable than gold or jewels.
16 Anyone stupid enough to promise to be responsible for a stranger's debts ought to have their own property held to guarantee payment.
17 What you get by dishonesty you

[g] *Probable text* No matter . . . any; *Hebrew unclear.* [h] If you . . . themselves; *or* But don't punish them so hard that you kill them. [i] get him out . . . again; *or* try to get him out of trouble, you only make things worse. [j] It . . . greedy; *or* Loyalty is what is desired in a person.

may enjoy like the finest food, but
sooner or later it will be like a mouthful
of sand.
18 Get good advice and you will succeed; don't go charging into battle without a plan.
19 A gossip can never keep a secret.
Stay away from people who talk too
much.
20 If you curse your parents, your life
will end like a lamp that goes out in the
dark.
21 The more easily you get your
wealth, the less good it will do you.
22 Don't take it on yourself to repay a
wrong. Trust the LORD and he will make
it right.
23 The LORD hates people who use dishonest scales and weights.
24 The LORD has determined our path;
how then can anyone understand the direction his own life is taking?
25 Think carefully before you promise
an offering to God. You might regret it
later.
26 A wise king will find out who is doing wrong, and will punish him without
pity.
27 The LORD gave us mind and conscience; we cannot hide from ourselves.
28 A king will remain in power as long
as his rule is honest, just, and fair.
29 We admire the strength of youth and
respect the gray hair of age.
30 Sometimes it takes a painful experience to make us change our ways.

21 The LORD controls the mind of a
king as easily as he directs the
course of a stream.
2 You may think that everything you
do is right, but remember that the LORD
judges your motives.
3 Do what is right and fair; that pleases
the LORD more than bringing him sacrifices.
4 Wicked people are controlled by
their conceit and arrogance, and this is
sinful.
5 Plan carefully and you will have
plenty; if you act too quickly, you will
never have enough.
6 The riches you get by dishonesty
soon disappear, but not before they lead
you into the jaws of death.
7 The wicked are doomed by their own
violence; they refuse to do what is right.
8 Guilty people walk a crooked path;
the innocent do what is right.
9 Better to live on the roof than share
the house with a nagging wife.
10 Wicked people are always hungry
for evil; they have no mercy on anyone.
11 When someone who is conceited
gets his punishment, even an unthinking
person learns a lesson. One who is wise
will learn from what he is taught.
12 God, the righteous one, knows what
goes on in the homes of the wicked, and
he will bring the wicked down to ruin.
13 If you refuse to listen to the cry of
the poor, your own cry for help will not
be heard.
14 If someone is angry with you, a gift
given secretly will calm him down.
15 When justice is done, good people
are happy, but evil people are brought to
despair.
16 Death is waiting for anyone who
wanders away from good sense.
17 Indulging in luxuries, wine, and rich
food will never make you wealthy.
18 The wicked bring on themselves the
suffering they try to cause good people.
19 Better to live out in the desert than
with a nagging, complaining wife.
20 Wise people live in wealth and luxury, but stupid people spend their
money as fast as they get it.
21 Be kind and honest and you will live
a long life; others will respect you and
treat you fairly.
22 A shrewd general can take a city defended by strong men, and destroy the
walls they relied on.
23 If you want to stay out of trouble, be
careful what you say.
24 Show me a conceited person and I
will show you someone who is arrogant,
proud, and inconsiderate.
25 Lazy people who refuse to work are
only killing themselves; 26 all they do is
think about what they would like to
have. The righteous, however, can give,
and give generously.
27 The LORD hates it when wicked people offer him sacrifices, especially if they
do it from evil motives.
28 The testimony of a liar is not believed, but the word of someone who
thinks matters through is accepted.
29 Righteous people are sure of themselves; the wicked have to pretend as
best they can.
30 Human wisdom, brilliance, insight—they are of no help if the LORD is
against you.

31 You can get horses ready for battle,
but it is the LORD who gives victory.

22 If you have to choose between
a good reputation and great
wealth, choose a good reputation.
2 The rich and the poor have this in
common: the LORD made them both.
3 Sensible people will see trouble coming and avoid it, but an unthinking person will walk right into it and regret it
later.
4 Obey the LORD, be humble, and you
will get riches, honor, and a long life.
5 If you love your life, stay away from
the traps that catch the wicked along
the way.
6 Teach children how they should live,
and they will remember it all their life.
7 Poor people are slaves of the rich.
Borrow money and you are the lender's
slave.
8 If you plant the seeds of injustice, disaster will spring up, and your oppression of others will end.
9 Be generous and share your food
with the poor. You will be blessed for it.
10 Get rid of a conceited person, and
then there will be no more arguments,
quarreling, or name-calling.
11 If you love purity of heart and gra-
ciousness of speech, the king will be
your friend.
12 The LORD sees to it that truth is kept
safe by disproving the words of liars.
13 Lazy people stay at home; they say a
lion might get them if they go outside.
14 Adultery is a trap—it catches those
with whom the LORD is angry.
15 Children just naturally do silly, careless things, but a good spanking will
teach them how to behave.
16 If you make gifts to rich people or
oppress the poor to get rich, you will become poor yourself.

The Thirty Wise Sayings

17 Listen, and I will teach you what the
wise have said. Study their teachings,
18 and you will be glad if you remember
them and can quote them. 19 I want you
to put your trust in the LORD; that is why
I am going to tell them to you now.
20 I have written down thirty sayings for
you. They contain knowledge and good
advice, 21 and will teach you what the
truth really is. Then when you are sent
to find it out, you will bring back the
right answer.

-1-

22 Don't take advantage of the poor
just because you can; don't take advantage of those who stand helpless in
court. 23 The LORD will argue their case
for them and threaten the life of anyone
who threatens theirs.

-2-

24 Don't make friends with people who
have hot, violent tempers. 25 You might
learn their habits and not be able to
change.

-3-

26 Don't promise to be responsible for
someone else's debts. 27 If you should be
unable to pay, they will take away even
your bed.

-4-

28 Never move an old property line that
your ancestors established.

-5-

29 Show me someone who does a good
job, and I will show you someone who is
better than most and worthy of the company of kings.

-6-

23 When you sit down to eat with
someone important, keep in
mind who he is.[k] 2 If you have a big appetite, restrain yourself. 3 Don't be
greedy for the fine food he serves; he
may be trying to trick you.

-7-

4 Be wise enough not to wear yourself
out trying to get rich. 5 Your money can
be gone in a flash, as if it had grown
wings and flown away like an eagle.

-8-

6 Don't eat at the table of a stingy person or be greedy for the fine food he
serves. 7 "Come on and have some
more," he says, but he doesn't mean it.
What he thinks is what he really is. 8 You
will vomit up what you have eaten, and
all your flattery will be wasted.

[k] keep ... is; *or* notice carefully what is before you.

-9-

9 Don't try to talk sense to a fool; he
can't appreciate it.

-10-

10 Never move an old property line or
take over land owned by orphans. 11 The
LORD is their powerful defender, and he
will argue their case against you.

-11-

12 Pay attention to your teacher and
learn all you can.

-12-

13 Don't hesitate to discipline children.
A good spanking won't kill them. 14 As a
matter of fact, it may save their lives.

-13-

15 My child, if you become wise, I will
be very happy. 16 I will be proud when I
hear you speaking words of wisdom.

-14-

17 Don't be envious of sinful people; let
reverence for the LORD be the concern of
your life. 18 If it is, you have a bright
future.

-15-

19 Listen, my child, be wise and give
serious thought to the way you live.
20 Don't associate with people who drink
too much wine or stuff themselves with
food. 21 Drunkards and gluttons will be
reduced to poverty. If all you do is eat
and sleep, you will soon be wearing
rags.

-16-

22 Listen to your father; without him
you would not exist. When your mother
is old, show her your appreciation.
23 Truth, wisdom, learning, and good
sense—these are worth paying for, but
too valuable for you to sell.
24 A righteous person's parents have
good reason to be happy. You can take
pride in a wise child.
25 Let your father and mother be proud
of you; give your mother that happiness.

-17-

26 Pay close attention, son, and let my
life be your example. 27 Prostitutes and
immoral women are a deadly trap.
28 They wait for you like robbers and
cause many men to be unfaithful.

-18-

29-30 Show me people who drink too
much, who have to try out fancy drinks,
and I will show you people who are miserable and sorry for themselves, always
causing trouble and always complaining. Their eyes are bloodshot, and they
have bruises that could have been
avoided. 31 Don't let wine tempt you,
even though it is rich red, and it sparkles
in the cup, and it goes down smoothly.
32 The next morning you will feel as if
you had been bitten by a poisonous
snake. 33 Weird sights will appear before
your eyes, and you will not be able to
think or speak clearly. 34 You will feel as
if you were out on the ocean, seasick,
swinging high up in the rigging of a tossing ship. 35 "I must have been hit," you
will say; "I must have been beaten up,
but I don't remember it. Why can't I
wake up? I need another drink."

-19-

24 Don't be envious of evil people,
and don't try to make friends
with them. 2 Causing trouble is all they
ever think about; every time they open
their mouth someone is going to be hurt.

-20-

3 Homes are built on the foundation of
wisdom and understanding.[l] 4 Where
there is knowledge, the rooms are furnished with valuable, beautiful things.

-21-

5 Being wise is better than being
strong;[m] yes, knowledge is more important than strength. 6 After all, you must
make careful plans before you fight a
battle, and the more good advice you
get, the more likely you are to win.

-22-

7 Wise sayings are too deep for stupid
people to understand. They have nothing to say when important matters are
being discussed.

[l] Homes . . . understanding; *or* It takes care to lay the foundations of a house, and skill to build it.
[m] *Some ancient translations* Being wise is better than being strong; *Hebrew* A person is wise in strength.

-23-

8 If you are always planning evil, you
will earn a reputation as a troublemaker.
9 Any scheme a fool thinks up is sinful.
People hate a person who has nothing
but scorn for others.

-24-

10 If you are weak in a crisis, you are
weak indeed.

-25-

11 Don't hesitate to rescue someone
who is about to be executed unjustly.
12 You may say that it is none of your
business, but God knows and judges
your motives. He keeps watch on you;
he knows. And he will reward you according to what you do.

-26-

13 My child, eat honey; it is good. And
just as honey from the comb is sweet on
your tongue, 14 you may be sure that wisdom is good for the soul. Get wisdom
and you have a bright future.

-27-

15 Don't be like the wicked who
scheme to rob honest people or to take
away their homes. 16 No matter how often honest people fall, they always get
up again; but disaster destroys the
wicked.

-28-

17 Don't be glad when your enemies
meet disaster, and don't rejoice when
they stumble. 18 The LORD will know if
you are gloating, and he will not like it;
and then maybe he won't punish them.

-29-

19 Don't let evil people worry you;
don't be envious of them. 20 A wicked
person has no future — nothing to look
forward to.

-30-

21 Have reverence for the LORD, my
child, and honor the king. Have nothing
to do with people who rebel against
them; 22 such people could be ruined in a
moment. Do you realize the disaster that
God or the king can cause?

More Wise Sayings

23 The wise have also said these things:
It is wrong for judges to be prejudiced.
24 If they pronounce a guilty person innocent, they will be cursed and hated by
everyone. 25 Judges who punish the
guilty, however, will be prosperous and
enjoy a good reputation.
26 An honest answer is a sign of true
friendship.
27 Don't build your house and establish
a home until your fields are ready, and
you are sure that you can earn a living.
28 Don't give evidence against others
without good reason, or say misleading
things about them. 29 Don't say, "I'll do to
them just what they did to me! I'll get
even with them!"
30 I walked through the fields and
vineyards of a lazy, stupid person.
31 They were full of thorn bushes and
overgrown with weeds. The stone wall
around them had fallen down.
32 I looked at this, thought about it, and
learned a lesson from it: 33 Go ahead and
take your nap; go ahead and sleep. Fold
your hands and rest awhile, 34 but while
you are asleep, poverty will attack you
like an armed robber.

More of Solomon's Proverbs

25 Here are more of Solomon's
proverbs, copied by scribes at
the court of King Hezekiah of Judah.
2 We honor God for what he conceals;
we honor kings for what they explain.
3 You never know what a king is thinking; his thoughts are beyond us, like the
heights of the sky or the depths of the
ocean.
4 Take the impurities out of silver and
the artist can produce a thing of beauty.
5 Keep evil advisers away from the king
and his government will be known for
its justice.
6 When you stand before the king,
don't try to impress him and pretend to
be important. 7 It is better to be asked to
take a higher position than to be told to
give your place to someone more important.
8 Don't be too quick to go to court
about something you have seen. If another witness later proves you wrong,
what will you do then?
9 If you and your neighbor have a difference of opinion, settle it between

yourselves and do not reveal any secrets. 10 Otherwise everyone will learn
that you can't keep a secret, and you will
never live down the shame.
11 An idea well-expressed is like a design of gold, set in silver.
12 A warning given by an experienced
person to someone willing to listen is
more valuable than gold rings or jewelry
made of the finest gold.
13 A reliable messenger is refreshing
to the one who sends him, like cold water in the heat of harvest time.
14 People who promise things that they
never give are like clouds and wind that
bring no rain.
15 Patient persuasion can break down
the strongest resistance and can even
convince rulers.
16 Never eat more honey than you
need; too much may make you vomit.
17 Don't visit your neighbors too often;
they may get tired of you and come to
hate you.
18 A false accusation is as deadly as a
sword, a club, or a sharp arrow.
19 Depending on an unreliable person
in a crisis is like trying to chew with a
loose tooth or walk with a crippled foot.
20 Singing to a person who is depressed is like taking off a person's
clothes on a cold day or like rubbing salt
in a wound.
21 If your enemies are hungry, feed
them; if they are thirsty, give them a
drink. 22 You will make them burn with
shame, and the LORD will reward you.
23 Gossip brings anger just as surely as
the north wind brings rain.
24 Better to live on the roof than share
the house with a nagging wife.
25 Finally hearing good news from a
distant land is like a drink of cold water
when you are dry and thirsty.
26 A good person who gives in to
someone who is evil reminds you of a
polluted spring or a poisoned well.
27 Too much honey is bad for you, and
so is trying to win too much praise.[n]
28 If you cannot control your anger,
you are as helpless as a city without
walls, open to attack.

26 Praise for a fool is out of place,
like snow in summer or rain at
harvest time.
2 Curses cannot hurt you unless you
deserve them. They are like birds that
fly by and never light.
3 You have to whip a horse, you have
to bridle a donkey, and you have to beat
a fool.
4 If you answer a silly question, you
are just as silly as the person who
asked it.
5 Give a silly answer to a silly question,
and the one who asked it will realize that
he's not as smart as he thinks.
6 If you let a fool deliver a message,
you might as well cut off your own feet;
you are asking for trouble.
7 A fool can use a proverb about as
well as crippled people can use their
legs.
8 Praising someone who is stupid
makes as much sense as tying a stone in
a sling.
9 A fool quoting a wise saying reminds
you of a drunk trying to pick a thorn out
of his hand.
10 An employer who hires any fool that
comes along is only hurting everybody
concerned.[o]
11 A fool doing some stupid thing a second time is like a dog going back to its
vomit.
12 The most stupid fool is better off
than those who think they are wise
when they are not.
13 Why don't lazy people ever get out
of the house? What are they afraid of?
Lions?
14 Lazy people turn over in bed. They
get no farther than a door swinging on
its hinges.
15 Some people are too lazy to put food
in their own mouths.
16 A lazy person will think he is
smarter than seven men who can give
good reasons for their opinions.
17 Getting involved in an argument
that is none of your business is like going down the street and grabbing a dog
by the ears.
18-19 Someone who tricks someone else
and then claims that he was only joking
is like a crazy person playing with a
deadly weapon.
20 Without wood, a fire goes out; without gossip, quarreling stops.
21 Charcoal keeps the embers glowing,
wood keeps the fire burning, and troublemakers keep arguments alive.

[n] *Probable text* and so ... praise; *Hebrew unclear.*

[o] *Verse 10 in Hebrew is unclear.*

22 Gossip is so tasty! How we love to
swallow it!
23 Insincere[p] talk that hides what you
are really thinking is like a fine glaze[q]
on a cheap clay pot.
24 A hypocrite hides hate behind flattering words. 25 They may sound fine,
but don't believe him, because his heart
is filled to the brim with hate. 26 He may
disguise his hatred, but everyone will
see the evil things he does.
27 People who set traps for others get
caught themselves. People who start
landslides get crushed.
28 You have to hate someone to want to
hurt him with lies. Insincere talk brings
nothing but ruin.

27 Never boast about tomorrow.
You don't know what will happen between now and then.
2 Let other people praise you—even
strangers; never do it yourself.
3 The weight of stone and sand is nothing compared to the trouble that stupidity can cause.
4 Anger is cruel and destructive, but it
is nothing compared to jealousy.
5 Better to correct someone openly
than to let him think you don't care for
him at all.
6 Friends mean well, even when they
hurt you. But when an enemy puts his
arm around your shoulder—watch out!
7 When you are full, you will refuse
honey, but when you are hungry, even
bitter food tastes sweet.
8 Anyone away from home is like a
bird away from its nest.
9 Perfume and fragrant oils make you
feel happier, but trouble shatters your
peace of mind.[r]
10 Do not forget your friends or your
father's friends. If you are in trouble,
don't ask a relative for help; a nearby
neighbor can help you more than relatives who are far away.
11 Be wise, my child, and I will be
happy; I will have an answer for anyone
who criticizes me.
12 Sensible people will see trouble
coming and avoid it, but an unthinking
person will walk right into it and regret
it later.
13 Any people stupid enough to promise to be responsible for a stranger's
debts[s] deserve to have their own property held to guarantee payment.
14 You might as well curse your friends
as wake them up early in the morning
with a loud greeting.
15 A nagging wife is like water going
drip-drip-drip on a rainy day. 16 How can
you keep her quiet? Have you ever tried
to stop the wind or ever tried to hold a
handful of oil?[t]
17 People learn from one another, just
as iron sharpens iron.
18 Take care of a fig tree and you will
have figs to eat. Servants who take care
of their master will be honored.
19 It is your own face that you see reflected in the water and it is your own
self that you see in your heart.
20 Human desires are like the world of
the dead—there is always room for
more.
21 Fire tests gold and silver; a person's
reputation can also be tested.
22 Even if you beat fools half to death,
you still can't beat their foolishness out
of them.
23 Look after your sheep and cattle as
carefully as you can, 24 because wealth is
not permanent. Not even nations last
forever. 25 You cut the hay and then cut
the grass on the hillsides while the next
crop of hay is growing. 26 You can make
clothes from the wool of your sheep and
buy land with the money you get from
selling some of your goats. 27 The rest of
the goats will provide milk for you and
your family, and for your servant
women as well.

28 The wicked run when no one is
chasing them, but an honest person is as brave as a lion.
2 When a nation sins, it will have one
ruler after another. But a nation will be
strong and endure when it has intelligent, sensible leaders.
3 Someone in authority who oppresses
poor people is like a driving rain that
destroys the crops.
4 If you have no regard for the law, you
are on the side of the wicked; but if you
obey it, you are against them.
5 Evil people do not know what justice

[p] *One ancient translation* Insincere; *Hebrew* Burning. [q] *Probable text* fine glaze; *Hebrew* unrefined silver. [r] *One ancient translation* but trouble . . . mind; *Hebrew unclear.*
[s] *One ancient translation* stranger's debts; *Hebrew* stranger's debts or those of an immoral woman. [t] *Probable text* or ever . . . oil; *Hebrew unclear.*

is, but those who worship the LORD
understand it well.
6 Better to be poor and honest than
rich and dishonest.
7 Young people who obey the law are
intelligent. Those who make friends
with good-for-nothings are a disgrace to
their parents.
8 If you get rich by charging interest
and taking advantage of people, your
wealth will go to someone who is kind to
the poor.
9 If you do not obey the law, God will
find your prayers too hateful to hear.
10 If you trick an honest person into
doing evil, you will fall into your own
trap.
The innocent will be well rewarded.
11 Rich people always think they are
wise, but a poor person who has insight
into character knows better.
12 When good people come to power,
everybody celebrates, but when bad
people rule, people stay in hiding.
13 You will never succeed in life if you
try to hide your sins. Confess them and
give them up; then God will show mercy
to you.
14 Always obey the LORD and you will
be happy. If you are stubborn, you will
be ruined.
15 Poor people are helpless against a
wicked ruler; he is as dangerous as a
growling lion or a prowling bear.
16 A ruler without good sense will be a
cruel tyrant. One who hates dishonesty
will rule a long time.
17 Someone guilty of murder is digging
his own grave as fast as he can. Don't try
to stop him.
18 Be honest and you will be safe. If
you are dishonest, you will suddenly
fall.
19 A hard-working farmer has plenty
to eat. People who waste time will always be poor.
20 Honest people will lead a full, happy
life. But if you are in a hurry to get rich,
you are going to be punished.
21 Prejudice is wrong. But some judges
will do wrong to get even the smallest
bribe.
22 Selfish people are in such a hurry to
get rich that they do not know when
poverty is about to strike.
23 Correct someone, and afterward he
will appreciate it more than flattery.
24 Anyone who thinks it isn't wrong to
steal from his parents is no better than a
common thief.
25 Selfishness only causes trouble. You
are much better off to trust the LORD.
26 It is foolish to follow your own opinions. Be safe, and follow the teachings of
wiser people.
27 Give to the poor and you will never
be in need. If you close your eyes to the
poor, many people will curse you.
28 People stay in hiding when the
wicked come to power. But when they
fall from power, the righteous will rule
again.

29

If you get more stubborn every
time you are corrected, one day
you will be crushed and never recover.
2 Show me a righteous ruler and I will
show you a happy people. Show me a
wicked ruler and I will show you a miserable people.
3 If you appreciate wisdom, your parents will be proud of you.
It is a foolish waste to spend money on
prostitutes.
4 When the king is concerned with justice, the nation will be strong, but when
he is only concerned with money, he will
ruin his country.
5 If you flatter your friends, you set a
trap for yourself.[u]
6 Evil people are trapped in their own
sins, while honest people are happy and
free.
7 A good person knows the rights of
the poor, but wicked people cannot
understand such things.
8 People with no regard for others can
throw whole cities into turmoil. Those
who are wise keep things calm.
9 When an intelligent person brings a
lawsuit against a fool, the fool only
laughs and becomes loud and abusive.
10 Bloodthirsty people hate anyone
who's honest, but righteous people will
protect[v] the life of such a person.
11 Stupid people express their anger
openly, but sensible people are patient
and hold it back.
12 If a ruler pays attention to false information, all his officials will be liars.
13 A poor person and his oppressor

[u] yourself; *or* them. [v] *Probable text* protect; *Hebrew* seek.

have this in common—the LORD gave
eyes to both of them.
14 If a king defends the rights of the
poor, he will rule for a long time.
15 Correction and discipline are good
for children. If they have their own way,
they will make their mothers ashamed
of them.
16 When evil people are in power,
crime increases. But the righteous will
live to see the downfall of such people.
17 Discipline your children and you
can always be proud of them. They will
never give you reason to be ashamed.
18 A nation without God's guidance is
a nation without order. Happy are those
who keep God's law!
19 You cannot correct servants just by
talking to them. They may understand
you, but they will pay no attention.
20 There is more hope for a stupid fool
than for someone who speaks without
thinking.
21 If you give your servants everything
they want from childhood on, some day
they will take over everything you
own.[w]
22 People with quick tempers cause a
lot of quarreling and trouble.
23 Arrogance will bring your downfall,
but if you are humble, you will be respected.
24 A thief's partner is his own worst
enemy. He will be punished if he tells the
truth in court, and God will curse him if
he doesn't.
25 It is dangerous to be concerned with
what others think of you, but if you trust
the LORD, you are safe.
26 Everybody wants the good will of
the ruler, but only from the LORD can you
get justice.
27 The righteous hate the wicked, and
the wicked hate the righteous.

The Words of Agur

30 These are the solemn words of
Agur son of Jakeh:
"God is not with me, God is not
with me,
and I am helpless.[x]
2 I am more like an animal than a
human being;
I do not have the sense we
humans should have.
3 I have never learned any wisdom,
and I know nothing at all
about God.
4 Have any ever mastered heavenly
knowledge?
Have any ever caught the wind
in their hands?
Or wrapped up water in a piece
of cloth?
Or fixed the boundaries of the
earth?
Who are they, if you know? Who
are their children?
5 "God keeps every promise he makes.
He is like a shield for all who seek his
protection. 6 If you claim that he said
something that he never said, he will
reprimand you and show that you are a
liar."

More Proverbs

7 I ask you, God, to let me have two
things before I die: 8 keep me from lying,
and let me be neither rich nor poor. So
give me only as much food as I need. 9 If
I have more, I might say that I do not
need you. But if I am poor, I might steal
and bring disgrace on my God.
10 Never criticize servants to their
master. You will be cursed and suffer
for it.
11 There are people who curse their
fathers and do not show their appreciation for their mothers.
12 There are people who think they are
pure when they are as filthy as they
can be.
13 There are people who think they are
so good—oh, how good they think
they are!
14 There are people who take cruel advantage of the poor and needy; that is
the way they make their living.
15 A leech has two daughters, and both
are named "Give me!"
There are four things that are never
satisfied:
16 the world of the dead,
a woman without children,
dry ground that needs rain,
and a fire burning out of control.
17 If you make fun of your father or despise your mother in her old age,[y] you
ought to be eaten by vultures or have
your eyes picked out by wild ravens.

[w] they . . . own; *or* you will not be able to control them. [x] *Probable text* "God . . . helpless; *Hebrew unclear.* [y] *One ancient translation* mother in her old age; *Hebrew* mother's obedience.

18There are four things that are too
mysterious for me to understand:
19an eagle flying in the sky,
a snake moving on a rock,
a ship finding its way over the sea,
and a man and a woman falling in
love.
20This is how an unfaithful wife acts:
she commits adultery, takes a bath, and
says, "But I haven't done anything
wrong!"
21There are four things that the earth
itself cannot tolerate:
22a slave who becomes a king,
a fool who has all he wants to
eat,
23a hateful woman who gets
married,
and a servant woman who takes
the place of her mistress.
24There are four animals in the world
that are small, but very, very clever:
25Ants: they are weak, but they
store up their food in the
summer.
26Rock badgers: they are not strong
either, but they make their
homes among the rocks.
27Locusts: they have no king, but
they move in formation.
28Lizards: you can hold one in your
hand, but you can find them in
palaces.
29There are four things that are impressive to watch as they walk:
30lions, strongest of all animals and
afraid of none;
31goats, strutting roosters,
and kings in front of their
people.[z]
32If you have been foolish enough to
be arrogant and plan evil, stop and
think! 33If you churn milk, you get but-
ter. If you hit someone's nose, it bleeds.
If you stir up anger, you get into trouble.

Advice to a King

31 These are the solemn words
which King Lemuel's mother
said to him:
2"You are my own dear son, the answer to my prayers. What shall I tell
you? 3Don't spend all your energy on
sex and all your money on women; they
have destroyed kings. 4Listen, Lemuel.
Kings should not drink wine or have a
craving for alcohol. 5When they drink,
they forget the laws and ignore the
rights of people in need. 6Alcohol is for
people who are dying, for those who are
in misery. 7Let them drink and forget
their poverty and unhappiness.
8"Speak up for people who cannot
speak for themselves. Protect the rights
of all who are helpless. 9Speak for them
and be a righteous judge. Protect the
rights of the poor and needy."

The Capable Wife

10How hard it is to find a capable wife!
She is worth far more than jewels!
11Her husband puts his confidence in
her, and he will never be poor.
12As long as she lives, she does him
good and never harm.
13She keeps herself busy making wool
and linen cloth.
14She brings home food from out-of-
the-way places, as merchant ships do.
15She gets up before daylight to prepare food for her family and to tell her
servant women what to do.
16She looks at land and buys it, and
with money she has earned she plants a
vineyard.
17She is a hard worker, strong and
industrious.
18She knows the value of everything
she makes, and works late into the
night.
19She spins her own thread and
weaves her own cloth.
20She is generous to the poor and
needy.
21She doesn't worry when it snows,
because her family has warm clothing.
22She makes bedspreads and wears
clothes of fine purple linen.
23Her husband is well known, one of
the leading citizens.
24She makes clothes and belts, and
sells them to merchants.
25She is strong and respected and not
afraid of the future.
26She speaks with a gentle wisdom.
27She is always busy and looks after
her family's needs.
28Her children show their appreciation, and her husband praises her.

[z] *Verse 31 in Hebrew is unclear.*

29 He says, "Many women are good wives, but you are the best of them all."
30 Charm is deceptive and beauty disappears, but a woman who honors the LORD should be praised.
31 Give her credit for all she does. She deserves the respect of everyone.

ECCLESIASTES

Introduction

The book of Ecclesiastes *contains the thoughts of "the Philosopher," a man who reflected deeply on how short and contradictory human life is, with its mysterious injustices and frustrations, and concluded that "life is useless." He could not understand the ways of God, who controls human destiny. Yet, in spite of this, he advised people to work hard, and to enjoy the gifts of God as much and as long as they could.*

Many of the Philosopher's thoughts appear negative and even depressing. But the fact that this book is in the Bible shows that biblical faith is broad enough to take into account such pessimism and doubt. Many have taken comfort in seeing themselves in the mirror of Ecclesiastes, *and have discovered that the same Bible which reflects these thoughts also offers the hope in God that gives life its greater meaning.*

Outline of Contents

Life Is Useless

1 These are the words of the Philosopher, David's son, who was king in
Jerusalem.
2 It is useless, useless, said the Philosopher. Life is useless, all useless. 3 You
spend your life working, laboring, and
what do you have to show for it? 4 Generations come and generations go, but the
world stays just the same. 5 The sun still
rises, and it still goes down, going wea-
rily back to where it must start all over
again. 6 The wind blows south, the wind
blows north—round and round and
back again. 7 Every river flows into the
sea, but the sea is not yet full. The water
returns to where the rivers began, and
starts all over again. 8 Everything leads
to weariness—a weariness too great for
words. Our eyes can never see enough to
be satisfied; our ears can never hear
enough. 9 What has happened before
will happen again. What has been done
before will be done again. There is nothing new in the whole world. 10 "Look,"
they say, "here is something new!"
But no, it has all happened before,
long before we were born. 11 No one remembers what has happened in the
past, and no one in days to come will remember what happens between now
and then.

The Philosopher's Experience

12 I, the Philosopher, have been king
over Israel in Jerusalem. 13 I determined
that I would examine and study all the
things that are done in this world.
God has laid a miserable fate upon us.
14 I have seen everything done in this
world, and I tell you, it is all useless. It is
like chasing the wind. 15 You can't
straighten out what is crooked; you can't
count things that aren't there.
16 I told myself, "I have become a great
man, far wiser than anyone who ruled
Jerusalem before me. I know what wisdom and knowledge really are." 17 I was
determined to learn the difference between knowledge and foolishness, wisdom and madness. But I found out that I
might as well be chasing the wind. 18 The
wiser you are, the more worries you
have; the more you know, the more it
hurts.

2 I decided to enjoy myself and find
out what happiness is. But I found
that this is useless, too. 2 I discovered
that laughter is foolish, that pleasure
does you no good. 3 Driven on by my desire for wisdom, I decided to cheer myself up with wine and have a good time.
I thought that this might be the best way
people can spend their short lives on
earth.

4 I accomplished great things. I built myself houses and planted vineyards. 5 I planted gardens and orchards, with all kinds of fruit trees in them; 6 I dug ponds to irrigate them. 7 I bought many slaves, and there were slaves born in my household. I owned more livestock than anyone else who had ever lived in Jerusalem. 8 I also piled up silver and gold from the royal treasuries of the lands I ruled. Men and women sang to entertain me, and I had all the women a man could want.

9 Yes, I was great, greater than anyone else who had ever lived in Jerusalem, and my wisdom never failed me. 10 Anything I wanted, I got. I did not deny myself any pleasure. I was proud of everything I had worked for, and all this was my reward. 11 Then I thought about all that I had done and how hard I had worked doing it, and I realized that it didn't mean a thing. It was like chasing the wind—of no use at all. 12 After all, a king can only do what previous kings have done.

So I started thinking about what it meant to be wise or reckless or foolish. 13 Oh, I know, "Wisdom is better than foolishness, just as light is better than darkness. 14 The wise can see where they are going, and fools cannot." But I also know that the same fate is waiting for us all. 15 I thought to myself, "What happens to fools is going to happen to me, too. So what have I gained from being so wise?" "Nothing," I answered, "not a thing." 16 No one remembers the wise, and no one remembers fools. In days to come, we will all be forgotten. We must all die—wise and foolish alike. 17 So life came to mean nothing to me, because everything in it had brought me nothing but trouble. It had all been useless; I had been chasing the wind.

18 Nothing that I had worked for and earned meant a thing to me, because I knew that I would have to leave it to my successor, 19 and he might be wise, or he might be foolish—who knows? Yet he will own everything I have worked for, everything my wisdom has earned for me in this world. It is all useless. 20 So I came to regret that I had worked so hard. 21 You work for something with all your wisdom, knowledge, and skill, and then you have to leave it all to someone who hasn't had to work for it. It is useless, and it isn't right! 22 You work and worry your way through life, and what do you have to show for it? 23 As long as you live, everything you do brings nothing but worry and heartache. Even at night your mind can't rest. It is all useless.

24 The best thing we can do is eat and drink and enjoy what we have earned. And yet, I realized that even this comes from God. 25 How else could you have anything to eat or enjoy yourself at all? 26 God gives wisdom, knowledge, and happiness to those who please him, but he makes sinners work, earning and saving, so that what they get can be given to those who please him. It is all useless. It is like chasing the wind.

A Time for Everything

3 Everything that happens in this world happens at the time God chooses.

2 He sets the time for birth and the time for death,
the time for planting and the time for pulling up,
3 the time for killing and the time for healing,
the time for tearing down and the time for building.
4 He sets the time for sorrow and the time for joy,
the time for mourning and the time for dancing,
5 the time for making love and the time for not making love,
the time for kissing and the time for not kissing.
6 He sets the time for finding and the time for losing,
the time for saving and the time for throwing away,
7 the time for tearing and the time for mending,
the time for silence and the time for talk.
8 He sets the time for love and the time for hate,
the time for war and the time for peace.

9 What do we gain from all our work? 10 I know the heavy burdens that God has laid on us. 11 He has set the right time for everything. He has given us a desire to know the future, but never gives us the satisfaction of fully understanding what he does. 12 So I realized that all we

can do is be happy and do the best we
can while we are still alive. 13 All of us
should eat and drink and enjoy what we
have worked for. It is God's gift.

14 I know that everything God does
will last forever. You can't add anything
to it or take anything away from it. And
one thing God does is to make us stand
in awe of him. 15 Whatever happens or
can happen has already happened before. God makes the same thing happen
again and again.

Injustice in the World

16 In addition, I have also noticed that
in this world you find wickedness where
justice and right ought to be. 17 I told myself, "God is going to judge the righteous
and the evil alike, because every thing,
every action, will happen at its own set
time."[a] 18 I decided that God is testing
us, to show us that we are no better than
animals. 19 After all, the same fate awaits
human beings and animals alike. One
dies just like the other. They are the
same kind of creature. A human being is
no better off than an animal, because life
has no meaning for either. 20 They are
both going to the same place — the dust.
They both came from it; they will both
go back to it. 21 How can anyone be sure
that the human spirit goes upward while
an animal's spirit goes down into the
ground? 22 So I realized then that the
best thing we can do is enjoy what we
have worked for. There is nothing else
we can do.[b] There is no way for us to
know what will happen after we die.

4 Then I looked again at all the injustice that goes on in this world. The
oppressed were crying, and no one
would help them. No one would help
them, because their oppressors had
power on their side. 2 I envy those who
are dead and gone; they are better off
than those who are still alive. 3 But better
off than either are those who have never
been born, who have never seen the injustice that goes on in this world.

4 I have also learned why people work
so hard to succeed: it is because they
envy the things their neighbors have.
But it is useless. It is like chasing the
wind. 5 They say that we would be fools
to fold our hands and let ourselves
starve to death. 6 Maybe so, but it is better to have only a little, with peace of
mind, than be busy all the time with both
hands, trying to catch the wind.

7 I have noticed something else in life
that is useless. 8 Here is someone who
lives alone. He has no son, no brother,
yet he is always working, never satisfied
with the wealth he has. For whom is he
working so hard and denying himself
any pleasure? This is useless, too — and a
miserable way to live.

9 Two are better off than one, because
together they can work more effectively.
10 If one of them falls down, the other can
help him up. But if someone is alone and
falls, it's just too bad, because there is no
one to help him. 11 If it is cold, two can
sleep together and stay warm, but how
can you keep warm by yourself? 12 Two
people can resist an attack that would
defeat one person alone. A rope made of
three cords is hard to break.

13-14 Someone may rise from poverty to
become king of his country, or go from
prison to the throne, but if in his old age
he is too foolish to take advice, he is not
as well off as a young man who is poor
but intelligent. 15 I thought about all the
people who live in this world, and I realized that somewhere among them there
is a young man who will take the king's
place. 16 There may be no limit to the
number of people a king rules; when he
is gone, no one will be grateful for what
he has done. It is useless. It is like chasing the wind.

Don't Make Rash Promises

5 Be careful about going to the Temple. It is better to go there to learn
than to offer sacrifices like foolish people who don't know right from wrong.
2 Think before you speak, and don't
make any rash promises to God. He is in
heaven and you are on earth, so don't
say any more than you have to. 3 The
more you worry, the more likely you are
to have bad dreams, and the more you
talk, the more likely you are to say
something foolish. 4 So when you make
a promise to God, keep it as quickly as
possible. He has no use for a fool. Do
what you promise to do. 5 Better not to
promise at all than to make a promise

[a] *Probable text* its own set time; *Hebrew* its own set time there. [b] what we have . . . do; *or* our work, because we are going to have to do it anyway.

and not keep it. 6 Don't let your own
words lead you into sin, so that you have
to tell God's priest that you didn't mean
it. Why make God angry with you? Why
let him destroy what you have worked
for? 7 No matter how much you dream,
how much useless work you do, or how
much you talk, you must still stand in
awe of God.

Life Is Useless

8 Don't be surprised when you see that
the government oppresses the poor and
denies them justice and their rights.
Every official is protected by someone
higher, and both are protected by still
higher officials.

9 Even a king depends on the
harvest.[c]

10 If you love money, you will never be
satisfied; if you long to be rich, you will
never get all you want. It is useless.
11 The richer you are, the more mouths
you have to feed. All you gain is the
knowledge that you are rich. 12 Workers
may or may not have enough to eat, but
at least they can get a good night's sleep.
The rich, however, have so much that
they stay awake worrying.

13 Here is a terrible thing that I have
seen in this world: people save up their
money for a time when they may need
it,[d] 14 and then lose it all in some bad
deal and end up with nothing left to pass
on to their children. 15 We leave this
world just as we entered it—with nothing. In spite of all our work there is nothing we can take with us. 16 It isn't right!
We go just as we came. We labor, trying
to catch the wind, and what do we get?
17 We get to live our lives in darkness
and grief,[e] worried, angry, and sick.

18 Here is what I have found out: the
best thing we can do is eat and drink and
enjoy what we have worked for during
the short life that God has given us; this
is our fate. 19 If God gives us wealth and
property and lets us enjoy them, we
should be grateful and enjoy what we
have worked for. It is a gift from God.
20 Since God has allowed us to be happy,
we will not worry too much about how
short life is.

6 I have noticed that in this world a
serious injustice is done. 2 God will
give us wealth, honor, and property, yes,
everything we want, but then will not let
us enjoy it. Some stranger will enjoy it
instead. It is useless, and it just isn't
right. 3 We may have a hundred children
and live a long time, but no matter how
long we live, if we do not get our share of
happiness and do not receive a decent
burial, then I say that a baby born dead
is better off. 4 It does that baby no good
to be born; it disappears into darkness,
where it is forgotten. 5 It never sees the
light of day or knows what life is like,
but at least it has found rest—6 more so
than the man who never enjoys life,
though he may live two thousand years.
After all, both of them are going to the
same place.

7 We do all our work just to get something to eat, but we never have enough.
8 How are the wise better off than fools?
What good does it do the poor to know
how to face life? 9 It is useless; it is like
chasing the wind. It is better to be satisfied with what you have than to be always wanting something else.

10 Everything that happens was already determined long ago, and we all
know that you[f] cannot argue with
someone who is stronger than you.
11 The longer you argue, the more useless it is, and you are no better off.
12 How can anyone know what is best for
us in this short, useless life of ours—a
life that passes like a shadow? How can
we know what will happen in the world
after we die?

Thoughts about Life

7 A good reputation is better than expensive perfume; and the day you
die is better than the day you are born.

2 It is better to go to a home where
there is mourning than to one where
there is a party, because the living
should always remind themselves that
death is waiting for us all.

3 Sorrow is better than laughter; it may
sadden your face, but it sharpens your
understanding.

4 Someone who is always thinking
about happiness is a fool. A wise person
thinks about death.

[c] *Verse 9 in Hebrew is unclear.* [d] for . . . it; *or* to their own hurt. [e] *Some ancient translations* in darkness and grief; *Hebrew* eating in darkness. [f] and we . . . you; *or* and our nature is already known; you.

5 It is better to have wise people reprimand you than to have stupid people
sing your praises.
6 When a fool laughs, it is like thorns
crackling in a fire. It doesn't mean a
thing.
7 You may be wise, but if you cheat
someone, you are acting like a fool. If
you take a bribe, you ruin your
character.
8 The end of something is better than
its beginning.
Patience is better than pride.
9 Keep your temper under control; it is
foolish to harbor a grudge.
10 Never ask, "Oh, why were things so
much better in the old days?" It's not an
intelligent question.
11 Everyone who lives ought to be
wise; it is as good as receiving an inheritance 12 and will give you as much security as money can. Wisdom keeps you
safe—this is the advantage of
knowledge.
13 Think about what God has done.
How can anyone straighten out what
God has made crooked? 14 When things
are going well for you, be glad, and
when trouble comes, just remember:
God sends both happiness and trouble;
you never know what is going to happen
next.[g]
15 My life has been useless, but in it I
have seen everything. Some good people
may die while others live on, even
though they are evil. 16 So don't be too
good or too wise—why kill yourself?
17 But don't be too wicked or too foolish,
either—why die before you have to?
18 Avoid both extremes. If you have reverence for God, you will be successful
anyway.
19 Wisdom does more for a person
than ten rulers can do for a city.
20 There is no one on earth who does
what is right all the time and never
makes a mistake.
21 Don't pay attention to everything
people say—you may hear your servant
insulting you, 22 and you know yourself
that you have insulted other people
many times.
23 I used my wisdom to test all of this.
I was determined to be wise, but it was
beyond me. 24 How can anyone discover
what life means? It is too deep for us, too
hard to understand. 25 But I devoted myself to knowledge and study; I was determined to find wisdom and the answers
to my questions, and to learn how
wicked and foolish stupidity is.
26 I found something more bitter than
death—the woman who is like a trap.
The love she offers you will catch you
like a net, and her arms around you will
hold you like a chain. A man who
pleases God can get away, but she will
catch the sinner. 27 Yes, said the Philosopher, I found this out little by little while
I was looking for answers. 28 I have
looked for other answers but have found
none. I found one man in a thousand
that I could respect, but not one woman.
29 This is all that I have learned: God
made us plain and simple, but we have
made ourselves very complicated.

8 Only the wise know what things really mean. Wisdom makes them
smile and makes their frowns disappear.

Obey the King

2 Do what the king says,[h] and don't
make any rash promises to God. 3 The
king can do anything he likes, so depart
from his presence; don't stay in such a
dangerous place. 4 The king acts with authority, and no one can challenge what
he does. 5 As long as you obey his commands, you are safe, and a wise person
knows how and when to do it. 6 There is
a right time and a right way to do everything, but we know so little! 7 None of us
knows what is going to happen, and
there is no one to tell us. 8 No one can
keep from dying or put off the day of
death. That is a battle we cannot escape;
we cannot cheat our way out.

The Wicked and the Righteous

9 I saw all this when I thought about
the things that are done in this world, a
world where some people have power
and others have to suffer under them.
10 Yes, I have seen the wicked buried and
in their graves, but on the way back
from the cemetery people praise them in
the very city where they did their evil.[i]
It is useless.
11 Why do people commit crimes so
readily? Because crime is not punished
quickly enough. 12 A sinner may commit

[g] *you . . . next; or* you cannot find fault with him. [h] *Some ancient translations* Do what the king says; *Hebrew unclear.* [i] *Verse 10 in Hebrew is unclear.*

a hundred crimes and still live. Oh yes, I know what they say: "If you obey God, everything will be all right, 13 but it will not go well for the wicked. Their life is like a shadow and they will die young, because they do not obey God." 14 But this is nonsense. Look at what happens in the world: sometimes the righteous get the punishment of the wicked, and the wicked get the reward of the righteous. I say it is useless.

15 So I am convinced that we should enjoy ourselves, because the only pleasure we have in this life is eating and drinking and enjoying ourselves. We can at least do this as we labor during the life that God has given us in this world.

16 Whenever I tried to become wise and learn what goes on in the world, I realized that you could stay awake night and day 17 and never be able to understand what God is doing. However hard you try, you will never find out. The wise may claim to know, but they don't.

9 I thought long and hard about all this and saw that God controls the actions of wise and righteous people, even their love and their hate. No one knows anything about what lies ahead. 2 It makes no difference.[j] The same fate comes to the righteous and the wicked, to the good and the bad,[k] to those who are religious and those who are not, to those who offer sacrifices and those who do not. A good person is no better off than a sinner; one who takes an oath is no better off than one who does not. 3 One fate comes to all alike, and this is as wrong as anything that happens in this world. As long as people live, their minds are full of evil and madness, and suddenly they die. 4 But anyone who is alive in the world of the living has some hope; a live dog is better off than a dead lion. 5 Yes, the living know they are going to die, but the dead know nothing. They have no further reward; they are completely forgotten. 6 Their loves, their hates, their passions, all died with them. They will never again take part in anything that happens in this world.

7 Go ahead—eat your food and be happy; drink your wine and be cheerful. It's all right with God. 8 Always look happy and cheerful. 9 Enjoy life with the one you love, as long as you live the useless life that God has given you in this world. Enjoy every useless day of it, because that is all you will get for all your trouble. 10 Work hard at whatever you do, because there will be no action, no thought, no knowledge, no wisdom in the world of the dead—and that is where you are going.

11 I realized another thing, that in this world fast runners do not always win the races, and the brave do not always win the battles. The wise do not always earn a living, intelligent people do not always get rich, and capable people do not always rise to high positions. Bad luck happens to everyone. 12 You never know when your time is coming. Like birds suddenly caught in a trap, like fish caught in a net, we are trapped at some evil moment when we least expect it.

Thoughts on Wisdom and Foolishness

13 There is something else I saw, a good example of how wisdom is regarded in this world. 14 There was a little town without many people in it. A powerful king attacked it. He surrounded it and prepared to break through the walls. 15 Someone lived there who was poor, but so clever that he could have saved the town. But no one thought about him.[l] 16 I have always said that wisdom is better than strength, but no one thinks of the poor as wise or pays any attention to what they say. 17 It is better to listen to the quiet words of someone wise than to the shouts of a ruler at a council of fools. 18 Wisdom does more good than weapons, but one sinner can undo a lot of good.

10 Dead flies can make a whole bottle of perfume stink, and a little stupidity can cancel out the greatest wisdom.

2 It is natural for the wise to do the right thing and for fools to do the wrong thing. 3 Their stupidity will be evident even to strangers they meet along the way; they let everyone know that they are fools.

[j] hate. No one . . . difference; *or* hate, but no one knows whether it is out of love or hate. 2 It makes no difference what lies ahead of us. [k] *Some ancient translations* and the bad; *Hebrew does not have these words.* [l] he could have . . . him; *or* he saved the town. But later on no one remembered him.

4 If your ruler becomes angry with
you, do not hand in your resignation; serious wrongs may be pardoned if you
keep calm.[m]
5 Here is an injustice I have seen in the
world—an injustice caused by rulers.
6 Stupid people are given positions of authority while the rich are ignored.
7 I have seen slaves on horseback while
noblemen go on foot like slaves.
8 If you dig a pit, you fall in it; if you
break through a wall, a snake bites you.
9 If you work in a stone quarry, you get
hurt by stones. If you split wood, you get
hurt doing it. 10 If your ax is dull and you
don't sharpen it, you have to work
harder to use it. It is smarter to plan
ahead. 11 Knowing how to charm a snake
is of no use if you let the snake bite first.
12 What the wise say brings them honor,
but fools are destroyed by their own
words. 13 They start out with silly talk
and end up with pure madness. 14 A fool
talks on and on.

No one knows what is going to happen
next, and no one can tell us what will
happen after we die.
15 Only someone too stupid to find his
way home would wear himself out with
work.
16 A country is in trouble when its king
is a youth and its leaders feast all night
long. 17 But a country is fortunate to have
a king who makes his own decisions and
leaders who eat at the proper time, who
control themselves and don't get drunk.
18 When you are too lazy to repair your
roof, it will leak, and the house will
fall in.
19 Feasting makes you happy and wine
cheers you up, but you can't have either
without money.
20 Don't criticize the king, even silently, and don't criticize the rich, even
in the privacy of your bedroom. A bird
might carry the message and tell them
what you said.

What a Wise Person Does

11 Invest your money in foreign
trade, and one of these days you
will make a profit. 2 Put your invest-
ments in several places—many places
even—because you never know what
kind of bad luck you are going to have in
this world.
3 No matter which direction a tree
falls, it will lie where it fell. When the
clouds are full, it rains. 4 If you wait until
the wind and the weather are just right,
you will never plant anything and never
harvest anything. 5 God made everything, and you can no more understand
what he does than you understand how
new life begins in the womb of a pregnant woman. 6 Do your planting in the
morning and in the evening, too. You
never know whether it will all grow well
or whether one planting will do better
than the other.
7 It is good to be able to enjoy the
pleasant light of day. 8 Be grateful for
every year you live. No matter how long
you live, remember that you will be dead
much longer. There is nothing at all to
look forward to.

Advice to Young People

9 Young people, enjoy your youth. Be
happy while you are still young. Do
what you want to do, and follow your
heart's desire. But remember that God is
going to judge you for whatever you do.
10 Don't let anything worry you or
cause you pain. You aren't going to be
young very long.

12 So remember your Creator[n]
while you are still young, before
those dismal days and years come when
you will say, "I don't enjoy life." 2 That is
when the light of the sun, the moon, and
the stars will grow dim for you, and the
rain clouds will never pass away. 3 Then
your arms, that have protected you, will
tremble, and your legs, now strong, will
grow weak. Your teeth will be too few to
chew your food, and your eyes too dim
to see clearly. 4 Your ears will be deaf to
the noise of the street. You will barely be
able to hear the mill as it grinds or music
as it plays, but even the song of a bird
will wake you from sleep. 5 You will be
afraid of high places, and walking will
be dangerous. Your hair will turn white;
you will hardly be able to drag yourself
along, and all desire will be gone.
We are going to our final resting
place, and then there will be mourning
in the streets. 6 The silver chain will

[m] keep calm; *or* submit to him. [n] *The Hebrew expression for* your Creator *sounds like the Hebrew for* your grave.

snap, and the golden lamp will fall and
break; the rope at the well will break,
and the water jar will be shattered. 7 Our
bodies will return to the dust of the
earth, and the breath of life will go back
to God, who gave it to us.
8 Useless, useless, said the Philosopher. It is all useless.

The Summing Up

9 But because the Philosopher was
wise, he kept on teaching the people
what he knew. He studied proverbs and
honestly tested their truth. 10 The Philosopher tried to find comforting words,
but the words he wrote were honest.
11 The sayings of the wise are like the
sharp sticks that shepherds use to guide
sheep, and collected proverbs are as
lasting as firmly driven nails. They have
been given by God, the one Shepherd of
us all.
12 My child, there is something else to
watch out for. There is no end to the
writing of books, and too much study
will wear you out.
13 After all this, there is only one thing
to say: Have reverence for God, and
obey his commands, because this is all
that we were created for. 14 God is going
to judge everything we do, whether good
or bad, even things done in secret.

SONG OF SONGS

Introduction

The Song of Songs *is a series of love poems, for the most part in the form of songs addressed by a man to a woman, and by the woman to the man. In some translations, the book is called* The Song of Solomon, *because it is attributed to Solomon in the Hebrew title.*

These songs have often been interpreted by Jews as a picture of the relationship between God and his people, and by Christians as a picture of the relationship between Christ and the Church.

Outline of Contents

---

1 The most beautiful of songs, by Solomon.[a]

The First Song

The Woman

2 Your lips cover me with kisses;
your love is better than wine.
3 There is a fragrance about you;
the sound of your name
recalls it.
No woman could keep from
loving you.
4 Take me with you, and we'll run
away;
be my king and take me to your
room.
We will be happy together,
drink deep, and lose ourselves in
love.
No wonder all women love
you!
5 Women of Jerusalem, I am dark
but[b] beautiful,
dark as the desert tents of
Kedar,

[a] by Solomon; *or* dedicated to Solomon, *or* about Solomon. [b] but; *or* and.

but beautiful as the draperies in
Solomon's palace.
6 Don't look down on me because of
my color,
because the sun has tanned me.
My brothers were angry with me
and made me work in the
vineyard.
I had no time to care for myself.
7 Tell me, my love,
Where will you lead your flock
to graze?
Where will they rest from the
noonday sun?
Why should I need to look for you
among the flocks of the other
shepherds?[c]

The Man

8 Don't you know the place,
loveliest of women?
Go and follow the flock;
find pasture for your goats
near the tents of the shepherds.

9 You, my love, excite men
as a mare excites the stallions of
Pharaoh's chariots.
10 Your hair is beautiful upon your
cheeks
and falls along your neck like
jewels.
11 But we will make for you a chain
of gold
with ornaments of silver.

The Woman

12 My king was lying on his couch,
and my perfume filled the air
with fragrance.
13 My lover has the scent of myrrh
as he lies upon my breasts.
14 My lover is like the wild flowers
that bloom in the vineyards at
Engedi.

The Man

15 How beautiful you are, my love;
how your eyes shine with love!

The Woman

16 How handsome you are, my
dearest;
how you delight me!
The green grass will be our bed;
17 the cedars will be the beams of
our house,
and the cypress trees the ceiling.

2 I am only a wild flower in Sharon,
a lily in a mountain valley.

The Man

2 Like a lily among thorns
is my darling among women.

The Woman

3 Like an apple tree among the trees
of the forest,
so is my dearest compared to
other men.
I love to sit in its shadow,
and its fruit is sweet to my taste.
4 He brought me to his banquet hall
and raised the banner of love
over me.
5 Restore my strength with raisins
and refresh me with apples!
I am weak from passion.
6 His left hand is under my head,
and his right hand caresses me.
7 Promise me, women of Jerusalem;
swear by the swift deer and the
gazelles
that you will not interrupt our
love.

The Second Song

The Woman

8 I hear my lover's voice.
He comes running over the
mountains,
racing across the hills to me.
9 My lover is like a gazelle,
like a young stag.
There he stands beside the wall.
He looks in through the window
and glances through the lattice.
10 My lover speaks to me.

The Man

Come then, my love;
my darling, come with me.
11 The winter is over; the rains have
stopped;
12 in the countryside the flowers
are in bloom.
This is the time for singing;
the song of doves is heard in the
fields.
13 Figs are beginning to ripen;

c *Probable text* Why should I . . . shepherds; *Hebrew unclear.*

the air is fragrant with
blossoming vines.
Come then, my love;
my darling, come with me.
14 You are like a dove that hides
in the crevice of a rock.
Let me see your lovely face
and hear your enchanting voice.

15 Catch the foxes, the little foxes,
before they ruin our vineyard in
bloom.

The Woman

16 My lover is mine, and I am his.
He feeds his flock among the lilies
17 until the morning breezes blow
and the darkness disappears.
Return, my darling, like a gazelle,
like a stag on the mountains of
Bether.[d]

3 Asleep on my bed, night after
night
I dreamed of the one I love;
I was looking for him, but
couldn't find him.
2 I went wandering through the city,
through its streets and alleys.
I looked for the one I love.
I looked, but couldn't find him.
3 The sentries patrolling the city
saw me.
I asked them, "Have you found
my lover?"
4 As soon as I left them, I
found him.
I held him and wouldn't let him go
until I took him to my mother's
house,
to the room where I was born.

5 Promise me, women of Jerusalem;
swear by the swift deer and the
gazelles
that you will not interrupt our
love.

The Third Song

The Woman

6 What is this coming from the
desert like a column of smoke,
fragrant with incense and
myrrh,
the incense sold by the traders?
7 Solomon is coming, carried on his
throne;
sixty soldiers form the
bodyguard,
the finest soldiers in Israel.
8 All of them are skillful with the
sword;
they are battle-hardened
veterans.
Each of them is armed with a
sword,
on guard against a night attack.
9 King Solomon is carried on a
throne
made of the finest wood.
10 Its posts are covered with silver;
over it is cloth embroidered with
gold.
Its cushions are covered with
purple cloth,
lovingly woven by the women of
Jerusalem.
11 Women of Zion, come and see
King Solomon.
He is wearing the crown that his
mother placed on his head
on his wedding day,
on the day of his gladness
and joy.

The Man

4 How beautiful you are, my love!
How your eyes shine with
love behind your veil.
Your hair dances like a flock of
goats
bounding down the hills of
Gilead.
2 Your teeth are as white as sheep
that have just been shorn and
washed.
Not one of them is missing;
they are all perfectly matched.
3 Your lips are like a scarlet ribbon;
how lovely they are when you
speak.
Your cheeks glow behind your
veil.
4 Your neck is like the tower of
David,
round and smooth,[e]
with a necklace like a thousand
shields hung around it.
5 Your breasts are like gazelles,
twin deer feeding among lilies.
6 I will stay on the hill of myrrh,
the hill of incense,
until the morning breezes blow

[d] mountains of Bether; *or* rugged mountains.
[e] round and smooth; *Hebrew unclear.*

and the darkness disappears.
7 How beautiful you are, my love;
how perfect you are!
8 Come with me from the Lebanon
Mountains, my bride;
come with me from Lebanon.
Come down from the top of Mount
Amana,
from Mount Senir and Mount
Hermon,
where the lions and leopards
live.
9 The look in your eyes, my
sweetheart and bride,
and the necklace you are
wearing
have stolen my heart.
10 Your love delights me,
my sweetheart and bride.
Your love is better than wine;
your perfume more fragrant
than any spice.
11 The taste of honey is on your lips,
my darling;
your tongue is milk and honey
for me.
Your clothing has all the fragrance
of Lebanon.
12 My sweetheart, my bride, is a
secret garden,
a walled garden, a private
spring;
13 there the plants flourish.
They grow like an orchard of
pomegranate trees
and bear the finest fruits.
There is no lack of henna and
nard,
14 of saffron, calamus, and
cinnamon,
or incense of every kind.
Myrrh and aloes grow there
with all the most fragrant
perfumes.
15 Fountains water the garden,
streams of flowing water,
brooks gushing down from the
Lebanon Mountains.

The Woman

16 Wake up, North Wind.
South Wind, blow on my garden;
fill the air with fragrance.
Let my lover come to his garden
and eat the best of its fruits.

The Man

5 I have entered my garden,
my sweetheart, my bride.
I am gathering my spices and
myrrh;
I am eating my honey and
honeycomb;
I am drinking my wine and milk.

The Women

Eat, lovers, and drink
until you are drunk with love!

The Fourth Song

The Woman

2 While I slept, my heart was
awake.
I dreamed my lover knocked at
the door.

The Man

Let me come in, my darling,
my sweetheart, my dove.
My head is wet with dew,
and my hair is damp from the
mist.

The Woman

3 I have already undressed;
why should I get dressed again?
I have washed my feet;
why should I get them dirty
again?

4 My lover put his hand to the door,
and I was thrilled that he was
near.
5 I was ready to let him come in.
My hands were covered with
myrrh,
my fingers with liquid myrrh,
as I grasped the handle of the
door.
6 I opened the door for my lover,
but he had already gone.
How I wanted to hear his
voice!
I looked for him, but couldn't
find him;
I called to him, but heard no
answer.

7 The sentries patrolling the city
found me;
they struck me and bruised me;
the guards at the city wall tore
off my cape.

8 Promise me, women of Jerusalem,
that if you find my lover,
you will tell him I am weak from passion.

The Women

9 Most beautiful of women,
is your lover different from everyone else?
What is there so wonderful about him
that we should give you our promise?

The Woman

10 My lover is handsome and strong;
he is one in ten thousand.
11 His face is bronzed and smooth;
his hair is wavy,
black as a raven.
12 His eyes are as beautiful as doves
by a flowing brook,
doves washed in milk and
standing by the stream.[f]
13 His cheeks are as lovely as a garden
that is full of herbs and spices.
His lips are like lilies,
wet with liquid myrrh.
14 His hands are well-formed,
and he wears rings set with gems.
His body is like smooth ivory,[g]
with sapphires set in it.
15 His thighs are columns of alabaster
set in sockets of gold.
He is majestic, like the Lebanon Mountains
with their towering cedars.
16 His mouth is sweet to kiss;
everything about him enchants me.
This is what my lover is like,
women of Jerusalem.

The Women

6 Most beautiful of women,
where has your lover gone?
Tell us which way your lover went,
so that we can help you find him.

The Woman

2 My lover has gone to his garden,
where the balsam trees grow.
He is feeding his flock in the garden
and gathering lilies.
3 My lover is mine, and I am his;
he feeds his flock among the lilies.

The Fifth Song

The Man

4 My love, you are as beautiful as Jerusalem,
as lovely as the city of Tirzah,
as breathtaking as these great cities.[h]
5 Turn your eyes away from me;
they are holding me captive.
Your hair dances like a flock of goats
bounding down the hills of Gilead.
6 Your teeth are as white as a flock of sheep
that have just been washed.
Not one of them is missing;
they are all perfectly matched.
7 Your cheeks glow behind your veil.
8 Let the king have sixty queens,
eighty concubines,
young women without number!
9 But I love only one,
and she is as lovely as a dove.
She is her mother's only daughter,
her mother's favorite child.
All women look at her and praise her;
queens and concubines sing her praises.

10 Who is this whose glance is like the dawn?
She is beautiful and bright,
as dazzling as the sun or the moon.[i]
11 I have come down among the almond trees
to see the young plants in the valley,
to see the new leaves on the vines
and the blossoms on the pomegranate trees.

[f] and standing by the stream; *Hebrew unclear.*
[g] like smooth ivory; *Hebrew unclear.*
[h] as breathtaking as . . . cities; *Hebrew unclear.*
[i] as dazzling as . . . moon; *Hebrew unclear.*

12 I am trembling; you have made me
as eager for love
as a chariot driver is for battle.[j]

The Women

13 Dance, dance,[k] girl of Shulam.
Let us watch you as you dance.

The Woman

Why do you want to watch me
as I dance between the rows of
onlookers?

The Man

7 What a magnificent young woman
you are!
How beautiful are your feet in
sandals.
The curve of your thighs
is like the work of an artist.
2 A bowl is there,
that never runs out of spiced
wine.
A sheaf of wheat is there,
surrounded by lilies.
3 Your breasts are like twin deer,
like two gazelles.
4 Your neck is like a tower of ivory.
Your eyes are like the pools in the
city of Heshbon,
near the gate of that great city.
Your nose is as lovely as the tower
of Lebanon
that stands guard at Damascus.
5 Your head is held high like Mount
Carmel.
Your braided hair shines like the
finest satin;
its beauty[l] could hold a king
captive.

6 How pretty you are, how beautiful;
how complete the delights of
your love.
7 You are as graceful as a palm tree,
and your breasts are clusters of
dates.
8 I will climb the palm tree
and pick its fruit.
To me your breasts are like
bunches of grapes,
your breath like the fragrance of
apples,
9 and your mouth like the finest
wine.

The Woman

Then let the wine flow straight to
my lover,
flowing over his lips and teeth.[m]
10 I belong to my lover, and he
desires me.
11 Come, darling, let's go out to the
countryside
and spend the night in the
villages.[n]
12 We will get up early and look at
the vines
to see whether they've started to
grow,
whether the blossoms are
opening
and the pomegranate trees are
in bloom.
There I will give you my love.
13 You can smell the scent of
mandrakes,
and all the pleasant fruits are
near our door.
Darling, I have kept for you
the old delights and the new.

8 I wish that you were my brother,
that my mother had nursed you
at her breast.
Then, if I met you in the street,
I could kiss you and no one
would mind.
2 I would take you to my mother's
house,
where you could teach me love.
I would give you spiced wine,
my pomegranate wine to drink.

3 Your left hand is under my head,
and your right hand
caresses me.

4 Promise me, women of Jerusalem,
that you will not interrupt our
love.

The Sixth Song

The Women

5 Who is this coming from the
desert,
arm in arm with her lover?

[j] *Verse 12 in Hebrew is unclear.* [k] Dance, dance; *or* Come back, come back.
[l] beauty; *Hebrew unclear.* [m] *Some ancient translations* lips and teeth; *Hebrew* lips of those who sleep. [n] villages; *or* fields.

The Woman

Under the apple tree I woke you,
in the place where you were born.
6 Close your heart to every love but mine;
hold no one in your arms but me.
Love is as powerful as death;
passion is as strong as death itself.
It bursts into flame
and burns like a raging fire.
7 Water cannot put it out;
no flood can drown it.
But if any tried to buy love with their wealth,
contempt is all they would get.

The Woman's Brothers

8 We have a young sister,
and her breasts are still small.
What will we do for her
when a young man comes courting?
9 If she is a wall,
we will build her a silver tower.
But if she is a gate,
we will protect her with panels of cedar.

The Woman

10 I am a wall,
and my breasts are its towers.
My lover knows that with him
I find contentment and peace.

The Man

11 Solomon has a vineyard
in a place called Baal Hamon.
There are farmers who rent it from him;
each one pays a thousand silver coins.
12 Solomon is welcome to his thousand coins,
and the farmers to two hundred as their share;
I have a vineyard of my own!
13 Let me hear your voice from the garden, my love;
my companions are waiting to hear you speak.

The Woman

14 Come to me, my lover, like a gazelle,
like a young stag on the mountains where spices grow.

The Book of
ISAIAH

Introduction

The Book of Isaiah *is named for a great prophet who lived in Jerusalem in the latter half of the eighth century B.C. This book may be divided into three principal parts:*

1) Chapters 1–39 *come from a time when Judah, the southern kingdom, was threatened by a powerful neighbor, Assyria. Isaiah saw that the real threat to the life of Judah was not simply the might of Assyria, but the nation's own sin and disobedience toward God, and their lack of trust in him. In vivid words and actions the prophet called the people and their leaders to a life of righteousness and justice, and warned that failure to listen to God would bring doom and destruction. Isaiah also foretold a time of world-wide peace and the coming of a descendant of David who would be the ideal king.*

2) Chapters 40–55 *speak to a time when many of the people of Judah were in exile in Babylon, crushed and without hope. The prophet proclaimed that God would set his people free and take them home to Jerusalem to begin a new life. A notable theme of these chapters is that God is the Lord of history, and his plan for his people includes their mission to all nations, who will be blessed through Israel. The passages about "the Servant of the Lord" are among the best known of the Old Testament.*

3) Chapters 56–66 *for the most part speak to a time when people were back in Jerusalem and needed reassurance that God was going to fulfill his promises to the nation. Concern is expressed for righteousness and justice, and also for Sabbath observance, sacrifice, and prayer. A notable passage is 61.1-2, words used by Jesus at the beginning of his ministry to express his calling.*

Outline of Contents

---

1 This book contains the messages
about Judah and Jerusalem which
God revealed to Isaiah son of Amoz dur-
ing the time when Uzziah, Jotham,
Ahaz, and Hezekiah were kings of
Judah.

God Reprimands His People

[2]The LORD said, "Earth and sky, listen
to what I am saying! The children I
brought up have rebelled against me.
[3]Cattle know who owns them, and donkeys know where their master feeds
them. But that is more than my people
Israel know. They don't understand
at all."

[4]You are doomed, you sinful nation,
you corrupt and evil people! Your sins
drag you down! You have rejected the
LORD, the holy God of Israel, and have
turned your backs on him. [5]Why do you
keep on rebelling? Do you want to be
punished even more? Israel, your head is
already covered with wounds, and your
heart and mind are sick. [6]From head to
foot there is not a healthy spot on your
body. You are covered with bruises and
sores and open wounds. Your wounds
have not been cleaned or bandaged. No
medicine has been put on them.

[7]Your country has been devastated,
and your cities have been burned to the
ground. While you look on, foreigners
take over your land and bring everything to ruin. [8]Jerusalem alone is left, a
city under siege — as defenseless as a
guard's hut in a vineyard or a shed in a
cucumber field. [9]If the LORD Almighty
had not let some of the people survive,
Jerusalem would have been totally destroyed, just as Sodom and Gomorrah
were.

[10]Jerusalem, your rulers and your
people are like those of Sodom and Go-

morrah. Listen to what the LORD is saying to you. Pay attention to what our
God is teaching you. 11 He says, "Do you
think I want all these sacrifices you keep
offering to me? I have had more than
enough of the sheep you burn as sacrifices and of the fat of your fine animals.
I am tired of the blood of bulls and sheep
and goats. 12 Who asked you to bring me
all this when you come to worship me?
Who asked you to do all this tramping
around in my Temple? 13 It's useless to
bring your offerings. I am disgusted with
the smell of the incense you burn. I cannot stand your New Moon Festivals,
your Sabbaths, and your religious gatherings; they are all corrupted by your
sins. 14 I hate your New Moon Festivals
and holy days; they are a burden that I
am tired of bearing.

15 "When you lift your hands in prayer,
I will not look at you. No matter how
much you pray, I will not listen, for your
hands are covered with blood. 16 Wash
yourselves clean. Stop all this evil that I
see you doing. Yes, stop doing evil 17 and
learn to do right. See that justice is
done—help those who are oppressed,
give orphans their rights, and defend
widows."

18 The LORD says, "Now, let's settle the
matter. You are stained red with sin, but
I will wash you as clean as snow.[a] Although your stains are deep red, you will
be as white as wool.[b] 19 If you will only
obey me, you will eat the good things the
land produces. 20 But if you defy me, you
are doomed to die. I, the LORD, have
spoken."

The Sinful City

21 The city that once was faithful is be-
having like a whore! At one time it was
filled with righteous people, but now
only murderers remain. 22 Jerusalem,
you were once like silver, but now you
are worthless; you were like good wine,
but now you are only water. 23 Your
leaders are rebels and friends of thieves;
they are always accepting gifts and
bribes. They never defend orphans in
court or listen when widows present
their case.

24 So now, listen to what the LORD
Almighty, Israel's powerful God, is saying: "I will take revenge on you, my enemies, and you will cause me no more
trouble. 25 I will take action against you.
I will purify you the way metal is refined, and will remove all your impurity.
26 I will give you rulers and advisers like
those you had long ago. Then Jerusalem
will be called the righteous, faithful
city."

27 Because the LORD is righteous, he
will save Jerusalem and everyone there
who repents. 28 But he will crush everyone who sins and rebels against him; he
will kill everyone who forsakes him.

29 You will be sorry that you ever worshiped trees and planted sacred gardens.[c] 30 You will wither like a dying
oak, like a garden that no one waters.
31 Just as straw is set on fire by a spark,
so powerful people will be destroyed by
their own evil deeds, and no one will be
able to stop the destruction.

Everlasting Peace

(Micah 4.1-3)

2 Here is the message which God
gave to Isaiah son of Amoz about
Judah and Jerusalem:

2 In days to come
the mountain where the Temple
stands
will be the highest one of all,
towering above all the hills.
Many nations will come streaming
to it,
3 and their people will say,
"Let us go up the hill of the LORD,[d]
to the Temple of Israel's God.
He will teach us what he wants us
to do;
we will walk in the paths he has
chosen.
For the LORD's teaching comes
from Jerusalem;
from Zion he speaks to his
people."

4 He will settle disputes among
great nations.
They will hammer their swords
into plows

[a] sin, but . . . snow; *or* sin; do you think I will wash you as clean as snow? [b] Although your . . . wool; *or* Your stains are deep red; do you think you will be as white as wool?

[c] SACRED GARDENS: *People believed that dedicating a garden to a fertility god would cause him to bless their crops.* [d] HILL OF THE LORD: *Mount Zion, the hill in Jerusalem which formed part of the area on which the Temple was built.*

and their spears into pruning
knives.
Nations will never again go
to war,
never prepare for battle again.
5 Now, descendants of Jacob, let us
walk in the light which the LORD
gives us!

Arrogance Will Be Destroyed

6 O God, you have forsaken your people, the descendants of Jacob! The land
is full of magic practices from the East
and from Philistia.[e] The people follow
foreign customs. 7 Their land is full of silver and gold, and there is no end to their
treasures. Their land is full of horses,
and there is no end to their chariots.
8 Their land is full of idols, and they worship objects that they have made with
their own hands.
9 Everyone will be humiliated and disgraced. Do not forgive them, LORD!
10 They will hide in caves in the rocky
hills or dig holes in the ground to try to
escape from the LORD's anger and to hide
from his power and glory! 11 A day is
coming when human pride will be ended
and human arrogance destroyed. Then
the LORD alone will be exalted. 12 On that
day the LORD Almighty will humble
everyone who is powerful, everyone
who is proud and conceited. 13 He will
destroy the tall cedars of Lebanon and
all the oaks in the land of Bashan. 14 He
will level the high mountains and hills,
15 every high tower, and the walls of
every fortress. 16 He will sink even the
largest and most beautiful ships.
17-18 Human pride will be ended, and human arrogance will be destroyed. Idols
will completely disappear, and the LORD
alone will be exalted on that day.
19 People will hide in caves in the
rocky hills or dig holes in the ground to
try to escape from the LORD's anger and
to hide from his power and glory, when
he comes to shake the earth. 20 When
that day comes, they will throw away
the gold and silver idols they have made,
and abandon them to the moles and the
bats. 21 When the LORD comes to shake
the earth, people will hide in holes and
caves in the rocky hills to try to escape
from his anger and to hide from his
power and glory.
22 Put no more confidence in mortals.
What are they worth?

Chaos in Jerusalem

3 Now the Lord, the Almighty LORD, is
about to take away from Jerusalem
and Judah everything and everyone that
the people depend on. He is going to
take away their food and their water,
2 their heroes and their soldiers, their
judges and their prophets, their fortunetellers and their statesmen, 3 their
military and civilian leaders, their
politicians and everyone who uses
magic to control events. 4 The LORD will
let the people be governed by immature
boys. 5 Everyone will take advantage of
everyone else. Young people will not respect their elders, and worthless people
will not respect their superiors.
6 A time will come when the members
of a clan will choose one of their number
and say to him, "You at least have something to wear, so be our leader in this
time of trouble."
7 But he will answer, "Not me! I can't
help you. I don't have any food or
clothes either. Don't make me your
leader!"
8 Yes, Jerusalem is doomed! Judah is
collapsing! Everything they say and do
is against the LORD; they openly insult
God himself. 9 Their prejudices will be
held against them. They sin as openly as
the people of Sodom did. They are
doomed, and they have brought it on
themselves.
10 The righteous will be happy,[f] and
things will go well for them. They will
get to enjoy what they have worked for.
11 But evil people are doomed; what they
have done to others will now be done to
them.
12 Moneylenders oppress my people,
and their creditors cheat them.
My people, your leaders are misleading you, so that you do not know which
way to turn.

The LORD Judges His People

13 The LORD is ready to state his case;
he is ready to judge his people.[g] 14 The
LORD is bringing the elders and leaders

[e] *Probable text* The land . . . Philistia; *Hebrew unclear.* [f] *Probable text* The righteous will be happy; *Hebrew* Say to the righteous. [g] *Some ancient translations* his people; *Hebrew* the peoples.

of his people to judgment. He makes this
accusation: "You have plundered vineyards, and your houses are full of what
you have taken from the poor. 15 You
have no right to crush my people and
take advantage of the poor. I, the
Sovereign LORD Almighty, have spoken."

A Warning to the Women of Jerusalem

16 The LORD said, "Look how proud the
women of Jerusalem are! They walk
along with their noses in the air. They
are always flirting. They take dainty little steps, and the bracelets on their ankles jingle. 17 But I will punish them—I
will shave their heads and leave them
bald."

18 A day is coming when the Lord will
take away from the women of Jerusalem
everything they are so proud of—the ornaments they wear on their ankles, on
their heads, on their necks, 19 and on
their wrists. He will take away their veils
20 and their hats; the magic charms they
wear on their arms and at their waists;
21 the rings they wear on their fingers
and in their noses; 22 all their fine robes,
gowns, cloaks, and purses; 23 their revealing garments, their linen handkerchiefs, and the scarves and long veils
they wear on their heads.

24 Instead of using perfumes, they will
stink; instead of fine belts, they will
wear coarse ropes; instead of having
beautiful hair, they will be bald; instead
of fine clothes, they will be dressed in
rags; their beauty will be turned to
shame!

25 The men of the city, yes, even the
strongest men, will be killed in war.
26 The city gates will mourn and cry, and
the city itself will be like a woman sitting
on the ground, stripped naked.

4 When that time comes, seven
women will grab hold of one man
and say, "We can feed and clothe ourselves, but please let us say you are our
husband, so that we won't have to endure the shame of being unmarried."

Jerusalem Will Be Restored

2 The time is coming when the LORD
will make every plant and tree in the
land grow large and beautiful. All the
people of Israel who survive will take
delight and pride in the crops that the
land produces. 3 Everyone who is left in
Jerusalem, whom God has chosen for
survival, will be called holy. 4 By his
power the Lord will judge and purify the
nation and wash away the guilt of Jerusalem and the blood that has been shed
there. 5 Then over Mount Zion and over
all who are gathered there, the LORD will
send a cloud in the daytime and smoke
and a bright flame at night. God's glory
will cover and protect the whole city.
6 His glory will shade the city from the
heat of the day and make it a place of
safety, sheltered from the rain and
storm.

The Song of the Vineyard

5 Listen while I sing you this song,
a song of my friend and his
vineyard:
My friend had a vineyard
on a very fertile hill.
2 He dug the soil and cleared it of
stones;
he planted the finest vines.
He built a tower to guard them,
dug a pit for treading the grapes.
He waited for the grapes to ripen,
but every grape was sour.

3 So now my friend says, "You people
who live in Jerusalem and Judah, judge
between my vineyard and me. 4 Is there
anything I failed to do for it? Then why
did it produce sour grapes and not the
good grapes I expected?

5 "Here is what I am going to do to my
vineyard: I will take away the hedge
around it, break down the wall that protects it, and let wild animals eat it and
trample it down. 6 I will let it be overgrown with weeds. I will not trim the
vines or hoe the ground; instead, I will
let briers and thorns cover it. I will even
forbid the clouds to let rain fall on it."

7 Israel is the vineyard of the LORD
Almighty;
the people of Judah are the
vines he planted.
He expected them to do what was
good,
but instead they committed
murder.
He expected them to do what was
right,
but their victims cried out for
justice.

The Evil That People Do

8 You are doomed! You buy more
houses and fields to add to those you already have. Soon there will be no place
for anyone else to live, and you alone
will live in the land. 9 I have heard the
LORD Almighty say, "All these big, fine
houses will be empty ruins. 10 The grapevines growing on five acres of land will
yield only five gallons of wine. Ten
bushels of seed will produce only one
bushel of grain."

11 You are doomed! You get up early in
the morning to start drinking, and you
spend long evenings getting drunk. 12 At
your feasts you have harps and tambourines and flutes—and wine. But you
don't understand what the LORD is doing,
13 and so you will be carried away as
prisoners. Your leaders will starve to
death, and the common people will die
of thirst. 14 The world of the dead is hungry for them, and it opens its mouth
wide. It gulps down the nobles of Jerusalem along with the noisy crowd of common people.

15 Everyone will be disgraced, and all
who are proud will be humbled. 16 But
the LORD Almighty shows his greatness
by doing what is right, and he reveals his
holiness by judging his people. 17 In the
ruins of the cities lambs will eat grass
and young goats will find pasture.[h]

18 You are doomed! You are unable to
break free from your sins. 19 You say,
"Let the LORD hurry up and do what he
says he will, so that we can see it. Let
Israel's holy God carry out his plans;
let's see what he has in mind."

20 You are doomed! You call evil good
and call good evil. You turn darkness
into light and light into darkness. You
make what is bitter sweet, and what is
sweet you make bitter.

21 You are doomed! You think you are
wise, so very clever.

22 You are doomed! Heroes of the wine
bottle! Brave and fearless when it comes
to mixing drinks! 23 But for just a bribe
you let the guilty go free, and you keep
the innocent from getting justice. 24 So
now, just as straw and dry grass shrivel
and burn in the fire, your roots will rot
and your blossoms will dry up and blow
away, because you have rejected what
the LORD Almighty, Israel's holy God,
has taught us. 25 The LORD is angry with
his people and has stretched out his
hand to punish them. The mountains
will shake, and the bodies of those who
die will be left in the streets like rubbish.
Yet even then the LORD's anger will not
be ended, but his hand will still be
stretched out to punish.

26 The LORD gives a signal to call for a
distant nation.[i] He whistles for them to
come from the ends of the earth. And
here they come, swiftly, quickly! 27 None
of them grow tired; none of them stumble. They never doze or sleep. Not a belt
is loose; not a sandal strap is broken.
28 Their arrows are sharp, and their
bows are ready to shoot. Their horses'
hoofs are as hard as flint, and their chariot wheels turn like a whirlwind. 29 The
soldiers roar like lions that have killed
an animal and are carrying it off where
no one can take it away from them.

30 When that day comes, they will roar
over Israel as loudly as the sea. Look at
this country! Darkness and distress! The
light is swallowed by darkness.

God Calls Isaiah to Be a Prophet

6 In the year that King Uzziah died, I
saw the Lord. He was sitting on his
throne, high and exalted, and his robe
filled the whole Temple. 2 Around him
flaming creatures were standing, each of
which had six wings. Each creature covered its face with two wings, and its
body with two, and used the other two
for flying. 3 They were calling out to each
other:

"Holy, holy, holy!
The LORD Almighty is holy!
His glory fills the world."

4 The sound of their voices made the
foundation of the Temple shake, and the
Temple itself became filled with smoke.

5 I said, "There is no hope for me! I am
doomed because every word that passes
my lips is sinful, and I live among a people whose every word is sinful. And yet,
with my own eyes I have seen the King,
the LORD Almighty."

6 Then one of the creatures flew down
to me, carrying a burning coal that he
had taken from the altar with a pair of
tongs. 7 He touched my lips with the
burning coal and said, "This has touched

[h] *Verse 17 in Hebrew is unclear.* [i] *Probable text* a distant nation; *Hebrew* distant nations.

your lips, and now your guilt is gone, and your sins are forgiven."

8 Then I heard the Lord say, "Whom shall I send? Who will be our messenger?"

I answered, "I will go! Send me!"

9 So he told me to go and give the people this message: "No matter how much you listen, you will not understand. No matter how much you look, you will not know what is happening." 10 Then he said to me, "Make the minds of these people dull, their ears deaf, and their eyes blind, so that they cannot see or hear or understand. If they did, they might turn to me and be healed."

11 I asked, "How long will it be like this, Lord?"

He answered, "Until the cities are ruined and empty—until the houses are uninhabited—until the land itself is a desolate wasteland. 12 I will send the people far away and make the whole land desolate. 13 Even if one person out of ten remains in the land, he too will be destroyed; he will be like the stump of an oak tree that has been cut down."

(The stump represents a new beginning for God's people.)

A Message for King Ahaz

7 When King Ahaz, the son of Jotham and grandson of Uzziah, ruled Judah, war broke out. Rezin, king of Syria, and Pekah son of Remaliah, king of Israel, attacked Jerusalem, but were unable to capture it.

2 When word reached the king of Judah that the armies of Syria were already in the territory of Israel, he and all his people were so terrified that they trembled like trees shaking in the wind.

3 The LORD said to Isaiah, "Take your son Shear Jashub,[j] and go to meet King Ahaz. You will find him on the road where the cloth makers work, at the end of the ditch that brings water from the upper pool. 4 Tell him to keep alert, to stay calm, and not to be frightened or disturbed. The anger of King Rezin and his Syrians and of King Pekah is no more dangerous than the smoke from two smoldering sticks of wood. 5 Syria, together with Israel and its king, has made a plot. 6 They intend to invade Judah, terrify the people into joining their side, and then put Tabeel's son on the throne.

7 "But I, the LORD, declare that this will never happen. 8 Why? Because Syria is no stronger than Damascus, its capital city, and Damascus is no stronger than King Rezin. As for Israel, within sixty-five years it will be too shattered to survive as a nation. 9 Israel is no stronger than Samaria, its capital city, and Samaria is no stronger than King Pekah.

"If your faith is not enduring, you will not endure."

The Sign of Immanuel

10 The LORD sent another message to Ahaz: 11 "Ask the LORD your God to give you a sign. It can be from deep in the world of the dead or from high up in heaven."

12 Ahaz answered, "I will not ask for a sign. I refuse to put the LORD to the test."

13 To that Isaiah replied, "Listen, now, descendants of King David. It's bad enough for you to wear out the patience of people—do you have to wear out God's patience too? 14 Well then, the Lord himself will give you a sign: a young woman[k] who is pregnant will have a son and will name him 'Immanuel.'[l] 15 By the time he is old enough to make his own decisions, people will be drinking milk and eating honey.[m] 16 Even before that time comes, the lands of those two kings who terrify you will be deserted.

17 "The LORD is going to bring on you, on your people, and on the whole royal family, days of trouble worse than any that have come since the kingdom of Israel separated from Judah—he is going to bring the king of Assyria.

18 "When that time comes, the LORD will whistle as a signal for the Egyptians to come like flies from the farthest branches of the Nile, and for the Assyrians to come from their land like bees. 19 They will swarm in the rugged valleys

[j] SHEAR JASHUB: *This name in Hebrew means "A few will come back" (see 10.20-22).*
[k] YOUNG WOMAN: *The Hebrew word here translated "young woman" is not the specific term for "virgin," but refers to any young woman of marriageable age. The use of "virgin" in Mt 1.23 reflects a Greek translation of the Old Testament, made some 500 years after Isaiah.*
[l] IMMANUEL: *This name in Hebrew means "God is with us."* [m] MILK AND HONEY: *These foods were associated with the earlier days of Israel's history.*

and in the caves in the rocks, and they will cover every thorn bush and every pasture.

20 "When that time comes, the Lord will hire a barber from across the Euphrates—the emperor of Assyria!—and he will shave off your beards and the hair on your heads and your bodies.

21 "When that time comes, even if a farmer has been able to save only one young cow and two goats, 22 they will give so much milk that he will have all he needs. Yes, the few survivors left in the land will have milk and honey to eat.

23 "When that time comes, the fine vineyards, each with a thousand vines and each worth a thousand pieces of silver, will be overgrown with thorn bushes and briers. 24 People will go hunting there with bows and arrows. Yes, the whole country will be full of briers and thorn bushes. 25 All the hills where crops were once planted will be so overgrown with thorns that no one will go there. It will be a place where cattle and sheep graze."

Isaiah's Son as a Sign to the People

8 The LORD said to me, "Take a large piece of writing material and write on it in large letters:[n] 'Quick Loot, Fast Plunder.' 2 Get two reliable men, the priest Uriah and Zechariah son of Jeberechiah, to serve as witnesses."

3 Some time later my wife became pregnant. When our son was born, the LORD said to me, "Name him 'Quick-Loot-Fast-Plunder.' 4 Before the boy is old enough to say 'Mamma' and 'Daddy,' all the wealth of Damascus and all the loot of Samaria will be carried off by the king of Assyria."

The Emperor of Assyria Is Coming

5 The LORD spoke to me again. 6 He said, "Because these people have rejected the quiet waters of Shiloah Brook[o] and tremble[p] before King Rezin and King Pekah, 7 I, the Lord, will bring the emperor of Assyria and all his forces to attack Judah. They will advance like the flood waters of the Euphrates River, overflowing all its banks. 8 They will sweep through Judah in a flood, rising shoulder high and covering everything."

God is with us! His outspread wings protect the land.[q]

9 Gather together in fear, you nations! Listen, you distant parts of the earth. Get ready to fight, but be afraid! Yes, get ready, but be afraid! 10 Make your plans! But they will never succeed. Talk all you want to! But it is all useless, because God is with us.

The LORD Warns the Prophet

11 With his great power the LORD warned me not to follow the road which the people were following. He said, 12 "Do not join in the schemes of the people and do not be afraid of the things that they fear. 13 Remember that I, the LORD Almighty, am holy; I am the one you must fear. 14 Because of my awesome holiness I am like a stone that people stumble over; I am like a trap that will catch the people of the kingdoms of Judah and Israel and the people of Jerusalem. 15 Many will stumble; they will fall and be crushed. They will be caught in a trap."

Warning against Consulting the Dead

16 You, my disciples, are to guard and preserve the messages that God has given me. 17 The LORD has hidden himself from his people, but I trust him and place my hope in him.

18 Here I am with the children the LORD has given me. The LORD Almighty, whose throne is on Mount Zion, has sent us as living messages to the people of Israel.

19 But people will tell you to ask for messages from fortunetellers and mediums, who chirp and mutter. They will say, "After all, people should ask for messages from the spirits and consult the dead on behalf of the living."

20 You are to answer them, "Listen to what the LORD is teaching you! Don't listen to mediums—what they tell you cannot keep trouble away."[r]

[n] large letters; *or* letters that everyone can read. [o] SHILOAH BROOK: *A stream which flowed from the large spring on the eastern side of Jerusalem.* [p] *Probable text* tremble; *Hebrew* rejoice.
[q] everything." God . . . land; *or* everything. They will spread out over the land. God be with us!"
[r] *Verse 20 in Hebrew is unclear.*

A Time of Trouble

21 The people will wander through the
land, discouraged and hungry. In their
hunger and their anger they will curse
their king and their God. They may look
up to the sky 22 or stare at the ground,
but they will see nothing but trouble and
darkness, terrifying darkness into which
9 they are being driven. 1 There will
be no way for them to escape from
this time of trouble.

The Future King

The land of the tribes of Zebulun and
Naphtali was once disgraced, but the future will bring honor to this region, from
the Mediterranean eastward to the land
on the other side of the Jordan, and even
to Galilee itself, where the foreigners
live.

2 The people who walked in
darkness
have seen a great light.
They lived in a land of shadows,
but now light is shining on
them.
3 You have given them great joy,[s]
Lord;
you have made them happy.
They rejoice in what you have
done,
as people rejoice when they
harvest grain
or when they divide captured
wealth.
4 For you have broken the yoke that
burdened them
and the rod that beat their
shoulders.
You have defeated the nation
that oppressed and exploited
your people,
just as you defeated the army of
Midian long ago.
5 The boots of the invading army
and all their bloodstained
clothing
will be destroyed by fire.
6 A child is born to us!
A son is given to us!
And he will be our ruler.
He will be called, "Wonderful[t]
Counselor,"
"Mighty God," "Eternal Father,"
"Prince of Peace."
7 His royal power will continue to
grow;
his kingdom will always be at
peace.
He will rule as King David's
successor,
basing his power on right and
justice,
from now until the end of time.
The LORD Almighty is determined
to do all this.

The LORD Will Punish Israel

8 The Lord has pronounced judgment
on the kingdom of Israel, on the
descendants of Jacob. 9 All the people of
Israel, everyone who lives in the city of
Samaria, will know that he has done
this. Now they are proud and arrogant.
They say, 10 "The brick buildings have
fallen down, but we will replace them
with stone buildings. The beams of sycamore wood have been cut down, but we
will replace them with the finest cedar."
11 The LORD has stirred up their enemies[u] to attack them. 12 Syria on the
east and Philistia on the west have
opened their mouths to devour Israel.
Yet even so the LORD's anger is not
ended; his hand is still stretched out to
punish.
13 The people of Israel have not repented; even though the LORD Almighty
has punished them, they have not returned to him. 14 In a single day the LORD
will punish Israel's leaders and its people; he will cut them off, head and tail.
15 The old and honorable men are the
head—and the tail is the prophets whose
teachings are lies! 16 Those who lead
these people have misled them and totally confused them. 17 And so the Lord
will not let any of the young men escape,
and he will not show pity on any of the
widows and orphans, because all the
people are godless and wicked and
everything they say is evil. Yet even so
the LORD's anger will not be ended, but
his hand will still be stretched out to
punish.
18 The wickedness of the people burns
like a fire that destroys thorn bushes and
thistles. It burns like a forest fire that
sends up columns of smoke. 19 Because

[s] *Probable text* You have given them great joy; *Hebrew* You have increased the nation.
[t] Wonderful; *or* Wise. [u] *Probable text* their enemies; *Hebrew* the enemies of Rezin.

the LORD Almighty is angry, his punishment burns like a fire throughout the
land and destroys the people, and it is
each of us for ourselves. 20 Everywhere
in the country people snatch and eat any
bit of food they can find, but their hunger is never satisfied. They even eat
their own children! 21 The people of Manasseh and the people of Ephraim attack
each other, and together they attack Judah. Yet even so the LORD's anger is not
ended; his hand is still stretched out to
punish.

10 You are doomed! You make unjust laws that oppress my people.
2 That is how you keep the poor from
having their rights and from getting justice. That is how you take the property
that belongs to widows and orphans.
3 What will you do when God punishes
you? What will you do when he brings
disaster on you from a distant country?
Where will you run to find help? Where
will you hide your wealth? 4 You will be
killed in battle or dragged off as prisoners. Yet even so the LORD's anger will not
be ended; his hand will still be stretched
out to punish.

The Emperor of Assyria as the Instrument of God

5 The LORD said, "Assyria! I use Assyria like a club to punish those with
whom I am angry. 6 I sent Assyria to attack a godless nation, people who have
made me angry. I sent them to loot and
steal and trample the people like dirt in
the streets."

7 But the Assyrian emperor has his
own violent plans in mind. He is determined to destroy many nations. 8 He
boasts, "Every one of my commanders is
a king! 9 I conquered the cities of Calno
and Carchemish, the cities of Hamath
and Arpad. I conquered Samaria and
Damascus. 10 I reached out to punish
those kingdoms that worship idols, idols
more numerous than those of Jerusalem
and Samaria. 11 I have destroyed Samaria and all its idols, and I will do the
same to Jerusalem and the images that
are worshiped there."

12 But the Lord says, "When I finish
what I am doing on Mount Zion and in
Jerusalem, I will punish the emperor of
Assyria for all his boasting and all his
pride."

13 The emperor of Assyria boasts, "I
have done it all myself. I am strong and
wise and clever. I wiped out the boundaries between nations and took the supplies they had stored. Like a bull I have
trampled the people who live there.
14 The nations of the world were like a
bird's nest, and I gathered their wealth
as easily as gathering eggs. Not a wing
fluttered to scare me off; no beak opened
to scream at me!"

15 But the LORD says, "Can an ax claim
to be greater than the one who uses it? Is
a saw more important than the one who
saws with it? A club doesn't lift up a person; a person lifts up a club."

16 The LORD Almighty is going to send
disease to punish those who are now
well-fed. In their bodies there will be a
fire that burns and burns. 17 God, the
light of Israel, will become a fire. Israel's
holy God will become a flame, which in
a single day will burn up everything,
even the thorns and thistles. 18 The rich
forests and farmlands will be totally destroyed, in the same way that a fatal
sickness destroys someone. 19 There will
be so few trees left that even a child will
be able to count them.

A Few Will Come Back

20 A time is coming when the people of
Israel who have survived will not rely
any more on the nation that almost destroyed them. They will truly put their
trust in the LORD, Israel's holy God.
21 A few of the people of Israel will come
back to their mighty God. 22 Even though
now there are as many people of Israel
as there are grains of sand by the sea,
only a few will come back. Destruction
is in store for the people, and it is fully
deserved. 23 Yes, throughout the whole
country the Sovereign LORD Almighty
will bring destruction, as he said he
would.

The LORD Will Punish Assyria

24 The Sovereign LORD Almighty says
to his people who live in Zion, "Do not
be afraid of the Assyrians, even though
they oppress you as the Egyptians used
to do. 25 In only a little while I will finish
punishing you, and then I will destroy
them. 26 I, the LORD Almighty, will beat
them with my whip as I did the people of
Midian at Oreb Rock. I will punish Assyria as I punished Egypt. 27 When that

time comes, I will free you from the
power of Assyria, and their yoke will no
longer be a burden on your shoulders."[v]

The Invader Attacks

28 The enemy army has captured the
city of Ai![w] They have passed through
Migron! They left their supplies at Michmash! 29 They have crossed the pass and
are spending the night at Geba! The people in the town of Ramah are terrified,
and the people in King Saul's hometown
of Gibeah have run away. 30 Shout, people of Gallim! Listen, people of Laishah!
Answer, people of Anathoth! 31 The people of Madmenah and Gebim are running for their lives. 32 Today the enemy
are in the town of Nob, and there they
are shaking their fists at Mount Zion, at
the city of Jerusalem.

33 The LORD Almighty will bring them
crashing down like branches cut off a
tree. The proudest and highest of them
will be cut down and humiliated. 34 The
LORD will cut them down as trees in the
heart of the forest are cut down with an
ax, as even the finest trees of Lebanon
fall!

The Peaceful Kingdom

11 The royal line of David is like a
tree that has been cut down; but
just as new branches sprout from a
stump, so a new king will arise from
among David's descendants.

2 The spirit of the LORD will give him
wisdom
and the knowledge and skill to
rule his people.
He will know the LORD's will and
honor him,
3 and find pleasure in
obeying him.
He will not judge by appearance
or hearsay;
4 he will judge the poor fairly
and defend the rights of the
helpless.
At his command the people will be
punished,
and evil persons will die.
5 He will rule his people with justice
and integrity.

6 Wolves and sheep will live
together in peace,
and leopards will lie down with
young goats.
Calves and lion cubs will feed[x]
together,
and little children will take care
of them.
7 Cows and bears will eat together,
and their calves and cubs will lie
down in peace.
Lions will eat straw as cattle do.
8 Even a baby will not be harmed
if it plays near a poisonous
snake.
9 On Zion, God's sacred hill,
there will be nothing harmful or
evil.
The land will be as full of
knowledge of the LORD
as the seas are full of water.

The Exiled People Will Return

10 A day is coming when the new king
from the royal line of David will be a
symbol to the nations. They will gather
in his royal city and give him honor.
11 When that day comes, the Lord will
once again use his power and bring back
home those of his people who are left in
Assyria and Egypt, in the lands of Pathros, Ethiopia,[y] Elam, Babylonia, and
Hamath, and in the coastlands and on
the islands of the sea. 12 The Lord will
raise a signal flag to show the nations
that he is gathering together again the
scattered people of Israel and Judah and
bringing them back from the four corners of the earth. 13 The kingdom of Israel will not be jealous of Judah any
more, and Judah will not be the enemy
of Israel. 14 Together they will attack the
Philistines on the west and plunder the
people who live to the east. They will
conquer the people of Edom and Moab,
and the people of Ammon will obey
them. 15 The LORD will dry up the Gulf of
Suez, and he will bring a hot wind to dry
up the Euphrates, leaving only seven

[v] *Hebrew has three additional words, the meaning of which is unclear.* [w] AI: *This and the other places mentioned in verses 28-32 were located near Jerusalem, along the way by which an invader would come to attack from the north.* [x] *Some ancient translations* will feed; *Hebrew* and well-fed cattle. [y] *Hebrew* Cush: *Cush is the ancient name of the extensive territory south of the First Cataract of the Nile River. This region was called Ethiopia in Graeco-Roman times, and included within its borders most of modern Sudan and some of present-day Ethiopia (Abyssinia).*

tiny streams, so that anyone can walk
across. 16 There will be a highway out of
Assyria for those of his people Israel
who have survived there, just as there
was for their ancestors when they left
Egypt.

Hymn of Thanksgiving

12 A day is coming when people
will sing,
"I praise you, LORD! You were
angry with me,
but now you comfort me and
are angry no longer.
2 God is my savior;
I will trust him and not be
afraid.
The LORD gives me power and
strength;
he is my savior.
3 As fresh water brings joy to the
thirsty,
so God's people rejoice when
he saves them."

4 A day is coming when people will
sing,
"Give thanks to the LORD! Call for
him to help you!
Tell all the nations what he has
done!
Tell them how great he is!
5 Sing to the LORD because of the
great things he has done.
Let the whole world hear the
news.
6 Let everyone who lives in Zion
shout and sing!
Israel's holy God is great,
and he lives among his people."

God Will Punish Babylon

13 This is a message about Babylon,
which Isaiah son of Amoz received from God.
2 On the top of a barren hill raise the
battle flag! Shout to the soldiers and
raise your arm as the signal for them to
attack the gates of the proud city. 3 The
LORD has called out his proud and confident soldiers to fight a holy war and
punish those he is angry with.
4 Listen to the noise on the mountains—the sound of a great crowd of people, the sound of nations and kingdoms gathering. The LORD of Armies is
preparing his troops for battle. 5 They
are coming from far-off countries at the
ends of the earth. In his anger the LORD is
coming to devastate the whole country.
6 Howl in pain! The day of the LORD is
near, the day when the Almighty brings
destruction. 7 Everyone's hands will
hang limp, and everyone's courage will
fail. 8 They will all be terrified and overcome with pain, like the pain of a
woman in labor. They will look at each
other in fear, and their faces will burn
with shame. 9 The day of the LORD is
coming—that cruel day of his fierce anger and fury. The earth will be made a
wilderness, and every sinner will be destroyed. 10 Every star and every constel-
lation will stop shining, the sun will be
dark when it rises, and the moon will
give no light.
11 The LORD says, "I will bring disaster
on the earth and punish all wicked people for their sins. I will humble everyone
who is proud and punish everyone who
is arrogant and cruel. 12 Those who survive will be scarcer than gold. 13 I will
make the heavens tremble, and the earth
will be shaken out of its place on that
day when I, the LORD Almighty, show my
anger.
14 "The foreigners living in Babylon
will run away to their homelands, scattering like deer escaping from hunters,
like sheep without a shepherd. 15 Anyone who is caught will be stabbed to
death. 16 While they look on helplessly,
their babies will be battered to death,
their houses will be looted, and their
wives will be raped."
17 The LORD says, "I am stirring up the
Medes [z] to attack Babylon. They care
nothing for silver and are not tempted
by gold. 18 With their bows and arrows
they will kill the young men. They will
show no mercy to babies and take no
pity on children. 19 Babylonia is the most
beautiful kingdom of all; it is the pride of
its people. But I, the LORD, will overthrow
Babylon as I did Sodom and Gomorrah!
20 No one will ever live there again. No
wandering Arab will ever pitch a tent
there, and no shepherd will ever pasture
a flock there. 21 It will be a place where
desert animals live and where owls build
their nests. Ostriches will live there, and
wild goats will prance through the ruins.

[z] MEDES: *People of a nation northeast of Babylonia, which became part of the Persian Empire.*

22 The towers and palaces will echo with
the cries of hyenas and jackals. Babylon's time has come! Her days are almost over."

The Return from Exile

14 The LORD will once again be merciful to his people Israel and
choose them as his own. He will let them
live in their own land again, and foreigners will come and live there with them.
2 Many nations will help the people of
Israel return to the land which the LORD
gave them, and there the nations will
serve Israel as slaves. Those who once
captured Israel will now be captured by
Israel, and the people of Israel will rule
over those who once oppressed them.

The King of Babylon in the World of the Dead

3 The LORD will give the people of Israel relief from their pain and suffering
and from the hard work they were
forced to do. 4 When he does this, they
are to mock the king of Babylon
and say:
"The cruel king has fallen! He will
never oppress anyone again! 5 The LORD
has ended the power of the evil rulers
6 who angrily oppressed the peoples and
never stopped persecuting the nations
they had conquered. 7 Now at last the
whole world enjoys rest and peace, and
everyone sings for joy. 8 The cypress
trees and the cedars of Lebanon rejoice
over the fallen king, because there is no
one to cut them down, now that he is
gone!
9 "The world of the dead is getting
ready to welcome the king of Babylon.
The ghosts of those who were powerful
on earth are stirring about. The ghosts of
kings are rising from their thrones.
10 They all call out to him, 'Now you are
as weak as we are! You are one of us!
11 You used to be honored with the music
of harps, but now here you are in the
world of the dead. You lie on a bed of
maggots and are covered with a blanket
of worms.'"
12 King of Babylon, bright morning
star, you have fallen from heaven! In the
past you conquered nations, but now
you have been thrown to the ground.
13 You were determined to climb up to
heaven and to place your throne above
the highest stars. You thought you
would sit like a king on that mountain in
the north where the gods assemble.
14 You said you would climb to the tops
of the clouds and be like the Almighty.
15 But instead, you have been brought
down to the deepest part of the world of
the dead.
16 The dead will stare and gape at you.
They will ask, "Is this the man who
shook the earth and made kingdoms
tremble? 17 Is this the man who destroyed cities and turned the world into
a desert? Is this the man who never freed
his prisoners or let them go home?"
18 All the kings of the earth lie in their
magnificent tombs, 19 but you have no
tomb, and your corpse is thrown out to
rot. It is covered by the bodies of soldiers
killed in battle, thrown with them into a
rocky pit, and trampled down. 20 Because you ruined your country and
killed your own people, you will not be
buried like other kings. None of your
evil family will survive. 21 Let the slaughter begin! The sons of this king will die
because of their ancestors' sins. None of
them will ever rule the earth or cover it
with cities.

God Will Destroy Babylon

22 The LORD Almighty says, "I will attack Babylon and bring it to ruin. I will
leave nothing—no children, no survivors at all. I, the LORD, have spoken.
23 I will turn Babylon into a marsh, and
owls will live there. I will sweep Babylon
with a broom that will sweep everything away. I, the LORD Almighty, have
spoken."

God Will Destroy the Assyrians

24 The LORD Almighty has sworn an
oath: "What I have planned will happen.
What I have determined to do will be
done. 25 I will destroy the Assyrians in
my land of Israel and trample them on
my mountains. I will free my people
from the Assyrian yoke and from the
burdens they have had to bear. 26 This is
my plan for the world, and my arm is
stretched out to punish the nations."
27 The LORD Almighty is determined to do
this; he has stretched out his arm to punish, and no one can stop him.

God Will Destroy the Philistines

28 This is a message that was proclaimed in the year that King Ahaz died.

29 People of Philistia, the rod that beat
you is broken, but you have no reason to
be glad. When one snake dies, a worse
one comes in its place. A snake's egg
hatches a flying dragon. 30 The LORD will
be a shepherd to the poor of his people
and will let them live in safety. But he
will send a terrible famine on you Philistines, and it will not leave any of you
alive.
31 Howl and cry for help, all you Philistine cities! Be terrified, all of you! A
cloud of dust is coming from the north—
it is an army with no cowards in its
ranks.
32 How shall we answer the messengers that come to us from Philistia? We
will tell them that the LORD has established Zion and that his suffering people
will find safety there.

God Will Destroy Moab

15 This is a message about Moab.
The cities of Ar and Kir are destroyed in a single night, and silence
covers the land of Moab. 2 The people of
Dibon[a] climb the hill to weep at the
shrine. The people of Moab wail in grief
over the cities of Nebo and Medeba; they
have shaved their heads and their
beards in grief. 3 The people in the
streets are dressed in sackcloth; in the
city squares and on the rooftops people
mourn and cry. 4 The people of Heshbon
and Elealeh cry out, and their cry can be
heard as far away as Jahaz. Even the
soldiers tremble; their courage is gone.
5 My heart cries out for Moab! The people have fled to the town of Zoar, and to
Eglath Shelishiyah. Some climb the road
to Luhith, weeping as they go; some escape to Horonaim, grieving loudly.
6 Nimrim Brook is dry, the grass beside it
has withered, and nothing green is left.
7 The people go across the Valley of Willows, trying to escape with all their possessions. 8 Everywhere at Moab's
borders the sound of crying is heard. It is
heard at the towns of Eglaim and Beer-
elim. 9 At the town of Dibon the river is
red with blood, and God has something
even worse in store for the people there.
Yes, there will be a bloody slaughter of
everyone left in Moab.

Moab's Hopeless Situation

16 From the city of Sela in the
desert the people of Moab send a
lamb as a present to the one who rules in
Jerusalem. 2 They wait on the banks of
the Arnon River and move aimlessly
back and forth, like birds driven from
their nest.
3 They say to the people of Judah, "Tell
us what to do. Protect us like a tree that
casts a cool shadow in the heat of noon,
and let us rest in your shade. We are refugees; hide us where no one can find us.
4 Let us stay in your land. Protect us
from those who want to destroy us."
(Oppression and destruction will end,
and those who are devastating the country will be gone. 5 Then one of David's
descendants will be king, and he will
rule the people with faithfulness and
love. He will be quick to do what is right,
and he will see that justice is done.)
6 The people of Judah say, "We have
heard how proud the people of Moab
are. We know that they are arrogant and
conceited, but their boasts are empty."
7 The people of Moab will weep because of the troubles they suffer. They
will all weep when they remember the
fine food they used to eat in the city of
Kir Heres. They will be driven to despair. 8 The farms near Heshbon and the
vineyards of Sibmah are destroyed—
those vineyards whose wine used to
make the rulers of the nations drunk. At
one time the vines spread as far as the
city of Jazer, and eastward into the
desert, and westward to the other side of
the Dead Sea. 9 Now I weep for Sibmah's
vines as I weep for Jazer. My tears fall
for Heshbon and Elealeh, because there
is no harvest to make the people glad.
10 No one is happy now in the fertile
fields. No one shouts or sings in the
vineyards. No one tramples grapes to
make wine; the shouts of joy are
ended.[b] 11 I groan with sadness for
Moab, with grief for Kir Heres. 12 The
people of Moab wear themselves out going to their mountain shrines and to
their temples to pray, but it will do them
no good.
13 That is the message the LORD gave
earlier about Moab. 14 And now the LORD

[a] *Probable text* people of Dibon; *Hebrew* people and Dibon. [b] *One ancient translation* the shouts of joy are ended; *Hebrew* I have ended the shouts of joy.

says, "In exactly three years Moab's
great wealth will disappear. Of its many
people, only a few will survive, and they
will be weak."

God Will Punish Syria and Israel

17 The LORD said, "Damascus will
not be a city any longer; it will be
only a pile of ruins. 2 The cities of Syria
will be deserted forever.[c] They will be a
pasture for sheep and cattle, and no one
will drive them away. 3 Israel will be
defenseless, and Damascus will lose its
independence. Those Syrians who survive will be in disgrace like the people
of Israel. I, the LORD Almighty, have
spoken."

4 The LORD said, "A day is coming
when Israel's greatness will come to an
end, and its wealth will be replaced by
poverty. 5 Israel will be like a field where
the grain has been cut and harvested, as
desolate as a field in Rephaim Valley
when it has been picked bare. 6 Only a
few people will survive, and Israel will
be like an olive tree from which all the
olives have been picked except two or
three at the very top, or a few that are
left on the lower branches. I, the LORD
God of Israel, have spoken."

7 When that day comes, people will
turn for help to their Creator, the holy
God of Israel. 8 They will no longer rely
on the altars they made with their own
hands, or trust in their own handi-
work—symbols of the goddess Asherah and altars for burning incense.

9 When that day comes, well-defended
cities will be deserted and left in ruins
like the cities that the Hivites and the
Amorites[d] abandoned as they fled from
the people of Israel.

10 Israel, you have forgotten the God
who rescues you and protects you like a
mighty rock. Instead, you plant sacred
gardens[e] in order to worship a foreign
god. 11 But even if they sprouted and
blossomed the very morning you
planted them, there would still be no
harvest. There would be only trouble
and incurable pain.

Enemy Nations Are Defeated

12 Powerful nations are in commotion
with a sound like the roar of the sea, like
the crashing of huge waves. 13 The nations advance like rushing waves, but
God reprimands them and they retreat,
driven away like dust on a mountainside, like straw in a whirlwind. 14 At evening they cause terror, but by morning
they are gone. That is the fate of everyone who plunders our land.

God Will Punish Ethiopia

18 Beyond the rivers of Ethiopia[f]
there is a land where the sound
of wings is heard. 2 From that land ambassadors come down the Nile in boats
made of reeds. Go back home, swift
messengers! Take a message back to
your land divided by rivers, to your
strong and powerful nation, to your tall
and smooth-skinned people, who are
feared all over the world.

3 Listen, everyone who lives on earth!
Look for a signal flag to be raised on the
mountaintops! Listen for the blowing of
the bugle! 4 The LORD said to me, "I will
look down from heaven as quietly as the
dew forms in the warm nights of harvest
time, as serenely as the sun shines in the
heat of the day. 5 Before the grapes are
gathered, when the blossoms have all
fallen and the grapes are ripening, the
enemy will destroy the Ethiopians[f] as
easily as a knife cuts branches from a
vine. 6 The corpses of their soldiers will
be left exposed to the birds and the wild
animals. In summer the birds will feed
on them, and in winter, the animals."

7 A time is coming when the LORD
Almighty will receive offerings from this
land divided by rivers, this strong and
powerful nation, this tall and smooth-
skinned people, who are feared all over
the world. They will come to Mount
Zion, where the LORD Almighty is
worshiped.

God Will Punish Egypt

19 This is a message about Egypt.
The LORD is coming to Egypt,
riding swiftly on a cloud. The Egyptian

[c] *One ancient translation* The cities . . . forever; *Hebrew* The cities of Aroer are deserted.
[d] *One ancient translation* the Hivites and the Amorites; *Hebrew* woodland and hill country.
[e] SACRED GARDENS: *See 1.29.* [f] *Hebrew* Cush(ites): *Cush is the ancient name of the extensive territory south of the First Cataract of the Nile River. This region was called Ethiopia in Graeco-Roman times, and included within its borders most of modern Sudan and some of present-day Ethiopia (Abyssinia).*

idols tremble before him, and the people
of Egypt lose their courage. 2The LORD
says, "I will stir up civil war in Egypt and
turn brother against brother and neighbor against neighbor. Rival cities will
fight each other, and rival kings will
struggle for power. 3I am going to frustrate the plans of the Egyptians and destroy their morale. They will ask their
idols to help them, and they will go and
consult mediums and ask the spirits of
the dead for advice. 4I will hand the
Egyptians over to a tyrant, to a cruel
king who will rule them. I, the LORD
Almighty, have spoken."
5The water will be low in the Nile, and
the river will gradually dry up. 6The
channels of the river will stink as they
slowly go dry. Reeds and rushes will
wither, 7and all the crops planted along
the banks of the Nile will dry up and be
blown away. 8Everyone who earns a living by fishing in the Nile will groan and
cry; their hooks and their nets will be
useless. 9Those who make linen cloth
will be in despair; 10weavers and skilled
workers will be broken and depressed.
11The leaders of the city of Zoan are
fools! Egypt's wisest people give stupid
advice! How do they dare to tell the king
that they are successors to the ancient
scholars and kings? 12King of Egypt,
where are those clever advisers of
yours? Perhaps they can tell you what
plans the LORD Almighty has for Egypt.
13The leaders of Zoan and Memphis are
fools. They were supposed to lead the
nation, but they have misled it. 14The
LORD has made them give confusing advice. As a result, Egypt does everything
wrong and staggers like a drunk slipping on his own vomit. 15No one in
Egypt, rich or poor, important or unknown, can offer help.

Egypt Will Worship the LORD

16A time is coming when the people of
Egypt will be as timid as women. They
will tremble in terror when they see that
the LORD Almighty has stretched out his
hand to punish them. 17The people of
Egypt will be terrified of Judah every
time they are reminded of the fate that
the LORD Almighty has prepared for
them.
18When that time comes, the Hebrew
language will be spoken in five Egyptian
cities. The people there will take their
oaths in the name of the LORD Almighty.
One of the cities will be called, "City of
the Sun."
19When that time comes, there will be
an altar to the LORD in the land of Egypt
and a stone pillar dedicated to him at the
Egyptian border. 20They will be symbols
of the LORD Almighty's presence in
Egypt. When the people there are oppressed and call out to the LORD for help,
he will send someone to rescue them.
21The LORD will reveal himself to the
Egyptian people, and then they will acknowledge and worship him, and bring
him sacrifices and offerings. They will
make solemn promises to him and do
what they promise. 22The LORD will punish the Egyptians, but then he will heal
them. They will turn to him, and he will
hear their prayers and heal them.
23When that time comes, there will be
a highway between Egypt and Assyria.
The people of these two countries will
travel back and forth between them, and
the two nations will worship together.
24When that time comes, Israel will rank
with Egypt and Assyria, and these three
nations will be a blessing to all the
world. 25The LORD Almighty will bless
them and say, "I will bless you, Egypt,
my people; you, Assyria, whom I created; and you, Israel, my chosen
people."

The Sign of the Naked Prophet

20 Under the orders of Emperor
Sargon of Assyria, the com-
mander-in-chief of the Assyrian
army attacked the Philistine city of Ashdod. 2Three years earlier the LORD had
told Isaiah son of Amoz to take off his
sandals and the sackcloth he was wearing. He obeyed and went around naked
and barefoot. 3When Ashdod was captured, the LORD said, "My servant Isaiah
has been going around naked and barefoot for three years. This is a sign of
what will happen to Egypt and Ethiopia.[f] 4The emperor of Assyria will lead

[f] *Hebrew* Cush(ites): *Cush is the ancient name of the extensive territory south of the First Cataract of the Nile River. This region was called Ethiopia in Graeco-Roman times, and included within its borders most of modern Sudan and some of present-day Ethiopia (Abyssinia).*

away naked the prisoners he captures
from those two countries. Young and
old, they will walk barefoot and naked,
with their buttocks exposed, bringing
shame on Egypt. 5 Those who have put
their trust in Ethiopia[f] and have
boasted about Egypt will be disillusioned, their hopes shattered. 6 When
that time comes, the people who live
along the coast of Philistia will say,
'Look at what has happened to the people we relied on to protect us from the
emperor of Assyria! How will we ever
survive?' "

A Vision of the Fall of Babylon

21 This is a message about
Babylonia.

Like a whirlwind sweeping across the
desert, disaster will come from a terrifying land. 2 I have seen a vision of cruel
events, a vision of betrayal and destruction.

Army of Elam, attack! Army of Media,
lay siege to the cities! God will put an
end to the suffering which Babylon has
caused.

3 What I saw and heard in the vision
has filled me with terror and pain, pain
like that of a woman in labor. 4 My head
is spinning, and I am trembling with
fear. I had been longing for evening to
come, but it has brought me nothing but
terror.

5 In the vision a banquet is ready; rugs
are spread for the guests to sit on. They
are eating and drinking. Suddenly the
command rings out: "Officers! Prepare
your shields!"

6 Then the Lord said to me, "Go and
post a sentry, and tell him to report what
he sees. 7 If he sees riders coming on
horseback, two by two, and riders on
donkeys and camels, he is to observe
them carefully."

8 The sentry calls out, "Sir, I have been
standing guard at my post day and
night."

9 Suddenly, here they come! Riders on
horseback, two by two. The sentry gives
the news, "Babylon has fallen! All the
idols they worshiped lie shattered on the
ground."

10 My people Israel, you have been
threshed like wheat, but now I have announced to you the good news that I
have heard from the LORD Almighty, the
God of Israel.

A Message about Edom

11 This is a message about Edom.

Someone calls to me from Edom,
"Sentry, how soon will the night be
over? Tell me how soon it will end."

12 I answer, "Morning is coming, but
night will come again. If you want to ask
again, come back and ask."

A Message about Arabia

13 This is a message about Arabia.

People of Dedan, you whose caravans
camp in the barren country of Arabia,
14 give water to the thirsty people who
come to you. You people of the land of
Tema, give food to the refugees. 15 People are fleeing to escape from swords
that are ready to kill them, from bows
that are ready to shoot, from all the dangers of war.

16 Then the Lord said to me, "In exactly
one year the greatness of the tribes of
Kedar will be at an end. 17 The archers
are the bravest warriors of Kedar, but
few of them will be left. I, the LORD God
of Israel, have spoken."

A Message about Jerusalem

22 This is a message about the Valley of Vision.

What is happening? Why are all the
people of the city celebrating on the
roofs of the houses? 2 The whole city is in
an uproar, filled with noise and excitement.

Your people who died in this war did
not die fighting. 3 All your leaders ran
away and were captured before they
shot a single arrow. 4 Now leave me
alone to weep bitterly over all those of
my people who have died. Don't try to
comfort me. 5 This is a time of panic, defeat, and confusion in the Valley of Vision, and the Sovereign LORD Almighty
has sent it on us. The walls of our city
have been battered down, and cries for
help have echoed among the hills.

6 The soldiers from the land of Elam
came riding on horseback, armed with

[f] *Hebrew* Cush(ites): *Cush is the ancient name of the extensive territory south of the First Cataract of the Nile River. This region was called Ethiopia in Graeco-Roman times, and included within its borders most of modern Sudan and some of present-day Ethiopia (Abyssinia).*

bows and arrows. Soldiers from the land
of Kir had their shields ready. 7The fertile valleys of Judah were filled with
chariots; soldiers on horseback stood in
front of Jerusalem's gates. 8All of Judah's defenses crumbled.

When that happened, you brought
weapons out of the arsenal. 9-10You
found the places where the walls of Jerusalem needed repair. You inspected all
the houses in Jerusalem and tore some
of them down to get stones to repair the
city walls. In order to store water, 11you
built a reservoir inside the city to hold
the water flowing down from the old
pool. But you paid no attention to God,
who planned all this long ago and who
caused it to happen.

12The Sovereign LORD Almighty was
calling you then to weep and mourn, to
shave your heads and wear sackcloth.
13Instead, you laughed and celebrated.
You killed sheep and cattle to eat, and
you drank wine. You said, "We might as
well eat and drink! Tomorrow we'll be
dead."

14The Sovereign LORD Almighty himself spoke to me and said, "This evil will
never be forgiven them as long as they
live. I, the Sovereign LORD Almighty,
have spoken."

A Warning to Shebna

15The Sovereign LORD Almighty told
me to go to Shebna, the manager of the
royal household, and say to him, 16"Who
do you think you are? What right do you
have to carve a tomb for yourself out of
the rocky hillside? 17You may be important, but the LORD will pick you up and
throw you away. 18He will pick you up
like a ball and throw you into a much
larger country. You will die there beside
the chariots you were so proud of. You
are a disgrace to your master's household. 19The LORD will remove you from
office and bring you down from your
high position."

20The LORD said to Shebna, "When
that happens, I will send for my servant
Eliakim son of Hilkiah. 21I will put your
official robe and belt on him and give
him all the authority you have had. He
will be like a father to the people of Jerusalem and Judah. 22I will give him complete authority under the king, the
descendant of David. He will have the
keys of office; what he opens, no one
will shut, and what he shuts, no one will
open. 23I will fasten him firmly in place
like a peg, and he will be a source of
honor to his whole family.

24"But all his relatives and dependents
will become a burden to him. They will
hang on him like pots and bowls hanging from a peg! 25When that happens,
the peg that was firmly fastened will pull
loose and fall. And that will be the end of
everything that was hanging on it." The
LORD has spoken.

A Message about Phoenicia

23 This is a message about Tyre.
Howl with grief, you sailors
out on the ocean! Your home port of
Tyre has been destroyed; its houses and
its harbor are in ruins. As your ships return from Cyprus, you learn the news.
2Wail, you merchants of Sidon! You
sent agents 3across the sea to buy and
sell the grain that grew in Egypt and to
do business with all the nations.

4City of Sidon, you are disgraced! The
sea and the great ocean depths disown
you and say, "I never had any children.
I never raised sons or daughters."
5Even the Egyptians will be shocked
and dismayed when they learn that Tyre
has been destroyed.

6Howl with grief, you people of Phoenicia! Try to escape to Spain! 7Can this
be the joyful city of Tyre, founded so
long ago? Is this the city that sent settlers across the sea to establish colonies?
8Who was it that planned to bring all
this on Tyre, that imperial city, whose
merchant princes were the most honored men on earth? 9The LORD Almighty
planned it. He planned it in order to put
an end to their pride in what they had
done and to humiliate their honored
ones.

10Go and farm the land, you people in
the colonies in Spain! There is no one to
protect you any more.[g] 11The LORD has
stretched out his hand over the sea and
overthrown kingdoms. He has commanded that the Phoenician centers of
commerce be destroyed. 12City of Sidon,
your happiness has ended, and your
people are oppressed. Even if they escape to Cyprus, they will still not be safe.

[g] *Verse 10 in Hebrew is unclear.*

(13 It was the Babylonians, not the Assyrians, who let the wild animals overrun Tyre. It was the Babylonians who
put up siege towers, tore down the fortifications of Tyre, and left the city in
ruins.[h])
14 Howl with grief, you sailors out on
the ocean! The city you relied on has
been destroyed.
15 A time is coming when Tyre will be
forgotten for seventy years, the lifetime
of a king. When those years are over,
Tyre will be like the prostitute in the
song:

16 Take your harp, go round the
town,
you poor forgotten whore!
Play and sing your songs again
to bring men back once more.

17 When the seventy years are over,
the LORD will let Tyre go back to her old
trade, and she will hire herself out to all
the kingdoms of the world. 18 The money
she earns by commerce will be dedicated to the LORD. She will not store it
away, but those who worship the LORD
will use her money to buy the food and
the clothing they need.

The LORD Will Punish the Earth

24 The LORD is going to devastate
the earth and leave it desolate.
He will twist the earth's surface and
scatter its people. 2 Everyone will meet
the same fate—the priests and the people, slaves and masters, buyers and sell-
ers, lenders and borrowers, rich and
poor. 3 The earth will lie shattered and
ruined. The LORD has spoken and it will
be done.
4 The earth dries up and withers; the
whole world grows weak; both earth
and sky decay. 5 The people have defiled
the earth by breaking God's laws and by
violating the covenant he made to last
forever. 6 So God has pronounced a
curse on the earth. Its people are paying
for what they have done. Fewer and
fewer remain alive. 7 The grapevines
wither, and wine is becoming scarce.
Everyone who was once happy is now
sad, 8 and the joyful music of their harps
and drums has ceased. 9 There is no
more happy singing over wine; no one
enjoys its taste any more. 10 In the city
everything is in chaos, and people lock
themselves in their houses for safety.
11 People shout in the streets because
there is no more wine. Happiness is gone
forever; it has been banished from the
land. 12 The city is in ruins, and its gates
have been broken down. 13 This is what
will happen in every nation all over the
world. It will be like the end of harvest,
when the olives have been beaten off
every tree and the last grapes picked
from the vines.
14 Those who survive will sing for joy.
Those in the West will tell how great the
LORD is, 15 and those in the East will
praise him. The people who live along
the sea will praise the LORD, the God of
Israel. 16 From the most distant parts of
the world we will hear songs in praise of
Israel, the righteous nation.
But there is no hope for me! I am wasting away! Traitors continue to betray,
and their treachery grows worse and
worse. 17 Listen to me, everyone! There
are terrors, pits, and traps waiting for
you. 18 Anyone who tries to escape from
the terror will fall in a pit, and anyone
who escapes from the pit will be caught
in a trap. Torrents of rain will pour from
the sky, and earth's foundations will
shake. 19 The earth will crack and shatter and split open. 20 The earth itself will
stagger like a drunk, sway like a hut in a
storm. The world is weighed down by its
sins; it will collapse and never rise
again.
21 A time is coming when the LORD will
punish the powers above and the rulers
of the earth. 22 God will crowd kings together like prisoners in a pit. He will
shut them in prison until the time of
their punishment comes. 23 The moon
will grow dark, and the sun will no
longer shine, for the LORD Almighty will
be king. He will rule in Jerusalem on
Mount Zion, and the leaders of the people will see his glory.

A Hymn of Praise

25 LORD, you are my God;
I will honor you and praise
your name.
You have done amazing things;
you have faithfully carried out
the plans you made long ago.
2 You have turned cities into ruins

[h] *Verse 13 in Hebrew is unclear.*

and destroyed their
fortifications.
The palaces which our enemies
built
are gone forever.
3 The people of powerful nations
will praise you;
you will be feared in the cities of
cruel nations.
4 The poor and the helpless have
fled to you
and have been safe in times of
trouble.
You give them shelter from storms
and shade from the burning
heat.
Cruel enemies attack like a winter
storm,[i]
5 like drought in a dry land.
But you, LORD, have silenced our
enemies;
you silence the shouts of cruel
people,
as a cloud cools a hot day.

God Prepares a Banquet

6 Here on Mount Zion the LORD
Almighty will prepare a banquet for all
the nations of the world—a banquet of
the richest food and the finest wine.
7 Here he will suddenly remove the cloud
of sorrow that has been hanging over all
the nations. 8 The Sovereign LORD will
destroy death forever! He will wipe
away the tears from everyone's eyes and
take away the disgrace his people have
suffered throughout the world. The LORD
himself has spoken.
9 When it happens, everyone will say,
"He is our God! We have put our trust in
him, and he has rescued us. He is the
LORD! We have put our trust in him, and
now we are happy and joyful because he
has saved us."

God Will Punish Moab

10 The LORD will protect Mount Zion,
but the people of Moab will be trampled
down the way straw is trampled in manure. 11 They will reach out their hands
as if they were trying to swim, but God
will humiliate them, and their hands will
sink helplessly. 12 He will destroy the
fortresses of Moab with their high walls
and bring them tumbling down into the
dust.

God Will Give His People Victory

26 A day is coming when the people will sing this song in the land
of Judah:
Our city is strong!
God himself defends its walls!
2 Open the city gates
and let the faithful nation enter,
the nation whose people do what
is right.
3 You, LORD, give perfect peace
to those who keep their purpose
firm
and put their trust in you.
4 Trust in the LORD forever;
he will always protect us.
5 He has humbled those who were
proud;
he destroyed the strong city they
lived in,
and sent its walls crashing into
the dust.
6 Those who were oppressed walk
over it now
and trample it under their feet.

7 LORD, you make the path smooth
for good people;
the road they travel is level.
8 We follow your will and put our
hope in you;
you are all that we desire.
9 At night I long for you with all my
heart;
when you judge the earth and its
people,
they will all learn what
justice is.
10 Even though you are kind to the
wicked,
they never learn to do what is
right.
Even here in a land of righteous
people
they still do wrong;
they refuse to recognize your
greatness.
11 Your enemies do not know that
you will punish them.
LORD, put them to shame and let
them suffer;
let them suffer the punishment
you have prepared.
Show them how much you love
your people.

[i] *Probable text* winter storm; *Hebrew* storm against a wall.

12 You will give us prosperity, LORD;
everything that we achieve
is the result of what you do.[j]
13 LORD our God, we have been ruled
by others,
but you alone are our LORD.
14 Now they are dead and will not
live again;
their ghosts will not rise,
for you have punished them and
destroyed them.
No one remembers them any
more.
15 LORD, you have made our nation
grow,
enlarging its territory on every
side;
and this has brought you honor.
16 You punished your people, LORD,
and in anguish they prayed
to you.[k]
17 You, LORD, have made us cry out,
as a woman in labor cries out in
pain.
18 We were in pain and agony,
but we gave birth to nothing.
We have won no victory for our
land;
we have accomplished nothing.[l]

19 Those of our people who have
died will live again!
Their bodies will come back to
life.
All those sleeping in their graves
will wake up and sing for joy.
As the sparkling dew refreshes the
earth,
so the LORD will revive those
who have long been dead.

Judgment and Restoration

20 Go into your houses, my people, and
shut the door behind you. Hide yourselves for a little while until God's anger
is over. 21 The LORD is coming from his
heavenly dwelling place to punish the
people of the earth for their sins. The
murders that were secretly committed
on the earth will be revealed, and the
ground will no longer hide those who
have been killed.

27 On that day the LORD will use his
powerful and deadly sword to
punish Leviathan, that wriggling, twist-
ing dragon, and to kill the monster[m]
that lives in the sea.
2 On that day the LORD will say of his
pleasant vineyard, 3 "I watch over it and
water it continually. I guard it night and
day so that no one will harm it. 4 I am no
longer angry with the vineyard. If there
were thorns and briers to fight against, I
would burn them up completely. 5 But if
the enemies of my people want my protection, let them make peace with me.
Yes, let them make peace with me."
6 In the days to come the people of Israel, the descendants of Jacob, will take
root like a tree, and they will blossom
and bud. The earth will be covered with
the fruit they produce.
7 Israel has not been punished by the
LORD as severely as its enemies nor lost
as many people. 8 The LORD punished his
people by sending them into exile. He
took them away with a cruel wind from
the east.[n] 9 But Israel's sins will be forgiven only when the stones of pagan altars are ground up like chalk, and no
more incense altars or symbols of the
goddess Asherah are left.
10 The fortified city lies in ruins. It is
deserted like an empty wilderness. It has
become a pasture for cattle, where they
can rest and graze. 11 The branches of
the trees are withered and broken, and
women gather them for firewood. Because the people have understood nothing, God their Creator will not pity them
or show them any mercy.
12 On that day, from the Euphrates to
the Egyptian border, the LORD will
gather his people one by one, as threshing separates the wheat from the chaff.
13 When that day comes, a trumpet will
be blown to call back from Assyria and
Egypt all the Israelites who are in exile
there. They will come and worship the
LORD in Jerusalem, on his sacred hill.[o]

A Warning to the Northern Kingdom

28 The kingdom of Israel is
doomed! Its glory is fading like
the crowns of flowers on the heads of its
drunken leaders. Their proud heads are

[j] everything that . . . do; *or* you treat us according to what we do. [k] *Verse 16 in Hebrew is unclear.* [l] We have won . . . nothing; *Hebrew unclear.* [m] LEVIATHAN . . . MONSTER: *Legendary monsters which were symbols of the nations oppressing Israel.* [n] *Verse 8 in Hebrew is unclear.* [o] SACRED HILL: *See 2.3.*

well perfumed, but there they lie, dead
drunk. 2The Lord has someone strong
and powerful ready to attack them,
someone who will come like a hailstorm,
like a torrent of rain, like a rushing,
overpowering flood, and will overwhelm
the land. 3The pride of those drunken
leaders will be trampled underfoot. 4The
fading glory of those proud leaders will
disappear like the first figs of the season,
picked and eaten as soon as they are
ripe.

5A day is coming when the LORD
Almighty will be like a glorious crown of
flowers for his people who survive. 6He
will give a sense of justice to those who
serve as judges, and courage to those
who defend the city gates from attack.

Isaiah and the Drunken Prophets of Judah

7Even the prophets and the priests are
so drunk that they stagger. They have
drunk so much wine and liquor that they
stumble in confusion. The prophets are
too drunk to understand the visions that
God sends, and the priests are too drunk
to decide the cases that are brought to
them. 8The tables where they sit are all
covered with vomit, and not a clean spot
is left.

9They complain about me. They say,
"Who does that man think he's teaching? Who needs his message? It's only
good for babies that have just stopped
nursing! 10He is trying to teach us letter
by letter, line by line, lesson by lesson."

11If you won't listen to me, then God
will use foreigners speaking some
strange-sounding language to teach you
a lesson. 12He offered rest and comfort
to all of you, but you refused to listen to
him. 13That is why the LORD is going to
teach you letter by letter, line by line,
lesson by lesson. Then you will stumble
with every step you take. You will be
wounded, trapped, and taken prisoner.

A Cornerstone for Zion

14Now you arrogant leaders who rule
here in Jerusalem over this people, listen
to what the LORD is saying. 15You boast
that you have made a treaty with death
and reached an agreement with the
world of the dead. You are certain that
disaster will spare you when it comes,
because you depend on lies and deceit to
keep you safe. 16This, now, is what the
Sovereign LORD says: "I am placing in
Zion a foundation that is firm and
strong. In it I am putting a solid cornerstone on which are written the words,
'Faith that is firm is also patient.' 17Jus-
tice will be the measuring line for the
foundation, and honesty will be its
plumb line."

Hailstorms will sweep away all the
lies you depend on, and floods will destroy your security. 18The treaty you
have made with death will be abolished,
and your agreement with the world of
the dead will be canceled. When disaster
sweeps down, you will be overcome. 19It
will strike you again and again, morning
after morning. You will have to bear it
day and night. Each new message from
God will bring new terror! 20You will be
like the person in the proverb, who tries
to sleep in a bed too short to stretch out
on, with a blanket too narrow to wrap
himself in. 21The LORD will fight as he
did at Mount Perazim and in the valley
of Gibeon, in order to do what he intends
to do—strange as his actions may seem.
He will complete his work, his mysterious work.

22Don't laugh at the warning I am giving you! If you do, it will be even harder
for you to escape. I have heard the LORD
Almighty's decision to destroy the whole
country.

God's Wisdom

23Listen to what I am saying; pay attention to what I am telling you. 24Farm-
ers don't constantly plow their fields and
keep getting them ready for planting.
25Once they have prepared the soil, they
plant the seeds of herbs such as dill and
cumin. They plant rows of wheat and
barley,[p] and at the edges of their fields
they plant other grain. 26They know
how to do their work, because God has
taught them. 27They never use a heavy
club to beat out dill seeds or cumin
seeds; instead they use light sticks of the
proper size. 28They do not ruin the
wheat by threshing it endlessly, and
they know how to thresh it by driving a
cart over it without bruising the grains.
29All this wisdom comes from the LORD

[p] *Hebrew has an additional word, the meaning of which is unclear.*

Almighty. The plans God makes are
wise, and they always succeed.

The Fate of Jerusalem

29 God's altar, Jerusalem itself, is
doomed! The city where David
camped is doomed! Let another year or
two come and go, with its feasts and festivals, 2 and then God will bring disaster
on the city that is called "God's altar."
There will be weeping and wailing, and
the whole city will be like an altar covered with blood. 3 God will attack the
city, surround it, and besiege it. 4 Jerusalem will be like a ghost struggling to
speak from under the ground, a muffled
voice coming from the dust.
5 Jerusalem, all the foreigners who attack you will be blown away like dust,
and their terrifying armies will fly away
like straw. Suddenly and unexpectedly
6 the LORD Almighty will rescue you with
violent thunderstorms and earthquakes.
He will send windstorms and raging fire;
7 then all the armies of the nations attacking the city of God's altar, all their
weapons and equipment—everything—
will vanish like a dream, like something
imagined in the night. 8 All the nations
that assemble to attack Jerusalem will
be like a starving person who dreams he
is eating and wakes up hungry, or like
someone dying of thirst who dreams he
is drinking and wakes with a dry throat.

Disregarded Warnings

9 Go ahead and be stupid! Go ahead
and be blind! Get drunk without any
wine! Stagger without drinking a drop!
10 The LORD has made you drowsy, ready
to fall into a deep sleep. The prophets
should be the eyes of the people, but God
has blindfolded them. 11 The meaning of
every prophetic vision will be hidden
from you; it will be like a sealed scroll. If
you take it to someone who knows how
to read and ask him to read it to you, he
will say he can't because it is sealed. 12 If
you give it to someone who can't read
and ask him to read it to you, he will
answer that he doesn't know how.
13 The Lord said, "These people claim
to worship me, but their words are
meaningless, and their hearts are somewhere else. Their religion is nothing but
human rules and traditions, which they
have simply memorized. 14 So I will star-
tle them with one unexpected blow after
another. Those who are wise will turn
out to be fools, and all their cleverness
will be useless."

Hope for the Future

15 Those who try to hide their plans
from the LORD are doomed! They carry
out their schemes in secret and think no
one will see them or know what they are
doing. 16 They turn everything upside
down. Which is more important, the potter or the clay? Can something you have
made say, "You didn't make me"? Or can
it say, "You don't know what you are
doing"?
17 As the saying goes, before long the
dense forest will become farmland, and
the farmland will go back to forest.
18 When that day comes, the deaf will
be able to hear a book being read aloud,
and the blind, who have been living in
darkness, will open their eyes and see.
19 Poor and humble people will once
again find the happiness which the LORD,
the holy God of Israel, gives. 20 It will be
the end of those who oppress others and
show contempt for God. Every sinner
will be destroyed. 21 God will destroy
those who slander others, those who
prevent the punishment of criminals,
and those who tell lies to keep honest
people from getting justice.
22 So now the LORD, the God of Israel,
who rescued Abraham from trouble,
says, "My people, you will not be disgraced any longer, and your faces will
no longer be pale with shame. 23 When
you see the children that I will give you,
then you will acknowledge that I am the
holy God of Israel. You will honor me
and stand in awe of me. 24 Foolish people
will learn to understand, and those who
are always grumbling will be glad to be
taught."

A Useless Treaty with Egypt

30 The LORD has spoken: "Those
who rule Judah are doomed because they rebel against me. They follow
plans that I did not make, and sign
treaties against my will, piling one sin
on another. 2 They go to Egypt for help
without asking for my advice. They
want Egypt to protect them, so they put
their trust in Egypt's king. 3 But the king
will be powerless to help them, and
Egypt's protection will end in disaster.
4 Although their ambassadors have

already arrived at the Egyptian cities of
Zoan and Hanes, 5 the people of Judah will regret that they ever trusted that
unreliable nation, a nation that fails
them when they expect help."
6 This is God's message about the animals of the southern desert: "The ambassadors travel through dangerous
country, where lions live and where
there are poisonous snakes and flying
dragons. They load their donkeys and
camels with expensive gifts for a nation
that cannot give them any help. 7 The
help that Egypt gives is useless. So I
have nicknamed Egypt, 'The Harmless
Dragon.' "

The Disobedient People

8 God told me to write down in a book
what the people are like, so that there
would be a permanent record of how
evil they are. 9 They are always rebelling
against God, always lying, always refusing to listen to the LORD's teachings.
10 They tell the prophets to keep quiet.
They say, "Don't talk to us about what's
right. Tell us what we want to hear. Let
us keep our illusions. 11 Get out of our
way and stop blocking our path. We
don't want to hear about your holy God
of Israel."
12 But this is what the holy God of Israel says: "You ignore what I tell you
and rely on violence and deceit. 13 You
are guilty. You are like a high wall with
a crack running down it; suddenly you
will collapse. 14 You will be shattered
like a clay pot, so badly broken that
there is no piece big enough to pick up
hot coals with or to dip water from a
cistern."
15 The Sovereign LORD, the Holy One of
Israel, says to the people, "Come back
and quietly trust in me. Then you will be
strong and secure." But you refuse to do
it. 16 Instead, you plan to escape from
your enemies by riding fast horses. And
you are right – escape is what you will
have to do! You think your horses are
fast enough, but those who pursue you
will be faster! 17 A thousand of you will
run away when you see one enemy soldier, and five soldiers will be enough to
make you all run away. Nothing will be
left of your army except a lonely flag-
pole on the top of a hill. 18 And yet the
LORD is waiting to be merciful to you. He
is ready to take pity on you because he
always does what is right. Happy are
those who put their trust in the LORD.

God Will Bless His People

19 You people who live in Jerusalem
will not weep any more. The LORD is
compassionate, and when you cry to
him for help, he will answer you. 20 The
Lord will make you go through hard
times, but he himself will be there to
teach you, and you will not have to
search for him any more. 21 If you wander off the road to the right or the left,
you will hear his voice behind you saying, "Here is the road. Follow it." 22 You
will take your idols plated with silver
and your idols covered with gold, and
will throw them away like filth, shouting, "Out of my sight!" 23 Whenever you
plant your crops, the Lord will send rain
to make them grow and will give you a
rich harvest, and your livestock will
have plenty of pasture. 24 The oxen and
donkeys that plow your fields will eat
the finest and best fodder. 25 On the day
when the forts of your enemies are captured and their people are killed,
streams of water will flow from every
mountain and every hill. 26 The moon
will be as bright as the sun, and the
sun will be seven times brighter than
usual, like the light of seven days in
one. This will all happen when the LORD
bandages and heals the wounds he has
given his people.

God Will Punish Assyria

27 The LORD's power and glory can be
seen in the distance. Fire and smoke
show his anger. He speaks, and his
words burn like fire. 28 He sends the
wind in front of him like a flood that carries everything away. It sweeps nations
to destruction and puts an end to their
evil plans. 29 But you, God's people, will
be happy and sing as you do on the night
of a sacred festival. You will be as happy
as those who walk to the music of flutes
on their way to the Temple of the LORD,
the defender of Israel.
30 The LORD will let everyone hear his
majestic voice and feel the force of his
anger. There will be flames, cloudbursts,
hailstones, and torrents of rain. 31 The
Assyrians will be terrified when they
hear the LORD's voice and feel the force
of his punishment. 32 As the LORD strikes

them again and again, his people will
keep time with the music of drums and
harps. God himself will fight against the
Assyrians. 33Long ago a place was prepared where a huge fire will burn the
emperor of Assyria. It is deep and wide,
and piled high with wood. The LORD will
breathe out a stream of flame to set it on
fire.

God Will Protect Jerusalem

31 Those who go to Egypt for help
are doomed! They are relying on
Egypt's vast military strength—horses,
chariots, and soldiers. But they do not
rely on the LORD, the holy God of Israel,
or ask him for help. 2He knows what he
is doing! He sends disaster. He carries
out his threats to punish evil people and
those who protect them. 3The Egyptians
are not gods—they are only human.
Their horses are not supernatural. When
the LORD acts, the strong nation will
crumble, and the weak nation it helped
will fall. Both of them will be destroyed.
4The LORD said to me, "No matter how
shepherds yell and shout, they can't
scare away a lion from an animal that it
has killed; in the same way, there is
nothing that can keep me, the LORD
Almighty, from protecting Mount Zion.
5Just as a bird hovers over its nest to
protect its young, so I, the LORD
Almighty, will protect Jerusalem and defend it."
6God said, "People of Israel, you have
sinned against me and opposed me. But
now, come back to me! 7A time is coming when all of you will throw away the
sinful idols you made out of silver and
gold. 8Assyria will be destroyed in war,
but not by human power. The Assyrians
will run from battle, and their young
men will be made slaves. 9Their emperor will run away in terror, and the
officers will be so frightened that they
will abandon their battle flags." The
LORD has spoken—the LORD who is worshiped in Jerusalem and whose fire
burns there for sacrifices.

A King with Integrity

32 Some day there will be a king
who rules with integrity, and national leaders who govern with justice.
2Each of them will be like a shelter from
the wind and a place to hide from
storms. They will be like streams flowing in a desert, like the shadow of a giant
rock in a barren land. 3Their eyes and
ears will be open to the needs of the people. 4They will not be impatient any
longer, but they will act with understanding and will say what they mean.
5No one will think that a fool is honorable or say that a scoundrel is honest.
6A fool speaks foolishly and thinks up
evil things to do. What he does and what
he says are an insult to the LORD, and he
never feeds the hungry or gives thirsty
people anything to drink. 7A stupid person is evil and does evil things; he plots
to ruin the poor with lies and to keep
them from getting their rights. 8But an
honorable person acts honestly and
stands firm for what is right.

Judgment and Restoration

9You women who live an easy life,
free from worries, listen to what I am
saying. 10You may be satisfied now, but
this time next year you will be in despair
because there will be no grapes for you
to gather. 11You have been living an
easy life, free from worries; but now,
tremble with fear! Strip off your clothes
and tie rags around your waist. 12Beat
your breasts in grief because the fertile
fields and the vineyards have been destroyed, 13and thorn bushes and briers
are growing on my people's land. Weep
for all the houses where people were
happy and for the city that was full of
life. 14Even the palace will be abandoned and the capital city totally deserted. Homes and the forts that guarded
them will be in ruins forever. Wild donkeys will roam there, and sheep will find
pasture there.
15But once more God will send us his
spirit. The wasteland will become fertile,
and fields will produce rich crops.
16Everywhere in the land righteousness
and justice will be done. 17Because
everyone will do what is right, there will
be peace and security forever. 18God's
people will be free from worries, and
their homes peaceful and safe. (19But
hail will fall on the forests, and the city
will be torn down.) 20How happy everyone will be with plenty of water for the
crops and safe pasture everywhere for
the donkeys and cattle.

A Prayer for Help

33 Our enemies are doomed! They
have robbed and betrayed, although no one has robbed them or betrayed them. But their time to rob and
betray will end, and they themselves
will become victims of robbery and
treachery.
2LORD, have mercy on us. We have put
our hope in you. Protect us day by day
and save us in times of trouble. 3When
you fight for us, nations run away from
the noise of battle. 4Their belongings are
pounced upon and taken as loot.
5How great the LORD is! He rules over
everything. He will fill Jerusalem with
justice and integrity 6and give stability
to the nation. He always protects his
people and gives them wisdom and
knowledge. Their greatest treasure is
their reverence for the LORD.
7The brave are calling for help. The
ambassadors who tried to bring about
peace are crying bitterly. 8The highways
are so dangerous that no one travels on
them. Treaties are broken and agreements are violated. No one is respected
any more. 9The land lies idle and deserted. The forests of Lebanon have
withered, the fertile valley of Sharon is
like a desert, and in Bashan and on
Mount Carmel the leaves are falling
from the trees.

The LORD Warns His Enemies

10The LORD says to the nations, "Now I
will act. I will show how powerful I am.
11You make worthless plans and everything you do is useless. My spirit is like
a fire that will destroy you.[q] 12You will
crumble like rocks burned to make lime,
like thorns burned to ashes. 13Let everyone near and far hear what I have done
and acknowledge my power."
14The sinful people of Zion are trembling with fright. They say, "God's judgment is like a fire that burns forever.
Can any of us survive a fire like that?"
15You can survive if you say and do
what is right. Don't use your power to
cheat the poor and don't accept bribes.
Don't join with those who plan to commit murder or to do other evil things.
16Then you will be safe; you will be as
secure as if in a strong fortress. You will
have food to eat and water to drink.

The Glorious Future

17Once again you will see a king ruling in splendor over a land that stretches
in all directions. 18Your old fears of foreign tax collectors and spies will be only
a memory. 19You will no longer see any
arrogant foreigners who speak a language that you can't understand. 20Look
at Zion, the city where we celebrate our
religious festivals. Look at Jerusalem!
What a safe place it will be to live in! It
will be like a tent that is never moved,
whose pegs are never pulled up and
whose ropes never break. 21The LORD
will show us his glory. We will live beside broad rivers and streams, but hostile ships will not sail on them.[r] 22-23All
the rigging on those ships is useless; the
sails cannot be spread! We will seize all
the wealth of enemy armies, and there
will be so much that even the lame can
get a share. The LORD himself will be our
king; he will rule over us and protect us.
24No one who lives in our land will ever
again complain of being sick, and all
sins will be forgiven.

God Will Punish His Enemies

34 Come, people of all nations!
Gather around and listen. Let the
whole earth and everyone living on it
come here and listen. 2The LORD is angry
with all the nations and all their armies.
He has condemned them to destruction.
3Their corpses will not be buried, but
will lie there rotting and stinking; and
the mountains will be red with blood.
4The sun, moon, and stars will crumble
to dust. The sky will disappear like a
scroll being rolled up, and the stars will
fall like leaves dropping from a vine or a
fig tree.
5The LORD has prepared his sword in
heaven, and now it will strike Edom,
those people whom he has condemned
to destruction. 6His sword will be covered with their blood and fat, like the
blood and fat of lambs and goats that are
sacrificed. The LORD will offer this sacrifice in the city of Bozrah; he will make
this a great slaughter in the land of
Edom. 7The people will fall like wild
oxen and young bulls, and the earth will

[q] *One ancient translation* My spirit . . . you; *Hebrew* You are destroying yourselves.
[r] *Verse 21 in Hebrew is unclear.*

be red with blood and covered with fat.
[8]This is the time when the LORD will rescue Zion and take vengeance on her
enemies.

[9]The rivers of Edom will turn into tar,
and the soil will turn into sulfur. The
whole country will burn like tar. [10]It will
burn day and night, and smoke will rise
from it forever. The land will lie waste
age after age, and no one will ever travel
through it again. [11]Owls and ravens will
take over the land. The LORD will make it
a barren waste again, as it was before
the creation. [12]There will be no king to
rule the country, and the leaders will all
be gone.[s] [13]Thorns and thistles will
grow up in all the palaces and walled
towns, and jackals and owls will live in
them. [14]Wild animals will roam there,
and demons will call to each other. The
night monster[t] will come there looking
for a place to rest. [15]Owls will build their
nests, lay eggs, hatch their young, and
care for them there. Vultures will gather
there, one after another.

[16]Search in the LORD's book of living
creatures and read what it says. Not one
of these creatures will be missing, and
not one will be without its mate. The
LORD has commanded it to be so; he himself will bring them together. [17]It is the
LORD who will divide the land among
them and give each of them a share.
They will live in the land age after age,
and it will belong to them forever.

The Road of Holiness

35 The desert will rejoice,
and flowers will bloom in the wastelands.
[2]The desert will sing and shout for joy;
it will be as beautiful as the Lebanon Mountains
and as fertile as the fields of Carmel and Sharon.
Everyone will see the LORD's splendor,
see his greatness and power.

[3]Give strength to hands that are tired
and to knees that tremble with weakness.
[4]Tell everyone who is discouraged,
"Be strong and don't be afraid!
God is coming to your rescue,
coming to punish your enemies."

[5]The blind will be able to see,
and the deaf will hear.
[6]The lame will leap and dance,
and those who cannot speak will shout for joy.
Streams of water will flow through the desert;
[7]the burning sand will become a lake,
and dry land will be filled with springs.
Where jackals used to live,
marsh grass and reeds will grow.

[8]There will be a highway there,
called "The Road of Holiness."
No sinner will ever travel that road;
no fools will mislead those who follow it.[u]
[9]No lions will be there;
no fierce animals will pass that way.
Those whom the LORD has rescued
will travel home by that road.
[10]They will reach Jerusalem with gladness,
singing and shouting for joy.
They will be happy forever,
forever free from sorrow and grief.

The Assyrians Threaten Jerusalem

(2 Kings 18.13-27; 2 Chronicles 32.1-19)

36 In the fourteenth year that Hezekiah was king of Judah, Sennacherib, the emperor of Assyria,
attacked the fortified cities of Judah and
captured them. [2]Then he ordered his
chief official to go from Lachish to Jerusalem with a large military force to demand that King Hezekiah surrender.
The official occupied the road where the
cloth makers work, by the ditch that
brings water from the upper pool.
[3]Three Judeans came out to meet him:
the official in charge of the palace, Eliakim son of Hilkiah; the court secretary,
Shebna; and the official in charge of the

[s] *Verse 12 in Hebrew begins with a word, the meaning of which is unclear.* [t] NIGHT MONSTER: *A female demon, believed to live in desolate places.* [u] *Probable text* no fools . . . follow it; *Hebrew unclear.*

records, Joah son of Asaph. 4The Assyrian official told them that the emperor wanted to know what made King
Hezekiah so confident. 5He demanded,
"Do you think that words can take the
place of military skill and might? Who
do you think will help you rebel against
Assyria? 6You are expecting Egypt to
help you, but that would be like using a
reed as a walking stick—it would break
and would jab your hand. That is what
the king of Egypt is like when anyone
relies on him."

7The Assyrian official went on, "Or
will you tell me that you are relying on
the LORD your God? It was the LORD's
shrines and altars that Hezekiah destroyed when he told the people of Judah and Jerusalem to worship at one
altar only. 8I will make a bargain with
you in the name of the emperor. I will
give you two thousand horses if you can
find that many riders. 9You are no
match for even the lowest ranking Assyrian official, and yet you expect the
Egyptians to send you chariots and
horsemen. 10Do you think I have attacked your country and destroyed it
without the LORD's help? The LORD himself told me to attack it and destroy it."

11Then Eliakim, Shebna, and Joah
told the official, "Speak Aramaic to us.
We understand it. Don't speak Hebrew;
all the people on the wall are listening."

12He replied, "Do you think you and
the king are the only ones the emperor
sent me to say all these things to? No, I
am also talking to the people who are
sitting on the wall, who will have to eat
their excrement and drink their urine,
just as you will."

13Then the official stood up and
shouted in Hebrew, "Listen to what the
emperor of Assyria is telling you. 14He
warns you not to let Hezekiah deceive
you. Hezekiah can't save you. 15And
don't let him persuade you to rely on the
LORD. Don't think that the LORD will save
you and that he will stop our Assyrian
army from capturing your city. 16Don't
listen to Hezekiah! The emperor of Assyria commands you to come out of the
city and surrender. You will all be allowed to eat grapes from your own vines
and figs from your own trees, and to
drink water from your own wells—
17until the emperor resettles you in a
country much like your own, where
there are vineyards to give wine and
there is grain for making bread. 18Don't
let Hezekiah fool you into thinking that
the LORD will rescue you. Did the gods of
any other nations save their countries
from the emperor of Assyria? 19Where
are they now, the gods of Hamath and
Arpad? Where are the gods of Sepharvaim? Did anyone save Samaria?
20When did any of the gods of all these
countries ever save their country from
our emperor? Then what makes you
think the LORD can save Jerusalem?"

21The people kept quiet, just as King
Hezekiah had told them to; they did not
say a word. 22Then Eliakim, Shebna,
and Joah tore their clothes in grief and
went and reported to the king what the
Assyrian official had said.

The King Asks Isaiah's Advice

(2 Kings 19.1-7)

37 As soon as King Hezekiah heard
their report, he tore his clothes in
grief, put on sackcloth, and went to the
Temple of the LORD. 2He sent Eliakim,
the official in charge of the palace,
Shebna, the court secretary, and the senior priests to the prophet Isaiah son of
Amoz. They also were wearing sackcloth. 3This is the message which he told
them to give to Isaiah: "Today is a day of
suffering; we are being punished and
are in disgrace. We are like a woman
who is ready to give birth, but is too
weak to do it. 4The Assyrian emperor
has sent his chief official to insult the
living God. May the LORD your God hear
these insults and punish those who
spoke them. So pray to God for those of
our people who survive."

5When Isaiah received King Hezekiah's message, 6he sent back this answer: "The LORD tells you not to let the
Assyrians frighten you by their claims
that he cannot save you. 7The LORD will
cause the emperor to hear a rumor that
will make him go back to his own country, and the LORD will have him killed
there."

The Assyrians Send Another Threat

(2 Kings 19.8-19)

8The Assyrian official learned that the
emperor had left Lachish and was fighting against the nearby city of Libnah; so
he went there to consult him. 9Word
reached the Assyrians that the Egyptian

army, led by King Tirhakah of Ethiopia,[v] was coming to attack them. When
the emperor heard this, he sent a letter
to King Hezekiah 10 of Judah to tell him:
“The god you are trusting in has told you
that you will not fall into my hands, but
don’t let that deceive you. 11 You have
heard what an Assyrian emperor does to
any country he decides to destroy. Do
you think that you can escape? 12 My ancestors destroyed the cities of Gozan,
Haran, and Rezeph, and killed the people of Betheden who lived in Telassar,
and none of their gods could save them.
13 Where are the kings of the cities of Hamath, Arpad, Sepharvaim, Hena, and
Ivvah?”

14 King Hezekiah took the letter from
the messengers and read it. Then he
went to the Temple, placed the letter
there in the presence of the LORD, 15 and
prayed, 16 “Almighty LORD, God of Israel,
seated above the winged creatures, you
alone are God, ruling all the kingdoms
of the world. You created the earth and
the sky. 17 Now, LORD, hear us and look
at what is happening to us. Listen to all
the things that Sennacherib is saying to
insult you, the living God. 18 We all
know, LORD, that the emperors of Assyria have destroyed many nations,
made their lands desolate, 19 and burned
up their gods—which were no gods at
all, only images of wood and stone made
by human hands. 20 Now, LORD our God,
rescue us from the Assyrians, so that all
the nations of the world will know that
you alone are God.”

Isaiah’s Message to the King

(2 Kings 19.20-37)

21 Then Isaiah sent a message telling
King Hezekiah that in answer to the
king’s prayer 22 the LORD had said, “The
city of Jerusalem laughs at you, Sennacherib, and makes fun of you.
23 Whom do you think you have been insulting and ridiculing? You have been
disrespectful to me, the holy God of Israel. 24 You sent your servants to boast
to me that with all your chariots you had
conquered the highest mountains of
Lebanon. You boasted that there you cut
down the tallest cedars and the finest cypress trees, and that you reached the
deepest parts of the forests. 25 You
boasted that you dug wells and drank
water in foreign lands, and that the feet
of your soldiers tramped the Nile
River dry.

26 “Have you never heard that I
planned all this long ago? And now I
have carried it out. I gave you the power
to turn fortified cities into piles of rubble. 27 The people who lived there were
powerless; they were frightened and
stunned. They were like grass in a field
or weeds growing on a roof when the hot
east wind blasts them.[w]

28 “But I know everything about you,
what you do and where you go. I know
how you rage against me. 29 I have received the report of that rage and that
pride of yours, and now I will put a hook
through your nose and a bit in your
mouth and will take you back by the
same road you came.”

30 Then Isaiah said to King Hezekiah,
“Here is a sign of what will happen. This
year and next you will have only wild
grain to eat, but the following year you
will be able to plant grain and harvest it,
and plant vines and eat grapes. 31 Those
in Judah who survive will flourish like
plants that send roots deep into the
ground and produce fruit. 32 There will
be people in Jerusalem and on Mount
Zion who will survive, because the LORD
Almighty is determined to make this
happen.

33 “And this is what the LORD has said
about the Assyrian emperor: ‘He will not
enter this city or shoot a single arrow
against it. No soldiers with shields will
come near the city, and no siege mounds
will be built around it. 34 He will go back
by the same road he came, without entering this city. I, the LORD, have spoken.
35 I will defend this city and protect it, for
the sake of my own honor and because
of the promise I made to my servant
David.’ ”

36 An angel of the LORD went to the As-
syrian camp and killed 185,000 soldiers.
At dawn the next day there they lay, all
dead! 37 Then the Assyrian emperor
Sennacherib withdrew and returned to
Nineveh. 38 One day when he was

[v] *Hebrew* Cush: *Cush is the ancient name of the extensive territory south of the First Cataract of the Nile River. This region was called Ethiopia in Graeco-Roman times, and included within its borders most of modern Sudan and some of present-day Ethiopia (Abyssinia).*
[w] *Probable text* when the hot east wind blasts them; *Hebrew* blasted before they are grown.

worshiping in the temple of his god Nisroch, two of his sons, Adrammelech and
Sharezer, killed him with their swords
and then escaped to the land of Ararat.
Another of his sons, Esarhaddon, succeeded him as emperor.

King Hezekiah's Illness and Recovery

(2 Kings 20.1-11; 2 Chronicles 32.24-26)

38 About this time King Hezekiah
became sick and almost died.
The prophet Isaiah son of Amoz went to
see him and said to him, "The LORD tells
you that you are to put everything in order because you will not recover. Get
ready to die."
2 Hezekiah turned his face to the wall
and prayed: 3 "Remember, LORD, that I
have served you faithfully and loyally,
and that I have always tried to do what
you wanted me to." And he began to cry
bitterly.
4 Then the LORD commanded Isaiah 5 to
go back to Hezekiah and say to him, "I,
the LORD, the God of your ancestor David, have heard your prayer and seen
your tears; I will let you live fifteen years
longer. 6 I will rescue you and this city of
Jerusalem from the emperor of Assyria,
and I will continue to protect the city."
21 Isaiah told the king to put a paste
made of figs on his boil, and he would
get well. 22 Then King Hezekiah asked,
"What is the sign to prove that I will be
able to go to the Temple?"[x]
7 Isaiah replied, "The LORD will give
you a sign to prove that he will keep his
promise. 8 On the stairway built by King
Ahaz, the LORD will make the shadow go
back ten steps." And the shadow moved
back ten steps.[y]
9 After Hezekiah recovered from his
illness, he wrote this song of praise:

10 I thought that in the prime of life
I was going to the world of the
dead,
Never to live out my life.
11 I thought that in this world of the
living
I would never again see the LORD
Or any living person.
12 My life was cut off and ended,
Like a tent that is taken down,
Like cloth that is cut from a loom.
I thought that God was ending my
life.[z]
13 All night I cried out with pain,
As if a lion were breaking my
bones.
I thought that God was ending my
life.[a]
14 My voice was thin and weak,
And I moaned like a dove.
My eyes grew tired from looking
to heaven.
LORD, rescue me from all this
trouble.
15 What can I say? The LORD has
done this.
My heart is bitter, and I cannot
sleep.[b]

16 Lord, I will live for you, for you
alone;
Heal me and let me live.[c]
17 My bitterness will turn into peace.
You save[d] my life from all
danger;
You forgive all my sins.
18 No one in the world of the dead
can praise you;
The dead cannot trust in your
faithfulness.
19 It is the living who praise you,
As I praise you now.
Parents tell their children how
faithful you are.
20 LORD, you have healed me.
We will play harps and sing your
praise,
Sing praise in your Temple as long
as we live.[e]

Messengers from Babylonia

(2 Kings 20.12-19)

39 About that same time the king of
Babylonia, Merodach Baladan,
son of Baladan, heard that King Hezekiah had been sick, so he sent him a letter and a present. 2 Hezekiah welcomed
the messengers and showed them his
wealth—his silver and gold, his spices
and perfumes, and all his military equipment. There was nothing in his storerooms or anywhere in his kingdom that

[x] *Verses 21-22 are moved here from the end of the chapter (see 2 K 20.6-9).* [y] stairway . . . ten steps . . . steps; *or* sundial . . . ten degrees . . . degrees *(see 2 K 20.9-11).* [z] I thought . . . my life; *Hebrew unclear.* [a] *Verse 13 in Hebrew is unclear.* [b] *One ancient translation suggests* I cannot sleep; *Hebrew unclear.* [c] *Verses 15 and 16 in Hebrew are unclear.* [d] *Some ancient translations* save; *Hebrew* love. [e] *Verses 21-22 are placed after verse 6.*

he did not show them. 3Then the prophet
Isaiah went to King Hezekiah and
asked, "Where did these messengers
come from and what did they say
to you?"
Hezekiah answered, "They came from
a very distant country, from Babylonia."
4"What did they see in the palace?"
"They saw everything. There is nothing in the storerooms that I didn't show
them."
5Isaiah then told the king, "The LORD
Almighty says that 6a time is coming
when everything in your palace, everything that your ancestors have stored up
to this day, will be carried off to Babylonia. Nothing will be left. 7Some of your
own direct descendants will be taken
away and made eunuchs to serve in the
palace of the king of Babylonia."
8King Hezekiah understood this to
mean that there would be peace and security during his lifetime, so he replied,
"The message you have given me from
the LORD is good."

Words of Hope

40 "Comfort my people," says our God. "Comfort them!
2Encourage the people of Jerusalem.
Tell them they have suffered long enough
and their sins are now forgiven.[f]
I have punished them in full for all their sins."

3A voice cries out,
"Prepare in the wilderness a road for the LORD!
Clear the way in the desert for our God!
4Fill every valley;
level every mountain.
The hills will become a plain,
and the rough country will be made smooth.
5Then the glory of the LORD will be revealed,
and all people will see it.
The LORD himself has promised this."

6A voice cries out, "Proclaim a message!"
"What message shall I proclaim?" I ask.
"Proclaim that all human beings are like grass;
they last no longer than wild flowers.
7Grass withers and flowers fade
when the LORD sends the wind blowing over them.
People are no more enduring than grass.
8Yes, grass withers and flowers fade,
but the word of our God endures forever."

9Jerusalem, go up on a high mountain
and proclaim the good news!
Call out with a loud voice, Zion;
announce the good news![g]
Speak out and do not be afraid.
Tell the towns of Judah
that their God is coming!

10The Sovereign LORD is coming to rule with power,
bringing with him the people he has rescued.[h]
11He will take care of his flock like a shepherd;
he will gather the lambs together
and carry them in his arms;
he will gently lead their mothers.

Israel's Incomparable God

12Can anyone measure the ocean by handfuls
or measure the sky with his hands?
Can anyone hold the soil of the earth in a cup
or weigh the mountains and hills on scales?
13Can anyone tell the LORD what to do?
Who can teach him or give him advice?

[f] and their sins are now forgiven; *or* they have paid for what they did. [g] Jerusalem, go up . . . news!; *or* Go up on a high mountain and proclaim the good news to Jerusalem! Call out with a loud voice and announce the good news to Zion! [h] the people he has rescued; *or* the rewards he has for his people.

14 With whom does God consult
in order to know and understand
and to learn how things should
be done?

15 To the LORD the nations are
nothing,
no more than a drop of water;
the distant islands are as light as
dust.
16 All the animals in the forests of
Lebanon
are not enough for a sacrifice to
our God,
and its trees are too few to
kindle the fire.
17 The nations are nothing at all
to him.

18 To whom can God be compared?
How can you describe what he
is like?
19 He is not like an idol that workers
make,
that metalworkers cover with
gold
and set in a base of silver.
20 Anyone who cannot afford silver
or gold[i]
chooses wood that will not rot.
He finds a skillful worker
to make an image that won't fall
down.

21 Do you not know?
Were you not told long ago?
Have you not heard how the
world began?
22 It was made by the one who sits
on his throne
above the earth and beyond
the sky;
the people below look as tiny as
ants.
He stretched out the sky like a
curtain,
like a tent in which to live.

23 He brings down powerful rulers
and reduces them to nothing.
24 They are like young plants,
just set out and barely rooted.
When the LORD sends a wind,
they dry up and blow away like
straw.

25 To whom can the holy God be
compared?
Is there anyone else like him?
26 Look up at the sky!
Who created the stars you see?
The one who leads them out like
an army,
he knows how many there are
and calls each one by name!
His power is so great—
not one of them is ever missing!

27 Israel, why then do you complain
that the LORD doesn't know your
troubles
or care if you suffer injustice?
28 Don't you know? Haven't you
heard?
The LORD is the everlasting God;
he created all the world.
He never grows tired or weary.
No one understands his
thoughts.
29 He strengthens those who are
weak and tired.
30 Even those who are young grow
weak;
young people can fall exhausted.
31 But those who trust in the LORD for
help
will find their strength renewed.
They will rise on wings like
eagles;
they will run and not get weary;
they will walk and not grow
weak.

God's Assurance to Israel

41 God says,
"Be silent and listen to me,
you distant lands!
Get ready to present your case
in court;
you will have your chance to
speak.
Let us come together to decide
who is right.

2 "Who was it that brought the
conqueror from the east[j]
and makes him triumphant
wherever he goes?
Who gives him victory over kings
and nations?

[i] *Verses 19-20a in Hebrew are unclear.* [j] THE CONQUEROR FROM THE EAST: *Cyrus, the emperor of Persia (see 45.1).*

His sword strikes them down as
if they were dust.
His arrows scatter them like
straw before the wind.
3 He follows in pursuit and marches
safely on,
so fast that he hardly touches
the ground!
4 Who was it that made this
happen?
Who has determined the course
of history?
I, the LORD, was there at the
beginning,
and I, the LORD, will be there at
the end.

5 "The people of distant lands have
seen what I have done;
they are frightened and tremble
with fear.
So they all assemble and come.
6 The skilled workers help and
encourage each other.
7 The carpenter says to the
goldsmith, 'Well done!'
The one who beats the idol
smooth
encourages the one who nails it
together.
They say, 'The soldering is
good'—
and they fasten the idol in place
with nails.

8 "But you, Israel my servant,
you are the people that I have
chosen,
the descendants of Abraham, my
friend.
9 I brought you from the ends of the
earth;
I called you from its farthest
corners
and said to you, 'You are my
servant.'
I did not reject you, but chose you.
10 Do not be afraid—I am with you!
I am your God—let nothing
terrify you!
I will make you strong and
help you;
I will protect you and save you.

11 "Those who are angry with you
will know the shame of defeat.
Those who fight against you
will die
12 and will disappear from the
earth.
13 I am the LORD your God;
I strengthen you and tell you,
'Do not be afraid; I will
help you.' "

14 The LORD says,
"Small and weak as you are,
Israel,
don't be afraid; I will help you.
I, the holy God of Israel, am the
one who saves you.
15 I will make you like a threshing
board,
with spikes that are new and
sharp.
You will thresh mountains and
destroy them;
hills will crumble into dust.
16 You will toss them in the air;
the wind will carry them off,
and they will be scattered by the
storm.
Then you will be happy because I
am your God;
you will praise me, the holy God
of Israel.

17 "When my people in their need
look for water,
when their throats are dry with
thirst,
then I, the LORD, will answer their
prayer;
I, the God of Israel, will never
abandon them.
18 I will make rivers flow among
barren hills
and springs of water run in the
valleys.
I will turn the desert into pools of
water
and the dry land into flowing
springs.
19 I will make cedars grow in the
desert,
and acacias and myrtles and
olive trees.
Forests will grow in barren land,
forests of pine and juniper and
cypress.
20 People will see this and know
that I, the LORD, have done it.
They will come to understand
that Israel's holy God has made
it happen."

The Lord's Challenge to False Gods

21 The LORD, the king of Israel, has this to say:

"You gods of the nations, present
your case.
Bring the best arguments you
have!
22 Come here and predict what will
happen,
so that we will know it when it
takes place.
Explain to the court the events of
the past,
and tell us what they
mean.
23 Tell us what the future holds—
then we will know that you are
gods!
Do something good or bring some
disaster;
fill us with fear and awe!
24 You and all you do are
nothing;
those who worship you are
disgusting!

25 "I have chosen a man who lives in
the east;[k]
I will bring him to attack from
the north.
He tramples on rulers as if they
were mud,
like a potter trampling
clay.
26 Which of you predicted that this
would happen,
so that we could say that you
were right?
None of you said a word about it;
no one heard you say a
thing!
27 I, the LORD, was the first to tell
Zion the news;
I sent a messenger to Jerusalem
to say,
'Your people are coming! They
are coming home!'[l]
28 When I looked among the gods,
none of them had a thing to
say;
not one could answer the
questions I asked.
29 All these gods are useless;
they can do nothing at all—
these idols are weak and
powerless."

The Lord's Servant

42 The LORD says,
"Here is my servant, whom I
strengthen—
the one I have chosen, with
whom I am pleased.
I have filled him with my Spirit,
and he will bring justice to every
nation.
2 He will not shout or raise his voice
or make loud speeches in the
streets.
3 He will not break off a bent reed
nor put out a flickering lamp.
He will bring lasting justice to all.
4 He will not lose hope or courage;
he will establish justice on the
earth.
Distant lands eagerly wait for
his teaching."

5 God created the heavens and
stretched them out;
he fashioned the earth and all
that lives there;
he gave life and breath to all its
people.
And now the LORD God says to his
servant,
6 "I, the LORD, have called you and
given you power
to see that justice is done on
earth.
Through you I will make a
covenant with all peoples;
through you I will bring light to
the nations.
7 You will open the eyes of the blind
and set free those who sit in
dark prisons.

8 "I alone am the LORD your God.
No other god may share my
glory;
I will not let idols share my
praise.
9 The things I predicted have now
come true.
Now I will tell you of new things
even before they begin to
happen."

A Song of Praise

10 Sing a new song to the LORD;
sing his praise, all the world!
Praise him, you that sail the sea;

[k] A MAN WHO LIVES IN THE EAST: *See 41.2.* [l] *Verse 27 in Hebrew is unclear.*

praise him, all creatures of
the sea!
Sing, distant lands and all who
live there!
11 Let the desert and its towns
praise God;
let the people of Kedar
praise him!
Let those who live in the city of
Sela
shout for joy from the tops of
the mountains!
12 Let those who live in distant lands
give praise and glory to the
LORD!
13 The LORD goes out to fight like a
warrior;
he is ready and eager for battle.
He gives a war cry, a battle
shout;
he shows his power against his
enemies.

God Promises to Help His People

14 God says,
"For a long time I kept silent;
I did not answer my people.
But now the time to act has come;
I cry out like a woman in labor.
15 I will destroy the hills and
mountains
and dry up the grass and trees.
I will turn the river valleys into
deserts[m]
and dry up the pools of water.

16 "I will lead my blind people
by roads they have never
traveled.
I will turn their darkness into light
and make rough country smooth
before them.
These are my promises,
and I will keep them without
fail.
17 All who trust in idols,
who call images their gods,
will be humiliated and
disgraced."

Israel's Failure to Learn

18 The LORD says,
"Listen, you deaf people!
Look closely, you that are blind!
19 Is anyone more blind than my
servant,
more deaf than the messenger I
send?
20 Israel, you have seen so much,
but what has it meant to you?
You have ears to hear with,
but what have you really
heard?"

21 The LORD is a God who is eager to
save,
so he exalted his laws and
teachings,
and he wanted his people to
honor them.
22 But now his people have been
plundered;
they are locked up in dungeons
and hidden away in prisons.
They were robbed and plundered,
with no one to come to their
rescue.

23 Will any of you listen to this?
From now on will you listen
with care?
24 Who gave Israel up to the looters?
It was the LORD himself, against
whom we sinned!
We would not live as he wanted us
to live
or obey the teachings he
gave us.
25 So he made us feel the force of his
anger
and suffer the violence of war.
Like fire his anger burned
throughout Israel,
but we never knew what was
happening;
we learned nothing at all
from it.

God Promises to Rescue His People

43 Israel, the LORD who created you
says,
"Do not be afraid — I will
save you.
I have called you by name — you
are mine.
2 When you pass through deep
waters, I will be with you;
your troubles will not
overwhelm you.
When you pass through fire, you
will not be burned;

[m] *Probable text* deserts; *Hebrew* coastlands.

the hard trials that come will not
hurt you.
3 For I am the LORD your God,
the holy God of Israel, who
saves you.
I will give up Egypt to set you
free;
I will give up Ethiopia[n] and
Seba.
4 I will give up whole nations to
save your life,
because you are precious to me
and because I love you and give
you honor.
5 Do not be afraid – I am with you!

"From the distant east and the
farthest west
I will bring your people home.
6 I will tell the north to let them go
and the south not to hold them
back.
Let my people return from distant
lands,
from every part of the world.
7 They are my own people,
and I created them to bring me
glory."

Israel Is the LORD's Witness

8 God says,
"Summon my people to court.
They have eyes, but they are
blind;
they have ears, but they are
deaf!
9 Summon the nations to come to
the trial.
Which of their gods can predict
the future?
Which of them foretold what is
happening now?
Let these gods bring in their
witnesses
to prove that they are right,
to testify to the truth of their
words.

10 "People of Israel, you are my
witnesses;
I chose you to be my servant,
so that you would know me and
believe in me
and understand that I am the
only God.
Besides me there is no other god;
there never was and never
will be.

11 "I alone am the LORD,
the only one who can save you.
12 I predicted what would happen,
and then I came to your aid.
No foreign god has ever done this;
you are my witnesses.
13 I am God and always will be.
No one can escape from my
power;
no one can change what I do."

Escape from Babylon

14 Israel's holy God, the LORD who
saves you, says,
"To save you, I will send an army
against Babylon;
I will break down the city gates,
and the shouts of her people will
turn into crying.
15 I am the LORD, your holy God.
I created you, Israel, and I am
your king."

16 Long ago the LORD made a road
through the sea,
a path through the swirling
waters.
17 He led a mighty army to
destruction,
an army of chariots and horses.
Down they fell, never to rise,
snuffed out like the flame of a
lamp!

18 But the LORD says,
"Do not cling to events of the past
or dwell on what happened
long ago.
19 Watch for the new thing I am
going to do.
It is happening already – you
can see it now!
I will make a road through the
wilderness
and give you streams of water
there.
20 Even the wild animals will
honor me;
jackals and ostriches will
praise me

n Hebrew Cush: *Cush is the ancient name of the extensive territory south of the First Cataract of the Nile River. This region was called Ethiopia in Graeco-Roman times, and included within its borders most of modern Sudan and some of present-day Ethiopia (Abyssinia).*

when I make rivers flow in the desert
to give water to my chosen people.
21 They are the people I made for myself,
and they will sing my praises!"

Israel's Sin

22 The LORD says,
"But you were tired of me, Israel;
you did not worship me.
23 You did not bring me your burnt offerings of sheep;
you did not honor me with your sacrifices.
I did not burden you by demanding offerings
or wear you out by asking for incense.
24 You didn't buy incense for me
or satisfy me with the fat of your animals.
Instead you burdened me with your sins;
you wore me out with the wrongs you have committed.
25 And yet, I am the God who forgives your sins,
and I do this because of who I am.
I will not hold your sins against you.

26 "Let us go to court; bring your accusation!
Present your case to prove you are in the right!
27 Your earliest ancestor[o] sinned;
your leaders sinned against me,
28 and your rulers profaned[p] my sanctuary.
So I brought destruction on Israel;
I let my own people be insulted."

The LORD Is the Only God

44 The LORD says,
"Listen now, Israel, my servant,
my chosen people, the descendants of Jacob.
2 I am the LORD who created you;
from the time you were born, I have helped you.
Do not be afraid; you are my servant,
my chosen people whom I love.

3 "I will give water to the thirsty land
and make streams flow on the dry ground.
I will pour out my spirit on your children
and my blessing on your descendants.
4 They will thrive like well-watered grass,
like willows by streams of running water.

5 "One by one, people will say, 'I am the LORD's.'
They will come to join the people of Israel.
They each will mark the name of the LORD on their arms
and call themselves one of God's people."

6 The LORD, who rules and protects Israel,
the LORD Almighty, has this to say:
"I am the first, the last, the only God;
there is no other god but me.
7 Could anyone else have done what I did?
Who could have predicted all that would happen
from the very beginning to the end of time?[q]
8 Do not be afraid, my people!
You know that from ancient times until now
I have predicted all that would happen,
and you are my witnesses.
Is there any other god?
Is there some powerful god I never heard of?"

Idolatry Is Ridiculed

9 All those who make idols are worthless, and the gods they prize so highly
are useless. Those who worship these
gods are blind and ignorant—and they
will be disgraced. 10 It does no good to

[o] YOUR EARLIEST ANCESTOR: *A reference to Jacob or to Abraham, or possibly to Adam.*
[p] *One ancient translation* your rulers profaned; *Hebrew* I profaned the rulers of. [q] *Verse 7 in Hebrew is unclear.*

make a metal image to worship as a god!
11 Everyone who worships it will be humiliated. The people who make idols are
human beings and nothing more. Let
them come and stand trial—they will be
terrified and will suffer disgrace.
12 The metalworker takes a piece of
metal and works with it over a fire. His
strong arm swings a hammer to pound
the metal into shape. As he works, he
gets hungry, thirsty, and tired.
13 The carpenter measures the wood.
He outlines a figure with chalk, carves it
out with his tools, and makes it in the
form of a man, a handsome human figure, to be placed in his house. 14 He
might cut down cedars to use, or choose
oak or cypress wood from the forest. Or
he might plant a laurel tree and wait for
the rain to make it grow. 15 A person
uses part of a tree for fuel and part of it
for making an idol. With one part he
builds a fire to warm himself and bake
bread; with the other part he makes a
god and worships it. 16 With some of the
wood he makes a fire; he roasts meat,
eats it, and is satisfied. He warms himself and says, "How nice and warm!
What a beautiful fire!" 17 The rest of the
wood he makes into an idol, and then he
bows down and worships it. He prays
to it and says, "You are my god—
save me!"
18 Such people are too stupid to know
what they are doing. They close their
eyes and their minds to the truth. 19 The
maker of idols hasn't the wit or the sense
to say, "Some of the wood I burned up. I
baked some bread on the coals, and I
roasted meat and ate it. And the rest of
the wood I made into an idol. Here I am
bowing down to a block of wood!"
20 It makes as much sense[r] as eating
ashes. His foolish ideas have so misled
him that he is beyond help. He won't admit to himself that the idol he holds in
his hand is not a god at all.

The Lord, the Creator and Savior

21 The Lord says,
"Israel, remember this;
remember that you are my
servant.
I created you to be my servant,
and I will never forget you.
22 I have swept your sins away like a
cloud.
Come back to me; I am the one
who saves you."
23 Shout for joy, you heavens!
Shout, deep places of the earth!
Shout for joy, mountains, and
every tree of the forest!
The Lord has shown his greatness
by saving his people Israel.

24 "I am the Lord, your savior;
I am the one who created you.
I am the Lord, the Creator of all
things.
I alone stretched out the
heavens;
when I made the earth, no one
helped me.
25 I make fools of fortunetellers
and frustrate the predictions of
astrologers.
The words of the wise I refute
and show that their wisdom is
foolishness.
26 But when my servant makes a
prediction,
when I send a messenger to
reveal my plans,
I make those plans and
predictions come true.
I tell Jerusalem that people will
live there again,
and the cities of Judah that they
will be rebuilt.
Those cities will rise from the
ruins.
27 With a word of command I dry up
the ocean.
28 I say to Cyrus, 'You are the one
who will rule for me;
you will do what I want you
to do:
you will order that Jerusalem be
rebuilt
and that the foundations of the
Temple be laid.'"

The Lord Appoints Cyrus

45 The Lord has chosen Cyrus to
be king.
He has appointed him to conquer
nations;
he sends him to strip kings of
their power;

[r] It makes as much sense; *or* It will do him as much good.

the LORD will open the gates of
cities for him.
To Cyrus the LORD says,
2 "I myself will prepare your way,
leveling mountains and hills.
I will break down bronze gates
and smash their iron bars.
3 I will give you treasures from
dark, secret places;
then you will know that I am the
LORD
and that the God of Israel has
called you by name.
4 I appoint you to help my servant
Israel,
the people that I have chosen.
I have given you great honor,
although you do not know me.

5 "I am the LORD; there is no
other god.
I will give you the strength you
need,
although you do not know me.
6 I do this so that everyone
from one end of the world to the
other
may know that I am the LORD
and that there is no other god.
7 I create both light and darkness;
I bring both blessing and
disaster.
I, the LORD, do all these things.
8 I will send victory from the sky
like rain;
the earth will open to receive it
and will blossom with freedom
and justice.
I, the LORD, will make this
happen."

The LORD of Creation and History

9 Does a clay pot dare argue with its
maker,
a pot that is like all the others?
Does the clay ask the potter what
he is doing?
Does the pot complain that its
maker has no skill?
10 Do we dare say to our parents,
"Why did you make me like
this?"
11 The LORD, the holy God of Israel,
the one who shapes the future,
says:
"You have no right to question me
about my children
or to tell me what I ought to do!
12 I am the one who made the earth
and created human beings to
live there.
By my power I stretched out the
heavens;
I control the sun, the moon, and
the stars.
13 I myself have stirred Cyrus to
action
to fulfill my purpose and put
things right.
I will straighten out every road
that he travels.
He will rebuild my city,
Jerusalem,
and set my captive people free.
No one has hired him or bribed
him to do this."
The LORD Almighty has spoken.

14 The LORD says to Israel,
"The wealth of Egypt and
Ethiopia[s] will be yours,
and the tall men of Seba will be
your slaves;
they will follow you in chains.
They will bow down to you and
confess,
'God is with you – he alone
is God.
15 The God of Israel, who saves his
people,
is a God who conceals himself.
16 Those who make idols will all be
ashamed;
all of them will be disgraced.
17 But Israel is saved by the LORD,
and her victory lasts forever;
her people will never be
disgraced.' "

18 The LORD created the heavens –
he is the one who is God!
He formed and made the earth –
he made it firm and lasting.
He did not make it a desolate
waste,
but a place for people to live.
It is he who says, "I am the LORD,
and there is no other god.
19 I have not spoken in secret
or kept my purpose hidden.

[s] *Hebrew* Cush: *Cush is the ancient name of the extensive territory south of the First Cataract of the Nile River. This region was called Ethiopia in Graeco-Roman times, and included within its borders most of modern Sudan and some of present-day Ethiopia (Abyssinia).*

I did not require the people of
Israel
to look for me in a desolate
waste.
I am the LORD, and I speak the
truth;
I make known what is right."

The LORD of the World and the Idols of Babylon

20 The LORD says,
"Come together, people of the
nations,
all who survive the fall of the
empire;
present yourselves for the trial!
The people who parade with their
idols of wood
and pray to gods that cannot
save them—
those people know nothing
at all!
21 Come and present your case in
court;
let the defendants consult one
another.
Who predicted long ago what
would happen?
Was it not I, the LORD, the God
who saves his people?
There is no other god.

22 "Turn to me now and be saved,
people all over the world!
I am the only God there is.
23 My promise is true,
and it will not be changed.
I solemnly promise by all that
I am:
Everyone will come and kneel
before me
and vow to be loyal to me.

24 "They will say that only
through me
are victory and strength to be
found;
but all who hate me will suffer
disgrace.
25 I, the LORD, will rescue all the
descendants of Jacob,
and they will give me praise.

46 "This is the end for Babylon's
gods!
Bel and Nebo once were
worshiped,
but now they are loaded on
donkeys,
a burden for the backs of tired
animals.
2 The idols cannot save
themselves;
they are captured and carried
away.
This is the end for Babylon's gods!

3 "Listen to me, descendants of
Jacob,
all who are left of my people.
I have cared for you from the time
you were born.
4 I am your God and will take care
of you
until you are old and your hair
is gray.
I made you and will care for you;
I will give you help and
rescue you.

5 "To whom will you compare me?"
says the LORD.
"Is there anyone else like me?
6 People open their purses and pour
out gold;
they weigh out silver on the
scales.
They hire a goldsmith to make
a god;
then they bow down and
worship it.
7 They lift it to their shoulders and
carry it;
they put it in place, and there it
stands,
unable to move from where it is.
If any pray to it, it cannot answer
or save them from disaster.

8 "Remember this, you sinners;
consider what I have done.
9 Remember what happened
long ago;
acknowledge that I alone
am God
and that there is no one else
like me.
10 From the beginning I predicted the
outcome;
long ago I foretold what would
happen.
I said that my plans would never
fail,
that I would do everything I
intended to do.

11 I am calling a man to come from
the east;[t]
he will swoop down like a hawk
and accomplish what I have
planned.
I have spoken, and it will be done.

12 "Listen to me, you stubborn people
who think that victory is far
away.
13 I am bringing the day of victory
near—
it is not far away at all.
My triumph will not be delayed.
I will save Jerusalem
and bring honor to Israel there."

Judgment on Babylon

47 The LORD says,
"Babylon, come down from
your throne,
and sit in the dust on the
ground.
You were once like a virgin, a city
unconquered,
but you are soft and delicate no
longer!
You are now a slave!
2 Turn the millstone! Grind the
flour!
Off with your veil! Strip off your
fine clothes!
Lift up your skirts to cross the
streams![u]
3 People will see you naked;
they will see you humbled and
shamed.
I will take vengeance, and no one
will stop me."

4 The holy God of Israel sets us
free—
his name is the LORD Almighty.

5 The LORD says to Babylon,
"Sit in silence and darkness;
no more will they call you the
queen of nations!
6 I was angry with my people;
I treated them as no longer
mine:
I put them in your power,
and you showed them no mercy;
even the aged you treated
harshly.
7 You thought you would always be
a queen,
and did not take these things to
heart
or think how it all would end.

8 "Listen to this, you lover of
pleasure,
you that think you are safe and
secure.
You claim you are as great
as God—
that there is no one else
like you.
You thought that you would never
be a widow
or suffer the loss of your
children.
9 But in a moment, in a single day,
both of these things will happen.
In spite of all the magic you use,
you will lose your husband and
children.

10 "You felt sure of yourself in your
evil;
you thought that no one could
see you.
Your wisdom and knowledge led
you astray,
and you said to yourself, 'I
am God—
there is no one else like me.'
11 Disaster will come upon you,
and none of your magic can
stop it.
Ruin will come on you suddenly—
ruin you never dreamed of!
12 Keep all your magic spells and
charms;
you have used them since you
were young.
Perhaps they will be of some help
to you;
perhaps you can frighten your
enemies.
13 You are powerless in spite of the
advice you get.
Let your astrologers come forward
and save you—
those people who study the
stars,
who map out the zones of the
heavens

[t] A MAN TO COME FROM THE EAST: *See 41.2.*
[u] CROSS THE STREAMS: *This probably refers to going into exile.*

and tell you from month to
month
what[v] is going to happen
to you.
14 "They will be like bits of straw,
and a fire will burn them up!
They will not even be able to save
themselves—
the flames will be too hot for
them,
not a cozy fire to warm
themselves by.
15 That is all the good they will
do you—
those astrologers you've
consulted all your life.
They all will leave you and go
their own way,
and none will be left to
save you."

God Is Lord of the Future

48 Listen to this, people of Israel,
you that are descended from
Judah:
You swear by the name of the
Lord
and claim to worship the God of
Israel—
but you don't mean a word
you say.
2 And yet you are proud to say
that you are citizens of the holy
city
and that you depend on
Israel's God,
whose name is the Lord
Almighty.

3 The Lord says to Israel,
"Long ago I predicted what would
take place;
then suddenly I made it happen.
4 I knew that you would prove to be
stubborn,
as rigid as iron and unyielding
as bronze.
5 And so I predicted your future
long ago,
announcing events before they
took place,
to keep you from claiming
that your idols and images made
them happen.
6 "All I foretold has now taken
place;
you have to admit my
predictions were right.
Now I will tell you of new things
to come,
events that I did not reveal
before.
7 Only now am I making them
happen;
nothing like this took place in
the past.
If it had, you would claim that you
knew all about it.
8 I knew that you couldn't be
trusted,
that you have always been
known as a rebel.
That is why you never heard of
this at all,
why no word of it ever came to
your ears.

9 "In order that people will praise
my name,
I am holding my anger in check;
I am keeping it back and will
not destroy you.
10 I have tested you in the fire of
suffering,
as silver is refined in a furnace.
But I have found that you are
worthless.
11 What I do is done for my own
sake—
I will not let my name be
dishonored
or let anyone else share the
glory
that should be mine and mine
alone."

Cyrus, the Lord's Chosen Leader

12 The Lord says,
"Listen to me, Israel, the people I
have called!
I am God, the first, the last, the
only God!
13 My hands made the earth's
foundations
and spread the heavens out.
When I summon earth and sky,
they come at once and present
themselves.

14 "Assemble and listen, all of you!

v *Some ancient translations* what; *Hebrew* from what.

None of the gods could predict
that the man I have chosen
would attack Babylon;
he will do what I want him
to do.
15 I am the one who spoke and
called him;
I led him out and gave him
success.

16 "Now come close to me and hear
what I say.
From the beginning I have
spoken openly
and have always made my
words come true."
(Now the Sovereign LORD has given me
his power and sent me.)

The LORD's Plan for His People

17 The holy God of Israel,
the LORD who saves you, says:
"I am the LORD your God,
the one who wants to teach you
for your own good
and direct you in the way you
should go.

18 "If only you had listened to my
commands!
Then blessings would have flowed
for you
like a stream that never
goes dry.
Victory would have come to you
like the waves that roll on the
shore.
19 Your descendants would be as
numerous as grains of sand,
and I would have made sure
they were never destroyed."
20 Go out from Babylon, go free!
Shout the news gladly; make it
known everywhere:
"The LORD has saved his servant
Israel!"
21 When the LORD led his people
through a hot, dry desert,
they did not suffer from thirst.
He made water come from a rock
for them;
he split the rock open, and water
flowed out.
22 "There is no safety for sinners,"
says the LORD.

Israel, A Light to the Nations

49 Listen to me, distant nations,
you people who live far
away!
Before I was born, the LORD
chose me
and appointed me to be his
servant.
2 He made my words as sharp as a
sword.
With his own hand he
protected me.[w]
He made me like an arrow,
sharp and ready for use.
3 He said to me, "Israel, you are my
servant;
because of you, people will
praise me."

4 I said, "I have worked, but how
hopeless it is!
I have used up my strength, but
have accomplished nothing."
Yet I can trust the LORD to defend
my cause;
he will reward me for what I do.

5 Before I was born, the LORD
appointed me;
he made me his servant to bring
back his people,
to bring back the scattered
people of Israel.
The LORD gives me honor;
he is the source of my strength.

6 The LORD said to me,
"I have a greater task for you, my
servant.
Not only will you restore to
greatness
the people of Israel who have
survived,
but I will also make you a light to
the nations—
so that all the world may be
saved."

7 Israel's holy God and savior says
to the one who is deeply
despised,
who is hated by the nations
and is the servant of rulers:

[w] With his own hand . . . me; *or* He kept me hidden in his hand.

"Kings will see you released
and will rise to show their
respect;
princes also will see it,
and they will bow low to
honor you."

This will happen because the LORD
has chosen his servant;
the holy God of Israel keeps his
promises.

The Restoration of Jerusalem

8 The LORD says to his people,
"When the time comes to save
you, I will show you favor
and answer your cries for help.
I will guard and protect you
and through you make a
covenant with all peoples.
I will let you settle once again
in your land that is now laid
waste.
9 I will say to the prisoners, 'Go
free!'
and to those who are in
darkness,
'Come out to the light!'
They will be like sheep that graze
on the hills;
10 they will never be hungry or
thirsty.
Sun and desert heat will not hurt
them,
for they will be led by one who
loves them.
He will lead them to springs of
water.

11 "I will make a highway across the
mountains
and prepare a road for my
people to travel.
12 My people will come from far
away,
from the north and the west,
and from Aswan[x] in the south."

13 Sing, heavens! Shout for joy,
earth!
Let the mountains burst into
song!
The LORD will comfort his people;
he will have pity on his suffering
people.

14 But the people of Jerusalem said,
"The LORD has abandoned us!
He has forgotten us."
15 So the LORD answers,
"Can a woman forget her own
baby
and not love the child she bore?
Even if a mother should forget her
child,
I will never forget you.
16 Jerusalem, I can never forget you!
I have written your name on the
palms of my hands.

17 "Those who will rebuild you are
coming soon,
and those who destroyed you
will leave.
18 Look around and see what is
happening!
Your people are assembling —
they are coming home!
As surely as I am the living God,
you will be proud of your
people,
as proud as a bride is of her
jewels.

19 "Your country was ruined and
desolate —
but now it will be too small
for those who are coming to live
there.
And those who left you in ruins
will be far removed from you.
20 Your people who were born in
exile
will one day say to you,
'This land is too small —
we need more room to live in!'
21 Then you will say to yourself,
'Who bore all these children
for me?
I lost my children and could have
no more.
I was exiled and driven away —
who brought these children up?
I was left all alone —
where did these children come
from?' "

22 The Sovereign LORD says to his
people:
"I will signal to the nations,
and they will bring your
children home.

[x] ASWAN: *A city in southern Egypt, where a large Jewish community had settled.*

[23]Kings will be like fathers to you;
queens will be like mothers.
They will bow low before you and honor you;
they will humbly show their respect for you.
Then you will know that I am the LORD;
no one who waits for my help will be disappointed."

[24]Can you take away a soldier's loot?
Can you rescue the prisoners of a tyrant?

[25]The LORD replies,
"That is just what is going to happen.
The soldier's prisoners will be taken away,
and the tyrant's loot will be seized.
I will fight against whoever fights you,
and I will rescue your children.
[26]I will make your oppressors kill each other;
they will be drunk with murder and rage.
Then all people will know that I am the LORD,
the one who saves you and sets you free.
They will know that I am Israel's powerful God."

50 The LORD says,
"Do you think I sent my people away
like a man who divorces his wife?
Where, then, are the papers of divorce?
Do you think I sold you into captivity
like a man who sells his children as slaves?
No, you went away captive because of your sins;
you were sent away because of your crimes.

[2]"Why did my people fail to respond
when I went to them to save them?
Why did they not answer when I called?
Am I too weak to save them?
I can dry up the sea with a command
and turn rivers into a desert,
so that the fish in them die for lack of water.
[3]I can make the sky turn dark,
as if it were in mourning for the dead."

The Obedience of the LORD's Servant

[4]The Sovereign LORD has taught me what to say,
so that I can strengthen the weary.
Every morning he makes me eager to hear what he is going to teach me.
[5]The LORD has given me understanding,
and I have not rebelled
or turned away from him.
[6]I bared my back to those who beat me.
I did not stop them when they insulted me,
when they pulled out the hairs of my beard
and spit in my face.

[7]But their insults cannot hurt me
because the Sovereign LORD gives me help.
I brace myself to endure them.
I know that I will not be disgraced,
[8]for God is near,
and he will prove me innocent.
Does anyone dare bring charges against me?
Let us go to court together!
Let him bring his accusation!
[9]The Sovereign LORD himself defends me—
who, then, can prove me guilty?
All my accusers will disappear;
they will vanish like moth-eaten cloth.

[10]All of you that honor the LORD
and obey the words of his servant,
the path you walk may be dark indeed,
but trust in the LORD, rely on your God.

11 All of you that plot to destroy
others
will be destroyed by your own
plots.
The LORD himself will make this
happen;
you will suffer a miserable fate.

Words of Comfort to Jerusalem

51 The LORD says,
"Listen to me, you that want
to be saved,
you that come to me for help.
Think of the rock from which you
came,
the quarry from which you
were cut.
2 Think of your ancestor, Abraham,
and of Sarah, from whom you
are descended.
When I called Abraham, he was
childless,
but I blessed him and gave him
children;
I made his descendants
numerous.

3 "I will show compassion to
Jerusalem,
to all who live in her ruins.
Though her land is a desert, I will
make it a garden,
like the garden I planted in
Eden.
Joy and gladness will be there,
and songs of praise and thanks
to me.

4 "Listen to me, my people,
listen to what I say:
I give my teaching to the nations;
my laws will bring them light.
5 I will come quickly and save them;
the time of my victory is near.
I myself will rule over the nations.
Distant lands wait for me to
come;
they wait with hope for me to
save them.
6 Look up at the heavens; look at
the earth!
The heavens will disappear like
smoke;
the earth will wear out like old
clothing,
and all its people will die like
flies.
But the deliverance I bring will
last forever;
my victory will be final.

7 "Listen to me, you that know what
is right,
who have my teaching fixed in
your hearts.
Do not be afraid when people
taunt and insult you;
8 they will vanish like moth-eaten
clothing!
But the deliverance I bring will
last forever;
my victory will endure for all
time."

9 Wake up, LORD, and help us!
Use your power and save us;
use it as you did in ancient
times.
It was you that cut the sea
monster Rahab[y] to pieces.
10 It was you also who dried up
the sea
and made a path through the
water,
so that those you were saving
could cross.
11 Those whom you have rescued
will reach Jerusalem with
gladness,
singing and shouting for joy.
They will be happy forever,
forever free from sorrow and
grief.

12 The LORD says,
"I am the one who
strengthens you.
Why should you fear mortals,
who are no more enduring than
grass?
13 Have you forgotten the LORD who
made you,
who stretched out the heavens
and laid the earth's foundations?
Why should you live in constant
fear
of the fury of those who
oppress you,
of those who are ready to
destroy you?

[y] RAHAB: *A legendary sea monster, which represented the forces of chaos and evil, was sometimes a symbol of Egypt.*

Their fury can no longer
touch you.
14 Those who are prisoners will soon
be set free;
they will live a long life
and have all the food they need.

15 "I am the LORD your God;
I stir up the sea
and make its waves roar.
My name is the LORD Almighty!
16 I stretched out[z] the heavens
and laid the earth's foundations;
I say to Jerusalem, 'You are my
people!
I have given you my teaching,
and I protect you with my
hand.' "

The End of Jerusalem's Suffering

17 Jerusalem, wake up!
Rouse yourself and get up!
You have drunk the cup of
punishment
that the LORD in his anger gave
you to drink;
you drank it down, and it made
you stagger.
18 There is no one to lead you,
no one among your people
to take you by the hand.

19 A double disaster has fallen
on you:
your land has been devastated
by war,
and your people have starved.
There is no one to show you
sympathy.
20 At the corner of every street
your people collapse from
weakness;
they are like deer caught in a
hunter's net.
They have felt the force of God's
anger.

21 You suffering people of Jerusalem,
you that stagger as though you
were drunk,
22 the LORD your God defends you
and says,
"I am taking away the cup
that I gave you in my anger.
You will no longer have to drink
the wine that makes you
stagger.
23 I will give it to those who
oppressed you,
to those who made you lie down
in the streets
and trampled on you as if you
were dirt."

God Will Rescue Jerusalem

52 Jerusalem, be strong and great
again!
Holy city of God, clothe yourself
with splendor!
The heathen will never enter your
gates again.
2 Shake yourself free, Jerusalem!
Rise from the dust and sit on
your throne!
Undo the chains that bind you,
captive people of Zion!

3 The Sovereign LORD says to his people, "When you became slaves, no
money was paid for you; in the same
way nothing will be paid to set you free.
4 When you went to live in Egypt as foreigners, you did so of your own free will;
Assyria, however, took you away by
force and paid nothing for you. 5 And
now in Babylonia the same thing has
happened: you are captives, and nothing
was paid for you. Those who rule over
you boast and brag and constantly show
contempt for me. 6 In time to come you
will acknowledge that I am God and that
I have spoken to you."

7 How wonderful it is to see
a messenger coming across the
mountains,
bringing good news, the news of
peace!
He announces victory and says to
Zion,
"Your God is king!"
8 Those who guard the city are
shouting,
shouting together for joy.
They can see with their own eyes
the return of the LORD to Zion.

9 Break into shouts of joy,
you ruins of Jerusalem!
The LORD will rescue his city
and comfort his people.

[z] *One ancient translation* stretched out; *Hebrew* planted.

10 The LORD will use his holy power;
he will save his people,
and all the world will see it.
11 Be sure to leave Babylonia,
all you that carry the Temple
equipment.
Touch no forbidden thing;[a]
keep yourselves holy and leave.
12 This time you will not have to
leave in a hurry;
you will not be trying to escape.
The LORD your God will lead you
and protect you on every side.

The Suffering Servant

13 The LORD says,
"My servant will succeed in his
task;
he will be highly honored.[b]
14 Many people were shocked when
they saw him;
he was so disfigured that he
hardly looked human.
15 But now many nations will marvel
at him,
and kings will be speechless
with amazement.
They will see and understand
something they had never
known."

53 The people reply,
"Who would have believed
what we now report?
Who could have seen the LORD's
hand in this?
2 It was the will of the LORD that his
servant
grow like a plant taking root in
dry ground.
He had no dignity or beauty
to make us take notice of him.
There was nothing attractive
about him,
nothing that would draw us
to him.
3 We despised him and
rejected him;
he endured suffering and pain.
No one would even look at him —
we ignored him as if he were
nothing.

4 "But he endured the suffering that
should have been ours,
the pain that we should have
borne.
All the while we thought that his
suffering
was punishment sent by God.
5 But because of our sins he was
wounded,
beaten because of the evil
we did.
We are healed by the punishment
he suffered,
made whole by the blows he
received.
6 All of us were like sheep that were
lost,
each of us going his own way.
But the LORD made the punishment
fall on him,
the punishment all of us
deserved.

7 "He was treated harshly, but
endured it humbly;
he never said a word.
Like a lamb about to be
slaughtered,
like a sheep about to be sheared,
he never said a word.
8 He was arrested and sentenced
and led off to die,
and no one cared about his fate.
He was put to death for the sins of
our people.
9 He was placed in a grave with
those who are evil,
he was buried with the rich,
even though he had never
committed a crime
or ever told a lie."

10 The LORD says,
"It was my will that he should
suffer;
his death was a sacrifice to
bring forgiveness.
And so he will see his
descendants;
he will live a long life,
and through him my purpose
will succeed.
11 After a life of suffering, he will
again have joy;
he will know that he did not
suffer in vain.

[a] FORBIDDEN THING: *Any object that was considered ritually unclean.* [b] he will be highly honored; *or* he will be restored to greatness and honor.

My devoted servant, with whom I
am pleased,
will bear the punishment of
many
and for his sake I will forgive
them.
12 And so I will give him a place of
honor,
a place among the great and
powerful.
He willingly gave his life
and shared the fate of evil men.
He took the place of many sinners
and prayed that they might be
forgiven."[c]

The Lord's Love for Israel

54 Jerusalem, you have been like a
childless woman,
but now you can sing and shout
for joy.
Now you will have more children
than a woman whose husband
never left her.
2 Make the tent you live in larger;
lengthen its ropes and
strengthen the pegs!
3 You will extend your boundaries
on all sides;
your people will get back the
land
that the other nations now
occupy.
Cities now deserted will be filled
with people.
4 Do not be afraid—you will not be
disgraced again;
you will not be humiliated.
You will forget your unfaithfulness
as a young wife,
and your desperate loneliness as
a widow.
5 Your Creator will be like a
husband to you—
the Lord Almighty is his name.
The holy God of Israel will
save you—
he is the ruler of all the world.
6 Israel, you are like a young wife,
deserted by her husband and
deeply distressed.
But the Lord calls you back to him
and says:
7 "For one brief moment I left you;
with deep love I will take you
back.
8 I turned away angry for only a
moment,
but I will show you my love
forever."
So says the Lord who saves you.

9 "In the time of Noah I promised
never again to flood the earth.
Now I promise not to be angry
with you again;
I will not reprimand or
punish you.
10 The mountains and hills may
crumble,
but my love for you will
never end;
I will keep forever my promise
of peace."
So says the Lord who loves you.

The Future Jerusalem

11 The Lord says,
"O Jerusalem, you suffering,
helpless city,
with no one to comfort you,
I will rebuild your foundations
with precious stones.
12 I will build your towers with
rubies,
your gates with stones that glow
like fire,
and the wall around you with
jewels.

13 "I myself will teach your people
and give them prosperity and
peace.
14 Justice and right will make you
strong.
You will be safe from
oppression and terror.
15 Whoever attacks you,
does it without my consent;
whoever fights against you will
fall.

16 "I create the blacksmith,
who builds a fire and forges
weapons.
I also create the soldier,
who uses the weapons to kill.
17 But no weapon will be able to
hurt you;

[c] prayed that they might be forgiven; *or* suffered the punishment they deserved.

you will have an answer for all
who accuse you.
I will defend my servants
and give them victory."

The LORD has spoken.

God's Offer of Mercy

55 The LORD says,
"Come, everyone who is
thirsty—
here is water!
Come, you that have no money—
buy grain and eat!
Come! Buy wine and milk—
it will cost you nothing!
2 Why spend money on what does
not satisfy?
Why spend your wages and still
be hungry?
Listen to me and do what I say,
and you will enjoy the best food
of all.

3 "Listen now, my people, and come
to me;
come to me, and you will have
life!
I will make a lasting covenant
with you
and give you the blessings I
promised to David.
4 I made him a leader and
commander of nations,
and through him I showed them
my power.
5 Now you will summon foreign
nations;
at one time they did not
know you,
but now they will come running
to join you!
I, the LORD your God, the holy God
of Israel,
will make all this happen;
I will give you honor and glory."

6 Turn to the LORD and pray to him,
now that he is near.
7 Let the wicked leave their way of
life
and change their way of
thinking.
Let them turn to the LORD,
our God;
he is merciful and quick to
forgive.

8 "My thoughts," says the LORD, "are
not like yours,
and my ways are different from
yours.
9 As high as the heavens are above
the earth,
so high are my ways and
thoughts above yours.

10 "My word is like the snow and the
rain
that come down from the sky to
water the earth.
They make the crops grow
and provide seed for planting
and food to eat.
11 So also will be the word that I
speak—
it will not fail to do what I plan
for it;
it will do everything I send it
to do.

12 "You will leave Babylon with
joy;
you will be led out of the city in
peace.
The mountains and hills will burst
into singing,
and the trees will shout for
joy.
13 Cypress trees will grow where
now there are briers;
myrtle trees will come up in
place of thorns.
This will be a sign that will last
forever,
a reminder of what I, the LORD,
have done."

God's People Will Include All Nations

56 The LORD says to his people, "Do
what is just and right, for soon I
will save you. 2 I will bless those who always observe the Sabbath and do not
misuse it. I will bless those who do nothing evil."
3 A foreigner who has joined the
LORD's people should not say, "The LORD
will not let me worship with his people."
A man who has been castrated should
never think that because he cannot have
children, he can never be part of God's
people. 4 The LORD says to such a man, "If
you honor me by observing the Sabbath
and if you do what pleases me and faith-

fully keep my covenant, 5 then your
name will be remembered in my Temple
and among my people longer than if you
had sons and daughters. You will never
be forgotten."
6 And the LORD says to those foreigners
who become part of his people, who love
him and serve him, who observe the
Sabbath and faithfully keep his covenant: 7 "I will bring you to Zion, my sacred hill,[d] give you joy in my house of
prayer, and accept the sacrifices you offer on my altar. My Temple will be called
a house of prayer for the people of all
nations."
8 The Sovereign LORD, who has
brought his people Israel home from exile, has promised that he will bring still
other people to join them.

Israel's Leaders Are Condemned

9 The LORD has told the foreign nations
to come like wild animals and devour his
people. 10 He says, "All the leaders, who
are supposed to warn my people, are
blind! They know nothing. They are like
watch dogs that don't bark—they only
lie around and dream. How they love to
sleep! 11 They are like greedy dogs that
never get enough. These leaders have no
understanding. They each do as they
please and seek their own advantage.
12 'Let's get some wine,' these drunkards
say, 'and drink all we can hold! Tomorrow will be even better than today!' "

Israel's Idolatry Is Condemned

57 Good people die, and no one
understands or even cares. But
when they die, no calamity can hurt
them. 2 Those who live good lives find
peace and rest in death.
3 Come here to be judged, you sinners!
You are no better than sorcerers, adulterers, and prostitutes. 4 Who are you
making fun of? Who are you liars jeer-
ing at? 5 You worship the fertility gods
by having sex under those sacred trees
of yours. You offer your children as sacrifices in the rocky caves near stream
beds. 6 You take smooth stones from
there and worship them as gods. You
pour out wine as offerings to them and
bring them grain offerings. Do you think
I am pleased with all this? 7 You go to the
high mountains to offer sacrifices and
have sex. 8 You set up your obscene idols
just inside your front doors. You forsake
me; you take off your clothes and climb
in your large beds with your lovers,
whom you pay to sleep with you. And
there you satisfy your lust. 9 You put on
your perfumes and ointments and go to
worship the god Molech. To find gods to
worship, you send messengers far and
wide, even to the world of the dead.
10 You wear yourselves out looking
for other gods, but you never give up.
You think your obscene idols give
you strength, and so you never grow
weak.
11 The LORD says, "Who are these gods
that make you afraid, so that you tell me
lies and forget me completely? Have you
stopped honoring me because I have
kept silent for so long? 12 You think that
what you do is right, but I will expose
your conduct, and your idols will not be
able to help you. 13 When you cry for
help, let those idols of yours save you! A
puff of wind will carry them off! But
those who trust in me will live in the
land and will worship me in my
Temple."

God's Promise of Help and Healing

14 The LORD says, "Let my people return to me. Remove every obstacle from
their path! Build the road and make it
ready!
15 "I am the high and holy God, who
lives forever. I live in a high and holy
place, but I also live with people who are
humble and repentant, so that I can restore their confidence and hope.
16 I gave my people life, and I will not
continue to accuse them or be angry
with them forever.[e] 17 I was angry with
them because of their sin and greed, and
so I punished them and abandoned
them. But they were stubborn and kept
on going their own way.
18 "I have seen how they acted, but I
will heal them. I will lead them and help
them, and I will comfort those who
mourn. 19 I offer peace to all, both near
and far! I will heal my people. 20 But evil
people are like the restless sea, whose
waves never stop rolling in, bringing
filth and muck. 21 There is no safety for
sinners," says the LORD.

[d] SACRED HILL: *See* 2.3. [e] I gave my people . . . forever; *or* I will not continue to accuse them or be angry with them forever, for then they would die—the very people to whom I gave life.

True Fasting

58 The Lord says, "Shout as loud as
you can! Tell my people Israel
about their sins! 2They worship me
every day, claiming that they are eager
to know my ways and obey my laws.
They say they want me to give them just
laws and that they take pleasure in worshiping me."
3The people ask, "Why should we fast
if the Lord never notices? Why should
we go without food if he pays no attention?"
The Lord says to them, "The truth is
that at the same time you fast, you pursue your own interests and oppress your
workers. 4Your fasting makes you violent, and you quarrel and fight. Do you
think this kind of fasting will make me
listen to your prayers? 5When you fast,
you make yourselves suffer; you bow
your heads low like a blade of grass and
spread out sackcloth and ashes to lie on.
Is that what you call fasting? Do you
think I will be pleased with that?
6"The kind of fasting I want is this:
Remove the chains of oppression and
the yoke of injustice, and let the oppressed go free. 7Share your food with
the hungry and open your homes to the
homeless poor. Give clothes to those
who have nothing to wear, and do not
refuse to help your own relatives.
8"Then my favor will shine on you like
the morning sun, and your wounds will
be quickly healed. I will always be with
you to save you; my presence will protect you on every side. 9When you pray,
I will answer you. When you call to me,
I will respond.
"If you put an end to oppression, to
every gesture of contempt, and to every
evil word; 10if you give food to the hungry and satisfy those who are in need,
then the darkness around you will turn
to the brightness of noon. 11And I will
always guide you and satisfy you with
good things. I will keep you strong and
well. You will be like a garden that has
plenty of water, like a spring of water
that never goes dry. 12Your people will
rebuild what has long been in ruins,
building again on the old foundations.
You will be known as the people who
rebuilt the walls, who restored the ruined houses."

The Reward for Keeping the Sabbath

13The Lord says, "If you treat the Sabbath as sacred and do not pursue your
own interests on that day; if you value
my holy day and honor it by not traveling, working, or talking idly on that day,
14then you will find the joy that comes
from serving me. I will make you honored all over the world, and you will enjoy the land I gave to your ancestor,
Jacob. I, the Lord, have spoken."

The Prophet Condemns the People's Sins

59 Don't think that the Lord is too
weak to save you or too deaf to
hear your call for help! 2It is because of
your sins that he doesn't hear you. It is
your sins that separate you from God
when you try to worship him. 3You are
guilty of lying, violence, and murder.
4You go to court, but you do not have
justice on your side. You depend on lies
to win your case. You carry out your
plans to hurt others. 5-6The evil plots you
make are as deadly as the eggs of a poisonous snake. Crush an egg, out comes a
snake! But your plots will do you no
good—they are as useless as clothing
made of cobwebs! 7You are always
planning something evil, and you can
hardly wait to do it. You never hesitate
to murder innocent people. You leave
ruin and destruction wherever you go,
8and no one is safe when you are
around. Everything you do is unjust.
You follow a crooked path, and no one
who walks that path will ever be safe.

The People Confess Their Sin

9The people say, "Now we know why
God does not save us from those who
oppress us. We hope for light to walk by,
but there is only darkness, 10and we
grope about like blind people. We stumble at noon, as if it were night, as if we
were in the dark world of the dead. 11We
are frightened and distressed. We long
for God to save us from oppression and
wrong, but nothing happens.
12"Lord, our crimes against you are
many. Our sins accuse us. We are well
aware of them all. 13We have rebelled
against you, rejected you, and refused to
follow you. We have oppressed others
and turned away from you. Our

thoughts are false; our words are lies.
14 Justice is driven away, and right cannot come near. Truth stumbles in the
public square, and honesty finds no
place there. 15 There is so little honesty
that those who stop doing evil find themselves the victims of crime."

The LORD Prepares to Rescue His People

The LORD has seen this, and he is displeased that there is no justice. 16 He is
astonished to see that there is no one to
help the oppressed. So he will use his
own power to rescue them and to win
the victory. 17 He will wear justice like a
coat of armor and saving power like a
helmet. He will clothe himself with the
strong desire to set things right and to
punish and avenge the wrongs that people suffer. 18 He will punish his enemies
according to what they have done, even
those who live in distant lands. 19 From
east to west everyone will fear him and
his great power. He will come like a
rushing river, like a strong wind.
20 The LORD says to his people, "I will
come to Jerusalem to defend you and to
save all of you that turn from your sins.
21 And I make a covenant with you: I
have given you my power and my teachings to be yours forever, and from now
on you are to obey me and teach your
children and your descendants to obey
me for all time to come."

The Future Glory of Jerusalem

60 Arise, Jerusalem, and shine like
the sun;
The glory of the LORD is shining
on you!
2 Other nations will be covered by
darkness,
But on you the light of the LORD
will shine;
The brightness of his presence will
be with you.
3 Nations will be drawn to your
light,
And kings to the dawning of your
new day.

4 Look around you and see what is
happening:
Your people are gathering to come
home!
Your sons will come from far
away;
Your daughters will be carried like
children.
5 You will see this and be filled
with joy;
You will tremble with excitement.
The wealth of the nations will be
brought to you;
From across the sea their riches
will come.

6 Great caravans of camels will
come, from Midian and Ephah.
They will come from Sheba,
bringing gold and incense.
People will tell the good news of
what the LORD has done!
7 All the sheep of Kedar and
Nebaioth
Will be brought to you as
sacrifices
And offered on the altar to please
the LORD.
The LORD will make his Temple
more glorious than ever.

8 What are these ships that skim
along like clouds,
Like doves returning home?
9 They are ships coming from
distant lands,
Bringing God's people home.
They bring with them silver and
gold
To honor the name of the LORD,
The holy God of Israel,
Who has made all nations honor
his people.

10 The LORD says to Jerusalem,
"Foreigners will rebuild your
walls,
And their kings will serve you.
In my anger I punished you,
But now I will show you my favor
and mercy.
11 Day and night your gates will be
open,
So that the kings of the nations
May bring you their wealth.
12 But nations that do not serve you
Will be completely destroyed.

13 "The wood of the pine, the juniper,
and the cypress,
The finest wood from the forests
of Lebanon,
Will be brought to rebuild you,
Jerusalem,

To make my Temple beautiful,
To make my city glorious.
14 The descendants of those who
oppressed you will come
And bow low to show their
respect.
All who once despised you will
worship at your feet.
They will call you 'The City of the
LORD,'
'Zion, the City of Israel's
Holy God.'

15 "You will no longer be forsaken
and hated,
A city deserted and desolate.
I will make you great and
beautiful,
A place of joy forever and ever.
16 Nations and kings will care
for you
As a mother nurses her child.
You will know that I, the LORD,
have saved you,
That the mighty God of Israel sets
you free.

17 "I will bring you gold instead of
bronze,
Silver and bronze instead of iron
and wood,
And iron instead of stone.
Your rulers will no longer
oppress you;
I will make them rule with justice
and peace.
18 The sounds of violence will be
heard no more;
Destruction will not shatter your
country again.
I will protect and defend you like
a wall;
You will praise me because I have
saved you.

19 "No longer will the sun be your
light by day
Or the moon be your light by
night;
I, the LORD, will be your eternal
light;
The light of my glory will shine
on you.
20 Your days of grief will come to
an end.
I, the LORD, will be your eternal
light,
More lasting than the sun and
moon.
21 Your people will all do what is
right,
And will possess the land forever.
I planted them, I made them,
To reveal my greatness to all.
22 Even your smallest and humblest
family
Will become as great as a
powerful nation.
When the right time comes,
I will make this happen quickly.
I am the LORD!"

The Good News of Deliverance

61 The Sovereign LORD has filled
me with his Spirit.
He has chosen me and sent me
To bring good news to the poor,
To heal the broken-hearted,
To announce release to captives
And freedom to those in prison.
2 He has sent me to proclaim
That the time has come
When the LORD will save his
people
And defeat their enemies.
He has sent me to comfort all who
mourn,
3 To give to those who mourn in
Zion
Joy and gladness instead of grief,
A song of praise instead of
sorrow.
They will be like trees
That the LORD himself has planted.
They will all do what is right,
And God will be praised for what
he has done.
4 They will rebuild cities that have
long been in ruins.

5 My people, foreigners will
serve you.
They will take care of your flocks
And farm your land and tend your
vineyards.
6 And you will be known as the
priests of the LORD,
The servants of our God.
You will enjoy the wealth of the
nations
And be proud that it is yours.
7 Your shame and disgrace are
ended.
You will live in your own land,
And your wealth will be doubled;

Your joy will last forever.
8 The LORD says,
"I love justice and I hate
oppression and crime.
I will faithfully reward my
people
And make an eternal covenant
with them.
9 They will be famous among the
nations;
Everyone who sees them will
know
That they are a people whom I
have blessed."

10 Jerusalem rejoices because of
what the LORD has done.
She is like a bride dressed for her
wedding.
God has clothed her with salvation
and victory.
11 As surely as seeds sprout and
grow,
The Sovereign LORD will save his
people,
And all the nations will
praise him.

62 I will speak out to encourage
Jerusalem;
I will not be silent until she is
saved,
And her victory shines like a torch
in the night.
2 Jerusalem, the nations will see you
victorious!
All their kings will see your glory.
You will be called by a new name,
A name given by the LORD
himself.
3 You will be like a beautiful crown
for the LORD.
4 No longer will you be called
"Forsaken,"
Or your land be called "The
Deserted Wife."
Your new name will be "God Is
Pleased with Her."
Your land will be called "Happily
Married,"
Because the LORD is pleased
with you
And will be like a husband to your
land.
5 Like a young man taking a virgin
as his bride,
He who formed you will
marry you.
As a groom is delighted with his
bride,
So your God will delight in you.

6 On your walls, Jerusalem, I have
placed sentries;
They must never be silent day or
night.
They must remind the LORD of his
promises
And never let him forget
them.
7 They must give him no rest until
he restores Jerusalem
And makes it a city the whole
world praises.

8 The LORD has made a solemn
promise,
And by his power he will carry
it out:
"Your grain will no longer be food
for your enemies,
And foreigners will no longer
drink your wine.
9 But you that planted and
harvested the grain
Will eat the bread and praise the
LORD.
You that tended and gathered the
grapes
Will drink the wine in the courts
of my Temple."

10 People of Jerusalem, go out of the
city
And build a road for your
returning people!
Prepare a highway; clear it of
stones!
Put up a signal so that the nations
can know
11 That the LORD is announcing to all
the earth:
"Tell the people of Jerusalem
That the LORD is coming to
save you,
Bringing with him the people he
has rescued."
12 You will be called "God's Holy
People,"
"The People the LORD Has Saved."
Jerusalem will be called "The City
That God Loves,"
"The City That God Did Not
Forsake."

The LORD's Victory over the Nations

63 "Who is this coming from the
city of Bozrah in Edom? Who is
this so splendidly dressed in red, marching along[f] in power and strength?"
It is the LORD, powerful to save, coming to announce his victory.
2 "Why is his clothing so red, like that
of someone who tramples grapes to
make wine?"
3 The LORD answers, "I have trampled
the nations like grapes, and no one came
to help me. I trampled them in my anger,
and their blood has stained all my clothing. 4 I decided that the time to save my
people had come; it was time to punish
their enemies. 5 I was amazed when I
looked and saw that there was no one to
help me. But my anger made me strong,
and I won the victory myself. 6 In my anger I trampled whole nations and shattered them. I poured out their lifeblood
on the ground."

The LORD's Goodness to Israel

7 I will tell of the LORD's unfailing
love;
I praise him for all he has done
for us.
He has richly blessed the people of
Israel
because of his mercy and
constant love.
8 The LORD said, "They are my people;
they will not deceive me." And so he
saved them 9 from all their suffering. It
was not an angel, but the LORD himself
who saved them. In his love and compassion he rescued them. He had always
taken care of them in the past, 10 but they
rebelled against him and made his holy
spirit sad. So the LORD became their enemy and fought against them.
11 But then they[g] remembered the
past, the days of Moses, the servant of
the LORD, and they asked, "Where now is
the LORD, who saved the leaders of his
people from the sea? Where is the LORD,
who gave his spirit to Moses? 12-13 Where
is the LORD, who by his power did great
things through Moses, dividing the waters of the sea and leading his people
through the deep water, to win everlasting fame for himself?"
Led by the LORD, they were as sure-
footed as wild horses, and never stumbled. 14 As cattle are led into a fertile
valley, so the LORD gave his people rest.
He led his people and brought honor to
his name.

A Prayer for Mercy and Help

15 LORD, look upon us from heaven,
where you live in your holiness and
glory. Where is your great concern for
us? Where is your power? Where are
your love and compassion? Do not ignore us. 16 You are our father. Our ancestors Abraham and Jacob do not
acknowledge us, but you, LORD, are our
father, the one who has always rescued
us. 17 Why do you let us stray from your
ways? Why do you make us so stubborn
that we turn away from you? Come
back, for the sake of those who serve
you, for the sake of the people who have
always been yours.
18 We, your holy people, were driven
out by our enemies for a little while; they
trampled down your sanctuary.[h] 19 You
treat us as though you had never been
our ruler, as though we had never been
your people.
64 Why don't you tear the sky open
and come down? The mountains
would see you and shake with fear.
2 They would tremble like water boiling
over a hot fire. Come and reveal your
power to your enemies, and make the
nations tremble at your presence!
3 There was a time when you came and
did terrifying things that we did not expect; the mountains saw you and shook
with fear. 4 No one has ever seen or
heard of a God like you, who does such
deeds for those who put their hope in
him. 5 You welcome those who find joy
in doing what is right, those who remember how you want them to live. You
were angry with us, but we went on sinning; in spite of your great anger we
have continued to do wrong since ancient times.[i] 6 All of us have been sinful;
even our best actions are filthy through
and through. Because of our sins we are
like leaves that wither and are blown
away by the wind. 7 No one turns to you
in prayer; no one goes to you for help.
You have hidden yourself from us and

[f] *Some ancient translations* marching along; *Hebrew* bowed down. [g] *Probable text* they; *Hebrew* he. [h] *Verse 18 in Hebrew is unclear.* [i] *Probable text* in spite of . . . ancient times; *Hebrew unclear.*

have abandoned[j] us because of our
sins.
8But you are our father, LORD. We are
like clay, and you are like the potter.
You created us, 9so do not be too angry
with us or hold our sins against us forever. We are your people; be merciful to
us. 10Your sacred cities are like a desert;
Jerusalem is a deserted ruin, 11and our
Temple, the sacred and beautiful place
where our ancestors praised you, has
been destroyed by fire. All the places we
loved are in ruins. 12LORD, are you un-
moved by all this? Are you going to do
nothing and make us suffer more than
we can endure?

God's Punishment of the Rebellious

65 The LORD said, "I was ready to
answer my people's prayers, but
they did not pray. I was ready for them
to find me, but they did not even try. The
nation did not pray to me, even though I
was always ready to answer, 'Here I am;
I will help you.' 2I have always been
ready to welcome my people, who stubbornly do what is wrong and go their
own way. 3They shamelessly keep on
making me angry. They offer pagan sacrifices at sacred gardens[k] and burn incense on pagan altars. 4At night they go
to caves and tombs to consult the spirits
of the dead. They eat pork and drink
broth made from meat offered in pagan
sacrifices. 5And then they say to others,
'Keep away from us; we are too holy for
you to touch!' I cannot stand people like
that—my anger against them is like a
fire that never goes out.
6"I have already decided on their punishment, and their sentence is written
down. I will not overlook what they have
done, but will repay them 7for their sins
and the sins of their ancestors. They
have burned incense at pagan hill
shrines and spoken evil of me. So I will
punish them as their past deeds
deserve."
8The LORD says, "No one destroys
good grapes; instead, they make wine
with them. Neither will I destroy all my
people—I will save those who serve me.
9I will bless the Israelites who belong to
the tribe of Judah, and their descendants
will possess my land of mountains. My
chosen people, who serve me, will live
there. 10They will worship me and will
lead their sheep and cattle to pasture in
the Plain of Sharon in the west and in
Trouble Valley in the east.
11"But it will be different for you that
forsake me, who ignore Zion, my sacred
hill,[l] and worship Gad and Meni, the
gods of luck and fate. 12It will be your
fate to die a violent death, because you
did not answer when I called you or listen when I spoke. You chose to disobey
me and do evil. 13And so I tell you that
those who worship and obey me will
have plenty to eat and drink, but you
will be hungry and thirsty. They will be
happy, but you will be disgraced. 14They
will sing for joy, but you will cry with a
broken heart. 15My chosen people will
use your name as a curse. I, the
Sovereign LORD, will put you to death.
But I will give a new name to those who
obey me. 16Anyone in the land who asks
for a blessing will ask to be blessed by
the faithful God. Whoever takes an oath
will swear by the name of the faithful
God. The troubles of the past will be
gone and forgotten."

The New Creation

17The LORD says, "I am making a new
earth and new heavens. The events of
the past will be completely forgotten.
18Be glad and rejoice forever in what I
create. The new Jerusalem I make will
be full of joy, and her people will be
happy. 19I myself will be filled with joy
because of Jerusalem and her people.
There will be no weeping there, no calling for help. 20Babies will no longer die
in infancy, and all people will live out
their life span. Those who live to be a
hundred will be considered young. To
die before that would be a sign that I had
punished them. 21-22People will build
houses and get to live in them—they will
not be used by someone else. They will
plant vineyards and enjoy the wine—it
will not be drunk by others. Like trees,
my people will live long lives. They will
fully enjoy the things that they have
worked for. 23The work they do will be
successful, and their children will not
meet with disaster. I will bless them and
their descendants for all time to come.

[j] *Some ancient translations* abandoned; *Hebrew* melted.
[k] SACRED GARDENS: *See 1.29.*
[l] SACRED HILL: *See 2.3.*

24 Even before they finish praying to me,
I will answer their prayers. 25 Wolves
and lambs will eat together; lions will
eat straw, as cattle do, and snakes will
no longer be dangerous. On Zion, my sacred hill,[l] there will be nothing harmful
or evil."

The LORD Judges the Nations

66 The LORD says, "Heaven is my
throne, and the earth is my footstool. What kind of house, then, could
you build for me, what kind of place for
me to live in? 2 I myself created the
whole universe! I am pleased with those
who are humble and repentant, who fear
me and obey me.

3 "The people do as they please. It's all
the same to them whether they kill a bull
as a sacrifice or sacrifice a human being;
whether they sacrifice a lamb or break a
dog's neck; whether they present a grain
offering or offer pigs' blood; whether
they offer incense or pray to an idol.
They take pleasure in disgusting ways of
worship. 4 So I will bring disaster upon
them—the very things they are afraid
of—because no one answered when I
called or listened when I spoke. They
chose to disobey me and do evil."

5 Listen to what the LORD says, you that
fear him and obey him: "Because you
are faithful to me, some of your own
people hate you and will have nothing to
do with you. They mock you and say,
'Let the LORD show his greatness and
save you, so that we may see you rejoice.' But they themselves will be disgraced! 6 Listen! That loud noise in the
city, that sound in the Temple, is the
sound of the LORD punishing his
enemies!

7 "My holy city is like a woman who
suddenly gives birth to a child without
ever going into labor. 8 Has anyone ever
seen or heard of such a thing? Has a
nation ever been born in a day? Zion
will not have to suffer long, before the nation is born. 9 Do not think that I will
bring my people to the point of birth
and not let them be born." The LORD has
spoken.

10 Rejoice with Jerusalem; be glad
for her,
all you that love this city!
Rejoice with her now,
all you that have mourned
for her!
11 You will enjoy her prosperity,
like a child at its mother's
breast.

12 The LORD says, "I will bring you lasting prosperity; the wealth of the nations
will flow to you like a river that never
goes dry. You will be like a child that is
nursed by its mother, carried in her
arms, and treated with love. 13 I will
comfort you in Jerusalem, as a mother
comforts her child. 14 When you see this
happen, you will be glad; it will make
you strong and healthy. Then you will
know that I, the LORD, help those who
obey me, and I show my anger against
my enemies."

15 The LORD will come with fire. He will
ride on the wings of a storm to punish
those he is angry with. 16 By fire and
sword he will punish all the people of the
world whom he finds guilty—and many
will be put to death.

17 The LORD says, "The end is near for
those who purify themselves for pagan
worship, who go in procession to sacred
gardens,[m] and who eat pork and mice
and other disgusting foods. 18 I know[n]
their thoughts and their deeds. I am
coming[o] to gather the people of all the
nations. When they come together, they
will see what my power can do 19 and
will know that I am the one who punishes them.

"But I will spare some of them and
send them to the nations and the distant
lands that have not heard of my fame or
seen my greatness and power: to Spain,
Libya,[p] and Lydia, with its skilled archers, and to Tubal and Greece. Among
these nations they will proclaim my
greatness. 20 They will bring back all
your people from the nations as a gift to
me. They will bring them to my sacred
hill[q] in Jerusalem on horses, mules, and
camels, and in chariots and wagons, just
as Israelites bring grain offerings to the
Temple in ritually clean containers.
21 I will make some of them priests and
Levites.

22 "Just as the new earth and the new
heavens will endure by my power, so
your descendants and your name will

[l] SACRED HILL: *See 2.3.* [m] SACRED GARDENS: *See 1.29.* [n] *Some ancient translations* I know; *Hebrew* I. [o] *Some ancient translations* I am coming; *Hebrew* He is coming.
[p] *One ancient translation* Libya; *Hebrew* Pul. [q] SACRED HILL: *See 2.3.*

endure. 23On every New Moon Festival
and every Sabbath people of every nation will come to worship me here in Jerusalem," says the LORD. 24"As they
leave, they will see the dead bodies of
those who have rebelled against me. The
worms that eat them will never die, and
the fire that burns them will never be put
out. The sight of them will be disgusting
to all people."

The Book of
JEREMIAH

Introduction

The prophet Jeremiah lived during the latter part of the seventh century and the first part of the sixth century B.C. During his long ministry he warned God's people of the catastrophe that was to fall upon the nation because of their idolatry and sin. He lived to see this prediction come true with the fall of Jerusalem to the Babylonian king, Nebuchadnezzar, the destruction of the city and the Temple, and the exile to Babylonia of Judah's king and many of the people. He also foretold the eventual return of the people from exile and the restoration of the nation.

The Book of Jeremiah *may be divided into the following parts: 1) The call of Jeremiah. 2) Messages from God to the nation of Judah and its rulers during the reigns of Josiah, Jehoiakim, Jehoiachin, and Zedekiah. 3) Material from the memoirs of Baruch, Jeremiah's secretary, including various prophecies and important events from the life of Jeremiah. 4) Messages from the Lord about various foreign nations. 5) A historical appendix, giving an account of the fall of Jerusalem, and the exile to Babylonia.*

Jeremiah was a sensitive man who deeply loved his people, and who hated to have to pronounce judgment upon them. In many passages he spoke with deep emotion about the things he suffered because God had called him to be a prophet. The word of the Lord was like fire in his heart—he could not keep it back.

Some of the greatest words in the book point beyond Jeremiah's own troubled time to the day when there would be a new covenant, one that God's people would keep without a teacher to remind them, because it would be written on their hearts (31.31-34).

Outline of Contents

The call of Jeremiah 1.1-19
Prophecies during the reigns of Josiah, Jehoiakim, Jehoiachin, and Zedekiah 2.1—25.38
Events in Jeremiah's life 26.1—45.5
Prophecies against the nations 46.1—51.64
The fall of Jerusalem 52.1-34

---

1 This book is the account of what
was said by Jeremiah son of Hilkiah, one of the priests of the town of
Anathoth in the territory of Benjamin.
2 The LORD spoke to Jeremiah in the thirteenth year that Josiah son of Amon was
king of Judah, 3 and he spoke to him
again when Josiah's son Jehoiakim was
king. After that, the LORD spoke to him
many times, until the eleventh year of
the reign of Zedekiah son of Josiah. In
the fifth month of that year the people of
Jerusalem were taken into exile.

The Call of Jeremiah

4 The LORD said to me, 5 "I chose you
before I gave you life, and before you
were born I selected you to be a prophet
to the nations."
6 I answered, "Sovereign LORD, I don't
know how to speak; I am too young."
7 But the LORD said to me, "Do not say
that you are too young, but go to the
people I send you to, and tell them
everything I command you to say. 8 Do
not be afraid of them, for I will be with
you to protect you. I, the LORD, have
spoken!"
9 Then the LORD reached out, touched
my lips, and said to me, "Listen, I am
giving you the words you must speak.
10 Today I give you authority over nations and kingdoms to uproot and to pull
down, to destroy and to overthrow, to
build and to plant."

Two Visions

11 The LORD asked me, "Jeremiah, what
do you see?"
I answered, "A branch of an almond
tree."
12 "You are right," the LORD said, "and I

am watching[a] to see that my words
come true."
13 Then the LORD spoke to me again.
"What else do you see?" he asked.
I answered, "I see a pot boiling in
the north, and it is about to tip over
this way."
14 He said to me, "Destruction will boil
over from the north on all who live in
this land, 15 because I am calling all the
nations in the north to come. Their kings
will set up their thrones at the gates of
Jerusalem and around its walls and also
around the other cities of Judah. 16 I will
punish my people because they have
sinned; they have abandoned me, have
offered sacrifices to other gods, and
have made idols and worshiped them.
17 Get ready, Jeremiah; go and tell them
everything I command you to say. Do
not be afraid of them now, or I will make
you even more afraid when you are with
them. 18-19 Listen, Jeremiah! Everyone in
this land—the kings of Judah, the officials, the priests, and the people—will
be against you. But today I am giving
you the strength to resist them; you will
be like a fortified city, an iron pillar, and
a bronze wall. They will not defeat you,
for I will be with you to protect you. I,
the LORD, have spoken."

God's Care for Israel

2 The LORD told me 2 to proclaim this
message to everyone in Jerusalem.
"I remember how faithful you
were when you were young,
how you loved me when we
were first married;
you followed me through the
desert,
through a land that had not been
planted.
3 Israel, you belonged to me alone;
you were my sacred possession.
I sent suffering and disaster
on everyone who hurt you.
I, the LORD, have spoken."

The Sin of Israel's Ancestors

4 Listen to the LORD's message, you
descendants of Jacob, you tribes of Israel. 5 The LORD says:
"What accusation did your
ancestors bring against me?
What made them turn away
from me?
They worshiped worthless idols
and became worthless
themselves.
6 They did not care about me,
even though I rescued them
from Egypt
and led them through the
wilderness:
a land of deserts and sand pits,
a dry and dangerous land
where no one lives
and no one will even travel.
7 I brought them into a fertile land,
to enjoy its harvests and its
other good things.
But instead they ruined my land;
they defiled the country I had
given them.
8 The priests did not ask, 'Where is
the LORD?'
My own priests did not
know me.
The rulers rebelled against me;
the prophets spoke in the name
of Baal
and worshiped useless idols.

The LORD's Case against His People

9 "And so I, the LORD, will state my
case against my people again.
I will bring charges against their
descendants.
10 Go west to the island of Cyprus,
and send someone eastward to
the land of Kedar.
You will see that nothing like
this has ever happened before.
11 No other nation has ever changed
its gods,
even though they were not real.
But my people have
exchanged me,
the God who has brought them
honor,
for gods that can do nothing for
them.
12 And so I command the sky to
shake with horror,
to be amazed and astonished,
13 for my people have committed
two sins:
they have turned away from me,
the spring of fresh water,
and they have dug cisterns,

[a] WATCHING: *This word in Hebrew sounds like the Hebrew for "almond."*

cracked cisterns that can hold
no water at all.

The Results of Israel's Unfaithfulness

14 "Israel is not a slave;
he was not born into slavery.
Why then do his enemies hunt
him down?
15 They have roared at him like
lions;
they have made his land a
desert,
and his towns lie in ruins,
completely abandoned.
16 Yes, the people of Memphis and
Tahpanhes
have cracked his skull.
17 Israel, you brought this on
yourself!
You deserted me, the LORD
your God,
while I was leading you along
the way.
18 What do you think you will gain
by going to Egypt
to drink water from the Nile?
What do you think you will gain
by going to Assyria
to drink water from the
Euphrates?
19 Your own evil will punish you,
and your turning from me will
condemn you.
You will learn how bitter and
wrong it is
to abandon me, the LORD
your God,
and no longer to remain faithful
to me.
I, the Sovereign LORD Almighty,
have spoken."

Israel Refuses to Worship the LORD

20 The Sovereign LORD says,
"Israel, long ago you rejected my
authority;
you refused to obey me and
worship me.
On every high hill
and under every green tree
you worshiped fertility gods.
21 I planted you like a choice vine
from the very best seed.
But look what you have become!
You are like a rotten, worthless
vine.
22 Even if you washed with the
strongest soap,
I would still see the stain of your
guilt.
23 How can you say you have not
defiled yourself,
that you have never worshiped
Baal?
Look how you sinned in the
valley;
see what you have done.
You are like a wild camel in heat,
running around loose,
24 rushing into the desert.[b]
When she is in heat, who can
control her?
No male that wants her has to
trouble himself;
she is always available in
mating season.
25 Israel, don't wear your feet out,
or let your throat become dry
from chasing after other gods.
But you say, 'No! I can't turn back.
I have loved foreign gods
and will go after them.'"

Israel Deserves to Be Punished

26 The LORD says, "Just as a thief is disgraced when caught, so all you people of
Israel will be disgraced—your kings and
officials, your priests and prophets.
27 You will all be disgraced—you that
say that a tree is your father and that a
rock is your mother. This will happen
because you turned away from me instead of turning to me. But when you are
in trouble, you ask me to come and
save you.
28 "Where are the gods that you made
for yourselves? When you are in trouble,
let them save you—if they can! Judah,
you have as many gods as you have cities. 29 What is your complaint? Why
have you rebelled against me? 30 I
punished you, but it did no good; you
would not let me correct you. Like a raging lion, you have murdered your prophets. 31 People of Israel, listen to what I am
saying. Have I been like a desert to you,
like a dark and dangerous land? Why,
then, do you say that you will do as you
please, that you will never come back to
me? 32 Does a young woman forget her
jewelry, or a bride her wedding dress?
But my people have forgotten me for

[b] *Probable text* rushing into the desert; *Hebrew* a wild donkey used to the desert.

more days than can be counted. 33 You
certainly know how to chase after lovers. Even the worst of women can learn
from you. 34 Your clothes are stained
with the blood of the poor and innocent,
not with the blood of burglars.
"But in spite of all this, 35 you say, 'I am
innocent; surely the LORD is no longer
angry with me.' But I, the LORD, will punish you because you deny that you have
sinned. 36 You have cheapened yourself
by turning to the gods of other nations.
You will be disappointed by Egypt, just
as you were by Assyria. 37 You will turn
away from Egypt, hanging your head in
shame. I, the LORD, have rejected those
you trust; you will not gain anything
from them."

Unfaithful Israel

3 The LORD says, "If a man divorces
his wife, and she leaves him and becomes another man's wife, he cannot
take her back again. This would completely defile the land. But, Israel, you
have had many lovers, and now you
want to return to me! 2 Look up at the
hilltops. Is there any place where you
have not acted like a prostitute? You
waited for lovers along the roadside, as
an Arab waits for victims in the desert.
You have defiled the land with your
prostitution. 3 That is why the rains were
held back, and the spring showers did
not come. You even look like a prostitute; you have no shame.
4 "And now you say to me, 'You are my
father, and you have loved me ever since
I was a child. 5 You won't always be angry; you won't be mad at me forever.'
Israel, that is what you said, but you did
all the evil you could."

Israel and Judah Must Repent

6 When Josiah was king, the LORD said
to me, "Have you seen what Israel, that
unfaithful woman, has done? She has
turned away from me, and on every high
hill and under every green tree she has
acted like a prostitute. 7 I thought that
after she had done all this, she would
surely return to me. But she did not return, and her unfaithful sister Judah saw
it all. 8 Judah also saw that I divorced
Israel and sent her away because she
had turned from me and had become a
prostitute. But Judah, Israel's unfaithful
sister, was not afraid. She too became a
prostitute 9 and was not at all ashamed.
She defiled the land, and she committed
adultery by worshiping stones and trees.
10 And after all this, Judah, Israel's unfaithful sister, only pretended to return
to me; she was not sincere. I, the LORD,
have spoken."
11 Then the LORD told me that, even
though Israel had turned away from
him, she had proved to be better than
unfaithful Judah. 12 He told me to go and
say to Israel, "Unfaithful Israel, come
back to me. I am merciful and will not be
angry; I will not be angry with you forever. 13 Only admit that you are guilty
and that you have rebelled against the
LORD, your God. Confess that under
every green tree you have given your
love to foreign gods and that you have
not obeyed my commands. I, the LORD,
have spoken.
14 "Unfaithful people, come back; you
belong to me. I will take one of you from
each town and two from each clan, and
I will bring you back to Mount Zion.
15 I will give you rulers who obey me,
and they will rule you with wisdom and
understanding. 16 Then when you have
become numerous in that land, people
will no longer talk about my Covenant
Box. They will no longer think about it
or remember it; they will not even need
it, nor will they make another one.
17 When that time comes, Jerusalem will
be called 'The Throne of the LORD,' and
all nations will gather there to worship
me. They will no longer do what their
stubborn and evil hearts tell them. 18 Israel will join with Judah, and together
they will come from exile in the country
in the north and will return to the land
that I gave your ancestors as a permanent possession."

The Idolatry of God's People

19 The LORD says,
"Israel, I wanted to accept you as
my child
and give you a delightful land,
the most beautiful land in all the
world.
I wanted you to call me father
and never again turn away
from me.
20 But like an unfaithful wife,
you have not been faithful
to me.
I, the LORD, have spoken."

21 A noise is heard on the hilltops:
it is the people of Israel crying
and pleading
because they have lived sinful
lives
and have forgotten the LORD
their God.
22 Return, all of you who have turned
away from the LORD;
he will heal you and make you
faithful.

You say, "Yes, we are coming to the
LORD because he is our God. 23 We were
not helped at all by our pagan worship
on the hilltops. Help for Israel comes
only from the LORD our God. 24 But the
worship of Baal, the god of shame, has
made us lose flocks and herds, sons and
daughters—everything that our ancestors have worked for since ancient
times. 25 We should lie down in shame
and let our disgrace cover us. We and
our ancestors have always sinned
against the LORD our God; we have never
obeyed his commands."

A Call to Repentance

4 The LORD says, "People of Israel, if
you want to turn, then turn back to
me. If you are faithful to me and remove
the idols I hate, 2 it will be right for you to
swear by my name. Then[c] all the nations will ask me to bless them, and they
will praise me."
3 The LORD says to the people of Judah
and Jerusalem, "Plow up your unplowed
fields; do not plant your seeds among
thorns. 4 Keep your covenant with me,
your LORD, and dedicate yourselves to
me, you people of Judah and Jerusalem.
If you don't, my anger will burn like fire
because of the evil things you have done.
It will burn, and there will be no one to
put it out."

Judah Is Threatened with Invasion

5 Blow the trumpet throughout the
land!
Shout loud and clear!
Tell the people of Judah and
Jerusalem
to run to the fortified cities.
6 Point the way to Zion!
Run for safety! Don't delay!
The LORD is bringing disaster
and great destruction from the
north.
7 Like a lion coming from its hiding
place,
a destroyer of nations has
set out.
He is coming to destroy Judah.
The cities of Judah will be left in
ruins,
and no one will live in them.
8 So put on sackcloth, and weep and
wail
because the fierce anger of the
LORD
has not turned away from
Judah.

9 The LORD said, "On that day kings
and officials will lose their courage;
priests will be shocked and prophets will
be astonished."
10 Then I said, "Sovereign LORD, you
have completely deceived the people of
Jerusalem! You have said there would
be peace, but a sword is at their throats."
11 The time is coming when the people
of Jerusalem will be told that a scorching wind is blowing in from the desert
toward them. It will not be a gentle wind
that only blows away the chaff—12 the
wind that comes at the LORD's command
will be much stronger than that! It is the
LORD himself who is pronouncing judgment on his people.

Judah Is Surrounded by Enemies

13 Look, the enemy is coming like
clouds. Their war chariots are like a
whirlwind, and their horses are faster
than eagles. We are lost! We are
doomed!
14 Jerusalem, wash the evil from your
heart, so that you may be saved. How
long will you go on thinking sinful
thoughts?
15 Messengers from the city of Dan and
from the hills of Ephraim announce the
bad news. 16 They have come to warn the
nations and to tell Jerusalem that enemies are coming from a country far
away. These enemies will shout against
the cities of Judah 17 and will surround
Jerusalem like men guarding a field, because her people have rebelled against
the LORD. The LORD has spoken.

[c] it will be right . . . name. Then; *or* and if you swear by my name and are truthful, just, and righteous, then.

18 Judah, you have brought this on yourself by the way you have lived and by the things you have done. Your sin has caused this suffering; it has stabbed you through the heart.

Jeremiah's Sorrow for His People

19 The pain! I can't bear the pain!
My heart! My heart is beating wildly!
I can't keep quiet;
I hear the trumpets
and the shouts of battle.
20 One disaster follows another;
the whole country is left in ruins.
Suddenly our tents are destroyed;
their curtains are torn to pieces.
21 How long must I see the battle raging
and hear the blasts of trumpets?
22 The LORD says, "My people are stupid;
they don't know me.
They are like foolish children;
they have no understanding.
They are experts at doing what is evil,
but failures at doing what is good."

Jeremiah's Vision of the Coming Destruction

23 I looked at the earth—it was a barren waste;
at the sky—there was no light.
24 I looked at the mountains—they were shaking,
and the hills were rocking back and forth.
25 I saw that there were no people;
even the birds had flown away.
26 The fertile land had become a desert;
its cities were in ruins
because of the LORD's fierce anger.

(27 The LORD has said that the whole earth will become a wasteland, but that he will not completely destroy it.)

28 The earth will mourn;
the sky will grow dark.
The LORD has spoken
and will not change his mind.
He has made his decision
and will not turn back.
29 At the noise of the cavalry and archers
everyone will run away.
Some will run to the forest;
others will climb up among the rocks.
Every town will be left empty,
and no one will live in them again.
30 Jerusalem, you are doomed!
Why do you dress in scarlet?
Why do you put on jewelry and paint your eyes?
You are making yourself beautiful for nothing!
Your lovers have rejected you
and want to kill you.
31 I heard a cry, like a woman in labor,
a scream like a woman bearing her first child.
It was the cry of Jerusalem
gasping for breath,
stretching out her hand and saying,
"I am doomed!
They are coming to kill me!"

The Sin of Jerusalem

5 People of Jerusalem, run through your streets!
Look around! See for yourselves!
Search the marketplaces!
Can you find one person
who does what is right
and tries to be faithful to God?
If you can, the LORD will forgive Jerusalem.
2 Even though you claim to worship the LORD,
you do not mean what you say.
3 Surely the LORD looks for faithfulness.
He struck you, but you paid no attention;
he crushed you, but you refused to learn.
You were stubborn and would not turn from your sins.
4 Then I thought, "These are only the poor and ignorant.
They behave foolishly;
they don't know what their God requires,
what the LORD wants them to do.
5 I will go to the people in power
and talk with them.
Surely they know what their God requires,

what the LORD wants them
to do."
But all of them have rejected the
LORD's authority
and refuse to obey him.
6 That is why lions from the forest
will kill them;
wolves from the desert will tear
them to pieces,
and leopards will prowl through
their towns.
If those people go out, they will be
torn apart
because their sins are numerous
and time after time they have
turned from God.
7 The LORD asked, "Why should I
forgive the sins of my people?
They have abandoned me
and have worshiped gods that
are not real.
I fed my people until they were
full,
but they committed adultery
and spent their time with
prostitutes.
8 They were like well-fed stallions
wild with desire,
each lusting for his neighbor's
wife.
9 Shouldn't I punish them for these
things
and take revenge on a nation
such as this?
10 I will send enemies to cut down
my people's vineyards,
but not to destroy them
completely.
I will tell them to strip away the
branches,
because those branches are not
mine.
11 The people of Israel and Judah
have betrayed me completely.
I, the LORD, have spoken."

The LORD Rejects Israel

12 The LORD's people have denied him
and have said, "He won't really do anything.[d] We won't have hard times; we
won't have war or famine." 13-14 They
have said that the prophets are nothing
but windbags and that they have no
message from the LORD. The LORD God
Almighty said to me, "Jeremiah, because
these people have said such things, I will
make my words like a fire in your
mouth. The people will be like wood,
and the fire will burn them up."
15 People of Israel, the LORD is bringing
a nation from far away to attack you. It
is a strong and ancient nation, a nation
whose language you do not know.
16 Their archers are mighty soldiers who
kill without mercy. 17 They will devour
your crops and your food; they will kill
your sons and your daughters. They will
slaughter your flocks and your herds
and destroy your vines and fig trees. The
fortified cities in which you trust will be
destroyed by their army.
18 The LORD says, "Yet even in those
days I will not completely destroy my
people. 19 When they ask why I did all
these things, tell them, Jeremiah, that
just as they turned away from me and
served foreign gods in their own land, so
they will serve strangers in a land that is
not theirs."

God Warns His People

20 The LORD says, "Tell the descendants
of Jacob, tell the people of Judah: 21 Pay
attention, you foolish and stupid people,
who have eyes, but cannot see, and have
ears, but cannot hear. 22 I am the LORD;
why don't you fear me? Why don't you
tremble before me? I placed the sand as
the boundary of the sea, a permanent
boundary that it cannot cross. The sea
may toss, but it cannot go beyond it; the
waves may roar, but they cannot break
through. 23 But you people! You are stubborn and rebellious; you have turned
aside and left me. 24 You never thought
to honor me, even though I send the autumn rains and the spring rains and give
you the harvest season each year. 25 Instead, your sins have kept these good
things from you.
26 "Evildoers live among my people;
they lie in wait like those who lay nets to
catch birds,[e] but they have set their
traps to catch people. 27 Just as a hunter
fills a cage with birds, they have filled
their houses with loot. That is why they
are powerful and rich, 28 why they are fat
and well fed. There is no limit to their
evil deeds. They do not give orphans

[d] He won't . . . anything; *or* We don't want anything to do with him. [e] *Probable text* they . . . birds; *Hebrew unclear.*

their rights or show justice to the oppressed.
29 "But I, the LORD, will punish them for
these things; I will take revenge on this
nation. 30 A terrible and shocking thing
has happened in the land: 31 prophets
speak nothing but lies; priests rule as the
prophets command, and my people offer
no objections. But what will they do
when it all comes to an end?"

Jerusalem Is Surrounded by Enemies

6 People of Benjamin, run for safety!
Escape from Jerusalem! Sound the
trumpet in Tekoa and build a signal fire
in Beth Haccherem. Disaster and destruction are about to come from the
north. 2 The city of Zion is beautiful, but
it will be destroyed; 3 kings will camp
there with their armies. They will pitch
their tents around the city, and each
of them will camp wherever they
want. 4 They will say, "Prepare to
attack Jerusalem! Get ready! We'll
attack at noon!" But then they will say,
"It's too late, the day is almost over,
and the evening shadows are growing
long. 5 We'll attack by night; we'll
destroy the city's fortresses."
6 The LORD Almighty has ordered these
kings to cut down trees and build
mounds in order to besiege Jerusalem.
He has said, "I will punish this city because it is full of oppression. 7 As a well
keeps its water fresh, so Jerusalem
keeps its evil fresh. I hear violence and
destruction in the city; sickness and
wounds are all I see. 8 People of Jerusalem, let these troubles be a warning to
you, or else I will abandon you; I will
turn your city into a desert, a place
where no one lives."

Rebellious Israel

9 The LORD Almighty said to me, "Israel
will be stripped clean like a vineyard
from which every grape has been
picked. So you must rescue everyone
you can while there is still time."
10 I answered, "Who would listen to
me if I spoke to them and warned them?
They are stubborn and refuse to listen to
your message; they laugh at what you
tell me to say. 11 Your anger against
them burns in me too, LORD, and I can't
hold it in any longer."
Then the LORD said to me, "Pour out
my anger on the children in the streets
and on the gatherings of the young people. Husbands and wives will be taken
away, and even the very old will not be
spared. 12 Their houses will be given to
others, and so will their fields and their
wives. I am going to punish the people of
this land. 13 Everyone, great and small,
tries to make money dishonestly; even
prophets and priests cheat the people.
14 They act as if my people's wounds
were only scratches. 'All is well,' they
say, when all is not well. 15 Were they
ashamed because they did these disgusting things? No, they were not at all
ashamed; they don't even know how to
blush. And so they will fall as others
have fallen; when I punish them, that
will be the end of them. I, the LORD, have
spoken."

Israel Rejects God's Way

16 The LORD said to his people, "Stand
at the crossroads and look. Ask for the
ancient paths and where the best road is.
Walk in it, and you will live in peace."
But they said, "No, we will not!"
17 Then the LORD appointed sentries to
listen for the trumpet's warning. But
they said, "We will not listen."
18 So the LORD said, "Listen, you nations, and learn what is going to happen
to my people. 19 Listen, earth! As punishment for all their schemes I am bringing
ruin on these people, because they have
rejected my teaching and have not
obeyed my words. 20 What do I care
about the incense they bring me from
Sheba, or the spices from a distant land?
I will not accept their offerings or be
pleased with their sacrifices. 21 And so I
will make these people stumble and fall.
Parents and children will die, and so will
friends and neighbors."

Invasion from the North

22 The LORD says, "People are coming
from a country in the north; a mighty
nation far away is preparing for war.
23 They have taken up their bows and
swords; they are cruel and merciless.
They sound like the roaring sea, as they
ride their horses. They are ready for battle against Jerusalem."
24 "We have heard the news," say the
people of Jerusalem, "and our hands
hang limp; we are seized by anguish and
pain like a woman in labor. 25 We don't
dare go to the countryside or walk on

the roads, because our enemies are
armed and terror is all around us."
26The LORD says to his people, "Put on
sackcloth and roll in ashes. Mourn with
bitter tears as you would for an only
child, because the one who comes to destroy you will suddenly attack. 27Jere-
miah, test my people, as you would test
metal, and find out what they are like.
28They are all stubborn rebels, hard as
bronze and iron. They are all corrupt,
going around and spreading gossip.
29The furnace burns fiercely, but the
waste metals do not melt and run off. It
is useless to go on refining my people,
because those who are evil are not taken
away. 30They will be called worthless
dross, because I, the LORD, have rejected
them."

Jeremiah Preaches in the Temple

7 1-3The LORD sent me to the gate of
the Temple where the people of Judah went in to worship. He told me to
stand there and announce what the LORD
Almighty, the God of Israel, had to say
to them: "Change the way you are living
and the things you are doing, and I will
let you go on living here. 4Stop believing
those deceitful words, 'We are safe! This
is the LORD's Temple, this is the LORD's
Temple, this is the LORD's Temple!'
5"Change the way you are living and
stop doing the things you are doing. Be
fair in your treatment of one another.
6Stop taking advantage of aliens, orphans, and widows. Stop killing innocent people in this land. Stop worshiping
other gods, for that will destroy you. 7If
you change, I will let you go on living
here in the land which I gave your ancestors as a permanent possession.
8"Look, you put your trust in deceitful
words. 9You steal, murder, commit adultery, tell lies under oath, offer sacrifices
to Baal, and worship gods that you had
not known before. 10You do these things
I hate, and then you come and stand in
my presence, in my own Temple, and
say, 'We are safe!' 11Do you think that
my Temple is a hiding place for robbers?
I have seen what you are doing. 12Go to
Shiloh,[f] the first place where I chose to
be worshiped, and see what I did to it
because of the sins of my people Israel.
13You have committed all these sins,
and even though I spoke to you over and
over again, you refused to listen. You
would not answer when I called you.
14And so, what I did to Shiloh I will do to
this Temple of mine, in which you trust.
Here in this place that I gave to your ancestors and you, I will do the same thing
that I did to Shiloh. 15I will drive you out
of my sight as I drove out your relatives,
the people of Israel. I, the LORD, have
spoken."

The People's Disobedience

16The LORD said, "Jeremiah, do not
pray for these people. Do not cry or pray
on their behalf; do not plead with me, for
I will not listen to you. 17Don't you see
what they are doing in the cities of Judah and in the streets of Jerusalem?
18The children gather firewood, the men
build fires, and the women mix dough to
bake cakes for the goddess they call the
Queen of Heaven. They also pour out offerings of wine to other gods, in order to
hurt me. 19But am I really the one they
are hurting? No, they are hurting themselves and bringing shame on themselves. 20And so I, the Sovereign LORD,
will pour out my fierce anger on this
Temple. I will pour it out on people and
animals alike, and even on the trees and
the crops. My anger will be like a fire
that no one can put out.
21"My people, some sacrifices you
burn completely on the altar, and some
you are permitted to eat. But what I, the
LORD, say is that you might as well eat
them all. 22I gave your ancestors no
commands about burnt offerings or any
other kinds of sacrifices when I brought
them out of Egypt. 23But I did command
them to obey me, so that I would be their
God and they would be my people. And
I told them to live the way I had commanded them, so that things would go
well for them. 24But they did not obey or
pay any attention. Instead, they did
whatever their stubborn and evil hearts
told them to do, and they became worse
instead of better. 25From the day that
your ancestors came out of Egypt until
this very day I have kept on sending to
you my servants, the prophets. 26Yet no
one listened or paid any attention. In-

[f] SHILOH: *The city where the Covenant Box was kept in the time of Eli (see 1 S 1.3). The city was destroyed, probably by the Philistines.*

stead, you became more stubborn and
rebellious than your ancestors.
27 "So, Jeremiah, you will speak all
these words to my people, but they will
not listen to you; you will call them, but
they will not answer. 28 You will tell
them that their nation does not obey me,
the LORD their God, or learn from their
punishment. Faithfulness is dead. No
longer is it even talked about.

Sinful Deeds in Hinnom Valley

29 "Mourn, people of Jerusalem;
cut off your hair and throw it
away.
Sing a funeral song on the
hilltops,
because I, the LORD, am angry
and have rejected my people.

30 "The people of Judah have done an
evil thing. They have placed their idols,
which I hate, in my Temple and have defiled it. 31 In Hinnom Valley they have
built an altar called Topheth, so that
they can sacrifice their sons and daughters in the fire. I did not command them
to do this—it did not even enter my
mind. 32 And so, the time will come when
it will no longer be called Topheth or
Hinnom Valley, but Slaughter Valley.
They will bury people there because
there will be nowhere else to bury them.
33 The corpses will be food for the birds
and wild animals, and there will be no
one to scare them off. 34 The land will
become a desert. In the cities of Judah
and in the streets of Jerusalem I will put
an end to the sounds of joy and gladness
and to the happy sounds of wedding
feasts.

8 "At that time the bones of the kings
and of the officials of Judah, as well
as the bones of the priests, of the prophets, and of the other people who lived in
Jerusalem, will be taken out of their
graves. 2 Instead of being gathered and
buried, their bones will be like manure
lying on the ground. They will be spread
out before the sun, the moon, and the
stars, which these people have loved and
served, and which they have consulted
and worshiped. 3 And the people of this
evil nation who survive, who live in the
places where I have scattered them, will
prefer to die rather than to go on living.
I, the LORD Almighty, have spoken."

Sin and Punishment

4 The LORD told me to say to his people,
"When someone falls down, doesn't he
get back up? If someone misses the road,
doesn't he turn back? 5 Why then, my
people, do you turn away from me without ever turning back? You cling to your
idols and refuse to return to me.
6 I listened carefully, but you did not
speak the truth. Not one of you has been
sorry for your wickedness; not one of
you has asked, 'What have I done
wrong?' Each of you keep on going your
own way, like a horse rushing into battle. 7 Even storks know when it is time to
return; doves, swallows, and thrushes
know when it is time to migrate. But, my
people, you do not know the laws by
which I rule you. 8 How can you say that
you are wise and that you know my
laws? Look, the laws have been changed
by dishonest scribes. 9 Your wise men
are put to shame; they are confused and
trapped. They have rejected my words;
what wisdom do they have now? 10 So I
will give their fields to new owners and
their wives to other men. Everyone,
great and small, tries to make money
dishonestly. Even prophets and priests
cheat the people. 11 They act as if my
people's wounds were only scratches.
'All is well,' they say, when all is not
well. 12 My people, were you ashamed
because you did these disgusting things?
No, you were not ashamed at all; you
don't even know how to blush! And so
you will fall as others have fallen; when
I punish you, that will be the end of you.
I, the LORD, have spoken.

13 "I wanted to gather my people, as a
farmer gathers a harvest; but they are
like a vine with no grapes, like a fig tree
with no figs; even the leaves have withered. Therefore, I have allowed outsiders to take over the land."[g]

14 "Why are we sitting still?" God's
people ask. "Come on, we will run to the
fortified cities and die there. The LORD
our God has condemned us to die; he has
given us poison to drink, because we
have sinned against him. 15 We hoped
for peace and a time of healing, but it
was no use; terror came instead. 16 Our
enemies are already in the city of Dan;
we hear the snorting of their horses. The
whole land trembles when their horses

[g] Therefore . . . land; *Hebrew unclear.*

neigh. Our enemies have come to destroy our land and everything in it, our
city and all its people."
17 "Watch out!" the LORD says, "I am
sending snakes among you, poisonous
snakes that cannot be charmed, and
they will bite you."

Jeremiah's Sorrow for His People

18 My sorrow cannot be healed;[h]
I am sick at heart.
19 Listen! Throughout the land
I hear my people crying out,
"Is the LORD no longer in Zion?
Is Zion's king no longer there?"
The LORD, their king, replies,
"Why have you made me angry by
worshiping your idols
and by bowing down to your
useless foreign gods?"
20 The people cry out,
"The summer is gone, the harvest
is over,
but we have not been saved."

21 My heart has been crushed
because my people are crushed;
I mourn; I am completely
dismayed.
22 Is there no medicine in Gilead?[i]
Are there no doctors there?
Why, then, have my people not
been healed?

9 I wish my head were a well of
water,
and my eyes a fountain of tears,
so that I could cry day and night
for my people who have been
killed.
2 I wish I had a place to stay in the
desert
where I could get away from my
people.
They are all unfaithful,
a mob of traitors.
3 They are always ready to tell lies;
dishonesty instead of truth rules
the land.

The LORD says,
"My people do one evil thing after
another
and do not acknowledge me as
their God."

4 Everyone must be on guard
against their friends,
and no one can trust their
relatives;
for all relatives are as deceitful as
Jacob,
and everyone slanders their
friends.
5-6 They all mislead their friends,
and no one tells the truth;
they have taught their tongues
to lie
and will not give up their
sinning.
They do one violent thing after
another,
and one deceitful act follows
another.

The LORD says that his people
reject him.
7 Because of this the LORD Almighty
says,
"I will refine my people like metal
and put them to the test.
My people have done evil—
what else can I do with them?
8 Their tongues are like deadly
arrows;
they always tell lies.
Everyone speaks friendly words to
their neighbors,
but they are really setting a trap
for them.
9 Will I not punish them for these
things?
Will I not take revenge on a
nation like this?
I, the LORD, have spoken."

10 I said, "I will mourn for the
mountains
and weep for the pastures,
because they have dried up,
and no one travels through
them.
The sound of livestock is no
longer heard;
birds and wild animals have fled
and gone."
11 The LORD says, "I will make
Jerusalem a pile of ruins,
a place where jackals live;

[h] *Probable text* My sorrow . . . healed; *Hebrew unclear.* [i] GILEAD: *A region east of the Jordan, famous for plants that were used for medicinal purposes.*

the cities of Judah will become a
desert,
a place where no one lives."

12 I asked, "LORD, why is the land devastated and dry as a desert, so that no
one travels through it? Who is wise
enough to understand this? To whom
have you explained it so that they can
tell others?"
13 The LORD answered, "This has happened because my people have abandoned the teaching that I gave them.
They have not obeyed me or done what
I told them. 14 Instead, they have been
stubborn and have worshiped the idols
of Baal as their ancestors taught them to
do. 15 So then, listen to what I, the LORD
Almighty, the God of Israel, will do: I
will give my people bitter plants to eat
and poison to drink. 16 I will scatter them
among nations that neither they nor
their ancestors have heard about, and I
will send armies against them until I
have completely destroyed them."

The People of Jerusalem Cry Out for Help

17 The LORD Almighty said,
"Think about what is happening!
Call for the mourners to come,
for the women who sing funeral
songs."

18 The people said,
"Tell them to hurry and sing a
funeral song for us,
until our eyes fill with tears,
and our eyelids are wet from
crying."

19 Listen to the sound of crying in
Zion:
"We are ruined!
We are completely disgraced!
We must leave our land;
our homes have been torn
down."

20 I said,
"Listen to the LORD, you women,
and pay attention to his words.
Teach your daughters how to
mourn,
and your friends how to sing a
funeral song.
21 Death has come in through our
windows
and entered our palaces;
it has cut down the children in the
streets
and the young men in the
marketplaces.
22 Dead bodies are scattered
everywhere,
like piles of manure on the
fields,
like grain cut and left behind by
the reapers,
grain that no one gathers.
This is what the LORD has told me
to say."

23 The LORD says,
"The wise should not boast of their
wisdom,
nor the strong of their strength,
nor the rich of their wealth.
24 If any want to boast,
they should boast that they
know and understand me,
because my love is constant,
and I do what is just and right.
These are the things that
please me.
I, the LORD, have spoken."

25-26 The LORD says, "The time is coming when I will punish the people of
Egypt, Judah, Edom, Ammon, Moab,
and the desert people, who have their
hair cut short.[j] All these people are circumcised, but have not kept the covenant it symbolizes. None of these people
and none of the people of Israel have
kept my covenant."

Idolatry and True Worship

10 People of Israel, listen to the
message that the LORD has for
you. 2 He says,
"Do not follow the ways of other
nations;
do not be disturbed by unusual
sights in the sky,
even though other nations are
terrified.
3 The religion of these people is
worthless.

[j] HAIR CUT SHORT: *The desert people cut their hair short in honor of their god, a pagan practice forbidden to the Israelites (see Lv 19.27).*

A tree is cut down in the forest;
it is carved by the tools of the woodworker
4 and decorated with silver and gold.
It is fastened down with nails
to keep it from falling over.
5 Such idols are like scarecrows in a field of melons;
they cannot speak;
they have to be carried
because they cannot walk.
Do not be afraid of them:
they can cause you no harm,
and they can do you no good."

6 LORD, there is no one like you;
you are mighty,
and your name is great and powerful.
7 Who would not honor you, the king of all nations?
You deserve to be honored.
There is no one like you
among all the wise men of the nations
or among any of their kings.
8 All of them are stupid and foolish.
What can they learn from wooden idols?[k]
9 Their idols are covered with silver from Spain
and with gold from Uphaz,
all the work of artists;
they are dressed in violet and purple cloth
woven by skilled weavers.
10 But you, LORD, are the true God,
you are the living God
and the eternal king.
When you are angry, the world trembles;
the nations cannot endure your anger.

(11 You people must tell them that the
gods who did not make the earth and the
sky will be destroyed. They will no
longer exist anywhere on earth.)

A Hymn of Praise to God

12 The LORD made the earth by his power;
by his wisdom he created the world
and stretched out the heavens.
13 At his command the waters above the sky[l] roar;
he brings clouds from the ends of the earth.
He makes lightning flash in the rain
and sends the wind from his storeroom.
14 At the sight of this, people feel stupid and senseless;
those who make idols are disillusioned,
because the gods they make are false and lifeless.
15 They are worthless and should be despised;
they will be destroyed when the LORD comes to deal with them.
16 The God of Jacob is not like them;
he is the one who made everything,
and he has chosen Israel to be his very own people.
The LORD Almighty is his name.

The Coming Exile

17 People of Jerusalem, you are under
siege! Gather up your belongings. 18 The
LORD is going to throw you out of this
land; he is going to crush you until not
one of you is left. The LORD has spoken.
19 The people of Jerusalem cried out,
"How badly we are hurt!
Our wounds will not heal.
And we thought this was
something we could endure!
20 Our tents are ruined;
the ropes that held them have broken.
Our children have all gone away;
there is no one left to put up our tents again;
there is no one to hang their curtains."

21 I answered, "Our leaders are stupid;
they do not ask the LORD for guidance.
This is why they have failed,
and our people have been scattered.
22 Listen! News has come!

[k] What can ... idols?; *or* What their idols teach is worthless. [l] WATERS ABOVE THE SKY: *See Gn 1.6-8.*

There is a great commotion in a
nation to the north;
its army will turn the cities of
Judah into a desert,
a place where jackals live."

23 LORD, I know that none of us are
in charge of our own destiny;
none of us have control over our
own life.
24 Correct your people, LORD,
but do not be too hard on us
or punish us when you are
angry;
that would be the end of us.
25 Turn your anger on the nations
that do not worship you
and on the people who
reject you.
They have killed your people;
they have destroyed us
completely
and left our country in ruins.

Jeremiah and the Covenant

11 The LORD said to me, 2 "Listen to
the terms of the covenant. Tell
the people of Judah and of Jerusalem
3 that I, the LORD God of Israel, have
placed a curse on everyone who does
not obey the terms of this covenant. 4 It is
the covenant I made with their ancestors
when I brought them out of Egypt, the
land that was like a blazing furnace to
them. I told them to obey me and to do
everything that I had commanded. I told
them that if they obeyed, they would be
my people and I would be their God.
5 Then I would keep the promise I made
to their ancestors that I would give them
the rich and fertile land which they now
have."

I said, "Yes, LORD."

6 Then the LORD said to me, "Go to the
cities of Judah and to the streets of Jerusalem. Proclaim my message there and
tell the people to listen to the terms of
the covenant and to obey them. 7 When I
brought their ancestors out of Egypt, I
solemnly warned them to obey me, and
I have kept on warning the people until
this day. 8 But they did not listen or obey.
Instead, everyone continued to be as
stubborn and evil as ever. I had commanded them to keep the covenant, but
they refused. So I brought on them all
the punishments described in it."

9 Then the LORD said to me, "The people of Judah and of Jerusalem are plotting against me. 10 They have gone back
to the sins of their ancestors, who refused to do what I said; they have worshiped other gods. Both Israel and Judah
have broken the covenant that I made
with their ancestors. 11 So now I, the
LORD, warn them that I am going to bring
destruction on them, and they will not
escape. And when they cry out to me for
help, I will not listen to them. 12 Then the
people of Judah and of Jerusalem will go
to the gods to whom they offer sacrifices
and will cry out to them for help. But
those gods will not be able to save them
when this destruction comes. 13 The people of Judah have as many gods as they
have cities, and the inhabitants of Jerusalem have set up as many altars for sacrifices to that disgusting god Baal as
there are streets in the city. 14 Jeremiah,
don't pray to me or plead with me on
behalf of these people. When they are in
trouble and call to me for help, I will not
listen to them."

15 The LORD says, "The people I love
are doing evil things. What right do they
have to be in my Temple? Do they think
they can prevent disaster by making
promises[m] and by offering animal sacrifices? Will they then rejoice? 16 I once
called them a leafy olive tree, full of
beautiful fruit; but now, with a roar like
thunder I will set its leaves on fire and
break its branches.

17 "I, the LORD Almighty, planted Israel
and Judah; but now I threaten them with
disaster. They have brought this on
themselves because they have done
wrong; they have made me angry by offering sacrifices to Baal."

A Plot against Jeremiah's Life

18 The LORD informed me of the plots
that my enemies were making against
me. 19 I was like a trusting lamb taken
out to be killed, and I did not know that
it was against me that they were planning evil things. They were saying,
"Let's chop down the tree while it is still
healthy;[n] let's kill him so that no one
will remember him any more."

[m] *One ancient translation* promises; *Hebrew* many. [n] *Probable text* while it is still healthy; *Hebrew* with its bread.

20 Then I prayed, "Almighty LORD, you
are a just judge; you test people's
thoughts and feelings. I have placed my
cause in your hands; so let me watch you
take revenge on these people."
21 The people of Anathoth wanted me
killed, and they told me that they would
kill me if I kept on proclaiming the
LORD's message. 22 So the LORD Almighty
said, "I will punish them! Their young
men will be killed in war; their children
will die of starvation. 23 I have set a time
for bringing disaster on the people of
Anathoth, and when that time comes,
none of them will survive."

Jeremiah Questions the LORD

12 "LORD, if I argued my case
with you,
you would prove to be right.
Yet I must question you about
matters of justice.
Why are the wicked so
prosperous?
Why do dishonest people
succeed?
2 You plant them, and they take
root;
they grow and bear fruit.
They always speak well of you,
yet they do not really care
about you.
3 But, LORD, you know me;
you see what I do
and how I love you.
Drag these evil people away like
sheep to be butchered;
guard them until it is time for
them to be slaughtered.
4 How long will our land be dry,
and the grass in every field be
withered?
Animals and birds are dying
because of the wickedness of
our people,
people who say, 'God doesn't
see what we are doing.' "[o]

5 The LORD said,
"Jeremiah, if you get tired racing
against people,
how can you race against
horses?
If you can't even stand up in open
country,
how will you manage in the
jungle by the Jordan?
6 Even your relatives, members of
your own family, have
betrayed you;
they join in the attacks
against you.
Do not trust them, even though
they speak friendly words."

The LORD's Sorrow because of His People

7 The LORD says,
"I have abandoned Israel;
I have rejected my chosen
nation.
I have given the people I love
into the power of their enemies.
8 My chosen people have turned
against me;
like a lion in the forest
they have roared at me,
and so I hate them.
9 My chosen people are like a bird
attacked from all sides by
hawks.
Call the wild animals
to come and join in the feast!
10 Many foreign rulers have
destroyed my vineyard;
they have trampled down my
fields;
they have turned my lovely land
into a desert.
11 They have made it a wasteland;
it lies desolate before me.
The whole land has become a
desert,
and no one cares.
12 Across all the desert highlands
people have come to plunder.
I have sent war to destroy the
entire land;
no one can live in peace.
13 My people planted wheat, but
gathered weeds;
they have worked hard, but got
nothing for it.
Because of my fierce anger
their crops have failed."

The LORD's Promise to Israel's Neighbors

14 The LORD says, "I have something to
say about Israel's neighbors who have
ruined the land I gave to my people Is-

[o] *Some ancient translations* what we are doing; *Hebrew* our latter end.

rael. I will take those wicked people
away from their countries like an uprooted plant, and I will rescue Judah
from them. 15 But after I have taken them
away, I will have mercy on them; I will
bring each nation back to its own land
and to its own country. 16 If with all their
hearts they will accept the religion of my
people and will swear, 'As the LORD
lives'—as they once taught my people to
swear by Baal—then they will also be a
part of my people and will prosper.
17 But if any nation will not obey, then I
will completely uproot it and destroy it.
I, the LORD, have spoken."

The Linen Shorts

13 The LORD told me to go and buy
myself some linen shorts and to
put them on; but he told me not to put
them in water. 2 So I bought them and
put them on. 3 Then the LORD spoke to me
again and said, 4 "Go to the Euphrates
River and hide the shorts in a hole in the
rocks." 5 So I went and hid them near the
Euphrates.
6 Some time later the LORD told me to
go back to the Euphrates and get the
shorts. 7 So I went back, and when I
found the place where I had hidden
them, I saw that they were ruined and
were no longer any good.
8 Then the LORD spoke to me again. He
said, 9 "This is how I will destroy the
pride of Judah and the great pride of Jerusalem. 10 These evil people have refused to obey me. They have been as
stubborn and wicked as ever, and have
worshiped and served other gods. So
then, they will become like these shorts
that are no longer any good. 11 Just as
shorts fit tightly around the waist, so I
intended all the people of Israel and Judah to hold tightly to me. I did this so
that they would be my people and would
bring praise and honor to my name; but
they would not obey me."

The Wine Jar

12 The LORD God said to me, "Jeremiah,
tell the people of Israel that every wine
jar should be filled with wine. They will
answer that they know every wine jar
should be filled with wine. 13 Then tell
them that I, the LORD, am going to fill the
people in this land with wine until they
are drunk: the kings, who are David's
descendants, the priests, the prophets,
and all the people of Jerusalem. 14 Then
I will smash them like jars against one
another, old and young alike. No pity,
compassion, or mercy will stop me from
killing them."

Jeremiah Warns against Pride

15 People of Israel, the LORD has
spoken!
Be humble and listen to him.
16 Honor the LORD, your God,
before he brings darkness,
and you stumble on the
mountains;
before he turns into deep darkness
the light you hoped for.
17 If you will not listen,
I will cry in secret because of
your pride;
I will cry bitterly, and my tears
will flow
because the LORD's people have
been taken away as captives.

18 The LORD said to me, "Tell the king
and his mother to come down from their
thrones, because their beautiful crowns
have fallen from their heads.[p] 19 The
towns of southern Judah are under
siege; no one can get through to them.
All the people of Judah have been taken
away into exile."
20 Jerusalem, look! Your enemies are
coming down from the north! Where are
the people entrusted to your care, your
people you were so proud of? 21 What
will you say when people you thought
were your friends conquer you and rule
over you?[q] You will be in pain like a
woman giving birth. 22 If you ask why all
this has happened to you—why your
clothes have been torn off and you have
been raped—it is because your sin is so
terrible. 23 Can people change the color
of their skin, or a leopard remove its
spots? If they could, then you that do
nothing but evil could learn to do what is
right. 24 The LORD will scatter you like
straw that is blown away by the desert
wind. 25 He has said that this will be your
fate. This is what he has decided to do
with you, because you have forgotten
him and have trusted in false gods.

[p] *Some ancient translations* from their heads; *Hebrew unclear.* [q] *Probable text* What . . . over you; *Hebrew unclear.*

26 The LORD himself will strip off your
clothes and expose you to shame. 27 He
has seen you do the things he hates. He
has seen you go after pagan gods on the
hills and in the fields, like a man lusting
after his neighbor's wife or like a stal-
lion after a mare. People of Jerusalem,
you are doomed! When will you ever be
pure?

The Terrible Drought

14 The LORD said to me concerning
the drought,

2 "Judah is in mourning;
its cities are dying,
its people lie on the ground in
sorrow,
and Jerusalem cries out for help.
3 The rich people send their
servants for water;
they go to the cisterns,
but find no water;
they come back with their jars
empty.
Discouraged and confused,
they hide their faces.
4 Because there is no rain
and the ground is dried up,
the farmers are sick at heart;
they hide their faces.
5 In the field the mother deer
abandons her newborn fawn
because there is no grass.
6 The wild donkeys stand on the
hilltops
and pant for breath like
jackals;
their eyesight fails them
because they have no food.
7 My people cry out to me,
'Even though our sins accuse us,
help us, LORD, as you have
promised.
We have turned away from you
many times;
we have sinned against you.
8 You are Israel's only hope;
you are the one who saves us
from disaster.
Why are you like a stranger in our
land,
like a traveler who stays for
only one night?
9 Why are you like someone taken
by surprise,
like a soldier powerless to help?
Surely, LORD, you are with us!
We are your people;
do not abandon us.'"

10 The LORD says about these people,
"They love to run away from me, and
they will not control themselves. So I am
not pleased with them. I will remember
the wrongs they have done and punish
them because of their sins."
11 The LORD said to me, "Do not ask me
to help these people. 12 Even if they fast,
I will not listen to their cry for help; and
even if they offer me burnt offerings and
grain offerings, I will not be pleased
with them. Instead, I will kill them in
war and by starvation and disease."
13 Then I said, "Sovereign LORD, you
know that the prophets are telling the
people that there will be no war or starvation, because you have promised, they
say, that there will be only peace in our
land."
14 But the LORD replied, "The prophets
are telling lies in my name; I did not
send them, nor did I give them any orders or speak one word to them. The visions they talk about have not come
from me; their predictions are worthless
things that they have imagined. 15 I, the
LORD, tell you what I am going to do to
those prophets whom I did not send but
who speak in my name and say war and
starvation will not strike this land—I
will kill them in war and by starvation.
16 The people to whom they have said
these things will be killed in the same
way. Their bodies will be thrown out
into the streets of Jerusalem, and there
will be no one to bury them. This will
happen to all of them—including their
wives, their sons, and their daughters.
I will make them pay for their
wickedness."
17 The LORD commanded me to tell the
people about my sorrow and to say:

"May my eyes flow with tears day
and night,
may I never stop weeping,
for my people are deeply wounded
and are badly hurt.
18 When I go out in the fields,
I see the bodies of men killed
in war;
when I go into the towns,
I see people starving to death.
Prophets and priests carry on their
work,

but they don't know what they
are doing."[r]

The People Plead with the LORD

19 LORD, have you completely rejected
Judah?
Do you hate the people of Zion?
Why have you hurt us so badly
that we cannot be healed?
We looked for peace, but nothing
good happened;
we hoped for healing, but terror
came instead.
20 We have sinned against you, LORD;
we confess our own sins
and the sins of our ancestors.
21 Remember your promises and do
not despise us;
do not bring disgrace on
Jerusalem,
the place of your glorious
throne.
Do not break the covenant you
made with us.
22 None of the idols of the nations
can send rain;
the sky by itself cannot make
showers fall.
We have put our hope in you,
O LORD our God,
because you are the one who
does these things.

Doom for the People of Judah

15 Then the LORD said to me, "Even
if Moses and Samuel were standing here pleading with me, I would not
show these people any mercy. Make
them go away; make them get out of my
sight. 2 When they ask you where they
should go, tell them that I have said:
Some are doomed to die by
disease —
that's where they will go!
Others are doomed to die in war —
that's where they will go!
Some are doomed to die of
starvation —
that's where they will go!
Others are doomed to be taken
away as prisoners —
that's where they will go!
3 I, the LORD, have decided that four terrible things will happen to them: they will
be killed in war; their bodies will be
dragged off by dogs; birds will eat them,
and wild animals will devour what is left
over. 4 I will make all the people of the
world horrified at them because of what
Hezekiah's son Manasseh did in Jerusalem when he was king of Judah."
5 The LORD says,
"Who will pity you, people of
Jerusalem,
and who will grieve over you?
Who will stop long enough
to ask how you are?
6 You people have rejected me;
you have turned your backs
on me.
So I reached out and crushed you
because I was tired of
controlling my anger.[s]
7 In every town in the land
I threw you to the wind like
straw.
I destroyed you, my people,
I killed your children
because you did not stop your
evil ways.
8 There are more widows in your
land
than grains of sand by the sea.
I killed your young men in their
prime
and made their mothers suffer.
I suddenly struck them
with anguish and terror.
9 The mother who lost her seven
children has fainted,
gasping for breath.
Her daylight has turned to
darkness;
she is disgraced and sick at
heart.
I will let your enemies kill
those of you who are still alive.
I, the LORD, have spoken."

Jeremiah Complains to the LORD

10 What an unhappy man I am! Why
did my mother bring me into the world?
I have to quarrel and argue with everyone in the land. I have not lent any
money or borrowed any; yet everyone
curses me. 11 LORD, may all their curses
come true if I have not served[t] you well,
if I have not pleaded with you on behalf
of my enemies when they were in trouble and distress. (12 No one can break

[r] Prophets . . . doing; *or* Prophets and priests have been dragged away to a land they know nothing about. [s] you because . . . anger; *or* you; I was tired of feeling sorry for you.
[t] *Probable text* LORD, . . . served; *Hebrew unclear.*

iron, especially the iron from the north
that is mixed with bronze.)
13 The LORD said to me, "I will send enemies to carry away the wealth and treasures of my people, in order to punish
them for the sins they have committed
throughout the land. 14 I will make them
serve their enemies in a land they know
nothing about, because my anger is like
fire, and it will burn forever."
15 Then I said, "LORD, you understand.
Remember me and help me. Let me have
revenge on those who persecute me. Do
not be so patient with them that they
succeed in killing me. Remember that it
is for your sake that I am insulted. 16 You
spoke to me, and I listened to every
word. I belong to you, LORD God
Almighty, and so your words filled my
heart with joy and happiness. 17 I did not
spend my time with other people, laughing and having a good time. In obedience to your orders I stayed by myself
and was filled with anger. 18 Why do I
keep on suffering? Why are my wounds
incurable? Why won't they heal? Do you
intend to disappoint me like a stream
that goes dry in the summer?"
19 To this the LORD replied, "If you return, I will take you back, and you will
be my servant again. If instead of talking
nonsense you proclaim a worthwhile
message, you will be my prophet again.
The people will come back to you, and
you will not need to go to them. 20 I will
make you like a solid bronze wall as far
as they are concerned. They will fight
against you, but they will not defeat you.
I will be with you to protect you and
keep you safe. 21 I will rescue you from
the power of wicked and violent people.
I, the LORD, have spoken."

The LORD's Will for Jeremiah's Life

16 Again the LORD spoke to me and
said, 2 "Do not marry or have
children in a place like this. 3 I will tell
you what is going to happen to the children who are born here and to their parents. 4 They will die of terrible diseases,
and no one will mourn for them or bury
them. Their bodies will lie like piles of
manure on the ground. They will be
killed in war or die of starvation, and
their bodies will be food for the birds
and the wild animals.
5 "You must not enter a house where
there is mourning. Do not grieve for
anyone. I will no longer bless my people
with peace or show them love and
mercy. 6 The rich and the poor will die in
this land, but no one will bury them or
mourn for them. Not one of you will
gash yourself or shave your head to
show your grief. 7 No one will eat or
drink with anyone to offer comfort when
a loved one dies. No one will show sympathy, not even for someone who has
lost a father or mother.
8 "Do not enter a house where people
are feasting. Do not sit down with them
to eat and drink. 9 Listen to what I, the
LORD Almighty, the God of Israel, have to
say. I will silence the sounds of joy and
gladness and the happy sounds of wedding feasts. The people here will live to
see this happen.
10 "When you tell them all this, they
will ask you why I have decided to punish them so harshly. They will ask what
crime they are guilty of and what sin
they have committed against the LORD
their God. 11 Then tell them that the LORD
has said, 'Your ancestors turned away
from me and worshiped and served
other gods. They abandoned me and did
not obey my teachings. 12 But you have
done even worse than your ancestors.
All of you are stubborn and evil, and you
do not obey me. 13 So then, I will throw
you out of this land into a land that neither you nor your ancestors have ever
known. And there you will serve other
gods day and night, and I will show you
no mercy.' "

The Return from Exile

14 The LORD says, "The time is coming
when people will no longer swear by me
as the living God who brought the people of Israel out of the land of Egypt.
15 Instead, they will swear by me as the
living God who brought the people of Israel out of a northern land and out of all
the other countries where I had scattered them. I will bring them back
to their own country, to the land that I
gave their ancestors. I, the LORD, have
spoken."

The Coming Punishment

16 The LORD says, "I am sending for
many fishermen to come and catch these
people. Then I will send for many hunters to hunt them down on every mountain and hill and in the caves among the

rocks. 17 I see everything they do. Nothing is hidden from me; their sins do not
escape my sight. 18 I will make them pay
double for their sin and wickedness, because they have defiled my land with
idols that are as lifeless as corpses, and
have filled it with their false gods."

Jeremiah's Prayer of Confidence in the LORD

19 LORD, you are the one who protects
me and gives me strength; you help me
in times of trouble. Nations will come to
you from the ends of the earth and say,
"Our ancestors had nothing but false
gods, nothing but useless idols. 20 Can
people make their own gods? No, if they
did, those would not really be gods."
21 "So then," says the LORD, "once and
for all I will make the nations know my
power and my might; they will know
that I am the LORD."

The Sin and Punishment of Judah

17 The LORD says, "People of Judah,
your sin is written with an iron
pen; it is engraved on your hearts with a
diamond point and carved on the corners of your altars. 2 Your people worship at the altars and the symbols that
have been set up for the goddess Asherah by every green tree and on the hilltops 3 and on the mountains in the open
country. I will have your enemies take
away your wealth and your treasures
because of all the sins you have committed[u] throughout your land. 4 You will
have to give up[v] the land I gave you,
and I will make you serve your enemies
in a land you know nothing about, because my anger is like a fire, and it will
burn forever."

Various Sayings

5 The LORD says,
"I will condemn those
who turn away from me
and put their trust in human
beings,
in the strength of mortals.
6 He is like a bush in the desert,
which grows in the dry
wasteland,
on salty ground where nothing
else grows.
Nothing good ever happens
to him.

7 "But I will bless the person
who puts his trust in me.
8 He is like a tree growing near a
stream
and sending out roots to the
water.
It is not afraid when hot weather
comes,
because its leaves stay green;
it has no worries when there is no
rain;
it keeps on bearing fruit.

9 "Who can understand the human
heart?
There is nothing else so
deceitful;
it is too sick to be healed.
10 I, the LORD, search the minds
and test the hearts of people.
I treat each of them according to
the way they live,
according to what they do."

11 The person who gets money
dishonestly
is like a bird that hatches eggs it
didn't lay.
In the prime of life he will lose his
riches,
and in the end he is nothing but
a fool.

12 Our Temple is like a glorious
throne,
standing on a high mountain
from the beginning.

13 LORD, you are Israel's hope;
all who abandon you will be put
to shame.
They will disappear like names
written in the dust,[w]
because they have abandoned
you, the LORD,
the spring of fresh water.

Jeremiah Asks the LORD for Help

14 LORD, heal me and I will be completely well; rescue me and I will be perfectly safe. You are the one I praise!
15 The people say to me, "Where are

[u] *Probable text* because of all the sins you have committed; *Hebrew* your high places for sins.
[v] *Probable text* You . . . give up; *Hebrew unclear.* [w] disappear . . . dust; *or* go to the world of the dead.

those threats the LORD made against us?
Let him carry them out now!"
16 But, LORD, I never urged you to bring
disaster on them;[x] I did not wish a time
of trouble for them. LORD, you know this;
you know what I have said. 17 Do not be
a terror to me; you are my place of safety
when trouble comes. 18 Bring disgrace
on those who persecute me, but spare
me, LORD. Fill them with terror, but do
not terrify me. Bring disaster on them
and break them to pieces.

On Observing the Sabbath

19 The LORD said to me, "Jeremiah, go
and announce my message at the People's Gate, through which the kings of
Judah enter and leave the city; then go
to all the other gates of Jerusalem. 20 Tell
the kings and all the people of Judah and
everyone who lives in Jerusalem and enters these gates, to listen to what I say.
21 Tell them that if they love their lives,
they must not carry any load on the Sabbath; they must not carry anything in
through the gates of Jerusalem 22 or
carry anything out of their houses on the
Sabbath. They must not work on the
Sabbath; they must observe it as a sacred day, as I commanded their ancestors. 23 Their ancestors did not listen to
me or pay any attention. Instead, they
became stubborn; they would not obey
me or learn from me.
24 "Tell these people that they must
obey all my commands. They must not
carry any load in through the gates of
this city on the Sabbath. They must observe the Sabbath as a sacred day and
must not do any work at all. 25 Then their
kings and princes will enter the gates of
Jerusalem and have the same royal
power that David had. Together with the
people of Judah and of Jerusalem, they
will ride in chariots and on horses, and
the city of Jerusalem will always be
filled with people. 26 People will come
from the towns of Judah and from the
villages around Jerusalem; they will
come from the territory of Benjamin,
from the foothills, from the mountains,
and from southern Judah. They will
bring to my Temple burnt offerings and
sacrifices, grain offerings and incense,
as well as thank offerings. 27 But they
must obey me and observe the Sabbath
as a sacred day. They must not carry any
load through the gates of Jerusalem on
that day, for if they do, I will set the
gates of Jerusalem on fire. Fire will burn
down the palaces of Jerusalem, and no
one will be able to put it out."

Jeremiah at the Potter's House

18 The LORD said to me, 2 "Go down
to the potter's house, where I will
give you my message." 3 So I went there
and saw the potter working at his wheel.
4 Whenever a piece of pottery turned out
imperfect, he would take the clay and
make it into something else.
5 Then the LORD said to me, 6 "Don't I
have the right to do with you people of
Israel what the potter did with the clay?
You are in my hands just like clay in the
potter's hands. 7 If at any time I say that
I am going to uproot, break down, or destroy any nation or kingdom, 8 but then
that nation turns from its evil, I will not
do what I said I would. 9 On the other
hand, if I say that I am going to plant or
build up any nation or kingdom, 10 but
then that nation disobeys me and does
evil, I will not do what I said I would.
11 Now then, tell the people of Judah and
of Jerusalem that I am making plans
against them and getting ready to punish them. Tell them to stop living sinful
lives — to change their ways and the
things they are doing. 12 They will answer, 'No, why should we? We will all be
just as stubborn and evil as we want
to be.' "

The People Reject the LORD

13 The LORD says,
"Ask every nation if such a thing
has ever happened before.
The people of Israel have done a
terrible thing!
14 Are Lebanon's rocky heights ever
without snow?
Do its cool mountain streams
ever run dry?
15 Yet my people have forgotten me;
they burn incense to idols.
They have stumbled in the way
they should go;
they no longer follow the old
ways;
they walk on unmarked paths.

[x] *Probable text* bring disaster on them; *Hebrew* from being a shepherd after you.

16 They have made this land a thing
of horror,
to be despised forever.
All who pass by will be shocked at
what they see;
they will shake their heads in
amazement.
17 I will scatter my people before
their enemies,
like dust blown by the east
wind.
I will turn my back on them;
I will not help them when the
disaster comes."

A Plot against Jeremiah

18 Then the people said, "Let's do
something about Jeremiah! There will
always be priests to instruct us, the wise
to give us counsel, and prophets to proclaim God's message. Let's bring
charges against him and stop listening
to what he says."
19 So I prayed, "LORD, hear what I am
saying and listen to what my enemies
are saying about me. 20 Is evil the payment for good? Yet they have dug a pit
for me to fall in. Remember how I came
to you and spoke on their behalf, so that
you would not deal with them in anger.
21 But now, LORD, let their children starve
to death; let them be killed in war. Let
the women lose their husbands and children; let the men die of disease and the
young men be killed in battle. 22 Send a
mob to plunder their homes without
warning; make them cry out in terror.
They have dug a pit for me to fall in and
have set traps to catch me. 23 But, LORD,
you know all their plots to kill me. Do
not forgive their evil or pardon their sin.
Throw them down in defeat and deal
with them while you are angry."

The Broken Jar

19 The LORD told me to go and buy a
clay jar. He also told me to take
some of the elders of the people and
some of the older priests, 2 and to go
through Potsherd Gate out to Hinnom
Valley. There I was to proclaim the message that he would give me. 3 The LORD
told me to say, "Kings of Judah and people of Jerusalem, listen to what I, the
LORD Almighty, the God of Israel, have to
say. I am going to bring such a disaster
on this place that everyone who hears
about it will be stunned. 4 I am going to
do this because the people have abandoned me and defiled this place by offering sacrifices here to other gods—gods
that neither they nor their ancestors nor
the kings of Judah have known anything
about. They have filled this place with
the blood of innocent people, 5 and they
have built altars for Baal in order to
burn their children in the fire as sacrifices. I never commanded them to do
this; it never even entered my mind. 6 So
then, the time will come when this place
will no longer be called Topheth or Hinnom Valley. Instead, it will be known as
Slaughter Valley. 7 In this place I will
frustrate all the plans of the people of
Judah and Jerusalem. I will let their enemies triumph over them and kill them in
battle. I will give their corpses to the
birds and the wild animals as food.
8 I will bring such terrible destruction on
this city that everyone who passes by
will be shocked and amazed. 9 The enemy will surround the city and try to kill
its people. The siege will be so terrible
that the people inside the city will eat
one another and even their own
children."
10 Then the LORD told me to break the
jar in front of those who had gone with
me 11 and to tell them that the LORD
Almighty had said, "I will break this
people and this city, and it will be like
this broken clay jar that cannot be put
together again. People will bury their
dead even in Topheth because there
will be nowhere else to bury them.
12 I promise that I will make this city and
its inhabitants like Topheth. 13 The
houses of Jerusalem, the houses of the
kings of Judah, and indeed all the
houses on whose roofs incense has been
burned to the stars and where wine has
been poured out as an offering to other
gods—they will all be as unclean as
Topheth."
14 Then I left Topheth, where the LORD
had sent me to proclaim his message. I
went and stood in the court of the Temple and told all the people 15 that the
LORD Almighty, the God of Israel, had
said, "I am going to bring on this city
and on every nearby town all the punishment that I said I would, because you
are stubborn and will not listen to what
I say."

Jeremiah's Conflict with Pashhur the Priest

20 When the priest Pashhur son of
Immer, who was the chief officer
of the Temple, heard me proclaim these
things, 2he had me beaten and placed in
chains near the upper Benjamin Gate in
the Temple. 3The next morning, after
Pashhur had released me from the
chains, I said to him, "The LORD did not
name you Pashhur. The name he has
given you is 'Terror Everywhere.' 4The
LORD himself has said, 'I am going to
make you a terror to yourself and to
your friends, and you will see them all
killed by the swords of their enemies. I
am going to put all the people of Judah
under the power of the king of Babylonia; he will take some away as prisoners
to his country and put others to death.
5I will also let their enemies plunder all
the wealth of this city and seize all its
possessions and property, even the
treasures of the kings of Judah, and
carry everything off to Babylonia. 6As
for you, Pashhur, you and all your family will also be captured and taken off to
Babylonia. There you will die and be
buried, along with all your friends to
whom you have told so many lies.' "

Jeremiah Complains to the LORD

7LORD, you have deceived me,
and I was deceived.
You are stronger than I am,
and you have overpowered me.
Everyone makes fun of me;
they laugh at me all day long.

8Whenever I speak, I have to
cry out
and shout, "Violence!
Destruction!"
LORD, I am ridiculed and scorned
all the time
because I proclaim your
message.
9But when I say, "I will forget the
LORD
and no longer speak in his
name,"
then your message is like a fire
burning deep within me.
I try my best to hold it in,
but can no longer keep it back.
10I hear everybody whispering,
"Terror is everywhere!
So let's report him to the
authorities!"
Even my close friends wait for my
downfall.
"Perhaps he can be tricked,"
they say;
"then we can catch him and get
revenge."
11But you, LORD, are on my side,
strong and mighty,
and those who persecute me will
fail.
They will be disgraced forever,
because they cannot succeed.
Their disgrace will never be
forgotten.
12But, Almighty LORD, you test
people justly;
you know what is in their hearts
and minds.
So let me see you take revenge on
my enemies,
for I have placed my cause in
your hands.
13Sing to the LORD!
Praise the LORD!
He rescues the oppressed from the
power of evil people.

14Curse the day I was born!
Forget the day my mother gave me
birth!
15Curse the one who made my
father glad
by bringing him the news,
"It's a boy! You have a son!"
16May he be like those cities
that the LORD destroyed without
mercy.
May he hear cries of pain in the
morning
and the battle alarm at noon,
17 for not killing me before I was
born.
Then my mother's womb would
have been my grave.
18Why was I born?
Was it only to have trouble and
sorrow,
to end my life in disgrace?

Jerusalem's Defeat Is Predicted

21 King Zedekiah of Judah sent to
me Pashhur son of Malchiah and
the priest Zephaniah son of Maaseiah
with this request: 2"Please speak to the
LORD for us, because King Nebuchadnezzar of Babylonia and his army are be-

sieging the city. Maybe the LORD will
perform one of his miracles for us and
force Nebuchadnezzar to retreat."
3 Then the LORD spoke to me, and I told
those who had been sent to me 4 to tell
Zedekiah that the LORD, the God of Israel, had said, "Zedekiah, I am going to
defeat your army that is fighting against
the king of Babylonia and his army. I
will pile up your soldiers' weapons in the
center of the city. 5 I will fight against
you with all my might, my anger, my
wrath, and my fury. 6 I will kill everyone
living in this city; people and animals
alike will die of a terrible disease. 7 But
as for you, your officials, and the people
who survive the war, the famine, and the
disease—I will let all of you be captured
by King Nebuchadnezzar and by your
enemies, who want to kill you. Nebuchadnezzar will put you to death. He will
not spare any of you or show mercy or
pity to any of you. I, the LORD, have
spoken."
8 Then the LORD told me to say to the
people, "Listen! I, the LORD, am giving
you a choice between the way that leads
to life and the way that leads to death.
9 Anyone who stays in the city will be
killed in war or by starvation or disease.
But those who go out and surrender to
the Babylonians, who are now attacking
the city, will not be killed; they will at
least escape with their life. 10 I have
made up my mind not to spare this city,
but to destroy it. It will be given over to
the king of Babylonia, and he will burn it
to the ground. I, the LORD, have spoken."

Judgment on the Royal House of Judah

11-12 The LORD told me to give this message to the royal house of Judah, the
descendants of David: "Listen to what I,
the LORD, am saying. See that justice is
done every day. Protect the person who
is being cheated from the one who is
cheating him. If you don't, the evil you
are doing will make my anger burn like
a fire that cannot be put out. 13 You, Jerusalem, are sitting[y] high above the valleys, like a rock rising above the plain.
But I will fight against you. You say that
no one can attack you or break through
your defenses. 14 But I will punish you
for what you have done. I will set your
palace on fire, and the fire will burn
down everything around it. I, the LORD,
have spoken."

Jeremiah's Message to the Royal House of Judah

22 1-2 The LORD told me to go to the
palace of the king of Judah, the
descendant of David, and there tell the
king, his officials, and the people of Jerusalem to listen to what the LORD had
said: 3 "I, the LORD, command you to do
what is just and right. Protect the person
who is being cheated from the one who
is cheating him. Do not mistreat or oppress aliens, orphans, or widows; and do
not kill innocent people in this holy
place. 4 If you really do as I have commanded, then David's descendants will
continue to be kings. And they, together
with their officials and their people, will
continue to pass through the gates of
this palace in chariots and on horses.
5 But if you do not obey my commands,
then I swear to you that this palace will
fall into ruins. I, the LORD, have spoken.
6 "To me, Judah's royal palace is as
beautiful as the land of Gilead and as the
Lebanon Mountains; but I will make it a
desolate place where no one lives. 7 I am
sending men to destroy it. They will all
bring their axes, cut down its beautiful
cedar pillars, and throw them into the
fire.
8 "Afterward many foreigners will
pass by and ask one another why I, the
LORD, have done such a thing to this
great city. 9 Then they will answer that it
is because you have abandoned your
covenant with me, your God, and have
worshiped and served other gods."

Jeremiah's Message concerning Joahaz

10 People of Judah, do not weep for
King Josiah;
do not mourn his death.
But weep bitterly for Joahaz,
his son;
they are taking him away, never
to return,
never again to see the land
where he was born.

11 The LORD says concerning Josiah's
son Joahaz, who succeeded his father as
king of Judah, "He has gone away from

[y] You, Jerusalem, are sitting; *or* You are enthroned.

here, never to return. 12 He will die in the
country where they have taken him, and
he will never again see this land."

Jeremiah's Message concerning Jehoiakim

13 Doomed is the one who builds his
house by injustice
and enlarges it by dishonesty;
who makes his people work for
nothing
and does not pay their wages.
14 Doomed is the one who says,
"I will build myself a mansion
with spacious rooms upstairs."
So he puts windows in his house,
panels it with cedar,
and paints it red.
15 Does it make you a better king
if you build houses of cedar,
finer than those of others?
Your father enjoyed a full life.
He was always just and fair,
and he prospered in everything
he did.
16 He gave the poor a fair trial,
and all went well with him.
That is what it means to know the
LORD.
17 But you can only see your selfish
interests;
you kill the innocent
and violently oppress your
people.
The LORD has spoken.

18 So then, the LORD says about Josiah's son Jehoiakim, king of Judah,
"No one will mourn his death
or say,
'How terrible, my friend, how
terrible!'
No one will weep for him or cry,
'My lord! My king!'
19 With the funeral honors of a
donkey,
he will be dragged away
and thrown outside Jerusalem's
gates."

Jeremiah's Message about the Fate of Jerusalem

20 People of Jerusalem, go to
Lebanon and shout,
go to the land of Bashan
and cry;
call out from the mountains of
Moab,
because all your allies have been
defeated.
21 The LORD spoke to you when you
were prosperous,
but you refused to listen.
That is what you've done all your
life;
you never would obey the LORD.
22 Your leaders will be blown away
by the wind,
your allies taken as prisoners
of war,
your city disgraced and put to
shame
because of all the evil you have
done.
23 You rest secure among the cedars
brought from Lebanon;
but how pitiful you'll be when
pains strike you,
pains like those of a woman in
labor.

God's Judgment on Jehoiachin

24 The LORD said to King Jehoiachin,
son of King Jehoiakim of Judah, "As
surely as I am the living God, even if you
were the signet ring on my right hand, I
would pull you off 25 and give you to
people you are afraid of, people who
want to kill you. I will give you to King
Nebuchadnezzar of Babylonia and
his soldiers. 26 I am going to force you
and your mother into exile. You will go
to a country where neither of you was
born, and both of you will die there.
27 You will long to see this country
again, but you will never return."

28 I said, "Has King Jehoiachin become like a broken jar that is thrown
away and that no one wants? Is that why
he and his children have been taken into
exile to a land they know nothing
about?"

29 O land, land, land!
Listen to what the LORD has said:
30 "This man is condemned to lose
his children,
to be a man who will never
succeed.
He will have no descendants
who will rule in Judah
as David's successors.
I, the LORD, have spoken."

Hope for the Future

23 How terrible will be the LORD's
judgment on those rulers who
destroy and scatter his people! 2This is
what the LORD, the God of Israel, says
about the rulers who were supposed to
take care of his people: "You have not
taken care of my people; you have scattered them and driven them away. Now
I am going to punish you for the evil you
have done. 3I will gather the rest of my
people from the countries where I have
scattered them, and I will bring them
back to their homeland. They will have
many children and increase in number.
4I will appoint rulers to take care of
them. My people will no longer be afraid
or terrified, and I will not punish them
again.[z] I, the LORD, have spoken."
5The LORD says, "The time is coming
when I will choose as king a righteous
descendant of David. That king will rule
wisely and do what is right and just
throughout the land. 6When he is king,
the people of Judah will be safe, and the
people of Israel will live in peace. He will
be called 'The LORD Our Salvation.'
7"The time is coming," says the LORD,
"when people will no longer swear by
me as the living God who brought the
people of Israel out of the land of Egypt.
8Instead, they will swear by me as the
living God who brought the people of Israel out of a northern land and out of all
the other countries where I had scattered them. Then they will live in their
own land."

Jeremiah's Message about the Prophets

9My heart is crushed,
and I am trembling.
Because of the LORD,
because of his holy words,
I am like a man who is drunk,
someone who has had too much
wine.
10The land is full of people
unfaithful to the LORD;
they live wicked lives and
misuse their power.
Because of the LORD's curse the
land mourns
and the pastures are dry.

11The LORD says,
"The prophets and the priests are
godless;
I have caught them doing evil in
the Temple itself.
12The paths they follow will be
slippery and dark;
I will make them stumble and
fall.
I am going to bring disaster on
them;
the time of their punishment is
coming.
I, the LORD, have spoken.
13I have seen the sin of Samaria's
prophets:
they have spoken in the name of
Baal
and have led my people astray.
14But I have seen the prophets in
Jerusalem do even worse:
they commit adultery and tell
lies;
they help people to do wrong,
so that no one stops doing what
is evil.
To me they are all as bad
as the people of Sodom and
Gomorrah.

15"So then, this is what I, the LORD
Almighty, say about the prophets of Jerusalem:
I will give them bitter plants to eat
and poison to drink,
because they have spread
ungodliness throughout the
land."
16The LORD Almighty said to the people of Jerusalem, "Do not listen to what
the prophets say; they are filling you
with false hopes. They tell you what they
have imagined and not what I have said.
17To the people who refuse to listen to
what I have said, they keep saying that
all will go well with them. And they tell
everyone who is stubborn that disaster
will never touch them."
18I said, "None of these prophets has
ever known the LORD's secret thoughts.
None of them has ever heard or understood his message, or ever listened or
paid attention to what he said. 19His anger is a storm, a furious wind that will
rage over the heads of the wicked, 20and
it will not end until he has done everything he intends to do. In days to come

[z] I will not punish them again; *or* not one of them will be missing.

his people will understand this clearly."
21 The LORD said, "I did not send these
prophets, but even so they went. I did
not give them any message, but still they
spoke in my name. 22 If they had known
my secret thoughts, then they could
have proclaimed my message to my people and could have made them give up
the evil lives they live and the wicked
things they do.

23 "I am a God who is everywhere and
not in one place only. 24 No one can hide
where I cannot see them. Do you not
know that I am everywhere in heaven
and on earth? 25 I know what those
prophets have said who speak lies in my
name and claim that I have given them
my messages in their dreams. 26 How
much longer will those prophets mislead
my people with the lies they have invented? 27 They think that the dreams
they tell will make my people forget me,
just as their ancestors forgot me and
turned to Baal. 28 The prophet who has
had a dream should say it is only a
dream, but the prophet who has heard
my message should proclaim that message faithfully. What good is straw compared with wheat? 29 My message is like
a fire and like a hammer that breaks
rocks in pieces. 30 I am against those
prophets who take each other's words
and proclaim them as my message.
31 I am also against those prophets who
speak their own words and claim they
came from me. 32 Listen to what I, the
LORD, say! I am against the prophets who
tell their dreams that are full of lies.
They tell these dreams and lead my people astray with their lies and their boasting. I did not send them or order them to
go, and they are of no help at all to the
people. I, the LORD, have spoken."

The LORD's Burden

33 The LORD said to me, "Jeremiah,
when one of my people or a prophet or a
priest asks you, 'What is the LORD's message?' you are to say, 'You are a burden[a] to the LORD, and he is going to get
rid of you.' 34 If any of my people or a
prophet or a priest even uses the words
'the LORD's burden,' I will punish them
and their families. 35 Instead, each one of
them should ask their friends and their
relatives, 'What answer has the LORD
given? What has the LORD said?' 36 So
they must no longer use the words 'the
LORD's burden,' because if any of them
do, I will make my message a real burden to them. The people have perverted
the words of their God, the living God,
the LORD Almighty. 37 Jeremiah, ask the
prophets, 'What answer did the LORD
give you? What did the LORD say?' 38 And
if they disobey my command and use the
words 'the LORD's burden,' then tell them
that 39 I will certainly pick them up[b] and
throw them far away from me, both
them and the city that I gave to them and
their ancestors. 40 I will bring on them
everlasting shame and disgrace that will
never be forgotten."

Two Baskets of Figs

24 The LORD showed me two baskets of figs placed in front of the
Temple. (This was after King Nebuchadnezzar of Babylonia had taken away Jehoiakim's son, King Jehoiachin of
Judah, as a prisoner from Jerusalem to
Babylonia, together with the leaders of
Judah, the craftworkers, and the skilled
workers.) 2 The first basket contained
good figs, those that ripen early; the
other one contained bad figs, too bad to
eat. 3 Then the LORD said to me, "Jeremiah, what do you see?"

I answered, "Figs. The good ones are
very good, and the bad ones are very
bad, too bad to eat."

4 So the LORD said to me, 5 "I, the LORD,
the God of Israel, consider that the people who were taken away to Babylonia
are like these good figs, and I will treat
them with kindness. 6 I will watch over
them and bring them back to this land. I
will build them up and not tear them
down; I will plant them and not pull
them up. 7 I will give them the desire to
know that I am the LORD. Then they will
be my people, and I will be their God,
because they will return to me with all
their heart.

8 "As for King Zedekiah of Judah, the
politicians around him, and the rest of
the people of Jerusalem who have
stayed in this land or moved to Egypt—I,
the LORD, will treat them all like these
figs that are too bad to be eaten. 9 I will

[a] *The Hebrew word for* message *and* burden *is the same.* [b] *The Hebrew verb for* pick up *comes from the same root as the Hebrew word for* message *and* burden.

bring such a disaster on them that all the
nations of the world will be terrified.
People will make fun of them, make
jokes about them, ridicule them, and use
their name as a curse everywhere I scatter them. 10 I will bring war, starvation,
and disease on them until there is not
one of them left in the land that I gave to
them and their ancestors."

The Enemy from the North

25 In the fourth year that Jehoiakim
son of Josiah was king of Judah,
I received a message from the LORD concerning all the people of Judah. (This
was the first year that Nebuchadnezzar
was king of Babylonia.) 2 I said to all the
people of Judah and of Jerusalem, 3 "For
twenty-three years, from the thirteenth
year that Josiah son of Amon was king
of Judah until this very day, the LORD has
spoken to me, and I have never failed to
tell you what he said. But you have paid
no attention. 4 You would not listen or
pay attention, even though the LORD has
continued to send you his servants the
prophets. 5 They told you to turn from
your wicked way of life and from the evil
things you are doing, so that you could
go on living in the land that the LORD
gave you and your ancestors as a permanent possession. 6 They told you not to
worship and serve other gods and not to
make the LORD angry by worshiping the
idols you had made. If you had obeyed
the LORD, then he would not have punished you. 7 But the LORD himself says
that you refused to listen to him. Instead,
you made him angry with your idols
and have brought his punishment on
yourselves.

8 "So then, because you would not listen to him, the LORD Almighty says, 9 'I
am going to send for all the peoples from
the north and for my servant, King Nebuchadnezzar of Babylonia. I am going to
bring them to fight against Judah and its
inhabitants and against all the neighboring nations. I am going to destroy this
nation and its neighbors and leave them
in ruins forever, a terrible and shocking
sight. I, the LORD, have spoken. 10 I will
silence their shouts of joy and gladness
and the happy sounds of wedding feasts.
They will have no oil for their lamps,
and there will be no more grain. 11 This
whole land will be left in ruins and will
be a shocking sight, and the neighboring
nations will serve the king of Babylonia
for seventy years. 12 After that I will punish Babylonia and its king for their sin. I
will destroy that country and leave it in
ruins forever. 13 I will punish Babylonia
with all the disasters that I threatened to
bring on the nations when I spoke
through Jeremiah – all the disasters recorded in this book. 14 I will pay the
Babylonians back for what they have
done, and many nations and great kings
will make slaves of them.' "

God's Judgment on the Nations

15 The LORD, the God of Israel, said to
me, "Here is a wine cup filled with my
anger. Take it to all the nations to whom
I send you, and make them drink from it.
16 When they drink from it, they will
stagger and go out of their minds because of the war I am sending against
them."

17 So I took the cup from the LORD's
hand, gave it to all the nations to whom
the LORD had sent me, and made them
drink from it. 18 Jerusalem and all the
towns of Judah, together with its kings
and leaders, were made to drink from it,
so that they would become a desert, a
terrible and shocking sight, and so that
people would use their name as a
curse – as they still do.

19-26 Here is the list of all the others
who had to drink from the cup:

the king of Egypt, his officials and
leaders;
all the Egyptians and all the
foreigners in Egypt;
all the kings of the land of Uz;
all the kings of the Philistine cities
of Ashkelon, Gaza, Ekron, and
what remains of Ashdod;
all the people of Edom, Moab, and
Ammon;
all the kings of Tyre and Sidon;
all the kings of the Mediterranean
lands;
the cities of Dedan, Tema,
and Buz;
all the people who cut their hair
short;
all the kings of Arabia;
all the kings of the desert tribes;
all the kings of Zimri, Elam, and
Media;
all the kings of the north, far and
near, one after another.

Every nation on the face of the earth

had to drink from it. Last of all, the king
of Babylonia will drink from it.
27 Then the LORD said to me, "Tell the
people that I, the LORD Almighty, the
God of Israel, am commanding them to
drink until they are drunk and vomit,
until they fall down and cannot get up,
because of the war that I am sending
against them. 28 And if they refuse to
take the cup from your hand and drink
from it, then tell them that the LORD
Almighty has said that they will still
have to drink from it. 29 I will begin my
work of destruction in my own city. Do
they think they will go unpunished? No,
they will be punished, for I am going to
send war on all the people on earth. I,
the LORD Almighty, have spoken.
30 "You, Jeremiah, must proclaim
everything I have said. You must tell
these people,

'The LORD will roar from heaven
and thunder from the heights of
heaven.
He will roar against his people;
he will shout like a man
treading grapes.
Everyone on earth will hear him,
31 and the sound will echo to the
ends of the earth.
The LORD has a case against the
nations.
He will bring all people to trial
and put the wicked to death.
The LORD has spoken.'"

32 The LORD Almighty says that disaster is coming on one nation after another, and a great storm is gathering at
the far ends of the earth. 33 On that day
the bodies of those whom the LORD has
killed will lie scattered from one end of
the earth to the other. No one will mourn
for them, and they will not be taken
away and buried. They will lie on the
ground like piles of manure.
34 Cry, you leaders, you shepherds of
my people, cry out loud! Mourn and roll
in the dust. The time has come for you to
be slaughtered,[c] and you will be butchered like rams.[d] 35 There will be no way
for you to escape. 36-37 You moan and cry
out in distress because the LORD in his
anger has destroyed your nation and left
your peaceful country in ruins. 38 The
LORD has abandoned his people[e] like a
lion that leaves its cave. The horrors of
war and the LORD's fierce anger have
turned the country into a desert.

Jeremiah Is Brought to Trial

26 Soon after Jehoiakim son of Josiah became king of Judah, 2 the
LORD said to me, "Stand in the court of
the Temple and proclaim all I have commanded you to say to the people who
come from the towns of Judah to worship there. Do not leave out anything.
3 Perhaps the people will listen and give
up their evil ways. If they do, then I will
change my mind about the destruction I
plan to bring on them for all their
wicked deeds."
4 The LORD told me to say to the people,
"I, the LORD, have said that you must
obey me by following the teaching that I
gave you, 5 and by paying attention to
the words of my servants, the prophets,
whom I have kept on sending to you.
You have never obeyed what they said.
6 If you continue to disobey, then I will
do to this Temple what I did to Shiloh,[f]
and all the nations of the world will use
the name of this city as a curse."
7 The priests, the prophets, and all the
people heard me saying these things in
the Temple, 8 and as soon as I had finished all that the LORD had commanded
me to speak, they grabbed me and
shouted, "You ought to be killed for this!
9 Why have you said in the LORD's name
that this Temple will become like Shiloh
and that this city will be destroyed and
no one will live in it?" Then the people
crowded around me.
10 When the leaders of Judah heard
what had happened, they hurried from
the royal palace to the Temple and took
their places at the New Gate. 11 Then the
priests and the prophets said to the leaders and to the people, "This man deserves to be sentenced to death because
he has spoken against our city. You
heard him with your own ears."
12 Then I said, "The LORD sent me to
proclaim everything that you heard me
say against this Temple and against this
city. 13 You must change the way you are
living and the things you are doing, and
must obey the LORD your God. If you do,

[c] *Hebrew has an additional word, the meaning of which is unclear.* [d] *One ancient translation* rams; *Hebrew* vessels. [e] The LORD . . . people; *or* The LORD's people run away.
[f] SHILOH: *See 7.12.*

he will change his mind about the destruction that he said he would bring on
you. 14 As for me, I am in your power! Do
with me whatever you think is fair and
right. 15 But be sure of this: if you kill me,
you and the people of this city will be
guilty of killing an innocent man, because it is the LORD who sent me to give
you this warning."

16 Then the leaders and the people said
to the priests and the prophets, "This
man spoke to us in the name of the LORD
our God; he should not be put to death."

17 After that, some of the elders stood
up and said to the people who had gathered, 18 "When Hezekiah was king of Judah, the prophet Micah of Moresheth
told all the people that the LORD
Almighty had said,

'Zion will be plowed like a field;
Jerusalem will become a pile of ruins,
and the Temple hill will become a forest.'

19 King Hezekiah and the people of Judah did not put Micah to death. Instead,
Hezekiah honored the LORD and tried to
win his favor. And the LORD changed his
mind about the disaster that he said he
would bring on them. Now we are about
to bring a terrible disaster on ourselves."

(20 There was another man, Uriah son
of Shemaiah from Kiriath Jearim, who
spoke in the name of the LORD against
this city and nation just as Jeremiah did.
21 When King Jehoiakim and his soldiers
and officials heard what Uriah had said,
the king tried to have him killed. But
Uriah heard about it; so he fled in terror
and escaped to Egypt. 22 King Jehoiakim, however, sent Elnathan son of Achbor and some other men to Egypt to get
Uriah. 23 They brought him back to King
Jehoiakim, who had him killed and his
body thrown into the public burial
ground.)

24 But because I had the support of
Ahikam son of Shaphan, I was not
handed over to the people and killed.

Jeremiah Wears an Ox Yoke

27 Soon after Josiah's son Zedekiah
became king of Judah, the LORD
told me 2 to make myself a yoke out of
leather straps and wooden crossbars
and to put it on my neck. 3 Then the LORD
told me to send a message[g] to the kings
of Edom, Moab, Ammon, Tyre, and Sidon through their ambassadors who had
come to Jerusalem to see King Zedekiah. 4 The LORD Almighty, the God of Israel, told me to command them to tell
their kings that the LORD had said: 5 "By
my great power and strength I created
the world, human beings, and all the animals that live on the earth; and I give it
to anyone I choose. 6 I am the one who
has placed all these nations under the
power of my servant, King Nebuchadnezzar of Babylonia, and I have made
even the wild animals serve him. 7 All
nations will serve him, and they will
serve his son and his grandson until the
time comes for his own nation to fall.
Then his nation will serve powerful nations and great kings.

8 "But if any nation or kingdom will
not submit to his rule, then I will punish
that nation by war, starvation, and disease until I have let Nebuchadnezzar destroy it completely. 9 Do not listen to
your prophets or to those who claim
they can predict the future, either by
dreams or by calling up the spirits of the
dead or by magic. They all tell you not to
submit to the king of Babylonia. 10 They
are deceiving you and will cause you to
be taken far away from your country. I
will drive you out, and you will be destroyed. 11 But if any nation submits to
the king of Babylonia and serves him,
then I will let it stay on in its own land,
to farm it and live there. I, the LORD, have
spoken."

12 I said the same thing to King Zedekiah of Judah, "Submit to the king of
Babylonia. Serve him and his people,
and you will live. 13 Why should you and
your people die in war or of starvation
or disease? That is what the LORD has
said will happen to any nation that does
not submit to the king of Babylonia.
14 Do not listen to the prophets who tell
you not to surrender to him. They are
deceiving you. 15 The LORD himself has
said that he did not send them and that
they are lying to you in his name. And so
he will drive you out, and you will be
killed, you and the prophets who are
telling you these lies."

16 Then I told the priests and the people that the LORD had said: "Do not listen

[g] *Probable text* a message; *Hebrew* them.

to the prophets who say that the Temple
treasures will soon be brought back
from Babylonia. They are lying to you.
17 Don't listen to them! Submit to the
king of Babylonia and you will live! Why
should this city become a pile of ruins?
18 If they are really prophets and if they
have my message, let them ask me, the
LORD Almighty, not to allow the treasures that remain in the Temple and
in the royal palace to be taken to
Babylonia."

(19-20 When King Nebuchadnezzar
took away to Babylonia the king of Judah, Jehoiachin son of Jehoiakim, and
the leading men of Judah and Jerusalem, he left the columns, the bronze
tank, the carts, and some of the other
Temple treasures.)

21 "Listen to what I, the LORD Almighty,
the God of Israel, say about the treasures that are left in the Temple and in
the royal palace in Jerusalem: 22 They
will be taken to Babylonia and will remain there until I turn my attention to
them. Then I will bring them back and
restore them to this place. I, the LORD,
have spoken."

Jeremiah and the Prophet Hananiah

28 That same year,[h] in the fifth
month of the fourth year that
Zedekiah was king, Hananiah son of Azzur, a prophet from the town of Gibeon,
spoke to me in the Temple. In the presence of the priests and of the people he
told me 2 that the LORD Almighty, the
God of Israel, had said: "I have broken
the power of the king of Babylonia.
3 Within two years I will bring back to
this place all the Temple treasures that
King Nebuchadnezzar took to Babylonia. 4 I will also bring back the king of
Judah, Jehoiachin son of Jehoiakim,
along with all of the people of Judah
who went into exile in Babylonia. Yes, I
will break the power of the king of Babylonia. I, the LORD, have spoken."

5 Then in the presence of the priests
and of all the people who were standing
in the Temple, I said to Hananiah,
6 "Wonderful! I hope the LORD will do
this! I certainly hope he will make your
prophecy come true and will bring back
from Babylonia all the Temple treasures
and all the people who were taken away
as prisoners. 7 But listen to what I say to
you and to the people. 8 The prophets
who spoke long ago, before my time and
yours, predicted that war, starvation,
and disease would come to many nations and powerful kingdoms. 9 But a
prophet who predicts peace can only be
recognized as a prophet whom the LORD
has truly sent when that prophet's predictions come true."

10 Then Hananiah took the yoke off my
neck, broke it in pieces, 11 and said in the
presence of all the people, "The LORD has
said that this is how he will break the
yoke that King Nebuchadnezzar has put
on the neck of all the nations; and he will
do this within two years." Then I left.

12 Some time after this the LORD told
me 13 to go and tell Hananiah: "The LORD
has said that you may be able to break a
wooden yoke, but he[i] will replace it
with an iron yoke. 14 The LORD Almighty,
the God of Israel, has said that he will
put an iron yoke on all these nations and
that they will serve King Nebuchadnezzar of Babylonia. The LORD has said that
he will make even the wild animals
serve Nebuchadnezzar."

15 Then I told Hananiah this, and
added, "Listen, Hananiah! The LORD did
not send you, and you are making these
people believe a lie. 16 And so the LORD
himself says that he is going to get rid of
you. Before this year is over you will die
because you have told the people to
rebel against the LORD."

17 And Hananiah died in the seventh
month of that same year.

Jeremiah's Letter to the Jews in Babylonia

29 I wrote a letter to the priests, the
prophets, the leaders of the people, and to all the others whom Nebuchadnezzar had taken away as
prisoners from Jerusalem to Babylonia.
2 I wrote it after King Jehoiachin, his
mother, the palace officials, the leaders
of Judah and of Jerusalem, the engravers, and the skilled workers had been
taken into exile. 3 I gave the letter to Elasah son of Shaphan and to Gemariah
son of Hilkiah, whom King Zedekiah of

[h] *One ancient translation* That same year; *Hebrew* That same year at the beginning of his reign.
[i] *One ancient translation* he; *Hebrew* you.

Judah was sending to King Nebuchadnezzar of Babylonia. It said:
4"The LORD Almighty, the God of
Israel, says to all those people whom
he allowed Nebuchadnezzar to take
away as prisoners from Jerusalem
to Babylonia: 5'Build houses and
settle down. Plant gardens and eat
what you grow in them. 6Marry and
have children. Then let your children get married, so that they also
may have children. You must increase in numbers and not decrease.
7Work for the good of the cities
where I have made you go as prisoners. Pray to me on their behalf, because if they are prosperous, you
will be prosperous too. 8I, the LORD,
the God of Israel, warn you not to
let yourselves be deceived by the
prophets who live among you or by
any others who claim they can predict the future. Do not pay any attention to their[j] dreams. 9They are
telling you lies in my name. I did not
send them. I, the LORD Almighty,
have spoken.'
10"The LORD says, 'When Babylonia's seventy years are over, I will
show my concern for you and keep
my promise to bring you back home.
11I alone know the plans I have for
you, plans to bring you prosperity
and not disaster, plans to bring
about the future you hope for.[k]
12Then you will call to me. You will
come and pray to me, and I will answer you. 13You will seek me, and
you will find me because you will
seek me with all your heart. 14Yes, I
say, you will find me, and I will restore you to your land. I will gather
you from every country and from
every place to which I have scattered you, and I will bring you back
to the land from which I had sent
you away into exile. I, the LORD,
have spoken.'
15"You say that the LORD has given
you prophets in Babylonia. 16Listen
to what the LORD says about the king
who rules the kingdom that David
ruled and about the people of this
city, that is, your relatives who were
not taken away as prisoners with
you. 17The LORD Almighty says, 'I
am bringing war, starvation, and
disease on them, and I will make
them like figs that are too rotten to
be eaten. 18I will pursue them with
war, starvation, and disease, and all
the nations of the world will be horrified at what they see. Everywhere
I scatter them, people will be
shocked and terrified at what has
happened to them. People will make
fun of them and use their name as a
curse. 19This will happen to them
because they did not obey the message that I kept on sending to them
through my servants the prophets.
They refused to listen. 20All of you
whom I sent into exile in Babylonia,
listen to what I, the LORD, say.'
21"The LORD Almighty, the God of
Israel, has spoken about Ahab son
of Kolaiah and Zedekiah son of Maaseiah, who are telling you lies in
his name. He has said that he will
hand them over to the power of King
Nebuchadnezzar of Babylonia, who
will put them to death before your
eyes. 22When the people who were
taken away as prisoners from Jerusalem to Babylonia want to bring a
curse on someone, they will say,
'May the LORD treat you like Zedekiah and Ahab, whom the king of
Babylonia roasted alive!' 23This will
be their fate because they are guilty
of terrible sins—they have committed adultery and have told lies in the
LORD's name. This was against the
LORD's will; he knows what they
have done, and he is a witness
against them.[l] The LORD has
spoken."

The Letter of Shemaiah

24-25The LORD Almighty, the God of Israel, gave me a message for Shemaiah of
Nehelam, who had sent a letter in his
own name to all the people of Jerusalem
and to the priest Zephaniah son of Maaseiah and to all the other priests. In this
letter Shemaiah wrote to Zephaniah:
26"The LORD made you a priest in
place of Jehoiada, and you are now
the chief officer[m] in the Temple. It is
your duty to see that every crazy

[j] *Probable text* their; *Hebrew* your. [k] the future you hope for; *or* a future full of hope.
[l] done, and he . . . them; *or* done; he saw them do it. [m] *Some ancient translations* officer; *Hebrew* officers.

person who pretends to be a prophet
is placed in chains with an iron collar around the neck. 27 Why haven't
you done this to Jeremiah of Anathoth, who has been speaking as a
prophet to the people? 28 He must be
stopped because he told the people
in Babylonia that they would be
prisoners there a long time and
should build houses, settle down,
plant gardens, and eat what they
grow."

29 Zephaniah read the letter to me,
30 and then the LORD told me 31-32 to send
to all the prisoners in Babylon this message about Shemaiah: "I, the LORD, will
punish Shemaiah and all of his descendants. I did not send him, but he spoke
to you as if he were a prophet, and he
made you believe lies. He will have no
descendants among you. He will not live
to see the good things that I am going to
do for my people, because he told them
to rebel against me. I, the LORD, have
spoken."

The LORD's Promises to His People

30 The LORD, the God of Israel, 2 said
to me, "Write down in a book
everything that I have told you, 3 because the time is coming when I will restore my people, Israel and Judah. I will
bring them back to the land that I gave
their ancestors, and they will take possession of it again. I, the LORD, have
spoken."

4 The LORD says to the people of Israel
and Judah,

5 "I heard a cry of terror,
a cry of fear and not of peace.
6 Now stop and think!
Can a man give birth to a child?
Why then do I see every man with
his hands on his stomach
like a woman in labor?
Why is everyone so pale?
7 A terrible day is coming;
no other day can compare
with it—
a time of distress for my people,
but they will survive."

8 The LORD Almighty says, "When that
day comes, I will break the yoke that is
around their neck and remove their
chains, and they will no longer be the
slaves of foreigners. 9 Instead, they will
serve me, the LORD their God, and a
descendant of David, whom I will en-
throne as king.

10 "My people, do not be afraid;
people of Israel, do not be
terrified.
I will rescue you from that
faraway land,
from the land where you are
prisoners.
You will come back home and live
in peace;
you will be secure, and no one
will make you afraid.
11 I will come to you and save you.
I will destroy all the nations
where I have scattered you,
but I will not destroy you.
I will not let you go unpunished;
but when I punish you, I will be
fair.
I, the LORD, have spoken."

12 The LORD says to his people,
"Your wounds are incurable,
your injuries cannot be healed.
13 There is no one to take care
of you,
no remedy for your sores,
no hope of healing for you.
14 All your lovers have forgotten you;
they no longer care about you.
I have attacked you like an enemy;
your punishment has been harsh
because your sins are many
and your wickedness is great.
15 Complain no more about your
injuries;
there is no cure for you.
I punished you like this
because your sins are many
and your wickedness is great.
16 But now, all who devour you will
be devoured,
and all your enemies will be
taken away as prisoners.
All who oppress you will be
oppressed,
and all who plunder you will be
plundered.
17 I will make you well again;
I will heal your wounds,
though your enemies say,
'Zion is an outcast;
no one cares about her.'
I, the LORD, have spoken."

18 The LORD says,

"I will restore my people to their
land
and have mercy on every family;
Jerusalem will be rebuilt,
and its palace restored.
19 The people who live there will
sing praise;
they will shout for joy.
By my blessing they will increase
in numbers;
my blessing will bring them
honor.
20 I will restore the nation's ancient
power
and establish it firmly again;
I will punish all who oppress
them.
21-22 Their ruler will come from their
own nation,
their prince from their own
people.
He will approach me when I
invite him,
for who would dare come
uninvited?
They will be my people,
and I will be their God.
I, the LORD, have spoken."

23-24 The LORD's anger is a storm, a furious wind that will rage over the heads of
the wicked. It will not end until he has
done all that he intends to do. In days to
come his people will understand this
clearly.

Israel's Return Home

31 The LORD says, "The time is coming when I will be the God of all
the tribes of Israel, and they will be my
people. 2 In the desert I showed mercy to
those people who had escaped death.
When the people of Israel longed for
rest, 3 I appeared to them[n] from far
away. People of Israel, I have always
loved you, so I continue to show you my
constant love. 4 Once again I will rebuild
you. Once again you will take up your
tambourines and dance joyfully. 5 Once
again you will plant vineyards on the
hills of Samaria, and those who plant
them will eat what the vineyards produce. 6 Yes, the time is coming when sentries will call out on the hills of Ephraim,
'Let's go up to Zion, to the LORD our
God.'"
7 The LORD says,
"Sing with joy for Israel,
the greatest of the nations.
Sing your song of praise,
'The LORD has saved his[o]
people;
he has rescued all who are left.'
8 I will bring them from the north
and gather them from the ends
of the earth.
The blind and the lame will come
with them,
pregnant women and those
about to give birth.
They will come back a great
nation.
9 My people will return weeping,
praying as I lead them back.
I will guide them to streams of
water,
on a smooth road where they
will not stumble.
I am like a father to Israel,
and Ephraim is my oldest son."

10 The LORD says,
"Nations, listen to me
and proclaim my words on the
far-off shores.
I scattered my people, but I will
gather them
and guard them as a shepherd
guards his flock.
11 I have set Israel's people free
and have saved them from a
mighty nation.
12 They will come and sing for joy on
Mount Zion
and be delighted with my gifts—
gifts of grain and wine and
olive oil,
gifts of sheep and cattle.
They will be like a well-watered
garden;
they will have everything they
need.
13 Then the young women will dance
and be happy,
and men, young and old, will
rejoice.
I will comfort them and turn their
mourning into joy,
their sorrow into gladness.

[n] *One ancient translation* them; *Hebrew* me. [o] *Some ancient translations* The LORD has saved his; *Hebrew* LORD, save your.

14 I will fill the priests with the
richest food
and satisfy all the needs of my
people.
I, the LORD, have spoken."

The LORD's Mercy on Israel

15 The LORD says,
"A sound is heard in Ramah,
the sound of bitter weeping.
Rachel is crying for her children;
they are gone,
and she refuses to be comforted.
16 Stop your crying
and wipe away your tears.
All that you have done for your
children
will not go unrewarded;
they will return from the
enemy's land.
17 There is hope for your future;
your children will come back
home.
I, the LORD, have spoken.

18 "I hear the people of Israel say in
grief,
'LORD, we were like an untamed
animal,
but you taught us to obey.
Bring us back;
we are ready to return to you,
the LORD our God.
19 We turned away from you,
but soon we wanted to return.
After you had punished us,
we hung our heads in grief.
We were ashamed and disgraced
because we sinned when we
were young.'

20 "Israel, you are my dearest child,
the one I love best.
Whenever I mention your name,
I think[p] of you with love.
My heart goes out to you;
I will be merciful.
21 Set up signs and mark the road;
find again the way by which you
left.
Come back, people of Israel,
come home to the towns you
left.
22 How long will you hesitate,
faithless people?
I have created something new and
different,
as different as a woman
protecting a man."[q]

The Future Prosperity of God's People

23 The LORD Almighty, the God of Israel, says, "When I restore the people to
their land, they will once again say in
the land of Judah and in its towns,
'May the LORD bless the sacred
hill[r] of Jerusalem,
the holy place where he lives.'
24 People will live in Judah and in all its
towns, and there will be farmers, and
shepherds with their flocks. 25 I will refresh those who are weary and will satisfy with food everyone who is weak
from hunger. 26 So then, people will say,
'I went to sleep and woke up refreshed.'
27 "I, the LORD, say that the time is coming when I will fill the land of Israel and
Judah with people and animals. 28 And
just as I took care to uproot, to pull
down, to overthrow, to destroy, and to
demolish them, so I will take care to
plant them and to build them up.
29 When that time comes, people will no
longer say,
'The parents ate the sour grapes,
But the children got the sour
taste.'
30 Instead, those who eat sour grapes will
have their own teeth set on edge; and
everyone will die because of their
own sin."
31 The LORD says, "The time is coming
when I will make a new covenant with
the people of Israel and with the people
of Judah. 32 It will not be like the old covenant that I made with their ancestors
when I took them by the hand and led
them out of Egypt. Although I was like a
husband to them, they did not keep that
covenant. 33 The new covenant that I will
make with the people of Israel will be
this: I will put my law within them and
write it on their hearts. I will be their
God, and they will be my people. 34 None
of them will have to teach a neighbor to
know the LORD, because all will know
me, from the least to the greatest. I will
forgive their sins and I will no longer

[p] I mention . . . I think; *or* I threaten to punish, I still think. [q] as different . . . man; *Hebrew unclear.* [r] SACRED HILL: *Mount Zion, the hill in Jerusalem which formed part of the Temple and palace area.*

remember their wrongs. I, the LORD,
have spoken."

35 The LORD provides the sun for light
by day,
the moon and the stars to shine
at night.
He stirs up the sea and makes it
roar;
his name is the LORD Almighty.
36 He promises that as long as the
natural order lasts,
so long will Israel be a nation.
37 If one day the sky could be
measured
and the foundations of the earth
explored,
only then would he reject the
people of Israel
because of all they have done.
The LORD has spoken.

38 "The time is coming," says the LORD,
"when all of Jerusalem will be rebuilt as
my city, from Hananel Tower west to the
Corner Gate. 39 And the boundary line
will continue from there on the west to
the hill of Gareb and then around to
Goah. 40 The entire valley, where the
dead are buried and garbage is dumped,
and all the fields above Kidron Brook as
far as the Horse Gate to the east, will be
sacred to me. The city will never again
be torn down or destroyed."

Jeremiah Buys a Field

32 The LORD spoke to me in the
tenth year that Zedekiah was
king of Judah, which was also the eighteenth year of King Nebuchadnezzar of
Babylonia. 2 At that time the army of the
king of Babylonia was attacking Jerusalem, and I was locked up in the courtyard of the royal palace. 3 King Zedekiah
had imprisoned me there and had accused me of announcing that the LORD
had said, "I am going to let the king of
Babylonia capture this city, 4 and King
Zedekiah will not escape. He will be
handed over to the king of Babylonia; he
will see him face-to-face and will speak
to him in person. 5 Zedekiah will be
taken to Babylonia, and he will remain
there until I deal with him. Even if he
fights the Babylonians, he will not be
successful. I, the LORD, have spoken."
6 The LORD told me 7 that Hanamel, my
uncle Shallum's son, would come to me
with the request to buy his field at Anathoth in the territory of Benjamin, because I was his nearest relative and had
the right to buy it for myself. 8 Then, just
as the LORD had said, Hanamel came to
me there in the courtyard and asked me
to buy the field. So I knew that the LORD
had really spoken to me. 9 I bought the
field from Hanamel and weighed out the
money to him; the price came to seventeen pieces of silver. 10 I signed and
sealed the deed, had it witnessed, and
weighed out the money on scales.
11 Then I took both copies of the deed of
purchase — the sealed copy containing
the contract and its conditions, and the
open copy — 12 and gave them to Baruch,
the son of Neriah and grandson of Mahseiah. I gave them to him in the presence
of Hanamel and of the witnesses who
had signed the deed of purchase and of
the people who were sitting in the courtyard. 13 Before them all I said to Baruch,
14 "The LORD Almighty, the God of Israel,
has ordered you to take these deeds,
both the sealed deed of purchase and the
open copy, and to place them in a clay
jar, so that they may be preserved for
years to come. 15 The LORD Almighty, the
God of Israel, has said that houses,
fields, and vineyards will again be
bought in this land."

Jeremiah's Prayer

16 After I had given the deed of purchase to Baruch, I prayed, 17 "Sovereign
LORD, you made the earth and the sky by
your great power and might; nothing is
too difficult for you. 18 You have shown
constant love to thousands, but you also
punish people for the sins of their parents. You are a great and powerful God;
you are the LORD Almighty. 19 You make
wise plans and do mighty things; you
see everything that people do, and you
reward them according to their actions.
20 Long ago you performed miracles and
wonders in Egypt, and you have continued to perform them to this day, both in
Israel and among all the other nations,
so that you are now known everywhere.
21 By means of miracles and wonders
that terrified our enemies, you used your
power and might to bring your people
Israel out of Egypt. 22 You gave them this
rich and fertile land, as you had promised their ancestors. 23 But when they
came into this land and took possession
of it, they did not obey your commands

or live according to your teaching; they
did nothing that you had ordered them
to do. And so you brought all this destruction on them.
24“The Babylonians have built siege
mounds around the city to capture it,
and they are attacking. War, starvation,
and disease will make the city fall into
their hands. You can see that all you
have said has come true. 25 Yet,
Sovereign LORD, you are the one who ordered me to buy the field in the presence
of witnesses, even though the city is
about to be captured by the Babylonians.”
26 Then the LORD said to me, 27 “I am the
LORD, the God of all people. Nothing is
too difficult for me. 28 I am going to give
this city over to King Nebuchadnezzar
of Babylonia and his army; they will
capture it 29 and set it on fire. They will
burn it down, together with the houses
where people have made me angry by
burning incense to Baal on the rooftops
and by pouring out wine offerings to
other gods. 30 From the very beginning of
their history the people of Israel and the
people of Judah have displeased me and
made me angry by what they have done.
31 The people of this city have made me
angry and furious from the day it was
built. I have decided to destroy it 32 because of all the evil that has been done
by the people of Judah and Jerusalem,
together with their kings and leaders,
their priests and prophets. 33 They
turned their backs on me; and though I
kept on teaching them, they would not
listen and learn. 34 They even placed
their disgusting idols in the Temple built
for my worship, and they have defiled it.
35 They have built altars to Baal in Hinnom Valley, to sacrifice their sons and
daughters to the god Molech. I did not
command them to do this, and it did not
even enter my mind that they would do
such a thing and make the people of Judah sin.”

A Promise of Hope

36 The LORD, the God of Israel, said to
me, “Jeremiah, the people are saying
that war, starvation, and disease will
make this city fall into the hands of the
king of Babylonia. Now listen to what
else I have to say. 37 I am going to gather
the people from all the countries where I
have scattered them in my anger and
fury, and I am going to bring them back
to this place and let them live here in
safety. 38 Then they will be my people,
and I will be their God. 39 I will give them
a single purpose in life: to honor me for
all time, for their own good and the good
of their descendants. 40 I will make an
eternal covenant with them. I will never
stop doing good things for them, and I
will make them fear me with all their
heart, so that they will never turn away
from me. 41 I will take pleasure in doing
good things for them, and I will establish
them permanently in this land.
42 “Just as I have brought this disaster
on these people, so I am going to give
them all the good things that I have
promised. 43 The people are saying that
this land will be like a desert where neither people nor animals live, and that it
will be given over to the Babylonians.
But fields will once again be bought in
this land. 44 People will buy them, and
the deeds will be signed, sealed, and witnessed. This will take place in the territory of Benjamin, in the villages around
Jerusalem, in the towns of Judah, and in
the towns in the hill country, in the foothills, and in southern Judah. I will restore the people to their land. I, the LORD,
have spoken.”

Another Promise of Hope

33 While I was still in prison in the
courtyard, the LORD’s message
came to me again. 2 The LORD, who made
the earth, who formed it and set it in
place, spoke to me. He whose name is
the LORD said, 3 “Call to me, and I will
answer you; I will tell you wonderful
and marvelous things that you know
nothing about. 4 I, the LORD, the God of
Israel, say that the houses of Jerusalem
and the royal palace of Judah will be
torn down as a result of the siege and the
attack. 5 Some will fight against the
Babylonians, who will fill the houses[s]
with the corpses of those whom I am going to strike down in my anger and fury.
I have turned away from this city because of the evil things that its people
have done. 6 But I will heal this city and
its people and restore them to health. I
will show them abundant peace and se-

[s] *In verses 4 and 5* as a result . . . houses; *Hebrew unclear.*

curity. 7I will make Judah and Israel
prosperous, and I will rebuild them as
they were before. 8I will purify them
from the sins that they have committed
against me, and I will forgive their sins
and their rebellion. 9Jerusalem will be a
source of joy, honor, and pride to me;
and every nation in the world will fear
and tremble when they hear about the
good things that I do for the people of
Jerusalem and about the prosperity that
I bring to the city."

10The LORD said, "People are saying
that this place is like a desert, that it has
no people or animals living in it. And
they are right; the towns of Judah and
the streets of Jerusalem are empty; no
people or animals live there. But in these
places you will hear again 11the shouts
of gladness and joy and the happy
sounds of wedding feasts. You will hear
people sing as they bring thank offerings to my Temple; they will say,

'Give thanks to the LORD Almighty,
because he is good
and his love is eternal.'

I will make this land as prosperous as it
was before. I, the LORD, have spoken."

12The LORD Almighty said, "In this
land that is like a desert and where no
people or animals live, there will once
again be pastures where shepherds can
take their sheep. 13In the towns in the
hill country, in the foothills, and in
southern Judah, in the territory of Benjamin, in the villages around Jerusalem,
and in the towns of Judah, shepherds
will once again count their sheep. I, the
LORD, have spoken."

14The LORD said, "The time is coming
when I will fulfill the promise that I
made to the people of Israel and Judah.
15At that time I will choose as king a
righteous descendant of David. That
king will do what is right and just
throughout the land. 16The people of Judah and of Jerusalem will be rescued
and will live in safety. The city will be
called 'The LORD Our Salvation.' 17I, the
LORD, promise that there will always be a
descendant of David to be king of Israel
18and that there will always be priests
from the tribe of Levi to serve me and to
offer burnt offerings, grain offerings,
and sacrifices."

19The LORD said to me, 20"I have made
a covenant with the day and with the
night, so that they always come at their
proper times; and that covenant can
never be broken. 21In the same way I
have made a covenant with my servant
David that he would always have a
descendant to be king, and I have made
a covenant with the priests from the
tribe of Levi that they would always
serve me; and those covenants can
never be broken. 22I will increase the
number of descendants of my servant
David and the number of priests from
the tribe of Levi, so that it will be as impossible to count them as it is to count
the stars in the sky or the grains of sand
on the seashore."

23The LORD said to me, 24"Have you
noticed how people are saying that I
have rejected Israel and Judah, the two
families that I chose? And so they look
with contempt on my people and no
longer consider them a nation. 25But I,
the LORD, have a covenant with day and
night, and I have made the laws that
control earth and sky. 26And just as
surely as I have done this, so I will maintain my covenant with Jacob's descendants and with my servant David. I will
choose one of David's descendants to
rule over the descendants of Abraham,
Isaac, and Jacob. I will be merciful to my
people and make them prosperous
again."

A Message for Zedekiah

34 The LORD spoke to me when King
Nebuchadnezzar of Babylonia
and his army, supported by troops from
all the nations and races that were subject to him, were attacking Jerusalem
and its nearby towns. 2The LORD, the
God of Israel, told me to go and say to
King Zedekiah of Judah, "I, the LORD,
will hand this city over to the king of
Babylonia, and he will burn it down.
3You will not escape; you will be captured and handed over to him. You will
see him face-to-face and talk to him in
person; then you will go to Babylonia.
4Zedekiah, listen to what I say about
you. You will not be killed in battle.
5You will die in peace, and as people
burned incense when they buried your
ancestors, who were kings before you,
in the same way they will burn incense
for you. They will mourn over you and
say, 'Our king is dead!' I, the LORD, have
spoken."

6Then I gave this message to King

Zedekiah in Jerusalem 7while the army
of the king of Babylonia was attacking
the city. The army was also attacking
Lachish and Azekah, the only other fortified cities left in Judah.

Deceitful Treatment of Slaves

8King Zedekiah and the people of Jerusalem had made an agreement to set
free 9their Hebrew slaves, both male
and female, so that no one would have
an Israelite as a slave. 10All the people
and their leaders agreed to free their
slaves and never to enslave them again.
They did set them free, 11but later they
changed their minds, took them back,
and forced them to become slaves again.

12Then the LORD, 13the God of Israel,
told me to say to the people: "I made a
covenant with your ancestors when I
rescued them from Egypt and set them
free from slavery. I told them that
14every seven years they were to set free
any Hebrew slave who had served them
for six years. But your ancestors would
not pay any attention to me or listen to
what I said. 15Just a few days ago you
changed your minds and did what
pleased me. All of you agreed to set all
Israelites free, and you made a covenant
in my presence, in the Temple where I
am worshiped. 16But then you changed
your minds again and dishonored me.
All of you took back the slaves whom
you had set free as they desired, and you
forced them into slavery again. 17So
now, I, the LORD, say that you have disobeyed me; you have not given all Israelites their freedom. Very well, then, I
will give you freedom: the freedom to
die by war, disease, and starvation. I will
make every nation in the world horrified
at what I do to you. 18-19The officials of
Judah and of Jerusalem, together with
the palace officials, the priests, and all
the leaders, made a covenant with me by
walking between the two halves of a bull
that they had cut in two. But they broke
the covenant and did not keep its terms.
So I will do to these people what they did
to the bull. 20I will hand them over to
their enemies, who want to kill them,
and their corpses will be eaten by birds
and wild animals. 21I will also hand over
King Zedekiah of Judah and his officials
to those who want to kill them. I will
hand them over to the Babylonian army,
which has stopped its attack against
you. 22I will give the order, and they will
return to this city. They will attack
it, capture it, and burn it down. I will
make the towns of Judah like a desert
where no one lives. I, the LORD, have
spoken."

Jeremiah and the Rechabites

35 When Jehoiakim son of Josiah
was king of Judah, the LORD said
to me, 2"Go to the members of the Rechabite clan and talk to them. Then bring
them into one of the rooms in the Temple and offer them some wine." 3So I
took the entire Rechabite clan—Jaazaniah (the son of another Jeremiah,
who was Habazziniah's son) and all his
brothers and sons—4and brought them
to the Temple. I took them into the room
of the disciples of the prophet Hanan
son of Igdaliah. This room was above
the room of Maaseiah son of Shallum,
an important official in the Temple, and
near the rooms of the other officials.
5Then I placed cups and bowls full of
wine before the Rechabites, and I said to
them, "Have some wine."

6But they answered, "We do not drink
wine. Our ancestor Jonadab son of Rechab told us that neither we nor our
descendants were ever to drink any
wine. 7He also told us not to build
houses or farm the land and not to plant
vineyards or buy them. He commanded
us always to live in tents, so that we
might remain in this land where we live
like strangers. 8We have obeyed all the
instructions that Jonadab gave us. We
ourselves never drink wine, and neither
do our wives, our sons, or our daughters.
9-10We do not build houses for homes—
we live in tents—and we own no vineyards, fields, or grain. We have fully
obeyed everything that our ancestor
Jonadab commanded us. 11But when
King Nebuchadnezzar invaded the
country, we decided to come to Jerusalem to get away from the Babylonian
and Syrian armies. That is why we are
living in Jerusalem."

12-13Then the LORD Almighty, the God
of Israel, told me to go and say to the
people of Judah and Jerusalem, "I, the
LORD, ask you why you refuse to listen to
me and to obey my instructions. 14Jona-
dab's descendants have obeyed his command not to drink wine, and to this very
day none of them drink any. But I have

kept on speaking to you, and you have
not obeyed me. 15 I have continued to
send you all my servants the prophets,
and they have told you to give up your
evil ways and to do what is right. They
warned you not to worship and serve
other gods, so that you could go on living in the land that I gave you and your
ancestors. But you would not listen to
me or pay any attention to me. 16 Jonadab's descendants have obeyed the command that their ancestor gave them, but
you people have not obeyed me. 17 So
now, I, the LORD Almighty, the God of
Israel, will bring on you people of Judah
and of Jerusalem all the destruction that
I promised. I will do this because you
would not listen when I spoke to you,
and you would not answer when I
called you."

18 Then I told the Rechabite clan that
the LORD Almighty, the God of Israel,
had said, "You have obeyed the command that your ancestor Jonadab gave
you; you have followed all his instructions, and you have done everything
he commanded you. 19 So I, the LORD
Almighty, the God of Israel, promise
that Jonadab son of Rechab will always
have a male descendant to serve me."

Baruch Reads the Scroll in the Temple

36 In the fourth year that Jehoiakim
son of Josiah was king of Judah,
the LORD said to me, 2 "Get a scroll and
write on it everything that I have told
you about Israel and Judah and all the
nations. Write everything that I have
told you from the time I first spoke to
you, when Josiah was king, up to the
present. 3 Perhaps when the people of
Judah hear about all the destruction that
I intend to bring on them, they will turn
from their evil ways. Then I will forgive
their wickedness and their sins."

4 So I called Baruch son of Neriah and
dictated to him everything that the LORD
had said to me. And Baruch wrote it all
down on a scroll. 5 Then I gave Baruch
the following instructions: "I am no
longer allowed to go into the Temple.
6 But I want you to go there the next time
the people are fasting. You are to read
the scroll aloud, so that they will hear
everything that the LORD has said to me
and that I have dictated to you. Do this
where everyone can hear you, including
the people of Judah who have come in
from their towns. 7 Perhaps they will
pray to the LORD and turn from their evil
ways, because the LORD has threatened
this people with his terrible anger and
fury." 8 So Baruch read the LORD's words
in the Temple exactly as I had told him
to do.

9 In the ninth month of the fifth year
that Jehoiakim was king of Judah, the
people fasted to gain the LORD's favor.
The fast was kept by all who lived in
Jerusalem and by all who came there
from the towns of Judah. 10 Then, while
all the people were listening, Baruch
read from the scroll everything that I
had said. He did this in the Temple, from
the room of Gemariah son of Shaphan,
the court secretary. His room was in the
upper court near the entrance of the
New Gate of the Temple.

The Scroll Is Read to the Officials

11 Micaiah, the son of Gemariah and
grandson of Shaphan, heard Baruch
read from the scroll what the LORD had
said. 12 Then he went to the royal palace,
to the room of the court secretary, where
all the officials were in session. Elishama, the court secretary, Delaiah son of
Shemaiah, Elnathan son of Achbor,
Gemariah son of Shaphan, Zedekiah
son of Hananiah, and all the other officials were there. 13 Micaiah told them
everything that he had heard Baruch
read to the people. 14 Then the officials
sent Jehudi (the son of Nethaniah,
grandson of Shelemiah, and great-
grandson of Cushi) to tell Baruch to
bring the scroll that he had read to the
people. Baruch brought them the scroll.
15 "Sit down," they said, "and read the
scroll to us." So Baruch did. 16 After he
had read it, they turned to one another in
alarm and said to Baruch, "We must report this to the king." 17 Then they asked
him, "Tell us, now, how did you come to
write all this? Did Jeremiah dictate it
to you?"

18 Baruch answered, "Jeremiah dictated every word of it to me, and I wrote
it down in ink on this scroll."

19 Then they told him, "You and Jeremiah must go and hide. Don't let anyone
know where you are."

The King Burns the Scroll

20 The officials put the scroll in the
room of Elishama, the court secretary,
and went to the king's court, where they
reported everything to the king. 21 Then
the king sent Jehudi to get the scroll. He
took it from the room of Elishama and
read it to the king and all the officials
who were standing around him. 22 It was
winter and the king was sitting in his
winter palace in front of the fire. 23 As
soon as Jehudi finished reading three or
four columns, the king cut them off with
a small knife and threw them into the
fire. He kept doing this until the entire
scroll was burned up. 24 But neither the
king nor any of his officials who heard
all this was afraid or showed any sign of
sorrow. 25 Although Elnathan, Delaiah,
and Gemariah begged the king not to
burn the scroll, he paid no attention to
them. 26 Then he ordered Prince Jerahmeel, together with Seraiah son of Azriel and Shelemiah son of Abdeel, to
arrest me and my secretary Baruch. But
the LORD had hidden us.

Jeremiah Writes Another Scroll

27 After King Jehoiakim had burned
the scroll that I had dictated to Baruch,
the LORD told me 28 to take another scroll
and write on it everything that had been
on the first one. 29 The LORD told me to
say to the king, "You have burned the
scroll, and you have asked Jeremiah
why he wrote that the king of Babylonia
would come and destroy this land and
kill its people and its animals. 30 So now,
I, the LORD, say to you, King Jehoiakim,
that no descendant of yours will ever
rule over David's kingdom. Your corpse
will be thrown out where it will be exposed to the sun during the day and to
the frost at night. 31 I will punish you,
your descendants, and your officials because of the sins all of you commit. Neither you nor the people of Jerusalem
and of Judah have paid any attention to
my warnings, and so I will bring on all of
you the disaster that I have threatened."

32 Then I took another scroll and gave
it to my secretary Baruch, and he wrote
down everything that I dictated. He
wrote everything that had been on the
first scroll and similar messages that I
dictated to him.

Zedekiah's Request to Jeremiah

37 King Nebuchadnezzar of Babylonia made Zedekiah son of Josiah king of Judah in the place of
Jehoiachin son of Jehoiakim. 2 But neither Zedekiah nor his officials nor the
people obeyed the message which the
LORD had given me.

3 King Zedekiah sent Jehucal son of
Shelemiah and the priest Zephaniah son
of Maaseiah to ask me to pray to the
LORD our God on behalf of our nation.
4 I had not yet been put in prison and
was still moving about freely among the
people. 5 The Babylonian army had been
besieging Jerusalem, but when they
heard that the Egyptian army had
crossed the Egyptian border, they retreated.

6 Then the LORD, the God of Israel, told
me 7 to say to Zedekiah, "The Egyptian
army is on its way to help you, but it will
return home. 8 Then the Babylonians
will come back, attack the city, capture
it, and burn it down. 9 I, the LORD, warn
you not to deceive yourselves into thinking that the Babylonians will not come
back, because they will. 10 Even if you
defeat the whole Babylonian army, so
that only wounded men are left, lying in
their tents, they would still get up and
burn this city to the ground."

Jeremiah Is Arrested and Imprisoned

11 The Babylonian army retreated
from Jerusalem because the Egyptian
army was approaching. 12 So I started to
leave Jerusalem and go to the territory
of Benjamin to take possession of my
share of the family property. 13 But when
I reached the Benjamin Gate, the officer
in charge of the soldiers on duty there, a
man by the name of Irijah, the son of
Shelemiah and grandson of Hananiah,
stopped me and said, "You are deserting
to the Babylonians!"

14 I answered, "That's not so! I'm not
deserting." But Irijah would not listen to
me. Instead, he arrested me and took me
to the officials. 15 They were furious with
me and had me beaten and locked up in
the house of Jonathan, the court secretary, whose house had been made into a
prison. 16 I was put in an underground
cell and kept there a long time.

17 Later on King Zedekiah sent for me,

and there in the palace he asked me privately, "Is there any message from the
LORD?"
"There is," I answered, and added,
"You will be handed over to the king of
Babylonia." 18 Then I asked, "What
crime have I committed against you or
your officials or this people, to make you
put me in prison? 19 What happened to
your prophets who told you that the king
of Babylonia would not attack you or the
country? 20 And now, Your Majesty, I
beg you to listen to me and do what I
ask. Please do not send me back to the
prison in Jonathan's house. If you do, I
will surely die there."
21 So King Zedekiah ordered me to be
locked up in the palace courtyard. I
stayed there, and each day I was given a
loaf of bread from the bakeries until all
the bread in the city was gone.

Jeremiah in a Dry Well

38 Shephatiah son of Mattan, Gedaliah son of Pashhur, Jehucal son
of Shelemiah, and Pashhur son of Malchiah heard that I was telling the people
that 2 the LORD had said, "Whoever stays
on in the city will die in war or of starvation or disease. But those who go out
and surrender to the Babylonians will
not be killed; they will at least escape
with their life." 3 I was also telling them
that the LORD had said, "I am going to
give the city to the Babylonian army,
and they will capture it."
4 Then the officials went to the king
and said, "This man must be put to
death. By talking like this he is making
the soldiers in the city lose their courage, and he is doing the same thing to
everyone else left in the city. He is not
trying to help the people; he only wants
to hurt them."
5 King Zedekiah answered, "Very well,
then, do what you want to with him; I
can't stop you." 6 So they took me and let
me down by ropes into Prince Malchiah's well, which was in the palace
courtyard. There was no water in the
well, only mud, and I sank down in it.
7 However, Ebedmelech the Ethiopian,[t] a eunuch who worked in the
royal palace, heard that they had put me
in the well. At that time the king was
holding court at the Benjamin Gate. 8 So
Ebedmelech went there and said to the
king, 9 "Your Majesty, what these men
have done is wrong. They have put Jeremiah in the well, where he is sure to die
of starvation, since there is no more food
in the city." 10 Then the king ordered
Ebedmelech to take with him three men
and to pull me out of the well before I
died. 11 So Ebedmelech went with the
men to the palace storeroom and got
some worn-out clothing which he let
down to me by ropes. 12 He told me to put
the rags under my arms, so that the
ropes wouldn't hurt me. I did this, 13 and
they pulled me up out of the well. After
that I was kept in the courtyard.

Zedekiah Asks Jeremiah's Advice

14 On another occasion King Zedekiah
had me brought to him at the third entrance to the Temple, and he said, "I am
going to ask you a question, and I want
you to tell me the whole truth."
15 I answered, "If I tell you the truth,
you will put me to death, and if I give
you advice, you won't pay any attention."
16 So King Zedekiah promised me in
secret, "I swear by the living God, the
God who gave us life, that I will not put
you to death or hand you over to the
men who want to kill you."
17 Then I told Zedekiah that the LORD
Almighty, the God of Israel, had said, "If
you surrender to the king of Babylonia's
officers, your life will be spared, and this
city will not be burned down. Both you
and your family will be spared. 18 But if
you do not surrender, then this city will
be handed over to the Babylonians, who
will burn it down, and you will not escape from them."
19 But the king answered, "I am afraid
of our own people who have deserted to
the Babylonians. I may be handed over
to them and tortured."
20 I said, "You will not be handed over
to them. I beg you to obey the LORD's
message; then all will go well with you,
and your life will be spared. 21 But the
LORD has shown me in a vision what will
happen if you refuse to surrender. 22 In it

[t] *Hebrew* Cushite: *Cush is the ancient name of the extensive territory south of the First Cataract of the Nile River. This region was called Ethiopia in Graeco-Roman times, and included within its borders most of modern Sudan and some of present-day Ethiopia (Abyssinia).*

I saw all the women left in Judah's royal
palace being led out to the king of Babylonia's officers. Listen to what they were
saying as they went:

'The king's best friends
misled him,
they overruled him.
And now that his feet have sunk
in the mud,
his friends have left him.' "

23 Then I added, "All your women and
children will be taken out to the Babylonians, and you yourself will not escape
from them. You will be taken prisoner
by the king of Babylonia, and this city
will be burned to the ground."
24 Zedekiah replied, "Don't let anyone
know about this conversation, and your
life will not be in danger. 25 If the officials hear that I have talked with you,
they will come and ask you what we
said. They will promise not to put you to
death if you tell them everything. 26 Just
tell them you were begging me not to
send you back to prison to die there."
27 Then all the officials came and questioned me, and I told them exactly what
the king had told me to say. There was
nothing else they could do, because no
one had overheard the conversation.
28 And I was kept in the palace courtyard
until the day Jerusalem was captured.

The Fall of Jerusalem

39 In the tenth month of the ninth
year that Zedekiah was king of
Judah, King Nebuchadnezzar of Babylonia came with his whole army and attacked Jerusalem. 2 On the ninth day of
the fourth month of Zedekiah's eleventh
year as king, the city walls were broken
through.
(3 When Jerusalem was captured,[u] all
the high officials of the king of Babylonia came and took their places at the
Middle Gate, including Nergal Sharezer,
Samgar Nebo, Sarsechim, and another
Nergal Sharezer.[v])
4 When King Zedekiah and all his soldiers saw what was happening, they
tried to escape from the city during the
night. They left by way of the royal garden, went through the gateway connecting the two walls, and escaped in the
direction of the Jordan Valley. 5 But the
Babylonian army pursued them and
captured Zedekiah in the plains near
Jericho. Then they took him to King
Nebuchadnezzar, who was in the city of
Riblah in the territory of Hamath, and
there Nebuchadnezzar passed sentence
on him. 6 At Riblah he put Zedekiah's
sons to death while Zedekiah was looking on, and he also had the officials of
Judah executed. 7 After that, he had Zedekiah's eyes put out and had him placed
in chains to be taken to Babylonia.
8 Meanwhile, the Babylonians burned
down the royal palace and the houses of
the people and tore down the walls of
Jerusalem. 9 Finally Nebuzaradan, the
commanding officer, took away as prisoners to Babylonia the people who were
left in the city, together with those who
had deserted to him. 10 He left in the land
of Judah some of the poorest people,
who owned no property, and he gave
them vineyards and fields.

Jeremiah's Release

11 But King Nebuchadnezzar commanded Nebuzaradan, the commanding
officer, to give the following order:
12 "Go and find Jeremiah and take good
care of him. Do not harm him, but do for
him whatever he wants." 13 So Nebuzaradan, together with the high officials
Nebushazban and Nergal Sharezer and
all the other officers of the king of Babylonia, 14 had me brought from the palace
courtyard. They put me under the care
of Gedaliah, the son of Ahikam and
grandson of Shaphan, who was to see
that I got home safely. And so I stayed
there among the people.

Hope for Ebedmelech

15 While I was still imprisoned in the
palace courtyard, the LORD told me 16 to
tell Ebedmelech the Ethiopian[w] that the
LORD Almighty, the God of Israel, had
said, "Just as I said I would, I am going
to bring upon this city destruction and
not prosperity. And when this happens,
you will be there to see it. 17 But I, the
LORD, will protect you, and you will not

[u] When Jerusalem was captured; *these words are moved here from the end of chapter 38.*
[v] *The names and titles of these men are unclear.* [w] *Hebrew* Cushite: *Cush is the ancient name of the extensive territory south of the First Cataract of the Nile River. This region was called Ethiopia in Graeco-Roman times, and included within its borders most of modern Sudan and some of present-day Ethiopia (Abyssinia).*

be handed over to the people you are
afraid of. 18 I will keep you safe, and
you will not be put to death. You will
escape with your life because you have
put your trust in me. I, the LORD, have
spoken."

Jeremiah Stays with Gedaliah

40 The LORD spoke to me after Nebuzaradan, the commanding officer, had set me free at Ramah. I had
been taken there in chains, along with
all the other people from Jerusalem and
Judah who were being taken away as
prisoners to Babylonia.
2 The commanding officer took me
aside and said, "The LORD your God
threatened this land with destruction,
3 and now he has done what he said he
would. All this happened because your
people sinned against the LORD and disobeyed him. 4 Now, I am taking the
chains off your wrists and setting you
free. If you want to go to Babylonia with
me, you may do so, and I will take care
of you. But if you don't want to go, you
don't have to. You have the whole country to choose from, and you may go
wherever you wish."
5 When I did not answer,[x] Nebuzaradan said, "Go back to Gedaliah, the son
of Ahikam and grandson of Shaphan,
whom the king of Babylonia has made
governor of the towns of Judah. You
may stay with him and live among the
people, or you may go anywhere you
think you should." Then he gave me a
present and some food to take with me,
and let me go on my way. 6 I went to stay
with Gedaliah in Mizpah and lived
among the people who were left in the
land.

Gedaliah, Governor of Judah

(2 Kings 25.22-24)

7 Some of the Judean officers and soldiers had not surrendered. They heard
that the king of Babylonia had made
Gedaliah governor of the land and had
placed him in charge of all those who
had not been taken away to Babylonia—
the poorest people in the land. 8 So Ishmael son of Nethaniah, Johanan son of
Kareah, Seraiah son of Tanhumeth, the
sons of Ephai from Netophah, and Jezaniah from Maacah went with their men
to Gedaliah at Mizpah. 9 Gedaliah said to
them, "I give you my word that there is
no need for you to be afraid to surrender
to the Babylonians. Settle in this land,
serve the king of Babylonia, and all will
go well with you. 10 I myself will stay in
Mizpah and be your representative
when the Babylonians come here. But
you can gather and store up wine, fruit,
and olive oil, and live in the villages you
occupy." 11 Meanwhile, all the Israelites
who were in Moab, Ammon, Edom, and
other countries, heard that the king of
Babylonia had allowed some Israelites
to stay on in Judah and that he had made
Gedaliah their governor. 12 So they left
the places where they had been scattered, and returned to Judah. They came
to Gedaliah at Mizpah, and there they
gathered in large amounts of wine and
fruit.

Gedaliah Is Murdered

(2 Kings 25.25, 26)

13 After this, Johanan and the leaders
of the soldiers who had not surrendered
came to Gedaliah at Mizpah 14 and said
to him, "Don't you know that King Baa-
lis of Ammon has sent Ishmael to murder you?" But Gedaliah did not believe it.
15 Then Johanan said privately to him,
"Let me go and kill Ishmael, and no one
will know who did it. Why should he be
allowed to murder you? That would
cause all the Jews who have gathered
around you to be scattered, and it would
bring disaster on all the people who are
left in Judah."
16 But Gedaliah answered, "Don't do it!
What you are saying about Ishmael is
not true!"

41 In the seventh month of that
year, Ishmael, the son of Nethaniah and grandson of Elishama, a member of the royal family and one of the
king's chief officers, went to Mizpah
with ten men to see Governor Gedaliah.
While they were all eating a meal together, 2 Ishmael and the ten men with
him pulled out their swords and killed
Gedaliah. 3 Ishmael also killed all the Israelites who were with Gedaliah at Mizpah and the Babylonian soldiers who
happened to be there.

[x] When I did not answer; *or* Then, before he left.

4 The next day, before anyone knew
about Gedaliah's murder, 5 eighty men
arrived from Shechem, Shiloh, and Samaria. They had shaved off their beards,
torn their clothes, and gashed themselves. They were taking grain and
incense to offer in the Temple. 6 So
Ishmael went out from Mizpah to meet
them, weeping as he went. When he
came to them, he said, "Please come in
to see Gedaliah." 7 As soon as they were
inside the city, Ishmael and his men
killed them and threw their bodies in a
well.

8 But there were ten men in the group
who said to Ishmael, "Please don't kill
us! We have wheat, barley, olive oil, and
honey hidden in the fields." So he spared
them. 9 The well into which Ishmael
threw the bodies of the men he had
killed was the large one[y] that King Asa
had dug when he was being attacked by
King Baasha of Israel. Ishmael filled the
well with the bodies. 10 Then he made
prisoners of the king's daughters and all
the rest of the people in Mizpah, whom
Nebuzaradan the commanding officer
had placed under the care of Gedaliah.
Ishmael took them prisoner and started
off in the direction of the territory of
Ammon.

11 Johanan and all the army leaders
with him heard of the crime that Ishmael
had committed. 12 So they went after him
with their men and overtook him near
the large pool at Gibeon. 13 When Ishmael's prisoners saw Johanan and the
leaders of the forces with him, they were
glad, 14 and turned and ran to them.
15 But Ishmael and eight of his men got
away from Johanan and escaped to the
land of Ammon.

16 Then Johanan and the leaders of the
forces with him took charge of the people whom Ishmael had taken away as
prisoners from Mizpah after murdering
Gedaliah — soldiers, women, children,
and eunuchs. 17-18 They were afraid of
the Babylonians because Ishmael had
murdered Gedaliah, whom the king of
Babylonia had made governor of the
land. So they set out for Egypt, in order
to get away from the Babylonians. On
the way they stopped at Chimham near
Bethlehem.

The People Ask Jeremiah to Pray for Them

42 Then all the army leaders, including Johanan son of Kareah
and Azariah[z] son of Hoshaiah, came
with people of every class 2 and said to
me, "Please do what we ask you! Pray to
the LORD our God for us. Pray for all of us
who have survived. Once there were
many of us; but now only a few of us are
left, as you can see. 3 Pray that the LORD
our God will show us the way we should
go and what we should do."

4 I answered, "Very well, then. I will
pray to the LORD our God, just as you
have asked, and whatever he says, I will
tell you. I will not keep back anything
from you."

5 Then they said to me, "May the LORD
be a true and faithful witness against us
if we do not obey all the commands that
the LORD our God gives you for us.
6 Whether it pleases us or not, we will
obey the LORD our God, to whom we are
asking you to pray. All will go well with
us if we obey him."

The LORD's Answer to Jeremiah's Prayer

7 Ten days later the LORD spoke to me;
8 so I called together Johanan, all the
army leaders who were with him, and all
the other people. 9 I said to them, "The
LORD, the God of Israel, to whom you
sent me with your request has said, 10 'If
you are willing to go on living in this
land, then I will build you up and not
tear you down; I will plant you and not
pull you up. The destruction I brought
on you has caused me great sorrow.
11 Stop being afraid of the king of Babylonia. I am with you, and I will rescue
you from his power. 12 Because I am
merciful, I will make him have mercy on
you and let you go back home. I, the
LORD, have spoken.'

13-15 "But you people who are left in Judah must not disobey the LORD your God
and refuse to live in this land. You must
not say, 'No, we will go and live in
Egypt, where we won't face war any
more or hear the call to battle or go hungry.' If you say this, then the LORD
Almighty, the God of Israel, says, 'If you
are determined to go and live in Egypt,

[y] *One ancient translation* was the large one; *Hebrew* by means of Gedaliah.
[z] *One ancient translation (see also 43.2)* Azariah; *Hebrew* Jezaniah.

16 then the war that you fear will overtake you, and the hunger you dread will
follow you, and you will die there in
Egypt. 17 All the people who are determined to go and live in Egypt will die
either in war or of starvation or disease.
Not one of them will survive, not one
will escape the disaster that I am going
to bring on them.'
18 "The LORD, the God of Israel, says,
'Just as my anger and fury were poured
out on the people of Jerusalem, so my
fury will be poured out on you if you go
to Egypt. You will be a horrifying sight;
people will make fun of you and use
your name as a curse. You will never see
this place again.'"
19 Then I continued, "The LORD has told
you people who are left in Judah not to
go to Egypt. And so I warn you now
20 that you are making a fatal mistake.
You asked me to pray to the LORD our
God for you, and you promised that you
would do everything that he commands.
21 And now I have told you, but you are
disobeying everything that the LORD our
God sent me to tell you. 22 So then, remember this: you will die in war or of
starvation or disease in the land where
you want to go and live."

Jeremiah Is Taken to Egypt

43 I finished telling the people
everything that the LORD their
God had sent me to tell them. 2 Then Azariah son of Hoshaiah and Johanan son
of Kareah and all the other arrogant
men said to me, "You are lying. The LORD
our God did not send you to tell us not to
go and live in Egypt. 3 Baruch son of Neriah has stirred you up against us, so
that the Babylonians will gain power
over us and can either kill us or take us
away to Babylonia." 4 So neither Johanan nor any of the army officers nor any
of the people would obey the LORD's
command to remain in the land of Judah. 5 Then Johanan and all the army officers took everybody left in Judah away
to Egypt, together with all the people
who had returned from the nations
where they had been scattered: 6 the
men, the women, the children, and the
king's daughters. They took everyone
whom Nebuzaradan the commanding
officer had left under the care of Gedaliah, including Baruch and me. 7 They
disobeyed the LORD's command and
went into Egypt as far as the city of
Tahpanhes.
8 There the LORD said to me, 9 "Get
some large stones and bury them in the
mortar of the pavement[a] in front of the
entrance to the government building
here in the city, and let some of the Israelites see you do it. 10 Then tell them that
I, the LORD Almighty, the God of Israel,
am going to bring my servant King Nebuchadnezzar of Babylonia to this place,
and he[b] will put his throne over these
stones that you[c] buried, and will spread
the royal tent over them. 11 Nebuchadnezzar will come and defeat Egypt.
Those people who are doomed to die of
disease will die of disease, those doomed
to be taken away as prisoners will be
taken away as prisoners, and those
doomed to be killed in war will be killed
in war. 12 I will set fire to the temples of
Egypt's gods, and the king of Babylonia
will either burn their gods or carry them
off. As shepherds pick their clothes
clean of lice, so the king of Babylonia
will pick the land of Egypt clean and
then leave victorious. 13 He will destroy
the sacred stone monuments at Heliopolis in Egypt and will burn down the temples of the Egyptian gods."

The LORD's Message to the Israelites in Egypt

44 The LORD spoke to me concerning all the Israelites living in
Egypt, in the cities of Migdol, Tahpanhes, and Memphis, and in the southern
part of the country. 2 The LORD Almighty,
the God of Israel, said, "You yourselves
have seen the destruction I brought on
Jerusalem and all the other cities of Judah. Even now they are still in ruins, and
no one lives in them 3 because their people had done evil and had made me angry. They offered sacrifices to other
gods and served gods that neither they
nor you nor your ancestors ever worshiped. 4 I kept sending you my servants
the prophets, who told you not to do this
terrible thing that I hate. 5 But you would
not listen or pay any attention. You
would not give up your evil practice of

[a] *Probable text* bury them . . . pavement; *Hebrew unclear.* [b] *Some ancient translations* he; *Hebrew* I. [c] *Some ancient translations* you; *Hebrew* I.

sacrificing to other gods. 6 So I poured
out my anger and fury on the towns of
Judah and on the streets of Jerusalem,
and I set them on fire. They were left in
ruins and became a horrifying sight, as
they are today.

7 "And so I, the LORD Almighty, the
God of Israel, now ask why you are doing such an evil thing to yourselves. Do
you want to bring destruction on men
and women, children and babies, so that
none of your people will be left? 8 Why
do you make me angry by worshiping
idols and by sacrificing to other gods
here in Egypt, where you have come to
live? Are you doing this just to destroy
yourselves, so that every nation on earth
will make fun of you and use your name
as a curse? 9 Have you forgotten all the
wicked things that have been done in the
towns of Judah and in the streets of Jerusalem by your ancestors, by the kings
of Judah and their wives, and by you
and your wives? 10 But to this day you
have not humbled yourselves. You have
not honored me or lived according to all
the laws that I gave you and your ancestors.

11 "So then, I, the LORD Almighty, the
God of Israel, will turn against you and
destroy all Judah. 12 As for the people of
Judah who are left and are determined
to go and live in Egypt, I will see to it
that all of them are destroyed. All of
them, great and small, will die in Egypt,
either in war or of starvation. They will
be a horrifying sight; people will make
fun of them and use their name as a
curse. 13 I will punish those who live in
Egypt, just as I punished Jerusalem—
with war, starvation, and disease.
14 None of the people of Judah who are
left and have come to Egypt to live will
escape or survive. Not one of them will
return to Judah, where they long to live
once again. No one will return except a
few refugees."

15 Then all the men who knew that
their wives offered sacrifices to other
gods, and all the women who were
standing there, including the Israelites
who lived in southern Egypt—a large
crowd in all—said to me, 16 "We refuse to
listen to what you have told us in the
name of the LORD. 17 We will do everything that we said we would. We will offer sacrifices to our goddess, the Queen
of Heaven, and we will pour out wine
offerings to her, just as we and our ancestors, our king and our leaders, used
to do in the towns of Judah and in the
streets of Jerusalem. Then we had
plenty of food, we were prosperous, and
had no troubles. 18 But ever since we
stopped sacrificing to the Queen of
Heaven and stopped pouring out wine
offerings to her, we have had nothing,
and our people have died in war and of
starvation."

19 And the women added, "When we
baked cakes shaped like the Queen of
Heaven, offered sacrifices to her, and
poured out wine offerings to her, our
husbands approved of what we were
doing."

20 Then I said to all the men and the
women who had answered me in this
way, 21 "As for the sacrifices which you
and your ancestors, your kings and your
leaders, and the people of the land offered in the towns of Judah and in the
streets of Jerusalem—do you think that
the LORD did not know about them or
that he forgot them? 22 This very day
your land lies in ruins and no one lives in
it. It has become a horrifying sight, and
people use its name as a curse because
the LORD could no longer endure your
wicked and evil practices. 23 This present
disaster has come on you because you
offered sacrifices to other gods and
sinned against the LORD by not obeying
all his commands."

24-25 I told all the people, especially the
women, what the LORD Almighty, the
God of Israel, was saying to the people
of Judah living in Egypt: "Both you and
your wives have made solemn promises
to the Queen of Heaven. You promised
that you would offer sacrifices to her
and pour out wine offerings to her, and
you have kept your promises. Very well,
then! Keep your promises! Carry out
your vows! 26 But now listen to the vow
that I, the LORD, have made in my mighty
name to all you Israelites in Egypt:
Never again will I let any of you use my
name to make a vow by saying, 'I swear
by the living Sovereign LORD!' 27 I will
see to it that you will not prosper, but
will be destroyed. All of you will die, either in war or of disease, until not one of
you is left. 28 But a few of you will escape
death and return from Egypt to Judah.
Then the survivors will know whose
words have come true, mine or theirs.

29I, the LORD, will give you proof that I
will punish you in this place and that my
promise to bring destruction on you will
come true. 30I will hand over King
Hophra of Egypt to his enemies who
want to kill him, just as I handed over
King Zedekiah of Judah to King Nebuchadnezzar of Babylonia, who was his
enemy and wanted to kill him."

God's Promise to Baruch

45 In the fourth year that Jehoiakim
son of Josiah was king of Judah,
Baruch wrote down what I had dictated
to him. Then I told him 2that the LORD,
the God of Israel, had said, "Baruch,
3you are saying, 'I give up! The LORD has
added sorrow to my troubles. I am worn
out from groaning, and I can't find any
rest!'
4"But I, the LORD, am tearing down
what I have built and pulling up what I
have planted. I will do this to the entire
earth. 5Are you looking for special treatment for yourself? Don't do it. I am
bringing disaster on all people, but you
will at least escape with your life, wherever you go. I, the LORD, have spoken."

Egypt's Defeat at Carchemish

46 The LORD spoke to me about the
nations, 2beginning with Egypt.
This is what he said about the army of
King Neco of Egypt, which King Nebuchadnezzar of Babylonia defeated at
Carchemish near the Euphrates River in
the fourth year that Jehoiakim was king
of Judah:

3"The Egyptian officers shout,
'Get your shields ready
and march into battle!
4Harness your horses and mount
them!
Fall in line and put on your
helmets!
Sharpen your spears!
Put on your armor!'

5"But what do I see?" asks the
LORD.
"They are turning back in terror.
Their soldiers are beaten back;
overcome with fear, they run as
fast as they can
and do not look back.
6Those who run fast cannot get
away;
the soldiers cannot escape.
In the north, by the Euphrates,
they stumble and fall.
7Who is this that rises like the Nile,
like a river flooding its banks?
8It is Egypt, rising like the Nile,
like a river flooding its banks.
Egypt said, 'I will rise and cover
the world;
I will destroy cities and the
people who live there.
9Command the horses to go
and the chariots to roll!
Send out the soldiers:
men from Ethiopia[d] and Libya,
carrying shields,
and skilled archers from
Lydia.'"

10This is the day of the Sovereign
LORD Almighty:
today he will take revenge;
today he will punish his
enemies.
His sword will eat them until it is
full,
and drink their blood until it is
satisfied.
Today the Almighty sacrifices his
victims
in the north, by the Euphrates.
11People of Egypt, go to Gilead[e]
and look for medicine!
All your medicine has proved
useless;
nothing can heal you.
12Nations have heard of your
shame;
everyone has heard you cry.
One soldier trips over another,
and both of them fall to the
ground.

The Coming of Nebuchadnezzar

13When King Nebuchadnezzar of
Babylonia came to attack Egypt, the
LORD spoke to me. He said,

14"Proclaim it in the towns of Egypt,
in Migdol, Memphis, and
Tahpanhes:
'Get ready to defend yourselves;

[d] *Hebrew* Cush: *Cush is the ancient name of the extensive territory south of the First Cataract of the Nile River. This region was called Ethiopia in Graeco-Roman times, and included within its borders most of modern Sudan and some of present-day Ethiopia (Abyssinia).*
[e] GILEAD: *See* 8.22.

all you have will be destroyed
in war!
15 Why has your mighty god Apis
fallen?
The LORD has struck him down!'
16 Your soldiers have stumbled and
fallen;[f]
each one says to the other,
'Hurry! Let's go home to our
people
and escape the enemy's sword!'

17 "Give the king of Egypt a new
name—
'Noisy Braggart Who Missed His
Chance.'
18 I, the LORD Almighty, am king.
I am the living God.
As Mount Tabor towers above the
mountains
and Mount Carmel stands high
above the sea,
so will be the strength of the one
who attacks you.
19 Get ready to be taken prisoner,
you people of Egypt!
Memphis will be made a desert,
a ruin where no one lives.
20 Egypt is like a splendid cow,
attacked by a stinging fly from
the north.
21 Even her hired soldiers
are helpless as calves.
They did not stand and fight;
all of them turned and ran.
The day of their doom had
arrived,
the time of their destruction.
22 Egypt runs away, hissing like a
snake,
as the enemy's army
approaches.
They attack her with axes,
like people cutting down trees
23 and destroying a thick forest.
Their soldiers are too many to
count;
they outnumber the locusts.
24 The people of Egypt are put to
shame;
they are conquered by the
people of the north.
I, the LORD, have spoken."

25 The LORD Almighty, the God of Israel, says, "I am going to punish Amon,
the god of Thebes, together with Egypt
and its gods and kings. I am going to
take the king of Egypt and all who put
their trust in him, 26 and hand them over
to those who want to kill them, to King
Nebuchadnezzar of Babylonia and his
army. But later on, people will live in
Egypt again, as they did in times past. I,
the LORD, have spoken.

The LORD Will Save His People

27 "My people, do not be afraid,
people of Israel, do not be
terrified.
I will rescue you from that
faraway land,
from the land where you are
prisoners.
You will come back home and live
in peace;
you will be secure, and no one
will make you afraid.
28 I will come to you and save you.
I will destroy all the nations
where I have scattered you,
but I will not destroy you.
I will not let you go unpunished;
but when I punish you, I will be
fair.
I, the LORD, have spoken."

The LORD's Message about Philistia

47 Before the king of Egypt attacked Gaza, the LORD spoke to
me about Philistia. 2 He said:
"Look! Waters are rising in the
north
and will rush like a river in
flood.
They will cover the land and
everything on it,
cities and the people who live
there.
People will call out for help;
everyone on earth will cry
bitterly.
3 They will hear the hoofbeats of
horses,
the clatter of chariots,
the rumble of wheels.
Parents will not turn back for their
children;
their hands will hang limp at
their sides.
4 The time has come to destroy
Philistia,

[f] *Probable text* Your soldiers . . . fallen; *Hebrew unclear.*

to cut off from Tyre and Sidon
all the help that remains.
I, the LORD, will destroy the
Philistines,
all who came from the shores of
Crete.
5 Great sorrow has come to the
people of Gaza,
and Ashkelon's people are silent.
How long will the rest of
Philistia mourn?
6 You cry out, 'Sword of the LORD!
How long will you go on
slashing?
Go back to your scabbard,
stay there and rest!'
7 But how can it rest,
when I have given it work to do?
I have commanded it to attack
Ashkelon
and the people who live on the
coast."

The Destruction of Moab

48 This is what the LORD Almighty
said about Moab:
"Pity the people of Nebo—
their town is destroyed!
Kiriathaim is captured,
its mighty fortress torn down,
and its people put to shame;
2 the splendor of Moab is gone.
The enemy have captured
Heshbon
and plot to destroy the nation of
Moab.
The town of Madmen will be
silenced;
armies will march against it.
3 The people of Horonaim cry out,
'Violence! Destruction!'

4 "Moab has been destroyed;
listen to the children crying.
5 Hear the sound of their sobs
along the road up to Luhith,
the cries of distress
on the way down to Horonaim.
6 'Quick, run for your lives!'
they say.
'Run like a wild desert donkey!'

7 "Moab, you trusted in your
strength and your wealth,
but now even you will be
conquered;
your god Chemosh will go into
exile,
along with his princes and
priests.
8 Not a town will escape the
destruction;
both valley and plain will be
ruined.
I, the LORD, have spoken.
9 Set up a tombstone for Moab;
it will soon be destroyed.
Its towns will be left in ruins,
and no one will live there
again."
(10 Curse those who do not do the
LORD's work with all their heart! Curse
those who do not slash and kill!)

The Cities of Moab Are Destroyed

11 The LORD said, "Moab has always
lived secure and has never been taken
into exile. Moab is like wine left to settle
undisturbed and never poured from jar
to jar. Its flavor has never been ruined,
and it tastes as good as ever.
12 "So now, the time is coming when I
will send people to pour Moab out like
wine. They will empty its wine jars and
break them in pieces. 13 Then the Moabites will be disillusioned with their god
Chemosh, just as the Israelites were disillusioned with Bethel, a god in whom
they trusted.
14 "Men of Moab, why do you claim
to be heroes,
brave soldiers tested in war?
15 Moab and its cities are destroyed;
its finest young men have been
slaughtered.
I am the king, the LORD Almighty,
and I have spoken.
16 Moab's doom approaches;
its ruin is coming soon.

17 "Mourn for that nation, you that
live nearby,
all of you that know its fame.
Say, 'Its powerful rule has been
broken;
its glory and might are no more.'
18 You that live in Dibon,
come down from your place of
honor
and sit on the ground in the
dust;
Moab's destroyer is here
and has left its forts in ruins.
19 You that live in Aroer,
stand by the road and wait;

ask those who are running
away,
find out from them what has
happened.
20 'Moab has fallen,' they will
answer,
'weep for it; it is disgraced.
Announce along the Arnon River
that Moab is destroyed!'

21 "Judgment has come on the cities of
the plateau: on Holon, Jahzah, Mephaath, 22 Dibon, Nebo, Beth Diblathaim,
23 Kiriathaim, Bethgamul, Bethmeon,
24 Kerioth, and Bozrah. Judgment has
come on all the cities of Moab, far and
near. 25 Moab's might has been crushed;
its power has been destroyed. I, the
LORD, have spoken."

Moab Will Be Humbled

26 The LORD said, "Make Moab drunk,
because it has rebelled against me.
Moab will roll in its own vomit, and
people will laugh. 27 Moab, remember
how you made fun of the people of
Israel? You treated them as though
they had been caught with a gang of
robbers.
28 "You people who live in Moab, leave
your towns! Go and live on the cliffs! Be
like the dove that makes its nest in the
sides of a ravine. 29 Moab is very proud!
I have heard how proud, arrogant, and
conceited the people are, how much they
think of themselves. 30 I, the LORD, know
of their arrogance. Their boasts amount
to nothing, and the things they do will
not last. 31 And so I will weep for everyone in Moab and for the people of Kir
Heres. 32 I will cry for the people of Sibmah, even more than for the people of
Jazer. City of Sibmah, you are like a
vine whose branches reach across the
Dead Sea and go as far as Jazer. But
now your summer fruits and your
grapes have been destroyed. 33 Happiness and joy have been taken away from
the fertile land of Moab. I have made the
wine stop flowing from the wine
presses; there is no one to make the wine
and shout for joy.
34 "The people of Heshbon and Elealeh
cry out,[g] and their cry can be heard as
far as Jahaz; it can be heard by the people in Zoar, and it is heard as far as Horonaim and Eglath Shelishiyah. Even
Nimrim Brook has dried up. 35 I will stop
the people of Moab from making burnt
offerings at their places of worship and
from offering sacrifices to their gods. I,
the LORD, have spoken.
36 "So my heart mourns for Moab and
for the people of Kir Heres, like someone
playing a funeral song on a flute, because everything they owned is gone.
37 All of them have shaved their heads
and cut off their beards. They have all
made gashes on their hands, and everyone is wearing sackcloth. 38 On all the
housetops of Moab and in all its public
squares there is nothing but mourning,
because I have broken Moab like a jar
that no one wants. 39 Moab has been
shattered! Cry out! Moab has been disgraced. It is in ruins, and all the surrounding nations make fun of it. I, the
LORD, have spoken."

No Escape for Moab

40 The LORD has promised that a nation
will swoop down on Moab like an eagle
with its outspread wings, 41 and the
towns and fortresses will be captured.
On that day Moab's soldiers will be as
frightened as a woman in labor. 42 Moab
will be destroyed and will no longer be a
nation, because it rebelled against me.
43 Terror, pits, and traps are waiting for
the people of Moab. The LORD has spoken. 44 Whoever tries to escape the terror
will fall into the pits, and whoever
climbs out of the pits will be caught in
the traps, because the LORD has set the
time for Moab's destruction. 45 Helpless
refugees try to find protection in Heshbon, the city that King Sihon once ruled,
but it is in flames.[h] Fire has burned
up the frontiers and the mountain
heights of the war-loving people of
Moab. 46 Pity the people of Moab! The
people who worshiped Chemosh have
been destroyed, and their sons and
daughters have been taken away as
prisoners.
47 But in days to come the LORD will
make Moab prosperous again. All of this
is what the LORD has said will happen to
Moab.

[g] *Probable text* Heshbon . . . cry out; *Hebrew unclear.* [h] Heshbon, the city . . . flames; *or* the city of Heshbon, but it is in flames and the palace of King Sihon is burning.

The LORD's Judgment on Ammon

49 This is what the LORD said about
Ammon: "Where are the men of
Israel? Is there no one to defend their
land? Why have they let the people who
worship Molech take the territory of the
tribe of Gad and settle there? 2 But the
time is coming when I will make the people of the capital city of Rabbah hear the
noise of battle, and it will be left in ruins
and its villages burned to the ground.
Then Israel will take its land back from
those who took it from them. 3 People of
Heshbon, cry out! Ai is destroyed!
Women of Rabbah, go into mourning!
Put on sackcloth and mourn. Run about
in confusion. Your god Molech will be
taken into exile, together with his priests
and princes. 4 Why do you unfaithful
people boast? Your strength is failing.
Why do you trust in your power and say
that no one would dare attack you?
5 I will bring terror on you from every
side. You will all run away. Each one
will run for his life, and there will be no
one to bring your troops together again.
6 "But later on I will make Ammon
prosperous again. I, the LORD, have
spoken."

The LORD's Judgment on Edom

7 This is what the LORD Almighty said
about Edom: "Have the people of Edom
lost their good judgment? Can their advisers no longer tell them what to do?
Has all their wisdom disappeared? 8 People of Dedan, turn and run! Hide! I am
going to destroy Esau's descendants because the time has come for me to punish them. 9 When people pick grapes,
they leave a few on the vines, and when
robbers come at night, they take only
what they want. 10 But I[l] have stripped
Esau's descendants completely and uncovered their hiding places, so that they
can no longer hide. All the people of
Edom are destroyed. Not one of them is
left. 11 Leave your orphans with me, and
I will take care of them. Your widows
can depend on me.
12 "If even those who did not deserve to
be punished had to drink from the cup of
punishment, do you think that you will
go unpunished? No, you must drink
from the cup! 13 I myself have sworn that
the city of Bozrah will become a horrifying sight and a desert; people will make
fun of it and use its name as a curse. All
the nearby villages will be in ruins forever. I, the LORD, have spoken."
14 I said, "Edom, I have received a message from the LORD. He has sent a messenger to tell the nations to assemble
their armies and to get ready to attack
you. 15 The LORD is going to make you
weak, and no one will respect you.
16 Your pride has deceived you. No one
fears you as much as you think they do.
You live on the rocky cliffs, high on top
of the mountain; but even though you
live as high up as an eagle, the LORD will
bring you down. The LORD has spoken."
17 The LORD said, "The destruction that
will come on Edom will be so terrible
that everyone who passes by will be
shocked and terrified. 18 The same thing
will happen to Edom that happened to
Sodom and Gomorrah, when they and
the nearby towns were destroyed. No
one will ever live there again. I, the LORD,
have spoken. 19 Like a lion coming out of
the thick woods along the Jordan River
up to the green pasture land, I will come
and make the Edomites run away suddenly from their country. Then the
leader I choose will rule the nation. Who
can be compared to me? Who would
dare challenge me? What ruler could oppose me? 20 So listen to the plan that I
have made against the people of Edom,
and to what I intend to do to the people
of the city of Teman. Even their children
will be dragged off, and everyone will be
horrified. 21 When Edom falls, there will
be such a noise that the entire earth will
shake, and the cries of alarm will be
heard as far away as the Gulf of Aqaba.
22 The enemy will attack Bozrah like an
eagle swooping down with outspread
wings. On that day Edom's soldiers will
be as frightened as a woman in labor."

The LORD's Judgment on Damascus

23 This is what the LORD said about Damascus: "The people in the cities of Hamath and Arpad are worried and
troubled because they have heard bad
news. Anxiety rolls over them like a
sea, and they cannot rest. 24 The people
of Damascus are weak and have fled in

[l] they leave a few . . . they take only what they want. 10 But I; *or* they leave nothing . . . they take everything. 10 And so I.

terror. They are in pain and misery like
a woman in labor. 25 The famous city
that used to be happy[j] is completely deserted. 26 On that day her young men will
be killed in the city streets, and all her
soldiers destroyed. 27 I will set the walls
of Damascus on fire and will burn down
King Benhadad's palaces. I, the LORD
Almighty, have spoken."

Judgment on the Tribe of Kedar and the City of Hazor

28 This is what the LORD said about the
tribe of Kedar and the districts controlled by Hazor, which were conquered
by King Nebuchadnezzar of Babylonia:
"Attack the people of Kedar and destroy
that tribe of eastern people! 29 Seize their
tents and their flocks, their tent curtains
and everything in their tents. Take their
camels and tell the people, 'Terror is all
around you!'

30 "People of Hazor, I, the LORD, warn
you to run far away and hide. King Nebuchadnezzar of Babylonia has plotted
against you, and this is what he says,
31 'Come on! We'll attack those people
that feel safe and secure! Their city has
no gates or locks and is completely un-
protected.'

32 "Take their camels and all their livestock! I will scatter in every direction
those people who cut their hair short,
and I will bring disaster on them from
every side. 33 Hazor will be made a
desert forever, a place where only jackals live. No one will ever live there
again. I, the LORD, have spoken."

The LORD's Judgment on Elam

34 Soon after Zedekiah became king of
Judah, the LORD Almighty spoke to me
about the country of Elam. 35 He said, "I
will kill all the archers who have made
Elam so powerful. 36 I will make winds
blow against Elam from all directions,
and I will scatter her people everywhere,
until there is no country where her refugees have not gone. 37 I will make the
people of Elam afraid of their enemies,
who want to kill them. In my great anger
I will destroy the people of Elam and
send armies against them until I have
wiped them out. 38 I will destroy their
kings and leaders, and set up my throne
there. 39 But later on I will make the people of Elam prosperous again. I, the
LORD, have spoken."

Babylon's Capture

50 This is the message that the LORD
gave me about the city of Babylon and its people:

2 "Tell the news to the nations!
Proclaim it!
Give the signal and announce
the news!
Do not keep it a secret!
Babylon has fallen!
Her god Marduk has been
shattered!
Babylon's idols are put to shame;
her disgusting images are
crushed!

3 "A nation from the north has come to
attack Babylonia and will make it a
desert. People and animals will run
away, and no one will live there."

Israel's Return

4 The LORD says, "When that time
comes, the people of both Israel and Judah will come weeping, looking for me,
their God. 5 They will ask the way to
Zion and then go in that direction. They
will make an eternal covenant with me
and never break it.

6 "My people are like sheep whose
shepherds have let them get lost in the
mountains. They have wandered like
sheep from one mountain to another,
and they have forgotten where their
home is. 7 They are attacked by all who
find them. Their enemies say, 'They
sinned against the LORD, and so what we
have done is not wrong. Their ancestors
trusted in the LORD, and they themselves
should have remained faithful to him.'

8 "People of Israel, run away from
Babylonia! Leave the country! Be the
first to leave! 9 I am going to stir up a
group of strong nations in the north and
make them attack Babylonia. They will
line up in battle against the country and
conquer it. They are skillful hunters,
shooting arrows that never miss the
mark. 10 Babylonia will be looted, and
those who loot it will take everything
they want. I, the LORD, have spoken."

[j] *Some ancient translations* happy; *Hebrew* my happiness.

Babylon's Fall

11 The LORD says, "People of Babylonia, you plundered my nation. You are
happy and glad, going about like a cow
threshing grain or like a neighing horse,
12 but your own great city will be humiliated and disgraced. Babylonia will be
the least important nation of all; it will
become a dry and waterless desert.
13 Because of my anger no one will live in
Babylon; it will be left in ruins, and all
who pass by will be shocked and
amazed.
14 "Archers, line up for battle against
Babylon and surround it. Shoot all your
arrows at Babylon, because it has sinned
against me, the LORD. 15 Raise the war cry
all around the city! Now Babylon has
surrendered. Its walls have been broken
through and torn down.[k] I am taking
my revenge on the Babylonians. So take
your revenge on them, and treat them as
they have treated others. 16 Do not let
seeds be planted in that country nor let a
harvest be gathered. Every foreigner living there will be afraid of the attacking
army and will go back home."

Israel's Return

17 The LORD says, "The people of Israel
are like sheep, chased and scattered by
lions. First, they were attacked by the
emperor of Assyria, and then King Nebuchadnezzar of Babylonia gnawed on
their bones. 18 Because of this, I, the LORD
Almighty, the God of Israel, will punish
King Nebuchadnezzar and his country,
just as I punished the emperor of Assyria. 19 I will restore the people of Israel
to their land. They will eat the food that
grows on Mount Carmel and in the region of Bashan, and they will eat all they
want of the crops that grow in the territories of Ephraim and Gilead. 20 When
that time comes, no sin will be found in
Israel and no wickedness in Judah, because I will forgive those people whose
lives I have spared. I, the LORD, have
spoken."

God's Judgment on Babylonia

21 The LORD says, "Attack the people of
Merathaim and of Pekod. Kill and destroy them.[l] Do everything I command
you. I, the LORD, have spoken. 22 The
noise of battle is heard in the land, and
there is great destruction. 23 Babylonia
hammered the whole world to pieces,
and now that hammer is shattered! All
the nations are shocked at what has happened to that country. 24 Babylonia, you
fought against me, and you have been
caught in the trap I set for you, even
though you did not know it. 25 I have
opened the place where my weapons are
stored, and in my anger I have taken
them out, because I, the Sovereign LORD
Almighty, have work to do in Babylonia.
26 Attack it from every side and break
open the places where its grain is stored!
Pile up the loot like piles of grain! Destroy the country! Leave nothing at all!
27 Kill all their soldiers! Slaughter them!
The people of Babylonia are doomed!
The time has come for them to be
punished!"
(28 Refugees escape from Babylonia
and come to Jerusalem, and they tell
how the LORD our God took revenge for
what the Babylonians had done to his
Temple.)
29 "Tell the archers to attack Babylon.
Send out everyone who knows how to
use the bow and arrow. Surround the
city and don't let anyone escape. Pay it
back for all it has done, and treat it as it
has treated others, because it acted with
pride against me, the Holy One of Israel.
30 So its young men will be killed in the
city streets, and all its soldiers will be
destroyed on that day. I, the LORD, have
spoken.
31 "Babylonia, you are filled with
pride, so I, the Sovereign LORD Almighty,
am against you! The time has come for
me to punish you. 32 Your proud nation
will stumble and fall, and no one will
help you up. I will set your cities on fire,
and everything around will be destroyed."
33 The LORD Almighty says, "The people of Israel and of Judah are oppressed.
All who captured them are guarding
them closely and will not let them go.
34 But the one who will rescue them is
strong—his name is the LORD Almighty.
He himself will take up their cause and
will bring peace to the earth, but trouble
to the people of Babylonia."
35 The LORD says,

[k] *Hebrew has an additional word, the meaning of which is unclear.* [l] *One ancient translation* them; *Hebrew* after them.

"Death to Babylonia!
Death to its people,
to its rulers, to its people of
wisdom.
36 Death to its lying prophets—
what fools they are!
Death to its soldiers—
how terrified they are!
37 Destroy its horses and chariots!
Death to its hired soldiers—
how weak they are!
Destroy its treasures;
plunder and loot.
38 Bring a drought on its land
and dry up its rivers.
Babylonia is a land of terrifying
idols
that have made fools of the
people.

39 "And so Babylon will be haunted by
demons and evil spirits,[m] and by unclean birds. Never again will people live
there, not for all time to come. 40 The
same thing will happen to Babylon that
happened to Sodom and Gomorrah,
when I destroyed them and the nearby
towns. No one will ever live there again.
I, the LORD, have spoken.

41 "People are coming from a country
in the north,
a mighty nation far away;
many kings are preparing
for war.
42 They have taken their bows and
swords;
they are cruel and merciless.
They sound like the roaring sea,
as they ride their horses.
They are ready for battle against
Babylonia.
43 The king of Babylonia hears the
news,
and his hands hang limp.
He is seized by anguish,
by pain like a woman in labor.

44 "Like a lion coming out of the thick
woods along the Jordan up to the green
pasture land, I, the LORD, will come and
make the Babylonians run away suddenly from their city. Then the leader I
choose will rule the nation. Who can be
compared to me? Who would dare challenge me? What ruler could oppose me?
45 So listen to the plan that I have made
against the city of Babylon and to what
I intend to do to its people. Even their
children will be dragged off, and everyone will be horrified. 46 When Babylon
falls, there will be such a noise that the
entire earth will shake, and the cries
of alarm will be heard by the other
nations."

Further Judgment on Babylonia

51 The LORD says, "I am bringing a
destructive wind[n] against Babylonia and its people. 2 I will send foreigners to destroy Babylonia like a wind that
blows straw away. When that day of destruction comes, they will attack from
every side and leave the land bare.
3 Don't give its soldiers time to shoot
their arrows or to put on their armor. Do
not spare the young men! Destroy the
whole army! 4 They will be wounded and
die in the streets of their cities. 5 I, the
LORD God Almighty, have not abandoned Israel and Judah, even though
they have sinned against me, the Holy
One of Israel. 6 Run away from Babylonia! Run for your lives! Do not be killed
because of Babylonia's sin. I am now
taking my revenge and punishing it as it
deserves. 7 Babylonia was like a gold cup
in my hand, making the whole world
drunk. The nations drank its wine and
went out of their minds. 8 Babylonia has
suddenly fallen and is destroyed! Mourn
over it! Get medicine for its wounds, and
maybe it can be healed. 9 Foreigners living there said, 'We tried to help Babylonia, but it was too late. Let's leave now
and go back home. God has punished
Babylonia with all his might and has destroyed it completely.' "

10 The LORD says, "My people shout,
'The LORD has shown that we are in the
right. Let's go and tell the people in Jerusalem what the LORD our God has
done.' "

11 The LORD has stirred up the kings of
Media, because he intends to destroy
Babylonia. That is how he will take re-
venge for the destruction of his Temple.

The attacking officers command,
"Sharpen your arrows! Get your shields
ready! 12 Give the signal to attack Babylon's walls. Strengthen the guard! Post
the sentries! Place troops in ambush!"

The LORD has done what he said he
would do to the people of Babylonia.
13 That country has many rivers and rich

[m] demons and evil spirits; *or* wildcats and jackals.

[n] destructive wind; *or* destroying spirit.

treasures, but its time is up, and its
thread of life is cut. 14 The LORD Almighty
has sworn by his own life that he will
bring many men to attack Babylonia like
a swarm of locusts, and they will shout
with victory.

A Hymn of Praise to God

15 The LORD made the earth by his power;
by his wisdom he created the world
and stretched out the heavens.
16 At his command the waters above the sky[o] roar;
he brings clouds from the ends of the earth.
He makes lightning flash in the rain
and sends the wind from his storeroom.
17 At the sight of this, people feel stupid and senseless;
those who make idols are disillusioned
because the gods they make are false and lifeless.
18 They are worthless and should be despised;
they will be destroyed when the LORD comes to deal with them.
19 The God of Jacob is not like them;
he is the one who made everything,
and he has chosen Israel to be his very own people.
The LORD Almighty is his name.

The LORD's Hammer

20 The LORD says,
"Babylonia, you are my hammer,
my weapon of war.
I used you to crush nations and kingdoms,
21 to shatter horses and riders,
to shatter chariots and their drivers,
22 to kill men and women,
to slay old and young,
to kill boys and girls,
23 to slaughter shepherds and their flocks,
to slaughter farmers and their plow horses,
to crush rulers and high officials."

Babylonia's Punishment

24 The LORD says, "You will see me repay Babylonia and its people for all the
evil they did to Jerusalem. 25 Babylonia,
you are like a mountain that destroys
the whole world, but I, the LORD, am your
enemy. I will take hold of you, level you
to the ground, and leave you in ashes.
26 None of the stones from your ruins
will ever be used again for building. You
will be like a desert forever. I, the LORD,
have spoken.

27 "Give the signal to attack! Blow the
trumpet so that the nations can hear!
Prepare the nations for war against
Babylonia! Tell the kingdoms of Ararat,
Minni, and Ashkenaz to attack. Appoint
an officer to lead the attack. Bring up the
horses like a swarm of locusts. 28 Prepare the nations for war against Babylonia. Send for the kings of Media, their
leaders and officials, and the armies of
all the countries they control. 29 The
earth trembles and shakes because the
LORD is carrying out his plan to make
Babylonia a desert, where no one lives.
30 The Babylonian soldiers have stopped
fighting and remain in their forts. They
have lost their courage and have become
helpless. The city gates are broken
down, and the houses are on fire. 31 Messenger after messenger runs to tell the
king of Babylonia that his city has been
broken into from every side. 32 The enemy have captured the river crossing
and have set the fortresses on fire. The
Babylonian soldiers have panicked.
33 Soon the enemy will cut them down
and trample them like grain on a threshing place. I, the LORD Almighty, the God
of Israel, have spoken."

34 The king of Babylonia cut Jerusalem up
and ate it.
He emptied the city like a jar;
like a monster he swallowed it.
He took what he wanted
and threw the rest away.
35 Let the people of Zion say,
"May Babylonia be held responsible
for the violence done to us!"
Let the people of Jerusalem say,
"May Babylonia be held responsible
for what we have suffered!"

[o] WATERS ABOVE THE SKY: *See Gn 1.6-8.*

The LORD Will Help Israel

36 And so the LORD said to the people of
Jerusalem, "I will take up your cause
and will make your enemies pay for
what they did to you. I will dry up the
source of Babylonia's water and make
its rivers go dry. 37 That country will become a pile of ruins where wild animals
live. It will be a horrible sight; no one
will live there, and all who see it will be
terrified. 38 The Babylonians all roar like
lions and growl like lion cubs. 39 Are
they greedy? I will prepare them a feast
and make them drunk and happy. They
will go to sleep and never wake up.
40 I will take them to be slaughtered, like
lambs, goats, and rams. I, the LORD, have
spoken."

Babylon's Fate

41 The LORD says about Babylon: "The
city that the whole world praised has
been captured! What a horrifying sight
Babylon has become to the nations!
42 The sea has rolled over Babylon and
covered it with roaring waves. 43 The
towns have become a horrifying sight
and are like a waterless desert, where no
one lives or even travels. 44 I will punish
Bel, the god of Babylonia, and make him
give up his stolen goods; the nations will
not worship him any more.

"Babylon's walls have fallen. 45 People
of Israel, run away from there! Run for
your life from my fierce anger. 46 Do not
lose courage or be afraid because of the
rumors you hear. Every year a different
rumor spreads—rumors of violence in
the land and of one king fighting another. 47 And so the time is coming when
I will deal with Babylonia's idols. The
whole country will be put to shame, and
all its people will be killed. 48 Everything
on earth and in the sky will shout for joy
when Babylonia falls to the people who
come from the north to destroy it.
49 Babylonia caused the death of people
all over the world, and now Babylonia
will fall because it caused the death of so
many Israelites. I, the LORD, have
spoken."

God's Message to the Israelites in Babylonia

50 The LORD says to his people in Babylonia: "You have escaped death! Now
go! Don't wait! Though you are far from
home, think about me, your LORD, and
remember Jerusalem. 51 You say, 'We've
been disgraced and made ashamed; we
feel completely helpless because foreigners have taken over the holy places
in the Temple.' 52 So then, I say that the
time is coming when I will deal with
Babylon's idols, and the wounded will
groan throughout the country. 53 Even if
Babylon could climb to the sky and build
a strong fortress there, I would still send
people to destroy it. I, the LORD, have
spoken."

Further Destruction on Babylon

54 The LORD says,
"Listen to the sound of crying in
Babylon,
of mourning for the destruction
in the land.
55 I am destroying Babylon
and putting it to silence.
The armies rush in like roaring
waves
and attack with noisy shouts.
56 They have come to destroy
Babylon;
its soldiers are captured,
and their bows are broken.
I am a God who punishes evil,
and I will treat Babylon as it
deserves.
57 I will make its rulers drunk—
men of wisdom, leaders, and
soldiers.
They will go to sleep and never
wake up.
I, the king, have spoken;
I am the LORD Almighty.
58 The walls of mighty Babylon will
be thrown to the ground,
and its towering gates burned
down.
The work of the nations is all for
nothing;
their efforts go up in flames.
I, the LORD Almighty, have
spoken."

Jeremiah's Message Is Sent to Babylonia

59 King Zedekiah's personal attendant
was Seraiah, the son of Neriah and
grandson of Mahseiah. In the fourth
year that Zedekiah was king of Judah,
Seraiah was going to Babylonia with
him, and I gave him some instructions.
60 I wrote in a book an account of all the

destruction that would come on Babylonia, as well as all these other things
about Babylonia. 61 I told Seraiah,
"When you get to Babylon, be sure to
read aloud to the people everything that
is written here. 62 Then pray, 'LORD, you
have said that you would destroy this
place, so that there would be no living
creatures in it, neither people nor animals, and it would be like a desert forever.' 63 Seraiah, when you finish
reading this book to the people, then tie
it to a rock and throw it into the Euphrates River 64 and say, 'This is what will
happen to Babylonia—it will sink and
never rise again because of the destruction that the LORD is going to bring
on it.' "[p]

The words of Jeremiah end here.

The Fall of Jerusalem

(2 Kings 24.18—25.7)

52 Zedekiah was twenty-one years
old when he became king of Judah, and he ruled in Jerusalem for
eleven years. His mother's name was
Hamutal, the daughter of the Jeremiah
who lived in the city of Libnah. 2 King
Zedekiah sinned against the LORD, just
as King Jehoiakim had done. 3 The LORD
became so angry with the people of Jerusalem and Judah that he banished
them from his sight.

Zedekiah rebelled against King Nebuchadnezzar of Babylonia, 4 and so Nebuchadnezzar came with all his army and
attacked Jerusalem on the tenth day of
the tenth month of the ninth year of Zedekiah's reign. They set up camp outside
the city, built siege walls around it, 5 and
kept it under siege until Zedekiah's eleventh year. 6 On the ninth day of the
fourth month of that same year, when
the famine was so bad that the people
had nothing left to eat, 7 the city walls
were broken through. Although the
Babylonians were surrounding the city,
all the soldiers escaped during the night.
They left by way of the royal garden,
went through the gateway connecting
the two walls, and fled in the direction of
the Jordan Valley. 8 But the Babylonian
army pursued King Zedekiah, captured
him in the plains near Jericho, and all
his soldiers deserted him. 9 Zedekiah
was taken to King Nebuchadnezzar,
who was in the city of Riblah in the territory of Hamath, and there Nebuchadnezzar passed sentence on him. 10 At
Riblah he put Zedekiah's sons to death
while Zedekiah was looking on and he
also had the officials of Judah executed.
11 After that, he had Zedekiah's eyes put
out and had him placed in chains and
taken to Babylon. Zedekiah remained in
prison in Babylon until the day he died.

The Destruction of the Temple

(2 Kings 25.8-17)

12 On the tenth day of the fifth month
of the nineteenth year of King Nebuchadnezzar of Babylonia, Nebuzaradan,
adviser to the king and commander of
his army, entered Jerusalem. 13 He
burned down the Temple, the palace,
and the houses of all the important people in Jerusalem; 14 and his soldiers tore
down the city walls. 15 Then Nebuzaradan took away to Babylonia[q] the people
who were left in the city, the remaining
skilled workers, and those who had deserted to the Babylonians. 16 But he left
in Judah some of the poorest people,
who owned no property, and he put
them to work in the vineyards and fields.

17 The Babylonians broke in pieces the
bronze columns and the carts that were
in the Temple, together with the large
bronze tank, and they took all the
bronze to Babylon. 18 They also took
away the shovels and the ash containers
used in cleaning the altar, the tools used
in tending the lamps, the bowls used for
catching the blood from the sacrifices,
the bowls used for burning incense, and
all the other bronze articles used in the
Temple service. 19 They took away
everything that was made of gold or silver: the small bowls, the pans used for
carrying live coals, the bowls for holding
the blood from the sacrifices, the ash
containers, the lampstands, the bowls
used for incense, and the bowls used for
pouring out wine offerings. 20 The
bronze objects that King Solomon had
made for the Temple—the two columns,
the carts, the large tank, and the twelve
bulls that supported it—were too heavy
to weigh. 21-22 The two columns were
identical: each one was 27 feet high and

[p] *One ancient translation* on it; *Hebrew* on it and they will become tired out.
[q] *Probable text* Babylonia; *Hebrew* Babylonia some of the poorest of the people.

18 feet around. They were hollow, and the metal was 3 inches thick. On top of each column was a bronze capital 7½ feet high, and all around it was a grill-work decorated with pomegranates, all of which was also made of bronze. 23 On
the grillwork of each column there were a hundred pomegranates in all, and ninety-six of these were visible from the ground.

The People of Judah Are Taken to Babylonia

(2 Kings 25.18-21, 27-30)

24 In addition, Nebuzaradan, the commanding officer, took away as prisoners Seraiah the High Priest, Zephaniah the priest next in rank, and the three other important Temple officials. 25 From the
city he took the officer who had been in command of the troops, seven of the king's personal advisers who were still in the city, the commander's assistant, who was in charge of military records, and sixty other important men. 26 Nebuzaradan took them to the king of Babylonia, who was in the city of Riblah 27 in
the territory of Hamath. There the king had them beaten and put to death.

So the people of Judah were carried away from their land into exile. 28 This is
the record of the people that Nebuchadnezzar took away as prisoners: in his seventh year as king he carried away 3,023; 29 in his eighteenth year, 832
from Jerusalem; 30 and in his twenty-
third year, 745—taken away by Nebuzaradan. In all, 4,600 people were taken away.

31 In the year that Evil-merodach became king of Babylonia, he showed kindness to King Jehoiachin of Judah by releasing him from prison. This happened on the twenty-fifth day of the twelfth month of the thirty-seventh year after Jehoiachin had been taken away as a prisoner. 32 Evilmerodach treated him
kindly and gave him a position of greater honor than he gave the other kings who were exiles with him in Babylonia. 33 So Jehoiachin was permitted to
change from his prison clothes and to dine at the king's table for the rest of his life. 34 Each day for as long as he lived,
he was given a regular allowance for his needs.

LAMENTATIONS

Introduction

The book of Lamentations *is a collection of five poems lamenting the destruction of Jerusalem in 586 B.C., and its aftermath of ruin and exile. In spite of the mournful nature of most of the book, there is also the note of trust in God and hope for the future. These poems are used by the Jews in worship on the annual days of fasting and mourning which commemorate the national disaster of 586 B.C.*

Outline of Contents

The Sorrows of Jerusalem

1 How lonely lies Jerusalem, once
so full of people!
Once honored by the world, she
is now like a widow;
The noblest of cities has fallen
into slavery.

2 All night long she cries; tears run
down her cheeks.
Of all her former friends, not
one is left to comfort her.
Her allies have betrayed her and
are all against her now.

3 Judah's people are helpless slaves,
forced away from home.[a]
They live in other lands, with no
place to call their own—
Surrounded by enemies, with no
way to escape.

4 No one comes to the Temple now
to worship on the holy days.
The young women who sang
there suffer, and the priests
can only groan.
The city gates stand empty, and
Zion is in agony.

5 Her enemies succeeded; they hold
her in their power.
The LORD has made her suffer
for all her many sins;
Her children have been captured
and taken away.

6 The splendor of Jerusalem is a
thing of the past.
Her leaders are like deer that
are weak from hunger,
Whose strength is almost gone
as they flee from the
hunters.

7 A lonely ruin now, Jerusalem
recalls her ancient splendor.
When she fell to the enemy,
there was no one to help her;
Her conquerors laughed at her
downfall.

8 Her honor is gone; she is naked
and held in contempt.
She groans and hides her face in
shame.
Jerusalem made herself filthy
with terrible sin.

9 Her uncleanness was easily seen,
but she showed no concern for
her fate.
Her downfall was terrible; no
one can comfort her.
Her enemies have won, and she
cries to the LORD for mercy.

10 The enemies robbed her of all her
treasures.
She saw them enter the Temple
itself,
Where the LORD had forbidden
Gentiles to go.

11 Her people groan as they look for
something to eat;
They exchange their treasures
for food to keep themselves
alive.
"Look at me, LORD," the city
cries; "see me in my
misery."

12 "Look at me!" she cries to
everyone who passes by.[b]
"No one has ever had pain like
mine,
Pain that the LORD brought on
me in the time of his anger.

13 "He sent fire from above, a fire
that burned inside me.
He set a trap for me and brought
me to the ground.
Then he abandoned me and left
me in constant pain.

14 "He took note of all my sins and
tied them all together;
He hung them around my neck,
and I grew weak beneath the
weight.
The Lord gave me to my foes,
and I was helpless against
them.

15 "The Lord laughed at all my
strongest soldiers;

[a] are helpless ... home; *or* fled from home, from the misery of slavery. [b] Look ... by; *or* May this not happen to you that pass by; *or* Does this mean nothing to you that pass by?

He sent an army to destroy my
young men.
He crushed my people like
grapes in a wine press.

16 "That is why my eyes are
overflowing with tears.
No one can comfort me; no one
can give me courage.
The enemy has conquered me;
my people have nothing left.

17 "I stretch out my hands, but no
one will help me.
The LORD has called enemies
against me from every side;
They treat me like some filthy
thing.

18 "But the LORD is just, for I have
disobeyed him.
Listen to me, people
everywhere; look at me in my
pain.
My young men and women have
been taken away captive.

19 "I called to my allies, but they
refused to help me.
The priests and the leaders died
in the city streets,
Looking for food to keep
themselves alive.

20 "Look, O LORD, at my agony, at the
anguish of my soul!
My heart is broken in sorrow for
my sins.
There is murder in the streets;
even indoors there is death.

21 "Listen[c] to my groans; there is no
one to comfort me.
My enemies are glad that you
brought disaster on me.
Bring[d] the day you promised;
make my enemies suffer as
I do.

22 "Condemn them for all their
wickedness;
Punish them as you punished me
for my sins.
I groan in misery, and I am sick
at heart."

The Lord's Punishment of Jerusalem

2 The Lord in his anger has covered
Zion with darkness.
Its heavenly splendor he has
turned into ruins.
On the day of his anger he
abandoned even his Temple.

2 The Lord destroyed without mercy
every village in Judah
And tore down the forts that
defended the land.
He brought disgrace on the
kingdom and its rulers.

3 In his fury he shattered the
strength of Israel;
He refused to help us when the
enemy came.
He raged against us like fire,
destroying everything.

4 He aimed his arrows at us like an
enemy;
He killed all those who were our
joy and delight.
Here in Jerusalem we felt his
burning anger.

5 Like an enemy, the Lord has
destroyed Israel;
He has left her forts and palaces
in ruins.
He has brought on the people of
Judah unending sorrow.

6 He smashed to pieces the Temple
where we worshiped him;
He has put an end to holy days
and Sabbaths.
King and priest alike have felt
the force of his anger.

7 The Lord rejected his altar and
deserted his holy Temple;
He allowed the enemy to tear
down its walls.
They shouted in victory where
once we had worshiped in joy.

8 The LORD was determined that the
walls of Zion should fall;
He measured them off to make
sure of total destruction.

[c] *One ancient translation* Listen; *Hebrew* They listened. [d] *One ancient translation* Bring; *Hebrew* You brought.

The towers and walls now lie in ruins together.

9 The gates lie buried in rubble, their bars smashed to pieces.
The king and the noblemen now are in exile.
The Law is no longer taught, and the prophets have no visions from the LORD.

10 Jerusalem's old men sit on the ground in silence,
With dust on their heads and sackcloth on their bodies.
Young women bow their heads to the ground.

11 My eyes are worn out with weeping; my soul is in anguish.
I am exhausted with grief at the destruction of my people.
Children and babies are fainting in the streets of the city.

12 Hungry and thirsty, they cry to their mothers;
They fall in the streets as though they were wounded,
And slowly die in their mothers' arms.

13 O Jerusalem, beloved Jerusalem, what can I say?
How can I comfort you? No one has ever suffered like this.
Your disaster is boundless as the ocean; there is no possible hope.

14 Your prophets had nothing to tell you but lies;
Their preaching deceived you by never exposing your sin.
They made you think you did not need to repent.

15 People passing by the city look at you in scorn.
They shake their heads and laugh at Jerusalem's ruins:
"Is this that lovely city? Is this the pride of the world?"

16 All your enemies mock you and glare at you with hate.
They curl their lips and sneer, "We have destroyed it!
This is the day we have waited for!"

17 The LORD has finally done what he threatened to do:
He has destroyed us without mercy, as he warned us long ago.
He gave our enemies victory, gave them joy at our downfall.

18 O Jerusalem, let your very walls cry out to the Lord![e]
Let your tears flow like rivers night and day;
Wear yourself out with weeping and grief!

19 All through the night get up again and again to cry out to the Lord;
Pour out your heart and beg him for mercy on your children—
Children starving to death on every street corner!

20 Look, O LORD! Why are you punishing us like this?
Women are eating the bodies of the children they loved!
Priests and prophets are being killed in the Temple itself!

21 Young and old alike lie dead in the streets,
Young men and women, killed by enemy swords.
You slaughtered them without mercy on the day of your anger.

22 You invited my enemies to hold a carnival of terror all around me,
And no one could escape on that day of your anger.
They murdered my children, whom I had raised and loved.

[e] *Probable text* O Jerusalem . . . Lord; *Hebrew* Their hearts cried out to the Lord, O wall of Jerusalem.

Punishment, Repentance, and Hope

3 I am one who knows what it is to
be punished by God.
2 He drove me deeper and deeper
into darkness
3 And beat me again and again
with merciless blows.

4 He has left my flesh open and raw,
and has broken my bones.
5 He has shut me in a prison of
misery and anguish.
6 He has forced me to live in the
stagnant darkness of death.

7 He has bound me in chains; I am a
prisoner with no hope of
escape.
8 I cry aloud for help, but God
refuses to listen;
9 I stagger as I walk; stone walls
block me wherever I turn.

10 He waited for me like a bear; he
pounced on me like a lion.
11 He chased me off the road, tore
me to pieces, and left me.
12 He drew his bow and made me
the target for his arrows.

13 He shot his arrows deep into my
body.
14 People laugh at me all day long;
I am a joke to them all.
15 Bitter suffering is all he has
given me for food and drink.

16 He rubbed my face in the ground
and broke my teeth on rocks.
17 I have forgotten what health and
peace and happiness are.
18 I do not have much longer to
live; my hope in the LORD is
gone.

19 The thought of my pain, my
homelessness, is bitter poison.
20 I think of it constantly, and my
spirit is depressed.
21 Yet hope returns when I
remember this one thing:

22 The LORD's unfailing love and
mercy still continue,
23 Fresh as the morning, as sure as
the sunrise.
24 The LORD is all I have, and so in
him I put my hope.

25 The LORD is good to everyone who
trusts in him,
26 So it is best for us to wait in
patience—to wait for him to
save us—
27 And it is best to learn this
patience in our youth.

28 When we suffer, we should sit
alone in silent patience;
29 We should bow in submission,
for there may still be hope.
30 Though beaten and insulted, we
should accept it all.

31 The Lord is merciful and will not
reject us forever.
32 He may bring us sorrow, but his
love for us is sure and strong.
33 He takes no pleasure in causing
us grief or pain.

34 The Lord knows when our spirits
are crushed in prison;
35 He knows when we are denied
the rights he gave us;
36 When justice is perverted in
court, he knows.

37 The will of the Lord alone is
always carried out.[f]
38 Good and evil alike take place at
his command.
39 Why should we ever complain
when we are punished for
our sin?[g]

40 Let us examine our ways and turn
back to the LORD.
41 Let us open our hearts to God in
heaven and pray,
42 "We have sinned and rebelled,
and you, O LORD, have not
forgiven us.

43 "You pursued us and killed us;
your mercy was hidden by
your anger,
44 By a cloud of fury too thick for
our prayers to get through.

[f] The will . . . out; *or* No one can make anything happen unless the Lord is willing.
[g] Why should . . . sin?; *or* Why should we complain about being punished for sin, as long as we are still alive?

45 You have made us the garbage
dump of the world.

46 "We are insulted and mocked by
all our enemies.
47 We have been through disaster
and ruin; we live in danger
and fear.
48 My eyes flow with rivers of tears
at the destruction of my
people.

49 "My tears will pour out in a
ceaseless stream
50 Until the LORD looks down from
heaven and sees us.
51 My heart is grieved when I see
what has happened to the
women of the city.

52 "I was trapped like a bird by
enemies who had no cause to
hate me.
53 They threw me alive into a pit
and closed the opening with a
stone.
54 Water began to close over me,
and I thought death was near.

55 "From the bottom of the pit,
O LORD, I cried out to you,
56 And when I begged you to listen
to my cry, you heard.
57 You answered me and told me
not to be afraid.

58 "You came to my rescue, Lord,
and saved my life.
59 Judge in my favor; you know
the wrongs done against me.
60 You know how my enemies hate
me and how they plot
against me.

61 "You have heard them insult me,
O LORD; you know all their
plots.
62 All day long they talk about me
and make their plans.
63 From morning till night they
make fun of me.

64 "Punish them for what they have
done, O LORD;
65 Curse them and fill them with
despair!
66 Hunt them down and wipe them
off the earth!"

Jerusalem after Its Fall

4 Our glittering gold has grown dull;
the stones of the Temple lie
scattered in the streets.

2 Zion's young people were as
precious to us as gold,
but now they are treated like
common clay pots.

3 Even a mother wolf will nurse her
cubs,
but my people are like ostriches,
cruel to their young.

4 They let their babies die of hunger
and thirst;
children are begging for food
that no one will give them.

5 People who once ate the finest
foods die starving in the
streets;
those raised in luxury are
pawing through garbage for
food.

6 My people have been punished
even more than the
inhabitants of Sodom,
which met a sudden downfall at
the hands of God.

7 Our princes[h] were undefiled and
pure as snow,
vigorous and strong, glowing
with health.

8 Now they lie unknown in the
streets, their faces blackened
in death;
their skin, dry as wood, has
shriveled on their bones.

9 Those who died in the war were
better off than those who died
later,
who starved slowly to death,
with no food to keep them
alive.

10 The disaster that came to my
people brought horror;

[h] princes; *or* Nazirites.

loving mothers boiled their own
children for food.

11 The LORD turned loose the full
force of his fury;
he lit a fire in Zion that burned
it to the ground.

12 No one anywhere, not even rulers
of foreign nations,
believed that any invader could
enter Jerusalem's gates.

13 But it happened, because her
prophets sinned and her
priests were guilty
of causing the death of innocent
people.

14 Her leaders wandered through the
streets as though blind,
so stained with blood that no
one would touch them.

15 "Get away!" people shouted.
"You're defiled! Don't
touch me!"
So they wandered from nation
to nation, welcomed by
no one.

16 The LORD had no more concern for
them; he scattered them
himself.
He showed no regard for our
priests and leaders.

17 For help that never came, we
looked until we could look no
longer.
We kept waiting for help from a
nation that had none to give.

18 The enemy was watching for us;
we could not even walk in the
streets.
Our days were over; the end had
come.

19 Swifter than eagles swooping from
the sky, they chased us down.
They tracked us down in the
hills; they took us by surprise
in the desert.

20 They captured the source of our
life, the king the LORD had
chosen,
the one we had trusted to
protect us from every invader.

21 Laugh on, people of Edom and Uz;
be glad while you can.
Your disaster is coming too; you
too will stagger naked in
shame.

22 Zion has paid for her sin; the LORD
will not keep us in exile any
longer.
But Edom, the LORD will punish
you; he will expose your guilty
acts.

A Prayer for Mercy

5 Remember, O LORD, what has
happened to us.
Look at us, and see our disgrace.

2 Our property is in the hands of
strangers;
foreigners are living in our
homes.

3 Our fathers have been killed by
the enemy,
and now our mothers are
widows.

4 We must pay for the water we
drink;
we must buy the wood we need
for fuel.

5 Driven hard like donkeys or
camels,
we are tired, but are allowed no
rest.

6 To get food enough to stay alive,
we went begging to Egypt and
Assyria.

7 Our ancestors sinned, but now
they are gone,
and we are suffering for their
sins.

8 Our rulers are no better than
slaves,
and no one can save us from
their power.

9 Murderers roam through the
countryside;

we risk our lives when we look
for food.

10 Hunger has made us burn with
fever
until our skin is as hot as an
oven.

11 Our wives have been raped on
Mount Zion itself;
in every Judean village our
daughters have been forced to
submit.

12 Our leaders have been taken and
hanged;
our elders are shown no respect.

13 Our young men are forced to grind
grain like slaves;
boys go staggering under heavy
loads of wood.

14 The old people no longer sit at the
city gate,
and the young people no longer
make music.

15 Happiness has gone out of our
lives;
grief has taken the place of our
dances.

16 Nothing is left of all we were
proud of.
We sinned, and now we are
doomed.

17 We are sick at our very hearts
and can hardly see through our
tears,

18 because Mount Zion lies lonely
and deserted,
and wild jackals prowl through
its ruins.

19 But you, O LORD, are king forever
and will rule to the end of time.

20 Why have you abandoned us so
long?
Will you ever remember us
again?

21 Bring us back to you, LORD! Bring
us back!
Restore our ancient glory.

22 Or have you rejected us forever?
Is there no limit to your anger?

The Book of

EZEKIEL

Introduction

The prophet Ezekiel lived in exile in Babylon during the period before and after the fall of Jerusalem in 586 B.C. His message was addressed both to the exiles in Babylonia and to the people of Jerusalem. The Book of Ezekiel has six principal parts: 1) God's call to Ezekiel to be a prophet. 2) Warnings to the people about God's judgment on them and about the coming fall and destruction of Jerusalem. 3) Messages from the Lord regarding his judgment upon the various nations that oppressed and misled his people. 4) Comfort for Israel after the fall of Jerusalem and the promise of a brighter future. 5) The prophecy against Gog. 6) Ezekiel's picture of a restored Temple and nation.

Ezekiel was a man of deep faith and great imagination. Many of his insights came in the form of visions, and many of his messages were expressed in vivid symbolic actions. Ezekiel emphasized the need for inner renewal of the heart and spirit, and the responsibility of each individual for his own sins. He also proclaimed his hope for the renewal of the life of the nation. As a priest, as well as prophet, he had special interest in the Temple and in the need for holiness.

Outline of Contents

EZEKIEL'S FIRST VISION OF GOD (1.1 – 7.27)

God's Throne

1 On the fifth day of the fourth month
of the thirtieth year,[a] I, Ezekiel the
priest, son of Buzi, was living with the
Jewish exiles by the Chebar River in
Babylonia. The sky opened, and I saw a
vision of God. (2 It was the fifth year
since King Jehoiachin had been taken
into exile.) 3 There in Babylonia beside
the Chebar River, I heard the LORD speak
to me, and I felt his power.
4 I looked up and saw a windstorm
coming from the north. Lightning was
flashing from a huge cloud, and the sky
around it was glowing. Where the lightning was flashing, something shone like
bronze. 5 At the center of the storm I saw
what looked like four living creatures in
human form, 6 but each of them had four
faces and four wings. 7 Their legs were
straight, and they had hoofs like those of
a bull. They shone like polished bronze.
8 In addition to their four faces and four
wings, they each had four human hands,
one under each wing. 9 Two wings of
each creature were spread out so that
the creatures formed a square, with their
wing tips touching. When they moved,
they moved as a group without turning
their bodies.
10 Each living creature had four different faces: a human face in front, a lion's
face at the right, a bull's face at the left,
and an eagle's face at the back. 11 Two
wings[b] of each creature were raised so
that they touched the tips of the wings of
the creatures next to it, and their other
two wings were folded against their bodies. 12 Each creature faced all four directions, and so the group could go
wherever they wished, without having
to turn.
13 Among[c] the creatures there was
something that looked like a blazing
torch, constantly moving. The fire would
blaze up and shoot out flashes of light-

[a] THIRTIETH YEAR: *It is not known to what year this refers.* [b] *Some ancient translations* Two wings; *Hebrew* Their faces, their wings. [c] *Some ancient translations* Among; *Hebrew* And the likeness of.

ning. 14 The creatures themselves darted back and forth with the speed of lightning.

15 As I was looking at the four creatures I saw four wheels touching the ground, one beside each of them.[d] 16 All four wheels were alike; each one shone like a precious stone, and each had another wheel intersecting it at right angles, 17 so that the wheels could move in any of the four directions. 18 The rims of the wheels were covered with eyes.[e] 19 Whenever the creatures moved, the wheels moved with them, and if the creatures rose up from the earth, so did the wheels. 20 The creatures went wherever they wished, and the wheels did exactly what the creatures did, because the creatures controlled them. 21 So every time the creatures moved or stopped or rose in the air, the wheels did exactly the same.

22 Above the heads of the creatures there was something that looked like a dome made of dazzling crystal. 23 There under the dome stood the creatures, each stretching out two wings toward the ones next to it and covering its body with the other two wings. 24 I heard the noise their wings made in flight; it sounded like the roar of the sea, like the noise of a huge army, like the voice of Almighty God. When they stopped flying, they folded their wings, 25 but there was still a sound coming from above the dome over their heads.

26 Above the dome there was something that looked like a throne made of sapphire, and sitting on the throne was a figure that looked like a human being. 27 The figure seemed to be shining like bronze in the middle of a fire. It shone all over with a bright light 28 that had in it all the colors of the rainbow. This was the dazzling light which shows the presence of the LORD.

God Calls Ezekiel to Be a Prophet

When I saw this, I fell face downward on the ground. Then I heard a voice

2 1 saying, "Mortal man, stand up. I want to talk to you." 2 While the voice was speaking, God's spirit entered me and raised me to my feet, and I heard the voice continue, 3 "Mortal man, I am sending you to the people of Israel. They have rebelled and turned against me and are still rebels, just as their ancestors were. 4 They are stubborn and do not respect me, so I am sending you to tell them what I, the Sovereign LORD, am saying to them. 5 Whether those rebels listen to you or not, they will know that a prophet has been among them.

6 "But you, mortal man, must not be afraid of them or of anything they say. They will defy and despise you; it will be like living among scorpions. Still, don't be afraid of those rebels or of anything they say. 7 You will tell them whatever I tell you to say, whether they listen or not. Remember what rebels they are.

8 "Mortal man, listen to what I tell you. Don't be rebellious like them. Open your mouth and eat what I am going to give you." 9 I saw a hand reaching out toward me, and it was holding a scroll. 10 The hand unrolled the scroll, and I saw that there was writing on both sides—cries of grief were written there, and wails and groans.

3 God said, "Mortal man, eat this scroll; then go and speak to the people of Israel."

2 So I opened my mouth, and he gave me the scroll to eat. 3 He said, "Mortal man, eat this scroll that I give you; fill your stomach with it." I ate it, and it tasted as sweet as honey.

4 Then God said, "Mortal man, go to the people of Israel and say to them whatever I tell you to say. 5 I am not sending you to a nation that speaks a difficult foreign language, but to the Israelites. 6 If I sent you to great nations that spoke difficult languages you didn't understand, they would listen to you. 7 But none of the people of Israel will be willing to listen; they will not even listen to me. All of them are stubborn and defiant. 8 Now I will make you as stubborn and as tough as they are. 9 I will make you as firm as a rock, as hard as a diamond; don't be afraid of those rebels."

10 God continued, "Mortal man, pay close attention and remember everything I tell you. 11 Then go to the people of your nation who are in exile and tell them what I, the Sovereign LORD, am saying to them, whether they pay attention to you or not."

12 Then God's spirit lifted me up, and I

[d] *Some ancient translations* them; *Hebrew* their faces. [e] *Verse 18 in Hebrew is unclear.*

heard behind me the loud roar of a voice
that said, "Praise the glory of the LORD in
heaven above!" 13I heard the wings of
the creatures beating together in the air,
and the noise of the wheels, as loud as
an earthquake. 14The power of the LORD
came on me with great force, and as his
spirit carried me off, I felt bitter and angry. 15So I came to Tel Abib beside the
Chebar River, where the exiles were living, and for seven days I stayed there,
overcome by what I had seen and heard.

The LORD Appoints Ezekiel as a Lookout

(Ezekiel 33.1-9)

16After the seven days had passed, the
LORD spoke to me. 17"Mortal man," he
said, "I am making you a lookout for the
nation of Israel. You will pass on to them
the warnings I give you. 18If I announce
that someone evil is going to die but you
do not warn him to change his ways so
that he can save his life, he will die, still
a sinner, but I will hold you responsible
for his death. 19If you do warn an evil
man and he doesn't stop sinning, he will
die, still a sinner, but your life will be
spared.

20"If someone truly good starts doing
evil and I put him in a dangerous situation, he will die if you do not warn him.
He will die because of his sins—I will
not remember the good he did—and I
will hold you responsible for his death.
21If you do warn a good man not to sin
and he listens to you and doesn't sin, he
will stay alive, and your life will also be
spared."

Ezekiel Will Be Unable to Talk

22I felt the powerful presence of the
LORD and heard him say to me, "Get up
and go out into the valley. I will talk to
you there."

23So I went out into the valley, and
there I saw the glory of the LORD, just as
I had seen it beside the Chebar River. I
fell face downward on the ground, 24but
God's spirit entered me and raised me to
my feet. The LORD said to me, "Go home
and shut yourself up in the house. 25You
will be tied with ropes, mortal man, and
you will not be able to go out in public.
26I will paralyze your tongue so that you
won't be able to warn these rebellious
people. 27Then, when I speak to you
again and give you back the power of
speech, you will tell them what I, the
Sovereign LORD, am saying. Some of
them will listen, but some will ignore
you, for they are a nation of rebels."

Ezekiel Acts Out the Siege of Jerusalem

4 God said, "Mortal man, get a brick,
put it in front of you, and scratch
lines on it to represent the city of Jerusalem. 2Then, to represent a siege, put
trenches, earthworks, camps, and battering rams all around it. 3Take an iron
pan and set it up like a wall between you
and the city. Face the city. It is under
siege, and you are the one besieging it.
This will be a sign to the nation of Israel.

4-5"Then lie down on your left side,
and I[f] will place on you the guilt of the
nation of Israel. For 390 days you will
stay there and suffer because of their
guilt. I have sentenced you to one day
for each year their punishment will last.
6When you finish that, turn over on your
right side and suffer for the guilt of Judah for forty days—one day for each
year of their punishment.

7"Fix your eyes on the siege of Jerusalem. Shake your fist at the city and
prophesy against it. 8I will tie you up so
that you cannot turn from one side to the
other until the siege is over.

9"Now take some wheat, barley,
beans, peas, millet, and spelt. Mix them
all together and make bread. That is
what you are to eat during the 390 days
you are lying on your left side. 10You
will be allowed eight ounces of bread a
day, and it will have to last until the next
day. 11You will also have a limited
amount of water to drink, two cups a
day. 12You are to build a fire out of dried
human excrement, bake bread on the
fire, and eat it where everyone can
see you."

13The LORD said, "This represents the
way the Israelites will have to eat food
which the Law forbids,[g] when I scatter
them to foreign countries."

14But I replied, "No, Sovereign LORD! I
have never defiled myself. From childhood on I have never eaten meat from

[f] *Probable text* I; *Hebrew* you. [g] FOOD WHICH THE LAW FORBIDS: *The Law of Moses prohibited the eating of certain foods as being ritually unclean (see Lv 11).*

any animal that died a natural death or was killed by wild animals. I have never eaten any food considered unclean."

15 So God said, "Very well. I will let you use cow dung instead, and you can bake your bread on that."

16 And he added, "Mortal man, I am going to cut off the supply of bread for Jerusalem. The people there will be distressed and anxious as they measure out the food they eat and the water they drink. 17 They will run out of bread and water; they will be in despair, and they will waste away because of their sins."

Ezekiel Cuts His Hair

5 The LORD said, "Mortal man, take a sharp sword and use it to shave off your beard and all your hair. Then weigh the hair on scales and divide it into three parts. 2 Burn up a third of it in the city when the siege is over. Take another third and chop it up with your sword as you move around outside the city. Scatter the remaining third to the winds, and I will pursue it with my sword. 3 Keep back a few hairs and wrap them in the hem of your clothes. 4 Then take a few of them out again, throw them in the fire, and let them burn up. From them fire will spread to the whole nation of Israel."

5 The Sovereign LORD said, "Look at Jerusalem. I put her at the center of the world, with other countries all around her. 6 But Jerusalem rebelled against my commands and showed that she was more wicked than the other nations, more disobedient than the countries around her. Jerusalem rejected my commands and refused to keep my laws. 7 Now listen, Jerusalem, to what I, the Sovereign LORD, am saying. By not obeying my laws or keeping my commands, you have caused more trouble than the nations around you. You have followed the customs of other nations. 8 And so I, the Sovereign LORD, am telling you that I am your enemy. I will pass judgment on you where all the nations can see it. 9 Because of all the things you do that I hate, I will punish Jerusalem as I have never done before and will never do again. 10 As a result, parents in Jerusalem will eat their children, and children will eat their parents. I will punish you and scatter in every direction any who are left alive.

11 "Therefore, as I am the living God—this is the word of the Sovereign LORD—because you defiled my Temple with all the evil, disgusting things you did, I will cut you down without mercy. 12 A third of your people will die from sickness and hunger in the city; a third will be cut down by swords outside the city; and I will scatter the last third to the winds and pursue them with a sword.

13 "You will feel all the force of my anger and rage until I am satisfied. When all this happens, you will be convinced that I, the LORD, have spoken to you because I am outraged at your unfaithfulness. 14 Everyone from the nations around you who passes by will sneer at you and keep their distance.

15 "When I am angry and furious with you and punish you, all the nations around you will be terrified. They will look at you with disgust and make fun of you. 16 I will cut off your supply of food and let you starve. You[h] will feel the pains of hunger like sharp arrows sent to destroy you. 17 I will send hunger and wild animals to kill your children, and will send sickness, violence, and war to kill you. I, the LORD, have spoken."

The LORD Condemns Idolatry

6 The LORD spoke to me. 2 "Mortal man," he said, "look toward the mountains of Israel and give them my message. 3 Tell the mountains of Israel to hear the Sovereign LORD's word—to hear what I, the Sovereign LORD, am telling the mountains, the hills, the gorges, and the valleys: I will send a sword to destroy the places where people worship idols. 4 The altars will be torn down and the incense altars broken. All the people there will be killed in front of their idols. 5 I will scatter the corpses of the people of Israel; I will scatter their bones all around the altars. 6 All the cities of Israel will be destroyed, so that all their altars and their idols will be smashed to pieces, their incense altars will be shattered, and everything they made will disappear. 7 People will be killed everywhere, and those who survive will acknowledge that I am the LORD.

8 "I will let some escape the slaughter

[h] *Probable text* You; *Hebrew* They.

and be scattered among the nations,
9 where they will live in exile. There they
will remember me and know that I have
punished them and disgraced them,[i]
because their faithless hearts deserted
me and they preferred idols to me. And
they will be disgusted with themselves
because of the evil and degrading things
they have done. 10 They will know that I
am the LORD and that my warnings were
not empty threats."

11 The Sovereign LORD said, "Wring
your hands! Stamp your feet! Cry in sorrow because of all the evil, disgusting
things the Israelites have done. They are
going to die in war or of starvation or
disease. 12 Those far away will get sick
and die; those nearby will be killed in
war; those who survive will starve to
death. They will feel all the force of my
anger. 13 Corpses will be scattered
among the idols and around the altars,
scattered on every high hill, on the top of
every mountain, under every green tree
and every large oak, in every place
where they burned sacrifices to their
idols. Then everyone will know that I am
the LORD. 14 Yes, I will reach out and destroy their country. I will make it a
wasteland from the southern desert to
the city of Riblah in the north, not sparing any place where the Israelites live.
Then everyone will know that I am the
LORD."

The End Is Near for Israel

7 The LORD spoke to me. 2 "Mortal
man," he said, "this is what I, the
Sovereign LORD, am saying to the land of
Israel: This is the end for the whole land!

3 "Israel, the end has come. You will
feel my anger, because I am judging you
for what you have done. I will pay you
back for all your disgusting conduct.
4 I will not spare you or show you any
mercy. I am going to punish you for the
disgusting things you have done, so that
you will know that I am the LORD."

5 This is what the Sovereign LORD is
saying: "One disaster after another is
coming on you. 6 It's all over. This is the
end. You are finished. 7 The end is coming for you people who live in the land.
The time is near when there will be no
more celebrations at the mountain
shrines, only confusion.[j]

8 "Very soon now you will feel all the
force of my anger. I am judging you for
what you have done, and I will pay you
back for all your disgusting conduct.
9 I will not spare you or show you any
mercy. I am going to punish you for the
disgusting things you have done, so that
you will know that I am the LORD and
that I am the one who punishes you."

10 The day of disaster is coming. Violence is flourishing. Pride is at its
height.[k] 11 Violence produces more
wickedness. Nothing of theirs will remain, nothing of their wealth, their
splendor, or their glory.

12 The time is coming. The day is near
when buying and selling will have no
more meaning, because God's punishment will fall on everyone alike. 13 No
merchants will live long enough to get
back what they have lost, because God's
anger is on everyone. Those who are evil
cannot survive.[l] 14 The trumpet blows,
and everyone gets ready. But no one
goes off to war, for God's anger will fall
on everyone alike.

Punishment for Israel's Sins

15 There is fighting in the streets, and
sickness and hunger in the houses. Anyone who is out in the country will die in
the fighting, and anyone in the city will
be a victim of sickness and hunger.
16 Some will escape to the mountains like
doves frightened from the valleys. All of
them will moan over their sins.[m]
17 Everyone's hands will be weak, and
their knees will shake. 18 They will put
on sackcloth and they will tremble all
over. Their heads will be shaved, and
they will all be disgraced. 19 They will
throw their gold and silver away in the
streets like garbage, because neither silver nor gold can save them when the
LORD pours out his fury. They cannot use
it to satisfy their desires or fill their
stomachs. Gold and silver led them into
sin. 20 Once they were proud of their
beautiful jewels, but they used them to
make disgusting idols. That is why the
LORD has made their wealth repulsive to
them.

21 "I will let foreigners rob them," says

[i] *Some ancient translations* disgraced them; *Hebrew* I am disgraced.
[j] *Probable text* celebrations . . . confusion; *Hebrew unclear.* [k] *Probable text* Pride is at its height; *Hebrew unclear.* [l] *Verse 13 in Hebrew is unclear.* [m] *Verse 16 in Hebrew is unclear.*

the LORD, "and lawbreakers will take all
their wealth and defile it. 22 I will not interfere when my treasured Temple is
profaned, when robbers break into it
and defile it.
23 "Everything is in confusion[n] — the
land is full of murders and the cities are
full of violence. 24 I will bring the most
evil nations here and let them have your
homes. Your strongest men will lose
their confidence when I let the nations
profane the places where you worship.
25 Despair is coming. You will look for
peace and never find it. 26 One disaster
will follow another, and a steady stream
of bad news will pour in. You will beg
the prophets to reveal what they foresee.
The priests will have nothing to teach
the people, and the elders will have no
advice to give. 27 The king will mourn,
the prince will give up hope, and the
people will shake with fear. I will punish
you for all you have done, and will judge
you in the same way as you have judged
others. This will show you that I am the
LORD."

EZEKIEL'S SECOND VISION OF GOD (8.1 – 10.22)

Idolatry in Jerusalem

8 On the fifth day of the sixth month
of the sixth year of our exile, the
leaders of the exiles from Judah were
sitting in my house with me. Suddenly
the power of the Sovereign LORD came
on me. 2 I looked up and saw a vision of
a fiery human form. From the waist
down his body looked like fire, and from
the waist up he was shining like polished bronze. 3 He reached out what
seemed to be a hand and grabbed me by
the hair. Then in this vision God's spirit
lifted me high in the air and took me to
Jerusalem. He took me to the inner entrance of the north gate of the Temple,
where there was an idol that was an outrage to God.
4 There I saw the dazzling light that
shows the presence of Israel's God, just
as I had seen it when I was by the Chebar River. 5 God said to me, "Mortal man,
look toward the north." I looked, and
there near the altar by the entrance of
the gateway I saw the idol that was an
outrage to God.
6 God said to me, "Mortal man, do you
see what is happening? Look at the disgusting things the people of Israel are
doing here, driving me farther and farther away from my holy place. You will
see even more disgraceful things than
this."
7 He took me to the entrance of the
outer courtyard and showed me a hole in
the wall. 8 He said, "Mortal man, break
through the wall here." I broke through
it and found a door. 9 He told me, "Go in
and look at the evil, disgusting things
they are doing there." 10 So I went in and
looked. The walls were covered with
drawings of snakes and other unclean
animals,[o] and of the other things which
the Israelites were worshiping. 11 Seventy Israelite leaders were there, including Jaazaniah son of Shaphan. Each one
was holding an incense burner, and
smoke was rising from the incense.
12 God asked me, "Mortal man, do you
see what the Israelite leaders are doing
in secret? They are all worshiping in a
room full of images. Their excuse is:
'The LORD doesn't see us! He has abandoned the country.' "
13 Then the LORD said to me, "You are
going to see them do even more disgusting things than that." 14 So he took me to
the north gate of the Temple and showed
me women weeping over the death of
the god Tammuz.[p]
15 He asked, "Mortal man, do you see
that? You will see even more disgusting
things." 16 So he took me to the inner
courtyard of the Temple. There near the
entrance of the sanctuary, between the
altar and the porch, were about twenty-
five men. They had turned their backs to
the sanctuary and were bowing low toward the east, worshiping the rising sun.
17 The LORD said to me, "Mortal man,
do you see that? These people of Judah
are not satisfied with merely doing all
the disgusting things you have seen here
and with spreading violence throughout
the country. No, they must come and do
them right here in the Temple and make
me even more angry. Look how they

[n] *One ancient translation* Everything is in confusion; *Hebrew unclear.* [o] UNCLEAN ANIMALS: *The Law of Moses prohibited the eating of certain animals as being ritually unclean (see 4.13; Lv 11).* [p] TAMMUZ: *A god who was thought to die when vegetation died and to come to life the next year. Women would mourn his ritual death.*

insult me in the most offensive way possible![q] 18 They will feel all the force
of my anger. I will not spare them or
show them any mercy. They will
shout prayers to me as loud as they
can, but I will not listen to them."

Jerusalem Is Punished

9 Then I heard God shout, "Come
here, you men who are going to
punish the city. Bring your weapons
with you." 2 At once six men came from
the outer north gate of the Temple, each
one carrying a weapon. With them was a
man dressed in linen clothes, carrying
something to write with. They all came
and stood by the bronze altar.
3 Then the dazzling light of the presence of the God of Israel rose up from
the winged creatures[r] where it had
been, and moved to the entrance of the
Temple. The LORD called to the man
dressed in linen, 4 "Go through the whole
city of Jerusalem and put a mark on the
forehead of everyone who is distressed
and troubled because of all the disgusting things being done in the city."
5 And I heard God say to the other
men, "Follow him through the city and
kill. Spare no one; have mercy on no
one. 6 Kill the old men, young men,
young women, mothers, and children.
But don't touch anyone who has the
mark on his forehead. Start here at my
Temple." So they began with the leaders
who were standing there at the Temple.
7 God said to them, "Defile the Temple.
Fill its courtyards with corpses. Get to
work!" So they began to kill the people
in the city.[s]
8 While the killing was going on, I was
there alone. I threw myself face downward on the ground and shouted,
"Sovereign LORD, are you so angry with
Jerusalem that you are going to kill
everyone left in Israel?"
9 God answered, "The people of Israel
and Judah are guilty of terrible sins.
They have committed murder all over
the land and have filled Jerusalem with
crime. They say that I, the LORD, have
abandoned their country and that I don't
see them. 10 But I will not have pity on
them; I will do to them what they have
done to others."
11 Then the man wearing linen clothes
returned and reported to the LORD, "I
have carried out your orders."

The Glory of the LORD Leaves the Temple

10 I looked at the dome over the
heads of the living creatures[t]
and above them was something that
seemed to be a throne made of sapphire.
2 God said to the man wearing linen
clothes, "Go between the wheels under
the creatures and fill your hands with
burning coals. Then scatter the coals
over the city."
I watched him go. 3 The creatures were
standing to the south of the Temple
when he went in, and a cloud filled the
inner courtyard. 4 The dazzling light of
the LORD's presence rose up from the
creatures and moved to the entrance of
the Temple. Then the cloud filled the
Temple, and the courtyard was blazing
with the light. 5 The noise made by the
creatures' wings was heard even in the
outer courtyard. It sounded like the
voice of Almighty God.
6 When the LORD commanded the man
wearing linen clothes to take some fire
from between the wheels that were under the creatures, the man went in and
stood by one of the wheels. 7 One of the
creatures reached his hand into the fire
that was there among them, picked up
some coals, and put them in the hands of
the man in linen. The man took the coals
and left.
8 I saw that each creature had what
looked like a human hand under each of
its wings. 9-10 I also saw that there were
four wheels, all alike, one beside each
creature. The wheels shone like precious
stones, and each one had another wheel
which intersected it at right angles.
11 When the creatures moved, they could
go in any direction without turning.
They all moved together in the direction
they wanted to go, without having to
turn around. 12 Their bodies, backs,
hands, wings, and wheels were covered
with eyes. 13 I heard a voice calling out,
"Whirling wheels."
14 Each creature had four faces. The
first was the face of a bull, the second a

[q] IN THE MOST OFFENSIVE WAY POSSIBLE: *A reference to a pagan rite of putting a branch to the nose.*
[r] WINGED CREATURES: *See 1.5-12.* [s] work!" So they . . . city.; *or* work! Go on and start killing the people in the city!" [t] LIVING CREATURES: *See 1.5-12.*

human face, the third the face of a lion, and the fourth the face of an eagle. 15 (They were the same creatures that I had seen by the Chebar River.) When the creatures rose in the air 16 and moved, the wheels went with them. Whenever they spread their wings to fly, the wheels still went with them. 17 When the creatures stopped, the wheels stopped; and when the creatures flew, the wheels went with them, because the creatures controlled them.

18 Then the dazzling light of the LORD's presence left the entrance of the Temple and moved to a place above the creatures. 19 They spread their wings and flew up from the earth while I was watching, and the wheels went with them. They paused at the east gate of the Temple, and the dazzling light was over them. 20 I recognized them as the same creatures which I had seen beneath the God of Israel at the Chebar River.

21 Each of them had four faces, four wings, and what looked like a human hand under each wing. 22 Their faces looked exactly like the faces[u] I had seen by the Chebar River. Each creature moved straight ahead.

Jerusalem Is Condemned

11 God's spirit lifted me up and took me to the east gate of the Temple. There near the gate I saw twenty-five men, including Jaazaniah son of Azzur and Pelatiah son of Benaiah, two leaders of the nation.

2 God said to me, "Mortal man, these men make evil plans and give bad advice in this city. 3 They say, 'We will soon be building houses again.[v] The city is like a cooking pot, and we are like the meat in it, but at least it protects us from the fire.' 4 Now then, denounce them, mortal man."

5 The spirit of the LORD took control of me, and the LORD told me to give the people this message: "People of Israel, I know what you are saying and what you are planning. 6 You have murdered so many people here in the city that the streets are full of corpses.

7 "So this is what I, the Sovereign LORD, am saying to you. This city is a cooking pot all right, but what is the meat? The corpses of those you have killed! You will not be here—I will throw you out of the city! 8 Are you afraid of swords? I will bring soldiers with swords to attack you. 9 I will take you out of the city and hand you over to foreigners. I have sentenced you to death, 10 and you will be killed in battle in your own country. Then everyone will know that I am the LORD. 11 This city will not protect you the way a pot protects the meat in it. I will punish you wherever you may be in the land of Israel. 12 You will know that I am the LORD and that while you were keeping the laws of the neighboring nations, you were breaking *my* laws and disobeying *my* commands."

13 While I was prophesying, Pelatiah dropped dead. I threw myself face downward on the ground and shouted, "No, Sovereign LORD! Are you going to kill everyone left in Israel?"

God's Promise to the Exiles

14 The LORD spoke to me. 15 "Mortal man," he said, "the people who live in Jerusalem are talking about you and those of your nation who are in exile. They say, 'The exiles are too far away to worship the LORD. He has given us possession of the land.'

16 "Now tell your fellow exiles what I am saying. I am the one who sent them to live in far-off nations and scattered them in other countries. Yet, for the time being I will be present with them in the lands where they have gone.

17 "So tell them what I, the Sovereign LORD, am saying. I will gather them out of the countries where I scattered them, and will give the land of Israel back to them. 18 When they return, they are to get rid of all the filthy, disgusting idols they find. 19 I will give them a new heart and a new mind. I will take away their stubborn heart of stone and will give them an obedient heart. 20 Then they will keep my laws and faithfully obey all my commands. They will be my people, and I will be their God. 21 But I will punish the people who love to worship filthy, disgusting idols. I will punish them for what they have done." The Sovereign LORD has spoken.

[u] *Probable text* the faces; *Hebrew* the faces and them. [v] We will . . . again; *or* We won't be building houses any time soon.

God's Glory Leaves Jerusalem

22 The living creatures began to fly,
and the wheels went with them. The dazzling light of the presence of the God of
Israel was over them. 23 Then the dazzling light left the city and moved to the
mountain east of it. 24 In the vision the
spirit of God lifted me up and brought
me back to the exiles in Babylonia. Then
the vision faded, 25 and I told the exiles
everything that the LORD had shown me.

The Prophet as a Refugee

12 The LORD spoke to me. 2 "Mortal
man," he said, "you are living
among rebellious people. They have
eyes, but they see nothing; they have
ears, but they hear nothing, because
they are rebellious.

3 "Now, mortal man, pack a bundle
just as a refugee would and start out before nightfall. Let everyone see you leaving and going to another place. Maybe
those rebels will notice you.[w] 4 While it
is still daylight, pack your bundle for exile, so that they can see you, and then let
them watch you leave in the evening as
if you were going into exile. 5 While they
are watching, break a hole through the
wall of your house and take your pack
out through it. 6 Let them watch you putting your pack on your shoulder and going out into the dark with your eyes
covered, so that you can't see where you
are going. What you do will be a warning to the Israelites."

7 I did what the LORD told me to do.
That day I packed a bundle as a refugee
would, and that evening as it was getting
dark I dug a hole in the wall with my
hands and went out. While everyone
watched, I put the pack on my shoulder
and left.

8 The next morning the LORD spoke to
me. 9 "Mortal man," he said, "now that
those Israelite rebels are asking you
what you're doing, 10 tell them what I,
the Sovereign LORD, am saying to them.
This message is for the prince ruling in
Jerusalem and for all the people who
live there. 11 Tell them that what you
have done is a sign of what will happen
to them—they will be refugees and captives. 12 The prince who is ruling them
will shoulder his pack in the dark and
escape through a hole that they dig for
him in the wall. He will cover his eyes
and not see where he is going. 13 But I
will spread out my net and trap him in it.
Then I will take him to the city of Babylon, where he will die without having
seen it. 14 I will scatter in every direction
all the members of his court and his advisers and bodyguards, and people will
search for them to kill them.

15 "When I scatter them among the
other nations and in foreign countries,
they will know that I am the LORD.
16 I will let a few of them survive the war,
the famine, and the diseases, so that
there among the nations they will realize
how disgusting their actions have been
and will acknowledge that I am the
LORD."

The Sign of the Trembling Prophet

17 The LORD spoke to me. 18 "Mortal
man," he said, "tremble when you eat,
and shake with fear when you drink.
19 Tell the whole nation that this is the
message of the Sovereign LORD to the
people of Jerusalem who are still living
in their land: They will tremble when
they eat and shake with fear when they
drink. Their land will be stripped bare,
because everyone who lives there is lawless. 20 Cities that are now full of people
will be destroyed, and the country will
be made a wilderness. Then they will
know that I am the LORD."

A Popular Proverb and an Unpopular Message

21 The LORD spoke to me. 22 "Mortal
man," he said, "why do the people of Israel repeat this proverb: 'Time goes by,
and predictions come to nothing'?
23 Now tell them what I, the Sovereign
LORD, have to say about that. I will put an
end to that proverb. It won't be repeated
in Israel any more. Tell them instead:
The time has come, and the predictions
are coming true!

24 "Among the people of Israel there
will be no more false visions or misleading prophecies. 25 I, the LORD, will speak
to them, and what I say will be done.
There will be no more delay. In your
own lifetime, you rebels, I will do what I
have warned you I would do. I have spoken," says the Sovereign LORD.

26 The LORD said to me, 27 "Mortal man,

[w] Maybe those . . . you; *or* Maybe they will then realize that they are rebels.

the Israelites think that your visions and
prophecies are about the distant future.
28 So tell them that I, the Sovereign LORD,
am saying: There will be no more delay.
What I have said will be done. I, the
Sovereign LORD, have spoken!"

Prophecy against False Male Prophets

13 The LORD spoke to me. 2 "Mortal
man," he said, "denounce the
prophets of Israel who make up their
own prophecies. Tell them to listen to
the word of the LORD."

3 This is what the Sovereign LORD says:
"These foolish prophets are doomed!
They provide their own inspiration and
invent their own visions. 4 People of Israel, your prophets are as useless as
foxes living among the ruins of a city.
5 They don't guard the places where the
walls have crumbled, nor do they rebuild the walls, and so Israel cannot be
defended when war comes on the day of
the LORD. 6 Their visions are false, and
their predictions are lies. They claim
that they are speaking my message, but
I have not sent them. Yet they expect
their words to come true! 7 I tell them:
Those visions you see are false, and the
predictions you make are lies. You say
that they are my words, but I haven't
spoken to you!"

8 So the Sovereign LORD says to them,
"Your words are false, and your visions
are lies. I am against you. 9 I am about to
punish you prophets who have false visions and make misleading predictions.
You will not be there when my people
gather to make decisions; your names
will not be included in the list of the citizens of Israel; you will never return to
your land. Then you will know that I am
the Sovereign LORD.

10 "The prophets mislead my people by
saying that all is well. All is certainly not
well! My people have put up a wall of
loose stones, and then the prophets have
come and covered it with whitewash.
11 Tell the prophets that their wall is going to fall down. I will send a pouring
rain. Hailstones will fall on it, and a
strong wind will blow against it. 12 The
wall will collapse, and everyone will ask
you what good the whitewash did."

13 Now this is what the Sovereign LORD
says: "In my anger I will send a strong
wind, pouring rain, and hailstones to destroy the wall. 14 I intend to break down
the wall they whitewashed, to shatter
it, and to leave the foundation stones
bare. It will collapse and kill you all.
Then everyone will know that I am the
LORD.

15 "The wall and those who covered it
with whitewash will feel the force of my
anger. Then I will tell you that the wall is
gone and so are those who whitewashed
it — 16 those prophets who assured Jerusalem that all was well, when all was not
well!" The Sovereign LORD has spoken.

Prophecy against False Female Prophets

17 The LORD said, "Now, mortal man,
look at the women among your people
who make up predictions. Denounce
them 18 and tell them what the Sovereign
LORD is saying to them:

"You women are doomed! You sew
magic wristbands for everyone and
make magic scarves for everyone to
wear on their heads, so that they can
have power over other people's lives.
You want to possess the power of life
and death over my people and to use it
for your own benefit. 19 You dishonor me
in front of my people in order to get a
few handfuls of barley and a few pieces
of bread. You kill people who don't deserve to die, and you keep people alive
who don't deserve to live. So you tell lies
to my people, and they believe you."

20 Now this is what the Sovereign LORD
says: "I hate the wristbands that you use
in your attempt to control life and death.
I will rip them off your arms and set free
the people that you were controlling.[x]
21 I will rip off your scarves and let my
people escape from your power once
and for all. Then you will know that I am
the LORD.

22 "By your lies you discourage good
people, whom I do not wish to hurt. You
prevent evil people from giving up evil
and saving their lives. 23 So now your
false visions and misleading predictions
are over. I am rescuing my people from
your power, so that you will know that I
am the LORD."

[x] *In verse 20 in Hebrew a word occurs twice, the meaning of which is unclear.*

God Condemns Idolatry

14 Some of the leaders of the Israelites came to consult me about the
LORD's will. 2 Then the LORD spoke to me.
3 "Mortal man," he said, "these men have
given their hearts to idols and are letting
idols lead them into sin. Do they think I
will give them an answer?
4 "Now speak to them and tell them
what I, the Sovereign LORD, am saying to
them: Each of you Israelites who have
given your heart to idols and let them
lead you into sin and who then come to
consult a prophet, will get an answer
from me—the answer that your many
idols deserve! 5 All those idols have
turned the Israelites away from me, but
by my answer I hope to win back their
loyalty.
6 "Now then, tell the Israelites what I,
the Sovereign LORD, am saying: Turn
back and leave your disgusting idols.
7 "Whenever one of you Israelites or
one of you foreigners who live in the Israelite community turn away from me
and worship idols, and then go to consult a prophet, I, the LORD, will give you
your answer! 8 I will oppose you. I will
make an example of you. I will remove
you from the community of my people,
so that all of you will know that I am the
LORD.
9 "If any prophets are deceived into
giving a false answer, it is because I, the
LORD, have deceived them. I will remove
them from the people of Israel. 10 Both
prophets and anyone who consults them
will get the same punishment. 11 I will do
this to keep the Israelites from deserting
me and defiling themselves by their sins.
They are to be my people, and I will be
their God." The Sovereign LORD has
spoken.

Noah, Danel, and Job

12 The LORD spoke to me. 13 "Mortal
man," he said, "if a country sins and is
unfaithful to me, I will reach out and destroy its supply of food. I will send a
famine and kill people and animals
alike. 14 Even if those three men, Noah,
Danel,[y] and Job, were living there, their
goodness would save only their own
lives." The Sovereign LORD has spoken.
15 "Or I might send wild animals to kill
the people, making the land so dangerous that no one could travel through it,
16 and even if those three men lived
there—as surely as I, the Sovereign
LORD, am the living God—they would
not be able to save even their own children. They would save only their own
lives, and the land would become a wilderness.
17 "Or I might bring war on that country and send destructive weapons to
wipe out people and animals alike, 18 and
even if those three men lived there—as
surely as I, the Sovereign LORD, am the
living God—they would not be able to
save even their children, but only their
own lives.
19 "If I send an epidemic on that country and in my anger take many lives,
killing people and animals, 20 even if
Noah, Danel, and Job lived there—as
surely as I, the Sovereign LORD, am the
living God—they would not be able to
save even their own children. Their
goodness would save only their own
lives."
21 This is what the Sovereign LORD is
saying: "I will send my four worst punishments on Jerusalem—war, famine,
wild animals, and disease—to destroy
people and animals alike. 22 If some survive and save their children, look at
them when they come to you. See how
evil they are, and be convinced that the
punishment I am bringing on Jerusalem
is justified; 23 then you will know that
there was good reason for everything I
did." The Sovereign LORD has spoken.

A Parable about a Vine

15 The LORD spoke to me. 2 "Mortal
man," he said, "how does a vine
compare with a tree? What good is a
branch of a grapevine compared with
the trees of the forest? 3 Can you use it to
make anything? Can you even make a
peg out of it to hang things on? 4 It is only
good for building a fire. And when the
ends are burned up and the middle is
charred, can you make anything out of
it? 5 It was useless even before it was
burned. Now that the fire has burned it
and charred it, it is even more useless."
6 Now this is what the Sovereign LORD
is saying: "Just as a vine is taken from
the forest and burned, so I will take the
people who live in Jerusalem 7 and will

[y] Danel; *or* Daniel *(see 28.3), an ancient hero, known for his righteous life.*

punish them. They have escaped one
fire, but now fire will burn them up.
When I punish them, you will know that
I am the LORD. 8They have been unfaithful to me, and so I will make the country
a wilderness." The Sovereign LORD has
spoken.

Jerusalem the Unfaithful

16 The LORD spoke to me again.
2"Mortal man," he said, "point
out to Jerusalem what disgusting things
she has done. 3Tell Jerusalem what the
Sovereign LORD is saying to her:

"You were born in the land of Canaan.
Your father was an Amorite, and your
mother was a Hittite.[z] 4When you were
born, no one cut your umbilical cord or
washed you[a] or rubbed you with salt or
wrapped you in cloths. 5No one took
enough pity on you to do any of these
things for you. When you were born, no
one loved you. You were thrown out in
an open field.

6"Then I passed by and saw you
squirming in your own blood. You were
covered with blood, but I wouldn't let
you die. 7I made you grow like a healthy
plant. You grew strong and tall and became a young woman.[b] Your breasts
were well-formed, and your hair had
grown, but you were naked.

8"As I passed by again, I saw that the
time had come for you to fall in love. I
covered your naked body with my coat
and promised to love you. Yes, I made a
marriage covenant with you, and you
became mine." This is what the
Sovereign LORD says.

9"Then I took water and washed the
blood off you. I rubbed olive oil on your
skin. 10I dressed you in embroidered
gowns and gave you shoes of the best
leather, a linen headband, and a silk
cloak. 11I put jewels on you—bracelets
and necklaces. 12I gave you a nose ring
and earrings and a beautiful crown to
wear. 13You had ornaments of gold and
silver, and you always wore clothes of
embroidered linen and silk. You ate
bread made from the best flour, and had
honey and olive oil to eat. Your beauty
was dazzling, and you became a queen.
14You became famous in every nation
for your perfect beauty, because I was
the one who made you so lovely." This is
what the Sovereign LORD says.

15"But you took advantage of your
beauty and fame to sleep with everyone
who came along.[c] 16You used some of
your clothes to decorate your places of
worship, and just like a prostitute,[d] you
gave yourself to everyone. 17You took
the silver and gold jewelry that I had
given you, used it to make male images,
and committed adultery with them.
18You took the embroidered clothes I
gave you and put them on the images,
and you offered to the images the olive
oil and incense I had given you. 19I gave
you food—the best flour, olive oil, and
honey—but you offered it as a sacrifice
to win the favor of idols." This is what
the Sovereign LORD says.

20"Then you took the sons and the
daughters you had borne me and offered
them as sacrifices to idols. Wasn't it bad
enough to be unfaithful to me, 21without
taking my children and sacrificing them
to idols? 22During your disgusting life as
a prostitute you never once remembered
your childhood—when you were naked,
squirming in your own blood."

Jerusalem's Life as a Prostitute

23The Sovereign LORD said, "You are
doomed! Doomed! You did all that evil,
and then 24by the side of every road you
built places to worship idols and practice prostitution. 25You dragged your
beauty through the mud. You offered
yourself to everyone who came by, and
you were more of a prostitute every day.
26You let your lustful neighbors, the
Egyptians, go to bed with you, and you
used your prostitution to make me
angry.

27"Now I have raised my hand to punish you and to take away your share of
my blessing. I have handed you over to
the Philistines, who hate you and are
disgusted with your immoral actions.

28"Because you were not satisfied by
the others, you went running after the
Assyrians. You were their prostitute,
but they didn't satisfy you either.
29You were also a prostitute for the

[z] AMORITE . . . HITTITE: *The Israelites regarded these people as immoral and idolatrous.*
[a] *Hebrew has an additional word, the meaning of which is unclear.* [b] *Probable text* young woman; *Hebrew unclear.* [c] *Hebrew has two additional words, the meaning of which is unclear.* [d] *Hebrew has four additional words, the meaning of which is unclear.*

Babylonians, that nation of merchants,
but they didn't satisfy you either."
30 This[e] is what the Sovereign LORD is
saying: "You have done all this like a
shameless prostitute. 31 On every street
you built places to worship idols and
practice prostitution. But you are not out
for money like a common prostitute.
32 You are like a woman who commits
adultery with strangers instead of loving
her husband. 33 A prostitute is paid, but
you gave presents to all your lovers and
bribed them to come from everywhere to
sleep with you. 34 You are a special kind
of prostitute. No one forced you to become one. You didn't get paid; you paid
them! Yes, you are different."

God's Judgment on Jerusalem

35 Now then, Jerusalem, you whore!
Hear what the LORD is saying.
36 This is what the Sovereign LORD
says: "You stripped off your clothes, and
like a prostitute, you gave yourself to
your lovers and to all your disgusting
idols, and you killed your children as
sacrifices to idols. 37 Because of this I
will bring all your former lovers
together—the ones you liked and the
ones you hated. I will bring them around
you in a circle, and then I will strip off
your clothes and let them see you naked.
38 I will condemn you for adultery and
murder, and in my anger and fury I will
punish you with death. 39 I will put you
in their power, and they will tear down
the places where you engage in prostitution and worship idols. They will take
away your clothes and jewels and leave
you completely naked.
40 "They will stir up a crowd to stone
you, and they will cut you to pieces with
their swords. 41 They will burn your
houses down and let crowds of women
see your punishment. I will make you
stop being a prostitute and make you
stop giving gifts to your lovers. 42 Then
my anger will be over, and I will be calm.
I will not be angry or jealous any more.
43 You have forgotten how I treated you
when you were young, and you have
made me angry by all the things you did.
That is why I have made you pay for
them all. Why did you add sexual immorality to all the other disgusting things
you did?" The Sovereign LORD has
spoken.

Like Mother, Like Daughter

44 The LORD said, "People will use this
proverb about you, Jerusalem: 'Like
mother, like daughter.' 45 You really are
your mother's daughter. She detested
her husband and her children. You are
like your sisters, who hated their husbands and their children. You and your
sister cities had a Hittite mother and an
Amorite[f] father.
46 "Your older sister, with her villages,
is Samaria, in the north. Your younger
sister, with her villages, is Sodom, in the
south. 47 Were you satisfied to follow in
their footsteps and copy their disgusting
actions? No, in only a little while you
were acting worse than they were in
everything you did.
48 "As surely as I am the living God,"
the Sovereign LORD says, "your sister
Sodom and her villages never did the
evil that you and your villages have
done. 49 She and her daughters were
proud because they had plenty to eat
and lived in peace and quiet, but they did
not take care of the poor and the under-
privileged. 50 They were proud and stubborn and did the things that I hate, so I
destroyed them, as you well know.
51 "Samaria did not sin half as much as
you have. You have acted more disgust-
ingly than she ever did. Your corruption
makes your sisters look innocent by
comparison. 52 And now you will have to
endure your disgrace. Your sins are so
much worse than those of your sisters
that they look innocent beside you. Now
blush and bear your shame, because you
make your sisters look pure."

Sodom and Samaria Will Be Restored

53 The LORD said to Jerusalem, "I will
make them prosperous again—Sodom
and her villages and Samaria and her
villages. Yes, I will make you prosperous too. 54 You will be ashamed of yourself, and your disgrace will show your
sisters how well-off they are. 55 They will
become prosperous again, and you and
your villages will also be restored.
56 Didn't you joke about Sodom in those

[e] *Verse 30 in Hebrew begins with three words, the meaning of which is unclear.* [f] HITTITE . . . AMORITE: *See 16.3.*

days when you were proud 57 and before
the evil you did had been exposed? Now
you are just like her—a joke to the
Edomites, the Philistines, and your other
neighbors who hate you. 58 You must
suffer for the obscene, disgusting things
you have done." The LORD has spoken.

A Covenant That Lasts Forever

59 The Sovereign LORD says, "I will
treat you the way you deserve, because
you ignored your promises and broke
the covenant. 60 But I will honor the covenant I made with you when you were
young, and I will make a covenant with
you that will last forever. 61 You will remember how you have acted, and be
ashamed of it when you get your older
sister and your younger sister back. I
will let them be like daughters to you,
even though this was not part of my covenant with you. 62 I will renew my covenant with you, and you will know that I
am the LORD. 63 I will forgive all the
wrongs you have done, but you will remember them and be too ashamed to
open your mouth." The Sovereign LORD
has spoken.

The Parable of the Eagles and the Vine

17 The LORD spoke to me. 2 "Mortal
man," he said, "tell the Israelites
a parable 3 to let them know what I, the
Sovereign LORD, am saying to them:
There was a giant eagle with beautiful
feathers and huge wings, spread wide.
He flew to the Lebanon Mountains and
broke off the top of a cedar tree, 4 which
he carried to a land of commerce and
placed in a city of merchants. 5 Then he
took a young plant from the land of Israel and planted it in a fertile field,[g]
where there was always water to make it
grow. 6 The plant sprouted and became a
low, wide-spreading grapevine. The
branches grew upward toward the eagle, and the roots grew deep. The vine
was covered with branches and leaves.
7 "There was another giant eagle with
huge wings and thick plumage. And now
the vine sent its roots toward him and
turned its leaves toward him, in the hope
that he would give it more water than
there was in the garden where it was
growing.[h] 8 But the vine had already
been planted in a fertile, well-watered
field so that it could grow leaves and
bear grapes and be a magnificent vine.
9 "So I, the Sovereign LORD, ask: Will
this vine live and grow? Won't the first
eagle pull it up by its roots, pull off the
grapes, and break off the branches and
let them wither? It will not take much
strength or a mighty nation to pull it up.
10 Yes, it is planted, but will it live and
grow? Won't it wither when the east
wind strikes it? Won't it wither there
where it is growing?"

The Parable Is Explained

11 The LORD said to me, 12 "Ask these
rebels if they know what the parable
means. Tell them that the king of Babylonia came to Jerusalem and took the
king and his officials back with him to
Babylonia. 13 He took one of the king's
family, made a treaty with him, and
made him swear to be loyal. He took important men as hostages 14 to keep the
nation from rising again and to make
sure that the treaty would be kept. 15 But
the king of Judah rebelled and sent
agents to Egypt to get horses and a large
army. Will he succeed? Can he get away
with that? He cannot break the treaty
and go unpunished!
16 "As surely as I am the living God,"
says the Sovereign LORD, "this king will
die in Babylonia because he broke his
oath and the treaty he had made with the
king of Babylonia, who put him on the
throne. 17 Even the powerful army of the
king of Egypt will not be able to help
him fight when the Babylonians build
earthworks and dig trenches in order to
kill many people. 18 He broke his oath
and the treaty he had made. He did all
these things, and now he will not
escape."
19 The Sovereign LORD says, "As surely
as I am the living God, I will punish him
for breaking the treaty which he swore
in my name to keep. 20 I will spread out a
hunter's net and catch him in it. I will
take him to Babylonia and punish him
there, because he was unfaithful to me.
21 His best soldiers will be killed in battle, and the survivors will be scattered in

[g] *Hebrew has an additional word, the meaning of which is unclear.* [h] And now the vine ... growing; *or* And now the vine turned away from the garden where it was growing and sent its roots toward him and turned its leaves toward him, in the hope that he would give it water.

every direction. Then you will know that
I, the LORD, have spoken."

God's Promise of Hope

22 This is what the Sovereign LORD
says:

"I will take the top of a tall cedar
and break off a tender sprout;
I will plant it on a high mountain,
23 on Israel's highest mountain.
It will grow branches and bear
seed
and become a magnificent cedar.
Birds of every kind will live there
and find shelter in its shade.
24 All the trees in the land will know
that I am the LORD.
I cut down the tall trees
and make small trees grow tall.
I wither up the green trees
and make the dry trees become
green.

I, the LORD, have spoken. I will do what I
have said I would do."

Individual Responsibility

18 The LORD spoke to me 2 and said,
"What is this proverb people
keep repeating in the land of Israel?

'The parents ate the sour grapes,
But the children got the sour
taste.'

3 "As surely as I am the living God,"
says the Sovereign LORD, "you will not
repeat this proverb in Israel any more.
4 The life of every person belongs to me,
the life of the parent as well as that of
the child. The person who sins is the one
who will die.

5 "Suppose there is a truly good man,
righteous and honest. 6 He doesn't worship the idols of the Israelites or eat the
sacrifices offered at forbidden shrines.
He doesn't seduce another man's wife or
have intercourse with a woman during
her period. 7 He doesn't cheat or rob anyone. He returns what a borrower gives
him as security; he feeds the hungry and
gives clothing to the naked. 8 He doesn't
lend money for profit. He refuses to do
evil and gives an honest decision in any
dispute. 9 Such a man obeys my commands and carefully keeps my laws. He
is righteous, and he will live," says the
Sovereign LORD.

10 "Then suppose this man has a son
who robs and kills, who does any[i] of
these things 11 that the father never did.
He eats sacrifices offered at forbidden
shrines and seduces other men's wives.
12 He cheats the poor, he robs, he keeps
what a borrower gives him as security.
He goes to pagan shrines, worships disgusting idols, 13 and lends money for
profit. Will he live? No, he will not. He
has done all these disgusting things, and
so he will die. He will be to blame for his
own death.

14 "Now suppose this second man has
a son. He sees all the sins his father
practiced, but does not follow his example. 15 He doesn't worship the idols of the
Israelites or eat the sacrifices offered at
forbidden shrines. He doesn't seduce another man's wife 16 or oppress anyone or
rob anyone. He returns what a borrower
gives him as security. He feeds the hungry and gives clothing to the naked.
17 He refuses to do evil[j] and doesn't
lend money for profit. He keeps my laws
and obeys my commands. He will not
die because of his father's sins, but he
will certainly live. 18 His father, on the
other hand, cheated and robbed[k] and
always did evil to everyone. And so he
died because of the sins he himself had
committed.

19 "But you ask, 'Why shouldn't the
son suffer because of his father's sins?'
The answer is that the son did what was
right and good. He kept my laws and followed them carefully, and so he will certainly live. 20 It is the one who sins who
will die. A son is not to suffer because of
his father's sins, nor a father because of
the sins of his son. Good people will be
rewarded for doing good, and evil people will suffer for the evil they do.

21 "If someone evil stops sinning and
keeps my laws, if he does what is right
and good, he will not die; he will certainly live. 22 All his sins will be forgiven,
and he will live, because he did what is
right. 23 Do you think I enjoy seeing evil
people die?" asks the Sovereign LORD.
"No, I would rather see them repent and
live.

24 "But if a righteous person stops doing good and starts doing all the evil,
disgusting things that evil people do,

[i] *Some ancient translations* who does any; *Hebrew unclear.* [j] *Some ancient translations (see also verse 8)* to do evil; *Hebrew* from the poor. [k] *Some ancient translations* robbed; *Hebrew unclear.*

will he go on living? No! None of the
good he did will be remembered. He will
die because of his unfaithfulness and his
sins.
25 "But you say, 'What the Lord does
isn't right.' Listen to me, you Israelites.
Do you think my way of doing things
isn't right? It is your way that isn't right.
26 When a righteous person stops doing
good and starts doing evil and then dies,
he dies because of the evil he has done.
27 When someone evil stops sinning and
does what is right and good, he saves his
life. 28 He realizes what he is doing and
stops sinning, so he will certainly not
die, but go on living. 29 And you Israelites say, 'What the Lord does isn't right.'
You think my way isn't right, do you? It
is your way that isn't right.
30 "Now I, the Sovereign LORD, am telling you Israelites that I will judge each
of you by what you have done. Turn
away from all the evil you are doing, and
don't let your sin destroy you. 31 Give up
all the evil you have been doing, and get
yourselves new minds and hearts. Why
do you Israelites want to die? 32 I do not
want anyone to die," says the Sovereign
LORD. "Turn away from your sins and
live."

A Song of Sorrow

19 The LORD told me to sing this song of sorrow for two princes of Israel:

2 What a lioness your mother was!
She raised her cubs among the
fierce male lions.
3 She raised a cub and taught him
to hunt;
he learned to eat people.
4 The nations heard about him
and trapped him in a pit.
With hooks they dragged him off
to Egypt.
5 She waited until she saw all hope
was gone.
Then she raised another of her
cubs,
and he grew into a fierce lion.
6 When he was full-grown,
he prowled with the other lions.
He too learned to hunt and eat
people.
7 He wrecked forts,[l] he ruined
towns.
The people of the land were
terrified
every time he roared.
8 The nations gathered to fight him;
people came from everywhere.
They spread their hunting nets
and caught him in their trap.
9 They put him in a cage
and took him to the king of
Babylonia.
They kept him under guard,
so that his roar would never be
heard again
on the hills of Israel.

10 Your mother was like a
grapevine[m]
planted near a stream.
Because there was plenty of water,
the vine was covered with leaves
and fruit.
11 Its branches were strong
and grew to be royal scepters.
The vine grew tall enough to reach
the clouds;
everyone saw how leafy and tall
it was.
12 But angry hands pulled it up by
the roots
and threw it to the ground.
The east wind dried up its fruit.
Its branches were broken off;
they dried up and were burned.
13 Now it is planted in the desert,
in a dry and waterless land.
14 The stem of the vine caught fire;
fire burned up its branches and
fruit.
The branches will never again be
strong,
will never be royal scepters.
This is a song of sorrow; it has been
sung again and again.

The LORD's Will and Human Defiance

20 It was the tenth day of the fifth month of the seventh year of our
exile. Some of the leaders of the Israelite
community came to consult me about
the LORD's will, and they sat down in
front of me. 2 Then the LORD spoke to me.
3 "Mortal man," he said, "speak to these
leaders and tell them that the Sovereign

[l] *One ancient translation* wrecked forts; *Hebrew unclear.* [m] *Hebrew has an additional word, the meaning of which is unclear.*

LORD is saying: You have come to ask my
will, have you? As surely as I am the living God, I will not let you ask me anything. I, the Sovereign LORD, have
spoken.
4 “Are you ready to pass sentence on
them, mortal man? Then do so. Remind
them of the disgusting things their ancestors did. 5 Tell them what I am saying.
When I chose Israel, I made them a
promise. I revealed myself to them in
Egypt and told them: I am the LORD your
God. 6 It was then that I promised to take
them out of Egypt and lead them to a
land I had chosen for them, a rich and
fertile land, the finest land of all. 7 I told
them to throw away the disgusting idols
they loved and not to make themselves
unclean with the false gods of Egypt, because I am the LORD their God. 8 But they
defied me and refused to listen. They did
not throw away their disgusting idols or
give up the Egyptian gods. I was ready
to let them feel the full force of my anger
there in Egypt. 9 But I did not, since that
would have brought dishonor to my
name, for in the presence of the people
among whom they were living I had announced to Israel that I was going to
lead them out of Egypt.
10 “And so I led them out of Egypt into
the desert. 11 I gave them my commands
and taught them my laws, which bring
life to anyone who obeys them. 12 I made
the keeping of the Sabbath a sign of the
agreement between us, to remind them
that I, the LORD, make them holy. 13 But
even in the desert they defied me. They
broke my laws and rejected my commands, which bring life to anyone who
obeys them. They completely profaned
the Sabbath. I was ready to let them feel
the force of my anger there in the desert
and to destroy them. 14 But I did not,
since that would have brought dishonor
to my name among the nations which
had seen me lead Israel out of Egypt.
15 So I made a vow in the desert that I
would not take them to the land I had
given them, a rich and fertile land, the
finest land of all. 16 I made the vow because they had rejected my commands,
broken my laws, and profaned the
Sabbath—they preferred to worship
their idols.
17 “But then I took pity on them. I decided not to kill them there in the desert.
18 Instead, I warned the young people
among them: Do not keep the laws your
ancestors made; do not follow their customs or defile yourselves with their
idols. 19 I am the LORD your God. Obey
my laws and my commands. 20 Make the
Sabbath a holy day, so that it will be a
sign of the covenant we made, and will
remind you that I am the LORD your God.
21 “But that generation also defied me.
They broke my laws and did not keep
my commands, which bring life to anyone who obeys them. They profaned the
Sabbath. I was ready to let them feel the
force of my anger there in the desert and
to kill them all. 22 But I did not, since that
would have brought dishonor to my
name among the nations which had seen
me bring Israel out of Egypt. 23 So I made
another vow in the desert. I vowed that I
would scatter them all over the world.
24 I did this because they had rejected
my commands, broken my laws, profaned the Sabbath, and worshiped the
same idols their ancestors had served.
25 “Then I gave them laws that are not
good and commands that do not bring
life. 26 I let them defile themselves with
their own offerings, and I let them sacrifice their first-born sons. This was to
punish them and show them that I am
the LORD.
27 “Now then, mortal man, tell the Israelites what I, the Sovereign LORD, am
saying to them. This is another way their
ancestors insulted me by their unfaithfulness. 28 I brought them to the land I
had promised to give them. When they
saw the high hills and green trees, they
offered sacrifices at all of them. They
made me angry by the sacrifices they
burned and by the wine they brought as
offerings. 29 I asked them: What are
these high places where you go? So they
have been called ‘High Places’[n] ever
since. 30 Now tell the Israelites what I am
saying: Why must you commit the same
sins your ancestors did and go running
after their idols? 31 Even today you offer
the same gifts and defile yourselves with
the same idols by sacrificing your children to them in the fire. And then you
Israelites still come to ask what my will

[n] HIGH PLACES: *Pagan places of worship which the Hebrews were forbidden to use. The Hebrew word translated “High Places” sounds like the Hebrew for “where you go.”*

is! As surely as I, the Sovereign LORD, am
the living God, I will not let you ask me
anything. 32 You have made up your
minds that you want to be like the other
nations, like the people who live in other
countries and worship trees and rocks.
But that will never be.

God Punishes and Forgives

33 "As surely as I, the Sovereign LORD,
am the living God, I warn you that in my
anger I will rule over you with a strong
hand, with all my power. 34 I will show
you my power and my anger when I
gather you together and bring you back
from all the countries where you have
been scattered. 35 I will bring you into
the 'Desert of the Nations,' and there I
will condemn you to your face. 36 I will
now condemn you just as I condemned
your ancestors in the Sinai Desert," says
the Sovereign LORD.

37 "I will take firm control of you and
make you obey my covenant. 38 I will
take away from among you those who
are rebellious and sinful. I will take them
out of the lands where they are living
now, but I will not let them return to the
land of Israel. Then you will know that I
am the LORD."

39 The Sovereign LORD says, "And now,
all you Israelites, suit yourselves! Go on
and serve your idols! But I warn you that
after this you will have to obey me and
stop dishonoring my holy name by offering gifts to your idols. 40 There in the
land, on my holy mountain,[o] the high
mountain of Israel, all you people of Israel will worship me. I will be pleased
with you and will expect you to bring me
your sacrifices, your best offerings, and
your holy gifts. 41 After I bring you out of
the countries where you have been scattered and gather you together, I will accept the sacrifices that you burn, and the
nations will see that I am holy. 42 When I
bring you back to Israel, the land that I
promised I would give to your ancestors,
then you will know that I am the LORD.
43 Then you will remember all the disgraceful things you did and how you defiled yourselves. You will be disgusted
with yourselves because of all the evil
things you did. 44 When I act to protect
my honor, you Israelites will know that I
am the LORD, because I do not deal with
you as your wicked, evil actions deserve." The Sovereign LORD has spoken.

Fire in the South

45 The LORD spoke to me. 46 "Mortal
man," he said, "look toward the south.
Speak against the south and prophesy
against the forest of the south. 47 Tell the
southern forest to hear what the
Sovereign LORD is saying: Look! I am
starting a fire, and it will burn up every
tree in you, whether green or dry. Nothing will be able to put it out. It will
spread from south to north, and everyone will feel the heat of the flames.
48 They will all see that I, the LORD, set it
on fire and that no one can put it out."

49 But I protested, "Sovereign LORD,
don't make me do it! Everyone is already
complaining that I always speak in
riddles."

The LORD's Sword

21 The LORD spoke to me. 2 "Mortal
man," he said, "denounce Jerusalem. Denounce the places where people worship. Warn the land of Israel
3 that I, the LORD, am saying: I am your
enemy. I will draw my sword and kill all
of you, good and evil alike. 4 I will use
my sword against everyone from south
to north. 5 Everyone will know that I, the
LORD, have drawn my sword and that I
will not put it away.

6 "Mortal man, groan as if your heart is
breaking with despair. Groan in sorrow
where everyone can watch you. 7 When
they ask you why you are groaning, tell
them it is because of the news that is
coming. When it comes, their hearts will
be filled with fear, their hands will hang
limp, their courage will fail, and their
knees will tremble. The time has come;
it is here." The Sovereign LORD has
spoken.

8 The LORD said to me, 9 "Mortal man,
prophesy. Tell the people what I, the
Lord, am saying:

A sword, a sword is sharpened
and polished.
10 It is sharpened to kill,
polished to flash like lightning.
There can be no rejoicing,

o HOLY MOUNTAIN: *Mount Zion, the hill in Jerusalem which formed part of the Temple and palace area.*

for my people have disregarded
every warning and
punishment.[p]
11 The sword is being polished,
to make it ready for use.
It is sharpened and polished,
to be put in the hands of a killer.
12 Howl in grief, mortal man;
this sword is meant for my
people
and for all the leaders of Israel.
They are going to be killed
with all the rest of my people.
Beat your breast in despair!
13 I am testing my people,
and if they refuse to repent,
all these things will happen to
them.[q]

14 "Now, mortal man, prophesy. Clap
your hands, and the sword will strike
again and again. It is a sword that kills,
a sword that terrifies[r] and slaughters.
15 It makes my people lose courage and
stumble. I am threatening their city with
a sword[s] that flashes like lightning and
is ready to kill. 16 Cut to the right and the
left, you sharp sword! Cut wherever you
turn.[t] 17 I also will clap my hands, and
my anger will be over. I, the LORD, have
spoken."

The Sword of the King of Babylonia

18 The LORD spoke to me. 19 "Mortal
man," he said, "mark out two roads by
which the king of Babylonia can come
with his sword. Both of them are to start
in the same country. Put up a signpost
where the roads fork.[u] 20 One will show
the king the way to the Ammonite city of
Rabbah, and the other the way to Judah,
to the fortified city, Jerusalem. 21 The
king of Babylonia stands by the signpost
at the fork of the road. To discover
which way to go, he shakes the arrows;[v] he consults his idols; he examines the liver of a sacrificed animal.
22 Now! His right hand holds the arrow
marked 'Jerusalem'! It tells him to go
and set up battering rams, to shout the
battle cry, to place battering rams
against the gates, to throw up earthworks, and to dig trenches. 23 The people
of Jerusalem won't believe this because
of the treaties they have made. But this
prediction is to remind them of their
sins and to warn them that they will be
captured. 24 This then is what I, the
Sovereign LORD, am saying: Your sins
are exposed. Everyone knows how
guilty you are. You show your sins in
your every action. You stand condemned, and I will hand you over to
your enemies.

25 "You wicked, unholy ruler of Israel,
your day, the day of your final punishment, is coming. 26 I, the Sovereign LORD,
have spoken. Take off your crown and
your turban. Nothing will be the same
again. Raise the poor to power! Bring
down those who are ruling! 27 Ruin, ruin!
Yes, I will make the city a ruin. But this
will not happen until the one comes
whom I have chosen to punish the city.
To him I will give it.

A Sword and the Ammonites

28 "Mortal man, prophesy. Announce
what I, the Sovereign LORD, am saying to
the Ammonites, who are insulting Israel.
Say to them:
'A sword is ready to destroy;
It is polished to kill, to flash like
lightning.
29 The visions that you see are false, and
the predictions you make are lies. You
are wicked and evil, and your day is
coming, the day of your final punishment. The sword is going to fall on your
necks.

30 " 'Put up the sword! I will judge you
in the place where you were created, in
the land where you were born. 31 You
will feel my anger when I turn it loose on
you like a blazing fire. And I will hand
you over to brutal men, experts at destruction. 32 You will be destroyed by
fire. Your blood will be shed in your own
country, and no one will remember you
any more.' " The LORD has spoken.

The Crimes of Jerusalem

22 The LORD spoke to me. 2 "Mortal
man," he said, "are you ready to
judge the city that is full of murderers?

[p] *Probable text* There ... punishment; *Hebrew unclear.* [q] *Verse 13 in Hebrew is unclear.*
[r] *Some ancient translations* terrifies; *Hebrew unclear.* [s] *Probable text* threatening ... sword; *Hebrew unclear.* [t] *Verse 16 in Hebrew is unclear.* [u] *Probable text* Put ... fork; *Hebrew unclear.* [v] SHAKES THE ARROWS: *When faced with a decision, people in ancient times would sometimes take a handful of arrows, throw them down, and study the pattern in which they fell, in order to learn what to do.*

Make clear to her all the disgusting
things she has done. 3 Tell the city what
I, the Sovereign LORD, am saying: Because you have murdered so many of
your own people and have defiled yourself by worshiping idols, your time is
coming. 4 You are guilty of those murders and are defiled by the idols you
made, and so your day is coming, your
time is up! That is why I have let the
nations make fun of you and all the
countries sneer at you. 5 Countries
nearby and countries far away sneer at
you because of your lawlessness. 6 All Israel's leaders trust in their own strength
and commit murder. 7 None of you in the
city honor your parents. You cheat foreigners and take advantage of widows
and orphans. 8 You have no respect for
the holy places, and you don't keep the
Sabbath. 9 Some of your people tell lies
about others in order to have them put to
death. Some of them eat sacrifices offered to idols. Some are always satisfying their lusts. 10 Some of them sleep
with their father's wife. Some force
women to have intercourse with them
during their period. 11 Some commit
adultery, and others seduce their
daughters-in-law or their half sisters.
12 Some of your people murder for pay.
Some charge interest on the loans they
make to other Israelites and get rich by
taking advantage of them. They have
forgotten me." The Sovereign LORD has
spoken.

13 "I will bring my fist down on your
robberies and murders. 14 Do you think
you will have any courage left or have
strength enough to lift your hand when I
am finished with you? I, the LORD, have
spoken, and I keep my word. 15 I will
scatter your people to every country and
nation and will put an end to your evil
actions. 16 And so the other nations will
dishonor you, but you will know that I
am the LORD."

God's Refining Furnace

17 The LORD said to me, 18 "Mortal man,
the Israelites are of no use to me. They
are like waste metal—copper, tin, iron,
and lead—left over after silver has been
refined in a furnace. 19 So now I, the
Sovereign LORD, am telling them that
they are just as useless as that. I will
bring them all together in Jerusalem 20 in
the same way that the ore of silver, copper, iron, lead, and tin is put in a refining
furnace. My anger and rage will melt
them the way fire melts ore. 21 Yes, I will
gather them in Jerusalem, build a fire
under them, and melt them with my anger. 22 They will be melted in Jerusalem
the way silver is melted in a furnace, and
then they will know that they are feeling
the anger of the LORD."

The Sins of Israel's Leaders

23 The LORD spoke to me again. 24 "Mortal man," he said, "tell the Israelites that
their land is unholy, and so I am punishing it in my anger. 25 The leaders[w] are
like lions roaring over the animals they
have killed. They kill the people, take all
the money and property they can get,
and by their murders leave many widows. 26 The priests break my law and
have no respect for what is holy. They
make no distinction between what is
holy and what is not. They do not teach
the difference between clean and unclean things, and they ignore the Sabbath. As a result the people of Israel do
not respect me. 27 The government officials are like wolves tearing apart the
animals they have killed. They commit
murder in order to get rich. 28 The prophets have hidden these sins like workers
covering a wall with whitewash. They
see false visions and make false predictions. They claim to speak the word of
the Sovereign LORD, but I, the LORD, have
not spoken to them. 29 The wealthy cheat
and rob. They mistreat the poor and take
advantage of foreigners. 30 I looked for
someone who could build a wall, who
could stand in the places where the walls
have crumbled and defend the land
when my anger is about to destroy it, but
I could find no one. 31 So I will turn my
anger loose on them, and like a fire I will
destroy them for what they have done."
The Sovereign LORD has spoken.

The Sinful Sisters

23 The LORD spoke to me. 2 "Mortal
man," he said, "there were once
two sisters. 3 When they were young, living in Egypt, they lost their virginity and
became prostitutes. 4 The older one was

[w] *One ancient translation* The leaders; *Hebrew* A conspiracy of her prophets.

named Oholah[x] (she represents Samaria), and the younger one was named
Oholibah[y] (she represents Jerusalem). I
married both of them, and they bore me
children. 5 Although she was mine, Oholah continued to be a prostitute and was
full of lust for her lovers from Assyria.
6 They were soldiers in uniforms of purple, noblemen and high-ranking officers; all of them were handsome young
cavalry officers. 7 She was the whore for
all the Assyrian officers, and her lust led
her to defile herself by worshiping Assyrian idols. 8 She continued what she
had begun as a prostitute in Egypt,
where she lost her virginity. From the
time she was a young woman, men slept
with her and treated her like a prostitute. 9 So I handed her over to her Assyrian lovers whom she wanted so
much. 10 They stripped her naked, seized
her sons and daughters, and then killed
her with a sword. Women everywhere
gossiped about her fate.

11 "Even though her sister Oholibah
saw this, she was wilder and more of a
prostitute than Oholah had ever been.
12 She too was full of lust for the Assyrian noblemen and officers—soldiers
in bright uniforms—and for the cavalry
officers, all of those handsome young
men. 13 I saw that she was completely
immoral, that the second sister was as
bad as the first.

14-15 "She sank deeper and deeper in
her immorality. She was attracted by the
images of high Babylonian officials
carved into the wall and painted bright
red, with sashes around their waists and
fancy turbans on their heads. 16 As soon
as she saw them, she was filled with lust
and sent messengers to them in Babylonia. 17 The Babylonians came to have sex
with her. They used her and defiled her
so much that finally she became disgusted with them. 18 She exposed herself
publicly and let everyone know she was
a whore. I was as disgusted with her as
I had been with her sister. 19 She became
more of a prostitute than ever, acting the
way she did as a young woman, when
she was a prostitute in Egypt. 20 She was
filled with lust for oversexed men who
had all the lustfulness of donkeys or
stallions." (21 Oholibah, you wanted to
repeat the immorality you were guilty o
as a young woman in Egypt, where me
played with your breasts and you los
your virginity.)

God's Judgment on the Younger Sister

22 "Now then, Oholibah, this is what I
the Sovereign LORD, am saying to you
You are tired of those lovers, but I wil
make them angry with you and brin
them to surround you. 23 I will bring al
the Babylonians and Chaldeans, me
from Pekod, Shoa, and Koa, and all th
Assyrians. I will gather all those hand
some young noblemen and officers, al
those important officials and high
ranking cavalry officers. 24 They will at
tack you from the north,[z] bringing
large army with chariots and suppl
wagons. Protected by shields and hel
mets, they will surround you. I will han
you over to them, and they will judg
you by their own laws. 25 Because I an
angry with you, I will let them deal wit
you in their anger. They will cut off you
nose and your ears and kill your chil
dren. Yes, they will take your sons an
daughters from you and burn the
alive. 26 They will tear off your clothe
and take your jewels. 27 I will put a sto
to your lust and to the obscenities yo
have committed ever since you were i
Egypt. You won't look at any more idol
or think about Egypt any more."

28 This is what the Sovereign LOR
says: "I will hand you over to people yo
hate and are disgusted with. 29 And be
cause they hate you, they will take awa
everything you have worked for an
leave you stripped naked, exposed like
prostitute. Your lust and your prostitu
tion 30 have brought this on you. Yo
were a prostitute for the nations and de
filed yourself with their idols. 31 You fol
lowed in your sister's footsteps, and so I
will give you the same cup of punish
ment to drink."

32 The Sovereign LORD says,

"You will drink from your
sister's cup;
it is large and deep.
Everyone will scorn and
mock you;
the cup is full.

[x] OHOLAH: *This name in Hebrew means "her sanctuary."* [y] OHOLIBAH: *This name in Hebrew means "my sanctuary is in her."* [z] *One ancient translation* north; *Hebrew unclear.*

33 It will make you miserable and
drunk,
that cup of fear and ruin,
your sister Samaria's cup.
34 You will drink and drain it dry,
and with its broken pieces
tear your breast.
I, the Sovereign LORD, have spoken."
35 Now this is what the Sovereign LORD
is saying: "Because you forgot me and
turned your back on me, you will suffer
for your lust and your prostitution."

God's Judgment on Both Sisters

36 The LORD said to me, "Mortal man,
are you ready to judge Oholah and Oholibah? Accuse them of the disgusting
things they have done. 37 They have
committed adultery and murder—
adultery with idols and murder of the
children they bore me. They sacrificed
my children to their idols. 38 And that is
not all they did. They profaned my Temple and broke the Sabbath, which I had
established. 39 The very day that they
killed my children as sacrifices to idols,
they came to my Temple and profaned it!
40 "Again and again they sent messengers to invite men to come from a great
distance, and the men came. The two sisters would bathe and put on eye shadow
and jewelry. 41 They would sit on a beautiful couch, and in front of them they
would have a table covered with good
things, including the incense and the olive oil that I had given them. 42 The
sound of a carefree crowd could be
heard, a group of men brought in from
the desert. They put bracelets on the
women's arms and beautiful crowns on
their heads. 43 And I said to myself that
they were using as a prostitute a woman
worn out by adultery.[a] 44 They went
back to these prostitutes again and
again. They went back to Oholah and
Oholibah, those immoral women.
45 Righteous men will condemn them on
the charge of adultery and murder, because they practice adultery and their
hands are stained with blood."
46 This is what the Sovereign LORD
says: "Bring a mob to terrorize them and
rob them. 47 Let the mob stone them and
attack them with swords, kill their children, and burn down their houses.
48 Throughout the land I will put a stop to
immorality, as a warning to every
woman not to commit adultery as they
did. 49 And you two sisters—I will punish
you for your immorality and your sin of
worshiping idols. Then you will know
that I am the Sovereign LORD."

The Corroded Cooking Pot

24 On the tenth day of the tenth
month of the ninth year of our
exile, the LORD spoke to me. 2 "Mortal
man," he said, "write down today's date,
because this is the day that the king of
Babylonia is beginning the siege of Jerusalem. 3 Tell my rebellious people this
parable that I, the Sovereign LORD, have
for them:
Set the pot on the fire
and fill it up with water.
4 Put in the best pieces of meat—
the shoulders and the legs—
fill it with choice bony
pieces too.
5 Use the meat of the finest
sheep;
pile the wood[b] under the pot.
Let the water boil;
boil the bones and the meat."
6 This is what the Sovereign LORD is
saying: "The city of murderers is
doomed! It is like a corroded pot that is
never cleaned. Piece after piece of meat
is taken out, and not one is left. 7 There
was murder in the city, but the blood
was not spilled on the ground where the
dust could hide it; it was spilled on a
bare rock. 8 I have left the blood there,
where it cannot be hidden, where it demands angry revenge."
9 This is what the Sovereign LORD is
saying: "The city of murderers is
doomed! I myself will pile up the firewood. 10 Bring more wood! Fan the
flames! Cook the meat! Boil away the
broth![c] Burn up the bones! 11 Now set
the empty bronze pot on the coals and
let it get red-hot. Then the pot will be
ritually pure again after the corrosion is
burned off, 12 although all that corrosion
will not disappear in the flames.[d] 13 Jerusalem, your immoral actions have defiled you. Although I tried to purify you,
you remained defiled. You will not be

[a] *Verses 42-43 in Hebrew are unclear.* [b] *Probable text* wood; *Hebrew* bones.
[c] *Some ancient translations* Boil away the broth!; *Hebrew unclear.* [d] *Verse 12 in Hebrew begins with two words, the meaning of which is unclear.*

pure again until you have felt the full force of my anger. 14 I, the LORD, have spoken. The time has come for me to act. I will not ignore your sins or show pity or be merciful. You will be punished for what you have done." The Sovereign LORD has spoken.

The Death of the Prophet's Wife

15 The LORD spoke to me. 16 "Mortal man," he said, "with one blow I am going to take away the person you love most. You are not to complain or cry or shed any tears. 17 Don't let your sobbing be heard. Do not go bareheaded or barefoot as a sign of mourning. Don't cover your face or eat the food that mourners eat."

18 Early in the day I was talking with the people. That evening my wife died, and the next day I did as I had been told. 19 The people asked me, "Why are you acting like this?"

20 So I said to them, "The LORD spoke to me and told me 21 to give you Israelites this message: You are proud of the strength of the Temple. You like to look at it and to visit it, but the LORD is going to profane it. And the younger members of your families who are left in Jerusalem will be killed in war. 22 Then you will do what I have done. You will not cover your faces or eat the food that mourners eat. 23 You will not go bareheaded or barefoot or mourn or cry. You will waste away because of your sins, and you will groan to one another. 24 Then I will be a sign to you; you will do everything I have done. The LORD says that when this happens, you will know that he is the Sovereign LORD."

25 The LORD said, "Now, mortal man, I will take away from them the strong Temple that was their pride and joy, which they liked to look at and to visit. And I will take away their sons and daughters. 26 On the day that I do this, some who escape the destruction will come and tell you about it. 27 That same day you will get back the power of speech which you had lost, and you will talk with them. In this way you will be a sign to the people, and they will know that I am the LORD."

Prophecy against Ammon

25 The LORD spoke to me. 2 "Mortal man," he said, "denounce the country of Ammon. 3 Tell them to listen to what I, the Sovereign LORD, am saying: You were delighted to see my Temple profaned, to see the land of Israel devastated, to see the people of Judah go into exile. 4 Because you were glad, I will let the tribes from the eastern desert conquer you. They will set up their camps in your country and settle there. They will eat the fruit and drink the milk that should have been yours. 5 I will turn the city of Rabbah into a place to keep camels, and the whole country of Ammon will become a place to keep sheep, so that you will know I am the LORD.

6 "This is what the Sovereign LORD is saying: You clapped your hands and jumped for joy. You despised the land of Israel. 7 Because you did, I will hand you over to other nations who will rob you and plunder you. I will destroy you so completely that you will not be a nation any more or have a country of your own. Then you will know that I am the LORD."

Prophecy against Moab

8 The Sovereign LORD said, "Because Moab[e] has said that Judah is like all the other nations, 9 I will let the cities that defend the border of Moab be attacked, including even the finest cities—Beth Jeshimoth, Baal Meon, and Kiriathaim. 10 I will let the tribes of the eastern desert conquer Moab, together with Ammon, so that Moab[f] will no longer be a nation. 11 I will punish Moab, and they will know that I am the LORD."

Prophecy against Edom

12 The Sovereign LORD said, "The people of Edom took cruel revenge on Judah, and that revenge has brought lasting guilt on Edom. 13 Now I announce that I will punish Edom and kill every person and animal there. I will make it a wasteland, from the city of Teman to the city of Dedan, and the people will be killed in battle. 14 My people Israel will take revenge on Edom for me, and they will make Edom feel my furious anger. Edom will know what it means to be the

[e] *Some ancient translations* Moab; *Hebrew* Moab and Seir. [f] *Probable text* Moab; *Hebrew* Ammon.

object of my revenge." The Sovereign
LORD has spoken.

Prophecy against Philistia

15 The Sovereign LORD said, "The Philistines have taken cruel revenge on
their agelong enemies and destroyed
them in their hate. 16 And so I am announcing that I will attack the Philistines and wipe them out. I will destroy
everyone left living there on the Philistine Plain. 17 I will punish them severely
and take full revenge on them. They will
feel my anger. Then they will know that
I am the LORD."

Prophecy against Tyre

26 On the first day of the . . .
month[g] of the eleventh year of
our exile, the LORD spoke to me. 2 "Mortal
man," he said, "this is what the people in
the city of Tyre are cheering about. They
shout, 'Jerusalem is shattered! Her commercial power is gone! She won't be our
rival any more!'
3 "Now then, this is what I, the
Sovereign LORD, am saying: I am your
enemy, city of Tyre. I will bring many
nations to attack you, and they will
come like the waves of the sea. 4 They
will destroy your city walls and tear
down your towers. Then I will sweep
away all the dust and leave only a bare
rock. 5 Fishermen will dry their nets on
it, there where it stands in the sea. I, the
Sovereign LORD, have spoken. The nations will plunder Tyre, 6 and with their
swords they will kill those who live in
her towns on the mainland. Then Tyre
will know that I am the LORD."
7 The Sovereign LORD says, "I am going
to bring the greatest king of all—King
Nebuchadnezzar of Babylonia—to attack Tyre. He will come from the north
with a huge army, with horses and chariots and with cavalry. 8 Those who live in
the towns on the mainland will be killed
in the fighting. The enemy will dig
trenches, build earthworks, and make a
solid wall of shields against you. 9 They
will pound in your walls with battering
rams and tear down your towers with
iron bars. 10 The clouds of dust raised by
their horses will cover you. The noise of
their horses pulling wagons and chariots
will shake your walls as they pass
through the gates of the ruined city.
11 Their cavalry will storm through your
streets, killing your people with their
swords. Your mighty pillars will be
thrown to the ground. 12 Your enemies
will help themselves to your wealth and
merchandise. They will pull down your
walls and shatter your luxurious houses.
They will take the stones and wood and
all the rubble, and dump them into the
sea. 13 I will put an end to all your songs,
and I will silence the music of your
harps. 14 I will leave only a bare rock
where fishermen can dry their nets.
The city will never be rebuilt. I, the
Sovereign LORD, have spoken."
15 The Sovereign LORD has this to say
to the city of Tyre: "When you are being
conquered, the people who live along
the coast will be terrified at the screams
of those who are slaughtered. 16 All the
kings of the seafaring nations will come
down from their thrones. They will take
off their robes and their embroidered
clothes and sit trembling on the ground.
They will be so terrified at your fate that
they will not be able to stop trembling.
17 They will sing this funeral song
for you:

The famous city is destroyed!
Her ships have been swept[h] from
the seas.
The people of this city ruled the
seas
And terrified all who lived on the
coast.
18 Now, on the day it has fallen,
The islands are trembling,
And their people are shocked at
such destruction."

19 The Sovereign LORD says: "I will
make you as desolate as ruined cities
where no one lives. I will cover you with
the water of the ocean depths. 20 I will
send you down to the world of the dead
to join the people who lived in ancient
times. I will make you stay in that underground world among eternal ruins,
keeping company with the dead. As a
result you will never again be inhabited
and take your place[i] in the land of the
living. 21 I will make you a terrifying example, and that will be the end of you.
People may look for you, but you will

[g] month; *the Hebrew text does not specify the month.* [h] *Some ancient translations* swept; *Hebrew* inhabited. [i] *One ancient translation* and take your place; *Hebrew unclear.*

never be found." The Sovereign LORD
has spoken.

A Funeral Song for Tyre

27 The LORD said to me, 2"Mortal
man, sing a funeral song for
Tyre, 3that city which stands at the edge
of the sea and does business with the
people living on every seacoast. Tell her
what the Sovereign LORD is saying:

"Tyre, you boasted of your perfect
beauty.
4Your home is the sea.
Your builders made you like a
beautiful ship;
5They used fir trees from Mount
Hermon for timber
And a cedar from Lebanon for
your mast.
6They took oak trees from Bashan
to make oars;
They made your deck out of pine
from Cyprus
And inlaid it with ivory.
7Your sails were made of linen,
Embroidered linen from Egypt,
Easily recognized from afar.
Your awnings were made of finest
cloth,
Of purple from the island of
Cyprus.
8Your oarsmen were from the cities
of Sidon and Arvad.
Your own skillful men were the
sailors.
9The ship's carpenters
Were well-trained men from
Byblos.
Sailors from every seagoing ship
Did business in your shops.

10"Soldiers from Persia, Lydia, and
Libya served in your army. They hung
their shields and their helmets in your
barracks. They are the men who won
glory for you. 11Soldiers from Arvad
guarded your walls, and troops from Ga-
mad guarded your towers. They hung
their shields on your walls. They are the
ones who made you beautiful.
12"You did business in Spain and took
silver, iron, tin, and lead in payment for
your abundant goods. 13You did business in Greece, Tubal, and Meshech and
traded your goods for slaves and for articles of bronze. 14You sold your goods
for workhorses, war-horses, and mules
from Beth Togarmah. 15The people of
Rhodes[j] traded with you; people of
many coastal lands gave you ivory and
ebony in exchange for your goods.
16The people of Syria bought your merchandise and your many products. They
gave emeralds, purple cloth, embroidery, fine linen, coral, and rubies in payment for your wares. 17Judah and Israel
paid for your goods with wheat,[k]
honey, olive oil, and spices. 18-19The people of Damascus bought your merchandise and your products, paying for them
with wine from Helbon and wool from
Sahar.[l] They traded wrought iron and
spices for your goods. 20The people of
Dedan traded saddle blankets for your
goods. 21The Arabians and the rulers of
the land of Kedar paid for your merchandise with lambs, sheep, and goats.
22For your goods the merchants of
Sheba and Raamah traded jewels, gold,
and the finest spices. 23The cities of Haran, Canneh, and Eden, the merchants
of Sheba, the cities of Asshur and
Chilmad—they all traded with you.
24They sold you luxurious clothing, purple cloth, and embroidery, brightly colored carpets, and well-made cords and
ropes. 25Your merchandise was carried
in fleets of the largest cargo ships.

"You were like a ship at sea
Loaded with heavy cargo.
26When your oarsmen brought you
out to sea,
An east wind wrecked you far
from land.
27All your wealth of merchandise,
All the sailors in your crew,
Your ship's carpenters and your
merchants,
Every soldier on board the ship—
All, all were lost at sea
When your ship was wrecked.
28The shouts of the drowning sailors
Echoed on the shore.

29"Every ship is now deserted,
And every sailor has gone ashore.
30They all mourn bitterly for you,
Throwing dust on their heads and
rolling in ashes.
31They shave their heads for you
And dress themselves in sackcloth.

[j] *One ancient translation* Rhodes; *Hebrew* Dedan. [k] *Hebrew has two additional words, the meaning of which is unclear.* [l] *Hebrew has three additional words, the meaning of which is unclear.*

Their hearts are bitter as they
weep.
32 They chant a funeral song for you:
'Who can be compared to Tyre,
To Tyre now silent in the sea?
33 When your merchandise went
overseas,
You filled the needs of every
nation.
Kings were made rich
By the wealth of your goods.
34 Now you are wrecked in the sea;
You have sunk to the ocean
depths.
Your goods and all who worked
for you
Have vanished with you in
the sea.'

35 "Everyone who lives along the coast
is shocked at your fate. Even their kings
are terrified, and fear is written on their
faces. 36 You are gone, gone forever, and
merchants all over the world are terrified, afraid that they will share your
fate."

Prophecy against the King of Tyre

28 The LORD spoke to me. 2 "Mortal
man," he said, "tell the ruler of
Tyre what I, the Sovereign LORD, am saying to him: Puffed up with pride, you
claim to be a god. You say that like a god
you sit on a throne, surrounded by the
seas. You may pretend to be a god, but,
no, you are mortal, not divine. 3 You
think you are wiser than Danel,[m] that no
secret can be kept from you. 4 Your wisdom and skill made you rich with treasures of gold and silver. 5 You made
clever business deals and kept on making profits. How proud you are of your
wealth!

6 "Now then, this is what I, the
Sovereign LORD, am saying: Because you
think you are as wise as a god, 7 I will
bring ruthless enemies to attack you.
They will destroy all the beautiful things
you have acquired by skill and wisdom.
8 They will kill you and send you to a
watery grave. 9 When they come to kill
you, will you still claim that you are a
god? When you face your murderers,
you will be mortal and not at all divine.
10 You will die like a dog at the hand of
godless foreigners. I, the Sovereign
LORD, have given the command."

The Fall of the King of Tyre

11 The LORD spoke to me again. 12 "Mortal man," he said, "grieve for the fate that
is waiting for the king of Tyre. Tell him
what I, the Sovereign LORD, am saying:
You were once an example of perfection. How wise and handsome you were!
13 You lived in Eden, the garden of God,
and wore gems of every kind: rubies and
diamonds; topaz, beryl, carnelian, and
jasper; sapphires, emeralds, and gar-
nets. You had ornaments of gold. They
were made for you[n] on the day you
were created. 14 I put a terrifying angel
there to guard you.[o] You lived on my
holy mountain and walked among sparkling gems. 15 Your conduct was perfect
from the day you were created until you
began to do evil. 16 You were busy buying and selling, and this led you to violence and sin. So I forced you to leave
my holy mountain, and the angel who
guarded you drove you away from the
sparkling gems. 17 You were proud of being handsome, and your fame made you
act like a fool. Because of this I hurled
you to the ground and left you as a warning to other kings. 18 You did such evil in
buying and selling that your places of
worship were corrupted. So I set fire to
the city and burned it to the ground. All
who look at you now see you reduced to
ashes. 19 You are gone, gone forever, and
all the nations that had come to know
you are terrified, afraid that they will
share your fate."

Prophecy against Sidon

20 The LORD said to me, 21 "Mortal man,
denounce the city of Sidon. 22 Tell the
people there what I, the Sovereign LORD,
say about them: I am your enemy, Sidon; people will praise me because of
what I do to you. They will know that I
am the LORD, when I show how holy I am
by punishing those who live in you.
23 I will send diseases on you and make
blood flow in your streets. You will be
attacked from every side, and your people will be killed. Then you will know
that I am the LORD."

[m] Danel; *or* Daniel *(see 14.14).* [n] *Probable text* They were made for you; *Hebrew unclear.*
[o] *One ancient translation* I put . . . you; *Hebrew unclear.*

Israel Will Be Blessed

24 The LORD said, "None of the surrounding nations that treated Israel with
scorn will ever again be like thorns and
briers to hurt Israel. And they will know
that I am the Sovereign LORD."
25 The Sovereign LORD said, "I will
bring back the people of Israel from the
nations where I scattered them, and all
the nations will know that I am holy. The
people of Israel will live in their own
land, the land that I gave to my servant
Jacob. 26 They will live there in safety.
They will build houses and plant vineyards. I will punish all their neighbors
who treated them with scorn, and Israel
will be secure. Then they will know that
I am the LORD their God."

Prophecy against Egypt

29 On the twelfth day of the tenth
month of the tenth year of our
exile, the LORD spoke to me. 2 "Mortal
man," he said, "denounce the king of
Egypt. Tell him how he and all the land
of Egypt will be punished. 3 Say that this
is what the Sovereign LORD is telling the
king of Egypt: I am your enemy, you
monster crocodile, lying in the river.
You say that the Nile is yours and that
you made it.[p] 4 I am going to put a hook
through your jaw and make the fish in
your river stick fast to you. Then I will
pull you up out of the Nile, with all the
fish sticking to you. 5 I will throw you
and all those fish into the desert. Your
body will fall on the ground and be left
unburied. I will give it to the birds and
animals for food. 6 Then all the people of
Egypt will know that I am the LORD."
The LORD says, "The Israelites relied
on you Egyptians for support, but you
were no better than a weak stick. 7 When
they leaned on you, you broke, pierced
their armpits, and made them wrench
their backs.[q] 8 Now then, I, the
Sovereign LORD, am telling you that I
will have troops attack you with swords,
and they will kill your people and your
animals. 9 Egypt will become an empty
wasteland. Then you will know that I am
the LORD.
"Because you said that the Nile is
yours and you made it, 10 I am your enemy and the enemy of your Nile. I will
make all of Egypt an empty wasteland,
from the city of Migdol in the north to
the city of Aswan in the south, all the
way to the Ethiopian[r] border. 11 No human being or animal will walk through
it. For forty years nothing will live there.
12 I will make Egypt the most desolate
country in the world. For forty years the
cities of Egypt will lie in ruins, ruins
worse than those of any other city. I will
make the Egyptians refugees. They will
flee to every country and live among
other peoples."
13 The Sovereign LORD says, "After
forty years I will bring the Egyptians
back from the nations where I have scattered them, 14 and I will let them live in
southern Egypt, their original home.
There they will be a weak kingdom,
15 the weakest kingdom of all, and they
will never again rule other nations. I will
make them so unimportant that they will
not be able to bend any other nation to
their will. 16 Israel will never again depend on them for help. Egypt's fate will
remind Israel how wrong it was to rely
on them. Then Israel will know that I am
the Sovereign LORD."

King Nebuchadnezzar Will Conquer Egypt

17 On the first day of the first month of
the twenty-seventh year of our exile, the
LORD spoke to me. 18 "Mortal man," he
said, "King Nebuchadnezzar of Babylonia launched an attack on Tyre. He
made his soldiers carry such heavy
loads that their heads were rubbed bald
and their shoulders were worn raw, but
neither the king nor his army got anything for all their trouble. 19 So now this
is what I, the Sovereign LORD, am saying:
I am giving the land of Egypt to King
Nebuchadnezzar. He will loot and plunder it and carry off all the wealth of
Egypt as his army's pay. 20 I am giving
him Egypt in payment for his services,
because his army was working for me. I,
the Sovereign LORD, have spoken.

[p] *Some ancient translations* you made it; *Hebrew* you made yourself.
[q] *One ancient translation* wrench their backs; *Hebrew* make their backs stand.
[r] *Hebrew* Cushite (Cush): *Cush is the ancient name of the extensive territory south of the First Cataract of the Nile River. This region was called Ethiopia in Graeco-Roman times, and included within its borders most of modern Sudan and some of present-day Ethiopia (Abyssinia).*

21 "When that happens, I will make the
people of Israel strong and let you, Ezekiel, speak out where everyone can hear
you, so that they will know that I am the
LORD."

The LORD Will Punish Egypt

30 The LORD spoke to me again.
2 "Mortal man," he said, "prophesy and announce what I, the Sovereign
LORD, am saying. You are to shout these
words:

A day of terror is coming!
3 The day is near, the day when the
LORD will act,
A day of clouds and trouble for
the nations.
4 There will be war in Egypt
And great distress in Ethiopia.[r]
Many in Egypt will be killed;
The country will be plundered
And left in ruins.

5 "That war will also kill the soldiers
hired from Ethiopia,[r] Libya, Lydia,
Arabia, Kub, and even from among my
own people."

6 The LORD says, "From Migdol in the
north to Aswan in the south, all Egypt's
defenders will be killed in battle. Egypt's
proud army will be destroyed. I, the
Sovereign LORD, have spoken. 7 The land
will be the most desolate in the world,
and its cities will be left totally in ruins.
8 When I set fire to Egypt and all her defenders are killed, then they will know
that I am the LORD.

9 "When that day comes and Egypt is
destroyed, I will send messengers in
ships to arouse the unsuspecting people
of Ethiopia,[r] and they will be terrified.
That day is coming!"

10 The Sovereign LORD says, "I will use
King Nebuchadnezzar of Babylonia to
put an end to Egypt's wealth. 11 He and
his ruthless army will come to devastate
the land. They will attack Egypt with
swords, and the land will be full of
corpses. 12 I will dry up the Nile and put
Egypt under the power of evil people.
Foreigners will devastate the whole
country. I, the LORD, have spoken."

13 The Sovereign LORD says, "I will destroy the idols and the false gods in
Memphis. There will be no one to rule
Egypt, and I will terrify all the people.
14 I will make southern Egypt desolate
and set fire to the city of Zoan in the
north. I will punish the capital city of
Thebes. 15 I will let the city of Pelusium,
Egypt's great fortress, feel my fury. I will
destroy the wealth of Thebes. 16 I will set
fire to Egypt, and Pelusium will be in agony. The walls of Thebes will be broken
down, and the city will be flooded.[s]
17 The young men of the cities of Heliopolis and Bubastis will die in the war, and
the other people will be taken prisoner.
18 Darkness will fall on Tahpanhes when
I break the power of Egypt and put an
end to the strength they were so proud
of. A cloud will cover Egypt, and the
people of all her cities will be taken prisoner. 19 When I punish Egypt in this way,
they will know that I am the LORD."

The Broken Power of the King of Egypt

20 On the seventh day of the first
month of the eleventh year of our exile,
the LORD spoke to me. 21 "Mortal man,"
he said, "I have broken the arm of the
king of Egypt. No one has bandaged it or
put it in a sling so that it could heal and
be strong enough to hold a sword again.
22 Now then, this is what I, the Sovereign
LORD, say: I am the enemy of the king of
Egypt. I am going to break both his
arms — the good one and the one already
broken — and the sword will fall from his
hand. 23 I am going to scatter the Egyptians throughout the world. 24 Then I will
make the arms of the king of Babylonia
strong and put my sword in his hands.
But I will break the arms of the king of
Egypt, and he will groan and die in front
of his enemy. 25 Yes, I will weaken him
and strengthen the king of Babylonia.
When I give him my sword and he points
it toward Egypt, everyone will know that
I am the LORD. 26 I will scatter the Egyptians throughout the world. Then they
will know that I am the LORD."

Egypt Is Compared to a Cedar Tree

31 On the first day of the third
month of the eleventh year of
our exile, the LORD spoke to me. 2 "Mortal

[r] *Hebrew* Cushite (Cush): *Cush is the ancient name of the extensive territory south of the First Cataract of the Nile River. This region was called Ethiopia in Graeco-Roman times, and included within its borders most of modern Sudan and some of present-day Ethiopia (Abyssinia).* [s] *One ancient translation* flooded; *Hebrew unclear.*

man," he said, "say to the king of Egypt
and all his people:
How powerful you are!
What can I compare you to?
3 You are like[t] a cedar in Lebanon,
With beautiful, shady branches,
A tree so tall it reaches the
clouds.[u]
4 There was water to make it grow,
And underground rivers to feed it.
They watered the place where the
tree was growing
And sent streams to all the trees
of the forest.
5 Because it was well-watered,
It grew taller than other trees.
Its branches grew thick and long.
6 Every kind of bird built nests in its
branches;
The wild animals bore their young
in its shelter;
The nations of the world rested in
its shade.
7 How beautiful the tree was—
So tall, with such long branches.
Its roots reached down to the
deep-flowing streams.
8 No cedar in God's garden could
compare with it.
No fir tree ever had such
branches,
And no plane tree such limbs.
No tree in God's own garden was
so beautiful.
9 I made it beautiful, with spreading
branches.
It was the envy of every tree in
Eden, the garden of God.

10 "Now then, I, the Sovereign LORD,
will tell you what is going to happen to
that tree that grew until it reached the
clouds.[u] As it grew taller it grew proud;
11 so I have rejected it and will let a foreign ruler have it. He will give that tree
what it deserves for its wickedness.
12 Ruthless foreigners will cut it down
and leave it. Its branches and broken
limbs will fall on every mountain and
valley in the country. All the nations that
have been living in its shade will go
away. 13 The birds will come and perch
on the fallen tree, and the wild animals
will walk over its branches. 14 And so
from now on, no tree, no matter how
well-watered it is, will grow that tall
again or push its top through the
clouds[u] and reach such a height. All of
them are doomed to die like mortals,
doomed to join those who go down to
the world of the dead."

15 This is what the Sovereign LORD
says: "On the day when the tree goes to
the world of the dead, I will make the
underground waters cover it as a sign of
mourning. I will hold back the rivers and
not let the many streams flow out. Because the tree has died, I will bring darkness over the Lebanon Mountains and
make all the trees of the forest wither.
16 When I send it down to the world of
the dead, the noise of its downfall will
shake the nations. All the trees of Eden
and all the choice, well-watered trees of
Lebanon who have gone to the world below will be pleased at its downfall.
17 They will go with it to the world of the
dead to join those that have already
fallen. And all who live under its shadow
will be scattered among the nations.[v]

18 "The tree is the king of Egypt and all
his people. Not even the trees in Eden
were so tall and impressive. But now,
like the trees of Eden, it will go down to
the world of the dead and join the ungodly and those killed in battle. I have
spoken," says the Sovereign LORD.

The King of Egypt Is Compared to a Crocodile

32 On the first day of the twelfth
month of the twelfth year of our
exile, the LORD spoke to me. 2 "Mortal
man," he said, "give a solemn warning to
the king of Egypt. Give him this message
from me: You act like a lion among the
nations, but you are more like a crocodile splashing through a river. You
muddy the water with your feet and pollute the rivers. 3 When many nations
gather, I will catch you in my net and let
them drag the net ashore. 4 I will throw
you out on the ground and bring all the
birds and animals of the world to feed on
you. 5 I will cover mountains and valleys
with your rotting corpse. 6 I will pour out
your blood until it spreads over the
mountains and fills the streams. 7 When
I destroy you, I will cover the sky and
blot out the stars. The sun will hide be-

[t] *Probable text* You are like; *Hebrew* Assyria is. [u] *One ancient translation* clouds; *Hebrew* thick branches. [v] *Probable text* And all . . . nations; *Hebrew unclear.*

hind the clouds, and the moon will give
no light. 8 I will put out all the lights of
heaven and plunge your world into
darkness. I, the Sovereign LORD, have
spoken.

9 "Many nations will be troubled when
I spread the news of your destruction
through countries you never heard of.
10 What I do to you will shock many nations. When I swing my sword, kings
will shudder with fright. On the day you
fall, all of them will tremble in fear for
their own lives."

11 The Sovereign LORD says to the king
of Egypt, "You will face the sword of the
king of Babylonia. 12 I will let soldiers
from cruel nations draw their swords
and kill all your people. All your people
and everything else that you are proud
of will be destroyed. 13 I will slaughter
your cattle at every water hole. There
will be no people or cattle to muddy the
water any more. 14 I will let your waters
settle and become clear and let your rivers run calm. I, the Sovereign LORD, have
spoken. 15 When I make Egypt a desolate
wasteland and destroy all who live
there, they will know that I am the LORD.
16 This solemn warning will become a funeral song. The women of the nations
will sing it to mourn for Egypt and all its
people. I, the Sovereign LORD, have
spoken."

The World of the Dead

17 On the fifteenth day of the first
month[w] of the twelfth year of our exile,
the LORD spoke to me. 18 "Mortal man,"
he said, "mourn for all the many people
of Egypt. Send them down with the
other powerful nations to the world of
the dead. 19 Say to them:

"Do you think you are more
beautiful than anyone else?
You will go down to the world of
the dead
and lie there among the
ungodly.

20 "The people of Egypt will fall with
those who are killed in battle. A sword is
ready to kill them all.[x] 21 The greatest
heroes and those who fought on the
Egyptian side welcome the Egyptians to
the world of the dead. They shout: 'The
ungodly who were killed in battle have
come down here, and here they lie!'

22 "Assyria is there, with the graves of
her soldiers all around. They were all
killed in battle, 23 and their graves are in
the deepest parts of the world of the
dead. All her soldiers fell in battle, and
their graves surround her tomb. Yet
once they terrified the land of the living.

24 "Elam is there, with the graves of
her soldiers all around. They were all
killed in battle, and they went down, uncircumcised, to the world of the dead. In
life they spread terror, but now they lie
dead and disgraced. 25 Elam lies down
among those killed in battle, and the
graves of her soldiers are all around her.
They are all uncircumcised, all killed in
battle. In life they spread terror, but now
they lie dead and disgraced, sharing the
fate of those killed in battle.

26 "Meshech and Tubal are there, with
the graves of their soldiers all around.
They are all uncircumcised, all killed in
battle. Yet once they terrified the living.
27 They were not given honorable burial
like the heroes of ancient times,[y] who
went fully armed to the world of the
dead, their swords placed under their
heads and their shields[z] over their bodies. These heroes were once powerful
enough to terrify the living.

28 "That is how the Egyptians will lie
crushed among the uncircumcised who
were killed in battle.

29 "Edom is there with her kings and
rulers. They were powerful soldiers, but
now they lie in the world of the dead
with the uncircumcised who were killed
in battle.

30 "All the princes of the north are
there, and so are the Sidonians. Their
power once spread terror, but now they
go down in disgrace with those killed in
battle and are laid to rest, uncircumcised. They share the disgrace of those
who go down to the world of the dead.

31 "The sight of all these who were
killed in battle will be a comfort to the
king of Egypt and his army," says the
Sovereign LORD.

32 "I caused the king of Egypt to terrorize the living, but he and all his army
will be killed and laid to rest with all the

[w] *One ancient translation* of the first month; *Hebrew does not have these words.*
[x] *Probable text* A sword . . . all; *Hebrew unclear.* [y] *Some ancient translations* of ancient times; *Hebrew* of the uncircumcised. [z] *Probable text* shields; *Hebrew* iniquities.

uncircumcised who die in battle." The
Sovereign LORD has spoken.

God Appoints Ezekiel as a Lookout

(Ezekiel 3.16-21)

33 The LORD spoke to me. 2"Mortal
man," he said, "tell your people
what happens when I bring war to a
land. The people of that country choose
one of their number to be a lookout.
3When he sees the enemy approaching,
he sounds the alarm to warn everyone.
4If someone hears it but pays no attention and the enemy comes and kills him,
then he is to blame for his own death.
5His death is his own fault, because he
paid no attention to the warning. If he
had paid attention, he could have escaped. 6If, however, the lookout sees the
enemy coming and does not sound the
alarm, the enemy will come and kill
those sinners, but I will hold the lookout
responsible for their death.
7"Now, mortal man, I am making you
a lookout for the nation of Israel. You
must pass on to them the warnings I give
you. 8If I announce that an evil person is
going to die but you do not warn him to
change his ways so that he can save his
life, then he will die, still a sinner, and I
will hold you responsible for his death.
9If you do warn an evil person and he
doesn't stop sinning, he will die, still a
sinner, but your life will be spared."

Individual Responsibility

10The LORD spoke to me. "Mortal
man," he said, "repeat to the Israelites
what they are saying: 'We are burdened
with our sins and the wrongs we have
done. We are wasting away. How can
we live?' 11Tell them that as surely as I,
the Sovereign LORD, am the living God, I
do not enjoy seeing sinners die. I would
rather see them stop sinning and live.
Israel, stop the evil you are doing. Why
do you want to die?
12"Now, mortal man, tell the Israelites
that when someone good sins, the good
he has done will not save him. If an evil
person stops doing evil, he won't be punished, and if a good man starts sinning,
his life will not be spared. 13I may promise life to someone good, but if he starts
thinking that his past goodness is
enough and begins to sin, I will not remember any of the good he did. He will
die because of his sins. 14I may warn
someone evil that he is going to die, but
if he stops sinning and does what is right
and good — 15for example, if he returns
the security he took for a loan or gives
back what he stole — if he stops sinning
and follows the laws that give life, he
will not die, but live. 16I will forgive the
sins he has committed, and he will live
because he has done what is right and
good.
17"And your people say that what I do
isn't right! No, it's their way that isn't
right. 18When someone righteous stops
doing good and starts doing evil, he will
die for it. 19When someone evil quits sinning and does what is right and good, he
has saved his life. 20But Israel, you say
that what I do isn't right. I am going to
judge you by what you do."

The News of Jerusalem's Fall

21On the fifth day of the tenth month
of the twelfth year of our exile, someone
who had escaped from Jerusalem came
and told me that the city had fallen.
22The evening before he came, I had felt
the powerful presence of the LORD. When
the man arrived the next morning, the
LORD gave me back the power of speech.

The Sins of the People

23The LORD spoke to me. 24"Mortal
man," he said, "the people who are living
in the ruined cities of the land of Israel
are saying: 'Abraham was only one
man, and he was given the whole land.
There are many of us, so now the land is
ours.'
25"Tell them what I, the Sovereign
LORD, am saying: You eat meat with the
blood still in it. You worship idols. You
commit murder. What makes you think
that the land belongs to you? 26You rely
on your swords. Your actions are disgusting. Everyone commits adultery.
What makes you think that the land is
yours?
27"Tell them that I, the Sovereign
LORD, warn them that as surely as I am
the living God, the people who live in the
ruined cities will be killed. Those living
in the country will be eaten by wild animals. Those hiding in the mountains and
in caves will die of disease. 28I will make
the country a desolate wasteland, and
the power they were so proud of will
come to an end. The mountains of Israel
will be so wild that no one will be able to

travel through them. 29 When I punish
the people for their sins and make the
country a wasteland, then they will
know that I am the LORD."

The Results of the Prophet's Message

30 The LORD said, "Mortal man, your
people are talking about you when they
meet by the city walls or in the doorways
of their houses. They say to one another,
'Let's go and hear what word has come
from the LORD now.' 31 So my people
crowd in to hear what you have to say,
but they don't do what you tell them to
do. Loving words are on their lips, but
they continue their greedy ways. 32 To
them you are nothing more than an en-
tertainer singing love songs or playing a
harp. They listen to all your words and
don't obey a single one of them. 33 But
when all your words come true—and
they will come true—then they will
know that a prophet has been among
them."

The Shepherds of Israel

34 The LORD spoke to me. 2 "Mortal
man," he said, "denounce the rulers of Israel. Prophesy to them, and tell
them what I, the Sovereign LORD, say to
them: You are doomed, you shepherds
of Israel! You take care of yourselves,
but never tend the sheep. 3 You drink the
milk, wear clothes made from the wool,
and kill and eat the finest sheep. But you
never tend the sheep. 4 You have not
taken care of the weak ones, healed the
ones that are sick, bandaged the ones
that are hurt, brought back the ones that
wandered off, or looked for the ones that
were lost. Instead, you treated them cruelly. 5 Because the sheep had no shepherd, they were scattered, and wild
animals killed and ate them. 6 So my
sheep wandered over the high hills and
the mountains. They were scattered over
the face of the earth, and no one looked
for them or tried to find them.

7 "Now, you shepherds, listen to what
I, the LORD, am telling you. 8 As surely as
I am the living God, you had better listen
to me. My sheep have been attacked by
wild animals that killed and ate them because there was no shepherd. My shepherds did not try to find the sheep. They
were taking care of themselves and not
the sheep. 9 So listen to me, you shepherds. 10 I, the Sovereign LORD, declare
that I am your enemy. I will take my
sheep away from you and never again
let you be their shepherds; never again
will I let you take care only of yourselves. I will rescue my sheep from you
and not let you eat them.

The Good Shepherd

11 "I, the Sovereign LORD, tell you that I
myself will look for my sheep and take
care of them 12 in the same way as shepherds take care of their sheep that were
scattered and are brought together
again. I will bring them back from all the
places where they were scattered on that
dark, disastrous day. 13 I will take them
out of foreign countries, gather them together, and bring them back to their own
land. I will lead them back to the mountains and the streams of Israel and will
feed them in pleasant pastures. 14 I will
let them graze in safety in the mountain
meadows and the valleys and in all the
green pastures of the land of Israel.
15 I myself will be the shepherd of my
sheep, and I will find them a place to
rest. I, the Sovereign LORD, have spoken.

16 "I will look for those that are lost,
bring back those that wander off, bandage those that are hurt, and heal those
that are sick; but those that are fat and
strong I will destroy, because I am a
shepherd who does what is right.

17 "Now then, my flock, I, the
Sovereign LORD, tell you that I will judge
each of you and separate the good from
the bad, the sheep from the goats.
18 Some of you are not satisfied with eating the best grass; you even trample
down what you don't eat! You drink the
clear water and muddy what you don't
drink! 19 My other sheep have to eat the
grass you trample down and drink the
water you muddy.

20 "So now, I, the Sovereign LORD, tell
you that I will judge between you strong
sheep and the weak sheep. 21 You
pushed the sick ones aside and butted
them away from the flock. 22 But I will
rescue my sheep and not let them be
mistreated any more. I will judge each of
my sheep and separate the good from
the bad. 23 I will give them a king like my
servant David to be their one shepherd,
and he will take care of them. 24 I, the
LORD, will be their God, and a king like
my servant David will be their ruler. I

have spoken. 25 I will make a covenant
with them that guarantees their security.
I will get rid of all the dangerous animals
in the land, so that my sheep can live
safely in the fields and sleep in the
forests.
26 "I will bless them and let them live
around my sacred hill.[a] There I will
bless them with showers of rain when
they need it. 27 The trees will bear fruit,
the fields will produce crops, and everyone will live in safety on his own land.
When I break my people's chains and
set them free from those who made them
slaves, then they will know that I am the
LORD. 28 The heathen nations will not
plunder them any more, and the wild animals will not kill and eat them. They
will live in safety, and no one will terrify
them. 29 I will give them fertile fields and
put an end to hunger in the land. The
other nations will not sneer at them any
more. 30 Everyone will know that I protect Israel and that they are my people. I,
the Sovereign LORD, have spoken.
31 "You, my sheep, the flock that I feed,
are my people, and I am your God," says
the Sovereign LORD.

God's Punishment of Edom

35 The LORD spoke to me. 2 "Mortal
man," he said, "denounce the
country of Edom. 3 Tell the people what
I, the Sovereign LORD, am saying:

"I am your enemy, mountains of
Edom!
I will make you a desolate
wasteland.
4 I will leave your cities in ruins
And your land desolate;
Then you will know that I am the
LORD.

5 "You were Israel's constant enemy
and let her people be slaughtered in the
time of her disaster, the time of final
punishment for her sins. 6 So then—as
surely as I, the Sovereign LORD, am the
living God—death is your fate, and you
cannot escape it. You are guilty of[b]
murder, and murder will follow you.
7 I will make the hill country of Edom a
wasteland and kill everyone who travels
through it. 8 I will cover the mountains
with corpses, and the bodies of those
who are killed in battle will cover the
hills and valleys. 9 I will make you desolate forever, and no one will live in your
cities again. Then you will know that I
am the LORD.
10 "You said that the two nations, Judah and Israel, together with their lands,
belonged to you and that you would possess them, even though I, the LORD, was
their God. 11 So then, as surely as I, the
Sovereign LORD, am the living God, I will
pay you back for your anger, your jealousy, and your hate toward my people.
They will know that I am punishing you
for what you did to them. 12 Then you
will know that I, the LORD, heard you say
with contempt that the mountains of Israel were desolate and that they were
yours to devour. 13 I have heard the
wild, boastful way you have talked
against me."
14 The Sovereign LORD says, "I will
make you so desolate that the whole
world will rejoice at your downfall,
15 just as you rejoiced at the devastation
of Israel, my own possession. The mountains of Seir, yes, all the land of Edom,
will be desolate. Then everyone will
know that I am the LORD."

God's Blessing on Israel

36 The LORD said, "Mortal man,
speak to the mountains of Israel
and tell them to listen to the message
which I, 2 the Sovereign LORD, have for
them: Israel's enemies gloated and said,
'Now those ancient hills are ours!'
3 "Prophesy, then, and announce what
I, the Sovereign LORD, am saying. When
the neighboring nations captured and
plundered the mountains of Israel,
everyone made fun of Israel. 4 So now
listen to what I, the Sovereign LORD, say
to you mountains and hills, to you
brooks and valleys, to you places that
were left in ruins, and to you deserted
cities which were plundered and
mocked by all the surrounding nations.
5 "I, the Sovereign LORD, have spoken
out in the heat of my anger against the
surrounding nations, and especially
against Edom. With glee and contempt
they captured my land and took possession of its pastures.
6 "So prophesy to the land of Israel; tell
the mountains, hills, brooks, and valleys
what I, the Sovereign LORD, am saying in
jealous anger because of the way the na-

[a] SACRED HILL: *See 20.40.* [b] *One ancient translation* are guilty of; *Hebrew* hate.

tions have insulted and humiliated them.
7 I, the Sovereign LORD, solemnly promise that the surrounding nations will be
humiliated. 8 But on the mountains of Israel the trees will again grow leaves and
bear fruit for you, my people Israel. You
are going to come home soon. 9 I am on
your side, and I will make sure that your
land is plowed again and crops are
planted on it. 10 I will make your population grow. You will live in the cities and
rebuild everything that was left in ruins.
11 I will make people and cattle increase
in number. There will be more of you
than ever before, and you will have
many children. I will let you live there as
you used to live, and I will make you
more prosperous than ever. Then you
will know that I am the LORD. 12 I will
bring you, my people Israel, back to live
again in the land. It will be your own
land, and it will never again let your
children starve.

13 "I, the Sovereign LORD, say: It is true
that people say that the land eats people
and that it robs the nation of its children.
14 But from now on it will no longer eat
people and rob you of your children. I,
the Sovereign LORD, have spoken. 15 The
land will no longer have to listen to the
nations making fun of it or see the peoples sneer at it. The land will no longer
rob the nation of its children. I, the
Sovereign LORD, have spoken."

Israel's New Life

16 The LORD spoke to me. 17 "Mortal
man," he said, "when the Israelites were
living in their land, they defiled it by the
way they lived and acted. I regarded
their behavior as being as ritually unclean as a woman is during her monthly
period.[c] 18 I let them feel the force of my
anger because of the murders they had
committed in the land and because of
the idols by which they had defiled it.
19 I condemned them for the way they
lived and acted, and I scattered them
through foreign countries. 20 Wherever
they went, they brought disgrace on my
holy name, because people would say,
'These are the people of the LORD, but
they had to leave his land.' 21 That made
me concerned for my holy name, since
the Israelites brought disgrace on it
everywhere they went.

22 "Now then, give the Israelites the
message that I, the Sovereign LORD, have
for them: What I am going to do is not
for the sake of you Israelites, but for the
sake of my holy name, which you have
disgraced in every country where you
have gone. 23 When I demonstrate to the
nations the holiness of my great name—
the name you disgraced among them—
then they will know that I am the LORD.
I, the Sovereign LORD, have spoken. I will
use you to show the nations that I am
holy. 24 I will take you from every nation
and country and bring you back to your
own land. 25 I will sprinkle clean water
on you and make you clean from all
your idols and everything else that has
defiled you. 26 I will give you a new heart
and a new mind. I will take away your
stubborn heart of stone and give you an
obedient heart. 27 I will put my spirit in
you and will see to it that you follow my
laws and keep all the commands I have
given you. 28 Then you will live in the
land I gave your ancestors. You will be
my people, and I will be your God.
29 I will save you from everything that
defiles you. I will command the grain to
be plentiful, so that you will not have
any more famines. 30 I will increase the
yield of your fruit trees and your fields,
so that there will be no more famines to
disgrace you among the nations. 31 You
will remember your evil conduct and the
wrongs that you committed, and you
will be disgusted with yourselves because of your sins and your iniquities.
32 Israel, I want you to know that I am
not doing all this for your sake. I want
you to feel the shame and disgrace of
what you are doing. I, the Sovereign
LORD, have spoken."

33 The Sovereign LORD says, "When I
make you clean from all your sins, I will
let you live in your cities again and let
you rebuild the ruins. 34 Everyone who
used to walk by your fields saw how
overgrown and wild they were, but I will
let you farm them again. 35 Everyone will
talk about how this land, which was
once a wilderness, has become like the
Garden of Eden, and how the cities
which were torn down, looted, and left

[c] RITUALLY UNCLEAN ... PERIOD: *This is based on the view of ritual uncleanness described in the Law of Moses (see Lv 15.19).*

in ruins, are now inhabited and fortified.
36 Then the neighboring nations that
have survived will know that I, the LORD,
rebuild ruined cities and replant waste
fields. I, the LORD, have promised that I
would do this—and I will."
37 The Sovereign LORD says, "I will
once again let the Israelites ask me for
help, and I will let them increase in numbers like a flock of sheep. 38 The cities
that are now in ruins will then be as full
of people as Jerusalem was once full of
the sheep which were offered as sacrifices at a festival. Then they will know
that I am the LORD."

The Valley of Dry Bones

37 I felt the powerful presence of
the LORD, and his spirit took me
and set me down in a valley where the
ground was covered with bones. 2 He led
me all around the valley, and I could see
that there were very many bones and
that they were very dry. 3 He said to me,
"Mortal man, can these bones come
back to life?"
I replied, "Sovereign LORD, only you
can answer that!"
4 He said, "Prophesy to the bones. Tell
these dry bones to listen to the word of
the LORD. 5 Tell them that I, the Sovereign
LORD, am saying to them: I am going to
put breath into you and bring you back
to life. 6 I will give you sinews and muscles, and cover you with skin. I will put
breath into you and bring you back to
life. Then you will know that I am the
LORD."
7 So I prophesied as I had been told.
While I was speaking, I heard a rattling
noise, and the bones began to join together. 8 While I watched, the bones
were covered with sinews and muscles,
and then with skin. But there was no
breath in the bodies.
9 God said to me, "Mortal man, prophesy to the wind.[d] Tell the wind that the
Sovereign LORD commands it to come
from every direction, to breathe into
these dead bodies, and to bring them
back to life."
10 So I prophesied as I had been told.
Breath entered the bodies, and they
came to life and stood up. There were
enough of them to form an army.
11 God said to me, "Mortal man, the
people of Israel are like these bones.
They say that they are dried up, without
any hope and with no future. 12 So
prophesy to my people Israel and tell
them that I, the Sovereign LORD, am going to open their graves. I am going to
take them out and bring them back to
the land of Israel. 13 When I open the
graves where my people are buried and
bring them out, they will know that I am
the LORD. 14 I will put my breath in them,
bring them back to life, and let them live
in their own land. Then they will know
that I am the LORD. I have promised that
I would do this—and I will. I, the LORD,
have spoken."

Judah and Israel in One Kingdom

15 The LORD spoke to me again. 16 "Mortal man," he said, "take a wooden stick
and write on it the words, 'The kingdom
of Judah.' Then take another stick and
write on it the words, 'The kingdom of
Israel.' 17 Then hold the two sticks end to
end in your hand so that they look like
one stick. 18 When your people ask you
to tell them what this means, 19 tell them
that I, the Sovereign LORD, am going to
take the stick representing Israel and
put it with the one that represents Judah.
Out of the two I will make one stick and
hold it in my hand.
20 "Hold in your hand the two sticks
and let the people see them. 21 Then tell
them that I, the Sovereign LORD, am going to take all my people out of the nations where they have gone, gather them
together, and bring them back to their
own land. 22 I will unite them into one
nation in the land, on the mountains of
Israel. They will have one king to rule
over them, and they will no longer be
divided into two nations or split into two
kingdoms. 23 They will not defile themselves with disgusting idols any more or
corrupt themselves with sin. I will free
them from all the ways in which they sin
and betray me. I will purify them; they
will be my people, and I will be their
God. 24 A king like my servant David will
be their king. They will all be united under one ruler and will obey my laws
faithfully. 25 They will live on the land I
gave to my servant Jacob, the land
where their ancestors lived. They will
live there forever, and so will their chil-

[d] wind; *or* spirit. *The same Hebrew word may mean* wind, *or* spirit, *or* breath.

dren and all their descendants. A king like my servant David will rule them forever. 26 I will make a covenant with them that guarantees their security forever. I will establish them and increase their population, and will see to it that my Temple stands forever in their land. 27 I will live there with them; I will be their God, and they will be my people. 28 When I place my Temple there to be among them forever, then the nations will know that I, the LORD, have chosen Israel to be my own people."

Gog as the Instrument of God

38 The LORD spoke to me. 2 "Mortal man," he said, "denounce Gog, chief ruler of the nations of Meshech and Tubal in the land of Magog. Denounce him 3 and tell him that I, the Sovereign LORD, am his enemy. 4 I will turn him around, put hooks in his jaws, and drag him and all his troops away. His army, with its horses and uniformed riders, is enormous, and every soldier carries a shield and is armed with a sword. 5 Troops from Persia, Ethiopia,[e] and Libya are with him, and all have shields and helmets. 6 All the fighting men of the lands of Gomer and Beth Togarmah in the north are with him, and so are men from many other nations. 7 Tell him to get ready and have all his troops ready at his command. 8 After many years I will order him to invade a country where the people were brought back together from many nations and have lived without fear of war. He will invade the mountains of Israel, which were desolate and deserted so long, but where all the people now live in safety. 9 He and his army and the many nations with him will attack like a storm and cover the land like a cloud."

10 This is what the Sovereign LORD says to Gog: "When that time comes, you will start thinking up an evil plan. 11 You will decide to invade a helpless country where the people live in peace and security in unwalled towns that have no defenses. 12 You will plunder and loot the people who live in cities that were once in ruins. They have been gathered from the nations, and now they have livestock and property and live at the crossroads of the world. 13 The people of Sheba and Dedan and the merchants from the towns of Spain will ask you, 'Have you assembled your army and attacked in order to loot and plunder? Do you intend to get silver and gold, livestock and property, and march off with all those spoils?' "

14 So the Sovereign LORD sent me to tell Gog what he was saying to him: "Now while my people Israel live in security, you will set out[f] 15 to come from your place in the far north, leading a large, powerful army of soldiers from many nations, all of them on horseback. 16 You will attack my people Israel like a storm moving across the land. When the time comes, I will send you to invade my land in order to show the nations who I am, to show my holiness by what I do through you. 17 You are the one I was talking about long ago, when I announced through my servants, the prophets of Israel, that in days to come I would bring someone to attack Israel." The Sovereign LORD has spoken.

God's Punishment of Gog

18 The Sovereign LORD says, "On the day when Gog invades Israel, I will become furious. 19 I declare in the heat of my anger that on that day there will be a severe earthquake in the land of Israel. 20 Every fish and bird, every animal large and small, and every human being on the face of the earth will tremble for fear of me. Mountains will fall, cliffs will crumble, and every wall will collapse. 21 I will terrify Gog with all sorts of calamities.[g] I, the Sovereign LORD, have spoken. His men will turn their swords against one another. 22 I will punish him with disease and bloodshed. Torrents of rain and hail, together with fire and sulfur, will pour down on him and his army and on the many nations that are on his side. 23 In this way I will show all the nations that I am great and that I am holy. They will know then that I am the LORD."

[e] *Hebrew* Cush: *Cush is the ancient name of the extensive territory south of the First Cataract of the Nile River. This region was called Ethiopia in Graeco-Roman times, and included within its borders most of modern Sudan and some of present-day Ethiopia (Abyssinia).*
[f] *One ancient translation* set out; *Hebrew* know. [g] *One ancient translation* terrify . . . calamities; *Hebrew unclear.*

The Defeat of Gog

39 The Sovereign LORD said, "Mortal man, denounce Gog, the chief
ruler of the nations of Meshech and Tubal, and tell him that I am his enemy.
2 I will turn him in a new direction and
lead him out of the far north until he
comes to the mountains of Israel. 3 Then
I will knock his bow out of his left hand
and his arrows out of his right hand.
4 Gog and his army and his allies will fall
dead on the mountains of Israel, and I
will let their bodies be food for all the
birds and wild animals. 5 They will fall
dead in the open field. I, the Sovereign
LORD, have spoken. 6 I will start a fire in
the land of Magog and along all the sea-
coasts where people live undisturbed,
and everyone will know that I am the
LORD. 7 I will make sure that my people
Israel know my holy name, and I will not
let my name be disgraced any more.
Then the nations will know that I, the
LORD, am the holy God of Israel."

8 The Sovereign LORD said, "The day I
spoke about is certain to come. 9 The
people who live in the cities of Israel will
go out and collect the abandoned weapons for firewood. They will build fires
with the shields, bows, arrows, spears,
and clubs, and have enough to last for
seven years. 10 They will not have to
gather firewood in the fields or cut down
trees in the forest, because they will
have the abandoned weapons to burn.
They will loot and plunder those who
looted and plundered them." The
Sovereign LORD has spoken.

The Burial of Gog

11 The LORD said, "When all this happens, I will give Gog a burial ground
there in Israel, in Travelers' Valley, east
of the Dead Sea.[h] Gog and all his army
will be buried there, and the valley will
be called 'The Valley of Gog's Army.'
12 It will take the Israelites seven months
to bury all the corpses and make the
land clean again. 13 Everyone in the land
will help bury them, and they will be
honored for this on the day of my victory. I, the Sovereign LORD, have spoken.
14 After the seven months are over, men
will be chosen to travel through the land
in order to find and bury those bodies[i]
remaining on the ground, so that they
can make the land clean. 15 As they go up
and down the country, every time they
find a human bone, they will put a
marker beside it so that the grave-
diggers can come and bury it in the Valley of Gog's Army. 16 (There will be a
town nearby named after the army.)
And so the land will be made clean
again."

17 The Sovereign LORD said to me,
"Mortal man, call all the birds and animals to come from all around to eat the
sacrifice I am preparing for them. It will
be a huge feast on the mountains of Israel, where they can eat meat and drink
blood. 18 They are to eat the bodies of
soldiers and drink the blood of the rulers
of the earth, all of whom will be killed
like rams or lambs or goats or fat bulls.
19 When I kill these people like sacrifices, the birds and animals are to eat all
the fat they can hold and to drink blood
until they are drunk. 20 At my table they
will eat all they can hold of horses and
their riders and of soldiers and fighting
men. I, the Sovereign LORD, have
spoken."

The Restoration of Israel

21 The LORD said, "I will let the nations
see my glory and show them how I use
my power to carry out my just decisions.
22 The Israelites will know from then on
that I am the LORD their God. 23 And the
nations will know that the Israelites
went into exile because of the sins which
they committed against me. I turned
away from them and let their enemies
defeat them and kill them in battle.
24 I gave them what they deserved for
their uncleanness and their wickedness,
and I turned away from them."

25 The Sovereign LORD said, "But now I
will be merciful to Jacob's descendants,
the people of Israel, and make them
prosperous again. I will protect my holy
name. 26 When they are once more living
in safety in their own land, with no one
to threaten them, they will be able to forget how they were disgraced for having
betrayed me. 27 In order to show to the
many nations that I am holy, I will bring
my people back from all the countries
where their enemies live. 28 Then my

[h] *Hebrew has four additional words, the meaning of which is unclear.*
[i] *Some ancient translations* those bodies; *Hebrew* the travelers.

people will know that I am the LORD their
God. They will know this, because I sent
them into captivity and now gather them
and bring them back into their own land,
not leaving even one of them behind.
29 I will pour out my spirit on the people
of Israel and never again turn away
from them. I, the Sovereign LORD, have
spoken."

A VISION OF THE FUTURE TEMPLE (40.1–48.35)

Ezekiel Is Taken to Jerusalem

40 It was the tenth day of the new
year, which was the twenty-fifth
year after we had been taken into exile
and the fourteenth year after Jerusalem
was captured. On that day I felt the powerful presence of the LORD, and he carried me away. 2 In a vision God took me
to the land of Israel and put me on a high
mountain. I saw in front of me[j] a group
of buildings that looked like a city. 3 He
took me closer, and I saw a man who
shone like bronze. He was holding a
linen tape measure and a measuring rod
and was standing by a gateway.
4 He said to me, "Watch, mortal man.
Listen carefully and pay close attention
to everything I show you, because this is
why you were brought here. You are to
tell the people of Israel everything
you see."

The East Gate

5 What I saw was the Temple, and
there was a wall around it. The man took
his measuring rod, which was 10 feet
long, and measured the wall. It was 10
feet high and 10 feet thick. 6 Then he
went to the gateway that faced east. He
went up the steps, and at the top he
measured the entrance; it was 10 feet
deep.[k] 7 Beyond it there was a passageway, which had three guardrooms on
each side. Each of the rooms was
square, 10 feet on each side, and the
walls between them were 8 feet thick.
Beyond the guardrooms there was a
passageway 10 feet long that led to an
entrance room which faced the Temple.
8-9 He measured this room and found it
was 14 feet deep. It formed that end of
the gateway which was nearest the Temple, and at its far end the walls were 4
feet thick. (10 These guardrooms on each
side of the passageway were all the
same size, and the walls between them
were all of the same thickness.)
11 Next, the man measured the width
of the passageway in the gateway. It was
22 feet altogether, and the space between the open gates was 16 feet. 12 In
front of each of the guardrooms there
was a low wall 20 inches high and 20
inches thick. (The rooms were 10 feet
square.) 13 Then he measured the distance from the back wall[l] of one room
to the back wall[l] of the room across the
passageway from it, and it was 42 feet.
14 The room at the far end led out to a
courtyard. He measured that room and
found it was 34 feet wide.[m] 15 The total
length of the gateway from the outside
wall of the gate to the far side of the last
room was 84 feet. 16 There were small
openings in the outside walls of all the
rooms and also in the inner walls between the rooms. There were palm trees
carved on the inner walls that faced the
passageway.

The Outer Courtyard

17 The man took me through the gateway into the courtyard. There were
thirty rooms built against the outer wall,
and in front of them there was an area
paved with stones, 18 which extended
around the courtyard. This outer courtyard was at a lower level than the inner
courtyard.
19 There was a gateway at a higher
level that led to the inner courtyard. The
man measured the distance between the
two gateways, and it was 168 feet.[n]

The North Gate

20 Then the man measured the gateway on the north side that led into the
outer courtyard. 21 The three guardrooms on each side of the passageway,
the walls between them, and the entrance room all had the same measurements as those in the east gateway. The
total length of the gateway was 84 feet
and the width 42 feet. 22 The entrance
room, the windows, and the carved palm

[j] *One ancient translation* in front of me; *Hebrew* in the south. [k] *One ancient translation* deep; *Hebrew* deep, one entrance 10 feet deep. [l] *Probable text* back wall; *Hebrew* roof. [m] *Verse 14 in Hebrew is unclear.* [n] *Hebrew has two additional words, the meaning of which is unclear.*

trees were like those in the east gate.
Here seven steps led up to the gate, and
the entrance room was at the end facing
the courtyard. 23 Across the courtyard
from this north gateway was another
gateway leading to the inner courtyard,
just as there was on the east side. The
man measured the distance between
these two gateways, and it was 168 feet.

The South Gate

24 Next, the man took me to the south
side, and there we saw another gateway.
He measured its inner walls and its entrance room, and they were the same as
the others. 25 There were windows in the
rooms of this gateway just as in the others. The total length of the gateway was
84 feet and the width 42 feet. 26 Seven
steps led up to it, and its entrance room
was also at the end facing the courtyard.
There were palm trees carved on the inner walls that faced the passageway.
27 Here, too, there was a gateway leading
to the inner courtyard. The man measured the distance to this second gateway, and it was 168 feet.

The Inner Courtyard: The South Gate

28 The man took me through the south
gateway into the inner courtyard. He
measured the gateway, and it was the
same size as the gateways in the outer
wall. 29-30 Its guardrooms, its entrance
room, and its inner walls were the same
size as those in the other gateways.
There were also windows in the rooms
of this gateway. The total length was 84
feet and the width 42 feet. 31 Its entrance
room faced the other courtyard, and
palm trees were carved on the walls
along the passageway. Eight steps led
up to this gate.

The Inner Courtyard: The East Gate

32 The man took me through the east
gateway into the inner courtyard. He
measured the gateway, and it was the
same size as the others. 33 Its guardrooms, its entrance room, and its inner
walls measured the same as those in the
other gateways. There were windows all
around, and in the entrance room also.
The total length was 84 feet and the
width 42 feet. 34 The entrance room
faced the outer courtyard. Palm trees
were carved on the walls along the
passageway. Eight steps led up to this
gate.

The Inner Courtyard: The North Gate

35 Then the man took me to the north
gateway. He measured it, and it was the
same size as the others. 36 Like them, it
also had guardrooms, decorated inner
walls, an entrance room, and windows
all around. Its total length was 84 feet
and its width 42 feet. 37 The entrance
room[o] faced the outer courtyard. Palm
trees were carved on the walls along the
passageway. Eight steps led up to this
gate.

Buildings Near the North Gate

38 In the outer courtyard there was an
annex attached to the inner gateway on
the north side. It opened into the entrance room that faced the courtyard,
and there they washed the carcasses of
the animals to be burned whole as sacrifices. 39 In this entrance room there were
four tables, two on each side of the
room. It was on these tables that they
killed the animals to be offered as sacrifices, either to be burned whole or to be
sacrifices for sin or as repayment offerings. 40 Outside the room there were four
similar tables, two on either side of the
entrance of the north gate. 41 Altogether
there were eight tables on which the animals to be sacrificed were killed: four
inside the room and four out in the
courtyard. 42 The four tables in the annex, used to prepare the offerings to be
burned whole, were of cut stone. They
were 20 inches high, and their tops were
30 inches square. All the equipment
used in killing the sacrificial animals
was kept on these tables. 43 Ledges 3
inches wide ran around the edge of the
tables. All the meat to be offered in sacrifice was placed on the tables.[p]

44 Then he brought me into the inner
court. There were two rooms opening on
the inner court, one facing south beside
the north gateway and the other facing
north beside the south gateway.[q] 45 The
man told me that the room which faced

[o] *Some ancient translations* entrance room; *Hebrew* inner wall. [p] *Verse 43 in Hebrew is unclear.* [q] *One ancient translation* Then . . . south gateway; *verse 44 in Hebrew is unclear.*

south was for the priests who served in the Temple, 46 and the room which faced north was for the priests who served at the altar. All the priests are descended from Zadok; they are the only members of the tribe of Levi who are permitted to go into the LORD's presence to serve him.

The Inner Courtyard and the Temple Building

47 The man measured the inner courtyard, and it was 168 feet square. The Temple was on the west side, and in front of it was an altar. 48 Then he took me into the entrance room of the Temple. He measured the entranceway: it was 9 feet deep and 24 feet wide,[r] with walls 5 feet thick on either side. 49 Steps led up to the entrance room, which was 34 feet wide and 20 feet deep.[s] There were two columns, one on each side of the entrance.

41 Next, the man took me into the central room, the Holy Place. He measured the passageway into it: it was 10 feet deep[t] 2 and 18 feet wide, with walls 8 feet thick on either side. He measured the room itself: it was 68 feet long and 34 feet wide.

3 Then he went to the innermost room. He measured the passageway into it: it was 3 feet deep and 10 feet wide, with walls on either side 12 feet thick.[u] 4 He measured the room itself, and it was 34 feet square. This room was beyond the central room. Then he said to me, "This is the Most Holy Place."

The Rooms Built against the Temple Walls

5 The man measured the thickness of the inner wall of the Temple building, and it was 10 feet. Against this wall, all around the Temple, was a series of small rooms 7 feet wide. 6 These rooms were in three stories, with thirty rooms on each floor. The Temple's outer wall on each floor was thinner than on the floor below, so that the rooms could rest on the wall without being anchored into it. 7 And so the Temple walls, when seen from the outside, seemed to have the same thickness all the way to the top. Against the Temple's outer wall, on the outside of the rooms, two wide stairways were built, so that it was possible to go from the lower story to the middle and the upper stories.[v] 8-11 The outside wall of these rooms was 8 feet thick; there was one door into the rooms on the north side of the Temple, and one into those on the south side. I saw that there was a terrace 8 feet wide around the Temple; it was 10 feet above the ground and it was level with the foundation of the rooms by the Temple walls. Between the terrace and the buildings used by the priests there was an open space 34 feet across, along the sides of the Temple.

The Building on the West

12 At the far end of the open space on the west side of the Temple there was a building 150 feet long and 116 feet wide; its walls were 9 feet thick all around.

The Total Measurements of the Temple Building

13 The man measured the outside of the Temple, and it was 168 feet long. And from the back of the Temple, across the open space to the far side of the building to the west, the distance was also 168 feet. 14 The distance across the front of the Temple, including the open space on either side, was also 168 feet. 15 He measured the length of the building to the west, including its galleries on both sides, and it was also 168 feet.

Details of the Temple Building

The entrance room of the Temple, the Holy Place, and the Most Holy Place 16 were all paneled with wood from the floor to the windows. These windows could be covered.[w] 17 The inside walls of the Temple, up as high as above the doors, were completely covered with carvings[x] 18 of palm trees and winged creatures. Palm trees alternated with creatures, one following the other, all the way around the room. Each creature had two faces: 19 a human face that was turned toward the palm tree on one side, and a lion's face that was turned toward the tree on the other side. It was like this

[r] *One ancient translation* and 24 feet wide; *Hebrew does not have these words.*
[s] *One ancient translation* 20 feet deep; *Hebrew* 18 feet deep. [t] *Hebrew has two additional words, the meaning of which is unclear.* [u] *One ancient translation* with walls on either side 12 feet thick; *Hebrew* and 12 feet thick. [v] *Verse 7 in Hebrew is unclear.* [w] *Verse 16 in Hebrew is unclear.* [x] *Verse 17 in Hebrew is unclear.*

all around the wall, 20 from the floor to
above the doors. 21 The doorposts of the
Holy Place were square.

The Wooden Altar

In front of the entrance of the Most
Holy Place there was something that
looked like 22 a wooden altar. It was 5
feet high and 4 feet wide. Its corner
posts, its base,[y] and its sides were all
made of wood. The man said to me,
"This is the table which stands in the
presence of the LORD."

The Doors

23 There was a door at the end of the
passageway to the Holy Place and one
also at the end of the passageway to the
Most Holy Place. 24 They were double
doors that swung open in the middle.
25 There were palm trees and winged
creatures carved on the doors of the
Holy Place, just as there were on the
walls. And there was a wooden covering
over the outside of the doorway of the
entrance room. 26 At the sides of this
room there were windows, and the walls
were decorated with palm trees.[z]

Two Buildings Near the Temple

42 Then the man took me into the
outer courtyard and led me to a
building on the north side of the Temple,
not far from the building at the west end
of the Temple. 2 This building was 168
feet long and 84 feet wide. 3 On one side
it faced the space 34 feet wide which was
alongside the Temple, and on the other
side it faced the pavement of the outer
courtyard. It was built on three levels,
each one set further back than the one
below it. 4 Along the north side of this
building was a passageway 16 feet wide
and 168 feet long,[a] with entrances on
that side. 5 The rooms at the upper level
of the building were narrower than
those at the middle and lower levels because they were set further back. 6 The
rooms at all three levels were on ter-
races and were not supported by columns like the other buildings in the
courtyard. 7-8 At the lower level the outer
wall of the building was solid for 84 feet,
half its length; and there were rooms in
the remaining 84 feet. At the top level
there were rooms in the entire length of
the building. 9-10 Below these rooms at
the east end of the building, where the
wall of the courtyard began,[b] there was
an entrance into the outer courtyard.

At the south[c] side of the Temple there
was an identical building not far from
the building at the west end of the Temple. 11 In front of the rooms there was a
passageway just like the one on the
north side. It had the same measurements, the same design, and the same
kind of entrances. 12 There was a door
under the rooms on the south side of the
building, at the east end where the wall
began.

13 The man said to me, "Both these
buildings are holy. In them the priests
who enter the LORD's presence eat the
holiest offerings. Because the rooms are
holy, the priests will place the holiest offerings there: the offerings of grain and
the sacrifices offered for sin or as repayment offerings. 14 When priests have
been in the Temple and want to go to the
outer courtyard, they must leave in these
rooms the holy clothing they wore while
serving the LORD. They must put on other
clothes before going out to the area
where the people gather."

The Measurements of the Temple Area

15 When the man had finished measuring inside the Temple area, he took me
out through the east gate and then measured the outside of the area. 16 He took
the measuring rod and measured the
east side, and it was 840 feet. 17-19 Then
he measured the north side, the south
side, and the west side; each side had the
same length, 840 feet,[d] 20 so that the
wall enclosed a square 840 feet on each
side. The wall served to separate what
was holy from what was not.

The LORD Returns to the Temple

43 The man took me to the gate that
faces east, 2 and there I saw coming from the east the dazzling light of
the presence of the God of Israel. God's

[y] *Some ancient translations* base; *Hebrew* length. [z] *Hebrew has three additional words, the meaning of which is unclear.* [a] *Some ancient translations* 168 feet long; *Hebrew* a way of 20 inches. [b] *One ancient translation* where the wall of the courtyard began; *Hebrew* in the breadth of the wall of the courtyard. [c] *One ancient translation* south; *Hebrew* east. [d] *Verses 16-19 in Hebrew are unclear.*

voice sounded like the roar of the sea,
and the earth shone with the dazzling
light. 3 This vision was like the one I had
seen when God came to destroy Jerusalem, and the one I saw by the Chebar
River. Then I threw myself face downward on the ground. 4 The dazzling light
passed through the east gate and went
into the Temple.

5 The LORD's spirit lifted me up and
took me into the inner courtyard, where
I saw that the Temple was filled with the
glory of the LORD. 6 The man stood beside
me there, and I heard the LORD speak to
me out of the Temple: 7 "Mortal man,
here is my throne. I will live here among
the people of Israel and rule them forever. Neither the people of Israel nor
their kings will ever again disgrace my
holy name by worshiping other gods or
by burying the corpses of[e] their dead
kings. 8 The kings built the doorsills and
doorposts of their palace right against
the doorsills and doorposts of my Temple, so that there was only a wall between us. They disgraced my holy name
by all the disgusting things they did, and
so in my anger I destroyed them. 9 Now
they must stop worshiping other gods
and remove the corpses of[f] their kings.
If they do, I will live among them
forever."

10 And the LORD continued, "Mortal
man, tell the people of Israel about the
Temple, and let them study its plan.
Make them ashamed of their sinful actions. 11 Then if they are ashamed of
what they have done, explain the plan of
the Temple to them: its design, its entrances and exits, its shape, the arrangement of everything, and all its rules and
regulations. Write all this down for them
so that they can see how everything is
arranged and can carry out all the rules.
12 This is the law of the Temple: All the
area surrounding it on the top of the
mountain is sacred and holy."

The Altar

13 These are the measurements of the
altar, using the same unit of measure as
in measuring the Temple. All around the
base of the altar there was a gutter 20
inches deep and 20 inches wide, with a
rim at the outside edge 10 inches high.
14 The lowest section of the altar, from
the top of the base, was 4 feet high. The
next section was set back from the edge
20 inches all around, and was 7 feet
high. The section after that was also set
back from the edge 20 inches all around.
15 This top section, on which the sacrifices were burned, was also 7 feet high.
The projections on the four corners were
higher than the rest of the top. 16 The top
of the altar was a square, 20 feet on each
side. 17 The middle section was also a
square, 24 feet on each side, with a rim
at the outside edge 10 inches high. (The
gutter was 20 inches wide.) The steps
going up the altar were on the east
side.

The Consecration of the Altar

18 The Sovereign LORD said to me,
"Mortal man, listen to what I tell you.
When the altar is built, you are to dedicate it by burning sacrifices on it and by
sprinkling on it the blood of the animals
that were sacrificed. 19 Those priests belonging to the tribe of Levi who are descended from Zadok are the only ones
who are to come into my presence to
serve me. I, the Sovereign LORD, command this. You will give them a young
bull to offer as a sacrifice for sin. 20 You
are to take some of its blood and put it
on the projections on the top corners of
the altar, on the corners of the middle
section of the altar, and all around its
edges. In this way you will purify the altar and consecrate it. 21 You are to take
the bull that is offered as a sacrifice for
sin and burn it at the specified place outside the Temple area. 22 The next day
you are to take a male goat without any
defects and offer it as a sacrifice for sin.
Purify the altar with its blood the same
way you did with the bull. 23 When you
have finished doing that, take a young
bull and a young ram, both of them without any defects, 24 and bring them to me.
The priests will sprinkle salt on them
and burn them as an offering to me.
25 Each day for seven days you are to offer a goat, a bull, and a ram as sacrifices
for sin. All of them must be without any
defects. 26 For seven days the priests are

[e] by burying the corpses of; *or* by putting up monuments to. [f] remove the corpses of; *or* remove the monuments to.

to consecrate the altar and make it ready
for use. 27 When the week is over, the
priests are to begin offering on the altar
the burnt offerings and the fellowship
offerings of the people. Then I will be
pleased with all of you. I, the Sovereign
LORD, have spoken."

The Use of the East Gate

44 The man led me to the outer gate
at the east side of the Temple
area. The gate was closed, 2 and the LORD
said to me, "This gate will stay closed
and will never be opened. No human being is allowed to use it, because I, the
LORD God of Israel, have entered through
it. It is to remain closed. 3 The ruling
prince, however, may go there to eat a
holy meal in my presence. He is to enter
and leave the gateway through the entrance room at the inner end."

Rules for Admission to the Temple

4 Then the man took me through the
north gate to the front of the Temple. As
I looked, I saw that the Temple of the
LORD was filled with the dazzling light of
his presence. I threw myself face downward on the ground, 5 and the LORD said
to me, "Mortal man, pay attention to
everything you see and hear. I am going
to tell you the rules and regulations for
the Temple. Note carefully which persons are allowed to go in and out of the
Temple, and which persons are not
allowed.
6 "Tell those rebellious people of Israel
that I, the Sovereign LORD, will no longer
tolerate the disgusting things that they
have been doing. 7 They have profaned
my Temple by letting uncircumcised foreigners, people who do not obey me, enter the Temple when the fat and the
blood of the sacrifices are being offered
to me. So my people have broken my
covenant by all the disgusting things
they have done. 8 They have not taken
charge of the sacred rituals in my Temple, but instead have put foreigners in
charge.
9 "I, the Sovereign LORD, declare that
no uncircumcised foreigner, no one who
disobeys me, will enter my Temple, not
even a foreigner who lives among the
people of Israel."

The Levites Are Excluded from the Priesthood

10 The LORD said to me, "I am punishing
those Levites who, together with the rest
of the people of Israel, deserted me and
worshiped idols. 11 They may serve me
in the Temple by taking charge of the
gates and by performing the work of the
Temple. They may kill the animals
which the people offer for burnt offerings and for sacrifices, and they are to
be on duty to serve the people. 12 But because they conducted the worship of
idols for the people of Israel and in this
way led the people into sin, I, the
Sovereign LORD, solemnly swear that
they must be punished. 13 They are not to
serve me as priests or to go near anything that is holy to me or to enter the
Most Holy Place. This is the punishment
for the disgusting things they have done.
14 I am assigning to them the menial
work that is to be done in the Temple."

The Priests

15 The Sovereign LORD said, "Those
priests belonging to the tribe of Levi
who are descended from Zadok, however, continued to serve me faithfully in
the Temple when the rest of the people
of Israel turned away from me. So now
they are the ones who are to serve me
and come into my presence to offer me
the fat and the blood of the sacrifices.
16 They alone will enter my Temple,
serve at my altar, and conduct the Temple worship. 17 When they enter the gateway to the inner courtyard of the
Temple, they are to put on linen clothing. They must not wear anything made
of wool when they are on duty in the
inner courtyard or in the Temple. 18 So
that they won't perspire, they are to
wear linen turbans and linen trousers,
but no belt. 19 Before they go to the outer
courtyard where the people are, they
must first take off the clothes they wore
on duty in the Temple and leave them in
the holy rooms. They are to put on other
clothing in order to keep their sacred
clothing from harming the people.[g]
20 "Priests must neither shave their
heads nor let their hair grow long. They
are to keep it a proper length. 21 Priests
must not drink any wine before going

[g] HARMING THE PEOPLE: *It was believed that ordinary people would be harmed by touching something holy.*

into the inner courtyard. 22 No priest
may marry a divorced woman; he is to
marry only an Israelite virgin or the
widow of another priest.
23 "The priests are to teach my people
the difference between what is holy and
what is not, and between what is ritually
clean and what is not. 24 When a legal
dispute arises, the priests are to decide
the case according to my laws. They are
to keep the religious festivals according
to my rules and regulations, and they
are to keep the Sabbaths holy.
25 "A priest is not to become ritually
unclean by touching a corpse, unless it is
one of his parents, one of his children or
a brother or an unmarried sister. 26 After
he has become clean again, he must wait
seven days 27 and then go into the inner
courtyard of the Temple and offer a sacrifice for his purification, so that he can
serve in the Temple again. I, the
Sovereign LORD, have spoken.
28 "The priests have the priesthood as
their share of what I have given Israel to
be handed down from one generation to
another. They are not to hold property in
Israel; I am all they need. 29 The grain
offerings, the sin offerings, and the repayment offerings will be the priests'
food, and they are to receive everything
in Israel that is set apart for me. 30 The
priests are to have the best of all the first
harvest and of everything else that is offered to me. Each time the people bake
bread, they are to give the priests the
first loaf as an offering, and my blessing
will rest on their homes. 31 The priests
must not eat any bird or animal that dies
a natural death or is killed by another
animal."

The LORD's Portion of the Country

45 When the land is divided to give
each tribe a share, one part is to
be dedicated to the LORD. It is to be 10
miles long by 8 miles[h] wide. The entire
area will be holy. 2 In this area there is to
be a square plot of land for the Temple,
840 feet on each side, entirely surrounded by an open space 84 feet wide.
3 Half of this area, a section 10 miles by
4 miles, is to be measured off; it will contain the Temple, the holiest place of all.
4 It will be a holy part of the country, set
aside for the priests who serve the LORD
in his Temple. It will contain their
houses and the section of land for the
Temple. 5 The other half of the area is to
be set aside as the possession of the Levites, who do the work in the Temple.
There will be towns there for them to
live in.[i]
6 Next to the holy area, another section, 10 miles long and 2 miles wide, is to
be set aside for a city where any of the
people of Israel may live.

Land for the Prince

7 Land is also to be set aside for the
ruling prince. From the west boundary
of the holy area it will extend west to the
Mediterranean Sea; and from the east
boundary it will extend to the eastern
border of the country, so that its length
will be the same as the length of one of
the areas allotted to the tribes of Israel.
8 This area will be the share the ruling
prince will have in the land of Israel, so
that he will no longer oppress the people, but will let the rest of the country
belong to the tribes of Israel.

Rules for the Prince

9 The Sovereign LORD said, "You have
sinned too long, you rulers of Israel!
Stop your violence and oppression. Do
what is right and just. You must never
again drive my people off their land. I,
the Sovereign LORD, am telling you this.
10 "Everyone must use honest weights
and measures:
11 "The *ephah* for dry measure is to be
equal to the *bath* for liquid measure. The
standard is the *homer*.[j] The resulting
measures are as follows:

1 *homer* = 10 *ephahs* = 10 *baths*

12 "Your weights are to be as follows:

20 *gerahs* = 1 *shekel*[k]
60 *shekels* = 1 *mina*

13-15 "This is the basis on which you are
to make your offerings:

Wheat: 1/60th of your harvest
Barley: 1/60th of your harvest
Olive oil: 1/100th of the yield of
your trees

(Measure it by the *bath*: 10 *baths* =
1 *homer* = 1 *kor*.)

[h] *One ancient translation* 8 miles; *Hebrew* 4 miles. [i] *One ancient translation* towns there for them to live in; *Hebrew* twenty rooms. [j] HOMER: *A unit of dry or liquid measure, about 5 bushels or 175 quarts; so an ephah or a bath would be about 1/2 bushel or 17.5 quarts.*
[k] SHEKEL: *In Ezekiel's time this unit of weight was about 0.4 ounce or 11.4 grams.*

Sheep: 1 sheep out of every 200
from the meadows of Israel
"You are to bring grain offerings, animals to be burned whole, and animals
for fellowship offerings, so that your
sins will be forgiven. I, the Sovereign
LORD, command it.
16 "All the people of the land must
take[l] these offerings to the ruling
prince of Israel. 17 It will be his duty to
provide the animals to be burned whole,
the grain offerings, and the wine offerings for the whole nation of Israel at the
New Moon Festivals, the Sabbaths, and
the other festivals. He is to provide the
sin offerings, the grain offerings, the offerings to be burned whole, and the fellowship offerings, to take away the sins
of the people of Israel."

The Festivals

(Exodus 12.1-20; Leviticus 23.33-43)

18 The Sovereign LORD said, "On the
first day of the first month you are to
sacrifice a bull without any defects and
purify the Temple. 19 The priest will take
some of the blood of this sin offering and
put it on the doorposts of the Temple, on
the four corners of the altar, and on the
posts of the gateways to the inner courtyard. 20 On the seventh day of the month
you are to do the same thing on behalf of
anyone who sins unintentionally or
through ignorance. In this way you will
keep the Temple holy.
21 "On the fourteenth day of the first
month you will begin the celebration of
the Passover Festival. For seven days
everyone will eat bread made without
yeast. 22 On the first day of the festival
the ruling prince must offer a bull as a
sacrifice for his sins and for those of all
the people. 23 On each of the seven days
of the festival he is to sacrifice to the
LORD seven bulls and seven rams without
any defects and burn them whole. He is
also to sacrifice a male goat each day as
a sin offering. 24 For each bull and each
ram that is sacrificed, there is to be an
offering of half a bushel of grain and
three quarts of olive oil.
25 "For the Festival of Shelters, which
begins on the fifteenth day of the seventh month, the prince will offer on each
of the seven days the same sacrifice for
sin, the same offerings to be burned
whole, and the same offerings of grain
and olive oil."

The Prince and the Festivals

46 The Sovereign LORD says, "The
east gateway to the inner courtyard must be kept closed during the six
working days, but it is to be opened on
the Sabbath and at the New Moon Festival. 2 The ruling prince will go from the
outer courtyard into the entrance room
of the gateway and stand beside the
posts of the gate while the priests burn
his sacrifices whole and offer his fellowship offerings. There at the gate he must
worship and then go back out. The gate
must not be shut until evening. 3 Each
Sabbath and each New Moon Festival all
the people are also to bow down and
worship the LORD in front of the gate.
4 On the Sabbath the prince is to bring to
the LORD, as sacrifices to be burned
whole, six lambs and one ram, all without any defects. 5 With each ram he is to
bring an offering of half a bushel of
grain, and with each lamb he is to bring
whatever he wants to give. For each
half-bushel of grain offering he is to
bring three quarts of olive oil. 6 At the
New Moon Festival he will offer a young
bull, six lambs, and a ram, all without
any defects. 7 With each bull and each
ram the offering is to be half a bushel of
grain, and with each lamb the offering is
to be whatever the prince wants to give.
Three quarts of olive oil are to be offered
with each half-bushel of grain. 8 The
prince must leave the entrance room of
the gateway and go out by the same way
he went in.
9 "When the people come to worship
the LORD at any festival, those who enter
by the north gate are to leave by the
south gate after they have worshiped,
and those who enter by the south gate
are to leave by the north gate. No one
may go out by the same way he entered,
but must leave by the opposite gate.
10 The prince is to come in when the people come, and leave when they leave.
11 On the feast days and at the festivals
the grain offering will be half a bushel
with each bull or ram, and whatever the
worshiper wants to give with each lamb.
Three quarts of olive oil are to be offered
with each half-bushel of grain.

[l] *Probable text* must take; *Hebrew unclear.*

12 "When the ruling prince wants to
make a voluntary offering to the LORD,
either an offering to be burned whole or
a fellowship offering, the east gate to the
inner courtyard will be opened for him.
He is to make the offering in the same
way he does on the Sabbath, and the
gate is to be closed after he goes
back out."

The Daily Offering

13 The LORD says, "Every morning a
one-year-old lamb without any defects is
to be burned whole as an offering to the
LORD. This offering must be made every
day. 14 Also an offering of five pounds of
flour is to be made every morning, along
with one quart of olive oil for mixing
with the flour. The rules for this offering
to the LORD are to be in force forever.
15 The lamb, the flour, and the olive oil
are to be offered to the LORD every morning forever."

The Prince and the Land

16 The Sovereign LORD commands: "If
the ruling prince gives any of the land he
owns to one of his sons as a present, it
will belong to that son as a part of his
family property. 17 But if the ruling
prince gives any of his land to anyone
who is in his service, it will become the
prince's property again when the Year
of Restoration[m] comes. It belongs to
him, and only he and his sons can own it
permanently. 18 The ruling prince must
not take any of the people's property
away from them. Any land he gives to
his sons must be from the land that is
assigned to him, so that he will not oppress any of my people by taking their
land."

The Temple Kitchens

19 Then the man took me to the entrance of the rooms facing north near
the gate on the south side of the inner
courtyard. These are holy rooms for the
priests. He pointed out a place on the
west side of the rooms 20 and said, "This
is the place where the priests are to boil
the meat offered as sacrifices for sin or
as repayment offerings, and to bake the
offerings of flour, so that nothing holy is
carried to the outer courtyard, where it
might harm the people."[n]
21-22 Then he led me to the outer courtyard and showed me that in each of its
four corners there was a smaller[o] courtyard, 68 feet long and 48 feet wide.
23 Each one had a stone wall around it,
with fireplaces built against the wall.
24 The man told me, "These are the kitch-
ens where the Temple servants are to
boil the sacrifices the people offer."

The Stream Flowing from the Temple

47 The man led me back to the entrance of the Temple. Water was
coming out from under the entrance and
flowing east, the direction the Temple
faced. It was flowing down from under
the south part of the Temple past the
south side of the altar. 2 The man then
took me out of the Temple area by way
of the north gate and led me around to
the gate that faces east. A small stream
of water was flowing out at the south
side of the gate. 3 With his measuring rod
the man measured 560 yards downstream to the east and told me to wade
through the stream there. The water
came only to my ankles. 4 Then he measured another 560 yards, and the water
came up to my knees. Another 560 yards
farther down, the water was up to my
waist. 5 He measured 560 yards more,
and there the stream was so deep I could
not wade through it. It was too deep to
cross except by swimming. 6 He said to
me, "Mortal man, note all this carefully."
Then the man took me back to the riverbank, 7 and when I got there, I saw that
there were very many trees on each
bank. 8 He said to me, "This water flows
through the land to the east and down
into the Jordan Valley and to the Dead
Sea. When it flows into the Dead Sea, it
replaces the salt water of that sea with
fresh water. 9 Wherever the stream
flows, there will be all kinds of animals
and fish. The stream will make the water
of the Dead Sea fresh, and wherever it
flows, it will bring life. 10 From the
Springs of Engedi all the way to the
Springs of Eneglaim, there will be fishermen on the shore of the sea, and they

[m] YEAR OF RESTORATION: *Every fifty years, all Israelites were required to give freedom to any Israelites who had become slaves because of debts; they were also to give back to the original owner, or his heirs, any ancestral land that had been sold for debt (see Lv 25.8-55).*
[n] HARM THE PEOPLE: *See 44.19.* [o] *One ancient translation* smaller; *Hebrew* enclosed.

will spread out their nets there to dry.
There will be as many different kinds of
fish there as there are in the Mediterranean Sea. 11 But the water in the marshes
and ponds along the shore will not be
made fresh. They will remain there as a
source of salt. 12 On each bank of the
stream all kinds of trees will grow to
provide food. Their leaves will never
wither, and they will never stop bearing
fruit. They will have fresh fruit every
month, because they are watered by the
stream that flows from the Temple. The
trees will provide food, and their leaves
will be used for healing people."

The Boundaries of the Land

13 The Sovereign LORD said, "These are
the boundaries of the land that is to be
divided among the twelve tribes, with
the tribe of Joseph receiving two sections.[p] 14 I solemnly promised your
ancestors that I would give them
possession of this land; now divide it
equally among you.
15 "The northern boundary runs eastward from the Mediterranean Sea to the
city of Hethlon, to Hamath Pass, to the
city of Zedad,[q] 16 to the cities of Bero-
thah and Sibraim (they are located between the territory of the kingdom of
Damascus and that of the kingdom of
Hamath), and to the city of Ticon (located by the border of the district of Hauran). 17 So the northern boundary runs
from the Mediterranean eastward to
Enon City, with the border regions of
Damascus and Hamath to the north of it.
18 "The eastern boundary runs south
from a point between the territory of
Damascus and that of Hauran, with the
Jordan River forming the boundary
between the land of Israel on the west
and Gilead on the east, as far as Tamar[r]
on the Dead Sea.
19 "The southern boundary runs southwest from Tamar to the oasis of Kadesh
Meribah and then northwest along the
Egyptian border to the Mediterranean Sea.
20 "The western boundary is formed by
the Mediterranean and runs north to a
point west of Hamath Pass.
21 "Divide this land among your tribes;
22 it is to be your permanent possession.
The foreigners who are living among
you and who have had children born
here are also to receive their share of the
land when you divide it. They are to be
treated like full Israelite citizens and are
to draw lots for shares of the land along
with the tribes of Israel. 23 All foreign
residents will receive their share with
the people of the tribe among whom
they are living. I, the Sovereign LORD,
have spoken."

The Division of the Land among the Tribes

48 1-7 The northern boundary of the
land runs eastward from the
Mediterranean Sea to the city of Hethlon, to Hamath Pass, to Enon City, to the
boundary between the kingdoms of Damascus and Hamath. Each tribe is to receive one section of land extending from
the eastern boundary west to the Mediterranean Sea,[s] in the following order
from north to south:

Dan
Asher
Naphtali
Manasseh
Ephraim
Reuben
Judah

The Special Section in the Center of the Land

8 The next section of the land is to be
set apart for special use. It is to be 10
miles wide from north to south, and the
same length from east to west as the sections given to the tribes. The Temple will
be located within this section.
9 In the center of this section, a special
area 10 miles by 8 miles[t] is to be dedicated to the LORD. 10 The priests are to
have a portion of this holy area. From
east to west their portion is to measure
10 miles, and from north to south, 4
miles. The Temple of the LORD is to be
located in the middle of this area. 11 This
holy area is to be for the priests who are
descendants of Zadok. They served me
faithfully and did not join the rest of the

[p] TWO SECTIONS: *The tribes of Manasseh and Ephraim, the sons of Joseph, were each given one section.* [q] *One ancient translation* Hamath Pass, to the city of Zedad; *Hebrew* Zedad Pass to the city of Hamath. [r] *Some ancient translations* Tamar; *Hebrew unclear.*
[s] *One ancient translation* extending . . . Sea; *Hebrew* having an eastern boundary and a western boundary. [t] *Probable text (see 45.1)* 8 miles; *Hebrew* 4 miles.

Israelites in doing wrong, as the other
members of the tribe of Levi did. 12 So
they are to have a special area next to
the area belonging to the Levites, and it
will be the holiest of all. 13 The Levites
also are to have a special area, south of
that of the priests. It too is to be 10 miles
from east to west, by 4 miles from north
to south. 14 The area dedicated to the
LORD is the best part of all the land, and
none of it may be sold or exchanged or
transferred to anyone else. It is holy and
belongs to the LORD.

15 The part of the special area that is
left, 10 miles by 2 miles, is not holy, but
is for the general use of the people. They
may live there and use the land. The city
is to be in the center of it, 16 and it will be
a square, 2,520 yards on each side. 17 All
around the city on each side there will be
an open space 140 yards across. 18 The
land that is left after the city has been
built in the area immediately to the
south of the holy area—4 miles by 2
miles on the east and 4 miles by 2 miles
on the west—is to be used as farmland
by the people who live in the city. 19 Anyone who lives in the city, no matter
which tribe he comes from, may farm
that land.

20 And so the total area in the center of
the section which was set apart will be a
square measuring 10 miles on each side,
and it will include the area occupied by
the city.

21-22 To the east and to the west of this
area which contains the Temple, the
priests' land, the Levites' land, and the
city, the remaining land belongs to the
ruling prince. It reaches east to the eastern boundary and west to the Mediterranean Sea, and is bounded on the north
by the section belonging to Judah and
on the south by the one belonging to
Benjamin.

Land for the Other Tribes

23-27 South of this special section, each
of the remaining tribes is to receive one
section of land running from the eastern
boundary west to the Mediterranean
Sea, in the following order from north to
south:

Benjamin
Simeon
Issachar
Zebulun
Gad

28 On the south side of the portion
given to the tribe of Gad, the boundary
runs southwest from Tamar to the oasis
of Kadesh, and then northwest along
the Egyptian border to the Mediterranean Sea.

29 The Sovereign LORD said, "That is
the way the land is to be divided into
sections for the tribes of Israel to
possess."

The Gates of Jerusalem

30-34 There are twelve entrances to the
city of Jerusalem. Each of the four walls
measures 2,520 yards and has three
gates in it, each named for one of the
tribes. The gates in the north wall are
named for Reuben, Judah, and Levi;
those in the east wall, for Joseph, Benjamin, and Dan; those in the south wall,
for Simeon, Issachar, and Zebulun; and
those in the west wall are named for
Gad, Asher, and Naphtali. 35 The total
length of the wall on all four sides of the
city is 10,080 yards. The name of the city
from now on will be "The-LORD-Is-Here!"

The Book of
DANIEL

Introduction

The Book of Daniel *was written during a time when the Jews were suffering greatly under the persecution and oppression of a pagan king. Using stories and accounts of visions, the writer encourages the people of his time with the hope that God will bring the tyrant down and restore sovereignty to God's people.*

The book has two main parts: 1) Stories about Daniel and some of his fellow exiles, who through their faith in God and obedience to him triumph over their enemies. These stories are set in the time of the Babylonian and Persian Empires. 2) A series of visions seen by Daniel, which in the form of symbols present the successive rise and fall of several empires, beginning with Babylonia, and predict the downfall of the pagan oppressor and the victory of God's people.

Outline of Contents

THE STORY OF DANIEL AND HIS FRIENDS (1.1 – 6.28)

The Young Men at Nebuchadnezzar's Court

1 In the third year that Jehoiakim
was king of Judah, King Nebuchadnezzar of Babylonia attacked Jerusalem
and surrounded the city. 2 The Lord let
him capture King Jehoiakim and seize
some of the Temple treasures. He took
some prisoners back with him to the
temple of his gods in Babylon, and put
the captured treasures in the temple
storerooms.
3 The king ordered Ashpenaz, his chief
official, to select from among the Israelite exiles some young men of the royal
family and of the noble families. 4 They
had to be handsome, intelligent, well-
trained, quick to learn, and free from
physical defects, so that they would be
qualified to serve in the royal court. Ashpenaz was to teach them to read and
write the Babylonian language. 5 The
king also gave orders that every day
they were to be given the same food and
wine as the members of the royal court.
After three years of this training they
were to appear before the king. 6 Among
those chosen were Daniel, Hananiah,
Mishael, and Azariah, all of whom were
from the tribe of Judah. 7 The chief official gave them new names: Belteshazzar, Shadrach, Meshach, and Abednego.
8 Daniel made up his mind not to let
himself become ritually unclean by eating the food and drinking the wine of the
royal court, so he asked Ashpenaz to
help him, 9 and God made Ashpenaz
sympathetic to Daniel. 10 Ashpenaz,
however, was afraid of the king, so he
said to Daniel, "The king has decided
what you are to eat and drink, and if you
don't look as fit as the other young men,
he may kill me."
11 So Daniel went to the guard whom
Ashpenaz had placed in charge of him
and his three friends. 12 "Test us for ten
days," he said. "Give us vegetables to eat
and water to drink. 13 Then compare us
with the young men who are eating the
food of the royal court, and base your
decision on how we look."
14 He agreed to let them try it for ten
days. 15 When the time was up, they
looked healthier and stronger than all
those who had been eating the royal
food. 16 So from then on the guard let
them continue to eat vegetables instead
of what the king provided.
17 God gave the four young men
knowledge and skill in literature and

philosophy. In addition, he gave Daniel
skill in interpreting visions and dreams.
18 At the end of the three years set by
the king, Ashpenaz took all the young
men to Nebuchadnezzar. 19 The king
talked with them all, and Daniel, Hananiah, Mishael, and Azariah impressed
him more than any of the others. So they
became members of the king's court.
20 No matter what question the king
asked or what problem he raised, these
four knew ten times more than any fortuneteller or magician in his whole kingdom. 21 Daniel remained at the royal
court until Cyrus, the emperor of Persia,
conquered Babylonia.

Nebuchadnezzar's Dream

2 In the second year that Nebuchadnezzar was king, he had a dream. It
worried him so much that he couldn't
sleep, 2 so he sent for his fortunetellers,
magicians, sorcerers, and wizards to
come and explain the dream to him.
When they came and stood before the
king, 3 he said to them, "I'm worried
about a dream I've had. I want to know
what it means."
4 They answered the king in Aramaic,[a] "May Your Majesty live forever!
Tell us your dream, and we will explain
it to you."
5 The king said to them, "I have made
up my mind that you must tell me the
dream and then tell me what it means. If
you can't, I'll have you torn limb from
limb and make your houses a pile of ruins. 6 But if you can tell me both the
dream and its meaning, I will reward
you with gifts and great honor. Now
then, tell me what the dream was and
what it means."
7 They answered the king again, "If
Your Majesty will only tell us what the
dream was, we will explain it."
8 At that, the king exclaimed, "Just as I
thought! You are trying to gain time, because you see that I have made up my
mind 9 to give all of you the same punishment if you don't tell me the dream. You
have agreed among yourselves to go on
telling me lies because you hope that in
time things will change. Tell me what
the dream was, and then I will know that
you can also tell me what it means."
10 The advisers replied, "There is no
one on the face of the earth who can tell
Your Majesty what you want to know.
No king, not even the greatest and most
powerful, has ever made such a demand
of his fortunetellers, magicians, and wizards. 11 What Your Majesty is asking for
is so difficult that no one can do it for
you except the gods, and they do not live
among human beings."
12 At that, the king flew into a rage and
ordered the execution of all the royal advisers in Babylon. 13 So the order was
issued for all of them to be killed,
including Daniel and his friends.

God Shows Daniel What the Dream Means

14 Then Daniel went to Arioch, commander of the king's bodyguard, who
had been ordered to carry out the execution. Choosing his words carefully, 15 he
asked Arioch why the king had issued
such a harsh order. So Arioch told Daniel what had happened.
16 Daniel went at once and obtained
royal permission for more time, so that
he could tell the king what the dream
meant. 17 Then Daniel went home and
told his friends Hananiah, Mishael, and
Azariah what had happened. 18 He told
them to pray to the God of heaven for
mercy and to ask him to explain the
mystery to them so that they would not
be killed along with the other advisers in
Babylon. 19 Then that same night the
mystery was revealed to Daniel in a vision, and he praised the God of heaven:

20 "God is wise and powerful!
Praise him forever and ever.
21 He controls the times and the
seasons;
he makes and unmakes kings;
it is he who gives wisdom and
understanding.
22 He reveals things that are deep
and secret;
he knows what is hidden in
darkness,
and he himself is surrounded by
light.
23 I praise you and honor you, God
of my ancestors.
You have given me wisdom and
strength;
you have answered my prayer

[a] *From here to the end of chapter 7, the language used is Aramaic, not Hebrew.*

and shown us what to tell the
king."

Daniel Tells the King the Dream and Explains It

24 So Daniel went to Arioch, whom the
king had commanded to execute the
royal advisers. He said to him, "Don't
put them to death. Take me to the king,
and I will tell him what his dream
means."
25 At once Arioch took Daniel into
King Nebuchadnezzar's presence and
told the king, "I have found one of the
Jewish exiles who can tell Your Majesty
the meaning of your dream."
26 The king said to Daniel (who was
also called Belteshazzar), "Can you tell
me what I dreamed and what it means?"
27 Daniel replied, "Your Majesty, there
is no wizard, magician, fortuneteller, or
astrologer who can tell you that. 28 But
there is a God in heaven, who reveals
mysteries. He has informed Your Majesty what will happen in the future. Now
I will tell you the dream, the vision you
had while you were asleep.
29 "While Your Majesty was sleeping,
you dreamed about the future; and God,
who reveals mysteries, showed you
what is going to happen. 30 Now, this
mystery was revealed to me, not because I am wiser than anyone else, but
so that Your Majesty may learn the
meaning of your dream and understand
the thoughts that have come to you.
31 "Your Majesty, in your vision you
saw standing before you a giant statue,
bright and shining, and terrifying to
look at. 32 Its head was made of the finest
gold; its chest and arms were made of
silver; its waist and hips of bronze, 33 its
legs of iron, and its feet partly of iron
and partly of clay. 34 While you were
looking at it, a great stone broke loose
from a cliff without anyone touching it,
struck the iron and clay feet of the
statue, and shattered them. 35 At once
the iron, clay, bronze, silver, and gold
crumbled and became like the dust on a
threshing place in summer. The wind
carried it all away, leaving not a trace.
But the stone grew to be a mountain that
covered the whole earth.
36 "This was the dream. Now I will tell
Your Majesty what it means. 37 Your
Majesty, you are the greatest of all
kings. The God of heaven has made you
emperor and given you power, might,
and honor. 38 He has made you ruler of
all the inhabited earth and ruler over all
the animals and birds. You are the head
of gold. 39 After you there will be another
empire, not as great as yours, and after
that a third, an empire of bronze, which
will rule the whole earth. 40 And then
there will be a fourth empire, as strong
as iron, which shatters and breaks
everything. And just as iron shatters
everything, it will shatter and crush all
the earlier empires. 41 You also saw that
the feet and the toes were partly clay
and partly iron. This means that it will
be a divided empire. It will have something of the strength of iron, because
there was iron mixed with the clay.
42 The toes—partly iron and partly
clay—mean that part of the empire will
be strong and part of it weak. 43 You also
saw that the iron was mixed with the
clay. This means that the rulers of that
empire will try to unite their families by
intermarriage, but they will not be able
to, any more than iron can mix with
clay. 44 At the time of those rulers the
God of heaven will establish a kingdom
that will never end. It will never be conquered, but will completely destroy all
those empires and then last forever.
45 You saw how a stone broke loose from
a cliff without anyone touching it and
how it struck the statue made of iron,
bronze, clay, silver, and gold. The great
God is telling Your Majesty what will
happen in the future. I have told you exactly what you dreamed, and have given
you its true meaning."

The King Rewards Daniel

46 Then King Nebuchadnezzar bowed
to the ground and gave orders for sacrifices and offerings to be made to Daniel.
47 The king said, "Your God is the greatest of all gods, the Lord over kings, and
the one who reveals mysteries. I know
this because you have been able to explain this mystery." 48 Then he gave
Daniel a high position, presented him
with many splendid gifts, put him in
charge of the province of Babylon, and
made him the head of all the royal advisers. 49 At Daniel's request the king put
Shadrach, Meshach, and Abednego in
charge of the affairs of the province of

Babylon; Daniel, however, remained at
the royal court.

Nebuchadnezzar Commands Everyone to Worship a Gold Statue

3 King Nebuchadnezzar had a gold
statue made, ninety feet high and
nine feet wide, and he had it set up in the
plain of Dura in the province of Babylon.
2 Then the king gave orders for all his
officials to come together—the princes,
governors, lieutenant governors, commissioners, treasurers, judges, magis-
trates, and all the other officials of the
provinces. They were to attend the dedication of the statue which King Nebuchadnezzar had set up. 3 When all these
officials gathered for the dedication and
stood in front of the statue, 4 a herald announced in a loud voice, "People of all
nations, races, and languages! 5 You will
hear the sound of the trumpets, followed
by the playing of oboes, lyres, zithers,
and harps; and then all the other instruments will join in. As soon as the music
starts, you are to bow down and worship
the gold statue that King Nebuchadnezzar has set up. 6 Anyone who does not
bow down and worship will immediately
be thrown into a blazing furnace." 7 And
so, as soon as they heard the sound of
the instruments, the people of all the nations, races, and languages bowed down
and worshiped the gold statue which
King Nebuchadnezzar had set up.

Daniel's Three Friends Are Accused of Disobedience

8 It was then that some Babylonians
took the opportunity to denounce the
Jews. 9 They said to King Nebuchadnezzar, "May Your Majesty live forever!
10 Your Majesty has issued an order that
as soon as the music starts, everyone is
to bow down and worship the gold
statue, 11 and that anyone who does not
bow down and worship it is to be thrown
into a blazing furnace. 12 There are some
Jews whom you put in charge of the
province of Babylon—Shadrach, Meshach, and Abednego—who are disobeying Your Majesty's orders. They do
not worship your god or bow down to
the statue you set up."

13 At that, the king flew into a rage and
ordered the three men to be brought before him. 14 He said to them, "Shadrach,
Meshach, and Abednego, is it true that
you refuse to worship my god and to
bow down to the gold statue I have set
up? 15 Now then, as soon as you hear the
sound of the trumpets, oboes, lyres, zithers, harps, and all the other instruments,
bow down and worship the statue. If you
do not, you will immediately be thrown
into a blazing furnace. Do you think
there is any god who can save you?"

16 Shadrach, Meshach, and Abednego
answered, "Your Majesty, we will not
try to defend ourselves. 17 If the God
whom we serve is able to save us from
the blazing furnace and from your
power, then he will.[b] 18 But even if he
doesn't, Your Majesty may be sure that
we will not worship your god, and we
will not bow down to the gold statue that
you have set up."

Daniel's Three Friends Are Sentenced to Death

19 Then Nebuchadnezzar lost his temper, and his face turned red with anger
at Shadrach, Meshach, and Abednego.
So he ordered the furnace to be heated
seven times hotter than usual. 20 And he
commanded the strongest men in his
army to tie the three men up and throw
them into the blazing furnace. 21 So they
tied them up, fully dressed—shirts,
robes, caps, and all—and threw them
into the blazing furnace. 22 Now because
the king had given strict orders for the
furnace to be made extremely hot, the
flames burned up the guards who took
the men to the furnace. 23 Then Shadrach, Meshach, and Abednego, still tied
up, fell into the heart of the blazing fire.

24 Suddenly Nebuchadnezzar leaped
to his feet in amazement. He asked his
officials, "Didn't we tie up three men and
throw them into the blazing furnace?"

They answered, "Yes, we did, Your
Majesty."

25 "Then why do I see four men walking around in the fire?" he asked. "They
are not tied up, and they show no sign of
being hurt—and the fourth one looks
like an angel."[c]

[b] If the God . . . will; *or* If it is true that we refuse to worship your god or bow down to the gold statue you set up, the God whom we serve is able to save us from the blazing furnace and from your power—and he will. [c] angel; *or* a son of the gods; *or* a son of God.

The Three Men Are Released and Promoted

26 So Nebuchadnezzar went up to the
door of the blazing furnace and called
out, "Shadrach! Meshach! Abednego!
Servants of the Supreme God! Come
out!" And they came out at once. 27 All
the princes, governors, lieutenant governors, and other officials of the king gathered to look at the three men, who had
not been harmed by the fire. Their hair
was not singed, their clothes were not
burned, and there was no smell of
smoke on them.

28 The king said, "Praise the God of
Shadrach, Meshach, and Abednego! He
sent his angel and rescued these men
who serve and trust him. They disobeyed my orders and risked their lives
rather than bow down and worship any
god except their own.

29 "And now I command that if anyone
of any nation, race, or language speaks
disrespectfully of the God of Shadrach,
Meshach, and Abednego, he is to be torn
limb from limb, and his house is to be
made a pile of ruins. There is no other
god who can rescue like this."

30 And the king promoted Shadrach,
Meshach, and Abednego to higher positions in the province of Babylon.

Nebuchadnezzar's Second Dream

4 King Nebuchadnezzar sent the following message to the people of all
nations, races, and languages in the
world:

"Greetings! 2 Listen to my account of
the wonders and miracles which the Supreme God has shown me.

3 "How great are the wonders God
shows us!
How powerful are the miracles he
performs!
God is king forever; he will rule
for all time.

4 "I was living comfortably in my palace, enjoying great prosperity. 5 But I
had a frightening dream and saw terrifying visions while I was asleep.
6 I ordered all the royal advisers in Babylon to be brought to me so that they
could tell me what the dream meant.
7 Then all the fortunetellers, magicians,
wizards, and astrologers were brought
in, and I told them my dream, but they
could not explain it to me. 8 Then Daniel
came in. (He is also called Belteshazzar,
after the name of my god.) The spirit of
the holy gods[d] is in him, so I told him
what I had dreamed. I said to him: 9 Belteshazzar, chief of the fortunetellers, I
know that the spirit of the holy gods[d] is
in you and that you understand all mysteries. This is[e] my dream. Tell me what
it means.

10 "While I was asleep, I had a vision of
a huge tree in the middle of the earth.
11 It grew bigger and bigger until it
reached the sky and could be seen by
everyone in the world. 12 Its leaves were
beautiful, and it was loaded down with
fruit—enough for the whole world to
eat. Wild animals rested in its shade,
birds built nests in its branches, and
every kind of living being ate its fruit.

13 "While I was thinking about the vision, I saw coming down from heaven an
angel, alert and watchful. 14 He proclaimed in a loud voice, 'Cut the tree
down and chop off its branches; strip off
its leaves and scatter its fruit. Drive the
animals from under it and the birds out
of its branches. 15 But leave the stump in
the ground with a band of iron and
bronze around it. Leave it there in the
field with the grass.

" 'Now let the dew fall on this man,
and let him live with the animals and the
plants. 16 For seven years he will not
have a human mind, but the mind of an
animal. 17 This is the decision of the alert
and watchful angels. So then, let all people everywhere know that the Supreme
God has power over human kingdoms
and that he can give them to anyone he
chooses—even to those who are least
important.'

18 "This is the dream I had," said King
Nebuchadnezzar. "Now, Belteshazzar,
tell me what it means. None of my royal
advisers could tell me, but you can, because the spirit of the holy gods[f] is
in you."

Daniel Explains the Dream

19 At this, Daniel, who is also called
Belteshazzar, was so alarmed that he
could not say anything. The king said to
him, "Belteshazzar, don't let the dream
and its message alarm you."

Belteshazzar replied, "Your Majesty, I

[d] gods; *or* God. [e] *Probable text* This is; *Aramaic* Visions of. [f] gods; *or* God.

wish that the dream and its explanation
applied to your enemies and not to you.
20 The tree, so tall that it reached the sky,
could be seen by everyone in the world.
21 Its leaves were beautiful, and it had
enough fruit on it to feed the whole
world. Wild animals rested under it, and
birds made their nests in its branches.

22 "Your Majesty, you are the tree, tall
and strong. You have grown so great
that you reach the sky, and your power
extends over the whole world. 23 While
Your Majesty was watching, an angel
came down from heaven and said, 'Cut
the tree down and destroy it, but leave
the stump in the ground. Wrap a band of
iron and bronze around it, and leave it
there in the field with the grass. Let the
dew fall on this man, and let him live
there with the animals for seven years.'

24 "This, then, is what it means, Your
Majesty, and this is what the Supreme
God has declared will happen to you.
25 You will be driven away from human
society and will live with wild animals.
For seven years you will eat grass like
an ox and sleep in the open air, where
the dew will fall on you. Then you will
admit that the Supreme God controls all
human kingdoms and that he can give
them to anyone he chooses. 26 The angel
ordered the stump to be left in the
ground. This means that you will become king again when you acknowledge
that God rules all the world. 27 So then,
Your Majesty, follow my advice. Stop
sinning, do what is right, and be merciful to the poor.[g] Then you will continue
to be prosperous."

28 All this did happen to King Nebuchadnezzar. 29 Only twelve months later,
while he was walking around on the roof
of his royal palace in Babylon, 30 he said,
"Look how great Babylon is! I built it as
my capital city to display my power and
might, my glory and majesty."

31 Before the words were out of his
mouth, a voice spoke from heaven,
"King Nebuchadnezzar, listen to what I
say! Your royal power is now taken
away from you. 32 You will be driven
away from human society, live with wild
animals, and eat grass like an ox for
seven years. Then you will acknowledge
that the Supreme God has power over
human kingdoms and that he can give
them to anyone he chooses."

33 The words came true immediately.
Nebuchadnezzar was driven out of human society and ate grass like an ox.
The dew fell on his body, and his hair
grew as long as eagle feathers and his
nails as long as bird claws.

Nebuchadnezzar Praises God

34 "When the seven years had passed,"
said the king, "I looked up at the sky,
and my sanity returned. I praised the Supreme God and gave honor and glory to
the one who lives forever.

"He will rule forever,
and his kingdom will last for
all time.
35 He looks on the people of the
earth as nothing;
angels in heaven and people
on earth
are under his control.
No one can oppose his will
or question what he does.

36 "When my sanity returned, my
honor, my majesty, and the glory of my
kingdom were given back to me. My officials and my noblemen welcomed me,
and I was given back my royal power
with even greater honor than before.

37 "And now, I, Nebuchadnezzar,
praise, honor, and glorify the King of
Heaven. Everything he does is right and
just, and he can humble anyone who
acts proudly."

Belshazzar's Banquet

5 One night King Belshazzar invited
a thousand noblemen to a great
banquet, and they drank wine together.
2 While they were drinking, Belshazzar
gave orders to bring in the gold and silver cups and bowls which his father[h]
Nebuchadnezzar had carried off from
the Temple in Jerusalem. The king sent
for them so that he, his noblemen, his
wives, and his concubines could drink
out of them. 3 At once the gold cups and
bowls were brought in, and they all
drank wine out of them 4 and praised
gods made of gold, silver, bronze, iron,
wood, and stone.

[g] Stop sinning . . . to the poor; *or* Make up for your sins by doing what is right and by being merciful to the poor. [h] *There were several kings of Babylonia between Nebuchadnezzar and Belshazzar.* Father *may mean predecessor, or the name* Nebuchadnezzar *may be used for* Nabonidus.

5 Suddenly a human hand appeared
and began writing on the plaster wall of
the palace, where the light from the
lamps was shining most brightly. And
the king saw the hand as it was writing.
6 He turned pale and was so frightened
that his knees began to shake. 7 He
shouted for someone to bring in the magicians, wizards, and astrologers. When
they came in, the king said to them,
"Anyone who can read this writing and
tell me what it means will be dressed in
robes of royal purple, wear a gold chain
of honor around his neck, and be the
third in power in the kingdom." 8 The
royal advisers came forward, but none
of them could read the writing or tell the
king what it meant. 9 In his distress King
Belshazzar grew even paler, and his noblemen had no idea what to do.

10 The queen mother heard the noise
made by the king and his noblemen and
entered the banquet hall. She said, "May
Your Majesty live forever! Please do not
be so disturbed and look so pale.
11 There is a man in your kingdom who
has the spirit of the holy gods[i] in him.
When your father was king, this man
showed good sense, knowledge, and
wisdom like the wisdom of the gods.
And King Nebuchadnezzar, your
father,[j] made him chief of the fortunetellers, magicians, wizards, and astrologers. 12 He has unusual ability and is
wise and skillful in interpreting dreams,
solving riddles, and explaining mysteries; so send for this man Daniel, whom
the king named Belteshazzar, and he
will tell you what all this means."

Daniel Explains the Writing

13 Daniel was brought at once into the
king's presence, and the king said to
him, "Are you Daniel, that Jewish exile
whom my father the king brought here
from Judah? 14 I have heard that the
spirit of the holy gods[k] is in you and
that you are skillful and have knowledge
and wisdom. 15 The advisers and magicians were brought in to read this writing and tell me what it means, but they
could not discover the meaning. 16 Now I
have heard that you can find hidden
meanings and explain mysteries. If you
can read this writing and tell me what it
means, you will be dressed in robes of
royal purple, wear a gold chain of honor
around your neck, and be the third in
power in the kingdom."

17 Daniel replied, "Keep your gifts for
yourself or give them to someone else. I
will read for Your Majesty what has
been written and tell you what it means.

18 "The Supreme God made your
father Nebuchadnezzar a great king and
gave him dignity and majesty. 19 He was
so great that people of all nations, races,
and languages were afraid of him and
trembled. If he wanted to kill someone,
he did; if he wanted to keep someone
alive, he did. He honored or disgraced
anyone he wanted to. 20 But because he
became proud, stubborn, and cruel, he
was removed from his royal throne and
lost his place of honor. 21 He was driven
away from human society, and his mind
became like that of an animal. He lived
with wild donkeys, ate grass like an ox,
and slept in the open air with nothing to
protect him from the dew. Finally he admitted that the Supreme God controls all
human kingdoms and can give them to
anyone he chooses.

22 "But you, his son, have not humbled
yourself, even though you knew all this.
23 You acted against the Lord of heaven
and brought in the cups and bowls taken
from his Temple. You, your noblemen,
your wives, and your concubines drank
wine out of them and praised gods made
of gold, silver, bronze, iron, wood, and
stone — gods that cannot see or hear and
that do not know anything. But you did
not honor the God who determines
whether you live or die and who controls
everything you do. 24 That is why God
has sent the hand to write these words.

25 "This is what was written: 'Number,
number, weight, divisions.' 26 And this is
what it means: *number,* God has numbered the days of your kingdom and
brought it to an end; 27 *weight,* you have
been weighed on the scales and found to
be too light; 28 *divisions,* your kingdom is
divided up and given to the Medes and
Persians."[l]

29 Immediately Belshazzar ordered his
servants to dress Daniel in a robe of
royal purple and to hang a gold chain of
honor around his neck. And he made

[i] gods; *or* God. [j] your father *(see 5.2).* [k] gods; *or* God. [l] PERSIANS: *In Aramaic the word for "Persians" sounds like the word for "division."*

him the third in power in the kingdom.
30 That same night Belshazzar, the king
of Babylonia, was killed; 31 and Darius
the Mede, who was then sixty-two years
old, seized the royal power.

Daniel in the Pit of Lions

6 Darius decided to appoint a hundred and twenty governors to hold
office throughout his empire. 2 In addition, he chose Daniel and two others to
supervise the governors and to look after the king's interests. 3 Daniel soon
showed that he could do better work
than the other supervisors or the governors. Because he was so outstanding,
the king considered putting him in
charge of the whole empire. 4 Then the
other supervisors and the governors
tried to find something wrong with the
way Daniel administered the empire, but
they couldn't, because Daniel was reliable and did not do anything wrong or
dishonest. 5 They said to each other, "We
are not going to find anything of which
to accuse Daniel unless it is something
in connection with his religion."

6 So they went to see the king and said,
"King Darius, may Your Majesty live
forever! 7 All of us who administer your
empire—the supervisors, the governors,
the lieutenant governors, and the other
officials—have agreed that Your Majesty should issue an order and enforce it
strictly. Give orders that for thirty days
no one be permitted to request anything
from any god or from any human being
except from Your Majesty. Anyone who
violates this order is to be thrown into a
pit filled with lions. 8 So let Your Majesty
issue this order and sign it, and it will be
in force, a law of the Medes and Persians, which cannot be changed." 9 And
so King Darius signed the order. 10 When
Daniel learned that the order had been
signed, he went home. In an upstairs
room of his house there were windows
that faced toward Jerusalem. There, just
as he had always done, he knelt down at
the open windows and prayed to God
three times a day.

11 When Daniel's enemies observed
him praying to God, 12 all of them went
together to the king to accuse Daniel.
They said, "Your Majesty, you signed an
order that for the next thirty days anyone who requested anything from any
god or from any human being except
you, would be thrown into a pit filled
with lions."

The king replied, "Yes, that is a strict
order, a law of the Medes and Persians,
which cannot be changed."

13 Then they said to the king, "Daniel,
one of the exiles from Judah, does not
respect Your Majesty or obey the order
you issued. He prays regularly three
times a day."

14 When the king heard this, he was
upset and did his best to find some way
to rescue Daniel. He kept trying until
sunset. 15 Then Daniel's enemies came
back to the king and said to him, "Your
Majesty knows that according to the
laws of the Medes and Persians no order
which the king issues can be changed."

16 So the king gave orders for Daniel to
be taken and thrown into the pit filled
with lions. He said to Daniel, "May your
God, whom you serve so loyally, rescue
you." 17 A stone was put over the mouth
of the pit, and the king placed his own
royal seal and the seal of his noblemen
on the stone, so that no one could rescue
Daniel. 18 Then the king returned to the
palace and spent a sleepless night, without food or any form of entertainment.

19 At dawn the king got up and hurried
to the pit. 20 When he got there, he called
out anxiously, "Daniel, servant of the
living God! Was the God you serve so
loyally able to save you from the lions?"

21 Daniel answered, "May Your Majesty live forever! 22 God sent his angel to
shut the mouths of the lions so that they
would not hurt me. He did this because
he knew that I was innocent and because I have not wronged you, Your
Majesty."

23 The king was overjoyed and gave
orders for Daniel to be pulled up out of
the pit. So they pulled him up and saw
that he had not been hurt at all, for he
trusted God. 24 Then the king gave orders to arrest all those who had accused
Daniel, and he had them thrown, together with their wives and children,
into the pit filled with lions. Before they
even reached the bottom of the pit, the
lions pounced on them and broke all
their bones.

25 Then King Darius wrote to the people of all nations, races, and languages
on earth:

"Greetings! 26 I command that

throughout my empire everyone should
fear and respect Daniel's God.

"He is a living God,
and he will rule forever.
His kingdom will never be
destroyed,
and his power will never come
to an end.
27 He saves and rescues;
he performs wonders and
miracles
in heaven and on earth.
He saved Daniel from being killed
by the lions."

28 Daniel prospered during the reign of
Darius and the reign of Cyrus the
Persian.

DANIEL DESCRIBES HIS VISIONS (7.1–12.13)

Daniel's Vision of the Four Beasts

7 In the first year that Belshazzar was
king of Babylonia, I had a dream
and saw a vision in the night. I wrote the
dream down, and this is the record 2 of
what I saw that night:
Winds were blowing from all directions and lashing the surface of the
ocean. 3 Four huge beasts came up out of
the ocean, each one different from the
others. 4 The first one looked like a lion,
but had wings like an eagle. While I was watching, the wings were torn off. The beast was lifted up and made to stand up straight. And then a human mind was given to it.
5 The second beast looked like a bear standing on its hind legs. It was holding three ribs between its teeth, and a voice said to it, "Go on, eat as much meat as you can!"
6 While I was watching, another beast appeared. It looked like a leopard, but on its back there were four wings, like the wings of a bird, and it had four heads. It had a look of authority about it.
7 As I was watching, a fourth beast appeared. It was powerful, horrible, terrifying. With its huge iron teeth it crushed its victims, and then it trampled on them. Unlike the other beasts, it had ten horns.
8 While I was staring at the horns, I saw
a little horn coming up among the others. It tore out three of the horns that were already there. This horn had human eyes and a mouth that was boasting proudly.

The Vision of the One Who Has Been Living Forever

9 While I was looking, thrones were put in place. One who had been living forever sat down on one of the thrones. His clothes were white as snow, and his hair was like pure wool. His throne, mounted on fiery wheels, was blazing
with fire, 10 and a stream of fire was
pouring out from it. There were many thousands of people there to serve him, and millions of people stood before him. The court began its session, and the books were opened.
11 While I was looking, I could still
hear the little horn bragging and boasting. As I watched, the fourth beast was killed, and its body was thrown into the
flames and destroyed. 12 The other
beasts had their power taken away, but they were permitted to go on living for a limited time.
13 During this vision in the night, I saw
what looked like a human being. He was approaching me, surrounded by clouds, and he went to the one who had been living forever and was presented to him.
14 He was given authority, honor, and
royal power, so that the people of all nations, races, and languages would serve him. His authority would last forever, and his kingdom would never end.

The Visions Are Explained

15 The visions I saw alarmed me, and I
was deeply disturbed.[m] 16 I went up to
one of those standing there and asked him to explain it all. So he told me the
meaning. 17 He said, "These four huge
beasts are four empires which will arise
on earth. 18 And the people of the Supreme God will receive royal power and keep it forever and ever."
19 Then I wanted to know more about
the fourth beast, which was not like any of the others—the terrifying beast which crushed its victims with its bronze claws and iron teeth and then trampled on
them. 20 And I wanted to know about the
ten horns on its head and the horn that had come up afterward and had made three of the horns fall. It had eyes and a mouth and was boasting proudly. It was

[m] *Aramaic has two additional words, the meaning of which is unclear.*

more terrifying than any of the others.
21 While I was looking, that horn made
war on God's people and conquered
them. 22 Then the one who had been living forever came and pronounced judgment in favor of[n] the people of the
Supreme God. The time had arrived for
God's people to receive royal power.
23 This is the explanation I was given:
"The fourth beast is a fourth empire that
will be on the earth and will be different
from all other empires. It will crush the
whole earth and trample it down. 24 The
ten horns are ten kings who will rule
that empire. Then another king will appear; he will be very different from the
earlier ones and will overthrow three
kings. 25 He will speak against the Supreme God and oppress God's people.
He will try to change their religious laws
and festivals, and God's people will be
under his power for three and a half
years. 26 Then the heavenly court will sit
in judgment, take away his power, and
destroy him completely. 27 The power
and greatness of all the kingdoms on
earth will be given to the people of the
Supreme God. Their royal power will
never end, and all rulers on earth will
serve and obey them."
28 This is the end of the account. I was
so frightened that I turned pale, and I
kept everything to myself.

Daniel's Vision of a Ram and a Goat

8 In the third year that Belshazzar
was king, I saw a second vision.[o]
2 In the vision I suddenly found myself in
the walled city of Susa in the province of
Elam. I was standing by the Ulai River,
3 and there beside the river I saw a ram
that had two long horns, one of which
was longer and newer than the other.
4 I watched the ram butting with his
horns to the west, the north, and the
south. No animal could stop him or escape his power. He did as he pleased and
grew arrogant.
5 While I was wondering what this
meant, a goat came rushing out of the
west, moving so fast that his feet didn't
touch the ground. He had one prominent
horn between his eyes. 6 He came toward
the ram, which I had seen standing beside the river, and rushed at him with all
his force. 7 I watched him attack the
ram. He was so angry that he smashed
into him and broke the two horns. The
ram had no strength to resist. He was
thrown to the ground and trampled on,
and there was no one who could
save him.
8 The goat grew more and more arrogant, but at the height of his power his
horn was broken. In its place four prominent horns came up, each pointing in a
different direction. 9 Out of one of these
four horns grew a little horn, whose
power extended toward the south and
the east and toward the Promised Land.
10 It grew strong enough to attack the
army of heaven, the stars themselves,
and it threw some of them to the ground
and trampled on them. 11 It even defied
the Prince of the heavenly army,
stopped the daily sacrifices offered to
him, and ruined the Temple. 12 People
sinned there instead of offering the
proper daily sacrifices,[p] and true religion was thrown to the ground. The
horn was successful in everything it did.
13 Then I heard one angel ask another,
"How long will these things that were
seen in the vision continue? How long
will an awful sin replace the daily sacrifices? How long will the army of heaven
and the Temple be trampled on?"
14 I heard the other angel answer, "It
will continue for 2,300 evenings and
mornings, during which sacrifices will
not be offered. Then the Temple will be
restored."

The Angel Gabriel Explains the Vision

15 I was trying to understand what the
vision meant, when suddenly someone
was standing in front of me. 16 I heard a
voice call out over the Ulai River, "Gabriel, explain to him the meaning of
what he saw." 17 Gabriel came and stood
beside me, and I was so terrified that I
fell to the ground.
He said to me, "Mortal man, understand the meaning. The vision has to do
with the end of the world." 18 While he
was talking, I fell to the ground unconscious. But he took hold of me, raised me
to my feet, 19 and said, "I am showing

[n] pronounced judgment in favor of; *or* gave the right to judge to. [o] *Beginning at 8.1, the rest of this book is in Hebrew (see 2.4).* [p] People . . . sacrifices; *Hebrew unclear.*

you what the result of God's anger will
be. The vision refers to the time of
the end.
20 “The ram you saw that had two
horns represents the kingdoms of Media
and Persia. 21 The goat represents the
kingdom of Greece, and the prominent
horn between his eyes is the first king.
22 The four horns that came up when the
first horn was broken represent the four
kingdoms into which that nation will be
divided and which will not be as strong
as the first kingdom.
23 “When the end of those kingdoms is
near and they have become so wicked
that they must be punished, there will be
a stubborn, vicious, and deceitful king.
24 He will grow strong—but not by his
own power. He will cause terrible destruction and be successful in everything he does. He will bring destruction
on powerful men and on God's own people. 25 Because he is cunning, he will succeed in his deceitful ways. He will be
proud of himself and destroy many people without warning. He will even defy
the greatest King of all, but he will be
destroyed without the use of any human
power. 26 This vision about the evening
and morning sacrifices which has been
explained to you will come true. But
keep it secret now, because it will be a
long time before it does come true.”
27 I was depressed and ill for several
days. Then I got up and went back to the
work that the king had assigned to me,
but I was puzzled by the vision and
could not understand it.

Daniel Prays for His People

9 Darius the Mede, who was the son
of Xerxes, ruled over the kingdom
of Babylonia. 2 In the first year of his
reign I was studying the sacred books
and thinking about the seventy years
that Jerusalem would be in ruins, according to what the LORD had told the
prophet Jeremiah. 3 And I prayed earnestly to the Lord God, pleading with
him, fasting, wearing sackcloth, and sitting in ashes. 4 I prayed to the LORD my
God and confessed the sins of my
people.
I said, “Lord God, you are great, and
we honor you. You are faithful to your
covenant and show constant love to
those who love you and do what you
command.
5 “We have sinned, we have been evil,
we have done wrong. We have rejected
what you commanded us to do and have
turned away from what you showed us
was right. 6 We have not listened to your
servants the prophets, who spoke in
your name to our kings, our rulers, our
ancestors, and our whole nation. 7 You,
Lord, always do what is right, but we
have always brought disgrace on ourselves. This is true of all of us who live in
Judea and in Jerusalem and of all the
Israelites whom you scattered in countries near and far because they were unfaithful to you. 8 Our kings, our rulers,
and our ancestors have acted shamefully and sinned against you, Lord. 9 You
are merciful and forgiving, although we
have rebelled against you. 10 We did not
listen to you, O LORD our God, when you
told us to live according to the laws
which you gave us through your servants the prophets. 11 All Israel broke
your laws and refused to listen to what
you said. We sinned against you, and so
you brought on us the curses that are
written in the Law of Moses, your servant. 12 You did what you said you would
do to us and our rulers. You punished
Jerusalem more severely than any other
city on earth, 13 giving us all the punishment described in the Law of Moses. But
even now, O LORD our God, we have not
tried to please you by turning from our
sins or by following your truth. 14 You,
O LORD our God, were prepared to punish us, and you did, because you always
do what is right, and we did not listen
to you.
15 “O Lord our God, you showed your
power by bringing your people out of
Egypt, and your power is still remembered. We have sinned; we have done
wrong. 16 You have defended us in the
past, so do not be angry with Jerusalem
any longer. It is your city, your sacred
hill.[q] All the people in the neighboring
countries look down on Jerusalem and
on your people because of our sins and
the evil our ancestors did. 17 O God, hear
my prayer and pleading. Restore your
Temple, which has been destroyed; restore it so that everyone will know that
you are God. 18 Listen to us, O God; look

[q] SACRED HILL: *Mount Zion (see Zion in Word List).*

at us and see the trouble we are in and the suffering of the city that bears your name. We are praying to you because you are merciful, not because we have done right. 19 Lord, hear us. Lord, forgive us. Lord, listen to us, and act! In order that everyone will know that you are God, do not delay! This city and these people are yours."

Gabriel Explains the Prophecy

20 I went on praying, confessing my sins and the sins of my people Israel and pleading with the LORD my God to restore his holy Temple. 21 While I was praying, Gabriel, whom I had seen in the earlier vision, came flying down to where I was. It was the time for the evening sacrifice to be offered. 22 He explained, "Daniel, I have come here to help you understand the prophecy. 23 When you began to plead with God, he answered you. He loves you, and so I have come to tell you the answer. Now pay attention while I explain the vision.

24 "Seven times seventy years is the length of time God has set for freeing your people and your holy city from sin and evil. Sin will be forgiven and eternal justice established, so that the vision and the prophecy will come true, and the holy Temple[r] will be rededicated. 25 Note this and understand it: From the time the command is given to rebuild Jerusalem until God's chosen leader comes, seven times seven years will pass. Jerusalem will be rebuilt with streets and strong defenses, and will stand for seven times sixty-two years, but this will be a time of troubles. 26 And at the end of that time God's chosen leader will be killed unjustly.[s] The city and the Temple will be destroyed by the invading army of a powerful ruler. The end will come like a flood, bringing the war and destruction which God has prepared. 27 That ruler will have a firm agreement with many people for seven years, and when half this time is past, he will put an end to sacrifices and offerings. The Awful Horror[t] will be placed on the highest point of the Temple and will remain there until the one who put it there meets the end which God has prepared for him."

Daniel's Vision by the Tigris River

10 In the third year that Cyrus was emperor of Persia, a message was revealed to Daniel, who is also called Belteshazzar. The message was true but extremely hard to understand.[u] It was explained to him in a vision.

2 At that time I was mourning for three weeks. 3 I did not eat any rich food or any meat, drink any wine, or comb my hair until the three weeks were past.

4 On the twenty-fourth day of the first month of the year I was standing on the bank of the mighty Tigris River. 5 I looked up and saw someone who was wearing linen clothes and a belt of fine gold. 6 His body shone like a jewel. His face was as bright as a flash of lightning, and his eyes blazed like fire. His arms and legs shone like polished bronze, and his voice sounded like the roar of a great crowd.

7 I was the only one who saw the vision. Those who were with me did not see anything, but they were terrified and ran and hid. 8 I was left there alone, watching this amazing vision. I had no strength left, and my face was so changed that no one could have recognized me. 9 When I heard his voice, I fell to the ground unconscious and lay there face downward. 10 Then a hand took hold of me and raised me to my hands and knees; I was still trembling.

11 The angel said to me, "Daniel, God loves you. Stand up and listen carefully to what I am going to say. I have been sent to you." When he had said this, I stood up, still trembling.

12 Then he said, "Daniel, don't be afraid. God has heard your prayers ever since the first day you decided to humble yourself in order to gain understanding. I have come in answer to your prayer. 13 The angel prince of the kingdom of Persia opposed me for twenty-one days. Then Michael, one of the chief angels, came to help me, because I had been left there alone in Persia. 14 I have come to make you understand what will happen to your people in the future. This is a vision about the future."

15 When he said this, I stared at the ground, speechless. 16 Then the angel,

[r] Temple; *or* altar. [s] *One ancient translation* unjustly; *Hebrew unclear.* [t] THE AWFUL HORROR: *A pagan image set up in the Jerusalem Temple by foreign conquerors (see 1 Macc 1.54-61).*
[u] but extremely hard to understand; *or* and it was about a great war.

who looked like a human being, reached
out and touched my lips. I said to him,
"Sir, this vision makes me so weak that
I can't stop trembling. 17 I am like a slave
standing before his master. How can I
talk to you? I have no strength or breath
left in me."
18 Once more he took hold of me, and I
felt stronger. 19 He said, "God loves you,
so don't let anything worry you or
frighten you."
When he had said this, I felt even
stronger and said, "Sir, tell me what you
have to say. You have made me feel
better."
20-21 He said, "Do you know why I
came to you? It is to reveal to you what
is written in the Book of Truth. Now I
have to go back and fight the guardian
angel of Persia. After that the guardian
angel of Greece will appear. There is no
one to help me except Michael, Israel's
11 guardian angel.[v] 1 He is[w] responsible for helping and defending me. 2 And what I am now going
to tell you is true."

The Kingdoms of Egypt and Syria

The angel said, "Three more kings will
rule over Persia, followed by a fourth,
who will be richer than all the others. At
the height of his power and wealth he
will challenge the kingdom of Greece.
3 "Then a heroic king will appear. He
will rule over a huge empire and do
whatever he wants. 4 But at the height of
his power his empire will break up and
be divided into four parts. Kings not descended from him will rule in his place,
but they will not have the power that
he had.
5 "The king of Egypt will be strong.
One of his generals, however, will be
even stronger and rule a greater kingdom. 6 After a number of years the king
of Egypt will make an alliance with the
king of Syria and give him his daughter
in marriage. But the alliance will not
last, and she, her husband, her child,[x]
and the servants who went with her will
all be killed. 7 Soon afterward one of her
relatives will become king. He will attack the army of the king of Syria, enter
their fortress, and defeat them. 8 He will
carry back to Egypt the images of their
gods and the articles of gold and silver
dedicated to those gods. After several
years of peace 9 the king of Syria will
invade Egypt, but he will be forced to
retreat.
10 "The sons of the king of Syria will
prepare for war and gather a large army.
One of them will sweep on like a flood
and attack an enemy fortress. 11 In his
anger the king of Egypt will go to war
against the king of Syria and capture his
huge army. 12 He will be proud of his victory and of the many soldiers he has
killed, but he will not continue to be victorious.
13 "The king of Syria will go back and
gather a larger army than he had before.
When the proper time comes, he will return with a large, well-equipped army.
14 Then many people will rebel against
the king of Egypt. And some violent people from your nation, Daniel, will rebel
because of a vision they have seen, but
they will be defeated. 15 So the king of
Syria will lay siege to a fortified city and
capture it. The soldiers of Egypt will not
continue to fight; even the best of them
will not have enough strength. 16 The
Syrian invader will do with them as he
pleases, without opposition. He will
stand in the Promised Land and have it
completely in his power.
17 "The king of Syria will plan an expedition, using his whole army. Then, in
order to destroy his enemy's kingdom,
he will make an alliance with him and
offer him his daughter[y] in marriage; but
his plan will not succeed. 18 After that he
will attack the nations by the sea and
conquer many of them. But a foreign
leader will defeat him and put an end to
his arrogance; indeed he will turn the arrogance of Syria's king back on him.[z]
19 The king will return to the fortresses
of his own land, but he will be defeated,
and that will be the end of him.
20 "He will be followed by another
king, who will send an officer to oppress
the people with taxes in order to increase the wealth of his kingdom. In a
short time that king will be killed, but
not publicly and not in battle."

[v] *Probable text* guardian angel; *Hebrew* guardian angel. And I, in the first year of Darius the Mede.
[w] *One ancient translation* He is; *Hebrew* I am. [x] *Some ancient translations* her child; *Hebrew* her father. [y] his daughter; *or* a young woman. [z] *Probable text* his arrogance . . . on him; *Hebrew unclear.*

The Evil King of Syria

21 The angel went on to explain: "The
next king of Syria will be an evil man
who has no right to be king, but he will
come unexpectedly and seize power by
trickery. 22 Anyone who opposes him,
even God's High Priest, will be swept
away and wiped out. 23 By making
treaties, he will deceive other nations,
and he will grow stronger and stronger,
even though he rules only a small nation. 24 He will invade a wealthy province without warning and will do things
that none of his ancestors ever did. Then
he will divide among his followers the
goods and property he has captured in
war. He will make plans to attack fortresses, but his time will soon run out.
25 "He will boldly raise a large army to
attack the king of Egypt, who will prepare to fight back with a huge and powerful army. But the king of Egypt will be
deceived and will not be successful.
26 His closest advisers will ruin him.
Many of his soldiers will be killed, and
his army will be wiped out. 27 Then the
two kings will sit down to eat at the
same table, but their motives will be evil,
and they will lie to each other. They will
not get what they want, because the time
for it has not yet come. 28 The king of
Syria will return home with all the loot
he has captured, determined to destroy
the religion of God's people. He will do
as he pleases and then return to his own
land.

29 "Later on he will invade Egypt
again, but this time things will turn out
differently. 30 The Romans will come in
ships and oppose him, and he will be
frightened.

"Then he will turn back in a rage and
try to destroy the religion of God's people. He will follow the advice of those
who have abandoned that religion.
31 Some of his soldiers will make the
Temple ritually unclean. They will stop
the daily sacrifices and set up The Awful
Horror.[a] 32 By deceit the king will win
the support of those who have already
abandoned their religion, but those who
follow God will fight back. 33 Wise leaders of the people will share their wisdom
with many others. But for a while some
of them will be killed in battle or be
burned to death, and some will be
robbed and made prisoners. 34 While the
killing is going on, God's people will receive a little help, even though many
who join them will do so for selfish reasons. 35 Some of those wise leaders will
be killed, but as a result of this the people will be purified. This will continue
until the end comes, the time that God
has set.

36 "The king of Syria will do as he
pleases. He will boast that he is greater
than any god, superior even to the Supreme God. He will be able to do this
until the time when God punishes him.
God will do exactly what he has
planned. 37 The king will ignore the god
his ancestors served, and also the god
that women love. In fact, he will ignore
every god, because he will think he is
greater than any of them. 38 Instead, he
will honor the god who protects fortresses. He will offer gold, silver, jewels,
and other rich gifts to a god his ancestors never worshiped. 39 To defend his
fortresses, he will use people who worship a foreign god. He will give great
honor to those who accept him as ruler,
put them into high offices, and give them
land as a reward.

40 "When the king of Syria's final hour
has almost come, the king of Egypt will
attack him, and the king of Syria will
fight back with all his power, using chariots, horses, and many ships. He will invade many countries, like the waters of
a flood. 41 He will even invade the Promised Land and kill tens of thousands, but
the countries of Edom, Moab, and what
is left of Ammon will escape. 42 When he
invades all those countries, even Egypt
will not be spared. 43 He will take away
Egypt's hidden treasures of gold and silver and its other prized possessions. He
will conquer Libya and Ethiopia.[b]
44 Then news that comes from the east
and the north will frighten him, and he
will fight furiously, killing many people.
45 He will even set up his huge royal tents
between the sea and the mountain on
which the Temple stands. But he will
die, with no one there to help him."

[a] THE AWFUL HORROR: *See 9.27.* [b] *Hebrew* Cush: *Cush is the ancient name of the extensive territory south of the First Cataract of the Nile River. This region was called Ethiopia in Graeco-Roman times, and included within its borders most of modern Sudan and some of present-day Ethiopia (Abyssinia).*

The Time of the End

12 The angel wearing linen clothes
said, "At that time the great angel Michael, who guards your people,
will appear. Then there will be a time of
troubles, the worst since nations first
came into existence. When that time
comes, all the people of your nation
whose names are written in God's book
will be saved. 2 Many of those who have
already died will live again: some will
enjoy eternal life, and some will suffer
eternal disgrace. 3 The wise leaders will
shine with all the brightness of the sky.
And those who have taught many people
to do what is right will shine like the
stars forever."
4 He said to me, "And now, Daniel,
close the book and put a seal on it until
the end of the world. Meanwhile, many
people will waste their efforts trying to
understand what is happening."
5 Then I saw two men standing by a
river, one on each bank. 6 One of them
asked the angel who was standing further upstream, "How long will it be until
these amazing events come to an end?"
7 The angel raised both hands toward
the sky and made a solemn promise in
the name of the Eternal God. I heard him
say, "It will be three and a half years.
When the persecution of God's people
ends, all these things will have happened."
8 I heard what he said, but I did not
understand it. So I asked, "But, sir, how
will it all end?"
9 He answered, "You must go now,
Daniel, because these words are to be
kept secret and hidden until the end
comes. 10 Many people will be purified.
Those who are wicked will not understand but will go on being wicked; only
those who are wise will understand.
11 "From the time the daily sacrifices
are stopped, that is, from the time of The
Awful Horror,[c] 1,290 days will pass.
12 Happy are those who remain faithful
until 1,335 days are over!
13 "And you, Daniel, be faithful to the
end. Then you will die, but you will rise
to receive your reward at the end of
time."

[c] THE AWFUL HORROR: *See 9.27.*

The Book of HOSEA

Introduction

The prophet Hosea preached in the northern kingdom of Israel, after the prophet Amos, during the troubled times before the fall of Samaria in 721 B.C. He was especially concerned about the idolatry of the people and their faithlessness toward God. Hosea boldly pictured this faithlessness in terms of his own disastrous marriage to an unfaithful woman. Just as his wife Gomer turned out to be unfaithful to him, so God's people had deserted the Lord. For this, judgment would fall on Israel. Yet in the end God's constant love for his people would prevail, and he would win the nation back to himself and restore the relationship. This love is expressed in the moving words: "How can I give you up, Israel? How can I abandon you? . . . My heart will not let me do it! My love for you is too strong" (11.8).

Outline of Contents

1 This is the message which the LORD
gave Hosea son of Beeri during the
time that Uzziah, Jotham, Ahaz, and
Hezekiah were kings of Judah, and Jeroboam son of Jehoash was king of Israel.

Hosea's Wife and Children

2 When the LORD first spoke to Israel
through Hosea, he said to Hosea, "Go
and get married; your wife will be unfaithful, and your children will be just
like her.[a] In the same way my people
have left me and become unfaithful."
3 So Hosea married a woman named
Gomer, the daughter of Diblaim. After
the birth of their first child, a son, 4 the
LORD said to Hosea, "Name him 'Jezreel,'
because it will not be long before I punish the king of Israel for the murders
that his ancestor Jehu committed at Jezreel.[b] I am going to put an end to Jehu's
dynasty.[c] 5 And in Jezreel Valley I will
at that time destroy Israel's military
power."
6 Gomer had a second child—this time
it was a daughter. The LORD said to Hosea, "Name her 'Unloved,' because I will
no longer show love to the people of Israel or forgive them. 7 But to the people
of Judah I will show love. I, the LORD
their God, will save them, but I will not
do it by war—with swords or bows and
arrows or with horses and horsemen."
8 After Gomer had weaned her daughter, she became pregnant again and had
another son. 9 The LORD said to Hosea,
"Name him 'Not-My-People,' because
the people of Israel are not my people,
and I am not their God."

Israel Is to Be Restored

10 The people of Israel will become like
the sand of the sea, more than can be
counted or measured. Now God says to
them, "You are not my people," but the
day is coming when he will say to them,
"You are the children of the living God!"
11 The people of Judah and the people of
Israel will be reunited. They will choose
for themselves a single leader, and once
again they will grow and prosper in their
land. Yes, the day of Jezreel[d] will be a

2 great day! 1 So call your fellow Israelites "God's People" and "Loved-
by-the-Lord."

Unfaithful Gomer — Unfaithful Israel

2 My children, plead with your
mother—though she is no longer a wife
to me, and I am no longer her husband.
Plead with her to stop her adultery and
prostitution. 3 If she does not, I will strip
her as naked as she was on the day she
was born. I will make her like a dry and
barren land, and she will die of thirst.
4-5 I will not show mercy to her children;
they are the children of a shameless
prostitute.[e] She herself said, "I will go
to my lovers—they give me food and
water, wool and linen, olive oil and
wine."
6 So I am going to fence her in with
thorn bushes and build a wall to block
her way. 7 She will run after her lovers
but will not catch them. She will look for
them but will not find them. Then she
will say, "I am going back to my first
husband—I was better off then than I
am now."
8 She would never acknowledge that I
am the one who gave her the grain, the
wine, the olive oil, and all the silver and
gold that she used in the worship of
Baal. 9 So at harvest time I will take back
my gifts of grain and wine, and will take
away the wool and the linen I gave her
for clothing. 10 I will strip her naked in
front of her lovers, and no one will be
able to save her from my power. 11 I will
put an end to all her festivities—her annual and monthly festivals and her Sabbath celebrations—all her religious
meetings. 12 I will destroy her grapevines and her fig trees, which she said
her lovers gave her for serving them. I
will turn her vineyards and orchards
into a wilderness; wild animals will destroy them. 13 I will punish her for the
times that she forgot me, when she
burned incense to Baal and put on her
jewelry to go chasing after her lovers.
The LORD has spoken.

[a] get married; your wife ... her; *or* marry a prostitute, and have children by her who will be just as bad as she is. [b] JEZREEL: *At this city Jehu assassinated the king of Israel and all the rest of the royal family, and became the first king of a new dynasty (see 2 K 9–10).* [c] Jehu's dynasty; *or* the kingdom of Israel. [d] JEZREEL: *This name in Hebrew means "God sows" and suggests growth and prosperity.* [e] the children of a shameless prostitute; *or* as shameless as their mother, a prostitute.

The LORD's Love for His People

14 So I am going to take her into the
desert again; there I will win her back
with words of love. 15 I will give back to
her the vineyards she had and make
Trouble Valley a door of hope. She will
respond to me there as she did when she
was young, when she came from Egypt.
16 Then once again she will call me her
husband—she will no longer call me her
Baal.[f] 17 I will never let her speak the
name of Baal again.

18 At that time I will make a covenant
with all the wild animals and birds, so
that they will not harm my people. I will
also remove all weapons of war from the
land, all swords and bows, and will let
my people live in peace and safety.

19 Israel, I will make you my wife;
I will be true and faithful;
I will show you constant love
and mercy
and make you mine forever.
20 I will keep my promise and make
you mine,
and you will acknowledge me as
LORD.
21-22 At that time I will answer the
prayers of my people Israel.[g]
I will make rain fall on the
earth,
and the earth will produce grain
and grapes and olives.
23 I will establish my people in the
land and make them prosper.
I will show love to those who were
called "Unloved,"
and to those who were called
"Not-My-People"
I will say, "You are my people,"
and they will answer, "You are
our God."

Hosea and the Unfaithful Woman

3 The LORD said to me, "Go again[h]
and show your love for a woman
who is committing adultery with a lover.
You must love her just as I still love the
people of Israel, even though they turn
to other gods and like to take offerings
of raisins to idols."[i]
2 So I paid fifteen pieces of silver and
seven bushels of barley to buy her.
3 I told her that for a long time she would
have to wait for me without being a
prostitute or committing adultery; and
during this time I would wait for her. 4 In
just this way the people of Israel will
have to live for a long time without kings
or leaders, without sacrifices or sacred
stone pillars, without idols or images to
use for divination. 5 But the time will
come when the people of Israel will once
again turn to the LORD their God and to a
descendant of David their king. Then
they will fear the LORD and will receive
his good gifts.

The LORD's Accusation against Israel

4 The LORD has an accusation to bring
against the people who live in this
land. Listen, Israel, to what he says:
"There is no faithfulness or love in the
land, and the people do not acknowledge me as God. 2 They make promises
and break them; they lie, murder, steal,
and commit adultery. Crimes increase,
and there is one murder after another.
3 And so the land will dry up, and everything that lives on it will die. All the animals and birds, and even the fish,
will die."

The LORD Accuses the Priests

4 The LORD says, "Let no one accuse the
people or reprimand them—my complaint is against you priests.[j] 5 Night
and day you blunder on, and the prophets do no better than you. I am going to
destroy Israel, your mother. 6 My people
are doomed because they do not acknowledge me. You priests have refused
to acknowledge me and have rejected
my teaching, and so I reject you and will
not acknowledge your sons as my
priests.

7 "The more of you priests there are,
the more you sin against me, and so I
will turn your honor into disgrace. 8 You
grow rich from the sins of my people,
and so you want them to sin more and
more. 9 You will suffer the same punishment as the people! I will punish you and

[f] BAAL: *This title of the Canaanite god means "Lord"; another meaning of the word is "husband."* [g] ISRAEL: *The Hebrew text here refers to Israel as Jezreel (see 1.4, 11).*
[h] The LORD . . . again; or The LORD spoke to me again. He said, "Go . . ." [i] OFFERINGS OF RAISINS TO IDOLS: *Dried grapes were used in the worship of fertility gods, who were believed to give abundant harvests to their worshipers.* [j] *Probable text* my complaint is against you priests; *Hebrew* your people are like those with a complaint against the priests.

make you pay for the evil you do. 10 You
will eat your share of the sacrifices, but
still be hungry. You will worship the fertility gods, but still have no children, because you have turned away from me to
follow other gods."

The Lord Condemns Pagan Worship

11 The Lord says, "Wine, both old and
new, is robbing my people of their
senses! 12 They ask for revelations from
a piece of wood! A stick tells them what
they want to know! They have left me.
Like a woman who becomes a prostitute, they have given themselves to other
gods. 13 At sacred places on the mountaintops they offer sacrifices, and on the
hills they burn incense under tall,
spreading trees, because the shade is so
pleasant!

"As a result, your daughters serve as
prostitutes, and your daughters-in-law
commit adultery. 14 Yet I will not punish
them for this, because you yourselves go
off with temple prostitutes,[k] and together with them you offer pagan sacrifices. As the proverb says, 'A people
without sense will be ruined.'

15 "Even though you people of Israel
are unfaithful to me, may Judah not be
guilty of the same thing. Don't worship
at Gilgal or Bethaven,[l] or make promises there in the name of the living Lord.
16 The people of Israel are as stubborn as
mules. How can I feed them like lambs
in a meadow? 17 The people of Israel are
under the spell of idols. Let them go
their own way. 18 After drinking much
wine, they delight in their prostitution,
preferring disgrace to honor. 19 They will
be carried away as by the wind, and they
will be ashamed of their pagan sacrifices.[m,n]

5 "Listen to this, you priests! Pay attention, people of Israel! Listen, you
that belong to the royal family! You are
supposed to judge with justice—so judgment will fall on you! You have become
a trap at Mizpah, a net spread on Mount
Tabor, 2 a deep pit at Acacia City,[o] and
I will punish all of you. 3 I know what
Israel is like—she cannot hide from me.
She has been unfaithful, and her people
are unfit to worship me."

Hosea Warns against Idolatry

4 The evil that the people have done
keeps them from returning to their God.
Idolatry has a powerful hold on them,
and they do not acknowledge the Lord.
5 The arrogance of the people of Israel
cries out against them. Their sins make
them stumble and fall, and the people of
Judah fall with them. 6 They take their
sheep and cattle to offer as sacrifices to
the Lord, but it does them no good. They
cannot find him, for he has left them.
7 They have been unfaithful to the Lord;
their children do not belong to him. So
now they and their lands will soon be
destroyed.

War between Judah and Israel

8 Blow the war trumpets in Gibeah!
Sound the alarm in Ramah! Raise the
war cry at Bethaven![p] Into battle, men
of Benjamin! 9 The day of punishment is
coming, and Israel will be ruined. People
of Israel, this will surely happen!

10 The Lord says, "I am angry because
the leaders of Judah have invaded Israel
and stolen land from her. So I will pour
out punishment on them like a flood.
11 Israel is suffering oppression; she has
lost land that was rightfully hers, because she insisted on going for help to
those who had none to give.[q] 12 I will
bring destruction on Israel and ruin on
the people of Judah.

13 "When Israel saw how sick she was
and when Judah saw her own wounds,
then Israel went to Assyria to ask the
great emperor for help, but he could not
cure them or heal their wounds. 14 I will
attack the people of Israel and Judah
like a lion. I myself will tear them to
pieces and then leave them. When I drag
them off, no one will be able to save
them.

15 "I will abandon my people until they

[k] TEMPLE PROSTITUTES: *These women were found in Canaanite temples, where fertility gods were worshiped. It was believed that intercourse with these prostitutes assured fertile fields and herds.* [l] BETHAVEN: *This name means "house of evil" or "house of idolatry" and in this passage refers to the city of Bethel, a name which means "house of God." See also 10.8.*
[m] sacrifices; *some ancient translations* altars. [n] *Verses 17-19 in Hebrew are unclear.*
[o] *Probable text* a deep pit at Acacia City; *Hebrew unclear.* [p] BETHAVEN: *This name means "house of evil" or "house of idolatry" and in this passage refers to the city of Bethel, a name which means "house of God." See also 10.8.* [q] *Probable text* those who had none to give; *Hebrew* command.

have suffered enough for their sins and
come looking for me. Perhaps in their
suffering they will try to find me."

The People's Insincere Repentance

6 The people say, "Let's return to the
LORD! He has hurt us, but he will be
sure to heal us; he has wounded us, but
he will bandage our wounds, won't he?
2 In two or three days he will revive us,
and we will live in his presence. 3 Let us
try to know the LORD. He will come to us
as surely as the day dawns, as surely as
the spring rains fall upon the earth."
4 But the LORD says, "Israel and Judah,
what am I going to do with you? Your
love for me disappears as quickly as
morning mist; it is like dew, that vanishes early in the day. 5 That is why I
have sent my prophets to you with my
message of judgment and destruction.
What I want from you is plain and clear:
6 I want your constant love, not your animal sacrifices. I would rather have my
people know me than burn offerings
to me.
7 "But as soon as they entered the land
at Adam,[r] they broke the covenant I
had made with them. 8 Gilead is a city
full of evil people and murderers. 9 The
priests are like a gang of robbers who
wait in ambush for someone. Even on
the road to the holy place at Shechem
they commit murder. And they do all
this evil deliberately! 10 I have seen a
horrible thing in Israel: my people have
defiled themselves by worshiping idols.
11 "And as for you, people of Judah, I
have set a time to punish you also for
what you are doing.

7 "Whenever I want to heal my people Israel and make them prosperous again, all I can see is their
wickedness and the evil they do. They
cheat one another; they break into
houses and steal; they rob people in the
streets. 2 It never enters their heads that
I will remember all this evil; but their
sins surround them, and I cannot avoid
seeing them."

Conspiracy in the Palace

3 The LORD says, "People deceive the
king and his officers by their evil plots.
4 They are all treacherous and disloyal.
Their hatred smolders like the fire in an
oven, which is not stirred by the baker
until the dough is ready to bake. 5 On the
day of the king's celebration they made
the king and his officials drunk and foolish with wine. 6 Yes, they burned[s] like
an oven with their plotting. All night
their anger smoldered, and in the morning it burst into flames.
7 "In the heat of their anger they murdered their rulers. Their kings have been
assassinated one after another, but no
one prays to me for help."

Israel and the Nations

8 The LORD says, "The people of Israel
are like a half-baked loaf of bread. They
rely on the nations around them 9 and do
not realize that this reliance on foreigners has robbed them of their strength.
Their days are numbered, but they don't
even know it. 10 The arrogance of the
people of Israel cries out against them.
In spite of everything that has happened,
they have not returned to me, the LORD
their God. 11 Israel flits around like a
silly pigeon; first her people call on
Egypt for help, and then they run to Assyria! 12 But I will spread out a net and
catch them like birds as they go by. I will
punish them for the evil they have
done.[t]
13 "They are doomed! They have left
me and rebelled against me. They will be
destroyed. I wanted to save them, but
their worship of me was false. 14 They
have not prayed to me sincerely, but instead they throw themselves down and
wail as the heathen do. When they pray
for grain and wine, they gash themselves like pagans. What rebels they are!
15 Even though I was the one who
brought them up and made them strong,
they plotted against me. 16 They keep on
turning away from me to a god that is
powerless.[u] They are as unreliable as a
crooked bow. Because their leaders talk
arrogantly, they will die a violent death,
and the Egyptians will laugh."

The LORD Condemns Israel for Idol Worship

8 The LORD says, "Sound the alarm!
Enemies are swooping down on my
land like eagles! My people have broken

[r] *Probable text* But . . . at Adam; *Hebrew* But like Adam. [s] *One ancient translation* burned; *Hebrew* drew near. [t] *Probable text* the evil they have done; *Hebrew* the report to their congregation. [u] *Probable text* a god that is powerless; *Hebrew unclear.*

the covenant I made with them and have
rebelled against my teaching. 2Even
though they call me their God and claim
that they are my people and that they
know me, 3they have rejected what is
good. Because of this their enemies will
pursue them.
4"My people chose kings, but they did
it on their own. They appointed leaders,
but without my approval. They took
their silver and gold and made idols—
for their own destruction. 5I hate the
gold bull worshiped by the people of the
city of Samaria. I am furious with them.
How long will it be before they give up
their idolatry? 6An Israelite craftsman
made the idol, and it is not a god at all!
The gold bull worshiped in Samaria will
be smashed to pieces! 7When they sow
the wind, they will reap a storm! A field
of grain that doesn't ripen can never
produce any bread. But even if it did,
foreigners would eat it up. 8Israel has
become like any other nation and is as
useless as a broken pot. 9Stubborn as
wild donkeys, the people of Israel
go their own way. They have gone
off to seek help from Assyria and
have paid other nations to protect
them. 10But now I am going to gather
them together and punish them.
Soon they will writhe in pain when the
emperor of Assyria oppresses
them.
11"The more altars the people of Israel
build for removing sin, the more places
they have for sinning! 12I write down
countless teachings for the people, but
they reject them as strange and foreign.
13They offer sacrifices to me and eat the
meat of the sacrifices.[v] But I, the LORD,
am not pleased with them, and now I
will remember their sin and punish
them for it; I will send them back to
Egypt!
14"The people of Israel have built palaces, but they have forgotten their own
Maker. The people of Judah have built
fortified cities. But I will send fire that
will burn down their palaces and their
cities."

Hosea Announces Punishment for Israel

9 People of Israel, stop celebrating
your festivals like pagans. You
have turned away from your God and
have been unfaithful to him. All over the
land you have sold yourselves like prostitutes to the god Baal and have loved
the grain you thought he paid you with!
2But soon you will not have enough
grain and olive oil, and there will be no
wine. 3The people of Israel will not remain in the LORD's land, but will have to
go back to Egypt and will have to eat
forbidden food[w] in Assyria. 4In those
foreign lands they will not be able to
make wine offerings to the LORD or bring
their sacrifices to him. Their food will
defile everyone who eats it, like food
eaten at funerals. It will be used only to
satisfy their hunger; none of it will be
taken as an offering to the LORD's Temple. 5And when the time comes for the
appointed festivals in honor of the LORD,
what will they do then? 6When the disaster comes and the people are scattered, the Egyptians will gather them
up—gather them for burial there at
Memphis! Their treasures of silver and
the places where their homes once stood
will be overgrown with weeds and thorn
bushes.
7The time for punishment has come,
the time when people will get what they
deserve. When that happens, Israel will
know it! "This prophet," you say, "is a
fool. This inspired man is insane." You
people hate me so much because your
sin is so great. 8God has sent me as a
prophet to warn his people Israel. Yet
wherever I go, you try to trap me like a
bird. Even in God's Temple the people
are the prophet's enemies. 9They are
hopelessly evil in what they do, just as
they were at Gibeah.[x] God will remember their sin and punish them for it.

Israel's Sin and Its Consequences

10The LORD says, "When I first found
Israel, it was like finding grapes growing in the desert. When I first saw your
ancestors, it was like seeing the first ripe
figs of the season. But when they came

[v] They offer . . . the sacrifices; *Hebrew unclear.* [w] FORBIDDEN FOOD: *The Law of Moses prohibited the eating of certain foods as being ritually unclean (see Lv 11).* [x] GIBEAH: *At this city some Israelites of the tribe of Benjamin raped a Levite's concubine; this caused a civil war that almost wiped out the Benjaminites (see Jg 19–21).*

to Mount Peor, they began to worship
Baal and soon became as disgusting as
the gods they loved. 11 Israel's greatness
will fly away like a bird, and there will
be no more children born to them, no
more women pregnant, no more children conceived. 12 But even if they did
bring up children, I would take them
away and not leave one alive. When I
abandon these people, terrible things
will happen to them."
13 LORD, I can see their children being
hunted down[y] and killed. 14 What shall I
ask you to do to these people? Make
their women barren! Make them unable
to nurse their babies!

The LORD's Judgment on Israel

15 The LORD says, "All their evildoing
began in Gilgal. It was there that I began
to hate them. And because of the evil
they have done, I will drive them out of
my land. I will not love them any more;
all their leaders have rebelled against
me. 16 The people of Israel are like a
plant whose roots have dried up and
which bears no fruit. They will have no
children, but even if they did, I would
kill the children so dear to them."

The Prophet Speaks about Israel

17 The God I serve will reject his people, because they have not listened to
him. They will become wanderers
10 among the nations. 1 The people
of Israel were like a grapevine
that was full of grapes. The more prosperous they were, the more altars they
built. The more productive their land
was, the more beautiful they made the
sacred stone pillars they worship. 2 The
people whose hearts are deceitful must
now suffer for their sins. God will break
down their altars and destroy their sacred pillars.
3 These people will soon be saying,
"We have no king because we did not
fear the LORD. But what could a king do
for us anyway?" 4 They utter empty
words and make false promises and useless treaties. Justice has become injustice, growing like poisonous weeds in a
plowed field.
5 The people who live in the city of Samaria will be afraid and will mourn the
loss of the gold bull[z] at Bethaven.[a]
They and the priests who serve the idol
will weep over it. They will wail when it
is stripped of its golden splendor. 6 The
idol will be carried off to Assyria as tribute to the great emperor. The people of
Israel will be disgraced and put to shame
because of the advice they followed.
7 Their king will be carried off, like a
chip of wood on water. 8 The hilltop
shrines of Aven,[a] where the people of
Israel worship idols, will be destroyed.
Thorns and weeds will grow up over
their altars. The people will call out to
the mountains, "Hide us!" and to the
hills, "Cover us!"

The LORD Pronounces Judgment on Israel

9 The LORD says, "The people of Israel
have not stopped sinning against me
since the time of their sin at Gibeah.[b] So
at Gibeah war will catch up with them.
10 I will attack[c] this sinful people and
punish them. Nations will join together
against them, and they will be punished
for their many sins.
11 "Israel was once like a well-trained
young cow, ready and willing to thresh
grain. But I decided to put a yoke[d] on
her beautiful neck and to harness her for
harder work. I made Judah pull the plow
and Israel pull the harrow. 12 I said,
'Plow new ground for yourselves, plant
righteousness, and reap the blessings
that your devotion to me will produce. It
is time for you to turn to me, your LORD,
and I will come and pour out blessings
upon you.' 13 But instead you planted evil
and reaped its harvest. You have eaten
the fruit produced by your lies.
"Because you trusted in your chariots[e] and in the large number of your
soldiers, 14 war will come to your people,
and all your fortresses will be destroyed.
It will be like the day when King Shal-
man destroyed the city of Betharbel in
battle, and mothers and their children

[y] *Probable text* being hunted down; *Hebrew unclear.* [z] *Some ancient translations* bull; *Hebrew* cows. [a] BETHAVEN: *This name means "house of evil" or "house of idolatry" and in this passage refers to the city of Bethel, a name which means "house of God." In verse 8, Bethaven is called Aven. See also 4.15 and 5.8.* [b] GIBEAH: *See 9.9.* [c] *One ancient translation* I will attack; *Hebrew* In my desire. [d] *Probable text* put a yoke; *Hebrew* spare.
[e] *One ancient translation* chariots; *Hebrew* way.

were crushed to death. 15 That is what
will happen to you, people of Bethel, because of the terrible evil that you have
done. As soon as the battle begins, the
king of Israel will die."

God's Love for His Rebellious People

11 The LORD says,
"When Israel was a child, I
loved him
and called him out of Egypt as
my son.[f]
2 But the more I[g] called to him,
the more he turned away
from me.[h]
My people sacrificed to Baal;
they burned incense to idols.
3 Yet I was the one who taught
Israel to walk.
I took my people up in my arms,[i]
but they did not acknowledge
that I took care of them.
4 I drew them to me with affection
and love.
I picked them up and held them
to my cheek;
I bent down to them and fed
them.[j]

5 "They refuse to return to me, and so
they must return to Egypt, and Assyria
will rule them. 6 War will sweep through
their cities and break down the city
gates. It will destroy my people because
they do what they themselves think best.
7 They insist on turning away from me.
They will cry out because of the yoke
that is on them, but no one will lift it
from them.[k]

8 "How can I give you up, Israel?
How can I abandon you?
Could I ever destroy you as I did
Admah,
or treat you as I did Zeboiim?
My heart will not let me do it!
My love for you is too strong.
9 I will not punish you in my anger;
I will not destroy Israel again.
For I am God and not a mere
human being.
I, the Holy One, am with you.
I will not come to you in anger.

10 "My people will follow me when I
roar like a lion at their enemies. They
will hurry to me from the west. 11 They
will come from Egypt, as swiftly as
birds, and from Assyria, like doves. I
will bring them to their homes again. I,
the LORD, have spoken."

Israel and Judah Are Condemned

12 The LORD says, "The people of Israel
have surrounded me with lies and deceit, and the people of Judah are still rebelling against me, the faithful and holy
12 God. 1 Everything that the people
of Israel do from morning to
night is useless and destructive. Treachery and acts of violence increase among
them. They make treaties with Assyria
and do business with Egypt."
2 The LORD has an accusation to bring
against the people of Judah; he is also
going to punish Israel for the way her
people act. He will pay them back for
what they have done. 3 Their ancestor
Jacob struggled with his twin brother
Esau while the two of them were still in
their mother's womb; when Jacob grew
up, he fought against God — 4 he fought
against an angel and won. He wept and
asked for a blessing. And at Bethel God
came to our ancestor Jacob and spoke
with him.[l] 5 This was the LORD God
Almighty — the LORD is the name by
which he is to be worshiped. 6 So now,
descendants of Jacob, trust in your God
and return to him. Be loyal and just, and
wait patiently for your God to act.

Further Words of Judgment

7 The LORD says, "The people of Israel
are as dishonest as the Canaanites; they
love to cheat their customers with false
scales. 8 'We are rich,' they say. 'We've
made a fortune. And no one can accuse
us of getting rich dishonestly.' 9 But I, the
LORD your God who led you out of Egypt,
I will make you live in tents again, as
you did when I came to you in the desert.
10 "I spoke to the prophets and gave
them many visions, and through the
prophets I gave my people warnings.
11 Yet idols are worshiped in Gilead, and
those who worship them will die. Bulls
are sacrificed in Gilgal, and the altars

[f] him, and called him . . . son; *or* him; from the time he left Egypt I have called him my son.
[g] *One ancient translation* I; *Hebrew* they. [h] *One ancient translation* me; *Hebrew* them.
[i] *One ancient translation* I . . . my arms; *Hebrew* He . . . his arms. [j] *Verse 4 in Hebrew is unclear.* [k] *Verse 7 in Hebrew is unclear.* [l] *Some ancient translations* him; *Hebrew* us.

there will become piles of stone in the open fields."

12 Our ancestor Jacob had to flee to Mesopotamia, where, in order to get a wife, he worked for another man and took care of his sheep. 13 The LORD sent a prophet to rescue the people of Israel from slavery in Egypt and to take care of them. 14 The people of Israel have made the LORD bitterly angry; they deserve death for their crimes. Their Lord will punish them for the disgrace they have brought on him.

Final Judgment on Israel

13 In the past, when the tribe of Ephraim spoke, the other tribes of Israel were afraid; they looked up to Ephraim. But the people sinned by worshiping Baal, and for this they will die. 2 They still keep on sinning by making metal images to worship—idols of silver, designed by human minds, made by human hands. And then they say, "Offer sacrifices to them!" How can anyone kiss those idols—idols in the shape of bulls![m] 3 And so these people will disappear like morning mist, like the dew that vanishes early in the day. They will be like chaff which the wind blows from the threshing place, like smoke from a chimney.

4 The LORD says, "I am the LORD your God, who led you out of Egypt. You have no God but me. I alone am your savior. 5 I took care of you in a dry, desert land. 6 But when you entered the good land, you became full and satisfied, and then you grew proud and forgot me. 7 So I will attack you like a lion. Like a leopard I will lie in wait along your path. 8 I will attack you like a bear that has lost her cubs, and I will tear you open. Like a lion I will devour you on the spot, and will tear you to pieces like a wild animal.

9 "I will destroy you, people of Israel! Then who can help you?[n] 10 You asked for a king and for leaders, but how can they save the nation?[o] 11 In my anger I have given you kings, and in my fury I have taken them away.

12 "Israel's sin and guilt are on record, and the records are safely stored away. 13 Israel has a chance to live, but is too foolish to take it—like a child about to be born, who refuses to come out of the womb. 14 I will not save this people from the world of the dead or rescue them from the power of death. Bring on[p] your plagues, death! Bring on[p] your destruction, world of the dead! I will no longer have pity for this people. 15 Even though Israel flourishes like weeds,[q] I will send a hot east wind from the desert, and it will dry up their springs and wells. It will take away everything of value. 16 Samaria must be punished for rebelling against me. Her people will die in war; babies will be dashed to the ground, and pregnant women will be ripped open."

Hosea's Plea to Israel

14 Return to the LORD your God, people of Israel. Your sin has made you stumble and fall. 2 Return to the LORD, and let this prayer be your offering to him: "Forgive all our sins and accept our prayer, and we will praise you as we have promised. 3 Assyria can never save us, and war horses cannot protect us. We will never again say to our idols that they are our God. O LORD, you show mercy to those who have no one else to turn to."

The LORD Promises New Life for Israel

4 The LORD says,
"I will bring my people back
to me.
I will love them with all my heart;
no longer am I angry with them.
5 I will be to the people of Israel
like rain in a dry land.
They will blossom like flowers;
they will be firmly rooted
like the trees of Lebanon.
6 They will be alive with new
growth,
and beautiful like olive trees.
They will be fragrant
like the cedars of Lebanon.
7 Once again they will live under
my protection.
They will grow crops of grain
and be fruitful like a vineyard.
They will be as famous as the
wine of Lebanon.

[m] *Probable text* And then they . . . bulls!; *Hebrew unclear.* [n] *One ancient translation* who can help you?; *Hebrew* in me is your help. [o] *Verse 10 in Hebrew is unclear.* [p] *Some ancient translations* Bring on; *Hebrew* I will be. [q] *Probable text* like weeds; *Hebrew* among brothers.

8 The people of Israel[r] will have
nothing more to do with idols;
I will answer their prayers and
take care of them.
Like an evergreen tree I will
shelter them;
I am the source of all their
blessings."

r One ancient translation The people of Israel; *Hebrew* Israel, I.

Conclusion

9 May those who are wise understand
what is written here, and may they take
it to heart. The LORD's ways are right,
and righteous people live by following
them, but sinners stumble and fall because they ignore them.

The Book of JOEL

Introduction

Little is known about the prophet Joel, and it is not clear just when he lived. But it seems likely that the book comes from the fifth or fourth century B.C., during the time of the Persian Empire. Joel describes a terrible invasion of locusts and a devastating drought in Palestine. In these events he sees a sign of the coming day of the Lord, a time when the Lord will punish those who oppose his righteous will. The prophet conveys the Lord's call to the people to repent, and his promise of restoration and blessing for his people. Noteworthy is the promise that God will send his Spirit upon all the people, men and women, young and old alike.

Outline of Contents

---

1 This is the LORD's message to Joel
son of Pethuel.

The People Mourn the Destruction of the Crops

2 Pay attention, you older people;
everyone in Judah, listen.
Has anything like this ever
happened
in your time or the time of your
ancestors?
3 Tell your children about it;
they will tell their children,
who in turn will tell the next
generation.

4 Swarm after swarm of locusts
settled on the crops;
what one swarm left, the next
swarm devoured.
5 Wake up and weep, you
drunkards;
cry, you wine-drinkers;
the grapes for making new wine
have been destroyed.

6 An army of locusts has attacked
our land;
they are powerful and too many
to count;
their teeth are as sharp as those
of a lion.
7 They have destroyed our
grapevines
and chewed up our fig trees.
They have stripped off the bark,
till the branches are white.

8 Cry, you people, like a young
woman who mourns the death
of the man she was going to
marry.
9 There is no grain or wine to offer
in the Temple;

the priests mourn because they
have no offerings for the LORD.
10 The fields are bare;
the ground mourns
because the grain is destroyed,
the grapes are dried up,
and the olive trees are withered.

11 Grieve, you farmers;
cry, you that take care of the
vineyards,
because the wheat, the barley,
yes all the crops are destroyed.
12 The grapevines and fig trees have
withered;
all the fruit trees have wilted
and died.
The joy of the people is gone.
13 Put on sackcloth and weep,
you priests who serve at the
altar!
Go into the Temple and mourn all
night!
There is no grain or wine to offer
your God.
14 Give orders for a fast;
call an assembly!
Gather the leaders
and all the people of Judah
into the Temple of the LORD
your God
and cry out to him!
15 The day of the LORD is near,
the day when the Almighty
brings destruction.
What terror that day will bring!

16 We look on helpless as our crops
are destroyed.
There is no joy in the Temple of
our God.
17 The seeds die in the dry earth.
There is no grain to be stored,
and so the empty granaries are
in ruins.
18 The cattle are bellowing in distress
because there is no pasture for
them;
the flocks of sheep also suffer.
19 I cry out to you, LORD,
because the pastures and trees
are dried up,
as though a fire had burned
them.
20 Even the wild animals cry out
to you
because the streams have
become dry.

The Locusts as a Warning of the Day of the LORD

2 Blow the trumpet; sound the
alarm
on Zion, God's sacred hill.[a]
Tremble, people of Judah!
The day of the LORD is coming
soon.
2 It will be a dark and gloomy day,
a black and cloudy day.
The great army of locusts
advances
like darkness spreading over the
mountains.
There has never been anything
like it,
and there never will be again.

3 Like fire they eat up the plants.
In front of them the land is like
the Garden of Eden,
but behind them it is a barren
desert.
Nothing escapes them.
4 They look like horses;
they run like war-horses.
5 As they leap on the tops of the
mountains,
they rattle like chariots;
they crackle like dry grass on
fire.
They are lined up like a great
army ready for battle.
6 As they approach, everyone is
terrified;
every face turns pale.
7 They attack like warriors;
they climb the walls like
soldiers.
They all keep marching straight
ahead
and do not change direction
8 or get in each other's way.
They swarm through defenses,
and nothing can stop them.
9 They rush against the city;
they run over the walls;
they climb up the houses
and go in through the windows
like thieves.

10 The earth shakes as they advance;
the sky trembles.

[a] SACRED HILL: *Mount Zion (see Zion in Word List).*

The sun and the moon grow dark,
and the stars no longer shine.
11 The LORD thunders commands to
his army.
The troops that obey him
are many and mighty.
How terrible is the day of the
LORD!
Who will survive it?

A Call to Repentance

12 "But even now," says the LORD,
"repent sincerely and return
to me
with fasting and weeping and
mourning.
13 Let your broken heart show your
sorrow;
tearing your clothes is not
enough."

Come back to the LORD your God.
He is kind and full of mercy;
he is patient and keeps his
promise;
he is always ready to forgive
and not punish.
14 Perhaps the LORD your God will
change his mind
and bless you with abundant
crops.
Then you can offer him grain and
wine.
15 Blow the trumpet on Mount Zion;
give orders for a fast and call an
assembly!
16 Gather the people together;
prepare them for a sacred
meeting;
bring the old people;
gather the children
and the babies too.
Even newly married couples
must leave their homes and
come.
17 The priests, serving the LORD
between the altar and the
entrance of the Temple,
must weep and pray:
"Have pity on your people, LORD.
Do not let other nations despise
us and mock us
by saying, 'Where is
your God?' "

God Restores Fertility to the Land

18 Then the LORD showed concern for
his land;
he had mercy on his people.
19 He answered them:
"Now I am going to give you
grain and wine and olive oil,
and you will be satisfied.
Other nations will no longer
despise you.
20 I will remove the locust army that
came from the north
and will drive some of them into
the desert.
Their front ranks will be driven
into the Dead Sea,
their rear ranks into the
Mediterranean.
Their dead bodies will stink.
I will destroy them because of all
they have done to you.
21 "Fields, don't be afraid,
but be joyful and glad
because of all the LORD has done
for you.
22 Animals, don't be afraid.
The pastures are green;
the trees bear their fruit,
and there are plenty of figs and
grapes.
23 "Be glad, people of Zion,
rejoice at what the LORD your
God has done for you.
He has given you the right
amount of autumn rain;[b]
he has poured down the winter
rain for you
and the spring rain as before.
24 The threshing places will be full of
grain;
the pits beside the presses will
overflow with wine and
olive oil.
25 I will give you back what you lost
in the years when swarms of
locusts ate your crops.
It was I who sent this army
against you.
26 Now you will have plenty to eat,
and be satisfied.
You will praise the LORD
your God,
who has done wonderful things
for you.

[b] right amount of autumn rain; *or* autumn rain because he is just.

My people will never be
despised again.
27 Then, Israel, you will know that
I am among you
and that I, the LORD, am
your God
and there is no other.
My people will never be
despised again.

The Day of the LORD

28 "Afterward I will pour out my
Spirit on everyone:
your sons and daughters will
proclaim my message;
your old people will have
dreams,
and your young people will see
visions.
29 At that time I will pour out my
Spirit
even on servants, both men and
women.

30 "I will give warnings of that day
in the sky and on the earth;
there will be bloodshed, fire, and
clouds of smoke.
31 The sun will be darkened,
and the moon will turn red as
blood
before the great and terrible day
of the LORD comes.
32 But all who ask the LORD for help
will be saved.
As the LORD has said,
'Some in Jerusalem will escape;
those whom I choose will
survive.' "

God Will Judge the Nations

3 The LORD says,
"At that time I will restore
the prosperity of Judah and
Jerusalem.
2 I will gather all the nations
and bring them to the Valley of
Judgment.
There I will judge them
for all they have done to my
people.
They have scattered the Israelites
in foreign countries
and divided Israel, my land.
3 They threw dice to decide
who would get the captives.
They sold boys and girls into
slavery
to pay for prostitutes and wine.

4 "What are you trying to do to me,
Tyre, Sidon, and all of Philistia? Are you
trying to pay me back for something? If
you are, I will quickly pay you back!
5 You have taken my silver and gold and
carried my rich treasures into your temples. 6 You have taken the people of Judah and Jerusalem far from their own
country and sold them to the Greeks.
7 Now I am going to bring them out of the
places to which you have sold them. I
will do to you what you have done to
them. 8 I will let your sons and daughters
be sold to the people of Judah; they will
sell them to the far-off Sabeans. I, the
LORD, have spoken.

9 "Make this announcement among
the nations:
'Prepare for war;
call your warriors;
gather all your soldiers and
march!
10 Hammer the points of your plows
into swords
and your pruning knives into
spears.
Even the weak must fight.
11 Hurry[c] and come,
all you surrounding nations,
and gather in the valley.' "

Send down, O LORD, your army to
attack them!

12 "The nations must get ready
and come to the Valley of
Judgment.
There I, the LORD, will sit to judge
all the surrounding nations.
13 They are very wicked;
cut them down like grain
at harvest time;
crush them as grapes are crushed
in a full wine press
until the wine runs over."

14 Thousands and thousands
are in the Valley of Judgment.
It is there that the day of the LORD
will soon come.

[c] *Probable text* Hurry; *Hebrew* Help.

15The sun and the moon grow dark,
and the stars no longer shine.

God Will Bless His People

16The LORD roars from Mount Zion;
his voice thunders from
Jerusalem;
earth and sky tremble.
But he will defend his people.
17"Then, Israel, you will know that I
am the LORD your God.
I live on Zion, my sacred hill.
Jerusalem will be a sacred city;
foreigners will never conquer it
again.
18At that time the mountains will be
covered with vineyards,
and cattle will be found on every
hill;
there will be plenty of water for
all of Judah.
A stream will flow from the
Temple of the LORD,
and it will water Acacia Valley.

19"Egypt will become a desert,
and Edom a ruined waste,
because they attacked the land of
Judah
and killed its innocent
people.
20-21I will avenge[d] those who were
killed;
I will not spare the guilty.
But Judah and Jerusalem will be
inhabited forever,
and I, the LORD, will live on
Mount Zion."

[d] *Some ancient translations* avenge; *Hebrew* declare innocent.

The Book of AMOS

Introduction

Amos was the first prophet in the Bible whose message was recorded at length. Although he came from a town in Judah, he preached to the people of the northern kingdom of Israel, about the middle of the eighth century B.C. It was a time of great prosperity, notable religious piety, and apparent security. But Amos saw that prosperity was limited to the wealthy, and that it fed on injustice and on oppression of the poor. Religious observance was insincere, and security more apparent than real. With passion and courage he preached that God would punish the nation. He called for justice to "flow like a stream," and said, "Perhaps the Lord will be merciful to the people of this nation who are still left alive" (5.15).

Outline of Contents

---

1 These are the words of Amos, a
shepherd from the town of Tekoa.
Two years before the earthquake, when
Uzziah was king of Judah and Jeroboam
son of Jehoash was king of Israel, God
revealed to Amos all these things about
Israel.
2Amos said,

"The LORD roars from Mount
Zion;
his voice thunders from
Jerusalem.
The pastures dry up,
and the grass on Mount Carmel
turns brown."

God's Judgment on Israel's Neighbors

Syria

3The LORD says, "The people of Damascus have sinned again and again,
and for this I will certainly punish them.
They treated the people of Gilead with
savage cruelty. 4So I will send fire upon
the palace built by King Hazael and I
will burn down the fortresses of King
Benhadad. 5I will smash the city gates
of Damascus and remove the inhabitants of Aven Valley and the ruler of
Betheden. The people of Syria will be
taken away as prisoners to the land
of Kir."

Philistia

6The LORD says, "The people of Gaza
have sinned again and again, and for
this I will certainly punish them. They
carried off a whole nation and sold them
as slaves to the people of Edom. 7So I
will send fire upon the city walls of Gaza
and burn down its fortresses. 8I will remove the rulers of the cities of Ashdod
and Ashkelon. I will punish the city of
Ekron, and all the Philistines who are
left will die."

Tyre

9The LORD says, "The people of Tyre
have sinned again and again, and for
this I will certainly punish them. They
carried off a whole nation into exile in
the land of Edom, and did not keep the
treaty of friendship they had made. 10So
I will send fire upon the city walls of
Tyre and burn down its fortresses."

Edom

11The LORD says, "The people of Edom
have sinned again and again, and for
this I will certainly punish them. They
hunted down their relatives,[a] the Israelites, and showed them no mercy. Their
anger had no limits, and they never let it
die. 12So I will send fire upon the city of
Teman and burn down the fortresses of
Bozrah."

Ammon

13The LORD says, "The people of Ammon have sinned again and again, and
for this I will certainly punish them. In
their wars for more territory they even
ripped open pregnant women in Gilead.
14So I will send fire upon the city walls
of Rabbah and burn down its fortresses.
Then there will be shouts on the day of
battle, and the fighting will rage like a
storm. 15Their king and his officers will
go into exile."

Moab

2 The LORD says, "The people of Moab
have sinned again and again, and
for this I will certainly punish them.
They dishonored the bones of the king
of Edom by burning them to ashes.
2I will send fire upon the land of Moab
and burn down the fortresses of Kerioth.
The people of Moab will die in the noise
of battle while soldiers are shouting and
trumpets are sounding. 3I will kill the
ruler of Moab and all the leaders of the
land."

Judah

4The LORD says, "The people of Judah
have sinned again and again, and for
this I will certainly punish them. They
have despised my teachings and have
not kept my commands. They have been
led astray by the same false gods that
their ancestors served. 5So I will send
fire upon Judah and burn down the fortresses of Jerusalem."

God's Judgment on Israel

6The LORD says, "The people of Israel
have sinned again and again, and for
this I will certainly punish them. They
sell into slavery honest people who cannot pay their debts, the poor who cannot
repay even the price of a pair of sandals.
7They trample[b] down the weak and
helpless and push the poor out of the
way. A man and his father have intercourse with the same slave woman, and
so profane my holy name. 8At every
place of worship people sleep on clothing that they have taken from the poor
as security for debts. In the temple of
their God they drink wine which they
have taken from those who owe them
money.
9"And yet, my people, it was for your
sake that I totally destroyed the Amorites, who were as tall as cedar trees and
as strong as oaks. 10I brought you out of

[a] THEIR RELATIVES: *The Israelites were descended from Jacob, who was the brother of Esau, the ancestor of the Edomites.* [b] trample; *Hebrew unclear.*

Egypt, led you through the desert for
forty years, and gave you the land of the
Amorites to be your own. 11 I chose some
of your sons to be prophets and some of
your young men to be nazirites.[c] Isn't
this true, people of Israel? I, the LORD,
have spoken. 12 But you made the nazirites drink wine, and ordered the prophets not to speak my message. 13 And now
I will crush you to the ground, and you
will groan like a cart loaded with grain.
14 Not even fast runners will escape;
strong men will lose their strength, and
soldiers will not be able to save their
own lives. 15 Archers will not stand their
ground, fast runners will not get away,
and men on horses will not escape with
their lives. 16 On that day even the bravest soldiers will drop their weapons and
run." The LORD has spoken.

3 People of Israel, listen to this message which the LORD has spoken
about you, the entire nation that he
brought out of Egypt: 2 "Of all the nations on earth, you are the only one I
have known and cared for. That is what
makes your sins so terrible, and that is
why I must punish you for them."

The Prophet's Task

3 Do two people start traveling together without arranging to meet?
4 Does a lion roar in the forest unless
he has found a victim?
Does a young lion growl in his den unless he has caught something?
5 Does a bird get caught in a trap if the
trap has not been baited?
Does a trap spring unless something
sets it off?
6 Does the war trumpet sound in a city
without making the people afraid?
Does disaster strike a city unless the
LORD sends it?
7 The Sovereign LORD never does anything without revealing his plan to his
servants, the prophets.
8 When a lion roars, who can keep
from being afraid?
When the Sovereign LORD speaks, who
can keep from proclaiming his message?

The Doom of Samaria

9 Announce to those who live in the
palaces of Egypt and Ashdod: "Gather
together in the hills around Samaria and
see the great disorder and the crimes being committed there."
10 The LORD says, "These people fill
their mansions with things taken by
crime and violence. They don't even
know how to be honest. 11 And so an enemy will surround their land, destroy
their defenses, and plunder their
mansions."
12 The LORD says, "As a shepherd re-
covers only two legs or an ear of a sheep
that a lion has eaten, so only a few will
survive of Samaria's people, who now
recline on luxurious couches.[d] 13 Listen
now, and warn the descendants of Jacob," says the Sovereign LORD Almighty.
14 "On the day when I punish the people
of Israel for their sins, I will destroy the
altars of Bethel. The corners of every altar will be broken off and will fall to the
ground. 15 I will destroy winter houses
and summer houses. The houses decorated with ivory will fall in ruins; every
large house will be destroyed."

4 Listen to this, you women of Samaria, who grow fat like the well-
fed cows of Bashan, who mistreat the
weak, oppress the poor, and demand
that your husbands keep you supplied
with liquor! 2 As the Sovereign LORD is
holy, he has promised, "The days will
come when they will drag you away
with hooks; every one of you will be like
a fish on a hook. 3 You will be dragged to
the nearest break in the wall and
thrown out."[e]

Israel's Failure to Learn

4 The Sovereign LORD says, "People of
Israel, go to the holy place in Bethel and
sin, if you must! Go to Gilgal and sin
with all your might! Go ahead and bring
animals to be sacrificed morning after
morning, and bring your tithes every
third day. 5 Go on and offer your bread
in thanksgiving to God, and brag about
the extra offerings you bring! This is the
kind of thing you love to do.
6 "I was the one who brought famine to
all your cities, yet you did not come back
to me. 7 I kept it from raining when your
crops needed it most. I sent rain on one
city, but not on another. Rain fell on one
field, but another field dried up. 8 Weak

[c] NAZIRITES: *Israelites who showed their devotion to God by taking vows not to drink wine or beer or cut their hair or touch corpses (see Nu 6.1-8).* [d] luxurious couches; *Hebrew unclear.* [e] *Hebrew has an additional word, the meaning of which is unclear.*

with thirst, the people of several cities
went to a city where they hoped to find
water, but there was not enough to
drink. Still you did not come back to me.
9 "I sent a scorching wind to dry up
your crops. The locusts ate up all your
gardens and vineyards, your fig trees
and olive trees. Still you did not come
back to me.
10 "I sent a plague on you like the one
I sent on Egypt. I killed your young men
in battle and took your horses away. I
filled your nostrils with the stink of dead
bodies in your camps. Still you did not
come back to me.
11 "I destroyed some of you as I destroyed Sodom and Gomorrah. Those of
you who survived were like a burning
stick saved from a fire. Still you did not
come back to me," says the LORD. 12 "So
then, people of Israel, I am going to punish you. And because I am going to do
this, get ready to face my judgment!"

13 God is the one who made the
 mountains
 and created the winds.
He makes his thoughts known to
 people;
 he changes day into night.
 He walks on the heights of the
 earth.
This is his name: the LORD God
 Almighty!

A Call to Repentance

5 Listen, people of Israel, to this funeral song which I sing over you:

2 Virgin Israel has fallen,
Never to rise again!
She lies abandoned on the ground,
And no one helps her up.

3 The Sovereign LORD says, "A city in
Israel sends out a thousand soldiers, but
only a hundred return; another city
sends out a hundred, but only ten come
back."
4 The LORD says to the people of Israel,
"Come to me, and you will live. 5 Do not
go to Beersheba to worship. Do not try
to find me at Bethel—Bethel will come
to nothing. Do not go to Gilgal—her people are doomed to exile."
6 Go to the LORD, and you will live. If
you do not go, he will sweep down like
fire on the people of Israel. The fire will
burn up the people of Bethel, and no one
will be able to put it out. 7 You are
doomed, you that twist justice and cheat
people out of their rights!

8 The LORD made the stars,
 the Pleiades and Orion.
He turns darkness into daylight
 and day into night.
He calls for the waters of the sea
 and pours them out on the earth.
His name is the LORD.
9 He brings destruction on the
 mighty and their strongholds.

10 You people hate anyone who challenges injustice and speaks the whole
truth in court. 11 You have oppressed the
poor and robbed them of their grain.
And so you will not live in the fine stone
houses you build or drink wine from the
beautiful vineyards you plant. 12 I know
how terrible your sins are and how
many crimes you have committed. You
persecute good people, take bribes, and
prevent the poor from getting justice in
the courts. 13 And so, keeping quiet in
such evil times is the smart thing to do!
14 Make it your aim to do what is right,
not what is evil, so that you may live.
Then the LORD God Almighty really will
be with you, as you claim he is. 15 Hate
what is evil, love what is right, and see
that justice prevails in the courts. Perhaps the LORD will be merciful to the people of this nation who are still left alive.
16 And so the Sovereign LORD Almighty
says, "There will be wailing and cries of
sorrow in the city streets. Even farmers
will be called to mourn the dead along
with those who are paid to mourn.
17 There will be wailing in all the vineyards. All this will take place because I
am coming to punish you." The LORD has
spoken.
18 How terrible it will be for you who
long for the day of the LORD! What good
will that day do you? For you it will be a
day of darkness and not of light. 19 It will
be like someone who runs from a lion
and meets a bear! Or like someone who
comes home and puts his hand on the
wall—only to be bitten by a snake!
20 The day of the LORD will bring darkness and not light; it will be a day of
gloom, without any brightness.
21 The LORD says, "I hate your religious
festivals; I cannot stand them! 22 When

you bring me burnt offerings and grain
offerings, I will not accept them; I will
not accept the animals you have fattened to bring me as offerings. 23 Stop
your noisy songs; I do not want to listen
to your harps. 24 Instead, let justice flow
like a stream, and righteousness like a
river that never goes dry.
25 "People of Israel, I did not demand
sacrifices and offerings during those
forty years that I led you through the
desert. 26 But now, because you have
worshiped images of Sakkuth, your king
god, and of Kaiwan, your star god, you
will have to carry those images 27 when I
take you into exile in a land beyond Damascus," says the LORD, whose name is
Almighty God.

The Destruction of Israel

6 How terrible it will be for you that
have such an easy life in Zion and
for you that feel safe in Samaria—you
great leaders of this great nation Israel,
you to whom the people go for help! 2 Go
and look at the city of Calneh. Then go
on to the great city of Hamath and on
down to the Philistine city of Gath. Were
they any better than the kingdoms of Judah and Israel? Was their territory
larger than yours? 3 You refuse to admit
that a day of disaster is coming, but
what you do only brings that day closer.
4 How terrible it will be for you that
stretch out on your luxurious couches,
feasting on veal and lamb! 5 You like to
compose songs, as David did, and play
them on harps. 6 You drink wine by the
bowlful and use the finest perfumes, but
you do not mourn over the ruin of Israel.
7 So you will be the first to go into exile.
Your feasts and banquets will come to
an end.
8 The Sovereign LORD Almighty has
given this solemn warning: "I hate the
pride of the people of Israel; I despise
their luxurious mansions. I will give
their capital city and everything in it to
the enemy."
9 If there are ten men left in a family,
they will die. 10 The dead man's relative,
the one in charge of the funeral, will
take the body out of the house. The relative will call to whoever is still left in the
house, "Is anyone else there with you?"
The person will answer, "No!"
Then the relative will say, "Be quiet!
We must be careful not even to mention
the LORD's name."[f]
11 When the LORD gives the command,
houses large and small will be smashed
to pieces. 12 Do horses gallop on rocks?
Does anyone plow the sea with oxen?
Yet you have turned justice into poison,
and right into wrong.
13 You brag about capturing the town
of Lodebar.[g] You boast, "We were
strong enough to take Karnaim."[h]
14 The LORD God Almighty himself
says, "People of Israel, I am going to
send a foreign army to occupy your
country. It will oppress you from Hamath Pass in the north to the Brook of
the Arabah in the south."

A Vision of Locusts

7 I had a vision from the Sovereign
LORD. In it I saw him create a swarm
of locusts just after the king's share of
the hay had been cut and the grass was
starting to grow again. 2 In my vision I
saw the locusts eat up every green thing
in the land, and then I said, "Sovereign
LORD, forgive your people! How can they
survive? They are so small and weak!"
3 The LORD changed his mind and said,
"What you saw will not take place."

A Vision of Fire

4 I had another vision from the
Sovereign LORD. In it I saw him preparing to punish his people with fire. The
fire burned up the great ocean under the
earth and started to burn up the land.
5 Then I said, "Stop, O Sovereign LORD!
How can your people survive? They are
so small and weak!"
6 The LORD changed his mind again
and said, "This will not take place
either."

A Vision of a Plumb Line

7 I had another vision from the LORD.
In it I saw him standing beside a wall
that had been built with the use of a
plumb line, and there was a plumb line
in his hand. 8 He asked me, "Amos, what
do you see?"
"A plumb line," I answered.
Then he said, "I am using it to show
that my people are like a wall that is out

[f] *Verse 10 in Hebrew is unclear.* [g] LODEBAR: *This name sounds like the Hebrew for "nothing."*
[h] KARNAIM: *The name of this small town means "horns," a symbol of strength.*

of line. I will not change my mind again
about punishing them. 9 The places
where Isaac's descendants worship will
be destroyed. The holy places of Israel
will be left in ruins. I will bring the dynasty of King Jeroboam to an end."

Amos and Amaziah

10 Amaziah, the priest of Bethel, then
sent a report to King Jeroboam of Israel:
"Amos is plotting against you among the
people. His speeches will destroy the
country. 11 This is what he says: 'Jeroboam will die in battle, and the people of
Israel will be taken away from their land
into exile.' "

12 Amaziah then said to Amos, "That's
enough, prophet! Go on back to Judah
and do your preaching there. Let *them*
pay you for it. 13 Don't prophesy here at
Bethel any more. This is the king's place
of worship, the national temple."

14 Amos answered, "I am not the kind
of prophet who prophesies for pay. I am
a herdsman, and I take care of fig trees.
15 But the LORD took me from my work as
a shepherd and ordered me to come and
prophesy to his people Israel. 16 So now
listen to what the LORD says. You tell me
to stop prophesying, to stop raving
against the people of Israel. 17 And so,
Amaziah, the LORD says to you, 'Your
wife will become a prostitute in the city,
and your children will be killed in war.
Your land will be divided up and given
to others, and you yourself will die in a
heathen country. And the people of Israel will certainly be taken away from
their own land into exile.' "

A Vision of a Basket of Fruit

8 I had another vision from the
Sovereign LORD. In it I saw a basket
of fruit. 2 The LORD asked, "Amos, what
do you see?"

"A basket of fruit," I answered.

The LORD said to me, "The end[i] has
come for my people Israel. I will not
change my mind again about punishing
them. 3 On that day the songs in the palace will become cries of mourning.
There will be dead bodies everywhere.
They will be cast out in silence."[j]

Israel's Doom

4 Listen to this, you that trample on the
needy and try to destroy the poor of the
country. 5 You say to yourselves, "We
can hardly wait for the holy days to be
over so that we can sell our grain. When
will the Sabbath end, so that we can
start selling again? Then we can over-
charge, use false measures, and fix the
scales to cheat our customers. 6 We can
sell worthless wheat at a high price.
We'll find someone poor who can't pay
his debts, not even the price of a pair of
sandals, and we'll buy him as a slave."

7 The LORD, the God of Israel, has
sworn, "I will never forget their evil
deeds. 8 And so the earth will quake, and
everyone in the land will be in distress.
The whole country will be shaken; it will
rise and fall like the Nile River. 9 The
time is coming when I will make the sun
go down at noon and the earth grow
dark in daytime. I, the Sovereign LORD,
have spoken. 10 I will turn your festivals
into funerals and change your glad
songs into cries of grief. I will make you
shave your heads and wear sackcloth,
and you will be like parents mourning
for their only child. That day will be bitter to the end.

11 "The time is coming when I will send
famine on the land. People will be hungry, but not for bread; they will be
thirsty, but not for water. They will hunger and thirst for a message from the
LORD. I, the Sovereign LORD, have spoken. 12 People will wander from the
Dead Sea to the Mediterranean and then
on around from the north to the east.
They will look everywhere for a message from the LORD, but they will not find
it. 13 On that day even healthy young
men and women will collapse from
thirst. 14 Those who swear by the idols of
Samaria, who say, 'By the god of Dan' or
'By the god of Beersheba'—those people
will fall and not rise again."

The LORD's Judgments

9 I saw the Lord standing by the altar. He gave the command: "Strike
the tops of the Temple columns so hard
that the foundation will shake. Break
them off and let them fall on the heads of
the people. I will kill the rest of the people in war. No one will get away; not one

[i] END: *The Hebrew words for "end" and "fruit" sound alike.* [j] out in silence; *or* out. Silence!

will escape. 2 Even if they dig their way
down to the world of the dead, I will
catch them. Even if they climb up to
heaven, I will bring them down. 3 If they
hide on the top of Mount Carmel, I will
search for them and catch them. If they
hide from me at the bottom of the sea, I
will command the sea monster[k] to bite
them. 4 If they are taken away into captivity by their enemies, I will order them
to be put to death. I am determined to
destroy them, not to help them."

5 The Sovereign LORD Almighty
touches the earth,
and it quakes;
all who live there mourn.
The whole world rises and falls
like the Nile River.
6 The LORD builds his home in the
heavens,
and over the earth he puts the
dome of the sky.
He calls for the waters of the sea
and pours them out on the earth.
His name is the LORD!

7 The LORD says, "People of Israel, I
think as much of the people of Ethiopia[l] as I do of you. I brought the Philistines from Crete and the Syrians from
Kir, just as I brought you from Egypt. 8 I,
the Sovereign LORD, am watching this
sinful kingdom of Israel, and I will destroy it from the face of the earth. But I
will not destroy all the descendants of
Jacob.
9 "I will give the command and shake
the people of Israel like grain in a sieve.
I will shake them among the nations to
remove all who are worthless. 10 The sinners among my people will be killed in
war—all those who say, 'God will not let
any harm come near us.' "

The Future Restoration of Israel

11 The LORD says, "A day is coming
when I will restore the kingdom of David, which is like a house fallen into ruins. I will repair its walls and restore it.
I will rebuild it and make it as it was long
ago. 12 And so the people of Israel will
conquer what is left of the land of Edom
and all the nations that were once mine,"
says the LORD, who will cause this to
happen.

13 "The days are coming," says the
LORD,
"when grain will grow faster
than it can be harvested,
and grapes will grow faster than
the wine can be made.
The mountains will drip with
sweet wine,
and the hills will flow with it.
14 I will bring my people back to
their land.
They will rebuild their ruined
cities and live there;
they will plant vineyards and
drink the wine;
they will plant gardens and eat
what they grow.
15 I will plant my people on the land
I gave them,
and they will not be pulled up
again."
The LORD your God has spoken.

[k] SEA MONSTER: *It was believed that the sea was inhabited by a great monster. This creature, like all others, was regarded as under God's control.* [l] *Hebrew* Cush: *Cush is the ancient name of the extensive territory south of the First Cataract of the Nile River. This region was called Ethiopia in Graeco-Roman times, and included within its borders most of modern Sudan and some of present-day Ethiopia (Abyssinia).*

The Book of
OBADIAH

Introduction

This short book comes from some undetermined time after the fall of Jerusalem in 586 B.C., when Edom, Judah's age-old enemy to the southeast, not only rejoiced over the fall of Jerusalem but took advantage of Judah's plight to loot the city and help the invader. Obadiah prophesied that Edom would be punished and defeated, along with other nations that were the enemies of Israel.

Outline of Contents

The punishment of Edom 1-14
The day of the Lord 15-21

---

1 This is the prophecy of Obadiah—what the Sovereign LORD said about the nation of Edom.

The LORD Will Punish Edom

The LORD has sent his messenger
to the nations,
and we have heard his message:
"Get ready! Let us go to war
against Edom!"
2 The LORD says to Edom,
"I will make you weak;
everyone will despise you.
3 Your pride has deceived you.
Your capital is a fortress of solid
rock;
your home is high in the
mountains,
and so you say to yourself,
'Who can ever pull me down?'
4 Even though you make your home
as high as an eagle's nest,
so that it seems to be among the
stars,
yet I will pull you down.

5 "When thieves come at night,
they take only what they want.
When people gather grapes,
they always leave a few.
But your enemies have wiped you
out completely.
6 Descendants of Esau, your
treasures have been looted.
7 Your allies have deceived you;
they have driven you from your
country.
People who were at peace with
you have now conquered you.
Those friends who ate with you
have laid a trap for you;
they say of you, 'Where is all
that cleverness he had?'

8 "On the day I punish Edom,
I will destroy their clever men
and wipe out all their wisdom.
9 The fighting men of Teman will be
terrified,
and every soldier in Edom will
be killed.

Reasons for Edom's Punishment

10 "Because you robbed and killed
your relatives,[a] the descendants
of Jacob,
you will be destroyed and
dishonored forever.
11 You stood aside on that day
when enemies broke down their
gates.
You were as bad as those
strangers
who carried off Jerusalem's
wealth
and divided it among
themselves.
12 You should not have gloated
over the misfortune of your
relatives in Judah.
You should not have been glad
on the day of their ruin.
You should not have laughed at
them
in their distress.

[a] YOUR RELATIVES: *The Israelites were descended from Jacob, who was the brother of Esau, the ancestor of the Edomites.*

13 You should not have entered the
city of my people
to gloat over their suffering
and to seize their riches
on the day of their disaster.
14 You should not have stood at the
crossroads
to catch those trying to escape.
You should not have handed them
over to the enemy
on the day of their distress.

God Will Judge the Nations

15 "The day is near when I, the LORD,
will judge all nations.
Edom, what you have done
will be done to you.
You will get back what you have
given.
16 My people have drunk a bitter cup
of punishment
on my sacred hill.[b]
But all the surrounding nations
will drink
a still more bitter cup of
punishment;
they will drink it all and vanish
away.

The Victory of Israel

17 "But on Mount Zion some will
escape,
and it will be a sacred place.
The people of Jacob will possess
the land that is theirs by right.
18 The people of Jacob and of Joseph
will be like fire;
they will destroy the people of
Esau
as fire burns stubble.
No descendant of Esau will
survive.
I, the LORD, have spoken.

19 "People from southern Judah will
occupy Edom;
those from the western foothills
will capture Philistia.
Israelites will possess the territory
of Ephraim and Samaria;
the people of Benjamin will take
Gilead.
20 The army of exiles from northern
Israel
will return and conquer
Phoenicia as far north as
Zarephath.
The exiles from Jerusalem who
are in Sardis
will capture the towns of
southern Judah.
21 The victorious men
of Jerusalem
will attack Edom and rule
over it.
And the LORD himself will be
king."

[b] SACRED HILL: *Mount Zion (see Zion in Word List).*

The Book of
JONAH

Introduction

The Book of Jonah *is unlike other prophetic books of the Bible in that it is a narrative, describing the adventures of a prophet who tried to disobey God's command. God told him to go to Nineveh, the capital of the great empire of Assyria, Israel's deadly enemy. But Jonah did not want to go there with God's message, because he was convinced that God would not carry out his threat to destroy the city. After a series of dramatic events, he reluctantly obeyed, and finally sulked when his message of doom did not come true.*

The book portrays God's absolute sovereignty over his creation. But above all it portrays God as a God of love and mercy, who would rather forgive and save even the enemies of his people, than punish and destroy them.

Outline of Contents

Jonah Disobeys the LORD

1 One day the LORD spoke to Jonah
son of Amittai. 2 He said, "Go to
Nineveh, that great city, and speak out
against it; I am aware of how wicked its
people are." 3 Jonah, however, set out in
the opposite direction in order to get
away from the LORD. He went to Joppa,
where he found a ship about to go to
Spain. He paid his fare and went aboard
with the crew to sail to Spain, where he
would be away from the LORD.

4 But the LORD sent a strong wind on
the sea, and the storm was so violent
that the ship was in danger of breaking
up. 5 The sailors were terrified and cried
out for help, each one to his own god.
Then, in order to lessen the danger,[a]
they threw the cargo[b] overboard.
Meanwhile, Jonah had gone below and
was lying in the ship's hold, sound
asleep.

6 The captain found him there and said
to him, "What are you doing asleep? Get
up and pray to your god for help. Maybe
he will feel sorry for us and spare our
lives."

7 The sailors said to each other, "Let's
draw lots and find out who is to blame
for getting us into this danger." They did
so, and Jonah's name was drawn. 8 So
they said to him, "Now, then, tell us!
Who is to blame for this? What are you
doing here? What country do you come
from? What is your nationality?"

9 "I am a Hebrew," Jonah answered. "I
worship the LORD, the God of heaven,
who made land and sea." 10 Jonah went
on to tell them that he was running away
from the LORD.

The sailors were terrified, and said to
him, "That was an awful thing to do!"[c]
11 The storm was getting worse all the
time, so the sailors asked him, "What
should we do to you to stop the storm?"

12 Jonah answered, "Throw me into
the sea, and it will calm down. I know it
is my fault that you are caught in this
violent storm."

13 Instead, the sailors tried to get the
ship to shore, rowing with all their
might. But the storm was becoming
worse and worse, and they got nowhere.
14 So they cried out to the LORD, "O LORD,
we pray, don't punish us with death for
taking this man's life! You, O LORD, are
responsible for all this; it is your doing."
15 Then they picked Jonah up and threw
him into the sea, and it calmed down at
once. 16 This made the sailors so afraid
of the LORD that they offered a sacrifice
and promised to serve him.

17 At the LORD's command a large fish
swallowed Jonah, and he was inside the
fish for three days and three nights.

Jonah's Prayer

2 From deep inside the fish Jonah
prayed to the LORD his God:

2 "In my distress, O LORD, I called
to you,
and you answered me.
From deep in the world of the
dead
I cried for help, and you
heard me.
3 You threw me down into the
depths,
to the very bottom of the sea,
where the waters were all
around me,
and all your mighty waves rolled
over me.
4 I thought I had been banished
from your presence
and would never see your holy
Temple again.
5 The water came over me and
choked me;
the sea covered me completely,
and seaweed wrapped around
my head.
6 I went down to the very roots of
the mountains,

[a] lessen the danger; *or* lighten the ship. [b] cargo; *or* equipment. [c] and said . . . to do!; *or* and asked him, "Why did you have to run away like that?"

into the land whose gates lock
shut forever.[d]
But you, O LORD my God,
brought me back from the
depths alive.
7 When I felt my life slipping away,
then, O LORD, I prayed to you,
and in your holy Temple you
heard me.
8 Those who worship worthless
idols
have abandoned their loyalty
to you.
9 But I will sing praises to you;
I will offer you a sacrifice
and do what I have promised.
Salvation comes from the LORD!"
10 Then the LORD ordered the fish to
spit Jonah up on the beach, and it did.

Jonah Obeys the LORD

3 Once again the LORD spoke to Jonah. 2 He said, "Go to Nineveh, that
great city, and proclaim to the people the
message I have given you." 3 So Jonah
obeyed the LORD and went to Nineveh, a
city so large that it took three days to
walk through it. 4 Jonah started through
the city, and after walking a whole day,
he proclaimed, "In forty days Nineveh
will be destroyed!"
5 The people of Nineveh believed
God's message. So they decided that
everyone should fast, and all the people,
from the greatest to the least, put on
sackcloth to show that they had
repented.
6 When the king of Nineveh heard
about it, he got up from his throne, took
off his robe, put on sackcloth, and sat
down in ashes. 7 He sent out a proclamation to the people of Nineveh: "This is an
order from the king and his officials: No
one is to eat anything; all persons, cattle,
and sheep are forbidden to eat or drink.
8 All persons and animals must wear
sackcloth. Everyone must pray earnestly to God and must give up their
wicked behavior and their evil actions.
9 Perhaps God will change his mind; perhaps he will stop being angry, and we
will not die!"
10 God saw what they did; he saw that
they had given up their wicked behavior. So he changed his mind and did not
punish them as he had said he would.

Jonah's Anger and God's Mercy

4 Jonah was very unhappy about this
and became angry. 2 So he prayed,
"LORD, didn't I say before I left home that
this is just what you would do? That's
why I did my best to run away to Spain!
I knew that you are a loving and merciful God, always patient, always kind,
and always ready to change your mind
and not punish. 3 Now then, LORD, let me
die. I am better off dead than alive."
4 The LORD answered, "What right do
you have to be angry?"
5 Jonah went out east of the city and
sat down. He made a shelter for himself
and sat in its shade, waiting to see what
would happen to Nineveh. 6 Then the
LORD God made a plant grow up over Jonah to give him some shade, so that he
would be more comfortable. Jonah was
extremely pleased with the plant. 7 But at
dawn the next day, at God's command, a
worm attacked the plant, and it died.
8 After the sun had risen, God sent a hot
east wind, and Jonah was about to faint
from the heat of the sun beating down
on his head. So he wished he were
dead.[e] "I am better off dead than alive,"
he said.
9 But God said to him, "What right do
you have to be angry about the plant?"
Jonah replied, "I have every right to be
angry—angry enough to die!"
10 The LORD said to him, "This plant
grew up in one night and disappeared
the next; you didn't do anything for it
and you didn't make it grow—yet you
feel sorry for it! 11 How much more, then,
should I have pity on Nineveh, that great
city. After all, it has more than 120,000
innocent children in it, as well as many
animals!"

[d] THE LAND WHOSE GATES LOCK SHUT FOREVER: *A reference to the world of the dead (see 2.2).*
[e] wished he were dead; *or* prayed that he would die.

The Book of
MICAH

Introduction

The prophet Micah, a contemporary of Isaiah, was from a country town in Judah, the southern kingdom. He was convinced that Judah was about to face the same kind of national catastrophe that Amos had predicted for the northern kingdom, and for the same reason God would punish the hateful injustice of the people. Micah's message, however, contains more clear and notable signs of hope for the future.

Passages especially worth noting are the picture of universal peace under God (4.1-4); the prediction of a great king who would come from the family line of David and bring peace to the nation (5.2-5a); and, in a single verse (6.8), the summary of much that the prophets of Israel had to say: "What he requires of us is this: to do what is just, to show constant love, and to live in humble fellowship with our God."

Outline of Contents

---

1 During the time that Jotham, Ahaz,
and Hezekiah were kings of Judah,
the LORD gave this message to Micah,
who was from the town of Moresheth.
The LORD revealed to Micah all these
things about Samaria and Jerusalem.

A Lament for Samaria and Jerusalem

2 Hear this, all you nations;
listen to this, all who live on earth!
The Sovereign LORD will testify against you.
Listen! He speaks from his heavenly temple.
3 The LORD is coming from his holy place;
he will come down and walk on the tops of the mountains.
4 Then the mountains will melt under him
like wax in a fire;
they will pour down into the valleys
like water pouring down a hill.

5 All this will happen because the people of Israel have sinned and rebelled
against God. Who is to blame for Israel's
rebellion? Samaria, the capital city itself! Who is guilty of idolatry in Judah?
Jerusalem itself! 6 So the LORD says, "I
will make Samaria a pile of ruins in the
open country, a place for planting grapevines. I will pour the rubble of the city
down into the valley, and will lay bare
the city's foundations. 7 All its precious
idols will be smashed to pieces, everything given to its temple prostitutes will
be destroyed by fire, and all its images
will become a desolate heap. Samaria
acquired these things for its fertility
rites, and now her enemies will carry
them off for temple prostitutes elsewhere."
8 Then Micah said, "Because of this I
will mourn and lament. To show my sorrow, I will walk around barefoot and naked. I will howl like a jackal and wail
like an ostrich. 9 Samaria's wounds cannot be healed, and Judah is about to suffer in the same way; destruction has
reached the gates of Jerusalem itself,
where my people live."

The Enemy Approaches Jerusalem

10 Don't tell our enemies in Gath about
our defeat; don't let them see you weeping. People of Beth Leaphrah,[a] show
your despair by rolling in the dust!
11 You people of Shaphir, go into exile,
naked and ashamed. Those who live in
Zaanan do not dare to come out of their

[a] BETH LEAPHRAH: *The prophet speaks of outlying towns (verses 10-14) which an enemy army approaching Jerusalem would attack.*

city. When you hear the people of Bethe-
zel mourn, you will know that there is no
refuge there. 12 The people of Maroth
anxiously wait for relief, because the
LORD has brought disaster close to Jerusalem. 13 You that live in Lachish, hitch
the horses to the chariots. You imitated
the sins of Israel and so caused Jerusalem to sin. 14 And now, people of Judah,
say good-bye to the town of Moresheth
Gath. The kings of Israel will get no help
from the town of Achzib.

15 People of Mareshah, the LORD will
hand you over to an enemy, who is going
to capture your town. The leaders of Israel will go and hide in the cave at Adullam. 16 People of Judah, cut off your hair
in mourning for the children you love.
Make yourselves as bald as vultures, because your children will be taken away
from you into exile.

The Fate of Those Who Oppress the Poor

2 How terrible it will be for those who
lie awake and plan evil! When
morning comes, as soon as they have the
chance, they do the evil they planned.
2 When they want fields, they seize
them; when they want houses, they take
them. No one's family or property is
safe.

3 And so the LORD says, "I am planning
to bring disaster on you, and you will not
be able to escape it. You are going to
find yourselves in trouble, and then you
will not walk so proudly any more.
4 When that time comes, people will use
the story about you as an example of disaster, and they will sing this song of despair about your experience:

We are completely ruined!
The LORD has taken our land away
And given it to those who took us
captive."[b]

5 So then, when the time comes for the
land to be given back to the LORD's people, there will be no share for any
of you.

6 The people preach at me and say,
"Don't preach at us. Don't preach about
all that. God is not going to disgrace us.
7 Do you think the people of Israel are
under a curse?[c] Has the LORD lost his
patience? Would he really do such
things? Doesn't he[d] speak kindly to
those who do right?"

8 The LORD replies, "You attack my
people[e] like enemies. Men return from
battle, thinking they are safe at home,
but there you are, waiting to steal the
coats off their backs. 9 You drive the
women of my people out of the homes
they love, and you have robbed their
children of my blessings forever. 10 Get
up and go; there is no safety here any
more. Your sins have doomed this place
to destruction.

11 "These people want the kind of
prophet who goes around full of lies and
deceit and says, 'I prophesy that wine
and liquor will flow for you.'

12 "But I will gather you together, all
you people of Israel that are left. I will
bring you together like sheep returning
to the fold. Like a pasture full of sheep,
your land will once again be filled with
many people."

13 God will open the way for them and
lead them out of exile. They will break
out of the city gates and go free. Their
king, the LORD himself, will lead
them out.

Micah Denounces Israel's Leaders

3 Listen, you rulers of Israel! You are
supposed to be concerned about
justice, 2 yet you hate what is good and
you love what is evil. You skin my people alive and tear the flesh off their
bones. 3 You eat my people up. You strip
off their skin, break their bones, and
chop them up like meat for the pot. 4 The
time is coming when you will cry out to
the LORD, but he will not answer you. He
will not listen to your prayers, for you
have done evil.

5 My people are deceived by prophets
who promise peace to those who pay
them, but threaten war for those who
don't. To these prophets the LORD says,
6 "Prophets, your day is almost over; the
sun is going down on you. Because you
mislead my people, you will have no
more prophetic visions, and you will not
be able to predict anything." 7 Those who

[b] *Probable text* those who took us captive; *Hebrew* rebels. [c] *Probable text* under a curse; *Hebrew unclear.* [d] *One ancient translation* Doesn't he; *Hebrew* Don't I. [e] *Probable text* You attack my people; *Hebrew* Recently my people have attacked.

predict the future will be disgraced by
their failure. They will all be humiliated
because God does not answer them.
8 But as for me, the LORD fills me with
his spirit and power, and gives me a
sense of justice and the courage to tell
the people of Israel what their sins are.
9 Listen to me, you rulers of Israel, you
that hate justice and turn right into
wrong. 10 You are building God's city,
Jerusalem, on a foundation of murder
and injustice. 11 The city's rulers govern
for bribes, the priests interpret the Law
for pay, the prophets give their revelations for money—and they all claim that
the LORD is with them. "No harm will
come to us," they say. "The LORD is
with us."
12 And so, because of you, Zion will be
plowed like a field, Jerusalem will become a pile of ruins, and the Temple hill
will become a forest.

The LORD's Universal Reign of Peace

(Isaiah 2.2-4)

4 In days to come
the mountain where the
Temple stands
will be the highest one of all,
towering above all the
hills.
Many nations will come streaming
to it,
2 and their people will say,
"Let us go up the hill of the
LORD,[f]
to the Temple of Israel's
God.
He will teach us what he wants us
to do;
we will walk in the paths he has
chosen.
For the LORD's teaching comes
from Jerusalem;
from Zion he speaks to his
people."

3 He will settle disputes among the
nations,
among the great powers near
and far.
They will hammer their swords
into plows
and their spears into pruning
knives.
Nations will never again go
to war,
never prepare for battle
again.
4 Everyone will live in peace
among their own vineyards and
fig trees,
and no one will make them
afraid.
The LORD Almighty has promised
this.

5 Each nation worships and obeys its
own god, but we will worship and obey
the LORD our God forever and ever.

Israel Will Return from Exile

6 "The time is coming," says the LORD,
"when I will gather together the people I
punished, those who have suffered in
exile. 7 They are crippled and far from
home, but I will make a new beginning
with those who are left, and they will
become a great nation. I will rule over
them on Mount Zion from that time on
and forever."
8 And you, Jerusalem, where God, like
a shepherd from his lookout tower,
watches over his people, will once again
be the capital of the kingdom that was
yours. 9 Why do you cry out so loudly?
Why are you suffering like a woman in
labor? Is it because you have no king,
and your counselors are dead? 10 Twist
and groan,[g] people of Jerusalem, like a
woman giving birth, for now you will
have to leave the city and live in the
open country. You will have to go to
Babylon, but there the LORD will save
you from your enemies. 11 Many nations
have gathered to attack you. They say,
"Jerusalem must be destroyed! We will
see this city in ruins!" 12 But these nations do not know what is in the LORD's
mind. They do not realize that they have
been gathered together to be punished
in the same way that grain is brought in
to be threshed.
13 The LORD says, "People of Jerusalem, go and punish your enemies! I will
make you as strong as a bull with iron
horns and bronze hoofs. You will crush
many nations, and the wealth they got
by violence you will present to me, the
Lord of the whole world."

[f] HILL OF THE LORD: *Mount Zion (see Zion in Word List).* [g] *Probable text* groan; *Hebrew* bring forth.

5 People of Jerusalem, gather your
forces![h] We are besieged! They are
attacking the leader of Israel!

God Promises a Ruler from Bethlehem

2 The LORD says, "Bethlehem Ephra-
thah, you are one of the smallest towns
in Judah, but out of you I will bring a
ruler for Israel, whose family line goes
back to ancient times."
3 So the LORD will abandon his people
to their enemies until the woman who is
to give birth has her son. Then those Israelites who are in exile will be reunited
with their own people. 4 When he comes,
he will rule his people with the strength
that comes from the LORD and with the
majesty of the LORD God himself. His
people will live in safety because people
all over the earth will acknowledge his
greatness, 5 and he will bring peace.

Deliverance and Punishment

When the Assyrians invade our country and break through our defenses, we
will send our strongest leaders to fight
them. 6 By force of arms they will conquer Assyria, the land of Nimrod, and
they[i] will save us from the Assyrians
when they invade our territory.
7 The people of Israel who survive will
be like refreshing dew sent by the LORD
for many nations, like showers on growing plants. They will depend on God, not
people. 8 Those who are left among the
nations will be like a lion hunting for
food in a forest or a pasture: it gets in
among the sheep, pounces on them, and
tears them to pieces—and there is no
hope of rescue. 9 Israel will conquer her
enemies and destroy them all.
10 The LORD says, "At that time I will
take away your horses and destroy your
chariots. 11 I will destroy the cities in
your land and tear down all your defenses. 12 I will destroy the magic
charms you use and leave you without
any fortunetellers. 13 I will destroy your
idols and sacred stone pillars; no longer
will you worship the things that you
yourselves have made. 14 I will pull
down the images of the goddess Asherah in your land and destroy your cities.
15 And in my great anger I will take revenge on all nations that have not
obeyed me."

The LORD's Case against Israel

6 Listen to the LORD's case against
Israel.
Arise, O LORD, and present your case;
let the mountains and the hills hear what
you say.
2 You mountains, you everlasting
foundations of the earth, listen to the
LORD's case! The LORD has a case against
his people. He is going to bring an accusation against Israel.
3 The LORD says, "My people, what
have I done to you? How have I been a
burden to you? Answer me. 4 I brought
you out of Egypt; I rescued you from
slavery; I sent Moses, Aaron, and Miriam to lead you. 5 My people, remember
what King Balak of Moab planned to do
to you and how Balaam son of Beor answered him. Remember the things that
happened on the way from the camp at
Acacia to Gilgal. Remember these things
and you will realize what I did in order
to save you."

What the LORD Requires

6 What shall I bring to the LORD, the
God of heaven, when I come to worship
him? Shall I bring the best calves to burn
as offerings to him? 7 Will the LORD be
pleased if I bring him thousands of
sheep or endless streams of olive oil?
Shall I offer him my first-born child to
pay for my sins? 8 No, the LORD has told
us what is good. What he requires of us
is this: to do what is just, to show constant love, and to live in humble fellowship with our God.
9 It is wise to fear the LORD. He calls to
the city, "Listen, you people who assemble in the city![j] 10 In the houses of evil
people are treasures which they got dishonestly. They use false measures, a
thing that I hate.[k] 11 How can I forgive
those who use false scales and weights?
12 Your rich people exploit the poor, and
all of you are liars. 13 So I have already
begun[l] your ruin and destruction because of your sins. 14 You will eat, but
not be satisfied—in fact you will still be
hungry. You will carry things off,
but you will not be able to save them;

[h] *Probable text* People . . . forces!; *Hebrew unclear.* [i] *Probable text* they; *Hebrew* he.
[j] *Probable text* who assemble in the city; *Hebrew* and who appointed it. Yet. [k] *Verse 10 in Hebrew is unclear.* [l] *Some ancient translations* begun; *Hebrew* made sick.

anything you do save I will destroy in
war. 15 You will sow grain, but not harvest the crop. You will press oil from
olives, but never get to use it. You will
make wine, but never drink it. 16 This will
happen because you have followed the
evil practices of King Omri and of his
son, King Ahab. You have continued
their policies, and so I will bring you to
ruin, and everyone will despise you.
People[m] everywhere will treat you
with contempt."[n]

Israel's Moral Corruption

7 It's hopeless! I am like a hungry
person who finds no fruit left on the
trees and no grapes on the vines. All the
grapes and all the tasty figs have been
picked. 2 There is not an honest person
left in the land, no one loyal to God.
Everyone is waiting for a chance to commit murder. Everyone hunts down their
own people. 3 They are all experts at doing evil. Officials and judges ask for
bribes. The influential people tell them
what they want, and so they scheme together.[o] 4 Even the best and most honest
of them are as worthless as weeds.

The day has come when God will punish the people, as he warned them
through their watchmen, the prophets.
Now they are in confusion. 5 Don't believe your neighbor or trust your friend.
Be careful what you say even to your
husband or wife. 6 In these times sons
treat their fathers like fools, daughters
oppose their mothers, and young
women quarrel with their mothers-in-
law; your enemies are the members of
your own family.

7 But I will watch for the LORD; I will
wait confidently for God, who will save
me. My God will hear me.

The LORD Brings Salvation

8 Our enemies have no reason to gloat
over us. We have fallen, but we will rise
again. We are in darkness now, but the
LORD will give us light. 9 We have sinned
against the LORD, so now we must endure his anger for a while. But in the end
he will defend us and right the wrongs
that have been done to us. He will bring
us out to the light; we will live to see him
save us. 10 Then our enemies will see this
and be disgraced—the same enemies
who taunted us by asking, "Where is the
LORD your God?" We will see them defeated, trampled[p] down like mud in the
streets.

11 People of Jerusalem, the time to rebuild the city walls is coming. At that
time your territory will be enlarged.
12 Your people will return to you from
everywhere—from Assyria in the east,
from Egypt in the south, from the region
of the Euphrates River, from distant seas
and far-off mountains. 13 But the earth
will become a desert because of the
wickedness of those who live on it.

The LORD's Compassion on Israel

14 Be a shepherd to your people, LORD,
the people you have chosen. Although
they live apart in the wilderness, there is
fertile land around them. Let them go
and feed in the rich pastures of Bashan
and Gilead, as they did long ago.

15 Work miracles for us,[q] LORD, as you
did in the days when you brought us out
of Egypt. 16 The nations will see this and
be frustrated in spite of all their
strength. In dismay they will close their
mouths and cover their ears. 17 They will
crawl in the dust like snakes; they will
come from their fortresses, trembling
and afraid. They will turn in fear to the
LORD our God.

18 There is no other god like you,
O LORD; you forgive the sins of your people who have survived. You do not stay
angry forever, but you take pleasure in
showing us your constant love. 19 You
will be merciful to us once again. You
will trample our sins underfoot and send
them to the bottom of the sea! 20 You will
show your faithfulness and constant
love to your people, the descendants of
Abraham and of Jacob, as you promised
our ancestors long ago.

[m] *One ancient translation* People; *Hebrew* My people. [n] People . . . contempt; *or* As my people you will everywhere be treated with contempt. [o] and so they scheme together; *Hebrew unclear.* [p] We will see . . . trampled; *or* We will gloat over them as they lie trampled. [q] *Probable text* Work miracles for us; *Hebrew* I will work miracles for him.

The Book of

NAHUM

Introduction

The Book of Nahum *is a poem celebrating the fall of Nineveh, the capital city of Israel's ancient and oppressive enemy, the Assyrians. The fall of Nineveh, near the end of the seventh century B.C., is seen as the judgment of God upon a cruel and arrogant nation.*

Outline of Contents

---

1 This is a message about Nineveh, the account of a vision seen by Nahum, who was from Elkosh.

The LORD's Anger against Nineveh

2 The LORD God tolerates no rivals;
he punishes those who
oppose him.
In his anger he pays them back.
3 The LORD does not easily become
angry,
but he is powerful
and never lets the guilty go
unpunished.

Where the LORD walks, storms
arise;
the clouds are the dust raised
by his feet!
4 He commands the sea, and it
dries up!
He makes the rivers go dry.
The fields of Bashan wither,
Mount Carmel turns brown,
and the flowers of Lebanon fade.
5 Mountains quake in the presence
of the LORD;
hills melt before him.
The earth shakes when the LORD
appears;
the world and all its people
tremble.
6 When he is angry, who can
survive?
Who can survive his terrible
fury?
He pours out his flaming anger;
rocks crumble to dust
before him.

7 The LORD is good;
he protects his people in times
of trouble;
he takes care of those who turn
to him.
8 Like a great rushing flood he
completely destroys his
enemies;[a]
he sends to their death those
who oppose him.
9 What are you plotting against the
LORD?
He will destroy you.
No one opposes him more than
once.
10 Like tangled thorns and dry straw
you drunkards will be
burned up!

11 From you, Nineveh, there came
someone full of wicked schemes, who
plotted against the LORD. 12 This is what
the LORD says to his people Israel: "Even
though the Assyrians are strong and numerous, they will be destroyed and disappear. My people, I made you suffer,
but I will not do it again. 13 I will now
end Assyria's power over you and break
the chains that bind you."

14 This is what the LORD has decreed
about the Assyrians: "They will have no descendants to carry on their name. I will destroy the idols that are in the temples of their gods. I am preparing a grave for the Assyrians—they don't deserve to live!"

15 Look, a messenger is coming over
the mountains with good news! He is on
his way to announce the victory! People

[a] *Some ancient translations* his enemies; *Hebrew* its place.

of Judah, celebrate your festivals and
give God what you solemnly promised
him. The wicked will never invade your
land again. They have been totally destroyed!

The Fall of Nineveh

2 Nineveh, you are under attack!
The power that will shatter
you has come.
Prepare the defenses!
Guard the road!
Prepare for battle!
(2 The LORD is about to restore the glory
of Israel, as it was before her enemies
plundered her.)
3 The enemy soldiers carry red
shields
and wear uniforms of red.
They are preparing to attack!
Their chariots flash like fire!
Their horses[b] prance!

4 Chariots dash wildly through the
streets,
rushing back and forth in the
city squares.
They flash like torches
and dart about like lightning.
5 The officers are summoned;
they stumble as they press
forward.

The attackers rush to the wall
and set up the shield for the
battering ram.
6 The gates by the river burst open;
the palace is filled with terror.
7 The queen is taken captive;
her servants moan like doves
and beat their breasts in sorrow.
8 Like water from a broken dam
the people rush from Nineveh![c]
"Stop! Stop!" the cry rings out—
but no one turns back.

9 Plunder the silver!
Plunder the gold!
The city is full of treasure!

10 Nineveh is destroyed, deserted,
desolate!
Hearts melt with fear;
knees tremble, strength is gone;
faces grow pale.

11 Where now is the city
that was like a den of lions,
the place where young lions
were fed,
where the lion and the lioness
would go
and their cubs would be safe?
12 The lion killed his prey
and tore it to pieces for his mate
and her cubs;
he filled his den with torn flesh.

13 "I am your enemy!" says the LORD
Almighty. "I will burn up your chariots.
Your soldiers will be killed in war, and I
will take away everything that you took
from others. The demands of your en-
voys will no longer be heard."

3 Doomed is the lying, murderous
city,
full of wealth to be looted and
plundered!
2 Listen! The crack of the whip,
the rattle of wheels,
the gallop of horses,
the jolting of chariots!
3 Cavalry troops charge,
swords flash, spears gleam!
Corpses are piled high,
dead bodies without number—
men stumble over them!
4 Nineveh the whore is being
punished.
Attractive and full of deadly
charms,
she enchanted nations and
enslaved[d] them.

5 The LORD Almighty says,
"I will punish you, Nineveh!
I will strip you naked
and let the nations see you,
see you in all your shame.
6 I will treat you with contempt
and cover you with filth.
People will stare at you in
horror.
7 All who see you will shrink back.
They will say, 'Nineveh lies in
ruins!
Who has any sympathy for her?
Who will want to comfort her?' "

8 Nineveh, are you any better than

[b] *Some ancient translations* horses; *Hebrew* cypresses. [c] *Probable text* Like water ... Nineveh; *Hebrew unclear.* [d] enslaved; *or* seduced.

Thebes, the capital of Egypt? She too had a river to protect her like a wall—the Nile was her defense. 9 She ruled Ethiopia[e] and Egypt, there was no limit to her power; Libya was her ally. 10 Yet the people of Thebes were carried off into exile. At every street corner their children were beaten to death. Their leading men were carried off in chains and divided among their captors.

11 Nineveh, you too will fall into a drunken stupor! You too will try to escape from your enemies. 12 All your fortresses will be like fig trees with ripe figs: shake the trees, and the fruit falls right into your mouth! 13 Your soldiers are helpless, and your country stands defenseless before your enemies. Fire will destroy the bars across your gates. 14 Draw water to prepare for a siege, and strengthen your fortresses! Trample the clay to make bricks, and get the brick molds ready! 15 No matter what you do, you will still be burned to death or killed in battle. You will be wiped out like crops eaten up by locusts.

You multiplied like locusts! 16 You produced more merchants than there are stars in the sky! But now they are gone, like locusts that spread their wings and fly away. 17 Your officials are like a swarm of locusts that stay in the walls on a cold day. But when the sun comes out, they fly away, and no one knows where they have gone!

18 Emperor of Assyria, your governors are dead, and your noblemen are asleep forever! Your people are scattered on the mountains, and there is no one to bring them home again. 19 There is no remedy for your injuries, and your wounds cannot be healed. All those who hear the news of your destruction clap their hands for joy. Did anyone escape your endless cruelty?

[e] *Hebrew* Cush: *Cush is the ancient name of the extensive territory south of the First Cataract of the Nile River. This region was called Ethiopia in Graeco-Roman times, and included within its borders most of modern Sudan and some of present-day Ethiopia (Abyssinia).*

The Book of HABAKKUK

Introduction

The words of the prophet Habakkuk come from near the end of the seventh century B.C., at a time when the Babylonians were in power. He was deeply disturbed by the violence of these cruel people, and asked the Lord, "So why are you silent while they destroy people who are more righteous than they are?" (1.13). The Lord's answer was that he would take action in his own good time, and meanwhile "those who are righteous will live because they are faithful to God" (2.4).

The rest of the book is a prophecy of doom on the unrighteous, with a concluding psalm celebrating the greatness of God and expressing the undying faith of the poet.

Outline of Contents

---

1 This is the message that the Lord revealed to the prophet Habakkuk.

Habakkuk Complains of Injustice

2 O Lord, how long must I call for help before you listen, before you save us from violence? 3 Why do you make me see such trouble? How can you stand to look on such wrongdoing? Destruction and violence are all around me, and there is fighting and quarreling everywhere. 4 The law is weak and useless,

and justice is never done. Evil people get
the better of the righteous, and so justice
is perverted.

The LORD's Reply

5 Then the LORD said to his people,
"Keep watching the nations around you,
and you will be astonished at what you
see. I am going to do something that you
will not believe when you hear about it.
6 I am bringing the Babylonians to
power, those fierce, restless people.
They are marching out across the world
to conquer other lands. 7 They spread
fear and terror, and in their pride they
are a law to themselves.
8 "Their horses are faster than leopards, fiercer than hungry wolves. Their
cavalry troops come riding from distant
lands; their horses paw the ground.
They come swooping down like eagles
attacking their prey.
9 "Their armies advance in violent conquest, and everyone is terrified as they
approach.[a] Their captives are as numerous as grains of sand. 10 They treat
kings with contempt and laugh at high
officials. No fortress can stop them—
they pile up earth against it and capture
it. 11 Then they sweep on like the wind
and are gone, these men whose power is
their god."

Habakkuk Complains to the LORD Again

12 LORD, from the very beginning you
are God. You are my God, holy and eternal. LORD, my God and protector, you
have chosen the Babylonians and made
them strong so that they can punish us.
13 But how can you stand these treacherous, evil men? Your eyes are too holy to
look at evil, and you cannot stand the
sight of people doing wrong. So why are
you silent while they destroy people who
are more righteous than they are?
14 How can you treat people like fish or
like a swarm of insects that have no
ruler to direct them? 15 The Babylonians
catch people with hooks, as though they
were fish. They drag them off in nets
and shout for joy over their catch!
16 They even worship their nets and offer
sacrifices to them, because their nets
provide them with the best of
everything.
17 Are they going to use their swords
forever and keep on destroying nations
without mercy?

The LORD's Answer to Habakkuk

2 I will climb my watchtower and
wait to see what the LORD will tell
me to say and what answer he[b] will give
to my complaint.
2 The LORD gave me this answer:
"Write down clearly on tablets what I reveal to you, so that it can be read at a
glance. 3 Put it in writing, because it is
not yet time for it to come true. But the
time is coming quickly, and what I show
you will come true. It may seem slow in
coming, but wait for it; it will certainly
take place, and it will not be delayed.
4 And this is the message: 'Those who
are evil will not survive,[c] but those who
are righteous will live because they are
faithful to God.'"

Doom on the Unrighteous

5 Wealth is deceitful. Greedy people
are proud and restless—like death itself
they are never satisfied. That is why
they conquer nation after nation for
themselves. 6 The conquered people will
taunt their conquerors and show their
scorn for them. They will say, "You take
what isn't yours, but you are doomed!
How long will you go on getting rich by
forcing your debtors to pay up?"
7 But before you know it, you that have
conquered others will be in debt yourselves and be forced to pay interest. Enemies will come and make you tremble.
They will plunder you! 8 You have plundered the people of many nations, but
now those who have survived will plunder you because of the murders you
have committed and because of your violence against the people of the world
and its cities.[d]
9 You are doomed! You have made
your family rich with what you took by
violence, and have tried to make your
own home safe from harm and danger!
10 But your schemes have brought shame
on your family; by destroying many nations you have only brought ruin on
yourself. 11 Even the stones of the walls

[a] *Probable text* and everyone . . . approach; *Hebrew unclear.* [b] *One ancient translation* he; *Hebrew* I. [c] *Probable text* will not survive; *Hebrew unclear.* [d] the people . . . cities; *or* the land, the city, and those who live in it.

cry out against you, and the rafters echo
the cry.
12 You are doomed! You founded a city
on crime and built it up by murder.
13 The nations you conquered wore
themselves out in useless labor, and all
they have built goes up in flames. The
LORD Almighty has done this. 14 But the
earth will be as full of the knowledge of
the LORD's glory as the seas are full of
water.
15 You are doomed! In your fury you
humiliated and disgraced your neighbors; you made them stagger as though
they were drunk. 16 You in turn will be
covered with shame instead of honor.
You yourself will drink and stagger. The
LORD will make you drink your own cup
of punishment, and your honor will be
turned to disgrace. 17 You have cut down
the forests of Lebanon; now you will be
cut down. You killed its animals; now
animals will terrify you. This will happen because of the murders you have
committed and because of your violence
against the people of the world and its
cities.[d]
18 What's the use of an idol? It is only
something that a human being has
made, and it tells you nothing but lies.
What good does it do for its maker to
trust it—a god that can't even talk!
19 You are doomed! You say to a piece of
wood, "Wake up!" or to a block of stone,
"Get up!" Can an idol reveal anything to
you? It may be covered with silver and
gold, but there is no life in it.
20 The LORD is in his holy Temple; let
everyone on earth be silent in his
presence.

A Prayer of Habakkuk

3 This is a prayer of the prophet Habakkuk:[e]

2 O LORD, I have heard of what you
have done,
and I am filled with awe.
Now do again in our times
the great deeds you used to do.
Be merciful, even when you are
angry.

3 God is coming again from Edom;
the holy God is coming from the
hills of Paran.
His splendor covers the heavens,
and the earth is full of his
praise.
4 He comes with the brightness of
lightning;
light flashes from his hand,
there where his power is hidden.
5 He sends disease before him
and commands death to
follow him.
6 When he stops, the earth shakes;
at his glance the nations
tremble.
The eternal mountains are
shattered;
the everlasting hills sink down,
the hills where he walked in
ancient times.

7 I saw the people of Cushan afraid
and the people of Midian
tremble.
8 Was it the rivers that made you
angry, LORD?
Was it the sea that made you
furious?
You rode upon the clouds;
the storm cloud was your
chariot,
as you brought victory to your
people.
9 You got ready to use your bow,
ready to shoot your arrows.[f]
Your lightning split open the
earth.
10 When the mountains saw you,
they trembled;
water poured down from the
skies.
The waters under the earth roared,
and their waves rose high.
11 At the flash of your speeding
arrows
and the gleam of your shining
spear,
the sun and the moon stood still.
12 You marched across the earth in
anger;
in fury you trampled the nations.
13 You went out to save your people,
to save your chosen king.
You struck down the leader of the
wicked

[d] the people . . . cities; *or* the land, the city, and those who live in it. [e] *Hebrew has an additional phrase, the meaning of which is unclear.* [f] *Probable text* ready to shoot your arrows; *Hebrew unclear.*

and completely destroyed his
followers.[g]
14 Your arrows pierced the
commander of his army
when it came like a storm to
scatter us,
gloating like those who secretly
oppress the poor.[h]
15 You trampled the sea with your
horses,
and the mighty waters foamed.

16 I hear all this, and I tremble;
my lips quiver with fear.
My body goes limp,
and my feet stumble[i]
beneath me.

I will quietly wait for the time to
come
when God will punish those who
attack us.

17 Even though the fig trees have no
fruit
and no grapes grow on the
vines,
even though the olive crop fails
and the fields produce no grain,
even though the sheep all die
and the cattle stalls are empty,
18 I will still be joyful and glad,
because the LORD God is my
savior.
19 The Sovereign LORD gives me
strength.
He makes me sure-footed as a
deer
and keeps me safe on the
mountains.

[g] *Probable text* completely . . . followers; *Hebrew unclear.* [h] *Verse 14 in Hebrew is unclear.*
[i] *Probable text* my feet stumble; *Hebrew* I am excited, because.

The Book of ZEPHANIAH

Introduction

The prophet Zephaniah preached in the latter part of the seventh century B.C., probably in the decade before King Josiah's religious reforms of 621 B.C. The book contains the familiar prophetic themes: A day of doom and destruction is threatened, when Judah will be punished for her worship of other gods. The Lord will punish other nations also. Although Jerusalem is doomed, in time the city will be restored, with a humble and righteous people living there.

Outline of Contents

---

1 This is the message that the LORD
gave to Zephaniah during the time
that Josiah son of Amon was king of Judah. (Zephaniah was descended from
King Hezekiah through Amariah, Gedaliah, and Cushi.)

The Day of the LORD's Judgment

2 The LORD said, "I am going to destroy
everything on earth, 3 all human beings
and animals, birds and fish. I will bring
about the downfall of[a] the wicked. I will
destroy everyone, and no survivors will
be left. I, the LORD, have spoken.
4 "I will punish the people of Jerusalem
and of all Judah. I will destroy the last
trace of the worship of Baal there, and
no one will even remember the pagan
priests who serve him. 5 I will destroy
anyone who goes up on the roof and

[a] *Probable text* I will bring about the downfall of; *Hebrew* the stumbling blocks.

worships the sun, the moon, and the stars. I will also destroy those who worship me and swear loyalty to me, but then take oaths in the name of the god Molech. 6 I will destroy those who have turned back and no longer follow me, those who do not come to me or ask me to guide them."

7 The day is near when the LORD will sit in judgment; so be silent in his presence. The LORD is preparing to sacrifice his people and has invited enemies to plunder Judah. 8 "On that day of slaughter," says the LORD, "I will punish the officials, the king's sons, and all who practice foreign customs. 9 I will punish all who worship like pagans and who steal and kill in order to fill their master's house[b] with loot.

10 "On that day," says the LORD, "you will hear the sound of crying at the Fish Gate in Jerusalem. You will hear wailing in the newer part of the city and a great crashing sound in the hills. 11 Wail and cry when you hear this, you that live in the lower part of the city, because all the merchants will be dead!

12 "At that time I will take a lamp and search Jerusalem. I will punish the people who are self-satisfied and confident, who say to themselves, 'The LORD never does anything, one way or the other.' 13 Their wealth will be looted and their houses destroyed. They will never live in the houses they are building or drink wine from the vineyards they are planting."

14 The great day of the LORD is near—very near and coming fast! That day will be bitter, for even[c] the bravest soldiers will cry out in despair! 15 It will be a day of fury, a day of trouble and distress, a day of ruin and destruction, a day of darkness and gloom, a black and cloudy day, 16 a day filled with the sound of war trumpets and the battle cry of soldiers attacking fortified cities and high towers.

17 The LORD says, "I will bring such disasters on the human race that everyone will grope about like someone blind. They have sinned against me, and now their blood will be poured out like water, and their dead bodies will lie rotting on the ground."

18 On the day when the LORD shows his fury, not even all their silver and gold will save them. The whole earth will be destroyed by the fire of his anger. He will put an end—a sudden end—to everyone who lives on earth.

A Plea for Repentance

2 Shameless nation, come to your senses 2 before you are driven away like chaff blown by the wind, before the burning anger of the LORD comes upon you, before the day when he shows his fury. 3 Turn to the LORD, all you humble people of the land, who obey his commands. Do what is right, and humble yourselves before the LORD. Perhaps you will escape punishment on the day when the LORD shows his anger.

The Doom of the Nations around Israel

4 No one will be left in the city of Gaza. Ashkelon will be deserted. The people of Ashdod will be driven out in half a day,[d] and the people of Ekron will be driven from their city. 5 You Philistines are doomed, you people who live along the coast. The LORD has passed sentence on you. He will destroy you, and not one of you will be left. 6 Your land by the sea will become open fields with shepherd's huts and sheep pens. 7 The people of Judah who survive will occupy your land. They will pasture their flocks there and sleep in the houses of Ashkelon. The LORD their God will be with them and make them prosper again.

8 The LORD Almighty says, "I have heard the people of Moab and Ammon insulting and taunting my people, and boasting that they would seize their land. 9 As surely as I am the living LORD, the God of Israel, I swear that Moab and Ammon are going to be destroyed like Sodom and Gomorrah. They will become a place of salt pits and everlasting ruin, overgrown with weeds. Those of my people who survive will plunder them and take their land."

10 That is how the people of Moab and Ammon will be punished for their pride and arrogance and for insulting the people of the LORD Almighty. 11 The LORD will terrify them. He will reduce the gods

[b] their master's house; *or* the temple of their god. [c] That day . . . even; *or* Listen! That terrible day is coming when even. [d] in half a day; *or* by a surprise attack at noontime.

of the earth to nothing, and then every
nation will worship him, each in its own
land.
12 The LORD will also put the people of
Ethiopia[e] to death.
13 The LORD will use his power to destroy Assyria. He will make the city of
Nineveh a deserted ruin, a waterless
desert. 14 It will be a place where flocks,
herds, and animals of every kind will lie
down. Owls will live among its ruins and
hoot from the windows. Crows[f] will
caw on the doorsteps. The cedar wood of
her buildings will be stripped away.
15 That is what will happen to the city
that is so proud of its own power and
thinks it is safe. Its people think that
their city is the greatest in the world.
What a desolate place it will become, a
place where wild animals will rest!
Everyone who passes by will shrink
back in horror.

Jerusalem's Sin and Redemption

3 Jerusalem is doomed, that corrupt,
rebellious city that oppresses its
own people. 2 It has not listened to the
LORD or accepted his discipline. It has
not put its trust in the LORD or asked for
his help. 3 Its officials are like roaring lions; its judges are like hungry wolves,
too greedy to leave a bone until morning. 4 The prophets are irresponsible and
treacherous; the priests defile what is sacred, and twist the law of God to their
own advantage. 5 But the LORD is still in
the city; he does what is right and never
what is wrong. Every morning without
fail, he brings justice to his people. And
yet the unrighteous people there keep on
doing wrong and are not ashamed.
6 The LORD says, "I have wiped out
whole nations; I have destroyed their cities and left their walls and towers in ruins. The cities are deserted; the streets
are empty—no one is left. 7 I thought
that then my people would have reverence for me and accept my discipline,
that they would never forget[g] the lesson
I taught them. But soon they were be-
having as badly as ever.
8 "Just wait," the LORD says. "Wait for
the day when I rise to accuse the nations. I have made up my mind to gather
nations and kingdoms in order to let
them feel the force of my anger. The
whole earth will be destroyed by the fire
of my fury.
9 "Then I will change the people of the
nations, and they will pray to me alone
and not to other gods. They will all obey
me. 10 Even from distant Ethiopia[h] my
scattered people will bring offerings to
me. 11 At that time you, my people, will
no longer need to be ashamed that you
rebelled against me. I will remove everyone who is proud and arrogant, and you
will never again rebel against me on my
sacred hill.[i] 12 I will leave there a humble and lowly people, who will come to
me for help. 13 The people of Israel who
survive will do no wrong to anyone, tell
no lies, nor try to deceive. They will be
prosperous and secure, afraid of
no one."

A Song of Joy

14 Sing and shout for joy, people of
Israel!
Rejoice with all your heart,
Jerusalem!
15 The LORD has stopped your
punishment;
he has removed all your
enemies.
The LORD, the king of Israel, is
with you;
there is no reason now to be
afraid.
16 The time is coming when they will
say to Jerusalem,
"Do not be afraid, city of Zion!
Do not let your hands hang
limp!
17 The LORD your God is with you;
his power gives you victory.
The LORD will take delight in you,
and in his love he will give you
new life.[j]

[e] *Hebrew* Cush: *Cush is the ancient name of the extensive territory south of the First Cataract of the Nile River. This region was called Ethiopia in Graeco-Roman times, and included within its borders most of modern Sudan and some of present-day Ethiopia (Abyssinia).*
[f] *Some ancient translations* Crows; *Hebrew* Desolation.
[g] *Some ancient translations* they would never forget; *Hebrew* their dwelling would not be cut off.
[h] *Hebrew* Cush: *Cush is the ancient name of the extensive territory south of the First Cataract of the Nile River. This region was called Ethiopia in Graeco-Roman times, and included within its borders most of modern Sudan and some of present-day Ethiopia (Abyssinia).*
[i] SACRED HILL: *Mount Zion (see Zion in Word List).*
[j] *Some ancient translations* give you new life; *Hebrew* be silent.

He will sing and be joyful
over you,
18 as joyful as people at a festival."
The LORD says,
"I have ended the threat of doom
and taken away your
disgrace.[k]
19 The time is coming!
I will punish your oppressors;
I will rescue all the lame
and bring the exiles home.
I will turn their shame to honor,
and all the world will praise
them.
20 The time is coming!
I will bring your scattered people
home;
I will make you famous
throughout the world
and make you prosperous once
again."
The LORD has spoken.

[k] *Verse 18 in Hebrew is unclear.*

The Book of HAGGAI

Introduction

The Book of Haggai *is a collection of brief messages that came from the Lord through the prophet Haggai in 520 B.C. The people had returned from exile and had lived in Jerusalem for some years, but the Temple still lay in ruins. The messages urge the leaders of the people to rebuild the Temple, and the Lord promises prosperity and peace in the future for a renewed and purified people.*

Outline of Contents

The LORD's Command to Rebuild the Temple

1 During the second year that Darius
was emperor of Persia, on the first
day of the sixth month, the LORD spoke
through the prophet Haggai. The message was for the governor of Judah, Zerubbabel son of Shealtiel, and for the
High Priest, Joshua son of Jehozadak.
2 The LORD Almighty said to Haggai,
"These people say that this is not the
right time to rebuild the Temple." 3 The
LORD then gave this message to the people through the prophet Haggai: 4 "My
people, why should you be living in well-
built houses while my Temple lies in ruins? 5 Don't you see what is happening to
you? 6 You have planted much grain, but
have harvested very little. You have
food to eat, but not enough to make you
full. You have wine to drink, but not
enough to get drunk on! You have clothing, but not enough to keep you warm.
And workers cannot earn enough to live
on. 7 Can't you see why this has happened? 8 Now go up into the hills, get
lumber, and rebuild the Temple; then I
will be pleased and will be worshiped as
I should be.
9 "You hoped for large harvests, but
they turned out to be small. And when
you brought the harvest home, I blew it
away.[a] Why did I do that? Because my
Temple lies in ruins while every one of
you is busy working on your own house.
10 That is why there is no rain and nothing can grow. 11 I have brought drought
on the land — on its hills, grainfields,
vineyards, and olive orchards — on every
crop the ground produces, on people
and animals, on everything you try to
grow."

[a] I blew it away; *or* I spoiled it.

The People Obey the LORD's Command

12 Then Zerubbabel and Joshua and all
the people who had returned from the
exile[b] in Babylonia, did what the LORD
their God told them to do. They were
afraid and obeyed the prophet Haggai,
the LORD's messenger. 13 Then Haggai
gave the LORD's message to the people: "I
will be with you—that is my promise."
14 The LORD inspired everyone to work
on the Temple: Zerubbabel, the governor of Judah; Joshua, the High Priest,
and all the people who had returned
from the exile.[b] They began working on
the Temple of the LORD Almighty, their
God, 15 on the twenty-fourth day of the
sixth month of the second year that Darius was emperor.

The Splendor of the New Temple

2 On the twenty-first day of the seventh month of that same year, the
LORD spoke again through the prophet
Haggai. 2 He told Haggai to speak to Zerubbabel, the governor of Judah, to
Joshua, the High Priest, and to the people, and to say to them, 3 "Is there anyone among you who can still remember
how splendid the Temple used to be?
How does it look to you now? It must
seem like nothing at all. 4 But now don't
be discouraged, any of you. Do the
work, for I am with you. 5 When you
came out of Egypt, I promised that I
would always be with you. I am still with
you, so do not be afraid.
6 "Before long I will shake heaven and
earth, land and sea. 7 I will overthrow all
the nations, and their treasures will be
brought here, and the Temple will be
filled with wealth. 8 All the silver and
gold of the world is mine. 9 The new
Temple will be more splendid than the
old one, and there I will give my people
prosperity and peace." The LORD
Almighty has spoken.

The Prophet Consults the Priests

10 On the twenty-fourth day of the
ninth month of the second year that Darius was emperor, the LORD Almighty
spoke again to the prophet Haggai. 11 He
said, "Ask the priests for a ruling on this
question: 12 Suppose someone takes a
piece of consecrated meat from a sacrifice and carries it in a fold of his robe. If
he then lets his robe touch any bread,
cooked food, wine, olive oil, or any kind
of food at all, will it make that food consecrated also?"
When the question was asked, the
priests answered, "No."
13 Then Haggai asked, "Suppose someone is defiled because he has touched a
dead body. If he then touches any of
these foods, will that make them defiled too?"
The priests answered, "Yes."
14 Then Haggai said, "The LORD says
that the same thing applies to the people
of this nation and to everything they
produce; and so everything they offer on
the altar is defiled."

The LORD Promises His Blessing

15 The LORD says, "Can't you see what
has happened to you? Before you started
to rebuild the Temple, 16 you would go to
a pile of grain expecting to find twenty
bushels, but there would be only ten.
You would go to draw fifty gallons of
wine from a vat, but find only twenty.
17 I sent scorching winds and hail to ruin
everything you tried to grow, but still
you did not repent. 18 Today is the
twenty-fourth day of the ninth month,
the day that the foundation of the Temple has been completed. See what is going to happen from now on. 19 Although
there is no grain left, and the grapevines,
fig trees, pomegranates, and olive trees
have not yet produced, yet from now on
I will bless you."

The LORD's Promise to Zerubbabel

20 On that same day, the twenty-fourth
of the month, the LORD gave Haggai a
second message 21 for Zerubbabel, the
governor of Judah: "I am about to shake
heaven and earth 22 and overthrow kingdoms and end their power. I will over-
turn chariots and their drivers; the
horses will die, and their riders will kill
one another. 23 On that day I will take
you, Zerubbabel my servant, and I will
appoint you to rule in my name. You are
the one I have chosen." The LORD
Almighty has spoken.

[b] who had returned from the exile; *or* who had not gone into exile.

The Book of
ZECHARIAH

Introduction

The Book of Zechariah *has two distinct parts: 1)* Chapters 1–8 *Prophecies from the prophet Zechariah, dated at various times in the years from 520 to 518 B.C. These are largely in the form of visions, and deal with the restoration of Jerusalem, the rebuilding of the Temple, the purification of God's people, and the messianic age to come. 2)* Chapters 9–14 *A collection of messages about the expected Messiah and the final judgment.*

Outline of Contents

The Lord Calls His People to Return to Him

1 In the eighth month of the second
year that Darius was emperor of
Persia, the Lord gave this message to the
prophet Zechariah, the son of Berechiah
and grandson of Iddo. 2 The Lord
Almighty told Zechariah to say to the
people, "I, the Lord, was very angry with
your ancestors, 3 but now I say to you,
'Return to me, and I will return to you.
4 Do not be like your ancestors. Long ago
the prophets gave them my message,
telling them not to live evil, sinful lives
any longer. But they would not listen to
me or obey me. 5 Your ancestors and
those prophets are no longer alive.
6 Through my servants the prophets I
gave your ancestors commands and
warnings, but they disregarded them
and suffered the consequences. Then
they repented and acknowledged that I,
the Lord Almighty, had punished them
as they deserved and as I had determined to do.' "

The Prophet's Vision of the Horses

7 In the second year that Darius was
emperor, on the twenty-fourth day of the
eleventh month (the month of Shebat),
the Lord gave me a message in a vision
at night. 8 I saw someone riding a red
horse. He had stopped among some
myrtle trees in a valley, and behind him
were other horses—red, dappled, and
white. 9 I asked him, "Sir, what do these
horses mean?"
He answered, "I will show you what
they mean. 10 The Lord sent them to go
and inspect the earth."
11 They reported to the angel: "We
have been all over the world and have
found that the whole world lies helpless
and subdued."
12 Then the angel said, "Almighty
Lord, you have been angry with Jerusalem and the cities of Judah for seventy
years now. How much longer will it be
before you show them mercy?"
13 The Lord answered the angel with
comforting words, 14 and the angel told
me to proclaim what the Lord Almighty
had said: "I have a deep love and concern for Jerusalem, my holy city, 15 and I
am very angry with the nations that enjoy quiet and peace. For while I was
holding back my anger against my people, those nations made the sufferings of
my people worse. 16 So I have come back
to Jerusalem to show mercy to the city.
My Temple will be restored, and the city
will be rebuilt."
17 The angel also told me to proclaim:
"The Lord Almighty says that his cities
will be prosperous again and that he will
once again help Jerusalem and claim the
city as his own."

The Vision of the Horns

18 In another vision I saw four ox
horns. 19 I asked the angel that had been
speaking to me, "What do these horns
mean?"
He answered, "They stand for the
world powers that have scattered the
people of Judah, Israel, and Jerusalem."
20 Then the Lord showed me four

workers with hammers. 21 I asked,
"What have they come to do?"
He answered, "They have come to terrify and overthrow the nations that completely crushed the land of Judah and
scattered its people."

The Vision of the Measuring Line

2 In another vision I saw a man with
a measuring line in his hand.
2 "Where are you going?" I asked.
"To measure Jerusalem," he answered, "to see how long and how wide
it is."
3 Then I saw the angel who had been
speaking to me step forward, and another angel came to meet him. 4 The first
one said to the other, "Run and tell that
young man with the measuring line that
there are going to be so many people
and so much livestock in Jerusalem that
it will be too big to have walls. 5 The LORD
has promised that he himself will be a
wall of fire around the city to protect it
and that he will live there in all his
glory."

The Exiles Are Called to Come Home

6-7 The LORD said to his people, "I scattered you in all directions. But now, you
exiles, escape from Babylonia and return to Jerusalem. 8 Anyone who strikes
you strikes what is most precious
to me."
So the LORD Almighty[a] sent me with
this message for the nations that had
plundered his people: 9 "The LORD himself will fight against you, and you will
be plundered by the people who were
once your servants."
When this happens, everyone will
know that the LORD Almighty sent
me.
10 The LORD said, "Sing for joy, people
of Jerusalem! I am coming to live
among you!"
11 At that time many nations will come
to the LORD and become his people. He
will live among you, and you will know
that he has sent me to you. 12 Once again
Judah will be the special possession of
the LORD in his sacred land, and Jerusalem will be the city he loves most of all.
13 Be silent, everyone, in the presence
of the LORD, for he is coming from his
holy dwelling place.

The Prophet's Vision of the High Priest

3 In another vision the LORD showed
me the High Priest Joshua standing
before the angel of the LORD. And there
beside Joshua stood Satan,[b] ready to
bring an accusation against him. 2 The
angel of the LORD[c] said to Satan, "May
the LORD condemn you, Satan! May the
LORD, who loves Jerusalem, condemn
you. This man is like a stick snatched
from the fire."
3 Joshua was standing there, wearing
filthy clothes. 4 The angel said to his
heavenly attendants, "Take away the
filthy clothes this man is wearing." Then
he said to Joshua, "I have taken away
your sin and will give you new clothes to
wear."
5 He commanded the attendants to
put[d] a clean turban on Joshua's head.
They did so, and then they put the new
clothes on him while the angel of the
LORD stood there.
6 Then the angel told Joshua that 7 the
LORD Almighty had said: "If you obey my
laws and perform the duties I have assigned you, then you will continue to be
in charge of my Temple and its courts,
and I will hear your prayers, just as I
hear the prayers of the angels who are in
my presence. 8 Listen then, Joshua, you
who are the High Priest; and listen, you
fellow priests of his, you that are the
sign of a good future: I will reveal my
servant, who is called The Branch! 9 I am
placing in front of Joshua a single stone
with seven facets. I will engrave an inscription on it, and in a single day I will
take away the sin of this land. 10 When
that day comes, each of you will invite
your neighbor to come and enjoy peace

[a] *Hebrew has two additional words, the meaning of which is unclear.* [b] SATAN: *A supernatural being whose name indicates he was regarded as the opponent of human beings.* [c] *One ancient translation* The angel of the LORD; *Hebrew* The LORD.
[d] *Some ancient translations* He commanded the attendants to put; *Hebrew* I said, "Let them put.

and security, surrounded by your vineyards and fig trees."

The Vision of the Lampstand

4 The angel who had been speaking to me came again and roused me as if I had been sleeping. 2 "What do you see?" he asked.

"A lampstand made of gold," I answered. "At the top is a bowl for the oil. On the lampstand are seven lamps, each one with places for seven wicks. 3 There are two olive trees beside the lampstand, one on each side of it." 4 Then I asked the angel, "What do these things stand for, sir?"

5 "Don't you know?" he asked me.

"No, I don't, sir," I replied.

10b The angel said to me, "The seven lamps are the seven eyes of the LORD, which see all over the earth."[e]

11 Then I asked him, "What do the two olive trees on either side of the lampstand mean? 12 And what is the meaning of the two olive branches beside the two gold pipes from which the olive oil pours?"

13 He asked me, "Don't you know?"

"No, I don't, sir," I answered.

14 Then he said, "These are the two men whom God has chosen and anointed to serve him, the Lord of the whole earth."

God's Promise to Zerubbabel

6 The angel told me to give Zerubbabel this message from the LORD: "You will succeed, not by military might or by your own strength, but by my spirit. 7 Obstacles as great as mountains will disappear before you. You will rebuild the Temple, and as you put the last stone in place, the people will shout, 'Beautiful, beautiful!' "

8 Another message came to me from the LORD. 9 He said, "Zerubbabel has laid the foundation of the Temple, and he will finish the building. When this happens, my people will know that it is I who sent you to them. 10a They are disappointed because so little progress is being made. But they will see Zerubbabel continuing to build the Temple, and they will be glad."

The Vision of the Flying Scroll

5 I looked again, and this time I saw a scroll flying through the air. 2 The angel asked me what I saw. I answered, "A scroll flying through the air; it is thirty feet long and fifteen feet wide."

3 Then he said to me, "On it is written the curse that is to go out over the whole land. On one side of the scroll it says that every thief will be removed from the land; and on the other side it says that everyone who tells lies under oath will also be taken away. 4 The LORD Almighty says that he will send this curse out, and it will enter the house of every thief and the house of everyone who tells lies under oath. It will remain in their houses and leave them in ruins."

The Vision of the Woman in the Basket

5 The angel appeared again and said, "Look! Something else is coming!"

6 "What is it?" I asked.

He replied, "It is a basket, and it stands for the sin[f] of the whole land."

7 The basket had a lid made of lead. As I watched, the lid was raised, and there in the basket sat a woman!

8 The angel said, "This represents wickedness." Then he pushed her down into the basket and put the lid back down. 9 I looked up and saw two women flying toward me with powerful wings like those of a stork. They picked up the basket and flew off with it.

10 I asked the angel, "Where are they taking it?"

11 He answered, "To Babylonia, where they will build a temple for it. When the temple is finished, the basket will be placed there to be worshiped."

The Vision of the Four Chariots

6 I had another vision. This time I saw four chariots coming out from between two bronze mountains. 2 The first chariot was pulled by red horses, the second by black horses, 3 the third by white horses, and the fourth by dappled horses. 4 Then I asked the angel, "Sir, what do these chariots mean?"

5 He answered, "These are the four winds; they have just come from the presence of the Lord of all the earth."

[e] *Verses 10b-14 are moved here from the end of the chapter in order to retain the natural sequence of the narrative.* [f] *Some ancient translations* sin; *Hebrew* eye.

6The chariot pulled by the black
horses was going north to Babylonia,
the white horses were going to the west,
and the dappled horses were going to
the country in the south. 7As the dappled horses came out, they were impatient to go and inspect the earth. The
angel said, "Go and inspect the earth!"—
and they did. 8Then the angel cried out
to me, "The horses that went north to
Babylonia have quieted the LORD's
anger."

The Command to Crown Joshua

9The LORD gave me this message. 10He
said, "Take the gifts given by the exiles
Heldai, Tobijah, and Jedaiah, and go at
once to the home of Josiah son of Zephaniah. All of them have returned from exile in Babylonia. 11Make a crown out of
the silver and gold they have given, and
put it on the head of the High Priest,
Joshua son of Jehozadak. 12Tell him
that the LORD Almighty says, 'The man
who is called The Branch will flourish
where he is and rebuild the LORD's Temple. 13He is the one who will build it and
receive the honor due a king, and he will
rule his people. A priest will stand by his
throne, and they will work together in
peace and harmony.' 14The crown will
be a memorial in the LORD's Temple in
honor of Heldai,[g] Tobijah, Jedaiah, and
Josiah."[h]

15Men who live far away will come
and help to rebuild the Temple of the
LORD. And when it is rebuilt, you will
know that the LORD Almighty sent me to
you. This will all happen if you fully
obey the commands of the LORD
your God.

The LORD Condemns Insincere Fasting

7 In the fourth year that Darius was
emperor, on the fourth day of the
ninth month (the month of Kislev), the
LORD gave me a message.

2The people of Bethel had sent Sharezer and Regemmelech and their men to
the Temple of the LORD Almighty to pray
for the LORD's blessing 3and to ask the
priests and the prophets this question:
"Should we continue to mourn because
of the destruction of the Temple, by fasting in the fifth month as we have done
for so many years now?"

4This is the message of the LORD that
came to me. 5He said, "Tell the people of
the land and the priests that when they
fasted and mourned in the fifth and seventh months during these seventy years,
it was not in honor of me. 6And when
they ate and drank, it was for their own
satisfaction."

7This is what the LORD said through
the earlier prophets at the time when Jerusalem was prosperous and filled with
people and when there were many people living not only in the towns around
the city but also in the southern region
and in the western foothills.

Disobedience, the Cause of Exile

8The LORD gave this message to Zechariah: 9"Long ago I gave these commands to my people: 'You must see that
justice is done, and must show kindness
and mercy to one another. 10Do not oppress widows, orphans, foreigners who
live among you, or anyone else in need.
And do not plan ways of harming one
another.'

11"But my people stubbornly refused
to listen. They closed their minds 12and
made their hearts as hard as rock. Because they would not listen to the teaching which I sent through the prophets
who lived long ago, I became very angry. 13Because they did not listen when I
spoke, I did not answer when they
prayed. 14Like a storm I swept them
away to live in foreign countries. This
good land was left a desolate place, with
no one living in it."

The LORD Promises to Restore Jerusalem

8 The LORD Almighty gave this message to Zechariah: 2"I have longed
to help Jerusalem because of my deep
love for her people, a love which has
made me angry with her enemies. 3I will
return to Jerusalem, my holy city, and
live there. It will be known as the faithful
city, and the hill of the LORD Almighty[i]
will be called the sacred hill. 4Once
again old men and women, so old that
they use canes when they walk, will be
sitting in the city squares. 5And the

[g] *One ancient translation* Heldai; *Hebrew* Helem. [h] *One ancient translation* Josiah; *Hebrew* Hen. [i] HILL OF THE LORD ALMIGHTY: *Mount Zion (see Zion in Word List).*

streets will again be full of boys and girls
playing.
6"This may seem impossible to those
of the nation who are now left, but it's
not impossible for me. 7I will rescue my
people from the lands where they have
been taken, 8and will bring them back
from east and west to live in Jerusalem.
They will be my people, and I will be
their God, ruling over them faithfully
and justly.
9"Have courage! You are now hearing
the same words the prophets spoke at
the time the foundation was being laid
for rebuilding my Temple. 10Before that
time no one could afford to hire either
men or animals, and no one was safe
from enemies. I turned people against
one another. 11But now I am treating the
survivors of this nation differently.
12They will plant their crops in peace.
Their vines will bear grapes, the earth
will produce crops, and there will be
plenty of rain. I will give all these blessings to the people of my nation who survive. 13People of Judah and Israel! In the
past foreigners have cursed one another
by saying, 'May the same disasters fall
on you that fell on Judah and Israel!' But
I will save you, and then those foreigners will say to one another, 'May you receive the same blessings that came to
Judah and Israel!' So have courage and
don't be afraid."
14The LORD Almighty says, "When
your ancestors made me angry, I
planned disaster for them and did not
change my mind, but carried out my
plans. 15But now I am planning to bless
the people of Jerusalem and Judah. So
don't be afraid. 16These are the things
you should do: Speak the truth to one
another. In the courts give real justice—
the kind that brings peace. 17Do not plan
ways of harming one another. Do not
give false testimony under oath. I hate
lying, injustice, and violence."
18The LORD Almighty gave this message to Zechariah: 19"The fasts held in
the fourth, fifth, seventh, and tenth
months will become festivals of joy and
gladness for the people of Judah. You
must love truth and peace."
20The LORD Almighty says, "The time
is coming when people from many[j] cities will come to Jerusalem. 21Those from
one city will say to those from another,
'We are going to worship the LORD
Almighty and pray for his blessing.
Come with us!' 22Many[j] peoples and
powerful nations will come to Jerusalem
to worship the LORD Almighty and to
pray for his blessing. 23In those days
ten foreigners will come to one Jew and
say, 'We want to share in your destiny,
because we have heard that God is
with you.' "

Judgment on Neighboring Nations

9 This is the LORD's message:
He has decreed punishment for
the land of Hadrach and for the city of
Damascus. Not only the tribes of Israel
but also the capital of Syria belong to the
LORD. 2Hamath, which borders on Hadrach, also belongs to him, and so do the
cities of Tyre and Sidon, with all their
skill. 3Tyre has built fortifications for
herself and has piled up so much silver
and gold that it is as common as dirt!
4But the Lord will take away everything
she has. He will throw her wealth into
the sea, and the city will be burned to the
ground.
5The city of Ashkelon will see this and
be afraid. The city of Gaza will see it and
suffer great pain. So will Ekron, and her
hopes will be shattered. Gaza will lose
her king, and Ashkelon will be left deserted. 6People of mixed race will live in
Ashdod. The LORD says, "I will humble
all these proud Philistines. 7They will no
longer eat meat with blood in it, or other
forbidden food. All the survivors will become part of my people and be like a
clan in the tribe of Judah. Ekron will become part of my people, as the Jebusites[k] did. 8I will guard my land and
keep armies from passing through it. I
will not allow tyrants to oppress my people any more. I have seen how my people have suffered."

The Future King

9Rejoice, rejoice, people of Zion!
Shout for joy, you people of
Jerusalem!
Look, your king is coming
to you!
He comes triumphant and
victorious,

[j] many; *or* great. [k] JEBUSITES: *The original inhabitants of Jerusalem, who became David's subjects after he captured the city.*

but humble and riding on a
donkey—
on a colt, the foal of a donkey.
10 The LORD says,
"I will remove the war chariots
from Israel
and take the horses from
Jerusalem;
the bows used in battle will be
destroyed.
Your king will make peace among
the nations;
he will rule from sea to sea,
from the Euphrates River to the
ends of the earth."

The Restoration of God's People

11 The LORD says,
"Because of my covenant with you
that was sealed by the blood of
sacrifices,
I will set your people free—
free from the waterless pit of
exile.
12 Return, you exiles who now have
hope;
return to your place of safety.
Now I tell you that I will repay
you twice over
with blessing for all you have
suffered.
13 I will use Judah like a
soldier's bow
and Israel like the arrows.
I will use the men of Zion like a
sword,
to fight the men of Greece."

14 The LORD will appear above his
people;
he will shoot his arrows like
lightning.
The Sovereign LORD will sound
the trumpet;
he will march in the storms
from the south.
15 The LORD Almighty will protect
his people,
and they will destroy their
enemies.
They will shout in battle like
drunk men
and will shed the blood of their
enemies;
it will flow like the blood of a
sacrifice
poured on the altar from a
bowl.[l]

16 When that day comes, the LORD
will save his people,
as a shepherd saves his flock
from danger.
They will shine in his land
like the jewels of a crown.
17 How good and beautiful the land
will be!
The young people will grow
strong on its grain and wine.

The LORD Promises Deliverance

10 Ask the LORD for rain in the
spring of the year. It is the LORD
who sends rain clouds and showers,
making the fields green for everyone.
2 People consult idols and fortunetellers,
but the answers they get are lies and
nonsense. Some interpret dreams, but
only mislead you; the comfort they give
is useless. So the people wander about
like lost sheep. They are in trouble because they have no leader.
3 The LORD says, "I am angry with
those foreigners who rule my people,
and I am going to punish them. The people of Judah are mine, and I, the LORD
Almighty, will take care of them. They
will be my powerful war-horses. 4 From
among them will come rulers, leaders,
and commanders to govern my people.[m]
5 The people of Judah will be victorious
like soldiers who trample their enemies
in the mud of the streets. They will fight
because the LORD is with them, and they
will defeat even the enemy cavalry.

6 "I will make the people of Judah
strong;
I will rescue the people of Israel.
I will have compassion on them
and bring them all back home.
They will be as though I had never
rejected them.
I am the LORD their God; I will
answer their prayers.
7 The people of Israel will be strong
like soldiers,
happy like those who have been
drinking wine.

[l] *Verse 15 in Hebrew is unclear.* [m] From among . . . people; *or* All oppressors—rulers, leaders, and commanders—will depart together from Judah.

Their descendants will remember
this victory
and be glad because of what the
LORD has done.

8 "I will call my people
and gather them together.
I will rescue them
and make them as numerous as
they used to be.
9 Though I have scattered them
among the nations,
yet in far-off places they will
remember me.
They and their children will
survive
and return home together.
10 From Egypt and Assyria I will
bring them home
and settle them in their own
country.
I will settle them in Gilead and
Lebanon also;
the whole land will be filled
with people.
11 When they pass through their sea
of trouble,
I, the LORD, will strike the waves,
and the depths of the Nile will
go dry.
Proud Assyria will be humbled,
and mighty Egypt will lose her
power.
12 I will make my people strong;
they will worship and obey me."
The LORD has spoken.

The Fall of the Tyrants

11 Open your doors, Lebanon,
so that fire can burn down
your cedar trees![n]
2 Weep and wail, cypress trees—
the cedars have fallen;
those glorious trees have been
destroyed!
Weep and wail, oaks of Bashan—
the dense forest has been cut
down!
3 The rulers cry out in grief;
their glory is gone!
Listen to the roaring of the lions;
their forest home along the
Jordan is destroyed!

The Two Shepherds

4 The LORD my God said to me, "Act the
part of the shepherd[o] of a flock of sheep
that are going to be butchered. 5 Their
owners kill them and go unpunished.
They sell the meat and say, 'Praise the
LORD! We are rich!' Even their own shepherds have no pity on them."
(6 The LORD said, "I will no longer pity
anyone on earth. I myself will put all the
people in the power of their rulers.
These rulers will devastate the earth,
and I will not save it from their power.")
7 Those who bought and sold the sheep
hired me, and I became the shepherd of
the sheep that were going to be butchered. I took two sticks: one I called "Favor" and the other "Unity." And I took
care of the flock. 8 I lost patience with
three other shepherds, who hated me,
and I got rid of them all in a single
month. 9 Then I said to the flock, "I will
not be your shepherd any longer. Let
those die who are to die. Let those be
destroyed who are to be destroyed.
Those who are left will destroy one another." 10 Then I took the stick called
"Favor" and broke it, to cancel the covenant which the LORD had made with all
the nations. 11 So the covenant was canceled on that day. Those who bought
and sold the sheep were watching me,
and they knew that the LORD was speaking through what I did. 12 I said to them,
"If you are willing, give me my wages.
But if not, keep them." So they paid me
thirty pieces of silver as my wages.
13 The LORD said to me, "Put them in
the Temple treasury."[p] So I took the
thirty pieces of silver—the magnificent
sum they thought I was worth—and put
them in the Temple treasury. 14 Then I
broke the second stick, the one called
"Unity," and the unity of Judah and Israel was shattered.
15 Then the LORD said to me, "Once
again act the part of a shepherd, this
time a worthless one. 16 I have put a
shepherd in charge of my flock, but he
does not help the sheep that are threatened by destruction; nor does he look
for the lost, or heal those that are hurt,
or feed the healthy. Instead, he eats the
meat of the fattest sheep and tears off

[n] CEDAR TREES: *Trees are used here as symbols of powerful nations or their kings.*
[o] SHEPHERD: *Shepherd is used here as a symbol of a king or leader, and sheep as symbols of his people or followers.* [p] *Some ancient translations* Put them in the Temple treasury; *Hebrew* Give them to the potter.

their hoofs. 17That worthless shepherd is doomed! He has abandoned his flock. War will totally destroy his power. His arm will wither, and his right eye will go blind."

The Future Deliverance of Jerusalem

12 This is a message about Israel from the LORD, the LORD who spread out the skies, created the earth, and gave life to man. He says, 2"I will make Jerusalem like a cup of wine; the nations around her will drink and stagger like drunks. And when they besiege Jerusalem, the cities of the rest of Judah will also be besieged. 3But when that time comes, I will make Jerusalem like a heavy stone—any nation that tries to lift it will be hurt. All the nations of the world will join forces to attack her. 4At that time I will terrify all their horses and make all their riders go crazy. I will watch over the people of Judah, but I will make the horses of their enemies blind. 5Then the clans of Judah will say to themselves, 'The LORD God Almighty gives strength to his people who live in Jerusalem.'

6"At that time I will make the clans of Judah like a fire in a forest or in a field of ripe grain—they will destroy all the surrounding nations. The people of Jerusalem will remain safe in the city.

7"I, the LORD, will give victory to the armies of Judah first, so that the honor which the descendants of David and the people of Jerusalem will receive will be no greater than that of the rest of Judah. 8At that time the LORD will protect those who live in Jerusalem, and even the weakest among them will become as strong as David was. The descendants of David will lead them like the angel of the LORD, like God himself. 9At that time I will destroy every nation that tries to attack Jerusalem.

10"I will fill the descendants of David and the other people of Jerusalem with the spirit of mercy and the spirit of prayer. They will look at the one whom they stabbed to death, and they will mourn for him like those who mourn for an only child. They will mourn bitterly, like those who have lost their first-born son. 11At that time the mourning in Jerusalem will be as great as the mourning for Hadad Rimmon[q] in the plain of Megiddo. 12-14Each family in the land will mourn by itself: the family descended from David, the family descended from Nathan, the family descended from Levi, the family descended from Shimei, and all the other families. Each family will mourn by itself, and the men of each family will mourn separately from the women.

13 "When that time comes," says the LORD Almighty, "a fountain will be opened to purify the descendants of David and the people of Jerusalem from their sin and idolatry. 2At that time I will remove the names of the idols from the land, and no one will remember them any more. I will get rid of anyone who claims to be a prophet and will take away the desire to worship idols. 3Then if anyone still insists on prophesying, his own father and mother will tell him that he must be put to death, because he claimed to speak the LORD's word, but spoke lies instead. When he prophesies, his own father and mother will stab him to death. 4When that time comes, no prophet will be proud of his visions or act like a prophet or wear a prophet's coarse garment in order to deceive people. 5Instead, he will say, 'I am not a prophet. I am a farmer—I have farmed the land all my life.' 6Then if someone asks him, 'What are those wounds on your chest?' he will answer, 'I got them at a friend's house.' "

The Command to Kill God's Shepherd

7The LORD Almighty says, "Wake up, sword, and attack the shepherd[r] who works for me! Kill him, and the sheep will be scattered. I will attack my people 8and throughout the land two-thirds of the people will die. 9And I will test the third that survives and will purify them as silver is purified by fire. I will test them as gold is tested. Then they will pray to me, and I will answer them. I will tell them that they are my people, and they will confess that I am their God."

[q] HADAD RIMMON: *Probably a name for Baal, the god of vegetation in Canaan and Syria. When the vegetation died each year, the worshipers thought that the god had died, and they mourned his death.* [r] SHEPHERD: *See 11.4.*

Jerusalem and the Nations

14 The day when the LORD will sit in
judgment is near. Then Jerusalem will be looted, and the loot will be
divided up before your eyes. 2 The LORD
will bring all the nations together to
make war on Jerusalem. The city will be
taken, the houses looted, and the women
raped. Half of the people will go into exile, but the rest of them will not be taken
away from the city. 3 Then the LORD will
go out and fight against those nations, as
he has fought in times past. 4 At that time
he will stand on the Mount of Olives, to
the east of Jerusalem. Then the Mount of
Olives will be split in two from east to
west by a large valley. Half of the mountain will move northward, and half of it
southward. 5 You will escape through
this valley that divides the mountain in
two.[s] You will flee as your ancestors
did when the earthquake struck in the
time of King Uzziah of Judah. The LORD
my God will come, bringing all the angels with him.

6 When that time comes, there will no
longer be cold or frost,[t] 7 nor any darkness. There will always be daylight,
even at nighttime. When this will happen is known only to the LORD.

8 When that day comes, fresh water
will flow from Jerusalem, half of it to the
Dead Sea and the other half to the Mediterranean. It will flow all year long, in
the dry season as well as the wet. 9 Then
the LORD will be king over all the earth;
everyone will worship him as God and
know him by the same name.

10 The whole region, from Geba in the
north to Rimmon in the south, will be
made level. Jerusalem will tower above
the land around it; the city will reach
from the Benjamin Gate to the Corner
Gate, where there had been an earlier
gate, and from the Tower of Hananel to
the royal wine presses. 11 The people will
live there in safety, no longer threatened
by destruction.

12 The LORD will bring a terrible disease on all the nations that make war on
Jerusalem. Their flesh will rot away
while they are still alive; their eyes and
their tongues will rot away.

13 At that time the LORD will make them
so confused and afraid that everyone
will seize the man next to him and attack
him. 14 The men of Judah will fight to defend Jerusalem. They will take as loot
the wealth of all the nations—gold, silver, and clothing in great abundance.

15 A terrible disease will also fall on
the horses, the mules, the camels, and
the donkeys—on all the animals in the
camps of the enemy.

16 Then all of the survivors from the
nations that have attacked Jerusalem
will go there each year to worship the
LORD Almighty as king and to celebrate
the Festival of Shelters. 17 If any nation
refuses to go and worship the LORD
Almighty as king, then rain will not fall
on their land. 18 If the Egyptians refuse to
celebrate the Festival of Shelters, then
they will be struck by the same disease
that the LORD will send on every nation
that refuses to go. 19 This will be the punishment that will fall on Egypt and on all
the other nations if they do not celebrate
the Festival of Shelters.

20 At that time even the harness bells
of the horses will be inscribed with the
words "Dedicated to the LORD." The
cooking pots in the Temple will be as
sacred as the bowls before the altar.
21 Every cooking pot in Jerusalem and in
all Judah will be set apart for use in the
worship of the LORD Almighty. The people who offer sacrifices will use them for
boiling the meat of the sacrifices. When
that time comes, there will no longer be
any merchant in the Temple of the LORD
Almighty.

[s] *Probable text* You will escape ... in two; *Hebrew unclear.* [t] *Probable text* cold or frost; *Hebrew unclear.*

The Book of
MALACHI

Introduction

The Book of Malachi *comes from some time in the fifth century B.C. after the Temple in Jerusalem was rebuilt. The prophet's main concern is to call priests and people to renew their faithfulness to their covenant with God. It is clear that there is laxity and corruption in the life and worship of God's people. Priests and people are cheating God by not giving him the offerings that are rightly due him, and by not living according to his teaching. But the Lord will come to judge and purify his people, sending ahead of him his messenger to prepare the way and to proclaim his covenant.*

Outline of Contents

Israel's sins 1.1 – 2.16
God's judgment and his mercy 2.17 – 4.6

---

1 This is the message that the LORD
gave Malachi to tell the people of
Israel.

The LORD's Love for Israel

2The LORD says to his people, "I have
always loved you."
But they reply, "How have you shown
your love for us?"
The LORD answers, "Esau and Jacob
were brothers, but I have loved Jacob
and his descendants, 3and have hated
Esau and his descendants. I have devastated Esau's hill country and abandoned
the land to jackals."
4If Esau's descendants, the Edomites,
say, "Our towns have been destroyed,
but we will rebuild them," then the LORD
will reply, "Let them rebuild – I will tear
them down again. People will call them
'The evil country' and 'The nation with
whom the LORD is angry forever.'"
5The people of Israel are going to see
this with their own eyes, and they will
say, "The LORD is mighty even outside
the land of Israel!"

The LORD Reprimands the Priests

6The LORD Almighty says to the
priests, "Children honor their parents,
and servants honor their masters. I am
your father – why don't you honor me? I
am your master – why don't you respect
me? You despise me, and yet you ask,
'How have we despised you?' 7This is
how – by offering worthless food on my
altar. Then you ask, 'How have we failed
to respect you?' I will tell you – by showing contempt for my altar. 8When you
bring a blind or sick or lame animal to
sacrifice to me, do you think there's
nothing wrong with that? Try giving an
animal like that to the governor! Would
he be pleased with you or grant you any
favors?"
9Now, you priests, try asking God to
be good to us. He will not answer your
prayer, and it will be your fault. 10The
LORD Almighty says, "I wish one of you
would close the Temple doors so as to
prevent you from lighting useless fires
on my altar. I am not pleased with you;
I will not accept the offerings you bring
me. 11People from one end of the world
to the other honor me. Everywhere they
burn incense to me and offer acceptable
sacrifices. All of them honor me! 12But
you dishonor me when you say that my
altar is worthless and when you offer on
it food that you despise. 13You say, 'How
tired we are of all this!' and you turn up
your nose at me. As your offering to me
you bring a stolen animal or one that is
lame or sick. Do you think I will accept
that from you? 14A curse on the cheater
who sacrifices a worthless animal to me,
when he has in his flock a good animal
that he promised to give me! For I am a
great king, and people of all nations
fear me."

2 The LORD Almighty says to the
priests, "This command is for you:
2You must honor me by what you do. If
you will not listen to what I say, then I
will bring a curse on you. I will put a
curse on the things you receive for your

support. In fact, I have already put a
curse on them, because you do not take
my command seriously. 3 I will punish
your children and rub your faces in the
dung of the animals you sacrifice—and
you will be taken out to the dung heap.
4 Then you will know that I have given
you this command, so that my covenant
with the priests, the descendants of Levi,
will not be broken.

5 "In my covenant I promised them life
and well-being, and this is what I gave
them, so that they might respect me. In
those days they did respect and fear me.
6 They taught what was right, not what
was wrong. They lived in harmony with
me; they not only did what was right
themselves, but they also helped many
others to stop doing evil. 7 It is the duty
of priests to teach the true knowledge of
God. People should go to them to learn
my will, because they are the messengers of the LORD Almighty.

8 "But now you priests have turned
away from the right path. Your teaching
has led many to do wrong. You have
broken the covenant I made with you.
9 So I, in turn, will make the people of
Israel despise you because you do not
obey my will, and when you teach my
people, you do not treat everyone alike."

The People's Unfaithfulness to God

10 Don't we all have the same father?
Didn't the same God create us all? Then
why do we break our promises to one
another, and why do we despise the covenant that God made with our ancestors? 11 The people of Judah have broken
their promise to God and done a horrible
thing in Jerusalem and all over the country. They have defiled the Temple which
the LORD loves. Men have married
women who worship foreign gods.
12 May the LORD remove from the community of Israel those who did this, and
never again let them participate in the
offerings our nation brings to the LORD
Almighty.[a]

13 This is another thing you do. You
drown the LORD's altar with tears, weeping and wailing because he no longer accepts the offerings you bring him. 14 You
ask why he no longer accepts them. It is
because he knows you have broken your
promise to the wife you married when
you were young. She was your partner,
and you have broken your promise to
her, although you promised before God
that you would be faithful to her.
15 Didn't God make you one body and
spirit with her?[b] What was his purpose
in this? It was that you should have children who are truly God's people. So
make sure that none of you breaks his
promise to his wife. 16 "I hate divorce,"
says the LORD God of Israel. "I hate it
when one of you does such a cruel thing
to his wife. Make sure that you do not
break your promise to be faithful to your
wife."

The Day of Judgment Is Near

17 You have tired the LORD out with
your talk. But you ask, "How have we
tired him?" By saying, "The LORD
Almighty thinks all evildoers are good;
in fact he likes them." Or by asking,
"Where is the God who is supposed to be
just?"

3 The LORD Almighty answers, "I will
send my messenger to prepare the
way for me. Then the Lord you are looking for will suddenly come to his Temple. The messenger you long to see will
come and proclaim my covenant."

2 But who will be able to endure the
day when he comes? Who will be able to
survive when he appears? He will be like
strong soap, like a fire that refines
metal. 3 He will come to judge like one
who refines and purifies silver. As a
metalworker refines silver and gold, so
the LORD's messenger will purify the
priests, so that they will bring to the
LORD the right kind of offerings. 4 Then
the offerings which the people of Judah
and Jerusalem bring to the LORD will be
pleasing to him, as they used to be in the
past.

5 The LORD Almighty says, "I will appear among you to judge, and I will testify at once against those who practice
magic, against adulterers, against those
who give false testimony, those who
cheat employees out of their wages, and
those who take advantage of widows,
orphans, and foreigners—against all
who do not respect me.

[a] *One ancient translation* May . . . Almighty; *Hebrew unclear.* [b] *Probable text* Didn't God . . . her; *Hebrew unclear.*

The Payment of Tithes

6 "I am the LORD, and I do not change.
And so you, the descendants of Jacob,
are not yet completely lost. 7 You, like
your ancestors before you, have turned
away from my laws and have not kept
them. Turn back to me, and I will turn to
you. But you ask, 'What must we do to
turn back to you?' 8 I ask you, is it right
for a person to cheat God? Of course not,
yet you are cheating me. 'How?' you ask.
In the matter of tithes and offerings.
9 A curse is on all of you because the
whole nation is cheating me. 10 Bring the
full amount of your tithes to the Temple,
so that there will be plenty of food there.
Put me to the test and you will see that I
will open the windows of heaven and
pour out on you in abundance all kinds
of good things. 11 I will not let insects destroy your crops, and your grapevines
will be loaded with grapes. 12 Then the
people of all nations will call you happy,
because your land will be a good place
to live.

God's Promise of Mercy

13 "You have said terrible things about
me," says the LORD. "But you ask, 'What
have we said about you?' 14 You have
said, 'It's useless to serve God. What's
the use of doing what he says or of trying to show the LORD Almighty that we
are sorry for what we have done? 15 As
we see it, proud people are the ones who
are happy. Evil people not only prosper,
but they test God's patience with their
evil deeds and get away with it.' "
16 Then the people who feared the LORD
spoke to one another, and the LORD listened and heard what they said. In his
presence, there was written down in a
book a record of those who feared the
LORD and respected him. 17 "They will be
my people," says the LORD Almighty. "On
the day when I act, they will be my very
own. I will be merciful to them as parents are merciful to the children who
serve them. 18 Once again my people will
see the difference between what happens to the righteous and to the wicked,
to the person who serves me and the one
who does not."

The Day of the LORD Is Coming

4 The LORD Almighty says, "The day
is coming when all proud and evil
people will burn like straw. On that day
they will burn up, and there will be nothing left of them. 2 But for you who obey
me, my saving power will rise on you
like the sun and bring healing like the
sun's rays. You will be as free and happy
as calves let out of a stall. 3 On the day
when I act, you will overcome the
wicked, and they will be like dust under
your feet.
4 "Remember the teachings of my servant Moses, the laws and commands
which I gave him at Mount Sinai for all
the people of Israel to obey.
5 "But before the great and terrible day
of the LORD comes, I will send you the
prophet Elijah. 6 He will bring fathers
and children together again; otherwise I
would have to come and destroy your
country."

HOLY BIBLE

Today's English Version

Deuterocanonicals/Apocrypha

DEUTEROCANONICALS / APOCRYPHA

Introduction

The following books: Tobit, Judith, Esther (the Greek text), Wisdom of Solomon, Sirach, Baruch, Letter of Jeremiah, Song of the Three Young Men, Susanna, Bel and the Dragon, 1 Maccabees, and 2 Maccabees, formed part of the Septuagint Greek text and were interspersed among other books of the Old Testament.

This Greek text was not only widely used by Jews but was known as well by numerous "God-fearing" Gentiles who were attracted to the high moral teachings of the Old Testament, even though they had not themselves become converts to Judaism. One can thus readily understand how and why early Christianity, as it spread among Greek-speaking Jews and Gentiles, employed this Greek text. In fact, the majority of Old Testament quotations in the New Testament are based on this translation.

Precisely when Jewish leadership officially adopted the traditional 39 books of the so-called "Hebrew Canon" is not known; nor is there agreement as to exactly what criteria were used in determining the canon. According to tradition the determination of the books of the Hebrew canon was made about A.D. 90, but there is evidence to believe that official and widespread agreement on this issue came somewhat later.

Among Christians it was apparently only in the fourth century that the issue of the canonicity of these books arose, a situation which is reflected in Jerome's placing these books in a separated section in his Vulgate translation of the Old Testament.

In 1546 at the Council of Trent the Roman Catholic Church officially declared these books to be sacred and canonical and to be accepted "with equal devotion and reverence."

At the time of the Reformation Martin Luther did not regard these books as Scripture but as "useful and good for reading." In his German translation of the Bible he followed the practice of Jerome in placing them at the end of the Old Testament with the superscription "Apocrypha." Protestants generally continued this practice in their translations of the Bible into such languages as Swedish, Norwegian, Danish, Slovenian, French, Spanish and English (King James Version).

Among Christians who do not accept these books as Scripture there is, however, widespread agreement as to their importance in providing much valuable information on Jewish history, life, thought, worship, and religious practice during the centuries immediately prior to the time of Christ. Accordingly, they make possible a clearer understanding of the historical and cultural situation in which Jesus lived and taught.

Catholics speak of these books as "deuterocanonical" to indicate that their canonical status as Scripture was settled later than that of the protocanonical books. Protestants usually refer to these books as Apocrypha.

The Book of
TOBIT

Introduction

The Book of Tobit, *originally written in Hebrew or Aramaic, is a story which tells of miraculous help to God's faithful people and teaches Jewish piety and morality. The book offers a vivid picture of Jewish religion and culture in the period prior to the New Testament.*

Outline of Contents

Tobit in Nineveh and Sarah in Media suffer and pray 1.1–3.15
Their prayers are answered 3.16–11.18
- a. *In answer to their prayers God sends the angel Raphael* 3.16-17
- b. *Tobit gives advice to his son, Tobias* 4.1-21
- c. *Raphael travels with Tobias to Media* 5.1–7.12
- d. *Tobias marries Sarah* 7.13–9.6
- e. *Raphael returns with Tobias and Sarah, and cures Tobit's blindness* 10.1–11.18

The angel Raphael reveals who he is 12.1-22
Tobit praises God and gives advice to Tobias 13.1–14.15

---

1 I am Tobit and this is the story of
my life. My father was Tobiel, my
grandfather was Ananiel, and my great-
grandfather was Aduel. Aduel's father
was Gabael; his grandfather was Raphael; and his great-grandfather was
Raguel, who belonged to the clan of
Asiel, a part of the tribe of Naphtali.
2 During the time that Shalmaneser was
emperor of Assyria, I was taken captive
in my hometown of Thisbe, located in
northern Galilee, south of Kadesh in
Naphtali, northwest of Hazor, and north
of Phogor.

Tobit's Early Life

3 All my life I have been honest and
have tried to do what was right. I often
gave money to help needy relatives and
other Jews who had been deported with
me to Nineveh, the capital of Assyria.
4 When I was young, I lived in northern Israel. All the tribes in Israel were
supposed to offer sacrifices in Jerusalem. It was the one city that God had
chosen from among all the Israelite cities as the place where his Temple was to
be built for his holy and eternal home.
But my entire tribe of Naphtali rejected
the city of Jerusalem and the kings descended from David. 5 Like everyone
else in this tribe, my own family used to
go to the city of Dan in the mountains of
northern Galilee to offer sacrifices to the
gold bull-calf which King Jeroboam of
Israel had set up there.

Tobit's Faithfulness to His Religion

6 I was the only one in my family who
regularly went to Jerusalem to celebrate
the religious festivals, as the Law of
Moses commands everyone to do. I
would hurry off to Jerusalem with the
first part of my harvest, the first-born of
my animals, a tenth of my cattle, and the
freshly clipped wool from my sheep.
Then I would stand before the altar in
the Temple, and give these offerings to
the priests, the descendants of Aaron.
7 I would give a tenth of my grain, wine,
olive oil, pomegranates, figs, and other
fruits to the Levites who served God in
Jerusalem. Every year, except the seventh year when the land was at rest,[a] I
would sell a second tenth of my possessions and spend the money in Jerusalem
on the festival meal.
8 But every third year, I would give a
third tithe[b] to widows and orphans and
to foreigners living among my people,
and we would eat the festival meal together. I did this in keeping with the Law
of Moses, which Deborah, the mother of
my grandfather Ananiel, had taught me

[a] THE LAND WAS AT REST: *See Lv 25.1-7.* [b] a third tithe; *some manuscripts have* the money.

to obey. (I had been left an orphan when
my father died.)

Tobit's Faithfulness in Exile

9 When I grew up, I married Anna, a
member of my own tribe. We had a
son and named him Tobias. 10 Later, I
was taken captive and deported to Assyria, and that is how I came to live in
Nineveh.

While we lived in Nineveh, all my relatives and the other Jews used to eat the
same kind of food as the other people
who lived there, 11 but I refused to do so.
12 Since I took seriously the commands
of the Most High God, 13 he made Emperor Shalmaneser respect me, and I
was placed in charge of purchasing all
the emperor's supplies.

14 Before the emperor died, I made regular trips to the land of Media to buy
things for him there. Once, when I was
in the city of Rages in Media, I left some
bags of money there with Gabael, Ga-
brias' brother, and asked him to keep
them for me. There were more than 600
pounds of silver coins in those bags.
15 When Shalmaneser died, his son Sennacherib succeeded him as emperor. It
soon became so dangerous to travel on
the roads in Media that I could no longer
go there.

Tobit Buries the Dead

16 While Shalmaneser was still emperor, I took good care of my own people whenever they were in need. 17 If
they were hungry, I shared my food with
them; if they needed clothes, I gave them
some of my own. Whenever I saw that
the dead body of one of my people had
been thrown outside the city wall, I gave
it a decent burial.

18 One day Sennacherib cursed God,
the King of Heaven; God punished him,
and Sennacherib had to retreat from Judah. On his way back to Media he was
so furious that he killed many Israelites.
But I secretly removed the bodies and
buried them; and when Sennacherib
later searched for the bodies, he could
not find them.

19 Then someone from Nineveh told
the emperor that I was the one who had
been burying his victims. As soon as I
realized that the emperor knew all about
me and that my life was in danger, I became frightened. So I ran away and hid.
20 Everything I owned was seized and
put in the royal treasury. My wife Anna
and my son Tobias were all I had left.

Tobit's Nephew Rescues Him

21 About six weeks later, two of Sennacherib's sons assassinated him and
then escaped to the mountains of Ararat.
Another son, Esarhaddon, became emperor and put Ahikar, my brother An-
ael's son, in charge of all the financial
affairs of the empire. 22 This was actually
the second time Ahikar was appointed
to this position, for when Sennacherib
was emperor of Assyria, Ahikar had
been wine steward, treasurer, and ac-
countant, and had been in charge of the
official seal. Since Ahikar was my
nephew, he put in a good word for me
with the emperor, and I was allowed to
return to Nineveh.

A Family Celebration

2 When I returned home I was reunited with my wife Anna and my
son Tobias. At the Harvest Festival,
which is also called the Festival of
Weeks, I sat down to a delicious meal.
2 When I saw how much food there was
on the table, I said to Tobias, "Son, go
out and find one of our people who is
living in poverty here in exile, someone
who takes God's commands seriously.
Bring him back with you, so that he can
share this festival meal with us. I won't
start eating until you come back."

A Murder in Nineveh

3 So Tobias went out to look for such a
person. But he quickly returned, shouting, "Father! Father!"

"Yes, what is it?" I asked.

"One of our people has just been murdered! Someone strangled him and
threw his body into the marketplace."

4 I jumped up and left the table without
even touching my food. I removed the
body from the street and carried it to a
little shed, where I left it until sunset,
when I could bury it. 5 Then I returned
home and washed, so as to purify myself. In deep sorrow I ate my dinner. 6 I
was reminded of what the prophet Amos
had said to the people of Bethel,

"Your festivals will be turned into
funerals,

and your glad songs will become
cries of grief."
I began to weep.
7 After sunset I went out, dug a grave,
and buried the man. 8 My neighbors
thought I was crazy. "Haven't you
learned anything?" they asked. "You
have already been hunted down once for
burying the dead, and you would have
been killed if you had not run away. But
here you are doing the same thing all
over again."

Tobit Is Blinded

9 That night I washed, so as to purify
myself, and went out into my courtyard
to sleep by the wall. It was a hot night,
and I did not pull the cover up over my
head. 10 Sparrows were on the wall right
above me, but I did not know it. Their
warm droppings fell into my eyes, causing a white film to form on them. I went
to one doctor after another, but the more
they treated me with their medicines, the
worse my eyes became, until finally I
was completely blind.

For four years I could see nothing. My relatives were deeply concerned about my condition, and Ahikar supported me for two years before he went to the land of Elam.

A Family Quarrel

11 After Ahikar left, my wife Anna had
to go to work, so she took up weaving,
like many other women. 12 The people
she worked for would pay her when she
delivered the cloth. One spring day, she
cut a finished piece of cloth from the
loom and took it to the people who had
ordered it. They paid her the full price
and also gave her a goat.
13 When Anna came home with the
goat, it began to bleat. I called out,
"Where did that goat come from? You
stole it, didn't you? Take it straight back
to its owners. It's not right to eat stolen
food!"
14 "No!" she replied. "It was given to
me as a gift in addition to what I got for
the cloth." But I didn't believe her, and I
blushed for shame for what she had
done. I ordered her to return the goat to
its owners, but she had the last word.
"Now I see what you are really like!" she
shouted. "Where is all that concern of
yours for others? What about all those
good deeds you used to do?"

Tobit's Prayer

3 I was so embarrassed and ashamed
that I sighed and began to cry.
Then, as I choked back my tears, I
prayed:

2 "You are righteous, O Lord!
You are merciful[c] in all you do,
faithful in all your ways.
You are the judge of this world.[d]
3-4 I beg you, treat me with
kindness.
Do not punish me for my sins,
not even for sins of which I am
unaware.
My ancestors rebelled and
disobeyed[e] your commands,
but do not punish me for their
sins.
You let our people be plundered,
taken captive and killed.
You made an example of our
people,
an object of contempt and
disgrace
in all the nations where you
scattered us.
5 You have often judged my
ancestors for their sins
and punished me for mine.
We were disloyal and rejected
your commands,
so our punishment has always
been just.

6 "Now treat me as you please.
Take my life away and free me
from this world;
let my body return to the earth.
I would be better off dead.
I am tormented by insults I don't
deserve,
and weighed down with despair.
Lord, give the command—
bring all my troubles to an end,
take me to my eternal rest.
Don't reject my prayer.
I would rather die than live in
misery
and face such cruel insults."

[c] merciful; *some manuscripts add* and just. [d] You are the judge of this world; *some manuscripts have* You are always fair and just when you judge. [e] My ancestors . . . disobeyed; *some manuscripts have* I disobeyed.

Sarah's Troubles

7 That same day in the city of Ecbatana
in Media, it happened that Sarah, the
daughter of a man named Raguel, was
insulted by one of her father's servant
women. 8 Sarah had been married seven
times, but the evil demon, Asmodeus,
killed each husband before the marriage
could be consummated. The servant
woman said to Sarah, "You husband
killer! Look at you! You've already had
seven husbands, but not one of them
lived long enough to give you a son.[f]
9 Why should you take it out on us? Why
don't you go and join your dead husbands? I hope we never see a child of
yours!"

10 Sarah was so depressed that she
burst into tears and went upstairs determined to hang herself. But when she
thought it over, she said to herself, "No,
I won't do it! People would insult my
father and say, 'You had only one child,
a daughter whom you loved dearly, but
she hanged herself because she felt so
miserable.' Such grief would bring my
gray-haired father to his grave, and I
would be responsible. I won't kill myself; I'll just beg the Lord to let me die.
Then I won't have to listen to those insults any longer!"

Sarah's Prayer

11 Then Sarah stood by the window,
raised her arms in prayer, and said,

"God of mercy, worthy of our
praise,
may your name always be
honored,
may all your creation praise you
forever.
12 "Lord, I look to you for help.
13 Speak the word and set me free
from this life;
then I will no longer have to
hear these insults.
14 You know, O Lord, that I'm still a
virgin;
I have never been defiled by
a man.
15 Never have I disgraced myself or
my father's name,
as long as we have lived in this
land of exile.
My father has no other child to be
his heir,
and there is no relative[g] whom
I can marry.
I have already lost seven
husbands,
so why should I live any longer?
But if it is not your will to take my
life,
at least show mercy to me.
Don't let me hear those insults
again!"[h]

God Hears the Prayers of Tobit and Sarah

16 As Tobit and Sarah were praying,
God in heaven heard their prayers 17 and
sent his angel Raphael to help them. He
was sent to remove the white film from
Tobit's eyes, so that he could see again,
and to arrange a marriage between
Sarah and Tobit's son Tobias, who, as
her cousin, had the right to marry her.
Raphael was also ordered to expel the
demon Asmodeus from Sarah. At the
very moment that Tobit went back into
his house from the courtyard, Sarah, in
her house in Ecbatana, was coming
downstairs.

Tobit's Advice to Tobias

4 That same day, Tobit remembered
the money that he had left with
Gabael at Rages in Media. 2 He thought
to himself, "Now that I have asked God
to let me die, I should call my son Tobias
and tell him about the money."

3-4 So Tobit called Tobias and said to
him, "Son, when I die, give me a proper
burial. And after I'm gone, show respect
to your mother. Take care of her for the
rest of her life, and when she dies, bury
her beside me. Remember, she risked
her life to bring you into this world, so
try to make her happy and never do anything that would worry her.

5 "Every day of your life, keep the Lord
our God in mind. Never sin deliberately
or disobey any of his commands. Always do what is right and never get involved in anything evil. 6 Be honest, and
you will succeed in whatever you do.
7 "Give generously to anyone who

[f] but . . . son; *some manuscripts have* but it hasn't done you a bit of good. [g] RELATIVE: *In Israel it was customary to marry within one's own tribe.* [h] at least . . . again; *some manuscripts have* at least listen to my complaint.

faithfully obeys God.[i] If you are stingy
in giving to the poor, God will be stingy
in giving to you. 8 Give according to
what you have. The more you have, the
more you should give. Even if you have
only a little, be sure to give something.
9 This is as good as money saved. You
will have your reward in a time of trouble. 10-11 Taking care of the poor is the
kind of offering that pleases God in
heaven. Do this, and you will be kept
safe from the dark world of the dead.
12 "Son, be on your guard against prostitutes. Above all, marry a woman of our
tribe, because we are descendants of the
prophets. Do not marry anyone who is
not related to us. Remember that Noah,
Abraham, Isaac and Jacob, our earliest
ancestors, all married relatives. God
blessed them with children, and so their
descendants will inherit the land of Israel. 13 Son, be loyal to your own relatives. Don't be too proud to marry one of
them. Such pride leads to terrible frustration and ruin, just as laziness brings
on severe poverty and causes starvation.
14 "Pay your workers each day; never
keep back their wages overnight. Honor
God in this way, and he will reward you.
Behave properly at all times. 15 Never do
to anyone else anything that you would
not want someone to do to you.
"Do not drink so much wine that you
get drunk, and do not let drinking become a habit.
16 "Give food to the hungry and clothes
to people in need. If you are prosperous,
give generously, and do it gladly!
17 "When one of God's faithful people
has died, prepare food for the family,[j]
but never do this when someone evil
dies.
18 "Take the advice of sensible people,
and never treat any useful advice lightly.
19 "Take advantage of every opportunity to praise the Lord your God. Ask
him to make you prosper in whatever
you set out to do. He does not give his
wisdom to the people of any other nation. He is the source of all good things,
but he can also destroy you and bring
you to certain death, if he wishes.
"Remember all my instructions. Don't
forget them for one minute.
20 "Tobias, I want you to know that I
once left a large sum of money with Ga-
brias' son, Gabael, at Rages in Media.
21 We're poor now, but don't worry. If
you obey God and avoid sin, he will be
pleased with you and make you
prosperous."

Travel Preparations

5 Then Tobias answered his father,
"I'll do everything you told me. 2 But
how can I get the money back from Gabael? We have never even met each other.
How can I prove to him who I am, so that
he will trust me and give me the money?
Besides that, I don't know how to get to
Media."
3 Tobit replied, "Gabael and I both
signed a document. I then tore it in two,
and we each took a half. I put his half
with the money. That was twenty years
ago! Now, go and find a reliable person
to travel with you to Media and back,
and we will pay him when you return.
But you must get the money that I left
with Gabael."

Tobias Meets Raphael

4 Tobias then went out to look for
someone who knew the way to Media
and would travel with him. Almost as
soon as he left the house, he found himself face-to-face with Raphael. Tobias
did not know that Raphael was an angel
of God, 5 so he asked him where he was
from.
"I am an Israelite," Raphael answered,
"one of your distant relatives, and I have
come here to Nineveh to find work."
"Do you know the way to Media?" Tobias asked.
6 "Yes, I do," Raphael replied. "I have
been there many times, and I know all
the roads well. I used to stay with our
relative Gabael, who lives there in the
town of Rages.[k] It takes at least two
days to travel there from Ecbatana, the
capital city, because Rages is up in the
mountains."
7 Then Tobias said to Raphael, "Wait
here for me, my friend, while I go in and
tell my father. I would like for you to
travel with me, and I will pay you for the
journey."
8 "All right," Raphael said, "I'll wait,
but don't take too long."

[i] *The translation of verses 7b-19b, accidentally omitted in the Greek manuscript that this translation normally follows, is based on other Greek manuscripts.* [j] prepare . . . family; *or* put food on his grave. [k] Rages; *Greek* Ecbatana.

9 Tobias went in and told his father,
"I have found an Israelite to travel
with me."

"Call the man in," Tobit replied. "I
would like to know what family and
tribe he belongs to, and whether he is a
reliable traveling companion for you."

Tobit Meets Raphael

So Tobias went out and called to Raphael, "My father would like to meet
you." When Raphael came in, Tobit
greeted him first.

Then Raphael returned the greeting, "I
hope all is well with you."

But Tobit replied, "How can all be well
with me? I'm blind and can't see a thing.
It's like being dead and no longer able to
see the light. I might as well be dead! I
can hear people talking, but I can't see
them."

"Cheer up!" Raphael said to him. "God
is going to cure you soon, so don't
worry!"

Tobit then said, "My son Tobias wants
to go to Media. Can you go with him and
show him the way? I will pay you, of
course."

Raphael replied, "Certainly I can go
with him. I have traveled there many
times and I know all the roads in the
mountains and on the plains."

10 Tobit questioned him further, "Tell
me, my friend, what family and tribe do
you belong to?"

11 But Raphael asked, "Why do you
need to know that?"

"Tell me the truth," said Tobit. "What
is your name, and who are you?"

12 Raphael replied, "My name is Azarias, and I am the son of the older Ananias, one of your relatives."

13 Then Tobit said to him, "Welcome to
our home! God bless you, my son. Please
don't be offended because I wanted to
know the truth about you and your family. As it turns out, you are from a good
family and a relative at that! I knew Ananias and Nathan, the two sons of the
older Shemaiah. They were always loyal
to their religion. We used to travel together to Jerusalem and worship there.
Your relatives are fine people, and you
come from good stock. Have a safe
journey."

14 Tobit continued, "I will pay the normal daily wage plus expenses for both of
you. 15 Be a good companion to Tobias,
and I will add a bonus to your wages."

16 "I will go with him," Raphael said.
"And don't worry; we will get there
and back safely. The roads are not
dangerous."

"God be with you!" Tobit replied. Then
he called Tobias and said to him, "Son,
get everything ready that you need for
the journey, so that the two of you can
be on your way. May God and his angel
watch over you both and bring you back
to me safe and sound."

Before leaving for Media, Tobias
kissed his father and mother good-bye.
Tobit said again, "Have a safe journey!"

17 Then his mother began to cry. "How
could you send my son away like this?"
she complained. "He's our only means of
support. Who will take care of us now?
18 Is that money so important to you that
you are willing to risk your own son's
life to get it back? 19 Why can't we be
content to live on what the Lord has
given us?"

20 "Calm down," Tobit said to her. "He
will get there and back safely, and with
your own eyes you will see him return
home safe and sound. 21 Now stop worrying about them, dear. A good angel
will go with Tobias. He will have a successful journey and will come back in
good health." At that, Anna calmed
down and stopped crying.

Tobias Catches a Fish

6 So Tobias and the angel started out
toward Media, taking Tobias' dog
along with them. They walked on until
sunset, then camped by the Tigris River.
2 Tobias had gone down to wash his feet
in the river, when suddenly a huge fish
jumped up out of the water and tried to
swallow one of his feet. Tobias let out a
yell, 3 and the angel called to him, "Grab
that fish! Don't let it get away."

Then Tobias grabbed the fish and
dragged it up on the bank.

4 "Cut the fish open," the angel instructed, "and take out its gall bladder,
heart, and liver. Keep these with you;
they can be used for medicine, but throw
away the guts."

5 Tobias did as the angel had told him.
Then he cooked the fish, ate part of
it, and salted the rest to take along
with him.

The two continued on together until
they were near Media. 6 Then Tobias

asked, "Azarias, my friend, what diseases can be cured by this gall bladder,
heart, and liver?"
7 The angel answered, "The heart and
liver can be burned and used to chase
away a demon or an evil spirit that is
tormenting someone. The attacks will
stop immediately, and the person will
never be troubled again. 8 You can use
the gall bladder to treat someone whose
eyes are covered with a white film. Just
rub it on his eyes and blow on the film,
and he will be able to see again."

On the Way to Ecbatana

9 When they had reached Media and
were approaching the city of Ecbatana,
10 Raphael said, "Tobias, my friend."
"Yes, what is it?" Tobias asked.
Raphael continued, "Tonight we will
stay at the home of your relative Raguel.
He has only one child, a daughter named
Sarah, 11 and since you are her closest
relative, you have the right to marry her.
You also have the right to inherit all her
father's property. 12 She is sensible,
brave, and very beautiful; and her father
is a good man. Tonight I'll discuss the
marriage proposal with her father, and
he will consent to give her to you as your
bride. Then, when we return home from
the town of Rages, we will celebrate the
marriage. Raguel cannot refuse to let
you marry her, and he cannot let any
other man have her. If he did, then according to the Law of Moses he would
deserve the death penalty. He knows
that you are the only man who has the
right to marry his daughter and receive
the inheritance, so follow my advice. Raguel and I will discuss the matter tonight
and arrange your engagement to Sarah.
When we get back from the city of
Rages, we will take her home with us."
13 Tobias then said to Raphael, "Azarias, my friend, I have already heard
about Sarah's seven former husbands,
and how each one dropped dead on his
wedding night, even before he could get
to bed. 14 According to the story I heard,
a demon killed them. He doesn't harm
Sarah, but he kills every man who tries
to get near her. I am afraid of this demon. I am an only child, and if I were to
die, the sorrow would send my parents
to their graves. They don't even have another son to bury them."
15 The angel replied, "Have you already forgotten your father's instructions? He told you to marry a woman
from your own tribe. So, listen carefully
to what I say. Don't worry about the demon. Marry Sarah! I know that tonight
Raguel will let Sarah marry you.
16 When you go into the bedroom, take
the fish's heart and liver with you and
place them on the burning incense, 17 so
that the odor will spread throughout the
room. When the demon smells it, he will
leave and never come near Sarah again.
But before you consummate the marriage, both of you must get up and pray
for the Lord in heaven to be merciful to
you and to protect you. Don't be afraid.
Sarah was meant to be yours from the
beginning of creation. You will rescue
her from the demon, and she will go with
you to your home. You and Sarah will
have many children, whom you will love
very much. So don't worry!"
Tobias listened very carefully to what
Raphael had to say. He knew that Sarah
was a relative on his father's side of the
family. He began to fall in love with her
and looked forward to marrying her.

At Raguel's House

7 When Tobias and the angel Raphael had entered the city of Ecbatana, Tobias said, "Azarias, my friend,
take me to see Raguel as quickly as you
can." The angel brought him to Raguel's
house, where they found him sitting at
the entrance to his courtyard. Raphael
and Tobias greeted him first; then he replied, "Come in, my friends. You are
welcome in my home."
Raguel brought them into his house
2 and said to his wife Edna, "Doesn't this
young man look just like my cousin
Tobit?"
3 Edna asked them, "Where do you
come from?"
"We are Israelites of the tribe of Naphtali," Tobias and Raphael answered,
"but we are now living in exile in the city
of Nineveh in Assyria."
4 Edna said, "Do you know our cousin
Tobit?"
"We certainly do know him," they
answered.
"How is he?" she asked.
5 "He is alive and well," they replied.
Then Tobias added, "Tobit is my
father." 6 At that Raguel got up, and with
tears of joy in his eyes he kissed Tobias.

7 Then he said, "God bless you, my child.
Your father is a good and noble man.
What a terrible tragedy that such an
honest and generous man should have
lost his sight!" He threw his arms around
Tobias' neck and wept on his shoulder.
8 His wife Edna and his daughter Sarah
also wept for Tobit.

Raguel gave Tobias and Raphael a
warm welcome and had one of his rams
slaughtered. After the guests had bathed
and were about to sit down to eat, Tobias said to Raphael, "Azarias, my
friend, when are you going to ask Raguel to let me marry Sarah?"
9 But Raguel overheard the question
and said to Tobias, 10 "Eat and drink
something first and enjoy yourself this
evening. You have the right to marry
Sarah, and I cannot let anyone else
marry her, because you are my closest
relative. But I must tell you the truth, my
son. 11 I have already given her to seven
men, all of them relatives. Each one died
on his wedding night, as soon as he entered the bedroom. But now, my son,
have something to eat and drink. The
Lord will take care of you both."

Tobias replied, "I won't eat or drink
until you give me your word."
12 Raguel agreed. "Certainly I will," he
said. "I will give her to you just as the
Law of Moses commands. God in
heaven has arranged this marriage, so
take her as your wife. From now on, you
belong to each other. Sarah is yours today and forever. May the Lord of heaven
keep both of you safe tonight. May he be
merciful and kind to you."

The Marriage Ceremony

13 Then Raguel called his daughter.
When she came in, he took her by the
hand and gave her to Tobias with his
blessing, "Take her to be your wife according to the teachings in the Law of
Moses. Take her safely with you to your
father's house. May the God of heaven
give you a happy life together."
14 Raguel asked his wife to bring him a
blank scroll so that he could write out
the marriage contract. Edna brought
him the scroll, and Raguel wrote out the
agreement, saying that Sarah was given
to Tobias according to the teachings in
the Law of Moses. 15 After the ceremony
they began the meal.
16 Raguel called his wife and said, "Get
the spare room ready, my dear, and take
Sarah there."
17 Edna made up the bed as Raguel had
told her. Then she took Sarah into the
room with her, and Sarah began to cry.[l]
But Edna wiped away her tears and said,
18 "Don't worry, Sarah. I'm sure the Lord
of heaven will make you happy this time
and not sad. So cheer up, my dear."
Then Edna left the room.

The Demon Is Expelled

8 When they had finished the meal,
and it was time to go to bed, Sarah's
parents led young Tobias to the bedroom. 2 He remembered Raphael's instructions, so he took the fish's liver and
heart out of the bag where he had been
keeping them. Then he placed them on
the burning incense. 3 The smell drove
the demon away from them, and he fled
to Egypt.[m] Raphael chased after him
and caught him there. At once he bound
him hand and foot.

The Prayer of Tobias

4 When Tobias and Sarah were alone
behind closed doors, Tobias got up from
the bed and said to his wife, "Get up,
dear. Let's pray for the Lord to be merciful and to protect us." 5 Sarah got up so
that they could pray together and ask
God for his protection. Then Tobias
prayed:

"God of our ancestors, you are
worthy of praise.
May your name be honored
forever and ever
by all your creatures in heaven
and on earth.
6 You created Adam and gave him
his wife Eve
to be his helper and support.
They became the parents of the
whole human race.
You said, 'It is not good for man
to live alone.
I will make a suitable helper
for him.'
7 Lord, I have chosen Sarah because
it is right,
not because I lusted for her.
Please be merciful to us

[l] and Sarah began to cry; *some manuscripts have* and she began to cry. [m] EGYPT: *Egypt was thought of as the most remote part of the world and the home of demons and evil spirits.*

and grant that we may grow old
together."
8Then they both said "Amen" 9and went
to bed for the night.

Anxious Parents

Later that night, Raguel called his
servants, and together they went out to
dig a grave, 10because Raguel thought,
"Tobias will probably die too, and people will laugh and make fun of us."
11When they finished digging the grave,
Raguel went back into the house and
said to his wife, 12"Send one of the servant women to find out if Tobias is still
alive. If he isn't, then we will bury him
before anyone finds out." 13They then
sent a servant woman to take a lamp and
see if he was still alive. As she opened
the door, she could see that both of them
were sound asleep. 14So she went back
and told Raguel and Edna that Tobias
was alive and unharmed. 15Then Raguel[n] praised the God of heaven:

Raguel's Prayer

"You are worthy of our praise,
O God.
May your people praise you
forever;
may they praise you with pure
hearts.
16I praise you because you have
made me glad;
you have been merciful to us,
and my worst fears did not come
true.
17You deserve our praise, O Lord;
you were merciful to this young
couple,
the only children of their
parents.
Now, grant them your mercy and
protection.
Let them live out their lives in
happiness and love."
18Then Raguel ordered his servants to
fill in the grave before dawn.

The Wedding Feast

19Raguel told his wife to bake enough
bread for a big feast. Then he went out to
the herd and brought back two oxen and
four rams, which he ordered his servants to slaughter in preparation for the
wedding feast. 20He called for Tobias
and vowed[o] that he would not let him
leave for two weeks. "Stay, and we will
eat and drink together," he said. "It will
do my daughter good after her terrible
suffering. 21Then you may take half of
what I own and go back to your parents
safe and sound. You will inherit the
other half when Edna and I die. Have no
doubts about our love for you; from now
on you are as much our son as Sarah is
our daughter. You can be sure of that,
my son."

The Journey to Rages

9 Then Tobias called Raphael and
said to him, 2"Azarias, take four of
the servants with you, and two camels,
and go to Gabael's house in the town of
Rages. Give him the signed document,
so that he will give you the money. Then
bring him back with you for the wedding
feast. 3-4You know that my father is
counting the days until I come home,
and he will be very upset if I am even
one day late. You know, too, how Raguel
insists that I must stay, and I cannot disappoint him."

5So Raphael and the four servants
went to Rages in Media, where they
stayed at Gabael's house. Raphael gave
him the signed document and told him
that Tobit's son Tobias had recently
married, and that Gabael was invited to
the wedding feast. At once Gabael
counted out the bags of money, which
were still sealed, and they loaded them
on the camels.[p] 6Very early the next
morning, they set out for the wedding
feast. When Raphael and Gabael came
to Raguel's house, they found Tobias at
dinner. Tobias immediately got up and
greeted Gabael. With tears in his eyes
Gabael returned the greeting and added,
"You are just like your honest and generous father. May the Lord in heaven
bless you and your wife, your mother-in-
law, and your father. Praise God! He has
let me live to see my cousin Tobias, who
looks so much like his father."

Tobit and Anna Are Worried

10 Meanwhile, every day Tobit was
keeping count of the time needed
to travel to Rages and back. When the
time was up and his son had not returned, Tobit said to his wife, 2"What

[n] Raguel; *some manuscripts have* they. [o] vowed; *some manuscripts have* said.
[p] loaded them on the camels; *some manuscripts have* stacked them up.

can be keeping him? Do you suppose
Gabael has died? Maybe there is no one
to give him the money." 3 Tobit was very
worried.
4 Then Anna said, "My son is dead. I'm
sure of it." She began to weep and to
mourn for Tobias, 5 "Oh, my son, the joy
of my life, why did I ever let you leave
home?"
6 Tobit tried to comfort her. "Calm
down, my dear," he said. "Don't worry.
He will be all right. Something unexpected is probably keeping them there
longer than we counted on. Besides, his
companion is a reliable man and a relative at that. Don't let yourself get so upset over him, dear. I'm sure he is already
on his way home."
7 But she replied, "Be quiet and leave
me alone! Don't try to fool me. My son is
dead." Each day she would rush out of
the house to the road which Tobias had
taken and would watch for him until
sunset. She would let no one comfort
her,[q] and when she returned home she
would weep and mourn for her son all
night long, without sleeping.

Departure from Ecbatana

The two-week wedding feast which
Raguel had promised to hold for his
daughter Sarah came to an end. So Tobias went to him and asked, "Please let
me go home now. I'm certain my parents
have given up all hope of ever seeing me
again. Please, Raguel, let me go home to
my father. I have already told you the
condition he was in when I left."
8 But Raguel answered, "Stay, my son.
Stay here with me. I will send messengers to your father to tell him that you
are all right."
9 But Tobias insisted, "No, I can't!
Please let me go back to my father."
10 So Raguel gave Tobias his bride
Sarah without further delay. He also
gave Tobias half of everything he
owned: slaves, cattle, sheep, donkeys,
camels, clothes, money, and furniture.
11 Raguel embraced Tobias and sent
them on their way with his blessing,
"Good-bye, my son. Have a safe journey.
May the Lord of heaven protect you and
Sarah. And may I live to see your children." 12 Raguel then said to Sarah, "Go
with your husband and live in his parents' house. From now on they are as
much your parents as your own mother
and I are. Let me hear only good things
about you as long as I live." After saying
good-bye he sent them on their way.
Then Edna said to Tobias, "Tobias my
dear child, may the Lord bring you
safely home. And may he let me live to
see your children. The Lord is my witness; I am placing my daughter in your
care. Never, at any time in your life, do
anything that would break her heart.
Have a safe journey, Tobias. From now
on, Sarah is your wife and I am your
mother. May we all prosper as long as
we live." Then Edna kissed them both
and sent them safely on their way.

11 When Tobias left, he was as
happy as could be. He praised
the Lord of heaven and earth, the King
of all the world, because his journey had
been so successful, and he promised to
honor Raguel and his wife as long as
they lived.[r]

The Homecoming

As they came near the city of Kaserin,
just outside Nineveh, 2 Raphael said,
"Tobias, you know the condition your
father was in when we left him. 3 We
should go on ahead of your wife and get
the house ready before everyone else ar-
rives. 4 Be sure to bring the fish's gall
bladder with you." So they went on
ahead, and Tobias' dog ran along with[s]
them.
5 Meanwhile, Anna sat looking down
the road for her son. 6 Suddenly she saw
him coming and she shouted out to Tobit, "Look! Our son is coming, and his
friend is with him!"
7 Before they reached Tobit, Raphael
said to Tobias, "Your father will be able
to see again. 8 Just put the fish's gall
bladder on his eyes like a plaster. The
medicine will make the white film
shrivel up so that you can peel it off, and
your father will then regain his
eyesight."
9 Anna ran to her son, threw her arms
around him, and exclaimed, "Now that I

[q] She would let no one comfort her; *some manuscripts have* She would not eat a bite.
[r] successful, and ... lived; *or* successful. And Raguel made Tobias promise to honor him and Edna as long as they lived. [s] Tobias' dog ... with; *some manuscripts have* the Lord accompanied.

have seen you alive, my child, I can die
in peace!" And she wept for joy.

Tobit's Cure

10 Tobit got up and stumbled out
through the entrance of the courtyard.
11 Tobias went up to him, holding the
fish's gall bladder in his hand. He blew
on his father's eyes and steadied him.
"Don't worry now, father," he said.
12-13 Tobias then applied the gall, and beginning from the corners of Tobit's eyes,
he peeled away the white film. 14 Tobit
threw his arms around Tobias' neck and
wept for joy. Then he exclaimed, "I can
see you! My son, the light of my eyes!

"Praise God. Praise him for his
greatness.
Praise all his holy angels.
May he continue to bless us.
Praise all his angels forever.
15 He brought this illness upon me,
but now I can see my son
Tobias!"

Then Tobias went happily into the
house, praising God at the top of his
voice. He told his father how successful
he had been, that he had not only
brought back the money, but had married Raguel's daughter Sarah, who was
on her way and would soon arrive.

Sarah's Arrival

16 Tobit was excited and praised God
as he went out to meet his son's bride at
the city gate. When the people of Nineveh saw him, they were amazed, because he was walking on his own, with
no one leading him by the hand. 17 Tobit
praised God and told everyone how God
in his mercy had restored his sight.

When Tobit met Sarah, he greeted
her, "Welcome, daughter! Praise God for
bringing you to us, my daughter. May
God bless your father, as well as you and
my son Tobias. Welcome to your new
home. May you always be blessed with
good health and happiness. Come in,
daughter!"

It was a day of great joy for all the
Jews of Nineveh. 18 Tobit's nephews Ahikar and Nadab came by to share Tobit's
happiness with him.

The Angel Raphael

12 When the wedding feast was
over, Tobit called his son Tobias
and said to him, "Son, be sure to pay
your traveling companion, and don't forget to give him a bonus."
2 Tobias asked him, "Father, how
much do you think I should pay him? I
wouldn't mind giving him half of everything we brought back with us. 3 He
brought me back home safe and sound;
he went to get the money for me from
Gabael; he rid my wife of a demon; and
he cured your blindness. How much of a
bonus should I give him?"
4 Tobit answered, "Give him half of
what he helped you bring back. He well
deserves that."
5 Tobias then called Raphael and said
to him, "Here is half of what you helped
me bring back. You have earned it; have
a safe journey home.
6 Then Raphael called the two men
aside and said to them, "Praise God and
tell everyone about the good things he
has done for you, so that they too will
honor him and sing his praises. Let
everyone know what God has done.
Never stop praising him.
7 "It's a good idea to keep a king's secret, but what God does should be told
everywhere, so that he may be praised
and honored.

"If you do good, no harm will come
to you.
8 "It is better to pray sincerely and to
please God by helping the poor than to
be rich and dishonest. It is better to give
to the poor than to store up gold. 9 Such
generosity will save you from death and
will wash away all your sins. Those who
give to the poor will live full lives, 10 but
those who live a life of sin and wickedness are their own worst enemies.
11 "I have already told you that a king's
secret ought to be kept, but the things
God does should be told to everyone.
Now I will reveal to you the full truth
and keep nothing back. 12 Tobit, when
you and Sarah prayed to the Lord, I was
the one who brought your prayers into
his glorious presence. I did the same
thing each time you buried the dead.
13 On the day you got up from the table
without eating your meal in order to
bury that corpse, God sent me to test
you. 14 But he also sent me to cure you
and to rescue your daughter-in-law,
Sarah, from her troubles. 15 I am Raphael, one of the seven angels who stand
in the glorious presence of the Lord,
ready to serve him."

16 Tobit and Tobias were terrified and
fell to the ground, trembling with fear.
17 But Raphael said to them, "Don't be
afraid; everything is all right. Always remember to praise God. 18 He wanted me
to come and help you; I did not come on
my own. So sing God's praises as long as
you live. 19 When you thought you saw
me eating, I did not really eat anything;
it only seemed so. 20 While you are on
this earth, you must praise the Lord God
and give him thanks. Now I must go
back to him who sent me. Write down
everything that has happened to you."
21 Then Raphael disappeared into the
sky. Tobit and Tobias stood up, but they
could no longer see him. 22 They began
to sing hymns of praise, giving thanks
for all the mighty deeds God had done
while his angel Raphael had been with
them.

Tobit's Song of Praise

13 Then Tobit prayed:

"Praise the eternal God,
praise the one who rules.
2 He punishes us; then he shows us
mercy.
He sends us down to the world
of the dead,
then he brings us up from the
grave.
No one can escape his power.

3 "People of Israel, give thanks
among the nations,
where he sent you into exile;
4 even there he showed his great
power.
Let all who live hear your praise.
The Lord is our God and father
forever.

5 "Though he punished you for your
wickedness,
he will be merciful and bring
you home
from among the nations where
he scattered you.

6 "Turn to him with all your heart
and soul,
live in loyal obedience to him.
Then he will turn to you to
help you
and will no longer hide himself.
Remember what God has done
for you,
and give thanks with all your
heart.
Praise the righteous Lord;
honor the eternal King.

"Although I live in exile in a
foreign land,
I will give thanks to the Lord
and will speak of his great
strength to a nation of sinners.
'Turn away from your sins, and do
what pleases God!
Perhaps he will be gracious
and show you his mercy.'

7 "I praise my God and rejoice in his
greatness;
my whole being honors the King
of heaven.

8 "Let everyone tell of his greatness
and sing his praises in
Jerusalem.

9 "Jerusalem, Holy City of our God,
he will punish you for the sins
of your people,
but he will be merciful to all
who do right.
10 So give thanks to the Lord, for he
is good.
Praise the eternal King.[t]
Your Temple will be rebuilt,
and your people will be happy
again.

"May the Lord make all your
exiles glad,
may he take care of your
suffering people
for as long as time shall last.

11 "Jerusalem, your light will shine
brightly for all the world,
and from far away many nations
will come to you.
Their people will come to honor
the Lord your God,
they will bring gifts for the King
of heaven.
In your streets many generations
will sing joyful praise,

t *Some manuscripts do not have verses 6b-10a* Although I live . . . Praise the eternal King.

your name will endure forever
as God's chosen city.
12 A curse will be on all who make
threats against you,
on all who destroy you and tear
down your walls,
on all who demolish your towers
and burn your homes.
But all who honor you will be
blessed forever.

13 "Rejoice, Jerusalem, because of
your righteous people;
they will be gathered together
from exile
to praise the Lord of the ages.

14 "Happy are all who love you
and are pleased to see you
prosper.
Those who mourn over your
suffering now
will one day be happy;
your happiness will bring them
joy forever.

15 "I praise the Lord, the great King;
16 Jerusalem will be rebuilt
and will be his home forever.

"Jerusalem, how happy I will be
when my descendants can see
your splendor
and give thanks to the King of
heaven.

"Your gates will be built with
sapphires and emeralds,
and all your walls with precious
stones.
Your towers will be made of gold,
and their fortifications of pure
gold.
17 Your streets will be paved with
rubies and precious jewels.
18 Joyful songs will ring out from
your gates,
and from all your houses people
will shout,
'Praise the Lord! Praise the God
of Israel!'
"Jerusalem, God will bless your
people,
and they will praise his holy
name forever."

With these words Tobit ended his
song of praise.

Tobit's Final Advice

14 1-2 Tobit was 62 years old when
he became blind, but after his
sight had been restored, he lived a very
full life. Once again he gave generously
to the poor, and he continued to praise
God and tell of his greatness. Tobit died
a peaceful death at the age of 112, and
was given an honorable burial in
Nineveh.
3 But just before Tobit died, he sent for
his son Tobias and told him, 4 "My son,
take your children and go at once to Media. I believe that God's judgment which
his prophet Nahum announced against
Nineveh is about to take place. Everything that God's prophets told Israel
about Nineveh and Assyria will happen.
It will all come true, every word of it,
when the right time comes. I am absolutely convinced that everything God
has said is sure to come true. God does
not break his promises. It will be safer
for you in Media than in Assyria or
Babylon.
"Those Jews who live in Israel will all
be scattered and taken from that good
land into exile. All Israel will become a
wasteland; Samaria and Jerusalem will
be abandoned cities. God's Temple will
be burned to the ground and will lie in
complete ruin for a while. 5 But God will
have mercy on his people again, and he
will bring them back to the land of Israel. They will rebuild the Temple, but it
will not be as splendid as the first Temple, not until the proper time has come.
But when that time does come, all the
people of Israel will return from exile,
and they will rebuild the city of Jerusalem in all its former splendor. They will
rebuild God's Temple in Jerusalem, just
as Israel's prophets have foretold.
6 "Then all the nations in the world will
come back to God. They will worship
him as the only true God and give up the
idols that led them into false worship.
7 The nations of the world will praise the
everlasting God by doing what he
demands.
"At that time God will save all the people of Israel who have been faithful to
him. He will bring them together to Jerusalem, and let them take possession of

the land of Abraham, and there they will
live securely forever. All who love God
with their heart and soul will rejoice, but
all sinners and evil people will be wiped
off the face of the earth.
8 "Now, my children, follow my instructions. Worship God sincerely and
do what is pleasing to him. 9 Bring up
your children to do what is right. Teach
them that they must give to the poor and
must always remember to praise God
with all sincerity.
10 "Tobias, my son, leave Nineveh
now. Do not stay here. As soon as you
bury your mother beside me, leave; do
not stay another night within the city
limits. It is a wicked city and full of immorality; the people here have no sense
of shame. Remember what Nadab did to
Ahikar his own uncle who had brought
him up. He tried to kill Ahikar and
forced him to go into hiding in a tomb.
Ahikar came back into the light of day,
but God sent Nadab down into everlasting darkness for what he had done.
Ahikar escaped the deadly trap which
Nadab had set for him, because Ahikar[u]
had given generously to the poor. But
Nadab fell into that fatal trap and it destroyed him. 11 So now, my children, you
see what happens to those who show
their concern for others, and how death
awaits those who treat others unjustly.
But now I am very weak."

Then they laid Tobit on his bed. He
died and was given an honorable burial.
12 Later on, Tobit's wife died and was
buried beside her husband. Then Tobias
and his wife moved to Ecbatana in Media, where they lived with Raguel, Tobias' father-in-law. 13 Tobias took care of
Edna and Raguel in their old age and
showed them great respect. When at last
they died, he buried them at Ecbatana.
Tobias inherited Raguel's estate, as he
had inherited the estate of his father
Tobit.
14 At the ripe old age of 117 Tobias
died, 15 having lived long enough to hear
about the destruction of Nineveh and to
see King Cyaxares[v] of Media take the
people away as captives. Tobias praised
God for the way that he had punished
the people of Nineveh and Assyria. As
long as he lived he gave thanks for what
God had done to Nineveh.

[u] Ahikar; *or* I. [v] *Probable text* Cyaxares; *Greek unclear.*

The Book of JUDITH

Introduction

The Book of Judith *depicts a time when the Jewish nation was about to be crushed by an enemy army. Judith, the heroine of the story, is a deeply religious widow who observes all the requirements of the Law of Moses. She depends on God to help her complete the dramatic rescue of the nation by killing Holofernes.*

Outline of Contents

The War between Nebuchadnezzar and Arphaxad

1 While King Nebuchadnezzar was
ruling over the Assyrians from his
capital city of Nineveh, King Arphaxad
ruled over the Medes from his capital
city of Ecbatana. 2 Around Ecbatana
King Arphaxad built a wall 105 feet high
and 75 feet thick of cut stones; each
stone was 4 1/2 feet thick and 9 feet long.
3 At each gate he built a tower 150 feet
high, with a foundation 90 feet thick.

4 Each gateway was 105 feet high and 60
feet wide – wide enough for his whole
army to march through, with the infantry in formation.
5 In the twelfth year of his reign King
Nebuchadnezzar went to war against
King Arphaxad in the large plain around
the city of Rages. 6 Many nations joined
forces with King Arphaxad – all the people who lived in the mountains, those
who lived along the Tigris, Euphrates,
and Hydaspes rivers, as well as those
who lived in the plain ruled by King Arioch of Elam. Many nations joined this
Chelodite alliance.
7 Then King Nebuchadnezzar of Assyria sent a message to the Persians and
to the people to the west, in the regions
of Cilicia, Damascus, Lebanon, Antileb-
anon, to those along the coast, 8 and in
the regions of Carmel, Gilead, northern
Galilee, and Jezreel Valley. 9-10 The message also went to the people living in Samaria and the nearby towns, to those in
the area west of the Jordan River as far
as the cities of Jerusalem, Bethany,
Chelous, and Kadesh, and to the district
of Goshen. The message was also taken
to the Egyptian cities of Tahpanhes,
Rameses, Tanis, and Memphis, and the
district up the Nile River to the Ethiopian[a] border. 11 But everyone in this
whole region ignored King Nebuchadnezzar's appeal and refused to take part
in the war. They thought that he had no
chance of winning the war, so they were
not afraid of him and sent his messengers back disgraced and empty-handed.
12 This made Nebuchadnezzar so furious that he vowed he would risk his entire kingdom to take revenge on all those
people. He vowed that he would put to
death the entire population of Cilicia,
Damascus, Syria, Moab, Ammon, Judah, and Egypt – everyone from the
Mediterranean Sea to the Persian Gulf.
13 In the seventeenth year of his reign
King Nebuchadnezzar led his army into
battle against King Arphaxad. He defeated all of Arphaxad's forces, including his entire cavalry, and all his
charioteers. 14 Then Nebuchadnezzar occupied all the towns in the land of Media
and advanced against the city of Ecbatana. He captured the city's towers,
looted its markets, and made that beautiful city a ruin. 15 He captured King Arphaxad in the mountains around Rages
and killed him. After Arphaxad's death,
16 Nebuchadnezzar and his entire army
returned to Nineveh with all the loot
taken in battle. There they relaxed and
feasted for four months.

The War against the Nations in the West

2 In the eighteenth year of Nebuchadnezzar's reign, on the twenty-
second day of the first month of that
year, he and his advisers decided to
carry out his threat to take revenge on
all those countries that had refused to
help him. 2-3 The king called his general
staff and senior officers together and reported in detail how those countries had
betrayed him. He and his officers agreed
that everyone who had refused to help
him in the war should be put to death.
Then he described to them his plan of
attack.
4 At the close of the meeting, Nebuchadnezzar gave the following command to Holofernes, who was the
general in command of his armies and
second in command to the king: 5 "I,
Nebuchadnezzar, the great king and
ruler of all the earth, command you to
choose some experienced soldiers:
120,000 infantry and 12,000 cavalry.
6 Then attack the lands to the west because they refused to respond to my appeal for help. 7 Warn them that they
must prepare their offerings of earth and
water to show that they have surrendered unconditionally. I will make them
feel the full force of my anger and completely destroy them. My armies will
march over every foot of their land and
plunder it as they go. 8 I will fill the valleys with their dead bodies and will
choke up every stream and river with so
many corpses that they will all overflow.
9 I will take captive all those who are left
alive and carry them off to the ends of
the earth.
10 "But you, Holofernes, are ordered to
go ahead of me and occupy all their territories in advance. If they surrender to

[a] Greek Ethiopian: *Ethiopia is the name given in Graeco-Roman times to the extensive territory south of the First Cataract of the Nile River. Cush was the ancient (Hebrew) name of this region which included within its borders most of modern Sudan and some of present-day Ethiopia (Abyssinia).*

you, hold them for me until I come to
punish them. 11 But if they resist, do not
spare them. Kill them and loot the entire
region under your control. 12 I have
taken a solemn vow, and at the risk of
my life and my royal power I am determined to do what I have vowed to do.
13 Do not disobey me in any way. I am
your king; remember that, and carry out
without delay every order that I have
given you."

The Campaign of Holofernes

14 So Holofernes left the king and
called together all the commanders, generals, and officers of the Assyrian army.
15 Just as the king had ordered, he chose
120,000 of the best infantrymen and
12,000 of the best mounted archers
16 and arranged them in battle formation. 17 He also took along a very large
number of camels, donkeys, and mules
to carry the equipment, as well as many
sheep, cattle, and goats for food. 18 Every soldier received plenty of rations
and a large payment of gold and silver
from the royal treasury.

19 Then Holofernes and his entire
army set out, advancing ahead of King
Nebuchadnezzar. The chariots, the cavalry, and the infantry marched out to
overrun the entire western region.
20 Other troops went with them. There
were so many that it was impossible to
count them—they were like a swarm of
locusts or like grains of sand in the
desert.

21 Three days after they had left the
city of Nineveh, they reached the plains
around Bectileth near the mountains
north of Cilicia, where they set up camp.
22 From there Holofernes advanced into
the hill country with his entire army, his
infantry, cavalry, and chariots. 23 He totally destroyed the countries of Libya
and Lydia, then plundered all the people
of Rassis and the Ishmaelites who lived
on the edge of the desert, south of the
land of the Chelleans.

24 Then Holofernes crossed the Euphrates River and marched through the
land of Mesopotamia, completely destroying all the walled towns along the
Abron River as far as the sea. 25 He
seized the territory of Cilicia, killing
everyone who resisted him, and went as
far as the southern borders of the land of
Japheth, near Arabia. 26 He surrounded
the Midianites, burned down their tents,
and slaughtered their sheep.

27 Holofernes went down into the
plains around Damascus during the
wheat harvest, burned all the fields,
slaughtered the flocks and herds, looted
the towns, devastated the entire
countryside, and killed all the young
men. 28 Panic seized all the people who
lived along the Mediterranean Sea,
and they shook with fear. Everyone in
the towns of Tyre, Sidon, Sur, Ocina,
Jamnia, Ashdod, and Ashkelon was
terrified.

The Peace Delegation to King Nebuchadnezzar

3 All these nations sent a peace delegation to King Nebuchadnezzar
with this message: 2 "We remain loyal to
you, great King Nebuchadnezzar; we
are ready to serve you and obey any
command that you may wish to give us.
3 Our buildings, all our land, our wheat
fields, our livestock, and our tents are at
your disposal; use them in any way you
wish. 4 Our people will be your slaves,
and you may use our towns as you
please."

5 After the peace delegation had
brought this message, 6 Holofernes led
Nebuchadnezzar's army down to the
Mediterranean coast. He stationed
guards in all the walled towns and selected certain local men in each of the
towns as reserve troops. 7 The people in
the towns and in the surrounding
countryside welcomed Holofernes by
wearing wreaths of flowers and dancing
to the beat of drums. 8 But Holofernes
destroyed all their places of worship[b]
and cut down their sacred trees. He had
been ordered to destroy all the gods of
the land so that all the nations and tribes
would worship only Nebuchadnezzar
and pray to him as a god.

9 Then Holofernes passed through Jezreel Valley near Dothan, which faces the
main ridge of the mountains of Judah,
10 and set up camp between Geba and
Scythopolis. He stayed there for a month
in order to get supplies for his army.

[b] *One ancient translation* places of worship; *Greek* territory.

The Israelite Plan for Defense

4 The people of Judah heard what
Holofernes, the commander of King
Nebuchadnezzar's armies, had done to
the other nations. They heard how he
had looted and destroyed all their temples, 2 and they were terrified of him and
afraid of what he might do to Jerusalem
and to the Temple of the Lord their God.
3 They had only recently returned home
to Judah from exile and had just rededicated the Temple and its utensils and its
altar after they had been defiled. 4 So
they sent a warning to the whole region
of Samaria and to the towns of Kona,
Beth Horon, Belmain, Jericho, Choba,
and Aesora, and to Salem Valley. 5 They
immediately occupied the mountaintops, fortified the villages on the mountains, and stored up food in preparation
for war. It was fortunate that they had
recently harvested their fields.
6 The High Priest Joakim, who was in
Jerusalem at that time, wrote to the people in the towns of Bethulia and Betomesthaim, which face Jezreel Valley
near Dothan. 7 He ordered them to occupy the mountain passes which led into
the land of Judah, where it would be
easy to withstand an attack, since the
approach was only wide enough for two
people at a time to pass. 8 The Israelites
carried out the orders given to them by
the High Priest Joakim and the Council
which met in Jerusalem.

Prayer before the War

9 The leaders of Israel prayed earnestly to God and fasted. 10 They put on
sackcloth—they and their wives, their
children, their livestock, and every resident foreigner, every slave and hired laborer. 11-12 They also covered the altar
with sackcloth. Then all the men,
women, and children in Jerusalem lay
face down on the ground in front of the
Temple; they lay there in the Lord's
presence, all in sackcloth, their heads
covered with ashes. They joined together in earnest prayer to the God of
Israel, begging him not to let their children be captured, their wives carried off,
or their home towns destroyed. They
pleaded with him not to give the Gentiles
the satisfaction of destroying the Temple and dishonoring it. 13 The Lord heard
their prayers and saw their distress. For
many days the people of Judah and Jerusalem continued their fast in front of
the Temple of the Lord Almighty. 14 The
High Priest Joakim, the priests, and all
the others who served in the Lord's
Temple, wore sackcloth when they offered the daily burnt offering, the freewill offerings of the people, and the
offerings made to fulfill a vow. 15 They
put ashes on their turbans and cried out
in prayer to the Lord, begging him to
have mercy on the whole nation.

The War Council in the Camp of Holofernes

5 When Holofernes, the Assyrian
general, heard that the Israelites
had prepared for war, blocked the
mountain passes, fortified the mountaintops, and set up roadblocks in the plains,
2 he boiled over with anger. He called together all the Moabite rulers, all the Ammonite generals, and all the governors
of the region along the Mediterranean
coast 3 and said to them, "You live in Canaan, so tell me about the people who
live in these mountains. Which cities do
they occupy? How large is their army?
What is the source of their power and
strength? Who is the king who leads
their army? 4 Why have they alone, of all
the people in the west, refused to come
out and surrender to me?"

The Speech of Achior

5 Then Achior, the leader of all the
Ammonites, answered Holofernes, "Sir,
if you will please be so kind as to listen
to me, I will tell you the truth about these
people who live in the mountains near
your camp. I will not lie to you. 6 These
people are the descendants of some
Babylonians 7-8 who abandoned the
ways of their ancestors in order to worship the God of heaven. Finally, they
were driven out of their land because
they refused to worship their ancestors'
gods. Then they fled to Mesopotamia,
where they settled and lived for a long
time.
9 "Afterward, their god told them to
leave Mesopotamia and go to the land of
Canaan, where they settled and became
very rich in gold, silver, and livestock.
10 Later, when a famine struck all the
land of Canaan, these Israelites, as they
were later called, went down to Egypt
and stayed there as long as there was

enough food. While they were there,
they became a large nation with so
many people that they could not be
counted. 11 So the king of Egypt turned
against them. He took advantage of
them and put them to work making
bricks. He oppressed them and made
them slaves. 12 But they prayed to their
god, and he sent disasters that left the
Egyptians helpless. When the Egyptians
drove them out of the country, 13 their
god dried up the Red Sea in front of
them, 14 and then led them along the way
to Sinai and Kadesh Barnea.

"The Israelites drove out all the people
who lived in the southern part of Canaan, 15 occupied the land of the Amorites, wiped out the people of Heshbon,
crossed the Jordan River, and took possession of the entire mountain region.
16 They drove out the Canaanites, the
Perizzites, the Jebusites, the Shechem-
ites, and all the Girgashites. The Israelites have now lived in these mountains
for a long time.

17 "Their god hates wickedness, and as
long as they did not sin against him, they
prospered. 18 But when they disobeyed
him, they suffered heavy losses in many
wars and were finally taken away as
captives to a foreign country. The temple of their god was leveled and their
cities were occupied by their enemies.
19 But now that they have returned to
their god, they have come back home
from the countries where they had been
scattered. They have again taken possession of the city of Jerusalem, where
their temple is, and have resettled in the
mountains that had remained uninhabited.

20 "Sir, if these people are now sinning
against their god, even unknowingly,
and if we can be sure that they are guilty
of some offense, we can successfully attack them. 21 But if they have not disobeyed the law of their god, then you
should leave them alone, or he will defend them, and we will be disgraced before the whole world."

The Reaction of the Crowd

22 When Achior had finished his
speech, all the people standing around
the tent began to protest. Holofernes'
own senior officers, as well as the Moabites and those from the Mediterranean
coast, demanded that Achior be put to
death.

23 "Why should we be afraid of these
Israelites?" they asked. "They are weak;
they can't put up a strong defense.
24 Let's go ahead! General Holofernes,
your great army will slaughter them
easily."

The Speech of Holofernes

6 When the noise of the crowd
around the council had subsided,
Holofernes spoke to Achior in front of
the entire group, those from the Mediterranean coast, the Moabites, and the Ammonite mercenaries.[c]

2 "Achior,[d] who do you think you are,
acting like a prophet? Who are you to
tell us not to go to war against the Israelites because some god will defend them?
Nebuchadnezzar is our god, and that's
all that matters. He will send his army
and wipe these Israelites off the face of
the earth. Their god can't help them.
3 But we serve Nebuchadnezzar, and we
will beat them as easily as if their whole
army were one man. They will not be
able to hold their ground against our
cavalry; 4 it will overwhelm them. The
mountains will be soaked with their
blood, and the valleys will be filled with
their corpses. After our attack, they will
be completely wiped out; not a trace of
them will be left. This is the command
of Nebuchadnezzar, the lord of the
whole earth, and he doesn't speak
idle words. 5 Achior, you are nothing
but an Ammonite mercenary, and
you talk like a traitor. You will not
see me again until I come and punish
this race of runaway slaves. 6 And
when I do, my soldiers will put you to
death. You will be just an other name
on the casualty list.

7 "Now my men will take you into the
mountains and leave you in one of the
Israelite towns, 8 and you will die with
the people there. 9 Why look so worried,
Achior? Don't you think the town can
stand against me? I will carry out all my
threats; you can be sure of that!"

[c] the Ammonite mercenaries; *some manuscripts do not have these words.*
[d] Achior; *some manuscripts add* you and your hired soldiers from Ephraim; *others add* you and your mercenaries from Ammon.

Achior Is Brought to Bethulia

10 Then Holofernes ordered his men,
who were waiting in his tent, to seize
Achior, take him to Bethulia, and hand
him over to the Israelites. 11 So the men
seized Achior and took him out of the
camp into the valley. From there they
led him into the mountains, as far as the
spring which was below Bethulia.
12 When the men of that town saw
them approaching, they picked up their
weapons and ran to the top of the hill.
Every man who used a sling as a weapon
rained stones down on Holofernes' soldiers, and this stopped them from coming any farther up the mountain. 13 The
Assyrians were forced to take cover
along the mountainside, where they tied
Achior up and left him lying at the foot
of the mountain. Then they returned to
Holofernes.
14 Later, when the Israelites came
down from Bethulia, they untied Achior,
brought him into the town, and took him
before the town officials, 15 who at that
time were Uzziah son of Micah, of the
tribe of Simeon, Chabris son of Gothoniel, and Charmis son of Melchiel. 16 The
officials called together the town elders,
and all the women and the young men
also ran to the assembly. Achior was
brought before the people, and Uzziah
began questioning him. 17 Achior told
them what had been said at Holofernes'
war council, what he himself had said to
the Assyrian officers, and how Holofernes had boasted about what he would do
to the Israelites. 18 When the people
heard this, they fell on their knees and
worshiped God. They prayed: 19 "O Lord
God of heaven, look how our boastful
enemies have humiliated your people!
Have pity on us and help us." 20 Then
they reassured Achior and praised him
for what he had done. 21 After the assembly was over, Uzziah took Achior home
with him, and gave a banquet there for
the elders. All that night they prayed to
the God of Israel for help.

The Siege of Bethulia

7 1-2 The next day Holofernes gathered his whole army together, as
well as his allied forces. It was an immense army, consisting of 170,000 infantry and 12,000 cavalry, not counting the
support troops who took care of the
equipment. He ordered them to march
on Bethulia, seize the mountain passes,
and attack the Israelites. So they moved
out 3 and set up camp beside the spring
in the valley near Bethulia. The camp
was so wide that it spread out toward the
town of Dothan as far as Balbaim, and
so long that it stretched from Bethulia to
Cyamon, which faces Jezreel Valley.
4 When the Israelites saw the size of
the army, they were terrified and said to
one another, "Those soldiers are going
to eat up everything in sight. There's not
enough food in the mountains, valleys,
and hills put together to feed an army
like that." 5 But in spite of their fear, all
the Israelites took up their weapons,
lighted signal fires on the towers, and
remained on guard duty all night. 6 The
next day Holofernes led out his entire
cavalry so that the Israelites in Bethulia
could see them. 7 He inspected the approaches to the town and the springs
that supplied its water. He seized the
springs and stationed guards there, before returning to camp.
8 All the leaders of the Edomite and
Moabite forces, along with the commanders of the troops from the Mediterranean coast, came to Holofernes and
said, 9 "Sir, if you listen to our advice,
your troops will not suffer heavy losses.
10 These Israelites do not rely on their
weapons for defense but rather on the
height of the mountains where they live,
since the mountains are not easy to
climb. 11 So then, General Holofernes, if
you do not make a direct attack on them,
your whole army will suffer no casualties. 12 Stay in your camp and keep your
soldiers in their quarters. Just command
your men to blockade the springs at the
foot of the mountains, 13 because that's
where the people of Bethulia come to
draw their water. Then, when they are
dying of thirst, they will surrender their
town to you. Meanwhile, we and our
men will go up to the tops of the surrounding mountains, where we will set
up camp and keep anyone from leaving
the town. 14 Everyone will starve to
death—men, women, and children.
Even before we attack, the streets will be
littered with their corpses. 15 In this way
you can make them pay for their rebellion and for refusing to surrender peacefully to you."
16 Holofernes and his entire staff were

pleased with this suggestion, so he gave
orders to put the plan into action. 17 The
Moabites and 5,000 Assyrians moved
their camp into the valley to control the
source of the town's water. 18 The Edomites and the Ammonites went up into the
mountains and set up their camp opposite the town of Dothan. They sent some
of their men to the southeast in the direction of Acraba, near Chusi, which is
beside the Mochmur River. The rest of
the Assyrian army set up camp in the
valley. Their camp was spread out over
the whole countryside, because the
number of tents and the amount of
equipment needed for such a large army
were immense.
19 Then the Israelites cried out to
the Lord their God for help. They had
lost their courage, for with the enemy
all around them there was no way
to escape. 20 The entire Assyrian
army—infantry, chariots, and
cavalry—blockaded Bethulia for thirty-
four days until the town ran out of water. 21 All the reservoirs and cisterns
went dry, so that the drinking water had
to be rationed, and not a day passed
when there was enough water to go
around. 22 Children were becoming
weak; everywhere throughout the town
women and young people were collapsing. No one had any strength left.
23 All the people of the town—men,
women, and children alike—gathered
around Uzziah and the town officials
and shouted in protest, 24 "God will punish you for what you have done to us!
You are to blame for what is happening,
because you did not make peace with
the Assyrians. 25 There is no one to help
us now! God has put us in their power.
We are exhausted and dying of thirst.
26 Call the Assyrians now and surrender
to them, and let Holofernes and his army
take the town and loot it. 27 We are better
off as prisoners of war. They will make
us slaves, but at least we will be alive,
and we won't have to watch our wives
and children dying before our eyes.
28 Heaven and earth are witnesses
against you, and so is our God, the Lord
of our ancestors, who is punishing us for
their sins as well as ours. We can only
hope and pray that he will not let these
terrible things happen to us today."[e]
29 Everyone there began to weep
loudly and to pray to the Lord their God.
30 Then Uzziah said to them, "Don't give
up, my friends! Let's wait five more days
to see if the Lord our God will be merciful to us. Surely he will not abandon us
completely. 31 But if no help comes after
five days, then I will do as you say." 32 So
Uzziah dismissed the people. All the
men returned to their guard posts on the
walls and towers, while the women and
children went back to their homes. The
morale of the entire town was very low.

Judith, the Israelite Widow

8 At that time, Judith heard about Uzziah's decision. She was the daughter of Merari, the granddaughter of Ox
and the great-granddaughter of Joseph.
Joseph's ancestors were Oziel, Elkiah,
Ananias, Gideon, Raphaim, Ahitub, Elijah, Hilkiah, Eliab, Nathanael, Salamiel,
Sarasadai, and Israel. 2 Judith's husband
Manasseh, who belonged to the same
tribe and clan, had died during the barley harvest. 3 He had suffered a sun-
stroke while in the fields supervising the
farm workers and later died in bed at
home in Bethulia. He was buried in the
family tomb in the field between Dothan
and Balamon.
4 For three years and four months, Judith had lived as a widow. 5 In her grief
she built a little shelter on the roof of her
house and lived there, wearing sackcloth. 6 She fasted during that entire period except when fasting was forbidden:
the day before the Sabbath and the Sabbath itself, the eve of the New Moon Festival and the Festival itself, and all the
festivals and holidays observed by the
people of Israel. 7 Judith was a very
beautiful woman. Her husband had left
her gold and silver, servants and slaves,
livestock and fields. She continued to supervise the estate, 8 and no one ever said
anything bad about Judith. She was a
very religious woman.

Judith Meets with the Town Officials

9 Judith heard how the people were
complaining bitterly against Uzziah,
now that the water shortage had broken
their morale. She learned that in answer

[e] We can ... today; *some Greek manuscripts and ancient translations have* We demand that you surrender, as we have asked you to do today.

to their complaints he had promised to surrender the town to the Assyrians after five days. 10 Judith sent a slave, the woman who managed her business affairs, to invite Uzziah,[f] Chabris, and Charmis, the town officials, to her home.

11 When the officials arrived, Judith said to them, "Please listen to me. You are the leaders of the people of Bethulia, but you were wrong to speak to the people as you did today. You should not have made a solemn promise before God that you would surrender the town to our enemies if the Lord did not come to our aid within a few days. 12 What right do you have to put God to the test as you have done today? Who are you to put yourselves in God's place in dealing with human affairs? 13 It is the Lord Almighty that you are putting to the test! Will you never learn? 14 There is no way that you can understand what is in the depths of a human heart or find out what a person is thinking. Yet you dare to read God's mind and interpret his thoughts! How can you claim to understand God, the Creator? No, my friends, you must stop arousing the anger of the Lord our God! 15 If he decides not to come to our aid within five days, he still may rescue us at any time he chooses. Or he may let our enemies destroy us. 16 But you must not lay down conditions for the Lord our God! Do you think that he is like one of us? Do you think you can bargain with him or force him to make a decision? 17 No! Instead, we should ask God for his help and wait patiently for him to rescue us. If he wants to, he will answer our cry for help. 18 We do not worship gods made with human hands. Not one of our clans, tribes, towns, or cities has ever done that, even though our ancestors used to do so. 19 That is why God let their enemies kill them and take everything they had. It was a great defeat! 20 But since we worship no other God but the Lord, we can hope that he will not reject us or any of our people.

21 "If our town is taken by the enemy, the entire region of Judah will then fall, and our Temple in Jerusalem will be looted. And God will make us pay with our lives for allowing the Temple to be defiled. 22 He will hold us responsible for the slaughter and captivity of our people and for the destruction of the land we have inherited. We will be despised and mocked by the people in those nations to which we will be taken as slaves. 23 We are not going to win the favor of our enemies by surrendering to them now.[g] If we do surrender, the Lord our God will see that we are put to shame.

24 "No, my friends, we should set an example for our own people. Not only their lives, but the fate of the Temple and the altar depend on us. 25 The Lord our God is putting us to the test, just as he tested our ancestors, and we should be thankful for that. 26 Remember how he put Abraham and Isaac to the test, and what happened to Jacob while he was working as a shepherd for his uncle Laban in Mesopotamia. 27 God is not testing our loyalty as severely as he did theirs. God is not sending this punishment on us as revenge, but as a warning to us who worship him."

28 Then Uzziah answered Judith, "Everything you have said makes good sense, and no one can argue with it. 29 This is not the first time you have shown wisdom. Ever since you were a child, all of us have recognized the soundness and maturity of your judgment. 30 But our people are dying of thirst. They forced us to say what we did and to make a solemn promise, which we cannot break. 31 So now, since you are a deeply religious woman, pray for our people; ask the Lord to send rain to fill our cisterns, so that we can get our strength back."

32 "All right," Judith replied, "I am going to do something which our Jewish people will never forget. 33 Tonight, the three of you must stand guard at the gate so that my slave woman and I can leave the town. And before the day comes on which you have promised to surrender, the Lord will use me to rescue the people of Israel. 34 But you must not ask me what I am going to do; I will explain it to you when it is all over."

35 Uzziah and the other officials said to her, "You have our blessing. May the Lord our God guide you as you take revenge on our enemies." Then they left

[f] Uzziah; *some Greek manuscripts do not have this word.* [g] We are not . . . now; *or* No good will ever come out of our slavery.

Judith's rooftop shelter and returned to their posts.

Judith's Prayer

9 Then Judith put ashes on her head, opened her robe to reveal the sackcloth she was wearing under her clothes, and bowed down with her face to the floor. It was the time that the evening incense was being offered in the Temple in Jerusalem, and Judith prayed in a loud voice: 2 "O Lord, the God of my ancestor Simeon, remember how you armed Simeon with a sword to take revenge on those foreigners who seized Dinah, who was a virgin, tore off her clothes,[h] and defiled her; they stripped her naked and shamed her; they raped her and disgraced her, even though you had forbidden this. 3 That is why you let their leaders be killed—put to death on the same bed where they had raped the woman.[i] You destroyed them all, slaves, princes, and rulers on their thrones. 4 You let their wives be carried off, their daughters taken captive, and their possessions plundered by the Israelites, your chosen people, who were eager to do your will. Dinah's brothers were furious because of this disgrace to their family, so they called on you for help.

"O my God, listen to my prayer, the prayer of a widow. 5 Your hand guided all that happened then, and all that happened before and after. You have planned it all—what is happening now, and what is yet to be. Your plans have always been carried out. 6 Whatever you want to be done is as good as done. You know in advance all that you will do and what decisions you will make. 7 Now the Assyrians are stronger than ever; they take pride in their cavalry and their infantry. They rely on their weapons, but they do not know that you, O Lord, are a warrior who ends war. The Lord is your name. 8 In your anger, use your power to shatter their mighty army. They plan to defile your Temple, where you are worshiped, and to hack off the corners of your altar with their swords. 9 Look how proud and boastful they are! Pour out your fury upon them! I am only a widow, but give me the strength to carry out my plan. 10 Use my deceitful words to strike them all dead, master and slave alike. Let a woman's strength break their pride. 11 Your power does not depend on the size and strength of an army. You are a God who cares for the humble and helps the oppressed. You give support and protection to people who are weak and helpless; you save those who have lost hope. 12 Now hear my prayer, O God of my ancestor Simeon, the God in whom Israel trusts, ruler of heaven and earth, creator of the rivers and the seas, king of all creation. Hear my prayer and 13 let my deceitful words wound and kill those who have planned such cruelty against your covenant and your holy Temple, against Mount Zion and the land you have given your people. 14 Make your whole nation and every tribe recognize that you are God, almighty and all-powerful, and that you alone protect the people of Israel!"

Judith Goes to the Camp of Holofernes

10 When Judith had finished her prayer to the God of Israel, 2 she stood up, called her slave woman, and went down into the house as she always did on Sabbaths and festival days. 3 She took off the sackcloth and her widow's clothes, took a bath, and put on rich perfumes. She brushed her hair, tied a ribbon around it, and dressed herself in the fine clothes she used to wear on joyful occasions when her husband Manasseh was still alive. 4 She put on sandals and all her finest jewelry: rings and earrings, and bracelets on her wrists and ankles. She made herself so beautiful that she was sure to attract the attention of any man who saw her. 5 Judith gave her slave woman a leather bag of wine and a jar of oil to carry. She filled a bag with roasted barley, cakes of dried figs, and several loaves of bread baked according to Jewish food laws. She carefully wrapped all the food and dishes and gave them to her slave. 6 Then the two women left the house and went to the gates of Bethulia, where they found Uzziah and the town officials, Chabris and Charmis, standing guard. 7 When the men saw Judith after she had changed

[h] *Probable text* clothes; *Greek unclear.* [i] *Probable text* put to death . . . woman; *Greek unclear.*

clothes and put on make-up, they were
struck by her beauty and said to her,
8 "May the God of our ancestors bless
you and make your plan successful, so
that you may bring glory to Jerusalem
and victory to Israel."

Judith prayed 9 and then said, "Order
the gates to be opened for me. I am on
my way to do what we were talking
about." Then they ordered the young
men to open the gates for her, 10 and Judith and her slave left the city. The men
watched her as she went down the
mountain into the valley, until she was
out of sight.

11 As the two women were walking
through the valley, an Assyrian patrol
met them. 12 They arrested Judith and
questioned her, "What is your nationality? Where did you come from, and
where are you going?"

"I am a Hebrew," she answered, "but I
am running away from the Israelites because God is going to let you destroy
them. 13 I am on my way to see Holofernes, the general in command of your
army, to give him some reliable information. I can show him how to advance into
the mountains and take control of the
entire region without a single casualty."

14 The men stared at her because she
was so beautiful. They listened to her
story and said, 15 "You have saved your
life by coming down here to see our general. Some of us will take you to his
headquarters and present you to him.
16 Do not be afraid of him. Just tell him
what you have told us, and he will treat
you well." 17 They assigned a hundred
men to escort Judith and her slave to the
headquarters of Holofernes.

18 There was great commotion in the
Assyrian camp as news of Judith's arrival spread from tent to tent. While she
stood outside the tent of Holofernes
waiting to be presented to him, many
Assyrian soldiers came and stood
around her. 19 They were greatly impressed by her beauty and wondered
what kind of people the Israelites were.
"Who can have contempt for people
whose women are so beautiful?" they
asked one another. "We had better kill
all the men, or else these Jews will be
able to charm the whole world."

20 Then Holofernes' bodyguard and his
personal servants came out and led Judith into the tent. 21 Holofernes was resting on his bed under a mosquito net
woven of purple and gold thread and
decorated with emeralds and other precious stones. 22 When the men told him
that Judith had arrived, he came to the
outer part of the tent. Silver lamps were
carried ahead of him. 23 When Judith
came near him and his servants, they
were all astonished at her beauty. She
bowed down to the ground before Holofernes, but his servants helped her to her
feet.

11 Holofernes said to Judith, "Don't
worry; there's no need for you to
be afraid. I have never hurt anyone who
was willing to serve Nebuchadnezzar,
king of the whole world. 2 Even now, if
your people up in the mountains had not
insulted me, I would not have declared
war on them. They have brought all this
trouble on themselves. 3 But tell me, why
have you left them and come to us? You
will be safe here. No need to be afraid!
We have spared your life tonight, and
you are in no danger for the future. 4 No
one here will harm you; everyone will
treat you well, like all other servants of
my master, Nebuchadnezzar."

5 Then Judith said to Holofernes, "Allow me to speak to you, my lord, and
please listen to what I have to say. I will
tell you the truth. 6 If you follow my advice, God will do something great with
you, and my lord will not fail in his plan.
7 For I swear to you by the life and
strength of Nebuchadnezzar, king of the
whole world, who sent you to bring order to all the subjects of his kingdom,
that not only have you made people
serve him, but because of you even the
wild animals, the livestock, and the
birds obey him. Because of you, Nebuchadnezzar and his entire kingdom will
prosper.[j] 8 We have heard how wise
and clever you are. The whole world
knows that you are the most competent,
skilled, and accomplished general in the
whole Assyrian Empire. 9 Achior was
rescued by the men of Bethulia, and has
told us what he said at your war council.
10 Please, sir, do not dismiss lightly what
Achior told you, but take it seriously,
because it is true. No one can harm or

[j] not only . . . prosper; *Greek unclear.*

conquer our people unless they sin
against their God.
11 "But you will not suffer any setbacks, nor will you fail to achieve your
goal. When the Israelites sin and make
their God angry, they will die. 12 Their
food supply has already run out, and the
water shortage has become serious, so
they have decided to kill their livestock
and eat foods that God's Law clearly forbids them to eat. 13 They have decided to
eat the wheat set aside from the early
harvest and the tithes of wine and oil,
which are holy and are reserved for the
priests who serve God in Jerusalem. The
rest of us are forbidden even to touch
this sacred food, 14 but since the people
in Jerusalem have already broken this
law, the people of our town have sent
messengers to the Council there requesting permission to do the same. 15 On the
day that they receive permission and actually eat the food, you will be able to
destroy them. 16 As soon as I learned
about this, I ran away from my people.
God has sent me to do something with
you that will amaze everyone in the entire world who hears about it. 17 Sir, I am
a religious woman; I worship the God of
heaven day and night. I will stay here in
your camp, and each night I will go out
into the valley to pray to God, and he
will tell me when the Israelites have
sinned. 18 As soon as I find out, I will
come and tell you, and you can march
out with your whole army. The Israelites
will not be able to defend themselves
against you. 19 I will guide you through
the central part of the land of Judah until
we come to Jerusalem, where I will
crown you king in the center of the city.
You will scatter the people of Jerusalem
like sheep without a shepherd. Not even
a dog will dare to growl at you. God has
revealed these things to me in advance
and has sent me to report them to you."
20 Holofernes and his personal servants were pleased with what Judith had
said, and they admired her wisdom.
21 "She must be the wisest and most
beautiful woman in the world," they
commented one to another.
22 Then Holofernes said to her, "It's a
good thing that God has sent you here to
bring us victory and to destroy those
who have insulted King Nebuchadnezzar. 23 Not only are you beautiful, but
you know how to make a speech. If you
do as you have promised, your God will
be my God. You will live in King Nebuchadnezzar's palace and will be famous
throughout the world."

Judith Remains Faithful to Her Religion

12 Holofernes commanded his men
to take Judith to the table which
was set with his silverware and to serve
her some of his own special food and
wine. 2 But Judith refused. "I cannot eat
your food," she said, "for I would be
breaking the laws of my God. I will eat
only what I have brought with me."
3 "But what will you do when your
food and wine are gone?" Holofernes
asked. "Where will we get more food for
you? There are no Israelites here in our
camp."
4 "Sir," Judith answered, "as surely as
you live, I have more than enough food
to last until the Lord has used me to
carry out his plan."
5 Then Holofernes' personal servants
led Judith to a tent. She slept there until
the time of the morning watch just before dawn, when she got up 6 and sent a
message to Holofernes requesting permission to go out into the valley to pray.
7 Holofernes ordered his guards to let Judith leave the camp. So for three days
Judith lived in the camp, and each night
she would go out to the valley near Bethulia and bathe at the spring. 8 After she
had bathed, she would pray to the Lord
God to guide her in her plan to bring
victory to Israel. 9 Then she would return
to the camp ritually pure and remain in
her tent until after the evening meal.

Holofernes' Banquet

10 On the fourth day of Judith's stay in
the camp, Holofernes gave a banquet for
his highest ranking officers, but he did
not invite any of the officers who were
on duty. 11 He said to Bagoas, the eunuch
who was in charge of his personal affairs, "Go and persuade the Hebrew
woman, who is in your care, to come to
my tent to eat and drink with us. 12 It
would be a shame to pass up an opportunity to make love to a woman like that. If
I don't try to seduce her, she will laugh
at me."
13 So Bagoas left Holofernes and went
to Judith. "Lovely lady," he said, "the
general invites you to his tent for some

drinks. Come and enjoy yourself like the
Assyrian women who serve in Nebuchadnezzar's palace. This is a great
honor."
14 "I shall be glad to accept," Judith answered. "How could I refuse? I'll remember this happy night as long as I live."
15 So Judith got up and put on her pret-
tiest clothes. Her slave woman went
ahead of her and placed on the ground
in front of Holofernes the lamb skins
that Bagoas had given Judith to sit on
when she ate. 16 Judith came into the tent
and sat down there. Holofernes was
aroused when he saw her and had an
uncontrollable desire to make love to
her. From the first day he had seen her,
he had been waiting for a chance to seduce her. 17 "Join us for a drink and enjoy yourself," he said to her.
18 "I'll be glad to, sir," Judith replied;
"this is the happiest day of my life."
19 But even then Judith ate and drank
only what her slave had prepared.
20 Holofernes was so charmed by her
that he drank more wine than he had
ever drunk at one time in his whole life.

13 Finally, when it got late, the
guests excused themselves and
left. Bagoas then closed up the tent from
the outside and prevented Holofernes'
servants from going in. So they all went
to bed; everyone was very tired because
the banquet had lasted so long. 2 Judith
was left alone in the tent with Holofernes who was lying drunk on his bed.
3 Judith's slave woman was waiting outside the tent for Judith to go and pray,
as she had done each night. Judith had
also told Bagoas that she would be
going out to pray as usual.
4 All the guests and servants were now
gone, and Judith and Holofernes were
alone in the tent. Judith stood by Holofernes' bed and prayed silently, "O Lord,
God Almighty, help me with what I am
about to do for the glory of Jerusalem.
5 Now is the time to rescue your chosen
people and to help me carry out my plan
to destroy the enemies who are threatening us." 6 Judith went to the bedpost by
Holofernes' head and took down his
sword. 7 She came closer, seized Holofernes by the hair of his head, and said,
"O Lord, God of Israel, give me strength
now." 8 Then Judith raised the sword
and struck him twice in the neck as hard
as she could, chopping off his head.
9 She rolled his body off the bed and took
down the mosquito net from the bed-
posts. Then she came out and gave Holofernes' head to her slave, 10 who put it in
the food bag.

Judith and Her Slave Return to Bethulia

Then the two women left together, as
they always did when they went to pray.
After they had walked through the Assyrian camp, they crossed the valley and
went up the mountainside until they
came to the gates of Bethulia. 11 When
they were a short distance away, Judith
called out to the guards at the gate,
"Open the gate! Open the gate! Our God
is still with us. Today he has once again
shown his strength in Israel and used his
power against our enemies."
12 When the men heard her voice, they
hurried down to the gates and called for
the town officials. 13 Everyone, young
and old, ran together to the gate. No one
could believe that Judith had come back.
They opened the gate for her and her
slave and welcomed them. Then, when
they had lit a fire to give some light and
had gathered around the two women,
14 Judith shouted, "Praise God, give him
praise! Praise God, who has not held
back his mercy from the people of Israel.
Tonight he has used me to destroy our
enemies." 15 She then took the head out
of the food bag and showed it to the people. "Here," she said, "is the head of Holofernes, the general of the Assyrian
army, and here is the mosquito net from
his bed, where he lay in a drunken stupor. The Lord used a woman to kill him.
16 As the Lord lives, I swear that Holofernes never touched me, although my
beauty deceived him and brought him to
his ruin. I was not defiled or disgraced;
the Lord took care of me through it all."
17 Everyone in the city was utterly
amazed. They bowed down and worshiped God, praying together, "Our God,
you are worthy of great praise. Today
you have triumphed over the enemies of
your people."
18 Then Uzziah said, "Judith, my dear,
the Most High God has blessed you
more than any other woman on earth.
How worthy of praise is the Lord God
who created heaven and earth! He
guided you as you cut off the head of our

deadliest enemy. 19 Your trust in God
will never be forgotten by those who tell
of God's power. 20 May God give you
everlasting honor for what you have
done. May he reward you with blessings, because you remained faithful to
him and did not hesitate to risk your
own life to relieve the oppression of your
people."
All the people replied, "Amen, amen!"

Judith's Plan

14 Then Judith said to them, "My
friends, please follow my advice.
In the morning, take this head and hang
it on the town wall. 2 Appoint a leader for
yourselves, and at sunrise have all your
able-bodied men take their weapons and
march out of the town with him, as if
they were going down into the valley to
attack the Assyrian outpost. 3 The Assyrian guards will grab their weapons
and rush back to camp to wake up their
officers. The officers will run to Holofernes' tent but will not find him, and the
whole army will be terrified and retreat
as you advance against them. 4 Then you
and all the other Israelites will be able to
follow them and kill them as they retreat. 5 But before you do any of this,
send Achior the Ammonite to me. I want
to see if he recognizes Holofernes, the
man who spoke of Israel with contempt
and sent Achior to us, thinking he would
be killed along with the rest of us."

Achior's Conversion

6 So they called Achior from Uzziah's
house. But when he came and saw the
head of Holofernes in the hands of one
of the men, Achior fainted and fell to the
floor. 7 When they had helped him up,
Achior bowed at Judith's feet in respect.
"May every family in the land of Judah
praise you," he said, "and may every nation tremble with terror when they hear
your name. 8 Please tell me how you
managed to do this."
While all the people were gathered
around, Judith told him everything that
she had done from the day she left the
town until that moment. 9 When she had
finished her story, the people cheered so
loudly that the whole town echoed with
sounds of joy. 10 When Achior heard
all that the God of Israel had done, he
became a firm believer. He was
circumcised and made a member of the
Israelite community, as his descendants
are to the present day.

Panic in Holofernes' Camp

11 The next morning the Israelites
hung the head of Holofernes on the wall
of the town. All of them took up their
weapons and went out in companies to
the slopes in front of the town. 12 When
the Assyrians saw what was happening,
they sent word to their officers, and
these reported the matter to their superiors. 13 These men then went to Holofernes' tent and said to Bagoas, "Wake up
the general! Those worthless Israelites
have dared to come down from the
mountain to attack us; they are just asking to be destroyed."
14 Bagoas went in and clapped his
hands in front of the sleeping quarters of
the tent, thinking that Holofernes was in
bed with Judith. 15 When there was no
answer, he drew the curtain aside and
went in, and there he found the head-
less body sprawled over a footstool.
16 Bagoas let out a yell. He screamed,
tore his clothes, and started groaning
and weeping. 17 He went into the tent
where Judith had stayed, but of course
he did not find her. He rushed out and
shouted to the officers, 18 "They have
tricked us! One Israelite woman has disgraced Nebuchadnezzar's whole kingdom. Look in there! Holofernes is lying
dead on the ground and his head is
gone!" 19 When the officers heard this,
they tore their clothes in grief; and as
the panic spread, wild cries and shouts
were heard throughout the camp.

Israel's Victory

15 When the soldiers heard what
had happened, they were horrified 2 and began to tremble with fear.
They all scattered in different directions
from the camp, making no effort to stay
together as they tried to escape along
the paths in the mountains and valleys.
3 The soldiers who had camped in the
mountains around Bethulia also began
to retreat. Then all the Israelite soldiers
came charging down on them.
4 Uzziah sent messengers to the towns
of Betomesthaim, Bebai, Choba, and
Kola, and throughout the land of Israel
to tell everyone what had happened and
to urge them to join in pursuing and destroying the enemy. 5 When they re-

ceived the message, they all attacked the
Assyrians and chased them as far as
Choba, slaughtering them as they went.
Even the people of Jerusalem and others
living in the mountains joined the attack
when the messengers told them what
had happened in the Assyrian camp.
The people of the regions of Gilead and
Galilee blocked the path of the retreating Assyrians and inflicted heavy losses
on them. They pursued them as far as
the region around Damascus.
6 The rest of the people in Bethulia
went down to the Assyrian camp, plundered it and carried away enough loot to
make themselves very rich. 7 When the
Israelite soldiers returned from the
slaughter, they helped themselves to
what was left. There was so much of it
that the people of the towns and villages
in the hill country also shared in the loot.

Israel Celebrates the Victory

8 The High Priest Joakim and the
Council of Israel came from Jerusalem
to see for themselves what great things
the Lord had done for his people and to
meet Judith and congratulate her.
9 When they arrived, they all praised her,
"You are Jerusalem's crowning glory,
the heroine of Israel, the pride and joy of
our people! 10 You have won this great
victory for Israel by yourself. God, the
Almighty, is pleased with what you have
done. May he bless you as long as you
live."
All the people responded, "Amen."
11 It took the people thirty days to finish looting the camp of the Assyrians.
Judith was given Holofernes' tent, all his
silver, his bowls, his couches, and all his
furniture. She took them and loaded as
much as she could on her mule; then she
brought her wagons and loaded them
too. 12 All the Israelite women came to
see her; they sang her praises and
danced in her honor. On this joyful occasion Judith and the other women waved
ivy-covered branches 13 and wore
wreaths of olive leaves on their heads.
Judith took her place at the head of the
procession to lead the women as they
danced. All the men of Israel followed,
wearing wreaths of flowers on their
heads, carrying their weapons, and singing songs of praise.

Judith's Song of Praise

16 Then Judith sang a song of
thanksgiving there with all Israel
present, and the people joined in this
song of praise. 2 She sang,

"Praise my God and sing to him;
praise the Lord with drums and
cymbals;
play a new song for him.
Praise him and call on him for
help.
3 The Lord is a warrior who
ends war.
He rescued me from my
pursuers
and brought me back to his
people's camp.
4 Down from the mountains of the
north came the Assyrians,
with their tens of thousands of
soldiers.
Their troops blocked the rivers in
the valleys;
their cavalry covered the
mountains.
5 They threatened to set fire to our
country,
slaughter our young men,
dash our babies to the ground,
take our children away as
captives,
and carry off all our young
women.
6 But the Lord Almighty tricked
them;
he used a woman to stop them.
7 Their hero was not slain by young
soldiers
or attacked and killed by mighty
giants.
It was Judith, the daughter of
Merari,
who brought him down with her
beauty.
8 She gave victory to the oppressed
people of Israel,
when she took off her widow's
clothes,
and put on a linen dress to
entice him.
She put on her rich perfumes
and tied a ribbon around her
hair.
9 Her dainty sandal caught his eye;
her beauty captured his heart.

Then the sword slashed through
his neck.
10 The Persians trembled at her
daring;
the Medes were amazed at her
bravery.
11 Then our people shouted in
victory.
They had been weak and
oppressed,
but they forced the enemy to
retreat in panic and fear.
12 We are the descendants of slaves,
but our enemies turned and ran;
we killed them like runaway
slaves.
They were destroyed by the army
of the Lord.

13 "I will sing a new song to my God.
O Lord, you are strong and
glorious!
You have never been defeated.
14 Let all your creatures serve you.
You gave the command,
and all of them came into being;
you breathed on them,
and all of them were created.
No one can oppose your
command.
15 The mountains and the seas
tremble,
and rocks melt like wax when
you come near.
But there is mercy for all who
obey you.
16 The Lord is more pleased with
those who obey him
than with all the choice meat on
the altar,
or with all the most fragrant
sacrifices.
17 The nations who rise up against
my people are doomed.
The Lord Almighty will punish
them on Judgment Day.
He will send fire and worms to
devour their bodies,
and they will weep in pain
forever."

Judith's Fame

18 When the people arrived in Jerusalem, they purified themselves and worshiped God. They presented their burnt
offerings, freewill offerings, and gifts.
19 Judith dedicated to God all of Holofernes' property, which the people had
given to her. And as a special offering in
fulfillment of a vow, she presented to the
Lord the mosquito net which she had
taken from Holofernes' bed. 20 For three
months the people continued to celebrate in front of the Temple in Jerusalem, and Judith stayed there with them.
21 When the celebrations had ended,
everyone returned home, and Judith
went back to Bethulia to live on her own
estate. For the rest of her life she was
famous throughout the land of Israel.
22 Many men wanted to marry her, but
she never remarried after the death of
her husband Manasseh. 23-24 Her fame
continued to spread, and she lived in the
house her husband had left her. Before
she died, Judith divided her property
among her husband's and her own close
relatives and set her slave woman free.
When she died in Bethulia at the age of
105, she was buried beside her husband,
and the people of Israel mourned her
death for seven days. 25 As long as Judith
lived, and for many years after her
death, no one dared to threaten the people of Israel.

The Book of
ESTHER
(The Greek Version)

Introduction

The Book of Esther *in Greek is a translation, adaptation, and expansion of* The Book of Esther *in Hebrew. The chain of events is much the same, but there are many variations in text, including different proper names and a strong religious tone. The six additions, shown as Chapters A–F in this translation, provide a different introduction and conclusion, introduce documents in an official style, and emphasize the religious elements by the addition of prayers and accounts of how they were answered.*

Outline of Contents

Mordecai's Strange Dream

A [a] 1-3 Mordecai, a Jew who belonged
to the tribe of Benjamin, was
taken into exile, along with King Jehoiachin of Judah, when King Nebuchadnezzar of Babylonia captured Jerusalem.
Mordecai was the son of Jair, a descendant of Kish and Shimei. He now lived in
the Persian city of Susa, where he was
an important official in the royal court of
Xerxes the great king.
During the second year of Xerxes'
reign, on the first day of the month of
Nisan, Mordecai had a dream. 4 He
dreamed that there was great noise and
confusion, loud thunder, and an earthquake, with terrible turmoil on the earth.
5 Then two huge dragons appeared,
ready to fight each other. 6 They made a
dreadful noise, and all the nations got
ready to make war against God's nation
of righteous people. 7 For the world it
was a day of darkness and gloom, trouble and distress, destruction and ruin.
8 All of God's righteous people were
troubled, in great fear of what was about
to happen to them. They prepared for
death, 9 but they cried out to God for
help. In the dream their prayer was answered by a great river which came
flowing out of a small spring. 10 The day
dawned, the sun rose, and the humble
people were made strong and destroyed
their arrogant enemies.
11 Mordecai woke up from this dream
in which he saw what God planned to
do. He thought about it all day and tried
to understand what it meant.

Mordecai Saves the King's Life

12 While Mordecai was resting in the
courtyard of the palace, where two of
the king's eunuchs, Gabatha and
Tharra, were on guard, 13 he overheard
them plotting together. He listened carefully to what they were saying and
learned that they were making plans to
kill the king. So Mordecai went to King
Xerxes and told him about the plot of the
two eunuchs. 14 The king had them questioned, and when they confessed, they
were led away and executed.
15 The king had an account of this written in the official records, and Mordecai
also wrote an account of it. 16 Then the
king appointed Mordecai to a position at
court and gave him many gifts as a reward for what he had done.
17 But Haman son of Hammedatha, a
Bougaean who was respected by the
king, tried to cause trouble for Mordecai
and his people the Jews, because Mordecai had been responsible for the death of
the two eunuchs.

[a] *Chapter A 1-17 corresponds to chapters 11.2–12.6 in a number of English translations.*

Queen Vashti Defies King Xerxes

1 1-2 These things happened in the
time of King Xerxes, who ruled 127
provinces, all the way from India to Ethiopia,[b] from his royal throne in Susa,
Persia's capital city. 3 In the third year of
his reign, the king gave a banquet for all
his advisers, the representatives of the
other countries, the noblemen from Persia and Media, and the governors of the
provinces. 4 For six whole months he
made a show of the riches of the imperial court with magnificent and expensive celebrations.
5 After the feast[c] the king gave a banquet for the people of other nations who
were in the city. It lasted a week and was
held in the palace courtyard, 6 which was
decorated with linen and cotton curtains, held by cords of purple linen attached to silver and gold blocks on
marble and stone columns. Couches
made of gold and silver had been placed
in the courtyard, which was paved with
green and white marble and mother-of-
pearl. The couches were spread with a
fine, thin fabric of many colors, with
roses around the edges. 7 There were
gold and silver cups, and one of them,
decorated with jewels worth more than
a thousand tons of silver, had been set
out for display. There was plenty of
good wine from the king's own supply.
8 There were no limits on the drinks. The
king had given orders to the palace servants that they should provide him and
his guests with as much as they wanted.
9 Meanwhile, inside the royal palace
Queen Vashti was giving a banquet for
the women.
10 On the seventh day of his banquet
the king was feeling happy, so he called
in the seven eunuchs who were his personal servants, Haman, Bazan, Tharra, Boraze, Zatholta, Abataza, and
Tharaba. 11 He ordered them to bring in
the queen, so that he could place the
royal crown on her head and show her
off to the officials and all his guests, for
she was a beautiful woman. 12 But Queen
Vashti refused to obey and would not
come with the servants. This embarrassed the king and made him furious.
13 He told his advisers about Vashti's
reply and asked them to give a legal
opinion about what he should do.
14-15 Three of them, who were closest to
the king and held the highest offices,
came and told him what the law required and what should be done to
Queen Vashti for disobeying the command he had given her through his
servants. They were Arkesaeus,
Sarsathaeus, and Malesear, officials of
Persia and Media.
16 Then the king told his officials and
the governors of Media and Persia how
the queen had defied him. So Muchaeus
said to the king and everyone present:
"Queen Vashti has insulted not only you
but all of us as well. 17-18 As soon as our
wives hear what the queen has done,
they will be bold enough to defy their
husbands and treat them with disrespect
in the same way that Vashti has treated
you. 19 If, then, it please Your Majesty,
issue a royal proclamation that Vashti
may never again appear before the king.
Have it written into the laws of Media
and Persia. Then give her place as queen
to some better woman. There is no other
way. 20 When your proclamation is made
known all over this empire, then every
woman will treat her husband with
proper respect, whether he is rich or
poor."
21 The king and his officials liked this
idea, and the king did as Muchaeus suggested. 22 To each of the royal provinces
he sent a message in the language of that
province, saying that every husband
must be respected in his own home.

Esther Becomes Queen

2 Later the king's anger cooled down.
Although he no longer mentioned
Vashti, he kept thinking about how he
had condemned her. 2 So some of the
king's advisers suggested, "Why don't
you make a search to find some beautiful young women of good character?
3 You can appoint officials in every province of the empire and have them bring
all these beautiful young virgins to your
harem here in Susa. Put them in the care
of Hegai, the eunuch who is in charge of
your women, and let them be given cosmetics and whatever else they may

[b] *Greek* Ethiopia: *Ethiopia is the name given in Graeco-Roman times to the extensive territory south of the First Cataract of the Nile River. Cush was the ancient (Hebrew) name of this region which included within its borders most of modern Sudan and some of present-day Ethiopia (Abyssinia).* [c] feast; *some manuscripts have* wedding feast.

need. 4 Then take the young woman you
like best and make her queen in Vashti's
place."

The king thought this was good advice, so he followed it.

5 There in Susa lived a Jew named
Mordecai son of Jair; he was from the
tribe of Benjamin and was a descendant
of Kish and Shimei. 6 He was among the
captives whom King Nebuchadnezzar of
Babylonia had taken into exile from Jerusalem. 7 Mordecai was the guardian of
Esther, the daughter of his uncle Aminadab. She was a beautiful young woman,
and after the death of her parents, Mordecai brought her up until she was
grown.[d]

8 When the king had issued his new
proclamation, many young women were
being brought to Susa, and Esther was
among them. She too was put in the
royal palace in the care of Hegai, who
had charge of the harem. 9 Hegai liked
Esther, and she won his favor. He lost no
time in beginning her beauty treatment
of massage and special diet. He assigned
seven young women specially chosen
from the royal palace to serve her, and
he treated her and her servants well.

10 Now, on the advice of Mordecai, Esther had kept secret the fact that she was
Jewish. 11 Every day Mordecai would
walk back and forth in front of the courtyard of the harem, watching to see what
was going to happen to her.

12 The regular beauty treatment for the
young women lasted a year: massages
with oil of myrrh for six months and
with beauty creams and cosmetics for
six more. 13 After that, each young
woman was handed over to the person
appointed to conduct her from the
harem to the palace, and she was taken
to the king. 14 She would go there in the
evening, and the next morning she
would be taken to another harem and
put in the care of Hegai, the eunuch in
charge. She would not go to the king
again unless he asked for her by name.

15 The time came for Esther, the
daughter of Aminadab the uncle of Mordecai, to go to the king. She had done
everything that Hegai had advised, and
she was admired by everyone who saw
her. 16 So in Xerxes' seventh year as
king, in the twelfth month, the month of
Adar, she was brought to the king. 17 He
fell in love with Esther, who pleased him
more than any of the others, and he
placed the queen's crown on her head.
18 Then the king gave a week-long banquet for all his advisers and administrators to celebrate his marriage to Esther.
He also granted a reduction of taxes for
the whole empire.

Mordecai Saves the King's Life

19 Meanwhile Mordecai had been appointed to a high administrative position. 20 As for Esther, she had still not let
it be known that she was Jewish. Mordecai had told her not to tell anyone, and
she obeyed him in this, just as she had
obeyed him when she was a little girl
under his care. She continued to worship God and carry out God's commands, without abandoning her Jewish
ways.

21 When the king promoted Mordecai
to a higher position, the two palace eunuchs who were officers of the king's
bodyguard became angry and plotted to
assassinate the king. 22 Mordecai
learned about it and told Queen Esther,
who then told the king the details of the
plot. 23 The king had the two men questioned, and both men were hanged. To
honor Mordecai, the king ordered an account of this to be written down in the
royal records, so that his valuable service would be remembered.

Haman Plots to Destroy the Jews

3 Some time later King Xerxes honored a man named Haman son of
Hammedatha, a Bougaean, by promoting him to the position of prime minister.
2 The king ordered all the officials in his
service to show their respect for Haman
by bowing to him. They all did so, except
Mordecai, who refused to bow to Haman. 3 The other officials in the royal
service asked him why he was disobeying the king's command. 4 Day after day
they urged him to give in, but he would
not listen to them. "I am a Jew," he explained, "and I cannot bow to Haman."
So they told Haman how Mordecai was
defying the king's orders. 5 Haman was
furious when he realized that Mordecai
was not going to bow to him, 6 and so he

[d] until she was grown; *or* and planned to marry her.

made plans to kill every Jew in the
whole Persian Empire.
7 In the twelfth year of King Xerxes'
reign, Haman ordered the lots to be cast
to find out the right day and month to
destroy the Jews, all in a single day. The
fourteenth day of the month of Adar was
the date chosen.
8 So Haman told the king, "There is a
certain race of people scattered among
the nations all over your empire. They
observe customs that are not like those
of any other people. Moreover, they do
not obey the laws of the empire, so it is
not in your best interests to tolerate
them. 9 If it please Your Majesty, issue a
decree that they are to be put to death. If
you do this, I promise to put 375 tons of
silver into the royal treasury."
10 The king took off his ring, which
was used to stamp official proclamations, and gave it to Haman to seal the
decree that was to be written against the
Jews. 11 The king told him, "Keep the
money, and do whatever you want with
that race of people."
12 So on the thirteenth day of the first
month, Haman called the king's secretaries and dictated a proclamation to be
translated into every language in the
empire and to be sent to all the rulers
and governors. It was issued in the name
of King Xerxes and sent to all the 127
provinces, which stretched from India to
Ethiopia.[e] 13 Runners took this proclamation to every province of the empire.
It contained the instructions that on a
single day in the twelfth month, the
month of Adar, all Jews were to be killed
and their belongings confiscated.[f]

Xerxes' Proclamation against the Jews

B[g] This is a copy of the decree:
"King Xerxes the Great sends
the following decree to the governors of
his 127 provinces, from India to Ethiopia,[h] and to their subordinate officials:
2 "After I became ruler of many nations and master of the whole world, I
resolved that my subjects should always
live at peace. I wanted this, not because
of pride in my power but because I was
always reasonable and governed my
subjects with kindness. I determined to
renew the peace that everyone longs for
and to do what was necessary to create
a civilized kingdom, safe for travel from
one border to another.
3 "I asked my advisers how to accomplish this goal, and Haman made a suggestion. He is distinguished among us as
a man of great wisdom, and at all times
he has demonstrated his concern for the
welfare of the kingdom. Because of his
unfailing loyalty, he has been raised to
the second highest position in the empire. 4 Recently Haman told us about a
certain unruly people scattered among
all the other peoples of the empire. He
explained to us that these people have
their own laws, are opposed to every
other nation, and constantly ignore
royal commands. As a result of their attitude, we are not able to establish the
kind of unified government which we
earnestly intend for the empire.
5 "These people are hostile to our government and commit terrible crimes
which threaten the security of the empire. They follow strange customs, obey
their own laws, and stand alone in their
constant opposition to all people. 6 In the
light of these facts, we recommend the
slaughter of the people referred to by
Haman, our prime minister. All of them,
including women and children, must be
put to death; no one is to be spared. They
are our enemies; we will show them no
pity. This order is to be carried out this
year on the fourteenth day of the twelfth
month, the month of Adar. 7 These people, who have caused so much trouble
for so long, will all die a violent death in
a single day. From then on, our government will be secure and stable."
3 14 The contents of the proclamation
were made public in every province, and everyone was ordered to be
prepared for that day.
15 The decree was also rapidly made
public in the capital city of Susa. And

[e] *Greek* Ethiopia: *Ethiopia is the name given in Graeco-Roman times to the extensive territory south of the First Cataract of the Nile River. Cush was the ancient (Hebrew) name of this region which included within its borders most of modern Sudan and some of present-day Ethiopia (Abyssinia).* [f] *Chapter 3 continues after chapter B.* [g] *Chapter B 1-7 corresponds to chapter 13.1-7 in a number of English translations.* [h] *Greek* Ethiopia: *Ethiopia is the name given in Graeco-Roman times to the extensive territory south of the First Cataract of the Nile River. Cush was the ancient (Hebrew) name of this region which included within its borders most of modern Sudan and some of present-day Ethiopia (Abyssinia).*

while the king and Haman got drunk,
the city of Susa was thrown into
confusion.

Mordecai Asks for Esther's Help

4 When Mordecai learned of all that
had been done, he tore his clothes
in anguish. Then he dressed in sackcloth, covered his head with ashes, and
ran through the city crying loudly, "An
innocent nation is being destroyed!"
2 When he came to the entrance of the
palace, he stopped. He did not go in because no one in sackcloth and ashes was
allowed inside. 3 Throughout all the
provinces, wherever the king's proclamation was made known, there was
loud mourning among the Jews. They
wept, wailed, and put on sackcloth and
ashes.
4 When Esther's servant women and
eunuchs told her what Mordecai was doing, she was deeply disturbed. She sent
Mordecai some clothes to put on instead
of the sackcloth, but he would not accept
them. 5 Then she called Hathach, one of
the palace eunuchs appointed as her
servant, and told him to go to Mordecai
and get the details of what was happening.[i] 7 Mordecai told him everything
that had happened and how Haman had
promised to put 375 tons of silver into
the royal treasury if all the Jews were
killed. 8 He gave Hathach a copy of the
proclamation that had been issued in
Susa, ordering the destruction of the
Jews. Mordecai asked him to take it to
Esther so that she might go and plead
with the king and beg him to have mercy
on her people. "Tell her," he said, "to remember the days when she was just an
ordinary person being brought up under
my care. Now, since Haman, the king's
prime minister, has spoken against us
and demands our death, she must pray
to the Lord and then speak to the king
about us. She must save us from death."
9 So Hathach did this, 10 and Esther
gave him this message to take back to
Mordecai: 11 "If anyone, man or woman,
goes to the inner courtyard and sees the
king without being summoned, that person will be sentenced to death. Everyone
in the empire knows that. Only if the
king holds out his gold scepter to him
can his life be spared. But it has been a
month now since the king has sent
for me."
12 When Mordecai received Esther's
message, 13 he sent her this warning:
"Esther, don't imagine that you are safer
than any of the other Jews in the empire.
14 If you keep quiet at a time like this,
help will come to the Jews in some other
way and they will be saved, but you will
die and your father's family will come to
an end. Yet, who knows? Maybe it was
for a time like this that you were made
queen!"
15 Esther sent Mordecai this reply:
16 "Go and gather all the Jews in Susa
together; hold a fast and pray for me.
Don't eat or drink anything for three
days and nights. My servant women and
I will be doing the same. After that, I will
go to the king, even though it is against
the law. If I must die for doing it, I
will die."
17 Mordecai then left and did everything that Esther had told him to do.

Mordecai's Prayer

C[j] Mordecai prayed to the Lord, calling to mind what the Lord had
done in the past: 2 "O Lord, you are the
Lord and King of all creation, and everything obeys your commands. If you wish
to save Israel, no one can stop you. 3 You
made heaven and earth and all the wonderful things on earth. 4 You are the Lord
of all, and there is no one who can stand
against you. 5 You know all things. You
know, Lord, that when I refused to bow
to that arrogant Haman, it was not because I was arrogant or trying to impress people. 6-7 I simply did not want to
honor any human being more than I
honor God. I refuse to bow to anyone but
you, my Lord; and this is not because of
pride. If it would help to save Israel, I
would be willing even to kiss the soles of
his feet.
8-9 "And now, O Lord, God and King,
God of Abraham, spare your people;
save us from our enemies. They are determined to destroy us; they are looking
for a chance. Long ago you chose us to
be your people and rescued us from the
land of Egypt. Do not abandon us now.
10 We are your chosen people, so listen to

[i] *Some manuscipts add verse 6:* Hathach went to Mordecai in the city square at the entrance to the palace. [j] *Chapter C 1-30 corresponds to chapters 13.8—14.19 in a number of English translations.*

my prayer and be gracious to us. Turn our misfortune into joy so that we may live to sing your praises. Save us from death so that we can keep on praising you."
11 And all the people of Israel prayed loudly and earnestly because they were sure that they were going to die.

Esther's Prayer

12 Queen Esther, in deep agony, turned
to the Lord. 13 She took off her splendid
robes and put on garments of mourning and grief. Instead of her rich perfumes, she put ashes and dung on her head. She did all she could to destroy any dignity in her appearance. She let her tangled and uncombed hair hang down over her body that she had always taken such
care to beautify. 14 She prayed to the
Lord God of Israel, "My Lord and King, only you are God. I am all alone, and I have no one to turn to but you. Help me!
15 I am about to risk my life. 16 O Lord, as
long as I can remember, my family has told me how you chose Israel from all the nations and how in ancient times you singled out our ancestors to be your people forever. You have kept all your promises to them.
17 "But we sinned against you. You
handed us over to our enemies because
we worshiped their gods. 18 We deserved
your punishment, O Lord. 19 But our en-
emies are no longer satisfied just to see us in slavery. They have made a solemn
promise to their idols 20 not only to de-
stroy the people who praise you, but to do away with your Law and to remove forever the glory of your house and altar. 21 They want the whole world to
praise worthless idols and stand in awe of mortal kings forever.
22 "Lord, these gods are nothing; do
not surrender your power to them or give our enemies the chance to laugh at our downfall. Instead, turn their evil plans against them, and make an example of that man who first planned our destruction.
23 "Remember us, O Lord. Come to us
in this time of trouble. Give me courage, King of all gods and Ruler over all
earthly powers. 24 Give me the right
words to say when I go in to face Xerxes, that savage lion. Change his heart so that he will turn against Haman, our enemy, and destroy him and his gang.
25 Come to our rescue, O Lord. Help me;
I am all alone, and I have no one to turn to but you.
26 "You know everything, Lord. You
know that I hate the honor I receive from these Gentiles. I detest the thought of having sex with any of these uncircumcised heathen. 27 But you know that
I have no choice. I hate the crown I have to wear as queen on official occasions. I never wear it unless I have to; it's as disgusting as last month's rag. 28 I refuse to
eat at Haman's table or honor the king by attending his parties, and I have never drunk any of the wine dedicated
to his gods. 29 Since I came here, the only
thing that has brought me joy is my worship of you, Lord God of Abraham.
30 "Almighty God, listen to the prayer
of your people. Rescue us from these evildoers, and take away my fear."

Esther Goes to the King

D[k] Queen Esther prayed for three days. Then she took off the clothes she had been wearing and put on
her splendid robes again. 2-3 In all her
royal splendor, she prayed again to her God and savior, who sees everything. Walking like a queen, she left her room accompanied by two servant women, one of them escorting her by the arm
and 4 the other holding up the train of
her robe. 5 Queen Esther's face was radi-
antly beautiful. She looked as cheerful as she was lovely, but in her heart she
was terror-stricken. 6 She passed
through all the doors and entered the throne room, where she stood before the king. He was seated on his royal throne, dressed in his glorious robes, which were covered with gold and precious jewels. It was an awe-inspiring sight.
7 His face glowed with splendor, but
when he saw Esther, he stared at her with fierce anger. She grew weak and turned pale; she almost fainted and had to lean her head on her attendant's shoulder.
8 But God changed the king's anger
into tender concern. He quickly rose from his throne and took her in his arms until she was able to stand. He calmed
her with comforting words. 9 "What is it,

[k] *Chapter D 1-15 corresponds to chapter 15.1-16 in a number of English translations.*

Esther?" he said to her. "I am your husband. There's no need to be afraid.
10 Our law applies only to ordinary people; you will not die. 11 Come here to
me." 12 He lifted his gold scepter and
touched her on the neck with it. Then he
kissed her and said, "Tell me what you
want."
13 "When I looked at you, my lord, I
thought I was seeing an angel of God,"
the queen answered, "and I was overcome by your awesome majesty. 14 You
are so marvelous and your face is so full
of kindness."
15 But while she was speaking, she
fainted again. 16 The king was concerned
about her, and all his attendants tried to
revive her.

Esther Invites the King and Haman to a Banquet

5 [l] 3 "What is it, Esther?" the king
asked. "Tell me what you want, and
you shall have it — even if it is half of my
empire."
4 Esther replied, "Today is a special
day for me. If it please my lord, I would
like you and Haman to be my guests tonight at a banquet I am preparing
for you."
5 The king then ordered Haman to
come quickly, so that they could be Esther's guests. So the king and Haman
went to Esther's banquet. 6 Over the
wine the king again said to her, "Tell me
what you want, Queen Esther."
7 Esther replied, 8 "If my lord is kind
enough to grant my request, I would like
you and Haman to be my guests tomorrow at another banquet that I will prepare for you. It will be just like this one."

Haman Plots to Kill Mordecai

9 When Haman left the king he was
happy and in a good mood, until he saw
Mordecai the Jew in the courtyard of the
palace. That made him furious, 10 but he
went on home. Then he invited his
friends to his house and asked his wife
Zeresh to join them. 11 He boasted to
them about how rich he was and about
the honor the king had paid him when
he promoted him to high office and
made him prime minister. 12 "What is
more," Haman said, "Queen Esther gave
a banquet for no one but the king and
me, and we are invited back tomorrow.
13 But none of this means a thing to me
as long as I see that Jew Mordecai sitting
in the courtyard of the palace."
14 Then his wife and all his friends suggested, "Why don't you have a gallows
put up, seventy-five feet high? Tomorrow morning you can ask the king to
have Mordecai hanged on it, and then
you can go with the king to the banquet
and enjoy yourself." Haman thought it
was a good idea, so he had the gallows
built.

The King Honors Mordecai

6 That night the Lord kept the king
from sleeping, so the king ordered
his private secretary to bring the official
records of the empire and read them to
him. 2 He read the account of how Mordecai had uncovered a plot to assassinate the king — the plot made by the
two eunuchs who served as palace
guards. 3 The king asked, "How have
we honored and rewarded Mordecai
for this?"
His servants answered, "You have
done nothing for him."
4 Now just as the king was inquiring
about Mordecai's good deed, Haman entered the courtyard. He had come to ask
the king to have Mordecai hanged on the
gallows that was now ready.
"Who is that in the courtyard?" the
king asked.
5 The servants answered, "It is Haman;
he is waiting to see you."
"Show him in," said the king.
6 So Haman came in, and the king said
to him, "There is someone I wish very
much to honor. What should I do for
this man?"
Haman thought to himself, "Now who
could the king want to honor so much?
Me, of course."
7-8 So he answered the king, "Let the
royal servants bring a fine linen robe for
this man — one that you yourself wear.
And let them bring a horse that you
yourself ride. 9 Then put that robe on the
man you like so much and then have
the nobleman lead him, mounted on the
horse, through the city square. Have the
nobleman announce as they go: 'See
how the king rewards a man whom he
wishes to honor!' "

[l] *In Greek, chapter D replaces verses 1 and 2 in Hebrew.*

10 Then the king said to Haman, "Fine!
Do all that for Mordecai the Jew, who
holds a high position in the palace; don't
leave out a thing."
11 So Haman got the robe and the
horse, and he put the robe on Mordecai.
Mordecai got on the horse, and Haman
led him through the city square, announcing to the people as they went:
"See how the king rewards a man whom
he wishes to honor!"
12 Mordecai then went back to the
courtyard while Haman hurried home,
covering his face in embarrassment.
13 He told his wife and all his friends
everything that had happened to him.
Then they all said to him, "You are beginning to lose power to Mordecai. He is
a Jew, and you cannot overcome him.
He will certainly defeat you, for the living God is with him!"

Haman Is Put to Death

14 While they were still talking, the
palace eunuchs arrived to take Haman
to Esther's banquet.
7 And so the king and Haman went to
eat with Esther 2 for a second time.
Over the wine the king asked her again,
"Now, Queen Esther, what do you want?
Tell me and you shall have it. I'll even
give you half the empire."
3 Queen Esther answered, "If it please
Your Majesty to grant my humble request, my wish is that I may live and that
my people may live. 4 My people and I
have been sold into slavery; our possessions have been plundered, and now we
are to be destroyed—all of us, including
our children, will be slaves—and so far I
have kept quiet. It isn't right that our enemy should be a member of the royal
court."
5 Then King Xerxes asked Esther,
"Who dares to do such a thing?"
6 Esther answered, "Our enemy is this
evil man Haman!"
In terror Haman faced the king and
queen. 7 The king got up from the table
and went outside to the palace gardens.
Haman could see that he was in a dangerous situation, so he stayed behind to
beg Queen Esther for his life. 8 He had
just thrown himself down on Esther's
couch to beg for mercy, when the king
came back into the room from the gardens. Seeing this, the king cried out,
"Are you going to rape my wife here in
my own palace?"
When Haman heard this, he turned
away in despair. 9 Then one of the eunuchs, whose name was Bougathan,
said, "Haman has even gone so far as to
build a gallows at his house so that he
can hang Mordecai, who warned Your
Majesty about the plot. And it's seventy-
five feet high!"
"Hang Haman on it!" the king commanded.
10 So Haman was hanged on the gallows that he had built for Mordecai.
Then the king's anger cooled down.

The Jews Are Told to Fight Back

8 That same day King Xerxes gave
Queen Esther all the property of
Haman, the enemy of the Jews. Esther
told the king that Mordecai was related
to her, and Mordecai was invited to enter the king's presence. 2 The king took
off his ring with his seal on it (which he
had taken back from Haman) and gave it
to Mordecai. Esther put Mordecai in
charge of Haman's property.
3 Then Esther spoke to the king again,
throwing herself at his feet. She begged
him to do something to stop the evil plot
that Haman had made against the Jews.
4 The king held out the gold scepter to
her, so she stood up 5 and said, "If it
please Your Majesty and if you care
about me, please issue a proclamation
to keep Haman's orders from being carried out—those orders he gave for
the destruction of all the Jews in the
empire. 6 How can I endure it if this
disaster comes on my people? How
can I go on living if my whole nation is
destroyed?"
7 Then the king said to Esther, "I have
hanged Haman for his plot against the
Jews, and I have given you his property.
If that is not enough, 8 you may write to
the Jews whatever you like; and you
may write it in my name and stamp it
with the royal seal, for a proclamation
issued in the king's name and stamped
with the royal seal cannot be revoked."
9 On the twenty-third day of the first
month, the month of Nisan, the king's
secretaries were called and letters were
written to the Jews and to the governors
and administrators of all 127 provinces

from India to Ethiopia.[m] The letters
were written to each province in its own
language. 10 They were written in the
name of the king and stamped with the
royal seal and they were delivered by
runners.

11 These letters explained that the king
would allow the Jews in every city of the
empire to live by their own laws and organize for self-defense. They were permitted to treat their opponents and
enemies in any way they liked. 12 This
decree was to take effect throughout the
Persian Empire on the thirteenth day of
Adar, the twelfth month.[n]

The King's Decree in Favor of the Jews

E[o] This is a copy of the decree:
"Greetings from King Xerxes
the Great to the governors of the 127
provinces, which extend from India to
Ethiopia,[p] and to all those who are loyal
to us.

2 "Many people become increasingly
arrogant when honors are given to them
and favors are done for them. 3 They do
not know what to do with so much good
fortune, so they not only try to harm our
subjects, but they even scheme against
those who grant them favors. 4 They are
never grateful for what people do for
them, and they even think they can escape the judgment of God, who hates
evil and sees everything. In their arrogance they listen to the flattery of ignorant, sinful people.

5 "It often happens also that friends
who have been entrusted with administrative responsibilities exert pressure on
those in authority. They make their leaders their partners in killing people and
bring about misfortunes that can never
be remedied. 6 These friends, by their
lies and deceitful ways, take advantage
of the good will of their rulers.

7 "You can see examples of this misuse
of power not only in the stories that have
been handed down to us from the past,
but in the more recent outrageous things
which have happened among you.

8 "I intend to make sure that in the future my kingdom will remain untroubled
and peaceful for all people. 9 This can be
done by changing certain policies and
by judging fairly each situation that
comes to my attention.

10 "Consider, for example, the case of
Haman son of Hammedatha, a Macedonian. He is a foreigner with no Persian
blood and with no trace of my generosity; but I welcomed him, 11 and he received the benefit of my concern and
love for all people. He was, in fact, proclaimed 'Father' of the empire and received more honor than anyone else,
except the king.

12 "But his arrogance knew no limits,
and he tried to murder me and take over
the empire. 13 In his crafty and deceitful
way, he asked that Mordecai be put to
death—Mordecai, who once saved my
life and who has always supported me.
He even asked for the death of Esther,
our blameless queen, and in fact, the
death of all the Jewish people. 14 His purpose was to leave us helpless and to allow the Macedonians to take over the
Persian Empire. 15 Even though this
wicked criminal plotted to wipe out the
Jews, I find that they are not traitors at
all but are governed by very just laws.
16 They worship the living God, the highest and greatest God, who has kept our
empire in its excellent condition from
the time of our ancestors until our
own day.

17 "Therefore I advise you not to carry
out the instructions issued in the letters
sent out by Haman. 18 He is the person
responsible for all of this, and he has
been hanged, along with his entire family, at the gates of Susa. God, who governs all things, has given him the speedy
punishment that he deserved.

19 "I order you to post copies of this
decree in every public place. Permit the
Jews to live by their own customs, 20 and
give them support when they defend
themselves against those who attack
them on the day set for their destruction,
the thirteenth day of Adar, the twelfth

[m] *Greek* Ethiopia: *Ethiopia is the name given in Graeco-Roman times to the extensive territory south of the First Cataract of the Nile River. Cush was the ancient (Hebrew) name of this region which included within its borders most of modern Sudan and some of present-day Ethiopia (Abyssinia).* [n] *Chapter 8 continues after chapter E.* [o] *Chapter E 1-24 corresponds to chapter 16.1-24 in a number of English translations.* [p] *Greek* Ethiopia: *Ethiopia is the name given in Graeco-Roman times to the extensive territory south of the First Cataract of the Nile River. Cush was the ancient (Hebrew) name of this region which included within its borders most of modern Sudan and some of present-day Ethiopia (Abyssinia).*

month. 21 God, who governs all things,
has turned that day of destruction into a
day of celebration for his chosen people.
22 "Include this day among your national holidays and celebrate it as a festival. 23 Now and in the future it will
remind us and all our allies of the way
God watches over our nation, and those
who plot against us will be reminded of
God's threat of destruction.
24 "Every province, every city, without
exception, which does not obey these orders will feel my anger. It will be destroyed in battle and burned to the
ground. No human being will ever go
there again, and even the birds and wild
animals will avoid it forever.

8 [q] 13 "Post copies of this decree in
plain view in every province, so
that all the Jews can be ready to fight
their enemies when that day comes."
14 Messengers on horses rode off at top
speed to carry out the orders of the king,
and the decree was also made public in
Susa.
15 Mordecai left the palace, wearing
royal robes, a turban of fine purple
linen, and a gold crown. When the people of Susa saw him, they cheered, 16 and
the Jews were happy and joyful. 17 They
held a joyful holiday with feasting and
happiness in every city and province,
wherever the king's proclamation was
posted. In fact, many Gentiles were circumcised and became Jews, because
they were now afraid of them.

The Jews Destroy Their Enemies

9 On the thirteenth day of Adar, the
day on which the royal proclamation was to take effect, 2 it was the enemies of the Jews who were wiped out.
People everywhere were afraid of the
Jews, and no one could stand against
them. 3 In fact, the provincial governors,
the administrators, and the royal scribes
showed respect for the Jews, because
they were all afraid of Mordecai. 4-5 The
royal decree had made his name known
throughout the empire.
6 In Susa, the capital city itself, the
Jews killed five hundred people 7-10 and
looted their property. Among them were
the ten sons of Haman son of Hammedatha, a Bougaean, the enemy of the Jews:
Pharsannestain, Delphon, Phasga,
Pharadatha, Barea, Sarbacha, Mar-
masima, Arouphaeus, Arsaeus, and
Zabouthaeus.
11 That same day the number of people
killed in Susa was reported to the king.
12 He then said to Esther, "In Susa alone
the Jews have killed five hundred people. What must they have done out in the
provinces! Tell me what else you want,
and you shall have it."
13 Esther answered, "Let the Jews in
Susa do again tomorrow what they were
allowed to do today. And have the bodies of Haman's ten sons hung up." 14 The
king agreed and permitted the Jews to
put the bodies of Haman's ten sons on
public display. 15 On the fourteenth day
of Adar the Jews of Susa got together
again and killed three hundred more
people in the city. But they did no
looting.
16 The Jews in the provinces also organized and defended themselves. They
rid themselves of their enemies by killing 15,000 people on the thirteenth day
of Adar, but they did no looting. 17 On
the next day, the fourteenth, there was
no more killing, and the Jews made it a
joyful holiday of rest and feasting. 18 The
Jews of Susa, however, made the fifteenth a holiday, since they had slaughtered their enemies on the thirteenth and
fourteenth and did not stop until the fifteenth. 19 This is why Jews who live in
small towns observe the fourteenth day
of the month of Adar as a holiday, a time
of giving gifts of food to one another,
while the Jews in the large cities celebrate the holiday in the same way on the
fifteenth.

The Festival of Purim

20 Mordecai had these events written
down in a book and sent it to all the
Jews, near and far, throughout the Persian Empire, 21 telling them to observe
the fourteenth and fifteenth days of
Adar as holidays. 22 These were the days
on which the Jews had rid themselves of
their enemies. The Jews were to observe
the whole month as a holiday, for this
was a month that had been turned from
a time of grief and despair into a time of
joy and happiness. They were told to observe these days with feasts and parties,
giving gifts of food to friends and to the

[q] *Verses 1-12 precede chapter E.*

poor. 23 So the Jews accepted all that
Mordecai had written.
24 Mordecai had recorded how Haman
son of Hammedatha, a Macedonian, had
fought against the Jewish people, how
he had made a decree and cast lots to
determine the day he would destroy
them, 25 and how he had gone to the king
to request that Mordecai be hanged. But
Haman suffered the same fate he had
planned for the Jews—he and his sons
were hanged from the gallows.
26-28 Because of Mordecai's letter, because of all they had suffered, and because of all that had happened to them,
the Jews accepted Mordecai's suggestion and made it a rule for themselves,
their descendants, and anyone that
might become a Jew, that these days
should be properly observed as a memorial, generation after generation, in
every city, province, and country. The
Jews were to remember and observe
these days of Purim for all time to come
and never neglect them. (The holidays
are called Purim because "purim" in
their language is the word for "lots.")
29-30 Then Queen Esther, the daughter
of Aminadab, along with Mordecai the
Jew, wrote down what they had done,
putting the queen's full authority behind
the letter about Purim. 31 They both took
responsibility for establishing the festival and made up their minds to observe
it at all costs.[r] 32 Esther established the
festival forever, and a written record
was made of her official decree.

The Greatness of Xerxes and Mordecai

10 King Xerxes imposed taxes on
the people of the coastal regions
of his empire as well as on those of the
interior. 2 His power and virtue, as well
as the wealth and splendor of his empire, are recorded in the official records
of the kings of Persia and Media. 3 Mordecai was second in rank only to King
Xerxes himself. He was a great man in
the empire and was honored by his fellow Jews. He was greatly loved, for he
sought the welfare of his people.

Mordecai Remembers His Dream

F[s] Then Mordecai said, "God has
caused all these things to happen!
2 And I am reminded of the dream I had
about all of this. Every detail of the
dream has come true: 3 the small spring
that became a river, the dawn that
turned into sunlight, and the abundance
of water. The river is Esther, whom the
king married and made his queen. 4 The
two dragons represent Haman and me.
5 The nations are all those who have
gathered together to destroy the Jews.
6 My nation is Israel, which cried out to
God for help and was saved. The Lord
saved his people! He rescued us from all
these evils and performed great miracles
and wonders that have never happened
among other nations. 7 That is because
God prepared one destiny for his own
people and another for all other nations.
8 Then came the day and the hour when
these two destinies were to be decided;
the time had come for God to make a
decision about the nations. 9 God remembered his chosen people and gave
the verdict in their favor. 10 So each year
for all time to come God's people will
gather together in his presence on the
fourteenth and fifteenth of the month of
Adar, and celebrate with joy and
happiness."

Postscript

During the fourth year of the reign of Ptolemy and Cleopatra, a man named Dositheus, who claimed to be a levitical priest, brought the preceding letter about the Purim festival. He was accompanied by his son Ptolemy, and they declared that the letter was genuine and that it had been translated by Lysimachus, son of Ptolemy, a member of a Jerusalem family.

[r] at all costs; *Greek unclear.* [s] *Chapter F 1-10 corresponds to chapters 10.4—11.1 in a number of English translations.*

THE WISDOM OF SOLOMON

Introduction

This book was originally written in Greek by an unknown Jewish author. The book makes use of traditional Jewish material, as well as ideas borrowed from Greek philosophy, in order to teach that God rewards those who are faithful to him.

Outline of Contents

The Search for Justice

1 Love justice, you rulers of the
world. Set your minds sincerely
on the Lord, and look for him with all
honesty. 2Those who do not try to test
him will find him; he will show himself
to those who trust him. 3Dishonest
thoughts separate people from God, and
if we are foolish enough to test him, his
power will put us to shame. 4Wisdom
will never be at home with anyone who
is deceitful or a slave of sin. 5Everyone
who is holy has learned to stay away
from deceitful people. He will not stay
around when foolish thoughts are being
expressed; he will not feel comfortable
when injustice is done.

God Is Aware of What We Say

6Wisdom is a spirit that is friendly to
people, but she will not forgive anyone
who speaks against God, for God knows
our feelings and thoughts, and hears our
every word. 7Since the Lord's spirit fills
the entire world, and holds everything in
it together, she knows every word that
people say. 8No one who speaks wickedly will escape notice; sooner or later
he will receive just punishment. 9The intentions of ungodly people will be
closely examined; their words will be reported to the Lord, and then they will get
the punishment that their wickedness
deserves. 10God will tolerate no challenge, and since he hears everything,
you cannot hide your complaining from
him. 11So be sure that you do not go
around complaining—it does no good—
and don't engage in bitter talk. The most
secret things you say will have their consequences, and lying will destroy your
soul.

God Did Not Create Death

12Do not bring on your own death by
sinful actions. 13God did not invent
death, and when living creatures die, it
gives him no pleasure. 14He created
everything so that it might continue to
exist, and everything he created is
wholesome and good. There is no deadly
poison in them. No, death does not rule
this world, 15for God's justice does
not die.
16Ungodly people have brought death
on themselves by the things they have
said and done. They yearn for death as if
it were a lover. They have gone into
partnership with death, and it is just
what they deserve.

Wicked Thinking

2 Wicked people are wrong when
they say to themselves, "Our life is
short and full of sorrow, and when its
end comes, there is no escape. No one
has ever been known to come back from
the world of the dead. 2We were born by
chance, and after life is over, we will be
as if we had never been born at all. Our
breath is no more than a puff of smoke;
our mind is nothing more than a spark
thrown off by the beating of our heart.
3When that spark dies, our body will
crumble into ashes, and our breath will
become part of the empty air. 4In time,
no one will remember anything we ever
did, and even our names will be forgot-

ten. Our lives will pass away like the
traces of clouds and vanish like fog in
the heat of the sun. 5Our time on earth is
like a passing shadow. There is no escape from the day of our death; it is
fixed, and no one can postpone it."
6The wicked say, "Come on, then, let's
enjoy the good things of life, and live in
this world the way we did when we were
young and free of care! 7Let's drink the
most expensive wines and use the finest
perfumes. Let's not miss a single flower
in the springtime! 8Before the roses
wither, let's pick them and wear them in
our hair! 9Let's all join in and leave
signs everywhere of our carefree rev-
elry! Life owes us that much!
10"We'll oppress the poor, even if they
are righteous. We'll show no respect for
widows or old people. 11We'll call ourselves right if we are strong enough to
get what we want. No one ever got anywhere by being weak! 12Righteous people are nothing but a nuisance, so let's
look for chances to get rid of them. They
are against what we do; they accuse us
of breaking the Law of Moses and violating the traditions of our ancestors.
13They claim to know God, and they call
themselves the Lord's children. 14We
can't stand the sight of people like that;
what they are contradicts our whole way
of thinking. 15They are not like other
people; they have strange ways. 16They
think that our moral standards are so
corrupt that everything we do should be
avoided. They boast of having God for
their Father, and believe that when all is
said and done, only the righteous will be
happy. 17But we'll see if that's true! Let's
see what will happen when it's time for
them to die! 18If the righteous really are
God's children, God will save them from
their enemies. 19So let's put them to the
test. We'll be cruel to them, and torment
them; then we'll find out how calm and
reasonable they are! We'll find out just
how much they can stand! 20We'll condemn them to a shameful death. After
all, they say that God will protect them."
21That is how evil people think, but
they are wrong. They are blinded by
their own wickedness. 22They have
never known God's secrets, never hoped
for the rewards of a holy and blameless
life. 23When God created us, he did not
intend for us to die; he made us like himself. 24It was the Devil's jealousy that
brought death into the world, and those
who belong to the Devil are the ones
who will die.

The Destiny of the Righteous

3 But righteous people are protected
by God and will never suffer torment. 2It is a foolish mistake to think
that righteous people die and that their
death is a terrible evil. 3They leave us,
but it is not a disaster. In fact, the righteous are at peace. 4It might appear that
they have suffered punishment, but they
have the confident hope of immortality.
5-6Their sufferings were minor compared with the blessings they will receive. God has tested them, like gold in a
furnace, and found them worthy to be
with him. He has accepted them, just as
he accepts the sacrifices which his worshipers burn on the altar.
7When God comes to reward the
righteous, they will blaze out against the
wicked like fire in dry straw. 8They will
rule over nations and peoples, and the
Lord will be their king forever. 9Those
who have put their trust in God will
come to understand the truth of his
ways. Those who have been faithful will
live with him in his love, for he is kind
and merciful to the ones whom he has
chosen.[a]

The Destiny of the Wicked

10The ungodly, however, will get the
punishment their wicked thoughts deserve, because they rebelled against the
Lord and ignored what was right.[b]
11A man who has no use for wisdom or
education has a miserable life in store
for him. He has nothing to hope for. His
labors are useless, and he will never accomplish anything worthwhile. 12The
woman he marries will turn out to be
irresponsible, and his children will go
wrong. 13All his descendants will be under a curse.

The Importance of Virtue

On Judgment Day God will reward the
woman who has never been able to have
a child, provided she has not been guilty
of adultery. Then she will be happy.

[a] *Some manuscripts add* and he protects his own people *(see 4.15).* [b] what was right; *or* righteous people.

14 On that day, even the man who has
been castrated will be rewarded with
happiness, if he has kept the Law and
has not stored up resentment against the
Lord. Because he has been faithful, he
will receive a special reward more precious than having children: a place in
the Lord's heavenly Temple. 15 Honest
deeds are like a tree that bears marvelous fruit. Wisdom is like a root that is
alive and can always send up new
shoots.

16 But children born of adultery or of a
forbidden union will die an early death.
17 Yet even if they do live a long time,
they will never amount to anything.
They will not be respected in their old
age, 18 and if they die young, they will
have no hope or comfort on Judgment
Day. 19 Children born of a forbidden
union suffer a miserable fate.

4 It is better to have virtue, even if it
means having no children. Your
virtue will be recognized by other people
and by God, and you will be remembered for it forever. 2 Virtue provides an
example for people to follow; when it is
not there, they miss it. It has always
been the finest prize a person can win,
and it always will be so. It is the noblest
of all the good qualities a person can
have.

3 No matter how many children are
born of a forbidden union, none of them
will ever amount to anything. They are
illegitimate; they can never lay a firm
foundation for themselves, never take
deep root. 4 Like trees with shallow
roots, they put out leaves for a while, but
they sway in the wind, and storms uproot them. 5 Their branches snap off before they mature; their fruit never
ripens, and it is good for nothing. 6 On
Judgment Day children born of a forbidden union will testify to the sin of their
parents and act as witnesses against
them.

7 Righteous people, however, will find
rest, even if they die young. 8 We honor
old age, but not just because a person
has lived a long time. 9 Wisdom and
righteousness are signs of the maturity
that should come with old age.

The Example of Enoch

10 Once there was a man named Enoch
who pleased God, and God loved him.
While Enoch was still living among sinners, God took him away, 11 so that evil
and falsehood could not corrupt his
mind and soul. (12 We all know that people can be so fascinated by evil that they
cannot recognize what is good even
when they are looking right at it. Innocent people can be so corrupted with desire that they can think of nothing but
what they want.) 13 This man Enoch
achieved in a few years' time a perfection that other people could never attain
in a complete lifetime. 14 The Lord was
pleased with Enoch's life and quickly
took him out of this wicked world. People were aware of his departure but
didn't understand. They never seemed to
learn the lesson 15 that God is kind and
merciful to his own people; he protects
those whom he has chosen.

The Fate of the Wicked

16 Even when righteous people are
dead and gone, they put to shame the
wicked people who live on after them. In
their old age the wicked will be disgraced by young people who have already achieved perfection. 17 The wise
may die young, but the wicked will
never understand that this is the Lord's
way of taking them off to safety. 18 They
make light of a wise person's death, but
the Lord will soon be laughing at them.
When they die, they will not be given an
honorable burial. Even the dead will
hold them in scorn and disgust forever.
19 God will throw them to the ground and
make them speechless. Like buildings
shaken from their foundations, they will
be reduced to piles of ruins. They will be
in torment. People will soon forget all
about them. 20 They will come in fear to
the Judgment, where their sins will be
counted; they will stand condemned by
their own lawless actions.

The Regrets of the Wicked

5 On that day someone righteous, full
of confidence, will stand before
those who oppressed him and made
light of his labors. 2 They will be amazed
to see him safe and will tremble with terrible fear. 3 Then they will regret what
they did, and groaning in anguish they
will say to each other: 4 "This is the one
we made fun of. We thought he was a
joke. What fools we were! We thought
he was crazy to live the way he did, and
when he died, we didn't honor him.

5 And now here he is, one of God's own
children, with a place of his own among
God's people. 6 We were the ones who
wandered off the right road. We never
lived in the light of righteousness; we
never caught the first glimmer of its
light. 7 All our lives we wandered across
unmarked deserts, instead of following
the road which the Lord wanted us to
travel. And this lawlessness led us to
ruin. 8 We were so proud of ourselves—
we bragged about how rich we were—
and now, what good has it done us? 9 All
those things are gone now; they have
disappeared like a shadow, like something you hear and then forget.

10 "A ship sails across the waves of the
ocean, but when it is gone, it leaves no
trace. You cannot tell it was ever there.
11 A bird flies through the air, but leaves
no sign that it has been there. It speeds
along, riding through the thin air by the
force of its wings, leaving behind no
trace of its passing. 12 An arrow splits the
air when it is shot at a target, but at once
the air closes up behind it, and no one
can tell where it passed. 13 It is the same
with us—we were born, and then we
ceased to be. We left no sign of virtue
behind us; we were destroyed by our
wickedness."

14 What hope do wicked people have?
Only the hope of straw blown about in
the wind, the hope of ocean foam[c] that
disappears in the storm, the hope of
smoke in the breeze. Their hope lasts no
longer than our memory of a guest who
stays one day and leaves the next.

15 But the righteous live on forever.
The Lord will reward them; the Most
High will protect them. 16 He will give
them royal splendor and a magnificent
crown. He will shield them with his powerful arm. 17 He will go out into battle
determined to defeat his enemies, and
use the creation itself as a weapon.
18 Righteousness will be his armor, genuine justice will be his helmet, 19 holiness
will be his invincible shield. 20 He will
sharpen his stern anger into a sword,
and the forces of nature will join him in
battle against those who are foolish
enough to oppose him. 21 Bolts of lightning will strike right on target, as if the
Lord had made a bow out of the clouds
and was shooting arrows. 22 Hailstones
will beat down on his enemies with terrible force. The oceans and rivers will
come rushing over them in a devastating
flood. 23 Great windstorms will blow
them away like straw. Lawlessness will
be the ruin of the whole world. Evil actions will cause governments to fall.

The Responsibility of Rulers

6 So then, you kings, you rulers the
world over, listen to what I say, and
learn from it. 2 You govern many lands
and are proud that so many people are
under your rule, 3 but this authority has
been given to you by the Lord Most
High. He will examine what you have
done and what you plan to do. 4 You rule
on behalf of God and his kingdom, and if
you do not govern justly, if you do not
uphold the law, if you do not live according to God's will, 5 you will suffer sudden
and terrible punishment. Judgment is
especially severe on those in power.
6 Common people may be mercifully forgiven for their wrongs, but those in
power will face a severe judgment. 7 The
Lord of all is not afraid of anyone, no
matter how great they are. He himself
made everyone, great and common
alike, and he provides for all equally,
8 but he will judge the conduct of rulers
more strictly. 9 It is for you, mighty
kings, that I write these words, so that
you may know how to act wisely and
avoid mistakes. 10 These are holy matters, and if you treat them in a holy manner, you yourselves will be considered
holy. If you have learned this lesson, you
will be able to defend yourselves at the
Judgment. 11 So then, make my teaching
your treasure and joy, and you will be
well instructed.

The Value of Wisdom

12 Wisdom shines bright and never
grows dim; those who love her and look
for her can easily find her. 13 She is quick
to make herself known to anyone who
desires her. 14 Get up early in the morning to find her, and you will have no
problem; you will find her sitting at your
door. 15 To fasten your attention on Wisdom is to gain perfect understanding. If
you look for her, you will soon find
peace of mind, 16 because she will be
looking for those who are worthy of her,

[c] ocean foam; *some manuscripts have* frost.

and she will find you wherever you are.
She is kind and will be with you in your
every thought.
17 Wisdom begins when you sincerely
want to learn. To desire Wisdom is to
love her; 18 to love her is to keep her
laws; to keep her laws is to be certain of
immortality; 19 immortality will bring
you close to God. 20 This desire for Wisdom can prepare you to rule a kingdom.
21 So then, you that rule the nations, if
you value your thrones and symbols of
authority, honor Wisdom so that you
may rule forever.

Solomon Wishes to Share His Wisdom

22 I will tell you what Wisdom is, and
how she came to be. I will not keep anything secret. I will trace her history from
the beginning and make knowledge of
her open to all. I will not ignore any part
of the truth. 23 No jealous desire to guard
my own knowledge will make me hold
back anything. Wisdom has nothing in
common with such an attitude. 24 No
indeed—the more wise people there are,
the safer the world will be. A sensible
king can be depended on to give his people this kind of security. 25 So then, learn
what I am about to teach you, and you
will profit from it.

A King Is Like Everyone Else

7 1-2 Like every human being, I am
mortal. I am a descendant of that
first man, who was made from the soil. I
was conceived from the sperm of a man,
in the pleasure of intercourse. For nine
months my flesh took shape in the blood
of my mother's womb. 3 When I was
born, I came into the world like anyone
else. I began to breathe the same air we
all breathe; and like everyone else, the
first sound I made was a cry. 4 I was
wrapped in cloths and cared for. 5 No
king ever began life differently. 6 For all
of us, there is one way into life, and
there is one way out.

Solomon Declares His Love for Wisdom

7 Realizing that I was only human, I
prayed and was given understanding.
The spirit of Wisdom came to me.
8 I regarded her more highly than any
throne or crown. Wealth was nothing
compared to her. 9 Precious jewels could
not equal her worth; beside Wisdom all
the gold in the world is a handful of
sand, and silver is nothing more than
clay. 10 I valued her more than health
and good looks. Hers is a brightness that
never grows dim, and I preferred it to
any other light.
11 When Wisdom came to me, all good
things came with her. She brought me
untold riches. 12 I was happy with them
all, because Wisdom had brought them
to me. I had not realized before that she
was the source of all these things.
13 I was sincere in learning from her, and
now I am glad to share what I learned.
14 No one can ever exhaust the treasures
of Wisdom. Use those treasures and you
are God's friends; he approves of what
you learn from her.
15 I pray to God that my thoughts may
be worthy of what I have learned, and
that I may speak according to his will.
He is Wisdom's guide; he gives correction to those who are wise. 16 We are
under his power and authority—we
ourselves, our words, all our understanding and skills. 17 It is he who gave
me true knowledge of the forces of nature: what the world is made of; how the
elements behave; 18 how the calendar is
determined by the movements of the
sun, the changing seasons, 19 the constellations, and the cycles of years. 20 He has
taught me about the nature of living
creatures, the behavior of wild animals,
the force of the winds, the reasoning
powers of human beings, the different
kinds of plants, and the use of their roots
as medicine. 21 I learned things that were
well known and things that had never
been known before, 22 because Wisdom,
who gave shape to everything that exists, was my teacher.

The Nature of Wisdom

The spirit of Wisdom is intelligent and
holy. It is of one nature but reveals itself
in many ways. It is not made of any material substance, and it moves about
freely. It is clear, clean, and confident; it
cannot be harmed.[d] It loves what is
good. It is sharp and unconquerable,
23 kind, and a friend of humanity. It is
dependable and sure, and has no wor-

[d] cannot be harmed; *or* does no harm.

ries. It has power over everything, and
sees everything. It penetrates every
spirit that is intelligent and pure, no matter how delicate its substance may be.
24 Wisdom moves more easily than
motion itself; she is so pure that she
penetrates everything. 25 She is a breath
of God's power—a pure and radiant
stream of glory from the Almighty.
Nothing that is defiled can ever steal its
way into Wisdom. 26 She is a reflection
of eternal light, a perfect mirror of God's
activity and goodness. 27 Even though
Wisdom acts alone, she can do anything.
She makes everything new, although
she herself never changes. From generation to generation she enters the souls of
holy people, and makes them God's
friends and prophets. 28 There is nothing
that God loves more than people who
are at home with Wisdom. 29 Wisdom is
more beautiful than the sun and all the
constellations. She is better than light itself, 30 because night always follows day,
8 but evil never overcomes Wisdom.
1 Her great power reaches into
every part of the world, and she sets
everything in useful order.

Solomon's Love for Wisdom

2 Wisdom has been my love. I courted
her when I was young and wanted to
make her my bride. I fell in love with her
beauty. 3 She glorifies her noble origin
by living with God, the Lord of all, who
loves her. 4 She is familiar with God's
mysteries and helps determine his
course of action.
5 Is it good to have riches in this life?
Nothing can make you richer than Wisdom, who makes everything function.
6 Is knowledge a useful thing to have?
Nothing is better than Wisdom, who has
given shape to everything that exists.
7 Do you love justice? All the virtues
are the result of Wisdom's work: justice
and courage, self-control and understanding. Life can offer us nothing more
valuable than these. 8 Do you want to
have wide experience? Wisdom knows
the lessons of history and can anticipate
the future. She knows how to interpret
what people say and how to solve problems. She knows the miracles that God
will perform, and how the movements of
history will develop.
9 So I decided to take Wisdom home to
live with me, because I knew that she
would give me good advice and encourage me in times of trouble and grief.
10 I thought to myself, "Because of her I
will be honored wherever people come
together. The old men will respect me,
even though I am young. 11 They will
find that my opinions show deep insight,
and those in power will admire me.
12 When I am silent, they will wait for me
to speak, and when I speak, they will
pay attention. Even when I speak at
length, they will listen with concentra-
tion. 13 Because of Wisdom I will gain
immortality; I will live forever in the
memory of those who come after me.
14 I will hold power over nations and
peoples; 15 dreaded tyrants will be seized
with fear at the mention of my name. I
will be famous, as a good king and as a
brave soldier. 16 When I come home to
Wisdom, I will find contentment because there is no conflict or pain in living with her, only happiness and joy."
17 And so I thought it over: to be wedded to Wisdom is to live forever, 18 to
love her is to be perfectly happy, to do
her work is to be rich beyond measure,
to share her company is to have sound
judgment, to converse with her is to be
honored. Then I was determined to take
Wisdom as my bride. 19 I had a pleasant
personality even as a child. I had been
fortunate enough to receive a good soul,
or rather, I was given a sound body to
live in because I was already good.
20 Still, I realized that I would never receive Wisdom unless God gave her to
me—and knowing that only God could
give her to me was itself a sign of understanding. So I prayed, begging the Lord
with all my heart:

Solomon Prays for Wisdom

9 "God of my ancestors, merciful
Lord, by your word you created
everything. 2 By your Wisdom you made
us humans to rule all creation, 3 to govern the world with holiness and righteousness, to administer justice with
integrity. 4 Give me the Wisdom that sits
beside your throne; give me a place
among your children. 5 I am your slave,
as was my mother before me. I am only
human. I am not strong, and my life will
be short. I have little understanding of
the Law or of how to apply it. 6 Even if
someone is perfect, he will be thought of
as nothing without the Wisdom that

comes from you. 7 You chose me over
everyone else to be the king of your own
people, to judge your sons and daughters. 8 You told me to build a temple on
your sacred mountain, an altar in Jerusalem, the city you chose as your home.
It is a copy of that temple in heaven,
which you prepared at the beginning.
9 Wisdom is with you and knows your
actions; she was present when you made
the world. She knows what pleases you,
what is right and in accordance with
your commands. 10 Send her from the
holy heavens, down from your glorious
throne, so that she may work at my side,
and I may learn what pleases you. 11 She
knows and understands everything, and
will guide me intelligently in what I do.
Her glory will protect me. 12 Then I will
judge your people fairly, and be worthy
of my father's throne. My actions will be
acceptable.
13 "Who can ever learn the will of God?
14 Human reason is not adequate for the
task, and our philosophies tend to mislead us, 15 because our mortal bodies
weigh our souls down. The body is a
temporary structure made of earth, a
burden to the active mind. 16 All we can
do is make guesses about things on
earth; we must struggle to learn about
things that are close to us. Who, then,
can ever hope to understand heavenly
things? 17 No one has ever learned your
will, unless you first gave him Wisdom,
and sent your holy spirit down to him.
18 In this way people on earth have been
set on the right path, have learned what
pleases you, and have been kept safe by
Wisdom."

Wisdom Protected Adam

10 Wisdom protected the father of
the world, the first man that was
ever formed, when he alone had been
created. She saved him from his own
sinful act 2 and gave him the strength
to master everything on earth.

Cain Abandoned Wisdom

3 But there was an unrighteous man
who abandoned Wisdom; he destroyed
himself by killing his brother in a fit of
anger.

Wisdom Protected Noah

4 Because of that sin, the earth was
flooded, but Wisdom saved it again. She
guided a righteous man in his flimsy
wooden boat.

Wisdom Helped Abraham

5 Once when the nations were frustrated in their wicked plans, Wisdom
recognized a righteous man and kept
him innocent in God's sight. She gave
him strength to obey God's command in
spite of his love for his son.

Wisdom Rescued Lot

6 Wisdom rescued a righteous man
while ungodly people were dying. He escaped the flames that destroyed the Five
Cities. 7 You can still see the evidence of
their wickedness. The land there is barren and smoking. The plants bear fruit
that never ripens, and a pillar of salt
stands as a monument to one who did
not believe. 8 The people of those cities
ignored Wisdom and could not tell right
from wrong. Not only that, but the remains of their cities still remind us of the
foolish way they lived, so that their failure can never be forgotten. 9 But Wisdom rescued her servants from the
danger.

Wisdom Protected Jacob

10 A righteous man once had to escape
from his brother's anger, and Wisdom
guided him in the right way. She showed
him God's kingdom and allowed him to
know about holy things.[e] She made him
prosperous and successful in his work.
11 When others were greedy for what he
had, and wanted to take it away from
him, Wisdom stood by him and made
him rich. 12 She protected him from his
enemies who were waiting for a chance
to attack him. She gave him victory in a
hard fight, so that he might realize that
nothing can make a person stronger
than serving God.

Wisdom Rescued Joseph

13 Once a righteous man was sold into
slavery, but Wisdom did not abandon
him. She kept him safe from sin. She
went to prison with him 14 and never left
him until she had given him power over
an empire and made him the ruler of

[e] holy things; *or* angels.

people who had once oppressed him.
She let it be known that a false accusation had been made against him, and she
gave him eternal honor.

Wisdom Led the Israelites Out of Egypt

15 Wisdom once rescued an innocent
and holy people from a nation of oppressors. 16 She entered the soul of one of
God's servants and[f] stood up to
dreaded kings by performing miracles.
17 She rewarded God's people for their
hardships. She guided them along a miraculous journey. She gave them shade
during the day and brilliant starlight
at night. 18 She led them through the
deep waters of the Red Sea, 19 but she
drowned their enemies and washed their
bodies up on the shore. 20 And so the
righteous looted the ungodly. They sang
hymns to your holy name, O Lord; together they praised you for defending
them. 21 Wisdom gave speech to those
who could not speak; she even caused
babies to speak clearly.

Wisdom Led the Israelites through the Desert

11 Wisdom brought success to the
people of Israel through a holy
prophet. 2 They traveled across a desert
where no one lived and camped in
places where no human being had ever
been. 3 They stood up to their enemies
and fought them off. 4 When your people
grew thirsty, they called to you, Lord,
and you gave them water flowing out of
solid rock. 5 The disasters that punished
the Egyptians saved your people when
they were in trouble.

The Punishment of the Egyptians

6-8 Because those enemies decreed that
the babies of your people should be
killed, you stirred up the sources of their
everflowing river and made it foul with
blood.

In the desert you let your people go
thirsty, to give them a taste of how you
had punished their enemies. And then,
when they least expected it, you gave
them plenty of water. 9 When they were
being tested, even though it was a merciful discipline, they learned how wicked
people were tortured when you judged
them in anger. 10 You tested your people,
as parents test their children, to warn
them. But you judged their enemies like
a stern king and condemned them.
11 They suffered, whether they were near
your people or far from them. 12 Their
sorrow was doubled; they groaned as
they looked back on what had happened. 13 When they learned that their
punishment had been of benefit to your
people, they realized that it was your
work, Lord. 14 The Egyptians had refused to have anything to do with that
man who, long before as a baby, had
been thrown out and exposed; but as
things worked out, they came to be
amazed at him. The righteous never suffered a thirst like theirs.

15 Their wickedness misled them into
silly ideas, so that they worshiped
snakes and other disgusting animals,
creatures without any powers of reason.
Because of this, you punished them with
millions of such animals, 16 and taught
them that punishment for sin takes the
same form as the sin itself. 17 Your
almighty power, Lord, created the world
out of material that had no form at all.
You could easily have punished those
people by sending an invasion of bears
or savage lions. 18 You could have created new and terrible animals, that
could breathe fire or roar and send out
clouds of smoke, or shoot out fearful
sparks from their eyes. 19 You could
have made animals like these that would
not have to attack those people to kill
them, but could scare them to death just
by looking at them. 20 But this was not
necessary. You could have pursued
them with your justice or struck them
dead at the slightest hint of your power.
But you have chosen to measure, count,
and weigh everything you do.

God Is Powerful and Merciful

21 You can show your great power any
time you wish, and no one can stand up
against it. 22 In your sight the whole
world is a grain of sand, barely heavy
enough to tip a pair of scales, a drop of
dew on the ground in the morning.
23 You are powerful enough to do anything, but you are merciful to everyone;
you overlook our sins and give us time
to repent. 24 You love everything that

[f] and; *or* who.

exists; you do not despise anything that
you have made. If you had not liked it,
you would not have made it in the first
place. 25How could anything last, if you
did not want it to? How could it endure,
if you had not created it? 26You have allowed it all to exist, O Lord, because it is
yours, and you love every living thing.

12 1Your immortal spirit is in every
one of them, 2and so you gently
correct those who sin against you. You
remind them of what they are doing, and
warn them about it, so that they may
abandon their evil ways and put their
trust in you, Lord.

The Sins of the Canaanites

3-4You hated the people who lived in
your holy land long ago, because they
did horrible things: they practiced magic
and conducted unholy worship; 5they
killed children without mercy and ate
the flesh and blood of human beings.
They were initiated into secret rituals[g]
6in which parents murdered their own
defenseless children. It was your will for
our ancestors to destroy these people,
7so that the land which you consider the
most precious of all lands would be a
suitable home for your people. 8But
even in this you showed mercy toward
their enemies, since they were only human beings. You sent hornets ahead of
your army, to destroy the enemy gradually. 9You could have allowed the righteous to destroy those ungodly people in
battle; you could have wiped them out
immediately with wild animals or with
one harsh command. 10But instead, you
carried out your sentence gradually, to
give them a chance to repent, even
though you knew that they came from
evil stock, that they had been wicked
since birth, and that they would never
change their way of thinking. 11Their
whole nation was cursed from the start,
and though you had not punished them
for their sins, it was not because you
were afraid of anyone.

God Is Sovereign

12You created those wicked people,
and no one can speak in their defense or
condemn you for destroying them. No
one can question what you have done or
challenge your judgment. 13All things
are under your care, and there is no
other god to whom you must justify your
decisions. 14No king or ruler on earth
can accuse you of punishing those people unfairly. 15You are righteous, and
you rule everything righteously. You
have never used your power to condemn
a person who does not deserve to be
punished. 16Your strength is the source
of justice. You can show mercy to everyone, because you are the Lord of all.
17You show your strength when people
doubt that your power is perfect, and
you punish anyone who knows your
power but dares to ignore it. 18Even
though you have absolute power, you
are a merciful judge. You could take action against us whenever you like, but
instead, you rule us with great patience.
19By the things you have done you
have taught your people that a person
who is righteous must also be kind. You
have given your people abundant hope
by allowing them to repent of their sins.
20You were very careful and patient in
punishing your people's enemies; even
when they deserved to die, you gave
them every opportunity to give up their
sinful ways. 21But you judged your own
people very strictly, even though you
had made covenants with their ancestors and had solemnly promised to give
them good things.
22Yes, you punish us, but you punish
our enemies ten thousand times more, so
that when we judge others, we may remember your goodness, and when we
are being judged, we may look for
mercy.

The Punishment of the Egyptians

23And so you tormented those who
were foolish enough to live wickedly—
you tormented them with the horrible
things they worshiped. 24They had wandered far away from the truth and worshiped the most disgusting and horrible
animals. They were deceived as easily as
little children. 25And so you punished
them for their stupidity, and your judgment made them look like fools. 26It was
a light punishment, but those who pay
no attention to such warnings deserve to
feel the full weight of God's judgment.
27When they were punished with those
creatures they considered gods, they be-

[g] They were ... rituals; *Greek unclear.*

came bitterly disillusioned and recognized that the true God was the one they
had always refused to acknowledge.
That is why they suffered the final punishment.

The Foolishness of Nature Worship

13 Anyone who does not know God
is simply foolish. Such people
look at the good things around them and
still fail to see the living God. They have
studied the things he made, but they
have not recognized the one who made
them. 2 Instead, they suppose that the
gods who rule the world are fire or wind
or storm or the circling stars or rushing
water or the heavenly bodies. 3 People
were so delighted with the beauty of
these things that they thought they must
be gods, but they should have realized
that these things have a master and that
he is much greater than all of them, for
he is the creator of beauty, and he created them. 4 Since people are amazed at
the power of these things, and how they
behave, they ought to learn from them
that their maker is far more powerful.
5 When we realize how vast and beautiful the creation is, we are learning about
the Creator at the same time.

6 But maybe we are too harsh with
these people. After all, they may have
really wanted to find God, but couldn't.
7 Surrounded by God's works, they keep
on looking at them, until they are finally
convinced that because the things they
see are so beautiful, they must be gods.
8 But still, these people really have no excuse. 9 If they had enough intelligence to
speculate about the nature of the universe, why did they never find the Lord
of all things?

The Foolishness of Idolatry

10 But the most miserable people of all
are those who rest their hopes on lifeless
things, who worship things that have
been made by human hands—images of
animals artistically made from gold and
silver, or some useless stone carved by
someone years ago. 11 A skilled woodworker may saw down some suitable
tree, carefully strip off the bark, and
then, with skillful craftsmanship, make
from it an object that will serve some
useful purpose. 12 He will take the leftover pieces and use them as firewood to
cook a meal that he can sit down to and
enjoy. 13 But among that scrap wood he
may take one piece that isn't good for
anything—maybe it's crooked and full
of knots—and carefully carve it in his
leisure time, using spare moments to
shape it into the crude image of a person, 14 or maybe of some worthless animal. He paints it all over with red,
covering up every flaw in the work.
15 Then he prepares a suitable place in
the wall for it and fastens it in place with
iron nails. 16 He is careful to keep it from
falling, because he knows it is only an
idol and needs help; it cannot help itself.
17 But he is not ashamed to pray to this
lifeless thing about his marriage, his
children, and his possessions. 18 It is
weak, but he prays to it for health. It is
dead, but he prays to it for life. It has no
experience, but he prays to it for help. It
cannot walk, but he prays to it for a successful journey. 19 Its hands have no
power, but he asks it to help him—in
business, in making money, and in his
work.

Wooden Idols Compared with Noah's Wooden Boat

14 In the same way, a man getting
ready to sail on the raging sea
will call for help from a piece of wood
that is not as strong as the ship he is
about to board. 2 Someone designed the
ship out of a desire for profit, and a
craftsman built it with skill. 3 But it is
your care, O Father, that steers it; you
give it a safe path through the waves of
the sea. 4 People may go to sea even if
they have no skill, because you can save
them from any danger. 5 It is your will
that the things you have made by your
wisdom should be put to use. And so
people can cross the sea in a boat and
come safely to land, because they trust
their lives to that small piece of wood.

6 This was how it was in ancient times,
when a proud race of giants was dying
away. The hope of the world escaped on
such a boat under your guidance and left
the world a new generation to carry on
the human race. 7 A blessing was on
Noah's wooden boat that allowed righteousness to survive, 8 but a curse is on an
idol made by human hands. A curse is
also on the one who makes it, because
he works on this perishable thing and
then calls it a god. 9 Ungodly people and

these ungodly things they make are
equally hated by God, 10who will punish
both the things made and the people
who made them. 11And so God's judgment will fall on pagan idols, because,
even though they are made from something God created, they became horrible
things that trap the souls of foolish
people.

The Origins of Idolatry

12Sexual immorality began when idols
were invented. They have corrupted human life ever since they were first made.
13Idols have not always existed, nor will
they exist forever. 14It was human pride
that brought them into the world, and
that is why a quick end has been
planned for them.

15Once there was a father who was
overwhelmed with grief at the untimely
death of his child, so he made an image
of that child who had been suddenly
taken from him. He then honored a dead
human being as a god, and handed on
secret rituals and ceremonies to those
who were under his authority. 16As time
went on, this ungodly custom became
stronger. Finally it became law, and
idols were being worshiped at the command of powerful rulers. 17When people
lived too far away to honor a ruler in his
presence but were eager to pay honor to
this absent king, they would imagine
what he must look like, and would then
make a likeness of him. 18The ambitious
artists who made these likenesses
caused this worship to spread, even
among people who did not know the
king. 19An artist might want to please
some ruler, and so he would use his skill
to make the likeness better looking than
the actual person. 20Then people would
be so attracted by the work of art, that
the one whom they had earlier honored
now became the object of their worship.
21So all this became a deadly trap,
because people who were grieving,
or under royal authority, would take
objects of stone or wood, and give
them the honor reserved for the One
God.

The Results of Idolatry

22One thing led to another. It was not
enough to be wrong about the knowledge of God. They lived in a state of evil
warfare, but they were so ignorant that
they called it peace. 23They murdered
children in their initiation rituals, celebrated secret mysteries, and held wild
ceremonial orgies with unnatural practices. 24They no longer kept their lives or
their marriages pure. A man might kill
another by an act of treachery or cause
him grief by committing adultery with
his wife. 25Everything was a complete
riot of bloody murder, robbery, deceit,
corruption, faithlessness, disorder,
falsehood, 26harassment of innocent
people, ingratitude, moral decay, sexual
perversion, broken marriages, adultery,
and immorality. 27The worship of idols,
whose names should never be spoken, is
the beginning and the end, the cause and
the result of every evil. 28People who
worship them lose control of themselves
in ecstasy, or pass off lies as prophecies,
or live wickedly, or break their word
without hesitation. 29They tell lies under
oath and expect no punishment, because
the idols they put their trust in are lifeless. 30But punishment will finally catch
up with them, for two reasons: first, they
were in error about God when they worshiped idols, and second, they had so little regard for holiness that they made
false statements to deceive people.
31When unrighteous people commit sin,
they will be hunted down, not by the
power of whatever thing they swear by,
but by the punishment that sinners
deserve.

The True God Gives Immortality

15 But you, our God, are kind and
true and patient. You rule the
universe with mercy. 2Even if we sin, we
know your power and are still yours. But
because we know that we belong to you,
we will not sin. 3Knowing you is perfect
righteousness. Recognizing your power
is where immortality begins. 4We have
not been misled by any evil product of
human skill, by any useless object
painted by some artist, or by any idol
smeared with different colors. 5The
sight of such things arouses the passions
of foolish people and makes them desire
a dead, lifeless image. 6Anyone who
makes such a thing or desires it or worships it is in love with something evil,
and gets what he deserves when he
places his hopes in it.

The Foolishness of Worshiping Clay Idols

7 A potter works the soft clay and
carefully shapes each object for our use.
Some things he makes are put to good
use, and some are not, but he makes
them all from the same clay, and shapes
them in the same manner. The potter
himself decides which objects shall be
used for what purposes. 8 He is a human
being who was himself formed from
earth only a short while earlier, and after a little while, when he must return
the soul that was lent to him, he will go
back to the same earth. He is a human
being, but he wastes his labor shaping a
useless god out of the same clay that he
uses to make pots. 9 His life will be short,
and he will soon have to die, but he is not
concerned about that. He wants to com-
pete with those who work in gold, silver,
and bronze, and make things like they
do. He takes great pride in the things he
makes, but they are counterfeit. 10 His
heart is made of ashes. His hope is
cheaper than dirt. His life is not worth as
much as his clay, 11 because he never
came to know the God who shaped him,
who breathed into him an active soul
and a living spirit. 12 He thinks of human
life as just a game, a market where he
can make a profit. He believes that he
must make money however he can, even
by evil ways. 13 This man, who makes
idols and fragile pots from the same
clay, knows better than anyone else that
he is sinning.

The Punishment of the Egyptians

14 But the most foolish of all people,
showing less sense than babies, were the
enemies who oppressed your people,
O Lord. 15 They thought that all their pagan idols were gods, even though idols
cannot see with their eyes, cannot
breathe through their nose, cannot hear
with their ears, cannot feel with their
fingers, and cannot walk on their legs.
16 Someone whose spirit is only borrowed made them. No one can ever
make a god that is equal to a human being. 17 Every person will sooner or later
die, but anything he makes with his
wicked hands is dead from the start. He
himself is better than what he worships.
He at least is alive, but what he worships
is not, and never has been. 18 Such people worship the most disgusting animals, including even the least intelligent
ones. 19 Even as animals they are not attractive enough to make anyone want
them. God himself passed them by when
he put his approval and blessing on the
16 rest of creation. 1 And so it was
appropriate that these people
were punished by such creatures—
tormented by swarms of them.
2 But you, O Lord, did not punish your
people in this way; instead, you showed
them kindness. You sent them quails to
eat, a rare, delicious food to satisfy their
hunger. 3 You did all this so that the idol-
aters, when they were hungry, would be
unable to eat because of the disgusting
creatures sent to them. Your people,
however, suffered hunger only a short
while, and then they ate the finest food.
4 It was necessary for the oppressors to
suffer relentless need, while your people
saw how their enemies were being
tormented.
5 When terrible, fierce snakes attacked
your people and were killing them with
their poison, you did not remain angry
long enough to destroy your people.
6 This trouble lasted for only a little
while, as a warning. Then you gave
them a healing symbol, the bronze
snake, to remind them of what your Law
requires. 7 If a person looked at that symbol, he was cured of the snakebite—not
by what he saw, but by you, the savior of
all mankind. 8 By doing this, you also
convinced our enemies that you are the
one who rescues people from every evil.
9 Our enemies died from the bites of locusts and flies; no way was found to cure
them, because they deserved to be punished by such creatures. 10 But even poisonous snakes could not overcome your
people, because you had mercy, helped
them, and cured them. 11 They were bitten so that they would remember your
commands, but they were quickly rescued, in order to keep them from forgetting you completely and depriving
themselves of your kindness. 12 No medicine or ointment cured them. They were
restored to health by your word, O Lord,
the word which heals all humanity.
13 You have power over life and death;
you can bring a person to the brink of
death and back again. 14 A wicked person may kill someone, but cannot bring

the dead person back to life or rescue a
soul imprisoned in the world of the dead.

Disastrous Storms Hit Egypt

15 No one can possibly escape from
you. 16 Look at those ungodly people:
they refused to recognize you as God, so
you punished them with your great
power. They were overtaken by terrible
storms of rain and hail and were completely destroyed by fire. 17 The most
amazing thing was that the fire burned
all the more fiercely in the water, which
usually puts fire out. All the forces of
nature fight to defend those who are
righteous. 18 At one point the flames died
down, so that they wouldn't destroy the
creatures sent to punish the ungodly.
Those people had to learn that they were
being overtaken by your judgment.
19 But at another point, when surrounded
by water, the flames burned more
fiercely than fire had ever burned before, and so destroyed the crops on the
land where those unrighteous people
lived.

The Israelites Receive Manna to Eat

20 But this disaster did not strike your
people. Instead, you gave them the food
of angels. From heaven you sent down
bread that was ready to eat, and they did
not have to prepare it. The food you gave
delighted everyone, no matter what his
taste. 21 All this showed how lovingly
you care for your children. That food
satisfied the desire of everyone who ate
it; it was changed to suit each person's
taste. 22 It was food that under normal
circumstances would vanish away like
snow or ice, but now it did not melt even
in the fire. This was meant to teach your
people that the same fire that was destroying their enemies' crops during the
heavy downpour of rain and hail 23 held
back its power, so that your own righteous people might have food.

24 You created the universe; it is at
your command. All creation uses its
power to punish unrighteous people, but
it becomes mild and kind to those who
put their trust in you. 25 Creation assumed all kinds of forms to show how
you provide generously for all who pray
to you.[h] 26 This happened so that the
people whom you loved, O Lord, might
learn that they are not fed by what they
can grow. It is your word that maintains
those who put their trust in you. 27 The
food that was not destroyed by the fire
melted when the first ray of sunlight
warmed it. 28 This was to teach us that
we must get up before daybreak to give
you thanks, and pray as the sun comes
up. 29 But an ungrateful person's hope
will melt away like frost, and drain away
like water that is not being used.

Terror Strikes the Egyptians at Night

17 O Lord, your acts of judgment
are marvelous and hard to explain; that is why people who had not
been taught about them went astray.
2 When lawless people imagined that
they had your holy nation in their
power, they were themselves imprisoned in a long night of darkness. They
lay in their own houses, shut off from
your eternal care. 3 They thought that
their sins had been secret and unnoticed,
shielded from view by a dark curtain of
forgetfulness, but now they were horri-
bly afraid, confused, and terrified by
ghostly forms. 4 Not even the dark corners where they lay could protect them
from fear. They were surrounded by
horrible noises; grim ghosts with
gloomy faces appeared before their
eyes. 5 No fire had power to give them
light, and the brilliant stars could do
nothing to relieve that deathly darkness.
6 There was only a dreadful fire, lit by no
human hand, that shone on them, and in
their terror they believed that the real
world was even worse than the things
they imagined. 7 The illusions produced
by their magic tricks were put to shame,
and all the wisdom they had boasted of
came to nothing. 8 They had claimed
they could drive away all the fears and
illnesses of sick minds, but now they
themselves were sick with silly, groundless fears. 9 Even though nothing dangerous had actually happened, they
were terrified by hissing snakes and animals advancing on them. 10 And so they
died, shaking with fear, afraid even to
open their eyes, yet unable to keep them
shut.

11 Wickedness is cowardly in itself and
stands self-condemned.[i] Someone with
a guilty conscience will always imagine

[h] pray to you; *or* are in need. [i] Wickedness . . . self-condemned: *Greek unclear.*

things to be worse than they really are.
12 Fear is nothing but the failure to use
the help that reason gives. 13 When you
lack the confidence to rely on reason,
you give in to the fears caused by ignorance.
14 All night long those people slept the
same restless sleep, even though the
night held no power over them, since it
came from the powerless depths of the
world of the dead. 15 They were chased
by hideous forms and lay paralyzed as
they surrendered themselves to the sudden, unexpected fear that came over
them. 16 People would suddenly collapse
and lie locked in the chains of their own
fear. 17 Farmers, shepherds, and laborers
out in the countryside were captured by
the same inevitable fate and bound in
the darkness by the same invisible
chain. 18-19 They were panic-stricken by
the sighing of the wind or by the singing
of birds in the trees or by the roar of
rushing water or by the rumble of falling
rock or by the sound of unseen creatures
running about or by the savage roaring
of wild animals or by the echoes from
the mountains. 20 In the full light of day,
the rest of the world went about its business undisturbed. 21 Only those people
were covered by this heavy night, a foretaste of the darkness of death that was
waiting for them. They were a burden to
themselves that was even heavier than
the darkness.

Light Shines on the Israelites

18 Yet all the while a brilliant light
was shining for your holy people. Their enemies heard their voices,
but couldn't see them. They envied the
good fortune of your people, who were
not suffering. 2 Those enemies could at
least be thankful that the people they
had wronged were not taking vengeance
on them now, and so they begged them
to leave.[j]
3 Then you guided your people as they
traveled through a country they did not
know. You guided them with a pillar of
fire. It was like a sun that would not
harm them on that glorious journey.
4 But their enemies, who were not allowed to see the light, deserved to be
prisoners in darkness, because they had
made prisoners of your people. And it
was through your people that the eternal
light of the Law was going to be given to
the world.

The Death of the Egyptian First-Born

5 When your enemies were carrying
out their resolve to kill the babies of
your holy people, there was one child
who was abandoned but later rescued.
Then you punished your enemies by killing a great number of their own children. You drowned their whole army at
one time in the rushing waters. 6 But our
ancestors had been told in advance of
what would happen that night, so that
they would be cheered and encouraged
by confident trust in your promises to
them. 7 Your people knew that you
would rescue the righteous nation and
destroy their enemies. 8 With the same
act you punished our enemies and did us
the glorious honor of calling us to
yourself.
9 During all this time devout people
from this righteous nation were secretly
offering sacrifices, giving their word to
each other that they would keep God's
law and share each other's blessings and
dangers. Already they were chanting
those ancient hymns of praise. 10 But
their enemies' pitiful cries of grief echoed everywhere, as they mourned for
their dead children. 11 Masters suffered
the same punishment as their slaves; the
king endured the same loss as the common people. 12 There were too many
dead bodies to count. There were not
enough people left to bury them all. In a
single moment their dearest children
died; all of them met death in the same
way. 13 These people had paid no attention to any warning, but relied instead
on their magical powers. But when their
first-born sons were killed, then they
recognized that Israel was God's son.
14 The short night was half over, and
all was quiet and peaceful, 15 when suddenly your threats were carried out! An
invincible word of judgment sped from
your royal throne in heaven, straight
down to that doomed land. It came like a
soldier in fierce attack, 16 carrying out
your firm command with a fearful
weapon, standing with feet on the
ground and head touching the sky,
filling the land with death. 17 At that

[j] begged them to leave; *or* begged their forgiveness for their past hostility.

moment the people who were about to
die had terrible nightmares and were
seized by sudden fear. 18 All over the
land they lay half-dead and let it be
known why they were dying. 19 They
knew why they were dying, because
their horrible dreams had told them.

Aaron's Prayer Saves the Israelites from Death

20 Death also came to the righteous nation, for an epidemic struck many of
them while they were in the desert, but
your anger did not last long. 21 There
was a certain blameless man who
quickly took action to defend them. Acting as their priest, Aaron offered
prayers and burned the incense used in
asking forgiveness of sins. With prayers
and incense as his weapons, he with-
stood your anger and ended the disaster.
By doing this he proved that he was your
servant. 22 He overcame the bitter difficulty,[k] but not by his own strength or by
military force. Instead, he used prayer to
stop the punishment, appealing to the
promises you solemnly gave to our ancestors. 23 Dead bodies were already lying in piles, but he stepped in to hold
your anger back and to keep it from
harming those who were left alive. 24 He
wore a long robe decorated with symbols of the universe. In honor of our ancestors he wore four rows of engraved
stones on his chest, and your own majesty was represented by the ornament
on his turban. 25 The Angel of Death was
afraid of these things, and gave up. It
was only a slight experience of your
wrath, but it was enough.

The Suicidal Stupidity of the Egyptians

19 But the godless continued to feel
your pitiless anger until the very
end. You knew what they would do before they did it. 2 You knew that even
though they let your people go and made
them leave quickly, they would change
their minds and pursue them. 3-4 While
the Egyptians were still mourning at the
graves of their dead, they forgot why all
this had happened, and they foolishly
decided that the people they had begged
to leave were runaways. So they chased
after them. They were led into this as
part of the punishment they deserved, so
that they would suffer the rest of the torments they were due to receive. 5 They
were to meet a strange death, while your
people continued on their miraculous
journey.

God Guides and Protects His People

6 The whole nature of the universe was
changed at your command so that your
people would not be harmed. 7 They saw
the cloud over their camp and dry land
where water had been. There was a
grass-covered plain between the stormy
waves of the Red Sea, making it easy for
them to cross over. 8 All your people, under your protection, saw this miracle
and went across. 9 They pranced about
like horses let out to pasture; they
skipped about like lambs and praised
you, Lord, for saving them. 10 They still
remembered what life had been like
when they were slaves—how the earth
bred gnats instead of cattle, how the
river produced huge numbers of frogs
instead of fish. 11-12 Later, when they
desperately wanted better food, quails
came up from the sea to satisfy their
hunger. The quail was a bird they had
never seen before.

The Punishment of the Egyptians

13 But violent thunder gave warning of
the punishment that was coming on
those sinners. They suffered a well-
deserved punishment for their great
wickedness. No nation had ever hated
strangers so bitterly. 14 Other people had
been known to refuse welcome to strangers who came to them, but these people
made slaves of those who were their
guests and who had shown them kindness. 15 Every nation will be punished if
it does not welcome foreigners, 16 but
these people, who had earlier welcomed
the foreigners with happy celebrations
and treated them as equals, later made
them suffer cruelly. 17 These people were
also struck with blindness, like the men
of Sodom who came to the door of that
righteous man Lot. They found themselves in total darkness, as each one
groped around to find his own door.

[k] *Probable text* bitter difficulty; *Greek* crowd.

God's Miraculous Power

18 On a harp each string keeps its own
pitch, but each sound can be combined
with others to make different melodies.
That is how it was in those days, when
the very elements entered into new com-
binations. Look at what happened!
19 Land animals took to the water, and
swimming creatures came up on the
land. 20 Fire burned even in water, which
could not put it out. 21 And yet the
flames could not burn the flesh of the
perishable creatures walking in them
and did not melt that heavenly food
that would ordinarily have melted like
frost.
22 Lord, you have made your people
great – glorious in all respects. You have
never neglected them. You have given
them help, always, everywhere.

SIRACH

THE WISDOM OF JESUS, SON OF SIRACH

(Ecclesiasticus)

Introduction

The Wisdom of Jesus, Son of Sirach, *also known as* Ecclesiasticus, *was written in Hebrew by a man named Joshua (or Jesus) and was later translated into Greek by his grandson. The book includes traditional Jewish wisdom material and makes a defense of Judaism by showing that God has given true wisdom to his people. Many subjects of a religious, moral, and practical nature are presented, sometimes at length and sometimes in short proverbial sayings.*

Outline of Contents

Foreword
In praise of wisdom (Part 1) 1.1 – 23.27
- *a. Duty, reward, and practical advice* 1.1 – 16.23
- *b. God's wisdom and human response* 16.24 – 23.27

In praise of wisdom (Part 2) 24.1 – 50.21
- *a. Wisdom and virtue* 24.1 – 32.13
- *b. God's wisdom and human worship and work* 32.14 – 42.14
- *c. God's glory in nature* 42.15 – 43.33
- *d. In praise of ancestors* 44.1 – 50.21

Epilogue and Appendices 50.22 – 51.30

Foreword

The Law, the Prophets, and the later writers have left us a wealth of valuable teachings, and we should praise Israel for the instruction and wisdom they provide. But it is not enough that those who read them should gain understanding for themselves. Anyone who values learning should be able to help others by what he himself says and writes. That is why my grandfather Jesus devoted himself to reading the Law, the Prophets, and the other books of our ancestors. After he had mastered them, he was led to write a book of his own in order to share his wisdom and learning with others, so that anyone who shared his love for learning should have his book available as well, and be all the more able to live according to the Law.

Let me urge you, then, to read this book carefully and with an open mind. And please be patient in those places where, in spite of all my diligent efforts, I may not have translated some phrases very well. What was originally written in Hebrew does not always have exactly the same sense when it is translated into another language.[a] That is true not only of this book, but even of the Law itself, the Prophets, and the other books. The translations differ quite a bit from the original.

I came to Egypt in the thirty-eighth year of King Euergetes' reign and stayed for some time. While I was there, I had the opportunity for a good deal of study and felt the necessity of translating the following book. I wanted to use all my diligence and skill to complete it and make it available for all those living in foreign lands who wish to learn and who have the strength of character to live by the Law of Moses.

In Praise of Wisdom

1 All wisdom comes from the Lord,
and Wisdom is with him forever.
2 Who can count raindrops or the
sand along the shore?
Who can count the days of
eternity?
3 How high is the sky? How wide is
the earth?
How deep is the ocean? How
profound is Wisdom?
Can anyone find answers to
these questions?
4 Wisdom was created before
anything else;
understanding has always
existed.[b]
6 Has anyone ever been shown
where Wisdom originates?
Does anyone understand her
subtle cleverness?[c]
8 There is only one who is wise,
and we must stand in awe
before his throne.
9 The Lord himself created Wisdom;
he saw her and recognized her
value,
and so he filled everything he
made with Wisdom.
10 He gave some measure of Wisdom
to everyone,
but poured her out on those who
love him.

11 If you fear the Lord, honor and
pride will be yours;
you will be crowned with
happiness and joy.
12 To honor the Lord is a heartfelt
delight;
it will give you a long and happy
life,
13 and at the end of your days all
will go well for you.
God will bless you on the day of
your death.
14 To fear the Lord is the first step to
Wisdom.
Wisdom is given to the faithful
in their mothers' wombs.
15 She has lived with us from ancient
times,
and generations to come will
rely on her.
16 To fear the Lord is Wisdom at her
fullest;
she satisfies us completely with
her gifts
17 and fills our homes and our barns
with all that our hearts can
desire.
18 To fear the Lord is the flower of
Wisdom
that blossoms with peace and
good health.[d]
19 She sends knowledge and
understanding like the rain,
and increases the honor of those
who receive her.
20 To fear the Lord is the root of
Wisdom;
her branches are long life.[e]

Self-control

22 There is no excuse for unjustified
anger; it can bring about your downfall.
23 Wait and be patient, and later you will
be glad you did. 24 Keep quiet until the
right time to speak, and you will gain a
reputation for good sense.

Wisdom and Reverence for God

25 Wisdom has a treasury of wise sayings, but sinners have nothing but contempt for godliness. 26 If you want to be
wise, keep the Lord's commands, and he

[a] *The book of Sirach was written in Hebrew, but the writer of this foreword translated it into Greek.* [b] *Some manuscripts add verse 5:* The source of Wisdom is the word of God on high; her ways are eternal commands. [c] *Some manuscripts add verse 7:* To whom has the knowledge of Wisdom been revealed? Who has understood her great experience?
[d] *Some manuscripts add:* He saw her and recognized her value *(see 1.9).* [e] *Some manuscripts add verse 21:* Honoring the Lord takes sin away; where the fear of the Lord is found, it turns away anger.

will give you Wisdom in abundance. 27 Fearing the Lord is Wisdom and an education in itself. He is pleased by loyalty and humility. 28 Be faithful in the practice of your religion; when you worship the Lord, do it with all your heart. 29 Be careful about what you say, and don't be a hypocrite. 30 Don't be arrogant; you may suffer a fall and be disgraced. The Lord will reveal your secrets and humble you in front of everyone in the synagogue, because you did not come there with reverence for the Lord, but with a heart full of hypocrisy.

Faithfulness to God

2 My child, if you are going to serve the Lord, be prepared for times when you will be put to the test. 2 Be sincere and determined. Keep calm when trouble comes. 3 Stay with the Lord; never abandon him, and you will be prosperous at the end of your days. 4 Accept whatever happens to you. Even if you suffer humiliation, be patient. 5 Gold is tested by fire, and human character is tested in the furnace of humiliation. 6 Trust the Lord, and he will help you. Walk straight in his ways, and put your hope in him.

7 All you that fear the Lord, wait for him to show you his mercy. Do not turn away from him, or you will fall. 8 All you that fear the Lord, trust him, and you will certainly be rewarded. 9 All you that fear the Lord, look forward to his blessings of mercy and eternal happiness.

10 Think back to the ancient generations and consider this: has the Lord ever disappointed anyone who put his hope in him? Has the Lord ever abandoned anyone who held him in constant reverence? Has the Lord ever ignored anyone who prayed to him? 11 The Lord is kind and merciful; he forgives our sins and keeps us safe in time of trouble. 12 But those who lose their nerve are doomed—all those sinners who try to have it both ways! 13 Doom is sure to come for those who lose their courage; they have no faith, and so they will have no protection. 14 Doom is sure to come for those who lose their hope. What will they do when the Lord comes to judge them?

15 Those who fear the Lord do not disobey his commands; those who love him will live as he wants them to live. 16 Those who fear and love the Lord will try to please him and devote themselves to the Law. 17 Those who fear the Lord are always ready to serve him. They humble themselves before him, and say, 18 "We place our destiny in the hands of the Lord, not in human hands, because his mercy is as great as his majesty."

Duties to Parents

3 Children, listen to me; I am your father. Do what I tell you and you will be safe, 2 for the Lord has given fathers authority over their children and given children the obligation to obey their mothers. 3 If you respect your father, you can make up for your sins, 4 and if you honor your mother, you are earning great wealth. 5 If you respect your father, one day your own children will make you happy; the Lord will hear your prayers. 6 If you obey the Lord by honoring your father and making your mother happy, you will live a long life. 7 Obey your parents as if you were their slave. 8 Honor your father in everything you do and say, so that you may receive his blessing. 9 When parents give their blessing, they give strength to their children's homes, but when they curse their children, they destroy the very foundations.

10 Never seek honor for yourself at your father's expense; it is not to your credit if he is dishonored. 11 Your own honor comes from the respect that you show to your father. If children do not honor their mothers, it is their own disgrace. 12 My child, take care of your father when he grows old; give him no cause for worry as long as he lives. 13 Be sympathetic even if his mind fails him; don't look down on him just because you are strong and healthy. 14 The Lord will not forget the kindness you show to your father; it will help you make up for your sins. 15 When you are in trouble, the Lord will remember your kindness and will help you; your sins will melt away like frost in warm sunshine. 16 Those who abandon their parents or give them cause for anger may as well be cursing the Lord; they are already under the Lord's curse.

Humility

17 My child, be humble in everything you do, and people will appreciate it

more than gifts.[f] 18The greater you become, the more humble you should be;
then the Lord will be pleased with you.[g]
20The Lord's power is great, and he is
honored by those who are humble.
21Don't try to understand things that are
too hard for you, or investigate matters
that are beyond your power to know.
22Concentrate on the Law, which has
been given to you. You do not need to
know about things which the Lord has
not revealed, 23so don't concern yourself
with them. After all, what has been
shown to you is beyond human power
to understand. 24Many people have
been misled by their own opinions;
their wrong ideas have warped their
judgment.[h]

26Stubbornness will get you into trouble at the end. If you live dangerously, it
will kill you. 27A stubborn person will
be burdened down with troubles. Sinners go on adding one sin to another.
28There is no cure for the troubles that
arrogant people have; wickedness has
taken deep root in them. 29Intelligent
people will learn from proverbs and parables. They listen well because they
want to learn.

Giving to the Poor

30Giving to the poor can make up for
sin, just as water can put out a blazing
fire. 31Anyone who responds to others
with acts of kindness is thinking of the
future, because he will find help if he
ever falls on hard times.

4 1My child,
don't prevent the poor from making
a living, or keep them waiting in their
need. 2Never give a hungry person any
cause for resentment or anger. 3Don't
add to the troubles of someone who is
already desperate. If he is in need, don't
put off giving to him. 4-5Don't refuse to
help a beggar who is in distress. Don't
turn your back on a poor person or give
him any reason to curse you. 6If he becomes so bitter that he does curse you,
his Creator will hear his prayer.

7Make yourself popular in the synagogue. Bow your head to men of authority. 8Listen to what the poor have to say,
and answer them politely. 9Protect people from those who want to wrong them,
and be firm in your judgments. 10Be like
a father to orphans, and provide widows
with the help their husbands can no
longer give them. Then you will be like a
child of the Most High, and he will love
you more than your own mother does.

Wisdom as a Teacher

11Wisdom takes care of those who
look for her; she raises them to greatness. 12Loving her is loving life itself;
rising early to look for her is pure joy.
13Anyone who obtains Wisdom will be
greatly honored. Wherever he goes, the
Lord will bless him. 14Wisdom's servants are the servants of the Holy One,
and the Lord loves everyone who loves
her. 15Those who obey her will give
sound judgments;[i] those who pay attention to her have true security. 16Put
your trust in Wisdom, and you will possess her and pass her on to your
descendants. 17At first, Wisdom will
lead you along difficult paths. She will
make you so afraid that you will think
you cannot go on. The discipline she demands will be tormenting, and she will
put you to the test with her requirements
until she trusts you[j] completely. 18Then
she will come to you with no delay, reveal her secrets to you, and make you
happy. 19But if you go astray, she will
abandon you and let you go to your own
ruin.

Self-confidence

20Take advantage of opportunities,
but guard yourself against evil. Don't
underrate yourself. 21Humility deserves
honor and respect, but a low opinion of
yourself leads to sin. 22Do not let others
have their way at your expense; do not
bring on your own ruin by giving up
your rights. 23Never hesitate to speak
out when the occasion[k] calls for it.

[f] *Hebrew* people . . . gifts; *Greek* those whom the Lord approves will love you.
[g] *Some Greek manuscripts add verse 19:* Many are exalted and esteemed, but God's secrets are revealed to the humble; *Hebrew:* God's mercy is great, and he reveals his secrets to those who are humble.
[h] *Some Greek manuscripts add verse 25:* If you have no eyes, you cannot see; don't claim to have knowledge if you don't have it; *Hebrew has, after verse 27:* If you have no eyes, you cannot see; if you have no knowledge, you cannot have Wisdom.
[i] *Hebrew* give sound judgments; *Greek* judge nations.
[j] she trusts you; *or* you trust her.
[k] *Probable text* the occasion; *Greek* safety.

Don't hide your wisdom.[l] 24 Your wisdom and education can be known only
by what you say. 25 Do not, however, go
against the truth, and remember that
you do not know everything. 26 Don't be
ashamed to confess your sins; there's no
point in trying to stop a river from flowing. 27 Don't allow yourself to be dominated by someone who is stupid or show
partiality to influential people. 28 Stand
up for what is right, even if it costs you
your life; the Lord God will be fighting
on your side.

29 Don't be quick to speak or lazy and
negligent in your work. 30 Don't act like
a lion at home or be suspicious of your
servants. 31 Don't stick out your hand to
get something if you're going to be tight-
fisted when the time comes to pay it
back.

Don't Be Presumptuous

5 Don't rely on money to make you
independent. 2 Don't think you have
to have everything you want, and then
spend your energy trying to get it.
3 Don't think that no one can exercise
authority over you; if you do, the Lord is
certain to punish you. 4 Don't think that
you can sin and get away with it; the
Lord does not mind waiting to punish
you. 5 Don't be so certain of the Lord's
forgiveness that you go on committing
one sin after another. 6 Don't think that
his mercy is so great that he will forgive
your sins no matter how many they are.
He does show mercy, but he also shows
his furious anger with sinners. 7 Come
back to the Lord quickly. Don't think
that you can keep putting it off. His anger can come upon you suddenly, and
you will die under his punishment.
8 Don't rely on dishonest wealth; it will
do you no good on that day of disaster.

Sincerity and Self-control

9-10 Be certain about what you believe
and consistent in what you say. Don't try
to please everyone or agree with everything people say.[m] 11 Always be ready to
listen, but take your time in answering.
12 Answer only if you know what to say,
and if you don't know what to say, keep
quiet. 13 Speaking can bring you either
honor or disgrace; what you say can
ruin you.

14 Don't get a reputation for being a
gossip, and don't tell tales that will hurt
people. Just as robbers will suffer disgrace, so liars will suffer severe condemnation. 15 Do nothing destructive,[n]
whether it seems insignificant or not,

6 1 and do not be an enemy when you
should be a friend. A bad reputation
brings you the disgrace that lying sinners deserve. 2 Do not let your passions
carry you away; this can tear your soul
to pieces like a bull.[o] 3 You will be left
like a dead tree without any leaves or
fruit. 4 Evil desire will destroy you and
make you a joke to your enemies.

Friendship

5 If you are polite and courteous, you
will enjoy the friendship of many people. 6 Exchange greetings with many, but
take advice from only one person out of
a thousand. 7 When you make friends,
don't be too quick to trust them; make
sure that they have proved themselves.
8 Some people will be your friends only
when it is convenient for them, but they
won't stand by you in trouble. 9 Others
will fall out with you over some argument, and then embarrass you by letting
everyone know about it. 10-11 Others will
sit at your table as long as things are
going well; they will stick to you like
your shadow and give orders to your
servants, but they will not stand by you
in trouble. 12 If your situation takes a
turn for the worse, they will turn against
you, and you won't be able to find them
anywhere.

13 Stay away from your enemies and
be on guard against your friends.
14 A loyal friend is like a safe shelter;
find one, and you have found a treasure.
15 Nothing else is as valuable; there is no
way of putting a price on it. 16 A loyal
friend is like a medicine that keeps
you in good health. Only those who fear
the Lord can find such a friend. 17 A person who fears the Lord can make real

[l] *Hebrew* Don't hide your wisdom; *most Greek manuscripts do not have these words; other Greek manuscripts* Don't hide your wisdom for the sake of appearances.
[m] *Hebrew* everything people say; *Greek adds* That is what double-tongued sinners do.
[n] *Hebrew* Do nothing destructive; *Greek* Do not be ignorant in anything. [o] *Verse 2 in both Greek and Hebrew is unclear.*

friendships, because he will treat his
friends as he does himself.[p]

Learn from Wisdom

18 My child, learn to value Wisdom
while you are young, and you will still be
able to find her when you grow old.
19 Work as hard to find Wisdom as a
farmer works to plow and plant his
fields; then you can expect a good harvest. You will have to work at it for a
while, but you will soon be enjoying
what you have earned. 20 Undisciplined
people find Wisdom's demands too hard
and don't have enough determination to
meet them. 21 Her requirements are a
burden heavier than they are willing to
bear, and they quickly lay them aside.
22 "Discipline" means just that—discipline,[q] and not many people are able
to discipline themselves.

23 My child, listen to me and take my
advice. 24 Put Wisdom's chains around
your feet and her yoke around your
neck. 25 Carry her on your shoulder and
don't be resentful of her bonds. 26 Follow
Wisdom, and keep to her ways with all
your heart. 27 Go looking for her, and she
will reveal herself to you. Take hold of
her and don't let go. 28 Then you will discover the peace of mind she offers, and
she will become your joy. 29-30 The signs
of slavery you wear will become signs of
royal majesty. Her chains will be your
protection, and you will wear her yoke
like a magnificent robe. 31 You will wear
Wisdom like a splendid crown.

32 My child, you can learn if you want
to. You can be clever if you are determined to be. 33 If you are willing to listen,
you will learn and become wise. 34 Go
where the old people are; find someone
who is wise, and stay with him. 35 Be
ready to listen when religious people
speak, and don't miss anything that
shows insight. 36 If you find someone
with understanding, get up early to call
on him; wear out his doorstep with your
visits.

37 Devote all your time to studying the
Lord's commands and thinking about
them. He will give you the insight and
wisdom you are looking for.

Miscellaneous Advice

7 1-2 If you do no wrong, no wrong
will ever come to you. 3 Do not plow
the ground to plant seeds of injustice;
you may reap a bigger harvest than you
expect.

4 Don't ask the Lord for a place of
honor or ask the king for an important
position. 5 Don't try to convince the Lord
that you are righteous or make a show of
your wisdom before the king. 6 Don't set
your heart on being a judge, unless you
have the strength of character it takes to
put an end to injustice. If you let yourself
be influenced by someone in a position
of power, your integrity will be damaged. 7 Don't commit any crime against
the general public, and don't disgrace
yourself among your townspeople.

8 Don't commit the same sin twice. The
punishment you get the first time ought
to be enough.

9 Don't think that God Most High is going to take into account how very generous you are and so accept any offering
you decide to make.

10 Never get tired of praying, and
never miss a chance to give to the poor.

11 Don't laugh at someone who has
been humiliated. It is the Lord who humbles a person, but the Lord also raises
him up again.

12 Don't think up lies to tell about your
friends. 13 Don't tell lies at all. It never
does any good.

14 In an official assembly, don't get up
and talk a lot of nonsense. And don't repeat yourself when you pray.

15 Don't try to avoid farm work or
other hard labor; the Most High has
given us these jobs to do.

16 Don't join up with a crowd of sinners; remember that the Lord's punishment is sure to come.

17 Be very humble, because the decay
of death awaits us all.[r]

Relations with Others

18 Don't betray a friend for money.
Don't betray a real friend for all the gold
in the world.

19 Don't miss your chance to marry a
wise and good woman. A gracious wife
is worth more than gold.

[p] because . . . himself; *or* because his friends will also fear the Lord. [q] *Hebrew* "Discipline" . . . discipline; *Greek* "Wisdom" . . . wisdom. [r] *Hebrew* the decay . . . all; *Greek* the punishment of the ungodly is fire and worms.

20 Don't mistreat servants who do their
work well, or employees who do their
best for you.
21 Show the same love to wise servants
that you would show to yourself,[s] and
let them have their freedom.
22 Take good care of any animals you
own. If they make money for you, keep
them.
23 If you have sons, educate them.
Teach them self-discipline while they
are young.
24 If you have daughters, keep them
virtuous, and don't be too indulgent with
them. 25 When you give your daughter in
marriage, you have finished a great task,
but give her to a sensible man.
26 If you have a good wife, do not divorce her, but do not trust yourself to
someone you don't love.
27 Honor your father with all your
heart, and never forget how your mother
suffered when you were born. 28 Remember that you owe your life to them. How
can you ever repay them for all they
have done for you?
29 Fear the Lord with all your heart,
and have respect for his priests. 30 Love
your Creator with all your strength, and
give his ministers your support. 31 Honor
the Lord and respect the priests. Supply
them with what you have been commanded to give: the first produce, the offering for sin, the shoulder of the
sacrificial animal—all the required sacrifices and offerings.
32 Give your help to the poor, and the
Lord will give you his perfect blessing.
33 Be generous to every living soul, and
be gracious to the memory of the dead.
34 Show sympathy to those who have lost
a loved one, and mourn with them. 35 Do
not hesitate to visit the sick. You will be
loved for things like these. 36 Whatever
you do, remember that some day you
must die. As long as you keep this in
mind, you will never sin.

Using Common Sense

8 Do not challenge a person who has
influence; you may fall into his
power. 2 Do not quarrel with someone
rich; he may bribe people to turn against
you. Gold has destroyed many people
and corrupted kings. 3 Don't argue with
someone who talks too much; you will
just be adding fuel to his fire. 4 Don't
make fun of someone who has bad manners; he may insult your ancestors.
5 Don't criticize someone if he is already
turning away from sin. Remember that
we are all guilty. 6 Never think less of
someone because he is old; some of us
are growing old, too. 7 Don't be happy
over the death of anyone; remember that
all of us must die.
8 Do not disregard what the wise have
said. Study their proverbs; from them
you can learn to be cultured and to serve
great people. 9 Pay attention to what old
people say, for they learned from those
who came before them. You can learn
from them, and they can teach you how
to have an answer ready when you
need one.
10 You should not provide a sinner
with more opportunity to sin. You might
get hurt yourself; it's as easy as getting
burned while adding logs to a fire. 11 You
should not get up and walk out on someone who is insolent. He might twist your
words and use them against you. 12 You
should not lend anything to someone
more powerful than you. If you do, you
might as well consider it lost. 13 You
should not guarantee anyone else's loan
to an extent that you cannot afford. You
must be prepared to pay any such guarantee. 14 You should not bring a lawsuit
against a judge. He will win because of
his position. 15 You should not travel
with anyone who is reckless. It will
cause you nothing but trouble. He will
do any foolish thing he pleases, and you
will die with him.
16 You should not get into an argument
with anyone who has a hot temper or go
to some place where the two of you will
be alone. Violence means nothing to
such a person, and he will attack you
when there is no one to help you. 17 You
should not ask a stupid person for advice. He will not be able to keep secret
what you tell him. 18 You should not do
anything in front of a stranger that
should be kept secret. There is no way of
knowing what will happen if you do.
19 You should not reveal your most private thoughts to anyone. If you do, you

[s] *Hebrew* Show the same love . . . yourself; *Greek* Show love to a wise servant.

may as well throw away any chance of happiness.[t]

Advice about Women

9 Don't be jealous of the wife you love. You will only be teaching her how to do you harm. 2 Do not surrender your dignity to any woman. 3 Keep away from other men's wives[u] or they will trap you. 4 Don't keep company with female musicians; they will trick you. 5 Don't look too intently at a virgin, or you may find yourself forced to pay a bride price. 6 Don't give yourself to prostitutes, or you may lose everything you own. 7 So don't go looking about in the streets or wandering around in the run-down parts of town. 8 When you see a good-looking woman, look the other way; don't let your mind dwell on the beauty of any woman who is not your wife. Many men have been led astray by a woman's beauty. It kindles passion as if it were fire. 9 Don't sit down to eat with another man's wife or join her for a drink. You may give in to the temptation of her charms and be destroyed by your passion.

Friendships with Others

10 Never abandon old friends; you will never find a new one who can take their place. Friendship is like wine; it gets better as it grows older. 11 Don't be jealous of a sinner's success; you don't know what kind of disaster is in store for him. 12 Don't take pleasure in the things that make ungodly people happy; remember that they will be held guilty as long as they live. 13 If you keep away from someone who has the power to put you to death, you will not have to fear for your life; but if you must go near him, be very careful, or he may kill you. Be conscious that you are walking among hidden traps, that you are an easy target.

14 Get to know the people around you as well as you can, and take advice only from those who are qualified to give it. 15 Engage in conversation with intelligent people, and let the Law of the Most High be the topic of your discussions. 16 Choose righteous people for your dinner companions. Your chief pride should be your fear of the Lord.

Rulers

17 A skilled worker is admired for the things he makes, and a leader's wisdom is proved by his words. 18 Someone who speaks rashly and recklessly is feared

10 and hated by everyone in town. 1 A wise ruler will educate his people, and his government will be orderly. 2 All the officials and all the citizens will be like their ruler. 3 An uneducated king will ruin his people, but a government will grow strong if its rulers are wise. 4 The Lord sees to the government of the world and brings the right person to power at the right time. 5 The success of that person is in the Lord's hands. The Lord is the source of the honor given to any official.

Pride

6 Don't be angry with someone for every little thing he does wrong. Don't do anything out of injured pride. 7 Arrogance and injustice are hated by both the Lord and people. 8 Injustice, arrogance, and wealth cause nations to fall from power, and others then rise to take their place. 9 We are only dust and ashes; what have we got to be proud of? Our body decays even while we are alive.[v] 10 A long illness puzzles the doctor.[w] Even a king may be alive today and dead tomorrow. 11 When a person dies, all he then possesses is worms, flies, and maggots.

12 Pride has its beginning when a person abandons the Lord, his maker. 13 Pride is like a fountain pouring out sin, and whoever persists in it will be full of wickedness. That is why the Lord brought terrible punishments on some people and completely destroyed them. 14 The Lord has overthrown kings and put humbler people in their place. 15 The Lord has pulled up nations by the roots and established humbler ones in their place. 16 The Lord has overthrown empires and completely devastated their lands. 17 He destroyed some so completely that they are not even remembered any more. 18 The Creator never intended for human beings to be arrogant and violent.

[t] *Hebrew* If . . . happiness; *Greek* And don't let anyone do you a favor. [u] *Hebrew* other men's wives; *Greek* immoral women. [v] Our body . . . alive; *this sentence in both Greek and Hebrew is unclear.* [w] A long . . . doctor; *this sentence in both Greek and Hebrew is unclear.*

People Who Should Be Honored

19 Who deserves honor? The human
race does, because people fear the Lord.
Who does not deserve honor? The human race does not, because people
break the Lord's commands. 20 A leader
should be honored by those who follow
him, and the Lord honors those who
fear him.[x]
22 Rich people, famous people, and
poor people all take pride in their fear of
the Lord. 23 It is not right to refuse honor
to a poor person who is intelligent, and it
is not right to give honor to a sinner.
24 People of influence, rulers, and judges
will be honored, but none of them is
greater than a person who fears the
Lord. 25 A slave who is wise will have
free citizens serving him; and if they are
sensible, they will not resent it.

Humility and Self-respect

26 When you do your work, don't make
a show of your skill, and don't try to put
on a show when you are in trouble. 27 It
is better to work and have more than
you need than to go around boasting but
hungry.
28 My child, keep your self-respect, but
remain modest. Value yourself at your
true worth. 29 There is no excuse for a
person to run himself down. No one respects a person who has no respect for
himself. 30 Poor people can be honored
for their good sense, and rich people can
be honored for their wealth. 31 If someone is honored while he is poor, think
how much he will be honored if he becomes rich! If someone is despised while
he is rich, think how much more he will
be despised if he becomes poor!

11

1 If a poor person is wise, he has
good reason to be proud, and he will be
thought of as someone great.

Appearances

2 Do not compliment a person on his
good looks. On the other hand, do not
look down on someone who is unattrac-
tive. 3 Compared to most flying things, a
bee is very small, but the honey it makes
is the sweetest of foods. 4 Don't make fun
of someone who has fallen on hard times
and is dressed in rags.[y] The Lord does
wonderful things that human beings
never notice. 5 Many are the kings who
have ended their careers sitting on the
ground, while their crowns were worn
by those no one had heard of before.
6 Many are the rulers who have suffered
disgrace. Many are the famous people
who have fallen into the power of others.

Be Cautious

7 Before you start criticizing, get your
facts straight and think the matter
through. 8 Don't interrupt while someone is speaking; hear what he has to say
before you answer. 9 Don't get into an
argument over something that is none of
your business. Don't take part in decisions that are being made by sinners.
10 My child, don't get involved in too
many things. If you try to do too much,
you will suffer for it. You won't be able
to finish your work, and you won't be
able to get away from it either. 11 For instance, here is someone who never stops
working like a slave, but gets further behind all the time. 12 On the other hand,
someone else may be very poor and not
up to his task. He may be slow, and he
may need help, but the Lord is pleased
with him and pulls him out of his bad
situation. 13 When he is back on his feet
again, everyone is astounded.
14 Everything comes from the Lord:
success and failure, poverty and wealth,
life and death. 15 Wisdom, understanding, knowledge of the Law, love,
and the doing of good deeds—all these
come from the Lord. 16 Error and darkness have been with sinners from the beginning, and those who enjoy evil will
have it with them into their old age.
17 The Lord's gifts to religious people are
gifts that endure. If he approves of you,
you will always be successful. 18 Someone may grow rich by working hard and
denying himself pleasure, but what does
he get for it? 19 He says to himself, "Now
I can finally sit back and enjoy what I
have worked for." But he has no idea
how long it will be before he must die
and leave his wealth to others.
20 Stand by your duty and stick to it;
grow old at your work. 21 Don't be jealous of what sinners achieve; just stick to
your own work, and trust the Lord. It is
very easy for the Lord to make a poor

[x] *Some manuscripts add verse 21:* Success begins with fear of the Lord, but failure begins with stubbornness and arrogance. [y] *Hebrew* Don't . . . rags; *Greek* Don't take pride in fine clothes, and don't let compliments go to your head.

person suddenly rich. 22 Devout people
will receive the Lord's blessing as their
reward, and that blessing can be given
in a moment. 23 Don't be concerned
about what you need, or what success
the future holds for you. 24 On the other
hand, don't think that you have everything you need or that nothing can go
wrong for you in the future. 25 When
things are going well, people don't think
about hard times; and when things are
going badly, they forget about prosperity. 26 The Lord can easily wait until the
day of our death to reward or punish us.
27 At that time our deeds are open for all
to see; all our happiness can be erased in
that one moment of misery. 28 So then,
don't think of anyone's life as happy until it is over, because all the evidence is
not in until the person is dead.[z]

Be Careful in Choosing Friends

29 Be careful about the kind of person
you invite into your home, because
clever people can fool you in many
ways. 30 A proud person is a decoy to
lure you into danger; like a spy, he will
look for your weaknesses.[a] 31 He will
make good appear evil and find fault
with the noblest actions. 32 A single
spark can set a pile of coals ablaze, and
a sinner is just waiting for a chance to do
violence. 33 Watch out for such people
and their evil plans; they will ruin you
permanently. 34 If you bring a stranger
home with you, it will only cause trouble, even between you and your own
family.

12 When you do a good deed, make
sure you know who is benefiting
from it; then what you do will not be
wasted.[b] 2 You will be repaid for any
kindness you show to a devout person. If
he doesn't repay you, the Most High will.
3 No good ever comes to a person who
gives comfort to the wicked; it is not a
righteous act.[c] 4 Give to religious people, but don't help sinners. 5 Do good to
humble people, but don't give anything
to those who are not devout. Don't give
them food, or they will use your kindness against you. Every good thing you
do for such people will bring you twice
as much trouble in return. 6 The Most
High himself hates sinners, and he will
punish them. 7 Give to good people, but
do not help sinners.

8 When things are going well, it is hard
to tell who your real friends are, but in
hard times you can recognize your enemies; 9 even your friends will leave you
then. But when you are successful, your
enemies will act like friends.[d] 10 Never
trust an enemy; his wickedness is as destructive as rust. 11 Watch out, and be on
guard against him, even if he acts ever
so humble. He is like a metal mirror that
rusts away if you don't keep it polished.
12 Seat an enemy at your right hand, and
the next thing you know he'll be trying
to get your own place of honor. Put him
next to you, and he will overthrow you.
Then you will realize the truth of my
words, and be stung with regret when
you remember them. 13 Nobody feels
sorry for snake charmers or wild animal
tamers who get bitten, 14 and nobody
will feel sorry for you if you run around
with sinners and get involved in their
wrongdoing.

15 An enemy will stay with you for a
while, but not when trouble comes. 16 He
will speak fine words while he plots how
to trap you. He will pretend to share
your sorrows, but he will kill you if he
gets a chance. 17 If trouble comes your
way, you will find him waiting, ready to
trip you up while he pretends to help
you. 18 He will be a different person then,
rubbing his hands, nodding his head,
and spreading rumors about you.

13 If you touch tar, it will stick to
you, and if you keep company
with arrogant people, you will come to
be just like them. 2 Don't try to lift something too heavy for you, and don't keep
company with people who are richer
and more powerful than you. You cannot keep a clay pot next to an iron kettle;
the pot will break if it hits the kettle. 3 If
a rich person wrongs someone, he can
afford to add insult to injury; but if a
poor person is wronged, he is forced to
apologize for himself. 4 A rich person
will use you as long as he can profit from
it, but when you need him, he will leave
you helpless. 5 He will live with you as
long as you have anything and will

[z] *Hebrew* all . . . dead; *Greek* a man will be known by his children. [a] *Hebrew* look . . . weaknesses; *Greek* wait for your downfall. [b] what you do . . . wasted; *or* you will be thanked for what you do. [c] *Hebrew* gives . . . act; *Greek* makes evil a habit or refuses to give to the poor. [d] *Hebrew* act like friends; *Greek* be sorry.

gladly drain you dry. 6 If he needs you, he will trick you with his smiles and cheerful, kindly words. "Do you need anything?" he will ask. 7 He will feed you until you are embarrassed. Finally, when he has drained you two or three times over, he will laugh at you. If you see him later, he will pretend he doesn't know you, and will pass you by.

8 Be careful not to be misled; you can be enjoying yourself and suddenly find yourself humiliated. 9 If you are invited to the home of someone influential, be reserved in your behavior. Then he will invite you more often. 10 If you push yourself on him, he will put you in your place. On the other hand, if you keep your distance from him, he will forget about you. 11 Don't pretend to be his equal or trust everything he says. In spite of all of his long and polite conversation, he is testing you.

12 If a person does not keep confidences, he is cruel; he will not hesitate to hurt you or have you put in jail. 13 Keep your secrets to yourself and be very careful, for you are always walking on dangerous ground.[e]

15 Every creature prefers its own kind, and people are no different. 16 Just as animals of the same species flock together, so people keep company with people like themselves. 17 A sinner has no more in common with a devout person than a wolf has with a lamb. 18 Rich people have no more in common with poor people than hyenas have with dogs. 19 The rich hunt down the poor just as lions hunt down wild donkeys in the open country. 20 Arrogant people have nothing but scorn for the humble, and the rich think of the poor in the same way. 21 When a rich person stumbles, his friends will steady him, but if a poor person falls, his friends will have nothing to do with him. 22 When someone rich makes a mistake, there are many people to cover up for him and explain away all the things he never should have said. But let someone poor make a mistake, and he gets nothing but criticism. Even if what he says makes good sense, nobody will listen. 23 When a rich person speaks, everyone is silent, and they praise him to the skies for what he says. But let a poor person speak, and everybody says, "Who is that?" They push him down if he so much as stumbles.

24 There is nothing wrong with being rich if you haven't sinned to get that way. But there is nothing sinful about being poor, either. Only the ungodly think so. 25 It's what is in your heart that makes the expression on your face happy or sad. 26 If you feel cheerful, you will look cheerful, although making up proverbs calls for some intense thought.

14 If a person never says anything carelessly, he is to be congratulated; he doesn't need to feel guilty. 2 If a person has a clear conscience and never gives up hope, he is certainly to be congratulated!

Responsible Use of Wealth

3 It isn't right for someone who is selfish to be rich. What use is money to a stingy person? 4 If you deny yourself in order to accumulate wealth, you are only accumulating it for someone else. Others will use your riches to live in luxury. 5 How can you be generous with others if you are stingy with yourself, if you are not willing to enjoy your own wealth? 6 No one is worse off than someone who is stingy with himself; it is a sin that brings its own punishment. 7 When such a person does something good, it is only by accident; his selfishness will sooner or later be evident. 8 A selfish person is evil; he turns his back on people's needs 9 and is never satisfied with what he has. Greed[f] will shrivel up a person's soul. 10 Some people are too stingy to put bread on their own table.

11 My child, treat yourself as well as you can, and bring worthy offerings to the Lord. 12 Remember that death is coming for you some day, and you haven't been told when that will be. 13 Before that day comes, be kind to your friends; be as generous as you can. 14 Don't deny yourself a single day's happiness. If there is something you want to do and it is lawful, go ahead! 15 Some day all that you have worked for will be divided up and given to others. 16 So be generous; but also be willing to receive from others. Enjoy yourself, for you will not find any pleasures in the world of

[e] *Some manuscripts add verses 13b-14:* When you hear this in your sleep, wake up! 14 As long as you live, love the Lord and call on him to rescue you. [f] *Probable text* Greed; *Greek* Wicked injustice.

the dead. 17 The human body wears out
like a piece of clothing. The ancient law
decrees that we must die. 18 Human beings are like leaves on a spreading tree.
New growth takes the place of the fallen
leaves; while some of us die, others are
being born. 19 Everything made by human hands will decay and perish, along
with the person who made it.

The Happiness of Having Wisdom

20 It is a happy person who is concerned with Wisdom and who uses good
sense. 21 Anyone who studies the ways
of Wisdom will also learn her secrets.
22 Go after Wisdom like a hunter looking
for game. 23 Look into her windows and
listen at her doors. 24 Camp as close to
her house as you can get, 25 and you will
have a fine place to live. 26-27 Build your
home there, safe beneath her protecting
branches, and shaded from the heat.[g]

15 If you fear the Lord, you will do
this. Master his Law, and you
will find Wisdom. 2 She will come to welcome you, like a mother or a young
bride. 3 She will give you wisdom and
knowledge like food and drink. 4 Rely on
her for support, and you will never know
the disgrace of failure. 5 She will make
you more honored than all your neighbors; when you speak in the assembly,
she will give you the right words. 6 You
will find happiness and genuine joy;
your name will be remembered forever.
7 But people who are foolish or sinful
will never even catch sight of Wisdom.
8 She will have nothing to do with conceited people; she never enters the mind
of liars. 9 It is not appropriate for a sinner to sing hymns of praise, because his
worship is insincere. 10 A hymn should
be an expression of wisdom, inspired by
the Lord himself.

Free Will

11 Don't blame the Lord for your sin;
the Lord does not cause what he hates.[h]
12 Don't claim that he has misled you; he
doesn't need the help of sinners to accomplish his purposes. 13 The Lord hates
evil in all its forms, and those who fear
the Lord find nothing attractive in evil.
14 When, in the beginning, the Lord created human beings, he left them free to
do as they wished. 15 If you want to, you
can keep the Lord's commands. You can
decide whether you will be loyal to him
or not. 16 He has placed fire and water
before you; reach out and take whichever you want. 17 You have a choice between life and death; you will get
whichever you choose. 18 The Lord's
wisdom and power are great and he sees
everything. 19 He is aware of everything
a person does, and he takes care of those
who fear him. 20 He has never commanded anyone to be wicked or given
anyone permission to sin.

God's Punishment of Sinners

16 A large family is nothing to be
desired if the children are worthless. Godless children are nothing to be
proud of. 2 No matter how many children
you have, don't look on them with pride
unless they fear the Lord. 3 Don't put
much hope in their future or expect them
to live a long time. One child who does
the Lord's will is better than a thousand
who do not.[i] It is better to go to your
grave with no children at all than to
have children who are godless.
4 A city's population may grow because of the wisdom of one person,
while a whole tribe of lawless people
disappears. 5 I have seen such things
many times and have heard of even
more striking examples. 6 The Lord's
flaming anger will break out against a
small gathering of sinners or a disobedient nation. 7 He did not forgive those ancient giants who rebelled against him,
confident of their own strength. 8 He detested the arrogance of the people
among whom Lot lived, and he did not
spare them. 9 He showed no mercy on
that nation which he doomed to destruction for its sins, 10 nor on those 600,000
people on the march through the wilderness who gathered together in stubborn
rebellion. 11 Even if there had been only
one stubborn person, it would have been
a miracle if he had escaped punishment.
The Lord is merciful, but he can also become angry. He can be overwhelming in
his forgiveness or in his anger. 12 His
punishment is as severe as his mercy is

[g] *Hebrew* Build . . . heat; *Greek* Let her protect your children. Live safe beneath her branches, shaded from the heat, surrounded by her glory. [h] *Hebrew* the Lord does not cause what he hates; *Greek* do not do what the Lord hates. [i] *Hebrew* who does . . . do not; *Greek* is better than a thousand.

great. He judges people by what they
have done. 13 No sinner can escape with
what he has stolen. The Lord will reward the patience of devout people.
14 Every righteous person will be rewarded;[j] everyone will get what he
deserves.[k]

17 Never say, "I will hide from the
Lord. Nobody up there is going to give
me a thought. How can I be noticed
among so many people? The creation is
so enormous, what am I worth? 18 When
the Lord comes, everything will tremble:
the earth and the great waters beneath
it, the sky and the heavens above it.
19 The mountains will shake, and the
foundations of the earth will shudder
when he looks at them. 20 The Lord isn't
going to give me a thought. Nobody
cares what I do. 21 If I sin and am secretly
disloyal, nobody will know it.[l] 22 If I do
what is right, nobody will tell the Lord
about it. Who wants to wait for him, anyway? He is too slow in doing what he has
said he would." 23 Only someone with
very little sense, and foolishly mis-
guided, would think things like that.

God's Wisdom in Creation

24 My child, listen and pay attention to
me; you will gain knowledge if you do.
25 I will give you diligent and accurate
instruction.

26 In the beginning the Lord did his
work of creation,[m]
and gave everything a place of
its own.
27 He arranged everything in an
eternal order
and decreed that it should be
that way forever.
Not one part of creation ever
grows hungry;
no part grows tired or stops its
work.
28 The parts do not crowd one
another,
and they never disobey his
word.
29 When the Lord had made all this,
he looked at the earth and filled
it with good things.
30 He covered it with all kinds of
creatures
that must die and return to the
dust.

17 Then the Lord formed human
beings from the dust
and sent each of them back to it
again.
2 He gave them only a limited time
to live,
but he gave them authority over
everything on earth.
3 He made them to be like himself,
and gave them his[n] own
strength.
4 He made all other creatures afraid
of them;
he gave them authority over all
the animals and birds.[o]
6 He gave them their tongues, their
eyes,
their ears, their minds, and their
consciences.
7 He filled them with knowledge
and understanding
and showed them the difference
between good and evil.
8 He gave them his own insight
to let them see the majesty of
his creation.[p]
10 They will praise his holy name
and proclaim the greatness of all
he does.
11 He made knowledge available to
them
and gave them the Law as a
source of life.
12 He made an eternal covenant with
them
and revealed his commands to
them.
13 They saw the splendor of his
majesty

[j] *Hebrew* Every . . . rewarded; *Greek* He makes room for every act of mercy.
[k] *Some manuscripts add verses 15-16:* The Lord made the king of Egypt so stubborn that he would not acknowledge the Lord, in order that the world might know the Lord's works. 16He shows his mercy to all creation; he has divided his light from darkness with a plumb line.
[l] *Hebrew* 20-21The Lord . . . know it; *Greek* 20It is altogether too big for the human mind to handle. No one can understand his ways. 21Most of his works are just as invisible as the storm wind.
[m] *Hebrew* In . . . creation; *Greek* In the judgment of the Lord his works are from the beginning.
[n] *Probable text* his; *Greek* their.
[o] *Some manuscripts add verse 5:* The Lord gave them the five senses, but he also gave them a sixth—intelligence, and a seventh—reason, which enables them to interpret what comes to them through the senses.
[p] *Some manuscripts add verse 9:* and he allowed them to take pride forever in his marvelous deeds.

and heard the glory of his voice.
14 He warned them against
unrighteousness
and taught each person how to
treat others.

God Is Judge

15 The Lord is always aware of what
people do; there is no way to hide from
him.[q] 17 He gave each nation its own
ruler, but Israel is the Lord's own possession.[r] 19 The Lord is always watching what people do; everything they do
is as clear as day to him. 20 None of their
sins are hidden from him; he is aware of
them all.[s] 22 When we give to the poor,
the Lord considers it as precious as a
valuable ring. Human kindness is as precious to him as life itself. 23 Later he will
judge the wicked and punish them; they
will get what they deserve. 24 But the
Lord will allow those who repent to return to him. He always gives encouragement to those who are losing hope.

A Call to Repentance

25 Come to the Lord, and leave your sin
behind. Pray sincerely that he will help
you live a better life. 26 Return to the
Most High and turn away from sin. Have
an intense hatred for wickedness.
27 Those who are alive can give thanks to
the Lord, but can anyone in the world of
the dead sing praise to the Most High?
28 A person who is alive and well can
sing the Lord's praises, but the dead,
who no longer exist, have no way to give
him thanks. 29 How great is the Lord's
merciful forgiveness of those who turn
to him! 30 But this is not the nature of
human beings;[t] not one of us is immortal. 31 Nothing is brighter than the sun,
but even the sun's light fails during an
eclipse. How much easier it is for human
thoughts to be eclipsed by evil! 32 The
Lord can look out over all the stars in the
sky. Human beings? They are dust and
ashes.

The Greatness of God

18 The Lord, who lives forever, created the whole universe, 2 and he
alone is just.[u] 4 He has given no one
enough power to describe what he has
done, and no one can investigate it completely. 5 Who can measure his majestic
power? Who can tell the whole story of
his merciful actions? 6 We cannot add to
them; we cannot subtract from them.
There is no way to comprehend the marvelous things the Lord has done. 7 When
we come to the end of that story, we
have not even begun; we are simply at a
loss for words.

Human Beings Are Nothing

8 What are human beings? Of what use
are we? The good that we do—the evil
that we do—what does it all mean? 9 If
we live a hundred years, we have lived
an unusually long time, 10 but compared
with all eternity, those years are like a
drop of water in the ocean, like a single
grain of sand. 11 That is why the Lord is
so patient with us, why he is so free with
his mercy. 12 He looks at us and knows
that we are doomed to die; that is why he
is so willing to forgive us. 13 We can
show compassion to someone we know,
but the Lord shows compassion for all
humanity. He corrects us; he disciplines
us; he teaches us. Like a shepherd tending sheep, he brings us back to himself.
14 He will have compassion on us if we
accept his guidance and are eager for
him to show us where we are wrong.

Kindness and Charity

15 My child, when you help someone,
don't reprimand him at the same time.
When you make a gift, don't say anything that hurts. 16 Your words count for
more than what you give. Even dew
gives some relief during a spell of hot
weather. 17 Yes, kind words are more effective than the best of gifts, and if you
are really concerned, you will give both.
18 It is stupid to be unkind and insulting.

[q] *Some manuscripts add verses 16-17a:* From childhood on they tend to be evil; their heart is like stone, and they don't seem to be able to make it more human. 17 He divided the nations of the whole earth. [r] *Some manuscripts add verse 18:* Israel is his first-born, whom he disciplines as he brings him up. He gives him the light of his love and never neglects him.
[s] *Some manuscripts add verse 21:* But the Lord is gracious and knows his creatures; so he has spared them rather than abandon them. [t] But . . . human beings; *or* People cannot have everything. [u] *Some manuscripts add verses 2b-3:* and there is no other besides him. 3 He guides the world with his hand, and everything obeys him. He is the king of all things, and his power separates what is holy from what is not.

No one's eyes are going to sparkle at a
gift that you resent giving.

Self-examination

19 Know what you are talking about
before you speak, and give attention to
your health before you get sick. 20 Examine your conscience before the Lord
judges you; then when that time comes,
he will forgive you. 21 Humble yourself
before you are punished with sickness.
When you have sinned, show repentance. 22 If you make a promise to the
Lord, keep it as soon as you can. Don't
wait until you are about to die to set
things straight. 23 But before you make
such a promise, be prepared to keep it.
Don't try to test the Lord's patience.
24 Think! Do you want him to be angry
with you on the day you die? When you
face his judgment, do you want him to
turn his back on you? 25 When you have
all you want, think what it is like to be
hungry, what it is to be poor. 26 Things
can change in a single day; the Lord can
act very quickly. 27 If you are wise, you
will be careful in everything you do.
When sin is all around you, be especially
careful that you do not become guilty.
28 Every intelligent person can recognize
wisdom and will honor anyone who
shows it. 29 If you appreciate wisdom
when you hear it, you will become wise
yourself, and your words will be a
source of wisdom for others.

Self-control

30 Don't be controlled by your lust;
keep your passions in check. 31 If you allow yourself to satisfy your every desire,
you will be a joke to your enemies.
32 Don't indulge in luxurious living; the
expense of it will ruin you. 33 Don't make
yourself a beggar by borrowing for expensive banquets when you don't have
19 enough money of your own. 1 If
you do, you[v] will never get rich;
if you don't pay attention to small matters, you will gradually ruin yourself.
2 Wine and women make sensible men
do foolish things. A man who goes to
prostitutes gets more and more careless,
3 and that carelessness will cost him his
life. Worms will feed on his decaying
body.

4 It is silly to trust people too quickly. If
you sin, you are hurting yourself. 5 If
wickedness makes you happy, you will
be condemned.

Loose Talk

6 Avoid idle talk, and you will avoid a
lot of trouble. 7 Never repeat what you
hear, and you will have no regrets.
8 Don't tell it to your friends or your enemies unless it would be sinful to keep it
to yourself. 9 Whoever hears you will
take note of it, and sooner or later will
hate you for it. 10 Have you heard a rumor? Let it die with you. Be brave! It
won't make you explode. 11 A foolish
person trying to keep a secret suffers
like a woman in labor. 12 Any time he
hears a secret, it's like an arrow stuck in
his leg.

13 If you hear that a friend has done
something wrong, ask him about it.
Maybe it isn't true. If it is true, he won't
do it again. 14 If you hear that a neighbor
has said something he shouldn't, ask
him about it. Maybe he didn't say it. If he
did, he won't say it again. 15 If you hear
something bad about a friend, ask him
about it. It might be a lie. Don't believe
everything you hear. 16 A person may
say something carelessly and not really
mean it. Everyone has sinned in this way
at one time or another. 17 If you hear
something that makes you angry with
your neighbor, ask him about it before
you threaten him. Leave the matter to
the Law of the Most High.[w]

Recognizing Real Wisdom

20 Fear the Lord and keep his Law; that
is what Wisdom is all about.[x] 22 You
may know everything there is to know
about wickedness, but that does not
make you wise. It is not sensible to follow the advice of sinners. 23 It is possible
to use cleverness for wicked purposes,
but some people act like fools because
they don't know any better. 24 A devout
person, even if he is not very intelligent,

[v] *Hebrew* If you do, you; *Greek* A worker who drinks too much. [w] *Some manuscripts add verses 17c-19:* and don't be angry. 18 Fearing the Lord is the first step toward his accepting you; he will love you if you are wise. 19 Learn the Lord's commands. It is a discipline that gives life. Those who do what pleases him enjoy the fruit of the tree of immortality. [x] *Some manuscripts add verses 20b-21:* and what the knowledge of his omnipotence means. 21 If a servant refuses to obey his master, but later does obey, the master is still angry.

is better off than the cleverest of sinners.
25 It is possible to be marvelously clever
and still be dishonest, or to get what you
want by being absurdly polite.

26 Then there are those wicked people
who go about looking very solemn and
mournful, but who are only trying to deceive you. 27 They will turn their faces
away and pretend not to hear you, but
they'll take advantage of you when you
least expect it. 28 If for some reason they
are unable to sin now, they'll get around
to it at the first opportunity. 29 You can
know people by their appearance. The
first time you look at them, you can tell
if they have good sense. 30 Their character shows in the way they dress, the way
they laugh, and the way they walk.

Knowing When to Talk

20 A person can be rebuked in the
wrong way; it may be wiser to
keep quiet than to speak. 2 But it is much
better to rebuke the person than to keep
your anger bottled up. 3 Admit when you
are wrong, and you will avoid embarrassment. 4 Using force to get a point
across is like a castrated man trying to
rape a young woman. 5 Some people are
thought to be wise because they don't
talk much; others are disliked because
they talk too much. 6 Some people keep
quiet because they don't have anything
to say; others keep quiet because they
know the right time to speak. 7 A wise
person will not speak until the right moment, but a bragging fool doesn't know
when that time is. 8 No one can stand a
person who talks too long and will not
give others a chance to speak.

Sudden Changes of Fortune

9 Bad luck can sometimes lead to success, and a stroke of good luck can
sometimes lead to loss.

10 Generosity will sometimes do you
no good, but at other times it will repay
you double.

11 Honor can be followed by disgrace,
but there are people who have risen
from obscurity to places of honor.

12 Sometimes what seems like a real
bargain can turn out to be a very expensive mistake.

13 When a person with good judgment
speaks, he wins friends. A stupid person,
though, can shower compliments on
everybody, and it won't help him a bit.
14 If such a person gives you something,
it won't do any good; it won't be as valuable as he thinks it is.[y] 15 He isn't generous with anything but criticism, which
he will shout for all the world to hear. If
he lends you something today, he'll want
it back tomorrow. (Don't you hate people like that?) 16 Then that fool will say,
"Nobody likes me. Nobody appreciates
what I do for them. They'll take what I
give them, but then talk about me behind my back." 17 And he's right—he's a
constant joke to everyone.

Inappropriate Talk

18 A slip of the tongue is worse than a
slip on the pavement; the wicked will go
to ruin just as suddenly as a person slips
and falls.

19 An impolite person is like one of
those off-color stories that ignorant people are always telling.

20 Nobody takes a proverb seriously
when some fool quotes it at the wrong
time.

21 If a person is too poor to afford sin,
he can rest without a guilty conscience.
22 You can lose all your self-respect by
being reluctant to speak up in the presence of stupidity.

23 If you promise a friend something
because you are too bashful to say no,
you're needlessly making an enemy.

24 Lying is an ugly blot on a person's
character, but ignorant people do it all
the time. 25 A thief is better than a habit-
ual liar, but both are headed for ruin.
26 A liar has no honor. He lives in constant disgrace.

Stewardship of Wisdom

27 Speak wisely, and you will get
ahead in the world. Influential people
appreciate good sense. 28 They will excuse your errors if they like you, so cultivate the soil and reap the harvest!

29 Gifts and bribes make even the wise
blind to the truth, and prevent them
from being honest in their criticism.

30 Wisdom that is not expressed is like
a treasure that has been hidden—both
are useless. 31 But a person who covers

[y] it won't be . . . it is; *or* he only expects to be repaid.

up his foolishness is better than one who
keeps his wisdom to himself.

Sin

21 My child, have you sinned?
Don't do it again, and pray for
forgiveness for what you have already
done. 2 Avoid sin as if it were a snake. If
you get too near, it will sink its teeth into
your soul like a lion, and destroy you.
3 Every lawless act leaves an incurable
wound, like one left by a double-edged
sword.
4 If a person is insolent and arrogant,
he may lose everything he has.
5 When poor people pray, God hears
them and quickly answers their prayers.
6 If you refuse to accept correction,
you are committing a sin; and if you fear
the Lord, you will make a sincere
change in your ways.
7 Someone may be famous as a good
speaker, but when he is wrong, a sensible person will detect it.
8 Anyone who borrows money to build
a house is just collecting stones for his
own tomb.[z]
9 A group of people who have no respect for the Law is like a pile of kin-
dling; they will meet a fiery end. 10 The
road that sinners walk is smooth and
paved, but it leads to the world of the
dead.

Wisdom and Foolishness

11 Whoever wants to keep the Law
must learn what the Law means. If you
fear the Lord in every sense of the term,
you will have wisdom. 12 You have to be
intelligent to learn anything; but there is
such a thing as just pretending to be intelligent, which only makes people bitter. 13 A wise person's knowledge is like
a river that never runs dry, like an everflowing stream of good advice.
14 A fool, on the other hand, has a
mind like a jar with a hole in it; anything
he learns is soon lost.
15 When an educated person hears
something that shows insight, it stimu-
lates his mind and leads him on to other
ideas. But when someone who is satisfied with ignorance hears it, he won't
like it, and will forget it as soon as he
can. 16 Listening to a foolish person talk
is like traveling with a heavy load on
your back, but it is a pleasure to hear
what intelligent people have to say.
17 The assembly will be eager to hear
from an intelligent person and will take
his opinion seriously.
18 To an ignorant person, wisdom is as
useless as a house gone to ruin. He has
never even thought about the things he
is so sure of. 19 To a person without any
sense, an education is like handcuffs,
20-21 but to a sensible person, it is like
gold bracelets. An intelligent person will
smile quietly while a fool roars with
laughter. 22-23 A stupid person will peep
into someone's house through the door
and then march right in, but someone
with experience and good manners will
have enough respect to wait outside.
24 Eavesdropping at doors is bad manners, and anyone with a sense of decency would be ashamed to do it.
25 Presumptuous people talk about
things that are none of their business,[a]
but the wise will consider the consequences of what they say. 26 Fools say
whatever comes to mind; wise people
think before they speak.
27 When a wicked person curses his
enemy[b] he is cursing himself.
28 A gossip ruins his own character,
and everyone in the neighborhood
hates him.

Laziness and Foolishness

22 1-2 Lazy people are no better than
dung; they are repulsive, and no
one wants to get near them.
3 It is a disgrace to a father to have an
undisciplined child, especially if it is a
daughter. 4 A sensible daughter will get
a husband, but a shameless daughter
brings her father grief. 5 A girl with no
sense of propriety will disgrace both her
husband and her father; neither will
have any respect for her.
6 Lecturing your children can sometimes be as out of place as singing to
people in mourning, but a whipping is a
wise choice of discipline at any time.
7 Trying to teach a fool is like gluing a
broken pot back together, like waking
someone out of a deep sleep. 8 Explaining something to a fool is like explaining
it to a sleepy person; when you have

[z] his own tomb; *some manuscripts have* the winter. [a] *Probable text* Presumptuous ... business; *Greek* The lips of strangers speak of these things. [b] his enemy; *or* Satan.

finished, he'll say, "What was that
again?"[c]
11 We mourn for the dead because they
have no access to light. We ought to
mourn for fools, because they have no
access to intelligence. In fact, we should
go into deeper mourning for fools, because the life they lead is worse than
death. The dead are at least at rest. 12 For
seven days we mourn the dead, but a
foolish or ungodly person causes a lifetime of grief.
13 Don't visit stupid people or spend a
lot of time talking with them. Avoid
them; then they can't contaminate you,
and you can live in peace without being
troubled or worn down by their foolishness. 14 Such people are a heavier burden to bear than lead; and the only word
that fits them is "fools." 15 It is easier to
carry a load of sand, salt, and iron than
to put up with a stupid person.
16 A wooden beam can be put into a
building so firmly that an earthquake
cannot shake it loose; a person can be
trained to use reason and good sense so
well that he keeps his head when a crisis
comes. 17 A mind that thinks things
through intelligently is like a firm wall,
finely decorated. 18 Small stones on top
of a wall[d] will not stay put when the
wind blows, and a person whose stupid
ideas have made him timid will not be
able to stand up to frightening situations.

Friendship

19 If you stick something in your eye,
tears will flow; and if you hurt a person
deeply, you will discover his true feelings. 20 If you throw rocks at birds, you
will scare them away; and if you insult a
friend, you will break up the friendship.
21-22 Even if you have a violent argument
with a friend, and speak sharply, all is
not lost. You can still make up with him.
But any friend will leave you if you insult him, if you are arrogant, if you reveal his secrets, or if you turn on him
unexpectedly.
23 Gain the confidence of your neighbor if he is poor; then you can share his
happiness if he becomes successful.
Stand by him when he is in trouble if you
want to share with him when better
times come his way.
24 Fumes and smoke appear before the
flames do; insults come before violence.
25 I will never be afraid to protect a
friend, and I will never turn a friend
away if he needs me. 26 If I suffer because of him, everyone who learns of it
will be on guard against him.

A Prayer for Help against Sin

27 I wish that a guard could be placed
at my mouth, that my lips could be
wisely sealed. It would keep me from
making mistakes and prevent me from
destroying myself with my own tongue!
23 O Lord, my Father and Master of
my life, do not leave me at the
mercy of my own words; don't let them
cause my downfall. 2 I wish I could be
whipped for my thoughts, so that Wisdom could discipline my mind. I would
not want to be spared when I am wrong;
I would not want a single sin to be overlooked! 3 Then I would not keep on sinning, making one mistake after another.
I could not fall to my enemies and be
humiliated by them.
4 O Lord, my Father, God of my life,
keep me from being arrogant; 5 protect
me from evil desires. 6 Keep me from being overcome by greed or lust; do not
leave me at the mercy of these shameless passions.

Taking Oaths

7 My children, listen to what I have to
say about proper speech; do as I teach
you and you will never get trapped.
8 Sinners are caught by their own arrogant, insulting words.
9 Don't fall into the habit of taking
oaths, and don't use God's holy name
too freely. 10 A slave who is constantly
beaten will never be free of bruises;
someone who is always taking an oath
by the Holy Name will never be free of
sin. 11 Anyone who takes oaths all the
time is sinful to the core, and punishment is never far away from his household. If he fails to fulfill his oath, he is
guilty. If he ignores his oath, he is twice
as guilty. If his oath was insincere in the

[c] *Some manuscripts add verses 9-10:* Children who are brought up well do not show the humble origin of their parents. 10 Children who are not brought up well, who are arrogant and conceited, are a stain on the noblest family. [d] Small . . . wall; *some manuscripts have* A fence on top of a hill.

first place, he cannot be pardoned and will have a house full of trouble.

Filthy Talk

12 There is one way of speaking that is like death itself—may no Israelite ever be guilty of it! Devout people do not wallow in such sin, and they will keep away from such behavior. 13 Don't fall into the habit of coarse, profane talk; it is sinful. 14 You might forget yourself while in the company of important people and make a fool of yourself with some foul word that comes to you naturally. Think how your parents would feel! You would curse the day you were born and wish you were dead! 15 If you fall into the habit of using offensive language, you will never break yourself of it as long as you live.

Sexual Sins

16 There are any number of ways to sin and bring down the Lord's anger, but sexual passion is a hot, blazing fire that cannot be put out at will; it can only burn itself out. A man who lives for nothing but sexual enjoyment will keep on until that fire destroys him. 17 To such a man all women are desirable, and he can never get enough as long as he lives.

18 The man who is unfaithful to his wife thinks to himself, "No one will ever know. It's dark in here, and no one sees me. I have nothing to worry about. As for the Most High, he won't even notice." 19 This man is only afraid of other people. He doesn't realize that the eyes of the Lord are 10,000 times brighter than the sun, that he sees everything we do, even when we try to hide it. 20 He knew everything before he created the world, as well as after. 21 That sinful man will be caught when he least expects it, and punished publicly.

22 The same is true of a woman who is unfaithful to her husband and presents him with a child by another man. 23 In the first place, she has broken the Law of the Most High. In the second place, she has wronged her husband. And in the third place, she has made a whore of herself by committing adultery and bearing the child of a man not her husband. 24-25 The children will suffer for her sin. They will not be able to find a place in society or establish families. She herself will be brought before the assembly 26 and permanently disgraced. There will be a curse on her memory. After she is gone, 27 everyone will realize that nothing is better than fearing the Lord, nothing is sweeter than keeping his commands.

In Praise of Wisdom

24 Listen to Wisdom! She proudly sings her own praises among the Israelites, her own people, 2 in the assembly of the Most High, in the presence of his power.[e]

3 "I am the word spoken by the
Most High.
I covered the earth like a mist.
4 I made my home in highest
heaven,
my throne on a pillar of cloud.
5 Alone I walked around the circle
of the sky
and walked through the ocean
beneath the earth.
6 I ruled over[f] all the earth and the
ocean waves,
over every nation, over every
people.
7 I looked everywhere for a place to
settle,
some part of the world to make
my home.
8 Then my Creator, who created the
universe,
told me where I was to live.
'Make your home in Israel,' he
said.
'The descendants of Jacob will
be your people.'
9 He created me in eternity, before
time began,
and I will exist for all eternity to
come.
10 I served him in the Sacred Tent
and then made my home on
Mount Zion.
11 He settled me in the Beloved City
and gave me authority over
Jerusalem.
12 I put down roots among an
honored people
whom the Lord had chosen as
his own.

[e] power; *or* angels. [f] ruled over; *some manuscripts have* gained possession of.

13 I grew tall, like the cedars in
Lebanon,
like the cypresses on Mount
Hermon,
14 like the palm trees of Engedi,[g]
like the roses of Jericho,
like beautiful olive trees in the
fields,
like plane trees growing by the
water.
15 My breath was the spicy smell of
cinnamon,
of sweet perfume and finest
myrrh,
of stacte, onycha, and galbanum,
the fragrant incense in the
Sacred Tent.
16 Like an oak I spread out my
branches,
magnificent and graceful.
17 Like a grapevine I put out lovely
shoots;
my blossoms gave way to rich
and glorious fruit.[h]
19 Come to me, all you that want me,
and eat your fill of my fruit.
20 You will remember me as sweeter
than honey,
better than honey from the
comb.
21 Eat me, and you will hunger for
more;
drink me, and you will thirst for
more.
22 Obey me, and you will never have
cause for embarrassment;
do as I say, and you will be safe
from sin."

Wisdom and the Law

23 Wisdom is the Law, the Law which
Moses commanded us to keep, the covenant of God Most High, the inheritance
of the synagogues of Israel.[i] 25 The Law
overflows with Wisdom like the Pishon
River, like the Tigris at fruit-picking
time. 26 The Law brims over with understanding like the Euphrates, like the Jordan at harvest time. 27 It sparkles with
teachings like the Nile,[j] like the Gihon
at grape-picking time.
28 The first human being ever created
never knew Wisdom completely, and the
last person on earth will be no more successful. 29 The possibilities of Wisdom
are vaster than the ocean; her resources
are more profound than the deepest waters beneath the earth.
30 As for me, I thought of myself as an
irrigation canal bringing water from a
river into a garden. 31 I only intended to
water my orchard and flower beds, but
the canal soon became a river, and the
river became a sea. 32 And so I present
you with my learning; I hold it high, so
that its light can be seen everywhere,
like that of the rising sun. 33 Like an inspired prophet, I pour out my teachings,
so that future generations can benefit
from them. 34 Please realize that I have
not done all this hard work for myself
alone, but to help anyone who wants to
be wise.

People Who Deserve Praise

25 There are three things in which I
take special delight—things that
are beautiful to the Lord and people
alike:[k]
brothers who get along with each
other,
neighbors who are friends,
and a married couple who are
happy together.
2 There are three kinds of people I cannot stand, whose behavior I find highly
offensive:
poor people who are arrogant,
rich people who lie,
and foolish old men who commit
adultery.
3 Unless you learn what you can while
you are young, you will never be wise
when you reach old age. 4 Sound judgment, good advice, and gray hair go
together beautifully. 5 Wisdom,
understanding, and sound counsel are
appropriate to the aged and the respected. 6 Elderly people wear the crown
of long experience, and they can boast
of nothing finer than their fear of the
Lord.
7 I will tell you about ten kinds of people that I feel fortunate to know, espe-

[g] of Engedi; *some manuscripts have* on the seashore. [h] *Some manuscripts add verse 18:* I am the mother of beautiful love, of fear, knowledge, and holy hope. Since I am eternal, I am given to all my children, who are named by him. [i] *Some manuscripts add verse 24:* Always be strong in the Lord; stay with him, so that he may make you strong. There is no God but the Lord Almighty, and no savior except him. [j] *One ancient translation* It sparkles . . . Nile; *Greek* It makes teachings shine like light. [k] *Some ancient translations* There are . . . alike; *Greek* I was made beautiful in three ways and I stood before the Lord and people in beauty.

cially fortunate in the case of the tenth:
someone who takes pride in his
children,
someone who lives to see his
enemies fall,
8 a man fortunate enough to have an
understanding wife,
a married couple who are
well-matched,[l]
a person who never speaks sinfully,
a person who doesn't have to work
for someone less competent than
himself,
9 someone fortunate enough to have
a real friend,[m]
a person that people are happy to
listen to,
10 and the really great one: someone
who is wise.
But the greatest one of all is the
person who fears the Lord.
11 Such a person has no equal, because
the fear of the Lord is the most important thing in the world.[n]

Advice about Women

13 No wound is as serious as wounded
love. No troubles are as serious as the
troubles that women cause. 14 No sufferings are worse than the sufferings
caused by people who hate you. No revenge is worse than revenge taken by an
enemy. 15 No poison is deadlier than the
poison of a snake, and no anger is deadlier than the anger of a woman.[o]
16 I would rather live in the same
house with a lion or a dragon than with
a bad wife. 17 When a wife is in a bad
mood, her expression changes until she
looks like an angry bear. 18 Her husband
has to go and eat with the neighbors,
where he can't hold back his bitter sighs.
19 Compared with the troubles caused
by a woman, any other trouble looks
small. May such women suffer the fate
of sinners!
20 A quiet man living with a nagging
wife is like an old man climbing up a
sandy hill.
21 Never lose your head over a
woman's beauty, and don't try to win a
woman because she is wealthy.[p]
22 When a man is supported by his wife,
there is sure to be anger, arrogance, and
humiliation. 23 A bad wife will make her
husband gloomy and depressed, and
break his heart. Show me a timid man
who can never make up his mind, and I
will show you a wife who doesn't make
her husband happy. 24 Sin began with a
woman, and we must all die because of
her. 25 Don't let a bad wife have her way,
any more than you would allow water to
leak from your cistern. 26 If she won't do
as you tell her, divorce her.

26 The husband of a good wife is a
fortunate man; he will live twice
as long because of her. 2 A fine wife is a
joy to her husband, and he can live out
his years in peace. 3 A good wife is
among the precious blessings given to
those who fear the Lord. 4 Whether such
men are rich or poor, they will be happy
and always look cheerful.
5 There are four things that scare me:
vicious rumors spread around town, a
gathering mob, false accusations—these
are all worse than death. 6 But a woman
jealous of another woman causes heartache and grief; her tongue lashes out at
everyone.
7 A bad wife is like a yoke that doesn't
fit. Trying to control her is like holding a
scorpion. 8 A drunken woman is an in-
furiating sight; she can't conceal her
shameless behavior. 9 You can tell an unfaithful wife by the bold and flirting look
in her eyes.
10 If your daughter is determined to
have her own way, keep a close watch
on her. If you don't, she'll take advantage of any chance she gets. 11 If she is
too self-willed, be on guard, and don't be
surprised if she disappoints you. 12 She'll
spread her legs anywhere for any man
who wants her, just as a thirsty traveler
will drink whatever water is available.
13 A gracious wife is her husband's delight; her abilities make him a stronger
man.[q] 14 A wife who doesn't talk too
much is a gift from the Lord. Such restraint is admirable beyond words.
15 A modest wife has endless charm; it is
a quality too precious to measure. 16 The

[l] *Hebrew and one ancient translation* a married couple . . . well-matched; *Greek does not have these words.* [m] *Some ancient translations* real friend; *Greek* good sense.
[n] *Some manuscripts add verse 12:* Fearing the Lord is the first step toward loving him, and faith is the first step toward loyalty to him. [o] *Some ancient translations* woman; *Greek* enemy. [p] *Hebrew* because she is wealthy; *Greek does not have these words.* [q] her abilities . . . man; *or* she knows how to keep him well-fed.

beauty of a good wife in her well-kept
home is like the noonday sun shining in
the Lord's sky. 17 Her beautiful face and
attractive figure are[r] as lovely as the
light from the sacred lampstand in the
Temple, 18 and like its gold shaft set on
its silver base are her shapely legs and
strong ankles.[s, t]

Sad Observations

28 There are two things that make me
sad, and a third that makes me angry:
a soldier who has become poor,
intelligent people who are not
respected,
and a righteous person who
turns to evil.
The Lord will punish such a person with
death!
29 A merchant can hardly avoid doing
wrong; every salesman is guilty of sin.
27 1 Many people have sinned while
looking for a profit; if you want
to be rich you have to keep blinders on
your eyes. 2 It is hard to remove a peg
that is stuck between two stones of a
house, and it is just as hard to remove
dishonesty from buying and selling.
3 Unless you are determined in your fear
of the Lord, your house is going to come
down on you.

Speech Reflects True Feelings

4 Your talk shows your faults; it is like
a sieve that separates out the rubbish.
5 The way you think shows your character just as surely as a kiln shows any
flaws in the pottery being fired. 6 You
can tell how well a tree has been cared
for by the fruit it bears, and you can tell
a person's feelings by the way he expresses himself. 7 Never praise anyone
before you hear him talk; that is the real
test.

Honesty

8 If you try to be honest, you can be,
and it will improve your character as
handsome clothing improves your appearance. 9 Birds come to roost with
those of their own kind, and the habit of
honesty comes to those who try to be
honest. 10 Sin waits for those looking for
a chance to sin, just as a lion waits for
prey.

Foolish Talk

11 When devout people talk, what they
say always makes sense, but foolish
people are always contradicting themselves. 12 When you find yourself with
stupid people, look for some excuse to
leave, but when you are with serious-
minded people, stay as long as you can.
13 The stories that foolish people tell
are offensive, and they make jokes
about the worst kinds of sin. 14 When
such people curse, it is enough to make
your hair stand on end, and when they
start arguing among themselves, all you
can do is to stop up your ears. 15 It is
painful to listen to them insult each
other, and such blustering can lead to
violence.

Betraying Secrets

16 If you repeat secrets that have been
told to you, you are destroying the confidence others have in you, and you will
never have a close friend. 17 Respect
your friends, and keep faith with them.
If you do betray a friend's confidence,
you may as well forget you have a
friend. 18 You have killed that friendship
just as surely as if you had taken a
weapon and killed an enemy. 19 Your
friend is gone. You can no more get him
back than you can get a bird to come
back to your hand once you let it go.
20 Don't bother going after him. It's too
late. He is gone, like a deer escaped from

[r] and attractive figure are; *or* as she grows older is. [s] strong ankles; *some manuscripts have* firm breasts *or* determined heart. [t] *Some manuscripts add verses 19-27:* My child, stay healthy while you are young, and don't give your strength to strangers. 20 Search the whole land for a fertile field, and plant it with your own seed, trusting your own good stock. 21 Then your children will survive and grow up confident of their good family. 22 A prostitute is like spit; a married woman who has affairs brings death to her lovers. 23 A lawless man will get a godless wife, as he deserves, but a man who honors the Lord will have a devout wife. 24 A shameless wife enjoys making a disgrace of herself, but a modest wife will act modestly even alone with her husband. 25 A self-willed woman is a bitch, but a woman with a sense of decency honors the Lord. 26 A wife who honors her husband will seem wise to everyone; but if she dishonors him by her overbearing attitude, everyone will know that she is ungodly. Fortunate is the husband of a good wife, because he will live twice as long. 27 A loud-mouthed, talkative woman is like a trumpet sounding the signal for attack, and any man who has such a wife will spend his life at war.

a trap. 21 Wounds can be bandaged and
insults can be forgiven, but if you betray
a confidence, it is hopeless.

Hypocrisy

22 When someone starts winking at
you, he has something bad in mind, and
nothing can stop him from going
through with it. 23 When he's with you,
his talk is so nice! He compliments you
on every word you say. But behind your
back it's a different story; he will take
what you have said and turn it against
you. 24 There is nothing in the world that
I hate as much as a person like that—
and the Lord hates him too.

25 Throw a stone straight up in the air
and it will come down on your head.
Strike a blow, and you yourself will be
wounded. 26 People who set traps fall
into them themselves. 27 People who hurt
others will be hurt by their own actions
and will have no idea why.

28 Arrogant people insult others and
make fun of them,[u] but someone is
waiting like a lion for a chance to take
revenge on them. 29 Those who are
happy to witness the downfall of devout
people are going to fall into a trap and
die a painful death.

Resentment

30 Anger and a hot temper are horrible
28 things, but sinners have both.
1 The Lord is taking note of your
sins, and if you take vengeance on someone, the Lord will take vengeance on
you. 2 But if you forgive someone who
has wronged you, your sins will be forgiven when you pray. 3 You cannot expect the Lord to pardon you while you
are holding a grudge against someone
else. 4 You yourself are a sinner, and if
you won't forgive another person, you
have no right to pray that the Lord will
forgive your sins. 5 If you cannot get rid
of your anger, you have no hope of
forgiveness—you are only a human being. 6 Think about it! Some day you will
die, and your body will decay. So give up
hate and live by the Lord's commands,
7 the commands in the covenant of the
Most High. Instead of getting upset over
your neighbor's faults, overlook them.

Arguments

8 If you stay out of arguments, you will
not sin so much, because a hot temper
gets them started. 9 It is sinful to break
up a friendship by creating hostility
among people who get along well together. 10 The more fuel, the hotter the
fire. The more stubbornness, the hotter
the argument. And the stronger or richer
people are, the angrier they can afford to
become. 11 An argument that blazes out
suddenly can lead to violence. 12 You can
blow on a spark to make it glow, or you
can spit on it to put it out. Either way,
you do it with your mouth.

Vicious Talk

13 Gossips and liars deserve to be
cursed, because they have been the ruin
of many people who were minding their
own business. 14 Many have had their
lives ruined and have been driven from
their homes because of people who med-
dled in their business. Such unwanted
interference has resulted in the destruction of strong cities and the homes of
respected people. 15 Meddlers have
caused faithful wives to be divorced,
robbed of everything they had worked
for. 16 Anyone who pays attention to
slander can never find peace of mind.
17 A whip can raise a welt, but a vicious
tongue can break bones. 18 More people
have died as a result of loose talk than
were ever killed by swords. 19-20 Count
yourself lucky if you have been spared
the experience of having irresponsible
talk directed against you—if you have
never had that iron yoke around your
neck or those heavy chains on your legs.
21 Slander leads to a miserable death; but
in fact, you'd be better off dead.

22 Devout people, however, cannot be
overcome by slander; they cannot be
burned by its flames. 23 Its victims are
those who have abandoned the Lord;
once the fire of slander has been lit
among them, it cannot be put out. Slander will pounce on them like a lion and
tear them to pieces like a leopard.

24 Don't you fence in your property?
Don't you lock up your money? 25 Well,
be just as careful with what you say.
Weigh every word, and have a lock
ready for your mouth. 26 Someone may
be waiting for you to slip, and if you are

[u] insult others . . . them; *or* will be insulted and mocked.

not careful, you will stumble over your
own words and fall down in front
of him.

Loans and Repayment

29 Be kind enough to lend to your
neighbor when he needs help.
You are keeping the Lord's commands if
you help him. 2If he needs something,
lend it to him. And when you are in debt,
pay it back as soon as you can. 3If you
meet your obligations, you will always
be able to borrow what you need. 4Many
people treat a loan as something they
found and can keep, causing embarrassment to those who helped them. 5Some
people will speak politely, bow, and
scrape until they get the loan they want,
but when the time comes to pay it back,
they'll put it off, say that it's inconven-
ient, and make a lot of worthless excuses. 6If the lender insists on being
paid, he can count himself lucky to get
back half. If he doesn't insist, the borrower has robbed him and made an unnecessary enemy. All the lender will get
from him are curses, insults, and disrespect, but never any gratitude.
7Many people refuse to lend at all, not
because they are stingy, but because[v]
they don't want to be cheated if they can
avoid it.

Generosity

8Nevertheless, be understanding with
those who are poor. Don't keep them
waiting for your generosity. 9The Lord
has commanded us to help the poor;
don't refuse them the help they need. 10It
is better to lose your money by helping a
relative or a friend than to lose it by letting it rust away under a rock somewhere. 11Use your wealth as the Most
High has commanded; this will do you
more good than keeping your money for
yourself. 12Count among your treasures
the fact that you give to the poor. It will
save you from all kinds of trouble 13and
will be a better defense against your enemies than the strongest shield or stout-
est spear.

Guaranteeing Debts

14A good man is willing to guarantee
his neighbor's debts. Only someone who
has lost all sense of decency would refuse to do so. 15If someone does this favor for you, don't forget it; he has risked
his good name for you. 16There are some
ungrateful sinners who abandon those
who stand behind them, and they cause
them loss of property. 17Guaranteeing
loans has ruined many prosperous people and caused them unsettling storms
of trouble. 18Influential people have lost
their homes over it and have had to go
wandering in foreign countries.
19A sinner who hopes to make a profit
by guaranteeing a loan is going to find
himself involved in lawsuits. 20So help
your neighbor as much as you can, but
protect yourself against the dangers
involved.

Home and Hospitality

21The necessities of life are water,
food, clothing, and a home where you
can have privacy. 22It is better to be poor
and live under your own crude roof than
to enjoy lavish banquets in other people's homes. 23Be happy with what you
have, even if it isn't very much, and
don't listen to anyone who would insult
your home and family.[w] 24Going from
house to house is a miserable way to
live. Anywhere you go, you don't dare
speak. 25You welcome the guests and
pour the drinks, and nobody thanks you.
Instead, people humiliate you by saying
things like: 26"Stranger! Come here and
set the table! I want to eat what you've
got there! Give it here! 27Go away, stranger! I've got an important guest! My
brother is coming to visit, and I need the
room!"
28Being denied hospitality or having a
moneylender hound you—these are
hard things for any sensitive person to
endure.

Bringing up Children

30 A father who loves his son will
whip him often, so that he can be
proud of him later. 2If a son is disciplined, he will be of some use, and his
father can boast of him to his friends.

[v] not because . . . stingy, but because; *some manuscripts have* therefore, because of this wickedness. [w] don't listen . . . family; *or* don't listen to insults from your family; *some manuscripts do not have these words; one ancient translation has* don't get a reputation for living off other people.

3 Anyone who gives good guidance to his
son cannot only take pride in him
among his friends, but he can make his
enemies jealous. 4-5 While the father is
alive, the sight of his son makes him
happy, and when he dies, he has no regrets. He is not really dead, because his
son is like him. 6 He has left someone to
take vengeance on his enemies and to
return the favors he owes his friends.

7 But anyone who spoils his son will
have to bandage his wounds.[x] His heart
will stop every time he hears a shout.
8 An untamed horse is going to be stubborn, and an undisciplined son is no different. 9 If you pamper your child and
play with him, he will be a disappointment and a source of grief. 10 Laugh with
him now, and one day you will have to
cry over him, grinding your teeth in regret. 11 Don't give him freedom while he
is young, and don't overlook what he
does wrong. 12 Whip him while he is still
a child, and make him respect your authority. If you don't, he will be stubborn
and disobedient and cause you nothing
but sorrow. 13 So discipline your son and
give him work to do, or else he will be an
embarrassment to you.

Health

14 It is better to be poor, but strong and
healthy, than to be rich, but in poor
health. 15 A sound, healthy body and a
cheerful attitude[y] are more valuable
than gold and jewels. 16 Nothing can
make you richer or give you greater happiness than those two things. 17 It would
be better to be dead, asleep forever, than
to live in the misery of chronic illness.
18 The finest food means nothing if you
are too sick to eat it; it might as well be
offered to an idol.[z] 19 But there is no
point in offering food to an idol; it can't
eat it or smell it. It is just the same with
someone whom the Lord has afflicted.
20 He looks at his food and sighs, like a
castrated man hugging a young woman.

Cheerfulness and Sadness

21 Don't deliberately torture yourself
by giving in to depression. 22 Happiness
makes for a long life and makes it worth
living. 23 Enjoy yourself and be happy;
don't worry all the time. Worry never
did anybody any good, and it has destroyed many people. 24 It will make you
old before your time. Jealousy and anger
will shorten your life. 25 A cheerful person with a good attitude will have a good
appetite and enjoy his food.

Problems Caused by Money

31 Worrying about money will
make you lose weight and lose
sleep. 2 Worrying about business[a] will
keep you from sleeping just as surely as
a serious illness does.

3 Rich people work hard to make a lot
of money; then they can sit back and live
in luxury. 4 Poor people work hard and
have nothing to show for it, and when
they rest, they are still poor.

5 No one who loves money can be
judged innocent; his efforts to get rich
have led him into sin.[b] 6 Many people
have been ruined because of money,
brought face-to-face with disaster.
7 Money is a trap for those who are fascinated by it, a trap that every fool falls
into.

8 A person who gets rich without sinfully chasing after money is fortunate.
9 Do you know anyone like that? If so,
we will congratulate him for performing
a miracle that no one else has ever been
able to do. 10 If anyone has ever passed
this test, he can well be proud. Has anyone ever known that he could get away
with cheating someone, and not taken
advantage of it? 11 If so, he deserves his
wealth, and everyone will praise him for
his generosity.

Behavior at Dinner Parties

12 When you sit down at a fancy banquet, don't let your mouth hang open,
and don't say, "Look at all that food!"
13 It is impolite to have a greedy eye; remember that. Nothing in creation is
greedier than the eye; that is why it
sheds tears so often.[c] 14 Don't reach out
for everything you see, and don't elbow
people out of the way to get at the food.
15 Be considerate of the other people at
the table and treat them the way you
want to be treated. 16 When you get your
food, eat it like a human being. Don't

[x] will have . . . wounds; *or* is going to be hurt. [y] *Hebrew* a cheerful attitude; *Greek* a strong body. [z] *Hebrew* offered to an idol; *Greek* placed on a grave. [a] *Hebrew* Worrying about business; *Greek* Sleepless worry. [b] *Hebrew* have . . . sin; *Greek* will destroy him. [c] *Hebrew* so often; *Greek* on every face.

smack and slurp; nobody can stand that.
17 It's good manners to be the first to stop
eating; stuffing yourself is offensive. 18 If
there are many people present, don't try
to be the first to be served. 19 A little bit
is plenty for anyone with good manners.
Besides, you won't be short of breath
when you go to bed. 20 People who eat
too much get stomach aches and cannot
sleep. If you don't overeat, you can get a
good night's sleep and wake up early the
next morning feeling fine. 21 But if you
do get a stomach ache from eating too
much, go off and vomit[d] and you will
feel better. 22 My child, if you listen to
what I am saying and put it into practice,
one of these days you will thank me for
it. Be moderate[e] in everything you do,
and you will never get sick.

23 People appreciate a generous host,
and he deserves their praise. 24 But
everybody in town will complain about a
host who is stingy with food, and their
complaints are justified.

25 Don't try to prove your manhood by
how much you can drink. Wine has been
the ruin of many. 26 An arrogant person's character shows through when he
is in a drunken argument, in the same
way that iron is tested when it is heated
red-hot and then dipped in water.
27 Wine can put new life into you if you
drink it in moderation. What would life
be like without it? Wine was created to
make us happy. 28 If you drink it in moderation and at the right time, it can lift
your spirits and make you cheerful,
29 but if you drink when you are angry
and upset, it leads to headaches, embarrassment, and disgrace.[f] 30 A drunken
fool can lose his temper and hurt himself. His drinking makes him weak and
an easy target for angry blows. 31 Never
rebuke a person when you have both
been drinking. Don't hurt his feelings
while he is having a good time. It's not
the time to criticize anyone, or to ask
him to pay back a debt.

32 If you are chosen to preside at a
banquet, don't put on airs. Just
be like everyone else. Look after the
guests before you sit down. 2 After you
have performed your duties, you can sit
down and enjoy yourself with the others. They will respect you for doing a
good job.

3 If you are older than most of the
guests, you may talk; that is your right.
But you should know what you are talking about and not interrupt the music.
4 If entertainment is being provided,
don't keep up a steady conversation; it's
the wrong time to show off your wit.
5 Music at a banquet where wine is
served is like a ruby set in gold. 6 Good
music and good wine—an emerald set in
gold.

7 If you are young, don't speak unless
you have to, but never more than twice,
and only if someone speaks to you first.
8 Come to the point and say it all in a
few words. Show that you are well-
informed, but stay quiet. 9 Don't treat important people as if you were their equal
and don't make a nuisance of yourself
by asking them a lot of questions.[g]
10 The reputation of a modest person
goes before him, as lightning before
thunder.

11 Leave the party at the right time and
never be the last to go. Don't linger at
the door; just go straight home. 12 There
you can enjoy yourself as you wish, but
don't commit the sin of bragging. 13 And
don't forget to thank your Creator for
letting you enjoy so many good things.

Interpreting the Law

14 If you fear the Lord, you will accept
his correction. He will bless those who
get up early in the morning to pray.
15 Study his Law, and you will master it,
unless you are insincere about it, in
which case you will fail. 16 If you fear the
Lord, you will know what is right, and
you will be famous for your fairness.
17 Sinners have no use for correction,
and will interpret the Law to suit themselves.

18 Sensible people will consider every
opinion, but arrogant[h] people will let
nothing stand in their way. 19 Never do
anything without thinking it through,
and once you have done something,
don't look back and wish you had done
something else. 20 Don't take a course of
action that is dangerous, and don't make

[d] go off and vomit; *some manuscripts have* get up in the middle of the meal. [e] *Hebrew* moderate; *Greek* industrious. [f] *Hebrew* when you are . . . disgrace; *Greek* too much, it leads to bitterness, offense, and stumbling. [g] *Hebrew* make . . . questions; *Greek* keep talking when someone else is speaking. [h] *Hebrew* arrogant; *Greek* foreign and arrogant.

the same mistake twice.[i] 21 Don't be too
sure of yourself, even when the way
looks easy. 22 Always watch where you
are going.[j] 23 Whatever you do be careful;[k] this is keeping the Lord's
commands.
24 Believing in the Law means keeping
the Lord's commands.
If you trust the Lord, you cannot lose.
33 1 No evil will ever come to a person who fears the Lord; however
often danger comes, the Lord will come
to the rescue. 2 A person who has no use
for the Law doesn't have good sense,
and anyone who is insincere about it is
going to be tossed about like a boat in a
storm. 3 If you are wise, you will believe
in the Law; you will find it as reliable as
the sacred lots.
4 Prepare what you are going to say
and people will listen to you. Use what
you have learned before you start talking. 5 A foolish person's mind works like
a cartwheel, going round and round in
circles. 6 A sarcastic friend is like a wild
horse that neighs no matter who tries to
ride him.

People Are Not Alike

7 Why are some days holier than others, even though the same sun rises on
every day of the year? 8 It is because the
Lord made them different by setting
them apart as religious holidays and festivals. 9 He made some days holy and important, and made other days ordinary.
10 Every human being was made from
the earth, just as Adam was. 11 But the
Lord, in his wisdom, made them all different and gave them different tasks.
12 He blessed some, making them honored and holy, keeping them near him.
Others he cursed, humbling them and
removing them from their positions.
13 Just as clay is in the potter's hands for
him to shape as he pleases, so we are in
the hands of our Creator for him to do
with as he wishes.
14 Good is the opposite of evil, life is
the opposite of death, and sin is the opposite of devotion to the Lord. 15 Think
about it: the Most High has made everything in pairs, each thing the opposite of
something else.
16 As for me, I have been the last to
come on duty, as if going through vineyards to gather whatever the grape-
pickers had left behind. But the Lord
blessed me, and I did well,[l] like a
grape-picker who has filled the wine
press. 17 But I want you to know that I
have not done all this work for myself
alone, but for everyone who wants to
learn. 18 Listen to me, all you great leaders! All you leaders of the assemblies,
hear what I have to say!

Be Independent

19 Never, as long as you live, give anyone power over you—whether son, wife,
brother, or friend. Don't give your property to anyone; you might change your
mind and have to ask for it back. 20 As
long as you have breath in your body,
don't let anyone lead your life for you.
21 It is better that your children be dependent on you than the other way
around. 22 Keep control over all that you
do; don't let anything stain your reputation. 23 Wait until the last moment of
your life, when you are breathing your
last, and then divide your property
among your heirs.

Treatment of Slaves

24 A donkey should be given its fodder
and its burden, and it should be beaten.
A slave should be given food and work,
and should be disciplined. 25 If you make
your slave work, you can set your mind
at ease. If you don't keep him busy, he
will be looking for freedom. 26 You can
use a harness and yoke to tame an animal, and a slave can be tortured in the
stocks. 27 Keep him at work, and don't let
him be idle; idleness can only teach him
how to make trouble. 28 Work is what he
needs. If he won't obey you, put him in
chains.
29 But don't be too severe with anyone,
and never be unfair. 30 If you have a
slave, treat him as you would want to be
treated; you bought him with your hard-
earned money. 31 Treat him as a brother;
you need him as you need yourself. If
you mistreat him and he runs away,
where are you going to look for him?

[i] *Hebrew* make . . . twice; *Greek* stumble on stones. [j] *Hebrew* watch . . . going; *Greek* look out for your children. [k] *Hebrew* be careful; *Greek* have confidence in yourself. [l] did well; *or* overtook the others.

Dreams Mean Nothing

34 Foolish people are deceived by
vain hopes, and dreams get them
all excited. 2 A person who pays any attention at all to dreams is like someone
who tries to catch shadows or chase the
wind. 3 What you see in a dream is no
more real than the reflection of your
face in a mirror. 4 What is unreal can no
more produce something real than what
is dirty can produce something clean.
5 Dreams, divination, and omens are all
nonsense. You see in them only what
you want to see.[m] 6 Unless the Most
High has sent you the dream, pay no attention to it. 7 Dreams have misled many
people; they put their faith in them, only
to be disappointed. 8 The Law is complete without such falsehood. Wisdom,
as spoken by the righteous, is also complete without it.

Travel

9 A well-traveled[n] person with wide
experience knows many things and
talks sense. 10 You can't know much if
you haven't experienced much, but
travel can make you more clever.
11 In my own travels I have seen many
things and learned more than I can
put into words. 12 I have been in danger
of death many times, but I have always
been able to escape by relying on past
experience.

Fear the Lord

13 Those who fear the Lord will live,
because they have put their trust in the
one who can save them. 14 Fear the Lord,
and you will have nothing else to fear. If
your trust is in him, you will never act
like a coward. 15 People who fear the
Lord are fortunate, because they know
where they can look for help. 16 The Lord
watches over those who love him; he is
their strong protection and firm support.
He shelters them from the heat, shades
them from the noonday sun, and keeps
them from stumbling and falling. 17 He
makes them cheerful and puts a sparkle
in their eyes. He blesses them with life
and health.

Offering Sacrifices

18 If you offer as a sacrifice an animal
that you have obtained dishonestly, it is
defective and unacceptable. 19 The Most
High gets no pleasure from sacrifices
made by ungodly people; no amount of
sacrifices can make up for their sins.
20 Anyone who steals an animal from the
poor to offer as a sacrifice is like someone who kills a boy before his father's
eyes. 21 Food means life itself to poor
people, and taking it away from them is
murder. 22 It is murder to deprive someone of his living or to cheat an employee
of his wages.
23 When one person builds and somebody else tears down, has anything been
accomplished but hard work? 24 When
one person blesses and somebody else
curses, which one is the Lord going to
listen to? 25 If you touch a dead body and
then purify yourself by washing, but
then go and touch it again, what good
did the washing do? 26 If you fast because of your sins, and then go out and
commit the same sins over again, what
have you gained by going without food?
Who do you think is going to listen to
your prayers?

35 Keeping the Law is worth many
offerings; it is a fellowship offering in itself. 2 Returning a kindness is
like a grain offering; giving to the poor is
like a thanksgiving offering. 3 Keeping
away from sin will please the Lord and
make atonement for sin. 4 But don't
come to the Temple without an offering;
5 the Law requires that you bring one.
6 When someone righteous offers a sacrifice and the fat drips down on the altar,
a pleasant smell rises to the Most High.
7 The Lord will accept the offerings
made by a righteous person and will not
forget them. 8 Praise the Lord by making
generous offerings to him; don't be
stingy with the first of your crops. 9 Be
cheerful with every gift you make, and
when you pay your tithes, do it gladly.
10 Give to the Most High as he has given
to you, just as generously as you can.
11 The Lord always repays and will do it
many times over. 12 But don't try to bribe
him or rely on offerings that you have
obtained dishonestly. He will not accept
them.

[m] *Probable text* You see . . . to see; *Greek* The mind has an imagination like a woman in labor.
[n] A well-traveled; *some manuscripts have* An educated.

God's Justice

The Lord is fair[o] and does not show
partiality. 13 He is not prejudiced against
the poor; when someone prays who has
been wronged, the Lord listens. 14 When
orphans and widows pour out their
prayers, he does not ignore them. 15 The
tears running down a widow's cheek cry
out in accusation against the one who
has caused her distress.

16 Serve the Lord willingly, and the
Lord will accept you; your prayers will
reach the skies. 17 The prayer of a humble person goes past the clouds and
keeps on going until it reaches the Lord
Most High, where it stays until he answers by seeing that justice is done and
that the guilty are punished.

18 And the Lord will act quickly. He
will show no patience with wicked people. He will take vengeance by crushing
the heathen. He will completely wipe out
the merciless and the arrogant, and will
destroy the authority of the wicked.
19 He will give each of us what our
thoughts and actions deserve. Because
of the Lord's mercy, his people will be
happy when he has judged their case.
20 In times of trouble his mercy is as welcome as rain after a long drought.

A Prayer for Israel

36 O Lord God of the universe, look
upon us and have mercy. 2 Make
every nation stand in fear of you. 3 Take
action against the foreign nations, and
let them witness your power! 4 You have
used us to show them how holy you are;
now use them to show us how great you
are. 5 Let them learn, as we have learned,
that there is no God, O Lord, but you.
6 Give new signs, perform new miracles;
show us your glorious strength! 7-9 Bring
on that appointed time when everyone
can talk about the great things you do.
Pour out your furious, flaming anger,
and let none of our enemies survive. Destroy those who have oppressed your
people. 10 Crush all those enemy rulers
who think they are the only people in the
world who matter! 11 Gather the tribes of
Israel together again, and give them
back their land as you gave it to them
long ago. 12 Lord, have mercy on Israel,
the people who are known by your
name, whom you called your first-born
son. 13 Take pity on Jerusalem, your holy
city, where you chose to stay. 14 Fill your
Temple[p] on Mount Zion with your glory
and with hymns of praise. 15 Testify for
your people, whom you created in the
beginning; fulfill the prophecies that
have been spoken in your name. 16 Reward those who have put their faith in
you, and vindicate your prophets. 17 You
have always been gracious to your people;[q] listen to your servants as we pray.
Then everyone on earth will recognize
that you are the Lord, the God of the
ages.

Choosing a Wife

18 Any kind of food can be eaten, but
some foods are better than others. 19 And
just as the tongue can distinguish the fla-
vors of different kinds of meat, so a
sharp mind can detect lies. 20 A person
with a warped mind causes trouble, but
an experienced person knows how to
pay it back.

21 A woman has to take any man as a
husband, but a man must choose his
wife carefully. 22 A woman's beauty
makes a man happy; there is no fairer
sight for the human eye to see. 23 If the
woman is kind and gentle in her speech,
her husband is the most fortunate of
men. 24 When a man marries, he gets the
finest thing he will ever have—a wife to
help and encourage him.

25 If property is not fenced in, thieves
will wander in and help themselves. And
if a man has no wife, he is a sighing wanderer; 26 people have no more trust in a
homeless person who sleeps in a different place every night than they have in a
wandering thief who goes from town to
town.

False Friends

37 Anyone can claim to be your
friend, but some people are
friends in name only. 2 The grief caused
when a close friendship turns sour is as
bad as death. 3 This evil impulse we
have! Why was it ever formed? How did
it manage to cover the earth with deceit?
4 Some people will be your friend as long
as things are going well, but they will
turn against you when trouble comes.

[o] *Hebrew* fair; *Greek* judge. [p] *Hebrew* Temple; *Greek* people. [q] *Hebrew* You have . . . people; *Greek* According to the blessing of Aaron on your people.

5 A real[r] friend will help you against your enemies[s] and protect you in the fight. 6 Never forget such companions in battle;[t] share the results of your victory with them.

Caution in Taking Advice

7 Anyone can give advice, but some people do so only in their own interest. 8 Be careful when somebody offers you advice. Find out first what his interest in the matter is, because you can be sure that he is thinking primarily of himself. Why should he come out on top instead of you?[u] 9 He will assure you that things look good, and then stand back to watch what happens to you.

10 Don't ask advice of anyone who doesn't trust you, and don't give advice to anyone who is jealous of you.

11 Don't ask a woman for advice about a rival of hers,
a coward about war,
a merchant about a bargain,
a buyer about selling,
a stingy person about gratitude,
a cruel person about kindness,
a lazy person about work,
a casual worker about finishing a job,
a lazy slave about a difficult task.
Pay no attention to any advice they may give.

12 Instead, rely on someone who is religious and known to keep the Lord's commands, someone who is sympathetic with you, who will be sorry to see you fail. 13 And trust your own judgment; no one's advice is more reliable. 14 Sometimes your own intuition can tell you more than seven watchmen on a high tower. 15 Above all, pray to the Most High that he will show you the right thing to do.

Wisdom and Confidence

16 Planning and thought lie behind everything that is done. 17-18 The mind concerns itself with four things: these are good and evil, life and death. They all begin in the mind,[v] but the tongue is their absolute ruler.

19 Someone may have the ability to teach, but still not be of much use to himself. 20 He may be clever with words, but end up starving because people hate him. 21 This may happen if he doesn't have good sense, if the Lord has not given him tact. 22 Someone may consider himself wise and let you know that he is certain about what he knows. 23 Anyone who really is wise will be the teacher of his people, and they can be certain that what he teaches is the truth. 24 Everyone will praise such a person and speak of him as fortunate. 25 A person's life has only a limited number of days, but the life of Israel cannot be measured in days at all. 26 The wise will win the confidence of others, and will be remembered forever.

Controlling the Appetite

27 My child, as you go through life, keep your appetite under control, and don't eat anything that you know is bad for you. 28 All food doesn't agree with everyone, and everyone doesn't like the same kinds of food. 29 Don't feel that you just have to have all sorts of fancy food, and don't be a glutton over any food. 30 If you eat too much, you'll get sick; if you do it all the time, you'll always have stomach trouble. 31 Gluttony has been the death of many people. Avoid it and live longer.

Sickness and Medicine

38 Give doctors the honor they deserve, for the Lord gave them their work to do.[w] 2 Their skill came from the Most High, and kings reward them for it. 3 Their knowledge gives them a position of importance, and powerful people hold them in high regard.

4 The Lord created medicines from the earth, and a sensible person will not hesitate to use them. 5 Didn't a tree once make bitter water fit to drink, so that the Lord's power[x] might be known? 6 He gave medical knowledge to human beings, so that we would praise him for the miracles he performs. 7-8 The druggist mixes these medicines, and the doctor will use them to cure diseases and ease pain. There is no end to the activities of

[r] *Hebrew* real; *Greek does not have this word.* [s] *Hebrew* against your enemies; *Greek* hoping to get a meal. [t] *Hebrew* in battle; *Greek* in your soul. [u] *Hebrew* Why . . . you?; *Greek* He may use his influence against you. [v] *Hebrew* The mind . . . the mind; *Greek* There are four things that show the changes of the heart: good and evil, life and death. [w] *Hebrew* gave them their work to do; *Greek* created them. [x] the Lord's power; *or* its healing properties.

the Lord, who gives health to the people
of the world.
9 My child, when you get sick, don't ignore it. Pray to the Lord, and he will
make you well. 10 Confess all your sins
and determine that in the future you will
live a righteous life. 11 Offer incense and
a grain offering, as fine as you can afford.[y] 12 Then call the doctor—for the
Lord created him—and keep him at your
side; you need him. 13 There are times
when you have to depend on his skill.
14 The doctor's prayer is that the Lord
will make him able to ease his patients'
pain and make them well again. 15 As for
the person who sins against his Creator,
he deserves to be sick.

Mourning for the Dead

16 My child, when someone dies, you
should mourn. Weep and wail to show
how deeply you feel the loss. Prepare the
body in the proper way, and be present
at the burial. 17 Weep bitterly and pas-
sionately; observe the proper period of
mourning for the person. Mourn for a
whole day or maybe two, to keep people
from talking, but then pull yourself together and reconcile yourself to the loss.
18 Grief can undermine your health and
even lead to your own death. 19 Grief lin-
gers on after the death of a loved one,
but it is not wise to let it lead you into
poverty.
20 Don't lose yourself in sorrow; drive
it away.[z] Remember that we must all
die sometime. 21 There is no way to bring
the dead person back. All your sorrow
does him no good, and it hurts you.
Don't forget that. 22 You will die, just as
he did. Today it was his turn; tomorrow
it will be yours. 23 When the dead have
been laid to rest, let the memory of them
fade. Once they are gone, take courage.

Scholarship and Other Occupations

24 Scholars must have time to study if
they are going to be wise; they must be
relieved of other responsibilities. 25 How
can a farm hand gain knowledge, when
his only ambition is to drive the oxen
and make them work, when all he
knows to talk about is livestock? 26 He
takes great pains to plow a straight fur-
row and will work far into the night to
feed the animals.
27 It is the same with the artist and the
craftsman, who work night and day engraving precious stones, carefully working out new designs. They take great
pains to produce a lifelike image, and
will work far into the night to finish the
work.
28 It is the same with the blacksmith at
his anvil, planning what he will make
from a piece of iron. The heat from the
fire sears his skin as he sweats away at
the forge. The clanging of the hammer
deafens him[a] as he carefully watches
the object he is working take shape. He
takes great pains to complete his task,
and will work far into the night to bring
it to perfection.
29 It is the same with the potter, sitting
at his wheel and turning it with his feet,
always concentrating on his work, concerned with how many objects he can
produce. 30 He works the clay with his
feet until he can shape it with his hands;
then he takes great pains to glaze it
properly, and will work far into the
night to clean out the kiln.
31 All of these people are skilled with
their hands, each of them an expert at
his own craft. 32 Without such people
there could be no cities; no one would
live or visit where these services were
not available. 33 These people are not
sought out to serve on the public coun-
cils, and they never attain positions of
great importance. They do not serve as
judges, and they do not understand legal
matters. They have no education and are
not known for their wisdom. You never
hear them quoting proverbs. 34 But the
work they do holds this world together.
When they do their work, it is the same
as offering prayer.[b]

39 But it is different with the person
who devotes himself to studying
the Law of the Most High. He examines
the wisdom of all the ancient writers and
concerns himself with the prophecies.
2 He memorizes the sayings of famous
men and is a skilled interpreter of parables. 3 He studies the hidden meaning of
proverbs and is able to discuss the obscure points of parables. 4 Great people
call on him for his services, and he is

[y] *Hebrew* as fine as you can afford; *Greek unclear.* [z] drive it away; *or* put the memory of the person aside. [a] *Probable text* deafens him; *Greek* renews his ears. [b] When . . . prayer; *or* When they pray, it is about their work.

seen in the company of rulers. He travels
to foreign lands in his efforts to learn
about human good and evil.
5 It is his
practice to get up early and pray aloud
to the Lord his Creator, asking the Most
High to forgive his sins.
6 Then, if the
great Lord is willing, he will be filled
with understanding. He will pour out a
stream of wise sayings, and give thanks
to the Lord in prayer.
7 He will have
knowledge to share and good advice to
give, as well as insight into the Lord's
secrets.
8 He will demonstrate his learning in what he teaches,[c] and his pride
will be in the Lord's Law and covenant.
9 He will be widely praised for his wisdom, and it will never be lost, because
people for generations to come will remember him.
10 The Gentiles will talk
about his wisdom, and he will be praised
aloud in the assembly.
11 If he lives to old
age, he will die famous, but if he is laid
to rest before he is famous, he will be
content.[d]

A Hymn in Praise of God

12 Like the moon, I am full—full of
more ideas to be discussed.
13 Listen to
me, you devout children of mine, and
blossom like a rosebush on a stream
bank.
14 Bloom like a sweet-smelling lily,
and send your fragrance into the air like
incense. Sing the Lord's praises, and
thank him for all that he has done.
15 Proclaim his glory in grateful praise!
To the music of the harp, sing this song:

16 All that the Lord has done is very
good;
all that he commands is sooner
or later done.
17 No one should ask why things are
as they are;
these questions will be answered
at the right time.
He commanded, and the water
piled up high,
great walls of water arose when
he spoke.
18 Whatever he commands is
promptly done;
there are no limits to his power
to save.
19 He sees all that every human
being does;
there is no way to hide from his
sight.
20 He sees the whole of time, from
beginning to end,
and nothing takes him by
surprise.[e]
21 No one should ask why things are
as they are;
everything in creation has its
purpose.

22 His blessings overflow like the
Nile,
enriching the world in a fertile
flood.[f]
23 He turns fresh water into salt
water,
and he turns his anger on the
nations.
24 For the devout, his ways are
straight;
for the wicked, they are laid
with traps.
25 From the beginning he has made
good things for the good
and terrible things for sinners.
26 The basic needs of life are these:
water, fire, iron, and salt,
flour, honey, and milk,
wine, clothing, and oil.
27 All these things are good for those
who are devout,
but they turn into evils for
sinners.

28 There are winds that were created
to bring punishment,
fierce enough to move
mountains.[g]
In times of judgment, they unleash
their strength
and calm the anger of their
maker.
29-30 Vicious animals, scorpions, and
snakes;
the sword that destroys the
wicked;
fire, hail, famine, and disease;
these have all been created as
punishments.
31 They are all glad to obey the
Lord's command

[c] his learning . . . teaches; *or* the wisdom of what he has been taught. [d] if he is . . . content; *Greek unclear.* [e] takes him by surprise; *or* is too marvelous for him. [f] *Hebrew* overflow . . . flood; *Greek* cover the dry land like a river and drench it like a flood. [g] *Hebrew* move mountains; *Greek* lash heavily.

and are ready to serve him here
on earth.
When their times of duty come,
they never disobey.
(32 I was long convinced of this, so after
thinking it over I put[h] it in writing.)
33 Everything made by the Lord is
good;
he meets every need at the
proper time.
34 No one can claim that some things
are worse than others,
for everything is good in its
proper place.
35 Now then, sing praises with all
your heart,
and praise the name of the Lord!

The Misery of Human Life

40 Every person has been given a
great deal of work to do. A heavy
burden lies on all of us from the day of
our birth until the day we go back to the
earth, the mother of us all. 2 We are confused and fearful, dreading the day of
our death—3-4 all of us from the king on
his splendid throne wearing royal robes
and a crown, to the humblest person
dressed in burlap and living in poverty.
5 All through our lives we meet anger,
jealousy, and trouble. Things disturb us;
we live with furious conflicts and with
the fear of death. Even when we go to
bed, we think up new troubles in our
sleep. 6 We get little rest, if any at all.
When we sleep, it is as if we were
awake, disturbed by our imaginations. If
we dream that we are running from an
enemy, 7 just as we are about to be
caught,[i] we wake up and are relieved to
find there is nothing to be afraid of.
8 Here is what all creatures, both human and animal, must face (but it is
seven times worse for sinners): 9 death,
violence, conflict, murder, disaster, famine, sickness, epidemic. 10 All these
things were created because of the
wicked; they are the ones who have
caused destruction.[j] 11 Everything that
comes from the earth goes back to the
earth, just as all water flows into the sea.

The Results of Evil

12 Nothing that comes from bribery or
injustice will last, but the effects of loyalty will remain forever. 13 Wealth that
has been obtained dishonestly is like a
stream that runs full during a thunderstorm, 14 tumbling rocks along as it
flows, but then suddenly goes dry.[k]
15 The children of ungodly people will
not leave large families; they are like
plants trying to take root on rock, 16 like
reeds along a river bank, withering[l] before any other plant. 17 Acts of kindness
and charity are as lasting as eternity.[m]

The Joys of Human Life

18 Being independently wealthy or
working for a living—both can make
life pleasant, but it is better to find a
treasure.
19 Your name can be preserved if you
have children or if you establish a city,
but finding Wisdom is a better way.
Owning livestock and orchards will
make you famous,[n] but it is better to
have a wife you love.[o]
20 Wine and music can make you
happy, but a happy marriage[p] is even
better.
21 Flutes and harps make fine music,
but a pleasant voice is better than either.
22 Gracefulness and beauty please the
eye, but not as much as new growth in
the spring.
23 You can't go wrong with a good
friend or neighbor, but an intelligent
wife is[q] better than either.
24 Relatives and helpers are good to
have in times of trouble, but it will be an
even greater help if you have made a
practice of giving to the poor.
25 Gold and silver provide security, but
good advice is better.
26 Wealth and strength give confidence, but the fear of the Lord can give
you even greater confidence. When you
fear the Lord you need nothing more; it
is all the support you need. 27 The fear of
the Lord is like a rich garden of blessings; you could not want a more glorious
shelter.

[h] put; *or* left. [i] *Probable text* caught; *Greek* rescued. [j] *Hebrew* have caused destruction; *Greek* caused the flood. [k] *Verses 13-14 are translated from Hebrew; verse 14 in Greek is unclear.* [l] *Hebrew* withering; *Greek* pulled up. [m] *Hebrew* Acts . . . eternity; *Greek* Kindness is a blessed garden, and charity lasts forever. [n] *Hebrew* but finding Wisdom . . . famous; *Greek does not have these words.* [o] *Hebrew* wife you love; *Greek* blameless wife. [p] *Hebrew* a happy marriage; *Greek* the love of Wisdom. [q] *Hebrew* an intelligent wife is; *Greek* a wife and a husband are.

Begging

28 My child, don't live the life of a beggar; it is better to die than to beg. 29 If
you have to depend on someone else for
your food, you are not really living your
own life. You pollute yourself by accepting food from another. Begging is torture to the soul of any sensitive person.[r]
30 A shameless person can make begging sound sweet, but something inside
him burns.

Death

41 Death! The very thought of it is
bitter to someone who is prosperous, living peacefully with his possessions, free of worries, and still able to
enjoy his food.
2 Death! Its sentence is welcome to
someone living in poverty, with failing
health, very old, burdened with worries,
blind, and without hope.[s]
3 Do not be afraid of death's decree.
Remember that it came to those before
you and will come to those after you.
4 The Lord has decreed it for every living
creature. Who are you to object to what
the Most High wishes? In the world
of the dead no one will care whether
you lived ten years, a hundred, or a
thousand.

The Fate of the Wicked

5 The children of sinners, brought up
in ungodly surroundings, turn out to be
hateful people. 6 They will lose whatever
they inherit, and their own descendants
will live in permanent disgrace. 7 The
children will put the blame for their disgrace on their ungodly parents.
8 You are doomed, you irreligious people who have abandoned the Law of the
Most High God. 9 When you have children, disaster will strike them and you
will be left with nothing but sorrow.
There will be great joy whenever you
stumble,[t] and even after your death you
will be cursed. 10 What comes into being
from nothing[u] will return to nothing;[u]
so it will be with the godless, doomed to
extinction.
11 A person's body amounts to nothing,[v] but a good reputation will last forever. 12 Protect your reputation; it will
outlive you and last longer than a thousand treasures of gold. 13 A good life
lasts only so long, but a good reputation
will last forever.

A Sense of Decency

14 My children, do as I teach you and
live at peace. Wisdom that is not expressed is like a treasure that has been
hidden—both are useless. 15 A person
who covers up his foolishness is better
than one who keeps his wisdom to
himself.
16 My children, listen and I will teach
you the circumstances when it is proper
to be ashamed.[w] Sometimes it is entirely
out of place.

17 Before your parents, be ashamed
of immoral behavior.
Before a ruler or an important
person, be ashamed of a lie.
18 Before a judge, be ashamed of
criminal behavior.
Before a public assembly, be
ashamed of breaking the law.
Before a friend or partner, be
ashamed of dishonesty.
19 Before your neighbors, be
ashamed of theft.
Be ashamed of breaking a
promise,[x]
of leaning on the dinner table
with your elbows,
of stinginess when you are
asked for something,
20 of not returning a greeting,
of staring at a prostitute,
of turning down a relative's
request,
of depriving someone of what
is rightly his,
of staring at another man's
wife,
22 of playing around with his
slave woman (keep away
from her bed!)
of insulting your friends,
of following up your gifts
with criticism,
23 of betraying secrets.

[r] *Hebrew* Begging . . . person; *Greek* An intelligent and understanding person will avoid it.
[s] *Hebrew* blind, and without hope; *Greek* rebellious and without patience. [t] *Hebrew* When you have . . . stumble; *Greek* You are born under a curse. [u] Hebrew nothing; *Greek* earth. [v] *Hebrew* A person's . . . nothing; *Greek* The death of a person's body is mourned. [w] *Hebrew* My children . . . ashamed; *Greek* Show respect for what I say.
[x] *Hebrew* of breaking a promise; *Greek* of yourself before the truth of God.

These are times when it is proper for you
to be ashamed, and people will respect
you for it.

A Sense of Pride

42 On the other hand, it is possible
to sin by giving in to other people too much. Here are some things you
should not be ashamed of:

2 the Law of the Most High and his
covenant,
judging even godless people fairly,
3 sharing expenses with a business
partner or a traveling
companion,
sharing an inheritance,
4 using accurate weights and
measures,
5 making a profit, whether great or
small,
bargaining with a merchant,
disciplining your children often,
beating a disloyal slave until the
blood flows.

6 It is wise to lock things up if you cannot trust your wife or if too many people
are around. 7 Keep an accurate record of
any deposits you make or of anything
you give or receive. 8 Don't hesitate to
correct someone who is acting foolishly
or an old man who goes around with
prostitutes. All of this is worthwhile advice, and if you follow it, everyone will
approve of your behavior.

Fathers and Daughters

9 Although he will not let his daughter
know it, a father will lie awake at night
worrying about her. If she is young, he
worries that she might not get married.
If she is already married, he worries
about her happiness. 10 If she is a virgin,
he worries that she might be seduced
and become pregnant while living in his
house. If she is married, he worries that
she might be unfaithful, or that she
might not be able to have children.

11 Keep a close watch over your
daughter if she is determined to have her
own way. If you don't, she may make a
fool of you in front of your enemies. You
will be a constant joke to everyone in
town, a public disgrace. Make sure that
her room has no windows or any place
where she can look out to the entrance
of the house.[y] 12 Don't let her show off
her beauty in front of men, or spend
her time talking with the women.[z]
13 Women hurt other women just as
moths damage clothing.

14 A man's wickedness is better than a
woman's goodness; women bring shame
and disgrace.

The Glory of God in Nature

15 Now I will remind you of the
works of the Lord
and describe the things I have
seen.
The words of the Lord brought his
works into being,
and the whole creation obeys his
commands.
16 The light of the sun shines down
on everything,
and everything is filled with the
Lord's glory.
17 Not even to his holy angels has
the Lord given power
to describe all his mighty deeds,
even though he has given them
power
to stand unharmed in his
glorious presence.[a]
18 He sees into the oceans and into
the human heart,
and he knows the secrets of
both.
The Most High knows everything
that can be known
and understands the signs of
the ages.
19 He knows all that has ever been
and all that ever will be;
he uncovers the deepest of
mysteries.
20 He takes notice of our every
thought
and hears our every word.
21 The orderly world shows the
greatness of his wisdom;
he is the same forever and
ever.[b]
Nothing can be added to him, and
nothing taken away;
he needs no one to give him
advice.
22 All his works are beautiful,

[y] *Hebrew* Make sure . . . house; *Greek does not have these words.* [z] *Hebrew* Don't let . . . women; *Greek unclear.* [a] *Hebrew* even though . . . presence; *Greek* which the Lord Almighty established so that everything may stand firm in his glory. [b] *Hebrew* he is . . . ever; *Greek* he is before eternity and is eternal.

down to the smallest and
faintest spark of light.[c]
23 All these things go on forever,
and all of them have their
purpose.
24 All things are in pairs, each the
opposite of the other,
but nothing the Lord made is
incomplete.
25 Everything completes the
goodness of something else.
Could anyone ever see enough
of this splendor?

43 How beautiful is the bright,
clear sky above us!
What a glorious sight it is!
2 The sun, when it appears,
proclaims as it rises
how marvelous a thing it is,
made by the Most High.
3 At noon it dries up the land;
no one can stand its blazing
heat.
4 The setting sun sets fire to the
hilltops,
like a metal furnace glowing
from the heat.[d]
It sends out fiery rays,
blinding the eyes with its
brightness.
5 The Lord, who made it, is great;
it speeds on its way at his
command.

6 There is also the moon, marking
the passage of time,[e]
an eternal sign of the changing
seasons.
7 The moon determines the holy
days.
Its light grows full and then
grows dim.
8 The "month" is named after the
moon,
marvelous to watch as it grows
fuller each night,
a signal light for the heavenly
armies,
shining out in the dome of
the sky.
9 The shining stars make the night
sky lovely,
brilliant ornaments in the Lord's
high heavens.
10 They stay in the places assigned to
them by the Holy One
and never relax their dutiful
watch.

11 Look at the rainbow and praise its
Creator!
How magnificent, how radiant,
its beauty!
12 Like a bow bent by the hands of
the Most High,
it spans the horizon in a circle
of glory.

13 He commands, and snow begins
to fall;
lightning strikes to carry out his
judgments.
14 The storerooms of the sky are
thrown open,
and the clouds roll out like
flying birds.
15 With his power he forms great
masses of clouds
and shatters the ice into
hailstones.
16-17 He speaks, and thunder twists the
earth in pain;
the mountains are shaken by his
strength.[f]
Whenever he wishes, the south
wind blows,
whirlwinds come, and
windstorms from the north.
He sends the snow fluttering down
like birds,
like locusts lighting on the
ground.
18 We marvel at its beautiful
whiteness,
and in fascination we watch it
fall.
19 He sprinkles frost over the ground
like salt,
and it freezes into thorny
flowers of ice.[g]
20 He sends the cold north wind
blowing
and the water hardens into ice;
every lake and pond freezes over,
putting on a coat of icy armor.

[c] *Hebrew* down to . . . spark of light; *Greek unclear.* [d] *Hebrew* The setting . . . heat; *Greek* A man at a furnace works with scorching heat, but the sun burns the hills three times as much. [e] *Hebrew* marking . . . time; *Greek unclear.* [f] *Hebrew* by his strength; *Greek* when he appears. [g] *Hebrew* flowers of ice; *Greek* points.

21 He scorches the wilderness hills
with drought,
and the grass turns brown from
its heat;
22 but a cloudy mist restores it all
to life
as the weather cools and dew
appears.

23 By his wisdom he calmed the
great oceans
and placed the islands there.
24 Sailors tell about the dangers of
the sea,
and we listen to their tales in
amazement.
25 In the sea are strange and
marvelous creatures:
huge monsters and all kinds of
living things.
26 Each of the Lord's messengers
succeeds at its task.
Everything is held together by
his word.

27 We could say much more and
never finish,
but it all means this: the Lord is
everything.
28 How can we find the power to
praise him?
He is greater than all his
creation.
29 The Lord is awesome in his
greatness;
his power is overwhelming.
30 Though you do your best to
praise him,
he is greater than you can ever
express.
Though you honor him tirelessly
and with all your strength,
you still cannot praise him
enough.
31 No one has seen him, no one can
describe him;
no one can praise him as he
deserves.
32 Mysteries greater than these are
still unknown;
we know only a fraction of his
works.
33 The Lord made the universe
and then gave wisdom to devout
people.

The Glory of God in History

44 So let us now give praise to
godly[h] men,
our ancestors of generations
past,
2 those whom the Lord honored
with great glory,
in whom his greatness has been
seen
from the beginning of time.
3 There were some who ruled
kingdoms,
and some who were known for
their strength.
Some were wise advisers,
and some spoke prophecies.
4 There were statesmen whose
policies governed the people,
rulers who issued decrees,[i]
scholars who spoke wise
words,[j]
and those who used pointed
proverbs,[k]
5 poets, and composers of music,
6 rich and powerful men living
peacefully at home.
7 All of these were famous in their
own times,
honored by the people of
their day.
8 Some of them left a reputation,
and people still praise them
today.
9 There are others who are not
remembered,
as if they had never lived,
who died and were forgotten,
they, and their children after
them.

10 But we will praise these
godly men,
whose righteous deeds have
never been forgotten.
11 Their reputations will be passed
on to their descendants,
and this will be their
inheritance.[l]
12 Their descendants continue to
keep the covenant
and always will, because of what
their ancestors did.
13 Their family line will go on
forever,

[h] *Hebrew* godly; *Greek* famous. [i] *Probable Hebrew text* rulers who issued decrees; *Greek unclear.* [j] *Hebrew* scholars ... words; *Greek unclear.* [k] *Hebrew* and those ... proverbs; *Greek does not have these words.* [l] *Verse 11 in Greek is unclear.*

and their fame will never fade.
14 Their bodies were laid to rest,
but their reputations will live
forever.
15 Nations will tell about their
wisdom,
and God's people will praise
them.

Enoch

16 Enoch pleased the Lord and was
taken up into heaven. He became an inspiration for repentance for all time to
come.

Noah

17 Noah was a perfectly righteous man.
After destruction came, he gave the human race a new start.[m] Because of him
there were people left on earth when the
flood was over. 18 The Lord made an
eternal covenant with him, promising
that life would never again be destroyed
by a flood.

Abraham

19 Abraham was the great ancestor of
many nations; his reputation was faultless.[n] 20 He kept the Law of the Most
High and made a covenant with him, a
covenant marked on his body. When he
was put to the test, he was found faithful. 21 And so the Lord made him a solemn promise that his descendants would
be a blessing to the world; that their
number would be countless, like the dust
of the earth; that they would be honored
more than any other people on earth;
and that their land would extend from
sea to sea, from the Euphrates to the
ends of the earth.

Isaac and Jacob

22-23 The Lord renewed that covenant
with Isaac, and then again with Jacob,
repeating the promise that Abraham's
descendants would be a blessing to the
whole human race. The Lord assured Jacob that he would bless him; he gave
him the land that would be his, dividing
it into twelve parts, one for each of the
tribes.

Moses

45 From Jacob's descendants the
Lord raised up a godly man who
won the favor of everyone, loved by God
and people alike. This man was Moses,
whose very memory is a blessing. 2 The
Lord made him as glorious as the angels
and made his enemies fear him. 3 There
in Egypt at his command the disaster
struck.[o] The Lord made kings hold him
in respect. The Lord gave him his commands for his people and showed him
the dazzling light of his presence. 4 The
Lord chose Moses out of the whole human race and consecrated him because
of his loyalty and humility. 5 He let him
hear his voice and led him into the dark
cloud, where, face-to-face, he gave him
the commandments, the Law that gives
life and knowledge, so that Moses might
teach the covenant regulations to the Israelites.

Aaron

6 The Lord raised up Aaron, a holy
man like his brother Moses, of the tribe
of Levi. 7 He made an eternal covenant
with him, giving him the privilege of
serving as priest to the Lord's people. He
honored him by clothing him with magnificent robes and fine ornaments, 8 perfect in their splendor. He granted him
the symbols of authority: the linen
shorts, the shirt, and the robe with the
pomegranates around the hem. 9 Gold
bells were also around its hem, so that
when he walked, their ringing would be
heard in the Temple, and the Lord would
remember his people. 10 The Lord gave
Aaron the sacred robe with the gold,
blue, and purple embroidery; the breastpiece with the Urim and Thummim;[p]
11 the red yarn, spun by an expert; the
precious stones with names engraved on
them, mounted in a gold setting by a
jeweler, placed on the breastpiece to remind the Lord of the twelve tribes of Israel. 12 He gave him the turban with the
gold ornament engraved with the words
"Dedicated to the Lord." It was expertly
crafted, a beautiful work of art, and it
was a high honor to wear it. 13 Before
Aaron's time such beautiful things were
never seen. No one but Aaron and his

[m] *Hebrew* gave ... start; *Greek* was taken in exchange for the human race.
[n] *Hebrew* his reputation was faultless; *Greek* there was no one like him in reputation.
[o] *Hebrew* struck; *Greek* stopped. [p] URIM AND THUMMIM: *Two objects used by the priest to determine God's will; it is not known precisely how they were used.*

descendants ever wore them, or ever
will. 14 The grain offering is to be presented twice a day and burned completely.
15 Moses ordained Aaron to office by
pouring the sacred anointing oil over his
head. An eternal covenant was made
with him and his descendants, that they
would serve the Lord as his priests and
bless the people in the Lord's name.
16 The Lord chose Aaron out of the
whole human race to offer sacrifices, to
burn fragrant incense to remind the
Lord of his people, and to take away
their sins. 17 He entrusted the commandments to Aaron's keeping and gave him
the authority to make legal decisions
and to teach Israel the Law.
18 Once, while the people were in the
wilderness, an angry group of jealous
outsiders conspired against Moses.
These were Dathan, Abiram, and Korah
with their supporters. 19 The Lord saw
what they were doing and became angry, so furious that he performed a miracle and destroyed them in a blazing fire.
20 Then he rewarded Aaron again, giving
him a special honor: the right to the offerings of the first produce, so that the
priests should have enough to eat.
21 Their food is the sacrifices offered to
the Lord; the Lord gave this to Aaron
and his descendants. 22 But Aaron, unlike the rest of the people, was to inherit
no land, no special portion of his own.
The Lord himself would be all he
needed.

Phinehas

23 Only Moses and Aaron were more
famous for their intense devotion to the
Lord than Phinehas son of Eleazar. He
brought about forgiveness for Israel's
sin by standing firm in brave determination when everyone else was in rebellion. 24 And so the Lord made a covenant
with him, valid for all time to come, that
he should be in charge of the sanctuary
and of his people, that he and his
descendants should hold the office of
High Priest forever. 25 Unlike the covenant made with David son of Jesse, from
the tribe of Judah, where the kingship
passed only from father to son, the
priesthood was to pass from Aaron to all
his descendants.
26 Now praise the Lord, who is good,
who has crowned you with glory![q] May
he give you wisdom to judge his people
fairly, so that their success and your authority[r] may continue for all time to
come.

Joshua

46 Joshua[s] son of Nun was a great
soldier and the next of the
prophets after Moses. He lived up to the
meaning of his name as the great deliverer of the Lord's chosen people. He defeated the enemies that attacked them,
so that Israel could claim its land. 2 How
magnificent it was when he raised his
arm and then led the attacks on the cities! 3 No one could stand up to him;[t] he
was fighting a holy war for the Lord.
4 Remember how he held back the sun
and made one day as long as two?
5 When his enemies were threatening
him from every side, he prayed to the
mighty Lord Most High, and his prayer
was answered with a hailstorm of devastating force. 6 The Lord hurled the hail
down on the enemy[u] and destroyed
them at the pass at Beth Horon, so that
the nations would realize how strong
Joshua was, since he was fighting as a
devoted follower of the Lord.

Caleb

7 Joshua was loyal as long as Moses
lived, both he and Caleb son of Jephunneh. They stood up to the whole community, made them stop their ungrateful
complaining, and kept them from sinning. 8 Out of the 600,000 Israelites who
marched through the wilderness, these
two were the only ones spared and allowed to enter the rich and fertile land
that was to be theirs. 9 The Lord made
Caleb strong, and when he was an old
man, he was still strong enough to go up
into the hill country and capture it for
himself and his descendants. 10 Then all
of Israel could see how good it is to follow the Lord.

[q] *Hebrew* Now praise . . . glory; *Greek does not have these words.* [r] *Probable Hebrew text* and your authority; *Greek unclear.* [s] JOSHUA: *This name in Hebrew means "the Lord saves."* [t] *Hebrew* no one . . . to him; *Greek* No one before had ever been so brave. [u] *Probable text* The Lord hurled . . . enemy; *Greek unclear.*

The Judges

11 Then there were the judges, each of
them famous in their own right, who
never fell into idolatry and never abandoned the Lord. 12 May their memory be
honored! May these whom we honor
spring from the grave to new life in their
descendants!

Samuel

13 Samuel was loved by the Lord. As
the Lord's prophet he established the
kingdom and appointed rulers for the
people. 14 He judged the nation in accordance with the Law of the Lord, and
the Lord protected Israel. 15 Because
Samuel was faithful, he was accepted as
a true prophet. People trusted him as a
seer because of his words. 16 When his
enemies were threatening him from
every side, he called upon the mighty
Lord and offered him a young lamb as a
sacrifice. 17 Then the Lord thundered
from heaven with a mighty roar 18 and
destroyed all the enemy[v] rulers of Philistia. 19 When Samuel was about to die,
he gave assurances before the Lord and
the anointed king that he had never
taken anyone's property, not even so
much as a pair of shoes, and no one contradicted him. 20 Even after he died, he
prophesied to King Saul how he would
die. Out of the grave he spoke as a
prophet, to blot out his people's
wickedness.

Nathan

47 After him came Nathan, who
was a prophet at the time of
David.

David

2 As the choice fat portion of the fellowship offering is reserved for the
Lord, so David was chosen from among
the Israelites. 3 He played with lions and
bears as if they were lambs or little
goats. 4 When he was still a boy, he
killed a giant to rescue his people. He
put a stone in his sling, took aim, and put
an end to Goliath's bragging. 5 He
prayed to the Lord, the Most High, and
was given the strength to kill that famous soldier, so that the nations would
have respect for the power of his people.
6 The people honored him for killing his
tens of thousands, and when he was
crowned king, they praised him for being chosen by the Lord. 7 He wiped out
all his enemies and permanently
crushed the Philistines, so that they
never again became a threat.

8 In everything David did, he gave
thanks and praise to the Holy Lord, the
Most High. He loved his Creator and
sang praises to him with all his heart.
9 He put singers at the altar to provide
beautiful music. 10 He set the times of the
festivals throughout the year and made
them splendid occasions; the Temple
rang with the Lord's praises all day long.
11 The Lord forgave David's sin and established his power forever. He made a
covenant with him that he and his
descendants would reign in splendor
over Israel.

Solomon

12 David prepared the way well for his
son, a wise man, to rule after him.
13 There was no war while Solomon was
king. God gave him peace on all his borders, so that he could build for the Lord
a Temple which would stand forever.
14 How wise you were, Solomon, when
you were young! Your knowledge was
like the Nile[w] in flood. 15 Your influence
reached over all the world; your proverbs and riddles were known everywhere. 16 You were famous everywhere,
and people loved you for bringing peace.
17 Nations around the world held you in
admiration for your songs, proverbs,
parables, and witty sayings. 18 You gathered silver and gold as if it were tin or
lead, all in the name of the Lord God of
Israel.

19 But your lust for women was your
downfall. 20 You stained your reputation
and that of your descendants. They suffered punishment for that foolishness of
yours, which caused them so much grief.
21 It divided the nation, and a rival kingdom arose in northern Israel. 22 But the
Lord will always be merciful and keep
all his promises.[x] He will never destroy
the descendants of David, whom he
chose and who loved him. So for Israel's
sake he allowed David's family to
survive.

[v] *Hebrew* enemy; *Greek* rulers of Tyre and. [w] *Hebrew* the Nile; *Greek* a river.
[x] *Hebrew* keep all his promises; *Greek* will not destroy what he made.

Rehoboam and Jeroboam

23 Solomon followed his ancestors in death and left one of his sons to rule after him. This was Rehoboam, a man of little intelligence and great foolishness,[y] whose policies caused a rebellion.

There was also the unspeakable[z] Jeroboam, who led northern Israel in sinful ways. 24 His people became so sinful that they were exiled from their land. 25 They tried all kinds of wickedness until the Lord took vengeance on them.

Elijah

48 Then there arose the fiery prophet Elijah, whose words blazed like a torch. 2 He brought a famine on the people, and many of them died because of his persistence. 3 Speaking in the name of the Lord, he kept the rain from coming, and on three occasions he called down fire. 4 Elijah, your miracles were marvelous! No one else can boast of such deeds! 5 In the name of the Most High, you brought a dead man back to life. 6 You brought a famous king down to sickness and death. 7 At Sinai you heard the Lord rebuke you and declare his determination to punish his enemies. 8 You anointed a king to be the instrument of that punishment, and a prophet to take your place. 9 You were taken up to heaven in a fiery whirlwind, a chariot drawn by fiery horses. 10 The scripture says that you are ready to appear at the designated time,[a] to cool God's anger before it breaks out in fury; that you "will bring parents and children together again," and restore the tribes of Israel. 11 Fortunate are those who live to see you come, as well as those who have already died in love, for we too shall live.[b]

Elisha

12 When Elijah was hidden by the whirlwind, Elisha was filled with his spirit. As long as he lived, he was not afraid of rulers, and they could not make him do as they wished. 13 Nothing was too hard for him. Even when he was dead, his body worked a miracle. 14 In life and in death he performed amazing miracles.

15 But in spite of all this, the people did not abandon their sinful ways until they were taken from their land as prisoners and scattered all over the world. This left the nation few in number, but those who remained were still ruled by the descendants of David. 16 Some of the people did what was pleasing to the Lord, but others committed sin after sin.

Hezekiah

17 Hezekiah prepared his city to resist a siege and provided it with a water supply. He had a tunnel built through solid rock with iron tools and had cisterns built to hold the water. 18 During his reign Sennacherib attacked the city and sent his chief official from Lachish. He challenged Jerusalem and boasted arrogantly. 19 The people lost their courage and shook with fear; they were in pain, like a woman in labor. 20 But they prayed to the merciful Lord, the Holy One in heaven, who quickly answered their prayers and sent Isaiah to save them. 21 The Lord struck the Assyrian camp; his angel wiped them out. 22 Yes, Hezekiah did what was pleasing to the Lord and firmly followed the example of his ancestor David. This was what was commanded by the great prophet Isaiah, whose visions were trusted. 23 He made the sun move backward and lengthened the king's life. 24 He comforted the mourners in Jerusalem. His powerful spirit looked into the future, 25 and he predicted what was to happen before the end of time, hidden things that had not yet occurred.

Josiah

49 The memory of Josiah is as sweet as the fragrance of expertly blended incense, sweet as honey to the taste,[c] like music with wine at a banquet. 2 He followed the correct policy of reforming the nation and removed the horrors of idolatry. 3 He was completely loyal to the Lord and strengthened true religion in those wicked times.

Jeremiah

4 All the kings, except David, Hezekiah, and Josiah, were terrible sinners, because they abandoned the Law of the

[y] *Hebrew* great foolishness; *Greek* the people's fool. [z] *Hebrew* the unspeakable (one); *Greek* Jeroboam son of Nebat. [a] *Hebrew* you are . . . time; *Greek unclear.* [b] *Verse 11 in Greek is unclear.* [c] *Hebrew* to the taste; *Greek* to everyone.

Most High to the very end of the kingdom.[d] 5 They surrendered their power
and honor to foreigners, 6 who set fire to
the holy city and left its streets deserted,
just as Jeremiah had predicted. 7 Jeremiah had been badly treated, even
though he was chosen as a prophet before he was born, "to uproot and to pull
down, to destroy and to overthrow," but
also "to build and to plant."

Ezekiel

8 It was Ezekiel who was shown the vision of the divine glory over the chariot
and the living creatures. 9 He also referred to the prophet Job, who always
did the right thing.[e]

The Twelve Prophets

10 May the bones of the twelve prophets rise to new life, because these men
encouraged the people of Israel and
saved them with confident hope.

Zerubbabel and Joshua

11 How can we praise Zerubbabel? He
was like a signet ring on the Lord's right
hand, 12 as was Joshua son of Jehozadak. They rebuilt the Lord's holy Temple, destined for eternal fame.

Nehemiah

13 The memory of Nehemiah is also
great. He rebuilt the ruined walls of Jerusalem, installing the gates and bars.
He rebuilt our homes.

The Patriarchs

14 No one else like Enoch has ever
walked the face of the earth, for he was
taken up from the earth. 15 No one else
like Joseph has ever been born;[f] even
his bones were honored.[g] 16 Shem, Seth,
and Enosh[h] were highly honored, but
Adam's glory was above that of any
other living being.

Simon Son of Onias

50 The greatest of his brothers and
the pride of his people[i] was the
High Priest Simon son of Onias, who repaired the Temple 2 and laid the foundation for the high double wall and the
fortifications of the Temple.[j] 3 The reservoir, as big as the bronze tank, was
dug[k] while he was in office. 4 He made
plans to protect his people from attack
and fortified the city so that it could
withstand a siege.

5 How glorious he was when he came
out of the Most Holy Place![l] 6 He was
like the morning star shining through
the clouds, like the full moon, 7 like the
sun shining on the Temple of the Most
High, like the rainbow gleaming in glory
against the clouds, 8 like roses in springtime, like lilies beside a stream, like the
cedars of Lebanon in summer, 9 like
burning incense, like a cup made of
hammered gold and decorated with all
kinds of jewels, 10 like an olive tree
loaded with fruit, like a cypress tree towering into the clouds.

11 When Simon put on his magnificent
robe and went up to the holy altar
dressed in perfect splendor, he made the
Temple courtyard a majestic sight.
12 When the priests handed him the portions of the sacrifice as he stood beside
the altar with his assistants circling him
like a wreath, he was like a young cedar
of Lebanon surrounded by palm trees.
13 Those were the descendants of Aaron
in their splendid garments, standing before the whole assembly of Israel, holding in their hands the offering made to
the Lord. 14 When he had finished the
service at the altar and had arranged the
sacrifice to the Most High, the Almighty,
15 he reached for a cup and poured out
sweet-smelling wine at the foot of the altar as an offering to the Most High, the
universal King. 16 Then the priests
shouted and blew their trumpets of hammered silver. They made a loud noise
that the Most High would hear. 17 All the
people immediately bowed down with
their faces to the ground to worship their
Lord, the Almighty, the Most High.
18 Then the choir began to sing his
praises, and the beautiful music rang
out. 19 The people kept praying to the
merciful Lord Most High until the serv-

[d] *Hebrew* to the very end of the kingdom; *Greek* and failed. [e] *Probable Hebrew text* He also . . . thing; *Greek unclear.* [f] *Greek adds* the greatest of his brothers and the pride of his people; *Hebrew and one ancient translation place these words in 50.1.* [g] even . . . honored; *or* the Lord watched over his body. [h] *Hebrew* Shem, Seth, and Enosh; *Greek* Shem and Seth among people. [i] The greatest . . . people; *Hebrew and one ancient translation place the words at this point; Greek places them at 49.15.* [j] *Verse 2 in Greek is unclear.* [k] *Hebrew* dug; *Greek* reduced. [l] *Hebrew* Most Holy Place; *Greek* Most Holy Place among the people.

ice of worship had come to a close.
20 Then Simon came down from the altar, raised his hands over the whole
assembly of Israel, and reverently
pronounced the blessing from the Lord,
21 while the people bowed a second time
in worship to receive that blessing from
the Most High.

A Benediction

22 Now then, give praise to the God of
the universe, who has done great things
everywhere, who brings us up[m] from
the time we are born, and deals with us
mercifully. 23 May he give us happiness
and allow us to have peace in Israel forever. 24 May he continue his mercy to us
and rescue us in our time of need.

Three Hated Nations

25 There are two nations that I detest,
and a third that does not even deserve to
be called a nation. 26 These are the
Edomites,[n] the inhabitants of the Philistine cities, and the stupid Samaritans.

The Wisdom of Jesus Son of Sirach

27 I, Jesus son of Sirach Eleazar[o] of
Jerusalem, put all my wisdom into writing this book to provide instruction and
knowledge for others. 28 May God bless
everyone who gives attention to these
teachings. Whoever takes them to heart
will become wise. 29 Whoever lives by
them will be strong enough for any occasion, because he will be walking in the
light of the Lord.

A Song of Thanksgiving

51 I give you thanks, O Lord and King;
I praise you as my God and Savior.
I give you thanks,
2 for you have helped me and protected me.
You have rescued me from death,
from dangerous lies and slander.
3 You helped me when no one else would;
in your great mercy you saved me
from the many troubles I have known:
from the glaring hatred of my enemies,
who wanted to put an end to my life;
4 from suffocation in oppressive smoke
rising from fires that I did not light;
5 from death itself;
from vicious slander reported to the king.
6 I was once brought face-to-face with death;
7 enemies surrounded me everywhere.
I looked for someone to help me,
but there was no one there.
8 But then, O Lord, I remembered
how merciful you are
and what you had done in times past.
I remembered that you rescue
those who rely on you,
that you save them from their enemies.
9 Then from here on earth I prayed to you
to rescue me from death.
10 I prayed, "O Lord, you are my father;[p]
do not abandon me to my troubles
when I am helpless against arrogant enemies.
11 I will always praise you
and sing hymns of thanksgiving."
You answered my prayer,
12 and saved me from the threat of destruction.
And so I thank you and praise you.
O Lord, I praise you!

The Search for Wisdom

13 When I was still young, before I
started out on my travels, I boldly
prayed for Wisdom. 14 I went to the Temple and asked for her, and I will look for
her as long as I live. 15 From my blossoming youth to my ripe old age she has
been my delight. I have followed directly
in her path ever since I was young.
16 I received Wisdom as soon as I began
listening for her, and I have been rewarded with great knowledge. 17 I have

[m] brings us up; *or* honors us. [n] *Hebrew* Edomites; *Greek* Samaritans. [o] Sirach Eleazar; *or* Sirach son of Eleazar. [p] *Hebrew* you are my father; *Greek* father of my Lord.

always been a learner and am grateful to
everyone who has been my teacher.
18 I was determined to live wisely and
was devoted to the cause of goodness. I
have no regrets. 19 I fought for Wisdom
and was strict in my conduct. When I
prayed, I sadly confessed how far short
of Wisdom I fell. 20 But I was determined
to have her, and I found her by keeping
myself free from sin. I have grown in
Wisdom since first I found her, and I will
never be without her. 21 Because I was
driven by the desire to find her, I have
been richly rewarded. 22 The Lord gave
me a gift for words, and I have used it in
his praise.

23 Come to me, all you that need instruction, and learn in my school. 24 Why
do you admit that you are ignorant and
do nothing about it? 25 Here is what I say:
It costs nothing to be wise. 26 Put on the
yoke, and be willing to learn. The opportunity is always near. 27 See for yourselves! I have really not studied very
hard, but I have found great contentment. 28 No matter how much it costs
you to get Wisdom, it will be well worth
it. 29 Be joyfully grateful for the Lord's
mercy, and never be ashamed to praise
him. 30 Do your duty at the proper time,
and the Lord, at the time he thinks
proper, will give you your reward.

The Book of BARUCH

Introduction

The Book of Baruch *is a collection of four distinct, short discourses, attributed to Baruch, the secretary of the prophet Jeremiah (Jeremiah 32.12; 36.4). These discourses, written at various times, probably in Hebrew originally, were later put together into a single document.*

Outline of Contents

Introduction

1 This book was written by Baruch
son of Neraiah, grandson of Mahseiah, and a descendant of Zedekiah, Hasadiah, and Hilkiah. It was written in
Babylon 2 on the seventh day of the
month[a] in the fifth year after the Babylonians captured Jerusalem and burned
it down. 3-4 Baruch read the book aloud
to Jehoiachin son of Jehoiakim, king of
Judah, and to all the people who lived in
Babylon by the Sud River. Everyone
came to hear it read—nobles, children of
royal families, elders, in fact, all the people, no matter what their status.
5 When the book was read, everyone
cried, fasted, and prayed to the Lord.
6 Then they all gave as much money as
they could, 7 and the collection was sent
to Jerusalem to Jehoiakim the High
Priest, son of Hilkiah and grandson of
Shallum, and to the other priests and to
all the people who were with him in Jerusalem.
8 On the tenth day of the month of Sivan, Baruch took the sacred utensils
which had been carried away from the
Temple and returned them to Judah.
These were the silver utensils which
Zedekiah son of King Josiah of Judah
had ordered made 9 after King Nebuchadnezzar of Babylonia had deported

[a] THE MONTH: *The month is probably the fifth month of the Hebrew calendar (see 2 K 25.8; Jr 52.12).*

Jehoiachin, the rulers, the skilled workers,[b] the nobles, and the common people and had taken them from Jerusalem
to Babylon.

A Letter to Jerusalem

10 The people wrote:
Please use the money we are sending you to buy animals for the burnt
offerings and the sin offerings, to buy
incense, and to provide the grain offerings. Offer them on the altar of the
Lord our God, 11 and pray for King
Nebuchadnezzar of Babylonia and his
son Belshazzar, that they may live as
long as the heavens last. 12 Then the
Lord will strengthen us and be our
guide. Nebuchadnezzar and his son
Belshazzar will protect us, and we will
be loyal to them as long as we live;
then they will be pleased with us.
13 We ask you also to pray to the Lord
God for us, because we have sinned
against him, and he is still angry with
us. 14 Please read this book that we are
sending you and make your own confession of sin in the Temple on the first
day of the Festival of Shelters and on
other holy days of assembly.

A Confession of Sin

15 This is the confession you should
make: "The Lord our God is righteous,
but we are still covered with shame.
All of us—the people of Judah, the
people of Jerusalem, 16 our kings, our
rulers, our priests, our prophets, and
our ancestors have been put to shame,
17 because we have sinned against the
Lord our God 18 and have disobeyed
him. We did not listen to him or live
according to his commandments.
19 From the day the Lord brought our
ancestors out of Egypt until the
present day, we have continued to be
unfaithful to him, and we have not
hesitated to disobey him. 20 Long ago,
when the Lord led our ancestors out of
Egypt, so that he could give us a rich
and fertile land, he pronounced curses
against us through his servant Moses.
And today we are suffering because of
those curses. 21 We refused to obey the
word of the Lord our God which he
spoke to us through the prophets. Instead, we all did as we pleased and
went on our own evil way. We turned
to other gods and did things the Lord
hates.

2 "So the Lord carried out the
threat he had made against us
and against our judges, our kings, our
rulers, and the people of Israel and Judah. 2 Nowhere else on earth have
such things happened as happened in
Jerusalem when the Lord carried out
the threats written in the Law of
Moses. 3 Things were so bad that we
even ate the flesh of our own sons and
daughters. 4 The Lord scattered our
people, handing us over to the control
of all the nations around us, and they
looked on us with reproach and horror. 5 We sinned against the Lord our
God and refused to obey him. Therefore, our nation was conquered, instead of being victorious.
6 "The Lord our God is always righteous, but we and our ancestors are
still burdened with our guilt. 7 Even
though the Lord punished us as he had
threatened, 8 we still did not turn to
him and pray that we would abandon
our evil thoughts. 9-10 We did not obey
him or live by his just commands, so
the Lord brought on us all the punishments he had kept ready for us.

The Prayer for Deliverance

11 "You, O Lord, are the God of Israel who brought your people out of
Egypt with great power and with
signs, miracles, and wonders. You
showed your mighty strength and
gained a glorious reputation, which is
still recognized today. 12 O Lord our
God, we have sinned; we have been
unfaithful; we have disobeyed all your
commands. 13 But do not be angry with
us any longer. Here among the nations
where you have scattered us, only a
few of us are left. 14 Listen to our
prayer of petition, Lord, and rescue us
for the sake of your own honor. Let
those who have taken us into exile be
pleased with us. 15 Then the whole
world will know that you are the Lord
our God and that you have chosen the
nation of Israel to be your own people.
16 "O Lord, look down from heaven
and see our misery. Listen to our
prayer. 17 Open your eyes and look

[b] skilled workers; *Greek* prisoners.

upon us. Those in the world of the
dead with no breath left in their bodies
cannot offer praises to you or proclaim how just you are. 18 Only the living, O Lord, can offer you praise and
acknowledge your justice, even
though they may be suffering greatly,
bent and weak, hungry and with failing eyesight.

19 “O Lord our God, we pray to you
for mercy, but not because of any
good things done by our ancestors and
our kings. 20 You turned your anger
and wrath against us, just as you had
threatened to do when your servants
the prophets spoke your word to us
and said, 21 ‘Bend your backs and
serve the king of Babylonia, and you
can remain in the land that I gave to
your ancestors. 22 But if you refuse to
obey my command to serve him,
23 I will bring to an end every sound of
joy and celebration in the towns of Judah and in Jerusalem. Even the happy
sounds of wedding feasts will no
longer be heard. The whole land will
be desolate and uninhabited.’

24 “But we did not obey your command to serve the king of Babylonia,
so you carried out the threat that you
had made when you spoke through
your servants the prophets, when you
said that the bones of our kings and of
our ancestors would be taken from
their tombs and scattered. 25 And now
here they lie exposed to the heat of the
day and to the frost of the night. They
died in torment from famine, war, and
disease. 26 And because of the sin of
the people of Israel and Judah, you
have reduced your own Temple to ruins, even as it is today.

27 “But, Lord, you have been patient
with us and have shown us great
mercy, 28 as you promised through
your servant Moses on the day you
commanded him to write your Law in
the presence of the Israelites. 29 ‘If you
do not obey me,’ you said, ‘you will be
reduced to a handful among the nations where I will scatter you.
30 I know that you will not obey me,
because you are a stubborn people.
But when you are taken into exile in
another land, you will come to your
senses. 31 Then you will realize that I
am the Lord your God, and I will give
you a desire to know and a mind with
which to understand. 32 There in the
land of your exile you will praise me
and remember me. 33 You will stop being so stubborn and wicked, for you
will remember what happened to your
ancestors when they sinned against
the Lord. 34 Then I will bring you back
to the land that I solemnly promised to
give to your ancestors, to Abraham,
Isaac, and Jacob, and it will be yours
again. I will increase your population,
and you will never again be reduced to
a small number. 35 I will make an everlasting covenant with you; I will be
your God and you will be my people. I
will never again remove you, the people of Israel, from the land that I
gave you.’

3 “O Lord Almighty, God of Israel,
from the depth of our troubled,
weary souls we cry out to you. 2 Hear
us, O Lord, and have mercy on us, because we have sinned against you.
3 You reign as king forever, but we die
and are gone forever. 4 O Lord
Almighty, God of Israel, hear our
prayer. We are no better off than the
dead. Our ancestors sinned against
you, the Lord their God. They refused
to obey you, and we are suffering the
consequences of their sin. 5 Forget the
sinful things that our ancestors did in
the past; at a time like this, think only
of your power and reputation, 6 for you
are the Lord our God, and we will
praise you. 7 You have made us fear
you, so that we might pray to you.
Here in exile we will praise you because we have turned away from the
sins of our ancestors. 8 You have scattered us among the nations, and you
have made them despise and curse us.
You are punishing us for the sins of
our ancestors when they rebelled
against you, the Lord our God.”

In Praise of Wisdom

9 Listen, Israel, to the commands that
promise life; pay attention, and you will
become wise. 10 Why is it, Israel, that you
find yourself in an enemy land? Why
have you grown old in a foreign country? You are ritually unclean, like the
dead; 11 you are already counted among
the dead. But why? 12 It is because you
have left the source of Wisdom! 13 If you
had walked in God’s ways, you would
have lived in peace forever. 14 Learn

where understanding, strength, and insight are to be found. Then you will
know where to find a long and full life,
light to guide you, and peace.
15 No one has ever found where Wisdom lives or has entered her treasure
house, 16-17 and those who have tried
have vanished: the rulers of the nations,
those who hunted wild animals and
birds for sport, those who accumulated
vast fortunes of silver and gold, which
everyone trusts and will do anything to
get, 18 and those who worried and
schemed to make money, but who left no
trace of their work behind. 19 They have
all disappeared and gone down to the
world of the dead. Others have come
along to take their place. 20 A later generation was born and lived in the land,
but they too did not discover the way to
knowledge. They did not find the path to
Wisdom or ever reach her. 21 Their children also failed. 22 Wisdom was not
found by the Canaanites. It has not been
discovered by the Edomites 23 although
they search after knowledge. The way to
Wisdom has not been found by the merchants of Merran and Tema or by those
who relate fables or by any others who
seek understanding.
24 O Israel, how great is the universe in
which God dwells! How vast is all that
he possesses! 25 There is no end to it;
there is no way to measure how wide or
how high it is. 26 Here in early times the
famous giants were born, a mighty race
skilled in war. 27 But God did not choose
them to be his people or show them the
way of knowledge. 28 They died out because they had neither understanding
nor insight.
29 No one has ever gone up into heaven
to get Wisdom and bring her down out
of the clouds. 30 No one has sailed across
the seas to find Wisdom or bought her
with precious gold. 31 No one knows how
to get to her or how to discover the path
that leads to her.
32 The only one who knows Wisdom is
God, and he knows all things. With his
understanding he found her. He established the earth for all time and filled it
with all kinds of animals. 33 The light
trembled and obeyed when he called. He
sent it forth, and it appeared. 34 He called
the stars, and they promptly answered;
they took their places and gladly shone
to please the one who made them. 35 He
is our God, and there is none like him.
36 He discovered the entire path leading
to understanding and gave Wisdom to
his servant Israel, whom he loved.
37 From that time on, Wisdom appeared
on earth and lived among us.

4 Wisdom is the book of God's commandments, the Law that will last
forever. All who hold onto her will live,
but those who abandon her will die.
2 Turn to Wisdom, people of Israel, and
take hold of her. Make your way toward
the splendor of her light. 3 Do not surrender our glorious privileges to any other
people. 4 How happy we are, people of
Israel; we have the advantage of knowing what is pleasing to God!

Comfort for Jerusalem

5 Take courage, my people, you are the
ones who keep Israel's name alive. 6 You
were sold to Gentile nations, but not to
be destroyed. Because you made God
angry, he handed you over to your enemies. 7 When you offered sacrifices to
demons instead of to God, you angered
the one who made you. 8 You forgot the
Eternal God, who had nourished you as
a child, and so you brought grief to Jerusalem, who had been like a mother to
you. 9 Jerusalem saw that God was punishing you because he was angry, and
she said to all the neighboring cities,
"Look at the great misery that God has
brought on me. 10 I saw my sons and
daughters taken into captivity, a captivity brought on them by the Eternal God.
11 I brought up my children with great
delight, but I cried and mourned when
they were taken from me. 12 Let no one
take pleasure in my suffering now that I
am a widow and so many of my children
have been taken from me. They turned
away from God's Law, and their sins
have made me a deserted city. 13 They
had no respect for his commandments
and would not live by them; they refused
to let him guide them in the way of righteousness.
14 "All you neighboring cities, come
and consider how the Eternal God has
sent my children into exile. 15 He
brought against them a nation from far
away, a shameless nation that speaks a
foreign language and has no respect for
the elderly and no pity for children.
16 These people carried off my beloved

sons and took away my daughters, and I was left a widow, completely alone.

17 "My children in exile, I can do nothing to help you. 18 Only the one who brought this punishment upon you can rescue you from your enemies. 19 Go your own way, my children; live your own life! I am all alone. 20 I have taken off the robes I wore during days of peace, and I have dressed myself like a person in mourning. I will cry out to the Eternal God for help as long as I live.

21 "Take courage, my children, and cry out to God for help. He will rescue you from oppression, from the power of your enemies. 22 I am confident that the Eternal God will soon set you free. The Holy One, your eternal savior, will make me happy when he shows you mercy. 23 I cried and wailed when you were taken away, but God will bring you back and will make me happy forever. 24 Just as the neighboring cities watched as you were taken captive, so they will soon see the Eternal God coming in glorious splendor to rescue you. 25 My children, endure God's punishment with patience. Your enemies have persecuted you, but you will soon see them destroyed and at your mercy. 26 My children, I spoiled you with love, but you have had to follow rugged paths; you were carried off like sheep caught in an enemy raid.

27 "Take courage, my children, and cry out to God for help. He punished you, but he will not forget you. 28 Just as you were once determined to turn away from God, now turn back and serve him with ten times more determination. 29 The one who brought these calamities upon you will rescue you and bring you everlasting joy."

Jerusalem Is Assured of Help

30 Take courage, Jerusalem. God, who gave you your name, will now bring comfort to you. 31 Misery will come to those who mistreated you and then rejoiced when you fell. 32 Misery will come to those cities that made your children slaves. Misery will be the fate of Babylon, that city which swallowed up your children. 33 Just as that city rejoiced when you fell and took delight in your ruin, so now she will mourn when she herself is deserted. 34 I will turn her proud boastings into mourning and take away her large population in which she took pride. 35 I, the Eternal God, will send down fire on her, and it will burn for many days. Her ruins will be haunted by demons for a long time to come.

36 Look to the east, Jerusalem, and see the joy that God is bringing to you. 37 Look, your children are coming home, the children that were taken from you. They have been gathered together from the east and from the west by the command of God, the Holy One. And now they are coming home, rejoicing in the glory of God.

5 Jerusalem, take off the clothes you have worn in your mourning and distress, and put on the eternal splendor of God's glory. 2 Put around you the cloak of God's righteousness. Place on your head the crown of the glory of the Eternal God. 3 God will show your splendor to every nation on earth. 4 Forever he will say to you: "Your security comes from your righteousness, and your splendor from your devotion to me."[c]

5 Get up, Jerusalem, stand on the mountaintop; see where God, the Holy One, is bringing your children together from the east and from the west. They are rejoicing that God has remembered them. 6 Jerusalem, your children were led away by their enemies; they left you on foot, but God is bringing them back to you, carried in royal splendor. 7 God has commanded that every high mountain and the everlasting hills shall be made low; he has commanded that the valleys shall be filled and the ground leveled, so that the people of Israel may come safely home in the glory of God. 8 At the command of God, forests of fragrant trees will spring up to provide shade for the people of Israel. 9 God will lead Israel home. They will return with great joy, guided by his mercy and righteousness, surrounded by the light of his glorious presence.

[c] Forever . . . devotion to me; *or* He will give you this name forever: "Peace from Righteousness and Glory from Godliness."

The Letter of
JEREMIAH

Introduction

The Letter of Jeremiah *is in the form of a letter, claiming to be written by the prophet Jeremiah to Jews who are about to be taken into exile. It consists primarily of a lengthy condemnation of idolatry.*

Outline of Contents

The helplessness of idols 1-40
The foolishness of worshiping idols 41-73

---

1 This is a copy of the letter sent by
Jeremiah to the people of Jerusalem just
before they were captured by the Babylonian king and taken to Babylon. It
contains the message that God had
commanded Jeremiah to give them.

The People Face a Long Captivity

2 You have sinned against God. That is
why you are about to be taken away as
prisoners to Babylon by King Nebuchadnezzar. 3 You will remain there in
exile for many years, as long as seven
generations; then God will lead you
peacefully home from Babylon.
4 There in Babylon you will see gods
made of wood, silver, and gold—gods
which people carry on their shoulders
and which fill the heathen with fear.
5 You must be careful never to imitate
those Gentiles. Don't let their gods fill
you with fear when you see them being
carried in procession and being worshiped. 6 Instead, say to yourselves, "It is
you alone, Lord, that we must worship."
7 God's angel will be there with you; he
will take care of you.

The Helplessness of Idols

8 Their idols are plated with silver and
gold and have tongues that were carved
by woodworkers. But they are not real
gods, and they cannot speak. 9 The people make gold crowns and put them on
the heads of their gods, as if these idols
were girls who love jewelry. 10 Sometimes the priests steal the silver and gold
from their gods and spend it on themselves; 11 they even give some of it to the
temple prostitutes. People take these
gods of wood, silver, and gold, and put
clothes on them, as if they were human.
12 But even though the gods are dressed
in purple robes like kings, they still cannot keep themselves from being tar-
nished or protect themselves from
termites. 13 When dust from the temple
settles on their faces, someone has to
wipe it off for them. 14 Like human
judges they hold scepters in their hands,
but they have no power to punish anyone who wrongs them. 15 Sometimes
they have daggers and axes in their
hands, but they cannot protect themselves from being destroyed in war or
from being carried off by thieves. 16 All
of this proves that they are not gods—do
not worship them.
17 Those gods sitting in their temples
are as useless as a broken bowl. Their
eyes are filled with the dust that people
kick up when they come in. 18 The priests
fortify the temples with doors and bars
and bolts, so that thieves cannot break
in. The gods are locked up as securely as
a prisoner about to be executed for a
crime against the king. 19 The priests
light lamps for the gods, far more than
they need for their own use, but the idols
can't see even one of them. 20 Their insides are eaten away by termites, just
like the wooden beams of the temple,
and their clothing is destroyed, but they
don't even know it. 21 Their faces are
blackened by the smoke in the temple.
22 Bats, swallows, and other birds perch
on them, and even cats sit on them. 23 All
of this proves that they are not gods—do
not worship them.
24 These idols have been plated with
gold to make them beautiful, but they do
not shine unless someone polishes them.
When they were being poured into
molds, they felt nothing. 25 It makes no
difference how high a price is paid for

them; they are still unable to breathe.
26 See how useless they are! They can't
walk on their own feet, but must be carried around. 27 Even those who take care
of them are embarrassed when one of
their gods falls to the ground and has to
be picked up again. When someone
stands one of them in a certain place, it
cannot move, and if it is leaning over, it
can never straighten itself up. Offering
gifts to them is like giving gifts to a
corpse. 28 Priests sell what is sacrificed
to their gods and use the money on
themselves. And the wives of the priests
preserve the sacrifices with salt for later
use, instead of sharing them with the
poor and helpless. 29 Even women who
are having their monthly period or
women who have just given birth are allowed to touch the sacrifices. All of this
proves that they are not gods – do not
worship them.

30 How can they ever be called gods,
when women are allowed to make offerings to these things made of wood, silver, and gold? 31 The priests even sit in
the temples when they are in mourning,
with torn clothes and shaved, uncovered
heads. 32 The priests roar and shout in
the presence of their gods as if they were
taking part in a funeral feast. 33 They
take the clothing off their gods and give
it to their wives and children. 34 It doesn't
matter whether a person helps or harms
these gods, since they cannot pay him
back. They are not able to make anyone
a king or to dethrone him, 35 and they
cannot make a person wealthy or give
him any money. If someone makes a
vow to them but does not keep it, they
will never make him pay. 36 They can
never rescue a person from death, and
they never help a weak person against
one who is strong. 37 They cannot restore
sight to the blind or save anyone in distress. 38 They cannot offer any mercy or
give help to widows or orphans. 39 These
things made of wood and covered with
silver and gold are as powerless as stone
taken from the mountains; and the people who worship them will be put to
shame. 40 How can anyone think that
they are gods or call them gods?

The Foolishness of Worshiping Idols

The Babylonians bring dishonor on
their own gods. 41 When someone cannot
speak, they take him to the temple and
ask Bel to give him the power of speech,
as if Bel could understand anything.
42 But even when the people realize that
their gods cannot help, they are stupid
enough to go on worshiping them. 43 Not
only that, but women wrap cords around
themselves and sit alongside the road
burning incense and offering themselves
as prostitutes. When one of them is
taken off for sex, she returns to ridicule
the woman next to her who was not
beautiful enough to be chosen. 44 Everything about these idols is false. How can
anyone think that they are gods or call
them gods?

45 Woodworkers and goldsmiths make
these gods, so they can never be anything other than what these people want
them to be. 46 Even their makers do not
live long lives, so how are they able to
create gods? 47 These people leave nothing but deceit and disgrace as an inheritance for future generations. 48 When
wars and disturbances come, the priests
plan where they can go into hiding with
their gods. 49 These idols are helpless in
the face of wars and disturbances. Why
can't people realize that these idols are
not gods?

50 These idols are nothing more than
wood covered with silver and gold; one
day it will be clear that they are really
not gods at all. 51 All nations and kings
will realize that idols are nothing more
than the work of human hands. They do
not have the power of a god, 52 and anyone should know that they are not really
gods.

53 These gods can never make anyone
a king or bring rain. 54 They can't make
decisions about their own affairs or give
justice to someone who has been
wronged; they can do absolutely nothing. They are as useless as crows flying
around in the air. 55 When a temple
catches on fire, the priests run away to
save themselves, while the gods made of
wood and covered with silver and gold
are left to burn like wooden beams.
56 They can't fight kings or go to war
against enemies. How can anyone believe that they are gods?

57 These gods of wood, covered with
silver and gold, cannot protect themselves from thieves and robbers 58 who
take off the silver and gold and the gods'
clothing and walk away with all of it.
The gods can do nothing to stop them.

59 Anything from a courageous king to a
useful piece of pottery is better than a
false god. Even a door is better than a
false god; a door at least protects the
things in the house. Even a wooden pillar in a palace is better than a false god.
60 God provided the sun, the moon,
and the stars to give light, and they obey
him. 61 The same is true of lightning and
wind. The lightning can be seen far and
wide, and the wind blows everywhere.
62 When God commands clouds to
spread out over the whole world, they
obey. 63 When God sends down fire from
heaven to burn up mountains and forests, it does what it is told. Idols cannot
do these things—they can't even do a
good imitation. 64 Why should they be
called gods, when they are not able to
help us or harm us in any way? 65 You
know that they are not gods—do not
worship them.
66 These gods have no power over
kings; they cannot pronounce curses on
them or grant them blessings. 67 They
cannot produce for the nations any signs
in the sky; they cannot shine like the sun
or the moon. 68 Even wild animals are
better off than these idols; animals can
at least run from danger to protect themselves. 69 So it is absolutely clear that
they are not gods—do not worship them.
70 These gods of theirs, made of wood
and covered with silver and gold, are
about as helpful as a scarecrow in a cucumber patch; they are no protection at
all. 71 They do as much good as a thorn
bush in a garden; instead of keeping
birds away, they provide a perch for
them. These gods are like a dead body
thrown out into the darkness. 72 The purple linen[a] robes they wear rot away, so
we know that they are not gods. Finally
they will be eaten by termites, and then
no one anywhere will have any use for
them.
73 The righteous person has an advantage over others; he does not own any
idols, and they can never make a fool
of him.

[a] linen; *Greek* marble.

THE PRAYER OF AZARIAH AND THE SONG OF

THE THREE YOUNG MEN

Introduction

The Prayer of Azariah and the Song of the Three Young Men *is one of the three major additions to* The Book of Daniel *in the Greek version. This insertion between 3.23 and 3.24 of* Daniel *gives the prayer of Azariah and the song of the three young men after King Nebuchadnezzar had them thrown into the blazing furnace.*

Outline of Contents

Prayer of Azariah 1-22
Description of the fiery furnace 23-27
The song of the three young men 28-68

The Prayer of Azariah

1 The three young men, Hananiah,
Mishael, and Azariah,[a] started walking
around in the flames, singing hymns to
God, and praising him as Lord. 2 Then
Azariah stood still and there in the fire
he prayed aloud: 3 "O Lord, the God of
our ancestors, we praise and adore you;
may your name be honored forever.
4 You have treated us as we deserve. In
everything you have done to us you are
always honest, and when you bring us to
judgment, you are always fair. 5 You did
what was right when you brought disas-

[a] HANANIAH, MISHAEL, AND AZARIAH: *These are the original names of Shadrach, Meshach, and Abednego (see Dn 1.6, 7).*

ter upon Jerusalem, the holy city of our
ancestors. We deserved that judgment
because of our sins. 6 We disobeyed you,
we turned our backs on you, and we are
guilty of every sin. 7 We did not do the
things that you commanded us to do. If
we had obeyed your laws, we would
have prospered, 8 but now we deserve
the judgment and punishment that you
have brought upon us. 9 You have
handed us over to lawless, hateful, and
defiant enemies—to the most wicked
king in the world. 10 And now all of us
who worship you are humiliated; we are
too ashamed to open our mouths.

11 "Yet for the sake of your own honor,
do not break your covenant with us and
abandon us forever. 12 Do not withhold
your mercy from us. Keep your promises
to Abraham, whom you loved, to Isaac,
your servant, and to Jacob, the father of
your holy people Israel. 13 You promised
to give them as many descendants as the
stars in the sky or as the grains of sand
along the seashore. 14 But now, Lord, we
are fewer in number than any other nation; wherever we are, we live in disgrace because of our sins. 15 We are left
without a king, without any prophets or
leaders. There is no longer a Temple
where we can go to offer you burnt offerings, sacrifices, gifts, or incense, no
place where we can make offerings to
you and find your mercy. 16 But we come
to you with repentant hearts and humble
spirits, begging you to accept us just as if
we had come with burnt offerings of
rams and bulls and thousands of fat
lambs. 17 Accept our repentance as our
sacrifice to you today, so that we may
obey you with all our hearts. No one
who trusts you will ever be disappointed. 18-19 Now with all our hearts we
promise to obey you, worship you, and
come to you in prayer. Treat us with
kindness and mercy, and let us never be
put to shame. 20 O Lord, rescue us with
one of your miracles; bring honor to
your name.

21 "Bring disgrace and shame on all
who harm us. Take away their might
and power and crush their strength.
22 Let them know that you alone are
Lord and God and that you rule in majesty over the whole world."

23 The king's servants who had thrown
the three men into the furnace kept the
fire hot by feeding it with oil, tar, flax,
and brushwood. 24 The flames blazed up
to a height of seventy-five feet 25 and
even spread out and burned up the
Babylonians standing near the furnace.
26 But an angel of the Lord came down
into the fire where the three men were.
He pushed aside the flames 27 so that it
felt as if a cool breeze were blowing, and
the fire did not touch the men at all or
hurt them in any way.

The Song of the Three Young Men

28 There in the furnace the three young
men again started singing together in
praise of God:

29 "We praise you, O Lord, the God
of our ancestors.
30 May your glorious, holy name
be held in honor and reverence
forever.
31 May hymns be sung to your glory
forever
and may your holy presence be
praised in that temple,
32 where you sit on your heavenly
throne above the winged
creatures
and look down to the world of
the dead.
May you be praised and honored
forever.
33 May you be praised as you sit on
your royal throne.
May hymns be sung to your
glory forever.
34 May you be praised in the dome of
the heavens.
May hymns be sung to your
glory forever.

35 "Praise the Lord, all creation;
sing his praise and honor him
forever.
36 Praise the Lord, skies above;
sing his praise and honor him
forever.
37 Praise the Lord, all angels of the
Lord;
sing his praise and honor him
forever.
38 Praise the Lord, all waters above
the sky;
sing his praise and honor him
forever.
39 Praise the Lord, all heavenly
powers;

sing his praise and honor him
forever.
40 Praise the Lord, sun and moon;
sing his praise and honor him
forever.
41 Praise the Lord, stars of heaven;
sing his praise and honor him
forever.
42 Praise the Lord, rain and dew;
sing his praise and honor him
forever.
43 Praise the Lord, all winds;
sing his praise and honor him
forever.
44 Praise the Lord, fire and heat;
sing his praise and honor him
forever.
45 Praise the Lord, bitter cold and
scorching heat;
sing his praise and honor him
forever.
46 Praise the Lord, dews and snows;
sing his praise and honor him
forever.
47 Praise the Lord, nights and days;
sing his praise and honor him
forever.
48 Praise the Lord, daylight and
darkness;
sing his praise and honor him
forever.
49 Praise the Lord, ice and cold;
sing his praise and honor him
forever.
50 Praise the Lord, frost and snow;
sing his praise and honor him
forever.
51 Praise the Lord, lightning and
storm clouds;
sing his praise and honor him
forever.

52 "Let the earth praise the Lord;
sing his praise and honor him
forever.
53 Praise the Lord, mountains and
hills;
sing his praise and honor him
forever.
54 Praise the Lord, everything that
grows;
sing his praise and honor him
forever.
55 Praise the Lord, lakes and rivers;
sing his praise and honor him
forever.
56 Praise the Lord, springs of water;
sing his praise and honor him
forever.
57 Praise the Lord, whales and sea
creatures;
sing his praise and honor him
forever.
58 Praise the Lord, all birds;
sing his praise and honor him
forever.
59 Praise the Lord, all cattle and wild
animals;
sing his praise and honor him
forever.

60 "Praise the Lord, all people on
earth;
sing his praise and honor him
forever.
61 Praise the Lord, people of Israel;
sing his praise and honor him
forever.
62 Praise the Lord, priests of the
Lord;
sing his praise and honor him
forever.
63 Praise the Lord, servants of the
Lord;
sing his praise and honor him
forever.
64 Praise the Lord, all faithful people;
sing his praise and honor him
forever.
65 Praise the Lord, all who are
humble and holy;
sing his praise and honor him
forever.
66 Praise the Lord, Hananiah,
Azariah, and Mishael;
sing his praise and honor him
forever.
He rescued us from the world of
the dead
and saved us from the power of
death.
He brought us out from the
burning furnace
and saved us from the fire.
67 Give thanks to the Lord, for he is
good
and his mercy lasts forever.
68 Praise the Lord, all who
worship him;
sing praise to the God of gods
and give him thanks,
for his mercy lasts forever."

The Book of
SUSANNA

Introduction

The Book of Susanna *is a story that was added to* The Book of Daniel, *evidently when the latter was translated into Greek. The book tells how the beautiful and virtuous Susanna, falsely charged with adultery, is cleared by the wisdom and courage of Daniel.*

Outline of Contents

Two wicked judges attempt to seduce Susanna 1-27
Susanna is condemned to death 28-41
Daniel rescues Susanna and the judges are condemned to death 42-64

Susanna's Beauty Attracts Two Judges

1 In Babylon there lived a man named
Joakim, 2 who was married to Susanna,
daughter of Hilkiah. Susanna was a
beautiful woman and deeply religious.
3 Her parents were devout Jews who had
brought up their daughter to live according to the Law of Moses. 4 Her husband
Joakim was very wealthy. Lovely gardens surrounded his house, and the
other Jews often gathered there for
meetings, because they all thought so
highly of him. 5-6 Everyone who had a legal case to present would also go to Joakim's house, where two judges held
court. These two leaders of the Jewish
community had recently been appointed
to office. They were the ones about
whom the Lord said, "There is wickedness in Babylon; judges are failing to
give guidance to the people."
7 Every day at noon, when all the people left for lunch, Susanna used to take a
walk in the gardens. 8 The two judges
were so attracted to her that they would
wait around and watch for her. 9 They
became so obsessed with their desire for
her that they lost interest both in prayer
and in their responsibility as judges.
10 They each wanted Susanna, but neither told the other how he felt, 11 for each
was ashamed to admit his lust. 12 So day
after day they watched eagerly to catch
sight of her.
13 One day at noon they said to each
other, "It's time for lunch; let's go
home." 14 So they both left and went
their separate ways, but soon each one
came back for a look at Susanna, and by
accident they met each other. At first
each tried to explain what he was doing
there, but finally they both confessed
their desire for Susanna. They decided
to watch for a time when they might find
her alone. 15-17 So they kept waiting for
the right opportunity.

The Judges Try to Seduce Susanna

One day Susanna went into the garden as usual with her two servant
women. No one else was there, except
the two judges, who had hidden themselves and were watching Susanna. It
was very hot and she decided to take a
bath. So she said to her servants, "Bring
me some bath oil and some perfume,
and lock the gates, so that I won't be disturbed." 18 The servants locked the main
gates and went out by the side door to
get what Susanna had asked for. They
did not notice the two men.
19 As soon as the servants had left, the
two judges jumped out from their hiding
place, ran to Susanna, 20 and said to her,
"The gates are locked and no one will
see us. We are burning to have sex with
you, so give us what we want. 21 If you
don't, we will go to court and swear that
we saw you send your servants away,
so that you could be alone with a
young man."
22 "There is no way out," Susanna
moaned. "If I give in to you, I could be
put to death for adultery. If I refuse, you
will still have me trapped. 23 But I would
rather be your innocent victim than sin
against the Lord." 24 So she started

screaming as loud as she could, and the
two judges began shouting accusations,
25 while one of them ran and unlocked
the gates.
26 As soon as the servants in the house
heard all the noise, they ran into the gardens through the side door to find out
what had happened to Susanna. 27 The
judges told their story, and the servants
were shocked and ashamed. Such a
thing had never before been said about
Susanna.

The Judges Testify against Susanna

28 The next day, when the people assembled at Joakim's house, the two
judges arrived, fully determined to carry
out their wicked plan to have Susanna
put to death. 29 In front of all the people
they said, "Send for Joakim's wife Susanna, the daughter of Hilkiah." When
she was called, 30 she came in with her
parents, her children, and all her other
relatives. 31 Susanna was so graceful and
beautiful 32 that the two wicked men ordered her veil to be removed, so that
they might enjoy looking at her. 33 Her
family and everyone else were in tears.
34 Then the two judges stood up in
front of the people, placed their hands
on Susanna's head, and began making
their accusations against her. 35 She was
crying, but she looked up to heaven because she trusted the Lord. 36 The two
men gave the following testimony: "We
were walking in the gardens when this
woman came in with her two servant
women. She locked the main gates and
asked the servants to leave. 37 Then a
young man who had been hiding in the
gardens came to her, and they lay down
together. 38 We were in a corner of the
gardens, and when we saw what was
happening, we ran over 39 and caught
them in the act. We tried to hold on to
the man, but he was too strong for us. He
ran and opened the gates and got away,
40 but we were able to hold the woman.
We asked her who the man was, but she
refused to tell us. We swear that our testimony is true." 41 Because the two men
were not only leaders in the community
but also judges, the people believed
their story and condemned Susanna to
death.

Daniel Rescues Susanna

42 Then Susanna cried out in a loud
voice, "Eternal God, nothing can be kept
secret from you; you know everything
before it happens. 43 Here I am about to
die, but you know that I am innocent,
that these men are lying. Why must
I die?"
44 The Lord heard her prayer 45 and led
a young man named Daniel to speak out,
just as Susanna was being taken away to
her death. 46 He shouted, "I refuse to be a
party to her death!"
47 Everyone turned around to look at
him and asked, "What are you talking
about?"
48 Daniel stood up before them and
said, "People of Israel, how foolish can
you be? Are you going to condemn an
Israelite woman to death on this kind of
evidence? You haven't even tried to find
out the truth. 49 Reopen the case. The testimony these men gave was a lie."
50 So all the people hurried back to
where the trial had taken place, and the
officials said to Daniel, "God has given
you wisdom beyond your years, so come
and join us and explain to us what you
mean."
51 Daniel said to them, "Separate the
two judges, and let me question them
one at a time." 52 Then Daniel called the
first judge and said, "You wicked old
man, now you will have to answer for all
the sins you have committed. 53 You
have been giving unjust sentences. You
have condemned the innocent and released the guilty, even though the Lord
has said, 'Do not put an innocent person
to death.' 54 Now if you really did see this
couple making love, tell me, what tree
were they under?"
"Under a small gum tree," he answered.
55 Daniel said, "All right! That lie will
cost you your life. God's angel has already been given orders to chop[a] you
in two."
56 Then the first judge was led away
and the second one was brought before
Daniel. "You are more like a Canaanite
than a Jew," Daniel said to him. "This
woman's beauty has warped your judgment, and lust has corrupted your thinking. 57 You are used to having your way
with the women of Israel because they

[a] CHOP: *This word in Greek sounds like the Greek for "a small gum tree."*

have been afraid of you, but here is a
Jewish woman, and she would not give
in. 58 Now, tell me what tree you saw
them under."
"Under a large oak tree," he answered.
59 Daniel said, "All right! That lie will
cost you your life; God's angel is waiting
with his sword in his hand, ready to
cut[b] you in two. Then we shall be rid of
you both."
60 Then all the people shouted and
praised God, who saves those who put
their trust in him. 61 They turned against
the two judges because Daniel had
proved that they had lied under oath.
62 The Law of Moses states that people
who give false testimony shall receive
the same punishment that the accused
person would have received. And so the
two judges were put to death, and the
life of an innocent woman was saved.
63 Susanna's parents, her husband, and
all her relatives praised God because she
had been proved innocent of the
charges. 64 From that day on, Daniel was
held in high regard.

[b] CUT: *This word in Greek sounds like the Greek for "a large oak tree."*

BEL AND THE DRAGON

Introduction

Bel and the Dragon, *consists of two stories which were added to the Greek translation of* The Book of Daniel. *The first tells of Daniel's wisdom and courage in revealing the falseness of the idol Bel, and the second describes how he destroyed a dragon which was worshiped by the Babylonians.*

Outline of Contents

Daniel and the Priests of Bel

1 After the death of King Astyages, Cyrus of Persia took over his kingdom.
2 Daniel was one of King Cyrus' closest
companions, and the king thought more
highly of Daniel than of any other of his
advisers.
3 The Babylonians had an idol named
Bel. Each day the people had to provide
Bel with an offering of twelve bushels of
fine flour, forty sheep, and fifty gallons
of wine. 4 King Cyrus believed that Bel
was a god, and each day he used to go
and worship it. But Daniel worshiped his
own God.
5 One day the king asked Daniel, "Why
don't you worship Bel?"
Daniel answered, "I do not worship
idols made with human hands. I worship
only the living God, who created heaven
and earth and is the Lord of all human
beings."
6 "And don't you believe that our god
Bel is really alive?" asked the king.
"Haven't you seen how much he eats
and drinks every day?"
7 Daniel laughed and said, "Don't be
fooled, Your Majesty. This god you call
Bel is nothing more than clay covered
with bronze; it has never eaten or drunk
anything."
8-10 At this the king became angry and
called in all seventy of the priests of Bel.
He said to them, "I warn you that you
will be put to death, unless you can show
me that it is Bel who is eating these offerings. If you prove to me that it is Bel,
then I will have Daniel put to death for
claiming that Bel is not a god."
Daniel agreed to this proposal.
11 Then they all went with the king into

Bel's temple, where the priests said to
the king, "Your Majesty, we will go out
and let you place the food on the table
and prepare the wine. When you leave,
you may lock the door behind you and
seal it with the royal seal. 12 In the morning when you return, if you find that Bel
has not eaten everything, you can put us
to death. But if he has, Daniel will die for
making false accusations against us."

13 But the priests were not worried, because they had made a secret entrance
underneath a table in the temple, so that
they could go in every night and eat the
offerings.

14 When the priests had left, the king
set out the food for Bel. Then Daniel ordered his servants to bring some ashes
and scatter them all over the floor of the
temple. No one except the king saw
them do this. After that they all went
out, locked the door, sealed it with the
royal seal, and left.

15 That night, as usual, the priests with
their wives and children came into the
temple by the secret entrance and ate all
the food and drank all the wine.

16 Early the next morning, the king
and Daniel went to the temple. 17 The
king asked, "Have the seals been broken, Daniel?"

"No, Your Majesty, they have not been
broken," he replied.

18 As soon as the door was opened, the
king saw the empty table and shouted,
"You are great, O Bel! You really are
a god."

19 But Daniel began to laugh and said
to the king, "Before you enter the temple, look at the floor and tell me whose
footprints you see there."

20 "I see the footprints of men, women,
and children," said the king, 21 and he
became so angry that he had the priests
and their families arrested and brought
to him. They showed him the secret
doors through which they had come in
each night to eat the food placed on the
table. 22 So the king had the priests put to
death, and he gave Bel to Daniel, who
destroyed the idol and tore down its
temple.

Daniel Kills the Dragon

23 There was also a huge dragon which
the Babylonians worshiped. 24 One day
the king said to Daniel, "You can't tell
me that this god is not alive. So worship him!"

25 "I worship the Lord," replied Daniel.
"He is the only living God. 26 And if Your
Majesty will give me permission, I will
kill this dragon of yours without using a
sword or a club."

"You have my permission," answered
the king.

27 So Daniel took some tar, some fat,
and some hair and boiled them all together. He made cakes out of the mixture and fed them to the dragon. When
the dragon ate them, it swelled up and
burst open. "That's the kind of thing you
Babylonians worship," said Daniel.

28 When the people of Babylon heard
what had happened, they staged an angry demonstration against the king.
"The king has become a Jew," they
shouted. "First he destroyed Bel and
slaughtered the priests, and now he has
killed our dragon." 29 They went to the
king and demanded that Daniel be
handed over to them. "If you refuse,"
they warned the king, "we will put you
and your family to death."

30 When the king saw that they meant
what they said, he was forced to hand
Daniel over to them. 31 They threw him
into a pit of lions, where they left him for
six days. 32 There were seven lions in the
pit, and normally they were fed two human bodies and two sheep each day. But
they were given nothing to eat during
these six days, in order to make sure
that Daniel would be eaten.

Daniel Is Rescued from the Pit of Lions

33 At that time the prophet Habakkuk
was in the land of Judah. He had cooked
a stew and crumbled bread into it. He
was carrying a bowl of it to the workers
who were out in the fields harvesting
grain, 34 when an angel of the Lord
spoke to him, "Take the food you are
carrying and give it to Daniel, who is in
Babylon in a pit of lions."

35 Habakkuk answered, "Sir, I have
never been to Babylon, and I don't know
where the pit of lions is."

36 So the angel grabbed the prophet by
the hair and took him to Babylon with

the speed of the wind.[a] He set him down
near the pit of lions. 37 Habakkuk called
out, "Daniel! Daniel! God has sent you
some food. Here, take it."

38 When Daniel heard Habakkuk, he
prayed, "God, you did remember me;
you never abandon those who love you."
39 Then he got up and ate the meal, and
God's angel immediately took Habakkuk home.

40 Seven days after Daniel had been
thrown to the lions, the king went to the
pit to mourn for him. When he got there
and looked in, there sat Daniel. 41 The
king shouted, "O Lord, the God of Daniel, how great you are. You alone are
God." 42 So he pulled Daniel out of the pit
and had those who had tried to kill Daniel thrown into it. And the lions ate them
immediately, while the king watched.

a with the speed of the wind; *or* by the power of his spirit.

The First Book of the
MACCABEES

Introduction

The First Book of the Maccabees *describes events in Jewish history from the time of Antiochus Epiphanes (175 B.C.) to the rise of John Hyrcanus (134 B.C.).*

The historical interest of the book centers in the Hasmonean, or Maccabean, family, and it supports the view that they are divinely chosen to save Israel. The book also has a strong religious theme: God is at work in history and will give victory as a reward to those who are faithful to him.

Outline of Contents

Alexander the Great

1 This history begins when Alexander the Great, son of Philip of Macedonia, marched from Macedonia and
attacked Darius, king of Persia and
Media. Alexander enlarged the Greek
Empire by defeating Darius and seiz-
ing his throne. 2 He fought many battles, captured fortified cities, and
put the kings of the region to death.
3 As he advanced to the ends of the
earth, he plundered many nations;
and when he had conquered the
world, he became proud and arrogant.
4 By building up a strong army, he
dominated whole nations and their
rulers, and forced everyone to pay him
taxes.
5-7 When Alexander had been emperor for twelve years, he fell ill and
realized that he was about to die. He
called together his generals, noblemen who had been brought up with
him since his early childhood, and he
divided his empire, giving a part to
each of them. 8 After his death, the
generals took control, 9 and each had
himself crowned king of his own
territory. The descendants of these
kings ruled for many generations and
brought a great deal of misery on the
world.

Antiochus Epiphanes and the Renegade Jews

(2 Maccabees 4.7-17)

10 The wicked ruler Antiochus Epiphanes, son of King Antiochus the Third of
Syria, was a descendant of one of Alexander's generals. Antiochus Epiphanes
had been a hostage in Rome before he
became king of Syria in the year 137.[a]
11 At that time there appeared in the
land of Israel a group of traitorous Jews
who had no regard for the Law and who
had a bad influence on many of our people. They said, "Let's come to terms with
the Gentiles, for our refusal to associate
with them has brought us nothing but
trouble." 12 This proposal appealed to
many people, 13 and some of them became so enthusiastic about it that they
went to the king and received from him
permission to follow Gentile customs.
14 They built in Jerusalem a stadium like
those in the Greek cities. 15 They had
surgery performed to hide their circumcision, abandoned the holy covenant,
started associating with[b] Gentiles, and
did all sorts of other evil things.

Antiochus Attacks Egypt

16 When Antiochus had firmly established himself as king, he decided to
conquer Egypt and rule that country as
well as Syria. 17 He invaded Egypt with a

[a] THE YEAR 137: *The dates in this book are counted from the beginning of the Syrian Kingdom in 312 B.C. The year 137 corresponds to 175 B.C.* [b] started associating with; *or* married.

large fleet of ships and a powerful army,
including chariots, elephants, and cavalry. 18 When the attack came, King Ptolemy of Egypt turned and fled, and many
of his soldiers were killed. 19 Antiochus
was able to capture the fortified cities of
Egypt and plunder the whole land.

Antiochus Persecutes the Jews

20 In the year 143,[c] after the conquest
of Egypt, Antiochus marched with a
great army against the land of Israel and
the city of Jerusalem. 21 In his arrogance,
he entered the Temple and took away
the gold altar, the lampstand with all its
equipment, 22 the table for the bread offered to the Lord, the cups and bowls,
the gold fire pans, the curtain, and the
crowns. He also stripped all the gold
from the front of the Temple 23 and carried off the silver and gold and everything else of value, including all the
treasures that he could find stored there.
24 Then he took it all to his own country.
He had also murdered many people and
boasted arrogantly about it. 25 There was
great mourning everywhere in the land
of Israel.

26 Rulers and leaders groaned in
sorrow.
Young men and young women
grew weak.
The beauty of our women faded.
27 Every bridegroom sang a funeral
song,
and every bride sat mourning in
her room.
28 All our people were clothed with
shame,
and our land trembled for them.

29 Two years later Antiochus sent a
large army from Mysia[d] against the
towns of Judea. When the soldiers entered Jerusalem, 30 their commander
spoke to the people, offering them terms
of peace and completely deceiving them.
Then he suddenly launched a fierce attack on the city, dealing it a major blow
and killing many of the people. 31 He
plundered the city, set it on fire, and tore
down its buildings and walls. 32 He and
his army took the women and children
as prisoners and seized the cattle.
33 Then Antiochus and his forces built
high walls and strong towers in the area
north of the Temple, turning it into a
fort. 34 They brought in a group of traitorous Jews and installed them there.
35 They also brought in arms and supplies and stored in the fort all the loot
that they had taken in Jerusalem. This
fort became a great threat to the city.

36 The fort was a threat to the
Temple,
a constant, evil menace for Israel.
37 Innocent people were murdered
around the altar;
the Holy Place was defiled by
murderers.
38 The people of Jerusalem fled in
fear,
and the city became a colony of
foreigners.
Jerusalem was foreign to its own
people,
who had been forced to abandon
the city.
39 Her Temple was as empty as a
wilderness;
her festivals were turned into days
of mourning,
her Sabbath joy into shame.
Her honor became an object of
ridicule.
40 Her shame was as great as her
former glory,
and her pride was turned into
deepest mourning.

41-43 Antiochus now issued a decree
that all nations in his empire should
abandon their own customs and become
one people. All the Gentiles and even
many of the Israelites submitted to this
decree. They adopted the official pagan
religion, offered sacrifices to idols, and
no longer observed the Sabbath.
44 The king also sent messengers with
a decree to Jerusalem and all the towns
of Judea, ordering the people to follow
customs that were foreign to the country. 45 He ordered them not to offer burnt
offerings, grain offerings, or wine offerings in the Temple, and commanded
them to treat Sabbaths and festivals as
ordinary work days. 46 They were even
ordered to defile the Temple and the
holy things in it.[e] 47 They were commanded to build pagan altars, temples,
and shrines, and to sacrifice pigs and

[c] THE YEAR 143: *This corresponds to 169 B.C.* [d] *Probable text* a large army from Mysia; *Greek* a tax collector with a large army. [e] the holy things in it; *or* the priests.

other unclean animals there. 48 They
were forbidden to circumcise their sons
and were required to make themselves
ritually unclean in every way they could,
49 so that they would forget the Law
which the Lord had given through
Moses and would disobey all its commands. 50 The penalty for disobeying the
king's decree was death.

51 The king not only issued the same
decree throughout his whole empire, but
he also appointed officials to supervise
the people and commanded each town
in Judea to offer pagan sacrifices.
52 Many of the Jews were ready to forsake the Law and to obey these officials.
They defiled the land with their evil,
53 and their conduct forced all true Israelites to hide wherever they could.

54 On the fifteenth day of the month of
Kislev in the year 145,[f] King Antiochus
set up "The Awful Horror" on the altar of
the Temple, and pagan altars were built
in the towns throughout Judea. 55 Pagan
sacrifices were offered in front of houses
and in the streets. 56 Any books of the
Law which were found were torn up and
burned, 57 and anyone who was caught
with a copy of the sacred books or who
obeyed the Law was put to death by order of the king. 58 Month after month
these wicked people used their power
against the Israelites caught in the
towns.

59 On the twenty-fifth of the month,
these same evil people offered sacrifices
on the pagan altar erected on top of the
altar in the Temple. 60 Mothers who had
allowed their babies to be circumcised
were put to death in accordance with the
king's decree. 61 Their babies were hung
around their necks, and their families
and those who had circumcised them
were put to death. 62 But many people in
Israel firmly resisted the king's decree
and refused to eat food that was ritually
unclean. 63 They preferred to die rather
than break the holy covenant and eat
unclean food—and many did die. 64 In
his anger God made Israel suffer
terribly.

The Faithfulness of Mattathias

2 During that time, a priest of the Jehoiarib family named Mattathias,
who was the son of John and the grandson of Simeon, moved from Jerusalem
and settled in Modein. 2 Mattathias had
five sons: John (also called Gaddi), 3 Simon (also called Thassi), 4 Judas (also
called Maccabeus), 5 Eleazar (also called
Avaran), and Jonathan (also called
Apphus).

6 When Mattathias saw all the sins that
were being committed in Judea and Jerusalem, 7 he said:

"Why was I born to see these
terrible things,
the ruin of my people and of the
holy city?
Must I sit here helpless
while the city is surrendered to
enemies
and the Temple falls into the
hands of foreigners?
8 The Temple is like someone
without honor.
9 Its splendid furnishings
have been carried away as loot.
Our children have been killed in
the streets,
and our young men by the
sword of the enemy.
10 Every nation in the world has
occupied the city
and robbed her of her
possessions.
11 All her ornaments have been
stripped away;
she is now a slave, no longer
free.
12 Look at our Temple, profaned by
the Gentiles,
emptied of all its splendor.
13 Why should we go on living?"

14 In their grief, Mattathias and his
sons tore their clothes, put on sackcloth,
and continued in deep mourning.
15 Then the king's officials, who were
forcing the people to turn from God,
came to the town of Modein to force the
people there to offer pagan sacrifices.
16 Many of the Israelites came to meet
them, including Mattathias and his sons.
17 The king's officials said to Mattathias,
"You are a respected leader in this town,
and you have the support of your sons
and relatives. 18 Why not be the first one
here to do what the king has commanded? All the Gentiles, the people of

[f] THE YEAR 145: *This corresponds to 167 B.C.*

Judea, and all the people left in Jerusalem have already done so. If you do, you
and your sons will be honored with the
title of 'Friends of the King,' and you will
be rewarded with silver and gold and
many gifts."
19 Mattathias answered in a loud voice,
"I don't care if every Gentile in this empire has obeyed the king and yielded to
the command to abandon the religion of
his ancestors. 20 My children, my relatives, and I will continue to keep the covenant that God made with our ancestors.
21 With God's help we will never abandon his Law or disobey his commands.
22 We will not obey the king's decree,
and we will not change our way of worship in the least."
23 Just as he finished speaking, one of
the men from Modein decided to obey
the king's decree and stepped out in
front of everyone to offer a pagan sacrifice on the altar that stood there. 24 When
Mattathias saw him, he became angry
enough to do what had to be done. Shaking with rage, he ran forward and killed
the man right there on the altar. 25 He
also killed the royal official who was
forcing the people to sacrifice, and then
he tore down the altar. 26 In this way
Mattathias showed his deep devotion for
the Law, just as Phinehas had done
when he killed Zimri son of Salu.

The Guerrilla Warfare of Mattathias

27 Then Mattathias went through the
town shouting, "Everyone who is faithful to God's covenant and obeys his
Law, follow me!" 28 With this, he and his
sons fled to the mountains, leaving behind all they owned.
29-30 At that time also many of the Israelites who were seeking to be right with
God through obedience to the Law went
out to live in the wilderness, taking their
children, their wives, and their livestock
with them, because of the terrible oppression they were suffering. 31 The report soon reached the king's officials
and the soldiers in the fort at Jerusalem
that some men who had defied the king's
command had gone into hiding in the
wilderness. 32 A large force of soldiers
pursued them, caught up with them, set
up camp opposite them, and prepared to
attack them on the Sabbath. 33 "There is
still time," they shouted out to the Jews.
"Come out and obey the king's command, and we will spare your lives."
34 "We will not come out," they answered. "We will not obey the king's
command, and we will not profane the
Sabbath."
35 The soldiers attacked them immediately, 36 but the Jews did nothing to resist; they did not even throw stones or
block the entrances to the caves where
they were hiding. 37 They said, "We will
all die with a clear conscience. Let
heaven and earth bear witness that you
are slaughtering us unjustly." 38 So the
enemy attacked them on the Sabbath
and killed the men, their wives, their
children, and their livestock. A thousand
people died.
39 When Mattathias and his friends
heard the news about this, they were
greatly saddened 40 and said to one another, "If all of us do as these other Jews
have done and refuse to fight the Gentiles to defend our lives and our religion,
we will soon be wiped off the face of the
earth." 41 On that day they decided that if
anyone attacked them on the Sabbath,
they would defend themselves, so that
they would not all die as those Jews had
died in the caves.
42 Then Mattathias and his friends
were joined by a group of devout and
patriotic Jews, the strongest and bravest
men in Israel, who had all volunteered to
defend the Law. 43 In addition, everyone
who was fleeing from the persecution
joined them and strengthened their
forces. 44 Now that they had an army,
they gave vent to their anger by attacking the renegade Jews. Those who escaped were forced to flee to the Gentiles
for safety. 45 Mattathias and his friends
went everywhere tearing down pagan
altars 46 and circumcising by force every
uncircumcised boy they found within
the borders of Israel. 47 They were also
successful in hunting down the arrogant
Gentile officials. 48 They rescued the
Law of Moses from the Gentiles and
their kings and broke the power of the
wicked King Antiochus.

The Death of Mattathias

49 When the time came for Mattathias
to die, he said to his sons, "These are
times of violence and distress. Arrogant
people are in control and have made us
an object of ridicule. 50 But you, my sons,

must be devoted to the Law and ready to
die to defend God's covenant with our
ancestors. 51 Remember what our ancestors did and how much they accomplished in their day. Follow their
example, and you will be rewarded with
great glory and undying fame. 52 Remember how Abraham put his trust in
the Lord when he was tested and how
the Lord was pleased with him and accepted him. 53 Joseph, in his time of
trouble, obeyed God's commands and
became ruler over the land of Egypt.
54 Phinehas, our ancestor, because of his
burning devotion, was given the promise
that his descendants would always be
priests. 55 Joshua was made a judge in
Israel because he obeyed the command
of Moses. 56 Caleb brought back a good
report to the community and was given a
part of the land as a reward. 57 David
was made king and was given the promise that his descendants would always
be kings because of his steadfast loyalty
to God. 58 Elijah, because of his great devotion to the Law, was taken up into
heaven. 59 Hananiah, Azariah, and Mishael were saved from the flames because
they had faith. 60 Daniel was a man of
integrity, and the Lord rescued him from
the mouth of the lions. 61 Take each of
these ancestors of ours as an example,
and you will realize that no one who
puts his trust in the Lord will ever lack
strength. 62 Don't be afraid of the threats
of a wicked man. Remember that he will
die and all his splendor will end with
worms feeding on his decaying body.
63 Today he may be highly honored, but
tomorrow he will disappear; his body
will return to the earth and his scheming
will come to an end. 64 But you, my sons,
be strong and courageous in defending
the Law, because it is through the Law
that you will earn great glory.

65 "Your brother Simon is wise, so always listen to him as you would to me.
66 Judas Maccabeus has been strong all
his life; he will be your commander and
will lead you in battle against the enemy.
67 Call everyone who obeys God's Law to
rally around you; then avenge the
wrongs done to your people. 68 Pay back
the Gentiles for what they have done,
and always obey the Law and its
commands."

69 Then Mattathias gave them his
blessing and died. 70 He was buried in
the family tomb at Modein, and all the
people of Israel went into deep mourning for him. This happened in the
year 146.[g]

The Early Victories of Judas

(2 Maccabees 8.1-7)

3 Judas Maccabeus took the place of
his father Mattathias. 2 All his
brothers and all the loyal followers of
his father gave him their support, and
they were happy to carry on Israel's war.

3 Judas brought greater glory to his
people.
In his armor, he was like a giant.
He took up his weapons and went
to war;
with his own sword he defended
his camp.
4 He was like a ferocious lion
roaring as it attacks.
5 Judas hunted down those who
broke the Law
and set fire to all who oppressed
his people.
6 In fear of him, lawless men
huddled together in terror,
not knowing which way to turn.
He advanced the cause of freedom
by what he did.
7 He made life miserable for many
kings,
but brought joy to the people
of Israel.
We will praise him forever for
what he did.
8 He went through the towns of
Judea
and destroyed all the
godless men.
He relieved Israel of its terrible
suffering.[h]
9 His fame spread to the ends of
the earth,
as he gathered together those
who were threatened with
death.

10 Then Apollonius assembled a Gentile army, including a large force from

[g] THE YEAR 146: *This corresponds to 166 B.C.* [h] relieved Israel of its terrible suffering; *or* saved Israel from God's anger.

Samaria, to attack the people of Israel.
11 When Judas learned of this, he
marched out to battle, defeated the
army, and killed Apollonius. Many Gentiles lost their lives, and the rest fled.
12 When the spoils of war were collected,
Judas took the sword of Apollonius and
used it in battle until the day he died.

13 Seron, the general of the Syrian
forces, learned that Judas had gathered
together an army, consisting of a band
of loyal men who were ready to fight under his command. 14 Seron said to himself, "I will make a reputation for myself
throughout the empire by defeating Judas and his men, who have no respect
for the king's command." 15 Then he began a new campaign against Judas and
was joined by a strong force of godless
men who were eager to help him take
vengeance on Israel. 16 When he approached the pass at Beth Horon, Judas
went out to meet him with a small group
of men. 17 When Judas' men saw the
army coming against them, they asked,
"How can our little group of men fight
an army as big as that? Besides, we have
not eaten all day, and we are tired!"

18 "It is not difficult," Judas answered,
"for a small group to overpower a large
one. It makes no difference to the Lord
whether we are rescued by many people
or by just a few. 19 Victory in battle does
not depend on who has the largest army;
it is the Lord's power that determines
the outcome. 20 Our enemies are coming
against us with great violence, intending
to plunder our possessions and kill our
wives and children. 21 But we are fighting for our lives and for our religion.
22 When we attack, the Lord will crush
our enemies, so don't be afraid of
them."

23 As soon as Judas had finished
speaking, he and his men made a sudden
attack against Seron and his army and
crushed them. 24 They pursued them
down the pass at Beth Horon to the plain
and killed about 800 men. Those who escaped fled to Philistia. 25 After that, Gentiles everywhere began to be afraid of
Judas and his brothers. 26 His fame
reached the ears of King Antiochus, and
people in every nation talked about Judas and his victories.

The King Appoints Lysias as Governor

27 When Antiochus heard what had
happened, he was furious. He ordered
all the armies of his empire to assemble
in one huge force. 28 From his treasury
he paid a full year's wages to his soldiers
and ordered them to be prepared for any
emergency. 29 But then he found that the
funds in his treasury were exhausted.
Income from taxes had decreased because of the disorder and the troubles
he had brought on the world by doing
away with the laws which had been
in force from the earliest times. 30 Antiochus had always given presents more
lavishly than earlier kings, but now
he was worried that he might not be
able to continue this, or even to meet
expenses—this had happened once or
twice before. 31 He was very disturbed;
but finally he decided to go to Persia,
collect the taxes from the provinces
there, and bring together a large sum of
ready cash.

32 He appointed Lysias, an important
man who had been granted the title
"Relative of the King," as governor to
take care of the king's affairs in the
whole territory between the Euphrates
River and the Egyptian border. 33 The
king also made Lysias the guardian of
his son Antiochus the Fifth until his own
return. 34 He put Lysias in charge of all
the elephants and of half his army, and
then gave him detailed instructions
about what he wanted done, and in particular, what he wanted done with the
inhabitants of Judea and Jerusalem.
35 Lysias was ordered to send an army
against the Jews, especially the Jews in
Jerusalem, to break their power and destroy them, so that no trace of them
would remain. 36 He was ordered to take
their land and give it to foreigners, who
would settle the whole area. 37 Taking
the other half of his army, the king set
out from Antioch, his capital city, in the
year 147.[i] He crossed the Euphrates
River and marched through Mesopotamia.

The Victories of Judas

(2 Maccabees 8.8-29, 34-36)

38 Lysias chose Nicanor, Gorgias, and
Ptolemy son of Dorymenes as army

[i] THE YEAR 147: *This corresponds to 165 B.C.*

commanders; all three were able men
who bore the title "Friend of the King."
39 He put them in charge of 40,000 infantry and 7,000 cavalry and ordered them
to invade the land of Judea and destroy
it as the king had commanded. 40 These
commanders set out with their entire
force, and when they came to the plains
near Emmaus, they made camp.
41 A force from Idumea[l] and Philistia
joined them. The merchants of the region heard about the strength of the
army, and they came to the camp with
chains and a large amount of money,
hoping to buy some Jewish slaves.

42 Judas and his brothers saw that
their situation was getting more and
more difficult, with foreign armies
camped within their own borders. They
also learned that the king had commanded the complete destruction of the
people. 43 So they determined to rebuild
their ruined nation and fight for their
country and the Temple. 44 Then the
whole community came together to
prepare for war and to pray for God's
mercy.

45 Jerusalem was as empty as a
 wilderness;
no citizens left or entered the city.
The holy Temple was profaned by
 foreigners,
and Gentiles camped in the city's
 fort;
so joy departed from the people
 of Israel,
and the sound of music was heard
 no more.

46 Then Judas and his men assembled
and marched to Mizpah, opposite Jerusalem, because the people of Israel had
previously had a place of worship there.
47 In deep mourning, they fasted all that
day, put on sackcloth, threw ashes on
their heads, and tore their clothes. 48 The
Gentiles would have consulted their
idols in such a situation, but the Israelites unrolled the book of the Law to
search for God's guidance. 49 They
brought the priests' robes, the offerings
of the first grain, and the tithes, and then
they brought in some Nazirites who had
completed their vows. 50 The whole community prayed, "Lord, what shall we do
with these things? Where shall we take
them, 51 now that your holy Temple has
been trampled and profaned by Gentiles, and your priests mourn in disgrace? 52 The Gentiles have come to
attack and destroy us. You know what
they plan to do! 53 If you don't help us,
how can we stand up against them?"
54 Then they blew trumpets and shouted
loudly.

55 After that, Judas divided his men
into groups of ten, fifty, a hundred, and
a thousand, placing officers in charge of
each group. 56 Then, in obedience to the
Law, he sent home everyone who had
recently been married, built a house, or
planted a vineyard, as well as anyone
who was afraid. 57 Finally, the army
marched out and took up positions south
of Emmaus, 58 where Judas said to them:
"Prepare yourselves for battle and be
courageous! Be ready early tomorrow
morning to fight these Gentiles who
have joined forces to attack us and destroy us and our Temple. 59 It is better for
us to die fighting than to stand idly by
and watch the destruction of our nation
and our Temple. 60 But the Lord will do
what he pleases."

4 Gorgias took 5,000 infantry and
1,000 of his most experienced cavalry and left camp by night, 2 with men
from the fort in Jerusalem as his guides.
He had planned to make a surprise attack on the Jewish army, 3 but Judas
learned of the plan and moved out with
his men to attack the king's army at
Emmaus 4 while Gorgias and his troops
were still away from the camp. 5 When
Gorgias and his army reached Judas'
camp that night, they found no one
there. They thought Judas and his men
were trying to escape, so they started
looking for them in the mountains.

6 At dawn Judas appeared in the plain
with 3,000 men, not all of them as well
armed as they would have liked. 7 They
saw the huge Gentile army of experienced troops wearing armor and protected by cavalry. 8 But Judas said to his
men, "Don't worry about the size of their
army, and don't be frightened when they
attack. 9 Remember how our ancestors
were saved at the Red Sea when the king
of Egypt was pursuing them with his
army! 10 Now let us ask the Lord to have
mercy on us. Let us pray that he will
honor his covenant with our ancestors

[l] *Probable text* Idumea; *Greek* Syria.

and crush this army when we attack today. 11 Then all the Gentiles will know
that Israel has a God who rescues and
saves them."
12 When the Gentiles saw Judas and
his men preparing for battle, 13 they
moved out of their camp to fight. Then
Judas and his men sounded their trumpets 14 and attacked. The Gentiles broke
ranks and fled to the plain, 15 but all the
stragglers were killed. The Israelites
pursued the enemy as far as Gezer, the
plains of Idumea, and the towns of Azotus and Jamnia. Altogether they killed
about 3,000 of the enemy.
16 When Judas and his army came
back from the pursuit, 17-18 he said to his
men, "Don't be greedy for loot. Gorgias
and his army are nearby in the mountains, so there is still heavy fighting
ahead of us. We must stand firm and
fight. After that, you can safely take all
the loot you want." 19 Judas was just finishing his speech when an enemy patrol
on a scouting mission looked down from
the mountains 20 and saw that their army
had been put to flight; they could tell
from the smoke that their camp was
burning. 21 When they saw all this, they
were terrified, and when they also saw
that Judas' army was in the plain ready
for battle, 22 they all fled to Philistia.
23 Then Judas returned to loot the enemy
camp; he took large amounts of gold and
silver, blue and purple cloth, and other
rich plunder. 24 When the Jews came
back to their own camp, they sang a
hymn: "The Lord is worthy of praise; his
mercy endures forever." 25 That day
brought a great victory to the people of
Israel.

Victory over Lysias

(2 Maccabees 11.1-12)

26 The Gentile troops that escaped
went to Lysias and reported all that had
happened. 27 When Lysias heard that his
troops had lost the battle, he was
shocked and disappointed that Israel
had not been defeated as the king had
commanded.
28 In the following year Lysias gathered an army of 60,000 well-trained infantry and 5,000 cavalry, intending to
conquer the Jews. 29 They marched into
Idumea and camped at Bethzur. Judas
came to meet them with 10,000 men.
30 When Judas saw how strong the enemy's army was, he prayed, "We will
praise you, Savior of Israel. You broke
the attack of the giant by the hand of
your servant David and you let Saul's
son Jonathan and the young man who
carried his weapons defeat the entire
Philistine army. 31 Now in the same way
let your people Israel defeat our enemy.
Put them to shame, in spite of all their
confidence in their infantry and cavalry.
32 Make them afraid; let their bold
strength melt away; let them tremble at
the prospect of defeat. 33 We love and
worship you; so let us kill our enemies,
that we may then sing your praises."
34 The battle began, and in the hand-
to-hand fighting about 5,000 of Lysias'
men were killed. 35 When Lysias saw
that his army was being defeated and
when he saw the reckless courage of Judas and his men, who showed that they
were ready to live or die with honor, he
returned to Antioch. There he recruited
some mercenaries and planned to return
to Judea later with a much larger army.

The Purification of the Temple

(2 Maccabees 10.1-8)

36 Judas and his brothers said, "Now
that our enemies have been defeated,
let's go to Jerusalem to purify the Temple and rededicate it." 37 So the whole
army was assembled and went up to
Mount Zion. 38 There they found the
Temple abandoned, the altar profaned,
the gates burned down, the courtyards
grown up in a forest of weeds, and the
priests' rooms torn down. 39 In their sorrow, they tore their clothes, cried loudly,
threw ashes on their heads, 40 and fell
face down on the ground. When the signal was given on the trumpets, everyone
cried out to the Lord.
41 Then Judas ordered some of his soldiers to attack the men in the fort, while
he purified the Temple. 42 He chose some
priests who were qualified and who
were devoted to the Law. 43 They purified the Temple and took the stones that
had been defiled and put them in an unclean place. 44 They discussed what
should be done with the altar of burnt
offerings, which had been desecrated
45 by the Gentiles, and decided to tear it
down, so that it would not stand there as
a monument to their shame. So they tore
down the altar 46 and put the stones in a
suitable place on the Temple hill, where

they were to be kept until a prophet
should appear and decide what to do
with them. 47 Then they took uncut
stones, as the Law of Moses required,
and built a new altar like the old one.
48 They repaired the Temple, inside and
out, and dedicated its courtyards.
49 They made new utensils for worship
and brought the lampstand, the altar of
incense, and the table for the bread into
the Temple. 50 They burned incense on
the altar and lit the lamps on the lampstand, and there was light in the Temple!
51 They placed the loaves of bread on the
table, hung the curtains, and completed
all the work.

52-54 The twenty-fifth day of the ninth
month, the month of Kislev, in the year
148[k] was the anniversary of the day the
Gentiles had desecrated the altar. On
that day a sacrifice was offered on the
new altar in accordance with the Law of
Moses. The new altar was dedicated and
hymns were sung to the accompaniment
of harps, lutes, and cymbals. 55 All the
people bowed down with their faces to
the ground and worshiped and praised
the Lord for giving them victory.

56 For eight days they celebrated the
rededication of the altar. With great joy
they brought burnt offerings and offered
fellowship offerings and thank offerings. 57 They decorated the front of the
Temple with gold crowns and shields,
rebuilt the gates and the priests' rooms
and put doors on them. 58 Now that the
Jews had removed the shame which the
Gentiles had brought, they held a great
celebration. 59 Then Judas, his brothers,
and the entire community of Israel decreed that the rededication of the altar
should be celebrated with a festival of
joy and gladness at the same time each
year, beginning on the twenty-fifth of
the month of Kislev and lasting for eight
days.

60 Then they built high walls and
strong towers around Mount Zion, so
that the Gentiles could not come in and
trample and defile it again. 61 Judas
placed a detachment of soldiers there to
guard the Temple. He also fortified the
town of Bethzur, so that the people of
Israel would have a fortress facing
Idumea.

Wars with Neighboring Nations

(2 Maccabees 10.14-33; 12.10-45)

5 When the neighboring nations
heard that the Jews had built the altar and restored the Temple as it had
been before, they were so furious 2 that
they made up their minds to destroy all
the Jews who were living among them.
So they began to murder and kill our
people.

3 The Idumeans were blockading the
Israelites, so Judas went to war against
them at Akrabattene, crushed them, and
looted them. 4 He also dealt with the people of Baean, who were a constant threat
to the people of Israel, because they
would lie in ambush waiting to trap Israelite travelers. 5 He shut the Baeanites up
in their forts, took a solemn oath that he
would destroy them, and burned their
forts with everyone in them. 6 Then he
marched against the land of Ammon,
where he met a large and powerful army
under the command of a man named
Timothy. 7 Judas won many battles
against them and finally defeated them.
8 He captured Jazer and its surrounding
villages and then returned to Judea.

9 The Gentiles in Gilead assembled to
attack and destroy the Israelites living in
their territory. But the Israelites fled to
the fortress of Dathema 10-11 and sent the
following letter to Judas and his brothers: "The Gentiles around us are joining
forces under Timothy. We have fled to
this fortress for protection, and now
they are getting ready to capture it and
destroy us. 12 Many of us have already
been killed. Come rescue us! 13 All the
Jewish men in the region of Tob[l] have
been killed, their wives and their children have been taken captive, and their
possessions have been carried off. A
force of about 1,000 men has been destroyed there."

14 This letter was still being read when
other messengers, who had torn their
clothes in sorrow, arrived with a report
from Galilee. 15 They said, "An army
from Ptolemais, Tyre, Sidon, and all of
Galilee has come together to destroy us."

16 When Judas and the people heard
all this, a great assembly was held to decide what should be done to help these

[k] THE YEAR 148: *This corresponds to 164 B.C.* [l] in the region of Tob; *or* who were fighting with Tobias.

countrymen, who were in such difficulty
under enemy attack. 17 Judas said to his
brother Simon, "Choose some men and
go rescue our fellow Jews in Galilee; our
brother Jonathan and I will go to Gilead." 18 Judas left the rest of his army to
defend Judea and put the two leaders,
Azariah and Joseph son of Zechariah, in
charge of the people. 19 He told them: "I
am leaving you in command here, but
don't go out and fight the Gentiles until
we get back." 20 Then 3,000 men joined
Simon for the march into Galilee, and
8,000 remained with Judas for the march
into Gilead.

21 Simon went into Galilee and fought
many battles with the Gentiles. He defeated them 22 and pursued them all the
way to the city of Ptolemais, killing
about 3,000 of them, and taking the loot.
23 Then he took the Jews who were in
Galilee and Arbatta, with their wives,
their children, and all they owned, and
brought them back to Judea with him.
There was great rejoicing.

24 During this time, Judas Maccabeus
and his brother Jonathan had crossed
the Jordan River and had marched for
three days through the desert. 25 They
met some friendly Nabateans who told
them all that had happened to the Jews
in Gilead. 26 They reported that many
Jews were imprisoned in the fortified
cities of Bozrah, Bosor, Alema, Chaspho, Maked, and Karnaim, 27 while others were imprisoned in the smaller
towns of Gilead. They also reported that
the enemy was drawn up to make an attack the next day on the Jewish fortresses, hoping to destroy all the Jews in
a single day.

28 So Judas and his army suddenly
turned and attacked Bozrah by the
desert road, captured the town, and
killed every man in it. They looted the
town and set it on fire. 29 They left there
and marched all night to the fortress at
Dathema. 30 At dawn Judas and his men
saw a vast army attacking the fortress;
they were bringing up ladders, siege
platforms, and battering rams in an effort to capture it. 31 When Judas heard
the noise, the shouts, and the sound of
trumpets coming from the city, he realized that the battle had begun, 32 so he
said to his men, "Fight today for our fellow Jews!"

33 He ordered his men to march in
three columns and attack the enemy
from the rear. As they moved forward,
they blew trumpets and shouted
prayers. 34 When the army under Timothy's command saw that it was Judas
Maccabeus, the soldiers turned and fled.
Judas crushed them and killed about
8,000 men that day.

35 Then Judas turned aside to attack
the town of Alema;[m] he captured it and
killed all the men in it. He looted the
town and set fire to it. 36 From there he
went on and captured Chaspho, Maked,
Bosor, and the other towns of Gilead.

37 After this, Timothy gathered another army and camped opposite Ra-
phon, on the other side of a river.
38 Judas sent some men to spy on the
camp, and they reported back to him
that all the Gentiles in the region had
joined Timothy and had formed a large
army. 39 Timothy had also hired Arab
mercenaries to help him, and these were
camped on the other side of the river
ready to attack Judas. So Judas went out
to meet them in battle.

40 As Judas and his army came closer
to the water, Timothy said to his officers,
"If he keeps on coming and crosses the
river, we won't be able to turn back his
attack, and he will defeat us. 41 But if he
is afraid and stops on the other side of
the river, we will cross over to attack
and defeat him." 42 When Judas reached
the bank of the river, he gave orders to
his officers to let no one stop but to push
everyone forward into battle. 43 Judas
was the first to cross the river against
the enemy, and all his men followed
him. The Gentiles broke ranks before
them, threw away their arms, and fled to
the pagan temple at Karnaim. 44 But Judas and his men took the city and
burned down the temple with all who
were in it. With Karnaim overthrown,
the Gentiles could no longer offer any
resistance to Judas.

45 Then Judas gathered together all the
Jews in Gilead to take them back to Judea with him. It was a large group of all
kinds of people, together with their
wives and children and all that they
owned. 46 They went as far as Ephron, a

[m] ALEMA: *The name of the town is not certain.*

large, well-fortified town. It was impossible to go around it on either side, and
the road passed directly through the
town. 47But the people there would not
let them pass and blocked the town
gates with stones. 48Then Judas sent a
friendly message to them: "Let us pass
through your territory to return home.
No one will harm you; we will just pass
through." But they still refused to open
the gates.
49So Judas told everyone in the group,
except the fighting men, to camp where
they were. 50The fighting men were ordered to take up their positions and attack the town. They fought all day and
all night, until they had taken it. 51Judas
had all the men of Ephron put to death,
plundered the town, and leveled it. Then
he and his army marched through the
town over the dead bodies. 52They
crossed the Jordan into the wide plain
opposite Beth Shan. 53Throughout the
whole march Judas kept gathering up
the stragglers and encouraging the people until they reached the land of Judea.
54With thanksgiving and rejoicing, they
went up to Mount Zion and sacrificed
burnt offerings because they had returned safely without a single loss.
55While Judas and Jonathan were in
Gilead and their brother Simon was attacking Ptolemais in Galilee, 56Joseph
and Azariah, the commanders of the
army in Judea, heard about their brave
deeds and victories. 57They said to one
another, "Let's go to war with the Gentiles around us and win some fame for
ourselves." 58So they and their men attacked Jamnia. 59Gorgias and his men
went out of the town to meet them in
battle. 60They defeated Joseph and Azariah and pursued them as far as the borders of Judea. At least 2,000 Israelite
men were killed that day. 61This great
defeat came about because the Jewish
commanders wanted to be heroes and
refused to obey Judas and his brothers.
62Besides, they did not belong to the
family of the Maccabees, whom God had
chosen to bring freedom to the people of
Israel.
63But Judas Maccabeus and his brothers won great respect among all the Israelites and all the Gentiles. When people
heard of their fame, 64large crowds
gathered to praise them.
65Then Judas and his brothers went to
war against the Edomites to the south.
He attacked Hebron and its surrounding
towns, destroyed its fortifications, and
burned down the towers around it.
66Then he marched into the land of the
Philistines and passed through Marisa.[n]
67That day a number of priests were
killed in battle because they wanted to
be heroes and foolishly went out to fight.
68Judas turned aside to Azotus in Philistia. He pulled down the altars, burned
the images of their gods, plundered their
towns, and then returned to Judea.

The Death of Antiochus the Fourth

(2 Maccabees 1.11-17; 9.1-29; 10.9-11)

6 As King Antiochus the Fourth was
passing through Mesopotamia, he
heard of a city in Persia, named Elymais,
which was famous for its riches in silver
and gold. 2The temple was very rich,
containing gold shields, armor, and
weapons left there by Alexander, son of
King Philip of Macedonia, who was the
first to rule the Greek Empire. 3Antio-
chus came and tried to take the city and
loot it, but he didn't succeed, because the
citizens had learned what he was planning to do, 4and they drew up their
troops to resist him. In great frustration
he withdrew to return to Babylonia.
5In Persia a messenger reached him
with the news that the armies he had
sent into Judea had been defeated. 6Lys-
ias and his strong army had been forced
to flee from the Jews, who were now reinforced by the additional weapons, supplies, and loot they had taken from the
defeated armies. 7The Jews had pulled
down the thing they called "The Awful
Horror" that Antiochus had built on the
altar in Jerusalem. They had also surrounded the Temple with high walls, as
it had been before, and had taken and
fortified the town of Bethzur, one of the
king's own towns.
8When the king heard this report, he
was so dumbfounded and terribly
shaken that he went to bed in a fit of
deep depression because things had not
turned out as he had hoped. 9He remained ill for a long time, as waves of
despair swept over him, until he finally

[n] *Some ancient translations* Marisa; *Greek* Samaria.

realized that he was going to die. 10He
called together all those to whom he had
given the title "Friends of the King" and
said to them, "I cannot sleep, and my
heart is broken with grief and worry.
11At first I asked myself why these great
waves of trouble were sweeping over
me, since I have been kind and well-
liked during my reign. 12But then I remembered the wrongs I did in Jerusalem
when I took all the silver and gold objects from the Temple and tried without
any good reason to destroy the inhabitants of Judea. 13I know this is why all
these terrible things have happened to
me and I am about to die in deep despair
here in this foreign land."

14Then he called Philip, one of his
most trusted advisers, and put him in
charge of his whole empire. 15He gave
him his crown, robe, and official ring,
and authorized him to educate his son
Antiochus the Fifth and bring him up to
be king. 16King Antiochus died there in
the year 149.[o]

17When Lysias learned that the king
had died, he made the young Antiochus
king in place of his father. He had
brought up Antiochus from childhood
and now gave him the name Eupator.

The Campaign of Antiochus the Fifth and Lysias

(2 Maccabees 13.1-26; 11.22-26)

18Meanwhile, the enemies in the fort
at Jerusalem had been blockading the
people of Israel in the area around the
Temple, constantly causing them trouble and giving support to the Gentiles.
19So Judas decided to get rid of them
and called all the people together to besiege the fort. 20The people assembled
and laid siege to the fort in the year
150.[p] They built siege platforms and
battering rams.

21But some of the men under siege escaped, and together with some of the
renegade Jews, they went to the king
and said, 22"How long are you going to
wait before you take revenge for what
was done to our countrymen? 23We
were willing to serve your father, follow
his orders, and obey his decrees. 24But
what good did it do us? Now our own
countrymen have become our enemies.[q] In fact, they have killed as many
of us as they could find and have stolen
our possessions. 25But we are not the
only ones they have harmed; they have
attacked all their neighbors. 26And now
they have laid siege to the fort in Jerusalem and are planning to take it. They
have also fortified the Temple and Bethzur. 27Unless you act immediately, they
will do even more, and you will not be
able to stop them."

28When the king heard this, he was furious. He brought together all the army
commanders, the cavalry officers, and
his most trusted advisers. 29He also
hired mercenary soldiers from other
countries and from the Greek islands.
30His forces numbered 100,000 infantry,
20,000 cavalry, and 32 elephants trained
for war. 31The king and his army passed
through Idumea and laid siege to Bethzur, where they fought for a long time.
They built battering rams and siege platforms, but the defenders fought bravely
and came out of the town and burned
down the platforms.

32Then Judas withdrew his troops
from the fort in Jerusalem and set up his
camp at Beth Zechariah, blocking the
advance of the king's army. 33Early the
next morning, the king rapidly moved
his army along the road to Beth Zechariah, where his troops took up battle positions and blew trumpets. 34They got
the elephants ready for battle by showing them grape juice and mulberry juice.
35The huge animals were distributed
among the infantry units. A thousand
men, protected by chain armor and
bronze helmets, were stationed with
each elephant. Each animal was also accompanied by a special force of 500 cavalry, 36which always remained with the
elephant. 37A strong, protected wooden
platform was securely fastened by a special harness to the back of each elephant. Three[r] soldiers rode on each
animal, in addition to the elephant
driver. 38Lysias placed the rest of the
cavalry on the two flanks of the army
where they could be protected by the infantry while harassing the enemy. 39The
sunlight, reflected off the bronze and
gold shields, shone on the mountains

[o] THE YEAR 149: *This corresponds to 163 B.C.* [p] THE YEAR 150: *This corresponds to 162 B.C.*
[q] enemies; *some manuscripts add* and besieged the fort. [r] *Probable text* Three; *Greek* Thirty *or* Thirty-two.

and flashed like burning torches. 40 Part
of the king's army was spread out over
the higher ground of the mountain
slopes and part over the lower land, but
they all moved forward steadily and in
good order. 41 All the people were terrified when they heard the noise made by
the clashing of weapons and the marching of that great and powerful army.

42 Judas and his army advanced into
battle, and immediately killed 600 of the
king's army. 43 When Eleazar Avaran
saw that one of the elephants was larger
than the others and that it was covered
with royal armor, he thought that the
king was riding on it. 44 Eleazar sacrificed his life to save his people and to
gain eternal fame. 45 He ran boldly toward the elephant, which was in the
middle of a battalion of infantry. He
rushed forward killing men to the right
and left, so that the enemy soldiers fell
back before him on both sides. 46 He
slipped in under the elephant and
stabbed it to death, and it fell on him and
killed him. 47 But when the Jews realized
how strong the royal army was and how
determined it was to fight, they retreated.

48 The king and his army advanced to
fight the Jews at Jerusalem and laid
siege to the whole of Judea and Jerusalem. 49 He made peace with the Jews of
Bethzur, who then left the town. There
had not been enough food in the town
for them to withstand the siege because
it was the sabbatical year, when no
crops were planted. 50 The king occupied
Bethzur and stationed a body of troops
there to guard it. 51 Then he surrounded
the Temple and besieged it for a long
time. He set up siege platforms, battering rams, catapults for throwing fire and
stones, and other weapons to throw
spears and rocks. 52 The defenders also
made war machines to oppose those of
the enemy, and so the battle went on for
a long time. 53 But there was no food left
in the Temple storage bins because it
was the sabbatical year, and the people
who had fled from the Gentiles and
taken refuge in Judea had eaten all the
food that had been stored there. 54 The
shortage of food had been so severe that
many people had scattered to their
homes, and only a few men were left in
the Temple.

55 Meanwhile, Philip, who had been
appointed by King Antiochus before his
death to educate his son to be king, 56 returned from Persia and Media. He had
come back with the royal army and
planned to take control of the government. When Lysias heard this news,
57 he made rapid preparations to depart.
He said to the young king, to his officers,
and to his men, "We are growing weaker
each day; we are short of provisions,
and this place we are besieging is
strong. Besides, there are pressing government affairs which need our attention. 58 So now let's arrange a truce and
make a peace treaty with the Jews and
their whole nation. 59 We will allow them
to follow their own laws and customs as
they did before. All this trouble started
when we provoked them by abolishing
their laws and customs."

60 This recommendation was well received by the king and the officers, so
Lysias proposed peace terms to the
Jews, and they accepted them. 61 When
the king and his officers solemnly
agreed to abide by these terms, the Jews
came out of their fortress. 62 But when
the king entered the Temple area on
Mount Zion and saw the strong fortifications, he broke his word and ordered the
walls surrounding the Temple to be torn
down. 63 Then he hurriedly left and returned to Antioch, where he found
Philip in control of the city. The king attacked the city and took it by force.

The High Priest Alcimus and the Campaign of Nicanor

(2 Maccabees 14.1-36; 15.1-36)

7 In the year 151,[s] Demetrius son of
Seleucus left Rome and with a few
men landed at a town on the Mediterranean coast, where he proclaimed himself king. 2 As he was making his way to
the royal palace of his ancestors, the soldiers arrested Antiochus the Fifth and
Lysias, planning to take them to Demetrius. 3 When Demetrius heard about it,
he said, "I don't want to see them." 4 So
the soldiers killed them, and Demetrius
took the throne.

5 Then all the godless traitorous Jews
led by Alcimus, who wanted to be High

[s] THE YEAR 151: *This corresponds to 161 B.C.*

Priest, went to Demetrius. 6 They
brought accusations against the other
Jews and said, "Judas and his brothers
have killed everybody who supported
you, and they have driven us out of our
country. 7 We advise you to send someone whom you can trust to go and inspect all the damage done to our
property and the king's territory and to
punish Judas, his brothers, and all who
support them."

8 King Demetrius chose one of his advisers, a man by the name of Bacchides,
who was the governor of Greater Syria.
He was an important man in the empire
and loyal to the king. 9 He was sent along
with the godless Alcimus, whom the
king had appointed High Priest; Alcimus
had orders to take revenge on the Jews.
10 They left Antioch and arrived in Judea
with a large army. Bacchides tried to
trick Judas and his brothers by sending
to them messengers with offers of peace.
11 But when Judas and his brothers saw
what a large army they had brought,
they did not believe what the messengers said.

12 A group of teachers of the Law
came to Alcimus and Bacchides, asking
for justice. 13 These devout and patriotic
men were the first of the Jews to try to
make peace with Alcimus and Bacchides. 14 They trusted Alcimus, who was a
priest descended from Aaron, and they
thought he would not cause them any
harm. 15 Alcimus assured them of his
peaceful intentions and solemnly promised that no harm would come to them or
their friends. 16 But as soon as they began to trust him, he arrested 60 of them
and put them all to death on the same
day. As the scripture says,

17 "The blood of your faithful people
was poured out,
their bodies were scattered around
Jerusalem,
and there was no one left to bury
the dead."

18 When this happened, all the people
were afraid of Alcimus and Bacchides,
and they said, "They don't know what
truth or justice means. They gave their
solemn word and then broke it!" 19 Bacchides left Jerusalem and set up his
headquarters at Beth Zaith. He ordered
the arrest of some of the faithful Jews
and even many of the renegades who
had willingly joined him; he had them
killed and thrown into a deep pit. 20 Bacchides put the country under the control
of Alcimus, left troops there to help him,
and returned to the king.

21 Alcimus then began his struggle to
establish himself as High Priest. 22 Every
troublemaker in the country joined him.
They gained control of the land of Judea
and caused great difficulties for the
Jews. 23 Judas saw that the trouble Alcimus and his men had caused was even
worse than the damage done by the Gentiles. 24 So he went around the whole
country of Judea taking revenge on all
the men who had willingly joined Alcimus and preventing them from leaving
the towns and going into the country.
25 When Alcimus saw that Judas and his
men were growing more powerful and
when he realized that he would not be
able to stand against them, he returned
to the king and accused them of great
crimes.

26 Then the king sent Nicanor, one of
his most honored officers, who hated the
Jews, with orders to exterminate them.
27 Nicanor came to Jerusalem with a big
army. He tried to trick Judas and his
brothers by sending peace offers. He
said, 28 "There need not be any quarrel
between you and me. I will come to you
with a small escort for a friendly private
conversation." 29 When he came to Judas, they exchanged polite greetings,
but Judas' enemies were ready to kidnap
him. 30 When Judas learned that Nicanor's visit was part of a plot against him,
he was afraid and decided not to meet
him again. 31 Nicanor realized that his
plan had been discovered, so he left Jerusalem to meet Judas in battle near
Capharsalama. 32 About 500 of Nicanor's
men were killed, and the rest of the army
escaped to the fort in Jerusalem.

33 Some time later Nicanor went to
Mount Zion. Some of the priests left the
Temple and, along with some of the
leaders of the people, went to welcome
him with words of peace and to show
him the burnt offering that was being
sacrificed on behalf of the king. 34 But he
ridiculed them and made them ceremonially unclean by spitting on them. He
spoke proudly 35 and angrily threatened
them with an oath, "Unless Judas and
his army are surrendered to me immediately, I will burn this Temple down as

soon as I return after my victory." And
he left in a rage.
36 The priests went into the courtyard
and stood facing the altar and the Temple. They started weeping and prayed,
37 "Lord, you chose this Temple to bear
your name and to be a place of prayer
and intercession for your people. 38 Now,
take vengeance on this man and his
army; let them die in battle. Remember
how they spoke evil of you, and let none
of them survive."
39 Nicanor left Jerusalem and set up
his headquarters at Beth Horon, where
the Syrian army joined him. 40 Meanwhile, Judas set up camp at Adasa with
3,000 men. There Judas prayed, 41 "Lord,
the Scriptures tell us that when a king
sent messengers to insult you, your angel went out and killed 185,000 of his
soldiers. 42 Now, in the same way, crush
this army before us today and let everyone know that Nicanor is being punished because he insulted your holy
Temple. Punish him as his wickedness
deserves."
43 The armies met in battle on the thirteenth day of the month of Adar, and
Nicanor's army was defeated. Nicanor
himself was the first to be killed in the
battle, 44 and when his soldiers saw that
he was dead, they threw down their
weapons and fled. 45 The Jews pursued
them all day long from Adasa to Gezer.
As they followed, they kept sounding
the call to battle on the trumpets, 46 and
from all the surrounding villages of Judea people came out and attacked the
fleeing enemy from the sides. This
forced them back toward the Jews who
were chasing them, and all of the enemy
were killed in the fight. Not one of them
survived.
47 The Jews took the loot and then cut
off Nicanor's head and his right arm,
which he had extended so arrogantly.
They brought his head and his arm to be
put on display outside Jerusalem.
48 There was great rejoicing among the
Jews. They set that day aside as a special day of celebration, 49 and decreed
that the thirteenth day of Adar should be
observed as an annual day of celebration. 50 There was peace in the land of
Judea for a little while.

The Treaty with the Romans

8 Judas had heard about the Romans
and their reputation as a military
power. He knew that they welcomed all
those who joined them as allies and that
those who came to them could be sure of
the friendship of Rome. 2 People had told
him about the wars the Romans had
fought and their heroic acts among the
Gauls, whom they had conquered and
forced to pay taxes. 3 He had been told
what they had done in Spain when they
captured the silver mines and the gold
mines there. 4 By careful planning and
persistence, they had conquered the
whole country, even though it was far
from Rome. They had overcome the
kings from distant lands who had fought
against them; they had defeated them so
badly that the survivors had to pay annual taxes. 5 They had fought and conquered Philip and Perseus, kings of
Macedonia, and all who had joined them
against Rome. 6 They had even defeated
Antiochus the Great, king of Syria, who
had attacked them with 120 elephants,
cavalry, chariots, and a powerful army.
7 They took him alive and forced him
and his successors to pay heavy taxes, to
give hostages, and to surrender 8 India,
Media, Lydia, and some of their best
lands. They took these and gave them to
King Eumenes.[t]
9 When the Greeks made plans to attack and destroy them, 10 the Romans
learned of the plans and sent a general
to fight against them. The Romans killed
many of the Greeks, took their wives
and children captive, plundered their
possessions, occupied their land, tore
down their fortresses, and made them
slaves, as they are today. 11 They also destroyed or made slaves of other kingdoms, the islands, and everyone who
had ever fought against them. 12 But they
maintained their friendship with their
allies and those who relied on them for
protection. They conquered kings near
and far, and everyone who heard of their
reputation was afraid of them. 13 They
helped some men to become kings,
while they deposed others; they had become a world power. 14 In spite of all
this, no Roman ever tried to advance his
own position by wearing a crown or putting on royal robes. 15 They created a

[t] KING EUMENES: *This is King Eumenes II, king of Pergamum from 197–158 B.C.*

senate, and each day 320 senators came
together to deliberate about the affairs
of the people and their well-being.
16 Each year they entrusted to one man
the responsibility of governing them and
controlling their whole territory. Everyone obeyed this one man, and there was
no envy or jealousy among them.
17 Judas chose Eupolemus, the son of
John and grandson of Accos, and Jason
son of Eleazar and sent them to Rome to
make a treaty of friendship and alliance
with the Romans. 18 He did this to eliminate Syrian oppression, since the Jews
clearly saw that they were being reduced to slavery. 19 After a long and difficult journey, Eupolemus and Jason
reached Rome and entered the Senate.
They addressed the assembly in these
terms: 20 "Judas Maccabeus, his brothers, and the Jewish people have sent us
here to make a mutual defense treaty
with you, so that we may be officially
recorded as your friends and allies."
21 The Romans accepted the proposal,
22 and what follows is a copy of the letter
which was engraved on bronze tablets
and sent to Jerusalem to remain there as
a record of the treaty:

23 "May things go well forever for
the Romans and for the Jewish nation
on land and sea! May they never have
enemies, and may they never go to
war! 24 But if war is declared first
against Rome or any of her allies anywhere, 25 the Jewish nation will come
to her aid with wholehearted support,
as the situation may require. 26 And to
those at war with her, the Jews shall
not give or supply food, arms, money,
or ships, as was agreed in Rome. The
Jews must carry out their obligations
without receiving anything in return.
27 "In the same way, if war is declared first against the Jewish nation,
the Romans will come to their aid with
hearty support, as the situation may
require. 28 And to their enemies there
shall not be given or supplied food,
arms, money, or ships, as was agreed
in Rome. The Romans must carry out
their obligations without deception.
29 "These are the terms of the treaty
that the Romans have made with the
Jewish people. 30 But if, in the future,
both parties shall agree to add or remove anything, they shall act on their
decision, and whatever they add or remove shall be valid.
31 "Furthermore, concerning the
wrongs which King Demetrius is doing against the Jews, we have written
him as follows, 'Why have you treated
our friends and allies, the Jews, so
harshly? 32 If they complain to us
about you one more time, we will support their cause and go to war against
you on land and sea.' "

The Death of Judas

9 When Demetrius heard that Nicanor and his army had been annihi-
lated, he again sent Bacchides and
Alcimus to the land of Judea, this time
with the Syrian wing of the army. 2 They
moved along Gilgal Road, laid siege to
Mesaloth in Arbela, captured it, and
killed many people. 3 In the first month
of the year 152,[u] they set up camp opposite Jerusalem. 4 From there they
marched to Berea with 20,000 infantry
and 2,000 cavalry.
5 Judas had camped at Elasa, with
3,000 experienced soldiers. 6 But when
they saw the enormous size of the enemy army, they were terrified. So many
men deserted that only 800 Jewish soldiers were left. 7 When Judas saw that
his army was dwindling away and that
the battle was about to begin, he was
worried because there was not enough
time to bring his army together. 8 He was
discouraged, but he said to those who
were still with him, "Let's prepare for
the attack; maybe we can still defeat
them."
9 His men tried to talk him out of it.
"We are not strong enough," they said.
"Let's retreat now and save our lives.
Then we can return with reinforcements
and fight the enemy. We don't have
enough men now."
10 Judas replied, "Never let it be said
that I ran from a battle. If our time has
come, let's die bravely for our fellow
Jews and not leave any stain on our
honor."
11 The Syrian army came out of the
camp and took up battle positions
against the Jews. The cavalry was divided into two parts. The shock troops
were in the front lines, but the archers

[u] THE YEAR 152: *This corresponds to 160 B.C.*

and those who used slings went ahead of the main formation. 12 Bacchides took his position on the right. The infantry advanced, protected on both sides by the cavalry, and the war trumpets were blown. The soldiers of Judas also sounded their trumpets. 13 The ground shook from the noise when the two armies met, and they fought from morning until evening.

14 When Judas saw that Bacchides and the main force of the Syrian army was on the right, all his bravest men joined him, 15 and they crushed the Syrians' right wing. They pursued them as far as the foothills.[v] 16 But when the Syrians on the left wing saw that their right wing had been crushed, they turned to attack Judas and his men from the rear. 17 The fighting became very fierce, and many on both sides were killed. 18 Finally Judas himself was killed. Then all his men fled. 19 Jonathan and Simon took their brother's body and buried it in the family tomb at Modein, 20 and there at the tomb they wept for him. All Israel mourned for him in great sorrow for many days. They said, 21 "It can't be! The mighty hero and savior of Israel has been killed!"

22 The other deeds of Judas, his battles, his courageous deeds, and his great accomplishments, were too many to write down.

Jonathan Succeeds Judas

23 After the death of Judas, the lawless traitors began to reappear everywhere in Judea, and all the wicked people returned. 24 Also at that time there was a severe famine, and the whole country went over to the side of the renegades. 25 Bacchides deliberately appointed some renegade Jews as rulers over the country. 26 These men hunted down the friends of Judas and brought them all before Bacchides, and he subjected them to torture and humiliation. 27 It was a time of great trouble for Israel, worse than anything that had happened to them since the time prophets ceased to appear among them.

28 Then all the friends of Judas came together and said to Jonathan, 29 "Since your brother Judas died, there has been no one like him to lead us against our enemies, against Bacchides and those of our own nation who oppose us. 30 So today we choose you to succeed him as our ruler and commander to carry on our war." 31 Jonathan accepted the leadership that day and took the place of his brother Judas.

The Campaigns of Jonathan

32 When Bacchides learned of this, he made up his mind to kill Jonathan. 33 But when this news reached Jonathan, he fled, with his brother Simon and their men, to the wilderness of Tekoa and set up camp at the pool of Asphar. (34 Bacchides learned about this on the Sabbath and crossed the Jordan with his whole army.[w]) 35 Jonathan sent his brother John, who was responsible for the soldiers' families, to ask the Nabateans, with whom he was on friendly terms, for permission to store with them the large amount of baggage they had. 36 But the Jambrites of Medeba attacked John, took him captive, and carried off all the baggage. 37 Some time later Jonathan and his brother Simon learned that the Jambrites were about to celebrate an important wedding and that there would be a bridal procession from the town of Nadabath. The bride was the daughter of one of the great princes of Canaan. 38 Jonathan and Simon had wanted revenge for the death of their brother John, so they and their men went up on one of the mountains and hid. 39 They kept watch and saw a noisy crowd loaded down with baggage. The bridegroom, his friends, and his relatives were on their way to meet the bride's party. They were heavily armed and were playing musical instruments and drums. 40 The Jews attacked from their ambush and killed many of them; the rest escaped into the mountains, while the Jews carried off all their possessions. 41 So the wedding was turned into a time of mourning and their joyful music into funeral songs. 42 Jonathan and Simon had taken full revenge for the death of their brother, and they returned to the marshes along the Jordan.

43 Bacchides heard about this and arrived on the Sabbath at the banks of the

[v] *Probable text* the foothills; *Greek* Mount Azotus.

[w] *Verse 34 is probably misplaced and belongs with verse 43.*

Jordan with a large army. 44 Jonathan
said to his men, "Now we must fight for
our lives. We are in a worse situation
than we have ever been in before. 45 The
enemy is in front of us, the river is behind us, and marshes and thickets are on
both sides of us; there is no way out.
46 So pray now for the Lord to save us
from our enemies."

47 The battle began and Jonathan and
his men were just about to kill Bacchides, when he escaped to the rear of the
army. 48 So Jonathan and his men
jumped into the Jordan and swam to the
other side to escape, and the Syrian
army did not cross the river to follow
them. 49 That day Bacchides lost about
1,000 men.

50 After Bacchides returned to Jerusalem, the Syrians built fortifications with
high walls and barred gates for a number of towns in Judea: Emmaus, Beth
Horon, Bethel, Timnath, Pirathon, Te-
phon, and the fortress in Jericho. 51 In all
of these he placed troops to harass the
Jews. 52 He also strengthened the fortifications of the towns of Bethzur and Gezer and of the fort in Jerusalem. He
placed army units in them and stored up
supplies there. 53 Then he took the sons
of the leading men of the country as hostages and imprisoned them in the fort.

54 In the second month of the year
153,[x] the High Priest Alcimus ordered
that the wall of the inner court of the Temple be torn down. This would have destroyed what the prophets had accomplished; but just as the work began, 55 he
had a stroke, and work was stopped.
Paralyzed and unable to open his mouth,
he could not speak or even make a will
for his family. 56 He died in great torment. 57 When Bacchides learned that
Alcimus was dead, he returned to King
Demetrius, and the land of Judea had
peace for two years.

58 Then all the renegades got together
and said, "Look, Jonathan and his men
are living in peace and security. If we
bring Bacchides here now, he can capture them all in a single night." 59 They
went to discuss the matter with Bacchides, 60 and he set out with a large army.
He sent secret letters to all his allies in
Judea, asking them to seize Jonathan
and his men. But they were not able to
do so because the plot was discovered.
61 Jonathan and his men captured 50 of
the traitorous leaders who had been involved in the plot and put them to death.
62 Then Jonathan, Simon, and their
forces withdrew to Bethbasi in the wilderness. They rebuilt the fallen fortifications and strengthened the town's
defenses. 63 When Bacchides learned
about all this, he got his whole army together and alerted his supporters in Judea. 64 He attacked Bethbasi from all
sides and built siege platforms. After the
battle had gone on for a long time,
65 Jonathan slipped out into the country
with a small body of men and left his
brother Simon in charge of the town.
66 Jonathan defeated Odomera and his
people, and then attacked and destroyed
the Phasirite camp. Once defeated, they
joined Jonathan and advanced with him
in his attack against Bacchides. 67 At the
same time, Simon and his men rushed
from the town and burned the siege platforms. 68 In the battle Bacchides was
pressed so hard that all his plans came
to nothing, and he was defeated. 69 He
was so furious with the traitorous Jews
who had urged him to come to Judea
that he put many of them to death.

Then Bacchides decided to return to
his own country, 70 but when Jonathan
learned of this, he sent ambassadors to
Bacchides to arrange for peace terms
and the return of Jewish prisoners.
71 Bacchides agreed to do as Jonathan
asked and gave him his solemn promise
that he would let him live in peace the
rest of his life. 72 Bacchides handed over
the prisoners and returned to his own
country. Never again did he come into
Jewish territory. 73 War came to an end
in Israel. Jonathan settled in Michmash
and began to govern the people and to
eliminate the renegade Jews from Israel.

Alexander Epiphanes Makes Jonathan High Priest

10 In the year 160,[y] Alexander
Epiphanes,[z] son of Antiochus
the Fourth, landed at Ptolemais and captured it. The people welcomed him as
their king. 2 When King Demetrius heard
of it, he gathered a large army and went

[x] THE YEAR 153: *This corresponds to 159 B.C.* [y] THE YEAR 160: *This corresponds to 152 B.C.*
[z] ALEXANDER EPIPHANES: *Alexander Epiphanes is more widely known as Alexander Balas.*

out to meet him in battle. 3 At that time
Demetrius sent Jonathan a friendly letter full of flattery, 4 in the hope of winning Jonathan over to his side and
making peace with the Jews before Alexander made a treaty with them
against him. 5 Demetrius thought that
Jonathan would certainly remember all
the wrongs he had done to him, his
brothers, and the entire Jewish nation.
6 And so Demetrius made Jonathan his
ally and gave him authority to raise an
army and equip it. He also ordered that
the hostages held in the fort at Jerusalem should be handed over to Jonathan.
7 So Jonathan went to Jerusalem and
read the letter to all the people and to the
men in the fort. 8 These men were terrified when they learned that the king had
given Jonathan authority to raise an
army. 9 They handed the hostages over
to him, and he returned them to their
parents.

10 Jonathan set up headquarters in Jerusalem and began to rebuild and restore the city. 11 He ordered the builders
to use squared stones for the city walls
and for the protecting wall around
Mount Zion. This was done. 12 The foreigners deserted the fortresses that Bacchides had built; 13 each man left his post
and returned to his own country. 14 But
some of the Jews who had abandoned
the Law of Moses and its commands
were still left in Bethzur, which served
as their last place of refuge.

15 King Alexander learned of the
promises Demetrius had made to Jonathan and he also learned about Jonathan
himself, about the battles he had fought,
his courageous deeds, and the troubles
he and his brothers had endured. 16 He
was certain that he would never find another man like Jonathan and so decided
to make him his friend and ally. 17 He
wrote Jonathan a letter:

18 "King Alexander to his friend Jonathan, greetings.

19 I have heard that you are a brave
man who has earned the right to be a
friend of the king. 20 I have this day
appointed you as High Priest of your
nation and conferred upon you the title of 'Friend of the King.' You are to
be our ally and give us your support."

He also sent him a royal robe and a gold
crown. 21 Jonathan put on the robes of
the High Priest in the seventh month of
the year 160 [a] at the Festival of Shelters.
He raised an army and stored up a large
supply of weapons.

Jonathan Supports Alexander Epiphanes

22 When Demetrius heard this, he was
distressed and said, 23 "How did we manage to let Alexander get ahead of us? He
has strengthened his position by making
an alliance with the Jews. 24 I also will
write them a friendly letter offering high
positions and gifts, so that they will support me."

25 He wrote:

"King Demetrius to the nation of the
Jews, greetings. 26 We are delighted to
learn that you have kept your obligations under our treaty, remained loyal
to us, and have not gone over to the
side of our enemies. 27 Now if you continue to remain loyal to us, we will reward you well. 28 We will grant you
exemptions from many taxes and allow you other privileges. 29 I hereby
grant all the Jewish people release
and exemption from payment of regular taxes, salt taxes, and other special
taxes. 30 Furthermore, from this day I
release you from your obligation to
pay me one third of the grain harvest
and one half of the fruit harvest. From
now on I will not demand these payments from Judea or from the three
districts that have been added to Judea from Samaria and Galilee. 31 Jerusalem and its surrounding territory is
to be recognized as a holy city and to
be exempt from the payment of all
taxes. 32 I also give up my authority
over the fort in Jerusalem and place
it under the High Priest, who may
station there anyone he wishes to
guard it. 33 I freely grant release to
all Jews who are prisoners of war anywhere in my kingdom. All of them
will be exempt from taxes, even on
their cattle. [b] 34 No taxes shall be
collected from any Jew anywhere
in my kingdom on Sabbaths, New
Moon Festivals, and other holy
days. Furthermore, no taxes shall
be collected three days before or
after the major holy days. 35 No one

[a] THE YEAR 160: *This corresponds to 152 B.C.* [b] *This sentence in Greek is unclear.*

has the right on any of these days to
demand payment or to trouble you in
any way.
36 "Jews may be enlisted in the royal
army up to a total of 30,000 men, and
they will receive the same pay as other
royal troops. 37 Some of them may be
stationed in the great royal fortresses,
and others assigned to responsible positions in the government. They shall
have Jews as their leaders and officers, and they shall be allowed to follow their own laws and customs, just
as the king has permitted for the people of Judea.
38 "The three districts added to Judea from the territory of Samaria will
be completely incorporated into Judea
and placed under the authority of the
High Priest alone. 39 I give to the Temple in Jerusalem for its operating expenses the revenues from the city of
Ptolemais and the lands belonging to
it. 40 I also promise to make an annual
gift of 15,000 silver coins from appropriate accounts within the royal treasury. 41 The total accumulated state
subsidy, which we have failed to pay
in recent years, shall be paid, and the
payments continued from now on for
the work of the Temple. 42 In addition
to this, we will no longer require the
5,000 silver coins annually from the
Temple income. This money belongs
to the priests serving in the Temple.
43 Whoever owes a debt to the king or
any other debt and takes refuge in the
Temple in Jerusalem or in any area
that belongs to it may not be arrested
nor may his property anywhere in my
kingdom be confiscated. 44 The expenses for rebuilding and renovating
the Temple shall be provided from
the royal treasury. 45 Likewise, the
expenses for rebuilding the walls of
Jerusalem and its surrounding
fortifications, as well as the walls of
designated towns in Judea, shall be
provided from the royal treasury."
46 When Jonathan and the people
heard the proposals made by King Demetrius, they refused to believe them or
accept them, because they remembered
how harshly he had treated them and
what terrible troubles he had caused
them. 47 They preferred to give their allegiance to Alexander because he had
been the first to open peace negotia-
tions, and they remained his allies as
long as he lived.
48 King Alexander raised a large army
and took up battle positions facing Demetrius. 49 But when the armies of the
two kings met in battle, the army of Alexander[c] turned and ran. Demetrius[d]
pursued them and won the battle. 50 Alexander[e] fought bitterly until sundown,
but Demetrius was killed that day.
51 Then Alexander sent ambassadors
to King Ptolemy the Sixth of Egypt with
this message:

52 "I have returned to my kingdom
and taken my seat on the throne of my
ancestors. I have taken over the government, and I am now in control of
the country. 53 I made war on Demetrius, defeated him and his army, and
I have taken over his kingdom. 54 Now
I am ready to make an alliance. Give
me your daughter in marriage, and I
will give both of you such gifts as you
deserve."

55 King Ptolemy replied, "It was a great
day when you returned to your country
and took the throne of your ancestors.
56 I agree to your proposals, but first
meet me at Ptolemais. We can get acquainted there, and I will give you my
daughter in marriage."
57 So in the year 162[f] Ptolemy and his
daughter Cleopatra[g] left Egypt and arrived at Ptolemais. 58 King Alexander
met them, and Ptolemy gave him his
daughter in marriage. The wedding was
celebrated there in Ptolemais with royal
splendor.
59 King Alexander wrote asking Jonathan to come to meet him. 60 So Jonathan, in a show of splendor, went to
Ptolemais and met the two kings. He
presented them with gifts of silver and
gold, and he also gave many gifts to the
high officials who had accompanied
them. Everyone was favorably impressed with him. 61 At the same time

[c] Alexander; *some manuscripts have* Demetrius. [d] Demetrius; *some manuscripts have* Alexander. [e] Alexander; *some manuscripts have* Demetrius. [f] THE YEAR 162: *This corresponds to 150 B.C.* [g] CLEOPATRA: *This was Cleopatra Thea, also known as Cleopatra the Third, and not to be confused with Cleopatra the Seventh (69–30 B.C.), who was involved in the history of Caesar and Mark Antony.*

some traitorous Jews who wanted to
make trouble for Jonathan made accusations against him, but King Alexander
paid no attention to them. 62 He gave orders that Jonathan should be given royal
robes to wear, 63 and he honored him by
letting him sit at his side. Alexander told
his officers to take Jonathan into the
center of the city and to announce that
no one was to bring charges against him
for any reason and no one was to cause
him any kind of trouble. 64 When his accusers saw the honors given to him,
heard the announcement, and saw him
clothed in royal robes, they all fled.
65 The king further honored Jonathan by
enrolling him in the First Order of the
"Friends of the King" and by making
him general and governor of his province. 66 Jonathan returned to Jerusalem
pleased and successful.

Jonathan's Victory over Apollonius

67 In the year 165[h] Demetrius the Second, the son of Demetrius the First, left
Crete and arrived in Syria, the land of
his ancestors. 68 When King Alexander
heard about this, he was worried and returned to Antioch, the capital of Syria.
69 Demetrius reappointed Apollonius
governor of Greater Syria. Apollonius
raised a large army, set up camp near
Jamnia, and sent the following message
to Jonathan the High Priest:

70 "Because of you I am being ridiculed, but why do you, there in your
mountains, continue this rebellion
when no one supports you? 71 If you
really have any confidence in your
army, come down here on the plain
and fight, where we can test each
other's strength. Study the situation,
and you will find that I have the support of the forces from the cities.
72 You will learn who I am and who
our allies are, and you will discover
that you have no chance of standing
against us. Your predecessors have
already been beaten twice on their
own ground; 73 so how do you expect
to defeat my cavalry and the kind
of army I have here on the plain?
Down here there is not so much as
a pebble to hide behind and no way
to escape."

74 When Jonathan received this message from Apollonius, he became angry.
He took 10,000 elite troops from Jerusalem; his brother Simon also brought
troops, and their two forces 75 set up
camp outside of Joppa. The men of the
city refused to let them in because there
was a detachment of Apollonius' troops
there, but Jonathan attacked, 76 and the
men in the city became so frightened
that they opened the gates, allowing
Jonathan to capture Joppa. 77 When Apollonius heard what had happened, he
took 3,000 cavalry and a large army of
infantry and pretended to retreat south
toward Azotus. However, relying upon
the strength of his cavalry, he marched
into the plain with his main force,
78-79 positioning 1,000 cavalry where
they could attack Jonathan's forces from
the rear. Jonathan continued his pursuit
as far as Azotus, where the two armies
met in battle. 80 Not until then did Jonathan realize that he was caught in an
ambush. His army was surrounded, and
enemy arrows rained down on them
from morning until evening. 81 But Jonathan's men stood firm, as he had ordered, and the attacking cavalry grew
tired. 82 Then, when the cavalry was exhausted, Simon appeared on the scene
with his forces and attacked and overwhelmed the enemy infantry, who broke
ranks and fled. 83 The cavalry, which by
now was scattered all over the battlefield, fled to Azotus, where they took refuge in the temple of Dagon, their god.
84 But Jonathan set fire to the city and to
the temple of Dagon, burning to death
all those who had taken refuge there.
Then he set fire to the surrounding
towns and looted them. 85 That day
about 8,000 were either killed in the battle or burned to death. 86 Jonathan left
and set up camp at Ascalon, where the
people of the city came out to welcome
him with great honors. 87 Jonathan and
his men returned to Jerusalem with
large quantities of loot.

88 When King Alexander heard what
Jonathan had done, he gave him even
greater honors. 89 He sent him a gold
shoulder buckle, which is given only to
those honored with the title "Relative of
the King." He also gave him the city of
Ekron and its surrounding territory.

[h] THE YEAR 165: *This corresponds to 147 B.C.*

The Fall of Alexander Epiphanes

11 King Ptolemy the Sixth of Egypt
assembled an army of soldiers
more numerous than the grains of sand
along the seashore, and he also gathered
a great fleet of ships. He intended to trap
Alexander, take his kingdom, and add it
to his own, 2 so he went to Syria with
promises of peace, and the citizens
opened their gates to him and welcomed
him. King Alexander had ordered them
to do this because Ptolemy was his
father-in-law. 3 But as Ptolemy moved
north, he stationed a detachment of
troops in each town. 4 When he reached
Azotus, the people there showed him the
burned ruins of the temple of Dagon and
all the destruction in the city and the surrounding towns. There were corpses
everywhere. The bodies of the men Jonathan had burned to death during the
battle were now stacked up along Ptolemy's route. 5 The people told him what
Jonathan had done, hoping that he
would hold him responsible, but Ptolemy said nothing. 6 Jonathan, with all
the proper ceremony, went to Joppa to
meet him. They exchanged greetings
and spent the night there. 7 Jonathan accompanied him as far as the Eleutherus
River before returning to Jerusalem. 8 In
this way King Ptolemy, in his plot
against Alexander, took control of the
towns along the coast as far north as
Seleucia-by-the-sea.

9 From there King Ptolemy sent this
message to King Demetrius: "Let's make
a treaty. My daughter is now Alexander's wife, but I will take her back and
give her to you and let you rule over
your father's kingdom. 10 I regret that I
ever gave her to Alexander, because he
has tried to kill me." 11 Ptolemy made
this accusation against Alexander because he wanted to take over his kingdom. 12 So he took his daughter away
from Alexander and gave her to Demetrius; he broke off all relations with Alexander, and they became open
enemies. 13 Then Ptolemy entered Antioch and assumed the crown of Syria; so
he wore both the crown of Egypt and the
crown of Syria.

14 King Alexander was in Cilicia at the
time because the people of that region
were in a state of rebellion. 15 But when
he heard what Ptolemy had done, he
moved to attack him. Ptolemy met him
with a large force and won a decisive
victory. 16 While Ptolemy reached the
peak of his power, Alexander fled to
Arabia to find protection, 17 but an Arab
named Zabdiel cut off his head and sent
it to Ptolemy. 18 Two days later Ptolemy
himself died, and the troops he had left
in the fortresses were then killed by the
local citizens. 19 So in the year 167[i] Demetrius the Second became king.

Jonathan Wins the Favor of Demetrius the Second

20 About that time Jonathan gathered
the men of Judea to attack the fort in
Jerusalem. They built many siege platforms to use in the attack. 21 But some
traitorous Jews who hated their own nation went to King Demetrius the Second
and told him that Jonathan was laying
siege to the fort in Jerusalem. 22 When
Demetrius heard this, he was furious
and immediately moved his headquarters to Ptolemais. He wrote to Jonathan and ordered him to lift the siege
and to meet him for a conference in Ptolemais without a moment's delay.

23 When Jonathan got the message, he
gave orders for the siege to continue,
and then chose some Jewish leaders and
some priests to go with him. At the risk
of his life, 24 he went to the king in Ptolemais, taking along robes, silver and
gold, and many other gifts. He made a
good impression on the king. 25 Although some lawless traitors of his own
nation had made accusations against
Jonathan, 26 the king still treated him
just as his predecessors had done. He
honored him in the presence of all his
advisers, 27 and confirmed him as High
Priest, restoring all his former honors
and appointing him to the highest rank
among the "Friends of the King."

28 Jonathan asked the king to release
the territory of Judea and the three regions of Samaria[j] from the payment of
taxes, promising that if Demetrius
would do that, he would pay him a lump
sum of 22,000 pounds of silver. 29 The
king agreed and wrote a letter to Jonathan to confirm all this:

[i] THE YEAR 167: *This corresponds to 145 B.C.* [j] *Probable text* three regions of Samaria; *Greek* three regions and Samaria.

30“King Demetrius to King Jonathan
and to the Jewish nation, greetings.
31“For your information I am sending a copy of the letter I have written to the Honorable Lasthenes about you:
32“ ‘King Demetrius to the Honorable Lasthenes, greetings. 33I have decided to grant the Jewish nation certain benefits because they are our loyal allies and keep their treaty obligations. 34I confirm their rights to the land of Judea and the three regions of Ephraim, Lydda, and Arimathea, which are hereby annexed to Judea from Samaria with all the lands belonging to them. This will be of benefit to everyone who goes to Jerusalem to offer sacrifice, since payments of the annual tax on produce and fruit from these lands will no longer be made to
the king, but to the Temple. 35And I
also grant them relief from the payment of revenues now due me from tithes, tolls, salt taxes, and special
taxes. 36None of the provisions mentioned in this letter shall ever be canceled in the future.
37“ ‘You are required to see that a complete copy of this decree is made and given to Jonathan, to be posted in a prominent place on the Temple hill.’ ”

Jonathan Helps Demetrius the Second

38When King Demetrius saw that the land was peaceful under his rule and there was no further resistance, he disbanded his whole army and sent everyone home, except the soldiers he had hired from the Greek islands. This made all the soldiers who had served under his predecessors hate him because they had
lost their source of income. 39One of Alexander's former supporters, Trypho, saw that all the soldiers were complaining about Demetrius, so he went to Imalkue, the Arab who was responsible for bringing up Alexander's young son Antiochus. 40Trypho stayed there for a long
time and kept urging Imalkue to hand the boy over to him, so that he could make him king in place of his father. He also told Imalkue about the decrees of Demetrius and how the soldiers hated him.

41Jonathan sent a message to King Demetrius asking him to remove his troops from the fort in Jerusalem and from the fortresses in Judea, since they
kept harassing the Jews. 42Demetrius
replied: “I will do what you request, and when the opportunity presents itself, I will bestow upon you and your nation
the highest honors. 43But now you can
help me by sending soldiers to fight for me, because all of my troops have revolted.”
44So Jonathan sent 3,000 trained soldiers to Antioch. The king was delighted
when they arrived, 45because a mob of
120,000 had gathered in the city determined to kill him. 46But he escaped to
the palace while the mob took control of
the streets and began to riot. 47Then the
king called on the Jewish soldiers for help, and they all rushed to his aid. They went through the whole city and killed
at least 100,000 people. 48They saved the
king's life, but they plundered and
burned the city. 49When the people saw
that the Jews had complete control of the city, they lost courage and appealed
to the king, requesting 50him to arrange
a truce and stop the Jewish attack. 51The
rebels threw down their arms and surrendered. The king and everyone in his kingdom now had great respect for the Jews, who returned to Jerusalem with a
great deal of loot. 52Demetrius was
firmly established as king, and the country was at peace under his rule, 53but he
broke all his promises and turned against Jonathan. He did not reward him for his loyal service, but instead continued to harass him.

Jonathan Supports Antiochus the Sixth

54Some time later, Trypho returned with the young boy Antiochus and
crowned him king. 55All the soldiers that
Demetrius had dismissed then came to the support of the young king. They defeated Demetrius, and he fled. 56Trypho
captured the elephants and took control
of Antioch. 57The young King Antiochus
wrote to Jonathan and confirmed him as High Priest and as ruler over the four regions and gave him the title “Friend of
the King.” 58He sent him a set of gold
tableware and authorized him to drink from gold cups, to wear a royal robe,

and to wear the gold shoulder buckle
awarded to "Relatives of the King." 59 He
also appointed Jonathan's brother Simon as governor of the territory from
the Phoenician coast to the Egyptian
border.

60 Jonathan then marched with his
army through the towns of Greater
Syria, and all the Syrian forces joined
him as allies. He went to Ascalon, where
the people welcomed him with great
honors. 61 Then he went to Gaza, but the
people there barred their gates against
him. So he laid siege to the city and
burned and looted the surrounding area.
62 The people of Gaza then asked for
peace, and Jonathan arranged a truce.
He took the sons of the leaders and sent
them to Jerusalem as hostages. After
that he marched on as far as Damascus.

63 Jonathan learned that the officers of
Demetrius had come to Kedesh in Galilee with a large army, intending to keep
him from carrying out his plan. 64 So he
left his brother Simon in Judea and set
out to meet them in battle. 65 Then Simon
laid siege to Bethzur and fought against
it for a long time. 66 The people asked for
peace terms, and Simon agreed. He then
took over the town, drove the people out,
and stationed a detachment of troops
there.

67 Jonathan and his army set up camp
by Lake Galilee. Early the next morning
he marched his troops to the plain of Hazor, 68 where the main force of the foreign army was advancing to meet him.
Unknown to Jonathan, they had left a
detachment of troops in ambush in the
mountains, 69 and when the men in ambush came out and attacked, 70 Jonathan's entire army turned and ran. No
one was left, except two officers, Mattathias son of Absalom and Judas son of
Chalphi. 71 Jonathan was humiliated, so
he tore his clothes, threw dust on his
head, and prayed. 72 Then he turned
back to the battle, crushed the enemy,
and put them to flight. 73 When his own
fleeing soldiers saw this, they turned
back and joined him in pursuit. They
chased the enemy all the way back to
their camp at Kedesh and then took over
the camp. 74 At least 3,000 enemy soldiers were killed that day. Jonathan
then returned to Jerusalem.

Alliances with Rome and Sparta

12 When Jonathan saw that things
were working out to his advantage, he chose ambassadors and sent
them to Rome to confirm and renew
friendship with the Romans. 2 He also
sent letters with a similar message to
Sparta and other places. 3 The ambassadors went to Rome, where they were admitted to the Senate chamber, and
reported that the High Priest Jonathan
and the Jewish nation had sent them to
renew the earlier ties of friendship and
alliance with Rome. 4 The Romans provided them with letters to the authorities
in each country through which they
would pass, guaranteeing them safe conduct in their return to the land of Judea.

5 Here is a copy of the letter Jonathan
wrote to the Spartans:

6 "Jonathan the High Priest, the national council of leaders, the priests,
and the rest of the people of Judea, to
our brothers in Sparta, greetings. 7 At
an earlier time, your King Arius sent a
letter to our High Priest Onias, stating
that our two nations are related, as the
attached copy shows. 8 Onias received
your ambassador with full honors and
acknowledged receipt of your letter,
which declared our alliance and
friendship. 9 And now, although we
are not in need of such alliances, since
we find our source of strength in the
holy books we possess, 10 we have
written to renew our ties of brotherhood and friendship with you. We do
not wish to become total strangers,
and it has now been many years since
your last communication. 11 Throughout the years we have taken every opportunity, on our festival days and
other suitable days, to remember you
when we have offered our sacrifices
and made our prayers, as it is fitting
and proper for brothers to do. 12 We
also are pleased that fame has come to
you. 13 But we have had one series of
troubles after another and have had to
fight many wars, because we have
been under constant attack by surrounding nations. 14 During this time
of war, we did not wish to trouble you
or our other allies and friends, 15 since
we do have the help of the Lord, who
has defeated our enemies and rescued
us from them. 16 So we have chosen

Numenius son of Antiochus together
with Antipater son of Jason and sent
them as ambassadors to Rome to renew our ties of friendship and alliance
with the Romans. 17 We have also ordered them to go to you with our
greetings and deliver this letter about
the renewal of our ties of brotherhood.
18 And now we request an answer to
this letter.
19 "The following is a copy of the earlier letter:
20 " 'King Arius of Sparta to Onias
the High Priest, greetings. 21 We have
found a document about the Spartans
and the Jews indicating that we are
related and that both of our nations
are descended from Abraham. 22 Now
that we have discovered this, please
send us a report about your situation.
23 In reply, we will send you a letter
indicating that we are willing to share
our possessions, including cattle and
property, if you will do the same. We
have given orders to our ambassadors
to give you a full report about these
matters.' "

Campaigns of Jonathan and Simon

24 Jonathan learned that the officers of
Demetrius had returned to attack him
with an even larger army than before.
25 Jonathan did not want to give them an
opportunity to penetrate his own territory, so he left Jerusalem and went to
meet them in the region of Hamath.
26 Jonathan sent spies into the enemy
camp, who reported to him that the enemy forces were making plans to attack
the Jews by night. 27 At sunset Jonathan
ordered all his soldiers to be on the alert
and to have their weapons ready for a
surprise attack any time during the
night. He also stationed guards all
around the camp. 28 When the enemy
soldiers learned that Jonathan and his
men were ready for battle, they were
panic-stricken and fled, leaving their
campfires burning. 29 Jonathan and his
men saw the campfires but did not realize what had happened until the next
morning. 30 Jonathan then set out after
them, but he could not overtake them
because they had already crossed the
Eleutherus River. 31 Then Jonathan
turned aside and attacked a tribe of Arabs called Zabadeans. He defeated them
and plundered their possessions. 32 Then
he broke camp and went to Damascus,
inspecting the entire area along
the way.
33 Meanwhile, Simon had also set out
on a campaign and had advanced as far
as Ascalon and the neighboring fortresses. Then he turned aside to Joppa
34 and stationed a detachment of soldiers
there because he had heard that the
people were planning to hand over the
fortress of Joppa to the soldiers of
Demetrius.
35 When Jonathan returned, he called
the council of the leaders together and
made plans with them to build fortresses
in Judea, 36 to increase the height of the
walls of Jerusalem, and to build a high
wall to separate the fort from the city.
This would isolate the fort, making it impossible for the enemy to buy or sell
anything. 37 The people worked together
to strengthen the city's defenses because
a part of the east wall along the Kidron
Valley had collapsed and the Chaphena-
tha section was in need of repair. 38 Simon also rebuilt the town of Adida in the
foothills. He fortified it and constructed
barred gates for it.

Trypho Captures Jonathan

39 Then Trypho plotted a rebellion
against King Antiochus so that he could
make himself king of Syria. 40 He was
afraid, however, that Jonathan would
not agree to this and would go to war
against him to prevent it. So Trypho got
his army ready and went to Beth Shan in
the hope of capturing Jonathan and putting him to death. 41 But Jonathan also
came to Beth Shan with 40,000 well-
trained soldiers. 42 When Trypho saw
how large an army Jonathan had
brought with him, he was afraid to take
action. 43 So he received Jonathan with
all honors, presented him to all his advisers, gave him gifts, and ordered his
advisers and soldiers to obey Jonathan
as they would him. 44 He asked Jonathan, "Why have you put these soldiers
to so much trouble when we are not at
war? 45 Why don't you send them home?
Choose a few men to stay with you, and
then accompany me to Ptolemais. I will
hand the city over to you, as well as the
rest of the fortresses, the troops, and all
the officials. Then I will turn around and
leave. In fact, that's why I am here."
46 Jonathan believed him, and following

his advice, sent his soldiers back to Judea. 47 He took 3,000 men with him, but
left 2,000 of them in Galilee, while only
1,000 accompanied him the rest of the
way. 48 But when Jonathan entered Ptolemais, the people of the city locked the
gates, arrested him, and killed everyone
who had come with him.

49 Trypho sent infantry and cavalry
units to Galilee and Jezreel Valley to kill
the rest of Jonathan's soldiers. 50 The
Jewish troops thought that Jonathan
had been captured and killed, along with
all those who had accompanied him, so
they encouraged one another and
marched out in battle formation.
51 When the approaching enemy forces
saw that the Jews were ready to fight for
their lives, they turned back. 52 Then the
Jewish soldiers returned to Judea safely,
but terribly afraid. The whole nation
was in deep mourning, assuming that
Jonathan and all his men had been
killed. 53 All the surrounding nations
now tried to destroy them. They thought
that the Jews had no leaders or allies
and that the time was ripe to annihilate
them and put an end to their history.

Simon Leads the Jews

13 Simon learned that Trypho had
assembled a large army and that
he had plans to invade Judea and devastate it. 2 He realized that this news had
brought panic and fear to the people, so
he went to Jerusalem, called the people
together, 3 and tried to encourage them
by saying, "You know how much my
father's family, my brothers, and I have
done for the sake of the Law of Moses
and the Temple. You also know about
the wars we have fought and the troubles we have had. 4 All my brothers have
been killed fighting for our Law, our
Temple, and our nation, and I am the
only one left. 5 But never let it be said
that I tried to save my own life in a time
of danger; I do not consider myself better than my brothers. 6 Not in the least! It
is true that in their hatred all the Gentile
nations have gathered together to destroy us, but I will fight to defend my
nation, the Temple, and your loved
ones."

7 These words immediately revived the
morale of the people, 8 and they answered with a loud shout, "You are now
our leader in place of your brothers Judas and Jonathan. 9 Fight our wars, and
we will do whatever you ask." 10 So Simon gathered together all the soldiers
and hurried to complete the walls of Jerusalem and to strengthen all its defenses. 11 He sent Jonathan son of
Absalom to Joppa with a large army.
This Jonathan drove out the people who
were there and occupied the town.

12 Trypho left Ptolemais with a large
army to invade Judea, taking Simon's
brother Jonathan along with him as a
prisoner. 13 Simon set up camp at Adida
at the edge of the plain. 14 When Trypho
learned that Simon had succeeded his
brother Jonathan and that he was ready
to meet him in battle, he sent this message to him: 15 "I am holding your
brother Jonathan under arrest because
while he was in office he did not pay his
debts to the royal treasury. 16 However, I
will release him if you will pay me 6,000
pounds of silver and send two of his sons
as hostages to guarantee that he will not
revolt against us when he is released."

17 Although Simon knew that they
were deceiving him, he sent for the
money and the two sons because he did
not want to arouse the hostility of the
Jews. 18 He was afraid that they might
later say that Jonathan was put to death
because Simon would not send the
money and the boys. 19 So he did as Trypho had demanded, but Trypho broke
his promise and did not release
Jonathan.

20 Then Trypho made his move to invade the land and destroy it, circling
around by the road to Adora. But Simon
and his army moved along facing him
wherever he went. 21 The enemy soldiers
in the fort in Jerusalem kept sending
messengers to Trypho urging him to
come to them quickly by way of the
desert and to send them supplies. 22 Trypho got all his cavalry ready for the invasion, but that night there was a heavy
snowstorm, and he was not able to move
up into the hills. So he withdrew and
went into Gilead. 23 When he was near
Baskama, he had Jonathan put to death
and his body buried there. 24 Then Trypho turned and went back to his own
country.

25 Simon had the body of his brother
Jonathan brought to Modein, to be buried in the town of their ancestors.
26 Everyone in Israel was in deep sorrow

at the loss of Jonathan, and they
mourned for him a long time. 27 Over the
tomb of his father and his brothers Simon built a high monument that could
be seen from a great distance. It was
covered front and back with polished
stone. 28 He constructed seven pyramids
side by side for his father, his mother,
and his four brothers. 29 For the pyramids he created a setting of tall columns
on which there were carvings. Some of
these carvings were of suits of armor
and some were of ships. It was a monument to their victories, which travelers
from overseas could visit.[k] 30 The tomb
which he built in Modein is still there
today.

31 Meanwhile, Trypho assassinated the
young king, Antiochus the Sixth, 32 and
took over his kingdom in Syria. He
brought that country great troubles.

33 Simon rebuilt the fortresses of Judea
with high towers, strong walls, and
barred gates; then he placed stores of
supplies there. 34 He sent ambassadors
to King Demetrius the Second to ask for
tax relief for the land, since Trypho was
doing nothing but robbing them. 35 King
Demetrius sent the following letter in
reply:

36 "King Demetrius to the High
Priest Simon, the friend of kings, to
the Jewish nation, and to their leaders,
greetings. 37 I have received the gold
crown and the gold palm branch
which you sent, and I am prepared to
make a peace treaty with you and to
instruct our tax officials to grant you
exemptions. 38 Our previous agreements with you are confirmed, and the
fortresses which you have built are to
remain yours. 39 I grant you pardon
for treaty violations committed up to
the present date, and I release you
from payment of the special tax still
due and any other taxes that have
been collected up to this time in Jerusalem. 40 All Jews who are qualified
may enroll in the royal service. Let us
have peace."

41 So in the year 170[l] the yoke of the
Gentile oppressors was removed from
the Jews. 42 People began to date their
documents and contracts with these
words: "In the first year of Simon, the
great High Priest, commander and
leader of the Jews."

43 At that time Simon laid siege to Gezer and surrounded it with his army. He
built a movable siege platform, brought
it up to the town wall, attacked one of
the towers, and captured it. 44 The men
who had been on the siege platform then
moved rapidly into the town, and this
created great confusion. 45 The men of
the town, their wives, and their children
tore their clothes in distress and climbed
up on the top of the town wall. They
pleaded loudly with Simon for a truce.
46 "Have mercy on us," they begged.
"Don't punish us as we deserve!"

47 So Simon came to terms with them
and ended the fighting. He made the
people leave the town; then he purified
the houses in which there had been
idols. When that was done, he and his
men entered the town singing hymns
and songs of praise. 48 He eliminated
everything that would make the town
ritually unclean and settled it with people who would obey every command
contained in the Law of Moses. He
strengthened the defenses of the town
and built himself a palace there.

49 Those in the fort in Jerusalem were
now prevented from leaving to buy or
sell anything. They were suffering from
severe hunger and many of them had
died of starvation. 50 Finally they appealed to Simon for a truce. He agreed,
removed them from the fort, and purified it. 51 On the twenty-third day of the
second month, in the year 171,[m] there
was a great celebration in the city because this terrible threat to the security
of Israel had come to an end. Simon and
his men entered the fort singing hymns
of praise and thanksgiving, while carrying palm branches and playing harps,
cymbals, and lyres. 52 Simon issued a decree that the day should be joyfully celebrated every year. He strengthened the
defenses of the Temple hill on the side
facing the fort, and he and his men made
their headquarters there. 53 Simon's son
John was now a grown man, so Simon
made him commander of the whole
army, and John set up headquarters at
Gezer.

[k] *Verses 28-29 in Greek are unclear.* [l] THE YEAR 170: *This corresponds to 142 B.C.*
[m] THE YEAR 171: *This corresponds to 141 B.C.*

In Praise of Simon

14 In the year 172[n] King Demetrius the Second gathered his army and went to Media to seek additional help for his war against Trypho. 2 When King Arsaces the Sixth of Persia and Media heard that Demetrius had entered his territory, he sent one of his commanders with some troops to capture Demetrius alive. 3 They attacked and defeated the army of Demetrius, took him captive, and brought him back to King Arsaces, who threw him in prison.

4 The land of Judea was at peace as long as Simon lived. During his entire reign, he used his position of power and influence to do what was good for his people, and they were always pleased with him as their ruler. 5 He added to his reputation when he captured the port of Joppa and opened up the route to the Greek islands. 6 He not only enlarged the territory of his nation and gained control of the whole country, 7 but he brought back many prisoners of war and captured Gezer, Bethzur, and the fort in Jerusalem. He purified the fort, and there was no one to oppose him.

8 The Jews farmed their land in peace; the land produced its crops and the trees bore fruit. 9 The young men showed off their splendid military uniforms, while the old men sat around the city squares and talked about the great things that had happened. 10 Simon supplied the cities with food and provided them with weapons of defense. His fame spread everywhere. 11 He brought peace to the country, and Israel's joy knew no bounds. 12 Everyone lived in peace among his own grapevines and fig trees, and no one made them afraid. 13 In those days all the enemy kings had been defeated, and there was no one left in the land to fight the Jews. 14 Simon provided help for all the poor among his people, and guided by the Law of Moses, he eliminated all wicked and lawless men. 15 He provided the Temple with splendid furnishings and added a large number of utensils for use in worship.

16 When the news that Jonathan had died reached Rome and Sparta, it brought great sorrow. 17 But when the Spartans heard that Simon had succeeded his brother as High Priest and that he was in control of the country and its towns, 18 they engraved on bronze tablets a renewal of the treaty of friendship which they had made with his brothers Judas and Jonathan and sent the tablets to him. 19 These were read to the assembly in Jerusalem. 20 What follows is a copy of the letter sent by the Spartans:

> "The people of Sparta and their rulers to Simon the High Priest, to the leaders and the priests of the Jews, and to all our Jewish brothers, greetings. 21 The delegation that you sent to our people has told us how respected and renowned you are. Their visit has been a source of joy for us, 22 and a report of their visit has been written down in our public records, as follows:
>
> 'Numenius son of Antiochus and Antipater son of Jason, honored representatives of the Jews, appeared before us to renew their treaty of friendship. 23 The assembly of the people was pleased to receive these men with all honors and to place a copy of their report in the public archives, so that the people of Sparta may have it on record. A copy of this document has been made for the High Priest Simon.' "

24 Later, Simon sent Numenius to Rome with the gift of a large gold shield weighing half a ton, to confirm the Jews' alliance with the Romans.

25 When the people of Israel heard about all this, they asked themselves, "How can we express our thanks to Simon and his sons? 26 He, his brothers, and his father's whole family have been towers of strength for our nation. They have fought off our enemies and set the nation free."

So they recorded this on bronze tablets and set them up on columns on Mount Zion. 27 The inscription read as follows:

> "On the eighteenth day of the month of Elul in the year 172,[n] that is, in the third year of Simon, the High Priest,[o] 28 at a great assembly of priests, people, officials, and national leaders the following facts were made known to us: 29 Often when wars broke out in the

[n] THE YEAR 172: *This corresponds to 140 B.C.* [o] *Greek has an additional word, the meaning of which is unclear.*

country, Simon son of Mattathias, a
priest of the Jehoiarib family, and his
brothers risked their lives in protecting our nation, our Temple, and our
Law against our enemies. They have
brought great glory to our nation.
30 Jonathan united our people and became the High Priest before he died.
31 The enemies of the Jews plotted to
invade the land and defile the Temple.
32 Then Simon assumed command and
fought for his country. He spent a
large amount of his own money to provide weapons and wages for his nation's armed forces. 33 He fortified the
towns of Judea, and especially Bethzur on the border, where enemy weapons had previously been stored. He
stationed a detachment of soldiers
there. 34 He fortified the seaport of
Joppa and the city of Gezer on the border of Azotus, which was previously
occupied by enemy soldiers. He settled Jews there and provided the
towns with everything that the people
needed.[p] 35 When the people saw Simon's patriotism and how he wanted
to bring glory to his nation, they made
him their leader and High Priest. They
did this because of all that he had accomplished through his loyalty and
because he had brought about justice
and had tried in every way to bring
glory to his nation.
36 "Under his leadership the Gentiles
were driven out of the land. Enemy
soldiers were forced out of the area
north of the Temple, where they had
built the fort, from which the soldiers
used to go out and defile the holy Temple. 37 Simon settled Jews in the fort,
strengthened it for the security of the
country and the city of Jerusalem, and
increased the height of the city walls.
38 As a result, King Demetrius confirmed him as High Priest, 39 gave him
the title of "Friend of the King," and
treated him with great honor. 40 Demetrius did this because he had heard
that the Romans were calling the Jews
their friends, allies, and brothers and
that they had received Simon's delegation with full honors.
41 "Therefore,[q] the Jews and their
priests are happy to have Simon and
his descendants as their leaders and
High Priests, until a true prophet appears. 42 Simon shall govern their
country, have charge of the Temple,
and shall be their military commander. He shall be in charge of military supplies, fortifications, and public
works. 43 The people must obey him in
everything. All government contracts
shall be drawn up in his name. He
shall have the right to wear royal
robes with the gold shoulder buckle.
44 "No one, priest or people, shall
have the legal right to annul any of
these decisions, to alter or change any
of Simon's orders, to convene any assembly in the country without his permission, or to wear royal robes with
the gold shoulder buckle. 45 Anyone
who disobeys or disregards these regulations shall be subject to punishment.
46 "The people gave their unanimous
approval to grant Simon the right to
act in accordance with these regulations. 47 Simon consented and agreed
to be supreme leader: High Priest,
commander of the armies, and governor of the Jews and the priests."
48 It was decided that this declaration
should be engraved on bronze tablets
and set up in a prominent place within
the Temple area 49 and that copies
should be placed in the Temple treasury,
where Simon and his sons would have
access to them.

Antiochus the Seventh Asks for Simon's Support

15 From the Greek islands Antiochus son of King Demetrius
wrote the following letter to Simon the
High Priest and governor of the Jews
and to the whole nation:
2 "King Antiochus to Simon, the
High Priest and governor, and to the
Jewish nation, greetings. 3 As you
know, the kingdom of my ancestors
has been seized by traitors. I have decided to reclaim it and restore its former greatness. I have raised a large
army of mercenary troops and have
fitted out warships. 4 I plan to invade
the land and to attack those who have

[p] that the people needed; *or* that was needed to keep them in repair.
[q] Therefore; *some manuscripts have* and that.

destroyed many of the towns and ruined the country.
5 "Now therefore, I confirm all exemptions from taxes and payments
granted you by former kings.
6 I authorize you to mint your own
coins as legal currency in your own
country. 7 Jerusalem and the Temple
shall be free of taxation. All the weapons that you have manufactured and
the defenses you have built and now
occupy shall remain yours. 8 In addition, all debts now owed to the royal
treasury, or which may in the future
fall due, are permanently canceled.
9 As soon as I have regained control of
my kingdom, I will confer upon you,
your nation, and the Temple such
great honors that the glory of your
country will be evident to the whole
world."
10 In the year 174[r] Antiochus invaded
the land of his ancestors. Most of the soldiers came over to his side, so that there
were very few left with Trypho. 11 Trypho, pursued by Antiochus, fled to the
coastal city of Dor, 12 realizing that he
was in a desperate situation, now that all
his troops had deserted him. 13 Then Antiochus laid siege to Dor with 120,000
well-trained soldiers and 8,000 cavalry.
14 With his ships joining the attack, he
completely surrounded the town and
brought such pressure on it that no one
was able to enter or leave.

Rome Supports the Jews

15 Meanwhile, Numenius and those
with him arrived in Jerusalem from
Rome with the following letter addressed to various kings and countries:
16 "From Lucius, consul of the Romans, to King Ptolemy, greetings.
17 A delegation from our friends and
allies the Jews has come to us to renew the earlier treaty of friendship
and alliance. They were sent by the
High Priest Simon and the Jewish people, 18 and they have brought as a gift
a gold shield weighing half a ton. 19 So
we have decided to write to various
kings and countries urging them not
to harm the Jews, their towns, or their
country in any way. They must not
make war against the Jews or give
support to those who attack them.
20 We have decided to accept the shield
and grant them protection. 21 Therefore if any traitors escape from Judea
and seek refuge in your land, hand
them over to Simon the High Priest, so
that he may punish them according to
Jewish law."
22 Lucius wrote the same letter to King
Demetrius, to Attalus, Ariarathes, and
Arsaces, 23 and to all the following countries: Sampsames, Sparta, Delos, Myn-
dos, Sicyon, Caria, Samos, Pamphylia,
Lycia, Halicarnassus, Rhodes, Phaselis,
Cos, Side, Aradus, Gortyna, Cnidus, Cyprus, and Cyrene. 24 A copy of the letter
was also sent to Simon the High Priest.

Antiochus the Seventh Breaks with Simon

25 King Antiochus laid siege to Dor for
a second time, keeping it under constant
attack. He built siege platforms, and his
blockade kept Trypho and his men from
going in or out. 26 Simon sent 2,000 well-
trained soldiers to help Antiochus, as
well as silver and gold and a great deal
of equipment. 27 But Antiochus refused
to accept them, canceled all the previous
agreements that he had made with Simon, and became his enemy. 28 Then Antiochus sent his trusted official
Athenobius to negotiate with Simon. He
told Simon, "You are occupying Joppa,
Gezer, and the fort in Jerusalem, cities
that belong to my kingdom. 29 You have
devastated those regions and brought
great trouble to the country. You have
seized control of many places in my
kingdom. 30 Now you must hand back
these cities that you have captured, and
you must give me the tax money that
you have taken from places that you occupied outside the territory of Judea. 31 If
you are unwilling to do this, then you
must pay me 30,000 pounds of silver,
and 30,000 additional pounds of silver to
compensate me for damages and for lost
taxes. If you refuse to do either of these,
we will go to war against you."
32 When Athenobius came to Jerusalem and saw the splendor of Simon's
court, the gold and silver tableware in
his banquet hall, and the rest of the display of great wealth, he was amazed. He
delivered the king's message to Simon,
33 and Simon answered, "We have never

[r] THE YEAR 174: *This corresponds to 138 B.C.*

taken land away from other nations or
confiscated anything that belonged to
other people. On the contrary, we have
simply taken back property that we inherited from our ancestors, land that
had been unjustly taken away from us
by our enemies at one time or another.
34 We are now only making use of this
opportunity to recover our ancestral
heritage. 35 As for Joppa and Gezer,
which you claim, we will give you 6,000
pounds of silver, in spite of the fact that
the people of those cities have done
great harm to our nation."

Athenobius made no reply, 36 but he
returned to the king in a rage. When he
told the king what Simon had said, and
reported on the splendor of Simon's
court and all that he had seen, the king
became violently angry.

John's Victory over Cendebeus

37 In the meantime, Trypho had
boarded a ship and escaped to the town
of Orthosia. 38 King Antiochus appointed
Cendebeus as commander of the coastal
area, provided him with infantry and
cavalry, 39 and gave him orders to move
against Judea. He also ordered him to
rebuild the town of Kedron and fortify
its gates, so that he could fight against
the Jewish people. The king himself continued to pursue Trypho.

40 Cendebeus then came to Jamnia and
began to harass the Jews by invading
Judea, capturing people, and murdering
them. 41 He rebuilt Kedron and stationed
some cavalry and infantry units there,
so that they could make attacks and patrol the roads of Judea, as the king had
ordered.

16 Simon's son John left Gezer and
went to report to his father what
Cendebeus had done. 2 Simon said to
John and Judas, his two oldest sons, "All
my father's family, my brothers, and I
have fought Israel's battles all our lives,
and many times we have been successful in saving Israel. 3 I am old now, but
you, thanks to God, are in the prime of
life. You must take my place and that of
my brother in fighting for our nation.
And may God himself be with you."

4 Then John raised an Israelite army of
20,000 trained soldiers and cavalry and
marched out against Cendebeus. They
spent the night in Modein, 5 and then
early the next morning they moved into
the plain. There a large army of infantry
and cavalry moved to meet them, but
there was a river between the two armies. 6 John and his army took up battle
positions facing the enemy, but when
John saw that his soldiers were afraid to
cross the river, he crossed ahead of
them, and his men saw him and followed. 7 John divided his army and
placed his cavalry in the middle of the
infantry, because there was a large number of enemy cavalry. 8 The trumpets
sounded the attack, and Cendebeus and
his army were defeated, and many of
them were killed. The rest ran back to
their fortress at Kedron. 9 Judas was
wounded in the battle, but his brother
John continued to pursue the enemy as
far as Kedron, which Cendebeus had rebuilt. 10 The escaping soldiers fled to the
towers in the fields at Azotus, and John
set fire to the city. On that day, 2,000
enemy soldiers were killed, and John returned safely to Judea.

The Murder of Simon and Two of His Sons

11 Simon the High Priest had appointed Ptolemy son of Abubus commander for the Plain of Jericho. Ptolemy
was very rich, 12 because he was Simon's
son-in-law. 13 But he became too ambitious and wanted to take over the country. So he devised a plan to assassinate
Simon and his sons. 14 Simon, together
with his sons Mattathias and Judas, was
visiting the towns in the area, in order to
take care of their needs. They arrived in
Jericho in the month of Shebat, the eleventh month, in the year 177.[s] 15 Ptolemy, still plotting to murder Simon and
his two sons, received them in a small
fortress called Dok, which he had built.
He gave a great banquet for them, but he
had men hidden within the fortress.
16 When Simon and his sons were drunk,
Ptolemy and his men came out of hiding
and with swords in hand rushed into the
banquet hall, where they killed Simon,
his two sons, and some of the servants.
17 With this horrible act of treachery,
Ptolemy returned evil for good.

18 Then Ptolemy wrote a report of what
he had done and sent it to the king. In

[s] THE YEAR 177: *This corresponds to 134 B.C.*

the letter he requested that troops be
sent to help him and that the country
and the cities be turned over to him.
19 He wrote a letter to the army officers
inviting them to join him and promising
them silver, gold, and gifts. Then he sent
some of his men to Gezer to kill John,
20 and others to take control of Jerusalem and the Temple hill. 21 But someone
ran to Gezer ahead of Ptolemy's men
and reported to John that his father and
his brothers had been killed and that
Ptolemy was sending his soldiers to kill
him. 22 John was horrified at this news,
but, because he had been warned in advance, he was able to capture and put to
death the men who had been sent to
kill him.

23 Now the rest of what John did from
the time he succeeded his father: his
wars, his deeds of courage, his rebuilding of walls, and his other accomplishments, 24 are all written in the chronicles
of his reign as High Priest.

The Second Book of the MACCABEES

Introduction

The Second Book of the Maccabees *is a condensation of a five-volume history by Jason of Cyrene. The book reports events in Jewish history from the time of the High Priest, Onias the Third (about 180 B.C.), to the death of Nicanor (161 B.C.), and parallels in part the events described in the early chapters of* 1 Maccabees. *There is a strong emphasis on loyalty to the law and on God's reward to martyrs who die for their faith.*

Outline of Contents

A Letter to the Jews in Egypt

1 "From the Jews of Jerusalem and
Judea to those in Egypt, warm
greetings.

2 "May God be good to you and keep
the covenant he made with Abraham,
Isaac, and Jacob, his faithful servants.
3 May he fill each of you with the desire
to worship him and to do his will eagerly
with all your heart and soul. 4 May he
enable you to understand his Law and
his commands. May he give you peace,
5 answer your prayers, forgive your sins,
and never abandon you in times of trouble. 6 Here in Judah we are now praying
for you.

7 "In the year 169,[a] when Demetrius
the Second was king of Syria, we wrote
to tell you about the persecution and the
hard times that came upon us in the
years after Jason revolted against authority in the Holy Land. 8 Jason and his
men set fire to the Temple gates and
slaughtered innocent people. Then we
prayed to the Lord and he answered our
prayers. So we sacrificed animals, gave
offerings of grain, lit the lamps in the
Temple, and set out the sacred loaves.
9 This is why we urge you to celebrate in
the month of Kislev a festival similar to
the Festival of Shelters. Written in the
year 188."[b]

A LETTER TO ARISTOBULUS

The Death of King Antiochus

10 "From the Jews of Jerusalem and Judea, the Jewish Senate, and Judas, to
Aristobulus, a descendant of priests and
the teacher of King Ptolemy, and to the

[a] THE YEAR 169: *This corresponds to 143 B.C.* [b] THE YEAR 188: *This corresponds to 124 B.C.*

Jews in Egypt, greetings and good
health.
11 "We thank God because he saved us
from great danger. We were like men
ready to fight against a king, 12 but God
drove the enemy from our holy city.
13 When King Antiochus arrived in Persia, his army seemed impossible to defeat, but they were cut to pieces in the
temple of the goddess Nanea by an act of
treachery on the part of her priests.
14 King Antiochus had gone to the temple with some of his most trusted advisers, so that he might marry the goddess
and then take away most of the temple
treasures as a wedding gift. 15 After the
priests had laid out the treasure, he and
a few of his men went into the temple to
collect it. But the priests closed the doors
behind him 16 and stoned him and his
men from trap doors hidden in the ceiling. Then they cut up the bodies and
threw the heads to the people outside.
17 Praise God for punishing those evil
men! Praise him for everything!

Fire Consumes Nehemiah's Sacrifice

18 "On the twenty-fifth day of the
month of Kislev we will celebrate the
Festival of Rededication just as we celebrate the Festival of Shelters. We
thought it important to remind you of
this, so that you too may celebrate this
festival. In this way you will remember
how fire appeared when Nehemiah offered sacrifices after he had rebuilt the
Temple and the altar. 19 At the time when
our ancestors were being taken to exile
in Persia, a few devout priests took some
fire from the altar and secretly hid it in
the bottom of a dry cistern. They hid the
fire so well that no one ever discovered
it. 20 Years later, when it pleased God,
the Persian emperor sent Nehemiah
back to Jerusalem, and Nehemiah told
the descendants of those priests to find
the fire. They reported to us that they
had found no fire but only some oily liquid. Nehemiah then told them to scoop
some up and bring it to him. 21 When
everything for the sacrifice had been
placed on the altar, he told the priests to
pour the liquid over both the wood and
the sacrifice. 22 After this was done and
some time had passed, the sun appeared
from behind the clouds, and suddenly
everything on the altar burst into flames.
Everyone looked on in amazement.
23 Then, while the fire was consuming
the sacrifice, Jonathan the High Priest
led the people in prayer, and Nehemiah
and all the people responded.

Nehemiah's Prayer

24 "Nehemiah's prayer went something
like this: 'Lord God, Creator of all
things, you are awesome and strong, yet
merciful and just. You alone are king.
No one but you is kind; 25 no one but you
is gracious and just. You are almighty
and eternal, forever ready to rescue Israel from trouble. You chose our ancestors to be your own special people.
26 Accept this sacrifice which we offer on
behalf of all Israel; protect your chosen
people and make us holy. 27 Free those
who are slaves in foreign lands and
gather together our scattered people.
Have mercy on our people, who are mistreated and despised, so that all other
nations will know that you are our God.
28 Punish the brutal and arrogant people
who have oppressed us, 29 and then establish your people in your holy land, as
Moses said you would.'

The Persian Emperor Hears about the Fire

30 "Then the priests sang hymns. 31 After the sacrifices had been consumed,
Nehemiah gave orders for the rest of the
liquid to be poured over some large
stones. 32 Immediately a fire blazed up,
but it was extinguished by a flame from
the fire on the altar.

33 "News of what had happened spread
everywhere. The Persian emperor heard
that a liquid had been found in the place
where the priests had hidden the altar
fire, just before they were taken into exile. He also heard that Nehemiah and his
friends had used this liquid to burn the
sacrifice on the altar. 34 When the emperor investigated the matter and found
out that this was true, he had the area
fenced off and made into a shrine. 35 It
became a substantial source of income
for him, and he used the money for
gifts to anyone who was in his good
favor. 36 Nehemiah and his friends
called the liquid *nephthar*, which means
'purification,' but most people call it
'naphtha.'

Jeremiah Hides the Tent of the Lord's Presence

2 "We know from the records that
Jeremiah the prophet instructed the
people who were being taken into exile
to hide some of the fire from the altar, as
we have just mentioned. 2 We also know
that he taught them God's Law and
warned them not to be deceived by the
ornamented gold and silver idols which
they would see in the land of their exile.
3 And then he urged them never to abandon the Law.
4 "These same records also tell us that
Jeremiah, acting under divine guidance,
commanded the Tent of the Lord's Presence and the Covenant Box to follow
him to the mountain where Moses had
looked down on the land which God had
promised our people. 5 When Jeremiah
got to the mountain, he found a huge
cave and there he hid the Tent of the
Lord's Presence, the Covenant Box, and
the altar of incense. Then he sealed up
the entrance.
6 "Some of Jeremiah's friends tried to
follow him and mark the way, but they
could not find the cave. 7 When Jeremiah
learned what they had done, he reprimanded them, saying, 'No one must
know about this place until God gathers
his people together again and shows
them mercy. 8 At that time he will reveal
where these things are hidden, and the
dazzling light of his presence will be
seen in the cloud, as it was in the time of
Moses and on the occasion when Solomon prayed that the Temple might be
dedicated in holy splendor.'

How Solomon Celebrated the Festival

9 "We are also told how the wise King
Solomon offered a sacrifice of dedication at the completion of the Temple,
10 and that when he prayed, fire came
down from heaven and consumed the
sacrifices, just as it had done earlier
when Moses prayed. 11 Moses had explained that the sin offering was consumed by fire because it was not eaten.
12 Solomon celebrated the festival for
eight days.

Nehemiah's Library

13 "These same facts are found in the
royal records and in the memoirs of Nehemiah, who established a library and
collected the writings of David, letters of
the kings concerning offerings, and
books about the kings and prophets.
14 Judas also collected the books that
had been scattered because of the war,
and we still have them. 15 If you ever
need any of these books, let us know,
and we will send them.

An Invitation to Celebrate the Festival

16 "Since we are about to celebrate the
Festival of Rededication, we are writing
to you, advising you to celebrate it as
well. 17 God has saved all his people and
has restored to all of us our holy land,
the kingship, the priesthood, and the
Temple services, 18 just as he promised
in his Law. He has rescued us from terrible evils and has purified the Temple,
and we are confident that in his mercy
he will soon gather us to his holy Temple
from every nation under the sun."

Author's Preface

19 Jason of Cyrene has recorded in five
volumes the story of Judas Maccabeus
and his brothers, the purification of the
great Temple, and the dedication of its
altar. 20 He has described the battles with
Antiochus Epiphanes and with his son
Eupator, 21 and he has told of the heavenly visions that appeared to those who
fought bravely and enthusiastically to
defend Judaism. Our forces were few in
number, but they plundered the entire
country and routed the heathen forces.
22 They recaptured the Temple famous
throughout the world, liberated Jerusalem, and restored the laws that were in
danger of being abolished. They were
able to do all these things because the
Lord was merciful and kind to them.
23 I will now try to summarize in a single book the five volumes written by Jason. 24 The number of details and the
bulk of material can be overwhelming
for anyone who wants to read an account of the events. 25 But I have attempted to simplify it for all readers;
those who read for sheer pleasure will
find enjoyment and those who want to
memorize the facts will not find it difficult. 26 Writing such a summary is a difficult task, demanding hard work and
sleepless nights. 27 It is as difficult as preparing a banquet that people of different

tastes will enjoy. But I am happy to
undergo this hardship in order to please
my readers. 28 I will leave the matter of
details to the original author and attempt to give only a summary of the
events. 29 I am not the builder of a new
house who is concerned with every detail of the structure, but simply a painter
whose only concern is to make the
house look attractive. 30 The historian
must master his subject, examine every
detail, and then explain it carefully,
31 but whoever is merely writing a summary should be permitted to give a brief
account without going into a detailed
discussion. 32 So then, without any further comment, I will begin my story. It
would be foolish to write such a long introduction that the story itself would
have to be cut short.

The Argument between Onias and Simon

3 When Onias[c] was High Priest in
Jerusalem, the holy city enjoyed
peace and prosperity, and its laws were
strictly obeyed, because he was devout
and hated evil. 2 The kings of Syria and
Egypt honored the Temple and presented it with expensive gifts, 3 and King
Seleucus,[d] ruler of all Asia, even used to
pay the costs of the Temple sacrifices
from the revenues he collected.

4 But a man by the name of Simon, of
the tribe of Bilgah,[e] the chief administrative official of the Temple, lost an argument he had with Onias over the
regulations governing the city market.
5 At this time Apollonius son of Thraseus
was the governor of Greater Syria. Simon went to him 6 and said that there
was so much money in the Temple treasury that it could not be counted, and
since the money was not needed for sacrifices, it might as well be placed under
the king's control.

Heliodorus Is Sent to Jerusalem

7 When Apollonius met with the king,
he told him about the money, and the
king ordered Heliodorus, his chief minister, to get it for him. 8 Heliodorus set
out at once on his mission, but he
claimed that he was only making a tour
of inspection of the cities of Greater
Syria. 9 After he had arrived in Jerusalem and had been warmly received by
the High Priest, he explained the real
reason for his visit and asked if what he
had been told was true. 10-11 The High
Priest then stated that Simon, that devil
of a man, had not been telling the truth.
There was indeed some money in the
Temple treasury, but part of it was set
aside for widows and orphans and part
of it belonged to Hyrcanus son of Tobias, a very important man. He also
pointed out that the total amount was
only 30,000 pounds of silver and 15,000
pounds of gold. 12 He added that it was
absolutely impossible that anyone
should be permitted to take the money
of those people who had placed their
trust in the sanctity and safety of this
world-famous Temple.

Heliodorus Plans to Enter the Temple

13 But Heliodorus insisted that the
money should be taken for the royal
treasury, as the king had ordered. 14 So
he set a day and went into the Temple to
supervise the counting of the money.
This caused an uproar throughout the
entire city. 15 Priests, wearing their
priestly robes, threw themselves face
downward before the altar and begged
God to keep the money safe, since he
had given the laws designed to protect
the money that people deposited in the
Temple. 16 It was heartbreaking to see
the High Priest. His face turned pale, revealing the agony of his soul, 17 and his
body was trembling with fear, reflecting
the pain in his heart. 18 People ran from
their houses to join together in prayer
that the Temple might not be defiled.
19 Women, wearing nothing but skirts of
sackcloth, crowded the streets. Young
girls whose parents had never allowed
them to be seen in public ran to the gates
or to the walls of the city, or just stared
out of their windows. 20 But wherever
they went, they lifted their hands to God
in prayer. 21 What a pitiful sight it was to
see the High Priest in such great agony
and frustration and to see everyone in
the city confused and lying face down on
the ground.

[c] ONIAS: *This is Onias the Third, son of Simon the Second (see 4.4-6; Si 50.1-21).*
[d] SELEUCUS: *This is Seleucus the Fourth, known as Philopator, son of Antiochus the Third, 187–175 B.C.*
[e] *Some ancient translations* Bilgah *(see Ne 12.5,18); Greek* Benjamin.

The Lord Protects His Temple

22 While everyone was begging the
Lord Almighty to protect the money that
had been entrusted to his care, 23 Heliodorus went on with his plan. 24 But at the
very moment that he and his bodyguards arrived at the treasury, the Lord
of all supernatural powers caused such a
vision to appear that everyone who had
dared to enter with Heliodorus was
panic-stricken and weak with fear at
this display of the Lord's power. 25 In the
vision they saw a horse and a rider. The
horse had a richly decorated bridle, and
its rider, dressed in gold armor, was
frightening. Suddenly the horse rushed
at Heliodorus, then reared up and struck
at him with its hoofs. 26 Heliodorus also
saw two unusually strong and handsome young men, wearing very fine
clothes. They stood on either side of him
and beat him unmercifully. 27 He immediately fell to the ground unconscious,
and his men put him on a stretcher 28 and
carried him out. Only a moment earlier
this man had entered the treasury with a
large group of men, including all his
bodyguards, but now he was being carried away helpless. So they all[f] openly
acknowledged the mighty power
of God.

Onias Prays for Heliodorus' Recovery

29 Heliodorus lay there unable to speak
and without hope of recovery from this
demonstration of God's power. 30 But the
Jews praised Almighty God because he
had miraculously protected his Temple
and had brought great happiness where
only minutes before there had been fear
and confusion. 31 Some of Heliodorus'
friends quickly asked Onias the High
Priest to pray that the Most High would
spare the life of this man who was at the
point of death. 32 So the High Priest offered a sacrifice in the hope that God
would save Heliodorus, for he did not
want the king to think that the Jews had
done this to the man he had sent.
33 While Onias was offering the sacrifice,
the two young men, wearing the same
clothes as before, again appeared to Heliodorus and said, "Be grateful to the
High Priest; the Lord has spared your
life because of him. 34 Remember that it
was the Lord of heaven who punished
you. Now go and tell everyone of his
great power." When they had said this,
they disappeared.

Heliodorus Praises God

35 So Heliodorus offered a sacrifice to
the Lord and made many promises, because the Lord had spared his life. Then
he said good-bye to Onias and returned
with his army to the king. 36 There he
told everyone what the Lord, the most
powerful of all gods, had done.
37 When the king asked Heliodorus
who would be the best man to send on
the next mission to Jerusalem, Heliodorus replied, 38 "If you have an enemy or
know of someone plotting against your
government, send him. He will come
back badly beaten, if he comes back at
all, for some strange power from God is
at work there. 39 The God of heaven
watches over the Temple; he strikes
down and destroys anyone who comes
to harm it." 40 That is the story of how the
Temple treasury was protected from Heliodorus.

Simon Accuses Onias

4 But Simon (mentioned earlier as the
one who informed Apollonius about
the money and brought trouble on the
nation) also lied about Onias, claiming
that he was responsible for the attack on
Heliodorus and for the difficulties that
followed. 2 He dared to accuse Onias of
plotting against the government—Onias
who not only had made donations to Jerusalem and had protected the Temple,
but who was eager to see that all our
laws were obeyed. 3-4 Apollonius son of
Menestheus, the governor of Greater
Syria, encouraged Simon in every evil
thing he did, and Simon's opposition finally grew so strong that one of his
trusted followers committed several
murders. Onias realized how dangerous
the situation had become, 5 so he went to
the king, not for the purpose of making
accusations against his own people, but
for the common good of all Jews, both in
their private and public lives. 6 He realized that without the king's cooperation
there was no hope for peace, and Simon
would keep on with his foolishness.

f they all; *some manuscripts have* he.

Jason Introduces Greek Customs

7 Later, when King Seleucus died and
Antiochus (known as Epiphanes) became king, Jason the brother of Onias
became High Priest by corrupt means.
8 He went to see[g] the king and offered
him 27,000 pounds of silver with 6,000
more pounds to be paid later. 9 Jason
also offered him an additional 11,250
pounds of silver for the authority to establish a stadium where young men
could train and to enroll the people of
Jerusalem as citizens of Antioch.[h]

10 The king gave his approval, and just
as soon as Jason took over the office of
High Priest, he made the people of Jerusalem change to the Greek way of life.
11 He began by abolishing the favors that
John had secured for the Jews from previous Syrian kings. (John was the father
of the Eupolemus who later went to
Rome to make an alliance and to establish ties of friendship.) Jason also
did away with our Jewish customs and
introduced new customs that were
contrary to our Law. 12 With great
enthusiasm he built a stadium near the
Temple hill and led our finest young
men to adopt the Greek custom of par-
ticipating in athletic events. 13 Because
of the unrivaled wickedness of Jason,
that ungodly and illegitimate High
Priest, the craze for the Greek way of life
and for foreign customs reached such a
point 14 that even the priests lost all interest in their sacred duties. They lost
interest in the Temple services and neglected the sacrifices. Just as soon as the
signal was given, they would rush off to
take part in the games that were forbidden by our Law. 15 They did not care
about anything their ancestors had valued; they prized only Greek honors.
16 And this turned out to be the source of
all their troubles, for the very people
whose ways they admired and whose
customs they tried to imitate became
their enemies and oppressed them. 17 It
is a serious thing to disregard God's
Law, as you will see from the following
events.

Jerusalem under Syrian Influence

18 Once when the king was present for
the athletic games that were held every
five[i] years in the city of Tyre, 19 that
worthless Jason sent some men there
from Jerusalem, who were also enrolled
as citizens of Antioch, to take 22,500
pounds of silver to pay for a sacrifice to
the god Hercules. But even these men
did not think it was fitting to use such a
large sum of money for a sacrifice, and
20 so the money originally intended as a
sacrifice to Hercules was used for the
construction of warships.

21 When Apollonius son of Menestheus
was sent to Egypt to attend the crowning
of Philometor as king, Antiochus
learned that Philometor was opposed to
his policies. Antiochus became concerned about the security of his own
kingdom, so he went to Joppa and then
on to Jerusalem. 22 There he was welcomed with great splendor by Jason and
the people of the city who went out to
greet him, shouting and carrying
torches. From Jerusalem Antiochus led
his army to Phoenicia.

Menelaus Becomes High Priest

23 Three years later, Jason sent Menelaus (brother of the Simon[j] mentioned
earlier) to take some money to the king
and to get his decision on several important matters. 24 But when he stood before
the king, Menelaus impressed him with
his show of authority and offered 22,500
pounds of silver more than Jason had
offered for his appointment to the office
of High Priest. 25 As a result Menelaus
returned to Jerusalem with papers from
the king, confirming him as High Priest.
But he possessed no other qualifica-
tions; he had the temper of a cruel tyrant
and could be as fierce as a wild animal.
26 So Jason, who had cheated his own
brother out of the office of High Priest,
was now forced to flee to the land of Ammon. 27 Menelaus continued to be High
Priest, but he never paid any of the
money he had promised the king.
28 However, Sostratus, the captain of the
fort in Jerusalem, kept demanding the
money, since it was his responsibility to
collect it. So finally, the two men were
summoned to appear before the king
concerning the matter. 29 Menelaus left
his brother Lysimachus as acting High
Priest, while Sostratus left the fort under

[g] went to see; *or* wrote to. [h] the people . . . Antioch; *or* the men of Jerusalem as supporters of King Antiochus. [i] five; *or* four. [j] SIMON: *See 3.4.*

the command of Crates, the commander
of the mercenary troops from Cyprus.

The Murder of Onias

30 Meanwhile, there was a revolt in the
Cilician cities of Tarsus and Mallus, because the king had given those cities to
Antiochis, his mistress. 31 So the king left
Andronicus, one of his high officials, in
command, while he hurried off to Cilicia
to restore order. 32 Menelaus took advantage of this opportunity and presented
Andronicus with some of the gold objects he had removed from the Temple in
Jerusalem. He had already sold some of
them to the city of Tyre and to other
nearby cities. 33 When Onias heard
about this, he fled for safety to a temple
at Daphne near the city of Antioch and
openly accused Menelaus. 34 Then Menelaus secretly persuaded Andronicus to
kill Onias. So Andronicus went to Onias
and deceived him with a friendly greeting and with promises of safety. Although Onias was suspicious, Andronicus finally lured him away from
the safety of the temple and immediately
murdered him in cold blood.

Andronicus Is Punished

35 The Jews and Gentiles were very angry because Onias had been murdered.
36 So when the king returned from the
territory of Cilicia, the Jews of Antioch
went to him and protested against this
senseless killing. Many Gentiles felt the
same way about the crime. 37 King Antiochus was deeply grieved and was so
filled with sorrow that he was moved to
tears when he recalled the wisdom and
self-control that Onias had shown
throughout his life. 38 Antiochus became
so angry that he tore off Andronicus'
royal robe, stripped him naked, and
marched him around the city to the very
spot where Onias had been murdered.
Then Antiochus had this bloodthirsty
murderer put to death. This was how the
Lord gave him the punishment he
deserved.

Lysimachus Is Killed

39 Meanwhile, with the support of his
brother Menelaus, Lysimachus had on
numerous occasions robbed the Jerusalem Temple and had taken many of its
gold objects. When word of this spread
around, crowds began to gather in protest against Lysimachus. 40 Finally, the
crowds were becoming dangerous and
were beginning to get out of control, so
Lysimachus sent 3,000 armed men to attack them. They were led by Auranus, a
man as stupid as he was old. 41 When the
Jews in the Temple courtyard realized
what was happening, they picked up
rocks, pieces of wood, or simply handfuls of ashes from the altar and threw
them at Lysimachus and his men in the
confusion. 42 They killed a few of Lysimachus' men, wounded many of them,
and all the rest ran for their lives. Lysimachus himself, that temple robber, was
killed near the Temple treasury.

Menelaus Is Brought to Trial

43 Because of this incident Menelaus
was brought to trial. 44 When the king
came to the city of Tyre, the Jewish authorities in Jerusalem sent three men to
bring charges against Menelaus.
45 When Menelaus saw that he was losing the case, he offered Ptolemy son of
Dorymenes a large bribe to persuade the
king to decide in his favor. 46 Ptolemy
then asked the king to go outside the
courtroom with him, as though to get
some fresh air, and there he persuaded
him to change his mind 47 and declare
Menelaus innocent of the charges
against him. So Menelaus was set free,
although he had caused the trouble; but
the three men, whom even the cruel
Scythians would have declared innocent, were sentenced to death. 48 The
three men had spoken in defense of Jerusalem, its people,[k] and the sacred objects stolen from the Temple, but they
were quickly and unjustly executed.
49 Some of the people of Tyre, however,
showed their disgust with this crime and
their respect for these men by giving
them a splendid funeral. 50 Menelaus
stayed on in his position because of the
greed of those in power. He grew more
evil every day and became the worst enemy of his own people.

Visions of a Battle

5 About this time Antiochus the
Fourth made a second attack
against Egypt. 2 For nearly forty days

[k] its people; *some manuscripts also have* the surrounding villages.

people all over Jerusalem saw visions of
cavalry troops in gold armor charging
across the sky. The riders were armed
with spears and their swords were
drawn. 3 They were lined up in battle
against one another, attacking and
counterattacking. Shields were clashing, there was a rain of spears, and arrows flew through the air. All the
different kinds of armor and the gold
bridles on the horses flashed in the sunlight. 4 Everyone in the city prayed that
these visions might be a good sign.

Jason Attacks Jerusalem

5 When a false report began to spread
that Antiochus had died, Jason took
more than a thousand men and suddenly
attacked Jerusalem. They drove back
those stationed on the city walls and finally captured the city. Menelaus fled
for safety to the fort, near the Temple
hill, 6 while Jason and his men went on
slaughtering their fellow Jews without
mercy. Jason did not realize that success
against one's own people is the worst
kind of failure. He even considered his
success a victory over enemies, rather
than a defeat of his own people. 7 But Jason did not take over the government.
Instead he was forced to flee once again
to the territory of the Ammonites, and in
the end his evil plot brought him nothing
but shame and disgrace, 8 and he died in
misery. Aretas, the ruler of the Arabs,
imprisoned him; he was looked upon as
a criminal and despised because he had
betrayed his own people; everyone was
hunting for him, and he had to run from
town to town. He fled to Egypt for
safety, 9 then to Greece, hoping to find
refuge among the Spartans, who were
related to the Jews. Finally, this man,
who had forced so many others to flee
from their own country, died as a fugitive in a foreign land. 10 Jason had killed
many people and left their bodies unburied, but now his own death was un-
mourned. He was not given a funeral or
even buried with his ancestors.

Antiochus Attacks Jerusalem

(1 Maccabees 1.20-63)

11 When the news of what had happened in Jerusalem reached Antiochus,
he thought the whole country of Judea
was in revolt, and he became as furious
as a wild animal. So he left Egypt and
took Jerusalem by storm, 12 giving his
men orders to cut down without mercy
everyone they met and to slaughter anyone they found hiding in the houses.
13 They murdered everyone—men and
women, boys and girls; even babies
were butchered. 14 Three days later Jerusalem had lost 80,000 people: 40,000
killed in the attack and at least that
many taken away to be sold as slaves.
15 But Antiochus was still not satisfied.
He even dared to enter the holiest Temple in all the world, guided by Menelaus,
who had become a traitor both to his religion and to his people. 16 With his filthy
and unholy hands, Antiochus swept
away the sacred objects of worship and
the gifts which other kings had given to
increase the glory and honor of the Temple. 17 He was so thrilled with his conquest that he did not realize that the
Lord had let his holy Temple be defiled
because the sin of the people of Jerusalem had made him angry for a while. 18 If
the people of Jerusalem had not been involved in so many sins, Antiochus would
have been punished immediately and
prevented from taking such a foolish action. He would have suffered the same
fate as Heliodorus, who was sent by
King Seleucus to inspect the treasury.
19 But the Lord did not choose his people
for the sake of his Temple; he established his Temple for the sake of his people. 20 So the Temple shared in the
people's suffering but also later shared
in their prosperity. The Lord abandoned
it when he became angry, but restored it
when his anger had cooled down.

Another Attack against Jerusalem

21 Antiochus took 135,000 pounds of
silver from the Temple and hurried off to
Antioch. Such was his arrogance that he
felt he could make ships sail across dry
land or troops march across the sea.
22 He appointed governors to cause trouble for the people. In Jerusalem he
placed Philip, a man from Phrygia who
was more evil than Antiochus himself.
23 At Mount Gerizim he placed Andronicus. In addition to these, there was Menelaus, who mistreated his fellow Jews
far worse than the governors did. Antiochus hated the Jews so much 24 that he
sent an army of 22,000 mercenary troops
from Mysia to Jerusalem under the command of a man named Apollonius, with

orders to kill every man in the city and
to sell the women and boys as slaves.
25 Apollonius arrived in Jerusalem, pretending to be on a peace mission. Then on a Sabbath, when all the Jews were observing the day of rest, he led his troops, who were fully armed, in a parade outside the city.
26 Suddenly he commanded his men to kill everyone who had come out to see them. They rushed into the city and murdered a great many people.

27 But Judas Maccabeus and about nine others escaped into the barren mountains, where they lived like wild animals. In order not to defile themselves, they ate only plants which they found growing there.

The Jews Are Persecuted Because of Their Faith

6 Not long after that, the king sent an elderly Athenian[l] to force the Jews to abandon their religion and the customs of their ancestors.
2 He was also to defile their Temple by dedicating it to the Olympian god Zeus.[m] The temple on Mount Gerizim was to be officially named "Temple of Zeus the God of Hospitality," as the people who lived there had requested.

3 The oppression was harsh and almost intolerable.
4 Gentiles filled the Temple with drinking parties and all sorts of immorality. They even had intercourse with prostitutes there. Forbidden objects were brought into the Temple,
5 and the altar was covered with detestable sacrifices prohibited by our Law.
6 It was impossible to observe the Sabbath, to celebrate any of the traditional festivals, or even so much as to admit to being a Jew.
7 Each month when the king's birthday was celebrated, the Jews were compelled by brute force to eat the intestines of sacrificial animals. Then, during the festival in honor of the wine god Dionysus, they were required to wear ivy wreaths on their heads and march in procession.
8 On the advice of Ptolemy,[n] the neighboring Greek cities were also instructed to require Jews to eat the sacrifices;
9 they were told to put to death every Jew who refused to adopt the Greek way of life. It was easy to see that hard times were ahead.
10 For example, two women were arrested for having their babies circumcised. They were paraded around the city with their babies hung from their breasts; then they were thrown down from the city wall.
11 On another occasion, Philip was told that some Jews had gathered in a nearby cave to observe the Sabbath in secret. Philip attacked and burned them all alive. They had such respect for the Sabbath that they would not fight to defend themselves.

The Lord Punishes and Shows Mercy

12 I beg you not to become discouraged as you read about the terrible things that happened. Consider that this was the Lord's way of punishing his people, not of destroying them.
13 In fact, it is a sign of kindness to punish a person immediately for his sins, rather than to wait a long time.
14 The Lord does not treat us as he does other nations: he waits patiently until they have become deeply involved in sin before he punishes them,
15 but he punishes us before we have sinned too much.
16 So the Lord is always merciful to us, his own people. Although he punishes us with disasters, he never abandons us.
17 I have made these few observations by way of reminder. We will now get on with the story.

Eleazar Dies for His Faith

18 There was an elderly and highly respected teacher of the Law by the name of Eleazar, whose mouth was being forced open to make him eat pork.
19-20 But he preferred an honorable death rather than a life of disgrace. So he spit out the meat and went willingly to the place of torture, showing how people should have courage to refuse unclean food, even if it costs them their lives.
21-22 Those in charge of the sacrifice had been friends of Eleazar for a long time, and because of this friendship they told him privately to bring meat that was lawful for him to eat. He need only pretend to eat the pork, they said, and in this way he would not be put to death.

[l] elderly Athenian; *or* an elder of Athens, *or* Athenaios the elder, *or* Geron an Athenian; *some manuscripts have* an elderly Antiochean; *or* an elder of Antioch. [m] ZEUS: *The supreme god of the Greeks; Mount Olympus was thought to be his home.* [n] Ptolemy *(see 4.45); some manuscripts have* the people of Ptolemais.

23 But Eleazar made a decision worthy
of his gray hair and advanced age. All
his life he had lived in perfect obedience
to God's holy laws, so he replied, "Kill
me, here and now. 24 Such deception is
not worthy of a man of my years. Many
young people would think that I had denied my faith after I was ninety years
old. 25 If I pretended to eat this meat, just
to live a little while longer, it would
bring shame and disgrace on me and
lead many young people astray. 26 For
the present I might be able to escape
what you could do to me, but whether I
live or die, I cannot escape Almighty
God. 27 If I die bravely now, it will show
that I deserved my long life. 28 It will also
set a good example of the way young
people should be willing and glad to die
for our sacred and respected laws."

As soon as he said these things, he
went[o] off to be tortured, 29 and the very
people who had treated him kindly a few
minutes before, now turned against him,
because they thought he had spoken like
a madman. 30 When they had beaten him
almost to the point of death, he groaned
and said, "The Lord possesses all holy
knowledge. He knows I could have escaped these terrible sufferings and
death, yet he also knows that I gladly
suffer these things, because I fear him."

31 So Eleazar died. But his courageous
death was remembered as a glorious example, not only by young people, but by
the entire nation as well.

A Mother and Her Sons Die for Their Faith

7 On another occasion a Jewish
mother and her seven sons were arrested. The king was having them
beaten to force them to eat pork. 2 Then
one of the young men said, "What do
you hope to gain by doing this? We
would rather die than abandon the traditions of our ancestors."

3 This made the king so furious that he
gave orders for huge pans and kettles to
be heated red hot, 4 and it was done immediately. Then he told his men to cut
off the tongue of the one who had spoken and to scalp him and chop off his
hands and feet, while his mother and six
brothers looked on. 5 After the young
man had been reduced to a helpless
mass of breathing flesh, the king gave
orders for him to be carried over and
thrown into one of the pans. As a cloud
of smoke streamed up from the pan, the
brothers and their mother encouraged
one another to die bravely, saying,
6 "The Lord God is looking on and understands our suffering. Moses made this
clear when he wrote a song condemning
those who had abandoned the Lord. He
said, 'The Lord will have mercy on those
who serve him.' "

7 After the first brother had died in this
way, the soldiers started amusing themselves with the second one by tearing
the hair and skin from his head. Then
they asked him, "Now will you eat this
pork, or do you want us to chop off your
hands and feet one by one?"

8 He replied in his native language, "I
will never eat it!" So the soldiers tortured him, just as they had the first one,
9 but with his dying breath he cried out
to the king, "You butcher! You may kill
us, but the King of the universe will raise
us from the dead and give us eternal life,
because we have obeyed his laws."

10 The soldiers began entertaining
themselves with the third brother. When
he was ordered to stick out his tongue,
he quickly did so. Then he bravely held
out his hands 11 and courageously said,
"God gave these to me. But his laws
mean more to me than my hands, and I
know God will give them back to me
again." 12 The king and those with him
were amazed at his courage and at his
willingness to suffer.

13 After he had died, the soldiers tortured the fourth one in the same cruel
way, 14 but his final words were, "I am
glad to die at your hands, because we
have the assurance that God will raise us
from death. But there will be no resurrection to life for you, Antiochus!"

15 When the soldiers took the fifth boy
and began torturing him, 16 he looked
the king squarely in the eye and said,
"You have the power to do whatever you
want with us, even though you also are
mortal. But do not think that God has
abandoned our people. 17 Just wait. God
will use his great power to torture you
and your descendants."

18 Then the soldiers took the sixth boy,
and just before he died he said, "Make

[o] went; *some manuscripts have* was dragged.

no mistake. We are suffering what we
deserve, because we have sinned against
our God. That's why all these terrible
things are happening to us. 19 But don't
think for a minute that you will avoid
being punished for fighting against
God."
20 The mother was the most amazing
one of them all, and she deserves a special place in our memory. Although she
saw her seven sons die in a single day,
she endured it with great courage because she trusted in the Lord. 21 She
combined womanly emotion with manly
courage and spoke words of encouragement to each of her sons in their native
language. 22 "I do not know how your life
began in my womb," she would say, "I
was not the one who gave you life and
breath and put together each part of
your body. 23 It was God who did it, God
who created the universe, the human
race, and all that exists. He is merciful
and he will give you back life and breath
again, because you love his laws more
than you love yourself."
24 Antiochus was sure that the mother
was making fun of him, so he did his
best to convince her youngest son to
abandon the traditions of his ancestors.
He promised not only to make the boy
rich and famous, but to place him in a
position of authority and to give him the
title "Friend of the King." 25 But the boy
paid no attention to him, so Antiochus
tried to persuade the boy's mother to
talk him into saving his life, 26 and after
much persuasion she agreed to do so.
27 Leaning over her son, she fooled the
cruel tyrant by saying in her native language, "My son, have pity on me. Remember that I carried you in my womb
for nine months and nursed you for
three years. I have taken care of you and
looked after all your needs up to the
present day. 28 So I urge you, my child, to
look at the sky and the earth. Consider
everything you see there, and realize
that God made it all from nothing, just as
he made the human race. 29 Don't be
afraid of this butcher. Give up your life
willingly and prove yourself worthy of
your brothers, so that by God's mercy I
may receive you back with them at the
resurrection."
30 Before she could finish speaking,
the boy said, "King Antiochus, what are
you waiting for? I refuse to obey your
orders. I only obey the commands in the
Law which Moses gave to our ancestors.
31 You have thought up all kinds of cruel
things to do to our people, but you won't
escape the punishment that God has in
store for you. 32-33 It is true that our living
Lord is angry with us and is making us
suffer because of our sins, in order to
correct and discipline us. But this will
last only a short while, for we are still his
servants, and he will forgive us. 34 But
you are the cruelest and most disgusting
thing that ever lived. So don't fool yourself with illusions of greatness while you
punish God's people. 35 There is no way
for you to escape punishment at the
hands of the almighty and all-seeing
God. 36 My brothers suffered briefly because of our faithfulness to God's covenant, but now they have entered eternal
life.[p] But you will fall under God's judgment and be punished as you deserve for
your arrogance. 37 I now give up my
body and my life for the laws of our ancestors, just as my brothers did. But I
also beg God to show mercy to his people quickly and to torture you until you
are forced to acknowledge that he alone
is God. 38 May my brothers and I be the
last to suffer the anger of Almighty God,
which he has justly brought upon our
entire nation."
39 These words of ridicule made Antiochus so furious that he had the boy tortured even more cruelly than his
brothers. 40 And so the boy died, with absolute trust in the Lord, never unfaithful
for a minute.
41 Last of all, the mother was put to
death.
42 But I have said enough about the
Jews being tortured and being forced to
eat the intestines of sacrificial animals.

Judas Maccabeus Revolts

(1 Maccabees 3.1-26)

8 Judas Maccabeus and his friends
went secretly from village to village
until they had gathered a force of about
6,000 Jewish men who had remained
faithful to their religion. 2 They begged
the Lord to help his people, now tram-

[p] briefly . . . life; *or* briefly, but now they have entered eternal life because of our covenant with God.

pled under foot by all nations, to take
pity on the Temple, now defiled by pagans, 3 and to have mercy on Jerusalem,
now destroyed and almost leveled to the
ground. 4 They also asked the Lord to
show his hatred of evil by taking revenge on those who were murdering his
people, mercilessly slaughtering innocent children, and saying evil things
against the Lord.

5 When Judas had finally organized
his forces, the Gentiles were unable to
stand against him, because the Lord's
anger against Israel had now turned to
mercy. 6-7 Judas would make sudden attacks on towns and villages and burn
them. He captured strategic positions
and routed many enemy troops, finding
that he was most successful at night.
People everywhere spoke of his bravery.

Ptolemy Sends Nicanor to Attack Judas

(1 Maccabees 3.38-41)

8 When Philip, governor of Jerusalem,
realized that Judas was gaining ground
little by little and that his victories were
becoming more and more frequent, he
wrote a letter to Ptolemy, governor of
Greater Syria, requesting his help in defending the royal interests. 9 Ptolemy immediately appointed Nicanor son of
Patroclus, who was also in the closest
circle of the King's Friends, and sent
him with more than 20,000 troops of various nationalities to wipe out the entire
Jewish race. Ptolemy also appointed
Gorgias, a general of wide military
experience, to go with him. 10 King Antiochus owed the Romans 150,000 pounds
of silver; Nicanor planned to pay off the
debt by selling Jewish prisoners of war
as slaves.

11 So he at once sent word to the towns
along the coast, informing them that he
would be selling Jews for less than a
pound of silver each. But he did not
know of the judgment that Almighty
God had in store for him.

Judas Learns of Nicanor's Plans

(1 Maccabees 3.42-54)

12 Judas learned that Nicanor was advancing with his army toward Judea, so
he informed his men. 13 Some were cowardly and did not believe in the justice of
God, and they ran away as fast as they
could. 14 But others sold all their remaining possessions so that the Lord would
consider them worthy to be saved from
the godless Nicanor, who had sold them
as slaves even before the battle had
taken place. 15 They prayed that if God
was not willing to do this for their sake
alone, he might be willing to rescue
them because of the covenants he had
made with their ancestors, and because
he, the great and wonderful God, had
called them to be his people. 16 Judas
brought together all 6,000 of his men
and encouraged them not to be frightened or to flee in panic at the sight of the
large number of Gentile troops who
were marching against them without
cause. Instead they should fight bravely,
17 never forgetting the crimes the Gentiles had committed against the Temple
and how they had made Jerusalem suffer terribly and had done away with
Jewish traditions. 18 "They rely on their
weapons and their daring," Judas said,
"but we trust in Almighty God, who is
able to destroy not only these troops,
but, if necessary, the entire world, with a
mere nod of his head."

19 Then Judas went on to remind them
of the ways God had helped their ancestors: during the time of Sennacherib
185,000 of the enemy had been destroyed; 20 and once in Babylonia 8,000
Jews came to the aid of 4,000 Macedonians, defeating 120,000 Galatians and
taking a great deal of loot, all because of
God's help.

Judas Defeats Nicanor

(1 Maccabees 3.55 – 4.27)

21 Judas' words encouraged his men
and made them willing to die for their
religion and their country. He then divided his army into four divisions 22 of
about 1,500 men each, with himself and
his brothers Simon, Joseph, and Jonathan each in charge of a division. 23 After
ordering Eleazar to read aloud[q] from
the holy book, he gave his men the battle
cry: "God will help us," and personally
led the attack against Nicanor.

24 Almighty God fought on their side,
and they killed more than 9,000 of the
enemy. They wounded many others and
put the entire enemy army to flight.

[q] *Probable text* After . . . aloud; *Greek unclear.*

25 They seized the money from the people who had come to buy them as slaves.
Then they pursued the enemy a long
way, until they had to return, 26 because
it was almost time for the Sabbath to begin. 27 When they had collected the enemy's weapons and looted the dead,
they celebrated the Sabbath, praising
the Lord and giving thanks to him, because he had brought them safely to that
day and had given them the first sign of
his mercy. 28 When the Sabbath was
over, they gave some of the loot to the
victims of persecution and to the widows
and orphans; then they divided the rest
among their own families. 29 Afterward
they joined together in prayer to the
merciful Lord, asking him to look favorably upon his servants.

Judas Defeats Timothy and Bacchides

30 The Jews later fought against the
forces of Timothy and Bacchides and
killed more than 20,000 of them. They
captured some very high fortresses and
took a lot of loot, which they divided
equally among themselves and the widows, orphans, old men, and the victims
of persecution. 31 They carefully collected all the enemy's weapons and
stored them in strategic places, but the
rest of the loot was taken to Jerusalem.
32 They executed the commanding officer of Timothy's forces, a godless man
who had caused the Jews much suffering. 33 While celebrating their victory in
the city of their ancestors, they burned
alive those men who had set fire to the
Temple gates. The dead included Callis-
thenes, who had hidden in a small
house; and so he received the punishment he deserved for his evil deeds.

34 In this way, the evil Nicanor, who
had brought a thousand merchants to
buy the Jews, 35 was defeated with the
help of the Lord by the very people he
despised so much. He threw off his
splendid uniform and fled all alone like
a runaway slave, until he reached Antioch. He had succeeded only in destroying his entire army. 36 This man, who
had tried to pay a debt to Rome by selling the people of Jerusalem, showed that
the Jews could not be defeated. God was
their mighty Defender, because they
obeyed the laws he had given them.

The Lord Punishes Antiochus

(1 Maccabees 6.1-7; 2 Maccabees 1.11-17)

9 About this time Antiochus was retreating in disorder from Persia,
2 where he had entered the city of Persepolis and had attempted to rob a temple and take control of the city. The
people took up arms and attacked Antiochus, forcing his army to retreat in disgrace. 3 When he reached Ecbatana, he
was told what had happened to the
forces of Nicanor and Timothy. 4 He became furious and decided to make the
Jews pay for the defeat he had suffered.
So he ordered his chariot driver not to
stop until they reached Jerusalem. With
great arrogance he said, "I will turn Jerusalem into a graveyard full of Jews."

But he did not know that he was heading straight for God's judgment. 5 In fact,
as soon as he had said these words, the
all-seeing Lord, the God of Israel, struck
him down with an invisible but fatal
blow. He was seized with sharp intestinal pains for which there was no relief—
6 a fitting punishment for the man who
had tortured others in so many terrible
ways! 7 But this in no way caused him to
give up his pride. Instead he became
more arrogant than ever, and breathing
out fiery threats against the Jews, he
gave orders to drive even faster. As a
result he fell out of his chariot with such
a thud that it made every bone in his
body ache. 8 His arrogant pride made
him think he had the superhuman
strength to make ocean waves obey him
and to weigh high mountains on a pair
of scales. But suddenly he fell flat on the
ground and had to be carried off on a
stretcher, a clear sign to everyone of
God's power. 9 Even the eyes of this godless man were crawling with worms and
he lived in terrible pain and agony. The
stink was so bad that his entire army
was sickened, 10 and no one was able to
come close enough to carry him around.
Yet only a short while before, he thought
he could take hold of the stars.

Antiochus Makes a Promise to God

(1 Maccabees 6.8-17)

11 Antiochus was deeply depressed
and suffered constant pain because of
the punishment that God had brought on
him, so he finally came to his senses and
gave up his arrogant pride. 12 Then,

when he could no longer endure his own
stink, he said, "It is right that all mortals
should be subject to God and not think
that they are his equal." 13 The time of
the Lord's mercy had come to an end for
Antiochus, but this worthless man made
the Lord a promise: 14 "I once intended to
level Jerusalem to the ground and make
that holy city a graveyard full of Jews,"
he said, "but now I declare it a free city.
15 I had planned to throw out the dead
bodies of the Jews and their children for
the wild animals and the birds to eat, for
I did not consider them worth burying.
But now I intend to grant them the same
privileges as the citizens of Athens enjoy. 16 I once looted the Temple and took
its sacred utensils, but I will fill it with
splendid gifts and with better utensils
than before, and I will pay the cost of the
sacrifices from my own resources. 17 Besides all this, I will become a Jew myself
and go wherever people live, telling
them of God's power."

Antiochus' Letter to the Jews

18 Antiochus was in despair and could
find no relief from his pain, because God
was punishing him as he deserved, so he
wrote the following letter to the Jews:

19 "King Antiochus to the Jews, my
most distinguished subjects. Warm
greetings and best wishes for your
health and prosperity.

20 "I hope that you and your families
are in good health and that all goes
well with you. My hope is in God,
21 and I remember with a deep sense of
joy the respect and kindness that you
have shown me.

"On my way home from Persia I fell
violently ill, and so I thought it best to
begin making plans for the general
welfare of the people. 22 I have not
given up hopes of getting well; in fact
I am fully confident that I will recover.
23 But I recall that my father used to
appoint a successor whenever he went
on a military campaign east of the Euphrates. 24 He did this so that if something unexpected happened, or if
some bad news came back, then his
subjects would not be afraid, for they
knew who had been left in command.
25 Also, I know how the rulers along
the frontiers of my kingdom are constantly on the lookout for any opportunity that may come along. That is
why I have appointed my son Antiochus to succeed me as king. I have frequently entrusted him to your care
and recommended him to you when I
went on my regular visits to the provinces east of the Euphrates. (He is receiving a copy of the letter which
follows.) 26 Now I strongly urge each
of you to keep in mind the good things
that I have done for you, both individually and as a nation, and to continue
in your good will toward me and my
son. 27 I am confident that he will treat
you with fairness and kindness, just as
I have always done."

28 And so, this murderer, who had
cursed God, suffered the same terrible
agonies he had brought on others, and
then died a miserable death in the mountains of a foreign land. 29 One of his close
friends, Philip, took his body home; but,
because he was afraid of Antiochus' son,
he went on to King Ptolemy Philometor
of Egypt.

The Rededication of the Temple

(1 Maccabees 4.36-61)

10 Judas Maccabeus and his followers, under the leadership of
the Lord, recaptured the Temple and the
city of Jerusalem. 2 They tore down the
altars which foreigners had set up in the
marketplace and destroyed the other
places of worship that had been built.
3 They purified the Temple and built a
new altar. Then, with new fire started by
striking flint, they offered sacrifice for
the first time in two years, burned incense, lighted the lamps, and set out the
sacred loaves. 4 After they had done all
this, they lay face down on the ground
and prayed that the Lord would never
again let such disasters strike them.
They begged him to be merciful when he
punished them for future sins and not
hand them over any more to barbaric,
pagan Gentiles. 5 They rededicated the
Temple on the twenty-fifth day of the
month of Kislev, the same day of the
same month on which the Temple had
been desecrated by the Gentiles. 6 The
happy celebration lasted eight days, like
the Festival of Shelters, and the people
remembered how only a short time before, they had spent the Festival of Shelters wandering like wild animals in the
mountains and living in caves. 7 But
now, carrying green palm branches and

sticks decorated with ivy, they paraded
around, singing grateful praises to him
who had brought about the purification
of his own Temple. 8 Everyone agreed
that the entire Jewish nation should celebrate this festival each year.

Ptolemy Macron Commits Suicide

9 The days of Antiochus Epiphanes
had come to an end. 10 Now we will tell
about Antiochus Eupator, the son of this
godless man, and give a summary of the
evil effects of his wars. 11 When he became king he appointed a man by the
name of Lysias to be in charge of the
affairs of state and to be chief governor
of Greater Syria, 12 replacing Ptolemy
Macron, who had been the first governor to treat the Jews fairly. Macron had
established peaceful relations with them
in an attempt to make up for the wrongs
they had suffered. 13 As a result the
King's Friends went to Eupator and accused Macron of treachery, because he
had abandoned the island of Cyprus,
which King Philometor of Egypt had
placed under his command, and had
gone over to Antiochus Epiphanes. In
fact, everyone called Macron a traitor.
No longer able to maintain the respect
that his office demanded, he committed
suicide by taking poison.

Judas Maccabeus Defeats the Idumeans

(1 Maccabees 5.1-8)

14 When Gorgias became governor of
Idumea, he kept a force of mercenaries
and attacked the Jews at every opportunity. 15 Not only this, but the Idumeans
themselves controlled certain strategic
fortresses and were constantly harassing the Jews. They welcomed those who
fled from Jerusalem and did everything
they could to keep the country in a perpetual state of war. 16 So Judas Maccabeus and his men, after offering prayers
for God's help, rushed out and made a
vigorous attack against the Idumean fortresses. 17 They beat back those who
were defending the walls and captured
the fortresses, killing everyone they
found, a total of about 20,000 people.

18 About 9,000 of the enemy, however,
managed to take refuge in two easily defended forts, with everything they
needed to withstand a siege. 19 Judas had
to go on to some other places in the
country, where he was more urgently
needed, but he left behind Simon and Joseph, together with Zacchaeus and his
men. This force was large enough to
continue the siege, 20 but some of Simon's men were greedy, and when they
were offered 140 pounds of silver, they
let some of the enemy escape from the
forts. 21 When Judas heard what had
happened, he called together the leaders
of his troops and accused those men of
selling their brothers by setting their enemies free to fight against them. 22 Then
he executed the traitors and immediately captured the two forts. 23 Judas was
always successful in battle, and in his
assault on those two forts he killed more
than 20,000 men.

Judas Defeats Timothy

24 Timothy, who had been defeated by
the Jews once before, had gathered a
large number of cavalry from Asia and a
tremendous force of mercenary troops
and was now advancing to take Judea
by armed attack. 25 But as the enemy
forces were approaching, Judas and his
men prayed to God. They put on sackcloth, threw dirt on their heads, 26 and
lay face downward on the steps of the
altar, begging God to help them by fighting against their enemies, as he had
promised in his Law.

27 When they had finished praying,
they took up their weapons, went out a
good distance from Jerusalem, and
stopped for the night not far from the
enemy. 28 At daybreak the two armies
joined in battle. The Jewish forces depended upon both their bravery and
their trust in the Lord for victory, while
the enemy relied only on their ability to
fight fiercely. 29 When the fighting was
at its worst, the enemy saw five handsome men riding on horses with gold
bridles and leading the Jewish forces.
30 These five men surrounded Judas,
protecting him with their own armor
and showering the enemy with arrows
and thunderbolts. The enemy forces
then became so confused and bewil-
dered that they broke ranks, and the
Jews cut them to pieces, 31 slaughtering
20,500 infantry and 600 cavalry.

32 Timothy himself escaped to the
strongly defended fort of Gezer, where
his brother Chaereas was in command.
33 Judas and his men besieged the fort

for four days with great enthusiasm,
34 but those inside trusted to the security
of their positions and shouted all sorts of
terrible insults against the Jews and
their God. 35 At dawn on the fifth day,
twenty of Judas' men, burning with anger at these insults, bravely climbed the
wall and with savage fury chopped
down everyone they met. 36 At the same
time, others climbed the walls on the
other side of the fort and set the towers
on fire. Many of the enemy were burned
to death as the flames spread. A third
force broke down the gates and let in the
rest of Judas' men to capture the city.
37 Timothy had hidden in a cistern, but
they killed him, as well as his brother
Chaereas and Apollophanes.
38 When it was over, the Jews celebrated by singing hymns and songs of
thanksgiving to the Lord, who had
shown them great kindness and had
given them victory.

Judas Maccabeus Defeats Lysias

(1 Maccabees 4.26-35)

11 Not long after Timothy was defeated, Lysias, the King's guardian and relative, and head of the
government, heard what had happened.
He became angry 2 and led 80,000 infantry and all his cavalry against the Jews
with the intention of turning Jerusalem
into a Greek city. 3 The Temple would be
taxed, as were all Gentile places of worship, and the office of High Priest would
be up for sale each year. 4 Lysias was so
pleased with his tens of thousands of infantry, his thousands of cavalry, and his
eighty elephants that he failed to take
into account the power of God. 5 He invaded Judea and attacked the fort of
Bethzur, about twenty miles south of Jerusalem.
6 When Judas and his men heard that
Lysias was laying siege to their forts,
they and all the people cried and wept,
begging the Lord to send a good angel to
save them. 7 Judas was the first to take
up his weapons, and he urged the others
to join him in risking their lives to help
the other Jews. So with great eagerness
they all set out together. 8 But they had
not gone far from Jerusalem, when suddenly they noticed they were being led
by a horseman dressed in white and carrying gold weapons. 9 Immediately all of
them together thanked God for his
mercy; he had made them brave enough
to attack not only men, but even the
most savage animals or even walls of
iron. 10 So they marched in battle formation, and with them went the one whom
the Lord in his mercy had sent to fight
on their side. 11 Then they charged into
the enemy like lions, killing 11,000 infantry and 1,600 cavalry, and forcing the
rest to run for their lives. 12 Most of those
who ran were wounded and had lost
their weapons, and Lysias himself managed to escape only because he ran
away like a coward.

Lysias Makes Peace with the Jews

(1 Maccabees 6.56-61)

13 Lysias was no fool. As he thought
about the defeat he had suffered, he realized it was because the mighty God had
fought for the Jews, making it impossible for them to be defeated. So he sent a
message to the Jews, 14 trying to persuade them to agree to a just settlement
and promising to do all he could to make
the king friendly toward them.[r] 15 Judas
Maccabeus considered what would be
best for the people, and so he agreed to
all the proposals Lysias had made, since
the king had granted every written request that Judas had presented to
Lysias.[s]

The Letter of Lysias to the Jews

16 Here is a copy of the letter which
Lysias wrote to the Jews:
"Lysias to the Jewish people, greetings. 17 Your representatives John and
Absalom have delivered to me the official document you sent with them, and
they have asked me to agree to what is
contained in it. 18 I have informed the
king of the matters that needed to be
brought to his attention, and he has
agreed to do whatever is possible.
19 If you continue to be loyal to the government, I will do everything I can
in the future to benefit your nation.
20 I have instructed your representatives and mine to meet with you to
discuss the details of these matters.
21 May all go well with you. Dated

[r] to do . . . them; *Greek unclear.* [s] since . . . Lysias; *or* and the king granted every written request that Judas presented to Lysias.

the twenty-fourth day of the month
of Dioscorinthius in the year 148."[t]

The King's Letter to Lysias

22 Here is a copy of the King's letter:
"King Antiochus to the honorable
Lysias, greetings. 23 Now that my
father has gone to be with the gods, I
want the subjects of my kingdom to
conduct their own affairs without interference. 24 I understand that the
Jews do not wish to adopt the Greek
way of life, as my father had intended,
but prefer their own way of life and
have requested that they be allowed to
live according to their own customs.
25 Since I desire that they live undisturbed like the other nations in my
empire, I hereby decree that their
Temple be restored to them and that
they be allowed to live according to
the customs of their ancestors.
26 Please inform them of this decision
and assure them of my friendship, so
that they may conduct their own affairs in peace, without anything to
worry about."
27 Here is a copy of the king's letter to
the Jewish people:
"King Antiochus to the Jewish leaders and all the Jews, greetings.
28 I hope that all is going well for you.
I am in good health. 29 Menelaus has
informed me of your desire to return
home and attend to your own affairs.
30 So then, those of you who return
home by the thirtieth of the month of
Xanthicus may rest assured that you
have nothing to fear. 31 You may continue to observe your food laws and
other laws, as you used to do, and no
Jew will be punished for any crime
done in ignorance. 32 I am sending
Menelaus to set your minds at ease.
33 May all go well with you. Dated the
fifteenth day of the month of Xanthicus in the year 148."[t]

The Letter of the Romans to the Jews

34 The Romans also sent the Jews the
following letter:
"Quintus Memmius and Titus Ma-
nius, representatives of the Romans,
to the Jews, greetings. 35 We are in
complete agreement with all that has
been granted to you by the honorable
Lysias. 36 We are now on our way to
Antioch, so please examine carefully
those matters that Lysias referred to
the king. Then send a reply to us immediately so that we can represent
your best interests before him. Do this
as soon as you can, 37 without delay, so
that we may know what you have decided. 38 May all go well with you.
Dated the fifteenth day of the month
of Xanthicus in the year 148."

The Jews of Joppa Are Murdered

12 When the peace agreement between the Jews and the Syrians
was completed, Lysias returned to the
king, and the Jews went back to their
farming. 2 But some of the local governors, Timothy and Apollonius son of
Gennaeus, as well as Hieronymus and
Demophon, would not let them live in
peace; and neither would Nicanor, the
commander of the mercenaries from
Cyprus.
3 About this time, the people of Joppa
did a cruel thing to the Jews of their city.
They pretended to be friendly to the
Jews and invited them and their families
to go sailing with them on ships they had
provided. 4 Since all the people of the
town had decided to do this, the Jews
suspected nothing and accepted the invitation out of a feeling of good will. But
when they were out at sea, the people of
Joppa drowned all two hundred of them.
5 As soon as Judas heard of this inhuman thing that had been done to those
Jews, he informed his men. 6 After they
had prayed to God, the just judge, they
attacked the murderers. Under cover of
darkness they set fire to the harbor,
burning all the ships, and killing everyone they found hiding there. 7 The gates
of the city were locked, so Judas withdrew; but he was determined to return at
some other time and wipe out everyone
living there.
8 Judas heard that the people of Jamnia had plans to kill the Jews of their city
also. 9 So he attacked Jamnia at night,
setting fire to its harbor and the ships
there. The flames could be seen as far as
Jerusalem, thirty miles away.

[t] THE YEAR 148: *This corresponds to 164 B.C.*

Judas' Victories in the Region of Gilead

(1 Maccabees 5.9-54)

10 When Judas and his men were about
a mile away from Jamnia on their way to
meet Timothy in battle, they were attacked by more than 5,000 Arabs, supported by 500 cavalry. 11 It was a hard
fight, but with the help of God they defeated these desert tribesmen, who then
asked to be on friendly terms with the
Jews, promising to give them some livestock and offering to help them in other
ways as well. 12 Judas thought their
friendship might prove useful in many
ways, so he agreed to make peace with
them; after that the Arabs returned to
their tents.

13 Judas also attacked the heavily fortified walled city of Caspin. The people
who lived there were a mixed population
of Gentiles 14 who relied on the strength
of their walls and felt confident that they
had enough food stored up to last
through a siege. So they made fun of Judas and his men, shouting out insults
against them and profanities against
their God. 15 But the Jews prayed to the
Almighty Lord of the universe, who had
torn down the walls of Jericho in the
days of Joshua without using battering
rams or siege weapons. Then they made
a fierce attack against the wall 16 and because it was God's will, they captured
the city. The Jews slaughtered so many
people that a nearby lake, which was
about a quarter of a mile wide, seemed
to be overflowing with blood.

Judas Defeats Timothy's Army

(1 Maccabees 5.37-44)

17 From the city of Caspin, Judas and
his men marched about 95 miles, until
they came to the Jewish settlement of
Charax, near the city of Tob. 18 But they
did not find Timothy there, because he
had already left the region. He had been
able to do nothing there except leave behind a strong garrison in one place.
19 Two of Judas' generals, Dositheus and
Sosipater, attacked the garrison and
killed all 10,000 men stationed there.
20 Then Judas divided his army into several divisions, placing Dositheus and Sosipater each in command of a division,
and hurried after Timothy, who had a
force of 120,000 infantry and 2,500 cavalry. 21 When Timothy found out that Judas was coming after him, he sent the
women and the children on ahead with
the baggage to the city of Karnaim,
which was almost impossible to besiege
or even to reach, because of the narrow
passes that led up to it. 22 But at the moment that Judas' first division came into
sight, the enemy forces were thrown
into panic by a vision sent by God, who
sees everything. In terror they began to
run wildly about and many of them were
wounded by the swords of their own
men. 23 So Judas and his men pursued
them as hard as they could, killing at
least 30,000 of the enemy. 24 Timothy
himself was captured by the troops of
Dositheus and Sosipater. But he was
very shrewd and managed to convince
them that many of their relatives were
his prisoners and would be put to death
if anything happened to him. 25 Finally,
after he had promised to send their relatives home safely, they let him go free.

Judas Wins Other Victories

(1 Maccabees 5.45-54)

26 Next, Judas attacked the city of Karnaim and the temple of the goddess
Atargatis there, killing 25,000 people
27 and completely destroying both the
city and the temple. Then he attacked
the fortified city of Ephron where Lysias
and[u] people of all nationalities were living. Strong young men took up their positions in front of the walls and fought
bravely, while inside the city were
stored large quantities of military supplies and weapons. 28 But the Jews
prayed for help to the Lord, who crushes
the power of his enemies. So they captured the city and killed about 25,000
people. 29 From there they hurried on to
the city of Beth Shan, seventy-five miles
north of Jerusalem. 30 The Jews there
told Judas how kindly the people of the
city had treated them, especially during
hard times. 31 So Judas and his men
thanked the people and urged them to
show the same good will toward the
Jews in the future. Then they left for Jerusalem, where they arrived shortly before the Harvest Festival.

[u] Lysias and; *some manuscripts do not have these words.*

Judas Defeats Gorgias

32After Pentecost (as the Harvest Festival is called in Greek) Judas and his
men quickly marched out against Gorgias, the governor of Idumea, 33who met
them with 3,000 infantry and 400 cavalry. 34In the battle that followed, a few
Jews were killed. 35Then a Jew from the
city of Tob,[v] a powerful cavalry soldier
by the name of Dositheus, grabbed Gorgias by his cloak and started dragging
him away by brute force, intending to
take the worthless man alive. But suddenly one from the Thracian cavalry
rushed at Dositheus and chopped off his
arm, allowing Gorgias to escape to the
city of Marisa.

36By now the Jewish men under the
command of Esdrias had been fighting
for a long time and were exhausted. So
Judas prayed that the Lord would show
that he was on their side and in command of their troops. 37Then, while Judas sang a hymn in his native language
as a battle cry, the Jews made a surprise
attack against Gorgias and his men and
put them to flight.

Prayers for Those Killed in Battle

38After the battle Judas led his men to
the town of Adullam. It was the day before the Sabbath, so they purified themselves according to Jewish custom and
then observed the holy day. 39By the following day it was urgent that they
gather up the bodies of the men who had
been killed in battle and bury them in
their family tombs. 40But on each of the
dead, hidden under their clothes, they
found small images of the gods worshiped in Jamnia, which the Law forbids
Jews to wear. Everyone then knew why
these men had been killed. 41So they
praised the ways of the Lord, the just
judge, who reveals what is hidden, 42and
they begged him that this sin might be
completely blotted out. Then, Judas, that
great man, urged the people to keep
away from sin, because they had seen
for themselves what had happened to
those men who had sinned. 43He also
took up a collection from all his men,
totaling about four pounds of silver, and
sent it to Jerusalem to provide for a sin
offering. Judas did this noble thing because he believed in the resurrection of
the dead. 44If he had not believed that
the dead would be raised, it would have
been foolish and useless to pray for
them. 45In his firm and devout conviction that all of God's faithful people
would receive a wonderful reward, Judas made provision for a sin offering to
set free from their sin those who had
died.

Menelaus Is Put to Death

13 In the year 149[w] Judas Maccabeus and his followers found out
that Antiochus Eupator was marching
against Judea with a large army 2and
that Lysias, the young king's guardian
and the head of his government, was
with him. They[x] had a force of Greek
troops consisting of 110,000 infantry,
5,300 cavalry, 22 elephants, and 300
chariots with sharp blades attached to
their wheels.

3Menelaus, trying to take advantage
of the situation, went over to their side
and urged them on, not because he was
concerned for the country, but because
he hoped to be confirmed as High Priest.
4But God, the King of kings, made Antiochus furious with Menelaus. Lysias
proved to Antiochus that this criminal
had been the source of all his troubles,
so Antiochus ordered him to be taken to
the city of Berea and put to death in the
way that it was done there. 5In that city
there is a tower about 75 feet high. It is
filled with ashes, and all around the inside of the tower is a platform sloping
down into the ashes. 6People accused of
crimes against the gods or of any other
serious crime are taken there and
thrown down to their death. 7Menelaus
was put to death in that way, without
even having the privilege of a burial,
8and that was just what he deserved. He
had often profaned the sacred ashes of
the altar fire in the Temple, and now he
met his death in ashes.

A Battle Near the City of Modein

9King Antiochus arrogantly continued
his barbaric invasion of Judah, intending to deal with the Jews more harshly
than his father had ever done. 10When
Judas learned of this, he told the people
to pray to the Lord day and night, be-

[v] a Jew from the city of Tob; *some manuscripts have* one of Bacenor's men. [w] THE YEAR 149: *This corresponds to 163 B.C.* [x] They; *Greek unclear.*

cause they were in danger of losing their
Law, their country, and their holy Temple. As never before, they needed his
help and protection 11 to keep their
newly restored country from falling into
the hands of godless Gentiles. 12 For
three days the people did nothing but lie
face down on the ground, fasting and
crying, begging the merciful Lord for his
help. Then Judas spoke words of encouragement to the people, urging them
to get ready for action.
13 Afterward, Judas met privately with
the Jewish leaders and decided to march
out with God's help to battle against the
king, rather than to wait for Antiochus
to invade Judea and besiege Jerusalem.
14 Then, leaving the outcome of the battle
to the Creator of the world, Judas encouraged his men to fight bravely and to
be willing to die for their laws, the Temple, Jerusalem, their country, and their
whole way of life. They set up camp near
the city of Modein. 15 Judas gave his men
the battle cry, "Victory comes from
God," and that night, with a picked force
of his bravest young men, he attacked
the area near the king's tent and killed
as many as 2,000 men. They also
stabbed to death[y] the lead elephant and
its keeper. 16 Everyone in camp was terrified and in panic when Judas and his
men finally left victoriously 17 just before
dawn. The help and protection of the
Lord had made all this possible.

Antiochus the Fifth Makes a Treaty with the Jews

(1 Maccabees 6.48-63)

18 This taste of Jewish daring was
enough to convince King Antiochus that
he had to find some better way of capturing the Jewish positions. 19 He attacked the strong Jewish fort of Bethzur,
but was repeatedly beaten back and finally defeated. 20 Judas sent supplies to
the men who were defending the fort,
21 but a Jewish soldier by the name of
Rhodocus gave some secret information
to the enemy. He was found out, however, caught, and put to death. 22 The
king made a second attempt to come to
terms with the people of Bethzur, and
when he had reached an agreement with
them, he withdrew his forces. Then he
went to attack Judas, but again he was
defeated. 23 Meanwhile, Philip had been
left at Antioch in charge of the government, but King Antiochus learned that
he had revolted. The king did not know
what to do, so he initiated peace talks
with the Jews, agreed to their terms, and
promised to be just in his treatment of
them. To put the treaty into effect, he
offered a sacrifice, gave a generous gift
to show his respect for the Temple,
24 and graciously received Judas Maccabeus. After that, the king appointed Heg-
emonides to be governor of the territory
between the cities of Ptolemais and Gerar, 25 and then he himself went on to
Ptolemais. The people there were angry
because of the treaty he had made with
the Jews—so angry, in fact, that they
wanted the treaty canceled. 26 But Lysias
made a public speech, defending the
treaty as well as he could. After he had
calmed the people down and convinced
them that he was right, he returned to
Antioch.
In this way King Antiochus' invasion
was turned into a retreat.

Alcimus Speaks against Judas

(1 Maccabees 7.1-21)

14 Three years later, Judas and his
men learned that Demetrius son
of Seleucus had sailed into the port of
Tripolis with a powerful army and a
fleet. 2 It was reported that he had killed
King Antiochus and his guardian Lysias
and had taken over the country.
3 There was a man by the name of Alcimus, who had formerly been High Priest
but who had gladly adopted the Greek
way of life during the revolt. Realizing
that he could never again be High Priest
and fearful of what the Jews might do to
him, 4 he went to see King Demetrius in
the year 151.[z] On this occasion he presented the king with a gold crown and a
palm branch, together with some olive
branches traditionally presented to the
Temple, but he said nothing about his
plans. 5 Later, however, he got the
chance to put his foolish plans into effect
when Demetrius summoned him to a
meeting of his advisers and asked him
what the Jews were intending to do.
Alcimus said, 6 "The followers of Judas Maccabeus think of themselves as
devout and patriotic; they love war and

[y] *Probable text* stabbed to death; *Greek unclear.*

[z] THE YEAR 151: *This corresponds to 161 B.C.*

are constantly inciting the people to rebellion and will never leave the nation in
peace. 7 It is their fault that I no longer
hold the glorious position of High Priest,
to which I am entitled by birth. And so I
have come here, 8 primarily out of a genuine concern for your interests as king,
but also out of consideration for my own
people, for the foolish policies of Judas
and his followers have brought terrible
suffering on our entire nation. 9 When
Your Majesty has examined all the details of these matters, please act in your
usual kind and generous manner to relieve the oppression of our nation and its
people. 10 As long as Judas is alive, it will
be impossible for our nation to enjoy
peace."

Demetrius Sends Nicanor to Attack Judas

11 As soon as Alcimus had finished his
speech, the other advisers quickly seized
this opportunity to arouse Demetrius'
anger against Judas, because they also
hated him. 12 So King Demetrius immediately appointed Nicanor, who was the
commander of his elephant forces, to be
governor of Judea, and sent him there
13 with orders to kill Judas, scatter his
followers, and make Alcimus High
Priest of the greatest Temple in all the
world. 14 All the foreigners in Judea, who
had fled from Judas' attacks, now
rushed to join forces with Nicanor, because they thought that any defeat or
trouble that came to the Jews would be
to their own advantage.

15 The Jews heard that Nicanor was attacking and that the foreigners in their
country were giving him their support.
So they threw dirt on themselves and
prayed to their God, who had chosen
their nation as his possession forever
and had never failed to help them in time
of need. 16 Then Judas, their leader, gave
the orders, and they immediately
marched out to engage the enemy in battle near the village of Adasa.[a] 17 Judas'
brother Simon was fighting Nicanor but
was gradually losing the battle because
of an unexpected move on the part of the
enemy. 18 However, when Nicanor heard
how bravely and courageously Judas
and his men were fighting for their
country, he decided not to settle the matter in battle. 19 Instead, he sent Posi-
donius, Theodotus, and Mattathias to
make a treaty with the Jews.

20 After the terms of the treaty had
been worked out in detail, Nicanor informed his troops, and they unanimously agreed. 21 Then a day was set on
which the leaders would meet in private.
Ceremonial chairs were brought out
from each camp and set up. 22 Judas had
taken the precaution of placing battle-
ready troops in strategic places, in case
of sudden treachery on the part of the
enemy. But the two leaders had a
friendly meeting. 23 Nicanor stayed on in
Jerusalem for some time after that. He
did not mistreat the Jews in any way,
and even sent away the people who had
come over to his side. 24 The two men
became the best of friends, and Judas
was Nicanor's constant companion.
25 Nicanor urged him to marry and start
a family. So Judas did this and settled
down to a peaceful life.

Nicanor Turns against Judas

26 When Alcimus noticed how well Nicanor and Judas were getting along, he
obtained a copy of the treaty and went to
see King Demetrius. He told the king
that Nicanor was disloyal to the government, because he had appointed the traitor Judas to be his successor. 27 These
false accusations infuriated the king,
and in his anger he wrote to Nicanor,
informing him that he was dissatisfied
with the treaty and ordering him to arrest Judas Maccabeus and send him to
Antioch at once.

28 When this message reached Nicanor, he was hurt and didn't know what
to do, because he did not like having to
break an agreement with a man who
had kept his part of the bargain. 29 Yet it
was impossible for him to ignore the
king's command, so he began looking
for a way to trap Judas. 30 Judas, however, noticed that Nicanor was becoming hostile and rude toward him, and he
knew that this was a bad sign. So he
gathered a large number of his followers
and went into hiding.

31 When Nicanor realized that Judas
had outsmarted him, he went to the
great and holy Temple at the time when
the priests were offering sacrifice and

[a] *Probable text* Adasa; *Greek* Dessau.

ordered them to surrender Judas to him.
32 But the priests declared under oath
that they had no idea where Judas was
hiding. 33 Then Nicanor raised his right
arm in the direction of the Temple and
made a solemn threat: "If you do not
hand Judas over to me as a prisoner, I
will level God's Temple to the ground,
demolish this altar, and on this spot
build a glorious temple to Dionysus."
34 Then he left, and immediately the
priests lifted their arms toward heaven
and prayed to God, the faithful Defender
of our nation: 35 "Lord, you are in need of
nothing, yet it has pleased you to place
your Temple here and to live among us.
36 You alone are holy, and your Temple
has only recently been purified, so now
protect its holiness forever."

Razis Dies for His Country

37 One of the leaders in Jerusalem, a
man by the name of Razis, was denounced to Nicanor. It was said that he
had helped his people in many ways and
was so highly respected by them that he
was known as "the Father of the Jews."
38 During the early days of the revolution
he had risked his life for Judaism and
had been brought to trial because of his
loyalty. 39 Wanting to show clearly how
much he disliked the Jews, Nicanor sent
more than 500 soldiers to arrest Razis,
40 because he thought his arrest would
be a crippling blow to the Jews. 41 The
soldiers were about to capture the tower
where Razis had gone. They were forcing open the gates to the courtyard, and
the order had been given to set the door
on fire. Razis realized there was no escape, so he tried to commit suicide with
his sword, 42 preferring to die with honor
rather than suffer humiliation at the
hands of evil men.
43 Under the pressure of the moment,
Razis misjudged the thrust of the sword,
and it did not kill him. So, while the soldiers were swarming into the room, he
rushed to the wall and jumped off like a
brave hero into the crowd below. 44 The
crowd quickly moved back, and he fell
in the space they left. 45 Still alive, and
burning with courage, he got up, and
with blood gushing from his wounds, he
ran through the crowd and finally
climbed a steep rock. 46 Now completely
drained of blood, he tore out his intestines with both hands and threw them at
the crowd, and as he did so, he prayed
for the Lord of life and breath to give
them back to him. That was how he died.

Nicanor's Cruel Plan

15 Nicanor learned that Judas and
his men were in the region of Samaria, and so he decided to attack them
on a Sabbath, when he could do so without any danger to himself. 2 The Jews
who were forced to accompany his army
begged him not to do such a cruel and
savage thing, but to respect the day that
the all-seeing God had honored and
made the most holy of all days. 3 Then
Nicanor, the lowest creature on earth,
asked if there was some sovereign ruler
in heaven who had commanded them to
honor the Sabbath. 4 And the Jews replied, "Yes; the living Lord, who rules in
heaven, commanded us to honor the
Sabbath."
5 But Nicanor answered, "I am the
ruler on earth, and I order you to take up
your weapons and to do what the king
commands." However, he did not succeed in carrying out his cruel plan.

Judas Prepares His Troops for Battle

6 In his arrogance Nicanor had
boasted that he would set up a monument in honor of his victory over Judas.
7 But Judas was fully confident that the
Lord would help him, 8 so he urged his
men not to be afraid of the enemy. He
encouraged them to remember how the
Almighty had helped them in times past
and to rest assured that he would give
them victory this time also. 9 He renewed
their hope by reading to them from the
Law and the Prophets and by reminding
them of the battles they had already
won. 10 When his men were ready for
battle, he gave them their orders and at
the same time pointed out how the Gentiles could not be trusted, because they
never kept their treaties. 11 He armed all
his men, not by encouraging them to
trust in shields and spears, but by inspir-
ing them with courageous words. He
also lifted their morale by telling them
about his dream, a kind of vision that
they could trust in.
12 He told them that he had seen a vision of Onias, the former High Priest,
that great and wonderful man of humble

and gentle disposition, who was an outstanding orator and who had been
taught from childhood how to live a virtuous life. With outstretched arms Onias
was praying for the entire Jewish nation. 13 Judas then saw an impressive
white-haired man of great dignity and
authority. 14 Onias said: "This is God's
prophet Jeremiah, who loves the Jewish
people and offers many prayers for us
and for Jerusalem, the holy city."

15 Then Jeremiah stretched out his
right hand and gave Judas a gold sword,
saying as he did so, 16 "This holy sword
is a gift from God. Take it and destroy
your enemies."

17 The eloquent words that Judas
spoke encouraged everyone to be brave,
and inspired boys to fight like men.
Their city, their religion, and their
Temple were in danger. So the Jews
made up their minds not to waste any
time, but to make a daring attack
against the enemy and bravely decide
their fate in hand-to-hand combat.
18 They were not so concerned about
their own families and relatives as
they were about their sacred Temple.
19 And the people who had to stay in
Jerusalem were deeply concerned
about how a battle on open ground
would turn out.

The Defeat and Death of Nicanor

20 Everyone was waiting to see who
would win the battle. The enemy troops
were already moving forward, with their
cavalry on each side of them, and their
elephants placed in strategic positions.
21 Judas Maccabeus looked at the huge
enemy force, the variety of their weapons, and their fierce elephants. Then he
raised his hands toward heaven and
prayed to the Lord, who works miracles,
because he knew that the Lord gives victory to those who deserve it, not to those
who have a strong army. 22 Judas said:
"Lord, when Hezekiah was king of Judah, you sent your angel, who killed
185,000 of King Sennacherib's men.
23 Now once again, Lord of heaven, send
your good angel to make our enemies
shake and tremble with fear. 24 With
your great power, destroy these people
who have slandered you and have come
out to attack your chosen people." So Judas ended his prayer.

25 Nicanor and his army moved forward to the sound of trumpets and battle
songs, 26 but Judas and his men went
into battle calling on God for help. 27 So
by fighting with their hands and praying
to God in their hearts, the Jews killed
more than 35,000 of the enemy. How
grateful they were for the help they had
received from God! 28 When the battle
was over and they were going home celebrating their victory, they noticed Nicanor in full armor lying dead on the
battlefield. 29 Then with loud shouts
they praised the Lord in their native
language.

30 Judas Maccabeus, who had always
fought with all his body and soul for his
own people, never losing the patriotism
of his youth, ordered his men to cut off
Nicanor's head and right arm and to
take them to Jerusalem. 31 When they arrived in the city, he called together all
the people, stationed the priests before
the altar, and sent for the men in the
fort. 32 He showed them the head of the
evil Nicanor and the arm which that
wicked man had arrogantly stretched
out against the sacred Temple of the
Almighty God. 33 Then he cut out the
tongue of that godless man, promising
to feed it bit by bit to the birds and to
hang up his head opposite the Temple,
as evidence of what his foolishness
did for him. 34 Everyone there looked
up to heaven and praised the Lord,
who had revealed his power and had
kept his Temple from being defiled.
35 Judas hung Nicanor's head from
the wall of the fort, as a clear proof to
everyone of the Lord's help. 36 By unanimous vote it was decided that this day
would never be forgotten, but would
be celebrated each year on the eve
of Mordecai's Day,[b] which is the thirteenth day of the twelfth month, called
Adar in Aramaic.

Concluding Words

37 That is how things turned out for Nicanor. The city of Jerusalem remained
in the possession of the Jewish people
from that time on, so I will end my story
here. 38 If it is well written and to the

[b] MORDECAI'S DAY: *The Festival of Purim (see Es 9.17-22).*

point, I am pleased; if it is poorly written
and uninteresting, I have still done my
best. 39 We know it is unhealthy to drink
wine or water alone, whereas wine
mixed with water makes a delightfully tasty drink. So also a good story skillfully written gives pleasure to those who read it. With this I conclude.

HOLY BIBLE

Today's English Version

Some Additional Books

SOME ADDITIONAL BOOKS

Introduction

The following books: 1 Esdras, 2 Esdras, and the Prayer of Manasseh, are included by many Protestants in the Apocrypha. However, they are not accepted as canonical by Roman Catholics. 1 Esdras and the Prayer of Manasseh constituted a part of the Septuagint Greek text of the Old Testament used by Christians during the early centuries of Christianity. The book of 2 Esdras may not have been in its final form until toward the end of the second century A.D.

The First Book of

ESDRAS

Introduction

The First Book of Esdras *parallels the account given in* 2 Chronicles 35–36, Ezra, *and* Nehemiah 6–8, *although there are omissions, additions, and variations in both order and detail. The most distinctive new material is the debate before the emperor in chapters 3 and 4.*

Outline of Contents

Josiah Celebrates the Passover

(2 Kings 23.21-23; 2 Chronicles 35.1-9)

1 King Josiah celebrated the Passover at Jerusalem in honor of the Lord; on the fourteenth day of the first month they killed the animals for the festival. 2 Josiah assigned the priests, dressed in their priestly robes, to serve in the Temple according to the daily order. 3 He also instructed the Levites, the Temple servants, to purify themselves for the Lord's service, so that they could put the sacred Covenant Box of the Lord in the Temple that King Solomon, the son of David, had built. 4 Josiah said to them, "You must no longer carry it from place to place, but you are to serve the Lord your God and minister to his people Israel. Get ready by family and clan to carry out your duties 5 according to the directions given by King David and the splendid way that they were carried out by his son King Solomon. Take your places in the Temple in proper order according to your family divisions as Levites serving the Lord for the people of Israel. 6 Kill the Passover lambs and goats and prepare the sacrifices for your people. Then celebrate the Passover according to the instructions that the Lord gave to Moses."

7 Josiah gave to the people who were present 30,000 young sheep and goats and 3,000 calves. These were a gift from the royal estates to carry out the promise he had made to the people, the priests, and the Levites. 8 The officials in charge of the Temple — Hilkiah, Zechariah, and Jehiel — also gave the priests 2,600 sheep and 300 calves for the sacrifices during the festival. 9 And the army commanders — Conaniah, Shemaiah and his brother Nethanel, Hashabiah, Ochiel, and Joram — contributed 5,000 sheep and 700 calves for the Levites to offer as sacrifices.

10-11 Here is what happened. The priests and the Levites, dressed in the proper manner and carrying the unleavened bread, came that morning to present the offerings to the Lord according to the instructions in the Law of Moses. They took their positions in front of the people in the order of tribal and family divisions. 12 The Levites roasted the Passover sacrifices and then boiled them in pots and kettles, making a pleasant smell. 13 Then they distributed the meat to all the people. After that was done, they took meat for themselves and for the priests, the descendants of Aaron, 14 because the priests were kept busy until night burning the fat of the sacrifices. 15-16 The guards at the Temple gates and the Temple singers of the Levite clan of Asaph (with Asaph, Zechariah, and Eddinus, who were representatives of the king) remained at the places assigned to them by King David's instructions. They did not need to leave their posts, because the other Levites prepared the Passover for them.

17-18 So, as King Josiah had commanded, everything that related to the sacrifices offered to the Lord was done

that day; the Passover Festival was celebrated, and the sacrifices were offered
on the altar. 19 All the people of Israel
who were present at that time kept the
Passover and observed the Festival of
Unleavened Bread for seven days.
20 Since the days of the prophet Samuel,
the Passover had never been celebrated
so well. 21-22 None of the former kings of
Israel had ever celebrated a Passover
like this one celebrated by King Josiah
in Jerusalem in the eighteenth year of
his reign; it was celebrated by the
priests, the Levites, and all the people of
Judah and Israel.

The End of Josiah's Reign

(2 Kings 23.28-30; 2 Chronicles 35.20-27)

23 The Lord was pleased with everything Josiah did, for he was a very religious man. 24 But the ancient records
also tell the story of those who sinned
and rebelled against the Lord during Josiah's reign. They sinned more than any
other nation or kingdom and did things
that offended the Lord so much that his
judgment fell on the people of Israel.
25 After Josiah had done all these
things, the king of Egypt led an army to
fight at Carchemish on the Euphrates
River. Josiah tried to stop him, 26 but the
king of Egypt sent Josiah this message:
"The war I am fighting does not concern
you, King of Judah. 27 The Lord God did
not send me to fight you; my battle is on
the Euphrates River. The Lord is with
me, and he is urging me on; so withdraw
your troops and don't oppose the Lord."
28 But Josiah did not go back to his chariot and withdraw. He refused to listen to
what the Lord had said through the
prophet Jeremiah and decided to fight.
29 He went into battle on the plain of Megiddo, and the Egyptian commanders attacked him.
30 King Josiah ordered his servants,
"Take me off the battlefield; I'm badly
hurt." So they took him out of the line of
battle immediately, 31 and he got into a
second chariot and was taken back to
Jerusalem. There he died and was buried in the royal tomb. 32 All the people of
Judah mourned his death.
The prophet Jeremiah composed a lament for King Josiah. It has become a
custom in Israel for the leaders and their
wives to sing this song when they mourn
for him. 33 These things are recorded in
The History of the Kings of Judah.
Everything that Josiah did, how he
gained his fame and his understanding
of the Law, what he did earlier and what
is told here, is all recorded in *The History of the Kings of Israel and Judah.*

King Joahaz of Judah

(2 Kings 23.30-35; 2 Chronicles 36.1-4)

34 The people of Judah chose Josiah's
son Joahaz[a] and made him king. Joahaz was twenty-three years old, 35 and
he ruled Judah and Jerusalem for three
months. Then the king of Egypt deposed
him 36 and made the nation pay 7,500
pounds of silver and 75 pounds of gold
as tribute. 37 The king of Egypt appointed Joahaz's brother Jehoiakim
king of Judah and Jerusalem. 38 Jehoiakim put the leading men of the nation in
prison, then had his brother Zarius arrested and brought back from Egypt.

King Jehoiakim of Judah

(2 Kings 23.36 – 24.7; 2 Chronicles 36.5-8)

39 Jehoiakim was twenty-five years old
when he became king of Judah and Jerusalem. He sinned against the Lord.
40 King Nebuchadnezzar of Babylonia
invaded Judah, captured Jehoiakim, and
took him to Babylonia in bronze chains.
41 Nebuchadnezzar also carried off some
of the sacred utensils from the Temple
and put them in his own temple in Babylon. 42 The stories about Jehoiakim, his
depravity, and the godless way he lived
are recorded in *The Chronicles of the
Kings.*

King Jehoiachin of Judah

(2 Kings 24.8-17; 2 Chronicles 36.9, 10)

43 Jehoiachin was eighteen years old
when he succeeded his father Jehoiakim
as king, 44 and he ruled in Jerusalem for
three months and ten days. He too
sinned against the Lord. 45 A year later
King Nebuchadnezzar had Jehoiachin
taken to Babylonia as a prisoner; Nebuchadnezzar also carried off sacred utensils from the Temple. 46 Then he made
Zedekiah king of Judah and Jerusalem.

[a] Joahaz; *some manuscripts have* Jeconiah.

King Zedekiah of Judah

*(2 Kings 24.18-20; 2 Chronicles 36.11, 12;
Jeremiah 52.1-3a)*

Zedekiah was then twenty-one years
old, and he ruled for eleven years. 47 He
sinned against the Lord and refused to
listen to the prophet Jeremiah, who
spoke the word of the Lord.

The Fall of Jerusalem

*(2 Kings 25.1-21; 2 Chronicles 36.13-21;
Jeremiah 52.3b-11)*

48 Although King Nebuchadnezzar
had forced Zedekiah to swear in the
Lord's name that he would be loyal to
him, Zedekiah broke his oath and rebelled against him. He stubbornly refused to obey the commands of the Lord,
the God of Israel. 49 In addition, the leaders of the people and even the chief
priests did more godless and lawless
things than all the corrupt heathen; they
defiled the Temple of the Lord, which he
had made holy. 50 The God of their ancestors had continued to send prophets
to call them back from their sins, because he wanted to spare them and the
Temple. 51 But when the Lord spoke
through his prophets, the people made
fun of them and laughed. 52 At last the
Lord became so angry with his people
and their depraved ways that he ordered
the kings of Babylonia to attack them.
53 The Babylonians killed the young men
of Judah all around the Temple and did
not spare anyone, young or old, man or
woman. The Lord handed them all over
to their enemies. 54 The Babylonians carried off all the sacred utensils from the
Temple, the treasure chests,[b] and the
wealth of the king; they took everything
away to Babylon, leaving nothing behind. 55 They burned down the Temple,
broke down the city wall, set fire to its
towers, 56 and completely destroyed all
its beauty. Nebuchadnezzar forced all
the survivors to be led away to Babylon,
57 where they served him and his
descendants as slaves until the rise of
the Persian Empire. And so what the
Lord had foretold through the prophet
Jeremiah was fulfilled: 58 "The land will
lie desolate for seventy years to make up
for the Sabbath rest[c] that has not been
observed."

Cyrus Commands the Jews to Return

(2 Chronicles 36.22, 23; Ezra 1.1-11)

2 In the first year that Cyrus of Persia
was emperor,[d] the Lord made
come true what he had said through the
prophet Jeremiah. 2 He prompted Cyrus
to issue the following command and
send it out in writing to be read aloud
everywhere in his empire:

3 "This is the command of Cyrus,
emperor of Persia. The Lord of Israel,
the Lord Most High, has appointed me
ruler over the whole world 4 and has
given me the responsibility of building
a Temple for him in Jerusalem in Judah. 5 May the Lord be with those of
you who are his people. You are to go
to Jerusalem and rebuild the Temple
of the Lord of Israel, the Lord who
lives in Jerusalem. 6 If any of his people in exile need help to return, their
neighbors must give them this help,
providing them with silver and gold
7 and other gifts, with horses and pack
animals, as well as anything else offered for the Temple of the Lord in Jerusalem in fulfillment of a vow."

8 Then the heads of the clans of the
tribes of Judah and Benjamin, the
priests and the Levites, and everyone
else whose heart the Lord had moved,
got ready to go and rebuild the Lord's
Temple in Jerusalem. 9 Their neighbors
helped them with everything, giving
them silver, gold, horses, and pack animals. Many of their neighbors were also
led to give a large number of other
things, in fulfillment of vows.

10 Emperor Cyrus gave them back the
sacred utensils that King Nebuchadnezzar had taken from Jerusalem and had
put in the temple of his idols. 11 He
brought them out and handed them over
to Mithredath, chief of the royal treasury, 12 who delivered them to Sheshbazzar, the governor of Judah. 13 Here is the
inventory of the utensils:

gold bowls for offerings	1,000
silver bowls for offerings	1,000
silver fire pans	29
small gold bowls	30

[b] treasure chests; *some manuscripts have* the equipment of the Covenant Box.

[c] SABBATH REST: *A reference to the requirement of the Law that every seventh year the land was not to be farmed (see Lv 25.1-7).* [d] EMPEROR: *King Cyrus of Persia occupied the city of Babylon in 539 B.C. and began to reign as the emperor of Babylonia.*

small silver bowls	2,410
other utensils	1,000

14 In all there were 5,469 gold and silver bowls and other utensils, 15 and
Sheshbazzar took these with him when
he and the other exiles went from Babylon to Jerusalem.

Opposition to Rebuilding Jerusalem

(*Ezra* 4.7-24)

16 In the reign of Emperor Artaxerxes
of Persia, Bishlam, Mithredath, Tabeel,
Rehum, Beltethmus, Shimshai the secretary of the province, and their associates
who lived in Samaria and elsewhere
wrote the following letter in protest
against the Jews who were living in Judah and Jerusalem:
17 "To Your Majesty Emperor Artaxerxes from your servants, the official
correspondent Rehum, the secretary
Shimshai, the other members of the
council, and the judges of Greater
Syria and Phoenicia.
18 "We want Your Majesty to know
that the Jews who came here from
your other territories have settled in
Jerusalem and are rebuilding that evil
and rebellious city. They are restoring
the marketplaces, repairing the walls,
and laying the foundations for a Temple. 19 If this city is rebuilt and its walls
are completed, the people will stop
paying taxes and will even rebel
against royal authority. 20 Since work
on the Temple has already begun, we
consider it appropriate not to overlook
such an important matter 21 but to
bring it to the attention of Your Majesty. Then, if it seems proper to you, a
search may be made in the records
your ancestors kept. 22 You will find
information about these matters in the
historical records, and you will discover that this city has always been
rebellious and given trouble to other
cities and kings. 23 The Jews have used
it from ancient times as a base for rebellions and wars. That is why the city
was destroyed. 24 We therefore declare
to you that if this city is rebuilt and its
walls are restored, Your Majesty will
no longer be able to enter Greater
Syria and Phoenicia."

25 The emperor sent the following answer to the official correspondent Rehum, Beltethmus, the secretary
Shimshai, and their associates who lived
in Samaria, Syria, and Phoenicia:
26 "After reading the letter which
you sent me, I gave orders for an investigation to be made, and it has indeed been found that from ancient
times Jerusalem has revolted against
royal authority, 27 and its people have
been involved in insurrections and
wars. Powerful and cruel kings have
reigned there and have ruled over
Greater Syria and Phoenicia, from
which they collected taxes. 28 Therefore I am now issuing orders that
those men be prevented from rebuilding the city and that necessary steps
be taken to insure that these orders
will not be disobeyed, 29 so that this
trouble spot will no longer be a threat
to the royal interests."
30 As soon as this letter from Emperor
Artaxerxes was read, Rehum, Shimshai
the secretary, and their associates hurried to Jerusalem with a force of cavalry
and a large number of armed troops and
began interfering with the rebuilding of
the Temple. The work had to stop, and
no more was done until the second year
of the reign of Emperor Darius of Persia.

The Debate of the Bodyguards before the Emperor

3 The Emperor Darius gave a great
banquet for all those under him, all
the members of his family and staff, all
the leading officials of Persia and Media,
2 all his chief officers, administrators,
and the governors of the 127 provinces
stretching from India to Ethiopia.[e]
3 When everyone had enough to eat and
drink, they left, and Darius went to bed.
He fell asleep but soon awoke.

A Contest Is Proposed

4 Then the three young men who
served Emperor Darius as his personal
bodyguard said to one another, 5 "Let
each one of us name the one thing that
he considers the strongest thing in the
world. The emperor will decide who has
given the wisest answer to this question

[e] *Greek* Ethiopia: *Ethiopia is the name given in Graeco-Roman times to the extensive territory south of the First Cataract of the Nile River. Cush was the ancient (Hebrew) name of this region which included within its borders most of modern Sudan and some of present-day Ethiopia (Abyssinia).*

and will give magnificent gifts and
prizes to the winner. 6 He will wear royal
robes, drink from a gold cup, and sleep
in a gold bed. He will have a chariot with
gold-studded bridles, wear a fine linen
turban, and have a gold necklace. 7 Because of his wisdom he will be an adviser to the emperor and will be given
the title "Relative of the Emperor."
8 Then each of them wrote down the
best answer he could think of, sealed it,
and put it under the emperor's pillow.
They said to one another, 9 "When the
emperor wakes up, the statements will
be given to him. He and the three leading officials of Persia will decide who
gave the wisest answer. The winner will
be given the prize on the basis of what
he has written." 10 The first wrote,
"There is nothing stronger than wine."
11 The second wrote, "There is nothing
stronger than the emperor." 12 And the
third wrote, "There is nothing stronger
than a woman, but truth can conquer
anything."
13 When the emperor woke up, the
written statements were given to him,
and he read them. 14 Then he sent messengers and called together all the leading officials of Persia and Media,
including the chief officers, administrators, governors, and commissioners.
15 He took his seat in the council chamber and had the three statements read
aloud. 16 "Bring in the three young men,"
he said, "and let them explain their answers." So when they were brought in,
17 they were asked to explain what they
had written.

The Speech about Wine

The bodyguard who had written about
the strength of wine spoke first: 18 "Gentlemen," he began, "wine is clearly the
strongest thing in the world. It confuses
the mind of everyone who drinks it. 19 It
has exactly the same effect on everyone:
king or orphan, slave or free, rich or
poor. 20 It makes every thought happy
and carefree, and makes one forget
every sorrow and responsibility. 21 It
makes everyone feel rich, ignore the
power of kings and officials, and talk as
if he owned the whole world. 22 When
men drink wine, they forget who their
friends and neighbors are, and then they
are soon drawing their swords to fight
them. 23 Then, when they sober up, they
don't remember what they have done.
24 Gentlemen," he concluded, "if wine
makes men act in this way, it certainly
must be the strongest thing in the
world."

The Speech about the Emperor

4 The bodyguard who had written
about the strength of the emperor
spoke next. 2 "Gentlemen," he began,
"nothing in the world is stronger than
men, since they rule over land and sea
and, in fact, over everything in the
world. 3 But the emperor is the strongest
of them all; he is their lord and master,
and men obey him, no matter what he
commands. 4 If he tells them to make
war on one another, they do it. If he
sends them out against his enemies, they
go, even if they have to break down
mountains, walls, or towers. 5 They may
kill or be killed, but they never disobey
the emperor's orders. If they are victorious, they bring him all their loot and
everything else they have taken in battle. 6 Farmers do not go out to war, but
even they bring to the emperor a part of
everything that they harvest, and they
compel one another to pay taxes to the
emperor. 7 Although the emperor is only
one man, if he orders people to kill, they
kill; if he orders them to set prisoners
free, they do it; 8 if he orders them to attack, they do; if he orders destruction,
they destroy; if he orders them to build,
they build; 9 if he orders crops to be destroyed or fields to be planted, it is done.
10 Everybody, soldier or civilian, obeys
the emperor. And when he sits down to
eat or drink and then falls asleep, 11 his
servants stand guard around him, without being able to go and take care of
their own affairs, for they never disobey
him. 12 Gentlemen," he concluded, "since
people obey the emperor like this, certainly nothing in the world is stronger
than he is."

The Speech about Women

13 The bodyguard who had written
about women and the truth — it was
Zerubbabel — spoke last. 14 "Gentlemen,"
he began, "the emperor is certainly powerful, men are numerous, and wine is
strong, but who rules and controls them
all? It is women! 15 Women gave birth to

the emperor and all the men who rule
over land and sea. 16 Women brought
them into the world. Women brought up
the men who planted the vineyards from
which wine comes. 17 Women make the
clothes that men wear; women bring
honor to men; in fact, without women,
men couldn't live.

18 "Men may accumulate silver or gold
or other beautiful things, but if they see
a woman with a pretty face or a good
figure, 19 they will leave it all to gape and
stare, and they will desire her more than
their wealth. 20 A man will leave his own
father, who brought him up, and leave
his own country to get married. 21 He
will forget his father, his mother, and his
country to spend the rest of his life with
his wife. 22 So you must recognize that
women are your masters. Don't you
work and sweat and then take all that
you have earned and give it to your
wives? 23 A man will take his sword and
go out to attack, rob and steal, and sail
the seas and rivers. 24 He may have to
face lions or travel in the dark, but when
he has robbed, stolen, and plundered, he
will bring the loot home to the woman
he loves.

25 "A man loves his wife more than his
parents. 26 Some men are driven out of
their minds on account of a woman, and
others become slaves for the sake of a
woman. 27 Others have been put to
death, have ruined their lives, or have
committed crimes because of a woman.
28 So now do you believe me?

"The emperor's power is certainly
great—no nation has the courage to attack him. 29 But once I saw him with
Apame, his concubine, the daughter of
the famous Bartacus. While sitting at the
emperor's right, 30 she took his crown off
his head, put it on her own, and then
slapped his face with her left hand. 31 All
the emperor did was look at her with his
mouth open. Whenever she smiles at
him, he smiles back; and when she gets
angry with him, he flatters her and
teases her until she is in a good mood
again. 32 Gentlemen, if women can do all
that, surely there can be nothing
stronger in the world." 33 The emperor
and his officials just looked at one
another.

The Speech about Truth

Then Zerubbabel began to speak
about truth. 34 "Yes, gentlemen," he said,
"women are very strong. But think of
how big the earth is, how high the sky is;
think how fast the sun moves, as it rapidly circles the whole sky in a single day.
35 If the sun can do this, it is certainly
great. But truth is greater and stronger
than all of these things. 36 Everyone on
earth honors truth; heaven praises it; all
creation trembles in awe before it.

"There is not the slightest injustice in
truth.[f] 37 You will find injustice in wine,
the emperor, women, all human beings,
in all they do, and in everything else.
There is no truth in them; they are unjust
and they will perish. 38 But truth endures
and is always strong; it will continue to
live and reign forever. 39 Truth shows no
partiality or favoritism; it does what is
right, rather than what is unjust or evil.
Everyone approves what truth does;
40 its decisions are always fair. Truth is
strong, royal, powerful, and majestic
forever. Let all things praise the God of
truth!"

The Response

41 When Zerubbabel had finished
speaking, all the people shouted, "Truth
is great—there is nothing stronger!"

42 Then the emperor said to him, "You
may ask anything you want, even more
than what was agreed, and I will give it
to you. You will be my adviser, and you
will be granted the title 'Relative of the
Emperor.' "

43 Zerubbabel replied, "Your Majesty,
permit me to remind you of the solemn
vow you took on the day you became
emperor. You promised to rebuild Jerusalem 44 and to send back all the treasures that had been taken from the city.
Remember that when Cyrus made a vow
to destroy Babylon, he set these things
aside and solemnly promised to send
them back to Jerusalem. 45 You also
promised to rebuild the Temple, which
the Edomites burned down when the
Babylonians devastated the land of Judah. 46 So, Your Majesty, because you
are a man of generosity, I beg you to
fulfill the solemn promise you made to
the King of heaven."

47 Then Emperor Darius stood up,

[f] in truth; *some manuscripts have* with God.

kissed Zerubbabel, and wrote letters for
him to all the treasurers, governors, and
administrators in the provinces, ordering them to provide safe conduct for him
and all those going with him to rebuild
Jerusalem. 48 He also wrote letters to all
the governors in Greater Syria and
Phoenicia, with special instructions to
those in Lebanon, to transport cedar
logs to Jerusalem and help Zerubbabel
rebuild the city.

49 The emperor also provided letters
for all the Jews who wished to return to
Jerusalem. These letters guaranteed
their freedom and ordered all governors,
treasurers, and other administrators not
to interfere with them in any way. 50 All
the land that they acquired was to be exempt from taxation, and the Edomites
were to surrender the villages they had
taken from the Jews. 51 Each year 1,500
pounds of silver would be given for the
construction of the Temple until it was
finished. 52 In addition, 750 pounds of silver would be given each year to provide
for the seventeen burnt offerings to be
offered in the Temple each day. 53 All the
Jews who left Babylonia to build the city
of Jerusalem would be granted their
freedom, together with their children
and the priests.

54 The emperor's orders gave specific
instructions, as follows: the priests must
be supported, their robes for the Temple
service must be provided, 55 the Levites
must be supported until the Temple and
Jerusalem are completely rebuilt, 56 and
land and wages must be provided for all
the guards of the city. 57 He also reaf-
firmed Cyrus' instructions that all the
small utensils and Temple treasures that
Cyrus had set aside should be returned
to Jerusalem.

58 Then the young man Zerubbabel left
the council chamber, turned toward Jerusalem, looked up to heaven, and
praised the King of heaven: 59 "Lord, all
praise belongs to you; you are the source
of all victory and wisdom, 60 and I thank
you, O Lord of our ancestors, for giving
wisdom to me, your servant."

61 Zerubbabel took the emperor's letters and went to Babylon, where he told
the other Jews everything that had happened. 62 They praised the God of their
ancestors because he had made it possible for them 63 to go and rebuild Jerusalem and the Temple which bears his
name. For seven days they held a joyful
celebration, accompanied by music.

The List of Those Who Returned from Exile

(Ezra 2.1-70; Nehemiah 7.4-73)

5 After this, the heads of clans were
chosen, tribe by tribe, to go to Jerusalem with their wives, children, slaves,
and animals. 2 Emperor Darius sent a
thousand cavalry troops to escort them
safely back to Jerusalem. 3 He sent them
off to the music of drums and flutes,
while all the rest of the Jewish people
danced for joy.

4 These are the names, by tribes, clans,
and families, of the men who returned:
5 Among the priests, descendants of
Phinehas son of Aaron, was Joshua, son
of Jozadak and grandson of Seraiah. He
was accompanied by Zerubbabel,[g] who
was the son of Shealtiel of the family of
David, of the line of Perez, of the tribe of
Judah. 6 He was the one who had spoken
the wise words before Emperor Darius
of Persia. They left Babylon in the second year of his reign in Nisan, the first
month.

7 These are the Jewish men who returned from exile. Their families had
been living in Babylonia since King Nebuchadnezzar had taken them there as
prisoners. 8 They returned to Jerusalem
and the rest of Judah, each to his own
hometown. Their leaders were Zerubbabel, Joshua, Nehemiah, Seraiah, Resa-
iah, Eneneus, Mordecai, Beelsarus,
Aspharasus, Reeliah, Rehum, and
Baanah.

9-17a The following is a list of the clans
of Israel, with the number of those from
each clan who returned with their leaders from exile:

Parosh	2,172
Shephatiah	472
Arah	756
Pahath Moab(descendants of Jeshua and Joab)	2,812
Elam	1,254
Zattu	945
Chorbe	705
Bani	648
Bebai	623

[g] *Probable text* He was accompanied by Zerubbabel; *Greek* and Joakim son of Zerubbabel.

Azgad	1,322
Adonikam	667
Bigvai	2,066
Adin	454
Ater (also called Hezekiah)	92
Kilan and Azetas	67
Azaru	432
Annias	101
Arom	—
Bezai	323
Arsiphurith	112
Baiterus	3,005

17b-23 People whose ancestors had lived
in the following towns also returned:

Bethlehem	123
Netophah	55
Anathoth	158
Beth Azmaveth	42
Kiriath Jearim	25
Chephirah and Beeroth	743
the towns of the Chadiasans and the Ammidians	422
Ramah and Geba	621
Michmash	122
Bethel	52
Magbish	156
The other Elam and Ono	725
Jericho	345
Senaah	3,330

24-25 The following is the list of the
priestly clans that returned from exile:

Jedaiah (descendants of Jeshua and Anasib)	972
Immer	1,052
Pashhur	1,247
Harim	1,017

26-28 Clans of Levites who returned
from exile:

Jeshua, Kadmiel, Bannas, and Sudias	74
Temple musicians (descendants of Asaph)	128
Temple guards (descendants of Shallum, Ater, Talmon, Akkub, Hatita, and Shobai)	139

29-32 Clans of Temple workmen who returned from exile:

Esau, Hasupha, Tabbaoth,
Keros, Siaha, Padon,
Lebanah, Hagabah, Akkub,
Uthai, Ketab, Hagab,
Shamlai, Hanan, Cathua,
Geddur, Jairus, Daisan,
Noeba, Chaseba, Gazera,
Uzza, Phinoe, Asara,
Besai, Asnah, Meunim,
Nephisim, Akub, Hakupha,
Asur, Pharakim, Bazluth,
Mehida, Cutha, Charea,
Barkos, Sisera, Temah,
Neziah, Hatipha

33-34 Clans of Solomon's servants who
returned from exile:

Hassophereth, Peruda, Jaalah,
Lozon, Giddel, Shephatiah,
Agia, Phochereth Hazzebaim,
Sarothie, Masiah, Gas,
Addus, Subas, Apherra,
Barodis, Shaphat, Adlon

35 The total number of descendants of
the Temple workmen and of Solomon's
servants who returned from exile
was 372.

36-37 There were 652 belonging to the
clans of Delaiah (descendants of Tobiah)
and Nekoda who returned from the
towns of Tel Melah and Tel Harsha, with
their leaders Cherub, Addan, and Immer; but these could not prove that they
were descendants of Israelites.

38-39 The following clans, who claimed
to be priestly clans, could find no record
to prove their ancestry: Habaiah, Hakkoz, Jaddus (the ancestor of the clan of
Jaddus had married Agia, one of the
daughters of Barzillai, and had taken the
name of his father-in-law's clan). Since
they were unable to prove who their ancestors were, they were not allowed to
function as priests. 40 Nehemiah the governor [h] told them that they could not eat
the food offered to God until there was a
High Priest who could use the Revelation and Truth. [i]

41-43 The total number of

Israelites (twelve years old or older, not counting servants)	42,360
Male and female servants	7,337
Male and female musicians	245
Camels	435
Horses	7,036
Mules	245
Donkeys	5,525

44 When the exiles arrived at the place
of God's Temple in Jerusalem, some of
the leaders of the clans took a vow to
rebuild the Temple on its old site, to the
best of their ability. 45 They promised to
contribute for the rebuilding and the

[h] *Probable meaning* the governor; *Greek* and Attharias. [i] REVELATION AND TRUTH: *This is the Greek translation of Urim and Thummim, two objects used by the priest to determine God's will; it is not known precisely how they were used.*

service of the Temple 1,000 pounds of
gold, 5,000 pounds of silver, and 100
robes for priests.
46 The priests, the Levites, and some of
the people settled in or near Jerusalem;
the musicians and the Temple guards
settled in nearby towns; and the rest of
the Israelites settled in the towns where
their ancestors had lived.

Worship Begins Again

(Ezra 3.1-6)

47 By the seventh month the people of
Israel were all settled in their towns.
Then they all assembled in the open
square in front of the first gate on the
east side of the Temple area. 48 Joshua
son of Jehozadak, his fellow priests, and
Zerubbabel son of Shealtiel, together
with his relatives, prepared the altar of
the God of Israel, 49 so that they could
burn sacrifices on it according to the instructions written in the Law of Moses,
the man of God. 50 Some of the local people, even though they were stronger
than the Jews and opposed to them,
joined them[j] in rebuilding the altar
where it had stood before. Then the
Jews began once again to burn the regular morning and evening sacrifices on
the altar. 51 They celebrated the Festival
of Shelters, according to the regulations,
each day offering the sacrifices required
for that day. 52 They also offered the normal daily sacrifices, as well as those required for the Sabbath, the New Moon
Festival, and the other regular assemblies for worship. 53 Although the people
had not yet rebuilt God's Temple, everyone who had made a vow to God began
to offer sacrifices on the first day of the
seventh month.

The Rebuilding of the Temple Begins

(Ezra 3.7-13)

54 The people gave money to pay the
stonemasons and the carpenters; they
gave food, drink, 55 and carts to be sent
to the cities of Tyre and Sidon in exchange for cedar logs from Lebanon,
which were to be floated to the harbor at
Joppa. All of this was done according to
the orders given by Emperor Cyrus of
Persia.
56-57 So in the second month of the year
after they came back to the site of the
Temple in Jerusalem, they started the
work and began laying the foundation.
Zerubbabel, Joshua, and the rest of the
Jewish people, the priests, and the
Levites—in fact, all the exiles who had
come back to Jerusalem, joined in the
work. 58 The Levites twenty years of age
or older were put in charge of rebuilding
the Temple for the Lord. The Levite
Jeshua and his sons and relatives, his
brother Kadmiel, the sons of Jeshua
Emadabun, the sons of Joda son of Ilia-
dun, and all their sons and relatives—in
fact, all the Levites joined together to
take charge of the rebuilding of the
Temple.
While the workers were building the
Temple of the Lord, 59 the priests in their
robes took their places with trumpets
and other musical instruments in their
hands, and the Levites of the clan of
Asaph stood there with cymbals. 60 They
praised the Lord and gave thanks to him
according to the instructions handed
down from the time of King David.
61 They sang psalms praising the Lord,
repeating the refrain: "The goodness of
the Lord and his glorious presence are
with all Israel forever." 62 All the people
blew trumpets and shouted with all their
might, praising the Lord because the
Temple was being rebuilt. 63 Some of the
older priests, Levites, and heads of clans
had seen the first Temple, and when
they came and saw the building of this
Temple, they cried and wailed. 64 Others
who were there blew trumpets and
shouted for joy. 65 The crowd blew the
trumpets so loud that the blast could be
heard far away, but no one nearby could
hear the blast of the trumpets because
the sound made by those who were crying and wailing was so loud.

Opposition to the Rebuilding of the Temple

(Ezra 4.1-5)

66 The enemies of the tribes of Judah
and Benjamin heard the sound of the
trumpets and came to see what it meant.
67 When they learned that those who had
returned from exile were rebuilding the
Temple of the Lord, the God of Israel,
68 they went to Zerubbabel, Joshua, and
the heads of the clans and said, "Let us
join you in building the Temple. 69 We

[j] Some of . . . joined them; *Greek unclear.*

worship the same Lord you worship and
we have been offering sacrifices to him
ever since Emperor Esarhaddon[k] of Assyria sent us here to live."
70 Zerubbabel, Joshua, and the heads
of the clans told them, "We don't need
your help in building the Temple for the
Lord our God. 71 We will build it ourselves, just as Emperor Cyrus of Persia
commanded us."
72 Then the people who had been living
in the land began to harass[l] the Jews;
they cut off their supplies and kept them
from building. 73 These people plotted,
agitated, and rioted so much that they
prevented the Temple from being completed during the reign of Emperor Cyrus. The work was halted until Darius
became emperor, two years later.

Work on the Temple Begins Again

(Ezra 5.1-17)

6 In the second year of the reign of
Emperor Darius, the two prophets,
Haggai and Zechariah son of Iddo, began to speak in the name of the Lord
God of Israel to the Jews who lived in
Judah and Jerusalem. 2 When Zerubbabel son of Shealtiel and Joshua son of
Jehozadak heard their messages, they
began to rebuild the Temple in Jerusalem, and the two prophets helped them.
3 Almost at once Governor Sisinnes of
Greater Syria and Phoenicia, with Shethar Bozenai and the other officials,
came to Jerusalem and demanded:
4 "Who gave you orders to build this
Temple and complete this roof and
everything else? Who is doing this
work?" 5 But the Lord was with the people who had returned from exile and
was watching over the Jewish leaders,
6 and they were allowed to continue
building until Emperor Darius could be
informed and his reply received. 7 Here
is the report that the Persian officials
sent to the emperor:
8 "To Emperor Darius, greetings.
"Your Majesty should know that we
went to Judah and to Jerusalem and
there we found the leaders of the Jews
who have returned from exile 9 building a large new Temple for the Lord
with expensive, shaped stone blocks
and with wooden beams set in the
walls. 10 The work is being done rapidly and is moving ahead steadily; yet
they are taking great care and doing
their work beautifully.
11 "We then asked the leaders of the
people to tell us who had given them
orders to rebuild the Temple and lay
the foundations for the buildings.
12 We also asked them who their leaders were and demanded a list of their
names, so that we could inform you.
13 "They answered, 'We are servants
of the Lord who created heaven and
earth. 14 This Temple was built and
equipped many years ago by a very
powerful king of Israel. 15 But because
our ancestors sinned against Israel's
Lord in heaven and made him angry,
he let them be conquered by King
Nebuchadnezzar of Babylonia, a king
of the Chaldean dynasty. 16 The Temple was demolished and burned, and
the people were taken into exile in
Babylonia. 17 Then, in the first year of
his reign as emperor of Babylonia, Cyrus issued orders for the Temple to be
rebuilt. 18 He gave back the sacred
gold and silver utensils which Nebuchadnezzar had taken from the Temple in Jerusalem and had placed in his
own temple in Babylon. Emperor
Cyrus turned these utensils over to
Zerubbabel and the governor,
Sheshbazzar. 19 The Emperor told
Sheshbazzar to take them and return
them to the Temple in Jerusalem, and
to rebuild the Temple where it had
stood before. 20 So Sheshbazzar came
and laid its foundation, and construction has continued from then until the
present, but the Temple is still not
finished.'
21 "Now, if it please Your Majesty,
have a search made in the royal
records in Babylon 22 to find whether
or not the building of this Temple in
Jerusalem had the approval of Emperor Cyrus, and then, if it please
Your Majesty, inform us what your
will is in this matter."

Emperor Cyrus' Order Is Rediscovered

(Ezra 6.1-5)

23 So Emperor Darius ordered a search
to be made in the royal records that were
kept in Babylon. It was, however, in the

[k] ESARHADDON: *Greek* Asbasareth. [l] *Probable text* harass; *Greek unclear.*

fortress of Ecbatana in the province of
Media that a scroll was found, containing the following record:
24 “In the first year of his reign Emperor Cyrus ordered the rebuilding of
the Temple in Jerusalem, where sacrifices are continually offered. 25 The
Temple is to be 90 feet high and 90 feet
wide. The walls must be built with one
layer of new local wood on top of each
three layers of shaped stone. All expenses are to be paid by the royal
treasury. 26 Also the gold and silver
utensils which King Nebuchadnezzar
brought to Babylon from the Temple
in Jerusalem are to be returned to
their proper place in the Jerusalem
Temple.”

Emperor Darius Orders the Work to Continue

(Ezra 6.6-12)

27 Then Emperor Darius gave strict orders to Sisinnes, governor of Greater
Syria and Phoenicia, Shethar Bozenai,
the other officials, and the local officials
to stay away from Jerusalem and let Zerubbabel, the servant of the Lord and
governor of Judah, and the other Jewish
leaders rebuild the Temple of the Lord
where it stood before. 28 “And I also
command,” he continued, “that it be
completely rebuilt and that, until it is
finished, every effort be made to help
the Jews who have returned from exile.
29 From the taxes received in Greater
Syria and Phoenicia a contribution shall
be made on a regular basis to these men,
payable to Governor Zerubbabel, for
bulls, sheep, and lambs to be used in
their sacrifices to the Lord. 30 In the same
way, each year and without further
question, wheat, salt, wine, and olive oil
are to be supplied, according to the daily
needs indicated by the priests. 31 This
must be done so that they can make
wine offerings to God Most High for me
and my children and pray for his blessing on our lives.” 32 He also gave these
orders: “If anyone disobeys the commands as written above or fails to carry
them out, he is to be hanged on a
wooden beam taken from his own
house, and his property is to be turned
over to the emperor. 33 May the Lord
who is worshiped at Jerusalem destroy
any king or nation that tries to stop the
work or damage the Temple there. 34 I,
Emperor Darius, issue the command
that these orders be carried out in every
detail.”

The Temple Is Dedicated

(Ezra 6.13-18)

7 Then Governor Sisinnes, Shethar
Bozenai, and the other officials did
exactly as the emperor had commanded
2 and gave careful supervision to the
work on the Temple, helping the Jewish
leaders and Temple officials. 3 The workers made good progress with the building of the Temple, encouraged by the
prophets Haggai and Zechariah. 4 The
Jews completed the building according
to the command of the Lord, the God of
Israel, and with the permission of Cyrus,
Darius, and Artaxerxes, emperors of
Persia. 5 The Temple was completed
on the twenty-third day of the month
of Adar in the sixth year of the reign of
Emperor Darius. 6 Then the people
of Israel – the priests, the Levites, and all
the others who had returned from exile
and joined them – carried out all the
commands in the Law of Moses. 7 For the
dedication they offered 100 bulls, 200
sheep, and 400 lambs as sacrifices, 8 and
12 goats as offerings for sin, one goat for
the leader of each tribe of Israel. 9 The
priests in their robes and the Levites
took their positions, family by family,
for the Temple services of the Lord, the
God of Israel, according to the instructions contained in the book of Moses.
The Temple guards stood at each gate.

The Passover

(Ezra 6.19-22)

10 The people of Israel who had returned from exile celebrated the Passover on the fourteenth day of the first
month of the following year. The priests
and Levites had purified themselves at
the same time. 11 Not all the Jews who
had returned purified themselves at that
time, but the Levites did.[m] 12 The Levites
killed the animals for the Passover
sacrifices for all the people who had
returned, for the priests, and for
themselves. 13 The sacrifices were eaten
by all the Israelites who had returned
from exile; they worshiped the Lord and

[m] *Verse 11 in Greek is unclear.*

rejected the pagan ways of the other
people who were living in the land. 14 For
seven days they celebrated the Festival
of Unleavened Bread. They rejoiced in
the presence of the Lord, 15 the God of
Israel, because he had made the plans of
the emperor of Assyria[n] favorable to
them and had supported them in their
work.

Ezra Arrives in Jerusalem

(Ezra 7.1-10)

8 Many years later, when Artaxerxes
was emperor of Persia, a man
named Ezra came from Babylon. He
traced his ancestry back to Aaron, the
High Priest, as follows: Ezra was the son
of Seraiah, son of Azariah, son of Hilkiah, son of Shallum, 2 son of Zadok, son
of Ahitub, son of Amariah, son of Azariah, son of Bukki, son of Abishua, son
of Phinehas, son of Eleazar, son of
Aaron.

3-4 Ezra was a scholar with a thorough
knowledge of the Law, which the God of
Israel had given to Moses. The emperor
had a high regard for him and approved
all the requests he made. Ezra set out
from Babylonia 5 for Jerusalem with a
group of Israelites which included
priests, Levites, Temple musicians, Temple guards, and workmen. 6 They left
Babylonia on the first day of the first
month in the seventh year of the reign of
Artaxerxes. God gave them a safe journey, and they arrived in Jerusalem on
the first day of the fifth month. 7 Ezra
had a thorough knowledge of the Law of
the Lord and neglected none of its details. As a result he could teach all its
laws and regulations to all the people of
Israel.

The Document That Emperor Artaxerxes Gave to Ezra

(Ezra 7.11-26)

8 The following is a copy of the decree
that Emperor Artaxerxes gave to Ezra,
the priest and scholar of the Law of the
Lord:

9 "From Emperor Artaxerxes to the
priest Ezra, scholar of the Law of the
Lord, greetings.

10 "In my generosity I have decided
to decree that throughout my empire
any of the Jews who so desire, including priests and Levites, may go with
you to Jerusalem. 11 I and the seven
counselors who have the title 'Friends
of the Emperor' have decided that all
who wish to do so may go with you.
12 Let them investigate the conditions
in Jerusalem and Judah to see how
well the Law of the Lord is being
obeyed. 13 Let them also take with
them to Jerusalem the gifts which I
and my counselors have vowed to give
to the Lord of Israel, including all the
silver and gold belonging to the Lord
which may be found in Babylonia,
14 and all that is given by the people of
Israel for the Temple of their Lord.
The silver and gold are to be collected
to buy bulls, rams, lambs, and everything else that is necessary, 15 so that
sacrifices may be offered on the altar
of the Lord in Jerusalem.

16 "You may use the silver and gold
for whatever you and the rest of your
people desire, in accordance with the
will of your God. 17-18 You may obtain
from the royal treasury the sacred vessels of the Lord that are being entrusted to you for use in the Temple of
your God in Jerusalem, as well as anything else you may need for the Temple service.

19 "I command all the treasury officials in Greater Syria and Phoenicia to
provide promptly for Ezra, the priest
and scholar of the Law of God Most
High, everything he asks for, 20 up to a
limit of 7,500 pounds of silver, 500
bushels of wheat, 550 gallons of wine,
and as much salt as may be needed.
21 You must be careful to do everything that the Law requires in order to
honor God Most High and so make
sure that he is never angry with me or
with those who reign after me. 22 You
are forbidden to collect any taxes from
the priests, Levites, musicians, guards,
workmen, or anyone else connected
with this Temple. No one has the right
to impose any burden on them.

23 "You, Ezra, using the wisdom that
comes from God, shall appoint administrators and judges to govern all the
people in Greater Syria and Phoenicia
who live by the Law of your God. You

[n] EMPEROR OF ASSYRIA: *Apparently a reference to the Persian emperor who then also ruled the territory once occupied by Assyria, Israel's ancient enemy.*

must teach that Law to anyone who
does not know it. 24 If anyone disobeys
the laws of your God or the laws of the
empire, he is to be punished promptly:
by death, by fine, by exile, or by some
other punishment."

Ezra Praises God

(Ezra 7.27, 28)

25 Ezra said, "Praise the Lord, the Lord
alone! He has made the emperor willing
to restore the glory of the Temple of the
Lord in Jerusalem. 26 By God's grace, I
have won the respect of the emperor, his
counselors, all his Friends, and all his
powerful officials. 27 The Lord my God
has given me courage, and I have been
able to persuade many men to return
with me."

The People Who Returned from Exile

(Ezra 8.1-14)

28 This is the list of the leaders of the
clans and families who had been in exile
in Babylonia and returned with Ezra
to Jerusalem when Artaxerxes was
emperor:

29-40 Gershom, of the clan of Phinehas
Gamael, of the clan of Ithamar
Hattush son of Shecaniah, of the
clan of David
Zechariah, of the clan of Parosh,
with 150 men of his clan (there
were records of their family line)
Eliehoenai son of Zechariah, of the
clan of Pahath Moab, with
200 men
Shecaniah son of Jehaziel, of the
clan of Zattu, with 300 men
Ebed son of Jonathan, of the clan of
Adin, with 250 men
Jeshaiah son of Gotholiah, of the
clan of Elam, with 70 men
Zeraiah son of Michael, of the clan
of Shephatiah, with 70 men
Obadiah son of Jehiel, of the clan of
Joab, with 212 men
Shelomith son of Josiphiah, of the
clan of Bani, with 160 men
Zechariah son of Bebai, of the clan
of Bebai, with 28 men
Johanan son of Hakkatan, of the
clan of Azgad, with 110 men
Eliphelet, Jeuel, and Shemaiah, of
the clan of Adonikam, with 70 men
(they returned at a later date)
Uthai son of Istalcurus, of the clan of
Bigvai, with 70 men

Ezra Finds Priests and Levites for the Temple

(Ezra 8.15-20)

41 I assembled the entire group at Theras River, and we camped there for three
days. I inspected them 42 and found that
there were no priests or Levites in the
group, 43-44 so I sent a message to ten of
the leaders who were competent men:
Eliezer, Iduel, Maasmas, Elnathan, Shemaiah, Jarib, Nathan, Elnathan, Zechariah, and Meshullam. 45 I told them to go
to Iddo, the chief official at the treasury,
46 and ask him, his associates, and the
treasury officials to send us priests to
serve in the Temple of our Lord. 47 With
God's help, they sent us some able men:
Sherebiah, a Levite from the clan of
Mahli, with eighteen of his sons and relatives, 48 and Hashabiah, Annunus, and
his brother Jeshaiah of the clan of Hananiah, with twenty of their sons. 49 There
were also 220 Temple workmen whose
ancestors had been designated by King
David and his officials to assist the Levites. They were all listed in the register
by name.

Ezra Leads the People in Fasting and Prayer

(Ezra 8.21-23)

50 There by Theras River I made a vow
that the young men should fast in the
presence of our Lord and ask him for a
safe journey for us, our children, and our
animals. 51 I would have been ashamed
to ask the emperor for infantry and cavalry to accompany us and protect us
from our enemies, 52 because I had told
him that our Lord by his strength blesses
and protects those who trust him. 53 So
once again we prayed for our Lord to
protect us, and he answered our prayers.

The Gifts for the Temple

(Ezra 8.24-30)

54 From among the leading priests I
chose Sherebiah, Hashabiah, and ten
others. 55 Then I weighed out the silver,
the gold, and the sacred utensils which
the emperor, his advisers and officials,
and the people of Israel had given to be
used in the Temple, and I gave it to the
priests. 56-57 This is what I gave them:

silver	25 tons
silver utensils	7,500 pounds

gold	7,500	pounds
gold bowls	20	
fine bronze bowls that looked like gold	12	

58 I said to the priests, "You are sacred
to the Lord, the Lord of our ancestors,
and so are the utensils and the silver and
gold brought to him in fulfillment of a
vow. 59 Guard them carefully until you
reach the Temple. There in the priests'
rooms, turn them over to the leaders of
the priests and the Levites and to the
leaders of the people of Israel in Jerusalem." 60 So the priests and the Levites
took charge of the silver, the gold, and
the utensils for Jerusalem and brought
them to the Temple.

The Return to Jerusalem

(Ezra 8.31-36)

61 It was on the twelfth day of the first
month that we left Theras River, and
with the Lord's presence and protection
we reached Jerusalem. He protected us
from all our enemies on our journey, and
we arrived safely. 62 After we had been
there three days, we went to the Temple,
weighed the silver and gold and turned it
all over to Meremoth the priest, son of
Uriah. 63 With him were Eleazar son of
Phinehas and two Levites, Jozabad son
of Jeshua and Moeth son of Sabannus.
64 Everything was counted and weighed,
and a complete record was made at the
same time.

65 All those who had returned from exile then offered sacrifices to the Lord,
the God of Israel. They offered 12 bulls
for all Israel, 96 rams, 66 and 72 lambs;
they also offered 12 goats as a fellowship offering. They sacrificed all these
animals to the Lord. 67 Then they took
the decree the emperor had given them
and gave it to the governors and officials
of Greater Syria and Phoenicia, who
then honored the Jewish people and the
Temple of the Lord.

Ezra Learns of Intermarriages with Non-Jews

(Ezra 9.1-15)

68 After all this had been done, some of
the leaders of the people of Israel came
and told me that 69 the people, the leaders, the priests, and the Levites had not
kept themselves separate from the people in the neighboring countries of
Edom, Moab, and Egypt, or from the Canaanites, Hittites, Perizzites, and Jebusites. They were doing the same
disgusting things which those people
did. 70 God's holy people had become
contaminated because Jewish men were
marrying foreign women. Even the leaders and the officials had taken part in
this breaking of the Law from the very
beginning. 71 As soon as I heard this, I
tore my clothes and my sacred robe in
despair. I also tore my hair and my
beard, and sat down crushed with anxiety and grief. 72 I sat there grieving
about this sin until it was time for the
evening sacrifice to be offered, when
people began to gather around me—all
those who were disturbed by what the
Lord of Israel had said.

73 Then I got up from where I had been
fasting, and still wearing my torn
clothes, I knelt in prayer and stretched
out my hands to the Lord. 74 I said,
"O Lord, I am ashamed and confused in
your presence. 75 Our sins tower over our
heads; they reach as high as the heavens. 76 This has been true from the days
of our ancestors until now; we, your people, have sinned greatly. 77 Because of
our sins and the sins of our ancestors,
we and our relatives, our kings, and our
priests have fallen into the hands of foreign kings, and we have been slaughtered, robbed, and carried away as
prisoners. We have been totally disgraced, as we still are today. 78 Now,
Lord, for a short time you have shown us
great mercy. You have allowed just a
few of us to survive in order to carry on
the name Israel here in your holy Temple. 79 You have let the light of our nation
shine again, after feeding us and taking
care of us during the time of our slavery.
80 Even when we were slaves you did not
abandon us; you made the emperors of
Persia favor us, so that they gave us
food, 81 restored the glory of your Temple, rebuilt the city of Jerusalem out of
its ruins, and gave us a place of security
here in Judah and Jerusalem.

82 "But now, Lord, what can we say,
after you have done all this for us? We
have again disobeyed the commands
that you gave us through your servants,
the prophets. They told us that 83 the
land we were to occupy was an impure
land because the heathen people who
lived in it filled it with their disgusting

deeds. 84 They told us that we should
never intermarry with those people
85 and never seek peaceful relations with
them if we wanted to be strong and enjoy the land and pass it on to our
descendants forever. 86 Even after everything that has happened to us in punishment for our sins, we know that you,
Lord, have punished us less than we deserve 87 and have allowed us to survive.
But we have rebelled again, broken your
Law, and intermarried with these
wicked people. 88 Yet you were not angry enough to destroy us completely and
leave none of us alive, with no descendants and without our name. 89 Lord of Israel, you are faithful; you have allowed
us to survive. 90 We confess our guilt to
you; we have no right to come into your
presence."

The Plan for Ending Mixed Marriages

(Ezra 10.1-17)

91 While Ezra was bowing in prayer in
front of the Temple, weeping and confessing these sins, a large group of people from Jerusalem—men, women, and
children—gathered around him, all of
them weeping bitterly. 92 Then Shecaniah son of Jehiel, one of the Israelites,
said to Ezra, "We have sinned against
the Lord by marrying foreign women,
but even so, there is still hope for Israel.
93 Now we must make a solemn promise
to the Lord that we will send all these
foreign women and their children away.
94 We will do what you and the others
who obey the Law of the Lord advise us
to do. 95 It is your responsibility to act.
We are behind you, so go ahead and get
it done."

96 So Ezra began by making the leaders of the priests, of the Levites, and of
the rest of the people take an oath that
they would divorce their foreign wives.

9 Then Ezra went from the court of
the Temple into the living quarters
of Jehohanan son of Eliashib 2 and spent
the night there grieving over the people's terrible violation of the Law. He did
not eat or drink anything.

3 A message was sent throughout Jerusalem and Judah, calling all those who
had returned from exile to meet in Jerusalem, 4 by order of the leaders of the
people. If anyone failed to come within
two or three days, his cattle would be
confiscated, and he would lose his right
to be a member of the community.

5 Within the three days, on the twentieth day of the ninth month, all the men
of the tribes of Judah and Benjamin
came to Jerusalem 6 and assembled in
the Temple square. Everyone was shiv-
ering from the cold because it was wintertime.

7 Then Ezra stood up and spoke to
them, "You have broken the Law and
brought guilt on Israel by marrying foreign women. 8 Now then, tell the truth
and confess your sins to the Lord, the
God of our ancestors, 9 and do what he
requires. Separate yourselves from the
foreigners living in our land and get rid
of your foreign wives."

10 The people shouted in reply, "We
will do whatever you say." 11 But they
added, "The crowd is too big, and it's
wintertime. We can't stand here in the
open like this. This isn't something that
can be settled in one or two days, since
so many of us are involved in this sin.
12 Let our officials stay in Jerusalem and
take charge of the matter. Then let anyone who has a foreign wife come at an
appointed time, 13 together with the leaders and the judges of his city. In this way
God's anger over this situation will be
turned away." 14 Jonathan son of Asahel
and Jahzeiah son of Tikvah assumed responsibility for the plan; and Meshullam, Levi, and Shabbethai served with
them as judges.

15 The returned exiles carried out the
investigation in full. 16 Ezra the priest appointed men from among the heads of
the clans and recorded their names. On
the first day of the tenth month they began their investigation. 17 And within the
next three months they investigated all
the cases of men with foreign wives.

The Men Who Had Foreign Wives

(Ezra 10.18-44)

18 The following is a list of the men
who had foreign wives:

Priests, listed by clans:

19 Clan of Joshua and his brothers,
sons of Jozadak: Maaseiah, Eliezar, Jarib, and Jodan. 20 They promised to divorce their wives, and they offered rams
as a sacrifice for their sins.

21 Clan of Immer: Hanani, Zebadiah,

Manes, Shemaiah, Jehiel, and Azariah
22 Clan of Pashhur: Elioenai, Maaseiah, Ishmael, Nathanael, Okidelus, and Elasah

23 *Levites:*
Jozabad, Shimei, Kelaiah (also called Kelita), Pethahiah, Judah, and Jonah

24 *Musicians:*
Eliashib and Bacchurus

25 *Temple guards:*
Shallum and Telem

26 *Others:*
Clan of Parosh: Ramiah, Izziah, Malchijah, Milelos, Eleazar, Asebiah, Benaiah
27 Clan of Elam: Mattaniah, Zechariah, Jezriel, Abdi, Jeremoth, and Elijah
28 Clan of Zattu: Elioenai, Eliashib, Othoniah, Jeremoth, Zabad, and Zerdaiah
29 Clan of Bebai: Jehohanan, Hananiah, Zabbai, and Emathis
30 Clan of Bani: Meshullam, Malluch, Adaiah, Jashub, Sheal, and Jeremoth
31 Clan of Addi: Naathus, Moossias, Laccunus, Naidus, Bescaspasmys, Sesthel, Belnuus, and Manasseas
32 Clan of Annan: Elionas, Asiah, Melchiah, Sabbaiah, and Simon Chosamaeus
33 Clan of Hashum: Mattenai, Mattattah, Zabad, Eliphelet, Manasseh, and Shimei
34 Clan of Bani: Jeremai, Maadai, Amram, Joel, Mamdai, Bedeiah, Vaniah, Carabasion, Eliashib, Machnadebai, Eliasis, Binnui, Elialis, Shimei, Shelemiah, and Nathaniah
Clan of Ezora: Shashai, Azarel, Azael, Shemaiah, Amariah, and Joseph
35 Clan of Nebo: Mattithiah, Zabad, Iddo, Joel, and Benaiah
36 All these men had foreign wives. They divorced them and sent them and their children away.

Ezra Reads the Law to the People

(Nehemiah 7.73–8.12)

37 The priests, the Levites, and many of
the ordinary people of Israel settled in
Jerusalem and its vicinity. By the seventh month the other Israelites were all settled in their towns. On the first day of
that month 38 they all assembled in Jerusalem in the square just inside the east
gate of the Temple. 39 They asked Ezra,
the High Priest and scholar of the Law which the Lord had given Israel through Moses, to bring the book of the
Law. 40 So Ezra brought it to the place where all the people—men, women, and all the priests—had gathered to
hear it. 41 There in the square by the gate he read the Law to them from dawn until noon, and they all listened attentively.
42 Ezra was standing on a wooden platform that had been built for the occa-
sion. 43 The following men stood at his right: Mattathiah, Shema, Ananiah, Azariah, Uriah, Hezekiah, and Baalsamos;
44 and the following stood at his left: Pedaiah, Mishael, Malchijah, Lothasubus, Nabariah, and Zechariah.
45 Ezra took his seat on the platform in a prominent place where everyone could see him. As soon as he took the book of
the Law 46 and opened it, all the people stood up. Ezra said, "Praise the Lord, God Most High, God Almighty, Ruler of all."
47 All the people raised their arms in the air and answered, "Amen!" They knelt down in worship, with their faces to the ground.
48 The following Levites taught the Law of the Lord to the people: Jeshua, Anniuth, Sherebiah, Jamin, Akkub, Shabbethai, Hodiah, Maiannas, Kelita, Azariah, Jozabad, Hanan, and Peliah. They read the Law to the people and explained what was read.
49-50 When the people heard what the Law required, they were so moved that they began to weep. The governor[o] said to Ezra, the priest and scholar of the Law, and to all the Levites who were teaching the people, "This day is holy to
the Lord; 51 go home and have a feast. Share your food and wine with those who don't have any. 52 Today is holy to
the Lord, so don't be sad. He will restore your former glory."

[o] *Probable meaning* The governor; *Greek* Attharates.

53 The Levites gave the command to all
the people: "This day is holy; do not be
sad." 54 So all the people went home and
joyfully ate and drank and shared what
they had with those who had nothing.
They celebrated 55 because they understood what had been read to them.
Then they assembled. . . .[p]

[p] *Originally the Greek text must have continued (see Ne 8.13).*

The Second Book of ESDRAS

Introduction

The Second Book of Esdras *is primarily an apocalypse (or series of visions and revelations) that was written by an unknown Jewish author in Hebrew or Aramaic. This was translated into Greek, and an introduction and appendix of Christian origin were added. The original and the Greek translation have disappeared, and the text is now preserved primarily in Latin. The main part of the work reports seven revelations that were given to Shealtiel (identified with Ezra) and answers questions about the problem of evil, suffering, persecution, the end of the world, judgment, and the new world.*

Outline of Contents

1 This is the second book of the
prophet Ezra. He was the son of Seraiah, the grandson of Azariah, and a
descendant of Hilkiah, Shallum, Zadok,
Ahitub, 2 Ahijah, Phinehas, Eli, Amariah, Azariah, Meraioth, Arna, Uzzi,
Borith, Abishua, Phinehas, Eleazar,
3 and Aaron, of the tribe of Levi.

The Rejection of Israel

When I, Ezra, was a captive in Media
during the reign of Artaxerxes, king of
Persia, 4 the Lord said to me, 5 "Go and
remind my people and their children of
the sins they have committed against
me, and let them tell their grandchildren. 6 My people have sinned even
more than their ancestors, for they have
forgotten me and offered sacrifices to
foreign gods. 7 I rescued them from
Egypt, where they were slaves, but they
have done things that made me angry
and have refused to listen to my
warnings.

8 "Ezra, tear your hair in grief and call
down on these people all the disasters
they deserve. They are rebellious and refuse to obey my Law. 9 How much longer
can I tolerate these people for whom I
have done so much? 10 For their sake I
overthrew many kings and crushed the
king of Egypt together with his officials
and all his army. 11 I destroyed all the
nations that opposed them, and in the
east I scattered the people of the provinces of Tyre and Sidon and killed all the
enemies of Israel.

12 "Ezra, tell them that the Lord says:
13 I brought you across the Red Sea and
made safe roads for you where there
were none. I made Moses your leader
and gave you Aaron as your priest. 14 I
provided you with light from a pillar
of fire and performed great miracles

among you, but you have forgotten me.
I, the Lord, have spoken.
15 "The Lord Almighty says: I sent you
quails as a sign of my care for you. I
provided you with camps where you
could be safe, but all you did there was
complain. 16 Even when I destroyed your
enemies, you did not appreciate what I
had done. You have never done anything but complain. 17 Have you forgotten the blessings I gave you? There in
the desert when you were hungry and
thirsty you cried out to me: 18 'Why have
you brought us out to this desert to kill
us? Being slaves to the Egyptians was
better than coming here to die.' 19 I was
moved by your bitter groans and gave
you manna, the bread of angels. 20 When
you were thirsty, I split the rock and all
the water you needed flowed out. To
protect you from the heat, I provided
you with shade trees. 21 I divided fertile
lands among you and drove out the Canaanites, the Perizzites, and the Philistines who opposed your advance. What
more could I have done for you?
22 "The Lord Almighty says: There in
the desert by the river of bitter water
when you were thirsty and cursed me,
23 in spite of your insults I did not send
fire upon you. Instead, I made the water
fit to drink by throwing wood into the
river. 24 People of Israel, what can I do
with you? People of Judah, you refuse to
obey me. So I will turn to other nations
and make them my people. They will
keep my laws. 25 Because you have abandoned me, I will abandon you. You will
beg me for mercy, but I will show you
none. 26 When you pray to me, I will not
hear you. You never hesitate to commit
murder; your hands are stained with the
blood of those you have killed. 27 It is not
me that you have betrayed; you have betrayed yourselves.

Israel Is to Be Replaced

28 "The Lord Almighty says: I have
pleaded with you as a father pleads with
his sons, as a mother pleads with her
daughters, or as a nursemaid pleads
with her small children. 29 I begged you
to be my people so that I could be your
God, to be my children so that I could be
your father. 30 I gathered you together as
a hen gathers her chicks under her
wings. But now what can I do with you?
I will banish you from my sight; 31 and
even when you offer sacrifices to me, I
will turn away from you. Your religious
festivals, your New Moon celebrations,
or your circumcision ceremonies mean
nothing to me. 32 I sent to you my servants, the prophets, but you killed them
and mutilated their corpses. I will make
you pay for murdering them.
33 "The Lord Almighty says: Your
Temple is abandoned. I will scatter you
like straw blown away by the wind.
34 Your children will have no descendants because they rejected my commandments and did what I hated, just as
you did. 35 I will give your home to a people that is about to appear. They will believe me, even though they have not yet
heard of me. They will do what I command, even though I never performed
any miracles for them. 36 They have not
seen the prophets, but they will live by
their ancient teachings. 37 I give my solemn promise that I will bless those people, and their little children will laugh
and shout for joy. Those people have
never seen me, but deep within them
they will believe my words.
38 "Now, Father Ezra, look with pride
at the people you see coming from the
east. 39 Look at the leaders I have given
them: Abraham, Isaac, Jacob, Hosea,
Amos, Micah, Joel, Obadiah, Jonah,
40 Nahum, Habakkuk, Zephaniah, Haggai, Zechariah, and Malachi (who is also
called the Lord's messenger).

2 "The Lord says: I led my people out
of slavery in Egypt; I gave them
commandments through my servants,
the prophets, but they refused to listen
and ignored my teachings. 2 Jerusalem,
the mother who brought them into the
world, says to them, 'Go your own way,
my children; I am now a widow left completely alone. 3 I took great delight in
bringing you up, but you sinned against
the Lord God and did what I knew was
wrong, so I mourned in deep grief when
I lost you. 4 What can I do for you, now
that I am a widow and left completely
alone? Go, my children, and ask the
Lord for mercy.'
5 "Father Ezra, I call on you to testify
against these people as their mother has
done, because they have refused to keep
my covenant. 6 Now bring confusion on
them and ruin on their mother, so that
they will have no descendants. 7 They
will be scattered among the nations, and

no one on earth will remember them any
longer, for they have despised my
covenant.
8“How terrible will be your punishment, Assyria. You have let wicked
people hide within your borders.
Remember, sinful nation, what I did to
Sodom and Gomorrah. 9Their land now
lies covered with lumps of tar and heaps
of ashes. That is what I do to people who
do not obey me.
10“The Lord says to Ezra: Announce
to my new people that I will give them
the kingdom of Jerusalem, which I had
planned to give to Israel. 11I will take the
dazzling light of my presence away from
Israel and will give to my new people the
eternal Temple that I had prepared for
Israel. 12The tree of life will fill the air
around them with its fragrance. They
will never have to work; they will never
grow tired. 13Ask, and you will receive.
Pray that the number of the days you
have to wait will be reduced. Even now
the kingdom has been prepared for you,
so stay alert. 14Call heaven and earth to
witness that I, the living God, have abolished evil and created good.
15“Mother Jerusalem, take your children in your arms. Guide their steps in
safe paths; raise them with the same delight that a dove has in raising her
young. I, the Lord, have chosen you.
16I will raise your dead from their
graves because I recognize them as my
people. 17Jerusalem, mother of these
people, do not be afraid; I, the Lord,
have chosen you.
18“I will send my servants Isaiah and
Jeremiah to help you. At their request I
have consecrated and prepared for you
twelve trees, heavy with different kinds
of fruit, 19twelve fountains flowing with
milk and honey, and seven high mountains covered with roses and lilies. I will
make your children very happy there.
20Now, Jerusalem, come to the defense
of widows, take the side of the fatherless, give to the poor, protect orphans,
give clothing to those who have none,
21take care of those who are broken and
weak, do not make fun of those who are
crippled, protect the disabled, and help
the blind to catch a vision of my dazzling
splendor. 22Keep both the old and the
young safe within your walls. 23When-
ever you find a dead body, bury it and
mark the grave, and I will give you a
place of honor when I raise the dead.
24“Be calm, my people; your time to
rest will come. 25Take care of your children like a faithful nursemaid and guide
their steps in safe paths, 26so that none
of them will be lost. When the time
comes, I will hold you responsible for
them. 27Don’t worry; when the day of
trouble and distress comes, others will
cry and mourn, but you will be happy
and rich. 28The other nations will be
jealous of you, but they will not be able
to harm you.
29“I will protect you with my power
and save your children from hell. 30Be
happy, Jerusalem, you and your children, because I, the Lord, will rescue
you. 31Remember your children who are
asleep in their graves; I, the Lord
Almighty, am merciful, and I will bring
them out from the place where they lie
hidden in the earth. 32Until I come, hold
your children close and tell them about
my grace and mercy, which are like a
spring that never runs dry.”

Ezra on Mount Sinai

33I, Ezra, was on Mount Sinai when
the Lord ordered me to go to the people
of Israel. But when I went to them, they
rejected me and refused to listen to what
the Lord commanded. 34That is why I
am speaking to you Gentiles. You are
ready to listen and understand: “Wait
for your shepherd who is coming very
soon, at the end of the age, to give you
eternal rest. 35Be ready to receive the
blessings of the kingdom, for eternal
light will shine on you forever. 36Flee
from the darkness of this present age
and accept the joyful splendor prepared
for you. I testify publicly for my savior.
37The Lord has appointed him, so accept
him and be happy. Give thanks to God,
who has called you into his heavenly
kingdom. 38Stand up and see the number of those who have received the
Lord’s mark and who share in his banquet. 39They have left the darkness of
this age and have received shining white
robes from the Lord. 40So now, Jerusalem, welcome these people who have
kept the Law of the Lord, and this will
complete the list of those whom God has
assigned to you. 41The children you
longed for have returned; their number
is now complete. So pray that the Lord’s

kingdom may come and that your people, whom God chose before he created
the world, may become holy."

Ezra on Mount Zion

42 I, Ezra, saw an enormous crowd on
Mount Zion, too many people to count.
They were all singing and praising the
Lord. 43 Standing in the middle of this
crowd was a very tall young man, taller
than any of the others. He was placing a
crown on the head of each person, but
he towered above them all. I was spell-
bound by the sight, 44 and I asked the angel, "Who are these people, sir?"

45 He replied, "These are people who
have taken off their mortal robes and
have put on immortal ones. They have
confessed their faith in God, and now
they are being given crowns and palm
branches as symbols of their victory."

46 Then I asked the angel, "Who is the
young man who is putting the crowns on
their heads and giving them the palms?"

47 "He is the Son of God," the angel replied, "and all these people confessed
their faith in him while they lived on
earth." Then I began to praise those who
had stood for the Lord so bravely. 48 And
the angel said to me, "Go and tell my
people what you have seen, the many
marvelous wonders of the Lord."

THE FIRST VISION

Ezra's Prayer of Complaint

3 Thirty years after the fall of Jerusalem, I, Shealtiel (also known as
Ezra), was in Babylon. I was lying on my
bed, troubled and disturbed, 2 as I
thought about the ruins of Jerusalem
and the prosperity of those who lived in
Babylon. 3 I was deeply disturbed and
began to express my fears to God Most
High. 4 "O Lord and Master," I said,
"you, and you alone, spoke the word at
the beginning of creation and formed
the world. At your command the dust
5 produced the lifeless body of Adam.
Then with your hands you shaped it, you
breathed into it the breath of life, and he
began to live. 6 You brought him into the
Garden of Eden, which you yourself had
planted before the earth was made.
7 You gave him just one commandment,
but he disobeyed it, and you immediately made him and his descendants
subject to death.

"From Adam were born more nations,
tribes, clans, and families than can be
counted. 8 All the nations did whatever
they wished; they sinned against you
and rejected your commands. But you
did nothing to stop them. 9 Then again,
after a while, you brought on the flood
and destroyed the world's population.
10 They all suffered the same fate: as
death had come to Adam, so now death
came to a whole generation in the flood.
11 But you spared one man, Noah, with
his family and all his righteous
descendants.

12 "The number of people living on
earth began to increase, and the number
of families, tribes, and nations grew.
They too fell into sin and were worse
than the generations before them. 13 But
then you chose Abraham. 14 You loved
him, and to him alone in the dead of
night, you secretly disclosed how the
world would end. 15 You made an everlasting covenant with him and promised
him that you would never abandon his
descendants. You gave him Isaac, and to
Isaac you gave Jacob and Esau. 16 You
chose Jacob, and his descendants became a great nation, but you rejected
Esau.

17 "You rescued the descendants of Jacob from Egypt and led them to Mount
Sinai. 18 There you bent down the skies,
shook[a] the earth, moved the world,
made the waters beneath the earth tremble, and brought disorder to the universe. 19 The dazzling light of your
presence passed through the four gates
of fire, earthquake, wind, and frost, in
order to give the Law and its commandments to Jacob's descendants, the people of Israel. 20 Yet you did not remove
their evil impulse, but let your Law
guide their lives. 21 The first man, Adam,
weighed down with an evil impulse,
sinned and was defeated, and the same
was true of all of his descendants. 22 So
the disease became permanent, and although the Law was in the hearts of the
people, so also was the root of evil! That
is why what was good passed away
while what was evil continued.

23 "Many years later you sent your
servant David 24 and told him to build a

[a] *Some ancient translations* shook; *Latin* steadied.

city which would bear your name and in
which sacrifices would be offered to
you. 25 This was done for many years,
but then the inhabitants of the city disobeyed you 26 and sinned just like Adam
and all his descendants, because they
had the same evil impulse. 27 So you
handed over your own city to your
enemies.

28 "I said to myself, 'Perhaps Babylon
has been allowed to conquer Jerusalem
because the people who live there are
better than we are.' 29 But when I got to
Babylon, I saw more sins than I could
count, and now for thirty years I have
seen many sinners here. So I was perplexed 30 when I saw how you tolerate
sinners and do not punish them, how
you protect your enemies and yet destroy your own people. 31 You haven't
given the faintest hint as to how these
ways of yours can be changed. Surely
Babylon is no better than Jerusalem.
32 No other nation, except Israel, has
ever known you or accepted your covenants. 33 But Israel was never rewarded,
and never profited from its labor. I have
traveled widely in the other nations, and
I have seen how prosperous they are, although they don't keep your commands.
34 Now then, Lord, if you would just
weigh our sins on the scales against
those of the rest of the world, it would be
perfectly clear that their sins are heavier. 35 There has never been a time when
the people of the world did not sin
against you; but has any other nation
kept your commands as well as Israel
has? 36 You may find individuals who
have, but you won't find a nation that
has done so."

The Human Mind Cannot Understand God's Ways

4 The angel Uriel, who had been sent
to me, replied, 2 "You can't even
understand what happens in this world.
Do you think you can understand the
ways of God Most High?"

3 "Yes, sir, I do!" I answered.

The angel continued, "I have been sent
to ask you to solve three riddles about
what happens in this world. 4 If you can
explain even one of them to me, I will
answer your questions about God's
ways and teach you why the human race
has an evil impulse."

5 "I agree, sir," I said.

Then he said to me, "Good! How do
you weigh out a pound of fire? How do
you measure a bushel[b] of wind? How do
you bring back a day that has passed?"

6 I answered, "Why do you ask me
such questions? No human being could
answer them."

7 Then he said, "What if I had asked
you how many dwelling places there are
at the bottom of the sea? How many rivers flow into the waters beneath the
earth? How many rivers are there above
the dome of the sky? Where are the exits
from the world of the dead? Where are
the entrances to[c] Paradise? 8 If I had
asked you these questions, you might
have answered, 'I have never gone down
into the waters beneath the earth, and I
have not yet entered the world of the
dead. I have never gone up to heaven.'
9 But all I have asked you about is fire,
wind, and the day that has just passed—
things that you have experienced. Yet
you have given me no answer. 10 You
can't even understand things that you
have been familiar with since you were a
child. 11 How then can your little mind
understand the ways of God Most High?
Can someone already worn down by
this corrupt world understand the ways
of the incorruptible God?"

When I heard this, I fell face downward on the ground[d] 12 and said to him,
"It would have been better if we had
never been born than to have to live in a
world of sin and suffering without
understanding why things happen as
they do."

13 The angel Uriel answered, "I once
went into the woods and heard the trees
plotting together. 14 They were saying,
'Let's go to war against the sea and push
it back, so that we may have more
room.' 15 But the waves of the sea also
plotted together and said, 'Let's conquer
the woods and extend our territory.'
16 But all the plotting of the trees was
useless because fire came and destroyed
them. 17 And the plotting of the sea was
just as useless because the sand stood
firm and blocked its advance. 18 Now, if
you were the judge and had to decide

[b] *Some ancient translations* bushel; *Latin* blast. [c] *Some ancient translations* exits from . . . entrances to; *Latin* exits from. [d] *Verse 11 in Latin is unclear.*

between them, which would you pronounce right?"
19 I replied, "They were both wrong, because trees belong on the land, and waves belong in the sea."
20 "You have given the right answer," he said. "So why can't you see the an-
swer to your own problems? 21 For just as trees have their place on land, and waves have their place in the sea, so the people of this world can understand only what goes on in this world, and only heavenly beings can understand what goes on in heaven."

The End of the Age

22 "Please tell me, sir," I asked, "why then was I given the ability to under-
stand anything? 23 I am not interested in asking questions about what goes on in the heavens; I am only concerned about things that go on around us. Why has God allowed Israel to be disgraced by foreign nations? Why has he let the nation he loves be handed over to the power of godless nations? Why do the Law and the covenant that were given to our ancestors mean nothing any more?
24 Why do we die as quickly as insects? Why is our life shorter than a breath? Why does God think us unworthy of his
mercy? 25 Why doesn't God do some-
thing to help his own people? These are the questions that I want to ask."
26 Uriel answered, "If you live long enough, you will be surprised at what you will see, because this age is rapidly
passing away. 27 This age is so full of misery and imperfection that it cannot hold all the blessings that God has promised the righteous in the time to come.
28 The evil about which you have asked me has already been planted, but the time for its harvesting has not yet arrived. 29 This evil must be harvested, and this world where it was planted must be removed, before the new age where the
good is to be planted can appear. 30 At the beginning of time one grain of evil seed was sown in the heart of Adam. See how much wickedness it has already produced! Think of how much more it will produce before it is cut down and
threshed out at Judgment Day. 31 You can see for yourself what a big crop this
one evil seed has produced. 32 How terri-
ble will be the harvest on Judgment Day when these countless heads of grain are threshed out!"
33 Then I asked, "How long do we have to wait before this happens? Why are our lives so short and so full of misery?"
34 Uriel answered, "Don't be in a greater hurry than God Most High! You are thinking only of yourself, but God has to be concerned about everybody.[e]
35 Your questions are the same ones asked by the souls of the righteous dead in the places where God is keeping them waiting: 'How long must we wait here? When will the day of judgment come,
when we will get our reward?' 36 The
archangel Jeremiel answers them, 'It will happen as soon as the complete number of those who have suffered as you have are here. For God has weighed
this age, 37 measured the years, and numbered the days. Nothing will be changed until time has run its predeter-
mined course.'"
38 "But, sir," I replied, "all of us here on
earth are such wicked sinners. 39 Is it possible that because of our sin the righteous dead are having to wait for their reward?"
40 His answer was, "Can a pregnant woman keep her child from being born after her nine months are up?"
41 "No, sir, she cannot," I answered.
And he continued, "In the world of the dead, the place where God has stored
the souls is like a womb. 42 It is as eager to return the souls entrusted to it from the beginning of the world as a woman
is to end her labor pains. 43 When that happens, you will have the answer to all your questions."
44 "Please, sir," I asked, "if you think I
am able to understand it, can you 45 tell me one more thing? Is the time that is still to come longer than the past that
has already gone by? 46 I know how long the past has been, but I don't know the future."
47 "Come here and stand at my right," he commanded, "and I will show you a
vision and explain its meaning." 48 So I stood by him and looked, and I saw a blazing fire pass by in front of me, and when it was gone, I saw that smoke was
still there. 49 Then a rain cloud passed by in front of me, bringing a heavy down-

[e] *Verse 34 in Latin is unclear.*

pour of rain; and when the downpour
was over, there was still a light rain.
50“Think about this,” said Uriel. “Just as
the downpour was greater than the light
rain that followed it and the fire was
greater than the smoke left behind, in
the same way the time that has passed is
much longer than the time to come. The
time that is left is like the light rain and
the smoke.”

The Signs of the End

51“Please tell me,” I asked, “do you
think I will live until that time? If not,
who will be alive when it happens?”
52He answered, “I can tell you some of
the signs of the end, if that is what you
are asking about; but I am not here to
tell you how long you will live, and in
any case, I don't know.
5 “But these are the signs: The time
will come when all people on earth
will be in the grip of great confusion.[f]
The way of truth will be hidden, and no
faith will be left in the land. 2Wicked-
ness will increase until it has become
worse than you have ever known it to
be. 3The country that you now see ruling
the world will lie in ruins, with no inhab-
itant or traveler there. 4After that,[g] if
God Most High lets you live long
enough, you will see that country in confusion. The sun will suddenly start shining at night, and the moon in the
daytime. 5Blood will drip from trees;
stones will speak; nations will be in confusion; the movement of the stars will be
changed. 6A king unwanted by anyone
will begin to rule, and the birds will fly
away. 7Fish will be washed up on the
shores of the Dead Sea. The voice of one
whom many do not know will be heard
at night; everyone will hear it. 8The
earth will break open[h] in many places
and begin spouting out flames. Wild animals will leave the fields and forests. At
their monthly periods women will bear
monsters. 9Fresh water will become
salty. Friends everywhere will attack
one another. Then understanding will
disappear, and reason will go into hiding, 10and they will not be found even
though many may look for them. Everywhere on earth wickedness and violence
will increase. 11One country will ask a
neighboring country if justice or anyone
who does right has come that way, but
the answer will always be ‘No.’ 12At that
time people will hope for much, but will
get nothing; they will work hard, but
will never succeed at anything. 13These
are the signs of the end that I am permitted to show you. But if you begin to pray
again and continue to weep and fast for
seven more days, you will hear even
greater things.”
14Then I woke up, and I was trembling
violently. I was so disturbed that I was
about to faint, 15but the angel that had
come to talk with me took hold of me,
strengthened me, and set me on my feet.
16The next night, Phaltiel, who was a
leader of the people, came to me and
asked, “Where have you been? And why
do you look so sad? 17Don't you know
that the people of Israel in the land of
their exile have been put in your care?
18So get up and eat. Do not abandon us
like a shepherd leaving his flock to the
attacks of savage wolves.”
19“Leave me alone,” I answered, “do
not come near me for the next seven
days. Then come back.” So he left.

THE SECOND VISION

Ezra's Prayer and Uriel's Answer

20Then, crying and mourning, I fasted
seven days, as the angel Uriel had commanded me to do. 21At the end of the
seven days, I was again deeply troubled,
22but I recovered my ability to think, and
again I began to speak with God Most
High. 23“Lord and Master,” I said, “from
all the forests and plants on earth you
have chosen this one vine. 24From all the
countries of the world, you have chosen
this one small land. From all the flowers
in the world, you have chosen this one
lily. 25From all the water in the deep
oceans, you have filled up this one river.
From all the cities that have ever been
built, you have set apart this one city,
Jerusalem, as your own. 26From all the
birds that were created, you chose this
one dove. From all the animals that were
made, you chose this one lamb. 27From
all the nations of the world, you chose
this one nation to be your own, and you
gave its people your Law, which is honored by people everywhere.

[f] *Some ancient translations* confusion; *Latin unclear.* [g] After that; *Latin unclear.*
[h] *One ancient translation* The earth will break open; *Latin* Chaos will appear.

28 "And now, Lord, since all of this is
true, why have you dishonored[i] this
one people more than all others by
handing them over to many nations?
Why have you scattered your own people, 29 who believed in your covenants?
Why have you let them be trampled by
people who rejected your promises?
30 If you are so angry with your own
people, you yourself ought to punish
them."

31 When I had finished speaking, the
angel who had come to me on a previous
night was sent to me again. 32 He said,
"Listen carefully to me, and I will teach
you more."

33 "Please go on, sir," I said.

So he continued, "Are you worried
about the people of Israel? Do you think
you love them more than God, who
made them?"

34 "No, sir," I replied. "I spoke as I did
because I was so confused and upset. I
am always troubled whenever I try to
think about the ways of God Most High
or to understand even a small part of
what he does."

35 "You cannot understand!" he answered.

And I asked, "Why not, sir? In that
case, why was I born? Why didn't I die
before I was born? Then I wouldn't have
seen the sufferings and troubles of the
people of Israel."

36 The angel said to me, "I will answer
you if you can do the following things:
Tell me how many people are yet to be
born; collect scattered raindrops for me;
make dead flowers bloom again; 37 open
the rooms where the winds are locked
up and make them blow for me; show
me the picture of a sound. If you can do
these things, I will answer your questions about the sufferings of the people
of Israel."

38 I answered, "Lord and master, no
one can do these things, except God,
who is not confined to this world. 39 How
can I give you any kind of answer? What
do I know?"

40 He continued, "You could not do
even one of the things that I asked you to
do. How can you expect to understand
God's judgments or why God has promised his love to his people?"

Descending Generations

41 Then I said, "But, Lord God, your
concern is with the people who will be
alive at the end of the world. What will
happen to those who live before that
time? What about us? What about those
who came before us, and those who will
live after us?"

42 He answered me, "The final judgment can be compared to a circle, and
just as a circle has no beginning or end,
so those who come early will not be too
early, and those who come late will not
be too late."

43 I replied, "But couldn't you have created all human beings, those of the past,
the present, and the future, so that they
would all live at the same time? In that
way, you could have had your final judgment sooner."

44 He answered, "The creation cannot
move faster than the Creator. And besides, the world wouldn't have been able
to hold all the people if everyone had
been created at the same time."

45 "Why, then," I asked, "did you just
now tell me that one day you would
bring back to life at the same time every
creature that ever lived? If the world
can hold them all then, it can hold
them now."

46 He answered, "That would be like
asking a woman who has given birth to
ten children why she didn't have them
all at once, instead of one at a time."

47 "That would be impossible," I answered. "She can't have them all at
once."

48 "In the same way," he continued, "I
have made the world like a womb so that
it produces human beings at regular intervals. 49 The rule that neither a young
child nor an old woman can give birth to
a baby also applies to the world that I
have created."

50 Then I said, "Since you have brought
up the subject, may I ask if the world you
have been talking about is still young or
is it approaching old age?"

51 He replied, "You can learn the answer from any woman who has given
birth to several children. 52 Ask her why
her younger children do not grow as tall
as her older children. 53 She will tell you
that those born while she was young and

[i] *Some ancient translations* dishonored; *Latin* prepared.

healthy are much stronger than those
born when she was getting old and becoming weak. 54 You will notice that you
are smaller than people of earlier generations; 55 those who come later will be
smaller still. This shows you that creation is already getting old and losing the
strength of her youth."

God Will Bring the End of the World

56 "If you please, Lord," I asked, "will
you show me the one through whom you
will bring judgment on your creation?"

6 He said to me, "I made this decision
before I created the world: before
the gates of the world were standing; before the winds were brought together to
blow, 2 or the lightning flashed, or the
thunder rolled; before the foundations of
Paradise were laid, 3 or the beautiful
flowers appeared; before the powers
that move the stars were established, or
the armies of angels assembled; 4 before
the air was piled up high, or the divisions of the heavens given their names;
before I chose Mount Zion as my footstool; 5 before the present age was
planned, or the scheming of its sinners
was rejected, or my seal was placed on
those who obeyed the Law and laid up a
treasure of faithfulness. 6 Even then, I
decided that since I, and I alone, had created the world, I, and I alone, would
bring it to an end."

7 Then I asked, "How long a period of
time will divide the ages? When will the
first age end and the next age begin?"

8 He answered, "The interval will be no
longer than that between Abraham and
Abraham.[j] He was the grandfather of
both Jacob and Esau, and when they
were born, Jacob was holding Esau's
heel. 9 Esau represents the end of this
age, and Jacob represents the beginning
of the new age. 10 So, if Jacob's hand is
the beginning and Esau's heel is the
end,[k] do not try to find a space in
between."

The Signs of the End

11 "Lord and Master," I said, "please
hear my request. 12 On that earlier night
you showed me some of the signs of the
end; now please show me the rest."

13 "Stand up," he said, "and you will
hear a very loud voice. 14 If the place
where you are standing is violently
shaken 15 while the voice is speaking,
don't be afraid. The message will be
about the end of the world, and the foundations of the world will understand
16 that the voice is speaking about them.
They will tremble and quake because
they know that they will undergo a
change when the end comes."

17 When he said this, I stood up and
listened. I heard a voice that sounded
like a roaring river. 18 It said, "The time
is near when I will come to judge the
people living on the earth. 19 I will punish those who have hurt others with
their injustice. Jerusalem's humiliation
will come to an end, 20 and this age
which is about to pass away will have
the final seal put on it. Then I will give
the following signs: the books will be
opened across the sky for all to see.
21 Children only a year old will speak.
Pregnant women will give birth after
only three or four months, and their premature babies will live and run about.
22 Planted fields will suddenly become
bare, and full barns will suddenly become empty. 23 Then the trumpet will
sound, and sudden terror will grip the
heart of everyone when they hear it.
24 Friends will fight like enemies, and the
earth and its people will be terrified. Rivers will stop flowing and stand still for
three hours.

25 "Those who survive all these things
that I have predicted will be rescued
when I bring to an end this world that I
created. 26 They will see those who never
died but were taken up alive into
heaven. The hearts and minds of people
on earth will be changed. 27 Evil will be
destroyed and deceit eliminated. 28 Faith
will grow strong, corruption will be
overcome, and truth, which has not produced fruit for so long, will make itself
felt again."

29 While the voice was speaking, the
ground beneath me began to rock back
and forth.[l] 30 Then the angel said to me,
"These are the things that I have come to
show you tonight.[m] 31 Now if you will
pray and fast for seven more days, I will
come back and tell you even greater

[j] Abraham; *some manuscripts have* Isaac. [k] *Some ancient translations* So . . . end; *Latin unclear.* [l] *Some ancient translations* the ground . . . forth; *Latin unclear.*
[m] *One ancient translation* tonight; *Latin unclear.*

things,[n] 32 because God Most High has
heard your prayer; the Mighty God has
seen the pure and righteous life that you
have lived since your youth. 33 That is
why he has sent me to show you all
these things and to tell you not to be
afraid but to trust him. 34 Do not be so
quick to raise useless questions in the
present age; then you will not be so
quick to do so in the final age."

THE THIRD VISION

Why God's People Suffer

35 After that, I mourned and fasted for
seven more days, as I had done before,
and so I completed the three weeks of
fasting that I had been commanded to
observe. 36 On the eighth night I was
again deeply troubled, and I began to
speak to God Most High. 37 I was very
tense and my heart was uneasy, 38 but I
said, "O Lord, at the beginning of creation you spoke the word. On the first day
you commanded, 'Let the universe be
made,' and your word carried out that
command. 39 At that time the spirit was
moving, darkness and silence were
everywhere, and no human voice was
yet heard.[o] 40 Then you commanded
that a ray of light shine out of the room
where it was stored, so that your works
could be seen. 41 On the second day you
created the angel of the sky and commanded him to separate the water, so
that part of it would move up above the
dome of the sky and part remain below.
42 On the third day you commanded the
water that covered the earth to come together in one place and cover one-
seventh of the earth's surface. Then you
dried out the rest of the earth's surface
to make dry land, so that it might be cultivated and planted and used in your
service. 43 Your word went out and completed the work immediately. 44 In an instant all kinds of fruits and vegetables
appeared, enough kinds to satisfy every
taste. There were flowers of indescrib-
able fragrances and of the most magnificent colors. These things were made on
the third day. 45 On the fourth day the
bright-shining sun, the light of the
moon, and the arrangement of the stars
were created by your command. 46 You
commanded them to serve the human
race, which would soon be created. 47 On
the fifth day you commanded the part of
the earth covered by water to produce
birds and fish; and it was done. 48 At
your command, the still and lifeless water brought forth living creatures, so that
the nations might proclaim your wonderful works. 49 Then you singled out
two of the living creatures; you named
one of them Behemoth and the other Leviathan. 50 You separated them from
each other because the sea wasn't big
enough to hold them both. 51 You let Behemoth live on a part of the land that
you dried up on the third day of creation; it is a land of a thousand mountains. 52 You let Leviathan live in the sea.
You kept them both alive, so that your
chosen people may feast on them at the
time you choose. 53 On the sixth day you
commanded the earth to produce the animals, domestic and wild, large and
small. 54 More important than all of
these, you created Adam and put him in
charge of everything that you had made.
And all of us, the people you have chosen, are descended from him.

55 "O Lord, I have told you all this because you said that you created this first
world for the sake of your people. 56 You
said that, in spite of their great numbers,
all the other nations which descended
from Adam are nothing, worth no more
than a drop of water, no more than spit.
57 But now, Lord, those nations that are
considered as nothing are ruling over us
and destroying us. 58 We are your people, and you have called us your first-
born, your only child, your witness, your
loved one, but we have been handed
over to the power of these other nations.
59 If this world was really created for the
sake of your people, why don't we have
possession of it? How much longer must
we wait?"

7 When I had finished speaking, the
same angel that had been sent to me
on the earlier nights appeared again.
2 He said, "Stand up, Ezra, and listen to
what I have come to tell you."

3 "Go ahead, sir," I said.

He continued, "Picture in your mind a
broad,[p] immense sea spreading over a
vast area, 4 but with an entrance no
wider than a river. 5 No one who wishes

[n] *Some ancient translations* things; *Latin adds* in the daytime. [o] *Some ancient translations* yet heard; *Latin adds* from you. [p] *Some ancient translations* broad; *Latin* deep.

to enter that sea, whether to visit it or
control it, can reach its broad expanse of
water without passing through the narrow entrance. 6 Or take another example: Picture a city built on a plain. The
city is full of all kinds of good things,
7 but the entrance to it is narrow and
steep, with fire on one side and deep water on the other. 8 The one path between
the fire and the water is so narrow that
only one person at a time may walk on
it. 9 If anyone inherits this city, he cannot
take possession of his inheritance without passing through this dangerous
entrance."
10 "That is right, sir," I said.
"That is how it is with the people of
Israel," he added. 11 "I made this world
for their sake, but when Adam broke my
commands, the world came under my
judgment. 12 Then the entrances into this
world were made narrow and difficult to
travel. They were rough, dangerous, and
few in number. 13 But the entrances to
the great world to come are wide and
safe and lead to immortality. 14 Everyone
who lives must walk the narrow and
meaningless ways of this world in order
to receive the blessings stored up in the
world to come. 15 So, Ezra, why are you
upset and disturbed by the thought
that[q] you are mortal and must die?
16 Why don't you think about the age to
come, rather than the present age?"
17 I answered, "Lord and master, in
your Law you said that the righteous
would receive all these blessings, but
that the wicked would perish. 18 The
righteous then can endure all the difficulties of this narrow way because they
look forward to the broad and open life
of the future, but the wicked must pass
through the narrow way without any
hope of seeing the broad open life."
19 The angel replied, "Do you think you
are a better judge than God? Do you
think you are wiser than God Most
High? 20 It is better to let many people of
the present age perish than to allow
them to neglect the Law that God has
given them. 21 God has given clear commandments to everyone coming into this
world, telling them what they should do
to obtain life and to avoid punishment.
22 But the wicked would not listen and
refused to obey him. In their foolishness
23 they have made their own wicked and
deceitful plans. They denied the existence of God Most High and refused to
follow his ways. 24 They have rejected
his Law, refused to accept his promises,
disobeyed his decrees, and failed to do
what he commanded. 25 That's the reason, Ezra, that there is emptiness for the
empty and fullness for the full.

The Messianic Kingdom and the Final Judgment

26 "The time is coming when these
signs will take place. The invisible city
will appear,[r] and the land that is now
hidden will be seen. 27 Everyone who
survives the calamities I have predicted
will also see the wonderful things I will
do. 28 My son the Messiah[s] will be revealed, together with those who come
with him. He will bring four hundred
years of happiness to all these survivors.
29 At the end of that time, my son the
Messiah and all human beings will die.
30 Then the world will return to its original silence, and for seven days it will be
like it was at the beginning. No one will
be left alive. 31 After seven days this corrupt age will pass out of existence and a
new age will be awakened. 32 The
ground will give up the dead who sleep
there in silence, and the souls of the
dead will be released from the places
where they have been kept. 33 God Most
High will appear on his judgment seat.
Mercy and patience will vanish completely 34 and be replaced by judgment.
Truth and faithfulness will once again
stand firm. 35 The good and bad that people have done will be fully revealed, and
reward and punishment will follow immediately.[t] 36 The pit of torment, the
fires of hell, will appear, and opposite
them the Paradise of joy and rest.
37 "Then God Most High will say to the
nations that have been raised from the
dead, 'Look! I am the one whom you
have denied and refused to serve; it is
my commands that you have rejected.
38 Look around you; there is joy and
peace in one direction, fire and torment

[q] by the thought that; *or* since. [r] *Some ancient translations* The invisible city will appear; *Latin* The bride will appear and the appearing city. [s] *Some ancient translations* the Messiah; *Latin* Jesus. [t] *Verses 36-105 are not found in the King James Version, but they have been restored from ancient sources.*

in the other.' That's what he will say to
them on Judgment Day.
39 "On Judgment Day there will be no
sun, moon, or stars; 40 no cloud, thunder,
or lightning; no wind, water, or air; no
darkness, evening, or morning; 41 no
summer, spring, or winter; no heat,
frost, or cold; no hail, rain, or dew; 42 no
noon, night, or dawn; no daylight,
brightness, or light. The only light will
be the dazzling brightness of God Most
High, making it possible for everyone to
see. 43 The judgment will last seven
years. 44 That's the arrangement I have
made for Judgment Day, but I have revealed these things only to you."

Only a Few Will Be Saved

45 Then I said, "Lord, I repeat what I
said earlier: How fortunate are the people who can live now and obey your
commands! 46 But what about those for
whom I have been praying? There is no
one in the present generation who has
not sinned, no one who has not broken
your covenant. 47 Now I understand that
the world to come will bring joy to only
a few, but torment to many. 48 The evil
impulse within us has grown and it has
led us away from God's ways, brought
us to ruin, put us on the way to death
and destruction, and taken us far from
life. It has destroyed not only a few, but
almost everyone who was ever created."
49 "Listen to me," the angel said, "and I
will teach you further and correct your
thinking. 50 Because only a few will be
saved, God created two worlds, instead
of only one. 51 As you say, only a few
people are righteous, but there are large
numbers of wicked people. But listen:
52 If you had only a few precious stones,
would you add lumps of lead and clay to
them in order to have more?"[u]
53 "Surely no one would do that, sir," I
answered.
54 "Take another illustration," he continued. "The earth itself will give you an
answer if you humbly ask it 55 whether it
produces more gold, silver, copper, iron,
lead, or clay. 56 There is more silver than
gold, more copper than silver, more iron
than copper, more lead than iron, and
more clay than lead. 57 So judge for yourself which are more desirable and valuable, common things or rare things."
58 I answered, "Lord and master, the
common things are cheap; it is the rare
things that are valuable."
59 "All right," he replied, "so draw the
logical conclusion: the person who has
what is scarce has more reason to be
pleased than the person who has what is
plentiful. 60 It's the same with the judgment[v] that I have promised: I will be
pleased with the few who will be saved,
because they are the ones who now
praise and honor me and make my name
known. 61 I will not be sad about the
large number of people who will be lost,
because even now they last no longer
than a vapor; they disappear like fire
and smoke; they catch fire, blaze up, and
quickly go out."
62 Then I said to the earth, "Look at
what you have done! When you gave
birth to the rest of creation you gave
birth to reason. 63 It would have been
better if you had never been created.
Then we humans would never have had
the power of reasoning! 64 But as it is
now, our reason grows up with us and
then torments us, because we realize
that we are going to die! 65 Compared to
us who must bear this sorrow, the dumb
animals must be happy. 66 They are
much better off than we are. They do not
have to look forward to the judgment;
they are not aware of any torment or salvation that is promised to them after
death. 67 What good is it to us that we are
going to be given life in the future if it is
to be a life of terrible torment? 68 Everyone who is born is caught in the web of
sin, is full of wickedness and burdened
with guilt. 69 I think it would be better if
after death we did not have to face
judgment."
70 The angel replied, "When God Most
High was creating the world, as well as
Adam and his descendants, the first
thing he did was to get everything ready
for the judgment. 71 So you ought to
learn from your own words. You said
that your reason grows up with you,
72 and that's the point. The people of this
world used their reason and sinned; they
received God's commands but did not
keep them; they accepted the Law and

[u] *One ancient translation* would you . . . more; *Latin unclear.* [v] *Some ancient translations* judgment; *Latin* creation.

then disobeyed it. And that's why they
will suffer torment. 73What excuse can
they offer at the judgment? How can
they answer at the last day? 74God Most
High has been very patient with the people of this world for a long time, but it
has not been for their sake. He has done
it for the sake of the age to come."

The Soul after Death

75Then I said, "Sir, may I ask you,
please, to explain to me what happens
when we die, when each of us must give
back our soul? Will we be kept at rest
until the time when you begin to make
your new creation, or will our torment
begin immediately?"

76"I will answer that question also," he
replied, "but do not include yourself
among those who will be tormented because they have no use for religion.
77After all, you have a treasure of good
works stored up with God Most High,
which will not be shown to you until the
last days. 78But to answer your question
about death: When God Most High has
pronounced the final decree that a person shall die, the soul leaves the body to
return to the one who gave it. Immediately it praises the glory of God Most
High. 79Let me explain first about people who had no use for the ways of God
Most High and hated those who worshiped him. 80There is no place where
their souls can go for rest; they must
wander around forever in torment, grief,
and sorrow. Their torment will progress
in seven stages. 81First, they ignore the
Law of God Most High. 82Second, they
can no longer make a sincere repentance and obtain life. 83Third, they see
the reward stored up for those who put
their faith in the covenants of God Most
High. 84Fourth, they think about the torment that has been stored up for them in
the last days. 85Fifth, they see angels
guarding the homes of other souls in
complete silence. 86Sixth, they recognize that they must soon be tormented.[w]
87Seventh, and worst of all, when they
see the glory of God Most High, they are
sick with remorse and shame. They
cringe in fear, because while they were
living they sinned against him. And now
they are about to come before him to be
judged on the last day.

88"Now let me explain about those
who followed the ways of God Most
High and what will happen when the
time comes for them to leave their mortal bodies. 89While they lived on earth,
through constant difficulty and danger,
they served God Most High and carefully kept the Law given by the Law-
giver. 90This is what they will receive:
91They will rejoice when they see the
great glory of God. He will receive them,
and they will enter their rest in seven
stages of joy. 92The first joy is to have
struggled hard and won the victory over
the evil impulse which was formed in
them, but which did not succeed in leading them from life into death. 93The second is to see the endless wandering of
the souls of the wicked and the punishment that is waiting for them. 94The
third is to know what a good report their
Maker has given about them, that during
their lifetime they kept the Law that was
entrusted to them. 95The fourth is to appreciate the rest that they are to enjoy in
the places where they have been
brought together, guarded by angels, in
complete silence, and with the glory that
is waiting for them at the last day. 96The
fifth is to rejoice that they have now escaped the corrupt world and that they
will receive the future life as their possession. They can see both the narrow,
troubled[x] world from which they have
been freed and the spacious world they
will receive and enjoy forever. 97The
sixth is to be shown how their faces will
shine like the sun and how they are to be
like the light of the stars that never die.
98The seventh joy, and best of all, is
when they rush to meet God face-to-
face, with perfect trust and happiness,
without any fear or shame. They served
him during their lifetime and now they
will receive from him their reward in
glory. 99These rewards that I have been
telling you about are those that have
been prepared for the souls of the righteous. I described to you earlier the torment that the rebellious will suffer."

100Then I asked, "When the souls of
the righteous are separated from their
bodies, will they be given time to see
what you have told me about?"

101"They will be free for seven days,"
he answered, "and during that time they

[w] *Verse 86 in Latin is unclear.* [x] *Some ancient translations* troubled; *Latin unclear.*

will be able to see the things I have told
you about. After that they will be
brought together with the other souls in
their homes."

The Finality of Judgment and the Salvation of the Few

102 Then I said, "Sir, please tell me
whether the righteous will be able to ask
God Most High to show mercy on the
unrighteous on Judgment Day. 103 Will
fathers be able to pray for their children,
children for parents, brothers for brothers, relatives for those near to them, and
friends[y] for those dear to them?"

104 "I will be happy to tell you," he replied. "Judgment Day is final[z] and sets
the final seal on truth for all to see. You
know that in this age a father cannot
send his son to be sick[a] for him or sleep
or eat or be healed for him. An owner
cannot send his slave to do these things
for him, nor can a person send his best
friend. 105 In the same way, on that day,
no one will be able to pray for another
person. Each person will receive the
punishment or reward for his own sinfulness or righteousness."[b]

106 "If that is so," I answered, "how can
we explain what we find in the Scriptures? Abraham prayed for the people of
Sodom, and Moses for our ancestors
who sinned in the desert. 107 Later,
Joshua prayed for the people of Israel in
the time of Achan, 108 and Samuel
prayed for them in the days of Saul.[c]
David prayed at the time of the epidemic, and Solomon prayed for those
who were going to worship in the Temple. 109 Elijah prayed that the people
might have rain and for a dead person to
come back to life. 110 Hezekiah prayed
for the people during the time of Sennacherib. And there are many other examples. 111 If righteous people prayed for
the unrighteous during such times when
corruption increased and injustice multiplied, why won't the same thing happen
at the Judgment Day?"

112 "The present age is not the end of
everything," the angel answered. "Even
in this age, the glorious presence of God
is not[d] always seen. That is why the
strong have prayed for the weak during
this age. 113 But the Judgment Day will
be the end of the present age and the
beginning of the future age. Then all corruption will end, 114 self-indulgence and
disloyalty will be eliminated. Righteousness and truth will reach their full maturity. 115 So on Judgment Day, no one will
be able to have mercy on those who
have been condemned, and no one will
be able to harm those who have been
acquitted."

116 I answered, "I made this point before, and I will make it again. It would
have been better if the earth had never
produced Adam, or when it had done so,
if it had made him so that he could not
sin. 117 What good is it for any of us to
have life in the present age, when it is
full of misery and when all we can look
forward to after death is punishment?
118 O Adam, what have you done? Your
sin was not only your own downfall; it
was also the downfall of all of us who
are your descendants. 119 What good is it
to us that we have the promise of immortal life, when we have committed sins
that condemn us to death? 120 What good
is the hope of eternity, when we find
ourselves in such a completely hopeless
situation? 121 What good is it that safe
and secure homes have been prepared
for us in the future world, when we have
lived such wicked lives? 122 What good is
the promise that the glorious presence of
God Most High will protect those who
have lived pure lives, when our own
lives have been so full of sin? 123 What
good is it that Paradise is shown to us,
that its imperishable fruit can heal us
and provide all we need? We can never
go there 124 because we have lived unacceptable lives.[e] 125 What good is it that
the faces of those who practice self-
control will shine more brightly than the
stars, when our own faces will be
blacker than the night? 126 Never in our
whole lives, when we sinned, did we
think about what we would have to suffer after death."

127 The angel replied, "Here is the
meaning of the conflict that every person on earth must endure: 128 If he is de-

[y] *Some ancient translations* friends; *Latin* the confident. [z] *One ancient translation* final; *Latin* bold. [a] *Some ancient translations* be sick; *Latin* understand. [b] *Verses 106-140 are the equivalent of verses 36-70 in the King James Version.* [c] *Some ancient translations* in the days of Saul; *Latin does not have these words.* [d] *Some ancient translations* is not; *Latin* is. [e] *Probable text* unacceptable lives; *Latin* in unacceptable places.

feated, he must suffer the things you
have just told me about, but if he is victorious, he will receive the rewards that I
have just mentioned. 129 That is why
Moses long ago urged the people to
choose life so that they might live. 130 But
they did not believe him or the prophets
who came after him, and they did not
believe me when I spoke to them. 131 So
the sadness over their destruction is
nothing compared to the great joy over
the salvation of those who believe."

132 I answered, "Sir, I know that God
Most High is spoken of as merciful because he shows mercy to those who
have not yet entered this world. 133 He is
called compassionate because he shows
compassion to those who repent and
obey his Law. 134 He is thought of as patient because he is patient with his own
creatures who have sinned. 135 He is
known as generous because he prefers
to give rather than to demand. 136 And he
is known as very forgiving because he
continues to forgive sinners of the past,
present, and future. 137 If he did not continue to forgive, there would be no life
for this world or the people in it. 138 He is
spoken of as pardoning because, if it
were not for his goodness in pardoning
sinners, not one person in ten thousand
would gain life. 139 He is called judge because he pardons and blots out the many
sins of those who were created by his
word. 140 If he did not, only a handful of
the whole human race would be left."[f]

8 The angel replied, "God Most High
made this world for many people,
but the future world for only a few.
2 Ezra, let me give you an illustration. If
you ask the earth, it will tell you that it
produces a large amount of clay for pots
but only a small amount of gold dust.
And that's the way it is with the present
world: 3 many have been created, but
only a few will be saved."

Ezra Prays for His People

4 I said to myself, "I must search for
wisdom and try to understand. 5 I was
brought into this world without my consent,[g] and I will leave it against my will.
God has given me only a few short years
as my span of life."

6 Then I prayed, "O Lord above, permit me, your humble servant, to offer
this prayer: Plant a seed within us, and
let it grow until it produces new hearts
and minds, so that sinful humanity may
have life. 7 For you alone are God, and
you created all of us, as the scripture
says. 8 You give life and provide arms
and legs to the body formed in the
womb, where it is kept safe in the elements of fire and water. The body which
you form is carried in the womb for nine
months, 9 and you alone provide safety
for the protecting womb and the protected body. Then when the womb delivers what was created in it, 10 your
command produces milk from the
breasts of the human body. 11 The infant
you created is fed in this way for a while,
and then you continue to provide your
mercy. 12 You raise the person on your
righteousness, teach him your Law, and
discipline him with your wisdom. 13 You
are his Creator and, as you wish, you
can take away his life or allow him to
live. 14 But if you are so ready to destroy
a person that was so carefully created at
your command, why was he created in
the first place?

15 "Now, Lord, I must say this: You
may know what is best in regard to the
rest of the human race, but I mourn for
your own people — 16 I am disturbed and
grieved for your own nation Israel, the
descendants of Jacob. 17 So I want to
pray for them and for myself, because I
can see how all of us who live on this
earth have failed, 18 and I know that
judgment will soon come upon us. 19 So
please hear me and listen to my prayer."

The prayer that Ezra prayed before he
was taken up into heaven begins here.
He prayed, 20 "O Lord, you live forever,
and the highest heavens are yours.
21 Your throne is more wonderful than
anything we can imagine; your glory
surpasses our understanding; the heavenly army of angels stands trembling before you. 22 They are ready to turn
themselves into wind or fire at your
command. Your word is everlastingly
true. 23 Your mighty commands accomplish fearful things. With one look, you
dry up the deep oceans, and you can
melt the mountains with your anger.
Your truth lasts forever.[h] 24 O Lord, you

[f] *Verses 106-140 are the equivalent of verses 36-70 in the King James Version.*
[g] *One ancient translation* without my consent; *Latin* to obey. [h] *Some ancient translations* lasts forever; *Latin* testifies.

created me, and I am your servant, so
listen to my prayer. 25 As long as I have
life and understanding, I cannot keep
silent.

26 "Do not take account of the sins of
your people; rather, consider those who
have served you faithfully. 27 Pay no attention to godless people and what they
do, but take into account those who have
kept your covenant in spite of all their
sufferings. 28 Do not think about those
who have lived wicked lives, but remember those who have gladly confessed
you as God. 29 Do not destroy your people because of those who have lived like
animals, but be mindful of those who
have taught your Law in such a wonderful way. 30 Do not be angry with those
you consider worse than animals, but
show your love to those who have always trusted in your glorious presence.

31 "It is true that we and our ancestors
have lived our lives in ways that bring
death, but it is because of us who are
sinners that you are called merciful.
32 You will surely be called merciful if
you choose to take pity on us—we are
sinners without any righteous deeds to
our credit. 33 Those who are righteous
will receive their reward on the basis of
the many good works that they have
stored up with you.

34 "What are human beings that you
should be angry with them? What is this
mortal race that you should be so bitter
against it? 35 To speak the truth, no person was ever born who did not sin; there
is no one living who is not guilty.
36 Therefore, Lord, your righteousness
and goodness will certainly be made
known when you show your mercy to
those who have no treasure of good
deeds."

37 The Lord answered me, "Part of
what you have said is correct, and things
will happen as you have indicated.
38 You can be sure that I will give no
thought to those who have sinned or to
their creation, death, judgment, or destruction. 39 Instead, I will find my joy in
the creation of the righteous, their
earthly journey, their salvation, and
their final reward. 40 Things will happen
just as I have said. 41 The farmer plants
many seeds and puts out many plants,
but not all of them take root or come up
at the right time. That's the way it is with
this world. Not everyone who has been
placed in this world will be saved."

42 Then I said, "Please let me speak.
43 The farmer's seed may not come up
because you did not send rain at the
right time, or it may be ruined by too
much rain. 44 But people are different.
You formed them with your own hands;
you created them to be like you; and you
made everything for their benefit. How
can you compare them to a farmer's
seed? 45 It's impossible, O Lord[i] above!
Spare the people who are your own.
Have pity on them. Show your mercy to
the people you have created."

46 He answered, "The present is for
those who live now, and the future for
those who are to come. 47 You are certainly not able to love what I have created more than I do. Never again
consider yourself among the unrighteous, as you have done so often. 48 Yet I
am very pleased 49 that you have shown
proper humility and not boasted by
thinking of yourself as righteous. 50 The
people of this world who have lived their
lives in pride and arrogance will suffer
many things in the last days. 51 But, Ezra,
you should be thinking about the glory
that is waiting for you and those like
you. 52 For all of you, Paradise has been
opened, the tree of life has been planted,
the world to come has been made ready,
all your needs have been provided, the
heavenly city has been built, full rest
from your labors has been offered, goodness and wisdom have been perfected.
53 The source of evil has been sealed off,
so that it cannot reach you; all sickness
has been removed, death[j] has been
taken away, hell is gone, and corruption
has disappeared. 54 All suffering has
been taken away, and the treasure of immortality is at last revealed.

55 "So don't ask any more questions
about the large number of people who
are lost. 56 For when they had the opportunity to choose, they despised God
Most High, had contempt for his Law,
and refused to follow his ways. 57 In addition, they mistreated the righteous
servants of God. 58 They even said to
themselves that there was no God, al-

i Some ancient translations O Lord; *Latin does not have these words.*
j Some ancient translations death; *Latin does not have this word.*

though they knew that they must die.
59 So the joys I have described are waiting for you, while thirst and torment are
in store for them. But God Most High did
not want anyone to perish. 60 He created
everyone and prepared life for everyone,
but those he created dishonored the
name of their Creator and were ungrateful to the one who offered them life.
61 That is why the day on which I will
judge them is near. 62 I have made this
known to you and a few others like you,
but not to everyone."

The Signs of the End

I answered, 63 "Sir, you have shown
me many signs which you will perform
in the last days, but you have not told me
how I can know when this will happen."

9 He answered, "Consider all these
things very carefully. When you see
that some of the signs I have told you
about have appeared, 2 you will know
that the time has come when God Most
High will bring judgment on the world
he has created. 3 There will be earthquakes, national rebellions, international intrigues, unstable leaders, and
confused rulers. When you see these
things happening, 4 you will know that
they are what God Most High has spoken about since the beginning of creation. 5 The beginning and the end[k] of
everything that happens in this world
are clear. 6 The same is true in the world
above:[l] wonders and miracles show the
beginning of events, and mighty signs
show when they end.

7 "Some people will escape destruction
and be saved by their good works or by
their faith. All of them 8 will survive the
dangers I have described and will enjoy
the salvation provided in the land that I
have set apart from eternity as my own.
9 Then those who have ignored my ways
and held them in contempt will be surprised when they find themselves in
continual torment. 10 This will include all
those who ignored me while they were
alive, even though they accepted the
blessings I gave them. 11 It will include
all those who scorned my Law during
the time they were free to do so and all
those who refused to repent when they
still had the chance. 12 The torment they
will have to suffer after death will force
them to recognize the truth. 13 Therefore,
Ezra, you should stop asking questions
about how the wicked will be punished.
Instead, be concerned about how and
when the righteous will be saved. The
world was created for them and belongs
to them."

14 I said, 15 "I must repeat what I said
before. The lost far outnumber those
who are saved — 16 it is like a wave compared with a drop of water."

17 He answered, "The seed to be
planted depends on the soil; the color of
the flower depends on the kind of
flower; the quality of a product depends
on the skill of the worker; and the size of
the harvest depends on how hard the
farmer has worked. 18 Before I created
this world or the people who would live
in it, no one opposed me, because no one
existed. 19 When I had created the world,
I supplied it with an abundance of food
and a Law of profound wisdom, but the
people I created lived corrupt lives.
20 I looked at my world and saw that it
was ruined. I saw that my earth was in
danger of being destroyed by the wicked
plans of the people who had come into it.
21 When I saw this, I found it very difficult to spare them, but I saved a few for
myself, one grape out of a bunch and
one tree out of a great forest.[m] 22 So let
them perish — all those people who were
born only to be lost. But let my chosen
people be kept safe — those for whom I
worked so hard to bring to perfection.

23 "And now, Ezra, you must wait
seven more days, but do not fast this
time. 24 Go to a field of wild flowers
where no one has ever lived and eat
nothing but the flowers — do not eat any
meat or drink any wine. 25 Pray the
whole time to God Most High. Then I
will come and talk with you again."

THE FOURTH VISION

The Law Remains

26 I obeyed the angel's command and
went to a field called Ardat. I sat there
among the flowers and ate the wild
plants, and that was enough food for me.
27 After seven days I was lying on the
grass, and once again my thoughts began to trouble me. 28 Then I began to

[k] *One ancient translation* The beginning and the end; *Latin unclear.* [l] The same . . . above; *Latin unclear.* [m] *Some ancient translations* a great forest; *Latin* great tribes.

speak and said to God Most High,
29 “O Lord, you revealed yourself to our
ancestors when they were traveling
through the trackless, barren desert after they had left Egypt. You said to them,
30 ‘Listen to me, people of Israel. 31 I am
giving you my Law. It will be like a seed
planted among you that produces fruit,
and it will be your crowning glory forever.’ 32 Our ancestors received the Law,
but they disobeyed its commands. Yet
the fruit of the Law was not destroyed—
it could not be destroyed because it was
yours. 33 Those who had received the
Law were destroyed because they did
not guard the good seed that was sown
in them. 34-35 The usual thing is that the
container remains after its contents
have been destroyed, for example, seed
in the ground, a ship on the sea, or food
in a bowl. But this is not the case with us
sinners. 36 The Law was placed in our
hearts, and we are the ones who will be
destroyed because we have sinned.
37 The Law will not be destroyed; it will
remain in all its glory.”

The Vision of the Weeping Woman

38 While I was saying these things to
myself, I looked around and saw a
woman on my right. She was weeping
and wailing, terribly upset; her clothes
were torn, and there were ashes on her
head. 39 I immediately put my own troubles out of my mind, turned to the
woman, 40 and asked, “Why are you crying? Why are you so upset?”

41 “Please, sir,” she answered, “leave
me alone and let me go on crying and
mourning; I am bitter and depressed.”

42 “Tell me what's wrong,” I said.

43 She answered, “Sir, I was married
for thirty years, but I was never able to
have a child. 44 During those thirty years
I prayed every day and every hour, day
and night, to God Most High for a child.
45 After thirty years God answered my
prayer; he saw my suffering, took away
my distress, and gave me a son. What
great joy this brought to my husband
and me and to all our neighbors! We
sang the praises of the Almighty.
46 I brought our son up with the greatest
care, 47 and when he was grown, I chose
a wife for him and prepared for the
wedding.

10 “On the wedding night when my
son entered the bedroom, he
dropped dead. 2 So we put out all the
wedding lamps, and all my neighbors
came to comfort me. I remained in control of myself until the evening of the
second day, 3 when they all left. That
night I got up and came out to this field,
as you see. 4 I have decided never to return to that town. I am going to stay here
in constant mourning, neither eating nor
drinking anything until I die.”

5 When she told me this, I put aside my
own thoughts and spoke sharply to her:
6 “You are the most foolish woman I ever
met. Don't you see what our people are
suffering? Don't you know all that has
happened to us? 7 Jerusalem, the mother
of us all, is overcome with grief and
shame. You ought to be mourning for
her 8 and sharing the grief and sorrow of
all of us. But you are mourning for that
one son of yours. 9 Ask the earth; let her
tell you that she is the one who ought to
be mourning for the vast multitudes of
people that she has brought to birth.
10 All of us who are living came originally from her, and there are more to
come. Almost all of us go straight to
destruction—the vast multitude of
earth's children are lost. 11 So who has
more right to mourn, you for your one
son, or the earth, which has lost so
many? 12-13 I know what you are thinking; you think that your sorrow is worse
than the earth's. You think that it is only
natural for earth's multitudes to live and
then die, but you have lost your own
flesh and blood which you brought to
birth with such trouble and pain. But let
me tell you 14 that from the time God created the earth she has suffered as much
in producing human beings for God as
you did in childbirth. 15 So keep your
tears to yourself, and be brave about
what has happened to you. 16 If you will
accept God's decision as just, you will
get your son back at the right time, and
you will receive the praise due a mother.
17 Go back to the city and to your
husband.”

18 “No,” she answered, “I will never go
back; I am going to stay here and die.”

19-20 “Don't do that,” I continued. “Consider the misfortunes and sorrows of Jerusalem, and you won't feel so sorry for
yourself. 21 You can see that our place of
worship is in ruins, our altar has been

torn down, our Temple has been destroyed, 22 our musical instruments lie
quiet, our hymns have been silenced,
our joy has ended, the light of the sacred
lamp has been put out, our Covenant
Box has been carried off, our sacred
utensils have been desecrated, the name
of our God has been profaned, our leaders have been dishonored, our priests
have been burned to death, our Levites
have been taken captive, our virgins
have been raped, our wives have been
violated, our devout men have been carried off, our children have been abandoned, our young people have been
made slaves, and our strong soldiers
have been made helpless. 23 Worst of all,
Jerusalem, once marked as God's own
city, has lost its glory and has been
handed over to our enemies. 24 So put
aside all your sorrow and grief. May
God Most High, the Almighty, be merciful to you and give you peace. May he
give you rest from your troubles."

25 While I was speaking to the woman,
her face suddenly began to shine with a
light that flashed like lightning. I was
afraid to stand near her and wondered
what all this meant. 26 Suddenly she let
out a loud and terrifying cry that shook
the earth. 27 When I looked up, I could no
longer see the woman, but there was a
city built[n] on huge foundations. I was
afraid and shouted, 28 "Where is the angel Uriel, who came to me earlier? It is
his fault that I am so confused. My
prayer is useless, and I have nothing to
hope for but death."

Uriel's Interpretation of the Vision

29 I was still speaking when the angel
Uriel appeared again. He saw me 30 lying
there unconscious like a corpse, so he
took hold of my right hand, gave me
strength, and stood me on my feet. Then
he asked, 31 "What's the matter? Why
are you so disturbed and confused?"

32 I answered, "You abandoned me
completely! I did as you told me and
came out to this field, but I cannot explain what I am seeing."

33 "Stand up straight," he answered,
"and I will explain it to you."

34 "Sir," I answered, "please explain it
to me. I will die in my frustration if you
leave me, 35 for I cannot understand
what I have seen and heard. 36 Or is my
mind playing tricks on me, and is this
just a bad dream? 37 I beg you, sir, tell
me what this vision means."

38 The angel said, "Now listen closely,
and I will explain the meaning of these
things that you fear. God Most High has
revealed many secrets to you 39 because
he has seen that you have lived a righteous life and have always grieved and
mourned for your people and for Jerusalem. 40 This is what the vision means: A
woman appeared to you a little while
ago, 41 and when you saw that she was
mourning, you tried to console her.
42-43 The woman told you about the death
of her son. Then she vanished from your
sight, and a whole city[o] appeared. This
is the meaning: 44 The woman you saw is
Jerusalem, which you now see as a completed city. 45 When she told you that for
thirty years she had had no children, it
meant that for three thousand[p] years no
offerings had yet been made there.
46 Then Solomon built the city, and sacrifices began to be offered there. At that
time the childless woman gave birth to
her son. 47 When she told you that she
took great care in bringing the son up,
that referred to the period when Jerusalem was inhabited. 48 When she told you
of the death of her son on his wedding
day, that meant the destruction of Jerusalem. 49 So in the vision you saw how
she mourned for her son, and you tried
to console her for what had happened—
this is what was to be revealed to you.
50 When God Most High saw that you
were grieving for the woman with all
your heart and soul, he showed you all
her glory and majestic beauty. 51 That is
why I told you to go and stay in the field
where no one had ever lived, 52 for I
knew that God Most High was going to
show you these things. 53 I told you to go
to the field where no foundation had
ever been built, 54 because nothing built
by human hands could stand in the place
where the city of God Most High was
about to be revealed.

55 "So don't be afraid. Go into the city
and look at its beautiful and majestic
buildings. See as much as you can. 56 After that, you will hear as much as you

[n] *Some ancient translations* built; *Latin* being built. [o] *Some ancient translations* whole city; *Latin* city being built. [p] *Some ancient translations* three thousand; *Latin* three.

can. 57 You are more fortunate than most
people, and only a few have the reputation with God Most High that you have.
58 Remain here until tomorrow night,
59 and he will show you in dreams and
visions what he plans to do for those
who will be living on the earth in the last
days." So I slept there that night and the
next, as I had been told.

THE FIFTH VISION

The Vision of an Eagle

11 The second night I had a dream.
I saw an eagle coming up out of
the sea. It had twelve wings and three
heads. 2 As I looked, it spread out its
wings over the whole world. Winds blew
on it from every direction, and clouds[q]
gathered over it. 3 Then from its wings I
saw rival wings begin to grow, but they
were small and insignificant. 4 All three
heads of the eagle were asleep, even the
middle one, which was larger than the
others. 5 While I was watching, the eagle
flew up in the air and became ruler of
the whole earth and all its people. 6 I saw
how everything on earth was brought
under the eagle's control—no one on
earth was able to oppose it. 7 Then I saw
the eagle stand up on its claws and say
to its wings, 8 "Not all of you are to wake
up at the same time; you must sleep
where you are and wake up when your
turn comes, 9 and the heads must wake
up last." 10 I looked again and saw that
the voice was not coming from any of
the eagle's heads but from the middle of
its body. 11 I counted its rival wings, and
there were eight of them.

12 I saw one of the wings on the right
side rise up and govern the whole world.
13 After its rule came to an end, it vanished so completely that it left no trace.
Then the next wing rose up and governed for a long time. 14 When its rule
was coming to an end and it was about
to vanish like the first wing, 15 a voice
said to it, 16 "Listen, you have ruled the
world for a long time, and I want you to
hear this message before you disappear:
17 No one after you will rule as long as
you did—not even half as long." 18 The
third wing rose up and governed as the
earlier ones had done; then it also vanished. 19 The same thing happened to all
the other wings: one after the other they
rose to power and then vanished.

20 I kept looking, and after a while the
other small wings on the right side rose
up to seize power. Some of them governed briefly and quickly disappeared,
21 while others rose up but were never
able to govern. 22 Then I noticed that the
twelve large wings and two of the small
wings had disappeared. 23 Nothing was
left on the eagle's body except the three
sleeping heads and the six small wings.
24 I kept watching, and suddenly two of
the six small wings left the others and
moved under the head on the right side,
while the other four remained where
they were. 25 Then I saw that these four
small wings were plotting to rise up and
seize power. 26 One of them rose up, but
it quickly disappeared. 27 The second
one also rose up, but it disappeared even
more quickly than the first. 28 I saw that
the two remaining small wings were
also plotting to seize control for themselves. 29 While they were making their
plans, one of the sleeping heads suddenly awoke. It was the one in the middle, the one that was larger than the
other two. 30 Then I saw that it was
joined by the other heads, 31 and when it
turned to eat up the two little wings that
were planning to seize power, the other
two heads helped it. 32 This head gained
power over the whole world, established
an oppressive rule over people everywhere, and exercised more power over
the world than any of the other wings
had done before. 33 Then, as I watched,
the middle head disappeared just as suddenly as the wings had done. 34 Two
heads were left, and they also gained
power over the earth and its people;
35 but while I was still watching, the head
on the right ate up the head on the left.

36 Then I heard a voice which said,
"Ezra, look straight ahead and think
about what you see."

37 I looked and saw what appeared to
be an angry lion come roaring out of the
forest. I heard it speak in human language to the eagle and say, 38 "Listen,
Eagle, to what I have to say to you; it is
the message of God Most High: 39 You
are the only one left of the four animals
that I appointed to govern my world and
to bring the ages of this world to an end.

[q] *Some ancient translations* clouds; *Latin does not have this word.*

[40]You are the fourth animal and you
have conquered all the animals that
came before you. As long as you have
been in this world, you have ruled it
through terror, oppression, and deceit,
[41]with a total disregard for truth. [42]You
have viciously attacked harmless people
who were living in peace; you have
hated those who spoke the truth, and
you have loved liars. You have destroyed the homes of those who were
prosperous and have torn down the
walls of those who did you no harm.
[43]God Most High knows how proud and
arrogant you are. The Almighty One
[44]has looked back over the world he established. The end has come; the final
age is over. [45]So, Eagle, the time has
come for you to vanish, along with your
big, terrible wings, your small, wicked
wings, your evil heads, your awful
claws, and your whole worthless body.
[46]The entire world will be set free from
your violence and renewed as it sets its
hope on the judgment and mercy of God,
who created it."

12 While the lion was speaking in
this way to the eagle, I looked
[2]and saw that the last head of the eagle
was gone. Then the two small wings that
had moved over to that head rose up to
govern, but their rule was short and full
of trouble. [3]They disappeared before my
eyes, and the whole body of the eagle
burst into flames, and the world was
terrified.

The Interpretation of the Vision

I was so disturbed and so afraid that I
woke up. I said, [4]"I have brought this on
myself, because I have tried to study the
ways of God Most High. [5]I am mentally
exhausted and completely worn out. The
terrible fears I have experienced this
night have taken my last bit of strength.
[6]All I can do now is pray to God Most
High to give me strength until the end."
[7]Then I prayed, "Master and Lord, if it is
true that you consider me more righteous than many others and if you hear
my prayers, then I beg you, [8]give me
strength. Show me, O Lord, the full
meaning of this terrifying vision, and set
my mind at ease. [9]After all, you did consider me worthy to be shown the end of
this age."

[10]God's angel said to me, "Here is the
interpretation of the vision you saw.
[11]The eagle you saw coming up out of
the sea represents the fourth kingdom in
the vision that your brother Daniel saw.
[12]But he was not given the same interpretation of it that I am giving you.
[13]The time is coming when an empire
will be established on earth that is more
terrible than any before it. [14]Twelve
kings will rule over it, one after the
other. [15]The second king will rule longer
than any of the others. [16]That is the
meaning of the twelve wings that
you saw.

[17]"You heard the voice speaking from
the middle of the eagle's body, instead of
from its heads. [18]That means that after
the rule of the second king, a great struggle for power will take place, and the
empire will be in danger of breaking up.
But that will not happen, and the empire
will regain its earlier power.

[19]"You saw the eight small wings
growing out of the eagle's big wings.
That means [20]that eight kings will rise
up in the empire, but their rule will be
brief and unimportant. [21]Two of them
will appear briefly near the middle of the
period, four of them will not appear until
near the end, and two will be left until
the very end.

[22]"You saw the three heads that were
asleep. That means [23]that in the last
days of the empire, God Most High will
raise up three kings; they[r] will restore
much of the empire and rule over the
world [24]and its people with more harshness than any before them. The reason
they are called the eagle's heads [25]is that
these three kings will bring to a head
and complete the godless work of the eagle. [26]You saw the largest head disappear. This means that one of the kings
will die in his bed, in great agony. [27]The
other two will die in battle. [28]One of
them will kill the other; then he also will
be killed in battle at the end of time.

[29]"You saw the two small wings moving under the head on the right side.
[30]That means that God Most High has
kept them until the end, but their rule
was short and full of trouble, as
you saw.

[31]"You saw the angry lion come roaring out of the forest, and you heard it

[r] *Some ancient translations* they; *Latin* he.

speak to the eagle and rebuke it for the
evil that it had done and for all that it
had said. 32 The lion represents the
Messiah, whom God Most High has held
back until the end. He will be a descendant of David and will come and speak[s]
to the rulers. He will rebuke them for
their wickedness, their sinfulness, and
their contempt for God's ways. 33 While
they are still living, he will bring them to
judgment, condemn them for their sin,
and destroy them. 34 But he will have
mercy on the rest of my people, those
who are left in my land; he will set them
free and make them happy until the end
comes, the Judgment Day about which I
told you at the beginning.

35 "That is the dream you had, and that
is its interpretation. 36 But you are the
only one that God Most High has considered worthy to reveal this secret to. 37 So
write in a book everything you saw, and
put it in a safe hiding place. 38 Then
teach these secrets to those who are wise
among your people, those who will be
able to understand them and keep them
secret. 39 But you must stay here seven
more days, so that God Most High may
reveal to you whatever he wishes." Then
the angel left me.

The People Come to Ezra

40 When the seven days had passed
and all the people heard that I had not
yet returned to the city, all of them, rich
and poor, came and asked me, 41 "What
wrong have we done to you? How have
we mistreated you? Why have you abandoned us and settled down in this place?
42 You are the only one of all our prophets who is left. You are like the last
bunch of grapes in a vineyard, like a lan-
tern in a dark place, like a safe harbor
for a ship in a storm. 43 Haven't we suffered enough already? 44 If you abandon
us, it would have been better if we had
died like the others in the fire that destroyed Jerusalem. 45 We are no better
than those who died." Then they all
started crying loudly.

I answered, 46 "Be brave, Israel, put
away your sorrow. 47 God Most High will
keep you in mind; the Almighty One has
not forgotten you in all your troubles.
48 And I haven't left you or abandoned
you. I came here to pray for Jerusalem in
her time of trouble and to ask mercy for
her and for your Temple, now in disgrace. 49 Please return to your homes, all
of you. I will come back to you in a few
days." 50 So they left me and went back
to the city.

THE SIXTH VISION

The Vision

51 I stayed in the field for seven days,
as the angel had commanded me. I ate
nothing but wild flowers; I was a vege-
tarian in those days.

13 The seven days passed, and the
following night I had a dream.
2 In my dream I saw a wind coming up
out of the sea and stirring up great
waves. 3 As I watched, the wind brought
with it out of the sea what looked like a
man,[t] and he was flying[u] on the
clouds. When he turned his face, everything he looked at began to tremble,
4 and when he spoke, everyone who
heard his voice melted like wax in a fire.

5 I looked again and saw a crowd too
large to count. They were people gathered together from all parts of the world
to fight against the man who had come
up out of the sea. 6 Then I watched the
man carve out a high mountain and fly
up on it. 7 I tried to see the place or the
region from which the mountain was
carved, but I couldn't. 8 Then I saw that
all the people who had come together to
make war against him were terrified, but
they still prepared to fight him. 9 When
the man saw the great crowd advancing
to attack him, he did not take up any
weapons. 10 The only thing I saw was
what looked like a stream of fire coming
out of his mouth. He sent a flaming wind
from his lips and a storm of sparks from
his tongue. The stream of fire, the flaming wind, and the great storm combined
11 and swept down on the crowd that was
coming to attack him, and burned them
all up. In a single moment, that crowd
too large to count vanished, and there
was nothing left but powdery ashes and
the smell of smoke. I was shocked when
I saw what had happened.

12 Then I saw the man come down
from the mountain and call another

[s] *Some ancient translations* He will . . . speak; *Latin does not have these words.*
[t] *Some ancient translations* the wind . . . man; *Latin does not have these words.*
[u] *Some ancient translations* flying; *Latin* growing strong.

large crowd to come to him—this was a
peace-loving crowd. 13All sorts of people came: some were happy, some were
sad, some had their hands and feet tied,
and some brought others as a gift to the
Lord.

The Interpretation of the Vision

I was so frightened that I woke up. I
prayed to God Most High and said,
14"Lord, you have been showing me all
these marvelous things. You have considered me worthy and have heard my
prayers. 15Now please show me the
meaning of this dream also. 16I have
been thinking how terrible it will be for
the people who will be living in those
days, but how much worse for those who
do not survive. 17They will be in great
sorrow 18because they will not enjoy
any of the pleasures reserved for the last
days. 19But how terrible also for those
who do survive; they will have to face
great dangers and many troubles, as
these dreams have shown. 20Neverthe-
less, it is better to pass through these
dangers and reach the end than to disappear like a cloud from this world and
never see what takes place in the last
days."

He answered, 21"I will explain to you
the meaning of the vision and answer
the questions you have asked. 22You
have raised questions about those who
will survive until the end. The answer is
that 23the one who brings the dangers in
those days will also protect from danger
the people who have stored up good
works and faithfulness with God the
Almighty One. 24You may be certain
that those who survive are far more fortunate than those who die.

25"This is the meaning of the vision.
The man you saw coming up out of the
sea 26represents the one whom God
Most High has kept ready for many
ages. He will free the world he created
and establish the new order for those
who survive. 27You saw the wind, fire,
and storm going out of the man's mouth,
28and you saw that without the use of a
spear or any other weapon he destroyed
the great crowd that was advancing to
attack him. This means that 29the time is
near when God Most High will begin to
free the people on earth. 30At that time
everyone will be close to panic. 31They
will begin to make war against one another, city against city, region against
region, nation against nation, and kingdom against kingdom. 32When that happens, the signs I told you about earlier
will take place, and then I will reveal my
son, whom you saw as a man coming out
of the sea. 33When they hear his voice,
all the nations will leave their own territory, forget their wars with one another,
34and come together in one great crowd
too large to count, as you saw in your
dream. The nations will unite with the
single purpose of making war on my
son. 35He will take his stand on the top
of Mount Zion, 36and the new Jerusalem
will be seen by everyone. It will be completed and fully built, just as in your
dream you saw the mountain carved out,
but not by human hands. 37Then my son
will condemn the assembled nations for
their godlessness. That is what the storm
meant. 38He will confront them with the
wicked plans they have made and also
with the torments they must endure.
That is what the flames meant. Then he
will easily destroy them by means of[v]
the Law. That is what the fire meant.

39"You saw him gather another great
crowd of peace-loving people. 40These
are the ten tribes of Israel who were
taken away into captivity in the time of
King Hoshea. King Shalmaneser of Assyria captured them and deported them
to a foreign land east of the Euphrates
River. 41But the ten tribes decided not to
stay in that land among the many Gentiles, so they moved farther east to a
country where no human beings had
ever lived before. 42There they hoped to
keep their laws, which they had failed to
keep in their own country. 43When they
had to make the difficult passage across
the Euphrates, 44God Most High performed miracles for them and blocked
the channels of the river until they had
crossed over. 45Their long journey
through that region, which is named Ar-
zareth, took a year and a half, 46and they
have lived there ever since. Now in these
last days they are coming back home,
47and once again God Most High will
block the channels of the river, so that
they may cross over. That is the meaning of the great crowd of peace-loving

[v] *One ancient translation* by means of; *Latin* and.

people you saw. 48 But they will also
have with them all of your own people
who are left and who are found within
the borders of my holy land. 49 When the
time comes for my son to destroy the
crowd that has gathered from every nation, he will protect his people who are
left 50 and perform many great miracles
for them."

51 Then I said, "Lord and Master,
please tell me why the man came up out
of the sea."

52 He answered, "No one can explore
the bottom of the sea to find out what is
there. In the same way, no human being
can see my son or those who come with
him until the day that has been fixed.
53 That is the meaning of your dream.
You alone have been given this information, 54 because you have given up your
own interests to devote yourself to mine
and to the study of my Law. 55 You have
dedicated your life to wisdom, and
understanding has been like a mother to
you. 56 That is why God Most High has
rewarded you by showing you these
things. After three days, I will come
back and tell you about other profound
wonders."

THE SEVENTH VISION

The Voice from the Bush

57 I went for a walk in the field, worshiping and praising God Most High for
the miracles he performs in his own
good time. 58 For he controls the ages
and what happens in them. I remained
there for three days.

14 On the third day, while I was sitting under an oak tree, 2 suddenly a voice came out of a bush near
me and called, "Ezra! Ezra!"

I stood up and answered, "Here I am,
Lord."

3 The voice continued, "I revealed myself from a bush and spoke to Moses
when my people were slaves in Egypt.
4 I sent him to lead them out of Egypt,
and I brought them to Mount Sinai. I
kept Moses with me there on the mountain for a long time, 5 while I told him the
secrets about the ages and the end of
time. I told him 6 what to make public
and what to keep secret. 7 Now I command you 8 to memorize the signs, visions, and interpretations that I have
given you. 9 You will be taken out of this
world into the heavenly world where
you and others like you will live with my
son until the end of time. 10 The world is
no longer young; it is rapidly approaching old age. 11 The whole history of the
world is divided into twelve periods, and
the tenth period has already arrived
12 and it is half over; only two and a half
parts remain. 13 So set your house in order, warn your people, comfort those
who are humble, and teach those who
are wise.[w] Then say good-bye to this
mortal life. 14 Put earthly cares away
from you, throw down your human burdens, and lay aside your weak human
nature. 15 Put all your anxieties aside,
and get ready to leave this world
quickly. 16 You have seen many evil
things already, but far worse things are
about to happen. 17 As the world grows
older and weaker, the evils that will
come upon its people will multiply.
18 Truth will depart and falsehood will
draw ever nearer. The eagle you saw in
your vision is just about to arrive."

Ezra Reproduces the Sacred Writings

19 I replied, "Let me speak[x] in your
presence, Lord. 20 I am ready to depart,
as you have commanded, and I will warn
the present generation; but who will
warn the people who have not yet been
born? This world is a dark place, and its
people have no light. 21 Your Law has
been destroyed by fire, so no one can
know what you have done in the past or
what you are planning to do in the future. 22 Please send your holy spirit to
me, so that I can write down everything
that has been done in this world from
the beginning, everything that was written in your Law. Then in these last days,
people will be able to find the right way
and obtain life if they want to."

23 He answered, "Go and call the people together and tell them not to look for
you for forty days. 24 Prepare a large
number of writing tablets, and take with
you these five men who can write fast:
Seraiah, Dabriah, Shelemiah, Ethan,
and Asiel. 25 Then come here, and I will
light the lamp of understanding in your

[w] *Some ancient translations* teach . . . wise; *Latin does not have these words.*
[x] *Some ancient translations* Let me speak; *Latin does not have these words.*

heart, and it will not go out until you
have finished what you are supposed to
write. 26 When you have finished your
work, you will make some of it public,
and you will give the rest to some wise
people, who will keep it secret. Tomorrow at this time you will begin to write."
27 I did as I was commanded and
called all the people together. I said,
28 "Listen to what I have to say, people of
Israel. 29 At first our ancestors lived as
foreigners in Egypt, but then they were
set free 30 and received from God the life-
giving Law. But they did not keep it, and
when your turn came, you did not keep
it either. 31 God gave you the holy land as
your own possession, but you were as
sinful as your ancestors and did not follow the ways that God Most High had
commanded. 32 God is a just judge, so after a while he took away what he had
given you. 33 Now you are in exile here,
but you are closer to Jerusalem than
some of your own people.[y] 34 But if you
will discipline your thoughts and be willing to learn, you will be kept safe in this
life and will be granted mercy after
death, 35 for Judgment Day comes after
death. We will be brought back to life,
and the righteous people will be made
known, while what the godless have
done will be exposed. 36 But now for
forty days, no one is to come near me or
try to find me."
37 As I had been commanded, I took
the five men, and we went to the field
and stayed there. 38 On the next day I
suddenly heard a voice saying, "Ezra,
open your mouth and drink what I am
giving you." 39 So I opened my mouth,
and I was handed a cup full of a fiery-
colored liquid, 40 which I took and drank.
When I had drunk it, my mind overflowed with understanding, and wisdom
increased within me as my memory became perfect. 41 I began to speak and
went on talking without stopping. 42 God
Most High also gave wisdom to the five
men with me, and they took turns writing down what I said. They used an alphabet[z] that they had not known
before, and worked for forty days, writing in the daytime and eating at night.
43 I spoke all day long, and I was not silent even at night. 44 During the forty
days, ninety-four[a] books were written.
45 At the end of the forty days, God
Most High said to me, "You are now to
make public the first twenty-four[b]
books[c] that you wrote, so that everyone, whether they are worthy or not,
may read them. 46 But the last seventy
books that you wrote are to be held back
and to be given only to those who are
wise among your people, 47 because
these books contain a flood of understanding, a fountain of wisdom, and a
river of knowledge." 48 Then I did as I
was told.

ADDITIONAL PROPHECIES

The Coming Disasters

15 The Lord says, "Proclaim to my
people the prophetic messages
that I will give you, 2 and then have them
written down, because they are true and
will be fulfilled. 3 Do not be afraid of
those who plot against you or be disturbed by their unbelief. 4 All unbelievers will die because of their unbelief."
5 The Lord says, "I am going to bring
terrible disasters on the whole world—
war and famine, death and destruction,
6 because wickedness has spread everywhere, and evil has reached its limit."
7 "Therefore," the Lord says, 8 "I will no
longer remain silent about the wickedness of these godless people; I will no
longer tolerate it. They have murdered
innocent people, and the blood they
have spilled cries out to me for revenge;
the souls of the righteous are constantly
pleading for vengeance. 9 Let there be no
doubt," says the Lord, "I will hear the
plea of all the innocent people who have
been murdered and I will take vengeance for what has been done to them.
10 "My people are being led to the
slaughter like a flock of sheep. They will
no longer have to live in Egypt; 11 I will
use all my strength and power to bring
them out of that land. I will bring disasters upon the Egyptians, as I did earlier,
and I will destroy their country. 12 The
whole land will be in mourning; it will be
shaken to its foundations when I, the
Lord, strike it and pound on it. 13 The

[y] but . . . own people; *Latin unclear.* [z] *Some ancient translations* an alphabet; *Latin unclear.*
[a] *Some ancient translations* ninety-four; *Latin unclear.* [b] *Some ancient translations* twenty-four; *Latin does not have this word.* [c] TWENTY-FOUR BOOKS: *The Hebrew Bible contains twenty-four books, corresponding to the thirty-nine books of the Christian Old Testament.*

farmers will mourn because their seed
will fail to sprout, and their trees will be
destroyed by blight, hail, and terrible
storms.
14 "The world and the people in it are
doomed. 15 The war that will bring their
destruction is very near. Nations will
arm themselves and fight against other
nations. 16 There will be great political
turmoil, with one group trying to overpower another and gain control, while
ignoring the legitimate government.
17 There will no longer be free access to
the cities, 18 because the struggle for
power will bring destruction, terror, and
total confusion wherever people live.
19 Driven by famine and terrible suffering, people will assault their neighbors
and mercilessly plunder their possessions."
20 God says, "I am calling together all
the kings of the earth to come from
north, south, east, and west to turn back
and restore what they have taken.
21 I will pay them back with the same
harsh treatment they have always given
to my chosen people." The Lord says,
22 "I will use my power, and there will be
no mercy for sinners; I will put to death
all who have murdered innocent people.
23 My anger has become so fierce that
fire has blazed out to burn up the foundations of the earth and to burn up sinners like straw. 24 Sinners who do not
keep my commands are doomed," says
the Lord. 25 "I will have no mercy on
them! Out of my sight, you rebels! Do
not defile my holy Temple."

A Terrifying Vision

26 God is aware of all those who sin
against him, and he will hand them over
to death and destruction. 27 Terrible disasters have already come upon the
world, and there is no escape. You have
sinned against God, and he will not rescue you.
28 Then in the east you will suddenly
see a fearsome sight. 29 Arab armies with
many chariots will advance like dragons. As soon as they start out, the sound
of their hissing will spread across the
world and bring fear and trembling to
everyone who hears it. 30 The Carmoni-
ans will come out of the forest in a fierce
rage like wild boars advancing in full
strength to attack the dragons. With
their tusks they will tear up a large part
of Assyria, 31 but the dragons will unite
their forces, regain their former
strength, and win the victory. They will
turn and pursue the wild boars, 32 who
will be thrown into panic, beaten into silence, and forced to turn and run. 33 The
wild boars will be ambushed in Assyria,
and one of them will be killed. This will
bring fear and panic to their army and
indecision to their kings.
34 Then suddenly clouds—terrible, angry storm clouds—will cover the sky
from one end to the other. 35 They will
collide head-on and release their violence upon the earth. The blood of war
will be as deep as a horse's belly 36 or
someone's thigh or a camel's knee.
37 Everywhere on earth people will tremble in fear at the horrible sight. 38 Then
great storm clouds will move in from the
north and the south, and others from the
west. 39 But the winds from the east will
prevail and push back those angry storm
clouds that were about to bring destruction.[d] 40-41 Huge, powerful, angry storm
clouds will arise and ruin the whole
world and its people. A terrible storm of
fire, hail, and flashing swords will come
sweeping down on those who have
power and authority.[e] Every river will
overflow into the fields, and the floods
42 will demolish cities, walls, mountains,
hills, forests, and crops. 43-44 This destruction will press on until it reaches
Babylon and engulfs it in a raging storm
of ruin. The dust and the smoke will
form a great cloud reaching to the sky,
and all the neighboring cities will mourn
for Babylon. 45 Anyone who survives
will become a slave to those who destroyed the city.

Asia Is Doomed

46-47 You, Asia, are to be pitied. You
are doomed! You have enjoyed the
splendor and glory of Babylon. You
have imitated her and dressed up your
daughters to look like prostitutes to
please and gratify your lovers, who have
always lusted for you. 48 Because you
have imitated that vile prostitute in
everything she has done or planned,

[d] *Verse 39 in Latin is unclear.* [e] those who have power and authority; *or* every hill and mountain.

God has this to say: 49“I will send disasters upon you. I will make you a widow
and send poverty, famine, war, and epidemics to destroy your homes and bring
ruin and death. 50The power of which
you boast will wither like a flower when
the burning heat is sent upon you. 51You
will be a wretched, weak woman so
bruised, beaten, and wounded that you
will no longer attract your wealthy lovers. 52I would not punish you so severely,” says the Lord, 53“if you had not
murdered my chosen people. But you
took great delight in striking them, and
when you were drunk, you boasted
about killing them.

54“Paint your face! 55You will be paid
for your work as a prostitute; you will
get what you have earned. 56I will pay
you back,” says the Lord, “for what you
have done to my chosen people. I will
bring disaster on you. 57You will be put
to death, and your children will starve.
Your cities will be torn down, and the
people out in the country will be killed.
58Those in the mountains will starve;
their hunger and thirst will drive them to
eat their own flesh and drink their own
blood. 59You will be more miserable
than anyone has ever been, but there
will be still more punishment to come.
60The army that destroyed Babylon will
march back through your country and
devastate your peaceful city; they will
destroy your beautiful country and leave
most of it in ruins. 61Your country will
be destroyed like straw in a fire. 62They
will burn up all your forests and orchards. All over your land, your cities
and mountains will be covered with ruins. 63Your splendor will vanish; your
children will be carried off as prisoners;
your possessions will be plundered.”

16 Babylonia, Asia, Egypt, and
Syria, you are doomed! 2Put on
your clothes of mourning, your sackcloth and goat’s hair. Cry and wail for
your children because the time for your
destruction is near. 3I am sending war
on you, and no one can stop it. 4I am
sending fire on you, and no one can put
it out. 5I am sending disasters on you,
and no one can stop them from coming.
6Can anyone stop a hungry lion in the
forest or put out a fire that is burning in
straw 7or turn back an arrow shot by a
strong archer? 8When the Lord God
sends disaster, no one can hold it back.
9No one can escape the blazing anger of
the Lord. 10When he sends lightning, no
one can keep from trembling; and when
it thunders, everyone is afraid. 11When
the Lord makes his threats, no one can
keep from falling to the ground in his
presence. 12The foundations of the earth
tremble. There is violent churning in the
deepest part of the sea. Even the creatures in the sea are in turmoil when the
Lord makes his glorious power felt. 13He
is like a mighty archer whose strong
right arm bends the bow. His arrows are
sharp and never miss their mark once
they are shot out toward any part of the
earth. 14He has already sent out his disasters toward the earth, and they will
not miss their target. 15The fire has been
lit, and it cannot be put out until it burns
up the foundations of the earth. 16The
disasters are on their way toward the
earth, and like an arrow shot by a strong
archer, they cannot be turned back.

17I’m doomed! I’m doomed! Who will
rescue me in those days? 18Troubles will
come, and many people will groan. Famine will come, and many will die. Wars
will come, and the world powers will
tremble. Disasters will come, and everyone will be terrified. What will people do
when these disasters come? 19Famine,
epidemics, troubles, and suffering are
sent to punish and correct people. 20But
in spite of all this, they will not turn
away from their sins; they soon forget
their punishment. 21The time is coming
when food will be so cheap that people
will think a time of peace and plenty has
arrived. But then disasters will spring up
everywhere—wars, famine, and great
confusion. 22Many people on earth will
starve to death, and those who escape
starvation will be killed in war. 23Their
corpses will be thrown out like garbage,
and there will be no one left to comfort
the living. The earth will be deserted and
its cities demolished. 24There will be no
one left to plow the land or plant it.
25Trees will bear their fruit, but there
will be no one left to pick it. 26Grapes
will ripen, but there will be no one left to
make wine. There will be desolation
everywhere, 27and a person will long to
see the face of another human being or
even to hear another person’s voice.
28Only ten will be left out of a whole city,
and in the countryside, only two, who
have hidden in the forest or in caves.

29 When an olive grove is harvested,
three or four olives may be left on each
tree. 30 When grapes in a vineyard are
picked, a few bunches may be left even
by those who look carefully. 31 That is
how it will be in those days. Three or
four will be missed by the soldiers who
search through the houses to kill everyone. 32 The land will be left empty; the
fields will be overgrown with briers; the
roads and paths will be covered with
weeds and thorns because there will be
no sheep to graze along them. 33 Young
women will be in mourning because
there is no one to marry them; wives will
be in mourning because they have lost
their husbands; daughters will be in
mourning because there is no one to
help them. 34 All the young men will be
killed in the war, and all the married
men will die in the famine.

God's People Must Prepare for the End

35 Now listen to my message, you people who serve the Lord. 36 It is the Lord's
message, so receive it and believe what
he says. 37 The disasters are approaching
rapidly, and they will not be delayed.
38 A woman in the ninth month of pregnancy may suffer labor pains for several
hours, but when the time comes for the
baby to be born, there is no longer any
delay. 39 In the same way, the disasters
that are coming on the earth will not be
delayed, and the world will groan when
it is caught in its labor pains.

40 Listen to my message, my people,
and get ready for the battle. When the
disasters come, you must live as people
whose home is not in this world.
41-42 Merchants must not expect to make
a profit from what they sell; they must
be ready to run for their lives. Their customers must expect to lose whatever
they buy. Whoever builds a house
should not plan to live in it. 43 Farmers
should not expect to harvest their crops
or pick their grapes. 44 Those who marry
must not expect to have children, and
those who don't marry must live as if
they had been widowed. 45 Anything that
is done will be useless. 46 Foreigners will
harvest the crops, seize the wealth, tear
down the houses, and carry off the children as slaves. Anyone who has children
will be bringing them up to be slaves or
to die of starvation. 47 Anyone who
makes money will do so only to see it
violently taken away. The more possessions people gather, the more they
spend on their cities and houses, the
more attention they give to their personal appearance, 48 the more angry the
Lord will become with them because of
their sin. This is what the Lord says.
49 Just as a respectable woman despises
a prostitute, 50 so righteousness despises
sinfulness, no matter how attractive it
may look. Righteousness will expose
every sin in the world and condemn it
face-to-face when her Defender comes.
51 So do not imitate sinfulness or what it
does, 52 for in a very short time sinfulness will be swept out of the world and
righteousness will rule among us.

53 Sinners must not deny their sins.
Those who say that they have not sinned
against God and his majesty are only
bringing fiery shame upon themselves.
54 The Lord certainly knows everything
that people do; he knows their plans and
innermost thoughts. 55 When the Lord
said, "Let the world be created," it was
done! When he said, "Let the sky be created," that was done too. 56 He set the
stars in place by his command, and he
knows how many of them there are.
57 He knows what is in the deepest part
of the sea and the treasures that are
there. He has measured the sea and
everything that is in it. 58 By his word he
confined the sea to its place and put the
land on top of the water. 59 The Lord
stretched out the sky and fixed it firmly
over the water like a dome. 60 He put
springs of water in the desert and lakes
in the high mountains, so that water
could flow down in the rivers and water
the land. 61 The Lord created human beings and gave each one of them a heart.
He gave them life, breath, and understanding, 62 which is the spirit of God the
Almighty, who created everything and
who knows all secrets and sees into all
hidden places. 63 My people, the Lord
knows everything you plan and the secret thoughts of your heart. Sinners who
try to hide their sins are doomed. 64 The
Lord will carefully examine everything
you have done and bring you to judgment. 65 On that day you will be thrown
into utter confusion; all your sins will be
publicly exposed and the wicked things
you have done will witness against you.

66 What will you do then? How will you
hide your sins from God and his angels?
67 God is your judge, so fear him! Abandon your sins, put away the evil you
have done, and never sin again. Then
God will save you from all these
disasters.

68 A vast mob of people is ready now
to descend on you and devour you like
flames. They will drag some of you off
and force you to eat pagan sacrifices.
69 If you give in to them, they will ridicule you, mock you, and humiliate you.
70 In many places near the cities[f] there
will be violent persecution against those
who fear the Lord. 71 The attackers will
act like wild people; they will plunder
and destroy without pity all those who
still fear the Lord. 72 They will turn them
out of their homes and take away all
their possessions. 73 This will be the time
of testing for my chosen people, and
they will prove to be as pure as refined
gold.

74 But listen to what the Lord says:
"My chosen people, the time of terrible
suffering is near, but I will rescue you.
75 Don't be afraid or have any doubts; I
am your God and I will lead you. 76 If you
keep my laws and commands," says the
Lord, "you must not let your sins weigh
you down or control you. 77 Those who
are chained by their sins, overwhelmed
by the evil they have done, are doomed.
They will be like a field overgrown with
brush, with the path across it so choked
with thorns that no one can get through.
78 It is abandoned and doomed to be destroyed by fire."

[f] In . . . cities; *Latin unclear.*

THE PRAYER OF MANASSEH

Introduction

The Prayer of Manasseh *is a beautiful short prayer of repentance. It is presented as a prayer by Manasseh, the wicked king of Judah, referred to in* 2 Chronicles 33.12,18,19.

---

1 Lord Almighty, God of our
ancestors,
God of Abraham, Isaac, and
Jacob,
God of their righteous
descendants,
2 you created the universe
and all the splendor that fills it.
3 The sea obeys your command
and never overflows its bounds.
The power of your wonderful,
glorious name
keeps the ocean depths in their
place.
4 When you show your power,
all creation trembles.
5 Your glorious splendor is
overwhelming,
and your anger is more than
sinners can endure.
6 But the mercy you promise is also
greater
than we can understand or
measure.
7 For you are the Lord Most High;
you are patient and show mercy
and compassion.
You make our punishment easier
to bear
when we suffer for our sins.
O Lord, in your great goodness
and mercy
you promise forgiveness and
salvation
to those who repent of their sin
against you.[a]

[a] O Lord . . . against you; *some manuscripts do not have these words.*

8 You, Lord, are the God of
righteous people.
Repentance was not necessary
for Abraham, Isaac, and Jacob,
for they did not sin against you.
But for sinners like me
you have made repentance
possible.
9 I have committed more sins
than there are grains of sand
along the seashore.
They are so many, Lord, they are
so many.
I have done so much that is wrong
that I am not worthy to turn my
face toward heaven.
10 I am crushed beneath the weight
of my sin;[b]
I am bowed down by its heavy
iron chain.
I can find no relief,
for I have made you angry.
I have set up idols everywhere;
I have done what you hate.
11 But now I bow in deep humility,
praying for your mercy.
12 I have sinned, Lord, I have sinned;
I confess the wicked things I
have done.
13 I beg you, Lord, I earnestly pray:
forgive me, forgive me.
Do not destroy me because of my
sins;
do not stay angry with me
forever
or store up punishment for me.
Do not condemn me to the world
of the dead,
for you, O Lord, forgive those
who repent.
14 Show me all your mercy and
kindness and save me,
even though I do not deserve it.
15 Then I will go on praising you as
long as I live.
All the heavenly powers sing your
praises,
and your glory endures forever.
Amen.

[b] *crushed* . . . my sin; *Greek unclear.*

HOLY BIBLE

Today's English Version

The New Testament

The Gospel according to
MATTHEW

Introduction

The Gospel according to Matthew *tells the good news that Jesus is the promised Savior, the one through whom God fulfilled the promises he made to his people in the Old Testament. This good news is not only for the Jewish people, among whom Jesus was born and lived, but for the whole world.*

Matthew *is carefully arranged. It begins with the birth of Jesus, describes his baptism and temptation, and then takes up his ministry of preaching, teaching, and healing in Galilee. After this the Gospel records Jesus' journey from Galilee to Jerusalem and the events of Jesus' last week, culminating in his crucifixion and resurrection.*

This Gospel presents Jesus as the great Teacher, who has the authority to interpret the Law of God, and who teaches about the Kingdom of God. Much of his teaching is gathered by subject matter into five collections: (1) the Sermon on the Mount, which concerns the character, duties, privileges, and destiny of the citizens of the Kingdom of heaven (chapters 5–7); (2) instructions to the twelve disciples for their mission (chapter 10); (3) parables about the Kingdom of heaven (chapter 13); (4) teaching on the meaning of discipleship (chapter 18); and (5) teaching about the end of the present age and the coming of the Kingdom of God (chapters 24–25).

Outline of Contents

The Ancestors of Jesus Christ
(Luke 3.23-38)

1 This is the list of the ancestors of
Jesus Christ, a descendant of David, who was a descendant of Abraham.
2-6a From Abraham to King David, the
following ancestors are listed: Abraham,
Isaac, Jacob, Judah and his brothers;
then Perez and Zerah (their mother was
Tamar), Hezron, Ram, Amminadab,
Nahshon, Salmon, Boaz (his mother was
Rahab), Obed (his mother was Ruth),
Jesse, and King David.
6b-11 From David to the time when the
people of Israel were taken into exile in
Babylon, the following ancestors are
listed: David, Solomon (his mother was
the woman who had been Uriah's wife),
Rehoboam, Abijah, Asa, Jehoshaphat,
Jehoram, Uzziah, Jotham, Ahaz, Hezekiah, Manasseh, Amon, Josiah, and Jehoiachin and his brothers.
12-16 From the time after the exile in
Babylon to the birth of Jesus, the following ancestors are listed: Jehoiachin,
Shealtiel, Zerubbabel, Abiud, Eliakim,
Azor, Zadok, Achim, Eliud, Eleazar,
Matthan, Jacob, and Joseph, who married Mary, the mother of Jesus, who was
called the Messiah.
17 So then, there were fourteen generations from Abraham to David, and fourteen from David to the exile in Babylon,
and fourteen from then to the birth of
the Messiah.

The Birth of Jesus Christ
(Luke 2.1-7)

18 This was how the birth of Jesus
Christ took place. His mother Mary was
engaged to Joseph, but before they were
married, she found out that she was going to have a baby by the Holy Spirit.
19 Joseph was a man who always did
what was right, but he did not want to
disgrace Mary publicly; so he made
plans to break the engagement privately. 20 While he was thinking about
this, an angel of the Lord appeared to
him in a dream and said, "Joseph,
descendant of David, do not be afraid to

take Mary to be your wife. For it is by
the Holy Spirit that she has conceived.
21 She will have a son, and you will name
him Jesus—because he will save his
people from their sins."

22 Now all this happened in order to
make come true what the Lord had said
through the prophet, 23 "A virgin will become pregnant and have a son, and he
will be called Immanuel" (which means,
"God is with us").

24 So when Joseph woke up, he married Mary, as the angel of the Lord had
told him to. 25 But he had no sexual relations with her before she gave birth to
her son. And Joseph named him Jesus.

Visitors from the East

2 Jesus was born in the town of Bethlehem in Judea, during the time
when Herod was king. Soon afterward,
some men who studied the stars came
from the East to Jerusalem 2 and asked,
"Where is the baby born to be the king of
the Jews? We saw his star when it came
up in the east, and we have come to worship him."

3 When King Herod heard about this,
he was very upset, and so was everyone
else in Jerusalem. 4 He called together all
the chief priests and the teachers of the
Law and asked them, "Where will the
Messiah be born?"

5 "In the town of Bethlehem in Judea,"
they answered. "For this is what the
prophet wrote:

6 'Bethlehem in the land of Judah,
you are by no means the least of
the leading cities of Judah;
for from you will come a leader
who will guide my people
Israel.' "

7 So Herod called the visitors from the
East to a secret meeting and found out
from them the exact time the star had
appeared. 8 Then he sent them to Bethlehem with these instructions: "Go and
make a careful search for the child; and
when you find him, let me know, so that
I too may go and worship him."

9-10 And so they left, and on their way
they saw the same star they had seen in
the East. When they saw it, how happy
they were, what joy was theirs! It went
ahead of them until it stopped over the
place where the child was. 11 They went
into the house, and when they saw the
child with his mother Mary, they knelt
down and worshiped him. They brought
out their gifts of gold, frankincense, and
myrrh, and presented them to him.

12 Then they returned to their country
by another road, since God had warned
them in a dream not to go back to Herod.

The Escape to Egypt

13 After they had left, an angel of the
Lord appeared in a dream to Joseph and
said, "Herod will be looking for the child
in order to kill him. So get up, take the
child and his mother and escape to
Egypt, and stay there until I tell you to
leave."

14 Joseph got up, took the child and his
mother, and left during the night for
Egypt, 15 where he stayed until Herod
died. This was done to make come true
what the Lord had said through the
prophet, "I called my Son out of Egypt."

The Killing of the Children

16 When Herod realized that the visitors from the East had tricked him, he
was furious. He gave orders to kill all the
boys in Bethlehem and its neighborhood
who were two years old and younger—
this was done in accordance with what
he had learned from the visitors about
the time when the star had appeared.

17 In this way what the prophet Jeremiah had said came true:

18 "A sound is heard in Ramah,
the sound of bitter weeping.
Rachel is crying for her children;
she refuses to be comforted,
for they are dead."

The Return from Egypt

19 After Herod died, an angel of the
Lord appeared in a dream to Joseph in
Egypt 20 and said, "Get up, take the child
and his mother, and go back to the land
of Israel, because those who tried to kill
the child are dead." 21 So Joseph got up,
took the child and his mother, and went
back to Israel.

22 But when Joseph heard that Arche-
laus had succeeded his father Herod as
king of Judea, he was afraid to go there.
He was given more instructions in a
dream, so he went to the province of
Galilee 23 and made his home in a town
named Nazareth. And so what the
prophets had said came true: "He will be
called a Nazarene."

The Preaching of John the Baptist

(Mark 1.1-8; Luke 3.1-18; John 1.19-28)

3 At that time John the Baptist came
to the desert of Judea and started
preaching. 2 "Turn away from your
sins," he said, "because the Kingdom of
heaven is near!" 3 John was the man the
prophet Isaiah was talking about when
he said,

"Someone is shouting in the
desert,
'Prepare a road for the Lord;
make a straight path for him to
travel!' "

4 John's clothes were made of camel's
hair; he wore a leather belt around his
waist, and his food was locusts and wild
honey. 5 People came to him from Jerusalem, from the whole province of Judea, and from all over the country near
the Jordan River. 6 They confessed their
sins, and he baptized them in the
Jordan.
7 When John saw many Pharisees and
Sadducees coming to him to be baptized,
he said to them, "You snakes—who told
you that you could escape from the punishment God is about to send? 8 Do those
things that will show that you have
turned from your sins. 9 And don't think
you can escape punishment by saying
that Abraham is your ancestor. I tell you
that God can take these rocks and make
descendants for Abraham! 10 The ax is
ready to cut down the trees at the roots;
every tree that does not bear good fruit
will be cut down and thrown in the fire.
11 I baptize you with water to show that
you have repented, but the one who will
come after me will baptize you with the
Holy Spirit and fire. He is much greater
than I am; and I am not good enough
even to carry his sandals. 12 He has his
winnowing shovel with him to thresh
out all the grain. He will gather his
wheat into his barn, but he will burn the
chaff in a fire that never goes out."

The Baptism of Jesus

(Mark 1.9-11; Luke 3.21, 22)

13 At that time Jesus arrived from Galilee and came to John at the Jordan to be
baptized by him. 14 But John tried to
make him change his mind. "I ought to
be baptized by you," John said, "and yet
you have come to me!"
15 But Jesus answered him, "Let it be
so for now. For in this way we shall do
all that God requires." So John agreed.
16 As soon as Jesus was baptized, he
came up out of the water. Then heaven
was opened to him, and he saw the Spirit
of God coming down like a dove and
lighting on him. 17 Then a voice said
from heaven, "This is my own dear Son,
with whom I am pleased."

The Temptation of Jesus

(Mark 1.12, 13; Luke 4.1-13)

4 Then the Spirit led Jesus into the
desert to be tempted by the Devil.
2 After spending forty days and nights
without food, Jesus was hungry. 3 Then
the Devil came to him and said, "If you
are God's Son, order these stones to turn
into bread."
4 But Jesus answered, "The scripture
says, 'Human beings cannot live on
bread alone, but need every word that
God speaks.' "
5 Then the Devil took Jesus to Jerusalem, the Holy City, set him on the highest point of the Temple, 6 and said to
him, "If you are God's Son, throw yourself down, for the scripture says,

'God will give orders to his angels
about you;
they will hold you up with their
hands,
so that not even your feet will be
hurt on the stones.' "

7 Jesus answered, "But the scripture
also says, 'Do not put the Lord your God
to the test.' "
8 Then the Devil took Jesus to a very
high mountain and showed him all the
kingdoms of the world in all their greatness. 9 "All this I will give you," the Devil
said, "if you kneel down and worship me."
10 Then Jesus answered, "Go away, Satan! The scripture says, 'Worship the
Lord your God and serve only him!' "
11 Then the Devil left Jesus; and angels
came and helped him.

Jesus Begins His Work in Galilee

(Mark 1.14, 15; Luke 4.14, 15)

12 When Jesus heard that John had
been put in prison, he went away to Galilee. 13 He did not stay in Nazareth, but
went to live in Capernaum, a town by
Lake Galilee, in the territory of Zebulun
and Naphtali. 14 This was done to make

come true what the prophet Isaiah had
said,
15 "Land of Zebulun and land of
Naphtali,
on the road to the sea, on the
other side of the Jordan,
Galilee, land of the Gentiles!
16 The people who live in darkness
will see a great light.
On those who live in the dark land
of death
the light will shine."
17 From that time Jesus began to
preach his message: "Turn away from
your sins, because the Kingdom of
heaven is near!"

Jesus Calls Four Fishermen

(Mark 1.16-20; Luke 5.1-11)

18 As Jesus walked along the shore of
Lake Galilee, he saw two brothers who
were fishermen, Simon (called Peter)
and his brother Andrew, catching fish in
the lake with a net. 19 Jesus said to them,
"Come with me, and I will teach you to
catch people." 20 At once they left their
nets and went with him.
21 He went on and saw two other
brothers, James and John, the sons of
Zebedee. They were in their boat with
their father Zebedee, getting their nets
ready. Jesus called them, 22 and at once
they left the boat and their father, and
went with him.

Jesus Teaches, Preaches, and Heals

(Luke 6.17-19)

23 Jesus went all over Galilee, teaching
in the synagogues, preaching the Good
News about the Kingdom, and healing
people who had all kinds of disease and
sickness. 24 The news about him spread
through the whole country of Syria, so
that people brought to him all those who
were sick, suffering from all kinds of
diseases and disorders: people with demons, and epileptics, and paralytics—
and Jesus healed them all. 25 Large
crowds followed him from Galilee and
the Ten Towns, from Jerusalem, Judea,
and the land on the other side of the
Jordan.

The Sermon on the Mount

5 Jesus saw the crowds and went up a
hill, where he sat down. His disciples gathered around him, 2 and he began to teach them:

True Happiness

(Luke 6.20-23)

3 "Happy are those who know they
are spiritually poor;
the Kingdom of heaven belongs
to them!
4 "Happy are those who mourn;
God will comfort them!
5 "Happy are those who are humble;
they will receive what God has
promised!
6 "Happy are those whose greatest
desire is to do what God
requires;
God will satisfy them fully!
7 "Happy are those who are merciful
to others;
God will be merciful to them!
8 "Happy are the pure in heart;
they will see God!
9 "Happy are those who work for
peace;
God will call them his children!
10 "Happy are those who are
persecuted because they do
what God requires;
the Kingdom of heaven belongs
to them!
11 "Happy are you when people insult
you and persecute you and tell all kinds
of evil lies against you because you are
my followers. 12 Be happy and glad, for a
great reward is kept for you in heaven.
This is how the prophets who lived before you were persecuted.

Salt and Light

(Mark 9.50; Luke 14.34, 35)

13 "You are like salt for the whole human race. But if salt loses its saltiness,
there is no way to make it salty again. It
has become worthless, so it is thrown
out and people trample on it.
14 "You are like light for the whole
world. A city built on a hill cannot be
hid. 15 No one lights a lamp and puts it
under a bowl; instead it is put on the
lampstand, where it gives light for
everyone in the house. 16 In the same
way your light must shine before people,
so that they will see the good things you
do and praise your Father in heaven.

Teaching about the Law

17 "Do not think that I have come to do
away with the Law of Moses and the
teachings of the prophets. I have not
come to do away with them, but to make

their teachings come true. 18Remember
that as long as heaven and earth last, not
the least point nor the smallest detail of
the Law will be done away with—not
until the end of all things.[a] 19So then,
whoever disobeys even the least important of the commandments and teaches
others to do the same, will be least in the
Kingdom of heaven. On the other hand,
whoever obeys the Law and teaches others to do the same, will be great in the
Kingdom of heaven. 20I tell you, then,
that you will be able to enter the Kingdom of heaven only if you are more
faithful than the teachers of the Law and
the Pharisees in doing what God
requires.

Teaching about Anger

21"You have heard that people were
told in the past, 'Do not commit murder;
anyone who does will be brought to
trial.' 22But now I tell you: if you are angry[b] with your brother you will be
brought to trial, if you call your brother
'You good-for-nothing!' you will be
brought before the Council, and if you
call your brother a worthless fool you
will be in danger of going to the fire of
hell. 23So if you are about to offer your
gift to God at the altar and there you remember that your brother has something against you, 24leave your gift there
in front of the altar, go at once and make
peace with your brother, and then come
back and offer your gift to God.

25"If someone brings a lawsuit against
you and takes you to court, settle the dispute while there is time, before you get
to court. Once you are there, you will be
turned over to the judge, who will hand
you over to the police, and you will be
put in jail. 26There you will stay, I tell
you, until you pay the last penny of your
fine.

Teaching about Adultery

27"You have heard that it was said,
'Do not commit adultery.' 28But now I
tell you: anyone who looks at a woman
and wants to possess her is guilty of
committing adultery with her in his
heart. 29So if your right eye causes you
to sin, take it out and throw it away! It is
much better for you to lose a part of your
body than to have your whole body
thrown into hell. 30If your right hand
causes you to sin, cut it off and throw it
away! It is much better for you to lose
one of your limbs than to have your
whole body go off to hell.

Teaching about Divorce

(Matthew 19.9; Mark 10.11, 12; Luke 16.18)

31"It was also said, 'Anyone who divorces his wife must give her a written
notice of divorce.' 32But now I tell you: if
a man divorces his wife for any cause
other than her unfaithfulness, then he is
guilty of making her commit adultery if
she marries again; and the man who
marries her commits adultery also.

Teaching about Vows

33"You have also heard that people
were told in the past, 'Do not break your
promise, but do what you have vowed to
the Lord to do.' 34But now I tell you: do
not use any vow when you make a promise. Do not swear by heaven, for it is
God's throne; 35nor by earth, for it is the
resting place for his feet; nor by Jerusalem, for it is the city of the great King.
36Do not even swear by your head, because you cannot make a single hair
white or black. 37Just say 'Yes' or 'No'—
anything else you say comes from the
Evil One.

Teaching about Revenge

(Luke 6.29, 30)

38"You have heard that it was said,
'An eye for an eye, and a tooth for a
tooth.' 39But now I tell you: do not take
revenge on someone who wrongs you. If
anyone slaps you on the right cheek, let
him slap your left cheek too. 40And if
someone takes you to court to sue you
for your shirt, let him have your coat as
well. 41And if one of the occupation
troops forces you to carry his pack one
mile, carry it two miles. 42When someone asks you for something, give it to
him; when someone wants to borrow
something, lend it to him.

Love for Enemies

(Luke 6.27, 28, 32-36)

43"You have heard that it was said,
'Love your friends, hate your enemies.'
44But now I tell you: love your enemies
and pray for those who persecute you,

[a] the end of all things; *or* all its teachings come true. [b] if you are angry; *some manuscripts have* if without cause you are angry.

45 so that you may become the children
of your Father in heaven. For he makes
his sun to shine on bad and good people
alike, and gives rain to those who do
good and to those who do evil. 46 Why
should God reward you if you love only
the people who love you? Even the tax
collectors do that! 47 And if you speak
only to your friends, have you done
anything out of the ordinary? Even the
pagans do that! 48 You must be
perfect—just as your Father in heaven is
perfect.

Teaching about Charity

6 "Make certain you do not perform
your religious duties in public so
that people will see what you do. If you
do these things publicly, you will not
have any reward from your Father in
heaven.

2 "So when you give something to a
needy person, do not make a big show of
it, as the hypocrites do in the houses of
worship and on the streets. They do it so
that people will praise them. I assure
you, they have already been paid in full.
3 But when you help a needy person, do
it in such a way that even your closest
friend will not know about it. 4 Then it
will be a private matter. And your
Father, who sees what you do in private,
will reward you.

Teaching about Prayer

(Luke 11.2-4)

5 "When you pray, do not be like the
hypocrites! They love to stand up and
pray in the houses of worship and on the
street corners, so that everyone will see
them. I assure you, they have already
been paid in full. 6 But when you pray, go
to your room, close the door, and pray to
your Father, who is unseen. And your
Father, who sees what you do in private,
will reward you.

7 "When you pray, do not use a lot of
meaningless words, as the pagans do,
who think that their gods will hear them
because their prayers are long. 8 Do not
be like them. Your Father already
knows what you need before you ask
him. 9 This, then, is how you should
pray:

'Our Father in heaven:
May your holy name be
honored;
10 may your Kingdom come;
may your will be done on earth
as it is in heaven.
11 Give us today the food we
need.[c]
12 Forgive us the wrongs we have
done,
as we forgive the wrongs that
others have done to us.
13 Do not bring us to hard testing,
but keep us safe from the
Evil One.'[d]

14 "If you forgive others the wrongs
they have done to you, your Father in
heaven will also forgive you. 15 But if you
do not forgive others, then your Father
will not forgive the wrongs you have
done.

Teaching about Fasting

16 "And when you fast, do not put on a
sad face as the hypocrites do. They neglect their appearance so that everyone
will see that they are fasting. I assure
you, they have already been paid in full.
17 When you go without food, wash your
face and comb your hair, 18 so that others cannot know that you are fasting—
only your Father, who is unseen, will
know. And your Father, who sees what
you do in private, will reward you.

Riches in Heaven

(Luke 12.33, 34)

19 "Do not store up riches for yourselves here on earth, where moths and
rust destroy, and robbers break in and
steal. 20 Instead, store up riches for yourselves in heaven, where moths and rust
cannot destroy, and robbers cannot
break in and steal. 21 For your heart will
always be where your riches are.

The Light of the Body

(Luke 11.34-36)

22 "The eyes are like a lamp for the
body. If your eyes are sound, your whole
body will be full of light; 23 but if your
eyes are no good, your body will be in
darkness. So if the light in you is darkness, how terribly dark it will be!

[c] we need; *or* for today, *or* for tomorrow. [d] *Some manuscripts add* For yours is the kingdom, and the power, and the glory forever. Amen.

God and Possessions

(Luke 16.13; 12.22-31)

24 “You cannot be a slave of two masters; you will hate one and love the
other; you will be loyal to one and despise the other. You cannot serve both
God and money.
25 “This is why I tell you: do not be
worried about the food and drink you
need in order to stay alive, or about
clothes for your body. After all, isn’t life
worth more than food? And isn’t the
body worth more than clothes? 26 Look
at the birds: they do not plant seeds,
gather a harvest and put it in barns; yet
your Father in heaven takes care of
them! Aren’t you worth much more
than birds? 27 Can any of you live a bit
longer[e] by worrying about it?
28 “And why worry about clothes?
Look how the wild flowers grow: they
do not work or make clothes for themselves. 29 But I tell you that not even King
Solomon with all his wealth had clothes
as beautiful as one of these flowers. 30 It
is God who clothes the wild grass—
grass that is here today and gone tomorrow, burned up in the oven. Won’t he be
all the more sure to clothe you? What
little faith you have!
31 “So do not start worrying: ‘Where
will my food come from? or my drink? or
my clothes?’ 32 (These are the things the
pagans are always concerned about.)
Your Father in heaven knows that you
need all these things. 33 Instead, be concerned above everything else with the
Kingdom of God and with what he requires of you, and he will provide you
with all these other things. 34 So do not
worry about tomorrow; it will have
enough worries of its own. There is no
need to add to the troubles each day
brings.

Judging Others

(Luke 6.37, 38, 41, 42)

7 “Do not judge others, so that God
will not judge you, 2 for God will
judge you in the same way you judge
others, and he will apply to you the same
rules you apply to others. 3 Why, then,
do you look at the speck in your
brother’s eye and pay no attention to
the log in your own eye? 4 How dare you
say to your brother, ‘Please, let me take
that speck out of your eye,’ when you
have a log in your own eye? 5 You hypocrite! First take the log out of your own
eye, and then you will be able to see
clearly to take the speck out of your
brother’s eye.
6 “Do not give what is holy to dogs—
they will only turn and attack you. Do
not throw your pearls in front of pigs—
they will only trample them underfoot.

Ask, Seek, Knock

(Luke 11.9-13)

7 “Ask, and you will receive; seek, and
you will find; knock, and the door will be
opened to you. 8 For everyone who asks
will receive, and anyone who seeks will
find, and the door will be opened to
those who knock. 9 Would any of you
who are fathers give your son a stone
when he asks for bread? 10 Or would you
give him a snake when he asks for a
fish? 11 As bad as you are, you know how
to give good things to your children.
How much more, then, will your Father
in heaven give good things to those who
ask him!
12 “Do for others what you want them
to do for you: this is the meaning of the
Law of Moses and of the teachings of the
prophets.

The Narrow Gate

(Luke 13.24)

13 “Go in through the narrow gate, because the gate to hell is wide and the
road that leads to it is easy, and there are
many who travel it. 14 But the gate to life
is narrow and the way that leads to it is
hard, and there are few people who
find it.

A Tree and Its Fruit

(Luke 6.43, 44)

15 “Be on your guard against false
prophets; they come to you looking like
sheep on the outside, but on the inside
they are really like wild wolves. 16 You
will know them by what they do. Thorn
bushes do not bear grapes, and briers do
not bear figs. 17 A healthy tree bears
good fruit, but a poor tree bears bad
fruit. 18 A healthy tree cannot bear bad
fruit, and a poor tree cannot bear good
fruit. 19 And any tree that does not bear
good fruit is cut down and thrown in the

[e] live a bit longer; *or* grow a bit taller.

fire. 20So then, you will know the false
prophets by what they do.

I Never Knew You

(Luke 13.25-27)

21"Not everyone who calls me 'Lord,
Lord' will enter the Kingdom of heaven,
but only those who do what my Father in
heaven wants them to do. 22When the
Judgment Day comes, many will say to
me, 'Lord, Lord! In your name we spoke
God's message, by your name we drove
out many demons and performed many
miracles!' 23Then I will say to them, 'I
never knew you. Get away from me, you
wicked people!'

The Two House Builders

(Luke 6.47-49)

24"So then, anyone who hears these
words of mine and obeys them is like a
wise man who built his house on rock.
25The rain poured down, the rivers
flooded over, and the wind blew hard
against that house. But it did not fall, because it was built on rock.

26"But anyone who hears these words
of mine and does not obey them is like a
foolish man who built his house on sand.
27The rain poured down, the rivers
flooded over, the wind blew hard against
that house, and it fell. And what a terrible fall that was!"

The Authority of Jesus

28When Jesus finished saying these
things, the crowd was amazed at the
way he taught. 29He wasn't like the
teachers of the Law; instead, he taught
with authority.

Jesus Heals a Man

(Mark 1.40-45; Luke 5.12-16)

8 When Jesus came down from the
hill, large crowds followed him.
2Then a man suffering from a dreaded
skin disease came to him, knelt down
before him, and said, "Sir, if you want to,
you can make me clean."[f]

3Jesus reached out and touched him.
"I do want to," he answered. "Be clean!"
At once the man was healed of his disease. 4Then Jesus said to him, "Listen!
Don't tell anyone, but go straight to the
priest and let him examine you; then in
order to prove to everyone that you are
cured, offer the sacrifice that Moses
ordered."

Jesus Heals a Roman Officer's Servant

(Luke 7.1-10)

5When Jesus entered Capernaum, a
Roman officer met him and begged for
help: 6"Sir, my servant is sick in bed at
home, unable to move and suffering
terribly."

7"I will go and make him well," Jesus
said.

8"Oh no, sir," answered the officer. "I
do not deserve to have you come into my
house. Just give the order, and my servant will get well. 9I, too, am a man under
the authority of superior officers, and I
have soldiers under me. I order this one,
'Go!' and he goes; and I order that one,
'Come!' and he comes; and I order my
slave, 'Do this!' and he does it."

10When Jesus heard this, he was surprised and said to the people following
him, "I tell you, I have never found anyone in Israel with faith like this. 11I assure you that many will come from the
east and the west and sit down with
Abraham, Isaac, and Jacob at the feast
in the Kingdom of heaven. 12But those
who should be in the Kingdom will be
thrown out into the darkness, where
they will cry and gnash their teeth."
13Then Jesus said to the officer, "Go
home, and what you believe will be done
for you."

And the officer's servant was healed
that very moment.

Jesus Heals Many People

(Mark 1.29-34; Luke 4.38-41)

14Jesus went to Peter's home, and
there he saw Peter's mother-in-law sick
in bed with a fever. 15He touched her
hand; the fever left her, and she got up
and began to wait on him.

16When evening came, people brought
to Jesus many who had demons in them.
Jesus drove out the evil spirits with a
word and healed all who were sick. 17He
did this to make come true what the
prophet Isaiah had said, "He himself
took our sickness and carried away our
diseases."

[f] MAKE ME CLEAN: *This disease was considered to make a person ritually unclean.*

The Would-Be Followers of Jesus

(Luke 9.57-62)

18 When Jesus noticed the crowd
around him, he ordered his disciples to
go to the other side of the lake.
19 A teacher of the Law came to him.
"Teacher," he said, "I am ready to go
with you wherever you go."
20 Jesus answered him, "Foxes have
holes, and birds have nests, but the Son
of Man has no place to lie down and
rest."
21 Another man, who was a disciple,
said, "Sir, first let me go back and bury
my father."
22 "Follow me," Jesus answered, "and
let the dead bury their own dead."

Jesus Calms a Storm

(Mark 4.35-41; Luke 8.22-25)

23 Jesus got into a boat, and his disciples went with him. 24 Suddenly a fierce
storm hit the lake, and the boat was in
danger of sinking. But Jesus was asleep.
25 The disciples went to him and woke
him up. "Save us, Lord!" they said. "We
are about to die!"
26 "Why are you so frightened?" Jesus
answered. "What little faith you have!"
Then he got up and ordered the winds
and the waves to stop, and there was a
great calm.
27 Everyone was amazed. "What kind
of man is this?" they said. "Even the
winds and the waves obey him!"

Jesus Heals Two Men with Demons

(Mark 5.1-20; Luke 8.26-39)

28 When Jesus came to the territory of
Gadara on the other side of the lake, he
was met by two men who came out of
the burial caves there. These men had
demons in them and were so fierce that
no one dared travel on that road. 29 At
once they screamed, "What do you want
with us, you Son of God? Have you come
to punish us before the right time?"
30 Not far away there was a large herd
of pigs feeding. 31 So the demons begged
Jesus, "If you are going to drive us out,
send us into that herd of pigs."
32 "Go," Jesus told them; so they left
and went off into the pigs. The whole
herd rushed down the side of the cliff
into the lake and was drowned.
33 The men who had been taking care
of the pigs ran away and went into the
town, where they told the whole story
and what had happened to the men with
the demons. 34 So everyone from the
town went out to meet Jesus; and when
they saw him, they begged him to leave
their territory.

Jesus Heals a Paralyzed Man

(Mark 2.1-12; Luke 5.17-26)

9 Jesus got into the boat and went
back across the lake to his own
town,[g] 2 where some people brought to
him a paralyzed man, lying on a bed.
When Jesus saw how much faith they
had, he said to the paralyzed man,
"Courage, my son! Your sins are forgiven."
3 Then some teachers of the Law said
to themselves, "This man is speaking
blasphemy!"
4 Jesus perceived what they were
thinking, and so he said, "Why are you
thinking such evil things? 5 Is it easier to
say, 'Your sins are forgiven,' or to say,
'Get up and walk'? 6 I will prove to you,
then, that the Son of Man has authority
on earth to forgive sins." So he said to
the paralyzed man, "Get up, pick up
your bed, and go home!"
7 The man got up and went home.
8 When the people saw it, they were
afraid, and praised God for giving such
authority to people.

Jesus Calls Matthew

(Mark 2.13-17; Luke 5.27-32)

9 Jesus left that place, and as he
walked along, he saw a tax collector,
named Matthew, sitting in his office. He
said to him, "Follow me."
Matthew got up and followed him.
10 While Jesus was having a meal in
Matthew's house,[h] many tax collectors
and other outcasts came and joined
Jesus and his disciples at the table.
11 Some Pharisees saw this and asked his
disciples, "Why does your teacher eat
with such people?"
12 Jesus heard them and answered,
"People who are well do not need a doctor, but only those who are sick. 13 Go
and find out what is meant by the scripture that says: 'It is kindness that I want,
not animal sacrifices.' I have not come to
call respectable people, but outcasts."

[g] HIS OWN TOWN: *Capernaum (see 4.13).* [h] in Matthew's house; *or* in his (*that is,* Jesus') house.

The Question about Fasting

(Mark 2.18-22; Luke 5.33-39)

14 Then the followers of John the Baptist came to Jesus, asking, "Why is it that
we and the Pharisees fast often, but your
disciples don't fast at all?"

15 Jesus answered, "Do you expect the
guests at a wedding party to be sad as
long as the bridegroom is with them? Of
course not! But the day will come when
the bridegroom will be taken away from
them, and then they will fast.

16 "No one patches up an old coat with
a piece of new cloth, for the new patch
will shrink and make an even bigger
hole in the coat. 17 Nor does anyone pour
new wine into used wineskins, for the
skins will burst, the wine will pour out,
and the skins will be ruined. Instead,
new wine is poured into fresh wineskins,
and both will keep in good condition."

The Official's Daughter and the Woman Who Touched Jesus' Cloak

(Mark 5.21-43; Luke 8.40-56)

18 While Jesus was saying this, a Jewish official came to him, knelt down before him, and said, "My daughter has
just died; but come and place your hands
on her, and she will live."

19 So Jesus got up and followed him,
and his disciples went along with him.

20 A woman who had suffered from severe bleeding for twelve years came up
behind Jesus and touched the edge of his
cloak. 21 She said to herself, "If only I
touch his cloak, I will get well."

22 Jesus turned around and saw her,
and said, "Courage, my daughter! Your
faith has made you well." At that very
moment the woman became well.

23 Then Jesus went into the official's
house. When he saw the musicians for
the funeral and the people all stirred up,
24 he said, "Get out, everybody! The little
girl is not dead—she is only sleeping!"
Then they all started making fun of him.
25 But as soon as the people had been put
out, Jesus went into the girl's room and
took hold of her hand, and she got up.
26 The news about this spread all over
that part of the country.

Jesus Heals Two Blind Men

27 Jesus left that place, and as he
walked along, two blind men started following him. "Have mercy on us, Son of
David!" they shouted.

28 When Jesus had gone indoors, the
two blind men came to him, and he
asked them, "Do you believe that I can
heal you?"

"Yes, sir!" they answered.

29 Then Jesus touched their eyes and
said, "Let it happen, then, just as you
believe!"—30 and their sight was restored. Jesus spoke sternly to them,
"Don't tell this to anyone!"

31 But they left and spread the news
about Jesus all over that part of the
country.

Jesus Heals a Man Who Could Not Speak

32 As the men were leaving, some people brought to Jesus a man who could
not talk because he had a demon. 33 But
as soon as the demon was driven out, the
man started talking, and everyone was
amazed. "We have never seen anything
like this in Israel!" they exclaimed.

34 But the Pharisees said, "It is the
chief of the demons who gives Jesus the
power to drive out demons."

Jesus Has Pity for the People

35 Jesus went around visiting all the
towns and villages. He taught in the synagogues, preached the Good News about
the Kingdom, and healed people with
every kind of disease and sickness. 36 As
he saw the crowds, his heart was filled
with pity for them, because they were
worried and helpless, like sheep without
a shepherd. 37 So he said to his disciples,
"The harvest is large, but there are few
workers to gather it in. 38 Pray to the
owner of the harvest that he will send
out workers to gather in his harvest."

The Twelve Apostles

(Mark 3.13-19; Luke 6.12-16)

10 Jesus called his twelve disciples
together and gave them author-
ity to drive out evil spirits and to heal
every disease and every sickness.
2 These are the names of the twelve
apostles: first, Simon (called Peter) and
his brother Andrew; James and his
brother John, the sons of Zebedee;
3 Philip and Bartholomew; Thomas and
Matthew, the tax collector; James son of
Alphaeus, and Thaddaeus; 4 Simon the

Patriot, and Judas Iscariot, who betrayed Jesus.

The Mission of the Twelve

(Mark 6.7-13; Luke 9.1-6)

5 These twelve men were sent out by
Jesus with the following instructions:
“Do not go to any Gentile territory or
any Samaritan towns. 6 Instead, you are
to go to the lost sheep of the people of
Israel. 7 Go and preach, ‘The Kingdom of
heaven is near!’ 8 Heal the sick, bring the
dead back to life, heal those who suffer
from dreaded skin diseases, and drive
out demons. You have received without
paying, so give without being paid. 9 Do
not carry any gold, silver, or copper
money in your pockets; 10 do not carry a
beggar’s bag for the trip or an extra shirt
or shoes or a walking stick. Workers
should be given what they need.

11 “When you come to a town or village, go in and look for someone who is
willing to welcome you, and stay with
him until you leave that place. 12 When
you go into a house, say, ‘Peace be with
you.’ 13 If the people in that house welcome you, let your greeting of peace remain; but if they do not welcome you,
then take back your greeting. 14 And if
some home or town will not welcome
you or listen to you, then leave that place
and shake the dust off your feet. 15 I assure you that on the Judgment Day God
will show more mercy to the people of
Sodom and Gomorrah than to the people
of that town!

Coming Persecutions

(Mark 13.9-13; Luke 21.12-17)

16 “Listen! I am sending you out just
like sheep to a pack of wolves. You must
be as cautious as snakes and as gentle as
doves. 17 Watch out, for there will be
those who will arrest you and take you
to court, and they will whip you in the
synagogues. 18 For my sake you will be
brought to trial before rulers and kings,
to tell the Good News to them and to the
Gentiles. 19 When they bring you to trial,
do not worry about what you are going
to say or how you will say it; when the
time comes, you will be given what you
will say. 20 For the words you will speak
will not be yours; they will come from
the Spirit of your Father speaking
through you.

21 “People will hand over their own
brothers to be put to death, and fathers
will do the same to their children; children will turn against their parents and
have them put to death. 22 Everyone will
hate you because of me. But whoever
holds out to the end will be saved.
23 When they persecute you in one town,
run away to another one. I assure you
that you will not finish your work in all
the towns of Israel before the Son of
Man comes.

24 “No pupil is greater than his teacher;
no slave is greater than his master. 25 So
a pupil should be satisfied to become
like his teacher, and a slave like his master. If the head of the family is called
Beelzebul, the members of the family
will be called even worse names!

Whom to Fear

(Luke 12.2-7)

26 “So do not be afraid of people.
Whatever is now covered up will be uncovered, and every secret will be made
known. 27 What I am telling you in the
dark you must repeat in broad daylight,
and what you have heard in private you
must announce from the housetops.
28 Do not be afraid of those who kill the
body but cannot kill the soul; rather be
afraid of God, who can destroy both
body and soul in hell. 29 For only a penny
you can buy two sparrows, yet not one
sparrow falls to the ground without
your Father’s consent. 30 As for you, even
the hairs of your head have all been
counted. 31 So do not be afraid; you are
worth much more than many sparrows!

Confessing and Rejecting Christ

(Luke 12.8, 9)

32 “Those who declare publicly that
they belong to me, I will do the same for
them before my Father in heaven. 33 But
those who reject me publicly, I will reject before my Father in heaven.

Not Peace, but a Sword

(Luke 12.51-53; 14.26, 27)

34 “Do not think that I have come to
bring peace to the world. No, I did not
come to bring peace, but a sword. 35 I
came to set sons against their fathers,
daughters against their mothers,
daughters-in-law against their mothers-
in-law; 36 your worst enemies will be the
members of your own family.

37 “Those who love their father or

mother more than me are not fit to be my
disciples; those who love their son or
daughter more than me are not fit to be
my disciples. 38 Those who do not take
up their cross and follow in my steps are
not fit to be my disciples. 39 Those who
try to gain their own life will lose it; but
those who lose their life for my sake will
gain it.

Rewards

(Mark 9.41)

40 "Whoever welcomes you welcomes
me; and whoever welcomes me welcomes the one who sent me. 41 Whoever
welcomes God's messenger because he
is God's messenger, will share in his reward. And whoever welcomes a good
man because he is good, will share in his
reward. 42 You can be sure that whoever
gives even a drink of cold water to one of
the least of these my followers because
he is my follower, will certainly receive
a reward."

The Messengers from John the Baptist

(Luke 7.18-35)

11 When Jesus finished giving
these instructions to his twelve
disciples, he left that place and went off
to teach and preach in the towns near
there.

2 When John the Baptist heard in
prison about the things that Christ was
doing, he sent some of his disciples to
him. 3 "Tell us," they asked Jesus, "are
you the one John said was going to
come, or should we expect someone
else?"

4 Jesus answered, "Go back and tell
John what you are hearing and seeing:
5 the blind can see, the lame can walk,
those who suffer from dreaded skin diseases are made clean,[i] the deaf hear,
the dead are brought back to life, and
the Good News is preached to the poor.
6 How happy are those who have no
doubts about me!"

7 While John's disciples were leaving,
Jesus spoke about him to the crowds:
"When you went out to John in the
desert, what did you expect to see? A
blade of grass bending in the wind?
8 What did you go out to see? A man
dressed up in fancy clothes? People who
dress like that live in palaces! 9 Tell me,
what did you go out to see? A prophet?
Yes indeed, but you saw much more
than a prophet. 10 For John is the one of
whom the scripture says: 'God said, I
will send my messenger ahead of you to
open the way for you.' 11 I assure you
that John the Baptist is greater than anyone who has ever lived. But the one who
is least in the Kingdom of heaven is
greater than John. 12 From the time John
preached his message until this very day
the Kingdom of heaven has suffered violent attacks,[j] and violent men try to
seize it. 13 Until the time of John all the
prophets and the Law of Moses spoke
about the Kingdom; 14 and if you are
willing to believe their message, John is
Elijah, whose coming was predicted.
15 Listen, then, if you have ears!

16 "Now, to what can I compare the
people of this day? They are like children sitting in the marketplace. One
group shouts to the other, 17 'We played
wedding music for you, but you
wouldn't dance! We sang funeral songs,
but you wouldn't cry!' 18 When John
came, he fasted and drank no wine, and
everyone said, 'He has a demon in him!'
19 When the Son of Man came, he ate and
drank, and everyone said, 'Look at this
man! He is a glutton and wine drinker, a
friend of tax collectors and other outcasts!' God's wisdom, however, is shown
to be true by its results."

The Unbelieving Towns

(Luke 10.13-15)

20 The people in the towns where Jesus
had performed most of his miracles did
not turn from their sins, so he re-
proached those towns. 21 "How terrible it
will be for you, Chorazin! How terrible
for you too, Bethsaida! If the miracles
which were performed in you had been
performed in Tyre and Sidon, the people
there would have long ago put on sackcloth and sprinkled ashes on themselves, to show that they had turned
from their sins! 22 I assure you that on
the Judgment Day God will show more
mercy to the people of Tyre and Sidon
than to you! 23 And as for you, Capernaum! Did you want to lift yourself up to
heaven? You will be thrown down to
hell! If the miracles which were per-

[i] MADE CLEAN: *See 8.2.* [j] has suffered violent attacks; *or* has been coming violently.

formed in you had been performed in
Sodom, it would still be in existence today! 24 You can be sure that on the Judgment Day God will show more mercy to
Sodom than to you!"

Come to Me and Rest

(Luke 10.21, 22)

25 At that time Jesus said, "Father,
Lord of heaven and earth! I thank you
because you have shown to the un-
learned what you have hidden from the
wise and learned. 26 Yes, Father, this was
how you were pleased to have it happen.
27 "My Father has given me all things.
No one knows the Son except the
Father, and no one knows the Father except the Son and those to whom the Son
chooses to reveal him.
28 "Come to me, all of you who are
tired from carrying heavy loads, and I
will give you rest. 29 Take my yoke and
put it on you, and learn from me, because I am gentle and humble in spirit;
and you will find rest. 30 For the yoke I
will give you is easy, and the load I will
put on you is light."

The Question about the Sabbath

(Mark 2.23-28; Luke 6.1-5)

12 Not long afterward Jesus was
walking through some wheat
fields on a Sabbath. His disciples were
hungry, so they began to pick heads of
wheat and eat the grain. 2 When the
Pharisees saw this, they said to Jesus,
"Look, it is against our Law for your disciples to do this on the Sabbath!"
3 Jesus answered, "Have you never
read what David did that time when he
and his men were hungry? 4 He went into
the house of God, and he and his men ate
the bread offered to God, even though it
was against the Law for them to eat it—
only the priests were allowed to eat that
bread. 5 Or have you not read in the Law
of Moses that every Sabbath the priests
in the Temple actually break the Sabbath law, yet they are not guilty? 6 I tell
you that there is something here greater
than the Temple. 7 The scripture says, 'It
is kindness that I want, not animal sacrifices.' If you really knew what this
means, you would not condemn people
who are not guilty; 8 for the Son of Man
is Lord of the Sabbath."

The Man with a Paralyzed Hand

(Mark 3.1-6; Luke 6.6-11)

9 Jesus left that place and went to a
synagogue, 10 where there was a man
who had a paralyzed hand. Some people
were there who wanted to accuse Jesus
of doing wrong, so they asked him, "Is
it against our Law to heal on the
Sabbath?"
11 Jesus answered, "What if one of you
has a sheep and it falls into a deep hole
on the Sabbath? Will you not take hold
of it and lift it out? 12 And a human being
is worth much more than a sheep! So
then, our Law does allow us to help
someone on the Sabbath." 13 Then he
said to the man with the paralyzed hand,
"Stretch out your hand."
He stretched it out, and it became well
again, just like the other one. 14 Then the
Pharisees left and made plans to kill
Jesus.

God's Chosen Servant

15 When Jesus heard about the plot
against him, he went away from that
place; and large crowds followed him.
He healed all the sick 16 and gave them
orders not to tell others about him. 17 He
did this so as to make come true what
God had said through the prophet
Isaiah:

18 "Here is my servant, whom I have
chosen,
the one I love, and with whom I
am pleased.
I will send my Spirit upon him,
and he will announce my
judgment to the nations.
19 He will not argue or shout,
or make loud speeches in the
streets.
20 He will not break off a bent reed,
nor put out a flickering lamp.
He will persist until he causes
justice to triumph,
21 and on him all peoples will put
their hope."

Jesus and Beelzebul

(Mark 3.20-30; Luke 11.14-23)

22 Then some people brought to Jesus
a man who was blind and could not talk
because he had a demon. Jesus healed
the man, so that he was able to talk and
see. 23 The crowds were all amazed at
what Jesus had done. "Could he be the
Son of David?" they asked.

24 When the Pharisees heard this, they
replied, "He drives out demons only because their ruler Beelzebul gives him
power to do so."
25 Jesus knew what they were thinking, and so he said to them, "Any country that divides itself into groups which
fight each other will not last very long.
And any town or family that divides itself into groups which fight each other
will fall apart. 26 So if one group is fighting another in Satan's kingdom, this
means that it is already divided into
groups and will soon fall apart! 27 You
say that I drive out demons because
Beelzebul gives me the power to do so.
Well, then, who gives your followers the
power to drive them out? What your
own followers do proves that you are
wrong! 28 No, it is not Beelzebul, but
God's Spirit, who gives me the power to
drive out demons, which proves that
the Kingdom of God has already come
upon you.
29 "No one can break into a strong
man's house and take away his belongings unless he first ties up the strong
man; then he can plunder his house.
30 "Anyone who is not for me is really
against me; anyone who does not help
me gather is really scattering. 31 For this
reason I tell you: people can be forgiven
any sin and any evil thing they say;[k]
but whoever says evil things against the
Holy Spirit will not be forgiven. 32 Anyone who says something against the Son
of Man can be forgiven; but whoever
says something against the Holy Spirit
will not be forgiven—now or ever.

A Tree and Its Fruit

(Luke 6.43-45)

33 "To have good fruit you must have a
healthy tree; if you have a poor tree, you
will have bad fruit. A tree is known by
the kind of fruit it bears. 34 You snakes—
how can you say good things when you
are evil? For the mouth speaks what the
heart is full of. 35 A good person brings
good things out of a treasure of good
things; a bad person brings bad things
out of a treasure of bad things.
36 "You can be sure that on the Judgment Day you will have to give account
of every useless word you have ever spoken. 37 Your words will be used to judge
you—to declare you either innocent or
guilty."

The Demand for a Miracle

(Mark 8.11, 12; Luke 11.29-32)

38 Then some teachers of the Law and
some Pharisees spoke up. "Teacher,"
they said, "we want to see you perform a
miracle."
39 "How evil and godless are the people
of this day!" Jesus exclaimed. "You ask
me for a miracle? No! The only miracle
you will be given is the miracle of the
prophet Jonah. 40 In the same way that
Jonah spent three days and nights in the
big fish, so will the Son of Man spend
three days and nights in the depths of
the earth. 41 On the Judgment Day the
people of Nineveh will stand up and accuse you, because they turned from their
sins when they heard Jonah preach; and
I tell you that there is something here
greater than Jonah! 42 On the Judgment
Day the Queen of Sheba will stand up
and accuse you, because she traveled all
the way from her country to listen to
King Solomon's wise teaching; and I assure you that there is something here
greater than Solomon!

The Return of the Evil Spirit

(Luke 11.24-26)

43 "When an evil spirit goes out of a
person, it travels over dry country looking for a place to rest. If it can't find one,
44 it says to itself, 'I will go back to my
house.' So it goes back and finds the
house empty, clean, and all fixed up.
45 Then it goes out and brings along
seven other spirits even worse than itself, and they come and live there. So
when it is all over, that person is in
worse shape than at the beginning. This
is what will happen to the evil people of
this day."

Jesus' Mother and Brothers

(Mark 3.31-35; Luke 8.19-21)

46 Jesus was still talking to the people
when his mother and brothers arrived.
They stood outside, asking to speak with
him. 47 So one of the people there said to
him, "Look, your mother and brothers
are standing outside, and they want to
speak with you."[l]

[k] evil thing they say; *or* evil thing they say against God. [l] *Some manuscripts do not have verse 47.*

48 Jesus answered, "Who is my
mother? Who are my brothers?" 49 Then
he pointed to his disciples and said,
"Look! Here are my mother and my
brothers! 50 Whoever does what my
Father in heaven wants is my brother,
my sister, and my mother."

The Parable of the Sower
(Mark 4.1-9; Luke 8.4-8)

13 That same day Jesus left the
house and went to the lakeside,
where he sat down to teach. 2 The crowd
that gathered around him was so large
that he got into a boat and sat in it, while
the crowd stood on the shore. 3 He used
parables to tell them many things.
"Once there was a man who went out
to sow grain. 4 As he scattered the seed
in the field, some of it fell along the path,
and the birds came and ate it up. 5 Some
of it fell on rocky ground, where there
was little soil. The seeds soon sprouted,
because the soil wasn't deep. 6 But when
the sun came up, it burned the young
plants; and because the roots had not
grown deep enough, the plants soon
dried up. 7 Some of the seed fell among
thorn bushes, which grew up and
choked the plants. 8 But some seeds fell
in good soil, and the plants bore grain:
some had one hundred grains, others
sixty, and others thirty."
9 And Jesus concluded, "Listen, then, if
you have ears!"

The Purpose of the Parables
(Mark 4.10-12; Luke 8.9, 10)

10 Then the disciples came to Jesus and
asked him, "Why do you use parables
when you talk to the people?"
11 Jesus answered, "The knowledge
about the secrets of the Kingdom of
heaven has been given to you, but not to
them. 12 For the person who has something will be given more, so that he will
have more than enough; but the person
who has nothing will have taken away
from him even the little he has. 13 The
reason I use parables in talking to them
is that they look, but do not see, and they
listen, but do not hear or understand.
14 So the prophecy of Isaiah applies to
them:

'This people will listen and listen,
but not understand;
they will look and look, but
not see,
15 because their minds are dull,
and they have stopped up their
ears
and have closed their eyes.
Otherwise, their eyes would see,
their ears would hear,
their minds would understand,
and they would turn to me,
says God,
and I would heal them.'

16 "As for you, how fortunate you are!
Your eyes see and your ears hear.
17 I assure you that many prophets and
many of God's people wanted very much
to see what you see, but they could not,
and to hear what you hear, but they
did not.

Jesus Explains the Parable of the Sower
(Mark 4.13-20; Luke 8.11-15)

18 "Listen, then, and learn what the
parable of the sower means. 19 Those
who hear the message about the Kingdom but do not understand it are like the
seeds that fell along the path. The Evil
One comes and snatches away what was
sown in them. 20 The seeds that fell on
rocky ground stand for those who receive the message gladly as soon as they
hear it. 21 But it does not sink deep into
them, and they don't last long. So when
trouble or persecution comes because of
the message, they give up at once. 22 The
seeds that fell among thorn bushes stand
for those who hear the message; but the
worries about this life and the love for
riches choke the message, and they
don't bear fruit. 23 And the seeds sown in
the good soil stand for those who hear
the message and understand it: they
bear fruit, some as much as one hundred, others sixty, and others thirty."

The Parable of the Weeds

24 Jesus told them another parable:
"The Kingdom of heaven is like this. A
man sowed good seed in his field. 25 One
night, when everyone was asleep, an enemy came and sowed weeds among the
wheat and went away. 26 When the
plants grew and the heads of grain began to form, then the weeds showed up.
27 The man's servants came to him and
said, 'Sir, it was good seed you sowed in
your field; where did the weeds come
from?' 28 'It was some enemy who did
this,' he answered. 'Do you want us to go

and pull up the weeds?' they asked him.
29 'No,' he answered, 'because as you
gather the weeds you might pull up
some of the wheat along with them.
30 Let the wheat and the weeds both
grow together until harvest. Then I will
tell the harvest workers to pull up the
weeds first, tie them in bundles and burn
them, and then to gather in the wheat
and put it in my barn.' "

The Parable of the Mustard Seed

(Mark 4.30-32; Luke 13.18, 19)

31 Jesus told them another parable:
"The Kingdom of heaven is like this. A
man takes a mustard seed and sows it in
his field. 32 It is the smallest of all seeds,
but when it grows up, it is the biggest of
all plants. It becomes a tree, so that birds
come and make their nests in its
branches."

The Parable of the Yeast

(Luke 13.20, 21)

33 Jesus told them still another parable: "The Kingdom of heaven is like this.
A woman takes some yeast and mixes it
with a bushel of flour until the whole
batch of dough rises."

Jesus' Use of Parables

(Mark 4.33, 34)

34 Jesus used parables to tell all these
things to the crowds; he would not say a
thing to them without using a parable.
35 He did this to make come true what
the prophet had said,

"I will use parables when I speak
to them;
I will tell them things unknown
since the creation of the
world."

Jesus Explains the Parable of the Weeds

36 When Jesus had left the crowd and
gone indoors, his disciples came to him
and said, "Tell us what the parable about
the weeds in the field means."

37 Jesus answered, "The man who
sowed the good seed is the Son of Man;
38 the field is the world; the good seed is
the people who belong to the Kingdom;
the weeds are the people who belong to
the Evil One; 39 and the enemy who
sowed the weeds is the Devil. The harvest is the end of the age, and the harvest workers are angels. 40 Just as the
weeds are gathered up and burned in the
fire, so the same thing will happen at the
end of the age: 41 the Son of Man will
send out his angels to gather up out of
his Kingdom all those who cause people
to sin and all others who do evil things,
42 and they will throw them into the fiery
furnace, where they will cry and gnash
their teeth. 43 Then God's people will
shine like the sun in their Father's Kingdom. Listen, then, if you have ears!

The Parable of the Hidden Treasure

44 "The Kingdom of heaven is like this.
A man happens to find a treasure hidden
in a field. He covers it up again, and is so
happy that he goes and sells everything
he has, and then goes back and buys
that field.

The Parable of the Pearl

45 "Also, the Kingdom of heaven is like
this. A man is looking for fine pearls,
46 and when he finds one that is unusually fine, he goes and sells everything he
has, and buys that pearl.

The Parable of the Net

47 "Also, the Kingdom of heaven is like
this. Some fishermen throw their net out
in the lake and catch all kinds of fish.
48 When the net is full, they pull it to
shore and sit down to divide the fish: the
good ones go into the buckets, the
worthless ones are thrown away. 49 It
will be like this at the end of the age: the
angels will go out and gather up the evil
people from among the good 50 and will
throw them into the fiery furnace, where
they will cry and gnash their teeth.

New Truths and Old

51 "Do you understand these things?"
Jesus asked them.

"Yes," they answered.

52 So he replied, "This means, then,
that every teacher of the Law who becomes a disciple in the Kingdom of
heaven is like a homeowner who takes
new and old things out of his storage
room."

Jesus Is Rejected at Nazareth

(Mark 6.1-6; Luke 4.16-30)

53 When Jesus finished telling these
parables, he left that place 54 and went
back to his hometown. He taught in the
synagogue, and those who heard him

were amazed. "Where did he get such
wisdom?" they asked. "And what about
his miracles? 55 Isn't he the carpenter's
son? Isn't Mary his mother, and aren't
James, Joseph, Simon, and Judas his
brothers? 56 Aren't all his sisters living
here? Where did he get all this?" 57 And
so they rejected him.

Jesus said to them, "A prophet is respected everywhere except in his hometown and by his own family." 58 Because
they did not have faith, he did not perform many miracles there.

The Death of John the Baptist

(Mark 6.14-29; Luke 9.7-9)

14 At that time Herod, the ruler of
Galilee, heard about Jesus. 2 "He
is really John the Baptist, who has come
back to life," he told his officials. "That is
why he has this power to perform
miracles."

3 For Herod had earlier ordered John's
arrest, and he had him tied up and put in
prison. He had done this because of Herodias, his brother Philip's wife. 4 For
some time John the Baptist had told
Herod, "It isn't right for you to be married to Herodias!" 5 Herod wanted to kill
him, but he was afraid of the Jewish people, because they considered John to be
a prophet.

6 On Herod's birthday the daughter of
Herodias danced in front of the whole
group. Herod was so pleased 7 that he
promised her, "I swear that I will give
you anything you ask for!"

8 At her mother's suggestion she asked
him, "Give me here and now the head of
John the Baptist on a plate!"

9 The king was sad, but because of the
promise he had made in front of all his
guests he gave orders that her wish be
granted. 10 So he had John beheaded in
prison. 11 The head was brought in on a
plate and given to the girl, who took it to
her mother. 12 John's disciples came,
carried away his body, and buried it;
then they went and told Jesus.

Jesus Feeds Five Thousand

(Mark 6.30-44; Luke 9.10-17; John 6.1-14)

13 When Jesus heard the news about
John, he left there in a boat and went to
a lonely place by himself. The people
heard about it, and so they left their
towns and followed him by land. 14 Jesus
got out of the boat, and when he saw the
large crowd, his heart was filled with
pity for them, and he healed their sick.

15 That evening his disciples came to
him and said, "It is already very late, and
this is a lonely place. Send the people
away and let them go to the villages to
buy food for themselves."

16 "They don't have to leave," answered Jesus. "You yourselves give
them something to eat!"

17 "All we have here are five loaves
and two fish," they replied.

18 "Then bring them here to me," Jesus
said. 19 He ordered the people to sit down
on the grass; then he took the five loaves
and the two fish, looked up to heaven,
and gave thanks to God. He broke the
loaves and gave them to the disciples,
and the disciples gave them to the people. 20 Everyone ate and had enough.
Then the disciples took up twelve baskets full of what was left over. 21 The
number of men who ate was about five
thousand, not counting the women and
children.

Jesus Walks on the Water

(Mark 6.45-52; John 6.15-21)

22 Then Jesus made the disciples get
into the boat and go on ahead to the
other side of the lake, while he sent the
people away. 23 After sending the people
away, he went up a hill by himself to
pray. When evening came, Jesus was
there alone; 24 and by this time the boat
was far out in the lake, tossed about by
the waves, because the wind was blowing against it.

25 Between three and six o'clock in the
morning Jesus came to the disciples,
walking on the water. 26 When they saw
him walking on the water, they were terrified. "It's a ghost!" they said, and
screamed with fear.

27 Jesus spoke to them at once. "Courage!" he said. "It is I. Don't be afraid!"

28 Then Peter spoke up. "Lord, if it is
really you, order me to come out on the
water to you."

29 "Come!" answered Jesus. So Peter
got out of the boat and started walking
on the water to Jesus. 30 But when he noticed the strong wind, he was afraid and
started to sink down in the water. "Save
me, Lord!" he cried.

31 At once Jesus reached out and
grabbed hold of him and said, "What little faith you have! Why did you doubt?"

32 They both got into the boat, and the
wind died down. 33 Then the disciples in
the boat worshiped Jesus. "Truly you are
the Son of God!" they exclaimed.

Jesus Heals the Sick in Gennesaret

(Mark 6.53-56)

34 They crossed the lake and came to
land at Gennesaret, 35 where the people
recognized Jesus. So they sent for the
sick people in all the surrounding country and brought them to Jesus. 36 They
begged him to let the sick at least touch
the edge of his cloak; and all who
touched it were made well.

The Teaching of the Ancestors

(Mark 7.1-13)

15 Then some Pharisees and teachers of the Law came from Jerusalem to Jesus and asked him, 2 "Why is
it that your disciples disobey the teaching handed down by our ancestors?
They don't wash their hands in the
proper way before they eat!"
3 Jesus answered, "And why do you
disobey God's command and follow
your own teaching? 4 For God said, 'Respect your father and your mother,' and
'If you curse your father or your mother,
you are to be put to death.' 5 But you
teach that if people have something they
could use to help their father or mother,
but say, 'This belongs to God,' 6 they do
not need to honor their father.[m] In this
way you disregard God's command, in
order to follow your own teaching. 7 You
hypocrites! How right Isaiah was when
he prophesied about you!

8 'These people, says God, honor me
with their words,
but their heart is really far away
from me.
9 It is no use for them to
worship me,
because they teach human rules
as though they were my
laws!' "

The Things That Make a Person Unclean

(Mark 7.14-23)

10 Then Jesus called the crowd to him
and said to them, "Listen and understand! 11 It is not what goes into your
mouth that makes you ritually unclean;
rather, what comes out of it makes you
unclean."
12 Then the disciples came to him and
said, "Do you know that the Pharisees
had their feelings hurt by what you
said?"
13 "Every plant which my Father in
heaven did not plant will be pulled up,"
answered Jesus. 14 "Don't worry about
them! They are blind leaders of the
blind; and when one blind man leads another, both fall into a ditch."
15 Peter spoke up, "Explain this saying
to us."
16 Jesus said to them, "You are still no
more intelligent than the others. 17 Don't
you understand? Anything that goes
into your mouth goes into your stomach
and then on out of your body. 18 But the
things that come out of the mouth come
from the heart, and these are the things
that make you ritually unclean. 19 For
from your heart come the evil ideas
which lead you to kill, commit adultery,
and do other immoral things; to rob, lie,
and slander others. 20 These are the
things that make you unclean. But to eat
without washing your hands as they say
you should—this doesn't make you
unclean."

A Woman's Faith

(Mark 7.24-30)

21 Jesus left that place and went off to
the territory near the cities of Tyre and
Sidon. 22 A Canaanite woman who lived
in that region came to him. "Son of David!" she cried out. "Have mercy on me,
sir! My daughter has a demon and is in
a terrible condition."
23 But Jesus did not say a word to her.
His disciples came to him and begged
him, "Send her away! She is following
us and making all this noise!"
24 Then Jesus replied, "I have been
sent only to the lost sheep of the people
of Israel."
25 At this the woman came and fell at
his feet. "Help me, sir!" she said.
26 Jesus answered, "It isn't right to take
the children's food and throw it to the
dogs."
27 "That's true, sir," she answered, "but
even the dogs eat the leftovers that fall
from their masters' table."
28 So Jesus answered her, "You are a

[m] their father; *some manuscripts have* their father or mother.

woman of great faith! What you want
will be done for you." And at that very
moment her daughter was healed.

Jesus Heals Many People

29 Jesus left there and went along by
Lake Galilee. He climbed a hill and sat
down. 30 Large crowds came to him,
bringing with them the lame, the blind,
the crippled, the dumb, and many other
sick people, whom they placed at Jesus'
feet; and he healed them. 31 The people
were amazed as they saw the dumb
speaking, the crippled made whole, the
lame walking, and the blind seeing; and
they praised the God of Israel.

Jesus Feeds Four Thousand

(Mark 8.1-10)

32 Jesus called his disciples to him and
said, "I feel sorry for these people, because they have been with me for three
days and now have nothing to eat. I
don't want to send them away without
feeding them, for they might faint on
their way home."

33 The disciples asked him, "Where
will we find enough food in this desert to
feed this crowd?"

34 "How much bread do you have?"
Jesus asked.

"Seven loaves," they answered, "and a
few small fish."

35 So Jesus ordered the crowd to sit
down on the ground. 36 Then he took the
seven loaves and the fish, gave thanks to
God, broke them, and gave them to the
disciples; and the disciples gave them to
the people. 37 They all ate and had
enough. Then the disciples took up
seven baskets full of pieces left over.
38 The number of men who ate was four
thousand, not counting the women and
children.

39 Then Jesus sent the people away,
got into a boat, and went to the territory
of Magadan.

The Demand for a Miracle

(Mark 8.11-13; Luke 12.54-56)

16 Some Pharisees and Sadducees
who came to Jesus wanted to
trap him, so they asked him to perform a
miracle for them, to show that God approved of him. 2 But Jesus answered,
"When the sun is setting, you say,
'We are going to have fine weather,
because the sky is red.' 3 And early in
the morning you say, 'It is going to
rain, because the sky is red and dark.'
You can predict the weather by looking
at the sky, but you cannot interpret the
signs concerning these times![n] 4 How
evil and godless are the people of this
day! You ask me for a miracle? No! The
only miracle you will be given is the
miracle of Jonah."

So he left them and went away.

The Yeast of the Pharisees and Sadducees

(Mark 8.14-21)

5 When the disciples crossed over to
the other side of the lake, they forgot to
take any bread. 6 Jesus said to them,
"Take care; be on your guard against the
yeast of the Pharisees and Sadducees."

7 They started discussing among themselves, "He says this because we didn't
bring any bread."

8 Jesus knew what they were saying,
so he asked them, "Why are you discussing among yourselves about not having
any bread? What little faith you have!
9 Don't you understand yet? Don't you
remember when I broke the five loaves
for the five thousand men? How many
baskets did you fill? 10 And what about
the seven loaves for the four thousand
men? How many baskets did you fill?
11 How is it that you don't understand
that I was not talking to you about
bread? Guard yourselves from the yeast
of the Pharisees and Sadducees!"

12 Then the disciples understood that
he was not warning them to guard themselves from the yeast used in bread but
from the teaching of the Pharisees and
Sadducees.

Peter's Declaration about Jesus

(Mark 8.27-30; Luke 9.18-21)

13 Jesus went to the territory near the
town of Caesarea Philippi, where he
asked his disciples, "Who do people say
the Son of Man is?"

14 "Some say John the Baptist," they
answered. "Others say Elijah, while others say Jeremiah or some other
prophet."

15 "What about you?" he asked them.
"Who do you say I am?"

[n] *Some manuscripts do not have the words of Jesus in verses 2-3.*

16 Simon Peter answered, "You are the
Messiah, the Son of the living God."
17 "Good for you, Simon son of John!"
answered Jesus. "For this truth did not
come to you from any human being, but
it was given to you directly by my Father
in heaven. 18 And so I tell you, Peter: you
are a rock, and on this rock foundation I
will build my church, and not even death
will ever be able to overcome it. 19 I will
give you the keys of the Kingdom of
heaven; what you prohibit on earth will
be prohibited in heaven, and what you
permit on earth will be permitted in
heaven."
20 Then Jesus ordered his disciples not
to tell anyone that he was the Messiah.

Jesus Speaks about His Suffering and Death

(Mark 8.31–9.1; Luke 9.22-27)

21 From that time on Jesus began to
say plainly to his disciples, "I must go to
Jerusalem and suffer much from the elders, the chief priests, and the teachers of
the Law. I will be put to death, but three
days later I will be raised to life."
22 Peter took him aside and began to
rebuke him. "God forbid it, Lord!" he
said. "That must never happen to you!"
23 Jesus turned around and said to Peter, "Get away from me, Satan! You are
an obstacle in my way, because these
thoughts of yours don't come from God,
but from human nature."
24 Then Jesus said to his disciples, "If
any of you want to come with me, you
must forget yourself, carry your cross,
and follow me. 25 For if you want to save
your own life, you will lose it; but if you
lose your life for my sake, you will find
it. 26 Will you gain anything if you win
the whole world but lose your life? Of
course not! There is nothing you can
give to regain your life. 27 For the Son of
Man is about to come in the glory of his
Father with his angels, and then he will
reward each one according to his deeds.
28 I assure you that there are some here
who will not die until they have seen the
Son of Man come as King."

The Transfiguration

(Mark 9.2-13; Luke 9.28-36)

17 Six days later Jesus took with
him Peter and the brothers
James and John and led them up a high
mountain where they were alone. 2 As
they looked on, a change came over
Jesus: his face was shining like the sun,
and his clothes were dazzling white.
3 Then the three disciples saw Moses and
Elijah talking with Jesus. 4 So Peter
spoke up and said to Jesus, "Lord, how
good it is that we are here! If you wish,
I will make three tents here, one for you,
one for Moses, and one for Elijah."
5 While he was talking, a shining cloud
came over them, and a voice from the
cloud said, "This is my own dear Son,
with whom I am pleased—listen
to him!"
6 When the disciples heard the voice,
they were so terrified that they threw
themselves face downward on the
ground. 7 Jesus came to them and
touched them. "Get up," he said. "Don't
be afraid!" 8 So they looked up and saw
no one there but Jesus.
9 As they came down the mountain,
Jesus ordered them, "Don't tell anyone
about this vision you have seen until the
Son of Man has been raised from death."
10 Then the disciples asked Jesus,
"Why do the teachers of the Law say
that Elijah has to come first?"
11 "Elijah is indeed coming first," answered Jesus, "and he will get everything ready. 12 But I tell you that Elijah
has already come and people did not
recognize him, but treated him just as
they pleased. In the same way they will
also mistreat the Son of Man."
13 Then the disciples understood that
he was talking to them about John the
Baptist.

Jesus Heals a Boy with a Demon

(Mark 9.14-29; Luke 9.37-43a)

14 When they returned to the crowd, a
man came to Jesus, knelt before him,
15 and said, "Sir, have mercy on my son!
He is an epileptic and has such terrible
attacks that he often falls in the fire or
into water. 16 I brought him to your disciples, but they could not heal him."
17 Jesus answered, "How unbelieving
and wrong you people are! How long
must I stay with you? How long do I
have to put up with you? Bring the boy
here to me!" 18 Jesus gave a command to
the demon, and it went out of the boy,
and at that very moment he was healed.
19 Then the disciples came to Jesus in
private and asked him, "Why couldn't
we drive the demon out?"

20 "It was because you do not have
enough faith," answered Jesus. "I assure
you that if you have faith as big as a
mustard seed, you can say to this hill,
'Go from here to there!' and it will go.
You could do anything!"[o]

Jesus Speaks Again about His Death
(Mark 9.30-32; Luke 9.43b-45)

22 When the disciples all came together
in Galilee, Jesus said to them, "The Son
of Man is about to be handed over to
those 23 who will kill him; but three days
later he will be raised to life."
The disciples became very sad.

Payment of the Temple Tax

24 When Jesus and his disciples came
to Capernaum, the collectors of the Temple tax came to Peter and asked, "Does
your teacher pay the Temple tax?"
25 "Of course," Peter answered.
When Peter went into the house, Jesus
spoke up first, "Simon, what is your
opinion? Who pays duties or taxes to the
kings of this world? The citizens of the
country or the foreigners?"
26 "The foreigners," answered Peter.
"Well, then," replied Jesus, "that
means that the citizens don't have to
pay. 27 But we don't want to offend these
people. So go to the lake and drop in a
line. Pull up the first fish you hook, and
in its mouth you will find a coin worth
enough for my Temple tax and yours.
Take it and pay them our taxes."

Who Is the Greatest?
(Mark 9.33-37; Luke 9.46-48)

18 At that time the disciples came to
Jesus, asking, "Who is the greatest in the Kingdom of heaven?"
2 So Jesus called a child to come and
stand in front of them, 3 and said, "I assure you that unless you change and become like children, you will never enter
the Kingdom of heaven. 4 The greatest in
the Kingdom of heaven is the one who
humbles himself and becomes like this
child. 5 And whoever welcomes in my
name one such child as this, welcomes me.

Temptations to Sin
(Mark 9.42-48; Luke 17.1, 2)

6 "If anyone should cause one of these
little ones to lose his faith in me, it would
be better for that person to have a large
millstone tied around his neck and be
drowned in the deep sea. 7 How terrible
for the world that there are things that
make people lose their faith! Such things
will always happen—but how terrible
for the one who causes them!
8 "If your hand or your foot makes you
lose your faith, cut it off and throw it
away! It is better for you to enter life
without a hand or a foot than to keep
both hands and both feet and be thrown
into the eternal fire. 9 And if your eye
makes you lose your faith, take it out
and throw it away! It is better for you to
enter life with only one eye than to keep
both eyes and be thrown into the fire of
hell.

The Parable of the Lost Sheep
(Luke 15.3-7)

10 "See that you don't despise any of
these little ones. Their angels in heaven,
I tell you, are always in the presence of
my Father in heaven.[p]
12 "What do you think a man does who
has one hundred sheep and one of them
gets lost? He will leave the other ninety-
nine grazing on the hillside and go and
look for the lost sheep. 13 When he finds
it, I tell you, he feels far happier over this
one sheep than over the ninety-nine that
did not get lost. 14 In just the same way
your[q] Father in heaven does not want
any of these little ones to be lost.

When Someone Sins

15 "If your brother sins against you,[r]
go to him and show him his fault. But do
it privately, just between yourselves. If
he listens to you, you have won your
brother back. 16 But if he will not listen to
you, take one or two other persons with
you, so that 'every accusation may be
upheld by the testimony of two or more
witnesses,' as the scripture says. 17 And
if he will not listen to them, then tell the
whole thing to the church. Finally, if he
will not listen to the church, treat him

[o] *Some manuscripts add verse 21:* But only prayer and fasting can drive this kind out; nothing else can *(see Mk 9.29).* [p] *Some manuscripts add verse 11:* For the Son of Man came to save the lost *(see Lk 19.10).* [q] your; *some manuscripts have* my. [r] *Some manuscripts do not have* against you.

as though he were a pagan or a tax
collector.

Prohibiting and Permitting

18 “And so I tell all of you: what you
prohibit on earth will be prohibited in
heaven, and what you permit on earth
will be permitted in heaven.
19 “And I tell you more: whenever two
of you on earth agree about anything
you pray for, it will be done for you by
my Father in heaven. 20 For where two or
three come together in my name, I am
there with them.”

The Parable of the Unforgiving Servant

21 Then Peter came to Jesus and asked,
“Lord, if my brother keeps on sinning
against me, how many times do I have to
forgive him? Seven times?”
22 “No, not seven times,” answered
Jesus, “but seventy times seven,[s] 23 because the Kingdom of heaven is like this.
Once there was a king who decided to
check on his servants' accounts. 24 He
had just begun to do so when one of
them was brought in who owed him millions of dollars. 25 The servant did not
have enough to pay his debt, so the king
ordered him to be sold as a slave, with
his wife and his children and all that he
had, in order to pay the debt. 26 The servant fell on his knees before the king. ‘Be
patient with me,’ he begged, ‘and I will
pay you everything!’ 27 The king felt
sorry for him, so he forgave him the debt
and let him go.
28 “Then the man went out and met one
of his fellow servants who owed him a
few dollars. He grabbed him and started
choking him. ‘Pay back what you owe
me!’ he said. 29 His fellow servant fell
down and begged him, ‘Be patient with
me, and I will pay you back!’ 30 But he
refused; instead, he had him thrown into
jail until he should pay the debt. 31 When
the other servants saw what had happened, they were very upset and went to
the king and told him everything. 32 So
he called the servant in. ‘You worthless
slave!’ he said. ‘I forgave you the whole
amount you owed me, just because you
asked me to. 33 You should have had
mercy on your fellow servant, just as I
had mercy on you.’ 34 The king was very
angry, and he sent the servant to jail to
be punished until he should pay back the
whole amount.”
35 And Jesus concluded, “That is how
my Father in heaven will treat every one
of you unless you forgive your brother
from your heart.”

Jesus Teaches about Divorce

(Mark 10.1-12)

19 When Jesus finished saying
these things, he left Galilee and
went to the territory of Judea on the
other side of the Jordan River. 2 Large
crowds followed him, and he healed
them there.
3 Some Pharisees came to him and
tried to trap him by asking, “Does our
Law allow a man to divorce his wife for
whatever reason he wishes?”
4 Jesus answered, “Haven't you read
the scripture that says that in the beginning the Creator made people male and
female? 5 And God said, ‘For this reason
a man will leave his father and mother
and unite with his wife, and the two will
become one.’ 6 So they are no longer
two, but one. No human being must separate, then, what God has joined
together.”
7 The Pharisees asked him, “Why,
then, did Moses give the law for a man to
hand his wife a divorce notice and send
her away?”
8 Jesus answered, “Moses gave you
permission to divorce your wives because you are so hard to teach. But it
was not like that at the time of creation.
9 I tell you, then, that any man who divorces his wife for any cause other than
her unfaithfulness, commits adultery if
he marries some other woman.”
10 His disciples said to him, “If this is
how it is between a man and his wife, it
is better not to marry.”
11 Jesus answered, “This teaching does
not apply to everyone, but only to those
to whom God has given it. 12 For there
are different reasons why men cannot
marry: some, because they were born
that way; others, because men made
them that way; and others do not marry
for the sake of the Kingdom of heaven.
Let him who can accept this teaching
do so.”

[s] seventy times seven; *or* seventy-seven times.

Jesus Blesses Little Children

(Mark 10.13-16; Luke 18.15-17)

13 Some people brought children to
Jesus for him to place his hands on them
and to pray for them, but the disciples
scolded the people. 14 Jesus said, "Let the
children come to me and do not stop
them, because the Kingdom of heaven
belongs to such as these."
15 He placed his hands on them and
then went away.

The Rich Young Man

(Mark 10.17-31; Luke 18.18-30)

16 Once a man came to Jesus.
"Teacher," he asked, "what good thing
must I do to receive eternal life?"
17 "Why do you ask me concerning
what is good?" answered Jesus. "There
is only One who is good. Keep the commandments if you want to enter life."
18 "What commandments?" he asked.
Jesus answered, "Do not commit murder; do not commit adultery; do not
steal; do not accuse anyone falsely;
19 respect your father and your mother;
and love your neighbor as you love
yourself."
20 "I have obeyed all these commandments," the young man replied. "What
else do I need to do?"
21 Jesus said to him, "If you want to be
perfect, go and sell all you have and give
the money to the poor, and you will have
riches in heaven; then come and follow me."
22 When the young man heard this, he
went away sad, because he was very
rich.
23 Jesus then said to his disciples, "I assure you: it will be very hard for rich
people to enter the Kingdom of heaven.
24 I repeat: it is much harder for a rich
person to enter the Kingdom of God
than for a camel to go through the eye of
a needle."
25 When the disciples heard this, they
were completely amazed. "Who, then,
can be saved?" they asked.
26 Jesus looked straight at them and
answered, "This is impossible for human
beings, but for God everything is
possible."
27 Then Peter spoke up. "Look," he
said, "we have left everything and followed you. What will we have?"
28 Jesus said to them, "You can be sure
that when the Son of Man sits on his glorious throne in the New Age, then you
twelve followers of mine will also sit on
thrones, to rule the twelve tribes of Israel. 29 And everyone who has left
houses or brothers or sisters or father or
mother or children or fields for my sake,
will receive a hundred times more
and will be given eternal life. 30 But
many who now are first will be last, and
many who now are last will be first.

The Workers in the Vineyard

20 "The Kingdom of heaven is like
this. Once there was a man who
went out early in the morning to hire
some men to work in his vineyard. 2 He
agreed to pay them the regular wage, a
silver coin a day, and sent them to work
in his vineyard. 3 He went out again to
the marketplace at nine o'clock and saw
some men standing there doing nothing,
4 so he told them, 'You also go and work
in the vineyard, and I will pay you a fair
wage.' 5 So they went. Then at twelve
o'clock and again at three o'clock he did
the same thing. 6 It was nearly five
o'clock when he went to the marketplace and saw some other men still
standing there. 'Why are you wasting
the whole day here doing nothing?' he
asked them. 7 'No one hired us,' they answered. 'Well, then, you go and work in
the vineyard,' he told them.
8 "When evening came, the owner told
his foreman, 'Call the workers and pay
them their wages, starting with those
who were hired last and ending with
those who were hired first.' 9 The men
who had begun to work at five o'clock
were paid a silver coin each. 10 So when
the men who were the first to be hired
came to be paid, they thought they
would get more; but they too were given
a silver coin each. 11 They took their
money and started grumbling against
the employer. 12 'These men who were
hired last worked only one hour,' they
said, 'while we put up with a whole day's
work in the hot sun—yet you paid them
the same as you paid us!' 13 'Listen,
friend,' the owner answered one of
them, 'I have not cheated you. After all,
you agreed to do a day's work for one
silver coin. 14 Now take your pay and go
home. I want to give this man who was
hired last as much as I gave you. 15 Don't
I have the right to do as I wish with my

own money? Or are you jealous because
I am generous?' "
16 And Jesus concluded, "So those who
are last will be first, and those who are
first will be last."

Jesus Speaks a Third Time about His Death

(Mark 10.32-34; Luke 18.31-34)

17 As Jesus was going up to Jerusalem,
he took the twelve disciples aside and
spoke to them privately, as they walked
along. 18 "Listen," he told them, "we are
going up to Jerusalem, where the Son of
Man will be handed over to the chief
priests and the teachers of the Law.
They will condemn him to death 19 and
then hand him over to the Gentiles, who
will make fun of him, whip him, and crucify him; but three days later he will be
raised to life."

A Mother's Request

(Mark 10.35-45)

20 Then the wife of Zebedee came to
Jesus with her two sons, bowed before
him, and asked him for a favor.
21 "What do you want?" Jesus
asked her.
She answered, "Promise me that these
two sons of mine will sit at your right
and your left when you are King."
22 "You don't know what you are asking for," Jesus answered the sons. "Can
you drink the cup of suffering that I am
about to drink?"
"We can," they answered.
23 "You will indeed drink from my
cup," Jesus told them, "but I do not have
the right to choose who will sit at my
right and my left. These places belong to
those for whom my Father has prepared
them."
24 When the other ten disciples heard
about this, they became angry with the
two brothers. 25 So Jesus called them all
together and said, "You know that the
rulers of the heathen have power over
them, and the leaders have complete authority. 26 This, however, is not the way
it shall be among you. If one of you
wants to be great, you must be the servant of the rest; 27 and if one of you wants
to be first, you must be the slave of the
others — 28 like the Son of Man, who did
not come to be served, but to serve and
to give his life to redeem many people."

Jesus Heals Two Blind Men

(Mark 10.46-52; Luke 18.35-43)

29 As Jesus and his disciples were leaving Jericho, a large crowd was following. 30 Two blind men who were sitting
by the road heard that Jesus was passing by, so they began to shout, "Son of
David! Have mercy on us, sir!"
31 The crowd scolded them and told
them to be quiet. But they shouted even
more loudly, "Son of David! Have mercy
on us, sir!"
32 Jesus stopped and called them.
"What do you want me to do for you?" he
asked them.
33 "Sir," they answered, "we want you
to give us our sight!"
34 Jesus had pity on them and touched
their eyes; at once they were able to see,
and they followed him.

The Triumphant Entry into Jerusalem

(Mark 11.1-11; Luke 19.28-40; John 12.12-19)

21 As Jesus and his disciples approached Jerusalem, they came
to Bethphage at the Mount of Olives.
There Jesus sent two of the disciples on
ahead 2 with these instructions: "Go to
the village there ahead of you, and at
once you will find a donkey tied up with
her colt beside her. Untie them and
bring them to me. 3 And if anyone says
anything, tell him, 'The Master[t] needs
them'; and then he will let them go at
once."
4 This happened in order to make
come true what the prophet had said:
5 "Tell the city of Zion,
Look, your king is coming
to you!
He is humble and rides on a
donkey
and on a colt, the foal of a
donkey."
6 So the disciples went and did what
Jesus had told them to do: 7 they brought
the donkey and the colt, threw their
cloaks over them, and Jesus got on.
8 A large crowd of people spread their
cloaks on the road while others cut
branches from the trees and spread
them on the road. 9 The crowds walking
in front of Jesus and those walking be-

[t] The Master; *or* Their owner.

hind began to shout, "Praise to David's
Son! God bless him who comes in the
name of the Lord! Praise be to God!"
10 When Jesus entered Jerusalem, the
whole city was thrown into an uproar.
"Who is he?" the people asked.
11 "This is the prophet Jesus, from
Nazareth in Galilee," the crowds
answered.

Jesus Goes to the Temple

(Mark 11.15-19; Luke 19.45-48; John 2.13-22)

12 Jesus went into the Temple and
drove out all those who were buying and
selling there. He overturned the tables of
the moneychangers and the stools of
those who sold pigeons, 13 and said to
them, "It is written in the Scriptures that
God said, 'My Temple will be called a
house of prayer.' But you are making it a
hideout for thieves!"
14 The blind and the crippled came to
him in the Temple, and he healed them.
15 The chief priests and the teachers of
the Law became angry when they saw
the wonderful things he was doing and
the children shouting in the Temple,
"Praise to David's Son!" 16 So they asked
Jesus, "Do you hear what they are
saying?"
"Indeed I do," answered Jesus.
"Haven't you ever read this scripture?
'You have trained children and babies to
offer perfect praise.' "
17 Jesus left them and went out of the
city to Bethany, where he spent the
night.

Jesus Curses the Fig Tree

(Mark 11.12-14, 20-24)

18 On his way back to the city early
next morning, Jesus was hungry. 19 He
saw a fig tree by the side of the road and
went to it, but found nothing on it except
leaves. So he said to the tree, "You will
never again bear fruit!" At once the fig
tree dried up.
20 The disciples saw this and were astounded. "How did the fig tree dry up so
quickly?" they asked.
21 Jesus answered, "I assure you that if
you believe and do not doubt, you will be
able to do what I have done to this fig
tree. And not only this, but you will even
be able to say to this hill, 'Get up and
throw yourself in the sea,' and it will. 22 If
you believe, you will receive whatever
you ask for in prayer."

The Question about Jesus' Authority

(Mark 11.27-33; Luke 20.1-8)

23 Jesus came back to the Temple; and
as he taught, the chief priests and the
elders came to him and asked, "What
right do you have to do these things?
Who gave you such right?"
24 Jesus answered them, "I will ask you
just one question, and if you give me an
answer, I will tell you what right I have
to do these things. 25 Where did John's
right to baptize come from: was it from
God or from human beings?"
They started to argue among themselves, "What shall we say? If we answer, 'From God,' he will say to us,
'Why, then, did you not believe John?'
26 But if we say, 'From human beings,'
we are afraid of what the people might
do, because they are all convinced that
John was a prophet." 27 So they answered Jesus, "We don't know."
And he said to them, "Neither will I
tell you, then, by what right I do these
things.

The Parable of the Two Sons

28 "Now, what do you think? There
was once a man who had two sons. He
went to the older one and said, 'Son, go
and work in the vineyard today.' 29 'I
don't want to,' he answered, but later he
changed his mind and went. 30 Then the
father went to the other son and said the
same thing. 'Yes, sir,' he answered, but
he did not go. 31 Which one of the two did
what his father wanted?"
"The older one," they answered.
So Jesus said to them, "I tell you: the
tax collectors and the prostitutes are going into the Kingdom of God ahead of
you. 32 For John the Baptist came to you
showing you the right path to take, and
you would not believe him; but the tax
collectors and the prostitutes believed
him. Even when you saw this, you did
not later change your minds and believe him.

The Parable of the Tenants in the Vineyard

(Mark 12.1-12; Luke 20.9-19)

33 "Listen to another parable," Jesus
said. "There was once a landowner who
planted a vineyard, put a fence around
it, dug a hole for the wine press, and
built a watchtower. Then he rented the

vineyard to tenants and left home on a
trip. 34 When the time came to gather the
grapes, he sent his slaves to the tenants
to receive his share of the harvest. 35 The
tenants grabbed his slaves, beat one,
killed another, and stoned another.
36 Again the man sent other slaves, more
than the first time, and the tenants
treated them the same way. 37 Last of all
he sent his son to them. 'Surely they will
respect my son,' he said. 38 But when the
tenants saw the son, they said to themselves, 'This is the owner's son. Come
on, let's kill him, and we will get his
property!' 39 So they grabbed him, threw
him out of the vineyard, and killed him.

40 "Now, when the owner of the vineyard comes, what will he do to those tenants?" Jesus asked.

41 "He will certainly kill those evil
men," they answered, "and rent the vineyard out to other tenants, who will give
him his share of the harvest at the right
time."

42 Jesus said to them, "Haven't you
ever read what the Scriptures say?

'The stone which the builders
rejected as worthless
turned out to be the most
important of all.
This was done by the Lord;
what a wonderful sight it is!'

43 "And so I tell you," added Jesus, "the
Kingdom of God will be taken away
from you and given to a people who will
produce the proper fruits."[u]

45 The chief priests and the Pharisees
heard Jesus' parables and knew that he
was talking about them, 46 so they tried
to arrest him. But they were afraid of the
crowds, who considered Jesus to be a
prophet.

The Parable of the Wedding Feast

(Luke 14.15-24)

22 Jesus again used parables in
talking to the people. 2 "The
Kingdom of heaven is like this. Once
there was a king who prepared a wedding feast for his son. 3 He sent his servants to tell the invited guests to come to
the feast, but they did not want to come.
4 So he sent other servants with this message for the guests: 'My feast is ready
now; my steers and prize calves have
been butchered, and everything is ready.
Come to the wedding feast!' 5 But the invited guests paid no attention and went
about their business: one went to his
farm, another to his store, 6 while others
grabbed the servants, beat them, and
killed them. 7 The king was very angry;
so he sent his soldiers, who killed those
murderers and burned down their city.
8 Then he called his servants and said to
them, 'My wedding feast is ready, but
the people I invited did not deserve it.
9 Now go to the main streets and invite to
the feast as many people as you find.'
10 So the servants went out into the
streets and gathered all the people they
could find, good and bad alike; and the
wedding hall was filled with people.

11 "The king went in to look at the
guests and saw a man who was not
wearing wedding clothes. 12 'Friend, how
did you get in here without wedding
clothes?' the king asked him. But the
man said nothing. 13 Then the king told
the servants, 'Tie him up hand and foot,
and throw him outside in the dark.
There he will cry and gnash his teeth.' "

14 And Jesus concluded, "Many are invited, but few are chosen."

The Question about Paying Taxes

(Mark 12.13-17; Luke 20.20-26)

15 The Pharisees went off and made a
plan to trap Jesus with questions.
16 Then they sent to him some of their
disciples and some members of Herod's
party. "Teacher," they said, "we know
that you tell the truth. You teach the
truth about God's will for people, without worrying about what others think
because you pay no attention to anyone's status. 17 Tell us, then, what do you
think? Is it against our Law to pay taxes
to the Roman Emperor, or not?"

18 Jesus, however, was aware of their
evil plan, and so he said, "You hypocrites! Why are you trying to trap me?
19 Show me the coin for paying the tax!"

They brought him the coin, 20 and he
asked them, "Whose face and name are
these?"

21 "The Emperor's," they answered.

So Jesus said to them, "Well, then, pay
to the Emperor what belongs to the

[u] *Some manuscripts add verse 44:* Whoever falls on this stone will be cut to pieces; and if the stone falls on someone, it will crush him to dust *(see Lk 20.18).*

Emperor, and pay to God what belongs
to God."
22 When they heard this, they were
amazed; and they left him and went
away.

The Question about Rising from Death

(Mark 12.18-27; Luke 20.27-40)

23 That same day some Sadducees
came to Jesus and claimed that people
will not rise from death. 24 "Teacher,"
they said, "Moses said that if a man who
has no children dies, his brother must
marry the widow so that they can have
children who will be considered the
dead man's children. 25 Now, there were
seven brothers who used to live here.
The oldest got married and died without
having children, so he left his widow to
his brother. 26 The same thing happened
to the second brother, to the third, and
finally to all seven. 27 Last of all, the
woman died. 28 Now, on the day when
the dead rise to life, whose wife will she
be? All of them had married her."
29 Jesus answered them, "How wrong
you are! It is because you don't know the
Scriptures or God's power. 30 For when
the dead rise to life, they will be like the
angels in heaven and will not marry.
31 Now, as for the dead rising to life:
haven't you ever read what God has told
you? He said, 32 'I am the God of Abraham, the God of Isaac, and the God of
Jacob.' He is the God of the living, not of
the dead."
33 When the crowds heard this, they
were amazed at his teaching.

The Great Commandment

(Mark 12.28-34; Luke 10.25-28)

34 When the Pharisees heard that
Jesus had silenced the Sadducees, they
came together, 35 and one of them, a
teacher of the Law, tried to trap him
with a question. 36 "Teacher," he asked,
"which is the greatest commandment in
the Law?"
37 Jesus answered, " 'Love the Lord
your God with all your heart, with all
your soul, and with all your mind.'
38 This is the greatest and the most important commandment. 39 The second
most important commandment is like it:
'Love your neighbor as you love yourself.' 40 The whole Law of Moses and the
teachings of the prophets depend on
these two commandments."

The Question about the Messiah

(Mark 12.35-37; Luke 20.41-44)

41 When some Pharisees gathered together, Jesus asked them, 42 "What do
you think about the Messiah? Whose
descendant is he?"
"He is David's descendant," they
answered.
43 "Why, then," Jesus asked, "did the
Spirit inspire David to call him 'Lord'?
David said,
44 'The Lord said to my Lord:
Sit here at my right side
until I put your enemies under
your feet.'
45 If, then, David called him 'Lord,'
how can the Messiah be David's
descendant?"
46 No one was able to give Jesus any
answer, and from that day on no one
dared to ask him any more questions.

Jesus Warns against the Teachers of the Law and the Pharisees

(Mark 12.38, 39; Luke 11.43, 46; 20.45, 46)

23 Then Jesus spoke to the crowds
and to his disciples. 2 "The teachers of the Law and the Pharisees are the
authorized interpreters of Moses' Law.
3 So you must obey and follow everything they tell you to do; do not, however, imitate their actions, because they
don't practice what they preach. 4 They
tie onto people's backs loads that are
heavy and hard to carry, yet they aren't
willing even to lift a finger to help them
carry those loads. 5 They do everything
so that people will see them. Look at the
straps with scripture verses on them
which they wear on their foreheads and
arms, and notice how large they are! Notice also how long are the tassels on
their cloaks![v] 6 They love the best places
at feasts and the reserved seats in the
synagogues; 7 they love to be greeted
with respect in the marketplaces and to
have people call them 'Teacher.' 8 You
must not be called 'Teacher,' because
you are all equal and have only one
Teacher. 9 And you must not call anyone

[v] TASSELS ON THEIR CLOAKS: *These tassels were worn as a sign of devotion to God (see Nu 15.37-41).*

here on earth 'Father,' because you have
only the one Father in heaven. 10 Nor
should you be called 'Leader,' because
your one and only leader is the Messiah.
11 The greatest one among you must be
your servant. 12 Whoever makes himself
great will be humbled, and whoever
humbles himself will be made great.

Jesus Condemns Their Hypocrisy

(Mark 12.40; Luke 11.39-42, 44, 52; 20.47)

13 "How terrible for you, teachers of
the Law and Pharisees! You hypocrites!
You lock the door to the Kingdom of
heaven in people's faces, but you yourselves don't go in, nor do you allow in
those who are trying to enter![w]
15 "How terrible for you, teachers of
the Law and Pharisees! You hypocrites!
You sail the seas and cross whole countries to win one convert; and when you
succeed, you make him twice as deserving of going to hell as you yourselves are!
16 "How terrible for you, blind guides!
You teach, 'If someone swears by the
Temple, he isn't bound by his vow; but if
he swears by the gold in the Temple, he
is bound.' 17 Blind fools! Which is more
important, the gold or the Temple which
makes the gold holy? 18 You also teach,
'If someone swears by the altar, he isn't
bound by his vow; but if he swears by
the gift on the altar, he is bound.' 19 How
blind you are! Which is the more important, the gift or the altar which makes
the gift holy? 20 So then, when a person
swears by the altar, he is swearing by it
and by all the gifts on it; 21 and when he
swears by the Temple, he is swearing by
it and by God, who lives there; 22 and
when someone swears by heaven, he is
swearing by God's throne and by him
who sits on it.
23 "How terrible for you, teachers of
the Law and Pharisees! You hypocrites!
You give to God one tenth even of the
seasoning herbs, such as mint, dill, and
cumin, but you neglect to obey the really
important teachings of the Law, such as
justice and mercy and honesty. These
you should practice, without neglecting
the others. 24 Blind guides! You strain a
fly out of your drink, but swallow a
camel!
25 "How terrible for you, teachers of
the Law and Pharisees! You hypocrites!
You clean the outside of your cup and
plate, while the inside is full of what you
have gotten by violence and selfishness.
26 Blind Pharisee! Clean what is inside
the cup first, and then the outside will be
clean too!
27 "How terrible for you, teachers of
the Law and Pharisees! You hypocrites!
You are like whitewashed tombs, which
look fine on the outside but are full of
bones and decaying corpses on the inside. 28 In the same way, on the outside
you appear good to everybody, but inside you are full of hypocrisy and sins.

Jesus Predicts Their Punishment

(Luke 11.47-51)

29 "How terrible for you, teachers of
the Law and Pharisees! You hypocrites!
You make fine tombs for the prophets
and decorate the monuments of those
who lived good lives; 30 and you claim
that if you had lived during the time of
your ancestors, you would not have
done what they did and killed the prophets. 31 So you actually admit that you are
the descendants of those who murdered
the prophets! 32 Go on, then, and finish
up what your ancestors started! 33 You
snakes and children of snakes! How do
you expect to escape from being condemned to hell? 34 And so I tell you that
I will send you prophets and wise men
and teachers; you will kill some of them,
crucify others, and whip others in the
synagogues and chase them from town
to town. 35 As a result, the punishment
for the murder of all innocent people
will fall on you, from the murder of innocent Abel to the murder of Zechariah
son of Berechiah, whom you murdered
between the Temple and the altar.
36 I tell you indeed: the punishment for
all these murders will fall on the people
of this day!

Jesus' Love for Jerusalem

(Luke 13.34, 35)

37 "Jerusalem, Jerusalem! You kill the
prophets and stone the messengers God

[w] *Some manuscripts add verse 14:* How terrible for you, teachers of the Law and Pharisees! You hypocrites! You take advantage of widows and rob them of their homes, and then make a show of saying long prayers! Because of this your punishment will be all the worse! *(see Mk 12.40).*

has sent you! How many times I wanted
to put my arms around all your people,
just as a hen gathers her chicks under
her wings, but you would not let me!
38 And so your Temple will be abandoned and empty. 39 From now on, I tell
you, you will never see me again until
you say, 'God bless him who comes in
the name of the Lord.' "

Jesus Speaks of the Destruction of the Temple

(Mark 13.1, 2; Luke 21.5, 6)

24 Jesus left and was going away
from the Temple when his disciples came to him to call his attention to
its buildings. 2 "Yes," he said, "you may
well look at all these. I tell you this: not
a single stone here will be left in its
place; every one of them will be thrown
down."

Troubles and Persecutions

(Mark 13.3-13; Luke 21.7-19)

3 As Jesus sat on the Mount of Olives,
the disciples came to him in private.
"Tell us when all this will be," they
asked, "and what will happen to show
that it is the time for your coming and
the end of the age."
4 Jesus answered, "Watch out, and do
not let anyone fool you. 5 Many men,
claiming to speak for me, will come and
say, 'I am the Messiah!' and they will
fool many people. 6 You are going to
hear the noise of battles close by and the
news of battles far away; but do not be
troubled. Such things must happen, but
they do not mean that the end has come.
7 Countries will fight each other; kingdoms will attack one another. There will
be famines and earthquakes everywhere. 8 All these things are like the first
pains of childbirth.
9 "Then you will be arrested and
handed over to be punished and be put
to death. Everyone will hate you because of me. 10 Many will give up their
faith at that time; they will betray one
another and hate one another. 11 Then
many false prophets will appear and
fool many people. 12 Such will be the
spread of evil that many people's love
will grow cold. 13 But whoever holds out
to the end will be saved. 14 And this Good
News about the Kingdom will be
preached through all the world for a witness to all people; and then the end will
come.

The Awful Horror

(Mark 13.14-23; Luke 21.20-24)

15 "You will see 'The Awful Horror' of
which the prophet Daniel spoke. It will
be standing in the holy place." (Note to
the reader: understand what this
means!) 16 "Then those who are in Judea
must run away to the hills. 17 Someone
who is on the roof of a house must not
take the time to go down and get any
belongings from the house. 18 Someone
who is in the field must not go back to
get a cloak. 19 How terrible it will be in
those days for women who are pregnant
and for mothers with little babies!
20 Pray to God that you will not have to
run away during the winter or on a Sabbath! 21 For the trouble at that time will
be far more terrible than any there has
ever been, from the beginning of the
world to this very day. Nor will there
ever be anything like it again. 22 But God
has already reduced the number of days;
had he not done so, nobody would survive. For the sake of his chosen people,
however, God will reduce the days.
23 "Then, if anyone says to you, 'Look,
here is the Messiah!' or 'There he is!'—
do not believe it. 24 For false Messiahs
and false prophets will appear; they will
perform great miracles and wonders in
order to deceive even God's chosen people, if possible. 25 Listen! I have told you
this ahead of time.
26 "Or, if people should tell you, 'Look,
he is out in the desert!'—don't go there;
or if they say, 'Look, he is hiding
here!'—don't believe it. 27 For the Son of
Man will come like the lightning which
flashes across the whole sky from the
east to the west.
28 "Wherever there is a dead body, the
vultures will gather.

The Coming of the Son of Man

(Mark 13.24-27; Luke 21.25-28)

29 "Soon after the trouble of those
days, the sun will grow dark, the moon
will no longer shine, the stars will fall
from heaven, and the powers in space
will be driven from their courses. 30 Then
the sign of the Son of Man will appear in
the sky; and all the peoples of earth will
weep as they see the Son of Man coming
on the clouds of heaven with power and

great glory. 31 The great trumpet will
sound, and he will send out his angels to
the four corners of the earth, and they
will gather his chosen people from one
end of the world to the other.

The Lesson of the Fig Tree

(Mark 13.28-31; Luke 21.29-33)

32 "Let the fig tree teach you a lesson.
When its branches become green and
tender and it starts putting out leaves,
you know that summer is near. 33 In the
same way, when you see all these things,
you will know that the time is near,
ready to begin.[x] 34 Remember that all
these things will happen before the people now living have all died. 35 Heaven
and earth will pass away, but my words
will never pass away.

No One Knows the Day and Hour

(Mark 13.32-37; Luke 17.26-30, 34-36)

36 "No one knows, however, when that
day and hour will come — neither the angels in heaven nor the Son;[y] the Father
alone knows. 37 The coming of the Son of
Man will be like what happened in the
time of Noah. 38 In the days before the
flood people ate and drank, men and
women married, up to the very day
Noah went into the boat; 39 yet they did
not realize what was happening until the
flood came and swept them all away.
That is how it will be when the Son of
Man comes. 40 At that time two men will
be working in a field: one will be taken
away, the other will be left behind.
41 Two women will be at a mill grinding
meal: one will be taken away, the other
will be left behind. 42 Watch out, then,
because you do not know what day your
Lord will come. 43 If the owner of a house
knew the time when the thief would
come, you can be sure that he would
stay awake and not let the thief break
into his house. 44 So then, you also must
always be ready, because the Son of
Man will come at an hour when you are
not expecting him.

The Faithful or the Unfaithful Servant

(Luke 12.41-48)

45 "Who, then, is a faithful and wise
servant? It is the one that his master has
placed in charge of the other servants to
give them their food at the proper time.
46 How happy that servant is if his master finds him doing this when he comes
home! 47 Indeed, I tell you, the master
will put that servant in charge of all his
property. 48 But if he is a bad servant, he
will tell himself that his master will not
come back for a long time, 49 and he will
begin to beat his fellow servants and to
eat and drink with drunkards. 50 Then
that servant's master will come back one
day when the servant does not expect
him and at a time he does not know.
51 The master will cut him in pieces[z]
and make him share the fate of the hypocrites. There he will cry and gnash his
teeth.

The Parable of the Ten Young Women

25 "At that time the Kingdom of
heaven will be like this. Once
there were ten young women who took
their oil lamps and went out to meet the
bridegroom. 2 Five of them were foolish,
and the other five were wise. 3 The foolish ones took their lamps but did not
take any extra oil with them, 4 while the
wise ones took containers full of oil for
their lamps. 5 The bridegroom was late
in coming, so they began to nod and fall
asleep.

6 "It was already midnight when the
cry rang out, 'Here is the bridegroom!
Come and meet him!' 7 The ten young
women woke up and trimmed their
lamps. 8 Then the foolish ones said to the
wise ones, 'Let us have some of your oil,
because our lamps are going out.' 9 'No,
indeed,' the wise ones answered, 'there
is not enough for you and for us. Go to
the store and buy some for yourselves.'
10 So the foolish ones went off to buy
some oil; and while they were gone, the
bridegroom arrived. The five who were
ready went in with him to the wedding
feast, and the door was closed.

11 "Later the others arrived. 'Sir, sir!
Let us in!' they cried out. 12 'Certainly
not! I don't know you,' the bridegroom
answered."

13 And Jesus concluded, "Watch out
then, because you do not know the day
or the hour.

[x] the time is near, ready to begin; *or* he is near, ready to come. [y] *Some manuscripts do not have* nor the Son. [z] cut him in pieces; *or* throw him out.

The Parable of the Three Servants

(Luke 19.11-27)

14 “At that time the Kingdom of heaven
will be like this. Once there was a man
who was about to leave home on a trip;
he called his servants and put them in
charge of his property. 15 He gave to
each one according to his ability: to one
he gave five thousand gold coins, to another he gave two thousand, and to another he gave one thousand. Then he left
on his trip. 16 The servant who had received five thousand coins went at once
and invested his money and earned another five thousand. 17 In the same way
the servant who had received two thousand coins earned another two thousand. 18 But the servant who had
received one thousand coins went off,
dug a hole in the ground, and hid his
master's money.

19 “After a long time the master of
those servants came back and settled accounts with them. 20 The servant who
had received five thousand coins came
in and handed over the other five thousand. ‘You gave me five thousand coins,
sir,’ he said. ‘Look! Here are another five
thousand that I have earned.’ 21 ‘Well
done, you good and faithful servant!’
said his master. ‘You have been faithful
in managing small amounts, so I will put
you in charge of large amounts. Come
on in and share my happiness!’ 22 Then
the servant who had been given two
thousand coins came in and said, ‘You
gave me two thousand coins, sir. Look!
Here are another two thousand that I
have earned.’ 23 ‘Well done, you good
and faithful servant!’ said his master.
‘You have been faithful in managing
small amounts, so I will put you in
charge of large amounts. Come on in
and share my happiness!’ 24 Then the
servant who had received one thousand
coins came in and said, ‘Sir, I know you
are a hard man; you reap harvests
where you did not plant, and you gather
crops where you did not scatter seed.
25 I was afraid, so I went off and hid your
money in the ground. Look! Here is
what belongs to you.’ 26 ‘You bad and
lazy servant!’ his master said. ‘You
knew, did you, that I reap harvests
where I did not plant, and gather crops
where I did not scatter seed? 27 Well,
then, you should have deposited my
money in the bank, and I would have
received it all back with interest when I
returned. 28 Now, take the money away
from him and give it to the one who has
ten thousand coins. 29 For to every person who has something, even more will
be given, and he will have more than
enough; but the person who has nothing,
even the little that he has will be taken
away from him. 30 As for this useless
servant — throw him outside in the darkness; there he will cry and gnash his
teeth.’

The Final Judgment

31 “When the Son of Man comes as
King and all the angels with him, he will
sit on his royal throne, 32 and the people
of all the nations will be gathered before
him. Then he will divide them into two
groups, just as a shepherd separates the
sheep from the goats. 33 He will put the
righteous people at his right and the others at his left. 34 Then the King will say to
the people on his right, ‘Come, you that
are blessed by my Father! Come and
possess the kingdom which has been
prepared for you ever since the creation
of the world. 35 I was hungry and you fed
me, thirsty and you gave me a drink; I
was a stranger and you received me in
your homes, 36 naked and you clothed
me; I was sick and you took care of me,
in prison and you visited me.’ 37 The
righteous will then answer him, ‘When,
Lord, did we ever see you hungry and
feed you, or thirsty and give you a
drink? 38 When did we ever see you a
stranger and welcome you in our homes,
or naked and clothe you? 39 When did we
ever see you sick or in prison, and visit
you?’ 40 The King will reply, ‘I tell you,
whenever you did this for one of the
least important of these followers of
mine, you did it for me!’

41 “Then he will say to those on his left,
‘Away from me, you that are under
God's curse! Away to the eternal fire
which has been prepared for the Devil
and his angels! 42 I was hungry but you
would not feed me, thirsty but you
would not give me a drink; 43 I was a
stranger but you would not welcome me
in your homes, naked but you would not
clothe me; I was sick and in prison but
you would not take care of me.’ 44 Then
they will answer him, ‘When, Lord, did
we ever see you hungry or thirsty or a

stranger or naked or sick or in prison,
and we would not help you?' 45 The King
will reply, 'I tell you, whenever you refused to help one of these least important ones, you refused to help me.'
46 These, then, will be sent off to eternal
punishment, but the righteous will go to
eternal life."

The Plot against Jesus

(Mark 14.1, 2; Luke 22.1, 2; John 11.45-53)

26 When Jesus had finished teaching all these things, he said to his
disciples, 2 "In two days, as you know, it
will be the Passover Festival, and the
Son of Man will be handed over to be
crucified."
3 Then the chief priests and the elders
met together in the palace of Caiaphas,
the High Priest, 4 and made plans to arrest Jesus secretly and put him to death.
5 "We must not do it during the festival,"
they said, "or the people will riot."

Jesus Is Anointed at Bethany

(Mark 14.3-9; John 12.1-8)

6 Jesus was in Bethany at the house of
Simon, a man who had suffered from a
dreaded skin disease. 7 While Jesus was
eating, a woman came to him with an
alabaster jar filled with an expensive
perfume, which she poured on his head.
8 The disciples saw this and became angry. "Why all this waste?" they asked.
9 "This perfume could have been sold for
a large amount and the money given to
the poor!"
10 Jesus knew what they were saying,
and so he said to them, "Why are you
bothering this woman? It is a fine and
beautiful thing that she has done for me.
11 You will always have poor people with
you, but you will not always have me.
12 What she did was to pour this perfume
on my body to get me ready for burial.
13 Now, I assure you that wherever this
gospel is preached all over the world,
what she has done will be told in memory of her."

Judas Agrees to Betray Jesus

(Mark 14.10, 11; Luke 22.3-6)

14 Then one of the twelve disciples—
the one named Judas Iscariot—went to
the chief priests 15 and asked, "What will
you give me if I betray Jesus to you?"
They counted out thirty silver coins and
gave them to him. 16 From then on Judas
was looking for a good chance to hand
Jesus over to them.

Jesus Eats the Passover Meal with His Disciples

(Mark 14.12-21; Luke 22.7-13, 21-23; John 13.21-30)

17 On the first day of the Festival of Unleavened Bread the disciples came to
Jesus and asked him, "Where do you
want us to get the Passover meal ready
for you?"
18 "Go to a certain man in the city," he
said to them, "and tell him: 'The Teacher
says, My hour has come; my disciples
and I will celebrate the Passover at your
house.' "
19 The disciples did as Jesus had told
them and prepared the Passover meal.
20 When it was evening, Jesus and the
twelve disciples sat down to eat. 21 During the meal Jesus said, "I tell you, one
of you will betray me."
22 The disciples were very upset and
began to ask him, one after the other,
"Surely, Lord, you don't mean me?"
23 Jesus answered, "One who dips his
bread in the dish with me will betray me.
24 The Son of Man will die as the Scriptures say he will, but how terrible for
that man who will betray the Son of
Man! It would have been better for that
man if he had never been born!"
25 Judas, the traitor, spoke up. "Surely,
Teacher, you don't mean me?" he asked.
Jesus answered, "So you say."

The Lord's Supper

(Mark 14.22-26; Luke 22.14-20; 1 Corinthians 11.23-25)

26 While they were eating, Jesus took a
piece of bread, gave a prayer of thanks,
broke it, and gave it to his disciples.
"Take and eat it," he said; "this is my
body."
27 Then he took a cup, gave thanks to
God, and gave it to them. "Drink it, all of
you," he said; 28 "this is my blood, which
seals God's covenant, my blood poured
out for many for the forgiveness of sins.
29 I tell you, I will never again drink this
wine until the day I drink the new wine
with you in my Father's Kingdom."
30 Then they sang a hymn and went
out to the Mount of Olives.

Jesus Predicts Peter's Denial

(Mark 14.27-31; Luke 22.31-34; John 13.36-38)

31 Then Jesus said to them, "This very
night all of you will run away and leave
me, for the scripture says, 'God will kill
the shepherd, and the sheep of the flock
will be scattered.' 32 But after I am raised
to life, I will go to Galilee ahead of you."
33 Peter spoke up and said to Jesus, "I
will never leave you, even though all the
rest do!"
34 Jesus said to Peter, "I tell you that
before the rooster crows tonight, you
will say three times that you do not
know me."
35 Peter answered, "I will never say
that, even if I have to die with you!"
And all the other disciples said the
same thing.

Jesus Prays in Gethsemane

(Mark 14.32-42; Luke 22.39-46)

36 Then Jesus went with his disciples
to a place called Gethsemane, and he
said to them, "Sit here while I go over
there and pray." 37 He took with him Peter and the two sons of Zebedee. Grief
and anguish came over him, 38 and he
said to them, "The sorrow in my heart is
so great that it almost crushes me. Stay
here and keep watch with me."
39 He went a little farther on, threw
himself face downward on the ground,
and prayed, "My Father, if it is possible,
take this cup of suffering from me! Yet
not what I want, but what you want."
40 Then he returned to the three disciples and found them asleep; and he said
to Peter, "How is it that you three were
not able to keep watch with me for even
one hour? 41 Keep watch and pray that
you will not fall into temptation. The
spirit is willing, but the flesh is weak."
42 Once more Jesus went away and
prayed, "My Father, if this cup of suffering cannot be taken away unless I drink
it, your will be done." 43 He returned
once more and found the disciples
asleep; they could not keep their eyes
open.
44 Again Jesus left them, went away,
and prayed the third time, saying the
same words. 45 Then he returned to the
disciples and said, "Are you still sleeping and resting? Look! The hour has
come for the Son of Man to be handed
over to the power of sinners. 46 Get up,
let us go. Look, here is the man who is
betraying me!"

The Arrest of Jesus

(Mark 14.43-50; Luke 22.47-53; John 18.3-12)

47 Jesus was still speaking when Judas, one of the twelve disciples, arrived.
With him was a large crowd armed with
swords and clubs and sent by the chief
priests and the elders. 48 The traitor had
given the crowd a signal: "The man I
kiss is the one you want. Arrest him!"
49 Judas went straight to Jesus and
said, "Peace be with you, Teacher," and
kissed him.
50 Jesus answered, "Be quick about it,
friend!"[a]
Then they came up, arrested Jesus,
and held him tight. 51 One of those who
were with Jesus drew his sword and
struck at the High Priest's slave, cutting
off his ear. 52 "Put your sword back in its
place," Jesus said to him. "All who take
the sword will die by the sword. 53 Don't
you know that I could call on my Father
for help, and at once he would send me
more than twelve armies of angels?
54 But in that case, how could the Scriptures come true which say that this is
what must happen?"
55 Then Jesus spoke to the crowd, "Did
you have to come with swords and clubs
to capture me, as though I were an outlaw? Every day I sat down and taught in
the Temple, and you did not arrest me.
56 But all this has happened in order to
make come true what the prophets
wrote in the Scriptures."
Then all the disciples left him and ran
away.

Jesus before the Council

(Mark 14.53-65; Luke 22.54, 55, 63-71; John 18.13, 14, 19-24)

57 Those who had arrested Jesus took
him to the house of Caiaphas, the High
Priest, where the teachers of the Law
and the elders had gathered together.
58 Peter followed from a distance, as far
as the courtyard of the High Priest's
house. He went into the courtyard and
sat down with the guards to see how it
would all come out. 59 The chief priests
and the whole Council tried to find some

[a] Be quick about it, friend!; *or* Why are you here, friend?

false evidence against Jesus to put him
to death; 60 but they could not find any,
even though many people came forward
and told lies about him. Finally two men
stepped up 61 and said, "This man said, 'I
am able to tear down God's Temple and
three days later build it back up.' "
62 The High Priest stood up and said to
Jesus, "Have you no answer to give to
this accusation against you?" 63 But
Jesus kept quiet. Again the High Priest
spoke to him, "In the name of the living
God I now put you under oath: tell us if
you are the Messiah, the Son of God."
64 Jesus answered him, "So you say.
But I tell all of you: from this time on you
will see the Son of Man sitting at the
right side of the Almighty and coming
on the clouds of heaven!"
65 At this the High Priest tore his
clothes and said, "Blasphemy! We don't
need any more witnesses! You have just
heard his blasphemy! 66 What do you
think?"
They answered, "He is guilty and
must die."
67 Then they spat in his face and beat
him; and those who slapped him 68 said,
"Prophesy for us, Messiah! Guess who
hit you!"

Peter Denies Jesus

(Mark 14.66-72; Luke 22.56-62; John 18.15-18, 25-27)

69 Peter was sitting outside in the
courtyard when one of the High Priest's
servant women came to him and said,
"You, too, were with Jesus of Galilee."
70 But he denied it in front of them all.
"I don't know what you are talking
about," he answered, 71 and went on out
to the entrance of the courtyard. Another
servant woman saw him and said
to the men there, "He was with Jesus of
Nazareth."
72 Again Peter denied it and answered,
"I swear that I don't know that man!"
73 After a little while the men standing
there came to Peter. "Of course you are
one of them," they said. "After all, the
way you speak gives you away!"
74 Then Peter said, "I swear that I am
telling the truth! May God punish me if I
am not! I do not know that man!"
Just then a rooster crowed, 75 and Peter
remembered what Jesus had told
him: "Before the rooster crows, you will
say three times that you do not know
me." He went out and wept bitterly.

Jesus Is Taken to Pilate

(Mark 15.1; Luke 23.1, 2; John 18.28-32)

27 Early in the morning all the chief
priests and the elders made their
plans against Jesus to put him to death.
2 They put him in chains, led him off, and
handed him over to Pilate, the Roman
governor.

The Death of Judas

(Acts 1.18, 19)

3 When Judas, the traitor, learned that
Jesus had been condemned, he repented
and took back the thirty silver coins to
the chief priests and the elders. 4 "I have
sinned by betraying an innocent man to
death!" he said.
"What do we care about that?" they
answered. "That is your business!"
5 Judas threw the coins down in the
Temple and left; then he went off and
hanged himself.
6 The chief priests picked up the coins
and said, "This is blood money, and it is
against our Law to put it in the Temple
treasury." 7 After reaching an agreement
about it, they used the money to buy Potter's
Field, as a cemetery for foreigners.
8 That is why that field is called "Field of
Blood" to this very day.
9 Then what the prophet Jeremiah had
said came true: "They took the thirty silver
coins, the amount the people of Israel
had agreed to pay for him, 10 and
used the money to buy the potter's field,
as the Lord had commanded me."

Pilate Questions Jesus

(Mark 15.2-5; Luke 23.3-5; John 18.33-38)

11 Jesus stood before the Roman governor,
who questioned him. "Are you the
king of the Jews?" he asked.
"So you say," answered Jesus. 12 But
he said nothing in response to the accusations
of the chief priests and elders.
13 So Pilate said to him, "Don't you
hear all these things they accuse
you of?"
14 But Jesus refused to answer a single
word, with the result that the Governor
was greatly surprised.

Jesus Is Sentenced to Death

(Mark 15.6-15; Luke 23.13-25; John 18.39—19.16)

15 At every Passover Festival the Roman
governor was in the habit of setting
free any one prisoner the crowd asked
for. 16 At that time there was a well-

known prisoner named Jesus Barabbas.
17 So when the crowd gathered, Pilate
asked them, "Which one do you want me
to set free for you? Jesus Barabbas or
Jesus called the Messiah?" 18 He knew
very well that the Jewish authorities had
handed Jesus over to him because they
were jealous.

19 While Pilate was sitting in the judgment hall, his wife sent him a message:
"Have nothing to do with that innocent
man, because in a dream last night I suffered much on account of him."

20 The chief priests and the elders persuaded the crowd to ask Pilate to set
Barabbas free and have Jesus put to
death. 21 But Pilate asked the crowd,
"Which one of these two do you want me
to set free for you?"

"Barabbas!" they answered.

22 "What, then, shall I do with Jesus
called the Messiah?" Pilate asked them.

"Crucify him!" they all answered.

23 But Pilate asked, "What crime has
he committed?"

Then they started shouting at the top
of their voices: "Crucify him!"

24 When Pilate saw that it was no use
to go on, but that a riot might break out,
he took some water, washed his hands
in front of the crowd, and said, "I am not
responsible for the death of this man!
This is your doing!"

25 The whole crowd answered, "Let the
responsibility for his death fall on us and
on our children!"

26 Then Pilate set Barabbas free for
them; and after he had Jesus whipped,
he handed him over to be crucified.

The Soldiers Make Fun of Jesus

(Mark 15.16-20; John 19.2, 3)

27 Then Pilate's soldiers took Jesus
into the governor's palace, and the
whole company gathered around him.
28 They stripped off his clothes and put a
scarlet robe on him. 29 Then they made a
crown out of thorny branches and
placed it on his head, and put a stick in
his right hand; then they knelt before
him and made fun of him. "Long live the
King of the Jews!" they said. 30 They spat
on him, and took the stick and hit him
over the head. 31 When they had finished
making fun of him, they took the robe
off and put his own clothes back on him.
Then they led him out to crucify him.

Jesus Is Crucified

(Mark 15.21-32; Luke 23.26-43; John 19.17-27)

32 As they were going out, they met a
man from Cyrene named Simon, and the
soldiers forced him to carry Jesus' cross.
33 They came to a place called Golgotha,
which means, "The Place of the Skull."
34 There they offered Jesus wine mixed
with a bitter substance; but after tasting
it, he would not drink it.

35 They crucified him and then divided
his clothes among them by throwing
dice. 36 After that they sat there and
watched him. 37 Above his head they put
the written notice of the accusation
against him: "This is Jesus, the King of
the Jews." 38 Then they crucified two
bandits with Jesus, one on his right and
the other on his left.

39 People passing by shook their heads
and hurled insults at Jesus: 40 "You were
going to tear down the Temple and build
it back up in three days! Save yourself if
you are God's Son! Come on down from
the cross!"

41 In the same way the chief priests
and the teachers of the Law and the elders made fun of him: 42 "He saved others,
but he cannot save himself! Isn't he the
king of Israel? If he will come down off
the cross now, we will believe in him!
43 He trusts in God and claims to be
God's Son. Well, then, let us see if God
wants to save him now!"

44 Even the bandits who had been crucified with him insulted him in the
same way.

The Death of Jesus

(Mark 15.33-41; Luke 23.44-49; John 19.28-30)

45 At noon the whole country was covered with darkness, which lasted for
three hours. 46 At about three o'clock
Jesus cried out with a loud shout, *"Eli,
Eli, lema sabachthani?"* which means,
"My God, my God, why did you abandon me?"

47 Some of the people standing there
heard him and said, "He is calling for
Elijah!" 48 One of them ran up at once,
took a sponge, soaked it in cheap wine,
put it on the end of a stick, and tried to
make him drink it.

49 But the others said, "Wait, let us see
if Elijah is coming to save him!"

50 Jesus again gave a loud cry and
breathed his last.

51 Then the curtain hanging in the
Temple was torn in two from top to bottom. The earth shook, the rocks split
apart, 52 the graves broke open, and
many of God's people who had died
were raised to life. 53 They left the
graves, and after Jesus rose from death,
they went into the Holy City, where
many people saw them.

54 When the army officer and the soldiers with him who were watching Jesus
saw the earthquake and everything else
that happened, they were terrified and
said, "He really was the Son of God!"

55 There were many women there,
looking on from a distance, who had followed Jesus from Galilee and helped
him. 56 Among them were Mary Magdalene, Mary the mother of James and Joseph, and the wife of Zebedee.

The Burial of Jesus

(Mark 15.42-47; Luke 23.50-56; John 19.38-42)

57 When it was evening, a rich man
from Arimathea arrived; his name was
Joseph, and he also was a disciple of
Jesus. 58 He went into the presence of Pilate and asked for the body of Jesus. Pilate gave orders for the body to be given
to Joseph. 59 So Joseph took it, wrapped
it in a new linen sheet, 60 and placed it in
his own tomb, which he had just recently dug out of solid rock. Then he
rolled a large stone across the entrance
to the tomb and went away. 61 Mary
Magdalene and the other Mary were sitting there, facing the tomb.

The Guard at the Tomb

62 The next day, which was a Sabbath,
the chief priests and the Pharisees met
with Pilate 63 and said, "Sir, we remember that while that liar was still alive he
said, 'I will be raised to life three days
later.' 64 Give orders, then, for his tomb
to be carefully guarded until the third
day, so that his disciples will not be able
to go and steal the body, and then tell the
people that he was raised from death.
This last lie would be even worse than
the first one."

65 "Take a guard," Pilate told them; "go
and make the tomb as secure as
you can."

66 So they left and made the tomb secure by putting a seal on the stone and
leaving the guard on watch.

The Resurrection

(Mark 16.1-10; Luke 24.1-12; John 20.1-10)

28 After the Sabbath, as Sunday
morning was dawning, Mary
Magdalene and the other Mary went to
look at the tomb. 2 Suddenly there was a
violent earthquake; an angel of the Lord
came down from heaven, rolled the
stone away, and sat on it. 3 His appearance was like lightning, and his clothes
were white as snow. 4 The guards were
so afraid that they trembled and became
like dead men.

5 The angel spoke to the women. "You
must not be afraid," he said. "I know you
are looking for Jesus, who was crucified.
6 He is not here; he has been raised, just
as he said. Come here and see the place
where he was lying. 7 Go quickly now,
and tell his disciples, 'He has been raised
from death, and now he is going to Galilee ahead of you; there you will see him!'
Remember what I have told you."

8 So they left the tomb in a hurry,
afraid and yet filled with joy, and ran to
tell his disciples.

9 Suddenly Jesus met them and said,
"Peace be with you." They came up to
him, took hold of his feet, and worshiped
him. 10 "Do not be afraid," Jesus said to
them. "Go and tell my brothers to go to
Galilee, and there they will see me."

The Report of the Guard

11 While the women went on their way,
some of the soldiers guarding the tomb
went back to the city and told the chief
priests everything that had happened.
12 The chief priests met with the elders
and made their plan; they gave a large
sum of money to the soldiers 13 and said,
"You are to say that his disciples came
during the night and stole his body while
you were asleep. 14 And if the Governor
should hear of this, we will convince him
that you are innocent, and you will have
nothing to worry about."

15 The guards took the money and did
what they were told to do. And so that is
the report spread around by the Jews to
this very day.

Jesus Appears to His Disciples

(Mark 16.14-18; Luke 24.36-49; John 20.19-23; Acts 1.6-8)

16 The eleven disciples went to the hill
in Galilee where Jesus had told them to
go. 17 When they saw him, they wor-

shiped him, even though some of them
doubted. 18 Jesus drew near and said to
them, "I have been given all authority in
heaven and on earth. 19 Go, then, to all
peoples everywhere and make them my
disciples: baptize them in the name of
the Father, the Son, and the Holy Spirit,
20 and teach them to obey everything I
have commanded you. And I will be with
you always, to the end of the age."

The Gospel according to
MARK

Introduction

The Gospel according to Mark *begins with the statement that it is "the Good News about Jesus Christ, the Son of God." Jesus is pictured as a man of action and authority. His authority is seen in his teaching, in his power over demons, and in forgiving people's sins. Jesus speaks of himself as the Son of Man, who came to give his life to set people free from sin.*

Mark *presents the story of Jesus in a straightforward, vigorous way, with emphasis on what Jesus did, rather than on his words and teachings. After a brief prologue about John the Baptist and the baptism and temptation of Jesus, the writer immediately takes up Jesus' ministry of healing and teaching. As time goes on, the followers of Jesus come to understand him better, but Jesus' opponents become more hostile. The closing chapters report the events of Jesus' last week of earthly life, especially his crucifixion and resurrection.*

The two endings to the Gospel, which are enclosed in brackets, are generally regarded as written by someone other than the author of Mark.

Outline of Contents

The Preaching of John the Baptist

(Matthew 3.1-12; Luke 3.1-18; John 1.19-28)

1 This is the Good News about Jesus
Christ, the Son of God.[a] 2 It began
as the prophet Isaiah had written:

"God said, 'I will send my
messenger ahead of you
to open the way for you.'
3 Someone is shouting in the desert,
'Get the road ready for the
Lord;
make a straight path for him to
travel!' "

4 So John appeared in the desert, baptizing and preaching.[b] "Turn away from
your sins and be baptized," he told the
people, "and God will forgive your sins."
5 Many people from the province of Judea and the city of Jerusalem went out to
hear John. They confessed their sins,
and he baptized them in the Jordan
River.
6 John wore clothes made of camel's
hair, with a leather belt around his
waist, and his food was locusts and wild
honey. 7 He announced to the people,
"The man who will come after me is
much greater than I am. I am not good
enough even to bend down and untie his
sandals. 8 I baptize you with water,
but he will baptize you with the Holy
Spirit."

The Baptism and Temptation of Jesus

(Matthew 3.13—4.11; Luke 3.21, 22; 4.1-13)

9 Not long afterward Jesus came from
Nazareth in the province of Galilee, and
was baptized by John in the Jordan.
10 As soon as Jesus came up out of the
water, he saw heaven opening and the
Spirit coming down on him like a dove.
11 And a voice came from heaven, "You
are my own dear Son. I am pleased
with you."
12 At once the Spirit made him go into
the desert, 13 where he stayed forty days,
being tempted by Satan. Wild animals
were there also, but angels came and
helped him.

[a] *Some manuscripts do not have* the Son of God. [b] John appeared in the desert, baptizing and preaching; *some manuscripts have* John the Baptist appeared in the desert, preaching.

Jesus Calls Four Fishermen

(Matthew 4.12-22; Luke 4.14, 15; 5.1-11)

14 After John had been put in prison,
Jesus went to Galilee and preached the
Good News from God. 15 "The right time
has come," he said, "and the Kingdom of
God is near! Turn away from your sins
and believe the Good News!"

16 As Jesus walked along the shore
of Lake Galilee, he saw two fishermen, Simon and his brother Andrew, catching fish with a net. 17 Jesus
said to them, "Come with me, and I
will teach you to catch people." 18 At
once they left their nets and went with
him.

19 He went a little farther on and saw
two other brothers, James and John,
the sons of Zebedee. They were in
their boat getting their nets ready. 20 As
soon as Jesus saw them, he called them;
they left their father Zebedee in the
boat with the hired men and went with
Jesus.

A Man with an Evil Spirit

(Luke 4.31-37)

21 Jesus and his disciples came to the
town of Capernaum, and on the next
Sabbath Jesus went to the synagogue
and began to teach. 22 The people who
heard him were amazed at the way he
taught, for he wasn't like the teachers of
the Law; instead, he taught with authority.

23 Just then a man with an evil spirit
came into the synagogue and screamed,
24 "What do you want with us, Jesus of
Nazareth? Are you here to destroy us? I
know who you are—you are God's holy
messenger!"

25 Jesus ordered the spirit, "Be quiet,
and come out of the man!"

26 The evil spirit shook the man hard,
gave a loud scream, and came out of
him. 27 The people were all so amazed
that they started saying to one another,
"What is this? Is it some kind of new
teaching? This man has authority to give
orders to the evil spirits, and they
obey him!"

28 And so the news about Jesus spread
quickly everywhere in the province of
Galilee.

Jesus Heals Many People

(Matthew 8.14-17; Luke 4.38-41)

29 Jesus and his disciples, including
James and John, left the synagogue and
went straight to the home of Simon and
Andrew. 30 Simon's mother-in-law was
sick in bed with a fever, and as soon as
Jesus arrived, he was told about her.
31 He went to her, took her by the hand,
and helped her up. The fever left her,
and she began to wait on them.

32 After the sun had set and evening
had come, people brought to Jesus all
the sick and those who had demons.
33 All the people of the town gathered in
front of the house. 34 Jesus healed many
who were sick with all kinds of diseases
and drove out many demons. He would
not let the demons say anything, because they knew who he was.

Jesus Preaches in Galilee

(Luke 4.42-44)

35 Very early the next morning, long
before daylight, Jesus got up and left the
house. He went out of town to a lonely
place, where he prayed. 36 But Simon
and his companions went out searching
for him, 37 and when they found him,
they said, "Everyone is looking for you."

38 But Jesus answered, "We must go on
to the other villages around here. I have
to preach in them also, because that is
why I came."

39 So he traveled all over Galilee,
preaching in the synagogues and driving
out demons.

Jesus Heals a Man

(Matthew 8.1-4; Luke 5.12-16)

40 A man suffering from a dreaded
skin disease came to Jesus, knelt down,
and begged him for help. "If you want
to," he said, "you can make me clean."[c]

41 Jesus was filled with pity,[d] and
reached out and touched him. "I do want
to," he answered. "Be clean!" 42 At once
the disease left the man, and he was
clean. 43 Then Jesus spoke sternly to him
and sent him away at once, 44 after saying to him, "Listen, don't tell anyone
about this. But go straight to the priest
and let him examine you; then in order
to prove to everyone that you are cured,
offer the sacrifice that Moses ordered."

[c] MAKE ME CLEAN: *This disease was considered to make a person ritually unclean.*
[d] pity; *some manuscripts have* anger.

45 But the man went away and began
to spread the news everywhere. Indeed,
he talked so much that Jesus could not
go into a town publicly. Instead, he
stayed out in lonely places, and people
came to him from everywhere.

Jesus Heals a Paralyzed Man

(Matthew 9.1-8; Luke 5.17-26)

2 A few days later Jesus went back to
Capernaum, and the news spread
that he was at home. 2 So many people
came together that there was no room
left, not even out in front of the door.
Jesus was preaching the message to
them 3 when four men arrived, carrying
a paralyzed man to Jesus. 4 Because of
the crowd, however, they could not get
the man to him. So they made a hole in
the roof right above the place where
Jesus was. When they had made an
opening, they let the man down, lying on
his mat. 5 Seeing how much faith they
had, Jesus said to the paralyzed man,
"My son, your sins are forgiven."
6 Some teachers of the Law who were
sitting there thought to themselves,
7 "How does he dare talk like this? This is
blasphemy! God is the only one who can
forgive sins!"
8 At once Jesus knew what they were
thinking, so he said to them, "Why do
you think such things? 9 Is it easier to say
to this paralyzed man, 'Your sins are
forgiven,' or to say, 'Get up, pick up your
mat, and walk'? 10 I will prove to you,
then, that the Son of Man has authority
on earth to forgive sins." So he said to
the paralyzed man, 11 "I tell you, get up,
pick up your mat, and go home!"
12 While they all watched, the man got
up, picked up his mat, and hurried away.
They were all completely amazed and
praised God, saying, "We have never
seen anything like this!"

Jesus Calls Levi

(Matthew 9.9-13; Luke 5.27-32)

13 Jesus went back again to the shore
of Lake Galilee. A crowd came to him,
and he started teaching them. 14 As he
walked along, he saw a tax collector,
Levi son of Alphaeus, sitting in his office. Jesus said to him, "Follow me." Levi
got up and followed him.
15 Later on Jesus was having a meal in
Levi's house.[e] A large number of tax
collectors and other outcasts was following Jesus, and many of them joined him
and his disciples at the table. 16 Some
teachers of the Law, who were Pharisees, saw that Jesus was eating with
these outcasts and tax collectors, so they
asked his disciples, "Why does he eat
with such people?"
17 Jesus heard them and answered,
"People who are well do not need a doctor, but only those who are sick. I have
not come to call respectable people, but
outcasts."

The Question about Fasting

(Matthew 9.14-17; Luke 5.33-39)

18 On one occasion the followers of
John the Baptist and the Pharisees were
fasting. Some people came to Jesus and
asked him, "Why is it that the disciples
of John the Baptist and the disciples of
the Pharisees fast, but yours do not?"
19 Jesus answered, "Do you expect the
guests at a wedding party to go without
food? Of course not! As long as the
bridegroom is with them, they will not
do that. 20 But the day will come when
the bridegroom will be taken away from
them, and then they will fast.
21 "No one uses a piece of new cloth to
patch up an old coat, because the new
patch will shrink and tear off some of
the old cloth, making an even bigger
hole. 22 Nor does anyone pour new wine
into used wineskins, because the wine
will burst the skins, and both the wine
and the skins will be ruined. Instead,
new wine must be poured into fresh
wineskins."

The Question about the Sabbath

(Matthew 12.1-8; Luke 6.1-5)

23 Jesus was walking through some
wheat fields on a Sabbath. As his disciples walked along with him, they began
to pick the heads of wheat. 24 So the
Pharisees said to Jesus, "Look, it is
against our Law for your disciples to do
that on the Sabbath!"
25 Jesus answered, "Have you never
read what David did that time when he
needed something to eat? He and his
men were hungry, 26 so he went into the
house of God and ate the bread offered
to God. This happened when Abiathar

[e] in Levi's house; *or* in his *(that is,* Jesus') house.

was the High Priest. According to our
Law only the priests may eat this
bread – but David ate it and even gave it
to his men."
27 And Jesus concluded, "The Sabbath
was made for the good of human beings;
they were not made for the Sabbath.
28 So the Son of Man is Lord even of the
Sabbath."

The Man with a Paralyzed Hand

(Matthew 12.9-14; Luke 6.6-11)

3 Then Jesus went back to the synagogue, where there was a man who
had a paralyzed hand. 2 Some people
were there who wanted to accuse Jesus
of doing wrong; so they watched him
closely to see whether he would cure the
man on the Sabbath. 3 Jesus said to the
man, "Come up here to the front." 4 Then
he asked the people, "What does our
Law allow us to do on the Sabbath? To
help or to harm? To save someone's life
or to destroy it?"
But they did not say a thing. 5 Jesus
was angry as he looked around at them,
but at the same time he felt sorry for
them, because they were so stubborn
and wrong. Then he said to the man,
"Stretch out your hand." He stretched it
out, and it became well again. 6 So the
Pharisees left the synagogue and met at
once with some members of Herod's
party, and they made plans to kill Jesus.

A Crowd by the Lake

7 Jesus and his disciples went away to
Lake Galilee, and a large crowd followed him. They had come from Galilee,
from Judea, 8 from Jerusalem, from the
territory of Idumea, from the territory
on the east side of the Jordan, and from
the region around the cities of Tyre and
Sidon. All these people came to Jesus
because they had heard of the things he
was doing. 9 The crowd was so large that
Jesus told his disciples to get a boat
ready for him, so that the people would
not crush him. 10 He had healed many
people, and all the sick kept pushing
their way to him in order to touch him.
11 And whenever the people who had evil
spirits in them saw him, they would fall
down before him and scream, "You are
the Son of God!"
12 Jesus sternly ordered the evil spirits
not to tell anyone who he was.

Jesus Chooses the Twelve Apostles

(Matthew 10.1-4; Luke 6.12-16)

13 Then Jesus went up a hill and called
to himself the men he wanted. They
came to him, 14 and he chose twelve,
whom he named apostles. "I have chosen you to be with me," he told them. "I
will also send you out to preach, 15 and
you will have authority to drive out
demons."
16 These are the twelve he chose: Simon (Jesus gave him the name Peter);
17 James and his brother John, the sons
of Zebedee (Jesus gave them the name
Boanerges, which means "Men of Thunder"); 18 Andrew, Philip, Bartholomew,
Matthew, Thomas, James son of Alphaeus, Thaddaeus, Simon the Patriot,
19 and Judas Iscariot, who betrayed
Jesus.

Jesus and Beelzebul

(Matthew 12.22-32; Luke 11.14-23; 12.10)

20 Then Jesus went home. Again such
a large crowd gathered that Jesus and
his disciples had no time to eat. 21 When
his family heard about it, they set out to
take charge of him, because people were
saying, "He's gone mad!"
22 Some teachers of the Law who had
come from Jerusalem were saying, "He
has Beelzebul in him! It is the chief of
the demons who gives him the power to
drive them out."
23 So Jesus called them to him and
spoke to them in parables: "How can Satan drive out Satan? 24 If a country divides itself into groups which fight each
other, that country will fall apart. 25 If a
family divides itself into groups which
fight each other, that family will fall
apart. 26 So if Satan's kingdom divides
into groups, it cannot last, but will fall
apart and come to an end.
27 "No one can break into a strong
man's house and take away his belongings unless he first ties up the strong
man; then he can plunder his house.
28 "I assure you that people can be forgiven all their sins and all the evil things
they may say.[f] 29 But whoever says evil
things against the Holy Spirit will never
be forgiven, because he has committed

[f] evil things they may say; *or* evil things they may say against God.

an eternal sin." (30 Jesus said this because some people were saying, "He has
an evil spirit in him.")

Jesus' Mother and Brothers

(Matthew 12.46-50; Luke 8.19-21)

31 Then Jesus' mother and brothers arrived. They stood outside the house and
sent in a message, asking for him.
32 A crowd was sitting around Jesus, and
they said to him, "Look, your mother
and your brothers and sisters are outside, and they want you."
33 Jesus answered, "Who is my
mother? Who are my brothers?" 34 He
looked at the people sitting around him
and said, "Look! Here are my mother
and my brothers! 35 Whoever does what
God wants is my brother, my sister, my
mother."

The Parable of the Sower

(Matthew 13.1-9; Luke 8.4-8)

4 Again Jesus began to teach beside
Lake Galilee. The crowd that gathered around him was so large that he got
into a boat and sat in it. The boat was out
in the water, and the crowd stood on the
shore at the water's edge. 2 He used parables to teach them many things, saying
to them:
3 "Listen! Once there was a man who
went out to sow grain. 4 As he scattered
the seed in the field, some of it fell along
the path, and the birds came and ate it
up. 5 Some of it fell on rocky ground,
where there was little soil. The seeds
soon sprouted, because the soil wasn't
deep. 6 Then, when the sun came up, it
burned the young plants; and because
the roots had not grown deep enough,
the plants soon dried up. 7 Some of the
seed fell among thorn bushes, which
grew up and choked the plants, and they
didn't bear grain. 8 But some seeds fell in
good soil, and the plants sprouted, grew,
and bore grain: some had thirty grains,
others sixty, and others one hundred."
9 And Jesus concluded, "Listen, then, if
you have ears!"

The Purpose of the Parables

(Matthew 13.10-17; Luke 8.9, 10)

10 When Jesus was alone, some of
those who had heard him came to him
with the twelve disciples and asked him
to explain the parables. 11 "You have
been given the secret of the Kingdom of
God," Jesus answered. "But the others,
who are on the outside, hear all things
by means of parables, 12 so that,

'They may look and look,
yet not see;
they may listen and listen,
yet not understand.
For if they did, they would turn
to God,
and he would forgive them.' "

Jesus Explains the Parable of the Sower

(Matthew 13.18-23; Luke 8.11-15)

13 Then Jesus asked them, "Don't you
understand this parable? How, then, will
you ever understand any parable? 14 The
sower sows God's message. 15 Some people are like the seeds that fall along the
path; as soon as they hear the message,
Satan comes and takes it away. 16 Other
people are like the seeds that fall on
rocky ground. As soon as they hear the
message, they receive it gladly. 17 But it
does not sink deep into them, and they
don't last long. So when trouble or persecution comes because of the message,
they give up at once. 18 Other people are
like the seeds sown among the thorn
bushes. These are the ones who hear the
message, 19 but the worries about this
life, the love for riches, and all other
kinds of desires crowd in and choke the
message, and they don't bear fruit. 20 But
other people are like seeds sown in good
soil. They hear the message, accept it,
and bear fruit: some thirty, some sixty,
and some one hundred."

A Lamp under a Bowl

(Luke 8.16-18)

21 Jesus continued, "Does anyone ever
bring in a lamp and put it under a bowl
or under the bed? Isn't it put on the
lampstand? 22 Whatever is hidden away
will be brought out into the open, and
whatever is covered up will be uncovered. 23 Listen, then, if you have ears!"
24 He also said to them, "Pay attention
to what you hear! The same rules you
use to judge others will be used by God
to judge you — but with even greater severity. 25 Those who have something will
be given more, and those who have
nothing will have taken away from them
even the little they have."

The Parable of the Growing Seed

26 Jesus went on to say, "The Kingdom
of God is like this. A man scatters seed
in his field. 27 He sleeps at night, is up
and about during the day, and all the
while the seeds are sprouting and growing. Yet he does not know how it happens. 28 The soil itself makes the plants
grow and bear fruit; first the tender stalk
appears, then the head, and finally the
head full of grain. 29 When the grain is
ripe, the man starts cutting it with his
sickle, because harvest time has come.

The Parable of the Mustard Seed

(Matthew 13.31, 32, 34; Luke 13.18, 19)

30 "What shall we say the Kingdom of
God is like?" asked Jesus. "What parable
shall we use to explain it? 31 It is like this.
A man takes a mustard seed, the smallest seed in the world, and plants it in the
ground. 32 After a while it grows up and
becomes the biggest of all plants. It puts
out such large branches that the birds
come and make their nests in its shade."

33 Jesus preached his message to the
people, using many other parables like
these; he told them as much as they
could understand. 34 He would not speak
to them without using parables, but
when he was alone with his disciples, he
would explain everything to them.

Jesus Calms a Storm

(Matthew 8.23-27; Luke 8.22-25)

35 On the evening of that same day
Jesus said to his disciples, "Let us go
across to the other side of the lake." 36 So
they left the crowd; the disciples got into
the boat in which Jesus was already sitting, and they took him with them. Other
boats were there too. 37 Suddenly a
strong wind blew up, and the waves began to spill over into the boat, so that it
was about to fill with water. 38 Jesus was
in the back of the boat, sleeping with his
head on a pillow. The disciples woke
him up and said, "Teacher, don't you
care that we are about to die?"

39 Jesus stood up and commanded the
wind, "Be quiet!" and he said to the
waves, "Be still!" The wind died down,
and there was a great calm. 40 Then
Jesus said to his disciples, "Why are you
frightened? Do you still have no faith?"

41 But they were terribly afraid and began to say to one another, "Who is this
man? Even the wind and the waves
obey him!"

Jesus Heals a Man with Evil Spirits

(Matthew 8.28-34; Luke 8.26-39)

5 Jesus and his disciples arrived on
the other side of Lake Galilee, in the
territory of Gerasa. 2 As soon as Jesus
got out of the boat, he was met by a man
who came out of the burial caves there.
This man had an evil spirit in him 3 and
lived among the tombs. Nobody could
keep him tied with chains any more;
4 many times his feet and his hands had
been tied, but every time he broke the
chains and smashed the irons on his
feet. He was too strong for anyone to
control him. 5 Day and night he wandered among the tombs and through the
hills, screaming and cutting himself with
stones.

6 He was some distance away when he
saw Jesus; so he ran, fell on his knees
before him, 7 and screamed in a loud
voice, "Jesus, Son of the Most High God!
What do you want with me? For God's
sake, I beg you, don't punish me!" (8 He
said this because Jesus was saying, "Evil
spirit, come out of this man!")

9 So Jesus asked him, "What is your
name!"

The man answered, "My name is
'Mob'—there are so many of us!" 10 And
he kept begging Jesus not to send the
evil spirits out of that region.

11 There was a large herd of pigs near
by, feeding on a hillside. 12 So the spirits
begged Jesus, "Send us to the pigs, and
let us go into them." 13 He let them go,
and the evil spirits went out of the man
and entered the pigs. The whole herd—
about two thousand pigs in all—rushed
down the side of the cliff into the lake
and was drowned.

14 The men who had been taking care
of the pigs ran away and spread the
news in the town and among the farms.
People went out to see what had happened, 15 and when they came to Jesus,
they saw the man who used to have the
mob of demons in him. He was sitting
there, clothed and in his right mind; and
they were all afraid. 16 Those who had
seen it told the people what had happened to the man with the demons, and
about the pigs.

17 So they asked Jesus to leave their
territory.

18 As Jesus was getting into the boat,
the man who had had the demons
begged him, "Let me go with you!"
19 But Jesus would not let him. Instead,
he told him, "Go back home to your family and tell them how much the Lord has
done for you and how kind he has been
to you."
20 So the man left and went all through
the Ten Towns, telling what Jesus had
done for him. And all who heard it were
amazed.

Jairus' Daughter and the Woman Who Touched Jesus' Cloak

(Matthew 9.18-26; Luke 8.40-56)

21 Jesus went back across to the other
side of the lake. There at the lakeside a
large crowd gathered around him. 22 Jairus, an official of the local synagogue,
arrived, and when he saw Jesus, he
threw himself down at his feet 23 and
begged him earnestly, "My little daughter is very sick. Please come and place
your hands on her, so that she will get
well and live!"
24 Then Jesus started off with him. So
many people were going along with
Jesus that they were crowding him from
every side.
25 There was a woman who had suffered terribly from severe bleeding for
twelve years, 26 even though she had
been treated by many doctors. She had
spent all her money, but instead of getting better she got worse all the time.
27 She had heard about Jesus, so she
came in the crowd behind him, 28 saying
to herself, "If I just touch his clothes, I
will get well."
29 She touched his cloak, and her
bleeding stopped at once; and she had
the feeling inside herself that she was
healed of her trouble. 30 At once Jesus
knew that power had gone out of him, so
he turned around in the crowd and
asked, "Who touched my clothes?"
31 His disciples answered, "You see
how the people are crowding you; why
do you ask who touched you?"
32 But Jesus kept looking around to see
who had done it. 33 The woman realized
what had happened to her, so she came,
trembling with fear, knelt at his feet, and
told him the whole truth. 34 Jesus said to
her, "My daughter, your faith has made
you well. Go in peace, and be healed of
your trouble."
35 While Jesus was saying this, some
messengers came from Jairus' house
and told him, "Your daughter has died.
Why bother the Teacher any longer?"
36 Jesus paid no attention to [g] what
they said, but told him, "Don't be afraid,
only believe." 37 Then he did not let anyone else go on with him except Peter and
James and his brother John. 38 They arrived at Jairus' house, where Jesus saw
the confusion and heard all the loud crying and wailing. 39 He went in and said to
them, "Why all this confusion? Why are
you crying? The child is not dead—she
is only sleeping!"
40 They started making fun of him, so
he put them all out, took the child's
father and mother and his three disciples, and went into the room where the
child was lying. 41 He took her by the
hand and said to her, *"Talitha, koum,"*
which means, "Little girl, I tell you to
get up!"
42 She got up at once and started walking around. (She was twelve years old.)
When this happened, they were completely amazed. 43 But Jesus gave them
strict orders not to tell anyone, and he
said, "Give her something to eat."

Jesus Is Rejected at Nazareth

(Matthew 13.53-58; Luke 4.16-30)

6 Jesus left that place and went back
to his hometown, followed by his
disciples. 2 On the Sabbath he began to
teach in the synagogue. Many people
were there; and when they heard him,
they were all amazed. "Where did he get
all this?" they asked. "What wisdom is
this that has been given him? How does
he perform miracles? 3 Isn't he the carpenter, the son of Mary, and the brother
of James, Joseph, Judas, and Simon?
Aren't his sisters living here?" And so
they rejected him.
4 Jesus said to them, "Prophets are respected everywhere except in their own
hometown and by their relatives and
their family."
5 He was not able to perform any miracles there, except that he placed his
hands on a few sick people and healed
them. 6 He was greatly surprised, because the people did not have faith.

[g] paid no attention to; *or* overheard.

Jesus Sends Out the Twelve Disciples

(Matthew 10.5-15; Luke 9.1-6)

Then Jesus went to the villages
around there, teaching the people. 7He
called the twelve disciples together and
sent them out two by two. He gave them
authority over the evil spirits 8and ordered them, "Don't take anything with
you on the trip except a walking stick—
no bread, no beggar's bag, no money in
your pockets. 9Wear sandals, but don't
carry an extra shirt." 10He also told
them, "Wherever you are welcomed,
stay in the same house until you leave
that place. 11If you come to a town
where people do not welcome you or
will not listen to you, leave it and shake
the dust off your feet. That will be a
warning to them!"
12So they went out and preached that
people should turn away from their sins.
13They drove out many demons, and
rubbed olive oil on many sick people
and healed them.

The Death of John the Baptist

(Matthew 14.1-12; Luke 9.7-9)

14Now King Herod[h] heard about all
this, because Jesus' reputation had
spread everywhere. Some people were
saying, "John the Baptist has come back
to life! That is why he has this power to
perform miracles."
15Others, however, said, "He is
Elijah."
Others said, "He is a prophet, like one
of the prophets of long ago."
16When Herod heard it, he said, "He is
John the Baptist! I had his head cut off,
but he has come back to life!" 17Herod
himself had ordered John's arrest, and
he had him tied up and put in prison.
Herod did this because of Herodias,
whom he had married, even though she
was the wife of his brother Philip.
18John the Baptist kept telling Herod,
"It isn't right for you to marry your
brother's wife!"
19So Herodias held a grudge against
John and wanted to kill him, but she
could not because of Herod. 20Herod
was afraid of John because he knew that
John was a good and holy man, and so
he kept him safe. He liked to listen to
him, even though he became greatly disturbed every time he heard him.
21Finally Herodias got her chance. It
was on Herod's birthday, when he gave
a feast for all the top government officials, the military chiefs, and the leading
citizens of Galilee. 22The daughter of
Herodias[i] came in and danced, and
pleased Herod and his guests. So the
king said to the girl, "What would you
like to have? I will give you anything you
want." 23With many vows he said to her,
"I swear that I will give you anything
you ask for, even as much as half my
kingdom!"
24So the girl went out and asked her
mother, "What shall I ask for?"
"The head of John the Baptist," she
answered.
25The girl hurried back at once to the
king and demanded, "I want you to give
me here and now the head of John the
Baptist on a plate!"
26This made the king very sad, but he
could not refuse her because of the vows
he had made in front of all his guests.
27So he sent off a guard at once with
orders to bring John's head. The guard
left, went to the prison, and cut John's
head off; 28then he brought it on a plate
and gave it to the girl, who gave it to her
mother. 29When John's disciples heard
about this, they came and got his body,
and buried it.

Jesus Feeds Five Thousand

(Matthew 14.13-21; Luke 9.10-17; John 6.1-14)

30The apostles returned and met with
Jesus, and told him all they had done
and taught. 31There were so many people coming and going that Jesus and his
disciples didn't even have time to eat. So
he said to them, "Let us go off by ourselves to some place where we will be
alone and you can rest a while." 32So
they started out in a boat by themselves
to a lonely place.
33Many people, however, saw them
leave and knew at once who they were;
so they went from all the towns and ran
ahead by land and arrived at the place
ahead of Jesus and his disciples. 34When
Jesus got out of the boat, he saw this
large crowd, and his heart was filled
with pity for them, because they were

[h] KING HEROD: *Herod Antipas, ruler of Galilee.* [i] The daughter of Herodias; *some manuscripts have* His daughter Herodias.

like sheep without a shepherd. So he began to teach them many things. 35 When
it was getting late, his disciples came to
him and said, "It is already very late, and
this is a lonely place. 36 Send the people
away, and let them go to the nearby
farms and villages in order to buy themselves something to eat."

37 "You yourselves give them something to eat," Jesus answered.

They asked, "Do you want us to go
and spend two hundred silver coins[j] on
bread in order to feed them?"

38 So Jesus asked them, "How much
bread do you have? Go and see."

When they found out, they told him,
"Five loaves and also two fish."

39 Jesus then told his disciples to make
all the people divide into groups and sit
down on the green grass. 40 So the people sat down in rows, in groups of a hundred and groups of fifty. 41 Then Jesus
took the five loaves and the two fish,
looked up to heaven, and gave thanks to
God. He broke the loaves and gave them
to his disciples to distribute to the people. He also divided the two fish among
them all. 42 Everyone ate and had
enough. 43 Then the disciples took up
twelve baskets full of what was left of
the bread and the fish. 44 The number of
men who were fed was five thousand.

Jesus Walks on the Water

(Matthew 14.22-33; John 6.15-21)

45 At once Jesus made his disciples get
into the boat and go ahead of him to
Bethsaida, on the other side of the lake,
while he sent the crowd away. 46 After
saying good-bye to the people, he went
away to a hill to pray. 47 When evening
came, the boat was in the middle of the
lake, while Jesus was alone on land.
48 He saw that his disciples were strain-
ing at the oars, because they were rowing against the wind; so sometime
between three and six o'clock in the
morning, he came to them, walking on
the water. He was going to pass them
by,[k] 49 but they saw him walking on the
water. "It's a ghost!" they thought, and
screamed. 50 They were all terrified
when they saw him.

Jesus spoke to them at once, "Courage!" he said. "It is I. Don't be afraid!"
51 Then he got into the boat with them,
and the wind died down. The disciples
were completely amazed, 52 because
they had not understood the real meaning of the feeding of the five thousand;
their minds could not grasp it.

Jesus Heals the Sick in Gennesaret

(Matthew 14.34-36)

53 They crossed the lake and came to
land at Gennesaret, where they tied up
the boat. 54 As they left the boat, people
recognized Jesus at once. 55 So they ran
throughout the whole region; and wherever they heard he was, they brought to
him the sick lying on their mats. 56 And
everywhere Jesus went, to villages,
towns, or farms, people would take their
sick to the marketplaces and beg him to
let the sick at least touch the edge of his
cloak. And all who touched it were made
well.

The Teaching of the Ancestors

(Matthew 15.1-9)

7 Some Pharisees and teachers of the
Law who had come from Jerusalem
gathered around Jesus. 2 They noticed
that some of his disciples were eating
their food with hands that were ritually
unclean—that is, they had not washed
them in the way the Pharisees said people should.

(3 For the Pharisees, as well as the rest
of the Jews, follow the teaching they received from their ancestors: they do not
eat unless they wash their hands in the
proper way; 4 nor do they eat anything
that comes from the market unless they
wash it first.[l] And they follow many
other rules which they have received,
such as the proper way to wash cups,
pots, copper bowls, and beds.[m])

5 So the Pharisees and the teachers of
the Law asked Jesus, "Why is it that
your disciples do not follow the teaching
handed down by our ancestors, but instead eat with ritually unclean hands?"

6 Jesus answered them, "How right
Isaiah was when he prophesied about
you! You are hypocrites, just as he
wrote:

[j] SILVER COINS: *A silver coin was the daily wage of a rural worker (see Mt 20.2).* [k] pass them by; *or* join them. [l] anything that comes from the market unless they wash it first; *or* anything after they come from the market unless they wash themselves first. [m] *Some manuscripts do not have* and beds.

'These people, says God, honor me
with their words,
but their heart is really far away
from me.
7 It is no use for them to
worship me,
because they teach human rules
as though they were my laws!'
8 "You put aside God's command and
obey human teachings."
9 And Jesus continued, "You have a
clever way of rejecting God's law in order to uphold your own teaching. 10 For
Moses commanded, 'Respect your father
and your mother,' and, 'If you curse your
father or your mother, you are to be put
to death.' 11 But you teach that if people
have something they could use to help
their father or mother, but say, 'This is
Corban' (which means, it belongs to
God), 12 they are excused from helping
their father or mother. 13 In this way the
teaching you pass on to others cancels
out the word of God. And there are
many other things like this that you do."

The Things That Make a Person Unclean

(Matthew 15.10-20)

14 Then Jesus called the crowd to him
once more and said to them, "Listen to
me, all of you, and understand. 15 There
is nothing that goes into you from the
outside which can make you ritually unclean. Rather, it is what comes out of
you that makes you unclean."[n]
17 When he left the crowd and went
into the house, his disciples asked him to
explain this saying. 18 "You are no more
intelligent than the others," Jesus said to
them. "Don't you understand? Nothing
that goes into you from the outside can
really make you unclean, 19 because it
does not go into your heart but into your
stomach and then goes on out of the
body." (In saying this, Jesus declared
that all foods are fit to be eaten.)
20 And he went on to say, "It is what
comes out of you that makes you unclean. 21 For from the inside, from your
heart, come the evil ideas which lead
you to do immoral things, to rob, kill,
22 commit adultery, be greedy, and do all
sorts of evil things; deceit, indecency,
jealousy, slander, pride, and folly—23 all
these evil things come from inside you
and make you unclean."

A Woman's Faith

(Matthew 15.21-28)

24 Then Jesus left and went away to the
territory near the city of Tyre. He went
into a house and did not want anyone to
know he was there, but he could not stay
hidden. 25 A woman, whose daughter
had an evil spirit in her, heard about
Jesus and came to him at once and fell at
his feet. 26 The woman was a Gentile,
born in the region of Phoenicia in Syria.
She begged Jesus to drive the demon out
of her daughter. 27 But Jesus answered,
"Let us first feed the children. It isn't
right to take the children's food and
throw it to the dogs."
28 "Sir," she answered, "even the dogs
under the table eat the children's
leftovers!"
29 So Jesus said to her, "Because of
that answer, go back home, where you
will find that the demon has gone out of
your daughter!"
30 She went home and found her child
lying on the bed; the demon had indeed
gone out of her.

Jesus Heals a Deaf-Mute

31 Jesus then left the neighborhood of
Tyre and went on through Sidon to Lake
Galilee, going by way of the territory of
the Ten Towns. 32 Some people brought
him a man who was deaf and could
hardly speak, and they begged Jesus to
place his hands on him. 33 So Jesus took
him off alone, away from the crowd, put
his fingers in the man's ears, spat, and
touched the man's tongue. 34 Then Jesus
looked up to heaven, gave a deep groan,
and said to the man, "*Ephphatha,*"
which means, "Open up!"
35 At once the man was able to hear,
his speech impediment was removed,
and he began to talk without any trouble. 36 Then Jesus ordered the people not
to speak of it to anyone; but the more he
ordered them not to, the more they told
it. 37 And all who heard were completely
amazed. "How well he does everything!"
they exclaimed. "He even causes the
deaf to hear and the dumb to speak!"

[n] *Some manuscripts add verse 16:* Listen, then, if you have ears! *(see 4.23).*

Jesus Feeds Four Thousand People

(Matthew 15.32-39)

8 Not long afterward another large
crowd came together. When the
people had nothing left to eat, Jesus
called the disciples to him and said, 2 "I
feel sorry for these people, because they
have been with me for three days and
now have nothing to eat. 3 If I send them
home without feeding them, they will
faint as they go, because some of them
have come a long way."

4 His disciples asked him, "Where in
this desert can anyone find enough food
to feed all these people?"

5 "How much bread do you have?"
Jesus asked.

"Seven loaves," they answered.

6 He ordered the crowd to sit down on
the ground. Then he took the seven
loaves, gave thanks to God, broke them,
and gave them to his disciples to distribute to the crowd; and the disciples did
so. 7 They also had a few small fish.
Jesus gave thanks for these and told
the disciples to distribute them too.
8-9 Everybody ate and had enough —
there were about four thousand people.
Then the disciples took up seven baskets
full of pieces left over. Jesus sent the
people away 10 and at once got into a
boat with his disciples and went to the
district of Dalmanutha.

The Pharisees Ask for a Miracle

(Matthew 16.1-4)

11 Some Pharisees came to Jesus and
started to argue with him. They wanted
to trap him, so they asked him to perform a miracle to show that God approved of him. 12 But Jesus gave a deep
groan and said, "Why do the people of
this day ask for a miracle? No, I tell you!
No such proof will be given to these
people!"

13 He left them, got back into the boat,
and started across to the other side of
the lake.

The Yeast of the Pharisees and of Herod

(Matthew 16.5-12)

14 The disciples had forgotten to bring
enough bread and had only one loaf
with them in the boat. 15 "Take care,"
Jesus warned them, "and be on your
guard against the yeast of the Pharisees
and the yeast of Herod."

16 They started discussing among
themselves: "He says this because we
don't have any bread."

17 Jesus knew what they were saying,
so he asked them, "Why are you discussing about not having any bread? Don't
you know or understand yet? Are your
minds so dull? 18 You have eyes — can't
you see? You have ears — can't you
hear? Don't you remember 19 when I
broke the five loaves for the five thousand people? How many baskets full of
leftover pieces did you take up?"

"Twelve," they answered.

20 "And when I broke the seven loaves
for the four thousand people," asked
Jesus, "how many baskets full of leftover pieces did you take up?"

"Seven," they answered.

21 "And you still don't understand?" he
asked them.

Jesus Heals a Blind Man at Bethsaida

22 They came to Bethsaida, where
some people brought a blind man to
Jesus and begged him to touch him.
23 Jesus took the blind man by the hand
and led him out of the village. After spitting on the man's eyes, Jesus placed his
hands on him and asked him, "Can you
see anything?"

24 The man looked up and said, "Yes, I
can see people, but they look like trees
walking around."

25 Jesus again placed his hands on the
man's eyes. This time the man looked
intently, his eyesight returned, and he
saw everything clearly. 26 Jesus then
sent him home with the order, "Don't go
back into the village."

Peter's Declaration about Jesus

(Matthew 16.13-20; Luke 9.18-21)

27 Then Jesus and his disciples went
away to the villages near Caesarea Philippi. On the way he asked them, "Tell
me, who do people say I am?"

28 "Some say that you are John the
Baptist," they answered; "others say that
you are Elijah, while others say that you
are one of the prophets."

29 "What about you?" he asked them.
"Who do you say I am?"

Peter answered, "You are the
Messiah."

30 Then Jesus ordered them, "Do not
tell anyone about me."

Jesus Speaks about His Suffering and Death

(Matthew 16.21-28; Luke 9.22-27)

31 Then Jesus began to teach his disciples: "The Son of Man must suffer much
and be rejected by the elders, the chief
priests, and the teachers of the Law. He
will be put to death, but three days later
he will rise to life." 32 He made this very
clear to them. So Peter took him aside
and began to rebuke him. 33 But Jesus
turned around, looked at his disciples,
and rebuked Peter. "Get away from me,
Satan," he said. "Your thoughts don't
come from God but from human
nature!"
34 Then Jesus called the crowd and his
disciples to him. "If any of you want to
come with me," he told them, "you must
forget yourself, carry your cross, and
follow me. 35 For if you want to save your
own life, you will lose it; but if you lose
your life for me and for the gospel, you
will save it. 36 Do you gain anything if
you win the whole world but lose your
life? Of course not! 37 There is nothing
you can give to regain your life. 38 If you
are ashamed of me and of my teaching
in this godless and wicked day, then the
Son of Man will be ashamed of you
when he comes in the glory of his Father
with the holy angels."
9 And he went on to say, "I tell you,
there are some here who will not
die until they have seen the Kingdom of
God come with power."

The Transfiguration

(Matthew 17.1-13; Luke 9.28-36)

2 Six days later Jesus took with him
Peter, James, and John, and led them up
a high mountain, where they were alone.
As they looked on, a change came over
Jesus, 3 and his clothes became shining
white – whiter than anyone in the world
could wash them. 4 Then the three disciples saw Elijah and Moses talking with
Jesus. 5 Peter spoke up and said to Jesus,
"Teacher, how good it is that we are
here! We will make three tents, one for
you, one for Moses, and one for Elijah."
6 He and the others were so frightened
that he did not know what to say.
7 Then a cloud appeared and covered
them with its shadow, and a voice came
from the cloud, "This is my own dear
Son – listen to him!" 8 They took a quick
look around but did not see anyone else;
only Jesus was with them.
9 As they came down the mountain,
Jesus ordered them, "Don't tell anyone
what you have seen, until the Son of
Man has risen from death."
10 They obeyed his order, but among
themselves they started discussing the
matter, "What does this 'rising from
death' mean?" 11 And they asked Jesus,
"Why do the teachers of the Law say
that Elijah has to come first?"
12 His answer was, "Elijah is indeed
coming first in order to get everything
ready. Yet why do the Scriptures say
that the Son of Man will suffer much and
be rejected? 13 I tell you, however, that
Elijah has already come and that people
treated him just as they pleased, as the
Scriptures say about him."

Jesus Heals a Boy with an Evil Spirit

(Matthew 17.14-21; Luke 9.37-43a)

14 When they joined the rest of the disciples, they saw a large crowd around
them and some teachers of the Law arguing with them. 15 When the people saw
Jesus, they were greatly surprised, and
ran to him and greeted him. 16 Jesus
asked his disciples, "What are you arguing with them about?"
17 A man in the crowd answered,
"Teacher, I brought my son to you, because he has an evil spirit in him and
cannot talk. 18 Whenever the spirit attacks him, it throws him to the ground,
and he foams at the mouth, grits his
teeth, and becomes stiff all over. I asked
your disciples to drive the spirit out, but
they could not."
19 Jesus said to them, "How unbelieving you people are! How long must I stay
with you? How long do I have to put up
with you? Bring the boy to me!" 20 They
brought him to Jesus.
As soon as the spirit saw Jesus, it
threw the boy into a fit, so that he fell on
the ground and rolled around, foaming
at the mouth. 21 "How long has he been
like this?" Jesus asked the father.
"Ever since he was a child," he replied.
22 "Many times the evil spirit has tried to
kill him by throwing him in the fire and
into water. Have pity on us and help us,
if you possibly can!"
23 "Yes," said Jesus, "if you yourself

can! Everything is possible for the person who has faith."
24 The father at once cried out, "I do
have faith, but not enough. Help me
have more!"
25 Jesus noticed that the crowd was
closing in on them, so he gave a command to the evil spirit. "Deaf and dumb
spirit," he said, "I order you to come out
of the boy and never go into him again!"
26 The spirit screamed, threw the boy
into a bad fit, and came out. The boy
looked like a corpse, and everyone said,
"He is dead!" 27 But Jesus took the boy by
the hand and helped him rise, and he
stood up.
28 After Jesus had gone indoors, his
disciples asked him privately, "Why
couldn't we drive the spirit out?"
29 "Only prayer can drive this kind
out," answered Jesus; "nothing else
can."

Jesus Speaks Again about His Death

(Matthew 17.22, 23; Luke 9.43b-45)

30 Jesus and his disciples left that place
and went on through Galilee. Jesus did
not want anyone to know where he was,
31 because he was teaching his disciples:
"The Son of Man will be handed over to
those who will kill him. Three days later,
however, he will rise to life."
32 But they did not understand what
this teaching meant, and they were
afraid to ask him.

Who Is the Greatest?

(Matthew 18.1-5; Luke 9.46-48)

33 They came to Capernaum, and after
going indoors Jesus asked his disciples,
"What were you arguing about on the
road?"
34 But they would not answer him, because on the road they had been arguing
among themselves about who was the
greatest. 35 Jesus sat down, called the
twelve disciples, and said to them,
"Whoever wants to be first must place
himself last of all and be the servant of
all." 36 Then he took a child and had him
stand in front of them. He put his arms
around him and said to them, 37 "Whoever welcomes in my name one of these
children, welcomes me; and whoever
welcomes me, welcomes not only me but
also the one who sent me."

Whoever Is Not against Us Is for Us

(Luke 9.49, 50)

38 John said to him, "Teacher, we saw
a man who was driving out demons in
your name, and we told him to stop, because he doesn't belong to our group."
39 "Do not try to stop him," Jesus told
them, "because no one who performs a
miracle in my name will be able soon
afterward to say evil things about me.
40 For whoever is not against us is for us.
41 I assure you that anyone who gives
you a drink of water because you belong
to me will certainly receive a reward.

Temptations to Sin

(Matthew 18.6-9; Luke 17.1, 2)

42 "If anyone should cause one of these
little ones to lose faith in me, it would be
better for that person to have a large
millstone tied around the neck and be
thrown into the sea. 43 So if your hand
makes you lose your faith, cut it off! It is
better for you to enter life without a
hand than to keep both hands and go off
to hell, to the fire that never goes out.[o]
45 And if your foot makes you lose your
faith, cut it off! It is better for you to
enter life without a foot than to keep
both feet and be thrown into hell.[p]
47 And if your eye makes you lose your
faith, take it out! It is better for you to
enter the Kingdom of God with only one
eye than to keep both eyes and be
thrown into hell. 48 There 'the worms
that eat them never die, and the fire that
burns them is never put out.'
49 "Everyone will be purified by fire as
a sacrifice is purified by salt.
50 "Salt is good; but if it loses its saltiness, how can you make it salty again?
"Have the salt of friendship among
yourselves, and live in peace with one
another."

Jesus Teaches about Divorce

(Matthew 19.1-12; Luke 16.18)

10 Then Jesus left that place, went
to the province of Judea, and
crossed the Jordan River. Crowds came
flocking to him again, and he taught
them, as he always did.

[o] *Some manuscripts add verse 44:* There 'the worms that eat them never die, and the fire that burns them is never put out' *(see verse 48).* [p] *Some manuscripts add verse 46:* There 'the worms that eat them never die, and the fire that burns them is never put out' *(see verse 48).*

2 Some Pharisees came to him and
tried to trap him. "Tell us," they asked,
"does our Law allow a man to divorce
his wife?"
3 Jesus answered with a question,
"What law did Moses give you?"
4 Their answer was, "Moses gave permission for a man to write a divorce notice and send his wife away."
5 Jesus said to them, "Moses wrote this
law for you because you are so hard to
teach. 6 But in the beginning, at the time
of creation, 'God made them male and
female,' as the scripture says. 7 'And for
this reason a man will leave his father
and mother and unite with his wife,[q]
8 and the two will become one.' So they
are no longer two, but one. 9 No human
being must separate, then, what God has
joined together."
10 When they went back into the
house, the disciples asked Jesus about
this matter. 11 He said to them, "A man
who divorces his wife and marries another woman commits adultery against
his wife. 12 In the same way, a woman
who divorces her husband and marries
another man commits adultery."

Jesus Blesses Little Children

(Matthew 19.13-15; Luke 18.15-17)

13 Some people brought children to
Jesus for him to place his hands on
them, but the disciples scolded the people. 14 When Jesus noticed this, he was
angry and said to his disciples, "Let the
children come to me, and do not stop
them, because the Kingdom of God belongs to such as these. 15 I assure you
that whoever does not receive the Kingdom of God like a child will never enter
it." 16 Then he took the children in his
arms, placed his hands on each of them,
and blessed them.

The Rich Man

(Matthew 19.16-30; Luke 18.18-30)

17 As Jesus was starting on his way
again, a man ran up, knelt before him,
and asked him, "Good Teacher, what
must I do to receive eternal life?"
18 "Why do you call me good?" Jesus
asked him. "No one is good except God
alone. 19 You know the commandments:
'Do not commit murder; do not commit
adultery; do not steal; do not accuse
anyone falsely; do not cheat; respect
your father and your mother.' "
20 "Teacher," the man said, "ever since
I was young, I have obeyed all these
commandments."
21 Jesus looked straight at him with
love and said, "You need only one thing.
Go and sell all you have and give the
money to the poor, and you will have
riches in heaven; then come and follow
me." 22 When the man heard this, gloom
spread over his face, and he went away
sad, because he was very rich.
23 Jesus looked around at his disciples
and said to them, "How hard it will be
for rich people to enter the Kingdom
of God!"
24 The disciples were shocked at these
words, but Jesus went on to say, "My
children, how hard it is to enter the
Kingdom of God! 25 It is much harder for
a rich person to enter the Kingdom of
God than for a camel to go through the
eye of a needle."
26 At this the disciples were completely
amazed and asked one another, "Who,
then, can be saved?"
27 Jesus looked straight at them and
answered, "This is impossible for human
beings but not for God; everything is
possible for God."
28 Then Peter spoke up, "Look, we
have left everything and followed you."
29 "Yes," Jesus said to them, "and I tell
you that those who leave home or brothers or sisters or mother or father or children or fields for me and for the gospel,
30 will receive much more in this present
age. They will receive a hundred times
more houses, brothers, sisters, mothers,
children, and fields—and persecutions
as well; and in the age to come they will
receive eternal life. 31 But many who are
now first will be last, and many who are
now last will be first."

Jesus Speaks a Third Time about His Death

(Matthew 20.17-19; Luke 18.31-34)

32 Jesus and his disciples were now on
the road going up to Jerusalem. Jesus
was going ahead of the disciples, who
were filled with alarm; the people who
followed behind were afraid. Once again
Jesus took the twelve disciples aside and
spoke of the things that were going to

[q] *Some manuscripts do not have* and unite with his wife.

happen to him. 33 “Listen,” he told them,
“we are going up to Jerusalem where the
Son of Man will be handed over to the
chief priests and the teachers of the
Law. They will condemn him to death
and then hand him over to the Gentiles,
34 who will make fun of him, spit on him,
whip him, and kill him; but three days
later he will rise to life.”

The Request of James and John

(Matthew 20.20-28)

35 Then James and John, the sons of
Zebedee, came to Jesus. “Teacher,” they
said, “there is something we want you to
do for us.”
36 “What is it?” Jesus asked them.
37 They answered, “When you sit on
your throne in your glorious Kingdom,
we want you to let us sit with you, one at
your right and one at your left.”
38 Jesus said to them, “You don't know
what you are asking for. Can you drink
the cup of suffering that I must drink?
Can you be baptized in the way I must
be baptized?”
39 “We can,” they answered.
Jesus said to them, “You will indeed
drink the cup I must drink and be baptized in the way I must be baptized.
40 But I do not have the right to choose
who will sit at my right and my left. It is
God who will give these places to those
for whom he has prepared them.”
41 When the other ten disciples heard
about it, they became angry with James
and John. 42 So Jesus called them all together to him and said, “You know that
those who are considered rulers of the
heathen have power over them, and the
leaders have complete authority. 43 This,
however, is not the way it is among you.
If one of you wants to be great, you must
be the servant of the rest; 44 and if one of
you wants to be first, you must be the
slave of all. 45 For even the Son of Man
did not come to be served; he came to
serve and to give his life to redeem many
people.”

Jesus Heals Blind Bartimaeus

(Matthew 20.29-34; Luke 18.35-43)

46 They came to Jericho, and as Jesus
was leaving with his disciples and a
large crowd, a blind beggar named Bar-
timaeus son of Timaeus was sitting by
the road. 47 When he heard that it was
Jesus of Nazareth, he began to shout,
“Jesus! Son of David! Have mercy
on me!”
48 Many of the people scolded him and
told him to be quiet. But he shouted even
more loudly, “Son of David, have mercy
on me!”
49 Jesus stopped and said, “Call him.”
So they called the blind man. “Cheer
up!” they said. “Get up, he is calling you.”
50 So he threw off his cloak, jumped
up, and came to Jesus.
51 “What do you want me to do for
you?” Jesus asked him.
“Teacher,” the blind man answered, “I
want to see again.”
52 “Go,” Jesus told him, “your faith has
made you well.”
At once he was able to see and followed Jesus on the road.

The Triumphant Entry into Jerusalem

(Matthew 21.1-11; Luke 19.28-40; John 12.12-19)

11 As they approached Jerusalem,
near the towns of Bethphage and
Bethany, they came to the Mount of Olives. Jesus sent two of his disciples on
ahead 2 with these instructions: “Go to
the village there ahead of you. As soon
as you get there, you will find a colt tied
up that has never been ridden. Untie it
and bring it here. 3 And if someone asks
you why you are doing that, say that the
Master[r] needs it and will send it back at
once.”
4 So they went and found a colt out in
the street, tied to the door of a house. As
they were untying it, 5 some of the bystanders asked them, “What are you doing, untying that colt?”
6 They answered just as Jesus had told
them, and the crowd let them go. 7 They
brought the colt to Jesus, threw their
cloaks over the animal, and Jesus got
on. 8 Many people spread their cloaks on
the road, while others cut branches in
the field and spread them on the road.
9 The people who were in front and those
who followed behind began to shout,
“Praise God! God bless him who comes
in the name of the Lord! 10 God bless the
coming kingdom of King David, our
father! Praise be to God!”
11 Jesus entered Jerusalem, went into

[r] the Master; *or* its owner.

the Temple, and looked around at everything. But since it was already late in the
day, he went out to Bethany with the
twelve disciples.

Jesus Curses the Fig Tree

(Matthew 21.18, 19)

12 The next day, as they were coming
back from Bethany, Jesus was hungry.
13 He saw in the distance a fig tree covered with leaves, so he went to see if he
could find any figs on it. But when he
came to it, he found only leaves, because
it was not the right time for figs. 14 Jesus
said to the fig tree, "No one shall ever eat
figs from you again!"
And his disciples heard him.

Jesus Goes to the Temple

(Matthew 21.12-17; Luke 19.45-48; John 2.13-22)

15 When they arrived in Jerusalem,
Jesus went to the Temple and began to
drive out all those who were buying and
selling. He overturned the tables of the
moneychangers and the stools of those
who sold pigeons, 16 and he would not let
anyone carry anything through the
Temple courtyards. 17 He then taught the
people: "It is written in the Scriptures
that God said, 'My Temple will be called
a house of prayer for the people of all
nations.' But you have turned it into a
hideout for thieves!"
18 The chief priests and the teachers of
the Law heard of this, so they began
looking for some way to kill Jesus. They
were afraid of him, because the whole
crowd was amazed at his teaching.
19 When evening came, Jesus and his
disciples left the city.

The Lesson from the Fig Tree

(Matthew 21.20-22)

20 Early next morning, as they walked
along the road, they saw the fig tree. It
was dead all the way down to its roots.
21 Peter remembered what had happened
and said to Jesus, "Look, Teacher, the
fig tree you cursed has died!"
22 Jesus answered them, "Have faith in
God. 23 I assure you that whoever tells
this hill to get up and throw itself in the
sea and does not doubt in his heart, but
believes that what he says will happen, it
will be done for him. 24 For this reason I
tell you: When you pray and ask for
something, believe that you have received it, and you will be given whatever
you ask for. 25 And when you stand and
pray, forgive anything you may have
against anyone, so that your Father in
heaven will forgive the wrongs you have
done."[s]

The Question about Jesus' Authority

(Matthew 21.23-27; Luke 20.1-8)

27 They arrived once again in Jerusalem. As Jesus was walking in the Temple, the chief priests, the teachers of the
Law, and the elders came to him 28 and
asked him, "What right do you have to
do these things? Who gave you such
right?"
29 Jesus answered them, "I will ask
you just one question, and if you give
me an answer, I will tell you what right
I have to do these things. 30 Tell me,
where did John's right to baptize come
from: was it from God or from human
beings?"
31 They started to argue among themselves: "What shall we say? If we answer, 'From God,' he will say, 'Why,
then, did you not believe John?' 32 But if
we say, 'From human beings . . .' " (They
were afraid of the people, because
everyone was convinced that John had
been a prophet.) 33 So their answer to
Jesus was, "We don't know."
Jesus said to them, "Neither will I tell
you, then, by what right I do these
things."

The Parable of the Tenants in the Vineyard

(Matthew 21.33-46; Luke 20.9-19)

12 Then Jesus spoke to them in parables: "Once there was a man
who planted a vineyard, put a fence
around it, dug a hole for the wine press,
and built a watchtower. Then he rented
the vineyard to tenants and left home on
a trip. 2 When the time came to gather
the grapes, he sent a slave to the tenants
to receive from them his share of the
harvest. 3 The tenants grabbed the slave,
beat him, and sent him back without a
thing. 4 Then the owner sent another

s *Some manuscripts add verse 26:* If you do not forgive others, your Father in heaven will not forgive the wrongs you have done *(see Mt 6.15).*

slave; the tenants beat him over the head
and treated him shamefully. 5 The owner
sent another slave, and they killed him;
and they treated many others the same
way, beating some and killing others.
6 The only one left to send was the man's
own dear son. Last of all, then, he sent
his son to the tenants. 'I am sure they
will respect my son,' he said. 7 But those
tenants said to one another, 'This is the
owner's son. Come on, let's kill him, and
his property will be ours!' 8 So they
grabbed the son and killed him and
threw his body out of the vineyard.
9 "What, then, will the owner of the
vineyard do?" asked Jesus. "He will
come and kill those tenants and turn the
vineyard over to others. 10 Surely you
have read this scripture?

'The stone which the builders
rejected as worthless
turned out to be the most
important of all.
11 This was done by the Lord;
what a wonderful sight it is!' "

12 The Jewish leaders tried to arrest
Jesus, because they knew that he had
told this parable against them. But they
were afraid of the crowd, so they left
him and went away.

The Question about Paying Taxes

(Matthew 22.15-22; Luke 20.20-26)

13 Some Pharisees and some members
of Herod's party were sent to Jesus to
trap him with questions. 14 They came to
him and said, "Teacher, we know that
you tell the truth, without worrying
about what people think. You pay no attention to anyone's status, but teach the
truth about God's will for people. Tell us,
is it against our Law to pay taxes to the
Roman Emperor? Should we pay them
or not?"
15 But Jesus saw through their trick
and answered, "Why are you trying to
trap me? Bring a silver coin, and let me
see it."
16 They brought him one, and he
asked, "Whose face and name are
these?"
"The Emperor's," they answered.
17 So Jesus said, "Well, then, pay to the
Emperor what belongs to the Emperor,
and pay to God what belongs to God."
And they were amazed at Jesus.

The Question about Rising from Death

(Matthew 22.23-33; Luke 20.27-40)

18 Then some Sadducees, who say that
people will not rise from death, came to
Jesus and said, 19 "Teacher, Moses wrote
this law for us: 'If a man dies and leaves
a wife but no children, that man's
brother must marry the widow so that
they can have children who will be considered the dead man's children.' 20 Once
there were seven brothers; the oldest got
married and died without having children. 21 Then the second one married the
woman, and he also died without having
children. The same thing happened to
the third brother, 22 and then to the rest:
all seven brothers married the woman
and died without having children. Last
of all, the woman died. 23 Now, when all
the dead rise to life on the day of resurrection, whose wife will she be? All
seven of them had married her."
24 Jesus answered them, "How wrong
you are! And do you know why? It is
because you don't know the Scriptures
or God's power. 25 For when the dead
rise to life, they will be like the angels in
heaven and will not marry. 26 Now, as for
the dead being raised: haven't you ever
read in the Book of Moses the passage
about the burning bush? There it is written that God said to Moses, 'I am the God
of Abraham, the God of Isaac, and the
God of Jacob.' 27 He is the God of the
living, not of the dead. You are completely wrong!"

The Great Commandment

(Matthew 22.34-40; Luke 10.25-28)

28 A teacher of the Law was there who
heard the discussion. He saw that Jesus
had given the Sadducees a good answer,
so he came to him with a question:
"Which commandment is the most important of all?"
29 Jesus replied, "The most important
one is this: 'Listen, Israel! The Lord our
God is the only Lord.[t] 30 Love the Lord
your God with all your heart, with all
your soul, with all your mind, and with
all your strength.' 31 The second most
important commandment is this: 'Love
your neighbor as you love yourself.'
There is no other commandment more
important than these two."

[t] The Lord our God is the only Lord; *or* The Lord is our God, the Lord alone.

32 The teacher of the Law said to Jesus,
"Well done, Teacher! It is true, as you
say, that only the Lord is God and that
there is no other god but he. 33 And
you must love God with all your heart
and with all your mind and with all
your strength; and you must love your
neighbor as you love yourself. It is
more important to obey these two
commandments than to offer on the
altar animals and other sacrifices to
God."
34 Jesus noticed how wise his answer
was, and so he told him, "You are not far
from the Kingdom of God."

After this nobody dared to ask Jesus
any more questions.

The Question about the Messiah

(Matthew 22.41-46; Luke 20.41-44)

35 As Jesus was teaching in the Temple,
he asked the question, "How can the
teachers of the Law say that the Messiah
will be the descendant of David? 36 The
Holy Spirit inspired David to say:

'The Lord said to my Lord:
Sit here at my right side
until I put your enemies under
your feet.'

37 David himself called him 'Lord'; so
how can the Messiah be David's
descendant?"

Jesus Warns against the Teachers of the Law

(Matthew 23.1-36; Luke 20.45-47)

A large crowd was listening to Jesus
gladly. 38 As he taught them, he said,
"Watch out for the teachers of the Law,
who like to walk around in their long
robes and be greeted with respect in the
marketplace, 39 who choose the reserved
seats in the synagogues and the best
places at feasts. 40 They take advantage
of widows and rob them of their homes,
and then make a show of saying long
prayers. Their punishment will be all the
worse!"

The Widow's Offering

(Luke 21.1-4)

41 As Jesus sat near the Temple treasury,
he watched the people as they
dropped in their money. Many rich men
dropped in a lot of money; 42 then a poor
widow came along and dropped in two
little copper coins, worth about a penny.
43 He called his disciples together and
said to them, "I tell you that this poor
widow put more in the offering box than
all the others. 44 For the others put in
what they had to spare of their riches;
but she, poor as she is, put in all she
had—she gave all she had to live on."

Jesus Speaks of the Destruction of the Temple

(Matthew 24.1, 2; Luke 21.5, 6)

13 As Jesus was leaving the Temple,
one of his disciples said,
"Look, Teacher! What wonderful stones
and buildings!"
2 Jesus answered, "You see these great
buildings? Not a single stone here will
be left in its place; every one of them will
be thrown down."

Troubles and Persecutions

(Matthew 24.3-14; Luke 21.7-19)

3 Jesus was sitting on the Mount of Olives,
across from the Temple, when Peter,
James, John, and Andrew came to
him in private. 4 "Tell us when this will
be," they said, "and tell us what will happen
to show that the time has come for
all these things to take place."
5 Jesus said to them, "Watch out, and
don't let anyone fool you. 6 Many men,
claiming to speak for me, will come and
say, 'I am he!' and they will fool many
people. 7 And don't be troubled when
you hear the noise of battles close by
and news of battles far away. Such
things must happen, but they do not
mean that the end has come. 8 Countries
will fight each other; kingdoms will attack
one another. There will be earthquakes
everywhere, and there will be
famines. These things are like the first
pains of childbirth.
9 "You yourselves must watch out. You
will be arrested and taken to court. You
will be beaten in the synagogues; you
will stand before rulers and kings for my
sake to tell them the Good News. 10 But
before the end comes, the gospel must
be preached to all peoples. 11 And when
you are arrested and taken to court, do
not worry ahead of time about what you
are going to say; when the time comes,
say whatever is then given to you. For
the words you speak will not be yours;
they will come from the Holy Spirit.

12 Men will hand over their own brothers
to be put to death, and fathers will do the
same to their children. Children will
turn against their parents and have them
put to death. 13 Everyone will hate you
because of me. But whoever holds out to
the end will be saved.

The Awful Horror

(Matthew 24.15-28; Luke 21.20-24)

14 "You will see 'The Awful Horror'
standing in the place where he should
not be." (Note to the reader: understand
what this means!) "Then those who are
in Judea must run away to the hills.
15 Someone who is on the roof of a house
must not lose time by going down into
the house to get anything to take along.
16 Someone who is in the field must not
go back to the house for a cloak. 17 How
terrible it will be in those days for
women who are pregnant and for mothers with little babies! 18 Pray to God that
these things will not happen in the winter! 19 For the trouble of those days will
be far worse than any the world has ever
known from the very beginning when
God created the world until the present
time. Nor will there ever be anything
like it again. 20 But the Lord has reduced
the number of those days; if he had not,
nobody would survive. For the sake of
his chosen people, however, he has reduced those days.

21 "Then, if anyone says to you, 'Look,
here is the Messiah!' or, 'Look, there
he is!'—do not believe it. 22 For false
Messiahs and false prophets will appear.
They will perform miracles and wonders
in order to deceive even God's chosen
people, if possible. 23 Be on your guard! I
have told you everything ahead of time.

The Coming of the Son of Man

(Matthew 24.29-31; Luke 21.25-28)

24 "In the days after that time of trouble the sun will grow dark, the moon will
no longer shine, 25 the stars will fall from
heaven, and the powers in space will be
driven from their courses. 26 Then the
Son of Man will appear, coming in the
clouds with great power and glory. 27 He
will send the angels out to the four corners of the earth to gather God's chosen
people from one end of the world to the
other.

The Lesson of the Fig Tree

(Matthew 24.32-35; Luke 21.29-33)

28 "Let the fig tree teach you a lesson.
When its branches become green and
tender and it starts putting out leaves,
you know that summer is near. 29 In the
same way, when you see these things
happening, you will know that the time
is near, ready to begin.[u] 30 Remember
that all these things will happen before
the people now living have all died.
31 Heaven and earth will pass away, but
my words will never pass away.

No One Knows the Day or Hour

(Matthew 24.36-44)

32 "No one knows, however, when that
day or hour will come—neither the angels in heaven, nor the Son; only the
Father knows. 33 Be on watch, be alert,
for you do not know when the time will
come. 34 It will be like a man who goes
away from home on a trip and leaves his
servants in charge, after giving to each
one his own work to do and after telling
the doorkeeper to keep watch. 35 Watch,
then, because you do not know when the
master of the house is coming—it might
be in the evening or at midnight or before dawn or at sunrise. 36 If he comes
suddenly, he must not find you asleep.
37 What I say to you, then, I say to all:
Watch!"

The Plot against Jesus

(Matthew 26.1-5; Luke 22.1, 2; John 11.45-53)

14 It was now two days before the
Festival of Passover and Unleavened Bread. The chief priests and the
teachers of the Law were looking for a
way to arrest Jesus secretly and put him
to death. 2 "We must not do it during the
festival," they said, "or the people might
riot."

Jesus Is Anointed at Bethany

(Matthew 26.6-13; John 12.1-8)

3 Jesus was in Bethany at the house of
Simon, a man who had suffered from a
dreaded skin disease. While Jesus was
eating, a woman came in with an alabaster jar full of a very expensive perfume
made of pure nard. She broke the jar
and poured the perfume on Jesus' head.
4 Some of the people there became angry
and said to one another, "What was the

[u] the time is near, ready to begin; *or* he is near, ready to come.

use of wasting the perfume? 5 It could
have been sold for more than three hundred silver coins[v] and the money given
to the poor!" And they criticized her
harshly.
6 But Jesus said, "Leave her alone!
Why are you bothering her? She has
done a fine and beautiful thing for me.
7 You will always have poor people with
you, and any time you want to, you can
help them. But you will not always have
me. 8 She did what she could; she poured
perfume on my body to prepare it ahead
of time for burial. 9 Now, I assure you
that wherever the gospel is preached all
over the world, what she has done will
be told in memory of her."

Judas Agrees to Betray Jesus

(Matthew 26.14-16; Luke 22.3-6)

10 Then Judas Iscariot, one of the
twelve disciples, went off to the chief
priests in order to betray Jesus to them.
11 They were pleased to hear what he
had to say, and promised to give him
money. So Judas started looking for a
good chance to hand Jesus over to them.

Jesus Eats the Passover Meal with His Disciples

(Matthew 26.17-25; Luke 22.7-14, 21-23; John 13.21-30)

12 On the first day of the Festival of Unleavened Bread, the day the lambs for
the Passover meal were killed, Jesus'
disciples asked him, "Where do you
want us to go and get the Passover meal
ready for you?"
13 Then Jesus sent two of them with
these instructions: "Go into the city, and
a man carrying a jar of water will meet
you. Follow him 14 to the house he enters, and say to the owner of the house:
'The Teacher says, Where is the room
where my disciples and I will eat the
Passover meal?' 15 Then he will show
you a large upstairs room, fixed up and
furnished, where you will get everything
ready for us."
16 The disciples left, went to the city,
and found everything just as Jesus had
told them; and they prepared the Passover meal.
17 When it was evening, Jesus came
with the twelve disciples. 18 While they
were at the table eating, Jesus said, "I
tell you that one of you will betray me—
one who is eating with me."
19 The disciples were upset and began
to ask him, one after the other, "Surely
you don't mean me, do you?"
20 Jesus answered, "It will be one of
you twelve, one who dips his bread in
the dish with me. 21 The Son of Man will
die as the Scriptures say he will; but how
terrible for that man who will betray the
Son of Man! It would have been better
for that man if he had never been born!"

The Lord's Supper

(Matthew 26.26-30; Luke 22.14-20; 1 Corinthians 11.23-25)

22 While they were eating, Jesus took a
piece of bread, gave a prayer of thanks,
broke it, and gave it to his disciples.
"Take it," he said, "this is my body."
23 Then he took a cup, gave thanks to
God, and handed it to them; and they all
drank from it. 24 Jesus said, "This is my
blood which is poured out for many, my
blood which seals God's covenant.
25 I tell you, I will never again drink this
wine until the day I drink the new wine
in the Kingdom of God."
26 Then they sang a hymn and went
out to the Mount of Olives.

Jesus Predicts Peter's Denial

(Matthew 26.31-35; Luke 22.31-34; John 13.36-38)

27 Jesus said to them, "All of you will
run away and leave me, for the scripture
says, 'God will kill the shepherd, and the
sheep will all be scattered.' 28 But after I
am raised to life, I will go to Galilee
ahead of you."
29 Peter answered, "I will never leave
you, even though all the rest do!"
30 Jesus said to Peter, "I tell you that
before the rooster crows two times tonight, you will say three times that you
do not know me."
31 Peter answered even more strongly,
"I will never say that, even if I have to
die with you!"
And all the other disciples said the
same thing.

Jesus Prays in Gethsemane

(Matthew 26.36-46; Luke 22.39-46)

32 They came to a place called Gethsemane, and Jesus said to his disciples,

[v] SILVER COINS: *See 6.37.*

"Sit here while I pray." 33 He took Peter,
James, and John with him. Distress and
anguish came over him, 34 and he said to
them, "The sorrow in my heart is so
great that it almost crushes me. Stay
here and keep watch."
35 He went a little farther on, threw
himself on the ground, and prayed
that, if possible, he might not have to
go through that time of suffering.
36 "Father," he prayed, "my Father! All
things are possible for you. Take this
cup of suffering away from me. Yet not
what I want, but what you want."
37 Then he returned and found the
three disciples asleep. He said to Peter,
"Simon, are you asleep? Weren't you
able to stay awake for even one hour?"
38 And he said to them, "Keep watch, and
pray that you will not fall into temptation. The spirit is willing, but the flesh is
weak."
39 He went away once more and
prayed, saying the same words. 40 Then
he came back to the disciples and found
them asleep; they could not keep their
eyes open. And they did not know what
to say to him.
41 When he came back the third time,
he said to them, "Are you still sleeping
and resting? Enough! The hour has
come! Look, the Son of Man is now being handed over to the power of sinners.
42 Get up, let us go. Look, here is the man
who is betraying me!"

The Arrest of Jesus

(Matthew 26.47-56; Luke 22.47-53; John 18.3-12)

43 Jesus was still speaking when Judas, one of the twelve disciples, arrived.
With him was a crowd armed with
swords and clubs and sent by the chief
priests, the teachers of the Law, and the
elders. 44 The traitor had given the crowd
a signal: "The man I kiss is the one you
want. Arrest him and take him away under guard."
45 As soon as Judas arrived, he went
up to Jesus and said, "Teacher!" and
kissed him. 46 So they arrested Jesus and
held him tight. 47 But one of those standing there drew his sword and struck at
the High Priest's slave, cutting off his
ear. 48 Then Jesus spoke up and said to
them, "Did you have to come with
swords and clubs to capture me, as
though I were an outlaw? 49 Day after
day I was with you teaching in the Temple, and you did not arrest me. But the
Scriptures must come true."
50 Then all the disciples left him and
ran away.
51 A certain young man, dressed only
in a linen cloth, was following Jesus.
They tried to arrest him, 52 but he
ran away naked, leaving the cloth
behind.

Jesus before the Council

(Matthew 26.57-68; Luke 22.54, 55, 63-71; John 18.13, 14, 19-24)

53 Then Jesus was taken to the High
Priest's house, where all the chief
priests, the elders, and the teachers of
the Law were gathering. 54 Peter followed from a distance and went into the
courtyard of the High Priest's house.
There he sat down with the guards,
keeping himself warm by the fire. 55 The
chief priests and the whole Council tried
to find some evidence against Jesus in
order to put him to death, but they could
not find any. 56 Many witnesses told lies
against Jesus, but their stories did not
agree.
57 Then some men stood up and told
this lie against Jesus: 58 "We heard him
say, 'I will tear down this Temple which
men have made, and after three days I
will build one that is not made by men.' "
59 Not even they, however, could make
their stories agree.
60 The High Priest stood up in front of
them all and questioned Jesus, "Have
you no answer to the accusation they
bring against you?"
61 But Jesus kept quiet and would not
say a word. Again the High Priest questioned him, "Are you the Messiah, the
Son of the Blessed God?"
62 "I am," answered Jesus, "and you
will all see the Son of Man seated at the
right side of the Almighty and coming
with the clouds of heaven!"
63 The High Priest tore his robes and
said, "We don't need any more witnesses! 64 You heard his blasphemy.
What is your decision?"
They all voted against him: he was
guilty and should be put to death.
65 Some of them began to spit on Jesus,
and they blindfolded him and hit him.
"Guess who hit you!" they said. And the
guards took him and slapped him.

Peter Denies Jesus

(Matthew 26.69-75; Luke 22.56-62;
John 18.15-18, 25-27)

66 Peter was still down in the courtyard
when one of the High Priest's servant
women came by. 67 When she saw Peter
warming himself, she looked straight at
him and said, "You, too, were with Jesus
of Nazareth."

68 But he denied it. "I don't know . . . I
don't understand what you are talking
about," he answered, and went out into
the passageway. Just then a rooster
crowed.[w]

69 The servant woman saw him there
and began to repeat to the bystanders,
"He is one of them!" 70 But Peter denied it
again.

A little while later the bystanders accused Peter again, "You can't deny that you are one of them, because you, too, are from Galilee."

71 Then Peter said, "I swear that I am
telling the truth! May God punish me if I
am not! I do not know the man you are
talking about!"

72 Just then a rooster crowed a second
time, and Peter remembered how Jesus
had said to him, "Before the rooster
crows two times, you will say three
times that you do not know me." And he
broke down and cried.

Jesus before Pilate

(Matthew 27.1, 2, 11-14; Luke 23.1-5; John 18.28-38)

15 Early in the morning the chief
priests met hurriedly with the
elders, the teachers of the Law, and the
whole Council, and made their plans.
They put Jesus in chains, led him away,
and handed him over to Pilate. 2 Pilate
questioned him, "Are you the king of the
Jews?"

Jesus answered, "So you say."

3 The chief priests were accusing Jesus
of many things, 4 so Pilate questioned
him again, "Aren't you going to answer?
Listen to all their accusations!"

5 Again Jesus refused to say a word,
and Pilate was amazed.

Jesus Is Sentenced to Death

(Matthew 27.15-26; Luke 23.13-25; John 18.39—19.16)

6 At every Passover Festival Pilate was
in the habit of setting free any one prisoner the people asked for. 7 At that time
a man named Barabbas was in prison
with the rebels who had committed murder in the riot. 8 When the crowd gathered and began to ask Pilate for the
usual favor, 9 he asked them, "Do you
want me to set free for you the king of
the Jews?" 10 He knew very well that the
chief priests had handed Jesus over to
him because they were jealous.

11 But the chief priests stirred up the
crowd to ask, instead, that Pilate set Barabbas free for them. 12 Pilate spoke again
to the crowd, "What, then, do you want
me to do with the one you call the king
of the Jews?"

13 They shouted back, "Crucify him!"

14 "But what crime has he committed?"
Pilate asked.

They shouted all the louder, "Crucify him!"

15 Pilate wanted to please the crowd,
so he set Barabbas free for them. Then
he had Jesus whipped and handed him
over to be crucified.

The Soldiers Make Fun of Jesus

(Matthew 27.27-31; John 19.2, 3)

16 The soldiers took Jesus inside to the
courtyard of the governor's palace and
called together the rest of the company.
17 They put a purple robe on Jesus, made
a crown out of thorny branches, and put
it on his head. 18 Then they began to sa-
lute him: "Long live the King of the
Jews!" 19 They beat him over the head
with a stick, spat on him, fell on their
knees, and bowed down to him. 20 When
they had finished making fun of him,
they took off the purple robe and put his
own clothes back on him. Then they led
him out to crucify him.

Jesus Is Crucified

(Matthew 27.32-44; Luke 23.26-43; John 19.17-27)

21 On the way they met a man named
Simon, who was coming into the city
from the country, and the soldiers forced
him to carry Jesus' cross. (Simon was
from Cyrene and was the father of Alexander and Rufus.) 22 They took Jesus to a
place called Golgotha, which means
"The Place of the Skull." 23 There they
tried to give him wine mixed with a drug
called myrrh, but Jesus would not drink
it. 24 Then they crucified him and divided
his clothes among themselves, throwing

[w] *Some manuscripts do not have* Just then a rooster crowed.

dice to see who would get which piece of
clothing. 25 It was nine o'clock in the
morning when they crucified him. 26 The
notice of the accusation against him
said: "The King of the Jews." 27 They also
crucified two bandits with Jesus, one on
his right and the other on his left.[x]
29 People passing by shook their heads
and hurled insults at Jesus: "Aha! You
were going to tear down the Temple and
build it back up in three days! 30 Now
come down from the cross and save
yourself!"
31 In the same way the chief priests
and the teachers of the Law made fun of
Jesus, saying to one another, "He saved
others, but he cannot save himself! 32 Let
us see the Messiah, the king of Israel,
come down from the cross now, and we
will believe in him!"

And the two who were crucified with Jesus insulted him also.

The Death of Jesus

(Matthew 27.45-56; Luke 23.44-49; John 19.28-30)

33 At noon the whole country was covered with darkness, which lasted for
three hours. 34 At three o'clock Jesus
cried out with a loud shout, *"Eloi, Eloi,
lema sabachthani?"* which means, "My
God, my God, why did you abandon me?"
35 Some of the people there heard him
and said, "Listen, he is calling for Elijah!" 36 One of them ran up with a
sponge, soaked it in cheap wine, and put
it on the end of a stick. Then he held it up
to Jesus' lips and said, "Wait! Let us see
if Elijah is coming to bring him down
from the cross!"
37 With a loud cry Jesus died.
38 The curtain hanging in the Temple
was torn in two, from top to bottom.
39 The army officer who was standing
there in front of the cross saw how Jesus
had died.[y] "This man was really the Son
of God!" he said.
40 Some women were there, looking on
from a distance. Among them were
Mary Magdalene, Mary the mother of
the younger James and of Joseph, and
Salome. 41 They had followed Jesus
while he was in Galilee and had helped
him. Many other women who had come
to Jerusalem with him were there also.

The Burial of Jesus

(Matthew 27.57-61; Luke 23.50-56; John 19.38-42)

42-43 It was toward evening when Joseph of Arimathea arrived. He was a respected member of the Council, who
was waiting for the coming of the Kingdom of God. It was Preparation day (that
is, the day before the Sabbath), so Joseph went boldly into the presence of Pilate and asked him for the body of Jesus.
44 Pilate was surprised to hear that Jesus
was already dead. He called the army
officer and asked him if Jesus had been
dead a long time. 45 After hearing the officer's report, Pilate told Joseph he could
have the body. 46 Joseph bought a linen
sheet, took the body down, wrapped it in
the sheet, and placed it in a tomb which
had been dug out of solid rock. Then he
rolled a large stone across the entrance
to the tomb. 47 Mary Magdalene and
Mary the mother of Joseph were watching and saw where the body of Jesus
was placed.

The Resurrection

(Matthew 28.1-8; Luke 24.1-12; John 20.1-10)

16 After the Sabbath was over,
Mary Magdalene, Mary the
mother of James, and Salome bought
spices to go and anoint the body of
Jesus. 2 Very early on Sunday morning,
at sunrise, they went to the tomb. 3-4 On
the way they said to one another, "Who
will roll away the stone for us from the
entrance to the tomb?" (It was a very
large stone.) Then they looked up and
saw that the stone had already been
rolled back. 5 So they entered the tomb,
where they saw a young man sitting at
the right, wearing a white robe—and
they were alarmed.
6 "Don't be alarmed," he said. "I know
you are looking for Jesus of Nazareth,
who was crucified. He is not here—he
has been raised! Look, here is the place
where he was placed. 7 Now go and give
this message to his disciples, including
Peter: 'He is going to Galilee ahead of
you; there you will see him, just as he
told you.' "
8 So they went out and ran from the
tomb, distressed and terrified. They said

[x] *Some manuscripts add verse 28:* In this way the scripture came true which says, "He shared the fate of criminals" *(see Lk 22.37).* [y] had died; *some manuscripts have* had cried out and died.

nothing to anyone, because they were
afraid.

AN OLD ENDING TO THE GOSPEL[z]

Jesus Appears to Mary Magdalene

(Matthew 28.9, 10; John 20.11-18)

[9 After Jesus rose from death early on
Sunday, he appeared first to Mary Magdalene, from whom he had driven out
seven demons. 10 She went and told his
companions. They were mourning and
crying; 11 and when they heard her say
that Jesus was alive and that she had
seen him, they did not believe her.

Jesus Appears to Two Followers

(Luke 24.13-35)

12 After this, Jesus appeared in a different manner to two of them while they
were on their way to the country. 13 They
returned and told the others, but these
would not believe it.

Jesus Appears to the Eleven

(Matthew 28.16-20; Luke 24.36-49; John 20.19-23; Acts 1.6-8)

14 Last of all, Jesus appeared to the
eleven disciples as they were eating. He
scolded them, because they did not have
faith and because they were too stubborn to believe those who had seen him
alive. 15 He said to them, "Go throughout
the whole world and preach the gospel
to all people. 16 Whoever believes and is
baptized will be saved; whoever does
not believe will be condemned. 17 Believers will be given the power to perform
miracles: they will drive out demons in
my name; they will speak in strange
tongues; 18 if they pick up snakes or
drink any poison, they will not be
harmed; they will place their hands on
sick people, and these will get well."

Jesus Is Taken Up to Heaven

(Luke 24.50-53; Acts 1.9-11)

19 After the Lord Jesus had talked with
them, he was taken up to heaven and sat
at the right side of God. 20 The disciples
went and preached everywhere, and the
Lord worked with them and proved that
their preaching was true by the miracles
that were performed.]

ANOTHER OLD ENDING[a]

[9 The women went to Peter and his
friends and gave them a brief account of
all they had been told. 10 After this, Jesus
himself sent out through his disciples
from the east to the west the sacred and
everliving message of eternal salvation.]

[z] Some manuscripts and ancient translations do not have this ending to the Gospel (verses 9-20).
[a] Some manuscripts and ancient translations have this shorter ending to the Gospel in addition to the longer ending (verses 9-20).

The Gospel according to
LUKE

Introduction

The Gospel according to Luke *presents Jesus as both the promised Savior of Israel and as the Savior of all people.* Luke *records that Jesus was called by the Spirit of the Lord to "bring good news to the poor," and this Gospel is filled with a concern for people with all kinds of need. The note of joy is also prominent in* Luke, *especially in the opening chapters that announce the coming of Jesus, and again at the conclusion, when Jesus ascends to heaven. The story of the growth and spread of the Christian faith after the ascension of Jesus is told by the same writer in the book of* Acts.

Parts 2 and 6 (see the outline below) contain much material that is found only in this Gospel, such as the stories about the song of the angels and the shepherds' visit at the birth of Jesus, Jesus in the Temple as a boy, and the parables of the Good Samaritan and the Lost Son. Throughout the Gospel great emphasis is placed on prayer, the Holy Spirit, the role of women in the ministry of Jesus, and God's forgiveness of sins.

Outline of Contents

Introduction 1.1-4
Birth and childhood of John the Baptist and of Jesus 1.5–2.52
The ministry of John the Baptist 3.1-20
The baptism and temptation of Jesus 3.21–4.13
Jesus' public ministry in Galilee 4.14–9.50
From Galilee to Jerusalem 9.51–19.27
The last week in and near Jerusalem 19.28–23.56
The resurrection, appearances, and ascension of the Lord 24.1-53

Introduction

1 Dear Theophilus:
Many people have done their best
to write a report of the things that have
taken place among us. [2]They wrote
what we have been told by those who
saw these things from the beginning and
who proclaimed the message. [3]And so,
Your Excellency, because I have carefully studied all these matters from their
beginning, I thought it would be good to
write an orderly account for you. [4]I do
this so that you will know the full truth
about everything which you have been
taught.

The Birth of John the Baptist Is Announced

[5]During the time when Herod was
king of Judea,[a] there was a priest
named Zechariah, who belonged to the
priestly order of Abijah. His wife's name
was Elizabeth; she also belonged to a
priestly family. [6]They both lived good
lives in God's sight and obeyed fully all
the Lord's laws and commands. [7]They
had no children because Elizabeth could
not have any, and she and Zechariah
were both very old.
[8]One day Zechariah was doing his
work as a priest in the Temple, taking
his turn in the daily service. [9]According
to the custom followed by the priests, he
was chosen by lot to burn incense on the
altar. So he went into the Temple of the
Lord, [10]while the crowd of people outside prayed during the hour when the
incense was burned. [11]An angel of the
Lord appeared to him, standing at the
right side of the altar where the incense
was burned. [12]When Zechariah saw
him, he was alarmed and felt afraid.
[13]But the angel said to him, "Don't be
afraid, Zechariah! God has heard your
prayer, and your wife Elizabeth will
bear you a son. You are to name him
John. [14]How glad and happy you will be,
and how happy many others will be
when he is born! [15]John will be great in
the Lord's sight. He must not drink any
wine or strong drink. From his very
birth he will be filled with the Holy

[a] JUDEA: *The term here refers to the whole land of Palestine.*

Spirit, 16 and he will bring back many of
the people of Israel to the Lord their
God. 17 He will go ahead of the Lord,
strong and mighty like the prophet Elijah. He will bring fathers and children
together again; he will turn disobedient
people back to the way of thinking of the
righteous; he will get the Lord's people
ready for him."

18 Zechariah said to the angel, "How
shall I know if this is so? I am an old
man, and my wife is old also."

19 "I am Gabriel," the angel answered.
"I stand in the presence of God, who sent
me to speak to you and tell you this good
news. 20 But you have not believed my
message, which will come true at the
right time. Because you have not believed, you will be unable to speak; you
will remain silent until the day my promise to you comes true."

21 In the meantime the people were
waiting for Zechariah and wondering
why he was spending such a long time in
the Temple. 22 When he came out, he
could not speak to them, and so they
knew that he had seen a vision in the
Temple. Unable to say a word, he made
signs to them with his hands.

23 When his period of service in the
Temple was over, Zechariah went back
home. 24 Some time later his wife Elizabeth became pregnant and did not leave
the house for five months. 25 "Now at last
the Lord has helped me," she said. "He
has taken away my public disgrace!"

The Birth of Jesus Is Announced

26 In the sixth month of Elizabeth's
pregnancy God sent the angel Gabriel to
a town in Galilee named Nazareth. 27 He
had a message for a young woman
promised in marriage to a man named
Joseph, who was a descendant of King
David. Her name was Mary. 28 The angel
came to her and said, "Peace be with
you! The Lord is with you and has
greatly blessed you!"

29 Mary was deeply troubled by the angel's message, and she wondered what
his words meant. 30 The angel said to
her, "Don't be afraid, Mary; God has
been gracious to you. 31 You will become
pregnant and give birth to a son, and
you will name him Jesus. 32 He will be
great and will be called the Son of the
Most High God. The Lord God will make
him a king, as his ancestor David was,
33 and he will be the king of the descendants of Jacob forever; his kingdom will
never end!"

34 Mary said to the angel, "I am a virgin. How, then, can this be?"

35 The angel answered, "The Holy
Spirit will come on you, and God's
power will rest upon you. For this reason
the holy child will be called the Son of
God. 36 Remember your relative Elizabeth. It is said that she cannot have children, but she herself is now six months
pregnant, even though she is very old.
37 For there is nothing that God cannot do."

38 "I am the Lord's servant," said Mary;
"may it happen to me as you have said."
And the angel left her.

Mary Visits Elizabeth

39 Soon afterward Mary got ready and
hurried off to a town in the hill country
of Judea. 40 She went into Zechariah's
house and greeted Elizabeth. 41 When
Elizabeth heard Mary's greeting, the
baby moved within her. Elizabeth was
filled with the Holy Spirit 42 and said in a
loud voice, "You are the most blessed of
all women, and blessed is the child you
will bear! 43 Why should this great thing
happen to me, that my Lord's mother
comes to visit me? 44 For as soon as I
heard your greeting, the baby within me
jumped with gladness. 45 How happy you
are to believe that the Lord's message to
you will come true!"

Mary's Song of Praise

46 Mary said,
"My heart praises the Lord;
47 my soul is glad because of God
my Savior,
48 for he has remembered me, his
lowly servant!
From now on all people will call
me happy,
49 because of the great things the
Mighty God has done for me.
His name is holy;
50 from one generation to another
he shows mercy to those who
honor him.
51 He has stretched out his
mighty arm
and scattered the proud with all
their plans.
52 He has brought down mighty
kings from their thrones,

and lifted up the lowly.
53 He has filled the hungry with good
things,
and sent the rich away with
empty hands.
54 He has kept the promise he made
to our ancestors,
and has come to the help of his
servant Israel.
55 He has remembered to show
mercy to Abraham
and to all his descendants
forever!"

56 Mary stayed about three months
with Elizabeth and then went back
home.

The Birth of John the Baptist

57 The time came for Elizabeth to have
her baby, and she gave birth to a son.
58 Her neighbors and relatives heard
how wonderfully good the Lord had
been to her, and they all rejoiced
with her.
59 When the baby was a week old, they
came to circumcise him, and they were
going to name him Zechariah, after his
father. 60 But his mother said, "No! His
name is to be John."
61 They said to her, "But you don't
have any relative with that name!"
62 Then they made signs to his father,
asking him what name he would like the
boy to have.
63 Zechariah asked for a writing pad
and wrote, "His name is John." How surprised they all were! 64 At that moment
Zechariah was able to speak again, and
he started praising God. 65 The neighbors were all filled with fear, and the
news about these things spread through
all the hill country of Judea. 66 Everyone
who heard of it thought about it and
asked, "What is this child going to be?"
For it was plain that the Lord's power
was upon him.

Zechariah's Prophecy

67 John's father Zechariah was filled
with the Holy Spirit, and he spoke God's
message:
68 "Let us praise the Lord, the God
of Israel!
He has come to the help of his
people and has set them free.
69 He has provided for us a mighty
Savior,
a descendant of his servant
David.
70 He promised through his holy
prophets long ago
71 that he would save us from our
enemies,
from the power of all those who
hate us.
72 He said he would show mercy to
our ancestors
and remember his sacred
covenant.
73-74 With a solemn oath to our
ancestor Abraham
he promised to rescue us from
our enemies
and allow us to serve him
without fear,
75 so that we might be holy and
righteous before him
all the days of our life.

76 "You, my child, will be called a
prophet of the Most High God.
You will go ahead of the Lord
to prepare his road for him,
77 to tell his people that they will be
saved
by having their sins forgiven.
78 Our God is merciful and tender.
He will cause the bright dawn of
salvation to rise on us
79 and to shine from heaven on all
those who live in the dark
shadow of death,
to guide our steps into the path
of peace."

80 The child grew and developed in
body and spirit. He lived in the desert
until the day when he appeared publicly
to the people of Israel.

The Birth of Jesus

(Matthew 1.18-25)

2 At that time Emperor Augustus ordered a census to be taken throughout the Roman Empire. 2 When this first
census took place, Quirinius was the
governor of Syria. 3 Everyone, then,
went to register himself, each to his own
hometown.
4 Joseph went from the town of Nazareth in Galilee to the town of Bethlehem
in Judea, the birthplace of King David.
Joseph went there because he was a
descendant of David. 5 He went to register with Mary, who was promised in
marriage to him. She was pregnant

6 and while they were in Bethlehem, the
time came for her to have her baby. 7 She
gave birth to her first son, wrapped him
in cloths and laid him in a manger—
there was no room for them to stay in
the inn.

The Shepherds and the Angels

8 There were some shepherds in that
part of the country who were spending
the night in the fields, taking care of
their flocks. 9 An angel of the Lord appeared to them, and the glory of the
Lord shone over them. They were terribly afraid, 10 but the angel said to them,
"Don't be afraid! I am here with good
news for you, which will bring great joy
to all the people. 11 This very day in David's town your Savior was born—
Christ the Lord! 12 And this is what will
prove it to you: you will find a baby
wrapped in cloths and lying in a
manger."
13 Suddenly a great army of heaven's
angels appeared with the angel, singing
praises to God:

14 "Glory to God in the highest
heaven,
and peace on earth to those with
whom he is pleased!"

15 When the angels went away from
them back into heaven, the shepherds
said to one another, "Let's go to Bethlehem and see this thing that has happened, which the Lord has told us."
16 So they hurried off and found Mary
and Joseph and saw the baby lying in
the manger. 17 When the shepherds saw
him, they told them what the angel had
said about the child. 18 All who heard it
were amazed at what the shepherds
said. 19 Mary remembered all these
things and thought deeply about them.
20 The shepherds went back, singing
praises to God for all they had heard and
seen; it had been just as the angel had
told them.

Jesus Is Named

21 A week later, when the time came
for the baby to be circumcised, he was
named Jesus, the name which the angel
had given him before he had been
conceived.

Jesus Is Presented in the Temple

22 The time came for Joseph and Mary
to perform the ceremony of purification,
as the Law of Moses commanded. So
they took the child to Jerusalem to
present him to the Lord, 23 as it is written
in the law of the Lord: "Every first-born
male is to be dedicated to the Lord."
24 They also went to offer a sacrifice of a
pair of doves or two young pigeons, as
required by the law of the Lord.
25 At that time there was a man named
Simeon living in Jerusalem. He was a
good, God-fearing man and was waiting
for Israel to be saved. The Holy Spirit
was with him 26 and had assured him
that he would not die before he had seen
the Lord's promised Messiah. 27 Led by
the Spirit, Simeon went into the Temple.
When the parents brought the child
Jesus into the Temple to do for him what
the Law required, 28 Simeon took the
child in his arms and gave thanks
to God:

29 "Now, Lord, you have kept your
promise,
and you may let your servant
go in peace.
30 With my own eyes I have seen
your salvation,
31 which you have prepared in the
presence of all peoples:
32 A light to reveal your will to the
Gentiles
and bring glory to your people
Israel."

33 The child's father and mother were
amazed at the things Simeon said about
him. 34 Simeon blessed them and said to
Mary, his mother, "This child is chosen
by God for the destruction and the salvation of many in Israel. He will be a sign
from God which many people will speak
against 35 and so reveal their secret
thoughts. And sorrow, like a sharp
sword, will break your own heart."
36-37 There was a very old prophet, a
widow named Anna, daughter of Pha-
nuel of the tribe of Asher. She had been
married for only seven years and was
now eighty-four years old.[b] She never
left the Temple; day and night she worshiped God, fasting and praying. 38 That
very same hour she arrived and gave
thanks to God and spoke about the child

[b] was now eighty-four years old; *or* had been a widow eighty-four years.

to all who were waiting for God to set
Jerusalem free.

The Return to Nazareth

39 When Joseph and Mary had finished
doing all that was required by the Law
of the Lord, they returned to their hometown of Nazareth in Galilee. 40 The child
grew and became strong; he was full of
wisdom, and God's blessings were
upon him.

The Boy Jesus in the Temple

41 Every year the parents of Jesus went
to Jerusalem for the Passover Festival.
42 When Jesus was twelve years old, they
went to the festival as usual. 43 When the
festival was over, they started back
home, but the boy Jesus stayed in Jerusalem. His parents did not know this;
44 they thought that he was with the
group, so they traveled a whole day and
then started looking for him among their
relatives and friends. 45 They did not find
him, so they went back to Jerusalem
looking for him. 46 On the third day they
found him in the Temple, sitting with the
Jewish teachers, listening to them and
asking questions. 47 All who heard him
were amazed at his intelligent answers.
48 His parents were astonished when
they saw him, and his mother said to
him, "Son, why have you done this to us?
Your father and I have been terribly
worried trying to find you."

49 He answered them, "Why did you
have to look for me? Didn't you know
that I had to be in my Father's house?"
50 But they did not understand his
answer.

51 So Jesus went back with them to
Nazareth, where he was obedient to
them. His mother treasured all these
things in her heart. 52 Jesus grew both in
body and in wisdom, gaining favor with
God and people.

The Preaching of John the Baptist

(Matthew 3.1-12; Mark 1.1-8; John 1.19-28)

3 It was the fifteenth year of the rule
of Emperor Tiberius; Pontius Pilate
was governor of Judea, Herod was ruler
of Galilee, and his brother Philip was
ruler of the territory of Iturea and Trach-
onitis; Lysanias was ruler of Abilene,
2 and Annas and Caiaphas were High
Priests. At that time the word of God
came to John son of Zechariah in the
desert. 3 So John went throughout the
whole territory of the Jordan River,
preaching, "Turn away from your sins
and be baptized, and God will forgive
your sins." 4 As it is written in the book
of the prophet Isaiah:

"Someone is shouting in the
desert:
'Get the road ready for the Lord;
make a straight path for him to
travel!
5 Every valley must be filled up,
every hill and mountain
leveled off.
The winding roads must be made
straight,
and the rough paths made
smooth.
6 The whole human race will see
God's salvation!'"

7 Crowds of people came out to John to
be baptized by him. "You snakes!" he
said to them. "Who told you that you
could escape from the punishment God
is about to send? 8 Do those things that
will show that you have turned from
your sins. And don't start saying among
yourselves that Abraham is your ancestor. I tell you that God can take these
rocks and make descendants for Abraham! 9 The ax is ready to cut down the
trees at the roots; every tree that does
not bear good fruit will be cut down and
thrown in the fire."

10 The people asked him, "What are we
to do, then?"

11 He answered, "Whoever has two
shirts must give one to the man who has
none, and whoever has food must
share it."

12 Some tax collectors came to be baptized, and they asked him, "Teacher,
what are we to do?"

13 "Don't collect more than is legal," he
told them.

14 Some soldiers also asked him,
"What about us? What are we to do?"

He said to them, "Don't take money
from anyone by force or accuse anyone
falsely. Be content with your pay."

15 People's hopes began to rise, and
they began to wonder whether John perhaps might be the Messiah. 16 So John
said to all of them, "I baptize you with
water, but someone is coming who is
much greater than I am. I am not good
enough even to untie his sandals. He will
baptize you with the Holy Spirit and fire.

17 He has his winnowing shovel with
him, to thresh out all the grain and
gather the wheat into his barn; but he
will burn the chaff in a fire that never
goes out."
18 In many different ways John
preached the Good News to the people
and urged them to change their ways.
19 But John reprimanded Governor
Herod, because he had married Herodias, his brother's wife, and had done
many other evil things. 20 Then Herod
did an even worse thing by putting John
in prison.

The Baptism of Jesus

(Matthew 3.13-17; Mark 1.9-11)

21 After all the people had been baptized, Jesus also was baptized. While he
was praying, heaven was opened, 22 and
the Holy Spirit came down upon him in
bodily form like a dove. And a voice
came from heaven, "You are my own
dear Son. I am pleased with you."

The Ancestors of Jesus

(Matthew 1.1-17)

23 When Jesus began his work, he was
about thirty years old. He was the son,
so people thought, of Joseph, who was
the son of Heli, 24 the son of Matthat, the
son of Levi, the son of Melchi, the son of
Jannai, the son of Joseph, 25 the son of
Mattathias, the son of Amos, the son of
Nahum, the son of Esli, the son of Nag-
gai, 26 the son of Maath, the son of Mattathias, the son of Semein, the son of
Josech, the son of Joda, 27 the son of Joa-
nan, the son of Rhesa, the son of Zerubbabel, the son of Shealtiel, the son of
Neri, 28 the son of Melchi, the son of
Addi, the son of Cosam, the son of Elma-
dam, the son of Er, 29 the son of Joshua,
the son of Eliezer, the son of Jorim, the
son of Matthat, the son of Levi, 30 the son
of Simeon, the son of Judah, the son of
Joseph, the son of Jonam, the son of Eliakim, 31 the son of Melea, the son of
Menna, the son of Mattatha, the son of
Nathan, the son of David, 32 the son of
Jesse, the son of Obed, the son of Boaz,
the son of Salmon, the son of Nahshon,
33 the son of Amminadab, the son of Ad-
min, the son of Arni, the son of Hezron,
the son of Perez, the son of Judah, 34 the
son of Jacob, the son of Isaac, the son of
Abraham, the son of Terah, the son of
Nahor, 35 the son of Serug, the son of
Reu, the son of Peleg, the son of Eber,
the son of Shelah, 36 the son of Cainan,
the son of Arphaxad, the son of Shem,
the son of Noah, the son of Lamech,
37 the son of Methuselah, the son of
Enoch, the son of Jared, the son of
Mahalaleel, the son of Kenan, 38 the son
of Enosh, the son of Seth, the son of
Adam, the son of God.

The Temptation of Jesus

(Matthew 4.1-11; Mark 1.12, 13)

4 Jesus returned from the Jordan full
of the Holy Spirit and was led by
the Spirit into the desert, 2 where he was
tempted by the Devil for forty days. In
all that time he ate nothing, so that he
was hungry when it was over.
3 The Devil said to him, "If you are
God's Son, order this stone to turn into
bread."
4 But Jesus answered, "The scripture
says, 'Human beings cannot live on
bread alone.' "
5 Then the Devil took him up and
showed him in a second all the kingdoms of the world. 6 "I will give you all
this power and all this wealth," the Devil
told him. "It has all been handed over to
me, and I can give it to anyone I choose.
7 All this will be yours, then, if you worship me."
8 Jesus answered, "The scripture says,
'Worship the Lord your God and serve
only him!' "
9 Then the Devil took him to Jerusalem
and set him on the highest point of the
Temple, and said to him, "If you are
God's Son, throw yourself down from
here. 10 For the scripture says, 'God will
order his angels to take good care of
you.' 11 It also says, 'They will hold you
up with their hands so that not even
your feet will be hurt on the stones.' "
12 But Jesus answered, "The scripture
says, 'Do not put the Lord your God to
the test.' "
13 When the Devil finished tempting
Jesus in every way, he left him for a
while.

Jesus Begins His Work in Galilee

(Matthew 4.12-17; Mark 1.14, 15)

14 Then Jesus returned to Galilee, and
the power of the Holy Spirit was with
him. The news about him spread
throughout all that territory. 15 He taught

in the synagogues and was praised by
everyone.

Jesus Is Rejected at Nazareth

(Matthew 13.53-58; Mark 6.1-6)

16 Then Jesus went to Nazareth, where
he had been brought up, and on the Sabbath he went as usual to the synagogue.
He stood up to read the Scriptures 17 and
was handed the book of the prophet Isaiah. He unrolled the scroll and found the
place where it is written,

18 "The Spirit of the Lord is upon me,
because he has chosen me to
bring good news to the poor.
He has sent me to proclaim liberty
to the captives
and recovery of sight to the
blind,
to set free the oppressed
19 and announce that the time has
come
when the Lord will save his
people."

20 Jesus rolled up the scroll, gave it
back to the attendant, and sat down. All
the people in the synagogue had their
eyes fixed on him, 21 as he said to them,
"This passage of scripture has come true
today, as you heard it being read."

22 They were all well impressed with
him and marveled at the eloquent words
that he spoke. They said, "Isn't he the
son of Joseph?"

23 He said to them, "I am sure that you
will quote this proverb to me, 'Doctor,
heal yourself.' You will also tell me to do
here in my hometown the same things
you heard were done in Capernaum. 24 I
tell you this," Jesus added, "prophets are
never welcomed in their hometown.
25 Listen to me: it is true that there were
many widows in Israel during the time
of Elijah, when there was no rain for
three and a half years and a severe famine spread throughout the whole land.
26 Yet Elijah was not sent to anyone in
Israel, but only to a widow living in Zarephath in the territory of Sidon. 27 And
there were many people suffering from a
dreaded skin disease who lived in Israel
during the time of the prophet Elisha;
yet not one of them was healed, but only
Naaman the Syrian."

28 When the people in the synagogue
heard this, they were filled with anger.
29 They rose up, dragged Jesus out of
town, and took him to the top of the hill
on which their town was built. They
meant to throw him over the cliff, 30 but
he walked through the middle of the
crowd and went his way.

A Man with an Evil Spirit

(Mark 1.21-28)

31 Then Jesus went to Capernaum, a
town in Galilee, where he taught the
people on the Sabbath. 32 They were all
amazed at the way he taught, because he
spoke with authority. 33 In the synagogue was a man who had the spirit of
an evil demon in him; he screamed out
in a loud voice, 34 "Ah! What do you
want with us, Jesus of Nazareth? Are
you here to destroy us? I know who you
are: you are God's holy messenger!"

35 Jesus ordered the spirit, "Be quiet
and come out of the man!" The demon
threw the man down in front of them
and went out of him without doing him
any harm.

36 The people were all amazed and
said to one another, "What kind of
words are these? With authority and
power this man gives orders to the evil
spirits, and they come out!" 37 And the
report about Jesus spread everywhere in
that region.

Jesus Heals Many People

(Matthew 8.14-17; Mark 1.29-34)

38 Jesus left the synagogue and went to
Simon's home. Simon's mother-in-law
was sick with a high fever, and they
spoke to Jesus about her. 39 He went and
stood at her bedside and ordered the fever to leave her. The fever left her, and
she got up at once and began to wait on
them.

40 After sunset all who had friends who
were sick with various diseases brought
them to Jesus; he placed his hands on
every one of them and healed them all.
41 Demons also went out from many
people, screaming, "You are the Son
of God!"

Jesus gave the demons an order and
would not let them speak, because they
knew he was the Messiah.

Jesus Preaches in the Synagogues

(Mark 1.35-39)

42 At daybreak Jesus left the town and
went off to a lonely place. The people
started looking for him, and when they
found him, they tried to keep him from

leaving. 43 But he said to them, "I must
preach the Good News about the Kingdom of God in other towns also, because
that is what God sent me to do."
44 So he preached in the synagogues
throughout the country.

Jesus Calls the First Disciples

(Matthew 4.18-22; Mark 1.16-20)

5 One day Jesus was standing on the
shore of Lake Gennesaret while the
people pushed their way up to him to
listen to the word of God. 2 He saw two
boats pulled up on the beach; the fishermen had left them and were washing the
nets. 3 Jesus got into one of the boats—it
belonged to Simon—and asked him to
push off a little from the shore. Jesus sat
in the boat and taught the crowd.
4 When he finished speaking, he said
to Simon, "Push the boat out further to
the deep water, and you and your partners let down your nets for a catch."
5 "Master," Simon answered, "we
worked hard all night long and caught
nothing. But if you say so, I will let down
the nets." 6 They let them down and
caught such a large number of fish that
the nets were about to break. 7 So they
motioned to their partners in the other
boat to come and help them. They came
and filled both boats so full of fish that
the boats were about to sink. 8 When Simon Peter saw what had happened, he
fell on his knees before Jesus and said,
"Go away from me, Lord! I am a sinful man!"
9 He and the others with him were all
amazed at the large number of fish they
had caught. 10 The same was true of Simon's partners, James and John, the
sons of Zebedee. Jesus said to Simon,
"Don't be afraid; from now on you will
be catching people."
11 They pulled the boats up on the
beach, left everything, and followed
Jesus.

Jesus Heals a Man

(Matthew 8.1-4; Mark 1.40-45)

12 Once Jesus was in a town where
there was a man who was suffering from
a dreaded skin disease. When he saw
Jesus, he threw himself down and
begged him, "Sir, if you want to, you can
make me clean!"[c]
13 Jesus reached out and touched him.
"I do want to," he answered. "Be clean!"
At once the disease left the man. 14 Jesus
ordered him, "Don't tell anyone, but go
straight to the priest and let him examine you; then to prove to everyone that
you are cured, offer the sacrifice as
Moses ordered."
15 But the news about Jesus spread all
the more widely, and crowds of people
came to hear him and be healed from
their diseases. 16 But he would go away
to lonely places, where he prayed.

Jesus Heals a Paralyzed Man

(Matthew 9.1-8; Mark 2.1-12)

17 One day when Jesus was teaching,
some Pharisees and teachers of the Law
were sitting there who had come from
every town in Galilee and Judea and
from Jerusalem. The power of the Lord
was present for Jesus to heal the sick.
18 Some men came carrying a paralyzed
man on a bed, and they tried to carry
him into the house and put him in front
of Jesus. 19 Because of the crowd, however, they could find no way to take him
in. So they carried him up on the roof,
made an opening in the tiles, and let him
down on his bed into the middle of the
group in front of Jesus. 20 When Jesus
saw how much faith they had, he said to
the man, "Your sins are forgiven, my
friend."
21 The teachers of the Law and the
Pharisees began to say to themselves,
"Who is this man who speaks such blasphemy! God is the only one who can forgive sins!"
22 Jesus knew their thoughts and said
to them, "Why do you think such things?
23 Is it easier to say, 'Your sins are forgiven you,' or to say, 'Get up and walk'?
24 I will prove to you, then, that the Son
of Man has authority on earth to forgive
sins." So he said to the paralyzed man, "I
tell you, get up, pick up your bed, and go
home!"
25 At once the man got up in front of
them all, took the bed he had been lying
on, and went home, praising God.
26 They were all completely amazed! Full
of fear, they praised God, saying, "What
marvelous things we have seen today!"

[c] MAKE ME CLEAN: *This disease was considered to make a person ritually unclean.*

Jesus Calls Levi

(Matthew 9.9-13; Mark 2.13-17)

27 After this, Jesus went out and saw a
tax collector named Levi, sitting in his
office. Jesus said to him, "Follow me."
28 Levi got up, left everything, and followed him.

29 Then Levi had a big feast in his
house for Jesus, and among the guests
was a large number of tax collectors and
other people. 30 Some Pharisees and
some teachers of the Law who belonged
to their group complained to Jesus' disciples. "Why do you eat and drink with
tax collectors and other outcasts?" they
asked.

31 Jesus answered them, "People who
are well do not need a doctor, but only
those who are sick. 32 I have not come to
call respectable people to repent, but
outcasts."

The Question about Fasting

(Matthew 9.14-17; Mark 2.18-22)

33 Some people said to Jesus, "The disciples of John fast frequently and offer
prayers, and the disciples of the Pharisees do the same; but your disciples eat
and drink."

34 Jesus answered, "Do you think you
can make the guests at a wedding party
go without food as long as the bridegroom is with them? Of course not!
35 But the day will come when the bridegroom will be taken away from them,
and then they will fast."

36 Jesus also told them this parable:
"You don't tear a piece off a new coat to
patch up an old coat. If you do, you will
have torn the new coat, and the piece of
new cloth will not match the old. 37 Nor
do you pour new wine into used wineskins, because the new wine will burst
the skins, the wine will pour out, and the
skins will be ruined. 38 Instead, new wine
must be poured into fresh wineskins!
39 And you don't want new wine after
drinking old wine. 'The old is better,'
you say."

The Question about the Sabbath

(Matthew 12.1-8; Mark 2.23-28)

6 Jesus was walking through some
wheat fields on a Sabbath. His disciples began to pick the heads of wheat,
rub them in their hands, and eat the
grain. 2 Some Pharisees asked, "Why are
you doing what our Law says you cannot do on the Sabbath?"

3 Jesus answered them, "Haven't you
read what David did when he and his
men were hungry? 4 He went into the
house of God, took the bread offered to
God, ate it, and gave it also to his men.
Yet it is against our Law for anyone except the priests to eat that bread."

5 And Jesus concluded, "The Son of
Man is Lord of the Sabbath."

The Man with a Paralyzed Hand

(Matthew 12.9-14; Mark 3.1-6)

6 On another Sabbath Jesus went into
a synagogue and taught. A man was
there whose right hand was paralyzed.
7 Some teachers of the Law and some
Pharisees wanted a reason to accuse
Jesus of doing wrong, so they watched
him closely to see if he would heal on the
Sabbath. 8 But Jesus knew their thoughts
and said to the man, "Stand up and come
here to the front." The man got up and
stood there. 9 Then Jesus said to them, "I
ask you: What does our Law allow us to
do on the Sabbath? To help or to harm?
To save someone's life or destroy it?"
10 He looked around at them all; then he
said[d] to the man, "Stretch out your
hand." He did so, and his hand became
well again.

11 They were filled with rage and began to discuss among themselves what
they could do to Jesus.

Jesus Chooses the Twelve Apostles

(Matthew 10.1-4; Mark 3.13-19)

12 At that time Jesus went up a hill to
pray and spent the whole night there
praying to God. 13 When day came, he
called his disciples to him and chose
twelve of them, whom he named apostles: 14 Simon (whom he named Peter)
and his brother Andrew; James and
John, Philip and Bartholomew, 15 Matthew and Thomas, James son of Alphaeus, and Simon (who was called the
Patriot), 16 Judas son of James, and Judas Iscariot, who became the traitor.

Jesus Teaches and Heals

(Matthew 4.23-25)

17 When Jesus had come down from
the hill with the apostles, he stood on a

[d] said; *some manuscripts have* said angrily.

level place with a large number of his
disciples. A large crowd of people was
there from all over Judea and from Jerusalem and from the coast cities of Tyre
and Sidon; 18 they had come to hear him
and to be healed of their diseases. Those
who were troubled by evil spirits also
came and were healed. 19 All the people
tried to touch him, for power was going
out from him and healing them all.

Happiness and Sorrow

(Matthew 5.1-12)

20 Jesus looked at his disciples and
said,

"Happy are you poor;
the Kingdom of God is yours!
21 "Happy are you who are
hungry now;
you will be filled!
"Happy are you who weep now;
you will laugh!

22 "Happy are you when people hate
you, reject you, insult you, and say that
you are evil, all because of the Son of
Man! 23 Be glad when that happens and
dance for joy, because a great reward is
kept for you in heaven. For their ancestors did the very same things to the
prophets.

24 "But how terrible for you who are
rich now;
you have had your easy life!
25 "How terrible for you who are
full now;
you will go hungry!
"How terrible for you who
laugh now;
you will mourn and weep!

26 "How terrible when all people speak
well of you; their ancestors said the very
same things about the false prophets.

Love for Enemies

(Matthew 5.38-48; 7.12a)

27 "But I tell you who hear me: Love
your enemies, do good to those who hate
you, 28 bless those who curse you, and
pray for those who mistreat you. 29 If
anyone hits you on one cheek, let him hit
the other one too; if someone takes your
coat, let him have your shirt as well.
30 Give to everyone who asks you for
something, and when someone takes
what is yours, do not ask for it back.
31 Do for others just what you want them
to do for you.

32 "If you love only the people who love
you, why should you receive a blessing?
Even sinners love those who love them!
33 And if you do good only to those who
do good to you, why should you receive
a blessing? Even sinners do that! 34 And
if you lend only to those from whom you
hope to get it back, why should you receive a blessing? Even sinners lend to
sinners, to get back the same amount!
35 No! Love your enemies and do good to
them; lend and expect nothing back.
You will then have a great reward, and
you will be children of the Most High
God. For he is good to the ungrateful and
the wicked. 36 Be merciful just as your
Father is merciful.

Judging Others

(Matthew 7.1-5)

37 "Do not judge others, and God will
not judge you; do not condemn others,
and God will not condemn you; forgive
others, and God will forgive you. 38 Give
to others, and God will give to you. Indeed, you will receive a full measure, a
generous helping, poured into your
hands — all that you can hold. The measure you use for others is the one that
God will use for you."

39 And Jesus told them this parable:
"One blind man cannot lead another
one; if he does, both will fall into a ditch.
40 No pupils are greater than their
teacher; but all pupils, when they have
completed their training, will be like
their teacher.

41 "Why do you look at the speck in
your brother's eye, but pay no attention
to the log in your own eye? 42 How can
you say to your brother, 'Please, brother,
let me take that speck out of your eye,'
yet cannot even see the log in your own
eye? You hypocrite! First take the log
out of your own eye, and then you will
be able to see clearly to take the speck
out of your brother's eye.

A Tree and Its Fruit

(Matthew 7.16-20; 12.33-35)

43 "A healthy tree does not bear bad
fruit, nor does a poor tree bear good
fruit. 44 Every tree is known by the fruit it
bears; you do not pick figs from thorn
bushes or gather grapes from bramble
bushes. 45 A good person brings good out
of the treasure of good things in his
heart; a bad person brings bad out of his

treasure of bad things. For the mouth
speaks what the heart is full of.

The Two House Builders

(Matthew 7.24-27)

46 "Why do you call me, 'Lord, Lord,'
and yet don't do what I tell you? 47 Anyone who comes to me and listens to my
words and obeys them — I will show you
what he is like. 48 He is like a man who,
in building his house, dug deep and laid
the foundation on rock. The river
flooded over and hit that house but
could not shake it, because it was well
built. 49 But anyone who hears my words
and does not obey them is like a man
who built his house without laying a
foundation; when the flood hit that
house it fell at once — and what a terrible
crash that was!"

Jesus Heals a Roman Officer's Servant

(Matthew 8.5-13)

7 When Jesus had finished saying all
these things to the people, he went
to Capernaum. 2 A Roman officer there
had a servant who was very dear to him;
the man was sick and about to die.
3 When the officer heard about Jesus, he
sent some Jewish elders to ask him to
come and heal his servant. 4 They came
to Jesus and begged him earnestly, "This
man really deserves your help. 5 He
loves our people and he himself built a
synagogue for us."

6 So Jesus went with them. He was not
far from the house when the officer sent
friends to tell him, "Sir, don't trouble
yourself. I do not deserve to have you
come into my house, 7 neither do I consider myself worthy to come to you in
person. Just give the order, and my servant will get well. 8 I, too, am a man
placed under the authority of superior
officers, and I have soldiers under me. I
order this one, 'Go!' and he goes; I order
that one, 'Come!' and he comes; and I
order my slave, 'Do this!' and he
does it."

9 Jesus was surprised when he heard
this; he turned around and said to the
crowd following him, "I tell you, I have
never found faith like this, not even in
Israel!"

10 The messengers went back to the
officer's house and found his servant
well.

Jesus Raises a Widow's Son

11 Soon afterward[e] Jesus went to a
town named Nain, accompanied by his
disciples and a large crowd. 12 Just as he
arrived at the gate of the town, a funeral
procession was coming out. The dead
man was the only son of a woman who
was a widow, and a large crowd from
the town was with her. 13 When the Lord
saw her, his heart was filled with pity for
her, and he said to her, "Don't cry."
14 Then he walked over and touched the
coffin, and the men carrying it stopped.
Jesus said, "Young man! Get up, I tell
you!" 15 The dead man sat up and began
to talk, and Jesus gave him back to his
mother.

16 They all were filled with fear and
praised God. "A great prophet has appeared among us!" they said; "God has
come to save his people!"

17 This news about Jesus went out
through all the country and the surrounding territory.

The Messengers from John the Baptist

(Matthew 11.2-19)

18 When John's disciples told him
about all these things, he called two of
them 19 and sent them to the Lord to ask
him, "Are you the one John said was going to come, or should we expect someone else?"

20 When they came to Jesus, they said,
"John the Baptist sent us to ask if you
are the one he said was going to come,
or should we expect someone else?"

21 At that very time Jesus healed many
people from their sicknesses, diseases,
and evil spirits, and gave sight to many
blind people. 22 He answered John's
messengers, "Go back and tell John
what you have seen and heard: the blind
can see, the lame can walk, those who
suffer from dreaded skin diseases are
made clean,[f] the deaf can hear, the
dead are raised to life, and the Good
News is preached to the poor. 23 How
happy are those who have no doubts
about me!"

[e] Soon afterward; *some manuscripts have* The next day. [f] MADE CLEAN: *See 5.12.*

24 After John's messengers had left,
Jesus began to speak about him to the
crowds: "When you went out to John in
the desert, what did you expect to see? A
blade of grass bending in the wind?
25 What did you go out to see? A man
dressed up in fancy clothes? People who
dress like that and live in luxury are
found in palaces! 26 Tell me, what did
you go out to see? A prophet? Yes indeed, but you saw much more than a
prophet. 27 For John is the one of whom
the scripture says: 'God said, I will send
my messenger ahead of you to open the
way for you.' 28 I tell you," Jesus added,
"John is greater than anyone who has
ever lived. But the one who is least
in the Kingdom of God is greater than
John."
29 All the people heard him; they and
especially the tax collectors were the
ones who had obeyed God's righteous
demands and had been baptized by
John. 30 But the Pharisees and the teachers of the Law rejected God's purpose
for themselves and refused to be baptized by John.
31 Jesus continued, "Now to what can I
compare the people of this day? What
are they like? 32 They are like children
sitting in the marketplace. One group
shouts to the other, 'We played wedding
music for you, but you wouldn't dance!
We sang funeral songs, but you wouldn't
cry!' 33 John the Baptist came, and he
fasted and drank no wine, and you said,
'He has a demon in him!' 34 The Son of
Man came, and he ate and drank, and
you said, 'Look at this man! He is a glutton and wine drinker, a friend of tax collectors and other outcasts!' 35 God's
wisdom, however, is shown to be true by
all who accept it."

Jesus at the Home of Simon the Pharisee

36 A Pharisee invited Jesus to have
dinner with him, and Jesus went to his
house and sat down to eat. 37 In that
town was a woman who lived a sinful
life. She heard that Jesus was eating in
the Pharisee's house, so she brought an
alabaster jar full of perfume 38 and stood
behind Jesus, by his feet, crying and
wetting his feet with her tears. Then she
dried his feet with her hair, kissed them,
and poured the perfume on them.
39 When the Pharisee saw this, he said
to himself, "If this man really were
a prophet, he would know who this
woman is who is touching him; he would
know what kind of sinful life she lives!"
40 Jesus spoke up and said to him, "Simon, I have something to tell you."
"Yes, Teacher," he said, "tell me."
41 "There were two men who owed
money to a moneylender," Jesus began.
"One owed him five hundred silver
coins, and the other owed him fifty.
42 Neither of them could pay him back,
so he canceled the debts of both. Which
one, then, will love him more?"
43 "I suppose," answered Simon, "that
it would be the one who was forgiven
more."
"You are right," said Jesus. 44 Then he
turned to the woman and said to Simon,
"Do you see this woman? I came into
your home, and you gave me no water
for my feet, but she has washed my feet
with her tears and dried them with her
hair. 45 You did not welcome me with a
kiss, but she has not stopped kissing my
feet since I came. 46 You provided no olive oil for my head, but she has covered
my feet with perfume. 47 I tell you, then,
the great love she has shown proves that
her many sins have been forgiven. But
whoever has been forgiven little shows
only a little love."
48 Then Jesus said to the woman,
"Your sins are forgiven."
49 The others sitting at the table began
to say to themselves, "Who is this, who
even forgives sins?"
50 But Jesus said to the woman, "Your
faith has saved you; go in peace."

Women Who Accompanied Jesus

8 Some time later Jesus traveled
through towns and villages, preaching the Good News about the Kingdom
of God. The twelve disciples went with
him, 2 and so did some women who had
been healed of evil spirits and diseases:
Mary (who was called Magdalene), from
whom seven demons had been driven
out; 3 Joanna, whose husband Chuza
was an officer in Herod's court; and Susanna, and many other women who
used their own resources to help Jesus
and his disciples.

The Parable of the Sower

(Matthew 13.1-9; Mark 4.1-9)

4 People kept coming to Jesus from
one town after another; and when a
great crowd gathered, Jesus told this
parable:

5 "Once there was a man who went out
to sow grain. As he scattered the seed in
the field, some of it fell along the path,
where it was stepped on, and the birds
ate it up. 6 Some of it fell on rocky
ground, and when the plants sprouted,
they dried up because the soil had no
moisture. 7 Some of the seed fell among
thorn bushes, which grew up with the
plants and choked them. 8 And some
seeds fell in good soil; the plants grew
and bore grain, one hundred grains
each."

And Jesus concluded, "Listen, then, if
you have ears!"

The Purpose of the Parables

(Matthew 13.10-17; Mark 4.10-12)

9 His disciples asked Jesus what this
parable meant, 10 and he answered, "The
knowledge of the secrets of the Kingdom
of God has been given to you, but to the
rest it comes by means of parables, so
that they may look but not see, and listen but not understand.

Jesus Explains the Parable of the Sower

(Matthew 13.18-23; Mark 4.13-20)

11 "This is what the parable means: the
seed is the word of God. 12 The seeds that
fell along the path stand for those who
hear; but the Devil comes and takes the
message away from their hearts in order
to keep them from believing and being
saved. 13 The seeds that fell on rocky
ground stand for those who hear the
message and receive it gladly. But it
does not sink deep into them; they believe only for a while but when the time
of testing comes, they fall away. 14 The
seeds that fell among thorn bushes stand
for those who hear; but the worries and
riches and pleasures of this life crowd in
and choke them, and their fruit never
ripens. 15 The seeds that fell in good soil
stand for those who hear the message
and retain it in a good and obedient
heart, and they persist until they bear
fruit.

A Lamp under a Bowl

(Mark 4.21-25)

16 "No one lights a lamp and covers it
with a bowl or puts it under a bed. Instead, it is put on the lampstand, so
that people will see the light as they
come in.

17 "Whatever is hidden away will be
brought out into the open, and whatever
is covered up will be found and brought
to light.

18 "Be careful, then, how you listen; because those who have something will be
given more, but whoever has nothing
will have taken away from them even
the little they think they have."

Jesus' Mother and Brothers

(Matthew 12.46-50; Mark 3.31-35)

19 Jesus' mother and brothers came to
him, but were unable to join him because of the crowd. 20 Someone said
to Jesus, "Your mother and brothers
are standing outside and want to see
you."

21 Jesus said to them all, "My mother
and brothers are those who hear the
word of God and obey it."

Jesus Calms a Storm

(Matthew 8.23-27; Mark 4.35-41)

22 One day Jesus got into a boat with
his disciples and said to them, "Let us go
across to the other side of the lake." So
they started out. 23 As they were sailing,
Jesus fell asleep. Suddenly a strong
wind blew down on the lake, and the
boat began to fill with water, so that
they were all in great danger. 24 The disciples went to Jesus and woke him up,
saying, "Master, Master! We are about
to die!"

Jesus got up and gave an order to the
wind and to the stormy water; they quieted down, and there was a great calm.
25 Then he said to the disciples, "Where
is your faith?"

But they were amazed and afraid, and
said to one another, "Who is this man?
He gives orders to the winds and waves,
and they obey him!"

Jesus Heals a Man with Demons

(Matthew 8.28-34; Mark 5.1-20)

26 Jesus and his disciples sailed on
over to the territory of Gerasa,[g] which

[g] Gerasa; *some manuscripts have* Gadara *(see Mt 8.28); others have* Gergesa.

is across the lake from Galilee. 27 As
Jesus stepped ashore, he was met by a
man from the town who had demons
in him. For a long time this man had
gone without clothes and would not
stay at home, but spent his time in
the burial caves. 28 When he saw Jesus,
he gave a loud cry, threw himself
down at his feet, and shouted, "Jesus,
Son of the Most High God! What do
you want with me? I beg you, don't
punish me!" 29 He said this because
Jesus had ordered the evil spirit to go
out of him. Many times it had seized
him, and even though he was kept
a prisoner, his hands and feet tied
with chains, he would break the chains
and be driven by the demon out into the
desert.

30 Jesus asked him, "What is your
name?"

"My name is 'Mob,'" he answered—
because many demons had gone into
him. 31 The demons begged Jesus not to
send them into the abyss.[h]

32 There was a large herd of pigs near
by, feeding on a hillside. So the demons
begged Jesus to let them go into the pigs,
and he let them. 33 They went out of the
man and into the pigs. The whole herd
rushed down the side of the cliff into the
lake and was drowned.

34 The men who had been taking care
of the pigs saw what happened, so they
ran off and spread the news in the town
and among the farms. 35 People went
out to see what had happened, and
when they came to Jesus, they found
the man from whom the demons had
gone out sitting at the feet of Jesus,
clothed and in his right mind; and they
were all afraid. 36 Those who had seen it
told the people how the man had been
cured. 37 Then all the people from that
territory asked Jesus to go away, because they were terribly afraid. So
Jesus got into the boat and left. 38 The
man from whom the demons had
gone out begged Jesus, "Let me go with
you."

But Jesus sent him away, saying,
39 "Go back home and tell what God has
done for you."

The man went through the town, telling what Jesus had done for him.

Jairus' Daughter and the Woman Who Touched Jesus' Cloak

(Matthew 9.18-26; Mark 5.21-43)

40 When Jesus returned to the other
side of the lake, the people welcomed
him, because they had all been waiting
for him. 41 Then a man named Jairus arrived; he was an official in the local synagogue. He threw himself down at Jesus'
feet and begged him to go to his home,
42 because his only daughter, who was
twelve years old, was dying.

As Jesus went along, the people were
crowding him from every side. 43 Among
them was a woman who had suffered
from severe bleeding for twelve years;
she had spent all she had on doctors,[i]
but no one had been able to cure her.
44 She came up in the crowd behind
Jesus and touched the edge of his cloak,
and her bleeding stopped at once.
45 Jesus asked, "Who touched me?"

Everyone denied it, and Peter said,
"Master, the people are all around you
and crowding in on you."

46 But Jesus said, "Someone touched
me, for I knew it when power went out of
me." 47 The woman saw that she had
been found out, so she came trembling
and threw herself at Jesus' feet. There in
front of everybody, she told him why she
had touched him and how she had been
healed at once. 48 Jesus said to her, "My
daughter, your faith has made you well.
Go in peace."

49 While Jesus was saying this, a messenger came from the official's house.
"Your daughter has died," he told Jairus;
"don't bother the Teacher any longer."

50 But Jesus heard it and said to Jairus,
"Don't be afraid; only believe, and she
will be well."

51 When he arrived at the house, he
would not let anyone go in with him except Peter, John, and James, and the
child's father and mother. 52 Everyone
there was crying and mourning for the
child. Jesus said, "Don't cry; the child is
not dead—she is only sleeping!"

53 They all made fun of him, because
they knew that she was dead. 54 But
Jesus took her by the hand and called
out, "Get up, child!" 55 Her life returned,
and she got up at once, and Jesus ordered them to give her something to eat.

[h] ABYSS: *It was thought that the demons were to be imprisoned in the depths of the earth until their final punishment.* [i] *Some manuscripts do not have* she had spent all she had on doctors.

56 Her parents were astounded, but Jesus
commanded them not to tell anyone
what had happened.

Jesus Sends Out the Twelve Disciples

(Matthew 10.5-15; Mark 6.7-13)

9 Jesus called the twelve disciples together and gave them power and
authority to drive out all demons and to
cure diseases. 2 Then he sent them out to
preach the Kingdom of God and to heal
the sick, 3 after saying to them, "Take
nothing with you for the trip: no walking stick, no beggar's bag, no food, no
money, not even an extra shirt. 4 Wherever you are welcomed, stay in the same
house until you leave that town; 5 wherever people don't welcome you, leave
that town and shake the dust off your
feet as a warning to them."
6 The disciples left and traveled
through all the villages, preaching the
Good News and healing people everywhere.

Herod's Confusion

(Matthew 14.1-12; Mark 6.14-29)

7 When Herod, the ruler of Galilee,
heard about all the things that were happening, he was very confused, because
some people were saying that John the
Baptist had come back to life. 8 Others
were saying that Elijah had appeared,
and still others that one of the prophets
of long ago had come back to life.
9 Herod said, "I had John's head cut off;
but who is this man I hear these things
about?" And he kept trying to see Jesus.

Jesus Feeds Five Thousand

(Matthew 14.13-21; Mark 6.30-44; John 6.1-14)

10 The apostles came back and told
Jesus everything they had done. He took
them with him, and they went off by
themselves to a town named Bethsaida.
11 When the crowds heard about it, they
followed him. He welcomed them, spoke
to them about the Kingdom of God, and
healed those who needed it.
12 When the sun was beginning to set,
the twelve disciples came to him and
said, "Send the people away so that they
can go to the villages and farms around
here and find food and lodging, because
this is a lonely place."
13 But Jesus said to them, "You yourselves give them something to eat."

They answered, "All we have are five
loaves and two fish. Do you want us to
go and buy food for this whole crowd?"
14 (There were about five thousand men
there.)
Jesus said to his disciples, "Make the
people sit down in groups of about fifty
each."
15 After the disciples had done so,
16 Jesus took the five loaves and two fish,
looked up to heaven, thanked God for
them, broke them, and gave them to the
disciples to distribute to the people.
17 They all ate and had enough, and the
disciples took up twelve baskets of what
was left over.

Peter's Declaration about Jesus

(Matthew 16.13-19; Mark 8.27-29)

18 One day when Jesus was praying
alone, the disciples came to him. "Who
do the crowds say I am?" he asked them.
19 "Some say that you are John the
Baptist," they answered. "Others say
that you are Elijah, while others say that
one of the prophets of long ago has come
back to life."
20 "What about you?" he asked them.
"Who do you say I am?"
Peter answered, "You are God's
Messiah."

Jesus Speaks about His Suffering and Death

(Matthew 16.20-28; Mark 8.30—9.1)

21 Then Jesus gave them strict orders
not to tell this to anyone. 22 He also told
them, "The Son of Man must suffer
much and be rejected by the elders, the
chief priests, and the teachers of the
Law. He will be put to death, but three
days later he will be raised to life."
23 And he said to them all, "If you want
to come with me, you must forget yourself, take up your cross every day, and
follow me. 24 For if you want to save your
own life, you will lose it, but if you lose
your life for my sake, you will save it.
25 Will you gain anything if you win the
whole world but are yourself lost or defeated? Of course not! 26 If you are
ashamed of me and of my teaching, then
the Son of Man will be ashamed of you
when he comes in his glory and in the
glory of the Father and of the holy angels. 27 I assure you that there are some
here who will not die until they have
seen the Kingdom of God."

The Transfiguration

(Matthew 17.1-8; Mark 9.2-8)

28 About a week after he had said these
things, Jesus took Peter, John, and
James with him and went up a hill to
pray. 29 While he was praying, his face
changed its appearance, and his clothes
became dazzling white. 30 Suddenly two
men were there talking with him. They
were Moses and Elijah, 31 who appeared
in heavenly glory and talked with Jesus
about the way in which he would soon
fulfill God's purpose by dying in Jerusalem. 32 Peter and his companions were
sound asleep, but they woke up and saw
Jesus' glory and the two men who were
standing with him. 33 As the men were
leaving Jesus, Peter said to him, "Master, how good it is that we are here! We
will make three tents, one for you, one
for Moses, and one for Elijah." (He did
not really know what he was saying.)
34 While he was still speaking, a cloud
appeared and covered them with its
shadow; and the disciples were afraid as
the cloud came over them. 35 A voice said
from the cloud, "This is my Son, whom I
have chosen — listen to him!"
36 When the voice stopped, there was
Jesus all alone. The disciples kept quiet
about all this and told no one at that time
anything they had seen.

Jesus Heals a Boy with an Evil Spirit

(Matthew 17.14-18; Mark 9.14-27)

37 The next day Jesus and the three
disciples went down from the hill, and a
large crowd met Jesus. 38 A man shouted
from the crowd, "Teacher! I beg you,
look at my son — my only son! 39 A spirit
attacks him with a sudden shout and
throws him into a fit, so that he foams at
the mouth; it keeps on hurting him and
will hardly let him go! 40 I begged your
disciples to drive it out, but they
couldn't."
41 Jesus answered, "How unbelieving
and wrong you people are! How long
must I stay with you? How long do I
have to put up with you?" Then he said
to the man, "Bring your son here."
42 As the boy was coming, the demon
knocked him to the ground and threw
him into a fit. Jesus gave a command to
the evil spirit, healed the boy, and gave
him back to his father. 43 All the people
were amazed at the mighty power
of God.

Jesus Speaks Again about His Death

(Matthew 17.22, 23; Mark 9.30-32)

The people were still marveling at
everything Jesus was doing, when he
said to his disciples, 44 "Don't forget
what I am about to tell you! The Son of
Man is going to be handed over to the
power of human beings." 45 But the disciples did not know what this meant. It
had been hidden from them so that they
could not understand it, and they were
afraid to ask him about the matter.

Who Is the Greatest?

(Matthew 18.1-5; Mark 9.33-37)

46 An argument broke out among the
disciples as to which one of them was
the greatest. 47 Jesus knew what they
were thinking, so he took a child, stood
him by his side, 48 and said to them,
"Whoever welcomes this child in my
name, welcomes me; and whoever welcomes me, also welcomes the one who
sent me. For the one who is least among
you all is the greatest."

Whoever Is Not against You Is for You

(Mark 9.38-40)

49 John spoke up, "Master, we saw a
man driving out demons in your name,
and we told him to stop, because he
doesn't belong to our group."
50 "Do not try to stop him," Jesus said
to him and to the other disciples, "because whoever is not against you is
for you."

A Samaritan Village Refuses to Receive Jesus

51 As the time drew near when Jesus
would be taken up to heaven, he made
up his mind and set out on his way to
Jerusalem. 52 He sent messengers ahead
of him, who went into a village in Samaria to get everything ready for him.
53 But the people there would not receive
him, because it was clear that he was on
his way to Jerusalem. 54 When the disciples James and John saw this, they said,
"Lord, do you want us to call fire down
from heaven to destroy them?"[j]

[j] *Some manuscripts add* as Elijah did.

55 Jesus turned and rebuked them.[k]
56 Then Jesus and his disciples went on
to another village.

The Would-Be Followers of Jesus

(Matthew 8.19-22)

57 As they went on their way, a man
said to Jesus, "I will follow you wherever
you go."
58 Jesus said to him, "Foxes have holes,
and birds have nests, but the Son of Man
has no place to lie down and rest."
59 He said to another man, "Follow me."
But that man said, "Sir, first let me go
back and bury my father."
60 Jesus answered, "Let the dead bury
their own dead. You go and proclaim the
Kingdom of God."
61 Someone else said, "I will follow
you, sir; but first let me go and say good-
bye to my family."
62 Jesus said to him, "Anyone who
starts to plow and then keeps looking
back is of no use for the Kingdom
of God."

Jesus Sends Out the Seventy-Two

10 After this the Lord chose another
seventy-two[l] men and sent
them out two by two, to go ahead of him
to every town and place where he himself was about to go. 2 He said to them,
"There is a large harvest, but few workers to gather it in. Pray to the owner of
the harvest that he will send out workers
to gather in his harvest. 3 Go! I am sending you like lambs among wolves.
4 Don't take a purse or a beggar's bag or
shoes; don't stop to greet anyone on the
road. 5 Whenever you go into a house,
first say, 'Peace be with this house.' 6 If
someone who is peace-loving lives
there, let your greeting of peace remain
on that person; if not, take back your
greeting of peace. 7 Stay in that same
house, eating and drinking whatever
they offer you, for workers should be
given their pay. Don't move around
from one house to another. 8 Whenever
you go into a town and are made welcome, eat what is set before you, 9 heal
the sick in that town, and say to the people there, 'The Kingdom of God has
come near you.' 10 But whenever you go
into a town and are not welcomed, go
out in the streets and say, 11 'Even the
dust from your town that sticks to our
feet we wipe off against you. But remember that the Kingdom of God has come
near you!' 12 I assure you that on the
Judgment Day God will show more
mercy to Sodom than to that town!

The Unbelieving Towns

(Matthew 11.20-24)

13 "How terrible it will be for you, Chorazin! How terrible for you too, Bethsaida! If the miracles which were performed in you had been performed in
Tyre and Sidon, the people there would
have long ago sat down, put on sackcloth, and sprinkled ashes on themselves, to show that they had turned
from their sins! 14 God will show more
mercy on the Judgment Day to Tyre and
Sidon than to you. 15 And as for you, Capernaum! Did you want to lift yourself
up to heaven? You will be thrown down
to hell!"
16 Jesus said to his disciples, "Whoever
listens to you listens to me; whoever rejects you rejects me; and whoever rejects me rejects the one who sent me."

The Return of the Seventy-Two

17 The seventy-two[m] men came back
in great joy. "Lord," they said, "even the
demons obeyed us when we gave them a
command in your name!"
18 Jesus answered them, "I saw Satan
fall like lightning from heaven. 19 Listen!
I have given you authority, so that you
can walk on snakes and scorpions and
overcome all the power of the Enemy,
and nothing will hurt you. 20 But don't be
glad because the evil spirits obey you;
rather be glad because your names are
written in heaven."

Jesus Rejoices

(Matthew 11.25-27; 13.16, 17)

21 At that time Jesus was filled with joy
by the Holy Spirit[n] and said, "Father,
Lord of heaven and earth! I thank you
because you have shown to the un-

[k] *Some manuscripts add* and said, "You don't know what kind of a Spirit you belong to; for the Son of Man did not come to destroy human lives, but to save them."
[l] seventy-two; *some manuscripts have* seventy.
[m] seventy-two; *some manuscripts have* seventy *(see verse 1).*
[n] by the Holy Spirit; *some manuscripts have* by the Spirit; *others have* in his spirit.

learned what you have hidden from the
wise and learned. Yes, Father, this was
how you were pleased to have it happen.
22 “My Father has given me all things.
No one knows who the Son is except the
Father, and no one knows who the
Father is except the Son and those to
whom the Son chooses to reveal him.”
23 Then Jesus turned to the disciples
and said to them privately, “How fortunate you are to see the things you see!
24 I tell you that many prophets and
kings wanted to see what you see, but
they could not, and to hear what you
hear, but they did not.”

The Parable of the Good Samaritan

25 A teacher of the Law came up and
tried to trap Jesus. “Teacher,” he asked,
“what must I do to receive eternal life?”
26 Jesus answered him, “What do the
Scriptures say? How do you interpret
them?”
27 The man answered, “ ‘Love the Lord
your God with all your heart, with all
your soul, with all your strength, and
with all your mind’; and ‘Love your
neighbor as you love yourself.’ ”
28 “You are right,” Jesus replied; “do
this and you will live.”
29 But the teacher of the Law wanted to
justify himself, so he asked Jesus, “Who
is my neighbor?”
30 Jesus answered, “There was once a
man who was going down from Jerusalem to Jericho when robbers attacked
him, stripped him, and beat him up,
leaving him half dead. 31 It so happened
that a priest was going down that road;
but when he saw the man, he walked on
by on the other side. 32 In the same way
a Levite also came there, went over and
looked at the man, and then walked on
by on the other side. 33 But a Samaritan
who was traveling that way came upon
the man, and when he saw him, his heart
was filled with pity. 34 He went over to
him, poured oil and wine on his wounds
and bandaged them; then he put the man
on his own animal and took him to an
inn, where he took care of him. 35 The
next day he took out two silver coins and
gave them to the innkeeper. ‘Take care
of him,’ he told the innkeeper, ‘and when
I come back this way, I will pay you
whatever else you spend on him.’ ”
36 And Jesus concluded, “In your opinion, which one of these three acted like a
neighbor toward the man attacked by
the robbers?”
37 The teacher of the Law answered,
“The one who was kind to him.”
Jesus replied, “You go, then, and do
the same.”

Jesus Visits Martha and Mary

38 As Jesus and his disciples went on
their way, he came to a village where a
woman named Martha welcomed him in
her home. 39 She had a sister named
Mary, who sat down at the feet of the
Lord and listened to his teaching. 40 Martha was upset over all the work she had
to do, so she came and said, “Lord, don't
you care that my sister has left me to do
all the work by myself? Tell her to come
and help me!”
41 The Lord answered her, “Martha,
Martha! You are worried and troubled
over so many things, 42 but just one is
needed. Mary has chosen the right thing,
and it will not be taken away from her.”

Jesus' Teaching on Prayer

(*Matthew 6.9-13; 7.7-11*)

11 One day Jesus was praying in a
certain place. When he had finished, one of his disciples said to him,
“Lord, teach us to pray, just as John
taught his disciples.”
2 Jesus said to them, “When you pray,
say this:

‘Father:
May your holy name be
honored;
may your Kingdom come.
3 Give us day by day the food we
need.[o]
4 Forgive us our sins,
for we forgive everyone who
does us wrong.
And do not bring us to hard
testing.’ ”

5 And Jesus said to his disciples, “Suppose one of you should go to a friend's
house at midnight and say, ‘Friend, let
me borrow three loaves of bread.
6 A friend of mine who is on a trip has
just come to my house, and I don't have
any food for him!’ 7 And suppose your
friend should answer from inside, ‘Don't
bother me! The door is already locked,

[o] the food we need; *or* food for the next day.

and my children and I are in bed. I can't
get up and give you anything.' 8 Well,
what then? I tell you that even if he will
not get up and give you the bread because you are his friend, yet he will get
up and give you everything you need because you are not ashamed to keep on
asking. 9 And so I say to you: Ask, and
you will receive; seek, and you will find;
knock, and the door will be opened to
you. 10 For those who ask will receive,
and those who seek will find, and the
door will be opened to anyone who
knocks. 11 Would any of you who are
fathers give your son a snake when he
asks for fish? 12 Or would you give him a
scorpion when he asks for an egg? 13 As
bad as you are, you know how to give
good things to your children. How much
more, then, will the Father in heaven
give the Holy Spirit to those who
ask him!"

Jesus and Beelzebul

(Matthew 12.22-30; Mark 3.20-27)

14 Jesus was driving out a demon that
could not talk; and when the demon
went out, the man began to talk. The
crowds were amazed, 15 but some of the
people said, "It is Beelzebul, the chief of
the demons, who gives him the power to
drive them out."
16 Others wanted to trap Jesus, so they
asked him to perform a miracle to show
that God approved of him. 17 But Jesus
knew what they were thinking, so he
said to them, "Any country that divides
itself into groups which fight each other
will not last very long; a family divided
against itself falls apart. 18 So if Satan's
kingdom has groups fighting each other,
how can it last? You say that I drive out
demons because Beelzebul gives me the
power to do so. 19 If this is how I drive
them out, how do your followers drive
them out? Your own followers prove
that you are wrong! 20 No, it is rather by
means of God's power that I drive out
demons, and this proves that the Kingdom of God has already come to you.
21 "When a strong man, with all his
weapons ready, guards his own house,
all his belongings are safe. 22 But when a
stronger man attacks him and defeats
him, he carries away all the weapons the
owner was depending on and divides up
what he stole.
23 "Anyone who is not for me is really
against me; anyone who does not help
me gather is really scattering.

The Return of the Evil Spirit

(Matthew 12.43-45)

24 "When an evil spirit goes out of a
person, it travels over dry country looking for a place to rest. If it can't find one,
it says to itself, 'I will go back to my
house.' 25 So it goes back and finds the
house clean and all fixed up. 26 Then it
goes out and brings seven other spirits
even worse than itself, and they come
and live there. So when it is all over, that
person is in worse shape than at the beginning."

True Happiness

27 When Jesus had said this, a woman
spoke up from the crowd and said to
him, "How happy is the woman who
bore you and nursed you!"
28 But Jesus answered, "Rather, how
happy are those who hear the word of
God and obey it!"

The Demand for a Miracle

(Matthew 12.38-42)

29 As the people crowded around
Jesus, he went on to say, "How evil are
the people of this day! They ask for a
miracle, but none will be given them except the miracle of Jonah. 30 In the same
way that the prophet Jonah was a sign
for the people of Nineveh, so the Son of
Man will be a sign for the people of this
day. 31 On the Judgment Day the Queen
of Sheba will stand up and accuse the
people of today, because she traveled all
the way from her country to listen to
King Solomon's wise teaching; and
there is something here, I tell you,
greater than Solomon. 32 On the Judgment Day the people of Nineveh will
stand up and accuse you, because they
turned from their sins when they heard
Jonah preach; and I assure you that
there is something here greater than
Jonah!

The Light of the Body

(Matthew 5.15; 6.22, 23)

33 "No one lights a lamp and then hides
it or puts it under a bowl;[p] instead, it is

[p] *Some manuscripts do not have* or puts it under a bowl.

put on the lampstand, so that people
may see the light as they come in.
34 Your eyes are like a lamp for the body.
When your eyes are sound, your whole
body is full of light; but when your eyes
are no good, your whole body will be in
darkness. 35 Make certain, then, that the
light in you is not darkness. 36 If your
whole body is full of light, with no part
of it in darkness, it will be bright all
over, as when a lamp shines on you with
its brightness."

Jesus Accuses the Pharisees and the Teachers of the Law

(Matthew 23.1-36; Mark 12.38-40)

37 When Jesus finished speaking, a
Pharisee invited him to eat with him; so
he went in and sat down to eat. 38 The
Pharisee was surprised when he noticed
that Jesus had not washed before eating.
39 So the Lord said to him, "Now then,
you Pharisees clean the outside of your
cup and plate, but inside you are full of
violence and evil. 40 Fools! Did not God,
who made the outside, also make the inside? 41 But give what is in your cups and
plates to the poor, and everything will be
ritually clean for you.

42 "How terrible for you Pharisees!
You give to God one tenth of the seasoning herbs, such as mint and rue and all
the other herbs, but you neglect justice
and love for God. These you should
practice, without neglecting the others.
43 "How terrible for you Pharisees!
You love the reserved seats in the synagogues and to be greeted with respect in
the marketplaces. 44 How terrible for
you! You are like unmarked graves
which people walk on without knowing it."

45 One of the teachers of the Law said
to him, "Teacher, when you say this, you
insult us too!"

46 Jesus answered, "How terrible also
for you teachers of the Law! You put
onto people's backs loads which are
hard to carry, but you yourselves will
not stretch out a finger to help them
carry those loads. 47 How terrible for
you! You make fine tombs for the
prophets—the very prophets your ancestors murdered. 48 You yourselves admit, then, that you approve of what your
ancestors did; they murdered the prophets, and you build their tombs. 49 For this
reason the Wisdom of God said, 'I will
send them prophets and messengers;
they will kill some of them and persecute others.' 50 So the people of this time
will be punished for the murder of all the
prophets killed since the creation of the
world, 51 from the murder of Abel to the
murder of Zechariah, who was killed between the altar and the Holy Place. Yes,
I tell you, the people of this time will be
punished for them all!

52 "How terrible for you teachers of the
Law! You have kept the key that opens
the door to the house of knowledge; you
yourselves will not go in, and you stop
those who are trying to go in!"

53 When Jesus left that place, the
teachers of the Law and the Pharisees
began to criticize him bitterly and ask
him questions about many things, 54 trying to lay traps for him and catch him
saying something wrong.

A Warning against Hypocrisy

(Matthew 10.26, 27)

12 As thousands of people crowded
together, so that they were step-
ping on each other, Jesus said first to his
disciples, "Be on guard against the yeast
of the Pharisees—I mean their hypocrisy. 2 Whatever is covered up will be uncovered, and every secret will be made
known. 3 So then, whatever you have
said in the dark will be heard in broad
daylight, and whatever you have whispered in private in a closed room will be
shouted from the housetops.

Whom to Fear

(Matthew 10.28-31)

4 "I tell you, my friends, do not be
afraid of those who kill the body but
cannot afterward do anything worse.
5 I will show you whom to fear: fear God,
who, after killing, has the authority to
throw into hell. Believe me, he is the one
you must fear!

6 "Aren't five sparrows sold for two
pennies? Yet not one sparrow is forgotten by God. 7 Even the hairs of your head
have all been counted. So do not be
afraid; you are worth much more than
many sparrows!

Confessing and Rejecting Christ

(Matthew 10.32, 33; 12.32; 10.19, 20)

8 "I assure you that those who declare
publicly that they belong to me, the Son

of Man will do the same for them before
the angels of God. 9 But those who reject
me publicly, the Son of Man will also
reject them before the angels of God.
10 "Whoever says a word against the
Son of Man can be forgiven; but whoever says evil things against the Holy
Spirit will not be forgiven.
11 "When they bring you to be tried in
the synagogues or before governors or
rulers, do not be worried about how you
will defend yourself or what you will
say. 12 For the Holy Spirit will teach you
at that time what you should say."

The Parable of the Rich Fool

13 A man in the crowd said to Jesus,
"Teacher, tell my brother to divide with
me the property our father left us."
14 Jesus answered him, "Friend, who
gave me the right to judge or to divide
the property between you two?" 15 And
he went on to say to them all, "Watch out
and guard yourselves from every kind of
greed; because your true life is not made
up of the things you own, no matter how
rich you may be."
16 Then Jesus told them this parable:
"There was once a rich man who had
land which bore good crops. 17 He began
to think to himself, 'I don't have a place
to keep all my crops. What can I do?
18 This is what I will do,' he told himself;
'I will tear down my barns and build bigger ones, where I will store the grain and
all my other goods. 19 Then I will say to
myself, Lucky man! You have all the
good things you need for many years.
Take life easy, eat, drink, and enjoy
yourself!' 20 But God said to him, 'You
fool! This very night you will have to
give up your life; then who will get
all these things you have kept for
yourself?' "
21 And Jesus concluded, "This is how it
is with those who pile up riches for
themselves but are not rich in God's
sight."

Trust in God

(Matthew 6.25-34)

22 Then Jesus said to the disciples,
"And so I tell you not to worry about the
food you need to stay alive or about the
clothes you need for your body. 23 Life is
much more important than food, and the
body much more important than clothes.
24 Look at the crows: they don't plant
seeds or gather a harvest; they don't
have storage rooms or barns; God feeds
them! You are worth so much more
than birds! 25 Can any of you live a bit
longer[q] by worrying about it? 26 If you
can't manage even such a small thing,
why worry about the other things?
27 Look how the wild flowers grow: they
don't work or make clothes for themselves. But I tell you that not even King
Solomon with all his wealth had clothes
as beautiful as one of these flowers. 28 It
is God who clothes the wild grass—
grass that is here today and gone tomorrow, burned up in the oven. Won't he be
all the more sure to clothe you? What
little faith you have!
29 "So don't be all upset, always concerned about what you will eat and
drink. 30 (For the pagans of this world
are always concerned about all these
things.) Your Father knows that you
need these things. 31 Instead, be concerned with his Kingdom, and he will
provide you with these things.

Riches in Heaven

(Matthew 6.19-21)

32 "Do not be afraid, little flock, for
your Father is pleased to give you the
Kingdom. 33 Sell all your belongings and
give the money to the poor. Provide for
yourselves purses that don't wear out,
and save your riches in heaven, where
they will never decrease, because no
thief can get to them, and no moth can
destroy them. 34 For your heart will always be where your riches are.

Watchful Servants

35 "Be ready for whatever comes,
dressed for action and with your lamps
lit, 36 like servants who are waiting for
their master to come back from a wedding feast. When he comes and knocks,
they will open the door for him at once.
37 How happy are those servants whose
master finds them awake and ready
when he returns! I tell you, he will take
off his coat, have them sit down, and will
wait on them. 38 How happy they are if
he finds them ready, even if he should
come at midnight or even later! 39 And
you can be sure that if the owner of a

q live a bit longer; *or* grow a bit taller.

house knew the time when the thief
would come, he would not let the thief
break into his house. 40 And you, too,
must be ready, because the Son of Man
will come at an hour when you are not
expecting him."

The Faithful or the Unfaithful Servant

(Matthew 24.45-51)

41 Peter said, "Lord, does this parable
apply to us, or do you mean it for
everyone?"
42 The Lord answered, "Who, then, is
the faithful and wise servant? He is the
one that his master will put in charge, to
run the household and give the other
servants their share of the food at the
proper time. 43 How happy that servant
is if his master finds him doing this
when he comes home! 44 Indeed, I tell
you, the master will put that servant in
charge of all his property. 45 But if that
servant says to himself that his master is
taking a long time to come back and if
he begins to beat the other servants,
both the men and the women, and eats
and drinks and gets drunk, 46 then the
master will come back one day when the
servant does not expect him and at a
time he does not know. The master will
cut him in pieces[r] and make him share
the fate of the disobedient.
47 "The servant who knows what his
master wants him to do, but does not get
himself ready and do it, will be punished
with a heavy whipping. 48 But the servant who does not know what his master
wants, and yet does something for
which he deserves a whipping, will be
punished with a light whipping. Much is
required from the person to whom much
is given; much more is required from the
person to whom much more is given.

Jesus the Cause of Division

(Matthew 10.34-36)

49 "I came to set the earth on fire, and
how I wish it were already kindled! 50 I
have a baptism to receive, and how distressed I am until it is over! 51 Do you
suppose that I came to bring peace to the
world? No, not peace, but division.
52 From now on a family of five will be
divided, three against two and two
against three. 53 Fathers will be against
their sons, and sons against their
fathers; mothers will be against their
daughters, and daughters against their
mothers; mothers-in-law will be against
their daughters-in-law, and daughters-
in-law against their mothers-in-law."

Understanding the Time

(Matthew 16.2, 3)

54 Jesus said also to the people, "When
you see a cloud coming up in the west, at
once you say that it is going to rain—
and it does. 55 And when you feel the
south wind blowing, you say that it is
going to get hot—and it does. 56 Hypocrites! You can look at the earth and the
sky and predict the weather; why, then,
don't you know the meaning of this
present time?

Settle with Your Opponent

(Matthew 5.25, 26)

57 "Why do you not judge for yourselves the right thing to do? 58 If someone brings a lawsuit against you and
takes you to court, do your best to settle
the dispute before you get to court. If
you don't, you will be dragged before the
judge, who will hand you over to the police, and you will be put in jail. 59 There
you will stay, I tell you, until you pay the
last penny of your fine."

Turn from Your Sins or Die

13 At that time some people were
there who told Jesus about the
Galileans whom Pilate had killed while
they were offering sacrifices to God.
2 Jesus answered them, "Because those
Galileans were killed in that way, do you
think it proves that they were worse sinners than all other Galileans? 3 No indeed! And I tell you that if you do not
turn from your sins, you will all die as
they did. 4 What about those eighteen
people in Siloam who were killed when
the tower fell on them? Do you suppose
this proves that they were worse than all
the other people living in Jerusalem?
5 No indeed! And I tell you that if you do
not turn from your sins, you will all die
as they did."

[r] cut him in pieces; *or* throw him out.

The Parable of the Unfruitful Fig Tree

6 Then Jesus told them this parable:
"There was once a man who had a fig
tree growing in his vineyard. He went
looking for figs on it but found none. 7 So
he said to his gardener, 'Look, for three
years I have been coming here looking
for figs on this fig tree, and I haven't
found any. Cut it down! Why should it
go on using up the soil?' 8 But the gardener answered, 'Leave it alone, sir, just
one more year; I will dig around it and
put in some fertilizer. 9 Then if the tree
bears figs next year, so much the better;
if not, then you can have it cut down.' "

Jesus Heals a Crippled Woman on the Sabbath

10 One Sabbath Jesus was teaching in
a synagogue. 11 A woman there had an
evil spirit that had kept her sick for
eighteen years; she was bent over and
could not straighten up at all. 12 When
Jesus saw her, he called out to her,
"Woman, you are free from your sickness!" 13 He placed his hands on her, and
at once she straightened herself up and
praised God.

14 The official of the synagogue was
angry that Jesus had healed on the Sabbath, so he spoke up and said to the people, "There are six days in which we
should work; so come during those days
and be healed, but not on the Sabbath!"

15 The Lord answered him, "You hypocrites! Any one of you would untie your
ox or your donkey from the stall and
take it out to give it water on the Sabbath. 16 Now here is this descendant of
Abraham whom Satan has kept in bonds
for eighteen years; should she not be released on the Sabbath?" 17 His answer
made his enemies ashamed of themselves, while the people rejoiced over all
the wonderful things that he did.

The Parable of the Mustard Seed

(Matthew 13.31, 32; Mark 4.30-32)

18 Jesus asked, "What is the Kingdom
of God like? What shall I compare it
with? 19 It is like this. A man takes a mustard seed and plants it in his field. The
plant grows and becomes a tree, and the
birds make their nests in its branches."

The Parable of the Yeast

(Matthew 13.33)

20 Again Jesus asked, "What shall I
compare the Kingdom of God with? 21 It
is like this. A woman takes some yeast
and mixes it with a bushel of flour until
the whole batch of dough rises."

The Narrow Door

(Matthew 7.13, 14, 21-23)

22 Jesus went through towns and villages, teaching the people and making
his way toward Jerusalem. 23 Someone
asked him, "Sir, will just a few people be
saved?"

Jesus answered them, 24 "Do your best
to go in through the narrow door; because many people will surely try to go
in but will not be able. 25 The master of
the house will get up and close the door;
then when you stand outside and begin
to knock on the door and say, 'Open the
door for us, sir!' he will answer you, 'I
don't know where you come from!'
26 Then you will answer, 'We ate and
drank with you; you taught in our town!'
27 But he will say again, 'I don't know
where you come from. Get away from
me, all you wicked people!' 28 How you
will cry and gnash your teeth when you
see Abraham, Isaac, and Jacob, and all
the prophets in the Kingdom of God,
while you are thrown out! 29 People will
come from the east and the west, from
the north and the south, and sit down at
the feast in the Kingdom of God. 30 Then
those who are now last will be first, and
those who are now first will be last."

Jesus' Love for Jerusalem

(Matthew 23.37-39)

31 At that same time some Pharisees
came to Jesus and said to him, "You
must get out of here and go somewhere
else, because Herod wants to kill you."

32 Jesus answered them, "Go and tell
that fox: 'I am driving out demons and
performing cures today and tomorrow,
and on the third day I shall finish my
work.' 33 Yet I must be on my way today,
tomorrow, and the next day; it is not
right for a prophet to be killed anywhere
except in Jerusalem.

34 "Jerusalem, Jerusalem! You kill the
prophets, you stone the messengers God
has sent you! How many times I wanted
to put my arms around all your people,
just as a hen gathers her chicks under

her wings, but you would not let me!
35 And so your Temple will be abandoned. I assure you that you will not see
me until the time comes when you say,
'God bless him who comes in the name
of the Lord.' "

Jesus Heals a Sick Man

14 One Sabbath Jesus went to eat a
meal at the home of one of the
leading Pharisees; and people were
watching Jesus closely. 2 A man whose
legs and arms were swollen came to
Jesus, 3 and Jesus spoke up and asked
the teachers of the Law and the Pharisees, "Does our Law allow healing on
the Sabbath or not?"
4 But they would not say a thing. Jesus
took the man, healed him, and sent him
away. 5 Then he said to them, "If any one
of you had a child or an ox that happened to fall in a well on a Sabbath,
would you not pull it out at once on the
Sabbath itself?"
6 But they were not able to answer him
about this.

Humility and Hospitality

7 Jesus noticed how some of the guests
were choosing the best places, so he told
this parable to all of them: 8 "When
someone invites you to a wedding feast,
do not sit down in the best place. It could
happen that someone more important
than you has been invited, 9 and your
host, who invited both of you, would
have to come and say to you, 'Let him
have this place.' Then you would be embarrassed and have to sit in the lowest
place. 10 Instead, when you are invited,
go and sit in the lowest place, so that
your host will come to you and say,
'Come on up, my friend, to a better
place.' This will bring you honor in the
presence of all the other guests. 11 For
those who make themselves great will
be humbled, and those who humble
themselves will be made great."
12 Then Jesus said to his host, "When
you give a lunch or a dinner, do not invite your friends or your brothers or
your relatives or your rich neighbors—
for they will invite you back, and in this
way you will be paid for what you did.
13 When you give a feast, invite the poor,
the crippled, the lame, and the blind;
14 and you will be blessed, because they
are not able to pay you back. God will
repay you on the day the good people
rise from death."

The Parable of the Great Feast

(Matthew 22.1-10)

15 When one of the guests sitting at the
table heard this, he said to Jesus, "How
happy are those who will sit down at the
feast in the Kingdom of God!"
16 Jesus said to him, "There was once a
man who was giving a great feast to
which he invited many people. 17 When
it was time for the feast, he sent his servant to tell his guests, 'Come, everything
is ready!' 18 But they all began, one after
another, to make excuses. The first one
told the servant, 'I have bought a field
and must go and look at it; please accept
my apologies.' 19 Another one said, 'I
have bought five pairs of oxen and am
on my way to try them out; please accept
my apologies.' 20 Another one said, 'I
have just gotten married, and for that
reason I cannot come.' 21 The servant
went back and told all this to his master.
The master was furious and said to his
servant, 'Hurry out to the streets and alleys of the town, and bring back the
poor, the crippled, the blind, and the
lame.' 22 Soon the servant said, 'Your order has been carried out, sir, but there is
room for more.' 23 So the master said to
the servant, 'Go out to the country roads
and lanes and make people come in, so
that my house will be full. 24 I tell you all
that none of those who were invited will
taste my dinner!' "

The Cost of Being a Disciple

(Matthew 10.37, 38)

25 Once when large crowds of people
were going along with Jesus, he turned
and said to them, 26 "Those who come to
me cannot be my disciples unless they
love me more than they love father and
mother, wife and children, brothers and
sisters, and themselves as well. 27 Those
who do not carry their own cross and
come after me cannot be my disciples.
28 If one of you is planning to build a
tower, you sit down first and figure out
what it will cost, to see if you have
enough money to finish the job. 29 If you
don't, you will not be able to finish the
tower after laying the foundation; and
all who see what happened will make
fun of you. 30 'You began to build but
can't finish the job!' they will say. 31 If a

king goes out with ten thousand men to
fight another king who comes against
him with twenty thousand men, he will
sit down first and decide if he is strong
enough to face that other king. 32 If he
isn't, he will send messengers to meet
the other king to ask for terms of peace
while he is still a long way off. 33 In the
same way," concluded Jesus, "none of
you can be my disciple unless you give
up everything you have.

Worthless Salt

(Matthew 5.13; Mark 9.50)

34 "Salt is good, but if it loses its saltiness, there is no way to make it salty
again. 35 It is no good for the soil or for
the manure pile; it is thrown away. Listen, then, if you have ears!"

The Lost Sheep

(Matthew 18.12-14)

15 One day when many tax collectors and other outcasts came to
listen to Jesus, 2 the Pharisees and the
teachers of the Law started grumbling,
"This man welcomes outcasts and even
eats with them!" 3 So Jesus told them this
parable:

4 "Suppose one of you has a hundred
sheep and loses one of them—what do
you do? You leave the other ninety-nine
sheep in the pasture and go looking for
the one that got lost until you find it.
5 When you find it, you are so happy that
you put it on your shoulders 6 and carry
it back home. Then you call your friends
and neighbors together and say to them,
'I am so happy I found my lost sheep. Let
us celebrate!' 7 In the same way, I tell
you, there will be more joy in heaven
over one sinner who repents than over
ninety-nine respectable people who do
not need to repent.

The Lost Coin

8 "Or suppose a woman who has ten
silver coins loses one of them—what
does she do? She lights a lamp, sweeps
her house, and looks carefully everywhere until she finds it. 9 When she finds
it, she calls her friends and neighbors
together, and says to them, 'I am so
happy I found the coin I lost. Let us celebrate!' 10 In the same way, I tell you, the
angels of God rejoice over one sinner
who repents."

The Lost Son

11 Jesus went on to say, "There was
once a man who had two sons. 12 The
younger one said to him, 'Father, give
me my share of the property now.' So
the man divided his property between
his two sons. 13 After a few days the
younger son sold his part of the property
and left home with the money. He went
to a country far away, where he wasted
his money in reckless living. 14 He spent
everything he had. Then a severe famine
spread over that country, and he was left
without a thing. 15 So he went to work
for one of the citizens of that country,
who sent him out to his farm to take care
of the pigs. 16 He wished he could fill
himself with the bean pods the pigs ate,
but no one gave him anything to eat.
17 At last he came to his senses and said,
'All my father's hired workers have
more than they can eat, and here I am
about to starve! 18 I will get up and go to
my father and say, "Father, I have
sinned against God and against you.
19 I am no longer fit to be called your
son; treat me as one of your hired workers." ' 20 So he got up and started back to
his father.

"He was still a long way from home
when his father saw him; his heart was
filled with pity, and he ran, threw his
arms around his son, and kissed him.
21 'Father,' the son said, 'I have sinned
against God and against you. I am no
longer fit to be called your son.' 22 But
the father called to his servants. 'Hurry!'
he said. 'Bring the best robe and put it on
him. Put a ring on his finger and shoes
on his feet. 23 Then go and get the prize
calf and kill it, and let us celebrate with
a feast! 24 For this son of mine was dead,
but now he is alive; he was lost, but now
he has been found.' And so the feasting
began.

25 "In the meantime the older son was
out in the field. On his way back, when
he came close to the house, he heard the
music and dancing. 26 So he called one of
the servants and asked him, 'What's going on?' 27 'Your brother has come back
home,' the servant answered, 'and your
father has killed the prize calf, because
he got him back safe and sound.' 28 The
older brother was so angry that he
would not go into the house; so his
father came out and begged him to come

in. 29 But he spoke back to his father,
'Look, all these years I have worked for
you like a slave, and I have never disobeyed your orders. What have you
given me? Not even a goat for me to
have a feast with my friends! 30 But this
son of yours wasted all your property on
prostitutes, and when he comes back
home, you kill the prize calf for him!'
31 'My son,' the father answered, 'you are
always here with me, and everything I
have is yours. 32 But we had to celebrate
and be happy, because your brother was
dead, but now he is alive; he was lost,
but now he has been found.' "

The Shrewd Manager

16 Jesus said to his disciples,
"There was once a rich man who
had a servant who managed his property. The rich man was told that the
manager was wasting his master's
money, 2 so he called him in and said,
'What is this I hear about you? Turn in a
complete account of your handling of
my property, because you cannot be my
manager any longer.' 3 The servant said
to himself, 'My master is going to dismiss me from my job. What shall I do? I
am not strong enough to dig ditches, and
I am ashamed to beg. 4 Now I know what
I will do! Then when my job is gone, I
shall have friends who will welcome me
in their homes.' 5 So he called in all the
people who were in debt to his master.
He asked the first one, 'How much do
you owe my master?' 6 'One hundred
barrels of olive oil,' he answered. 'Here
is your account,' the manager told him;
'sit down and write fifty.' 7 Then he
asked another one, 'And you—how
much do you owe?' 'A thousand bushels
of wheat,' he answered. 'Here is your account,' the manager told him; 'write
eight hundred.' 8 As a result the master
of this dishonest manager praised him
for doing such a shrewd thing; because
the people of this world are much more
shrewd in handling their affairs than the
people who belong to the light."

9 And Jesus went on to say, "And so I
tell you: make friends for yourselves
with worldly wealth, so that when it
gives out, you will be welcomed in the
eternal home. 10 Whoever is faithful in
small matters will be faithful in large
ones; whoever is dishonest in small matters will be dishonest in large ones. 11 If,
then, you have not been faithful in handling worldly wealth, how can you be
trusted with true wealth? 12 And if you
have not been faithful with what belongs
to someone else, who will give you what
belongs to you?

13 "No servant can be the slave of two
masters; such a slave will hate one and
love the other or will be loyal to one and
despise the other. You cannot serve both
God and money."

Some Sayings of Jesus

(Matthew 11.12, 13; 5.31, 32; Mark 10.11, 12)

14 When the Pharisees heard all this,
they made fun of Jesus, because they
loved money. 15 Jesus said to them, "You
are the ones who make yourselves look
right in other people's sight, but God
knows your hearts. For the things that
are considered of great value by people
are worth nothing in God's sight.

16 "The Law of Moses and the writings
of the prophets were in effect up to the
time of John the Baptist; since then the
Good News about the Kingdom of God is
being told, and everyone forces their
way in. 17 But it is easier for heaven and
earth to disappear than for the smallest
detail of the Law to be done away with.

18 "Any man who divorces his wife and
marries another woman commits adultery; and the man who marries a divorced woman commits adultery.

The Rich Man and Lazarus

19 "There was once a rich man who
dressed in the most expensive clothes
and lived in great luxury every day.
20 There was also a poor man named
Lazarus, covered with sores, who used
to be brought to the rich man's door,
21 hoping to eat the bits of food that fell
from the rich man's table. Even the dogs
would come and lick his sores. 22 The
poor man died and was carried by the
angels to sit beside Abraham at the feast
in heaven. The rich man died and was
buried, 23 and in Hades,[s] where he was
in great pain, he looked up and saw
Abraham, far away, with Lazarus at his
side. 24 So he called out, 'Father Abraham! Take pity on me, and send Lazarus
to dip his finger in some water and cool

[s] HADES: *The world of the dead.*

off my tongue, because I am in great
pain in this fire!' 25 But Abraham said,
'Remember, my son, that in your lifetime you were given all the good things,
while Lazarus got all the bad things. But
now he is enjoying himself here, while
you are in pain. 26 Besides all that, there
is a deep pit lying between us, so that
those who want to cross over from here
to you cannot do so, nor can anyone
cross over to us from where you are.'
27 The rich man said, 'Then I beg you,
father Abraham, send Lazarus to my
father's house, 28 where I have five
brothers. Let him go and warn them so
that they, at least, will not come to this
place of pain.' 29 Abraham said, 'Your
brothers have Moses and the prophets to
warn them; your brothers should listen
to what they say.' 30 The rich man answered, 'That is not enough, father
Abraham! But if someone were to rise
from death and go to them, then they
would turn from their sins.' 31 But Abraham said, 'If they will not listen to Moses
and the prophets, they will not be convinced even if someone were to rise
from death.' "

Sin

(Matthew 18.6, 7, 21, 22; Mark 9.42)

17 Jesus said to his disciples,
"Things that make people fall
into sin are bound to happen, but how
terrible for the one who makes them
happen! 2 It would be better for him if a
large millstone were tied around his
neck and he were thrown into the sea
than for him to cause one of these little
ones to sin. 3 So watch what you do!
"If your brother sins, rebuke him, and
if he repents, forgive him. 4 If he sins
against you seven times in one day, and
each time he comes to you saying, 'I repent,' you must forgive him."

Faith

5 The apostles said to the Lord, "Make
our faith greater."
6 The Lord answered, "If you had faith
as big as a mustard seed, you could say
to this mulberry tree, 'Pull yourself up
by the roots and plant yourself in the
sea!' and it would obey you.

A Servant's Duty

7 "Suppose one of you has a servant
who is plowing or looking after the
sheep. When he comes in from the field,
do you tell him to hurry along and eat
his meal? 8 Of course not! Instead, you
say to him, 'Get my supper ready, then
put on your apron and wait on me while
I eat and drink; after that you may have
your meal.' 9 The servant does not deserve thanks for obeying orders, does
he? 10 It is the same with you; when you
have done all you have been told to do,
say, 'We are ordinary servants; we have
only done our duty.' "

Jesus Heals Ten Men

11 As Jesus made his way to Jerusalem, he went along the border between
Samaria and Galilee. 12 He was going
into a village when he was met by ten
men suffering from a dreaded skin disease. They stood at a distance 13 and
shouted, "Jesus! Master! Have pity
on us!"
14 Jesus saw them and said to them,
"Go and let the priests examine you."
On the way they were made clean.[t]
15 When one of them saw that he was
healed, he came back, praising God in a
loud voice. 16 He threw himself to the
ground at Jesus' feet and thanked him.
The man was a Samaritan. 17 Jesus
spoke up, "There were ten who were
healed; where are the other nine? 18 Why
is this foreigner the only one who came
back to give thanks to God?" 19 And
Jesus said to him, "Get up and go; your
faith has made you well."

The Coming of the Kingdom

(Matthew 24.23-28, 37-41)

20 Some Pharisees asked Jesus when
the Kingdom of God would come. His
answer was, "The Kingdom of God does
not come in such a way as to be seen.
21 No one will say, 'Look, here it is!' or,
'There it is!'; because the Kingdom of
God is within you."[u]
22 Then he said to the disciples, "The
time will come when you will wish you
could see one of the days of the Son of
Man, but you will not see it. 23 There will
be those who will say to you, 'Look, over
there!' or, 'Look, over here!' But don't go
out looking for it. 24 As the lightning

[t] MADE CLEAN: *See* 5.12. [u] within you; *or* among you, *or* will suddenly appear among you.

flashes across the sky and lights it up from one side to the other, so will the Son of Man be in his day. 25 But first he must suffer much and be rejected by the people of this day. 26 As it was in the time of Noah so shall it be in the days of the Son of Man. 27 Everybody kept on eating and drinking, and men and women married, up to the very day Noah went into the boat and the flood came and killed them all. 28 It will be as it was in the time of Lot. Everybody kept on eating and drinking, buying and selling, planting and building. 29 On the day Lot left Sodom, fire and sulfur rained down from heaven and killed them all. 30 That is how it will be on the day the Son of Man is revealed.

31 "On that day someone who is on the roof of a house must not go down into the house to get any belongings; in the same way anyone who is out in the field must not go back to the house. 32 Remember Lot's wife! 33 Those who try to save their own life will lose it; those who lose their life will save it. 34 On that night, I tell you, there will be two people sleeping in the same bed: one will be taken away, the other will be left behind. 35 Two women will be grinding meal together: one will be taken away, the other will be left behind."[v]

37 The disciples asked him, "Where, Lord?"

Jesus answered, "Wherever there is a dead body, the vultures will gather."

The Parable of the Widow and the Judge

18 Then Jesus told his disciples a parable to teach them that they should always pray and never become discouraged. 2 "In a certain town there was a judge who neither feared God nor respected people. 3 And there was a widow in that same town who kept coming to him and pleading for her rights, saying, 'Help me against my opponent!' 4 For a long time the judge refused to act, but at last he said to himself, 'Even though I don't fear God or respect people, 5 yet because of all the trouble this widow is giving me, I will see to it that she gets her rights. If I don't, she will keep on coming and finally wear me out!' "

6 And the Lord continued, "Listen to what that corrupt judge said. 7 Now, will God not judge in favor of his own people who cry to him day and night for help? Will he be slow to help them? 8 I tell you, he will judge in their favor and do it quickly. But will the Son of Man find faith on earth when he comes?"

The Parable of the Pharisee and the Tax Collector

9 Jesus also told this parable to people who were sure of their own goodness and despised everybody else. 10 "Once there were two men who went up to the Temple to pray: one was a Pharisee, the other a tax collector. 11 The Pharisee stood apart by himself and prayed,[w] 'I thank you, God, that I am not greedy, dishonest, or an adulterer, like everybody else. I thank you that I am not like that tax collector over there. 12 I fast two days a week, and I give you one tenth of all my income.' 13 But the tax collector stood at a distance and would not even raise his face to heaven, but beat on his breast and said, 'God, have pity on me, a sinner!' 14 I tell you," said Jesus, "the tax collector, and not the Pharisee, was in the right with God when he went home. For those who make themselves great will be humbled, and those who humble themselves will be made great."

Jesus Blesses Little Children

(Matthew 19.13-15; Mark 10.13-16)

15 Some people brought their babies to Jesus for him to place his hands on them. The disciples saw them and scolded them for doing so, 16 but Jesus called the children to him and said, "Let the children come to me and do not stop them, because the Kingdom of God belongs to such as these. 17 Remember this! Whoever does not receive the Kingdom of God like a child will never enter it."

The Rich Man

(Matthew 19.16-30; Mark 10.17-31)

18 A Jewish leader asked Jesus, "Good Teacher, what must I do to receive eternal life?"

19 "Why do you call me good?" Jesus

[v] *Some manuscripts add verse 36:* Two men will be working in a field: one will be taken away, the other will be left behind *(see Mt 24.40).* [w] stood apart by himself and prayed; *some manuscripts have* stood up and prayed to himself.

asked him. "No one is good except God
alone. 20 You know the commandments:
'Do not commit adultery; do not commit
murder; do not steal; do not accuse anyone falsely; respect your father and your
mother.'"

21 The man replied, "Ever since I was
young, I have obeyed all these commandments."

22 When Jesus heard this, he said to
him, "There is still one more thing you
need to do. Sell all you have and give the
money to the poor, and you will have
riches in heaven; then come and follow
me." 23 But when the man heard this, he
became very sad, because he was very
rich.

24 Jesus saw that he was sad and said,
"How hard it is for rich people to enter
the Kingdom of God! 25 It is much harder
for a rich person to enter the Kingdom of
God than for a camel to go through the
eye of a needle."

26 The people who heard him asked,
"Who, then, can be saved?"

27 Jesus answered, "What is humanly
impossible is possible for God."

28 Then Peter said, "Look! We have left
our homes to follow you."

29 "Yes," Jesus said to them, "and I assure you that anyone who leaves home
or wife or brothers or parents or children for the sake of the Kingdom of God
30 will receive much more in this present
age and eternal life in the age to come."

Jesus Speaks a Third Time about His Death

(Matthew 20.17-19; Mark 10.32-34)

31 Jesus took the twelve disciples aside
and said to them, "Listen! We are going
to Jerusalem where everything the
prophets wrote about the Son of Man
will come true. 32 He will be handed over
to the Gentiles, who will make fun of
him, insult him, and spit on him. 33 They
will whip him and kill him, but three
days later he will rise to life."

34 But the disciples did not understand
any of these things; the meaning of the
words was hidden from them, and they
did not know what Jesus was talking
about.

Jesus Heals a Blind Beggar

(Matthew 20.29-34; Mark 10.46-52)

35 As Jesus was coming near Jericho,
there was a blind man sitting by the
road, begging. 36 When he heard the
crowd passing by, he asked, "What is
this?"

37 "Jesus of Nazareth is passing by,"
they told him.

38 He cried out, "Jesus! Son of David!
Have mercy on me!"

39 The people in front scolded him and
told him to be quiet. But he shouted even
more loudly, "Son of David! Have mercy
on me!"

40 So Jesus stopped and ordered the
blind man to be brought to him. When
he came near, Jesus asked him, 41 "What
do you want me to do for you?"

"Sir," he answered, "I want to see
again."

42 Jesus said to him, "Then see! Your
faith has made you well."

43 At once he was able to see, and
he followed Jesus, giving thanks to
God. When the crowd saw it, they all
praised God.

Jesus and Zacchaeus

19 Jesus went on into Jericho and
was passing through. 2 There
was a chief tax collector there named
Zacchaeus, who was rich. 3 He was trying to see who Jesus was, but he was a
little man and could not see Jesus because of the crowd. 4 So he ran ahead of
the crowd and climbed a sycamore tree
to see Jesus, who was going to pass that
way. 5 When Jesus came to that place, he
looked up and said to Zacchaeus, "Hurry
down, Zacchaeus, because I must stay in
your house today."

6 Zacchaeus hurried down and welcomed him with great joy. 7 All the people who saw it started grumbling, "This
man has gone as a guest to the home of
a sinner!"

8 Zacchaeus stood up and said to the
Lord, "Listen, sir! I will give half my
belongings to the poor, and if I have
cheated anyone, I will pay back four
times as much."

9 Jesus said to him, "Salvation has
come to this house today, for this man,
also, is a descendant of Abraham. 10 The
Son of Man came to seek and to save the
lost."

The Parable of the Gold Coins

(Matthew 25.14-30)

11 While the people were listening to
this, Jesus continued and told them a

parable. He was now almost at Jerusalem, and they supposed that the
Kingdom of God was just about to
appear. 12 So he said, "There was once
a man of high rank who was going
to a country far away to be made king,
after which he planned to come back
home. 13 Before he left, he called his
ten servants and gave them each a
gold coin and told them, 'See what
you can earn with this while I am gone.'
14 Now, his own people hated him, and
so they sent messengers after him to
say, 'We don't want this man to be our
king.'

15 "The man was made king and came
back. At once he ordered his servants to
appear before him, in order to find out
how much they had earned. 16 The first
one came and said, 'Sir, I have earned
ten gold coins with the one you gave
me.' 17 'Well done,' he said; 'you are a
good servant! Since you were faithful
in small matters, I will put you in charge
of ten cities.' 18 The second servant
came and said, 'Sir, I have earned five
gold coins with the one you gave me.'
19 To this one he said, 'You will be in
charge of five cities.' 20 Another servant
came and said, 'Sir, here is your gold
coin; I kept it hidden in a handkerchief.
21 I was afraid of you, because you are
a hard man. You take what is not yours
and reap what you did not plant.' 22 He
said to him, 'You bad servant! I will
use your own words to condemn you!
You know that I am a hard man, taking
what is not mine and reaping what
I have not planted. 23 Well, then, why
didn't you put my money in the bank?
Then I would have received it back
with interest when I returned.' 24 Then
he said to those who were standing
there, 'Take the gold coin away from
him and give it to the servant who has
ten coins.' 25 But they said to him, 'Sir, he
already has ten coins!' 26 'I tell you,' he
replied, 'that to those who have something, even more will be given; but those
who have nothing, even the little that
they have will be taken away from them.
27 Now, as for those enemies of mine
who did not want me to be their king,
bring them here and kill them in my
presence!' "

The Triumphant Approach to Jerusalem

(Matthew 21.1-11; Mark 11.1-11; John 12.12-19)

28 After Jesus said this, he went on in
front of them toward Jerusalem. 29 As he
came near Bethphage and Bethany at
the Mount of Olives, he sent two disciples ahead 30 with these instructions:
"Go to the village there ahead of you; as
you go in, you will find a colt tied up that
has never been ridden. Untie it and
bring it here. 31 If someone asks you why
you are untying it, tell him that the Master[x] needs it."

32 They went on their way and found
everything just as Jesus had told them.
33 As they were untying the colt, its owners said to them, "Why are you untying it?"

34 "The Master needs it," they answered, 35 and they took the colt to
Jesus. Then they threw their cloaks over
the animal and helped Jesus get on. 36 As
he rode on, people spread their cloaks
on the road.

37 When he came near Jerusalem, at
the place where the road went down the
Mount of Olives, the large crowd of his
disciples began to thank God and praise
him in loud voices for all the great things
that they had seen: 38 "God bless the king
who comes in the name of the Lord!
Peace in heaven and glory to God!"

39 Then some of the Pharisees in the
crowd spoke to Jesus. "Teacher," they
said, "command your disciples to be
quiet!"

40 Jesus answered, "I tell you that if
they keep quiet, the stones themselves
will start shouting."

Jesus Weeps over Jerusalem

41 He came closer to the city, and when
he saw it, he wept over it, 42 saying, "If
you only knew today what is needed for
peace! But now you cannot see it! 43 The
time will come when your enemies will
surround you with barricades, blockade
you, and close in on you from every side.
44 They will completely destroy you and
the people within your walls; not a single stone will they leave in its place, because you did not recognize the time
when God came to save you!"

[x] the Master; *or* its owner.

Jesus Goes to the Temple

(Matthew 21.12-17; Mark 11.15-19; John 2.13-22)

45 Then Jesus went into the Temple
and began to drive out the merchants,
46 saying to them, "It is written in the
Scriptures that God said, 'My Temple
will be a house of prayer.' But you have
turned it into a hideout for thieves!"
47 Every day Jesus taught in the Temple. The chief priests, the teachers of the
Law, and the leaders of the people
wanted to kill him, 48 but they could not
find a way to do it, because all the people
kept listening to him, not wanting to
miss a single word.

The Question about Jesus' Authority

(Matthew 21.23-27; Mark 11.27-33)

20 One day when Jesus was in the
Temple teaching the people and
preaching the Good News, the chief
priests and the teachers of the Law, together with the elders, came 2 and said to
him, "Tell us, what right do you have to
do these things? Who gave you such
right?"
3 Jesus answered them, "Now let me
ask you a question. Tell me, 4 did John's
right to baptize come from God or from
human beings?"
5 They started to argue among themselves, "What shall we say? If we say,
'From God,' he will say, 'Why, then, did
you not believe John?' 6 But if we say,
'From human beings,' this whole crowd
here will stone us, because they are convinced that John was a prophet." 7 So
they answered, "We don't know where it
came from."
8 And Jesus said to them, "Neither will
I tell you, then, by what right I do these
things."

The Parable of the Tenants in the Vineyard

(Matthew 21.33-46; Mark 12.1-12)

9 Then Jesus told the people this parable: "There was once a man who planted
a vineyard, rented it out to tenants, and
then left home for a long time. 10 When
the time came to gather the grapes, he
sent a slave to the tenants to receive
from them his share of the harvest. But
the tenants beat the slave and sent him
back without a thing. 11 So he sent another slave; but the tenants beat him
also, treated him shamefully, and sent
him back without a thing. 12 Then he sent
a third slave; the tenants wounded him,
too, and threw him out. 13 Then the
owner of the vineyard said, 'What shall
I do? I will send my own dear son; surely
they will respect him!' 14 But when the
tenants saw him, they said to one another, 'This is the owner's son. Let's kill
him, and his property will be ours!' 15 So
they threw him out of the vineyard and
killed him.

"What, then, will the owner of the
vineyard do to the tenants?" Jesus
asked. 16 "He will come and kill those
men, and turn the vineyard over to other
tenants."

When the people heard this, they said,
"Surely not!"
17 Jesus looked at them and asked,
"What, then, does this scripture mean?

'The stone which the builders
rejected as worthless
turned out to be the most
important of all.'

18 Everyone who falls on that stone will
be cut to pieces; and if that stone falls on
someone, that person will be crushed to
dust."

The Question about Paying Taxes

(Matthew 22.15-22; Mark 12.13-17)

19 The teachers of the Law and the
chief priests tried to arrest Jesus on the
spot, because they knew that he had told
this parable against them; but they were
afraid of the people. 20 So they looked for
an opportunity. They bribed some men
to pretend they were sincere, and they
sent them to trap Jesus with questions,
so that they could hand him over to
the authority and power of the Roman
Governor. 21 These spies said to Jesus,
"Teacher, we know that what you say
and teach is right. We know that you
pay no attention to anyone's status, but
teach the truth about God's will for people. 22 Tell us, is it against our Law for us
to pay taxes to the Roman Emperor,
or not?"
23 But Jesus saw through their trick
and said to them, 24 "Show me a silver
coin. Whose face and name are these
on it?"

"The Emperor's," they answered.
25 So Jesus said, "Well, then, pay to the
Emperor what belongs to the Emperor,
and pay to God what belongs to God."
26 There before the people they could

not catch him in a thing, so they kept
quiet, amazed at his answer.

The Question about Rising from Death

(Matthew 22.23-33; Mark 12.18-27)

27 Then some Sadducees, who say that
people will not rise from death, came to
Jesus and said, 28 "Teacher, Moses wrote
this law for us: 'If a man dies and leaves
a wife but no children, that man's
brother must marry the widow so that
they can have children who will be considered the dead man's children.' 29 Once
there were seven brothers; the oldest got
married and died without having children. 30 Then the second one married the
woman, 31 and then the third. The same
thing happened to all seven—they died
without having children. 32 Last of all,
the woman died. 33 Now, on the day
when the dead rise to life, whose wife
will she be? All seven of them had married her."
34 Jesus answered them, "The men and
women of this age marry, 35 but the men
and women who are worthy to rise from
death and live in the age to come will not
then marry. 36 They will be like angels
and cannot die. They are the children of
God, because they have risen from
death. 37 And Moses clearly proves that
the dead are raised to life. In the passage
about the burning bush he speaks of the
Lord as 'the God of Abraham, the God of
Isaac, and the God of Jacob.' 38 He is the
God of the living, not of the dead, for to
him all are alive."
39 Some of the teachers of the Law
spoke up, "A good answer, Teacher!"
40 For they did not dare ask him any
more questions.

The Question about the Messiah

(Matthew 22.41-46; Mark 12.35-37)

41 Jesus asked them, "How can it be
said that the Messiah will be the
descendant of David? 42 For David himself says in the book of Psalms,
'The Lord said to my Lord:
Sit here at my right side
43 until I put your enemies as a
footstool under your feet.'
44 David called him 'Lord'; how, then,
can the Messiah be David's
descendant?"

Jesus Warns against the Teachers of the Law

(Matthew 23.1-36; Mark 12.38-40)

45 As all the people listened to him,
Jesus said to his disciples, 46 "Be on your
guard against the teachers of the Law,
who like to walk around in their long
robes and love to be greeted with respect
in the marketplace; who choose the reserved seats in the synagogues and the
best places at feasts; 47 who take advantage of widows and rob them of their
homes, and then make a show of saying
long prayers! Their punishment will be
all the worse!"

The Widow's Offering

(Mark 12.41-44)

21 Jesus looked around and saw
rich people dropping their gifts
in the Temple treasury, 2 and he also saw
a very poor widow dropping in two little
copper coins. 3 He said, "I tell you that
this poor widow put in more than all the
others. 4 For the others offered their gifts
from what they had to spare of their
riches; but she, poor as she is, gave all
she had to live on."

Jesus Speaks of the Destruction of the Temple

(Matthew 24.1, 2; Mark 13.1, 2)

5 Some of the disciples were talking
about the Temple, how beautiful it
looked with its fine stones and the gifts
offered to God. Jesus said, 6 "All this you
see—the time will come when not a single stone here will be left in its place;
every one will be thrown down."

Troubles and Persecutions

(Matthew 24.3-14; Mark 13.3-13)

7 "Teacher," they asked, "when will
this be? And what will happen in order
to show that the time has come for it to
take place?"
8 Jesus said, "Watch out; don't be
fooled. Many men, claiming to speak for
me, will come and say, 'I am he!' and,
'The time has come!' But don't follow
them. 9 Don't be afraid when you hear of
wars and revolutions; such things must
happen first, but they do not mean that
the end is near."
10 He went on to say, "Countries will
fight each other; kingdoms will attack
one another. 11 There will be terrible

earthquakes, famines, and plagues
everywhere; there will be strange and
terrifying things coming from the sky.
12 Before all these things take place,
however, you will be arrested and persecuted; you will be handed over to be
tried in synagogues and be put in prison;
you will be brought before kings and rulers for my sake. 13 This will be your
chance to tell the Good News. 14 Make up
your minds ahead of time not to worry
about how you will defend yourselves,
15 because I will give you such words and
wisdom that none of your enemies will
be able to refute or contradict what you
say. 16 You will be handed over by your
parents, your brothers, your relatives,
and your friends; and some of you will
be put to death. 17 Everyone will hate you
because of me. 18 But not a single hair
from your heads will be lost. 19 Stand
firm, and you will save yourselves.

Jesus Speaks of the Destruction of Jerusalem

(Matthew 24.15-21; Mark 13.14-19)

20 "When you see Jerusalem surrounded by armies, then you will know
that it will soon be destroyed. 21 Then
those who are in Judea must run away to
the hills; those who are in the city must
leave, and those who are out in the country must not go into the city. 22 For those
will be 'The Days of Punishment,' to
make come true all that the Scriptures
say. 23 How terrible it will be in those
days for women who are pregnant and
for mothers with little babies! Terrible
distress will come upon this land, and
God's punishment will fall on this people. 24 Some will be killed by the sword,
and others will be taken as prisoners to
all countries; and the heathen will trample over Jerusalem until their time is up.

The Coming of the Son of Man

(Matthew 24.29-31; Mark 13.24-27)

25 "There will be strange things happening to the sun, the moon, and the
stars. On earth whole countries will be
in despair, afraid of the roar of the sea
and the raging tides. 26 People will faint
from fear as they wait for what is coming over the whole earth, for the powers
in space will be driven from their
courses. 27 Then the Son of Man will appear, coming in a cloud with great
power and glory. 28 When these things
begin to happen, stand up and raise your
heads, because your salvation is near."

The Lesson of the Fig Tree

(Matthew 24.32-35; Mark 13.28-31)

29 Then Jesus told them this parable:
"Think of the fig tree and all the other
trees. 30 When you see their leaves beginning to appear, you know that summer is near. 31 In the same way, when
you see these things happening, you will
know that the Kingdom of God is about
to come.

32 "Remember that all these things will
take place before the people now living
have all died. 33 Heaven and earth will
pass away, but my words will never pass
away.

The Need to Watch

34 "Be careful not to let yourselves become occupied with too much feasting
and drinking and with the worries of
this life, or that Day may suddenly catch
you 35 like a trap. For it will come upon
all people everywhere on earth. 36 Be on
watch and pray always that you will
have the strength to go safely through
all those things that will happen and to
stand before the Son of Man."

37 Jesus spent those days teaching in
the Temple, and when evening came, he
would go out and spend the night on the
Mount of Olives. 38 Early each morning
all the people went to the Temple to listen to him.

The Plot against Jesus

(Matthew 26.1-5; Mark 14.1, 2; John 11.45-53)

22 The time was near for the Festival of Unleavened Bread, which
is called the Passover. 2 The chief priests
and the teachers of the Law were afraid
of the people, and so they were trying to
find a way of putting Jesus to death
secretly.

Judas Agrees to Betray Jesus

(Matthew 26.14-16; Mark 14.10, 11)

3 Then Satan entered into Judas, called
Iscariot, who was one of the twelve disciples. 4 So Judas went off and spoke
with the chief priests and the officers of
the Temple guard about how he could
betray Jesus to them. 5 They were
pleased and offered to pay him money.
6 Judas agreed to it and started looking
for a good chance to hand Jesus over to

them without the people knowing
about it.

Jesus Prepares to Eat the Passover Meal

(Matthew 26.17-25; Mark 14.12-21; John 13.21-30)

7 The day came during the Festival of
Unleavened Bread when the lambs for
the Passover meal were to be killed.
8 Jesus sent Peter and John with these
instructions: "Go and get the Passover
meal ready for us to eat."
9 "Where do you want us to get it
ready?" they asked him.
10 He answered, "As you go into the
city, a man carrying a jar of water will
meet you. Follow him into the house that
he enters, 11 and say to the owner of the
house: 'The Teacher says to you, Where
is the room where my disciples and I will
eat the Passover meal?' 12 He will show
you a large furnished room upstairs,
where you will get everything ready."
13 They went off and found everything
just as Jesus had told them, and they
prepared the Passover meal.

The Lord's Supper

(Matthew 26.26-30; Mark 14.22-26; 1 Corinthians 11.23-25)

14 When the hour came, Jesus took his
place at the table with the apostles. 15 He
said to them, "I have wanted so much to
eat this Passover meal with you before I
suffer! 16 For I tell you, I will never eat it
until it is given its full meaning in the
Kingdom of God."
17 Then Jesus took a cup, gave thanks
to God, and said, "Take this and share it
among yourselves. 18 I tell you that from
now on I will not drink this wine until
the Kingdom of God comes."
19 Then he took a piece of bread, gave
thanks to God, broke it, and gave it to
them, saying, "This is my body, which is
given for you. Do this in memory of me."
20 In the same way, he gave them the cup
after the supper, saying, "This cup is
God's new covenant sealed with my
blood, which is poured out for you.[y]
21 "But, look! The one who betrays me
is here at the table with me! 22 The Son of
Man will die as God has decided, but
how terrible for that man who betrays him!"
23 Then they began to ask among
themselves which one of them it could
be who was going to do this.

The Argument about Greatness

24 An argument broke out among the
disciples as to which one of them should
be thought of as the greatest. 25 Jesus
said to them, "The kings of the pagans
have power over their people, and the
rulers claim the title 'Friends of the People.' 26 But this is not the way it is with
you; rather, the greatest one among you
must be like the youngest, and the leader
must be like the servant. 27 Who is
greater, the one who sits down to eat or
the one who serves? The one who sits
down, of course. But I am among you as
one who serves.
28 "You have stayed with me all
through my trials; 29 and just as my
Father has given me the right to rule, so
I will give you the same right. 30 You will
eat and drink at my table in my Kingdom, and you will sit on thrones to rule
over the twelve tribes of Israel.

Jesus Predicts Peter's Denial

(Matthew 26.31-35; Mark 14.27-31; John 13.36-38)

31 "Simon, Simon! Listen! Satan has
received permission to test all of you, to
separate the good from the bad, as a
farmer separates the wheat from the
chaff. 32 But I have prayed for you, Simon, that your faith will not fail. And
when you turn back to me, you must
strengthen your brothers."
33 Peter answered, "Lord, I am ready
to go to prison with you and to die
with you!"
34 "I tell you, Peter," Jesus said, "the
rooster will not crow tonight until you
have said three times that you do not
know me."

Purse, Bag, and Sword

35 Then Jesus asked his disciples,
"When I sent you out that time without
purse, bag, or shoes, did you lack
anything?"
"Not a thing," they answered.
36 "But now," Jesus said, "whoever has
a purse or a bag must take it; and whoever does not have a sword must sell his
coat and buy one. 37 For I tell you that the
scripture which says, 'He shared the fate

[y] *Some manuscripts do not have the words of Jesus after* This is my body *in verse 19, and all of verse 20.*

of criminals,' must come true about me,
because what was written about me is
coming true."
38 The disciples said, "Look! Here are
two swords, Lord!"
"That is enough!"[z] he replied.

Jesus Prays on the Mount of Olives

(Matthew 26.36-46; Mark 14.32-42)

39 Jesus left the city and went, as he
usually did, to the Mount of Olives; and
the disciples went with him. 40 When he
arrived at the place, he said to them,
"Pray that you will not fall into temptation."
41 Then he went off from them about
the distance of a stone's throw and knelt
down and prayed. 42 "Father," he said, "if
you will, take this cup of suffering away
from me. Not my will, however, but your
will be done." 43 An angel from heaven
appeared to him and strengthened him.
44 In great anguish he prayed even more
fervently; his sweat was like drops of
blood falling to the ground.[a]
45 Rising from his prayer, he went
back to the disciples and found them
asleep, worn out by their grief. 46 He said
to them, "Why are you sleeping? Get up
and pray that you will not fall into
temptation."

The Arrest of Jesus

(Matthew 26.47-56; Mark 14.43-50; John 18.3-11)

47 Jesus was still speaking when a
crowd arrived, led by Judas, one of the
twelve disciples. He came up to Jesus to
kiss him. 48 But Jesus said, "Judas, is it
with a kiss that you betray the Son
of Man?"
49 When the disciples who were with
Jesus saw what was going to happen,
they asked, "Shall we use our swords,
Lord?" 50 And one of them struck the
High Priest's slave and cut off his
right ear.
51 But Jesus said, "Enough of this!" He
touched the man's ear and healed him.
52 Then Jesus said to the chief priests
and the officers of the Temple guard and
the elders who had come there to get
him, "Did you have to come with swords
and clubs, as though I were an outlaw?
53 I was with you in the Temple every
day, and you did not try to arrest me. But
this is your hour to act, when the power
of darkness rules."

Peter Denies Jesus

(Matthew 26.57, 58, 69-75; Mark 14.53, 54, 66-72; John 18.12-18, 25-27)

54 They arrested Jesus and took him
away into the house of the High Priest;
and Peter followed at a distance. 55 A fire
had been lit in the center of the courtyard, and Peter joined those who were
sitting around it. 56 When one of the
servant women saw him sitting there at
the fire, she looked straight at him and
said, "This man too was with Jesus!"
57 But Peter denied it, "Woman, I don't
even know him!"
58 After a little while a man noticed Peter and said, "You are one of them, too!"
But Peter answered, "Man, I am not!"
59 And about an hour later another
man insisted strongly, "There isn't any
doubt that this man was with Jesus, because he also is a Galilean!"
60 But Peter answered, "Man, I don't
know what you are talking about!"
At once, while he was still speaking, a
rooster crowed. 61 The Lord turned
around and looked straight at Peter, and
Peter remembered that the Lord had
said to him, "Before the rooster crows
tonight, you will say three times that you
do not know me." 62 Peter went out and
wept bitterly.

Jesus Is Mocked and Beaten

(Matthew 26.67, 68; Mark 14.65)

63 The men who were guarding Jesus
made fun of him and beat him. 64 They
blindfolded him and asked him, "Who
hit you? Guess!" 65 And they said many
other insulting things to him.

Jesus before the Council

(Matthew 26.59-66; Mark 14.55-64; John 18.19-24)

66 When day came, the elders, the chief
priests, and the teachers of the Law met
together, and Jesus was brought before
the Council. 67 "Tell us," they said, "are
you the Messiah?"
He answered, "If I tell you, you will not
believe me; 68 and if I ask you a question,
you will not answer. 69 But from now on
the Son of Man will be seated at the right
side of Almighty God."
70 They all said, "Are you, then, the
Son of God?"

[z] That is enough; *or* Enough of this. [a] *Some manuscripts do not have verses 43-44.*

He answered them, "You say that
I am."
71 And they said, "We don't need any
witnesses! We ourselves have heard
what he said!"

Jesus before Pilate

(Matthew 27.1, 2, 11-14; Mark 15.1-5; John 18.28-38)

23 The whole group rose up and
took Jesus before Pilate, 2 where
they began to accuse him: "We caught
this man misleading our people, telling
them not to pay taxes to the Emperor
and claiming that he himself is the
Messiah, a king."
3 Pilate asked him, "Are you the king
of the Jews?"
"So you say," answered Jesus.
4 Then Pilate said to the chief priests
and the crowds, "I find no reason to condemn this man."
5 But they insisted even more strongly,
"With his teaching he is starting a riot
among the people all through Judea. He
began in Galilee and now has come
here."

Jesus before Herod

6 When Pilate heard this, he asked, "Is
this man a Galilean?" 7 When he learned
that Jesus was from the region ruled by
Herod, he sent him to Herod, who was
also in Jerusalem at that time. 8 Herod
was very pleased when he saw Jesus, because he had heard about him and had
been wanting to see him for a long time.
He was hoping to see Jesus perform
some miracle. 9 So Herod asked Jesus
many questions, but Jesus made no answer. 10 The chief priests and the teachers of the Law stepped forward and
made strong accusations against Jesus.
11 Herod and his soldiers made fun of
Jesus and treated him with contempt;
then they put a fine robe on him and sent
him back to Pilate. 12 On that very day
Herod and Pilate became friends; before
this they had been enemies.

Jesus Is Sentenced to Death

(Matthew 27.15-26; Mark 15.6-15; John 18.39—19.16)

13 Pilate called together the chief
priests, the leaders, and the people,
14 and said to them, "You brought this
man to me and said that he was misleading the people. Now, I have examined
him here in your presence, and I have
not found him guilty of any of the crimes
you accuse him of. 15 Nor did Herod find
him guilty, for he sent him back to us.
There is nothing this man has done to
deserve death. 16 So I will have him
whipped and let him go."[b]
18 The whole crowd cried out, "Kill
him! Set Barabbas free for us!" (19 Barabbas had been put in prison for a riot
that had taken place in the city, and for
murder.)
20 Pilate wanted to set Jesus free, so he
appealed to the crowd again. 21 But they
shouted back, "Crucify him! Crucify him!"
22 Pilate said to them the third time,
"But what crime has he committed? I
cannot find anything he has done to deserve death! I will have him whipped
and set him free."
23 But they kept on shouting at the top
of their voices that Jesus should be crucified, and finally their shouting succeeded. 24 So Pilate passed the sentence
on Jesus that they were asking for. 25 He
set free the man they wanted, the one
who had been put in prison for riot and
murder, and he handed Jesus over for
them to do as they wished.

Jesus Is Crucified

(Matthew 27.32-44; Mark 15.21-32; John 19.17-27)

26 The soldiers led Jesus away, and as
they were going, they met a man from
Cyrene named Simon who was coming
into the city from the country. They
seized him, put the cross on him, and
made him carry it behind Jesus.
27 A large crowd of people followed
him; among them were some women
who were weeping and wailing for him.
28 Jesus turned to them and said,
"Women of Jerusalem! Don't cry for me,
but for yourselves and your children.
29 For the days are coming when people
will say, 'How lucky are the women who
never had children, who never bore babies, who never nursed them!' 30 That
will be the time when people will say to
the mountains, 'Fall on us!' and to the
hills, 'Hide us!' 31 For if such things as
these are done when the wood is green,
what will happen when it is dry?"
32 Two other men, both of them crimi-

[b] *Some manuscripts add verse 17:* At every Passover Festival Pilate had to set free one prisoner for them *(see Mk 15.6)*.

nals, were also led out to be put to death
with Jesus. 33 When they came to the
place called "The Skull," they crucified
Jesus there, and the two criminals, one
on his right and the other on his left.
34 Jesus said, "Forgive them, Father!
They don't know what they are doing."[c]
They divided his clothes among themselves by throwing dice. 35 The people
stood there watching while the Jewish
leaders made fun of him: "He saved others; let him save himself if he is the
Messiah whom God has chosen!"
36 The soldiers also made fun of him:
they came up to him and offered him
cheap wine, 37 and said, "Save yourself if
you are the king of the Jews!"
38 Above him were written these
words: "This is the King of the Jews."
39 One of the criminals hanging there
hurled insults at him: "Aren't you the
Messiah? Save yourself and us!"
40 The other one, however, rebuked
him, saying, "Don't you fear God? You
received the same sentence he did.
41 Ours, however, is only right, because
we are getting what we deserve for what
we did; but he has done no wrong."
42 And he said to Jesus, "Remember me,
Jesus, when you come as King!"
43 Jesus said to him, "I promise you
that today you will be in Paradise
with me."

The Death of Jesus

(Matthew 27.45-56; Mark 15.33-41; John 19.28-30)

44-45 It was about twelve o'clock when
the sun stopped shining and darkness
covered the whole country until three
o'clock; and the curtain hanging in the
Temple was torn in two. 46 Jesus cried
out in a loud voice, "Father! In your
hands I place my spirit!" He said this and
died.
47 The army officer saw what had happened, and he praised God, saying, "Certainly he was a good man!"
48 When the people who had gathered
there to watch the spectacle saw what
happened, they all went back home,
beating their breasts in sorrow. 49 All
those who knew Jesus personally, including the women who had followed
him from Galilee, stood at a distance to
watch.

The Burial of Jesus

(Matthew 27.57-61; Mark 15.42-47; John 19.38-42)

50-51 There was a man named Joseph
from Arimathea, a town in Judea. He
was a good and honorable man, who
was waiting for the coming of the Kingdom of God. Although he was a member
of the Council, he had not agreed with
their decision and action. 52 He went into
the presence of Pilate and asked for the
body of Jesus. 53 Then he took the body
down, wrapped it in a linen sheet, and
placed it in a tomb which had been dug
out of solid rock and which had never
been used. 54 It was Friday, and the Sabbath was about to begin.
55 The women who had followed Jesus
from Galilee went with Joseph and saw
the tomb and how Jesus' body was
placed in it. 56 Then they went back
home and prepared the spices and perfumes for the body.
On the Sabbath they rested, as the
Law commanded.

The Resurrection

(Matthew 28.1-10; Mark 16.1-8; John 20.1-10)

24 Very early on Sunday morning
the women went to the tomb,
carrying the spices they had prepared.
2 They found the stone rolled away from
the entrance to the tomb, 3 so they went
in; but they did not find the body of the
Lord Jesus. 4 They stood there puzzled
about this, when suddenly two men in
bright shining clothes stood by them.
5 Full of fear, the women bowed down to
the ground, as the men said to them,
"Why are you looking among the dead
for one who is alive? 6 He is not here; he
has been raised. Remember what he said
to you while he was in Galilee: 7 'The
Son of Man must be handed over to sinners, be crucified, and three days later
rise to life.' "
8 Then the women remembered his
words, 9 returned from the tomb, and
told all these things to the eleven disciples and all the rest. 10 The women were
Mary Magdalene, Joanna, and Mary the
mother of James; they and the other
women with them told these things to
the apostles. 11 But the apostles thought
that what the women said was nonsense,
and they did not believe them. 12 But Pe-

c *Some manuscripts do not have* Jesus said, "Forgive them, Father! They don't know what they are doing."

ter got up and ran to the tomb; he bent
down and saw the grave cloths but nothing else. Then he went back home
amazed at what had happened.[d]

The Walk to Emmaus

(Mark 16.12, 13)

13 On that same day two of Jesus' followers were going to a village named
Emmaus, about seven miles from Jerusalem, 14 and they were talking to each
other about all the things that had happened. 15 As they talked and discussed,
Jesus himself drew near and walked
along with them; 16 they saw him, but
somehow did not recognize him. 17 Jesus
said to them, "What are you talking
about to each other, as you walk along?"
They stood still, with sad faces. 18 One
of them, named Cleopas, asked him,
"Are you the only visitor in Jerusalem
who doesn't know the things that have
been happening there these last few
days?"
19 "What things?" he asked.
"The things that happened to Jesus of
Nazareth," they answered. "This man
was a prophet and was considered by
God and by all the people to be powerful
in everything he said and did. 20 Our
chief priests and rulers handed him over
to be sentenced to death, and he was
crucified. 21 And we had hoped that he
would be the one who was going to set
Israel free! Besides all that, this is now
the third day since it happened. 22 Some
of the women of our group surprised us;
they went at dawn to the tomb, 23 but
could not find his body. They came back
saying they had seen a vision of angels
who told them that he is alive. 24 Some of
our group went to the tomb and found it
exactly as the women had said, but they
did not see him."
25 Then Jesus said to them, "How foolish you are, how slow you are to believe
everything the prophets said! 26 Was it
not necessary for the Messiah to suffer
these things and then to enter his glory?"
27 And Jesus explained to them what was
said about himself in all the Scriptures,
beginning with the books of Moses and
the writings of all the prophets.
28 As they came near the village to
which they were going, Jesus acted as if
he were going farther; 29 but they held
him back, saying, "Stay with us; the day
is almost over and it is getting dark." So
he went in to stay with them. 30 He sat
down to eat with them, took the bread,
and said the blessing; then he broke the
bread and gave it to them. 31 Then their
eyes were opened and they recognized
him, but he disappeared from their sight.
32 They said to each other, "Wasn't it like
a fire burning in us when he talked to us
on the road and explained the Scriptures
to us?"
33 They got up at once and went back
to Jerusalem, where they found the
eleven disciples gathered together with
the others 34 and saying, "The Lord is
risen indeed! He has appeared to
Simon!"
35 The two then explained to them
what had happened on the road, and
how they had recognized the Lord when
he broke the bread.

Jesus Appears to His Disciples

(Matthew 28.16-20; Mark 16.14-18; John 20.19-23; Acts 1.6-8)

36 While the two were telling them this,
suddenly the Lord himself stood among
them and said to them, "Peace be
with you."[e]
37 They were terrified, thinking that
they were seeing a ghost. 38 But he said
to them, "Why are you alarmed? Why
are these doubts coming up in your
minds? 39 Look at my hands and my feet,
and see that it is I myself. Feel me, and
you will know, for a ghost doesn't have
flesh and bones, as you can see I have."
40 He said this and showed them his
hands and his feet.[f] 41 They still could
not believe, they were so full of joy and
wonder; so he asked them, "Do you have
anything here to eat?" 42 They gave him
a piece of cooked fish, 43 which he took
and ate in their presence.
44 Then he said to them, "These are the
very things I told you about while I was
still with you: everything written about
me in the Law of Moses, the writings of
the prophets, and the Psalms had to
come true."
45 Then he opened their minds to
understand the Scriptures, 46 and said to

[d] *Some manuscripts do not have verse 12.* [e] *Some manuscripts do not have* and said to them, "Peace be with you." [f] *Some manuscripts do not have verse 40.*

them, "This is what is written: the
Messiah must suffer and must rise from
death three days later, 47 and in his name
the message about repentance and the
forgiveness of sins must be preached to
all nations, beginning in Jerusalem.
48 You are witnesses of these things.
49 And I myself will send upon you what
my Father has promised. But you must
wait in the city until the power from
above comes down upon you."

Jesus Is Taken Up to Heaven

(Mark 16.19, 20; Acts 1.9-11)

50 Then he led them out of the city as
far as Bethany, where he raised his
hands and blessed them. 51 As he was
blessing them, he departed from them
and was taken up into heaven.[g] 52 They
worshiped him and went back into Jerusalem, filled with great joy, 53 and spent
all their time in the Temple giving
thanks to God.

[g] *Some manuscripts do not have* and was taken up into heaven.

The Gospel according to

JOHN

Introduction

The Gospel according to John *presents Jesus as the eternal Word of God, who "became a human being and lived among us." As the book itself says, this Gospel was written so that its readers might believe that Jesus is the promised Savior, the Son of God, and that through their faith in him they may have life (20.31).*

After an introduction that identifies the eternal Word of God with Jesus, the first part of the Gospel presents various miracles which show that Jesus is the promised Savior, the Son of God. These are followed by discourses that explain what is revealed by the miracles. This part of the book tells how some people believed in Jesus and became his followers, while others opposed him and refused to believe. Chapters 13–17 record at length the close fellowship of Jesus with his disciples on the night of his arrest, and his words of preparation and encouragement to them on the eve of his crucifixion. The closing chapters tell of Jesus' arrest and trial, his crucifixion and resurrection, and his appearances to his disciples after the resurrection.

The story of the woman caught in adultery (8.1-11) is placed in brackets because many manuscripts and early translations omit it, while others include it in other places.

John emphasizes the gift of eternal life through Christ, a gift which begins now and which comes to those who respond to Jesus as the way, the truth, and the life. A striking feature of John is the symbolic use of common things from everyday life to point to spiritual realities, such as water, bread, light, the shepherd and his sheep, and the grapevine and its fruit.

Outline of Contents

The Word of Life

1 In the beginning the Word already
existed; the Word was with God,
and the Word was God. 2 From the very
beginning the Word was with God.
3 Through him God made all things; not
one thing in all creation was made without him. 4 The Word was the source of
life,[a] and this life brought light to people. 5 The light shines in the darkness,
and the darkness has never put it out.
6 God sent his messenger, a man
named John, 7 who came to tell people
about the light, so that all should hear
the message and believe. 8 He himself
was not the light; he came to tell about
the light. 9 This was the real light—the
light that comes into the world and
shines on all people.
10 The Word was in the world, and
though God made the world through
him, yet the world did not recognize
him. 11 He came to his own country, but
his own people did not receive him.
12 Some, however, did receive him and
believed in him; so he gave them the
right to become God's children. 13 They
did not become God's children by natural means, that is, by being born as the
children of a human father; God himself
was their Father.
14 The Word became a human being
and, full of grace and truth, lived among
us. We saw his glory, the glory which he
received as the Father's only Son.
15 John spoke about him. He cried out,
"This is the one I was talking about
when I said, 'He comes after me, but he
is greater than I am, because he existed
before I was born.' "
16 Out of the fullness of his grace he
has blessed us all, giving us one blessing

[a] The Word was the source of life; *or* What was made had life in union with the Word.

after another. 17 God gave the Law
through Moses, but grace and truth
came through Jesus Christ. 18 No one has
ever seen God. The only Son, who is the
same as God and is at the Father's side,
he has made him known.

John the Baptist's Message

(Matthew 3.1-12; Mark 1.1-8; Luke 3.1-18)

19 The Jewish authorities in Jerusalem
sent some priests and Levites to John to
ask him, "Who are you?"

20 John did not refuse to answer, but
spoke out openly and clearly, saying: "I
am not the Messiah."

21 "Who are you, then?" they asked.
"Are you Elijah?"

"No, I am not," John answered.

"Are you the Prophet?"[b] they asked.

"No," he replied.

22 "Then tell us who you are," they
said. "We have to take an answer back
to those who sent us. What do you say
about yourself?"

23 John answered by quoting the
prophet Isaiah:

"I am 'the voice of someone
shouting in the desert:
Make a straight path for the
Lord to travel!' "

24 The messengers, who had been sent
by the Pharisees, 25 then[c] asked John,
"If you are not the Messiah nor Elijah
nor the Prophet, why do you baptize?"

26 John answered, "I baptize with water, but among you stands the one you
do not know. 27 He is coming after me,
but I am not good enough even to untie
his sandals."

28 All this happened in Bethany on the
east side of the Jordan River, where
John was baptizing.

The Lamb of God

29 The next day John saw Jesus coming to him, and said, "There is the Lamb
of God, who takes away the sin of the
world! 30 This is the one I was talking
about when I said, 'A man is coming after me, but he is greater than I am, because he existed before I was born.'
31 I did not know who he would be, but I
came baptizing with water in order to
make him known to the people of
Israel."

32 And John gave this testimony: "I
saw the Spirit come down like a dove
from heaven and stay on him. 33 I still
did not know that he was the one, but
God, who sent me to baptize with water,
had said to me, 'You will see the Spirit
come down and stay on a man; he is the
one who baptizes with the Holy Spirit.'
34 I have seen it," said John, "and I tell
you that he is the Son of God."

The First Disciples of Jesus

35 The next day John was standing
there again with two of his disciples,
36 when he saw Jesus walking by. "There
is the Lamb of God!" he said.

37 The two disciples heard him say this
and went with Jesus. 38 Jesus turned,
saw them following him, and asked,
"What are you looking for?"

They answered, "Where do you live,
Rabbi?" (This word means "Teacher.")

39 "Come and see," he answered. (It
was then about four o'clock in the afternoon.) So they went with him and saw
where he lived, and spent the rest of that
day with him.

40 One of them was Andrew, Simon Peter's brother. 41 At once he found his
brother Simon and told him, "We have
found the Messiah." (This word means
"Christ.") 42 Then he took Simon to
Jesus.

Jesus looked at him and said, "Your
name is Simon son of John, but you will
be called Cephas." (This is the same as
Peter and means "a rock.")

Jesus Calls Philip and Nathanael

43 The next day Jesus decided to go to
Galilee. He found Philip and said to him,
"Come with me!" (44 Philip was from
Bethsaida, the town where Andrew and
Peter lived.) 45 Philip found Nathanael
and told him, "We have found the one
whom Moses wrote about in the book of
the Law and whom the prophets also
wrote about. He is Jesus son of Joseph,
from Nazareth."

46 "Can anything good come from Nazareth?" Nathanael asked.

"Come and see," answered Philip.

---

[b] THE PROPHET: *The one who was expected to appear and announce the coming of the Messiah.*

[c] The messengers, who had been sent by the Pharisees, then; *or* Those who had been sent were Pharisees; they.

47 When Jesus saw Nathanael coming
to him, he said about him, "Here is a real
Israelite; there is nothing false in him!"
48 Nathanael asked him, "How do you
know me?"
Jesus answered, "I saw you when you
were under the fig tree before Philip
called you."
49 "Teacher," answered Nathanael,
"you are the Son of God! You are the
King of Israel!"
50 Jesus said, "Do you believe just because I told you I saw you when you
were under the fig tree? You will see
much greater things than this!" 51 And he
said to them, "I am telling you the truth:
you will see heaven open and God's angels going up and coming down on the
Son of Man."

The Wedding in Cana

2 Two days later there was a wedding
in the town of Cana in Galilee.
Jesus' mother was there, 2 and Jesus and
his disciples had also been invited to the
wedding. 3 When the wine had given out,
Jesus' mother said to him, "They are out
of wine."
4 "You must not tell me what to do,"
Jesus replied. "My time has not yet
come."
5 Jesus' mother then told the servants,
"Do whatever he tells you."
6 The Jews have rules about ritual
washing, and for this purpose six stone
water jars were there, each one large
enough to hold between twenty and
thirty gallons. 7 Jesus said to the servants, "Fill these jars with water." They
filled them to the brim, 8 and then he told
them, "Now draw some water out and
take it to the man in charge of the feast."
They took him the water, 9 which now
had turned into wine, and he tasted it.
He did not know where this wine had
come from (but, of course, the servants
who had drawn out the water knew); so
he called the bridegroom 10 and said to
him, "Everyone else serves the best wine
first, and after the guests have drunk a
lot, he serves the ordinary wine. But you
have kept the best wine until now!"
11 Jesus performed this first miracle in
Cana in Galilee; there he revealed his
glory, and his disciples believed in him.
12 After this, Jesus and his mother,
brothers, and disciples went to Capernaum and stayed there a few days.

Jesus Goes to the Temple

(Matthew 21.12, 13; Mark 11.15-17; Luke 19.45, 46)

13 It was almost time for the Passover
Festival, so Jesus went to Jerusalem.
14 There in the Temple he found people
selling cattle, sheep, and pigeons, and
also the moneychangers sitting at their
tables. 15 So he made a whip from cords
and drove all the animals out of the
Temple, both the sheep and the cattle; he
overturned the tables of the moneychangers and scattered their coins;
16 and he ordered those who sold the pigeons, "Take them out of here! Stop
making my Father's house a marketplace!" 17 His disciples remembered that
the scripture says, "My devotion to your
house, O God, burns in me like a fire."
18 The Jewish authorities came back at
him with a question, "What miracle can
you perform to show us that you have
the right to do this?"
19 Jesus answered, "Tear down this
Temple, and in three days I will build it
again."
20 "Are you going to build it again in
three days?" they asked him. "It has
taken forty-six years to build this
Temple!"
21 But the temple Jesus was speaking
about was his body. 22 So when he was
raised from death, his disciples remembered that he had said this, and they believed the scripture and what Jesus had
said.

Jesus' Knowledge of Human Nature

23 While Jesus was in Jerusalem during the Passover Festival, many believed
in him as they saw the miracles he performed. 24 But Jesus did not trust himself
to them, because he knew them all.
25 There was no need for anyone to tell
him about them, because he himself
knew what was in their hearts.

Jesus and Nicodemus

3 There was a Jewish leader named
Nicodemus, who belonged to the
party of the Pharisees. 2 One night he
went to Jesus and said to him, "Rabbi,
we know that you are a teacher sent by
God. No one could perform the miracles
you are doing unless God were
with him."
3 Jesus answered, "I am telling you the

truth: no one can see the Kingdom of
God without being born again."[d]
4 "How can a grown man be born
again?" Nicodemus asked. "He certainly
cannot enter his mother's womb and be
born a second time!"
5 "I am telling you the truth," replied
Jesus, "that no one can enter the Kingdom of God without being born of water
and the Spirit. 6 A person is born physically of human parents, but is born spiritually of the Spirit. 7 Do not be surprised
because I tell you that you must all be
born again.[d] 8 The wind blows wherever
it wishes; you hear the sound it makes,
but you do not know where it comes
from or where it is going. It is like that
with everyone who is born of the Spirit."
9 "How can this be?" asked Nicodemus.
10 Jesus answered, "You are a great
teacher in Israel, and you don't know
this? 11 I am telling you the truth: we
speak of what we know and report what
we have seen, yet none of you is willing
to accept our message. 12 You do not believe me when I tell you about the things
of this world; how will you ever believe
me, then, when I tell you about the
things of heaven? 13 And no one has ever
gone up to heaven except the Son of
Man, who came down from heaven."[e]
14 As Moses lifted up the bronze snake
on a pole in the desert, in the same way
the Son of Man must be lifted up, 15 so
that everyone who believes in him may
have eternal life. 16 For God loved the
world so much that he gave his only
Son, so that everyone who believes in
him may not die but have eternal life.
17 For God did not send his Son into the
world to be its judge, but to be its savior.
18 Those who believe in the Son are not
judged; but those who do not believe
have already been judged, because they
have not believed in God's only Son.
19 This is how the judgment works: the
light has come into the world, but people
love the darkness rather than the light,
because their deeds are evil. 20 Those
who do evil things hate the light and will
not come to the light, because they do
not want their evil deeds to be shown up.
21 But those who do what is true come to
the light in order that the light may show
that what they did was in obedience
to God.

Jesus and John

22 After this, Jesus and his disciples
went to the province of Judea, where he
spent some time with them and baptized. 23 John also was baptizing in Aenon, not far from Salim, because there
was plenty of water in that place. People
were going to him, and he was baptizing
them. (24 This was before John had been
put in prison.)
25 Some of John's disciples began arguing with a Jew[f] about the matter of
ritual washing. 26 So they went to John
and told him, "Teacher, you remember
the man who was with you on the east
side of the Jordan, the one you spoke
about? Well, he is baptizing now, and
everyone is going to him!"
27 John answered, "No one can have
anything unless God gives it. 28 You
yourselves are my witnesses that I said,
'I am not the Messiah, but I have been
sent ahead of him.' 29 The bridegroom is
the one to whom the bride belongs; but
the bridegroom's friend, who stands by
and listens, is glad when he hears the
bridegroom's voice. This is how my own
happiness is made complete. 30 He must
become more important while I become
less important."

He Who Comes from Heaven

31 He who comes from above is greater
than all. He who is from the earth belongs to the earth and speaks about
earthly matters, but he who comes from
heaven is above all. 32 He tells what he
has seen and heard, yet no one accepts
his message. 33 But whoever accepts his
message confirms by this that God is
truthful. 34 The one whom God has sent
speaks God's words, because God gives
him the fullness of his Spirit. 35 The
Father loves his Son and has put everything in his power. 36 Whoever believes
in the Son has eternal life; whoever disobeys the Son will not have life, but will
remain under God's punishment.

Jesus and the Samaritan Woman

4 The Pharisees heard that Jesus was
winning and baptizing more disciples than John. (2 Actually, Jesus him-

[d] again; *or* from above. [e] *The quotation may continue through verse 21.* [f] a Jew; *some manuscripts have* some Jews.

self did not baptize anyone; only his
disciples did.) 3 So when Jesus heard
what was being said, he left Judea and
went back to Galilee; 4 on his way there
he had to go through Samaria.

5 In Samaria he came to a town named
Sychar, which was not far from the field
that Jacob had given to his son Joseph.
6 Jacob's well was there, and Jesus, tired
out by the trip, sat down by the well. It
was about noon.

7 A Samaritan woman came to draw
some water, and Jesus said to her, "Give
me a drink of water." (8 His disciples had
gone into town to buy food.)

9 The woman answered, "You are a
Jew, and I am a Samaritan — so how can
you ask me for a drink?" (Jews will not
use the same cups and bowls that Samaritans use.)[g]

10 Jesus answered, "If you only knew
what God gives and who it is that is asking you for a drink, you would ask him,
and he would give you life-giving
water."

11 "Sir," the woman said, "you don't
have a bucket, and the well is deep.
Where would you get that life-giving
water? 12 It was our ancestor Jacob who
gave us this well; he and his children
and his flocks all drank from it. You
don't claim to be greater than Jacob,
do you?"

13 Jesus answered, "Those who drink
this water will get thirsty again, 14 but
those who drink the water that I will
give them will never be thirsty again.
The water that I will give them will become in them a spring which will provide them with life-giving water and
give them eternal life."

15 "Sir," the woman said, "give me that
water! Then I will never be thirsty again,
nor will I have to come here to draw
water."

16 "Go and call your husband," Jesus
told her, "and come back."

17 "I don't have a husband," she
answered.

Jesus replied, "You are right when you
say you don't have a husband. 18 You
have been married to five men, and the
man you live with now is not really your
husband. You have told me the truth."

19 "I see you are a prophet, sir," the
woman said. 20 "My Samaritan ancestors
worshiped God on this mountain, but
you Jews say that Jerusalem is the place
where we should worship God."

21 Jesus said to her, "Believe me,
woman, the time will come when people
will not worship the Father either on this
mountain or in Jerusalem. 22 You Samaritans do not really know whom you worship; but we Jews know whom we
worship, because it is from the Jews that
salvation comes. 23 But the time is coming and is already here, when by the
power of God's Spirit people will worship the Father as he really is, offering
him the true worship that he wants.
24 God is Spirit, and only by the power of
his Spirit can people worship him as he
really is."

25 The woman said to him, "I know that
the Messiah will come, and when he
comes, he will tell us everything."

26 Jesus answered, "I am he, I who am
talking with you."

27 At that moment Jesus' disciples returned, and they were greatly surprised
to find him talking with a woman. But
none of them said to her, "What do you
want?" or asked him, "Why are you talking with her?"

28 Then the woman left her water jar,
went back to the town, and said to the
people there, 29 "Come and see the man
who told me everything I have ever
done. Could he be the Messiah?" 30 So
they left the town and went to Jesus.

31 In the meantime the disciples were
begging Jesus, "Teacher, have something to eat!"

32 But he answered, "I have food to eat
that you know nothing about."

33 So the disciples started asking
among themselves, "Could somebody
have brought him food?"

34 "My food," Jesus said to them, "is to
obey the will of the one who sent me and
to finish the work he gave me to do.
35 You have a saying, 'Four more months
and then the harvest.' But I tell you, take
a good look at the fields; the crops are
now ripe and ready to be harvested!
36 The one who reaps the harvest is being
paid and gathers the crops for eternal
life; so the one who plants and the one
who reaps will be glad together. 37 For

[g] Jews will not use the same cups and bowls that Samaritans use; *or* Jews will have nothing to do with Samaritans.

the saying is true, 'Someone plants,
someone else reaps.' 38 I have sent you to
reap a harvest in a field where you did
not work; others worked there, and you
profit from their work."
39 Many of the Samaritans in that town
believed in Jesus because the woman
had said, "He told me everything I have
ever done." 40 So when the Samaritans
came to him, they begged him to stay
with them, and Jesus stayed there two
days.
41 Many more believed because of his
message, 42 and they told the woman,
"We believe now, not because of what
you said, but because we ourselves have
heard him, and we know that he really is
the Savior of the world."

Jesus Heals an Official's Son

43 After spending two days there, Jesus
left and went to Galilee. 44 For he himself
had said, "Prophets are not respected in
their own country." 45 When he arrived
in Galilee, the people there welcomed
him, because they had gone to the Passover Festival in Jerusalem and had seen
everything that he had done during the
festival.
46 Then Jesus went back to Cana in
Galilee, where he had turned the water
into wine. A government official was
there whose son was sick in Capernaum.
47 When he heard that Jesus had come
from Judea to Galilee, he went to him
and asked him to go to Capernaum and
heal his son, who was about to die.
48 Jesus said to him, "None of you will
ever believe unless you see miracles and
wonders."
49 "Sir," replied the official, "come with
me before my child dies."
50 Jesus said to him, "Go; your son will
live!"
The man believed Jesus' words and
went. 51 On his way home his servants
met him with the news, "Your boy is going to live!"
52 He asked them what time it was
when his son got better, and they answered, "It was one o'clock yesterday
afternoon when the fever left him."
53 Then the father remembered that it
was at that very hour when Jesus had
told him, "Your son will live." So he and
all his family believed.
54 This was the second miracle that
Jesus performed after coming from Judea to Galilee.

The Healing at the Pool

5 After this, Jesus went to Jerusalem
for a religious festival. 2 Near the
Sheep Gate in Jerusalem there is a
pool[h] with five porches; in Hebrew it is
called Bethzatha.[i] 3 A large crowd of
sick people were lying on the porches—
the blind, the lame, and the paralyzed.[j]
5 A man was there who had been sick for
thirty-eight years. 6 Jesus saw him lying
there, and he knew that the man had
been sick for such a long time; so he
asked him, "Do you want to get well?"
7 The sick man answered, "Sir, I don't
have anyone here to put me in the pool
when the water is stirred up; while I am
trying to get in, somebody else gets there
first."
8 Jesus said to him, "Get up, pick up
your mat, and walk." 9 Immediately the
man got well; he picked up his mat and
started walking.
The day this happened was a Sabbath,
10 so the Jewish authorities told the man
who had been healed, "This is a Sabbath, and it is against our Law for you to
carry your mat."
11 He answered, "The man who made
me well told me to pick up my mat and
walk."
12 They asked him, "Who is the man
who told you to do this?"
13 But the man who had been healed
did not know who Jesus was, for there
was a crowd in that place, and Jesus had
slipped away.
14 Afterward, Jesus found him in the
Temple and said, "Listen, you are well
now; so stop sinning or something
worse may happen to you."
15 Then the man left and told the Jewish authorities that it was Jesus who had
healed him. 16 So they began to persecute Jesus, because he had done this
healing on a Sabbath. 17 Jesus answered

[h] Near the Sheep Gate . . . a pool; *or* Near the Sheep Pool . . . a place.
[i] Bethzatha; *some manuscripts have* Bethesda. [j] *Some manuscripts add verses 3b-4:* They were waiting for the water to move, 4 because every now and then an angel of the Lord went down into the pool and stirred up the water. The first sick person to go into the pool after the water was stirred up was healed from whatever disease he had.

them, "My Father is always working,
and I too must work."
18This saying made the Jewish authorities all the more determined to kill him;
not only had he broken the Sabbath law,
but he had said that God was his own
Father and in this way had made himself
equal with God.

The Authority of the Son

19So Jesus answered them, "I tell you
the truth: the Son can do nothing on his
own; he does only what he sees his
Father doing. What the Father does, the
Son also does. 20For the Father loves the
Son and shows him all that he himself is
doing. He will show him even greater
things to do than this, and you will all be
amazed. 21Just as the Father raises the
dead and gives them life, in the same
way the Son gives life to those he wants
to. 22Nor does the Father himself judge
anyone. He has given his Son the full
right to judge, 23so that all will honor the
Son in the same way as they honor the
Father. Whoever does not honor the Son
does not honor the Father who sent him.
24"I am telling you the truth: those
who hear my words and believe in him
who sent me have eternal life. They will
not be judged, but have already passed
from death to life. 25I am telling you the
truth: the time is coming—the time has
already come—when the dead will hear
the voice of the Son of God, and those
who hear it will come to life. 26Just as
the Father is himself the source of life, in
the same way he has made his Son to be
the source of life. 27And he has given the
Son the right to judge, because he is the
Son of Man. 28Do not be surprised at
this; the time is coming when all the
dead will hear his voice 29and come out
of their graves: those who have done
good will rise and live, and those who
have done evil will rise and be condemned.

Witnesses to Jesus

30"I can do nothing on my own authority; I judge only as God tells me, so my
judgment is right, because I am not trying to do what I want, but only what he
who sent me wants.
31"If I testify on my own behalf, what
I say is not to be accepted as real proof.
32But there is someone else who testifies
on my behalf, and I know that what he
says about me is true. 33John is the one
to whom you sent your messengers, and
he spoke on behalf of the truth. 34It is
not that I must have a human witness; I
say this only in order that you may be
saved. 35John was like a lamp, burning
and shining, and you were willing for a
while to enjoy his light. 36But I have a
witness on my behalf which is even
greater than the witness that John gave:
what I do, that is, the deeds my Father
gave me to do, these speak on my behalf
and show that the Father has sent me.
37And the Father, who sent me, also testifies on my behalf. You have never
heard his voice or seen his face, 38and
you do not keep his message in your
hearts, for you do not believe in the one
whom he sent. 39You study the Scriptures, because you think that in them
you will find eternal life. And these very
Scriptures speak about me! 40Yet you
are not willing to come to me in order to
have life.
41"I am not looking for human praise.
42But I know what kind of people you
are, and I know that you have no love for
God in your hearts. 43I have come with
my Father's authority, but you have not
received me; when, however, someone
comes with his own authority, you will
receive him. 44You like to receive praise
from one another, but you do not try to
win praise from the one who alone is
God; how, then, can you believe me?
45Do not think, however, that I am the
one who will accuse you to my Father.
Moses, in whom you have put your
hope, is the very one who will accuse
you. 46If you had really believed Moses,
you would have believed me, because he
wrote about me. 47But since you do not
believe what he wrote, how can you believe what I say?"

Jesus Feeds Five Thousand

(Matthew 14.13-21; Mark 6.30-44; Luke 9.10-17)

6 After this, Jesus went across Lake
Galilee (or, Lake Tiberias, as it is
also called). 2A large crowd followed
him, because they had seen his miracles
of healing the sick. 3Jesus went up a hill
and sat down with his disciples. 4The
time for the Passover Festival was near.
5Jesus looked around and saw that a
large crowd was coming to him, so he
asked Philip, "Where can we buy
enough food to feed all these people?"

(6 He said this to test Philip; actually he
already knew what he would do.)
7 Philip answered, "For everyone to
have even a little, it would take more
than two hundred silver coins[k] to buy
enough bread."
8 Another one of his disciples, Andrew,
who was Simon Peter's brother, said,
9 "There is a boy here who has five
loaves of barley bread and two fish. But
they will certainly not be enough for all
these people."
10 "Make the people sit down," Jesus
told them. (There was a lot of grass
there.) So all the people sat down; there
were about five thousand men. 11 Jesus
took the bread, gave thanks to God, and
distributed it to the people who were sitting there. He did the same with the fish,
and they all had as much as they
wanted. 12 When they were all full, he
said to his disciples, "Gather the pieces
left over; let us not waste a bit." 13 So
they gathered them all and filled twelve
baskets with the pieces left over from
the five barley loaves which the people
had eaten.
14 Seeing this miracle that Jesus had
performed, the people there said,
"Surely this is the Prophet[l] who was to
come into the world!" 15 Jesus knew that
they were about to come and seize him
in order to make him king by force; so
he went off again to the hills by himself.

Jesus Walks on the Water

(Matthew 14.22-33; Mark 6.45-52)

16 When evening came, Jesus' disciples went down to the lake, 17 got into a
boat, and went back across the lake toward Capernaum. Night came on, and
Jesus still had not come to them. 18 By
then a strong wind was blowing and stirring up the water. 19 The disciples had
rowed about three or four miles when
they saw Jesus walking on the water,
coming near the boat, and they were terrified. 20 "Don't be afraid," Jesus told
them, "it is I!" 21 Then they willingly took
him into the boat, and immediately the
boat reached land at the place they were
heading for.

The People Seek Jesus

22 Next day the crowd which had
stayed on the other side of the lake realized that there had been only one boat
there. They knew that Jesus had not
gone in it with his disciples, but that they
had left without him. 23 Other boats,
which were from Tiberias, came to shore
near the place where the crowd had
eaten the bread after the Lord had given
thanks. 24 When the crowd saw that
Jesus was not there, nor his disciples,
they got into those boats and went to Capernaum, looking for him.

Jesus the Bread of Life

25 When the people found Jesus on the
other side of the lake, they said to him,
"Teacher, when did you get here?"
26 Jesus answered, "I am telling you
the truth: you are looking for me because you ate the bread and had all you
wanted, not because you understood my
miracles. 27 Do not work for food that
spoils; instead, work for the food that
lasts for eternal life. This is the food
which the Son of Man will give you, because God, the Father, has put his mark
of approval on him."
28 So they asked him, "What can we do
in order to do what God wants us to do?"
29 Jesus answered, "What God wants
you to do is to believe in the one he
sent."
30 They replied, "What miracle will
you perform so that we may see it and
believe you? What will you do? 31 Our
ancestors ate manna in the desert, just
as the scripture says, 'He gave them
bread from heaven to eat.'"
32 "I am telling you the truth," Jesus
said. "What Moses gave you was not[m]
the bread from heaven; it is my Father
who gives you the real bread from
heaven. 33 For the bread that God gives is
he who comes down from heaven and
gives life to the world."
34 "Sir," they asked him, "give us this
bread always."
35 "I am the bread of life," Jesus told
them. "Those who come to me will never
be hungry; those who believe in me will
never be thirsty. 36 Now, I told you that
you have seen me but will not believe.
37 Everyone whom my Father gives me
will come to me. I will never turn away
anyone who comes to me, 38 because I
have come down from heaven to do not

[k] SILVER COINS: *A silver coin was the daily wage of a rural worker (see Mt 20.2).*
[l] THE PROPHET: *See 1.21.* [m] What Moses gave you was not; *or* It was not Moses who gave you.

my own will but the will of him who sent
me. 39 And it is the will of him who sent
me that I should not lose any of all those
he has given me, but that I should raise
them all to life on the last day. 40 For
what my Father wants is that all who see
the Son and believe in him should have
eternal life. And I will raise them to life
on the last day."
41 The people started grumbling about
him, because he said, "I am the bread
that came down from heaven." 42 So they
said, "This man is Jesus son of Joseph,
isn't he? We know his father and
mother. How, then, does he now say he
came down from heaven?"
43 Jesus answered, "Stop grumbling
among yourselves. 44 People cannot
come to me unless the Father who sent
me draws them to me; and I will raise
them to life on the last day. 45 The prophets wrote, 'Everyone will be taught by
God.' Anyone who hears the Father and
learns from him comes to me. 46 This
does not mean that anyone has seen the
Father; he who is from God is the only
one who has seen the Father. 47 I am telling you the truth: he who believes has
eternal life. 48 I am the bread of life.
49 Your ancestors ate manna in the
desert, but they died. 50 But the bread
that comes down from heaven is of such
a kind that whoever eats it will not die.
51 I am the living bread that came down
from heaven. If you eat this bread, you
will live forever. The bread that I will
give you is my flesh, which I give so that
the world may live."
52 This started an angry argument
among them. "How can this man give us
his flesh to eat?" they asked.
53 Jesus said to them, "I am telling you
the truth: if you do not eat the flesh of
the Son of Man and drink his blood, you
will not have life in yourselves. 54 Those
who eat my flesh and drink my blood
have eternal life, and I will raise them to
life on the last day. 55 For my flesh is the
real food; my blood is the real drink.
56 Those who eat my flesh and drink my
blood live in me, and I live in them.
57 The living Father sent me, and because
of him I live also. In the same way whoever eats me will live because of me.
58 This, then, is the bread that came
down from heaven; it is not like the
bread that your ancestors ate, but then
later died. Those who eat this bread will
live forever."
59 Jesus said this as he taught in the
synagogue in Capernaum.

The Words of Eternal Life

60 Many of his followers heard this and
said, "This teaching is too hard. Who
can listen to it?"
61 Without being told, Jesus knew that
they were grumbling about this, so he
said to them, "Does this make you want
to give up? 62 Suppose, then, that you
should see the Son of Man go back up to
the place where he was before? 63 What
gives life is God's Spirit; human power is
of no use at all. The words I have spoken
to you bring God's life-giving Spirit.
64 Yet some of you do not believe." (Jesus
knew from the very beginning who were
the ones that would not believe and
which one would betray him.) 65 And he
added, "This is the very reason I told you
that no people can come to me unless the
Father makes it possible for them to
do so."
66 Because of this, many of Jesus' followers turned back and would not go
with him any more. 67 So he asked the
twelve disciples, "And you—would you
also like to leave?"
68 Simon Peter answered him, "Lord,
to whom would we go? You have the
words that give eternal life. 69 And now
we believe and know that you are the
Holy One who has come from God."
70 Jesus replied, "I chose the twelve of
you, didn't I? Yet one of you is a devil!"
71 He was talking about Judas, the son of
Simon Iscariot. For Judas, even though
he was one of the twelve disciples, was
going to betray him.

Jesus and His Brothers

7 After this, Jesus traveled in Galilee;
he did not want to travel in Judea,
because the Jewish authorities there
were wanting to kill him. 2 The time for
the Festival of Shelters was near, 3 so
Jesus' brothers said to him, "Leave this
place and go to Judea, so that your followers will see the things that you are
doing. 4 People don't hide what they are
doing if they want to be well known.
Since you are doing these things, let the
whole world know about you!" (5 Not
even his brothers believed in him.)
6 Jesus said to them, "The right time

for me has not yet come. Any time is
right for you. 7The world cannot hate
you, but it hates me, because I keep telling it that its ways are bad. 8You go on
to the festival. I am not going[n] to this
festival, because the right time has not
come for me." 9He said this and then
stayed on in Galilee.

Jesus at the Festival of Shelters

10After his brothers had gone to the
festival, Jesus also went; however, he
did not go openly, but secretly. 11The
Jewish authorities were looking for him
at the festival. "Where is he?" they
asked.

12There was much whispering about
him in the crowd. "He is a good man,"
some people said. "No," others said, "he
fools the people." 13But no one talked
about him openly, because they were
afraid of the Jewish authorities.

14The festival was nearly half over
when Jesus went to the Temple and began teaching. 15The Jewish authorities
were greatly surprised and said, "How
does this man know so much when he
has never been to school?"

16Jesus answered, "What I teach is not
my own teaching, but it comes from
God, who sent me. 17Whoever is willing
to do what God wants will know
whether what I teach comes from God or
whether I speak on my own authority.
18Those who speak on their own authority are trying to gain glory for themselves. But he who wants glory for the
one who sent him is honest, and there is
nothing false in him. 19Moses gave you
the Law, didn't he? But not one of you
obeys the Law. Why are you trying to
kill me?"

20"You have a demon in you!" the
crowd answered. "Who is trying to
kill you?"

21Jesus answered, "I performed one
miracle, and you were all surprised.
22Moses ordered you to circumcise your
sons (although it was not Moses but
your ancestors who started it), and so
you circumcise a boy on the Sabbath.
23If a boy is circumcised on the Sabbath
so that Moses' Law is not broken, why
are you angry with me because I made a
man completely well on the Sabbath?
24Stop judging by external standards,
and judge by true standards."

Is He the Messiah?

25Some of the people of Jerusalem
said, "Isn't this the man the authorities
are trying to kill? 26Look! He is talking
in public, and they say nothing against
him! Can it be that they really know
that he is the Messiah? 27But when the
Messiah comes, no one will know where
he is from. And we all know where this
man comes from."

28As Jesus taught in the Temple, he
said in a loud voice, "Do you really know
me and know where I am from? I have
not come on my own authority. He who
sent me, however, is truthful. You do not
know him, 29but I know him, because I
come from him and he sent me."

30Then they tried to seize him, but no
one laid a hand on him, because his hour
had not yet come. 31But many in the
crowd believed in him and said, "When
the Messiah comes, will he perform
more miracles than this man has?"

Guards Are Sent to Arrest Jesus

32The Pharisees heard the crowd
whispering these things about Jesus, so
they and the chief priests sent some
guards to arrest him. 33Jesus said, "I
shall be with you a little while longer,
and then I shall go away to him who sent
me. 34You will look for me, but you will
not find me, because you cannot go
where I will be."

35The Jewish authorities said among
themselves, "Where is he about to go so
that we shall not find him? Will he go to
the Greek cities where our people live,
and teach the Greeks? 36He says that we
will look for him but will not find him,
and that we cannot go where he will be.
What does he mean?"

Streams of Life-Giving Water

37On the last and most important day
of the festival Jesus stood up and said in
a loud voice, "Whoever is thirsty should
come to me, and 38whoever believes in
me should drink. As the scripture says,
'Streams of life-giving water will pour
out from his side.' "[o] 39Jesus said this
about the Spirit, which those who be-

[n] I am not going; *some manuscripts have* I am not yet going. [o] *Jesus' words in verses 37-38 may be translated:* "Whoever is thirsty should come to me and drink. 38As the scripture says, 'Streams of life-giving water will pour out from within anyone who believes in me.' "

lieved in him were going to receive. At
that time the Spirit had not yet been
given, because Jesus had not been
raised to glory.

Division among the People

40 Some of the people in the crowd
heard him say this and said, "This man
is really the Prophet!"[p]
41 Others said, "He is the Messiah!"
But others said, "The Messiah will not
come from Galilee! 42 The scripture says
that the Messiah will be a descendant of
King David and will be born in Bethlehem, the town where David lived." 43 So
there was a division in the crowd because of Jesus. 44 Some wanted to seize
him, but no one laid a hand on him.

The Unbelief of the Jewish Authorities

45 When the guards went back, the
chief priests and Pharisees asked them,
"Why did you not bring him?"
46 The guards answered, "Nobody has
ever talked the way this man does!"
47 "Did he fool you, too?" the Pharisees
asked them. 48 "Have you ever known
one of the authorities or one Pharisee to
believe in him? 49 This crowd does not
know the Law of Moses, so they are under God's curse!"
50 One of the Pharisees there was Nicodemus, the man who had gone to see
Jesus before. He said to the others,
51 "According to our Law we cannot condemn people before hearing them and
finding out what they have done."
52 "Well," they answered, "are you also
from Galilee? Study the Scriptures and
you will learn that no prophet ever
comes[q] from Galilee."

The Woman Caught in Adultery

8 [Then everyone went home, but
Jesus went to the Mount of Olives.
2 Early the next morning he went back to
the Temple. All the people gathered
around him, and he sat down and began
to teach them. 3 The teachers of the Law
and the Pharisees brought in a woman
who had been caught committing adultery, and they made her stand before
them all. 4 "Teacher," they said to Jesus,
"this woman was caught in the very act
of committing adultery. 5 In our Law
Moses commanded that such a woman
must be stoned to death. Now, what do
you say?" 6 They said this to trap Jesus,
so that they could accuse him. But he
bent over and wrote on the ground with
his finger. 7 As they stood there asking
him questions, he straightened up and
said to them, "Whichever one of you has
committed no sin may throw the first
stone at her." 8 Then he bent over again
and wrote on the ground. 9 When they
heard this, they all left, one by one, the
older ones first. Jesus was left alone,
with the woman still standing there.
10 He straightened up and said to her,
"Where are they? Is there no one left to
condemn you?"
11 "No one, sir," she answered.
"Well, then," Jesus said, "I do not condemn you either. Go, but do not sin
again."][r]

Jesus the Light of the World

12 Jesus spoke to the Pharisees again.
"I am the light of the world," he said.
"Whoever follows me will have the light
of life and will never walk in darkness."
13 The Pharisees said to him, "Now you
are testifying on your own behalf; what
you say proves nothing."
14 "No," Jesus answered, "even though
I do testify on my own behalf, what I say
is true, because I know where I came
from and where I am going. You do not
know where I came from or where I am
going. 15 You make judgments in a
purely human way; I pass judgment on
no one. 16 But if I were to do so, my judgment would be true, because I am not
alone in this; the Father who sent me is
with me. 17 It is written in your Law that
when two witnesses agree, what they
say is true. 18 I testify on my own behalf,
and the Father who sent me also testifies
on my behalf."
19 "Where is your father?" they
asked him.
"You know neither me nor my
Father," Jesus answered. "If you knew
me, you would know my Father also."
20 Jesus said all this as he taught in the
Temple, in the room where the offering
boxes were placed. And no one arrested
him, because his hour had not come.

[p] THE PROPHET: *See 1.21.* [q] no prophet ever comes; *one manuscript has* the Prophet will not come. [r] *Many manuscripts and early translations do not have this passage (8.1-11); others have it after Jn 21.24; others have it after Lk 21.38; one manuscript has it after Jn 7.36.*

You Cannot Go Where I Am Going

21 Again Jesus said to them, "I will go
away; you will look for me, but you will
die in your sins. You cannot go where I
am going."
22 So the Jewish authorities said, "He
says that we cannot go where he is going. Does this mean that he will kill
himself?"
23 Jesus answered, "You belong to this
world here below, but I come from
above. You are from this world, but I am
not from this world. 24 That is why I told
you that you will die in your sins. And
you will die in your sins if you do not
believe that 'I Am Who I Am'."
25 "Who are you?" they asked him.

Jesus answered, "What I have told you
from the very beginning.[s] 26 I have
much to say about you, much to condemn you for. The one who sent me,
however, is truthful, and I tell the world
only what I have heard from him."
27 They did not understand that Jesus
was talking to them about the Father.
28 So he said to them, "When you lift up
the Son of Man, you will know that 'I
Am Who I Am'; then you will know that
I do nothing on my own authority, but I
say only what the Father has instructed
me to say. 29 And he who sent me is with
me; he has not left me alone, because I
always do what pleases him."
30 Many who heard Jesus say these
things believed in him.

The Truth Will Set You Free

31 So Jesus said to those who believed
in him, "If you obey my teaching, you
are really my disciples; 32 you will know
the truth, and the truth will set you free."
33 "We are the descendants of Abraham," they answered, "and we have
never been anybody's slaves. What do
you mean, then, by saying, 'You will be
free'?"
34 Jesus said to them, "I am telling you
the truth: everyone who sins is a slave of
sin. 35 A slave does not belong to a family permanently, but a son belongs there
forever. 36 If the Son sets you free, then
you will be really free. 37 I know you are
Abraham's descendants. Yet you are
trying to kill me, because you will not
accept my teaching. 38 I talk about what
my Father has shown me, but you do
what your father has told you."
39 They answered him, "Our father is
Abraham."

"If you really were Abraham's children," Jesus replied, "you would do[t] the
same things that he did. 40 All I have ever
done is to tell you the truth I heard from
God, yet you are trying to kill me. Abraham did nothing like this! 41 You are doing what your father did."

"God himself is the only Father we
have," they answered, "and we are his
true children."
42 Jesus said to them, "If God really
were your Father, you would love me,
because I came from God and now I am
here. I did not come on my own authority, but he sent me. 43 Why do you not
understand what I say? It is because you
cannot bear to listen to my message.
44 You are the children of your father,
the Devil, and you want to follow your
father's desires. From the very beginning he was a murderer and has never
been on the side of truth, because there
is no truth in him. When he tells a lie, he
is only doing what is natural to him, because he is a liar and the father of all
lies. 45 But I tell the truth, and that is why
you do not believe me. 46 Which one of
you can prove that I am guilty of sin? If
I tell the truth, then why do you not believe me? 47 He who comes from God listens to God's words. You, however, are
not from God, and that is why you will
not listen."

Jesus and Abraham

48 They asked Jesus, "Were we not
right in saying that you are a Samaritan
and have a demon in you?"
49 "I have no demon," Jesus answered.
"I honor my Father, but you dishonor
me. 50 I am not seeking honor for myself.
But there is one who is seeking it and
who judges in my favor. 51 I am telling
you the truth: whoever obeys my teaching will never die."
52 They said to him, "Now we know for
sure that you have a demon! Abraham
died, and the prophets died, yet you say
that whoever obeys your teaching will
never die. 53 Our father Abraham died;
you do not claim to be greater than

[s] What I have told you from the very beginning; *or* Why should I speak to you at all?
[t] If you really were . . . you would do; *some manuscripts have* If you are . . . do.

Abraham, do you? And the prophets
also died. Who do you think you are?"
54 Jesus answered, "If I were to honor
myself, that honor would be worth nothing. The one who honors me is my
Father—the very one you say is your
God. 55 You have never known him, but I
know him. If I were to say that I do not
know him, I would be a liar like you. But
I do know him, and I obey his word.
56 Your father Abraham rejoiced that he
was to see the time of my coming; he
saw it and was glad."
57 They said to him, "You are not even
fifty years old—and you have seen
Abraham?"[u]
58 "I am telling you the truth," Jesus
replied. "Before Abraham was born,
'I Am'."
59 Then they picked up stones to throw
at him, but Jesus hid himself and left the
Temple.

Jesus Heals a Man Born Blind

9 As Jesus was walking along, he saw
a man who had been born blind.
2 His disciples asked him, "Teacher,
whose sin caused him to be born blind?
Was it his own or his parents' sin?"
3 Jesus answered, "His blindness has
nothing to do with his sins or his parents' sins. He is blind so that God's
power might be seen at work in him. 4 As
long as it is day, we must do the work of
him who sent me; night is coming when
no one can work. 5 While I am in the
world, I am the light for the world."
6 After he said this, Jesus spat on the
ground and made some mud with the
spittle; he rubbed the mud on the man's
eyes 7 and told him, "Go and wash your
face in the Pool of Siloam." (This name
means "Sent.") So the man went,
washed his face, and came back
seeing.
8 His neighbors, then, and the people
who had seen him begging before this,
asked, "Isn't this the man who used to sit
and beg?"
9 Some said, "He is the one," but others
said, "No he isn't; he just looks like
him."
So the man himself said, "I am
the man."
10 "How is it that you can now see?"
they asked him.
11 He answered, "The man called Jesus
made some mud, rubbed it on my eyes,
and told me to go to Siloam and wash
my face. So I went, and as soon as I
washed, I could see."
12 "Where is he?" they asked.
"I don't know," he answered.

The Pharisees Investigate the Healing

13 Then they took to the Pharisees the
man who had been blind. 14 The day that
Jesus made the mud and cured him of
his blindness was a Sabbath. 15 The
Pharisees, then, asked the man again
how he had received his sight. He told
them, "He put some mud on my eyes; I
washed my face, and now I can see."
16 Some of the Pharisees said, "The
man who did this cannot be from God,
for he does not obey the Sabbath
law."
Others, however, said, "How could a
man who is a sinner perform such miracles as these?" And there was a division
among them.
17 So the Pharisees asked the man
once more, "You say he cured you of
your blindness—well, what do you say
about him?"
"He is a prophet," the man answered.
18 The Jewish authorities, however,
were not willing to believe that he had
been blind and could now see, until they
called his parents 19 and asked them, "Is
this your son? You say that he was born
blind; how is it, then, that he can
now see?"
20 His parents answered, "We know
that he is our son, and we know that he
was born blind. 21 But we do not know
how it is that he is now able to see, nor
do we know who cured him of his blindness. Ask him; he is old enough, and he
can answer for himself!" 22 His parents
said this because they were afraid of the
Jewish authorities, who had already
agreed that anyone who said he believed
that Jesus was the Messiah would be expelled from the synagogue. 23 That is
why his parents said, "He is old enough;
ask him!"
24 A second time they called back the
man who had been born blind, and said
to him, "Promise before God that you

[u] you have seen Abraham?; *some manuscripts have* has Abraham seen you?

will tell the truth! We know that this
man who cured you is a sinner."
25 "I do not know if he is a sinner or
not," the man replied. "One thing I do
know: I was blind, and now I see."
26 "What did he do to you?" they asked.
"How did he cure you of your blindness?"
27 "I have already told you," he answered, "and you would not listen. Why
do you want to hear it again? Maybe
you, too, would like to be his disciples?"
28 They insulted him and said, "You
are that fellow's disciple; but we are
Moses' disciples. 29 We know that God
spoke to Moses; as for that fellow, however, we do not even know where he
comes from!"
30 The man answered, "What a strange
thing that is! You do not know where he
comes from, but he cured me of my
blindness! 31 We know that God does not
listen to sinners; he does listen to people
who respect him and do what he wants
them to do. 32 Since the beginning of the
world nobody has ever heard of anyone
giving sight to a person born blind.
33 Unless this man came from God, he
would not be able to do a thing."
34 They answered, "You were born and
brought up in sin—and you are trying to
teach us?" And they expelled him from
the synagogue.

Spiritual Blindness

35 When Jesus heard what had happened, he found the man and asked him,
"Do you believe in the Son of Man?"
36 The man answered, "Tell me who he
is, sir, so that I can believe in him!"
37 Jesus said to him, "You have already
seen him, and he is the one who is talking with you now."
38 "I believe, Lord!" the man said, and
knelt down before Jesus.
39 Jesus said, "I came to this world to
judge, so that the blind should see and
those who see should become blind."
40 Some Pharisees who were there
with him heard him say this and asked
him, "Surely you don't mean that we are
blind, too?"
41 Jesus answered, "If you were blind,
then you would not be guilty; but since
you claim that you can see, this means
that you are still guilty."

The Parable of the Shepherd

10 Jesus said, "I am telling you the
truth: the man who does not enter the sheep pen by the gate, but climbs
in some other way, is a thief and a robber. 2 The man who goes in through the
gate is the shepherd of the sheep. 3 The
gatekeeper opens the gate for him; the
sheep hear his voice as he calls his own
sheep by name, and he leads them out.
4 When he has brought them out, he goes
ahead of them, and the sheep follow
him, because they know his voice. 5 They
will not follow someone else; instead,
they will run away from such a person,
because they do not know his voice."
6 Jesus told them this parable, but they
did not understand what he meant.

Jesus the Good Shepherd

7 So Jesus said again, "I am telling you
the truth: I am the gate for the sheep.
8 All others who came before me are
thieves and robbers, but the sheep did
not listen to them. 9 I am the gate. Those
who come in by me will be saved; they
will come in and go out and find pasture.
10 The thief comes only in order to steal,
kill, and destroy. I have come in order
that you might have life—life in all its
fullness.
11 "I am the good shepherd, who is
willing to die for the sheep. 12 When the
hired man, who is not a shepherd and
does not own the sheep, sees a wolf coming, he leaves the sheep and runs away;
so the wolf snatches the sheep and scatters them. 13 The hired man runs away
because he is only a hired man and does
not care about the sheep. 14-15 I am the
good shepherd. As the Father knows me
and I know the Father, in the same way
I know my sheep and they know me.
And I am willing to die for them. 16 There
are other sheep which belong to me that
are not in this sheep pen. I must bring
them, too; they will listen to my voice,
and they will become[v] one flock with
one shepherd.
17 "The Father loves me because I am
willing to give up my life, in order that I
may receive it back again. 18 No one
takes my life away from me. I give it up
of my own free will. I have the right to
give it up, and I have the right to take it

[v] they will become; *some manuscripts have* there will be.

back. This is what my Father has commanded me to do."
19 Again there was a division among
the people because of these words.
20 Many of them were saying, "He has a
demon! He is crazy! Why do you listen
to him?"
21 But others were saying, "A man with
a demon could not talk like this! How
could a demon give sight to blind
people?"

Jesus Is Rejected

22 It was winter, and the Festival of the
Dedication of the Temple was being celebrated in Jerusalem. 23 Jesus was walking in Solomon's Porch in the Temple,
24 when the people gathered around him
and asked, "How long are you going to
keep us in suspense? Tell us the plain
truth: are you the Messiah?"
25 Jesus answered, "I have already told
you, but you would not believe me. The
deeds I do by my Father's authority
speak on my behalf; 26 but you will not
believe, for you are not my sheep. 27 My
sheep listen to my voice; I know them,
and they follow me. 28 I give them eternal life, and they shall never die. No one
can snatch them away from me. 29 What
my Father has given me is greater[w] than
everything, and no one can snatch them
away from the Father's care. 30 The
Father and I are one."
31 Then the people again picked up
stones to throw at him. 32 Jesus said to
them, "I have done many good deeds in
your presence which the Father gave me
to do; for which one of these do you
want to stone me?"
33 They answered, "We do not want to
stone you because of any good deeds,
but because of your blasphemy! You are
only a man, but you are trying to make
yourself God!"
34 Jesus answered, "It is written in
your own Law that God said, 'You are
gods.' 35 We know that what the scripture says is true forever; and God called
those people gods, the people to whom
his message was given. 36 As for me, the
Father chose me and sent me into the
world. How, then, can you say that I
blaspheme because I said that I am the
Son of God? 37 Do not believe me, then, if
I am not doing the things my Father
wants me to do. 38 But if I do them, even
though you do not believe me, you
should at least believe my deeds, in order that you may know once and for all
that the Father is in me and that I am in
the Father."
39 Once more they tried to seize Jesus,
but he slipped out of their hands.
40 Jesus then went back again across
the Jordan River to the place where
John had been baptizing, and he stayed
there. 41 Many people came to him.
"John performed no miracles," they
said, "but everything he said about this
man was true." 42 And many people
there believed in him.

The Death of Lazarus

11 A man named Lazarus, who
lived in Bethany, became sick.
Bethany was the town where Mary and
her sister Martha lived. (2 This Mary was
the one who poured the perfume on the
Lord's feet and wiped them with her
hair; it was her brother Lazarus who
was sick.) 3 The sisters sent Jesus a message: "Lord, your dear friend is sick."
4 When Jesus heard it, he said, "The
final result of this sickness will not be
the death of Lazarus; this has happened
in order to bring glory to God, and it will
be the means by which the Son of God
will receive glory."
5 Jesus loved Martha and her sister
and Lazarus. 6 Yet when he received the
news that Lazarus was sick, he stayed
where he was for two more days. 7 Then
he said to the disciples, "Let us go back
to Judea."
8 "Teacher," the disciples answered,
"just a short time ago the people there
wanted to stone you; and are you planning to go back?"
9 Jesus said, "A day has twelve hours,
doesn't it? So those who walk in broad
daylight do not stumble, for they see the
light of this world. 10 But if they walk
during the night they stumble, because
they have no light." 11 Jesus said this and
then added, "Our friend Lazarus has
fallen asleep, but I will go and wake
him up."
12 The disciples answered, "If he is
asleep, Lord, he will get well."

[w] What my Father has given me is greater; *some manuscripts have* My Father, who gave them to me, is greater.

13 Jesus meant that Lazarus had died,
but they thought he meant natural sleep.
14 So Jesus told them plainly, "Lazarus is
dead, 15 but for your sake I am glad that
I was not with him, so that you will believe. Let us go to him."

16 Thomas (called the Twin) said to his
fellow disciples, "Let us all go along with
the Teacher, so that we may die
with him!"

Jesus the Resurrection and the Life

17 When Jesus arrived, he found that
Lazarus had been buried four days before. 18 Bethany was less than two miles
from Jerusalem, 19 and many Judeans
had come to see Martha and Mary to
comfort them about their brother's
death.

20 When Martha heard that Jesus was
coming, she went out to meet him, but
Mary stayed in the house. 21 Martha said
to Jesus, "If you had been here, Lord, my
brother would not have died! 22 But I
know that even now God will give you
whatever you ask him for."

23 "Your brother will rise to life," Jesus
told her.

24 "I know," she replied, "that he will
rise to life on the last day."

25 Jesus said to her, "I am the resurrection and the life. Those who believe in
me will live, even though they die; 26 and
those who live and believe in me will
never die. Do you believe this?"

27 "Yes, Lord!" she answered. "I do believe that you are the Messiah, the Son
of God, who was to come into the
world."

Jesus Weeps

28 After Martha said this, she went
back and called her sister Mary privately. "The Teacher is here," she told
her, "and is asking for you." 29 When
Mary heard this, she got up and hurried
out to meet him. (30 Jesus had not yet arrived in the village, but was still in the
place where Martha had met him.) 31 The
people who were in the house with Mary
comforting her followed her when they
saw her get up and hurry out. They
thought that she was going to the grave
to weep there.

32 Mary arrived where Jesus was, and
as soon as she saw him, she fell at his
feet. "Lord," she said, "if you had been
here, my brother would not have died!"

33 Jesus saw her weeping, and he saw
how the people with her were weeping
also; his heart was touched, and he was
deeply moved. 34 "Where have you buried him?" he asked them.

"Come and see, Lord," they answered.

35 Jesus wept. 36 "See how much he
loved him!" the people said.

37 But some of them said, "He gave
sight to the blind man, didn't he? Could
he not have kept Lazarus from dying?"

Lazarus Is Brought to Life

38 Deeply moved once more, Jesus
went to the tomb, which was a cave with
a stone placed at the entrance. 39 "Take
the stone away!" Jesus ordered.

Martha, the dead man's sister, answered, "There will be a bad smell, Lord.
He has been buried four days!"

40 Jesus said to her, "Didn't I tell you
that you would see God's glory if you
believed?" 41 They took the stone away.
Jesus looked up and said, "I thank you,
Father, that you listen to me. 42 I know
that you always listen to me, but I say
this for the sake of the people here, so
that they will believe that you sent me."
43 After he had said this, he called out in
a loud voice, "Lazarus, come out!" 44 He
came out, his hands and feet wrapped in
grave cloths, and with a cloth around his
face. "Untie him," Jesus told them, "and
let him go."

The Plot against Jesus

(Matthew 26.1-5; Mark 14.1, 2; Luke 22.1, 2)

45 Many of the people who had come to
visit Mary saw what Jesus did, and they
believed in him. 46 But some of them returned to the Pharisees and told them
what Jesus had done. 47 So the Pharisees
and the chief priests met with the Council and said, "What shall we do? Look at
all the miracles this man is performing!
48 If we let him go on in this way, everyone will believe in him, and the Roman
authorities will take action and destroy
our Temple and our nation!"

49 One of them, named Caiaphas, who
was High Priest that year, said, "What
fools you are! 50 Don't you realize that it
is better for you to have one man die for
the people, instead of having the whole
nation destroyed?" 51 Actually, he did
not say this of his own accord; rather, as
he was High Priest that year, he was
prophesying that Jesus was going to die

for the Jewish people, 52 and not only for
them, but also to bring together into one
body all the scattered people of God.
53 From that day on the Jewish authorities made plans to kill Jesus. 54 So Jesus
did not travel openly in Judea, but left
and went to a place near the desert, to a
town named Ephraim, where he stayed
with the disciples.
55 The time for the Passover Festival
was near, and many people went up
from the country to Jerusalem to perform the ritual of purification before the
festival. 56 They were looking for Jesus,
and as they gathered in the Temple, they
asked one another, "What do you think?
Surely he will not come to the festival,
will he?" 57 The chief priests and the
Pharisees had given orders that if anyone knew where Jesus was, he must report it, so that they could arrest him.

Jesus Is Anointed at Bethany

(Matthew 26.6-13; Mark 14.3-9)

12 Six days before the Passover,
Jesus went to Bethany, the home
of Lazarus, the man he had raised from
death. 2 They prepared a dinner for him
there, which Martha helped serve; Lazarus was one of those who were sitting at
the table with Jesus. 3 Then Mary took a
whole pint of a very expensive perfume
made of pure nard, poured it on Jesus'
feet, and wiped them with her hair. The
sweet smell of the perfume filled the
whole house. 4 One of Jesus' disciples,
Judas Iscariot—the one who was going
to betray him—said, 5 "Why wasn't this
perfume sold for three hundred silver
coins[x] and the money given to the
poor?" 6 He said this, not because he
cared about the poor, but because he
was a thief. He carried the money bag
and would help himself from it.
7 But Jesus said, "Leave her alone! Let
her keep what she has for the day of my
burial. 8 You will always have poor people with you, but you will not always
have me."

The Plot against Lazarus

9 A large number of people heard that
Jesus was in Bethany, so they went
there, not only because of Jesus but also
to see Lazarus, whom Jesus had raised
from death. 10 So the chief priests made
plans to kill Lazarus too, 11 because on
his account many Jews were rejecting
them and believing in Jesus.

The Triumphant Entry into Jerusalem

(Matthew 21.1-11; Mark 11.1-11; Luke 19.28-40)

12 The next day the large crowd that
had come to the Passover Festival heard
that Jesus was coming to Jerusalem.
13 So they took branches of palm trees
and went out to meet him, shouting,
"Praise God! God bless him who comes
in the name of the Lord! God bless the
King of Israel!"
14 Jesus found a donkey and rode on it,
just as the scripture says,

15 "Do not be afraid, city of Zion!
Here comes your king,
riding on a young donkey."

16 His disciples did not understand this
at the time; but when Jesus had been
raised to glory, they remembered that
the scripture said this about him and
that they had done this for him.
17 The people who had been with Jesus
when he called Lazarus out of the grave
and raised him from death had reported
what had happened. 18 That was why the
crowd met him—because they heard
that he had performed this miracle.
19 The Pharisees then said to one another, "You see, we are not succeeding
at all! Look, the whole world is following him!"

Some Greeks Seek Jesus

20 Some Greeks were among those
who had gone to Jerusalem to worship
during the festival. 21 They went to Philip
(he was from Bethsaida in Galilee) and
said, "Sir, we want to see Jesus."
22 Philip went and told Andrew, and
the two of them went and told Jesus.
23 Jesus answered them, "The hour has
now come for the Son of Man to receive
great glory. 24 I am telling you the truth:
a grain of wheat remains no more than a
single grain unless it is dropped into the
ground and dies. If it does die, then it
produces many grains. 25 Those who
love their own life will lose it; those who
hate their own life in this world will keep
it for life eternal. 26 Whoever wants to
serve me must follow me, so that my
servant will be with me where I am. And

[x] SILVER COINS: *See* 6.7.

my Father will honor anyone who
serves me.

Jesus Speaks about His Death

27 "Now my heart is troubled—and
what shall I say? Shall I say, 'Father, do
not let this hour come upon me'? But
that is why I came—so that I might go
through this hour of suffering. 28 Father,
bring glory to your name!"

Then a voice spoke from heaven, "I
have brought glory to it, and I will do so
again."

29 The crowd standing there heard the
voice, and some of them said it was
thunder, while others said, "An angel
spoke to him!"

30 But Jesus said to them, "It was not
for my sake that this voice spoke, but for
yours. 31 Now is the time for this world to
be judged; now the ruler of this world
will be overthrown. 32 When I am lifted
up from the earth, I will draw everyone
to me." (33 In saying this he indicated the
kind of death he was going to suffer.)

34 The crowd answered, "Our Law tells
us that the Messiah will live forever.
How, then, can you say that the Son of
Man must be lifted up? Who is this Son
of Man?"

35 Jesus answered, "The light will be
among you a little longer. Continue on
your way while you have the light, so
that the darkness will not come upon
you; for the one who walks in the dark
does not know where he is going. 36 Believe in the light, then, while you have it,
so that you will be the people of the
light."

The Unbelief of the People

After Jesus said this, he went off and
hid himself from them. 37 Even though
he had performed all these miracles in
their presence, they did not believe in
him, 38 so that what the prophet Isaiah
had said might come true:

"Lord, who believed the message
we told?
To whom did the Lord reveal his
power?"

39 And so they were not able to believe,
because Isaiah also said,

40 "God has blinded their eyes
and closed their minds,
so that their eyes would not see,
and their minds would not
understand,
and they would not turn to me,
says God,
for me to heal them."

41 Isaiah said this because he saw
Jesus' glory and spoke about him.

42 Even then, many Jewish authorities
believed in Jesus; but because of the
Pharisees they did not talk about it
openly, so as not to be expelled from the
synagogue. 43 They loved human approval rather than the approval of God.

Judgment by Jesus' Words

44 Jesus said in a loud voice, "Whoever
believes in me believes not only in me
but also in him who sent me. 45 Whoever
sees me sees also him who sent me.
46 I have come into the world as light, so
that everyone who believes in me should
not remain in the darkness. 47 If people
hear my message and do not obey it, I
will not judge them. I came, not to judge
the world, but to save it. 48 Those who
reject me and do not accept my message
have one who will judge them. The
words I have spoken will be their judge
on the last day! 49 This is true, because I
have not spoken on my own authority,
but the Father who sent me has commanded me what I must say and speak.
50 And I know that his command brings
eternal life. What I say, then, is what the
Father has told me to say."

Jesus Washes His Disciples' Feet

13 It was now the day before the
Passover Festival. Jesus knew
that the hour had come for him to leave
this world and go to the Father. He had
always loved those in the world who
were his own, and he loved them to the
very end.

2 Jesus and his disciples were at supper. The Devil had already put into the
heart of Judas, the son of Simon Iscariot,
the thought of betraying Jesus.[y] 3 Jesus
knew that the Father had given him
complete power; he knew that he had
come from God and was going to God.
4 So he rose from the table, took off his
outer garment, and tied a towel around
his waist. 5 Then he poured some water
into a washbasin and began to wash the
disciples' feet and dry them with the

[y] The Devil . . . betraying Jesus; *or* The Devil had already decided that Judas, the son of Simon Iscariot, would betray Jesus.

towel around his waist. 6 He came to Simon Peter, who said to him, "Are you
going to wash my feet, Lord?"
7 Jesus answered him, "You do not
understand now what I am doing, but
you will understand later."
8 Peter declared, "Never at any time
will you wash my feet!"
"If I do not wash your feet," Jesus answered, "you will no longer be my
disciple."
9 Simon Peter answered, "Lord, do not
wash only my feet, then! Wash my
hands and head, too!"
10 Jesus said, "Those who have taken a
bath are completely clean and do not
have to wash themselves, except for
their feet.[z] All of you are clean—all except one." (11 Jesus already knew who
was going to betray him; that is why he
said, "All of you, except one, are clean.")
12 After Jesus had washed their feet, he
put his outer garment back on and returned to his place at the table. "Do you
understand what I have just done to
you?" he asked. 13 "You call me Teacher
and Lord, and it is right that you do so,
because that is what I am. 14 I, your Lord
and Teacher, have just washed your
feet. You, then, should wash one another's feet. 15 I have set an example for
you, so that you will do just what I have
done for you. 16 I am telling you the
truth: no slaves are greater than their
master, and no messengers are greater
than the one who sent them. 17 Now that
you know this truth, how happy you will
be if you put it into practice!
18 "I am not talking about all of you; I
know those I have chosen. But the scripture must come true that says, 'The man
who shared my food turned against me.'
19 I tell you this now before it happens,
so that when it does happen, you will
believe that 'I Am Who I Am.' 20 I am
telling you the truth: whoever receives
anyone I send receives me also; and
whoever receives me receives him who
sent me."

Jesus Predicts His Betrayal

(Matthew 26.20-25; Mark 14.17-21; Luke 22.21-23)

21 After Jesus had said this, he was
deeply troubled and declared openly, "I
am telling you the truth: one of you is
going to betray me."
22 The disciples looked at one another,
completely puzzled about whom he
meant. 23 One of the disciples, the one
whom Jesus loved, was sitting next to
Jesus. 24 Simon Peter motioned to him
and said, "Ask him whom he is talking
about."
25 So that disciple moved closer to
Jesus' side and asked, "Who is it, Lord?"
26 Jesus answered, "I will dip some
bread in the sauce and give it to him; he
is the man." So he took a piece of bread,
dipped it, and gave it to Judas, the son of
Simon Iscariot. 27 As soon as Judas took
the bread, Satan entered into him. Jesus
said to him, "Hurry and do what you
must!" 28 None of the others at the table
understood why Jesus said this to him.
29 Since Judas was in charge of the
money bag, some of the disciples
thought that Jesus had told him to go
and buy what they needed for the festival, or to give something to the poor.
30 Judas accepted the bread and went
out at once. It was night.

The New Commandment

31 After Judas had left, Jesus said,
"Now the Son of Man's glory is revealed;
now God's glory is revealed through
him. 32 And if God's glory is revealed
through him, then God will reveal the
glory of the Son of Man in himself, and
he will do so at once. 33 My children, I
shall not be with you very much longer.
You will look for me; but I tell you now
what I told the Jewish authorities, 'You
cannot go where I am going.' 34 And now
I give you a new commandment: love
one another. As I have loved you, so you
must love one another. 35 If you have
love for one another, then everyone will
know that you are my disciples."

Jesus Predicts Peter's Denial

(Matthew 26.31-35; Mark 14.27-31; Luke 22.31-34)

36 "Where are you going, Lord?" Simon Peter asked him.
"You cannot follow me now where I
am going," answered Jesus; "but later
you will follow me."
37 "Lord, why can't I follow you now?"
asked Peter. "I am ready to die for you!"
38 Jesus answered, "Are you really
ready to die for me? I am telling you
the truth: before the rooster crows you

[z] *Some manuscripts do not have* except for their feet.

will say three times that you do not
know me.

Jesus the Way to the Father

14 "Do not be worried and upset,"
Jesus told them. "Believe[a] in
God and believe also in me. 2 There are
many rooms in my Father's house, and I
am going to prepare a place for you. I
would not tell you this if it were not so.[b]
3 And after I go and prepare a place for
you, I will come back and take you to
myself, so that you will be where I am.
4 You know the way that leads to the
place where I am going."

5 Thomas said to him, "Lord, we do not
know where you are going; so how can
we know the way to get there?"

6 Jesus answered him, "I am the way,
the truth, and the life; no one goes to the
Father except by me. 7 Now that you
have known me," he said to them, "you
will know[c] my Father also, and from
now on you do know him and you have
seen him."

8 Philip said to him, "Lord, show us the
Father; that is all we need."

9 Jesus answered, "For a long time I
have been with you all; yet you do not
know me, Philip? Whoever has seen me
has seen the Father. Why, then, do you
say, 'Show us the Father'? 10 Do you not
believe, Philip, that I am in the Father
and the Father is in me? The words that
I have spoken to you," Jesus said to his
disciples, "do not come from me. The
Father, who remains in me, does his own
work. 11 Believe me when I say that I am
in the Father and the Father is in me. If
not, believe because of the things I do.
12 I am telling you the truth: those who
believe in me will do what I do—yes,
they will do even greater things, because
I am going to the Father. 13 And I will do
whatever you ask for in my name, so
that the Father's glory will be shown
through the Son. 14 If you ask me[d] for
anything in my name, I will do it.

The Promise of the Holy Spirit

15 "If you love me, you will obey my
commandments. 16 I will ask the Father,
and he will give you another Helper,
who will stay with you forever. 17 He is
the Spirit, who reveals the truth about
God. The world cannot receive him, because it cannot see him or know him.
But you know him, because he remains
with you and is[e] in you.

18 "When I go, you will not be left all
alone; I will come back to you. 19 In a
little while the world will see me no
more, but you will see me; and because
I live, you also will live. 20 When that day
comes, you will know that I am in my
Father and that you are in me, just as I
am in you.

21 "Those who accept my commandments and obey them are the ones who
love me. My Father will love those who
love me; I too will love them and reveal
myself to them."

22 Judas (not Judas Iscariot) said,
"Lord, how can it be that you will reveal
yourself to us and not to the world?"

23 Jesus answered him, "Those who
love me will obey my teaching. My
Father will love them, and my Father
and I will come to them and live with
them. 24 Those who do not love me do
not obey my teaching. And the teaching
you have heard is not mine, but comes
from the Father, who sent me.

25 "I have told you this while I am still
with you. 26 The Helper, the Holy Spirit,
whom the Father will send in my name,
will teach you everything and make you
remember all that I have told you.

27 "Peace is what I leave with you; it is
my own peace that I give you. I do not
give it as the world does. Do not be worried and upset; do not be afraid. 28 You
heard me say to you, 'I am leaving, but I
will come back to you.' If you loved me,
you would be glad that I am going to the
Father; for he is greater than I. 29 I have
told you this now before it all happens,
so that when it does happen, you will
believe. 30 I cannot talk with you much
longer, because the ruler of this world is
coming. He has no power over me, 31 but
the world must know that I love the
Father; that is why I do everything as he
commands me.

"Come, let us go from this place.

[a] Believe; *or* You believe. [b] There are . . . were not so; *or* There are many rooms in my Father's house; if it were not so, would I tell you that I am going to prepare a place for you? [c] Now that you have known me . . . you will know; *some manuscripts have* If you had known me . . . you would know. [d] *Some manuscripts do not have* me. [e] is; *some manuscripts have* will be.

Jesus the Real Vine

15 "I am the real vine, and my
Father is the gardener. 2He
breaks off every branch in me that does
not bear fruit, and he prunes every
branch that does bear fruit, so that it will
be clean and bear more fruit. 3You have
been made clean already by the teaching
I have given you. 4Remain united to me,
and I will remain united to you. A
branch cannot bear fruit by itself; it can
do so only if it remains in the vine. In the
same way you cannot bear fruit unless
you remain in me.

5"I am the vine, and you are the
branches. Those who remain in me, and
I in them, will bear much fruit; for you
can do nothing without me. 6Those who
do not remain in me are thrown out like
a branch and dry up; such branches are
gathered up and thrown into the fire,
where they are burned. 7If you remain in
me and my words remain in you, then
you will ask for anything you wish, and
you shall have it. 8My Father's glory is
shown by your bearing much fruit; and
in this way you become my disciples.
9I love you just as the Father loves me;
remain in my love. 10If you obey my
commands, you will remain in my love,
just as I have obeyed my Father's commands and remain in his love.

11"I have told you this so that my joy
may be in you and that your joy may be
complete. 12My commandment is this:
love one another, just as I love you.
13The greatest love you can have for
your friends is to give your life for them.
14And you are my friends if you do what
I command you. 15I do not call you servants any longer, because servants do not
know what their master is doing. Instead, I call you friends, because I have
told you everything I heard from my
Father. 16You did not choose me; I chose
you and appointed you to go and bear
much fruit, the kind of fruit that endures.
And so the Father will give you whatever you ask of him in my name. 17This,
then, is what I command you: love one
another.

The World's Hatred

18"If the world hates you, just remember that it has hated me first. 19If you
belonged to the world, then the world
would love you as its own. But I chose
you from this world, and you do not belong to it; that is why the world hates
you. 20Remember what I told you:
'Slaves are not greater than their master.' If people persecuted me, they will
persecute you too; if they obeyed my
teaching, they will obey yours too. 21But
they will do all this to you because you
are mine; for they do not know the one
who sent me. 22They would not have
been guilty of sin if I had not come and
spoken to them; as it is, they no longer
have any excuse for their sin. 23Who-
ever hates me hates my Father also.
24They would not have been guilty of sin
if I had not done among them the things
that no one else ever did; as it is, they
have seen what I did, and they hate both
me and my Father. 25This, however, was
bound to happen so that what is written
in their Law may come true: 'They hated
me for no reason at all.'

26"The Helper will come—the Spirit,
who reveals the truth about God and
who comes from the Father. I will send
him to you from the Father, and he will
speak about me. 27And you, too, will
speak about me, because you have been
with me from the very beginning.

16 "I have told you this, so that you
will not give up your faith. 2You
will be expelled from the synagogues,
and the time will come when those who
kill you will think that by doing this they
are serving God. 3People will do these
things to you because they have not
known either the Father or me. 4But I
have told you this, so that when the time
comes for them to do these things, you
will remember what I told you.

The Work of the Holy Spirit

"I did not tell you these things at the
beginning, for I was with you. 5But now
I am going to him who sent me, yet none
of you asks me where I am going. 6And
now that I have told you, your hearts are
full of sadness. 7But I am telling you the
truth: it is better for you that I go away,
because if I do not go, the Helper will not
come to you. But if I do go away, then I
will send him to you. 8And when he
comes, he will prove to the people of the
world that they are wrong about sin and
about what is right and about God's
judgment. 9They are wrong about sin,
because they do not believe in me;
10they are wrong about what is right,

because I am going to the Father and
you will not see me any more; 11 and they
are wrong about judgment, because the
ruler of this world has already been
judged.
12 "I have much more to tell you, but
now it would be too much for you to
bear. 13 When, however, the Spirit
comes, who reveals the truth about God,
he will lead you into all the truth. He will
not speak on his own authority, but he
will speak of what he hears and will tell
you of things to come. 14 He will give me
glory, because he will take what I say
and tell it to you. 15 All that my Father
has is mine; that is why I said that the
Spirit will take what I give him and tell it
to you.

Sadness and Gladness

16 "In a little while you will not see me
any more, and then a little while later
you will see me."
17 Some of his disciples asked among
themselves, "What does this mean? He
tells us that in a little while we will not
see him, and then a little while later we
will see him; and he also says, 'It is because I am going to the Father.' 18 What
does this 'a little while' mean? We don't
know what he is talking about!"
19 Jesus knew that they wanted to
question him, so he said to them, "I said,
'In a little while you will not see me, and
then a little while later you will see me.'
Is this what you are asking about among
yourselves? 20 I am telling you the truth:
you will cry and weep, but the world will
be glad; you will be sad, but your sadness will turn into gladness. 21 When a
woman is about to give birth, she is sad
because her hour of suffering has come;
but when the baby is born, she forgets
her suffering, because she is happy that
a baby has been born into the world.
22 That is how it is with you: now you are
sad, but I will see you again, and your
hearts will be filled with gladness, the
kind of gladness that no one can take
away from you.
23 "When that day comes, you will not
ask me for anything. I am telling you the
truth: the Father will give you whatever
you ask of him in my name.[f] 24 Until
now you have not asked for anything in
my name; ask and you will receive, so
that your happiness may be complete.

Victory over the World

25 "I have used figures of speech to tell
you these things. But the time will come
when I will not use figures of speech, but
will speak to you plainly about the
Father. 26 When that day comes, you will
ask him in my name; and I do not say
that I will ask him on your behalf, 27 for
the Father himself loves you. He loves
you because you love me and have believed that I came from God. 28 I did
come from the Father, and I came into
the world; and now I am leaving the
world and going to the Father."
29 Then his disciples said to him, "Now
you are speaking plainly, without using
figures of speech. 30 We know now that
you know everything; you do not need to
have someone ask you questions. This
makes us believe that you came
from God."
31 Jesus answered them, "Do you believe now? 32 The time is coming, and is
already here, when all of you will be
scattered, each of you to your own
home, and I will be left all alone. But I
am not really alone, because the Father
is with me. 33 I have told you this so that
you will have peace by being united to
me. The world will make you suffer. But
be brave! I have defeated the world!"

Jesus Prays for His Disciples

17 After Jesus finished saying this,
he looked up to heaven and said,
"Father, the hour has come. Give glory
to your Son, so that the Son may give
glory to you. 2 For you gave him authority over all people, so that he might give
eternal life to all those you gave him.
3 And eternal life means to know you,
the only true God, and to know Jesus
Christ, whom you sent. 4 I have shown
your glory on earth; I have finished the
work you gave me to do. 5 Father! Give
me glory in your presence now, the
same glory I had with you before the
world was made.
6 "I have made you known to those you
gave me out of the world. They belonged
to you, and you gave them to me. They
have obeyed your word, 7 and now they
know that everything you gave me

[f] the Father will give you whatever you ask of him in my name; *some manuscripts have* if you ask the Father for anything, he will give it to you in my name.

comes from you. 8 I gave them the message that you gave me, and they received it; they know that it is true that I
came from you, and they believe that
you sent me.
9 "I pray for them. I do not pray for the
world but for those you gave me, for
they belong to you. 10 All I have is yours,
and all you have is mine; and my glory is
shown through them. 11 And now I am
coming to you; I am no longer in the
world, but they are in the world. Holy
Father! Keep them safe by the power of
your name, the name you gave me,[g] so
that they may be one just as you and I
are one. 12 While I was with them, I kept
them safe by the power of your name,
the name you gave me.[h] I protected
them, and not one of them was lost, except the man who was bound to be lost—
so that the scripture might come true.
13 And now I am coming to you, and I say
these things in the world so that they
might have my joy in their hearts in all
its fullness. 14 I gave them your message,
and the world hated them, because they
do not belong to the world, just as I do
not belong to the world. 15 I do not ask
you to take them out of the world, but I
do ask you to keep them safe from the
Evil One. 16 Just as I do not belong to the
world, they do not belong to the world.
17 Dedicate them to yourself by means of
the truth; your word is truth. 18 I sent
them into the world, just as you sent me
into the world. 19 And for their sake I
dedicate myself to you, in order that
they, too, may be truly dedicated to you.
20 "I pray not only for them, but also
for those who believe in me because of
their message. 21 I pray that they may all
be one. Father! May they be in us, just as
you are in me and I am in you. May they
be one, so that the world will believe that
you sent me. 22 I gave them the same
glory you gave me, so that they may be
one, just as you and I are one: 23 I in
them and you in me, so that they may be
completely one, in order that the world
may know that you sent me and that you
love them as you love me.
24 "Father! You have given them to me,
and I want them to be with me where I
am, so that they may see my glory, the
glory you gave me; for you loved me before the world was made. 25 Righteous
Father! The world does not know you,
but I know you, and these know that you
sent me. 26 I made you known to them,
and I will continue to do so, in order that
the love you have for me may be in
them, and so that I also may be in them."

The Arrest of Jesus

(Matthew 26.47-56; Mark 14.43-50; Luke 22.47-53)

18 After Jesus had said this prayer,
he left with his disciples and
went across Kidron Brook. There was a
garden in that place, and Jesus and his
disciples went in. 2 Judas, the traitor,
knew where it was, because many times
Jesus had met there with his disciples.
3 So Judas went to the garden, taking
with him a group of Roman soldiers, and
some Temple guards sent by the chief
priests and the Pharisees; they were
armed and carried lanterns and torches.
4 Jesus knew everything that was going
to happen to him, so he stepped forward
and asked them, "Who is it you are looking for?"
5 "Jesus of Nazareth," they answered.
"I am he," he said.
Judas, the traitor, was standing there
with them. 6 When Jesus said to them, "I
am he," they moved back and fell to the
ground. 7 Again Jesus asked them, "Who
is it you are looking for?"
"Jesus of Nazareth," they said.
8 "I have already told you that I am he,"
Jesus said. "If, then, you are looking for
me, let these others go." (9 He said this so
that what he had said might come true:
"Father, I have not lost even one of those
you gave me.")
10 Simon Peter, who had a sword, drew
it and struck the High Priest's slave, cutting off his right ear. The name of the
slave was Malchus. 11 Jesus said to Peter,
"Put your sword back in its place! Do
you think that I will not drink the cup
of suffering which my Father has
given me?"

Jesus before Annas

12 Then the Roman soldiers with their
commanding officer and the Jewish
guards arrested Jesus, tied him up,

[g] Keep them safe by the power of your name, the name you gave me; *some manuscripts have* By the power of your name keep safe those you have given me. [h] I kept them safe by the power of your name, the name you gave me; *some manuscripts have* By the power of your name I kept safe those you have given me.

13 and took him first to Annas. He was
the father-in-law of Caiaphas, who was
High Priest that year. 14 It was Caiaphas
who had advised the Jewish authorities
that it was better that one man should
die for all the people.

Peter Denies Jesus

(Matthew 26.69, 70; Mark 14.66-68; Luke 22.55-57)

15 Simon Peter and another disciple
followed Jesus. That other disciple was
well known to the High Priest, so he
went with Jesus into the courtyard of the
High Priest's house, 16 while Peter stayed
outside by the gate. Then the other disciple went back out, spoke to the girl at
the gate, and brought Peter inside. 17 The
girl at the gate said to Peter, "Aren't you
also one of the disciples of that man?"
"No, I am not," answered Peter.
18 It was cold, so the servants and
guards had built a charcoal fire and
were standing around it, warming themselves. So Peter went over and stood
with them, warming himself.

The High Priest Questions Jesus

(Matthew 26.59-66; Mark 14.55-64; Luke 22.66-71)

19 The High Priest questioned Jesus
about his disciples and about his teaching. 20 Jesus answered, "I have always
spoken publicly to everyone; all my
teaching was done in the synagogues
and in the Temple, where all the people
come together. I have never said anything in secret. 21 Why, then, do you
question me? Question the people who
heard me. Ask them what I told them—
they know what I said."
22 When Jesus said this, one of the
guards there slapped him and said,
"How dare you talk like that to the High
Priest!"
23 Jesus answered him, "If I have said
anything wrong, tell everyone here what
it was. But if I am right in what I have
said, why do you hit me?"
24 Then Annas sent him, still tied up, to
Caiaphas the High Priest.

Peter Denies Jesus Again

(Matthew 26.71-75; Mark 14.69-72; Luke 22.58-62)

25 Peter was still standing there keeping himself warm. So the others said to
him, "Aren't you also one of the disciples
of that man?"
But Peter denied it. "No, I am not," he
said.
26 One of the High Priest's slaves, a relative of the man whose ear Peter had cut
off, spoke up. "Didn't I see you with him
in the garden?" he asked.
27 Again Peter said "No"—and at once
a rooster crowed.

Jesus before Pilate

(Matthew 27.1, 2, 11-14; Mark 15.1-5; Luke 23.1-5)

28 Early in the morning Jesus was
taken from Caiaphas' house to the governor's palace. The Jewish authorities
did not go inside the palace, for they
wanted to keep themselves ritually
clean, in order to be able to eat the Passover meal. 29 So Pilate went outside to
them and asked, "What do you accuse
this man of?"
30 Their answer was, "We would not
have brought him to you if he had not
committed a crime."
31 Pilate said to them, "Then you yourselves take him and try him according to
your own law."
They replied, "We are not allowed to
put anyone to death." (32 This happened
in order to make come true what Jesus
had said when he indicated the kind of
death he would die.)
33 Pilate went back into the palace and
called Jesus. "Are you the king of the
Jews?" he asked him.
34 Jesus answered, "Does this question
come from you or have others told you
about me?"
35 Pilate replied, "Do you think I am a
Jew? It was your own people and the
chief priests who handed you over to
me. What have you done?"
36 Jesus said, "My kingdom does not
belong to this world; if my kingdom belonged to this world, my followers
would fight to keep me from being
handed over to the Jewish authorities.
No, my kingdom does not belong here!"
37 So Pilate asked him, "Are you a
king, then?"
Jesus answered, "You say that I am a
king. I was born and came into the world
for this one purpose, to speak about the
truth. Whoever belongs to the truth listens to me."
38 "And what is truth?" Pilate asked.

Jesus Is Sentenced to Death

(Matthew 27.15-31; Mark 15.6-20; Luke 23.13-25)

Then Pilate went back outside to the
people and said to them, "I cannot find

any reason to condemn him. 39But according to the custom you have, I always
set free a prisoner for you during the
Passover. Do you want me to set free for
you the king of the Jews?"
40They answered him with a shout,
"No, not him! We want Barabbas!" (Barabbas was a bandit.)

19 Then Pilate took Jesus and had
him whipped. 2The soldiers
made a crown out of thorny branches
and put it on his head; then they put a
purple robe on him 3and came to him
and said, "Long live the King of the
Jews!" And they went up and
slapped him.
4Pilate went back out once more and
said to the crowd, "Look, I will bring him
out here to you to let you see that I cannot find any reason to condemn him."
5So Jesus came out, wearing the crown
of thorns and the purple robe. Pilate said
to them, "Look! Here is the man!"
6When the chief priests and the Temple guards saw him, they shouted, "Crucify him! Crucify him!"
Pilate said to them, "You take him,
then, and crucify him. I find no reason to
condemn him."
7The crowd answered back, "We have
a law that says he ought to die, because
he claimed to be the Son of God."
8When Pilate heard this, he was even
more afraid. 9He went back into the palace and asked Jesus, "Where do you
come from?"
But Jesus did not answer. 10Pilate said
to him, "You will not speak to me? Remember, I have the authority to set you
free and also to have you crucified."
11Jesus answered, "You have authority over me only because it was given to
you by God. So the man who handed me
over to you is guilty of a worse sin."
12When Pilate heard this, he tried to
find a way to set Jesus free. But the
crowd shouted back, "If you set him free,
that means that you are not the Emperor's friend! Anyone who claims to be
a king is a rebel against the Emperor!"
13When Pilate heard these words, he
took Jesus outside and sat down on the
judge's seat in the place called "The
Stone Pavement." (In Hebrew the name
is "Gabbatha.") 14It was then almost
noon of the day before the Passover. Pilate said to the people, "Here is your
king!"
15They shouted back, "Kill him! Kill
him! Crucify him!"
Pilate asked them, "Do you want me to
crucify your king?"
The chief priests answered, "The only
king we have is the Emperor!"
16Then Pilate handed Jesus over to
them to be crucified.

Jesus Is Crucified

(Matthew 27.32-44; Mark 15.21-32; Luke 23.26-43)

So they took charge of Jesus. 17He
went out, carrying his cross, and came to
"The Place of the Skull," as it is called.
(In Hebrew it is called "Golgotha.")
18There they crucified him; and they
also crucified two other men, one on
each side, with Jesus between them.
19Pilate wrote a notice and had it put on
the cross. "Jesus of Nazareth, the King
of the Jews," is what he wrote. 20Many
people read it, because the place where
Jesus was crucified was not far from the
city. The notice was written in Hebrew,
Latin, and Greek. 21The chief priests
said to Pilate, "Do not write 'The King of
the Jews,' but rather, 'This man said, I
am the King of the Jews.' "
22Pilate answered, "What I have written stays written."
23After the soldiers had crucified
Jesus, they took his clothes and divided
them into four parts, one part for each
soldier. They also took the robe, which
was made of one piece of woven cloth
without any seams in it. 24The soldiers
said to one another, "Let's not tear it;
let's throw dice to see who will get it."
This happened in order to make the
scripture come true:

"They divided my clothes among
themselves
and gambled for my robe."

And this is what the soldiers did.
25Standing close to Jesus' cross were
his mother, his mother's sister, Mary the
wife of Clopas, and Mary Magdalene.
26Jesus saw his mother and the disciple
he loved standing there; so he said to his
mother, "He is your son."
27Then he said to the disciple, "She is
your mother." From that time the disciple took her to live in his home.

The Death of Jesus

(Matthew 27.45-56; Mark 15.33-41; Luke 23.44-49)

28Jesus knew that by now everything
had been completed; and in order to

make the scripture come true, he said, "I
am thirsty."
29 A bowl was there, full of cheap
wine; so a sponge was soaked in the
wine, put on a stalk of hyssop, and lifted
up to his lips. 30 Jesus drank the wine
and said, "It is finished!"
Then he bowed his head and gave up
his spirit.

Jesus' Side Is Pierced

31 Then the Jewish authorities asked
Pilate to allow them to break the legs of
the men who had been crucified, and to
take the bodies down from the crosses.
They requested this because it was Friday, and they did not want the bodies to
stay on the crosses on the Sabbath, since
the coming Sabbath was especially holy.
32 So the soldiers went and broke the
legs of the first man and then of the
other man who had been crucified with
Jesus. 33 But when they came to Jesus,
they saw that he was already dead, so
they did not break his legs. 34 One of the
soldiers, however, plunged his spear
into Jesus' side, and at once blood and
water poured out. (35 The one who saw
this happen has spoken of it, so that you
also may believe.[i] What he said is true,
and he knows that he speaks the truth.)
36 This was done to make the scripture
come true: "Not one of his bones will be
broken." 37 And there is another scripture that says, "People will look at him
whom they pierced."

The Burial of Jesus

(Matthew 27.57-61; Mark 15.42-47; Luke 23.50-56)

38 After this, Joseph, who was from the
town of Arimathea, asked Pilate if he
could take Jesus' body. (Joseph was a
follower of Jesus, but in secret, because
he was afraid of the Jewish authorities.)
Pilate told him he could have the body,
so Joseph went and took it away. 39 Nicodemus, who at first had gone to see
Jesus at night, went with Joseph, taking
with him about one hundred pounds of
spices, a mixture of myrrh and aloes.
40 The two men took Jesus' body and
wrapped it in linen cloths with the spices
according to the Jewish custom of preparing a body for burial. 41 There was a
garden in the place where Jesus had
been put to death, and in it there was a
new tomb where no one had ever been
buried. 42 Since it was the day before the
Sabbath and because the tomb was close
by, they placed Jesus' body there.

The Empty Tomb

(Matthew 28.1-8; Mark 16.1-8; Luke 24.1-12)

20 Early on Sunday morning, while
it was still dark, Mary Magdalene went to the tomb and saw that the
stone had been taken away from the entrance. 2 She went running to Simon Peter and the other disciple, whom Jesus
loved, and told them, "They have taken
the Lord from the tomb, and we don't
know where they have put him!"
3 Then Peter and the other disciple
went to the tomb. 4 The two of them were
running, but the other disciple ran faster
than Peter and reached the tomb first.
5 He bent over and saw the linen cloths,
but he did not go in. 6 Behind him came
Simon Peter, and he went straight into
the tomb. He saw the linen cloths lying
there 7 and the cloth which had been
around Jesus' head. It was not lying with
the linen cloths but was rolled up by itself. 8 Then the other disciple, who had
reached the tomb first, also went in; he
saw and believed. (9 They still did not
understand the scripture which said that
he must rise from death.) 10 Then the disciples went back home.

Jesus Appears to Mary Magdalene

(Matthew 28.9, 10; Mark 16.9-11)

11 Mary stood crying outside the tomb.
While she was still crying, she bent over
and looked in the tomb 12 and saw two
angels there dressed in white, sitting
where the body of Jesus had been, one at
the head and the other at the feet.
13 "Woman, why are you crying?" they
asked her.
She answered, "They have taken my
Lord away, and I do not know where
they have put him!"
14 Then she turned around and saw
Jesus standing there; but she did not
know that it was Jesus. 15 "Woman, why
are you crying?" Jesus asked her. "Who
is it that you are looking for?"
She thought he was the gardener, so
she said to him, "If you took him away,
sir, tell me where you have put him, and
I will go and get him."

[i] believe; *some manuscripts have* continue to believe.

16 Jesus said to her, "Mary!"
She turned toward him and said in
Hebrew, "Rabboni!" (This means
"Teacher.")
17 "Do not hold on to me," Jesus told
her, "because I have not yet gone back
up to the Father. But go to my brothers
and tell them that I am returning to him
who is my Father and their Father, my
God and their God."
18 So Mary Magdalene went and told
the disciples that she had seen the Lord
and related to them what he had
told her.

Jesus Appears to His Disciples

(Matthew 28.16-20; Mark 16.14-18; Luke 24.36-49)

19 It was late that Sunday evening, and
the disciples were gathered together behind locked doors, because they were
afraid of the Jewish authorities. Then
Jesus came and stood among them.
"Peace be with you," he said. 20 After
saying this, he showed them his hands
and his side. The disciples were filled
with joy at seeing the Lord. 21 Jesus said
to them again, "Peace be with you. As
the Father sent me, so I send you."
22 Then he breathed on them and said,
"Receive the Holy Spirit. 23 If you forgive
people's sins, they are forgiven; if you
do not forgive them, they are not
forgiven."

Jesus and Thomas

24 One of the twelve disciples, Thomas
(called the Twin), was not with them
when Jesus came. 25 So the other disciples told him, "We have seen the Lord!"
Thomas said to them, "Unless I see the
scars of the nails in his hands and put
my finger on those scars and my hand in
his side, I will not believe."
26 A week later the disciples were together again indoors, and Thomas was
with them. The doors were locked, but
Jesus came and stood among them and
said, "Peace be with you." 27 Then he
said to Thomas, "Put your finger here,
and look at my hands; then reach out
your hand and put it in my side. Stop
your doubting, and believe!"
28 Thomas answered him, "My Lord
and my God!"
29 Jesus said to him, "Do you believe
because you see me? How happy are
those who believe without seeing me!"

The Purpose of This Book

30 In his disciples' presence Jesus performed many other miracles which are
not written down in this book. 31 But
these have been written in order that
you may believe[i] that Jesus is the
Messiah, the Son of God, and that
through your faith in him you may have
life.

Jesus Appears to Seven Disciples

21 After this, Jesus appeared once
more to his disciples at Lake Tiberias. This is how it happened. 2 Simon
Peter, Thomas (called the Twin), Nathanael (the one from Cana in Galilee),
the sons of Zebedee, and two other disciples of Jesus were all together. 3 Simon
Peter said to the others, "I am going
fishing."
"We will come with you," they told
him. So they went out in a boat, but all
that night they did not catch a thing. 4 As
the sun was rising, Jesus stood at the
water's edge, but the disciples did not
know that it was Jesus. 5 Then he asked
them, "Young men, haven't you caught
anything?"
"Not a thing," they answered.
6 He said to them, "Throw your net out
on the right side of the boat, and you will
catch some." So they threw the net out
and could not pull it back in, because
they had caught so many fish.
7 The disciple whom Jesus loved said
to Peter, "It is the Lord!" When Peter
heard that it was the Lord, he wrapped
his outer garment around him (for he
had taken his clothes off) and jumped
into the water. 8 The other disciples
came to shore in the boat, pulling the net
full of fish. They were not very far from
land, about a hundred yards away.
9 When they stepped ashore, they saw a
charcoal fire there with fish on it and
some bread. 10 Then Jesus said to them,
"Bring some of the fish you have just
caught."
11 Simon Peter went aboard and
dragged the net ashore full of big fish, a
hundred and fifty-three in all; even
though there were so many, still the net
did not tear. 12 Jesus said to them, "Come

[i] believe; *some manuscripts have* continue to believe.

and eat." None of the disciples dared ask
him, "Who are you?" because they knew
it was the Lord. 13 So Jesus went over,
took the bread, and gave it to them; he
did the same with the fish.

14 This, then, was the third time Jesus
appeared to the disciples after he was
raised from death.

Jesus and Peter

15 After they had eaten, Jesus said to
Simon Peter, "Simon son of John, do you
love me more than these others do?"

"Yes, Lord," he answered, "you know
that I love you."

Jesus said to him, "Take care of my
lambs." 16 A second time Jesus said to
him, "Simon son of John, do you
love me?"

"Yes, Lord," he answered, "you know
that I love you."

Jesus said to him, "Take care of my
sheep." 17 A third time Jesus said, "Simon son of John, do you love me?"

Peter became sad because Jesus asked
him the third time, "Do you love me?"
and so he said to him, "Lord, you know
everything; you know that I love you!"

Jesus said to him, "Take care of my
sheep. 18 I am telling you the truth: when
you were young, you used to get ready
and go anywhere you wanted to; but
when you are old, you will stretch out
your hands and someone else will tie
you up and take you where you don't
want to go." 19 (In saying this, Jesus was
indicating the way in which Peter would
die and bring glory to God.) Then Jesus
said to him, "Follow me!"

Jesus and the Other Disciple

20 Peter turned around and saw behind
him that other disciple, whom Jesus
loved—the one who had leaned close to
Jesus at the meal and had asked, "Lord,
who is going to betray you?" 21 When Peter saw him, he asked Jesus, "Lord, what
about this man?"

22 Jesus answered him, "If I want him
to live until I come, what is that to you?
Follow me!"

23 So a report spread among the followers of Jesus that this disciple would
not die. But Jesus did not say he would
not die; he said, "If I want him to live
until I come, what is that to you?"

24 He is the disciple who spoke of these
things, the one who also wrote them
down; and we know that what he said is
true.

Conclusion

25 Now, there are many other things
that Jesus did. If they were all written
down one by one, I suppose that the
whole world could not hold the books
that would be written.

THE ACTS
of the Apostles

Introduction

The Acts of the Apostles *is a continuation of* The Gospel according to Luke. *Its chief purpose is to tell how Jesus' early followers, led by the Holy Spirit, spread the Good News about him "in Jerusalem, in all of Judea and Samaria, and to the ends of the earth" (1.8). It is the story of the Christian movement as it began among the Jewish people and went on to become a faith for the whole world. The writer was also concerned to reassure his readers that the Christians were not a subversive political threat to the Roman Empire, and that the Christian faith was the fulfillment of the Jewish religion.*

Acts *may be divided into three principal parts, reflecting the ever widening area in which the Good News about Jesus was proclaimed and the church established: (1) the beginning of the Christian movement in Jerusalem following the ascension of Jesus; (2) expansion into other parts of Palestine; and (3) further expansion, into the Mediterranean world as far as Rome.*

An important feature of Acts *is the activity of the Holy Spirit, who comes with power upon the believers in Jerusalem on the day of Pentecost and continues to guide and strengthen the church and its leaders throughout the events reported in the book. The early Christian message is summarized in a number of sermons, and the events recorded in* Acts *show the power of this message in the lives of the believers and in the fellowship of the church.*

Outline of Contents

---

1 Dear Theophilus:
In my first book I wrote about all
the things that Jesus did and taught from
the time he began his work 2 until the
day he was taken up to heaven. Before
he was taken up, he gave instructions by
the power of the Holy Spirit to the men
he had chosen as his apostles. 3 For forty
days after his death he appeared to them
many times in ways that proved beyond
doubt that he was alive. They saw him,
and he talked with them about the Kingdom of God. 4 And when they came together,[a] he gave them this order: "Do
not leave Jerusalem, but wait for the gift
I told you about, the gift my Father
promised. 5 John baptized with water,
but in a few days you will be baptized
with the Holy Spirit."

Jesus Is Taken Up to Heaven

6 When the apostles met together with
Jesus, they asked him, "Lord, will you at
this time give the Kingdom back to
Israel?"
7 Jesus said to them, "The times and
occasions are set by my Father's own
authority, and it is not for you to know
when they will be. 8 But when the Holy
Spirit comes upon you, you will be filled
with power, and you will be witnesses
for me in Jerusalem, in all of Judea and
Samaria, and to the ends of the earth."
9 After saying this, he was taken up to

[a] when they came together; *or* while he was staying with them, *or* while he was eating with them.

heaven as they watched him, and a
cloud hid him from their sight.
10 They still had their eyes fixed on the
sky as he went away, when two men
dressed in white suddenly stood beside
them 11 and said, "Galileans, why are
you standing there looking up at the
sky? This Jesus, who was taken from
you into heaven, will come back in the
same way that you saw him go to
heaven."

Judas' Successor

12 Then the apostles went back to Jerusalem from the Mount of Olives, which
is about half a mile away from the city.
13 They entered the city and went up to
the room where they were staying: Peter, John, James and Andrew, Philip and
Thomas, Bartholomew and Matthew,
James son of Alphaeus, Simon the Patriot, and Judas son of James. 14 They
gathered frequently to pray as a group,
together with the women and with Mary
the mother of Jesus and with his
brothers.
15 A few days later there was a meeting of the believers, about a hundred and
twenty in all, and Peter stood up to
speak. 16 "My friends," he said, "the
scripture had to come true in which the
Holy Spirit, speaking through David,
made a prediction about Judas, who was
the guide for those who arrested Jesus.
17 Judas was a member of our group, for
he had been chosen to have a part in our
work."
(18 With the money that Judas got for
his evil act he bought a field, where he
fell to his death; he burst open and all his
insides spilled out. 19 All the people living in Jerusalem heard about it, and so
in their own language they call that field
Akeldama, which means "Field of
Blood.")
20 "For it is written in the book of
Psalms,

'May his house become empty;
may no one live in it.'

It is also written,

'May someone else take his place
of service.'

21-22 "So then, someone must join us as
a witness to the resurrection of the Lord
Jesus. He must be one of the men who
were in our group during the whole time
that the Lord Jesus traveled about with
us, beginning from the time John
preached his message of baptism[b] until
the day Jesus was taken up from us to
heaven."
23 So they proposed two men: Joseph,
who was called Barsabbas (also known
as Justus), and Matthias. 24 Then they
prayed, "Lord, you know the thoughts of
everyone, so show us which of these two
you have chosen 25 to serve as an apostle
in the place of Judas, who left to go to
the place where he belongs." 26 Then
they drew lots to choose between the
two men, and the one chosen was Matthias, who was added to the group of
eleven apostles.

The Coming of the Holy Spirit

2 When the day of Pentecost came,
all the believers were gathered together in one place. 2 Suddenly there
was a noise from the sky which sounded
like a strong wind blowing, and it filled
the whole house where they were sitting. 3 Then they saw what looked like
tongues of fire which spread out and
touched each person there. 4 They were
all filled with the Holy Spirit and began
to talk in other languages, as the Spirit
enabled them to speak.
5 There were Jews living in Jerusalem,
religious people who had come from
every country in the world. 6 When they
heard this noise, a large crowd gathered.
They were all excited, because all of
them heard the believers talking in their
own languages. 7 In amazement and
wonder they exclaimed, "These people
who are talking like this are Galileans!
8 How is it, then, that all of us hear them
speaking in our own native languages?
9 We are from Parthia, Media, and Elam;
from Mesopotamia, Judea, and Cappadocia; from Pontus and Asia, 10 from
Phrygia and Pamphylia, from Egypt and
the regions of Libya near Cyrene. Some
of us are from Rome, 11 both Jews and
Gentiles converted to Judaism, and
some of us are from Crete and Arabia—
yet all of us hear them speaking in our
own languages about the great things
that God has done!" 12 Amazed and confused, they kept asking each other,
"What does this mean?"

[b] John preached his message of baptism; *or* John baptized him.

13 But others made fun of the believers,
saying, "These people are drunk!"

Peter's Message

14 Then Peter stood up with the other
eleven apostles and in a loud voice began to speak to the crowd: "Fellow Jews
and all of you who live in Jerusalem, listen to me and let me tell you what this
means. 15 These people are not drunk, as
you suppose; it is only nine o'clock in
the morning. 16 Instead, this is what the
prophet Joel spoke about:

17 'This is what I will do in the last
days, God says:
I will pour out my Spirit on
everyone.
Your sons and daughters will
proclaim my message;
your young men will see visions,
and your old men will have
dreams.
18 Yes, even on my servants, both
men and women,
I will pour out my Spirit in those
days,
and they will proclaim my
message.
19 I will perform miracles in the sky
above
and wonders on the earth below.
There will be blood, fire, and thick
smoke;
20 the sun will be darkened,
and the moon will turn red as
blood,
before the great and glorious
Day of the Lord comes.
21 And then, whoever calls out to the
Lord for help will be saved.'

22 "Listen to these words, fellow Israelites! Jesus of Nazareth was a man whose
divine authority was clearly proven to
you by all the miracles and wonders
which God performed through him. You
yourselves know this, for it happened
here among you. 23 In accordance with
his own plan God had already decided
that Jesus would be handed over to you;
and you killed him by letting sinful men
crucify him. 24 But God raised him from
death, setting him free from its power,
because it was impossible that death
should hold him prisoner. 25 For David
said about him,

'I saw the Lord before me at all
times;
he is near me, and I will not be
troubled.
26 And so I am filled with gladness,
and my words are full of joy.
And I, mortal though I am,
will rest assured in hope,
27 because you will not abandon me
in the world of the dead;
you will not allow your faithful
servant to rot in the grave.
28 You have shown me the paths that
lead to life,
and your presence will fill me
with joy.'

29 "My friends, I must speak to you
plainly about our famous ancestor King
David. He died and was buried, and his
grave is here with us to this very day.
30 He was a prophet, and he knew what
God had promised him: God had made a
vow that he would make one of David's
descendants a king, just as David was.
31 David saw what God was going to do
in the future, and so he spoke about the
resurrection of the Messiah when he
said,

'He was not abandoned in the
world of the dead;
his body did not rot in the
grave.'

32 God has raised this very Jesus from
death, and we are all witnesses to this
fact. 33 He has been raised to the right
side of God, his Father, and has received
from him the Holy Spirit, as he had
promised. What you now see and hear is
his gift that he has poured out on us.
34 For it was not David who went up into
heaven; rather he said,

'The Lord said to my Lord:
Sit here at my right side
35 until I put your enemies as a
footstool under your feet.'

36 "All the people of Israel, then, are to
know for sure that this Jesus, whom you
crucified, is the one that God has made
Lord and Messiah!"

37 When the people heard this, they
were deeply troubled and said to Peter
and the other apostles, "What shall we
do, brothers?"

38 Peter said to them, "Each one of you
must turn away from your sins and be
baptized in the name of Jesus Christ, so
that your sins will be forgiven; and you
will receive God's gift, the Holy Spirit.
39 For God's promise was made to you
and your children, and to all who are far

away — all whom the Lord our God calls
to himself."
40 Peter made his appeal to them and
with many other words he urged them,
saying, "Save yourselves from the punishment coming on this wicked people!"
41 Many of them believed his message
and were baptized, and about three
thousand people were added to the
group that day. 42 They spent their time
in learning from the apostles, taking
part in the fellowship, and sharing in the
fellowship meals and the prayers.

Life among the Believers

43 Many miracles and wonders were
being done through the apostles, and
everyone was filled with awe. 44 All the
believers continued together in close fellowship and shared their belongings
with one another. 45 They would sell
their property and possessions, and distribute the money among all, according
to what each one needed. 46 Day after
day they met as a group in the Temple,
and they had their meals together in
their homes, eating with glad and humble hearts, 47 praising God, and enjoying
the good will of all the people. And every
day the Lord added to their group those
who were being saved.

A Lame Beggar Is Healed

3 One day Peter and John went to the
Temple at three o'clock in the afternoon, the hour for prayer. 2 There at the
Beautiful Gate, as it was called, was a
man who had been lame all his life.
Every day he was carried to the gate to
beg for money from the people who
were going into the Temple. 3 When he
saw Peter and John going in, he begged
them to give him something. 4 They
looked straight at him, and Peter said,
"Look at us!" 5 So he looked at them, expecting to get something from them.
6 But Peter said to him, "I have no money
at all, but I give you what I have: in the
name of Jesus Christ of Nazareth I order
you to get up and walk!" 7 Then he took
him by his right hand and helped him
up. At once the man's feet and ankles
became strong; 8 he jumped up, stood on
his feet, and started walking around.
Then he went into the Temple with
them, walking and jumping and praising
God. 9 The people there saw him walking
and praising God, 10 and when they recognized him as the beggar who had sat
at the Beautiful Gate, they were all surprised and amazed at what had happened to him.

Peter's Message in the Temple

11 As the man held on to Peter and
John in Solomon's Porch, as it was
called, the people were amazed and ran
to them. 12 When Peter saw the people,
he said to them, "Fellow Israelites, why
are you surprised at this, and why do
you stare at us? Do you think that it was
by means of our own power or godliness
that we made this man walk? 13 The God
of Abraham, Isaac, and Jacob, the God
of our ancestors, has given divine glory
to his Servant Jesus. But you handed
him over to the authorities, and you rejected him in Pilate's presence, even after Pilate had decided to set him free.
14 He was holy and good, but you rejected him, and instead you asked Pilate
to do you the favor of turning loose a
murderer. 15 You killed the one who
leads to life, but God raised him from
death — and we are witnesses to this. 16 It
was the power of his name that gave
strength to this lame man. What you see
and know was done by faith in his name;
it was faith in Jesus that has made him
well, as you can all see.
17 "And now, my friends, I know that
what you and your leaders did to Jesus
was due to your ignorance. 18 God announced long ago through all the prophets that his Messiah had to suffer; and he
made it come true in this way. 19 Repent,
then, and turn to God, so that he will
forgive your sins. If you do, 20 times of
spiritual strength will come from the
Lord, and he will send Jesus, who is the
Messiah he has already chosen for you.
21 He must remain in heaven until the
time comes for all things to be made
new, as God announced through his
holy prophets of long ago. 22 For Moses
said, 'The Lord your God will send you a
prophet, just as he sent me,[c] and he will
be one of your own people. You are to
obey everything that he tells you to do.
23 Anyone who does not obey that
prophet shall be separated from God's
people and destroyed.' 24 And all the

[c] just as he sent me; *or* like me.

prophets who had a message, including
Samuel and those who came after him,
also announced what has been happening these days. 25 The promises of God
through his prophets are for you, and
you share in the covenant which God
made with your ancestors. As he said to
Abraham, 'Through your descendants I
will bless all the people on earth.' 26 And
so God chose his Servant and sent him
to you first, to bless you by making
every one of you turn away from your
wicked ways."

Peter and John before the Council

4 Peter and John were still speaking
to the people when some priests,[d]
the officer in charge of the Temple
guards, and some Sadducees arrived.
2 They were annoyed because the two
apostles were teaching the people that
Jesus had risen from death, which
proved that the dead will rise to life. 3 So
they arrested them and put them in jail
until the next day, since it was already
late. 4 But many who heard the message
believed; and the number grew to about
five thousand.

5 The next day the Jewish leaders, the
elders, and the teachers of the Law gathered in Jerusalem. 6 They met with the
High Priest Annas and with Caiaphas,
John, Alexander, and the others who belonged to the High Priest's family. 7 They
made the apostles stand before them
and asked them, "How did you do this?
What power do you have or whose name
did you use?"

8 Peter, full of the Holy Spirit, answered them, "Leaders of the people and
elders: 9 if we are being questioned today
about the good deed done to the lame
man and how he was healed, 10 then you
should all know, and all the people of
Israel should know, that this man stands
here before you completely well through
the power of the name of Jesus Christ of
Nazareth — whom you crucified and
whom God raised from death. 11 Jesus is
the one of whom the scripture says,

'The stone that you the builders
despised
turned out to be the most
important of all.'

12 Salvation is to be found through him
alone; in all the world there is no one
else whom God has given who can
save us."

13 The members of the Council were
amazed to see how bold Peter and John
were and to learn that they were ordinary men of no education. They realized
then that they had been companions of
Jesus. 14 But there was nothing that they
could say, because they saw the man
who had been healed standing there
with Peter and John. 15 So they told them
to leave the Council room, and then they
started discussing among themselves.
16 "What shall we do with these men?"
they asked. "Everyone in Jerusalem
knows that this extraordinary miracle
has been performed by them, and we
cannot deny it. 17 But to keep this matter
from spreading any further among the
people, let us warn these men never
again to speak to anyone in the name of
Jesus."

18 So they called them back in and told
them that under no condition were they
to speak or to teach in the name of Jesus.
19 But Peter and John answered them,
"You yourselves judge which is right in
God's sight — to obey you or to obey
God. 20 For we cannot stop speaking of
what we ourselves have seen and
heard." 21 So the Council warned them
even more strongly and then set them
free. They saw that it was impossible to
punish them, because the people were
all praising God for what had happened.
22 The man on whom this miracle of
healing had been performed was over
forty years old.

The Believers Pray for Boldness

23 As soon as Peter and John were set
free, they returned to their group and
told them what the chief priests and the
elders had said. 24 When the believers
heard it, they all joined together in
prayer to God: "Master and Creator of
heaven, earth, and sea, and all that is in
them! 25 By means of the Holy Spirit you
spoke through our ancestor David, your
servant, when he said,

'Why were the Gentiles furious;
why did people make their
useless plots?
26 The kings of the earth prepared
themselves,
and the rulers met together

[d] priests; *some manuscripts have* chief priests.

against the Lord and his
Messiah.'
27For indeed Herod and Pontius Pilate
met together in this city with the Gentiles and the people of Israel against
Jesus, your holy Servant, whom you
made Messiah. 28They gathered to do
everything that you by your power and
will had already decided would happen.
29And now, Lord, take notice of the
threats they have made, and allow us,
your servants, to speak your message
with all boldness. 30Reach out your hand
to heal, and grant that wonders and miracles may be performed through the
name of your holy Servant Jesus."
31When they finished praying, the
place where they were meeting was
shaken. They were all filled with the
Holy Spirit and began to proclaim God's
message with boldness.

The Believers Share Their Possessions

32The group of believers was one in
mind and heart. None of them said that
any of their belongings were their own,
but they all shared with one another
everything they had. 33With great power
the apostles gave witness to the resurrection of the Lord Jesus, and God
poured rich blessings on them all.
34There was no one in the group who
was in need. Those who owned fields or
houses would sell them, bring the money
received from the sale, 35and turn it over
to the apostles; and the money was distributed according to the needs of the
people.
36And so it was that Joseph, a Levite
born in Cyprus, whom the apostles
called Barnabas (which means "One
who Encourages"), 37sold a field he
owned, brought the money, and turned it
over to the apostles.

Ananias and Sapphira

5 But there was a man named Ananias, who with his wife Sapphira
sold some property that belonged to
them. 2But with his wife's agreement he
kept part of the money for himself and
turned the rest over to the apostles. 3Pe-
ter said to him, "Ananias, why did you
let Satan take control of you and make
you lie to the Holy Spirit by keeping part
of the money you received for the property? 4Before you sold the property, it
belonged to you; and after you sold it,
the money was yours. Why, then, did
you decide to do such a thing? You have
not lied to people — you have lied to
God!" 5As soon as Ananias heard this,
he fell down dead; and all who heard
about it were terrified. 6The young men
came in, wrapped up his body, carried
him out, and buried him.
7About three hours later his wife, not
knowing what had happened, came in.
8Peter asked her, "Tell me, was this the
full amount you and your husband received for your property?"
"Yes," she answered, "the full
amount."
9So Peter said to her, "Why did you
and your husband decide to put the
Lord's Spirit to the test? The men who
buried your husband are at the door
right now, and they will carry you out
too!" 10At once she fell down at his feet
and died. The young men came in and
saw that she was dead, so they carried
her out and buried her beside her husband. 11The whole church and all the
others who heard of this were terrified.

Miracles and Wonders

12Many miracles and wonders were
being performed among the people by
the apostles. All the believers met together in Solomon's Porch. 13Nobody
outside the group dared join them, even
though the people spoke highly of them.
14But more and more people were added
to the group — a crowd of men and
women who believed in the Lord. 15As a
result of what the apostles were doing,
sick people were carried out into the
streets and placed on beds and mats so
that at least Peter's shadow might fall on
some of them as he passed by. 16And
crowds of people came in from the
towns around Jerusalem, bringing those
who were sick or who had evil spirits in
them; and they were all healed.

The Apostles Are Persecuted

17Then the High Priest and all his
companions, members of the local party
of the Sadducees, became extremely
jealous of the apostles; so they decided
to take action. 18They arrested the apostles and put them in the public jail. 19But
that night an angel of the Lord opened
the prison gates, led the apostles out,
and said to them, 20"Go and stand in the

Temple, and tell the people all about this
new life." 21 The apostles obeyed, and at
dawn they entered the Temple and
started teaching.

The High Priest and his companions
called together all the Jewish elders for
a full meeting of the Council; then they
sent orders to the prison to have the
apostles brought before them. 22 But
when the officials arrived, they did not
find the apostles in prison, so they returned to the Council and reported,
23 "When we arrived at the jail, we found
it locked up tight and all the guards on
watch at the gates; but when we opened
the gates, we found no one inside!"
24 When the chief priests and the officer
in charge of the Temple guards heard
this, they wondered what had happened
to the apostles. 25 Then a man came in
and said to them, "Listen! The men you
put in prison are in the Temple teaching
the people!" 26 So the officer went off
with his men and brought the apostles
back. They did not use force, however,
because they were afraid that the people
might stone them.

27 They brought the apostles in, made
them stand before the Council, and the
High Priest questioned them. 28 "We
gave you strict orders not to teach in the
name of this man," he said; "but see
what you have done! You have spread
your teaching all over Jerusalem, and
you want to make us responsible for his
death!"

29 Peter and the other apostles answered, "We must obey God, not men.
30 The God of our ancestors raised Jesus
from death, after you had killed him by
nailing him to a cross. 31 God raised him
to his right side as Leader and Savior, to
give the people of Israel the opportunity
to repent and have their sins forgiven.
32 We are witnesses to these things—we
and the Holy Spirit, who is God's gift to
those who obey him."

33 When the members of the Council
heard this, they were so furious that they
wanted to have the apostles put to death.
34 But one of them, a Pharisee named Gamaliel, who was a teacher of the Law
and was highly respected by all the people, stood up in the Council. He ordered
the apostles to be taken out for a while,
35 and then he said to the Council, "Fellow Israelites, be careful what you do to
these men. 36 You remember that Theu-
das appeared some time ago, claiming to
be somebody great, and about four hundred men joined him. But he was killed,
all his followers were scattered, and his
movement died out. 37 After that, Judas
the Galilean appeared during the time of
the census; he drew a crowd after him,
but he also was killed, and all his followers were scattered. 38 And so in this case,
I tell you, do not take any action against
these men. Leave them alone! If what
they have planned and done is of human
origin, it will disappear, 39 but if it comes
from God, you cannot possibly defeat
them. You could find yourselves fighting
against God!"

The Council followed Gamaliel's advice. 40 They called the apostles in, had
them whipped, and ordered them never
again to speak in the name of Jesus; and
then they set them free. 41 As the apostles left the Council, they were happy,
because God had considered them worthy to suffer disgrace for the sake of
Jesus. 42 And every day in the Temple
and in people's homes they continued to
teach and preach the Good News about
Jesus the Messiah.

The Seven Helpers

6 Some time later, as the number of
disciples kept growing, there was a
quarrel between the Greek-speaking
Jews and the native Jews. The Greek-
speaking Jews claimed that their widows were being neglected in the daily
distribution of funds. 2 So the twelve
apostles called the whole group of believers together and said, "It is not right
for us to neglect the preaching of God's
word in order to handle finances. 3 So
then, friends, choose seven men among
you who are known to be full of the Holy
Spirit and wisdom, and we will put them
in charge of this matter. 4 We ourselves,
then, will give our full time to prayer and
the work of preaching."

5 The whole group was pleased with
the apostles' proposal, so they chose
Stephen, a man full of faith and the Holy
Spirit, and Philip, Prochorus, Nicanor,
Timon, Parmenas, and Nicolaus, a Gentile from Antioch who had earlier been
converted to Judaism. 6 The group presented them to the apostles, who prayed
and placed their hands on them.

7 And so the word of God continued
to spread. The number of disciples in

Jerusalem grew larger and larger, and
a great number of priests accepted the
faith.

The Arrest of Stephen

8 Stephen, a man richly blessed by God
and full of power, performed great miracles and wonders among the people.
9 But he was opposed by some men who
were members of the synagogue of the
Freedmen[e] (as it was called), which had
Jews from Cyrene and Alexandria. They
and other Jews from the provinces of Cilicia and Asia started arguing with Stephen. 10 But the Spirit gave Stephen such
wisdom that when he spoke, they could
not refute him. 11 So they bribed some
men to say, "We heard him speaking
against Moses and against God!" 12 In
this way they stirred up the people, the
elders, and the teachers of the Law.
They seized Stephen and took him before the Council. 13 Then they brought in
some men to tell lies about him. "This
man," they said, "is always talking
against our sacred Temple and the Law
of Moses. 14 We heard him say that this
Jesus of Nazareth will tear down the
Temple and change all the customs
which have come down to us from
Moses!" 15 All those sitting in the Council
fixed their eyes on Stephen and saw that
his face looked like the face of an angel.

Stephen's Speech

7 The High Priest asked Stephen, "Is
this true?"
2 Stephen answered, "Brothers and
fathers, listen to me! Before our ancestor
Abraham had gone to live in Haran, the
God of glory appeared to him in Mesopotamia 3 and said to him, 'Leave your
family and country and go to the land
that I will show you.' 4 And so he left his
country and went to live in Haran. After
Abraham's father died, God made him
move to this land where you now live.
5 God did not then give Abraham any
part of it as his own, not even a square
foot of ground, but God promised to give
it to him, and that it would belong to him
and to his descendants. At the time God
made this promise, Abraham had no
children. 6 This is what God said to him:
'Your descendants will live in a foreign
country, where they will be slaves and
will be badly treated for four hundred
years. 7 But I will pass judgment on the
people that they will serve, and afterward your descendants will come out of
that country and will worship me in this
place.' 8 Then God gave to Abraham the
ceremony of circumcision as a sign of
the covenant. So Abraham circumcised
Isaac a week after he was born; Isaac
circumcised his son Jacob, and Jacob
circumcised his twelve sons, the famous
ancestors of our race.
9 "Jacob's sons became jealous of their
brother Joseph and sold him to be a
slave in Egypt. But God was with him
10 and brought him safely through all his
troubles. When Joseph appeared before
the king of Egypt, God gave him a pleasing manner and wisdom, and the king
made Joseph governor over the country
and the royal household. 11 Then there
was a famine all over Egypt and Canaan, which caused much suffering. Our
ancestors could not find any food, 12 and
when Jacob heard that there was grain
in Egypt, he sent his sons, our ancestors,
on their first visit there. 13 On the second
visit Joseph made himself known to his
brothers, and the king of Egypt came to
know about Joseph's family. 14 So Joseph sent a message to his father Jacob,
telling him and the whole family,
seventy-five people in all, to come to
Egypt. 15 Then Jacob went to Egypt,
where he and his sons died. 16 Their bodies were taken to Shechem, where they
were buried in the grave which Abraham had bought from the clan of Hamor
for a sum of money.
17 "When the time drew near for God
to keep the promise he had made to
Abraham, the number of our people in
Egypt had grown much larger. 18 At last
a king who did not know about Joseph
began to rule in Egypt. 19 He tricked our
ancestors and was cruel to them, forcing
them to put their babies out of their
homes, so that they would die. 20 It was
at this time that Moses was born, a very
beautiful child. He was cared for at
home for three months, 21 and when he
was put out of his home, the king's
daughter adopted him and brought him
up as her own son. 22 He was taught all
the wisdom of the Egyptians and became a great man in words and deeds.

[e] FREEDMEN: *These were Jews who had been slaves, but had bought or been given their freedom.*

23 “When Moses was forty years old,
he decided to find out how his fellow Israelites were being treated. 24 He saw
one of them being mistreated by an
Egyptian, so he went to his help and
took revenge on the Egyptian by killing
him. (25 He thought that his own people
would understand that God was going to
use him to set them free, but they did not
understand.) 26 The next day he saw two
Israelites fighting, and he tried to make
peace between them. ‘Listen, men,’ he
said, ‘you are fellow Israelites; why are
you fighting like this?’ 27 But the one
who was mistreating the other pushed
Moses aside. ‘Who made you ruler and
judge over us?’ he asked. 28 ‘Do you want
to kill me, just as you killed that Egyptian yesterday?’ 29 When Moses heard
this, he fled from Egypt and went to live
in the land of Midian. There he had two
sons.

30 “After forty years had passed, an angel appeared to Moses in the flames of a
burning bush in the desert near Mount
Sinai. 31 Moses was amazed by what he
saw, and went near the bush to get a better look. But he heard the Lord’s voice:
32 ‘I am the God of your ancestors, the
God of Abraham, Isaac, and Jacob.’
Moses trembled with fear and dared not
look. 33 The Lord said to him, ‘Take your
sandals off, for the place where you are
standing is holy ground. 34 I have seen
the cruel suffering of my people in
Egypt. I have heard their groans, and I
have come down to set them free. Come
now; I will send you to Egypt.’

35 “Moses is the one who was rejected
by the people of Israel. ‘Who made you
ruler and judge over us?’ they asked. He
is the one whom God sent to rule the
people and set them free with the help of
the angel who appeared to him in the
burning bush. 36 He led the people out of
Egypt, performing miracles and wonders in Egypt and at the Red Sea and for
forty years in the desert. 37 Moses is the
one who said to the people of Israel,
‘God will send you a prophet, just as he
sent me,[f] and he will be one of your
own people.’ 38 He is the one who was
with the people of Israel assembled in
the desert; he was there with our ancestors and with the angel who spoke to
him on Mount Sinai, and he received
God’s living messages to pass on to us.

39 “But our ancestors refused to obey
him; they pushed him aside and wished
that they could go back to Egypt. 40 So
they said to Aaron, ‘Make us some gods
who will lead us. We do not know what
has happened to that man Moses, who
brought us out of Egypt.’ 41 It was then
that they made an idol in the shape of a
bull, offered sacrifice to it, and had a
feast in honor of what they themselves
had made. 42 So God turned away from
them and gave them over to worship the
stars of heaven, as it is written in the
book of the prophets:

‘People of Israel! It was not to me
that you slaughtered and
sacrificed animals
for forty years in the desert.
43 It was the tent of the god Molech
that you carried,
and the image of Rephan, your
star god;
they were idols that you had
made to worship.
And so I will send you into exile
beyond Babylon.’

44 “Our ancestors had the Tent of
God’s presence with them in the desert.
It had been made as God had told Moses
to make it, according to the pattern that
Moses had been shown. 45 Later on, our
ancestors who received the tent from
their fathers carried it with them when
they went with Joshua and took over the
land from the nations that God drove out
as they advanced. And it stayed there
until the time of David. 46 He won God’s
favor and asked God to allow him to provide a dwelling place for the God of Jacob.[g] 47 But it was Solomon who built
him a house.

48 “But the Most High God does not
live in houses built by human hands; as
the prophet says,

49 ‘Heaven is my throne, says the
Lord,
and the earth is my footstool.
What kind of house would you
build for me?
Where is the place for me to
live in?
50 Did not I myself make all these
things?’

[f] just as he sent me; *or* like me. [g] the God of Jacob; *some manuscripts have* the people of Israel.

51 "How stubborn you are!" Stephen
went on to say. "How heathen your
hearts, how deaf you are to God's message! You are just like your ancestors:
you too have always resisted the Holy
Spirit! 52 Was there any prophet that
your ancestors did not persecute? They
killed God's messengers, who long ago
announced the coming of his righteous
Servant. And now you have betrayed
and murdered him. 53 You are the ones
who received God's law, that was
handed down by angels—yet you have
not obeyed it!"

The Stoning of Stephen

54 As the members of the Council listened to Stephen, they became furious
and ground their teeth at him in anger.
55 But Stephen, full of the Holy Spirit,
looked up to heaven and saw God's
glory and Jesus standing at the right
side of God. 56 "Look!" he said. "I see
heaven opened and the Son of Man
standing at the right side of God!"

57 With a loud cry the Council members covered their ears with their hands.
Then they all rushed at him at once,
58 threw him out of the city, and stoned
him. The witnesses left their cloaks in
the care of a young man named Saul.
59 They kept on stoning Stephen as he
called out to the Lord, "Lord Jesus, receive my spirit!" 60 He knelt down and
cried out in a loud voice, "Lord! Do not
remember this sin against them!" He
said this and died.

8 And Saul approved of his murder.

Saul Persecutes the Church

That very day the church in Jerusalem
began to suffer cruel persecution. All the
believers, except the apostles, were scattered throughout the provinces of Judea
and Samaria. 2 Some devout men buried
Stephen, mourning for him with loud
cries.

3 But Saul tried to destroy the church;
going from house to house, he dragged
out the believers, both men and women,
and threw them into jail.

The Gospel Is Preached in Samaria

4 The believers who were scattered
went everywhere, preaching the message. 5 Philip went to the principal city[h]
in Samaria and preached the Messiah to
the people there. 6 The crowds paid close
attention to what Philip said, as they listened to him and saw the miracles that
he performed. 7 Evil spirits came out
from many people with a loud cry, and
many paralyzed and lame people were
healed. 8 So there was great joy in that
city.

9 A man named Simon lived there,
who for some time had astounded the
Samaritans with his magic. He claimed
that he was someone great, 10 and everyone in the city, from all classes of society, paid close attention to him. "He is
that power of God known as 'The Great
Power,'" they said. 11 They paid this attention to him because for such a long
time he had astonished them with his
magic. 12 But when they believed Philip's
message about the good news of the
Kingdom of God and about Jesus Christ,
they were baptized, both men and
women. 13 Simon himself also believed;
and after being baptized, he stayed close
to Philip and was astounded when he
saw the great wonders and miracles that
were being performed.

14 The apostles in Jerusalem heard that
the people of Samaria had received the
word of God, so they sent Peter and
John to them. 15 When they arrived, they
prayed for the believers that they might
receive the Holy Spirit. 16 For the Holy
Spirit had not yet come down on any of
them; they had only been baptized in the
name of the Lord Jesus. 17 Then Peter
and John placed their hands on them,
and they received the Holy Spirit.

18 Simon saw that the Spirit had been
given to the believers when the apostles
placed their hands on them. So he offered money to Peter and John, 19 and
said, "Give this power to me too, so that
anyone I place my hands on will receive
the Holy Spirit."

20 But Peter answered him, "May you
and your money go to hell, for thinking
that you can buy God's gift with money!
21 You have no part or share in our work,
because your heart is not right in God's
sight. 22 Repent, then, of this evil plan of
yours, and pray to the Lord that he will
forgive you for thinking such a thing as
this. 23 For I see that you are full of bitter
envy and are a prisoner of sin."

[h] the principal city; *some manuscripts have* a city.

24 Simon said to Peter and John,
"Please pray to the Lord for me, so that
none of these things you spoke of will
happen to me."
25 After they had given their testimony
and proclaimed the Lord's message, Peter and John went back to Jerusalem. On
their way they preached the Good News
in many villages of Samaria.

Philip and the Ethiopian Official

26 An angel of the Lord said to Philip,
"Get ready and go south[i] to the road
that goes from Jerusalem to Gaza." (This
road is not used nowadays.)[j] 27-28 So
Philip got ready and went. Now an Ethiopian eunuch, who was an important official in charge of the treasury of the
queen of Ethiopia, was on his way home.
He had been to Jerusalem to worship
God and was going back home in his
carriage. As he rode along, he was reading from the book of the prophet Isaiah.
29 The Holy Spirit said to Philip, "Go over
to that carriage and stay close to it."
30 Philip ran over and heard him reading
from the book of the prophet Isaiah. He
asked him, "Do you understand what
you are reading?"
31 The official replied, "How can I
understand unless someone explains it
to me?" And he invited Philip to climb up
and sit in the carriage with him. 32 The
passage of scripture which he was reading was this:

"He was like a sheep that is taken
to be slaughtered,
like a lamb that makes no sound
when its wool is cut off.
He did not say a word.
33 He was humiliated, and justice
was denied him.
No one will be able to tell about
his descendants,
because his life on earth has
come to an end."

34 The official asked Philip, "Tell me,
of whom is the prophet saying this? Of
himself or of someone else?" 35 Then
Philip began to speak; starting from this
passage of scripture, he told him the
Good News about Jesus. 36 As they traveled down the road, they came to a place
where there was some water, and the official said, "Here is some water. What is
to keep me from being baptized?"[k]
38 The official ordered the carriage to
stop, and both Philip and the official
went down into the water, and Philip
baptized him. 39 When they came up out
of the water, the Spirit of the Lord took
Philip away. The official did not see him
again, but continued on his way, full of
joy. 40 Philip found himself in Azotus; he
went on to Caesarea, and on the way he
preached the Good News in every town.

The Conversion of Saul

(Acts 22.6-16; 26.12-18)

9 In the meantime Saul kept up his
violent threats of murder against
the followers of the Lord. He went to the
High Priest 2 and asked for letters of introduction to the synagogues in Damascus, so that if he should find there any
followers of the Way of the Lord, he
would be able to arrest them, both men
and women, and bring them back to Jerusalem.
3 As Saul was coming near the city of
Damascus, suddenly a light from the sky
flashed around him. 4 He fell to the
ground and heard a voice saying to him,
"Saul, Saul! Why do you persecute me?"
5 "Who are you, Lord?" he asked.
"I am Jesus, whom you persecute," the
voice said. 6 "But get up and go into the
city, where you will be told what you
must do."
7 The men who were traveling with
Saul had stopped, not saying a word;
they heard the voice but could not see
anyone. 8 Saul got up from the ground
and opened his eyes, but could not see a
thing. So they took him by the hand and
led him into Damascus. 9 For three days
he was not able to see, and during that
time he did not eat or drink anything.
10 There was a believer in Damascus
named Ananias. He had a vision, in
which the Lord said to him, "Ananias!"
"Here I am, Lord," he answered.
11 The Lord said to him, "Get ready
and go to Straight Street, and at the
house of Judas ask for a man from Tarsus named Saul. He is praying, 12 and in
a vision he has seen a man named Ananias come in and place his hands on him
so that he might see again."

[i] south; *or* at midday. [j] This road is not used nowadays; *or* This is the desert road.
[k] *Some manuscripts add verse 37:* Philip said to him, "You may be baptized if you believe with all your heart." "I do," he answered; "I believe that Jesus Christ is the Son of God."

13 Ananias answered, "Lord, many
people have told me about this man and
about all the terrible things he has done
to your people in Jerusalem. 14 And he
has come to Damascus with authority
from the chief priests to arrest all who
worship you."
15 The Lord said to him, "Go, because I
have chosen him to serve me, to make
my name known to Gentiles and kings
and to the people of Israel. 16 And I myself will show him all that he must suffer
for my sake."
17 So Ananias went, entered the house
where Saul was, and placed his hands
on him. "Brother Saul," he said, "the
Lord has sent me—Jesus himself, who
appeared to you on the road as you were
coming here. He sent me so that you
might see again and be filled with the
Holy Spirit." 18 At once something like
fish scales fell from Saul's eyes, and he
was able to see again. He stood up and
was baptized; 19 and after he had eaten,
his strength came back.

Saul Preaches in Damascus

Saul stayed for a few days with the
believers in Damascus. 20 He went
straight to the synagogues and began to
preach that Jesus was the Son of God.
21 All who heard him were amazed and
asked, "Isn't he the one who in Jerusalem was killing those who worship that
man Jesus? And didn't he come here for
the very purpose of arresting those people and taking them back to the chief
priests?"
22 But Saul's preaching became even
more powerful, and his proofs that Jesus
was the Messiah were so convincing
that the Jews who lived in Damascus
could not answer him.
23 After many days had gone by, the
Jews met together and made plans to kill
Saul, 24 but he was told of their plan. Day
and night they watched the city gates in
order to kill him. 25 But one night Saul's
followers took him and let him down
through an opening in the wall, lowering
him in a basket.

Saul in Jerusalem

26 Saul went to Jerusalem and tried to
join the disciples. But they would not believe that he was a disciple, and they
were all afraid of him. 27 Then Barnabas
came to his help and took him to the
apostles. He explained to them how Saul
had seen the Lord on the road and that
the Lord had spoken to him. He also told
them how boldly Saul had preached in
the name of Jesus in Damascus. 28 And
so Saul stayed with them and went all
over Jerusalem, preaching boldly in the
name of the Lord. 29 He also talked and
disputed with the Greek-speaking Jews,
but they tried to kill him. 30 When the
believers found out about this, they took
Saul to Caesarea and sent him away to
Tarsus.
31 And so it was that the church
throughout Judea, Galilee, and Samaria
had a time of peace. Through the help of
the Holy Spirit it was strengthened and
grew in numbers, as it lived in reverence
for the Lord.

Peter in Lydda and Joppa

32 Peter traveled everywhere, and on
one occasion he went to visit God's people who lived in Lydda. 33 There he met a
man named Aeneas, who was paralyzed
and had not been able to get out of bed
for eight years. 34 "Aeneas," Peter said to
him, "Jesus Christ makes you well. Get
up and make your bed." At once Aeneas
got up. 35 All the people living in Lydda
and Sharon saw him, and they turned to
the Lord.
36 In Joppa there was a woman named
Tabitha, who was a believer. (Her name
in Greek is Dorcas, meaning "a deer.")
She spent all her time doing good and
helping the poor. 37 At that time she got
sick and died. Her body was washed and
laid in a room upstairs. 38 Joppa was not
very far from Lydda, and when the believers in Joppa heard that Peter was in
Lydda, they sent two men to him with
the message, "Please hurry and come to
us." 39 So Peter got ready and went with
them. When he arrived, he was taken to
the room upstairs, where all the widows
crowded around him, crying and showing him all the shirts and coats that Dorcas had made while she was alive.
40 Peter put them all out of the room, and
knelt down and prayed; then he turned
to the body and said, "Tabitha, get up!"
She opened her eyes, and when she saw
Peter, she sat up. 41 Peter reached over
and helped her get up. Then he called all
the believers, including the widows, and
presented her alive to them. 42 The news
about this spread all over Joppa, and

many people believed in the Lord. 43 Peter stayed on in Joppa for many days
with a tanner of leather named Simon.

Peter and Cornelius

10 There was a man in Caesarea
named Cornelius, who was a
captain in the Roman army regiment
called "The Italian Regiment." 2 He was a
religious man; he and his whole family
worshiped God. He also did much to
help the Jewish poor people and was
constantly praying to God. 3 It was about
three o'clock one afternoon when he had
a vision, in which he clearly saw an angel of God come in and say to him,
"Cornelius!"

4 He stared at the angel in fear and
said, "What is it, sir?"

The angel answered, "God is pleased
with your prayers and works of charity,
and is ready to answer you. 5 And now
send some men to Joppa for a certain
man whose full name is Simon Peter.
6 He is a guest in the home of a tanner of
leather named Simon, who lives by the
sea." 7 Then the angel went away, and
Cornelius called two of his house servants and a soldier, a religious man who
was one of his personal attendants. 8 He
told them what had happened and sent
them off to Joppa.

9 The next day, as they were on their
way and coming near Joppa, Peter went
up on the roof of the house about noon
in order to pray. 10 He became hungry
and wanted something to eat; while the
food was being prepared, he had a vision. 11 He saw heaven opened and
something coming down that looked like
a large sheet being lowered by its four
corners to the earth. 12 In it were all
kinds of animals, reptiles, and wild
birds. 13 A voice said to him, "Get up, Peter; kill and eat!"

14 But Peter said, "Certainly not, Lord!
I have never eaten anything ritually unclean or defiled."

15 The voice spoke to him again, "Do
not consider anything unclean that God
has declared clean." 16 This happened
three times, and then the thing was
taken back up into heaven.

17 While Peter was wondering about
the meaning of this vision, the men sent
by Cornelius had learned where Simon's
house was, and they were now standing
in front of the gate. 18 They called out
and asked, "Is there a guest here by the
name of Simon Peter?"

19 Peter was still trying to understand
what the vision meant, when the Spirit
said, "Listen! Three[l] men are here looking for you. 20 So get ready and go down,
and do not hesitate to go with them, for
I have sent them." 21 So Peter went down
and said to the men, "I am the man you
are looking for. Why have you come?"

22 "Captain Cornelius sent us," they
answered. "He is a good man who worships God and is highly respected by all
the Jewish people. An angel of God told
him to invite you to his house, so that he
could hear what you have to say." 23 Peter invited the men in and had them
spend the night there.

The next day he got ready and went
with them; and some of the believers
from Joppa went along with him. 24 The
following day he arrived in Caesarea,
where Cornelius was waiting for him, together with relatives and close friends
that he had invited. 25 As Peter was
about to go in, Cornelius met him, fell at
his feet, and bowed down before him.
26 But Peter made him rise. "Stand up,"
he said, "I myself am only a man." 27 Peter kept on talking to Cornelius as he
went into the house, where he found
many people gathered. 28 He said to
them, "You yourselves know very well
that a Jew is not allowed by his religion
to visit or associate with Gentiles. But
God has shown me that I must not consider any person ritually unclean or defiled. 29 And so when you sent for me, I
came without any objection. I ask you,
then, why did you send for me?"

30 Cornelius said, "It was about this
time three days ago that I was praying[m]
in my house at three o'clock in the afternoon. Suddenly a man dressed in shining clothes stood in front of me 31 and
said: 'Cornelius! God has heard your
prayer and has taken notice of your
works of charity. 32 Send someone to
Joppa for a man whose full name is Simon Peter. He is a guest in the home of
Simon the tanner of leather, who lives
by the sea.' 33 And so I sent for you at

[l] Three; *some manuscripts have* Some; *one manuscript has* Two.
[m] praying; *some manuscripts have* fasting and praying.

once, and you have been good enough to
come. Now we are all here in the presence of God, waiting to hear anything
that the Lord has instructed you to say."

Peter's Speech

34 Peter began to speak: "I now realize
that it is true that God treats everyone
on the same basis. 35 Those who fear him
and do what is right are acceptable to
him, no matter what race they belong to.
36 You know the message he sent to the
people of Israel, proclaiming the Good
News of peace through Jesus Christ,
who is Lord of all. 37 You know of the
great event that took place throughout
the land of Israel, beginning in Galilee
after John preached his message of baptism. 38 You know about Jesus of Nazareth and how God poured out on him the
Holy Spirit and power. He went everywhere, doing good and healing all who
were under the power of the Devil, for
God was with him. 39 We are witnesses
of everything that he did in the land of
Israel and in Jerusalem. Then they put
him to death by nailing him to a cross.
40 But God raised him from death three
days later and caused him to appear,
41 not to everyone, but only to the witnesses that God had already chosen,
that is, to us who ate and drank with him
after he rose from death. 42 And he commanded us to preach the gospel to the
people and to testify that he is the one
whom God has appointed judge of the
living and the dead. 43 All the prophets
spoke about him, saying that all who believe in him will have their sins forgiven
through the power of his name."

The Gentiles Receive the Holy Spirit

44 While Peter was still speaking, the
Holy Spirit came down on all those who
were listening to his message. 45 The
Jewish believers who had come from
Joppa with Peter were amazed that God
had poured out his gift of the Holy Spirit
on the Gentiles also. 46 For they heard
them speaking in strange tongues and
praising God's greatness. Peter spoke
up: 47 "These people have received the
Holy Spirit, just as we also did. Can anyone, then, stop them from being baptized with water?" 48 So he ordered them
to be baptized in the name of Jesus
Christ. Then they asked him to stay with
them for a few days.

Peter's Report to the Church at Jerusalem

11 The apostles and the other believers throughout Judea heard
that the Gentiles also had received the
word of God. 2 When Peter went to Jerusalem, those who were in favor of circumcising Gentiles criticized him,
saying, 3 "You were a guest in the home
of uncircumcised Gentiles, and you even
ate with them!" 4 So Peter gave them a
complete account of what had happened
from the very beginning:

5 "While I was praying in the city of
Joppa, I had a vision. I saw something
coming down that looked like a large
sheet being lowered by its four corners
from heaven, and it stopped next to me.
6 I looked closely inside and saw domes-
ticated and wild animals, reptiles, and
wild birds. 7 Then I heard a voice saying
to me, 'Get up, Peter; kill and eat!' 8 But
I said, 'Certainly not, Lord! No ritually
unclean or defiled food has ever entered
my mouth.' 9 The voice spoke again from
heaven, 'Do not consider anything unclean that God has declared clean.'
10 This happened three times, and finally
the whole thing was drawn back up into
heaven. 11 At that very moment three
men who had been sent to me from
Caesarea arrived at the house where I
was[n] staying. 12 The Spirit told me to go
with them without hesitation. These six
fellow believers from Joppa accompanied me to Caesarea, and we all went
into the house of Cornelius. 13 He told us
how he had seen an angel standing in
his house, who said to him, 'Send someone to Joppa for a man whose full name
is Simon Peter. 14 He will speak words to
you by which you and all your family
will be saved.' 15 And when I began to
speak, the Holy Spirit came down on
them just as on us at the beginning.
16 Then I remembered what the Lord had
said: 'John baptized with water, but you
will be baptized with the Holy Spirit.'
17 It is clear that God gave those Gentiles
the same gift that he gave us when we
believed in the Lord Jesus Christ; who
was I, then, to try to stop God!"

18 When they heard this, they stopped

[n] I was; *some manuscripts have* we were.

their criticism and praised God, saying,
"Then God has given to the Gentiles also
the opportunity to repent and live!"

The Church at Antioch

19 Some of the believers who were
scattered by the persecution which took
place when Stephen was killed went as
far as Phoenicia, Cyprus, and Antioch,
telling the message to Jews only. 20 But
other believers, who were from Cyprus
and Cyrene, went to Antioch and proclaimed the message to Gentiles[o] also,
telling them the Good News about the
Lord Jesus. 21 The Lord's power was
with them, and a great number of people
believed and turned to the Lord.
22 The news about this reached the
church in Jerusalem, so they sent Barnabas to Antioch. 23 When he arrived and
saw how God had blessed the people, he
was glad and urged them all to be faithful and true to the Lord with all their
hearts. 24 Barnabas was a good man, full
of the Holy Spirit and faith, and many
people were brought to the Lord.
25 Then Barnabas went to Tarsus to
look for Saul. 26 When he found him, he
took him to Antioch, and for a whole
year the two met with the people of the
church and taught a large group. It was
at Antioch that the believers were first
called Christians.
27 About that time some prophets went
from Jerusalem to Antioch. 28 One of
them, named Agabus, stood up and by
the power of the Spirit predicted that a
severe famine was about to come over
all the earth. (It came when Claudius
was emperor.) 29 The disciples decided
that they each would send as much as
they could to help their fellow believers
who lived in Judea. 30 They did this,
then, and sent the money to the church
elders by Barnabas and Saul.

More Persecution

12 About this time King Herod[p] began to persecute some members
of the church. 2 He had James, the
brother of John, put to death by the
sword. 3 When he saw that this pleased
the Jews, he went ahead and had Peter
arrested. (This happened during the
time of the Festival of Unleavened
Bread.) 4 After his arrest Peter was put in
jail, where he was handed over to be
guarded by four groups of four soldiers
each. Herod planned to put him on trial
in public after Passover. 5 So Peter was
kept in jail, but the people of the church
were praying earnestly to God for him.

Peter Is Set Free from Prison

6 The night before Herod was going to
bring him out to the people, Peter was
sleeping between two guards. He was
tied with two chains, and there were
guards on duty at the prison gate. 7 Suddenly an angel of the Lord stood there,
and a light shone in the cell. The angel
shook Peter by the shoulder, woke him
up, and said, "Hurry! Get up!" At once
the chains fell off Peter's hands. 8 Then
the angel said, "Tighten your belt and
put on your sandals." Peter did so, and
the angel said, "Put your cloak around
you and come with me." 9 Peter followed
him out of the prison, not knowing, however, if what the angel was doing was
real; he thought he was seeing a vision.
10 They passed by the first guard station
and then the second, and came at last to
the iron gate that opens into the city. The
gate opened for them by itself, and they
went out. They walked down a street,
and suddenly the angel left Peter.
11 Then Peter realized what had happened to him, and said, "Now I know
that it is really true! The Lord sent his
angel to rescue me from Herod's power
and from everything the Jewish people
expected to happen."
12 Aware of his situation, he went to
the home of Mary, the mother of John
Mark, where many people had gathered
and were praying. 13 Peter knocked at
the outside door, and a servant named
Rhoda came to answer it. 14 She recognized Peter's voice and was so happy
that she ran back in without opening the
door, and announced that Peter was
standing outside. 15 "You are crazy!"
they told her. But she insisted that it was
true. So they answered, "It is his angel."
16 Meanwhile Peter kept on knocking.
At last they opened the door, and when
they saw him, they were amazed. 17 He
motioned with his hand for them to be
quiet, and he explained to them how the
Lord had brought him out of prison.

[o] Gentiles; *some manuscripts have* Greek-speaking Jews *or* Greek-speaking people.
[p] KING HEROD: *Herod Agrippa I, ruler of all Palestine.*

"Tell this to James and the rest of the
believers," he said; then he left and went
somewhere else.
18 When morning came, there was a
tremendous confusion among the
guards—what had happened to Peter?
19 Herod gave orders to search for him,
but they could not find him. So he had
the guards questioned and ordered them
put to death.
After this, Herod left Judea and spent
some time in Caesarea.

The Death of Herod

20 Herod was very angry with the people of Tyre and Sidon, so they went in a
group to see him. First they convinced
Blastus, the man in charge of the palace,
that he should help them. Then they
went to Herod and asked him for peace,
because their country got its food supplies from the king's country.
21 On a chosen day Herod put on his
royal robes, sat on his throne, and made
a speech to the people. 22 "It isn't a man
speaking, but a god!" they shouted. 23 At
once the angel of the Lord struck Herod
down, because he did not give honor to
God. He was eaten by worms and died.
24 Meanwhile the word of God continued to spread and grow.
25 Barnabas and Saul finished their
mission and returned from[q] Jerusalem,
taking John Mark with them.

Barnabas and Saul Are Chosen and Sent

13 In the church at Antioch there
were some prophets and teachers: Barnabas, Simeon (called the
Black), Lucius (from Cyrene), Manaen
(who had been brought up with Governor Herod[r]), and Saul. 2 While they
were serving the Lord and fasting, the
Holy Spirit said to them, "Set apart for
me Barnabas and Saul, to do the work to
which I have called them."
3 They fasted and prayed, placed their
hands on them, and sent them off.

In Cyprus

4 Having been sent by the Holy Spirit,
Barnabas and Saul went to Seleucia and
sailed from there to the island of Cyprus.
5 When they arrived at Salamis, they
preached the word of God in the synagogues. They had John Mark with them
to help in the work.
6 They went all the way across the island to Paphos, where they met a certain
magician named Bar-Jesus, a Jew who
claimed to be a prophet. 7 He was a
friend of the governor of the island, Ser-
gius Paulus, who was an intelligent man.
The governor called Barnabas and Saul
before him because he wanted to hear
the word of God. 8 But they were opposed by the magician Elymas (that is
his name in Greek), who tried to turn the
governor away from the faith. 9 Then
Saul—also known as Paul—was filled
with the Holy Spirit; he looked straight
at the magician 10 and said, "You son of
the Devil! You are the enemy of everything that is good. You are full of all
kinds of evil tricks, and you always keep
trying to turn the Lord's truths into lies!
11 The Lord's hand will come down on
you now; you will be blind and will not
see the light of day for a time."
At once Elymas felt a dark mist cover
his eyes, and he walked around trying to
find someone to lead him by the hand.
12 When the governor saw what had happened, he believed; for he was greatly
amazed at the teaching about the Lord.

In Antioch in Pisidia

13 Paul and his companions sailed
from Paphos and came to Perga, a city in
Pamphylia, where John Mark left them
and went back to Jerusalem. 14 They
went on from Perga and arrived in Antioch in Pisidia, and on the Sabbath they
went into the synagogue and sat down.
15 After the reading from the Law of
Moses and from the writings of the
prophets, the officials of the synagogue
sent them a message: "Friends, we want
you to speak to the people if you have a
message of encouragement for them."
16 Paul stood up, motioned with his hand,
and began to speak:
"Fellow Israelites and all Gentiles here
who worship God: hear me! 17 The God
of the people of Israel chose our ancestors and made the people a great nation
during the time they lived as foreigners
in Egypt. God brought them out of Egypt
by his great power, 18 and for forty years

[q] from; *some manuscripts have* to. [r] HEROD: *Herod Antipas, ruler of Galilee (see Lk 3.1).*

he endured[s] them in the desert. 19 He
destroyed seven nations in the land of
Canaan and made his people the owners
of the land. 20 All of this took about 450
years.

"After this[t] he gave them judges until
the time of the prophet Samuel. 21 And
when they asked for a king, God gave
them Saul son of Kish from the tribe of
Benjamin, to be their king for forty
years. 22 After removing him, God made
David their king. This is what God said
about him: 'I have found that David son
of Jesse is the kind of man I like, a man
who will do all I want him to do.' 23 It was
Jesus, a descendant of David, whom
God made the Savior of the people of
Israel, as he had promised. 24 Before
Jesus began his work, John preached to
all the people of Israel that they should
turn from their sins and be baptized.
25 And as John was about to finish his
mission, he said to the people, 'Who do
you think I am? I am not the one you are
waiting for. But listen! He is coming after me, and I am not good enough to take
his sandals off his feet.'

26 "My fellow Israelites, descendants of
Abraham, and all Gentiles here who
worship God: it is to us that this message
of salvation has been sent! 27 For the
people who live in Jerusalem and their
leaders did not know that he is the
Savior, nor did they understand the
words of the prophets that are read
every Sabbath. Yet they made the
prophets' words come true by condemning Jesus. 28 And even though they could
find no reason to pass the death sentence on him, they asked Pilate to have
him put to death. 29 And after they had
done everything that the Scriptures say
about him, they took him down from the
cross and placed him in a tomb. 30 But
God raised him from death, 31 and for
many days he appeared to those who
had traveled with him from Galilee to
Jerusalem. They are now witnesses for
him to the people of Israel. 32-33 And we
are here to bring the Good News to you:
what God promised our ancestors he
would do, he has now done for us, who
are their descendants, by raising Jesus
to life. As it is written in the second
Psalm,

'You are my Son;
today I have become your
Father.'

34 And this is what God said about raising him from death, never to rot away in
the grave:

'I will give you the sacred and
sure blessings
that I promised to David.'

35 As indeed he says in another passage,

'You will not allow your faithful
servant to rot in the grave.'

36 For David served God's purposes in
his own time, and then he died, was buried with his ancestors, and his body rotted in the grave. 37 But this did not
happen to the one whom God raised
from death. 38-39 All of you, my fellow Israelites, are to know for sure that it is
through Jesus that the message about
forgiveness of sins is preached to you;
you are to know that everyone who believes in him is set free from all the sins
from which the Law of Moses could not
set you free. 40 Take care, then, so that
what the prophets said may not happen
to you:[u]

41 'Look, you scoffers! Be astonished
and die!
For what I am doing today
is something that you will not
believe,
even when someone explains it
to you!' "

42 As Paul and Barnabas were leaving
the synagogue, the people invited them
to come back the next Sabbath and tell
them more about these things. 43 After
the people had left the meeting, Paul and
Barnabas were followed by many Jews
and by many Gentiles who had been
converted to Judaism. The apostles
spoke to them and encouraged them to
keep on living in the grace of God.

44 The next Sabbath nearly everyone
in the town came to hear the word of the
Lord. 45 When the Jews saw the crowds,
they were filled with jealousy; they disputed what Paul was saying and insulted
him. 46 But Paul and Barnabas spoke out
even more boldly: "It was necessary that
the word of God should be spoken first
to you. But since you reject it and do not
consider yourselves worthy of eternal
life, we will leave you and go to the

[s] he endured; *some manuscripts have* he took care of. [t] All of this took about 450 years. After this; *or* Some 450 years later. [u] *Some manuscripts do not have* to you.

Gentiles. 47For this is the commandment
that the Lord has given us:

'I have made you a light for the
Gentiles,
so that all the world may be
saved.' "

48When the Gentiles heard this, they
were glad and praised the Lord's message; and those who had been chosen
for eternal life became believers.

49The word of the Lord spread everywhere in that region. 50But the Jews
stirred up the leading men of the city
and the Gentile women of high social
standing who worshiped God. They
started a persecution against Paul and
Barnabas and threw them out of their
region. 51The apostles shook the dust off
their feet in protest against them and
went on to Iconium. 52The believers in
Antioch were full of joy and the Holy
Spirit.

In Iconium

14 The same thing happened in Iconium: Paul and Barnabas went
to the synagogue and spoke in such a
way that a great number of Jews and
Gentiles became believers. 2But the
Jews who would not believe stirred up
the Gentiles and turned them against the
believers. 3The apostles stayed there for
a long time, speaking boldly about the
Lord, who proved that their message
about his grace was true by giving them
the power to perform miracles and wonders. 4The people of the city were divided: some were for the Jews, others
for the apostles.

5Then some Gentiles and Jews, together with their leaders, decided to mistreat the apostles and stone them.
6When the apostles learned about it,
they fled to the cities of Lystra and
Derbe in Lycaonia and to the surrounding territory. 7There they preached the
Good News.

In Lystra and Derbe

8In Lystra there was a crippled man
who had been lame from birth and had
never been able to walk. 9He sat there
and listened to Paul's words. Paul saw
that he believed and could be healed, so
he looked straight at him 10and said in a
loud voice, "Stand up straight on your
feet!" The man jumped up and started
walking around. 11When the crowds
saw what Paul had done, they started
shouting in their own Lycaonian language, "The gods have become like men
and have come down to us!" 12They gave
Barnabas the name Zeus, and Paul the
name Hermes, because he was the chief
speaker. 13The priest of the god Zeus,
whose temple stood just outside the
town, brought bulls and flowers to the
gate, for he and the crowds wanted to
offer sacrifice to the apostles.

14When Barnabas and Paul heard
what they were about to do, they tore
their clothes and ran into the middle of
the crowd, shouting, 15"Why are you doing this? We ourselves are only human
beings like you! We are here to announce the Good News, to turn you
away from these worthless things to the
living God, who made heaven, earth,
sea, and all that is in them. 16In the past
he allowed all people to go their own
way. 17But he has always given evidence
of his existence by the good things he
does: he gives you rain from heaven and
crops at the right times; he gives you
food and fills your hearts with happiness." 18Even with these words the apostles could hardly keep the crowd from
offering a sacrifice to them.

19Some Jews came from Antioch in Pisidia and from Iconium; they won the
crowds over to their side, stoned Paul
and dragged him out of the town, thinking that he was dead. 20But when the believers gathered around him, he got up
and went back into the town. The next
day he and Barnabas went to Derbe.

The Return to Antioch in Syria

21Paul and Barnabas preached the
Good News in Derbe and won many disciples. Then they went back to Lystra, to
Iconium, and on to Antioch in Pisidia.
22They strengthened the believers and
encouraged them to remain true to the
faith. "We must pass through many troubles to enter the Kingdom of God," they
taught. 23In each church they appointed
elders, and with prayers and fasting
they commended them to the Lord, in
whom they had put their trust.

24After going through the territory of
Pisidia, they came to Pamphylia.
25There they preached the message in
Perga and then went to Attalia, 26and
from there they sailed back to Antioch,
the place where they had been com-

mended to the care of God's grace for
the work they had now completed.
27 When they arrived in Antioch, they
gathered the people of the church together and told them about all that God
had done with them and how he had
opened the way for the Gentiles to believe. 28 And they stayed a long time
there with the believers.

The Meeting at Jerusalem

15 Some men came from Judea to
Antioch and started teaching the
believers, "You cannot be saved unless
you are circumcised as the Law of
Moses requires." 2 Paul and Barnabas
got into a fierce argument with them
about this, so it was decided that Paul
and Barnabas and some of the others in
Antioch should go to Jerusalem and see
the apostles and elders about this
matter.
3 They were sent on their way by the
church; and as they went through Phoenicia and Samaria, they reported how
the Gentiles had turned to God; this
news brought great joy to all the believers. 4 When they arrived in Jerusalem,
they were welcomed by the church, the
apostles, and the elders, to whom they
told all that God had done through them.
5 But some of the believers who belonged
to the party of the Pharisees stood up
and said, "The Gentiles must be circumcised and told to obey the Law of
Moses."
6 The apostles and the elders met together to consider this question. 7 After a
long debate Peter stood up and said, "My
friends, you know that a long time ago
God chose me from among you to
preach the Good News to the Gentiles,
so that they could hear and believe.
8 And God, who knows the thoughts of
everyone, showed his approval of the
Gentiles by giving the Holy Spirit to
them, just as he had to us. 9 He made no
difference between us and them; he forgave their sins because they believed.
10 So then, why do you now want to put
God to the test by laying a load on the
backs of the believers which neither our
ancestors nor we ourselves were able to
carry? 11 No! We believe and are saved
by the grace of the Lord Jesus, just as
they are."
12 The whole group was silent as they
heard Barnabas and Paul report all the
miracles and wonders that God had performed through them among the Gentiles. 13 When they had finished
speaking, James spoke up: "Listen to
me, my friends! 14 Simon has just explained how God first showed his care
for the Gentiles by taking from among
them a people to belong to him. 15 The
words of the prophets agree completely
with this. As the scripture says,

16 'After this I will return, says the
Lord,
and restore the kingdom of
David.
I will rebuild its ruins
and make it strong again.
17 And so all the rest of the human
race will come to me,
all the Gentiles whom I have
called to be my own.
18 So says the Lord, who made this
known long ago.'

19 "It is my opinion," James went on,
"that we should not trouble the Gentiles
who are turning to God. 20 Instead, we
should write a letter telling them not to
eat any food that is ritually unclean because it has been offered to idols; to
keep themselves from sexual immorality; and not to eat any animal that has
been strangled, or any blood. 21 For the
Law of Moses has been read for a very
long time in the synagogues every Sabbath, and his words are preached in
every town."

The Letter to the Gentile Believers

22 Then the apostles and the elders, together with the whole church, decided to
choose some men from the group and
send them to Antioch with Paul and Barnabas. They chose two men who were
highly respected by the believers, Judas,
called Barsabbas, and Silas, 23 and they
sent the following letter by them:

"We, the apostles and the elders,
your brothers, send greetings to all
our brothers of Gentile birth who live
in Antioch, Syria, and Cilicia. 24 We
have heard that some who went from
our group have troubled and upset
you by what they said; they had not,
however, received any instruction
from us. 25 And so we have met together and have all agreed to choose
some messengers and send them to
you. They will go with our dear friends
Barnabas and Paul, 26 who have risked

their lives in the service of our Lord
Jesus Christ. 27 We send you, then, Judas and Silas, who will tell you in person the same things we are writing.
28 The Holy Spirit and we have agreed
not to put any other burden on you besides these necessary rules: 29 eat no
food that has been offered to idols; eat
no blood; eat no animal that has been
strangled; and keep yourselves from
sexual immorality. You will do well if
you take care not to do these things.
With our best wishes."

30 The messengers were sent off and
went to Antioch, where they gathered
the whole group of believers and gave
them the letter. 31 When the people read
it, they were filled with joy by the message of encouragement. 32 Judas and Silas, who were themselves prophets,
spoke a long time with them, giving
them courage and strength. 33 After
spending some time there, they were
sent off in peace by the believers and
went back to those who had sent them.[v]
35 Paul and Barnabas spent some time
in Antioch, and together with many others they taught and preached the word
of the Lord.

Paul and Barnabas Separate

36 Some time later Paul said to Barnabas, "Let us go back and visit the believers in every town where we preached
the word of the Lord, and let us find out
how they are getting along." 37 Barnabas
wanted to take John Mark with them,
38 but Paul did not think it was right to
take him, because he had not stayed
with them to the end of their mission,
but had turned back and left them in
Pamphylia. 39 There was a sharp argument, and they separated: Barnabas
took Mark and sailed off for Cyprus,
40 while Paul chose Silas and left, commended by the believers to the care of
the Lord's grace. 41 He went through
Syria and Cilicia, strengthening the
churches.

Timothy Goes with Paul and Silas

16 Paul traveled on to Derbe and
Lystra, where a Christian named
Timothy lived. His mother, who was also
a Christian, was Jewish, but his father
was a Greek. 2 All the believers in Lystra
and Iconium spoke well of Timothy.
3 Paul wanted to take Timothy along
with him, so he circumcised him. He did
so because all the Jews who lived in
those places knew that Timothy's father
was Greek. 4 As they went through the
towns, they delivered to the believers
the rules decided upon by the apostles
and elders in Jerusalem, and they told
them to obey those rules. 5 So the
churches were made stronger in the
faith and grew in numbers every day.

In Troas: Paul's Vision

6 They traveled through the region of
Phrygia and Galatia because the Holy
Spirit did not let them preach the message in the province of Asia. 7 When they
reached the border of Mysia, they tried
to go into the province of Bithynia, but
the Spirit of Jesus did not allow them.
8 So they traveled right on through[w]
Mysia and went to Troas. 9 That night
Paul had a vision in which he saw a
Macedonian standing and begging him,
"Come over to Macedonia and help us!"
10 As soon as Paul had this vision, we got
ready to leave for Macedonia, because
we decided that God had called us to
preach the Good News to the people
there.

In Philippi: the Conversion of Lydia

11 We left by ship from Troas and
sailed straight across to Samothrace,
and the next day to Neapolis. 12 From
there we went inland to Philippi, a city
of the first district of Macedonia;[x] it is
also a Roman colony. We spent several
days there. 13 On the Sabbath we went
out of the city to the riverside, where we
thought there would be a place where
Jews gathered for prayer. We sat down
and talked to the women who gathered
there. 14 One of those who heard us was
Lydia from Thyatira, who was a dealer
in purple cloth. She was a woman who
worshiped God, and the Lord opened
her mind to pay attention to what Paul
was saying. 15 After she and the people
of her house had been baptized, she invited us, "Come and stay in my house if
you have decided that I am a true be-

[v] *Some manuscripts add verse 34:* But Silas decided to stay there. [w] traveled right on through; *or* passed by. [x] a city of the first district of Macedonia; *some manuscripts have* a leading city of the district of Macedonia, *or* a leading city of that district in Macedonia.

liever in the Lord." And she persuaded
us to go.

In Prison at Philippi

16 One day as we were going to the
place of prayer, we were met by a young
servant woman who had an evil spirit
that enabled her to predict the future.
She earned a lot of money for her owners by telling fortunes. 17 She followed
Paul and us, shouting, "These men are
servants of the Most High God! They announce to you how you can be saved!"
18 She did this for many days, until Paul
became so upset that he turned around
and said to the spirit, "In the name of
Jesus Christ I order you to come out of
her!" The spirit went out of her that very
moment. 19 When her owners realized
that their chance of making money was
gone, they seized Paul and Silas and
dragged them to the authorities in the
public square. 20 They brought them before the Roman officials and said,
"These men are Jews, and they are causing trouble in our city. 21 They are teaching customs that are against our law; we
are Roman citizens, and we cannot accept these customs or practice them."
22 And the crowd joined in the attack
against Paul and Silas.

Then the officials tore the clothes off
Paul and Silas and ordered them to be
whipped. 23 After a severe beating, they
were thrown into jail, and the jailer was
ordered to lock them up tight. 24 Upon
receiving this order, the jailer threw
them into the inner cell and fastened
their feet between heavy blocks of wood.

25 About midnight Paul and Silas were
praying and singing hymns to God, and
the other prisoners were listening to
them. 26 Suddenly there was a violent
earthquake, which shook the prison to
its foundations. At once all the doors
opened, and the chains fell off all the
prisoners. 27 The jailer woke up, and
when he saw the prison doors open, he
thought that the prisoners had escaped;
so he pulled out his sword and was
about to kill himself. 28 But Paul shouted
at the top of his voice, "Don't harm yourself! We are all here!"

29 The jailer called for a light, rushed
in, and fell trembling at the feet of Paul
and Silas. 30 Then he led them out and
asked, "Sirs, what must I do to be
saved?"

31 They answered, "Believe in the Lord
Jesus, and you will be saved—you and
your family." 32 Then they preached the
word of the Lord to him and to all the
others in the house. 33 At that very hour
of the night the jailer took them and
washed their wounds; and he and all his
family were baptized at once. 34 Then he
took Paul and Silas up into his house
and gave them some food to eat. He and
his family were filled with joy, because
they now believed in God.

35 The next morning the Roman authorities sent police officers with the order, "Let those men go."

36 So the jailer told Paul, "The officials
have sent an order for you and Silas to
be released. You may leave, then, and go
in peace."

37 But Paul said to the police officers,
"We were not found guilty of any crime,
yet they whipped us in public—and we
are Roman citizens! Then they threw us
in prison. And now they want to send us
away secretly? Not at all! The Roman
officials themselves must come here and
let us out."

38 The police officers reported these
words to the Roman officials; and when
they heard that Paul and Silas were Roman citizens, they were afraid. 39 So they
went and apologized to them; then they
led them out of the prison and asked
them to leave the city. 40 Paul and Silas
left the prison and went to Lydia's
house. There they met the believers,
spoke words of encouragement to them,
and left.

In Thessalonica

17 Paul and Silas traveled on
through Amphipolis and Apollo-
nia and came to Thessalonica, where
there was a synagogue. 2 According to
his usual habit Paul went to the synagogue. There during three Sabbaths he
held discussions with the people, quoting 3 and explaining the Scriptures, and
proving from them that the Messiah had
to suffer and rise from death. "This Jesus
whom I announce to you," Paul said, "is
the Messiah." 4 Some of them were convinced and joined Paul and Silas; so did
many of the leading women and a large
group of Greeks who worshiped God.

5 But some Jews were jealous and
gathered worthless loafers from the
streets and formed a mob. They set the

whole city in an uproar and attacked the
home of a man named Jason, in an attempt to find Paul and Silas and bring
them out to the people. 6 But when they
did not find them, they dragged Jason
and some other believers before the city
authorities and shouted, "These men
have caused trouble everywhere! Now
they have come to our city, 7 and Jason
has kept them in his house. They are all
breaking the laws of the Emperor, saying that there is another king, whose
name is Jesus." 8 With these words they
threw the crowd and the city authorities
in an uproar. 9 The authorities made Jason and the others pay the required
amount of money to be released, and
then let them go.

In Berea

10 As soon as night came, the believers
sent Paul and Silas to Berea. When they
arrived, they went to the synagogue.
11 The people there were more open-
minded than the people in Thessalonica.
They listened to the message with great
eagerness, and every day they studied
the Scriptures to see if what Paul said
was really true. 12 Many of them believed; and many Greek women of high
social standing and many Greek men
also believed. 13 But when the Jews in
Thessalonica heard that Paul had
preached the word of God in Berea also,
they came there and started exciting and
stirring up the mobs. 14 At once the believers sent Paul away to the coast; but
both Silas and Timothy stayed in Berea.
15 The men who were taking Paul went
with him as far as Athens and then returned to Berea with instructions from
Paul that Silas and Timothy should join
him as soon as possible.

In Athens

16 While Paul was waiting in Athens
for Silas and Timothy, he was greatly
upset when he noticed how full of idols
the city was. 17 So he held discussions in
the synagogue with the Jews and with
the Gentiles who worshiped God, and
also in the public square every day with
the people who happened to come by.
18 Certain Epicurean and Stoic teachers
also debated with him. Some of them
asked, "What is this ignorant show-off
trying to say?"

Others answered, "He seems to be
talking about foreign gods." They said
this because Paul was preaching about
Jesus and the resurrection.[y] 19 So they
took Paul, brought him before the city
council, the Areopagus, and said, "We
would like to know what this new teaching is that you are talking about. 20 Some
of the things we hear you say sound
strange to us, and we would like to know
what they mean." (21 For all the citizens
of Athens and the foreigners who lived
there liked to spend all their time telling
and hearing the latest new thing.)

22 Paul stood up in front of the city
council and said, "I see that in every way
you Athenians are very religious. 23 For
as I walked through your city and
looked at the places where you worship,
I found an altar on which is written, 'To
an Unknown God.' That which you worship, then, even though you do not know
it, is what I now proclaim to you. 24 God,
who made the world and everything in
it, is Lord of heaven and earth and does
not live in temples made by human
hands. 25 Nor does he need anything that
we can supply by working for him, since
it is he himself who gives life and breath
and everything else to everyone. 26 From
one human being he created all races of
people and made them live throughout
the whole earth. He himself fixed
beforehand the exact times and the limits of the places where they would live.
27 He did this so that they would look for
him, and perhaps find him as they felt
around for him. Yet God is actually not
far from any one of us; 28 as someone has
said,

'In him we live and move and
exist.'

It is as some of your poets have said,

'We too are his children.'

29 Since we are God's children, we
should not suppose that his nature is
anything like an image of gold or silver
or stone, shaped by human art and skill.
30 God has overlooked the times when
people did not know him, but now he
commands all of them everywhere to
turn away from their evil ways. 31 For he
has fixed a day in which he will judge

[y] JESUS AND THE RESURRECTION: *In Greek, the feminine noun "resurrection" could be understood to be the name of a goddess.*

the whole world with justice by means of
a man he has chosen. He has given proof
of this to everyone by raising that man
from death!"
32 When they heard Paul speak about a
raising from death, some of them made
fun of him, but others said, "We want to
hear you speak about this again." 33 And
so Paul left the meeting. 34 Some men
joined him and believed, among whom
was Dionysius, a member of the council;
there was also a woman named Dama-
ris, and some other people.

In Corinth

18 After this, Paul left Athens and
went on to Corinth. 2 There he
met a Jew named Aquila, born in Pontus, who had recently come from Italy
with his wife Priscilla, for Emperor
Claudius had ordered all the Jews to
leave Rome. Paul went to see them, 3 and
stayed and worked with them, because
he earned his living by making tents,
just as they did. 4 He held discussions in
the synagogue every Sabbath, trying to
convince both Jews and Greeks.
5 When Silas and Timothy arrived
from Macedonia, Paul gave his whole
time to preaching the message, testifying to the Jews that Jesus is the Messiah.
6 When they opposed him and said evil
things about him, he protested by shaking the dust from his clothes and saying
to them, "If you are lost, you yourselves
must take the blame for it! I am not responsible. From now on I will go to the
Gentiles." 7 So he left them and went to
live in the house of a Gentile named Ti-
tius Justus, who worshiped God; his
house was next to the synagogue. 8 Crispus, who was the leader of the synagogue, believed in the Lord, together
with all his family; and many other people in Corinth heard the message, believed, and were baptized.
9 One night Paul had a vision in which
the Lord said to him, "Do not be afraid,
but keep on speaking and do not give up,
10 for I am with you. No one will be able
to harm you, for many in this city are my
people." 11 So Paul stayed there for a
year and a half, teaching the people the
word of God.
12 When Gallio was made the Roman
governor of Achaia, Jews there got together, seized Paul, and took him into
court. 13 "This man," they said, "is trying
to persuade people to worship God in a
way that is against the law!"
14 Paul was about to speak when Gallio
said to the Jews, "If this were a matter of
some evil crime or wrong that has been
committed, it would be reasonable for
me to be patient with you Jews. 15 But
since it is an argument about words and
names and your own law, you yourselves must settle it. I will not be the
judge of such things!" 16 And he drove
them out of the court. 17 They all grabbed
Sosthenes, the leader of the synagogue,
and beat him in front of the court. But
that did not bother Gallio a bit.

The Return to Antioch

18 Paul stayed on with the believers in
Corinth for many days, then left them
and sailed off with Priscilla and Aquila
for Syria. Before sailing from Cenchreae
he had his head shaved because of a vow
he had taken.[z] 19 They arrived in Ephesus, where Paul left Priscilla and Aquila.
He went into the synagogue and held
discussions with the Jews. 20 The people
asked him to stay longer, but he would
not consent. 21 Instead, he told them as
he left, "If it is the will of God, I will
come back to you." And so he sailed
from Ephesus.
22 When he arrived at Caesarea, he
went to Jerusalem and greeted the
church, and then went to Antioch. 23 After spending some time there, he left and
went through the region of Galatia and
Phrygia, strengthening all the believers.

Apollos in Ephesus and Corinth

24 At that time a Jew named Apollos,
who had been born in Alexandria, came
to Ephesus. He was an eloquent speaker
and had a thorough knowledge of the
Scriptures. 25 He had been instructed in
the Way of the Lord, and with great enthusiasm he proclaimed and taught correctly the facts about Jesus. However, he
knew only the baptism of John. 26 He began to speak boldly in the synagogue.
When Priscilla and Aquila heard him,
they took him home with them and explained to him more correctly the Way
of God. 27 Apollos then decided to go to

[z] A VOW HE HAD TAKEN: *This refers to the Jewish custom of shaving the head as a sign that a vow has been kept.*

Achaia, so the believers in Ephesus
helped him by writing to the believers in
Achaia, urging them to welcome him.
When he arrived, he was a great help to
those who through God's grace had become believers. 28 For with his strong arguments he defeated the Jews in public
debates by proving from the Scriptures
that Jesus is the Messiah.

Paul in Ephesus

19 While Apollos was in Corinth,
Paul traveled through the interior of the province and arrived in Ephesus. There he found some disciples 2 and
asked them, "Did you receive the Holy
Spirit when you became believers?"
"We have not even heard that there is
a Holy Spirit," they answered.
3 "Well, then, what kind of baptism did
you receive?" Paul asked.
"The baptism of John," they answered.
4 Paul said, "The baptism of John was
for those who turned from their sins;
and he told the people of Israel to believe
in the one who was coming after him—
that is, in Jesus."
5 When they heard this, they were baptized in the name of the Lord Jesus.
6 Paul placed his hands on them, and the
Holy Spirit came upon them; they spoke
in strange tongues and also proclaimed
God's message. 7 They were about
twelve men in all.
8 Paul went into the synagogue and for
three months spoke boldly with the people, holding discussions with them and
trying to convince them about the Kingdom of God. 9 But some of them were
stubborn and would not believe, and before the whole group they said evil
things about the Way of the Lord. So
Paul left them and took the believers
with him, and every day[a] he held discussions in the lecture hall of Tyrannus.
10 This went on for two years, so that all
the people who lived in the province of
Asia, both Jews and Gentiles, heard the
word of the Lord.

The Sons of Sceva

11 God was performing unusual miracles through Paul. 12 Even handkerchiefs
and aprons he had used were taken to
the sick, and their diseases were driven
away, and the evil spirits would go out of
them. 13 Some Jews who traveled around
and drove out evil spirits also tried to
use the name of the Lord Jesus to do
this. They said to the evil spirits, "I command you in the name of Jesus, whom
Paul preaches." 14 Seven brothers, who
were the sons of a Jewish High Priest
named Sceva, were doing this.
15 But the evil spirit said to them, "I
know Jesus, and I know about Paul; but
you—who are you?"
16 The man who had the evil spirit in
him attacked them with such violence
that he overpowered them all. They ran
away from his house, wounded and with
their clothes torn off. 17 All the Jews and
Gentiles who lived in Ephesus heard
about this; they were all filled with fear,
and the name of the Lord Jesus was
given greater honor. 18 Many of the believers came, publicly admitting and revealing what they had done. 19 Many of
those who had practiced magic brought
their books together and burned them in
public. They added up the price of the
books, and the total came to fifty thousand silver coins.[b] 20 In this powerful
way the word of the Lord[c] kept spreading and growing stronger.

The Riot in Ephesus

21 After these things had happened,
Paul made up his mind[d] to travel
through Macedonia and Achaia and go
on to Jerusalem. "After I go there," he
said, "I must also see Rome." 22 So he
sent Timothy and Erastus, two of his
helpers, to Macedonia, while he spent
more time in the province of Asia.
23 It was at this time that there was serious trouble in Ephesus because of the
Way of the Lord. 24 A certain silversmith
named Demetrius made silver models of
the temple of the goddess Artemis, and
his business brought a great deal of
profit to the workers. 25 So he called
them all together with others whose
work was like theirs and said to them,
"Men, you know that our prosperity
comes from this work. 26 Now, you can
see and hear for yourselves what this
fellow Paul is doing. He says that hand-
made gods are not gods at all, and he has
succeeded in convincing many people,

[a] *Some manuscripts add* from 11:00 a.m. until 4:00 p.m. [b] SILVER COINS: *A silver coin was the daily wage of a rural worker (see Mt 20.2).* [c] In this . . . Lord; *or* And so, by the power of the Lord, the message. [d] Paul made up his mind; *or* Paul, led by the Spirit, decided.

both here in Ephesus and in nearly the
whole province of Asia. 27There is the
danger, then, that this business of ours
will get a bad name. Not only that, but
there is also the danger that the temple
of the great goddess Artemis will come
to mean nothing and that her greatness
will be destroyed—the goddess worshiped by everyone in Asia and in all the
world!"
28As the crowd heard these words,
they became furious and started shouting, "Great is Artemis of Ephesus!"
29The uproar spread throughout the
whole city. The mob grabbed Gaius and
Aristarchus, two Macedonians who
were traveling with Paul, and rushed
with them to the theater. 30Paul himself
wanted to go before the crowd, but the
believers would not let him. 31Some of
the provincial authorities, who were his
friends, also sent him a message begging
him not to show himself in the theater.
32Meanwhile the whole meeting was in
an uproar: some people were shouting
one thing, others were shouting something else, because most of them did not
even know why they had come together.
33Some of the people concluded that Alexander was responsible, since the Jews
made him go up to the front. Then Alexander motioned with his hand for the
people to be silent, and he tried to make
a speech of defense. 34But when they
recognized that he was a Jew, they all
shouted together the same thing for two
hours: "Great is Artemis of Ephesus!"
35At last the city clerk was able to
calm the crowd. "Fellow Ephesians!" he
said. "Everyone knows that the city of
Ephesus is the keeper of the temple of
the great Artemis and of the sacred
stone that fell down from heaven. 36No-
body can deny these things. So then, you
must calm down and not do anything
reckless. 37You have brought these men
here even though they have not robbed
temples or said evil things about our
goddess. 38If Demetrius and his workers
have an accusation against anyone, we
have the authorities and the regular
days for court; charges can be made
there. 39But if there is something more
that you want, it will have to be settled in
a legal meeting of citizens. 40For after
what has happened today, there is the
danger that we will be accused of a riot.
There is no excuse for all this uproar,
and we would not be able to give a good
reason for it." 41After saying this, he dismissed the meeting.

To Macedonia and Achaia

20 After the uproar died down, Paul
called together the believers and
with words of encouragement said good-
bye to them. Then he left and went on to
Macedonia. 2He went through those regions and encouraged the people with
many messages. Then he came to
Achaia, 3where he stayed three months.
He was getting ready to go to Syria
when he discovered that there were
Jews plotting against him; so he decided
to go back through Macedonia. 4Sopater
son of Pyrrhus, from Berea, went with
him; so did Aristarchus and Secundus,
from Thessalonica; Gaius, from Derbe;
Tychicus and Trophimus, from the province of Asia; and Timothy. 5They went
ahead and waited for us in Troas. 6We
sailed from Philippi after the Festival of
Unleavened Bread, and five days later
we joined them in Troas, where we spent
a week.

Paul's Last Visit to Troas

7On Saturday[e] evening we gathered
together for the fellowship meal. Paul
spoke to the people and kept on speaking until midnight, since he was going to
leave the next day. 8Many lamps were
burning in the upstairs room where we
were meeting. 9A young man named
Eutychus was sitting in the window, and
as Paul kept on talking, Eutychus got
sleepier and sleepier, until he finally
went sound asleep and fell from the
third story to the ground. When they
picked him up, he was dead. 10But Paul
went down and threw himself on him
and hugged him. "Don't worry," he said,
"he is still alive!" 11Then he went back
upstairs, broke bread, and ate. After
talking with them for a long time, even
until sunrise, Paul left. 12They took the
young man home alive and were greatly
comforted.

From Troas to Miletus

13We went on ahead to the ship and
sailed off to Assos, where we were going

[e] Saturday; *or* Sunday.

to take Paul aboard. He had told us to do
this, because he was going there by land.
14 When he met us in Assos, we took him
aboard and went on to Mitylene. 15 We
sailed from there and arrived off Chios
the next day. A day later we came to Samos, and the following day we reached
Miletus. 16 Paul had decided to sail on by
Ephesus, so as not to lose any time in the
province of Asia. He was in a hurry to
arrive in Jerusalem by the day of Pentecost, if at all possible.

Paul's Farewell Speech to the Elders of Ephesus

17 From Miletus Paul sent a message to
Ephesus, asking the elders of the church
to meet him. 18 When they arrived, he
said to them, "You know how I spent the
whole time I was with you, from the first
day I arrived in the province of Asia.
19 With all humility and many tears I did
my work as the Lord's servant during
the hard times that came to me because
of the plots of some Jews. 20 You know
that I did not hold back anything that
would be of help to you as I preached
and taught in public and in your homes.
21 To Jews and Gentiles alike I gave solemn warning that they should turn from
their sins to God and believe in our Lord
Jesus. 22 And now, in obedience to the
Holy Spirit I am going to Jerusalem, not
knowing what will happen to me there.
23 I only know that in every city the Holy
Spirit has warned me that prison and
troubles wait for me. 24 But I reckon my
own life to be worth nothing to me; I
only want to complete my mission and
finish the work that the Lord Jesus gave
me to do, which is to declare the Good
News about the grace of God.

25 "I have gone about among all of you,
preaching the Kingdom of God. And
now I know that none of you will ever
see me again. 26 So I solemnly declare to
you this very day: if any of you should
be lost, I am not responsible. 27 For I
have not held back from announcing to
you the whole purpose of God. 28 So
keep watch over yourselves and over all
the flock which the Holy Spirit has
placed in your care. Be shepherds of the
church of God,[f] which he made his own
through the blood of his Son.[g] 29 I know
that after I leave, fierce wolves will come
among you, and they will not spare the
flock. 30 The time will come when some
men from your own group will tell lies to
lead the believers away after them.
31 Watch, then, and remember that with
many tears, day and night, I taught
every one of you for three years.

32 "And now I commend you to the
care of God and to the message of his
grace, which is able to build you up and
give you the blessings God has for all his
people. 33 I have not wanted anyone's
silver or gold or clothing. 34 You yourselves know that I have worked with
these hands of mine to provide everything that my companions and I have
needed. 35 I have shown you in all things
that by working hard in this way we
must help the weak, remembering the
words that the Lord Jesus himself said,
'There is more happiness in giving than
in receiving.'"

36 When Paul finished, he knelt down
with them and prayed. 37 They were all
crying as they hugged him and kissed
him good-bye. 38 They were especially
sad because he had said that they would
never see him again. And so they went
with him to the ship.

Paul Goes to Jerusalem

21 We said good-bye to them and
left. After sailing straight across,
we came to Cos; the next day we
reached Rhodes, and from there we
went on to Patara. 2 There we found a
ship that was going to Phoenicia, so we
went aboard and sailed away. 3 We came
to where we could see Cyprus, and then
sailed south of it on to Syria. We went
ashore at Tyre, where the ship was going to unload its cargo. 4 There we found
some believers and stayed with them a
week. By the power of the Spirit they
told Paul not to go to Jerusalem. 5 But
when our time with them was over, we
left and went on our way. All of them,
together with their wives and children,
went with us out of the city to the beach,
where we all knelt and prayed. 6 Then
we said good-bye to one another, and we
went on board the ship while they went
back home.

7 We continued our voyage, sailing

[f] God; *some manuscripts have* the Lord. [g] through the blood of his Son; *or* through the sacrificial death of his Son; *or* through his own blood.

from Tyre to Ptolemais, where we
greeted the believers and stayed with
them for a day. 8 On the following day
we left and arrived in Caesarea. There
we stayed at the house of Philip the
evangelist, one of the seven men who
had been chosen as helpers in Jerusalem. 9 He had four unmarried daughters
who proclaimed God's message. 10 We
had been there for several days when a
prophet named Agabus arrived from Judea. 11 He came to us, took Paul's belt,
tied up his own feet and hands with it,
and said, "This is what the Holy Spirit
says: The owner of this belt will be tied
up in this way by the Jews in Jerusalem,
and they will hand him over to the
Gentiles."
12 When we heard this, we and the others there begged Paul not to go to Jerusalem. 13 But he answered, "What are
you doing, crying like this and breaking
my heart? I am ready not only to be tied
up in Jerusalem but even to die there for
the sake of the Lord Jesus."
14 We could not convince him, so we
gave up and said, "May the Lord's will
be done."
15 After spending some time there, we
got our things ready and left for Jerusalem. 16 Some of the disciples from Caesarea also went with us and took us to
the house of the man we were going
to stay with[h]—Mnason, from Cyprus,
who had been a believer since the early
days.

Paul Visits James

17 When we arrived in Jerusalem, the
believers welcomed us warmly. 18 The
next day Paul went with us to see James;
and all the church elders were present.
19 Paul greeted them and gave a complete report of everything that God had
done among the Gentiles through his
work. 20 After hearing him, they all
praised God. Then they said, "Brother
Paul, you can see how many thousands
of Jews have become believers, and how
devoted they all are to the Law. 21 They
have been told that you have been teaching all the Jews who live in Gentile countries to abandon the Law of Moses,
telling them not to circumcise their children or follow the Jewish customs.
22 They are sure to hear that you have
arrived. What should be done, then?
23 This is what we want you to do. There
are four men here who have taken a
vow. 24 Go along with them and join
them in the ceremony of purification
and pay their expenses; then they will be
able to shave their heads.[i] In this way
everyone will know that there is no truth
in any of the things that they have been
told about you, but that you yourself live
in accordance with the Law of Moses.
25 But as for the Gentiles who have become believers, we have sent them a letter telling them we decided that they
must not eat any food that has been offered to idols, or any blood, or any animal that has been strangled, and that
they must keep themselves from sexual
immorality."
26 So Paul took the men and the next
day performed the ceremony of purification with them. Then he went into the
Temple and gave notice of how many
days it would be until the end of the period of purification, when a sacrifice
would be offered for each one of them.

Paul Is Arrested in the Temple

27 But just when the seven days were
about to come to an end, some Jews
from the province of Asia saw Paul in
the Temple. They stirred up the whole
crowd and grabbed Paul. 28 "People of Israel!" they shouted. "Help! This is the
man who goes everywhere teaching
everyone against the people of Israel,
the Law of Moses, and this Temple. And
now he has even brought some Gentiles
into the Temple and defiled this holy
place!" (29 They said this because they
had seen Trophimus from Ephesus with
Paul in the city, and they thought that
Paul had taken him into the Temple.)
30 Confusion spread through the whole
city, and the people all ran together,
grabbed Paul, and dragged him out of
the Temple. At once the Temple doors
were closed. 31 The mob was trying to
kill Paul, when a report was sent up to
the commander of the Roman troops
that all of Jerusalem was rioting. 32 At
once the commander took some officers

[h] and took us to the house of the man we were going to stay with; *or* bringing with them the man at whose house we were going to stay. [i] SHAVE THEIR HEADS: *See* 18.18.

and soldiers and rushed down to the
crowd. When the people saw him with
the soldiers, they stopped beating Paul.
33 The commander went over to Paul, arrested him, and ordered him to be bound
with two chains. Then he asked, "Who
is this man, and what has he done?"
34 Some in the crowd shouted one thing,
others something else. There was such
confusion that the commander could not
find out exactly what had happened, so
he ordered his men to take Paul up into
the fort. 35 They got as far as the steps
with him, and then the soldiers had to
carry him because the mob was so wild.
36 They were all coming after him and
screaming, "Kill him!"

Paul Defends Himself

37 As the soldiers were about to take
Paul into the fort, he spoke to the commander: "May I say something to you?"

"You speak Greek, do you?" the commander asked. 38 "Then you are not that
Egyptian fellow who some time ago
started a revolution and led four thousand armed terrorists out into the
desert?"

39 Paul answered, "I am a Jew, born in
Tarsus in Cilicia, a citizen of an important city. Please let me speak to the
people."

40 The commander gave him permission, so Paul stood on the steps and motioned with his hand for the people to be
silent. When they were quiet, Paul spoke
to them in Hebrew:

22 "My fellow Jews, listen to me as
I make my defense before you!"
2 When they heard him speaking to them
in Hebrew, they became even quieter;
and Paul went on:

3 "I am a Jew, born in Tarsus in Cilicia,
but brought up here in Jerusalem as a
student of Gamaliel. I received strict instruction in the Law of our ancestors
and was just as dedicated to God as are
all of you who are here today. 4 I persecuted to the death the people who followed this Way. I arrested men and
women and threw them into prison.
5 The High Priest and the whole Council
can prove that I am telling the truth.
I received from them letters written
to fellow Jews in Damascus, so I went
there to arrest these people and bring
them back in chains to Jerusalem to be
punished.

Paul Tells of His Conversion

(Acts 9.1-19; 26.12-18)

6 "As I was traveling and coming near
Damascus, about midday a bright light
from the sky flashed suddenly around
me. 7 I fell to the ground and heard a
voice saying to me, 'Saul, Saul! Why do
you persecute me?' 8 'Who are you,
Lord?' I asked. 'I am Jesus of Nazareth,
whom you persecute,' he said to me.
9 The men with me saw the light, but did
not hear the voice of the one who was
speaking to me. 10 I asked, 'What shall I
do, Lord?' and the Lord said to me, 'Get
up and go into Damascus, and there you
will be told everything that God has determined for you to do.' 11 I was blind because of the bright light, and so my
companions took me by the hand and
led me into Damascus.

12 "In that city was a man named Ananias, a religious man who obeyed our
Law and was highly respected by all the
Jews living there. 13 He came to me,
stood by me, and said, 'Brother Saul, see
again!' At that very moment I saw again
and looked at him. 14 He said, 'The God
of our ancestors has chosen you to know
his will, to see his righteous Servant, and
to hear him speaking with his own voice.
15 For you will be a witness for him to tell
everyone what you have seen and heard.
16 And now, why wait any longer? Get up
and be baptized and have your sins
washed away by praying to him.'

Paul's Call to Preach to the Gentiles

17 "I went back to Jerusalem, and while
I was praying in the Temple, I had a vision, 18 in which I saw the Lord, as he
said to me, 'Hurry and leave Jerusalem
quickly, because the people here will not
accept your witness about me.' 19 'Lord,'
I answered, 'they know very well that I
went to the synagogues and arrested
and beat those who believe in you.
20 And when your witness Stephen was
put to death, I myself was there, approv-
ing of his murder and taking care of the
cloaks of his murderers.' 21 'Go,' the
Lord said to me, 'for I will send you far
away to the Gentiles.'"

22 The people listened to Paul until he
said this; but then they started shouting
at the top of their voices, "Away with
him! Kill him! He's not fit to live!"
23 They were screaming, waving their

clothes, and throwing dust up in the air.
24 The Roman commander ordered his
men to take Paul into the fort, and he
told them to whip him in order to find
out why the Jews were screaming like
this against him. 25 But when they had
tied him up to be whipped, Paul said to
the officer standing there, "Is it lawful
for you to whip a Roman citizen who
hasn't even been tried for any crime?"
26 When the officer heard this, he went
to the commander and asked him,
"What are you doing? That man is a Roman citizen!"
27 So the commander went to Paul and
asked him, "Tell me, are you a Roman
citizen?"
"Yes," answered Paul.
28 The commander said, "I became one
by paying a large amount of money."
"But I am one by birth," Paul
answered.
29 At once the men who were going to
question Paul drew back from him; and
the commander was frightened when he
realized that Paul was a Roman citizen
and that he had put him in chains.

Paul before the Council

30 The commander wanted to find out
for sure what the Jews were accusing
Paul of; so the next day he had Paul's
chains taken off and ordered the chief
priests and the whole Council to meet.
Then he took Paul and made him stand
before them.

23

Paul looked straight at the Council and said, "My fellow Israelites! My conscience is perfectly clear
about the way in which I have lived before God to this very day." 2 The High
Priest Ananias ordered those who were
standing close to Paul to strike him on
the mouth. 3 Paul said to him, "God will
certainly strike you—you whitewashed
wall! You sit there to judge me according to the Law, yet you break the Law by
ordering them to strike me!"
4 The men close to Paul said to him,
"You are insulting God's High Priest!"
5 Paul answered, "My fellow Israelites,
I did not know that he was the High
Priest. The scripture says, 'You must not
speak evil of the ruler of your people.' "
6 When Paul saw that some of the
group were Sadducees and the others
were Pharisees, he called out in the
Council, "Fellow Israelites! I am a Pharisee, the son of Pharisees. I am on trial
here because of the hope I have that the
dead will rise to life!"
7 As soon as he said this, the Pharisees
and Sadducees started to quarrel, and
the group was divided. (8 For the Sadducees say that people will not rise from
death and that there are no angels or
spirits; but the Pharisees believe in all
three.) 9 The shouting became louder,
and some of the teachers of the Law who
belonged to the party of the Pharisees
stood up and protested strongly: "We
cannot find a thing wrong with this man!
Perhaps a spirit or an angel really did
speak to him!"
10 The argument became so violent
that the commander was afraid that Paul
would be torn to pieces. So he ordered
his soldiers to go down into the group,
get Paul away from them, and take him
into the fort.
11 That night the Lord stood by Paul
and said, "Don't be afraid! You have
given your witness for me here in Jerusalem, and you must also do the same in
Rome."

The Plot against Paul's Life

12 The next morning some Jews met together and made a plan. They took a
vow that they would not eat or drink
anything until they had killed Paul.
13 There were more than forty who
planned this together. 14 Then they went
to the chief priests and elders and said,
"We have taken a solemn vow together
not to eat a thing until we have killed
Paul. 15 Now then, you and the Council
send word to the Roman commander to
bring Paul down to you, pretending that
you want to get more accurate information about him. But we will be ready to
kill him before he ever gets here."
16 But the son of Paul's sister heard
about the plot; so he went to the fort and
told Paul. 17 Then Paul called one of the
officers and said to him, "Take this
young man to the commander; he has
something to tell him." 18 The officer
took him, led him to the commander,
and said, "The prisoner Paul called me
and asked me to bring this young man to
you, because he has something to say
to you."
19 The commander took him by the
hand, led him off by himself, and asked
him, "What do you have to tell me?"

20 He said, "The Jewish authorities
have agreed to ask you tomorrow to
take Paul down to the Council, pretending that the Council wants to get more
accurate information about him. 21 But
don't listen to them, because there are
more than forty men who will be hiding
and waiting for him. They have taken a
vow not to eat or drink until they have
killed him. They are now ready to do it
and are waiting for your decision."
22 The commander said, "Don't tell
anyone that you have reported this to
me." And he sent the young man away.

Paul Is Sent to Governor Felix

23 Then the commander called two of
his officers and said, "Get two hundred
soldiers ready to go to Caesarea, together with seventy horsemen and two
hundred spearmen, and be ready to
leave by nine o'clock tonight. 24 Provide
some horses for Paul to ride and get him
safely through to Governor Felix."
25 Then the commander wrote a letter
that went like this:
26 "Claudius Lysias to His Excellency, Governor Felix: Greetings.
27 The Jews seized this man and were
about to kill him. I learned that he is a
Roman citizen, so I went with my soldiers and rescued him. 28 I wanted to
know what they were accusing him of,
so I took him down to their Council.
29 I found out that he had not done a
thing for which he deserved to die or
be put in prison; the accusation
against him had to do with questions
about their own law. 30 And when I
was informed that there was a plot
against him, at once I decided to send
him to you. I have told his accusers to
make their charges against him before you."
31 The soldiers carried out their orders.
They got Paul and took him that night as
far as Antipatris. 32 The next day the foot
soldiers returned to the fort and left the
horsemen to go on with him. 33 They
took him to Caesarea, delivered the letter to the governor, and turned Paul over
to him. 34 The governor read the letter
and asked Paul what province he was
from. When he found out that he was
from Cilicia, 35 he said, "I will hear you
when your accusers arrive." Then he
gave orders for Paul to be kept under
guard in the governor's headquarters.

The Case Against Paul

24 Five days later the High Priest
Ananias went to Caesarea with
some elders and a lawyer named Tertul-
lus. They appeared before Governor Felix and made their charges against Paul.
2 Then Paul was called in, and Tertul-
lus began to make his accusation, as
follows:
"Your Excellency! Your wise leadership has brought us a long period of
peace, and many necessary reforms are
being made for the good of our country.
3 We welcome this everywhere and at all
times, and we are deeply grateful to you.
4 I do not want to take up too much of
your time, however, so I beg you to be
kind and listen to our brief account. 5 We
found this man to be a dangerous nuisance; he starts riots among Jews all
over the world and is a leader of the
party of the Nazarenes. 6 He also tried to
defile the Temple, and we arrested
him.[j] 8 If you question this man, you
yourself will be able to learn from him
all the things that we are accusing him
of." 9 The Jews joined in the accusation
and said that all this was true.

Paul's Defense before Felix

10 The governor then motioned to Paul
to speak, and Paul said,
"I know that you have been a judge
over this nation for many years, and so I
am happy to defend myself before you.
11 As you can find out for yourself, it was
no more than twelve days ago that I
went to Jerusalem to worship. 12 The
Jews did not find me arguing with anyone in the Temple, nor did they find me
stirring up the people, either in the synagogues or anywhere else in the city.
13 Nor can they give you proof of the accusations they now bring against me.
14 I do admit this to you: I worship the
God of our ancestors by following that
Way which they say is false. But I also
believe in everything written in the Law
of Moses and the books of the prophets.
15 I have the same hope in God that these
themselves have, namely, that all peo-

[j] *Some manuscripts add verses 6b-8a:* We planned to judge him according to our own law, 7 but the commander Lysias came, and with great violence took him from us. 8 Then Lysias gave orders that his accusers should come before you.

ple, both the good and the bad, will rise
from death. 16And so I do my best always to have a clear conscience before
God and people.
17"After being away from Jerusalem
for several years, I went there to take
some money to my own people and to
offer sacrifices. 18It was while I was doing this that they found me in the Temple after I had completed the ceremony
of purification. There was no crowd with
me and no disorder. 19But some Jews
from the province of Asia were there;
they themselves ought to come before
you and make their accusations if they
have anything against me. 20Or let these
who are here tell what crime they found
me guilty of when I stood before the
Council—21except for the one thing I
called out when I stood before them: 'I
am being tried by you today for believing that the dead will rise to life.' "
22Then Felix, who was well informed
about the Way, brought the hearing to a
close. "When the commander Lysias ar-
rives," he told them, "I will decide your
case." 23He ordered the officer in charge
of Paul to keep him under guard, but to
give him some freedom and allow his
friends to provide for his needs.

Paul before Felix and Drusilla

24After some days Felix came with his
wife Drusilla, who was Jewish. He sent
for Paul and listened to him as he talked
about faith in Christ Jesus. 25But as Paul
went on discussing about goodness, self-
control, and the coming Day of Judgment, Felix was afraid and said, "You
may leave now. I will call you again
when I get the chance." 26At the same
time he was hoping that Paul would give
him some money; and for this reason
he would call for him often and talk
with him.
27After two years had passed, Porcius
Festus succeeded Felix as governor. Felix wanted to gain favor with the Jews so
he left Paul in prison.

Paul Appeals to the Emperor

25 Three days after Festus arrived
in the province, he went from
Caesarea to Jerusalem, 2where the chief
priests and the Jewish leaders brought
their charges against Paul. They begged
Festus 3to do them the favor of having
Paul come to Jerusalem, for they had
made a plot to kill him on the way. 4Fes-
tus answered, "Paul is being kept a prisoner in Caesarea, and I myself will be
going back there soon. 5Let your leaders
go to Caesarea with me and accuse the
man if he has done anything wrong."
6Festus spent another eight or ten
days with them and then went to Caesarea. On the next day he sat down in the
judgment court and ordered Paul to be
brought in. 7When Paul arrived, the
Jews who had come from Jerusalem
stood around him and started making
many serious charges against him,
which they were not able to prove. 8But
Paul defended himself: "I have done
nothing wrong against the Law of the
Jews or against the Temple or against
the Roman Emperor."
9But Festus wanted to gain favor with
the Jews, so he asked Paul, "Would you
be willing to go to Jerusalem and be
tried on these charges before me there?"
10Paul said, "I am standing before the
Emperor's own judgment court, where I
should be tried. I have done no wrong to
the Jews, as you yourself well know. 11If
I have broken the law and done something for which I deserve the death penalty, I do not ask to escape it. But if there
is no truth in the charges they bring
against me, no one can hand me over to
them. I appeal to the Emperor."
12Then Festus, after conferring with
his advisers, answered, "You have appealed to the Emperor, so to the Emperor you will go."

Paul before Agrippa and Bernice

13Some time later King Agrippa and
Bernice came to Caesarea to pay a visit
of welcome to Festus. 14After they had
been there several days, Festus explained Paul's situation to the king:
"There is a man here who was left a prisoner by Felix; 15and when I went to Jerusalem, the Jewish chief priests and
elders brought charges against him and
asked me to condemn him. 16But I told
them that we Romans are not in the
habit of handing over any who are accused of a crime before they have met
their accusers face-to-face and have had
the chance of defending themselves
against the accusation. 17When they
came here, then, I lost no time, but on
the very next day I sat in the judgment
court and ordered the man to be brought

in. 18 His opponents stood up, but they
did not accuse him of any of the evil
crimes that I thought they would. 19 All
they had were some arguments with him
about their own religion and about a
man named Jesus, who has died; but
Paul claims that he is alive. 20 I was undecided about how I could get information on these matters, so I asked Paul if
he would be willing to go to Jerusalem
and be tried there on these charges.
21 But Paul appealed; he asked to be kept
under guard and to let the Emperor decide his case. So I gave orders for him to
be kept under guard until I could send
him to the Emperor."
22 Agrippa said to Festus, "I would like
to hear this man myself."

"You will hear him tomorrow," Festus
answered.

23 The next day Agrippa and Bernice
came with great pomp and ceremony
and entered the audience hall with the
military chiefs and the leading men of
the city. Festus gave the order, and Paul
was brought in. 24 Festus said, "King
Agrippa and all who are here with us:
You see this man against whom all the
Jewish people, both here and in Jerusalem, have brought complaints to me.
They scream that he should not live any
longer. 25 But I could not find that he had
done anything for which he deserved the
death sentence. And since he himself
made an appeal to the Emperor, I have
decided to send him. 26 But I have nothing definite about him to write to the
Emperor. So I have brought him here before you — and especially before you,
King Agrippa! — so that, after investigat-
ing his case, I may have something to
write. 27 For it seems unreasonable to me
to send a prisoner without clearly indicating the charges against him."

Paul Defends Himself before Agrippa

26 Agrippa said to Paul, "You have
permission to speak on your own
behalf." Paul stretched out his hand and
defended himself as follows:
2 "King Agrippa! I consider myself fortunate that today I am to defend myself
before you from all the things these
Jews accuse me of, 3 particularly since
you know so well all the Jewish customs
and disputes. I ask you, then, to listen to
me with patience.

4 "All the Jews know how I have lived
ever since I was young. They know how
I have spent my whole life, at first in my
own country and then in Jerusalem.
5 They have always known, if they are
willing to testify, that from the very first
I have lived as a member of the strictest
party of our religion, the Pharisees.
6 And now I stand here to be tried because of the hope I have in the promise
that God made to our ancestors — 7 the
very thing that the twelve tribes of our
people hope to receive, as they worship
God day and night. And it is because of
this hope, Your Majesty, that I am being
accused by these Jews! 8 Why do you
who are here find it impossible to believe that God raises the dead?

9 "I myself thought that I should do
everything I could against the cause of
Jesus of Nazareth. 10 That is what I did in
Jerusalem. I received authority from the
chief priests and put many of God's people in prison; and when they were sentenced to death, I also voted against
them. 11 Many times I had them punished
in the synagogues and tried to make
them deny their faith. I was so furious
with them that I even went to foreign
cities to persecute them.

Paul Tells of His Conversion

(Acts 9.1-19; 22.6-16)

12 "It was for this purpose that I went
to Damascus with authority and orders
from the chief priests. 13 It was on the
road at midday, Your Majesty, that I saw
a light much brighter than the sun, coming from the sky and shining around me
and the men traveling with me. 14 All of
us fell to the ground, and I heard a voice
say to me in Hebrew, 'Saul, Saul! Why
are you persecuting me? You are hurting
yourself by hitting back, like an ox kick-
ing against its owner's stick.' 15 'Who are
you, Lord?' I asked. And the Lord answered, 'I am Jesus, whom you persecute. 16 But get up and stand on your feet.
I have appeared to you to appoint you as
my servant. You are to tell others what
you have seen of me[k] today and what I
will show you in the future. 17 I will rescue you from the people of Israel and
from the Gentiles to whom I will send

[k] *Some manuscripts do not have* of me.

you. 18 You are to open their eyes and
turn them from the darkness to the light
and from the power of Satan to God, so
that through their faith in me they will
have their sins forgiven and receive
their place among God's chosen people.'

Paul Tells of His Work

19 "And so, King Agrippa, I did not disobey the vision I had from heaven.
20 First in Damascus and in Jerusalem
and then in the whole country of Israel
and among the Gentiles, I preached that
they must repent of their sins and turn to
God and do the things that would show
they had repented. 21 It was for this reason that these Jews seized me while I
was in the Temple, and they tried to kill
me. 22 But to this very day I have been
helped by God, and so I stand here giving my witness to all, to small and great
alike. What I say is the very same thing
which the prophets and Moses said was
going to happen: 23 that the Messiah
must suffer and be the first one to rise
from death, to announce the light of salvation to the Jews and to the Gentiles."

24 As Paul defended himself in this
way, Festus shouted at him, "You are
mad, Paul! Your great learning is driving you mad!"

25 Paul answered, "I am not mad, Your
Excellency! I am speaking the sober
truth. 26 King Agrippa! I can speak to
you with all boldness, because you know
about these things. I am sure that you
have taken notice of every one of them,
for this thing has not happened hidden
away in a corner. 27 King Agrippa, do
you believe the prophets? I know that
you do!"

28 Agrippa said to Paul, "In this short
time do you think you will make me a
Christian?"

29 "Whether a short time or a long
time," Paul answered, "my prayer to
God is that you and all the rest of you
who are listening to me today might become what I am—except, of course, for
these chains!"

30 Then the king, the governor, Bernice, and all the others got up, 31 and after leaving they said to each other, "This
man has not done anything for which he
should die or be put in prison." 32 And
Agrippa said to Festus, "This man could
have been released if he had not appealed to the Emperor."

Paul Sails for Rome

27 When it was decided that we
should sail to Italy, they handed
Paul and some other prisoners over to
Julius, an officer in the Roman army
regiment called "The Emperor's Regiment." 2 We went aboard a ship from Ad-
ramyttium, which was ready to leave for
the seaports of the province of Asia, and
we sailed away. Aristarchus, a Macedonian from Thessalonica, was with us.
3 The next day we arrived at Sidon. Julius was kind to Paul and allowed him to
go and see his friends, to be given what
he needed. 4 We went on from there, and
because the winds were blowing against
us, we sailed on the sheltered side of the
island of Cyprus. 5 We crossed over the
sea off Cilicia and Pamphylia and came
to Myra in Lycia. 6 There the officer
found a ship from Alexandria that was
going to sail for Italy, so he put us
aboard.

7 We sailed slowly for several days and
with great difficulty finally arrived off
the town of Cnidus. The wind would not
let us go any farther in that direction, so
we sailed down the sheltered side of the
island of Crete, passing by Cape Sal-
mone. 8 We kept close to the coast and
with great difficulty came to a place
called Safe Harbors, not far from the
town of Lasea.

9 We spent a long time there, until it
became dangerous to continue the voyage, for by now the Day of Atonement[l]
was already past. So Paul gave them this
advice: 10 "Men, I see that our voyage
from here on will be dangerous; there
will be great damage to the cargo and to
the ship, and loss of life as well." 11 But
the army officer was convinced by what
the captain and the owner of the ship
said, and not by what Paul said. 12 The
harbor was not a good one to spend the
winter in; so almost everyone was in favor of putting out to sea and trying to
reach Phoenix, if possible, in order to
spend the winter there. Phoenix is a harbor in Crete that faces southwest and
northwest.[m]

[l] DAY OF ATONEMENT: *This was celebrated toward the end of September or beginning of October, at which time bad weather made sailing dangerous.* [m] southwest and northwest; *or* northeast and southeast.

The Storm at Sea

13 A soft wind from the south began to
blow, and the men thought that they
could carry out their plan, so they pulled
up the anchor and sailed as close as possible along the coast of Crete. 14 But soon
a very strong wind—the one called
"Northeaster"—blew down from the island. 15 It hit the ship, and since it was
impossible to keep the ship headed into
the wind, we gave up trying and let it be
carried along by the wind. 16 We got
some shelter when we passed to the
south of the little island of Cauda. There,
with some difficulty we managed to
make the ship's boat secure. 17 They
pulled it aboard and then fastened some
ropes tight around the ship. They were
afraid that they might run into the sand-
banks off the coast of Libya, so they lowered the sail and let the ship be carried
by the wind. 18 The violent storm continued, so on the next day they began to
throw some of the ship's cargo overboard, 19 and on the following day they
threw part of the ship's equipment overboard. 20 For many days we could not see
the sun or the stars, and the wind kept
on blowing very hard. We finally gave
up all hope of being saved.
21 After everyone had gone a long time
without food, Paul stood before them
and said, "You should have listened to
me and not have sailed from Crete; then
we would have avoided all this damage
and loss. 22 But now I beg you, take courage! Not one of you will lose your life;
only the ship will be lost. 23 For last night
an angel of the God to whom I belong
and whom I worship came to me 24 and
said, 'Don't be afraid, Paul! You must
stand before the Emperor. And God in
his goodness to you has spared the lives
of all those who are sailing with you.'
25 So take courage, men! For I trust in
God that it will be just as I was told.
26 But we will be driven ashore on some
island."
27 It was the fourteenth night, and we
were being driven in the Mediterranean
by the storm. About midnight the sailors
suspected that we were getting close to
land. 28 So they dropped a line with a
weight tied to it and found that the water
was one hundred and twenty feet deep; a
little later they did the same and found
that it was ninety feet deep. 29 They were
afraid that the ship would go on the
rocks, so they lowered four anchors
from the back of the ship and prayed for
daylight. 30 Then the sailors tried to escape from the ship; they lowered the
boat into the water and pretended that
they were going to put out some anchors
from the front of the ship. 31 But Paul
said to the army officer and soldiers, "If
the sailors don't stay on board, you have
no hope of being saved." 32 So the soldiers cut the ropes that held the boat and
let it go.
33 Just before dawn, Paul begged them
all to eat some food: "You have been
waiting for fourteen days now, and all
this time you have not eaten a thing.
34 I beg you, then, eat some food; you
need it in order to survive. Not even a
hair of your heads will be lost." 35 After
saying this, Paul took some bread, gave
thanks to God before them all, broke it,
and began to eat. 36 They took courage,
and every one of them also ate some
food. 37 There was a total of 276[n] of us
on board. 38 After everyone had eaten
enough, they lightened the ship by
throwing all the wheat into the sea.

The Shipwreck

39 When day came, the sailors did not
recognize the coast, but they noticed a
bay with a beach and decided that, if
possible, they would run the ship
aground there. 40 So they cut off the anchors and let them sink in the sea, and at
the same time they untied the ropes that
held the steering oars. Then they raised
the sail at the front of the ship so that the
wind would blow the ship forward, and
we headed for shore. 41 But the ship hit a
sandbank and went aground; the front
part of the ship got stuck and could not
move, while the back part was being
broken to pieces by the violence of the
waves.
42 The soldiers made a plan to kill all
the prisoners, in order to keep them
from swimming ashore and escaping.
43 But the army officer wanted to save
Paul, so he stopped them from doing
this. Instead, he ordered everyone who
could swim to jump overboard first and
swim ashore; 44 the rest were to follow,
holding on to the planks or to some bro-

[n] 276; *some manuscripts have* 275; *others have* about 76.

ken pieces of the ship. And this was how we all got safely ashore.

In Malta

28 When we were safely ashore, we learned that the island was called Malta. 2The natives there were very friendly to us. It had started to rain and was cold, so they built a fire and made us all welcome. 3Paul gathered up a bundle of sticks and was putting them on the fire when a snake came out on account of the heat and fastened itself to his hand. 4The natives saw the snake hanging on Paul's hand and said to one another, "This man must be a murderer, but Fate will not let him live, even though he escaped from the sea." 5But Paul shook the snake off into the fire without being harmed at all. 6They were waiting for him to swell up or suddenly fall down dead. But after waiting for a long time and not seeing anything unusual happening to him, they changed their minds and said, "He is a god!"

7Not far from that place were some fields that belonged to Publius, the chief of the island. He welcomed us kindly and for three days we were his guests. 8Publius' father was in bed, sick with fever and dysentery. Paul went into his room, prayed, placed his hands on him, and healed him. 9When this happened, all the other sick people on the island came and were healed. 10They gave us many gifts, and when we sailed, they put on board what we needed for the voyage.

From Malta to Rome

11After three months we sailed away on a ship from Alexandria, called "The Twin Gods," which had spent the winter in the island. 12We arrived in the city of Syracuse and stayed there for three days. 13From there we sailed on and arrived in the city of Rhegium. The next day a wind began to blow from the south, and in two days we came to the town of Puteoli. 14We found some believers there who asked us to stay with them a week. And so we came to Rome. 15The believers in Rome heard about us and came as far as the towns of Market of Appius and Three Inns to meet us. When Paul saw them, he thanked God and was greatly encouraged.

In Rome

16When we arrived in Rome, Paul was allowed to live by himself with a soldier guarding him.

17After three days Paul called the local Jewish leaders to a meeting. When they had gathered, he said to them, "My fellow Israelites, even though I did nothing against our people or the customs that we received from our ancestors, I was made a prisoner in Jerusalem and handed over to the Romans. 18After questioning me, the Romans wanted to release me, because they found that I had done nothing for which I deserved to die. 19But when the Jews opposed this, I was forced to appeal to the Emperor, even though I had no accusation to make against my own people. 20That is why I asked to see you and talk with you. As a matter of fact, I am bound in chains like this for the sake of him for whom the people of Israel hope."

21They said to him, "We have not received any letters from Judea about you, nor have any of our people come from there with any news or anything bad to say about you. 22But we would like to hear your ideas, because we know that everywhere people speak against this party to which you belong."

23So they set a date with Paul, and a large number of them came that day to the place where Paul was staying. From morning till night he explained to them his message about the Kingdom of God, and he tried to convince them about Jesus by quoting from the Law of Moses and the writings of the prophets. 24Some of them were convinced by his words, but others would not believe. 25So they left, disagreeing among themselves, after Paul had said this one thing: "How well the Holy Spirit spoke through the prophet Isaiah to your ancestors! 26For he said,

'Go and say to this people:
You will listen and listen, but not understand;
you will look and look, but not see,
27because this people's minds are dull,
and they have stopped up their ears
and closed their eyes.

Otherwise, their eyes would see,
their ears would hear,
their minds would understand,
and they would turn to me,
says God,
and I would heal them.' "
28 And Paul concluded: "You are to
know, then, that God's message of salvation has been sent to the Gentiles. They
will listen!"o
30 For two years Paul lived in a place
he rented for himself, and there he welcomed all who came to see him. 31 He
preached about the Kingdom of God and
taught about the Lord Jesus Christ,
speaking with all boldness and freedom.

o *Some manuscripts add verse 29:* After Paul said this, the Jews left, arguing violently among themselves.

Paul's Letter to the

ROMANS

Introduction

Paul's Letter to the Romans *was written to prepare the way for a visit Paul planned to make to the church at Rome. His plan was to work among the Christians there for a while and then, with their support, to go on to Spain. He wrote to explain his understanding of the Christian faith and its practical implications for the lives of Christians. The book contains Paul's most complete statement of his message.*

After greeting the people of the church at Rome and telling them of his prayers for them, Paul states the theme of the letter: "The gospel reveals how God puts people right with himself: it is through faith from beginning to end" (1.17).

Paul then develops this theme. All people, both Jews and Gentiles, need to be put right with God, for all alike are under the power of sin. People are put right with God through faith in Jesus Christ. Next Paul describes the new life in union with Christ that results from this new relation with God. The believer has peace with God and is set free by God's Spirit from the power of sin and death. In chapters 5–8 Paul also discusses the purpose of the Law of God and the power of God's Spirit in the believer's life. Then the apostle wrestles with the question of how Jews and Gentiles fit into the plan of God for all people. He concludes that the Jewish rejection of Jesus is part of God's plan for bringing all people within the reach of God's grace in Jesus Christ, and he believes that the Jews will not always reject Jesus. Finally Paul writes about how the Christian life should be lived, especially about the way of love in relations with others. He takes up such themes as service to God, the duty of Christians to the state and to one another, and questions of conscience. He ends the letter with personal messages and with words of praise to God.

Outline of Contents

Introduction and theme 1.1-17
The universal human need of salvation 1.18–3.20
God's way of salvation 3.21–4.25
The new life in Christ 5.1–8.39
Israel in the plan of God 9.1–11.36
Christian conduct 12.1–15.13
Conclusion and personal greetings 15.14–16.27

---

1 From Paul, a servant of Christ Jesus
and an apostle chosen and called by
God to preach his Good News.
2 The Good News was promised long
ago by God through his prophets, as
written in the Holy Scriptures. 3 It is
about his Son, our Lord Jesus Christ: as
to his humanity, he was born a descendant of David; 4 as to his divine holiness,
he was shown with great power to be the
Son of God by being raised from death.
5 Through him God gave me the privilege of being an apostle for the sake of
Christ, in order to lead people of all nations to believe and obey. 6 This also includes you who are in Rome, whom God
has called to belong to Jesus Christ.
7 And so I write to all of you in Rome
whom God loves and has called to be his
own people:

May God our Father and the Lord
Jesus Christ give you grace and peace.

Prayer of Thanksgiving

8 First, I thank my God through Jesus
Christ for all of you, because the whole
world is hearing about your faith. 9 God
is my witness that what I say is true—
the God whom I serve with all my heart
by preaching the Good News about his
Son. God knows that I remember you
10 every time I pray. I ask that God in his
good will may at last make it possible for
me to visit you now. 11 For I want very
much to see you, in order to share a spiritual blessing with you to make you
strong. 12 What I mean is that both you
and I will be helped at the same time,
you by my faith and I by yours.
13 You must remember, my friends,

that many times I have planned to visit
you, but something has always kept me
from doing so. I want to win converts
among you also, as I have among other
Gentiles. 14 For I have an obligation to all
peoples, to the civilized and to the savage, to the educated and to the ignorant.
15 So then, I am eager to preach the Good
News to you also who live in Rome.

The Power of the Gospel

16 I have complete confidence in the
gospel; it is God's power to save all who
believe, first the Jews and also the Gentiles. 17 For the gospel reveals how God
puts people right with himself: it is
through faith from beginning to end. As
the scripture says, "The person who is
put right with God through faith shall
live."[a]

Human Guilt

18 God's anger is revealed from heaven
against all the sin and evil of the people
whose evil ways prevent the truth from
being known. 19 God punishes them, because what can be known about God is
plain to them, for God himself made it
plain. 20 Ever since God created the
world, his invisible qualities, both his
eternal power and his divine nature,
have been clearly seen; they are perceived in the things that God has made.
So those people have no excuse at all!
21 They know God, but they do not give
him the honor that belongs to him, nor
do they thank him. Instead, their
thoughts have become complete nonsense, and their empty minds are filled
with darkness. 22 They say they are wise,
but they are fools; 23 instead of worshiping the immortal God, they worship images made to look like mortals or birds
or animals or reptiles.

24 And so God has given those people
over to do the filthy things their hearts
desire, and they do shameful things with
each other. 25 They exchange the truth
about God for a lie; they worship and
serve what God has created instead of
the Creator himself, who is to be praised
forever! Amen.

26 Because they do this, God has given
them over to shameful passions. Even
the women pervert the natural use of
their sex by unnatural acts. 27 In the
same way the men give up natural sexual relations with women and burn with
passion for each other. Men do shameful
things with each other, and as a result
they bring upon themselves the punishment they deserve for their wrongdoing.

28 Because those people refuse to keep
in mind the true knowledge about God,
he has given them over to corrupted
minds, so that they do the things that
they should not do. 29 They are filled
with all kinds of wickedness, evil, greed,
and vice; they are full of jealousy, murder, fighting, deceit, and malice. They
gossip 30 and speak evil of one another;
they are hateful to God, insolent,[b]
proud, and boastful; they think of more
ways to do evil; they disobey their parents; 31 they have no conscience; they do
not keep their promises, and they show
no kindness or pity for others. 32 They
know that God's law says that people
who live in this way deserve death. Yet,
not only do they continue to do these
very things, but they even approve of
others who do them.

God's Judgment

2 Do you, my friend, pass judgment
on others? You have no excuse at
all, whoever you are. For when you
judge others and then do the same
things which they do, you condemn
yourself. 2 We know that God is right
when he judges the people who do such
things as these. 3 But you, my friend, do
those very things for which you pass
judgment on others! Do you think you
will escape God's judgment? 4 Or perhaps you despise his great kindness, tol-
erance, and patience. Surely you know
that God is kind, because he is trying to
lead you to repent. 5 But you have a hard
and stubborn heart, and so you are making your own punishment even greater
on the Day when God's anger and righteous judgments will be revealed. 6 For
God will reward each of us according to
what we have done. 7 Some people keep
on doing good, and seek glory, honor,
and immortal life; to them God will give
eternal life. 8 Other people are selfish
and reject what is right, in order to follow what is wrong; on them God will
pour out his anger and fury. 9 There will

[a] put right with God through faith shall live; *or* put right with God shall live through faith.
[b] are hateful to God, insolent; *or* hate God, and are insolent.

be suffering and pain for all those who
do what is evil, for the Jews first and
also for the Gentiles. 10 But God will give
glory, honor, and peace to all who do
what is good, to the Jews first and also to
the Gentiles. 11 For God judges everyone
by the same standard.
12 The Gentiles do not have the Law of
Moses; they sin and are lost apart from
the Law. The Jews have the Law; they
sin and are judged by the Law. 13 For it is
not by hearing the Law that people are
put right with God, but by doing what
the Law commands. 14 The Gentiles do
not have the Law; but whenever they do
by instinct what the Law commands,
they are their own law, even though they
do not have the Law. 15 Their conduct
shows that what the Law commands is
written in their hearts. Their consciences also show that this is true, since
their thoughts sometimes accuse them
and sometimes defend them. 16 And so,
according to the Good News I preach,
this is how it will be on that Day when
God through Jesus Christ will judge the
secret thoughts of all.

The Jews and the Law

17 What about you? You call yourself a
Jew; you depend on the Law and boast
about God; 18 you know what God wants
you to do, and you have learned from
the Law to choose what is right; 19 you
are sure that you are a guide for the
blind, a light for those who are in darkness, 20 an instructor for the foolish, and
a teacher for the ignorant. You are certain that in the Law you have the full
content of knowledge and of truth.
21 You teach others—why don't you
teach yourself? You preach, "Do not
steal"—but do you yourself steal? 22 You
say, "Do not commit adultery"—but do
you commit adultery? You detest idols—
but do you rob temples? 23 You boast
about having God's law—but do you
bring shame on God by breaking his
law? 24 The scripture says, "Because of
you Jews, the Gentiles speak evil
of God."
25 If you obey the Law, your circumcision is of value; but if you disobey the
Law, you might as well never have been
circumcised. 26 If the Gentile, who is not
circumcised, obeys the commands of the
Law, will not God regard him as though
he were circumcised? 27 And so you Jews
will be condemned by the Gentiles because you break the Law, even though
you have it written down and are circumcised; but they obey the Law, even
though they are not physically circumcised. 28 After all, who is a real Jew, truly
circumcised? It is not the man who is a
Jew on the outside, whose circumcision
is a physical thing. 29 Rather, the real
Jew is the person who is a Jew on the
inside, that is, whose heart has been circumcised, and this is the work of God's
Spirit, not of the written Law. Such a
person receives praise from God, not
from human beings.

3 Do the Jews then have any advantage over the Gentiles? Or is there
any value in being circumcised? 2 Much,
indeed, in every way! In the first place,
God trusted his message to the Jews.
3 But what if some of them were not
faithful? Does this mean that God will
not be faithful? 4 Certainly not! God must
be true, even though all human beings
are liars. As the scripture says,

"You must be shown to be right
when you speak;
you must win your case when
you are being tried."

5 But what if our doing wrong serves to
show up more clearly God's doing right?
Can we say that God does wrong when
he punishes us? (This would be the natural question to ask.) 6 By no means! If
God is not just, how can he judge the
world?
7 But what if my untruth serves God's
glory by making his truth stand out
more clearly? Why should I still be condemned as a sinner? 8 Why not say, then,
"Let us do evil so that good may come"?
Some people, indeed, have insulted me
by accusing me of saying this very thing!
They will be condemned, as they
should be.

No One Is Righteous

9 Well then, are we Jews in any better
condition than the Gentiles? Not at all![c]
I have already shown that Jews and
Gentiles alike are all under the power of
sin. 10 As the Scriptures say:

[c] any better condition than the Gentiles? Not at all!; *or* any worse condition than the Gentiles? Not altogether.

"There is no one who is righteous,
11 no one who is wise
or who worships God.
12 All have turned away from God;
they have all gone wrong;
no one does what is right, not
even one.
13 Their words are full of deadly
deceit;
wicked lies roll off their tongues,
and dangerous threats, like
snake's poison, from their lips;
14 their speech is filled with bitter
curses.
15 They are quick to hurt and kill;
16 they leave ruin and destruction
wherever they go.
17 They have not known the path of
peace,
18 nor have they learned reverence
for God."
19 Now we know that everything in the
Law applies to those who live under the
Law, in order to stop all human excuses
and bring the whole world under God's
judgment. 20 For no one is put right in
God's sight by doing what the Law requires; what the Law does is to make us
know that we have sinned.

How We Are Put Right with God

21 But now God's way of putting people right with himself has been revealed.
It has nothing to do with law, even
though the Law of Moses and the prophets gave their witness to it. 22 God puts
people right through their faith in Jesus
Christ. God does this to all who believe
in Christ, because there is no difference
at all: 23 everyone has sinned and is far
away from God's saving presence. 24 But
by the free gift of God's grace all are put
right with him through Christ Jesus,
who sets them free. 25-26 God offered
him, so that by his blood[d] he should become the means by which people's sins
are forgiven through their faith in him.
God did this in order to demonstrate that
he is righteous. In the past he was patient and overlooked people's sins; but
in the present time he deals with their
sins, in order to demonstrate his righteousness. In this way God shows that he
himself is righteous and that he puts
right everyone who believes in Jesus.
27 What, then, can we boast about?
Nothing! And what is the reason for
this? Is it that we obey the Law? No, but
that we believe. 28 For we conclude that a
person is put right with God only
through faith, and not by doing what the
Law commands. 29 Or is God the God of
the Jews only? Is he not the God of the
Gentiles also? Of course he is. 30 God is
one, and he will put the Jews right with
himself on the basis of their faith, and
will put the Gentiles right through their
faith. 31 Does this mean that by this faith
we do away with the Law? No, not at all;
instead, we uphold the Law.

The Example of Abraham

4 What shall we say, then, of Abraham, the father of our race? What
was his experience? 2 If he was put right
with God by the things he did, he would
have something to boast about—but not
in God's sight. 3 The scripture says,
"Abraham believed God, and because of
his faith God accepted him as righteous." 4 A person who works is paid
wages, but they are not regarded as a
gift; they are something that has been
earned. 5 But those who depend on faith,
not on deeds, and who believe in the
God who declares the guilty to be innocent, it is this faith that God takes into
account in order to put them right with
himself. 6 This is what David meant
when he spoke of the happiness of the
person whom God accepts as righteous,
apart from anything that person does:
7 "Happy are those whose wrongs
are forgiven,
whose sins are pardoned!
8 Happy is the person whose sins
the Lord will not keep
account of!"
9 Does this happiness that David spoke
of belong only to those who are circumcised? No indeed! It belongs also to
those who are not circumcised. For we
have quoted the scripture, "Abraham believed God, and because of his faith God
accepted him as righteous." 10 When did
this take place? Was it before or after
Abraham was circumcised? It was before, not after. 11 He was circumcised
later, and his circumcision was a sign to
show that because of his faith God had
accepted him as righteous before he had
been circumcised. And so Abraham is

[d] by his blood; *or* by his sacrificial death.

the spiritual father of all who believe in
God and are accepted as righteous by
him, even though they are not circumcised. 12 He is also the father of those
who are circumcised, that is, of those
who, in addition to being circumcised,
also live the same life of faith that our
father Abraham lived before he was circumcised.

God's Promise Is Received through Faith

13 When God promised Abraham and
his descendants that the world would
belong to him, he did so, not because
Abraham obeyed the Law, but because
he believed and was accepted as righteous by God. 14 For if what God promises
is to be given to those who obey the Law,
then faith means nothing and God's
promise is worthless. 15 The Law brings
down God's anger; but where there is no
law, there is no disobeying of the law.
16 And so the promise was based on
faith, in order that the promise should be
guaranteed as God's free gift to all of
Abraham's descendants—not just to
those who obey the Law, but also to
those who believe as Abraham did. For
Abraham is the spiritual father of us all;
17 as the scripture says, "I have made you
father of many nations." So the promise
is good in the sight of God, in whom
Abraham believed—the God who brings
the dead to life and whose command
brings into being what did not exist.
18 Abraham believed and hoped, even
when there was no reason for hoping,
and so became "the father of many nations." Just as the scripture says, "Your
descendants will be as many as the
stars." 19 He was then almost one hundred years old; but his faith did not
weaken when he thought of his body,
which was already practically dead, or
of the fact that Sarah could not have
children. 20 His faith did not leave him,
and he did not doubt God's promise; his
faith filled him with power, and he gave
praise to God. 21 He was absolutely sure
that God would be able to do what he
had promised. 22 That is why Abraham,
through faith, "was accepted as righteous by God." 23 The words "he was accepted as righteous" were not written for
him alone. 24 They were written also for
us who are to be accepted as righteous,
who believe in him who raised Jesus our
Lord from death. 25 Because of our sins
he was given over to die, and he was
raised to life in order to put us right
with God.

Right with God

5 Now that we have been put right
with God through faith, we have[e]
peace with God through our Lord Jesus
Christ. 2 He has brought us by faith into
this experience of God's grace, in which
we now live. And so we boast[f] of the
hope we have of sharing God's glory!
3 We also boast[g] of our troubles, because we know that trouble produces
endurance, 4 endurance brings God's approval, and his approval creates hope.
5 This hope does not disappoint us, for
God has poured out his love into our
hearts by means of the Holy Spirit, who
is God's gift to us.
6 For when we were still helpless,
Christ died for the wicked at the time
that God chose. 7 It is a difficult thing for
someone to die for a righteous person. It
may even be that someone might dare to
die for a good person. 8 But God has
shown us how much he loves us—it was
while we were still sinners that Christ
died for us! 9 By his blood[h] we are now
put right with God; how much more,
then, will we be saved by him from
God's anger! 10 We were God's enemies,
but he made us his friends through the
death of his Son. Now that we are God's
friends, how much more will we be
saved by Christ's life! 11 But that is not
all; we rejoice because of what God has
done through our Lord Jesus Christ,
who has now made us God's friends.

Adam and Christ

12 Sin came into the world through one
man, and his sin brought death with it.
As a result, death has spread to the
whole human race because everyone
has sinned. 13 There was sin in the world
before the Law was given; but where
there is no law, no account is kept of
sins. 14 But from the time of Adam to the
time of Moses, death ruled over all human beings, even over those who did not

[e] we have; *some manuscripts have* let us have. [f] we boast; *or* let us boast. [g] We also boast; *or* Let us also boast. [h] By his blood; *or* By his sacrificial death.

sin in the same way that Adam did when
he disobeyed God's command.

Adam was a figure of the one who was
to come. 15 But the two are not the same,
because God's free gift is not like
Adam's sin. It is true that many people
died because of the sin of that one man.
But God's grace is much greater, and so
is his free gift to so many people through
the grace of the one man, Jesus Christ.
16 And there is a difference between
God's gift and the sin of one man. After
the one sin, came the judgment of
"Guilty"; but after so many sins, comes
the undeserved gift of "Not guilty!" 17 It
is true that through the sin of one man
death began to rule because of that one
man. But how much greater is the result
of what was done by the one man, Jesus
Christ! All who receive God's abundant
grace and are freely put right with him
will rule in life through Christ.

18 So then, as the one sin condemned
all people, in the same way the one
righteous act sets all people free and
gives them life. 19 And just as all people
were made sinners as the result of the
disobedience of one man, in the same
way they will all be put right with God
as the result of the obedience of the
one man.

20 Law was introduced in order to increase wrongdoing; but where sin increased, God's grace increased much
more. 21 So then, just as sin ruled by
means of death, so also God's grace
rules by means of righteousness, leading
us to eternal life through Jesus Christ
our Lord.

Dead to Sin but Alive in Union with Christ

6 What shall we say, then? Should we
continue to live in sin so that God's
grace will increase? 2 Certainly not! We
have died to sin — how then can we go on
living in it? 3 For surely you know that
when we were baptized into union with
Christ Jesus, we were baptized into
union with his death. 4 By our baptism,
then, we were buried with him and
shared his death, in order that, just as
Christ was raised from death by the glorious power of the Father, so also we
might live a new life.

5 For since we have become one with
him in dying as he did, in the same way
we shall be one with him by being raised
to life as he was. 6 And we know that our
old being has been put to death with
Christ on his cross, in order that the
power of the sinful self might be destroyed, so that we should no longer be
the slaves of sin. 7 For when we die, we
are set free from the power of sin. 8 Since
we have died with Christ, we believe
that we will also live with him. 9 For we
know that Christ has been raised from
death and will never die again — death
will no longer rule over him. 10 And so,
because he died, sin has no power over
him; and now he lives his life in fellowship with God. 11 In the same way you
are to think of yourselves as dead, so far
as sin is concerned, but living in fellowship with God through Christ Jesus.

12 Sin must no longer rule in your mortal bodies, so that you obey the desires
of your natural self. 13 Nor must you surrender any part of yourselves to sin to be
used for wicked purposes. Instead, give
yourselves to God, as those who have
been brought from death to life, and surrender your whole being to him to be
used for righteous purposes. 14 Sin must
not be your master; for you do not live
under law but under God's grace.

Slaves of Righteousness

15 What, then? Shall we sin, because
we are not under law but under God's
grace? By no means! 16 Surely you know
that when you surrender yourselves as
slaves to obey someone, you are in fact
the slaves of the master you obey —
either of sin, which results in death, or of
obedience, which results in being put
right with God. 17 But thanks be to God!
For though at one time you were slaves
to sin, you have obeyed with all your
heart the truths found in the teaching
you received. 18 You were set free from
sin and became the slaves of righteousness. 19 (I use everyday language because of the weakness of your natural
selves.) At one time you surrendered
yourselves entirely as slaves to impurity
and wickedness for wicked purposes. In
the same way you must now surrender
yourselves entirely as slaves of righteousness for holy purposes.

20 When you were the slaves of sin,
you were free from righteousness.
21 What did you gain from doing the
things that you are now ashamed of?

The result of those things is death! 22 But
now you have been set free from sin and
are the slaves of God. Your gain is a life
fully dedicated to him, and the result is
eternal life. 23 For sin pays its wage—
death; but God's free gift is eternal life in
union with Christ Jesus our Lord.

An Illustration from Marriage

7 Certainly you will understand what
I am about to say, my friends, because all of you know about law. The
law rules over people only as long as
they live. 2 A married woman, for example, is bound by the law to her husband
as long as he lives; but if he dies, then
she is free from the law that bound her
to him. 3 So then, if she lives with another man while her husband is alive,
she will be called an adulteress; but if
her husband dies, she is legally a free
woman and does not commit adultery if
she marries another man. 4 That is how it
is with you, my friends. As far as the
Law is concerned, you also have died because you are part of the body of Christ;
and now you belong to him who was
raised from death in order that we might
be useful in the service of God. 5 For
when we lived according to our human
nature, the sinful desires stirred up by
the Law were at work in our bodies, and
all we did ended in death. 6 Now, however, we are free from the Law, because
we died to that which once held us prisoners. No longer do we serve in the old
way of a written law, but in the new way
of the Spirit.

Law and Sin

7 Shall we say, then, that the Law itself
is sinful? Of course not! But it was the
Law that made me know what sin is. If
the Law had not said, "Do not desire
what belongs to someone else," I would
not have known such a desire. 8 But by
means of that commandment sin found
its chance to stir up all kinds of selfish
desires in me. Apart from law, sin is a
dead thing. 9 I myself was once alive
apart from law; but when the commandment came, sin sprang to life, 10 and I
died. And the commandment which was
meant to bring life, in my case brought
death. 11 Sin found its chance, and by
means of the commandment it deceived
me and killed me.
12 So then, the Law itself is holy, and
the commandment is holy, right, and
good. 13 But does this mean that what is
good caused my death? By no means! It
was sin that did it; by using what is
good, sin brought death to me, in order
that its true nature as sin might be revealed. And so, by means of the commandment sin is shown to be even more
terribly sinful.

The Conflict in Us

14 We know that the Law is spiritual;
but I am a mortal, sold as a slave to sin.
15 I do not understand what I do; for I
don't do what I would like to do, but instead I do what I hate. 16 Since what I do
is what I don't want to do, this shows
that I agree that the Law is right. 17 So I
am not really the one who does this
thing; rather it is the sin that lives in me.
18 I know that good does not live in me—
that is, in my human nature. For even
though the desire to do good is in me, I
am not able to do it. 19 I don't do the good
I want to do; instead, I do the evil that I
do not want to do. 20 If I do what I don't
want to do, this means that I am no
longer the one who does it; instead, it is
the sin that lives in me.
21 So I find that this law is at work:
when I want to do what is good, what is
evil is the only choice I have. 22 My inner
being delights in the law of God. 23 But I
see a different law at work in my body—
a law that fights against the law which
my mind approves of. It makes me a
prisoner to the law of sin which is at
work in my body. 24 What an unhappy
man I am! Who will rescue me from this
body that is taking me to death?
25 Thanks be to God, who does this
through our Lord Jesus Christ!
This, then, is my condition: on my own
I can serve God's law only with my
mind, while my human nature serves the
law of sin.

Life in the Spirit

8 There is no condemnation now for
those who live in union with Christ
Jesus. 2 For the law of the Spirit, which
brings us life in union with Christ Jesus,
has set me[l] free from the law of sin and

[l] me; *some manuscripts have* you; *others have* us.

death. 3 What the Law could not do, because human nature was weak, God did.
He condemned sin in human nature by
sending his own Son, who came with a
nature like our sinful nature, to do away
with sin. 4 God did this so that the righteous demands of the Law might be fully
satisfied in us who live according to the
Spirit, and not according to human nature. 5 Those who live as their human nature tells them to, have their minds
controlled by what human nature wants.
Those who live as the Spirit tells them
to, have their minds controlled by what
the Spirit wants. 6 To be controlled by
human nature results in death; to be
controlled by the Spirit results in life and
peace. 7 And so people become enemies
of God when they are controlled by their
human nature; for they do not obey
God's law, and in fact they cannot obey
it. 8 Those who obey their human nature
cannot please God.

9 But you do not live as your human
nature tells you to; instead, you live as
the Spirit tells you to—if, in fact, God's
Spirit lives in you. Whoever does not
have the Spirit of Christ does not belong
to him. 10 But if Christ lives in you, the
Spirit is life for you[j] because you have
been put right with God, even though
your bodies are going to die because of
sin. 11 If the Spirit of God, who raised
Jesus from death, lives in you, then he
who raised Christ from death will also
give life to your mortal bodies by the
presence of his Spirit in you.

12 So then, my friends, we have an obligation, but it is not to live as our human
nature wants us to. 13 For if you live according to your human nature, you are
going to die; but if by the Spirit you put
to death your sinful actions, you will
live. 14 Those who are led by God's Spirit
are God's children. 15 For the Spirit that
God has given you does not make you
slaves and cause you to be afraid; instead, the Spirit makes you God's children, and by the Spirit's power we cry
out to God, "Father! my Father!" 16 God's
Spirit joins himself to our spirits to declare that we are God's children. 17 Since
we are his children, we will possess the
blessings he keeps for his people, and
we will also possess with Christ what
God has kept for him; for if we share
Christ's suffering, we will also share his
glory.

The Future Glory

18 I consider that what we suffer at this
present time cannot be compared at all
with the glory that is going to be revealed to us. 19 All of creation waits with
eager longing for God to reveal his children. 20 For creation was condemned to
lose its purpose, not of its own will, but
because God willed it to be so. Yet there
was the hope 21 that creation itself would
one day be set free from its slavery to
decay and would share the glorious freedom of the children of God. 22 For we
know that up to the present time all of
creation groans with pain, like the pain
of childbirth. 23 But it is not just creation
alone which groans; we who have the
Spirit as the first of God's gifts also
groan within ourselves as we wait for
God to make us his children and[k] set
our whole being free. 24 For it was by
hope that we were saved; but if we see
what we hope for, then it is not really
hope. For who of us hopes for something
we see? 25 But if we hope for what we do
not see, we wait for it with patience.

26 In the same way the Spirit also
comes to help us, weak as we are. For we
do not know how we ought to pray; the
Spirit himself pleads with God for us in
groans that words cannot express.
27 And God, who sees into our hearts,
knows what the thought of the Spirit is;
because the Spirit pleads with God on
behalf of his people and in accordance
with his will.

28 We know that in all things God
works for good with those who love
him,[l] those whom he has called according to his purpose. 29 Those whom God
had already chosen he also set apart to
become like his Son, so that the Son
would be the first among many believers. 30 And so those whom God set apart,
he called; and those he called, he put
right with himself, and he shared his
glory with them.

God's Love in Christ Jesus

31 In view of all this, what can we say?
If God is for us, who can be against us?

[j] the Spirit is life for you; *or* your spirit is alive. [k] *Some manuscripts do not have* make us his children and. [l] in all things God works for good with those who love him; *some manuscripts have* all things work for good for those who love God.

32 Certainly not God, who did not even
keep back his own Son, but offered him
for us all! He gave us his Son—will he
not also freely give us all things? 33 Who
will accuse God's chosen people? God
himself declares them not guilty! 34 Who,
then, will condemn them? Not Christ
Jesus, who died, or rather, who was
raised to life and is at the right side of
God, pleading with him for us! 35 Who,
then, can separate us from the love of
Christ? Can trouble do it, or hardship or
persecution or hunger or poverty or danger or death? 36 As the scripture says,

"For your sake we are in danger of
death at all times;
we are treated like sheep that
are going to be slaughtered."

37 No, in all these things we have complete victory through him who loved us!
38 For I am certain that nothing can separate us from his love: neither death nor
life, neither angels nor other heavenly
rulers or powers, neither the present nor
the future, 39 neither the world above nor
the world below—there is nothing in all
creation that will ever be able to separate us from the love of God which is
ours through Christ Jesus our Lord.

God and His People

9 I am speaking the truth; I belong to
Christ and I do not lie. My conscience, ruled by the Holy Spirit, also assures me that I am not lying 2 when I say
how great is my sorrow, how endless the
pain in my heart 3 for my people, my
own flesh and blood! For their sake I
could wish that I myself were under
God's curse and separated from Christ.
4 They are God's people; he made them
his children and revealed his glory to
them; he made his covenants[m] with
them and gave them the Law; they have
the true worship; they have received
God's promises; 5 they are descended
from the famous Hebrew ancestors; and
Christ, as a human being, belongs to
their race. May God, who rules over all,
be praised forever![n] Amen.

6 I am not saying that the promise of
God has failed; for not all the people of
Israel are the people of God. 7 Nor are all
of Abraham's descendants the children
of God. God said to Abraham, "It is
through Isaac that you will have the
descendants I promised you." 8 This
means that the children born in the
usual way[o] are not the children of God;
instead, the children born as a result of
God's promise are regarded as the true
descendants. 9 For God's promise was
made in these words: "At the right time[p]
I will come back, and Sarah will have
a son."

10 And this is not all. For Rebecca's two
sons had the same father, our ancestor
Isaac. 11-12 But in order that the choice of
one son might be completely the result
of God's own purpose, God said to her,
"The older will serve the younger." He
said this before they were born, before
they had done anything either good or
bad; so God's choice was based on his
call, and not on anything they had done.
13 As the scripture says, "I loved Jacob,
but I hated Esau."

14 Shall we say, then, that God is unjust? Not at all. 15 For he said to Moses, "I
will have mercy on anyone I wish; I will
take pity on anyone I wish." 16 So then,
everything depends, not on what we humans want or do, but only on God's
mercy. 17 For the scripture says to the
king of Egypt, "I made you king in order
to use you to show my power and to
spread my fame over the whole world."
18 So then, God has mercy on anyone he
wishes, and he makes stubborn anyone
he wishes.

God's Anger and Mercy

19 But one of you will say to me, "If this
is so, how can God find fault with anyone? Who can resist God's will?" 20 But
who are you, my friend, to talk back to
God? A clay pot does not ask the man
who made it, "Why did you make me
like this?" 21 After all, the man who
makes the pots has the right to use the
clay as he wishes, and to make two pots
from the same lump of clay, one for special occasions and the other for ordinary use.

22 And the same is true of what God
has done. He wanted to show his anger
and to make his power known. But he
was very patient in enduring those who

[m] covenants; *some manuscripts have* covenant. [n] May God, who rules over all, be praised forever!; *or* And may he, who is God ruling over all, be praised forever! [o] CHILDREN BORN IN THE USUAL WAY: *This refers to the descendants Abraham had through Ishmael, his son by Hagar (see Ga 4.22-23).* [p] At the right time; *or* At this time next year.

were the objects of his anger, who were
doomed to destruction. 23 And he also
wanted to reveal his abundant glory,
which was poured out on us who are the
objects of his mercy, those of us whom
he has prepared to receive his glory.
24 For we are the people he called, not
only from among the Jews but also from
among the Gentiles. 25 This is what he
says in the book of Hosea:

"The people who were not mine
I will call 'My People.'
The nation that I did not love
I will call 'My Beloved.'
26 And in the very place where they
were told, 'You are not my
people,'
there they will be called the
children of the living God."

27 And Isaiah exclaims about Israel:
"Even if the people of Israel are as many
as the grains of sand by the sea, yet only
a few of them will be saved; 28 for the
Lord will quickly settle his full account
with the world." 29 It is as Isaiah had said
before, "If the Lord Almighty had not
left us some descendants, we would
have become like Sodom, we would
have been like Gomorrah."

Israel and the Gospel

30 So we say that the Gentiles, who
were not trying to put themselves right
with God, were put right with him
through faith; 31 while God's people, who
were seeking a law that would put them
right with God, did not find it. 32 And
why not? Because they did not depend
on faith but on what they did. And so
they stumbled over the "stumbling
stone" 33 that the scripture speaks of:

"Look, I place in Zion a stone
that will make people stumble,
a rock that will make them fall.
But whoever believes in him will
not be disappointed."

10 My friends, how I wish with all
my heart that my own people
might be saved! How I pray to God for
them! 2 I can assure you that they are
deeply devoted to God; but their devotion is not based on true knowledge.
3 They have not known the way in which
God puts people right with himself, and
instead, they have tried to set up their
own way; and so they did not submit
themselves to God's way of putting people right. 4 For Christ has brought the
Law to an end, so that everyone who believes is put right with God.

Salvation Is for All

5 Moses wrote this about being put
right with God by obeying the Law:
"Whoever obeys the commands of the
Law will live." 6 But what the scripture
says about being put right with God
through faith is this: "You are not to ask
yourself, Who will go up into heaven?"
(that is, to bring Christ down). 7 "Nor are
you to ask, Who will go down into the
world below?" (that is, to bring Christ up
from death). 8 What it says is this: "God's
message is near you, on your lips and in
your heart"—that is, the message of
faith that we preach. 9 If you confess that
Jesus is Lord and believe that God
raised him from death, you will be
saved. 10 For it is by our faith that we are
put right with God; it is by our confession that we are saved. 11 The scripture
says, "Whoever believes in him will not
be disappointed." 12 This includes everyone, because there is no difference between Jews and Gentiles; God is the
same Lord of all and richly blesses all
who call to him. 13 As the scripture says,
"Everyone who calls out to the Lord for
help will be saved."

14 But how can they call to him for help
if they have not believed? And how can
they believe if they have not heard the
message? And how can they hear if the
message is not proclaimed? 15 And how
can the message be proclaimed if the
messengers are not sent out? As the
scripture says, "How wonderful is the
coming of messengers who bring good
news!" 16 But not all have accepted the
Good News. Isaiah himself said, "Lord,
who believed our message?" 17 So then,
faith comes from hearing the message,
and the message comes through preaching Christ.

18 But I ask: Is it true that they did not
hear the message? Of course they did—
for as the scripture says:

"The sound of their voice went out
to all the world;
their words reached the ends of
the earth."

19 Again I ask: Did the people of Israel
not understand? Moses himself is the
first one to answer:

"I will use a so-called nation
to make my people jealous;

and by means of a nation of fools
I will make my people angry."
20And Isaiah is even bolder when he
says,
"I was found by those who were
not looking for me;
I appeared to those who were
not asking for me."
21But concerning Israel he says, "All day
long I held out my hands to welcome a
disobedient and rebellious people."

God's Mercy on Israel

11 I ask, then: Did God reject his
own people? Certainly not! I myself am an Israelite, a descendant of
Abraham, a member of the tribe of Benjamin. 2God has not rejected his people,
whom he chose from the beginning. You
know what the scripture says in the passage where Elijah pleads with God
against Israel: 3"Lord, they have killed
your prophets and torn down your altars; I am the only one left, and they are
trying to kill me." 4What answer did
God give him? "I have kept for myself
seven thousand men who have not worshiped the false god Baal." 5It is the
same way now: there is a small number
left of those whom God has chosen because of his grace. 6His choice is based
on his grace, not on what they have
done. For if God's choice were based on
what people do, then his grace would
not be real grace.
7What then? The people of Israel did
not find what they were looking for. It
was only the small group that God chose
who found it; the rest grew deaf to God's
call. 8As the scripture says, "God made
their minds and hearts dull; to this very
day they cannot see or hear." 9And David says,
"May they be caught and trapped
at their feasts;
may they fall, may they be
punished!
10May their eyes be blinded so that
they cannot see;
and make them bend under their
troubles at all times."
11I ask, then: When the Jews stumbled, did they fall to their ruin? By no
means! Because they sinned, salvation
has come to the Gentiles, to make the
Jews jealous of them. 12The sin of the
Jews brought rich blessings to the
world, and their spiritual poverty
brought rich blessings to the Gentiles.
Then, how much greater the blessings
will be when the complete number of
Jews is included!

The Salvation of the Gentiles

13I am speaking now to you Gentiles:
As long as I am an apostle to the Gentiles, I will take pride in my work. 14Per-
haps I can make the people of my own
race jealous, and so be able to save some
of them. 15For when they were rejected,
all other people were changed from
God's enemies into his friends. What
will it be, then, when they are accepted?
It will be life for the dead!
16If the first piece of bread is given to
God, then the whole loaf is his also; and
if the roots of a tree are offered to God,
the branches are his also. 17Some of the
branches of the cultivated olive tree
have been broken off, and a branch of a
wild olive tree has been joined to it. You
Gentiles are like that wild olive tree, and
now you share the strong spiritual life of
the Jews. 18So then, you must not despise those who were broken off like
branches. How can you be proud? You
are just a branch; you don't support the
roots—the roots support you.
19But you will say, "Yes, but the
branches were broken off to make room
for me." 20That is true. They were broken off because they did not believe,
while you remain in place because you
do believe. But do not be proud of it; instead, be afraid. 21God did not spare the
Jews, who are like natural branches; do
you think he will spare you? 22Here we
see how kind and how severe God is. He
is severe toward those who have fallen,
but kind to you—if you continue in his
kindness. But if you do not, you too will
be broken off. 23And if the Jews abandon their unbelief, they will be put back
in the place where they were; for God is
able to do that. 24You Gentiles are like
the branch of a wild olive tree that is
broken off and then, contrary to nature,
is joined to a cultivated olive tree. The
Jews are like this cultivated tree; and it
will be much easier for God to join these
broken-off branches to their own tree
again.

God's Mercy on All

25There is a secret truth, my friends,
which I want you to know, for it will

keep you from thinking how wise you
are. It is that the stubbornness of the
people of Israel is not permanent, but
will last only until the complete number
of Gentiles comes to God. 26 And this is
how all Israel will be saved. As the scripture says,

"The Savior will come from Zion
and remove all wickedness from
the descendants of Jacob.
27 I will make this covenant with
them
when I take away their sins."

28 Because they reject the Good News,
the Jews are God's enemies for the sake
of you Gentiles. But because of God's
choice, they are his friends because of
their ancestors. 29 For God does not
change his mind about whom he
chooses and blesses. 30 As for you Gentiles, you disobeyed God in the past; but
now you have received God's mercy because the Jews were disobedient. 31 In
the same way, because of the mercy that
you have received, the Jews now disobey God, in order that they also may
now[q] receive God's mercy. 32 For God
has made all people prisoners of disobedience, so that he might show mercy to
them all.

Praise to God

33 How great are God's riches! How
deep are his wisdom and knowledge!
Who can explain his decisions? Who can
understand his ways? 34 As the scripture
says,

"Who knows the mind of the
Lord?
Who is able to give him advice?
35 Who has ever given him anything,
so that he had to pay it back?"

36 For all things were created by him,
and all things exist through him and for
him. To God be the glory forever! Amen.

Life in God's Service

12 So then, my friends, because of
God's great mercy to us I appeal
to you: Offer yourselves as a living sacrifice to God, dedicated to his service and
pleasing to him. This is the true worship
that you should offer. 2 Do not conform
yourselves to the standards of this
world, but let God transform you inwardly by a complete change of your
mind. Then you will be able to know the
will of God—what is good and is pleasing to him and is perfect.

3 And because of God's gracious gift to
me I say to every one of you: Do not
think of yourself more highly than you
should. Instead, be modest in your
thinking, and judge yourself according
to the amount of faith that God has given
you. 4 We have many parts in the one
body, and all these parts have different
functions. 5 In the same way, though we
are many, we are one body in union with
Christ, and we are all joined to each
other as different parts of one body. 6 So
we are to use our different gifts in accordance with the grace that God has
given us. If our gift is to speak God's
message, we should do it according to
the faith that we have; 7 if it is to serve,
we should serve; if it is to teach, we
should teach; 8 if it is to encourage others, we should do so. Whoever shares
with others should do it generously;
whoever has authority should work
hard; whoever shows kindness to others
should do it cheerfully.

9 Love must be completely sincere.
Hate what is evil, hold on to what is
good. 10 Love one another warmly as
Christians, and be eager to show respect
for one another. 11 Work hard and do not
be lazy. Serve the Lord with a heart full
of devotion. 12 Let your hope keep you
joyful, be patient in your troubles, and
pray at all times. 13 Share your belongings with your needy fellow Christians,
and open your homes to strangers.

14 Ask God to bless those who persecute you—yes, ask him to bless, not to
curse. 15 Be happy with those who are
happy, weep with those who weep.
16 Have the same concern for everyone.
Do not be proud, but accept humble
duties.[r] Do not think of yourselves as
wise.

17 If someone has done you wrong, do
not repay him with a wrong. Try to do
what everyone considers to be good.
18 Do everything possible on your part to
live in peace with everybody. 19 Never
take revenge, my friends, but instead let
God's anger do it. For the scripture says,
"I will take revenge, I will pay back, says
the Lord." 20 Instead, as the scripture

[q] *Some manuscripts do not have* now. [r] accept humble duties; *or* make friends with humble people.

says: "If your enemies are hungry, feed
them; if they are thirsty, give them a
drink; for by doing this you will make
them burn with shame." 21 Do not let evil
defeat you; instead, conquer evil with
good.

Duties toward State Authorities

13 Everyone must obey state authorities, because no authority
exists without God's permission, and the
existing authorities have been put there
by God. 2 Whoever opposes the existing
authority opposes what God has ordered; and anyone who does so will
bring judgment on himself. 3 For rulers
are not to be feared by those who do
good, but by those who do evil. Would
you like to be unafraid of those in authority? Then do what is good, and they
will praise you, 4 because they are God's
servants working for your own good.
But if you do evil, then be afraid of them,
because their power to punish is real.
They are God's servants and carry out
God's punishment on those who do evil.
5 For this reason you must obey the
authorities — not just because of God's
punishment, but also as a matter of conscience.

6 That is also why you pay taxes, because the authorities are working for
God when they fulfill their duties. 7 Pay,
then, what you owe them; pay them your
personal and property taxes, and show
respect and honor for them all.

Duties toward One Another

8 Be under obligation to no one — the
only obligation you have is to love one
another. Whoever does this has obeyed
the Law. 9 The commandments, "Do not
commit adultery; do not commit murder;
do not steal; do not desire what belongs
to someone else" — all these, and any
others besides, are summed up in the
one command, "Love your neighbor as
you love yourself." 10 If you love others,
you will never do them wrong; to love,
then, is to obey the whole Law.

11 You must do this, because you know
that the time has come for you to wake
up from your sleep. For the moment
when we will be saved is closer now
than it was when we first believed. 12 The
night is nearly over, day is almost here.
Let us stop doing the things that belong
to the dark, and let us take up weapons
for fighting in the light. 13 Let us conduct
ourselves properly, as people who live in
the light of day — no orgies or drunkenness, no immorality or indecency, no
fighting or jealousy. 14 But take up the
weapons of the Lord Jesus Christ, and
stop paying attention to your sinful nature and satisfying its desires.

Do Not Judge Others

14 Welcome those who are weak in
faith, but do not argue with them
about their personal opinions. 2 Some
people's faith allows them to eat anything, but the person who is weak in the
faith eats only vegetables. 3 The person
who will eat anything is not to despise
the one who doesn't; while the one who
eats only vegetables is not to pass judgment on the one who will eat anything;
for God has accepted that person. 4 Who
are you to judge the servants of someone
else? It is their own Master who will decide whether they succeed or fail. And
they will succeed, because the Lord is
able to make them succeed.

5 Some people think that a certain day
is more important than other days, while
others think that all days are the same.
We each should firmly make up our own
minds. 6 Those who think highly of a certain day do so in honor of the Lord;
those who will eat anything do so in
honor of the Lord, because they give
thanks to God for the food. Those who
refuse to eat certain things do so in
honor of the Lord, and they give thanks
to God. 7 We do not live for ourselves
only, and we do not die for ourselves
only. 8 If we live, it is for the Lord that we
live, and if we die, it is for the Lord that
we die. So whether we live or die, we
belong to the Lord. 9 For Christ died and
rose to life in order to be the Lord of the
living and of the dead. 10 You then, who
eat only vegetables — why do you pass
judgment on others? And you who eat
anything — why do you despise other believers? All of us will stand before God
to be judged by him. 11 For the scripture
says,

"As surely as I am the living God,
says the Lord,
everyone will kneel before me,
and everyone will confess that I
am God."

12 Every one of us, then, will have to give
an account to God.

Do Not Make Others Fall

13 So then, let us stop judging one another. Instead, you should decide never
to do anything that would make others
stumble or fall into sin. 14 My union with
the Lord Jesus makes me certain that no
food is of itself ritually unclean; but if
you believe that some food is unclean,
then it becomes unclean for you. 15 If you
hurt others because of something you
eat, then you are no longer acting from
love. Do not let the food that you eat ruin
the person for whom Christ died! 16 Do
not let what you regard as good get a
bad name. 17 For God's Kingdom is not a
matter of eating and drinking, but of the
righteousness, peace, and joy which the
Holy Spirit gives. 18 And when you serve
Christ in this way, you please God and
are approved by others.

19 So then, we must always aim[s] at
those things that bring peace and that
help strengthen one another. 20 Do not,
because of food, destroy what God has
done. All foods may be eaten, but it is
wrong to eat anything that will cause
someone else to fall into sin. 21 The right
thing to do is to keep from eating meat,
drinking wine, or doing anything else
that will make other believers fall.
22 Keep what you believe about this matter, then, between yourself and God.
Happy are those who do not feel guilty
when they do something they judge is
right! 23 But if they have doubts about
what they eat, God condemns them
when they eat it, because their action is
not based on faith. And anything that is
not based on faith is sin.

Please Others, Not Yourselves

15 We who are strong in the faith
ought to help the weak to carry
their burdens. We should not please ourselves. 2 Instead, we should all please
other believers for their own good, in order to build them up in the faith. 3 For
Christ did not please himself. Instead, as
the scripture says, "The insults which
are hurled at you have fallen on me."
4 Everything written in the Scriptures
was written to teach us, in order that we
might have hope through the patience
and encouragement which the Scriptures give us. 5 And may God, the source
of patience and encouragement, enable
you to have the same point of view
among yourselves by following the example of Christ Jesus, 6 so that all of you
together may praise with one voice the
God and Father of our Lord Jesus Christ.

The Gospel to the Gentiles

7 Accept one another, then, for the
glory of God, as Christ has accepted you.
8 For I tell you that Christ's life of service
was on behalf of the Jews, to show that
God is faithful, to make his promises to
their ancestors come true, 9 and to enable even the Gentiles to praise God for
his mercy. As the scripture says,

"And so I will praise you among
the Gentiles;
I will sing praises to you."

10 Again it says,

"Rejoice, Gentiles, with God's
people!"

11 And again,

"Praise the Lord, all Gentiles;
praise him, all peoples!"

12 And again, Isaiah says,

"A descendant of Jesse will
appear;
he will come to rule the Gentiles,
and they will put their hope
in him."

13 May God, the source of hope, fill you
with all joy and peace by means of your
faith in him, so that your hope will continue to grow by the power of the Holy
Spirit.

Paul's Reason for Writing So Boldly

14 My friends: I myself feel sure that
you are full of goodness, that you have
all knowledge, and that you are able to
teach one another. 15 But in this letter I
have been quite bold about certain subjects of which I have reminded you. I
have been bold because of the privilege
God has given me 16 of being a servant of
Christ Jesus to work for the Gentiles. I
serve like a priest in preaching the Good
News from God, in order that the Gentiles may be an offering acceptable to
God, dedicated to him by the Holy Spirit.
17 In union with Christ Jesus, then, I can
be proud of my service for God. 18 I will
be bold and speak only about what
Christ has done through me to lead the
Gentiles to obey God. He has done this
by means of words and deeds, 19 by the

[s] we must always aim; *some manuscripts have* we always aim.

power of miracles and wonders, and by the power of the Spirit of God. And so, in traveling all the way from Jerusalem to Illyricum, I have proclaimed fully the Good News about Christ. 20 My ambition has always been to proclaim the Good News in places where Christ has not been heard of, so as not to build on a foundation laid by someone else. 21 As the scripture says,

"Those who were not told about
him will see,
and those who have not heard
will understand."

Paul's Plan to Visit Rome

22 And so I have been prevented many times from coming to you. 23 But now that I have finished my work in these regions and since I have been wanting for so many years to come to see you, 24 I hope to do so now. I would like to see you on my way to Spain, and be helped by you to go there, after I have enjoyed visiting you for a while. 25 Right now, however, I am going to Jerusalem in the service of God's people there. 26 For the churches in Macedonia and Achaia have freely decided to give an offering to help the poor among God's people in Jerusalem. 27 That decision was their own; but, as a matter of fact, they have an obligation to help them. Since the Jews shared their spiritual blessings with the Gentiles, the Gentiles ought to use their material blessings to help the Jews. 28 When I have finished this task and have turned over to them all the money that has been raised for them, I shall leave for Spain and visit you on my way there. 29 When I come to you, I know that I shall come with a full measure of the blessing of Christ.

30 I urge you, friends, by our Lord Jesus Christ and by the love that the Spirit gives: join me in praying fervently to God for me. 31 Pray that I may be kept safe from the unbelievers in Judea and that my service in Jerusalem may be acceptable to God's people there. 32 And so I will come to you full of joy, if it is God's will, and enjoy a refreshing visit with you. 33 May God, our source of peace, be with all of you. Amen.

Personal Greetings

16 I recommend to you our sister Phoebe, who serves the church at Cenchreae. 2 Receive her in the Lord's name, as God's people should, and give her any help she may need from you; for she herself has been a good friend to many people and also to me.

3 I send greetings to Priscilla and Aquila, my fellow workers in the service of Christ Jesus; 4 they risked their lives for me. I am grateful to them—not only I, but all the Gentile churches as well. 5 Greetings also to the church that meets in their house.

Greetings to my dear friend Epaenetus, who was the first in the province of Asia to believe in Christ. 6 Greetings to Mary, who has worked so hard for you. 7 Greetings also to Andronicus and Junia,[t] fellow Jews who were in prison with me; they are well known among the apostles, and they became Christians before I did.

8 My greetings to Ampliatus, my dear friend in the fellowship of the Lord. 9 Greetings also to Urbanus, our fellow worker in Christ's service, and to Stachys, my dear friend. 10 Greetings to Apelles, whose loyalty to Christ has been proved. Greetings to those who belong to the family of Aristobulus. 11 Greetings to Herodion, a fellow Jew, and to the Christians in the family of Narcissus.

12 My greetings to Tryphaena and Tryphosa, who work in the Lord's service, and to my dear friend Persis, who has done so much work for the Lord. 13 I send greetings to Rufus, that outstanding worker in the Lord's service, and to his mother, who has always treated me like a son. 14 My greetings to Asyncritus, Phlegon, Hermes, Patrobas, Hermas, and all the other Christians with them. 15 Greetings to Philologus and Julia, to Nereus and his sister, to Olympas and to all of God's people who are with them.

16 Greet one another with the kiss of peace. All the churches of Christ send you their greetings.

Final Instructions

17 I urge you, my friends: watch out for those who cause divisions and upset

[t] Junia; *or* Junias; *some manuscripts have* Julia.

people's faith and go against the teaching which you have received. Keep away
from them! 18 For those who do such
things are not serving Christ our Lord,
but their own appetites. By their fine
words and flattering speech they deceive innocent people. 19 Everyone has
heard of your loyalty to the gospel, and
for this reason I am happy about you. I
want you to be wise about what is good,
but innocent in what is evil. 20 And God,
our source of peace, will soon crush Satan under your feet.
The grace of our Lord Jesus be with
you.[u]
21 Timothy, my fellow worker, sends
you his greetings; and so do Lucius, Jason, and Sosipater, fellow Jews.
22 I, Tertius, the writer of this letter,
send you Christian greetings.
23 My host Gaius, in whose house the
church meets, sends you his greetings;
Erastus, the city treasurer, and our
brother Quartus send you their
greetings.[v]

Concluding Prayer of Praise

25 Let us give glory to God! He is able
to make you stand firm in your faith, according to the Good News I preach
about Jesus Christ and according to the
revelation of the secret truth which was
hidden for long ages in the past. 26 Now,
however, that truth has been brought
out into the open through the writings of
the prophets; and by the command of
the eternal God it is made known to all
nations, so that all may believe and
obey.
27 To the only God, who alone is all-
wise, be glory through Jesus Christ forever! Amen.[w]

[u] *Some manuscripts omit this sentence.* [v] *Some manuscripts add verse 24:* The grace of our Lord Jesus Christ be with you all. Amen; *others add this after verse 27.*
[w] *Some manuscripts have verses 25-27 here and after 14.23; others have them only after 14.23; one has them after 15.33.*

Paul's First Letter to the CORINTHIANS

Introduction

Paul's First Letter to the Corinthians *was written to deal with problems of Christian life and faith that had arisen in the church which Paul had established at Corinth. At that time Corinth was a great cosmopolitan Greek city, the capital of the Roman province of Achaia. It was noted for its thriving commerce, proud culture, widespread immorality, and variety of religions.*

The apostle's chief concerns are with problems such as divisions and immorality in the church, and with questions about sex and marriage, matters of conscience, church order, gifts of the Holy Spirit, and the resurrection. With deep insight he shows how the Good News speaks to these questions.

Chapter 13, which presents love as the best of God's gifts to his people, is probably the most widely known passage in the book.

Outline of Contents

Introduction 1.1-9
Factions in the church 1.10—4.21
Sexual morality and family life 5.1—7.40
Christians and pagans 8.1—11.1
Church life and worship 11.2—14.40
The resurrection of Christ and of believers 15.1-58
The offering for the Christians in Judea 16.1-4
Personal matters and conclusion 16.5-24

1 From Paul, who was called by the
will of God to be an apostle of
Christ Jesus, and from our brother
Sosthenes—
2 To the church of God which is in Corinth, to all who are called to be God's
holy people, who belong to him in union
with Christ Jesus, together with all people everywhere who worship our Lord
Jesus Christ, their Lord and ours:
3 May God our Father and the Lord
Jesus Christ give you grace and peace.

Blessings in Christ

4 I always give thanks to my God for
you because of the grace he has given
you through Christ Jesus. 5 For in union
with Christ you have become rich in all
things, including all speech and all
knowledge. 6 The message about Christ
has become so firmly established in you
7 that you have not failed to receive a single blessing, as you wait for our Lord
Jesus Christ to be revealed. 8 He will also
keep you firm to the end, so that you will
be faultless on the Day of our Lord Jesus
Christ. 9 God is to be trusted, the God
who called you to have fellowship with
his Son Jesus Christ, our Lord.

Divisions in the Church

10 By the authority of our Lord Jesus
Christ I appeal to all of you, my friends,
to agree in what you say, so that there
will be no divisions among you. Be completely united, with only one thought
and one purpose. 11 For some people
from Chloe's family have told me quite
plainly, my friends, that there are quarrels among you. 12 Let me put it this way:
each one of you says something different. One says, "I follow Paul"; another, "I
follow Apollos"; another, "I follow Peter"; and another, "I follow Christ."
13 Christ has been divided[a] into groups!
Was it Paul who died on the cross for
you? Were you baptized as Paul's
disciples?
14 I thank God that I did not baptize
any of you except Crispus and Gaius.
15 No one can say, then, that you were
baptized as my disciples. (16 Oh yes, I
also baptized Stephanas and his family;
but I can't remember whether I baptized
anyone else.) 17 Christ did not send me to
baptize. He sent me to tell the Good
News, and to tell it without using the
language of human wisdom, in order to
make sure that Christ's death on the
cross is not robbed of its power.

Christ the Power and the Wisdom of God

18 For the message about Christ's
death on the cross is nonsense to those
who are being lost; but for us who are
being saved it is God's power. 19 The
scripture says,

> "I will destroy the wisdom of the
> wise
> and set aside the understanding
> of the scholars."

20 So then, where does that leave the
wise? or the scholars? or the skillful de-
baters of this world? God has shown that
this world's wisdom is foolishness!
21 For God in his wisdom made it impossible for people to know him by
means of their own wisdom. Instead, by
means of the so-called "foolish" message
we preach, God decided to save those
who believe. 22 Jews want miracles for
proof, and Greeks look for wisdom. 23 As
for us, we proclaim the crucified Christ,
a message that is offensive to the Jews
and nonsense to the Gentiles; 24 but for
those whom God has called, both Jews
and Gentiles, this message is Christ,
who is the power of God and the wisdom
of God. 25 For what seems to be God's
foolishness is wiser than human wisdom, and what seems to be God's weakness is stronger than human strength.
26 Now remember what you were, my
friends, when God called you. From the
human point of view few of you were
wise or powerful or of high social standing. 27 God purposely chose what the
world considers nonsense in order to
shame the wise, and he chose what the
world considers weak in order to shame
the powerful. 28 He chose what the world
looks down on and despises and thinks
is nothing, in order to destroy what the
world thinks is important. 29 This means
that no one can boast in God's presence.
30 But God has brought you into union
with Christ Jesus, and God has made
Christ to be our wisdom. By him we are
put right with God; we become God's
holy people and are set free. 31 So then,
as the scripture says, "Whoever wants to

[a] Christ has been divided; *some manuscripts have* Christ cannot be divided.

boast must boast of what the Lord has
done."

The Message about the Crucified Christ

2 When I came to you, my friends, to
preach God's secret truth,[b] I did
not use big words and great learning.
2 For while I was with you, I made up my
mind to forget everything except Jesus
Christ and especially his death on the
cross. 3 So when I came to you, I was
weak and trembled all over with fear,
4 and my teaching and message were not
delivered with skillful words of human
wisdom, but with convincing proof of
the power of God's Spirit. 5 Your faith,
then, does not rest on human wisdom
but on God's power.

God's Wisdom

6 Yet I do proclaim a message of wisdom to those who are spiritually mature.
But it is not the wisdom that belongs to
this world or to the powers that rule this
world — powers that are losing their
power. 7 The wisdom I proclaim is God's
secret wisdom, which is hidden from human beings, but which he had already
chosen for our glory even before the
world was made. 8 None of the rulers of
this world knew this wisdom. If they had
known it, they would not have crucified
the Lord of glory. 9 However, as the
scripture says,

"What no one ever saw or heard,
what no one ever thought could
happen,
is the very thing God prepared
for those who love him."

10 But[c] it was to us that God made
known his secret by means of his Spirit.
The Spirit searches everything, even the
hidden depths of God's purposes. 11 It is
only our own spirit within us that knows
all about us; in the same way, only God's
Spirit knows all about God. 12 We have
not received this world's spirit; instead,
we have received the Spirit sent by God,
so that we may know all that God has
given us.
13 So then, we do not speak in words
taught by human wisdom, but in words
taught by the Spirit, as we explain spiritual truths to those who have the Spirit.[d]
14 Whoever does not have the Spirit cannot receive the gifts that come from
God's Spirit. Such a person really does
not understand them, and they seem to
be nonsense, because their value can be
judged only on a spiritual basis. 15 Whoever has the Spirit, however, is able to
judge the value of everything, but no one
is able to judge him. 16 As the scripture
says,

"Who knows the mind of the
Lord?
Who is able to give him advice?"

We, however, have the mind of Christ.

Servants of God

3 As a matter of fact, my friends, I
could not talk to you as I talk to people who have the Spirit; I had to talk to
you as though you belonged to this
world, as children in the Christian faith.
2 I had to feed you milk, not solid food,
because you were not ready for it. And
even now you are not ready for it, 3 because you still live as the people of this
world live. When there is jealousy
among you and you quarrel with one another, doesn't this prove that you belong
to this world, living by its standards?
4 When one of you says, "I follow Paul,"
and another, "I follow Apollos" — aren't
you acting like worldly people?
5 After all, who is Apollos? And who is
Paul? We are simply God's servants, by
whom you were led to believe. Each one
of us does the work which the Lord gave
him to do: 6 I planted the seed, Apollos
watered the plant, but it was God who
made the plant grow. 7 The one who
plants and the one who waters really do
not matter. It is God who matters, because he makes the plant grow. 8 There
is no difference between the one who
plants and the one who waters; God will
reward each one according to the work
each has done. 9 For we are partners
working together for God, and you are
God's field.
You are also God's building. 10 Using
the gift that God gave me, I did the work
of an expert builder and laid the foundation, and someone else is building on it.
But each of you must be careful how you
build. 11 For God has already placed
Jesus Christ as the one and only founda-

[b] God's secret truth; *some manuscripts have* the testimony about God.
[c] But; *some manuscripts have* For. [d] to those who have the Spirit; *or* with words given by the Spirit.

tion, and no other foundation can be
laid. 12 Some will use gold or silver or
precious stones in building on the foundation; others will use wood or grass or
straw. 13 And the quality of each person's work will be seen when the Day of
Christ exposes it. For on that Day fire
will reveal everyone's work; the fire will
test it and show its real quality. 14 If what
was built on the foundation survives the
fire, the builder will receive a reward.
15 But if your work is burnt up, then you
will lose it; but you yourself will be
saved, as if you had escaped through the
fire.

16 Surely you know that you are God's
temple and that God's Spirit lives in you!
17 God will destroy anyone who destroys
God's temple. For God's temple is holy,
and you yourselves are his temple.

18 You should not fool yourself. If any
of you think that you are wise by this
world's standards, you should become a
fool, in order to be really wise. 19 For
what this world considers to be wisdom
is nonsense in God's sight. As the scripture says, "God traps the wise in their
cleverness"; 20 and another scripture
says, "The Lord knows that the thoughts
of the wise are worthless." 21 No one,
then, should boast about what human
beings can do. Actually everything belongs to you: 22 Paul, Apollos, and Peter;
this world, life and death, the present
and the future—all these are yours,
23 and you belong to Christ, and Christ
belongs to God.

Apostles of Christ

4 You should think of us as Christ's
servants, who have been put in
charge of God's secret truths. 2 The one
thing required of such servants is that
they be faithful to their master. 3 Now, I
am not at all concerned about being
judged by you or by any human standard; I don't even pass judgment on myself. 4 My conscience is clear, but that
does not prove that I am really innocent.
The Lord is the one who passes judgment on me. 5 So you should not pass
judgment on anyone before the right
time comes. Final judgment must wait
until the Lord comes; he will bring to
light the dark secrets and expose the
hidden purposes of people's minds. And
then all will receive from God the praise
they deserve.

6 For your sake, my friends, I have applied all this to Apollos and me, using
the two of us as an example, so that you
may learn what the saying means, "Observe the proper rules." None of you
should be proud of one person and despise another. 7 Who made you superior
to others? Didn't God give you everything you have? Well, then, how can you
boast, as if what you have were not a
gift?

8 Do you already have everything you
need? Are you already rich? Have you
become kings, even though we are not?
Well, I wish you really were kings, so
that we could be kings together with
you. 9 For it seems to me that God has
given the very last place to us apostles,
like people condemned to die in public
as a spectacle for the whole world of angels and of human beings. 10 For Christ's
sake we are fools; but you are wise in
union with Christ! We are weak, but you
are strong! We are despised, but you are
honored! 11 To this very moment we go
hungry and thirsty; we are clothed in
rags; we are beaten; we wander from
place to place; 12 we wear ourselves out
with hard work. When we are cursed,
we bless; when we are persecuted, we
endure; 13 when we are insulted, we answer back with kind words. We are no
more than this world's garbage; we are
the scum of the earth to this very
moment!

14 I write this to you, not because I
want to make you feel ashamed, but to
instruct you as my own dear children.
15 For even if you have ten thousand
guardians in your Christian life, you
have only one father. For in your life in
union with Christ Jesus I have become
your father by bringing the Good News
to you. 16 I beg you, then, to follow my
example. 17 For this purpose I am sending to you Timothy, who is my own dear
and faithful son in the Christian life. He
will remind you of the principles which I
follow in the new life in union with
Christ Jesus and which I teach in all the
churches everywhere.

18 Some of you have become proud because you have thought that I would not
be coming to visit you. 19 If the Lord is
willing, however, I will come to you
soon, and then I will find out for myself
the power which these proud people
have, and not just what they say. 20 For

the Kingdom of God is not a matter of
words but of power. 21 Which do you
prefer? Shall I come to you with a whip,
or in a spirit of love and gentleness?

Immorality in the Church

5 Now, it is actually being said that
there is sexual immorality among
you so terrible that not even the heathen
would be guilty of it. I am told that a man
is sleeping with his stepmother! 2 How,
then, can you be proud? On the contrary,
you should be filled with sadness, and
the man who has done such a thing
should be expelled from your fellowship. 3-4 And even though I am far away
from you in body, still I am there with
you in spirit; and as though I were there
with you, I have in the name of our Lord
Jesus already passed judgment on the
man who has done this terrible thing. As
you meet together, and I meet with you
in my spirit, by the power of our Lord
Jesus present with us, 5 you are to hand
this man over to Satan for his body to be
destroyed, so that his spirit may be
saved in the Day of the Lord.

6 It is not right for you to be proud!
You know the saying, "A little bit of
yeast makes the whole batch of dough
rise." 7 You must remove the old yeast of
sin so that you will be entirely pure.
Then you will be like a new batch of
dough without any yeast, as indeed I
know you actually are. For our Passover
Festival is ready, now that Christ, our
Passover lamb, has been sacrificed. 8 Let
us celebrate our Passover, then, not with
bread having the old yeast of sin and
wickedness, but with the bread that has
no yeast, the bread of purity and truth.

9 In the letter that I wrote you I told
you not to associate with immoral people. 10 Now I did not mean pagans who
are immoral or greedy or are thieves, or
who worship idols. To avoid them you
would have to get out of the world completely. 11 What I meant was that you
should not associate with a person who
calls himself a believer but is immoral or
greedy or worships idols or is a slan-
derer or a drunkard or a thief. Don't
even sit down to eat with such a person.

12-13 After all, it is none of my business
to judge outsiders. God will judge them.
But should you not judge the members
of your own fellowship? As the scripture
says, "Remove the evil person from your
group."

Lawsuits against Fellow Christians

6 If any of you have a dispute with
another Christian, how dare you go
before heathen judges instead of letting
God's people settle the matter? 2 Don't
you know that God's people will judge
the world? Well, then, if you are to judge
the world, aren't you capable of judging
small matters? 3 Do you not know that
we shall judge the angels? How much
more, then, the things of this life! 4 If
such matters come up, are you going to
take them to be settled by people who
have no standing in the church? 5 Shame
on you! Surely there is at least one wise
person in your fellowship who can settle a dispute between fellow Christians.
6 Instead, one Christian goes to court
against another and lets unbelievers
judge the case!

7 The very fact that you have legal disputes among yourselves shows that you
have failed completely. Would it not be
better for you to be wronged? Would it
not be better for you to be robbed? 8 Instead, you yourselves wrong one another and rob one another, even other
believers! 9 Surely you know that the
wicked will not possess God's Kingdom.
Do not fool yourselves; people who are
immoral or who worship idols or are
adulterers or homosexual perverts 10 or
who steal or are greedy or are drunkards or who slander others or are
thieves—none of these will possess
God's Kingdom. 11 Some of you were like
that. But you have been purified from
sin; you have been dedicated to God;
you have been put right with God by the
Lord Jesus Christ and by the Spirit of
our God.

Use Your Bodies for God's Glory

12 Someone will say, "I am allowed to
do anything." Yes; but not everything is
good for you. I could say that I am allowed to do anything, but I am not going
to let anything make me its slave.
13 Someone else will say, "Food is for the
stomach, and the stomach is for food."
Yes; but God will put an end to both. The
body is not to be used for sexual immorality, but to serve the Lord; and the
Lord provides for the body. 14 God raised

the Lord from death, and he will also
raise us by his power.
15 You know that your bodies are parts
of the body of Christ. Shall I take a part
of Christ's body and make it part of the
body of a prostitute? Impossible! 16 Or
perhaps you don't know that the man
who joins his body to a prostitute becomes physically one with her? The
scripture says quite plainly, "The two
will become one body." 17 But he who
joins himself to the Lord becomes spiritually one with him.
18 Avoid immorality. Any other sin a
man commits does not affect his body;
but the man who is guilty of sexual immorality sins against his own body.
19 Don't you know that your body is the
temple of the Holy Spirit, who lives in
you and who was given to you by God?
You do not belong to yourselves but to
God; 20 he bought you for a price. So use
your bodies for God's glory.

Questions about Marriage

7 Now, to deal with the matters you
wrote about.
A man does well not to marry.[e] 2 But
because there is so much immorality,
every man should have his own wife,
and every woman should have her own
husband. 3 A man should fulfill his duty
as a husband, and a woman should fulfill her duty as a wife, and each should
satisfy the other's needs. 4 A wife is not
the master of her own body, but her husband is; in the same way a husband is
not the master of his own body, but his
wife is. 5 Do not deny yourselves to each
other, unless you first agree to do so for
a while in order to spend your time in
prayer; but then resume normal marital
relations. In this way you will be kept
from giving in to Satan's temptation because of your lack of self-control.
6 I tell you this not as an order, but
simply as a permission. 7 Actually I
would prefer that all of you were as I am;
but each one has a special gift from God,
one person this gift, another one that
gift.
8 Now, to the unmarried and to the
widows I say that it would be better for
you to continue to live alone as I do. 9 But
if you cannot restrain your desires, go
ahead and marry—it is better to marry
than to burn with passion.
10 For married people I have a command which is not my own but the
Lord's: a wife must not leave her husband; 11 but if she does, she must remain
single or else be reconciled to her husband; and a husband must not divorce
his wife.
12 To the others I say (I, myself, not the
Lord): if a Christian man has a wife who
is an unbeliever and she agrees to go on
living with him, he must not divorce her.
13 And if a Christian woman is married
to a man who is an unbeliever and he
agrees to go on living with her, she must
not divorce him. 14 For the unbelieving
husband is made acceptable to God by
being united to his wife, and the unbelieving wife is made acceptable to God
by being united to her Christian husband. If this were not so, their children
would be like pagan children; but as it is,
they are acceptable to God. 15 However,
if the one who is not a believer wishes to
leave the Christian partner, let it be so.
In such cases the Christian partner,
whether husband or wife, is free to act.
God has called you to live in peace.
16 How can you be sure, Christian wife,
that you will not save[f] your husband?
Or how can you be sure, Christian husband, that you will not save[f] your wife?

Live As God Called You

17 Each of you should go on living according to the Lord's gift to you, and as
you were when God called you. This is
the rule I teach in all the churches. 18 If a
circumcised man has accepted God's
call, he should not try to remove the
marks of circumcision; if an uncircumcised man has accepted God's call, he
should not get circumcised. 19 For
whether or not a man is circumcised
means nothing; what matters is to obey
God's commandments. 20 Each of you
should remain as you were when you accepted God's call. 21 Were you a slave
when God called you? Well, never mind;
but if you have a chance to become
free, use it.[g] 22 For a slave who has
been called by the Lord is the Lord's free

[e] A man does well not to marry; *or* You say that a man does well not to marry.
[f] How can you be sure . . . that you will not save; *or* How do you know . . . that you will save.
[g] but if you have a chance to become free, use it; *or* but even if you have a chance to become free, choose rather to make the best of your condition as a slave.

person; in the same way a free person
who has been called by Christ is his
slave. 23 God bought you for a price; so
do not become slaves of people. 24 My
friends, each of you should remain in fellowship with God in the same condition
that you were when you were called.

Questions about the Unmarried and the Widows

25 Now, concerning what you wrote
about unmarried people: I do not have a
command from the Lord, but I give my
opinion as one who by the Lord's mercy
is worthy of trust.
26 Considering the present distress, I
think it is better for a man to stay as he
is. 27 Do you have a wife? Then don't try
to get rid of her. Are you unmarried?
Then don't look for a wife. 28 But if you
do marry, you haven't committed a sin;
and if an unmarried woman marries, she
hasn't committed a sin. But I would
rather spare you the everyday troubles
that married people will have.
29 What I mean, my friends, is this:
there is not much time left, and from
now on married people should live as
though they were not married; 30 those
who weep, as though they were not sad;
those who laugh, as though they were
not happy; those who buy, as though
they did not own what they bought;
31 those who deal in material goods, as
though they were not fully occupied
with them. For this world, as it is now,
will not last much longer.
32 I would like you to be free from
worry. An unmarried man concerns
himself with the Lord's work, because
he is trying to please the Lord. 33 But a
married man concerns himself with
worldly matters, because he wants to
please his wife; 34 and so he is pulled in
two directions. An unmarried woman or
a virgin concerns herself with the Lord's
work, because she wants to be dedicated
both in body and spirit; but a married
woman concerns herself with worldly
matters, because she wants to please her
husband.
35 I am saying this because I want to
help you. I am not trying to put restrictions on you. Instead, I want you to do
what is right and proper, and to give
yourselves completely to the Lord's
service without any reservation.
36 In the case of an engaged couple
who have decided not to marry: if the
man feels that he is not acting properly
toward the young woman and if his passions are too strong and he feels that
they ought to marry, then they should
get married, as he wants to.[h] There is no
sin in this. 37 But if a man, without being
forced to do so, has firmly made up his
mind not to marry,[i] and if he has his
will under complete control and has already decided in his own mind what to
do—then he does well not to marry the
young woman.[j] 38 So the man who marries[k] does well, but the one who doesn't
marry[l] does even better.
39 A married woman is not free as long
as her husband lives; but if her husband
dies, then she is free to be married to any
man she wishes, but only if he is a Christian. 40 She will be happier, however, if
she stays as she is. That is my opinion,
and I think that I too have God's Spirit.

The Question about Food Offered to Idols

8 Now, concerning what you wrote
about food offered to idols.
It is true, of course, that "all of us have
knowledge," as they say. Such knowledge, however, puffs a person up with
pride; but love builds up. 2 Those who
think they know something really don't
know as they ought to know. 3 But the
person who loves God is known by him.
4 So then, about eating the food offered to idols: we know that an idol
stands for something that does not really
exist; we know that there is only the one
God. 5 Even if there are so-called "gods,"
whether in heaven or on earth, and even
though there are many of these "gods"
and "lords," 6 yet there is for us only one
God, the Father, who is the Creator of all
things and for whom we live; and there
is only one Lord, Jesus Christ, through
whom all things were created and
through whom we live.
7 But not everyone knows this truth.

[h] an engaged couple . . . as he wants to; *or* a man and his unmarried daughter: if he feels that he is not acting properly toward her, and if she is at the right age to marry, then he should do as he wishes and let her get married. [i] not to marry; *or* not to let his daughter get married.
[j] marry the young woman; *or* let her get married. [k] marries; *or* lets his daughter get married.
[l] doesn't marry; *or* doesn't let her get married.

Some people have been so used to idols
that to this day when they eat such food
they still think of it as food that belongs
to an idol; their conscience is weak, and
they feel they are defiled by the food.
8 Food, however, will not improve our relation with God; we shall not lose anything if we do not eat, nor shall we gain
anything if we do eat.

9 Be careful, however, not to let your
freedom of action make those who are
weak in the faith fall into sin. 10 Suppose
a person whose conscience is weak in
this matter sees you, who have so-called
"knowledge," eating in the temple of an
idol; will not this encourage him to eat
food offered to idols? 11 And so this weak
person, your brother for whom Christ
died, will perish because of your "knowledge"! 12 And in this way you will be sinning against Christ by sinning against
other Christians and wounding their
weak conscience. 13 So then, if food
makes a believer sin, I will never eat
meat again, so as not to make a believer
fall into sin.

Rights and Duties of an Apostle

9 Am I not a free man? Am I not an
apostle? Haven't I seen Jesus our
Lord? And aren't you the result of my
work for the Lord? 2 Even if others do
not accept me as an apostle, surely you
do! Because of your life in union with
the Lord you yourselves are proof of the
fact that I am an apostle.

3 When people criticize me, this is how
I defend myself: 4 Don't I have the right
to be given food and drink for my work?
5 Don't I have the right to follow the example of the other apostles and the
Lord's brothers and Peter, by taking a
Christian wife with me on my trips? 6 Or
are Barnabas and I the only ones who
have to work for our living? 7 What soldiers ever have to pay their own expenses in the army? What farmers do
not eat the grapes from their own vineyard? What shepherds do not use the
milk from their own sheep?

8 I don't have to limit myself to these
everyday examples, because the Law
says the same thing. 9 We read in the
Law of Moses, "Do not muzzle an ox
when you are using it to thresh grain."
Now, is God concerned about oxen?
10 Didn't he really mean us when he said
that? Of course that was written for us.
Anyone who plows and anyone who
reaps should do their work in the hope
of getting a share of the crop. 11 We have
sown spiritual seed among you. Is it too
much if we reap material benefits from
you? 12 If others have the right to expect
this from you, don't we have an even
greater right?

But we haven't made use of this right.
Instead, we have endured everything in
order not to put any obstacle in the way
of the Good News about Christ. 13 Surely
you know that the men who work in the
Temple get their food from the Temple
and that those who offer the sacrifices
on the altar get a share of the sacrifices.
14 In the same way, the Lord has ordered
that those who preach the gospel should
get their living from it.

15 But I haven't made use of any of
these rights, nor am I writing this now in
order to claim such rights for myself. I
would rather die first! Nobody is going
to turn my rightful boast into empty
words! 16 I have no right to boast just because I preach the gospel. After all, I am
under orders to do so. And how terrible
it would be for me if I did not preach the
gospel! 17 If I did my work as a matter of
free choice, then I could expect to be
paid; but I do it as a matter of duty, because God has entrusted me with this
task. 18 What pay do I get, then? It is the
privilege of preaching the Good News
without charging for it, without claiming
my rights in my work for the gospel.

19 I am a free man, nobody's slave; but
I make myself everybody's slave in order to win as many people as possible.
20 While working with the Jews, I live
like a Jew in order to win them; and
even though I myself am not subject to
the Law of Moses, I live as though I were
when working with those who are, in order to win them. 21 In the same way,
when working with Gentiles, I live like a
Gentile, outside the Jewish Law, in order to win Gentiles. This does not mean
that I don't obey God's law; I am really
under Christ's law. 22 Among the weak
in faith I become weak like one of them,
in order to win them. So I become all
things to all people, that I may save
some of them by whatever means are
possible.

23 All this I do for the gospel's sake, in
order to share in its blessings. 24 Surely
you know that many runners take part

in a race, but only one of them wins the
prize. Run, then, in such a way as to win
the prize. 25 Every athlete in training
submits to strict discipline, in order to be
crowned with a wreath that will not last;
but we do it for one that will last forever.
26 That is why I run straight for the finish
line; that is why I am like a boxer who
does not waste his punches. 27 I harden
my body with blows and bring it under
complete control, to keep myself from
being disqualified after having called
others to the contest.

Warnings against Idols

10 I want you to remember, my
friends, what happened to our
ancestors who followed Moses. They
were all under the protection of the
cloud, and all passed safely through the
Red Sea. 2 In the cloud and in the sea
they were all baptized as followers of
Moses. 3 All ate the same spiritual bread
4 and drank the same spiritual drink.
They drank from the spiritual rock that
went with them; and that rock was
Christ himself. 5 But even then God was
not pleased with most of them, and so
their dead bodies were scattered over
the desert.

6 Now, all of this is an example for us,
to warn us not to desire evil things, as
they did, 7 nor to worship idols, as some
of them did. As the scripture says, "The
people sat down to a feast which turned
into an orgy of drinking and sex." 8 We
must not be guilty of sexual immorality,
as some of them were — and in one day
twenty-three thousand of them fell dead.
9 We must not put the Lord[m] to the test,
as some of them did — and they were
killed by snakes. 10 We must not complain, as some of them did — and they
were destroyed by the Angel of Death.

11 All these things happened to them as
examples for others, and they were written down as a warning for us. For we
live at a time when the end is about to
come.

12 If you think you are standing firm
you had better be careful that you do not
fall. 13 Every test that you have experienced is the kind that normally comes to
people. But God keeps his promise, and
he will not allow you to be tested beyond
your power to remain firm; at the time
you are put to the test, he will give you
the strength to endure it, and so provide
you with a way out.

14 So then, my dear friends, keep away
from the worship of idols. 15 I speak to
you as sensible people; judge for yourselves what I say. 16 The cup we use in
the Lord's Supper and for which we give
thanks to God: when we drink from it,
we are sharing in the blood of Christ.
And the bread we break: when we eat it,
we are sharing in the body of Christ.
17 Because there is the one loaf of bread,
all of us, though many, are one body, for
we all share the same loaf.

18 Consider the people of Israel; those
who eat what is offered in sacrifice
share in the altar's service to God. 19 Do
I imply, then, that an idol or the food
offered to it really amounts to anything?
20 No! What I am saying is that what is
sacrificed on pagan altars is offered to
demons, not to God. And I do not want
you to be partners with demons. 21 You
cannot drink from the Lord's cup and
also from the cup of demons; you cannot
eat at the Lord's table and also at the
table of demons. 22 Or do we want to
make the Lord jealous? Do we think that
we are stronger than he?

23 "We are allowed to do anything," so
they say. That is true, but not everything
is good. "We are allowed to do anything" — but not everything is helpful.
24 None of you should be looking out
for your own interests, but for the interests of others.

25 You are free to eat anything sold in
the meat market, without asking any
questions because of your conscience.
26 For, as the scripture says, "The earth
and everything in it belong to the Lord."

27 If an unbeliever invites you to a meal
and you decide to go, eat what is set before you, without asking any questions
because of your conscience. 28 But if
someone tells you, "This food was offered to idols," then do not eat that food,
for the sake of the one who told you and
for conscience' sake — 29 that is, not your
own conscience, but the other person's
conscience.

"Well, then," someone asks, "why
should my freedom to act be limited by
another person's conscience? 30 If I
thank God for my food, why should any-

[m] the Lord; *some manuscripts have* Christ.

one criticize me about food for which I
give thanks?"
31 Well, whatever you do, whether you
eat or drink, do it all for God's glory.
32 Live in such a way as to cause no trouble either to Jews or Gentiles or to the
church of God. 33 Just do as I do; I try to
please everyone in all that I do, not
thinking of my own good, but of the
good of all, so that they might be saved.
11 Imitate me, then, just as I imitate
Christ.

Covering the Head in Worship

2 I praise you because you always remember me and follow the teachings
that I have handed on to you. 3 But I want
you to understand that Christ is supreme
over every man, the husband is supreme
over his wife, and God is supreme over
Christ. 4 So a man who prays or proclaims God's message in public worship
with his head covered disgraces Christ.
5 And any woman who prays or proclaims God's message in public worship
with nothing on her head disgraces her
husband; there is no difference between
her and a woman whose head has been
shaved. 6 If the woman does not cover
her head, she might as well cut her hair.
And since it is a shameful thing for a
woman to shave her head or cut her
hair, she should cover her head. 7 A man
has no need to cover his head, because
he reflects the image and glory of God.
But woman reflects the glory of man;
8 for man was not created from woman,
but woman from man. 9 Nor was man
created for woman's sake, but woman
was created for man's sake. 10 On account of the angels, then, a woman
should have a covering over her head to
show that she is under her husband's authority. 11 In our life in the Lord, however, woman is not independent of man,
nor is man independent of woman. 12 For
as woman was made from man, in the
same way man is born of woman; and it
is God who brings everything into existence.
13 Judge for yourselves whether it is
proper for a woman to pray to God in
public worship with nothing on her
head. 14 Why, nature itself teaches you
that long hair on a man is a disgrace,
15 but on a woman it is a thing of beauty.
Her long hair has been given her to
serve as a covering. 16 But if anyone
wants to argue about it, all I have to say
is that neither we nor the churches of
God have any other custom in worship.

The Lord's Supper

(Matthew 26.26-29; Mark 14.22-25; Luke 22.14-20)

17 In the following instructions, however, I do not praise you, because your
meetings for worship actually do more
harm than good. 18 In the first place, I
have been told that there are opposing
groups in your meetings; and this I believe is partly true. (19 No doubt there
must be divisions among you so that the
ones who are in the right may be clearly
seen.) 20 When you meet together as a
group, it is not the Lord's Supper that
you eat. 21 For as you eat, you each go
ahead with your own meal, so that some
are hungry while others get drunk.
22 Don't you have your own homes in
which to eat and drink? Or would you
rather despise the church of God and put
to shame the people who are in need?
What do you expect me to say to you
about this? Shall I praise you? Of course
I don't!
23 For I received from the Lord the
teaching that I passed on to you: that the
Lord Jesus, on the night he was betrayed, took a piece of bread, 24 gave
thanks to God, broke it, and said, "This
is my body, which is for you. Do this in
memory of me." 25 In the same way, after
the supper he took the cup and said,
"This cup is God's new covenant, sealed
with my blood. Whenever you drink it,
do so in memory of me."
26 This means that every time you eat
this bread and drink from this cup you
proclaim the Lord's death until he
comes. 27 It follows that if one of you eats
the Lord's bread or drinks from his cup
in a way that dishonors him, you are
guilty of sin against the Lord's body and
blood. 28 So then, you should each examine yourself first, and then eat the bread
and drink from the cup. 29 For if you do
not recognize the meaning of the Lord's
body when you eat the bread and drink
from the cup, you bring judgment on
yourself as you eat and drink. 30 That is
why many of you are sick and weak, and
several have died. 31 If we would examine ourselves first, we would not come
under God's judgment. 32 But we are
judged and punished by the Lord, so that

we shall not be condemned together
with the world.
33 So then, my friends, when you
gather together to eat the Lord's Supper,
wait for one another. 34 And if any of you
are hungry, you should eat at home, so
that you will not come under God's judgment as you meet together. As for the
other matters, I will settle them when I
come.

Gifts from the Holy Spirit

12 Now, concerning what you
wrote about the gifts from the
Holy Spirit.
I want you to know the truth about
them, my friends. 2 You know that while
you were still heathen, you were led
astray in many ways to the worship of
lifeless idols. 3 I want you to know that
no one who is led by God's Spirit can say
"A curse on Jesus!" and no one can confess "Jesus is Lord," without being
guided by the Holy Spirit.
4 There are different kinds of spiritual
gifts, but the same Spirit gives them.
5 There are different ways of serving, but
the same Lord is served. 6 There are different abilities to perform service, but
the same God gives ability to all for their
particular service. 7 The Spirit's presence is shown in some way in each person for the good of all. 8 The Spirit gives
one person a message full of wisdom,
while to another person the same Spirit
gives a message full of knowledge. 9 One
and the same Spirit gives faith to one
person, while to another person he gives
the power to heal. 10 The Spirit gives one
person the power to work miracles; to
another, the gift of speaking God's message; and to yet another, the ability to
tell the difference between gifts that
come from the Spirit and those that do
not. To one person he gives the ability to
speak in strange tongues, and to another
he gives the ability to explain what is
said. 11 But it is one and the same Spirit
who does all this; as he wishes, he gives
a different gift to each person.

One Body with Many Parts

12 Christ is like a single body, which
has many parts; it is still one body, even
though it is made up of different parts.
13 In the same way, all of us, whether
Jews or Gentiles, whether slaves or free,
have been baptized into the one body by
the same Spirit, and we have all been
given the one Spirit to drink.
14 For the body itself is not made up of
only one part, but of many parts. 15 If the
foot were to say, "Because I am not a
hand, I don't belong to the body," that
would not keep it from being a part of
the body. 16 And if the ear were to say,
"Because I am not an eye, I don't belong
to the body," that would not keep it from
being a part of the body. 17 If the whole
body were just an eye, how could it
hear? And if it were only an ear, how
could it smell? 18 As it is, however, God
put every different part in the body just
as he wanted it to be. 19 There would not
be a body if it were all only one part!
20 As it is, there are many parts but one
body.
21 So then, the eye cannot say to the
hand, "I don't need you!" Nor can the
head say to the feet, "Well, I don't need
you!" 22 On the contrary, we cannot do
without the parts of the body that seem
to be weaker; 23 and those parts that we
think aren't worth very much are the
ones which we treat with greater care;
while the parts of the body which don't
look very nice are treated with special
modesty, 24 which the more beautiful
parts do not need. God himself has put
the body together in such a way as to
give greater honor to those parts that
need it. 25 And so there is no division in
the body, but all its different parts have
the same concern for one another. 26 If
one part of the body suffers, all the other
parts suffer with it; if one part is praised,
all the other parts share its happiness.
27 All of you are Christ's body, and
each one is a part of it. 28 In the church
God has put all in place: in the first place
apostles, in the second place prophets,
and in the third place teachers; then
those who perform miracles, followed
by those who are given the power to heal
or to help others or to direct them or to
speak in strange tongues. 29 They are not
all apostles or prophets or teachers. Not
everyone has the power to work miracles 30 or to heal diseases or to speak in
strange tongues or to explain what is
said. 31 Set your hearts, then, on the
more important gifts.
Best of all, however, is the following way.

Love

13 I may be able to speak the languages of human beings and
even of angels, but if I have no love, my
speech is no more than a noisy gong or
a clanging bell. 2 I may have the gift of
inspired preaching; I may have all
knowledge and understand all secrets; I
may have all the faith needed to move
mountains – but if I have no love, I am
nothing. 3 I may give away everything I
have, and even give up my body to be
burned[n] – but if I have no love, this does
me no good.
4 Love is patient and kind; it is not jealous or conceited or proud; 5 love is not
ill-mannered or selfish or irritable; love
does not keep a record of wrongs; 6 love
is not happy with evil, but is happy with
the truth. 7 Love never gives up; and its
faith, hope, and patience never fail.
8 Love is eternal. There are inspired
messages, but they are temporary; there
are gifts of speaking in strange tongues,
but they will cease; there is knowledge,
but it will pass. 9 For our gifts of knowledge and of inspired messages are only
partial; 10 but when what is perfect
comes, then what is partial will disappear.
11 When I was a child, my speech, feelings, and thinking were all those of a
child; now that I am an adult, I have no
more use for childish ways. 12 What we
see now is like a dim image in a mirror;
then we shall see face-to-face. What I
know now is only partial; then it will be
complete – as complete as God's knowledge of me.
13 Meanwhile these three remain:
faith, hope, and love; and the greatest of
these is love.

More about Gifts from the Spirit

14 It is love, then, that you should
strive for. Set your hearts on
spiritual gifts, especially the gift of proclaiming God's message. 2 Those who
speak in strange tongues do not speak
to others but to God, because no one
understands them. They are speaking
secret truths by the power of the Spirit.
3 But those who proclaim God's message
speak to people and give them help, encouragement, and comfort. 4 Those who
speak in strange tongues help only
themselves, but those who proclaim
God's message help the whole church.
5 I would like for all of you to speak in
strange tongues; but I would rather that
you had the gift of proclaiming God's
message. For the person who proclaims
God's message is of greater value than
the one who speaks in strange
tongues – unless there is someone
present who can explain what is said, so
that the whole church may be helped.
6 So when I come to you, my friends,
what use will I be to you if I speak in
strange tongues? Not a bit, unless I bring
you some revelation from God or some
knowledge or some inspired message or
some teaching.
7 Take such lifeless musical instruments as the flute or the harp – how will
anyone know the tune that is being
played unless the notes are sounded distinctly? 8 And if the one who plays the
bugle does not sound a clear call, who
will prepare for battle? 9 In the same
way, how will anyone understand what
you are talking about if your message
given in strange tongues is not clear?
Your words will vanish in the air!
10 There are many different languages in
the world, yet none of them is without
meaning. 11 But if I do not know the language being spoken, those who use it
will be foreigners to me and I will be a
foreigner to them. 12 Since you are eager
to have the gifts of the Spirit, you must
try above everything else to make
greater use of those which help to build
up the church.
13 The person who speaks in strange
tongues, then, must pray for the gift to
explain what is said. 14 For if I pray in
this way, my spirit prays indeed, but my
mind has no part in it. 15 What should I
do, then? I will pray with my spirit, but I
will pray also with my mind; I will sing
with my spirit, but I will sing also with
my mind. 16 When you give thanks to
God in spirit only, how can ordinary
people taking part in the meeting say
"Amen" to your prayer of thanksgiving?
They have no way of knowing what you
are saying. 17 Even if your prayer of
thanks to God is quite good, other people are not helped at all.
18 I thank God that I speak in strange
tongues much more than any of you.

[n] to be burned; *some manuscripts have* in order to boast.

19 But in church worship I would rather
speak five words that can be understood, in order to teach others, than
speak thousands of words in strange
tongues.
20 Do not be like children in your
thinking, my friends; be children so far
as evil is concerned, but be grown up in
your thinking. 21 In the Scriptures it is
written,

"By means of people speaking
strange languages
I will speak to my people, says
the Lord.
I will speak through lips of
foreigners,
but even then my people will not
listen to me."

22 So then, the gift of speaking in strange
tongues is proof for unbelievers, not for
believers, while the gift of proclaiming
God's message is proof for believers, not
for unbelievers.
23 If, then, the whole church meets together and everyone starts speaking in
strange tongues—and if some ordinary
people or unbelievers come in, won't
they say that you are all crazy? 24 But if
everyone is proclaiming God's message
when some unbelievers or ordinary people come in, they will be convinced of
their sin by what they hear. They will be
judged by all they hear, 25 their secret
thoughts will be brought into the open,
and they will bow down and worship
God, confessing, "Truly God is here
among you!"

Order in the Church

26 This is what I mean, my friends.
When you meet for worship, one person
has a hymn, another a teaching, another
a revelation from God, another a message in strange tongues, and still another the explanation of what is said.
Everything must be of help to the
church. 27 If someone is going to speak in
strange tongues, two or three at the most
should speak, one after the other, and
someone else must explain what is being
said. 28 But if no one is there who can
explain, then the one who speaks in
strange tongues must be quiet and speak
only to himself and to God. 29 Two or
three who are given God's message
should speak, while the others are to
judge what they say. 30 But if someone
sitting in the meeting receives a message
from God, the one who is speaking
should stop. 31 All of you may proclaim
God's message, one by one, so that
everyone will learn and be encouraged.
32 The gift of proclaiming God's message
should be under the speaker's control,
33 because God does not want us to be in
disorder but in harmony and peace.
As in all the churches of God's people,
34 the women should keep quiet in the
meetings. They are not allowed to
speak; as the Jewish Law says, they
must not be in charge. 35 If they want to
find out about something, they should
ask their husbands at home. It is a disgraceful thing for a woman to speak in a
church meeting.
36 Or could it be that the word of God
came from you? Or are you the only
ones to whom it came? 37 If anyone sup-
poses he is God's messenger or has a
spiritual gift, he must realize that what I
am writing to you is the Lord's command. 38 But if he does not pay attention
to this, pay no attention to him.
39 So then, my friends, set your heart
on proclaiming God's message, but do
not forbid the speaking in strange
tongues. 40 Everything must be done in a
proper and orderly way.

The Resurrection of Christ

15 And now I want to remind you,
my friends, of the Good News
which I preached to you, which you received, and on which your faith stands
firm. 2 That is the gospel, the message
that I preached to you. You are saved by
the gospel if you hold firmly to it—
unless it was for nothing that you
believed.
3 I passed on to you what I received,
which is of the greatest importance: that
Christ died for our sins, as written in the
Scriptures; 4 that he was buried and that
he was raised to life three days later, as
written in the Scriptures; 5 that he appeared to Peter and then to all twelve
apostles. 6 Then he appeared to more
than five hundred of his followers at
once, most of whom are still alive, although some have died. 7 Then he appeared to James, and afterward to all the
apostles.
8 Last of all he appeared also to me—
even though I am like someone whose

birth was abnormal.[o] 9 For I am the least
of all the apostles — I do not even deserve to be called an apostle, because I
persecuted God's church. 10 But by God's
grace I am what I am, and the grace that
he gave me was not without effect. On
the contrary, I have worked harder than
any of the other apostles, although it
was not really my own doing, but God's
grace working with me. 11 So then,
whether it came from me or from them,
this is what we all preach, and this is
what you believe.

Our Resurrection

12 Now, since our message is that
Christ has been raised from death, how
can some of you say that the dead will
not be raised to life? 13 If that is true, it
means that Christ was not raised; 14 and
if Christ has not been raised from death,
then we have nothing to preach and you
have nothing to believe. 15 More than
that, we are shown to be lying about
God, because we said that he raised
Christ from death — but if it is true that
the dead are not raised to life, then he
did not raise Christ. 16 For if the dead are
not raised, neither has Christ been
raised. 17 And if Christ has not been
raised, then your faith is a delusion and
you are still lost in your sins. 18 It would
also mean that the believers in Christ
who have died are lost. 19 If our hope in
Christ is good for this life only and no
more,[p] then we deserve more pity than
anyone else in all the world.

20 But the truth is that Christ has been
raised from death, as the guarantee that
those who sleep in death will also be
raised. 21 For just as death came by
means of a man, in the same way the
rising from death comes by means of a
man. 22 For just as all people die because
of their union with Adam, in the same
way all will be raised to life because of
their union with Christ. 23 But each one
will be raised in proper order: Christ,
first of all; then, at the time of his coming, those who belong to him. 24 Then the
end will come; Christ will overcome all
spiritual rulers, authorities, and powers,
and will hand over the Kingdom to God
the Father. 25 For Christ must rule until
God defeats all enemies and puts them
under his feet. 26 The last enemy to be
defeated will be death. 27 For the scripture says, "God put *all* things under his
feet." It is clear, of course, that the words
"all things" do not include God himself,
who puts all things under Christ. 28 But
when all things have been placed under
Christ's rule, then he himself, the Son,
will place himself under God, who
placed all things under him; and God
will rule completely over all.

29 Now, what about those people who
are baptized for the dead? What do they
hope to accomplish? If it is true, as some
claim, that the dead are not raised to life,
why are those people being baptized for
the dead? 30 And as for us — why would
we run the risk of danger every hour?
31 My friends, I face death every day!
The pride I have in you, in our life in
union with Christ Jesus our Lord, makes
me declare this. 32 If I have, as it were,
fought "wild beasts" here in Ephesus
simply from human motives, what have
I gained? But if the dead are not raised to
life, then, as the saying goes, "Let us eat
and drink, for tomorrow we will die."

33 Do not be fooled. "Bad companions
ruin good character." 34 Come back to
your right senses and stop your sinful
ways. I declare to your shame that some
of you do not know God.

The Resurrection Body

35 Someone will ask, "How can the
dead be raised to life? What kind of body
will they have?" 36 You fool! When you
plant a seed in the ground, it does not
sprout to life unless it dies. 37 And what
you plant is a bare seed, perhaps a grain
of wheat or some other grain, not the
full-bodied plant that will later grow up.
38 God provides that seed with the body
he wishes; he gives each seed its own
proper body.

39 And the flesh of living beings is not
all the same kind of flesh; human beings
have one kind of flesh, animals another,
birds another, and fish another.

40 And there are heavenly bodies and
earthly bodies; the beauty that belongs
to heavenly bodies is different from the
beauty that belongs to earthly bodies.
41 The sun has its own beauty, the moon
another beauty, and the stars a different

[o] whose birth was abnormal; *or* who was born at the wrong time. [p] If our hope in Christ is good for this life only and no more; *or* If all we have in this life is our hope in Christ.

beauty; and even among stars there are
different kinds of beauty.
42 This is how it will be when the dead
are raised to life. When the body is buried, it is mortal; when raised, it will be
immortal. 43 When buried, it is ugly and
weak; when raised, it will be beautiful
and strong. 44 When buried, it is a physical body; when raised, it will be a spiritual body. There is, of course, a physical
body, so there has to be a spiritual body.
45 For the scripture says, "The first man,
Adam, was created a living being"; but
the last Adam is the life-giving Spirit.
46 It is not the spiritual that comes first,
but the physical, and then the spiritual.
47 The first Adam, made of earth, came
from the earth; the second Adam came
from heaven. 48 Those who belong to the
earth are like the one who was made of
earth; those who are of heaven are like
the one who came from heaven. 49 Just
as we wear the likeness of the man made
of earth, so we will wear[q] the likeness
of the Man from heaven.
50 What I mean, friends, is that what is
made of flesh and blood cannot share in
God's Kingdom, and what is mortal cannot possess immortality.
51-52 Listen to this secret truth: we shall
not all die, but when the last trumpet
sounds, we shall all be changed in an
instant, as quickly as the blinking of an
eye. For when the trumpet sounds, the
dead will be raised, never to die again,
and we shall all be changed. 53 For what
is mortal must be changed into what is
immortal; what will die must be changed
into what cannot die. 54 So when this
takes place, and the mortal has been
changed into the immortal, then the
scripture will come true: "Death is destroyed; victory is complete!"
55 "Where, Death, is your victory?
Where, Death, is your power to
hurt?"
56 Death gets its power to hurt from sin,
and sin gets its power from the Law.
57 But thanks be to God who gives us the
victory through our Lord Jesus Christ!
58 So then, my dear friends, stand firm
and steady. Keep busy always in your
work for the Lord, since you know that
nothing you do in the Lord's service is
ever useless.

The Offering for Needy Believers

16 Now, concerning what you
wrote about the money to be
raised to help God's people in Judea.
You must do what I told the churches in
Galatia to do. 2 Every Sunday each of
you must put aside some money, in proportion to what you have earned, and
save it up, so that there will be no need
to collect money when I come. 3 After I
come, I shall give letters of introduction
to those you have approved, and send
them to take your gift to Jerusalem. 4 If it
seems worthwhile for me to go, then
they can go along with me.

Paul's Plans

5 I shall come to you after I have gone
through Macedonia—for I have to go
through Macedonia. 6 I shall probably
spend some time with you, perhaps the
whole winter, and then you can help me
to continue my trip, wherever it is I shall
go next. 7 I want to see you more than
just briefly in passing; I hope to spend
quite a long time with you, if the Lord
allows.
8 I will stay here in Ephesus until the
day of Pentecost. 9 There is a real opportunity here for great and worthwhile
work, even though there are many opponents.
10 If Timothy comes your way, be sure
to make him feel welcome among you,
because he is working for the Lord, just
as I am. 11 No one should look down on
him, but you must help him continue his
trip in peace, so that he will come back
to me; for I am expecting him back with
the believers.
12 Now, about brother Apollos. I have
often encouraged him to visit you with
the other believers, but he is not completely convinced[r] that he should go at
this time. When he gets the chance, however, he will go.

Final Words

13 Be alert, stand firm in the faith, be
brave, be strong. 14 Do all your work in
love.
15 You know about Stephanas and his
family; they are the first Christian converts in Achaia and have given them-

[q] we will wear; *some manuscripts have* let us wear. [r] he is not completely convinced; *or* it is not at all God's will.

selves to the service of God's people. I
beg you, my friends, 16 to follow the leadership of such people as these, and of
anyone else who works and serves with
them.
17 I am happy about the coming of
Stephanas, Fortunatus, and Achaicus;
they have made up for your absence
18 and have cheered me up, just as they
cheered you up. Such men as these deserve notice.
19 The churches in the province of Asia
send you their greetings; Aquila and
Priscilla and the church that meets in
their house send warm Christian greetings. 20 All the believers here send
greetings.
Greet one another with the kiss of
peace.
21 With my own hand I write this:
Greetings from Paul.
22 Whoever does not love the Lord—a
curse on him!
Marana tha—Our Lord, come!
23 The grace of the Lord Jesus be
with you.
24 My love be with you all in Christ
Jesus.

Paul's Second Letter to the CORINTHIANS

Introduction

Paul's Second Letter to the Corinthians *was written during a difficult period in his relation with the church at Corinth. Some members of the church had evidently made strong attacks against Paul, but he shows his deep longing for reconciliation and expresses his great joy when this is brought about.*

In the first part of the letter Paul discusses his relationship with the church at Corinth, explaining why he had responded with severity to insult and opposition in the church and expressing his joy that this severity had resulted in repentance and reconciliation. Then he appeals to the church for a generous offering to help the needy Christians in Judea. In the final chapters Paul defends his apostleship against a few people at Corinth who had set themselves up as true apostles, while accusing Paul of being a false one.

Outline of Contents

---

1 From Paul, an apostle of Christ
Jesus by God's will, and from our
brother Timothy—
To the church of God in Corinth, and
to all God's people throughout Achaia:
2 May God our Father and the Lord
Jesus Christ give you grace and peace.

Paul Gives Thanks to God

3 Let us give thanks to the God and
Father of our Lord Jesus Christ, the merciful Father, the God from whom all help
comes! 4 He helps us in all our troubles,
so that we are able to help others who
have all kinds of troubles, using the
same help that we ourselves have received from God. 5 Just as we have a
share in Christ's many sufferings, so
also through Christ we share in God's
great help. 6 If we suffer, it is for your
help and salvation; if we are helped,
then you too are helped and given the
strength to endure with patience the
same sufferings that we also endure. 7 So
our hope in you is never shaken; we
know that just as you share in our sufferings, you also share in the help we
receive.

8 We want to remind you, friends, of
the trouble we had in the province of
Asia. The burdens laid upon us were so
great and so heavy that we gave up all
hope of staying alive. 9 We felt that the
death sentence had been passed on us.
But this happened so that we should
rely, not on ourselves, but only on God,
who raises the dead. 10 From such terrible dangers of death[a] he saved us, and
will save us; and we have placed our
hope in him that he will save us again,
11 as you help us by means of your
prayers for us. So it will be that the
many prayers for us will be answered,
and God will bless us; and many will
raise their voices to him in thanksgiving
for us.

The Change in Paul's Plans

12 We are proud that our conscience
assures us that our lives in this world,
and especially our relations with you,
have been ruled by God-given frankness[b] and sincerity, by the power of
God's grace and not by human wisdom.
13-14 We write to you only what you can
read and understand. But even though
you now understand us only in part, I
hope that you will come to understand
us completely, so that in the Day of our
Lord Jesus you can be as proud of us as
we shall be of you.
15 I was so sure of all this that I made
plans at first to visit you, in order that
you might be blessed twice. 16 For I
planned to visit you on my way to Macedonia and again on my way back, in order to get help from you for my trip to
Judea. 17 In planning this, did I appear
fickle? When I make my plans, do I
make them from selfish motives, ready
to say "Yes, yes" and "No, no" at the
same time? 18 As surely as God speaks
the truth, my promise to you was not a
"Yes" and a "No." 19 For Jesus Christ, the
Son of God, who was preached among
you by Silas, Timothy, and myself, is not
one who is "Yes" and "No." On the contrary, he is God's "Yes"; 20 for it is he
who is the "Yes" to all of God's promises. This is why through Jesus Christ
our "Amen" is said to the glory of God.
21 It is God himself who makes us, together with you, sure of our life in union
with Christ; it is God himself who has set
us apart, 22 who has placed his mark of
ownership upon us, and who has given
us the Holy Spirit in our hearts as the
guarantee of all that he has in store
for us.
23 I call God as my witness – he knows
my heart! It was in order to spare you
that I decided not to go to Corinth. 24 We
are not trying to dictate to you what you
must believe; we know that you stand
firm in the faith. Instead, we are working with you for your own happiness.
2 So I made up my mind not to come
to you again to make you sad. 2 For
if I were to make you sad, who would be
left to cheer me up? Only the very persons I had made sad. 3 That is why I
wrote that letter to you – I did not want
to come to you and be made sad by the
very people who should make me glad.
For I am convinced that when I am
happy, then all of you are happy too.
4 I wrote you with a greatly troubled and
distressed heart and with many tears;
my purpose was not to make you sad,
but to make you realize how much I love
you all.

Forgiveness for the Offender

5 Now, if anyone has made somebody
sad, he has not done it to me but to all of
you – in part, at least. (I say this because
I do not want to be too hard on him.) 6 It
is enough that this person has been punished in this way by most of you. 7 Now,
however, you should forgive him and
encourage him, in order to keep him
from becoming so sad as to give up completely. 8 And so I beg you to let him
know that you really do love him.
9 I wrote you that letter because I wanted
to find out how well you had stood the
test and whether you are always ready
to obey my instructions. 10 When you
forgive people for what they have done,
I forgive them too. For when I forgive –
if, indeed, I need to forgive anything – I
do it in Christ's presence because of you,
11 in order to keep Satan from getting the
upper hand over us; for we know what
his plans are.

Paul's Anxiety in Troas

12 When I arrived in Troas to preach
the Good News about Christ, I found

[a] terrible dangers of death; *some manuscripts have* terrible death.
[b] frankness; *some manuscripts have* holiness.

that the Lord had opened the way for the
work there. 13 But I was deeply worried,
because I could not find our brother Titus. So I said good-bye to the people
there and went on to Macedonia.

Victory through Christ

14 But thanks be to God! For in union
with Christ we are always led by God as
prisoners in Christ's victory procession.
God uses us to make the knowledge
about Christ spread everywhere like a
sweet fragrance. 15 For we are like a
sweet-smelling incense offered by Christ
to God, which spreads among those who
are being saved and those who are being
lost. 16 For those who are being lost, it is
a deadly stench that kills; but for those
who are being saved, it is a fragrance
that brings life. Who, then, is capable for
such a task? 17 We are not like so many
others, who handle God's message as if
it were cheap merchandise; but because
God has sent us, we speak with sincerity
in his presence, as servants of Christ.

Servants of the New Covenant

3 Does this sound as if we were again
boasting about ourselves? Could it
be that, like some other people, we need
letters of recommendation to you or
from you? 2 You yourselves are the letter
we have, written on our hearts for everyone to know and read. 3 It is clear that
Christ himself wrote this letter and sent
it by us. It is written, not with ink but
with the Spirit of the living God, and not
on stone tablets but on human hearts.
4 We say this because we have confidence in God through Christ. 5 There is
nothing in us that allows us to claim that
we are capable of doing this work. The
capacity we have comes from God; 6 it is
he who made us capable of serving the
new covenant, which consists not of a
written law but of the Spirit. The written
law brings death, but the Spirit gives
life.

7 The Law was carved in letters on
stone tablets, and God's glory appeared
when it was given. Even though the
brightness on Moses' face was fading, it
was so strong that the people of Israel
could not keep their eyes fixed on him. If
the Law, which brings death when it is
in force, came with such glory, 8 how
much greater is the glory that belongs to
the activity of the Spirit! 9 The system
which brings condemnation was glorious; how much more glorious is the activity which brings salvation! 10 We may
say that because of the far brighter glory
now the glory that was so bright in the
past is gone. 11 For if there was glory in
that which lasted for a while, how much
more glory is there in that which lasts
forever!

12 Because we have this hope, we are
very bold. 13 We are not like Moses, who
had to put a veil over his face so that the
people of Israel would not see the brightness fade and disappear. 14 Their minds,
indeed, were closed; and to this very day
their minds are covered with the same
veil as they read the books of the old
covenant. The veil is removed only when
a person is joined to Christ. 15 Even today, whenever they read the Law of
Moses, the veil still covers their minds.
16 But it can be removed, as the scripture
says about Moses: "His veil was removed when he turned to the Lord."[c]
17 Now, "the Lord" in this passage is the
Spirit; and where the Spirit of the Lord
is present, there is freedom. 18 All of us,
then, reflect the glory of the Lord with
uncovered faces; and that same glory,
coming from the Lord, who is the Spirit,
transforms us into his likeness in an
ever greater degree of glory.

Spiritual Treasure in Clay Pots

4 God in his mercy has given us this
work to do, and so we do not become discouraged. 2 We put aside all secret and shameful deeds; we do not act
with deceit, nor do we falsify the word of
God. In the full light of truth we live in
God's sight and try to commend ourselves to everyone's good conscience.
3 For if the gospel we preach is hidden, it
is hidden only from those who are being
lost. 4 They do not believe, because their
minds have been kept in the dark by the
evil god of this world. He keeps them
from seeing the light shining on them,
the light that comes from the Good News
about the glory of Christ, who is the exact likeness of God. 5 For it is not ourselves that we preach; we preach Jesus
Christ as Lord, and ourselves as your
servants for Jesus' sake. 6 The God who

[c] *Verse 16 may be translated:* But the veil is removed whenever someone turns to the Lord.

said, "Out of darkness the light shall
shine!" is the same God who made his
light shine in our hearts, to bring us the
knowledge of God's glory shining in the
face of Christ.
7 Yet we who have this spiritual treasure are like common clay pots, in order
to show that the supreme power belongs
to God, not to us. 8 We are often troubled, but not crushed; sometimes in
doubt, but never in despair; 9 there are
many enemies, but we are never without
a friend; and though badly hurt at times,
we are not destroyed. 10 At all times we
carry in our mortal bodies the death of
Jesus, so that his life also may be seen in
our bodies. 11 Throughout our lives we
are always in danger of death for Jesus'
sake, in order that his life may be seen in
this mortal body of ours. 12 This means
that death is at work in us, but life is at
work in you.
13 The scripture says, "I spoke because
I believed." In the same spirit of faith we
also speak because we believe. 14 We
know that God, who raised the Lord
Jesus to life, will also raise us up with
Jesus and take us, together with you,
into his presence. 15 All this is for your
sake; and as God's grace reaches more
and more people, they will offer to
the glory of God more prayers of
thanksgiving.

Living by Faith

16 For this reason we never become
discouraged. Even though our physical
being is gradually decaying, yet our
spiritual being is renewed day after day.
17 And this small and temporary trouble
we suffer will bring us a tremendous and
eternal glory, much greater than the
trouble. 18 For we fix our attention, not
on things that are seen, but on things
that are unseen. What can be seen lasts
only for a time, but what cannot be seen
lasts forever.

5 For we know that when this tent we
live in—our body here on earth—is
torn down, God will have a house in
heaven for us to live in, a home he himself has made, which will last forever.
2 And now we sigh, so great is our desire
that our home which comes from heaven
should be put on over us; 3 by being
clothed with it we shall not be without a
body. 4 While we live in this earthly tent,
we groan with a feeling of oppression; it
is not that we want to get rid of our
earthly body, but that we want to have
the heavenly one put on over us, so that
what is mortal will be transformed by
life. 5 God is the one who has prepared
us for this change, and he gave us his
Spirit as the guarantee of all that he has
in store for us.
6 So we are always full of courage. We
know that as long as we are at home in
the body we are away from the Lord's
home. 7 For our life is a matter of faith,
not of sight. 8 We are full of courage and
would much prefer to leave our home in
the body and be at home with the Lord.
9 More than anything else, however, we
want to please him, whether in our home
here or there. 10 For all of us must appear
before Christ, to be judged by him. We
will each receive what we deserve, according to everything we have done,
good or bad, in our bodily life.

Friendship with God through Christ

11 We know what it means to fear the
Lord, and so we try to persuade others.
God knows us completely, and I hope
that in your hearts you know me as well.
12 We are not trying again to recommend
ourselves to you; rather, we are trying to
give you a good reason to be proud of us,
so that you will be able to answer those
who boast about people's appearance
and not about their character. 13 Are we
really insane? It is for God's sake. Or are
we sane? Then it is for your sake. 14 We
are ruled by the love of Christ, now that
we recognize that one man died for
everyone, which means that they all
share in his death. 15 He died for all, so
that those who live should no longer live
for themselves, but only for him who
died and was raised to life for their sake.
16 No longer, then, do we judge anyone
by human standards. Even if at one time
we judged Christ according to human
standards, we no longer do so. 17 Anyone
who is joined to Christ is a new being;
the old is gone, the new has come. 18 All
this is done by God, who through Christ
changed us from enemies into his
friends and gave us the task of making
others his friends also. 19 Our message is
that God was making all human beings

his friends through Christ.[d] God did not
keep an account of their sins, and he has
given us the message which tells how he
makes them his friends.
20 Here we are, then, speaking for
Christ, as though God himself were
making his appeal through us. We plead
on Christ's behalf: let God change you
from enemies into his friends! 21 Christ
was without sin, but for our sake God
made him share our sin in order that in
union with him we might share the
righteousness of God.

6 In our work together with God,
then, we beg you who have received
God's grace not to let it be wasted. 2 Hear
what God says:

"When the time came for me to
show you favor,
I heard you;
when the day arrived for me to
save you,
I helped you."

Listen! This is the hour to receive God's
favor; today is the day to be saved!
3 We do not want anyone to find fault
with our work, so we try not to put obstacles in anyone's way. 4 Instead, in
everything we do we show that we are
God's servants by patiently enduring
troubles, hardships, and difficulties.
5 We have been beaten, jailed, and
mobbed; we have been overworked and
have gone without sleep or food. 6 By our
purity, knowledge, patience, and kindness we have shown ourselves to be
God's servants—by the Holy Spirit, by
our true love, 7 by our message of truth,
and by the power of God. We have righteousness as our weapon, both to attack
and to defend ourselves. 8 We are honored and disgraced; we are insulted and
praised. We are treated as liars, yet we
speak the truth; 9 as unknown, yet we
are known by all; as though we were
dead, but, as you see, we live on. Although punished, we are not killed; 10 although saddened, we are always glad;
we seem poor, but we make many people rich; we seem to have nothing, yet
we really possess everything.
11 Dear friends in Corinth! We have
spoken frankly to you; we have opened
our hearts wide. 12 It is not we who have
closed our hearts to you; it is you who
have closed your hearts to us. 13 I speak
now as though you were my children:
show us the same feelings that we have
for you. Open your hearts wide!

Warning against Pagan Influences

14 Do not try to work together as
equals with unbelievers, for it cannot be
done. How can right and wrong be partners? How can light and darkness live
together? 15 How can Christ and the
Devil agree? What does a believer have
in common with an unbeliever? 16 How
can God's temple come to terms with pagan idols? For we are the temple of the
living God! As God himself has said,

"I will make my home with my
people
and live among them;
I will be their God,
and they shall be my people."

17 And so the Lord says,

"You must leave them
and separate yourselves from
them.
Have nothing to do with what is
unclean,
and I will accept you.
18 I will be your father,
and you shall be my sons and
daughters,
says the Lord Almighty."

7 All these promises are made to us,
my dear friends. So then, let us purify ourselves from everything that
makes body or soul unclean, and let us
be completely holy by living in awe
of God.

Paul's Joy

2 Make room for us in your hearts. We
have wronged no one; we have ruined
no one, nor tried to take advantage of
anyone. 3 I do not say this to condemn
you; for, as I have said before, you are so
dear to us that we are always together,
whether we live or die. 4 I am so sure of
you; I take such pride in you! In all our
troubles I am still full of courage; I am
running over with joy.
5 Even after we arrived in Macedonia,
we did not have any rest. There were
troubles everywhere, quarrels with others, fears in our hearts. 6 But God, who
encourages the downhearted, encouraged us with the coming of Titus. 7 It was

[d] God was making all human beings his friends through Christ; *or* God was in Christ making all human beings his friends.

not only his coming that cheered us, but
also his report of how you encouraged
him. He told us how much you want to
see me, how sorry you are, how ready
you are to defend me; and so I am even
happier now.
8For even if that letter of mine made
you sad, I am not sorry I wrote it. I could
have been sorry when I saw that it made
you sad for a while. 9But now I am
happy—not because I made you sad, but
because your sadness made you change
your ways. That sadness was used by
God, and so we caused you no harm.
10For the sadness that is used by God
brings a change of heart that leads to
salvation—and there is no regret in that!
But sadness that is merely human
causes death. 11See what God did with
this sadness of yours: how earnest it has
made you, how eager to prove your innocence! Such indignation, such alarm,
such feelings, such devotion, such readiness to punish wrongdoing! You have
shown yourselves to be without fault in
the whole matter.
12So, even though I wrote that letter, it
was not because of the one who did
wrong or the one who was wronged. Instead, I wrote it to make plain to you, in
God's sight, how deep your devotion to
us really is. 13That is why we were encouraged.
Not only were we encouraged; how
happy Titus made us with his happiness
over the way in which all of you helped
to cheer him up! 14I did boast of you to
him, and you have not disappointed me.
We have always spoken the truth to you,
and in the same way the boast we made
to Titus has proved true. 15And so his
love for you grows stronger, as he remembers how all of you were ready to
obey his instructions, how you welcomed him with fear and trembling.
16How happy I am that I can depend on
you completely!

Christian Giving

8 Our friends, we want you to know
what God's grace has accomplished
in the churches in Macedonia. 2They
have been severely tested by the troubles they went through; but their joy was
so great that they were extremely generous in their giving, even though they are
very poor. 3I can assure you that they
gave as much as they could, and even
more than they could. Of their own free
will 4they begged us and pleaded for the
privilege of having a part in helping
God's people in Judea. 5It was more
than we could have hoped for! First they
gave themselves to the Lord; and then,
by God's will they gave themselves to us
as well. 6So we urged Titus, who began
this work, to continue it and help you
complete this special service of love.
7You are so rich in all you have: in faith,
speech, and knowledge, in your eagerness to help and in your love for us.[e]
And so we want you to be generous also
in this service of love.
8I am not laying down any rules. But
by showing how eager others are to
help, I am trying to find out how real
your own love is. 9You know the grace
of our Lord Jesus Christ; rich as he was,
he made himself poor for your sake, in
order to make you rich by means of his
poverty.
10My opinion is that it is better for you
to finish now what you began last year.
You were the first, not only to act, but
also to be willing to act. 11On with it,
then, and finish the job! Be as eager to
finish it as you were to plan it, and do it
with what you now have. 12If you are
eager to give, God will accept your gift
on the basis of what you have to give,
not on what you don't have.
13-14I am not trying to relieve others
by putting a burden on you; but since
you have plenty at this time, it is only
fair that you should help those who are
in need. Then, when you are in need and
they have plenty, they will help you. In
this way both are treated equally. 15As
the scripture says, "The one who gathered much did not have too much, and
the one who gathered little did not have
too little."

Titus and His Companions

16How we thank God for making Titus
as eager as we are to help you! 17Not
only did he welcome our request; he was
so eager to help that of his own free will
he decided to go to you. 18With him we
are sending the brother who is highly
respected in all the churches for his
work in preaching the gospel. 19And be-

[e] your love for us; *some manuscripts have* our love for you.

sides that, he has been chosen and appointed by the churches to travel with us
as we carry out this service of love for
the sake of the Lord's glory and in order
to show that we want to help.
20 We are being careful not to stir up
any complaints about the way we handle
this generous gift. 21 Our purpose is to do
what is right, not only in the sight of the
Lord, but also in the sight of others.
22 So we are sending our brother with
them; we have tested him many times
and found him always very eager to
help. And now that he has so much confidence in you, he is all the more eager to
help. 23 As for Titus, he is my partner and
works with me to help you; as for the
other brothers who are going with him,
they represent the churches and bring
glory to Christ. 24 Show your love to
them, so that all the churches will be
sure of it and know that we are right in
boasting about you.

Help for Needy Believers

9 There is really no need for me to
write you about the help being sent
to God's people in Judea. 2 I know that
you are willing to help, and I have
boasted of you to the people in Macedonia. "The believers in Achaia," I said,
"have been ready to help since last
year." Your eagerness has stirred up
most of them. 3 Now I am sending these
believers, so that our boasting about you
in this matter may not turn out to be
empty words. But, just as I said, you will
be ready with your help. 4 However, if
the people from Macedonia should come
with me and find out that you are not
ready, how ashamed we would be—not
to speak of your shame—for feeling so
sure of you! 5 So I thought it was necessary to urge these believers to go to you
ahead of me and get ready in advance
the gift you promised to make. Then it
will be ready when I arrive, and it will
show that you give because you want to,
not because you have to.
6 Remember that the person who
plants few seeds will have a small crop;
the one who plants many seeds will have
a large crop. 7 You should each give,
then, as you have decided, not with regret or out of a sense of duty; for God
loves the one who gives gladly. 8 And
God is able to give you more than you
need, so that you will always have all
you need for yourselves and more than
enough for every good cause. 9 As the
scripture says,

"He gives generously to the needy;
his kindness lasts forever."

10 And God, who supplies seed for the
sower and bread to eat, will also supply
you with all the seed you need and will
make it grow and produce a rich harvest
from your generosity. 11 He will always
make you rich enough to be generous at
all times, so that many will thank God
for your gifts which they receive from
us. 12 For this service you perform not
only meets the needs of God's people,
but also produces an outpouring of gratitude to God. 13 And because of the proof
which this service of yours brings, many
will give glory to God for your loyalty to
the gospel of Christ, which you profess,
and for your generosity in sharing with
them and everyone else. 14 And so with
deep affection they will pray for you because of the extraordinary grace God
has shown you. 15 Let us thank God for
his priceless gift!

Paul Defends His Ministry

10 I, Paul, make a personal appeal
to you—I who am said to be
meek and mild when I am with you, but
harsh with you when I am away. By the
gentleness and kindness of Christ 2 I beg
you not to force me to be harsh when I
come; for I am sure I can deal harshly
with those who say that we act from
worldly motives. 3 It is true that we live
in the world, but we do not fight from
worldly motives. 4 The weapons we use
in our fight are not the world's weapons
but God's powerful weapons, which we
use to destroy strongholds. We destroy
false arguments; 5 we pull down every
proud obstacle that is raised against the
knowledge of God; we take every
thought captive and make it obey Christ.
6 And after you have proved your complete loyalty, we will be ready to punish
any act of disloyalty.
7 You are looking at the outward appearance of things. Are there some there
who reckon themselves to belong to
Christ? Well, let them think again about
themselves, because we belong to Christ
just as much as they do. 8 For I am not
ashamed, even if I have boasted somewhat too much about the authority that
the Lord has given us—authority to

build you up, not to tear you down. 9I do
not want it to appear that I am trying to
frighten you with my letters. 10Someone
will say, "Paul's letters are severe and
strong, but when he is with us in person,
he is weak, and his words are nothing!"
11Such a person must understand that
there is no difference between what we
write in our letters when we are away
and what we will do when we are there
with you.

12Of course we would not dare classify
ourselves or compare ourselves with
those who rate themselves so highly.
How stupid they are! They make up
their own standards to measure themselves by, and they judge themselves by
their own standards! 13As for us, however, our boasting will not go beyond
certain limits; it will stay within the limits of the work which God has set for us,
and this includes our work among you.
14And since you are within those limits,
we were not going beyond them when
we came to you, bringing the Good
News about Christ. 15So we do not boast
about the work that others have done
beyond the limits God set for us. Instead, we hope that your faith may grow
and that we may be able to do a much
greater work among you, always within
the limits that God has set. 16Then we
can preach the Good News in other
countries beyond you and shall not have
to boast about work already done in
someone else's field.

17But as the scripture says, "Whoever
wants to boast must boast about what
the Lord has done." 18For it is when the
Lord thinks well of us that we are really
approved, and not when we think well of
ourselves.

Paul and the False Apostles

11 I wish you would tolerate me,
even when I am a bit foolish.
Please do! 2I am jealous for you, just as
God is; you are like a pure virgin whom
I have promised in marriage to one man
only, Christ himself. 3I am afraid that
your minds will be corrupted and that
you will abandon your full and pure devotion to Christ—in the same way that
Eve was deceived by the snake's clever
lies. 4For you gladly tolerate anyone
who comes to you and preaches a different Jesus, not the one we preached; and
you accept a spirit and a gospel completely different from the Spirit and the
gospel you received from us!

5I do not think that I am the least bit
inferior to those very special so-called
"apostles" of yours! 6Perhaps I am an
amateur in speaking, but certainly not in
knowledge; we have made this clear to
you at all times and in all conditions.

7I did not charge you a thing when I
preached the Good News of God to you;
I humbled myself in order to make you
important. Was that wrong of me?
8While I was working among you, I was
paid by other churches. I was robbing
them, so to speak, in order to help you.
9And during the time I was with you I
did not bother you for help when I
needed money; the believers who came
from Macedonia brought me everything
I needed. As in the past, so in the future:
I will never be a burden to you! 10By
Christ's truth in me, I promise that this
boast of mine will not be silenced anywhere in all of Achaia. 11Do I say this
because I don't love you? God knows I
love you!

12I will go on doing what I am doing
now, in order to keep those other "apostles" from having any reason for boasting and saying that they work in the
same way that we do. 13Those men are
not true apostles—they are false apostles, who lie about their work and disguise themselves to look like real
apostles of Christ. 14Well, no wonder!
Even Satan can disguise himself to look
like an angel of light! 15So it is no great
thing if his servants disguise themselves
to look like servants of righteousness. In
the end they will get exactly what their
actions deserve.

Paul's Sufferings as an Apostle

16I repeat: no one should think that I
am a fool. But if you do, at least accept
me as a fool, just so I will have a little to
boast of. 17Of course what I am saying
now is not what the Lord would have me
say; in this matter of boasting I am really
talking like a fool. 18But since there are
so many who boast for merely human
reasons, I will do the same. 19You yourselves are so wise, and so you gladly tolerate fools! 20You tolerate anyone who
orders you around or takes advantage of
you or traps you or looks down on you
or slaps you in the face. 21I am ashamed

to admit that we were too timid to do
those things!

But if anyone dares to boast about
something—I am talking like a fool—I
will be just as daring. 22 Are they Hebrews? So am I. Are they Israelites? So
am I. Are they Abraham's descendants?
So am I. 23 Are they Christ's servants? I
sound like a madman—but I am a better
servant than they are! I have worked
much harder, I have been in prison more
times, I have been whipped much more,
and I have been near death more often.
24 Five times I was given the thirty-nine
lashes by the Jews; 25 three times I was
whipped by the Romans; and once I was
stoned. I have been in three shipwrecks,
and once I spent twenty-four hours in
the water. 26 In my many travels I have
been in danger from floods and from
robbers, in danger from my own people
and from Gentiles; there have been dangers in the cities, dangers in the wilds,
dangers on the high seas, and dangers
from false friends. 27 There has been
work and toil; often I have gone without
sleep; I have been hungry and thirsty; I
have often been without enough food,
shelter, or clothing. 28 And not to mention other things, every day I am under
the pressure of my concern for all the
churches. 29 When someone is weak,
then I feel weak too; when someone is
led into sin, I am filled with distress.

30 If I must boast, I will boast about
things that show how weak I am. 31 The
God and Father of the Lord Jesus—
blessed be his name forever!—knows
that I am not lying. 32 When I was in Damascus, the governor under King Aretas
placed guards at the city gates to arrest
me. 33 But I was let down in a basket
through an opening in the wall and escaped from him.

Paul's Visions and Revelations

12 I have to boast, even though it
doesn't do any good. But I will
now talk about visions and revelations
given me by the Lord. 2 I know a certain
Christian man who fourteen years ago
was snatched up to the highest heaven (I
do not know whether this actually happened or whether he had a vision—only
God knows). 3-4 I repeat, I know that this
man was snatched to Paradise (again, I
do not know whether this actually happened or whether it was a vision—only
God knows), and there he heard things
which cannot be put into words, things
that human lips may not speak. 5 So I
will boast about this man—but I will not
boast about myself, except the things
that show how weak I am. 6 If I wanted to
boast, I would not be a fool, because I
would be telling the truth. But I will not
boast, because I do not want any of you
to have a higher opinion of me than you
have as a result of what you have seen
me do and heard me say.

7 But to keep me from being puffed up
with pride because of the many wonderful things I saw, I was given a painful
physical ailment, which acts as Satan's
messenger to beat me and keep me from
being proud. 8 Three times I prayed to
the Lord about this and asked him to
take it away. 9 But his answer was: "My
grace is all you need, for my power is
greatest when you are weak." I am most
happy, then, to be proud of my weaknesses, in order to feel the protection of
Christ's power over me. 10 I am content
with weaknesses, insults, hardships,
persecutions, and difficulties for Christ's
sake. For when I am weak, then I am
strong.

Paul's Concern for the Corinthians

11 I am acting like a fool—but you
have made me do it. You are the ones
who ought to show your approval of me.
For even if I am nothing, I am in no way
inferior to those very special "apostles"
of yours. 12 The many miracles and wonders that prove that I am an apostle were
performed among you with much patience. 13 How were you treated any
worse than the other churches, except
that I did not bother you for financial
help? Please forgive me for being so
unfair!

14 This is now the third time that I am
ready to come to visit you—and I will
not make any demands on you. It is you
I want, not your money. After all, children should not have to provide for their
parents, but parents should provide for
their children. 15 I will be glad to spend
all I have, and myself as well, in order to
help you. Will you love me less because
I love you so much?

16 You will agree, then, that I was not
a burden to you. But someone will say
that I was tricky, and trapped you with
lies. 17 How? Did I take advantage of you

through any of the messengers I sent?
18 I begged Titus to go, and I sent the
other believer with him. Would you say
that Titus took advantage of you? Do not
he and I act from the very same motives
and behave in the same way?
19 Perhaps you think that all along we
have been trying to defend ourselves before you. No! We speak as Christ would
have us speak in the presence of God,
and everything we do, dear friends, is
done to help you. 20 I am afraid that
when I get there I will find you different
from what I would like you to be and you
will find me different from what you
would like me to be. I am afraid that I
will find quarreling and jealousy, hot
tempers and selfishness, insults and gossip, pride and disorder. 21 I am afraid
that the next time I come my God will
humiliate me in your presence, and I
shall weep over many who sinned in the
past and have not repented of the immoral things they have done—their lust
and their sexual sins.

Final Warnings and Greetings

13 This is now the third time that I
am coming to visit you. "Any accusation must be upheld by the evidence
of two or more witnesses"—as the scripture says. 2 I want to tell those of you
who have sinned in the past, and all the
others; I said it before during my second
visit to you, but I will say it again now
that I am away: the next time I come nobody will escape punishment. 3 You will
have all the proof you want that Christ
speaks through me. When he deals with
you, he is not weak; instead, he shows
his power among you. 4 For even though
it was in weakness that he was put to
death on the cross, it is by God's power
that he lives. In union with him we also
are weak; but in our relations with you
we shall share God's power in his life.
5 Put yourselves to the test and judge
yourselves, to find out whether you are
living in faith. Surely you know that
Christ Jesus is in you?—unless you have
completely failed. 6 I trust you will know
that we are not failures. 7 We pray to
God that you will do no wrong—not in
order to show that we are a success, but
so that you may do what is right, even
though we may seem to be failures. 8 For
we cannot do a thing against the truth,
but only for it. 9 We are glad when we
are weak but you are strong. And so we
also pray that you will become perfect.
10 That is why I write this while I am
away from you; it is so that when I arrive
I will not have to deal harshly with you
in using the authority that the Lord has
given me—authority to build you up, not
to tear you down.
11 And now, my friends, good-bye!
Strive for perfection; listen to my appeals; agree with one another; live in
peace. And the God of love and peace
will be with you.
12 Greet one another with the kiss of
peace.
All of God's people send you their
greetings.
13 The grace of the Lord Jesus Christ,
the love of God, and the fellowship of the
Holy Spirit be with you all.

Paul's Letter to the
GALATIANS

Introduction

As the good news about Jesus began to be preached and welcomed among people who were not Jews, the question arose as to whether a person must obey the Law of Moses in order to be a true Christian. Paul had argued that this was not necessary — that in fact, the only sound basis for life in Christ was faith, by which all are put right with God. But among the churches of Galatia, a Roman province in Asia Minor, there had come people who opposed Paul and claimed that one must also observe the Law of Moses in order to be right with God.

Paul's Letter to the Galatians *was written in order to bring back to true faith and practice those people who were being misled by this false teaching. Paul begins by defending his right to be called an apostle of Jesus Christ. He insists that his call to be an apostle came from God, not from any human authority, and that his mission was especially to the non-Jews. Then he develops the argument that it is by faith alone that people are put right with God. In the concluding chapters Paul shows that Christian conduct flows naturally from the love that results from faith in Christ.*

Outline of Contents

---

1 From Paul, whose call to be an
apostle did not come from human
beings or by human means, but from
Jesus Christ and God the Father, who
raised him from death. 2 All the believers
who are here join me in sending greetings to the churches of Galatia:
3 May God our Father and the Lord
Jesus Christ give you grace and peace.
4 In order to set us free from this
present evil age, Christ gave himself for
our sins, in obedience to the will of our
God and Father. 5 To God be the glory
forever and ever! Amen.

The One Gospel

6 I am surprised at you! In no time at
all you are deserting the one who called
you by the grace of Christ,[a] and are accepting another gospel. 7 Actually, there
is no "other gospel," but I say this because there are some people who are upsetting you and trying to change the
gospel of Christ. 8 But even if we or an
angel from heaven should preach to you
a gospel that is different from the one we
preached to you, may he be condemned
to hell! 9 We have said it before, and now
I say it again: if anyone preaches to you
a gospel that is different from the one
you accepted, may he be condemned to
hell!
10 Does this sound as if I am trying to
win human approval? No indeed! What I
want is God's approval! Am I trying to
be popular with people? If I were still
trying to do so, I would not be a servant
of Christ.

How Paul Became an Apostle

11 Let me tell you, my friends, that the
gospel I preach is not of human origin.
12 I did not receive it from any human
being, nor did anyone teach it to me. It
was Jesus Christ himself who revealed it
to me.
13 You have been told how I used to
live when I was devoted to the Jewish
religion, how I persecuted without
mercy the church of God and did my
best to destroy it. 14 I was ahead of most
other Jews of my age in my practice of
the Jewish religion, and was much more
devoted to the traditions of our ancestors.
15 But God in his grace chose me even
before I was born, and called me to serve
him. And when he decided 16 to reveal

[a] by the grace of Christ; *some manuscripts have* by his grace.

his Son to me, so that I might preach the
Good News about him to the Gentiles, I
did not go to anyone for advice, 17 nor
did I go to Jerusalem to see those who
were apostles before me. Instead, I went
at once to Arabia, and then I returned to
Damascus. 18 It was three years later that
I went to Jerusalem to obtain information from Peter, and I stayed with him
for two weeks. 19 I did not see any other
apostle except James,[b] the Lord's
brother.

20 What I write is true. God knows that
I am not lying!

21 Afterward I went to places in Syria
and Cilicia. 22 At that time the members
of the churches in Judea did not know
me personally. 23 They knew only what
others were saying: "The man who used
to persecute us is now preaching the
faith that he once tried to destroy!"
24 And so they praised God because
of me.

Paul and the Other Apostles

2 Fourteen years later I went back to
Jerusalem with Barnabas, taking
Titus along with me. 2 I went because
God revealed to me that I should go. In a
private meeting with the leaders I explained the gospel message that I preach
to the Gentiles. I did not want my work
in the past or in the present to be a failure. 3 My companion Titus, even though
he is Greek, was not forced to be circumcised, 4 although some wanted it done.
Pretending to be believers, these men
slipped into our group as spies, in order
to find out about the freedom we have
through our union with Christ Jesus.
They wanted to make slaves of us, 5 but
in order to keep the truth of the gospel
safe for you, we did not give in to them
for a minute.

6 But those who seemed to be the
leaders—I say this because it makes no
difference to me what they were; God
does not judge by outward appearances—those leaders, I say, made
no new suggestions to me. 7 On the
contrary, they saw that God had given
me the task of preaching the gospel to
the Gentiles, just as he had given Peter
the task of preaching the gospel to the
Jews. 8 For by God's power I was made
an apostle to the Gentiles, just as Peter
was made an apostle to the Jews.
9 James, Peter, and John, who seemed to
be the leaders, recognized that God had
given me this special task; so they shook
hands with Barnabas and me, as a sign
that we were all partners. We agreed
that Barnabas and I would work among
the Gentiles and they among the Jews.
10 All they asked was that we should remember the needy in their group, which
is the very thing I have[c] been eager
to do.

Paul Rebukes Peter at Antioch

11 But when Peter came to Antioch, I
opposed him in public, because he was
clearly wrong. 12 Before some men who
had been sent by James arrived there,
Peter had been eating with the Gentile
believers. But after these men arrived,
he drew back and would not eat with the
Gentiles, because he was afraid of those
who were in favor of circumcising them.
13 The other Jewish believers also
started acting like cowards along with
Peter; and even Barnabas was swept
along by their cowardly action. 14 When
I saw that they were not walking a
straight path in line with the truth of the
gospel, I said to Peter in front of them
all, "You are a Jew, yet you have been
living like a Gentile, not like a Jew. How,
then, can you try to force Gentiles to live
like Jews?"

Jews and Gentiles Are Saved by Faith

15 Indeed, we are Jews by birth and not
"Gentile sinners," as they are called.
16 Yet we know that a person is put right
with God only through faith in Jesus
Christ, never by doing what the Law requires. We, too, have believed in Christ
Jesus in order to be put right with God
through our faith in Christ, and not by
doing what the Law requires. For no one
is put right with God by doing what the
Law requires. 17 If, then, as we try to be
put right with God by our union with
Christ, we are found to be sinners, as
much as the Gentiles are—does this
mean that Christ is serving the cause of
sin? By no means! 18 If I start to rebuild

[b] any other apostle except James; *or* any other apostle; the only other person I saw was James.
[c] have; *or* had.

the system of Law that I tore down, then
I show myself to be someone who
breaks the Law. 19 So far as the Law is
concerned, however, I am dead—killed
by the Law itself—in order that I might
live for God. I have been put to death
with Christ on his cross, 20 so that it is no
longer I who live, but it is Christ who
lives in me. This life that I live now, I live
by faith in the Son of God, who loved me
and gave his life for me. 21 I refuse to reject the grace of God. But if a person is
put right with God through the Law, it
means that Christ died for nothing!

Law or Faith

3 You foolish Galatians! Who put a
spell on you? Before your very eyes
you had a clear description of the death
of Jesus Christ on the cross! 2 Tell me
this one thing: did you receive God's
Spirit by doing what the Law requires or
by hearing the gospel and believing it?
3 How can you be so foolish! You began
by God's Spirit; do you now want to finish by your own power? 4 Did all your
experience mean nothing at all? Surely
it meant something! 5 Does God give you
the Spirit and work miracles among you
because you do what the Law requires
or because you hear the gospel and believe it?
6 Consider the experience of Abraham; as the scripture says, "He believed
God, and because of his faith God accepted him as righteous." 7 You should
realize, then, that the real descendants
of Abraham are the people who have
faith. 8 The scripture predicted that God
would put the Gentiles right with himself through faith. And so the scripture
announced the Good News to Abraham:
"Through you God will bless all people."
9 Abraham believed and was blessed; so
all who believe are blessed as he was.
10 Those who depend on obeying the
Law live under a curse. For the scripture
says, "Whoever does not always obey
everything that is written in the book of
the Law is under God's curse!" 11 Now, it
is clear that no one is put right with God
by means of the Law, because the scripture says, "Only the person who is put
right with God through faith shall
live."[d] 12 But the Law has nothing to do
with faith. Instead, as the scripture says,
"Whoever *does* everything the Law requires will live."
13 But by becoming a curse for us
Christ has redeemed us from the curse
that the Law brings; for the scripture
says, "Anyone who is hanged on a tree is
under God's curse." 14 Christ did this in
order that the blessing which God promised to Abraham might be given to the
Gentiles by means of Christ Jesus, so
that through faith we might receive the
Spirit promised by God.

The Law and the Promise

15 My friends, I am going to use an
everyday example: when two people
agree on a matter and sign an agreement, no one can break it or add anything to it. 16 Now, God made his
promises to Abraham and to his
descendant. The scripture does not use
the plural "descendants," meaning many
people, but the singular "descendant,"
meaning one person only, namely,
Christ. 17 What I mean is that God made
a covenant with Abraham and promised
to keep it. The Law, which was given
four hundred and thirty years later, cannot break that covenant and cancel
God's promise. 18 For if God's gift depends on the Law, then it no longer depends on his promise. However, it was
because of his promise that God gave
that gift to Abraham.
19 What, then, was the purpose of the
Law? It was added in order to show
what wrongdoing is, and it was meant to
last until the coming of Abraham's
descendant, to whom the promise was
made. The Law was handed down by angels, with a man acting as a go-between.
20 But a go-between is not needed when
only one person is involved; and God
is one.[e]

The Purpose of the Law

21 Does this mean that the Law is
against God's promises? No, not at all!
For if human beings had received a law
that could bring life, then everyone
could be put right with God by obeying
it. 22 But the scripture says that the whole
world is under the power of sin; and so
the gift which is promised on the basis of

[d] put right with God through faith shall live; *or* put right with God shall live through faith.
[e] and God is one; *or* and God acts alone.

faith in Jesus Christ is given to those
who believe.
23 But before the time for faith came,
the Law kept us all locked up as prisoners until this coming faith should be revealed. 24 And so the Law was in charge
of us until Christ came, in order that we
might then be put right with God
through faith. 25 Now that the time for
faith is here, the Law is no longer in
charge of us.
26 It is through faith that all of you are
God's children in union with Christ
Jesus. 27 You were baptized into union
with Christ, and now you are clothed, so
to speak, with the life of Christ himself.
28 So there is no difference between Jews
and Gentiles, between slaves and free
people, between men and women; you
are all one in union with Christ Jesus.
29 If you belong to Christ, then you are
the descendants of Abraham and will receive what God has promised.

4 But now to continue—the son who
will receive his father's property is
treated just like a slave while he is
young, even though he really owns
everything. 2 While he is young, there
are men who take care of him and manage his affairs until the time set by his
father. 3 In the same way, we too were
slaves of the ruling spirits of the universe before we reached spiritual maturity. 4 But when the right time finally
came, God sent his own Son. He came as
the son of a human mother and lived under the Jewish Law, 5 to redeem those
who were under the Law, so that we
might become God's children.
6 To show that you are[f] his children,
God sent the Spirit of his Son into our
hearts, the Spirit who cries out, "Father,
my Father." 7 So then, you are no longer
a slave but a child. And since you are his
child, God will give you all that he has
for his children.

Paul's Concern for the Galatians

8 In the past you did not know God,
and so you were slaves of beings who
are not gods. 9 But now that you know
God—or, I should say, now that God
knows you—how is it that you want to
turn back to those weak and pitiful ruling spirits? Why do you want to become
their slaves all over again? 10 You pay
special attention to certain days,
months, seasons, and years. 11 I am worried about you! Can it be that all my
work for you has been for nothing?
12 I beg you, my friends, be like me. After all, I am like you. You have not done
me any wrong. 13 You remember why I
preached the gospel to you the first time;
it was because I was sick. 14 But even
though my physical condition was a
great trial to you, you did not despise or
reject me. Instead, you received me as
you would an angel from heaven; you
received me as you would Christ Jesus.
15 You were so happy! What has happened? I myself can say that you would
have taken out your own eyes, if you
could, and given them to me. 16 Have I
now become your enemy by telling you
the truth?
17 Those other people show a deep interest in you, but their intentions are not
good. All they want is to separate you
from me, so that you will have the same
interest in them as they have in you.
18 Now, it is good to have such a deep
interest if the purpose is good—this is
true always, and not merely when I am
with you. 19 My dear children! Once
again, just like a mother in childbirth, I
feel the same kind of pain for you until
Christ's nature is formed in you. 20 How
I wish I were with you now, so that I
could take a different attitude toward
you. I am so worried about you!

The Example of Hagar and Sarah

21 Let me ask those of you who want to
be subject to the Law: do you not hear
what the Law says? 22 It says that Abraham had two sons, one by a slave
woman, the other by a free woman.
23 His son by the slave woman was born
in the usual way, but his son by the free
woman was born as a result of God's
promise. 24 These things can be understood as a figure: the two women represent two covenants. The one whose
children are born in slavery is Hagar,
and she represents the covenant made at
Mount Sinai. 25 Hagar, who stands for
Mount Sinai in Arabia, is[g] a figure of
the present city of Jerusalem, in slavery
with all its people. 26 But the heavenly

[f] To show that you are; *or* Because you are. [g] Hagar . . . is; *some manuscripts have* Sinai is a mountain in Arabia, and it is.

Jerusalem is free, and she is our mother.
27 For the scripture says,
"Be happy, you childless woman!
Shout and cry with joy, you who
never felt the pains of
childbirth!
For the woman who was deserted
will have more children
than the woman whose husband
never left her."
28 Now, you, my friends, are God's
children as a result of his promise, just
as Isaac was. 29 At that time the son who
was born in the usual way persecuted
the one who was born because of God's
Spirit; and it is the same now. 30 But
what does the scripture say? It says,
"Send the slave woman and her son
away; for the son of the slave woman
will not have a part of the father's property along with the son of the free
woman." 31 So then, my friends, we are
not the children of a slave woman but of
a free woman.

Preserve Your Freedom

5 Freedom is what we have—Christ
has set us free! Stand, then, as free
people, and do not allow yourselves to
become slaves again.
2 Listen! I, Paul, tell you that if you allow yourselves to be circumcised, it
means that Christ is of no use to you at
all. 3 Once more I warn any man who allows himself to be circumcised that he is
obliged to obey the whole Law. 4 Those
of you who try to be put right with God
by obeying the Law have cut yourselves
off from Christ. You are outside God's
grace. 5 As for us, our hope is that God
will put us right with him; and this is
what we wait for by the power of God's
Spirit working through our faith. 6 For
when we are in union with Christ Jesus,
neither circumcision nor the lack of it
makes any difference at all; what matters is faith that works through love.
7 You were doing so well! Who made
you stop obeying the truth? How did he
persuade you? 8 It was not done by God,
who calls you. 9 "It takes only a little
yeast to make the whole batch of dough
rise," as they say. 10 But I still feel confident about you. Our life in union with
the Lord makes me confident that you
will not take a different view and that
whoever is upsetting you will be punished by God.
11 But as for me, my friends, if I continue to preach that circumcision is necessary, why am I still being persecuted?
If that were true, then my preaching
about the cross of Christ would cause no
trouble. 12 I wish that the people who are
upsetting you would go all the way; let
them go on and castrate themselves!
13 As for you, my friends, you were
called to be free. But do not let this freedom become an excuse for letting your
physical desires control you. Instead, let
love make you serve one another. 14 For
the whole Law is summed up in one
commandment: "Love your neighbor as
you love yourself." 15 But if you act like
wild animals, hurting and harming each
other, then watch out, or you will completely destroy one another.

The Spirit and Human Nature

16 What I say is this: let the Spirit direct your lives, and you will not satisfy
the desires of the human nature. 17 For
what our human nature wants is opposed to what the Spirit wants, and what
the Spirit wants is opposed to what our
human nature wants. These two are enemies, and this means that you cannot do
what you want to do. 18 If the Spirit leads
you, then you are not subject to the Law.
19 What human nature does is quite
plain. It shows itself in immoral, filthy,
and indecent actions; 20 in worship of
idols and witchcraft. People become
enemies and they fight; they become
jealous, angry, and ambitious. They
separate into parties and groups; 21 they
are envious, get drunk, have orgies, and
do other things like these. I warn you
now as I have before: those who do these
things will not possess the Kingdom
of God.
22 But the Spirit produces love, joy,
peace, patience, kindness, goodness,
faithfulness, 23 humility, and self-
control. There is no law against such
things as these. 24 And those who belong
to Christ Jesus have put to death their
human nature with all its passions and
desires. 25 The Spirit has given us life; he
must also control our lives. 26 We must
not be proud or irritate one another or
be jealous of one another.

Bear One Another's Burdens

6 My friends, if someone is caught in
any kind of wrongdoing, those of
you who are spiritual should set him

right; but you must do it in a gentle way.
And keep an eye on yourselves, so that
you will not be tempted, too. 2 Help carry
one another's burdens, and in this way
you will obey[h] the law of Christ. 3 If you
think you are something when you really are nothing, you are only deceiving
yourself. 4 You should each judge your
own conduct. If it is good, then you can
be proud of what you yourself have
done, without having to compare it with
what someone else has done. 5 For each
of you have to carry your own load.

6 If you are being taught the Christian
message, you should share all the good
things you have with your teacher.

7 Do not deceive yourselves; no one
makes a fool of God. You will reap exactly what you plant. 8 If you plant in the
field of your natural desires, from it you
will gather the harvest of death; if you
plant in the field of the Spirit, from the
Spirit you will gather the harvest of eternal life. 9 So let us not become tired of
doing good; for if we do not give up, the
time will come when we will reap the
harvest. 10 So then, as often as we have
the chance, we should do good to everyone, and especially to those who belong
to our family in the faith.

[h] you will obey; *some manuscripts have* obey.

Final Warning and Greeting

11 See what big letters I make as I write
to you now with my own hand! 12 The
people who are trying to force you to be
circumcised are the ones who want to
show off and boast about external matters. They do it, however, only so that
they may not be persecuted for the cross
of Christ. 13 Even those who practice circumcision do not obey the Law; they
want you to be circumcised so that they
can boast that you submitted to this
physical ceremony. 14 As for me, however, I will boast only about the cross of
our Lord Jesus Christ; for by means of
his cross the world is dead to me, and I
am dead to the world. 15 It does not matter at all whether or not one is circumcised; what does matter is being a new
creature. 16 As for those who follow this
rule in their lives, may peace and mercy
be with them — with them and with all of
God's people!

17 To conclude: let no one give me any
more trouble, because the scars I have
on my body show that I am the slave of
Jesus.

18 May the grace of our Lord Jesus
Christ be with you all, my friends.
Amen.

Paul's Letter to the
EPHESIANS

Introduction

Paul's Letter to the Ephesians *is concerned first of all with "God's plan . . . to bring all creation together, everything in heaven and on earth, with Christ as head" (1.10). It is also an appeal to God's people to live out the meaning of this great plan for the unity of the whole human race through oneness with Jesus Christ.*

In the first part of Ephesians *the writer develops the theme of unity by speaking of the way in which God the Father has chosen his people, how they are forgiven and set free from their sins through Jesus Christ the Son, and how God's great promise is guaranteed by the Holy Spirit. In the second part he appeals to the readers to live in such a way that their oneness in Christ may become real in their life together.*

Several figures of speech are used to show the oneness of God's people in union with Christ: the church is like a body, with Christ as the head; or like a building, with Christ as the cornerstone; or like a wife, with Christ as the husband. This letter rises to great heights of expression as the writer is moved by the thought of God's grace in Christ. Everything is seen in the light of Christ's love, sacrifice, forgiveness, grace, and purity.

Outline of Contents

---

1 From Paul, who by God's will is an
apostle of Christ Jesus—
To God's people in Ephesus,[a] who are
faithful in their life in union with Christ
Jesus:
2 May God our Father and the Lord
Jesus Christ give you grace and peace.

Spiritual Blessings in Christ

3 Let us give thanks to the God and
Father of our Lord Jesus Christ! For in
our union with Christ he has blessed us
by giving us every spiritual blessing in
the heavenly world. 4 Even before the
world was made, God had already chosen us to be his through our union with
Christ, so that we would be holy and
without fault before him.
Because of his love 5 God[b] had already decided that through Jesus Christ
he would make us his children—this
was his pleasure and purpose. 6 Let us
praise God for his glorious grace, for the
free gift he gave us in his dear Son! 7 For
by the blood of Christ[c] we are set free,
that is, our sins are forgiven. How great
is the grace of God, 8 which he gave to us
in such large measure!
In all his wisdom and insight 9 God did
what he had purposed, and made known
to us the secret plan he had already decided to complete by means of Christ.
10 This plan, which God will complete
when the time is right, is to bring all creation together, everything in heaven and
on earth, with Christ as head.
11 All things are done according to
God's plan and decision; and God chose
us to be his own people in union with
Christ because of his own purpose,
based on what he had decided from the
very beginning. 12 Let us, then, who were
the first to hope in Christ, praise God's
glory!
13 And you also became God's people
when you heard the true message, the
Good News that brought you salvation.
You believed in Christ, and God put his
stamp of ownership on you by giving
you the Holy Spirit he had promised.
14 The Spirit is the guarantee that we
shall receive what God has promised his
people, and this assures us that God will
give complete freedom to those who are
his. Let us praise his glory!

Paul's Prayer

15 For this reason, ever since I heard of
your faith in the Lord Jesus and your
love for all of God's people, 16 I have not
stopped giving thanks to God for you. I
remember you in my prayers 17 and ask
the God of our Lord Jesus Christ, the
glorious Father, to give you the Spirit,
who will make you wise and reveal God
to you, so that you will know him.
18 I ask that your minds may be opened
to see his light, so that you will know
what is the hope to which he has called
you, how rich are the wonderful blessings he promises his people, 19 and how
very great is his power at work in us
who believe. This power working in us is
the same as the mighty strength 20 which
he used when he raised Christ from
death and seated him at his right side in
the heavenly world. 21 Christ rules there
above all heavenly rulers, authorities,
powers, and lords; he has a title superior
to all titles of authority in this world and
in the next. 22 God put all things under
Christ's feet and gave him to the church
as supreme Lord over all things. 23 The
church is Christ's body, the completion
of him who himself completes all things
everywhere.[d]

---

[a] *Some manuscripts do not have* in Ephesus. [b] before him. Because of his love God; *or* before him, and to live in love. God. [c] by the blood of Christ; *or* by the sacrificial death of Christ.
[d] who himself completes all things everywhere; *or* who is himself completely filled with God's fullness.

From Death to Life

2 In the past you were spiritually
dead because of your disobedience
and sins. 2 At that time you followed the
world's evil way; you obeyed the ruler of
the spiritual powers in space, the spirit
who now controls the people who disobey God. 3 Actually all of us were like
them and lived according to our natural
desires, doing whatever suited the
wishes of our own bodies and minds. In
our natural condition we, like everyone
else, were destined to suffer God's
anger.
4 But God's mercy is so abundant, and
his love for us is so great, 5 that while we
were spiritually dead in our disobedience he brought us to life with Christ. It
is by God's grace that you have been
saved. 6 In our union with Christ Jesus
he raised us up with him to rule with him
in the heavenly world. 7 He did this to
demonstrate for all time to come the extraordinary greatness of his grace in the
love he showed us in Christ Jesus. 8-9 For
it is by God's grace that you have been
saved through faith. It is not the result of
your own efforts, but God's gift, so that
no one can boast about it. 10 God has
made us what we are, and in our union
with Christ Jesus he has created us for a
life of good deeds, which he has already
prepared for us to do.

One in Christ

11 You Gentiles by birth—called "the
uncircumcised" by the Jews, who call
themselves the circumcised (which refers to what men do to their bodies)—
remember what you were in the past.
12 At that time you were apart from
Christ. You were foreigners and did not
belong to God's chosen people. You had
no part in the covenants, which were
based on God's promises to his people,
and you lived in this world without hope
and without God. 13 But now, in union
with Christ Jesus you, who used to be far
away, have been brought near by the
blood of Christ.[e] 14 For Christ himself
has brought us peace by making Jews
and Gentiles one people. With his own
body he broke down the wall that separated them and kept them enemies. 15 He
abolished the Jewish Law with its commandments and rules, in order to create
out of the two races one new people in
union with himself, in this way making
peace. 16 By his death on the cross Christ
destroyed their enmity; by means of the
cross he united both races into one body
and brought them back to God. 17 So
Christ came and preached the Good
News of peace to all—to you Gentiles,
who were far away from God, and to the
Jews, who were near to him. 18 It is
through Christ that all of us, Jews and
Gentiles, are able to come in the one
Spirit into the presence of the Father.
19 So then, you Gentiles are not foreigners or strangers any longer; you are
now citizens together with God's people
and members of the family of God.
20 You, too, are built upon the foundation
laid by the apostles and prophets,[f] the
cornerstone being Christ Jesus himself.
21 He is the one who holds the whole
building together and makes it grow into
a sacred temple dedicated to the Lord.
22 In union with him you too are being
built together with all the others into a
place where God lives through his Spirit.

Paul's Work for the Gentiles

3 For this reason I, Paul, the prisoner
of Christ Jesus for the sake of you
Gentiles, pray to God. 2 Surely you have
heard that God in his grace has given me
this work to do for your good. 3 God revealed his secret plan and made it
known to me. (I have written briefly
about this, 4 and if you will read what I
have written, you can learn about my
understanding of the secret of Christ.)
5 In past times human beings were not
told this secret, but God has revealed it
now by the Spirit to his holy apostles
and prophets. 6 The secret is that by
means of the gospel the Gentiles have a
part with the Jews in God's blessings;
they are members of the same body and
share in the promise that God made
through Christ Jesus.
7 I was made a servant of the gospel by
God's special gift, which he gave me
through the working of his power. 8 I am
less than the least of all God's people;
yet God gave me this privilege of taking
to the Gentiles the Good News about the

[e] by the blood of Christ; *or* by the sacrificial death of Christ. [f] the foundation laid by the apostles and prophets; *or* the foundation, that is, the apostles and prophets.

infinite riches of Christ, 9 and of making
all people see how God's secret plan is to
be put into effect. God, who is the Creator of all things, kept his secret hidden
through all the past ages, 10 in order that
at the present time, by means of the
church, the angelic rulers and powers in
the heavenly world might learn of his
wisdom in all its different forms. 11 God
did this according to his eternal purpose,
which he achieved through Christ Jesus
our Lord. 12 In union with Christ and
through our faith in him we have the
boldness to go into God's presence with
all confidence. 13 I beg you, then, not to
be discouraged because I am suffering
for you; it is all for your benefit.

The Love of Christ

14 For this reason I fall on my knees
before the Father, 15 from whom every
family in heaven and on earth receives
its true name. 16 I ask God from the
wealth of his glory to give you power
through his Spirit to be strong in your
inner selves, 17 and I pray that Christ will
make his home in your hearts through
faith. I pray that you may have your
roots and foundation in love, 18 so that
you, together with all God's people, may
have the power to understand how
broad and long, how high and deep, is
Christ's love. 19 Yes, may you come to
know his love—although it can never be
fully known—and so be completely
filled with the very nature of God.

20 To him who by means of his power
working in us is able to do so much more
than we can ever ask for, or even think
of: 21 to God be the glory in the church
and in Christ Jesus for all time, forever
and ever! Amen.

The Unity of the Body

4 I urge you, then—I who am a prisoner because I serve the Lord: live a
life that measures up to the standard
God set when he called you. 2 Be always
humble, gentle, and patient. Show your
love by being tolerant with one another.
3 Do your best to preserve the unity
which the Spirit gives by means of the
peace that binds you together. 4 There is
one body and one Spirit, just as there is
one hope to which God has called you.
5 There is one Lord, one faith, one baptism; 6 there is one God and Father of
all people, who is Lord of all, works
through all, and is in all.

7 Each one of us has received a special
gift in proportion to what Christ has
given. 8 As the scripture says,

"When he went up to the very
heights,
he took many captives with him;
he gave gifts to people."

9 Now, what does "he went up" mean? It
means that first he came down to the
lowest depths of the earth.[g] 10 So the
one who came down is the same one
who went up, above and beyond the
heavens, to fill the whole universe with
his presence. 11 It was he who "gave gifts
to people"; he appointed some to be
apostles, others to be prophets, others to
be evangelists, others to be pastors and
teachers. 12 He did this to prepare all
God's people for the work of Christian
service, in order to build up the body of
Christ. 13 And so we shall all come together to that oneness in our faith and in
our knowledge of the Son of God; we
shall become mature people, reaching to
the very height of Christ's full stature.
14 Then we shall no longer be children,
carried by the waves and blown about
by every shifting wind of the teaching of
deceitful people, who lead others into error by the tricks they invent. 15 Instead,
by speaking the truth in a spirit of love,
we must grow up in every way to Christ,
who is the head. 16 Under his control all
the different parts of the body fit together, and the whole body is held together by every joint with which it is
provided. So when each separate part
works as it should, the whole body
grows and builds itself up through love.

The New Life in Christ

17 In the Lord's name, then, I warn
you: do not continue to live like the heathen, whose thoughts are worthless
18 and whose minds are in the dark. They
have no part in the life that God gives,
for they are completely ignorant and
stubborn. 19 They have lost all feeling of
shame; they give themselves over to vice
and do all sorts of indecent things without restraint.

20 That was not what you learned

[g] the lowest depths of the earth; *or* the lower depths, the earth itself.

about Christ! 21 You certainly heard about him, and as his followers you were taught the truth that is in Jesus. 22 So get rid of your old self, which made you live as you used to—the old self that was being destroyed by its deceitful desires. 23 Your hearts and minds must be made completely new, 24 and you must put on the new self, which is created in God's likeness and reveals itself in the true life that is upright and holy.

25 No more lying, then! Each of you must tell the truth to the other believer, because we are all members together in the body of Christ. 26 If you become angry, do not let your anger lead you into sin, and do not stay angry all day. 27 Don't give the Devil a chance. 28 If you used to rob, you must stop robbing and start working, in order to earn an honest living for yourself and to be able to help the poor. 29 Do not use harmful words, but only helpful words, the kind that build up and provide what is needed, so that what you say will do good to those who hear you. 30 And do not make God's Holy Spirit sad; for the Spirit is God's mark of ownership on you, a guarantee that the Day will come when God will set you free. 31 Get rid of all bitterness, passion, and anger. No more shouting or insults, no more hateful feelings of any sort. 32 Instead, be kind and tenderhearted to one another, and forgive one another, as God has forgiven you through Christ.

Living in the Light

5 Since you are God's dear children, you must try to be like him. 2 Your life must be controlled by love, just as Christ loved us and gave his life for us as a sweet-smelling offering and sacrifice that pleases God.

3 Since you are God's people, it is not right that any matters of sexual immorality or indecency or greed should even be mentioned among you. 4 Nor is it fitting for you to use language which is obscene, profane, or vulgar. Rather you should give thanks to God. 5 You may be sure that no one who is immoral, indecent, or greedy (for greed is a form of idolatry) will ever receive a share in the Kingdom of Christ and of God.

6 Do not let anyone deceive you with foolish words; it is because of these very things that God's anger will come upon those who do not obey him. 7 So have nothing at all to do with such people. 8 You yourselves used to be in the darkness, but since you have become the Lord's people, you are in the light. So you must live like people who belong to the light, 9 for it is the light[h] that brings a rich harvest of every kind of goodness, righteousness, and truth. 10 Try to learn what pleases the Lord. 11 Have nothing to do with the worthless things that people do, things that belong to the darkness. Instead, bring them out to the light. (12 It is really too shameful even to talk about the things they do in secret.) 13 And when all things are brought out to the light, then their true nature is clearly revealed; 14 for anything that is clearly revealed becomes light.[i] That is why it is said,

"Wake up, sleeper,
and rise from death,
and Christ will shine on you."

15 So be careful how you live. Don't live like ignorant people, but like wise people. 16 Make good use of every opportunity you have, because these are evil days. 17 Don't be fools, then, but try to find out what the Lord wants you to do.

18 Do not get drunk with wine, which will only ruin you; instead, be filled with the Spirit. 19 Speak to one another with the words of psalms, hymns, and sacred songs; sing hymns and psalms to the Lord with praise in your hearts. 20 In the name of our Lord Jesus Christ, always give thanks for everything to God the Father.

Wives and Husbands

21 Submit yourselves to one another because of your reverence for Christ.

22 Wives, submit yourselves to your husbands as to the Lord. 23 For a husband has authority over his wife just as Christ has authority over the church; and Christ is himself the Savior of the church, his body. 24 And so wives must submit themselves completely to their husbands just as the church submits itself to Christ.

[h] the light; *some manuscripts have* the Spirit. [i] anything that is clearly revealed becomes light; *or* it is light that clearly reveals everything.

25 Husbands, love your wives just as
Christ loved the church and gave his life
for it. 26 He did this to dedicate the
church to God by his word, after making
it clean by washing it in water, 27 in order to present the church to himself in
all its beauty—pure and faultless, without spot or wrinkle or any other imperfection. 28 Men ought to love their wives
just as they love their own bodies. A
man who loves his wife loves himself.
(29 None of us ever hate our own bodies.
Instead, we feed them, and take care of
them, just as Christ does the church;
30 for we are members of his body.) 31 As
the scripture says, "For this reason a
man will leave his father and mother
and unite with his wife, and the two will
become one." 32 There is a deep secret
truth revealed in this scripture, which I
understand as applying to Christ and the
church. 33 But it also applies to you:
every husband must love his wife as
himself, and every wife must respect her
husband.

Children and Parents

6 Children, it is your Christian duty
to[l] obey your parents, for this is
the right thing to do. 2 "Respect your
father and mother" is the first commandment that has a promise added: 3 "so that
all may go well with you, and you may
live a long time in the land."

4 Parents, do not treat your children in
such a way as to make them angry. Instead, raise them with Christian discipline and instruction.

Slaves and Masters

5 Slaves, obey your human masters
with fear and trembling; and do it with a
sincere heart, as though you were serving Christ. 6 Do this not only when they
are watching you, because you want to
gain their approval; but with all your
heart do what God wants, as slaves of
Christ. 7 Do your work as slaves cheerfully, as though you served the Lord,
and not merely human beings. 8 Remember that the Lord will reward each of us,
whether slave or free, for the good work
we do.

9 Masters, behave in the same way toward your slaves and stop using threats.
Remember that you and your slaves belong to the same Master in heaven, who
judges everyone by the same standard.

The Whole Armor of God

10 Finally, build up your strength in
union with the Lord and by means of his
mighty power. 11 Put on all the armor
that God gives you, so that you will be
able to stand up against the Devil's evil
tricks. 12 For we are not fighting against
human beings but against the wicked
spiritual forces in the heavenly world,
the rulers, authorities, and cosmic powers of this dark age. 13 So put on God's
armor now! Then when the evil day
comes, you will be able to resist the enemy's attacks; and after fighting to the
end, you will still hold your ground.

14 So stand ready, with truth as a belt
tight around your waist, with righteousness as your breastplate, 15 and as your
shoes the readiness to announce the
Good News of peace. 16 At all times carry
faith as a shield; for with it you will be
able to put out all the burning arrows
shot by the Evil One. 17 And accept salvation as a helmet, and the word of God
as the sword which the Spirit gives you.
18 Do all this in prayer, asking for God's
help. Pray on every occasion, as the
Spirit leads. For this reason keep alert
and never give up; pray always for all
God's people. 19 And pray also for me,
that God will give me a message when I
am ready to speak, so that I may speak
boldly and make known the gospel's secret. 20 For the sake of this gospel I am an
ambassador, though now I am in prison.
Pray that I may be bold in speaking
about the gospel as I should.

Final Greetings

21 Tychicus, our dear brother and
faithful servant in the Lord's work, will
give you all the news about me, so that
you may know how I am getting along.
22 That is why I am sending him to you—
to tell you how all of us are getting along
and to encourage you.

23 May God the Father and the Lord
Jesus Christ give to all Christians peace
and love with faith. 24 May God's grace
be with all those who love our Lord
Jesus Christ with undying love.

[l] *Some manuscripts do not have* it is your Christian duty to.

Paul's Letter to the
PHILIPPIANS

Introduction

Paul's Letter to the Philippians *was written to the first church that Paul established on European soil, in the Roman province of Macedonia. It was written while the apostle was in prison, and at a time when he was troubled by the opposition of other Christian workers toward himself and was distressed by false teaching in the church at Philippi. Yet this letter breathes a joy and confidence that can be explained only by Paul's deep faith in Jesus Christ.*

The immediate reason for writing the letter was to thank the Philippian Christians for the gift which they had sent to help him in his time of need. He uses this opportunity to reassure them, so that they may have courage and confidence in spite of all his troubles and their own as well. He pleads with them to have the humble attitude of Jesus, rather than to be controlled by selfish ambition and pride. He reminds them that their life in union with Christ is a gift of God's grace which they have received through faith, not through obedience to the ceremonies of the Jewish Law. He writes of the joy and peace that God gives to those who live in union with Christ.

This letter is marked by its emphasis on joy, confidence, unity, and perseverance in the Christian faith and life. It also reveals the deep affection Paul had for the church at Philippi.

Outline of Contents

---

1 From Paul and Timothy, servants of
Christ Jesus—
To all God's people in Philippi who are
in union with Christ Jesus, including the
church leaders and helpers:
2 May God our Father and the Lord
Jesus Christ give you grace and peace.

Paul's Prayer for His Readers

3 I thank my God for you every time I
think of you; 4 and every time I pray for
you all, I pray with joy 5 because of the
way in which you have helped me in the
work of the gospel from the very first
day until now. 6 And so I am sure that
God, who began this good work in you,
will carry it on until it is finished on the
Day of Christ Jesus. 7 You are always in
my heart! And so it is only right for me
to feel as I do about you. For you have all
shared with me in this privilege that God
has given me, both now that I am in
prison and also while I was free to defend the gospel and establish it firmly.
8 God is my witness that I tell the truth
when I say that my deep feeling for you
all comes from the heart of Christ Jesus
himself.
9 I pray that your love will keep on
growing more and more, together with
true knowledge and perfect judgment,
10 so that you will be able to choose what
is best. Then you will be free from all
impurity and blame on the Day of
Christ. 11 Your lives will be filled with
the truly good qualities which only Jesus
Christ can produce, for the glory and
praise of God.

To Live Is Christ

12 I want you to know, my friends, that
the things that have happened to me
have really helped the progress of the
gospel. 13 As a result, the whole palace
guard and all the others here know that
I am in prison because I am a servant of
Christ. 14 And my being in prison has
given most of the believers more confidence in the Lord, so that they grow

bolder all the time to preach the message[a] fearlessly.
15 Of course some of them preach
Christ because they are jealous and
quarrelsome, but others from genuine
good will. 16 These do so from love, because they know that God has given me
the work of defending the gospel. 17 The
others do not proclaim Christ sincerely,
but from a spirit of selfish ambition; they
think that they will make more trouble
for me while I am in prison.
18 It does not matter! I am happy about
it—just so Christ is preached in every
way possible, whether from wrong or
right motives. And I will continue to be
happy, 19 because I know that by means
of your prayers and the help which
comes from the Spirit of Jesus Christ I
shall be set free. 20 My deep desire and
hope is that I shall never fail in my duty,
but that at all times, and especially right
now, I shall be full of courage, so that
with my whole being I shall bring honor
to Christ, whether I live or die. 21 For
what is life? To me, it is Christ. Death,
then, will bring more. 22 But if by continuing to live I can do more worthwhile
work, then I am not sure which I should
choose. 23 I am pulled in two directions. I
want very much to leave this life and be
with Christ, which is a far better thing;
24 but for your sake it is much more important that I remain alive. 25 I am sure
of this, and so I know that I will stay. I
will stay on with you all, to add to your
progress and joy in the faith, 26 so that
when I am with you again, you will have
even more reason to be proud of me in
your life in union with Christ Jesus.
27 Now, the important thing is that
your way of life should be as the gospel
of Christ requires, so that, whether or
not I am able to go and see you, I will
hear that you are standing firm with one
common purpose and that with only one
desire you are fighting together for the
faith of the gospel. 28 Don't be afraid of
your enemies; always be courageous,
and this will prove to them that they will
lose and that you will win, because it is
God who gives you the victory. 29 For
you have been given the privilege of
serving Christ, not only by believing in
him, but also by suffering for him.
30 Now you can take part with me in the
battle. It is the same battle you saw me
fighting in the past, and as you hear, the
one I am fighting still.

Christ's Humility and Greatness

2 Your life in Christ makes you
strong, and his love comforts you.
You have fellowship with the Spirit,[b]
and you have kindness and compassion
for one another. 2 I urge you, then, to
make me completely happy by having
the same thoughts, sharing the same
love, and being one in soul and mind.
3 Don't do anything from selfish ambition or from a cheap desire to boast, but
be humble toward one another, always
considering others better than yourselves. 4 And look out for one another's
interests, not just for your own. 5 The attitude you should have is the one that
Christ Jesus had:

6 He always had the nature of God,
but he did not think that by
force he should try to remain[c]
equal with God.
7 Instead of this, of his own free will
he gave up all he had,
and took the nature of a servant.
He became like a human being
and appeared in human likeness.
8 He was humble and walked the
path of obedience all the way
to death—
his death on the cross.
9 For this reason God raised him to
the highest place above
and gave him the name that is
greater than any other name.
10 And so, in honor of the name of
Jesus
all beings in heaven, on earth,
and in the world below[d]
will fall on their knees,
11 and all will openly proclaim that
Jesus Christ is Lord,
to the glory of God the Father.

Shining as Lights in the World

12 So then, dear friends, as you always
obeyed me when I was with you, it is
even more important that you obey me
now while I am away from you. Keep on

[a] the message; *some manuscripts have* God's message. [b] You have fellowship with the Spirit; *or* The Spirit has brought you into fellowship with one another. [c] remain; *or* become.
[d] WORLD BELOW: *It was thought that the dead continued to exist in a dark world under the ground.*

working with fear and trembling to complete your salvation, 13 because God is
always at work in you to make you willing and able to obey his own purpose.
14 Do everything without complaining
or arguing, 15 so that you may be innocent and pure as God's perfect children,
who live in a world of corrupt and sinful
people. You must shine among them like
stars lighting up the sky, 16 as you offer
them the message of life. If you do so, I
shall have reason to be proud of you on
the Day of Christ, because it will show
that all my effort and work have not
been wasted.
17 Perhaps my life's blood is to be
poured out like an offering on the sacrifice that your faith offers to God. If that
is so, I am glad and share my joy with
you all. 18 In the same way, you too must
be glad and share your joy with me.

Timothy and Epaphroditus

19 If it is the Lord's will, I hope that I
will be able to send Timothy to you soon,
so that I may be encouraged by news
about you. 20 He is the only one who
shares my feelings and who really cares
about you. 21 Everyone else is concerned
only with their own affairs, not with the
cause of Jesus Christ. 22 And you yourselves know how he has proved his
worth, how he and I, like a son and his
father, have worked together for the
sake of the gospel. 23 So I hope to send
him to you as soon as I know how things
are going to turn out for me. 24 And I
trust in the Lord that I myself will be
able to come to you soon.
25 I have thought it necessary to send
to you our brother Epaphroditus, who
has worked and fought by my side and
who has served as your messenger in
helping me. 26 He is anxious to see you
all and is very upset because you had
heard that he was sick. 27 Indeed he was
sick and almost died. But God had pity
on him, and not only on him but on me,
too, and spared me an even greater sorrow. 28 I am all the more eager, then, to
send him to you, so that you will be glad
again when you see him, and my own
sorrow will disappear. 29 Receive him,
then, with joy, as a believer in the Lord.
Show respect to all such people as he,
30 because he risked his life and nearly
died for the sake of the work of Christ, in
order to give me the help that you yourselves could not give.

The True Righteousness

3 In conclusion, my friends, be joyful
in your union with the Lord. I don't
mind repeating what I have written before, and you will be safer if I do so.
2 Watch out for those who do evil things,
those dogs, those who insist on cutting
the body. 3 It is we, not they, who have
received the true circumcision, for we
worship God by means of his Spirit and
rejoice in our life in union with Christ
Jesus. We do not put any trust in external ceremonies. 4 I could, of course, put
my trust in such things. If any of you
think you can trust in external ceremonies, I have even more reason to feel that
way. 5 I was circumcised when I was a
week old. I am an Israelite by birth, of
the tribe of Benjamin, a pure-blooded
Hebrew. As far as keeping the Jewish
Law is concerned, I was a Pharisee, 6 and
I was so zealous that I persecuted the
church. As far as a person can be righteous by obeying the commands of the
Law, I was without fault. 7 But all those
things that I might count as profit I now
reckon as loss for Christ's sake. 8 Not
only those things; I reckon everything as
complete loss for the sake of what is so
much more valuable, the knowledge of
Christ Jesus my Lord. For his sake I
have thrown everything away; I consider it all as mere garbage, so that I may
gain Christ 9 and be completely united
with him. I no longer have a righteousness of my own, the kind that is gained
by obeying the Law. I now have the
righteousness that is given through faith
in Christ, the righteousness that comes
from God and is based on faith. 10 All I
want is to know Christ and to experience the power of his resurrection, to
share in his sufferings and become like
him in his death, 11 in the hope that I myself will be raised from death to life.

Running toward the Goal

12 I do not claim that I have already
succeeded or have already become perfect. I keep striving to win the prize for
which Christ Jesus has already won me
to himself. 13 Of course, my friends, I re-

ally do not[e] think that I have already
won it; the one thing I do, however, is
to forget what is behind me and do my
best to reach what is ahead. 14 So I run
straight toward the goal in order to win
the prize, which is God's call through
Christ Jesus to the life above.
15 All of us who are spiritually mature
should have this same attitude. But if
some of you have a different attitude,
God will make this clear to you. 16 However that may be, let us go forward according to the same rules we have
followed until now.
17 Keep on imitating me, my friends.
Pay attention to those who follow the
right example that we have set for you.
18 I have told you this many times before, and now I repeat it with tears: there
are many whose lives make them enemies of Christ's death on the cross.
19 They are going to end up in hell, because their god is their bodily desires.
They are proud of what they should be
ashamed of, and they think only of
things that belong to this world. 20 We,
however, are citizens of heaven, and we
eagerly wait for our Savior, the Lord
Jesus Christ, to come from heaven. 21 He
will change our weak mortal bodies and
make them like his own glorious body,
using that power by which he is able to
bring all things under his rule.

Instructions

4 So then, my friends, how dear you
are to me and how I miss you! How
happy you make me, and how proud I
am of you!—this, dear friends, is how
you should stand firm in your life in the
Lord.
2 Euodia and Syntyche, please, I beg
you, try to agree as sisters in the Lord.
3 And you too, my faithful partner, I
want you to help these women; for they
have worked hard with me to spread the
gospel, together with Clement and all
my other fellow workers, whose names
are in God's book of the living.
4 May you always be joyful in your
union with the Lord. I say it again:
rejoice!
5 Show a gentle attitude toward everyone. The Lord is coming soon. 6 Don't
worry about anything, but in all your
prayers ask God for what you need, always asking him with a thankful heart.
7 And God's peace, which is far beyond
human understanding, will keep your
hearts and minds safe in union with
Christ Jesus.
8 In conclusion, my friends, fill your
minds with those things that are good
and that deserve praise: things that are
true, noble, right, pure, lovely, and honorable. 9 Put into practice what you
learned and received from me, both
from my words and from my actions.
And the God who gives us peace will be
with you.

Thanks for the Gift

10 In my life in union with the Lord it is
a great joy to me that after so long a time
you once more had the chance of showing that you care for me. I don't mean
that you had stopped caring for me—
you just had no chance to show it. 11 And
I am not saying this because I feel neglected, for I have learned to be satisfied
with what I have. 12 I know what it is to
be in need and what it is to have more
than enough. I have learned this secret,
so that anywhere, at any time, I am content, whether I am full or hungry,
whether I have too much or too little.
13 I have the strength to face all conditions by the power that Christ gives me.
14 But it was very good of you to help
me in my troubles. 15 You Philippians
know very well that when I left Macedonia in the early days of preaching the
Good News, you were the only church to
help me; you were the only ones who
shared my profits and losses. 16 More
than once when I needed help in Thessalonica, you sent it to me. 17 It is not that
I just want to receive gifts; rather, I want
to see profit added to your account.
18 Here, then, is my receipt for everything you have given me—and it has
been more than enough! I have all I need
now that Epaphroditus has brought me
all your gifts. They are like a sweet-
smelling offering to God, a sacrifice
which is acceptable and pleasing to him.
19 And with all his abundant wealth
through Christ Jesus, my God will supply all your needs. 20 To our God and

[e] not; *some manuscripts have* not yet.

Father be the glory forever and ever!
Amen.

Final Greetings

21 Greetings to each one of God's people who belong to Christ Jesus. The believers here with me send you their
greetings. 22 All God's people here send
greetings, especially those who belong
to the Emperor's palace.
23 May the grace of the Lord Jesus
Christ be with you all.

Paul's Letter to the COLOSSIANS

Introduction

Paul's Letter to the Colossians *was written to the church at Colossae, a town in Asia Minor east of Ephesus. This church had not been established by Paul, but was in an area for which Paul felt responsible, as he sent out workers from Ephesus, the capital of the Roman province of Asia. Paul had learned that there were false teachers in the church at Colossae who insisted that in order to know God and have full salvation one must worship certain "spiritual rulers and authorities." In addition, these teachers said, one must submit to special rites such as circumcision and must observe strict rules about foods and other matters.*

Paul writes to oppose these teachings with the true Christian message. The heart of his reply is that Jesus Christ is able to give full salvation and that these other beliefs and practices actually lead away from him. Through Christ, God created the world and through him he is bringing it back to himself. Only in union with Christ is there hope of salvation for the world. Paul then spells out the implications of this great teaching for the lives of believers.

It is noteworthy that Tychicus, who took this letter to Colossae for Paul, was accompanied by Onesimus, the slave on whose behalf Paul wrote Philemon.

Outline of Contents

Introduction 1.1-8
The nature and work of Christ 1.9—2.19
The new life in Christ 2.20—4.6
Conclusion 4.7-18

---

1 From Paul, who by God's will is an
apostle of Christ Jesus, and from
our brother Timothy—
2 To God's people in Colossae, who are
our faithful friends in union with Christ:
May God our Father give you grace
and peace.

Prayer of Thanksgiving

3 We always give thanks to God, the
Father of our Lord Jesus Christ, when
we pray for you. 4 For we have heard of
your faith in Christ Jesus and of your
love for all God's people. 5 When the true
message, the Good News, first came to
you, you heard about the hope it offers.
So your faith and love are based on what
you hope for, which is kept safe for you
in heaven. 6 The gospel keeps bringing
blessings and is spreading throughout
the world, just as it has among you ever
since the day you first heard about the
grace of God and came to know it as it
really is. 7 You learned of God's grace
from Epaphras, our dear fellow servant,
who is Christ's faithful worker on our[a]
behalf. 8 He has told us of the love that
the Spirit has given you.
9 For this reason we have always
prayed for you, ever since we heard
about you. We ask God to fill you with
the knowledge of his will, with all the

[a] our; *some manuscripts have* your.

wisdom and understanding that his
Spirit gives. 10 Then you will be able to
live as the Lord wants and will always
do what pleases him. Your lives will produce all kinds of good deeds, and you
will grow in your knowledge of God.
11-12 May you be made strong with all the
strength which comes from his glorious
power, so that you may be able to endure everything with patience. And with
joy give thanks to[b] the Father, who has
made you fit to have your share of what
God has reserved for his people in the
kingdom of light. 13 He rescued us from
the power of darkness and brought us
safe into the kingdom of his dear Son,
14 by whom we are set free, that is, our
sins are forgiven.

The Person and Work of Christ

15 Christ is the visible likeness of the
invisible God. He is the first-born Son,
superior to all created things. 16 For
through him God created everything in
heaven and on earth, the seen and the
unseen things, including spiritual powers, lords, rulers, and authorities. God
created the whole universe through him
and for him. 17 Christ existed before all
things, and in union with him all things
have their proper place. 18 He is the head
of his body, the church; he is the source
of the body's life. He is the first-born
Son, who was raised from death, in order that he alone might have the first
place in all things. 19 For it was by God's
own decision that the Son has in himself
the full nature of God. 20 Through the
Son, then, God decided to bring the
whole universe back to himself. God
made peace through his Son's blood[c]
on the cross and so brought back to himself all things, both on earth and in
heaven.

21 At one time you were far away from
God and were his enemies because of
the evil things you did and thought.
22 But now, by means of the physical
death of his Son, God has made you his
friends, in order to bring you, holy, pure,
and faultless, into his presence. 23 You
must, of course, continue faithful on a
firm and sure foundation, and must not
allow yourselves to be shaken from the
hope you gained when you heard the
gospel. It is of this gospel that I, Paul,
became a servant—this gospel which
has been preached to everybody in the
world.

Paul's Work as a Servant of the Church

24 And now I am happy about my sufferings for you, for by means of my
physical sufferings I am helping to complete what still remains of Christ's sufferings on behalf of his body, the church.
25 And I have been made a servant of the
church by God, who gave me this task to
perform for your good. It is the task of
fully proclaiming his message, 26 which
is the secret he hid through all past ages
from all human beings but has now revealed to his people. 27 God's plan is to
make known his secret to his people,
this rich and glorious secret which he
has for all peoples. And the secret is that
Christ is in you, which means that you
will share in the glory of God. 28 So we
preach Christ to everyone. With all possible wisdom we warn and teach them in
order to bring each one into God's presence as a mature individual in union
with Christ. 29 To get this done I toil and
struggle, using the mighty strength
which Christ supplies and which is at
work in me.

2 Let me tell you how hard I have
worked for you and for the people
in Laodicea and for all others who do
not know me personally. 2 I do this in order that they may be filled with courage
and may be drawn together in love, and
so have the full wealth of assurance
which true understanding brings. In this
way they will know God's secret, which
is Christ himself.[d] 3 He is the key that
opens all the hidden treasures of God's
wisdom and knowledge.

4 I tell you, then, do not let anyone deceive you with false arguments, no matter how good they seem to be. 5 For even
though I am absent in body, yet I am
with you in spirit, and I am glad as I see
the resolute firmness with which you
stand together in your faith in Christ.

[b] with patience. And with joy give thanks to; *or* with patience and joy. And give thanks to.
[c] his Son's blood; *or* his Son's sacrificial death. [d] God's secret, which is Christ himself; *some manuscripts have* God's secret; *others have* the secret of God the Father of Christ; *others have* the secret of the God and Father, and of Christ.

Fullness of Life in Christ

6 Since you have accepted Christ Jesus
as Lord, live in union with him. 7 Keep
your roots deep in him, build your lives
on him, and become stronger in your
faith, as you were taught. And be filled
with thanksgiving.

8 See to it, then, that no one enslaves
you by means of the worthless deceit of
human wisdom, which comes from the
teachings handed down by human beings and from the ruling spirits of the
universe, and not from Christ. 9 For the
full content of divine nature lives in
Christ, in his humanity, 10 and you have
been given full life in union with him. He
is supreme over every spiritual ruler and
authority.

11 In union with Christ you were circumcised, not with the circumcision that
is made by human beings, but with the
circumcision made by Christ, which
consists of being freed from the power of
this sinful self. 12 For when you were
baptized, you were buried with Christ,
and in baptism you were also raised
with Christ through your faith in the active power of God, who raised him from
death. 13 You were at one time spiritually
dead because of your sins and because
you were Gentiles without the Law. But
God has now brought you to life with
Christ. God forgave us all our sins; 14 he
canceled the unfavorable record of our
debts with its binding rules and did
away with it completely by nailing it to
the cross. 15 And on that cross Christ
freed himself from the power of the spiritual rulers and authorities;[e] he made a
public spectacle of them by leading them
as captives in his victory procession.

16 So let no one make rules about what
you eat or drink or about holy days or
the New Moon Festival or the Sabbath.
17 All such things are only a shadow of
things in the future; the reality is Christ.
18 Do not allow yourselves to be condemned by anyone who claims to be superior because of special visions and
who insists on false humility and the
worship of angels. For no reason at all,
such people are all puffed up by their
human way of thinking 19 and have
stopped holding on to Christ, who is the
head of the body. Under Christ's control
the whole body is nourished and held together by its joints and ligaments, and it
grows as God wants it to grow.

Dying and Living with Christ

20 You have died with Christ and are
set free from the ruling spirits of the universe. Why, then, do you live as though
you belonged to this world? Why do you
obey such rules as 21 "Don't handle this,"
"Don't taste that," "Don't touch the
other"? 22 All these refer to things which
become useless once they are used; they
are only human rules and teachings.
23 Of course such rules appear to be
based on wisdom in their forced worship
of angels, and false humility, and severe
treatment of the body; but they have no
real value in controlling physical
passions.

3 You have been raised to life with
Christ, so set your hearts on the
things that are in heaven, where Christ
sits on his throne at the right side of
God. 2 Keep your minds fixed on things
there, not on things here on earth. 3 For
you have died, and your life is hidden
with Christ in God. 4 Your real life is
Christ and when he appears, then you
too will appear with him and share his
glory!

The Old Life and the New

5 You must put to death, then, the
earthly desires at work in you, such as
sexual immorality, indecency, lust, evil
passions, and greed (for greed is a form
of idolatry). 6 Because of such things
God's anger will come upon those who
do not obey him.[f] 7 At one time you
yourselves used to live according to such
desires, when your life was dominated
by them.

8 But now you must get rid of all these
things: anger, passion, and hateful feelings. No insults or obscene talk must
ever come from your lips. 9 Do not lie to
one another, for you have put off the old
self with its habits 10 and have put on the
new self. This is the new being which
God, its Creator, is constantly renewing

[e] **Christ freed himself from the power of the spiritual rulers and authorities;** *or* **Christ stripped the spiritual rulers and authorities of their power.** [f] *Some manuscripts do not have* **upon those who do not obey him.**

in his own image, in order to bring you
to a full knowledge of himself. 11 As a
result, there is no longer any distinction
between Gentiles and Jews, circumcised
and uncircumcised, barbarians, savages, slaves, and free, but Christ is all,
Christ is in all.

12 You are the people of God; he loved
you and chose you for his own. So then,
you must clothe yourselves with compassion, kindness, humility, gentleness,
and patience. 13 Be tolerant with one another and forgive one another whenever
any of you has a complaint against
someone else. You must forgive one another just as the Lord has forgiven you.
14 And to all these qualities add love,
which binds all things together in perfect unity. 15 The peace that Christ gives
is to guide you in the decisions you
make; for it is to this peace that God has
called you together in the one body. And
be thankful. 16 Christ's message in all its
richness must live in your hearts. Teach
and instruct one another with all wisdom. Sing psalms, hymns, and sacred
songs; sing to God with thanksgiving in
your hearts. 17 Everything you do or say,
then, should be done in the name of the
Lord Jesus, as you give thanks through
him to God the Father.

Personal Relations in the New Life

18 Wives, submit yourselves to your
husbands, for that is what you should do
as Christians.

19 Husbands, love your wives and do
not be harsh with them.

20 Children, it is your Christian duty to
obey your parents always, for that is
what pleases God.

21 Parents, do not irritate your children, or they will become discouraged.
22 Slaves, obey your human masters in
all things, not only when they are watching you because you want to gain their
approval; but do it with a sincere heart
because of your reverence for the Lord.
23 Whatever you do, work at it with all
your heart, as though you were working
for the Lord and not for people. 24 Remember that the Lord will give you as a
reward what he has kept for his people.
For Christ is the real Master you serve.
25 And all wrongdoers will be repaid for
the wrong things they do, because God
judges everyone by the same standard.

4 Masters, be fair and just in the way
you treat your slaves. Remember
that you too have a Master in heaven.

Instructions

2 Be persistent in prayer, and keep
alert as you pray, giving thanks to God.
3 At the same time pray also for us, so
that God will give us a good opportunity
to preach his message about the secret
of Christ. For that is why I am now in
prison. 4 Pray, then, that I may speak, as
I should, in such a way as to make it
clear.

5 Be wise in the way you act toward
those who are not believers, making
good use of every opportunity you have.
6 Your speech should always be pleasant
and interesting, and you should know
how to give the right answer to everyone.

Final Greetings

7 Our dear friend Tychicus, who is a
faithful worker and fellow servant in the
Lord's work, will give you all the news
about me. 8 That is why I am sending
him to you, in order to cheer you up by
telling you how all of us are getting
along. 9 With him goes Onesimus, that
dear and faithful friend, who belongs to
your group. They will tell you everything that is happening here.

10 Aristarchus, who is in prison with
me, sends you greetings, and so does
Mark, the cousin of Barnabas. (You
have already received instructions to
welcome Mark if he comes your way.)
11 Joshua, also called Justus, sends
greetings too. These three are the only
Jewish believers who work with me for
the Kingdom of God, and they have been
a great help to me.

12 Greetings from Epaphras, another
member of your group and a servant of
Christ Jesus. He always prays fervently
for you, asking God to make you stand
firm, as mature and fully convinced
Christians, in complete obedience to
God's will. 13 I can personally testify to
his hard work for you and for the people
in Laodicea and Hierapolis. 14 Luke, our
dear doctor, and Demas send you their
greetings.

15 Give our best wishes to the believers
in Laodicea and to Nympha and the

church that meets in her house.[g] 16After
you read this letter, make sure that it is
read also in the church at Laodicea. At
the same time, you are to read the letter
that the believers in Laodicea will send
you. 17And tell Archippus, "Be sure to
finish the task you were given in the
Lord's service."
18With my own hand I write this:
Greetings from Paul. Do not forget my
chains!

May God's grace be with you.

[g] Nympha . . . her house; *some manuscripts have* Nymphas . . . his house.

Paul's First Letter to the THESSALONIANS

Introduction

Thessalonica was the capital city of the Roman province of Macedonia. Paul established a church there after he left Philippi. Soon, however, there was opposition from Jews who were jealous of Paul's success in preaching the Christian message among the non-Jews who had become interested in Judaism. Paul was forced to leave Thessalonica and go on to Berea. Later on, after he reached Corinth, Paul received a personal report from his companion and fellow worker Timothy about the situation in the church at Thessalonica.

Paul's First Letter to the Thessalonians *was then written to encourage and reassure the Christians there. He gives thanks for the news about their faith and love; he reminds them of the kind of life he had lived while he was with them, and then answers questions that had arisen in the church about the return of Christ: Could a believer who died before Christ's return still share in the eternal life that his return will bring? And when will Christ come again? Paul takes this occasion to tell them to go on working quietly while waiting in hope for Christ's return.*

Outline of Contents

Introduction 1.1
Gratitude and praise 1.2–3.13
Exhortation to Christian conduct 4.1-12
Instructions about the coming of Christ 4.13–5.11
Final exhortations 5.12-22
Conclusion 5.23-28

---

1 From Paul, Silas, and Timothy—
To the people of the church in
Thessalonica, who belong to God the
Father and the Lord Jesus Christ:

May grace and peace be yours.

The Life and Faith of the Thessalonians

2We always thank God for you all and
always mention you in our prayers. 3For
we remember before our God and Father
how you put your faith into practice,
how your love made you work so hard,
and how your hope in our Lord Jesus
Christ is firm. 4Our friends, we know
that God loves you and has chosen you
to be his own. 5For we brought the Good
News to you, not with words only, but
also with power and the Holy Spirit, and
with complete conviction of its truth.
You know how we lived when we were
with you; it was for your own good.
6You imitated us and the Lord; and even
though you suffered much, you received
the message with the joy that comes
from the Holy Spirit. 7So you became an
example to all believers in Macedonia
and Achaia. 8For not only did the message about the Lord go out from you
throughout Macedonia and Achaia, but
the news about your faith in God has
gone everywhere. There is nothing,
then, that we need to say. 9All those people speak about how you received us

when we visited you, and how you
turned away from idols to God, to serve
the true and living God 10 and to wait for
his Son to come from heaven—his Son
Jesus, whom he raised from death and
who rescues us from God's anger that is
coming.

Paul's Work in Thessalonica

2 Our friends, you yourselves know
that our visit to you was not a failure. 2 You know how we had already
been mistreated and insulted in Philippi
before we came to you in Thessalonica.
And even though there was much opposition, our God gave us courage to tell
you the Good News that comes from
him. 3 Our appeal to you is not based on
error or impure motives, nor do we try to
trick anyone. 4 Instead, we always speak
as God wants us to, because he has
judged us worthy to be entrusted with
the Good News. We do not try to please
people, but to please God, who tests our
motives. 5 You know very well that we
did not come to you with flattering talk,
nor did we use words to cover up
greed—God is our witness! 6 We did not
try to get praise from anyone, either
from you or from others, 7 even though
as apostles of Christ we could have
made demands on you. But we were
gentle when we were with you, like a
mother[a] taking care of her children.
8 Because of our love for you we were
ready to share with you not only the
Good News from God but even our own
lives. You were so dear to us! 9 Surely
you remember, our friends, how we
worked and toiled! We worked day and
night so that we would not be any trouble to you as we preached to you the
Good News from God.

10 You are our witnesses, and so is
God, that our conduct toward you who
believe was pure, right, and without
fault. 11 You know that we treated each
one of you just as parents treat their own
children. 12 We encouraged you, we
comforted you, and we kept urging you
to live the kind of life that pleases God,
who calls you to share in his own Kingdom and glory.

13 And there is another reason why we
always give thanks to God. When we
brought you God's message, you heard it
and accepted it, not as a message from
human beings but as God's message,
which indeed it is. For God is at work in
you who believe. 14 Our friends, the same
things happened to you that happened to
the churches of God in Judea, to the people there who belong to Christ Jesus.
You suffered the same persecutions
from your own people that they suffered
from the Jews, 15 who killed the Lord
Jesus and the prophets, and persecuted
us. How displeasing they are to God!
How hostile they are to everyone!
16 They even tried to stop us from
preaching to the Gentiles the message
that would bring them salvation. In this
way they have brought to completion all
the sins they have always committed.
And now God's anger has at last come
down on them!

Paul's Desire to Visit Them Again

17 As for us, friends, when we were
separated from you for a little while—
not in our thoughts, of course, but only
in body—how we missed you and how
hard we tried to see you again! 18 We
wanted to return to you. I myself tried to
go back more than once, but Satan
would not let us. 19 After all, it is you—
you, no less than others!—who are our
hope, our joy, and our reason for boasting of our victory in the presence of our
Lord Jesus when he comes. 20 Indeed,
you are our pride and our joy!

3 Finally, we could not bear it any
longer. So we decided to stay on
alone in Athens 2 while we sent Timothy,
our brother who works with us for God
in preaching the Good News about
Christ. We sent him to strengthen you
and help your faith, 3 so that none of you
should turn back because of these persecutions. You yourselves know that such
persecutions are part of God's will for
us. 4 For while we were still with you, we
told you ahead of time that we were going to be persecuted; and as you well
know, that is exactly what happened.
5 That is why I had to send Timothy. I
could not bear it any longer, so I sent
him to find out about your faith. Surely
it could not be that the Devil had

[a] we were gentle when we were with you, like a mother; *some manuscripts have* we were like children when we were with you; we were like a mother.

tempted you and all our work had been
for nothing!
6 Now Timothy has come back, and he
has brought us the welcome news about
your faith and love. He has told us that
you always think well of us and that you
want to see us just as much as we want
to see you. 7 So, in all our trouble and
suffering we have been encouraged
about you, friends. It was your faith that
encouraged us, 8 because now we really
live if you stand firm in your life in union
with the Lord. 9 Now we can give thanks
to our God for you. We thank him for the
joy we have in his presence because of
you. 10 Day and night we ask him with all
our heart to let us see you personally
and supply what is needed in your faith.
11 May our God and Father himself and
our Lord Jesus prepare the way for us to
come to you! 12 May the Lord make your
love for one another and for all people
grow more and more and become as
great as our love for you. 13 In this way
he will strengthen you, and you will be
perfect and holy in the presence of our
God and Father when our Lord Jesus
comes with all who belong to him.[b]

A Life That Pleases God

4 Finally, our friends, you learned
from us how you should live in order to please God. This is, of course, the
way you have been living. And now we
beg and urge you in the name of the
Lord Jesus to do even more. 2 For you
know the instructions we gave you by
the authority of the Lord Jesus. 3 God
wants you to be holy and completely
free from sexual immorality. 4 Each of
you should know how to live with your
wife[c] in a holy and honorable way, 5 not
with a lustful desire, like the heathen
who do not know God. 6 In this matter,
then, none of you should do wrong to
other Christians or take advantage of
them. We have told you this before, and
we strongly warned you that the Lord
will punish those who do that. 7 God did
not call us to live in immorality, but in
holiness. 8 So then, whoever rejects this
teaching is not rejecting a human being,
but God, who gives you his Holy Spirit.
9 There is no need to write you about
love for each other. You yourselves have
been taught by God how you should love
one another. 10 And you have, in fact, behaved like this toward all the believers
in all of Macedonia. So we beg you, our
friends, to do even more. 11 Make it your
aim to live a quiet life, to mind your own
business, and to earn your own living,
just as we told you before. 12 In this way
you will win the respect of those who are
not believers, and you will not have to
depend on anyone for what you need.

The Lord's Coming

13 Our friends, we want you to know
the truth about those who have died, so
that you will not be sad, as are those
who have no hope. 14 We believe that
Jesus died and rose again, and so we believe that God will take back with Jesus
those who have died believing in him.
15 What we are teaching you now is
the Lord's teaching: we who are alive on
the day the Lord comes will not go
ahead of those who have died. 16 There
will be the shout of command, the archangel's voice, the sound of God's trumpet, and the Lord himself will come
down from heaven. Those who have
died believing in Christ will rise to life
first; 17 then we who are living at that
time will be gathered up along with
them in the clouds to meet the Lord in
the air. And so we will always be with
the Lord. 18 So then, encourage one another with these words.

Be Ready for the Lord's Coming

5 There is no need to write you,
friends, about the times and occasions when these things will happen.
2 For you yourselves know very well that
the Day of the Lord will come as a thief
comes at night. 3 When people say,
"Everything is quiet and safe," then suddenly destruction will hit them! It will
come as suddenly as the pains that come
upon a woman in labor, and people will
not escape. 4 But you, friends, are not in
the darkness, and the Day should not
take you by surprise like a thief. 5 All of
you are people who belong to the light,
who belong to the day. We do not belong
to the night or to the darkness. 6 So then,
we should not be sleeping like the others; we should be awake and sober. 7 It is
at night when people sleep; it is at night
when they get drunk. 8 But we belong to

[b] all who belong to him; *or* all his angels. [c] live with your wife; *or* control your body.

the day, and we should be sober. We
must wear faith and love as a breastplate, and our hope of salvation as a helmet. 9 God did not choose us to suffer his
anger, but to possess salvation through
our Lord Jesus Christ, 10 who died for us
in order that we might live together with
him, whether we are alive or dead when
he comes. 11 And so encourage one another and help one another, just as you
are now doing.

Final Instructions and Greetings

12 We beg you, our friends, to pay
proper respect to those who work
among you, who guide and instruct you
in the Christian life. 13 Treat them with
the greatest respect and love because of
the work they do. Be at peace among
yourselves.

14 We urge you, our friends, to warn
the idle, encourage the timid, help the
weak, be patient with everyone. 15 See
that no one pays back wrong for wrong,
but at all times make it your aim to do
good to one another and to all people.

16 Be joyful always, 17 pray at all times,
18 be thankful in all circumstances. This
is what God wants from you in your life
in union with Christ Jesus.

19 Do not restrain the Holy Spirit; 20 do
not despise inspired messages. 21 Put all
things to the test: keep what is good
22 and avoid every kind of evil.

23 May the God who gives us peace
make you holy in every way and keep
your whole being—spirit, soul, and
body—free from every fault at the coming of our Lord Jesus Christ. 24 He who
calls you will do it, because he is faithful.

25 Pray also for us, friends.

26 Greet all the believers with the kiss
of peace.

27 I urge you by the authority of the
Lord to read this letter to all the believers.

28 The grace of our Lord Jesus Christ
be with you.

Paul's Second Letter to the

THESSALONIANS

Introduction

Confusion over the expected return of Christ continued to cause disturbances in the church at Thessalonica. Paul's Second Letter to the Thessalonians *deals with the belief that the day of the Lord's coming had already arrived. Paul corrects this idea, pointing out that before Christ returns, evil and wickedness will reach a climax under the leadership of a mysterious figure called "the Wicked One," who would be opposed to Christ.*

The apostle emphasizes the need for his readers to remain steady in their faith in spite of trouble and suffering, to work for a living as did Paul and his fellow workers, and to persevere in doing good.

Outline of Contents

Introduction 1.1-2
Praise and commendation 1.3-12
Instructions about the coming of Christ 2.1-17
Exhortation to Christian conduct 3.1-15
Conclusion 3.16-18

---

1 From Paul, Silas, and Timothy—
To the people of the church in
Thessalonica, who belong to God our
Father and the Lord Jesus Christ:

2 May God our Father and the Lord
Jesus Christ give you grace and peace.

The Judgment at Christ's Coming

3 Our friends, we must thank God at all
times for you. It is right for us to do so,
because your faith is growing so much
and the love each of you has for the others is becoming greater. 4 That is why
we ourselves boast about you in the
churches of God. We boast about the
way you continue to endure and believe
through all the persecutions and sufferings you are experiencing.
5 All of this proves that God's judgment is just and as a result you will become worthy of his Kingdom, for which
you are suffering. 6 God will do what is
right: he will bring suffering on those
who make you suffer, 7 and he will give
relief to you who suffer and to us as well.
He will do this when the Lord Jesus appears from heaven with his mighty angels, 8 with a flaming fire, to punish
those who reject God and who do not
obey the Good News about our Lord
Jesus. 9 They will suffer the punishment
of eternal destruction, separated from
the presence of the Lord and from his
glorious might, 10 when he comes on that
Day to receive glory from all his people
and honor from all who believe. You too
will be among them, because you have
believed the message that we told you.
11 That is why we always pray for
you. We ask our God to make you worthy
of the life he has called you to live. May
he fulfill by his power all your desire
for goodness and complete your work
of faith. 12 In this way the name of our
Lord Jesus will receive glory from you,
and you from him, by the grace of our
God and of the Lord[a] Jesus Christ.

The Wicked One

2 Concerning the coming of our Lord
Jesus Christ and our being gathered
together to be with him: I beg you, my
friends, 2 not to be so easily confused in
your thinking or upset by the claim that
the Day of the Lord has come. Perhaps it
is thought that we said this while prophesying or preaching, or that we wrote it
in a letter. 3 Do not let anyone deceive
you in any way. For the Day will not
come until the final Rebellion takes
place and the Wicked One appears, who
is destined to hell. 4 He will oppose every
so-called god or object of worship and
will put himself above them all. He will
even go in and sit down in God's Temple
and claim to be God.
5 Don't you remember? I told you all
this while I was with you. 6 Yet there is
something that keeps this from happening now, and you know what it is. At the
proper time, then, the Wicked One will
appear. 7 The Mysterious Wickedness is
already at work, but what is going to
happen will not happen until the one
who holds it back is taken out of the
way. 8 Then the Wicked One will be revealed, but when the Lord Jesus comes,
he will kill him with the breath from his
mouth and destroy him with his dazzling presence. 9 The Wicked One will
come with the power of Satan and perform all kinds of false miracles and wonders, 10 and use every kind of wicked
deceit on those who will perish. They
will perish because they did not welcome and love the truth so as to be
saved. 11 And so God sends the power of
error to work in them so that they believe what is false. 12 The result is that all
who have not believed the truth, but
have taken pleasure in sin, will be
condemned.

You Are Chosen for Salvation

13 We must thank God at all times for
you, friends, you whom the Lord loves.
For God chose you as the first[b] to be
saved by the Spirit's power to make you
his holy people and by your faith in the
truth. 14 God called you to this through
the Good News we preached to you; he
called you to possess your share of the
glory of our Lord Jesus Christ. 15 So
then, our friends, stand firm and hold on
to those truths which we taught you,
both in our preaching and in our letter.
16 May our Lord Jesus Christ himself
and God our Father, who loved us and in
his grace gave us unfailing courage and
a firm hope, 17 encourage you and
strengthen you to always do and say
what is good.

Pray for Us

3 Finally, our friends, pray for us that
the Lord's message may continue to
spread rapidly and be received with
honor, just as it was among you. 2 Pray

[a] our God and of the Lord; *or* our God and Lord.

[b] as the first; *some manuscripts have* from the beginning.

also that God will rescue us from wicked
and evil people; for not everyone believes the message.
3 But the Lord is faithful, and he will
strengthen you and keep you safe from
the Evil One. 4 And the Lord gives us
confidence in you, and we are sure that
you are doing and will continue to do
what we tell you.
5 May the Lord lead you into a greater
understanding of God's love and the endurance that is given by Christ.

The Obligation to Work

6 Our friends, we command you in the
name of our Lord Jesus Christ to keep
away from all believers who are living a
lazy life and who do not follow the instructions that we gave them. 7 You
yourselves know very well that you
should do just what we did. We were not
lazy when we were with you. 8 We did
not accept anyone's support without
paying for it. Instead, we worked and
toiled; we kept working day and night so
as not to be an expense to any of you.
9 We did this, not because we do not
have the right to demand our support;
we did it to be an example for you to
follow. 10 While we were with you, we
used to tell you, "Whoever refuses to
work is not allowed to eat."
11 We say this because we hear that
there are some people among you who
live lazy lives and who do nothing except meddle in other people's business.
12 In the name of the Lord Jesus Christ
we command these people and warn
them to lead orderly lives and work to
earn their own living.
13 But you, friends, must not become
tired of doing good. 14 It may be that
some there will not obey the message we
send you in this letter. If so, take note of
them and have nothing to do with them,
so that they will be ashamed. 15 But do
not treat them as enemies; instead, warn
them as believers.

Final Words

16 May the Lord himself, who is our
source of peace, give you peace at all
times and in every way. The Lord be
with you all.
17 With my own hand I write this:
Greetings from Paul. This is the way I
sign every letter; this is how I write.
18 May the grace of our Lord Jesus
Christ be with you all.

Paul's First Letter to
TIMOTHY

Introduction

Timothy, a young Christian from Asia Minor, was the son of a Jewish mother and a Greek father. He became a companion and assistant to Paul in his missionary work. Paul's First Letter to Timothy *deals with three main concerns.*

The letter is first of all a warning against false teaching in the church. This teaching, a mixture of Jewish and non-Jewish ideas, was based on the belief that the physical world is evil and that one can attain salvation only by special secret knowledge and by practices such as avoiding certain foods and not marrying. The letter also contains instructions about church administration and worship, with a description of the kind of character that church leaders and helpers should have. Finally, Timothy is advised how to be a good servant of Jesus Christ and about the responsibilities that he has toward various groups of believers.

Outline of Contents

Introduction 1.1-2
Instructions concerning the church and its officers 1.3–3.16
Instructions to Timothy about his work 4.1–6.21

1 From Paul, an apostle of Christ
Jesus by order of God our Savior
and Christ Jesus our hope—
2 To Timothy, my true son in the faith:
May God the Father and Christ Jesus
our Lord give you grace, mercy, and
peace.

Warnings against False Teaching

3 I want you to stay in Ephesus, just as
I urged you when I was on my way to
Macedonia. Some people there are
teaching false doctrines, and you must
order them to stop. 4 Tell them to give up
those legends and those long lists of ancestors, which only produce arguments;
they do not serve God's plan, which is
known by faith. 5 The purpose of this order is to arouse the love that comes from
a pure heart, a clear conscience, and a
genuine faith. 6 Some people have
turned away from these and have lost
their way in foolish discussions. 7 They
want to be teachers of God's law, but
they do not understand their own words
or the matters about which they speak
with so much confidence.
8 We know that the Law is good if it is
used as it should be used. 9 It must be
remembered, of course, that laws are
made, not for good people, but for lawbreakers and criminals, for the godless
and sinful, for those who are not religious or spiritual, for those who kill their
fathers or mothers, for murderers, 10 for
the immoral, for sexual perverts, for kid-
nappers, for those who lie and give false
testimony or who do anything else contrary to sound doctrine. 11 That teaching
is found in the gospel that was entrusted
to me to announce, the Good News from
the glorious and blessed God.

Gratitude for God's Mercy

12 I give thanks to Christ Jesus our
Lord, who has given me strength for my
work. I thank him for considering me
worthy and appointing me to serve him,
13 even though in the past I spoke evil of
him and persecuted and insulted him.
But God was merciful to me because I
did not yet have faith and so did not
know what I was doing. 14 And our Lord
poured out his abundant grace on me
and gave me the faith and love which
are ours in union with Christ Jesus.
15 This is a true saying, to be completely
accepted and believed: Christ Jesus
came into the world to save sinners. I am
the worst of them, 16 but God was merciful to me in order that Christ Jesus might
show his full patience in dealing with
me, the worst of sinners, as an example
for all those who would later believe in
him and receive eternal life. 17 To the
eternal King, immortal and invisible, the
only God—to him be honor and glory
forever and ever! Amen.
18 Timothy, my child, I entrust to you
this command, which is in accordance
with the words of prophecy spoken in
the past about you. Use those words as
weapons in order to fight well, 19 and
keep your faith and a clear conscience.
Some people have not listened to their
conscience and have made a ruin of
their faith. 20 Among them are Hymenaeus and Alexander, whom I have punished by handing them over to the power
of Satan; this will teach them to stop
their blasphemy.

Church Worship

2 First of all, then, I urge that petitions, prayers, requests, and
thanksgivings be offered to God for all
people; 2 for kings and all others who are
in authority, that we may live a quiet and
peaceful life with all reverence toward
God and with proper conduct. 3 This is
good and it pleases God our Savior,
4 who wants everyone to be saved and to
come to know the truth. 5 For there is one
God, and there is one who brings God
and human beings together, the man
Christ Jesus, 6 who gave himself to redeem the whole human race. That was
the proof at the right time that God
wants everyone to be saved, 7 and that is
why I was sent as an apostle and teacher
of the Gentiles, to proclaim the message
of faith and truth. I am not lying; I am
telling the truth!
8 In every church service I want the
men to pray, men who are dedicated to
God and can lift up their hands in prayer
without anger or argument. 9 I also want
the women to be modest and sensible
about their clothes and to dress properly; not with fancy hair styles or with
gold ornaments or pearls or expensive
dresses, 10 but with good deeds, as is
proper for women who claim to be religious. 11 Women should learn in silence
and all humility. 12 I do not allow them to

teach or to have authority over men;
they must keep quiet. 13 For Adam was
created first, and then Eve. 14 And it was
not Adam who was deceived; it was the
woman who was deceived and broke
God's law. 15 But a woman will be saved
through having children,[a] if she perseveres[b] in faith and love and holiness,
with modesty.

Leaders in the Church

3 This is a true saying: If a man is eager to be a church leader, he desires
an excellent work. 2 A church leader
must be without fault; he must have only
one wife,[c] be sober, self-controlled, and
orderly; he must welcome strangers in
his home; he must be able to teach; 3 he
must not be a drunkard or a violent man,
but gentle and peaceful; he must not
love money; 4 he must be able to manage
his own family well and make his children obey him with all respect. 5 For if a
man does not know how to manage his
own family, how can he take care of the
church of God? 6 He must be mature in
the faith, so that he will not swell up
with pride and be condemned, as the
Devil was. 7 He should be a man who is
respected by the people outside the
church, so that he will not be disgraced
and fall into the Devil's trap.

Helpers in the Church

8 Church helpers must also have a
good character and be sincere; they
must not drink too much wine or be
greedy for money; 9 they should hold to
the revealed truth of the faith with a
clear conscience. 10 They should be
tested first, and then, if they pass the
test, they are to serve. 11 Their wives[d]
also must be of good character and must
not gossip; they must be sober and honest in everything. 12 A church helper
must have only one wife,[e] and be able
to manage his children and family well.
13 Those helpers who do their work well
win for themselves a good standing and
are able to speak boldly about their faith
in Christ Jesus.

The Great Secret

14 As I write this letter to you, I hope to
come and see you soon. 15 But if I delay,
this letter will let you know how we
should conduct ourselves in God's
household, which is the church of the
living God, the pillar and support of the
truth. 16 No one can deny how great is
the secret of our religion:

He appeared in human form,
was shown to be right by the Spirit,[f]
and was seen by angels.
He was preached among the nations,
was believed in throughout the world,
and was taken up to heaven.

False Teachers

4 The Spirit says clearly that some
people will abandon the faith in
later times; they will obey lying spirits
and follow the teachings of demons.
2 Such teachings are spread by deceitful
liars, whose consciences are dead, as if
burnt with a hot iron. 3 Such people
teach that it is wrong to marry and to eat
certain foods. But God created those
foods to be eaten, after a prayer of
thanks, by those who are believers and
have come to know the truth. 4 Everything that God has created is good; nothing is to be rejected, but everything is to
be received with a prayer of thanks, 5 because the word of God and the prayer
make it acceptable to God.

A Good Servant of Christ Jesus

6 If you give these instructions to the
believers, you will be a good servant of
Christ Jesus, as you feed yourself spiritually on the words of faith and of the
true teaching which you have followed.
7 But keep away from those godless legends, which are not worth telling. Keep
yourself in training for a godly life.
8 Physical exercise has some value, but
spiritual exercise is valuable in every
way, because it promises life both for
the present and for the future. 9 This is a
true saying, to be completely accepted

[a] will be saved through having children; *or* will be kept safe through childbirth.
[b] if she perseveres; *or* if they persevere. [c] have only one wife; *or* be married only once.
[d] Their wives; *or* Women helpers. [e] have only one wife; *or* be married only once.
[f] was shown to be right by the Spirit; *or* and, in spiritual form, was shown to be right.

and believed. 10 We struggle[g] and work hard, because we have placed our hope in the living God, who is the Savior of all and especially of those who believe.

11 Give them these instructions and these teachings. 12 Do not let anyone look down on you because you are young, but be an example for the believers in your speech, your conduct, your love, faith, and purity. 13 Until I come, give your time and effort to the public reading of the Scriptures and to preaching and teaching. 14 Do not neglect the spiritual gift that is in you, which was given to you when the prophets spoke and the elders laid their hands on you. 15 Practice these things and devote yourself to them, in order that your progress may be seen by all. 16 Watch yourself and watch your teaching. Keep on doing these things, because if you do, you will save both yourself and those who hear you.

Responsibilities toward Believers

5 Do not rebuke an older man, but appeal to him as if he were your father. Treat the younger men as your brothers, 2 the older women as mothers, and the younger women as sisters, with all purity.

3 Show respect for widows who really are all alone. 4 But if a widow has children or grandchildren, they should learn first to carry out their religious duties toward their own family and in this way repay their parents and grandparents, because that is what pleases God. 5 A widow who is all alone, with no one to take care of her, has placed her hope in God and continues to pray and ask him for his help night and day. 6 But a widow who gives herself to pleasure has already died, even though she lives. 7 Give them these instructions, so that no one will find fault with them. 8 But if any do not take care of their relatives, especially the members of their own family, they have denied the faith and are worse than an unbeliever.

9 Do not add any widow to the list of widows unless she is over sixty years of age. In addition, she must have been married only once[h] 10 and have a reputation for good deeds: a woman who brought up her children well, received strangers in her home, performed humble duties for other Christians, helped people in trouble, and devoted herself to doing good.

11 But do not include younger widows in the list; because when their desires make them want to marry, they turn away from Christ, 12 and so become guilty of breaking their earlier promise to him. 13 They also learn to waste their time in going around from house to house; but even worse, they learn to be gossips and busybodies, talking of things they should not. 14 So I would prefer that the younger widows get married, have children, and take care of their homes, so as to give our enemies no chance of speaking evil of us. 15 For some widows have already turned away to follow Satan. 16 But if any Christian woman has widows in her family, she must take care of them and not put the burden on the church, so that it may take care of the widows who are all alone.

17 The elders who do good work as leaders should be considered worthy of receiving double pay, especially those who work hard at preaching and teaching. 18 For the scripture says, "Do not muzzle an ox when you are using it to thresh grain" and "Workers should be given their pay." 19 Do not listen to an accusation against an elder unless it is brought by two or more witnesses. 20 Rebuke publicly all those who commit sins, so that the rest may be afraid.

21 In the presence of God and of Christ Jesus and of the holy angels I solemnly call upon you to obey these instructions without showing any prejudice or favor to anyone in anything you do. 22 Be in no hurry to lay hands on people to dedicate them to the Lord's service. Take no part in the sins of others; keep yourself pure.

23 Do not drink water only, but take a little wine to help your digestion, since you are sick so often.

24 The sins of some people are plain to see, and their sins go ahead of them to judgment; but the sins of others are seen only later. 25 In the same way good deeds are plainly seen, and even those that are not so plain cannot be hidden.

[g] struggle; *some manuscripts have* are reviled.

[h] married only once; *or* faithful to her husband.

6 Those who are slaves must consider
their masters worthy of all respect,
so that no one will speak evil of the
name of God and of our teaching.
2 Slaves belonging to Christian masters
must not despise them, for they are believers too. Instead, they are to serve
them even better, because those who
benefit from their work are believers
whom they love.

False Teaching and True Riches

You must teach and preach these
things. 3 Whoever teaches a different
doctrine and does not agree with the
true words of our Lord Jesus Christ and
with the teaching of our religion 4 is
swollen with pride and knows nothing.
He has an unhealthy desire to argue and
quarrel about words, and this brings on
jealousy, disputes, insults, evil suspicions, 5 and constant arguments from
people whose minds do not function and
who no longer have the truth. They
think that religion is a way to become
rich.

6 Well, religion does make us very
rich, if we are satisfied with what we
have. 7 What did we bring into the
world? Nothing! What can we take out
of the world? Nothing! 8 So then, if we
have food and clothes, that should be
enough for us. 9 But those who want to
get rich fall into temptation and are
caught in the trap of many foolish and
harmful desires, which pull them down
to ruin and destruction. 10 For the love of
money is a source of all kinds of evil.
Some have been so eager to have it that
they have wandered away from the faith
and have broken their hearts with many
sorrows.

Personal Instructions

11 But you, man of God, avoid all these
things. Strive for righteousness, godliness, faith, love, endurance, and gentleness. 12 Run your best in the race of faith,
and win eternal life for yourself; for it
was to this life that God called you when
you firmly professed your faith before
many witnesses. 13 Before God, who
gives life to all things, and before Christ
Jesus, who firmly professed his faith before Pontius Pilate, I command you 14 to
obey your orders and keep them faithfully until the Day when our Lord Jesus
Christ will appear. 15 His appearing will
be brought about at the right time by
God, the blessed and only Ruler, the
King of kings and the Lord of lords. 16 He
alone is immortal; he lives in the light
that no one can approach. No one has
ever seen him; no one can ever see him.
To him be honor and eternal power!
Amen.

17 Command those who are rich in the
things of this life not to be proud, but to
place their hope, not in such an uncertain thing as riches, but in God, who
generously gives us everything for our
enjoyment. 18 Command them to do
good, to be rich in good works, to be
generous and ready to share with others.
19 In this way they will store up for themselves a treasure which will be a solid
foundation for the future. And then they
will be able to win the life which is true
life.

20 Timothy, keep safe what has been
entrusted to your care. Avoid the profane talk and foolish arguments of what
some people wrongly call "Knowledge."
21 For some have claimed to possess it,
and as a result they have lost the way of
faith.

God's grace be with you all.

Paul's Second Letter to
TIMOTHY

Introduction

Paul's Second Letter to Timothy *consists largely of personal advice to Timothy, as a younger colleague and assistant. The main theme is endurance. Timothy is advised and encouraged to keep on witnessing faithfully to Jesus Christ, to hold to the true teaching of the Good News and the Old Testament, and to do his duty as teacher and evangelist, all in the face of suffering and opposition.*

Timothy is especially warned about the dangers of becoming involved in "foolish and ignorant arguments" that do no good, but only ruin the people who listen to them.

In all this, Timothy is reminded of the example of the writer's own life and purpose—his faith, patience, love, endurance, and suffering in persecution.

Outline of Contents

---

1 From Paul, an apostle of Christ
Jesus by God's will, sent to proclaim the promised life which we have in
union with Christ Jesus—
2 To Timothy, my dear son:
May God the Father and Christ Jesus
our Lord give you grace, mercy, and
peace.

Thanksgiving and Encouragement

3 I give thanks to God, whom I serve
with a clear conscience, as my ancestors
did. I thank him as I remember you always in my prayers night and day.
4 I remember your tears, and I want to
see you very much, so that I may be
filled with joy. 5 I remember the sincere
faith you have, the kind of faith that
your grandmother Lois and your mother
Eunice also had. I am sure that you have
it also. 6 For this reason I remind you to
keep alive the gift that God gave you
when I laid my hands on you. 7 For the
Spirit that God has given us does not
make us timid; instead, his Spirit fills us
with power, love, and self-control.
8 Do not be ashamed, then, of witnessing for our Lord; neither be ashamed of
me, a prisoner for Christ's sake. Instead,
take your part in suffering for the Good
News, as God gives you the strength for
it. 9 He saved us and called us to be his
own people, not because of what we
have done, but because of his own purpose and grace. He gave us this grace by
means of Christ Jesus before the beginning of time, 10 but now it has been revealed to us through the coming of our
Savior, Christ Jesus. He has ended the
power of death and through the gospel
has revealed immortal life.
11 God has appointed me as an apostle
and teacher to proclaim the Good News,
12 and it is for this reason that I suffer
these things. But I am still full of confidence, because I know whom I have
trusted, and I am sure that he is able to
keep safe until that Day what he has entrusted to me.[a] 13 Hold firmly to the true
words that I taught you, as the example
for you to follow, and remain in the faith
and love that are ours in union with
Christ Jesus. 14 Through the power of the
Holy Spirit, who lives in us, keep the
good things that have been entrusted
to you.
15 You know that everyone in the province of Asia, including Phygelus and
Hermogenes, has deserted me. 16 May
the Lord show mercy to the family of
Onesiphorus, because he cheered me up
many times. He was not ashamed that I
am in prison, 17 but as soon as he arrived
in Rome, he started looking for me until

[a] what he has entrusted to me; *or* what I have entrusted to him.

he found me. 18 May the Lord grant him
his mercy on that Day! And you know
very well how much he did for me in
Ephesus.

A Loyal Soldier of Christ Jesus

2 As for you, my son, be strong
through the grace that is ours in
union with Christ Jesus. 2 Take the
teachings that you heard me proclaim in
the presence of many witnesses, and entrust them to reliable people, who will be
able to teach others also.

3 Take your part in suffering, as a loyal
soldier of Christ Jesus. 4 A soldier on active duty wants to please his commanding officer and so does not get mixed up
in the affairs of civilian life. 5 An athlete
who runs in a race cannot win the prize
unless he obeys the rules. 6 The farmer
who has done the hard work should
have the first share of the harvest.
7 Think about what I am saying, because
the Lord will enable you to understand
it all.

8 Remember Jesus Christ, who was
raised from death, who was a descendant of David, as is taught in the Good
News I preach. 9 Because I preach the
Good News, I suffer and I am even
chained like a criminal. But the word of
God is not in chains, 10 and so I endure
everything for the sake of God's chosen
people, in order that they too may obtain
the salvation that comes through Christ
Jesus and brings eternal glory. 11 This is
a true saying:

"If we have died with him,
we shall also live with him.
12 If we continue to endure,
we shall also rule with him.
If we deny him,
he also will deny us.
13 If we are not faithful,
he remains faithful,
because he cannot be false to
himself."

An Approved Worker

14 Remind your people of this, and give
them a solemn warning in God's presence not to fight over words. It does no
good, but only ruins the people who listen. 15 Do your best to win full approval
in God's sight, as a worker who is not
ashamed of his work, one who correctly
teaches the message of God's truth.
16 Keep away from profane and foolish
discussions, which only drive people farther away from God. 17 Such teaching is
like an open sore that eats away the
flesh. Two men who have taught such
things are Hymenaeus and Philetus.
18 They have left the way of truth and are
upsetting the faith of some believers by
saying that our resurrection has already
taken place. 19 But the solid foundation
that God has laid cannot be shaken; and
on it are written these words: "The Lord
knows those who are his" and "Those
who say that they belong to the Lord
must turn away from wrongdoing."

20 In a large house there are dishes and
bowls of all kinds: some are made of silver and gold, others of wood and clay;
some are for special occasions, others
for ordinary use. 21 Those who make
themselves clean from all those evil
things, will be used for special purposes,
because they are dedicated and useful to
their Master, ready to be used for every
good deed. 22 Avoid the passions of
youth, and strive for righteousness,
faith, love, and peace, together with
those who with a pure heart call out to
the Lord for help. 23 But keep away from
foolish and ignorant arguments; you
know that they end up in quarrels. 24 As
the Lord's servant, you must not quarrel.
You must be kind toward all, a good and
patient teacher, 25 who is gentle as you
correct your opponents, for it may be
that God will give them the opportunity
to repent and come to know the truth.
26 And then they will come to their
senses and escape from the trap of the
Devil, who had caught them and made
them obey his will.

The Last Days

3 Remember that there will be difficult times in the last days. 2 People
will be selfish, greedy, boastful, and conceited; they will be insulting, disobedient to their parents, ungrateful, and
irreligious; 3 they will be unkind, merciless, slanderers, violent, and fierce; they
will hate the good; 4 they will be treacherous, reckless, and swollen with pride;
they will love pleasure rather than God;
5 they will hold to the outward form of
our religion, but reject its real power.
Keep away from such people. 6 Some of
them go into people's houses and gain
control over weak women who are burdened by the guilt of their sins and

driven by all kinds of desires, 7 women
who are always trying to learn but who
can never come to know the truth. 8 As
Jannes and Jambres were opposed to
Moses, so also these people are opposed
to the truth—people whose minds do not
function and who are failures in the
faith. 9 But they will not get very far, because everyone will see how stupid they
are. That is just what happened to Jannes and Jambres.

Last Instructions

10 But you have followed my teaching,
my conduct, and my purpose in life; you
have observed my faith, my patience,
my love, my endurance, 11 my persecutions, and my sufferings. You know all
that happened to me in Antioch, Iconium, and Lystra, the terrible persecutions I endured! But the Lord rescued me
from them all. 12 Everyone who wants to
live a godly life in union with Christ
Jesus will be persecuted; 13 and evil persons and impostors will keep on going
from bad to worse, deceiving others and
being deceived themselves. 14 But as for
you, continue in the truths that you were
taught and firmly believe. You know
who your teachers were, 15 and you remember that ever since you were a
child, you have known the Holy Scriptures, which are able to give you the wisdom that leads to salvation through faith
in Christ Jesus. 16 All Scripture is inspired by God and is useful[b] for teaching the truth, rebuking error, correcting
faults, and giving instruction for right
living, 17 so that the person who serves
God may be fully qualified and equipped
to do every kind of good deed.

4 In the presence of God and of Christ
Jesus, who will judge the living and
the dead, and because he is coming to
rule as King, I solemnly urge you 2 to
preach the message, to insist upon proclaiming it (whether the time is right or
not), to convince, reproach, and encourage, as you teach with all patience. 3 The
time will come when people will not listen to sound doctrine, but will follow
their own desires and will collect for
themselves more and more teachers
who will tell them what they are itching
to hear. 4 They will turn away from listening to the truth and give their attention to legends. 5 But you must keep
control of yourself in all circumstances;
endure suffering, do the work of a
preacher of the Good News, and perform your whole duty as a servant
of God.

6 As for me, the hour has come for me
to be sacrificed; the time is here for me
to leave this life. 7 I have done my best in
the race, I have run the full distance, and
I have kept the faith.[c] 8 And now there is
waiting for me the victory prize of being
put right with God, which the Lord, the
righteous Judge, will give me on that
Day—and not only to me, but to all
those who wait with love for him to
appear.

Personal Words

9 Do your best to come to me soon.
10 Demas fell in love with this present
world and has deserted me, going off to
Thessalonica. Crescens went to Galatia,
and Titus to Dalmatia. 11 Only Luke is
with me. Get Mark and bring him with
you, because he can help me in the
work. 12 I sent Tychicus to Ephesus.
13 When you come, bring my coat that I
left in Troas with Carpus; bring the
books too, and especially the ones made
of parchment.

14 Alexander the metalworker did me
great harm; the Lord will reward him according to what he has done. 15 Be on
your guard against him yourself, because he was violently opposed to our
message.

16 No one stood by me the first time I
defended myself; all deserted me. May
God not count it against them! 17 But the
Lord stayed with me and gave me
strength, so that I was able to proclaim
the full message for all the Gentiles to
hear; and I was rescued from being sentenced to death. 18 And the Lord will rescue me from all evil and take me safely
into his heavenly Kingdom. To him be
the glory forever and ever! Amen.

Final Greetings

19 I send greetings to Priscilla and Aquila and to the family of Onesiphorus.
20 Erastus stayed in Corinth, and I left

[b] All Scripture is inspired by God and is useful; *or* Every scripture inspired by God is also useful. [c] kept the faith; *or* been true to my promise.

Trophimus in Miletus, because he was
sick. 21 Do your best to come before
winter.
Eubulus, Pudens, Linus, and Claudia
send their greetings, and so do all the
other Christians.
22 The Lord be with your spirit.
God's grace be with you all.

Paul's Letter to
TITUS

Introduction

Titus was a Gentile convert to Christianity who became a fellow worker and assistant to Paul in his missionary work. Paul's Letter to Titus *is addressed to his young helper in Crete, who had been left there to supervise the work of the church. The letter expresses three main concerns.*

First, Titus is reminded of the kind of character that church leaders should have, especially in view of the bad character of many Cretans. Next, Titus is advised how to teach the various groups in the church, the older men, the older women (who are, in turn, to teach the younger women), the young men, and the slaves. Finally, the writer gives Titus advice regarding Christian conduct, especially the need to be peaceful and friendly, and to avoid hatred, argument, and division in the church.

Outline of Contents

---

1 From Paul, a servant of God and an
apostle of Jesus Christ.
I was chosen and sent to help the faith
of God's chosen people and to lead
them to the truth taught by our religion,
2 which is based on the hope for eternal
life. God, who does not lie, promised us
this life before the beginning of time,
3 and at the right time he revealed it in
his message. This was entrusted to me,
and I proclaim it by order of God our
Savior.
4 I write to Titus, my true son in the
faith that we have in common.
May God the Father and Christ Jesus
our Savior give you grace and peace.

Titus' Work in Crete

5 I left you in Crete, so that you could
put in order the things that still needed
doing and appoint church elders in
every town. Remember my instructions:
6 an elder must be without fault; he must
have only one wife,[a] and his children
must be believers and not have the reputation of being wild or disobedient. 7 For
since a church leader is in charge of
God's work, he should be without fault.
He must not be arrogant or quick-
tempered, or a drunkard or violent or
greedy for money. 8 He must be hospita-
ble and love what is good. He must be
self-controlled, upright, holy, and disciplined. 9 He must hold firmly to the message which can be trusted and which
agrees with the doctrine. In this way he
will be able to encourage others with the
true teaching and also to show the error
of those who are opposed to it.
10 For there are many, especially the
converts from Judaism, who rebel and
deceive others with their nonsense. 11 It
is necessary to stop their talk, because
they are upsetting whole families by
teaching what they should not, and all
for the shameful purpose of making
money. 12-13 It was a Cretan himself, one
of their own prophets, who spoke the

[a] have only one wife; *or* be married only once.

truth when he said, "Cretans are always
liars, wicked beasts, and lazy gluttons."
For this reason you must rebuke them
sharply, so that they may have a healthy
faith 14 and no longer hold on to Jewish
legends and to human commandments
which come from people who have rejected the truth. 15 Everything is pure to
those who are themselves pure; but
nothing is pure to those who are defiled
and unbelieving, for their minds and
consciences have been defiled. 16 They
claim that they know God, but their actions deny it. They are hateful and disobedient, not fit to do anything good.

Sound Doctrine

2 But you must teach what agrees
with sound doctrine. 2 Instruct the
older men to be sober, sensible, and self-
controlled; to be sound in their faith,
love, and endurance. 3 In the same way
instruct the older women to behave as
women should who live a holy life. They
must not be slanderers or slaves to wine.
They must teach what is good, 4 in order
to train the younger women to love their
husbands and children, 5 to be self-
controlled and pure, and to be good
housewives who submit themselves to
their husbands, so that no one will
speak evil of the message that comes
from God.

6 In the same way urge the young men
to be self-controlled. 7 In all things you
yourself must be an example of good behavior. Be sincere and serious in your
teaching. 8 Use sound words that cannot
be criticized, so that your enemies may
be put to shame by not having anything
bad to say about us.

9 Slaves are to submit themselves to
their masters and please them in all
things. They must not talk back to them
10 or steal from them. Instead, they must
show that they are always good and
faithful, so as to bring credit to the
teaching about God our Savior in all
they do.

11 For God has revealed his grace for
the salvation of all people. 12 That grace
instructs us to give up ungodly living
and worldly passions, and to live self-
controlled, upright, and godly lives in
this world, 13 as we wait for the blessed
Day we hope for, when the glory of our
great God and Savior Jesus Christ[b] will
appear. 14 He gave himself for us, to rescue us from all wickedness and to make
us a pure people who belong to him
alone and are eager to do good.

15 Teach these things and use your full
authority as you encourage and rebuke
your hearers. Let none of them look
down on you.

Christian Conduct

3 Remind your people to submit to
rulers and authorities, to obey
them, and to be ready to do good in
every way. 2 Tell them not to speak evil
of anyone, but to be peaceful and
friendly, and always to show a gentle attitude toward everyone. 3 For we ourselves were once foolish, disobedient,
and wrong. We were slaves to passions
and pleasures of all kinds. We spent our
lives in malice and envy; others hated us
and we hated them. 4 But when the kindness and love of God our Savior was revealed, 5 he saved us. It was not because
of any good deeds that we ourselves had
done, but because of his own mercy that
he saved us, through the Holy Spirit,
who gives us new birth and new life by
washing us. 6 God poured out the Holy
Spirit abundantly on us through Jesus
Christ our Savior, 7 so that by his grace
we might be put right with God and
come into possession of the eternal life
we hope for. 8 This is a true saying.

I want you to give special emphasis to
these matters, so that those who believe
in God may be concerned with giving
their time to doing good deeds, which
are good and useful for everyone. 9 But
avoid stupid arguments, long lists of ancestors, quarrels, and fights about the
Law. They are useless and worthless.
10 Give at least two warnings to those
who cause divisions, and then have
nothing more to do with them. 11 You
know that such people are corrupt, and
their sins prove that they are wrong.

Final Instructions

12 When I send Artemas or Tychicus to
you, do your best to come to me in Ni-
copolis, because I have decided to spend
the winter there. 13 Do your best to help

[b] our great God and Savior Jesus Christ; *or* the great God and our Savior Jesus Christ.

Zenas the lawyer and Apollos to get
started on their travels, and see to it that
they have everything they need. 14 Our
people must learn to spend their time doing good, in order to provide for real
needs; they should not live useless lives.
15 All who are with me send you greetings. Give our greetings to our friends in
the faith.
God's grace be with you all.

Paul's Letter to PHILEMON

Introduction

Philemon was a prominent Christian, probably a member of the church at Colossae and the owner of a slave named Onesimus. This slave had run away from his master, and then somehow he had come in contact with Paul, who was then in prison. Through Paul, Onesimus became a Christian. Paul's Letter to Philemon *is an appeal to Philemon to be reconciled to his slave, whom Paul is sending back to him, and to welcome him not only as a forgiven slave but as a Christian brother.*

Outline of Contents

Introduction 1-3
Praise for Philemon 4-7
Appeal for Onesimus 8-22
Conclusion 23-25

---

1 From Paul, a prisoner for the sake of
Christ Jesus, and from our brother
Timothy—
To our friend and fellow worker Philemon, 2 and the church that meets in
your house, and our sister Apphia, and
our fellow soldier Archippus:
3 May God our Father and the Lord
Jesus Christ give you grace and peace.

Philemon's Love and Faith

4 Brother Philemon, every time I pray,
I mention you and give thanks to my
God. 5 For I hear of your love for all of
God's people and the faith you have in
the Lord Jesus. 6 My prayer is that our
fellowship with you as believers will
bring about a deeper understanding of
every blessing which we have in our life
in union with Christ. 7 Your love, dear
brother, has brought me great joy and
much encouragement! You have
cheered the hearts of all of God's people.

A Request for Onesimus

8 For this reason I could be bold
enough, as your brother in Christ, to order you to do what should be done. 9 But
because I love you, I make a request instead. I do this even though I am Paul,
the ambassador of Christ Jesus, and at
present also a prisoner for his sake.[a]
10 So I make a request to you on behalf of
Onesimus, who is my own son in Christ;
for while in prison I have become his
spiritual father. 11 At one time he was of
no use to you, but now he is useful[b]
both to you and to me.
12 I am sending him back to you now,
and with him goes my heart. 13 I would
like to keep him here with me, while I
am in prison for the gospel's sake, so
that he could help me in your place.
14 However, I do not want to force you to
help me; rather, I would like for you to
do it of your own free will. So I will not
do anything unless you agree.

[a] the ambassador of Christ Jesus, and at present also a prisoner for his sake; *or* an old man, and at present a prisoner for the sake of Christ Jesus. [b] *The Greek name Onesimus means "useful."*

15 It may be that Onesimus was away
from you for a short time so that you
might have him back for all time. 16 And
now he is not just a slave, but much
more than a slave: he is a dear brother in
Christ. How much he means to me! And
how much more he will mean to you,
both as a slave and as a brother in the
Lord!

17 So, if you think of me as your partner, welcome him back just as you
would welcome me. 18 If he has done you
any wrong or owes you anything,
charge it to my account. 19 Here, I will
write this with my own hand: *I, Paul, will
pay you back.* (I should not have to remind you, of course, that you owe your
very self to me.) 20 So, my brother, please
do me this favor for the Lord's sake; as
a brother in Christ, cheer me up!

21 I am sure, as I write this, that you
will do what I ask—in fact I know that
you will do even more. 22 At the same
time, get a room ready for me, because I
hope that God will answer the prayers of
all of you and give me back to you.

Final Greetings

23 Epaphras, who is in prison with me
for the sake of Christ Jesus, sends you
his greetings, 24 and so do my co-
workers Mark, Aristarchus, Demas, and
Luke.

25 May the grace of the Lord Jesus
Christ be with you all.

The Letter to the
HEBREWS

Introduction

The Letter to the Hebrews *was written to a group of Christians who, faced with increasing opposition, were in danger of abandoning the Christian faith. The writer encourages them in their faith primarily by showing that Jesus Christ is the true and final revelation of God. In doing this he emphasizes three truths: (1) Jesus is the eternal Son of God, who learned true obedience to the Father through the suffering that he endured. As the Son of God, Jesus is superior to the prophets of the Old Testament, to the angels, and to Moses himself. (2) Jesus has been declared by God to be an eternal priest, superior to the priests of the Old Testament. (3) Through Jesus the believer is saved from sin, fear, and death; and Jesus, as High Priest, provides the true salvation, which was only foreshadowed by the rituals and animal sacrifices of the Hebrew religion.*

By citing the example of the faith of some famous persons in Israel's history (chapter 11), the writer appeals to his readers to remain faithful, and in chapter 12 he urges his readers to continue faithful to the end, with eyes fixed on Jesus, and to endure whatever suffering and persecution may come to them. The book closes with words of advice and warning.

Outline of Contents

Introduction: Christ the complete revelation of God 1.1-3
Christ's superiority over the angels 1.4 – 2.18
Christ's superiority over Moses and Joshua 3.1 – 4.13
The superiority of Christ's priesthood 4.14 – 7.28
The superiority of Christ's covenant 8.1 – 9.22
The superiority of Christ's sacrifice 9.23 – 10.39
The primacy of faith 11.1 – 12.29
Pleasing God 13.1-19
Closing prayer 13.20-21
Final words 13.22-25

God's Word through His Son

1 In the past God spoke to our ancestors many times and in many ways
through the prophets, 2but in these last
days he has spoken to us through his
Son. He is the one through whom God
created the universe, the one whom God
has chosen to possess all things at
the end. 3He reflects the brightness of
God's glory and is the exact likeness
of God's own being, sustaining the universe with his powerful word. After
achieving forgiveness for the sins of
all human beings, he sat down in heav-
en at the right side of God, the Supreme
Power.

The Greatness of God's Son

4The Son was made greater than the
angels, just as the name that God gave
him is greater than theirs. 5For God
never said to any of his angels,

"You are my Son;
today I have become your
Father."

Nor did God say about any angel,

"I will be his Father,
and he will be my Son."

6But when God was about to send his
first-born Son into the world, he said,

"All of God's angels must
worship him."

7But about the angels God said,

"God makes his angels winds,
and his servants flames of fire."

8About the Son, however, God said:

"Your kingdom, O God, will last[a]
forever and ever!
You rule over your[b] people with
justice.

[a] Your kingdom, O God, will last; *or* God is your kingdom. [b] your; *some manuscripts have* his.

[9]You love what is right and hate
what is wrong.
That is why God, your God, has
chosen you
and has given you the joy of an
honor far greater
than he gave to your
companions."
[10]He also said,
"You, Lord, in the beginning
created the earth,
and with your own hands you
made the heavens.
[11]They will disappear, but you will
remain;
they will all wear out like
clothes.
[12]You will fold them up like a coat,
and they will be changed like
clothes.
But you are always the same,
and your life never ends."
[13]God never said to any of his angels:
"Sit here at my right side
until I put your enemies
as a footstool under your feet."
[14]What are the angels, then? They are
spirits who serve God and are sent by
him to help those who are to receive
salvation.

The Great Salvation

2 That is why we must hold on all the
more firmly to the truths we have
heard, so that we will not be carried
away. [2]The message given to our ancestors by the angels was shown to be true,
and those who did not follow it or obey
it received the punishment they deserved. [3]How, then, shall we escape if
we pay no attention to such a great salvation? The Lord himself first announced this salvation, and those who
heard him proved to us that it is true. [4]At
the same time God added his witness to
theirs by performing all kinds of miracles and wonders and by distributing the
gifts of the Holy Spirit according to his
will.

The One Who Leads Us to Salvation

[5]God has not placed the angels as rulers over the new world to come—the
world of which we speak. [6]Instead, as it
is said somewhere in the Scriptures:
"What are human beings, O God,
that you should think of them;
mere human beings, that you
should care for them?
[7]You made them for a little while
lower than the angels;
you crowned them with glory
and honor,[c]
[8] and made them rulers over all
things."
It says that God made them "rulers over
all things"; this clearly includes everything. We do not, however, see human
beings ruling over all things now. [9]But
we do see Jesus, who for a little while
was made lower than the angels, so that
through God's grace he should die for
everyone. We see him now crowned
with glory and honor because of the
death he suffered. [10]It was only right
that God, who creates and preserves all
things, should make Jesus perfect
through suffering, in order to bring
many children to share his glory. For
Jesus is the one who leads them to
salvation.
[11]He purifies people from their sins,
and both he and those who are made
pure all have the same Father. That is
why Jesus is not ashamed to call them
his family. [12]He says to God,
"I will tell my people what you
have done;
I will praise you in their
meeting."
[13]He also says, "I will put my trust in
God." And he also says, "Here I am with
the children that God has given me."
[14]Since the children, as he calls them,
are people of flesh and blood, Jesus himself became like them and shared their
human nature. He did this so that
through his death he might destroy the
Devil, who has the power over death,
[15]and in this way set free those who
were slaves all their lives because of
their fear of death. [16]For it is clear that it
is not the angels that he helps. Instead,
he helps the descendants of Abraham.
[17]This means that he had to become like
his people in every way, in order to be
their faithful and merciful High Priest in
his service to God, so that the people's
sins would be forgiven. [18]And now he
can help those who are tempted, be-

[c] *Many manuscripts add:* You made them rulers over everything you made *(see Ps 8.6).*

cause he himself was tempted and
suffered.

Jesus Is Greater than Moses

3 My Christian friends, who also
have been called by God! Think of
Jesus, whom God sent to be the High
Priest of the faith we profess. 2 He was
faithful to God, who chose him to do
this work, just as Moses was faithful in
his work in God's house. 3 A man who
builds a house receives more honor than
the house itself. In the same way Jesus is
worthy of much greater honor than
Moses. 4 Every house, of course, is built
by someone—and God is the one who
has built all things. 5 Moses was faithful
in God's house as a servant, and he
spoke of the things that God would say
in the future. 6 But Christ is faithful as
the Son in charge of God's house. We
are his house if we keep up our courage
and our confidence in what we hope for.

A Rest for God's People

7 So then, as the Holy Spirit says,
"If you hear God's voice today,
8 do not be stubborn, as your
ancestors were when they
rebelled against God,
as they were that day in the
desert when they put him to
the test.
9 There they put me to the test and
tried me, says God,
although they had seen what I
did for forty years.
10 And so I was angry with those
people and said,
'They are always disloyal
and refuse to obey my
commands.'
11 I was angry and made a solemn
promise:
'They will never enter the land
where I would have given
them rest!' "
12 My friends, be careful that none of
you have a heart so evil and unbelieving
that you will turn away from the living
God. 13 Instead, in order that none of you
be deceived by sin and become stubborn, you must help one another every
day, as long as the word "Today" in the
scripture applies to us. 14 For we are all
partners with Christ if we hold firmly to
the end the confidence we had at the beginning.
15 This is what the scripture says:
"If you hear God's voice today,
do not be stubborn, as your
ancestors were
when they rebelled
against God."
16 Who were the people who heard
God's voice and rebelled against him?
All those who were led out of Egypt by
Moses. 17 With whom was God angry
for forty years? With the people who
sinned, who fell down dead in the desert.
18 When God made his solemn promise,
"They will never enter the land where I
would have given them rest"—of whom
was he speaking? Of those who rebelled.
19 We see, then, that they were not able
to enter the land, because they did not
believe.

4 Now, God has offered us the promise that we may receive that rest he
spoke about. Let us take care, then, that
none of you will be found to have failed
to receive that promised rest. 2 For we
have heard the Good News, just as they
did. They heard the message, but it did
them no good, because when they heard
it, they did not accept it with faith. 3 We
who believe, then, do receive that rest
which God promised. It is just as he said,
"I was angry and made a solemn
promise:
'They will never enter the land
where I would have given
them rest!' "
He said this even though his work had
been finished from the time he created
the world. 4 For somewhere in the Scriptures this is said about the seventh day:
"God rested on the seventh day from all
his work." 5 This same matter is spoken
of again: "They will never enter that
land where I would have given them
rest." 6 Those who first heard the Good
News did not receive that rest, because
they did not believe. There are, then,
others who are allowed to receive it.
7 This is shown by the fact that God sets
another day, which is called "Today."
Many years later he spoke of it through
David in the scripture already quoted:
"If you hear God's voice today,
do not be stubborn."
8 If Joshua had given the people the
rest that God had promised, God would
not have spoken later about another
day. 9 As it is, however, there still remains for God's people a rest like God's

resting on the seventh day. 10 For those who receive that rest which God promised will rest from their own work, just as God rested from his. 11 Let us, then, do our best to receive that rest, so that no one of us will fail as they did because of their lack of faith.

12 The word of God is alive and active, sharper than any double-edged sword. It cuts all the way through, to where soul and spirit meet, to where joints and marrow come together. It judges the desires and thoughts of the heart. 13 There is nothing that can be hid from God; everything in all creation is exposed and lies open before his eyes. And it is to him that we must all give an account of ourselves.

Jesus the Great High Priest

14 Let us, then, hold firmly to the faith we profess. For we have a great High Priest who has gone into the very presence of God—Jesus, the Son of God. 15 Our High Priest is not one who cannot feel sympathy for our weaknesses. On the contrary, we have a High Priest who was tempted in every way that we are, but did not sin. 16 Let us have confidence, then, and approach God's throne, where there is grace. There we will receive mercy and find grace to help us just when we need it.

5 Every high priest is chosen from his fellow-men and appointed to serve God on their behalf, to offer sacrifices and offerings for sins. 2 Since he himself is weak in many ways, he is able to be gentle with those who are ignorant and make mistakes. 3 And because he is himself weak, he must offer sacrifices not only for the sins of the people but also for his own sins. 4 No one chooses for himself the honor of being a high priest. It is only by God's call that a man is made a high priest—just as Aaron was.

5 In the same way, Christ did not take upon himself the honor of being a high priest. Instead, God said to him,

"You are my Son;
today I have become your
Father."

6 He also said in another place,

"You will be a priest forever,
in the priestly order of
Melchizedek."[d]

7 In his life on earth Jesus made his prayers and requests with loud cries and tears to God, who could save him from death. Because he was humble and devoted, God heard him. 8 But even though he was God's Son, he learned through his sufferings to be obedient. 9 When he was made perfect, he became the source of eternal salvation for all those who obey him, 10 and God declared him to be high priest, in the priestly order of Melchizedek.[d]

Warning against Abandoning the Faith

11 There is much we have to say about this matter, but it is hard to explain to you, because you are so slow to understand. 12 There has been enough time for you to be teachers—yet you still need someone to teach you the first lessons of God's message. Instead of eating solid food, you still have to drink milk. 13 Anyone who has to drink milk is still a child, without any experience in the matter of right and wrong. 14 Solid food, on the other hand, is for adults, who through practice are able to distinguish between good and evil.

6 Let us go forward, then, to mature teaching and leave behind us the first lessons of the Christian message. We should not lay again the foundation of turning away from useless works and believing in God; 2 of the teaching about baptisms[e] and the laying on of hands; of the resurrection of the dead and the eternal judgment. 3 Let us go forward! And this is what we will do, if God allows.

4 For how can those who abandon their faith be brought back to repent again? They were once in God's light; they tasted heaven's gift and received their share of the Holy Spirit; 5 they knew from experience that God's word is good, and they had felt the powers of the coming age. 6 And then they abandoned their faith! It is impossible to bring them back to repent again, because they are again crucifying the Son of God and exposing him to public shame.

[d] in the priestly order of Melchizedek; *or* like Melchizedek; *or* in the line of succession to Melchizedek. [e] baptisms; *or* purification ceremonies.

7 God blesses the soil which drinks in
the rain that often falls on it and which
grows plants that are useful to those for
whom it is cultivated. 8 But if it grows
thorns and weeds, it is worth nothing; it
is in danger of being cursed by God and
will be destroyed by fire.
9 But even if we speak like this, dear
friends, we feel sure about you. We
know that you have the better blessings
that belong to your salvation. 10 God is
not unfair. He will not forget the work
you did or the love you showed for him
in the help you gave and are still giving
to other Christians. 11 Our great desire is
that each of you keep up your eagerness
to the end, so that the things you hope
for will come true. 12 We do not want you
to become lazy, but to be like those who
believe and are patient, and so receive
what God has promised.

God's Sure Promise

13 When God made his promise to
Abraham, he made a vow to do what he
had promised. Since there was no one
greater than himself, he used his own
name when he made his vow. 14 He said,
"I promise you that I will bless you and
give you many descendants." 15 Abraham was patient, and so he received
what God had promised. 16 When we
make a vow, we use the name of someone greater than ourselves, and the vow
settles all arguments. 17 To those who
were to receive what he promised, God
wanted to make it very clear that he
would never change his purpose; so he
added his vow to the promise. 18 There
are these two things, then, that cannot
change and about which God cannot lie.
So we who have found safety with him
are greatly encouraged to hold firmly to
the hope placed before us. 19 We have
this hope as an anchor for our lives. It is
safe and sure, and goes through the curtain of the heavenly temple into the inner sanctuary. 20 On our behalf Jesus has
gone in there before us and has become
a high priest forever, in the priestly order of Melchizedek.[f]

The Priest Melchizedek

7 This Melchizedek was king of Salem and a priest of the Most High
God. As Abraham was coming back
from the battle in which he defeated the
four kings, Melchizedek met him and
blessed him, 2 and Abraham gave him
one tenth of all he had taken. (The first
meaning of Melchizedek's name is
"King of Righteousness"; and because
he was king of Salem, his name also
means "King of Peace.") 3 There is no
record of Melchizedek's father or
mother or of any of his ancestors; no
record of his birth or of his death. He is
like the Son of God; he remains a priest
forever.
4 You see, then, how great he was.
Abraham, our famous ancestor, gave
him one tenth of all he got in the battle.
5 And those descendants of Levi who are
priests are commanded by the Law to
collect one tenth from the people of Israel, that is, from their own people, even
though they are also descendants of
Abraham. 6 Melchizedek was not descended from Levi, but he collected one
tenth from Abraham and blessed him,
the man who received God's promises.
7 There is no doubt that the one who
blesses is greater than the one who is
blessed. 8 In the case of the priests the
tenth is collected by men who die; but
as for Melchizedek the tenth was collected by one who lives, as the scripture says. 9 And, so to speak, when
Abraham paid the tenth, Levi (whose
descendants collect the tenth) also paid
it. 10 For Levi had not yet been born,
but was, so to speak, in the body of his
ancestor Abraham when Melchizedek
met him.
11 It was on the basis of the levitical
priesthood that the Law was given to
the people of Israel. Now, if the work
of the levitical priests had been perfect, there would have been no need
for a different kind of priest to appear,
one who is in the priestly order of Melchizedek,[f] not of Aaron. 12 For when the
priesthood is changed, there also has to
be a change in the law. 13 And our Lord,
of whom these things are said, belonged
to a different tribe, and no member of
his tribe ever served as a priest. 14 It is
well known that he was born a member
of the tribe of Judah; and Moses did
not mention this tribe when he spoke
of priests.

[f] in the priestly order of Melchizedek *(see 5.6).*

Another Priest, like Melchizedek

15 The matter becomes even plainer; a
different priest has appeared, who is like
Melchizedek. 16 He was made a priest,
not by human rules and regulations, but
through the power of a life which has no
end. 17 For the scripture says, "You will
be a priest forever, in the priestly order
of Melchizedek."[f] 18 The old rule, then,
is set aside, because it was weak and
useless. 19 For the Law of Moses could
not make anything perfect. And now a
better hope has been provided through
which we come near to God.

20 In addition, there is also God's vow.
There was no such vow when the others
were made priests. 21 But Jesus became a
priest by means of a vow when God said
to him,

"The Lord has made a solemn
promise
and will not take it back:
'You will be a priest forever.' "

22 This difference, then, also makes
Jesus the guarantee of a better covenant.

23 There is another difference: there
were many of those other priests, because they died and could not continue
their work. 24 But Jesus lives on forever,
and his work as priest does not pass on
to someone else. 25 And so he is able,
now and always, to save those who
come to God through him, because he
lives forever to plead with God for them.

26 Jesus, then, is the High Priest that
meets our needs. He is holy; he has no
fault or sin in him; he has been set apart
from sinners and raised above the heavens. 27 He is not like other high priests;
he does not need to offer sacrifices every
day for his own sins first and then for
the sins of the people. He offered one
sacrifice, once and for all, when he offered himself. 28 The Law of Moses appoints men who are imperfect to be high
priests; but God's promise made with
the vow, which came later than the Law,
appoints the Son, who has been made
perfect forever.

Jesus Our High Priest

8 The whole point of what we are saying is that we have such a High
Priest, who sits at the right of the throne
of the Divine Majesty in heaven. 2 He
serves as high priest in the Most Holy
Place, that is, in the real tent which was
put up by the Lord, not by human hands.

3 Every high priest is appointed to
present offerings and animal sacrifices
to God, and so our High Priest must also
have something to offer. 4 If he were on
earth, he would not be a priest at all,
since there are priests who offer the gifts
required by the Jewish Law. 5 The work
they do as priests is really only a copy
and a shadow of what is in heaven. It is
the same as it was with Moses. When he
was about to build the Sacred Tent, God
told him, "Be sure to make everything
according to the pattern you were
shown on the mountain." 6 But now,
Jesus has been given priestly work
which is superior to theirs, just as the
covenant which he arranged between
God and his people is a better one, because it is based on promises of better
things.

7 If there had been nothing wrong with
the first covenant, there would have
been no need for a second one. 8 But God
finds fault with his people when he says,

"The days are coming, says the
Lord,
when I will draw up a new
covenant with the people of
Israel and with the people of
Judah.
9 It will not be like the covenant
that I made with their
ancestors
on the day I took them by the
hand and led them out of
Egypt.
They were not faithful to the
covenant I made with them,
and so I paid no attention to
them.
10 Now, this is the covenant that I
will make with the people
of Israel
in the days to come, says the
Lord:
I will put my laws in their minds
and write them on their hearts.
I will be their God,
and they will be my people.
11 None of them will have to teach
their friends
or tell their neighbors,
'Know the Lord.'
For they will all know me,

[f] in the priestly order of Melchizedek *(see 5.6)*.

from the least to the greatest.
12 I will forgive their sins
and will no longer remember
their wrongs."
13 By speaking of a new covenant, God
has made the first one old; and anything
that becomes old and worn out will soon
disappear.

Earthly and Heavenly Worship

9 The first covenant had rules for
worship and a place made for worship as well. 2 A tent was put up, the
outer one, which was called the Holy
Place. In it were the lampstand and the
table with the bread offered to God. 3 Behind the second curtain was the tent
called the Most Holy Place. 4 In it were
the gold altar for the burning of incense
and the Covenant Box all covered with
gold and containing the gold jar with the
manna in it, Aaron's stick that had
sprouted leaves, and the two stone tablets with the commandments written on
them. 5 Above the Box were the winged
creatures representing God's presence,
with their wings spread over the place
where sins were forgiven. But now is not
the time to explain everything in detail.
6 This is how those things have been
arranged. The priests go into the outer
tent every day to perform their duties,
7 but only the high priest goes into the
inner tent, and he does so only once a
year. He takes with him blood which he
offers to God on behalf of himself and
for the sins which the people have committed without knowing they were sinning. 8 The Holy Spirit clearly teaches
from all these arrangements that the
way into the Most Holy Place has not yet
been opened as long as the outer tent
still stands. 9 This is a symbol which
points to the present time. It means that
the offerings and animal sacrifices presented to God cannot make the worshiper's heart perfect, 10 since they have
to do only with food, drink, and various
purification ceremonies. These are all
outward rules, which apply only until
the time when God will establish the
new order.
11 But Christ has already come as the
High Priest of the good things that are
already here.[g] The tent in which he
serves is greater and more perfect; it is
not a tent made by human hands, that is,
it is not a part of this created world.
12 When Christ went through the tent
and entered once and for all into the
Most Holy Place, he did not take the
blood of goats and bulls to offer as a sacrifice; rather, he took his own blood and
obtained eternal salvation for us. 13 The
blood of goats and bulls and the ashes of
a burnt calf are sprinkled on the people
who are ritually unclean, and this purifies them by taking away their ritual impurity. 14 Since this is true, how much
more is accomplished by the blood of
Christ! Through the eternal Spirit he offered himself as a perfect sacrifice to
God. His blood will purify our consciences from useless rituals, so that we
may serve the living God.
15 For this reason Christ is the one who
arranges a new covenant, so that those
who have been called by God may receive the eternal blessings that God has
promised. This can be done because
there has been a death which sets people
free from the wrongs they did while the
first covenant was in effect.
16 In the case of a will it is necessary to
prove that the person who made it has
died, 17 for a will means nothing while
the person who made it is alive; it goes
into effect only after his death. 18 That is
why even the first covenant[h] went into
effect only with the use of blood. 19 First,
Moses proclaimed to the people all the
commandments as set forth in the Law.
Then he took the blood of bulls and
goats, mixed it with water, and sprinkled it on the book of the Law and all the
people, using a sprig of hyssop and some
red wool. 20 He said, "This is the blood
which seals the covenant that God has
commanded you to obey." 21 In the same
way Moses also sprinkled the blood on
the Sacred Tent and over all the things
used in worship. 22 Indeed, according to
the Law almost everything is purified by
blood, and sins are forgiven only if
blood is poured out.

Christ's Sacrifice Takes Away Sins

23 Those things, which are copies of
the heavenly originals, had to be purified in that way. But the heavenly things

[g] already here; *some manuscripts have* coming.

[h] COVENANT: *In Greek the same word means "will" and "covenant."*

themselves require much better sacrifices. 24 For Christ did not go into a Holy
Place made by human hands, which was
a copy of the real one. He went into
heaven itself, where he now appears on
our behalf in the presence of God. 25 The
Jewish high priest goes into the Most
Holy Place every year with the blood of
an animal. But Christ did not go in to
offer himself many times, 26 for then he
would have had to suffer many times
ever since the creation of the world. Instead, now when all ages of time are
nearing the end, he has appeared once
and for all, to remove sin through the
sacrifice of himself. 27 Everyone must die
once, and after that be judged by God.
28 In the same manner Christ also was
offered in sacrifice once to take away
the sins of many. He will appear a second time, not to deal with sin, but to save
those who are waiting for him.

10 The Jewish Law is not a full and
faithful model of the real things;
it is only a faint outline of the good
things to come. The same sacrifices are
offered forever, year after year. How
can the Law, then, by means of these
sacrifices make perfect the people who
come to God? 2 If the people worshiping
God had really been purified from their
sins, they would not feel guilty of sin any
more, and all sacrifices would stop. 3 As
it is, however, the sacrifices serve year
after year to remind people of their sins.
4 For the blood of bulls and goats can
never take away sins.

5 For this reason, when Christ was
about to come into the world, he said
to God:

"You do not want sacrifices and
offerings,
but you have prepared a body
for me.
6 You are not pleased with animals
burned whole on the altar
or with sacrifices to take away
sins.
7 Then I said, 'Here I am,
to do your will, O God,
just as it is written of me in the
book of the Law.' "

8 First he said, "You neither want nor are
you pleased with sacrifices and offerings or with animals burned on the altar
and the sacrifices to take away sins." He
said this even though all these sacrifices
are offered according to the Law. 9 Then
he said, "Here I am, O God, to do your
will." So God does away with all the old
sacrifices and puts the sacrifice of Christ
in their place. 10 Because Jesus Christ
did what God wanted him to do, we are
all purified from sin by the offering that
he made of his own body once and
for all.

11 Every Jewish priest performs his
services every day and offers the same
sacrifices many times; but these sacrifices can never take away sins. 12 Christ,
however, offered one sacrifice for sins,
an offering that is effective forever, and
then he sat down at the right side of God.
13 There he now waits until God puts his
enemies as a footstool under his feet.
14 With one sacrifice, then, he has made
perfect forever those who are purified
from sin.

15 And the Holy Spirit also gives us his
witness. First he says,

16 "This is the covenant that I will
make with them
in the days to come, says the
Lord:
I will put my laws in their hearts
and write them on their minds."

17 And then he says, "I will not remember
their sins and evil deeds any longer."
18 So when these have been forgiven, an
offering to take away sins is no longer
needed.

Let Us Come Near to God

19 We have, then, my friends, complete
freedom to go into the Most Holy Place
by means of the death of Jesus. 20 He
opened for us a new way, a living way,
through the curtain—that is, through his
own body. 21 We have a great priest in
charge of the house of God. 22 So let us
come near to God with a sincere heart
and a sure faith, with hearts that have
been purified from a guilty conscience
and with bodies washed with clean water. 23 Let us hold on firmly to the hope
we profess, because we can trust God to
keep his promise. 24 Let us be concerned
for one another, to help one another to
show love and to do good. 25 Let us not
give up the habit of meeting together, as
some are doing. Instead, let us encourage one another all the more, since you
see that the Day of the Lord is coming
nearer.

26 For there is no longer any sacrifice
that will take away sins if we purposely

go on sinning after the truth has been
made known to us. 27 Instead, all that is
left is to wait in fear for the coming
Judgment and the fierce fire which will
destroy those who oppose God! 28 Anyone who disobeys the Law of Moses is
put to death without any mercy when
judged guilty from the evidence of two
or more witnesses. 29 What, then, of
those who despise the Son of God? who
treat as a cheap thing the blood of God's
covenant which purified them from sin?
who insult the Spirit of grace? Just think
how much worse is the punishment they
will deserve! 30 For we know who said, "I
will take revenge, I will repay"; and who
also said, "The Lord will judge his people." 31 It is a terrifying thing to fall into
the hands of the living God!

32 Remember how it was with you in
the past. In those days, after God's light
had shone on you, you suffered many
things, yet were not defeated by the
struggle. 33 You were at times publicly
insulted and mistreated, and at other
times you were ready to join those who
were being treated in this way. 34 You
shared the sufferings of prisoners, and
when all your belongings were seized,
you endured your loss gladly, because
you knew that you still possessed something much better, which would last forever. 35 Do not lose your courage, then,
because it brings with it a great reward.
36 You need to be patient, in order to do
the will of God and receive what he
promises. 37 For, as the scripture says,

"Just a little while longer,
and he who is coming will come;
he will not delay.
38 My righteous people, however, will
believe and live;
but if any of them turns back,
I will not be pleased with them."

39 We are not people who turn back and
are lost. Instead, we have faith and are
saved.

Faith

11 To have faith is to be sure of the
things we hope for, to be certain
of the things we cannot see. 2 It was by
their faith that people of ancient times
won God's approval.

3 It is by faith that we understand that
the universe was created by God's word,
so that what can be seen was made out
of what cannot be seen.

4 It was faith that made Abel offer to
God a better sacrifice than Cain's.
Through his faith he won God's approval as a righteous man, because God
himself approved of his gifts. By means
of his faith Abel still speaks, even
though he is dead.

5 It was faith that kept Enoch from dying. Instead, he was taken up to God,
and nobody could find him, because God
had taken him up. The scripture says
that before Enoch was taken up, he had
pleased God. 6 No one can please God
without faith, for whoever comes to God
must have faith that God exists and rewards those who seek him.

7 It was faith that made Noah hear
God's warnings about things in the future that he could not see. He obeyed
God and built a boat in which he and his
family were saved. As a result, the world
was condemned, and Noah received
from God the righteousness that comes
by faith.

8 It was faith that made Abraham obey
when God called him to go out to a country which God had promised to give him.
He left his own country without knowing where he was going. 9 By faith he
lived as a foreigner in the country that
God had promised him. He lived in tents,
as did Isaac and Jacob, who received the
same promise from God. 10 For Abraham
was waiting for the city which God has
designed and built, the city with permanent foundations.

11 It was faith that made Abraham able
to become a father, even though he was
too old and Sarah herself could not have
children. He[i] trusted God to keep his
promise. 12 Though Abraham was practically dead, from this one man came as
many descendants as there are stars in
the sky, as many as the numberless
grains of sand on the seashore.

13 It was in faith that all these persons
died. They did not receive the things
God had promised, but from a long way
off they saw them and welcomed them,
and admitted openly that they were foreigners and refugees on earth. 14 Those
who say such things make it clear that

[i] It was faith . . . children. He; *some manuscripts have* It was faith that made Sarah herself able to conceive, even though she was too old to have children. She.

they are looking for a country of their
own. 15 They did not keep thinking about
the country they had left; if they had,
they would have had the chance to return. 16 Instead, it was a better country
they longed for, the heavenly country.
And so God is not ashamed for them to
call him their God, because he has prepared a city for them.

17 It was faith that made Abraham offer his son Isaac as a sacrifice when God
put Abraham to the test. Abraham was
the one to whom God had made the
promise, yet he was ready to offer his
only son as a sacrifice. 18 God had said to
him, "It is through Isaac that you will
have the descendants I promised."
19 Abraham reckoned that God was able
to raise Isaac from death—and, so to
speak, Abraham did receive Isaac back
from death.

20 It was faith that made Isaac promise
blessings for the future to Jacob and
Esau.

21 It was faith that made Jacob bless
each of the sons of Joseph just before he
died. He leaned on the top of his walking
stick and worshiped God.

22 It was faith that made Joseph, when
he was about to die, speak of the departure of the Israelites from Egypt, and
leave instructions about what should be
done with his body.

23 It was faith that made the parents of
Moses hide him for three months after
he was born. They saw that he was a
beautiful child, and they were not afraid
to disobey the king's order.

24 It was faith that made Moses, when
he had grown up, refuse to be called the
son of the king's daughter. 25 He preferred to suffer with God's people rather
than to enjoy sin for a little while. 26 He
reckoned that to suffer scorn for the
Messiah was worth far more than all the
treasures of Egypt, for he kept his eyes
on the future reward.

27 It was faith that made Moses leave
Egypt without being afraid of the king's
anger. As though he saw the invisible
God, he refused to turn back. 28 It was
faith that made him establish the Passover and order the blood to be sprinkled
on the doors, so that the Angel of Death
would not kill the first-born sons of the
Israelites.

29 It was faith that made the Israelites
able to cross the Red Sea as if on dry
land; when the Egyptians tried to do it,
the water swallowed them up.

30 It was faith that made the walls of
Jericho fall down after the Israelites had
marched around them for seven days.
31 It was faith that kept the prostitute Rahab from being killed with those who
disobeyed God, for she gave the Israelite
spies a friendly welcome.

32 Should I go on? There isn't enough
time for me to speak of Gideon, Barak,
Samson, Jephthah, David, Samuel, and
the prophets. 33 Through faith they
fought whole countries and won. They
did what was right and received what
God had promised. They shut the
mouths of lions, 34 put out fierce fires, escaped being killed by the sword. They
were weak, but became strong; they
were mighty in battle and defeated the
armies of foreigners. 35 Through faith
women received their dead relatives
raised back to life.

Others, refusing to accept freedom,
died under torture in order to be raised
to a better life. 36 Some were mocked and
whipped, and others were put in chains
and taken off to prison. 37 They were
stoned, they were sawed in two, they
were killed by the sword. They went
around clothed in skins of sheep or
goats—poor, persecuted, and mistreated. 38 The world was not good
enough for them! They wandered like
refugees in the deserts and hills, living in
caves and holes in the ground.

39 What a record all of these have won
by their faith! Yet they did not receive
what God had promised, 40 because God
had decided on an even better plan for
us. His purpose was that only in company with us would they be made
perfect.

God Our Father

12 As for us, we have this large
crowd of witnesses around us.
So then, let us rid ourselves of everything that gets in the way, and of the sin
which holds on to us so tightly, and let
us run with determination the race that
lies before us. 2 Let us keep our eyes
fixed on Jesus, on whom our faith depends from beginning to end. He did not
give up because of the cross! On the contrary, because of the joy that was waiting for him, he thought nothing of the
disgrace of dying on the cross, and he is

now seated at the right side of God's
throne.
3 Think of what he went through; how
he put up with so much hatred from sinners! So do not let yourselves become
discouraged and give up. 4 For in your
struggle against sin you have not yet had
to resist to the point of being killed.
5 Have you forgotten the encouraging
words which God speaks to you as his
children?

"My child, pay attention when the
Lord corrects you,
and do not be discouraged when
he rebukes you.
6 Because the Lord corrects
everyone he loves,
and punishes everyone he
accepts as a child."

7 Endure what you suffer as being a
father's punishment; your suffering
shows that God is treating you as his
children. Was there ever a child who
was not punished by his father? 8 If you
are not punished, as all his children are,
it means you are not real children, but
bastards. 9 In the case of our human
fathers, they punished us and we respected them. How much more, then,
should we submit to our spiritual Father
and live! 10 Our human fathers punished
us for a short time, as it seemed right to
them; but God does it for our own good,
so that we may share his holiness.
11 When we are punished, it seems to us
at the time something to make us sad,
not glad. Later, however, those who
have been disciplined by such punishment reap the peaceful reward of a
righteous life.

Instructions and Warnings

12 Lift up your tired hands, then, and
strengthen your trembling knees!
13 Keep walking on straight paths, so
that the lame foot may not be disabled,
but instead be healed.

14 Try to be at peace with everyone,
and try to live a holy life, because no one
will see the Lord without it. 15 Guard
against turning back from the grace of
God. Let no one become like a bitter
plant that grows up and causes many
troubles with its poison. 16 Let no one become immoral or unspiritual like Esau,
who for a single meal sold his rights as
the older son. 17 Afterward, you know,
he wanted to receive his father's blessing; but he was turned back, because he
could not find any way to change what
he had done, even though in tears he
looked for it.[j]

18 You have not come, as the people of
Israel came, to what you can feel, to
Mount Sinai with its blazing fire, the
darkness and the gloom, the storm, 19 the
blast of a trumpet, and the sound of a
voice. When the people heard the voice,
they begged not to hear another word,
20 because they could not bear the order
which said, "If even an animal touches
the mountain, it must be stoned to
death." 21 The sight was so terrifying that
Moses said, "I am trembling and afraid!"

22 Instead, you have come to Mount
Zion and to the city of the living God, the
heavenly Jerusalem, with its thousands
of angels. 23 You have come to the joyful
gathering of God's first-born, whose
names are written in heaven. You have
come to God, who is the judge of all people, and to the spirits of good people
made perfect. 24 You have come to Jesus,
who arranged the new covenant, and to
the sprinkled blood that promises much
better things than does the blood of
Abel.

25 Be careful, then, and do not refuse to
hear him who speaks. Those who refused to hear the one who gave the divine message on earth did not escape.
How much less shall we escape, then, if
we turn away from the one who speaks
from heaven! 26 His voice shook the
earth at that time, but now he has promised, "I will once more shake not only
the earth but heaven as well." 27 The
words "once more" plainly show that the
created things will be shaken and removed, so that the things that cannot be
shaken will remain.

28 Let us be thankful, then, because we
receive a kingdom that cannot be
shaken. Let us be grateful and worship
God in a way that will please him, with
reverence and awe; 29 because our God
is indeed a destroying fire.

How to Please God

13 Keep on loving one another as
Christians. 2 Remember to welcome strangers in your homes. There

[j] he looked for it; *or* he tried to get the blessing.

were some who did that and welcomed
angels without knowing it. 3 Remember
those who are in prison, as though you
were in prison with them. Remember
those who are suffering, as though you
were suffering as they are.
4 Marriage is to be honored by all, and
husbands and wives must be faithful to
each other. God will judge those who
are immoral and those who commit
adultery.
5 Keep your lives free from the love of
money, and be satisfied with what you
have. For God has said, "I will never
leave you; I will never abandon you."
6 Let us be bold, then, and say,

"The Lord is my helper,
I will not be afraid.
What can anyone do to me?"

7 Remember your former leaders, who
spoke God's message to you. Think back
on how they lived and died, and imitate
their faith. 8 Jesus Christ is the same yesterday, today, and forever. 9 Do not let
all kinds of strange teachings lead you
from the right way. It is good to receive
inner strength from God's grace, and not
by obeying rules about foods; those who
obey these rules have not been helped
by them.
10 The priests who serve in the Jewish
place of worship have no right to eat any
of the sacrifice on our altar. 11 The Jewish high priest brings the blood of the
animals into the Most Holy Place to offer
it as a sacrifice for sins; but the bodies of
the animals are burned outside the
camp. 12 For this reason Jesus also died
outside the city, in order to purify the
people from sin with his own blood.
13 Let us, then, go to him outside the
camp and share his shame. 14 For there is
no permanent city for us here on earth;
we are looking for the city which is to
come. 15 Let us, then, always offer praise
to God as our sacrifice through Jesus,
which is the offering presented by lips
that confess him as Lord. 16 Do not forget
to do good and to help one another, because these are the sacrifices that
please God.
17 Obey your leaders and follow their
orders. They watch over your souls
without resting, since they must give to
God an account of their service. If you
obey them, they will do their work
gladly; if not, they will do it with sadness, and that would be of no help
to you.
18 Keep on praying for us. We are sure
we have a clear conscience, because we
want to do the right thing at all times.
19 And I beg you even more earnestly to
pray that God will send me back to you
soon.

Closing Prayer

20-21 God has raised from death our
Lord Jesus, who is the Great Shepherd
of the sheep as the result of his blood,[k]
by which the eternal covenant is sealed.
May the God of peace provide you with
every good thing you need in order to do
his will, and may he, through Jesus
Christ, do in us what pleases him. And to
Christ be the glory forever and ever!
Amen.

Final Words

22 I beg you, my friends, to listen patiently to this message of encouragement; for this letter I have written you is
not very long. 23 I want you to know that
our brother Timothy has been let out of
prison. If he comes soon enough, I will
have him with me when I see you.
24 Give our greetings to all your leaders and to all God's people. The believers from Italy send you their greetings.
25 May God's grace be with you all.

[k] his blood; *or* his sacrificial death.

The Letter from

JAMES

Introduction

The Letter from James *is a collection of practical instructions, written to "all God's people scattered over the whole world." The writer uses many vivid figures of speech to present instructions regarding practical wisdom and guidance for Christian attitudes and conduct. From the Christian perspective he deals with a variety of topics such as riches and poverty, temptation, good conduct, prejudice, faith and actions, the use of the tongue, wisdom, quarreling, pride and humility, judging others, boasting, patience, and prayer.*

The letter emphasizes the importance of actions along with faith, in the practice of the Christian religion.

Outline of Contents

---

1 From James, a servant of God and
of the Lord Jesus Christ:
Greetings to all God's people scattered
over the whole world.

Faith and Wisdom

2 My friends, consider yourselves fortunate when all kinds of trials come your
way, 3 for you know that when your faith
succeeds in facing such trials, the result
is the ability to endure. 4 Make sure that
your endurance carries you all the way
without failing, so that you may be perfect and complete, lacking nothing. 5 But
if any of you lack wisdom, you should
pray to God, who will give it to you; because God gives generously and graciously to all. 6 But when you pray, you
must believe and not doubt at all. Whoever doubts is like a wave in the sea that
is driven and blown about by the wind.
7-8 If you are like that, unable to make up
your mind and undecided in all you do,
you must not think that you will receive
anything from the Lord.

Poverty and Riches

9 Those Christians who are poor must
be glad when God lifts them up, 10 and
the rich Christians must be glad when
God brings them down. For the rich will
pass away like the flower of a wild plant.
11 The sun rises with its blazing heat and
burns the plant; its flower falls off, and
its beauty is destroyed. In the same way
the rich will be destroyed while they go
about their business.

Testing and Tempting

12 Happy are those who remain faithful under trials, because when they succeed in passing such a test, they will
receive as their reward the life which
God has promised to those who love
him. 13 If we are tempted by such trials,
we must not say, "This temptation
comes from God." For God cannot be
tempted by evil, and he himself tempts
no one. 14 But we are tempted when we
are drawn away and trapped by our own
evil desires. 15 Then our evil desires conceive and give birth to sin; and sin, when
it is full-grown, gives birth to death.
16 Do not be deceived, my dear friends!
17 Every good gift and every perfect
present comes from heaven; it comes
down from God, the Creator of the heavenly lights, who does not change or

cause darkness by turning. 18 By his own
will he brought us into being through the
word of truth, so that we should have
first place among all his creatures.

Hearing and Doing

19 Remember this, my dear friends!
Everyone must be quick to listen, but
slow to speak and slow to become angry.
20 Human anger does not achieve God's
righteous purpose. 21 So get rid of every
filthy habit and all wicked conduct. Submit to God and accept the word that he
plants in your hearts, which is able to
save you.

22 Do not deceive yourselves by just
listening to his word; instead, put it into
practice. 23 If you listen to the word, but
do not put it into practice you are like
people who look in a mirror and see
themselves as they are. 24 They take a
good look at themselves and then go
away and at once forget what they look
like. 25 But if you look closely into the
perfect law that sets people free, and
keep on paying attention to it and do not
simply listen and then forget it, but put it
into practice—you will be blessed by
God in what you do.

26 Do any of you think you are religious? If you do not control your tongue,
your religion is worthless and you deceive yourself. 27 What God the Father
considers to be pure and genuine religion is this: to take care of orphans and
widows in their suffering and to keep
oneself from being corrupted by the
world.

Warning against Prejudice

2 My friends, as believers in our Lord
Jesus Christ, the Lord of glory, you
must never treat people in different
ways according to their outward appearance. 2 Suppose a rich man wearing a
gold ring and fine clothes comes to your
meeting, and a poor man in ragged
clothes also comes. 3 If you show more
respect to the well-dressed man and say
to him, "Have this best seat here," but
say to the poor man, "Stand over there,
or sit here on the floor by my feet," 4 then
you are guilty of creating distinctions
among yourselves and of making judgments based on evil motives.

5 Listen, my dear friends! God chose
the poor people of this world to be rich
in faith and to possess the kingdom
which he promised to those who love
him. 6 But you dishonor the poor! Who
are the ones who oppress you and drag
you before the judges? The rich! 7 They
are the ones who speak evil of that good
name which has been given to you.

8 You will be doing the right thing if
you obey the law of the Kingdom, which
is found in the scripture, "Love your
neighbor as you love yourself." 9 But if
you treat people according to their outward appearance, you are guilty of sin,
and the Law condemns you as a lawbreaker. 10 Whoever breaks one commandment is guilty of breaking them
all. 11 For the same one who said, "Do
not commit adultery," also said, "Do not
commit murder." Even if you do not
commit adultery, you have become a
lawbreaker if you commit murder.
12 Speak and act as people who will be
judged by the law that sets us free. 13 For
God will not show mercy when he
judges the person who has not been
merciful; but mercy triumphs over
judgment.

Faith and Actions

14 My friends, what good is it for one of
you to say that you have faith if your
actions do not prove it? Can that faith
save you? 15 Suppose there are brothers
or sisters who need clothes and don't
have enough to eat. 16 What good is there
in your saying to them, "God bless you!
Keep warm and eat well!"—if you don't
give them the necessities of life? 17 So it
is with faith: if it is alone and includes no
actions, then it is dead.

18 But someone will say, "One person
has faith, another has actions." My answer is, "Show me how anyone can have
faith without actions. I will show you my
faith by my actions." 19 Do you believe
that there is only one God? Good! The
demons also believe—and tremble with
fear. 20 You fool! Do you want to be
shown that faith without actions is useless?[a] 21 How was our ancestor Abraham put right with God? It was through
his actions, when he offered his son
Isaac on the altar. 22 Can't you see? His
faith and his actions worked together;
his faith was made perfect through his

[a] useless; *some manuscripts have* dead.

actions. 23 And the scripture came true
that said, "Abraham believed God, and
because of his faith God accepted him as
righteous." And so Abraham was called
God's friend. 24 You see, then, that it is
by our actions that we are put right with
God, and not by our faith alone.
25 It was the same with the prostitute
Rahab. She was put right with God
through her actions, by welcoming the
Israelite spies and helping them to escape by a different road.
26 So then, as the body without the
spirit is dead, also faith without actions
is dead.

The Tongue

3 My friends, not many of you should
become teachers. As you know, we
teachers will be judged with greater
strictness than others. 2 All of us often
make mistakes. But if a person never
makes a mistake in what he says, he is
perfect and is also able to control his
whole being. 3 We put a bit into the
mouth of a horse to make it obey us, and
we are able to make it go where we
want. 4 Or think of a ship: big as it is and
driven by such strong winds, it can be
steered by a very small rudder, and it
goes wherever the pilot wants it to go.
5 So it is with the tongue: small as it is, it
can boast about great things.
Just think how large a forest can be
set on fire by a tiny flame! 6 And the
tongue is like a fire. It is a world of
wrong, occupying its place in our bodies
and spreading evil through our whole
being. It sets on fire the entire course of
our existence with the fire that comes to
it from hell itself. 7 We humans are able
to tame and have tamed all other
creatures—wild animals and birds, reptiles and fish. 8 But no one has ever been
able to tame the tongue. It is evil and
uncontrollable, full of deadly poison.
9 We use it to give thanks to our Lord
and Father and also to curse other people, who are created in the likeness of
God. 10 Words of thanksgiving and cursing pour out from the same mouth. My
friends, this should not happen! 11 No
spring of water pours out sweet water
and bitter water from the same opening.
12 A fig tree, my friends, cannot bear olives; a grapevine cannot bear figs, nor
can a salty spring produce sweet water.

The Wisdom from Above

13 Are there any of you who are wise
and understanding? You are to prove it
by your good life, by your good deeds
performed with humility and wisdom.
14 But if in your heart you are jealous,
bitter, and selfish, don't sin against the
truth by boasting of your wisdom.
15 Such wisdom does not come down
from heaven; it belongs to the world, it is
unspiritual and demonic. 16 Where there
is jealousy and selfishness, there is also
disorder and every kind of evil. 17 But the
wisdom from above is pure first of all; it
is also peaceful, gentle, and friendly; it is
full of compassion and produces a harvest of good deeds; it is free from prejudice and hypocrisy. 18 And goodness is
the harvest that is produced from the
seeds the peacemakers plant in peace.

Friendship with the World

4 Where do all the fights and quarrels
among you come from? They come
from your desires for pleasure, which
are constantly fighting within you. 2 You
want things, but you cannot have them,
so you are ready to kill; you strongly desire things, but you cannot get them, so
you quarrel and fight. You do not have
what you want because you do not ask
God for it. 3 And when you ask, you do
not receive it, because your motives are
bad; you ask for things to use for your
own pleasures. 4 Unfaithful people!
Don't you know that to be the world's
friend means to be God's enemy? If you
want to be the world's friend, you make
yourself God's enemy. 5 Don't think that
there is no truth in the scripture that
says, "The spirit that God placed in us is
filled with fierce desires."[b] 6 But the
grace that God gives is even stronger. As
the scripture says, "God resists the
proud, but gives grace to the humble."
7 So then, submit yourselves to God.
Resist the Devil, and he will run away
from you. 8 Come near to God, and he
will come near to you. Wash your hands,
you sinners! Purify your hearts, you
hypocrites! 9 Be sorrowful, cry, and
weep; change your laughter into crying,

[b] The spirit . . . fierce desires; *or* God yearns jealously over the spirit that he placed in us.

your joy into gloom! 10 Humble yourselves before the Lord, and he will lift
you up.

Warning against Judging One Another

11 Do not criticize one another, my
friends. If you criticize or judge another
Christian, you criticize and judge the
Law. If you judge the Law, then you are
no longer one who obeys the Law, but
one who judges it. 12 God is the only law-
giver and judge. He alone can save and
destroy. Who do you think you are, to
judge someone else?

Warning against Boasting

13 Now listen to me, you that say, "Today or tomorrow we will travel to a certain city, where we will stay a year and
go into business and make a lot of
money." 14 You don't even know what
your life tomorrow will be! You are like
a puff of smoke, which appears for a moment and then disappears. 15 What you
should say is this: "If the Lord is willing,
we will live and do this or that." 16 But
now you are proud, and you boast; all
such boasting is wrong.

17 So then, if we do not do the good we
know we should do, we are guilty of sin.

Warning to the Rich

5 And now, you rich people, listen to
me! Weep and wail over the miser-
ies that are coming upon you! 2 Your
riches have rotted away, and your
clothes have been eaten by moths.
3 Your gold and silver are covered with
rust, and this rust will be a witness
against you and will eat up your flesh
like fire. You have piled up riches in
these last days. 4 You have not paid any
wages to those who work in your fields.
Listen to their complaints! The cries of
those who gather in your crops have
reached the ears of God, the Lord
Almighty. 5 Your life here on earth has
been full of luxury and pleasure. You
have made yourselves fat for the day of
slaughter. 6 You have condemned and
murdered innocent people, and they do
not resist you.[c]

Patience and Prayer

7 Be patient, then, my friends, until the
Lord comes. See how patient farmers
are as they wait for their land to produce precious crops. They wait patiently
for the autumn and spring rains. 8 You
also must be patient. Keep your hopes
high, for the day of the Lord's coming is
near.

9 Do not complain against one another, my friends, so that God will not
judge you. The Judge is near, ready to
appear. 10 My friends, remember the
prophets who spoke in the name of the
Lord. Take them as examples of patient
endurance under suffering. 11 We call
them happy because they endured. You
have heard of Job's patience, and you
know how the Lord provided for him in
the end. For the Lord is full of mercy and
compassion.

12 Above all, my friends, do not use an
oath when you make a promise. Do not
swear by heaven or by earth or by anything else. Say only "Yes" when you
mean yes, and "No" when you mean no,
and then you will not come under God's
judgment.

13 Are any among you in trouble? They
should pray. Are any among you happy?
They should sing praises. 14 Are any
among you sick? They should send for
the church elders, who will pray for
them and rub olive oil on them in the
name of the Lord. 15 This prayer made in
faith will heal the sick; the Lord will restore them to health, and the sins they
have committed will be forgiven. 16 So
then, confess your sins to one another
and pray for one another, so that you
will be healed. The prayer of a good person has a powerful effect. 17 Elijah was
the same kind of person as we are. He
prayed earnestly that there would be no
rain, and no rain fell on the land for
three and a half years. 18 Once again he
prayed, and the sky poured out its rain
and the earth produced its crops.

19 My friends, if any of you wander
away from the truth and another one
brings you back again, 20 remember this:
whoever turns a sinner back from the
wrong way will save that sinner's soul[d]
from death and bring about the forgiveness of many sins.

[c] people, and they do not resist you; *or* people. Will God not resist you? [d] that sinner's soul; *or* his own soul.

The First Letter from
PETER

Introduction

The First Letter from Peter *was addressed to Christians, here called "God's chosen people," who were scattered throughout the northern part of Asia Minor. The main purpose of the letter is to encourage the readers, who were facing persecution and suffering for their faith. The writer does this by reminding his readers of the Good News about Jesus Christ, whose death, resurrection, and promised coming gave them hope. In the light of this they are to accept and endure their suffering, confident that it is a test of the genuineness of their faith and that they will be rewarded on "the Day when Jesus Christ is revealed."*

Along with his encouragement in time of trouble, the writer also urges his readers to live as people who belong to Christ.

Outline of Contents

---

1 From Peter, apostle of Jesus
Christ—
To God's chosen people who live as
refugees scattered throughout the provinces of Pontus, Galatia, Cappadocia,
Asia, and Bithynia. 2 You were chosen
according to the purpose of God the
Father and were made a holy people by
his Spirit, to obey Jesus Christ and be
purified by his blood.
May grace and peace be yours in full
measure.

A Living Hope

3 Let us give thanks to the God and
Father of our Lord Jesus Christ! Because
of his great mercy he gave us new life by
raising Jesus Christ from death. This
fills us with a living hope, 4 and so we
look forward to possessing the rich
blessings that God keeps for his people.
He keeps them for you in heaven, where
they cannot decay or spoil or fade away.
5 They are for you, who through faith are
kept safe by God's power for the salvation which is ready to be revealed at the
end of time.
6 Be glad about this, even though it
may now be necessary for you to be sad
for a while because of the many kinds of
trials you suffer. 7 Their purpose is to
prove that your faith is genuine. Even
gold, which can be destroyed, is tested
by fire; and so your faith, which is much
more precious than gold, must also be
tested, so that it may endure. Then you
will receive praise and glory and honor
on the Day when Jesus Christ is revealed. 8 You love him, although you
have not seen him, and you believe in
him, although you do not now see him.
So you rejoice with a great and glorious
joy which words cannot express, 9 because you are receiving the salvation of
your souls, which is the purpose of your
faith in him.
10 It was concerning this salvation that
the prophets made careful search and
investigation, and they prophesied
about this gift which God would give
you. 11 They tried to find out when the
time would be and how it would come.[a]
This was the time to which Christ's
Spirit in them was pointing, in predict-
ing the sufferings that Christ would have
to endure and the glory that would follow. 12 God revealed to these prophets
that their work was not for their own

[a] when the time would be and how it would come; *or* who the person would be and when he would come.

benefit, but for yours, as they spoke
about those things which you have now
heard from the messengers who announced the Good News by the power of
the Holy Spirit sent from heaven. These
are things which even the angels would
like to understand.

A Call to Holy Living

13 So then, have your minds ready for
action. Keep alert and set your hope
completely on the blessing which will be
given you when Jesus Christ is revealed.
14 Be obedient to God, and do not allow
your lives to be shaped by those desires
you had when you were still ignorant.
15 Instead, be holy in all that you do, just
as God who called you is holy. 16 The
scripture says, "Be holy because I am
holy."

17 You call him Father, when you pray
to God, who judges all people by the
same standard, according to what each
one has done; so then, spend the rest of
your lives here on earth in reverence for
him. 18 For you know what was paid to
set you free from the worthless manner
of life handed down by your ancestors. It
was not something that can be destroyed, such as silver or gold; 19 it was
the costly sacrifice of Christ, who was
like a lamb without defect or flaw. 20 He
had been chosen by God before the creation of the world and was revealed in
these last days for your sake. 21 Through
him you believe in God, who raised him
from death and gave him glory; and so
your faith and hope are fixed on God.

22 Now that by your obedience to the
truth you have purified yourselves and
have come to have a sincere love for
other believers, love one another earnestly with all your heart.[b] 23 For
through the living and eternal word of
God you have been born again as the
children of a parent who is immortal, not
mortal. 24 As the scripture says,

"All human beings are like grass,
and all their glory is like wild
flowers.
The grass withers, and the flowers
fall,
25 but the word of the Lord
remains forever."

This word is the Good News that was
proclaimed to you.

The Living Stone and the Holy Nation

2 Rid yourselves, then, of all evil; no
more lying or hypocrisy or jealousy
or insulting language. 2 Be like newborn
babies, always thirsty for the pure spiritual milk, so that by drinking it you may
grow up and be saved. 3 As the scripture
says, "You have found out for yourselves how kind the Lord is."

4 Come to the Lord, the living stone rejected by people as worthless but chosen
by God as valuable. 5 Come as living
stones, and let yourselves be used in
building the spiritual temple, where you
will serve as holy priests to offer spiritual and acceptable sacrifices to God
through Jesus Christ. 6 For the scripture
says,

"I chose a valuable stone,
which I am placing as the
cornerstone in Zion;
and whoever believes in him will
never be disappointed."

7 This stone is of great value for you that
believe; but for those who do not
believe:

"The stone which the builders
rejected as worthless
turned out to be the most
important of all."

8 And another scripture says,

"This is the stone that will make
people stumble,
the rock that will make them
fall."

They stumbled because they did not believe in the word; such was God's will
for them.

9 But you are the chosen race, the
King's priests, the holy nation, God's
own people, chosen to proclaim the
wonderful acts of God, who called you
out of darkness into his own marvelous
light. 10 At one time you were not God's
people, but now you are his people; at
one time you did not know God's mercy,
but now you have received his mercy.

Slaves of God

11 I appeal to you, my friends, as strangers and refugees in this world! Do not
give in to bodily passions, which are al-

[b] with all your heart; *some manuscripts have* with a pure heart.

ways at war against the soul. 12 Your
conduct among the heathen should be so
good that when they accuse you of being
evildoers, they will have to recognize
your good deeds and so praise God on
the Day of his coming.

13 For the sake of the Lord submit
yourselves to every human authority: to
the Emperor, who is the supreme authority, 14 and to the governors, who
have been appointed by him to punish
the evildoers and to praise those who do
good. 15 For God wants you to silence the
ignorant talk of foolish people by the
good things you do. 16 Live as free people; do not, however, use your freedom
to cover up any evil, but live as God's
slaves. 17 Respect everyone, love other
believers, honor God, and respect the
Emperor.

The Example of Christ's Suffering

18 You servants must submit yourselves to your masters and show them
complete respect, not only to those who
are kind and considerate, but also to
those who are harsh. 19 God will bless
you for this, if you endure the pain of
undeserved suffering because you are
conscious of his will. 20 For what credit is
there if you endure the beatings you deserve for having done wrong? But if you
endure suffering even when you have
done right, God will bless you for it. 21 It
was to this that God called you, for
Christ himself suffered for you and left
you an example, so that you would follow in his steps. 22 He committed no sin,
and no one ever heard a lie come from
his lips. 23 When he was insulted, he did
not answer back with an insult; when he
suffered, he did not threaten, but placed
his hopes in God, the righteous Judge.
24 Christ himself carried our sins in his
body to the cross, so that we might die to
sin and live for righteousness. It is by his
wounds that you have been healed.
25 You were like sheep that had lost their
way, but now you have been brought
back to follow the Shepherd and Keeper
of your souls.

Wives and Husbands

3 In the same way you wives must
submit yourselves to your husbands, so that if any of them do not believe God's word, your conduct will win
them over to believe. It will not be necessary for you to say a word, 2 because
they will see how pure and reverent your
conduct is. 3 You should not use outward
aids to make yourselves beautiful, such
as the way you fix your hair, or the jewelry you put on, or the dresses you wear.
4 Instead, your beauty should consist of
your true inner self, the ageless beauty
of a gentle and quiet spirit, which is of
the greatest value in God's sight. 5 For
the devout women of the past who
placed their hope in God used to make
themselves beautiful by submitting
themselves to their husbands. 6 Sarah
was like that; she obeyed Abraham and
called him her master. You are now her
daughters if you do good and are not
afraid of anything.

7 In the same way you husbands must
live with your wives with the proper
understanding that they are more delicate than you. Treat them with respect,
because they also will receive, together
with you, God's gift of life. Do this so
that nothing will interfere with your
prayers.

Suffering for Doing Right

8 To conclude: you must all have the
same attitude and the same feelings;
love one another, and be kind and humble with one another. 9 Do not pay back
evil with evil or cursing with cursing; instead, pay back with a blessing, because
a blessing is what God promised to give
you when he called you. 10 As the scripture says,

"If you want to enjoy life
 and wish to see good times,
 you must keep from speaking
  evil
 and stop telling lies.
11 You must turn away from evil and
  do good;
 you must strive for peace with
  all your heart.
12 For the Lord watches over the
  righteous
 and listens to their prayers;
 but he opposes those who do
  evil."

13 Who will harm you if you are eager
to do what is good? 14 But even if you
should suffer for doing what is right,
how happy you are! Do not be afraid of
anyone, and do not worry. 15 But have
reverence for Christ in your hearts, and
honor him as Lord. Be ready at all times

to answer anyone who asks you to explain the hope you have in you, 16 but do
it with gentleness and respect. Keep
your conscience clear, so that when you
are insulted, those who speak evil of
your good conduct as followers of Christ
will become ashamed of what they say.
17 For it is better to suffer for doing good,
if this should be God's will, than for doing evil. 18 For Christ died[c] for sins once
and for all, a good man on behalf of sinners, in order to lead you to God. He was
put to death physically, but made alive
spiritually, 19 and in his spiritual existence he went and preached to the imprisoned spirits. 20 These were the spirits
of those who had not obeyed God when
he waited patiently during the days that
Noah was building his boat. The few
people in the boat—eight in all—were
saved by the water, 21 which was a symbol pointing to baptism, which now
saves you. It is not the washing off of
bodily dirt, but the promise made to God
from a good conscience. It saves you
through the resurrection of Jesus Christ,
22 who has gone to heaven and is at the
right side of God, ruling over all angels
and heavenly authorities and powers.

Changed Lives

4 Since Christ suffered physically,
you too must strengthen yourselves
with the same way of thinking that he
had; because whoever suffers physically
is no longer involved with sin. 2 From
now on, then, you must live the rest of
your earthly lives controlled by God's
will and not by human desires. 3 You
have spent enough time in the past doing what the heathen like to do. Your
lives were spent in indecency, lust,
drunkenness, orgies, drinking parties,
and the disgusting worship of idols.
4 And now the heathen are surprised
when you do not join them in the same
wild and reckless living, and so they insult you. 5 But they will have to give an
account of themselves to God, who is
ready to judge the living and the dead.
6 That is why the Good News was
preached also to the dead, to those who
had been judged in their physical existence as everyone is judged; it was
preached to them so that in their spiritual existence they may live as God lives.

c died; *many manuscripts have* suffered.

Good Managers of God's Gifts

7 The end of all things is near. You
must be self-controlled and alert, to be
able to pray. 8 Above everything, love
one another earnestly, because love covers over many sins. 9 Open your homes
to each other without complaining.
10 Each one, as a good manager of God's
different gifts, must use for the good of
others the special gift he has received
from God. 11 Those who preach must
preach God's messages; those who serve
must serve with the strength that God
gives them, so that in all things praise
may be given to God through Jesus
Christ, to whom belong glory and power
forever and ever. Amen.

Suffering as a Christian

12 My dear friends, do not be surprised
at the painful test you are suffering, as
though something unusual were happening to you. 13 Rather be glad that you
are sharing Christ's sufferings, so that
you may be full of joy when his glory is
revealed. 14 Happy are you if you are insulted because you are Christ's followers; this means that the glorious Spirit,
the Spirit of God, is resting on you. 15 If
you suffer, it must not be because you
are a murderer or a thief or a criminal or
a meddler in other people's affairs.
16 However, if you suffer because you are
a Christian, don't be ashamed of it, but
thank God that you bear Christ's name.
17 The time has come for judgment to
begin, and God's own people are the
first to be judged. If it starts with us, how
will it end with those who do not believe
the Good News from God? 18 As the
scripture says,

"It is difficult for good people to
be saved;
what, then, will become of
godless sinners?"

19 So then, those who suffer because it is
God's will for them, should by their good
actions trust themselves completely to
their Creator, who always keeps his
promise.

The Flock of God

5 I, who am an elder myself, appeal to
the church elders among you. I am
a witness of Christ's sufferings, and I

will share in the glory that will be revealed. I appeal to you 2 to be shepherds
of the flock that God gave you and to
take care of it willingly, as God wants
you to, and not unwillingly. Do your
work, not for mere pay, but from a real
desire to serve. 3 Do not try to rule over
those who have been put in your care,
but be examples to the flock. 4 And when
the Chief Shepherd appears, you will receive the glorious crown which will
never lose its brightness.

5 In the same way you younger people
must submit yourselves to your elders.
And all of you must put on the apron of
humility, to serve one another; for the
scripture says, "God resists the proud,
but shows favor to the humble." 6 Humble yourselves, then, under God's
mighty hand, so that he will lift you up in
his own good time. 7 Leave all your worries with him, because he cares for you.

8 Be alert, be on watch! Your enemy,
the Devil, roams around like a roaring
lion, looking for someone to devour. 9 Be
firm in your faith and resist him, because you know that other believers in
all the world are going through the same
kind of sufferings. 10 But after you have
suffered for a little while, the God of all
grace, who calls you to share his eternal
glory in union with Christ, will himself
perfect you and give you firmness,
strength, and a sure foundation. 11 To
him be the power forever! Amen.

Final Greetings

12 I write you this brief letter with the
help of Silas, whom I regard as a faithful
Christian. I want to encourage you and
give my testimony that this is the true
grace of God. Stand firm in it.

13 Your sister church in Babylon,[d]
also chosen by God, sends you greetings, and so does my son Mark. 14 Greet
one another with the kiss of Christian
love.

May peace be with all of you who belong to Christ.

[d] BABYLON: *As in the book of Revelation, this probably refers to Rome.*

The Second Letter from PETER

Introduction

The Second Letter from Peter *is addressed to a wide circle of early Christians. Its main concern is to combat the work of false teachers and the immorality which results from such teaching. The answer to these problems is found in holding to the true knowledge of God and of the Lord Jesus Christ, knowledge which has been conveyed by persons who themselves have seen Jesus and have heard him teach. The writer is especially concerned with the teaching of those who claim that Christ will not return again. He says that the apparent delay in Christ's return is due to the fact that God "does not want anyone to be destroyed, but wants all to turn away from their sins."*

Outline of Contents

Introduction 1.1-2
The Christian calling 1.3-21
False teachers 2.1-22
The final coming of Christ 3.1-18

1 From Simon Peter, a servant and
apostle of Jesus Christ—
To those who through the righteousness of our God and Savior Jesus Christ
have been given a faith as precious as
ours:

2 May grace and peace be yours in full
measure through your knowledge of
God and of Jesus our Lord.

God's Call and Choice

3 God's divine power has given us
everything we need to live a truly religious life through our knowledge of the
one who called us to share in his own[a]
glory and goodness. 4 In this way he has
given us the very great and precious
gifts he promised, so that by means of
these gifts you may escape from the destructive lust that is in the world, and
may come to share the divine nature.
5 For this very reason do your best to add
goodness to your faith; to your goodness
add knowledge; 6 to your knowledge add
self-control; to your self-control add endurance; to your endurance add godliness; 7 to your godliness add Christian
affection; and to your Christian affection add love. 8 These are the qualities
you need, and if you have them in abundance, they will make you active and effective in your knowledge of our Lord
Jesus Christ. 9 But if you do not have
them, you are so shortsighted that you
cannot see and have forgotten that you
have been purified from your past sins.
10 So then, my friends, try even harder
to make God's call and his choice of you
a permanent experience; if you do so,
you will never abandon your faith.[b] 11 In
this way you will be given the full right
to enter the eternal Kingdom of our Lord
and Savior Jesus Christ.
12 And so I will always remind you of
these matters, even though you already
know them and are firmly grounded in
the truth you have received. 13 I think it
only right for me to stir up your memory
of these matters as long as I am still
alive. 14 I know that I shall soon put off
this mortal body, as our Lord Jesus
Christ plainly told me. 15 I will do my
best, then, to provide a way for you to
remember these matters at all times after my death.

Eyewitnesses of Christ's Glory

16 We have not depended on made-up
stories in making known to you the
mighty coming of our Lord Jesus Christ.
With our own eyes we saw his greatness. 17 We were there when he was
given honor and glory by God the
Father, when the voice came to him
from the Supreme Glory, saying, "This is
my own dear Son, with whom I am
pleased!" 18 We ourselves heard this
voice coming from heaven, when we
were with him on the holy mountain.
19 So we are even more confident of
the message proclaimed by the prophets. You will do well to pay attention to
it, because it is like a lamp shining in a
dark place until the Day dawns and the
light of the morning star shines in your
hearts. 20 Above all else, however, remember that none of us can explain by
ourselves a prophecy in the Scriptures.
21 For no prophetic message ever came
just from the human will, but people
were under the control of the Holy Spirit
as they spoke the message that came
from God.

False Teachers

2 False prophets appeared in the past
among the people, and in the same
way false teachers will appear among
you. They will bring in destructive, un-
true doctrines, and will deny the Master
who redeemed them, and so they will
bring upon themselves sudden destruction. 2 Even so, many will follow their
immoral ways; and because of what they
do, others will speak evil of the Way of
truth. 3 In their greed these false teachers
will make a profit out of telling you
made-up stories. For a long time now
their Judge has been ready, and their
Destroyer has been wide awake!
4 God did not spare the angels who
sinned, but threw them into hell, where
they are kept chained in darkness,[c]
waiting for the Day of Judgment. 5 God
did not spare the ancient world, but
brought the flood on the world of godless people; the only ones he saved were
Noah, who preached righteousness, and
seven other people. 6 God condemned
the cities of Sodom and Gomorrah, destroying them with fire, and made them
an example of what will happen to the
godless. 7 He rescued Lot, a good man,
who was distressed by the immoral conduct of lawless people. 8 That good man
lived among them, and day after day he

[a] to share in his own; *some manuscripts have* through his. [b] abandon your faith; *or* fall into sin. [c] chained in darkness; *some manuscripts have* in dark pits.

suffered agony as he saw and heard
their evil actions. 9 And so the Lord
knows how to rescue godly people from
their trials and how to keep the wicked
under punishment for the Day of Judgment,
10 especially those who follow
their filthy bodily lusts and despise
God's authority.

These false teachers are bold and arrogant,
and show no respect for the glorious
beings above; instead, they insult
them. 11 Even the angels, who are so
much stronger and mightier than these
false teachers, do not accuse them with
insults in the presence of the Lord. 12 But
these people act by instinct, like wild animals
born to be captured and killed;
they attack with insults anything they do
not understand. They will be destroyed
like wild animals, 13 and they will be
paid with suffering for the suffering they
have caused. Pleasure for them is to do
anything in broad daylight that will satisfy
their bodily appetites; they are a
shame and a disgrace as they join you in
your meals, all the while enjoying their
deceitful ways! 14 They want to look for
nothing but the chance to commit adultery;
their appetite for sin is never satisfied.
They lead weak people into a trap.
Their hearts are trained to be greedy.
They are under God's curse! 15 They
have left the straight path and have lost
their way; they have followed the path
taken by Balaam son of Beor, who loved
the money he would get for doing wrong
16 and was rebuked for his sin. His donkey
spoke with a human voice and
stopped the prophet's insane action.

17 These people are like dried-up
springs, like clouds blown along by a
storm; God has reserved a place for
them in the deepest darkness. 18 They
make proud and stupid statements, and
use immoral bodily lusts to trap those
who are just beginning to escape from
among people who live in error. 19 They
promise them freedom while they themselves
are slaves of destructive habits—
for we are slaves of anything that has
conquered us. 20 If people have escaped
from the corrupting forces of the world
through their knowledge of our Lord
and Savior Jesus Christ, and then are
again caught and conquered by them,
such people are in worse condition at the
end than they were at the beginning. 21 It
would have been much better for them
never to have known the way of righteousness
than to know it and then turn
away from the sacred command that
was given them. 22 What happened to
them shows that the proverbs are true:
"A dog goes back to what it has vomited"
and "A pig that has been washed
goes back to roll in the mud."

The Promise of the Lord's Coming

3 My dear friends, this is now the second
letter I have written you. In
both letters I have tried to arouse pure
thoughts in your minds by reminding
you of these things. 2 I want you to remember
the words that were spoken
long ago by the holy prophets, and the
command from the Lord and Savior
which was given you by your apostles.
3 First of all, you must understand that in
the last days some people will appear
whose lives are controlled by their own
lusts. They will make fun of you 4 and
will ask, "He promised to come, didn't
he? Where is he? Our ancestors have already
died, but everything is still the
same as it was since the creation of the
world!" 5 They purposely ignore the fact
that long ago God gave a command, and
the heavens and earth were created. The
earth was formed out of water and by
water, 6 and it was also by water, the water
of the flood, that the old world was
destroyed. 7 But the heavens and the
earth that now exist are being preserved
by the same command of God, in order
to be destroyed by fire. They are being
kept for the day when godless people
will be judged and destroyed.

8 But do not forget one thing, my dear
friends! There is no difference in the
Lord's sight between one day and a
thousand years; to him the two are the
same. 9 The Lord is not slow to do what
he has promised, as some think. Instead,
he is patient with you, because he
does not want anyone to be destroyed,
but wants all to turn away from their
sins.

10 But the Day of the Lord will come
like a thief. On that Day the heavens
will disappear with a shrill noise, the
heavenly bodies will burn up and be
destroyed, and the earth with everything

in it will vanish.[d] 11 Since all these things
will be destroyed in this way, what kind
of people should you be? Your lives
should be holy and dedicated to God,
12 as you wait for the Day of God and do
your best to make it come soon—the
Day when the heavens will burn up and
be destroyed, and the heavenly bodies
will be melted by the heat. 13 But we wait
for what God has promised: new heavens and a new earth, where righteousness will be at home.

14 And so, my friends, as you wait for
that Day, do your best to be pure and
faultless in God's sight and to be at
peace with him. 15 Look on our Lord's
patience as the opportunity he is giving
you to be saved, just as our dear friend
Paul wrote to you, using the wisdom that
God gave him. 16 This is what he says in
all his letters when he writes on the subject. There are some difficult things in
his letters which ignorant and unstable
people explain falsely, as they do with
other passages of the Scriptures. So they
bring on their own destruction.

17 But you, my friends, already know
this. Be on your guard, then, so that you
will not be led away by the errors of lawless people and fall from your safe position. 18 But continue to grow in the grace
and knowledge of our Lord and Savior
Jesus Christ. To him be the glory, now
and forever! Amen.

[d] vanish; *some manuscripts have* be found; *others have* be burned up; *one has* be found destroyed.

The First Letter of JOHN

Introduction

The First Letter of John *has two main purposes: to encourage its readers to live in fellowship with God and with his Son, Jesus Christ, and to warn them against following false teaching that would destroy this fellowship. This teaching was based on the belief that evil results from contact with the physical world, and so Jesus, the Son of God, could not really have been a human being. Those teachers claimed that to be saved was to be set free from concern with life in this world; and they also taught that salvation had nothing to do with matters of morality or of love for others.*

In opposition to this teaching the writer clearly states that Jesus Christ was a real human being, and he emphasizes that all who believe in Jesus and love God must also love one another.

Outline of Contents

Introduction 1.1-4
Light and darkness 1.5–2.29
Children of God and children of the Devil 3.1-24
Truth and error 4.1-6
The duty of love 4.7-21
Victorious faith 5.1-21

The Word of Life

1 We write to you about the Word of
life, which has existed from the
very beginning. We have heard it, and
we have seen it with our eyes; yes, we
have seen it, and our hands have
touched it. 2 When this life became visible, we saw it; so we speak of it and tell
you about the eternal life which was
with the Father and was made known to
us. 3 What we have seen and heard we
announce to you also, so that you will
join with us in the fellowship that we
have with the Father and with his Son
Jesus Christ. 4 We write this in order that
our[a] joy may be complete.

[a] our; *some manuscripts have* your.

God Is Light

5 Now the message that we have heard
from his Son and announce is this: God
is light, and there is no darkness at all in
him. 6 If, then, we say that we have fellowship with him, yet at the same time
live in the darkness, we are lying both in
our words and in our actions. 7 But if we
live in the light—just as he is in the
light—then we have fellowship with one
another, and the blood of Jesus, his Son,
purifies us from every sin.
8 If we say that we have no sin, we deceive ourselves, and there is no truth in
us. 9 But if we confess our sins to God, he
will keep his promise and do what is
right: he will forgive us our sins and purify us from all our wrongdoing. 10 If we
say that we have not sinned, we make a
liar out of God, and his word is not in us.

Christ Our Helper

2 I am writing this to you, my children, so that you will not sin; but if
anyone does sin, we have someone who
pleads with the Father on our behalf—
Jesus Christ, the righteous one. 2 And
Christ himself is the means by which our
sins are forgiven, and not our sins only,
but also the sins of everyone.
3 If we obey God's commands, then we
are sure that we know him. 4 If we say
that we know him, but do not obey his
commands, we are liars and there is no
truth in us. 5 But if we obey his word, we
are the ones whose love for God has really been made perfect. This is how we
can be sure that we are in union with
God: 6 if we say that we remain in union
with God, we should live just as Jesus
Christ did.

The New Command

7 My dear friends, this command I am
writing you is not new; it is the old command, the one you have had from the
very beginning. The old command is the
message you have already heard. 8 However, the command I now write you is
new, because its truth is seen in Christ
and also in you. For the darkness is
passing away, and the real light is already shining.
9 If we say that we are in the light, yet
hate others, we are in the darkness to
this very hour. 10 If we love others, we
live in the light, and so there is nothing
in us that will cause someone else[b] to
sin. 11 But if we hate others, we are in the
darkness; we walk in it and do not know
where we are going, because the darkness has made us blind.
12 I write to you, my children, because
your sins are forgiven for the sake of
Christ. 13 I write to you, fathers, because
you know him who has existed from the
beginning. I write to you, young people,
because you have defeated the Evil One.
14 I write to you, my children, because
you know the Father. I write to you,
fathers, because you know him who has
existed from the beginning. I write to
you, young people, because you are
strong; the word of God lives in you, and
you have defeated the Evil One.
15 Do not love the world or anything
that belongs to the world. If you love the
world, you do not love the Father.
16 Everything that belongs to the world—
what the sinful self desires, what people
see and want, and everything in this
world that people are so proud of—none
of this comes from the Father; it all
comes from the world. 17 The world and
everything in it that people desire is
passing away; but those who do the will
of God live forever.

The Enemy of Christ

18 My children, the end is near! You
were told that the Enemy of Christ
would come; and now many enemies of
Christ have already appeared, and so we
know that the end is near. 19 These people really did not belong to our fellowship, and that is why they left us; if they
had belonged to our fellowship, they
would have stayed with us. But they left
so that it might be clear that none of
them really belonged to us.
20 But you have had the Holy Spirit
poured out on you by Christ, and so all
of you know the truth. 21 I write you,
then, not because you do not know the
truth; instead, it is because you do know
it, and you also know that no lie ever
comes from the truth.
22 Who, then, is the liar? It is those who
say that Jesus is not the Messiah. Such
people are the Enemy of Christ—they
reject both the Father and the Son. 23 For
those who reject the Son reject also the

[b] someone else; *or* us.

Father; those who accept the Son have
the Father also.
24 Be sure, then, to keep in your hearts
the message you heard from the beginning. If you keep that message, then you
will always live in union with the Son
and the Father. 25 And this is what Christ
himself promised to give us—eternal
life.
26 I am writing this to you about those
who are trying to deceive you. 27 But as
for you, Christ has poured out his Spirit
on you. As long as his Spirit remains in
you, you do not need anyone to teach
you. For his Spirit teaches you about
everything, and what he teaches is true,
not false. Obey the Spirit's teaching,
then, and remain in union with Christ.
28 Yes, my children, remain in union
with him, so that when he appears we
may be full of courage and need not hide
in shame from him on the Day he comes.
29 You know that Christ is righteous; you
should know, then, that everyone who
does what is right is God's child.

Children of God

3 See how much the Father has loved
us! His love is so great that we are
called God's children—and so, in fact,
we are. This is why the world does not
know us: it has not known God. 2 My
dear friends, we are now God's children,
but it is not yet clear what we shall become. But we know that when Christ appears, we shall be like him, because we
shall see him as he really is. 3 Everyone
who has this hope in Christ keeps himself pure, just as Christ is pure.
4 Whoever sins is guilty of breaking
God's law, because sin is a breaking of
the law. 5 You know that Christ appeared in order to take away sins,[c] and
that there is no sin in him. 6 So everyone who lives in union with Christ does
not continue to sin; but whoever continues to sin has never seen him or known
him.
7 Let no one deceive you, my children!
Whoever does what is right is righteous,
just as Christ is righteous. 8 Whoever
continues to sin belongs to the Devil, because the Devil has sinned from the very
beginning. The Son of God appeared for
this very reason, to destroy what the
Devil had done.
9 Those who are children of God do not
continue to sin, for God's very nature is
in them; and because God is their
Father, they cannot continue to sin.
10 Here is the clear difference between
God's children and the Devil's children:
those who do not do what is right or do
not love others are not God's children.

Love One Another

11 The message you heard from the
very beginning is this: we must love one
another. 12 We must not be like Cain; he
belonged to the Evil One and murdered
his own brother Abel. Why did Cain
murder him? Because the things he himself did were wrong, and the things his
brother did were right.
13 So do not be surprised, my friends, if
the people of the world hate you. 14 We
know that we have left death and come
over into life; we know it because we
love others. Those who do not love are
still under the power of death. 15 Those
who hate others are murderers, and you
know that murderers do not have eternal life in them. 16 This is how we know
what love is: Christ gave his life for us.
We too, then, ought to give our lives for
others! 17 If we are rich and see others in
need, yet close our hearts against them,
how can we claim that we love God?
18 My children, our love should not be
just words and talk; it must be true love,
which shows itself in action.

Courage before God

19 This, then, is how we will know that
we belong to the truth; this is how we
will be confident in God's presence. 20 If
our conscience condemns us, we know
that God is greater than our conscience
and that he knows everything. 21 And so,
my dear friends, if our conscience does
not condemn us, we have courage in
God's presence. 22 We receive from him
whatever we ask, because we obey his
commands and do what pleases him.
23 What he commands is that we believe
in his Son Jesus Christ and love one another, just as Christ commanded us.
24 Those who obey God's commands live
in union with God and God lives in
union with them. And because of the
Spirit that God has given us we know
that God lives in union with us.

[c] sins; *some manuscripts have* our sins.

The True Spirit and the False Spirit

4 My dear friends, do not believe all
who claim to have the Spirit, but
test them to find out if the spirit they
have comes from God. For many false
prophets have gone out everywhere.
2 This is how you will be able to know
whether it is God's Spirit: anyone who
acknowledges that Jesus Christ came as
a human being has the Spirit who comes
from God. 3 But anyone who denies this
about Jesus does not have the Spirit
from God. The spirit that he has is from
the Enemy of Christ; you heard that it
would come, and now it is here in the
world already.
4 But you belong to God, my children,
and have defeated the false prophets,
because the Spirit who is in you is more
powerful than the spirit in those who belong to the world. 5 Those false prophets
speak about matters of the world, and
the world listens to them because they
belong to the world. 6 But we belong to
God. Whoever knows God listens to us;
whoever does not belong to God does
not listen to us. This, then, is how we can
tell the difference between the Spirit of
truth and the spirit of error.

God Is Love

7 Dear friends, let us love one another,
because love comes from God. Whoever
loves is a child of God and knows God.
8 Whoever does not love does not know
God, for God is love. 9 And God showed
his love for us by sending his only Son
into the world, so that we might have life
through him. 10 This is what love is: it is
not that we have loved God, but that he
loved us and sent his Son to be the
means by which our sins are forgiven.
11 Dear friends, if this is how God
loved us, then we should love one another. 12 No one has ever seen God, but if
we love one another, God lives in union
with us, and his love is made perfect
in us.
13 We are sure that we live in union
with God and that he lives in union with
us, because he has given us his Spirit.
14 And we have seen and tell others that
the Father sent his Son to be the Savior
of the world. 15 If we declare that Jesus is
the Son of God, we live in union with
God and God lives in union with us.
16 And we ourselves know and believe
the love which God has for us.
God is love, and those who live in love
live in union with God and God lives in
union with them. 17 Love is made perfect
in us in order that we may have courage
on the Judgment Day; and we will have
it because our life in this world is the
same as Christ's. 18 There is no fear in
love; perfect love drives out all fear. So
then, love has not been made perfect in
anyone who is afraid, because fear has
to do with punishment.
19 We love because God first loved us.
20 If we say we love God, but hate others,
we are liars. For we cannot love God,
whom we have not seen, if we do not
love others, whom we have seen. 21 The
command that Christ has given us is
this: whoever loves God must love others also.

Our Victory over the World

5 Whoever believes that Jesus is the
Messiah is a child of God; and whoever loves a father loves his child also.
2 This is how we know that we love
God's children: it is by loving God and
obeying his commands. 3 For our love for
God means that we obey his commands.
And his commands are not too hard for
us, 4 because every child of God is able to
defeat the world. And we win the victory
over the world by means of our faith.
5 Who can defeat the world? Only the
person who believes that Jesus is the
Son of God.

The Witness about Jesus Christ

6 Jesus Christ is the one who came
with the water of his baptism and the
blood of his death. He came not only
with the water, but with both the water
and the blood. And the Spirit himself
testifies that this is true, because the
Spirit is truth. 7 There are three witnesses: 8 the Spirit, the water, and the
blood; and all three give the same testimony. 9 We believe human testimony;
but God's testimony is much stronger,
and he has given this testimony about
his Son. 10 So those who believe in the
Son of God have this testimony in their
own heart; but those who do not believe

God, have made a liar of him, because
they have not believed what God has
said about his son. [11]The testimony is
this: God has given us eternal life, and
this life has its source in his Son. [12]Who-
ever has the Son has this life; whoever
does not have the Son of God does not
have life.

Eternal Life

[13]I am writing this to you so that you
may know that you have eternal life—
you that believe in the Son of God. [14]We
have courage in God's presence, because we are sure that he hears us if we
ask him for anything that is according to
his will. [15]He hears us whenever we ask
him; and since we know this is true, we
know also that he gives us what we ask
from him.

[16]If you see a believer commit a sin
that does not lead to death, you should
pray to God, who will give that person
life. This applies to those whose sins do
not lead to death. But there is sin which
leads to death, and I do not say that you
should pray to God about that. [17]All
wrongdoing is sin, but there is sin which
does not lead to death.

[18]We know that no children of God
keep on sinning, for the Son of God
keeps them safe, and the Evil One cannot harm them.

[19]We know that we belong to God
even though the whole world is under
the rule of the Evil One.

[20]We know that the Son of God has
come and has given us understanding,
so that we know the true God. We live in
union with the true God—in union with
his Son Jesus Christ. This is the true
God, and this is eternal life.

[21]My children, keep yourselves safe
from false gods!

The Second Letter of JOHN

Introduction

The Second Letter of John *was written by "the Elder" to "the dear Lady and to her children," probably meaning a local church and its members. The brief message is an appeal to love one another and a warning against false teachers and their teachings.*

Outline of Contents

Introduction 1-3
The primacy of love 4-6
Warning against false doctrine 7-11
Conclusion 12-13

---

[1]From the Elder—
To the dear Lady and to her children,[a] whom I truly love. And I am not
the only one, but all who know the truth
love you, [2]because the truth remains in
us and will be with us forever.

[3]May God the Father and Jesus Christ,
the Father's Son, give us grace, mercy,
and peace; may they be ours in truth and
love.

Truth and Love

[4]How happy I was to find that some of
your children live in the truth, just as the
Father commanded us. [5]And so I ask
you, dear Lady: let us all love one another. This is no new command I am
writing you; it is the command which we
have had from the beginning. [6]This love
I speak of means that we must live in
obedience to God's commands. The

[a] LADY AND . . . HER CHILDREN: *This probably refers to a church and its members (also in verses 4, 5).*

command, as you have all heard from
the beginning, is that you must all live in
love.
7 Many deceivers have gone out over
the world, people who do not acknowledge that Jesus Christ came as a human
being. Such a person is a deceiver and
the Enemy of Christ. 8 Be on your guard,
then, so that you will not lose what we[b]
have worked for, but will receive your
reward in full.
9 Anyone who does not stay with the
teaching of Christ, but goes beyond it,
does not have God. Whoever does stay
with the teaching has both the Father
and the Son. 10 So then, if some come to
you who do not bring this teaching, do
not welcome them in your homes; do not
even say, "Peace be with you." 11 For
anyone who wishes them peace becomes their partner in the evil things
they do.

Final Words

12 I have so much to tell you, but I
would rather not do it with paper and
ink; instead, I hope to visit you and talk
with you personally, so that we shall be
completely happy.
13 The children of your dear Sister[c]
send you their greetings.

[b] we; *some manuscripts have* you. [c] CHILDREN OF YOUR DEAR SISTER: *This probably refers to the members of the church to which the writer belonged.*

The Third Letter of JOHN

Introduction

The Third Letter of John *was written by "the Elder" to a church leader named Gaius. The writer praises Gaius because of his help to other Christians, and warns against a man named Diotrephes.*

Outline of Contents

Introduction 1-4
Gaius is praised 5-8
Diotrephes is condemned 9-10
Demetrius is commended 11-12
Conclusion 13-15

---

1 From the Elder—
To my dear Gaius, whom I truly love.
2 My dear friend, I pray that everything may go well with you and that you
may be in good health—as I know you
are well in spirit. 3 I was so happy when
some Christians arrived and told me
how faithful you are to the truth—just as
you always live in the truth. 4 Nothing
makes me happier than to hear that my
children live in the truth.

Gaius Is Praised

5 My dear friend, you are so faithful in
the work you do for other Christians,
even when they are strangers. 6 They
have spoken to the church here about
your love. Please help them to continue
their trip in a way that will please God.
7 For they set out on their trip in the service of Christ without accepting any help
from unbelievers. 8 We Christians, then,
must help these people, so that we may
share in their work for the truth.

Diotrephes and Demetrius

9 I wrote a short letter to the church;
but Diotrephes, who likes to be their
leader, will not pay any attention to
what I say. 10 When I come, then, I will

bring up everything he has done: the terrible things he says about us and the lies
he tells! But that is not enough for him;
he will not receive the Christians when
they come, and even stops those who
want to receive them and tries to drive
them out of the church!
11 My dear friend, do not imitate what
is bad, but imitate what is good. Whoever does good belongs to God; whoever
does what is bad has not seen God.
12 Everyone speaks well of Demetrius;
truth itself speaks well of him. And we
add our testimony, and you know that
what we say is true.

Final Greetings

13 I have so much to tell you, but I do
not want to do it with pen and ink.
14 I hope to see you soon, and then we
will talk personally.
15 Peace be with you.
All your friends send greetings. Greet
all our friends personally.

The Letter from JUDE

Introduction

The Letter from Jude *was written to warn against false teachers who claimed to be believers. In this brief letter, which is similar in content to* 2 Peter, *the writer encourages his readers "to fight on for the faith which once and for all God has given to his people."*

Outline of Contents

Introduction 1-2
Character, teaching, and doom of the false teachers 3-16
Admonition to keep the faith 17-23
Benediction 24-25

---

1 From Jude, servant of Jesus Christ,
and brother of James—
To those who have been called by
God, who live in the love of God the
Father and the protection of Jesus
Christ:
2 May mercy, peace, and love be yours
in full measure.

False Teachers

3 My dear friends, I was doing my best
to write to you about the salvation we
share in common, when I felt the need of
writing at once to encourage you to fight
on for the faith which once and for all
God has given to his people. 4 For some
godless people have slipped in unnoticed among us, persons who distort the
message about the grace of our God in
order to excuse their immoral ways, and
who reject Jesus Christ, our only Master
and Lord. Long ago the Scriptures predicted the condemnation they have
received.
5 For even though you know all this, I
want to remind you of how the Lord[a]
once rescued the people of Israel from
Egypt, but afterward destroyed those
who did not believe. 6 Remember the angels who did not stay within the limits of
their proper authority, but abandoned
their own dwelling place: they are
bound with eternal chains in the darkness below, where God is keeping them
for that great Day on which they will be
condemned. 7 Remember Sodom and
Gomorrah, and the nearby towns, whose
people acted as those angels did and in-
dulged in sexual immorality and perversion: they suffer the punishment of
eternal fire as a plain warning to all.
8 In the same way also, these people
have visions which make them sin

[a] the Lord; *some manuscripts have* Jesus, *which in Greek is the same as* Joshua.

against their own bodies; they despise God's authority and insult the glorious beings above. 9 Not even the chief angel Michael did this. In his quarrel with the Devil, when they argued about who would have the body of Moses, Michael did not dare condemn the Devil with insulting words, but said, "The Lord rebuke you!" 10 But these people attack with insults anything they do not understand; and those things that they know by instinct, like wild animals, are the very things that destroy them. 11 How terrible for them! They have followed the way that Cain took. For the sake of money they have given themselves over to the error that Balaam committed. They have rebelled as Korah rebelled, and like him they are destroyed. 12 With their shameless carousing they are like dirty spots in your fellowship meals. They take care only of themselves. They are like clouds carried along by the wind, but bringing no rain. They are like trees that bear no fruit, even in autumn, trees that have been pulled up by the roots and are completely dead. 13 They are like wild waves of the sea, with their shameful deeds showing up like foam. They are like wandering stars, for whom God has reserved a place forever in the deepest darkness.

14 It was Enoch, the seventh[b] direct descendant from Adam, who long ago prophesied this about them: "The Lord will come with many thousands of his holy angels 15 to bring judgment on all, to condemn them all for the godless deeds they have performed and for all the terrible words that godless sinners have spoken against him!"

16 These people are always grumbling and blaming others; they follow their own evil desires; they brag about themselves and flatter others in order to get their own way.

Warnings and Instructions

17 But remember, my friends, what you were told in the past by the apostles of our Lord Jesus Christ. 18 They said to you, "When the last days come, people will appear who will make fun of you, people who follow their own godless desires." 19 These are the people who cause divisions, who are controlled by their natural desires, who do not have the Spirit. 20 But you, my friends, keep on building yourselves up on your most sacred faith. Pray in the power of the Holy Spirit, 21 and keep yourselves in the love of God, as you wait for our Lord Jesus Christ in his mercy to give you eternal life.

22 Show mercy toward those who have doubts; 23 save others by snatching them out of the fire; and to others show mercy mixed with fear, but hate their very clothes, stained by their sinful lusts.

Prayer of Praise

24 To him who is able to keep you from falling and to bring you faultless and joyful before his glorious presence— 25 to the only God our Savior, through Jesus Christ our Lord, be glory, majesty, might, and authority, from all ages past, and now, and forever and ever! Amen.

[b] SEVENTH: *This numbering includes both the first and the last in the series of seven names from Adam to Enoch.*

THE REVELATION
to John

Introduction

The Revelation to John *was written at a time when Christians were being persecuted because of their faith in Jesus Christ as Lord. The writer's main concern is to give his readers hope and encouragement, and to urge them to remain faithful during times of suffering and persecution.*

For the most part the book consists of several series of revelations and visions presented in symbolic language that would have been understood by Christians of that day, but would have remained a mystery to all others. As with the themes of a symphony, the themes of this book are repeated again and again in different ways through the various series of visions. Although there are differences of opinion regarding the details of interpretation of the book, the central theme is clear: through Christ the Lord, God will finally and totally defeat all of his enemies, including Satan, and will reward his faithful people with the blessings of a new heaven and a new earth when this victory is complete.

Outline of Contents

Introduction 1.1-8
Opening vision and the letters to the seven churches 1.9–3.22
The scroll with seven seals 4.1–8.1
The seven trumpets 8.2–11.19
The dragon and the two beasts 12.1–13.18
Various visions 14.1–15.8
The seven bowls of God's anger 16.1-21
The destruction of Babylon, and the defeat of the beast, the false prophet, and the Devil 17.1–20.10
The final judgment 20.11-15
The new heaven, the new earth, the new Jerusalem 21.1–22.5
Conclusion 22.6-21

---

1 This book is the record of the events
that Jesus Christ revealed. God
gave him this revelation in order to
show to his servants what must happen
very soon. Christ made these things
known to his servant John by sending
his angel to him, 2 and John has told all
that he has seen. This is his report concerning the message from God and the
truth revealed by Jesus Christ. 3 Happy
is the one who reads this book, and
happy are those who listen to the words
of this prophetic message and obey what
is written in this book! For the time is
near when all these things will happen.

Greetings to the Seven Churches

4 From John to the seven churches in
the province of Asia:

Grace and peace be yours from God,
who is, who was, and who is to come,
and from the seven spirits in front of his
throne, 5 and from Jesus Christ, the
faithful witness, the first to be raised
from death and who is also the ruler of
the kings of the world.

He loves us, and by his sacrificial
death he has freed us from our sins 6 and
made us a kingdom of priests to serve
his God and Father. To Jesus Christ be
the glory and power forever and ever!
Amen.

7 Look, he is coming on the clouds!
Everyone will see him, including those
who pierced him. All peoples on earth
will mourn over him. So shall it be!

8 "I am the first and the last," says the
Lord God Almighty, who is, who was,
and who is to come.

A Vision of Christ

9 I am John, your brother, and as a follower of Jesus I am your partner in patiently enduring the suffering that comes
to those who belong to his Kingdom. I
was put on the island of Patmos because
I had proclaimed God's word and the
truth that Jesus revealed. 10 On the

Lord's day the Spirit took control of me,
and I heard a loud voice, that sounded
like a trumpet, speaking behind me. 11 It
said, "Write down what you see, and
send the book to the churches in these
seven cities: Ephesus, Smyrna, Pergamum, Thyatira, Sardis, Philadelphia,
and Laodicea."
12 I turned around to see who was talking to me, and I saw seven gold lampstands, 13 and among them there was
what looked like a human being, wearing a robe that reached to his feet, and a
gold band around his chest. 14 His hair
was white as wool, or as snow, and his
eyes blazed like fire; 15 his feet shone
like brass that has been refined and polished, and his voice sounded like a roaring waterfall. 16 He held seven stars in
his right hand, and a sharp two-edged
sword came out of his mouth. His face
was as bright as the midday sun.
17 When I saw him, I fell down at his feet
like a dead man. He placed his right
hand on me and said, "Don't be afraid! I
am the first and the last. 18 I am the living one! I was dead, but now I am alive
forever and ever. I have authority over
death and the world of the dead.
19 Write, then, the things you see, both
the things that are now and the things
that will happen afterward. 20 Here is the
secret meaning of the seven stars that
you see in my right hand, and of the
seven gold lampstands: the seven stars
are the angels of the seven churches,
and the seven lampstands are the seven
churches.

The Message to Ephesus

2 "To the angel of the church in Ephesus write:
"This is the message from the one who
holds the seven stars in his right hand
and who walks among the seven gold
lampstands. 2 I know what you have
done; I know how hard you have
worked and how patient you have been.
I know that you cannot tolerate evil people and that you have tested those who
say they are apostles but are not, and
have found out that they are liars. 3 You
are patient, you have suffered for my
sake, and you have not given up. 4 But
this is what I have against you: you do
not love me now as you did at first.
5 Think how far you have fallen! Turn
from your sins and do what you did at
first. If you don't turn from your sins, I
will come to you and take your lampstand from its place. 6 But this is what
you have in your favor: you hate what
the Nicolaitans do, as much as I do.
7 "If you have ears, then, listen to what
the Spirit says to the churches!
"To those who win the victory I will
give the right to eat the fruit of the tree
of life that grows in the Garden of God.

The Message to Smyrna

8 "To the angel of the church in
Smyrna write:
"This is the message from the one who
is the first and the last, who died and
lived again. 9 I know your troubles; I
know that you are poor—but really you
are rich! I know the evil things said
against you by those who claim to be
Jews but are not; they are a group that
belongs to Satan! 10 Don't be afraid of
anything you are about to suffer. Listen!
The Devil will put you to the test by having some of you thrown into prison, and
your troubles will last ten days. Be faithful to me, even if it means death, and I
will give you life as your prize of victory.
11 "If you have ears, then, listen to
what the Spirit says to the churches!
"Those who win the victory will not be
hurt by the second death.

The Message to Pergamum

12 "To the angel of the church in Pergamum write:
"This is the message from the one
who has the sharp two-edged sword.
13 I know where you live, there where
Satan has his throne. You are true to me,
and you did not abandon your faith in
me even during the time when Antipas,
my faithful witness, was killed there
where Satan lives. 14 But there are a few
things I have against you: there are
some among you who follow the teaching of Balaam, who taught Balak how to
lead the people of Israel into sin by per-
suading them to eat food that had been
offered to idols and to practice sexual
immorality. 15 In the same way you have
people among you who follow the teaching of the Nicolaitans. 16 Now turn from
your sins! If you don't, I will come to you
soon and fight against those people with
the sword that comes out of my mouth.

17 "If you have ears, then, listen to
what the Spirit says to the churches!
"To those who win the victory I will
give some of the hidden manna. I will
also give each of them a white stone on
which is written a new name that no one
knows except the one who receives it.

The Message to Thyatira

18 "To the angel of the church in Thyatira write:
"This is the message from the Son of
God, whose eyes blaze like fire, whose
feet shine like polished brass. 19 I know
what you do. I know your love, your
faithfulness, your service, and your patience. I know that you are doing more
now than you did at first. 20 But this is
what I have against you: you tolerate
that woman Jezebel, who calls herself a
messenger of God. By her teaching she
misleads my servants into practicing
sexual immorality and eating food that
has been offered to idols. 21 I have given
her time to repent of her sins, but she
does not want to turn from her immorality. 22 And so I will throw her on a bed
where she and those who committed
adultery with her will suffer terribly. I
will do this now unless they repent of the
wicked things they did with her. 23 I will
also kill her followers, and then all the
churches will know that I am the one
who knows everyone's thoughts and
wishes. I will repay each of you according to what you have done.
24 "But the rest of you in Thyatira have
not followed this evil teaching; you have
not learned what the others call 'the
deep secrets of Satan.' I say to you that
I will not put any other burden on you.
25 But until I come, you must hold firmly
to what you have. 26-28 To those who win
the victory, who continue to the end to
do what I want, I will give the same authority that I received from my Father: I
will give them authority over the nations, to rule them with an iron rod and
to break them to pieces like clay pots. I
will also give them the morning star.
29 "If you have ears, then, listen to
what the Spirit says to the churches!

The Message to Sardis

3 "To the angel of the church in Sardis write:
"This is the message from the one who
has the seven spirits of God and the
seven stars. I know what you are doing;
I know that you have the reputation of
being alive, even though you are dead!
2 So wake up, and strengthen what you
still have before it dies completely. For I
find that what you have done is not yet
perfect in the sight of my God. 3 Remember, then, what you were taught and
what you heard; obey it and turn from
your sins. If you do not wake up, I will
come upon you like a thief, and you will
not even know the time when I will
come. 4 But a few of you there in Sardis
have kept your clothes clean. You will
walk with me, clothed in white, because
you are worthy to do so. 5 Those who win
the victory will be clothed like this in
white, and I will not remove their names
from the book of the living. In the presence of my Father and of his angels I will
declare openly that they belong to me.
6 "If you have ears, then, listen to what
the Spirit says to the churches!

The Message to Philadelphia

7 "To the angel of the church in Philadelphia write:
"This is the message from the one who
is holy and true. He has the key that belonged to David, and when he opens a
door, no one can close it, and when he
closes it, no one can open it. 8 I know
what you do; I know that you have a little power; you have followed my teaching and have been faithful to me. I have
opened a door in front of you, which no
one can close. 9 Listen! As for that group
that belongs to Satan, those liars who
claim that they are Jews but are not, I
will make them come and bow down at
your feet. They will all know that I love
you. 10 Because you have kept my command to endure, I will also keep you safe
from the time of trouble which is coming
upon the world to test all the people on
earth. 11 I am coming soon. Keep safe
what you have, so that no one will rob
you of your victory prize. 12 I will make
those who are victorious pillars in the
temple of my God, and they will never
leave it. I will write on them the name
of my God and the name of the city
of my God, the new Jerusalem, which
will come down out of heaven from my
God. I will also write on them my new
name.
13 "If you have ears, then, listen to
what the Spirit says to the churches!

The Message to Laodicea

14“To the angel of the church in Laodicea write:
“This is the message from the Amen,
the faithful and true witness, who is the
origin[a] of all that God has created.
15I know what you have done; I know
that you are neither cold nor hot. How I
wish you were either one or the other!
16But because you are lukewarm, neither hot nor cold, I am going to spit you
out of my mouth! 17You say, ‘I am rich
and well off; I have all I need.’ But you
do not know how miserable and pitiful
you are! You are poor, naked, and blind.
18I advise you, then, to buy gold from
me, pure gold, in order to be rich. Buy
also white clothing to dress yourself and
cover up your shameful nakedness. Buy
also some ointment to put on your eyes,
so that you may see. 19I rebuke and punish all whom I love. Be in earnest, then,
and turn from your sins. 20Listen! I
stand at the door and knock; if any hear
my voice and open the door, I will come
into their house and eat with them, and
they will eat with me. 21To those who
win the victory I will give the right to sit
beside me on my throne, just as I have
been victorious and now sit by my
Father on his throne.
22“If you have ears, then, listen to
what the Spirit says to the churches!”

Worship in Heaven

4 At this point I had another vision
and saw an open door in heaven.
And the voice that sounded like a
trumpet, which I had heard speaking to
me before, said, “Come up here, and I
will show you what must happen after
this.” 2At once the Spirit took control of
me. There in heaven was a throne with
someone sitting on it. 3His face gleamed
like such precious stones as jasper and
carnelian, and all around the throne
there was a rainbow the color of an emerald. 4In a circle around the throne
were twenty-four other thrones, on
which were seated twenty-four elders
dressed in white and wearing crowns of
gold. 5From the throne came flashes of
lightning, rumblings, and peals of thunder. In front of the throne seven lighted
torches were burning, which are the
seven spirits of God. 6Also in front of the
throne there was what looked like a sea
of glass, clear as crystal.
Surrounding the throne on each of its
sides, were four living creatures covered
with eyes in front and behind. 7The first
one looked like a lion; the second looked
like a bull; the third had a face like a
human face; and the fourth looked like
an eagle in flight. 8Each one of the four
living creatures had six wings, and they
were covered with eyes, inside and out.
Day and night they never stop singing:

“Holy, holy, holy, is the Lord God
Almighty,
who was, who is, and who is to
come.”

9The four living creatures sing songs
of glory and honor and thanks to the one
who sits on the throne, who lives forever
and ever. When they do so, 10the twenty-
four elders fall down before the one who
sits on the throne, and worship him who
lives forever and ever. They throw their
crowns down in front of the throne
and say,

11“Our Lord and God! You are
worthy
to receive glory, honor, and
power.
For you created all things,
and by your will they were
given existence and life.”

The Scroll and the Lamb

5 I saw a scroll in the right hand of
the one who sits on the throne; it
was covered with writing on both sides
and was sealed with seven seals. 2And I
saw a mighty angel, who announced in a
loud voice, “Who is worthy to break the
seals and open the scroll?” 3But there
was no one in heaven or on earth or in
the world below[b] who could open the
scroll and look inside it. 4I cried bitterly
because no one could be found who was
worthy to open the scroll or look inside
it. 5Then one of the elders said to me,
“Don’t cry. Look! The Lion from Judah’s
tribe, the great descendant of David, has
won the victory, and he can break the
seven seals and open the scroll.”
6Then I saw a Lamb standing in the
center of the throne, surrounded by the
four living creatures and the elders. The
Lamb appeared to have been killed. It
had seven horns and seven eyes, which

[a] origin; *or* ruler. [b] WORLD BELOW: *The world of the dead (see 1.18).*

are the seven spirits of God that have
been sent through the whole earth. 7 The
Lamb went and took the scroll from the
right hand of the one who sits on the
throne. 8 As he did so, the four living
creatures and the twenty-four elders fell
down before the Lamb. Each had a harp
and gold bowls filled with incense,
which are the prayers of God's people.
9 They sang a new song:

"You are worthy to take the scroll
and to break open its seals.
For you were killed, and by your
sacrificial death you bought
for God
people from every tribe,
language, nation, and race.
10 You have made them a kingdom
of priests to serve our God,
and they shall rule on earth."

11 Again I looked, and I heard angels,
thousands and millions of them! They
stood around the throne, the four living
creatures, and the elders, 12 and sang in a
loud voice:

"The Lamb who was killed is
worthy
to receive power, wealth,
wisdom, and strength,
honor, glory, and praise!"

13 And I heard every creature in heaven,
on earth, in the world below, and in the
sea—all living beings in the universe—
and they were singing:

"To him who sits on the throne
and to the Lamb,
be praise and honor, glory and
might,
forever and ever!"

14 The four living creatures answered,
"Amen!" And the elders fell down and
worshiped.

The Seals

6 Then I saw the Lamb break open
the first of the seven seals, and I
heard one of the four living creatures
say in a voice that sounded like thunder,
"Come!" 2 I looked, and there was a
white horse. Its rider held a bow, and he
was given a crown. He rode out as a conqueror to conquer.

3 Then the Lamb broke open the second seal; and I heard the second living
creature say, "Come!" 4 Another horse
came out, a red one. Its rider was given
the power to bring war on the earth, so
that people should kill each other. He
was given a large sword.

5 Then the Lamb broke open the third
seal; and I heard the third living creature
say, "Come!" I looked, and there was a
black horse. Its rider held a pair of
scales in his hand. 6 I heard what
sounded like a voice coming from
among the four living creatures, which
said, "A quart of wheat for a day's
wages, and three quarts of barley for a
day's wages. But do not damage the olive trees and the vineyards!"

7 Then the Lamb broke open the fourth
seal; and I heard the fourth living creature say, "Come!" 8 I looked, and there
was a pale-colored horse. Its rider was
named Death, and Hades[c] followed
close behind. They were given authority
over one fourth of the earth, to kill by
means of war, famine, disease, and wild
animals.

9 Then the Lamb broke open the fifth
seal. I saw underneath the altar the souls
of those who had been killed because
they had proclaimed God's word and
had been faithful in their witnessing.
10 They shouted in a loud voice,
"Almighty Lord, holy and true! How
long will it be until you judge the people
on earth and punish them for killing us?"
11 Each of them was given a white robe,
and they were told to rest a little while
longer, until the complete number of
other servants and believers were killed,
as they had been.

12 And I saw the Lamb break open the
sixth seal. There was a violent earthquake, and the sun became black like
coarse black cloth, and the moon turned
completely red like blood. 13 The stars
fell down to the earth, like unripe figs
falling from the tree when a strong wind
shakes it. 14 The sky disappeared like a
scroll being rolled up, and every mountain and island was moved from its
place. 15 Then the kings of the earth, the
rulers and the military chiefs, the rich
and the powerful, and all other people,
slave and free, hid themselves in caves
and under rocks on the mountains.
16 They called out to the mountains and
to the rocks, "Fall on us and hide us from
the eyes of the one who sits on the
throne and from the anger of the Lamb!

[c] HADES: *The world of the dead (see 1.18).*

17 The terrible day of their anger is here,
and who can stand up against it?"

The 144,000 People of Israel

7 After this I saw four angels standing at the four corners of the earth, holding back the four winds so that no wind should blow on the earth or the sea or against any tree.
2 And I saw another angel coming up from the east with the seal of the living God. He called out in a loud voice to the four angels to whom God had given the power to damage the earth and the sea.
3 The angel said, "Do not harm the earth, the sea, or the trees, until we mark the servants of our God with a seal on their foreheads."
4 And I was told that the number of those who were marked with God's seal on their foreheads was 144,000. They were from the twelve tribes of Israel,
5-8 twelve thousand from each tribe: Judah, Reuben, Gad, Asher, Naphtali, Manasseh, Simeon, Levi, Issachar, Zebulun, Joseph, and Benjamin.

The Enormous Crowd

9 After this I looked, and there was an enormous crowd—no one could count all the people! They were from every race, tribe, nation, and language, and they stood in front of the throne and of the Lamb, dressed in white robes and holding palm branches in their hands.
10 They called out in a loud voice: "Salvation comes from our God, who sits on the throne, and from the Lamb!"
11 All the angels stood around the throne, the elders, and the four living creatures. Then they threw themselves face downward in front of the throne and worshiped God,
12 saying, "Amen! Praise, glory, wisdom, thanksgiving, honor, power, and might belong to our God forever and ever! Amen!"

13 One of the elders asked me, "Who are these people dressed in white robes, and where do they come from?"

14 "I don't know, sir. You do," I answered.

He said to me, "These are the people who have come safely through the terrible persecution. They have washed their robes and made them white with the blood of the Lamb.
15 That is why they stand before God's throne and serve him day and night in his temple. He who sits on the throne will protect them with his presence.
16 Never again will they hunger or thirst; neither sun nor any scorching heat will burn them,
17 because the Lamb, who is in the center of the throne, will be their shepherd, and he will guide them to springs of life-giving water. And God will wipe away every tear from their eyes."

The Seventh Seal

8 When the Lamb broke open the seventh seal, there was silence in heaven for about half an hour.
2 Then I saw the seven angels who stand before God, and they were given seven trumpets.

3 Another angel, who had a gold incense container, came and stood at the altar. He was given a lot of incense to add to the prayers of all God's people and to offer it on the gold altar that stands before the throne.
4 The smoke of the burning incense went up with the prayers of God's people from the hands of the angel standing before God.
5 Then the angel took the incense container, filled it with fire from the altar, and threw it on the earth. There were rumblings and peals of thunder, flashes of lightning, and an earthquake.

The Trumpets

6 Then the seven angels with the seven trumpets prepared to blow them.

7 The first angel blew his trumpet. Hail and fire, mixed with blood, came pouring down on the earth. A third of the earth was burned up, a third of the trees, and every blade of green grass.

8 Then the second angel blew his trumpet. Something that looked like a huge mountain on fire was thrown into the sea. A third of the sea was turned into blood,
9 a third of the living creatures in the sea died, and a third of the ships were destroyed.

10 Then the third angel blew his trumpet. A large star, burning like a torch, dropped from the sky and fell on a third of the rivers and on the springs of water.
11 (The name of the star is "Bitterness.") A third of the water turned bitter, and many people died from drinking the water, because it had turned bitter.

12 Then the fourth angel blew his trumpet. A third of the sun was struck, and a third of the moon, and a third of the stars, so that their light lost a third of its

brightness; there was no light during a
third of the day and a third of the night
also.

13 Then I looked, and I heard an eagle
that was flying high in the air say in a
loud voice, "O horror! horror! How horrible it will be for all who live on earth
when the sound comes from the trumpets that the other three angels must
blow!"

9 Then the fifth angel blew his trumpet. I saw a star which had fallen
down to the earth, and it was given the
key to the abyss.[d] 2 The star opened the
abyss, and smoke poured out of it, like
the smoke from a large furnace; the sunlight and the air were darkened by the
smoke from the abyss. 3 Locusts came
down out of the smoke upon the earth,
and they were given the same kind of
power that scorpions have. 4 They were
told not to harm the grass or the trees or
any other plant; they could harm only
the people who did not have the mark of
God's seal on their foreheads. 5 The locusts were not allowed to kill these people, but only to torture them for five
months. The pain caused by the torture
is like the pain caused by a scorpion's
sting. 6 During those five months they
will seek death, but will not find it; they
will want to die, but death will flee from
them.

7 The locusts looked like horses ready
for battle; on their heads they had what
seemed to be crowns of gold, and their
faces were like human faces. 8 Their hair
was like women's hair, their teeth were
like lions' teeth. 9 Their chests were covered with what looked like iron breastplates, and the sound made by their
wings was like the noise of many horse-
drawn chariots rushing into battle.
10 They have tails and stings like those of
a scorpion, and it is with their tails that
they have the power to hurt people for
five months. 11 They have a king ruling
over them, who is the angel in charge of
the abyss. His name in Hebrew is Abad-
don; in Greek the name is Apollyon
(meaning "The Destroyer").

12 The first horror is over; after this
there are still two more horrors to come.

13 Then the sixth angel blew his trumpet. I heard a voice coming from the four
corners of the gold altar standing before
God. 14 The voice said to the sixth angel,
"Release the four angels who are bound
at the great Euphrates River!" 15 The four
angels were released; for this very hour
of this very day of this very month and
year they had been kept ready to kill a
third of all the human race. 16 I was told
the number of the mounted troops: it
was two hundred million. 17 And in my
vision I saw the horses and their riders:
they had breastplates red as fire, blue as
sapphire, and yellow as sulfur. The
horses' heads were like lions' heads, and
from their mouths came out fire, smoke,
and sulfur. 18 A third of the human race
was killed by those three plagues: the
fire, the smoke, and the sulfur coming
out of the horses' mouths. 19 For the
power of the horses is in their mouths
and also in their tails. Their tails are like
snakes with heads, and they use them to
hurt people.

20 The rest of the human race, all those
who had not been killed by these
plagues, did not turn away from what
they themselves had made. They did not
stop worshiping demons, nor the idols of
gold, silver, bronze, stone, and wood,
which cannot see, hear, or walk. 21 Nor
did they repent of their murders, their
magic, their sexual immorality, or their
stealing.

The Angel and the Little Scroll

10 Then I saw another mighty angel
coming down out of heaven. He
was wrapped in a cloud and had a rainbow around his head; his face was like
the sun, and his legs were like columns
of fire. 2 He had a small scroll open in his
hand. He put his right foot on the sea
and his left foot on the land, 3 and called
out in a loud voice that sounded like the
roar of lions. After he had called out, the
seven thunders answered with a roar.
4 As soon as they spoke, I was about to
write. But I heard a voice speak from
heaven, "Keep secret what the seven
thunders have said; do not write it
down!"

5 Then the angel that I saw standing on
the sea and on the land raised his right
hand to heaven 6 and took a vow in the
name of God, who lives forever and

d ABYSS: *The place in the depths of the earth where the demons were imprisoned until their final punishment.*

ever, who created heaven, earth, and the
sea, and everything in them. The angel
said, "There will be no more delay! 7 But
when the seventh angel blows his trumpet, then God will accomplish his secret
plan, as he announced to his servants,
the prophets."

8 Then the voice that I had heard
speaking from heaven spoke to me
again, saying, "Go and take the open
scroll which is in the hand of the angel
standing on the sea and on the land."

9 I went to the angel and asked him to
give me the little scroll. He said to me,
"Take it and eat it; it will turn sour in
your stomach, but in your mouth it will
be sweet as honey."

10 I took the little scroll from his hand
and ate it, and it tasted sweet as honey in
my mouth. But after I swallowed it, it
turned sour in my stomach. 11 Then I was
told, "Once again you must proclaim
God's message about many nations,
races, languages, and kings."

The Two Witnesses

11 I was then given a stick that
looked like a measuring-rod, and
was told, "Go and measure the temple of
God and the altar, and count those who
are worshiping in the temple. 2 But do
not measure the outer courts, because
they have been given to the heathen,
who will trample on the Holy City for
forty-two months. 3 I will send my two
witnesses dressed in sackcloth, and they
will proclaim God's message during
those 1,260 days."

4 The two witnesses are the two olive
trees and the two lamps that stand before the Lord of the earth. 5 If anyone
tries to harm them, fire comes out of
their mouths and destroys their enemies; and in this way whoever tries to
harm them will be killed. 6 They have authority to shut up the sky so that there
will be no rain during the time they proclaim God's message. They have authority also over the springs of water, to turn
them into blood; they have authority
also to strike the earth with every kind
of plague as often as they wish.

7 When they finish proclaiming their
message, the beast that comes up out of
the abyss will fight against them. He will
defeat them and kill them, 8 and their
bodies will lie in the street of the great
city, where their Lord was crucified. The
symbolic name of that city is Sodom, or
Egypt. 9 People from all nations, tribes,
languages, and races will look at their
bodies for three and a half days and will
not allow them to be buried. 10 The people of the earth will be happy because of
the death of these two. They will celebrate and send presents to each other,
because those two prophets brought
much suffering upon the whole human
race. 11 After three and a half days a life-
giving breath came from God and entered them, and they stood up; and all
who saw them were terrified. 12 Then the
two prophets heard a loud voice say to
them from heaven, "Come up here!" As
their enemies watched, they went up
into heaven in a cloud. 13 At that very
moment there was a violent earthquake;
a tenth of the city was destroyed, and
seven thousand people were killed. The
rest of the people were terrified and
praised the greatness of the God of
heaven.

14 The second horror is over, but the
third horror will come soon!

The Seventh Trumpet

15 Then the seventh angel blew his
trumpet, and there were loud voices in
heaven, saying, "The power to rule over
the world belongs now to our Lord and
his Messiah, and he will rule forever and
ever!" 16 Then the twenty-four elders
who sit on their thrones in front of God
threw themselves face downward and
worshiped God, 17 saying:

"Lord God Almighty, the one who
is and who was!
We thank you that you have taken
your great power
and have begun to rule!
18 The heathen were filled with rage,
because the time for your anger
has come,
the time for the dead to be
judged.
The time has come to reward your
servants, the prophets,
and all your people, all who
have reverence for you,
great and small alike.
The time has come to destroy
those who destroy the earth!"

19 God's temple in heaven was opened,
and the Covenant Box was seen there.
Then there were flashes of lightning,

rumblings and peals of thunder, an
earthquake, and heavy hail.

The Woman and the Dragon

12 Then a great and mysterious
sight appeared in the sky. There
was a woman, whose dress was the sun
and who had the moon under her feet
and a crown of twelve stars on her head.
2 She was soon to give birth, and the
pains and suffering of childbirth made
her cry out.
3 Another mysterious sight appeared
in the sky. There was a huge red dragon
with seven heads and ten horns and a
crown on each of his heads. 4 With his
tail he dragged a third of the stars out of
the sky and threw them down to the
earth. He stood in front of the woman, in
order to eat her child as soon as it was
born. 5 Then she gave birth to a son, who
will rule over all nations with an iron
rod. But the child was snatched away
and taken to God and his throne. 6 The
woman fled to the desert, to a place God
had prepared for her, where she will be
taken care of for 1,260 days.
7 Then war broke out in heaven. Michael and his angels fought against the
dragon, who fought back with his angels; 8 but the dragon was defeated, and
he and his angels were not allowed to
stay in heaven any longer. 9 The huge
dragon was thrown out—that ancient
serpent, named the Devil, or Satan, that
deceived the whole world. He was
thrown down to earth, and all his angels
with him.
10 Then I heard a loud voice in heaven
saying, "Now God's salvation has come!
Now God has shown his power as King!
Now his Messiah has shown his authority! For the one who stood before our
God and accused believers day and
night has been thrown out of heaven.
11 They won the victory over him by the
blood of the Lamb and by the truth
which they proclaimed; and they were
willing to give up their lives and die.
12 And so be glad, you heavens, and all
you that live there! But how terrible for
the earth and the sea! For the Devil has
come down to you, and he is filled with
rage, because he knows that he has only
a little time left."
13 When the dragon realized that he
had been thrown down to the earth, he
began to pursue the woman who had
given birth to the boy. 14 She was given
the two wings of a large eagle in order to
fly to her place in the desert, where she
will be taken care of for three and a half
years, safe from the dragon's attack.
15 And then from his mouth the dragon
poured out a flood of water after the
woman, so that it would carry her away.
16 But the earth helped the woman; it
opened its mouth and swallowed the water that had come from the dragon's
mouth. 17 The dragon was furious with
the woman and went off to fight against
the rest of her descendants, all those
who obey God's commandments and are
faithful to the truth revealed by Jesus.
18 And the dragon stood[e] on the seashore.

The Two Beasts

13 Then I saw a beast coming up
out of the sea. It had ten horns
and seven heads; on each of its horns
there was a crown, and on each of its
heads there was a name that was insulting to God. 2 The beast looked like a
leopard, with feet like a bear's feet and a
mouth like a lion's mouth. The dragon
gave the beast his own power, his
throne, and his vast authority. 3 One of
the heads of the beast seemed to have
been fatally wounded, but the wound
had healed. The whole earth was
amazed and followed the beast. 4 Everyone worshiped the dragon because he
had given his authority to the beast.
They worshiped the beast also, saying,
"Who is like the beast? Who can fight
against it?"
5 The beast was allowed to make
proud claims which were insulting to
God, and it was permitted to have authority for forty-two months. 6 It began
to curse God, his name, the place where
he lives, and all those who live in
heaven. 7 It was allowed to fight against
God's people and to defeat them, and it
was given authority over every tribe, nation, language, and race. 8 All people living on earth will worship it, except those
whose names were written before the
creation of the world in the book of the

[e] And the dragon stood; *some manuscripts have* And I stood, *connecting this verse with what follows.*

living which belongs to the Lamb that
was killed.
9 “Listen, then, if you have ears!
10 Whoever is meant to be captured will
surely be captured; whoever is meant to
be killed by the sword will surely be
killed by the sword. This calls for endurance and faith on the part of God's
people.”
11 Then I saw another beast, which
came up out of the earth. It had two
horns like a lamb's horns, and it spoke
like a dragon. 12 It used the vast authority of the first beast in its presence. It
forced the earth and all who live on it to
worship the first beast, whose wound
had healed. 13 This second beast performed great miracles; it made fire come
down out of heaven to earth in the sight
of everyone. 14 And it deceived all the
people living on earth by means of the
miracles which it was allowed to perform in the presence of the first beast.
The beast told them to build an image in
honor of the beast that had been
wounded by the sword and yet lived.
15 The second beast was allowed to
breathe life into the image of the first
beast, so that the image could talk and
put to death all those who would not
worship it. 16 The beast forced all the
people, small and great, rich and poor,
slave and free, to have a mark placed on
their right hands or on their foreheads.
17 No one could buy or sell without this
mark, that is, the beast's name or the
number that stands for the name.
18 This calls for wisdom. Whoever is
intelligent can figure out the meaning of
the number of the beast, because the
number stands for the name of someone.
Its number is 666.

The Lamb and His People

14 Then I looked, and there was the
Lamb standing on Mount Zion;
with him were 144,000 people who have
his name and his Father's name written
on their foreheads. 2 And I heard a voice
from heaven that sounded like a roaring
waterfall, like a loud peal of thunder. It
sounded like the music made by musicians playing their harps. 3 The 144,000
people stood before the throne, the four
living creatures, and the elders; they
were singing a new song, which only
they could learn. Of the whole human
race they are the only ones who have
been redeemed. 4 They are the men who
have kept themselves pure by not having sexual relations with women; they
are virgins. They follow the Lamb wherever he goes. They have been redeemed
from the rest of the human race and are
the first ones to be offered to God and to
the Lamb. 5 They have never been
known to tell lies; they are faultless.

The Three Angels

6 Then I saw another angel flying high
in the air, with an eternal message of
Good News to announce to the peoples
of the earth, to every race, tribe, language, and nation. 7 He said in a loud
voice, “Honor God and praise his greatness! For the time has come for him to
judge all people. Worship him who
made heaven, earth, sea, and the springs
of water!”
8 A second angel followed the first one,
saying, “She has fallen! Great Babylon
has fallen! She made all peoples drink
her wine—the strong wine of her immoral lust!”
9 A third angel followed the first two,
saying in a loud voice, “Those who worship the beast and its image and receive
the mark on their forehead or on their
hand 10 will themselves drink God's
wine, the wine of his fury, which he has
poured at full strength into the cup of his
anger! All who do this will be tormented
in fire and sulfur before the holy angels
and the Lamb. 11 The smoke of the fire
that torments them goes up forever and
ever. There is no relief day or night for
those who worship the beast and its image, for anyone who has the mark of its
name.”
12 This calls for endurance on the part
of God's people, those who obey God's
commandments and are faithful to
Jesus.
13 Then I heard a voice from heaven
saying, “Write this: Happy are those
who from now on die in the service of
the Lord!”

“Yes indeed!” answers the Spirit.
“They will enjoy rest from their hard
work, because the results of their service
go with them.”

The Harvest of the Earth

14 Then I looked, and there was a white
cloud, and sitting on the cloud was what
looked like a human being, with a crown

of gold on his head and a sharp sickle in
his hand. 15 Then another angel came out
from the temple and cried out in a loud
voice to the one who was sitting on the
cloud, "Use your sickle and reap the harvest, because the time has come; the
earth is ripe for the harvest!" 16 Then the
one who sat on the cloud swung his
sickle on the earth, and the earth's harvest was reaped.

17 Then I saw another angel come out
of the temple in heaven, and he also had
a sharp sickle.

18 Then another angel, who is in
charge of the fire, came from the altar.
He shouted in a loud voice to the angel
who had the sharp sickle, "Use your
sickle, and cut the grapes from the vineyard of the earth, because the grapes are
ripe!" 19 So the angel swung his sickle on
the earth, cut the grapes from the vine,
and threw them into the wine press of
God's furious anger. 20 The grapes were
squeezed out in the wine press outside
the city, and blood came out of the wine
press in a flood two hundred miles long
and about five feet deep.

The Angels with the Last Plagues

15 Then I saw in the sky another
mysterious sight, great and
amazing. There were seven angels with
seven plagues, which are the last ones,
because they are the final expression of
God's anger.

2 Then I saw what looked like a sea of
glass mixed with fire. I also saw those
who had won the victory over the beast
and its image and over the one whose
name is represented by a number. They
were standing by the sea of glass, holding harps that God had given them 3 and
singing the song of Moses, the servant of
God, and the song of the Lamb:

"Lord God Almighty,
how great and wonderful are
your deeds!
King of the nations,[f]
how right and true are your
ways!
4 Who will not stand in awe of you,
Lord?
Who will refuse to declare your
greatness?
You alone are holy.
All the nations will come
and worship you,
because your just actions are
seen by all."

5 After this I saw the temple in heaven
open, with the Sacred Tent in it. 6 The
seven angels who had the seven plagues
came out of the temple, dressed in clean
shining linen and with gold bands tied
around their chests. 7 Then one of the
four living creatures gave the seven angels seven gold bowls full of the anger of
God, who lives forever and ever. 8 The
temple was filled with smoke from the
glory and power of God, and no one
could go into the temple until the seven
plagues brought by the seven angels had
come to an end.

The Bowls of God's Anger

16 Then I heard a loud voice speaking from the temple to the seven
angels: "Go and pour out the seven
bowls of God's anger on the earth!"

2 The first angel went and poured out
his bowl on the earth. Terrible and painful sores appeared on those who had the
mark of the beast and on those who had
worshiped its image.

3 Then the second angel poured out his
bowl on the sea. The water became like
the blood of a dead person, and every
living creature in the sea died.

4 Then the third angel poured out his
bowl on the rivers and the springs of water, and they turned into blood. 5 I heard
the angel in charge of the waters say,
"The judgments you have made are just,
O Holy One, you who are and who were!
6 They poured out the blood of God's
people and of the prophets, and so you
have given them blood to drink. They
are getting what they deserve!" 7 Then I
heard a voice from the altar saying,
"Lord God Almighty! True and just indeed are your judgments!"

8 Then the fourth angel poured out his
bowl on the sun, and it was allowed to
burn people with its fiery heat. 9 They
were burned by the fierce heat, and they
cursed the name of God, who has authority over these plagues. But they
would not turn from their sins and
praise his greatness.

10 Then the fifth angel poured out his
bowl on the throne of the beast. Darkness fell over the beast's kingdom, and

[f] nations; *some manuscripts have* ages.

people bit their tongues because of their
pain, 11 and they cursed the God of
heaven for their pains and sores. But
they did not turn from their evil ways.
12 Then the sixth angel poured out his
bowl on the great Euphrates River. The
river dried up, to provide a way for the
kings who come from the east. 13 Then I
saw three unclean spirits that looked
like frogs. They were coming out of the
mouth of the dragon, the mouth of the
beast, and the mouth of the false
prophet. 14 They are the spirits of demons that perform miracles. These
three spirits go out to all the kings
of the world, to bring them together
for the battle on the great Day of
Almighty God.
15 "Listen! I am coming like a thief!
Happy is he who stays awake and
guards his clothes, so that he will not
walk around naked and be ashamed in
public!"
16 Then the spirits brought the kings
together in the place that in Hebrew is
called Armageddon.
17 Then the seventh angel poured out
his bowl in the air. A loud voice came
from the throne in the temple, saying, "It
is done!" 18 There were flashes of lightning, rumblings and peals of thunder,
and a terrible earthquake. There has
never been such an earthquake since the
creation of human beings; this was the
worst earthquake of all! 19 The great city
was split into three parts, and the cities
of all countries were destroyed. God remembered great Babylon and made her
drink the wine from his cup—the wine
of his furious anger. 20 All the islands
disappeared, all the mountains vanished. 21 Huge hailstones, each weighing
as much as a hundred pounds, fell from
the sky on people, who cursed God on
account of the plague of hail, because it
was such a terrible plague.

The Famous Prostitute

17 Then one of the seven angels
who had the seven bowls came
to me and said, "Come, and I will show
you how the famous prostitute is to be
punished, that great city that is built
near many rivers. 2 The kings of the
earth practiced sexual immorality with
her, and the people of the world became
drunk from drinking the wine of her immorality."
3 The Spirit took control of me, and the
angel carried me to a desert. There I saw
a woman sitting on a red beast that had
names insulting to God written all over
it; the beast had seven heads and ten
horns. 4 The woman was dressed in purple and scarlet, and covered with gold
ornaments, precious stones, and pearls.
In her hand she held a gold cup full of
obscene and filthy things, the result of
her immorality. 5 On her forehead was
written a name that has a secret meaning: "Great Babylon, the mother of all
prostitutes and perverts in the world."
6 And I saw that the woman was drunk
with the blood of God's people and the
blood of those who were killed because
they had been loyal to Jesus.
When I saw her, I was completely
amazed. 7 "Why are you amazed?" the
angel asked me. "I will tell you the secret
meaning of the woman and of the beast
that carries her, the beast with seven
heads and ten horns. 8 That beast was
once alive, but lives no longer; it is about
to come up from the abyss and will go
off to be destroyed. The people living on
earth whose names have not been written before the creation of the world in
the book of the living, will all be amazed
as they look at the beast. It was once
alive; now it no longer lives, but it will
reappear.
9 "This calls for wisdom and understanding. The seven heads are seven
hills, on which the woman sits. They are
also seven kings: 10 five of them have
fallen, one still rules, and the other one
has not yet come; when he comes, he
must rule only a little while. 11 And the
beast that was once alive, but lives no
longer, is itself an eighth king who is one
of the seven and is going off to be destroyed.
12 "The ten horns you saw are ten
kings who have not yet begun to rule,
but who will be given authority to rule as
kings for one hour with the beast.
13 These ten all have the same purpose,
and they give their power and authority
to the beast. 14 They will fight against the
Lamb; but the Lamb, together with his
called, chosen, and faithful followers,
will defeat them, because he is Lord of
lords and King of kings."
15 The angel also said to me, "The waters you saw, on which the prostitute
sits, are nations, peoples, races, and

languages. 16 The ten horns you saw and
the beast will hate the prostitute; they
will take away everything she has and
leave her naked; they will eat her flesh
and destroy her with fire. 17 For God has
placed in their hearts the will to carry
out his purpose by acting together and
giving to the beast their power to rule
until God's words come true.
18 "The woman you saw is the great
city that rules over the kings of the
earth."

The Fall of Babylon

18 After this I saw another angel
coming down out of heaven. He
had great authority, and his splendor
brightened the whole earth. 2 He cried
out in a loud voice: "She has fallen!
Great Babylon has fallen! She is now
haunted by demons and unclean spirits;
all kinds of filthy and hateful birds live
in her. 3 For all the nations have drunk
her wine—the strong wine of her immoral lust. The kings of the earth practiced sexual immorality with her, and
the merchants of the world grew rich
from her unrestrained lust."
4 Then I heard another voice from
heaven, saying,

"Come out, my people! Come out
from her!
You must not take part in her
sins;
you must not share in her
punishment!
5 For her sins are piled up as high
as heaven,
and God remembers her wicked
ways.
6 Treat her exactly as she has
treated you;
pay her back double for all she
has done.
Fill her cup with a drink twice as
strong
as the drink she prepared
for you.
7 Give her as much suffering and
grief
as the glory and luxury she gave
herself.
For she keeps telling herself:
'Here I sit, a queen!
I am no widow,
I will never know grief!'
8 Because of this, in one day she
will be struck with plagues—
disease, grief, and famine.
And she will be burned with fire,
because the Lord God, who
judges her, is mighty."

9 The kings of the earth who took part
in her immorality and lust will cry and
weep over the city when they see the
smoke from the flames that consume
her. 10 They stand a long way off, because they are afraid of sharing in her
suffering. They say, "How terrible! How
awful! This great and mighty city Babylon! In just one hour you have been
punished!"
11 The merchants of the earth also cry
and mourn for her, because no one buys
their goods any longer; 12 no one buys
their gold, silver, precious stones, and
pearls; their goods of linen, purple cloth,
silk, and scarlet cloth; all kinds of rare
woods and all kinds of objects made of
ivory and of expensive wood, of bronze,
iron, and marble; 13 and cinnamon,
spice, incense, myrrh, and frankincense;
wine and oil, flour and wheat, cattle and
sheep, horses and carriages, slaves, and
even human lives. 14 The merchants say
to her, "All the good things you longed
to own have disappeared, and all your
wealth and glamor are gone, and you
will never find them again!" 15 The merchants, who became rich from doing
business in that city, will stand a long
way off, because they are afraid of sharing in her suffering. They will cry and
mourn, 16 and say, "How terrible! How
awful for the great city! She used to
dress herself in linen, purple, and scarlet, and cover herself with gold ornaments, precious stones, and pearls!
17 And in one hour she has lost all this
wealth!"
All the ships' captains and passengers,
the sailors and all others who earn their
living on the sea, stood a long way off,
18 and cried out as they saw the smoke
from the flames that consumed her:
"There never has been another city like
this great city!" 19 They threw dust on
their heads, they cried and mourned,
saying, "How terrible! How awful for the
great city! She is the city where all who
have ships sailing the seas became rich
on her wealth! And in one hour she has
lost everything!"
20 Be glad, heaven, because of her destruction! Be glad, God's people and the

apostles and prophets! For God has condemned her for what she did to you!
21 Then a mighty angel picked up a
stone the size of a large millstone and
threw it into the sea, saying, "This is
how the great city Babylon will be violently thrown down and will never be
seen again. 22 The music of harps and of
human voices, of players of the flute and
the trumpet, will never be heard in you
again! No workman in any trade will
ever be found in you again; and the
sound of the millstone will be heard no
more! 23 Never again will the light of a
lamp be seen in you; no more will the
voices of brides and grooms be heard in
you. Your merchants were the most
powerful in all the world, and with your
false magic you deceived all the peoples
of the world!"
24 Babylon was punished because the
blood of prophets and of God's people
was found in the city; yes, the blood of
all those who have been killed on earth.

19 After this I heard what sounded
like the roar of a large crowd of
people in heaven, saying, "Praise God!
Salvation, glory, and power belong to
our God! 2 True and just are his judgments! He has condemned the prostitute
who was corrupting the earth with her
immorality. God has punished her because she killed his servants." 3 Again
they shouted, "Praise God! The smoke
from the flames that consume the great
city goes up forever and ever!" 4 The
twenty-four elders and the four living
creatures fell down and worshiped God,
who was seated on the throne. They
said, "Amen! Praise God!"

The Wedding Feast of the Lamb

5 Then there came from the throne the
sound of a voice, saying, "Praise our
God, all his servants and all people, both
great and small, who have reverence for
him!" 6 Then I heard what sounded like a
crowd, like the sound of a roaring waterfall, like loud peals of thunder. I heard
them say, "Praise God! For the Lord, our
Almighty God, is King! 7 Let us rejoice
and be glad; let us praise his greatness!
For the time has come for the wedding of
the Lamb, and his bride has prepared
herself for it. 8 She has been given clean
shining linen to wear." (The linen is the
good deeds of God's people.)
9 Then the angel said to me, "Write
this: Happy are those who have been invited to the wedding feast of the Lamb."
And the angel added, "These are the true
words of God."
10 I fell down at his feet to worship
him, but he said to me, "Don't do it! I am
a servant together with you and with
other believers, all those who hold to
the truth that Jesus revealed. Worship God!"
For the truth that Jesus revealed is what inspires the prophets.

The Rider on the White Horse

11 Then I saw heaven open, and there
was a white horse. Its rider is called
Faithful and True; it is with justice that
he judges and fights his battles. 12 His
eyes were like a flame of fire, and he
wore many crowns on his head. He had
a name written on him, but no one except himself knows what it is. 13 The
robe he wore was covered with blood.
His name is "The Word of God." 14 The
armies of heaven followed him, riding
on white horses and dressed in clean
white linen. 15 Out of his mouth came a
sharp sword, with which he will defeat
the nations. He will rule over them with
a rod of iron, and he will trample out the
wine in the wine press of the furious anger of the Almighty God. 16 On his robe
and on his thigh was written the name:
"King of kings and Lord of lords."
17 Then I saw an angel standing on the
sun. He shouted in a loud voice to all the
birds flying in midair: "Come and gather
together for God's great feast! 18 Come
and eat the flesh of kings, generals, and
soldiers, the flesh of horses and their riders, the flesh of all people, slave and
free, great and small!"
19 Then I saw the beast and the kings
of the earth and their armies gathered to
fight against the one who was riding the
horse and against his army. 20 The beast
was taken prisoner, together with the
false prophet who had performed miracles in his presence. (It was by those miracles that he had deceived those who
had the mark of the beast and those who
had worshiped the image of the beast.)
The beast and the false prophet were
both thrown alive into the lake of fire
that burns with sulfur. 21 Their armies
were killed by the sword that comes out
of the mouth of the one who was riding

the horse; and all the birds ate all they
could of their flesh.

The Thousand Years

20 Then I saw an angel coming
down from heaven, holding in
his hand the key of the abyss and a
heavy chain. 2 He seized the dragon, that
ancient serpent—that is, the Devil, or
Satan—and chained him up for a thousand years. 3 The angel threw him into
the abyss, locked it, and sealed it, so that
he could not deceive the nations any
more until the thousand years were
over. After that he must be set loose for
a little while.

4 Then I saw thrones, and those who
sat on them were given the power to
judge. I also saw the souls of those who
had been executed because they had
proclaimed the truth that Jesus revealed
and the word of God. They had not worshiped the beast or its image, nor had
they received the mark of the beast on
their foreheads or their hands. They
came to life and ruled as kings with
Christ for a thousand years. 5 (The rest of
the dead did not come to life until the
thousand years were over.) This is the
first raising of the dead. 6 Happy and
greatly blessed are those who are included in this first raising of the dead.
The second death has no power over
them; they shall be priests of God and of
Christ, and they will rule with him for a
thousand years.

The Defeat of Satan

7 After the thousand years are over,
Satan will be set loose from his prison,
8 and he will go out to deceive the nations scattered over the whole world,
that is, Gog and Magog. Satan will bring
them all together for battle, as many as
the grains of sand on the seashore.
9 They spread out over the earth and surrounded the camp of God's people and
the city that he loves. But fire came
down from heaven and destroyed them.
10 Then the Devil, who deceived them,
was thrown into the lake of fire and sulfur, where the beast and the false
prophet had already been thrown; and
they will be tormented day and night
forever and ever.

The Final Judgment

11 Then I saw a great white throne and
the one who sits on it. Earth and heaven
fled from his presence and were seen no
more. 12 And I saw the dead, great and
small alike, standing before the throne.
Books were opened, and then another
book was opened, the book of the living.
The dead were judged according to what
they had done, as recorded in the books.
13 Then the sea gave up its dead. Death
and the world of the dead also gave up
the dead they held. And all were judged
according to what they had done.
14 Then death and the world of the dead
were thrown into the lake of fire. (This
lake of fire is the second death.) 15 Those
who did not have their name written in
the book of the living were thrown into
the lake of fire.

The New Heaven and the New Earth

21 Then I saw a new heaven and a
new earth. The first heaven and
the first earth disappeared, and the sea
vanished. 2 And I saw the Holy City, the
new Jerusalem, coming down out of
heaven from God, prepared and ready,
like a bride dressed to meet her husband. 3 I heard a loud voice speaking
from the throne: "Now God's home is
with people! He will live with them, and
they shall be his people. God himself
will be with them, and he will be their
God. 4 He will wipe away all tears from
their eyes. There will be no more death,
no more grief or crying or pain. The old
things have disappeared."

5 Then the one who sits on the throne
said, "And now I make all things new!"
He also said to me, "Write this, because
these words are true and can be trusted."
6 And he said, "It is done! I am the first
and the last, the beginning and the end.
To anyone who is thirsty I will give the
right to drink from the spring of the water of life without paying for it. 7 Those
who win the victory will receive this
from me: I will be their God, and they
will be my children. 8 But cowards, traitors, perverts, murderers, the immoral,
those who practice magic, those who
worship idols, and all liars—the place
for them is the lake burning with fire
and sulfur, which is the second death."

The New Jerusalem

9 One of the seven angels who had the
seven bowls full of the seven last
plagues came to me and said, "Come,
and I will show you the Bride, the wife of
the Lamb." 10 The Spirit took control of
me, and the angel carried me to the top
of a very high mountain. He showed me
Jerusalem, the Holy City, coming down
out of heaven from God 11 and shining
with the glory of God. The city shone
like a precious stone, like a jasper, clear
as crystal. 12 It had a great, high wall
with twelve gates and with twelve angels in charge of the gates. On the gates
were written the names of the twelve
tribes of the people of Israel. 13 There
were three gates on each side: three on
the east, three on the south, three on the
north, and three on the west. 14 The city's
wall was built on twelve foundation
stones, on which were written the names
of the twelve apostles of the Lamb.
15 The angel who spoke to me had a gold
measuring stick to measure the city,
its gates, and its wall. 16 The city was
perfectly square, as wide as it was long.
The angel measured the city with his
measuring stick: it was fifteen hundred
miles long and was as wide and as high
as it was long. 17 The angel also measured the wall, and it was 216 feet high,[g]
according to the standard unit of
measure which he was using.[h] 18 The
wall was made of jasper, and the city
itself was made of pure gold, as clear
as glass. 19 The foundation stones of
the city wall were adorned with all
kinds of precious stones. The first foundation stone was jasper, the second
sapphire, the third agate, the fourth
emerald, 20 the fifth onyx, the sixth carnelian, the seventh yellow quartz, the
eighth beryl, the ninth topaz, the tenth
chalcedony, the eleventh turquoise,
the twelfth amethyst. 21 The twelve
gates were twelve pearls; each gate
was made from a single pearl. The street
of the city was of pure gold, transpar-
ent as glass.

22 I did not see a temple in the city, because its temple is the Lord God
Almighty and the Lamb. 23 The city has
no need of the sun or the moon to shine
on it, because the glory of God shines on
it, and the Lamb is its lamp. 24 The peoples of the world will walk by its light,
and the kings of the earth will bring
their wealth into it. 25 The gates of the
city will stand open all day; they will
never be closed, because there will be no
night there. 26 The greatness and the
wealth of the nations will be brought
into the city. 27 But nothing that is impure will enter the city, nor anyone who
does shameful things or tells lies. Only
those whose names are written in the
Lamb's book of the living will enter the
city.

22 The angel also showed me the
river of the water of life, sparkling like crystal, and coming from the
throne of God and of the Lamb 2 and
flowing down the middle of the city's
street. On each side of the river was the
tree of life, which bears fruit twelve
times a year, once each month; and its
leaves are for the healing of the nations.
3 Nothing that is under God's curse will
be found in the city.

The throne of God and of the Lamb
will be in the city, and his servants will
worship him. 4 They will see his face,
and his name will be written on their
foreheads. 5 There shall be no more
night, and they will not need lamps or
sunlight, because the Lord God will be
their light, and they will rule as kings
forever and ever.

The Coming of Jesus

6 Then the angel said to me, "These
words are true and can be trusted. And
the Lord God, who gives his Spirit to the
prophets, has sent his angel to show his
servants what must happen very soon."

7 "Listen!" says Jesus. "I am coming
soon! Happy are those who obey the
prophetic words in this book!"

8 I, John, have heard and seen all these
things. And when I finished hearing and
seeing them, I fell down at the feet of the
angel who had shown me these things,
and I was about to worship him. 9 But he
said to me, "Don't do it! I am a servant
together with you and with your brothers the prophets and of all those who
obey the words in this book. Worship

[g] high; or thick. [h] *In verses 16 and 17 the Greek text speaks of "12,000 furlongs" and "144 cubits" which may have symbolic significance.*

God!” 10 And he said to me, “Do not
keep the prophetic words of this book
a secret, because the time is near
when all this will happen. 11 Whoever is
evil must go on doing evil, and whoever is filthy must go on being filthy;
whoever is good must go on doing good,
and whoever is holy must go on being
holy.”
12 “Listen!” says Jesus. “I am coming
soon! I will bring my rewards with me,
to give to each one according to what he
has done. 13 I am the first and the last,
the beginning and the end.”
14 Happy are those who wash their
robes clean and so have the right to eat
the fruit from the tree of life and to go
through the gates into the city. 15 But
outside the city are the perverts and
those who practice magic, the immoral
and the murderers, those who worship
idols and those who are liars both in
words and deeds.
16 “I, Jesus, have sent my angel to announce these things to you in the
churches. I am descended from the family of David; I am the bright morning
star.”
17 The Spirit and the Bride say,
“Come!”

Everyone who hears this must also
say, “Come!”

Come, whoever is thirsty; accept the
water of life as a gift, whoever wants it.

Conclusion

18 I, John, solemnly warn everyone
who hears the prophetic words of this
book: if any add anything to them, God
will add to their punishment the plagues
described in this book. 19 And if any take
anything away from the prophetic
words of this book, God will take away
from them their share of the fruit of the
tree of life and of the Holy City, which
are described in this book.
20 He who gives his testimony to all
this says, “Yes indeed! I am coming
soon!”

So be it. Come, Lord Jesus!
21 May the grace of the Lord Jesus be
with everyone.[i]

[i] everyone; *some manuscripts have* God’s people; *others have* all of God’s people.

Word List

WORD LIST

This Word List identifies many objects or cultural features whose meaning may not be known to all readers.

Abib The first month of the Hebrew calendar, corresponding to the period from about mid-March to about mid-April. This month is also called Nisan.

Abyss The place in the depths of the earth where the demons were imprisoned until their final punishment.

Acacia A flowering tree, a type of mimosa, with hard and durable wood.

Adar The twelfth month of the Hebrew calendar, corresponding to the period from about mid-February to about mid-March.

Agate A semiprecious stone of various colors, but usually white and brown.

Alabaster A soft stone of usually light creamy color, from which vases and jars were made.

Aloes A sweet-smelling substance, derived from a plant. It was used medicinally and as a perfume.

Amen A Hebrew word which means "it is so" or "may it be so." It can also be translated "certainly," "truly," or "surely." In Revelation 3.14 it is used as a title for Christ.

Amethyst A semiprecious stone, usually purple or violet in color.

Anoint To pour or rub olive oil on someone in order to honor him or to appoint him to some special work. The Israelite kings were anointed as a sign of their taking office, and so the king could be called "the anointed one." In a figurative sense, "The Anointed One" is the title of the one whom God chose and appointed as Savior and Lord.

Apostle Principally one of the group of twelve men whom Jesus chose to be his special followers and helpers. It is also used in the New Testament to refer to Paul and other Christian workers. The word may have the sense of "messenger."

Areopagus A hill in Athens where the city council used to meet. For this reason the council itself was called Areopagus, even after it no longer met on the hill.

Artemis The Greek name of an ancient goddess of fertility, worshiped especially in Asia Minor.

Asherah A goddess of fertility worshiped by the Canaanites; her male counterpart was Baal. After the Hebrews invaded Canaan, many of them began worshiping these two gods.

Astarte A goddess of fertility and war who was widely worshiped in the ancient Near East.

Atonement, Day of The most important of Israel's holy days, when the High Priest would offer sacrifice for the sins of the people of Israel (Leviticus 16). It was held on the 10th day of the seventh month of the Hebrew calendar (around October 1). The Jewish name for this day is Yom Kippur.

Baal The god of fertility worshiped by the Canaanites; his female counterpart was Asherah. After the Hebrews invaded Canaan, many of them began worshiping these two gods.

Baal-of-the-Covenant A name by which the god Baal was known by the people of Shechem.

Balsam A tree from which sweet-smelling resin was obtained; the resin was used for perfume and medicine.

Barley A cultivated grain similar to wheat, grown as a food crop.

Beelzebul A New Testament name given to the Devil as the chief of the evil spirits.

Beryl A semiprecious stone, usually green or bluish green in color.

Breastplate Part of a soldier's armor, made of leather or metal; it covered the chest and sometimes the back as a protection against arrows and the blows of a sword.

Bul The eighth month of the Hebrew calendar, corresponding to the period from about mid-October to about mid-November.

Burnt offering A type of sacrifice in which all the parts of the animal were completely burned on the altar; in other sacrifices only certain parts of the animal were burned.

Calamus A sweet-smelling reed-like plant.

Capital The top part of a column supporting a roof.

Carnelian A semiprecious stone, usually red in color.

Cassia A spice made from the bark of a tree; it closely resembles cinnamon.

Chalcedony A semiprecious stone, usually milky or gray in color.

Christ Originally a title, the Greek equivalent of the Hebrew word "Messiah." It means "the anointed one." Jesus was called the Christ because he was the one whom God chose and sent as Savior and Lord.

Circumcise To cut off the foreskin of the penis. As a sign of God's covenant with his people Israelite boys were circumcised eight days after they were born (Genesis 17.9-14).

Concubine A servant woman who, although not a wife, had sexual relations with her master. She had important legal rights, and her master was referred to as her husband.

Coral A brightly colored stony substance found in the sea; it was used as jewelry.

Council The supreme religious court of the Jews, composed of seventy leaders of the Jewish people and presided over by the High Priest.

Covenant An agreement, either between persons or between God and a person or a people. God made a covenant with Noah (Genesis 9.8-17) and with Abraham (Genesis 17.1-8), but in the Old Testament the term usually refers to the covenant made between God and the people of Israel at the time of Moses (Exodus 24.4-8).

Covenant Box The wooden chest covered with gold, in which were kept the two stone tablets on which were written the Ten Commandments. It has traditionally been called the Ark of the Covenant.

Cumin A small plant whose seeds are ground up and used for seasoning foods.

Cush The term "Cush" in the Old Testament Hebrew text normally designates the territory extending south from the First Cataract of the Nile River at Aswan. It was known in Graeco-Roman times as Ethiopia (Gk., *Aithiopia*), and later as Nubia. This extensive region included within its borders most of modern Sudan and some of present-day Ethiopia (Abyssinia). In Genesis 10, the Table of Nations, verses 8-12 are included under the genealogy of Egyptian Cush, yet all the peoples named are in Mesopotamia. Apparently the Hebrew designation for the Babylonian Kassites was "Cush" as well, thus resulting in the mixing of the two regions. Genesis 2.13 may be another reference to Babylonian Cush.

Cymbals A pair of thin pieces of metal held in the hands and struck together rhythmically in music.

David's City In the Old Testament the reference is generally to that part of the city of Jerusalem which was captured from the Jebusites by King David. In the New Testament the reference is to the town of Bethlehem, David's boyhood home, where Jesus was born.

Dedication, Festival of The Jewish festival, lasting eight days, which celebrated the restoration and rededication in 165 B.C. of the Temple altar by the Jewish patriot Judas Maccabeus. The festival began on the 25th day of the month Kislev (around December 10). The Jewish name for this festival is Hanukkah.

Defile To make ritually unclean or impure. Certain foods and practices were prohibited by the Law of Moses because they were thought to make a person ritually or ceremonially unclean. Such a person could not take part in the public worship until he had performed certain rituals which would remove the defilement.

Demon An evil spirit with the power to harm people; it was regarded as a messenger and servant of the Devil.

Dill A small garden plant whose stems, leaves, and seeds are used for seasoning food.

Dipper: Big Dipper and ***Little Dipper*** Two groups of stars which in the Northern Hemisphere are visible in the northern sky. The star at the end of the "handle" of the Little Dipper is Polaris, the North Star.

Disciple A person who follows and learns from someone else. In the New Testament the word is used of the followers of John the Baptist and especially of the followers of Jesus, particularly the twelve apostles.

Divination The attempt to discover a message from God or the gods by examining such things as marked stones or the liver of a sacrificed animal.

Dragon A legendary beast, thought to be like a huge lizard. It is also called a serpent and appears as a figure of the Devil (Revelation 12.3—13.4; 20.2, 3).

Elders In the Old Testament this is a name given to certain respected leaders of a tribe, nation, or city. In the New Testament three different groups are called elders: (1) in the Gospels the elders are influential Jewish religious leaders, some of whom were members of the supreme Council; (2) in Acts 11—21 and the Letters the elders are Christian church officers who had general responsibility for the work of the church; (3) in Revelation the twenty-four elders are part of God's court in heaven, perhaps as representatives of God's people.

Elul The sixth month of the Hebrew calendar, corresponding to the period from about mid-August to about mid-September.

Ephod The Hebrew term traditionally transliterated as "ephod" is of uncertain meaning in a number of contexts. Generally it refers to some type of priestly garment which was worn over the shoulder by the High Priest and with which the Urim and Thummim were associated. In certain contexts, however, the Hebrew term refers to an object of worship, and in some other passages, it evidently refers to an object used to foretell future events.

Epicureans Those who followed the teaching of Epicurus (died 270 B.C.), a Greek philosopher who taught that happiness is the highest good in life.

Epileptic A person who suffers from a nervous disease causing convulsions and fainting.

Ethanim The seventh month of the Hebrew calendar, corresponding to the period from about mid-September to about mid-October; it was later called Tishri.

Ethiopia See "Cush."

Eunuch A man who has been made physically incapable of having normal sexual relations. Eunuchs were often important officials in the courts of ancient kings, and the term may have come to be used of such officials in general, regardless of their sexual condition.

Fast To go without food for a while as a religious duty.

Feldspar A colorful, rather hard rock, often glassy in appearance.

Fellowship offerings A type of sacrifice offered to insure a right relationship with God. Only a portion of the animal was burned on the altar; the rest was eaten by the worshipers or the priests.

Flax A small cultivated plant; the fibers of its stem are spun into thread used in making linen cloth.

Frankincense A valuable incense, made from the sap of a certain tree. This incense was probably imported from Arabia.

Garnet A semiprecious stone, usually red in color.

Gazelle A kind of antelope, known for its beauty and gracefulness.

Gentile A person who is not a Jew.

Hades The Greek name used in the New Testament to refer to the world of the dead.

Harrow A farm implement used to break up the ground and level it after plowing.

Harvest Festival The Israelite festival celebrating the wheat harvest, held in the latter part of May, fifty days after Passover. The Jewish name for this festival is Shavuoth (the Feast of Weeks). It has also been called Pentecost.

Hermes The name of a Greek god who served as messenger of the gods.

Herod's party A political party in New Testament times composed of Jews who favored being ruled by one of the descendants of Herod the Great rather than by the Roman governor.

High Priest The priest who occupied the highest office in the Jewish priestly system and was president of the supreme Council of the Jews. Once a year (on the Day of Atonement) he would enter the Most Holy Place in the Temple and offer sacrifice for himself and for the sins of the people of Israel.

Hyssop A small bushy plant, used in religious ceremonies to sprinkle liquids.

Incense Material which is burned in order to produce a pleasant smell. The Israelites used it in their worship.

Jackal A small wild animal resembling a fox.

Jasper A semiprecious stone of various colors. The jasper mentioned in the Bible was probably green, or else clear.

Javelin A short, light spear used by soldiers in ancient times.

Kislev The ninth month of the Hebrew calendar, corresponding to the period from about mid-November to about mid-December.

Law The name which the Jews applied to the first five books of the Old Testament, also called "The Books of Moses." Sometimes, however, the name is applied in a more general way to the entire Old Testament.

Leviathan A legendary animal associated with water, in some passages identified by some scholars as the crocodile. In a figurative sense it may represent the chaos that existed before God created the world (Isaiah 27.1; Psalm 74.14).

Levite (1) A member of the tribe of Levi; (2) a man who assisted the priest in the performance of religious duties.

Levitical priest A Hebrew priest descended from the tribe of Levi. All priests were supposed to be members of the tribe of Levi, but in later times not all members of the tribe of Levi were priests.

Living creatures (also referred to as "winged creatures" and traditionally called "cherubim") symbols of God's majesty and associated with his presence. For a description of such creatures see Exodus 25.18-20; Ezekiel 1.5-13; 10; Revelation 4.6-9.

Lord in this translation represents the Hebrew name Yahweh (traditionally represented by Jehovah), corresponding either to the occurrence of the name itself or to a pronoun standing for the name.

Lyre A kind of harp.

Mandrake A small plant; it was believed that eating its root or fruit would make a woman more easily able to have children.

Manna A food eaten by the Israelites during their travels in the wilderness. It was white and flaky and looked like small seeds (Exodus 16.14-21; Numbers 11.7-9).

Medium A person who believes that he or she can communicate with the dead.

Messiah A Hebrew title (meaning "the anointed one") given to the promised Savior, whose coming was foretold by the Hebrew prophets; the corresponding Greek term "the Christ" has the same meaning.

Mildew A fungus that appears on various objects, especially in damp weather.

Millet A cultivated grain that was grown as a food crop.

Molech One of the gods of the ancient people of Canaan.

Most Holy Place The innermost room of the Tent of the LORD's presence or the Temple. The Covenant Box was kept there. Only the High Priest could enter the Most Holy Place, and he did so only once a year, on the Day of Atonement.

Mustard A large plant which grows from a very small seed. The seeds were ground into powder and used as spice on food.

Myrrh A sweet-smelling resin that was highly prized. It served as a medicine (Mark 15.23) and was used by the Jews in preparing bodies for burial (John 19.39).

Myrtle A kind of evergreen shrub or tree.

Nard An expensive perfume made from a plant.

Nazarene Someone from the town of Nazareth. The name was used as a title for Jesus and also as a name for the early Christians (Acts 24.5).

Nazirite A person who took a special vow of self-dedication. Such a person was not to drink beer or wine, cut his hair, or touch a dead body (Numbers 6.1-21). The vow could be taken for a certain period of time, but some persons were dedicated to God as Nazirites from their birth.

New Moon Festival A religious observance held by the Israelites on the day of each new moon.

New Year Festival The Jewish name for this festival is "Rosh Hashanah."

Nisan The first month of the Hebrew calendar, corresponding to the period from about mid-March to about mid-April. The month is also called Abib.

Onyx A semiprecious stone of various colors.

Orion A group of prominent stars visible during winter evenings.

Outcasts In the Gospels this name, which in many translations appears as "sinners," refers to those Jews who had been excluded from synagogue worship because they violated rules about foods that should not be eaten and about associating with people who were not Jews. Such outcasts were despised by many of their fellow Jews, and Jesus was criticized for associating with them (Mark 2.15-17; Luke 7.34; 15.1, 2).

Parable A story which teaches spiritual truth; it was often used by Jesus.

Paradise A name for heaven (Luke 23.43; 2 Corinthians 12.3).

Paralytic Someone who suffers from a disease that prevents him from moving part or all of his body.

Passover The Israelite festival, on the 14th day of the month Nisan (around April 1), which celebrated the deliverance of the ancient Hebrews from their captivity in Egypt. The Angel of Death killed the first-born in the Egyptian homes but passed over the Hebrew homes (Exodus 12.23-27). The Jewish name for this festival is Pesach.

Pentecost, Day of The Greek name for the Israelite festival of wheat harvest (see Harvest Festival). The name Pentecost (meaning "fiftieth") comes from the fact that the feast was held fifty days after Passover.

Pervert One who commits unnatural sexual acts.

Pharisees A Jewish religious party during the time of Jesus. They were strict in obeying the Law of Moses and other regulations which had been added to it through the centuries.

Pistachio nut A small greenish nut.

Pleiades A small group of stars visible during winter evenings.

Pomegranate A reddish fruit about the size of a large apple; it has a hard rind and is full of tasty seeds.

Preparation, Day of The sixth day of the week (Friday), on which the Jews made the required preparations to observe the Sabbath (Saturday).

Prophet A person who proclaims a message from God. The term usually refers to certain men in the Old Testament, but the New Testament speaks of prophets in the early church. John the Baptist is also called a prophet.

Purim The Jewish religious holiday

held on the 14th day of the month Adar (around March 1), celebrating the deliverance of the Jews from Haman by Esther and Mordecai. The story is told in the book of Esther.

Quartz A semiprecious stone of various colors, but usually clear.

Rabbi A Hebrew word which means "my teacher."

Red Sea Evidently referred originally to (1) a series of lakes and marshes between the head of the Gulf of Suez and the Mediterranean, the region generally regarded as the site of the events described in Exodus 13, and was also used to designate (2) the Gulf of Suez, (3) the Gulf of Aqaba.

Rephan The name of an ancient god that was worshiped as the ruler of the planet Saturn.

Resin A fragrant, gummy substance produced from the sap of certain trees and shrubs.

Restoration, Year of The year, coming every fifty years, when the ancient Israelites returned to the original owner any property they were holding, freed their Israelite slaves, and did not cultivate their fields.

Sabbath The seventh day of the Jewish week (from sundown on Friday to sundown on Saturday), a holy day on which no work was permitted.

Sackcloth A coarse cloth made of goats' hair, which was worn as a sign of mourning or distress.

Sadducees A small Jewish religious party in New Testament times, composed largely of priests. They based their beliefs primarily on the first five books of the Old Testament and differed in several matters of belief and practice from the larger party of the Pharisees.

Samaritan A name used to refer to a native of Samaria, the region between Judea and Galilee. Because of differences in politics, race, customs, and religion (including especially the central place of worship), there was much bad feeling between the Jews and the Samaritans.

Sanctuary A building dedicated to the worship of God. Sometimes the word refers to the central place of worship and not to the whole building.

Sapphire A very valuable stone, usually blue in color.

Scepter A short rod held by kings to symbolize their authority.

Scorpion A small creature which has eight legs and a long tail with a poisonous sting. It can inflict a very painful, and sometimes fatal, wound.

Scribe A person whose business it was to write documents for others or to copy written material. Some scribes were employed by ancient kings to prepare official documents, and some of them became important officials.

Scriptures In the New Testament the word refers to the collected body of Hebrew sacred writings, known to Christians as the Old Testament. Various names are used: the Law (or the Law of Moses) and the prophets (Matthew 5.17; 7.12; Luke 2.22; 24.44; Acts 13.15; 28.23); the Holy Scriptures (Romans 1.2; 2 Timothy 3.15); the old covenant (2 Corinthians 3.14). The singular "scripture" refers to a single passage of the Old Testament.

Serpent A name given to the dragon, which appears in the New Testament as a figure of the Devil (Revelation 12.3-17; 20.2, 3).

Seventh year The year, coming every seventh year, when the ancient Israelites did not cultivate their fields and when debts were canceled.

Shebat The eleventh month of the Hebrew calendar, corresponding to the period from about mid-January to about mid-February.

Shelters, Festival of A joyous festival celebrated by the Israelites in the fall after the completion of the harvest. In order to help them remember the years when their ancestors wandered through the wilderness, the Israelites constructed rough shelters to live in during the festival. The Jewish name for this festival is Sukkoth. It has been traditionally called the Feast of Tabernacles or the Feast of Booths.

Sickle A tool consisting of a curved

metal blade and a wooden handle, used for cutting wheat and other crops.

Sivan The third month of the Hebrew calendar, corresponding to the period from about mid-May to about mid-June.

Snuffer The Hebrew word translated "snuffer" apparently identifies an implement used to trim the oil lamps used in the Tent of the LORD's presence or the Temple.

Sorcerer A person who works magic for evil purposes.

Stoics Those who followed the teachings of the Greek philosopher Zeno (died 265 B.C.), who taught that happiness is to be found in being free from pleasure and pain.

Sulfur In the Bible this refers to a sulfur compound which burns with great heat and produces an unpleasant smell.

Synagogue A place where Jews met every Sabbath day for their public worship. It probably also served as a center for Jewish social life and a school for Jewish children.

Tambourine A small drum with pieces of metal in the rim, held in the hand and shaken. In biblical times it was generally used by women.

Tassel A group of threads or cords, fastened together at one end and loose at the other. The Israelites were commanded to wear these on their clothes (Numbers 15.37-41).

Teachers of the Law Men who in New Testament times taught and interpreted the teachings of the Old Testament, especially the first five books.

Tebeth The tenth month of the Hebrew calendar, corresponding to the period from about mid-December to about mid-January.

Tenant A man who grows crops on land owned by someone else, and turns over a part of the harvest to the owner to pay for the use of his land.

Tent of the LORD's presence The large tent described in detail in Exodus 26, where the Israelites worshiped God until Solomon built the Temple. It has traditionally been called the Tabernacle or Tent of meeting.

Tithe A tenth part of a person's produce or income, given for religious purposes.

Topaz A semiprecious stone, usually yellow in color.

Turban A head covering worn by men, made of cloth wrapped around the head.

Turquoise A semiprecious stone, blue or bluish green in color.

Unleavened Bread, Festival of The Israelite festival, lasting seven days after Passover; it also celebrated the deliverance of the ancient Hebrews from Egypt. The name came from the practice of not using leaven (yeast) in making bread during that week (Exodus 12.14-20). It was held from the 15th to the 22nd day of the month Nisan (around the first week of April).

Urim and Thummim Two small objects used by Israelite priests to determine God's will.

Vow A strong declaration or promise, usually made while calling upon God to punish the speaker if the statement should prove to be not true or if the promise were not kept.

Winged creatures (also referred to as "living creatures" and traditionally called "cherubim") symbols of God's majesty and associated with his presence. For a description of such creatures see Exodus 25.18-20; Ezekiel 1.5-13; 10; Revelation 4.6-9.

Winnowing shovel A tool like a shovel or a large fork, used to separate the wheat from the chaff.

Wreath Flowers or leaves arranged in a circle, to be placed on a person's head. In ancient times a wreath of leaves was the prize given to winners in athletic contests.

Yeast A substance, also called leaven, which is added to dough made from the flour of wheat or barley to make it rise before being baked into bread.

Yoke A heavy bar of wood fitted over

the necks of two oxen to make it possible for them to pull a plow or a cart. The word is used figuratively to describe the moral lessons that a teacher passes on to his pupils.

Zeus The name of the supreme god of the Greeks.

Zion Originally a designation for "David's City," the Jebusite stronghold captured by King David's forces. The term "Zion" was later extended in meaning to refer to the hill on which the Temple stood.

Ziv The second month of the Hebrew calendar, corresponding to the period from about mid-April to about mid-May.

NEW TESTAMENT PASSAGES QUOTED OR PARAPHRASED FROM THE SEPTUAGINT

The writers of the New Testament generally quoted or paraphrased the ancient Greek translation of the Old Testament, commonly known as the Septuagint Version (LXX), made some two hundred years before the time of Christ. In a number of instances this version differs significantly in meaning from the Masoretic Hebrew text, and as a special help to the reader such occurrences of LXX quotations, paraphrases, or evident allusions are listed here. The following translations of the LXX passages reflect in general the wording of *Today's English Version* of the New Testament. When, however, a LXX quotation occurs several times in the New Testament, the TEV wording of the translation may vary because of evident differences in meaning or emphasis reflected in the different contexts. Chapter and verse numbers are those of the English Bible.

Matthew 1.23 (Isaiah 7.14) A virgin will become pregnant and have a son.

Matthew 3.3 (Isaiah 40.3) Someone is shouting in the desert, "Prepare a road for the Lord; make a straight path for our God to travel!"

Matthew 12.21 (Isaiah 42.4) And on him all people will put their hope.

Matthew 13.14, 15 (Isaiah 6.9, 10) This people will listen and listen, but not understand; they will look and look, but not see, because their minds are dull, and they have stopped up their ears, and have closed their eyes. Otherwise, their eyes would see, their ears would hear, their minds would understand, and they would turn to me, says God, and I would heal them.

Matthew 15.8, 9 (Isaiah 29.13) These people, says God, . . . honor me with their words, but their heart is really far away from me. It is no use for them to worship me, because they teach man-made rules and laws.

Matthew 21.16 (Psalm 8.2) You have trained children and babies to offer perfect praise.

Mark 1.3 (Isaiah 40.3) Someone is shouting in the desert, "Get the road ready for the Lord; make a straight path for our God to travel!"

Mark 4.12 (Isaiah 6.9, 10) This people will listen and listen, but not understand; they will look and look, but not see . . .; for if they did . . ., they would turn to me, says God, and I would heal them.

Mark 7.6, 7 (Isaiah 29.13) These people, says God, . . . honor me with their words, but their heart is really far away from me. It is no use for them to worship me, because they teach man-made rules and laws.

Luke 3.4-6 (Isaiah 40.3-5) Someone is shouting in the desert: "Get the road ready for the Lord, make a straight path for our God to travel! Every valley must be filled up, every hill and mountain leveled off. All the winding roads must be made straight, and the rough paths made smooth. . . . All people will see God's salvation!"

Luke 4.18 (Isaiah 61.1) The Spirit of the Lord is upon me, because he has chosen me to bring good news to the poor. He has sent me . . . to proclaim liberty to the captives and recovery of sight to the blind.

Luke 8.10 (Isaiah 6.9) You will listen and listen, but not understand; you will look and look, but not see.

John 1.23 (Isaiah 40.3) The voice of someone shouting in the desert: . . .

"Make a straight path for our God to travel!"

John 12.38 (Isaiah 53.1) Lord, who believed the message we told?

John 12.40 (Isaiah 6.10) This people's minds are dull, and they have stopped up their ears and have closed their eyes. Otherwise, their eyes would see, and their ears would hear, their minds would understand, and they would turn to me, says God, for me to heal them.

Acts 2.19, 20 (Joel 2.30, 31) There will be blood, fire, and thick smoke; the sun will be darkened, and the moon will turn red as blood, before the great and glorious Day of the Lord comes.

Acts 2.25-28 (Psalm 16.8-11) I saw the Lord before me at all times. He is near me, and I will not be troubled. And so I am filled with gladness, and my words are full of joy. And I, mortal though I am, will rest assured in hope, because you will not abandon me in the world of the dead; you will not allow your faithful servant to rot in the grave. You have shown me the paths that lead to life, and your presence will fill me with joy.

Acts 3.22 (Deuteronomy 18.15) You are to obey him in all things.

Acts 4.25, 26 (Psalm 2.1, 2) Why were the Gentiles furious; why did people make their useless plots? The kings of the earth prepared themselves, and the rulers met together.

Acts 7.14 (Genesis 46.27) Seventy-five people.

Acts 7.42, 43 (Amos 5.25-27) People of Israel! It was not to me that you slaughtered and sacrificed animals for forty years in the desert. It was the tent of the god Molech that you carried, and the image of Rephan, your star god; they were idols that you had made for yourselves. And so I will send you into exile beyond Damascus.

Acts 8.33 (Isaiah 53.8) He was humiliated, and justice was denied him. No one will be able to tell about his descendants, because his life on earth has come to an end.

Acts 13.34 (Isaiah 55.3) I will make an everlasting covenant with you, the sacred and sure blessings I promised to David.

Acts 13.41 (Habakkuk 1.5) Look, you scoffers! Be much astonished and die!

Acts 15.16, 17 (Amos 9.11, 12) In that day, says the Lord, I will restore the kingdom of David. I will rebuild its ruins, and make it strong again. . . . And so all the rest of the human race will come to me, all the Gentiles whom I have called to be my own.

Acts 28.26, 27 (Isaiah 6.9, 10) Go and say to this people: You will listen and listen, but not understand; you will look and look, but not see, because this people's minds are dull, and they have stopped up their ears and closed their eyes. Otherwise, their eyes would see, their ears would hear, their minds would understand, and they would turn to me, says God, and I would heal them.

Romans 2.24 (Isaiah 52.5) Because of you Jews, the Gentiles continually speak evil of God.

Romans 3.4 (Psalm 51.4) You must be shown to be right when you speak; you must win your case when you are being tried.

Romans 3.12 (Psalms 14.3; 53.3) All have turned away from God; they have all gone wrong.

Romans 3.13 (Psalm 5.9) Wicked lies roll off their tongues.

Romans 3.14 (Psalm 10.7) Their speech is filled with bitter curses and guile.

Romans 9.17 (Exodus 9.16) To use you to show my power.

Romans 9.27, 28 (Isaiah 10.22, 23) Even if the people of Israel are as many as the grains of sand by the sea, yet only a few of them will be saved; for God will quickly and justly settle his full account with all the world.

Romans 9.29 (Isaiah 1.9) If the Lord Almighty had not left us some descendants.

Romans 9.33 (Isaiah 28.16) Whoever believes in him will not be disappointed.

Romans 10.11 (Isaiah 28.16) Whoever believes in him will not be disappointed.

Romans 10.16 (Isaiah 53.1) Lord, who believed our message?

Romans 10.18 (Psalm 19.4) The sound of their voice went out to all the world; their words reached the ends of the earth.

Romans 10.20 (Isaiah 65.1) I appeared to those who were not looking for me, I was found by those who were not asking for me.

Romans 10.21 (Isaiah 65.2) All day long I held out my hands to welcome a disobedient and rebellious people.

Romans 11.9, 10 (Psalm 69.22, 23) May they fall, may they be punished! . . . Make them bend under their troubles at all times.

Romans 11.26, 27 (Isaiah 59.20, 21) The Savior will come for the sake of Zion, and remove all wickedness from the descendants of Jacob. I will make this covenant with them, (Isaiah 27.9) when I take away their sins.

Romans 11.34 (Isaiah 40.13) Who knows the mind of the Lord?

Romans 12.20 (Proverbs 25.21, 22) If your enemies are hungry, feed them; if they are thirsty, give them a drink; for by doing this you will make them burn with shame.

Romans 14.11 (Isaiah 45.23) Everyone will kneel before me, and everyone will confess that I am God.

Romans 15.12 (Isaiah 11.10) On that day a descendant of Jesse will appear; he will come to rule the Gentiles, and they will put their hope in him.

Romans 15.21 (Isaiah 52.15) Those who were not told about him will see, and those who have not heard will understand.

1 Corinthians 1.19 (Isaiah 29.14) I will destroy the wisdom of the wise, and hide the understanding of the scholars.

1 Corinthians 2.16 (Isaiah 40.13) Who knows the mind of the Lord?

1 Corinthians 5.13 (Deuteronomy 17.7) Remove the evil man from your group.

1 Corinthians 10.20 (Deuteronomy 32.17) What is sacrificed on pagan altars is offered to demons, not to God.

1 Corinthians 15.55 (Hosea 13.14) Where, Death, is your punishment? Where, Hades, is your power to hurt?

2 Corinthians 4.13 (Psalm 116.10) I spoke because I believed.

2 Corinthians 8.21 (Proverbs 3.4) Make it your purpose to do what is right, not only in the sight of the Lord, but also in the sight of man.

Galatians 3.10 (Deuteronomy 27.26) Whoever does not always obey everything that is written in this Law is under God's curse.

Ephesians 4.26 (Psalm 4.4) If you become angry, do not let your anger lead you into sin.

Philippians 2.11 (Isaiah 45.23) And all will openly proclaim God.

Hebrews 1.6 (Deuteronomy 32.43) All of God's sons must worship him.

Hebrews 1.7 (Psalm 104.4) God makes his angels winds, and his servants a flaming fire.

Hebrews 1.10-12 (Psalm 102.25-27) You, Lord, in the beginning created the earth. . . . You will fold them up like a coat, and they will be changed.

Hebrews 2.7 (Psalm 8.5) You made him for a little while lower than the angels.

Hebrews 3.7-9 (Psalm 95.7-9) If you hear God's voice today, do not be stubborn as your ancestors were when they rebelled against God, as they were that day in the desert when they put him to the test. There they put me to the test and tried me, says God, although they saw what I did.

Hebrews 3.15 (Psalm 95.7, 8) If you hear God's voice today, do not be stubborn as your ancestors were when they rebelled against God.

Hebrews 4.7 (Psalm 95.7, 8) If you hear God's voice today, do not be stubborn.

Hebrews 8.9 (Jeremiah 31.32) They were not faithful to the covenant I made with them, and so I paid no attention to them.

Hebrews 10.5 (Psalm 40.6) You do not want sacrifices and offerings, but you have prepared a body for me.

Hebrews 10.27 (Isaiah 26.11) The fierceness . . . and now fire will destroy those who oppose God.

Hebrews 10.38b (Habakkuk 2.4a) If he turns back, I will not be pleased with him.

Hebrews 11.5 (Genesis 5.24) Enoch pleased God, and nobody could find him, because God had taken him up.

Hebrews 11.21 (Genesis 47.31) He leaned on the top of his walking stick and worshiped God.

Hebrews 12.5, 6 (Proverbs 3.11, 12) Son, pay attention when the Lord corrects you, and do not be discouraged when he rebukes you. Because the Lord corrects everyone he loves, and punishes everyone he accepts as a son.

Hebrews 12.13 (Proverbs 4.26) Keep walking on straight paths.

Hebrews 12.15 (Deuteronomy 29.18) A bitter plant that grows up.

Hebrews 12.26 (Haggai 2.6) I will once more shake heaven and earth.

Hebrews 13.6 (Psalm 118.6) The Lord is my helper; I will not fear what anyone may do to me.

James 1.10, 11 (Isaiah 40.6, 7) Like the flower of a wild plant. . . . Its flower falls off.

James 4.6 (Proverbs 3.34) The Lord resists the proud, but gives grace to the humble.

1 Peter 1.24 (Isaiah 40.6, 7) All human beings are like grass, and all their glory is like wild flowers. The grass withers, and the flowers fall.

1 Peter 2.6 (Isaiah 28.16) I chose a valuable and costly stone, which I am placing as the cornerstone in the foundations of Zion, and whoever believes in him will never be disappointed.

1 Peter 2.9 (Isaiah 43.20) The chosen race, (Exodus 19.5, 6) the King's priests, the holy nation, (Isaiah 43.21) my own people, chosen to proclaim my wonderful acts.

1 Peter 3.10 (Psalm 34.12) Whoever wishes life and wants to see good times.

1 Peter 4.18 (Proverbs 11.31) It is difficult for good people to be saved; what, then, will become of godless sinners?

1 Peter 5.5 (Proverbs 3.34) The Lord resists the proud, but shows favor to the humble.

Revelation 2.7 (Ezekiel 28.13; 31.8, 9) The Garden of God.

Revelation 2.27 (Psalm 2.9) You will rule them with an iron rod.

Bible Study Notes

Chronology of the Bible

Time scales represent varied number of years

B.C. = Before Christ ca. = circa (around)[†]

Year	
PREHISTORY	THE BEGINNINGS: EVENTS IN PREHISTORY • Creation • Adam and Eve in the Garden • Cain and Abel • Noah and the Flood • The Tower of Babel
2000 B.C.	THE ANCESTORS OF THE ISRAELITES • Abraham comes to Palestine. ca. 1900 • Isaac is born to Abraham. • Jacob is born to Isaac. • Jacob has twelve sons, who become the ancestors of the twelve
1800 B.C.	tribes of Israel. The most prominent of these sons is Joseph, who becomes adviser to the King of Egypt. THE ISRAELITES IN EGYPT • The descendants of Jacob are enslaved in Egypt. ca. 1700—ca. 1290
1600 B.C.	• Moses leads the Israelites out of Egypt. ca. 1290 The Israelites wander in the wilderness. During this time Moses receives the Law on Mount Sinai. ca. 1290 — ca. 1250
1250 B.C.	THE CONQUEST AND SETTLEMENT OF CANAAN • Joshua leads the first stage of the invasion of Canaan. ca. 1250 • Israel remains a loose confederation of tribes, and leadership is exercised by heroic figures known as the Judges.
1000 B.C.	THE UNITED ISRAELITE KINGDOM • Reign of Saul ca. 1030—ca. 1010 • Reign of David ca. 1010—ca. 970 • Reign of Solomon ca. 970—ca. 931

[†]A circa date is only an approximation. Generally speaking, the earlier the time, the less precise is the dating. From the time of the death of Solomon in 931 B.C. to the Edict of Cyrus in 538 B.C., the dates given are fairly accurate, but even in the epoch a possible error of a year or two must be allowed for.

Chronology of the Bible

The Two Israelite Kingdoms

Prophets	**Year**	JUDAH (Southern Kingdom)	ISRAEL (Northern Kingdom)
	950 B.C.		
		Kings	*Kings*
		Rehoboam 931-913	Jeroboam 931-910
		Abijah 913-911	Nadab 910-909
			Baasha 909-886
	900 B.C.	Asa 911-870	Elah 886-885
			Zimri 7 days in 885
		Jehoshaphat 870-848	Omri 885-874
Elijah	**850 B.C.**	Jehoram 848-841	Ahab 874-853
		Ahaziah 841	Ahaziah 853-852
		Queen Athaliah 841-835	Joram 852-841
Elisha		Joash 835-796	Jehu 841-814
	800 B.C.	Amaziah 796-781	Jehoahaz 814-798
			Jehoash 798-783
		Uzziah 781-740	Jeroboam II 783-743
Jonah Amos Hosea Micah Isaiah	**750 B.C.**		Zechariah 6 months in 743
		Jotham 740-736	Shallum 1 month in 743
		Ahaz 736-716	Menahem 743-738
		Hezekiah 716-687	Pekahiah 738-737
			Pekah 737-732
	700 B.C.		Hosea 732-723
			Fall of Samaria 722
		THE LAST YEARS OF THE KINGDOM OF JUDAH	
		Manasseh 687-642	
	650 B.C.		
		Amon 642-640	
		Josiah 640-609	
Zephaniah Nahum Jeremiah Habakkuk? Ezekiel	**600 B.C.**	Joahaz 3 months in 609	
		Jehoiakim 609-598	
		Jehoiachin 3 months in 598	
		Zedekiah 598-587	
		Fall of Jerusalem July 587 or 586	

Chronology of the Bible

Prophets	Year	
		THE EXILE AND THE RESTORATION
	550 B.C.	The Jews taken into exile in Babylonia after the fall of Jerusalem
Haggai Obadiah Malachi Joel? Zechariah Daniel		• Persian Rule begins 539 • Edict of Cyrus allows Jews to return. 538 • Foundations of New Temple laid. 520 • Restoration of the walls of Jerusalem 445-443
	400 B.C.	THE TIME BETWEEN THE TESTAMENTS
		• Alexander the Great establishes Greek rule in Palestine. 333 • Palestine is ruled by the Ptolemies, descendants of one of Alexander's generals, who had been given the position of ruler over Egypt. 323 to 198
	200 B.C.	• Palestine is ruled by the Seleucids, descendants of one of Alexander's generals, who had acquired the rule of Syria. 198 to 166 • Jewish revolt under Judas Maccabeus reestablishes Jewish independence. Palestine is ruled by Judas' family and descendants, the Hasmoneans. 166 to 63 • The Roman general Pompey takes Jerusalem 63 B.C. Palestine is ruled by puppet kings appointed by Rome. One of these is Herod the Great, who rules from 37 B.C. to 4 B.C.
	A.D. 1	THE TIME OF THE NEW TESTAMENT *Birth of Jesus*[†] Ministry of John the Baptist; baptism of Jesus and beginning of his public ministry
	A.D. 30	• Death and resurrection of Jesus • Conversion of Paul (Saul of Tarsus) ca. A.D. 37 • Ministry of Paul ca. A.D. 41 to A.D. 65 • Final imprisonment of Paul ca. A.D. 65

[†] The present era was calculated to begin with the birth of Jesus Christ, that is, in A.D. 1 (A.D. standing for *Anno Domini* 'in the year of the Lord'). However, the original calculation was later found to be wrong by a few years, so that the birth of Christ took place perhaps about 6 B.C.

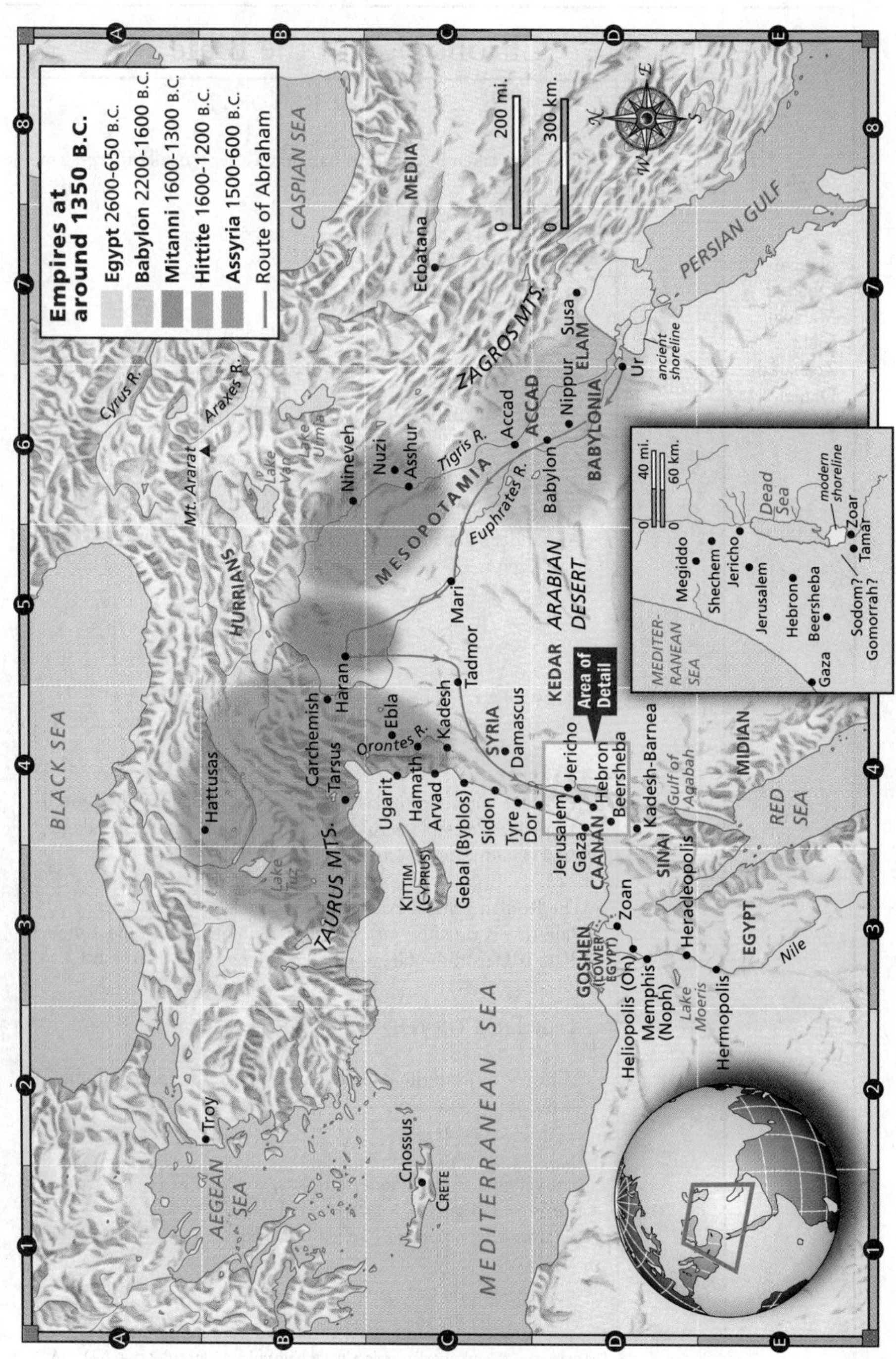

Map 1 The Ancient Near East, 1800 to 1400 B.C.

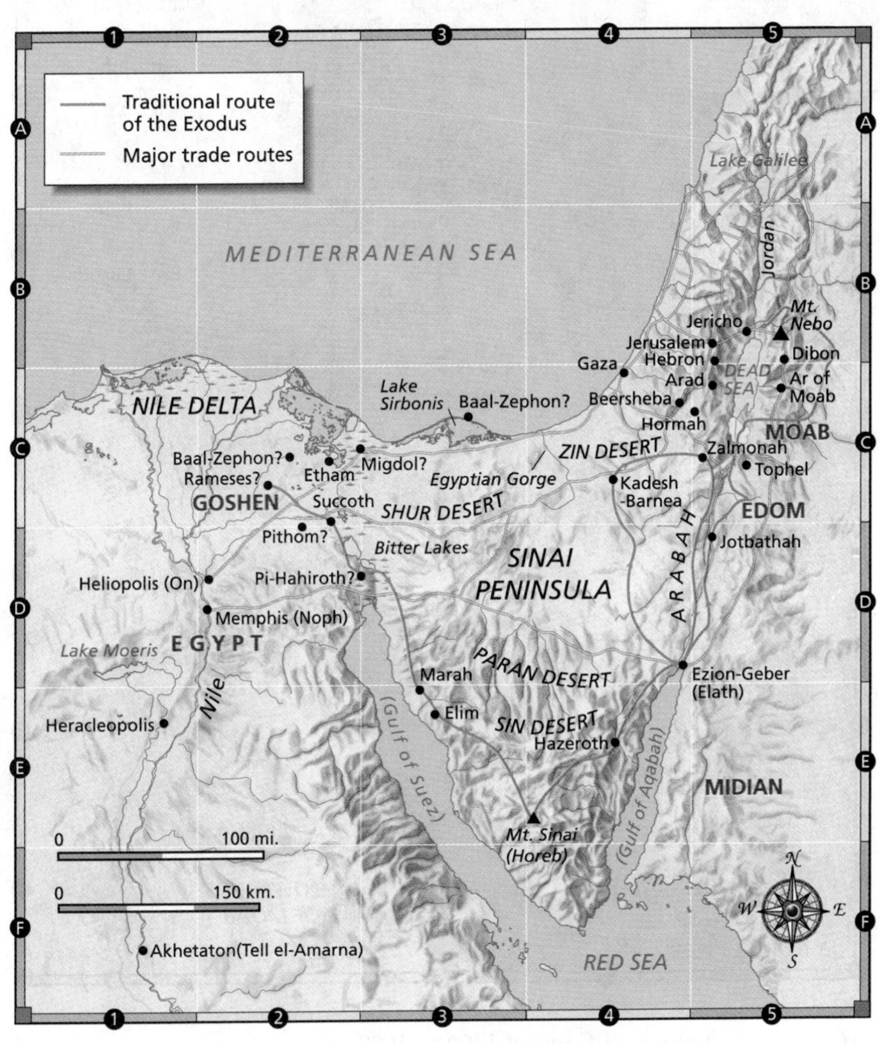

Map 2 Egypt and Sinai, 1400 to1200 B.C.

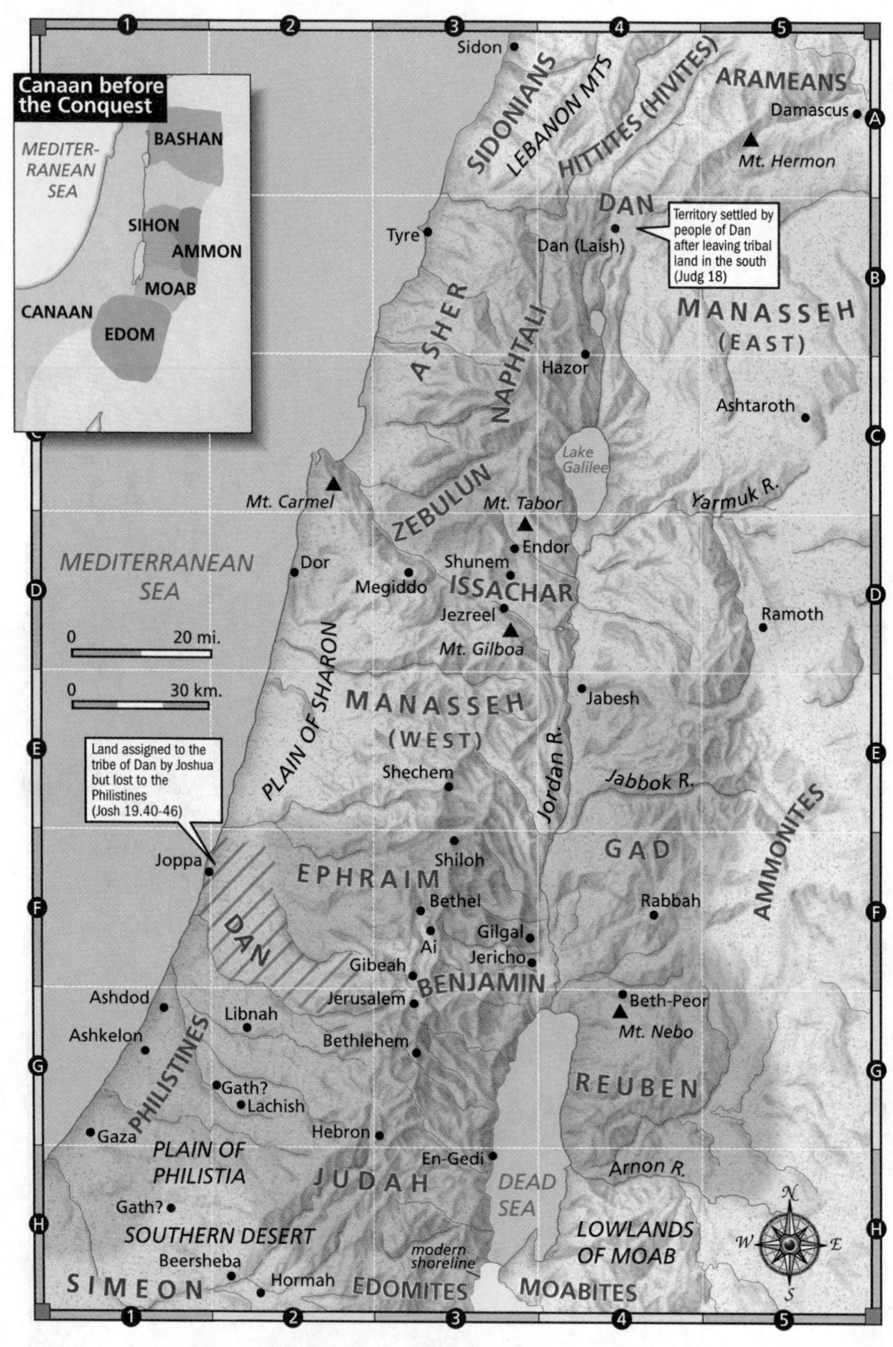

Canaan before the Conquest
MEDITER-RANEAN SEA
BASHAN
SIHON
AMMON
MOAB
CANAAN
EDOM
Sidon
SIDONIANS
LEBANON MTS
HITTITES (HIVITES)
ARAMEANS
Damascus
Mt. Hermon
DAN
Dan (Laish)
Territory settled by people of Dan after leaving tribal land in the south (Judg 18)
Tyre
ASHER
NAPHTALI
MANASSEH (EAST)
Hazor
Ashtaroth
Lake Galilee
Yarmuk R.
Mt. Carmel
ZEBULUN
Mt. Tabor
Endor
MEDITERRANEAN SEA
Dor
Shunem
Megiddo
ISSACHAR
Jezreel
Ramoth
Mt. Gilboa
0 20 mi.
0 30 km.
PLAIN OF SHARON
MANASSEH (WEST)
Jabesh
Land assigned to the tribe of Dan by Joshua but lost to the Philistines (Josh 19.40-46)
Shechem
Jordan R.
Jabbok R.
AMMONITES
Joppa
Shiloh
GAD
EPHRAIM
Bethel
Rabbah
DAN
Ai
Gilgal
Jericho
Gibeah
BENJAMIN
Ashdod
Jerusalem
Beth-Peor
Libnah
Mt. Nebo
Ashkelon
Bethlehem
PHILISTINES
Gath?
Lachish
REUBEN
Gaza
Hebron
PLAIN OF PHILISTIA
En-Gedi
Arnon R.
JUDAH
DEAD SEA
Gath?
SOUTHERN DESERT
LOWLANDS OF MOAB
Beersheba
modern shoreline
SIMEON
Hormah
EDOMITES
MOABITES
N
W
E
S

Map 3 Division of Canaan, 1200 to 1000 B.C.

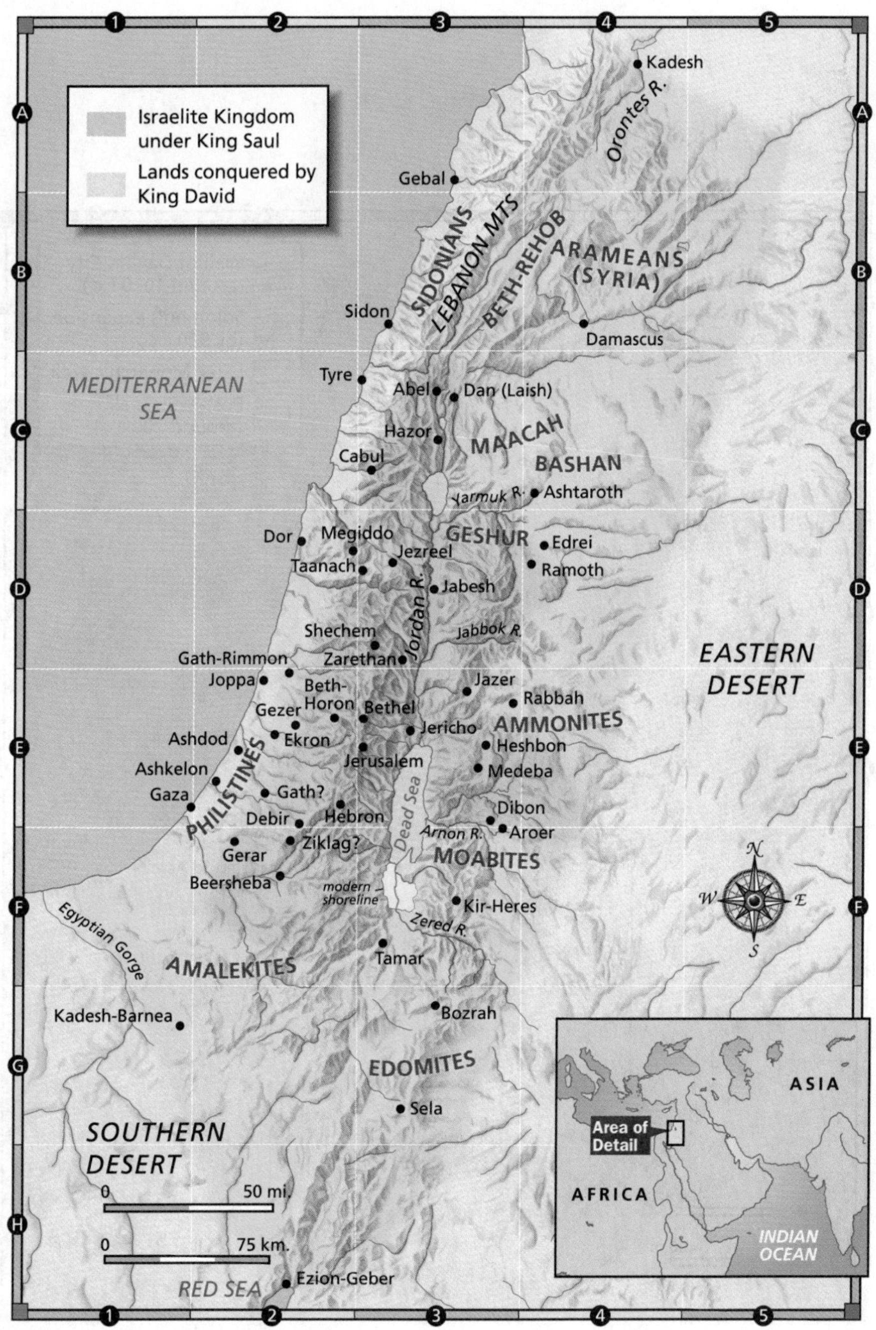

Map 4 United Israelite Kingdom, Israel in the time of King David and Solomon, 1000 to 924 B.C.

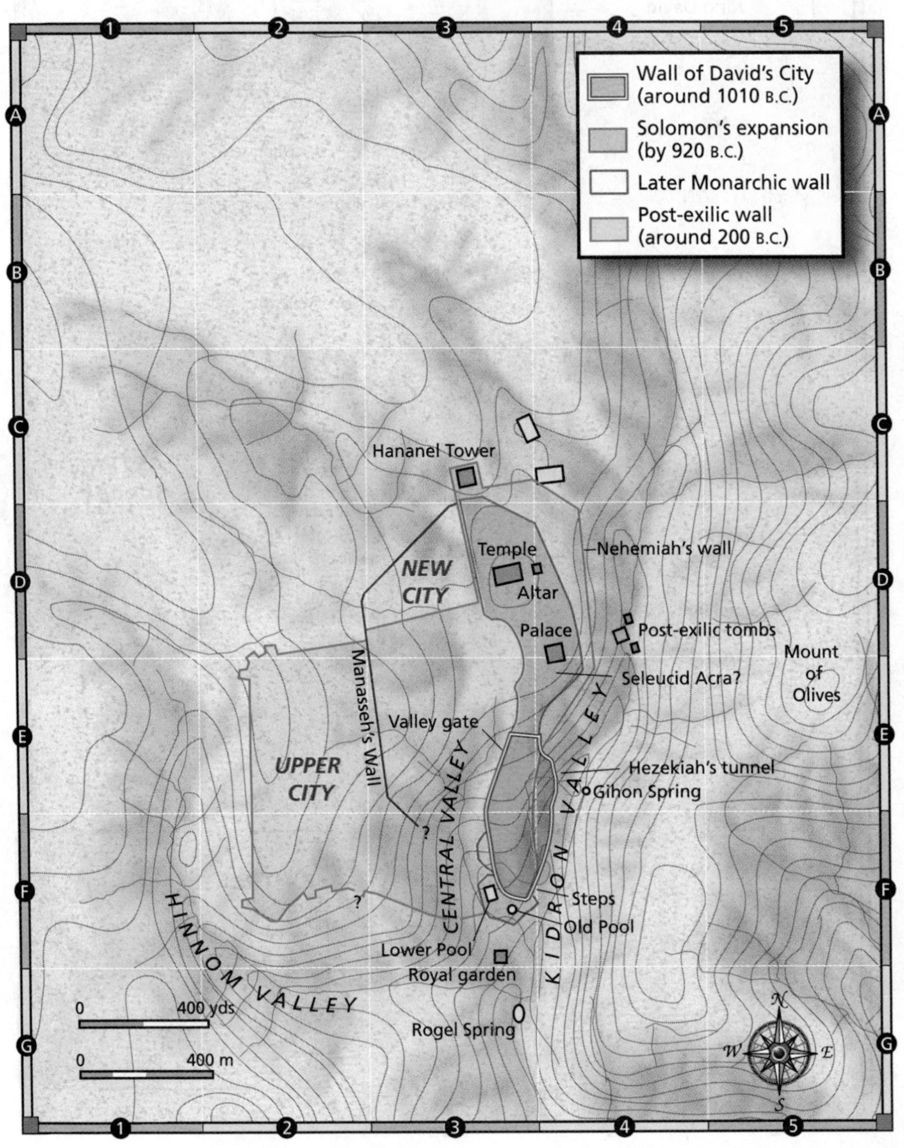

Map 5 Jerusalem in Old Testament Times, The Growth of David's City, 1010 to 200 B.C.

Map 6 The Kingdoms of Israel and Judah, 924 to 722 B.C.

Map 7 Assyrian and Babylonian Kingdoms, 9th to 6th Centuries B.C.

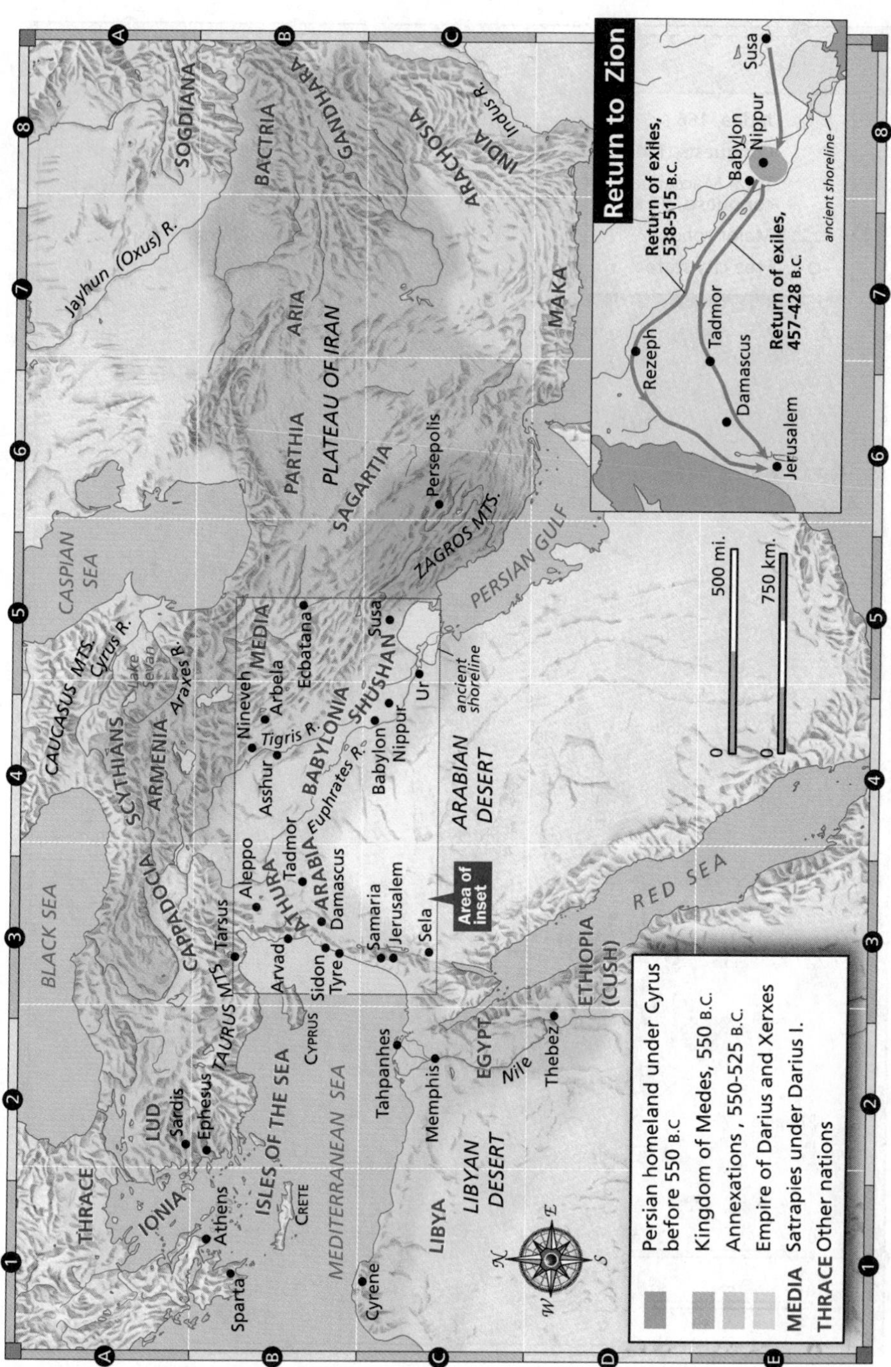

Return to Zion
Return of exiles, 538-515 B.C.
Return of exiles, 457-428 B.C.
Rezeph
Tadmor
Damascus
Jerusalem
Babylon
Nippur
Susa
ancient shoreline
BLACK SEA
CASPIAN SEA
MEDITERRANEAN SEA
PERSIAN GULF
RED SEA
CAUCASUS MTS.
TAURUS MTS.
ZAGROS MTS.
THRACE
IONIA
LUD
ISLES OF THE SEA
CAPPADOCIA
SCYTHIANS
ARMENIA
MEDIA
BABYLONIA
SHUSHAN
ATHURA
ARABIA
ARABIAN DESERT
LIBYA
LIBYAN DESERT
EGYPT
ETHIOPIA (CUSH)
PARTHIA
PLATEAU OF IRAN
SAGARTIA
ARIA
BACTRIA
SOGDIANA
GANDHARA
ARACHOSIA
INDIA
MAKA
Sparta
Athens
Sardis
Ephesus
Crete
Cyprus
Cyrene
Memphis
Tahpanhes
Thebez
Nile
Tarsus
Arvad
Sidon
Tyre
Samaria
Jerusalem
Sela
Aleppo
Tadmor
Damascus
Asshur
Nineveh
Arbela
Ecbatana
Babylon
Nippur
Ur
Susa
Persepolis
Tigris R.
Euphrates R.
Cyrus R.
Araxes R.
Lake Sevan
Jayhun (Oxus) R.
Indus R.
Area of inset
500 mi.
750 km.
Persian homeland under Cyrus before 550 B.C
Kingdom of Medes, 550 B.C.
Annexations , 550-525 B.C.
Empire of Darius and Xerxes
MEDIA Satrapies under Darius I.
THRACE Other nations

Map 8 Persian Kingdom, 550 to 330 B.C.

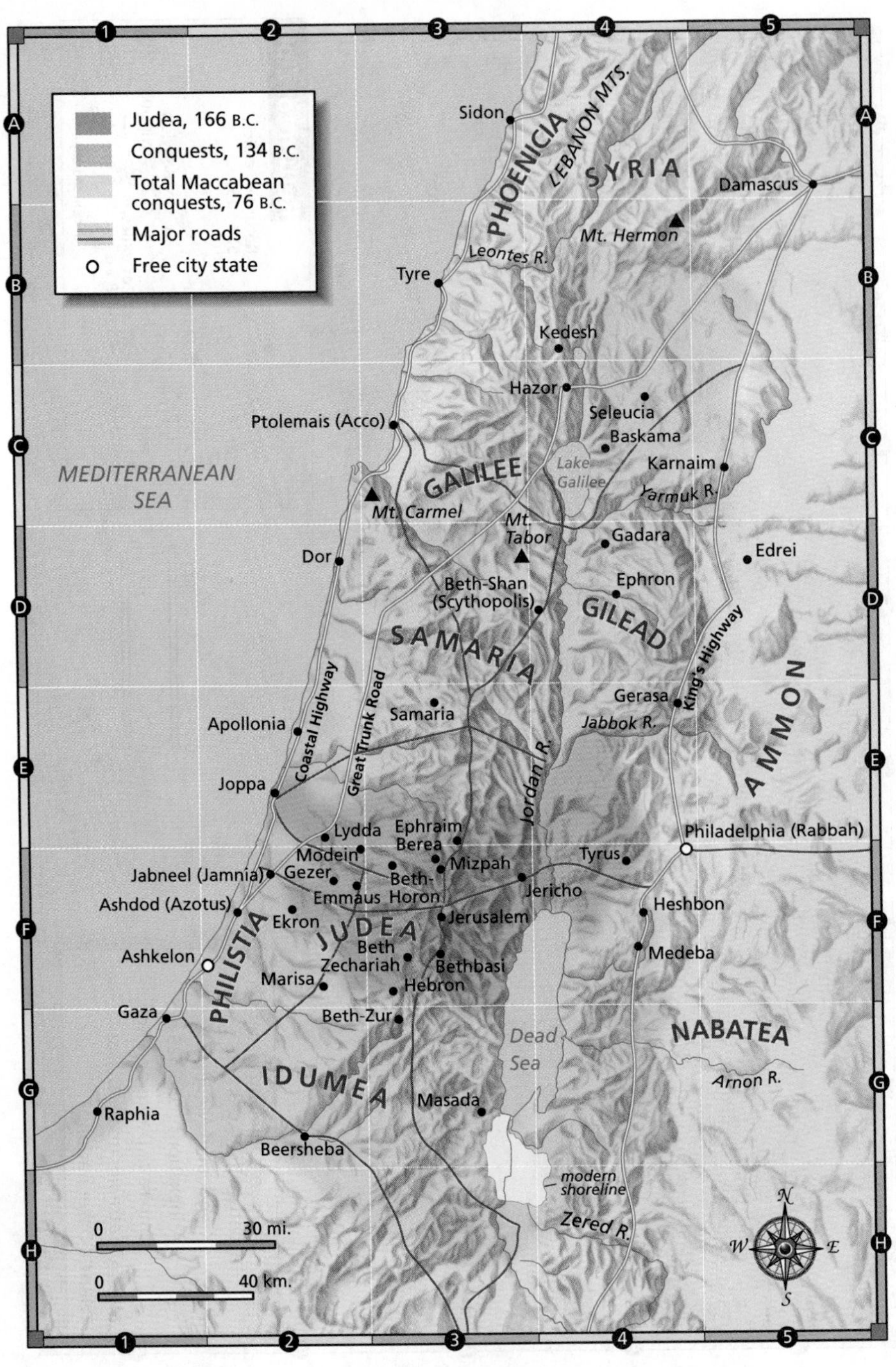

Map 9 Palestine in the Time of the Maccabees, 175 to 63 B.C.

Jesus in Galilee
Chorazin
Capernaum
Cana
Lake Galilee
Magadan
Tiberias
Hippos
Nazereth
Yarmuk R.
Mt. Tabor
Nain
Gadara
Mt.Moreh
Jordan R.
Sidon
PHOENICIA
LEBANON MTS.
Abila
ABILENE
Zarephath
Damascus
SYRIA
Mt. Hermon
Leontes R.
Tyre
ITURAEA
Caesarea Philippi
BATANEA
Ptolemais (Acco)
Capernaum
Area of Detail
Raphana
Lake Galilee
AURANITIS
Mt. Carmel
GALILEE
Tiberias
Hippos
Dion
MEDITERRANEAN SEA
Nazareth
Yarmuk R.
Abila
Gadara
Dor
Mt. Tabor
DECAPOLIS
SAMARIA
Scythopolis
Caesarea
Salim
Pella
Aenon
Samaria
Mt. Ebal
Gerasa
Mt.Gerizim
Sychar
Jabbok R.
Jordan R.
PEREA
Joppa
Arimathea?
Lydda
Ephraim
Philadelphia
Jabneel (Jamnia)
Jericho
Emmaus
Ashdod (Azotus)
Jerusalem
Bethany
Qumran
Bethlehem
Ascalon
JUDEA
Hebron
Gaza
Dead Sea
Arnon R.
IDUMEA
Raphia
Beersheba
NABATEA
modern shoreline
0
30 mi.
0
40 km.
Zered R.
N
W
E
S

Map 10 Palestine in the Time of Jesus, A.D. 6 to 30

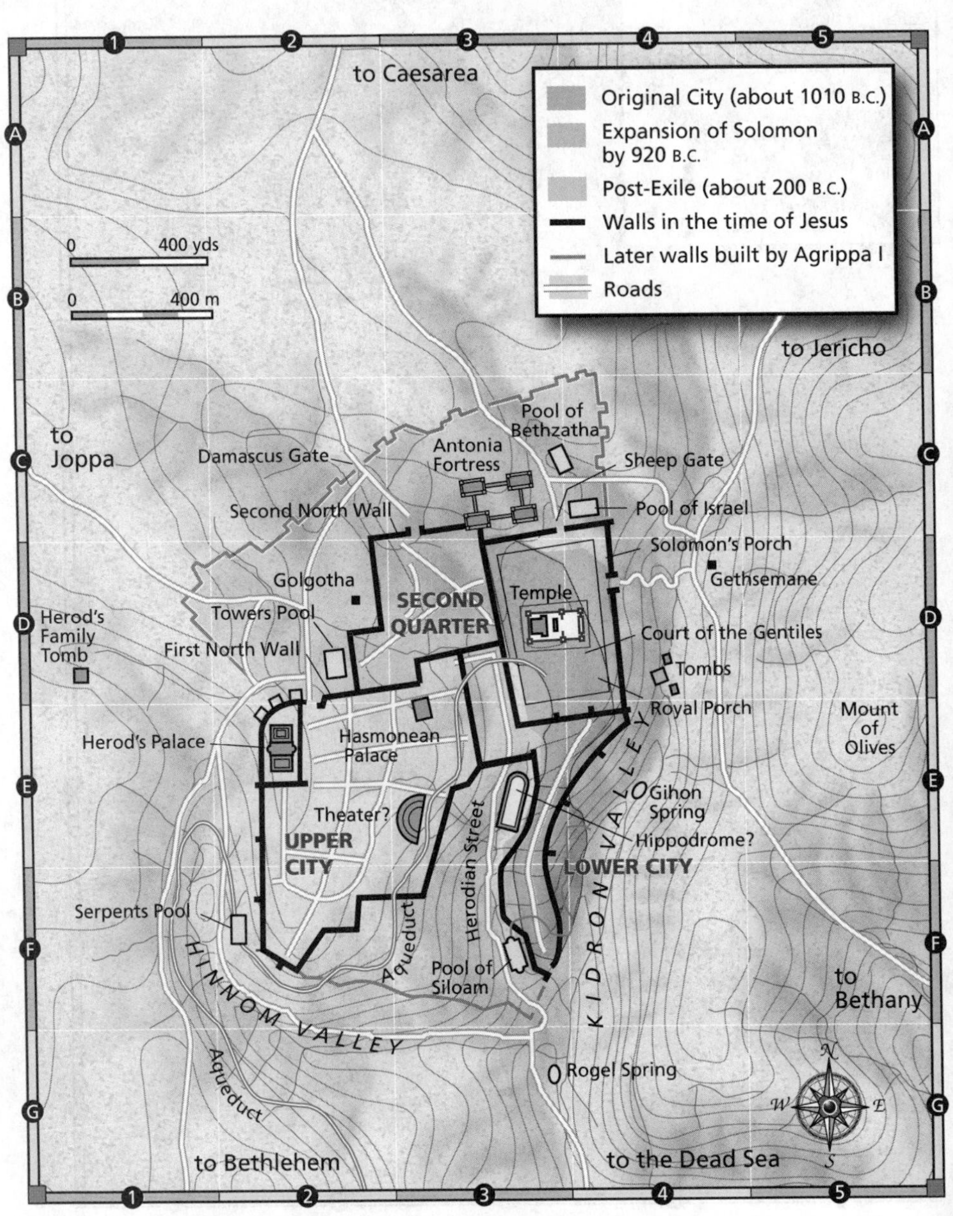

to Caesarea
Original City (about 1010 B.C.)
Expansion of Solomon by 920 B.C.
Post-Exile (about 200 B.C.)
Walls in the time of Jesus
Later walls built by Agrippa I
Roads
0 400 yds
0 400 m
to Jericho
to Joppa
Damascus Gate
Antonia Fortress
Pool of Bethzatha
Sheep Gate
Second North Wall
Pool of Israel
Solomon's Porch
Golgotha
Gethsemane
SECOND QUARTER
Temple
Herod's Family Tomb
Towers Pool
First North Wall
Court of the Gentiles
Tombs
Royal Porch
Mount of Olives
Herod's Palace
Hasmonean Palace
Gihon Spring
Theater?
Hippodrome?
UPPER CITY
Herodian Street
LOWER CITY
Serpents Pool
Aqueduct
Pool of Siloam
KIDRON VALLEY
HINNOM VALLEY
to Bethany
Rogel Spring
Aqueduct
to Bethlehem
to the Dead Sea
N
W
E
S

Map 11 Jerusalem in the Time of Jesus, around A.D. 30

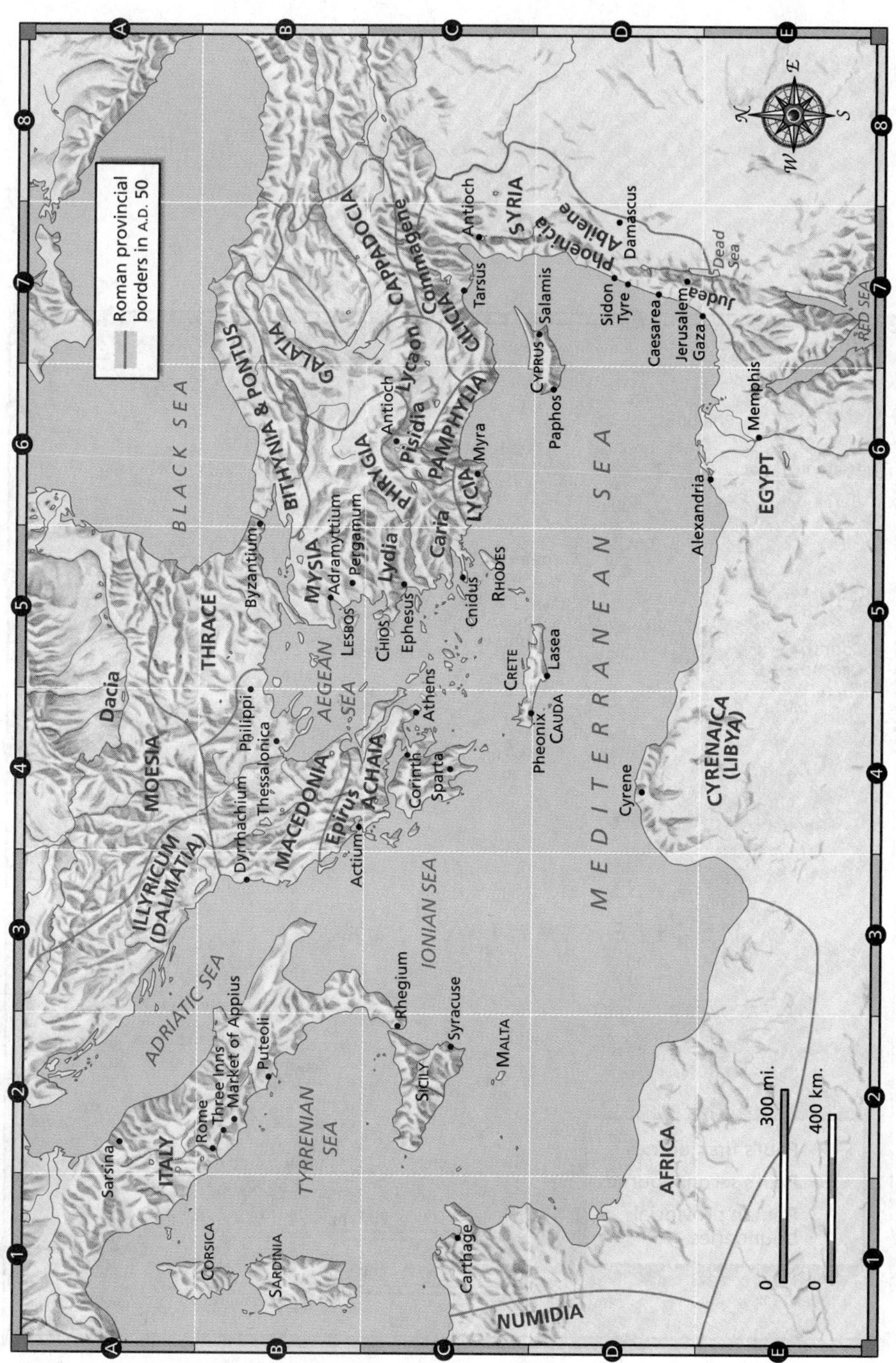

Map 12 World of the New Testament, around A.D. 50

Map 13 Paul's First and Second Journeys

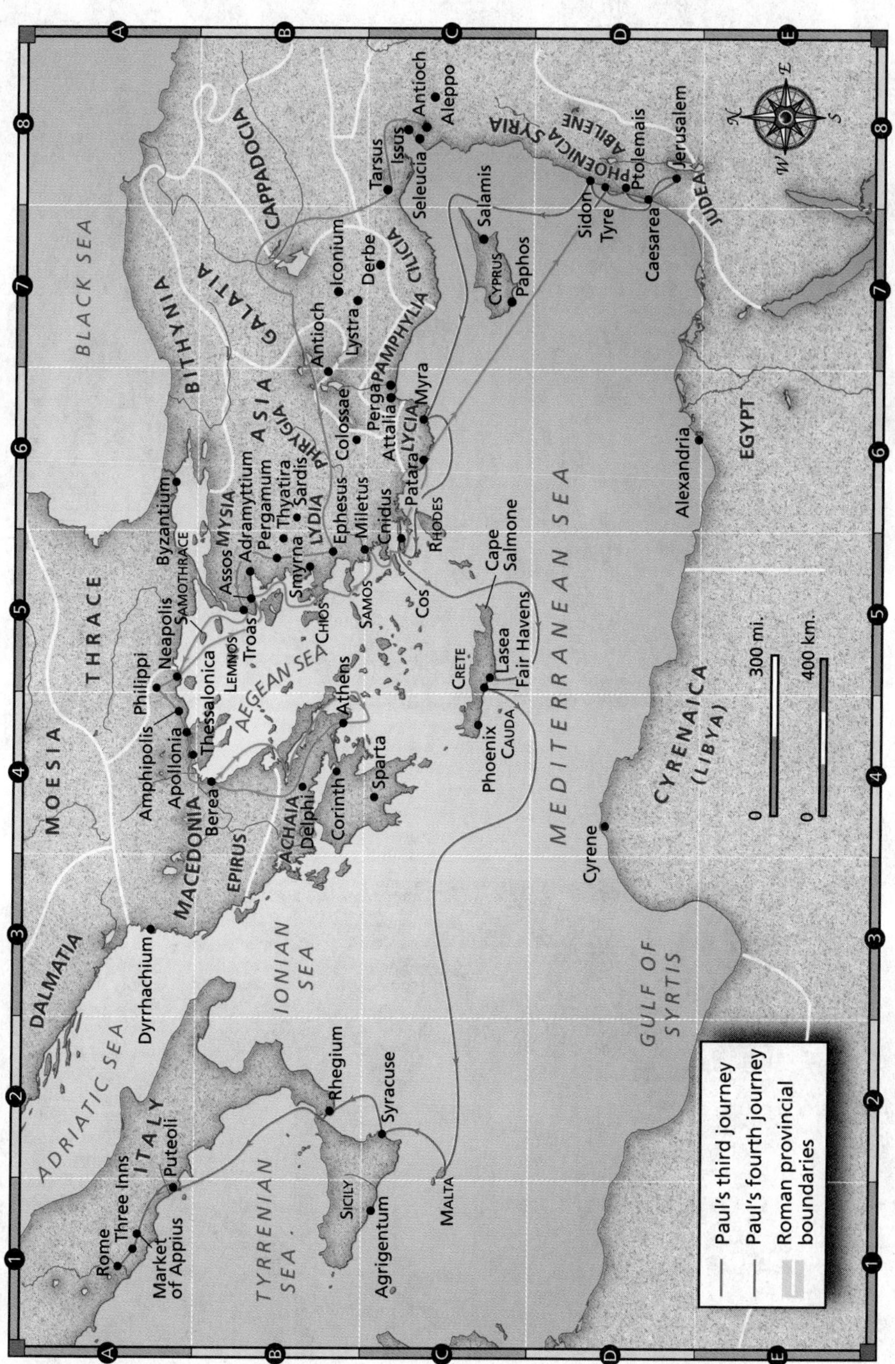

Map 14 Paul's Third Journey and His Journey to Rome

Bible Study Notes

The Bible is one of the most precious books the world has ever seen. It is a book full of profound wisdom and insight about human nature and the character and purpose of the God who created all things. Throughout the centuries people from many lands have opened the Bible and read from it in their own language. Here they have learned about God's love and justice. Great leaders and thinkers have searched its pages and explored its truths, looking for the answers to life's problems and challenges.

You are invited to make that same exploration. The following reading helps can assist you to begin this rewarding journey.

What's in the Bible gives a brief summary of every book in the Bible, and is preceded by a chart giving an overview of all the books that make up the Bible.

How to Read the Bible provides simple suggestions on how to read the Bible devotionally and to keep notes on the many lessons you'll learn.

Read through the Bible in a Year is a reading plan that is easy to follow and guides you through the entire Old and New Testaments in exactly one year.

Some Readings for Special Days guides you to passages you may want to read on special days like Christmas, Easter, Mother's Day — and even your own birthday.

Famous Passages of the Bible helps you locate those famous Bible stories you've heard time and again, but may never have read for yourself.

Finding Help in the Bible leads you to those passages that can help you when you're facing a difficult problem or special challenge.

What the Bible Says about God's Forgiveness leads you to places in the Bible where you can learn how much God loves each one of us and what he has done to put us right with himself.

It really doesn't matter where you begin, but it does matter that you begin. Use any one of the above sections to get you started on a daily habit of reading the Bible. Discover for yourself the help and hope it has to offer.

Chart of the Bible

The word "Bible" comes from the Greek word *biblia*, which means "books." So the Bible is really a collection or library of many books. These books are divided into two main parts, the Old Testament and the New Testament.

Old Testament

The Old Testament tells the history of the people of Israel. This history is based on their faith in the God of Israel and on their religious life as the people of God. The authors of these books wrote about what God had done for them as a people and how they were to worship and obey God in return. The following chart shows the different groups of books that make up the Old Testament.

The Law	History	Poetry & Wisdom	Major Prophets	Minor Prophets
Genesis	Joshua	Job	Isaiah	Hosea
Exodus	Judges	Psalms	Jeremiah	Joel
Leviticus	Ruth	Proverbs	Lamentations	Amos
Numbers	1 Samuel	Ecclesiastes	Ezekiel	Obadiah
Deuteronomy	2 Samuel	Songs of Songs	Daniel	Jonah
	1 Kings			Micah
	2 Kings			Nahum
	1 Chronicles			Habakkuk
	2 Chronicles			Zephaniah
	Ezra			Haggai
	Nehemiah			Zechariah
	Esther			Malachi

Deuterocanonicals/Apocrypha

The Deuterocanonicals/Apocrypha books form part of the ancient Greek translation of the Old Testament known as the Septuagint. They were located at various places among the other books of the Old Testament. They cover the period in between the Old Testament and New Testament and provide significant knowledge of development during this period.

History	Letters	Wisdom	Devotional	Teaching Stories	Prophecy
1 Esdras	Baruch	Wisdom of Solomon	Prayer of Azariah and Song of the Three Young Men	Tobit Judith Susanna Bel and the Dragon	2 Esdras
Additions to Book of Esther	Letter of Jeremiah	Sirach (Ecclesiasticus)			
1 Maccabees 2 Maccabees			Prayer of Manasseh		

New Testament

The books of the New Testament were written by the followers of Jesus Christ. These followers wanted others to know the Good News about Jesus Christ and the possibility of a "new" life available to them through his death and resurrection. The following chart shows the different groups of books that make up the New Testament. Although scholarly opinion has varied, Paul has traditionally been identified as the author of the letters indicated below.

The Gospels	Paul's Letters	History	Prophecy	General Letters
Matthew Mark Luke John	Romans 1 Corinthians 2 Corinthians Galatians Ephesians Philippians Colossians 1 Thessalonians 2 Thessalonians 1 Timothy 2 Timothy Titus Philemon	Acts	Revelation	Hebrews James 1 Peter 2 Peter 1 John 2 John 3 John Jude

What's in the Bible

The following are summaries for each book of the Bible. It will be obvious from how brief the descriptions are that they are not complete. They should, however, serve as a quick and handy guide to the content of the whole Bible.

Old Testament

Genesis: In this book of beginnings the stories are about creation, early relationships between God and people, and God's promise to bless Abraham and his descendants.

Exodus: The name Exodus means "departure" and this book tells how God led the Israelites out of a life of hardship and slavery in Egypt. God made a covenant with them and gave them the Law to order their lives.

Leviticus: This book is named for the priestly tribe of Levi and is made up of laws concerning rituals and ceremonies.

Numbers: The Israelites wandered in the wilderness for 40 years before entering Canaan, the promised land. The name of the book comes from two censuses taken during the journey.

Deuteronomy: Moses gave three farewell speeches shortly before he died. In them he reviewed the laws of God for the Israelites. This book gets its name—"second law"—from this review.

Joshua: Joshua led the Israelite armies to victory over the Canaanites. The book ends with the division of the land among the tribes of Israel.

Judges: The Israelites often fell away from God and into the hands of oppressors. God sent "judges" to lead and deliver them.

Ruth: Love and dedication between Ruth and her mother-in-law, Naomi, are the focus of this story.

1 Samuel: Samuel was the leader of Israel between the time of Judges and the time of Saul, the first King of Israel. When Saul's leadership failed, David was anointed by Samuel to be king.

2 Samuel: Under David's rule, the new nation was strong and unified. But after David committed adultery and murder, his family and nation suffered.

1 Kings: This book starts with stories about Solomon's reign over Israel. After the death of Solomon, the kingdom went to war with itself, north against south. The result was two nations, Israel in the north and Judah in the south.

2 Kings: Israel was conquered by Assyria in 721 B.C. Judah was defeated by Babylon in 586 B.C. These events were seen as judgment upon the people because they did not follow the laws of God.

1 Chronicles: This book begins with genealogies from Adam to David and then recounts the incidents of David's reign.

2 Chronicles: This book covers the same period as 2 Kings but the emphasis is on Judah, the southern kingdom, and its rulers.

Ezra: God's people returned to Jerusalem after being held captive in Babylon for several decades. One of the leaders was Ezra. This book contains his charge to the people to be true to the Law of God.

Nehemiah: After the Temple was rebuilt, the protective wall around Jerusalem was restored. Nehemiah brought this effort to completion. He also worked with Ezra to restore religious fervor among the people.

Esther: This book tells the story of the Jewish queen of Persia who exposed a plot to destroy her people and thus saved all the Jews in that country from destruction.

Job: The question, "Why do innocent people suffer?" is addressed in the story of Job.

Psalms: These 150 prayers and hymns were used by the Hebrew people to express their relationship with God. They cover the whole range of human emotions from joy to anger, from hope to despair.

Proverbs: This is a book of wise sayings and ethical and common sense teachings on how to live a godly life.

Ecclesiastes: In a quest for happiness and the meaning of life, this writer, known as "the Philosopher," asks many questions that are still raised in today's society.

Song of Songs: This poem describes the joy and ecstasy of love. It has been understood both as a picture of God's love for Israel and of Christ's love for the Church.

Isaiah: The prophet Isaiah brought the message of God's judgment on the nations, pointed to a future king like David, and promised a time of comfort and peace.

Jeremiah: Before Babylon destroyed Judah, Jeremiah foretold God's judgment. While his message was largely of destruction, he also pointed toward a new covenant with God.

Lamentations: As Jeremiah had warned, Jerusalem fell to the Babylonians. This book records five "laments" for the fallen city.

Ezekiel: Ezekiel's message was given to the Jews held captive in Babylon. He used stories and parables to speak about judgment, hope and restoration.

Daniel: Daniel remained faithful to God while facing many pressures as a captive in Babylon. This book includes Daniel's prophetic visions.

Hosea: Hosea used his commitment to his wife in the face of her unfaithfulness to illustrate the "adultery" Israel had committed against God, whose faithful love never ceased.

Joel: After a locust plague in Judah, Joel urged the people to repent.

Amos: During an era of prosperity, this Judean prophet preached judgment on the rich leaders of Israel. Amos urged them to consider the poor and oppressed rather than their own self-satisfaction.

Obadiah: Obadiah prophesied judgment on Edom, a neighboring country.

Jonah: Jonah did not want to preach to the Ninevites, an enemy people. When he finally brought God's message to them, they repented.

Micah: Micah's message to Judah was a prophecy of judgment as well as forgiveness and hope for restoration. Especially notable is his single verse summary of what God requires of us (6.8).

Nahum: Nahum announced that God would destroy the people of Nineveh because of their cruelty in war.

Habakkuk: Habakkuk's book features a dialogue between Habakkuk and God about suffering and justice.

Zephaniah: Zephaniah announced the day of the Lord, which would bring judgment on Judah and other surrounding nations. This coming day would be one of doom for many, but a humble and faithful remnant would survive to bless the whole world.

Haggai: After the people returned from exile, Haggai reminded them to give God their highest priority and to rebuild the Temple before working on their own homes.

Zechariah: Like Haggai, Zechariah urged the people to rebuild the Temple, assuring them of God's help and blessings. His visions pointed to a glorious future.

Malachi: After the exiles returned, they became complacent about their religious life. Malachi tried to stir them up by preaching about the day of the Lord.

Deuterocanonicals/Apocrypha

Tobit: The book of Tobit provides a clear picture of Jewish culture and religious life in the centuries before the time of Jesus. It weaves together two stories about Jewish life in Persia after the exile—that of the pious Tobit in Nineveh and the long-suffering Sarah in Ecbatana.

Judith: This book tells the story of Judith, a woman of great courage and faith in God who was able to carry out a bold plan to rescue her people by driving out the enemy troops who were attacking her city.

Additions to Book of Esther: The book of Esther in Greek is a translation, adaptation, and expansion of the book of Esther in Hebrew. The new material helps the reader better to see the religious dimensions of Esther's story.

Wisdom of Solomon: This book uses both traditional Jewish material and ideas from Greek philosophy to teach that God will reward the faithful and punish the wicked.

Sirach (Ecclesiasticus): This book is a lengthy collection of wise advice on a wide variety of practical problems. It is very similar in style to the Old Testament book of Proverbs.

Baruch: This book is set in the time of the Babylonian exile. It is comprised of a national prayer of confession, a wisdom hymn and a consolation poem in the style of Isaiah.

Letter of Jeremiah: While written in the form of a letter, this book is really more of a sermon about the foolishness of idolatry.

The Prayer of Azariah and Song of the Three Young Men: This is an addition to the book of Daniel. It includes the prayer of Azariah followed by a hymn of praise that the three friends of Daniel sang in the midst of the fiery furnace.

Susanna: This book is also an addition to the book of Daniel. It is the story of a narrow escape by an innocent victim of lust and lying, and is the basis of Daniel's enduring reputation as a brilliant judge.

Bel and the Dragon: This is the third of the additions to Daniel. It consists of two stories attacking idolatry. In each one Daniel shows that there is only one true and living God.

1 Maccabees: This is a history of the Jewish revolt (168 B.C.) against the Seleucid rulers of Syria. It tells of the priestly family of Judas Maccabeus and the establishment of an independent Judea under Maccabean kings (134 B.C.). This book seeks to show that God, who had led and rescued Israel in former times of crisis, is just as active in their present day, and in the same ways.

2 Maccabees: This book is not a continuation of the history given in 1 Maccabees. Instead, it is a parallel account of the period covered in 1 Maccabees 1–7. The author is deeply interested in the meaning of martyrdom and resurrection.

1 Esdras: Esdras is the Greek form of the name Ezra and this book closely parallels the canonical Old Testament book of Ezra. It is a history of the Jews from the time of Josiah to that of Ezra. The author's purpose is to encourage the reform and renewal of Israel's worship life.

2 Esdras: This book is not related to 1 Esdras. It is a series of visions and revelations which aims to reveal the future in ways that will help believers bear up under the suffering and persecution they must endure.

The Prayer of Manasseh: This brief prayer is an excellent example of a Psalm of repentance.

New Testament

Matthew: This Gospel includes many Old Testament quotations, thus appealing to a Jewish audience and presenting Jesus as the Messiah promised in the Hebrew Scriptures. Matthew told the story of Jesus from birth to resurrection and placed emphasis on his teaching.

Mark: Mark wrote a short, action-packed Gospel. He emphasized Jesus' miracles and his life of suffering. His aim was to deepen the faith and commitment of the believers in the community to which he wrote.

Luke: In this Gospel, the availability of salvation for all people is emphasized. Luke proclaimed this message by showing Jesus' involvement with people who are poor, needy, and on the fringes of society.

John: John's Gospel stands apart from the others. John organized his message around seven signs that point to Jesus as the Son of God. His writing style is reflective and filled with striking images.

Acts: When Jesus left his disciples, the Holy Spirit came to abide with them. Written by Luke as the sequel to his Gospel, Acts records key events in the history of the work of the early Christian Church to spread the Gospel throughout the Mediterranean world.

Romans: In this important letter, Paul wrote to the Romans about life in the Spirit, which is given to believers in Christ through faith. The apostle tells them about God's great kindness and declares that because of Jesus Christ, God accepts us and sets us free from our sins.

1 Corinthians: This letter deals with the problems the church in Corinth was experiencing: dissension, immorality, public worship, and confusion about spiritual gifts.

2 Corinthians: In this letter, Paul wrote about his relationship with the church of Corinth and the effects of certain false apostles on his ministry.

Galatians: This letter addresses freedom from the law through Christ. Paul declares that it is by faith that all who believe are put right with God.

Ephesians: A central theme to this letter is that God's eternal purpose is to bring together from many nations and peoples the universal church of Jesus Christ.

Philippians: This letter emphasizes the joy found in any situation when a person believes in Christ. Paul wrote it while in prison.

Colossians: In this letter Paul tells the people of Colossae to make Christ the center of their faith and to put aside their superstitions.

1 Thessalonians: In this letter Paul gives advice to the people of Thessalonica concerning Christ's return.

2 Thessalonians: This letter discusses the same topics as the first. Paul teaches the people a way to be ready for the Lord.

1 Timothy: This letter served as a guide for Timothy, a young leader in the church. It contains advice about worship, ministry, and relationships within the church.

2 Timothy: This is Paul's last letter. In it he offers a final challenge to his co-worker.

Titus: Titus was ministering in Crete. In this letter, Paul gave him advice on how to help Christians follow Christ.

Philemon: In this letter, Philemon is urged to forgive his runaway slave, Onesimus, and accept him as a friend in Christ.

Hebrews: The letter to the Hebrews challenges new Christians to move beyond their traditional rituals and ceremonies and believe that Christ has fulfilled them all.

James: James advises putting beliefs into practice and offers practical ways for Christians to live out their faith.

1 Peter: This letter was written to comfort early Christians who were being persecuted for their faith.

2 Peter: In this letter Peter warned against false teachers and urged Christians to stay loyal to God.

1 John: This letter explains basic truths about the Christian life, with emphasis on the command to love one another.

2 John: This letter, addressed to "the elect lady and her children," warns against false teachers.

3 John: In contrast to 2 John, this letter states the need to welcome people who preach Christ.

Jude: Jude warns against the influence of evil ones outside the fellowship of believers.

Revelation: This book was written to encourage persecuted believers and affirm their faith that God will care for them. Using visions and symbols, the writer illustrates the triumph of good over evil and the creation of a new heaven and new earth.

How to Read the Bible

Set aside time each day to read from your Bible. Try to make it the same time each day. Be realistic. Commit yourself only to as much time as you honestly feel that you can stick to on an ongoing basis. Before you begin reading ask for God's guidance and blessing. Some people have found that keeping a daily notebook is helpful. Use the following steps to get the most out of your daily Bible reading:

1. **Select** a passage (perhaps one from the "Read through the Bible in a Year" section that follows).

2. **Examine** its context:

   a. What kind of book is it drawn from? A biographical book such as one of the Gospel accounts of Jesus' life; a long historical book, such as The Second Book of Samuel, which tells of the reign of King David; a brief letter to a person (The Letters of Paul to Timothy) or to a specific church (The Letters of Paul to the Corinthians).

   b. What is the overall purpose/intent of this book? (Do not do lengthy research, but feel free to read the opening and closing paragraphs as well as section headings and introductions if your Bible has them.)

   c. What occurs, or is discussed in the passages immediately preceding and following the passage you chose?

3. **Read** the passage quickly for sense.

4. **Identify** key words or phrases. Are there words or thoughts that are repeated throughout the passage? Are any cause and effect relationships established? (These are often signaled by words like *if* and *then*, *therefore*, *because*, *since*, and *so*.) Are any comparisons made or similarities pointed out? Are any two people, things or concepts contrasted?

5. **Read** the passage again and ask yourself what is the intent or purpose of the passage. Try to find out what the author is saying. Be honest; don't just look for what you want to hear. The Bible has many strong messages that can change lives!

6. **What do you learn about God from this passage?** What do you learn about human nature? Ask yourself how this message applies to you. Is there anything you need to change in your life in order to be a more faithful child of God or more loving to your neighbor? Ask for God's help in making this change.

7. **Re-read** the passage one more time. Is there one verse you would like to commit to memory? Why not write it on an index card and carry it with you throughout the day as a study aid?

8. **Thank God** for what he has shown you, and ask for his help as you seek to apply this lesson in your life.

9. **Share** what you have learned with someone else.

Read through the Bible in a Year

Have you ever read the entire Bible all the way through? By committing just twenty or thirty minutes a day you can use the following daily reading plan to help you do just that in one year. The abbreviations used here are explained at the end of this section. For help in finding the passages refer to "How to Look Up a Bible Reference" box. Begin today and discover the riches of God's Word!

How to Look Up a Bible Reference

Every verse in this Bible is marked by its own *verse number*. To find any one of the passages listed in these reader's helps, you need to find the book, the chapter in the book, and the verse or verses within that chapter. The chapter number immediately follows the name of the book. This is followed by a period (.) which is followed by the number or range of numbers for the verses you seek. For example: 1 Corinthians 12.1-11 is the First Letter of Paul to the Corinthians, chapter twelve, verses one through eleven.

January

1 ❑Lk 5.27-39 ❑Gen 1–2 ❑Ps 1 ❑Tob 1
2 ❑Lk 6.1-26 ❑Gen 3–5 ❑Ps 2 ❑Tob 2
3 ❑Lk 6.27-49 ❑Gen 6–7 ❑Ps 3
4 ❑Lk 7.1-17 ❑Gen 8–10 ❑Ps 4 ❑Tob 3
5 ❑Lk 7.18-50 ❑Gen 11 ❑Ps 5 ❑Tob 4
6 ❑Lk 8.1-25 ❑Gen 12 ❑Ps 6
7 ❑Lk 8.26-56 ❑Gen 13–14 ❑Ps 7 ❑Tob 5
8 ❑Lk 9.1-27 ❑Gen 15 ❑Ps 8 ❑Tob 6
9 ❑Lk 9.28-62 ❑Gen 16 ❑Ps 9
10 ❑Lk 10.1-20 ❑Gen 17 ❑Ps 10
11 ❑Lk 10.21-42 ❑Gen 18 ❑Ps 11 ❑Tob 7
12 ❑Lk 11.1-28 ❑Gen 19 ❑Ps 12 ❑Tob 8
13 ❑Lk 11.29-54 ❑Gen 20 ❑Ps 13
14 ❑Lk 12.1-31 ❑Gen 21 ❑Ps 14 ❑Tob 9
15 ❑Lk 12.32-59 ❑Gen 22 ❑Ps 15 ❑Tob 10
16 ❑Lk 13.1-17 ❑Gen 23 ❑Ps 16
17 ❑Lk 13.18-35 ❑Gen 24 ❑Ps 17 ❑Tob 11
18 ❑Lk 14.1-24 ❑Gen 25 ❑Ps 18 ❑Tob 12
19 ❑Lk 14.25-35 ❑Gen 26 ❑Ps 19
20 ❑Lk 15 ❑Gen 27.1-45 ❑Ps 20 ❑Tob 13
21 ❑Lk 16 ❑Gen 27.46–28.22 ❑Ps 21 ❑Tob 14
22 ❑Lk 17 ❑Gen 29.1-30 ❑Ps 22
23 ❑Lk 18.1-17 ❑Gen 29.31–30.43 ❑Ps 23 ❑Jdt 1
24 ❑Lk 18.18-43 ❑Gen 31 ❑Ps 24 ❑Jdt 2
25 ❑Lk 19.1-27 ❑Gen 32–33 ❑Ps 25
26 ❑Lk 19.28-48 ❑Gen 34 ❑Ps 26 ❑Jdt 3
27 ❑Lk 20.1-26 ❑Gen 35–36 ❑Ps 27 ❑Jdt 4
28 ❑Lk 20.27-47 ❑Gen 37 ❑Ps 28
29 ❑Lk 21 ❑Gen 38 ❑Ps 29 ❑Jdt 5
30 ❑Lk 22.1-38 ❑Gen 39 ❑Ps 30 ❑Jdt 6
31 ❑Lk 22.39-71 ❑Gen 40 ❑Ps 31

February

1 ❑Lk 23.1-25 ❑Gen 41 ❑Ps 32 ❑Jdt 7
2 ❑Lk 23.26-56 ❑Gen 42 ❑Ps 33 ❑Jdt 8
3 ❑Lk 24.1-12 ❑Gen 43 ❑Ps 34
4 ❑Lk 24.13-53 ❑Gen 44 ❑Ps 35 ❑Jdt 9
5 ❑Heb 1 ❑Gen 45.1–46.27 ❑Ps 36 ❑Jdt 10
6 ❑Heb 2 ❑Gen 46.28–47.31 ❑Ps 37
7 ❑Heb 3.1–4.13 ❑Gen 48 ❑Ps 38 ❑Jdt 11
8 ❑Heb 4.14–6.12 ❑Gen 49–50 ❑Ps 39 ❑Jdt 12
9 ❑Heb 6.13-20 ❑Ex 1–2 ❑Ps 40
10 ❑Heb 7 ❑Ex 3–4 ❑Ps 41 ❑Jdt 13
11 ❑Heb 8 ❑Ex 5.1–6.27 ❑Prov 1 ❑Jdt 14
12 ❑Heb 9.1-22 ❑Ex 6.28–8.32 ❑Prov 2
13 ❑Heb 9.23–10.18 ❑Ex 9–10 ❑Prov 3 ❑Jdt 15
14 ❑Heb 10.19-39 ❑Ex 11–12 ❑Prov 4 ❑Jdt 16
15 ❑Heb 11.1-22 ❑Ex 13–14 ❑Prov 5
16 ❑Heb 11.23-40 ❑Ex 15 ❑Prov 6.1–7.5 ❑Wis 1
17 ❑Heb 12 ❑Ex 16–17 ❑Prov 7.6-27 ❑Wis 2
18 ❑Heb 13 ❑Ex 18–19 ❑Prov 8
19 ❑Mt 1 ❑Ex 20–21 ❑Prov 9 ❑Wis 3
20 ❑Mt 2 ❑Ex 22–23 ❑Prov 10 ❑Wis 4
21 ❑Mt 3 ❑Ex 24 ❑Prov 11
22 ❑Mt 4 ❑Ex 25–27 ❑Prov 12 ❑Wis 5
23 ❑Mt 5.1-20 ❑Ex 28–29 ❑Prov 13 ❑Wis 6
24 ❑Mt 5.21-48 ❑Ex 30–32 ❑Prov 14
25 ❑Mt 6.1-18 ❑Ex 33–34 ❑Prov 15 ❑Wis 7
26 ❑Mt 6.19-34 ❑Ex 35–36 ❑Prov 16 ❑Wis 8
27 ❑Mt 7 ❑Ex 37–38 ❑Prov 17
28 ❑Mt 8.1-13 ❑Ex 39–40 ❑Prov 18 ❑Wis 9

March

1 ❑Mt 8.14-34 ❑Lev 1–2 ❑Prov 19 ❑Wis 10
2 ❑Mt 9.1-17 ❑Lev 3–4 ❑Prov 20
3 ❑Mt 9.18-38 ❑Lev 5–6 ❑Prov 21 ❑Wis 11
4 ❑Mt 10.1-25 ❑Lev 7–8 ❑Prov 22 ❑Wis 12
5 ❑Mt 10.26-42 ❑Lev 9–10 ❑Prov 23
6 ❑Mt 11.1-19 ❑Lev 11–12 ❑Prov 24 ❑Wis 13
7 ❑Mt 11.20-30 ❑Lev 13 ❑Prov 25 ❑Wis 14
8 ❑Mt 12.1-21 ❑Lev 14 ❑Prov 26
9 ❑Mt 12.22-50 ❑Lev 15–16 ❑Prov 27 ❑Wis 15
10 ❑Mt 13.1-23 ❑Lev 17–18 ❑Prov 28 ❑Wis 16
11 ❑Mt 13.24-58 ❑Lev 19 ❑Prov 29 ❑Hos 4.1-11a

12 ❑Mt 14.1-21 ❑Lev 20–21 ❑Prov 30 ❑Wis 17
13 ❑Mt 14.22-36 ❑Lev 22–23 ❑Prov 31 ❑Wis 18
14 ❑Mt 15.1-20 ❑Lev 24–25 ❑Eccl 1.1-11
15 ❑Mt 15.21-39 ❑Lev 26–27 ❑Eccl 1.12—2.26 ❑Wis 19
16 ❑Mt 16 ❑Num 1–2 ❑Eccl 3.1-15 ❑Sir 1
17 ❑Mt 17 ❑Num 3–4 ❑Eccl 3.16—4.16
18 ❑Mt 18.1-20 ❑Num 5–6 ❑Eccl 5 ❑Sir 2
19 ❑Mt 18.21-35 ❑Num 7–8 ❑Eccl 6 ❑Sir 3
20 ❑Mt 19.1-15 ❑Num 9–10 ❑Eccl 7
21 ❑Mt 19.16-30 ❑Num 11–12 ❑Eccl 8 ❑Sir 4
22 ❑Mt 20.1-16 ❑Num 13–14 ❑Eccl 9.1-12 ❑Sir 5–6
23 ❑Mt 20.17-34 ❑Num 15–16 ❑Eccl 9.13—10.20
24 ❑Mt 21.1-27 ❑Num 17–18 ❑Eccl 11.1-8 ❑Sir 7
25 ❑Mt 21.28-46 ❑Num 19–20 ❑Eccl 11.9—12.14 ❑Sir 8–9
26 ❑Mt 22.1-22 ❑Num 21 ❑Song 1.1—2.7
27 ❑Mt 22.23-46 ❑Num 22.1-40 ❑Song 2.8—3.5 ❑Sir 10
28 ❑Mt 23.1-12 ❑Num 22.41—23.26 ❑Song 3.6—5.1 ❑Sir 11
29 ❑Mt 23.13-39 ❑Num 23.27—24.25 ❑Song 5.2—6.3
30 ❑Mt 24.1-31 ❑Num 25–27 ❑Song 6.4—8.4 ❑Sir 12–13
31 ❑Mt 24.32-51 ❑Num 28–29 ❑Song 8.5-14 ❑Sir 14–15

April

1 ❑Mt 25.1-30 ❑Num 30–31 ❑Job 1 ❑Sir 16–17
2 ❑Mt 25.31-46 ❑Num 32–34 ❑Job 2
3 ❑Mt 26.1-25 ❑Num 35–36 ❑Job 3 ❑Sir 18–19
4 ❑Mt 26.26-46 ❑Deut 1–2 ❑Job 4 ❑Sir 20
5 ❑Mt 26.47-75 ❑Deut 3–4 ❑Job 5
6 ❑Mt 27.1-31 ❑Deut 5–6 ❑Job 6 ❑Sir 21
7 ❑Mt 27.32-66 ❑Deut 7–8 ❑Job 7 ❑Sir 22–23
8 ❑Mt 28 ❑Deut 9–10 ❑Job 8 ❑Sir 24
9 ❑Acts 1 ❑Deut 11–12 ❑Job 9
10 ❑Acts 2.1-13 ❑Deut 13–14 ❑Job 10 ❑Sir 25
11 ❑Acts 2.14-47 ❑Deut 15–16 ❑Job 11
12 ❑Acts 3 ❑Deut 17–18 ❑Job 12 ❑Sir 26
13 ❑Acts 4.1-22 ❑Deut 19–20 ❑Job 13 ❑Sir 27
14 ❑Acts 4.23-37 ❑Deut 21–22 ❑Job 14
15 ❑Acts 5.1-16 ❑Deut 23–24 ❑Job 15 ❑Sir 28
16 ❑Acts 5.17-42 ❑Deut 25–27 ❑Job 16
17 ❑Acts 6 ❑Deut 28 ❑Job 17 ❑Sir 29
18 ❑Acts 7.1-22 ❑Deut 29–30 ❑Job 18 ❑Sir 30
19 ❑Acts 7.23—8.1a ❑Deut 31–32 ❑Job 19 ❑Sir 31
20 ❑Acts 8.1b-25 ❑Deut 33–34 ❑Job 20
21 ❑Acts 8.26-40 ❑Josh 1–2 ❑Job 21 ❑Sir 32
22 ❑Acts 9.1-25 ❑Josh 3.1—5.1 ❑Job 22 ❑Sir 33
23 ❑Acts 9.26-43 ❑Josh 5.2—6.27 ❑Job 23
24 ❑Acts 10.1-33 ❑Josh 7–8 ❑Job 24 ❑Sir 34
25 ❑Acts 10.34-48 ❑Josh 9–10 ❑Job 25 ❑Sir 35
26 ❑Acts 11.1-18 ❑Josh 11–12 ❑Job 26
27 ❑Acts 11.19-30 ❑Josh 13–14 ❑Job 27 ❑Sir 36
28 ❑Acts 12 ❑Josh 15–17 ❑Job 28 ❑Sir 37
29 ❑Acts 13.1-25 ❑Josh 18–19 ❑Job 29
30 ❑Acts 13.26-52 ❑Josh 20–21 ❑Job 30 ❑Sir 38

May

1 ❑Acts 14 ❑Josh 22 ❑Job 31 ❑Sir 39
2 ❑Acts 15.1-21 ❑Josh 23–24 ❑Job 32
3 ❑Acts 15.22-41 ❑Judg 1 ❑Job 33 ❑Sir 40
4 ❑Acts 16.1-15 ❑Judg 2–3 ❑Job 34 ❑Sir 41
5 ❑Acts 16.16-40 ❑Judg 4–5 ❑Job 35 ❑Sir 42
6 ❑Acts 17.1-15 ❑Judg 6 ❑Job 36

7 ❑Acts 17.16-34 ❑Judg 7–8 ❑Job 37 ❑Sir 43
8 ❑Acts 18 ❑Judg 9 ❑Job 38 ❑Sir 44
9 ❑Acts 19.1-20 ❑Judg 10.1–11.3 ❑Job 39
10 ❑Acts 19.21-41 ❑Judg 11.34–12.15 ❑Job 40 ❑Sir 45
11 ❑Acts 20.1-16 ❑Judg 13 ❑Job 41 ❑Sir 46
12 ❑Acts 20.17-38 ❑Judg 14–15 ❑Job 42
13 ❑Acts 21.1-36 ❑Judg 16 ❑Ps 42 ❑Sir 47
14 ❑Acts 21.37–22.29 ❑Judg 17–18 ❑Ps 43 ❑Sir 48
15 ❑Acts 22.30–23.22 ❑Judg 19 ❑Ps 44 ❑Sir 49
16 ❑Acts 23.23–24.9 ❑Judg 20 ❑Ps 45
17 ❑Acts 24.10-27 ❑Judg 21 ❑Ps 46 ❑Sir 50
18 ❑Acts 25 ❑Ruth 1–2 ❑Ps 47 ❑Sir 51
19 ❑Acts 26.1-18 ❑Ruth 3–4 ❑Ps 48
20 ❑Acts 26.19-32 ❑1 Sam 1.1–2.10 ❑Ps 49 ❑Gk Est 1
21 ❑Acts 27.1-12 ❑1 Sam 2.11-36 ❑Ps 50
22 ❑Acts 27.13-44 ❑1 Sam 3 ❑Ps 51
23 ❑Acts 28.1-16 ❑1 Sam 4–5 ❑Ps 52 ❑Gk Est 2
24 ❑Acts 28.17-31 ❑1 Sam 6–7 ❑Ps 53 ❑Gk Est 3.1-13
25 ❑Rom 1.1-15 ❑1 Sam 8 ❑Ps 54
26 ❑Rom 1.16-32 ❑1 Sam 9.1–10.16 ❑Ps 55 ❑Gk Est 13.1-7
27 ❑Rom 2.1–3.8 ❑1 Sam 10.17–11.15 ❑Ps 56 ❑Gk Est 3.14–4.17
28 ❑Rom 3.9-31 ❑1 Sam 12 ❑Ps 57 ❑Gk Est 13.8-18
29 ❑Rom 4 ❑1 Sam 13 ❑Ps 58 ❑Gk Est 14
30 ❑Rom 5 ❑1 Sam 14 ❑Ps 59 ❑Gk Est 15
31 ❑Rom 6 ❑1 Sam 15 ❑Ps 60

June

1 ❑Rom 7 ❑1 Sam 16 ❑Ps 61 ❑Gk Est 5.3–6.14
2 ❑Rom 8 ❑1 Sam 17.1-54 ❑Ps 62 ❑Gk Est 7.1–8.12
3 ❑Rom 9.1-29 ❑1 Sam 17.55–18.30 ❑Ps 63
4 ❑Rom 9.30–10.21 ❑1 Sam 19 ❑Ps 64 ❑Gk Est 16
5 ❑Rom 11.1-24 ❑1 Sam 20 ❑Ps 65 ❑Gk Est 8.13–9.19
6 ❑Rom 11.25-36 ❑1 Sam 21–22 ❑Ps 66
7 ❑Rom 12 ❑1 Sam 23–24 ❑Ps 67 ❑Gk Est 9.20–10.3
8 ❑Rom 13 ❑1 Sam 25 ❑Ps 68 ❑Gk Est 10.4–11.1
9 ❑Rom 14 ❑1 Sam 26 ❑Ps 69
10 ❑Rom 15.1-13 ❑1 Sam 27–28 ❑Ps 70 ❑Bar 1.1–3.8
11 ❑Rom 15.14-33 ❑1 Sam 29–31 ❑Ps 71 ❑Bar 3.9–5.9
12 ❑Rom 16 ❑2 Sam 1 ❑Ps 72
13 ❑Mk 1.1-20 ❑2 Sam 2.1–3.1 ❑Dan 1 ❑Let Jer 6.1-40a
14 ❑Mk 1.21-45 ❑2 Sam 3.2-39 ❑Dan 2.1-23 ❑Let Jer 6.40b-73
15 ❑Mk 2 ❑2 Sam 4–5 ❑Dan 2.24-49
16 ❑Mk 3.1-19 ❑2 Sam 6 ❑Dan 3 ❑Azar/Song Thr 1-34
17 ❑Mk 3.20-35 ❑2 Sam 7–8 ❑Dan 4 ❑Azar/Song Thr 35-68
18 ❑Mk 4.1-20 ❑2 Sam 9–10 ❑Dan 5
19 ❑Mk 4.21-41 ❑2 Sam 11–12 ❑Dan 6 ❑Sus 1-41
20 ❑Mk 5.1-20 ❑2 Sam 13 ❑Dan 7 ❑Sus 42-64
21 ❑Mk 5.21-43 ❑2 Sam 14 ❑Dan 8
22 ❑Mk 6.1-29 ❑2 Sam 15 ❑Dan 9 ❑Bel 1-22
23 ❑Mk 6.30-56 ❑2 Sam 16 ❑Dan 10.1-21 ❑Bel 23-42
24 ❑Mk 7.1-13 ❑2 Sam 17 ❑Dan 11.1-19
25 ❑Mk 7.14-37 ❑2 Sam 18 ❑Dan 11.20-45 ❑1 Macc 1
26 ❑Mk 8.1-21 ❑2 Sam 19 ❑Dan 12 ❑1 Macc 2.1-26
27 ❑Mk 8.22–9.1 ❑2 Sam 20–21 ❑Hos 1.1–2.1
28 ❑Mk 9.2-50 ❑2 Sam 22 ❑Hos 2.2-23 ❑1 Macc 2.27-48
29 ❑Mk 10.1-31 ❑2 Sam 23 ❑Hos 3 ❑1 Macc 2.49-70
30 ❑Mk 10.32-52 ❑2 Sam 24

July

1 ❑Mk 11.1-14 ❑1 Kings 1 ❑Hos 4.11b–5.4 ❑1 Macc 3.1-37
2 ❑Mk 11.15-33 ❑1 Kings 2 ❑Hos 5.5-15 ❑1 Macc 3.38–4.25
3 ❑Mk 12.1-27 ❑1 Kings 3 ❑Hos 6.1–7.2

4 ❑Mk 12.28-44 ❑1 Kings 4–5 ❑Hos 7.3-16 ❑1 Macc 4.26-61
5 ❑Mk 13.1-13 ❑1 Kings 6 ❑Hos 8 ❑1 Macc 5.1-34
6 ❑Mk 13.14-37 ❑1 Kings 7 ❑Hos 9.1-16
7 ❑Mk 14.1-31 ❑1 Kings 8 ❑Hos 9.17—10.15 ❑1 Macc 5.35-68
8 ❑Mk 14.32-72 ❑1 Kings 9 ❑Hos 11.1-11 ❑1 Macc 6.1-17
9 ❑Mk 15.1-20 ❑1 Kings 10 ❑Hos 11.12—12.14
10 ❑Mk 15.21-47 ❑1 Kings 11 ❑Hos 13 ❑1 Macc 6.18-39
11 ❑Mk 16 ❑1 Kings 12.1-31 ❑Hos 14 ❑1 Macc 6.40-63
12 ❑1 Cor 1.1-17 ❑1 Kings 12.32—13.34 ❑Joel 1
13 ❑1 Cor 1.18-31 ❑1 Kings 14 ❑Joel 2.1-11 ❑1 Macc 7.1-20
14 ❑1 Cor 2 ❑1 Kings 15.1-32 ❑Joel 2.12-32 ❑1 Macc 7.21-50
15 ❑1 Cor 3 ❑1 Kings 15.33—16.34 ❑Joel 3
16 ❑1 Cor 4 ❑1 Kings 17 ❑Am 1 ❑1 Macc 8.1-16
17 ❑1 Cor 5 ❑1 Kings 18 ❑Am 2.1—3.2 ❑1 Macc 8.17-32
18 ❑1 Cor 6 ❑1 Kings 19 ❑Am 3.3—4.3
19 ❑1 Cor 7.1-24 ❑1 Kings 20 ❑Am 4.4-13 ❑1 Macc 9.1-22
20 ❑1 Cor 7.25-40 ❑1 Kings 21 ❑Am 5 ❑1 Macc 9.23-49
21 ❑1 Cor 8 ❑1 Kings 22 ❑Am 6
22 ❑1 Cor 9 ❑2 Kings 1–2 ❑Am 7 ❑1 Macc 9.50-73
23 ❑1 Cor 10 ❑2 Kings 3 ❑Am 8 ❑1 Macc 10.1-66
24 ❑1 Cor 11.1-16 ❑2 Kings 4 ❑Am 9
25 ❑1 Cor 11.17-34 ❑2 Kings 5 ❑Ob ❑1 Macc 10.67-89
26 ❑1 Cor 12 ❑2 Kings 6.1—7.2 ❑Jon 1 ❑1 Macc 11.1-37
27 ❑1 Cor 13 ❑2 Kings 7.3-20 ❑Jon 2
28 ❑1 Cor 14.1-25 ❑2 Kings 8 ❑Jon 3 ❑1 Macc 11.38-74
29 ❑1 Cor 14.26-40 ❑2 Kings 9 ❑Jon 4 ❑1 Macc 12.1-23
30 ❑1 Cor 15.1-34 ❑2 Kings 10 ❑Mic 1
31 ❑1 Cor 15.35-58 ❑2 Kings 11 ❑Mic 2 ❑1 Macc 12.24-53

August

1 ❑1 Cor 16 ❑2 Kings 12–13 ❑Mic 3 ❑1 Macc 13.30
2 ❑2 Cor 1.1—2.4 ❑2 Kings 14 ❑Mic 4.1—5.1
3 ❑2 Cor 2.5—3.18 ❑2 Kings 15–16 ❑Mic 5.2-15 ❑1 Macc 13.31-53
4 ❑2 Cor 4.1—5.10 ❑2 Kings 17 ❑Mic 6 ❑1 Macc 14.1-24
5 ❑2 Cor 5.11—6.13 ❑2 Kings 18 ❑Mic 7
6 ❑2 Cor 6.14—7.16 ❑2 Kings 19 ❑Nah 1 ❑1 Macc 14.25-49
7 ❑2 Cor 8 ❑2 Kings 20–21 ❑Nah 2 ❑1 Macc 15.1-36
8 ❑2 Cor 9 ❑2 Kings 22.1—23.35 ❑Nah 3
9 ❑2 Cor 10 ❑2 Kings 23.36—24.20 ❑Hab 1 ❑1 Macc 15.37—16.24
10 ❑2 Cor 11 ❑2 Kings 25 ❑Hab 2 ❑2 Macc 1
11 ❑2 Cor 12 ❑1 Chr 1–2 ❑Hab 3
12 ❑2 Cor 13 ❑1 Chr 3–4 ❑Zeph 1 ❑2 Macc 2
13 ❑Jn 1.1-18 ❑1 Chr 5–6 ❑Zeph 2 ❑2 Macc 3.1-21
14 ❑Jn 1.19-34 ❑1 Chr 7–8 ❑Zeph 3
15 ❑Jn 1.35-51 ❑1 Chr 9 ❑Hag 1–2 ❑2 Macc 3.22-40
16 ❑Jn 2 ❑1 Chr 10–11 ❑Zech 1 ❑2 Macc 4.1-29
17 ❑Jn 3.1-21 ❑1 Chr 12 ❑Zech 2 ❑2 Macc 4.30-50
18 ❑Jn 3.22-36 ❑1 Chr 13–14 ❑Zech 3
19 ❑Jn 4.1-26 ❑1 Chr 15.1—16.6 ❑Zech 4 ❑2 Macc 5
20 ❑Jn 4.27-42 ❑1 Chr 16.7-43 ❑Zech 5 ❑2 Macc 6
21 ❑Jn 4.43-54 ❑1 Chr 17 ❑Zech 6
22 ❑Jn 5.1-18 ❑1 Chr 18–19 ❑Zech 7 ❑2 Macc 7.1-23
23 ❑Jn 5.19-47 ❑1 Chr 20.1—22.1 ❑Zech 8 ❑2 Macc 7.24-42
24 ❑Jn 6.1-21 ❑1 Chr 22.2—23.32 ❑Zech 9
25 ❑Jn 6.22-59 ❑1 Chr 24 ❑Zech 10 ❑2 Macc 8

26 ❑Jn 6.60-71 ❑1 Chr 25–26 ❑Zech 11 ❑2 Macc 9
27 ❑Jn 7.1-24 ❑1 Chr 27–28 ❑Zech 12
28 ❑Jn 7.25-52 ❑1 Chr 29 ❑Zech 13 ❑2 Macc 10
29 ❑Jn 8.1-20 ❑2 Chr 1.1—2.16 ❑Zech 14 ❑2 Macc 11
30 ❑Jn 8.21-47 ❑2 Chr 2.17—5.1 ❑Mal 1.1—2.9
31 ❑Jn 8.48-59 ❑2 Chr 5.2-14 ❑Mal 2.10-16

September

1 ❑Jn 9.1-23 ❑2 Chr 6 ❑Mal 2.17—3.18 ❑2 Macc 12.1-25
2 ❑Jn 9.24-41 ❑2 Chr 7 ❑Mal 4 ❑2 Macc 12.26-45
3 ❑Jn 10.1-21 ❑2 Chr 8 ❑Ps 73
4 ❑Jn 10.22-42 ❑2 Chr 9 ❑Ps 74 ❑2 Macc 13
5 ❑Jn 11.1-27 ❑2 Chr 10–11 ❑Ps 75 ❑2 Macc 14.1-25
6 ❑Jn 11.28-57 ❑2 Chr 12–13 ❑Ps 76
7 ❑Jn 12.1-26 ❑2 Chr 14–15 ❑Ps 77 ❑2 Macc 14.26-46
8 ❑Jn 12.27-50 ❑2 Chr 16–17 ❑Ps 78.1-20 ❑2 Macc 15
9 ❑Jn 13.1-20 ❑2 Chr 18 ❑Ps 78.21-37
10 ❑Jn 13.21-38 ❑2 Chr 19 ❑Ps 78.38-55 ❑1 Esd 1.1-22
11 ❑Jn 14.1-14 ❑2 Chr 20.1—21.1 ❑Ps 78.56-72 ❑1 Esd 1.23-46a
12 ❑Jn 14.15-31 ❑2 Chr 21.2—22.12 ❑Ps 79
13 ❑Jn 15.1—16.4a ❑2 Chr 23 ❑Ps 80 ❑1 Esd 1.46b-58
14 ❑Jn 16.4b-33 ❑2 Chr 24 ❑Ps 81 ❑1 Esd 2
15 ❑Jn 17 ❑2 Chr 25 ❑Ps 82
16 ❑Jn 18.1-18 ❑2 Chr 26 ❑Ps 83 ❑1 Esd 3
17 ❑Jn 18.19-38a ❑2 Chr 27–28 ❑Ps 84 ❑1 Esd 4.1-41
18 ❑Jn 18.38b—19.16a ❑2 Chr 29 ❑Ps 85
19 ❑Jn 19.16b-42 ❑2 Chr 30 ❑Ps 86 ❑1 Esd 4.42-63
20 ❑Jn 20.1-18 ❑2 Chr 31 ❑Ps 87 ❑1 Esd 5.1-46
21 ❑Jn 20.19-31 ❑2 Chr 32 ❑Ps 88
22 ❑Jn 21 ❑2 Chr 33 ❑Ps 89.1-18 ❑1 Esd 5.47-73
23 ❑1 Jn 1 ❑2 Chr 34 ❑Ps 89.19-37 ❑1 Esd 6
24 ❑1 Jn 2 ❑2 Chr 35 ❑Ps 89.38-52
25 ❑1 Jn 3 ❑2 Chr 36 ❑Ps 90 ❑1 Esd 7
26 ❑1 Jn 4 ❑Ezra 1–2 ❑Ps 91 ❑1 Esd 8.1-40
27 ❑1 Jn 5 ❑Ezra 3–4 ❑Ps 92
28 ❑2 Jn ❑Ezra 5–6 ❑Ps 93 ❑1 Esd 8.41-90
29 ❑3 Jn ❑Ezra 7–8 ❑Ps 94 ❑1 Esd 8.91—9.36
30 ❑Jude ❑Ezra 9–10 ❑Ps 95

October

1 ❑Rev 1 ❑Neh 1–2 ❑Ps 96 ❑1 Esd 9.37-55
2 ❑Rev 2 ❑Neh 3 ❑Ps 97 ❑2 Esd 1
3 ❑Rev 3 ❑Neh 4 ❑Ps 98
4 ❑Rev 4 ❑Neh 5.1—7.4 ❑Ps 99 ❑2 Esd 2
5 ❑Rev 5 ❑Neh 7.5—8.12 ❑Ps 100 ❑2 Esd 3
6 ❑Rev 6 ❑Neh 8.13—9.37 ❑Ps 101
7 ❑Rev 7 ❑Neh 9.38—10.39 ❑Ps 102 ❑2 Esd 4.1-21
8 ❑Rev 8 ❑Neh 11 ❑Ps 103 ❑2 Esd 4.22-50
9 ❑Rev 9 ❑Neh 12 ❑Ps 104.1-23
10 ❑Rev 10 ❑Neh 13 ❑Ps 104.24-35 ❑2 Esd 4.51—5.20
11 ❑Rev 11 ❑Esth 1 ❑Ps 105.1-25 ❑2 Esd 5.21-55
12 ❑Rev 12 ❑Esth 2 ❑Ps 105.26-45
13 ❑Rev 13 ❑Esth 3–4 ❑Ps 106.1-23 ❑2 Esd 5.56—6.34
14 ❑Rev 14 ❑Esth 5.1—6.13 ❑Ps 106.24-48 ❑2 Esd 6.35—7.25
15 ❑Rev 15 ❑Esth 6.14—8.17 ❑Ps 107.1-22
16 ❑Rev 16 ❑Esth 9–10 ❑Ps 107.23-43 ❑2 Esd 7.26-74
17 ❑Rev 17 ❑Isa 1–2 ❑Ps 108 ❑2 Esd 7.75-101
18 ❑Rev 18 ❑Isa 3–4 ❑Ps 109.1-19
19 ❑Rev 19 ❑Isa 5–6 ❑Ps 109.20-31 ❑2 Esd 7.102—8.3
20 ❑Rev 20 ❑Isa 7–8 ❑Ps 110 ❑2 Esd 8.4-30
21 ❑Rev 21–22 ❑Isa 9–10 ❑Ps 111
22 ❑1 Thess 1 ❑Isa 11–13 ❑Ps 112 ❑2 Esd 8.31-62a

23 ❑1 Thess 2.1-16 ❑Isa 14–16 ❑Ps 113
❑2 Esd 8.62b—9.25
24 ❑1 Thess 2.17—3.13 ❑Isa 17–19
❑Ps 114
25 ❑1 Thess 4 ❑Isa 20–22 ❑Ps 115
❑2 Esd 9.26—10.28
26 ❑1 Thess 5 ❑Isa 23–24 ❑Ps 116
❑2 Esd 10.29-59
27 ❑2 Thess 1 ❑Isa 25–26 ❑Ps 117
28 ❑2 Thess 2 ❑Isa 27–28 ❑Ps 118
❑2 Esd 11.1—12.6
29 ❑2 Thess 3 ❑Isa 29–30 ❑Ps 119.1-32
❑2 Esd 12.7-50
30 ❑1 Tim 1 ❑Isa 31–33 ❑Ps 119.33-64
31 ❑1 Tim 2 ❑Isa 34–35 ❑Ps 119.65-96
❑2 Esd 12.51—13.56

November

1 ❑1 Tim 3 ❑Isa 36–37 ❑Ps 119.97-120
❑2 Esd 13.57—14.48
2 ❑1 Tim 4 ❑Isa 38–39 ❑Ps 119.121-144
3 ❑1 Tim 5.1-22 ❑Jer 1–2 ❑Ps
119.145-176 ❑2 Esd 15.1-45
4 ❑1 Tim 5.23—6.21 ❑Jer 3–4 ❑Ps 120
❑2 Esd 15.46—16.34
5 ❑2 Tim 1 ❑Jer 5–6 ❑Ps 121
6 ❑2 Tim 2 ❑Jer 7–8 ❑Ps 122
❑2 Esd 16.35-78
7 ❑2 Tim 3 ❑Jer 9–10 ❑Ps 123 ❑Pr Man
8 ❑2 Tim 4 ❑Jer 11–12 ❑Ps 124
9 ❑Titus 1 ❑Jer 13–14 ❑Ps 125
10 ❑Titus 2 ❑Jer 15–16 ❑Ps 126
11 ❑Titus 3 ❑Jer 17–18 ❑Ps 127
12 ❑Philem ❑Jer 19–20 ❑Ps 128
13 ❑Jas 1 ❑Jer 21–22 ❑Ps 129
14 ❑Jas 2 ❑Jer 23–24 ❑Ps 130
15 ❑Jas 3 ❑Jer 25–26 ❑Ps 131
16 ❑Jas 4 ❑Jer 27–28 ❑Ps 132
17 ❑Jas 5 ❑Jer 29–30 ❑Ps 133
18 ❑1 Pet 1 ❑Jer 31–32 ❑Ps 134
19 ❑1 Pet 2 ❑Jer 33–34 ❑Ps 135
20 ❑1 Pet 3 ❑Jer 35–36 ❑Ps 136
21 ❑1 Pet 4 ❑Jer 37–38 ❑Ps 137
22 ❑1 Pet 5 ❑Jer 39–40 ❑Ps 138
23 ❑2 Pet 1 ❑Jer 41–42 ❑Ps 139
24 ❑2 Pet 2 ❑Jer 43–44 ❑Ps 140
25 ❑2 Pet 3 ❑Jer 45–46 ❑Ps 141
26 ❑Gal 1 ❑Jer 47–48 ❑Ps 142
27 ❑Gal 2 ❑Jer 49–50 ❑Ps 143
28 ❑Gal 3.1-18 ❑Jer 51–52 ❑Ps 144
29 ❑Gal 3.19—4.20 ❑Lam 1–2 ❑Ps 145
30 ❑Gal 4.21-31 ❑Lam 3–4 ❑Ps 146

December

1 ❑Gal 5.1-15 ❑Lam 5 ❑Ps 147
2 ❑Gal 5.16-26 ❑Ezek 1 ❑Ps 148
3 ❑Gal 6 ❑Ezek 2–3 ❑Ps 149
4 ❑Eph 1 ❑Ezek 4–5 ❑Ps 150
5 ❑Eph 2 ❑Ezek 6–7 ❑Isa 40
6 ❑Eph 3 ❑Ezek 8–9 ❑Isa 41
7 ❑Eph 4.1-16 ❑Ezek 10–11 ❑Isa 42
8 ❑Eph 4.17-32 ❑Ezek 12–13 ❑Isa 43
9 ❑Eph 5.1-20 ❑Ezek 14–15 ❑Isa 44
10 ❑Eph 5.21-33 ❑Ezek 16 ❑Isa 45
11 ❑Eph 6 ❑Ezek 17 ❑Isa 46
12 ❑Phil 1.1-11 ❑Ezek 18 ❑Isa 47
13 ❑Phil 1.12-30 ❑Ezek 19 ❑Isa 48
14 ❑Phil 2.1-11 ❑Ezek 20 ❑Isa 49
15 ❑Phil 2.12-30 ❑Ezek 21–22 ❑Isa 50
16 ❑Phil 3 ❑Ezek 23 ❑Isa 51
17 ❑Phil 4 ❑Ezek 24 ❑Isa 52
18 ❑Col 1.1-23 ❑Ezek 25–26 ❑Isa 53
19 ❑Col 1.24—2.19 ❑Ezek 27–28 ❑Isa 54
20 ❑Col 2.20—3.17 ❑Ezek 29–30 ❑Isa 55
21 ❑Col 3.18—4.18 ❑Ezek 31–32 ❑Isa 56
22 ❑Lk 1.1-25 ❑Ezek 33 ❑Isa 57
23 ❑Lk 1.26-56 ❑Ezek 34 ❑Isa 58
24 ❑Lk 1.57-80 ❑Ezek 35–36 ❑Isa 59
25 ❑Lk 2.1-20 ❑Ezek 37 ❑Isa 60
26 ❑Lk 2.21-52 ❑Ezek 38–39 ❑Isa 61
27 ❑Lk 3.1-20 ❑Ezek 40–41 ❑Isa 62
28 ❑Lk 3.21-38 ❑Ezek 42–43 ❑Isa 63
29 ❑Lk 4.1-30 ❑Ezek 44–45 ❑Isa 64
30 ❑Lk 4.31-44 ❑Ezek 46–47 ❑Isa 65
31 ❑Lk 5.1-26 ❑Ezek 48 ❑Isa 66

Abbreviations

The following abbreviations are used for the books of the Bible:

Old Testament

Gen	Genesis	2 Chr	2 Chronicles	Dan	Daniel
Ex	Exodus	Ezra	Ezra	Hos	Hosea
Lev	Leviticus	Neh	Nehemiah	Joel	Joel
Num	Numbers	Esth	Esther	Am	Amos
Deut	Deuteronomy	Job	Job	Ob	Obadiah
Josh	Joshua	Ps (pl: Pss)	Psalms	Jon	Jonah
Judg	Judges	Prov	Proverbs	Mic	Micah
Ruth	Ruth	Eccl	Ecclesiastes	Nah	Nahum
1 Sam	1 Samuel	Song	Song of Solomon	Hab	Habakkuk
2 Sam	2 Samuel	Isa	Isaiah	Zeph	Zephaniah
1 Kings	1 Kings	Jer	Jeremiah	Hag	Haggai
2 Kings	2 Kings	Lam	Lamentations	Zech	Zechariah
1 Chr	1 Chronicles	Ezek	Ezekiel	Mal	Malachi

Deuterocanonicals/Apocrypha

Tob	Tobit	Let Jer	Letter of Jeremiah	Bel	Bel and the Dragon
Jdt	Judith	Azar/Song Thr	Prayer of Azariah and Song of the Three Young Men	1 Macc	1 Maccabees
Gk Est	Esther (Greek)			2 Macc	2 Maccabees
Wis	Wisdom of Solomon			1 Esd	1 Esdras
				Pr Man	Prayer of Manasseh
Sir	Sirach				
Bar	Baruch	Sus	Susanna	2 Esd	2 Esdras

New Testament

Mt	Matthew	Eph	Ephesians	Heb	Hebrews
Mk	Mark	Phil	Philippians	Jas	James
Lk	Luke	Col	Colossians	1 Pet	1 Peter
Jn	John	1 Thess	1 Thessalonians	2 Pet	2 Peter
Acts	Acts of the Apostles	2 Thess	2 Thessalonians	1 Jn	1 John
Rom	Romans	1 Tim	1 Timothy	2 Jn	2 John
1 Cor	1 Corinthians	2 Tim	2 Timothy	3 Jn	3 John
2 Cor	2 Corinthians	Titus	Titus	Jude	Jude
Gal	Galatians	Philem	Philemon	Rev	Revelation

What's a Parable?

Parables are stories that use typical, everyday situations in order to teach important truths. Jesus used many parables to teach his followers about the Kingdom of God.

Some Readings for Special Days

New Year's Day
Colossians 3.5-17

Epiphany
Matthew 2.1-12

Martin Luther King, Jr. Day
Exodus 3.1-22

Christian Unity Sunday
John 17

Valentine's Day
1Corinthians 13; 1 John 4.7-21

Presidents' Day
Isaiah 32.1-8

Ash Wednesday
Psalm 51; Joel 2.12-19; Matthew 6.1-6; James 1.12-18

St. Patrick's Day
Isaiah 52.7-12

Palm Sunday
Mark 11.1-11; John 12.12-19; Philippians 2.5-11

Holy (Maundy) Thursday
Matthew 26.26-30; John 13.1-35; Psalm 116

Good Friday
John 18.1—19.42; Psalm 22; Isaiah 52.13—53.12

Easter
Matthew 28; Luke 24; John 20; Acts 10.34-43; Psalm 33

Passover
Exodus 12

Mother's Day
1 Samuel 1.1-28; Proverbs 23.22-25; 31.10-31; Luke 1.26-56

Memorial Day
Isaiah 26.1-19

Pentecost
Acts 2.1-11

Father's Day
Proverbs 4; 20.7; Luke 15.11-32

Independence Day
Psalm 33

Labor Day
Genesis 1.26 — 2.4

Yom Kippur
Jeremiah 31.31-34

Grandparent's Day
Psalm 128

World Communion Sunday
1 Corinthians 11.23-34

All Saints Day
Hebrews 11

Stewardship Day
Matthew 25.14-29; 2 Corinthians 9.1-15

Election Day
1 Peter 2.13-17

Veterans' Day
Isaiah 2.1-5

Bible Sunday
2 Timothy 3.10-17

Thanksgiving
Deuteronomy 8.1-10; Psalm 65; 67

First Sunday in Advent
Isaiah 63.15—64.12; Matthew 24.36-44; Luke 21.25-36; Psalm 25

Second Sunday in Advent
Malachi 3.1-5; Matthew 3.1-12; Psalm 85

Third Sunday in Advent
Isaiah 12.1-6; Matthew 11.2-19; Luke 3.7-18; Philippians 4.4-9

Fourth Sunday in Advent
Isaiah 7.10-17; Micah 5.2-5; Luke 1.26-56; Psalm 89.1-18

Christmas
Luke 2.1-20; Matthew 1.18-25; John 1.1-18; Titus 3.4-7

Personal Birthday
Psalm 145

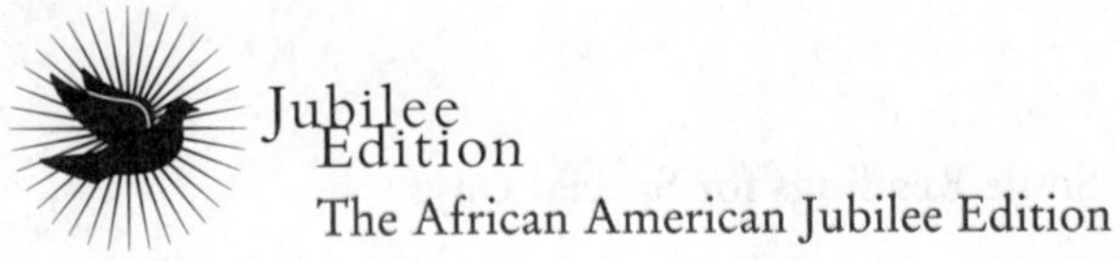

The African American Jubilee Edition

Famous Passages of the Bible

Stories from the Old Testament

Early Beginnings

Creation and Sin
Genesis 2.4—3.24

The First Murder
Genesis 4.1-15

Noah and the Flood
Genesis 6.1—9.17

The Tower of Babylon (Babel)
Genesis 11.1-9

The Call of Abraham
Genesis 12.1-9

The Destruction of Sodom and Gomorrah
Genesis 19.1-28

Hagar and Ishmael
Genesis 16.1-15; 21.9-21

The Birth of Isaac
Genesis 21.1-8

Abraham's Offering of Isaac
Genesis 22.1-19

The Story of Jacob
Genesis 25.19—35.29

Moses in Egypt
Exodus 1–14

Moses' Wilderness Wanderings
Exodus 15.22— 20.26; 31.18—34.35; Numbers 20.1—21.25

The Ten Commandments
Exodus 20.1-17; Deuteronomy 5.1-21

The King of Moab and Balaam
Numbers 22–24

People of Great Faith in the Old Testament

Rahab Helps the Israelite Spies
Joshua 2

Joshua, Military Strategist
Joshua 3; 6

Deborah, a Woman of Power and Judgment
Judges 4–5

Gideon, the Conqueror
Judges 6.11— 8.32

Samson, a Man of Great Strength
Judges 13–16

Ruth, a Woman of Loyalty and Devotion
Ruth 1–4

Samuel, a Prophet Who Listened to God
1 Samuel 1–3; 7–10; 12; 15; 16

Saul, Israel's First King
1 Samuel 8–11; 13; 15; 28; 31

David, the Shepherd King
1 Samuel 16-27; 29.1—30.25; 2 Samuel 2;11; 12; 15.1-8; 18; 1 Kings 1.1-31; 2.1-11

Solomon, the Wise King
1 Kings 2.12—11.43

Elijah, a Great Prophet
1 Kings 17–19; 21; 2 Kings 1

Elisha, His Successor
2 Kings 2; 4.1—7.2; 13.14-21

Nehemiah, a Heroic Builder
Nehemiah 1; 2; 4

Esther, a Brave Queen
Esther 1–10

Daniel, a Prophet of Courage
Daniel 1–6

Jonah, the Reluctant Missionary
Jonah 1–4

Stories from the Deuterocanonicals/Apocrypha

Moral Counsel to a Son
Tobit 4.1-21

A Hymn of Praise to God
Tobit 13.1-18

A Song of Thanksgiving
Judith 16.1-17

Solomon's Prayer for Wisdom
Wisdom of Solomon 9.1-18

God's Wisdom in Creation
Sirach 16.24—17.14

God's Great Majesty
Sirach 18.1-14

In Praise of Wisdom
Sirach 24.1-34

In Praise of the Faithful
Sirach 44.1—50.24

A Hymn of Thanksgiving
Sirach 50.22-24

Song of the Three Young Men
Prayer of Azariah and Song of the Three Young Men 23–68

The Faithful Martyrs
2 Maccabees 7

The Three Royal Guards
1 Esdras 3.1—5.6

A Prayer of Confession
Prayer of Manasseh

Ezra Copies the Scriptures
2 Esdras 14.37-48

Stories from the New Testament

The Life of Jesus

The Birth of Jesus
Matthew 1.18—2.15; Luke 2.1-20

Jesus Is Named and Presented in the Temple
Luke 2.21-40

The Young Jesus
Luke 2.41-52

The Baptism of Jesus
Matthew 3; Mark 1.1-11; Luke 3.21,22

The Temptation of Jesus
Matthew 4.1-11; Mark 1.12,13; Luke 4.1-13

Jesus Calls His First Disciples
Matthew 4.18-22; Mark 1.16-20; Luke 5.1-11

Jesus Chooses Twelve Apostles
Matthew 10.1-4; Mark 3.13-19; Luke 6.12-16

The Transfiguration of Jesus
Matthew 17.1-13; Mark 9.2-13

Jesus' Death and Resurrection

Jesus' Entry into Jerusalem
Matthew 21.1-11; Mark 11.1-11; Luke 19.29-44; John 12.12-19

The Last Supper of Jesus
Matthew 26.17-35; Mark 14.12-26; Luke 22.1-38

Jesus Prays in Gethsemane
Matthew 26.36-46; Mark 14.32-42; Luke 22.39-46

Jesus' Trial and Crucifixion
Matthew 26.47—27.66; Mark 14.43—15.47; Luke 22.47—23.56; John 18; 19

The Resurrection of Jesus
Matthew 28.1-10; Mark 16; Luke 24.1-12; John 20

The Great Commission
Matthew 28.16-20

The Ascension of Jesus
Luke 24.50-53; Acts 1.1-12

Miracles and Healings of Jesus

Jesus Turns Water into Wine
John 2.1-11

Jesus Feeds Many People
Matthew 14.13-21; 15.32-39; Mark 6.30-44; 8.1-10; Luke 9.10-17; John 6.1-15

Jesus Calms a Storm
Matthew 8.23-27; Mark 4.35-41; Luke 8.22-25

The Great Catch of Fish
Luke 5.1-11

Jesus Walks on Water
Matthew 14.22-33; Mark 6.45-52; John 6.16-21

Jesus Heals People with Skin Diseases
Matthew 8.1-4; Mark 1.40-45; Luke 5.12-16; 17.11-19

Jesus Casts Out Demons
Matthew 8.28-34; 12.22-37; 17.14-21; Mark 1.21-28; 3.20-30; 5.1-20; 9.14-29; Luke 4.31-37; 8.26-39; 9.37-43; 11.14-23

Jesus Heals the Blind
Matthew 9.27-31; 20.29-34; Mark 10.46-52; Luke 18.35-43

Jesus Heals a Deaf Man
Mark 7.31-37

Jesus Heals the Paralyzed and Crippled
Matthew 9.1-8; 12.9-14; Mark 2.1-12; 3.1-6; Luke 5.17-26; 6.6-11; 14.1-6; John 5.1-9

Jesus Heals Many Women
Matthew 9.18-26; 15.21-28; Mark 5.21-43; 7.24-30; Luke 8.1-3; 8.40-56; 13.10-17

Jesus Heals the Centurion's Servant
Matthew 8.5-13; Luke 7.1-10

Jesus Heals Peter's Mother-in-law
Matthew 8.14,15; Mark 1.29-31; Luke 4.38, 39

Jesus Heals an Official's Son
John 4.46-54

Jesus Revives an Official's Daughter
Matthew 9.18,19,23-26; Mark 5.21-24, 35-42; Luke 8.40-42, 49-56

Jesus Raises the Dead
Luke 7.11-17; John 11.1-44

The Teachings and Parables of Jesus

The Sermon on the Mount
Matthew 5–7; Luke 6.20-49

The Beatitudes
Matthew 5.3-11; Luke 6.20-26

The Great Commandment
Matthew 22.37-39; Mark 12.29-31; Luke 10.27

The Golden Rule
Matthew 7.12; Luke 6.31

The Grain of Mustard Seed
Matthew 13.31,32; Mark 4.30-32; Luke13.18, 19

The Parable of the Sower
Matthew 13.1-23; Mark 4.1-20; Luke 8.4-15

The Parable of the Growing Seed
Mark 4.26-29

Some Parables about the Kingdom of Heaven
Matthew 13.24-52

The Parable of the Unforgiving Servant
Matthew 18.23-35

The Parable of the Workers in the Vineyard
Matthew 20.1-16

The Parable of the Tenants in the Vineyard
Matthew 21.33-46; Mark 12.1-11; Luke 20.9-18

The Parable of the Wedding Feast
Matthew 22.1-14; Luke 14.15-24

The Parable of the Ten Young Women (Virgins) *Matthew 25.1-13*

The Parable of the Three Servants and Their Coins
Matthew 25.14-30; Luke 19.11-27

The Parable of the Sheep and the Goats
Matthew 25.31-46

The Parable of the Good Samaritan
Luke 10.25-37

The Parable of the Shepherd
John 10.1-21

The Parable of the Rich Fool
Luke 12.16-21

The Parable of the Watchful Servants
Luke 12.35-48

The Parable of the Barren Fig Tree
Luke 13.6-9

The Parable of the Lost Sheep
Matthew 18.12-14; Luke15.3-7

The Parable of the Lost Coin
Luke 15.8-10

The Parable of the Lost Son
Luke 15.11-32

The Parable of the Shrewd Manager
Luke 16.1-13

The Rich Man and Lazarus
Luke 16.19-31

The Parable of the Widow and the Judge
Luke 18.1-8

The Parable of the Pharisee and the Tax Collector
Luke 18.9-14

Other New Testament Stories

The Birth of John the Baptist
Luke 1.57-66

John the Baptist Is Executed
Matthew 14.1-12; Mark 6.14-29

Peter Receives the Keys of the Kingdom
Matthew 16.13-20

The Holy Spirit Comes on Pentecost
Acts 2

Stephen, the First Martyr
Acts 6.5-15; 7.54-60

Philip Baptizes the Ethiopian Official
Acts 8.26-39

The Conversion of Paul
Acts 9.1-31

Peter and Cornelius
Acts 10

Peter in Prison
Acts 12.1-19

The Baptism of Lydia
Acts 16.11-15

Paul in Prison
Acts 16.16-40

The Riot at Ephesus
Acts 19.23-41

Paul's Voyage to Rome
Acts 27; 28

Other Famous Passages

Songs of the Bible

Moses' Song of Deliverance
Exodus 15.1-18

Deborah and Barak's Song of Victory
Judges 51-31

Hannah's Song of Praise
1 Samuel 2.1-10

David's Song of Lament
2 Samuel 1.17-27

David's Song of Victory
2 Samuel 22; Psalm 18

Solomon's Love Song
Song of Solomon 2.10-15

Mary's Song of Praise
Luke 1.46-55

A Hymn to Christ Jesus
Philippians 2.6-11

Prayers of the Bible

Solomon's Personal Prayer
1 Kings 3.5-10

Solomon's Public Prayer
1 Kings 8.22-61; 2 Chronicles 6.12-42

Hezekiah's Temple Prayer
2 Kings 19.15-19; Isaiah 37.14-20

David's Prayer of Thanksgiving
2 Samuel 7.18-29; 1 Chronicles 17.16-27

Job's Prayer
Job 42.1-6

Jeremiah's Prayer
Jeremiah 32.16-25

Daniel's Prayer
Daniel 9.3-19

Jonah's Prayer
Jonah 2.1-9

The Lord's Prayer
Matthew 6.9-13

Jesus' Prayer in Gethsemane
Matthew 26.36-44

Jesus' Prayer for His Disciples
John 17

The Disciples' Prayer
Acts 4.24-31

Paul's Prayer for Believers
Ephesians 3.14-21

Special Blessings from the Bible

Invocations and Openings
Psalm 19.14; 1 Corinthians 1.3; 1 Timothy 1.2; 2 John 3; Revelation 1.4-6

Dismissals and Closings
Numbers 6.24-26; 1 Kings 8.57,58; Romans 15.5; 6.13; 16.25-27; 2 Corinthians 13.13; Ephesians 6.23,24; Philippians 4.7; Hebrews 13.20,21; Jude 24,25

Finding Help in the Bible

Help in Special Circumstances

Being a friend
Proverbs 17.17; Luke 10.25-37; John 15.11-17; Romans 16.1, 2

Being a leader
Isaiah 11.1-9; 32.1-8; 1 Timothy 3.1-7; 2 Timothy 2.14-26; Titus 1.5-9

Caring for the aged and widowed
Genesis 47.1-12; Ruth 1; Proverbs 23.22; 1 Timothy 5.3-8

Celebrating the birth/adoption of a child
Psalm 100; Proverbs 22.6; Luke 18.15-17; John 16.16-22

Celebrating a graduation
Psalm 119.105,106; Proverbs 9.10-12; Galatians 5.16-26; Philippians 4.4-9

Celebrating a marriage
Genesis 2.18-24; Song of Songs 8.6,7; Ephesians 5.21-33; Colossians 2.6,7

Celebrating a wedding anniversary
Psalm 100; 1 Corinthians 13

Controlling your temper
Proverbs 14.17, 29; 15.18; 19.11; 29.22; Ecclesiastes 7.9; Galatians 5.16-26

Controlling your tongue
Psalm 12; 19.14; Proverbs 11.13; 26.20; 2 Thessalonians 2.16,17; James 3.1-12

Discovering God's will
Psalm 15; Micah 6.6-8; Matthew 5.14-16; Luke 9.21-27; Romans 13.8-14; 2 Peter 1.3-9; 1 John 4.7-21

Facing a divorce
Psalm 25; Matthew 19.1-9; Philippians 3.1-11

Encountering a cult
Matthew 7.15-20; 2 Peter 2; 1 John 4.1-6; Jude

Encountering peer pressure
Proverbs 1.7-19; Romans 12.1,2; Galatians 6.1-5; Ephesians 5.1-20

Entering college
Proverbs 2.1-8; 3.1-18; 4.1-27; 23.12; Romans 8.1-17; 1 Corinthians 1.18-31

Entering military service
2 Samuel 22.2-51; Psalm 91; Ephesians 6.10-20; 2 Timothy 2.1-13

Experiencing the death of a loved one
Job 19.25-27; John 11.25-27; 14.1-7; Romans 8.31-39; 14.7-9; 1 Thessalonians 4.13-18

Experiencing illness
Psalm 23; Mark 1.29-34; 6.53-56; James 5.14-16

Experiencing suffering and persecution
Psalm 109; 119.153-160; Matthew 5.3-12; John 15.18—16.4; Romans 8.18-30; 2 Corinthians 4.1-15; Hebrews 12.1-11; 1 Peter 4.12-19

Facing a difficult decision
1 Kings 3; Esther 4–7; Psalm 139; Daniel 2.14-23; Colossians 3.12-17

Facing homelessness
Psalm 90.1, 2; Isaiah 65.17-25; Lamentations 3.19-24; Luke 9.57-62; Revelation 21.1-4

Facing imprisonment
Lamentations 3.34-36; Matthew 25.31-46; Luke 4.16-21

Facing life alone
1 Corinthians 7.25-38; 12.1-31

Facing a natural disaster
Genesis 8.1—9.17; Job 36.22—37.13; Psalm 29; 36.5-9; 124; Jeremiah 31.35-37; Romans 8.31-39; 1 Peter 1.3-12

Facing a trial or lawsuit
Psalm 26; Isaiah 50.4-11; Matthew 5.25,26; Luke 18.1-8

Losing your job
Jeremiah 29.10-14; Luke 16.1-13; Philippians 4.10-13

Losing your property and possessions
Job 1.13-22; 42.7-17; Isaiah30.19-26; 41.17-20; Romans 8.18-39

Managing your time
Proverbs 12.11; 28.19; Mark 13.32-37; Luke 21.34-36; 1 Timothy 4.11-16; Titus 3.8-14

Moving into a new home
Psalm 127.1,2; Proverbs 24.3,4; John 14.1-7; Ephesians 3.14-21; Revelation 3.20,21

Overcoming addiction
Psalm 40.1-5, 11-17; 116.1-7; Proverbs 23.29-35; 2 Corinthians 5.16-21; Ephesians 4.22-24

Overcoming a grudge
Leviticus 19.17,18; Matthew 5.23-26; Luke 6.27-36; Ephesians 4.25-32

Overcoming prejudice
Matthew 7.1-5; Acts 10.34-36; Galatians 3.26-29; Ephesians 2.11-22; Colossians 3.5-11; James 2.1-13

Overcoming pride
Psalm 131; Mark 9.33-37; Luke 14.7-11; Luke 18.9-14; 22.24-27; Romans 12.14-16; 1 Corinthians 1.18-31; 2 Corinthians 12.1-10

Overcoming procrastination
Matthew 22.1-14; 25.1-13; 2 Corinthians 6.1, 2

Raising children
Proverbs 22.6; Ephesians 6.4; Colossians 3.21

Respecting civil authorities
Mark 12.13-17; Romans 13.1-7; Titus 3.1,2; 1 Peter 2.13-17

Respecting parents
Exodus 20.12; Proverbs 23.22; Ephesians 6.1-3; Colossians 3.20

Retiring from your job
Numbers 6.24-26; Psalm 145; Matthew 25.31-46; Romans 12.1,2; Philippians 3.12-21; 2 Peter 1.2

Seeking forgiveness
Psalm 32.1-5; 51; Proverbs 28.13; Joel 2.12-17; Matthew 6.14,15; Luke 15; Philemon; Hebrews 4.14-16; 1 John 1.5-10

Seeking God's help
Psalm 5; 57; 86; 119.169-176; 121; 130; Matthew 7.7-12

Seeking justice
Psalm 10; 17; 75; 94; Isaiah 42.1-7; 61.1-9; Amos 5.21-24; Habakkuk 1.1—2.4

Seeking salvation
John 3.1-21; Romans 1.16,17; 3.21-31; 5.1-11; 10.5-13; Ephesians 1.3-14; 2.1-10

Seeking strength
Psalms 46; 138; Isaiah 40.27-31; 51.12-16; Ephesians 6.10-20; 2 Thessalonians 2.16, 17

Seeking truth
Psalm 119.153-160; John 8.31-47; 14.6-14; 16.4b-15; 1 Timothy 2.1-7

Sharing your gifts
Exodus 35.20-29; Malachi 3.6-12; Luke 21.1-4; Acts 2.43-47; 4.32-37; Romans 12.9-13; 1 Corinthians 16.1-4; 2 Corinthians 8.1-15; 9.6-15

Starting a new job
Proverbs 11.3; 22.29; Romans 12.3-11; 1 Thessalonians 5.12-18; 2 Thessalonians 3.6-13; 1 Peter 4.7-11

Understanding your relationship with God
Deuteronomy 5.1-22; Psalm 139; John 15.1-17; Romans 5.1-11; 8.1-17

Understanding your relationship with others
Deuteronomy 5.16-21; Proverbs 3.27-35; Matthew 18.15-17; 18.21-35; Romans 14.13-23; 15.1-6; Galatians 6.1-10; Colossians 3.12-17; 1 John 4.7-12

Worrying about the future
Isaiah 35; 60; Jeremiah 29.10-14; 1 Peter 1.3-5; Revelation 21.1-8

Worrying about growing old
Psalm 37.23-29; Isaiah 46.3, 4

Worrying about money
Proverbs 11.7; Ecclesiastes 5.10-20; Matthew 6.24-34; Luke 12.13-21; 1Timothy 6.6-10

Experiencing Troublesome Feelings

Afraid?
Psalms 27; 91; Isaiah 41.5-13; Mark 4.35-41; Hebrews 13.5,6; 1 John 4.13-18

Afraid of death?
Psalm 23; 63.1-8; John 6.35-40; Romans 8.18-39; 1 Corinthians 15.35-57; 2 Corinthians 5.1-10; 2 Timothy 1.8-10

Angry?
Proverbs 15.1; Matthew 5.21-24; Romans 12.17-21; Ephesians 4.26-32; James 1.19-21

Anxious? Worried?
Psalm 25; Matthew 6.24-34; 10.26-31; 1 Peter 1.3-5; 5.7

Depressed?
Psalm 16; 43; 130; Isaiah 61.1-4; Jeremiah 15.10-21; Lamentations 3.55-57; John 3.14-17; Ephesians 3.14-21

Disappointed? Let down?
Psalm 55; 62.1-8; Jeremiah 20.7-18

Discouraged?
Psalm 34; Isaiah 12.1-6; Romans 15.13; 2 Corinthians 4.16-18; Philippians 4.10-13; Colossians 1.9-14; Hebrews 6.9-12

Doubting your faith in God?
Psalm 8; 146; Proverbs 30.5; Matthew 7.7-12; Luke 17.5,6; John 20.24-31; Romans 4.13-25; Hebrews 11; 1 John 5.13-1

Frustrated?
Job 21.1-16; 24.1-17; 36.1-26;Matthew 7.13,14

Impatient?
Psalm 13; 37.1-7; 40.1-5; Ecclesiastes 3.1-15; Lamentations 3.25-33; Hebrews 6.13-20; James 5.7-11

Insecure? Lacking confidence?
Deuteronomy 31.1-8; Psalm 73.21-26; 108; Philippians 4.10-20; 1 John 3.19-24

Jealous?
Psalm 49; Proverbs 23.17; James 3.13-18

Lonely?
Psalm 22; 42; John 14.15-31a

Overwhelmed?
Experiencing stress?
Isaiah 55.1-9; Matthew 11.25-30; John 4.1-30; 2 Corinthians 6.3-10; Revelation 22.17

Rejected?
Psalm 38; Isaiah 52.13—53.12; Matthew 9.9-13; Luke 4.16-30; John 15.18—16.4; Ephesians 1.3-14; 1 Peter 2.1-10

Tempted?
Psalm 19.12-14; 141; Luke 4.1-13; Hebrews 2.11-18; 4.14-16; James 1.12-18

Tempted by sex?
2 Samuel 11.1—12.25; 1 Corinthians 6.12-20; Galatians 5.16-26

Tired? Weary?
Psalm 3.5,6; 4.4-8; Isaiah 35.1-10; Matthew 11.25-30; 2 Thessalonians 3.16; Hebrews 4.1-11

Feeling useless? Inferior?
Isaiah 6.1-8; Jeremiah 1.4-10; Galatians 1.11-24; Ephesians 4.1-16; 1 Peter 2.4-10

Vengeful?
Matthew 5.38-42; Romans 12.17-21

What the Bible Says about God's Forgiveness

Every person is separated from God because of sin.

Isaiah 59.1-15
Romans 3.9-20
Romans 5.12-21
Ecclesiastes 7.20
Romans 7.14-25

God has always sought to form a close relationship with people.

Exodus 19.3b-8
Jeremiah 31.31-34
Isaiah 54.1-10
1 Peter 1.1-10
1 John 3.1-10

God has reached out to people in a personal way by sending Jesus Christ.

Colossians 1.15-23
Romans 5.1-11
1 Peter 2.10-25
John 3.1-21
2 Timothy 1.3-10
Ephesians 2.1-10

God's forgiveness through Jesus Christ is available to every person.

Psalm 51.1-17
1 John 1.5-10
Romans 10. 5-13
Psalm 32.1-11
Romans 8.31-39
Romans 3.21-26

New life in Christ calls a person to live in a Christ-like way.

Romans 6.1-14
Matthew 20.20-28
Ephesians 4.17-32
Galatians 5.16-26
1 John 4.7-21
Romans 12.1-21

Lectionary Reading Guide

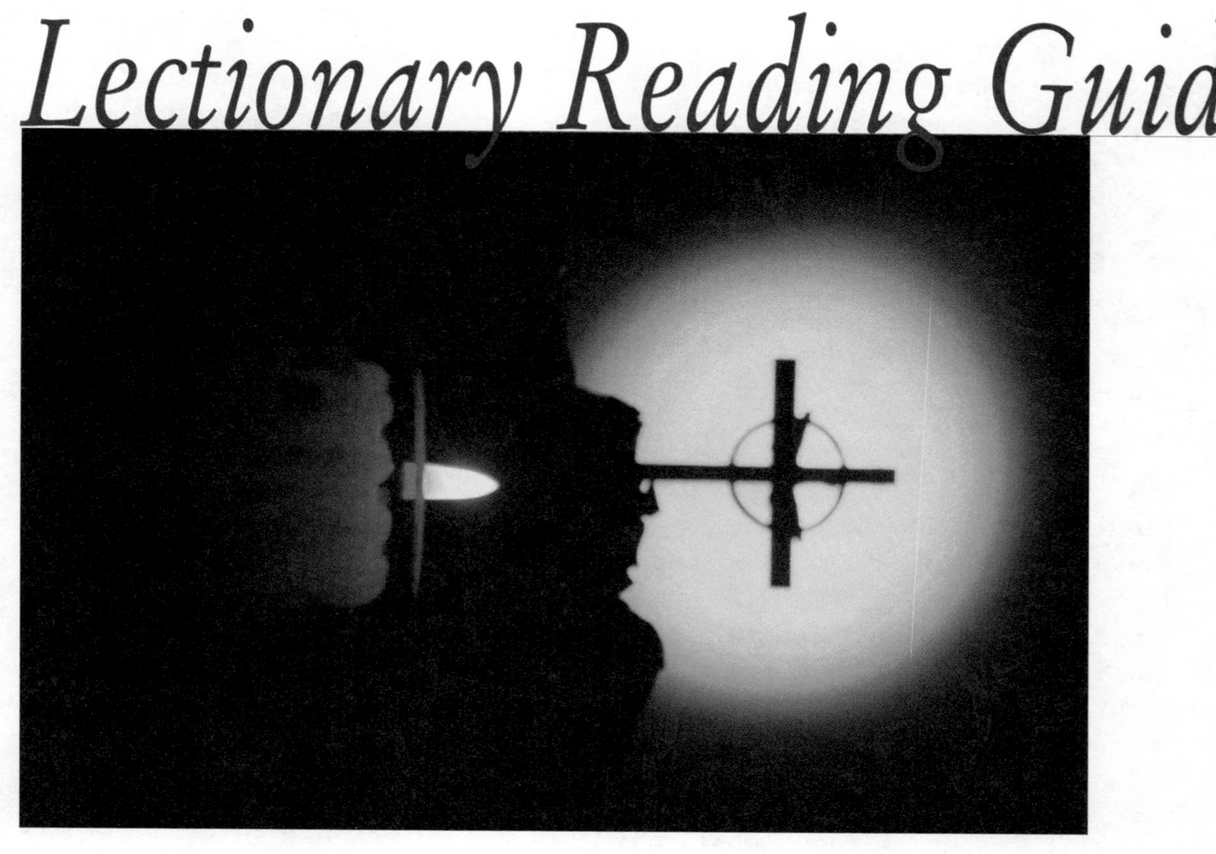

Photography Credits

Page 51, PhotoDisc

Pages 20, 54, 68, 81, Courtesy Our Lady of Victory Roman Catholic Church, Brooklyn, N.Y., Michael Scott Studios, NY.

Lectionary Reading Guide

Contents

The 3-Year Cycle of Readings For Sunday Mass

Year A

Advent Season

1st Sunday of Advent
1. Isa 2.1-5
2. Rom 13.11-14
3. Matt 24.37-44

2nd Sunday of Advent
1. Isa 11.1-10
2. Rom 15.4-9
3. Matt 3.1-12

3rd Sunday of Advent
1. Isa 35.1-6a, 10
2. Jas 5.7-10
3. Matt 11.2-11

4th Sunday of Advent
1. Isa 7.10-14
2. Rom 1.1-7
3. Matt 1.18-24

Christmas Season

Christmas Vigil
1. Isa 62.1-5
2. Acts 13.16, 17, 22-25
3. Matt 1.1-25

Christmas (Midnight)
1. Isa 9.1-6
2. Titus 2.11-14
3. Luke 2.1-14

Christmas (Dawn)
1. Isa 62.11, 12
2. Titus 3.4-7
3. Luke 2.15-20

Christmas (Day)
1. Isa 52.7-10
2. Heb 1.1-6
3. John 1.1-18

Sunday after Christmas (Holy Family)
1. Si 3.3-7, 14-17a
2. Col 3.12-21
3. Matt 2.13-15, 19-23

January 1 (Solemnity of Mary, Mother of God)
1. Num 6.22-27
2. Gal 4.4-7
3. Luke 2.16-21

2nd Sunday after Christmas
1. Si 24.1-4, 12-16
2. Eph 1.3-6, 15-18
3. John 1.1-18

Epiphany
1. Isa 60.1-6
2. Eph 3.2-3a, 5, 6
3. Matt 2.1-12

Sunday after Epiphany (Baptism of the Lord)
1. Isa 42.1-4, 6, 7
2. Acts 10.34-38
3. Matt 3.13-17

Lenten Season

Ash Wednesday
1. Joel 2.12-18
2. 2 Cor 5.20—6.2
3. Matt 6.1-6, 16-18

1st Sunday of Lent
1. Gen 2.7-9; 3.1-7
2. Rom 5. 12-19
3. Matt 4.1-11

2nd Sunday of Lent
1. Gen 12.1-4a
2. 2 Tim 1.8b-10
3. Matt 17.1-9

3rd Sunday of Lent
1. Exod 17.3-7
2. Rom 5.1, 2, 5-8
3. John 4. 5-42

4th Sunday of Lent
1. 1 Sam 16.1b; 6, 7, 10-13a
2. Eph 5.8-14
3. John 9.1-41

5th Sunday of Lent
1. Ezek 37.12-14
2. Rom 8.8-11
3. John 11.1-45

Passion Sunday (Palm Sunday)
Procession: Matt 21.1-11
1. Isa 50.4-7
2. Phil 2.6-11
3. Matt 26.14—27.66

Easter Triduum and Easter Season

Mass of Lord's Supper
1. Exod 12.1-8, 11-14
2. 1 Cor 11.23-26
3. John 13.1-15

Good Friday
1. Isa 52.13—53.12
2. Heb 4.14-16; 5.7-9
3. John 18.1—19.42

Easter Vigil
1. Gen 1.1—2.2
Gen 22.1-18
Exod 14.15—15.1
Isa 54.5-14
Isa 55.1-11
Ba 3.9-15
Ba 3.32—4.4
Ezek 36.16-17a, 18-28
2. Rom 6.3-11
3. Matt 28.1-10

Easter Sunday
1. Acts 10.34a, 37-43
2. Col 3.1-4 or
1 Cor 5.6b-8
3. John 20.1-9 or
Matt 28.1-10
Evening:
3. Luke 24.13-35

2nd Sunday of Easter
1. Acts 2.42-47
2. 1 Pet 1.3-9
3. John 20.19-31

3rd Sunday of Easter
1. Acts 2.14, 22-33
2. 1 Pet 1.17-21
3. Luke 24.13-35

4th Sunday of Easter
1. Acts 2.14a, 36-41
2. 1 Pet 2.20b-25
3. John 10.1-10

5th Sunday of Easter
1. Acts 6.1-7
2. 1 Pet 2.4-9
3. John 14.1-12

6th Sunday of Easter
1. Acts 8.5-8, 14-17
2. 1 Pet 3.15-18
3. John 14.15-21

Ascension of Our Lord
1. Acts 1.1-11
2. Eph 1.17-23
3. Matt 28.16-20

7th Sunday of Easter
1. Acts 1.12-14
2. 1 Pet 4.13-16
3. John 17.1-11a

Pentecost Vigil
1. Gen 11.1-9 or
Exod 19.3-8a, 16-20b
or Ezra 37.1-14 or
1 John 3.1-5
2. Rom 8.22-27
3. John 7.37-39

Mass of the Day
1. Acts 2.1-11
2. 1 Cor 12.3b-7, 12, 13
3. John 20.19-23

Solemnities of the Lord During Ordinary Time

Trinity Sunday (Sunday after Pentecost)
1. Exod 34.4b-6, 8, 9
2. 2 Cor 13.11-13
3. John 3.16-18

Corpus Christi
1. Deut 8.2, 3, 14b-16a
2. 1 Cor 10.16, 17
3. John 6.51-58

Sacred Heart of Jesus
1. Deut 7.6-11
2. 1 John 4.7-16
3. Matt 11.25-30

Ordinary Time

1st Sunday
(See Baptism of the Lord, page 55)

2nd Sunday
1. Isa 49.3, 5, 6
2. 1 Cor 1.1-3
3. John 1.29-34

3rd Sunday
1. Isa 8.23b—9.3
2. 1 Cor 1.10-13, 17
3. Matt 4.12-23

4th Sunday
1. Zeph 2.3; 3.12, 13
2. 1 Cor 1.26-31
3. Matt 5.1-12a

5th Sunday
1. Isa 58.7-10
2. 1 Cor 2.1-5
3. Matt 5.13-16

6th Sunday
1. Si 15.16-21
2. 1 Cor 2.6-10
3. Matt 5.17-37

7th Sunday
1. Lev 19.1, 2, 17, 18
2. 1 Cor 3.16-23
3. Matt 5.38-48

8th Sunday
1. Isa 49.14, 15
2. 1 Cor 4.1-5
3. Matt 6.24-34

9th Sunday
1. Deut 11.18,26-28, 32
2. Rom 3.21-25a, 28
3. Matt 7.21-27

10th Sunday
1. Hos 6.3-6
2. Rom 4.18-25
3. Matt 9.9-13

11th Sunday
1. Exod 19.2-6a
2. Rom 5.6-11
3. Matt 9.36—10.8

12th Sunday
1. Jer 20.10-13
2. Rom 5.12-15
3. Matt 10.26-33

13th Sunday
1. 2 Kgs 4.8-11, 14-16a
2. Rom 6.3, 4, 8-11
3. Matt 10.37-42

14th Sunday
1. Zech 9.9, 10
2. Rom 8.9, 11-13
3. Matt 11.25-30

15th Sunday
1. Isa 55.10, 11
2. Rom 8.18-23
3. Matt 13.1-23

16th Sunday
1. Ws 12.13, 16-19
2. Rom 8.26, 27
3. Matt 13.24-43

17th Sunday
1. 1 Kgs 3.5, 7-12
2. Rom 8.28-30
3. Matt 13.44-52

18th Sunday
1. Isa 55.1-3
2. Rom 8.35, 37-39
3. Matt 14.13-21

19th Sunday
1. 1 Kgs 19.9a, 11-13a
2. Rom 9.1-5
3. Matt 14.22-33

20th Sunday
1. Isa 56.1, 6, 7
2. Rom 11.13-15, 29-32
3. Matt 15.21-28

21st Sunday
1. Isa 22.19-23
2. Rom 11.33-36
3. Matt 16.13-20

22nd Sunday
1. Jer 20.7-9
2. Rom 12.1, 2
3. Matt 16.21-27

23rd Sunday
1. Ezek 33.7-9
2. Rom 13.8-10
3. Matt 18.15-20

24th Sunday
1. Si 27.30—28.7
2. Rom 14.7-9
3. Matt 18.21-35

25th Sunday
1. Isa 55.6-9
2. Phil 1.20c-24, 27a
3. Matt 20.1-16a

26th Sunday
1. Ezek 18.25-28
2. Phil 2.1-11
3. Matt 21.28-32

27th Sunday
1. Isa 5.1-7
2. Phil 4.6-9
3. Matt 21.33-43

28th Sunday
1. Isa 25.6-10a
2. Phil 4.12-14, 19, 20
3. Matt 22.1-14

29th Sunday
1. Isa 45.1, 4-6
2. 1 Thes 1.1-5b
3. Matt 22.15-21

30th Sunday
1. Exod 22.20-26
2. 1 Thes 1.5c-10
3. Matt 22.34-40

31st Sunday
1. Mal 1.14b—2.2b, 8-10
2. 1 Thes 2.7b—9.13
3. Matt 23.1-12

32nd Sunday
1. Ws 6.12-16
2. 1 Thes 4.13-18
3. Matt 25.1-13

33rd Sunday
1. Prov 31.10-13, 19, 20, 30, 31
2. 1 Thes 5.1-6
3. Matt 25.14-30

34th Sunday (Christ the King)
1. Ezek 34.11, 12, 15-17
2. 1 Cor 15.20-26, 28
3. Matt 25.31-46

The 3-Year Cycle of Readings for Sunday Mass

Year B

Advent Season

1st Sunday of Advent
1. Isa 63.16b, 17, 19b; 64.2b-7
2. 1 Cor 1.3-9
3. Mark 13.33-37

2nd Sunday of Advent
1. Isa 40.1-5, 9-11
2. 2 Pet 3.8-14
3. Mark 1.1-8

3rd Sunday of Advent
1. Isa 61.1,2a, 10, 11
2. 1 Thes 5.16-24
3. John 1.6-8, 19-28

4th Sunday of Advent
1. 2 Sam 7.1-5, 8b-12, 14a, 16
2. Rom 16.25-27
3. Luke 1.26-38

Christmas Season

Christmas Vigil
1. Isa 62.1-5
2. Acts 13.16, 17; 22-25
3. Matt 1.1-25

Christmas (Midnight)
1. Isa 9.1-6
2. Titus 2.11-14
3. Luke 2.1-14

Christmas (Dawn)
1. Isa 62.11, 12
2. Titus 3.4-7
3. Luke 2.15-20

Christmas (Day)
1. Isa 52.7-10
2. Heb 1.1-6
3. John 1.1-18

Sunday after Christmas (Holy Family)
1. Gen 15.1-6; 21.1-3
2. Heb 11.8, 11, 12, 17-19
3. Luke 2.22-40 or 2.22, 39, 40

January 1 (Solemnity of Mary, Mother of God)
1. Num 6.22-27
2. Gal 4.4-7
3. Luke 2.16-21

2nd Sunday after Christmas
1. Si 24.1, 2, 8-12
2. Eph 1.3-6, 15-18
3. John 1.1-18

Epiphany
1. Isa 60.1-6
2. Eph 3.2, 3a, 5, 6
3. Matt 2.1-12

Sunday after Epiphany (Baptism of the Lord)
1. Isa 55.1-11
2. 1 John 5.1-9
3. Mark 1.7-11

Lenten Season

Ash Wednesday
1. Joel 2.12-18
2. 2 Cor 5.20—6.2
3. Matt 6.1-6, 16-18

1st Sunday of Lent
1. Gen 9.8-15
2. 1 Pet 3.18-22
3. Mark 1.12-15

2nd Sunday of Lent
1. Gen 22.1, 2, 9a, 10-13, 15-18
2. Rom 8.31b-34
3. Mark 9.2-10

3rd Sunday of Lent
1. Exod 20.1-17
2. 1 Cor 1.22-25
3. John 2.13-25

4th Sunday of Lent
1. 2 Chr 36.14-16, 19-23
2. Eph 2.4-10
3. John 3.14-21

5th Sunday of Lent
1. Jer 31.31-34
2. Heb 5.7-9
3. John 12.20-33

Passion Sunday (Palm Sunday)
Procession: Mark 11.1-10 or John 12.12-16
1. Isa 50.4-7
2. Phil 2.6-11
3. Mark 14.1—15.47

Easter Triduum and Easter Season

Mass of Lord's Supper
1. Exod 12.1-8,11-14
2. 1 Cor 11.23-26
3. John 13.1-15

Good Friday
1. Isa 52.13—53.12
2. Heb 4.14-16, 5.7-9
3. John 18.1—19.42

Easter Vigil
1. Gen 1.1—2.2
Gen 22.1-18
Exod 14.15—15.1
Isa 54.5-14
Isa 55.1-11
Ba 3.9-15
Ba 3.32—4.4
Ezek 36.16-28
2. Rom 6.3-11
3. Mark 16.1-7

Easter Sunday
1. Acts 10.34a, 37-43
2. Col 3.1-4 or 1 Cor 5.6b-8
3. John 20.1-9 or Mark 16.1-8
Evening:
3. Luke 24.13-35

2nd Sunday of Easter
1. Acts 4.32-35
2. 1 John 5.1-6
3. John 20.19-31

3rd Sunday of Easter
1. Acts 3.13-15, 17-19
2. 1 John 2.1-5a
3. Luke 24.35-48

4th Sunday of Easter
1. Acts 4.8-12
2. 1 John 3.1,2
3. John 10.11-18

5th Sunday of Easter
1. Acts 9.26-31
2. 1 John 3.18-24
3. John 15.1-8

6th Sunday of Easter
1. Acts 10.25, 26, 34, 35, 44-48
2. 1 John 4.7-10
3. John 15.9-17

Ascension of Our Lord
1. Acts 1.1-11
2. Eph 1.17-23 or 4.1-13
3. Mark 16.15-20

7th Sunday of Easter
1. Acts 1.15-17, 20a, 20c-26
2. 1 John 4.11-16
3. John 17.11b-19

Pentecost Vigil
1. Gen 11.1-9 or Exod 19.3-8a, 16-20b or Ezek 37.1-14 or Joel 3.1-5
2. Rom 8.22-27
3. John 7.37-39

Mass of the Day
1. Acts 2.1-11
2. 1 Cor 12.3b-7, 12, 13
3. John 20.19-23

Pentecost-Optional
2. Gal 5.16-25
3. John 15.26, 27; 16.12-15

Solemnities of the Lord During Ordinary Time

Trinity Sunday (Sunday after Pentecost)
1. Deut 4.32-34, 39, 40
2. Rom 8.14-17
3. Matt 28.16-20

Corpus Christi
1. Exod 24.3-8
2. Heb 9.11-15
3. Mark 14.12-16, 22-26

Sacred Heart of Jesus
1. Hos 11.1, 3, 4, 8c, 9
2. Eph 3.8-12, 14-19
3. John 19.31-37

Ordinary Time

1st Sunday
(See Baptism of the Lord, page 59)

2nd Sunday
1. 1 Sam 3.3b-10, 19
2. 1 Cor 6.13c-15a, 17-20
3. John 1.35-42

3rd Sunday
1. Jonah 3.1-5, 10
2. 1 Cor 7.29-31
3. Mark 1.14-20

4th Sunday
1. Deut 18.15-20
2. 1 Cor 7.32-35
3. Mark 1.21-28

5th Sunday
1. Job 7.1-4, 6, 7
2. 1 Cor 9.16-19, 22, 23
3. Mark 1.29-39

6th Sunday
1. Lev 13.1, 2, 45, 46
2. 1 Cor 10.31—11.1
3. Mark 1.40-45

7th Sunday
1. Isa 43.18, 19, 21, 22, 24b, 25
2. 2 Cor 1.18-22
3. Mark 2.1-12

8th Sunday
1. Hos 2.16b, 17b, 21, 22
2. 2 Cor 3.1b-6
3. Mark 2.18-22

9th Sunday
1. Deut 5.12-15
2. 2 Cor 4.6-11
3. Mark 2.23—3.6

10th Sunday
1. Gen 3.9-15
2. 2 Cor 4.13—5.1
3. Mark 3.20-35

11th Sunday
1. Ezek 17.22-24
2. 2 Cor 5.6-10
3. Mark 4.26-34

12th Sunday
1. Job 38.1, 8-11
2. 2 Cor 5.14-17
3. Mark 4.35-41

13th Sunday
1. Ws 1.13-15, 2.23, 24
2. 2 Cor 8.7, 9, 13-15
3. Mark 5.21-43

14th Sunday
1. Ezek 2.2-5
1. 2 Cor 12.7-10
2. Mark 6.1-6

15th Sunday
1. Amos 7.12-15
2. Eph 1.3-14
3. Mark 6.7-13

16th Sunday
1. Jer 23.1-6
2. Eph 2.13-18.
3. Mark 6.30-34

17th Sunday
1. 2 Kgs 4.42-44
2. Eph 4.1-6
3. John 6.1-15

18th Sunday
1. Exod 16.2-4, 12-15
2. Eph 4.17, 20-24
3. John 6.24-35

19th Sunday
1. 1 Kgs 19.4-8
2. Eph 4.30—5.2
3. John 6.41-51

20th Sunday
1. Prov 9.1-6
2. Eph 5.15-20
3. John 6.51-58

21st Sunday
1. Jas 24.1, 2a, 15-17, 18b
2. Eph 5.21-32
3. John 6.60-69

22nd Sunday
1. Deut 4.1, 2, 6-8
2. Jas 1.17, 18, 21b, 22, 27
3. Mark 7.1-8, 14, 15, 21-23

23rd Sunday
1. Isa 35.4-7a
2. Jas 2.1-5
3. Mark 7.31-37

24th Sunday
1. Isa 50.5-9a
2. Jas 2.14—18
3. Mark 8.27-35

25th Sunday
1. Ws 2.12, 17-20
2. Jas 3.16—4.3
3. Mark 9.30-37

26th Sunday
1. Num 11.25-29
2. Jas 5.1-6
3. Mark 9.38-43, 45, 47, 48

27th Sunday
1. Gen 2.18-24
2. Heb 2.9-11
3. Mark 10.2-16

28th Sunday
1. Ws 7.7-11
2. Heb 4.12, 13
3. Mark 10.17-30

29th Sunday
1. Isa 53.10, 11
2. Heb 4.14-16
3. Mark 10.35-45

30th Sunday
1. Jer 31.7-9
2. Heb 5.1-6
3. Mark 10.46-52

31st Sunday
1. Deut 6.2-6
2. Heb 7.23-28
3. Mark 12.28b-34

32nd Sunday
1. 1 Kgs 17.10-16
2. Heb 9.24-28
3. Mark 12.38-44

33rd Sunday
1. Dan 12.1-3
2. Heb 10.11-14, 18
3. Mark 13.24-32

34th Sunday (Christ the King)
1. Dan 7.13, 14
2. Rev 1.5-8
3. John 18.33b-37

The 3-Year Cycle of Readings for Sunday Mass

Year C

Advent Season

1st Sunday of Advent
1. Jer 33.14-16
2. 1 Thes 3.12—4.2
3. Luke 21.25-28, 34-36

2nd Sunday of Advent
1. Ba 5.1-9
2. Phil 1.4-6, 8-11
3. Luke 3.1-6

3rd Sunday of Advent
1. Zeph 3.14-18a
2. Phil 4.4-7
3. Luke 3.10-18

4th Sunday of Advent
1. Mic 5.1-4a
2. Heb 10.5-10
3. Luke 1.39-45

Christmas Season

Christmas Vigil
1. Isa 62.1-6
2. Acts 13.16, 17; 22-25
3. Matt 1.1-25

Christmas (Midnight)
1. Isa 9.1-6
2. Titus 2.11-14
3. Luke 2.1-14

Christmas (Dawn)
1. Isa 62.11, 12
2. Titus 3.4-7
3. Luke 2.15-20

Christmas (Day)
1. Isa 57.7-10
2. Heb 1.1-6
3. John 1.1-18

Sunday after Christmas (Holy Family)
1. 1 Sam 1.20-22, 24-28
2. 1 John 3.1, 2, 21-24
3. Luke 2.41-52

January 1 (Solemnity of Mary, Mother of God)
1. Num 6.22-27
2. Gal 4.4-7
3. Luke 2.16-21

2nd Sunday after Christmas
1. Si 24.1, 2, 8-12
2. Eph 1.3-6, 15-18
3. John 1.1-18

Epiphany
1. Isa 60.1-6
2. Eph 3.2, 3a, 5, 6
3. Matt 2.1-12

Sunday after Epiphany (Baptism of the Lord)
1. Isa 40.1-5, 9-11
2. Titus 2.11-14; 3.4-7
3. Luke 3.15, 16, 21, 22

Lenten Season

Ash Wednesday
1. Joel 2.12-18
2. 2 Cor 5.20—6.2
3. Matt 6.1-6, 16-18

1st Sunday of Lent
1. Deut 26.4-10
2. Rom 10.8-13
3. Luke 4.1-13

2nd Sunday of Lent
1. Gen 15.5-12, 17, 18
2. Phil 3.17—4.1
3. Luke 9.28b-36

3rd Sunday of Lent
1. Exod 3.1-8a, 13-15
2. 1 Cor 10.1-6, 10-12
3. Luke 13.1-9

4th Sunday of Lent
1. Jas 5.9a, 10-12
2. 2 Cor 5.17-21
3. Luke 15.1-3, 11-32

5th Sunday of Lent
1. Isa 43.16-21
2. Phil 3.8-14
3. John 8.1-11

Passion Sunday (Palm Sunday)
Procession: Luke 19.28-40
1. Isa 50.4-7
2. Phil 2.6-11
3. Luke 22.14-23, 56

Easter Triduum and Easter Season

Mass of Lord's Supper
1. Exod 12.1-8, 11-14
2. 1 Cor 11.23-26
3. John 13.1-15

Good Friday
1. Isa 52.13—53.12
2. Heb 4.14-16; 5.7-9
3. John 18.1-19, 42

Easter Vigil
1. Gen 1.1—2.2
   Gen 22.1-18
   Exod 14.15—15.1
   Isa 54.5-14
   Isa 55.1-11
   Ba 3.9-15
   Ba 3.32—4.4
   Ezek 36.16-28
2. Rom 6.3-11
3. Luke 24.1-12

Easter Sunday
1. Acts 10.34a, 37-43
2. Col 3.1-4 or
   1 Cor 5.6b-8
3. John 20.1-9 or
   Luke 24.1-12
   Evening:
3. Luke 24.13-35

2nd Sunday of Easter
1. Acts 5.12-16
2. Rev 1.9-11a, 12, 13, 17-19
3. John 20.19-31

3rd Sunday of Easter
1. Acts 5.27b-32, 40b, 41
2. Rev 5.11-14
3. John 21.1-19 or 1-14

4th Sunday of Easter
1. Acts 13.14, 43-52
2. Rev 7.9, 14b-17
3. John 10.27-30

5th Sunday of Easter
1. Acts 14.21b-27
2. Rev 21.1-5a
3. John 13.31-33a, 34, 35

6th Sunday of Easter
1. Acts 15.1, 2, 22-29
2. Rev 21.10-14, 22, 23
3. John 14.23-29

Ascension of the Lord
1. Acts 1.1-11
2. Eph 1.17-23 or
   Heb 9.24-28; 10.19-23
3. Luke 24.46-53

7th Sunday of Easter
1. Acts 7.55-60
2. Rev 22.12-14, 16, 17, 20
3. John 17.20-26

Pentecost Vigil
1. Gen 11.1-9 or Exod 19.3-8a, 16-20b, or Ezek 37.1-14, or Joel 3.1-5
2. Rom 8.22-27
3. John 7.37-39

Mass of the Day
1. Acts 2.1-11
2. 1 Cor 12.3b-7, 12, 13 or Rom 8.8-27
3. John 20.19-23 or John 14.15, 16, 23b-26

Solemnities of the Lord During Ordinary Time

Trinity Sunday (Sunday after Pentecost)
1. Prov 8.22-31
2. Rom 5.1-5
3. John 16.12-15

Corpus Christi
1. Gen 14.18-20
2. 1 Cor 11.23-26
3. Luke 9.11b-17

Sacred Heart of Jesus
1. Ezek 34.11-16
2. Rom 5.5b-11
3. Luke 15.3-7

Ordinary Time

1st Sunday
(See Baptism of the Lord, page 63)

2nd Sunday
1. Isa 62.1-5
2. 1 Cor 12.4-11
3. John 2.1-12

3rd Sunday
1. Neh 8.2-4a, 5, 6, 8-10
2. 1 Cor 12.12-30
3. Luke 1.1-4; 4.14-21

4th Sunday
1. Jer 1.4, 5, 17-19
2. 1 Cor 12.31—13.13
3. Luke 4.21-30

5th Sunday
1. Isa 6.1, 2a, 3-8
2. 1 Cor 15.1-11
3. Luke 5.1-11

6th Sunday
1. Jer 17.5-8
2. 1 Cor 15.12, 16-20
3. Luke 6.17, 20-26

7th Sunday
1. 1 Sam 26.2,7-9, 12, 13, 22, 23
2. 1 Cor 15.45-49
3. Luke 6.27-38

8th Sunday
1. Si 27.5-8
2. 1 Cor 15.54-58
3. Luke 6.39-45

9th Sunday
1. 1 Kgs 8.41-43
2. Gal 1.1, 2, 6-10
3. Luke 7.1-10

10th Sunday
1. 1 Kgs 17.17-24
2. Gal 1.11-19
3. Luke 7.11-17

11th Sunday
1. 2 Sam 12.7-10, 13
2. Gal 2.16, 19-21
3. Luke 7.36—8.3

12th Sunday
1. Zech 12.10,11
2. Gal 3.26-29
3. Luke 9.18-24

13th Sunday
1. 1 Kgs 19.16b, 19-21
2. Gal 5.1, 13-18
3. Luke 9.51-62

14th Sunday
1. Isa 66.10-14c
2. Gal 6.14-18
3. Luke 10.1-12, 17-20

15th Sunday
1. Deut 30.10-14
2. Col 1.15-20
3. Luke 10.25-37

16th Sunday
1. Gen 18.1-10a
2. Col 1.24-28
3. Luke 10.38-42

17th Sunday
1. Gen 18.20-32
2. Col 2.12-14
3. Luke 11.1-13

18th Sunday
1. Eccl 1.2; 2.21-23
2. Col 3.1-5, 9-11
3. Luke 12.13-31

19th Sunday
1. Ws 18.6-9
2. Heb 11.1, 2, 8-19
3. Luke 12.32-48

20th Sunday
1. Jer 38.4-6, 8-10
2. Heb 12.1-4
3. Luke 12.49-53

21st Sunday
1. Isa 66.18-21
2. Heb 12.5-7, 11-13
3. Luke 13.22-30

22nd Sunday
1. Si 3.19-21, 30, 31
2. Heb 12.18, 19, 22-24a
3. Luke 14.1, 7-14

23rd Sunday
1. Ws 9.13-19
2. Phlm 9b, 10, 12-17
3. Luke 14.25-33

24th Sunday
1. Exod 32.7-11, 13, 14
2. 1 Tim 1.12-17
3. Luke 15.1-32

25th Sunday
1. Amos 8.4-7
2. 1 Tim 2.1-8
3. Luke 16.1-13

26th Sunday
1. Amos 6.1a, 4-7
2. 1 Tim 6.11-16
3. Luke 16.19-31

27th Sunday
1. Hab 1.2, 3; 2.2-4
2. 2 Tim 1.6-8, 13, 14
3. Luke 17.5-10

28th Sunday
1. 2 Kgs 5.14-17
2. 2 Tim 2.8-13
3. Luke 17.11-19

29th Sunday
1. Exod 17.8-13
2. 2 Tim 3.14—4.2
3. Luke 18.1-8

30th Sunday
1. Si 35.15b-17, 20-22a
2. 2 Tim 4.6-8, 16-18
3. Luke 18.9-14

31st Sunday
1. Ws 11.23—12.2
2. 2 Thes 1.11—2.2
3. Luke 19.1-10

32nd Sunday
1. 1 Macc 7.1, 2, 9-14
2. 2 Thes 2.16—3.5
3. Luke 20.27-38

33rd Sunday
1. Mal 3.19, 20a
2. 2 Thes 3.7-12
3. Luke 21.5-19

34th Sunday
(Christ the King)
1. 2 Sam 5.1-3
2. Col 1.12-20
3. Luke 23.35-43

Readings for the Major Feasts of the Year

February 2:
Presentation of the Lord
1. Mal 3.1-4
2. Heb 2.14-18
3. Luke 2.22-40

March 19:
Joseph, Husband of Mary
1. 2 Sam 7.4, 5a, 12-14a, 16
2. Rom 4.13, 16-18, 22
3. Matt 1.16, 18-21, 24a
   or Luke 2.41-51a

March 25:
Annunciation
1. Isa 7.10-14
2. Heb 10.4-10
3. Luke 1.26-28

June 24:
John the Baptist Vigil
1. Jer 1.4-10
2. 1 Pet 1.8-12
3. Luke 1.5-17

Mass of the Day
1. Isa 49.1-6
2. Acts13.22-26
3. Luke 1.57-66, 80

June 29:
Peter and Paul Vigil
1. Acts 3.1-10
2. Gal 1.11-20
3. John 21.15-19

Mass of the Day
1. Acts 12.1-11
2. 2 Tim 4.6-8, 17, 18
3. Matt 16.13-19

August 6:
Transfiguration
1. Dan 7.9, 10, 13, 14
2. 2 Pet 1.16-19
3. (YA) Matt 7.1-9,
   (YB) Mark 9.2-10,
   (YB) Luke 9.28b-36

August15:
Assumption Vigil
1. 1 Chr 15.3, 4,
   15;16.1, 2
2. 1 Cor 15.54-57
3. Luke 11.27, 28

Mass of the Day
1. Rev 11.19a;
   12.1-6a, 10ab
2. 1 Cor 15.20-26
3. Luke 1.39-56

September 14:
Triumph of the Cross
1. Num 21.4-9
2. Phil 2.6-11
3. John 3.13-17

November 1:
All Saints
1. Rev 7.2-4, 9-14
2. 1 John 3.1-3
3. Matt 5.1-12a

November 2:
All Souls First Mass
1. Job 19.1, 23-27
2. 1 Cor 15.51-57
3. John 6.37-40

Second Mass
1. Ws 3.1-9
2. Phil 3.20, 21
3. John 11.17-27

Third Mass
1. 2 Macc 12.43-46
2. Rev 14.13
3. John 14.1-6

(Other Readings may be chosen)

November 9:
Dedication of St. John Lateran
1. 2 Chr 5.6-10; 5.13—6.2
2. 1 Cor 3.9-13, 16, 17
3. Luke 19.1-10

(Other Readings may be chosen)

December 8:
Immaculate Conception
1. Gen 3.9-15, 20
2. Eph 1.3-6, 11, 12
3. Luke 1.26-38

Weekday Lectionary

Advent Season

First Week of Advent
Monday: Isa 2.1-5 (Year 1: Isa 4.2-6); Matt 8.5-11
Tuesday: Isa 11.1-10; Luke 10.21-24
Wednesday: Isa 25.6-10a; Matt 15.29-37
Thursday: Isa 26.1-6; Matt 7.21, 24-27
Friday: Isa 29.17-24; Matt 9.27-31
Saturday: Isa 30.19-21, 23-26;
Matt 9.35—10.1, 6-8

Second Week of Advent
Monday: Isa 35.1-10; Luke 5.17-26
Tuesday: Isa 40.1-11; Matt 18.12-14
Wednesday: Isa 40.25-31; Matt 11.28-30
Thursday: Isa 41.13-20; Matt 11.11-15
Friday: Isa 48.17-19; Matt 11.16-19
Saturday: Si 48.1-4, 9-11; Matt 17.10-13

Third Week of Advent
Monday: Num 24.2-7, 15-17a; Matt 21.23-27
Tuesday: Zeph 3.1, 2, 9-13; Matt 21.28-32
Wednesday: Isa 45.6b-8, 18, 21b-25;
Luke 7.18b-23
Thursday: Isa 54.1-10; Luke 7.24-30
Friday: Isa 56.1-3a, 6-8; John 5.33-36

December 17: Gen 49.2, 8-10; Matt 1.1-17
December 18: Jer 23.5-8; Matt 1.18-24
December 19: Judg 13.2-7, 24,25a; Luke 1.5-25
December 20: Isa 7.10-14; Luke 1.26-38
December 21: Song 2.8-14 or Zeph 3.14-18a;
Luke 1.39-45
December 22: 1 Sam 1.24-28; Luke 1.46-56
December 23: Mal 3.1-4, 23, 24; Luke 1.57-66
December 24: 2 Sam 7.1-5, 8b-11, 16;
Luke 1.67-79

Christmas Season

Octave of Christmas
Second Day (St. Stephen): Acts 6.8-10;
7.54-59; Matt 10.17-22
Third Day (St. John): 1 John 1.1-4; John 20.2-8
Fourth Day (Holy Innocents): 1 John 1.5—2.2;
Matt 2.13-18
Fifth Day: 1 John 2.3-11; Luke 2.22-35
Sixth Day: 1 John 2.12-17; Luke 2.36-40
Seventh Day: 1 John 2.18-21; John 1.1-18

January 2: 1 John 2.22-28; John 1.19-28
January 3: 1 John 2.29—3.6; John 1.29-34
January 4: 1 John 3.7-10; John 1.35-42
January 5: 1 John 3.11-21; John 1.43-51
January 6 (if Epiphany not celebrated):
1 John 5.5-13; Mark 1.6b-11

Readings may vary slightly depending on when Epiphany is celebrated

Week after Epiphany
Monday after Epiphany: 1 John 3.22—4.6;
Matt 4.12-17, 23-25
Tuesday after Epiphany: 1 John 4.7-10;
Mark 6.34-44
Wednesday after Epiphany: 1 John 4.11-18;
Mark 6.45-52
Thursday after Epiphany: 1 John 4.19—5.4;
Luke 4.14-22a
Friday after Epiphany: 1 John 5.5-13;
Luke 5.12-16
Saturday after Epiphany: 1 John 5.14-21;
John 3.22-30

Lenten Season

Ash Wednesday: Joel 2.12-18; 2 Cor 5.20—6.2;
Matt 6.1-6, 16-18
Thursday after Ash Wednesday:
Deut 30.15-20; Luke 9.22-25
Friday after Ash Wednesday: Isa 58.1-9a;
Matt 9.14,15
Saturday after Ash Wednesday: Isa 58.9b-14;
Luke 5.27-32

First Week of Lent
Monday: Lev 19.1, 2, 11-18; Matt 25.31-46
Tuesday: Isa 55.10,11; Matt 6.7-15
Wednesday: Jonah 3.1-10; Luke 11.29-32
Thursday: Gr Est C. 12,14-16, 23-25; Matt 7.7-12
Friday: Ezek 18.21-28; Matt 5.20-26
Saturday: Deut 26.16-19; Matt 5.43-48

Second Week of Lent
Monday: Dan 9.4b-10; Luke 6.36-38
Tuesday: Isa 1.10, 16-20; Matt 23.1-12
Wednesday: Jer 18.18-20; Matt 20.17-28
Thursday: Jer 17.5-10; Luke 16.19-31
Friday: Gen 37.3, 4, 12, 13a, 17b-28;
Matt 21.33-43, 45,46
Saturday: Mic 7.14, 15, 18-20;
Luke 15.1-3, 11-32

Third Week of Lent
Monday: 2 Kgs 5.1-15a; Luke 4.24-30
Tuesday: Dan 3.25, 34-43; Matt 18.21-35
Wednesday: Deut 4.1, 5-9; Matt 5.17-19
Thursday: Jer 7.23-28; Luke 11.14-23
Friday: Hos 14.2-10; Mark 12.28b-34
Saturday: Hos 6.1-6; Luke 18.19-24

Fourth Week of Lent
Monday: Isa 65.17-21; John 4.43-54
Tuesday: Ezek 47.1-9, 12; John 5.1-3a, 5-16
Wednesday: Isa 49.8-15; John 5.17-30
Thursday: Exod 32.7-14; John 5.31-47
Friday: Ws 2.1a, 12-22; John 7.1, 2, 10, 25-30
Saturday: Jer 11.18-20; John 7.40-53

Fifth Week of Lent
Monday: Sus 13.1-9, 15-17, 19-30, 33-62;
John 8.1-11 (Year 3: John 8.12-20)
Tuesday: Num 21.4-9; John 8.21-30
Wednesday: Dan 3.14-20, 24, 25, 28;
John 8.31-42
Thursday: Gen 17.3-9; John 8.51-59
Friday: Jer 20.10-13; John 10.31-42
Saturday: Ezek 37.21-28; John 11.45-56

Holy Week
Monday: Isa 42.1-7; John 12.1-11
Tuesday: Isa 49.1-6; John 13.21-33, 36-38
Wednesday: Isa 50.4-9a; Matt 26.14-25
Thursday Chrism Mass: Isa 61.1, 3a, 6a, 8b, 9;
Rev 1.5-8; Luke 4.16-21

Easter Season

Octave of Easter
Monday: Acts 2.14, 22-32; Matt 28.8-15
Tuesday: Acts 2.36-41; John 20.11-18
Wednesday: Acts 3.1-10; Luke 24.13-35
Thursday: Acts 3.11-26; Luke 24.35-48
Friday: Acts 4.1-12; John 21.1-14
Saturday: Acts 4.13-21; Mark 16.9-15

Second Week of Easter
Monday: Acts 4.23-31; John 3.1-8
Tuesday: Acts 4.32-37; John 3.7-15
Wednesday: Acts 5.17-26; John 3.16-21
Thursday: Acts 5.27-33; John 3.31-36
Friday: Acts 5.34-42; John 6.1-15
Saturday: Acts 6.1-7; John 6.16-21

Third Week of Easter
Monday: Acts 6.8-15; John 6.22-29
Tuesday: Acts 7.51—8.1a; John 6.30-35
Wednesday: Acts 8.1-8; John 6.35-40
Thursday: Acts 8.26-40; John 6.44-51
Friday: Acts 9.1-20; John 6.52-59
Saturday: Acts 9.31-42; John 6.60-69

Fourth Week of Easter
Monday: Acts 11.1-18; John 10.1-10
(Year 1: John 10.11-18)
Tuesday: Acts 11.19-26; John 10.22-30
Wednesday: Acts 12.24—13.5a;
John 12.44-50
Thursday: Acts 13.13-25; John 13.16-20
Friday: Acts 13.26-33; John 14.1-6
Saturday: Acts 13.44-52; John 14.7-14

Fifth Week of Easter
Monday: Acts 14.5-18; John 14.21-26
Tuesday: Acts 14.19-28; John 14.27-31a
Wednesday: Acts 15.1-6; John 15.1-8
Thursday: Acts 15.7-21; John 15.9-11
Friday: Acts 15.22-31; John 15.12-17
Saturday: Acts 16.1-10; John 15.18-21

Sixth Week of Easter
Monday: Acts 16.11-15; John 15.26—16.4a
Tuesday: Acts 16.22-34; John 16.5-11
Wednesday: Acts 17.15; 17.22—18.1;
John 16.12-15
Thursday: Acts 18.1-8; John 16.16-20
Friday: Acts 18.9-18; John 16.20-23a
Saturday: Acts 18.23-28; John 16.23b-28

Seventh Week of Easter

Monday: Acts 19.1-8; John 16.29-33
Tuesday: Acts 20.17-27; John 17.1-11a
Wednesday: Acts 20.28-38; John 17.11b-19
Thursday: Acts 22.30; 23.6-11; John 17.20-26
Friday: Acts 25.13-21; John 21.15-19
Saturday: Acts 28.16-20, 30, 31; John 21.20-25

Season of the Year

(I is the reading for Year 1; II is the reading for Year 2; the Gospel is the same each year)

Week One

Monday: I: Heb 1.1-6; II: 1 Sam 1.1-8; Mark 1.14-20
Tuesday: I: Heb 2.5-12; II: 1 Sam 1.9-20; Mark 1.21-28
Wednesday: I: Heb 2.14-18; II: 1 Sam 3.1-10, 19, 20; Mark 1.29-39
Thursday: I: Heb 3.7-14; II: 1 Sam 4.1-11; Mark 1.40-45
Friday: I: Heb 4.1-5, 11; II: 1 Sam 8.4-7, 10-22a; Mark 2.1-12
Saturday: I: Heb 4.12-16; II: 1 Sam 9.1-14, 17-19; 10.1a; Mark 2.13-17

Week Two

Monday: I: Heb 5.1-10; II: 1 Sam 15.16-23; Mark 2.18-22
Tuesday: I: Heb 6.10-20; II: 1 Sam 16.1-13; Mark 2.23-28
Wednesday: I: Heb 7.1-3, 15-17; II: 1 Sam 17.32, 33, 37, 40-51; Mark 3.1-6
Thursday: I: Heb 7.25—8.6; II: 1 Sam 18.6-9; 19.1-7; Mark 3.7-12
Friday: I: Heb 8.6-13; II: 1 Sam 24.3-21; Mark 3.13-19
Saturday: I: Heb 9.2, 3, 11-14; II: 2 Sam 1.1-4, 11, 12, 19, 23-27; Mark 3.20, 21

Week Three

Monday: I: Heb 9.15, 24-28; II: 2 Sam 5.1-7, 10; Mark 3.22-30
Tuesday: I: Heb 10.1-10; II: 2 Sam 6.12b-15, 17-19; Mark 3.31-35
Wednesday: I: Heb 10.11-18; II: 2 Sam 7.4-17; Mark 4.1-20
Thursday: I: Heb 10.19-25; II: 2 Sam 7.18, 19, 24-29; Mark 4.21-25
Friday: I: Heb 10.32-39; II: 2 Sam 11.1-4a, 5-10a,13-17; Mark 4.26-34
Saturday: I: Heb 11.1,2, 8,9; II: 2 Sam 12.1-7a, 10-17; Mark 4.35-41

Week Four

Monday: I: Heb 11.32-40; II: 2 Sam 15.13, 14, 30;16.5-13a; Mark 5.1-20
Tuesday: I: Heb 12.1-4; II: 2 Sam 18.9,10, 14b, 24, 25a; 18.30—19.3; Mark 5.21-43
Wednesday: I: Heb 12.4-7, 11-15; II: 2 Sam 24.2, 9-17; Mark 6.1-6
Thursday: I: Heb 12.18, 19, 21-24; II: 1 Kgs 2.1-4, 10-12; Mark 6.7-13
Friday: I: Heb 13.1-8; II: Si 47.2-11; Mark 6.14-29
Saturday: I: Heb 13.15-17, 20, 21; II: 1 Kgs 3.4-13; Mark 6.30-34

Week Five

Monday: I: Gen 1.1-19; II: 1 Kgs 8.1-7, 9-13; Mark 6.53-56
Tuesday: I: Gen 1.20—2.4a; II: 1 Kgs 8.22, 23, 27-30; Mark 7.1-13
Wednesday: I: Gen 2.4b-9, 15-17; II: 1 Kgs 10.1-10; Mark 7.14-23
Thursday: I: Gen 2.18-25; II: 1 Kgs 11.4-13; Mark 7.24-30
Friday: I: Gen 3.1-8; II: 1 Kgs 11.29-32; 12.19; Mark 7.31-37
Saturday: I: Gen 3.9-24; II: 1 Kgs 12.26-32; 13.33, 34; Mark 8.1-10

Week Six

Monday: I: Gen 4.1-15, 25; II: Jas 1.1-11; Mark 8.11-13
Tuesday: I: Gen 6.5-8; 7.1-5, 10; II: Jas 1.12-18; Mark 8.14-21
Wednesday: I: Gen 8.6-13, 20-22; II: Jas 1.19-27; Mark 8.22-26
Thursday: I: Gen 9.1-13; II: Jas 2.1-9; Mark 8.27-33
Friday: I: Gen 11.1-9; II: Jas 2.14-24, 26; Mark 8.34—9.1
Saturday: I: Heb 11.1-7; II: Jas 3.1-10; Mark 9.2-13

Week Seven
Monday: I: Si 1.1-10; II: Jas 3.13-18; Mark 9.14-29
Tuesday: I: Si 2.1-11; II: Jas 4.1-10; Mark 9.30-37
Wednesday: I: Si 4.11-19; II: Jas 4.13-17; Mark 9.38-40
Thursday: I: Si 5.1-8; II: Jas 5.1-6; Mark 9.41-50
Friday: I: Si 6.5-17; II: Jas 5.9-12; Mark 10.1-12
Saturday: I: Si 17.1-15; II: Jas 5.13-20; Mark 10.13-16

Week Eight
Monday: I: Si 17.19-27; II: 1 Pet 1.3-9; Mark 10.17-27
Tuesday: I: Si 35.1-12; II: 1 Pet 1.10-16; Mark 10.28-31
Wednesday: I: Si 36.1, 5, 6, 10-17; II:1 Pet 1.18-25; Mark 10.32-45
Thursday: I: Si 42.15-25; II: 1 Pet 2.2-5, 9-12; Mark 10.46-52
Friday: I: Si 44.1, 9-13; II: 1 Pet 4.7-13; Mark 11.11-26
Saturday: I: Si 51.12b-20; II: Jdt 17.20b-25; Mark 11.27-33

Week Nine
Monday: I: Tb 1.1a,2; 2.1-9; II: 2 Pet 1.2-7; Mark 12.1-12
Tuesday: I: Tb 2.9-14; II: 2 Pet 3.12-15a,17,18; Mark 12.13-17
Wednesday: I: Tb 3.1-11, 16; II: 2 Tim 1.1-3, 6-12; Mark 12.18-27
Thursday: I: Tb 6.10,11; 7.1, 9-17; 8.4-7; II: 2 Tim 2.8-15; Mark 12.28b-34
Friday: I: Tb 11.5-17; II: 2 Tim 3.10-17; Mark 12.35-37
Saturday: I: Tb 12.1, 5-15, 20; II: 2 Tim 4.1-8; Mark 12.38-44

Week Ten
Monday: I: 2 Cor 1.1-7; II: 1 Kgs 17.1-6; Matt 5.1-12
Tuesday: I: 2 Cor 1.18-22; II: 1 Kgs 17.7-16; Matt 5.13-16
Wednesday: I: 2 Cor 3.4-11; II:1 Kgs 18.20-39; Matt 5.17-19
Thursday: I: 2 Cor 3.15—4.1, 3-6; II: 1 Kgs 18.41-46; Matt 5.20-26
Friday: I: 2 Cor 4.7-15; II: 1 Kgs 19.9a, 11-16; Matt 5.27-32
Saturday: I: 2 Cor 5.14-21; II: 1 Kgs 19.19-21; Matt 5.33-37

Week Eleven
Monday: I: 2 Cor 6.1-10; II: 1 Kgs 21.1-16; Matt 5.38-42
Tuesday: I: 2 Cor 8.1-9; II: 1 Kgs 21.17-29; Matt 5.43-48
Wednesday: I: 2 Cor 9.6-11; II: 1 Kgs 2.1, 6-14; Matt 6.1-6, 16-18
Thursday: I: 2 Cor 11.1-11; II: Si 48.1-15; Matt 6.7-15
Friday: I: 2 Cor 11.18, 21b-30; II: 2 Kgs 11. 1-4, 9-18, 20; Matt 6.19-23
Saturday: I: 2 Cor 12.1-10; II: 2 Chr 24.17-25; Matt 6.24-34

Week Twelve
Monday: I: Gen 12.1-9; II: 2 Kgs 17.5-8, 13-15a, 18; Matt 7.1-5
Tuesday: I: Gen 13.2, 5-8; II: 2 Kgs 19.9b-11, 14-21, 31-35a, 36; Matt 7.6, 12-14
Wednesday: I: Gen 15.1-12, 17,18; II: 2 Kgs 22.8-13; 23.1-3; Matt 7.15-20
Thursday: I: Gen 16.1-12, 15,16; II: 2 Kgs 24.8-17; Matt 7.21-29
Friday: Gen 17.1, 9,10, 15-22; II: 2 Kgs 25.1-12; Matt 8.1-4
Saturday: I: Gen 18.1-15; II: Lam 2.2, 10-14, 18,19; Matt 8.5-17

Week Thirteen
Monday: I: Gen 18.16-33; II: Amos 2.6-10, 13-16; Matt 8.18-22
Tuesday: I: Gen 19.15-29; II: Amos 3.1-8; 4.11,12; Matt 8.23-27
Wednesday: I: Gen 21.5, 8-20; II: Amos 5.14,15, 21-24; Matt 8.28-34
Thursday: I: Gen 22.1-19; II: Amos 7.10-17; Matt 9.1-8
Friday: I: Gen 23.1-4, 19; 24.1-8, 62-67; II: Amos 8.4-6, 9-12; Matt 9.9-13
Saturday: I: Gen 27.1-5, 15-29; II: Amos 9.11-15; Matt 9.14-17

Week Fourteen

Monday: I: Gen 28.10-22a; II: Hos 2.16, 17b,18, 21,22; Matt 9.18-26

Tuesday: I: Gen 32.22-33; II: Hos 8.4-7, 11-13; Matt 9.32-38

Wednesday: I: Gen 41.51-57; 42.5-7a, 17-24a; II: Hos 10.1-3, 7, 8, 12; Matt 10.1-7

Thursday: I: Gen 44.18-21, 23b-29; 45.1-5; II: Hos 11.1, 3,4, 8c, 9; Matt 10.7-15

Friday: I: Gen 46.1-7, 28-30; II: Hos 14.2-10; Matt 10.16-23

Saturday: I: Gen 49.29-33; 50.15-24; II:Isa 6.1-8; Matt 10.24-33

Week Fifteen

Monday: I: Exod 1.8-14, 22; II: Isa 1.10-17; Matt 10.34—11.1

Tuesday: I: Exod 2.1-15a; II: Isa 7.1-9; Matt 11.20-24

Wednesday: I: Exod 3.1-6, 9-12; II: Isa 10.5-7, 13-16; Matt 11.25-27

Thursday: I: Exod 3.13-20; II: Isa 26.7-9, 12, 16-19; Matt 11.28-30

Friday: I: Exod 11.10-12, 14; II: Isa 38.1-6, 21, 22, 7, 8; Matt 12.1-8

Saturday: I: Exod 12.37-42; II: Mic 2.1-5; Matt 12.14-21

Week Sixteen

Monday: I: Exod 14.5-18; II: Mic 6.1-4, 6-8; Matt 12.38-42

Tuesday: I: Exod 14.21—15.2; II: Mic 7.14, 15, 18-20; Matt 12.46-50

Wednesday: I: Exod 16.1-5, 9-15; II: Jer 1.1, 4-10; Matt 13.1-9

Thursday: I: Exod 19.1, 2, 9-11, 16-20b; II: Jer 2.1-3, 7, 8, 12, 13; Matt 13.10-17

Friday: I: Exod 20.1-17; II: Jer 3.14-17; Matt 13.18-23

Saturday: I: Exod 24.3-8; II: Jer 7.1-11; Matt 13.24-30

Week Seventeen

Monday: I: Exod 32.15-24, 30-34; II: Jer 13.1-11; Matt 13.31-35

Tuesday: I: Exod 33.7-11; 34.5b-9, 28; II: Jer 14.17-22; Matt 13.36-43

Wednesday: I: Exod 34.29-34; II: Jer 15.10, 16-21; Matt 13.44-46

Thursday: I: Exod 40.16-21, 34-38; II: Jer 18.1-6; Matt. 13.47-53

Friday: I: Lev 23.1, 4-11, 15, 16, 27, 34b-37; II: Jer 26.1-9; Matt 13.54-58

Saturday: I: Lev 25.1, 8-17; II: Jer 26.11-16, 24; Matt 14.1-12

Week Eighteen

Monday: I: Num 11.4b-15; II: Jer 28.1-17; Matt 14.13-21 or Matt 14.22-36

Tuesday: I: Num 12.1-13; II: Jer 30.1, 2, 12-15, 18-22; Matt 14.22-36 or Matt 15.1,2, 10-14

Wednesday: I: Num 13.1, 2a; 13.25—14.1, 26-29, 34,35; II: Jer 31.1-7; Matt 15.21-28

Thursday: I: Num 20.1-13; II: Jer 31.31-34; Matt 16.13-23

Friday: I: Deut 4.32-40; II: Neh 2.1, 3; 3.1-3, 6,7; Matt 16.24-28

Saturday: I: Deut 6.4-13; II: Hab 1.12—2.4; Matt 17.14-20

Week Nineteen

Monday: I: Deut 10.12-22; II: Ezek 1.2-5, 24-28c; Matt 17.22-27

Tuesday: I: Deut 31.1-8; II: Ezek 2.8—3.4; Matt 18.1-5, 10, 12-14

Wednesday: I: Deut 34.1-12; Ezek 9.1-7; 10.18-22; Matt 18.15-20

Thursday: I: Josh 3.7-10a, 11, 13-17; II: Ezek 12.1-12; Matt 18.21—19.1

Friday: I: Josh 24.1-13; II: Ezek 16.1-15, 60, 63; Matt 19.3-12

Saturday: I: Josh 24.14-29; II: Ezek 18.1-10, 13b, 30-32; Matt 19.13-15

Week Twenty

Monday: I: Judg 2.11-19; II: Ezek 24.15-24; Matt 19.16-22

Tuesday: I: Judg 6.11-24a; II: Ezek 28.1-10; Matt 19.23-30

Wednesday: I: Judg 9.6-15; II: Ezek 34.1-11; Matt 20.1-16a

Thursday: I: Judg 11.29-39a; II: Ezek 36.23-28; Matt 22.1-14

Friday: I: Ruth 1.1, 3-6, 14b-16, 22; II: Ezek 37.1-14; Matt 22.34-40

Saturday: I: Ruth 2.1-3, 8-11; 4.13-17; II: Ezek 43.1-7a; Matt 23.1-12

Week Twenty-one
Monday: I: Thes 1.2b-5, 8b-10; II: 2 Thes 1.1-5, 11b,12; Matt 23.13-22
Tuesday: I: 1 Thes 2.1-18; II: 2 Thes 2.1-3a, 13-17; Matt 23.23-26
Wednesday: I: 1 Thes 2.9-13; II: 2 Thes 3.6-10, 16-18; Matt 23.27-32
Thursday: I: 1 Thes 3.7-13; II: 1 Cor 1.1-9; Matt 24.42-51
Friday: I: 1 Thes 4.1-8; II: 1 Cor 1.17-25; Matt 25.1-13
Saturday: I: 1 Thes 4.9-12; II: 1 Cor 1.26-31; Matt 25.14-30

Week Twenty-two
Monday: I: 1 Thes 4.13-18; II: 1 Cor 2.1-5; Luke 4.16-30
Tuesday: I: 1 Thes 5.1-6, 9-11; II: 1 Cor 2.10b-16; Luke 4.31-37
Wednesday: I: Col 1.1-8; II: 1 Cor 3.1-9; Luke 4.38-44
Thursday: I: Col 1.9-14; II: 1 Cor 3.18-23; Luke 5.1-11
Friday: I: Col 1.15-20; II: 1 Cor 4.1-5; Luke 5.33-39
Saturday: I: Col 1.21-23; II: 1 Cor 4.9-15; Luke 6.1-5

Week Twenty-three
Monday: I: Col 1.24–2.3; II: 1 Cor 5.1-8, Luke 6.1-11
Tuesday: I: Col 2.6-15; II: 1 Cor 6.1-11; Luke 6.12-19
Wednesday: I: Col 3.1-11; II: 1 Cor 7.25-31; Luke 6.20-26
Thursday: I: Col 3.12-17; II: 1 Cor 8.1b-7, 11-13;Luke 6.27-38
Friday: I: 1 Tim 1.1, 2, 12-14; II: 1 Cor 9.16-19, 22b-27; Luke 6.39-42
Saturday: I: 1 Tim 1.15-17; II: 1 Cor 10.14-22a; Luke 6.43-49

Week Twenty-four
Monday: I: 1 Tim 2.1-8; II: 1 Cor 11.17-26, 33; Luke 7.1-10
Tuesday: I: 1 Tim 3.1-13; II: 1 Cor 12.12-14, 27-31a; Luke 7.11-17
Wednesday: I: 1 Tim 3.14-16; II: 1 Cor 12.31–13.13; Luke 7.31-35
Thursday: I: 1 Tim 4.12-16; II: 1 Cor 15.1-11; Luke 7.36-50
Friday: I: 1 Tim 6.2c-12; II: 1 Cor 15.12-20; Luke 8.1-3
Saturday: I: 1 Tim 6.13-16; II: 1 Cor 15.36, 37, 42-49; Luke 8.4-15

Week Twenty-five
Monday: I: Ezra 1.1-6; II: Prov 3.27-34; Luke 8.16-18
Tuesday: I: Ezra 6.7, 8, 12b, 14-20; II: Prov 21.1-6, 10-13; Luke 8.19-21
Wednesday: I: Ezra 9.5-9; II: Prov 30.5-9; Luke 9.1-6
Thursday: I: Hag 1.1-8; II: Eccl 1.2-11; Luke 9.7-9
Friday: I: Hag 1.15b–2.9; II: Eccl 3.1-11; Luke 9.18-22
Saturday: I: Zech 2.5-9a, 14, 15a; II: Eccl 11.9–12.8; Luke 9.43b-45

Week Twenty-six
Monday: I: Zech 8.1-8; II: Job 1.6-22; Luke 9.46-50
Tuesday: I: Zech 8.20-23; II: Job 3.1-3, 11-17, 20-23; Luke 9.51-56
Wednesday: I: Neh 2.1-8; II: Job 9.1-12, 14-16; Luke 9.57-62
Thursday: I: Neh 8.1-4a, 5,6, 7b-12; II: Job 19.12-27; Luke 10.1-12
Friday: I: Ba 1.15-21; II: Job 38.1, 12-21; 40.3-5; Luke 10.13-16
Saturday: I: Ba 4.5-12, 27-29; II: Job 42.1-3, 5, 6, 12-17; Luke 10.17-24

Week Twenty-seven
Monday: I: Jonah 1.1–2.1, 11; II: Gal 1.6-12; Luke 10.25-37
Tuesday: I: Jonah 3.1-10; II: Gal 1.13-24; Luke 10.38-42
Wednesday: I: Jonah 4.1-11; II: Gal 2.1, 2, 7-14; Luke 11.1-4
Thursday: I: Mal 3.13-20a; II: Gal 3.1-5; Luke 11.5-13
Friday: I: Joel 1.13-15; 2.1,2; II: Gal 3.7-14; Luke 11.15-26
Saturday: I: Joel 4.12-21; II: Gal 3.22-29; Luke 11.27, 28

Week Twenty-eight
Monday: I: Rom 1.1-7; II: Gal 4.22-24, 26, 27; Luke 11.29-32
Tuesday: I: Rom 1.16-25; II: Gal 5.1-6; Luke 11.37-41
Wednesday: I: Rom 2.1-11; II: Gal 5.18-25; Luke 11.42-46
Thursday: I: Rom 3.21-29; II: Eph 1.3-10; Luke 11.47-54
Friday: I: Rom 4.1-8; II: Eph 1.11-14; Luke 12.1-7
Saturday: I: Rom 4.13, 16-18; II: Eph 1.15-23; Luke 12.8-12

Week Twenty-nine
Monday: I: Rom 4.20-25; II: Eph 2.1-10; Luke 12.13-21
Tuesday: I: Rom 5.12, 15b, 17-19, 20b, 21; II: Eph 2.12-22; Luke 12.35-38
Wednesday: I: Rom 6.12-18; II: Eph 3.2-12; Luke 12.39-48
Thursday: I: Rom 6.19-23; II: Eph 3.14-21; Luke 12.49-53
Friday: I: Rom 7.18-25a; II: Eph 4.1-6; Luke 12.54-59
Saturday: I: Rom 8.1-11; II: Eph 4.7-16; Luke 13.1-9

Week Thirty
Monday: I: Rom 8.12-17; II: Eph 4.32—5.8; Luke 13.10-17
Tuesday: I: Rom 8.18-25; II: Eph 5.21-33; Luke 13.18-21
Wednesday: I: Rom 8.26-30; II: Eph 6.1-9; Luke 13.22-30
Thursday: I: Rom 3.31b-39; II: Eph 6.10-20; Luke 13.31-35
Friday: I: Rom 9.1-5; II: Phil 1.1-11; Luke 14.1-6
Saturday: I: Rom 11.1, 2a, 11, 12, 25-29; II:Phil 1.18b-26; Luke 14.1, 7-11

Week Thirty-one
Monday: I: Rom 11.29-36; II: Phil 2.1-4; Luke 14.12-14
Tuesday: I: Rom 12.5-16a; II: Phil 2.5-11; Luke 14.15-24
Wednesday: I: Rom 13.8-10; II: Phil 2.12-18; Luke 14.25-33
Thursday: I: Rom 14.7-12; II: Phil 3.3-8a; Luke 15.1-10
Friday: I: Rom 15.14-21; II: Phil 3.17—4.1; Luke 16.1-8
Saturday: I: Rom 16.3-9, 16, 22-27; II: Phil 4.10-19; Luke 16.9-15

Week Thirty-two
Monday: I: Ws 1.1-7; II: Titus 1.1-9; Luke 17.1-6
Tuesday: I: Ws 2.23—3.9; II: Titus 2.1-8, 11-14; Luke 17.7-10
Wednesday: I: Ws 6.1-11; II: Titus 3.1-7; Luke 17.11-19
Thursday: I: Ws 7.22—8.1; II: Phlm 7-20; Luke 17.20-25
Friday: I: Ws 13.1-9; II: 2 John 4-9; Luke 17.26-37
Saturday: I: Ws 18.14-16; 19.6-9; II: 3 John 5-8; Luke 18.1-8

Week Thirty-three
Monday: I: 1 Macc 1.10-15, 41-43, 54, 57, 62, 64; II: Rev 1.1-4; 2.1-5a; Luke 18.35-43
Tuesday: I: 2 Macc 6.18-31; II: Rev 3.1-6, 14-22; Luke 19.1-10
Wednesday: I: 2 Macc 7.1, 20-31; II: Rev 4.1-11; Luke 19.11-28
Thursday: I: 1 Macc 2.15-29; II: Rev 5.1-10; Luke 19.41-44
Friday: I: 1 Macc 4.36,37, 52-59; II: Rev 10.8-11; Luke 19.45-48
Saturday: I: 1 Macc 6.1-13; II: Rev 11.4-12; Luke 20.27-40

Week Thirty-four
Monday: I: Dan 1.1-6, 8-20; II: Rev 14.1-3, 4b, 5; Luke 21.1-4
Tuesday: I: Dan 2.31-45; II: Rev 14.14-19; Luke 21.5-11
Wednesday: I: Dan 5.1-6, 13, 14, 16, 17, 23-28; II: Rev 15.1-4; Luke 21.12-19
Thursday: I: Dan 6.11-28; II: Rev 18.1, 2, 21-23; 19.1-3, 9a; Luke 21.20-28
Friday: I: Dan 7.2-14; II: Rev 20.1-4; 20.11—21.2; Luke 21.29-33
Saturday: I: Dan 7.15-27; II: Rev 22.1-7; Luke 21.34-36

Principal Celebrations of the Liturgical Year

Table 1

Year	Lectionary Cycle		Ash Wednesday	Holy Thursday	Good Friday
	Sunday	Weekday			
1999	A	I	17 February	1 April	2 April
2000	B	II	8 March	20 April	21 April
2001	C	I	28 February	12 April	13 April
2002	A	II	13 February	28 March	29 March
2003	B	I	5 March	17 April	18 April
2004	C	II	25 February	8 April	9 April
2005	A	I	9 February	24 March	25 March
2006	B	II	1 March	13 April	14 April
2007	C	I	21 February	5 April	6 April
2008	A	II	6 February	20 March	21 March
2009	B	I	25 February	9 April	10 April
2010	C	II	17 February	1 April	2 April
2011	A	I	9 March	21 April	22 April
2012	B	II	22 February	5 April	6 April
2013	C	I	13 February	28 March	29 March
2014	A	II	5 March	17 April	18 April
2015	B	I	18 February	2 April	3 April
2016	C	II	10 February	24 March	25 March
2017	A	I	1 March	13 April	14 April
2018	B	II	14 February	29 March	30 March
2019	C	I	6 March	18 April	19 April
2020	A	II	26 February	9 April	10 April
2021	B	I	17 February	1 April	2 April
2022	C	II	2 March	14 April	15 April
2023	A	I	22 February	6 April	7 April
2024	B	II	14 February	28 March	29 March
2025	C	I	5 March	17 April	18 April

Easter	Ascension Thursday	Pentecost	The Body and Blood of Christ
4 April	13 May	23 May	6 June
23 April	1 June	11 June	25 June
15 April	24 May	3 June	17 June
31 March	9 May	19 May	2 June
20 April	29 May	8 June	22 June
11 April	20 May	30 May	13 June
27 March	5 May	15 May	29 May
16 April	25 May	4 June	18 June
8 April	17 May	27 May	10 June
23 March	1 May	11 May	25 May
12 April	21 May	31 May	14 June
4 April	13 May	23 May	6 June
24 April	2 June	12 June	26 June
8 April	17 May	27 May	10 June
31 March	9 May	19 May	2 June
20 April	29 May	8 June	22 June
5 April	14 May	24 May	7 June
27 March	5 May	15 May	29 May
16 April	25 May	4 June	18 June
1 April	10 May	20 May	3 June
21 April	30 May	9 June	23 June
12 April	21 May	31 May	14 June
4 April	13 May	23 May	6 June
17 April	26 May	5 June	19 June
9 April	18 May	28 May	11 June
31 March	9 May	19 May	2 June
20 April	29 May	8 June	22 June

Principal Celebrations of the Liturgical Year

Table 2

Year	Lectionary Cycle		Weeks in Ordinary Time Before Lent	
	Sunday	Weekday	Number of Weeks	Ending
1999	A	I	6	16 February
2000	B	II	9	7 March
2001	C	I	8	27 February
2002	A	II	5	12 February
2003	B	I	8	4 March
2004	C	II	7	24 February
2005	A	I	5	8 February
2006	B	II	8	28 February
2007	C	I	7	20 February
2008	A	II	4	5 February
2009	B	I	7	24 February
2010	C	II	6	16 February
2011	A	I	9	8 March
2012	B	II	7	21 February
2013	C	I	5	12 February
2014	A	II	8	4 March
2015	B	I	6	17 February
2016	C	II	5	9 February
2017	A	I	8	28 February
2018	B	II	6	14 February
2019	C	I	8	5 March
2020	A	II	7	25 February
2021	B	I	6	16 February
2022	C	II	8	1 March
2023	A	I	7	21 February
2024	B	II	6	13 February
2025	C	I	8	4 March

After Easter Season		
Ending	Week Number	First Sunday of Advent
24 May	8	28 November
12 June	10	3 December
4 June	9	2 December
20 May	7	1 December
9 June	10	30 November
31 May	9	28 November
16 May	7	27 November
5 June	9	3 December
28 May	8	2 December
12 May	6	30 November
1 June	9	29 November
24 May	8	28 November
13 June	11	27 November
28 May	8	2 December
20 May	7	1 December
9 June	10	30 November
25 May	8	29 November
16 May	7	27 November
5 June	9	3 December
21 May	7	2 December
10 June	10	1 December
1 June	9	29 November
24 May	8	28 November
6 June	10	27 November
29 May	8	3 December
20 May	7	1 December
9 June	10	30 November

Order of the Second Reading for Sundays in Ordinary Time

Table 3

Sunday	Year One	Year Two	Year Three
2	1 Corinthians, 1-4	1 Corinthians, 6-11	1 Corinthians, 12-15
3	1 Corinthians, 1-4	1 Corinthians, 6-11	1 Corinthians, 12-15
4	1 Corinthians, 1-4	1 Corinthians, 6-11	1 Corinthians, 12-15
5	1 Corinthians, 1-4	1 Corinthians, 6-11	1 Corinthians, 12-15
6	1 Corinthians, 1-4	1 Corinthians, 6-11	1 Corinthians, 12-15
7	1 Corinthians, 1-4	2 Corinthians	1 Corinthians, 12-15
8	1 Corinthians, 1-4	2 Corinthians	1 Corinthians, 12-15
9	Romans	2 Corinthians	Galatians
10	Romans	2 Corinthians	Galatians
11	Romans	2 Corinthians	Galatians
12	Romans	2 Corinthians	Galatians
13	Romans	2 Corinthians	Galatians
14	Romans	2 Corinthians	Galatians
15	Romans	Ephesians	Colossians
16	Romans	Ephesians	Colossians
17	Romans	Ephesians	Colossians
18	Romans	Ephesians	Colossians
19	Romans	Ephesians	Hebrews, 11-12
20	Romans	Ephesians	Hebrews, 11-12
21	Romans	Ephesians	Hebrews, 11-12
22	Romans	James	Hebrews, 11-12
23	Romans	James	Philemon
24	Romans	James	1 Timothy
25	Philippians	James	1 Timothy
26	Philippians	James	1 Timothy
27	Philippians	Hebrews, 1-10	2 Timothy
28	Philippians	Hebrews, 1-10	2 Timothy
29	1 Thessalonians	Hebrews, 1-10	2 Timothy
30	1 Thessalonians	Hebrews, 1-10	2 Timothy
31	1 Thessalonians	Hebrews, 1-10	2 Thessalonians
32	1 Thessalonians	Hebrews, 1-10	2 Thessalonians
33	1 Thessalonians	Hebrews, 1-10	2 Thessalonians

I.N.
R.I.

Abbreviations

The following abbreviations are used for the books of the Bible:

Old Testament

Genesis	Gen	Ecclesiastes	Eccl
Exodus	Exod	Song of Songs	Song
Leviticus	Lev	Wisdom	Ws
Numbers	Num	Sirach	Si
Deuteronomy	Deut	(Ecclesiasticus)	
Joshua	Josh	Isaiah	Isa
Judges	Judg	Jeremiah	Jer
Ruth	Ruth	Lamentations	Lam
1 Samuel	1 Sam	Baruch	Ba
2 Samuel	2 Sam	Ezekiel	Ezek
1 Kings	1 Kgs	Daniel	Dan
2 Kings	2 Kgs	Hosea	Hos
1 Chronicles	1 Chr	Joel	Joel
2 Chronicles	2 Chr	Amos	Amos
Ezra	Ezra	Obadiah	Obad
Nehemiah	Neh	Jonah	Jonah
Tobit	Tb	Micah	Mic
Judith	Jdt	Nahum	Nah
Esther	Esth	Habakkuk	Hab
1 Maccabees	1 Macc	Zephaniah	Zeph
2 Maccabees	2 Macc	Haggai	Hag
Job	Job	Zechariah	Zech
Psalms	Ps	Malachi	Mal
Proverbs	Prov		

New Testament

Matthew	Matt	1 Timothy	1 Tim
Mark	Mark	2 Timothy	2 Tim
Luke	Luke	Titus	Titus
John	John	Philemon	Phlm
Acts	Acts	Hebrews	Heb
Romans	Rom	James	Jas
1 Corinthians	1 Cor	1 Peter	1 Pet
2 Corinthians	2 Cor	2 Peter	2 Pet
Galatians	Gal	1 John	1 John
Ephesians	Eph	2 John	2 John
Philippians	Phil	3 John	3 John
Colossians	Col	Jude	Jude
1 Thessalonians	1 Thes	Revelation	Rev
2 Thessalonians	2 Thes		

Notes

Notes

Notes

Notes

Notes

Notes